RANDOM HOUSE
WEBSTER'S

spanish-english
english-spanish
dictionary

SECOND EDITION

RANDOM HOUSE
REFERENCE

NEW YORK TORONTO LONDON SYDNEY AUCKLAND

This work was published in 1999 as *Random House Spanish-English English-Spanish Dictionary, Second Edition*. This is a completely revised and updated edition of volumes published in 1995 and 1997 as the *Random House Spanish-English English-Spanish Dictionary*.

RANDOM HOUSE is a registered trademark of Random House, Inc.

Please address inquiries about electronic licensing of any products for use on a network, in software or on CD-ROM to the Subsidiary Rights Department, Random House Information Group, fax 212-572-6003.

This book is available at special discounts for bulk purchases for sales promotions or premiums. Special editions, including personalized covers, excerpts of existing books, and corporate imprints, can be created in large quantities for special needs. For more information, write to Random House, Inc., Special Markets/Premium Sales, 1745 Broadway, MD 6-2, New York, NY, 10019 or e-mail specialmarkets@randomhouse.com.

Visit the Random House Reference Web site: www.randomwords.com

Printed in the United States of America

10 9 8 7 6 5 4 3

Library of Congress Cataloging in Publication Data is available

ISBN-10: 0-375-72196-7

ISBN-13: 978-0-375-72196-0

Contents

Preface

New Second Edition

This is a revised Second Edition of *Random House Spanish–English English–Spanish Dictionary,* first published in 1995. New to this edition are pronunciations for all Spanish and English main entries, using IPA (International Phonetic Alphabet) symbols. The IPA symbols are explained in the pronunciation key for English on page viii and for Spanish on page xiv. Also included in this dictionary are detailed guides to the pronunciation of both languages.

Selection of Vocabulary

The aim of this dictionary is to cover as much current vocabulary as possible, as well as certain terms found in standard works of modern Spanish and English literature.

This dictionary includes items often omitted in other bilingual dictionaries—road and street signs, for example—though few things could be as frustrating (and, sometimes, as dangerous) as seeing such signs but not knowing what they mean (in this dictionary, all kinds of public notices are enclosed by the symbols << >> in Spanish and by quotation marks in English). Also, many vocabulary items consisting of more than one word have been covered here (see for instance **do** in the English–Spanish section).

Spanish Spelling and Alphabetization

On January 1, 1959, the Spanish language academies changed certain spelling rules and on April 27, 1994, they eliminated **ch** and **ll** as separate letters of the alphabet. Thus, whereas words like **chico** and **chocolate** were formerly alphabetized under their own letter (**ch**, which came between **c** and **d**) and words like **llamar** and **llegar** were formerly alphabetized under their own letter (**ll**, which came between **l** and **m**), words containing **ch** or **ll**, in whatever part of the word they may appear, are now alphabetized as they would be in English (**chico** therefore now appears under **c** and **llegar** under **l**).

Field Labels

Only essential field labels are given in this dictionary. For example, the label *medicine* or *pathology* is unnecessary at **flebitis** "phlebitis" (in the Spanish–English section) because both the Spanish and English words refer only to the medical condition so called in those languages.

In contrast to that entry, we do need a label at **foca** "seal" (in the Spanish–English section) because English **seal** has several meanings and only the zoological one is intended here. English speakers looking up **foca** thus need the label *zoology* (Spanish speakers need no label because they know that **foca** is the name of an animal, and so they will correctly assume that **seal** is intended only in its zoological sense).

Regional Labels for Spanish

Regional labels are given in this dictionary when a less than universal usage is found in a certain region or country. A regional label should be interpreted as meaning that the usage so labeled is found in that particular place, but it may also be found elsewhere. For instance, the regional label *Mexican* means that the usage so labeled is found in Mexico, but further research would be necessary to determine whether the usage is present or absent in other countries. The label *West. Hem.* is used for Spanish terms that are in general use throughout the Western Hemisphere.

Subentries

If a main entry head is repeated in a subentry in exactly the same form, it is abbreviated to its first letter (for instance, at **fin** in the Spanish–English section we find **a f. de,** which stands for **a fin de**). If the main entry head appears in any other form, the full form is given in the subentry (thus, at **fin,** the subentry head **a fines de** is spelled without abbreviation).

Irregular Spanish Verbs and the Direction "See . . ."

If a Spanish verb is irregular, it has been treated in one of two ways: either its principal parts are shown (see for example the end of the entry for **caber**) or you are referred to an analogous irregular verb for guidance (see for example the end of the entry for **comparecer,** where you are directed to **conocer**). Thus, since the irregular form **conozco** is shown at **conocer** (it being irregular in the sense that it has a **z**), you may infer that **comparecer** has the irregular form **comparezco.**

One of the consequences of the changes in Spanish spelling is that a new kind of orthographically irregular verb has come into existence (for example, **ahijar, ahincar, ahitar, ahuchar, ahumar, ahusar, cohibir, desahuciar, prohibir, prohijar, rehilar, rehusar, sahumar, sobrehilar,** and **trashumar**).

If "See . . ." is all you find at an entry, you are being directed to a synonym. Thus, "**descompasarse** See **descomedirse**" means that the translations of **descomedirse** are those of **descompasarse** too.

Spanish Equivalents of "you"

Today's Spanish, when taken as a whole, has at least six equivalents of "you": **tú, vos, usted** (abbreviated to **Vd.**), **su merced** (all of which are used in addressing one person), **ustedes** (abbreviated to **Vds.**), **vosotros, vosotras,** and **sus mercedes** (all used in addressing more than one person).

When **you** occurs in this dictionary, usually only one of those words has been chosen to translate it, though three are never used here: **su merced, sus mercedes,** because they are now limited to only a small area of the Spanish-speaking world (the Cundinamarca Savanna, in Colombia) and even there they are now obsolescent, and **vos,** because the verb forms corresponding to this pronoun often vary from country to country.

Usually, the selection of one pronoun or another in this dictionary has been arbitrary, in which case any of the others could just as easily have been chosen. For example, for **How are you?** the translation "¿Cómo está Vd.?" is offered, yet any of the other pronouns could appear instead (with, in certain cases, a different verb form, for instance "¿Cómo están Vds.?").

In certain cases, however, not all pronouns (whether actually used or just implicit) would be appropriate. For example, among the translations of **please** . . . are imperative forms of **servirse.** . . . Because **servirse** in this sense is a formal usage (found mostly in impersonal writing like application blanks), it is not found in any familiar form of the imperative. The dictionary therefore gives ¡**sírvase . . .** ! (where the understood subject is **usted,** a formal pronoun). It could also have given ¡**sírvanse . . .** ! (where the understood subject is **ustedes,** likewise a formal pronoun), but not any form in which the subject were an informal pronoun.

Masculine and Feminine, Male and Female

As women engage in more and more activities once the domain of men, a growing number of Spanish nouns formerly used only in the masculine gender are being used in the feminine too. This dictionary thus labels **nauta, paracaidista, púgil, pugilista, recluta, reservista,** and **seminarista,** for example, as both masculine and feminine (the gender to be chosen depending on the gender of the person in question). For the user's convenience, the gender of Spanish nouns is indicated not only in the Spanish–English section but also in the English–Spanish one.

Many sample Spanish phrases and sentences in this dictionary can refer to people of either gender. For example, under **wish** in the English–Spanish section the sample sentence **I wished him a Merry Christmas** is translated "Le deseé unas Pascuas muy felices" and "Le felicité las Pascuas." Since they both also mean "I wished her a Merry Christmas," the sentence could as easily have contained **her** rather than **him.** In this dictionary, male and female references have been chosen randomly, hopefully in about equal number.

In other cases, a slight change is needed to turn a male reference into a female one or vice versa. For instance, **He was within an inch of being killed** (under **within,** in the English–Spanish section) is rendered by "Por poco le matan." Changing **he** to **she** and **le** to **la** will yield a correct equivalence referring to a female. With just an elementary knowledge of both languages, users of this dictionary will be able to make the necessary changes and thus have at their disposal many more sample phrases and sentences than it supplies.

Símbolos de Pronunciacíon por los Sonidos del inglés

Pronunciation Symbols for the Sounds of English

Símbolos del AFI IPA Symbols	Ejemplos Key Words
/æ/	*Eng.* hat
/ei/	*Eng.* stay; *Fr.* cité; *Ger.* bequem; *It.* fréccia; *Sp.* reina
/ɛə/ [followed by /r/]	*Eng.* hair; *Fr.* frère; *Ger.* mehr; *It.* mercante; *Sp.* ver
/ɑ/	*Eng.* father; *Fr.* tasse; *Ger.* Vater; *It.* pasta; *Sp.* casa
/ɛ/	*Eng.* bet; *Fr.* gazelle; *Ger.* Bett; *It.* freschezza; *Sp.* entre
/i/	*Eng.* bee; *Fr.* difficile; *Ger.* Wiegen; *It.* limone; *Sp.* vida
/ɪə/ [followed by /r/]	*Eng.* hear; *Fr.* rire; *Ger.* hier
/ɪ/	*Eng.* sit; *Ger.* ist
/ai/	*Eng.* try; *Ger.* zeigen; *It.* operaio; *Sp.* ay
/ɒ/	*Eng.* hot
/o/	*Eng.* boat; *Fr.* chapeau; *Ger.* Mond
/ɔ/	*Eng.* saw; *Fr.* donner; *Ger.* doch; *It.* oglio; *Sp.* nota
/ɔi/	*Eng.* toy; *Ger.* Deutsch; *Sp.* hoy
/ʊ/	*Eng.* book
/u/	*Eng.* too; *Fr.* tout; *Ger.* tun; *It.* inutile; *Sp.* luna
/au/	*Eng.* cow; *Ger.* aus; *Sp.* pausa
/ʌ/	*Eng.* up
/ɜ/ [followed by /r/]	*Eng.* burn; *Fr.* fleur; *Ger.* böse
/ə/	*Eng.* alone; *Fr.* demain; *Ger.* stehen
/ᵊ/	*Eng.* fire (fiᵊr); *Fr.* bastille
/œ̃/, /ɔ̃/, /ɛ̃/, /ɑ̃/ [A tilde over a vowel shows that it is nasalized]	As in *Fr.* un bon vin blanc
/b/	*Eng.* boy; *Fr.* bête; *Ger.* backen; *It.* buio; *Sp.* boca
/tʃ/	*Eng.* child; *It.* cibo; *Sp.* mucho
/d/	*Eng.* dad; *Fr.* danse; *Ger.* dieser; *It.* destra; *Sp.* doy
/f/	*Eng.* for; *Fr.* fête; *Ger.* fahren; *It.* fretta; *Sp.* fecha
/g/	*Eng.* give; *Fr.* garde; *Ger.* gut; *It.* seguito; *Sp.* gato

Símbolos del AFI IPA Symbols	Ejemplos Key Words
/h/	*Eng.* happy; *Ger.* heben; *It.* hascisc
/dʒ/	*Eng.* just; *It.* giugno
/k/	*Eng.* kick; *Fr.* capable; *Ger.* Kirche; *It.* amichevole; *Sp.* kilogramo
/l/	*Eng.* love; *Fr.* lait; *Ger.* lieben; *It.* lira; *Sp.* libro
/m/	*Eng.* mother; *Fr.* manger; *Ger.* Mann; *It.* meandro; *Sp.* limbo
/n/	*Eng.* now; *Fr.* noble; *Ger.* nach; *It.* nulla; *Sp.* noche
/ŋ/	*Eng.* sing; *Ger.* singen; *It.* vengo
/p/	*Eng.* pot; *Fr.* parfum; *Ger.* Post; *It.* pace; *Sp.* papa
/r/	*Eng.* read; *Fr.* rouge; *Ger.* Rat; *It.* ricco; *Sp.* para
/s/	*Eng.* see; *Fr.* santé; *Ger.* essen; *It.* sérpo; *Sp.* hasta
/ʃ/	*Eng.* shop; *Fr.* chercher; *Ger.* Schlaf; *It.* scelto
/t/	*Eng.* ten; *Fr.* tête; *Ger.* Teil; *It.* topo; *Sp.* tomar
/θ/	*Eng.* thing; *Sp.* (in Spain) cerdo
/ð/	*Eng.* father; *Sp.* codo
/v/	*Eng.* victory; *Fr.* vie; *Ger.* was; *It.* voi; *Sp.* verdad
/w/	*Eng.* witch; *Fr.* oui; *It.* guardare
/y/	*Eng.* yes; *Fr.* yeux; *Ger.* jung; *Sp.* yacer
/z/	*Eng.* zipper; *Fr.* zéro; *Ger.* Sieg
/ʒ/	*Eng.* pleasure; *Fr.* jeune

Los sonidos del inglés americano

Vocales y diptongos

a Cuando representa el sonido /æ/, se pronuncia más cerrada que la *a* de *paro* (por ejemplo: **act, at, bat, hat, marry**); también se encuentra este sonido en palabras deletreadas con: -ah- (d*ah*lia), -ai- (pl*ai*d), -al- (h*al*f), -au- (l*au*gh), -ua- (g*ua*rantee).

a Cuando representa el sonido /ei/, se pronuncia más cerrada que la *e* de *hablé* y como si fuera seguido de *i* (por ejemplo: **age, gate, rate**); también se encuentra este sonido en palabras deletreadas con: -ai- (r*ai*n, *ai*r), -aigh- (str*aigh*t), -au- (g*au*ge), -ay- (s*ay*), -ea- (st*ea*k), -ei- (v*ei*l, w*ei*gh), -ey- (ob*ey*).

a /ɑ/ Equivale aproximadamente a la *a* de *sentado* y *bajo* (por ejemplo: **ah, father, part**); también se encuentra este sonido en palabras deletreadas con: -al- (c*al*m), -e(r)- (s*er*geant), -ea(r)- (h*ear*t), -ua- (g*ua*rd).

a /ə/ Equivale aproximadamente a la *e* de las palabras francesas *de* y *le* (por ejemplo: **alone, about**); también se encuentra este sonido en palabras deletreadas con: -e- (syst*e*m), -i- (eas*i*ly), -o- (gallop), -u- (circ*u*s), -y- (mart*y*r).

e /ɛ/ Equivale aproximadamente a la *e* de *templo* y *perro* (por ejemplo: **edge, set, merry**); también se encuentra este sonido en palabras deletreadas con: a-, -a- (*a*ny, m*a*ny), -ai- (s*ai*d), -ay- (s*ay*s), -ea- (l*ea*ther), -ei- (h*ei*fer), -eo- (j*eo*pardy), -ie- (fr*ie*nd).

e /i/ Equivale aproximadamente a la *i* de *Chile* (por ejemplo: **be, equal, secret**); también se encuentra este sonido en palabras deletreadas con: ea- (*ea*ch, t*ea*), -ee- (f*ee*, k*ee*p), -ei- (rec*ei*ve), -eo- (p*eo*ple), -ey (k*ey*), -ie- (f*ie*ld), -y (cit*y*).

i /ɪ/ Se pronuncia menos cerrada que la *i* de *Chile* (por ejemplo: **if, big, fit, mirror**); también se encuentra este sonido en palabras deletreadas con: e- (*E*ngland), -ee- (b*ee*n), -ei- (counterf*ei*t), -ia- (carr*ia*ge), -ie- (s*ie*ve), -o- (w*o*man), (b)u(s)- (b*u*siness), -y- (s*y*mpathetic).

i /ai/ Equivale aproximadamente a la *ai* de *aire, baile* (por ejemplo: **bite, ice, pirate**); también se encuentra este sonido en palabras deletreadas con: ais- (*ai*sle), -ei- (h*ei*ght, st*ei*n), -eye- (*eye*), -ie (p*ie*), -igh (h*igh*), is- (*i*sland), -uy (b*uy*), -y (cycle, sk*y*), -ye (l*ye*).

o /ou/ Se pronuncia más cerrada que la *o* de *supo* (por ejemplo: **hope, go, oh, over**); también se encuentra este sonido en palabras deletreadas con: -au- (m*au*ve), -aux (f*aux* pas), -eau (b*eau*), -ew (s*ew*), -oa- (r*oa*d), -oe- (t*oe*), -oo- (br*oo*ch), -ot (dep*o*t), -ou- (s*ou*l), -ow (fl*ow*), -owe- (*owe*).

o /ɔ/ Se pronuncia más cerrada que la *o* de *corre* (por ejemplo: **alcohol, order, raw**); también se encuentra este sonido en palabras deletreadas con: -a- (t*a*ll), -al- (w*a*lk), au- (*au*thor, v*au*lt), -augh- (c*augh*t), -oa- (br*oa*d), -oo- (fl*oo*r), -ough- (s*ough*t).

oi /oi/ Equivqale aproximadamente a la *oy* de *doy* (por ejemplo: **oil, joint, voice**); también se encuentra este sonido en palabras deletreadas con: -awy- (l*awy*er), -oy- (b*oy*).

oo /ʊ/ Se pronuncia menos cerrada que la *u* de *insulto* (por ejemplo: **book, foot**); también se encuentra este sonido en palabras deletreadas con: -o- (w*o*lf), -ou- (t*ou*r), -u- (p*u*ll).

oo /u/	Se pronuncia más larga que la *u* de *susto* (por ejemplo: **too, ooze, fool**); también se encuentra este sonido en palabras deletreadas con: -eu- (man*eu*ver), -ew (gr*ew*), -o (wh*o*), -o. . .*e* (m*o*ve), -oe (can*oe*), -ou- (tr*ou*pe), -u. . .*e* (r*u*le), -ue (fl*ue*), -ui- (s*ui*t).
ou /au/	Equivale aproximadamente a la *au* de *aurora* (por ejemplo: **loud, out**); también se encuentra este sonido en palabras deletreadas con -ow (br*ow*, c*ow*, pl*ow*).
u /iu/	Equivale aproximadamente a la *iu* de *ciudad* (por ejemplo: **cue, use, utility**); también se encuentra este sonido en palabras deletreadas con: -eau- (b*eau*ty), -eu- (f*eu*d), -ew (f*ew*), (h)u- (h*u*man), (h)u. . .*e* (h*u*ge), -iew (v*iew*), you (*you*), yu. . .*e* (*yu*le).
u /ʌ/	Es sonido intermedio entre la *o* de *borro* y la *a* de *barro*, algo parecido a la pronunciación de la *eu* francesa de *peur;* (por ejemplo: **up, sun, mud**); también se encuentra este sonido en palabras deletreadas con: o- (*o*ther), -o- (s*o*n), -oe- (d*oe*s), o. . .*e* (l*o*ve), -oo- (bl*oo*d), -ou (tr*ou*ble).

Consonantes

b	Se pronuncia igual que la *p* española salvo que en la pronunciación de la *b* suenan las cuerdas vocales. La *b* inglesa es más fuerte (más aspirada) que la española. Se encuentra en palabras escritas con b (**bed, amber, rub**) y también en palabras deletreadas con -bb- (ho**bb**y).
c	Como la *c* española, lleva dos sonidos, /s/ y /k/. La /s/ se pronuncia igual que la *s* española y se encuentra en palabras deletreadas con ce- (**center**) y ci- (**city**). La /k/ es semejante a la *c* española cuando aparece delante de -a, -o, y -u (*católica, cómo, cuándo*) pero se pronuncia más fuerte (más aspirada). La /k/ se encuentra en palabras deletreadas con ca-, co-, y cu- (**cat, account, cut**).
ch	Equivale aproximadamente a la *ch* española (por ejemplo: **chief, beach**); también se encuentra en palabras deletreadas con: -tch- (ca*tch*, bu*tch*er), -te- (righ*te*ous), -ti- (ques*ti*on), -tu- (na*tu*ral). A veces equivale a la /š/ de la palabra francese *chèrie* (**chef**), o a la /k/ de *cómo* (**character**).
d	Equivale aproximadamente a la *d* de *onda* (por ejemplo: **do, odor, red**); también se encuentra en palabras deletreadas con -dd- (la**dd**er) y -de- (fa**de**). La *d* inglesa es siempre más fuerte (más aspirada) que la española y no se pronuncia nunca /dʒ/ como la *d* de *padre* o las *d*'s de *Madrid*.
f	Equivale aproximadamente a la *f* española (por ejemplo: **feed, safe**); también se encuentra en palabras deletreadas con -ff- (mu**ff**in) y -fe (li**fe**).
g	Equivale aproximadamente a la *g* de *globo* (por ejemplo: **give, fog**); también se encuentra en palabras deletreadas con -gg (e**gg**), gh- (**gh**ost), y -gue (pla**gue**). La *g* cuando cae delante de -i y -e se pronuncia /dʒ/ (**George, gem, legitimate**). El sonido /dʒ/ es semejante a, pero más fuerte que, la *y* y la *ll* españolas de *yo* y *llevar*. Véase *j*.
h	Se pronuncia más aspirada pero menos áspera que la *j* española en *jabón* (por ejemplo: **hit, hope**); también se encuentra en palabras deletreadas con wh- (**wh**o).

j Equivale aproximadamente a la *y* de *yo* en su pronunciación enfática (p.ej. . . . *yo, y yo sólo soy el dueño aquí!*) o como la *y* de *cónyuge* en ciertas modalidades del español (por ejemplo: **just, joke**); también se encuentra en palabras deletreadas con: -dg- (ju*dg*e), -di- (sol*di*er), -ge (sa*ge*), -gg- (exa*gg*erate), gi- (*gi*n). La pronunciación de la *j* y de la *g* delante de -i y -e /ʤ/ es igual que la de la *ch* española, salvo que suenan las cuerdas vocales en la pronunciación del sonido /ʤ/.

k (Por ejemplo: **keep, make, token**) equivale a la *qui-* y *que* españolas pero se pronuncia más fuerte (más aspirada). La *k* inglesa no se pronuncia cuando cae delante de una *n* (**knife, knight, knee**).

l Se pronuncia aproximadamente como la *l* de *lago* (por ejemplo: **leap, sail**); también se encuentra en palabras deletreadas con -le (mi*le*) y -ll (ca*ll*).

m Equivale aproximadamente a la *m* española (por ejemplo: **more, drum, him, summer**). Tengan cuidado de pronunciar la *m* al final de una palabra igual que se pronuncia en medio de la palabra y de no convertir el sonido en *n*.

n Equivale aproximadamente a la *n* de *bueno* (por ejemplo: **now, sunny**); tambièn se encuentra en palabras deletreadas con gn- (*gn*at) y kn- (*kn*ife).

ng (Por ejemplo: **sing, Washington**) equivale aproximadamente a la *n* de *blanco*.

p (Por ejemplo: **pool, spool, supper, stop**) tras consonante equivale aproximadamente a la *p* española, pero lleva más aspiración. La *p* delante de una *s* (**psychologist, psyche**) no se pronuncia.

r Se pronuncia con la punta de la lengua elevada hacia el paladar (sin tocarlo) y doblada para atrás (por ejemplo: **red, hurry, near**); también se encuentra en palabras deletreadas con: -re (pu*re*), rh- (*rh*ythm), y wr- (*wr*ong).

s Equivale aproximadamente a la *s* de *salir*, pero algo más tensa y larga (por ejemplo: **see, kiss**).

sh Equivale aproximadamente a la *ch* de las palabras francesas *changer* and *chapeau* (por ejemplo: **ship, wash**); también se encuentra en palabras deletreadas con: -ce- (o*ce*an), -ch- (ma*ch*ine), -ci- (spe*ci*al), s(u)- (*s*ugar), -sci- (con*sci*ence), -si- (man*si*on), -ss- (ti*ss*ue, mi*ss*ion), -ti- (cap*ti*on).

t (Por ejemplo: **team, ten, steam, bit**) tras consonante equivale aproximadamente a la *t* española salvo con más aspiración; también se encuentra en palabras deletreadas con: -bt (dou*bt*), -cht (ya*cht*), -ed (talk*ed*), -ght (bou*ght*), -te (bi*te*), th- (*th*yme), -tt- (bo*tt*om), tw- (*tw*o).

th (Por ejemplo: **thin, ether, path**) equivale aproximadamente a la *z* española en el norte de España.

th (Por ejemplo: **that, the, either, smooth**) equivale aproximadamente a la *d* de *adoptar*.

v (Por ejemplo: **voice, river, live**) equivale aproximadamente a la *b* de *haba* pero es labiodental en vez de bilabial. La pronunciación de la *v* inglesa es igual que la de la *f*, salvo que suenan las cuerdas vocales en la pronunción de la *v*.

w (Por ejemplo: **west, witch, away**) equivale aproximadamente a la *u* de *puesto*.

y (Por ejemplo: **yes, beyond**) equivale aproximadamente a la *i* de *bien;* también se encuentra en palabras deletreadas con -i- (on*i*on, un*i*on), -j- (halleu*j*ah), y -ll- (torti*ll*a).

z Tiene dos sonidos: /z/ y /zh/. La /z/, la más común (por ejemplo: **zoo, lazy, zone**), equivale aproximadamente a la *s* de *isla* y *mismo* en ciertas modalidades del español, pero con más sonoridad. Este sonido se pronuncia igual que la *s* española, salvo que en la pronunciación de la /z/ suenan las cuerdas vocales. Se encuentra el sonido /z/ en algunas palabras deletreadas con: -s- (ha*s*), -se (ri*se*), x- (*x*ylophone), y -zz- (bu*zz*ard, fu*zz*). El sonido /zh/ que se encuentra en **azure** y **brazier** equivale aproximadamente a la *ll* del español de la gente mayor de la cuidad de Buenos Aires (o sea, como la *j* de la palabra francesa *bonjour*). El sonido /zh/ también se encuentra en ciertas palabras deletreadas con -ge (gara*ge*, mira*ge*), -si- (vi*si*on), y su- (plea*su*re).

Pronunciation Symbols for the Sounds of Spanish
Símbolos de Pronunciacíon por los Sonidos del español

IPA Symbols / Símbolos del AFI	Key Words / Ejemplos	Key Words / Ejemplos
a	albo, banco, cera	father, depart
e	esto, del, parte	rain, eight
i	ir, fino, adiós, muy	beet, conceive
o	oler, flor, grano	telephone, goal
u	un, luna, cuento	fool, group
b	bajo, vaca	by, abet
β	hablar, escribir, lavar	
d	dar, desde, dos, dueña	deal, adept
ð	pedir, Pedro, verdad	that, gather
f	fecha, afectar, golf	fan, after
g	gato, grave, gusto, largo	garden, ugly
h	gemir, giro, junta, bajo, relojes	horse, loch
k	cacao, claro, cura, cuenta, que, quinto	kind, actor
l	lado, lente, habla, papel	lot, altar
ʎ	llamar, calle, olla	million, civilian
m	mal, amor	more, commit
n	nada, nuevo, mano, bien	not, enter
ɲ	ñaques, año	canyon, companion
ŋ	angosto, aunque	ring, anchor
p	peso, guapo	pill, applaud
r	real, faro, deber	rice, carpet
s	sala, espejo, mas	say, clasp
θ	cena, hacer, cierto, cine, zarzuela, lazo, vez	thin, myth
t	tocar, estado, cenit	table, attract
y	ya, ayer	you, voyage
tʃ	chica, mucho	chill, batch

Diphthongs

ai, ay	baile, hay	high, rye
au	auditor, laudar	out, round
ei	veinte, seis	aim, ray
eu	euscaro, deuda	
oi, oy	roido, hoy	coin, loyal
ue	buena, suerte	sway, quaint
ie	miel, tambien	fiesta, pieta

The Basics of Standard Spanish Pronunciation

Whereas the fit between English spelling and pronunciation has for centuries been less than ideal (think, for example, of the various pronunciations of -ough, as in **although, bough, cough,** and **slough**), the fit between today's Spanish spelling and pronunciation is quite good, thanks to the regulatory efforts of the Spanish academies.

The following instructions thus take spelling as their starting point. Pronunciation is described in two ways: with phonetic symbols (enclosed in slashes) and by way of approximate comparisons with English. A wavy line separates variants (like **esnob ~ snob**). A stress mark (') means that the syllable following it is stressed (as in /re'lo/). An asterisk indicates a nonexistent form (like English *llion). A right-facing "arrow" (>), or "greater than" sign, means "became in Spanish" (as in English **rum** and French **rhum** > **ron ~ romo**).

As may be expected of a language that has been used for many centuries, over a vast area, and by many diverse people, Spanish is now pronounced in various ways. Of the many current pronunciations, two are offered as most suitable for speakers of Spanish as a second language. The two standards are identical to a large extent, differing chiefly with respect to the pronunciation of **c** before **e**; **c** before **i**; **z** in any position; and, optionally, **ll, g,** and **j.**

To the extent that the two standards differ, features belonging to just one of them are labeled either *Standard 1* or *Standard 2* below.

Features labeled *Standard 1* are accepted as standard in Spain but not in the Western Hemisphere. Features labeled *Standard 2* are accepted as standard in the Western Hemisphere but not in Spain. If you speak Spanish mostly with Spaniards or mostly with people from the Western Hemisphere, your choice of standard will thus be straightforward. If you speak with people from both areas, you can either try to master both standards or, if you want to follow just one of them no matter to whom you speak, pick Standard 2.

a is pronounced /a/, which is similar to the second vowel of the English interjection **aha!** and the vowel of the English interjection **ah,** although much shorter in duration. See also "Diphthongs and Triphthongs" below.

b has three pronunciations. At the beginning of an utterance, after /m/ (whether represented by **m** or by **n**), or after /n/ (whether represented by **n** or by **m**), the letter **b** is pronounced /b/, which is similar to the pronunciation of the first consonant of English **beach, broth, pebble,** etc. For example, in the sentence **Bulgaria envió a ambos embajadores en un barco japonés,** each of the four instances of **b** (and the one instance of **v**) is pronounced in this way.

At the end of a word, more than one pronunciation of **b** may be heard. For example, **club** may be /klub/, /kluβ/, or /klu/. Its plural, **clubs,** may be /klups/, /klus/, and possibly /kluβs/, unless the plural **clubes** is used, whose universal pronunciation is /kluβɛs/ (see the next paragraph for interpreting /β/, and **e** for interpreting /ɛ/). All of the foregoing holds for compounds of **club,** like **aeroclub.** In **esnob ~ snob,** the final **b** is pronounced /b/.

In all other positions (for example, **hablas, hablar,** and **habré**), **b** is pronounced /β/, a sound absent in English, which is made by bringing the lips close together without letting them touch each other (as if you were blowing dust away or blowing out a match or candle), expelling air through the mouth, and vibrating the vocal cords. This sound is thus similar to /v/ (as in English **very** and **vowel**), except that the latter is made by making the lower lip touch the upper teeth. English-speakers should not mistake Spanish /β/ for English /v/.

It follows from the foregoing that if the position of **b** in the utterance changes, its pronunciation may change. For example, when the word **baba** is pronounced in isolation, the first **b** is rendered /b/ and the second one /β/, but in the phrase **la baba**, the first **b** is no longer at the beginning of an utterance (nor is it preceded by the sounds /m/ or /n/), hence the phrase is pronounced /laβaβa/.

These rules of pronunciation also hold true for the letter **v**, which is pronounced /b/ at the beginning of words, and /β/ in the middle. See also **v**.

c has several pronunciations. If it is followed by **e** or **i**, the letter **c** is pronounced /θ/ in Standard 1 and /s/ in Standard 2. The pronunciation of /θ/ in Spanish is similar to that of **th** in English **thatch, think,** etc., but made with somewhat more protrusion of the tongue. The sound /s/ is similar to the pronunciation of **s** in English **say, simple,** etc.

Although Standard 1 has /θ/ for **c** before **e** or **i**, people who use that pronunciation will not be put off if they hear you pronounce the **c** as /s/, because the latter is widespread (though not standard) in Spain. In the Western Hemisphere, **c** before **e** or **i** is always pronounced /s/ and never /θ/. Speakers of Western Hemispheric Spanish will react to /θ/ either as "the correct pronunciation" ("though we don't use it") or as a pretentious pronunciation (unless it comes from people to the manner born, i.e., many Spaniards). Thus, whereas it is desirable though not obligatory that you use Standard 1 in Spain, you would be well advised to use only Standard 2 in the Western Hemisphere, where /θ/ is bound to elicit a sharp reaction of one kind or another (as sharp as British **drawing pin, lorry,** or **trunk call** instead of **thumbtack, truck,** and **long-distance call** would probably elicit in the United States).

ch, wherever it is found, is always pronounced as /tʃ/, which is similar to the pronunciation of **ch** in English **church, child,** etc.

If **c** ends a syllable (for instance, **accionista, facsimíl,** and **técnico**), **c** is pronounced as /k/. Spanish /k/ is similar to the pronunciation of **c** in English **escape, scandal,** etc. To achieve a good rendition of Spanish /k/, hold your open palm in front of your mouth and pronounce first **cape** and **coop,** then **escape** and **scandal.** When pronouncing the first two words, you felt a noticeable puff of air on your palm, but in the last two words you felt almost no puff at all. A noticeable puff of air accompanying a speech sound is called *aspiration;* sounds pronounced with aspiration are *aspirated,* and those pronounced without it are *unaspirated.* Spanish /k/ (like Spanish /p/ and /t/) is always unaspirated, wherever it occurs. Thus, you should have no trouble with Spanish **escapar** and **escandalo** because here /k/ occurs after /s/, and as an English speaker you will automatically pronounce it as unaspirated, just as you would the **c** of the English cognates of those words: **escape** and **scandal.** It is in other positions that you have to be careful not to aspirate: **claro, crear,** etc. (contrast them with their English cognates, both of which have an aspirated /k/: **clear, create**).

See also **k, ll** (under **l**), **q, s,** and **z.**

d has several pronunciations. At the beginning of an utterance, after /n/, or after /l/, this letter is pronounced /d/, which is similar to the pronunciation of **d** in English **dear, dust,** etc., with this difference: in the production of Spanish /d/, the tongue touches the lower edge of the upper front incisors.

When between two vowels, when preceded by a vowel and followed by **r,** or when at the end of a word and not preceded by **r** (as in **pedir, Pedro,** and

libertad), the letter **d** is pronounced /ð/, which is similar to the pronunciation of **th** in English **that, there,** etc., but less interdental than English /ð/ (in the production of the Spanish sound, the tip of the tongue gently touches the lower edge of the upper incisors).

It follows from the foregoing that if the position of **d** in the utterance changes, its pronunciation may change. Contrast, for example, these three utterances: (1) **Dinamarca mandó embajadores a doce países,** (2) **En Dinamarca viven unos cuantos americanos,** and (3) **Iremos a Dinamarca.** In (1), the **d** of **Dinamarca** is pronounced /d/ because it comes at the beginning of an utterance; in (2) the same **d** is also pronounced /d/ because it comes after /n/; but in (3) the same **d** is pronounced /ð/ because none of the conditions for pronouncing it /d/ is met. Similarly, when the word **dedo** is pronounced in isolation, the first **d** is rendered /d/ (and the second one /ð/), but in the phrase **mi dedo,** the first **d** is no longer at the beginning of an utterance (nor is it preceded by /n/ or /l/); hence the phrase is pronounced /miðeðo/.

e has two pronunciations. The instruction given in some books that **e** is pronounced /e/ when stressed and /ɛ/ when unstressed does not hold true for today's Spanish and may never have been an accurate description of its pronunciation in any variety of the language.

Here are better guidelines for **e** (except when it is part of a diphthong or triphthong):

If **e** is found in a syllable ending in a consonant (see "Syllabification" below), it is pronounced /ɛ/, which is similar to the pronunciation of **è** in French or to the vowel of **bet, let, met,** etc., as pronounced in Standard English, that is, with considerable lowering of the jaw, for example, **embaldosar, fresco, hablen,** and **mestizo.**

If **e** ends a syllable and the next one begins with **r, rr,** or **t,** it is pronounced /ɛ/, for instance, **pero, caballete** (the first **e**), **cerrar,** and **jinete.**

Otherwise, **e** is pronounced /e/, which is similar to the pronunciation of **é** in French, that is, the jaw is lowered only minimally (the closest English comes to having a sound like /e/ is the vowel of **ache, rake, stake,** etc.), for example, **caballete** (the second **e**), **hablé,** and **mesa.** In this dictionary, the sounds /e/ and /ɛ/ are both represented by /e/.

See also "Diphthongs and Triphthongs" below.

f is pronounced /f/, which is similar to the pronunciation of **f** in English **fate, feet,** etc., for example, **afectar, fecha, golf, golfo, ¡uf!.**

g has several pronunciations. At the beginning of an utterance and when followed by **a, o, u,** or a consonant letter except **n** (as in **gato, goma, gusto,** or **glaciar**), **g** is pronounced /g/, which is similar to the pronunciation of **g** in English **get, go, gumption,** etc.

At the beginning of a word and when followed by **n,** the letter **g** is silent (as in **gnomo**). That pronunciation is in fact so widespread and reputable that a **g**-less spelling is now acceptable and is in fact preferred in this dictionary (see "Miscellaneous" below).

When **g** occurs at the end of a syllable and is preceded by **n,** it is silent, as in **búmerang.** In older borrowings from other languages, that **g** was systematically or sometimes omitted, as in **sterling > esterlina, pudding > pudín.**

Before **e** or **i** (as in **gemir** and **gigante**), except if it comes at the end of a word, the letter **g** is pronounced /x/, which is absent in most varieties of current English. This sound is similar to the pronunciation of **ch** in German **Bach,** that of **ch** in Israeli Hebrew **zecher,** and that of **ch** in Scots English **loch, Lochaber,** etc. Press the back of the tongue against the soft palate, expel air (as if coughing), and do not vibrate the vocal chords. **g** before **e** or **i** can also be pronounced /h/, as in English **"house,"** which is common in Latin America and in southern Spain. In this dictionary, both /x/ and /h/ are represented by /h/.

If **g** ends a syllable that is not the last syllable of the word (as in **dogma** and the first syllable of **zigzag**), this letter is pronounced /g/. In such cases, the next syllable always begins with a consonant.

Otherwise, **g** is pronounced /ɣ/, a sound absent in English, which is made by bringing the back of the tongue close to the soft palate (without letting them touch), expelling air through the mouth, and vibrating the vocal chords. Examples are **hago** and **hígado**. In this dictionary, both sounds, /g/ and /ɣ/, are represented by /g/.

h is silent.

i is pronounced /i/, which is similar to the vowel of English **beet, feet, sheen,** etc., but shorter (for instance, **dicho, isla,** and **cursi**). See also **y**.

j is almost always pronounced /x/, although a pronunciation as /h/ is also acceptable in parts of Latin America and southern Spain (see **g** for interpreting these symbols). A notable exception is **reloj,** which many speakers pronounce /re'lo/. That pronunciation of **reloj** is so widespread that **reló** is an alternate spelling of the singular form, but only in informal writing. In the plural, everyone pronounces /x/ or /h/ and therefore writes the **j: relojes.** See **x**.

k, which is now found only in recent borrowings from other languages, is pronounced /k/ (see **c** for interpreting that symbol). The letter combination **ck** (as in **crack, flashback, shock, snack, stock**) is pronounced /k/.

l when not doubled is pronounced /l/, which is formed by putting the tip of the tongue against the sockets of the upper incisors, the remainder of the tongue lying flat. Spanish /l/ thus does not have the hollow sound of English /l/, in whose formation the back of the tongue rises toward the palate.

ll has two pronunciations, /ʎ/ and /y/, which vary by region and class rather than by placement within a word. /ʎ/, a sound similar to the Italian **gli,** has no real equivalent in English, although the **lli** of **million** comes close. While /λ/ is held to be the "correct" pronunciation by Spanish radio and television guidelines, it is almost never used in Latin America, except among some academics and the very wealthy. In Spain it is only heard in the northern regions of Castile. Much more common, and almost universally accepted today, is the pronunciation /y/, which is similar to our **y** in **yes** or **yam**.

In the Southern Cone of Latin America, a third pronunciation, /ʒ/ (like the French **Geneviève**), is also used.

m is pronounced /m/, which is similar to the pronunciation of **m** in English **make, might,** etc.

Traditionally, Spanish does not have /m/ at the end of a word when it is pronounced in isolation. However, a few words (all learned borrowings from other languages) end in **m** (for example, **álbum, factótum, ídem, médium, memorándum, ultimátum,** and **vademécum**), and that letter always appears in the Spanish names of many places outside Spanish-speaking areas, like **Bírmingham, Búckingham, Siam,** and **Vietnam.** Both /m/ and /n/ are heard in such words, depending on people's ability to pronounce /m/ at the end of a word (as more and more Spanish-speakers study other languages, they find it easier to produce that sound in that position) and their interest in maintaining the supposedly "correct" (i.e., non-Spanish) pronunciation of that letter.

n has several pronunciations. If immediately followed by a labial consonant (represented by **b, f, m, p,** or **v**) whether in the same word or in the next one, it is pronounced /m/ (as in the words **anfitrión, inmediato, anverso,** or the sentences **insiste en bucear, insiste en pelear,** and **en muchos casos hay más**). Since /m/ + /m/ is reduced to a single /m/, **en muchos casos** actually has just one /m/.

However, /m/ + /n/ (as in **insomne**) is not reduced.

Before /k/ or /g/ (as in **aunque** and **angosto**), **n** is pronounced /ŋ/, which is similar to the final consonant of **sing, long,** and **song** as pronounced in English.

In all other positions (as in **Anatolia, andan,** and **nombrar**), **n** is pronounced /n/, which is similar to the pronunciation of **n** in English **hand, near,** etc.

See also **m,** "Stress," and, "Miscellaneous" below.

ñ is pronounced /ɲ/, which is similar to the pronunciation of **ny** in English **canyon** or **ni** in English **onion.**

o is pronounced similarly to the **o** in the English words **tote** and **gloat.** English speakers, however, must be careful not to end the pronunciation of this vowel with an "off-glide" (an "off-glide," in this case, would close the **o** into a **u** sound at the end of the vowel). Thus, the Spanish **no** and the English **no** are not exactly alike, as the Spanish ends in a pure /o/ sound, while the English "off-glides" into a /u/, producing /nou/.

p, where it is pronounced, stands for /p/, which is similar to the pronunciation of **p** in English **space, spare, spook,** etc., but different from that of **p** in English **pike, peak, poke,** etc., in that it is not aspirated (see **c** for definitions of aspirated and unaspirated sounds).

Spanish **ps** at the beginning of a word is pronounced /s/.

q is always followed by **ue** or **ui.** The sequence **que** is pronounced /ke/ and **qui** is pronounced /ki/ (for example, **quince**).

To represent the sound sequences /kue/ and /kui/, Spanish has **cue** and **cui** respectively (as in **cueva** and **cuidar**).

Because **q** is always followed by **u,** if Spanish-speakers borrow words containing just **q** from other languages, that letter is changed to **k.** Thus, the Spanish names of Iraq and Qatar, for example, are **Irak** and **Katar.**

r has two pronunciations. At the beginning of a word or when it comes after **l, n,** or **s** (for example, **reir, alrededor, enrojecer,** and **Israel**), this letter has the same pronunciation as **rr** (see below).

In all other positions, **r** is pronounced with one flip of the upper part of the tongue against the sockets of the upper incisors (for instance, **leer, para, pera, pero, tercero,** and **treinta**).

rr is pronounced with a trill (several flips) of the upper front part of the tongue against the sockets of the upper incisors (for instance, **parra, perra, perro,** and **sierra**). Thus, **para** and **parra** are different words, with different meanings. The same applies to **caro** and **carro, pera** and **perra, pero** and **perro, torero** and **torrero,** and other pairs of words.

s has several pronunciations. When it represents the plural ending of nouns recently borrowed from other languages, it is silent in certain words, like **cabarets, carnets, complots, conforts, superávits, tíckets, trusts, vermuts.**

Before the letters **b, v, d, g** (but only when the letter is not followed by **e** or **i**), **l, m, n,** or **r** (whether any of those eight letters appear in the same word as **s** or they appear in the next word), you have an alternative in both standards if **s** is not the last letter of the word: it may be pronounced /z/ (a sound similar to the pronunciation of **z** in English **zebra, zoo,** etc.) or /s/ (see **c** for interpreting that symbol): **esbelto, esdrújulo, esgrimir, isla, esmalte, Israel, los baúles, los varones, los dedos, los guantes, los lagos, los maestros, los nervios, los ratones,** etc. If **s** is the last letter, only /s/ is found (for instance, in the family name **Pons**).

If **s** is followed by **r** (whether in the same word or in the next one), besides the two pronunciations suggested above, /s/ or /z/, a third possibility is not to pronounce the **s** at all and, as compensation, trill the **r** more. The word **Israel** (and its derivatives) thus has three pronunciations: /isrrael/, /izrrael/, and /irrrael/.

Otherwise, **s** is pronounced /s/ (as in **ese, especial, hablas, hasta, insistir, seco**).

If **s** is followed by **h,** the foregoing paragraph applies, except in the case of Spanish words recently borrowed from other languages or words modeled on such recently borrowed words, in which **sh** constitutes a unit, to be pronounced /ʃ/ (a sound similar to the pronunciation of **sh** in English **shall, sheet, should,** etc.). Thus, in **deshacer,** an old Spanish word not recently borrowed from another language, the instructions about **s** apply and the **h** is silent (hence the first two syllables of that word are /desa/), whereas in **riksha, sh** is pronounced /ʃ/.

See also **b, c, t, z,** and "Syllabification" below.

t is pronounced /t/, which is similar to the pronunciation of **t** in English **stoop, stake, steer,** etc., but different from that of **t** in English **take, teak, took,** etc., in that it is less aspirated (see **c**).

The Spanish /t/ is made by touching the tip of the tongue against the upper incisors (in contrast to English /t/, in whose production the tongue touches the gums). In two positions, **t** may not be pronounced as described above. First, before **l** or **m** in the same word (as in **atleta, aritmético,** and **ritmo**) you have an alternative: **t** may be pronounced as described or it may be pronounced /ð/ (see **d** for interpreting that symbol).

Second, the **t** at the end of a word may be silent. Probably many, most, or all Spanish-speakers pronounce it in **cenit, déficit, fagot, mamut, superavít,** and **Tíbet ~ el Tibet,** whereas in other words the **t** is silent, for instance **cabaret, carnet, complot, tícket, trust,** and **vermut,** which are pronounced as if written *cabaré, *carné, *compló, *tique, *trus, and *vermú (the plurals are pronounced identically to their singulars). In still other words you have an alternative: **confort** is pronounced either /kom'for/ or /kom'fort/ (the plural **conforts** has both variants too).

u has two pronunciations. In the combinations **gue, gui, que,** and **qui,** the letter **u** is silent, for example, **guedeja** /geðeha/, **quedar** /keðar/, and **quien** /kien/ (see **q** and **e** on the pronunciation of those letters).

In all other cases, it is pronounced /u/, which is similar to the vowel sound of English **who** and **cool.** Thus, **puesto** and **seudonónimo,** for example, are pronounced /puesto/ and /seuðonónimo/.

v has two pronunciations. At the beginning of an utterance or after **n** (which in this position is pronounced /m/), the letter **v** is pronounced /b/, which is similar to the first consonant of English **beach, broth,** etc. In all other positions, this letter is pronounced /β/ (see **b** for interpreting that symbol). For example, in the sentence **¿Es verdad que en el anverso de la medalla se ve un pavo real?,** the second and sixth words have /b/ and the eleventh and thirteenth have /β/.

The instructions for pronouncing **b** and those for pronouncing **v** are identical (depending on the position of those letters in the utterance), as a consequence of which pairs of words like **baca** and **vaca** or **hube** and **uve** are homophones in today's Spanish and, as a further consequence of which, if you hear /b/ or /β/, you cannot tell whether it is to be represented by **b** or by **v** unless you know how to spell the word.

See also **b.**

w, which is found only in borrowings from Germanic languages and French, has several pronunciations. In several words, it is pronounced as if it were **b** or **v** and in such cases alternate spellings with **v** are found too: **wagneriano ~ vagneriano, Westfalia ~ Vestfalia.** The forms with **v** are preferable.

In at least a few words, **w** is pronounced /w/ (a sound similar to the first sound of English **win** and **won**), and for one of them an alternate spelling with **u** exists: **Malawi, Taiwán, Zimbabwe.**

In **whisky,** the letter combination **wh** is pronounced /w/ by those who want to show off their knowledge of English or, alternatively, /gw/.

x has several pronunciations. If **x** occurs before a consonant (as in **experiencia, extremidad,** and **mixto**), pronounce it /ks/. That pronunciation is probably the most frequent in words beginning with the prefix **ex-** followed by a consonant, for example **excelente,** widely pronounced /eksselente/ in Latin America, or /eksθelente/ in Castile.

If **x** occurs between vowels, you have an alternative in certain words (**examen** and **exiguo,** for example, may be pronounced with /ks/ or /gz/, but not in others (for instance, all Spanish-speakers, it seems, now pronounce **sexo** with /ks/).

At the end of a word, the pronunciation of **x** is in flux. In **ántrax, Benelux, dux, fénix, látex,** and **tórax,** /ks/ seems to be the most frequent if not universal pronunciation today, although /s/ is also heard.

At least some exceptions to those pronunciations are heard in words of Native American origin: for example, in **México** and **mexicano,** the **x** is now always pronounced /x/ (those are the spellings official and universal in Mexico; elsewhere, **Méjico** and **mejicano** are used); in **Xochimilco** (a Mexican place name), the **x** is always pronounced /s/.

Further exceptions are certain given and family names, which are found in two variants: one preserving a now archaic spelling with **x** (like **Xavier** and **Ximénez**) and the other spelled in modern fashion with **j** (**Javier** and **Jiménez**). Here, **x** is pronounced /h/, that is, just like **j.**

y has several pronunciations. In the word **y,** it is pronounced /i/ (see **i** for interpreting that symbol).

When it represents the first or last segment of a diphthong or triphthong (see "Diphthongs and Triphthongs" below), as in **ya, yegua, yunque, ley, rey, soy,** and **Paraguay,** the letter **y** is pronounced /y/ (see **ll** for interpreting that symbol).

In certain varieties of Spanish, **y** is pronounced with more occlusion, so that it has come to be close to /ʒ/ if not actually that sound (see **ll** for interpreting the latter symbol); and in still other varieties it is pronounced with so much occlusion that is has come to be close to /dʒ/ if not actually that (/dʒ/ is similar to the first consonant of English **Jacob, Jerusalem, Jew,** etc.)

Certain family names have two spelling variants, an archaic one with **y** and one spelled in modern fashion with **i** (like **Yglesias ~ Iglesias**). Here, **y** is pronounced /i/, that is, just like **i.**

z has several pronunciations. In Standard 1, you have an alternative: (1) In all positions, pronounce it /θ/ (see **c** for interpreting that symbol). Or, (2) Before the letters **b, v, d, g, l, m, n,** or **r** (whether in the same word or in the next one), pronounce it /ð/ (see **d** for interpreting that symbol), and in all other positions pronounce is /θ/.

In Standard 2, you have an alternative: (3) In all positions, pronounce it /s/ (see **c** for interpreting that symbol). Or, (4) Before the letters **b, v, d, g, l, m, n,** or **r** (whether in the same word or in the next one), pronounce it /z/, and in all other positions pronounce it /s/.

Diphthongs and Triphthongs

Spanish has fifteen diphthongs and eight triphthongs.

Eight of the diphthongs begin with a semivowel:

ia /ia/ is spelled **ya** at the beginning of a word, e.g., **desahuciar, yámbico.**

ua /ua/, e.g., **guardar.**

ie /ie/ is spelled **ye** at the beginning of a word, e.g., **agüero, bien, higiene, siete, yema.**

ue /ue/ is spelled **üe** after **g** that is not pronounced /h/, e.g., **huelga, hueste, huevo, vergüenza.**

io /io/ e.g., **biombo, piojo.** The spelling **io** at the beginning of a word is an imitation of Greek.

uo /uo/, e.g., **arduo.**

iu /iu/ is spelled **yu** at the beginning of a word, e.g., **yuca, yugo, triunfo.**

ui /ui/ (spelled **uy** in **muy**), e.g., **cuidar, muy.** For **uy** representing /uy/, see **uy** in the next section.

Take care to pronounce diphthongs beginning with a semivowel as diphthongs and not as two syllables. Thus, whereas English **barrio** has three syllables, Spanish **barrio** has two (**ba-rrio**), pronounced /barrio/.

Seven of the diphthongs end in a semivowel:

ai /ai/ is spelled **ay** at the end of most words; rarely, **ay** is found in the middle of a word, e.g., **aimará ~ aymará, hay, Raimundo, Seychelles.** If **ay** occurs before a vowel in the same word, it represents not a diphthong but /a/ + /y/, and each of those sounds belongs to a different syllable (thus, **aya** and **haya** for example are syllabified **a-ya** and **ha-ya**).

au /au/, e.g., **caudillo.**

ei is almost always pronounced /ey/ and is almost always spelled **ey** at the end of a word, e.g., **reina, rey.** A pronunciation exception is **reir,** which is pronounced as if it is spelled *reír. If **ey** occurs before a vowel in the same word, it represents not a diphthong but /e/ + /y/, and each of those sounds belongs to a different syllable (thus, **reyes** and **leyenda** for instance are syllabified **re-yes** and **le-yen-da**).

eu /eu/, e.g., **seudonónimo.**

oi is almost always pronounced /oi/ and is spelled **oy** at the end of a word, e.g., **hoy,** and in certain family names in other positions too (like **Goytisolo**). A pronunciation exception is **oir,** which is pronounced as if spelled *oír. If **oy** occurs before a vowel in the same word, it represents not a diphthong but /o/ + /y/ and each of those sounds belongs to a different syllable (thus, **Goya** is syllabified **Go-ya**).

uy, which always occurs at the end of a word, is almost always pronounced /ui/ (as in ¡**huy!, Jujuy**). The exception is **muy,** whose pronunciation is given in the previous section. If **uy** occurs before a vowel in the same word, it represents not a diphthong but /u/ + /y/ and each of those sounds belongs to a different syllable (thus, **cuyo** and **tuyas** are syllabified **cu-yo** and **tu-yas**).

The triphthongs are:
iai /iai/ e.g., **despreciáis.**
iau /iau/ e.g., **miau.**
iei /iei/ e.g., **despreciéis.**
uai /uai/ (spelled **uay** at the end of a word), e.g., **evaluáis, Uruguay.**
uau /uau/ e.g., **guau.**
uei /uei/ (spelled **uey** at the end of a word), e.g., **evaluéis, buey.**

Syllabification

Spanish is a consonant-vowel language, that is, syllables preferably end in a vowel (though many exceptions are found). Therefore, a single consonant and the vowel following it usually form a syllable or, expressed otherwise, a single consonant between two vowels usually goes with the following vowel (thus, **ba-jo, ad-he-sión**). Since **ch, ll, ñ,** and **rr** represent a single consonant, the syllabification is, for example, **mu-cha-cho, ha-llar, ni-ño, ba-rrio,** and **haz-me-rreír.**

The consonant clusters **bl, cl, dl, fl, gl, pl, tl, br, cr, dr, fr, gr, pr,** and **tr** form a syllable with the following vowel, for instance, **ha-blar, a-cla-rar, a-flo-jar, a-glo-me-rar, a-pla-zar, a-tle-ta, a-bra-zar, a-cre-di-tar, a-dre-de, a-fran-ce-sar, a-gre-gar,** and **a-pren-der.**

When representing /ʃ/, **sh** is not divided, whereas if a consonant letter + **h** is found in the middle of a word and the **h** is silent, the **h** begins a new syllable: **al-ha-ra-ca, clor-hi-dra-to, des-hi-dra-tar, in-hu-ma-ción.**

All other clusters of two consonants between vowels (including diphthongs and triphthongs) are usually divided, so that the first consonant belongs to the preceding syllable and the second consonant to the following syllable, for example, **a-cos-tar-se, ac-tuar, cuer-do, en-car-gar, es-la-vo, fras-co, Is-ra-el, llan-ta, per-di-ción, sol-da-du-ra,** and **der-vi-che.** Subject to that rule are also instances of double **c** or **n,** as in **per-fec-ción** and **en-ne-gre-cer.**

If a cluster of three or more consonants stands between vowels, the last two consonants are usually **bl, cl, fl, gl, pl, tl, br, cr, dr, fr, gr, pr,** or **tr** and they go with the following syllable, for instance, **tem-blar, ten-dré, ex-plo-tar, tem-pra-no.**

If a cluster of three or more consonants stands between vowels and if the second consonant is **s,** the **s** goes with the preceding syllable, for example **ins-tan-te** and **pers-pec-ti-va.**

If one vowel follows another and they do not constitute a diphthong (see above), they belong to separate syllables, for instance, **ma-es-tro, cre-o, le-er, to-a-lla.** Accordingly, if **i** or **u** (which represent respectively /i/ or /u/ in diphthongs and triphthongs) represents a vowel, it belongs in a separate syllable and that fact is indicated by a stress mark. Thus, **ahínco** (three syllables: **a-hín-co**), **búho** (two syllables: **bú-ho**), **desahúcio** (four syllables: **de-sa-hú-cio**), **traído** (three syllables: **tra-í-do**), **prohíbo** (three syllables: **pro-hí-bo**), **Raúl** (two syllables: **Ra-úl**), **haría** (three syllables: **ha-rí-a**), **haríais** (three syllables: **ha-rí-ais**), etc.

If **y** is preceded and followed by a vowel, it forms a diphthong with the following one and therefore belongs in the following syllable, for instance **ca-yó, tu-yo, cre-yó.** In fact, all diphthongs and triphthongs (see the list above) form syllables of their own. In contrast, identical contiguous vowels (as in **creer**) and vowels that do not form diphthongs or triphthongs (as in **leal**), as well as diphthongs or triphthongs dissolved by the stress mark (see the examples from **ahínco** to **haríais** in the previous paragraph), form separate syllables (thus, **cre-er, le-al,** etc.).

It is permissible but not obligatory to set aside the foregoing rules in the case of prefixes, which one may consider as forming syllables of their own (whether or not such would be the case if the rules were followed) or which one may subject to the rules. For example, **ab-ro-ga-ción** or **a-bro** . . ., **des-a-bro-char** or **de-sa** . . ., **ex-a-cer-ba-ción** or **e-xa** . . ., **sub-li-mar** or **su-bli** . . . (in each pair, the first variant reflects treatment of the prefix as a syllable in its own right, no matter what the rules should require, and the second variant shows syllabification when the rules are applied). The same applies to solid compounds: **no-so-tros, vos-o-tras** or **vo-so-tras**, etc.

The foregoing paragraph notwithstanding, the rules must be followed with respect to a succession of three consonant letters, the second of which is **s**, in which case **s** belongs with the preceding, not the following letter (thus, as already noted, **ins-tan-te, pers-pect-ti-va**, not **in-st** . . ., **per-sp** . . .) and with respect to prefixes if the first letter immediately following them is **h** (thus, **des-ha-cer** and **des-hi-dra-tar**, not **de-sha** . . . or **de-shi** . . .).

Stress

Most Spanish words have only one primary stress, which can be determined from the spelling according to these rules:

(1) If a word is spelled with a stress mark, stress the syllable in which it is found (like **águila, bíceps, fórceps, hablarán, Martínez**).

(2) If a word contains no stress mark:

[2.A] Stress the last syllable if the word ends in:

    [2.A.i] a vowel letter + **y** (like **convoy, Uruguay, virrey**),

    [2.A.ii] a consonant letter other than **n** or **s** (like **consentir, David, lateral**),

    [2.A.iii] **n** not preceded by a vowel letter (like **Isern**),

    [2.A.iv] **s** not preceded by a vowel letter (like **Fontanals, Casals**).

[2.B] Stress the next-to-last syllable if the word ends in:

    [2.B.i] a vowel letter other than **y** (like **casi, habla, hable, hablo, fatuo, patria, sitio**),

    [2.B.ii] a vowel letter + **n** (like **consienten, hablan**),

    [2.B.iii] a vowel letter + **s** (like **consientes, hablas**).

The triplets **árbitro, arbitro, arbitró; público, publico, publicó; término, termino, terminó; tráfago, trafago, trafagó;** and **válido, valido, validó** illustrate several possibilities.

Miscellaneous

It is noted above that /m/ + /m/, /n/ + /n/, /p/ + /p/, and /s/ + /s/ are respectively reduced to one /m/, /p/, and /s/. Since the number of instances of /s/ + /s/ is not the same in all varieties of Spanish, the number of reductions to /s/ varies accordingly. For example, **absceso** is pronounced /apseso/ only where **c** before **e** (or **i**) is pronounced /s/ (otherwise it is rendered /apθeso/); see also **excelente** in the remarks on **x**.

Reduction of identical contiguous sounds (whether vowels or consonants) is widespread in Spanish, whether within a word or between two words. Thus, /a/ + /a/ is reduced to /a/ both in the word **portaaviones** and in a phrase like **a ambos**; or, /e/ + /e/ is reduced to /e/ in the word **sobreexcitar**. The spellings **guardagujas, guardalmacén, remplazar, sobrentender**, etc., are in fact used too and they are preferable. In many cases, only spellings reflecting a reduction are now found, for example, **aprensión, prensil,** and **reprensible** (contrast those forms with their English cognates: **apprehension, prehensile,** and **reprehensible**).

English, especially British English, is a stress-timed language (it has a rhythm in which stressed syllables tend to occur at regular intervals of time, regardless of the number of intervening unstressed syllables) whereas Spanish is a syllable-timed language (with rhythm in which syllables are approximately equal in duration and thus tend to follow one another at regular intervals). Consequently, speakers of English, especially British English, tend to reduce unstressed syllables (as in the British pronunciation of **momentary, pattern, secretary**), whereas Spanish-speakers tend to pronounce each syllable distinctly and do not often slur over any of them. Spanish-speakers thus often react to English-accented Spanish as one in which **se comen las vocales** 'the vowels are swallowed up' and speakers of English (especially British English) tend to react to Spanish-accented English as "overly precise." To get an idea of the difference between stress- and syllable-timed languages, contrast American and British pronunciations of **momentary** and **secretary:** Americans pronounce each syllable of those words with more or less the same degree of distinctiveness, whereas the British pronounce only the first syllable distinctly and slur over the others; thus, American English is more syllable-timed and British English more stress-timed. To pronounce Spanish correctly, English-speakers should therefore give each vowel its full value.

Formerly, in the Spanish-speaking world, the pronunciation and spelling of words borrowed from other languages were routinely changed so that they conformed to Spanish norms. Thus for example, **bowline > bolina, coolie > culi, goal > gol,** and **kerosene > kerosen.**

Now, however, the trend is to retain non-Spanish spellings, though not necessarily non-Spanish pronunciations, with the result that the good fit between the Spanish spelling and pronunciation is in certain words absent.

List of Abbreviations Used in This Dictionary

a adjective
Abbr. abbreviation
acc accusative
adv adverb
Aer. aeronautics
Agr. agriculture
Anat. anatomy
Archit. architecture
Archeol. archeology
art. article
art art
Astron. astronomy
Astrol. astrology
Auto. automobiles
aux auxiliary
Biol. biology
Bot. botany
Cards. card games
Chem. chemistry
Com. commerce
Compar. comparative
condit conditional
conjunc conjunction
Culin. culinary
Dance. dancing
dat dative
dim diminutive
Eccl. ecclesiastical
Educ. education
Elec. electricity
Engin. engineering
Ent. entomology
Euph. euphemism
f feminine
Fig. figurative
Fig. Inf. used
  figuratively in
  informal speech
  or writing
fut future
gen generally; genitive

Geog. geography
Geol. geology
Geom. geometry
Gram. grammar
Gym. gymnastics
Herald. heraldry
Hist. history
Ichth. ichthyology
imperf imperfect
impers impersonal
indic indicative
indef art indefinite
  article
Inf. informal
infin infinitive
insep inseparable
interj interjection,
  exclamation
interr interrogative
Ironic. ironical
irr irregular
Law. law
Ling. linguistics
Lit. literature
m masculine
Mas. masonry
Math. mathematics
Mech. mechanics
Med. medical
Metall. metallurgy
mf masculine or femi-
  nine
Mil. military
Mineral. mineralogy
Mus. music
Myth. mythology
n noun
Naut. nautical
Nav. naval
neut neuter
Obs obsolete

Opt. optics
Ornith. ornithology
part participle
Pers. personal; person
Pharm. pharmacy
Philos. philosophy
Phonet. phonetics
Photo. photography
Phys. physics
Physiol. physiology
pl plural
Poet. poetic
Polit. political
Polit. Econ. political
  economy
poss possessive
prep preposition
pres present
Print. printing
pron pronoun
Psychol. psychology
Radio. radio
Rail. railway
Sew. sewing
sing singular
Spirit. spiritualism
Sports. sports
subjunc subjunctive
Superl superlative
Surg. surgery
Surv. surveying
Tan. tanning
Theat. theater
Theol. theology
v aux auxiliary verb
vi intransitive verb
vr reflexive verb
vt transitive verb
West. Hem. Western
  Hemispheric Spanish
Zool. zoology

Spanish-English
Dictionary

A

a /a/ *f,* name of the letter A

a /a/ *prep* to; at; on; by; in, into; up to; according to; if, etc. 1. Denotes the direct complement of verb before objects representing specified persons or animals, personified nouns, pronouns referring to specific persons (**alguien, entrambos, cualquiera,** etc.), demonstrative or relative pronouns, collective nouns representing persons (**el público, la muchedumbre,** etc.), names of countries, cities, rivers, etc., except where these invariably take the def. art., e.g. *Dejé a Varsovia,* I left Warsaw, *but Dejé el Perú,* I left Peru. 2. Introduces indirect obj. when this is a noun governed by a verb implying motion, or an emphatic pers. pron., e.g. *Nos conviene a ti y a mí,* It suits both you and me. It is also used before indirect obj. to avoid ambiguity when there is both an indirect and direct obj. 3. Denotes the complement of verb when this is an infin., e.g. *Enseñó a pintar a María,* He taught Mary to paint. 4. Indicates direction or destination, e.g. *Vamos a Edimburgo,* We are going to Edinburgh. 5. Signifies location, or point of time when action takes place, e.g. *Vinieron a las doce.* They came at twelve o'clock. 6. Describes position of persons or things, e.g. *Se sentaron a la puerta,* They sat down at the door. *La casa queda a la derecha,* The house is on the right. 7. Denotes interval of time or place between one thing and another, e.g. *de tres a cinco de la tarde,* from three to five in the afternoon, *de calle a calle,* from street to street. 8. Expresses manner of action, e.g. *a la francesa,* in the French way, *bordado a mano,* embroidered by hand. 9. Indicates rate or price, e.g. *a cuatro pesetas la libra,* at four pesetas the lb. 10. Indicates difference or comparison, e.g. *Va mucho de querer a hacer,* There's a difference between wishing and doing. 11. Sometimes is synonymous with *hasta, según, hacia* and governs almost all parts of speech. Has many idiomatic uses. 12. Before infin. sometimes has conditional sense, e.g. *A haber sabido las noticias no lo hubiéramos hecho,* If we had heard the news we would not have done it. 13. With nouns and adjectives forms adverbial phrases, e.g. *poco a poco,* little by little, *a veces,* sometimes, *a ciegas,* blindly, etc. *A* + *el* becomes *al,* e.g. *al rey,* to the king. *Al* + infin. means when or on, e.g. *al marcharme yo,* when I left (on my leaving)

abacería /aβaθe'ria/ *f,* grocery shop

abacero /aβa'θero; aβa'sero/ **(-ra)** *n* grocer

ábaco /'aβako/ *m, Archit.* abacus; counting frame

abad /a'βað/ *m,* abbot

abadesa /aβa'ðesa/ *f,* abbess

abadía /aβa'ðia/ *f,* abbacy; abbey

abajamiento /a,βaha'miento/ *m,* lowering; letting down

abajar /aβa'har/ *vt* to lower

abajo /a'βaho/ *adv* under; underneath; below; down. Used immediately after noun in adverbial phrases, e.g. *cuesta a., escalera a.,* downhill, downstairs —*interj* Down with! e.g., *¡A. el rey!* Down with the king! *venirse a.,* to fall down; *Fig.* collapse

abalanzamiento /aβa,lanθa'miento; aβa,lansa-'miento/ *m,* balancing; rushing upon; dashing

abalanzar /aβalan'θar; aβalan'sar/ *vt* to balance; impel violently; —*vr* throw oneself upon; attack, rush upon; *(with prep a)* rush into, risk. **Se abalanzó hacia ellos,** He rushed toward them

abalorio /aβa'lorio/ *m,* glass bead; bead work

abanderado /aβande'raðo/ *m,* standardbearer; (Argentina) valedictorian

abanderar /aβande'rar/ *vt* to register (a ship)

abanderizar /aβanderi'θar; aβanderi'sar/ *vt* to organize in groups; —*vr* band together

abandonado /aβando'naðo/ *a* deserted; forlorn; helpless; indolent, careless; slovenly

abandonamiento /a,βandona'miento/ *m,* desertion; forlornness; helplessness; carelessness; slovenliness

abandonar /aβando'nar/ *vt* to forsake, desert; neglect; leave; give up; renounce; —*vr* neglect oneself; grow discouraged; *(with prep a)* give oneself over to

abandono /aβan'dono/ *m,* abandonment; defenselessness; forlornness; dilapidation; renunciation; neglect; slovenliness; debauchery

abanicar /aβani'kar/ *vt* to fan

abanico /aβa'niko/ *m,* fan; anything fan-shaped; *Inf.* sword; railway signal; *Naut.* derrick. **en a.,** fanshaped

abaniqueo /aβani'keo/ *m,* fanning; swinging; oscillation; gesticulation

abaratar /aβara'tar/ *vt* to cheapen, make less expensive; —*vr* fall in price

abarca /a'βarka/ *f,* leather sandal, worn chiefly in the Basque provinces

abarcador /aβarka'ðor/ **(-ra)** *n* one who clasps or embraces; monopolist

abarcadura /aβarka'ðura/ *f,* **abarcamiento** /aβarka-'miento/ *m,* inclusion; scope

abarcar /aβar'kar/ *vt* to clasp, encircle; include, comprise; undertake, attempt; monopolize

abarquillar /aβarki'ʎar; aβarki'yar/ *vt* to shape into a roll; curl

abarracar /aβarra'kar/ **(se)** *vi* and *vr Mil.* to go into barracks

abarrancadero /aβarranka'ðero/ *m,* rough road; ravine, precipice; *Fig.* difficult situation

abarrancar /aβarran'kar/ *vt* to ditch; make a ravine; —*vr* fall into a pit; stick (in the mud, etc.); get into difficulties; *Naut.* run aground

abastar /aβas'tar/ see **abastecer**

abastecedor /aβasteθe'ðor; aβastese'ðor/ **(-ra)** *a* provisioning, supplying —*n* provider; purveyor, supplier; caterer

abastecer /aβaste'θer; aβaste'ser/ *vt irr* to supply, provide; purvey. See **conocer**

abastecimiento /aβasteθi'miento; aβastesi'miento/ *m,* providing; supply, provision; catering; supplies

abasto /a'βasto/ *m,* provisions, food; *Com.* supply —*adv* plentifully, abundantly

abatanar /aβata'nar/ *vt* to full (cloth)

abate /a'βate/ *m,* abbé

abatido /aβa'tiðo/ *a* dejected, depressed; spiritless; discouraged; crushed, humbled; *Com.* depreciated

abatimiento /aβati'miento/ *m,* dejection, depression; humiliation; discouragement; falling; lowering; (*Aer. Naut.*) drift

abatir /aβa'tir/ *vt* to knock down; overthrow; demolish; lower, take down; droop; humiliate; discourage; *Naut.* dismantle; —*vi* (*Naut. Aer.*) drift; —*vr* be despondent, despair; humble oneself; swoop down (of birds). **a. el vuelo,** to fly down

ABC /aβe'θe; aβe'se/ *m,* ABCs (e.g. *el ABC de la física,* the ABCs of physics)

abdicación /aβðika'θion; aβðika'sion/ *f,* abdication

abdicar /aβði'kar/ *vt* to abdicate; revoke, cancel; give up (rights, opinions)

abdomen /aβ'ðomen/ *m,* abdomen

abdominal /aβðomi'nal/ *a* abdominal

abecé /aβe'θe; aβe'se/ *m,* ABCs

abecedario /aβeθe'ðario; aβese'ðario/ *m,* ABC, alphabet; reading book, primer

abedul /aβe'ðul/ *m,* birch tree; birch wood

abeja /a'βeha/ *f,* bee. **a. maestra,** queen bee. **a. obrera,** worker

abejar /aβe'har/ *m,* beehive

abejero /aβe'hero/ **(-ra)** *n* beekeeper

abejón /aβe'hon/ *m,* drone; hornet

abejorro /aβe'horro/ *m,* bumblebee

abellacar /aβeʎa'kar; aβeya'kar/ *vt* to make a rogue of; —*vr* become a rogue

aberración /aβerra'θion; aβerra'sion/ *f,* deviation; error, lapse; (*Astron. Phys. Biol.*) aberration

abertura /aβer'tura/ *f,* opening; aperture, gap, hole; fissure, cleft; mountain pass; naturalness, frankness

abeto /a'βeto/ *m,* yew-leaved fir

abetunado /aβetu'naðo/ a bituminous

abiertamente /aβierta'mente/ adv openly; frankly.

abierto /a'βierto/ a free, unobstructed; open, not enclosed; open, full-blown (flowers); frank, sincere —adv openly

abigarrado /aβiga'rraðo/ a variegated; varied; speckled

abigarrar /aβiga'rrar/ vt to variegate; vary; speckle; fleck; spot; dapple

abigotado /aβigo'taðo/ a having a thick moustache

abintestato /aβintes'tato/ a Law. intestate

abiselar /aβisel'ar/ vt to bevel

abismal /aβis'mal/ a abysmal

abismar /aβis'mar/ vt to plunge into an abyss; depress, sadden; —vr despair; be plunged in thought, be abstracted; be amazed

abismo /a'βismo/ m, chasm, abyss, gulf; hell

abjuración /aβhura'θion; aβhura'sion/ f, abjuration

abjurar /aβhu'rar/ vt to forswear, retract

ablactar /aβlak'tar/ vt to wean

ablandamiento /aβlanda'miento/ m, softening; placating

ablandante /aβlan'dante/ a softening; placatory

ablandar /aβlan'dar/ vt to soften; appease, placate; loosen; relax; —vi and vr be softened; be appeased; grow less stormy; (elements) decrease in force

ablandecer /aβlande'θer; aβlande'ser/ vt irr to soften. See **conocer**

ablución /aβlu'θion; aβlu'sion/ f, ablution

abnegación /aβnega'θion; aβnega'sion/ f, abnegation, self-sacrifice

abnegado /aβne'gaðo/ a self-sacrificing

abnegarse /aβne'garse/ vr irr to deprive oneself, sacrifice oneself. See **cegar**

abobado /aβo'βaðo/ a bewildered; foolish-looking, silly

abobar /aβo'βar/ vt to daze, bewilder; make stupid

abocado /aβo'kaðo/ a full-flavored, pleasant (of wine)

abocar /aβo'kar/ vt to seize with the mouth; bring nearer; transfer (contents of one jug to another); —vr meet, assemble; —vi Naut. enter (a channel, port, etc.). **abocarse (con...),** to contact (...), get in touch (with...)

abocetado /aβoθe'taðo; aβose'taðo/ a Art. unfinished; sketchy

abochornado /aβotʃor'naðo/ a flushed (of the face); ashamed; embarrassed

abochornar /aβotʃor'nar/ vt to overheat, make flushed; shame; embarrass; —vr (plants) dry up

abofetear /aβofete'ar/ vt to slap, hit; buffet

abogacía /aβoga'θia; aβoga'sia/ f, legal profession; practice of law; advocacy

abogado /aβo'gaðo/ (-da) n lawyer

abogar /aβo'gar/ vi to defend at law; intercede for; advocate, champion

abolengo /aβo'leŋgo/ m, lineage, descent, family; inheritance

abolición /aβoli'θion; aβoli'sion/ f, abolition

abolir /aβo'lir/ vt to abolish; cancel; annul

abolladura /aβoʎa'ðura; aβoya'ðura/ f, bruise; dent; embossment

abollar /aβo'ʎar; aβo'yar/ vt to bruise; dent

abollonar /aβoʎo'nar; aβoyo'nar/ vt to emboss, do raised work on; —vr (vines) sprout

abombado /aβom'baðo/ a convex; domed

abombar /aβom'bar/ vt to make convex; Inf. deafen, bewilder; —vr begin to putrefy; get intoxicated

abominable /aβomi'naβle/ a abominable

abominación /aβomina'θion; aβomina'sion/ f, abomination; loathing, detestation

abominar /aβomi'nar/ vt to abominate, loathe, detest

abonable /aβo'naβle/ a subscribable; payable

abonado /aβo'naðo/ (-da) a trustworthy, reliable; ready, prepared, inclined —n subscriber; season ticket holder (for concerts, etc.)

abonanzar /aβonan'θar; aβonan'sar/ vi impers to clear up, be fine (weather)

abonar /aβo'nar/ vt to guarantee; go surety for; improve, better; manure; ratify, confirm; pay; Com.

place to the credit of; —vr subscribe, become a subscriber; take out (season tickets, etc.)

abonaré /aβona're/ m, Com. due bill; promissory note, I.O.U.

abono /a'βono/ m, subscription; voucher; guarantee; manure. **a. verde,** leaf mold. **en a. de,** in payment of; in support of

aboquillado /aβoki'ʎaðo; aβoki'yaðo/ a tipped (of cigarettes)

abordaje /aβor'ðahe/ m, Naut. boarding of a ship

abordar /aβor'ðar/ vt Naut. to board a ship; Naut. collide, run into; accost, tackle; undertake; —vi Naut. put into port

aborigen /aβor'ihen/ a aboriginal

aborígenes /aβo'rihenes/ m pl, aborigines

aborrachado /aβorra'tʃaðo/ a bright red; highly colored; flushed

aborrascarse /aβorras'karse/ vr to grow stormy

aborrecedor /aβorreθe'ðor; aβorrese'ðor/ (-ra) a hateful, loather

aborrecer /aβorre'θer; aβorre'ser/ vt irr to hate, loathe; desert offspring (animals, birds). See **conocer**

aborrecible /aβorre'θiβle; aβorre'siβle/ a hateful, detestable

aborrecimiento /aβorreθi'miento; aβorresi'miento/ m, hate, detestation; dislike

abortar /aβor'tar/ vt to abort; foil (a plot); —vi Med. miscarry; fail, go awry

abortivo /aβor'tiβo/ a abortive

aborto /a'βorto/ m, abortion; miscarriage; monster; failure

abotagarse /aβota'garse/ vr to swell up, become bloated

abotonador /aβotona'ðor/ m, button-hook

abotonar /aβoto'nar/ vt to button; —vi bud, sprout

abozalar /aβoθa'lar; aβosa'lar/ vt to muzzle

abra /'aβra/ f, cove, small bay; narrow gorge; fissure, cleft

abrasador /aβrasa'ðor/ a burning, flaming

abrasamiento /aβrasa'miento/ m, burning; ardor, heat

abrasar /aβra'sar/ vt to burn; dry up, parch (plants); squander, waste; shame; —vi burn; —vr be very hot, glow; burn with passion

abrasión /aβra'sion/ f, abrasion

abrasivo /aβra'siβo/ a and m, abrasive

abrazadera /aβraθa'ðera; aβrasa'ðera/ f, clasp; clamp

abrazamiento /aβraθa'miento; aβrasa'miento/ m, embracing

abrazar /aβra'θar; aβra'sar/ vt to embrace, clasp in one's arms; follow, adopt; engage in; seize, take advantage of; comprise, include; surround; take in hand; clamp; clasp. **abrazarse a,** to clutch, hang on to

abrazo /a'βraθo; a'βraso/ m, embrace

abrelatas /aβre'latas/ m, can opener

abrevadero /aβreβa'ðero/ m, watering place (for cattle)

abrevar /aβre'βar/ vt to water cattle; irrigate, water

abreviación /aβreβia'θion; aβreβia'sion/ f, abbreviation, shortening; summary; hastening

abreviador /aβreβia'ðor/ m, abridger, condenser

abreviar /aβre'βiar/ vt to abbreviate, shorten; hasten, accelerate; condense, abridge. **a. tiempo,** to save time. **Y para a....,** And, to cut a long story short...

abreviatura /aβreβia'tura/ f, abbreviation, contraction; shorthand

abridor /aβri'ðor/ m, opener; ear-ring (for keeping holes in ears open). **a. de guantes,** glove-stretcher. **a. de láminas,** engraving needle. **a. de latas,** can opener

abridura /aβri'ðura/ f, (act of) opening (e.g. of a trunk)

abrigada /aβri'gaða/ f, **abrigadero** m, sheltered place

abrigar /aβri'gar/ vt to shelter, protect (against the cold, etc.); defend, help; hold (opinions); nurse (a hope, etc.); cover; —vr take shelter; wrap oneself up

abrigo /a'βrigo/ m, shelter; defense; protection; help; sheltered place; wrap, coat; Naut. haven

abril /a'βril/ m, April; youth; pl Poet. years

abrillantar /aβriʎan'tar; aβriyan'tar/ vt to cut in

facets like a diamond; polish, burnish; cause to shine; *Fig.* improve, add luster to

abrir /a'βrir/ *vt* to open; reveal; unlock; slide the bolt of; extend, spread out; cleave; engrave; clear (the way, etc.); begin; head, lead; separate; dig; inaugurate —*vi* unfold (flowers); expand; **en un abrir y cerrar de ojos,** in the twinkling of an eye, in the wink of an eye; —*vr* open; expand; (*with con*) confide in. **a. el camino (a...),** to pave the way (for...). **abrirse camino,** to make one's way; **abrirse paso a codazos,** to elbow one's way out, (or through)

abrochador /aβrotʃa'ðor/ *m,* button-hook

abrochamiento /aβrotʃa'miento/ *m,* buttoning; fastening

abrochar /aβro'tʃar/ *vt* to button; fasten, clasp; hook up (a dress, etc.); buckle

abrogación /aβroga'θion; aβroga'sion/ *f,* repeal, annulment

abrogar /aβro'gar/ *vt* to repeal, annul

abrojo /a'βroho/ *m,* thistle; *Bot.* caltrops; thorn, prickle; *pl* submerged rocks in sea

abroncar /aβron'kar/ *vt Inf.* to bore, annoy

abrumador /aβruma'ðor/ *a* burdensome, crushing, oppressive; troublesome, tiresome; exhausting

abrumar /aβru'mar/ *vt* to weigh down; overwhelm, oppress; weary, exhaust; —*vr* grow misty

abrupto /a'βrupto/ *a* steep; rough, broken (ground); rugged

absceso /aβs'θeso; aβs'sseso/ *m,* abscess

absentismo /aβsen'tismo/ *m,* absenteeism

ábside /'aβsiðe/ *mf, Archit.* apse. *m, Astron.* apsis

absolución /aβsolu'θion; aβsolu'sion/ *f,* (*Eccl.* and *Law.*) absolution; remission, pardon

absoluta /aβso'luta/ *f, Mil.* discharge

absolutismo /aβsolu'tismo/ *m,* absolutism

absolutista /aβsolu'tista/ *mf* absolutist

absoluto /aβso'luto/ *a* absolute; categorical; *Inf.* despotic. **en a.,** absolutely

absolver /aβsol'βer/ *vt irr* to absolve; acquit (of a charge). *Law.* **a. de la instancia,** to dismiss the case. See **mover**

absorbente /aβsor'βente/ *a* and *m,* absorbent

absorber /aβsor'βer/ *vt* to absorb; consume, use up; attract, hold (the attention, etc.); imbibe

absorción /aβsor'θion; aβsor'sion/ *f,* absorption

absortar /aβsor'tar/ *vt* to amaze, dumbfound

absorto /aβ'sorto/ *a* amazed, astounded; abstracted, lost in thought

abstemio /aβs'temio/ *a* abstemious

abstención /aβsten'θion; aβsten'sion/ *f,* abstention

abstenerse /aβste'nerse/ *vr irr* to refrain; abstain. See **tener**

abstinencia /aβsti'nenθia; aβsti'nensia/ *f,* abstinence; fasting

abstinente /aβsti'nente/ *a* abstemious; temperate

abstracción /aβstrak'θion; aβstrak'sion/ *f,* abstraction; preoccupation; absent-mindedness

abstracto /aβ'strakto/ *a* abstract. **en a.,** in the abstract

abstraer /aβstra'er/ *vt irr* to abstract; consider separately; —*vi* (*with de*) do without, exclude; —*vr* be preoccupied; let one's thoughts wander. See **traer**

abstraído /aβstra'iðo/ *a* retired, recluse; preoccupied; absent-minded

abstruso /aβ'struso/ *a* abstruse

absurdidad /aβsurði'ðað/ *f,* absurdity; folly, nonsense

absurdo /aβ'surðo/ *a* ridiculous, absurd. *m,* piece of folly, nonsense

abuchear /aβutʃe'ar/ *vt vi* to boo, hoot, jeer

abuela /a'βuela/ *f,* grandmother; old woman, dame

abuelo /a'βuelo/ *m,* grandfather; ancestor (gen. *pl*); old man; *pl* grandparents

abulia /a'βulia/ *f,* lack of will-power, abulia

abúlico /a'βuliko/ *a* abulic, lacking will-power

abultado /aβul'taðo/ *a* bulky, large; voluminous; exaggerated

abultamiento /aβulta'miento/ *m,* bulkiness; enlargement, increase; mound; exaggeration

abultar /aβul'tar/ *vt* to enlarge, increase; exaggerate; model in rough (sculpture); —*vi* be bulky; be large

abundancia /aβun'danθia; aβun'dansia/ *f,* abundance, plenty

abundante /aβun'dante/ *a* abundant, plentiful; abounding (in)

abundar /aβun'dar/ *vi* to be plentiful, abound

abundoso /aβun'doso/ *a* See **abundante**

aburrido /aβu'rriðo/ *a* boring, tedious, dull; tired, weary

aburrimiento /aβurri'miento/ *m,* boredom, dullness; wearisomeness, tediousness

aburrir /aβu'rrir/ *vt* to bore; *Inf.* spend (time, money); (birds) desert the nest; —*vr* grow bored; be weary

abusar /aβu'sar/ *vi* to abuse; exceed one's rights, go too far; (*with de*) take advantage of

abusivo /aβu'siβo/ *a* abusive

abuso /a'βuso/ *m,* abuse. **a. de confianza,** abuse of trust

abyección /aβyek'θion; aβyek'sion/ *f,* degradation, misery; abjectness, servility

abyecto /aβ'yekto/ *a* abject, wretched; servile

acá /a'ka/ *adv* hither, here; at this time, now. **a. y acullá,** hither and thither. **desde ayer a.,** from yesterday until now

acabable /aka'βaβle/ *a* terminable, finishable; achievable

acabado /aka'βaðo/ *a* complete; perfect; expert, consummate; old, worn out; ill, infirm. *m,* finish

acabamiento /akaβa'miento/ *m,* finishing, completion; end; death, decease

acabar /aka'βar/ *vt* to end, terminate; finish; complete, perfect; kill; (*with con*) destroy, finish off; suppress; squander; —*vi* end; die; be destroyed; (*with de* + *infin*) to have just (e.g. *Acaba de salir,* He has just gone out); —*vr* end, be exhausted, run out of (e.g. *Se le acabó el dinero,* His money ran out); fade, grow weak; be destroyed. **Se les acabaron las dudas,** Their doubts were cleared up. **a. de desconcertar,** to nonplus completely; **a. de decidirse,** to come to a decision; **a. de saber,** to finally learn

acacia /a'kaθia; a'kasia/ *f, Bot.* acacia

academia /aka'ðemia/ *f,* academy

academicismo /akaðemi'θismo; akaðemi'sismo/ *m,* academicism, academism

académico /aka'ðemiko/ **(-ca)** *a* academic —*n* academician. **a. de la lengua,** member of the Royal Spanish Academy

acaecer /akae'θer; akae'ser/ *vi irr* to happen, occur. See **conocer**

acaecimiento /akaeθi'miento; akaesi'miento/ *m,* happening, occurrence, event

acalambrarse /akalam'brarse/ (muscle) to contract with cramps. **Estar acalambrado,** to have cramps

acalenturarse /akalentu'rarse/ *vr* to grow feverish

acallar /aka'ʎar; aka'yar/ *vt* to quieten, hush; soothe, appease

acalorado /akalo'raðo/ *a* hot; fervent; *Fig.* heated

acaloramiento /akalora'miento/ *m,* excitement, agitation, vehemence; ardor

acalorar /akalo'rar/ *vt* to warm; aid, encourage; excite, stimulate; stir, move (to enthusiasm); inflame, rouse; tire (by exercise); —*vr* grow hot; become agitated or excited; become heated (arguments)

acamar /aka'mar/ *vt* to lay flat (plants by the wind); —*vr* be flattened (plants); lie down (animals); go rotten (fruit)

acampar /akam'par/ *vi* and *vt* to encamp

acanalar /akana'lar/ *vt* to groove; striate, flute; corrugate; furrow, channel

acantilado /akanti'laðo/ *a* steep, precipitous; shelving (ocean-bed). *m,* cliff

acanto /a'kanto/ *m,* (*Archit. Bot.*) acanthus

acantonamiento /akantona'miento/ *m,* billeting; cantonment

acantonar /akanto'nar/ *vt* to billet or quarter troops

acaparador /akapara'ðor/ **(-ra)** *n* monopolist

acaparar /akapa'rar/ *vt Com.* to monopolize, corner; seize, take possession of

acápite /a'kapite/ *m, West. Hem.* new paragraph

acaracolado /akarako'laðo/ *a* spiral, winding, twisting

acardenalar /akarðena'lar/ *vt* to bruise; —*vr* be bruised; be covered with livid marks

acarear /akare'ar/ *vt* to face; face up to, meet with courage

acariciador /akariθia'ðor; akarisia'ðor/ **(-ra)** *a* caressing, loving —*n* fondler

acariciar /akari'θiar; akari'siar/ *vt* to caress; brush, touch lightly; cherish, treat affectionately; toy with (a suggestion)

acarreador /akarrea'ðor/ **(-ra)** *n* carrier, carter

acarreamiento, acarreo /akarrea'miento, aka'reo/ *m*, cartage, carting; transport, carriage; occasioning

acarrear /akarre'ar/ *vt* to cart, transport; occasion, bring (gen. evil). **La guerra acarreó la carestía,** The war brought scarcity

acartonado /akarto'naðo/ *a* shriveled; shrunken; of cardboard; *Fig.* forced (dialogue)

acaso /a'kaso/ *m*, chance —*adv* by chance; perhaps, perchance. **por si a.,** in case (e.g. *Por si a. venga,* In case he comes)

acatable /aka'taβle/ *a* venerable, worthy

acatadamente /akataða'mente/ *adv* with respect, humbly

acatamiento /akata'miento/ *m*, respect; reverence; observance

acatar /aka'tar/ *vt* to treat with respect, honor, revere; observe

acatarrarse /akata'rrarse/ *vr* to catch a cold

acaudalado /akauða'laðo/ *a* wealthy, well-to-do

acaudalar /akauða'lar/ *vt* to make money; hoard up wealth; acquire (learning, etc.)

acaudillar /akauði'ʎar; akauði'yar/ *vt Mil.* to command, lead; head (a party, etc.)

acceder /akθe'ðer; akse'ðer/ *vi* (*with prep a*) to concede, grant; accede to, agree to

accesibilidad /ak,θesiβili'ðað; ak,sesiβili'ðað/ *f*, accessibility; approachableness

accesible /akθe'siβle; akse'siβle/ *a* accessible; approachable

accesión /akθe'sion; akse'sion/ *f*, agreement, acquiescence; accession; accessory; feverish attack

acceso /ak'θeso; ak'seso/ *m*, access; paroxysm, outburst; *Med.* attack

accesorio /akθe'sorio; akse'sorio/ *a* accessory

accesorios /akθe'sorios; akse'sorios/ *m pl*, accessories; *Theat.* properties

accidentado /akθiðen'taðo; aksiðen'taðo/ *a* rough, uneven; stormy, troubled (life, etc.)

accidental /akθiðen'tal; aksiðen'tal/ *a* accidental; *m*, *Mus.* accidental

accidentar /akθiðen'tar; aksiðen'tar/ *vt* to cause (someone) an accident; —*vr* be the victim of an accident; be seized by a fit

accidente /akθi'ðente; aksi'ðente/ *m*, chance; accident, mishap; illness, indisposition; *Med.* fit; *Gram.* accidence; *Mus.* accidental. **a. del trabajo,** accident at work. **por a.,** by chance, accidentally

acción /ak'θion; ak'sion/ *f*, action; battle; skirmish; *Mech.* drive; *Com.* share; gesture; lawsuit; *Lit.* action (of play, etc.); *Art.* posture, pose. **a. de gracias,** thanksgiving; *Com.* **a. liberada,** paid-up share. **a. privilegiada,** preference share

accionar /akθio'nar; aksio'nar/ *vi* to gesture, gesticulate

accionista /akθio'nista; aksio'nista/ *mf Com.* shareholder

acechar /aθe'tʃar; ase'tʃar/ *vt* to spy upon, watch; lie in ambush for

acecho /a'θetʃo; a'setʃo/ *m*, spying upon, watch; waylaying, ambush. **al a.,** in ambush; on the watch

acechona /aθe'tʃona; ase'tʃona/ *f*, waylaying; ambush

acecinar /aθeθi'nar; asesi'nar/ *vt* to salt and dry (meat); —*vr* (persons) wither, dry up

acedar /aθe'ðar; ase'ðar/ *vt* to make bitter, sour; embitter, displease; —*vr* turn sour; wither (plants)

acedía /aθe'ðia; ase'ðia/ *f*, acidity; heartburn

acedo /a'θeðo; a'seðo/ *a* sour, acid; *Fig.* harsh, disagreeable

acefalía /aθefa'lia; asefa'lia/ *f*, acephalia, headlessness

acéfalo /a'θefalo; a'sefalo/ *a* acephalous

aceitar /aθei'tar; asei'tar/ *vt* to oil, lubricate; rub with oil

aceite /a'θeite; a'seite/ *m*, olive oil; oil. **a. de hígado**

de bacalao, cod-liver oil. **a. de linaza,** linseed oil. **a. de ricino,** castor-oil. **a. de trementina,** oil of turpentine

aceitera /aθei'tera; asei'tera/ *f*, woman who sells oil; oil can; oil bottle; *pl* cruet

aceitero /aθei'tero; asei'tero/ *m*, oil seller —*a* oil

aceitoso /aθei'toso; asei'toso/ *a* oily

aceituna /aθei'tuna; asei'tuna/ *f*, *Bot.* olive

aceitunado /aθeitu'naðo; aseitu'naðo/ *a* olive-colored

aceitunero /aθeitu'nero; aseitu'nero/ **(-ra)** *n* olive picker; olive seller. *m*, warehouse for storing olives

aceituno /aθei'tuno; asei'tuno/ *m*, olive tree

aceleración /aθelera'θion; aselera'sion/ *f*, speed, haste; acceleration

aceleradamente /aθele,raða'mente; asele,raða-'mente/ *adv* hastily, swiftly

acelerador /aθelera'ðor; aselera'ðor/ *a* accelerating. *m*, accelerator; *Auto.* accelerator

acelerar /aθele'rar; asele'rar/ *vt* to hasten, speed up; accelerate

acémila /a'θemila; a'semila/ *f*, beast of burden, mule

acendrado /aθen'draðo; asen'draðo/ *a* pure, unblemished, spotless

acendrar /aθen'drar; asen'drar/ *vt* to refine (metals); purify, make spotless

acento /a'θento; a'sento/ *m*, accent; tone, inflection; *Poet.* voice, words. **a. agudo,** acute accent. **a. circunflejo,** circumflex accent. **a. grave,** grave accent. **a. ortográfico,** graphic accent, written accent. **a. tónico,** tonic accent

acentuación /aθentua'θion; asentua'sion/ *f*, accentuation, stress; emphasis

acentuar /aθen'tuar; asen'tuar/ *vt* to accent; stress, emphasize; —*vr* become evident, become marked, be noticeable

aceña /a'θeɲa; a'seɲa/ *f*, water-mill; irrigation waterwheel; chain-well

acepción /aθep'θion; asep'sion/ *f*, meaning, significance, acceptation. **a. de personas,** partiality, preference

acepilladura /aθe,piʎa'ðura; ase,piya'ðura/ *f*, sweeping, brushing; planing; wood-shaving

acepillar /aθepi'ʎar; asepi'yar/ *vt* to sweep, brush; plane. *Inf.* brush up, polish up

aceptabilidad /a,θeptaβili'ðað; a,septaβili'ðað/ *f*, acceptability

aceptable /aθep'taβle; asep'taβle/ *a* acceptable

aceptación /aθepta'θion; asepta'sion/ *f*, acceptance; popularity; approval

aceptador /aθepta'ðor; asepta'ðor/ **(-ra)** *a* accepting —*n* acceptor

aceptar /aθep'tar; asep'tar/ *vt* to accept; approve; accept a challenge; *Com.* honor

acequia /aθe'kia; ase'kia/ *f*, ditch, trench; irrigation channel

acequiero /aθe'kiero; ase'kiero/ *m*, keeper of irrigation ditches

acera /a'θera; a'sera/ *f*, sidewalk, pavement. **a. del sol,** sunny side of the street

acerado /aθe'raðo; ase'raðo/ *a* steel; steel-like; strong, tough; mordant, incisive

acerar /aθe'rar; ase'rar/ *vt* to steel; treat (liquids) with steel; harden, make obdurate

acerbidad /aθerβi'ðað; aserβi'ðað/ *f*, bitterness, acerbity, sourness; harshness, cruelty

acerbo /a'θerβo; a'serβo/ *a* sour, tart, bitter; cruel, harsh

acerca de /a'θerka de; a'serka de/ *adv* about, concerning

acercamiento /aθerka'miento; aserka'miento/ *m*, approach

acercar /aθer'kar; aser'kar/ *vt* to bring nearer; —*vr* be near at hand, draw near; (*with prep a*) approach

acerico /aθe'riko; ase'riko/ *m*, small cushion; pincushion

acero /a'θero; a'sero/ *m*, steel; blade, sword; *pl* bravery, spirit; *Inf.* good appetite. **a. inoxidable,** stainless steel

acérrimo /a'θerrimo; a'serrimo/ *a superl* extremely strong, mighty; most harsh; most resolute, unflinching; very strong (taste, smell)

acerrojar /aθerroˈhar; aserroˈhar/ *vt* to lock, padlock; bolt

acertado /aθerˈtaðo; aserˈtaðo/ *a* well-aimed; fitting, suitable; wise; successful

acertar /aθerˈtar; aserˈtar/ *vt irr* to hit the mark; find, come across; succeed (in), achieve; guess, find out; **No acertaba a explicármelo,** I couldn't quite understand it. **a. por chambra,** to make a lucky guess —*vi* be successful; thrive (of plants); (*with prep* a + *infin*) happen, occur, come to pass —*Pres. Indic.* **acierto, aciertas, acierta, aciertan.** *Pres. Subjunc.* **acierte, aciertes, acierte, acierten**

acertijo /aθerˈtiho; aserˈtiho/ *m*, riddle

acervo /aˈθerβo; aˈserβo/ *m*, pile, heap; *Fig.* storehouse, wealth (e.g. of words)

acetato /aθeˈtato; aseˈtato/ *m*, acetate

acético /aˈθetiko; aˈsetiko/ *a* acetic

acetileno /aθetiˈleno; asetiˈleno/ *m*, acetylene

achacar /atʃaˈkar/ *vt* to attribute, impute, assign. **achacable a,** imputable to

achacoso /atʃaˈkoso/ *a* ailing, ill, sickly

achantarse /atʃanˈtarse/ *vr Inf.* to hide from danger; put up with, bear

achaparrado /atʃapaˈrraðo/ *a* stocky

achaque /aˈtʃake/ *m*, ailment, illness (permanent); *Inf.* period, menstruation; pregnancy; matter, affair; pretext; failing, bad habit. **En a. de...,** Re..., concerning...

achatamiento /atʃataˈmiento/ *m*, flattening

achatar /atʃaˈtar/ *vt* to flatten, make flat

achicado /atʃiˈkaðo/ *a* childish

achicar /atʃiˈkar/ *vt* to make smaller, diminish; drain, bail out; depreciate, belittle

achicarse /atʃiˈkarse/ *Inf.* to sing small

achicharrar /atʃitʃaˈrrar/ *vt Cul.* to overcook; overheat; annoy, importune

achicoria /atʃiˈkoria/ *f*, chicory

achique /aˈtʃike/ *m*, bailing, draining

achispado /atʃisˈpaðo/ *a Inf.* tipsy

achubascarse /atʃuβasˈkarse/ *vr* to become overcast, grow stormy

achuchar /atʃuˈtʃar/ *vt Inf.* to squeeze, hug; jostle, push against

achuchón /atʃuˈtʃon/ *m*, *Inf.* shove, push; hug, squeeze

achulado /atʃuˈlaðo/ *a Inf.* brazen, tough

aciago /aˈθiago; aˈsiago/ *a* unhappy, ill-omened; fateful

acíbar /aˈθiβar; aˈsiβar/ *m*, aloe tree; bitter aloes; sorrow, bitterness

acibarar /aθiβaˈrar; asiβaˈrar/ *vt* to add bitter aloes to; embitter, sadden

acicalado /aθikaˈlaðo; asikaˈlaðo/ *a* polished; neat; well-groomed. *m*, polishing, burnishing (of weapons)

acicalador /aθikalaˈðor; asikalaˈðor/ **(-ra)** *a* polishing —*n* polisher. *m*, burnisher (machine)

acicalar /aθikaˈlar; asikaˈlar/ *vt* to burnish (weapons); adorn, deck; —*vr* dress oneself with care

acicate /aθiˈkate; asiˈkate/ *m*, Moorish spur; incitement, stimulus

acicatear /aθikateˈar; asikateˈar/ *vt* to induce, spur on. **a. la curiosidad,** arouse curiosity

acidez /aθiˈðeθ; asiˈðes/ *f*, acidity, bitterness

acidia /aˈθiðia; aˈsiðia/ *f*, indolence; sluggishness

ácido /ˈaθiðo; ˈasiðo/ *a* sour; harsh. *m*, acid. **a. fénico,** carbolic acid. **a. graso,** fatty acid

acidular /aθiðuˈlar; asiðuˈlar/ *vt Chem.* to acidulate

acídulo /aˈθiðulo; aˈsiðulo/ *a Chem.* acidulous

acierto /aˈθierto; aˈsierto/ *m*, good hit, bull's-eye; success; achievement; cleverness; dexterity; skill; wisdom, sense; tact

acimut /aθiˈmut; asiˈmut/ *m*, *Astron.* azimuth

aclamación /aklamaˈθion; aklamaˈsion/ *f*, acclamation; shout of acclamation. **por a.,** unanimously

aclamador /aklamaˈðor/ **(-ra)** *a* acclaiming —*n* applauder, acclaimer

aclamar /aklaˈmar/ *vt* to acclaim; applaud

aclaración /aklaraˈθion; aklaraˈsion/ *f*, explanation; elucidation

aclarado /aklaˈraðo/ *m*, rinse; rinsing

aclarador, aclaratorio /aklaraˈðor, aklaraˈtorio/ *a* explanatory

aclarar /aklaˈrar/ *vt* to clarify, purify; clear; rinse (clothes); explain; thin; —*vi* clear; (sky) clear up; dawn

aclimatación /aklimataˈθion; aklimataˈsion/ *f*, acclimatization

aclimatar /aklimaˈtar/ *vt* to acclimatize

acné /akˈne/ *m*, acne

acobardar /akoβarˈðar/ *vt* to intimidate, frighten

acocear /akoθeˈar; akoseˈar/ *vt* to kick; *Inf.* insult, humiliate

acocharse /akoˈtʃarse/ *vr* to squat, crouch

acodalar /akoðaˈlar/ *vt* to prop

acodiciar /akoðiˈθiar; akoðiˈsiar/ *vt* to yearn for, covet, desire

acogedizo /akoheˈðiθo; akoheˈðiso/ *a* gathered haphazardly

acogedor /akoheˈðor/ **(-ra)** *a* welcoming, friendly; inviting (e.g. a chair or room); —*n* protector

acoger /akoˈher/ *vt* to receive, welcome, admit; protect, harbor; —*vr* take refuge; (*with prep* a) make use of, resort to; **acogerse a sagrado,** seek sanctuary

acogida /akoˈhiða/ *f*, reception, welcome; protection, shelter; meeting place; confluence (of waters). **tener buena a.,** to be well received

acogollar /akogoˈʎar/ *vt* to protect, cover (plants); —*vi* sprout, shoot

acogotar /akogoˈtar/ *vt* to fell by a blow on the neck; *Inf.* knock out

acolada /akoˈlaða/ *f*, accolade

acolitar /akoliˈtar/ *vi* to serve as an altar boy, serve as an altar girl

acólito /aˈkolito/ *m*, acolyte

acometedor /akometeˈðor/ **(-ra)** *a* capable, enterprising; aggressive —*n* aggressor, attacker

acometer /akomeˈter/ *vt* to attack furiously; undertake; take in hand; overcome (of sleep, etc.)

acometida /akomeˈtiða/ *f*, **acometimiento** *m*, assault, onrush; undertaking

acometividad /akometiβiˈðað/ *f*, aggressiveness

acomodable /akomoˈðaβle/ *a* easily arranged

acomodación /akomoðaˈθion; akomoðaˈsion/ *f*, adjustment; adaptation; accommodation

acomodadizo /akomoðaˈðiθo; akomoðaˈðiso/ *a* accommodating, easy-going

acomodado /akomoˈðaðo/ *a* suitable; convenient; wealthy, well-off; comfort-loving; moderate, low (of price)

acomodador /akomoðaˈðor/ **(-ra)** *n* theater attendant, usher

acomodamiento /akomoðaˈmiento/ *m*, agreement, transaction; accommodation

acomodar /akomoˈðar/ *vt* to arrange, adjust, accommodate; adapt; appoint; place; reconcile; employ; take on; equip, provide; lodge; —*vi* suit, be convenient; —*vr* compromise, agree

acomodaticio /akomoðaˈtiθio; akomoðaˈtisio/ *a* accommodating

acomodo /akoˈmoðo/ *m*, post, employment; arrangement; settlement

acompañamiento /akompaɲaˈmiento/ *m*, accompaniment; following, retinue; *Mus.* accompaniment; *Theat.* crowd, chorus

acompañanta /akompaˈɲanta/ *f*, chaperon; maid, servant

acompañante /akompaˈɲante/ *m*, *Mus.* accompanist

acompañar /akompaˈɲar/ *vt* to accompany; follow, escort; enclose (a letter, etc.); *Mus.* accompany

acompasado /akompaˈsaðo/ *a* rhythmic; deliberate, slow

acondicionado /akondiθioˈnaðo; akondisioˈnaðo/ *a* conditioned; (*with* **bien** *or* **mal**) in good or bad condition; of good or bad quality; good- or ill-natured. **reflejo acondicionado** *Med.* conditioned reflex

acondicionar /akondiθioˈnar; akondisioˈnar/ *vt* to prepare; mend, repair; —*vr* condition oneself

acongojar /akongoˈhar/ *vt* to sadden, grieve; oppress

aconsejable /akonseˈhaβle/ *a* advisable

aconsejar /akonseˈhar/ *vt* to advise; —*vr* (*with con*) consult, ask advice of

aconsonantar /akonsonan'tar/ *vt* and *vi* to rhyme

acontecedero /akonteθe'ðero; akontese'ðero/ *a* possible

acontecer /akonte'θer; akonte'ser/ *vi irr impers* to happen. See **conocer**

acontecimiento /akonteθi'miento; akontesi'miento/ *m,* event, occurrence

acopiar /ako'piar/ *vt* to collect, amass, gather

acopio /a'kopio/ *m,* collection, store; accumulation, gathering

acopladura /akopla'ðura/ *f,* **acoplamiento** *m,* (*Mech.*) joint; coupling; yoking; mating (of animals)

acoplar /ako'plar/ *vt* to join, couple; yoke; mate (animals); reconcile (opinions); —*vr Inf.* fall in love

acoquinar /akoki'nar/ *vt Inf.* to intimidate, terrify

acorazado /akora'θaðo; akora'saðo/ *a* (*Nav. Mil.*) armored, iron-clad. *m,* iron-clad, battleship

acorazar /akora'θar; akora'sar/ *vt* (*Nav. Mil.*) to armor

acorcharse /akor'tʃarse/ *vr* to dry up, shrivel; go numb (limbs)

acordadamente /akor,ðaða'mente/ *adv* by common consent, unanimously; deliberately, after due thought

acordar /akor'ðar/ *vt irr* to decide unanimously; resolve; remind; tune; harmonize (colors); —*vi* agree; —*vr* remember; come to an agreement. **Si mal no me acuerdo,** If memory serves me right —*Pres. Indic.* **acuerdo, acuerdas, acuerda, acuerdan.** *Pres. Subjunc.* **acuerde, acuerdes, acuerde, acuerden**

acorde /a'korðe/ *a* agreed; in harmony; in agreement. *m, Mus.* chord; harmony

acordeón /akorðe'on/ *m,* accordion; (slang) crib sheet

acordonar /akorðo'nar/ *vt* to lace; cordon off, surround; mill (coins)

acornear /akorne'ar/ *vt* to butt, toss (bulls)

acorralado /akorra'laðo/ *a* at bay, intimidated

acorralamiento /akorrala'miento/ *m,* corralling, penning

acorralar /akorra'lar/ *vt* to corral, pen; confine; corner, silence (in argument); frighten; harass

acorrer /ako'rrer/ *vt* to aid, assist; —*vi* run, hasten; —*vr* take refuge

acortamiento /akorta'miento/ *m,* shortening

acortar /akor'tar/ *vt* to shorten; —*vr* be speechless, be shy. **a. las velas,** to take in sail

acosador /akosa'ðor/ **(-ra)** *a* persecuting —*n* persecutor

acosamiento /akosa'miento/ *m,* persecution

acosar /ako'sar/ *vt* to persecute relentlessly; annoy, harass

acostado /akos'taðo/ *a* in bed; stretched out; *Herald.* couchant

acostar /akos'tar/ *vt irr* to lay down, stretch out; put to bed; —*vi* lean, tilt; —*vr* lie down; go to bed; *Naut.* come alongside. See **contar**

acostumbrado /akostum'braðo/ *a* accustomed, usual

acostumbrar /akostum'brar/ *vt* to habituate, accustom; —*vi* be in the habit of (e.g. *Acostumbramos ir a la playa en el verano,* We generally go to the seashore in summer); —*vr* (*with prep a*) become used to

acotación /akota'θion; akota'sion/ *f,* noting; marginal note; stage direction; ordnance survey number

acotar /ako'tar/ *vt* to annotate; mark out boundaries; fix, establish; accept; *Inf.* choose; testify; fill in elevation figures (on a map); —*vr* seek refuge

acotillo /ako'tiʎo; ako'tiyo/ *m,* sledgehammer

acre /'akre/ *a* bitter, sour; harsh; biting, mordant. *m,* acre (land measure)

acrecencia /akre'θenθia; akre'sensia/ *f,* **acrecentamiento** *m,* increase; addition

acrecentar /akreθen'tar; akresen'tar/ *vt irr* to increase; augment; promote, prefer. See **acertar**

acrecer /akre'θer; akre'ser/ *vt irr* to increase; augment. See **conocer**

acreción /akre'θion; akre'sion/ *f,* accretion

acreditado /akreði'taðo/ *a* accredited, well-reputed; respected

acreditar /akreði'tar/ *vt* to prove; verify; accredit; recommend; sanction, authorize; vouch for, guarantee; *Com.* credit

acreedor /akree'ðor/ **(-ra)** *n* creditor; claimant —*a* deserving. **a. hipotecario,** mortgagee

acreencia /akre'enθia; akre'ensia/ *f,* debt; *Com.* claim

acribillar /akriβi'ʎar; akriβi'yar/ *vt* to riddle with holes; wound repeatedly; pelt; torment; *Inf.* pester, harass

acriminación /akrimina'θion; akrimina'sion/ *f,* accusation

acriminador /akrimina'ðor/ **(-ra)** *a* incriminating —*n* accuser

acriminar /akrimi'nar/ *vt* to accuse, charge

acrimonia /akri'monia/ *f,* acrimony

acrisolar /akriso'lar/ *vt* to refine, purify (metals); perfect; clarify, elucidate

acrobacia /akro'βaθia; akro'βasia/ *f,* acrobatics

acróbata /a'kroβata/ *mf* acrobat

acrobático /akro'βatiko/ *a* acrobatic

acromatópsico /akroma'topsiko/ *a* color-blind

acrópolis /a'kropolis/ *f,* acropolis

acróstico /a'krostiko/ *a* and *m,* acrostic

acta /'akta/ *f,* minutes, record; certificate of election (as deputy to Cortes, etc.); *pl* deeds (of a martyr). **a. matrimonial,** marriage register

actitud /akti'tuð/ *f,* attitude

activar /akti'βar/ *vt* to stimulate, make active; accelerate, hasten

actividad /aktiβi'ðað/ *f,* activity; movement, bustle. **en a.,** in action; at work

activo /ak'tiβo/ *a* active. *m, Com.* assets

acto /'akto/ *m,* act, deed, action; act, law; act (of a play); public ceremony; *pl* minutes (of a meeting), proceedings (of a conference). **a. continuo** *or* **a. seguido,** immediately afterwards. **a. vandálico,** act of vandalism. **los Actos de los Apóstoles,** Acts of the Apostles. **en a.,** in the act (of doing). **en el a.,** in the act; immediately

actor /ak'tor/ *m,* actor; *Law.* plaintiff

actriz /ak'triθ; ak'tris/ *f,* actress

actuación /aktua'θion; aktua'sion/ *f,* operation, functioning; action; *pl* legal functions, judicial acts

actual /ak'tual/ *a* present; contemporary

actualidad /aktuali'ðað/ *f,* present, present time; topic of interest. **actualidades,** current events. **en la a.,** at the present time

actuar /ak'tuar/ *vt* to operate, set in motion; —*vi* act; exercise legal functions

actuario /ak'tuario/ (**de seguros**) *m,* actuary

acuarela /akua'rela/ *f,* water-color painting

acuarelista /akuare'lista/ *mf* water-colorist

acuario /a'kuario/ *m,* aquarium; Aquarius

acuartelamiento /a,kuartela'miento/ *m,* billeting (of troops); billet, quarters

acuartelar /akuarte'lar/ *vt* to billet

acuático, acuátil /a'kuatiko, a'kuatil/ *a* aquatic

acuatinta /akua'tinta/ *f,* aquatint

acuchillado /akutʃi'ʎaðo; akutʃi'yaðo/ *a* taught by experience, schooled

acuchillar /akutʃi'ʎar; akutʃi'yar/ *vt* to hack, cut about; stab, put to the sword; slash (sleeves, etc.); —*vr* fight with swords, daggers

acucia /a'kuθia; a'kusia/ *f,* fervor, zeal; yearning, longing

acuciar /aku'θiar; aku'siar/ *vt* to incite; goad; stimulate; encourage

acuciosidad /akuθiosi'ðað; akusiosi'ðað/ *f,* eagerness, fervor, zeal

acucioso /aku'θioso; aku'sioso/ *a* eager, fervent, keen, assiduous

acuclillarse /akukli'ʎarse; akukli'yarse/ *vr* to squat, crouch

acudir /aku'ðir/ *vi* to go, repair (to); come; go or come to the aid of; attend, be present; **No me acude ningún ejemplo a la memoria,** No example comes to mind; resort (to), seek protection; reply, respond

acueducto /akue'ðukto/ *m,* aqueduct

acuerdo /a'kuerðo/ *m,* motion, resolution; decision; harmony, agreement; opinion, belief; remembrance; report; meeting (of members of a tribunal); *Art.* harmony (of colors). **de a.,** in agreement, in conformity; unanimously. **estar de a. (con),** to agree (with). **es-**

tar de acuerdo en (+ inf.), to agree to (+ inf.)
ponerse de a., to come to an understanding
acuitar /akui'tar/ vt to distress, trouble; grieve
acullá /aku'ʎa; aku'ya/ adv afar, yonder, in the distance
acumulación /akumula'θion; akumula'sion/ f, accumulation, collection
acumulador /akumula'ðor/ **(-ra)** a accumulative. m, accumulator, storage battery —n collector, accumulator
acumulamiento /akumula'miento/ m, accumulation (act)
acumular /akumu'lar/ vt to accumulate, amass, collect; accuse, charge with
acuñación /akuɲa'θion; akuɲa'sion/ f, minting, coining; wedging
acuñador /akuɲa'ðor/ **(-ra)** n coiner, stamper; wedge. m, coining machine
acuñar /aku'ɲar/ vt to mint, stamp, coin; wedge
acuosidad /akuosi'ðað/ f, wateriness
acuoso /a'kuoso/ a aqueous, watery
acurrucarse /akurru'karse/ vr to huddle; curl up; crouch
acusación /akusa'θion; akusa'sion/ f, accusation; Law. charge; Law. prosecution
acusado /aku'saðo/ **(-da)** a accused; prominent; well-defined; —n accused; Law. defendant
acusador /akusa'ðor/ **(-ra)** a accusing —n accuser; Law. prosecutor
acusar /aku'sar/ vt to accuse; blame; denounce; Com. acknowledge receipt; Law. prosecute; Law. charge.
acusarle a uno las cuarenta, Inf. to give someone a piece of one's mind
acusatorio /akusa'torio/ a accusatory
acusón /aku'son/ **(-ona)** n Inf. telltale, sneak, informer
acústica /a'kustika/ f, acoustics
acústico /a'kustiko/ a acoustic
adagio /a'ðahio; also for 2 a'dadʒio/ m, adage; Mus. adagio
adalid /aða'lið/ m, chieftain; head, leader
adamado /aða'maðo/ a effeminate; refined; genteel
adamantino /aðaman'tino/ a adamantine
adaptabilidad /aðaptaβili'ðað/ f, adaptability
adaptación /aðapta'θion; aðapta'sion/ f, adaptation
adaptar /aðap'tar/ vt to adapt, make suitable; —vr adapt oneself
adarme /a'ðarme/ m, tittle, jot. **por adarmes,** in bits and pieces, in drabs and driblets
adecentar /aðeθen'tar; aðesen'tar/ vt to make decent; tidy up; —vr tidy oneself
adecuación /aðekua'θion; aðekua'sion/ f, adequacy; suitability
adecuado /aðe'kuaðo/ a adequate; suitable
adecuar /aðe'kuar/ vt to proportion, fit; Fig. tailor
adefesio /aðe'fesio/ m, Inf. folly, absurdity (gen. pl); extravagant attire; guy, sight
adelantado /aðelan'taðo/ a precocious; forward, pert; fast (clocks); early (of fruit); excellent; capable, proficient. m, Obs. provincial governor or chief justice or captain-general (Spanish history). **por a.,** in advance
adelantamiento /aðelanta'miento/ m, promotion, furtherance; progress, advancement; betterment, improvement; Obs. office of **adelantado;** anticipation
adelantar /aðelan'tar/ vt to advance, move on; hasten; forestall; overtake; put on (the hands of clocks); improve, better; beat, excel; place in front; —vi progress, advance; be fast (clocks); grow, develop; —vr come forward
adelante /aðe'lante/ adv on, forward; further on; straight ahead. **¡A.!** Onward!; Come in! **de hoy en a.,** henceforth, from today
adelanto /aðe'lanto/ m, anticipation; progress; Com. payment in advance. **el a. de la hora,** moving the clock forward
adelfa /a'ðelfa/ f, Bot. rose-bay, oleander
adelgazamiento /aðel,gaθa'miento; aðel,gasa'miento/ m, loss of weight; slenderness; thinness
adelgazar /aðelga'θar; aðelga'sar/ vt to make slender or thin; Fig. split hairs; whittle, taper; —vi grow slender or thin

ademán /aðe'man/ m, posture, attitude; gesture; pl behavior, manners
además /aðe'mas/ adv besides, in addition; moreover. **a. de,** as well as
adentellar /aðente'ʎar; aðente'yar/ vt to bite, sink the teeth into
adentro /a'ðentro/ adv inside, within
adentros /a'ðentros/ m pl, private thoughts (e.g. Pensé para mis adentros, I thought to myself) —interj **¡Adentro!** Come in!; Go in!
adepto /a'ðepto/ a affiliated; adept, proficient
aderezamiento /aðe,reθa'miento; aðe,resa'miento/ m, dressing; seasoning; embellishment
aderezar /aðere'θar; aðere'sar/ vt to deck, embellish; cook; Cul. season; Cul. dress; prepare; repair, mend; guide, direct; dress (cloth)
aderezo /aðe're θo; aðe'reso/ m, dressing, adornment; beautifying; finery, ornament; preparation; seasoning; set of jewels; horse's trappings; gum starch (for dressing cloth); equipment
adeudar /aðeu'ðar/ vt to owe; be dutiable (goods); Com. debit; —vi become related (by marriage); —vr run into debt
adeudo /a'ðeuðo/ m, debt; customs duty; Com. debit
adherencia /aðe'renθia; aðe'rensia/ f, adherence; adhesion
adherente /aðe'rente/ a adhesive; connected, attached. mf adherent, follower; m pl. **adherentes,** accessories, requisites
adherirse /aðe'rirse/ vr irr to adhere, stick; follow; believe (in). See **herir**
adhesión /aðe'sion/ f, adhesion; adherence
adhesivo /aðe'siβo/ a adhesive
adición /aði'θion; aði'sion/ f, addition
adicional /aðiθio'nal; aðisio'nal/ a additional, extra
adicionar /aðiθio'nar; aðisio'nar/ vt to add up; add to
adicto /a'ðikto/ **(-ta)** a addicted, fond; joint —n addict; follower, disciple
adiestrador /aðiestra'ðor/ **(-ra)** n trainer, coach; guide, teacher
adiestrar /aðies'trar/ vt to train, coach; guide, teach; lead; —vr practice, perfect oneself
adietar /aðie'tar/ vt Med. to put on a diet
adinerado /aðine'raðo/ a wealthy, well-off, rich
adiós /a'ðios/ interj Good-bye!; Hello, God be with you! (used as greeting). m, farewell
adiposo /aði'poso/ a adipose
aditamento /aðita'mento/ m, addition
adive /a'ðiβe/ m, jackal
adivinación /aðiβina'θion; aðiβina'sion/ f, divination; guess
adivinador /aðiβina'ðor/ **(-ra)** a prophesying, divining —n soothsayer
adivinanza /aðiβi'nanθa; aðiβi'nansa/ f, divination; riddle; puzzle. **adivinanzas,** guessing games. **no estar para jugar a las a.,** to be in no mood for guessing games
adivinar /aðiβi'nar/ vt to prophesy, foretell; divine, guess; solve, guess (riddles, etc.)
adivino /aði'βino/ **(-na)** n soothsayer, prophet
adjetivo /aðhe'tiβo/ a adjectival. m, adjective
adjudicación /aðhuðika'θion; aðhuðika'sion/ f, adjudication, award
adjudicador /aðhuðika'ðor/ **(-ra)** n adjudicator
adjudicar /aðhuði'kar/ vt to adjudge; award; —vr appropriate
adjudicatario /aðhuðika'tario/ **(-ia)** n recipient (of a prize, etc.); grantee
adjuntar /aðhun'tar/ vt to enclose (with a letter, etc.)
adjunto /að'hunto/ a attached; enclosed, accompanying; assistant, deputy; adjectival. m, addition, supplement
administración /aðministra'θion; aðministra'sion/ f, administration; direction, control; administratorship
administrador /aðministra'ðor/ **(-ra)** a administrative —n administrator. **a. de correos,** postmaster
administrar /aðminis'trar/ vt to control, manage; provide, supply; administer. **administrarse el tiempo,** to budget one's time

administrativo /aðministra'tiβo/ *a* administrative, executive

admirable /aðmi'raβle/ *a* admirable

admirablemente /aðmi,raβle'mente/ *adv* admirably, excellently

admiración /aðmira'θion; aðmira'sion/ *f*, amazement; admiration; wonder; exclamation mark

admirador /aðmira'ðor/ **(-ra)** *a* admiring —*n* admirer

admirar /aðmi'rar/ *vt* to admire; surprise, amaze (e.g. *Me admira su acción*, His action surprises me); to see (e.g. *Desde la colina se pueden admirar varios edificios de la ciudad*, From the hill several buildings in the city can be seen); —*vr* (*with de*) be surprised at or by

admirativo /aðmira'tiβo/ *a* admiring; admirable, excellent

admisibilidad /aðmisiβili'ðað/ *f*, allowability, permissibility

admisible /aðmi'siβle/ *a* admissible; permissible

admisión /aðmi'sion/ *f*, admission; acceptance; allowance

admitir /aðmi'tir/ *vt* to admit; receive, accept; tolerate, brook; allow, permit

admonición /aðmoni'θion; aðmoni'sion/ *f*, admonition, warning; reprimand

adobar /aðo'βar/ *vt* to prepare; *Cul.* garnish; pickle (meat); cook; dress (hides)

adobo /a'ðoβo/ *m*, repairing; dressing (for cloth, leather); *Cul.* savory sauce; pickling sauce; make-up, cosmetic

adocenado /aðoθe'naðo; aðose'naðo/ *a* ordinary; narrow-minded

adoctrinar /aðoktri'nar/ *vt* to instruct

adolecer /aðole'θer; aðole'ser/ *vi irr* to fall ill; (*with de*) suffer from (diseases, defects); —*vr* be sorry for, regret. See **conocer**

adolescencia /aðoles'θenθia; aðoles'sensia/ *f*, adolescence

adolescente /aðoles'θente; aðoles'sente/ *a* and *mf* adolescent

adonde /a'ðonde/ *adv* (*interr a dónde*) where to, whither (e.g. *¿A dónde fuiste?* Where did you go to?)

adondequiera /a,ðonde'kiera/ *adv* wherever

adopción /aðop'θion; aðop'sion/ *f*, adoption

adoptador /aðopta'ðor/ **(-ra)** *a* adopting —*n* adopter

adoptar /aðop'tar/ *vt* to adopt (children); make one's own, embrace (opinions); take (decisions)

adoptivo /aðop'tiβo/ *a* adoptive

adoquín /aðo'kin/ *m*, cobble-stone; *Fig.* blockhead

adoquinado /aðoki'naðo/ *m*, cobbling, paving. *m*, cobbled pavement

adoquinar /aðoki'nar/ *vt* to pave with cobble-stones

adorable /aðo'raβle/ *a* adorable

adoración /aðora'θion; aðora'sion/ *f*, worship, adoration. **A. de los Reyes,** Adoration of the Magi; Epiphany

adorador /aðora'ðor/ **(-ra)** *a* adoring —*n* adorer

adorar /aðo'rar/ *vt* to adore; worship; (*with en*) dote on; —*vr* pray

adormecedor /aðormeθe'ðor; aðormese'ðor/ *a* soporific, drowsy

adormecer /aðorme'θer; aðorme'ser/ *vt irr* to make drowsy; soothe, lull; hush to sleep; —*vr* go to sleep; (limbs) fall asleep; (*with en*) persist in. See **conocer**

adormecimiento /aðormeθi'miento; aðormesi'miento/ *m*, sleepiness; lulling asleep; numbness

adormitarse /aðormi'tarse/ *vr* to doze, take a nap, snooze

adornamiento /aðorna'miento/ *m*, adornment, decoration

adornar /aðor'nar/ *vt* to deck, beautify; decorate; trim, embellish; adorn (of virtues, etc.)

adorno /a'ðorno/ *m*, decoration, adornment; ornament; trimming. **de a.,** ornamental; flowering (shrubs)

adquiridor /aðkiri'ðor/ **(-ra)** *a* acquiring —*n* acquirer

adquirir /aðki'rir/ *vt irr* to acquire, get; achieve, obtain —*Pres. Indic.* **adquiero, adquieres, adquiere, adquieren.** *Pres. Subjunc.* **adquiera, adquieras, adquiera, adquieran**

adquisición /aðkisi'θion; aðkisi'sion/ *f*, acquirement; acquisition. **poder de a.,** purchasing power

adquisidor /aðkisi'ðor/ **(-ra)** *a* acquiring —*n* acquirer, obtainer

adquisitivo /aðkisi'tiβo/ *a* acquisitive

adquisividad /aðkisiβi'ðað/ *f*, acquisitiveness

adrazo /a'ðraθo; a'ðraso/ *m*, salt-water still

adrede /a'ðreðe/ *adv* on purpose, intentionally

adrenalina /aðrena'lina/ *f*, adrenaline

adriático /a'ðriatiko/ *a* Adriatic

adscribir /aðskri'βir/ *vt* to ascribe, attribute; appoint (to a post, etc.)

adscripción /aðskrip'θion; aðskrip'sion/ *f*, ascription, attribution; appointment

aduana /a'ðuana/ *f*, customs house, customs. **pasar por la a.,** to go through customs

aduanero /aðua'nero/ *a* customs. *m*, customs officer

aducir /aðu'θir; aðu'sir/ *vt irr* to adduce, allege, cite; add. See **conducir**

adueñarse /aðue'ɲarse/ **(-de)** *vr* to appropriate, take possession (of)

adulación /aðula'θion; aðula'sion/ *f*, adulation, flattery

adulador /aðula'ðor/ **(-ra)** *a* fawning —*n* flatterer

adular /aðu'lar/ *vt* to flatter, fawn upon, adulate

adulteración /aðultera'θion; aðultera'sion/ *f*, adulteration; falsification

adulterador /aðultera'ðor/ **(-ra)** *a* adulterant —*n* adulterator; falsifier; coiner

adulterar /aðulte'rar/ *vi* to commit adultery; —*vt* adulterate; falsify

adulterino /aðulte'rino/ *a* adulterous; false

adulterio /aðul'terio/ *m*, adultery

adúltero /a'ðultero/ **(-ra)** *a* adulterous; corrupt —*n* adulterer

adulto /a'ðulto/ **(-ta)** *a* and *n* adult

adunar /aðu'nar/ *vt* to join, unite; unify, combine

adusto /a'ðusto/ *a* extremely hot (of climate); grave, austere; standoffish, reserved

advenedizo /aðβene'ðiθo; aðβene'ðiso/ *a* foreign, alien; strange, unknown; upstart; newly rich

advenimiento /aðβeni'miento/ *m*, advent, arrival; ascension (to the throne)

advenir /aðβe'nir/ *vi irr* to come, arrive; happen, befall. See **venir**

adventicio /aðβen'tiθio; aðβen'tisio/ *a* casual, accidental; *Bot.* adventitious

adverbio /að'βerβio/ *m*, adverb

adversario /aðβer'sario/ **(-ia)** *n* adversary, rival; opponent

adversidad /aðβersi'ðað/ *f*, adversity, misfortune, sorrow

adverso /að'βerso/ *a* unfavorable, contrary, adverse; opposite

advertencia /aðβer'tenθia; aðβer'tensia/ *f*, warning; introduction, preface; remark

advertido /aðβer'tiðo/ *a* capable, clever; experienced; expert

advertir /aðβer'tir/ *vt irr* to observe, notice; warn; advise; feel, be conscious of; point out, indicate; inform; discover. See **sentir**

Adviento /að'βiento/ *m*, *Eccl.* Advent

adyacente /aðya'θente; aðya'sente/ *a* adjacent, near-by, neighboring

aedo /a'eðo/ *m*, *Poet.* poet

aeración /aera'θion; aera'sion/ *f*, aeration

aéreo /'aereo/ *a* aerial; airborne; airy; air; aeronautic; unsubstantial, fantastic. **correo a.,** airmail. **linea aérea** airline

aerobismo /aero'βismo/ *m*, aerobics

aerodinámica /aeroði'namika/ *f*, aerodynamics

aeronauta /aero'nauta/ *mf* aeronaut, balloonist

aeronáutica /aero'nautika/ *f*, aeronautics

aeronáutico /aero'nautiko/ *a* aeronautic

aeropuerto /aero'puerto/ *m*, airport

aeróstato /ae'rostato/ *m*, dirigible

afabilidad /afaβili'ðað/ *f*, affability, geniality, friendliness

afable /a'faβle/ *a* affable, genial, pleasant

afamado /afa'maðo/ *a* famous, well-known

afamar /afa'mar/ *vt* to make famous

afán /a'fan/ *m*, effort; manual labor; desire, anxiety **a. de mando,** thirst for power

afanar /afa'nar/ vt to press, urge on; filch; —vr toil, labor; (with por) work hard to, try to

afanoso /afa'noso/ a hard, laborious; hard-working, painstaking; eager, anxious

afasia /a'fasia/ f, Med. aphasia

afear /afe'ar/ vt to make ugly; distort, deform; blame; criticize

afección /afek'θion; afek'sion/ f, fondness, affection; complaint, ailment, trouble

afectación /afekta'θion; afekta'sion/ f, affectation

afectado /afek'taðo/ a affected

afectar /afek'tar/ vt to feign, assume; affect; move, touch; Law. encumber

afectivo /afek'tiβo/ a affective

afecto /a'fekto/ a fond, affectionate; Law. encumbered; (with prep a) addicted to. m, emotion, sentiment; affection

afectuosidad /afektuosi'ðað/ f, affectionateness

afectuoso /afek'tuoso/ a affectionate, fond

afeitada /afei'taða/ f, shave, shaving

afeitar /afei'tar/ vt to shave; make up (one's face); adorn, beautify

afeite /a'feite/ m, cosmetic; make-up (for the complexion)

afelpado /afel'paðo/ a velvet-like, plushy

afeminación /afemina'θion; afemina'sion/ f, effeminacy; weakness, languor

afeminado /afemi'naðo/ a effeminate

afeminar /afemi'nar/ vt to make effeminate; weaken; —vr grow effeminate

aferradamente /aferraða'mente/ adv tenaciously, persistently, obstinately

aferramiento /aferra'miento/ m, seizing, clutching; Naut. furling; Naut. grappling; mooring, anchoring; obstinacy

aferrar /afe'rrar/ vt to seize, clutch; Naut. take in, furl; Naut. grapple; —vi Naut. anchor; —vr (with con, en, a) persist in, insist on

afestonado /afesto'naðo/ a festooned

Afganistán /afganis'tan/ Afghanistan

afgano /af'gano/ (**-na**) a and n Afghan

afianzamiento /afianθa'miento; afiansa'miento/ m, fastening, fixing; propping; grasping; guarantee, security

afianzar /afian'θar; afian'sar/ vt to fasten, fix; prop; consolidate (e.g. one's power); guarantee, be security for; grasp

afición /afi'θion; afi'sion/ f, propensity, inclination; fondness. **tomar a. (a),** to take a liking to

aficionado /afiθio'naðo; afisio'naðo/ (**-da**) a amateur —n amateur, fan, enthusiast. **ser a a.,** to be fond of, have a liking for

aficionar /afiθio'nar; afisio'nar/ vt to inspire liking or affection; —vr (with prep a) take a liking to, grow fond of; become an enthusiast of

afijo /a'fiho/ m, Gram. affix

afiladera /afila'ðera/ f, whetstone, grindstone

afilado /afi'laðo/ a sharp, keen (of edges)

afilador /afila'ðor/ m, grinder (of scissors, etc.); razor strop

afilalápices /afila'lapiθes; afila'lapises/ m, pencil sharpener

afilar /afi'lar/ vt to sharpen; grind, whet; taper; —vr grow thin; taper

afiliación /afilia'θion; afilia'sion/ f, affiliation

afiliar /afi'liar/ vt (with prep a) to affiliate with; —vr (with prep a) become affiliated with; join, become a member of

afiligranado /afiligra'naðo/ a filigree; delicate, fine; slender

afilón /afi'lon/ m, steel, knife sharpener; razor-strop

afín /a'fin/ a nearby, contiguous; similar, related. mf relative by marriage

afinador /afina'ðor/ m, tuning key; tuner (of pianos, etc.)

afinar /afi'nar/ vt to finish, perfect; Fig. polish, refine; tune (musical instruments); refine (metals); —vi sing in tune; —vr grow refined

afinidad /afini'ðað/ f, affinity, analogy; relationship (by marriage); Chem. affinity

afirmación /afirma'θion; afirma'sion/ f, affirmation, statement

afirmadamente /afir,maða'mente/ adv firmly

afirmar /afir'mar/ vt to make firm; fix, fasten; affirm; —vr steady oneself; hold on to

afirmativa /afirma'tiβa/ f, affirmative

afirmativo /afirma'tiβo/ a affirmative

aflicción /aflik'θion; aflik'sion/ f, affliction, grief

aflictivo /aflik'tiβo/ a sorrowful, grievous

afligidamente /afli,hiða'mente/ adv sorrowfully

afligir /afli'hir/ vt to sadden; afflict, trouble; —vr lament, mourn

aflojamiento /afloha'miento/ m, slackening; loosening; diminution

aflojar /aflo'har/ vt to slacken; loosen; —vi relax, weaken; abate, diminish. **a. el paso,** to slow down

afluencia /a'fluenθia; a'fluensia/ f, crowd, concourse; eloquence, fluency

afluente /a'fluente/ a fluent, eloquent. m, tributary (river)

afluir /aflu'ir/ vi irr to crowd, swarm; flow (into). See **huir**

afonía /afo'nia/ f, Med. aphonia, loss of voice; hoarseness

afónico /a'foniko/ a hoarse

aforismo /afo'rismo/ m, aphorism

aforrador /aforra'ðor/ (**-ra**) n one who lines jackets, etc.

aforrar /afo'rrar/ vt to line (clothes, etc.); —vr wrap oneself up; Inf. gormandize

afortunadamente /afortu,naða'mente/ adv luckily, fortunately

afortunado /afortu'naðo/ a lucky, fortunate; happy; stormy

afortunar /afortu'nar/ vt to bring luck to, make happy

afrancesado /afranθe'saðo; afranse'saðo/ (**-da**) a Francophile; Frenchified —n Francophile

afrancesamiento /afranθesa'miento; afranse-sa'miento/ m, adoption of the French way of life; servile imitation of everything French

afrancesar /afranθe'sar; afranse'sar/ vt to make French, gallicize; Frenchify; —vr become a Francophile

afrenta /a'frenta/ f, insult, affront; disgrace

afrentar /afren'tar/ vt to insult; —vr be ashamed

afrentoso /afren'toso/ a insulting, outrageous; disgraceful

África /'afrika/ Africa

africanismo /,afrikan'ismo/ m, Africanism

africano /afri'kano/ (**-na**) a and n African

afrodisíaco /afroði'siako/ a and m, aphrodisiac

afrontar /afron'tar/ vt to place opposite; confront; face (danger, etc.)

afuera /a'fuera/ adv outside, out.

afueras /a'fueras/ f pl, suburbs, outskirts

agachada /aga'tʃaða/ f, crouch, duck; jerk

agachar /aga'tʃar/ vt Inf. bend, bow; —vr Inf. crouch down; lie low, hide

agalla /a'gaʎa; a'gaya/ f, oak-apple; tonsil (gen. pl); Zool. gill; Inf. gall, cheek

ágape /'agape/ m, agape; banquet, feast

Agar /a'gar/ Hagar

agárico /a'gariko/ m, Bot. agaric

agarrada /aga'rraða/ f, Inf. brawl, scuffle

agarradero /agarra'ðero/ m, handle; heft; Inf. influence, pull

agarrado /aga'rraðo/ a Inf. tight-fisted, mean

agarrar /aga'rrar/ vt to grip, grasp; seize, take; Inf. nab (jobs); —vr grip, hold on

agarro /a'garro/ m, hold; grip, grasp

agarrotar /agarro'tar/ vt to garrotte; tighten (ropes, etc.); press, squeeze; —vr (limbs) go numb

agasajar /agasa'har/ vt to indulge, spoil, pet; receive kindly; entertain; caress

agasajo /aga'saho/ m, indulgence, kindness; affability, geniality; entertainment; gift, offering

agauchado /agau'tʃaðo/ a gaucho-like

agazapar /agaθa'par; agasa'par/ vt Inf. to nab, catch; —vr Inf. squat, crouch

agencia /a'henθia; a'hensia/ f, influence, agency
agenciar /ahen'θiar; ahen'siar/ vt to negotiate, arrange; procure, manage
agenda /a'henda/ f, notebook; agenda
agente /a'hente/ m, agent. **a. de bolsa** or **a. de cambio**, bill broker. **a. de negocios**, business agent. **a. de policía**, police officer. **a. fiscal**, revenue officer
agerasia /ahe'rasia/ f, sickness-free old age
agestado /ahes'taðo/ a used generally with advs. **bien** or **mal**, well or ill-featured
agigantado /ahigan'taðo/ a enormous, gigantic; outstanding, extraordinary
ágil /'ahil/ a agile, nimble; easy to use (e.g. un libro ágil, a book easy to use)
agilidad /ahili'ðað/ f, agility, nimbleness
agilizar /ahili'θar; ahili'sar/ vt to make agile, limber; refresh one's knowledge of (e.g. Quiero agilizar mi español, I want to refresh my knowledge of Spanish); to enable; —vr limber up
agitación /ahita'θion; ahita'sion/ f, shaking; agitation, excitement
agitador /ahita'ðor/ (**-ra**) a stirring; agitating —n agitator. m, stirrer, stirring rod
agitar /ahi'tar/ vt to stir; shake; agitate, excite **a. una cuestión**, raise a question; discuss a question
aglomeración /aglomera'θion; aglomera'sion/ f, agglomeration
aglomerado /aglome'raðo/ m, briquette
aglomerar /aglome'rar/ vt to agglomerate, amass
aglutinación /aglutina'θion; aglutina'sion/ f, agglutination
aglutinar(se) /agluti'nar/ vt and vr to stick, agglutinate
agnosticismo /agnosti'θismo; agnosti'sismo/ m, agnosticism
agnóstico /ag'nostiko/ (**-ca**) a and n agnostic
agobiar /ago'βiar/ vt to bow, bend down; Fig. weigh down, oppress; —vr bend (beneath a weight)
agobio /a'goβio/ m, bowing, bending down; oppression, burden, weight
agolparse /agol'parse/ vr to rush, crowd, swarm
agonía /ago'nia/ f, agony, anguish
agónico /a'goniko/ a dying; agonizing
agonizante /agoni'θante; agoni'sante/ a dying
agonizar /agoni'θar; agoni'sar/ vt to attend a dying person; Inf. pester, annoy; —vi be dying (gen. **estar agonizando**)
agorar /ago'rar/ vt to prophesy, foretell
agorero /ago'rero/ (**-ra**) a prophetic; ill-boding —n seer, augur
agostarse /agos'tarse/ vt and vr to dry up, shrivel
agosto /a'gosto/ m, August; harvest. Inf. **hacer su a.**, to make hay while the sun shines
agotable /ago'taβle/ a exhaustible
agotado /ago'taðo/ a exhausted; out of print (of books)
agotador /agota'ðor/ a exhausting; exhaustive
agotamiento /a,gota'miento/ m, exhaustion
agotar /ago'tar/ vt to drain off (water); empty (a glass); exhaust; run through (money); study thoroughly, examine closely (a subject)
agraciado /agra'θiaðo; agra'siaðo/ a graceful; pretty
agraciar /agra'θiar; agra'siar/ vt to lend grace to; make pretty; favor
agradable /agra'ðaβle/ a agreeable, pleasant
agradar /agra'ðar/ vi to be pleasing, like, please (e.g. Me agrada su sinceridad, I like his sincerity)
agradecer /agraðe'θer; agraðe'ser/ vt irr to be grateful for; thank for; Fig. repay, requite. See **conocer**
agradecido /agraðe'θiðo; agraðe'siðo/ a grateful; thankful
agradecimiento /agraðeθi'miento; agraðesi'miento/ m, gratitude; thankfulness
agrado /a'graðo/ m, pleasure; desire, liking; amiability, affability
agrandar /agran'dar/ vt to enlarge
agrario /a'grario/ a agrarian
agravación /agraβa'θion; agraβa'sion/ f, **agravamiento** m, aggravation, worsening
agravador /agraβa'ðor/ a aggravating; worsening; increasing

agravar /agra'βar/ vt to aggravate, increase; oppress (taxes, responsibilities); make worse; exaggerate; —vr grow worse
agraviador /agraβia'ðor/ **-ra** a offensive —n offender
agraviar /agra'βiar/ vt to offend; wrong; —vr take offense, be insulted
agravio /a'graβio/ m, offense, insult; wrong, injury
agraz /a'graθ; a'gras/ m, unripened grape; verjuice; Fig. bitterness
agredir /agre'ðir/ vt to attack
agregación /agrega'θion; agrega'sion/ f, association, aggregation; total, collection, aggregate
agregado /agre'gaðo/ m, aggregate; assistant; attaché
agregar /agre'gar/ vt to add; collect, amass; appoint (to a post). **agregarse a...**, to join... (e.g. an association)
agresión /agre'sion/ f, aggression
agresivo /agre'siβo/ a aggressive
agresor /agre'sor/ (**-ra**) a and n aggressor
agreste /a'greste/ a rural, rustic; wild; uncouth, rude
agriar /a'griar/ vt to make bitter or sour; exasperate, provoke
agrícola /a'grikola/ a agricultural; mf agriculturalist, farmer
agricultura /agrikul'tura/ f, agriculture
agridulce /agri'ðulθe; agri'ðulse/ a bitter-sweet
agrietarse /agrie'tarse/ vr to crack, split
agrimensor /agrimen'sor/ m, surveyor
agrimensura /agrimen'sura/ f, surveying
agrio /'agrio/ a bitter, sour; rough, uneven (ground); brittle; sharp (of color contrast); unsociable; disagreeable
agrisetado /agrise'taðo/ a flowered (of materials)
agronomía /agrono'mia/ f, agronomy
agrónomo /a'gronomo/ a agronomic. m, agronomist
agrupación /agrupa'θion; agrupa'sion/ f, congregation, assembly; group; crowd; crowding, grouping
agrupar /agru'par/ vt to assemble, group; —vr crowd, cluster
agrura /a'grura/ f, bitterness; sourness; asperity
agua /'agua/ f, water; rain; slope of a roof; pl shot or watered effect on silks, etc.; medicinal waters; waves; water (of precious stones). **a. abajo**, down-stream. **a. arriba**, upstream. **a. bendita**, holy water. **a. cruda**, hard water. **a. de colonia**, eau de Cologne. **a. dulce**, fresh water. **a. fresca**, cold water. **a. nieve**, sleet. **a. oxigenada**, hydrogen peroxide. Fig. Inf. **estar con el a. al cuello**, to be in low water. Fig. Inf. **estar entre dos aguas**, to be between two fires. Naut. **hacer a.**, to leak. **Todo eso es ya a. pasada**, That's all water under the bridge
aguacero /agua'θero; agua'sero/ m, heavy rainfall, shower
aguada /a'guaða/ f, water supply on board ship; flood (in mines); watering station; Art. water color
aguadero /agua'ðero/ m, (animals') watering place
aguado /a'guaðo/ a watery; abstemious; watered
aguador /agua'ðor/ (**-ra**) n water carrier, water seller; drawer (of water)
aguafiestas /,agua'fiestas/ mf Fig. Inf. wet blanket
aguafuerte /,agua'fuerte/ f, etching
aguaje /a'guahe/ m, tide, waves; sea current; water supply (on board ship); wake (of a ship)
aguamanil /aguama'nil/ m, washstand; pitcher, ewer
aguamanos /agua'manos/ m, water for washing hands; pitcher
aguamarina /aguama'rina/ f, aquamarine
aguamiel /agua'miel/ f, honey and water, hydromel
aguantable /aguan'taβle/ a tolerable, bearable
aguantar /aguan'tar/ vt to bear, tolerate, endure; restrain, resist, oppose; —vr bear in silence, keep quiet
aguante /a'guante/ m, patience, endurance; resistance
aguar /a'guar/ vt to water down (wine, etc.); spoil (fun, etc.); —vr be filled with water; be flooded; become watery or thin
aguardar /aguar'ðar/ vt to await; expect; allow time to (debtors)
aguardentería /aguar,ðente'ria/ f, liquor shop

aguardentoso /aguarðen'toso/ *a* spirituous, containing; **aguardiente** hoarse, husky (of the voice)

aguardiente /aguar'ðiente/ *m*, liquor. **a. de caña,** rum

aguardo /a'guarðo/ *m*, ambush (for a hunter)

aguarrás /agua'rras/ *m*, oil of turpentine

aguatinta /agua'tinta/ *f*, aquatint

aguatocha /agua'totʃa/ *f*, pump (for water, etc.)

aguaturma /agua'turma/ *f*, Jerusalem artichoke

agudeza /agu'ðeθa; agu'ðesa/ *f*, sharpness; keenness; distinctness; alertness, cleverness; witty sally, repartee; wit; swiftness

agudo /a'guðo/ *a* sharp; alert, clever; (*Geom. Med.*) acute; fine, keen; rapid; high-pitched; strong (of scents, etc.)

agüero /a'guero/ *m*, omen, sign; prophecy, prediction

aguerrido /age'rriðo/ *a* veteran, war-hardened

aguerrir /age'rrir/ *vt defective* to harden to war; toughen

aguijada /agi'haða/ *f*, goad, spur

aguijar /agi'har/ *vt* to prick (with a goad); urge on, encourage (animals); incite, instigate; spur on; —*vi* walk swiftly

aguijón /agi'hon/ *m*, goad; sting; thorn, prickle; spur; incitement, stimulus. **tener aguijones,** to be on pins and needles

aguijonazo /agiho'naθo; agiho'naso/ *m*, prick (with a goad)

águila /'agila/ *f*, eagle; master mind. **a. caudal** *or* **a. real,** royal eagle. **á. o sol,** heads or tails (Mexico)

aguileña /agi'leɲa/ *f*, *Bot.* columbine

aguileño /agi'leɲo/ *a* aquiline

aguilón /agi'lon/ *m*, *Archit.* gable; boom (of a crane)

aguinaldo /agi'naldo/ *m*, Christmas present; New Year's gift

aguja /a'guha/ *f*, needle; hand, pointer; hatpin; engraver's burin; switch; *Rail.* point; *Rail.* rail; obelisk; spire; bodkin; knitting needle; crochet hook; (compass) needle *pl Bot.* plumelet. **a. capotera, a. de zurcir,** darning needle. **a. de marear** *Naut.,* binnacle; mariner's compass. **a. de media,** knitting needle. **a. espartera,** packing needle

agujerear /aguhere'ar/ *vt* to perforate, make holes in

agujero /agu'hero/ *m*, hole, aperture; needle maker or seller; needle case

agujeta /agu'heta/ *f*, lace (for shoes, etc.); *pl* muscular pains, aches; tip, gratuity

agusanarse /agusa'narse/ *vr* to become worm-infested

aguzadura /aguθa'ðura; agusa'ðura/ *f*, sharpening, grinding, whetting

aguzar /agu'θar; agu'sar/ *vt* to sharpen; grind, whet; stimulate, encourage; incite

ahechadura /aetʃa'ðura/ *f*, chaff (of grain)

ahembrado /aem'braðo/ *a* effeminate

aherrojar /aerro'har/ *vt* to put (a prisoner) in irons; oppress

aherrumbrar /aerrum'brar/ *vt* to give the color or taste of iron to; —*vr* taste or look like iron; go rusty

ahí /a'i/ *adv* there; over there. **de a.,** thus, so. **por a.,** somewhere about, near at hand.

ahidalgado /aiðal'gaðo/ *a* gentlemanly; noble, generous

ahijado /ai'haðo/ **(-da)** *n* godchild; protégé

ahijar /ai'har/ *vt* to adopt (children); mother (animals); attribute, impute; —*vi* bring forth offspring; *Bot.* sprout. See **prohibir**

ahincado /ain'kaðo/ *a* earnest, eager

ahincar /ain'kar/ *vt* to urge, press; —*vr* hurry, hasten. See **prohibir**

ahínco /a'inko/ *m*, earnestness, eagerness

ahitar /ai'tar/ *vt* to stuff with food; bore, disgust. See **prohibir**

ahíto /a'ito/ *a* full of food; *Fig.* fed up. *m*, indigestion

ahogado /ao'gaðo/ **(-da)** *a* drowned; suffocated; stuffy, unventilated; stifling —*n* drowned person; victim of suffocation

ahogamiento /aoga'miento/ *m*, drowning; suffocation

ahogar /ao'gar/ *vt* to drown; suffocate; put out (the fire); stifle (yawns, etc.); suppress, extinguish; tire; overwater (plants); —*vr Naut.* sink, founder; drown; suffocate

ahogo /a'ogo/ *m*, anxiety, grief; difficulty in breathing, oppression; asthma; embarrassment; suffocation; straitened circumstances

ahondamiento /aonda'miento/ *m*, in-depth treatment (e.g. *el a. de un problema,* in-depth treatment of a problem)

ahondar /aon'dar/ *vt* to deepen; excavate, dig; go into thoroughly; go deep into, penetrate; —*vr* (earth) subside

ahora /a'ora/ *adv* now; very soon; just now, a short time ago —*conjunc* whether; now. **a. bien,** well now, given that. **a. mismo,** immediately, at once. **por a.,** for the present

ahorcado /aor'kaðo/ **(-da)** *n* hanged man

ahorcar /aor'kar/ *vt* to execute by hanging, hang. *Inf.* **a. los hábitos,** to leave the priesthood, cease to be an ecclesiastic

ahormar /aor'mar/ *vt* to adjust, shape; break in (new shoes); make (a person) see reason

ahorquillar /aorki'ʎar; aorki'yar/ *vt* to prop up (trees) with forks; —*vr* grow forked

ahorrar /ao'rrar/ *vt* to free (slaves); save, economize; avoid, eschew; —*vr* avoid; remove clothing

ahorro /a'orro/ *m*, economy, thrift; *pl* savings

ahuchar /au'tʃar/ *vt* to hoard; expel, drive away. See **desahuciar**

ahuciar /au'θiar; au'siar/ *vt* take possession of (a house)

ahuecar /aue'kar/ *vt* to hollow out; loosen; shake out; puff out, inflate; put on a solemn voice; hoe, dig; *Inf.* *vr* puff oneself out; put on airs

ahumada /au'maða/ *f*, smoke signal

ahumado /au'maðo/ *a* smoked; smoky

ahumar /au'mar/ *vt* to smoke (herrings, etc.); fill with smoke; —*vi* smoke, burn; —*vr* be full of smoke; taste smoked; *Inf.* get drunk. See **desahuciar**

ahusado /au'saðo/ *a* spindle-shaped

ahuyentar /auyen'tar/ *vt* to frighten off; drive away; dismiss, banish (anxiety, etc.); —*vr* flee

airadamente /airaða'mente/ *adv* wrathfully, angrily

airado /ai'raðo/ *a* angry

airar /ai'rar/ *vt* to annoy, anger; —*vr* grow annoyed

aire /'aire/ *m*, air; atmosphere (sometimes *pl*); breeze, wind; bearing, appearance; vanity; (horse's) gait; futility, frivolity; grace, charm; gracefulness; *Mus.* air; *Mus.* tempo. **a. popular,** popular tune. **al a. libre,** in the open air, outdoors. *Inf.* **beber los aires (por),** to yearn (for)

aireación /airea'θion; airea'sion/ *f*, airing; ventilation

airear /aire'ar/ *vt* to air; ventilate; aerate; —*vr* take the air; catch a chill

airosidad /airosi'ðað/ *f*, gracefulness; jauntiness

airoso /ai'roso/ *a* airy, open; windy, breezy, fresh; graceful; handsome; jaunty; victorious, successful

aislacionismo /aislaθiona'mismo; aislasiona'mismo/ *m*, *Polit.* isolationism

aislacionista /aislaθion'ista; aislasion'ista/ *mf Polit.* isolationist

aislado /ais'laðo/ *a* isolated; remote; individual; single; *Elec.* insulated

aislador /aisla'ðor/ *m*, *Phys.* insulator

aislamiento /aisla'miento/ *m*, isolation; *Phys.* insulation

aislante /ais'lante/ *a* isolating; insulating

aislar /ais'lar/ *vt* to isolate; *Elec.* insulate; —*vr* become a recluse; become isolated

¡ajá! /a'ha/ *interj Inf.* Aha! Good!

ajaquecarse /ahake'karse/ *vr* to have a headache

ajar /a'har/ *vt* to crease, crumple, spoil; humiliate; —*vr* fade, wither (flowers)

ajear /ahe'ar/ *vi* (partridge) to squawk (when cornered)

ajedrecista /aheðre'θista; aheðre'sista/ *mf* chess player

ajedrez /ahe'ðreθ; ahe'ðres/ *m*, chess

ajenjo /a'henho/ *m*, *Bot.* wormwood; absinthe

ajeno /a'heno/ *a* alien; belonging to another; various, diverse; free, exempt; unsuitable; irrelevant

ajetrear /ahetre'ar/ *vt* to tire out, exhaust; —*vr* be overtired

ajetreo /ahe'treo/ *m*, exhaustion, fatigue

ajo /'aho/ *m*, garlic; *Inf.* make up, paint; disreputable affair, shady business; curse, oath. *Inf.* **revolver el a.**, to stir up trouble

ajorca /a'horka/ *f*, bracelet; slave bangle

ajornalar /ahorna'lar/ *vt* to hire by the day

ajuar /ahu'ar/ *m*, trousseau; household equipment

ajustado /ahus'taðo/ *a* exact; tight-fitting; trim

ajustador /ahusta'ðor/ **(-ra)** *a* adjusting —*n* adjuster. *m*, tight-fitting jacket

ajustamiento /ahusta'miento/ *m*, adjustment; agreement

ajustar /ahus'tar/ *vt* to adjust; fit; arrange; make an agreement about; reconcile; settle (accounts); engage, employ; retain (a barrister); regulate; tune up (a motor); —*vi* fit; —*vr* adapt oneself. *Inf.* **a. cuentas viejas,** to settle old accounts

ajuste /a'huste/ *m*, fitting; adjustment; agreement; arrangement; *Print.* make-up. reconciliation; settlement; regulation; engagement, appointment

ajusticiado /ahusti'θiaðo; ahusti'siaðo/ **(-da)** *n* executed person

ajusticiar /ahusti'θiar; ahusti'siar/ *vt* to put to death

al /al/ (contraction of *a* + *el*). 1 —*prep a* + *m. def. art.*, to the, e.g. *Han ido al mar*, They have gone to the sea. 2 —*prep a* + *el* used as *dem. pron* to that, to the one, e.g. *Mi sombrero se parece mucho al que tiene Vd.*, My hat is very similar to the one you have. *al* + *infin.* means when, as, at the same time as, e.g. *Al llamar a la puerta la vi en el jardín*, As I was knocking at the door, I saw her in the garden

ala /'ala/ *f*, *Zool.* wing; row, line; brim (of a hat); eaves; (*Archit. Aer. Mil. Bot.*) wing; blade (of propeller); fin (of fish); *pl* courage. **a. del corazón,** *Anat.* auricle. **arrastrar el a.,** to woo, flirt with. *Fig.* **cortar (or quebrar) las alas (a),** to clip a person's wings

Alá /a'la/ *m*, Allah

alabador /alaβa'ðor/ **(-ra)** *a* praiser, extoller

alabanza /ala'βanθa; ala'βansa/ *f*, praise; eulogy

alabar /ala'βar/ *vt* to praise; —*vr* brag, boast

alabarda /ala'βarða/ *f*, halberd

alabardero /alaβar'ðero/ *m*, halberdier; *Theat.* claque, clapper

alabastrino /alaβas'trino/ *a* alabastrine, alabaster

alabastro /ala'βastro/ *m*, alabaster

alacena /ala'θena; ala'sena/ *f*, cupboard; recess; closet; safe (for food)

alacrán /ala'kran/ *m*, scorpion

alacridad /alakri'ðað/ *f*, alacrity, eagerness

alado /a'laðo/ *a* winged; feathered; *Fig.* soaring

alambicado /alambi'kaðo/ *a* sparing, frugal; subtle; euphuistic

alambicar /alambi'kar/ *vt* to distil; examine carefully, scrutinize; make over-subtle or euphuistic (of style)

alambique /alam'bike/ *m*, still

alambrada /alam'braða/ *f*, *Mil.* wire-entanglement

alambrado /alam'braðo/ *m*, wire-netting; *Mil.* wire-entanglement; wire cover

alambrar /alam'brar/ *vt* to wire (fence)

alambre /a'lambre/ *m*, wire; sheep bells. **a. espinoso,** barbed wire

alambrera /alam'brera/ *f*, wire fence; wire-netting; wire cover

alambrista /alam'brista/ *mf* tight-rope walker; (Mexico) wetback

alameda /ala'meða/ *f*, poplar wood or grove; avenue of poplars

álamo /'alamo/ *m*, poplar. **a. temblón,** aspen tree

alano /a'lano/ *m*, mastiff

alarde /a'larðe/ *m*, *Mil.* parade; display, ostentation. **hacer a. de,** to brag about

alargamiento /alarga'miento/ *m*, lengthening; stretching

alargar /alar'gar/ *vt* to lengthen; prolong; pass, hand (things); pay out (ropes, etc.); increase; —*vr* go away, depart; be wordy, spread oneself; lengthen

alarido /ala'riðo/ *m*, yell, shout; shriek, scream; howl; yelp; cry (of a seagull)

alarma /a'larma/ *f*, alarm. **a. aérea,** air-raid warning

alarmante /alar'mante/ *a* alarming

alarmar /alar'mar/ *vt* to give the alarm; frighten; —*vr* be alarmed

alarmista /alar'mista/ *mf* alarmist

alazán /ala'θan; ala'san/ *a* sorrel-colored. *m*, sorrel horse

alazo /a'laθo; a'laso/ *m*, flap or stroke of the wings

alba /'alβa/ *f*, dawn; *Eccl.* alb, vestment. **al a.,** at dawn

albacea /alβa'θea; alβa'sea/ *mf* executor, executrix; testator

albanés /alβa'nes/ **(-esa)** *a* and *n* Albanian. *m*, Albanian language

albañil /alβa'ɲil/ *m*, mason, bricklayer

albañilería /alβaɲile'ria/ *f*, masonry; bricklaying

albarda /al'βarða/ *f*, pack-saddle

albardilla /alβar'ðiʎa; alβar'ðiya/ *f*, small saddle; pad; small pillow; *Archit.* coping

albaricoque /alβari'koke/ *m*, apricot

albaricoquero /alβariko'kero/ *m*, apricot tree

albarrada /alβa'rraða/ *f*, stone wall; mud fence

albatros /alβa'tros/ *m*, albatross

albear /alβe'ar/ *vi* to become white, whiten

albedrío /alβe'ðrio/ *m*, free will; fancy, caprice

albéitar /al'βeitar/ *m*, veterinary surgeon; farrier

alberca /al'βerka/ *f*, reservoir, tank; vat; artificial lake

albergar /alβer'gar/ *vt* to shelter; nourish, harbor; —*vi* and *vr* take refuge or shelter; lodge

albergue /al'βerge/ *m*, shelter, refuge; den, lair; hospitality; lodging; asylum

albo /'alβo/ *a* pure white

albóndiga /al'βondiga/ *f*, forced meat ball, rissole

albor /al'βor/ *m*, whiteness; dawnlight, dawn. **a. de la vida,** life's dawning, childhood

alborada /alβo'raða/ *f*, dawn; reveille; *Mil.* dawn attack; *Mus.* aubade

alborear /alβore'ar/ *vi* to grow light, dawn

albornoz /alβor'noθ; alβor'nos/ *m*, burnouse

alborotado /alβoro'taðo/ *a* impulsive; turbulent; noisy; excitable

alborotar /alβoro'tar/ *vt* to disturb; —*vi* make a noise; be gay; —*vr* riot; grow rough (sea)

alboroto /alβo'roto/ *m*, noise; confusion; tumult; riot; rejoicing, gaiety; *pl* popcorn

alborozar /alβoro'θar; alβoro'sar/ *vt* to overjoy, gladden; —*vr* rejoice, be glad

alborozo /alβo'roθo; alβo'roso/ *m*, gladness, rejoicing, joy

albricias /al'βriθias; al'βrisias/ *f pl*, reward for bringer of good tidings —*interj* **¡A.!** Joy! Congratulations!

álbum /'alβum/ *m*, album

albúmina /al'βumina/ *f*, albumin

albur /al'βur/ *m*, *Ichth.* dace; chance, risk. **al a. de,** at the risk of

alcachofa /alka'tʃofa/ *f*, artichoke

alcahueta /alka'ueta/ *f*, procuress, go-between

alcahuete /alka'uete/ *m*, procurer, go-between, pimp, pander; *Fig. Inf.* protector, screen; *Inf.* scandalmonger

alcahuetear /alkauete'ar/ *vt* to procure, act as a go-between for; —*vi* be a pimp or a procuress

alcaide /al'kaiðe/ *m*, governor of a fortress *Obs.*; governor of a prison

alcalde /al'kalde/ *m*, mayor; magistrate. *Inf.* **tener el padre a.,** to have a friend at court

alcaldesa /alkal'desa/ *f*, mayoress

alcaldía /alkal'dia/ *f*, office or authority of an alcalde

álcali /'alkali/ *m*, *Chem.* alkali

alcalino /alka'lino/ *a* alkaline

alcaloide /alka'loiðe/ *m*, *Chem.* alkaloid

alcance /al'kanθe; al'kanse/ *m*, reaching, attainment; range (of firearms, etc.); scope; arm's length or reach; pursuit; stop press *or* extra edition (newspapers); *Com.* deficit; importance; *pl* talent; capacity. **al a. de la voz,** within call. **hombre de cortos alcances,** a limited, dull man. **poner al a. de,** to make available to; make intelligible to

alcancía /alkan'θia; alkan'sia/ *f*, money-box; coin bank, piggy bank

alcanfor /alkan'for/ *m*, camphor

alcanforado /alkanfo'raðo/ *a* camphorated

alcantarilla /alkanta'riʎa; alkanta'riya/ f, little bridge; sewer; culvert; bed for electric cable

alcantarillado /alkantari'ʎaðo; alkantari'yaðo/ m, sewage system; main sewer

alcanzable /alkan'θaβle; alkan'saβle/ a obtainable; attainable

alcanzadizo /alkanθa'ðiθo; alkansa'ðiso/ a attainable, easily reached

alcanzar /alkan'θar; alkan'sar/ vt to overtake; reach; range (of guns, etc.); attain, achieve; understand; Fig. equal (in attainments); live at the same time as, be contemporaneous with; be capable of, be able; —vi reach; share, participate in; be enough

alcaparra /alka'parra/ f, Bot. caper; caper bush

alcaucil /alkau'θil; alkau'sil/ m, (in most places) wild artichoke; (in some places) cultivated artichoke

alcazaba /alka'θaβa; alka'saβa/ f, fortress (within a walled town or city), casbah

alcázar /al'kaθar; al'kasar/ m, fortress; royal residence, castle; Naut. quarterdeck

alción /al'θion; al'sion/ m, Ornith. kingfisher

alcista /al'θista; al'sista/ mf speculator (on Stock Exchange)

alcoba /al'koβa/ f, bedroom; alcove, recess; Moorish flute

alcohol /al'kool/ m, alcohol; galena; eye black (cosmetic); spirits of wine. **a. desnaturalizado**, industrial alcohol, methylated spirit. **a. metílico**, wood alcohol

alcohólico /alko'oliko/ a alcoholic

alcoholismo /alkool'ismo/ m, alcoholism

alcor /al'kor/ m, hill; slope

Alcorán /alko'ran/ m, Koran

alcornoque /alkor'noke/ m, cork tree; dunderhead, dolt

alcorza /al'korθa; al'korsa/ f, Cul. icing, sugar-paste

alcorzar /alkor'θar; alkor'sar/ vt Cul. to ice, cover with sugar; decorate, adorn

alcurnia /al'kurnia/ f, lineage, family, descent

alcuza /al'kuθa; al'kusa/ f, oil-bottle; oil-can; cruet

aldaba /al'daβa/ f, door knocker; bolt, latch; pl protectors, influential helpers. Inf. **tener buenas aldabas,** to have plenty of pull

aldabada /alda'βaða/ f, rap with the knocker; sudden shock

aldabeo /alda'βeo/ m, knocking

aldea /al'dea/ f, village

aldeano /alde'ano/ **(-na)** a village; country, ignorant —n villager; countryman, peasant

aldehído /alde'iðo/ m, Chem. aldehyde

aleación /alea'θion; alea'sion/ f, alloy

alear /ale'ar/ vi to flutter, beat the wings; flap one's arms; recuperate, grow well; —vt alloy

aleatorio /alea'torio/ a accidental, fortuitous

aleccionamiento /alekθiona'miento; aleksiona'miento/ m, teaching, training, coaching

aleccionar /alekθio'nar; aleksio'nar/ vt to teach, train, coach

aledaño /ale'ðaɲo/ a adjoining; border. m, boundary, border

alegación /alega'θion; alega'sion/ f, allegation, statement

alegar /ale'gar/ vt to allege, state; cite; —vi Law. bring forward, adduce

alegato /ale'gato/ m, Law. speech (for the prosecution or defense)

alegoría /alego'ria/ f, allegory

alegórico /ale'goriko/ a allegorical

alegorizar /alegori'θar; alegori'sar/ vt to interpret allegorically, treat as an allegory

alegrar /ale'grar/ vt to make happy, gladden, rejoice; adorn, beautify; stir (fires); —vr be glad, rejoice; Inf. be merry (tipsy)

alegre /a'legre/ a joyful, glad; cheerful, gay; bright (colors, etc.); pretty, attractive; Inf. risqué; Inf. flirtatious, light

alegría /ale'gria/ f, joy, gladness; cheerfulness, gaiety; pl public rejoicings

alegrón /ale'gron/ m, sudden unexpected joy; Inf. flash of light —a Inf. flirtatious

alejamiento /aleha'miento/ m, placing at a distance, removal; withdrawal

Alejandría /alehan'dria/ Alexandria

alejar /ale'har/ vt to place at a distance, remove; withdraw; ward off (dangers, etc.); —vr depart, go away; withdraw. **alejarse de,** to abandon (a belief, custom, superstition, etc.)

alelar /ale'lar/ vt to make silly or stupid

aleluya /ale'luya/ mf, alleluia. m, Eastertide. f, small Easter cake; Inf. daub, poor painting; Inf. doggerel; joy, rejoicing

alemán /ale'man/ **(-ana)** a and n German. m, German language.

Alemania /ale'mania/ Germany

alentada /alen'taða/ f, deep breath

alentado /alen'taðo/ a valiant, spirited; proud

alentador /alenta'ðor/ a encouraging, inspiring, stimulating

alentar /alen'tar/ vi irr to breathe; —vt encourage, inspire; —vr be encouraged. See **sentar**

alerce /a'lerθe; a'lerse/ m, larch tree and wood

alergia /a'ler'hia/ f, allergy

alergólogo /aler'gologo/ m, allergist

alero /a'lero/ m, projecting roof; splashboard (of carriages); eaves; gable end

alerón /ale'ron/ m, Aer. aileron

alerta /a'lerta/ adv watchfully —interj Take care! Look out! **estar ojo a.,** to be on the watch

alerto /a'lerto/ a watchful, alert

aleta /a'leta/ f, dim. small wing; fin

aletargado /aletar'gaðo/ a lethargic; comatose

aletargamiento /aletarga'miento/ m, lethargy

aletargar /aletar'gar/ vt to cause lethargy; —vr become lethargic

aletazo /ale'taθo; ale'taso/ m, flapping, beating (of wings); Inf. theft

aletear /alete'ar/ vi to flap the wings, flutter; move the arms up and down; become convalescent

aleteo /ale'teo/ m, fluttering, flapping of wings; beating, palpitation (of heart)

aleve /a'leβe/ a See **alevoso**

alevosía /aleβo'sia/ f, Law. malice; treachery

alevoso /ale'βoso/ a Law. malicious; treacherous

alfabético /alfa'βetiko/ a alphabetical

alfabetización /alfaβetiθa'θion; alfaβetisa'sion/ f, literacy work

alfabetizador /alfaβetiθa'ðor; alfaβetisa'ðor/ m, literacy worker

alfabeto /alfa'βeto/ m, alphabet. **a. manual,** sign language

alfalfa /al'falfa/ f, Bot. lucerne

alfar /al'far/ m, potter's workshop; pottery, earthenware

alfarería /alfare'ria/ f, pottery shop; potter's workshop; potter's craft

alfarero /alfa'rero/ m, potter

alfeñique /alfe'ɲike/ m, Cul. icing, sugarpaste; Inf. affectation

alférez /al'fereθ; al'feres/ m, Mil. ensign; second lieutenant; lieutenant. Nav. **a. de fragata,** sub-lieutenant. Nav. **a. de navío,** lieutenant

alfil /al'fil/ m, bishop (in chess)

alfiler /alfi'ler/ m, pin; brooch with a pin; tiepin; pl pin-money, dress-allowance; Fig. Inf. **no estar uno con sus alfileres,** to have a slate loose. Inf. **vestido de veinticinco alfileres,** dressed to the nines

alfiletero /alfile'tero/ m, needle-case

alfombra /al'fombra/ f, carpet; rug

alfombrado /alfom'braðo/ m, carpeting

alfombrar /alfom'brar/ vt to carpet

alfombrilla eléctrica /alfom'briʎa e'lektrika; alfom'briya e'lektrika/ f, electric pad or blanket

alfombrista /alfom'brista/ m, carpet merchant; layer of carpets

alforja /al'forha/ f, saddle-bag; Mil. knapsack

alforza /al'forθa; al'forsa/ f, Sew. tuck; Inf. scar

alforzar /alfor'θar; alfor'sar/ vt Sew. to tuck

alga /'alga/ f, alga, seaweed

algalia /al'galia/ f, civet

algarabía /algara'βia/ f, Arabic; Inf. gibberish; din of voices, uproar

algarada /alga'raða/ f, troop of horse; uproar, hubbub; outcry

algarroba /alga'rroβa/ *f*, *Bot.* carob bean

algazara /alga'θara; alga'sara/ *f*, Moorish war cry; rejoicing, merriment; noise, clamor

álgebra /'alheβra/ *f*, algebra; art of bone setting

algebraico /alhe'βraiko/ *a* algebraic

algebrista /alhe'βrista/ *mf* bonesetter; algebraist

álgido /'alhiðo/ *a* icy cold

algo /'algo/ *indef pron* some, something (e.g. *Se ve que hay a. que le molesta*, You can see that something is irritating him) —*adv* somewhat, a bit. **en a.**, in some way

algodón /algo'ðon/ *m*, cotton plant; cotton flower; cotton fabric; candy floss (UK), cotton candy (USA). **a. en rama**, cotton-wool. **a. hidró-filo**, absorbent cotton wool. **a. pólvora**, nitrocellulose

algodonal /algoðo'nal/ *m*, cotton plantation

algodonero /algoðo'nero/ **(-ra)** *a* cotton —*n* cotton merchant

alguacil /algua'θil; algua'sil/ *m*, policeman, constable; *Obs.* city governor; short-legged spider

alguien /'algien/ *indef pron* someone, somebody, e.g. *Dime si viene a.*, Tell me if anyone comes

algún /al'gun/ *Abbr.* of **alguno** bef. *m sing* noun, e.g. *a. libro*

alguno /al'guno/ *a* (*Abbr.* **algún** bef. *m*, *sing*) some, any —*indef pron* someone, somebody; *pl* some, some people. **alguno que otro**, a few

alhaja /al'aha/ *f*, jewel; ornament; treasure, precious object; *Inf.* gem, excellent person (also ironic, e.g. *Es una a.*, He's a fine fellow)

alhajar /ala'har/ *vt* to adorn with jewels, bejewel; furnish, equip

alharaca /alar'aka/ *f*, vehemence, demonstration, fuss (gen. *pl*)

alheña /al'eɲa/ *f*, *Bot.* privet; henna

alhóndiga /al'ondiga/ *f*, corn exchange; public granary

aliado /a'liaðo/ *a* allied —*da* ally

alianza /a'lianθa; a'liansa/ *f*, alliance; pact, agreement; relationship (by marriage); sum total, whole (of factions, etc.); wedding-ring

aliarse /a'liarse/ *vr* to join together, become allies; be associated

alicaído /alika'iðo/ *a* drooping; *Inf.* weak, exhausted; discouraged, downhearted; come down in the world

alicates /ali'kates/ *m pl*, pincers, pliers

aliciente /ali'θiente; ali'siente/ *m*, attraction, inducement

alícuota /a'likuota/ *f*, *a* aliquot; proportional. **partes alícuotas**, aliquot parts

alienación /aliena'θion; aliena'sion/ *f*, alienation

alienado /alie'naðo/ *a* insane, mad

alienar /alie'nar/ *vt* See **enajenar**

alienista /alie'nista/ *mf* *Med.* alienist

aliento /a'liento/ *m*, breathing; breath; courage, spirit; encouragement. **el posterior a.**, one's last breath. **cobrar a.**, to regain one's breath; take heart. **de un a.**, in one breath; without stopping

alifafe /ali'fafe/ *m*, *Inf.* ailment; tumor on horse's hock

aligación /aliga'θion; aliga'sion/ *f*, binding together, alligation

aligeramiento /a,lihera'miento/ *m*, lightening, reduction in weight

aligerar /alihe'rar/ *vt* to lighten, make less heavy; quicken, hasten; ease, alleviate; moderate; shorten, abbreviate

alígero /a'lihero/ *a* *Poet.* winged; fleet, swift

alimaña /ali'maɲa/ *f*, destructive animal

alimentación /alimenta'θion; alimenta'sion/ *f*, nourishment; feeding

alimentar /alimen'tar/ *vt* to feed; nourish; encourage, foment; assist, aid; keep, support

alimenticio /alimen'tiθio; alimen'tisio/ *a* nourishing; feeding

alimento /ali'mento/ *m*, food, nourishment; stimulus, encouragement; *pl* alimony; allowance

alindar /alin'dar/ *vt* to mark the boundary of; beautify, adorn; —*vi* border, be contiguous

alineación /alinea'θion; alinea'sion/ *f*, alignment

alinear /aline'ar/ *vt* to align, range in line; dress (troops); —*vr* fall into line

aliñar /ali'ɲar/ *vt* to decorate, adorn; *Cul.* season; prepare; set (bones)

aliño /a'liɲo/ *m*, decoration, ornament; preparation; condiment, seasoning; setting (bones)

aliquebrado /alike'βraðo/ *a* broken-winged; *Inf.* down in the mouth

alisador /alisa'ðor/ **(-ra)** *a* smoothing; polishing —*n* polisher

alisar /ali'sar/ *vt* to smooth; polish; sleek; plane; comb lightly

alisios /a'lisios/ *m pl*, trade winds

aliso /a'liso/ *m*, alder tree and wood

alistador /alista'ðor/ *m*, enroller

alistamiento /alista'miento/ *m*, enlistment; conscription; enrolment

alistar /alis'tar/ *vt* to enroll, list; enlist; conscript; prepare, get ready; —*vr* enroll; *Mil.* enlist; get ready

aliviar /ali'βiar/ *vt* to lighten; alleviate, mitigate; relieve; ease; quicken (one's step); hasten, speed up; steal

alivio /a'liβio/ *m*, lightening; relief; alleviation; ease

aljaba /al'haβa/ *f*, quiver (for arrows)

aljibe /al'hiβe/ *m*, tank, cistern; watership or tanker

aljófar /al'hofar/ *m*, small irregular shaped pearl; dew-drop, raindrop, tear drop

aljofifa /alho'fifa/ *f*, floorcloth

allá /a'ʎa; a'ya/ *adv* there; to that place. **más a.**, farther on, beyond. Used in conjunction with phrases of time, indicates remoteness, e.g. *a. en tiempos de los Reyes Católicos*, long ago in the time of the Catholic Monarchs. *a. por 1900*, way back in 1900

allanamiento /aʎana'miento; ayana'miento/ *m*, leveling, flattening; condescension, affability; (police) raid, (police) search acceptance of a judicial finding

allanar /aʎa'nar; aya'nar/ *vt* to level, flatten; overcome (difficulties); soothe; break into (a house, etc.); give entrance to the police; —*vr* collapse (buildings, etc.); abide by, adapt oneself (to); condescend, be affable. **a. el camino (a...)**, to pave the way (for...)

allegado /aʎe'gaðo; aye'gaðo/ **(-da)** *a* near, allied; related —*n* follower, ally

allegar /aʎe'gar; aye'gar/ *vt* to gather, collect; draw nearer; *Agr.* reap; add; —*vi* arrive

allende /a'ʎende; a'yende/ *adv* beyond; besides. **de a. el mar**, from beyond the sea

allí /a'ʎi; a'yi/ *adv* there; to that place, thereto; thereupon, then. **por a.**, through there; that way

alma /'alma/ *f*, soul; living person; essence, core; vivacity, animation; energy, vitality; spirit, ghost; core (of a rope). **a. de cántaro**, fool, ninny. **a. de Dios**, simple soul, kind person. **a. en pena**, soul in purgatory. **¡A. mía!** My darling! **con todo el a.**, with all my heart. **Lo siento en el a.**, I feel it deeply

almacén /alma'θen; alma'sen/ *m*, warehouse; store, shop

almacenaje /almaθe'nahe; almase'nahe/ *m*, cost of storage

almacenar /almaθe'nar; almase'nar/ *vt* to store; put in store; hoard

almacenero /almaθe'nero; almase'nero/ *m*, warehouseman, storekeeper

almacenista /almaθe'nista; almase'nista/ *mf* owner of a store; assistant, salesman (saleswoman)

almáciga /al'maθiga; al'masiga/ *f*, mastic; tree plantation or nursery

almagre /al'magre/ *m*, *Mineral.* red ocher; stain, mark

almanaque /alma'nake/ *m*, calendar, almanac

almeja /al'meha/ *f*, *Ichth.* clam

almenara /alme'nara/ *f*, beacon fire

almendra /al'mendra/ *f*, almond; kernel; crystal drop (of chandeliers, etc.); cocoon; bean (of cocoa tree, etc.). **a. garapiñada**, sugar almond

almendro /al'mendro/ *m*, almond tree

almendruco /almen'druko/ *m*, green almond

almete /al'mete/ *m*, casque, helmet; helmeted soldier

almiar /al'miar/ *m*, haystack, hayrick

almíbar /al'miβar/ *m*, sugar syrup; nectar

almibarado /almiβa'raðo/ *a* syrupy; *Inf.* sugary

almibarar /almiβa'rar/ *vt* to coat with sugar; preserve (fruit) in syrup; flatter with sweet words

almidón /almi'ðon/ *m*, starch

almidonado /almiðo'naðo/ *a* starched; *Fig. Inf.* stiff, unbending; prim, starchy

almidonar /almiðo'nar/ *vt* to starch

alminar /almi'nar/ *m*, minaret (of mosque)

almiranta /almi'ranta/ *f*, admiral's wife; flagship

almirantazgo /almiran'taθgo; almiran'tasgo/ *m*, Admiralty; admiralship; Admiralty Court

almirante /almi'rante/ *m*, admiral

almizcle /al'miθkle; al'miskle/ *m*, musk

almizcleño /almiθ'kleɲo; almis'kleɲo/ *a* musk (of scents)

almizclero /almiθ'klero; almis'klero/ *a* musky. *m*, *Zool.* musk-deer

almocafre /almo'kafre/ *m*, *Agr.* hoe; trowel, dibble

almohada /almo'aða/ *f*, pillow; pillowcase; cushion. *Inf.* **aconsejarse** *or* **consultar con la a.**, to think over (a matter) carefully, sleep on it

almohadilla /almoa'ðiʎa; almoa'ðiya/ *f*, *dim* small cushion; lace or sewing cushion; pin cushion

almohadillado /almoaðiʎ'aðo; almoaðiʎ'yaðo/ *a* cushioned; padded

almoneda /almo'neða/ *f*, auction; furniture sale

almonedear /almoneðe'ar/ *vt* to auction; sell off (furniture)

almorranas /almo'rranas/ *f pl*, hemorrhoids

almorzar /almor'θar; almor'sar/ *vi irr* to lunch; breakfast. See **forzar**

almuecín, almuédano /almue'θin, al'mueðano; almue'sin, al'mueðano/ *m*, muezzin

almuerzo /al'muerθo; al'muerso/ *m*, luncheon; breakfast (not so usual)

alocado /alo'kaðo/ *a* feather-brained, reckless; crazy, wild

alocución /aloku'θion; aloku'sion/ *f*, allocution, address, harangue

áloe /'aloe/ *m*, *Bot.* aloe

alojado /alo'haðo/ **(-da)** *m*, billeted soldier —*n* lodger

alojamiento /aloha'miento/ *m*, lodging; dwelling; *Mil.* billeting; *Naut.* steerage; camp, encampment

alojar /alo'har/ *vt* to lodge; billet, quarter (troops); insert, introduce; —*vi* and *vr* lodge; live, dwell

alondra /a'londra/ *f*, *Ornith.* lark

alopatía /alopa'tia/ *f*, *Med.* allopathy

alpaca /al'paka/ *f*, alpaca (animal and fabric); nickel silver

alpargata /alpar'gata/ *f*, sandal with hemp sole

alpargatero /alparga'tero/ **(-ra)** *n* manufacturer or seller of alpargatas

Alpes, los /'alpes, los/ the Alps

alpestre /al'pestre/ *a* Alpine; rock (of plants); mountainous, lofty

alpinismo /alpi'nismo/ *m*, mountaineering

alpinista /alpi'nista/ *mf* mountaineer; climber

alpino /al'pino/ *a* Alpine

alpiste /al'piste/ *m*, bird seed

alpro /'alpro/ *f*, (Alianza para el Progreso)

alquería /alke'ria/ *f*, farmstead

alquiladizo /alkila'ðiθo; alkila'ðiso/ *a* rentable, hirable

alquilador /alkila'ðor/ **(-ra)** *n* hirer

alquilamiento /alkila'miento/ *m*, See **alquiler**

alquilar /alki'lar/ *vt* to rent; hire out; hire; —*vr* hire oneself out, serve on a wage basis

alquiler /alki'ler/ *m*, hiring out; renting; rental; hire; wages. **de a.**, for hire, on hire

alquimia /al'kimia/ *f*, alchemy

alquímico /al'kimiko/ *a* alchemic

alquimista /alki'mista/ *mf* alchemist

alquitrán /alki'tran/ *m*, tar, pitch. **a. mineral**, coal tar

alquitranado /alkitra'naðo/ *a* tarred. *m*, *Naut.* tarpaulin

alrededor /alreðe'ðor/ *adv* around, round about. **a. de**, around; approximately, about (e.g. *a. de cinco dólares*, about $5)

alrededores /alreðe'ðores/ *m pl*, environs, surrounding country

Alsacia /al'saθia; al'sasia/ Alsace

alsaciano /alsa'θiano; alsa'siano/ **(-na)** *a* and *n* Alsatian

alta /'alta/ *f*, certificate of discharge from hospital

altanería /altane'ria/ *f*, hawking; haughtiness, disdain; superciliousness

altanero /alta'nero/ *a* soaring, high-flying (of birds); supercilious; haughty, disdainful

altar /al'tar/ *m*, altar. **a. mayor**, high altar

altavoz /ˌalta'βoθ; ˌalta'βos/ *m*, loudspeaker; megaphone

altearse /alte'arse/ *vr* to rise, grow steep (of land)

alterabilidad /alteraβili'ðað/ *f*, alterability, changeability

alteración /altera'θion; altera'sion/ *f*, alteration, change; debasement (of coinage); agitation

alterar /alte'rar/ *vt* to change, alter; debase (coinage); disturb, agitate; —*vr* grow angry; become excited

altercación, /alterka'θion; alterka'sion/ *f*. **altercado** *m*, altercation, quarrel

altercar /alter'kar/ **(se)** *vi* and *vr* to quarrel, dispute, altercate

alternación /alterna'θion; alterna'sion/ *f*, alternation

alternado /alter'naðo/ *a* alternate

alternador /alterna'ðor/ *a* alternating. *m*, *Elec.* alternator

alternante /alter'nante/ *a* alternating

alternar /alter'nar/ *vt* to alternate; make one's debut as a **matador**; —*vi* alternate; (*with con*) have dealings with, know

alternativa /alterna'tiβa/ *f*, alternative, option; service performed by turns; alternation

alternativo /alterna'tiβo/ *a* alternative

alterno /al'terno/ *a* alternative; *Bot.* alternate

alteza /al'teθa; al'tesa/ *f*, altitude, height; sublimity, perfection; **(A.)** Highness (title)

altibajo /alti'βaho/ *m*, embossed velvet; *pl Inf.* rough ground; *Inf.* vicissitudes of fortune

altillo /al'tiʎo; al'tiyo/ *m*, hillock, eminence; garret, attic

altímetro /al'timetro/ *m*, *Aer.* altimeter

altiplanicie /altipla'niθie; altipla'nisie/ *f*, plateau; highland

altisonante /altiso'nante/ *a* sonorous; sublime; high-flown, pompous

altitud /alti'tuð/ *f*, altitude, height

altivez /alti'βeθ; alti'βes/ *f*, arrogance, haughtiness

altivo /al'tiβo/ *a* arrogant, haughty

alto /'alto/ *a* high; tall; difficult, arduous; sublime; deep; most serious (of crimes, etc.); dear (of price); small, early (hours). *m*, height; eminence, hill; story, floor; *Mil.* halt; red light (traffic light) —*adv* up, above, on high; loudly —*interj* **¡A.!** *Mil.* Halt! *Mil.* **A. Mando**, High Command. **las altas horas de la noche**, the small (or early) hours. **en alta voz**, in a loud voice. **en alto**, on high; up above. **hacer alto**, to halt, stop

altoparlante /ˌaltopar'lante/ *m*, *Radio.* loudspeaker

altozano /alto'θano; alto'sano/ *m*, mound, hillock; viewpoint, open space

altruismo /altru'ismo/ *m*, altruism

altruista /altru'ista/ *a* altruistic. *mf* altruist

altura /al'tura/ *f*, height; altitude; *Geom.* altitude or height; top, peak; sublimity; latitude

alucinación /aluθina'θion; alusina'sion/ *f*, **alucinamiento**, *m*, hallucination

alucinado /aluθi'naðo; alusi'naðo/ *m*, person suffering from hallucinations

alucinador /aluθina'ðor; alusina'ðor/ *a* hallucinatory, deceptive

alucinar /aluθi'nar; alusi'nar/ *vt* to dazzle, fascinate; deceive

alud /a'luð/ *m*, avalanche

aludir /alu'ðir/ *vi* to allude (to); refer (to), cite

alumbrado /alum'braðo/ *m*, lighting; *pl* illuminati

alumbramiento /alumbra'miento/ *m*, lighting, supply of light; childbirth

alumbrar /alum'brar/ *vt* to light, illuminate; give sight to the blind; instruct, teach; inflict (blows); hoe vine roots; —*vi* give birth to a child; —*vr Inf.* grow tipsy

alumbre /a'lumbre/ *m,* alum

aluminio /alu'minio/ *m,* aluminum

alumno /a'lumno/ **(-na)** *n* ward, adopted child; pupil. **a. externo,** day pupil. **a. interno,** boarder

alunizaje /aluni'θahe; aluni'sahe/ *m,* landing on the moon, moon-landing

alunizar /aluni'θar; aluni'sar/ *vi* to land on the moon

alusión /alu'sion/ *f,* allusion

alusivo /alu'siβo/ *a* allusive, suggestive; hinting

aluvial /alu'βial/ *a* alluvial

aluvión /alu'βion/ *m,* alluvium. **de a.,** alluvial

alza /'alθa; 'alsa/ *f,* rise (of temperature, etc.); increase (in price); front sight (of guns)

alzacuello /alθa'kueʎo; alsa'kueyo/ *m,* high collar, clerical collar; neck stock

alzada /al'θaða; al'saða/ *f,* horse's stature; mountain pasture; *Law.* appeal

alzado /al'θaðo; al'saðo/ *a* fraudulent (of bankruptcy); fixed (of price). *m,* theft; *Archit.* front elevation

alzamiento /alθa'miento; alsa'miento/ *m,* raising, lifting; higher bid (at auction); rising, rebellion; fraudulent bankruptcy

alzaprima /alθa'prima; alsa'prima/ *f,* lever; wedge; bridge (of string instruments)

alzar /al'θar; al'sar/ *vt* to raise; lift up; elevate (the Host); steal, remove; hide; gather in the harvest; build, construct; *Naut.* heave; —*vr* rise (of temperature, mercury, price, etc.); make a fraudulent bankruptcy; *Law.* appeal; (*with con*) run off with, steal. *Naut.* **a. la vela,** to set sail

ama /'ama/ *f,* mistress of the house; owner; housekeeper; wet nurse. **a. de casa,** homemaker, housewife. **a. de leche,** foster-mother. **a. de llaves** *or* **a. de gobierno,** housekeeper. **a. seca,** children's nurse

amabilidad /amaβili'ðað/ *f,* lovableness; kindness; niceness, goodness, helpfulness

amable /a'maβle/ *a* lovable; kind; nice, good, helpful

amador /ama'ðor/ **(-ra)** *a* loving —*n* lover, admirer

amadrigar /amaðri'gar/ *vt* to welcome, receive well; —*vr* go into a burrow or lair; go into seclusion

amaestrar /amaes'trar/ *vt* to train, instruct; tame; break in (horses)

amagar /ama'gar/ *vt* and *vi* to threaten; —*vt* show signs of (diseases, etc.); —*vr Inf.* hide

amago (contra...), /a'mago/ threat (to...), menace (to...)

amainar /amai'nar/ *vt Naut.* to take in the sails; —*vi* drop (of the wind); —*vi* and *vt* relax (efforts, etc.)

amaine /a'maine/ *m,* dropping, abatement (of the wind)

amalgama /amal'gama/ *f, Chem.* amalgam

amalgamación /amalgama'θion; amalgama'sion/ *f,* amalgamation

amalgamar /amalga'mar/ *vt* to amalgamate; —*vr* be amalgamated

amamantamiento /amamanta'miento/ *m,* suckling, nursling

amamantar /amaman'tar/ *vt* to suckle

amancebado /amanθe'βaðo; amanse'βaðo/ *m,* concubine

amancillar /amanθi'ʎar; amansi'yar/ *vt* to discredit, dishonor; tarnish; stain

amanecer /amane'θer; amane'ser/ *vi irr* to dawn; arrive *or* be somewhere *or* be doing, at dawn (e.g. *Amanecimos en el barco,* Dawn came while we were on the ship. *Amanecimos escribiendo la carta,* The day broke as we were writing the letter); appear at daybreak; begin to appear. *m,* dawn, daybreak. See **conocer**

amanerado /amane'raðo/ *a* mannered; affected

amaneramiento /amanera'miento/ *m,* manneredness; mannerism

amanerarse /amane'rarse/ *vr* to acquire mannerisms or tricks of style; become affected

amansador /amansa'ðor/ **(-ra)** *a* soothing, calming —*n* appeaser

amansamiento /amansa'miento/ *m,* taming; appeasement; soothing; breaking in (horses)

amansar /aman'sar/ *vt* to tame; appease, moderate; soothe, pacify; break in (horses)

amante /a'mante/ *a* loving. *mf* lover

amanuense /ama'nuense/ *mf* amanuensis, secretary, clerk

amanzanar /amanθa'nar; amansa'nar/ to lay out the streets of

amañar /ama'ɲar/ *vt* to execute with skill; —*vr* grow skillful

amaño /a'maɲo/ *m,* skill, dexterity; *pl* schemes, intrigues; tools, equipment

amapola /ama'pola/ *f,* poppy

amar /a'mar/ *vt* to love

amaranto /ama'ranto/ *m, Bot.* amaranth

amarar /ama'rar/ *vi* to alight on the water (of hydroplanes)

amargar /amar'gar/ *vi* to taste or be bitter; —*vt* make bitter; embitter

amargo /a'margo/ *a* bitter; embittered; grievous, sad. *m,* bitterness; *pl* bitters

amargor /amar'gor/ *m,* **amargura,** /amar'gura/ *f,* bitter taste, bitterness; trouble, affliction, pain

amaricado /amari'kaðo/ *a Inf.* effeminate

amarilis /ama'rilis/ *f, Bot.* amaryllis; *Poet.* shepherdess

amarillear /amariʎe'ar; amariye'ar/ *vi* to look yellow; turn yellow; tend to yellow

amarillento /amari'ʎento; amari'yento/ *a* yellowish, turning yellow

amarilleo /amari'ʎeo; amari'yeo/ *m,* yellowing

amarillez /amari'ʎeθ; amari'yes/ *f,* yellowness

amarillo /ama'riʎo; ama'riyo/ *a* and *m,* yellow

amarra /a'marra/ *f, Naut.* cable, thick rope

amarradero /amarra'ðero/ *m, Naut.* mooring berth; mooring-post; hitchingpost or ring

amarraje /ama'rrahe/ *m, Naut.* mooring charge

amarrar /ama'rrar/ *vt* to tie up, hitch; moor

amarre /a'marre/ *m,* mooring; hitching

amartelar /amarte'lar/ *vt* to make jealous; court, woo, make love to; —*vr* be jealous; fall madly in love

amartillar /amarti'ʎar; amarti'yar/ *vt* to hammer, knock; cock (firearms)

amasadera /amasa'ðera/ *f,* kneading-trough

amasador /amasa'ðor/ **(-ra)** *a* kneading —*n* kneader

amasar /ama'sar/ *vt* to knead; massage; scheme, plot

amasia /a'masia/ *f,* concubine

amasiato /ama'siato/ *m,* concubinage

amasijo /ama'siho/ *m, Cul.* dough; kneading; portion of plaster or mortar; *Inf.* hotchpotch, mixture; scheme, plot

amatista /ama'tista/ *f,* amethyst

amatorio /ama'torio/ *a* amatory

amazacotado /a,maθako'taðo; a,masako'taðo/ *a* heavy, dense; *Fig.* stodgy (of writings, etc.)

amazona /ama'θona; ama'sona/ *f,* Amazon; independent woman; woman rider; woman's riding habit

ambages /am'bahes/ *m pl,* maze, intricate paths; circumlocutions

ámbar /'ambar/ *m,* amber. **a. gris,** ambergris

ambarino /amba'rino/ *a* amber

Amberes /am'beres/ Antwerp

ambición /ambi'θion; ambi'sion/ *f,* ambition

ambicionar /ambiθio'nar; ambisio'nar/ *vt* to long for; desire eagerly; be ambitious to

ambicioso /ambi'θioso; ambi'sioso/ *a* ambitious; eager, desirous

ambidextro /ambi'ðekstro/ *a* ambidextrous

ambiente /am'biente/ *a* ambient, surrounding. *m,* air, atmosphere; environment

ambigú /ambi'gu/ *m,* cold buffet; buffet (in theaters, etc.)

ambigüedad /ambigue'ðað/ *f,* ambiguity

ambiguo /am'biguo/ *a* ambiguous

ámbito /'ambito/ *m,* precincts; boundary, limit; compass, scope

amblar /am'blar/ *vi* to pace (of a horse)

ambos, /'ambos,/ *a m pl,* **ambas** *a f pl,* both, e.g. *ambas casas,* both houses

ambulancia /ambu'lanθia; ambu'lansia/ *f,* ambulance. **a. de correos,** railway post office. **a. fija,** field-hospital

ambulante /ambu'lante/ *a* walking; traveling, wandering

amedrentador /ameðrenta'ðor/ *a* frightening; terrible; intimidating

amedrentar /ameðren'tar/ *vt* to frighten, scare; intimidate

ameliorar /amelio'rar/ *vt* to better, improve

amelonado /amelo'naðo/ *a* melon-shaped; *Inf.* madly in love

amén /a'men/ *m*, amen, so be it. **a. de,** besides, in addition to. *Inf.* **en un decir a.,** in a trice

amenaza /ame'naθa; ame'nasa/ *f*, threat

amenazador, amenazante /amenaθa'ðor, amena-'θante; amenasa'ðor, amena'sante/ *a* menacing, threatening

amenazar /amena'θar; amena'sar/ *vt* to threaten; —*vt* and *vi* presage, be pending

amenguamiento /amengua'miento/ *m*, lessening, diminution; discredit; loss of prestige

amenguar /amen'guar/ *vt* to lessen, decrease; dishonor, discredit

amenidad /ameni'ðað/ *f*, amenity; agreeableness

amenizar /ameni'θar; ameni'sar/ *vt* to make pleasant or attractive

ameno /a'meno/ *a* pleasant; entertaining; agreeable, delightful

América /a'merika/ America

América del Norte /a'merika del 'norte/ North America

América del Sur /a'merika del sur/ South America

americana /ameri'kana/ *f*, (man's) jacket

americanismo /amerika'nismo/ *m*, usage typical of Western-Hemisphere Spanish

americano /ameri'kano/ *a* American

ameritar /ameri'tar/ *vt West. Hem.* to deserve, merit

ametrallador /ametraʎa'ðor; ametraya'ðor/ *m*, machine-gunner

ametralladora /ametraʎa'ðora; ametraya'ðora/ *f*, machine-gun

amianto /a'mianto/ *m*, *Mineral.* amianthus, asbestos

amiba /a'miβa/ *f*, *Zool.* ameba

amicísimo /ami'θisimo; ami'sisimo/ *a superl* **amigo,** most friendly

amiga /a'miga/ *f*, woman friend; mistress, lover; dame, schoolmistress; dame school

amigabilidad /amigaβili'ðað/ *f*, friendliness, amicability

amigable /ami'gaβle/ *a* friendly, amicable; harmonious; suitable

amígdala /a'migðala/ *f*, tonsil

amigdalitis /amigða'litis/ *f*, tonsillitis

amigo /a'migo/ **(-ga)** *a* friendly; fond, addicted —*n* friend. *m*, lover. *Inf.* **ser muy a. de,** to be very friendly with; be very keen on or fond of

amilanado /amila'naðo/ *a* cowed, spiritless

amilanar /amila'nar/ *vt* to terrify, intimidate; —*vr* grow discouraged

aminorar /amino'rar/ *vt* to diminish, lessen

amir /a'mir/ *m*, emir, Arab prince or chief

amistad /amis'tað/ *f*, friendship; liaison; favor; *pl* acquaintances, friends

amistar /amis'tar/ *vt* to introduce, make known to each other; bring about a reconciliation between or with

amistoso /amis'toso/ *a* friendly

amnesia /am'nesia/ *f*, amnesia

amnistía /amnis'tia/ *f*, amnesty

amnistiar /amnisti'ar/ *vt* to concede an amnesty, pardon

amo /'amo/ *m*, head of the house; master; owner; overlord; overseer. **a. de huéspedes,** keeper of a boarding house. **Nuestro A.** Our Lord. *Inf.* **ser el a. del cotarro,** to rule the roost

amodorramiento /amoðorra'miento/ *m*, stupor, deep sleep

amodorrarse /amoðo'rrarse/ *vr* to fall into a stupor; fall into a heavy sleep

amoladera /amola'ðera/ *f*, whetstone

amolador /amola'ðor/ *m*, scissors grinder; knife grinder; sharpener

amoladura /amola'ðura/ *f*, grinding, whetting, sharpening

amolar /amo'lar/ *vt irr* to grind, sharpen; *Inf.* pester, annoy. See **colar**

amoldar /amol'dar/ *vt* to mold; adjust; —*vr* adapt oneself

amonedación /amoneða'θion; amoneða'sion/ *f*, coinage, minting

amonedar /amone'ðar/ *vt* to coin, mint

amonestación /amonesta'θion; amonesta'sion/ *f*, warning; advice. **correr las amonestaciones,** to publish bans of marriage

amonestador /amonesta'ðor/ **(-ra)** *a* warning, admonitory —*n* admonisher

amonestar /amones'tar/ *vt* to warn; advise; rebuke; *Eccl.* publish bans of marriage

amoníaco /amo'niako/ *m*, ammonia

amontillado /amonti'ʎaðo; amonti'yaðo/ *m*, kind of pale, dry sherry

amontonamiento /amontona'miento/ *m*, accumulation; gathering, collection; piling up, heaping

amontonar /amonto'nar/ *vt* to pile up, heap; gather; collect; accumulate; —*vr Inf.* fly into a rage

amor /a'mor/ *m*, love; beloved; willingness, pleasure; *pl* love affairs; caresses. **a. propio,** self-esteem; vanity. *Inf.* **con mil amores,** with great pleasure. **por a. de,** for love of; for the sake of

amoral /amo'ral/ *a* amoral

amoralidad /amorali'ðað/ *f*, amorality

amoratado /amora'taðo/ *a* livid, bluish

amorcillo /amor'θiʎo; amor'siyo/ *m*, *dim* little love; unimportant love affair; Cupid

amordazamiento /amorðaθa'miento; amorðasa-'miento/ *m*, muzzling; gagging

amordazar /amorða'θar; amorða'sar/ *vt* to muzzle; gag; prevent speaking

amorfo /a'morfo/ *a* amorphous

amorío /amo'rio/ *m*, *Inf.* wooing, love making; *pl* love affairs

amoroso /amo'roso/ *a* loving; gentle; mild, balmy

amorrar /amo'rrar/ *vi Inf.* to hang one's head; sulk, be sullen

amortajar /amorta'har/ *vt* to wrap in a shroud; enshroud

amortiguador /amortigua'ðor/ *m*, *Mech.* shock absorber. *Auto.* **a. de los muelles,** shock-absorber

amortiguamiento /amortigua'miento/ *m*, softening, deadening; mitigation, lessening

amortiguar /amorti'guar/ *vt* to soften, deaden; absorb (shocks); moderate, mitigate; soften (colors)

amortización /amortiθa'θion; amortisa'sion/ *f*, amortization

amortizar /amorti'θar; amorti'sar/ *vt* to amortize; recover, redeem; suppress, abolish (posts)

amoscarse /amos'karse/ *vr Inf.* to be piqued or annoyed; become agitated

amostazar /amosta'θar; amosta'sar/ *vt Inf.* to annoy; —*vi* become peeved

amotinador /amotina'ðor/ **(-ra)** *a* mutinous, rebellious —*n* rebel, mutineer; rioter

amotinar /amoti'nar/ *vt* to incite to rebellion; unbalance, unhinge (mind); —*vr* rebel; riot; *Fig.* be unhinged

amovible /amo'βiβle/ *a* movable, removable; removable (of officials, etc.)

amovilidad /amoβili'ðað/ *f*, movability, removability; liability to discharge or dismissal

amparador /ampara'ðor/ **(-ra)** *a* protective; sheltering —*n* protector, defender, helper; shelterer

amparar /ampa'rar/ *vt* to protect, favor, help; shelter; —*vr* take refuge, take shelter; defend oneself

amparo /am'paro/ *m*, shelter, refuge; protection, favor, help; defense

amper /am'per/ *m*, *Elec.* ampere

amperímetro /ampe'rimetro/ *m*, *Elec.* ammeter

amperio /am'perio/ *m*, *Elec.* ampere

ampliable /am'pliaβle/ *a* amplifiable

ampliación /amplia'θion; amplia'sion/ *f*, enlargement, increase, extension; *Photo.* enlargement

ampliador /amplia'ðor/ **(-ra)** *a* enlarging —*n* enlarger

ampliadora /amplia'ðora/ *f*, *Photo.* enlarger

ampliar /amp'liar/ *vt* to extend, enlarge, increase; *Photo.* enlarge

amplificación /amplifika'θion; amplifika'sion/ *f*, extension, amplification; *Photo.* enlargement

amplificar /amplifi'kar/ *vt* to enlarge; extend; increase; amplify, expatiate upon

amplio /'amplio/ *a* wide; extensive; roomy, ample; prolix

amplitud /ampli'tuð/ *f*, extension; width; spaciousness, amplitude

ampolla /am'poʎa; am'poya/ *f*, blister; ampoule; bubble; *Elec.* bulb

ampulosidad /ampulosi'ðað/ *f*, pomposity, redundancy (of style)

ampuloso /ampu'loso/ *a* pompous, high-flown (style)

amputación /amputa'θion; amputa'sion/ *f*, amputation

amputar /ampu'tar/ *vt* to amputate

amuchachado /amutʃa'tʃaðo/ *a* boyish

amueblar /amue'βlar/ *vt* to furnish; provide with furniture

amuleto /amu'leto/ *m*, amulet, charm

amurallar /amura'ʎar; amura'yar/ *vt* to surround with a wall, wall

amusgar /amus'gar/ *vt* and *vi* to flatten the ears (animals); —*vt* screw up the eyes (to see better)

ana /'ana/ *f*, ell (measure)

anabaptismo /anaβap'tismo/ *m*, Anabaptism

anabaptista /anaβap'tista/ *mf* Anabaptist

anacardo /ana'karðo/ *m*, cashew (nut)

anacoreta /anako'reta/ *mf* anchorite, hermit

anacreóntico /anakre'ontiko/ *a* Anacreontic

anacrónico /ana'kroniko/ *a* anachronous

anacronismo /anakro'nismo/ *m*, anachronism

ánade /'anaðe/ *mf* duck

anadear /anaðe'ar/ *vi* to waddle (like a duck)

anadeo /ana'ðeo/ *m*, waddle

anadino /ana'ðino/ **(-na)** *n* duckling

anadón /ana'ðon/ *m*, drake

anáfora /a'nafora/ *f*, anaphora

anafrodisíaco /anafroði'siako/ *a* anaphrodisiac

anagrama /ana'grama/ *m*, anagram

analectas /ana'lektas/ *f*, *pl* analects

anales /a'nales/ *m*, *pl* annals

analfabetismo /analfaβe'tismo/ *m*, illiteracy

analfabeto /analfa'βeto/ **(-ta)** *a* and *n* illiterate

analgesia /anal'hesia/ *f*, analgesia

analgésico /anal'hesiko/ *a* and *m*, *Med.* analgesic

análisis /a'nalisis/ *m*, analysis; *Gram.* parsing

analista /ana'lista/ *mf* analyst

analizar /anali'θar; anali'sar/ *vt* to analyse

analogía /analo'hia/ *f*, analogy

analógico, análogo /ana'lohiko, a'nalogo/ *a* analogous

ananás /ana'nas/ *m*, pineapple

anaquel /ana'kel/ *m*, shelf, ledge

anaranjado /anaran'haðo/ *a* and *m*, orange (color)

anarquía /anar'kia/ *f*, anarchy

anárquico /a'narkiko/ *a* anarchical

anarquismo /anar'kismo/ *m*, anarchism

anarquista /anar'kista/ *mf* anarchist

anatema /ana'tema/ *mf*. anathema

anatematizar /anatemati'θar; anatemati'sar/ *vt* to anathematize, denounce

anatomía /anato'mia/ *f*, anatomy

anatómico /ana'tomiko/ *a* anatomical

anatomista /anato'mista/ *mf* anatomist

anca /'anka/ *f*, croup, hindquarters of a horse

ancho /'antʃo/ *a* wide, broad. *m*, width, breadth. *Inf.* **a mis (tus, sus,** etc.) **anchas** *or* **anchos,** at my (your, his, etc.) ease, with complete freedom

anchoa /an'tʃoa/ *f*, anchovy

anchura /an'tʃura/ *f*, width, breadth; ease, freedom; extent

anchuroso /antʃu'roso/ *a* very wide; extensive; spacious

ancianidad /anθiani'ðað; ansiani'ðað/ *f*, old age; seniority; oldness

anciano /an'θiano; an'siano/ **(-na)** *a* old; ancient —*n* old person

ancla /'ankla/ *f*, anchor. **a. de la esperanza,** sheet anchor. **echar anclas,** to anchor

ancladero, anclaje /ankla'ðero, an'klahe/ *m*, anchorage

anclar /an'klar/ *vi* to anchor

áncora /'ankora/ *f*, anchor; refuge, haven

andada /an'daða/ *f*, wandering, roving; hard bread roll; pasture; *pl* trail, tracks. *Fig. Inf.* **volver a las andadas,** to return to one's old tricks

andaderas /anda'ðeras/ *f pl*, go-cart (for learning to walk)

andadoba /anda'ðoβa/ *f*, lansquenet (card game)

andador /anda'ðor/ *a* walking; swift walking; wandering. *m*, walker; garden path; *pl* leading-strings, reins

andadura /anda'ðura/ *f*, walk, gait; pace, step

Andalucía /andalu'θia; andalu'sia/ Andalusia

andaluz /anda'luθ; anda'lus/ **(-za)** *a* and *n* Andalusian

andaluzada /andalu'θaða; andalu'saða/ *f*, *Inf.* exaggeration, tall story

andamio /an'damio/ *m*, scaffolding; stand, platform

andanada /anda'naða/ *f*, *Naut.* broadside; cheapest priced seat in a bullring; *Inf.* dressing-down, scolding

andante /an'dante/ *a* walking, strolling; errant (of knights) —*a* and *m*, *Mus.* andante

andanza /an'danθa; an'dansa/ *f*, happening, occurrence; *pl* doings, deeds. **buena a.,** good fortune

andar /an'dar/ *vi irr* to walk; move; work, operate, run (machines, etc.); progress, get along (negotiations, etc.); be, feel; elapse (of time); be occupied; behave; (*with prep a*) administer (blows, etc.); (*with en*) upset, turn over (papers, etc.); ride in or on (cars, bicycles, etc.); be engaged in; (*with con*) use, handle; —*vt* traverse. *m*, gait, walk. **a. por los cuarenta,** to be in one's forties. **a. con paños tibios,** not to be firm. **a. con pies de plomo,** to be extremely cautious. **a. tras,** to follow, go after; persecute; desire ardently (things). **andarse a la flor del berro,** to sow one's wild oats. *Fig. Inf.* **andarse por las ramas,** to beat about the bush. **¡Anda!** Get along with you!; Hurry up!; You don't say so! **¡Andando!** Let's get going!, Let's get a move on it! *Preterite* **anduve,** etc —*imperf subjunc* **anduviese,** etc.

andariego /anda'riego/ *a* swift walking; wandering, vagrant

andarín (-ina) /anda'rin/ *n* good walker; professional walker

andas /'andas/ *f pl*, kind of stretcher; bier

andén /an'den/ *m*, railway platform

andero /an'dero/ *m*, bearer (of a bier)

andino /an'dino/ *a* Andean

andorrano (-na) /ando'rrano/ *a* and *n* Andorran

andrajo /an'draho/ *m*, rag, wisp of cloth, tatter

andrajoso /andra'hoso/ *a* ragged, tattered

andurriales /andu'rriales/ *m pl*, byways, unfrequented paths; remote places

anécdota /a'nekðota/ *f*, anecdote

anecdótico /anek'ðotiko/ *a* anecdotal

anegación /anega'θion; anega'sion/ *f*, drowning; flooding, inundation

anegar /ane'gar/ *vt* to drown; inundate; shipwreck; —*vr* drown; be flooded

anejo /a'neho/ *a* attached, annexed. *m*, annexed borough

anemia /a'nemia/ *f*, anemia

anémico /a'nemiko/ *a* anemic

anémona, anémone /a'nemona, a'nemone/ *f*, anemone. **anémona de mar,** sea-anemone

anestesia /anes'tesia/ *f*, anesthesia

anestesiador (-ra) /anestesia'ðor/ *n* anesthetist

anestesiar /aneste'siar/ *vt* to anesthetize

anestésico /anes'tesiko/ *a* and *m*, anesthetic

aneurisma /aneu'risma/ *mf Med.* aneurism

anexar /anek'sar/ *vt* to annex

anexión /anek'sion/ *f*, annexation

anexo /a'nekso/ *a* attached, joined. *m*, annex

anfibio /an'fiβio/ *a* amphibious. *m*, amphibian

anfiteatro /anfite'atro/ *m*, amphitheater; operating theater; dissecting room; morgue; *Theat.* dress-circle

anfitrión /anfitri'on/ *m*, *Inf.* host, one who entertains guests

ánfora /'anfora/ *f*, amphora

angarillas /aŋga'riʎas; aŋga'riyas/ *f pl*, hand barrow; table cruet; yoke and panniers

ángel /'anhel/ *m*, angel. **á. de la guarda**, guardian angel. **estar con los ángeles**, to be in Heaven (euphem. for "to be dead")

angelical, angélico /anheli'kal, an'heliko/ *a* angelic; divine, excellent

angina /an'hina/ *f*, *Med.* angina, tonsillitis. **a. de pecho**, angina pectoris

anglicanismo /aŋglika'nismo/ *m*, Anglicanism

anglicano (-na) /aŋgli'kano/ *a* and *n* Anglican

anglicismo /aŋgli'sismo/ *m*, anglicism

anglo (-la) /'aŋglo/ *a* and *n* Angle —*a* Anglo-

angloamericano (-na) /ˌaŋgloameri'kano/ *a* and *n* Anglo-American

anglófilo (-la) /aŋ'glofilo/ *n* Anglophile

anglosajón (-ona) /aŋglosa'hon/ *a* and *n* Anglo-Saxon. *m*, Anglo-Saxon language

angostar /aŋgos'tar/ *vi* and *vt* to narrow; tighten

angosto /aŋ'gosto/ *a* narrow; tight

angostura /aŋgos'tura/ *f*, narrowness; tightness; narrow pass; strait; *Fig.* tight corner, fix

anguila /aŋ'gila/ *f*, *Ichth.* eel; *pl Naut.* slipway, slips

angula /aŋ'gula/ *f*, *Ichth.* elver (young eel)

angular /aŋgu'lar/ *a* angular

ángulo /'aŋgulo/ *m*, angle. **á. inferior izquierdo**, lower lefthand corner. **á. inferior derecho**, lower righthand corner. **á. superior izquierdo**, upper lefthand corner. **á. superior derecho**, upper righthand corner. **á. recto**, right angle

anguloso /aŋgu'loso/ *a* angulate; angular, gaunt; cornered

angustia /aŋ'gustia/ *f*, anguish, grief

angustiante /aŋgus'tiante/ *a* distressing

angustiar /aŋgus'tiar/ *vt* to grieve; afflict; —*vr* be full of anguish

anhelación /anela'θion; anela'sion/ *f*, panting, hard breathing; yearning, longing

anhelar /ane'lar/ *vi* to pant, breathe with difficulty; —*vi* and *vt* long for, yearn for, desire

anhélito /a'nelito/ *m*, pant, hard breathing

anhelo (de) /a'nelo/ *m*, longing (for), desire (for), yearning (for)

anheloso /ane'loso/ *a* difficult, labored (of breathing); anxious, longing

anidar /ani'ðar/ *vi* to nest (birds); swell; —*vt* shelter, protect; —*vr* nest; dwell; nestle

anilla /a'niʎa; a'niya/ *f*, curtain ring; *pl* gymnastic rings

anillo /a'niʎo; a'niyo/ *m*, finger ring; small ring; coil (of serpents and ropes). *Inf.* **venir como a. al dedo**, to fit like a glove; come just at the right moment

ánima /'anima/ *f*, soul, spirit; soul in purgatory; bore (of firearms); *pl* prayer bell for the souls of the departed

animación /anima'θion; anima'sion/ *f*, liveliness, gaiety, animation, vivacity; bustle, movement

animal /ani'mal/ *m*, animal; *Inf.* dolt, brute —*a* animal; *Inf.* brutish, doltish

animalada /anima'laða/ *f*, *Inf.* stupidity, foolishness

animalidad /animali'ðað/ *f*, animalism

animar /ani'mar/ *vt* to animate; encourage, incite; invigorate, enliven; make gay, cheer up; make attractive, adorn; —*vr* take heart; make up one's mind; cheer up; grow gay

animismo /ani'mismo/ *m*, animism

ánimo /'animo/ *m*, soul, spirit; courage; endurance, fortitude; will, intention; mind. **con ánimo de + inf.**, with the intention of + *ger.* **¡Á.!** Courage!

animosidad /animosi'ðað/ *f*, hatred, animosity, dislike

animoso /ani'moso/ *a* spirited, lively; valiant

aniñado /ani'ɲaðo/ *a* childlike, childish

aniquilable /aniki'laβle/ *a* destructible

aniquilación /anikila'θion; anikila'sion/ *f*, destruction, annihilation; suppression; decay

aniquilador (-ra) /anikila'ðor/ *a* destructive, annihilating —*n* destroyer

aniquilamiento /anikila'miento/ *m*, See **aniquilación**

aniquilar /aniki'lar/ *vt* to annihilate, destroy completely; —*vr* waste away, decay

anís /a'nis/ *m*, aniseed, anise; anisette (liqueur)

anisar /ani'sar/ *vt* to flavor with aniseed

anisete /ani'sete/ *m*, anisette

aniversario /aniβer'sario/ *a* annual. *m*, anniversary

Anjeo /an'heo/ Anjou

ano /'ano/ *m*, anus

anoche /a'notʃe/ *adv* last night; the previous night

anochecer /anotʃe'θer; anotʃe'ser/ *vi irr* to grow night; become dark; be in a place *or* be doing something at nightfall (e.g. *Anochecimos en Lérida*, We were in Lerida at nightfall) —*vr Poet.* be obscured or darkened. *m*, nightfall, dusk. See **conocer**

anochecida /anotʃe'θiða; anotʃe'siða/ *f*, dusk, late twilight

anodino /ano'ðino/ *a Med.* anodyne; ineffective, useless; inoffensive. *m*, anodyne

anomalía /anoma'lia/ *f*, anomaly, inconstancy, irregularity; *Astron.* anomaly

anómalo /a'nomalo/ *a* anomalous, abnormal, unusual

anonadar /anona'ðar/ *vt* to destroy, annihilate; suppress; *Fig.* overwhelm, depress; humble

anónimo /a'nonimo/ *a* anonymous. *m*, anonymity; anonymous letter; unsigned literary work

anormal /anor'mal/ *a* abnormal; irregular, unusual. *mf* abnormal person

anormalidad /anormali'ðað/ *f*, abnormality; irregularity, inconsistency

anotación /anota'θion; anota'sion/ *f*, annotation

anotador (-ra) /anota'ðor/ *n* annotator

anotar /ano'tar/ *vt* to annotate; note down

anquilostoma /ankilos'toma/ *m*, *Med.* hookworm

ánsar /an'sar/ *m*, goose; drake

ansarino /ansa'rino/ *a* goose. *m*, gosling

anseático /anse'atiko/ *a* Hanseatic

ansia (de) /'ansia/ *f*, anxiety, trouble; grief; longing (for), yearning (for); greed

ansiar /an'siar/ *vt* to long for, yearn for; covet, desire

ansiedad /ansie'ðað/ *f*, anxiety, anguish, worry

ansión /an'sion/ *f*, intense desire

ansioso /an'sioso/ *a* anxious; grievous, painful; eager, desirous; greedy

anta /'anta/ *f*, *Zool.* elk; obelisk

antagónico /anta'goniko/ *a* antagonistic

antagonismo /antago'nismo/ *m*, antagonism

antagonista /antago'nista/ *mf* antagonist, adversary

antaño /an'taɲo/ *adv* last year, yesteryear; long ago

antártico /an'tartiko/ *a* antarctic

ante /'ante/ *m*, *Zool.* elk; suede; buffalo

ante /'ante/ *prep* in the presence of, before; regarding, in the face of (e.g. *a. deber tan alto*, in the face of so noble a duty)

anteado /ante'aðo/ *a* beige, buff-colored, fawn

anteanoche /antea'notʃe/ *adv* the night before last

anteayer /antea'yer/ *adv* the day before yesterday

antebrazo /ante'βraθo; ante'βraso/ *m*, forearm

antecámara /ante'kamara/ *f*, antechamber

antecedente /anteθe'ðente; antese'ðente/ *m*, antecedent. **antecedentes** *m pl* background (of a case, situation, etc.)

antecedentemente /anteθe,ðente'mente; antese,ðente'mente/ *adv* previously

anteceder /anteθe'ðer; antese'ðer/ *vt* to precede

antecesor (-ra) /anteθe'sor; antese'sor/ *a* previous —*n* predecessor. *m*, forebear, ancestor

antecoger /anteko'her/ *vt* to carry in front, lead before; pick too soon

antecomedor /antekome'ðor/ *m*, breakfast nook, breakfast room

antedata /ante'ðata/ *f*, antedate

antedatar /anteða'tar/ *vt* to antedate

antedicho /ante'ðitʃo/ *a* aforementioned, aforesaid

antediluviano /anteðilu'βiano/ *a* antediluvian

antelación /antela'θion; antela'sion/ *f*, advance, anticipation

antemano, de /ante'mano, de/ *adv* in advance, beforehand

antemeridiano /antemeri'ðiano/ *a* antemeridian, forenoon

antena /an'tena/ *f*, antenna; *Radio.* aerial

antenacido /antena'θiðo; antena'siðo/ a born prematurely

antenombre /ante'nombre/ m, title (placed before name)

anteojera /anteo'hera/ f, horse's blinker; eyeglass case

anteojo /ante'oho/ m, spy-glass, small telescope; pl horse's blinkers; eyeglasses, glasses; spectacles; goggles

antepagar /antepa'gar/ vt to pay in advance

antepalco /ante'palko/ m, vestibule of a box in a theater

antepasado /antepa'saðo/ a previous, past. m, ancestor (gen. pl)

antepecho /ante'petʃo/ m, parapet; windowsill; railing, balustrade; front (of a theater box, etc.); Naut. bulwark

antepenúltimo /antepe'nultimo/ a antepenultimate, second from the last

anteponer /antepo'ner/ vt irr to place before; prefer, favor. See **poner**

anteproyecto /antepro'yekto/ m, first sketch, preliminary work or plan

antepuerta /ante'puerta/ f, door-curtain, portiere; Mil. anteport

anterior /ante'rior/ a previous, former; anterior; aforementioned, preceding

anteriormente /anterior'mente/ adv beforehand, previously

antes /'antes/ adv before; rather, on the contrary; previously. **a. bien,** rather, sooner. **a. con a.** or **cuanto a.,** as soon as possible

antesala /ante'sala/ f, antechamber

antevíspera /ante'βispera/ f, two days previously

antiaéreo /anti'aereo/ a antiaircraft. m pl. **(cañones) antiaéreos,** A.A. guns

anticiclón /antiθi'klon; antisi'klon/ m, anticyclone

anticipación /antiθipa'θion; antisipa'sion/ f, anticipation; advance

anticipada /antiθi'paða; antisi'paða/ f, foul thrust (in fencing, etc.)

anticipadamente /antiθi,paða'mente; antisi,paða-'mente/ adv in advance; prematurely

anticipado /antiθi'paðo; antisi'paðo/ a in advance; premature

anticipador /antiθipa'ðor; antisipa'ðor/ a anticipatory

anticipar /antiθi'par; antisi'par/ vt to anticipate; foresee; forestall; advance (money); lend; —vr happen before time; (with prep a) act in advance of, anticipate; get ahead of oneself

anticipo /anti'θipo; anti'sipo/ m, anticipation, advance; advance payment; sum of money lent

anticlerical /antikleri'kal/ a anticlerical

anticlímax /anti'klimaks/ m, anticlimax

anticonstitucional /antikonstituθio'nal; antikonstitusio'nal/ a unconstitutional

Anticristo /anti'kristo/ m, Antichrist

anticuado /anti'kuaðo/ a antiquated, ancient

anticuario /anti'kuario/ m, antiquarian, antique dealer

antídoto /an'tiðoto/ m, antidote

antiesclavista /antieskla'βista/ a antislavery. mf antislavist

antiespasmódico /antiespas'moðiko/ a and m, Med. antispasmodic

antiestético /anties'tetiko/ a unesthetic

antietimológico /antietimo'lohiko/ a non-etymological, unetymological

antifaz /anti'faθ; anti'fas/ m, mask; face-covering

antiflogístico /antiflo'histiko/ a and m, Med. antiphlogistic

antigramatical /antigramati'kal/ a ungrammatical

antigualla /anti'guaʎa; anti'guaya/ f, antique; ancient custom; anything out-of-date

antiguamente /antigua'mente/ adv in time past, formerly

antiguamiento /antigua'miento/ m, seniority

antigüedad /antigue'ðaθ/ f, antiquity; ancients; length of service (in an employment); pl antiquities

antiguo /an'tiguo/ a ancient, very old; antique; senior (in an employment); former. m, senior member (of a community, etc.). m pl, ancients. **A. Testamento,** Old Testament. **de a.,** from ancient times. **en lo antiguo,** in ancient times; in former times, in days of yore

antillano /anti'ʎano; anti'yano/ **(-na)** a and n of or from the Antilles

Antillas, las /an'tiʎas, las; an'tiyas, las/ the Antilles

antílope /an'tilope/ m, antelope

antimacasar /antimaka'sar/ m, antimacassar

antimilitarismo /antimilita'rismo/ m, antimilitarism

antimilitarista /antimilita'rista/ a antimilitaristic

antimonárquico /antimo'narkiko/ a antimonarchical

antimonio /anti'monio/ m, Metall. antimony

antipalúdico /antipa'luðiko/ a antimalarial

antipapa /anti'papa/ m, antipope

antipara /anti'para/ f, screen, shield

antiparras /anti'parras/ f pl, Inf. spectacles, eyeglasses, glasses

antipatía /antipa'tia/ f, antipathy

antipático /anti'patiko/ a disagreeable; unattractive

antipatriótico /antipa'triotiko/ a unpatriotic

antípoda /an'tipoða/ a and m, or f, antipode

antiquísimo /anti'kisimo/ a superl, antiguo, most ancient

antirrepublicano /antirrepuβli'kano/ a antirepublican

antisemita /antise'mita/ a anti-Semitic. mf anti-Semite

antisemitismo /antisemi'tismo/ m, anti-Semitism

antiséptico /anti'septiko/ a and m, antiseptic

antisifilítico /antisifi'litiko/ a Med. anti-syphilitic

antisocial /antiso'θial; antiso'sial/ a antisocial

antítesis /an'titesis/ f, antithesis

antitético /anti'tetiko/ a antithetic, contrasted

antófago /an'tofago/ a anthophagous, flower-eating

antojadizo /antoha'ðiθo; antoha'ðiso/ a capricious, fanciful, whimsical

antojarse /anto'harse/ vr to have a fancy for, want (e.g. Se me antoja marcharme al campo, I have a yen to go to the country); suspect, imagine

antojo /an'toho/ m, caprice, fancy, whim; desire, will; pl birthmark

antología /antolo'hia/ f, anthology

antólogo /an'tologo/ m, anthologist

antonomasia /antono'masia/ f, antonomasia. **por a.,** by analogy, by transference

antorcha /an'tortʃa/ f, torch, flambeau

antracita /antra'θita; antra'sita/ f, anthracite

ántrax /'antraks/ m, Med. anthrax

antro /'antro/ m, cave, cavern; Anat. antrum

antropofagia /antropo'fahia/ f, cannibalism, anthropophagy

antropófago /antro'pofago/ **(-ga)** a cannibalistic —n cannibal

antropología /antropolo'hia/ f, anthropology

antropológico /antropo'lohiko/ a anthropological

antropólogo /antro'pologo/ m, anthropologist

antropometría /antropome'tria/ f, anthropometry

antropomorfo /antropo'morfo/ a anthropomorphous

antroposofía /antroposo'fia/ f, anthroposophy

antruejo /antru'eho/ m, three days of carnival before Lent

anual /a'nual/ a yearly, annual

anualidad /anuali'ðaθ/ f, annuity

anuario /a'nuario/ m, directory, yearbook, handbook

anubarrado /anuβa'rraðo/ a covered with clouds, cloudy

anublado /anu'βlaðo/ a lowering, overcast; clouded

anublar /anu'βlar/ vt to cloud; darken, obscure; blight (plants); —vr cloud over; become blighted or mildewed

anudar /anu'ðar/ vt to knot; tie, fasten; join; continue; **a. amistad de,** to strike up a friendship with. **a. la corbata,** to put on one's tie, tie one's tie; —vr grow stunted

anulable /anu'laβle/ a annulable, voidable

anulación /anula'θion; anula'sion/ f, annulment, abrogation

anular /anu'lar/ a annular, ring-shaped —vt to annul; Math. cancel out

anuloso /anu'loso/ *a* annulate, formed of rings

anunciación /anunθia'θion; anunsia'sion/ *f, Eccl.* Annunciation; announcement

anunciador /anunθia'ðor; anunsia'ðor/ **(-ra)**, *n* **anunciante** /anun'θiante; anun'siante/ *mf* announcer; advertiser

anunciar /anun'θiar; anun'siar/ *vt* to announce; publish, proclaim; advertise; foretell, presage. **Anuncian lluvia,** The forecast calls for rain

anuncio /a'nunθio; a'nunsio/ *m,* announcement; publication, proclamation; advertisement; presage, omen. **a. luminoso,** sky-sign

anverso /am'berso/ *m,* obverse, face

anzuelo /an'θuelo; an'suelo/ *m,* fish-hook; *Cul.* fritter; *Inf.* attraction, inducement

añadido /aɲa'ðiðo/ *m,* hair-switch; make-weight

añadidura /aɲaði'ðura/ *f,* addition; make-weight, extra

añadir /aɲa'ðir/ *vt* to add; increase

añagaza /aɲa'gaθa; aɲa'gasa/ *f,* decoy bird; enticement, lure

añejo /a'ɲeho/ *a* very old

añicos /a'ɲikos/ *m pl,* fragments, small pieces. **hacer a.,** to break into fragments

añil /a'ɲil/ *m,* indigo; indigo blue

año /'aɲo/ *m,* year; *pl* birthday. **a. bisiesto,** leap-year. **a. económico,** fiscal year. **A. Nuevo,** New Year. **tener (siete) años,** to be (seven) years old. **los Años Bobos,** the period from 1874 to 1898 in Spain

añoranza /aɲo'ranθa; aɲo'ransa/ *f,* homesickness, loneliness; nostalgia

añorar /aɲo'rar/ *vi* to be homesick or lonely

añoso /a'ɲoso/ *a* very old, full of years

añublo /a'ɲuβlo/ *m,* mildew

aojamiento /aoha'miento/ *m,* evil eye, wicked spell

aojar /ao'har/ *vt* to bewitch, place under a spell; spoil, frustrate

aojo /a'oho/ *m,* evil eye; magic spell

aorta /a'orta/ *f, Anat.* aorta

aovillarse /aoβi'ʎarse; aoβi'yarse/ *vr* to roll oneself into a ball; curl up

apabullante /apaβu'ʎante; apaβu'yante/ *a* crushing, flattening

apacentadero /apaθenta'ðero; apasenta'ðero/ *m,* grazing land, pasture

apacentamiento /apaθenta'miento; apasenta-'miento/ *m,* pasturage; grazing

apacentar /apaθen'tar; apasen'tar/ *vt irr* to put out to grass; teach, instruct; satisfy (one's desires); —*vr* graze (cattle). See **acertar**

apacibilidad /apaθiβili'ðað; apasiβili'ðað/ *f,* agreeableness; mildness; peaceableness

apacible /apa'θiβle; apa'siβle/ *a* agreeable; mild; peaceable; calm, peaceful

apaciguamiento /a,paθigua'miento; a,pasigua-'miento/ *m,* appeasement; soothing, pacification

apaciguar /apaθi'guar; apasi'guar/ *vt* to appease, pacify; calm

apadrinar /apaðri'nar/ *vt* to act as godfather to; be best man to (at a wedding); act as a second for (in a duel); sponsor; favor

apagable /apa'gaβle/ *a* extinguishable

apagado /apa'gaðo/ *a* timid, nervous; pale (of colors); dull, lusterless

apagador /apaga'ðor/ **(-ra)** *a* quenching —*n* extinguisher. *m,* candle-snuffer; damper (of a piano)

apagaincendios /apagain'θendios; apagain-'sendios/ *m,* ship's fire-extinguisher

apagamiento /apaga'miento/ *m,* quenching, extinguishment

apagar /apa'gar/ *vt* to extinguish, put out; *Fig.* quench, moderate; slake (lime); *Art.* tone down (colors); shut off (engines)

apagarrisas /apaga'rrisas/ *mf* crapehanger, killjoy, wet blanket

apagavelas /apaga'βelas/ *m,* candle-snuffer

apalabrar /apala'βrar/ *vt* to make an appointment with; discuss, consider

apaleamiento /apalea'miento/ *m,* beating, thrashing

apalear /apale'ar/ *vt* to beat, thrash; knock down with a stick

apandillarse /apandi'ʎarse; apandi'yarse/ *vr* to form a gang or group

apañar /apa'ɲar/ *vt* to take away, remove; seize; steal; dress; get ready; *Inf.* wrap up; patch, repair; —*vr Inf.* grow skillful

apaño /a'paɲo/ *m,* dexterity; skill; craft, guile

aparador /apara'ðor/ *m,* shop window; sideboard; workshop; *Eccl.* credence (table)

aparato /apa'rato/ *m,* apparatus; equipment, utensils; pomp, ostentation; symptoms; sign, circumstance, token. **a. digestivo,** digestive system; digestive tract. **a. fonador,** speech apparatus

aparatoso /apara'toso/ *a* showy, ostentatious. **incendio. a.,** a conflagration, large fire

aparcería /aparθe'ria; aparse'ria/ *f,* partnership (in a farm)

aparear /apare'ar/ *vt* to match, make equal; pair; mate (animals); —*vr* form up in pairs

aparecer /apare'θer; apare'ser/ **(se)** *vi* and *vr irr* to appear; seem; be. See **conocer**

aparecido /apare'θiðo; apare'siðo/ *m,* apparition, specter

aparejador /apareha'ðor/ *m,* overseer, foreman; *Naut.* rigger

aparejar /apare'har/ *vt* to prepare, make ready; saddle (horses); prime, size; rig (a ship)

aparejo /apa'reho/ *m,* preparation, arrangement; harness, trappings; *Naut.* rigging; *Naut.* gear; priming, sizing; *Mech.* tackle; *pl* equipment

aparentar /aparen'tar/ *vt* to pretend, simulate

aparente /apa'rente/ *a* seeming, apparent; obvious, visible; suitable, proper

aparición /apari'θion; apari'sion/ *f,* appearance, arrival; apparition, phantom

apariencia /apa'rienθia; apa'riensia/ *f,* appearance, looks, probability, likelihood; outward semblance; *pl Theat.* scenery

apartadamente /apartaða'mente/ *adv* apart, in private; secretly

apartadero /aparta'ðero/ *m,* passing place for cars; railway siding; grass verge. **a. ferroviario,** railway marshaling yard

apartado /apar'taðo/ *a* distant, far off; secluded; different. *m,* post-office box; secluded room; smelting house; sorting of cattle; selection of bulls for a bullfight

apartamiento /aparta'miento/ *m,* separation; withdrawal, retiral; seclusion; apartment, flat; *Law.* withdrawal of an action

apartar /apar'tar/ *vt* to separate; remove (e.g. an obstacle), take away; *Rail.* shunt; dissuade; sort; —*vr* obtain a divorce; *Law.* withdraw an action. **apartarse de la tradición,** to depart from tradition

aparte /a'parte/ *adv* aside, on one side; separately; *Theat.* aside; besides; beyond. *m, Theat.* aside; paragraph; space between words. **¡Aparte!** Move to one side!

apartidario /aparti'ðario/ *a* non-partisan

apasionado /apasio'naðo/ **(-da)** *a* impassioned; fervent, devoted; passionate; enthusiastic —*n* admirer, lover; enthusiast

apasionamiento /apasiona'miento/ *m,* passion

apasionar /apasio'nar/ *vt* to arouse to passion; pain; —*vr (with por)* grow passionately fond of; become enthusiastic for

apatía /apa'tia/ *f,* apathy

apático /a'patiko/ *a* apathetic

apeadero /apea'ðero/ *m,* mounting-block; halt, stopping place; wayside railway station; pied-à-terre, occasional dwelling

apear /ape'ar/ *vt* to dismount; hobble (horse); survey, map out; fell a tree; *Fig.* overcome (difficulties); *Inf.* dissuade; prop; remove, bring down; scotch (a wheel); —*vr* dismount; alight, step off

apechugar /apetʃu'gar/ *vi* to push with the breast; *Inf.* put up with reluctantly

apedazar /apeða'θar; apeða'sar/ *vt* to tear; break; mend, repair

apedrear /apeðre'ar/ *vt* to stone; stone to death; —*vi impers* hail; —*vr* be damaged by hail (crops)

apegarse /ape'garse/ *vr* to grow fond (of), become attached (to)

apego /a'pego/ *m,* fondness, inclination; affection, attachment

apelación /apela'θion; apela'sion/ *f, Law.* appeal; *Inf.* doctor's consultation

apelante /ape'lante/ *a* and *mf Law.* appellant

apelar /ape'lar/ *vi Law.* to appeal; (*with prep a*) have recourse to; —*vi* be of the same color (horses)

apellidar /apeʌi'ðar; apeyi'ðar/ *vt* to name, call; acclaim; call to arms; —*vr* be named

apellido /ape'ʌiðo; ape'yiðo/ *m,* surname; nickname; call to arms; clamor; name

apenar /ape'nar/ *vt* to grieve, afflict; cause sorrow

apenas /a'penas/ *adv* scarcely; immediately, as soon as; with trouble or difficulty

apéndice /a'pendiθe; a'pendise/ *m,* appendix, supplement; *Anat.* appendix

apendicitis /apendi'θitis; apendi'sitis/ *f,* appendicitis

Apeninos, los /ape'ninos, los/ the Apennines

apeo /a'peo/ *m,* survey; scaffolding; prop, support

apercibimiento /aperθiβi'miento; apersiβi'miento/ *m,* preparation; provision; warning; *Law.* summons

apercibir /aperθi'βir; apersi'βir/ *vt* to prepare, furnish; warn; *Law.* summon

apergaminado /apergami'naðo/ *a* parchment; parchment-like

apergaminarse /apergami'narse/ *vr Inf.* to shrivel, dry up (with old age, etc.)

aperitivo /aperi'tiβo/ *a* aperitive. *m,* aperient; aperitive, appetizer

apertura /aper'tura/ *f,* opening; inauguration; reading (of a will)

apesadumbrar /apesaðum'brar/ *vt* to sadden, afflict, grieve

apestar /apes'tar/ *vt* to infect with the plague; catch the plague; *Fig.* corrupt; *Inf.* pester, annoy; —*vi* stink

apestoso /apes'toso/ *a* stinking, putrid

apetecer /apete'θer; apete'ser/ *vt irr* to want, desire; attract. See **conocer**

apetecible /apete'θiβle; apete'siβle/ *a* attractive, desirable

apetencia /ape'tenθia; ape'tensia/ *f,* appetite; desire

apetito /ape'tito/ *m,* appetite

apetitoso /apeti'toso/ *a* appetising; tasty, savory; attractive

apiadarse /apia'ðarse/ *vr* (*with de*) to have compassion on, be sorry for

ápice /'apiθe; 'apise/ *m,* apex; peak, summit, top; orthographic accent; iota, tittle; crux (of a problem)

apicultor /apikul'tor/ (**-ra**) *n* apiarist, beekeeper

apicultura /apikul'tura/ *f,* apiculture, beekeeping

apilar /api'lar/ *vt* to pile, heap

apiñado /api'ɲaðo/ *a* crowded, serried

apiñamiento /apiɲa'miento/ *m,* crowding; congestion

apiñar /api'ɲar/ *vt* to group together, crowd; —*vr* crowd

apio /'apio/ *m,* celery

apisonadora /apisona'ðora/ *f,* steam-roller; roller

apisonar /apiso'nar/ *vt* to roll, stamp, flatten, ram down; tamp, pack down (e.g. tobacco in a pipe)

apizarrado /apiθa'rraðo; apisa'rraðo/ *a* slate-colored

aplacable /apla'kaβle/ *a* appeasable, placable

aplacamiento /aplaka'miento/ *m,* appeasement

aplacar /apla'kar/ *vt* to appease, calm; moderate, mitigate

aplacible /apla'θiβle; apla'siβle/ *a* agreeable, pleasant

aplanar /apla'nar/ *vt* to flatten, level; roll (pastry); *Inf.* dumbfound, overwhelm; —*vr* collapse (buildings); lose heart

aplastar /aplas'tar/ *vt* to flatten, squash, crush; *Inf.* squash flat, floor

aplaudir /aplau'ðir/ *vt* to applaud, clap; praise, commend, approve

aplauso /a'plauso/ *m,* applause; clapping, plaudit; approbation, commendation

aplazamiento /aplaθa'miento; aplasa'miento/ *m,* postponement; appointment, summons

aplazar /apla'θar; apla'sar/ *vt* to summon, arrange a meeting; postpone; adjourn

aplicabilidad /aplikaβili'ðað/ *f,* applicability

aplicable /apli'kaβle/ *a* applicable

aplicación /aplika'θion; aplika'sion/ *f,* application; diligence, assiduity; appliqué, ornamentation

aplicado /apli'kaðo/ *a* diligent, hardworking; appliqué

aplicar /apli'kar/ *vt* to apply; impute; intend, destine (for processions); *Law.* adjudge; —*vr* engage in; apply oneself. **a. el oído,** to listen intently. **a. sanciones,** *Polit.* to impose sanctions

aplomado /aplo'maðo/ *a* self-possessed, dignified; leaden, lead-colored

aplomar /aplo'mar/ *vt* and *vi* to plumb, test with a plumb-line; —*vr* collapse, fall down

aplomo /a'plomo/ *m,* self-possession, dignity; sangfroid

apocado /apo'kaðo/ *a* spiritless, timid; base, mean

Apocalipsis /apoka'lipsis/ *m,* Apocalypse

apocalíptico /apoka'liptiko/ *a* apocalyptic

apocamiento /apoka'miento/ *m,* timidity, pusillanimity; depression, discouragement; shyness; baseness, meanness

apocar /apo'kar/ *vt* to diminish, reduce; humiliate, scorn

apócrifo /a'pokrifo/ *a* fictitious, false; apocryphal. **Apócrifos,** Apocrypha

apodar /apo'ðar/ *vt* to nickname

apoderado /apoðe'raðo/ *a* authorized. *m,* attorney; deputy; proxy

apoderar /apoðe'rar/ *vt* to authorize; grant powers of attorney to; —*vr* (*with de*) seize, take possession of

apodo /a'poðo/ *m,* nickname

apogeo /apo'heo/ *m, Astron.* apogee; *Fig.* zenith, peak (of fame, etc.)

apolillar /apoli'ʌar; apoli'yar/ *vt* to eat clothes (moths); —*vr* be moth-eaten

apolíneo /apo'lineo/ *a* Apollo-like

apologético /apolo'hetiko/ *a* apologetic

apologista /apolo'hista/ *mf* apologist

apólogo /a'pologo/ *m,* apologue, moral fable

apoltronarse /apoltro'narse/ *vr* to grow idle

apoplejía /apople'hia/ *f,* apoplexy

apoplético /apo'pletiko/ (**-ca**) *a* and *n* apoplectic

aporrear /aporre'ar/ *vt* to beat, cudgel; —*vr* work hard, slog away

aportación /aporta'θion; aporta'sion/ *f,* contribution; occasionnar

aportar /apor'tar/ *vt* to cause, occasion; contribute; —*vi Naut.* reach port; **El buque aportó a Nueva York,** The ship reached New York, The ship sailed into New York harbor; arrive at an unexpected place

aposentador /aposenta'ðor/ *m,* usher; *Mil.* billeting officer

aposentar /aposen'tar/ *vt* to lodge, give hospitality to; —*vr* lodge, settle down

aposento /apo'sento/ *m,* room; suite, apartments; lodging, accommodation; *Theat.* box

aposición /aposi'θion; aposi'sion/ *f, Gram.* apposition

apósito /a'posito/ *m,* poultice, external application; (medical) dressing

apostadero /aposta'ðero/ *m, Naut.* naval station; placing or stationing (of soldiers)

apostar /apos'tar/ *vt irr* to bet; station (soldiers); —*vi* compete, rival. See **contar**

apostasía /aposta'sia/ *f,* apostasy

apóstata /a'postata/ *mf* apostate

apostilla /apos'tiʌa; apos'tiya/ *f,* marginal note, gloss

apóstol /a'postol/ *m,* apostle

apostólico /apos'toliko/ *a* apostolic

apóstrofe /a'postrofe/ *m,* or *f,* apostrophe, hortatory exclamation

apóstrofo /a'postrofo/ *m, Gram.* apostrophe

apostura /apos'tura/ *f,* neatness, spruceness

apotegma /apo'tegma/ *m,* apothegm, maxim

apoteosis /apote'osis/ *f,* apotheosis

apoyar /apo'yar/ *vt* (*with en*) to lean against; rest upon; —*vt* uphold, favor; confirm, bear out; droop the head (horses); second (a motion); —*vi* (*with en*) rest on; lean against; —*vr* (*with en*) rest on; lean against; **apoyarse de codos,** to lean on one's elbows; be upheld by; *Fig.* be founded on; *Fig.* depend on, lean on

apoyo /a'poyo/ *m*, support, prop; windowsill, sill; assistance; backing, support

apreciable /apreθia'βle; apresia'βle/ *a* appreciable; estimable; important

apreciación /apreθia'θion; apresia'sion/ *f*, appreciation; valuation, estimate

apreciador /apreθia'ðor; apresia'ðor/ **(-ra)** *a* appreciatory —*n* appreciator

apreciar /apre'θiar; apre'siar/ *vt* to estimate (values); appreciate; like, esteem, have a regard for

apreciativo /apreθia'tiβo; apresia'tiβo/ *a* appreciative

aprecio /a'preθio; a'presio/ *m*, valuation; appreciation, regard

aprehender /apreen'der/ *vt* to apprehend, catch; seize (contraband); understand, grasp

aprehensión /apreen'sion/ *f*, seizure, apprehension

apremiador, apremiante /apremia'ðor, apre'miante/ *a* urgent, pressing

apremiar /apre'miar/ *vt* to hurry; urge, press; force, oblige; burden, oppress (with taxes)

apremio /a'premio/ *m*, insistence, pressure; compulsion; demand note

aprendedor /aprende'ðor/ **(-ra)** *n* learner

aprender /apren'der/ *vt* to learn. **a. de memoria,** to learn by heart

aprendiz /apren'diθ; apren'dis/ **(-za)** *n* apprentice

aprendizaje /aprendi'θahe; aprendi'sahe/ *m*, apprenticeship. **hacer el a.,** to serve an apprenticeship

aprensión /apren'sion/ *f*, capture; fear, apprehension; suspicion, fancy; prejudice, scruple

aprensivo /apren'siβo/ *a* apprehensive, nervous, fearful

apresar /apre'sar/ *vt* to nab, catch; capture (a ship); imprison; fetter

aprestar /apres'tar/ *vt* to prepare, arrange; dress (fabrics)

apresto /a'presto/ *m*, preparation, arrangement; dressing (for cloth)

apresurar /apresu'rar/ *vt* to quicken; —*vr* hasten, be quick

apretado /apre'taðo/ *a* difficult, dangerous; tight; crabbed (of handwriting); clustered (e.g. *casas apretadas alrededor de la sinagoga,* houses clustered around the synagogue). *Inf.* mean, close-fisted. *m*, small close handwriting

apretadura /apreta'ðura/ *f*, tightening, compression

apretar /apre'tar/ *vt irr* to tighten; compress; urge on, press; harass, vex; trouble, worry; speed up; squeeze; press (bells, gun triggers, etc.); —*vi* increase, grow worse (storms, heat, etc.); pinch, hurt (shoes). **a. los pasos,** to quicken one's pace. *Inf.* **a. a correr,** to take to one's heels. **¡Aprieta!** *Inf.* Nonsense! It can't be! See **acertar**

apretón /apre'ton/ *m*, squeeze, grip, pressure; *Inf.* sprint, spurt; *Inf.* fix, pickle. **a. de manos,** handshake

apretujamiento /apretuha'miento/ *m*, squeezing together

apretujar /apretu'har/ *vt Inf.* to squeeze, hug

aprieto /a'prieto/ *m*, crowd, crush; urgency; *Inf.* jam, trouble, fix

aprisa /a'prisa/ *adv* quickly, in a hurry

aprisco /a'prisko/ *m*, cattle-shed; sheepfold

aprisionar /aprisio'nar/ *vt* to imprison; bind, fetter; tie

aprobación /aproβa'θion; aproβa'sion/ *f*, approbation, approval, commendation; ratification (of a bill); pass (in an examination)

aprobado /apro'βaðo/ *m*, pass certificate (in examinations)

aprobar /apro'βar/ *vt irr* to approve; pass (in an examination). See **contar**

apropiación /apropia'θion; apropia'sion/ *f*, appropriation; application; adaptation

apropiado /apro'piaðo/ *a* appropriate, suitable, proper

apropiar /apro'piar/ *vt* to appropriate; adapt, fit; —*vr* appropriate, take possession

aprovechable /aproβe'tʃaβle/ *a* usable, available

aprovechado /aproβe'tʃaðo/ *a* advantageous; assiduous, conscientious; capable; thrifty

aprovechador /aproβetʃa'ðor/ *a* self-seeking

aprovechamiento /aproβetʃa'miento/ *m*, utilization, employment; exploitation; profitable use

aprovechar /aproβe'tʃar/ *vi* to be advantageous or useful; be beneficial; make progress (in studies, etc.); —*vt* use; profit by; —*vr* take advantage of, make use of. **¡Que aproveche!** May it do you good! (said to anyone eating)

aprovisionar /aproβi'sionar/ *vt* to provision, supply

aproximación /aproksima'θion; aproksima'sion/ *f*, approximation; consolation prize (in a lottery)

aproximadamente /aproksimaða'mente/ *adv* approximately; nearly, almost

aproximar /aproksi'mar/ *vt* to bring or draw nearer; —*vr* approach; be almost, be approximately; draw closer

aptitud /apti'tuð/ *f*, aptitude, ability; fitness; propensity

apto /'apto/ *a* suitable, fitting; competent. **no apta para menores,** not suitable for children (of films, etc.)

apuesta /a'puesta/ *f*, bet, wager; competition

apuestas benéficas de fútbol /a'puestas be'nefikas de 'futβol/ football pools

apuesto /a'puesto/ *a* elegant; handsome, well set-up

apuntación /apunta'θion; apunta'sion/ *f*, noting down; note; *Mus.* notation

apuntador /apunta'ðor/ **(-ra)** *n* note-taker; observer. *m*, *Theat.* prompter; *Theat.* stage-manager

apuntalar /apunta'lar/ *vt* to prop, prop up, underpin, bolster

apuntamiento /apunta'miento/ *m*, summary; *Law.* indictment, minute

apuntar /apun'tar/ *vt* to aim (a gun, etc.); point to, indicate; note down; mark; sketch; sharpen; bet (at cards); fasten temporarily; *Inf.* mend; *Theat.* prompt; suggest, hint (e.g. *La fecha está apuntada en vanos manuscritos,* The date is hinted at in various manuscripts); —*vi* begin to appear. *Inf.* **a. y no dar,** to promise and do nothing

apunte /a'punte/ *m*, abstract; note; annotation; sketch; *Theat.* prompt or prompter or prompt book or cue; stake in a card game

apuñalado /apuɲa'laðo/ *a* dagger-shaped

apuñalar /apuɲa'lar/ *vt* to stab, attack with a dagger

apurado /apu'raðo/ *a* poor, needy; dangerous; difficult; accurate, exact; hurried

apurar /apu'rar/ *vt* to purify; drain; exhaust; finish, conclude; examine closely, scrutinize (e.g. *apurar una materia,* to exhaust a subject, examine a subject thoroughly); irritate, make impatient; urge on, hasten; —*vr* be anxious, fret

apuro /a'puro/ *m*, difficulty, fix; poverty, want; anxiety, worry. **pasar apuros,** to have a hard time

aquejar /ake'har/ *vt* to afflict; weary, beset, harass; —*vr* complain; hurry

aquel, aquella, *a* *m* **aquella,** *a* *f* **aquellos,** *a* *m pl* **aquellas** *a* *f pl*, that, those; that or those over there (farther off than **ese**)

aquel /a'kel/ *m*, charm, attraction, it

aquél, aquélla, aquéllos, aquéllas /a'kel, a'keʎa, a'keʎos, a'keʎas; a'kel, a'keʎas, a'keyos, a'keyas/ *dem pron m, f,* sing. and pl., that, the one, those, those ones; the former. e.g. *La casa que ve usted a lo lejos aquélla es la vivienda de mi tío,* The house that you see in the distance, that is my uncle's dwelling. *Éste no me gusta pero aquél sí,* I do not like the latter, but I like the former

aquelarre /ake'larre/ *m*, witches' sabbath

aquello /a'keʎo; a'keyo/ *dem pron neut* that; the fact; the matter, the affair, the former (remark, idea, etc.). e.g. *Todo a. por fin acabó,* All that came to an end at last. *a. de,* the fact that

aquende /a'kende/ *adv* on this side (rarely used)

aquí /a'ki/ *adv* here. **de a.,** hence the fact that. **¡He a.!** Behold!

aquiescencia /akies'θenθia; akies'sensia/ *f*, consent, acquiescence

aquietar /akie'tar/ *vt* to calm, soothe

aquilatar /akila'tar/ *vt* to assay; scrutinize; examine, weigh up (persons)

aquistar /akis'tar/ *vt* to attain, acquire

ara /'ara/ *f*, altar; **en aras de,** in honor of; for the sake of

árabe /'araβe/ *a* Arab, Arabic. *mf* Arab. *m*, Arabic (language)

arabesco /ara'βesko/ *a* Arabic. *m*, *Art*. arabesque

Arabia Saudita /a'raβia sau'ðita/ Saudi Arabia

arábigo /a'raβigo/ *a* Arabic. *m*, Arabic (language)

arácnido /a'rakniðo/ *m*, *Zool*. arachnid

arado /a'raðo/ *m*, plow

arador /ara'ðor/ *a* plowing. *m*, plowman. **a. de la sarna, **Ent*. scabies mite

aragonés /arago'nes/ **(-esa)** *a* and *n* Aragonese

arahuaco /ara'uako/ *a* and *n* Arawak, Arawakian

arancel /aran'θel; aran'sel/ *m*, tariff, duty, tax

arancelar /aranθe'lar; aranse'lar/ to charge tuition for (e.g. *a. la universidad,* charge tuition for college studies)

arancelario /aranθe'lario; aranse'lario/ *a* tariff, tax; customs

arándano /a'randano/ *m*, *Bot*. bilberry

arandela /aran'dela/ *f*, candle-dripper; *Mech*. washer; wall candelabrum

araña /a'raɲa/ *f*, spider; chandelier

arañacielos /a,raɲa'θielos; a,raɲa'sielos/ *m*, skyscraper

arañar /ara'ɲar/ *vt* to scratch; *Inf*. scrape together, hoard

arañazo /ara'ɲaθo; ara'ɲaso/ *m*, scratch

arar /a'rar/ *vt* to plough. **a. en el mar,** to labor in vain

arbitrador /arβitra'ðor/ **(-ra)** *n* arbitrator

arbitraje /arβi'trahe/ *m*, arbitration; arbitrament, decision

arbitrar /arβi'trar/ *vt* to judge freely; *Law*. arbitrate, mediate; devise; invent; marshal (money, resources, etc.); draft (a law) *vr* make shift, contrive

arbitrariedad /arβitrarie'ðað/ *f*, arbitrariness

arbitrario /arβi'trario/ *a* arbitral, mediatory; arbitrary, capricious

arbitrio /ar'βitrio/ *m*, free will; arbitration; means, way; discretion; arbitrament, judgment; *pl* rates, municipal taxes

árbitro /'arβitro/ **(-ra)** *a* arbitrary —*n* arbiter. *m*, *Sports*. umpire; referee

árbol /'arβol/ *m*, tree; *Mech*. shaft; *Naut*. mast; axis of a winding stair. **a. de amor** *or* **a. de Judas,** Judas tree. **a. de la ciencia (del bien y del mal),** Tree of Knowledge (of good and evil). **a. de levas,** *Mech*. camshaft. **a. del pan,** breadfruit tree. *Naut*. **a. mayor,** mainmast. **a. motor** *Mech*., drivingshaft

arbolado /arβo'laðo/ *a* tree-covered, wooded. *m*, copse, woodland

arboladura /arβola'ðura/ *f*, *Naut*. masts and spars

arbolar /arβo'lar/ *vt* to hoist (flags); *Naut*. fit with masts; place upright; —*vr* rear, prance (horses)

arboleda /arβo'leða/ *f*, copse, grove, spinney

arbotante /arβo'tante/ *m*, flying buttress

arbusto /ar'βusto/ *m*, shrub, woody plant

arca /'arka/ *f*, chest; money-box, coffer; ark; *pl* (treasury) vaults. **a. caudal,** strong box. **a. de agua,** water-tower. **a. de la alianza.** *or* **a. del testamento,** Ark of the Covenant (Bible). **a. de Noé,** Noah's Ark; lumber box

arcabucero /arkaβu'θero; arkaβu'sero/ *m*, arquebusier; maker of arquebuses

arcabuz /arka'βuθ; arka'βus/ *m*, arquebus

arcada /ar'kaða/ *f*, arcade; series of arches; *pl* sickness, nausea

árcade /ar'kaðe/ *a* and *mf* Arcadian

arcaico /ar'kaiko/ *a* archaic

arcaísmo /arka'ismo/ *m*, archaism

arcángel /ar'kanhel/ *m*, archangel

arcano /ar'kano/ *a* secret. *m*, mystery, arcanum

arce /'arθe; 'arse/ *m*, *Bot*. maple tree

archifeliz /artʃife'liθ; artʃife'lis/ *a* extremely happy, in bliss

archimandrita /artʃiman'drita/ *m*, archimandrite

archimillonario /artʃimiʎo'nario; artʃimiyo'nario/ **(-ia)** *a* and *n* multimillionaire

archipiélago /artʃi'pielago/ *m*, archipelago

Archipiélago de Colón /artʃi'pielago de ko'lon/ *m*, Galapagos Islands

archivar /artʃi'βar/ *vt* to place in an archive; file (papers)

archivero /artʃi'βero/ *m*, archivist, keeper of the archives; librarian; registrar; (Mexico) file cabinet, filing cabinet

archivista /artʃi'βista/ *mf* archivist; file clerk, filing clerk

archivo /ar'tʃiβo/ *m*, archives

arcilla /ar'θiʎa; ar'siya/ *f*, clay

arcilloso /arθi'ʎoso; arsi'yoso/ *a* clayey, like or full of clay

arcipreste /arθi'preste; arsi'preste/ *m*, archpriest

arco /'arko/ *m*, *Geom*. arc; *Mil*. bow; bow (of a stringed instrument); hoop (of casks, etc.); *Archit*. arch. **a. del cielo** *or* **a. de San Martín** *or* **a. iris,** rainbow. **a. voltaico,** electric arc. *Mus*. **para a.,** for strings

arder /ar'ðer/ *vi* to burn; shine, gleam; *Fig*. burn (with passion, etc.); —*vt* to set alight, burn

ardid /ar'ðið/ *a* crafty. *m*, trick, stratagem

ardiente /ar'ðiente/ *a* burning; ardent, passionate; vehement; enthusiastic; flame-colored; fiery-red

ardilla /ar'ðiʎa; ar'ðiya/ *f*, squirrel

ardite /ar'ðite/ *m*, ancient Spanish coin of little value; *Fig*. farthing, fig, straw. **no valer un a.,** to be not worth a straw

ardor /ar'ðor/ *m*, great heat; zeal, earnestness; passion, ardor; courage

ardoroso /arðo'roso/ *a* ardorous

arduo /'arðuo/ *a* arduous

área /'area/ *f*, area; small plot of ground; common threshing floor; arc (surface measure)

arena /a'rena/ *f*, sand; arena; grit, gravel. **a. mo"**z·**za,** quicksand

arenal /are'nal/ *m*, quicksand; sand pit; sandy place

arenero /are'nero/ **(-ra)** *n* sand merchant. *m*, sandbox (carried by railway engines)

arenga /a'renga/ *f*, harangue, discourse

arenilla /are'niʎa; are'niya/ *f*, sand (for drying writing)

arenisca /are'niska/ *f*, sandstone

arenisco /are'nisko/ *a* sandy

arenque /a'renke/ *m*, herring

arete /a'rete/ *m*, earring

argamasa /arga'masa/ *f*, mortar

argayo /ar'gayo/ *m*, landslide; (Asturias) **a. de nieve,** avalanche

Árgel /'arhel/ Algiers

Argelia /ar'helia/ Algeria

argelino /arhe'lino/ **(-na)** *a* and *n* Algerian

argentado /arhen'taðo/ *a* silvered; silvery

argénteo /ar'henteo/ *a* silver; silvery

argentífero /arhen'tifero/ *a* silver-yielding

argentino /arhen'tino/ **(-na)** *a* silvery —*a* and *n* Argentinian. *m*, Argentinian gold coin

argento /ar'hento/ *m*, silver. **a. vivo,** mercury

argolla /ar'goʎa; ar'goya/ *f*, thick metal ring (for hitching, etc.); croquet (game); stocks, pillory; hoop, iron arch

argonauta /argo'nauta/ *m*, *Myth*. Argonaut; *Zool*. paper nautilus, argonaut

argucia /ar'guθia; ar'gusia/ *f*, sophism, quibble; subtlety

argüir /ar'guir/ *vt irr* to deduce, imply; prove; reveal, manifest; accuse; —*vi* argue, debate; dispute, oppose. See **huir**

argumentador /argumenta'ðor/ **(-ra)** *a* argumentative —*n* arguer

argumentar /argumen'tar/ *vi* to argue; dispute; oppose

argumento /argu'mento/ *m*, contention, case; theme (of a book, etc.); argument, discussion

aridez /ari'ðeθ; ari'ðes/ *f*, aridity, dryness; drought; sterility, barrenness; dullness, lack of interest

árido /'ariðo/ *a* dry, arid; sterile, barren; uninteresting, dull

ariete /a'riete/ *m*, *Mil*. battering ram

ario /'ario/ **(-ia)** *a* and *n* Aryan

arisco /a'risko/ *a* unsociable, surly; wild, shy (animals)

arista /a'rista/ *f, Bot.* arista, awn, beard; pebble; edge, side

aristocracia /aristo'kraθia; aristo'krasia/ *f,* aristocracy

aristócrata /aris'tokrata/ *mf* aristocrat

aristocrático /aristo'kratiko/ *a* aristocratic

aristotélico /aristo'teliko/ *a* Aristotelian

aristotelismo /aristote'lismo/ *m,* Aristotelianism

aritmética /arit'metika/ *f,* arithmetic

aritmético /arit'metiko/ **(-ca)** *a* arithmetical —*n* arithmetician

arlequín /arle'kin/ *m,* harlequin; *Inf.* fool, buffoon; Neapolitan ice-cream

arlequinada /arleki'naða/ *f,* harlequinade; buffoonery

arma /'arma/ *f,* weapon; *Mil.* arm, branch; bull's horn; *pl* troops, army; means, way; arms, coat of arms. **a. arrojadiza,** missile. **a. blanca,** steel weapon. **a. de fuego,** fire-arm. **¡Armas al hombro!** Shoulder Arms! **armas portátiles,** small arms. *Inf.* **de armas tomar,** belligerent; resolute. **pasar por las armas,** *Mil.* to shoot. **presentar las armas,** *Mil.* to present arms. **ser a. de dos filos,** *Fig.* to cut both ways

armada /ar'maða/ *f,* navy, armada; fleet, squadron

armadía /arma'ðia/ *f,* raft, pontoon

armador /arma'ðor/ **(-ra)** *n* supplier, outfitter. *m,* shipowner; pirate, privateer; jacket; assembler, fitter

armadura /arma'ðura/ *f,* armature, armor; frame, framework; skeleton (of a building); skeleton (of vertebrates); *Phys.* armature; plate armor (of persons)

armamento /arma'mento/ *m, Mil.* armament; arms, military equipment

armar /ar'mar/ *vt* to arm; *Mech.* mount; man (guns); put together, assemble; roll (a cigarette); reinforce (concrete); *Inf.* arrange, prepare; *Inf.* occasion (quarrels); *Inf.* outfit; *Naut.* equip; commission (a ship); —*vr* prepare oneself, arm oneself. **a. caballero,** to knight. **a. los remos,** to ship the oars. *Inf.* **armarla,** to cause a row or quarrel

armario /ar'mario/ *m,* cupboard; wardrobe. **a. de luna,** wardrobe with a mirror

armatoste /arma'toste/ *m,* unwieldy piece of furniture; *Fig. Inf.* dead weight, clumsy person; snare

armazón /arma'θon; arma'son/ *f,* frame, framework; ship's hulk. *m, Anat.* skeleton

armenio /ar'menio/ **(-ia)** *a* and *n* Armenian. *m,* Armenian language

armería /arme'ria/ *f,* armory; heraldry; gunsmith's craft or shop

armero /ar'mero/ *m,* gunsmith, armorer; stand for weapons. **a. mayor,** Royal Armorer

armiño /ar'mino/ *m,* ermine

armisticio /armis'tiθio; armis'tisio/ *m,* armistice

armón de artillería /ar'mon de arti'ʎeria; ar'mon de artiye'ria/ *m,* gun-carriage

armonía /armo'nia/ *f,* harmony; friendship, concord; *Mus.* harmony

armónica /ar'monika/ **(de boca)** *f,* mouth-organ

armónico /ar'moniko/ *a* harmonious —*a* and *m, Mus.* harmonic

armonio /ar'monio/ *m,* harmonium

armonioso /armo'nioso/ *a* harmonious

armonización /armoniθa'θion; armonisa'sion/ *f, Mus.* harmonization

armonizar /armoni'θar; armoni'sar/ *vt* to bring into harmony; *Mus.* harmonize

arnés /ar'nes/ *m,* armor; harness; *pl* horse trappings; *Inf.* equipment, tools

aro /'aro/ *m,* hoop; rim (of wheel, etc.); napkin-ring; croquet hoop; *Bot.* wild arum; child's hoop. **a. de empaquetadura,** *Mech.* gasket

aroma /a'roma/ *m,* aroma, fragrance; balsam; sweet-smelling herb

aromático /aro'matiko/ *a* aromatic

arpa /'arpa/ *f,* harp. **a. eolia,** Eolian harp

arpar /ar'par/ *vt* to scratch, claw; tear, rend

arpegio /ar'pehio/ *m, Mus.* arpeggio

arpía /ar'pia/ *f,* harpy

arpicordio /arpi'korðio/ *m,* harpsichord

arpista /ar'pista/ *mf* harpist, harp player

arpón /ar'pon/ *m,* harpoon

arponear /arpone'ar/ *vt* to harpoon

arponero /arpo'nero/ *m,* harpooner; harpoon maker

arquear /arke'ar/ *vt* to arch; bend; beat (wool); gauge (ship's capacity); —*vi* retch

arqueo /ar'keo/ *m,* arching; bending, curving; *Naut.* tonnage; gauging (of ship's capacity); *Com.* examination of deposits and contents of safe

arqueología /arkeolo'hia/ *f,* archeology

arqueológico /arkeo'lohiko/ *a* archeological

arqueólogo /arke'ologo/ *m,* archeologist

arquero /ar'kero/ *m, Com.* cashier, treasurer; *Mil.* archer

arquitecto /arki'tekto/ *m,* architect. **a. de jardines,** landscape gardener

arquitectónico /arkitek'toniko/ *a* architectural

arquitectura /arkitek'tura/ *f,* architecture

arquitrabe /arki'traβe/ *m,* architrave

arrabal /arra'βal/ *m,* suburb, district; *pl* outskirts

arracada /arra'kaða/ *f,* pendant-earring

arracimarse /arraθi'marse; arrasi'marse/ *vr* to cluster; group

arraigadamente /arrai,gaða'mente/ *adv* deeply, firmly

arraigado /arrai'gaðo/ *a* deep-rooted; firm; convinced

arraigar /arrai'gar/ *vi* to take root; —*vi* and *vr Fig.* become established, take hold; —*vr* settle; take up residence

arraigo /a'rraigo/ *m,* rooting; settlement, establishment; landed property

arrancaclavos /a,rranka'klaβos/ *m,* nail-puller

arrancadero /a,rranka'ðero/ *m, Sports.* starting-point

arrancar /arran'kar/ *vt* to uproot; pull out; wrench; tear off; extirpate; obtain by threats; clear one's throat; —*vt* and *vi Naut.* put on speed; —*vi* start (a race); *Inf.* leave, quit; derive, originate **¡Arrancan!** And they're off! (races)

arranque /a'rranke/ *m,* uprooting; extirpation; wrenching, pulling, seizing; stimulus (of passion); sudden impulse; *Mech.* start; *Mech.* starter. **a. automático,** self-starter

arras /'arras/ *f pl,* dowry; coins given by bridegroom to his bride; earnest money, token

arrasamiento /arrasa'miento/ *m,* demolition, destruction; leveling

arrasar /arra'sar/ *vt* to demolish, destroy; level; fill to the brim; —*vi* and *vr* clear up (sky). **ojos arrasados de lágrimas,** eyes brimming with tears

arrastrado /arras'traðo/ *a Inf.* poverty-stricken, wretched; *Inf.* knavish; unhappy, unfortunate

arrastrar /arras'trar/ *vt* to drag; trail; convince; haul; —*vi* trail along or touch the ground; trump (at cards); —*vr* crawl, creep; shuffle along; humble oneself

arrastre /a'rrastre/ *m,* dragging, trailing; haulage; trumping (at cards)

¡arre! /'arre/ *interj* Gee up! Get along!

arrear /arre'ar/ *vt* to spur on, whip up (horses, etc.) —*interj Inf.* **¡Arrea!** Hurry up! Get on!

arrebañar /arreβa'ɲar/ *vt* to pick clean, clear; eat or drink up

arrebatado /arreβa'taðo/ *a* precipitate, headlong; rash; flushed, red

arrebatador /arreβata'ðor/ *a* overwhelming; violent; bewitching, captivating; delighting

arrebatamiento /arreβata'miento/ *m,* abduction; seizure; fury; ecstasy

arrebatar /arreβa'tar/ *vt* to abduct, carry off; seize, grab; attract, charm; grip (the attention); —*vr* be overcome with rage

arrebatiña /arreβa'tiɲa/ *f,* grab; scuffle, scrimmage

arrebato /arre'βato/ *m,* fit (gen. of anger); ecstasy, rapture

arrebol /arre'βol/ *m,* red flush in the sky; rouge; *pl* red clouds

arrebozar /arreβo'θar; arreβo'sar/ *vt* to muffle; envelop

arrebujarse /arreβu'harse/ *vr* to huddle; wrap oneself up

arrechucho /arre'tʃutʃo/ *m, Inf.* fit of rage; sudden slight ailment

arreciar /arre'θiar; arre'siar/ *vi* to increase in intensity; —*vr* grow strong

arrecife /arre'θife; arre'sife/ *m*, reef (in the sea); stone-paved road

arredrar /arre'ðrar/ *vt* to separate, remove; force back, repel; terrify

arregazar /arrega'θar; arrega'sar/ **(se)** *vt* and *vr* to tuck up one's skirts

arreglado /arre'glaðo/ *a* regular; regulated; ordered; methodical

arreglar /arre'glar/ *vt* to regulate; arrange; adjust, put right; tidy; make up (the face); —*vr* (*with prep a*) conform to; (*with con*) reach an agreement with. **Me voy a a.**, I am going to make myself presentable. *Inf.* **arreglárselas,** to shift for oneself

arreglo /a'rreglo/ *m*, arrangement; rule; regulation; method, order; agreement; adjustment; compromise

arrellanarse /arreʎa'narse; arreya'narse/ *vr* to settle comfortably in one's chair; be happy in one's work

arremangar /arreman̠'gar/ *vt* to roll up (sleeves, trousers, etc.); —*vr Inf.* make a decision

arremango /arre'man̠go/ *m*, rolling or tucking up (of sleeve, etc.)

arremetedor /arremete'ðor/ **(-ra)** *n* attacker, assailant

arremeter /arreme'ter/ *vt* to attack, assail; —*vr* launch oneself (at); *Fig.* spoil the view, shock the eye

arremetida /arreme'tiða/ *f*, attack, assault

arremolinarse /arremoli'narse/ *vr* to crowd, cluster, group

arrendador /arrenda'ðor/ **(-ra)** *n* landlord; renter; hirer; tenant

arrendamiento /arrenda'miento/ *m*, letting, renting; hiring; rental; agreement, lease

arrendar /arren'dar/ *vt irr* to let, lease; hire; rent (as a tenant); train (horses); tie up (horses); restrain; mimic, imitate. See **recomendar**

arrendatario /arrenda'tario/ **(-ia)** *a* rent, lease —*n* tenant; lessee; hirer. **a. de contribuciones,** tax farmer

arreo /a'rreo/ *m*, ornament; apparel; *pl* horse trappings; appurtenances, equipment

¡Arrepa! /a'rrepa/ But look!, Hold on!, Hold your horses!, Not so fast!

arrepentimiento /arrepenti'miento/ *m*, repentance

arrepentirse /arrepen'tirse/ *vr irr* to repent. See **sentir**

arrestado /arres'taðo/ *a* courageous, audacious, bold

arrestar /arres'tar/ *vt* to arrest, detain; —*vr* be bold, dare

arresto /a'rresto/ *m*, arrest; detention; imprisonment; audacity, boldness

arriada /a'rriaða/ *f*, lowering (of a boat); taking in (of sail)

arriar /a'rriar/ *vt Naut.* to strike (colors); take in (sail); pay out (ropes, etc.); lower (boats); flood, inundate

arriate /a'rriate/ *m*, garden border; avenue, walk; trellis (for plants)

arriba /a'rriβa/ *adv* up, above; overhead; upstairs; earlier, before; upwards (with prices) —*interj* **¡A.!** Up with!; Long live! **de a. abajo,** from head to foot, from one end to the other; completely, wholly

arribada /arri'βaða/ *f*, *Naut.* arrival. **de a.,** emergency (port)

arribar /arri'βar/ *vi Naut.* to arrive; put into an emergency port; reach, arrive at; *Inf.* convalesce; attain; *Naut.* drift

arribista /arri'βista/ *mf* social climber

arribo /a'rriβo/ *m*, arrival

arriero /a'rriero/ *m*, farrier; muleteer

arriesgado /arries'gaðo/ *a* dangerous, risky; rash, daring

arriesgar /arries'gar/ *vt* to risk; —*vr* run into danger; dare, risk

arrimar /arri'mar/ *vt* to bring or draw near; abandon (professions, etc.); lay aside, discard; *Inf.* administer (blows); *Naut.* stow (cargo); —*vr* (*with prep a*) lean against, rest on; join, go with; seek the protection of. **Cada cual se arrima a su cada cual,** Birds of a feather flock together

arrimo /a'rrimo/ *m*, bringing or placing near; leaning

or resting against; abandonment, giving up; protection; staff, support

arrinconado /arrinko'naðo/ *a* remote, secluded; forgotten, neglected

arrinconar /arrinko'nar/ *vt* to discard, lay aside; corner, besiege; set aside, dismiss; forsake; —*vr* go into retirement, withdraw

arriscado /arris'kaðo/ *a* craggy, rugged; bold, resolute; sprightly, handsome

arro, arro, arro /'arro, 'arro, 'arro/ purrrr (echoic of a cat's purr)

arroba /a'rroβa/ *f*, weight of 25 lb.; variable liquid measure

arrobamiento /arroβa'miento/ *m*, ecstasy, rapture; trance

arrobar /arro'βar/ *vt* to charm, entrance; —*vr* be enraptured; be in ecstasy

arrodillar /arroði'ʎar; arroði'yar/ *vt* to cause to kneel down; —*vi* and *vr* kneel down

arrogancia /arro'ganθia; arro'gansia/ *f*, arrogance; courage; majesty, pride

arrogante /arro'gante/ *a* arrogant, haughty; courageous; proud, majestic

arrogar /arro'gar/ *vt* to adopt (as a son); —*vr* usurp, appropriate

arrojadizo /arroha'ðiθo; arroha'ðiso/ *a* easily cast or hurled; projectile

arrojado /arro'haðo/ *a* bold, determined; rash

arrojar /arro'har/ *vt* to throw, hurl, cast; shed (light, etc.); e.g. *La cuenta arroja un total de cien dólares,* The bill shows a total of a hundred dollars); *Com.* show (a balance, etc.); put out (sprouts); dismiss, send away; —*vr* cast oneself; (*with prep a*) hurl oneself against or upon; undertake, venture upon. **a. de sí (a),** to get rid of, dismiss

arrojo /a'rroho/ *m*, daring, intrepidity; boldness

arrollar /arro'ʎar; arro'yar/ *vt* to roll; make into a roll, roll up; defeat (the enemy); silence, confound; rock to sleep; bear along, carry off

arromar /arro'mar/ *vt* to blunt; flatten

arropamiento /arropa'miento/ *m*, wrapping up, covering, muffling

arropar /arro'par/ *vt* to wrap up, cover

arrostrar /arros'trar/ *vt* to confront, defy, face up to; —*vr* fight hand to hand. **a. las consecuencias,** *Fig.* to face the music

arroyada /arro'yaða/ *f*, gorge, gully; course, channel; flood

arroyo /a'rroyo/ *m*, stream, brook; street gutter; road, street; *Fig.* flood, plenty

arroz /a'rroθ; a'rros/ *m*, rice

arrozal /arro'θal; arro'sal/ *m*, rice field

arruga /a'rruga/ *f*, wrinkle; fold, pleat; crease

arrugamiento /arruga'miento/ *m*, wrinkling; fold, pleating; crumpling, creasing; corrugation

arrugar /arru'gar/ *vt* to wrinkle; pleat; corrugate; crumple, crease. **a. el ceño,** to knit one's brow, scowl

arruinamiento /arruina'miento/ *m*, ruin, decay, decline

arruinar /arrui'nar/ *vt* to ruin; destroy, damage severely

arrullar /arru'ʎar; arru'yar/ *vt* to bill and coo (doves); lull to sleep; *Inf.* whisper sweet words to, make love to

arrullo /a'rruʎo; a'rruyo/ *m*, cooing of doves; lullaby

arrumaco /arru'mako/ *m*, *Inf.* embrace, caress (gen. *pl*); ornament in bad taste

arrumaje /arru'mahe/ *m*, *Naut.* stowage; clouds on the horizon

arrurruz /arru'rruθ; arru'rrus/ *m*, arrowroot

arsenal /arse'nal/ *m*, dockyard; arsenal; *Fig.* store (of information, etc.)

arsénico /ar'seniko/ *m*, arsenic

arte /'arte/ *mf*, art; skill; ability; talent; guile, craftiness. **las bellas artes,** fine arts. *Inf.* **no tener a. ni parte en,** to have nothing to do with, have no part in

artefacto /arte'fakto/ *m*, machine, mechanism, apparatus; device, appliance. **a. atómico,** atomic bomb

arteria /ar'teria/ *f*, *Med.* artery; main line of (communication)

artería /arte'ria/ *f*, craftiness, guile

arterial /arte'rial/ *a* arterial

artesa /ar'tesa/ *f,* wooden trough; kneading bowl

artesano /arte'sano/ **(-na)** *n* artisan; mechanic

artesiano /arte'sjano/ *a* artesian

artesón /arte'son/ *m,* bucket, pail; *Archit.* curved ceiling-panel; paneled ceiling

artesonado /arteso'naðo/ *a Archit.* paneled (ceiling). *m,* paneled ceiling

ártico /'artiko/ *a* Arctic

articulación /artikula'θion; artikula'sion/ *f,* joint, articulation; jointing; enunciation, pronunciation

articular /artiku'lar/ *vt* to joint, articulate; enunciate, pronounce clearly

articulista /artiku'lista/ *mf* article writer

artículo /ar'tikulo/ *m,* finger knuckle; heading; article; *Anat.* joint; *Gram.* article; *pl* goods, things. **a. de fondo,** leading article (in a newspaper). **a. de primera necesidad,** prime necessity, essential

artífice /ar'tifiθe; ar'tifise/ *mf* craftsman, artificer; author, creator; forger

artificial /artifi'θial; artifi'sial/ *a* artificial

artificio /arti'fiθio; arti'fiçio/ *m,* skill, art; appliance, contraption, mechanism; trick, cunning device; guile, craftiness

artificioso /artifi'θioso; artifi'sioso/ *a* skilful; artificial; crafty, cunning

artillería /artiʎe'ria; artiye'ria/ *f,* artillery. **a. de costa,** coastal guns. **a. ligera, a. montada, a. rodada** *or* **a. volante,** field artillery

artillero /arti'ʎero; arti'yero/ *m,* gunner

artimaña /arti'maɲa/ *f,* trick, ruse, stratagem

artista /ar'tista/ *mf* artist; performer

artístico /ar'tistiko/ *a* artistic

artrítico /ar'tritiko/ *a Med.* arthritic

artritis /ar'tritis/ *f, Med.* arthritis

arveja /ar'βeha/ *f, Bot.* vetch

arzobispado /arθoβis'paðo; arsoβis'paðo/ *m,* archbishopric

arzobispo /arθo'βispo; arso'βispo/ *m,* archbishop

as /as/ *m,* Roman copper coin; ace (*Aer.* cards, etc.)

asa /'asa/ *f,* handle; pretext, excuse

asado /a'saðo/ *m, Cul.* roast

asador /asa'ðor/ *m, Cul.* roasting-spit; roaster

asadura /asa'ðura/ *f, Cul.* chitterlings; offal

asalariar /asala'riar/ *vt* to fix a salary for

asaltador /asalta'ðor/ **(-ra)** *a* attacking —*n* assailant, attacker

asaltar /asal'tar/ *vt* to storm, besiege; assault, attack; occur to (ideas); come on suddenly (illness)

asalto /a'salto/ *m,* storming, besieging; assault, attack; bout (in fencing, boxing, wrestling); round (in a fight)

asamblea /asam'βlea/ *f,* congregation, assembly; meeting; legislative assembly; *Mil.* assembly (bugle call)

asambleísta /asamble'ista/ *mf* member of an assembly

asar /a'sar/ *vt Cul.* to roast; grill; —*vr* be burning-hot; *Fig.* burn (with enthusiasm)

asaz /a'saθ; a'sas/ *adv* sufficiently, enough; very; in abundance —*a* sufficient; many

asbesto /as'βesto/ *m,* asbestos

ascalonia /aska'lonia/ *f, Bot.* shallot

ascendencia /asθen'denθia; assen'densia/ *f,* lineage, ancestry, origin

ascendente /asθen'dente; assen'dente/ *a* ascending

ascender /asθen'der; assen'der/ *vi irr* to ascend, climb; be promoted; (*with prep a*) amount to (bills, etc.); —*vt* promote. See **entender**

ascendiente /asθen'diente; assen'diente/ *mf* ancestor, forbear. *m,* influence, ascendancy

ascensión /asθen'sion; assen'sion/ *f,* ascension; promotion; *Astron.* exaltation

ascenso /as'θenso; as'senso/ *m,* ascent; promotion, preferment

ascensor /asθen'sor; assen'sor/ *m,* lift, elevator

ascensorista /asθenso'rista; assenso'rista/ *mf* elevator operator

asceta /as'θeta; as'seta/ *mf* ascetic

ascético /as'θetiko; as'setiko/ *a* ascetic

ascetismo /asθe'tismo; asse'tismo/ *m,* asceticism

asco /'asko/ *m,* nausea; repugnance, loathing; revolting thing. *Inf.* **Me da a.,** It sickens me

ascua /'askua/ *f,* live coal, ember. **estar como una a. de oro,** to be as bright as a new pin. **estar en ascuas,** *Fig.* to be on pins

aseado /ase'aðo/ *a* clean, tidy

asear /ase'ar/ *vt* to tidy, make neat; clean up; decorate, adorn

asechanza /ase'tʃanθa; ase'tʃansa/ *f,* ambush; trick, snare, stratagem

asechar /ase'tʃar/ *vt* to ambush, waylay; *Fig.* lay snares for

asediador /aseðia'ðor/ **(-ra)** *n* besieger

asediar /ase'ðiar/ *vt* to besiege; pester, importune

asedio /a'seðio/ *m,* siege; importunity

asegurado /asegu'raðo/ **(-da)** *a* insured —*n* insured person

asegurador /asegura'ðor/ **(-ra)** *a* insuring —*n* insurer

asegurar /asegu'rar/ *vt* to fasten, make secure; pinion, grip; reassure, soothe; assert, state; *Com.* insure; guarantee; ensure, secure; —*vr Com.* insure oneself; (*with de*) make sure of

asemejar /aseme'har/ *vt* to imitate, copy; make similar to; —*vr* (*with prep a*) be like, be similar to

asenderear /asendere'ar/ *vt* to make a pathway through; persecute, harass

asenso /a'senso/ *m,* assent. **dar a.,** to believe, give credence (to)

asentaderas /asenta'ðeras/ *f pl, Inf.* buttocks, seat

asentado /asen'taðo/ *a* prudent, circumspect; permanent, stable

asentamiento /asenta'miento/ *m,* seating; settlement, residence; prudence, judgment

asentar /asen'tar/ *vt irr* to seat; place; fasten, fix; found; plant (flags); pitch (a tent); establish, make firm; smooth; hone (razors); estimate, budget, arrange, set forth; note down; affirm, believe; *Com.* enter (in an account); —*vi* fit (clothes); —*vr* seat oneself; alight (birds); settle (liquids); *Archit.* settle, subside; to be located (e.g. *El edificio se asienta en una esquina,* The building is located on a corner). **a. la mano en,** to strike hard. See **acertar**

asentimiento /asenti'miento/ *m,* assent; consent, approval

asentir /asen'tir/ *vi irr* to assent, agree; (*with en*) consent to. See **sentir**

aseñorado /aseɲo'raðo/ *a* refined, gentlemanly; ladylike; presumptuous

aseo /a'seo/ *m,* cleanliness, neatness

asepsia /a'sepsia/ *f,* asepsis

asequible /ase'kiβle/ *a* attainable; obtainable

aserción /aser'θion; aser'sion/ *f,* assertion

aserradero /ase'rraðero/ *m,* sawmill; saw-pit

aserrador /aserra'ðor/ **(-ra)** *n* sawyer

aserrar /ase'rrar/ *vt irr* to saw. See **acertar**

aserrín /ase'rrin/ *m,* sawdust

asertivo /aser'tiβo/ *a* assertive

aserto /a'serto/ *m,* assertion

asesinar /asesi'nar/ *vt* to assassinate, murder

asesinato /asesi'nato/ *m,* assassination, murder

asesino /ase'sino/ *mf* assassin, murderer; murderess

asesor /ase'sor/ **(-ra)** *n* assessor

asesorar /aseso'rar/ *vt* to give advice; —*vr* take legal advice; seek advice

asestar /ases'tar/ *vt* to aim (firearms); fire; deal (a blow)

aseveración /aseβera'θion; aseβera'sion/ *f,* assertion, statement

aseveradamente /aseβeraða'mente/ *adv* affirmatively

aseverar /aseβe'rar/ *vt* to affirm, assert

asfaltado /asfal'taðo/ *m,* asphalting; asphalt pavement

asfaltar /asfal'tar/ *vt* to asphalt

asfalto /as'falto/ *m,* asphalt

asfixia /as'fiksia/ *f, Med.* asphyxia

asfixiante /asfik'siante/ *a* asphyxiating

asfixiar /asfik'siar/ *vt* to asphyxiate

asfódelo /as'foðelo/ *m, Bot.* asphodel

así /a'si/ *adv* thus, so, in this way; like this (e.g. *en días a.,* on days like this); even if; so that, therefore. **a. a.,** middling, so-so. **a. como a.,** as well as; as soon as. **a. las cosas,** that being the case, **a. que,** as soon as, immediately; consequently, thus

Asia Menor /'asia me'nor/ Asia Minor

asiático /a'siatiko/ **(-ca)** *a* and *n* Asiatic

asidero /asi'ðero/ *m,* hold, grasp; handle, haft; pretext, excuse

asido a /a'siðo a/ wedded to (e.g. a belief)

asiduidad /asiðui'ðað/ *f,* assiduity

asiduo /a'siðuo/ *a* assiduous

asiento /a'siento/ *m,* seat; place, position; site; base (of a vase, etc.); lees, sediment; indigestion; *Archit.* subsidence, settling; treaty, pact; contract; note, reminder; *Com.* entry; permanence, stability; prudence; bit (of a bridle); *pl* buttocks, seat. **estar de a.,** to be established (in a place)

asignación /asigna'θion; asigna'sion/ *f,* assignation; appropriation (of money); salary; portion, share

asignar /asig'nar/ *vt* to assign; apportion; destine, intend; appoint

asignatura /asigna'tura/ *f,* subject (of study in schools, etc.)

asilar /asi'lar/ *vt* to give shelter to, receive; put into an institution

asilo /a'silo/ *m,* shelter, refuge; sanctuary, asylum; *Fig.* protection, defense; home, institution

asimetría /asime'tria/ *f,* asymmetry

asimétrico /asi'metriko/ *a* asymmetrical

asimiento /asi'miento/ *m,* hold, grasp; attachment, affection

asimilable /asimi'laβle/ *a* assimilable

asimilación /asimila'θion; asimila'sion/ *f,* assimilation

asimilar /asimi'lar/ *vt* to compare, liken; (*Bot. Zool. Gram.*) assimilate; —*vi* resemble, be like; *Fig.* assimilate, digest (ideas)

asimismo /asi'mismo/ *adv* similarly, likewise

asir /a'sir/ *vt irr* to grasp, take hold of; seize; —*vi* take root (plants); —*vr* (*with de*) lay hold of; take advantage of; make an excuse to —*Pres. Indic.* **asgo, ases,** etc —*Pres. Subjunc.* **asga,** etc.

asirio /a'sirio/ **(-ia)** *a* and *n* Assyrian. *m,* Assyrian language

asistencia /asis'tenθia; asisten'sia/ *f,* presence, attendance; minimal attendance required (e.g. *Los alumnos tienen que completar una a.,* Pupils must attend a certain number of classes) assistance, help; service, attendance; medical treatment; remuneration; *pl* allowance. **a. pública,** Public Assistance. **a. social,** social work

asistenta /asis'tenta/ *f,* daily maid; waiting-maid

asistente /asis'tente/ *m,* assistant; *Mil.* orderly

asistir /asis'tir/ *vt* to accompany; assist, help; attend, treat; (*with de*) act as; —*vi* (*with prep a*) be present at, attend; follow suit (in cards)

asma /'asma/ *f,* asthma

asmático /as'matiko/ **(-ca)** *a* asthmatic —*n* asthma sufferer

asnal /as'nal/ *a* asinine; brutish, stupid

asno /'asno/ *m,* ass

asociación /asoθia'θion; asosia'sion/ *f,* association; company, partnership; society, fellowship

asociado /aso'θiaðo; aso'siaðo/ **(-da)** *n* associate; member; partner

asociar /aso'θiar; aso'siar/ *vt* to associate; —*vr* associate oneself; join together; form a partnership

asolar /aso'lar/ *vt irr* to destroy, devastate, lay flat; —*vr* wither; settle (liquids). See **contar**

asoldar /asol'dar/ *vt irr* to employ, engage, hire. See **contar**

asolear /asole'ar/ *vt* to expose to the sun; —*vr* sun oneself; become sunburnt

asomada /aso'maða/ *f,* brief appearance; vantage point

asomar /aso'mar/ *vt* to show, allow to appear, put forth; —*vi* begin to show; —*vr* show oneself, appear; *Inf.* be flushed (with wine); (*with prep a, por*) look out of. **asomarse a la ventana,** to show oneself at, or look out of, the window

asombrar /asom'βrar/ *vt* to shade, shadow; darken (a color); terrify; amaze

asombro /a'sombro/ *m,* fright, terror; amazement; wonder, marvel

asombroso /asom'βroso/ *a* amazing; marvelous, wonderful

asonancia /aso'nanθia; aso'nansia/ *f,* assonance; congruity, harmony

asonante /aso'nante/ *a* and *m,* assonant

asordar /asor'ðar/ *vt* to deafen

aspa /'aspa/ *f,* cross; sail of a windmill

aspaviento /aspa'βiento/ *m,* exaggerated display of emotion; gesture (of horror, etc.); **hacer aspavientos,** to make a fuss

aspecto /as'pekto/ *m,* look, appearance; aspect, outlook

aspereza /aspe'reθa; aspe'resa/ *f,* roughness, harshness; ruggedness, rockiness; severity, asperity

áspero /'aspero/ *a* rough, harsh; uneven, rocky; jarring, grating; hard, severe

aspersión /asper'sion/ *f, Eccl.* aspersion; sprinkling

áspid /'aspið/ *m,* asp, viper

aspiración /aspira'θion; aspira'sion/ *f,* breath; breathing; aspiration, desire; *Mus.* pause

aspirador /aspira'ðor/ **(de polvo)** *m,* vacuum cleaner

aspirante /aspi'rante/ *m,* aspirant, novice; office-seeker; applicant

aspirar /aspi'rar/ *vt* to breathe in, inhale; *Gram.* aspirate; (*with prep a*) aspire to, desire

aspirina /aspi'rina/ *f,* aspirin

asquear /aske'ar/ *vi* and *vt* to hate, loathe

asquerosidad /askerosi'ðað/ *f,* filthiness, loathsomeness; vileness, hatefulness

asqueroso /aske'roso/ *a* nauseating; loathsome, revolting; vile, hateful

asta /'asta/ *f,* lance, spear, pike; horn (of bull); antler; flagstaff; shaft. **a media a.,** at half-mast

asterisco /aste'risko/ *m,* asterisk

astigmático /astig'matiko/ *a* astigmatic

astigmatismo /astigma'tismo/ *m,* astigmatism

astil /as'til/ *m,* handle, pole, shaft; bar of a balance; beam feather

astilla /as'tiʎa; as'tiya/ *f,* splinter

astillar /asti'ʎar; asti'yar/ *vt* to splinter, chip

astillero /asti'ʎero; asti'yero/ *m,* shipyard; rack for lances and pikes

astilloso /asti'ʎoso; asti'yoso/ *a* splintery, fragile

astracán /astra'kan/ *m,* astrakhan

astringente /astrin'hente/ *a* astringent

astringir /astrin'hir/ *vt* to tighten up; compress; constrain

astro /'astro/ *m,* heavenly body

astrolatría /astrola'tria/ *f,* astrolatry, star worship

astrología /astrolo'hia/ *f,* astrology

astrológico /astro'lohiko/ *a* astrological

astrólogo /as'trologo/ **(-ga)** *n* astrologist

astronauta /astro'nauta/ *m,* astronaut

astronomía /astrono'mia/ *f,* astronomy

astronómico /astro'nomiko/ *a* astronomical

astrónomo /as'tronomo/ *m,* astronomer

astucia /as'tuθia; as'tusia/ *f,* astuteness, guile, craftiness

asturiano /astu'riano/ **(-na)** *a* and *n* Asturian

astuto /as'tuto/ *a* guileful, crafty, astute

Asuero /a'suero/ Ahasuerus

asueto /a'sueto/ *m,* day's holiday

asumir /asu'mir/ *vt* to assume; adopt, appropriate

asunción /asun'θion; asun'sion/ *f,* assumption

asunto /a'sunto/ *m,* matter, theme, subject; business, affair

asustadizo /asusta'ðiθo; asusta'ðiso/ *a* timid, nervous, easily frightened

asustar /asus'tar/ *vt* to frighten; **que asusta,** terribly (e.g. *Es de una ñoñería que asusta,* It's a terribly timid thing to do) *vr* be frightened

atablar /ata'βlar/ *vt* to roll, flatten (earth)

atacado /ata'kaðo/ *a Inf.* hesitant; mean, stingy

atacador /ataka'ðor/ **(-ra)** *a* attacking —*n* aggressor, attacker

atacar /ata'kar/ *vt* to attack; fasten, button; fit (clothes); ram (guns); *Fig.* press hard, corner (persons). **a. a los nervios,** to jar on the nerves

atadero /ata'ðero/ *m,* rope, tie, cord; hook, ring, etc. (for hitching); hindrance, impediment; hitching or fastening point

atado /a'taðo/ *m*, bundle, roll

atadura /ata'ðura/ *f*, tying, stringing, fastening, tie; knot; connection

atajar /ata'har/ *vi* to take a short cut; —*vt* intercept, cut off; screen off, divide; impede, stop; interrupt (people); **atajarle la palabra a uno,** to cut somebody off, interrupt *vr* be overcome (by fear, shame, etc.)

atajo /a'taho/ *m*, short cut, quick way; cutting, abbreviation; division. *Inf.* **echar por el a.,** to go to the root of (a matter)

atalaya /ata'laya/ *f*, look out, watch tower; observation point. *m*, lookout

atalayar /atala'yar/ *vt* to scan, watch; spy upon

atalón /ata'lon/ *m*, atoll, coral island

atañadero: en lo atañadero a /atana'ðero en lo atana'ðero a/ with regard to, with respect to

atañer /ata'ner/ *vi impers* to concern, affect; belong, pertain

ataque /a'take/ *m*, (*Mil. Med.*) attack; quarrel, fight

atar /a'tar/ *vt* to tie; fasten; lace; strap, paralyse; —*vr* get in a fix; confine oneself. **a. cabos,** to put two and two together

atardecer /atarðe'θer; atarðe'ser/ *vi irr impers* to grow dusk. See **conocer**

atardecer /atarðe'θer; atarðe'ser/ *m*, dusk, evening

atarear /atare'ar/ *vt* to set to work, assign work to; —*vr* work hard

atarugar /ataru'gar/ *vt* to wedge; stop up; plug; block; *Inf.* silence, shut up; stuff, cram; —*vr Fig. Inf.* lose one's head

atasajar /atasa'har/ *vt* to cut up, jerk (beef, etc.)

atascadero /ataska'ðero/ *m*, deep rut, boggy place; impediment, obstacle

atascar /atas'kar/ *vt* to plug; block up; stop (a leak); hinder, obstruct; —*vr* stick in the mud; be held up or delayed; *Inf.* get stuck in a speech

atasco /a'tasko/ *m*, obstruction, block

ataúd /ata'uð/ *m*, coffin

Ataulfo /a'taulfo/ Ataulf

ataviar /ata'βiar/ *vt* to deck, apparel, adorn

atavío /ata'βio/ *m*, get-up, dress, apparel; *pl* ornaments

atavismo /ata'βismo/ *m*, atavism

ate /'ate/ *m*, (Mexico) kind of Turkish delight

ateísmo /ate'ismo/ *m*, atheism

atelaje /ate'lahe/ *m*, team, yoke (of horses); trappings, harness; *Inf.* trousseau

atemperación /atempera'θion; atempera'sion/ *f*, moderation, mitigation; tempering

atemperar /atempe'rar/ *vt* to moderate, mitigate; adapt, adjust; temper, cool. **atemperarse a la realidad,** to adjust to reality

Atenas /a'tenas/ Athens

atenazar /atena'θar; atena'sar/ *vt* to grip, grasp; torture

atención /aten'θion; aten'sion/ *f*, attention; solicitude, kindness; courtesy, civility; *pl* business affairs —*interj* ¡**A.**! Take care! Look out!; *Mil.* Attention! **en a.** (**a**), taking into consideration. **estar en a.,** (patient) to be under treatment

atender /aten'der/ *vt irr* to await, expect; take care of, look after; —*vi* (*with prep a*) attend to, listen to; —*vi* remember. See **entender**

ateneo /ate'neo/ *m*, atheneum —*a* Athenian

atenerse /ate'nerse/ *vr irr* (*with prep a*) to abide by; resort to, rely on. See **tener**

ateniense /ate'niense/ *a* and *mf* Athenian

atentado /aten'taðo/ *a* prudent, sensible; secret, silent. *m*, infringement, violation; attempt (on a person's life); crime

atentar /aten'tar/ *vt irr* to do illegally; attempt a crime; —*vr* proceed cautiously; restrain oneself. See **acertar**

atento /a'tento/ *a* attentive; courteous, civil —*adv* taking into consideration. **su atenta** (**atta**), *Com.* your favor

atenuación /atenua'θion; atenua'sion/ *f*, attenuation, diminution

atenuante /ate'nuante/ *a* attenuating; extenuating (of circumstances)

atenuar /ate'nuar/ *vt* to attenuate, diminish; extenuate

ateo /a'teo/ (**-ea**) *a* atheistic —*n* atheist

aterciopelado /aterθiope'laðo; atersiope'laðo/ *a* velvety

aterirse /ate'rirse/ *vr defective* to grow stiff with cold

aterrador /aterra'ðor/ *a* terrifying, dreadful

aterraje /ate'rrahe/ *m*, (*Aer. Naut.*) landing

aterramiento /aterra'miento/ *m*, horror, terror; terrorization; *Naut.* landing; ruin, demolition

aterrar /ate'rrar/ *vt irr* to demolish; discourage; cover with earth; —*vi* land; —*vr Naut.* draw near to land. See **acertar**

aterrizaje /aterri'θahe; aterri'sahe/ *m*, *Aer.* landing. **a. forzoso,** forced landing. **campo de a.,** landing field

aterrizar /aterri'θar; aterri'sar/ *vi Aer.* to land, touch down

aterrorizar /aterrori'θar; aterrori'sar/ *vt* to terrify; terrorize

atesorar /ateso'rar/ *vt* to hoard, treasure up

atestación /atesta'θion; atesta'sion/ *f*, attestation, affidavit

atestar /ates'tar/ *vt irr* to stuff, cram; insert; *Inf.* stuff with food; crowd, fill with people. See **acertar**

atestar /ates'tar/ *vt* to attest, testify

atestiguación /atestigua'θion; atestigua'sion/ *f*, deposition, testimony

atestiguar /atesti'guar/ *vt* to testify, attest

atetar /ate'tar/ *vt* to suckle; —*vi* suck

atezado /ate'θaðo; ate'saðo/ *a* bronzed, sunburnt; black

ático /'atiko/ *a* Attic; *m*, penthouse

atiesar /atie'sar/ *vt* to stiffen

atildar /atil'dar/ *vt* to place a tilde over; blame, criticize; decorate, ornament

atimia /a'timia/ *f*, loss of status

atinado /ati'naðo/ *a* pertinent, relevant

atinar /ati'nar/ *vi* to find by touch; discover by chance; guess; hit the mark

atinente a... /ati'nente a / concerning...

atisbadura /atisβa'ðura/ *f*, watching, spying, prying

atisbar /atis'βar/ *vt* to spy upon, watch

atisbo /a'tisβo/ *m*, prying, watching; suspicion, hint

atisbón /atis'βon/ *a* penetrating (mind, vision)

atizador /atiθa'ðor; atisa'ðor/ *m*, poker (for the fire)

atizar /ati'θar; ati'sar/ *vt* to poke (the fire); dowse, snuff; trim (lamps); excite, rouse; *Inf.* slap, wallop

atlántico /at'lantiko/ *a* Atlantic. *m*, Atlantic Ocean

Atlántida /at'lantiða/ Atlantis

atleta /at'leta/ *m*, athlete

atlético /at'letiko/ *a* athletic

atletismo /atle'tismo/ *m*, athletics

atmósfera /at'mosfera/ *f*, atmosphere

atmosférico /atmos'feriko/ *a* atmospheric

atolladero /atoʎa'ðero; atoya'ðero/ *m*, rut; mud; bog

atolón /ato'lon/ *m*, atoll, coral island

atolondrado /atolon'draðo/ *a* scatter-brained, flighty

atolondramiento /atolondra'miento/ *m*, rashness, recklessness; bewilderment

atolondrar /atolon'drar/ *vt* to bewilder, confuse

atómico /a'tomiko/ *a* atomic

atomización /atomiθa'θion; atomisa'sion/ *f*, atomization

átomo /'atomo/ *m*, atom; speck, particle

atónito /a'tonito/ *a* amazed, astounded

atontar /aton'tar/ *vt* to confuse, daze; make stupid; stun

atormentador /atormenta'ðor/ (**-ra**) *a* torturing —*n* tormentor; torturer

atormentar /atormen'tar/ *vt* to torment; torture; grieve, harass

atorrante /ato'rrante/ *a* and *mf* (Argentina) good-for-nothing

atracadero /atraka'ðero/ *m*, jetty, landingstage

atracar /atra'kar/ *vt Inf.* to stuff with food; *Naut.* tie up, moor; hold up, rob; —*vi Naut.* moor, stop; —*vr Inf.* guzzle, gorge

atracción /atrak'θion; atrak'sion/ *f*, attraction

atraco /a'trako/ (**a**) *m*, hold up (of), ambush (of)

atracón /atra'kon/ *m*, *Inf.* gorge, fill; surfeit. **darse atracones de,** to gorge oneself on

atractivo /atrak'tiβo/ *a* attractive. *m*, attraction, charm

atractriz /atrak'triθ; atrak'tris/ *a* attracting; *f*, force of attraction; (fig.) lure

atraer /atra'er/ *vt irr* to attract; charm, enchant. See **traer**

atragantarse /atragan'tarse/ *vr* to choke; *Inf*. be at a loss, dry up (in conversation)

atraíble /atra'iβle/ *a* attractable, able to be attracted

atrancar /atran'kar/ *vt* to bar the door; obstruct, block; hinder; —*vi Inf*. stride; skip (in reading)

atrapar /atra'par/ *vt Inf*. grab, seize, catch; net, obtain; deceive

atrás /a'tras/ *adv* behind, back; past; previously. **¡A.!** Back! **años a.,** years ago

atrasado /atra'saðo/ *a* slow (of clocks); backward; old-fashioned; hard-up, poor. **a. mental,** retarded person

atrasar /atra'sar/ *vt* to delay, retard; fix a later date than the true one; put back (clocks) —*vi* be slow (clocks); —*vr* be late; be left behind

atraso /a'traso/ *m*, delay; backwardness, dullness; slowness (clocks); lateness; *pl* arrears. **El reloj lleva cinco minutos de a.,** The watch is five minutes slow

atravesado /atraβe'saðo/ *a* slightly squint-eyed; mongrel, crossbreed; half-caste; ill-intentioned

atravesar /atraβe'sar/ *vt irr* to lay across, put athwart; cross, traverse; pierce; obstruct; *Naut*. lie to; —*vr* be among, mingle (with); interrupt; interfere, take part; quarrel; occur, arise. See **confesar**

atrayente /atra'yente/ *a* attractive

atreverse /atre'βerse/ *vr* to dare, risk, venture; be overbold or insolvent

atrevido /atre'βiðo/ *a* bold, audacious; hazardous, dangerous; brazen, impudent

atribución /atriβu'θion; atriβu'sion/ *f*, attribution; perquisite, attribute

atribuible /atri'βuiβle/ *a* attributable

atribuir /atri'βuir/ *vt irr* to impute, attribute; assign, turn over to; —*vr* take upon oneself, assume. See **huir**

atributo /atri'βuto/ *m*, attribute, quality

atril /a'tril/ *m*, lectern, reading desk; music stand

atrincherar /atrintʃe'rar/ *vt* to protect with entrenchments; —*vr* entrench oneself

atrio /'atrio/ *m*, atrium; hall, vestibule; *Archit*. parvis

atrocidad /atroθi'ðað; atrosi'ðað/ *f*, atrocity, cruelty; *Inf*. terrific amount; enormity, crime

atrofia /a'trofia/ *f*, atrophy

atrofiarse /atro'fiarse/ *vr* to atrophy

atronado /atro'naðo/ *a* harebrained, foolish

atronar /atro'nar/ *vt irr* to deafen, stun with noise; confuse, daze. See **tronar**

atropelladamente /atropeʎaða'mente; atropeya-ða'mente/ *adv* in disorder, helter-skelter

atropellado /atrope'ʎaðo; atrope'yaðo/ *a* rash, foolhardy

atropellar /atrope'ʎar; atrope'yar/ *vt* to trample upon; thrust out of the way; knock down; disregard, violate (feelings); insult, abuse; transgress; do hastily; —*vr* act rashly

atropello /atro'peʎo; atro'peyo/ *m*, trampling; road accident; knocking over; upsetting; violation; outrage

atroz /a'troθ; a'ntros/ *a* atrocious, savage; monstrous, outrageous; *Inf*. terrific, enormous

atufar /atu'far/ *vt* to irritate, vex; —*vr* grow irritated; turn sour (wine, etc.)

atún /a'tun/ *m*, tuna

aturdido /atur'ðiðo/ *a* reckless, scatterbrained, silly; thoughtless; stunned

aturdimiento /aturði'miento/ *m*, daze; confusion, bewilderment

aturdir /atur'ðir/ *vt* to daze; confuse, bewilder; amaze; stun

atusar /atu'sar/ *vt* to trim (hair, beard); *Agr*. prune; smooth down (hair); —*vr* dress over-carefully

audacia /au'ðaθia; au'ðasia/ *f*, audacity

audaz /au'ðaθ; au'ðas/ *a* audacious, daring

audibilidad /auðiβili'ðað/ *f*, audibility

audición /auði'θion; auði'sion/ *f*, audition

audiencia /au'ðienθia; au'ðiensia/ *f*, audience, hearing; *Law*. audience; audience chamber

audífono /au'ðifono/ *m*, hearing aid

audioteca /auðio'teka/ *f*, audio library

auditivo /auði'tiβo/ *a* auditory

auditor /auði'tor/ *m*, magistrate, judge

auditorio /auði'torio/ *a* auditory. *m*, audience

auge /'auhe/ *m*, *Fig*. zenith, height; *Astron*. apogee

augusto /au'gusto/ *a* august, awesome

aula /'aula/ *f*, lecture or class room; *Poet*. palace

aullador /auʎa'ðor; auya'ðor/ *a* howling

aullar /au'ʎar; au'yar/ *vi* to howl; bay

aullido /au'ʎiðo; au'yiðo/ *m*, howl; baying

aumentar /aumen'tar/ **(se)** *vt vi vr* to increase, augment

aumentativo /aumenta'tiβo/ *a Gram*. augmentative

aumento /au'mento/ *m*, increase; progress; enlargement. **ir en a.,** to increase; advance, progress; prosper

aun /a'un/ *adv* even. **A. los que viven lejos han de oíros,** Even those who live far must hear you. **a. así** *or* **a. siendo así,** even so. **a. ayer,** only yesterday. **a. cuando,** even if. **más a.,** even more. **ni a. si,** not even if.

aún /a'un/ *adv* still, yet. **A. no te creen** *or* **No te creen a.,** They still don't believe you **¿A. se lo darás?** *or* **¿Se lo darás a.?** Will you still give it to her?

aunque /'aunke/ *conjunc* although, even if, even though. It takes the Indicative referring to statement of fact and Subjunctive referring to a hypothesis, e.g. *A. vino, no lo hizo,* Although he came, he did not do it. *A. él cantase yo no iría allí,* Even though he sang (were to sing), I should not go there

aura /'aura/ *f*, zephyr, gentle breeze; popularity, approbation; aura. **a. epiléptica,** *Med*. epileptic aura

áureo /'aureo/ *a* gold, gilt; golden

auricular /auriku'lar/ *a* auricular. *m*, little finger; receiver, ear-piece (of a telephone); earphone (radio)

aurífero /au'rifero/ *a* gold-yielding, auriferous

auriga /au'riga/ *m*, charioteer

aurora /au'rora/ *f*, dawn; genesis, beginnings. **a. boreal,** aurora borealis, Northern Lights

auscultación /auskulta'θion; auskulta'sion/ *f*, *Med*. auscultation

auscultar /auskul'tar/ *vt Med*. to auscultate

ausencia /au'senθia; au'sensia/ *f*, absence. **en ausencia de,** in the absence of

ausentar /ausen'tar/ *vt* to send away; —*vr* absent oneself

ausente /au'sente/ *a* absent. *mf* absent person

auspicio /aus'piθio; aus'pisio/ *m*, augury, prediction; favor, patronage; *pl* auspices

austeridad /austeri'ðað/ *f*, austerity; mortification of the flesh

austero /aus'tero/ *a* austere, ascetic; severe, harsh; honest, upright

austral /aus'tral/ *a* southerly, austral

australiano /austra'liano/ *a* **(-na)** *a* and *n* Australian

austríaco /aus'triako/ **(-ca)** *a* and *n* Austrian

Austrias, los /'austrias, los/ the Hapsburgs (ruling house of Spain, 1516–1700)

austrófilo /aus'trofilo/ *a* and *n* Austrophile

autenticación /autentika'θion; autentika'sion/ *f*, authentication

autenticar /autenti'kar/ *vt* to authenticate, attest; prove genuine

autenticidad /autentiθi'ðað; autentisi'ðað/ *f*, authenticity

auténtico /au'tentiko/ *a* authentic

auto /'auto/ *m*, *Law*. sentence, decision; *Theat*. one-act allegory (gen. religious); *pl* proceedings. **a. de fe,** auto-da-fé. **a. de reconocimiento,** search-warrant. **a. sacramental,** one-act religious drama on theme of mystery of the Eucharist. **hacer a. de fe,** to burn

autobiografía /autoβiogra'fia/ *f*, autobiography

autobús /auto'βus/ *m*, motor bus, bus

autocitarse /autoθi'tarse; autosi'tarse/ *vr* to quote from one's own works

autoclave /auto'klaβe/ *m*, pressure cooker

autocracia /auto'kraθia; auto'krasia/ *f*, autocracy

autócrata /au'tokrata/ *mf* autocrat

autocrático /auto'kratiko/ *a* autocratic

autocrueldad /autokruel'dað/ *f*, self-inflicted pain

autodescubrimiento /autoðeskuβri'miento/ *m*, self-discovery

autodidacto /auto'ðiðakto/ *a* autodidactic; self-educated, self-taught

autódromo /au'toðromo/ *m*, speedway

autógeno /au'toheno/ *a* autogenous, self-generating

autogiro /auto'hiro/ *m*, *Aer.* autogyro

autografía /autogra'fia/ *f*, autography

autográfico /auto'grafiko/ *a* autographic, in lithographic reproduction

autógrafo /au'tografo/ *a* autographical. *m*, autograph

autoinducción /autoinduk'θion; autoinduk'sion/ *f*, self-induction

autómata /au'tomata/ *m*, automaton

automático /auto'matiko/ *a* automatic. *m*, *Sew.* press stud

automatismo /automa'tismo/ *m*, automatism

automejoramiento /autome,hora'miento/ *m*, self-improvement

automóvil /auto'moβil/ *m*, automobile, motor car —*a* automatic

automovilismo /automoβi'lismo/ *m*, motoring

automovilista /automoβi'lista/ *mf* motorist

autonombrarse /autonom'βrarse/ *vr* to call oneself, go by the name of

autonomía /autono'mia/ *f*, autonomy

autónomo /au'tonomo/ *a* autonomous

autopista /auto'pista/ *f*, motor road

autopsia /au'topsia/ *f*, *Med.* autopsy, post-mortem

autor /au'tor/ **(-ra)** *n* agent, originator; author; inventor; *Law.* perpetrator

autoridad /autori'ðað/ *f*, authority; pomp, show

autoritario /autori'tario/ *a* authoritarian; authoritative

autorización /autoriθa'θion; autorisa'sion/ *f*, authorization

autorizado /autori'θaðo; autori'saðo/ *a* approved, authorized, responsible

autorizar /autori'θar; autori'sar/ *vt* to authorize; *Law.* attest, testify; cite, prove by reference; approve; exalt

autorretratarse /autorretra'tarse/ *vr* to have one's portrait painted, sit for one's portrait

autorretrato /autorre'trato/ *m*, self-portrait

autostopista /autosto'pista/ *mf* hitchhiker (Spain)

autosugestión /autosuhes'tion/ *f*, autosuggestion

auxiliador /auksilia'ðor/ **(-ra)** *a* assistant; helpful —*n* helper, assistant

auxiliar /auksi'liar/ *vt* to help, aid; attend (the dying). *m*, *Educ.* lecturer —*a* assisting

auxiliaría /auksilia'ria/ *f*, *Educ.* lectureship

auxilio /auk'silio/ *m*, help, aid, assistance

aval /a'βal/ *m*, *Com.* endorsement; voucher

avalar /aβa'lar/ *vt* to enhance. **avalado por la tradición**, hallowed by tradition

avalentado /aβalen'taðo/ *a* boastful, bragging

avalorar /aβalo'rar/ *vt* to value, estimate; put spirit into, encourage

avance /a'βanθe; a'βanse/ *m*, advance; advance payment; balance sheet; attack

avanzada /aβan'θaða; aβan'saða/ *f*, *Mil.* advance guard

avanzado /aβan'θaðo; aβan'saðo/ *a* advanced, progressive

avanzar /aβan'θar; aβan'sar/ *vt* to advance; promote; —*vi* advance; attack; grow late (time)

avanzo /a'βanθo; a'βanso/ *m*, balance sheet; price estimate

avaricia /aβa'riθia; aβa'risia/ *f*, greed, avarice

avaricioso, avariento /aβari'θioso; aβari'riento; aβari'sioso, aβa'riento/ *a* avaricious, greedy

avaro /a'βaro/ **(-ra)** *a* miserly; greedy —*n* miser

avasallador /aβasaʎa'ðor; aβasaya'ðor/ *a* dominating; *Fig.* overwhelming; enslaving

avasallar /aβasa'ʎar; aβasa'yar/ *vt* to subdue, dominate; —*vr* become a vassal; surrender, yield

ave /'aβe/ *f*, bird. **a. de paso**, migratory bird; *Fig.* bird of passage. **a. de rapiña**, bird of prey. **a. fría**, *Ornith.* plover. **ave cantora**, songbird

avecinarse /aβeθi'narse; aβesi'narse/ *vr* to be approaching (e.g. *el año que avecina*, the coming year)

avellana /aβe'ʎana; aβe'yana/ *f*, hazel nut

avellanarse /aβeʎa'narse; aβeya'narse/ *vr* to shrivel

avellano /aβe'ʎano; aβe'yano/ *m*, *Bot.* hazel

avemaría /aβema'ria/ *f*, Hail Mary (prayer); Angelus; rosary bead. *Inf.* **en un a.**, in a trice

avena /a'βena/ *f*, oats; *Poet.* oaten pipe. **a. loca**, wild oats

avenal /aβe'nal/ *m*, oatfield

avenar /aβe'nar/ *vt* to drain (land); drain off (liquids)

avenencia /aβe'nenθia; aβe'nensia/ *f*, agreement, arrangement; transaction; conformity, harmony

avenida /aβe'niða/ *f*, flood, spate; avenue; abundance; way, approach (to a place)

avenido /aβe'niðo/ *a* (*with bien or mal*) well *or* ill-suited

avenidor /aβeni'ðor/ **(-ra)** *n* arbitrator, mediator

avenir /aβe'nir/ *vt irr* to reconcile; —*vi* happen (used in infinitive and third singular and plural); —*vr* be reconciled; agree; compromise, give way; harmonize (things); (*with con*) get on with, agree with. See **venir**

aventador /aβenta'ðor/ *m*, *Agr.* winnower; pitchfork

aventajado /aβenta'haðo/ *a* outstanding, talented; advantageous. *m*, *Mil.* private who enjoys extra pay

aventajar /aβenta'har/ *vt* to improve, better; promote, prefer; excel; —*vr* (*with prep a*) surpass, excel. **Te aventajo en diez años**, I'm ten years older than you

aventamiento /aβenta'miento/ *m*, winnowing

aventar /aβen'tar/ *vt irr* to fan; air, ventilate; winnow; *Inf.* drive away, expel; —*vr* be inflated; *Inf.* flee; smell (bad meat). See **sentar**

aventura /aβen'tura/ *f*, adventure; chance, luck; risk, danger

aventurar /aβentu'rar/ *vt* to risk, hazard

aventurero /aβentu'rero/ **(-ra)** *a* adventurous; unscrupulous, intriguing; undisciplined (of troops) —*n* adventurer

avergonzar /aβergon'θar; aβergon'sar/ *vt irr* to shame; make shy, abash; —*vr* be ashamed; be shy or sheepish —*Pres. Indic.* **avergüenzo, avergüenzas, avergüenza, avergüenzan**. *Pres. Subjunc.* **avergüence, avergüences, avergüence, avergüencen**

avería /aβe'ria/ *f*, aviary; damage (to merchandise); loss, harm; *Elec.* fault; breakdown. **a. gruesa**, general average (marine insurance)

averiarse /aβe'riarse/ *vr* to be damaged; deteriorate; break down

averiguable /aβeri'guaβle/ *a* examinable, investigable; discoverable

averiguación /aβerigua'θion; aβerigua'sion/ *f*, inquiry, investigation; discovery

averiguar /aβeri'guar/ *vt* to investigate, inquire into; discover, ascertain. **¡averígüelo Vargas!** Beats me!, Search me!

averío /aβe'rio/ *m*, flock of birds

Averno /a'βerno/ *m*, *Poet.* Avernus, Hades

aversión /aβer'sion/ *f*, aversion, repugnance

avestruz /aβes'truθ; aβes'trus/ *m*, ostrich

avetado /aβe'taðo/ *a* veined, mottled, streaked

avezar /aβe'θar; aβe'sar/ *vt* to accustom; —*vr* grow accustomed (to)

aviación /aβia'θion; aβia'sion/ *f*, aviation

aviador /aβia'ðor/ *m*, aviator

aviar /a'βiar/ *vt* to outfit, equip; prepare, make ready; *Inf.* speed up; caulk (ship). *Fig. Inf.* **estar aviado**, to be in a mess

avidez /aβi'ðeθ; aβi'ðes/ *f*, avidity, greed; longing, desire

ávido /'aβiðo/ *a* avid, greedy

avieso /a'βieso/ *a* twisted, crooked; ill-natured; sinister

avillanado /aβiʎa'naðo; aβiya'naðo/ *a* countrified; gross, vulgar; boorish

avinagrado /aβina'graðo/ *a Inf.* crabbed, sour, testy

avío /a'βio/ *m*, preparation, provision; picnic lunch; money advanced (to miners or laborers); *pl Inf.* equipment, tools. **avíos de pesca**, fishing tackle

avión /a'βion/ *m*, airplane; *Ornith.* martin or swift. **a. de bombardeo**, bomber. **a. de caza**, fighter plane. **a. de combate nocturno**, night fighter. **a. de hostigamiento**, interceptor. **a. de reacción**, jet airplane. **a. de transporte**, *Aer.* transport. **a. en picado**, dive-bomber. **a. taxi,** air taxi. **por a.,** by airmail «Avión» "Airmail"

avioneta /aβio'neta/ f, light airplane, small airplane

avisado /aβi'saðo/ a shrewd, sensible. **mal a.,** ill-advised, imprudent

avisar /aβi'sar/ vt to inform, acquaint; warn; advise

aviso /a'βiso/ m, notice, announcement; warning; advice; care, caution; attention; shrewdness, prudence. **estar sobre a.,** to be on call; be on the alert

avispa /a'βispa/ f, wasp

avispado /aβis'paðo/ a Inf. smart, clever, quick; wide-awake

avispar /aβis'par/ vt to goad, prick; Inf. rouse, incite; —vr be uneasy, fret

avispero /aβis'pero/ m, wasp's nest; swarm of wasps; Fig. Inf. hornet's nest

avispón /aβis'pon/ m, hornet

avistamiento /aβista'miento/ m, sighting, spotting (e.g. of a ship)

avistar /aβis'tar/ vt to descry, sight, spot; —vr **avistarse con,** to interview

avituallar /aβitua'ʎar/ aβitua'yar/ vt to victual, supply with food

avivar /aβi'βar/ vt to enliven; stimulate, encourage; stir (fire); trim (wicks); brighten (colors); inflame; vivify, invigorate; —vi revive, recover

avizor /aβi'θor/ aβi'sor/ m, watcher, spy —a watchful, vigilant

avizorar /aβiθo'rar/ aβiso'rar/ vt to watch, spy upon

avutarda /aβu'tarða/ f, bustard

axila /ak'sila/ f, Bot. axil; Anat. axilla, armpit

axioma /ak'sioma/ m, axiom

axiomático /aksio'matiko/ a axiomatic

¡ay! /ai/ interj Alas! Woe is me! m, complaint, sigh

aya /'aya/ f, governess

ayer /a'yer/ adv yesterday; a short while ago; in the past. m, past

ayo /'ayo/ m, tutor

ayuda /a'yuða/ f, help, assistance; enema; clyster; watch dog. m, **a. de cámara,** valet

ayudador /ayuða'ðor/ **(-ra)** a helping, assisting —n helper

ayudante /ayu'ðante/ m, assistant; teaching assistant; Mil. adjutant. **a. a cátedra,** Educ. assistant lecturer. **a. de plaza,** post adjutant

ayudar /ayu'ðar/ vt to assist; help, aid; —vr make an effort; avail oneself of another's help

ayunador /ayuna'ðor/ **(-ra)** a fasting —n faster; abstainer

ayunar /ayu'nar/ vi to fast

ayuno /a'yuno/ m, fast —a fasting; ignorant, unaware. **en a.** or **en ayunas,** before breakfast, fasting; Inf. ignorant, unaware

ayuntamiento /ayunta'miento/ m, meeting, assembly; municipal government; town hall; sexual union

azabache /aθa'βatʃe/ asaβatʃe/ m, Mineral. jet

azada /a'θaða/ a'saða/ f, Agr. spade; hoe

azadón /aθa'ðon/ asa'ðon/ m, Agr. hoe

azafata /aθa'fata/ asa'fata/ f, queen's waiting-maid Obs.; flight attendant

azafate /aθa'fate/ asa'fate/ m, flat basket; small tray

azafrán /aθa'fran/ asa'fran/ m, Bot. saffron; crocus

azafranado /aθafra'naðo/ asafra'naðo/ a saffron-colored

azahar /a'θaar/ a'saar/ m, flower of orange, lemon or sweet lime tree

azar /a'θar/ a'sar/ m, chance, hazard; unexpected misfortune; losing card or throw of dice

azararse /aθa'rarse/ asa'rarse/ vr to go wrong, fail (negotiations, etc.); grow nervous; become confused; blush

azaroso /aθa'roso/ asa'roso/ a unlucky, ill-omened; hazardous

ázimo /'aθimo/ 'asimo/ a unleavened (bread)

ázoe /'aθoe/ 'asoe/ m, nitrogen

azogar /aθo'gar/ aso'gar/ vt to silver (mirrors, etc.); slake lime; —vr suffer from mercury poisoning; Inf. grow uneasy, be agitated

azogue /a'θoge/ a'soge/ m, Mineral. mercury, quicksilver; market-place

azolve /a'θolβe/ a'solβe/ m, silt

azoramiento /aθora'miento; asora'miento/ m, alarm, terror; confusion, stupefaction; incitement

azorar /aθo'rar/ aso'rar/ vt to alarm, terrify; confuse, stun, dumbfound; excite, stimulate; encourage

azotacalles /aθota'kaʎes; asota'kayes/ mf Inf. idler, street loafer

azotaina /aθo'taina/ aso'taina/ f, Inf. whipping, spanking

azotamiento /aθota'miento; asota'miento/ m, flogging, beating, whipping

azotar /aθo'tar/ aso'tar/ vt to whip, beat, flog; scourge, ravage; knock against or strike repeatedly

azotazo /aθo'taθo; aso'taso/ m, spank

azote /a'θote; a'sote/ m, whip; scourge; lash, blow with a whip; spank, slap; misfortune, disaster. Inf. **azotes y galeras,** monotonous diet

azotea /aθo'tea; aso'tea/ f, flat terrace roof

azozador /aθoθa'ðor; asosa'ðor/ party whip, whip

azteca /aθ'teka; as'teka/ a and mf Aztec

azúcar /a'θukar; a'sukar/ m, sugar. **a. blanco** or **a. de flor,** white sugar. **a. de pilón,** loaf sugar. **a. moreno,** brown sugar. **a. quebrado,** brown sugar. **a. y canela,** sorrel gray (of horses)

azucarado /aθuka'raðo; asuka'raðo/ a sugary; sugared, sugar-coated; Inf. honeyed, flattering

azucarar /aθuka'rar; asuka'rar/ vt to coat with sugar; sweeten; Inf. soften, mitigate; —vr crystallize; go sugary (jam)

azucarera /aθuka'rera; asuka'rera/ f, sugar-basin

azucarero /aθuka'rero; asuka'rero/ a sugar-producing (e.g. province)

azucarillo /aθuka'riʎo; asuka'riyo/ m, Cul. bar made of white of egg and sugar for sweetening water

azucena /aθu'θena; asu'sena/ f, white lily. **a. de agua,** water-lily

azuela /aθu'ela; a'suela/ f, adze

azufrar /aθu'frar; asu'frar/ vt to sulphurate

azufre /a'θufre; a'sufre/ m, sulphur

azufroso /aθu'froso; asu'froso/ a sulphurous

azul /a'θul; a'sul/ a and m, blue. **a. celeste,** sky blue, azure. **a. de mar** or **a. marino,** navy blue. **a. de ultramar,** ultramarine. **a. turquí,** indigo

azulado /aθu'laðo; asu'laðo/ a bluish, blue

azulear /aθule'ar; asule'ar/ vi to look bluish, have a blue tint

azulejo /aθu'leho; asu'leho/ m, ornamental glazed tile

azumbre /a'θumbre; a'sumbre/ f, liquid measure (just over 2 liters)

azuzar /aθu'θar; asu'sar/ vt to set on (dogs); irritate, provoke; incite, urge

B

baba /'baβa/ f, saliva; secretion (of snails, etc.); viscous fluid (of plants). *Inf.* **caérsele (a uno) la b.**, to ooze satisfaction; be dumbfounded

babador, babero /baβa'ðor, ba'βero/ m, bib, feeder

babear /baβe'ar/ vi to dribble, slaver; *Fig. Inf.* slobber over, be sloppy

babel /ba'βel/ m, babel

babélico /ba'βeliko/ a Babelian, Babel-like confusion; unintelligible

Babia, estar en /'baβia, es'tar en/ to be daydreaming

babieca /ba'βieka/ mf *Inf.* stupid person. **Babieca** f, the Cid's horse

Babilonia /baβi'lonia/ Babylon

babilónico /baβi'loniko/ a Babylonian

bable /'baβle/ m, Asturian (language)

babor /ba'βor/ m, *Naut.* larboard, port

babosa /ba'βosa/ f, slug; young onion

baboso /ba'βoso/ a slavering; *Fig. Inf.* "sloppy"; *Inf.* incompetent, useless

babucha /ba'βutʃa/ f, heelless slipper, babouche

babuino /ba'βuino/ m, *Zool.* baboon

baca /'baka/ f, luggage carrier (on roof of bus, etc.)

bacalao /baka'lao/ m, codfish

bacanales /baka'nales/ f pl, Bacchanalia

bacante /ba'kante/ f, Bacchante

bacará /baka'ra/ m, baccarat (card game)

baceta /ba'θeta; ba'seta/ f, pool (in card games)

bache /'batʃe/ m, rut (in road); pothole

bacheo /ba'tʃeo/ m, repairing of streets

bachiller /batʃi'ʎer; batʃi'yer/ mf high-school graduate. m, *Inf.* babbler. f, **bachillera**, *Inf.* blue-stocking; garrulous woman

bachillerarse /batʃiʎe'rarse; batʃiye'rarse/ vr to graduate as a bachelor

bachillerato /batʃiʎe'rato; batʃiye'rato/ m, baccalaureate, bachelor's degree

bacía /ba'θia; ba'sia/ f, bowl; barber's circular shaving-dish; barber's trade sign

bacilar /baθi'lar; basi'lar/ a bacillary

bacilo /ba'θilo; ba'silo/ m, bacillus

bacterial, bacteriano /bakteri'rial, bakte'riano/ a bacterial

bactericida /bakteri'θiða; bakteri'siða/ m, bactericide

bacteriología /bakteriolo'hia/ f, bacteriology

bacteriológico /bakterio'lohiko/ a bacteriological

bacteriólogo /bakte'riologo/ m, bacteriologist

báculo /'bakulo/ m, staff; walking-stick; *Fig.* support. **b. episcopal**, bishop's crozier

badajo /ba'ðaho/ m, clapper (of a bell); chatterbox, gossip

badana /ba'ðana/ f, cured sheepskin, chamois leather, washleather; sweat band; *Inf.* **zurrar (a uno) la b.**, to take the hide off; insult

badén /ba'ðen/ m, channel made by rain, furrow; conduit

badil /ba'ðil/ m, fire-shovel

badulaque /baðu'lake/ m, *Inf.* good-for-nothing

bagaje /ba'gahe/ m, *Mil.* baggage; beast of burden, transport animal; luggage

bagatela /baga'tela/ f, trifle, oddment, bagatelle

bagazo /ba'gaθo; ba'gaso/ m, oilcake, bagasse

bagual /ba'gual/ a *West. Hem.* untamed, wild; doltish, dull. m, untamed horse, wild horse

bahía /ba'ia/ f, bay, harbor

bailable /bai'laβle/ a dance (of music). m, *Theat.* dance number

bailador /baila'ðor/ (-ra) n dancer

bailar /bai'lar/ vi to dance; spin around. **b. al son que le toca**, to adapt oneself to circumstances

bailarín /baila'rin/ a dancing. m, professional dancer. **b. de cuerda, bailarín de la cuerda floja**, tightrope dancer

bailarina /baila'rina/ f, ballerina

baile /'baile/ m, dance; ball; ballet. **b. de máscaras**, **b. de trajes**, fancy-dress ball. **b. de San Vito**, St. Vitus' dance. **b. ruso**, ballet

bailotear /bailote'ar/ vi to jig about; dance

baja /'baha/ f, drop, diminution; fall (in price, etc.); *Mil.* casualty; discharge. *Inf.* **darse de b.**, to leave an employment

bajada /ba'haða/ f, descent, fall; slope, incline; hollow, depression. **b. de aguas**, roof gutter

bajalato /baha'lato/ m, pashalik

bajamar /baha'mar/ f, low tide

bajamente /baha'mente/ adv basely, abjectly

bajar /ba'har/ vi to descend; go down; get off; drop; fall, decrease; —vt lower, take down, bring down; let down; dismount, alight; bend, droop; drop; reduce (price); *Fig.* lower (voices); humiliate, humble; **b. a tierra**, to step ashore; **b. la cabeza ante**, to submit to (e.g. a judgment) vr alight, dismount; humble oneself

bajel /ba'hel/ m, *Naut.* galley, ship

bajeza /ba'heθa; ba'hesa/ f, base action; meanness; *Fig.* humble estate, lowliness. **b. de ánimo**, timorousness

bajío /ba'hio/ m, *Naut.* shallows, shoal; depression, hollow

bajista /ba'hista/ mf speculator, bear (Stock Exchange)

bajo /'baho/ a low; short, not tall; downcast; under; subordinate; pale (of colors); humble (origin); base; coarse, vulgar; cheap (price); low (sounds). m, depth; shoal, sand bank; *Mus.* bass; pl petticoats, skirts; horses' hoofs —adv beneath, below —prep under, beneath. **b. juramento**, upon oath. **bajo relieve**, bas relief. **en voz baja**, in a low voice. **planta baja**, ground floor. **por lo b.**, in a whisper; in secret, on the sly

bajolatino /bahola'tino/ a Low Latin

bajón /ba'hon/ m, *Mus.* bassoon; bassoon player; *Fig. Inf.* downfall

bajonista /baho'nista/ mf bassoon player

bala /'bala/ f, bullet, ball; bale. **b. fría**, spent bullet. **b. luminosa**, tracer bullet. **b. perdida**, stray bullet. *Inf.* **como una b.**, like a shot

balada /ba'laða/ f, ballad, song

baladí /bala'ði/ a worthless, insignificant

baladro /ba'laðro/ m, yell, outcry, shout

baladrón /bala'ðron/ a braggart

baladronada /balaðro'naða/ f, bravado, bragging

balagar /bala'gar/ m, straw rick

bálago /'balago/ m, straw; soap-ball; straw rick

balance /ba'lanθe; ba'lanse/ m, balance; swinging; oscillation; rolling, rocking (of a ship, etc.); doubt, insecurity, *Com.* balance; *Com.* balance sheet

balancear /balanθe'ar; balanse'ar/ vi to swing; oscillate; vacillate, hesitate; —vt balance; —vr balance oneself; rock or swing oneself

balanceo /balan'θeo; balan'seo/ m, balancing; rocking; swinging; rolling (of a ship, etc.)

balancín /balan'θin; balan'sin/ m, swing-bar; whipple-tree; balance beam; tight-rope dancer's pole; minting-mill; yoke (for carrying pails); pl *Naut.* lifts

balandra /ba'landra/ f, *Naut.* sloop, cutter

balanza /ba'lanθa; ba'lansa/ f, balance; scale; judgment; comparison. **b. de comercio**, balance of trade. **en balanzas**, in doubt or danger, in the balance

balar /ba'lar/ vi to bleat (sheep)

balasto /ba'lasto/ m, *Rail.* ballast

balaustrada /balaus'traða/ f, balustrade

balaustre /bala'ustre/ m, baluster

balazo /ba'laθo; ba'laso/ m, shot; bullet wound

balbuceo /balβu'θeo; balβu'seo/ m, stammering; babbling; lisping; **balbuceos** *Fig.* beginnings, early stages (e.g. *los b. de la literatura yídica*, the beginnings of Yiddish literature)

balbuciente /balβu'θiente; balβu'siente/ a stammering; babbling; lisping

balbucir /balβu'θir; balβu'sir/ vi irr *defective* to stammer; lisp; babble; read hesitantly. See **lucir**

Balcanes, los /bal'kanes, los/ the Balkans

balcánico /bal'kaniko/ a Balkan

balcón /bal'kon/ *m*, balcony
baldaquín /balda'kin/ *m*, canopy, baldachin
baldar /bal'dar/ *vt* to cripple; impede, obstruct
balde /'balde/ *m*, bucket
balde /'balde/ **(en)** *adv* in vain. **de b.**, gratis, free of charge
baldear /balde'ar/ *vt Naut.* to wash the decks
baldío /bal'dio/ *a* untilled; fallow; useless, worthless; vagrant
baldón /bal'don/ *m*, insult; dishonor
baldonar /baldo'nar/ *vt* to insult
baldosa /bal'dosa/ *f*, paving stone; tile
baldrufa /bal'drufa/ *f*, top, spinning top
balduque /bal'duke/ *m*, red tape
Baleares, las Islas /bale'ares, las 'islas/ the Balearic Islands
baleárico /bale'ariko/ *a* Balearic
balido /ba'liðo/ *m*, bleat, bleating
balística /ba'listika/ *f*, ballistics
baliza /ba'liθa; ba'lisa/ *f, Naut.* buoy, beacon
balizamiento /baliθa'miento; balisa'miento/ *m*, marking with beacons, marking with buoys; traffic signs and signals
ballena /ba'ʎena; ba'yena/ *f*, whale; whalebone
ballenero /baʎe'nero; baye'nero/ *a* whaling. *m*, whaler
ballesta /ba'ʎesta; ba'yesta/ *f*, crossbow; spring (of carriages)
ballestería /baʎeste'ria; bayeste'ria/ *f*, archery; crossbowmen
ballestero /baʎes'tero; bayes'tero/ *m*, archer; crossbowman; crossbow maker
balneario /balne'ario/ *a* pertaining to public baths; bathing; holiday; spa. *m*, watering place, spa
balompié /balom'pie/ *m*, football (game)
balón /ba'lon/ *m*, large ball; football; *Chem.* balloon; bundle; bale. **b. de ensayo**, *Fig.* feeler
baloncesto /balon'θesto; balon'sesto/ *m, Sports.* basketball
balota /ba'lota/ *f*, ballot
balotaje /balo'tahe/ *m*, balloting; run-off election
balotar /balo'tar/ *vi* to ballot
balsa /'balsa/ *f*, pond; raft
balsadera /balsa'ðera/ *f*, ferry
balsámico /bal'samiko/ *a* balmy
bálsamo /'balsamo/ *m*, balm
balsero /bal'sero/ *m*, ferryman; rafter (person fleeing a country by raft, rowboat, etc.)
balso /'balso/ *m, Naut.* sling
báltico /'baltiko/ *a* Baltic. **el Mar Báltico** the Baltic Sea
baluarte /ba'luarte/ *m*, bulwark; bastion; protection, defense
bambalina /bamba'lina/ *f*, fly (theatrical scenery)
bamboleante /bambole'ante/ *a* swaying, swinging; *Fig.* tottering (e.g. empire)
bambolearse /bambole'arse/ *vr* to sway; swing; totter; be shaky; stagger
bamboleo /bambo'leo/ *m*, rocking; swinging; tottering; staggering; reeling
bambolla /bam'βoʎa; bam'βoya/ *f, Inf.* ostentation, swank
bambú /bam'βu/ *m*, bamboo
banal /ba'nal/ *a* banal, commonplace
banana /ba'nana/ *f*, banana
banasta /ba'nasta/ *f*, big basket
banastero /banas'tero/ **(-ra)** *n* basket maker or dealer
banasto /ba'nasto/ *m*, big round basket
banca /'banka/ *f*, bench; card game; stall; *Com.* banking
bancada /ban'kaða/ *f*, rowing seat
bancal /ban'kal/ *m*, oblong garden plot; terrace
bancario /ban'kario/ *a* banking, bank
bancarrota /banka'rrota/ *f*, bankruptcy. **hacer b.**, to go bankrupt
banco /'banko/ *m*, form, bench; rowing seat; settle; seat; bench; *Com.* bank; *Naut.* bar, shoal; school (of fish). **b. azul**, government benches in Spanish Parliament. **b. de arena**, sand-bank. **b. de descuento**, discount bank. **b. de emisión, banco emisor**, bank of issue. **b. de hielo**, iceberg. **b. de nivel**, benchmark

banda /'banda/ *f*, wide ribbon; sash; ribbon, insignia; strip; border; party, group; gang; flock (of birds); zone, belt; side (of ship); *Mus.* band; cushion (billiards); *Herald.* bar, bend. **b. elástica**, rubber band. *Naut.* **dar a la b.**, to lie along
bandada /ban'daða/ *f*, flock (of birds)
bandeja /ban'deha/ *f*, tray, salver
bandera /ban'dera/ *f*, banner, flag; colors, standard. **b. de popa**, ensign. **jurar la b.**, (*Mil. Nav.*) to take the oath of allegiance
banderilla /bande'riʎa; bande'riya/ *f*, banderilla (bullfighting)
banderillear /banderiʎe'ar; banderiye'ar/ *vt* to put banderillas on bulls
banderillero /banderi'ʎero; banderi'yero/ *m*, man who puts banderillas on bulls
banderín /bande'rin/ *m, dim* small flag; recruiting post
banderizo /bande'riθo; bande'riso/ *a* factious; vehement, excitable
banderola /bande'rola/ *f*, banderole, pennon; bannerole
bandido /ban'diðo/ **(-da)** *a* and *n* outlaw, fugitive. *m*, bandit; highwayman; rogue, desperado
bando /'bando/ *m*, proclamation, order; faction, group, party
bandola /ban'dola/ *f, Mus.* pandora, pandore
bandolerismo /bandole'rismo/ *m*, brigandage
bandolero /bando'lero/ *m*, robber, footpad, brigand
bandolín /bando'lin/ *m*, mandolin
bandurria /ban'durria/ *f, Mus.* mandolin
banjo /'banho/ *m*, banjo
banquero /ban'kero/ *m*, banker
banqueta /ban'keta/ *f*, three-legged stool; seat; footstool
banquete /ban'kete/ *m*, banquet, feast
banquetear /bankete'ar/ *vt* and *vi* to banquet
banqueteo /banke'teo/ *m*, banqueting, feasting
bañado /ba'ɲaðo/ *m*, chamber pot; *West. Hem.* marshy land, marsh; **bañados** *pl* marsh
bañador /baɲa'ðor/ **(-ra)** *a* bathing —*n* bather. *m*, bathing dress; bath, vat
bañar /ba'ɲar/ *vt* to bathe; coat, cover; dip; lave, wash; *Fig.* bathe (of sunlight, etc.) —*vr* take a bath; bathe
bañera /ba'ɲera/ *f*, bath attendant; bathtub
bañista /ba'ɲista/ *mf* bather; one who takes spa waters
baño /'baɲo/ *m*, bathing; bath; bathroom; bathtub; bagnio, Turkish prison; covering, coat; *pl* mineral baths, spa. **b. de mar**, sea bath. **b. de María**, double saucepan. **b. de sol**, sunbath. **casa de baños**, public baths. **cuarto de b.**, bathroom
bao /'bao/ *m, Naut.* beam
baptisterio /baptis'terio/ *m*, baptistery; *Eccl.* font
baquelita /bake'lita/ *f*, bakelite
baqueta /ba'keta/ *f*, ramrod; *pl* drumsticks; *Mil.* gauntlet
bar /bar/ *m*, bar; café
barahúnda /bara'unda/ *f*, See **baraúnda**
baraja /ba'raha/ *f*, pack (of cards); game of cards
barajar /bara'har/ *vt* to shuffle (cards); jumble, mix; —*vi* quarrel
baranda /ba'randa/ *f*, handrail, banister; cushion (of billiard table)
barandilla /baran'diʎa; baran'diya/ *f, dim* railing
baratija /bara'tiha/ *f*, (gen. *pl*) trifle, oddment
baratillo /bara'tiʎo; bara'tiyo/ *m*, second-hand article, frippery; second-hand shop or stall; bargain counter
barato /ba'rato/ *a* cheap; easy. *m*, bargain sale —*adv* cheaply
baratura /bara'tura/ *f*, cheapness
baraúnda /bara'unda/ *f*, uproar, confusion
barba /'barβa/ *f*, chin; beard; whiskers; fin; barb (of a feather); *m*, actor who plays old men. *f pl*, fibers of plants. **b. bien poblada**, a thick beard. **barbas de ballena**, whalebone. *Fig. Inf.* **echar a las barbas**, to throw in a person's face. **en la barba, en las barbas**, to ones face (e.g. *Me lo dijeron en las barbas*. They

told me so to my face). **hacer la b.,** to shave; *Inf.* annoy

barbacoa /barβa'koa/ *f, West Hem.* barbecue; trellis (for climbing plants)

barbado /bar'βaðo/ *a* bearded. *m,* shoot; sucker; transplanted plant

barbárico /bar'βariko/ *a* barbarian; barbaric

barbaridad /barβari'ðað/ *f,* barbarity; blunder; atrocity; outrage; *Inf.* huge amount. **¡Qué b.!** How awful! You don't say so!

barbarie /bar'βarie/ *f,* barbarism; barbarity, cruelty

barbarismo /barβa'rismo/ *m,* barbarism; cruelty; barbarians

bárbaro /'barβaro/ **(-ra)** *a* and *n* barbarian —*a* fierce; headstrong; uncivilized. **como un b.,** like crazy (e.g. *estudiar como un b.,* to study like crazy)

barbechar /barβe'tʃar/ *vt* to plow; leave fallow

barbecho /bar'βetʃo/ *m, Agr.* fallow; first plowing

barbería /barβe'ria/ *f,* barber shop

barbero /bar'βero/ *m,* barber

barbihecho /barβi'etʃo/ *a* fresh-shaved

barbilampiño /barβilam'piɲo/ *a* smooth-faced, beardless, clean-shaven

barbilindo /barβi'lindo/ *a* dandified, dappy; *m,* dandy

barbilla /bar'βiʎa; bar'βiya/ *f,* point of the chin; chin. **acariciar la b. (de),** to chuck under the chin

barbiquejo /barβi'keho/ *m, Naut.* bobstay; hat-guard

barbudo /bar'βuðo/ *a* heavily bearded

barbulla /bar'βuʎa; bar'βuya/ *f, Inf.* babble, chatter, murmur of voices

barca /'barka/ *f,* small boat, bark; barge. **b. de pasaje,** ferryboat. **b. plantaminas** minelayer

barcada /bar'kaða/ *f,* boat-load; ferry crossing

barcaza /bar'kaθa; bar'kasa/ *f, Naut.* lighter; barge. **b. de desembarco,** landingcraft

barcelonés /barθelo'nes; barselo'nes/ **(-esa)** *a* and *n* of or from Barcelona

barcino /bar'θino; bar'sino/ *a* ruddy (of animals); fawn and white; *Inf.* turncoat (of politicians)

barco /'barko/ *m,* boat; ship; hollow, rut. **b. barredero,** trawler. **b. siembraminas,** minelayer

barda /'barða/ *f,* horse armor; thatch; shingle; (Mexico) cement fence, cement wall

bardal /bar'ðal/ *m,* thatched wall; mud wall

bardar /bar'ðar/ *vt* to thatch

bardo /'barðo/ *m,* poet, bard

bario /'bario/ *m,* barium

barítono /ba'ritono/ *m,* baritone

barloventear /barloβente'ar/ *vi Naut.* to tack; ply to windward; *Inf.* wander about

barlovento /barlo'βento/ *m, Naut.* windward

barnacla /bar'nakla/ *m,* barnacle

barniz /bar'niθ; bar'nis/ *m,* varnish; glaze; smattering, veneer

barnizar /barni'θar; barni'sar/ *vt* to varnish; glaze

barométrico /baro'metriko/ *a* barometric

barómetro /ba'rometro/ *m,* barometer

barón /ba'ron/ *m,* baron

baronesa /baro'nesa/ *f,* baroness

baronía /baro'nia/ *f,* barony

barquero /bar'kero/ *m,* boatman; bargee; *Ent.* waterboatman

barquillero /barki'ʎero; barki'yero/ *m,* seller of wafers; waffle-iron

barquillo /bar'kiʎo; bar'kiyo/ *m,* wafer, cornet

barquín /bar'kin/ *m,* furnace bellows

barra /'barra/ *f,* bar; ingot; railing (in courtroom); sandbank; fault (in cloth); lever, crossbar; (in cricket) bail; *Mus.* bar. **b. de jabón de afeitar,** shaving-stick. **a barras derechas,** without deceit

barrabasada /barraβa'saða/ *f, Inf.* wilfulness, escapade

barraca /ba'rraka/ *f,* cabin, hut; stall; sideshow. **b. de tiro,** shooting gallery

barracón /barra'kon/ *m,* side-show; stall

barragana /barra'gana/ *f,* concubine, mistress

barranca /ba'rranka/ *f,* **barranco** *m,* furrow, channel, rut; gorge; difficulty, fix

barrancoso /barran'koso/ *a* rutty, uneven

barredor /barre'ðor/ **(-ra)** *n* sweeper

barredura /barre'ðura/ *f,* sweeping; *pl* sweepings; rubbish

barrena /ba'rrena/ *f,* borer, gimlet, drill, auger. *Aer.* **b. de cola,** tail-spin

barrenar /barre'nar/ *vt* to drill, bore; blast (in quarries)

barrendero /barren'dero/ **(-ra)** *n* sweeper, scavenger

barrenero /barre'nero/ *m,* driller; blaster

barreno /ba'rreno/ *m,* blast hole; bore, drill; vanity

barreño /ba'rreɲo/ *m,* earthenware bowl (for dish washing, etc.)

barrer /ba'rrer/ *vt* to sweep; *Fig.* clear, make a clean sweep

barrera /ba'rrera/ *f,* barrier; barricade; *Fig.* obstacle. **b. de golpe,** automatic gate (at level crossings, etc.). **b. de minas,** minefield

barriada /barri'aða/ *f,* district; quarter (of a city)

barrica /ba'rrika/ *f,* cask; barrel

barricada /barri'kaða/ *f,* barricade

barriga /ba'rriga/ *f, Inf.* belly

barrigón, barrigudo /barri'gon, barri'guðo/ *a* pot-bellied

barril /ba'rril/ *m,* barrel; cask; water-butt

barrilero /barri'lero/ *m,* cooper

barrilete /barri'lete/ *m, dim* keg; clamp; *Naut.* mouse

barrio /'barrio/ *m,* district, quarter; suburb. **barrios bajos,** slums, back streets. **el otro b.,** the other world, Eternity

barrizal /barri'θal; barri'sal/ *m,* muddy place; claypit

barro /'barro/ *m,* mud; clay; earthenware drinking vessel; *Inf.* money

barroco /ba'rroko/ *a* baroque

barroso /ba'rroso/ *a* muddy; pimpled; mud-colored

barrote /ba'rrote/ *m,* thick iron bar; stave, bond

barruntar /barrun'tar/ *vt* to conjecture; suspect

barrunto /ba'rrunto/ *m,* conjecture; indication, sign

bártulos /'bartulos/ *m pl,* household goods; *Fig.* means, wherewithal

barullo /ba'ruʎo; ba'ruyo/ *m, Inf.* confusion, disorder; mob

basa /'basa/ *f,* base; *Archit.* pedestal; foundation, basis

basalto /ba'salto/ *m,* basalt

basar /ba'sar/ *vt* to base, place on a base; *Fig.* found, base; —*vr* (*with en*) rely upon, base oneself on

basca /'baska/ *f,* (gen. *pl*) nausea; retching; wave of anger

báscula /'baskula/ *f,* weighing-machine, platform-scale; weigh-bridge

base /'base/ *f,* base; (*Chem. Geom. Mil.*) base; basis; *Archit.* pedestal; *Mus.* root. **sin b.,** baseless

básico /'basiko/ *a* basic

Basilea /basi'lea/ Basel, Basle

basílica /ba'silika/ *f,* palace; church, basilica

basilisco /basi'lisko/ *m,* basilisk; antique cannon

basquear /baske'ar/ *vi* to retch; feel squeamish

bastante /bas'tante/ *a* sufficient, enough —*adv* sufficiently; enough; fairly; a good deal; somewhat. **Hace b. calor,** It is quite hot. **Tengo b.,** I have enough. **Tenemos b. tiempo,** We have sufficient time

bastar /bas'tar/ *vi* to suffice. **¡Basta!** Enough! No more! Stop! **¡Basta de...!** Enough of...! **Basta decir que...,** Suffice it to say that...

bastardía /bastar'ðia/ *f,* bastardy, illegitimacy; baseness, meanness

bastardilla /bastar'ðiʎa; bastar'ðiya/ *f, Print.* italics

bastardo /bas'tarðo/ **(-da)** *a* bastard; spurious —*n* bastard

bastear /baste'ar/ *vt Sew.* to baste

bastidor /basti'ðor/ *m,* embroidery frame; *Art.* stretcher (for canvas); *Theat.* wing; *Mech.* underframe; chassis, carriage; frame (of a window). *Fig.* **entre bastidores,** behind the scenes

bastilla /bas'tiʎa; bas'tiya/ *f, Sew.* hem; bastille

bastimentar /bastimen'tar/ *vt* to provision; supply

bastimento /basti'mento/ *m,* supplies; provisioning

bastión /bas'tion/ *m,* bastion

basto /'basto/ *m,* pack-saddle; ace of clubs; clubs (cards) —*a* rude; tough; *Fig.* unpolished, rough

bastón /bas'ton/ *m,* cane, walking-stick; rod (of office); truncheon. **b. de junquillo,** Malacca cane. **empuñar el b.,** to take control, take over. **meter el b.,** to mediate

bastonear /bastone'ar/ vt to cane; stir with a stick

basura /ba'sura/ f, rubbish, refuse; dung; sweepings

basurero /basu'rero/ m, dustman; dunghill, rubbish dump; kitchen middens; dust-bin

bata /'bata/ f, dressing-gown; smoking-jacket; old-fashioned dress; overall, smock

batacazo /bata'kaθo; bata'kaso/ m, bump, noise of a fall; Polit. dark horse

batahola /bata'ola/ f, Inf. hurly-burly, hubbub

batalla /ba'taʎa; ba'taya/ f, battle; Fig. struggle, conflict; tournament; Art. battle-piece. **b. campal,** pitched battle

batallador /bataʎa'ðor; bataya'ðor/ a fighting, warlike

batallar /bata'ʎar; bata'yar/ vi to battle, fight; dispute, argue; hesitate

batallón /bata'ʎon; bata'yon/ m, battalion

batanero /bata'nero/ m, fuller

batata /ba'tata/ f, sweet potato

batayola /bata'yola/ f, Naut. rail

batea /ba'tea/ f, wooden tray; punt

batería /bate'ria/ f, (Mil. Elec. Naut.) battery. **b. de cocina,** kitchen utensils. **b. de pilas secas,** dry battery. **b. de teatro,** stage lights. **b. eléctrica,** electric battery

baticola /bati'kola/ f, crupper

batida /ba'tiða/ f, game drive; attack; Metall. beating

batido /ba'tiðo/ a beaten (of metals); shot (of silk); trodden, worn (roads, etc.). m, Cul. batter; hunting party

batidor /bati'ðor/ m, beater; scout; outrider; hair comb; Cul. whisk. **b. de oro** (or **de plata**), gold (or silver) beater

batiente /ba'tiente/ m, jamb (of door, etc.); damper (piano); leaf (of door); place where sea beats against cliffs, etc.

batihoja /bati'oha/ m, gold beater; metal worker

batimiento /bati'miento/ m, beating

batín /ba'tin/ m, smoking-jacket; man's dressing-gown

batintín /batin'tin/ m, Chinese gong

batir /ba'tir/ vt to beat, slap; demolish; dismantle, take down (stall, etc.); hammer, flatten; batter; Fig. beat (of sun, etc.); stir; pound; churn; comb (hair); vanquish, defeat; coin; reconnoiter, beat; throw down or drop; —vr fight; swoop (birds of prey). **b. palmas,** to clap, applaud

batista /ba'tista/ f, cambric, batiste

baturrillo /batu'rriʎo; batu'rriyo/ m, hotchpotch (gen. food); Inf. farrago, medley

batuta /ba'tuta/ f, baton, conductor's wand. **llevar la b.,** Inf. boss the show, call the music, be in charge, to rule the roost

baúl /ba'ul/ m, trunk; Inf. belly. **b. escaparate** or **b. mundo,** wardrobe trunk

bauprés /bau'pres/ m, Naut. bowsprit

bausán /bau'san/ **(-ana)** n guy, strawman; puppet; fool, idiot; lazybones

bautismo /bau'tismo/ m, baptism

bautista /bau'tista/ m, baptizer, baptist. **San Juan B.,** St. John the Baptist

bautisterio /bautis'terio/ m, baptistery

bautizar /bauti'θar; bauti'sar/ vt to baptize, christen; Inf. nickname; Inf. water (wine); accidentally shower with water

bautizo /bau'tiθo; bau'tiso/ m, baptism; christening party

bávaro /'baβaro/ **(-ra)** a and n Bavarian

baya /'baia/ f, berry

bayadera /baya'ðera/ f, Indian dancing girl

bayeta /ba'yeta/ f, baize; flannel

bayo /'bayo/ **(-ya)** a bay (of horses)

Bayona /ba'yona/ Bayonne

bayoneta /bayo'neta/ f, bayonet. **b. calada,** fixed bayonet

bayonetazo /bayone'taθo; bayone'taso/ m, bayonet thrust

baza /'baθa; 'basa/ f, tricks taken (playing cards). Fig. Inf. **meter b.,** to stick one's oar in

bazar /ba'θar; ba'sar/ m, bazaar; shop, store; department store

bazo /'baθo; 'baso/ m, Anat. spleen —a yellow-brown

bazucar, bazuquear /baθu'kar, baθuke'ar; basu'kar, basuke'ar/ vt to shake or stir (liquids)

bazuqueo /baθu'keo; basu'keo/ m, shaking or stirring of liquids

be /be/ f, letter B. m, baa

beata /be'ata/ f, devout woman; Inf. pious hypocrite, prude; Sister of Mercy; over-religious woman

beatería /beate'ria/ f, sanctimoniousness; bigotry

beatificación /beatifika'θion; beatifika'sion/ f, beatification

beatificar /beatifi'kar/ vt to make happy; sanctify; beatify

beatífico /bea'tifiko/ a beatific

beatitud /beati'tuð/ f, blessedness, beatitude; happiness

beato /be'ato/ **(-ta)** a happy; blessed, beatified; devout; prudish —n devout person; over-pious person

bebé /be'βe/ m, baby

bebedero /beβe'ðero/ a drinkable. m, drinking trough or place

bebedizo /beβe'ðiθo; beβe'ðiso/ a drinkable. m, draught of medicine; love-potion; poisonous drink

bebedor /beβe'ðor/ **(-ra)** a drinkable —n drinker; toper

beber /be'βer/ vt to drink; absorb; —vi toast, drink to the health (of); tipple. m, drinking; drink

bebida /be'βiða/ f, drink; beverage; alcoholic liquor

beca /'beka/ f, academic scarf or sash; scholarship, exhibition

becado, becario /be'kaðo, be'kario/ m, exhibitioner, scholarship holder

becerra /be'θerra; be'serra/ f, calf; Bot. snapdragon

becerro /be'θerro; be'serro/ m, bullock; bull calf; calf-skin. **b. marino,** Zool. seal

Beda el Venerable /'beða el bene'raβle/ the Venerable Bede

bedel /be'ðel/ m, beadle; servitor, university porter

beduino /be'ðuino/ **(-na)** a and n Bedouin. m, savage, bloodthirsty man

befar /be'far/ vt to mock, ridicule

befo /'befo/ a thick-lipped; knock-kneed. m, animal's lip

begonia /be'gonia/ f, Bot. begonia

bejín /be'hin/ m, Bot. puff-ball; spoiled child

bejuco /be'huko/ m, rattan

beldad /bel'dað/ f, beauty; belle

beldar /bel'dar/ vt Agr. to winnow

Belén /be'len/ Bethlehem

belén /be'len/ m, nativity, manger; Inf. bedlam; Inf. gossip

belfo /'belfo/ a thick-lipped

belga /'belga/ a and mf Belgian

Bélgica /'belhika/ Belgium

bélgico /'belhiko/ a Belgian

Belgrado /bel'graðo/ Belgrade

Belice /be'liðe; be'lise/ Belize

belicista /beli'θista; beli'sista/ adj war, militaristic; mf warmonger

bélico /'beliko/ a warlike, military

belicosidad /belikosi'ðað/ f, bellicosity

belicoso /beli'koso/ a bellicose, aggressive; warlike

beligerancia /belihe'ranθia; belihe'ransia/ f, belligerency

beligerante /belihe'rante/ a and mf belligerent

belitre /be'litre/ a Inf. knavish, cunning

bellaco /be'ʎako; be'yako/ **(-ca)** a artful, cunning —n knave

belladona /beʎa'ðona; beya'ðona/ f, belladonna

bellaquería /beʎake'ria; beyake'ria/ f, roguery, knavery, cunning

bellasombra /beʎa'sombra; beya'sombra/ f, umbra tree

belleza /be'ʎeθa; be'yesa/ f, beauty, loveliness, fairness

bello /'beʎo; 'beyo/ a beautiful

bellota /be'Aota; be'yota/ *f*, acorn; carnation bud; ornamental button, knob

bellote /be'Aote; be'yote/ *m*, round-headed nail

bemol /be'mol/ *a* and *m*, *Mus*. flat. *Inf*. **tener bemoles**, to be thorny, be difficult

bencina /ben'θina; ben'sina/ *f*, benzine; gasoline

bendecir /bende'θir; bende'sir/ *vt irr* to praise, extol; bless; dedicate, consecrate. See **decir**

bendición /bendi'θion; bendi'sion/ *f*, benediction; blessing; consecration; *pl* marriage ceremony. **b. de la mesa**, grace before meals

bendito /ben'dito/ *a* holy, blessed; fortunate; simple. **ser un b.**, to be a simpleton; be a good soul. **¡Benditos los ojos que te ven!** It's so nice to see you!

benedictino /beneδik'tino/ **(-na)** *a* and *n* Benedictine. *m*, Benedictine liqueur

beneficencia /benefi'θenθia; benefi'sensia/ *f*, beneficence; charitable institutions

beneficiación /benefiθia'θion; benefisia'sion/ *f*, benefaction

beneficiado /benefi'θiaδo; benefi'siaδo/ **(-da)** *n* beneficiary. *m*, incumbent of a benefice

beneficiador /benefiθia'δor; benefisia'δor/ **(-ra)** *n* benefactor

beneficiar /benefi'θiar; benefi'siar/ *vt* to benefit; improve; cultivate (land); exploit (mine); purchase (directorship, etc.); sell at a loss (bonds, etc.)

beneficiario /benefi'θiario; benefi'siario/ **(-ia)** *n* beneficiary

beneficiencia /benefi'θienθia; benefi'siensia/ *f*, beneficence, charity

beneficio /bene'fiθio; bene'fisio/ *m*, benefit; profit; cultivation (land, etc.); working (mine); *Eccl*. benefice; *Theat*. benefit

beneficioso /benefi'θioso; benefi'sioso/ *a* beneficial; useful

benéfico /be'nefiko/ *a* beneficent; kind, helpful; charitable

benemérito /bene'merito/ *a* benemeritus, worthy, meritorious

beneplácito /bene'plaθito; bene'plasito/ *m*, approbation; consent

benevolencia /beneβo'lenθia; beneβo'lensia/ *f*, benevolence, goodwill

benévolo /be'neβolo/ *a* benevolent, kind

Bengala /ben'gala/ Bengal

bengalí /benga'li/ *a* and *mf* Bengali

benignidad /benigni'δaδ/ *f*, kindness; mildness (of the weather, etc.)

benigno /be'nigno/ *a* kind; benign; mild; balmy

beodo /be'oδo/ **(-da)** *a* drunk, intoxicated —*n* drunkard

Berbería /berβe'ria/ Barbary

bereber /bere'βer/ *a* and *mf* Berber

berenjena /beren'hena/ *f*, eggplant

bergante /ber'gante/ *m*, rascal, rogue

bergantín /bergan'tin/ *m*, *Naut*. brig, brigantine

berilo /be'rilo/ *m*, beryl

Berlín /ber'lin/ Berlin

berlinés /ber'lines/ **(-esa)** *a* and *n* of or from Berlin

bermejear /bermehe'ar/ *vi* to be or look reddish

bermejo /ber'meho/ *a* reddish; red; redgold; carroty (of hair)

bermellón /berme'Aon; berme'yon/ *m*, vermilion

Berna /'berna/ Berne

bernardina /bernar'δina/ *f*, lie; boast; gibberish

bernardo /ber'narδo/ **(-da)** *a* and *n* *Eccl*. Bernardine (Order of St. Bernard)

berquelio /ber'kelio/ *m*, berkelium

berrear /berre'ar/ *vi* to low, bellow; yell, squall; shriek; —*vr* reveal, confess

berrido /be'rriδo/ *m*, lowing, bellowing; *Inf*. yell

berrinche /be'rrintʃe/ *m*, *Inf*. tantrum, fit, fit of sulks

berro /'berro/ *m*, watercress

berroqueña /berro'keɲa/ *f*, granite

berza /'berθa; 'bersa/ *f*, cabbage

besamanos /besa'manos/ *m*, ceremony of kissing royal hand, levee; kissing fingers (in salute)

besar /be'sar/ *vt* to kiss; *Inf*. brush against, touch (of things); —*vr* kiss one another; *Inf*. bang into, knock against one another

beso /'beso/ *m*, kiss; knock, collision

bestia /'bestia/ *f*, quadruped (especially horses or mules); beast. *mf Inf*. nasty piece of work. **b. de carga**, beast of burden. **como una b.**, like a dog (e.g. *Trabajo como una b*. I work like a dog)

bestial /bes'tial/ *a* bestial; brutal; beastly

bestialidad /bestiali'δaδ/ *f*, brutality; bestiality; beastliness

bestialismo /bestia'lismo/ *m*, bestiality (sexual orientation)

besuquear /besuke'ar/ *vt Inf*. to cover with kisses; —*vr Inf*. spoon, make love

besuqueo /besu'keo/ *m*, *Inf*. kissing and spooning

bético /'betiko/ *a* Andalusian

betún /be'tun/ *m*, bitumen; shoe blacking; kind of cement. **b. de Judea** or **b. judaico**, asphalt

bey /bei/ *m*, bey

bezo /'beθo; 'beso/ *m*, blubber lip; proud flesh (of a wound)

bezudo /be'θuδo; be'suδo/ *a* thick-lipped

biberón /biβe'ron/ *m*, feeding bottle

Biblia /'biβlia/ *f*, Bible

bíblico /'biβliko/ *a* biblical

bibliófilo /biβli'ofilo/ *m*, bibliophile

bibliografía /biβliogra'fia/ *f*, bibliography

bibliográfico /biβlio'grafiko/ *a* bibliographical

biblioteca /biβlio'teka/ *f*, library; book series. **b. por subscripción**, circulating library

bibliotecario /biβliote'kario/ **(-ia)** *n* librarian

bibliotecnia, **bibliotecología**, **biblioteconomía** /biβlio'teknia, biβlioteko'lohia, biβliotekono'mia/ *f*, library science

bicarbonato /bikarβo'nato/ *m*, bicarbonate

bíceps /'biθeps; 'biseps/ *m*, biceps

bicho /'bitʃo/ *m*, any small animal or reptile; quadruped; fighting bull; scarecrow, sight. **b. viviente**, *Inf*. living soul. **mal b.**, rogue

bicicleta /biθi'kleta; bisi'kleta/ *f*, bicycle, bike. **ir** (or **andar** or **montar**) **en b.**, to bicycle, bike, go by bicycle, go by bike

bicoca /bi'koka/ *f*, *Inf*. trifle, bagatelle

bicolor /biko'lor/ *a* bicolored

bidé /bi'δe/ *m*, bidet

biela /'biela/ *f*, axle-tree; connecting-rod; big-end

bielda /'bielda/ *f*, pitchfork; *Agr*. winnowing

bien /bien/ *m*, ideal goodness, perfection; benefit; advantage; welfare; *pl* property, wealth —*adv* well; willingly; happily; perfectly; easily; enough, sufficient; all right! very well! **b. que**, although. **b. de equipo**, capital good. **bienes muebles**, movables, goods and chattels. **bienes raíces**, real estate. **B. y el Mal**, Good and Evil. **¡Está b.!** All right! **no b.**, scarcely, as soon as. **si b.**, although, even if. **¿Y b.?** And so what? Well, then; What next?

bienal /bie'nal/ *a* biennial

bienamado /biena'maδo/ *a* dearly beloved

bienandante /bienan'dante/ *a* prosperous; happy

bienandanza /bienan'danθa; bienan'dansa/ *f*, happiness, welfare; prosperity

bienaventurado /bienaβentu'raδo/ *a* blessed, holy; happy; *Inf*. over-simple, innocent, foolish

bienaventuranza /bienaβentu'ranθa; bienaβentu'ransa/ *f*, blessedness

bienestar /bienes'tar/ *m*, wellbeing; ease; comfort

bienhablado /biena'βlaδo/ *a* well-spoken; civil, polite

bienhadado /biena'δaδo/ *a* fortunate, happy

bienhechor /biene'tʃor/ **(-ra)** *a* kind, helpful —*n* benefactor

bienintencionado /bieninten θio'naδo; bieninten sio'naδo/ *a* well-meaning

bienio /'bienio/ *m*, biennium, space of two years, period of two years

bienquisto /bien'kisto/ *a* respected; generally esteemed

bienvenida /biembe'niδa/ *f*, safe or happy arrival; welcome. **dar la b.**, to welcome

bienvivir /biembi'βir/ *vi* to live comfortably; live decently or uprightly

bies /bies/ *m*, bias, cross; slant

biftec /bif'tek/ *m*, beefsteak

bifurcación /bifurka'θion; bifurka'sion/ f, bifurcation; fork, branch, junction

bifurcarse /bifur'karse/ vr to fork, branch

bigamia /bi'gamia/ f, bigamy

bígamo /'bigamo/ (-ma) a bigamous —n bigamist

bigornia /bi'gornia/ f, anvil

bigote /bi'gote/ m, moustache; pl whiskers

bigotudo /bigo'tuðo/ a moustached, whiskered

bikini /bi'kini/ m, bikini

bilateral /bilate'ral/ a bilateral

bilbaíno /bilβa'ino/ a pertaining to or native of Bilbao

bilingüe /bi'lingue/ a bilingual

bilioso /bi'lioso/ a bilious

bilis /'bilis/ f, bile

billar /bi'ʎar; bi'yar/ m, billiards; billiard table

billete /bi'ʎete; bi'yete/ m, note, short letter; ticket; banknote. **b. circular,** excursion ticket. **b. de abono,** season ticket. **b. de andén,** platform ticket. **b. de banco,** banknote. **b. de favor,** free ticket. **b. de ida y vuelta,** round trip ticket. **b. entero,** full fare. **b. kilométrico,** tourist ticket. **b. sencillo,** one-way. **medio b.,** half-fare

billón /bi'ʎon; bi'yon/ m, billion

bimestral /bimes'tral/ a bimonthly

bimestre /bi'mestre/ a bimonthly. m, two months' duration; money paid or received at two-monthly intervals

bimotor /bimo'tor/ a two-motor. m, twin-engined aircraft

binario /bi'nario/ a binary

binóculo /bi'nokulo/ m, opera glasses

binomio /bi'nomio/ a and m, binomial

biodiversidad f, biodiversity

biofísica /bio'fisika/ f, biophysics

biografía /biogra'fia/ f, biography

biográfico /bio'grafiko/ a biographical

biógrafo /'biografo/ (-fa) n biographer; (Chile) movie theater (e.g. ¡Vamos al biógrafo! Let's go to the movies!)

biología /biolo'hia/ f, biology

biológico /bio'lohiko/ a biological

biólogo /'biologo/ m, biologist

biombo /'biombo/ m, screen

bioquímica /bio'kimika/ f, biochemistry

bioquímico /bio'kimiko/ m, biochemist

bipartido /bipar'tiðo/ a bipartite

bípedo /'bipeðo/ a and m, biped

biplano /bi'plano/ m, biplane

biplaza /bi'plaθa; biplasa/ a two-seater

birla /'birla/ f, skittle

birlar /bir'lar/ vt to bowl from where the bowl stopped; Inf. knock down; snatch away; Inf. rob

birlocha /bir'lotʃa/ f, child's kite

birlocho /bir'lotʃo/ m, barouche

Birmania /bir'mania/ Burma

birmano /bir'mano/ (-na) a and n Burmese

birreta /bi'rreta/ f, biretta

birrete /bi'rrete/ m, biretta; university cap; cap

bis /bis/ adv twice; repeat; encore —a duplicate; **B** (in addresses, e.g., Calle de Alcalá 18bis, 18b Alcalá St.)

bisabuela /bisa'βuela/ f, great-grandmother

bisabuelo /bisa'βuelo/ m, great-grandfather

bisagra /bi'sagra/ f, hinge; shoemaker's polisher

bisbís /bis'βis/ m, game of chance

bisbisar /bisβi'sar/ vt Inf. to mutter; whisper

bisbiseo /bisβi'seo/ m, Inf. muttering; murmuring; whispering

bisecar /bise'kar/ vt to bisect

bisección /bisek'θion; bisek'sion/ f, Geom. bisection

bisectriz /bisek'triθ; bisek'tris/ f, bisector

bisel /bi'sel/ m, bevel, chamfer

bisiesto /bi'siesto/ a leap and m, leap (year)

bisílabo /bi'silaβo/ a two-syllabled

bismuto /bis'muto/ m, bismuth

bisnieto /bis'nieto/ (-ta) n great-grandchild

bisonte /bi'sonte/ m, bison

bisoño /bi'soɲo/ (-ña) a inexperienced, raw —n recruit; Inf. greenhorn

bistec /bis'tek/ m, beef steak

bisturí /bistu'ri/ m, surgical knife

bisunto /bi'sunto/ a grubby, greasy

bisutería /bisute'ria/ f, imitation jewelry

bituminoso /bitumi'noso/ a bituminous

bivalvo /bi'βalβo/ a bivalve

Bizancio /bi'θanθio; bi'sansio/ Byzantium

bizantinismo /biθanti'nismo; bisanti'nismo/ m, Byzantinism

bizantino /biθan'tino; bisan'tino/ a Byzantine

bizarría /biθa'rria; bisa'rria/ f, handsomeness; dash; verve; gallantry, courage; magnificence; liberality; whim, caprice

bizarro /bi'θarro; bi'sarro/ a handsome; dashing; gallant, courageous; liberal; splendid, magnificent

bizcaitarrismo /biθkaita'rrismo; biskaita'rrismo/ m, doctrine of Basque autonomy; Basque autonomy movement

bizco /'biθko; 'bisko/ a squint-eyed, cross-eyed

bizcocho /biθ'kotʃo; bis'kotʃo/ m, biscuit; sponge-cake; bisque

bizma /'biθma; 'bisma/ f, poultice. **poner bizmas,** to poultice

biznieto /biθ'nieto; bis'nieto/ n See **bisnieto**

blanca /'blanka/ f, old Spanish coin; Inf. penny; Mus. minim. **sin b.,** penniless

blanco /'blanko/ a white; fair-skinned; blank, vacant; Inf. cowardly. m, target; blank left in writing; white person; interval. **b. de España,** whiting. **b. de la uña,** half-moon of the nail. **dar en el b.,** to hit the mark. **en b.,** blank, unused; Inf. in vain; uncomprehendingly; (of nights) sleepless

blancor, /blan'kor,/ m. **blancura** f, whiteness; fairness (of skin)

blandear /blande'ar/ vt to moderate, soothe; brandish; —vi Fig. give way, yield

blandir /blan'dir/ vt to brandish, wield, flourish

blando /'blando/ a soft; mild (weather); delicate; kind; peaceable; delicate, effeminate; Inf. cowardly

blandón /blan'don/ m, wax taper

blandura /blan'dura/ f, softness; poultice; blandishment, compliment; mildness (of weather); gentleness, affability; luxury

blanquear /blanke'ar/ vt to bleach; whitewash; whiten; —vi appear white; show white

blanquecino /blanke'θino; blanke'sino/ a whitish

blanqueo /blan'keo/ m, whitening; whitewashing; bleaching

blanquizal /blanki'θal; blanki'sal/ m, pipe-clay

blasfemador /blasfema'ðor/ (-ra) a blaspheming —n blasphemer

blasfemar /blasfe'mar/ vi to blaspheme; curse, swear

blasfemia /blas'femia/ f, blasphemy; insult

blasfemo /blas'femo/ (-ma) n blasphemer —a blasphemous

blasón /bla'son/ m, heraldry; escutcheon; glory, honor. **una familia con antiguos blasones,** a family of ancient lineage

blasonar /blaso'nar/ vt to blazon; —vi boast, brag, blazon abroad

bledo /'bleðo/ m, blade, leaf. **no importar un b.,** not to matter a straw

blenda /'blenda/ f, Mineral. blende

blindado /blin'daðo/ a Nav. armored, ironclad

blindaje /blin'dahe/ m, Nav. armor-plating; Mil. blindage

blindar /blin'dar/ vt to plate with armor, to case with steel

blocao /blo'kao/ m, Mil. blockhouse

blonda /'blonda/ f, blonde (of lace)

blondo /'blondo/ a fair, blond, flaxen-haired

bloque /'bloke/ m, block, slab

bloquear /bloke'ar/ vt to blockade; besiege

bloqueo /blo'keo/ m, blockade; siege; blocking; freezing (of assets). **violar el b.,** to run the blockade

blusa /'blusa/ f, blouse

boa /'boa/ f, boa, large snake. m, boa (fur)

boato /bo'ato/ m, outward show, ostentation

bobería /boβe'ria/ f, foolishness, stupidity

bóbilis, bóbilis /'boβilis, 'boβilis/ (de) adv Inf. free of charge; without effort

bobina /bo'βina/ f, bobbin, spool, reel; *Elec.* coil; spool (of fishing rod)

bobo /'boβo/ **(-ba)** a stupid, idiotic; simple, innocent —n fool. m, clown, jester

boca /'boka/ f, mouth; pincers (of crustaceans); entrance or exit; mouth (of a river), gulf, inlet; orifice, opening; muzzle (of guns); cutting edge (of tools); taste (of wine, etc.). **b. abajo**, face down, prone. **b. arriba**, on one's back, face up, supine. **b. del estómago**, pit of the stomach. **b. rasgada**, large mouth. **a b.**, verbally. **a b. de jarro**, point-blank. **a pedir de b.**, just as one would wish. **de b.**, by word of mouth. *Inf.* **sin decir esta b. es mía**, without a word, in silence

bocacalle /boka'kaʎe; boka'kaye/ f, entrance (to a street); street junction

Bocacio /bo'kaθio/ Bocaccio

bocadillo /boka'ðiʎo; boka'ðiyo/ m, narrow ribbon; sandwich

bocado /bo'kaðo/ m, mouthful. **b. de reyes**, delicacy, exquisite dish (of food); snack; bite; (horse's) bit; bridle; pl preserved fruit cut up

bocamanga /boka'manga/ f, wrist (of sleeve)

bocanada /boka'naða/ f, mouthful (of liquid); cloud (of smoke). **b. de aire**, gust of wind

boceto /bo'θeto; bo'seto/ m, sketch; outline; roughcast model

bocha /'botʃa/ f, *Sports.* bowl; pl bowls

bochorno /bo'tʃorno/ m, sultry weather; heat, stuffiness; blush, hot flush; shame

bochornoso /botʃor'noso/ a sultry; shameful

bocina /bo'θina; bo'sina/ f, trumpet; megaphone; foghorn; hooter; *Auto.* horn; horn (of gramophone); *Astron.* Ursa Minor

bocio /'boθio; 'bosio/ m, *Med.* goiter

bocoy /bo'koi/ m, hogshead; large cask

boda /'boða/ f, wedding, marriage. **bodas de oro**, fiftieth (golden) anniversary. **bodas de plata**, silver wedding anniversary

bodega /bo'ðega/ f, wine-cellar; storeroom; stockroom; granary; *West Hem.* grocery store; *Naut.* hold (of ship)

bodegón /boðe'gon/ m, eating-house; tavern; *Art.* still-life; genre picture

bóer /'boer/ a and mf Boer

bofes /'bofes/ m pl, lungs, lights. *Inf.* **echar los b.**, to work oneself to death

bofetada /bofe'taða/ f, **bofetón** m, blow, slap; box on the ear

boga /'boga/ f, rowing; fashion, vogue; *Mech.* bogie. mf oarsman, rower. **estar en b.**, to be fashionable

bogador /boga'ðor/ **(-ra)** n rower, oarsman

bogar /bo'gar/ vi to row

bogavante /boga'βante/ m, lobster

bogotano /bogo'tano/ **(-na)** a and n of or from Bogotá

bohemio /bo'emio/ **(-ia)** a and n gipsy; bohemian; Bohemian. m, archer's short cloak

boicot, boicoteo /boi'kot, boiko'teo/ m, boycott

boicotear /boikote'ar/ vt to boycott

boina /'boina/ f, Basque cap; beret

boj /boh/ m, box tree; boxwood, box oak; shoemaker's tool

bola /'bola/ f, globe; ball; *Sports.* bowl; *Archit.* balloon; *Inf.* trick, lie; (Cuba) rumor. **b. de nieves**, snowball. *Inf.* **dejar rodar la b.**, to let things slide

bolardo /bo'larðo/ m, bollard

bolchevique /boltʃe'βike/ a and mf bolshevist

bolchevismo /boltʃe'βismo/ m, Bolshevism

bolchevista /boltʃe'βista/ mf bolshevist

bolea /bo'lea/ f, (tennis) volley; throw

bolera /bo'lera/ f, bowling alley

bolero /bo'lero/ m, bolero; dancer; *Inf.* top hat

boleta /bo'leta/ f, admission ticket; billet ticket; warrant, voucher; summons, ticket, traffic ticket

boletín /bole'tin/ m, bulletin; admission ticket; pay warrant; *Com.* price list; learned periodical. **b. de noticias**, news bulletin. **b. meteorológico**, weather report

boliche /bo'litʃe/ m, jack (in bowls); cup-and-ball

toy; small oven (for charcoal); dragnet. **juego de b.** bowls

bólido /'boliðo/ m, *Astron.* bolide, meteor

bolígrafo /bo'ligrafo/ f, ballpoint pen

bolillo /bo'liʎo; bo'liyo/ m, bobbin (lace making)

bolina /bo'lina/ f, *Naut.* bowline; *Naut.* sounder; *Inf.* uproar, tumult

bolita /bo'lita/ f, pellet

boliviano /boli'βiano/ **(-na)** a and n Bolivian. m, silver coin

bollo /'boʎo; 'boyo/ m, bread roll; bun; bulge, bruise (in metal); *Med.* lump

bollón /bo'ʎon; bo'yon/ m, round-headed or brassheaded nail; *Bot.* bud (especially vines)

bolo /'bolo/ m, skittle, ninepin; pillow (for lace making); Cuban coin; *Med.* large pill; *Fig. Inf.* blockhead; pl skittles (game of)

boloñés /bolo'ɲes/ **(-esa)** a and n Bolognese

bolsa /'bolsa/ f, purse; bag; footmuff; fold, pucker; pouch; exchange, stock exchange, capital, money; prize money; *Med.* sac; *Mineral.* pocket. **b. de estudio**, scholarship grant. **b. de trabajo**, labor exchange. **b. de valores**, stock exchange. **bajar (or subir) la b.**, to fall (or rise) (of stock exchange quotations). **jugar a la b.**, to speculate on the stock exchange

bolsillo /bol'siʎo; bol'siyo/ m, pocket; purse; money

bolsista /bol'sista/ mf stock-broker; speculator (on the stock exchange)

bomba /'bomba/ f, *Mech.* pump; pumping engine; bomb; *Mil.* shell; lamp globe; *Inf.* improvised verses; *Inf.* drinking bout. **¡B.!** Listen! Here goes! **b. de incendios**, fire-engine. **b. marina**, waterspout. **b. de mecha atrasada**, time bomb. **b. volante**, flyingbomb. **a prueba de b.**, bombproof. **arrojar bombas**, to bomb. *Inf.* **caer como una b.**, to be a bombshell

bombachos /bom'batʃos/ a baggy, loose-fitting; m pl, plus fours

bombardear /bombarðe'ar/ vt to bombard; bomb; shell

bombardeo /bombar'ðeo/ m, bombardment, bombing; shelling

bombardero /bombar'ðero/ m, gunner, bombardier; *Aer.* bomber. **b. pesado**, *Aer.* heavy bomber. **Servicio de b.**, Bomber Command

bombástico /bom'βastiko/ a bombastic, high sounding

bombazo /bom'βaθo; bom'βaso/ m, bombshell; bomb crater; noise of an exploding bomb

bombear /bombe'ar/ vt to pump; bombard, shell; praise

bombero /bom'βero/ m, worker of a pressure pump; fireman; mortar, howitzer

bombilla /bom'βiʎa; bom'βiya/ f, *Naut.* lantern; (*Elec. Phys.*) bulb; small pump; straw for drinking maté *West Hem.*

bombillo /bom'βiʎo; bom'βiyo/ m, w.c. siphon; handpump

bombo /'bombo/ m, big drum or player of it; *Naut.* barge, ferry; ballot box; exaggerated praise

bombón /bom'βon/ m, bonbon, sweet

bombonera /bombo'nera/ f, box for toffee, etc.

Bona /'bona/ Bonn

bonachón /bona'tʃon/ a *Inf.* genial, good-natured

bonaerense /bonae'rense/ a and mf of or from the Province of Buenos Aires

Bonaira /bo'naira/ Bonaire

bonancible /bonan'θiβle; bonan'siβle/ a calm (of weather, sea)

bonanza /bo'nanθa; bo'nansa/ f, fair weather; prosperity

bondad /bon'dað/ f, goodness; kindness, helpfulness. **Tenga la b. de...**, Be good enough to..., Please...

bondadoso /bonda'ðoso/ a good, kind

bonete /bo'nete/ m, academic cap; *Zool.* reticulum (ruminants); *Eccl.* biretta. **gran b.**, important person. *Inf.* **a tente b.**, insistently

bonetero /bone'tero/ **(-ra)** n seller or maker of caps and birettas

bonificación /bonifika'θion; bonifika'sion/ f, bonus; allowance, discount

bonito /bo'nito/ a pretty; graceful; (ironical) fine. m, *Ichth.* bonito

bono /'bono/ *m*, voucher; *Com.* bond, certificate. **b. postal**, postal money order. **bono del gobierno**, government bond

boñiga /bo'niga/ *f*, cow-dung, animal manure

boqueada /boke'aða/ *f*, gasp, opening of the mouth. **dar las boqueadas, estar en las últimas boqueadas**, to be at the last gasp

boquear /boke'ar/ *vi* to gasp; be dying; *Inf.* be at last gasp (of things); —*vt* say, utter

boquera /bo'kera/ *f*, sluice (in irrigation canal)

boquerón /boke'ron/ *m*, large opening; *Ichth.* anchovy (fish); whitebait

boquete /bo'kete/ *m*, narrow entrance, aperture; gap, breach; hole

boquiabierto /bokia'βierto/ *a* open-mouthed; amazed

boquiancho /bo'kiantʃo/ *a* wide-mouthed

boquiasombrado /bokiasom'braðo/ *a* gaping

boquilla /bo'kiʎa; bo'kiya/ *f*, *dim* small mouth; mouthpiece (of wind instruments, etc.); cigar- or cigarette-holder; gas-burner; nozzle; tip (of cigarettes)

boquirroto /boki'rroto/ *a Inf.* loquacious, indiscreet

borbollar /borβo'ʎar; borβo'yar/ *vi* to bubble, foam, froth

borbollón, borbotón /borβo'ʎon, borβo'ton; borβo'yon, borβo'ton/ *m*, gushing, bubbling, welling up. **a borbollones**, in a torrent; hastily, impetuously

borbónico /bor'βoniko/ *a* Bourbon

borbotar /borβo'tar/ *vi* to gush out, well up

borceguí /borθe'gi; borse'gi/ *m*, buskin, boot

borda /'borða/ *f*, hut, cabin; *Naut.* gunwale

bordado /bor'ðaðo/ *m*, embroidery

bordador /borða'nðor/ **(-ra)** *n* embroiderer

bordar /bor'ðar/ *vt* to embroider; *Fig.* perform perfectly

borde /'borðe/ *m*, edge; fringe; verge; rim; mount (of a picture); brim (of a hat); side (of ship) —*a* wild (of plants); illegitimate. **estar lleno hasta los bordes**, to be full to the brim

bordear /borðe'ar/ *vt* to border, trim with a bordear; line (a street, e.g. *Diez mil personas bordearon las calles durante el desfile*, Ten thousand people lined the streets during the parade)

bordelés /bor'ðeles/ **(-esa)** *a* and *n* of or from Bordeaux

bordillo /bor'ðiʎo; bor'ðiyo/ *m*, curbstone, curb.

bordo /'borðo/ *m*, side (of ships); border, edge. **a b.**, on board

bordón /bor'ðon/ *m*, pilgrim's staff; monotonous repetition; refrain; *Mus.* bass string; *Fig.* guide, stay

borgoña /bor'goŋa/ *m*, Burgundy wine

borgoñón /borgo'ŋon/ **(-ona)** *a* and *n* Burgundian

bórico /'boriko/ *a* boric

borla /'borla/ *f*, tassel; puff (for powder). *Fig.* **tomar la b.**, to take one's doctorate, graduate

borne /'borne/ *m*, tip (of lance); *Elec.* terminal

bornear /borne'ar/ *vt* to bend, twist; *Archit.* hoist into position; —*vr* warp (wood)

borra /'borra/ *f*, yearling ewe; thickest wool; wad-stuffing; lees, sediment; fluff, dust; *Inf.* trash. **b. de algodón**, cotton-waste

borrachera /borra'tʃera/ *f*, drunkenness; orgy, carousal; *Inf.* blunder

borrachín /borra'tʃin/ **(-ina)** *n* tippler, toper

borrachito /borra'tʃito/ *a* high (on liquor), tipsy

borracho /bo'rratʃo/ **(de)** *a* drunk (on), intoxicated (with); *Inf.* blind (with rage, etc.) —*n* tippler, drunkard

borrador /borra'ðor/ *m*, rough draft. **en borrador**, in the works (e.g. *Tiene dos ensayos en borrador*, She has two essays in the works). **estar en borrador**, to be in the works

borradura /borra'ðura/ *f*, erasure

borrajear /borrahe'ar/ *vt* to scribble

borrar /bo'rrar/ *vt* to erase; cross out; blot out; *Fig.* obliterate

borrasca /bo'rraska/ *f*, storm, tempest; peril, danger; *Inf.* orgy

borrascosidad /borraskosi'ðað/ *f*, storminess

borrascoso /borras'koso/ *a* stormy; disordered, turbulent

borrego /bo'rrego/ **(-ga)** *n* lamb; *Inf.* nincompoop, simpleton; *m pl*, fleecy clouds; white horses (waves)

borrico /bo'rriko/ **(-ca)** *n* donkey; fool. *m*, sawing-horse

borrón /bo'rron/ *m*, blot; rough draft; defect; *Fig.* stigma

borroso /bo'rroso/ *a* blurred, indistinct; full of dregs, muddy

boscaje /bos'kahe/ *m*, grove, group of trees, thicket

Bósforo, el /'bosforo, el/ the Bosporus

bosque /'boske/ *m*, wood, forest

bosquejar /boske'har/ *vt Art.* to sketch out; sketch; draft; model in rough (sculpture); outline

bosquejo /bos'keho/ *m*, outline, sketch; rough plan or idea; unfinished work. **en bosquejo**, grosso modo

bostar /bos'tar/ *m*, ox barn

bostezar /boste'θar; boste'sar/ *vi* to yawn

bostezo /bos'teθo; bos'teso/ *m*, yawning; yawn

bota /'bota/ *f*, small wineskin; barrel, butt; boot. **b. de montar**, riding boot. **botas de campaña**, top-boots. **botas de vadear**, waders

botada, botadura /bo'taða, bota'ðura/ *f*, launching (of a ship)

botador /bota'ðor/ *m*, thrower; boating-pole; nail-puller

botafuego /bota'fuego/ *m*, *Mil.* linstock; *Inf.* quick-tempered, irascible person

botalón /bota'lon/ *m*, *Naut.* boom. **b. de foque**, jib-boom

botánica /bo'tanika/ *f*, botany

botánico /bo'taniko/ **(-ca)** *a* botanical —*n* botanist

botar /bo'tar/ *vt* to fling; launch (boat); *Naut.* shift the helm; —*vi* jump; bounce, rebound; rear, prance (horses)

botarate /bota'rate/ *m*, *Inf.* madcap, devil-may-care

botarel, botarete /bota'rel, bota'rete/ *m*, *Archit.* abutment, buttress, flying buttress

botarga /bo'targa/ *f*, motley; harlequin

bote /'bote/ *m*, thrust (with lance, etc.); rearing (of horse); rebound; *Aer.* bump; open boat; small bottle, jar. **b. salvavidas**, lifeboat. *Inf.* **de b. en b.**, chockfull

botella /bo'teʎa; bo'teya/ *f*, bottle; bottleful; flask

botica /bo'tika/ *f*, chemist's shop; medicines, remedies; physic; store, shop; medicine chest

boticario /boti'kario/ *m*, apothecary, chemist

botija /bo'tiha/ *f*, earthen jug; *Slang* chunky person

botijo /bo'tiho/ *m*, earthenware jar with spout and handle

botillería /botiʎe'ria; botiye'ria/ *f*, ice-cream bar

botín /bo'tin/ *m*, gaiter; buskin; booty

botiquín /boti'kin/ *m*, first-aid kit; medicine chest

botón /bo'ton/ *m*, bud; button; knob, handle; switch (electric); press button (bell); *Bot.* center; button (on a foil); *Mech.* stud

botonero /boto'nero/ **(-ra)** *n* button maker or seller

bóveda /b'oβeða/ *f*, *Archit.* vault, arch; crypt; cavern. **b. celeste**, sky

bovino /bo'βino/ *a* bovine

boxeador /boksea'ðor/ *m*, boxer

boxear /bokse'ar/ *vi Sports.* to box

boxeo /bok'seo/ *m*, *Sports.* boxing

boya /'boya/ *f*, *Naut.* buoy; float

boyante /bo'yante/ *a* floating; light, buoyant; prosperous

boyar /bo'yar/ *vi Naut.* to float

boyera /bo'yera/ *f*, ox-stall

boyero /bo'yero/ *m*, cowherd

boza /'boθa; 'bosa/ *f*, painter (of a boat)

bozal /bo'θal; bo'sal/ *m*, muzzle; nosebag; harness bells. *mf Inf.* greenhorn; —*a* wild, untamed (horses)

bozo /'boθo; 'boso/ *m*, down which precedes beard; muzzle; headstall; lips, snout

bracero /bra'θero; bra'sero/ *m*, one who offers his arm (to a lady); day laborer; strong man. **de b.**, arm-in-arm

bracete /bra'θete; bra'sete/ *m*, small arm. **de b.**, arm-in-arm

bracmán /brak'man/ *m*, Brahmin

braga /'braga/ *f*, (gen. *pl*) breeches; knickerbockers; hoist or pulley rope

bragazas /bra'gaθas; bra'gasas/ m, Inf. weak-willed, fellow, soft specimen

braguero /bra'gero/ m, Med. truss

bragueta /bra'geta/ f, fly (of breeches)

brahmanismo /brama'nismo/ m, Brahmanism

bramante /bra'mante/ a roaring. m, twine, pack-thread

bramar /bra'mar/ vi to roar; rage; Fig. howl (of the wind, etc.)

bramido /bra'miðo/ m, bellowing; roaring; yell of rage; Fig. howling (wind, sea, etc.)

brancada /bran'kaða/ f, drag net

branquia /'brankia/ f, (gen. pl) Ichth. gill

branquial /bran'kial/ a branchiate

braquicefalia /bra,kiθe'falia; bra,kise'falia/ f, brachycephaly

braquiotomía /brakioto'mia/ f, Surg. brachiotomy, amputation of the arms

brasa /'brasa/ f, live coal. **estar como en brasas,** to be like a cat on hot bricks

brasero /bra'sero/ m, brazier

Brasil /bra'sil/ Brazil

brasileño /brasi'leɲo/ (-ña) a and n Brazilian

bravata /bra'βata/ f, bravado; threat

braveza /bra'βeθa; bra'βesa/ f, ferocity, savageness; valor; violence, fury (of elements)

bravío /bra'βio/ a savage, untamed; wild (plants); uncultured

bravo /'braβo/ a valiant; surly, rude; independent, strong-minded, good, excellent; savage (animals); stormy (sea); rough, rugged; violent, angry; Inf. sumptuous, magnificent.

bravura /bra'βura/ f, ferocity (animals); courage (persons); boastful threat

braza /'braθa; 'brasa/ f, Naut. fathom; stroke (in swimming)

brazado /bra'θaðo; bra'saðo/ m, armful

brazal /bra'θal; bra'sal/ m, armlet, brassard

brazalete /braθa'lete; brasa'lete/ m, bracelet; brassard

brazo /'braθo; 'braso/ m, arm; upper arm; front paw; Mech. arm; branch (of chandelier, etc.); bough; arm (of chair); power, courage; pl protectors; workmen, hands. **b. de mar,** firth, arm of the sea. **a b. partido,** in unarmed fight, man to man. **con los brazos abiertos,** welcomingly; willingly, gladly. **dar los brazos(a),** to embrace. Inf. **hecho un b. de mar,** dressed up to the nines

brea /'brea/ f, pitch, tar; sacking, canvas

brebaje /bre'βahe/ m, beverage; unpleasant drink; Naut. draft (of beer, grog, etc.)

brecha /'bretʃa/ f, Mil. breach; opening; Fig. impression (on mind). **morir en la b.,** to fight to the last ditch; die in harness

brécol /'brekol/ m, Bot. broccoli

brega /'breɡa/ f, fight; quarrel; disappointment, trick. **andar a la b.,** to work hard. **dar b.,** to play a trick

bregar /bre'ɡar/ vi to fight; work hard; Fig. struggle; **bregarse con,** to tackle (a problem)

Brema /'brema/ Bremen

breña /'breɲa/ f, rough ground, bramble patch

breñal /bre'ɲal/ m, scrub, brushwood

breñoso /bre'ɲoso/ a rugged, rocky

Bretaña /bre'taɲa/ Brittany

brete /'brete/ m, fetters, shackles; Fig. fix, squeeze, tight spot, tight squeeze (e.g. Estoy en un brete. I'm in a tight spot)

bretón /bre'ton/ (-ona) a and n Breton. m, Breton (language)

breva /'breβa/ f, early fig; early acorn; Fig. advantage, "plum"; Inf. peach (girl); Inf. windfall, piece of luck; Havana cigar

breve /'breβe/ a brief; concise. m, papal brief. f, Mus. breve. **en b.,** shortly, concisely; in a short while, soon

brevedad /breβe'ðað/ f, brevity

breviario /bre'βiario/ m, breviary

brezal /bre'θal; bre'sal/ m, heath, moor

brezo /'breθo; 'breso/ m, Bot. heath

bribón /bri'βon/ (-ona) n rogue, ruffian —a knavish, dishonest; lazy

bribonada /briβo'naða/ f, knavery, mischievous trick

bribonear /briβone'ar/ vi to idle; play tricks, be a rogue

bribonería /briβone'ria/ f, rascality, vagrant life

brida /'briða/ f, bridle

brigada /bri'ɡaða/ f, Mil. brigade; Naut. division of fleet; beasts of burden. **brigada millonaria,** (Castroist Cuba) team of thirty sugarcane cutters who cut a million or more arrobas in one harvest

brigadier /briɡa'ðier/ m, brigadier-general

brillante /bri'ʎante; bri'yante/ a sparkling, brilliant; Fig. outstanding. m, diamond

brillantez /briʎan'teθ; briyan'tes/ f, brightness, luster; fame; Fig. brilliance

brillantina /briʎan'tina; briyan'tina/ f, brilliantine

brillar /bri'ʎar; bri'yar/ vi to shine, sparkle, gleam, glisten; Fig. be brilliant or outstanding

brillo /'briʎo; 'briyo/ m, brilliancy, brightness, shine; fame, glory; distinction, brilliance, splendor

brincar /brin'kar/ vi to spring, leap, skip, frisk; Fig. Inf. skip, omit; Inf. grow angry; —vt jump a child up and down

brinco /'brinko/ m, leap, spring; skip, frolicking

brindar /brin'dar/ vi to invite, provoke (of things); (with prep a or por) drink the health of, toast; —vt and vi give, present; offer; —vr offer one's services

brindis /'brindis/ m, toast (drink)

brío /'brio/ m, vigor; spirit, courage; gusto, verve

brioso /'brioso/ a vigorous, enterprising; spirited, courageous; dashing, lively

briqueta /bri'keta/ f, briquette

brisa /'brisa/ f, breeze; grape pressings

británico /bri'taniko/ a British

brizna /'briθna; 'brisna/ f, shred, paring; blade (grass); filament, fiber; string (of bean-pod, etc.); splinter, chip

broca /'broka/ f, reel; tack (shoemaker's); Mech. drill, bit

brocado /bro'kaðo/ m, brocade —a brocade or embroidered like brocade

brocal /bro'kal/ m, puteal (of a well); mouthpiece (of wineskin); metal ring (of sword-sheath)

brocamantón /brokaman'ton/ m, large jeweled brooch

brocatel /broka'tel/ m, imitation brocade

brocha /'brotʃa/ f, brush. **b. de afeitar,** shaving brush. **de b. gorda,** crudely painted. **pintor de b. gorda,** decorator

brochada /bro'tʃaða/ f, stroke (of the brush)

brochado /bro'tʃaðo/ a brocaded, embossed

brochadura /brotʃa'ðura/ f, fastening, set of hooks and eyes

broche /'brotʃe/ m, clasp, fastening; brooch; hooks and eyes

brochón /bro'tʃon/ m, whitewash brush

broma /'broma/ f, merriment; joke, jest; ship-worm. **b. literaria,** literary hoax

bromear /brome'ar/ (se) vi and vr to joke, make fun

bromista /bro'mista/ a joking, jesting; mischievous. mf genial person; prankster, tease

bromo /'bromo/ m, bromine

bromuro /bro'muro/ m, bromide

bronca /'bronka/ f, Inf. shindy

bronce /'bronθe; 'bronse/ m, bronze; brass; Poet. gun, bell, trumpet; bronze statue; sunburn

bronceado /bronθe'aðo; bronse'aðo/ a bronzed; sunburned. m, sunburn

broncear /bronθe'ar; bronse'ar/ vt to bronze; sunburn

bronco /'bronko/ a rough, coarse; brittle; (of metals); harsh (voice, musical instruments); rigid, stiff; surly

bronconeumonía /,bronkoneumo'nia/ f, bronchopneumonia

bronquial /bron'kial/ a bronchial

bronquio /'bronkio/ m, (gen. pl) bronchi

bronquitis /bron'kitis/ f, bronchitis

broquel /bro'kel/ m, shield; Fig. protection

broquelero /broke'lero/ m, shield maker; quarrelsome man

broqueta /bro'keta/ f, skewer

brotadura /brota'ðura/ *f*, budding

brotar /bro'tar/ *vi* to germinate, sprout; gush forth (water); issue forth, burst out; *Fig.* appear (of rash); *Fig.* begin to appear; —*vt* to bring forth; produce (of earth)

brote /'brote/ *m*, bud, sprout; *Fig.* germ, genesis; iota, jot, atom

broza /'broθa; 'brosa/ *f*, garden rubbish; debris; thicket

bruces /'bruθes; 'bruses/ (**a** *or* **de**) *adv* face downwards. **caer de b.**, to fall flat. Also with other verbs: **dar, echarse,** etc.

bruja /'bruha/ *f*, witch; owl; *Inf.* hag

Brujas /'bruhas/ Bruges

brujear /bruhe'ar/ *vi* to practice witchcraft

brujería /bruhe'ria/ *f*, witchcraft

brujo /'bruho/ *m*, magician, wizard

brújula /'bruhula/ *f*, magnetic needle; compass; mariner's compass. **b. de bolsillo,** pocket compass. **b. giroscópica,** gyrocompass

bruma /'bruma/ *f*, haze; sea-mist

brumoso /bru'moso/ *a* misty, hazy

bruno /'bruno/ *a* dark brown

bruñido /bru'ɲiðo/ *m*, polishing; burnish

bruñidor /bruɲi'ðor/ (**-ra**) *a* polishing —*n* burnisher. *m*, polisher (instrument)

bruñir /bru'ɲir/ *vt* to polish, burnish; *Inf.* apply make up

brusco /'brusko/ *a* brusque, rude; blunt; sudden, unexpected; sharp (of bends)

Bruselas /bru'selas/ Brussels

bruselense /bruse'lense/ *a* and *mf* of or from Brussels

brusquedad /bruske'ðað/ *f*, brusquerie, rudeness; bluntness; suddenness, unexpectedness; sharpness (of a bend)

brutal /bru'tal/ *a* brutal

brutalidad /brutali'ðað/ *f*, brutality; *Fig.* brutishness; viciousness

bruto /'bruto/ *a* stupid, unreasonable; vicious; unpolished, rough. *m*, animal (gen. quadruped). **en b.,** in the rough; *Com.* in bulk. **diamante en b.,** an uncut diamond

bruza /'bruθa; 'brusa/ *f*, strong brush; scrubbing brush

Bs. As. /,buenos 'aires/ abbrev. of Buenos Aires

bu /bu/ *m*, *Inf.* bogey man

buba /'buβa/ *f*, pustule; *pl* buboes

bubónico /bu'βoniko/ *a* bubonic

bucal /bu'kal/ *a* buccal

bucanero /buka'nero/ *m*, buccaneer

Bucarest /buka'rest/ Bucharest

búcaro /'bukaro/ *m*, arsenican clay; jar made of arsenican clay

buceador /buθea'ðor; busea'ðor/ *m*, diver

bucear /buθe'ar; buse'ar/ *vi* to work as a diver; swim under water; *Fig.* investigate

bucéfalo /bu'θefalo; bu'sefalo/ *m*, bucephalus; *Inf.* fool, blockhead

buceo /bu'θeo; bu'seo/ *m*, diving; dive; *Fig.* investigation

buche /'butʃe/ *m*, craw or crop; mouthful; wrinkle, pleat; *Inf.* stomach, belly. *Fig. Inf.* inmost heart

bucle /'bukle/ *m*, ringlet, curl

bucólico /bu'koliko/ *a* bucolic

búdico /'buðiko/ *a* Buddhist

budín /bu'ðin/ *m*, pudding

budismo /bu'ðismo/ *m*, Buddhism

budista /bu'ðista/ *a* and *mf* Buddhist

buen /buen/ *a* Abbr. of **bueno**, good. Used before *m*, singular nouns and infinitives used as nouns, e.g. *un b. libro,* a good book. *el b. cantar,* good singing

buenamente /buena'mente/ *adv* easily; comfortably, conveniently; willingly

buenaventura /buenaβen'tura/ *f*, good luck; fortune told from hand

bueno /'bueno/ (see **buen**) *a* good; kind; useful; convenient; pleasant; healthy; large (drink, etc.); simple, innocent; suitable; sufficient; opportune. ¡B.! Good!; Enough!; All right! **a buenas,** willingly. **de**

buenas a primeras, at first sight, from the beginning. **hacer bueno,** to prove, justify (a claim)

buey /buei/ *m*, ox. **b. suelto,** *Inf.* freelance; bachelor

búfalo /'bufalo/ (**-la**) *n* buffalo

bufanda /bu'fanda/ *f*, scarf

bufar /bu'far/ *vi* to bellow; snort; *Inf.* snort with rage

bufete /bu'fete/ *m*, desk, writing table; lawyer's office or practice; sideboard

bufido /bu'fiðo/ *m*, snort; bellow

bufo /'bufo/ *a* comic. *m*, clown, buffoon

bufón /bu'fon/ *m*, buffoon, clown; jester —*a* comical, clownish

bufonada /bufo'naða/ *f*, buffoonery, clowning; raillery, taunt

bufonear /bufone'ar/ (**se**) *vr* and *vi* to joke, jest, parody

bufonería. /bufone'ria/ See **bufonada**

buhardilla /buar'ðiʎa; buar'ðiya/ *f*, garret; skylight

búho /'buo/ *m*, owl; *Inf.* hermit, unsociable person

buhonería /buone'ria/ *f*, peddling, hawking; peddler's wares

buhonero /buo'nero/ *m*, pedler

buido /'buiðo/ *a* sharp-pointed; sharp

buitre /'buitre/ *m*, vulture

bujía /bu'hia/ *f*, candle; candlestick; *Elec.* candlepower; *Auto.* sparking plug

bula /'bula/ *f*, (Papal) bull

bulbo /'bulβo/ *m*, *Bot.* bulb. **b. dentario,** pulp (of teeth)

bulboso /bul'βoso/ *a* bulbous

bulevar /bule'βar/ *m*, boulevard, promenade

búlgaro /'bulgaro/ (**-ra**) *a* and *n* Bulgarian

bulla /'buʎa; 'buya/ *f*, noise; bustle; confusion; fuss. *Inf.* **meter a b.,** to throw into great confusion

bullebulle /buʎe'βuʎe; buye'βuye/ *mf* busybody; madcap

bullente /bu'ʎente; bu'yente/ *adj* boiling, bubbling; frothy (beer); swarming, teeming. **b. de sol,** drenched in sunlight, sun-drenched

bullicio /bu'ʎiθio; buyi'sio/ *m*, noise, bustle; rioting; uproar

bullicioso /buʎi'θioso; buyi'sioso/ *a* noisy, merry, boisterous; rebellious; lively, restless

bullir /bu'ʎir; bu'yir/ *vi* to boil; foam, bubble; *Fig.* seethe; *Fig.* swarm (insects); bustle; —*vt* move, stir; —*vr* stir, give signs of life

bulto /'bulto/ *m*, bulk, mass, size; form of person, etc., seen indistinctly; swelling; bust, statue; bundle, package, piece of luggage; pillowcase. *Fig. Inf.* **poner de b.,** to put clearly, emphasize. **ser de b.,** to be obvious

bumerang /bume'raŋ/ *m*, boomerang

buñolería /buɲole'ria/ *f*, bun or waffle shop

buñuelo /bu'ɲuelo/ *m*, bun; waffle, fritter; *Fig.* botch

buque /'buke/ *m*, ship, vessel; capacity of ship; ship's hull. **b. barreminas,** minesweeper. **b. de guerra,** battleship, man-of-war. **b. de vapor,** steamer. **b. de vela,** sailing ship. **b. escuela,** trainingship. **b. mercante,** merchant vessel. **b. submarino,** submarine. **b. transbordador,** train-ferry

burbuja /bur'βuha/ *f*, bubble

burbujear /burβuhe'ar/ *vi* to bubble

burdel /bur'ðel/ *m*, brothel; *Inf.* untidy, noisy place —*a* lascivious

burdo /'burðo/ *a* coarse, tough

burgalés /burga'les/ (**-esa**) *a* and *n* of or from Burgos

burgo /'burgo/ *m*, borough, burgh

burgomaestre /burgoma'estre/ *m*, burgomaster

burgués /bur'ges/ (**-esa**) *a* and *n* bourgeois

burguesía /burge'sia/ *f*, bourgeoisie

buriel /bu'riel/ *a* dark red

buril /bu'ril/ *m*, burin, engraver's tool

burla /'burla/ *f*, mockery; joke, jest; trick. **b. burlando,** without effort; negligently. **de burlas,** in fun. **entre burlas y veras,** half-jokingly

burlador /burla'ðor/ *a* mocking. *m*, libertine, rake; deceiver

burlar /bur'lar/ *vt* to play a trick on; deceive; disappoint; —*vr* and *vi* (*with de*) make fun of, laugh at, ridicule

burlesco /bur'lesko/ *a* jocular, comic, burlesque

burlón /bur'lon/ (**-ona**) a joking; mocking, scoffing —n joker; scoffer

buró /bu'ro/ m, bureau, writing-desk

burocracia /buro'kraθia; buro'krasia/ f, bureaucracy

burócrata /bu'rokrata/ mf bureaucrat

burocrático /buro'kratiko/ a bureaucratic

burocratismo /burokra'tismo/ m, bureaucracy, red tape

burra /'burra/ f, she-ass; foolish, unteachable woman; painstaking, patient woman

burrajo /bu'rraho/ m, dry stable dung used as fuel

burro /'burro/ m, ass, donkey; sawing-horse; card game

bursátil /bur'satil/ a Com. relating to the stock exchange; financial

busca /'buska/ f, search; hunting party; research; pursuit

buscado /bus'kaðo/ adj deliberate, intentional (negligence, etc.)

buscador /buska'ðor/ (**-ra**) n searcher; investigator. m, finder (of a camera, etc.)

buscapié /buska'pie/ m, hint or suggestion; Fig. feeler

buscapiés /buska'pies/ m, squib, cracker

buscar /bus'kar/ vt to search, look for; pursue. **ir a b.**, to go to look for, go and get; bring, fetch

buscarruidos /buska'rruiðos/ mf Inf. quarrel maker

buscavidas /buska'βiðas/ mf Inf. busybody; Inf. go-getter

buscón /bus'kon/ (**-ona**) n searcher; pickpocket, thief, swindler, rogue

buscona /bus'kona/ f, prostitute

busilis /bu'silis/ m, Inf. knotty problem, snag; **ahí está el b.**, there's the rub; core, main point

búsqueda /'buskeða/ (**de**) f, search (for)

busto /'busto/ m, Art. bust, head and shoulders

butaca /bu'taka/ f, armchair; Theat. orchestra stall; seat (in movies, etc.)

butifarra /bu'tifarra/ f, sausage made principally in Catalonia and the Balearic Islands; Inf. badly fitting stocking

buzo /buθ; bus/ m, respectful kiss

buzo /'buθo; 'buso/ m, diver

buzón /bu'θon; bu'son/ m, mailbox; letter-box; canal, channel; sluice

C

C. /k/ abbrev. of ciudadano

¡ca! /ka/ *interj* Fancy! Oh no!

cabal /ka'βal/ *a* just, exact; perfect; complete; faultless —*interj* Exactly! **por sus cabales,** according to plan; perfectly

cábala /'kaβala/ *f,* cabala; divination; *Inf.* intrigue. **hacer cábalas,** to venture a guess

cabalgada /kaβal'gaða/ *f,* cavalcade; foray, raid

cabalgador /kaβalga'ðor/ **(-ra)** *n* rider, horseman

cabalgadura /kaβalga'ðura/ *f,* riding horse; beast of burden

cabalgar /kaβal'gar/ *vi* to ride a horse; ride in procession

cabalgata /kaβal'gata/ *f,* cavalcade; troop of horse

cabalístico /kaβa'listiko/ *a* cabalistic; mysterious

caballa /ka'βaʎa; ka'βaya/ *f,* mackerel

caballada /kaβa'ʎaða; kaβa'yaða/ *f,* pack of horses; stud (of horses)

caballeresco /kaβaʎe'resko; kaβaye'resko/ *a* gentlemanly; knightly; chivalrous

caballerete /kaβaʎe'rete; kaβaye'rete/ *m, dim Inf.* foppish young man, dandy

caballería /kaβaʎe'ria; kaβaye'ria/ *f,* riding animal; cavalry; knightly deed or quest; any of Spanish Military Orders; knight-errantry; knighthood; chivalry; share of the spoils of war; horsemanship. **c. andante,** knight-errantry. **c. ligera,** *Mil.* light horse. **c. mayor,** horses, mares, mules. **c. menor,** asses, donkeys

caballeriza /kaβaʎe'riθa; kaβaye'risa/ *f,* stable; stud of horses; staff of a stable

caballerizo /kaβaʎe'riθo; kaβaye'riso/ *m,* head stable-groom. **c. mayor del rey,** Master of the King's Horse

caballero /kaβa'ʎero; kaβa'yero/ *m,* gentleman; cavalier; knight. **c. andante,** knight-errant. *Inf.* **c. de industria,** adventurer, sharper. **el C. de la Mancha,** the Knight of La Mancha. **el C. Sin Miedo y Sin Tacha,** the Seigneur de Bayart. **c. del hábito,** knight of one of the Spanish Military Orders. **c. novel,** untried knight. **armar c.,** to dub a knight

caballerosidad /kaβaʎerosi'ðað; kaβayerosi'ðað/ *f,* gentlemanliness; nobility; generosity; chivalry

caballeroso /kaβaʎe'roso; kaβaye'roso/ *a* gentlemanly; noble; generous; chivalrous

caballete /kaβa'ʎete; kaβa'yete/ *m,* ridge (of a roof); *Mil.* wooden horse; brake (for flax and hemp); *Agr.* furrow; easel; sawing-frame; trestle; bridge (of the nose)

caballito /kaβa'ʎito; kaβa'yito/ *m, dim* little horse; *pl* merry-go-round; automatic horse gambling game; circus equestrian act. **c. del diablo,** dragonfly

caballo /ka'βaʎo; ka'βayo/ *m,* horse; (chess) knight; (Spanish cards) queen; sawing-frame; *pl* cavalry. **c. balancín,** rocking horse. **c. de batalla,** war-horse; *Fig.* hobby-horse; forte; crux. **c. de cartón,** hobbyhorse; rocking horse. **c. de carrera,** racehorse. **c. de tiro,** draft-horse. **c. de vapor,** horsepower. **c. marino,** sea-horse. **a c.,** on horseback. **A c. regalado no le mires el diente,** Never look a gift horse in the mouth. **caer bien a c.,** to have a good seat (on a horse). **ser un c. loco en una cacharrería,** to be like a bull in a china shop

cabaña /ka'βaɲa/ *f,* hut, cabin, cottage; flock (of sheep); drove (of mules); *Art.* pastoral scene; balk (billiards)

cabaret /kaβa'ret/ *m,* cabaret, nightclub

cabaretero /kaβare'tero/ *m,* nightclub owner

cabecear /kaβeθe'ar; kaβese'ar/ *vi* to nod; shake the head in disapproval; move the head from side to side; toss the head (horses); (*Aer. Naut.*) pitch; sway (of a carriage); lean; —*vt* refoot (socks); head (wine)

cabeceo /kaβe'θeo; kaβe'seo/ *m,* nod, shake (of head); (*Naut. Aer.*) pitching; lurching (of a carriage, etc.); bight (of river)

cabecera /kaβe'θera; kaβe'sera/ *f,* top, upper portion, head; seat of honor; bed-head; river source; capital (country or county); illustrated chapter heading; pillow; inscription, heading

cabecilla /kaβe'θiʎa; kaβe'siya/ *dim f,* small head. *mf Inf.* hothead. *m,* rebel leader

cabellera /kaβe'ʎera; kaβe'yera/ *f,* head of long hair; hair-switch; tail (of comet)

cabello /ka'βeʎo; ka'βeyo/ *m,* hair; head of hair; silk (of maize). *Fig. Inf.* **asirse de un c.,** to clutch at a straw

cabelludo /kaβe'ʎuðo; kaβe'yuðo/ *a* hairy; *Bot.* fibrous

caber /ka'βer/ *vi irr* to be room for, contain; fit into, go into (e.g. *No cabemos todos en este coche,* There isn't room for all of us in this car); happen, befall, have (e.g. *No les cupo tal suerte,* They did not have such luck--Such luck did not befall them); be possible (e.g. *Todo cabe en Dios,* All things are possible with God). **No cabe más,** There's no room for anything else; *Fig.* That's the limit. *Fig.* **no c. en sí,** to be beyond oneself (with joy, pride, etc.). **No cabe duda de que,** There's no doubt that —*Pres. Indic.* **quepo, cabes,** etc —*Fut.* **cabré,** etc —*Conditional* **cabría,** etc —*Preterite* **cupe, cupiste,** etc —*Pres. Subjunc.* **quepa, quepas,** etc —*Imperf. Subjunc.* **cupiese,** etc.

cabestrar /kaβes'trar/ *vt* to halter

cabestrillo /kaβes'triʎo; kaβes'triyo/ *m,* sling; thin chain (for ornament). **en c.,** in a sling (e.g. *Tenía el brazo en c.,* His arm was in a sling)

cabestro /ka'βestro/ *m,* halter; sling; leading ox

cabeza /ka'βeθa; ka'βesa/ *f,* head; top, upper end; nail-head; brain; mind; judgment; self-control; edge (of book); peak, summit; source, origin; individual, person; head of cattle; capital city. *m,* leader, chief, head. *Mech.* **c. de biela,** big-end. *Inf.* **c. de chorlito,** scatterbrain (person). **c. de hierro,** blockhead. *Mil.* **c. de puente,** bridgehead. **c. de partido,** principal town of a region. **c. de turco,** scapegoat. **irse la c. (** a alguien), to feel giddy. *Fig. Inf.* **meter a uno en la c.,** to put into someone's head. *Inf.* **quebrarse la c.,** to rack one's brains. *Inf.* **quitar a uno de la c. (** una cosa), to dissuade; get an idea out of someone's head

cabezada /kaβe'θaða; kaβe'saða/ *f,* blow with or on the head; nod; headshake; headstall; *Naut.* pitching. **dar cabezadas,** to nod, go to sleep

cabezal /kaβe'θal; kaβe'sal/ *m,* small head pillow; *Surg.* pad; bolster; narrow mattress; *Mech.* head

cabezo /ka'βeθo; ka'βeso/ *m,* summit (of mountain); hill; *Naut.* reef

cabezón /kaβe'θon; kaβe'son/ *m,* tax-register; collar-band; head-opening (of a garment)

cabezudo /kaβe'θuðo; kaβe'suðo/ *a* large-headed; *Inf.* obstinate; *Inf.* heady (of wine). *m,* carnival grotesque

cabida /ka'βiða/ *f,* space, capacity; extent, area

cabildear /kaβilde'ar/ *vi* to canvass votes, lobby

cabildo /ka'βildo/ *m, Eccl.* chapter; municipal council; meeting, or meeting place of council. **c. abierto,** town meeting

cabina /ka'βina/ *f,* cabin. **c. telefónica** phone booth

cabizbajo /kaβiβ'βaho; kaβis'βaho/ *a* crestfallen; pensive, melancholy

cable /'kaβle/ *m,* cable; string (of bridge); cable's length; **c. aéreo,** overhead cable. **c. alimentario,** feed line. **c. eléctrico,** electric cable

cabo /'kaβo/ *m,* end, extremity; stump, stub; handle, shaft, haft; leader; *Geog.* cape; end, conclusion; *Naut.* rope; ply (of wool, etc.); *Mil.* corporal; *pl* accessories (clothes); horse's tail and mane. **c. de maestranza,** foreman. **c. de mar,** naval quartermaster. **c. furriel,** *Mil.* quartermaster. **al c.,** in the end. **llevar a c.,** to finish

Cabo de Buena Esperanza /'kaβo de 'buena espe'ranθa; 'kaβo de 'buena espe'ransa/ Cape of Good Hope

Cabo de Hornos /'kaβo de 'ornos/ Cape Horn

cabotaje /kaβo'tahe/ *m, Naut.* coasting trade

cabra /'kaβra/ f, nanny-goat; goat. **c. montesa,** wild goat

cabrahigo /kaβra'igo/ m, wild fig; wild fig tree

cabrerizo /kaβre'riθo/ kaβreriso/ **(-za)** a goatish. m, goatherd

cabrero /ka'βrero/ **(-ra)** m, goatherd

cabrestante /kaβres'tante/ m, Naut. capstan

cabria /'kaβria/ f, winch, hoist

cabrilla /ka'βriʎa/ ka'βriya/ f, saw-horse; pl Astron. Pleiades; burn marks on legs from sitting too near fire; white crests (of waves)

cabrillear /kaβriʎe'ar/ kaβriye'ar/ vi to foam, froth (the sea)

cabrío /ka'βrio/ a goatish. m, herd of goats. **macho c.,** male goat, he-goat

cabriola /ka'βriola/ f, fouetté (in dancing); spin in the air (acrobats); curvet (horses); caper

cabriolar /kaβrio'lar/ vi to curvet; caper, skip

cabriolé /kaβrio'le/ m, cabriolet; short cape with or without sleeves

cabritilla /kaβri'tiʎa/ kaβri'tiya/ f, dressed kid; lambskin, etc.

cabrito /ka'βrito/ m, Zool. kid; pl toasted maize, popcorn

cabrón /ka'βron/ m, billy goat, buck, he-goat; Inf. complaisant husband, cuckold; Chile owner or operator of a brothel

cabrona /ka'βrona/ f, Chile bawd, madam

cabruno /ka'βruno/ a goatish

cabujón /kaβu'hon/ m, Mineral. uncut gem; unpolished ruby; pl vignettes

cacahual /kaka'ual/ m, cacao plantation

cacahuete /kaka'uete/ m, Bot. peanut, monkey nut

cacao /ka'kao/ m, Bot. cacao tree; cacaonut

cacarear /kakare'ar/ vi to crow, cackle; —vt Inf. boast

cacareo /kaka'reo/ m, crowing, cackling; Inf. boast

cacatúa /kaka'tua/ f, cockatoo

cacera /ka'θera/ ka'sera/ f, irrigation channel

cacería /kaθe'ria/ kase'ria/ f, hunting party; hunting bag, booty; Art. hunting scene

cacerola /kaθe'rola/ kase'rola/ f, stew-pot, casserole

cachalote /katʃa'lote/ m, sperm whale

cachano /ka'tʃano/ m, Old Nick

cachar /ka'tʃar/ vt to break in fragments; split (wood)

cacharrería /katʃarre'ria/ f, crockery store

cacharro /ka'tʃarro/ m, coarse earthenware vessel; Inf. decrepit, worthless object

cachazudo /katʃa'θuðo/ katʃa'suðo/ a phlegmatic, slow

cachear /katʃe'ar/ vt to search (a person) for weapons

Cachemira /katʃe'mira/ Kashmir

cachemira /katʃe'mira/ f, cashmere

cacheo /ka'tʃeo/ m, search (of persons) for weapons

cachete /ka'tʃete/ m, blow on the head or face with one's fist; cheek (especially fat one)

cachetero /katʃe'tero/ m, dagger

cachetina /katʃe'tina/ f, hand-to-hand fight

cachiporra /katʃi'porra/ f, club, bludgeon

cachivache /katʃi'βatʃe/ m, Inf. (gen. pl) trash; pots, pans, utensils

cacho /'katʃo/ m, small slice (gen. of bread or fruit)

cachón /ka'tʃon/ m, breaker, wave; small waterfall

cachorro /ka'tʃorro/ **(-rra)** n puppy; cub. m, small pistol

cachuela /ka'tʃuela/ f, Extremaduran pork stew

cacillo /ka'θiʎo/ ka'siyo/ m, ladle; basting spoon

cacique /ka'θike/ ka'sike/ m, Indian chief, cacique; Inf. political "boss"

caciquismo /kaθi'kismo/ kasi'kismo/ m, political "bossism"

caco /'kako/ m, pickpocket, thief; Inf. poltroon

cacofonía /kakofo'nia/ f, cacophony

cacografía /kakogra'fia/ f, cacography

cacto /'kakto/ m, cactus

cacumen /ka'kumen/ m, Inf. brains, acumen

cada /'kaða/ a every, each. **c. cual,** each. **c. que,** whenever; every time that. **c. y cuando que,** whenever

cadalso /ka'ðalso/ m, scaffold; platform, stand

cadáver /ka'ðaβer/ m, corpse

cadavérico /kaða'βeriko/ a cadaverous, ghastly

cadena /ka'ðena/ f, chain; link, tie; Fig. bond; Fig. sequence (of events); Law. imprisonment; Archit. buttress; grand chain (dancing); **c. de montañas,** range of mountains. **c. perpetua,** life imprisonment

cadencia /ka'ðenθia/ ka'ðensia/ f, cadence; rhythm; Mus. measure, time; Mus. cadenza

cadencioso /kaðen'θioso; kaðen'sioso/ a rhythmic

cadente /ka'ðente/ a falling, declining; decaying, dying; rhythmic

cadera /ka'ðera/ f, hip; flank

caderillas /kaðe'riʎas; kaðe'riyas/ f pl, bustle, panniers

cadete /ka'ðete/ m, Mil. cadet

cadi /'kaði/ mf caddy

Cádiz /'kaðiθ/ /'kaðis/ Cadiz

caducar /kaðu'kar/ vi to become senile; become invalid, be annulled; expire, lapse; Fig. be worn out

caduceo /kaðu'θeo; kaðu'seo/ m, Mercury's wand

caducidad /kaðuθi'ðað/ kaðusi'ðað/ f, decrepitude; lapse, expiry

caduco /ka'ðuko/ a senile; decrepit; perishable; lapsed; obsolete

caduquez /kaðu'keθ; kaðu'kes/ f, senility

caedizo /kae'ðiθo; kae'ðiso/ a ready to fall; timid, cowardly, weak

caer /ka'er/ vi irr to fall, drop; drop out or off; suit, fit, become; fail; fade (colors); Fig. drop (voice); (with sobre) attack, fall upon; (with en) fall in or on to; decay, collapse; understand; (with preps. a, hacia) Fig. look on to, face; (with por, en) Fig. fall on, occur on; —vr Aer. crash; fly off (buttons, etc.). **c. de cabeza,** to fall head foremost. **c. en conflicto (con),** to come into conflict (with). **c. en las manos de uno,** to come into somebody's possession (come to be owned by somebody). **c. en gracia,** to make a good impression, arouse affection. **caerse de suyo,** to be self-evident. **c. por tierra,** (plan, etc.) to fall through. **Cayó enfermo,** He was taken ill. **cayendo y levantado,** dying. Pres. Indic. **caigo, caes,** etc —Pres. Part. **cayendo.** Preterite **cayó cayeron.** Pres. Subjunc. **caiga,** etc.

café /ka'fe/ m, coffee (tree, berry, drink); café, coffee-house. **c. con leche,** café au lait

cafeína /kafe'ina/ f, caffeine

cafetal /kafe'tal/ m, coffee plantation

cafetera /kafe'tera/ f, coffeepot; Peru cab, taxi

cafeto /ka'feto/ m, coffee tree

cafiche /ka'fitʃe/ m, Argentina, Chile pimp

caficultor /kafikul'tor/ m, coffee-grower

caficultura /kafikul'tura/ f, coffee-growing

cafúa /ka'fua/ f, Argentina clink, slammer

cagadas /ka'gaðas/ f pl, droppings, dung

cagar /ka'gar/ **(se)** vi vt vr to evacuate (bowels); —vt Inf. spoil, make a botch of

cagarruta /kaga'rruta/ f, dung of sheep, deer, rabbits, etc.

caída /ka'iða/ f, falling; fall; ruin; failure; close (of day); Fig. falling off; hanging (curtains, etc.); diminution; incline; pl coarse wool; Inf. repartee. **a la c. de la tarde,** at the end of the afternoon. **a la c. del sol,** at sunset

caído /ka'iðo/ **(-da)** a debilitated, languid; lapsed; (of a shoulder) sloping. **los caídos,** the fallen, the dead (in war, etc.)

caimán /kai'man/ m, alligator; Inf. shark, astute person

caja /'kaha/ f, box; safe, cash box; coffin; (of a vehicle) body; Mus. drum; case (of piano, watch, etc.); cavity; well (of a stair); Com. cash; cash-desk; cashier's office; Bot. sheath. **c. de ahorros,** savings bank. **c. de caudales,** strong-box. Print. **c. de imprenta,** type case. **c. de música,** musical box. **c. de reclutamiento,** recruiting office. **c. de velocidades,** gearbox. **c. registradora,** cash register. **c. torácica,** rib cage, thoracic cage

cajero /ka'hero/ **(-ra)** m, boxmaker; —n Com. cashier; pedler **c. automático,** automatic teller, automatic teller machine, bank machine, money machine

cajetilla /kahe'tiʎa/ kahe'tiya/ f, packet (cigarettes, etc.)

cajista /ka'hista/ mf Print. compositor

cajón /ka'hon/ *m*, chest, locker, case; drawer. **c. de municiones**, ammunition-box
cajonera /kaho'nera/ *f*, *Eccl.* chest of drawers in sacristy; *Agr.* frame
cal /kal/ *f*, lime. **c. muerta**, slaked lime. **c. viva**, quicklime. *Fig. Inf.* **de c. y canto**, tough, strong
cala /'kala/ *f*, sample slice (of fruit); *Naut.* hold; *Surg.* probe; cove, small bay; *Bot.* iris
calabacera /kalaβa'θera; kalaβa'sera/ *f*, *Bot.* pumpkin or gourd plant
calabacín /kalaβa'θin; kalaβa'sin/ *m*, kind of vegetable marrow; *Inf.* dolt
calabaza /kala'βaθa; kala'βasa/ *f*, *Bot.* pumpkin (plant and fruit); gourd; *Inf.* dolt. **dar calabazas**, to refuse (suitor); flunk (an examinee). *Inf.* **llevar calabazas**, to get the sack; be jilted
calabobos /kala'βoβos/ *m*, drizzle
calabocero /kalaβo'θero; kalaβo'sero/ *m*, jailer
calabozo /kala'βoθo; kala'βoso/ *m*, dungeon; prison cell; pruning knife
calabrés /kala'βres/ **(-esa)** *a* and *n* Calabrian
calada /ka'laða/ *f*, soaking, wetting through; flight of bird of prey; swoop. **dar una c.**, *Fig. Inf.* to dress down
calado /ka'laðo/ *a* soaked, wet through. *m*, *Sew.* open-work; fretwork; *Naut.* draft of a ship; water level; *pl* lace. **c. hasta los huesos**, soaked to the skin; madly in love
calador /kala'ðor/ *m*, one who does open or fretwork; caulking iron; borer; *Surg.* probe
calafate /kala'fate/ *m*, caulker
calafatear /kalafate'ar/ *vt* *Naut.* to caulk
calamar /kala'mar/ *m*, *Zool.* squid, calamary
calambre /ka'lambre/ *m*, cramp. **c. del escribiente**, writer's cramp
calamidad /kalami'ðað/ *f*, misfortune, calamity
calamina /kala'mina/ *f*, *Mineral.* calamine
calamitoso /kalami'toso/ *a* calamitous; unfortunate, unhappy
cálamo /'kalamo/ *m*, ancient flute; stalk (of grass); *Poet.* pen
calamocano /kalamo'kano/ *a* maudlin, tipsy
calandria /ka'landria/ *f*, *Ornith.* calender, lark; *Mech.* calender; treadmill. *mf Inf.* malingerer
calaña /ka'laɲa/ *f*, sample; model; pattern; kind, quality; temperament; cheap fan
calar /ka'lar/ *vt* to permeate, soak through; pierce; do openwork (in cloth, paper, metal); cut a sample slice from fruit; pull (hat, etc.) well down on head; put down (an eyeshade or visor); fix (bayonets, etc.); *Inf.* understand (persons); *Inf.* guess, realize; *Naut.* let down; —*vi Naut.* draw (water); —*vr* be drenched, wet through; swoop (birds of prey); *Inf.* sneak in —*a* calcareous
calar /ka'lar/ *m*, limestone deposit or region
calavera /kala'βera/ *f*, skull. *m*, dare-devil, madcap; roué
calaverada /kalaβe'raða/ *f*, *Inf.* dare-devilment, foolishness; escapade
calcañar /kalka'ɲar/ *m*, heel (of foot)
calcar /kal'kar/ *vt* to trace (drawing); press with foot; copy servilely, imitate
calcáreo /kal'kareo/ *a* calcareous
calce /'kalθe; 'kalse/ *m*, rim of a wheel; wedge; tire
calcés /kal'θes; kal'ses/ *m*, *Naut.* masthead
calceta /kal'θeta; kal'seta/ *f*, stocking; fetter. *Inf.* **hacer c.**, to knit
calcetería /kalθete'ria; kalsete'ria/ *f*, hosiery shop; hosiery trade
calcetero /kalθe'tero; kalse'tero/ **(-ra)** *n* hosier; hose maker or darner
calcetín /kalθe'tin; kalse'tin/ *m*, sock
calcificación /kalθifika'θion; kalsifika'sion/ *f*, *Med.* calcification
calcinación /kalθina'θion; kalsina'sion/ *f*, calcination
calcinar /kalθi'nar; kalsi'nar/ *vt* to calcine
calcio /'kalθio; 'kalsio/ *m*, calcium
calco /'kalko/ *m*, tracing (drawing)
calcografía /kalkogra'fia/ *f*, chalcography
calcografiar /kalkogra'fiar/ *vt* to transfer; make chalcographies of

calcomanía /kalkoma'nia/ *f*, transfer
calculación /kalkula'θion; kalkula'sion/ *f*, calculation
calculadamente /kalkulaða'mente/ *adv* calculatedly
calculado /kalku'laðo/ *a* calculated
calculador /kalkula'ðor/ *a* calculating. *m*, calculating machine, comptometer
calcular /kalku'lar/ *vt* to calculate
cálculo /'kalkulo/ *m*, calculation; *Math.* estimate; investigation; conjecture; *(Math Med.)* calculus. **c. hepático**, *Med.* gallstone
Calcuta /kal'kuta/ Calcutta
calda /'kalda/ *f*, heating; *pl* hot mineral baths
Caldea /kal'dea/ Chaldea
caldear /kalde'ar/ *vt* to heat
caldeo /kal'deo/ **(-ea)** *a* and *n* Chaldean
caldeo /kal'deo/ *m*, heating
caldera /kal'dera/ *f*, cauldron; cauldron full; *West Hem.* teapot; *Engin.* boiler. **c. de vapor**, steam-boiler
calderería /kaldere'ria/ *f*, coppersmith's trade and shop
calderero /kalde'rero/ *m*, boiler maker; coppersmith; tinker
calderilla /kalde'riʎa; kalde'riya/ *f*, holy water stoup; any copper coin
caldero /kal'dero/ *m*, small cauldron; casserole; kettle
calderón /kalde'ron/ *m*, large cauldron; *Mus.* rest; *Mus.* trill; pause
caldo /'kaldo/ *m*, broth; salad dressing; *pl Agr.* oil, wine, vegetable juices
calefacción /kalefak'θion; kalefak'sion/ *f*, heating. **c. central**, central heating
calendario /kalen'dario/ *m*, calendar. **c. deportivo**, fixture card. **c. gregoriano**, Gregorian calendar
calendas /ka'lendas/ *f pl*, calends. **en las c. griegas**, at the Greek calends
caléndula /ka'lendula/ *f*, marigold
calentador /kalenta'ðor/ *a* heating, warming. *m*, heater; warming-pan
calentamiento /kalenta'miento/ *m*, heating, warming
calentar /kalen'tar/ *vt irr* to heat, warm; rev-up (an engine); hasten; *Inf.* spank; —*vr* warm oneself; be in heat (animals); grow excited. See **acertar**
calentura /kalen'tura/ *f*, fever
calenturiento /kalentu'riento/ *a* feverish
calera /ka'lera/ *f*, lime-pit; lime-kiln; fishing smack
calesa /ka'lesa/ *f*, calash, calèche, chaise (two-wheeled carriage)
caleta /ka'leta/ *f*, cove, creek
caletre /ka'letre/ *m*, *Inf.* discernment, head, sense
calibrar /kali'βrar/ *vt* to calibrate; gauge
calibre /ka'liβre/ *m*, *Mech.* gauge; bore, caliber; diameter (tubes, pipes, etc.)
calidad /kali'ðað/ *f*, quality; role; character, temperament; condition, requisite; importance, gravity; personal particulars; nobility; *pl* qualities of the mind. **c. originaria**, rank and birth. **c. de oficio**, justification for action. **en c. de**, in the capacity of
cálido /'kaliðo/ *a* warm, hot; warming, heating; vehement, ardent; *Art.* warm
calidoscópico /kaliðos'kopiko/ *a* kaleidoscopic
calidoscopio /kaliðos'kopio/ *m*, kaleidoscope
calientalibros /kalienta'liβros/ *m*, bookworm (person)
calientapiés /kalienta'pies/ *m*, footwarmer
calientaplatos /kalienta'platos/ *m*, hot plate, plate-warmer
caliente /ka'liente/ *a* warm, hot; excited; *Art.* warm
calientito /kalien'tito/ *a* piping hot
califa /ka'lifa/ *m*, caliph
califal /kali'fal/ *a* caliphal
califato /kali'fato/ *m*, caliphate
calificable /kalifi'kaβle/ *a* classifiable; qualifiable
calificación /kalifika'θion; kalifika'sion/ *f*, classification; qualification; judgment; mark, place (examinations)
calificar /kalifi'kar/ *vt* to class; authorize; judge (qualities); *Fig.* ennoble; —*vr* prove noble descent
calificativo /kalifika'tiβo/ *a* *Gram.* qualifying. *m*, epithet

californio /kaliˈfornio/ **(-ia)** *a* and *n* Californian

caliginoso /kalihiˈnoso/ *a* murky, dark

caligrafía /kaligraˈfia/ *f*, calligraphy

calígrafo /kaˈligrafo/ *m*, calligraphist

calinoso /kaliˈnoso/ *a* hazy

caliqueño /kaliˈkeɲo/ *m*, cheroot

calistenia /kalisˈtenia/ *f*, callisthenics

cáliz /ˈkaliθ; ˈkalis/ *m*, chalice; *Poet.* cup; *Bot.* calyx

caliza /kaˈliθa; kaˈlisa/ *f*, limestone

calizo /kaˈliθo; kaˈliso/ *a* calcareous

callado /kaˈʎaðo; kaˈyaðo/ *a* silent; reserved; secret

callar /kaˈʎar; kaˈyar/ **(se)** *vi* and *vr* to say nothing, keep silent; stop speaking; stop making any sound (persons, animals, things); —*vt* conceal, keep secret; omit, leave out; *Inf.* interj **¡Calle!** You don't say so! **Quien calla otorga,** Silence gives consent

calle /ˈkaʎe; ˈkaye/ *f*, street. *Inf.* **abrir c.,** to clear the way. *Inf.* **dejar en la c.,** to leave destitute. *Inf.* **echar a la c.,** put out of the house, to throw out of the house; make known, publish. **ponerse en la c.,** to go out

calleja, callejuela /kaˈʎeha, kaʎeˈhuela; kaˈyeha, kayeˈhuela/ *f*, small street, alley, side street

callejear /kaʎeheˈar; kayeheˈar/ *vi* to walk the streets, wander about the streets, loaf around the streets

callejero /kaʎeˈhero; kayeˈhero/ *a* fond of gadding. *m*, street directory

callejón /kaʎeˈhon; kayeˈhon/ *m*, alley, lane. **c. sin salida,** cul-de-sac; *Fig.* impasse

callicida /kaʎiˈθiða; kayiˈsiða/ *m*, corn cure

callista /kaˈʎista; kaˈyista/ *mf* chiropodist

callo /ˈkaʎo; ˈkayo/ *m*, corn, callosity; *Med.* callus; *pl* tripe

calloso /kaˈʎoso; kaˈyoso/ *a* callous, horny

calma /ˈkalma/ *f*, calm, airlessness; serenity, composure; quiet, tranquillity, peace. **c. chicha,** dead calm. **en c.,** at peace; tranquil; calm (of the sea)

calmante /kalˈmante/ *a* calming, soothing. *Med. a* and *m*, sedative, tranquilizer

calmar /kalˈmar/ *vt* to soothe, calm; moderate, mitigate; pacify; quench (thirst); —*vi* grow calm; moderate; be becalmed

calmoso /kalˈmoso/ *a* calm, tranquil; *Inf.* sluggish, lazy; imperturbable

calor /kaˈlor/ *m*, heat; ardor, vehemence; cordiality; *Fig.* heat (of battle); excitement

caloría /kaloˈria/ *f*, *Phys.* calorie

calórico /kaˈloriko/ *a Phys.* caloric, thermic

calorífero /kaloˈrifero/ *a* heat-giving. *m*, heater, radiator

calorífico /kaloˈrifiko/ *a* calorific

calumnia /kaˈlumnia/ *f*, calumny; *Law.* slander

calumniador /kalumniaˈðor/ **(-ra)** *a* slandering —*n* calumniator, slanderer

calumniar /kalumniˈar/ *vt* to calumniate; *Law.* slander

calumnioso /kalumˈnioso/ *a* calumnious, slanderous

caluroso /kaluˈroso/ *a* hot, warm; cordial, friendly; enthusiastic; ardent, impassioned; excited

calva /ˈkalβa/ *f*, bald patch on head; worn place (cloth, etc.); bare spot, clearing (trees, etc.)

Calvario /kalˈβario/ *m*, Calvary; *Inf.* series of disasters; *Inf.* debts

calvero /kalˈβero/ *m*, clearing (in a wood); chalk or marl pit

calvicie /kalˈβiθie; kalˈβisie/ *f*, baldness

calvinismo /kalβiˈnismo/ *m*, Calvinism

calvinista /kalβiˈnista/ *mf* Calvinist —*a* Calvinistic

calvo /ˈkalβo/ *a* bald; bare, barren (land); worn (cloth, etc.)

calza /ˈkalθa; ˈkalsa/ *f*, breeches (gen. *pl*); wedge; *Inf.* stocking. *Inf.* **tomar calzas,** to beat it

calzada /kalˈθaða; kalˈsaða/ *f*, roadway. **c. romana,** Roman road

calzado /kalˈθaðo; kalˈsaðo/ *m*, footwear, shoes

calzador /kalθaˈðor; kalsaˈðor/ *m*, shoehorn

calzadura /kalθaˈðura; kalsaˈðura/ *f*, wedging (of a wheel); act of putting on shoes; felloe of a wheel

calzar /kalˈθar; kalˈsar/ *vt* to put on shoes; wear (spurs, gloves, etc.); wedge, block (wheel); scotch (a

wheel). *Fig. Inf.* **c. el coturno,** don the buskin; write in the sublime style; write a tragedy, write tragedies.

calzarse a una persona, to have a person in one's pocket

calzón /kalˈθon; kalˈson/ *m*, breeches (gen. *pl*). *Fig. Inf.* **ponerse los calzones,** to wear the breeches (of a woman)

calzonazos /kalθoˈnaθos; kalsoˈnasos/ *m*, *Inf.* weak-willed, easily led fellow

calzoncillos /kalθonˈθiʎos; kalsonˈsiyos/ *m pl*, drawers, pants

cama /ˈkama/ *f*, bed; bedstead; bedhanging; lair, form; floor (of a cart); check (of bridle) (gen. *pl*). **c. de campaña,** camp bed. **c. de matrimonio,** double bed. **c. de monja,** single bed. **c. de operaciones,** operating table. **c. turca,** settee-bed. **guardar c.,** to stay in bed

camada /kaˈmaða/ *f*, brood, litter; *Inf.* gang

camafeo /kamaˈfeo/ *m*, cameo

camaleón /kamaleˈon/ *m*, chameleon; *Inf.* changeable person

cámara /ˈkamara/ *f*, chamber; hall; house (of deputies); granary; *Naut.* state room; chamber (firearms, mines); *Phys.* camera; human excrement; *Auto.* inner tube. **c. acorazada,** strong-room. **c. alta,** Upper House, **c. baja** or **c. de los comunes,** lower house, house of commons. **c. de comercio,** chamber of commerce. **c. oscura,** (optics) dark room

camarada /kamaˈraða/ *mf* pal, companion, comrade

camaradería /kamaraðeˈria/ *f*, comradeship, companionship

camarera /kamaˈrera/ *f*, waiting-maid; waitress; chambermaid; stewardess

camarero /kamaˈrero/ *m*, waiter; papal chamberlain; chamberlain; steward; valet. **c. mayor,** lord chamberlain

camarilla /kamaˈriʎa; kamaˈriya/ *f*, palace or other clique, coterie; *Inf.* back-scratch

camarín /kamaˈrin/ *m*, *Theat.* dressing-room; closet; boudoir; cage (of a lift); niche

camarón /kamaˈron/ *m*, prawn, shrimp; tip, reward

camarote /kamaˈrote/ *m*, cabin; berth

cambalachear /kambalatʃeˈar/ *vt Inf.* to barter

cámbaro /ˈkambaro/ *m*, sea-crab

cambiable /kamˈβiaβle/ *a* exchangeable; changeable

cambiante /kamˈβiante/ *a* exchanging; changing. *m*, sheen, luster (gen. *pl*); money changer

cambiar /kamˈβiar/ *vt* to exchange; convert —*vt* and *vi* change, alter; —*vi* and *vr* to veer (wind). **c. de aguas,** *Poet.* to move (change one's residence). **c. de aire,** get a change of scenery. **c. de frente,** to face about; *Fig.* change front

cambio /ˈkambio/ *m*, exchange; change; *Com.* rate of exchange; money change; *Com.* premium on bills of exchange. **a c. de, en c. de,** in exchange for; instead of. **en c.,** instead, on the other hand. **c. de velocidad,** *Auto.* gear-changing. **letra de c.,** bill of exchange. **libre c.,** free trade

cambista /kamˈβista/ *mf* money changer. *m*, banker

Camboya /kamˈβoia/ Cambodia

Cambrige /kamˈβrihe/ Cambridge

camelar /kameˈlar/ *vt Inf.* to woo; seduce

camelia /kaˈmelia/ *f*, camelia. **c. japonesa,** japonica

camellero /kameˈʎero; kameˈyero/ *m*, camel keeper or driver

camello /kaˈmeʎo; kaˈmeyo/ *m*, camel. **c. pardal,** giraffe

camellón /kameˈʎon; kameˈyon/ *m*, furrow; drinking trough; *Mexico* island, traffic island, median strip

camelo /kaˈmelo/ *m*, *Inf.* eyewash

Camerún /kameˈrun/ Cameroon

camilla /kaˈmiʎa; kaˈmiya/ *f*, couch; small round skirted table with brazier underneath; stretcher, litter

camillero /kamiˈʎero; kamiˈyero/ *m*, *Mil.* stretcher-bearer

caminador /kaminaˈðor/ *a* in the habit of walking a great deal

caminante /kamiˈnante/ *mf* walker, traveler

caminar /kamiˈnar/ *vi* to travel; walk; *Fig.* move on, go (inanimate things). *Fig. Inf.* **c. derecho,** to walk uprightly

caminata /kamiˈnata/ *f*, long, tiring walk; excursion

caminejo /kami'neho/ *m*, worn path
camino /ka'mino/ *m*, road; route; journey; way; means; **c. de hierro**, railway. **c. de mesa**, table-runner. **c. de sirga**, towpath. **c. real**, highway, main road. **de c.**, on the way, in passing. **ponerse en c.**, to set out
camión /ka'mion/ *m*, truck. **c. de volteo, c. volquete** dump truck; *Mexico* bus
camioneta /kamio'neta/ *f*, light truck, pick-up truck; *West. Hem.* station wagon
camisa /ka'misa/ *f*, shirt, stiff shirt; thin skin (of fruit); sloughed skin of snakes; coat (of whitewash, etc.); *Mech.* jacket; mantle (gas). **c. de fuerza**, straitjacket. **dejar sin c.**, *Inf.* to leave penniless
camisería /kamise'ria/ *f*, shirt shop or factory
camisero /kami'sero/ **(-ra)** *n* shirt maker or seller
camiseta /kami'seta/ *f*, vest, T-shirt. **c. de fútbol**, soccer player's jersey
camisola /kami'sola/ *f*, stiff shirt; ruffled shirt
camisón /kami'son/ *m*, large wide shirt; night shirt
camomila /kamo'mila/ *f*, chamomile
camorra /ka'morra/ *f*, *Inf.* brawl, shindy. **armar c.**, to start a row
campal /kam'pal/ *a* field, country
campamento /kampa'mento/ *m*, camping; *Mil.* encampment; camp; jamboree
campana /kam'pana/ *f*, bell; anything bell-shaped; church, parish. **c. de chimenea**, mantelpiece. **c. de hogar**, hood, shutter (of a fireplace)
campanada /kampa'naða/ *f*, peal of a bell; scandal
campanario /kampa'nario/ *m*, belfry, bell tower
campanear /kampane'ar/ *vi* to ring bells frequently
campaneo /kampa'neo/ *m*, bell-ringing; chime
campanero /kampa'nero/ *m*, bell-founder; bell ringer
campanil /kampa'nil/ *m*, small belfry, campanile
campanilla /kampa'niʎa; kampa'niya/ *f*, hand-bell; bubble; any bell-shaped flower
campanillazo /kampani'ʎaθo; kampani'yaso/ *m*, loud peal of a bell
campante /kam'pante/ *a* outstanding; *Inf.* proud, satisfied
campanudo /kampa'nuðo/ *a* bell-shaped; sonorous (of words); pompous (of speech)
campaña /kam'paɲa/ *f*, level country; campaign. *Naut.* voyage, cruise. **correr la c.**, to reconnoiter. **la C. del Desierto**, the War against the Gauchos (in Argentina)
campar /kam'par/ *vi* to camp. *Inf.* **c. por sus respetos**, to stand on one's own feet
campeador /kampea'ðor/ *a* mighty in battle
campear /kampe'ar/ *vi* to go out to graze; grow green (crops); excel; *Mil.* be engaged in a campaign, reconnoiter
campechano /kampe'tʃano/ *a Inf.* hearty; frank; cheerful; generous
campeche /kam'petʃe/ *m*, *Bot.* logwood
campeón /kampe'on/ *m*, champion; advocate, defender
campeonato /kampeo'nato/ *m*, championship
campesinado /kampesi'naðo/ *m*, peasantry
campesino /kampe'sino/ **(-na)** *a* rural, rustic —*n* country dweller
campestre /kam'pestre/ *a* rural
campiña /kam'piɲa/ *f*, expanse of cultivated land; countryside, landscape
campo /'kampo/ *m*, country (as opposed to urban areas); field; *Fig.* sphere, province; (*Phys. Herald. Mil.*) field; *Art.* ground; *Mil.* camp, army; plain ground (of silks, etc.). **«C. Abierto»**, "Miscellaneous" (e.g. as the title of a section in a book catalog). **c. de aterrizaje**, *Aer.* landing-field. **c. de batalla**, battlefield. **c. de concentración**, concentration camp. **c. de experimentación**, testing ground. **c. de golf**, golf course. **c. de prisioneros** *Mil.* prison camp. **c. de tiro**, riflerange. **c. santo**, graveyard. **c. visual**, field of vision. **a c. abierto**, in the open air. **a c. travieso**, cross-country
camuflaje /kamu'flahe/ *m*, camouflage
camuflar /kamu'flar/ *vt* to camouflage
can /kan/ *m*, dog; trigger; *Archit.* modillion; *Astron.* Dog Star
cana /'kana/ *f*, gray hair

Canadá /kana'ða/ Canada
canadiense /kana'ðiense/ *a* and *mf* Canadian
canal /ka'nal/ *m*, canal. *mf*, *Geol.* subterranean waterway; channel; *Anat.* canal, duct; defile, narrow valley; gutter; drinking trough; animal carcass. **abrir en c.**, to open up, split open
Canal de la Mancha /ka'nal de la 'mantʃa/ English Channel
canalera /kana'lera/ *f*, roof gutter
canaleta /kana'leta/ *f*, (wooden) trough; gutter (on roof)
canalete /kana'lete/ *m*, paddle
canalización /kanaliθa'θion; kanalisa'sion/ *f*, canalization; *Elec.* main, mains; piping, tubing
canalizar /kanali'θar; kanali'sar/ *vt* to make canals or channels; regulate waters of rivers, etc.; canalize
canalla /ka'naʎa; ka'naya/ *f*, *Inf.* mob, rabble. *m*, *Inf.* scoundrel
canallesco /kana'ʎesko; kana'yesko/ *a* scoundrelly, knavish; despicable
canalón /kana'lon/ *m*, gutter, spout; shovel hat; pantile
canana /ka'nana/ *f*, cartridge belt
canapé /kana'pe/ *m*, sofa
Canarias, las Islas /ka'narias, las 'islas/ the Canary Islands
canario /ka'nario/ **(-ia)** *m*, canary —*a* and *n* pertaining to or native of the Canary Islands.
canasta /ka'nasta/ *f*, hamper, basket; card game
canastilla /kanas'tiʎa; kanas'tiya/ *f*, small basket; layette
canastillo /kanas'tiʎo; kanas'tiyo/ *m*, basket-work tray
cáncamo /'kankamo/ *m*, ring-bolt
cancamusa /kanka'musa/ *f*, *Inf.* trick, deception
cancel /kan'θel; kan'sel/ *m*, draftscreen; *Eccl.* screen
cancela /kan'θela; kan'sela/ *f*, wrought-iron door
cancelación /kanθela'θion; kansela'sion/ *f*, cancellation; expunging
cancelar /kanθe'lar; kanse'lar/ *vt* to cancel; expunge, annul; abolish, blot out; pay off, clear (a mortgage)
cancelaría /kanθe'laria; kanse'laria/ *f*, papal chancery
cancelario /kanθe'lario; kanse'lario/ *m*, chancellor (universities)
cáncer /'kanθer; 'kanser/ *m*, cancer
cancerar /kanθe'rar; kanse'rar/ *vt* to consume; weaken; mortify; —*vr* suffer from cancer; become cancerous
cancerbero /kanθer'βero; kanser'βero/ *m*, *Myth.* Cerberus; *Fig.* unbribable guard
canceroso /kanθe'roso; kanse'roso/ *a* cancerous
cancha /'kantʃa/ *f*, *Sports.* fronton; (tennis) court; cockpit; yard; hippodrome; widest part of a river; road; toasted maize
canciller /kanθi'ʎer; kansi'yer/ *m*, chancellor; foreign minister; assistant vice-consul
cancillería /kanθiʎe'ria; kansiye'ria/ *f*, chancellorship; chancellery; foreign ministry
canción /kan'θion; kan'sion/ *f*, song; lyric poem; musical accompaniment; old name for any poetical composition. **volver a la misma c.**, *Fig.* to be always harping on the same theme
cancionero /kanθio'nero; kansio'nero/ *m*, collection of songs and verses; songbook
cancionista /kanθio'nista; kansio'nista/ *mf* singer; song writer
candado /kan'daðo/ *m*, padlock; earring
candeal /kande'al/ *a* white (of bread)
candela /kan'dela/ *f*, candle; horse-chestnut flower; candlestick; *Inf.* fire. **en c.**, *Naut.* vertical (of masts, etc.)
candelabro /kande'laβro/ *m*, candelabrum
candelaria /kande'laria/ *f*, Candlemas
candelero /kande'lero/ *m*, candlestick; lamp; candle maker or seller; *Naut.* stanchion
candente /kan'dente/ *a* candescent, red-hot
candidatear /kandiðate'ar/ *vi* to run (for office)
candidato /kandi'ðato/ **(-ta)** *a* candidate
candidatura /kandiða'tura/ *f*, candidature
candidez /kandi'ðeθ; kandi'ðes/ *f*, simplicity, ingenuousness; candidness

cándido /'kandiðo/ *a* white; simple, ingenuous; candid, frank

candil /kan'dil/ *m*, oil lamp; Greek lamp; tips of stag's horns; *Inf.* cock of a hat

candileja /kandi'leha/ *f*, oil reservoir of lamp; *pl* footlights, floats

candor /kan'dor/ *m*, extreme whiteness; sincerity, candor; simplicity, innocence

candoroso /kando'roso/ *a* candid, open; simple, honest

canela /ka'nela/ *f*, *Bot.* cinnamon; *Fig.* anything exquisitely perfect

canelo /ka'nelo/ *m*, cinnamon tree —*a* cinnamon-colored

cangilón /kanhi'lon/ *m*, pitcher, jar; bucket (for water); dredging bucket

cangreja /kaŋ'greha/ *f*, *Naut.* gaffsail. **c. de mesana,** *Naut.* jigger

cangrejo /kaŋ'greho/ *m*, crab. **c. de mar,** sea-crab. **c. ermitaño,** hermit crab

canguro /kaŋ'guro/ *m*, kangaroo

caníbal /ka'niβal/ *a* and *mf* cannibal

canibalismo /kaniβa'lismo/ *m*, cannibalism

canica /ka'nika/ *f*, marble (for playing with)

canícula /ka'nikula/ *f*, dog days; *Astron.* Dog star

caniculares /kaniku'lares/ *m pl* dog days

canijo /ka'niho/ *a Inf.* delicate, sickly; anemic, stunted

canilla /ka'niʎa; ka'niya/ *f*, long bone of leg or arm; any principal bones in bird's wing; tap, faucet; spool, reel; fault (in cloth)

canino /ka'nino/ *a* canine

canje /'kanhe/ *m*, (diplomacy, *Mil.*, *Com.*) exchange, substitution. **c. de prisioneros,** exchange of prisoners

canjear /kanhe'ar/ *vt* to exchange

cano /'kano/ *a* white-haired, hoary; ancient; *Poet.* white

canoa /ka'noa/ *f*, canoe; launch. **c. automóvil,** motor launch

canódromo /ka'noðromo/ *m*, dog-race track

canoero /kano'ero/ **(-ra)** *n* canoeist

canon /'kanon/ *m*, rule; (*Eccl. Print.*) canon; catalog; part of the Mass; *Mus.* canon, catch; tax *pl* canon law

canonesa /kano'nesa/ *f*, canoness

canónico /ka'noniko/ *a* canonic, canonical

canónigo /ka'nonigo/ *m*, canon; prebendary

canonización /kanoniθa'θion; kanonisa'sion/ *f*, canonization

canonizar /kanoni'θar; kanoni'sar/ *vt* to canonize; extol, exalt; approve, acclaim

canonjía /kanon'hia/ *f*, canonry, canonship; *Inf.* sinecure

canoso /ka'noso/ *a* white-haired, hoary

cansado /kan'saðo/ **(-da)** *a* tired; weary; exhausted; decadent; tiresome; *Inf.* fed up —*n* bore, tedious person

cansancio /kan'sanθio; kan'sansio/ *m*, fatigue, weariness

cansar /kan'sar/ *vt* to tire, weary; *Agr.* exhaust soil; bore; badger, annoy; —*vr* be tired; grow weary

cansino /kan'sino/ *a* worn-out (of horses, etc.)

cantable /kan'taβle/ *a* singable; *Mus.* cantabile

cantábrico /kan'taβriko/ **(-ca)** *a* and *n* Cantabrian

cantante /kan'tante/ *a* singing. *mf* professional singer

cantar /kan'tar/ *vi* to sing; twitter, chirp; extol; *Inf.* squeak, creak; *Fig.* call (cards); *Inf.* squeal, confess. *m*, song. **C. de los Cantares,** Song of Songs. **cantarlas claras,** to call a spade a spade

cántara /'kantara/ *f*, pitcher, jug

cantárida /kan'tariða/ *f*, Spanish fly

cántaro /'kantaro/ *m*, pitcher, jug; jugful; varying wine measure; ballot box; tax on spirits and oil

cantata /kan'tata/ *f*, cantata

cantatriz /kanta'triθ; kanta'tris/ *f*, singer, prima donna

cante /'kante/ *m*, song; singing

cantera /kan'tera/ *f*, *Mineral.* quarry; capacity, talent

cantería /kante'ria/ *f*, stone-cutting; quarrying; building made of hewn stone

cantero /kan'tero/ *m*, stone-cutter; quarryman

cántico /'kantiko/ *m*, *Eccl.* canticle; *Poet.* poem

cantidad /kanti'ðað/ *f*, quantity; large part; portion; sum of money; quantity (prosody). **c. llovida,** rainfall

cantiga /kan'tiga/ *or* **cántiga** /'kantiga/ *f*, old poetic form designed to be sung

cantil /kan'til/ *m*, cliff; steep rock

cantimplora /kantim'plora/ *f*, water cooler; canteen (of water); siphon

cantina /kan'tina/ *f*, wine cellar; canteen; refreshment room

cantinero /kanti'nero/ *m*, sutler; owner of a canteen

canto /'kanto/ *m*, singing; song; canto; epic or other poem; end, rim, edge; non-cutting edge (knives, swords); pebble, stone; angle (of a building). *Mus.* **c. llano,** plain-song. **al c. del gallo,** at cockcrow. **de c.,** on edge

cantón /kan'ton/ *m*, province, region; corner (of a street); cantonment; *Herald.* canton, quartering

cantonera /kanto'nera/ *f*, corner-piece (books, furniture, etc., as ornament); angle-iron; bracket, small shelf

cantor /kan'tor/ **(-ra)** *a* singing —*n* singer; song-bird

Cantórbery /kan'torβeri/ Canterbury

canturía /kantu'ria/ *f*, singing exercise; vocal music; monotonous song; droning; *Mus.* execution, technique

canturreo, /kantu'rreo,/ *m*, **canturria** *f*, humming; droning

canturriar /kantu'rriar/ *vi Inf.* to hum, sing under one's breath

caña /'kaɲa/ *f*, stalk; reed; bone of arm or leg; leg (of a trouser, stocking, boot, etc.); marrow; *Bot.* cane; tumbler, glass; wine measure; gallery (of mine); *pl* mock joust on horseback using **cañas** as spears. **c. de azúcar,** sugar-cane. **c. de pescar,** fishing rod. **c. del timón,** tiller *Naut.*

cañada /ka'ɲaða/ *f*, glen, gulch, gully, hollow, ravine, vale, cattle path; *West. Hem.* brook, cattle track

cañal /ka'ɲal/ *m*, cane-break; weir (for fish)

cañamazo /kaɲa'maθo; kaɲa'maso/ *m*, hempen canvas; embroidery canvas; embroidered canvas

cañamelar /kaɲame'lar/ *m*, sugar-cane plantation

cáñamo /'kaɲamo/ *m*, hemp

cañamón /kaɲa'mon/ *m*, hemp-seed

cañar /ka'ɲar/ *m*, canebrake; growth of reeds; fishgarth made of reeds

cañavalera /kaɲaβa'lera/ *f*, canefield

cañaveral /kaɲaβe'ral/ *m*, cane-brake; *West. Hem.* bamboo field

cañazo /ka'ɲaθo; ka'ɲaso/ *m*, blow with a cane

cañería /kaɲe'ria/ *f*, conduit; pipe; piping

cañero /ka'ɲero/ *m*, pipe layer

caño /'kaɲo/ *m*, pipe, tube, sewer; organ pipe; jet (of water); mine gallery

cañón /ka'ɲon/ *m*, pipe, cylindrical tube; flue; quill (of birds); cannon; soft down; *Archit.* shaft (of column); stack (of a chimney). **c. antiaéreo,** A.A. gun. **c. antitanque,** anti-tank gun. **c. de escalera,** well of a staircase; *Slang.* terrific-looking; absolutely gorgeous (e.g. mujer cañón)

cañonazo /kaɲo'naθo; kaɲo'naso/ *m*, cannon shot; roar of a cannon

cañonear /kaɲone'ar/ *vt* to bombard

cañoneo /kaɲo'neo/ *m*, cannonade; bombardment

cañonera /kaɲo'nera/ *f*, embrasure (for cannon)

cañonería /kaɲone'ria/ *f*, *Mil.* group of cannon; *Mus.* set of organ pipes

cañonero /kaɲo'nero/ *m*, gunboat

cañuto /ka'ɲuto/ *m*, *Bot.* internode; small pipe or tube; *Inf.* tale-bearer

caoba /ka'oβa/ *f*, *Bot.* mahogany

caos /'kaos/ *m*, chaos; confusion

caótico /ka'otiko/ *a* chaotic

capa /'kapa/ *f*, cloak; cape; *Eccl.* cope; coating; layer; cover; coat (animals); *Fig.* cloak, disguise; *Geol.* stratum. **la c. del cielo,** the canopy of heaven. *Fig. Inf.* **echar la c. al toro,** to throw one's cap over the windmill. *Naut.* **estarse** (*or* **ponerse) a la c.,** to lie to

capacete /kapa'θete; kapa'sete/ *m*, helmet

capacidad /kapaθi'ðað; kapasi'ðað/ *f*, capacity; extension, space; mental capacity, talent; opportunity, means; *Law.* capacity. **c. de compra,** buying power, purchasing power. **c. de producción,** output

capacitación /kapaθita'θion; kapasita'sion/ *f,* qualification, (act of) qualifying; (act of) training

capacitar /kapaθi'tar; kapasi'tar/ *vt* to capacitate, qualify, enable

capadura /kapa'ðura/ *f,* castration

capar /ka'par/ *vt* to castrate, geld; *Inf.* diminish, reduce

caparazón /kapara'θon; kapara'son/ *m,* caparison, horse blanket; waterproof cover; hood (of carriages); nosebag; shell (insects, crustaceans)

capataz /kapa'taθ; kapa'tas/ *m,* foreman; steward; overseer

capaz /ka'paθ; ka'pas/ *a* capacious; large, spacious; capable, competent; *Law.* able

capcioso /kap'θioso; kap'sioso/ *a* deceitful, artful; captious, carping

capear /kape'ar/ *vt* to steal a cape; play the bull with a cape (bullfighting); *Inf.*. put off with excuses, deceive; *Naut.* lie to

capellán /kape'ʎan; kape'yan/ *m,* chaplain; any ecclesiastic

capellanía /kapeʎa'nia; kapeya'nia/ *f,* chaplaincy

capelo /ka'pelo/ *m,* cardinal's hat; cardinalate

capeo /ka'peo/ *m,* playing the bull with a cape (bullfighting)

caperuza /kape'ruθa; kape'rusa/ *f,* hood, pointed cap; *Archit.* coping-stone

capigorrón /kapigo'rron/ *a Inf.* loafing. *m,* loafer, idler

capilar /kapi'lar/ *a* capillary

capilaridad /kapilari'ðað/ *f,* capillarity

capilla /ka'piʎa; ka'piya/ *f,* cowl, hood; chapel; *Eccl.* chapter; *Eccl.* choir. **c. ardiente,** chapelle ardente. **estar en c.,** to await execution (criminals); *Inf.* be in suspense, await anxiously

capillero /kapi'ʎero; kapi'yero/ *m,* sexton; churchwarden

capillo /ka'piʎo; ka'piyo/ *m,* baby's bonnet; cocoon of silkworm; flowerbud

capirotazo /kapiro'taθo; kapiro'taso/ *m,* box on the ear; fillip

capirote /kapi'rote/ *m,* academic hood and cap; hood (falconry); tall pointed cap. **ser tonto de c.,** *Inf.* to be a complete fool

capitación /kapita'θion; kapita'sion/ *f,* poll-tax, capitation

capital /kapi'tal/ *a* relating to the head; capital (sins, etc.); main, principal. *m,* capital, patrimony; *Com.* capital stock. *f,* capital (city). **c. pagado,** paid-in capital stock

capitalismo /kapita'lismo/ *m,* capitalism

capitalista /kapita'lista/ *a* capitalistic. *mf* capitalist

capitalización /kapitaliθa'θion; kapitalisa'sion/ *f,* capitalization

capitalizar /kapitali'θar; kapitali'sar/ *vt* to capitalize

capitán /kapi'tan/ *m,* captain, skipper; chief, leader; ringleader. *Aer.* **c. de aviación,** group captain. **c. de fragata,** *Nav.* commander. **c. de puerto,** harbor master. **c. general de ejército,** field-marshal

capitana /kapi'tana/ *f,* admiral's ship; *Inf.* captain's wife

capitanear /kapitane'ar/ *vt* to captain, command; *Fig.* guide, lead

capitanía /kapita'nia/ *f,* captaincy; captainship

capitel /kapi'tel/ *m,* *Archit.* capital

capitolio /kapi'tolio/ *m,* dignified building; *Archit.* acropolis; Capitol

capitulación /kapitula'θion; kapitula'sion/ *f,* agreement, pact; capitulation; *pl* marriage articles

capitular /kapitu'lar/ *a* capitulary, belonging to a Chapter. *m,* capitular, member of a Chapter —*vi* to make an agreement; capitulate; sing prayers; arrange order

capítulo /ka'pitulo/ *m,* *Eccl.* Chapter; meeting of town council, etc.; chapter (of book); item (in a budget); determination, decision

capó /ka'po/ *m,* *Auto.* hood

capón /ka'pon/ *a* castrated; gelded. *m,* capon; bundle of firewood or vines

caponera /kapo'nera/ *f,* coop for fattening capons;

Inf. gaol; *Inf.* place where one lives well free of charge

capota /ka'pota/ *f,* *Bot.* head of teasel; bonnet; hood (of vehicles)

capote /ka'pote/ *m,* short, brightly colored cape (used by bullfighters); cape coat; (cards) slam; *Inf.* scowl

capricho /ka'pritʃo/ *m,* caprice, fancy; strong desire

caprichoso /kapri'tʃoso/ *a* capricious; whimsical

caprichudo /kapri'tʃuðo/ *a* headstrong; capricious

Capricornio /kapri'kornio/ *m,* Capricorn

cápsula /'kapsula/ *f,* cartridge-case; bottlecap; (*Bot.* *Med. Chem. Zool.*) capsule

captar /kap'tar/ *vt* gain, attract (goodwill, attention, etc.); *Mech.* collect; monitor (foreign broadcasts)

captor /kap'tor/ *m,* capturer

captura /kap'tura/ *f,* *Law.* capture; seizing, arrest

capturar /kaptu'rar/ *vt* to capture; arrest, apprehend

capucha /ka'putʃa/ *f,* hood; cowl; *Print.* circumflex accent

capuchina /kapu'tʃina/ *f,* Capuchin nun; *Bot.* nasturtium; table-lamp with an extinguisher

capuchino /kapu'tʃino/ (**-na**) *a* and *n* Capuchin

capucho /ka'putʃo/ *m,* cowl

capullo /ka'puʎo; ka'puyo/ *m,* cocoon; flower bud; acorn cup; *Anat.* prepuce

caqui /'kaki/ *m,* khaki; khaki color

cara /'kara/ *f,* face; likeness, aspect; façade; front; surface; side (of metal, etc.); mien. **c. a c.,** face to face; frankly; openly. *Inf.* **c. de juez,** severe face. *Inf.* **c. de pascua,** smiling face. *Inf.* **c. de vinagre,** sour face. **c. o cruz,** heads or tails. **de c.,** opposite. **hacer a dos caras,** to be deceitful, be two-faced. **hacer c.(a),** to stand up to

caraba /ka'raβa/ *f,* *Slang.* 25-centimo coin

cárabe /'karaβe/ *m,* amber

carabina /kara'βina/ *f,* carbine; rifle

carabinazo /karaβi'naθo; karaβi'naso/ *m,* report of a carbine

carabinero /karaβi'nero/ *m,* carabineer; customs' guard, revenue guard; customs officer, customs official

caracol /kara'kol/ *m,* snail; snail's shell; cure; *Zool.* cochlea; winding stair. **c. marino,** periwinkle. **¡Caracoles!** Fancy!

caracola /kara'kola/ *f,* conch shell used as a horn

caracolear /karakole'ar/ *vi* to prance from side to side (horses)

carácter /ka'rakter/ *m,* sign, mark; character, writing (gen. *pl*); style of writing; brand (animals); nature, temperament; character, individuality, strongmindedness, energy, firmness; condition, state, capacity. **comedia de c.,** psychological play. **en su c. de,** as in one's capacity as. **caracteres de imprenta,** printing types

característica /karakte'ristika/ *f,* quality, characteristic; *Math.* characteristic; actress who plays the part of an old woman

característico /karakte'ristiko/ *a* characteristic, distinctive. *m,* actor who plays roles of old men

caracterización /karakteriθa'θion; karakterisa'sion/ *f,* characterization; *Theat.* make-up

caracterizar /karakteri'θar; karakteri'sar/ *vt* to characterize; confer an office, honor, dignity, on; *Theat.* create a character; —*vr Theat.* to make up, dress as, a character

caraísmo /kara'ismo/ *m,* Karaism

caraíta /kara'ita/ *a* and *mf* Karaite

¡caramba! /ka'ramba/ *interj* gosh!; blast!

carámbano /ka'rambano/ *m,* icicle

carambola /karam'βola/ *f,* cannon (billiards); *Inf.* double effect; *Inf.* trick, deception

caramelo /kara'melo/ *m,* caramel; toffee

caramillo /kara'miʎo; kara'miyo/ *m,* flageolet; small flute, pipe; gossip, intrigue

carantamaula /karanta'maula/ *f,* *Inf.* hideous mask; ugly person

carapacho /kara'patʃo/ *m,* carapace, shell

carátula /ka'ratula/ *f,* mask; *Fig.* dramatic art, the theater

caravana /kara'βana/ *f,* caravan, group of traders, pilgrims, etc. (especially in East); *Inf.* crowd of excursionists, picnickers, etc.

¡caray! /ka'rai/ *interj* blast!; gosh!

carbólico /kar'βoliko/ *a* carbolic

carbón /kar'βon/ *m*, coal; charcoal; black chalk, crayon. **c. bituminoso**, soft coal. **c. de coque**, coke. **c. de leña**, charcoal. **c. mineral**, coal, anthracite. **mina de c.**, coal-mine

carboncillo /karβon'θiʎo; karβon'siyo/ *m*, charcoal crayon

carbonear /karβone'ar/ *vt* to turn into charcoal; *Naut.* coal

carboneo /karβo'neo/ *m*, coaling

carbonera /karβo'nera/ *f*, coal-cellar, coal-house, etc.; coal-scuttle; woman who sells charcoal or coal; charcoal burner

carbonería /karβone'ria/ *f*, coal or charcoal merchant's office

carbonero /karβo'nero/ *a* relating to coal or charcoal. *m*, collier; charcoal maker; coal merchant; *Naut.* coal-ship

carbónico /kar'βoniko/ *a Chem.* carbonic

carbonífero /karβo'nifero/ *a* carboniferous

carbonizar /karβoni'θar; karβoni'sar/ *vt* to carbonize

carbono /kar'βono/ *m*, *Chem.* carbon

carbonoso /karβo'noso/ *a* carbonaceous; coaly

carbunco /kar'βunko/ *m*, *Med.* carbuncle

carbúnculo /kar'βunkulo/ *m*, carbuncle, ruby

carburador /karβura'ðor/ *m*, carburetor

carcaj /kar'kah/ *m*, quiver (for arrows)

carcajada /karka'haða/ *f*, burst of laughter, guffaw. **reírse a carcajadas**, to roar with laughter

carcajearse /karkahe'arse/ *vi* to guffaw

carcamal /karka'mal/ *m*, *Inf.* dotard

cárcel /'karθel; 'karsel/ *f*, prison, jail

carcelario /karθe'lario; karse'lario/ *a* prison, jail

carcelero /karθe'lero; karse'lero/ **(-ra)** *a* jail —*n* jailer

cárcola /'karkola/ *f*, treadle (of a loom)

carcoma /kar'koma/ *f*, wood-worm; dry rot; *Fig.* gnawing care; spendthrift

carcomer /karko'mer/ *vt* to gnaw wood (worms); *Fig.* undermine (health, etc.); —*vr* be worm-eaten

carda /'karða/ *f*, card, carding; teasel head; card brush; *Inf.* reprimand

cardador /karða'ðor/ **(-ra)** *n* carder, comber

cardadura /karða'ðura/ *f*, carding; carding frame

cardar /kar'ðar/ *vt* to card, tease; brush up (felt, etc.)

cardenal /karðe'nal/ *m*, cardinal; cardinal bird; bruise

cardenalato /karðena'lato/ *m*, cardinalate, cardinalship

cardenillo /karðe'niʎo; karðe'niyo/ *m*, verdigris; *Art.* verditer

cárdeno /'karðeno/ *a* livid

cardíaco /kar'ðiako/ *a Med.* cardiac

cardinal /karði'nal/ *a* principal; cardinal (point); *Gram.* cardinal (number)

cardiógrafo /kar'ðiografo/ *m*, *Med.* cardiograph

cardiograma /karðio'grama/ *m*, *Med.* cardiogram

cardizal /karði'θal; karði'sal/ *m*, waste land covered with thistles and weeds

cardo /'karðo/ *m*, *Bot.* thistle

carear /kare'ar/ *vt* to confront; compare; —*vi* turn towards, face; —*vr* meet; come together

carecer /kare'θer; kare'ser/ *vi irr* to be short; lack, need (e.g. *Carece de las condiciones necesarias*, It lacks the necessary conditions). See **conocer**

carena /ka'rena/ *f*, *Naut.* bottom; careening

carenar /kare'nar/ *vt* to careen

carencia /ka'renθia; ka'rensia/ *f*, shortage, lack

carestía /kares'tia/ *f*, shortage, scarcity; famine; dearness, high price

careta /ka'reta/ *f*, mask; beekeeper's veil; fencing mask. *Fig.* **quitar la c.** (a), to unmask

carey /ka'rei/ *m*, *Zool.* shell turtle; tortoise-shell

carga /'karga/ *f*, loading; *Elec.* charging, charge; load; burden, weight; cargo; explosive charge; *Fig.* imposition; tax; duty, obligation. *Naut.* **c. de profundidad**, depth charge

cargadero /karga'ðero/ *m*, place where goods are loaded or unloaded

cargado /kar'gaðo/ *a* loaded; heavy, sultry; strong (tea, coffee). **c. de cadenas**, (prisoner, etc.) in chains. **c. de espaldas**, round-shouldered

cargador /karga'ðor/ *m*, loader; porter; dockhand; pitchfork; rammer; *Mech.* stoker; *Elec.* charger

cargamento /karga'mento/ *m*, *Naut.* cargo, freight, shipload

cargar /kar'gar/ *vt* to load; charge (guns, etc.); stoke; overburden; tax, impose; blame for, charge with; *Inf.* annoy, bore; *Argentina Inf.* to kid, tease; *Com.* charge, book; *Mil.* attack; (football) tackle; —*vi* tip, slope; (*with con*) carry away; be loaded with (fruit); assume responsibility; (*with sobre*) importune, urge; lean against; —*vr* turn (head, etc.); lower, grow darker (sky); (*with de*) be abundant (in or with); load oneself with

cargazón /karga'θon; karga'son/ *f*, cargo; loading; heaviness; darkness (of the sky)

cargo /'kargo/ *m*, loading; load, weight; post, office; duty, obligation; management, charge; care; *Com.* debit; accusation. *Com.* **el c. y la data**, debit and credit. **hacerse c. de**, to take charge of; understand; consider carefully. **ser en c.** (a), to be debtor (to)

cariacontecido /kariakonte'θiðo; kariakonte'siðo/ *a* crestfallen, disappointed; glum

cariancho /kari'antʃo/ *a Inf.* broadfaced

cariarse /ka'riarse/ *vr* to become carious

cariátide /ka'riatiðe/ *f*, *Archit.* caryatid

caribe /ka'riβe/ *a* Caribbean. *mf* cannibal, savage

caricatura /karika'tura/ *f*, caricature

caricaturesco /karikatu'resko/ *a* caricaturish

caricaturista /karikatu'rista/ *mf* caricaturist

caricaturizar /karikaturi'θar; karikaturi'sar/ *vt* to caricature

caricia /ka'riθia; ka'risia/ *f*, caress

caridad /kari'ðað/ *f*, charity; charitableness; alms

caries /'karies/ *f*, caries

carilargo /kari'largo/ *a Inf.* long-faced

carilla /ka'riʎa; ka'riya/ *f*, *dim* small face; mask; page (of a book)

carilleno /kari'ʎeno; kari'yeno/ *a Inf.* plump-faced, round-faced

carillón /kari'ʎon; kari'yon/ *m*, peal (of bells)

cariño /ka'riɲo/ *m*, affection; love; caress affectionately (gen. *pl*); fondness, inclination. **con c.**, affectionately

cariñoso /kari'ɲoso/ *a* affectionate; loving; kind

carirredondo /karirre'ðondo/ *a Inf.* roundfaced

carismático /karis'matiko/ *a* charismatic

caritativo /karita'tiβo/ *a* charitable

cariz /ka'riθ; ka'ris/ *m*, appearance of the sky; look, face; aspect; *Inf.* outlook (for a business deal, etc.)

carlista /kar'lista/ *a* and *mf* Carlist

carmelita /karme'lita/ *a* and *mf* Carmelite

carmen /'karmen/ *m*, country house and garden (Granada); song; poem

carmesí /karme'si/ *a* crimson. *m*, crimson color; cramoisy

carmín /kar'min/ *m*, red, carmine color; red wild rose-tree and flower

carnada /kar'naða/ *f*, bait

carnaje /kar'nahe/ *m*, salted meat

carnal /kar'nal/ *a* carnal; lascivious; materialistic, worldly; related by blood

carnalidad /karnali'ðað/ *f*, carnality

carnaval /karna'βal/ *m*, carnival. **martes de c.**, Shrove Tuesday

carnavalesco /karnaβa'lesko/ *a* carnival

carne /'karne/ *f*, flesh; meat; pulpy part of fruit; carnality. **c. concentrada**, meat extract. **c. congelada**, frozen meat. **c. de gallina** *Fig.* gooseflesh. **c. de membrillo**, quince cheese or conserve. **c. y hueso**, *Fig.* flesh and blood. *Inf.* **cobrar carnes**, to put on weight. **poner toda la c. en el asador**, *Inf.* to put all one's eggs in one basket

carnerada /karne'raða/ *f*, flock of sheep

carnerero /karne'rero/ **(-ra)** *n* shepherd

carnero /kar'nero/ *m*, sheep; mutton; mortuary; charnel-house; family burial vault. **c. marino**, *Zool.* seal

carnestolendas /karnesto'lendas/ f pl three days of carnival before Ash Wednesday

carnet /kar'net/ m, notebook, diary; identity card; membership card, pass. **c. de chófer,** driving license

carnicería /karniθe'ria; karnise'ria/ f, butcher's shop; carnage, slaughter

carnicero /karni'θero; karni'sero/ a carnivorous; inhuman, cruel. m, butcher

carnívoro /kar'niβoro/ a carnivorous. m, carnivore

carnosidad /karnosi'ðað/ f, proud flesh; local fat; fatness

carnoso /kar'noso/ a meaty; fleshy; full of marrow; Bot. pulpy, juicy

caro /'karo/ a beloved; expensive; dear —adv expensively; dear

carolingio /karo'linhio/ **(-ia)** a and n Carolingian

carótida /ka'rotiða/ f, carotid artery

carpa /'karpa/ f, Ichth. carp. **c. dorada,** goldfish

carpanta /kar'panta/ f, Inf. violent hunger

Cárpatos, los Montes /'karpatos, los 'montes/ the Carpathian Mountains

carpeta /kar'peta/ f, table or chest cover, doily; writing case; portfolio; docket, letter file

carpetazo, dar /karpe'taθo, dar; karpe'taso, dar/ vt to shelve (a project, etc.)

carpintear /karpinte'ar/ vi to carpenter

carpintería /karpinte'ria/ f, carpenter's shop; carpentry

carpinteril /karpinte'ril/ a carpentering

carpintero /karpin'tero/ m, carpenter, joiner; Theat. scene-shifter. **c. de carretas,** wheelwright. **c. de ribera,** shipwright

carraca /ka'rraka/ f, rattle; ratchet-drill

Carrapempe /karra'pempe/ m, Old Nick

carrascal /karras'kal/ m, field of pinoaks

carraspear /karraspe'ar/ vi to clear one's throat, cough

carraspera /karras'pera/ f, Inf. hoarseness

carraspique /karras'pike/ m, Bot. candytuft

carrera /ka'rrera/ f, run; race; racing; racecourse; Astron. course; high road; route; Mas. layer, course; line, row; Fig. ladder (in stockings, etc.); course; duration (of life); career, profession; conduct; girder. **c. de fondo,** long-distance race. **c. de relevos, c. de equipos,** relay race. **a c. abierta, a c. tendida,** at full speed

carrerista /karre'rista/ mf racing enthusiast; professional racer

carreta /ka'rreta/ f, long, narrow two-wheeled cart; wagon; tumbril

carretada /karre'taða/ f, cart-load; Inf. great deal, mass

carretaje /karre'tahe/ m, cartage; carriage, transport

carrete /ka'rrete/ m, spool, reel, bobbin; fishing reel; Elec. coil; Photo. film spool

carretear /karrete'ar/ vt to cart; drive a cart

carretela /karre'tela/ f, calash

carretera /karre'tera/ f, high road

carretería /karre'teria/ f, number of carts; carting trade; cartwright's yard

carretero /karre'tero/ m, cartwright; carter, driver

carretilla /karre'tiʎa; karre'tiya/ f, wheelbarrow; hand cart; railway truck; squib. **de c.,** Inf. mechanically, without thought; (with saber, repetir, etc.) by rote

carretón /karre'ton/ m, truck, trolley; hand cart

carril /ka'rril/ m, wheel mark; furrow, rut; cart road, narrow road; rail (railways, etc.)

carrillera /karri'ʎera; karri'yera/ f, jaw (of some animals); chin strap; pl bonnet strings, etc.

carrillo /ka'rriʎo; ka'rriyo/ m, cheek; jowl

carriola /ka'rriola/ f, truckle bed; curricle

carro /'karro/ m, cart; cartload; car, chariot; carriage (of a typewriter, etc.); chassis; Astron. Plow, Great Bear. Mil. **c. blindado,** armored car. Mil. **c. de asalto,** tank. **c. de mudanzas,** moving van. **c. de regar,** watercart

carrocería /karroθe'ria; karrose'ria/ f, place where carriages are made, sold, repaired; Auto. coachwork, body shop

carrocha /ka'rrotʃa/ f, eggs (of insects)

carrochar /karro'tʃar/ vi to lay eggs (insects)

carromato /karro'mato/ m, road wagon; covered wagon

carroña /ka'rroɲa/ f, putrid flesh; carrion

carroza /ka'rroθa; ka'rrosa/ f, elegant coach; state coach; carriage; float (for tableaux, etc.); Naut. awning

carruaje /ka'rruahe/ m, carriage; any vehicle

carta /'karta/ f, letter; charter; royal order; playing card; chart, map. **c. certificada,** registered letter. **c. de amparo,** safe-conduct. **c. de crédito,** Com. letter of credit. **c. de marear,** sea chart. **c. de naturaleza,** naturalization papers. **c. de pésame,** letter of condolence. **c. de venta,** Com. bill of sale. **c. ejecutoria de hidalguía,** letters patent of nobility. **carta-poder,** letter of proxy, proxy. **cartas rusas,** (game of) consequences. **poner las cartas boca arriba,** Fig. to lay one's cards on the table

cartabón /karta'βon/ m, set-square; shoemaker's slide; quadrant

cartaginés /kartahi'nes/ **(-esa)** a and n Carthaginian

Cartago /'kartago/ Carthage

cartapacio /karta'paθio; karta'pasio/ m, note-book; schoolbag, satchel; file, batch of papers

cartear /karte'ar/ vi Cards. to play low; —vr to correspond by letter

cartel /kar'tel/ m, placard, poster; cartel; pasquinade, lampoon. **fijar carteles,** to placard

cartela /kar'tela/ f, tablet (for writing); slip (of paper, etc.); Archit. console, bracket

cartelera /karte'lera/ f, billboard

cartelero /karte'lero/ m, billpaster, billsticker

carteo /kar'teo/ m, correspondence (by letter)

cartera /kar'tera/ f, pocketbook; wallet; dispatch-case; portfolio; notebook; pocket flap; office of a cabinet minister; Com. shares

cartería /karte'ria/ f, sorting room (in a post-office)

carterista /karte'rista/ mf pickpocket

cartero /kar'tero/ m, mail carrier, postman

cartesiano /karte'siano/ **(-na)** a and n Cartesian

Cartesio /kar'tesio/ Descartes

carteta /kar'teta/ f, lansquenet (card game)

cartilaginoso /kartilahi'noso/ a cartilaginous

cartílago /kar'tilago/ m, cartilage

cartilla /kar'tiʎa; kar'tiya/ f, first reading book; primer; certificate of ordination; note-book; liturgical calendar. **c. de racionamiento,** ration book

cartografía /kartogra'fia/ f, cartography

cartógrafo /kar'tografo/ m, map maker

cartón /kar'ton/ m, pasteboard, cardboard; Archit. bracket; Art. cartoon, design

cartuchera /kartu'tʃera/ f, cartridge-pouch; cartridge-belt

cartucho /kar'tutʃo/ m, cartridge; paper cone

cartuja /kar'tuha/ f, Carthusian Order or monastery

cartujano /kartu'hano/ a Carthusian

cartujo /kar'tuho/ m, Carthusian monk; Inf. taciturn, reserved man

cartulina /kartu'lina/ f, Bristol board, oaktag, pasteboard, card

carúncula /ka'runkula/ f, caruncle, comb of cock, etc.

casa /'kasa/ f, house; home; household; residence, dwelling; family house; Com. firm. **c. consistorial,** town hall. **c. cuna,** crèche. **c. de campo,** country-house. **c. de empeño,** pawnshop. **c. de huéspedes,** boarding house, lodging-house. **c. de los sustos,** haunted house (at amusement park). **c. de moneda,** mint. **c. de socorro,** First Aid Post. **c. de vecindad,** tenement. **c. mala,** house of ill repute. **c. solar** or **c. solariega,** family seat. **en c.,** at home (also sport usage). **poner c.,** to set up house

casaca /ka'saka/ f, dress coat. **volver la c.,** to become a turncoat, change one's allegiance

casación /kasa'θion; kasa'sion/ f, Law. cassation

casadero /kasa'ðero/ a marriageable

casadoro /kasa'ðoro/ m, Costa Rica bus

casamata /kasa'mata/ f, Mil. casemate

casamiento /kasa'miento/ m, marriage; wedding

casar /ka'sar/ vt to marry (of a priest); Law. repeal; Inf. marry off; join; match, harmonize; —vi and vr (with con) to get married

casar /ka'sar/ *m*, group of houses

casca /'kaska/ *f*, grape skin; tan (bark); shell, peel, rind

cascabel /kaska'βel/ *m*, small bell (for harness, etc.). **serpiente de c.**, rattlesnake. *Inf.* **ser un c.**, to be feather-brained

cascabeleo /kaska'βeleo/ *m*, jingling of bells

cascabillo /kaska'βiʎo; kaska'βiyo/ *m*, husk (of cereals)

cascada /kas'kaða/ *f*, cascade; waterfall

cascadura /kaska'ðura/ *f*, cracking, crack

cascajo /kas'kaho/ *m*, gravel, shingle; *Inf.* broken, old things, junk; nuts

cascanueces /kaska'nueθes; kaska'nueses/ *m*, nutcrackers

cascar /kas'kar/ *vt* to crack, split, break; *Inf.* beat; *Fig. Inf.* break down (of health); —*vi Inf.* talk, chatter

cáscara /'kaskara/ *f*, shell; peel, rind; bark. *Med.* **c. sagrada**, cascara

cascarón /kaska'ron/ *m*, eggshell; *Archit.* vault

cascarrabias /kaska'rraβias/ *mf Inf.* spitfire

casco /'kasko/ *m*, cranium; broken fragment of china, glass, etc.; crown of hat; helmet; tree of saddle; bottle; tank, pipe; barrel; *Naut.* hull; hoof; quarter (of fruit); *pl Inf.* head. **c. colonial**, sun-helmet. **c. respiratorio**, smoke-helmet

cascote /kas'kote/ *m*, rubble, ruins

caseoso /kase'oso/ *a* cheesy

caserío /kase'rio/ *m*, group of houses; country house

casero /ka'sero/ *a* home made; home bred; familiar; informa; *Inf.* domesticated, home-loving; domestic. *m*, *landlord*; caretaker; tenant

caserón /kase'ron/ *m*, large tumbledown house, mansion, hall

caseta /ka'seta/ *f*, hut; cottage; booth, stall. **c. de baños**, bathing van

casi /'kasi/ *adv* almost, nearly. **c. c.**, very nearly

casilla /ka'siʎa; ka'siya/ *f*, hut; cabin; lodge; ticket office; pigeon-hole. *Aer.* **c. del piloto**, cockpit

casillero /kasi'ʎero; kasi'yero/ *m*, file cabinet, filing cabinet; locker (as in a locker room); set of pigeonholes; *Sports.* scoreboard; *Rail.* crossing guard

casino /ka'sino/ *m*, casino; club

caso /'kaso/ *m*, happening, event; chance, hazard; occasion, opportunity; case, matter; (*Med. Gram.*) case. **en el c. de**, in a position to (e.g. *No estamos en el c. de pagar tanto dinero*. We are in no position to pay so much money). **en tal c.**, in such a case. **en todo c.**, in any case. **no hacer c. de**, to take no notice of. **venir al c.**, to be opportune

caspa /'kaspa/ *f*, dandruff; scab

caspio /'kaspio/ *a* Caspian

¡cáspita! /'kaspita/ *interj* Amazing! Wonderful!

casquete /kas'kete/ *m*, helmet; skullcap; half wig

casquijo /kas'kiho/ *m*, gravel

casquillo /kas'kiʎo; kas'kiyo/ *m*, tip, cap, ferrule; socket; arrow-head; metal cartridge-case

casquivano /kaski'βano/ *a Inf.* giddy, feather-brained

casta /'kasta/ *f*, race; caste; breed (animals); kind, species, quality. **de buena c.**, pedigree (e.g. *perros de buena c.*, pedigree dogs)

castaña /kas'taɲa/ *f, Bot.* chestnut; knot, bun (of hair)

castañar /kasta'ɲar/ *m*, chestnut plantation or grove

castañetear /kastaɲete'ar/ *vi* to play the castanets; snap one's fingers; chatter (of teeth); knock together (of knees)

castaño /kas'taɲo/ *a* chestnut-colored. *m*, chestnut tree; chestnut wood. **c. de Indias**, horse-chestnut tree

castañuela /kasta'ɲuela/ *f*, castanet. **tocar las castañuelas**, to play the castanets

castellán /kaste'ʎan; kaste'yan/ *m*, castellan

castellano /kaste'ʎano; kaste'yano/ **(-na)** *n* Castilian; Spaniard. *m*, Spanish (language); castellan —*a* Castilian; Spanish

casticismo /kasti'θismo; kasti'sismo/ *m*, purity (of language); Spanish spirit; traditionalism

castidad /kasti'ðað/ *f*, chastity

castigador /kastiga'ðor/ *a* punishing. *m*, punisher; *Inf.* lady-killer

castigadora /kastiga'ðora/ *f, Inf.* man-hunter

castigar /kasti'gar/ *vt* to punish; chastise; chasten, advise; pain, grieve; correct, edit; decrease (expenses); *Com.* allow a discount

castigo /kas'tigo/ *m*, punishment; emendation, correction

Castilla /kas'tiʎa; kas'tiya/ Castile

castillo /kas'tiʎo; kas'tiyo/ *m*, castle; howdah. **c. de naipes**, house of cards. **c. de proa**, *Naut.* forecastle. **c. fuerte**, fortified castle. *Inf.* **hacer castillos en el aire**, to build castles in the air or in Spain

castizo /kas'tiθo; kas'tiso/ *a* pure-blooded; prolific; pure (of language); typically Spanish; traditional

casto /'kasto/ *a* chaste; pure, unsullied

castor /kas'tor/ *m*, *Zool.* beaver (animal and fur); soft, woollen cloth

castración /kastra'θion; kastra'sion/ *f*, castration, gelding

castrado /kas'traðo/ *a* castrated. *m*, *Inf.* eunuch

castrador /kastra'ðor/ *m*, castrator, gelder

castrapo /kas'trapo/ *m*, mixed Spanish and Galician spoken in Galicia, Spain

castrar /kas'trar/ *vt* to castrate, geld; prune; remove honeycomb from hives; weaken

castrense /kas'trense/ *a* military

castrista /kas'trista/ *a* and *mf* Castroite

casual /ka'sual/ *a* accidental, casual

casualidad /kasuali'ðað/ *f*, chance, coincidence. **por c.**, by chance. **ser mucha c. que...**, to be too much of a coincidence that...

casucha /ka'sutʃa/ *f, Inf.* tumbledown hut

casuista /ka'suista/ *a* casuistic. *mf* casuist

casuística /ka'suistika/ *f*, casuistry

casulla /ka'suʎa; ka'suya/ *f*, chasuble

cata /'kata/ *f*, tasting; taste, sample

catabolismo /kataβo'lismo/ *m*, catabolism

cataclismo /kata'klismo/ *m*, cataclysm

catacumbas /kata'kumbas/ *f pl*, catacombs

catador /kata'ðor/ *m*, taster, sampler

catadura /kata'ðura/ *f*, tasting; look, countenance (gen. qualified)

catafalco /kata'falko/ *m*, catafalque

catalán /kata'lan/ **(-ana)** *a* and *n* Catalan, Catalonian. *m*, Catalan (language)

catalejo /kata'leho/ *m*, telescope

cataléptico /kata'leptiko/ *a* cataleptic

catálisis /ka'talisis/ *f, Chem.* catalysis

catalítico /kata'litiko/ *a* catalytic

catalogar /katalo'gar/ *vt* to catalog, list

catálogo /ka'talogo/ *m*, catalog, list

Cataluña /kata'luɲa/ Catalonia

cataplasma /kata'plasma/ *f*, cataplasm

catapulta /kata'pulta/ *f*, catapult

catar /ka'tar/ *vt* to taste, sample; see, examine; inspect; regard

catarata /kata'rata/ *f*, cataract, waterfall; *Med.* cataract (of the eyes)

catarral /kata'rral/ *a* catarrhal

catarro /ka'tarro/ *m*, catarrh; common cold

catástrofe /ka'tastrofe/ *f, Lit.* tragic climax; catastrophe

catastrófico /katas'trofiko/ *a* catastrophic

catavino /kata'βino/ *m*, taster (cup)

catavinos /kata'βinos/ *m*, professional wine taster; *Inf.* tippler, tavern haunter

cate /'kate/ *m, Slang* flunk (failure in a course at school)

catecismo /kate'θismo; kate'sismo/ *m*, catechism

catecúmeno /kate'kumeno/ **(-na)** *n* catechumen

cátedra /'kateðra/ *f*, university chair; chair in a Spanish **instituto**; professorship; university lecture room; subject taught by professor; reading desk, lectern; *Eccl.* throne; *Eccl.* see. **c. del espíritu santo**, pulpit. **c. de San Pedro**, Holy See

catedral /kate'ðral/ *f*, and *a* cathedral

catedrático /kate'ðratiko/ **(-ca)** *n* professor

categoría /katego'ria/ *f, Philos.* category; class, rank

categórico /kate'goriko/ *a* categorical, downright

cateo /ka'teo/ *m, West. Hem.* sampling; prospecting; house search (by the police)

catequismo /kate'kismo/ *m*, catechism; question and answer method of teaching

catequista /kate'kista/ *mf* catechist

catequizar /kateki'θar; kateki'sar/ *vt* to catechize; persuade, induce

caterva /ka'terβa/ *f,* crowd, throng; jumble, collection

catéter /ka'teter/ *m, Surg.* probe; catheter

catódico /ka'toðiko/ *a Elec.* cathodic

cátodo /'katoðo/ *m,* cathode

catolicidad /katoliθi'ðað; katolisi'ðað/ *f,* catholicity; catholic world

catolicismo /katoli'θismo; katoli'sismo/ *m,* Catholicism

católico /ka'toliko/ **(-ca)** *a* universal, catholic; infallible —*a* and *n* Catholic (by religion)

catorce /ka'torθe; ka'torse/ *a* fourteen; fourteenth. *m,* number fourteen; fourteenth (of days of month)

catorzavo /kator'θaβo; kator'saβo/ *a* fourteenth

catre /'katre/ *m,* camp-bed; truckle-bed; cot

caucáseo /kau'kaseo/ **(-ea)** *a* and *n* Caucasian

Cáucaso, el /'kaukaso, el/ the Caucasus

cauce /'kauθe; 'kause/ *m,* river or stream bed; ditch, irrigation canal

cauchal /kau'tʃal/ *m,* rubber plantation

cauchera /kau'tʃera/ *f,* rubber tree

cauchero /kau'tʃero/ *m,* rubber planter

caucho /'kautʃo/ *m,* caoutchouc, rubber

caución /kau'θion; kau'sion/ *f,* caution, precaution; surety; security

caucional /kauθio'nal; kausio'nal/ *a* See **libertad**

caudal /kau'ðal/ *m,* wealth, capital; flow, volume (of water); plenty, abundance (e.g. *un c. de conocimientos,* a wealth of knowledge)

caudaloso /kauða'loso/ *a* carrying much water; wealthy; abundant

caudillo /kau'ðiʎo; kau'ðiyo/ *m,* head, leader; chief tain. **el C.,** (title of Francisco Franco)

causa /'kausa/ *f,* cause; reason, motive; lawsuit; *Law.* trial. **c. final,** *Philos.* final cause. **c. pública,** public welfare. **ser c. bastante para...,** to be reason enough to...

causador /kausa'ðor/ **(-ra)** *a* motivating —*n* occasioner, originator

causalidad /kausali'ðað/ *f,* causality

causante /kau'sante/ *a* causative, causing. *m, Law.* principal; *Mexico* taxpayer

causar /kau'sar/ *vt* to cause; occasion .

causticidad /kaustiθi'ðað; kaustisi'ðað/ *f,* causticity; mordacity

cáustico /'kaustiko/ *a* burning, caustic; scathing; mordant; *Surg.* caustic

cautela /kau'tela/ *f,* caution; astuteness, cunning

cauteloso /kaute'loso/ *a* cautious; cunning

cauterio /kau'terio/ *m,* cautery

cauterización /kauteriθa'θion; kauterisa'sion/ *f,* cauterization

cauterizar /kauteri'θar; kauteri'sar/ *vt* to cauterize

cautivar /kauti'βar/ *vt* to capture; captivate, charm; attract; —*vi* become a prisoner

cautiverio /kauti'βerio/ *m,* captivity

cautivo /kau'tiβo/ **(-va)** *a* and *n* captive

cauto /'kauto/ *a* cautious; prudent; sly

cava /'kaβa/ *f,* digging (especially vines); wine cellar in royal palaces

cavador /kaβa'ðor/ **(-ra)** *n* digger, hoer

cavadura /kaβa'ðura/ *f,* digging, hoeing; sinking (wells)

cavar /ka'βar/ *vt* to dig, hoe; sink (wells); —*vi* hollow; *Fig.* go deeply into a thing

caverna /ka'βerna/ *f,* cavern, cave; *Med.* cavity (generally in the lung)

cavernícola /kaβer'nikola/ *a* cave. **hombre c.,** caveman

cavernoso /kaβer'noso/ *a* cavernous; caverned; *Fig.* hollow (cough, etc.); deaf

cavidad /kaβi'ðað/ *f,* cavity; sinus; cell

cavilación /kaβila'θion; kaβila'sion/ *f,* caviling

cavilar /kaβi'lar/ *vt* to cavil; criticize

caviloso /kaβi'loso/ *a* captious

cayado /ka'yaðo/ *m,* crook; bishop's crozier

caz /kaθ; kas/ *m,* channel, canal; head-race, flume

caza /'kaθa; 'kasa/ *f,* hunting; hunt, chase; game. *m, Aer.* fighter. *Aer.* **c. lanzacohetes,** rocket-launching aircraft. **c. nocturno,** night fighter. *Naut.* **dar c.,** to pursue

cazaautógrafos /,kaθaau'tografos; ,kasaau'tografos/ *m,* autograph hunter

cazabombardero /,kaθaβombar'ðero; ,kasaβombar-'ðero/ *m, Aer.* fighter bomber

cazadero /kaθa'ðero; kasa'ðero/ *m,* hunting ground

cazador /kaθa'ðor; kasa'ðor/ *a* hunting. *m, Mil.* chasseur; huntsman

cazadora /kaθa'ðora; kasa'ðora/ *f,* huntress; jacket; forage cap

cazadotes /kaθa'ðotes; kasa'ðotes/ *m,* dowry hunter

cazafortunas /kaθafor'tunas; kasafor'tunas/ *mf* fortune hunter

cazar /ka'θar; ka'sar/ *vt* to hunt, chase; *Fig. Inf.* run to earth; *Fig. Inf.* catch out; *Inf.* overcome by flattery

cazasubmarino /kaθasuβma'rino; kasasuβma'rino/ *m,* submarine chaser

cazatorpedero /kaθatorpe'ðero; kasatorpe'ðero/ *m, Naut.* torpedo-boat destroyer

cazo /'kaθo; 'kaso/ *m,* ladle; dipper

cazolada /kaθo'laða; kaso'laða/ *f,* panful

cazoleta /kaθo'leta; kaso'leta/ *f,* small pan; bowl (of pipe, etc.); sword guard; boss of a shield; pan (of a firelock)

cazuela /ka'θuela; ka'suela/ *f,* earthenware cooking dish; stew-pot; part of theater formerly reserved for women; *Theat.* gallery

cazumbrón /kaθum'βron; kasum'βron/ *m,* cooper

cazurro /ka'θurro; ka'surro/ *a Inf.* unsociable; surly, boorish

c.c.p. /θeθe'pe; sese'pe/ abbrev. of **con copia para**

ce /θe; se/ *f,* name of the letter C —*interj* Look! Chist! **ce por be,** in detail

cebada /θe'βaða; se'βaða/ *f,* barley (plant and grain). **c. perlada,** pearl barley

cebadal /θeβa'ðal; seβa'ðal/ *m,* barley field

cebadera /θeβa'ðera; seβa'ðera/ *f,* nose-bag; barley bin

cebadero /θeβa'ðero; seβa'ðero/ *m,* barley dealer

cebado /θe'βaðo; se'βaðo/ *a* on the prowl; having tasted human flesh (animal)

cebar /θe'βar; se'βar/ *vt* to feed or fatten (animals); fuel, feed (furnace, etc.); prime, charge (firearms, etc.); start up (machines); bait (fish hook); stimulate (passion, etc.); —*vi* stick in, penetrate (nails, screws, etc.); —*vr* put one's mind to; grow angry. **cebarse en vanas esperanzas,** to nurture vain hopes

cebo /'θeβo; 'seβo/ *m,* fodder; detonator; encouragement, food; bait

cebolla /θe'βoʎa; se'βoya/ *f,* onion; onion bulb; any bulbous stem; oil bulb (of lamp). **c. escalonia,** shallot

cebollana /θeβo'ʎana; seβo'yana/ *f,* chive

cebollero /θeβo'ʎero; seβo'yero/ **(-ra)** *n* onion seller

cebolleta /θeβo'ʎeta; seβo'yeta/ *f,* leek; young onion

cebollino /θeβo'ʎino; seβo'yino/ *m,* onion seed; onion bed; chive

cebra /'θeβra; 'seβra/ *f,* zebra

ceca /'θeka; 'seka/ *f,* mint (for coining money); name of mosque in Cordova. **de C. en Meca,** from pillar to post, hither and thither

cecear /θeθe'ar; sese'ar/ *vi* to lisp

ceceo /θe'θeo; se'seo/ *m,* lisping

ceceoso /θeθe'oso; sese'oso/ *a* lisping

cecial /θe'θial; se'sial/ *m,* dried fish

cecina /θe'θina; se'sina/ *f,* dried salt meat

cedazo /θe'ðaθo; se'ðaso/ *m,* sieve, strainer

ceder /θe'ðer; se'ðer/ *vt* to cede, give up; transfer; —*vi* give in, yield; diminish, decrease (fever, storm, etc.); fail, end; happen, turn out; sag, give, stretch. **No c. la fama a,** to be no less famous than

cedro /'θeðro; 'seðro/ *m,* cedar tree; cedar wood. **c. dulce,** red cedar

cédula /'θeðula; 'seðula/ *f,* document, certificate, card. *Eccl.* **c. de comunión,** Communion card. **c. personal,** identity card. **c. real,** royal letters patent

céfiro /'θefiro; 'sefiro/ *m,* west wind; *Poet.* zephyr

cegajoso /θega'hoso; sega'hoso/ *a* blear-eyed

cegar /θe'gar; se'gar/ *vi irr* to become blind; —*vt* to put out the eyes; *Fig.* blind; wall up, close up, stop up; infatuate —*Pres. Indic.* **ciego, ciegas, ciega, ciegan.** *Pres. Subjunc.* **ciegue, ciegues, ciegue, cieguen**

cegato /θe'gato; se'gato/ *a Inf.* short-sighted

ceguedad, ceguera /θege'δaδ, θe'gera; sege'δaδ, se'gera/ *f,* blindness; delusion; ignorance

Ceilán /θei'lan; sei'lan/ Ceylon

ceja /'θeha; 'seha/ *f,* eyebrow; cloud cap; mountain peak; *Mus.* bridge (of stringed instruments). *Fig.* **quemarse las cejas,** to burn the midnight oil

cejar /θe'har; se'har/ *vi* to go backwards; give way, hesitate

cejijunto /θehi'hunto; sehi'hunto/ *a* having eyebrows that almost meet, beetle-browed

cejo /'θeho; 'seho/ *m,* river mist

cejudo /θe'huδo; se'huδo/ *a* having long thick eyebrows

celada /θe'laδa; se'laδa/ *f,* helmet; ambush; fraud, trick

celador /θela'δor; sela'δor/ **(-ra)** *a* watchful, zealous —*n* supervisor; caretaker; guard (at a museum, etc.)

celaje /θe'lahe; se'lahe/ *m,* sky with scudding clouds (gen. *pl*); skylight, window; promising sign, presage

celar /θe'lar; se'lar/ *vt* to be zealous in discharge of duties; spy upon; watch; oversee, superintend; conceal; engrave

celda /'θelda; 'selda/ *f,* cell

celdilla /θel'diʎa; sel'diya/ *f,* cell (bees, wasps, etc.); (*Zool. Bot.*) cell; *Bot.* capsule

celebérrimo, célebre /θele'βerrimo; sele'βerrimo,/ *a superl* most celebrated

celebración /θeleβra'θion; seleβra'sion/ *f,* celebration; applause

celebrador /θeleβra'δor; seleβra'δor/ **(-ra)** *n* celebrator; applauder

celebrante /θele'βrante; sele'βrante/ *a* celebrating. *m, Eccl.* celebrant

celebrar /θele'βrar; sele'βrar/ *vt* to celebrate; applaud; praise; venerate; hold, conduct; **c. que** + *subj,* to be happy that, be glad that —*vt* and *vi Eccl.* officiate; —*vr* take place

célebre /'θeleβre; 'seleβre/ *a* famous

celebridad /θeleβri'δaδ; seleβri'δaδ/ *f,* fame, celebrity; magnificence, show, pomp

celeridad /θeleri'δaδ; seleri'δaδ/ *f,* celerity

celeste /θe'leste; se'leste/ *a* celestial, heavenly

celestial /θeles'tial; seles'tial/ *a* celestial, heavenly; perfect, delightful; *Inf.* foolish (ironical)

celestina /θeles'tina; seles'tina/ *f,* procuress (allusion to *Tragicomedia de Calixto y Melibea*)

celestinaje /θelesti'nahe; selesti'nahe/ *m,* pandering, procuring

celibato /θeli'βato; seli'βato/ *m,* celibacy; *Inf.* bachelor

célibe /'θeliβe; 'seliβe/ *a* celibate, unmarried. *mf* unmarried person

celo /'θelo; 'selo/ *m,* enthusiasm, ardor; religious zeal; devotion; jealousy; heat, rut; *pl* jealousy, suspicion. **dar celos (a),** to make jealous

celosía /θelo'sia; selo'sia/ *f,* lattice; Venetian blind

celoso /θe'loso; se'loso/ *a* zealous; jealous; suspicious

celta /'θelta; 'selta/ *a* Celtic. *mf* Celt

célula /'θelula; 'selula/ *f,* cell

celular /θelu'lar; selu'lar/ *a* cellular —*m,* cellular phone.

celuloide /θelu'loiδe; selu'loiδe/ *f,* celluloid

celulosa /θelu'losa; selu'losa/ *f,* cellulose

celuloso /θelu'loso; selu'loso/ *a* cellular

cementación /θementa'θion; sementa'sion/ *f,* cementation

cementar /θemen'tar; semen'tar/ *vt* to cement

cementerio /θemen'terio; semen'terio/ *m,* cemetery

cemento /θe'mento; se'mento/ *m,* cement

cena /'θena; 'sena/ *f,* evening meal; supper; Last Supper

cenacho /θe'natʃo; se'natʃo/ *m,* marketing bag

cenáculo /θe'nakulo; se'nakulo/ *m,* cenacle

cenador /θena'δor; sena'δor/ *m,* diner out; arbor, pergola

cenagal /θena'gal; sena'gal/ *m,* quagmire; *Fig.* impasse

cenagoso /θena'goso; sena'goso/ *a* miry, muddy

cenar /θe'nar; se'nar/ *vi* to dine, sup; —*vt* eat for evening meal, sup off

cenceño /θen'θeɲo; sen'seɲo/ *a* slim, thin

cencerrada /θenθe'rraδa; sense'rraδa/ *f,* noisy mock serenade given to widows or widowers on the first night of their new marriage

cencerrear /θenθerre'ar; senserre'ar/ *vi* to jingle; *Inf.* play out of tune; bang in the wind, rattle; squeak

cencerreo /θenθe'rreo; sense'rreo/ *m,* jingling; jangle; rattling; squeaking

cencerro /θen'θerro; sen'serro/ *m,* cow-bell

cendal /θen'dal; sen'dal/ *m,* gauze; *Eccl.* stole; barbs of a feather

cenefa /θe'nefa; se'nefa/ *f,* border; valance, flounce; edging

cenicero /θeni'θero; seni'sero/ *m,* ash-pan; ash-pit; ash-tray

ceniciento /θeni'θiento; seni'siento/ *a* ash colored, ashen. **la Cenicienta,** Cinderella

cenit /'θenit; 'senit/ *m, Astron.* zenith; *Fig.* peak, summit

ceniza /θe'niθa; se'nisa/ *f,* ash, cinders

cenotafio /θeno'tafio; seno'tafio/ *m,* cenotaph

censo /'θenso; 'senso/ *m,* census; agreement for settlement of an annuity; annual ground rent; leasehold

censor /θen'sor; sen'sor/ *m,* censor; censorious person; *Educ.* proctor

censual /θen'sual; sen'sual/ *a* pertaining to census, annuity, rents

censualista /θensua'lista; sensua'lista/ *mf* annuitant

censura /θen'sura; sen'sura/ *f,* censorship; criticism; blame, reproach; scandal, gossip; *Psychol.* censorship

censurable /θensu'raβle; sensu'raβle/ *a* reprehensible; censorable

censurar /θensu'rar; sensu'rar/ *vt* to judge; censure; criticize

centauro /θen'tauro; sen'tauro/ *m, Myth.* centaur

centavo /θen'taβo; sen'taβo/ *m,* hundredth part; cent

centella /θen'teʎa; sen'teya/ *f,* lightning; spark; flash; *Fig.* spark (of anger, affection, etc.)

centellador /θenteʎa'δor; senteya'δor/ *a* flashing

centellear /θenteʎe'ar; senteye'ar/ *vi* to flash; twinkle; sparkle

centelleo /θente'ʎeo; sente'yeo/ *m,* scintillation; sparkle; flash

centén /θen'ten; sen'ten/ *m,* Spanish gold coin once worth 100 reals and later 25 pesetas

centena /θen'tena; sen'tena/ *f,* hundred

centenal, centenar /θente'nal, θente'nar; sente'nal, sente'nar/ *m,* hundred; centenary; rye field. **a centenares,** by the hundred, in crowds

centenario /θente'nario; sente'nario/ **(-ia)** *a* centenary —*n* centenarian. *m,* centenary

centeno /θen'teno; sen'teno/ *m, Bot.* rye

centésimo /θen'tesimo; sen'tesimo/ *a* and *m,* hundredth

centígrado /θen'tigraδo; sen'tigraδo/ *a* centigrade

centigramo /θenti'gramo; senti'gramo/ *m,* centigram

centilitro /θenti'litro; senti'litro/ *m,* centiliter

centímetro /θenti'metro; senti'metro/ *m,* centimeter. **c. cúbico,** cubic centimeter, milliliter

céntimo /'θentimo; 'sentimo/ *a* hundredth. *m,* centime (coin)

centinela /θenti'nela; senti'nela/ *mf Mil.* sentry, sentinel; person on watch. **estar de c.,** to be on sentry duty; be on guard

centolla /θen'toʎa; sen'toya/ *f,* marine crab

centón /θen'ton; sen'ton/ *m,* patchwork quilt

central /θen'tral; sen'tral/ *a* central; centric. *f,* head office; central depot; mother house. **c. de fuerza,** power-house. **c. telefónica,** telephone exchange

centralilla, centralita /θentra'liʎa, θentra'lita; sentra'liya, sentra'lita/ *f,* local exchange, private exchange

centralismo /θentra'lismo; sentra'lismo/ *m,* centralism

centralista /θentra'lista; sentra'lista/ *a* centralistic. *mf* centralist

centralización /θentraliθa'θion; sentralisa'sion/ *f,* centralization

centralizador /θentraliθa'ðor; sentralisa'ðor/ *a* centralizing

centralizar /θentrali'θar; sentrali'sar/ *vt* to centralize

centrar /θen'trar; sen'trar/ *vt* to center

céntrico /'θentriko; 'sentriko/ *a* central, centric; centrally located; downtown

centrífugo /θen'trifugo; sen'trifugo/ *a* centrifugal

centrípeto /θen'tripeto; sen'tripeto/ *a* centripetal

centro /'θentro; 'sentro/ *m,* center; headquarters, meeting place, club; center, hub; middle; core (of a rope); *Fig.* focus. *Phys.* **c. de gravedad,** center of gravity. **c. de mesa,** table center-piece. *Anat.* **centro nervioso,** nerve center

centroamericano /θentroameri'kano; sentroameri'kano/ **(-na)** *a* and *n* Central American

céntuplo /'θentuplo; 'sentuplo/ *a* centuple

centuria /θen'turia; sen'turia/ *f,* century

centurión /θentu'rion; sentu'rion/ *m,* centurion

ceñidamente /θeɲiða'mente; seɲiða'mente/ tightly (e.g. *un argumento c. organizado,* a tightly organized plot)

ceñido /θe'ɲiðo; se'ɲiðo/ *a* thrifty; wasp-waisted, slender waisted; fitting (of garments)

ceñidor /θeɲi'ðor; seɲi'ðor/ *m,* girdle, belt

ceñir /θe'ɲir; se'ɲir/ *vt irr* to girdle; surround; shorten, abbreviate; —*vr* be moderate (speech, expenditure, etc.); conform, confine oneself (to). **ceñirse a las reglas,** to abide by the rules —*Pres. Indic.* **ciño, ciñes, ciñen.** *Pres. Part.* **ciñendo.** *Preterite* **ciñó, ciñeron.** *Pres. Subjunc.* **ciña,** etc —*Imperf. Subjunc.* **ciñese,** etc.

ceño /'θeɲo; 'seɲo/ *m,* band, hoop; frown; *Fig.* dark outlook

ceñudo /θe'ɲuðo; se'ɲuðo/ *a* frowning

cepa /'θepa; 'sepa/ *f,* stump; vine-stock; root (tails, antlers, etc.); *Fig.* origin, trunk (of a family); *Biol.* strain. **de la más pura c.,** of the best quality

cepillar /θepi'ʎar; sepi'yar/ *vt* to brush; plane; smooth

cepillo /θe'piʎo; se'piyo/ *m,* brush; plane; poor-box, offertory-box. **c. para los dientes,** toothbrush. **c. para ropa,** clothes-brush. **c. para el suelo,** scrubbing-brush. **c. para las uñas,** nail-brush

cepo /'θepo; 'sepo/ *m,* bough; wooden stocks; snare; trap; poor-box; collecting-box

cera /'θera; 'sera/ *f,* beeswax; wax; wax candles, etc., used at a function. *Inf.* **ser como una c.,** to be like wax (in the hands of)

cerador /θera'ðor; sera'ðor/ *m,* floor waxer (person)

ceradora /θera'ðora; sera'ðora/ *f,* floor waxer (machine)

cerámica /θe'ramika; se'ramika/ *f,* ceramics; ceramic art, pottery

cerámico /θe'ramiko; se'ramiko/ *a* ceramic

cerbatana /θerβa'tana; serβa'tana/ *f,* blow-pipe, pop-gun; pea-shooter; ear-trumpet

cerca /'θerka; 'serka/ *f,* fence, wall

cerca /'θerka; 'serka/ *adv* near. **c. de,** near to; almost, nearly (e.g. *c. de las once,* nearly eleven o'clock)

cercado /θer'kaðo; ser'kaðo/ *m,* enclosure, fenced in place; fence

cercanía /θerka'nia; serka'nia/ *f,* nearness, proximity; (gen. *pl*) outskirts, surroundings

cercano /θer'kano; ser'kano/ *a* near, neighboring; impending, early

cercar /θer'kar; ser'kar/ *vt* to enclose; build a wall or fence round; to lay siege to; crowd round; *Mil.* surround

cercenamiento /θerθena'miento; sersena'miento/ **(a)** *m,* curtailment (of)

cercenar /θerθe'nar; serse'nar/ *vt* to lop off the ends, clip; curtail, diminish; abridge; whittle

cerciorar /θerθio'rar; sersio'rar/ *vt* to assure, confirm; —*vr* make sure

cerco /'θerko; 'serko/ *m,* ring, hoop; fence; siege; small conversational circle; spin, circling; halo (sun, moon); frame; sash (of a window). **poner c.** (a), to lay siege to, blockade

cerda /'θerða; 'serða/ *f,* sow; bristle

Cerdeña /θer'ðeɲa; ser'ðeɲa/ Sardinia

cerdo /'θerðo; 'serðo/ *m,* pig, hog

cerdoso /θer'ðoso; ser'ðoso/ *a* bristly

cereal /θere'al; sere'al/ *a* and *m,* cereal

cerebelo /θere'βelo; sere'βelo/ *m, Anat.* cerebellum

cerebral /θere'βral; sere'βral/ *a* cerebral

cerebro /θe'reβro; se'reβro/ *m,* cerebrum; brain; intelligence

cerebro-espinal /θe'reβro-espi'nal; se'reβro-espi'nal/ *a* cerebrospinal

ceremonia /θere'monia; sere'monia/ *f,* ceremony; function, display; formality. **de c.,** ceremonial; formally. **por c.,** for politeness' sake

ceremonial /θeremo'nial; seremo'nial/ *a* ceremonial. *m,* ceremony; rite; protocol (rules of behavior)

ceremonioso /θeremo'nioso; seremo'nioso/ *a* ceremonious; formal, over-courteous

cerero /θe'rero; se'rero/ *m,* wax-chandler

cereza /θe'reθa; se'resa/ *f,* cherry

cerezal /θere'θal; sere'sal/ *m,* cherry orchard

cerezo /θe'reθo; se'reso/ *m,* cherry tree; cherry wood

cerilla /θe'riʎa; se'riya/ *f,* wax taper; match; ear wax

cerner /θer'ner; ser'ner/ *vt irr* to sieve; watch, observe; *Fig.* sift, clarify; —*vi* bolt (of plants); drizzle; —*vr* waddle; hover; threaten (of evil, etc.) —*Pres. Indic.* **cierno, ciernes, cierne, ciernen.** *Pres. Subjunc.* **cierna, ciernas, cierna, ciernan**

cernícalo /θer'nikalo; ser'nikalo/ *m, Ornith.* kestrel; *Inf.* lout

cernidillo /θerni'ðiʎo; serni'ðiyo/ *m,* drizzle; teetering walk

cernido /θer'niðo; ser'niðo/ *m,* sifting, sieving; sifted flour

cerniduras /θerni'ðuras; serni'ðuras/ *f pl,* siftings

cero /'θero; 'sero/ *m, Math.* zero; naught; (tennis) love. *Fig. Inf.* **ser un c.,** to be a mere cipher

cerote /θe'rote; se'rote/ *m,* cobbler's wax. *Inf.* fear

cerquillo /θer'kiʎo; ser'kiyo/ *m,* tonsure; welt (of a shoe)

cerquita /θer'kita; ser'kita/ *adv* very near, hard by

cerradero, /θerra'ðero; serra'ðero,/ *m,* **cerradera** *f,* bolt staple; catch of a lock; clasp or strings of a purse

cerradizo /θerra'ðiθo; serra'ðiso/ *a* closable, lockable

cerrado /θe'rraðo; se'rraðo/ *a* closed; compact; incomprehensible, obscure; overcast, cloudy; *Inf.* taciturn; secretive. *m,* enclosure

cerradura /θerra'ðura; serra'ðura/ *f,* fastening, lock; closing, locking

cerraja /θe'rraha; se'rraha/ *f,* lock (of a door); bolt

cerrajería /θerrahe'ria; serrahe'ria/ *f,* locksmith's craft; locksmith's workshop or shop

cerrajero /θerra'hero; serra'hero/ *m,* locksmith

cerramiento /θerra'miento; serra'miento/ *m,* closing, locking up; fence; enclosure, shooting preserve; partition wall

cerrar /θe'rrar; se'rrar/ *vt irr* to close; lock, fasten, bolt; shut up; *Mech.* shut off, turn off; fold up; block or stop up; seal (letters, etc.); close down; terminate; obstruct; (*with con*) attack; —*vi* close; close in (of night, etc.); —*vr* heal up (wounds); close (flowers); *Radio.* close down; crowd together; *Fig.* stand firm. *Inf.* **cerrarse la espuela,** to take a nightcap, have a last drink. **c. la marcha,** to bring up the rear. **al c. la edición,** stop press. See **acertar**

cerrazón /θerra'θon; serra'son/ *f,* dark, overcast sky heralding a storm

cerril /θe'rril; se'rril/ *a* rough, rocky; wild, untamed (cattle, horses); *Inf.* boorish

cerrillar /θerri'ʎar; serri'yar/ *vt* to mill coins

cerro /'θerro; 'serro/ *m,* neck of an animal; spine, backbone; hill. *Fig.* **irse por los cerros de Úbeda,** to go off the track, indulge in irrelevancies

cerrojo /θe'rroho; se'rroho/ *m,* bolt (of a door, etc.); lock (of a door, gun, etc.)

certamen /θer'tamen; ser'tamen/ *m,* contest; competition; match

certero /θer'tero; ser'tero/ *a* well-aimed; sure, well-timed; knowledgeable, sure

certeza, certidumbre /θer'teθa, θerti'ðumbre; ser'tesa, serti'ðumbre/ *f,* certitude, assurance

certificación /θertifika'θion; sertifika'sion/ *f,* certification; certificate; affidavit

certificado /θertifi'kaðo; sertifi'kaðo/ *a* certified; registered. *m*, registered letter; certificate

certificar /θertifi'kar; sertifi'kar/ *vt* to certify; register (letter, etc.)

certificatorio /θertifika'torio; sertifika'torio/ *a* certifying or serving to certify

certísimo /θer'tisimo; ser'tisimo/ *a* learned form of the superlative of **cierto** (see **certísimo**)

certitud /θerti'tuð; serti'tuð/ *f*, certitude

cervantino /θerβan'tino; serβan'tino/ *a* Cervantine

cervato /θer'βato; ser'βato/ *m*, fawn

cervecería /θerβeθe'ria; serβese'ria/ *f*, brewery; alehouse

cervecero /θerβe'θero; serβe'sero/ **(-ra)** *n* brewer; beer seller

cerveza /θer'βeθa; ser'βesa/ *f*, beer, ale. **c. negra,** stout

cerviz /θer'βiθ; ser'βis/ *f*, cervix, nape (of neck). **doblar** (*or* **bajar**) **la c.,** to humble oneself

cesación /θesa'θion; sesa'sion/ *f*, cessation, stopping

cesante /θe'sante; se'sante/ *a* dismissed; pensioned off. **declarar c.** (**a**), to dismiss (a person from a post). **estar c.,** to be out of a job

cesantía /θesan'tia; sesan'tia/ *f*, status of dismissed or retired official; retirement pension

cesar /θe'sar; se'sar/ *vi* to cease, stop, end; leave an employment; desist; retire

cesáreo /θe'sareo; se'sareo/ *a* Cesarean; imperial

cese /'θese; 'sese/ *m*, stopping of payment for an employment

cesión /θe'sion; se'sion/ *f*, cession; transfer; resignation; *Law.* release

cesionario /θesio'nario; sesio'nario/ **(-ia)** *n* cessionary, transferee

cesionista /θesio'nista; sesio'nista/ *mf* grantor, transferer

césped /'θespeð; 'sespeð/ *m*, grass, sward; sod, lawn

cesta /'θesta; 'sesta/ *f*, basket, hamper; *Sports.* racket; cradle (for a wine bottle)

cestada /θes'taða; ses'taða/ *f*, basketful

cestería /θeste'ria; seste'ria/ *f*, basketmaking, basketweaving; basket factory; basket shop; basketwork

cestero /θes'tero; ses'tero/ **(-ra)** *n* basket maker or seller

cesto /'θesto; 'sesto/ *m*, basket, hamper, skip

cesura /θe'sura; se'sura/ *f*, cesura

cetáceo /θe'taθeo; se'taseo/ *a* and *m*, *Zool.* cetacean

cetorrino /θeto'rrino; seto'rrino/ *m*, basking shark

cetrería /θetre'ria; setre'ria/ *f*, falconry

cetrino /θe'trino; se'trino/ *a* greenish-yellow; sallow; citrine; melancholy; reserved, aloof

cetro /'θetro; 'setro/ *m*, scepter; verge; reign

Cevenes, los /θe'βenes, los; se'βenes, los/ the Cevennes

chabacanería /tʃaβakane'ria/ *f*, bad taste; vulgarity

chabacano /tʃaβa'kano/ *a* vulgar, common; rude, uncouth

chacal /tʃa'kal/ *m*, *Zool.* jackal

cháchara /'tʃatʃara/ *f*, *Inf.* empty chatter; verbiage

chacharear /tʃatʃare'ar/ *vi* to chatter; gabble, cackle

chacharero /tʃatʃa'rero/ *a Inf.* chattering; talkative

chacolotear /tʃakolote'ar/ *vi* to clatter, clink (loose horseshoe)

chacota /tʃa'kota/ *f*, merriment, mirth

chacotear /tʃakote'ar/ *vi Inf.* to be merry, have fun

chacotón /tʃako'ton/ *a* of a boisterous humor

chafado /tʃa'faðo/ *a* taken aback; disappointed

chafallar /tʃafa'ʎar; tʃafa'yar/ *vt Inf.* to mend carelessly, botch

chafandín /tʃafan'din/ *m*, vain fool

chafar /tʃa'far/ *vt* to flatten; crumple, crease (clothes); *Inf.* heckle

chafarrinar /tʃafarri'nar/ *vt* to stain, mark, blot

chaflán /tʃa'flan/ *m*, bevel edge, chamfer

chagrén /tʃa'gren/ *m*, shagreen leather

chal /tʃal/ *m*, shawl

chalán /tʃa'lan/ *m*, horse-dealer

chalana /tʃa'lana/ *f*, *Naut.* wherry, lighter

chalanear /tʃalane'ar/ *vt* to bargain; indulge in sharp practice

chalar /tʃa'lar/ *vt* to drive mad; enamor

chaleco /tʃa'leko/ *m*, waistcoat; cardigan

chalina /tʃa'lina/ *f*, flowing scarf, artist's bow

Chalo /'tʃalo/ pet form of the male given name *Carlos* "Charles', hence = English *Chuck; Bud, Mac* (in direct address to a male whose name one does not know)

chalote /tʃa'lote/ *m*, shallot

chalupa /tʃa'lupa/ *f*, shallop; launch; canoe; long boat, ship's boat

chamar /tʃa'mar/ *vt Inf.* to palm off, barter

chamarasca /tʃama'raska/ *f*, brushwood, tinder

chamarilero /tʃamari'lero/ **(-ra)** *n* secondhand dealer

chamarreta /tʃama'rreta/ *f*, sheepskin jacket; *Mexico* jacket

chambelán /tʃambe'lan/ *m*, court chamberlain

chambergo /tʃam'βergo/ *a* pertaining to the Chambergo regiment. *m*, broad-brimmed hat

chambón /tʃam'βon/ *a Inf.* awkward, clumsy; lucky

chambonada /tʃambo'naða/ *f*, *Inf.* blunder; fluke, chance

chambra /'tʃambra/ *f*, dressing-jacket, peignoir, negligee

chamicera /tʃami'θera; tʃami'sera/ *f*, piece of scorched earth (woodland, etc.)

chamorro /tʃa'morro/ *a* close-cropped, shorn (hair)

champán /tʃam'pan/ *m*, champagne. **c. obrero,** humorous cider

champaña /tʃam'paɲa/ *m*, champagne

champar /tʃam'par/ *vt Inf.* to cast in a person's face, remind

champú /tʃam'pu/ *m*, shampoo

chamuscar /tʃamus'kar/ *vt* to scorch; singe

chamusquina /tʃamus'kina/ *f*, scorching; singeing; *Inf.* brawl

chanada /tʃa'naða/ *f*, *Inf.* trick, mischievous act

chancearse /tʃanθe'arse; tʃanse'arse/ *vr* to joke

chancero /tʃan'θero; tʃan'sero/ *a* joking, facetious

chanchollada /tʃantʃo'ʎaða; tʃantʃo'yaða/ *f*, dirty trick, foul play, trick

chanchullo /tʃan'tʃuʎo; tʃan'tʃuyo/ *m*, *Inf.* fraud

chanciller /tʃanθi'ʎer; tʃansi'yer/ *m*, chancellor

chancillería /tʃanθiʎe'ria; tʃansiye'ria/ *f*, chancery

chancla /'tʃankla/ *f*, down at heel shoe; heelless slipper

chancleta /tʃan'kleta/ *f*, heelless slipper, babouche. *mf Inf.* ninny

chancleteo /tʃankle'teo/ *m*, clicking of heelless slippers

chanclo /'tʃanklo/ *m*, overshoe; Wellington

chanfaina /tʃan'faina/ *f*, *Cul.* savory fricassee

chanflón /tʃan'flon/ *a* tough, coarse; ungainly

chantaje /tʃan'tahe/ *m*, blackmail

chantajista /tʃanta'hista/ *mf* blackmailer

chantar /tʃan'tar/ *vt* to put on, clothe; *Inf.* tell plainly. *Inf.* **c. sus verdades,** to tell hometruths

chanza /'tʃanθa; 'tʃansa/ *f*, joke, jest

chanzoneta /tʃanθo'neta; tʃanso'neta/ *f*, canzonetta; *Inf.* joke

chapa /'tʃapa/ *f*, plate, sheet; veneer; clasp; *Inf.* prudence, common sense; rouge. **c. de hierro,** sheetiron. **c. de identidad,** number plate

chapado a la antigua /tʃa'paðo a la an'tigua/ *a* oldfashioned

chapalear /tʃapale'ar/ *vi* to dabble in water; splash; clatter (of a horseshoe)

chapaleo /tʃapa'leo/ *m*, dabbling, paddling; splash; clattering, clink (of a horseshoe)

chapaleteo /tʃapale'teo/ *m*, lapping of water; splashing (of rain)

chaparrear /tʃaparre'ar/ *vi* to pour with rain

chaparrón /tʃapa'rron/ *m*, heavy shower of rain, downpour

chapear /tʃape'ar/ *vt* to veneer; —*vi* clatter (loose horseshoe)

chapeo /tʃa'peo/ *m*, hat

chaperón /tʃape'ron/ *m*, hood

chapeta /tʃa'peta/ *f*, *dim* clasp; red flush or spot on cheek

chapetón /tʃape'ton/ **(-ona)** *n West Hem.* recently arrived European, especially Spaniard

chapín /tʃa'pin/ m, cork-soled leather overshoe (for women) Obs.

chapino /tʃa'pino/ a and m, Mexico contemptuous Guatemalan

chapitel /tʃapi'tel/ m, Archit. capital; spire

chapodar /tʃapo'ðar/ vt to prune, lop off branches; cut down, reduce

chapotear /tʃapote'ar/ vt to sponge, moisten, damp; —vi paddle, splash; dabble or trail the hands (in water)

chapoteo /tʃapo'teo/ m, moistening, sponging; paddling, splashing; dabbling

chapucear /tʃapuθe'ar/ tʃapuse'ar/ vt to botch, do badly; bungle

chapuceramente /tʃapuθera'mente; tʃapusera'mente/ adv awkwardly. **hablar el japonés c.,** to speak broken Japanese

chapucería /tʃapuθe'ria; tʃapuse'ria/ f, roughness, poor workmanship; botch

chapucero /tʃapu'θero; tʃapu'sero/ a rough, badly finished; bungling, clumsy, awkward

chapurrado /tʃapu'rraðo/ a broken (e.g. hablar un italiano c., to speak broken Italian)

chapurrar, chapurrear /tʃapu'rrar, tʃapurre'ar/ vt to speak badly (a language); jabber; Inf. mix (drinks)

chapuz /tʃa'puθ; tʃa'pus/ m, ducking, submerging; plunge; unimportant job; clumsiness

chapuzar /tʃapu'θar; tʃapu'sar/ vt to duck, submerge; plunge

chaqué /tʃa'ke/ m, morning coat; morning suit

chaqueta /tʃa'keta/ f, jacket; Mech. casing

chaquete /tʃa'kete/ m, backgammon

chaquetilla /tʃake'tiʎa; tʃake'tiya/ f, short jacket; coatee; blazer

chaquetón /tʃake'ton/ m, short coat. **c. de piloto,** Aer. pea-jacket

charabán /tʃara'βan/ m, charabanc

charada /tʃa'raða/ f, charade

charanguero /tʃaraŋ'guero/ a rough, badly finished; clumsy. m, Andalusian boat

charca /'tʃarka/ f, pond, pool; reservoir

charco /'tʃarko/ m, puddle; Inf. sea

charla /'tʃarla/ f, Inf. chatter; conversation; talk, informal lecture

charlar /tʃar'lar/ vi Inf. to prattle, chatter; chat, converse; give a talk (on)

charlatán /tʃarla'tan/ (-ana) a loquacious, garrulous; indiscreet; fraudulent, false —n charlatan; chatterer

charlatanería /tʃarlatane'ria/ f, loquacity, garrulity; quackery

charlatanismo /tʃarlata'nismo/ m, charlatanism, quackery

charnela /tʃar'nela/ f, hinge; hinged joint

charol /tʃa'rol/ m, japan, varnish; patent leather

charolar /tʃaro'lar/ vt to japan, varnish

charolista /tʃaro'lista/ m, varnisher

charpa /'tʃarpa/ f, pistol-belt; sling

charrán /tʃa'rran/ (-ana) n rogue, trickster

charranada /tʃarra'naða/ f, roguery, knavery

charrería /tʃarre'ria/ f, tawdriness; gaudiness

charretera /tʃarre'tera/ f, Mil. epaulet; garter

charro /'tʃarro/ a churlish, coarse; flashy, tawdry

chasca /'tʃaska/ f, brushwood, firewood

chascar /tʃas'kar/ vi to creak, crack; clack (the tongue); swallow

chascarrillo /tʃaska'rriʎo; tʃaska'rriyo/ m, Inf. amusing anecdote, good story

chasco /'tʃasko/ m, trick, practical joke; disappointment. **llevarse un c.,** to meet with a disappointment

chasis /'tʃasis/ m, Auto. chassis; Photo. plate-holder; Mech. underframe

chasquear /tʃaske'ar/ vt to play a trick on; wag (one's tongue); crack (a whip, one's knuckles); break a promise, disappoint; —vi creak, crack; meet with a disappointment

chasquido /tʃas'kiðo/ m, crack (of whip); creaking (of wood); click (of the tongue)

chatarra /tʃa'tarra/ f, scrap iron; junk

chato /'tʃato/ a flat-nosed; flat

chauvinismo /tʃauβi'nismo/ m, chauvinism

chaval /tʃa'βal/ a Inf. young. m, lad

chaveta /tʃa'βeta/ f, Mech. bolt, pin, peg, cotter, key

che /tʃe/ f, name of the letter ch

checo /'tʃeko/ (-ca) a and n Czech. Czech (language)

checoslovaco /tʃekoslo'βako/ (-ca) a Czechoslovakian —n Czechoslovak

Checoslovaquia /tʃekoslo'βakia/ Czechoslovakia

Chejov /tʃe'hoβ/ Chekov

chelín /tʃe'lin/ m, shilling

Chengis-Jan /tʃenhis-'han/ Genghis Khan

chepa /'tʃepa/ f, Inf. hunch (back); hump

cheque /'tʃeke/ m, check. **c. cruzado,** crossed check

chica /'tʃika/ f, girl; Inf. dear

chicana /tʃi'kana/ f, chicanery

chicano /tʃi'kano/ (-na) a and n Chicano, American of Mexican ancestry

chícharo /'tʃitʃaro/ m, pea

chicharrón /tʃitʃa'rron/ m, Cul. crackling; burnt meat; Inf. sunburnt person

chichón /tʃi'tʃon/ m, bruise, bump

chichonera /tʃitʃo'nera/ f, child's protective hat (something like a straw crash-helmet)

chicle /'tʃikle/ m, chewing gum

chiclero /tʃi'klero/ m, chicle-gatherer

chico /'tʃiko/ a little, small; young. m, little boy; youth; Inf. old boy, dear. **Es un buen c.,** He's a good fellow

chicoleo /tʃiko'leo/ m, Inf. compliment

chicote /tʃi'kote/ mf sturdy child. m, Inf. cigar

chifla /'tʃifla/ f, whistling, whistle; tanner's paring knife

chiflado /tʃi'flaðo/ a Inf. cracked, daft; crack-brained

chifladura /tʃifla'ðura/ f, whistling; Inf. whim, mania, hobby

chiflar /tʃi'flar/ vi to whistle; —vt to make fun of, hiss; pare or scrape leather; Inf. swill, tipple; —vr Inf. have a slate loose; be slightly mad; Inf. lose one's head over, adore

chifle /'tʃifle/ m, whistle, whistling; decoy call (birds)

chile /'tʃile/ m, Bot. red pepper, chilli

chileno /tʃi'leno/ (-na) a and n Chilean

chillador /tʃiʎa'ðor; tʃiya'ðor/ a screaming, shrieking

chillar /tʃi'ʎar; tʃi'yar/ vi to scream, shriek; creak; squeak; jabber (monkeys, etc.); Art. be strident (of colors)

chillería /tʃiʎe'ria; tʃiye'ria/ f, shrieking, screaming

chillido /tʃi'ʎiðo; tʃi'yiðo/ m, scream, shriek; squeak (of mice, etc.); jabber (of monkeys, etc.)

chillón /tʃi'ʎon; tʃi'yon/ a Inf. screaming, yelling; strident, piercing; crude, loud (colors)

chimenea /tʃime'nea/ f, chimney; funnel; fireplace; kitchen range

chimpancé /tʃimpan'θe; tʃimpan'se/ m, chimpanzee

china /'tʃina/ f, pebble; porcelain, china; Chinese silk

chinche /'tʃintʃe/ f, bedbug; thumbtack, drawing-pin. mf Inf. bore

chinchona /tʃin'tʃona/ f, quinine

chinchorrería /tʃintʃorre'ria/ f, Inf. impertinence, tediousness; gossip

chinela /tʃi'nela/ f, mule, slipper; overshoe, patten Obs.

chinero /tʃi'nero/ m, china cupboard

chinesco /tʃi'nesko/ a Chinese. **a la chinesca,** in Chinese fashion

chino /'tʃino/ (-na) a and n Chinese. m, Chinese (language)

Chipre /'tʃipre/ Cyprus

chipriota /tʃi'priota/ a and mf Cypriot

chiquero /tʃi'kero/ m, pigsty; stable for bulls

chiquillada /tʃiki'ʎaða; tʃiki'yaða/ f, childishness, puerility

chiquillería /tʃikiʎe'ria; tʃikiye'ria/ f, Inf. crowd of children

chiquillo /tʃi'kiʎo; tʃi'kiyo/ (-lla) n small boy

chiquito /tʃi'kito/ (-ta) a dim chico, tiny, very small —n little one, small boy

chirimía /tʃiri'mia/ f, flageolet. m, flageolet player

chiripa /tʃi'ripa/ f, (billiards) fluke; Inf. happy coincidence, stroke of luck; lucky guess

chirivía /tʃiri'βia/ f, Bot. parsnip; Ornith. wagtail

chirlar /tʃir'lar/ vi Inf. to gabble, talk loudly

chirlo /'tʃirlo/ m, knife wound, sabre cut; knife scar

chirona /tʃi'rona/ *f, Inf.* jail

chirriador /tʃirria'ðor/ *a* sizzling, crackling; creaking, squeaking

chirriar /tʃi'rriar/ *vi* to sizzle, crackle; creak, squeak; squawk; *Inf.* croak, sing out of tune

chirrido /tʃi'rriðo/ *m,* squawk; croaking; noise of grasshoppers; squeaking; creaking, creak

¡chis! /tʃis/ *interj* Shh! Silence!

chisme /'tʃisme/ *m,* gossip, tale; *Inf.* small household utensil, trifle

chismear /tʃisme'ar/ *vt* to tell tales, gossip

chismero /tʃis'mero/ **(-ra), chismoso (-sa)** *a* gossiping, talebearing —*n* gossip, tale bearer

chispa /'tʃispa/ *f,* spark; ember; *Elec.* spark; tiny diamond; small particle; wit; quickwittedness; *Inf.* drunkenness. **c. del encendido,** ignition spark

chispazo /tʃis'paθo/ tʃis'paso/ *m,* flying out of a spark, sparking; damage done by spark; *Inf.* gossip, rumor

chispeante /tʃispe'ante/ *a* sparking; sparkling; *Fig.* scintillating (with wit etc.)

chispear /tʃispe'ar/ *vi* to throw out sparks, spark; sparkle, gleam; *Fig.* scintillate; drizzle gently

chisporrotear /tʃisporrote'ar/ *vi Inf.* to sputter; fizz

chisporroteo /tʃisporro'teo/ *m, Inf.* sputtering; fizz

chisposo /tʃis'poso/ *a* sputtering, throwing out sparks

chistar /tʃis'tar/ *vi* to speak, break silence (gen. used negatively)

chiste /'tʃiste/ *m,* witticism, bon mot; amusing incident; joke

chistera /tʃis'tera/ *f,* creel (for fish); *Inf.* top-hat, tile

chistoso /tʃis'toso/ *a* joking; amusing, funny

chiticallando /tʃitika'ʎando/ tʃitika'yando/ *adv* quietly, stealthily; *Fig.* on the quiet, in secret

¡chito! ¡chitón! /'tʃito; tʃi'ton/ *interj* Hush! Sh!

chiva /'tʃiβa/ *f,* Panama bus

chivo /'tʃiβo/ *n Zool.* kid. **c. expiatorio,** scapegoat

chocante /tʃo'kante/ *a* colliding; provoking; shocking; surprising

chocar /tʃo'kar/ *vi* to collide; strike (against); run into; fight, clash; —*vt* clink (glasses); provoke, annoy; surprise, shock. **¡Choca cinco!** Clasp five!, Gimme five!, Put it there!, Give some skin! (invitation to shake hands)

chocarrería /tʃokarre'ria/ *f,* coarse joke

chochear /tʃotʃe'ar/ *vi* to be senile; *Fig. Inf.* dote (on)

chocho /'tʃotʃo/ *a* senile; *Fig. Inf.* doting

choco /'tʃoko/ *m,* small hump, hunchback

chocolate /tʃoko'late/ *m,* chocolate; drinking chocolate. **c. a la española,** thick chocolate. **c. a la francesa,** French drinking chocolate

chocolatería /tʃokolate'ria/ *f,* chocolate factory or shop

chocolatero /tʃokola'tero/ **(-ra)** *a* fond of chocolate —*n* chocolate maker or seller

chófer /'tʃofer/ *m,* chauffeur; driver

chopera /tʃo'pera/ *f,* grove or plantation of black poplar trees

chopo /'tʃopo/ *m, Bot.* black poplar; *Inf.* gun

choque /'tʃoke/ *m,* collision; shock; jar; *Med.* concussion; fight; clink (of glasses); clash; *Mil.* skirmish

choricera /tʃori'θera/ tʃori'sera/ *f,* sausage-making machine

choricero /tʃori'θero/ tʃori'sero/ **(-ra)** *n* sausage maker

chorizo /tʃo'riθo/ tʃo'riso/ *m,* kind of pork sausage; counterweight

chorrear /tʃorre'ar/ *vi* to spout, jet; drip; *Fig. Inf.* trickle, arrive slowly

chorreo /tʃo'rreo/ *m,* drip, dripping; spouting, gushing

chorrera /tʃo'rrera/ *f,* spout; drip; jabot, lace front

chorro /'tʃorro/ *m,* jet; stream (of water, etc.); *Fig.* shower. **a chorros,** in a stream; in abundance, plentifully

chova /'tʃoβa/ *f,* rook; carrion crow; jackdaw

choza /'tʃoθa/ 'tʃosa/ *f,* hut, cabin; cottage

chubasco /tʃu'βasko/ *m,* squall, downpour; storm; transitory misfortune

chuchería /tʃutʃe'ria/ *f,* gewgaw, trinket; savory titbit; snaring, trapping

chucruta /tʃu'kruta/ *f,* sauerkraut

chueca /tʃu'eka/ *f,* round head of a bone; small ball; game like shinty; *Inf.* practical joke

chufa /'tʃufa/ *f, Bot.* chufa; *Inf.* joke, trick

chufería /tʃufe'ria/ *f,* place where drink made of **chufas** is sold

chufla /'tʃufla/ *f,* flippant remark

chufleta /tʃu'fleta/ *f, Inf.* joke; taunt

chulada /tʃu'laða/ *f,* mean trick, base action; drollery

chulería /tʃule'ria/ *f,* drollness; attractive personality

chuleta /tʃu'leta/ *f, Cul.* cutlet, chop; mutton-chop; *Inf.* slap

chulo /'tʃulo/ *a* droll, amusing; attractive. *m,* slaughterhouse worker; bullfighter's assistant; pimp; rogue

chumbera /tʃum'βera/ *f,* prickly pear; Indian fig

chunga /'tʃunga/ *f, Inf.* banter, teasing

chupada /tʃu'paða/ *f,* sucking; suck; suction

chupado de cara, c. de mofletes /tʃu'paðo de 'kara, mof'letes/ *a* lantern-jawed

chupador /tʃupa'ðor/ *a* sucking. *m,* baby's comforter or dummy

chupar /tʃu'par/ *vt* to suck; absorb (of plants); *Fig. Inf.* drain, rob; —*vr* grow thin. **chuparse los dedos,** *Inf.* to lick one's lips; be delighted

chupatintas /tʃupa'tintas/ *m, Inf.* scrivener, clerk (scornful)

churdón /tʃur'ðon/ *m,* raspberry cane; raspberry; raspberry vinegar

churrería /tʃurre'ria/ *f,* place where **churros** are made or sold

churrero /tʃu'rrero/ **(-ra)** *n* maker or seller of **churros**

churrigueresco /tʃurrige'resko/ *a* Churrigueresque

churro /'tʃurro/ *a* coarse (of wool). *m, Cul.* a kind of fritter eaten with chocolate, coffee, etc.

churumbela /tʃurum'βela/ *f, Mus.* pipe; reed for drinking mate *West Hem.*

chusco /'tʃusko/ *a* droll, witty, amusing

chusma /'tʃusma/ *f,* galley hands, crew; rabble, mob

chutar /tʃu'tar/ *vt Sports.* to shoot (a goal)

chuzo /'tʃuθo/ 'tʃuso/ *m, Mil.* pike

chuzón /tʃu'θon/ tʃu'son/ *a* wily, suspicious, cunning

cianuro /θia'nuro/ sia'nuro/ *m,* cyanide

ciar /θiar/ siar/ *vi* to go backwards; *Naut.* row backwards; *Fig.* make no headway (negotiations)

ciática /'θiatika/ 'siatika/ *f,* sciatica

ciático /'θiatiko/ 'siatiko/ *a* sciatic

ciberespacio *m,* cyberspace

ciborio /θi'βorio/ si'βorio/ *m,* ciborium

cicatería /θikate'ria/ sikate'ria/ *f,* niggardliness, avarice

cicatero /θika'tero/ sika'tero/ *a* avaricious, niggardly, mean

cicatriz /θika'triθ/ sika'tris/ *f,* cicatrice; *Fig.* scar, mark, impression

cicatrización /θikatriθa'θion/ sikatrisa'sion/ *f,* cicatrization

cicatrizar /θikatri'θar/ sikatri'sar/ *vt* to cicatrize, heal; —*vr* scar over

ciclamino /θikla'mino/ sikla'mino/ *m,* cyclamen

cíclico /'θikliko/ 'sikliko/ *a* cyclic, cyclical

ciclismo /θi'klismo/ si'klismo/ *m,* bicycling

ciclista /θi'klista/ si'klista/ *mf* cyclist

ciclo /'θiklo/ 'siklo/ *m,* cycle (of time). **c. artúrico, c. de Artús,** Arthurian Cycle. **c. de conferencias,** series of lectures

ciclón /θi'klon/ si'klon/ *m,* cyclone

ciclópeo /θi'klopeo/ si'klopeo/ *a* cyclopean

ciclostilo /θiklos'tilo/ siklos'tilo/ *m,* cyclostyle

cicuta /θi'kuta/ si'kuta/ *f,* hemlock

cid /θið/ sið/ *m,* great warrior, chief. **el Cid,** national hero of Spanish wars against the Moors

cidra /'θiðra/ 'siðra/ *f,* citron

cidro /'θiðro/ 'siðro/ *m,* citron tree

ciego /'θiego/ 'siego/ *a* blind; dazed, blinded; choked up. *m,* blind man; *Anat.* cæcum. **a ciegas,** blindly; heedlessly

cielo /'θielo/ 'sielo/ *m,* sky, firmament; atmosphere; climate; paradise; Providence; bliss, glory; roof, canopy; *Inf.* darling. **a c. abierto,** in the open air. **parecer un c.,** to be heavenly

ciempiés /θiem'pies/ siem'pies/ *m,* centipede

cien /θien; sien/ *a* abb. **ciento,** hundred. Used always before substantives (e.g. *c. hombres,* 100 men)

ciénaga /'θienaga; 'sienaga/ *f,* swamp; morass

ciencia /'θienθia; 'siensia/ *f,* science; knowledge; erudition, ability. **ciencias naturales,** natural science. **a c. cierta,** for certain, without doubt (gen. with *saber*)

cienmilésimo /θiemi'lesimo; siemi'lesimo/ *a* hundred-thousandth

cieno /'θieno; 'sieno/ *m,* slime, mud; silt

científico /θien'tifiko; sien'tifiko/ *a* scientific. *m,* scientist

ciento /'θiento; 'siento/ (cf. **cien**) *a* hundred; hundredth. *m,* hundred. **por c.,** per cent.

cierne, en /'θierne, en; 'sierne, en/ in flower; *Fig.* in the early stages, in embryo

cierre /'θierre; 'sierre/ *m,* closing, shutting; closing time of shops, etc.; fastening; fastener; clasp (of a necklace, handbag, etc.). **c. cremallera,** zip fastener. **c. metálico,** doorshutter

ciertamente /θierta'mente; sierta'mente/ *adv* certainly; undoubtedly; indeed

ciertísimo /θier'tisimo; sier'tisimo/ *a* everyday form of the superlative of **cierto** (see **certísimo**)

cierto /'θierto; 'sierto/ *a* certain, sure; true; particular (e.g. *c. hombre,* a certain man (note no *def. art.*)). **un c. sabor,** a special flavor. **una cosa cierta,** something certain. **no, por c.,** no, certainly not. **por c.,** truly, indeed

cierva /'θierβa; 'sierβa/ *f,* hind

ciervo /'θierβo; 'sierβo/ *m,* stag. **c. volante,** stag-beetle

cierzo /'θierθo; 'sierso/ *m,* northerly wind

cifra /'θifra; 'sifra/ *f,* number; figure; sum total; cipher, code; monogram; abbreviation

cifrar /θi'frar; si'frar/ *vt* to write in cipher; summarize, abridge; (*with en*) be dependent on; depend on

cigarra /θi'garra; si'garra/ *f, Ent.* cicada, harvest fly

cigarral /θiga'rral; siga'rral/ *m,* (Toledo) country-house and garden or orchard

cigarrera /θiga'rrera; siga'rrera/ *f,* woman who makes or sells cigars; cigar-cabinet; cigar-case

cigarrillo /θiga'rriʎo; siga'rriyo/ *m,* cigarette

cigarro /θi'garro; si'garro/ *m,* cigar

cigüeña /θi'gueɲa; si'gueɲa/ *f, Ornith.* stork; *Mech.* crank

ciliar /θi'liar; si'liar/ *a* ciliary

cilicio /θi'liθio; si'lisio/ *m,* hairshirt

cilindrar /θilin'drar; silin'drar/ *vt* to roll; calendar; bore

cilindrero /θilin'drero; silin'drero/ *m,* organ grinder

cilíndrico /θi'lindriko; si'lindriko/ *a* cylindrical

cilindro /θi'lindro; si'lindro/ *m,* cylinder; roller

cima /'θima; 'sima/ *f,* summit; top of trees; apex; *Archit.* coping; head (thistle, etc.); *Fig.* aim, goal, end

cimbalero /θimba'lero; simba'lero/ **(-ra)** *n* cymbalist

címbalo /'θimbalo; 'simbalo/ *m,* cymbal

cimborrio /θim'βorrio; sim'βorrio/ *m, Archit.* cupola; cimborium

cimbrar, cimbrear /θim'βrar, θimbre'ar; sim'βrar, simbre'ar/ *vt* to bend; brandish; —*vr* sway (in walking)

cimbreño /θim'βreɲo; sim'βreɲo/ *a* graceful, lithe, willowy

cimbreo /θim'βreo; sim'βreo/ *m,* swaying, bending

cimentar /θimen'tar; simen'tar/ *vt irr* to lay foundations; refine (gold, metals, etc.); found; *Fig.* ground (in virtue, etc.). See **acertar**

cimera /θi'mera; si'mera/ *f,* crest of helmet

cimiento /θi'miento; si'miento/ *m,* foundation (of a building); bottom; groundwork; origin, base. **abrir los cimientos,** to lay the foundations

cimitarra /θimi'tarra; simi'tarra/ *f,* scimitar

cinabrio /θi'naβrio; si'naβrio/ *m,* cinnabar; vermilion

cinc /θink; sink/ *m,* zinc

cincel /θin'θel; sin'sel/ *m,* chisel; burin, engraver

cincelador /θinθela'ðor; sinsela'ðor/ **(-ra)** *n* engraver; chiseler

cincelar /θinθe'lar; sinse'lar/ *vt* to chisel; carve; engrave

cincha /'θintʃa; 'sintʃa/ *f,* girth of a saddle

cinchar /θin'tʃar; sin'tʃar/ *vt* to tighten the saddle girths

cincho /'θintʃo; 'sintʃo/ *m,* belt, girdle; iron hoop

cinco /'θinko; 'sinko/ *a* and *m,* five; fifth. **a las c.,** at five o'clock

cincuenta /θin'kuenta; sin'kuenta/ *a* and *m,* fifty; fiftieth

cincuentavo /θinkuen'taβo; sinkuen'taβo/ *a* fiftieth

cincuentenario /θinkuente'nario; sinkuente'nario/ *m,* fiftieth anniversary

cincuentón /θinkuen'ton; sinkuen'ton/ **(-ona)** *a* and *n* fifty years old (person)

cine, cinema /'θine, θi'nema; 'sine, si'nema/ *m,* cinema, movies. **c. sonoro,** sound film

cinemática /θine'matika; sine'matika/ *f, Phys.* kinematics

cinematografía /θinematogra'fia; sinematogra'fia/ *f,* cinematography

cinematografiar /θinematogra'fiar; sinematogra-'fiar/ *vt* to film

cinematográfico /θinemato'grafiko; sinemato-'grafiko/ *a* cinematographic

cinematógrafo /θinema'tografo; sinema'tografo/ *m,* motion-picture camera; cinema

cínico /'θiniko; 'siniko/ *a* cynical; impudent; untidy. *m,* cynic

cinismo /θi'nismo; si'nismo/ *m,* cynicism

cinta /'θinta; 'sinta/ *f,* ribbon; tape; strip; film (cinematograph). **c. métrica,** tape-measure

cintillo /θin'tiʎo; sin'tiyo/ *m,* hatband; small ring set with gems

cinto /'θinto; 'sinto/ *m,* belt, girdle. **c. de pistolas,** pistol-belt

cintoteca /θinto'teka; sinto'teka/ *f,* tape library

cintura /θin'tura; sin'tura/ *f,* waist; belt, girdle

cinturón /θintu'ron; sintu'ron/ *m,* large waist; belt girdle; sword-belt; that which encircles or surrounds. **c. de seguridad,** seat belt

ciprés /θi'pres; si'pres/ *m, Bot.* cypress tree or wood

cipresal /θipre'sal; sipre'sal/ *m,* cypress grove

cipresino /θipre'sino; sipre'sino/ *a* cypress; cypress-like

circasiano /θirka'siano; sirka'siano/ **(-na)** *a* and *n* Circassian

circo /'θirko; 'sirko/ *m,* circus; amphitheater

circón /θir'kon; sir'kon/ *m,* zircon

circuir /θir'kuir; sir'kuir/ *vt. irr* to surround, encircle. See **huir**

circuito /θir'kuito; sir'kuito/ *m,* periphery; contour; (*Elec. Phys.*) circuit. **corto c.,** short circuit

circulación /θirkula'θion; sirkula'sion/ *f,* circulation; traffic. **c. de la sangre,** circulation of the blood. **calle de gran c.,** busy street

circular /θirku'lar; sirku'lar/ *a* circular. *f,* circular —*vt* to pass round; —*vi* circle; circulate; move in a circle; move about; run, travel (traffic)

circulatorio /θirkula'torio; sirkula'torio/ *a* circulatory

círculo /'θirkulo; 'sirkulo/ *m,* circle; circumference; circuit; casino, social club

circuncidar /θirkunθi'ðar; sirkunsi'ðar/ *vt* to circumcise; modify, reduce

circuncisión /θirkunθi'sion; sirkunsi'sion/ *f,* circumcision

circunciso /θirkun'θiso; sirkun'siso/ *a* circumcised

circundar /θirkun'dar; sirkun'dar/ *vt* to surround

circunferencia /θirkunfe'renθia; sirkunfe'rensia/ *f,* circumference

circunflejo /θirkun'fleho; sirkun'fleho/ *a* circumflex. **acento c.,** circumflex accent

circunlocución /θirkunloku'θion; sirkunloku'sion/ *f,* circumlocution

circunnavegación /θirkunnaβega'θion; sirkunnaβega'sion/ *f,* circumnavigation

circunnavegar /θirkunnaβe'gar; sirkunnaβe'gar/ *vt* to circumnavigate

circunscribir /θirkunskri'βir; sirkunskri'βir/ *vt* to circumscribe —*Past Part.* **circunscrito**

circunscripción /θirkunskrip'θion; sirkunskrip'sion/ *f,* circumscription

circunspección /θirkunspek'θion; sirkunspek'sion/ *f,* circumspection; seriousness, dignity

circunspecto /θirkuns'pekto; sirkuns'pekto/ *a* circumspect; serious, dignified

circunstancia /θirkuns'tanθia; sirkuns'tansia/ *f*, circumstance; incident, detail; condition. **c. agravante,** aggravating circumstance. **c. atenuante,** extenuating circumstance. **bajo las circunstancias,** in the circumstances. **de circunstancias,** occasional (e.g. *poesías de circunstancias,* occasional verse). **estar al nivel de las circunstancias,** to rise to the occasion

circunstanciado /θirkunstan'θiaðo; sirkunstan'siaðo/ *a* circumstantiated, detailed

circunstancial /θirkunstan'θial; sirkunstan'sial/ *a* circumstantial; occasional (e.g. *poesías circunstanciales,* occasional verse)

circunstante /θirkuns'tante; sirkuns'tante/ *a* surrounding; present. *mf* person present, bystander

circunvecino /θirkumbe'θino; sirkumbe'sino/ *a* adjacent, neighboring

circunvolución /θirkumbolu'θion; sirkumbolu'sion/ *f*, circumvolution

cirial /θi'rial; si'rial/ *m*, processional candlestick

cirio /'θirio; 'sirio/ *m*, wax candle

cirro /'θirro; 'sirro/ *m*, *Med.* scirrhus; *Bot.* tendril; *Zool.* cirrus

cirrosis /θi'rrosis; si'rrosis/ *f*, cirrhosis

cirroso /θi'rroso; si'rroso/ *a* *Med.* scirrhous; (*Zool. Bot.*) cirrose

ciruela /θi'ruela; si'ruela/ *f*, plum; prune. **c. claudia, c. veidal,** greengage. **c. damascena,** damson

ciruelo /θi'ruelo; si'ruelo/ *m*, plum tree

cirugía /θiru'hia; siru'hia/ *f*, surgery

cirujano /θiru'hano; siru'hano/ *m*, surgeon

cisco /'θisko; 'sisko/ *m*, coal dust, slack coal; *Inf.* hubbub, quarrel

cisma /'θisma; 'sisma/ *m*, or *f*, schism; disagreement, discord. **el C. de Occidente,** the Western Schism

cismático /θis'matiko; sis'matiko/ *a* schismatic; discordant, inharmonious

cisne /'θisne; 'sisne/ *m*, swan

cisterciense /θister'θiense; sister'siense/ *a* Cistercian

cisterna /θis'terna; sis'terna/ *f*, water-tank, cistern

cístico /'θistiko; 'sistiko/ *a* cystic

cistitis /θis'titis; sis'titis/ *f*, cystitis

cita /'θita; 'sita/ *f*, appointment; quotation, citation

citable /θi'taβle; si'taβle/ *a* quotable

citación /θita'θion; sita'sion/ *f*, quotation; *Law.* summons

citar /θi'tar; si'tar/ *vt* to make an appointment; cite, quote; *Law.* summon. **c. en comparecencia,** to summon to appear in court

cítara /'θitara; 'sitara/ *f*, *Mus.* zither

citatorio /θita'torio; sita'torio/ *m*, summons

citerior /θite'rior; site'rior/ *a* hither, nearer

citrato /θi'trato; si'trato/ *m*, *Chem.* citrate

cítrico /'θitriko; 'sitriko/ *a* citric

ciudad /θiu'ðað; siu'ðað/ *f*, city; municipal body. **la c. señorial,** the Aristocratic City (Ponce, Puerto Rico)

ciudadanía /θiuðaða'nia; siuðaða'nia/ *f*, citizenship

ciudadano /θiuða'ðano; siuða'ðano/ **(-na)** *a* city; civic, born in or belonging to a city —*n* citizen; burgess; bourgeois. **c. de honor,** freeman (of a city)

ciudadela /θiuða'ðela; siuða'ðela/ *f*, citadel

cívico /'θiβiko; 'siβiko/ *a* civic; patriotic

civicultura /θiβikul'tura; siβikul'tura/ *f*, raising of civets

civil /θi'βil; si'βil/ *a* civil; civilian; polite

civilidad /θiβili'ðað; siβili'ðað/ *f*, politeness, civility

civilización /θiβiliθa'θion; siβilisa'sion/ *f*, civilization

civilizador /θiβiliθa'ðor; siβilisa'ðor/ *a* civilizing

civilizar /θiβili'θar; siβili'sar/ *vt* to civilize; educate; —*vr* grow civilized; be educated

civismo /θi'βismo; si'βismo/ *m*, civism; patriotism; civics

cizalla /θi'θaʎa; si'saya/ *f*, shears, shearing machine; metal filings

cizaña /θi'θaɲa; si'saɲa/ *f*, *Bot.* darnel, tare; vice, evil; dissension, discord (gen. with *meter* and *sembrar*)

clac /klak/ *m*, opera-hat; tricorne

clamar /kla'mar/ *vi* to cry out; *Fig.* demand (of inanimate things); vociferate; speak solemnly

clamor /kla'mor/ *m*, outcry, shouting; shriek, complaint; knell, tolling of bells

clamorear /klamore'ar/ *vt* to implore, clamor (for); —*vi* toll (of bells)

clamoroso /klamo'roso/ *a* noisy, clamorous

clandestino /klandes'tino/ *a* clandestine, secret

clangor /klaŋ'gor/ *m*, *Poet.* blare, bray (of trumpet)

claqué /kla'ke/ *m*, tap-dance

clara /'klara/ *f*, white of egg; bald patch (in fur); *Inf.* fair interval on a rainy day

claraboya /klara'βoya/ *f*, skylight; *Archit.* clerestory

claramente /klara'mente/ *adv* clearly, evidently

clarear /klare'ar/ *vt* to clear; give light to; —*vi* to dawn; grow light; —*vr* be transparent; *Inf.* reveal secrets unwittingly

clarete /kla'rete/ *m*, claret (wine); claret color —*a* claret; claret-colored

claridad /klari'ðað/ *f*, clearness, transparency; lightness, brightness; distinctness; clarity; good reputation, renown; plain truth, home truth (gen. *pl*)

clarificación /klarifika'θion; klarifika'sion/ *f*, clarification; purifying, refining

clarificar /klarifi'kar/ *vt* to illuminate; clarify, purify; refine (sugar, etc.)

clarín /kla'rin/ *m*, bugle; clarion; organ stop; bugler

clarinete /klari'nete/ *m*, clarinet; clarinet player

clarión /kla'rion/ *m*, white chalk, crayon

clarividencia /klariβi'ðenθia; klariβi'ðensia/ *f*, perspicuity, clear-sightedness

clarividente /klariβi'ðente/ *a* perspicacious, clear-sighted

claro /'klaro/ *a* clear; light, bright; distinct; pure, clean; transparent, translucent; light (of colors); easily understood; evident, obvious; frank; cloudless; shrewd, quick-thinking; famous. *m*, skylight; space between words; break in a speech; space in procession, etc.; *Art.* (gen. *pl*) high lights —*interj* ¡C.! or ¡C. está! Of course! **a las claras,** openly, frankly

claroscuro /klaros'kuro/ *m*, chiaroscuro; monochrome

clase /'klase/ *f*, class, group; kind, sort, quality; class (school, university); lecture room; lecture, lesson; order, family. **c. dirigente,** ruling class. **c. media,** middle class. **c. social,** social class

clasicismo /klasi'θismo; klasi'sismo/ *m*, classicism

clasicista /klasi'θista; klasi'sista/ *a* and *mf* classicist

clásico /'klasiko/ *a* classic; notable; classical. *m*, classic

clasificación /klasifika'θion; klasifika'sion/ *f*, classification

clasificador /klasifika'ðor/ **(-ra)** *n* classifier. **c. de billetes,** ticket-punch

clasificar /klasifi'kar/ *vt* to classify, arrange. **c. correspondencia,** to file letters

claudicación /klauðika'θion; klauðika'sion/ *f*, limping; negligence; hesitancy, weakness; backing down

claudicar /klauði'kar/ *vi* to limp; be negligent; hesitate, give way

claustral /klaus'tral/ *a* cloistral

claustro /'klaustro/ *m*, cloister; council, faculty, senate (of university); monastic rule

claustrofobia /klaustro'foβia/ *f*, claustrophobia

cláusula /'klausula/ *f*, clause. **c. de negación implícita,** contrary-to-fact clause. **c. principal,** main clause. **c. subordinada,** dependent clause, subordinate clause. **c. sustantiva,** noun clause

clausura /klau'sura/ *f*, sanctum of convent; claustration; solemn ending ceremony of tribunal, etc. **la vida de c.,** monastic or conventual life

clava /'klaβa/ *f*, club, truncheon; *Naut.* scupper

clavadizo /klaβa'ðiθo; klaβa'ðiso/ *a* nail-studded (doors, etc.)

clavar /kla'βar/ *vt* to nail; fasten with nails; pierce, prick; set gems (jeweler); spike (cannon, gum); *Fig.* fix (eyes, attention, etc.); *Inf.* cheat

clave /'klaβe/ *m*, clavichord. *f*, code, key; *Mus.* clef; *Archit.* keystone; plug (telephones); **c. (de),** key to. *Mus.* **c. de sol,** treble clef

clavel /kla'βel/ *m*, *Bot.* carnation plant and flower

clavelito /klaβe'lito/ *m*, *Bot.* pink plant and flower

clavero /kla'βero/ **(-ra)** *n* keeper of the keys. *m*, clove tree

clavetear /klaβete'ar/ *vt* to stud with nails; *Fig.* round off (business affairs)
clavicordio /klaβi'korðio/ *m*, clavichord
clavícula /kla'βikula/ *f*, clavicle
clavija /kla'βiha/ *f*, peg, pin; plug; peg of stringed instrument; axle-pin
clavo /'klaβo/ *m*, nail, spike, peg; corn (on foot); anguish. **c. de especia,** clove. **c. de herradura,** hob-nail
claymore /klai'more/ *f*, claymore
clemátide /kle'matiðe/ *f, Bot.* clematis
clemencia /kle'menθia; kle'mensia/ *f*, mildness; clemency; mercy
clemente /kle'mente/ *a* mild; clement; merciful
cleptomanía /kleptoma'nia/ *f*, kleptomania
cleptómano /klep'tomano/ **(-na)** *a* and *n* kleptomaniac
clerecía /klere'θia; klere'sia/ *f*, clergy
clerical /kleri'kal/ *a* belonging to the clergy; clerical
clericalismo /klerika'lismo/ *m*, clericalism
clerigalla /kleri'gaʎa; kleri'gaya/ *f*, (*contemptuous*) dog-collar men
clérigo /'klerigo/ *m*, cleric, clergyman; clerk (in Middle Ages)
clero /'klero/ *m*, clergy
cliente /'kliente/ *mf* client, customer; protégé, ward
clientela /klien'tela/ *f*, patronage, protection; clientele
clima /'klima/ *m*, climate, clime
climatérico /klima'teriko/ *a* climacteric
climático /kli'matiko/ *a* climatic
climatología /klimatolo'hia/ *f*, climatology
clímax /'klimaks/ *m*, climax
clínica /'klinika/ *f*, clinic, nursing home; department of medicine or surgery
clínico /'kliniko/ *a* clinical
clíper /'kliper/ *m*, (*Aer.* and *Naut.*) clipper
clisar /kli'sar/ *vt Print.* to cast from a mold, stereotype
clisé /kli'se/ *m, Print.* stereotype plate
cloaca /klo'aka/ *f*, sewer, drain; *Zool.* cloaca
cloquear /kloke'ar/ *vi* to go broody (hen); cluck
cloqueo /klo'keo/ *m*, cluck, clucking
cloquera /klo'kera/ *f*, broodiness (hens)
clorato /klo'rato/ *m*, chlorate
clorhidrato /klori'ðrato/ *m*, hydrochloride
clorhídrico /klor'iðriko/ *a* hydrochloric
cloro /'kloro/ *m*, chlorine
clorofila /kloro'fila/ *f*, chlorophyll
cloroformizar /kloroformi'θar; kloroformi'sar/ *vt* to chloroform
cloroformo /kloro'formo/ *m*, chloroform
clorosis /klo'rosis/ *f*, chlorosis
cloruro /klo'ruro/ *m*, chloride
club /kluβ/ *m*, club
clueca /'klueka/ *f*, broody hen
clueco /'klueko/ *a* broody (hens); *Inf.* doddering
C.N.T. /knt/ initialism of Confederación Nacional de Trabajo
coacción /koak'θion; koak'sion/ *f*, coercion
coactivo /koak'tiβo/ *a* coercive
coadjutor /koaðhu'tor/ *m*, co-worker, assistant
coadunar /koaðu'nar/ *vt* to join or mingle together
coadyuvar /koaðyu'βar/ *vt* to assist
coagulación /koagula'θion; koagula'sion/ *f*, coagulation
coagular /koagu'lar/ *vt* to coagulate; clot; curdle
coágulo /ko'agulo/ *m*, clot; coagulation; congealed blood
coalición /koali'θion; koali'sion/ *f*, coalition
coartada /koar'taða/ *f*, alibi. **probar la c.,** to prove an alibi
coartar /koar'tar/ *vt* to limit, restrict
coautor /koau'tor/ **(-ra)** *n* co-author
cobalto /ko'βalto/ *m*, cobalt
cobarde /ko'βarðe/ *a* cowardly; irresolute. *m*, coward
cobardía /koβar'ðia/ *f*, cowardice
cobayo /ko'βayo/ *m*, guinea-pig
cobertera /koβer'tera/ *f*, lid, cover
cobertizo /koβer'tiθo; koβer'tiso/ *m*, overhanging roof; shack, shed, hut. **c. de aeroplanos,** *Aer.* hangar
cobertura /koβer'tura/ *f*, covering; coverlet; wrapping

cobija /ko'βiha/ *f*, imbrex tile; cover
cobijar /koβi'har/ *vt* to cover; shelter
cobra /'koβra/ *f, Zool.* cobra; rope or thong for yoking oxen; retrieval (of game)
cobradero /koβra'ðero/ *a* that which can be collected, recoverable
cobrador /koβra'ðor/ *m*, collector, receiver —*a* collecting. **c. de tranvía,** tram conductor
cobranza /ko'βranθa; ko'βransa/ *f*, receiving, collecting; collection of fruit or money
cobrar /ko'βrar/ *vt* to collect (what is owed); charge; earn; regain, recover; feel, experience (emotions); wind, pull in (ropes, etc.); gain, acquire; retrieve (game); —*vr* recuperate. **c. ánimo,** to take courage. **c. cariño (a),** to grow fond of. **c. fuerzas,** to gather strength. **c. importancia,** to gain importance. **¿Cuánto cobra Vd.?** How much do you charge?; How much do you earn?
cobre /'koβre/ *m, Mineral.* copper; copper kitchen utensils; *pl Mus.* brass
cobrizo /ko'βriθo; ko'βriso/ *a* containing copper; copper-colored
cocacolismo /kokako'lismo/ *n Inf.* economic dependence on the United States and adoption of its pop culture
cocacolonización /kokakoloniθa'θion; kokakolonisa'sion/ *f*, economic domination by the United States and introduction of its pop culture
cocacolonizar /kokakoloni'θar; kokakoloni'sar/ *vt* (United States) to gain economic control of... and introduce into its pop culture
cocaína /koka'ina/ *f*, cocaine
cocción /kok'θion; kok'sion/ *f*, coction
coceador /koθea'ðor; kosea'ðor/ *a* inclined to kick; kicking (animals)
coceadura /koθea'ðura; kosea'ðura/ *f*, kicking
cocear /koθe'ar; kose'ar/ *vi* to kick; *Inf.* kick against, oppose
cocedero /koθe'ðero; kose'ðero/ *a* easily cooked
cocer /ko'θer; ko'ser/ *vt. irr* to boil; cook; bake (bricks, etc.); digest; *Surg.* suppurate; —*vi* boil (of a liquid); ferment; —*vr* suffer pain or inconvenience over a long period —*Pres. Indic.* **cuezo, cueces, cuece, cuecen.** *Pres. Subjunc.* **cueza, cuezas, cueza, cuezan**
coche /'kotʃe/ *m*, carriage, car. **c. camas,** sleeping car. **c. -camioneta,** station wagon. **c. cerrado,** *Auto.* sedan. **c. de muchos caballos,** high-powered car. **c. de plaza,** hackney-carriage. **c. fúnebre,** hearse. **c. -línea,** intercity bus. *f, Ecuador* puddle
cochera /ko'tʃera/ *f*, coach house; tramway depot
cochero /ko'tʃero/ *m*, coachman; driver —*a* easily cooked
¡cochi! /'kotʃi/ (call to pigs)
cochina /ko'tʃina/ *f*, sow
cochinería /kotʃine'ria/ *f, Inf.* filthiness; mean trick
cochinilla /kotʃi'niʎa; kotʃi'niya/ *f*, wood louse; cochineal insect; cochineal
cochinillo /kotʃi'niʎo; kotʃi'niyo/ *m*, sucking-pig. **c. de Indias,** guinea-pig
cochino /ko'tʃino/ *m*, pig; *Inf.* filthy person —*a* filthy
cocido /ko'θiðo; ko'siðo/ *a* boiled, cooked, baked. *m*, dish of stewed meat, pork, chicken, with peas, etc.
cociente /ko'θiente; ko'siente/ *m*, quotient
cocimiento /koθi'miento; kosi'miento/ *m*, cooking; decoction
cocina /ko'θina; ko'sina/ *f*, kitchen; pottage; broth; cookery. **c. de campaña,** field-kitchen. **c. económica,** cooking range
cocinar /koθi'nar; kosi'nar/ *vt* to cook; —*vi Inf.* meddle, interfere
cocinería /koθine'ria; kosine'ria/ *f, Naut.* galley
cocinero /koθi'nero; kosi'nero/ **(-ra)** *n* cook, chef
cocinilla /koθi'niʎa; kosi'niya/ *f*, spirit-stove
coco /'koko/ *m, Bot.* coconut tree and fruit; coconut shell; grub, maggot; bogeyman; hobgoblin; *Inf.* grimace. *Inf.* **ser un c.,** to be hideously ugly
cocodrilo /koko'ðrilo/ *m*, crocodile
cócora /'kokora/ *mf Inf.* bore, nosy Parker
cocotal /koko'tal/ *m*, grove of coconut palms
cocotero /koko'tero/ *m*, coconut palm
coctel /kok'tel/ *m*, cocktail

cocuyo /ko'kuyo/ *m*, firefly

codal /ko'ðal/ *a* cubital. *m*, shoot of a vine; prop, strut; frame of a hand-saw

codazo /ko'ðaθo; ko'ðaso/ *m*, blow or nudge of the elbow. **dar codazos,** to elbow, shoulder out of the way

codear /koðe'ar/ *vi* to jostle; elbow, nudge; —*vr* be on terms of equality with

codeína /koðe'ina/ *f*, codeine

codelincuente /koðelin'kuente/ *mf* partner in crime, accomplice

codera /ko'ðera/ *f*, elbow rash; elbow-piece or patch

codeso /ko'ðeso/ *m*, laburnum

códice /'koðiθe; 'koðise/ *m*, codex

codicia /ko'ðiθia; ko'ðisia/ *f*, covetousness; greed

codiciar /koðiθi'ar; koðisi'ar/ *vt* to covet

codicilo /koðiθ'θilo; koði'silo/ *m*, codicil

codicioso /koðiθi'oso; koðisi'oso/ **(-sa)** *a* covetous; *Inf.* hardworking —*n* covetous person

codificación /koðifika'θion; koðifika'sion/ *f*, codification

codificar /koðifi'kar/ *vt* to codify, compile

código /'koðigo/ *m*, code of laws. **c. civil,** civil laws. **c. de la circulación, c. de la vía pública,** highway code, traffic code. *Naut.* **c. de señales,** signal code. **c. penal,** criminal laws. **c. postal,** zip code

codillo /ko'ðiʎo; ko'ðiyo/ *m*, knee (of quadrupeds); shaft (of branch); bend (pipe, tube); stirrup

codo /'koðo/ *m*, elbow; angle, bend (pipe, tube); cubit. *Inf.* **hablar por los codos,** to chatter

codorniz /koðor'niθ; koðor'nis/ *f*, *Ornith.* quail

coeducación /koeðuka'θion; koeðuka'sion/ *f*, co-education

coeficiente /koefi'θiente; koefi'siente/ *m*, coefficient

coercer /koer'θer; koer'ser/ *vt* to restrain, coerce

coerción /koer'θion; koer'sion/ *f*, *Law.* coercion

coercitivo /koerθi'tiβo; koersi'tiβo/ *a* coercive

coetáneo /koe'taneo/ **(-ea)** *a* contemporaneous —*n* contemporary

coevo /ko'eβo/ *a* coeval

coexistencia /koeksis'tenθia; koeksis'tensia/ *f*, co-existence

coexistir /koeksis'tir/ *vi* to co-exist

cofia /'kofia/ *f*, hairnet; coif

cofín /ko'fin/ *m*, basket

cofradía /kofra'ðia/ *f*, confraternity, brotherhood or sisterhood **c. de gastronomía,** eating club (US), dining society (UK)

cofre /'kofre/ *m*, trunk, chest (for clothes); coffer

cogedor /kohe'ðor/ *m*, collector, gatherer; dustpan; coal-shovel

coger /ko'her/ *vt* to seize, hold; catch; take, collect, gather; have room for; take up or occupy space; find; catch in the act; attack, surprise; touch; **c. un berrinche,** have a fit, have a tantrum —*vi* have room, fit

cogida /ko'hiða/ *f*, gathering, picking; *Inf.* fruit harvest; toss (bullfighting)

cogido /ko'hiðo/ *m*, pleat, fold; crease. **estar c. de tiempo,** to be pressed for time.

cogitabundo /kohita'βundo/ *a* very pensive

cognación /kogna'θion; kogna'sion/ *f*, cognation; kinship

cognoscitivo /kognosθi'tiβo; kognossi'tiβo/ *a* cognitive

cogollo /ko'goʎo; ko'goyo/ *m*, heart (of lettuce, etc.); shoot; topmost branches of pine tree

cogote /ko'gote/ *m*, nape (of neck)

cogulla /ko'guʎa; ko'guya/ *f*, monk's habit

cohabitación /koaβita'θion; koaβita'sion/ *f*, cohabitation

cohabitar /koaβi'tar/ *vt* to cohabit

cohechador /koetʃa'ðor/ **(-ra)** *a* bribing —*n* briber

cohechar /koe'tʃar/ *vt* to bribe, corrupt, suborn

cohecho /ko'etʃo/ *m*, bribing; bribe

coheredero /koere'ðero/ **(-ra)** *n* co-heir

coherencia /koe'renθia; koe'rensia/ *f*, coherence, connection

coherente /koe'rente/ *a* coherent

cohesión /koe'sion/ *f*, cohesion

cohesivo /koe'siβo/ *a* cohesive

cohete /ko'ete/ *m*, rocket

cohetero /koe'tero/ *m*, firework manufacturer

cohibir /koi'βir/ *vt* to restrain; repress. See **Prohibir.**

cohombrillo /koom'briʎo; koom'briyo/ *m*, *dim* gherkin

cohombro /ko'ombro/ *m*, cucumber

cohonestar /koones'tar/ *vt Fig.* to gloss over, cover up; make appear decent (actions, etc.)

cohorte /ko'orte/ *f*, cohort

coincidencia /koinθi'ðenθia; koinsi'ðensia/ *f*, coincidence

coincidir /koinθi'ðir; koinsi'ðir/ *vt* to coincide; (two or more people) be in the same place at the same time. **c. con que...** to agree that...

coito /'koito/ *m*, coitus

cojear /kohe'ar/ *vi* to limp; wobble, be unsteady (of furniture); *Fig. Inf.* go wrong or astray; *Inf.* suffer from (vice, bad habit)

cojera /ko'hera/ *f*, lameness, limp

cojijoso /kohi'hoso/ *a* peevish

cojín /ko'hin/ *m*, cushion; pad; pillow (for lace-making)

cojinete /kohi'nete/ *m*, small cushion; *Mech.* bearing. **c. de bolas,** ball-bearing

cojo /'koho/ *a* lame; unsteady, wobbly (of furniture, etc.)

col /kol/ *f*, cabbage. **c. de Bruselas,** Brussels sprouts

cola /'kola/ *f*, tail; train (of gown); shank (of a button); queue; tailpiece (of a violin, etc.); appendage; glue. **c. de milano,** dovetail. **c. de pescado,** isinglass. **formar c.,** to line up, queue up

colaboración /kolaβora'θion; kolaβora'sion/ *f*, collaboration. **en c.,** joint (e.g. *obra en colaboración,* joint work)

colaboracionista /kolaβoraθio'nista; kolaβorasio'nista/ *mf* collaborationist

colaborador /kolaβora'ðor/ **(-ra)** *n* collaborator

colaborar /kolaβo'rar/ *vt* to collaborate

colación /kola'θion; kola'sion/ *f*, conferment of a degree; collation (of texts); light repast; cold supper; area of a parish

colada /ko'laða/ *f*, wash; bleaching; mountain path; *Metall.* casting; *Inf.* trusty sword (allusion to name of one of the Cid's swords)

coladero /kola'ðero/ *m*, colander, sieve, strainer; narrow path

colador /kola'ðor/ *m*, colander

coladura /kola'ðura/ *f*, straining, filtration; *Inf.* untruth; *Inf.* howler, mistake

colapso /ko'lapso/ *m*, *Med.* prostration, collapse

colar /ko'lar/ *vt irr* to filter, strain; bleach; *Metall.* cast; —*vi* go through a narrow place; *Inf.* drink wine; —*vr* thread one's way; *Inf.* enter by stealth, steal in; *Inf.* tell untruths —*Pres. Indic.* **cuelo, cuelas, cuela, cuelan.** *Pres. Subjunc.* **cuele, cueles, cuele, cuelen**

colateral /kolate'ral/ *a* collateral

colcha /'koltʃa/ *f*, bedspread, counterpane, quilt

colchadura /koltʃa'ðura/ *f*, quilting

colchero /kol'tʃero/ *m*, quilt maker

colchón /kol'tʃon/ *m*, mattress. **c. de muelles,** spring-mattress. **c. de viento,** air-bed

colchonero /koltʃo'nero/ *m*, mattress maker or seller

colchoneta /koltʃo'neta/ *f*, pad, thin mattress

coleada /kole'aða/ *f*, wag of the tail

colear /kole'ar/ *vi* to wag the tail

colección /kolek'θion; kolek'sion/ *f*, collection

coleccionador /kolekθiona'ðor; koleksiona'ðor/ **(-ra)** *n* collector

coleccionar /kolekθio'nar; koleksio'nar/ *vt* to collect

coleccionista /kolekθio'nista; koleksio'nista/ *mf* collector

colecta /ko'lekta/ *f*, assessment; collection (of donations); *Eccl.* collect; voluntary offering

colectivero /kolekti'βero/ *m*, bus driver

colectividad /kolektiβi'ðað/ *f*, collectivity; body of people

colectivismo /kolekti'βismo/ *m*, collectivism

colectivista /kolekti'βista/ *a* collectivist

colectivo /kolek'tiβo/ *a* collective; *Argentina* (local) bus

colector /kolek'tor/ *m*, gatherer; collector; tax-collector; water-pipe; water-conduit; *Elec.* commutator, collector

colega /ko'lega/ *m,* colleague

colegiado /kole'hiaðo/ *a* collegiate

colegial **(-la)** *a* college, collegiate —*n* student; pupil; *Fig. Inf.* novice.

colegiarse /kole'hiarse/ *vr* to meet as an association (professional, etc.)

colegiata /kole'hiata/ *f,* college church

colegiatura /kolehia'tura/ *f,* scholarship, fellowship (money granted a student); tuition (fee paid by a student), tuition fee, tuition fees

colegio /ko'lehio/ *m,* college; school; academy; association (professional); council, convocation; college or school buildings. **c. de abogados,** bar association. **c. de cardenales,** College of Cardinals. **c. electoral,** polling-booth. **c. militar,** military academy

colegir /kole'hir/ *vt irr* to collect, gather; deduce, infer. See **elegir**

cólera /'kolera/ *f,* bile, anger. *m,* cholera. **montar en c.,** to fly into a rage

colérico /ko'leriko/ *a* angry; choleric; suffering from cholera

colesterina /koleste'rina/ *f, Chem.* cholesterol

coleta /ko'leta/ *f,* pigtail; queue; *Inf.* postscript

coletazo /kole'taðo; kole'taso/ *m,* blow with one's tail, lash with one's tail; lash of a dying fish; *Fig.* last hurrah

coleto /ko'leto/ *m,* leather jerkin; *Inf.* body of a man

colgadero /kolga'ðero/ *a* able to be hung up. *m,* coat-hanger, hook

colgadizo /kolga'ðiθo; kolga'ðiso/ *a* hanging. *m,* overhanging roof

colgadura /kolga'ðura/ *f,* hangings, drapery, tapestries. **c. de cama,** bedhangings

colgajo /kol'gaho/ *m,* tatter; bunch (of grapes, etc.); *Surg.* skin lap

colgar /kol'gar/ *vt irr* to hang up; decorate with hangings; *Inf.* hang, kill; —*vi* hang, be suspended; *Fig.* be dependent. See **contar**

colibrí /koli'βri/ *m,* hummingbird

cólico /'koliko/ *m,* colic

colicuar /koli'kuar/ *vt* to dissolve

coliflor /koli'flor/ *f,* cauliflower

coligarse /koli'garse/ *vr* to confederate, unite

colilla /ko'liʎa; ko'liya/ *f,* stub (of a cigar or cigarette)

colina /ko'lina/ *f,* hill; cabbage seed; *Chem.* choline

colindante /kolin'dante/ *a* adjacent, contiguous

coliseo /koli'seo/ *m,* coliseum; theater

colisión /koli'sion/ *f,* collision; abrasion, bruise; *Fig.* clash (of ideas)

colitis /ko'litis/ *f,* colitis

collado /ko'ʎaðo; ko'yaðo/ *m,* hill, hillock

collar /ko'ʎar; ko'yar/ *m,* necklace; chain of office or honor; collar (dogs, etc.)

collera /ko'ʎera; ko'yera/ *f,* **collerón,** *m,* horse collar

colmado /kol'maðo/ *a* abundant. *m,* provision shop

colmar /kol'mar/ *vt* to fill to overflowing; bestow generously, heap upon

colmena /kol'mena/ *f,* beehive

colmenero **(-ra)** *n* beekeeper

colmillo /kol'miʎo; kol'miyo/ *m,* canine tooth; tusk; fang

colmilludo /kolmi'ʎuðo; kolmi'yuðo/ *a* having large canine teeth; tusked; fanged; sagacious

colmo /'kolmo/ *m,* overflow; highest point; completion, limit, end. **ser el c.,** *Inf.* to be the last straw. **el c. de los colmos,** the absolute limit

colocación /koloka'θion; koloka'sion/ *f,* placing, putting; situation, place; employment; *Sports.* placing; order, arrangement; *Ling.* collocation

colocar /kolo'kar/ *vt* to place, put, arrange; place in employment. **c. bajo banderas,** to draft (into the armed forces) —*vr* place oneself

colofón /kolo'fon/ *m, Print.* colophon

colofonia /kolo'fonia/ *f,* solid resin (for bows of stringed instruments, etc.)

coloide /ko'loiðe/ *a* and *m,* colloid

colombiano /kolom'biano/ **(-na)** *a* and *n* Colombian

colombina /kolom'bina/ *f,* columbine

colombofilia /kolombo'filia/ *f,* pigeon fancying

colonia /ko'lonia/ *f,* colony; plantation

colonial /kolo'nial/ *a* colonial

colonización /koloniθa'θion; kolonisa'sion/ *f,* colonization

colonizador /koloniθa'ðor; kolonisa'ðor/ **(-ra)** *a* colonizing —*n* colonizer

colonizar /koloni'θar; koloni'sar/ *vt* to colonize; settle

colono /ko'lono/ *m,* settler, colonist; farmer

coloquio /ko'lokio/ *m,* colloquy, conversation, talk; colloquium

color /ko'lor/ *m,* color; dye; paint; rouge; coloring; pretext, excuse; character, individuality; *pl* natural colors. **c. estable, c. sólido,** fast color. **mudar de c.,** to change color. **de c.,** colored. **so c.,** under the pretext. **ver las cosas c. de rosa,** to see things through rose-colored glasses

coloración /kolora'θion; kolora'sion/ *f,* coloration, painting

colorado /kolo'raðo/ *a* colored. *West Hem.* red, reddish; *Inf.* blue, obscene; becoming

colorante /kolo'rante/ *a* coloring. *m,* dyestuff; coloring (substance)

colorar /kolo'rar/ *vt* to color; dye

colorear /kolore'ar/ *vt* to color; pretext; *Fig.* whitewash, excuse; —*vi* show color; be reddish; grow red, ripe (tomatoes, cherries, etc.)

colorero /kolo'rero/ *m,* dyer

colorete /kolo'rete/ *m,* rouge

colorido /kolo'riðo/ *m,* coloring, color

colorín /kolo'rin/ *m,* goldfinch; bright color

colorista /kolo'rista/ *a* and *mf* colorist

colosal /kolo'sal/ *a* colossal, enormous; extraordinary, excellent

coloso /ko'loso/ *m,* colossus; *Fig.* outstanding person or thing, giant; **el C. del Norte, el Gran C. del Norte,** (contemptuous epithet for the United States of America)

columbino /kolum'bino/ *a* pertaining to a dove; dovelike; candid, innocent; purply-red

columbrar /kolum'brar/ *vt* to discern in the distance, glimpse; conjecture, guess

columna /ko'lumna/ *f, Mil. Archit. Print.* column; *Fig.* protection, shelter; *Naut.* stanchion. **c. cerrada,** *Mil.* etc. mass formation. **c. de los suspiros,** agony column (in a newspaper)

columnata /kolum'nata/ *f,* colonnade

columpiar /kolum'piar/ *vt* to swing; dangle (one's feet); —*vr Inf.* sway in walking; swing

columpio /ko'lumpio/ *m,* swing

colusión /kolu'sion/ *f,* collusion

colusorio /kolu'sorio/ *a* collusive

coma /'koma/ *f, Gram.* comma. *m, Med.* coma

comadre /ko'maðre/ *f,* midwife; *Inf.* procuress, go-between; *Inf.* pal, gossip

comadrear /komaðre'ar/ *vi Inf.* to gossip

comadreja /koma'ðreha/ *f, Zool.* weasel

comadrón /koma'ðron/ *m,* accoucheur

comadrona /koma'ðrona/ *f,* midwife

comandancia /koman'danθia; koman'dansia/ *f, Mil.* command; commandant's H.Q.

comandante /koman'dante/ *m,* commandant; commander; major; squadron-leader —*a Mil.* commanding. **c. en jefe,** commanding officer

comandar /koman'dar/ *vt Mil.* to command

comandita /koman'dita/ *f, Com.* sleeping partnership; private company

comando /ko'mando/ *m, Mil.* commando

comarca /ko'marka/ *f,* district, region

comatoso /koma'toso/ *a* comatose

comba /'komba/ *f,* bend, warping; jump rope, skipping-rope; camber (of road)

combadura /komba'ðura/ *f,* curvature; warping; camber (of a road)

combar /kom'bar/ *vt* to bend; twist; warp; camber

combate /kom'bate/ *m,* fight, combat; mental strife; contradiction, opposition. **c. judicial,** trial by combat. **dejar fuera de c.,** (a) (boxing) to knock out

combatiente /komba'tiente/ *m,* combatant, soldier

combatir /komba'tir/ *vi* to fight; —*vt* attack; struggle against (winds, water, etc.); contradict, oppose; *Fig.* disturb, trouble (emotions)

combinación /kombina'θion; kombina'sion/ *f,* combination; list of words beginning with same letter; project; concurrence; underskirt, petticoat. **estar en c.** (**con**), to be in cahoots (with), connive (with)

combinar /kombi'nar/ *vt* to combine; (*Mil. Nav.*) join forces; arrange, plan; *Chem.* combine; **combinar para + inf.** (two or more people) to make arrangements to + inf.

combustible /kombus'tiβle/ *a* combustible. *m,* fuel

combustión /kombus'tion/ *f,* combustion. **c. activa,** rapid combustion. **c. espontánea,** spontaneous combustion

comedero /kome'ðero/ *a* edible. *m,* feeding-trough; dining-room

comedia /ko'meðia/ *f,* comedy; play; theater; comic incident; *Fig.* play-acting, theatricalism. **c. alta,** art theater. **c. de costumbres,** comedy of manners. **c. de enredo,** play with very involved plot. *Inf.* **hacer la c.,** to play-act, pretend

comedianta /kome'ðianta/ *f,* actress

comediante /kome'ðiante/ *m,* actor; *Inf.* dissembler.

comedido /kome'ðiðo/ *a* courteous; prudent; moderate

comedimiento /komeði'miento/ *m,* courtesy; moderation; prudence

comedir /kome'ðir/ *vt irr* to prepare, premeditate; —*vr* restrain oneself, be moderate; offer one's services. See **pedir**

comedor /kome'ðor/ *a* voracious. *m,* dining-room

comendador /komenda'ðor/ *m,* knight commander

comendatorio /komenda'torio/ *a* commendatory (of letters)

Comenio /ko'menio/ Comenius

comensal /komen'sal/ *mf* table companion

comentador /komenta'ðor/ **(-ra)** *n* commentator

comentar /komen'tar/ *vt* explain (document); *Inf.* comment

comentario /komen'tario/ **(a)** *m,* commentary (on)

comentarista /komenta'rista/ *mf* commentator

comento /ko'mento/ *m,* comment; commentary

comenzante /komen'θante; komen'sante/ *mf* beginner, novice —*a* initial

comenzar /komen'θar; komen'sar/ *vt vi irr* to begin, commence. See **empezar**

comer /ko'mer/ *m,* eating; food —*vi* to eat; feed; dine —*vt* eat; *Inf.* enjoy an income; waste (patrimony); consume, exhaust; fade (of colors); —*vr* be troubled, uneasy, remorseful. **ser de buen c.,** to have a good appetite; taste good. **tener que c.,** to be obliged to eat; have to eat; have enough to eat

comerciable /komer'θiaβle; komer'siaβle/ *a* marketable; sociable, pleasant (of persons)

comercial /komer'θial; komer'sial/ *a* commercial

comerciante /komer'θiante; komer'siante/ *a* trading. *mf* merchant, trader

comerciar /komer'θiar; komer'siar/ *vt* to trade; have dealings (with)

comercio /ko'merθio; ko'mersio/ *m,* trade, commerce; intercourse, traffic; illicit sexual intercourse; shop, store; tradesmen; commercial quarter of town

comestible /komes'tiβle/ *a* edible, eatable. *m,* (gen. *pl*) provisions

cometa /ko'meta/ *m,* *Astron.* comet. *f,* kite (toy). **c. celular,** box-kite

cometedor /komete'ðor/ **(-ra)** *n* perpetrator

cometer /kome'ter/ *vt* to entrust, hand over to; commit (crime, sins, etc.); *Com.* order

cometido /kome'tiðo/ *m,* charge, commission; moral obligation; function

comezón /kome'θon; kome'son/ *f,* itching, irritation; hankering, longing

comicidad /komiθi'ðað; komisi'ðað/ *f,* comic element; comic spirit

cómico /'komiko/ *a* comic; funny, comical. *m,* actor; comedian. **c. de la legua,** strolling player

comida /ko'miða/ *f,* food; meal; dinner; eating. **c. de gala,** state banquet. **c. de prueba,** *Med.* test meal

comienzo /ko'mienθo; ko'mienso/ *m,* beginning, origin

comillas /ko'miʎas; ko'miyas/ *f pl,* *Gram.* inverted commas

comilón /komi'lon/ **(-ona)** *a* *Inf.* gluttonous —*n* glutton

comino /ko'mino/ *m,* *Bot.* cumin. **no valer un c.,** to be not worth a jot

comisar /komi'sar/ *vt* to confiscate, sequestrate

comisaría /komisa'ria/ *f,* commissaryship; commissariat. **c. de policía,** police station

comisario /komi'sario/ *m,* deputy, agent; commissary, head of police; commissioner. **alto c.,** high commissioner. **c. propietario,** stockholders' representative

comisión /komi'sion/ *f,* perpetration, committal; commission; committee; *Com.* commission

comisionado /komisio'naðo/ **(-da)** *a* commissioned. *m,* commissary

comisionar /komisio'nar/ *vt* to commission

comisionista /komisio'nista/ *mf* *Com.* commission agent

comiso /ko'miso/ *m,* *Law.* confiscation, sequestration; contraband

comité /komi'te/ *m,* committee

comitiva /komi'tiβa/ *f,* retinue, following

como /'komo/ *adv* like, as; in the same way; thus, accordingly; in the capacity of; so that; since —*conjunc* if (*followed by subjunc.*); because. **c. no,** unless. ¿**Cómo?** How? In what way? Why? Pardon? What did you say? *interj* ¡**Cómo!** What! You don't say! ¡**Cómo no!** Why not! Of course! Surely! ¿**Cómo que...?** What do you mean that...?

cómo /'komo/ *m,* the wherefore. **no saber el porqué ni el c.,** not to know the why or wherefore

cómoda /'komoða/ *f,* chest of drawers

comodidad /komoði'ðað/ *f,* comfort; convenience; advantage; utility, interest

comodín /komo'ðin/ *m,* (in cards) joker

cómodo /'komoðo/ *a* comfortable; convenient; opportune

comodón /komo'ðon/ *a* *Inf.* comfort-loving; easygoing; egoistical

comodoro /komo'ðoro/ *m,* *Naut.* commodore

comoquiera que /komo'kiera ke/ *adv* by any means that, anyway; whereas, given that

compacidad /kompaθi'ðað; kompasi'ðað/ *f,* compactness

compacto /kom'pakto/ *a* compact, dense; close (type)

compadecer /kompaðe'θer; kompaðe'ser/ *vt irr* to pity; —*vr* (*with* **de**) sympathize with; pity; harmonize, agree with. See **conocer**

compadre /kom'paðre/ *m,* *Inf.* pal

compaginación /kompahina'θion; kompahina'sion/ *f,* joining, fixing; *Print.* making-up

compaginar /kompahi'nar/ *vt* to fit together; join, put in order; harmonize, square (e.g. *compaginé una cuenta con la otra,* I squared one account with the other); *Print.* make up

compañero /kompa'ɲero/ **(-ra)** *m,* companion, comrade; fellow-member; partner (games); *Fig.* pair, fellow, mate (things). **c. de armas,** brother-in-arms, companion-at-arms. **c. de cabina,** boothmate. **c. de exilio,** companion in exile, fellow exile. **c. de generación,** contemporary, person of the same generation. **c. de viaje,** traveling companion; *Polit.* fellow traveler (communist sympathizer)

compañía /kompa'ɲia/ *f,* company; society, association; theatrical company; (*Com. Mil.*) company. **C. de Jesús,** Order of Jesus. **c. de la zarza,** guild of guards and woodcutters for autos de fe. **c. de navegación,** shipping company. **c. por acciones,** joint stock company

comparable /kompa'raβle/ *a* comparable

comparación /kompara'θion; kompara'sion/ *f,* comparison

comparar /kompa'rar/ *vt* to compare; collate

comparativo /kompara'tiβo/ *a* comparative

comparecencia /kompare'θenθia; kompare'sensia/ *f,* (gen. *Law.*) appearance

comparecer /kompare'θer; kompare'ser/ *vi irr Law.* to appear (before tribunal, etc.); present oneself. See **conocer**

comparendo /kompa'rendo/ *m,* *Law.* summons

comparsa /kom'parsa/ *f*, retinue; *Theat.* chorus; troop of carnival revelers dressed alike. *mf Theat.* supernumerary actor

comparte /kom'parte/ *mf Law.* partner; accomplice

compartimiento /komparti'miento/ *m*, share, division; railway carriage. *Naut.* **c. estanco**, compartment

compartir /kompar'tir/ *vt* to share out, divide; participate

compás /kom'pas/ *m*, compasses; callipers; size; compass, time; range of voice; (*Naut. Mineral.*) compass; *Mus.* time, rhythm, bar, marking time. **c. de mar,** mariner's compass. **c. de puntas,** dividers, callipers. **fuera de c.,** *Mus.* out of time; out of joint (of the times). *Mus.* **llevar el c.,** to beat time

compasar /kompa'sar/ *vt* to measure with compasses; arrange or apportion accurately; *Mus.* put into bars

compasillo /kompa'siʎo; kompa'siyo/ *m*, *Mus.* $\frac{4}{4}$ measure

compasivo /kompa'siβo/ *a* compassionate; tenderhearted

compatibilidad /kompatiβili'ðað/ *f*, compatibility

compatible /kompa'tiβle/ *a* compatible

compatriota /kompa'triota/ *mf* compatriot

compeler /kompe'ler/ *vt* to compel, force

compendiar /kompen'diar/ *vt* to abridge, summarize

compendio /kom'pendio/ *m*, compendium. **en c.,** briefly

compendioso /kompen'dioso/ *a* summary, condensed; compendious

compenetración /kompenetra'θion; kompenetra'sion/ *f*, co-penetration; intermingling

compenetrado /kompene'traðo/ **(de)** *a* thoroughly convinced (of)

compenetrarse /kompene'trarse/ *vr* to co-penetrate; intermingle

compensación /kompensa'θion; kompensa'sion/ *f*, compensating; compensation

compensar /kompen'sar/ *vt* to equalize, counterbalance; compensate

compensatorio /kompensa'torio/ *a* compensatory; equalizing

competencia /kompe'tenθia; kompe'tensia/ *f*, competition, contest; rivalry; competence; aptitude; *Law.* jurisdiction

competente /kompe'tente/ *a* adequate, opportune; rightful, correct; apt, suitable; learned, competent

competer /kompe'ter/ *vi irr* to belong to; devolve on; concern. See **pedir**

competición /kompeti'θion; kompeti'sion/ *f*, competition

competidor /kompeti'ðor/ **(-ra)** *n* competitor

competir /kompe'tir/ *vi irr* to compete, contest; be equal (to), vie (with). See **pedir**

compilación /kompila'θion; kompila'sion/ *f*, compilation

compilador /kompila'ðor/ **(-ra)** *n* compiler —*a* compiling

compilar /kompi'lar/ *vt* to compile

compinche /kom'pintʃe/ *mf Inf.* pal, chum

complacencia /kompla'θenθia; kompla'sensia/ *f*, satisfaction, pleasure

complacer /kompla'θer; kompla'ser/ *vt irr* to oblige, humor; —*vr* (*with en*) be pleased or satisfied with; delight in, like to. See **nacer**

complaciente /kompla'θiente; kompla'siente/ *a* pleasing; obliging, helpful

complejidad /komplehi'ðað/ *f*, complexity

complejo /kom'pleho/ *a* complex; intricate. *m*, complex. **c. de inferioridad,** inferiority complex

complementario /komplemen'tario/ *a* complementary

complemento /komple'mento/ *m*, complement (all meanings)

completar /komple'tar/ *vt* to complete; perfect

completo /kom'pleto/ *a* full; finished; perfect

complexión /komplek'sion/ *f*, physical constitution

complexo /kom'plekso/ *a* complex; intricate

complicación /komplika'θion; komplika'sion/ *f*, complication

complicar /kompli'kar/ *vt* to complicate; muddle,

confuse; —*vr* be complicated; be muddled or confused

cómplice /'kompliθe; 'komplise/ *mf* accomplice

complicidad /kompliθi'ðað; komplisi'ðað/ *f*, complicity

complot /kom'plot/ *m*, *Inf.* conspiracy, plot, intrigue

complutense /komplu'tense/ *a* a native of, or belonging to, Alcalá de Henares

componedor /kompone'ðor/ **(-ra)** *n* repairer; arbitrator; bone-setter; *Mus.* composer; writer, author, compiler; *Print.* compositor

componenda /kompo'nenda/ *f*, mending, repair; *Inf.* settlement; compromise, arbitration; *Inf.* shady business

componente /kompo'nente/ *a* and *m*, component

componer /kompo'ner/ *vt irr* to construct, form; *Mech.* resolve; compose, create; *Print.* compose; prepare, concoct, mend, repair; settle (differences); remedy; trim; correct, adjust; *Lit. Mus.* compose; add up to, amount to; —*vi* write (verses); *Mus.* compose; —*vr* dress oneself up. **c. el semblante,** to compose one's features; *Inf.* **componérselas,** to fix matters, use one's wits. See **poner**

componible /kompo'niβle/ *a* reparable, mendable; able to be arranged or adjusted

comportamiento /komporta'miento/ *m*, conduct; deportment

comportar /kompor'tar/ *vt* to tolerate; —*vr* behave, comport oneself

composición /komposi'θion; komposi'sion/ *f*, composition; repair; arrangement, compromise; *Print.* composition; *Gram.* compound; *Chem.* constitution; *Mech.* resolution

compositor /komposi'tor/ **(-ra)** *n Mus.* composer; *Print.* compositor

Compostela /kompos'tela/ Compostella

compostura /kompos'tura/ *f*, composition, structure; repair; neatness (of person); adulteration; arrangement, agreement; discretion, modesty

compota /kom'pota/ *f*, fruit preserve, compote; thick sauce

compotera /kompo'tera/ *f*, jam or preserve dish

compra /'kompra/ *f*, buying; marketing, shopping; purchase. **estar de compras,** *Euph.* to be in the family way. **ir de compras,** to go shopping

comprable /kom'praβle/ *a* purchasable

comprador /kompra'ðor/ **(-ra)** *a* purchasing —*n* purchaser; buyer; shopper

comprar /kom'prar/ *vt* to buy; bribe

comprender /kompren'der/ *vt* to encircle, surround; include, comprise, contain; understand

comprensible /kompren'siβle/ *a* comprehensible

comprensión /kompren'sion/ *f*, comprehension, understanding

comprensivo /kompren'siβo/ *a* understanding; comprehensive

compresa /kom'presa/ *f*, *Med.* compress, swab; pack (for the face, etc.)

compresión /kompre'sion/ *f*, compression; squeeze

compresivo /kompre'siβo/ *a* compressive

compresor /kompre'sor/ *m*, compressor; *Auto. Aer.* supercharger

comprimido /kompri'miðo/ *m*, tablet, pill

comprimir /kompri'mir/ *vt* to compress; squeeze; restrain; —*vr* restrain oneself

comprobación /komproβa'θion; komproβa'sion/ *f*, verification; checking; proof

comprobante /kompro'βante/ *a* verifying; confirmatory

comprobar /kompro'βar/ *vt irr* to verify, check; confirm, prove. See **probar**

comprobatorio /komproβa'torio/ *a* confirmatory; verifying; testing

comprometedor /kompromete'ðor/ *a Inf.* compromising; jeopardizing

comprometer /komprome'ter/ *vt* to submit to arbitration; compromise; imperil, jeopardize; —*vr* pledge oneself; *Inf.* compromise oneself

comprometido /komprome'tiðo/ *a* awkward, embarrassing; (e.g. literature of a writer) committed, engagé

compromiso /kompro'miso/ *m*, compromise, agree-

ment, arbitration, commitment, obligation; appointment, engagement; jeopardy; difficulty

compuerta /kom'puerta/ f, half-door, wicket, hatch; floodgate, sluice. **c. flotante,** floating dam

compuesto /kom'puesto/ a and past part made-up, built-up; composite; circumspect; Bot. Gram. compound. m, composite; preparation, compound

compulsar /kompul'sar/ vt to collate; Law. make a transcript of

compulsivo /kompul'siβo/ a compelling

compunción /kompun'θion; kompun'sion/ f, compunction

compungir /kompun'hir/ vt to cause remorse or pity; —vr repent; sympathize with, pity

computable /kompu'taβle/ a computable

computación /komputa'θion; komputa'sion/ f, **cómputo** m, calculation, computation

computador /komputa'ðor/ **(-ra)** n computer

computar /kompu'tar/ vt to compute

computista /kompu'tista/ mf computer

cómputo /'komputo/ m, computation; estimate

comulgar /komul'gar/ vt to administer Holy Communion; —vi receive Holy Communion

comulgatorio /komulga'torio/ m, communion rail, altar rail

común /ko'mun/ a general, customary, ordinary; public, communal; universal, common; vulgar, low. m, community, population; water-closet. **en c.,** in common; generally. **por lo c.,** generally. **sentido c.,** common sense

comunal /komu'nal/ a communal; common. m, commonalty

comunero /komu'nero/ a popular, affable, democratic. m, joint owner; commoner; Hist. commune

comunicable /komuni'kaβle/ a communicable; communicative, sociable

comunicación /komunika'θion; komunika'sion/ f, communication; (telephone) call, message; letter (to the press); Mil. communiqué; pl lines of communication, transport

comunicado /komuni'kaðo/ m, official communication, communiqué; letter (to the press)

comunicante /komuni'kante/ a communicating

comunicar /komuni'kar/ vt to communicate; transmit; impart, share; —vr **comunicarse con,** (door) to open onto (e.g. Esta puerta se comunica con el jardín. This door opens onto the garden); communicate, converse, correspond with each other

comunicativo /komunika'tiβo/ a communicative; talkative, not reserved

comunidad /komuni'ðað/ f, the common people; community; generality, majority; pl Hist. Commune

comunión /komu'nion/ f, communion; intercourse, fellowship; Eccl. Communion

comunismo /komu'nismo/ m, communism

comunista /komu'nista/ a and mf communist

comunistófilo, comunistoide /komunis'tofilo, komunis'toiðe/ a fellow-traveling; —n fellow traveler

comúnmente /komu'mente/ adv commonly, generally; frequently

con /kon/ prep with; by means of; in the company of; towards, to; although (followed by infin., but generally translated by an inflected verb, e.g. C. ser almirante, no le gusta el mar, Although he is an admiral, he doesn't like the sea); by (followed by infin. and generally translated by a gerund, e.g. c. hacer todo esto, by doing all this). **c. bien,** safe and sound, safely (e.g. Llegamos con bien. We arrived safely.) **c. cuentagotas,** sparingly; stingily. **c. que,** so, then. **c. tal que,** provided that, on condition that. **c. todo,** nevertheless. **¿Con...?** Is this...? (on the telephone, e.g. ¿Con el Sr. Piñangos? Is this Mr. Piñangos?)

conato /ko'nato/ m, effort, endeavor; tendency; Law. attempted crime

concatenación /konkatena'θion; konkatena'sion/ f, concatenation

concavidad /konkaβi'ðað/ f, concavity; hollow

cóncavo /'konkaβo/ a concave. m, concavity; hollow

concebible /konθe'βiβle; konse'βiβle/ a conceivable

concebimiento /konθeβi'miento; konseβi'miento/ m. See **concepción**

concebir /konθe'βir; konse'βir/ vi irr to become pregnant; conceive, imagine; understand; —vt conceive, acquire (affection, etc.). See **pedir**

concedente /konθe'ðente; konse'ðente/ a conceding

conceder /konθe'ðer; konse'ðer/ vt to confer, grant; concede; agree to

concejal /konθe'hal; konse'hal/ m, councillor; alderman

concejil /konθe'hil; konse'hil/ a pertaining to a municipal council; public

concejo /kon'θeho; kon'seho/ m, town council; town hall; council meeting

concentración /konθentra'θion; konsentra'sion/ f, concentration

concentrado /konθen'traðo; konsen'traðo/ a concentrated; (of persons) reserved

concentrar /konθen'trar; konsen'trar/ vt to concentrate

concéntrico /kon'θentriko; kon'sentriko/ a concentric

concepción /konθep'θion; konsep'sion/ f, conception; idea, concept; Eccl. Immaculate Conception

conceptismo /konθep'tismo; konsep'tismo/ m, Lit. Conceptism (cf. **Euphuism**)

conceptista /konθep'tista; konsep'tista/ a and mf conceptist

concepto /kon'θepto; kon'septo/ m, idea, concept; epigram; opinion. **en mi c.,** in my opinion; judgment. **por c. de,** in payment of

conceptualismo /konθeptua'lismo; konseptua'lismo/ m, conceptualism

conceptuar /konθep'tuar; konsep'tuar/ vt to judge, take to be; believe; imagine

conceptuoso /konθep'tuoso; konsep'tuoso/ a witty, ingenious

concernencia /konθer'nenθia; konser'nensia/ f, respect, relation

concerniente /konθer'niente; konser'niente/ a concerning

concernir /konθer'nir; konser'nir/ vi irr defective to concern. See **discernir**

concertadamente /konθertaða'mente; konsertaða'mente/ adv methodically, orderly; by arrangement, or agreement

concertar /konθer'tar; konser'tar/ vt irr to arrange, settle, adjust; bargain; conclude (business deal); harmonize; compare, correlate; tune instruments; —vi reach an agreement. See **acertar**

concertina /konθer'tina; konser'tina/ f, concertina

concertista /konθer'tista; konser'tista/ mf Mus. performer, soloist; Mus. manager. **c. de piano,** concert pianist

concesión /konθe'sion; konse'sion/ f, conceding, grant; concession; lease

concesionario /konθesio'nario; konsesio'nario/ m, Law. concessionaire, leaseholder

concha /'kontʃa/ f, shell; turtle-shell; prompter's box; cove, creek; anything shell-shaped. Fig. **meterse en su c.,** to retire into one's shell. Inf. **tener más conchas que un galápago,** to be very cunning

conchado /kon'tʃaðo/ a scaly, having a shell

conciencia /kon'θienθia; kon'siensia/ f, consciousness; conscience; conscientiousness. **c. doble,** dual personality. **ancho de c.,** broad-minded. **a c.,** conscientiously

concienzudo /konθien'θuðo; konsien'suðo/ a of a delicate conscience, scrupulous; conscientious

concierto /kon'θierto; kon'sierto/ m, methodical arrangement; agreement; Mus. concert; Mus. concerto. **de c.,** by common consent

conciliable /konθi'liaβle; konsi'liaβle/ a reconcilable, compatible

conciliábulo /konθi'liaβulo; konsi'liaβulo/ m, conclave, private meeting; secret meeting

conciliación /konθilia'θion; konsilia'sion/ f, conciliation; similarity, affinity; protection, favor

conciliador /konθilia'ðor; konsilia'ðor/ a conciliatory

conciliar /konθi'liar; konsi'liar/ m, councilor —vt to conciliate; Fig. reconcile (opposing theories, etc.). **c. el sueño,** to induce sleep, woo sleep —vr win liking (or sometimes dislike)

concilio /kon'θilio; kon'silio/ m, council; Eccl. assembly; conciliary decree; findings of council

concinidad /konθini'ðað; konsini'ðað/ f, concinnity

concino /kon'θino; kon'sino/ a concinnous

concisión /konθi'sion; konsi'sion/ f, conciseness, brevity

conciso /kon'θiso; kon'siso/ a concise

concitar /konθi'tar; konsi'tar/ vt to stir up, foment

conciudadano /konθiuða'ðano; konsiuða'ðano/ (**-na**) n fellow citizen; fellow countryman

cónclave /'konklaβe/ m, conclave; meeting

concluir /kon'kluir/ vt irr to conclude, finish; come to a conclusion, decide; infer, deduce; convince by reasoning; Law. close legal proceedings; —vr expire, terminate. **c. con**, to put an end to. See **huir**

conclusión /konklu'sion/ f, finish, end; decision; close, denouement; theory, proposition (gen. pl); deduction, inference; Law. close. **en c.**, in conclusion

conclusivo /konklu'siβo/ a final; conclusive

concluyente /konklu'yente/ a concluding; convincing; conclusive

concomer /konko'mer/ vi Inf. to give a shrug, shrug one's shoulders; fidget with an itch. **c. de placer**, to itch with pleasure

concomitancia /konkomi'tanθia; konkomi'tansia/ f, concomitance

concomitante /konkomi'tante/ a and m, concomitant

concordable /konkor'ðaβle/ a conformable

concordador /konkorðo'ðor/ (**-ra**) a peacemaking —n peacemaker

concordancia /konkor'ðanθia; konkor'ðansia/ f, harmony, agreement; (Mus. Gram.) concord; pl concordance

concordar /konkor'ðar/ vt irr to bring to agreement; —vi agree. See **acordar**

concordato /konkor'ðato/ m, concordat

concorde /kon'korðe/ a agreeing; harmonious

concordia /kon'korðia/ f, concord, agreement, harmony; written agreement

concreción /konkre'θion; konkre'sion/ f, concretion

concretar /konkre'tar/ vt to combine, bring together; make concise; resume; —vr Fig. confine oneself (to a subject) to hammer out, work out (an agreement)

concreto /kon'kreto/ a concrete, real, not abstract. **en c.**, in definite terms; finally, to sum up

concubina /konku'βina/ f, concubine, mistress

concubinato /konkuβi'nato/ m, concubinage

conculcación /konkulka'θion; konkulka'sion/ f, trampling, treading; violation

conculcador /konkulka'ðor/ m, violator

conculcar /konkul'kar/ vt to trample under foot, tread on; break, violate

concupiscencia /konkupis'θenθia; konkupis'sensia/ f, concupiscence, lust; greed

concupiscente /konkupis'θente; konkupis'sente/ a concupiscent, lustful; greedy

concurrencia /konku'rrenθia; konku'rrensia/ f, assembly; coincidence; attendance; help, influence

concurrido /konku'rriðo/ a crowded; busy; frequented

concurrir /konku'rrir/ vi to coincide; contribute; meet together; agree, be of same opinion; compete (in an examination, etc.)

concurso /kon'kurso/ m, crowd, concourse; conjunction, coincidence; help; competition; (tennis) tournament; competitive examination; invitation to offer tenders. **c. de acreedores**, creditors' meeting. **c. interno**, competitive examination for a position open to staff members only

concusión /konku'sion/ f, concussion; shock; extortion

condado /kon'daðo/ m, earldom; county

condal /kon'dal/ a of an earl, earl's; of a count, count's; of Barcelona

conde /'konde/ m, earl; king of the gypsies

condecir /konde'θir; konde'sir/ vi (**con**) to agree (with)

condecoración /kondekora'θion; kondekora'sion/ f, conferment of an honor, decoration; medal

condecorar /kondeko'rar/ vt to confer a decoration or medal

condena /kon'dena/ f, Law. sentence; punishment; penalty

condenable /konde'naβle/ a culpable, guilty; worthy of damnation

condenado /konde'naðo/ (**-da**) a damned; wicked, harmful —n Law. convicted criminal

condenador /kondena'ðor/ a condemning; incriminating; blaming

condenar /konde'nar/ vt Law. to pronounce sentence (on), convict; condemn; disapprove; wall or block or close up. **c. a galeras**, to condemn to the gallies —vr blame oneself; be eternally damned

condenatorio /kondena'torio/ a condemnatory; incriminating

condensación /kondensa'θion; kondensa'sion/ f, condensation

condensador /kondensa'ðor/ a condensing. m, (Elec. Mech. Chem.) condenser

condensante /konden'sante/ a condensing

condensar /konden'sar/ vt to condense; thicken; abridge

condesa /kon'desa/ f, countess

condescendencia /kondesθen'denθia; kondessen'densia/ f, affability, graciousness

condescender /kondesθen'der; kondessen'der/ vi irr to be obliging, helpful, agreeable. See **entender**

condescendiente /kondesθen'diente; kondessen'diente/ a affable, gracious

condestable /kondes'taβle/ m, Hist. constable, commander-in-chief

condición /kondi'θion; kondi'sion/ f, condition; quality; temperament, character; (social) position; rank, family; nobility, circumstance; stipulation, condition, requirement. **estar en condiciones de**, to be in a position to. **no estar en condiciones de**, to be in no condition to

condicional /kondiθio'nal; kondisio'nal/ a conditional

condicionar /kondiθio'nar; kondisio'nar/ vi to come to an agreement, arrange; —vt impose conditions

condigno /kon'digno/ a condign

condimentación /kondimenta'θion; kondimenta-'sion/ f, Cul. seasoning

condimentar /kondimen'tar/ vt to flavor, season (food)

condimento /kondi'mento/ m, condiment, flavoring

condiscípulo /kondis'θipulo; kondis'sipulo/ m, schoolfellow

condolencia /kondo'lenθia; kondo'lensia/ f, compassion; condolence

condolerse /kondo'lerse/ vr (with de) to sympathize with, be sorry for. See **doler**

condonar /kondo'nar/ vt to condone

conducción /konduk'θion; konduk'sion/ f. **conducencia**, f, transport, conveyance, carriage; guiding; direction, management; Phys. conduction; Mech. control-gear. Auto. **c. a izquierda**, left-hand drive

conducente /kondu'θente; kondu'sente/ a conducting, conducive

conducir /kondu'θir; kondu'sir/ vt irr to transport, convey, carry; Phys. conduct; guide, lead; manage, direct; Auto. drive; conduce; —vi be suitable; —vr behave, conduct oneself —Pres. Indic. **conduzco, conduces**, etc —Preterite **conduje, condujiste**, etc —Pres. Subjunc. **conduzca, conduzcas**, etc —Imperf. Subjunc. **condujese**, etc.

conducta /kon'dukta/ f, transport, conveyance; management, conduct, direction; behavior

conductibilidad /konduktiβili'ðað/ f, Phys. conductivity

conductivo /konduk'tiβo/ a conductive

conducto /kon'dukto/ m, pipe, conduit, drain, duct; Fig. channel, means; Anat. tube

conductor /konduk'tor/ (**-ra**) n guide; leader; driver (vehicles); m, Phys. conductor. **c. de entrada**, Radio. lead-in. **c. del calor**, heat-conductor. **c. eléctrico**, electric wire or cable

conectar /konek'tar/ vt Elec. to connect, switch on; couple; attach, join

conectivo /konek'tiβo/ a connective; (Elec. Mech.) connecting

conejera /kone'hera/ *f*, rabbit-warren; *Inf*. low dive or haunt

conejillo de Indias /kone'hiʎo de 'indias; kone'hiyo de 'indias/ *m*, guineapig

conejo /ko'neho/ *m*, rabbit

conejuna /kone'huna/ *f*, rabbit fur, coney

conejuno /kone'huno/ *a* rabbit, rabbit-like

conexión /konek'sion/ *f*, connection; *Elec*. switching on, connection; joint; joining; *pl* friends, connections; *Elec*. wiring

conexo /ko'nekso/ *a* connected

confabulación /konfaβula'θion; konfaβula'sion/ *f*, confabulation, conspiracy

confabular /konfaβu'lar/ *vi* to confer; —*vr* scheme, plot

confalón /konfa'lon/ *m*, standard, banner

confección /konfek'θion; konfek'sion/ *f*, making; confection; making-up; concoction, remedy; ready-made garment

confeccionador /konfekθiona'ðor; konfeksiona'ðor/ **(-ra)** *n* maker (of clothes, etc.)

confeccionar /konfekθio'nar; konfeksio'nar/ *vt* to make; prepare; make up (pharmaceuticals)

confederación /konfeðera'θion; konfeðera'sion/ *f*, alliance, pact; confederacy, federation

confederarse /konfeðe'rarse/ *vr* to confederate, be allied

conferencia /konfe'renθia; konfe'rensia/ *f*, conference, meeting; lecture; (telephone) long-distance call (US), trunk call (UK)

conferenciante /konferen'θiante; konferen'siante/ *mf* lecturer

conferenciar /konferen'θiar; konferen'siar/ *vi* to confer

conferir /konfe'rir/ *vt irr* to grant, concede; consider, discuss; compare, correlate. See **herir**

confesable /konfe'saβle/ *a* acknowledgeable, avowable

confesar /konfe'sar/ *vt irr* to avow, declare; acknowledge, admit; *Eccl*. hear confession; —*vr Eccl*. confess —*Pres. Indic*. **confieso, confiesas, confiesa, confiesan**. *Pres. Subjunc*. **confiese, confieses, confiese, confiesen**

confesión /konfe'sion/ *f*, confession

confesional /konfesio'nal/ *a* confessional

confesionario, confesonario, confesorio /konfesio'nario, konfeso'nario, konfe'sorio/ *m*, *Eccl*. confessional

confeso /kon'feso/ *a* confessed; converted (of Jews). *m*, *Eccl*. lay brother

confesor /konfe'sor/ *m*, confessor

confeti /kon'feti/ *m*, confetti

confianza /kon'fianθa; kon'fiansa/ *f*, confidence, trust; assurance, courage; over-confidence, conceit; intimacy; familiarity. **de c.,** reliable (e.g. *persona de c.,* reliable person); informal (e.g. *reunión de c.,* informal meeting). **en c.,** in confidence, confidentially

confianzudo /konfian'θuðo; konfian'suðo/ *a Inf.* overconfident

confiar /kon'fiar/ *vi* (*with en*) to trust in, hope; —*vt* (*with prep a or en*) entrust, commit to the care of; confide in

confidencia /konfi'ðenθia; konfi'ðensia/ *f*, trust; confidence; confidential information

confidencial /konfiðen'θial; konfiðen'sial/ *a* confidential

confidente /konfi'ðente/ **(-ta)** *a* trustworthy, true. *m*, seat for two —*n* confidant(e); spy

configuración /konfigura'θion; konfigura'sion/ *f*, configuration, form, lie

configurar /konfigu'rar/ *vt* to shape

confín /kon'fin/ *m*, boundary, frontier; limit —*a* boundary

confinado /konfi'naðo/ *a* banished. *m*, *Law*. prisoner

confinar /konfi'nar/ *vi* (*with con*) to be bounded by, contiguous to; —*vt* banish; place in confinement

confirmación /konfirma'θion; konfirma'sion/ *f*, corroboration; *Eccl*. confirmation

confirmar /konfir'mar/ *vt* to corroborate; uphold; *Eccl*. confirm

confirmatorio /konfirma'torio/ *a* confirmatory

confiscación /konfiska'θion; konfiska'sion/ *f*, confiscation

confiscar /konfis'kar/ *vt* to confiscate

confitar /konfi'tar/ *vt* to candy, crystallize or preserve (fruit, etc.); *Fig*. sweeten

confite /kon'fite/ *m*, bonbon, sugared almond, etc.

confitería /konfite'ria/ *f*, confectionery

confitero /konfi'tero/ **(-ra)** *n* confectioner

confitura /konfi'tura/ *f*, preserve, jam

conflagración /konflagra'θion; konflagra'sion/ *f*, conflagration, blaze; uprising, rebellion

conflicto /kon'flikto/ *m*, strife, struggle; spiritual conflict; *Fig*. difficult situation

confluencia /kon'fluenθia; kon'fluensia/ *f*, confluence; crowd

confluir /kon'fluir/ *vi irr* to meet, flow together (rivers); run together (roads); crowd. See **huir**

conformación /konforma'θion; konforma'sion/ *f*, conformation; make-up, structure (e.g. of an organization)

conformar /konfor'mar/ *vt* to fit, adjust; —*vr* agree, be of the same opinion; submit, comply; to make up (e.g. *los grupos sociales que conforman este país,* the social groups who make up this country)

conforme /kon'forme/ *a* similar, alike; consistent; in agreement; long-suffering, resigned —*adv* according (to), in proportion (to)

conformidad /konformi'ðað/ *f*, conformity; similarity; resignation; agreement, harmony; proportion, symmetry. **de c.,** by common consent. **en c.,** according to

confort /kon'fort/ *m*, comfort

confortante /konfor'tante/ *a* comforting; consoling; strengthening (of beverages)

confortar /konfor'tar/ *vt* to comfort, reassure; encourage; console

confortativo /konforta'tiβo/ *a* comforting; comfortable; strengthening, warming (of beverages); encouraging, cheering

confrontación /konfronta'θion; konfronta'sion/ *f*, confrontment; comparison (of texts, etc.)

confrontar /konfron'tar/ *vt* to bring face to face; compare, correlate; —*vi* face; (*with con*) be contiguous to, border on

confucianismo /konfuθia'nismo; konfusia'nismo/ *m*, Confucianism

confundible /konfun'diβle/ *a* mistakable, liable to be confused

confundimiento /konfundi'miento/ *m*, confounding; mistaking; confusion

confundir /konfun'dir/ *vt* to mix, confuse; jumble together; mistake; *Fig*. confound (in argument); humble; bewilder, perplex; —*vr* be mixed together; mistake, confuse; be ashamed; be bewildered

confusión /konfu'sion/ *f*, confusion; perplexity; shame; jumble

confuso /kon'fuso/ *a* mixed, upset; jumbled; obscure; indistinct; blurred; bewildered

confutación /konfuta'θion; konfuta'sion/ *f*, confutation

confutar /konfu'tar/ *vt* to confute

conga /'koŋga/ *f*, conga (dance; drum)

congelación /konhela'θion; konhela'sion/ *f*, freezing; congealment. **punto de c.,** freezing point

congelar /konhe'lar/ *vt* to congeal; freeze

congeniar /konhe'niar/ *vi* to be congenial

congénito /kon'henito/ *a* congenital

congestión /konhes'tion/ *f*, *Med*. congestion

congestionar /konhestio'nar/ *vt* to congest; —*vr Med*. be overcharged (with blood)

conglomeración /konglomera'θion; konglomera'sion/ *f*, conglomeration

conglomerar /konglome'rar/ *vt* to conglomerate

congoja /koŋ'goha/ *f*, anguish, anxiety, grief

congraciarse /koŋgra'θiarse; koŋgra'siarse/ *vr* to ingratiate oneself (with), get into the good graces (of)

congratulación /koŋgratula'θion; koŋgratula'sion/ *f*, congratulation

congratular /koŋgratu'lar/ *vt* to congratulate; —*vr* congratulate oneself

congratulatorio /koŋgratula'torio/ *a* congratulatory

congregación /koŋgrega'θion; koŋgrega'sion/ *f*, gathering, meeting, congregation; brotherhood, guild

congregar /koŋgre'gar/ **(se)** *vt* and *vr* to meet, assemble

congresista /koŋgre'sista/ *mf* member of a congress

congreso /koŋ'greso/ *m*, congress; conference, meeting; sexual intercourse

congrio /'koŋgrio/ *m*, conger eel

congruencia /koŋ'gruenθia; koŋ'gruensia/ *f*, suitability, convenience; *Math.* congruence

congruente /koŋ'gruente/ *a* convenient, opportune; *Math.* congruent

cónico /'koniko/ *a* conical, tapering *Math.* conic

conífera /ko'nifera/ *f*, conifer

conífero /ko'nifero/ *a* coniferous

conjetura /konhe'tura/ *f*, conjecture

conjetural /konhetu'ral/ *a* conjectural

conjeturar /konhetu'rar/ *vt* to conjecture, surmise

conjugación /konhuga'θion; konhuga'sion/ *f*, conjugation

conjugar /konhu'gar/ *vt* to conjugate

conjunción /konhun'θion; konhun'sion/ *f*, connection, union association; (*Astron. Gram.*) conjunction

conjuntivitis /konhunti'βitis/ *f*, conjunctivitis

conjunto /kon'hunto/ *a* united, associated adjoining; mingled, mixed (with) bound, affiliated. *m*, whole; combo, ensemble (of musicians). **c. habitacional,** housing complex, housing project

conjura, conjuración /kon'hura, konhura'θion; kon'hura, konhura'sion/ *f*, conspiracy, plot

conjurador /konhura'ðor/ **(-ra)** *n* conspirator, plotter; exorcist

conjurar /konhu'rar/ *vi* to conspire, plot *vt* swear, take an oath; exorcise; implore, beg; ward off (danger)

conjuro /kon'huro/ *m*, plot, conspiracy, spell, incantation; entreaty

conllevar /konʎe'βar; konye'βar/ *vt* to share (troubles) bear, put up with; endure

conmemoración /komemora'θion; komemora'sion/ *f*, commemoration

conmemorar /komemo'rar/ *vt* to commemorate

conmemorativo /komemora'tiβo/ *a* commemorative

conmensurable /komensu'raβle/ *a* commensurable

conmigo /ko'migo/ *pers pron* 1st pers. sing. *mf* with myself, with me

conminar /komi'nar/ *vt* to threaten

conminatorio /komina'torio/ *a* threatening

conmiseración /komisera'θion; komisera'sion/ *f*, commiseration, compassion, pity

conmoción /komo'θion; komo'sion/ *f*, disturbance (mind or body); upheaval, commotion. **c. eléctrica,** electric shock

conmovedor /komoβe'ðor/ *a* moving, pitiful; stirring, thrilling

conmover /komo'βer/ *vt irr* to perturb, stir; move to pity. **c. los cimientos de,** to shake the foundations of; —*vr* be emotionally moved. See **mover**

conmutable /komu'taβle/ *a* commutable

conmutación /komuta'θion; komuta'sion/ *f*, commutation

conmutador /komuta'ðor/ *m*, *Elec.* commutator; change-over switch

conmutar /komu'tar/ *vt* to commute; *Elec.* switch, convert

conmutatriz /komuta'triθ; komuta'tris/ *f*, *Elec.* converter

connato /kon'nato/ *a* contemporary

connatural /konnatu'ral/ *a* innate, inborn

connaturalizar /konnaturali'θar; konnaturali'sar/ *vt* to connaturalize

connaturalizarse /konnaturali'θarse; konnaturali'sarse/ **(con)** *vr* to become accustomed (to), become acclimated (to)

connivencia /konni'βenθia; konni'βensia/ *f*, connivance

connotación /konnota'θion; konnota'sion/ *f*, connotation

connotar /konno'tar/ *vt* to connote

cono /'kono/ *m*, (*Geom. Bot.*) cone. **el C. Sur,** the Southern Cone

conocedor /konoθe'ðor; konose'ðor/ **(-ra)** *n* one who knows; connoisseur; expert

conocer /kono'θer; kono'ser/ *vt irr* to know; understand; observe, perceive; be acquainted (with); conjecture; confess, acknowledge; know carnally; —*vr* know oneself; know one another. **conocerle a uno la voz,** to recognize somebody's voice (e.g. *Le conozco la voz.* I recognize her by her voice.) **conocerle a uno en su manera de andar,** to recognize somebody by his gait, recognize somebody by his walk —*Pres. Indic.* **conozco, conoces,** etc —*Pres. Subjunc.* **conozca,** etc.

conocido /kono'θiðo; kono'siðo/ **(-da)** *a* illustrious, distinguished —*n* acquaintance

conocimiento /konoθi'miento; konosi'miento/ *m*, knowledge; understanding; intelligence; acquaintance (*not friend*); consciousness; *Com.* bill of lading; *pl* knowledge, learning

conque /'konke/ *conjunc* so, so that (e.g. *¿C. Juan se va?* So John's going away?)

conquista /kon'kista/ *f*, conquest

conquistador /konkista'ðor/ **(-ra)** *a* conquering —*n* conqueror

conquistar /konkis'tar/ *vt* to conquer; *Fig.* captivate, win

consabido /konsa'βiðo/ *a* aforesaid, beforementioned

consagración /konsagra'θion; konsagra'sion/ *f*, consecration; dedication

consagrar /konsa'grar/ *vt* to consecrate; dedicate, devote; deify; —*vr* (*with prep a*) dedicate oneself to, engage in

consanguíneo /konsaŋ'guineo/ *a* consanguineous

consanguinidad /konsaŋguini'ðað/ *f*, consanguinity

consciente /kons'θiente; kons'siente/ *a* conscious; aware; sane. *m*, *Psychol.* conscious

conscripción /konskrip'θion; konskrip'sion/ *f*, conscription

conscripto /kons'kripto/ *m*, conscript

consecución /konseku'θion; konseku'sion/ *f*, obtainment; attainment

consecuencia /konse'kuenθia; konse'kuensia/ *f*, consequence, outcome; logical consequence, conclusion; importance; consistence (of people)

consecuente /konse'kuente/ *a* consequent, resultant; consistent. **c. consigo mismo,** self-consistent *m*, consequence; *Math.* consequent

consecutivo /konseku'tiβo/ *a* consecutive, successive

conseguir /konse'gir/ *vt irr* to obtain, achieve. See **seguir**

conseja /kon'seha/ *f*, story, fairy-tale; old wives' tale

consejero /konse'hero/ **(-ra)** *n* adviser; member of council. *m*, **c. de estado,** counselor of state

consejo /kon'seho/ *m*, advice; council, commission; board; council chamber or building. **c. de administración,** board of directors. **c. de guerra,** council of war. **c. del reino,** council of the realm. **c. privado,** privy council

consenso /kon'senso/ *m*, consensus of opinion, unanimity

consentido /konsen'tiðo/ *a* complaisant (of husband); spoiled, over-indulged

consentimiento /konsenti'miento/ *m*, consent; assent

consentir /konsen'tir/ *vt irr* to permit, allow; believe; tolerate, put up with; over-indulge, spoil; —*vr* crack, give way (furniture, etc.). **c. en,** to consent to; to agree to. See **sentir**

conserje /kon'serhe/ *m*, concierge, porter; warden or keeper (of castle, etc.)

conserjería /konserhe'ria/ *f*, conciergerie, porter's lodge; warden's dwelling (in castles, etc.)

conserva /kon'serβa/ *f*, jam; preserve; pickles; *Naut.* convoy. **en c.,** preserved, tinned

conservación /konserβa'θion; konserβa'sion/ *f*, upkeep; preservation, maintenance; *Cul.* preserving; conservation. **c. refrigerada,** cold storage

conservador /konserβa'ðor/ **(-ra)** *a* keeping, preserving —*a* and *n* preserver; *Polit.* conservative; traditionalist. *m*, curator

conservadurismo /konserβaðu'rismo/ *m*, conservatism

conservar /konser'βar/ *vt* to keep, maintain, preserve; keep up (custom, etc.); guard; *Cul.* preserve. **c. en buen estado**, to keep in repair

conservatorio /konserβa'torio/ *m*, conservatoire; academy. **c. de música**, academy of music, conservatoire

considerable /konsiðe'raβle/ *a* considerable; worthy of consideration; powerful; numerous; large; important

consideración /konsiðera'θion; konsiðera'sion/ *f*, consideration, attention; reflection, thought; civility; importance. **en c. de**, considering

considerado /konsiðe'raðo/ *a* considerate; prudent; distinguished; important

considerar /konsiðe'rar/ *vt* to consider, reflect upon; treat with consideration (persons); judge, estimate, feel (e.g. *Considero que...* I feel that...)

consigna /kon'signa/ *f*, *Mil.* watchword; left luggage office

consignador /konsigna'ðor/ (**-ra**) *n Com.* consigner, sender

consignar /konsig'nar/ *vt* to assign, lay aside; deposit; *Com.* consign; entrust, commit; put in writing; *Law.* deposit in trust; book (a suspect)

consignatario /konsigna'tario/ *m*, *Law.* trustee; mortgagee; *Com.* consignee. **c. de buques**, shipping agent

consigo /kon'sigo/ *pers pron* 3rd sing. and pl. *mf* with himself, herself, oneself, yourself, yourselves, themselves

consiguiente /konsi'giente/ *a* consequent, resulting. *m*, consequence. **por c.**, in consequence

consistencia /konsis'tenθia; konsis'tensia/ *f*, solidity; consistence, density; consistency, congruity, relevance

consistente /konsis'tente/ *a* of a certain consistency; solid

consistir /konsis'tir/ *vi* (*with en*) to consist in; be comprised of; be the result of

consistorio /konsis'torio/ *m*, consistory; municipal council (in some Spanish towns); town hall

consola /kon'sola/ *f*, console table; piertable; *Mech.* bracket

cónsola /'konsola/ *f*, radio cabinet

consolable /konso'laβle/ *a* consolable

consolación /konsola'θion; konsola'sion/ *f*, consolation

consolador /konsola'ðor/ (**-ra**) *n* comforter, consoler

consolar /konso'lar/ *vt irr* to comfort, console. **consolarse de + inf.**, to console oneself for + *pp*. See **contar**

consolidación /konsoliða'θion; konsoliða'sion/ *f*, consolidation; stiffening

consolidar /konsoli'ðar/ *vt* to consolidate; strengthen; combine, unite; —*vr Law.* unite

consomé /konso'me/ *m*, consommé

consonancia /konso'nanθianb; konso'nansia/ *f*, harmony; agreement

consonante /konso'nante/ *a* consonant, consistent. *m*, rhyme. *f*, *Gram.* consonant

consonantismo /konsonan'tismo/ *m*, consonantism, consonant system

consorcio /kon'sorθio; kon'sorsio/ *m*, partnership; trust; intimacy, common life

consorte /kon'sorte/ *mf* consort; companion, associate, partner; spouse

conspicuo /kons'pikuo/ *a* outstanding, distinguished; conspicuous

conspiración /konspira'θion; konspira'sion/ *f*, conspiracy

conspirador /konspira'ðor/ (**-ra**) *n* conspirator

conspirar /konspi'rar/ *vi* to conspire; plot, scheme; tend, combine

constancia /kons'tanθia; kons'tansia/ *f*, constancy, steadfastness; stability, steadiness; transcript (of grades). **c. de estudios**, transcript (of grades)

constante /kons'tante/ *a* constant; durable; *Mech.* steady, non-oscillating. *m*, constant

Constantinopla /konstanti'nopla/ Constantinople

Constanza /kons'tanθa; kons'tansa/ Constance (female given name and lake)

constar /kons'tar/ *vi* to be evident, be clear; (*with de*) be composed of, consist of, comprise

constelación /konstela'θion; konstela'sion/ *f*, *Astron.* constellation; climate

consternación /konsterna'θion; konsterna'sion/ *f*, dismay, alarm

consternarse /konster'narse/ *vr* to be dismayed or alarmed

constipado /konsti'paðo/ *m*, *Med.* cold; chill

constiparse /konsti'parse/ *vr* to catch a cold or chill

constitución /konstitu'θion; konstitu'sion/ *f*, constitution; composition, make-up (e.g. *la c. del suelo*, the make-up of the soil)

constitucional /konstituθio'nal; konstitusio'nal/ *a* constitutional

constituir /konsti'tuir/ *vt irr* to constitute, form; found, establish; (*with en*) appoint, nominate; *Fig.* place in (a difficult situation, etc.); —*vr* (*with en* or *por*) be appointed or authorized; be under (an obligation). See **huir**

constituyente, constitutivo /konstitu'yente, konstitu'tiβo/ *a* and *m*, constituent

constreñir /konstre'ɲir/ *vt irr* to constrain, oblige; constrict; constipate. See **ceñir**

constricción /konstrik'θion; konstrik'sion/ *f*, constriction; contraction, shrinkage

construcción /konstruk'θion; konstruk'sion/ *f*, construction; art or process of construction; fabric, structure; *Gram.* construction; building, erection. **c. de caminos**, road making. **c. naval**, shipbuilding

constructor /konstruk'tor/ (**-ra**) *a* building, constructive —*n* builder; constructor

construir /kons'truir/ *vt irr* to construct; build, make; *Gram.* construct. See **huir**

consuelo /kon'suelo/ *m*, consolation; comfort, solace; joy, delight

cónsul /'konsul/ *m*, consul

consulado /konsu'laðo/ *m*, consulate. **c. general**, consulate general

consulta /kon'sulta/ *f*, deliberation, consideration; advice; reference; conference, consultation

consultar /konsul'tar/ *vt* to discuss, consider; seek advice, consult. **consultarlo con la almohada**, *Fig.* to sleep on it, think it over, mull it over

consultor /konsul'tor/ (**-ra**) *a* consultative, advisory; consulting —*n* consultant; adviser. **c. externo**, outside consultant

consultorio /konsul'torio/ *m*, *Med.* consulting rooms; surgery; technical information bureau

consumación /konsuma'θion; konsuma'sion/ *f*, consummation; completion, attainment; extinction, end

consumado /konsu'maðo/ *a* consummate; *Inf.* thorough, perfect

consumar /konsu'mar/ *vt* to consummate; complete, accomplish, perfect

consumido /konsu'miðo/ *a Inf.* emaciated, wasted away; timid, spiritless

consumidor /konsumi'ðor/ (**-ra**) *a* consuming —*n* consumer, user

consumir /konsu'mir/ *vt* to destroy; consume, use; waste away, wear away; *Eccl.* take communion; *Inf.* grieve; —*vr* be destroyed; *Inf.* be consumed with grief

consumo /kon'sumo/ *m*, consumption; demand. **c. de combustible**, fuel consumption

contabilidad /kontaβili'ðað/ *f*, bookkeeping; accounts; accounting

contable /kon'taβle/ *m*, bookkeeper

contacto /kon'takto/ *m*, contact (also *Elec. Mil.*). **en c.**, in common (e.g. *Los dos libros tienen mucho en c.* The two books have much in common.)

contado /kon'taðo/ *a* few; infrequent; rare. **al c.**, *Com.* cash down. **por de c.**, presumably; of course, naturally

contador /konta'ðor/ *a* counting. *m*, accountant; *Law.* auditor; counter (in banks); *Elec.* meter, counter; *Naut.* purser. **c. oficial**, *Argentina* certified public accountant. **c. público titulado**, certified public accountant

contaduría /kontaðu'ria/ *f*, accountancy; counting house; accountant's office; auditorship; *Theat.* box-office; *Naut.* purser's office

contagiar /konta'hiar/ *vt* to infect; corrupt, pervert; —*vr* (*with con, de or por*) be infected by or through

contagio /kon'tahio/ *m*, infection; contagious disease; *Fig.* contagion, perversion, corruption

contagioso /konta'hioso/ *a* infectious; *Fig.* catching, contagious

contaminación /kontamina'θion; kontamina'sion/ *f*, contamination, pollution

contaminar /kontami'nar/ *vt* to pollute, contaminate; infect; *Fig.* corrupt

contante /kon'tante/ *a* ready (of money)

contar /kon'tar/ *vt irr* to count; recount, tell; place to account; include, count among; —*vi* calculate, compute. **contarle a uno las cuarenta,** *Inf.* to give someone a piece of one's mind. **c. con,** to rely upon; reckon upon —*Pres. Indic.* **cuento, cuentas, cuenta, cuentan.** *Pres. Subjunc.* **cuente, cuentes, cuente, cuenten**

contemplación /kontempla'θion; kontempla'sion/ *f*, meditation, contemplation; consideration

contemplar /kontem'plar/ *vt* to consider, reflect upon; look at, contemplate; indulge, please

contemplativo /kontempla'tiβo/ *a Eccl.* contemplative; reflective, thoughtful; kind, indulgent

contemporáneo /kontempo'raneo/ **(de)** *a* contemporaneous (to *or* with) *n* contemporary

contemporizar /kontempori'θar; kontempori'sar/ *vi* to temporize, gain time

contencioso /konten'θioso; konten'sioso/ *a* contentious, argumentative; *Law.* litigious

contender /konten'der/ *vi irr* to contain; restrain, hold back; comprise; —*vr* control oneself. See **entender**

contendiente /konten'diente/ *mf* contestant

contener /konte'ner/ *vt irr* to contain; include; comprise; hold back; restrain; check, repress; hold down, subdue; suppress, put down; —*vr* contain oneself; keep one's temper; keep quiet; refrain. See **tener**

contenido /konte'niðo/ *m*, contents —*a* contained; *Fig.* restrained; reserved (of persons)

contentamiento /kontenta'miento/ *m*, contentment

contentar /konten'tar/ *vt* to satisfy, please; *Com.* endorse; —*vr* be pleased or satisfied

contento /kon'tento/ *a* happy; content; satisfied; pleased. *m*, pleasure; contentment. **no caber de c.,** to be overjoyed

contestación /kontesta'θion; kontesta'sion/ *f*, reply, answer; discussion, argument, dispute

contestar /kontes'tar/ *vt* to reply, answer; confirm, attest; —*vi* accord, harmonize

contexto /kon'teksto/ *m*, context

contextura /konteks'tura/ *f*, structure; context; physique, frame

contienda /kon'tienda/ *f*, struggle, fight; quarrel, dispute; discussion

contigo /kon'tigo/ *pers pron* 2nd *sing. mf* with thee, with you

contigüidad /kontigui'ðað/ *f*, proximity, nearness

contiguo /kon'tiguo/ *a* adjacent, near

continencia /konti'nenθia; konti'nensia/ *f*, moderation, self-restraint; continence; chastity; containing

continental /konti'nental/ *a* continental. *m*, express messenger service; *Puerto Rico* person from the mainland United States

continente /konti'nente/ *a* continent. *m*, container; demeanor, bearing; *Geog.* continent; mainland

contingencia /kontin'henθia; kontin'hensia/ *f*, contingency; risk, danger

contingente /kontin'hente/ *a* incidental; fortuitous; dependent; *m*, *Mil.* taskforce, contingent

continuación /kontinua'θion; kontinua'sion/ *f*, continuation; prolongation; sequel (of a story, etc.)

continuador /kontinua'ðor/ **(-ra)** *n* continuer

continuar /konti'nuar/ *vt* to continue; —*vi* continue; last, remain, go on; —*vr* be prolonged

continuidad /kontinui'ðað/ *f*, continuity

continuo /kon'tinuo/ *a* continuous, steady, uninterrupted; persevering, tenacious; persistent, lasting, unremitting. *m*, a united whole. **de c.,** continuously

contonearse /kontone'arse/ *vr* to swing the hips (in walking); strut

contorno /kon'torno/ *m*, contour, outline; (gen. *pl*) environs, surrounding district

contorsión /kontor'sion/ *f*, contortion

contorsionista /kontorsio'nista/ *mf* contortionist

contra /'kontra/ *prep* against, counter, athwart; opposed to, hostile to; in front of, opposite; towards. *m*, opposite view or opinion. *f*, *Inf.* difficulty, trouble. **c. la corriente,** upstream. **el pro y el c.,** the pros and cons. **en c.,** in opposition, against

contraalmirante /kontraalmi'rante/ *m*, rear admiral

contraataque /kontraa'take/ *m*, counterattack

contraaviso /kontraa'βiso/ *m*, countermand

contrabajo /kontra'βaho/ *m*, doublebass; player of this instrument; deep bass voice

contrabalancear /kontraβalanθe'ar; kontraβalanse'ar/ *vt* to counterbalance; *Fig.* compensate

contrabandista /kontraβan'dista/ *a* smuggling. *mf* smuggler

contrabando /kontra'βando/ *m*, contraband; smuggling

contracción /kontrak'θion; kontrak'sion/ *f*, contraction; shrinkage; abridgment; abbreviation

contracubierta /kontraku'βierta/ *f*, book jacket, jacket

contradanza /kontra'ðanθa; kontra'ðansa/ *f*, square dance

contradecir /kontraðe'θir; kontraðe'sir/ *vt irr* to contradict; —*vr* contradict oneself. See **decir**

contradicción /kontraðik'θion; kontraðik'sion/ *f*, contradiction

contradictorio /kontraðik'torio/ *a* contradictory

contraer /kontra'er/ *vt irr* to shrink, reduce in size, shorten; abridge; contract (matrimony, obligations); *Fig.* acquire (diseases, habits); —*vr* shorten, contract, shrink. See **traer**

contrafuerte /kontra'fuerte/ *m*, buttress, counterfort, abutment; *Geog.* spur

contrahacer /kontraa'θer; kontraa'ser/ *vt irr* to forge, counterfeit; mimic; imitate. See **hacer**

contrahecho /kontra'etʃo/ *a* deformed

contralor /kontra'lor/ *m*, comptroller

contraloría /kontralo'ria/ *f*, comptrollership, office of comptroller (position); comptroller's office (place)

contralto /kon'tralto/ *m*, contralto (voice)

contraluz /kontra'luθ; kontra'lus/ *f*, counterlight

contramaestre /kontrama'estre/ *m*, *Naut.* boatswain; overseer, superintendent, foreman

contramarcha /kontra'martʃa/ *f*, retrogression; *Mil.* countermarch

contramedida /kontrame'ðiða/ *f*, counter-measure

contraorden /kontra'orðen/ *f*, countermand

contrapedalear /kontrapeðale'ar/ *vi* to backpedal

contrapelo /kontra'pelo/ *a adv* the wrong way of the hair, against the grain; *Inf.* reluctantly, distastefully

contrapeso /kontra'peso/ *m*, counterpoise, counterweight; balancing-pole (acrobats); *Fig.* counterbalance; makeweight

contraponer /kontrapo'ner/ *vt irr* to compare; place opposite; oppose. See **poner**

contraproducente /kontraproðu'θente; kontraproðu'sente/ *a* counteractive, counterproductive, unproductive, self-deceiving; self-defeating

contrapuesto /kontra'puesto/ *a* opposing, divergent

contrapunto /kontra'punto/ *m*, counterpoint

contrariar /kontra'riar/ *vt* to counter, oppose; impede; vex, annoy

contrariedad /kontrarie'ðað/ *f*, contrariety, opposition; obstacle; vexation, trouble

contrario /kon'trario/ **(-ia)** *a* opposite; hostile, opposed; harmful; adverse, contrary —*n* adversary; opponent. *m*, obstacle. *f*. **contraria,** contrary, opposite. **al contrario,** on the contrary. **llevar la contraria (a),** to oppose; contradict

contrarreforma /kontrarre'forma/ *f*, counter-Reformation

contrasentido /kontrasen'tiðo/ *m*, wrong sense, opposite sense (of words); contradiction of initial premise; self-contradiction; nonsense

contraseña /kontra'seɲa/ *f*, countersign; *Mil.* password

contrastar /kontras'tar/ *vt* to contrast; oppose; resist;

check (weights and measures); assay; *Mech.* calibrate, gauge; —*vi* contrast

contraste /kon'traste/ *m*, contrast; opposition, difference; weights and measures inspector; dispute, clash. **en c. a,** in contrast to

contrata /kon'trata/ *f*, **contrato,** *m*, contract. **contrato de arrendamiento,** lease

contratación /kontrata'θion; kontrata'sion/ *f*, hiring; *Com.* transaction; commerce, trade

contratapa /kontra'tapa/ *f*, back cover (of a periodical, etc.)

contratar /kontra'tar/ *vt* to contract, enter into an agreement; make a bargain (with), deal (with); hire, contract

contratiempo /kontra'tiempo/ *m*, mishap, accident

contratista /kontra'tista/ *mf* contractor

contratorpedero /kontratorpe'ðero/ *m*, torpedoboat destroyer

contravención /kontraβen'θion; kontraβen'sion/ *f*, contravention; violation. **en c. a,** in violation of

contraveneno /kontraβe'neno/ *m*, *Med.* antidote; remedy, precaution

contravenir /kontraβe'nir/ *vt irr* to infringe, contravene. See **venir**

contraventana /kontraβen'tana/ *f*, shutter (for windows)

contravidriera /kontraβið'riera/ *f*, storm window

contrayente /kontra'yente/ *a* contracting. *mf* contracting party (used of matrimony)

contribución /kontriβu'θion; kontriβu'sion/ *f*, contribution; tax. **c. sobre la propiedad,** property tax

contribuir /kontri'βuir/ *vt irr* to pay (taxes); contribute. See **huir**

contribuyente /kontriβu'yente/ *a* contributing; contributory. *mf* contributor; taxpayer

contrición /kontri'θion; kontri'sion/ *f*, contrition

contrincante /kontrin'kante/ *m*, competitor, candidate (public examinations); rival, opponent

contrito /kon'trito/ *a* contrite

control /kon'trol/ *m*, control; checking. **c. de precios,** price control

controlar /kontro'lar/ *vt* to control

controversia /kontro'βersia/ *f*, controversy

controvertir /kontroβer'tir/ *vi* and *vt irr* to dispute, argue against, deny. See **sentir**

contumacia /kontu'maθia; kontu'masia/ *f*, obstinacy; *Law.* contumacy

contumaz /kontu'maθ; kontu'mas/ *a* stubborn; impenitent; *Law.* contumacious; *Med.* obstinate, resistant (to cure)

contumelia /kontu'melia/ *f*, contumely

conturbar /kontur'βar/ *vt* to perturb, make anxious, disturb; —*vr* be perturbed

contuso /kon'tuso/ *a* contused, bruised

convalecencia /kombale'θenθia; kombale'sensia/ *f*, convalescence; convalescent home

convalecer /kombale'θer; kombale'ser/ *vi irr* to convalesce, get better; *Fig.* recover, regain (influence, etc.). See **conocer**

convaleciente /kombale'θiente; kombale'siente/ *a* and *mf* convalescent

convalidar /kombali'ðar/ *vt* to ratify, confirm

convecino /kombe'θino; kombe'sino/ *a* nearby; neighboring

convencedor /kombenθe'ðor; kombense'ðor/ *a* convincing

convencer /komben'θer; komben'ser/ *vt* to convince; prove beyond doubt, demonstrate to (persons); be convincing (e.g. *No convence,* It's not convincing; He's not convincing.) *vr* be convinced

convencimiento /kombenθi'miento; kombensi'miento/ *m*, conviction, belief, assurance

convención /komben'θion; komben'sion/ *f*, pact, formal agreement; harmony, conformity; convention

convencional /kombenθio'nal; kombensio'nal/ *a* conventional (all meanings)

convencionalismo /kombenθiona'lismo; kombensiona'lismo/ *m*, conventionality

convenido /kombe'niðo/ *a* agreed

conveniencia /kombe'nienθia; kombe'niensia/ *f*, conformity, harmony; adjustment; experience, suitability, convenience; advantage; agreement, pact; post as domestic; ease, comfort; *pl* income; social conventions

conveniente /kombe'niente/ *a* convenient, opportune; suitable, fitting; profitable; useful; decorous. **tener por c. + inf,** to think it fitting to + *inf,* find it appropriate to + *Inf.*

convenio /kom'benio/ *m*, pact, treaty; *Com.* agreement, contract

convenir /kombe'nir/ *vi irr* to agree; assemble, congregate; belong; be suitable; —*vr* agree; suit oneself. **No me conviene salir esta tarde,** It does not suit me to go out this afternoon. **Me convendría pasar un mes allí,** It would be a good idea (or a wise thing) for me to spend a month there. See **venir**

convento /kom'bento/ *m*, convent; monastery; religious community

conventual /komben'tual/ *a* conventual; monastic. *m*, *Eccl.* conventual

convergencia /komber'henθia; komber'hensia/ *f*, convergence

convergir /komber'hir/ *vi* to converge; *Fig.* coincide (views, etc.)

conversación /kombersa'θion; kombersa'sion/ *f*, conversation; intercourse, company; *Law.* criminal conversation

conversar /komber'sar/ *vi* to converse; chat; live with others; know socially

conversión /komber'sion/ *f*, conversion; change, transformation; *Com.* conversion; *Mil.* wheel; wheeling

converso /kom'berso/ **(-sa)** *n* convert

convertible /komber'tiβle/ *a* convertible

convertir /komber'tir/ *vt irr* to change, transform; convert; reform; —*vr* be transformed; be converted; be reformed. See **sentir**

convexidad /kombeksi'ðað/ *f*, convexity

convexo /kom'bekso/ *a* convex

convicción /kombik'θion; kombik'sion/ *f*, conviction; certitude; *Law.* conviction

convicto /kom'bikto/ **(-ta)** *a* and *n* *Law.* convict

convidado /kombi'ðaðo/ **(-da)** *n* guest

convidar /kombi'ðar/ *vt* to invite (persons); encourage, provoke; entice, attract; —*vr* invite oneself; offer one's services

convincente /kombin'θente; kombin'sente/ *a* convincing

convite /kom'bite/ *m*, invitation; banquet; party

convivencia /kombi'βenθia; kombi'βensia/ *f*, coexistence, common life, life together. **c. pacífica,** peaceful coexistence

convivial /kombi'βial/ *a* convivial

convivir /kombi'βir/ *vi* to live together, live under the same roof

convocación /komboka'θion; komboka'sion/ *f*, convocation

convocar /kombo'kar/ *vt* to convene, convoke

convoy /kom'boi/ *m*, convoy; escort; following; cruet-stand

convoyar /kombo'yar/ *vt* to convoy, escort

convulsión /kombul'sion/ *f*, convulsion

convulsivo /kombul'siβo/ *a* convulsive

conyugal /konyu'gal/ *a* conjugal

cónyuge /'konyuhe/ *mf* husband or (and) wife (used gen. in *pl*)

coñac /ko'ɲak/ *m*, brandy

cooperación /koopera'θion; koopera'sion/ *f*, cooperation

cooperador /koopera'ðor/ **(-ra)** *a* cooperative —*n* cooperator, collaborator

cooperar /koope'rar/ *vi* to cooperate

cooperativa /koopera'tiβa/ *f*, cooperative society

cooperativo /koopera'tiβo/ *a* cooperative

coordenada /koorðe'naða/ *f*, coordinate

coordinación /koorðina'θion; koorðina'sion/ *f*, coordination

coordinar /koorði'nar/ *vt* to coordinate, classify

copa /'kopa/ *f*, wineglass, goblet; glassful; top branches (of trees); crown (of hat); *Cards.* heart; gill (liquid measure); *Inf.* drink, glass; *pl* *Cards.* hearts (in Spanish pack, goblets)

copartícipe /kopar'tiθipe; kopar'tisipe/ *mf* co-partner, partaker, participant

copec /'kopek/ *m,* kopeck

Copenhague /kope'nage/ Copenhagen

copernicano /koperni'kano/ *a* Copernican

copero /ko'pero/ *m,* cupbearer; sideboard; cocktail cabinet

copete /ko'pete/ *m,* lock, tress (hair); tuft, crest; forelock (horses); head, top (ice-cream, drinks); *Inf.* **de alto c.,** aristocratic; socially prominent

copia /'kopia/ *f,* abundance, plenty; copy, reproduction; transcript; imitation

copiador /kopia'ðor/ **(-ra)** *a* copying —*n* copier; transcriber. *m,* copybook

copiar /ko'piar/ *vt* to copy

copioso /ko'pioso/ *a* abundant, plentiful

copla /'kopla/ *f,* couplet; popular four-line poem; couple, pair; *pl Inf.* verses

coplero /kop'lero/ **(-ra)** *n* balladmonger; poetaster

copo /'kopo/ *m,* cop (of a spindle); snowflake

copón /ko'pon/ *m,* large goblet; *Eccl.* ciborium, chalice

coprófago /ko'profago/ *a* coprophagous

copropietario /kopropie'tario/ **(-ia)** *n* coproprietor, coowner

cóptico /'koptiko/ *a* Coptic. *m,* Coptic (language)

copto /'kopto/ **(-ta)** *n* Copt

cópula /'kopula/ *f,* connection; coupling; joining; copulation

copularse /kopu'larse/ *vr* to copulate

coque /'koke/ *m,* coke

coqueluche /koke'lutʃe/ *f,* whooping cough

coqueta /ko'keta/ *f,* coquette, flirt

coquetear /kokete'ar/ *vi* to flirt

coqueteo /koke'teo/ *m,* coquetry; flirtation

coquetería /kokete'ria/ *f,* coquetry

coquetón /koke'ton/ *a* coquettish

coracero /kora'θero; kora'sero/ *m,* cuirassier

coraje /ko'rahe/ *m,* courage, valor; anger

coral /ko'ral/ *m,* coral. *f,* coral snake. *m, Bot.* coral tree; *pl* coral beads

coral /ko'ral/ *a* choral

coralina /kora'lina/ *f,* coral (polyp).

coraza /ko'raθa; ko'rasa/ *f,* cuirass; shell (of tortoise); armor-plate, armor (ships, etc.)

corazón /kora'θon; kora'son/ *m,* heart; courage, spirit; love, tenderness; goodwill, benevolence; core (of a fruit); *Fig.* palm. **de c.,** sincerely. **tener el c. en la mano,** to wear one's heart on one's sleeve

corazonada /koraθo'naða; koraso'naða/ *f,* feeling, instinct; presentiment, apprehension

corbata /kor'βata/ *f,* necktie; scarf; ribbon (insignia)

corbatería /korβate'ria/ *f,* necktie shop

corbatero /korβa'tero/ *m,* necktie maker; necktie dealer; tie rack

corbeta /kor'βeta/ *f,* corvette

Córcega /'korθega; 'korsega/ Corsica

corcel /kor'θel; kor'sel/ *m,* charger or battle horse

corchea /kor'tʃea/ *f, Mus.* quaver

corchete /kor'tʃete/ *m, Sew.* hook and eye; hook

corcho /'kortʃo/ *m, Bot.* cork, cork bark; stopper, cork; cork mat; bee hive

corcova /kor'koβa/ *f,* hump, abnormal protuberance

corcovado /korko'βaðo/ **(-da)** *a* hunchbacked, crooked —*n* hunchback

corcovear /korkoβe'ar/ *vi* to curvet, caper

cordaje /kor'ðahe/ *m, Naut.* cordage, tackling, rope

cordel /kor'ðel/ *m,* cord; *Naut.* line. **a c.,** in a straight line

cordelería /korðele'ria/ *f,* rope making; ropeyard; cordage

cordelero /korðe'lero/ **(-ra)** *n* rope maker

cordera /kor'ðera/ *f,* ewe lamb; sweet, gentle woman

cordero /kor'ðero/ *m,* lamb; dressed lambskin; peaceable, mild man; Jesus (gen. **Divino C.**)

cordial /kor'ðial/ *a* warming, invigorating; affectionate, loving, friendly. *m, Med.* cordial

cordialidad /korðiali'ðað/ *f,* cordiality, friendliness

cordillera /korði'ʎera; korði'yera/ *f,* mountain range

Córdoba /'korðoβa/ Cordova

cordobán /korðo'βan/ *m,* cured goatskin; Cordovan leather, Spanish leather

cordobés /korðo'βes/ **(-esa)** *a* and *n* Cordovan

cordón /kor'ðon/ *m,* cord; cordon; *Eccl.* rope girdle; *Archit.* string-course

cordoncillo /korðon'θiʎo; korðon'siyo/ *m,* rib (in cloth); ridge, milling (of coins); *Sew.* piping

cordura /kor'ðura/ *f,* good sense, prudence

Corea /ko'rea/ Korea

corego, corega /ko'rego, ko'rega/ *m,* choragus

coreografía /koreogra'fia/ *f,* choreography; art of dancing

coreográfico /koreo'grafiko/ *a* choreographic

coreógrafo /kore'ografo/ *m,* choreographer

corintio /ko'rintio/ **(-ia)** *a* and *n* Corinthian

Corinto /ko'rinto/ Corinth

corista /ko'rista/ *m, Eccl.* chorister. *mf Theat.* member of the chorus

cornada /kor'naða/ *f,* horn thrust or wound (bulls, etc.)

cornalina /korna'lina/ *f, Mineral.* cornelian

cornamenta /korna'menta/ *f,* horns (bulls, deer, etc.)

córnea /'kornea/ *f,* cornea

corneja /kor'neha/ *f,* carrion or black crow

córneo /'korneo/ *a* horny, corneous

corneta /kor'neta/ *f, Mus.* bugle; *Mus.* cornet; swineherd's horn; *Mil.* pennon. *m,* bugler; *Mil.* cornet. **c. de monte,** hunting horn

cornetín /korne'tin/ *m, dim* **corneta,** *Mus.* cornet; cornet player

cornezuelo /korne'θuelo; korne'suelo/ *m, dim* little horn; *Med.* ergot; *Bot.* variety of olive

cornisa /kor'nisa/ *f,* cornice

cornucopia /kornu'kopia/ *f,* cornucopia, horn of plenty; sconce; mirror

cornudo /kor'nuðo/ *a* horned. *m,* cuckold. **el C.,** the Devil

coro /'koro/ *m,* choir; chorus; *Archit.* choir. **hacer c. (a),** to listen to, support. **saber de c.,** to know by heart

corolario /koro'lario/ *m,* corollary

corona /ko'rona/ *f,* garland, wreath; halo; (*Astron. Archit.*) corona; crown (of tooth); crown (of head); tonsure; crown (coin); royal power; kingdom; triumph; reward; summit, height, peak; circlet (for candles)

coronación /korona'θion; korona'sion/ *f,* coronation; coping stone

coronamiento /korona'miento/ *m,* coronation; coping stone; *Fig.* crowning touch; *Naut.* taffrail

coronar /koro'nar/ *vt* to crown; crown (in draughts); complete, round off; —*vr* be crowned; crown oneself; be tipped or capped

coronel /koro'nel/ *m,* colonel

coronela /koro'nela/ *f, Inf.* colonel's wife

coronelía /korone'lia/ *f,* colonelcy

coronilla /koro'niʎa; koro'niya/ *f, dim* small crown; crown of head; *Fig. Inf.* **estar hasta la c.,** to be fed up

coroza /ko'roθa; ko'rosa/ *f,* dunce's cap

corpiño /kor'piɲo/ *m,* bodice

corporación /korpora'θion; korpora'sion/ *f,* corporation, body, association

corporal /korpo'ral/ *a* and *m, Eccl.* corporal

corporativo /korpora'tiβo/ *a* corporate, corporative

corpóreo /kor'poreo/ *a* corporeal

corporizar /korpori'θar; korpori'sar/ *vt* to embody

corpulento /korpu'lento/ *a* corpulent, stout

Corpus /'korpus/ *m,* Corpus Christi

corpúsculo /kor'puskulo/ *m,* corpuscle

corral /ko'rral/ *m,* yard; pen, enclosure, corral; old-time theater. **c. de madera,** timber yard. *Inf.* **hacer corrales,** to play truant

correa /ko'rrea/ *f,* leather strap or thong; flexibility; *Mech.* belt, band

corrección /korrek'θion; korrek'sion/ *f,* correction; correctness; punishment; emendation. **c. de pruebas,** proofreading, proofing, reading proof

correccional /korre'θional; korre'sional/ *a* correctional. *m,* reformatory

correctivo /korrek'tiβo/ *a* and *m,* corrective

correcto /ko'rrekto/ *a* correct; well-bred; unexceptionable, irreproachable; regular (of features)

corredera /korre'ðera/ *f*, link (engines); *Mech.* slide; *Naut.* log; racecourse; *Inf.* procuress

corredizo /korre'ðiθo; korre'ðiso/ *a* easy to untie; running (of knots); sliding

corredor /korre'ðor/ **(-ra)** *n* runner. *m*, *Com.* broker; corridor; *Inf.* meddler; *Inf.* procurer, pimp —*a* running. **c. de bolsa**, stockbroker

corregible /korre'hiβle/ *a* corrigible

corregidor /korrehi'ðor/ *m*, Spanish magistrate; *Obs.* mayor

corregidora /korrehi'ðora/ *f*, wife of corregidor; mayoress

corregir /korre'hir/ *vt irr* to correct; scold, punish; moderate, counteract; *Mech.* adjust; —*vr* mend one's ways. **c. pruebas**, to read proof —*Pres. Indic.* **corrijo, corriges, corrige, corrigen.** *Pres. Part.* **corrigiendo.** *Pres. Subjunc.* **corrija, corrijas**, etc —*Imperf. Subjunc.* **corrigiese**, etc.

correlación /korrela'θion; korrela'sion/ *f*, correlation

correligionario /korrelihio'nario/ **(-ia)** *n* coreligionist; fellow-supporter or believer

correo /ko'rreo/ *m*, courier; mail; post-office; letters. **c. aéreo**, air-mail. **c. certificado**, registered mail. **c. electrónico**, e-mail. **a vuelta de c.**, by return of mail. **tren c.**, mail train

correr /ko'rrer/ *vi* to run; race; sail, steam; flow; blow; flood; extend, stretch; pass (of time); fall due (salary, etc.); be current or general; (*with con*) be in charge of or responsible for; —*vt* run (a horse); fasten, slide (bolts, etc.); draw (curtains); undergo, suffer; sell, auction; *Inf.* steal; *Fig.* embarrass; spread (a rumor, etc.); catch, make (bus, train, etc.); —*vr* slide, glide, slip; run (of colors); *Inf.* spread oneself, talk too much. **c. cañas**, to participate in a mock joust using reeds as spears

correría /korre'ria/ *f*, raid, foray; excursion, trip

correspondencia /korrespon'denθia; korrespon'densia/ *f*, relationship, connection; intercourse, communication; correspondence; letters; equivalence, exact translation

corresponder /korrespon'der/ *vi* to requite, repay; be grateful; belong to, concern; devolve upon, fall to; suit, harmonize (with); fit; —*vr* correspond by letters; like or love each other

correspondiente /korrespon'diente/ *a* suitable; proportionate; corresponding. *mf* correspondent

corresponsal /korrespon'sal/ *mf* correspondent (especially professional); *Com.* agent

corretear /korrete'ar/ *vi* to wander about the streets; gad

correveidile /korreβei'ðile/ *mf Inf.* tale-bearer, gossip

corrida /ko'rriða/ *f*, race, run; *Aer.* taxying; bull fight (abb. for **c. de toros**)

corrido /ko'rriðo/ *a* extra, over (of weight); embarrassed; experienced

corriente /ko'rriente/ *a* current, present; well-known; usual, customary; fluent (style); ordinary, average; easy. *f*, flow, stream; *Fig.* course (of events, etc.); *Elec.* current —*adv* quite, exactly. *Elec.* **c. alterna**, alternating current. **c. continua**, direct current. **c. de aire**, draft. **estar al c.**, to be informed (of something)

Corriente del Golfo /ko'rriente del 'golfo/ Gulf Stream

corrillo /ko'rriʎo; ko'rriyo/ *m*, knot, group, huddle (of people)

corro /'korro/ *m*, circle, ring (for children's games)

corroboración /korroβora'θion; korroβora'sion/ *f*, corroboration, confirmation

corroborar /korroβo'rar/ *vt* to fortify; corroborate, support

corroborativo /korroβora'tiβo/ *a* corroborative

corroer /korro'er/ *vt irr* to corrode, waste away; *Fig.* gnaw. See **roer**

corromper /korrom'per/ *vt* to rot; mar; spoil, ruin; seduce; corrupt (texts); bribe; *Fig.* contaminate, corrupt; —*vi* stink; —*vr* putrefy, rot; be spoiled; *Fig.* be corrupted

corrosión /korro'sion/ *f*, corrosion

corrosivo /korro'siβo/ *a* corrosive

corrugación /korruga'θion; korruga'sion/ *f*, corrugation, wrinkling

corrupción /korrup'θion; korrup'sion/ *f*, rot, putrefaction; corruption, depravity; decay; stink; bribery; falsification (of texts); corruption (of language, etc.)

corrupto /ko'rrupto/ *a* corrupt

corruptor /korrup'tor/ **(-ra)** *n* corrupter

corsario /kor'sario/ *m*, pirate; privateer

corsé /kor'se/ *m*, corset

corsetería /korsete'ria/ *f*, corset shop or manufactory

corso /'korso/ **(-sa)** *a* and *n* Corsican

corta /'korta/ *f*, felling, cutting

cortacircuitos /kortaθir'kuitos; kortasir'kuitos/ *m*, *Elec.* circuit breaker, cut-out; disconnecting switch

cortado /kor'taðo/ *a* fitting, proportioned; disjointed (style); confused, shamefaced

cortador /korta'ðor/ *m*, cutter; cutter-out (dresses, etc.); butcher

cortadura /korta'ðura/ *f*, cut, wound; cutting (from periodicals); defile; *pl* clippings, cuttings

cortafrío /korta'frio/ *m*, cold chisel; hammer-head chisel

cortalápices /korta'lapiθes; korta'lapises/ *m*, pencil sharpener

cortante /kor'tante/ *a* cutting; sharp; piercing (of wind, etc.); trenchant

cortapapel /kortapa'pel/ *m*, paper-knife

cortapisa /korta'pisa/ *f*, condition, stipulation

cortaplumas /korta'plumas/ *m*, penknife

cortapuros /korta'puros/ *m*, cigar cutter

cortar /kor'tar/ *vt* to cut; cut out (dresses, etc.); switch off, shut off (water, electricity, etc.); cleave, divide; cut (cards); pierce (wind, etc.); interrupt, impede; omit, cut; *Fig.* interrupt (conversation); decide, determine; —*vr* be confused or shamefaced; curdle, turn sour (e.g. *Se cortó la leche*, The milk turned sour); split, fray; chap

cortavidrios /korta'βiðrios/ *m*, diamond, glasscutter

cortaviento /korta'βiento/ *m*, windscreen

corte /'korte/ *f*, court (royal); retinue; yard; *pl* Spanish parliament. *m*, cutting, cut; blade, cutting edge; cutting out, dressmaking; length, material required for garment, shoes, etc.; cut, fit; style; book edge; *Archit.* section; means, expedient; counting of money (in a till). **c. de caja**, counting of money (in a till). **c. trasversal**, side view

cortedad /korte'ðað/ *f*, shortness, brevity; smallness; stupidity, dullness; timidity, shyness. **c. de fuerzas**, lack of strength

cortejar /korte'har/ *vt* to accompany, escort; woo, court

cortejo /kor'teho/ *m*, courtship, wooing; suite, accompaniment; gift, present; homage, attention; *Inf.* lover, beau

cortés /kor'tes/ *a* polite, attentive, courteous, civil

cortesana /korte'sana/ *f*, courtesan

cortesano /korte'sano/ *a* court; courtly. *m*, courtier

cortesía /korte'sia/ *f*, politeness, courtesy; attentiveness; civility; gift, present; favor. **c. internacional**, courtesy of nations. **c. de boca mucho vale y poco cuesta.** Courtesy is worth much and costs little

corteza /kor'teθa; kor'tesa/ *f*, *Bot.* bark; *Anat.* cortex; skin, peel, crust; aspect, appearance; roughness. **c. terrestre**, Earth's crust, crust of the Earth. **de c.**, superficial (e.g. explanation)

cortijo /kor'tiho/ *m*, farmhouse and land

cortina /kor'tina/ *f*, curtain; *Fig.* veil; *Inf.* heel taps; *Mil.* curtain, screen. **c. de fuego de artillería**, anti-aircraft barrage. **c. de globos de intercepción**, balloon barrage. **c. de humo**, smoke screen. **c. metálica**, metal shutter

cortinaje /korti'nahe/ *m*, curtains, hangings

corto /'korto/ *a* short, brief; timid, bashful; concise; defective; stupid, dull; tongue-tied, inarticulate. **c. circuito**, *Elec.* short-circuit. **c. de alcances**, dull-witted. **c. de vista**, short-sighted

coruscar /korus'kar/ *vi* to glitter, shine

corvadura /korβa'ðura/ *f*, bend; curvature

corvea /kor'βea/ *f*, corvée

corveta /kor'βeta/ *f*, curvet, prancing

corvetear /korβete'ar/ *vi* to curvet

corzo /'korθo; 'korso/ *m*, roe-deer, fallow-deer

cosa /'kosa/ f, thing. **c. rara**, strange to relate; an extraordinary thing. **como si tal c.**, as though nothing had happened. Inf. **poquita c.**, a person of no account

cosaco /ko'sako/ **(-ca)** a and n Cossack

coscorrón /kosko'rron/ m, blow on the head, cuff

cosecha /ko'setʃa/ f, harvest; harvest time; reaping, gathering, lifting; yield, produce; crop, shower (of honors, etc.). **c. de vino**, vintage

cosechar /kose'tʃar/ vi and vt to harvest, reap

coseno /ko'seno/ m, cosine

coser /ko'ser/ vt to sew, stitch; join, unite; press together (lips, etc.). **c. a puñaladas**, to stab repeatedly

Cosme /'kosme/ Cosmo

cosmético /kos'metiko/ a and m, cosmetic

cósmico /'kosmiko/ a cosmic

cosmografía /kosmogra'fia/ f, cosmography

cosmógrafo /kos'mografo/ m, cosmographer

cosmonave /kosmo'naβe/ f, spaceship

cosmopolita /kosmopo'lita/ a and mf cosmopolitan

cosmopolitismo /kosmopoli'tismo/ m, cosmopolitanism

cosmos /'kosmos/ m, cosmos

cospel /kos'pel/ m, blank (from which to stamp coins); to ken; subway to ken

cosquillas /kos'kiʎas; kos'kiyas/ f pl, tickling. **hacer c. (a)**, to tickle

cosquillear /koskiʎe'ar; koskiye'ar/ vt to tickle

cosquilleo /koski'ʎeo; koski'yeo/ m, tickle, tickling

cosquilloso /koski'ʎoso; koski'yoso/ a ticklish; hypersensitive, touchy

costa /'kosta/ f, cost; expense; coast; pl Law. costs. **a c. de**, by dint of; at the cost of. **a toda c.**, at all costs

Costa del Oro, la /'kosta del 'oro, la/ the Gold Coast

Costa de Marfil /'kosta de mar'fil/ Ivory Coast

costado /kos'taðo/ m, Anat. side; Mil. flank; side; pl line of descent, genealogy. Naut. **dar el c.**, to be broadside on

costal /kos'tal/ m, sack, bag

costanero /kosta'nero/ a sloping; coast, coastal

costar /kos'tar/ vi irr to cost; cause. See **contar**

costarriqueño /kostarri'keɲo/ **(-ña)** a and n Costa Rican

coste /'koste/ m, cost, price

costear /koste'ar/ vt to pay for, defray the expense of; Naut. coast; —vr pay (for itself)

costilla /kos'tiʎa; kos'tiya/ f, (Anat. Aer. Naut. Archit.) rib; Fig. Inf. better half, wife; pl Inf. back, behind

costillaje, costillar /kosti'ʎahe, kosti'ʎar; kosti'yahe, kosti'yar/ m, Anat. ribs; Naut. ship's frame

costoso /kos'toso/ a expensive, costly; valuable; dear, costly; difficult

costra /'kostra/ f, crust; scab; rind (of cheese)

costumbre /kos'tumbre/ f, habit; custom

costumbrista /kostum'brista/ mf writer on everyday life and customs —a (of literary work) dealing with life and customs

costura /kos'tura/ f, sewing; seam; needlework; joint; riveting

costurera /kostu'rera/ f, seamstress

costurero /kostu'rero/ m, work-box, sewing bag

cota /'kota/ f, Surv. elevation, height; coat (of mail); quota. **c. de malla**, chain-mail

cotangente /kotan'hente/ f, cotangent

cotejar /kote'har/ vt to compare; collate

cotejo /ko'teho/ m, comparison; collation

cótel /'kotel/ m, cocktail, drink

cotelera /kote'lera/ f, cocktail shaker

cotí /ko'ti/ m, ticking (cloth)

cotidiano /koti'ðiano/ a daily

cotillón /koti'ʎon; koti'yon/ m, cotillion

cotizable /koti'θaβle; koti'saβle/ a valued at; (of prices, shares) quoted

cotización /kotiθa'θion; kotisa'sion/ f, Com. quotation; Com. rate. **boletín de c.**, price list (of shares, etc.)

cotizar /koti'θar; koti'sar/ vt Com. to quote (prices, rates)

coto /'koto/ m, enclosed ground; boundary stone;

preserve, covert; hand's breadth; end, stop, limit. **c. de caza**, game preserve

cotorra /ko'torra/ f, small green parrot; magpie; Inf. chatterbox

cotufa /ko'tufa/ f, earthnut; titbit; Inf. **pedir cotufas en el golfo**, to ask for the moon

coturno /ko'turno/ m, buskin

coyote /ko'yote/ m, coyote, prairie wolf; Mexico fixer (anyone who can pull strings to cut red tape or achieve something illegally); smuggler (of goods or people)

coyuntura /koyun'tura/ f, Anat. joint; juncture, occasion

coz /koθ; kos/ f, kick, recoil (of gun); butt (of a rifle); Inf. slap in the face, unprovoked rudeness. **dar coces**, to kick

craneal /krane'al/ a cranial

cráneo /'kraneo/ m, cranium, skull

crápula /'krapula/ f, drunkenness; depravity, immorality, debauchery

craquear /krake'ar/ vt to crack (petroleum)

crasitud /krasi'tuð/ f, greasiness; fatness; crassness

craso /'kraso/ a fat, greasy; thick; unpardonable, crass (often with ignorancia). m, fatness; ignorance

creación /krea'θion; krea'sion/ f, creation; universe, world; foundation; establishment; appointment (dignitaries)

creador /krea'ðor/ **(-ra)** n creator, originator. m, God —a creative

crear /kre'ar/ vt to create; found, institute, establish; make, appoint

crecer /kre'θer; kre'ser/ vi irr to grow; grow up; increase in size; grow longer; wax (moon); come in (of the tide); increase in value (money); —vr become more sure of oneself; swell with pride; grow in authority. See **nacer**

creces /'kreθes; 'kreses/ f pl, increase, interest. **con c.**, fully, amply. **pagar con c.**, Fig. to pay with interest

crecida /kre'θiða; kre'siða/ f, swollen river or stream; food; rising (of the tide)

crecido /kre'θiðo; kre'siðo/ a grown up; considerable; abundant, plentiful; large; full; serious, important

crecidos /kre'θiðos; kre'siðos/ m pl, widening stitches (knitting)

creciente /kre'θiente; kre'siente/ a growing; rising (of the tide); crescent (moon). m, Herald. crescent. f, rising of the tide; crescent moon

crecimiento /kreθi'miento; kresi'miento/ m, growing; growth, development; increase (in value, money); waxing (of moon)

credencial /kreðen'θial; kreðen'sial/ a accrediting

credenciales /kreðen'θiales; kreðen'siales/ f pl, credentials

credibilidad /kreðiβili'ðað/ f, credibility

crédito /'kreðito/ m, belief, credence; assent, acquiescence; reputation, name; favor, popularity, acceptance; Com. credit; Com. letter of credit. **créditos activos**, assets. **créditos pasivos**, liabilities. **a c.**, on credit

credo /'kreðo/ m, creed. Inf. **en un c.**, in a jiffy

credulidad /kreðuli'ðað/ f, credulity

crédulo /'kreðulo/ a credulous

creencia /kre'enθia; kre'ensia/ f, belief; religion, sect, faith

creer /kre'er/ vt irr to believe; think, consider, opine; think likely or probable. **¡Ya lo creo!** I should just think so! Rather! **creerse la divina garza**, Mexico to think one is God's gift to the world. **creerse descender del sobaco de Jesucristo**, to think one is God's gift to the world —Pres. Part. **creyendo**. Preterite **creyó, creyeron**. Imperf. Subjunc. **creyese**, etc.

creíble /kre'iβle/ a credible

crema /'krema/ f, cream (off milk); custard mold, cream, shape; face cream; cold cream; elect, flower (of society, etc.)

cremación /krema'θion; krema'sion/ f, cremation; burning, incineration

cremallera /krema'ʎera; krema'yera/ f, Mech. rack, ratch; zip fastener. **colgar la c.**, to give a house-warming

crematístico /krema'tistiko/ a economic, financial

crematorio /krema'torio/ *m*, crematorium —*a* burning; cremating

cremor /kre'mor/ *m*, *Chem.* cream of tartar

cremoso /kre'moso/ *a* creamy

crencha /'krentʃa/ *f*, parting (of the hair); each side of parting

creosota /kreo'sota/ *f*, creosote

crepitación /krepita'θion; krepita'sion/ *f*, crackling, sputtering; hissing; roar (of a fire); *Med.* crepitation

crepitar /krepi'tar/ *vi* to crackle; sputter; hiss; roar (of a fire); *Med.* crepitate

crepuscular /krepusku'lar/ *a* twilight

crepúsculo /kre'puskulo/ *m*, twilight, half light

cresa /'kresa/ *f*, maggot; cheese-mite; fly's egg

Creso /'kreso/ Croesus

crespo /'krespo/ *a* curly, frizzy (hair); rough (of animal's fur); curled (leaves); artificial, involved (style)

crespón /kres'pon/ *m*, crape

cresta /'kresta/ *f*, comb (of cock, etc.); tuft, topknot (birds); plume; summit, top (of mountains); crest (of a wave); *Herald.* crest

crestado /kres'taðo/ *a* crested

Creta /'kreta/ Crete

creta /'kreta/ *f*, chalk

cretense /kre'tense/ *a* Cretan

cretinismo /kreti'nismo/ *m*, cretinism

cretino /kre'tino/ **(-na)** *a* and *n* cretin

creyente /kre'yente/ *a* believing; religious. *mf* believer

cría /'kria/ *f*, rearing; bringing up; nursing; suckling; breeding; brood; litter

criada /kri'aða/ *f*, servant, maid

criadero /kria'ðero/ *m*, *Mineral.* vein, deposit; tree nursery, plantation; breeding farm or place —*a* prolific

criado /kri'aðo/ *m*, servant —*a* bred, brought up (used with *bien* or *mal*, well or badly brought up)

criador /kria'ðor/ **(-ra)** *n* breeder, keeper, raiser —*a* creating; rearing; creative; fertile, rich

crianza /kri'anθa; kri'ansa/ *f*, feeding, suckling; lactation; manners. **buena** (or **mala**) **c.**, good (or bad) breeding or upbringing

criar /kri'ar/ *vt* to create; procreate; rear, educate, bring up; feed, nurse, suckle; raise (birds, animals); inspire, give rise to. **Me crié raquítico,** I grew up delicate

criatura /kria'tura/ *f*, being, creature; man, human being; infant; small child; fetus; *Fig.* puppet, tool

criba /'kriβa/ *f*, sieve, cribble

cribar /kri'βar/ *vt* to sieve; riddle (earth, etc.)

crimen /'krimen/ *m*, crime. **c. pasional,** crime of passion

criminal /krimi'nal/ *a* and *m*, criminal

criminalidad /kriminali'ðað/ *f*, guilt; crime ratio; delinquency

criminalista /krimina'lista/ *mf* criminal lawyer; criminologist

criminología /kriminolo'hia/ *f*, criminology

crin /krin/ *f*, horsehair; (gen. *pl*) mane

crinolina /krino'lina/ *f*, crinoline

crío /'krio/ *m*, *Inf.* kid, brat

criollo /'krioʎo; 'krioyo/ **(-lla)** *a* and *n* creole —*a* indigenous, native

cripta /'kripta/ *f*, crypt

criptografía /kriptogra'fia/ *f*, cryptography

criquet /kri'ket/ *m*, *Sports.* cricket

crisálida /kri'saliða/ *f*, chrysalis

crisantemo /krisan'temo/ *m*, chrysanthemum

crisis /'krisis/ *f*, crisis. **c. de vivienda,** housing shortage. **c. de desarrollo,** growing pains.

crisma /'krisma/ *m*, or *f*, chrism

crisol /kri'sol/ *m*, crucible; melting pot

crispado /kris'paðo/ *a* stiffened

crispar /kris'par/ *vt* to cause to contract or twitch; —*vr* twitch. *Inf.* **Se me crispan los nervios,** My nerves are all on edge

cristal /kris'tal/ *m*, crystal; glass; windowpane; mirror; water. **c. tallado,** cut glass

cristalería /kristale'ria/ *f*, glassware; glass manufacture; glass panes; glass and china shop

cristalino /krista'lino/ *a* crystalline. *m*, lens (of the eye)

cristalización /kristaliθa'θion; kristalisa'sion/ *f*, crystallization

cristalizar /kristali'θar; kristali'sar/ *vi* to crystallize; *Fig.* take shape; —*vt* cause to crystallize

cristalografía /kristalogra'fia/ *f*, crystallography

cristiandad /kristian'dað/ *f*, Christendom

cristianismo /kristia'nismo/ *m*, Christianity; Christendom

cristianizar /kristiani'θar; kristiani'sar/ *vt* to convert to Christianity, christianize

cristiano /kris'tiano/ **(-na)** *a* and *n* Christian —*a Inf.* watered (of wine). *m*, *Inf.* Spanish (contrasted with other languages); *Inf.* soul, person

cristino /kris'tino/ **(-na)** *a* and *n* supporting, or follower of, Queen Regent Maria Cristina during Carlist wars

cristo /'kristo/ *m*, Christ; crucifix. *Inf.* **donde C. dio las tres voces,** in the middle of nowhere

cristus /'kristus/ *m*, Christ-cross; alphabet. **no saber el c.,** to be extremely ignorant

criterio /kri'terio/ *m*, criterion, standard; judgment, discernment; opinion. **a c. de,** in the opinion of. **según mi c.,** in my opinion

crítica /'kritika/ **(a)** *f*, criticism (of)

criticar /kriti'kar/ *vt* to criticize; censure, find fault with, blame

crítico /'kritiko/ *a* critical; censorious; dangerous, difficult; *Med.* critical. *m*, critic; fault-finder

criticón /kriti'kon/ **(-ona)** *a* censorious, hyper-critical —*n* fault-finder

Croacia /kro'aθia; kro'asia/ Croatia

croar /kro'ar/ *vi* (frog) to croak

croata /kro'ata/ *a* and *mf* Croatian

croché /kro'tʃe/ *m*, crochet work

crol /krol/ *m*, crawl (swimming)

cromado /kro'maðo/ *a* chromium-plated

cromático /kro'matiko/ *a* chromatic

cromato /kro'mato/ *m*, chromate

crómico /'kromiko/ *a* chromic

cromo /'kromo/ *m*, chrome; chromium; chromolithograph

crónica /'kronika/ *f*, chronicle; diary of events

crónico /'kroniko/ *a* chronic; inveterate

cronista /kro'nista/ *mf* chronicler

cronología /kronolo'hia/ *f*, chronology

cronológico /krono'lohiko/ *a* chronological

cronómetro /kro'nometro/ *m*, stop-watch

croqueta /kro'keta/ *f*, croquette

croquis /'krokis/ *m*, sketch, outline, drawing. **c. de nivel,** (optical) foresight

crótalo /'krotalo/ *m*, rattlesnake; snapper (kind of castanet)

cruce /'kruθe; 'kruse/ *m*, crossing; point of intersection; crossroads

crucero /kru'θero; kru'sero/ *m*, *Eccl.* cross-bearer; crossroads; *Archit.* transept; *Astron.* Cross; *Naut.* cruiser

crucificar /kruθifi'kar; krusifi'kar/ *vt* to crucify; *Fig. Inf.* torment, torture

crucifijo /kruθi'fiho; krusi'fiho/ *m*, crucifix

crucifixión /kruθifik'sion; krusifik'sion/ *f*, crucifixion

cruciforme /kruθi'forme; krusi'forme/ *a* cruciform

crucigrama /kruθi'grama; krusi'grama/ *m*, crossword puzzle

cruda /'kruða/ *f*, *Mexico* hangover

crudelísimo /kruðe'lisimo/ *a superl* cruel, most cruel, exceedingly cruel

crudeza /kru'ðeθa; kru'ðesa/ *f*, rawness, uncookedness; unripeness; rawness (silk, etc.); crudeness; harshness; *Inf.* boasting

crudo /'kruðo/ *a* uncooked, raw; green, unripe; indigestible; raw, natural, unbleached; harsh, cruel; cold, raw; *Inf.* boastful. **crudos de petróleo,** *m pl* crude oil

crueldad /kruel'dað/ *f*, cruelty; harshness

cruento /'kruento/ *a* bloody

crujía /kru'hia/ *f*, passage, corridor; *Naut.* midship gangway

crujidero /kruhi'ðero/ *a* crackling; creaking; crispy; clattering; rustling; chattering

crujido /kru'hiðo/ *m*, creak, crack, crackling, rustle

crujir /kru'hir/ *vi* to creak, crackle, rustle

crup /krup/ *m*, croup

crupié /kru'pje/ *m*, croupier

crustáceo /krus'taθeo; krus'taseo/ *a* and *m*, crustacean

crux /kruks/ *f*, cross; tails (of coin); withers (of animals); insignia, decoration; affliction, trouble; *Astron.* Southern Cross; *Print.* dagger, obelisk, obelus. **c. doble**, diesis, double dagger. **c. de mayo**, May cross. **c. gamada**, swastika. *Inf.* **¡C. y raya!** An end to this! **en c.**, in the shape of a cross. *Inf.* **hacerse cruces**, to be left speechless, be dumbfounded

cruzada /kru'θaða; kru'saða/ *f*, crusade; crossroads; campaign

cruzado /kru'θaðo; kru'saðo/ *a* cross; double-breasted (of coats). *m*, crusader; member of military order

cruzamiento /kruθa'mjento; krusa'mjento/ *m*, crossing; intersection

cruzar /kru'θar; kru'sar/ *vt* to cross; intersect; interbreed; bestow a cross upon; *Naut.* cruise; —*vr* take part in a crusade; cross one another; coincide; *Geom.* intersect

cu /ku/ *f*, name of the letter Q

cuacuac /kua'kuak/ *m*, quack (of a duck)

cuaderna /kua'ðerna/ *f*, *Naut.* ship's frame, timber; double fours (backgammon)

cuaderno /kua'ðerno/ *m*, notebook, jotter, account book; *Inf.* card pack. *Naut.* **c. de bitácora**, logbook

cuadra /'kuaðra/ *f*, stable; ward, dormitory; hall, large room; quarter of a mile

cuadrado /kua'ðraðo/ *a* square; perfect, exact. *m*, square; (*Mil. Math.*) square; window-frame; clock (of a stocking)

cuadragenario /kuaðrahe'nario/ *a* forty years old

cuadragésima /kuaðra'hesima/ *f*, Quadragesima

cuadragésimo /kuaðra'hesimo/ *a* fortieth

cuadrángulo /kua'ðrangulo/ *m*, quadrangle

cuadrante /kua'ðrante/ *m*, quadrant; dial, face

cuadrar /kua'ðrar/ *vt* (*Math.*) to square; make square; —*vi* correspond, tally; fit, be appropriate —*vr Mil.* stand at attention; *Fig. Inf.* dig one's heels in

cuadrática /kua'ðratika/ *f*, quadratic equation

cuadrático /kua'ðratiko/ *a* quadratic

cuadratura /kuaðra'tura/ *f*, squareness; (*Math. Astron.*) quadrature

cuadrienio /kua'ðrienio/ *m*, space of four years

cuadriga /kua'ðriga/ *f*, quadriga

cuadrilátero /kuaðri'latero/ *m*, quadrilateral; boxing ring —*a* quadrilateral

cuadrilla /kua'ðriʎa; kua'ðriya/ *f*, gang; company, band, group; police patrol; quadrille (dance); matadors and their assistants (at a bull fight). **c. carrillana**, track gang

cuadrilongo /kuaðri'longo/ *a* and *m*, oblong

cuadrimotor /kuaðrimo'tor/ *a Aer.* four-engined

cuadrivio /kua'ðriβio/ *m*, quadrivium

cuadro /'kuaðro/ *m*, square; picture-frame; frame (of bicycle); flowerbed; *Theat.* tableau, scene; spectacle, sight; board (of instruments); description (in novel, etc.); *Mil.* command, officers; square (of troops). **c. de distribución**, *Elec.* main switchboard. **c. enrejado**, play pen. **cuadro de costumbres**, word-picture of everyday life and customs. **cuadro vivo**, tableau vivant. **a cuadros**, checked, in squares

cuadrúpedo /kua'ðrupeðo/ **(-da)** *a* and *n* quadruped

cuadruple /kua'ðruple/ *a* quadruple

cuadruplicar /kuaðrupli'kar/ *vt* to quadruple

cuajada /kua'haða/ *f*, curd (of milk)

cuajar /kua'har/ *m*, maw (of a ruminant)

cuajar /kua'har/ *vt* to coagulate; curdle; —*vi Inf.* achieve, get away with; —*vr* be coagulated or curdled; *Inf.* be packed or chock full; get stuck (e.g. a piece of food in one's throat)

cuajarón /kuaha'ron/ *m*, clot (of blood, etc.)

cuajo /'kuaho/ *m*, rennet; coagulation; curdling; *Anat.* abomasum

cual /kual/ *rel pron* sing. *mf* and *neut pl* **cuales**, which; who; such as (e.g. *Le detuvieron sucesos cuales suelen ocurrir*, He was detained by events such as usually happen). **a c. mas**, vying (with) (e.g. *Los*

dos canónigos a c. más grueso, The two canons each fatter (vying in fatness) than the other). **c.** is used with *def art* **el (la, lo, los, las) cual(es)**; who; which, when the antecedent is a noun (e.g. *Juan saltó en el barco, el c. zarpó en seguida*, John jumped into the boat which sailed at once). **por lo c.**, for which reason —*adv* like (gen. literary or poet.). **¿cuál?** *interr. pron* (no article) which? what? e.g. *Aquí tienes dos cuadros, ¿cuál de ellos te gusta?* Here are two pictures, which one do you like? Also expresses an implicit question, e.g. *No sé cuál te guste*, I don't know which you will like. **¡cuál!** *adv interj* how! *c.... c.* indef *pron* some... some

cualesquier /kuales'kier/ *a pl* of **cualquier**

cualesquiera /kuales'kiera/ *a pl* of **cualquiera**

cualidad /kuali'ðað/ *f*, quality; characteristic; talent

cualitativo /kualita'tiβo/ *a* qualitative

cualquier /kual'kier/ *Abbr.* **of cualquiera**, any; *pl* **cualesquier**. Only used as abb. *before noun*

cualquiera /kual'kiera/ *a mf* any, e.g. *una canción c.*, any song —*pron* anybody, each, anyone whatsoever, whoever (e.g. *¡C. diría que no te gusta!* Anyone would say you don't like it!) *Inf.* **un c.**, a nobody

cuán /ku'an/ *adv* how (e.g. *¡C. bello es!* How beautiful it is). Used only before *a* or *adv*. Abb. of **cuánto**

cuando /'kuando/ *adv* when; if —*interr* **¿cuándo?** *conjunc* although; since; sometimes; —*prep* during (e.g. *c. la guerra*, during the war) **c. más**, at most, at best. **c. menos**, at the least. **c. no**, if not (e.g. *Es agnóstica cuando no atea*, She's an agnostic, if not an atheist) **de c. en c.**, from time to time

cuandoquiera /kuando'kiera/ *adv* whenever

cuanta, teoría de la /'kuanta, teo'ria de la/ *f*, quantum theory

cuantía /kuan'tia/ *f*, quantity, amount; importance, rank, distinction

cuantiar /kuan'tiar/ *vt* to value, estimate; tax

cuantidad /kuanti'ðað/ *f*, quantity

cuantioso /kuan'tioso/ *a* large, considerable; numerous; plentiful, abundant

cuantitativo /kuantita'tiβo/ *a* quantitative

cuanto /'kuanto/ *a* as much as, all the; *pl* as many as, all the (e.g. *Te daré cuantas muñecas veas allí*, I'll give you all the dolls you see there) —*a correlative* the... the, as... as (e.g. *C. más tanto, mejor*, The more the better). **cuánto**, *a* and *pron interr* and *interj* how much; *pl* how many (e.g. *¡Cuánto tiempo sin verla!* How long without seeing her!) *pron neut* **cuanto**, as much as, all that (e.g. *Te daré c. quieras*, I shall give you all that you wish) —*adv* cuanto, as soon as. **c. antes**, as soon as possible. **c. a** or **en c. a**, concerning —*adv* and *conjunc* **c. más**, all the more (e.g. *Se lo diré c. más que tenía esa intención*, I shall tell him all the more because I meant to do so) —*adv* **en c.**, as soon as, immediately (e.g. *Lo haré en c. venga*, I shall do it immediately he comes). **en c. a**, with regard to. **por c.**, inasmuch, for this reason —*adv interr* **¿Cuánto?** How much? How long? *adv interj* How! How much! (e.g. *¡Cuánto me gustaría ir!* How much I should like to go!)

cuaquerismo /kuake'rismo/ *m*, Quakerism

cuáquero /'kuakero/ **(-ra)** *n* Quaker

cuarenta /kua'renta/ *a* and *m*, forty; fortieth

cuarentena /kuaren'tena/ *f*, fortieth; period of forty days, months or years; Lent; quarantine

cuarentón /kuaren'ton/ **(-ona)** *n* person forty years old

cuaresma /kua'resma/ *f*, Lent

cuaresmal /kuares'mal/ *a* Lenten

cuarta /'kuarta/ *f*, quarter, fourth; hand's breadth; *Mus.* fourth; *Astron.* quadrant

cuartana /kuar'tana/ *f*, quartan (fever)

cuarteadura /kuartea'ðura/ *f*, crack

cuartear /kuarte'ar/ *vt* to quarter, divide into quarters; cut or divide into pieces

cuartel /kuar'tel/ *m*, barracks; *Naut.* hatch; quarter, fourth; *Herald.* quarter; district, ward; flowerbed; *Inf.* house, accommodation; *Mil.* quarter, mercy; *Mil.* billet, station. *Mil.* **c. general**, general headquarters

cuartelada /kuarte'laða/ *f*, *Naut.* quarter; military rebellion, military uprising, mutiny

cuartelar /kuarte'lar/ *vt Herald.* to quarter

cuartelazo /kuarte'laθo; kuarte'laso/ *m*, military rebellion, military uprising, mutiny

cuarterón /kuarte'ron/ **(-ona)** *n* quadroon

cuarteta /kuar'teta/ *f*, quatrain

cuarteto /kuar'teto/ *m*, *Mus.* quartet; *Poet.* quatrain

cuartilla /kuar'tiʎa; kuar'tiya/ *f*, sheet of paper; liquid measure; quarter of an arroba; pastern (horses)

cuarto /'kuarto/ *m*, room; quarter, fourth; point (of compass); watch (on battleships); *Astron.* quarter, phase; portion, quarter; joint (of meat); *pl* quarters (of animals); *Inf.* penny, farthing —a quarter, fourth. **c. creciente,** first phase (of moon). **c. de hora,** quarter of an hour. **en c.,** *Print.* in quarto. *Inf.* **no tener un c.,** to be broke

cuarzo /'kuarθo; 'kuarso/ *m*, quartz

cuasi /'kuasi/ *adv* almost, nearly, quasi

cuasidelito /kuasiðe'lito/ *m*, *Law.* technical offense

cuasimodo /kuasi'moðo/ *m*, *Eccl.* Low Sunday, Quasimodo

cuaterna /kua'terna/ *f*, quaternion

cuatrillón /kuatri'ʎon; kuatri'yon/ *m*, quadrillion

cuatrimestre /kuatri'mestre/ *a* of four months' duration. *m*, space of four months

cuatrimotor /kuatrimo'tor/ *m*, *Aer.* four-engine airplane

cuatrisílabo /kuatri'silaβo/ *a* quadrisyllabic

cuatro /'kuatro/ *a* four; fourth. *m*, figure four; fourth (of days of months); playing-card with four spots; *Mus.* quartet. **el c. de mayo,** the fourth of May. **Son las c.,** It is four o'clock

cuatrocientos /kuatro'θientos; kuatro'sientos/ *a* four hundred; four hundredth

cuba /'kuβa/ *f*, barrel, cask; tub, vat; *Inf.* pot-bellied person; *Inf.* drunkard, toper

cubano /ku'βano/ **(-na)** *a* and *n* Cuban

cubería /kuβe'ria/ *f*, cooperage

cubeta /ku'βeta/ *f*, *dim* keg, small cask; bucket, pail; *Photo.* developing dish

cubicar /kuβi'kar/ *vt* *Math.* to cube; *Geom.* measure the volume of

cúbico /'kuβiko/ *a* cubic

cubículo /ku'βikulo/ *m*, cubicle

cubierta /ku'βierta/ *f*, cover; envelope; casing; deck (of ship); tire cover; book-jacket; pretext, excuse. **c. de escotilla,** *Naut.* companion-hatch. **c. de paseo,** promenade deck

cubierto /ku'βierto/ *m*, cover, place at table; course (of a meal); table d'hôte, complete meal; roof. **un c. de doscientas pesetas,** a two hundred peseta meal

cubil /ku'βil/ *m*, lair, den (of animals)

cubilete /kuβi'lete/ *m*, *Cul.* mold; dice box; conjurer's cup

cubismo /ku'βismo/ *m*, cubism

cubista /ku'βista/ *mf* cubist —*a* cubistic

cubo /'kuβo/ *m*, bucket, pail; *Mech.* socket; *Math.* cube; hub (of a wheel); mill-pond

cubrecama /kuβre'kama/ *m*, bedspread

cubrecorsé /kuβrekor'se/ *m*, camisole

cubrimiento /kuβri'miento/ *m*, covering

cubrir /ku'βrir/ *vt* to cover; *Mil.* defend; spread over, extend over; conceal, hide; *Com.* cover; dissemble; *Archit.* roof; —*vr* cover one's head; pay, meet (debts, etc.); cover or protect oneself (by insurance, etc.) —*Past Part.* **cubierto**

cucaña /ku'kaɲa/ *f*, greasy pole; *Inf.* snip, cinch, bargain

cucaracha /kuka'ratʃa/ *f*, cockroach

cuchara /ku'tʃara/ *f*, spoon; ladle; *Naut.* boat scoop; scoop, dipper. *Fig.* **meter c.,** to stick one's oar in

cucharada /kutʃa'raða/ *f*, spoonful; ladleful

cuchicheador /kutʃitʃea'ðor/ **(-ra)** *n* whisperer

cuchichear /kutʃitʃe'ar/ *vi* to whisper

cuchicheo /kutʃi'tʃeo/ *m*, whisper; whispering; murmur

cuchillada /kutʃi'ʎaða; kutʃi'yaða/ *f*, knife thrust or wound; *pl* (in sleeves, etc.) slashes; fight, blows

cuchillería /kutʃiʎe'ria; kutʃiye'ria/ *f*, cutlery; cutler's shop

cuchillero /kutʃi'ʎero; kutʃi'yero/ *m*, cutler

cuchillo /ku'tʃiʎo; ku'tʃiyo/ *m*, knife; *Sew.* gore, gus-

set (gen. *pl*); authority, power; anything triangular in shape. **pasar a c.,** to put to the sword

cuclillas, en /ku'kliʎas, en; ku'kliyas, en/ *adv* in a squatting position

cuclillo /ku'kliʎo; ku'kliyo/ *m*, *Ornith.* cuckoo; *Inf.* cuckold

cuco /'kuko/ *a* *Inf.* pretty, cute; crafty, smart

cucú /ku'ku/ *m*, cry of the cuckoo

Cucufo /ku'kufo/ *m*, the Devil

cuculla /ku'kuʎa; ku'kuya/ *f*, cowl, hood

cucurucho /kuku'rutʃo/ *m*, paper cornet

cuello /'kueʎo; 'kueyo/ *m*, *Anat.* neck; neck (of bottle, etc.); *Sew.* neck; collar; necklet (of fur, etc.)

cuenca /'kuenka/ *f*, socket (of eye); *Geog.* catchment-basin; gorge, deep valley. **c. de un río,** river-basin

cuenta /'kuenta/ *f*, count, counting; calculation; account; bead; charge, responsibility; reckoning; explanation, reason; *Com.* bill. **c. a cero, c. a la inversa, c. atrás,** countdown. **c. corriente,** current account. **cuentas alegres, cuentas galanas,** *Inf.* idle dreams, illusions. **c. pendiente,** outstanding account. *Inf.* **caer en la c.,** to tumble to, realize. **llevar la c.,** to reckon, keep account. **sin c.,** countless. **tener en c.,** to bear in mind

cuentacorrentista /kuentakorren'tista/ *mf* one who has a bank account

cuentagotas /kuenta'gotas/ *m*, dropper, dropping tube

cuentakilómetros /kuentaki'lometros/ *m*, speedometer

cuentapasos /kuenta'pasos/ *m*, pedometer

cuentista /kuen'tista/ *mf* storyteller; *Inf.* gossip

cuento /'kuento/ *m*, story, tale; narrative; calculation; *Inf.* gossip, fairytale; *Math.* million. **c. de viejas,** old wives' tale. *Fig. Inf.* **dejarse de cuentos,** to go straight to the point. *Inf.* **Va de c.,** It is told, they say

cuerda /'kuerða/ *f*, rope; cord; string; *Geom.* chord; *Mus.* string; catgut; chain (of clock); *Mus.* chord; vocal range. **dar c.** (**a**), to wind up (a watch); lead on, make talk. **de cuerdas cruzadas,** overstrung (of a piano)

cuerdo /'kuerðo/ *a* sane; prudent; levelheaded

cuerno /'kuerno/ *m*, *Anat.* horn; feeler, antenna; *Mus.* horn; horn (of the moon). **c. de abundancia,** horn of plenty. *Inf.* **poner en los cuernos de la luna,** to praise to the skies

cuero /'kuero/ *m*, hide, pelt; leather. **c. charolado,** patent leather. **en cueros,** stark naked

cuerpo /'kuerpo/ *m*, *Anat.* body or trunk; flesh (as opposed to spirit); bodice; volume, book; main portion; collection; size, volume; physical appearance; corpse; group, assembly; corporation, association; *Geom.* solid; *Chem.* element; thickness, density; *Mil.* corps. **c. de bomberos,** fire brigade. **c. de guardia,** guardhouse. **c. de la vida,** staff of life; *Inf.* **dar con el c. en tierra,** to fall flat. **de c. entero,** *Art.* full-length (portrait). **en c.,** without a coat, lightly clad. **un c. a c.,** a clinch (in wrestling)

cuervo /'kuerβo/ *m*, raven; crow

cuesco /'kuesko/ *m*, stone, seed, pip

cuesta /'kuesta/ *f*, slope, incline, gradient. **c. abajo** (**arriba**), down (up) hill. **a cuestas,** on one's back; having the responsibility of

cuestión /kues'tion/ *f*, problem, question; quarrel; disagreement; affair, matter; torture

cuestionable /kuestio'naβle/ *a* doubtful, questionable

cuestionar /kuestio'nar/ *vt* to discuss, debate

cuestionario /kuestio'nario/ *m*, questionnaire

cueva /'kueβa/ *f*, cave, cavern; basement, cellar. *Fig.* **c. de ladrones,** den of thieves

cuévano /'kueβano/ *m*, hamper, basket

cuidado /kui'ðaðo/ *m*, carefulness, pains; attention; charge, care, responsibility; anxiety, fear —*interj* **¡C.!** Careful! Look out! **Me tiene sin c. su opinión,** I am not interested in his (your) opinion. *Inf.* **estar al c. de,** to be under the direction of. **estar de c.,** to be dangerously ill

cuidadoso /kuiða'ðoso/ **(de)** *a* careful (about *or* with); anxious (about); concerned (with); watchful; conscientious

cuidar /kui'ðar/ *vt* to care for; tend; take care of, look after; mind, be careful of; —*vr* look after oneself

cuita /'kuita/ *f*, misfortune, anxiety, trouble

cuitado /kui'taðo/ *a* unfortunate, worried; timid, bashful, humble

culata /ku'lata/ *f*, *Anat.* haunch; butt (of fire-arms); back, rear; *Auto.* sump

culatazo /kula'taθo; kula'taso/ *m*, recoil (of fire-arms)

culebra /ku'leβra/ *f*, snake; *Inf.* trick, joke; *Inf.* sudden uproar. **hacer c.**, to stagger along

culebrear /kuleβre'ar/ *vi* to wriggle; grovel; meander, wind

culebreo /kule'βreo/ *m*, wriggling; meandering, winding

culí /ku'li/ *m*, coolie

culinario /kuli'nario/ *a* culinary

culminación /kulmina'θion; kulmina'sion/ *f*, culmination, peak; *Astron.* zenith

culminante /kulmi'nante/ *a* culminating; *Fig.* outstanding

culminar /kulmi'nar/ *vi* to culminate (in)

culo /'kulo/ *m*, buttocks, seat; rump; anus; base, bottom. **c. de lámpara**, *Archit.* pendant; *Print.* tail-piece

culpa /'kulpa/ *f*, fault; blame. **echar la c.** (**a**), to blame. **por c. de**, through the fault of. **tener la c.**, to be to blame

culpabilidad /kulpaβili'ðað/ *f*, guilt

culpable /kul'paβle/ *a* culpable

culpado /kul'paðo/ **(-da)** *n* culprit

culpar /kul'par/ *vt* to blame, accuse; criticize, censure

culteranismo, cultismo /kultera'nismo, kul'tismo/ *m*, involved literary style (cf. **Euphuism**)

cultígeno /kul'tiheno/ *m*, cultigen

cultismo /kul'tismo/ *m*, cultism (Gongorism); learned form, learnedism, learned word

cultivable /kulti'βaβle/ *a* cultivable

cultivación /kultiβa'θion; kultiβa'sion/ *f*, cultivation; culture

cultivador /kultiβa'ðor/ **(-ra)** *n* cultivator; planter

cultivar /kulti'βar/ *vt* to cultivate; develop; exercise, practice (professions); culture (bacteriology)

cultivo /kul'tiβo/ *m*, cultivation; farming; culture (bacteriological)

culto /'kulto/ *a* cultivated; educated; cultured; elegant, artificial (style). *m*, worship; cult; religion, creed; homage

cultura /kul'tura/ *f*, cultivation; culture. **de c. universitaria**, college-educated

cultural /kultu'ral/ *a* cultural

cumbre /'kumbre/ *f*, peak, crest, summit; *Fig.* zenith, acme

cumpleaños /kumple'anos/ *m*, birthday

cumplidamente /kumpliða'mente/ *adv* fully, completely

cumplido /kum'pliðo/ *a* complete; thorough; long; plentiful; courteous, punctilious; fulfilled. *m*, courtesy, attention; formality. **gastar cumplidos**, to stand on ceremony; be formal

cumplimentar /kumplimen'tar/ *vt* to congratulate; perform, carry out

cumplimentero /kumplimen'tero/ *a* over-complimentary; *Inf.* gushing

cumplimiento /kumpli'miento/ *m*, fulfillment, performance; courtesy, formality; completion; complement

cumplir /kum'plir/ *vt* to perform, carry into effect; reach (of age); keep (promises). **c. su palabra**, to keep one's word; —*vi* perform a duty; expire, fall due; serve the required term of military service; be necessary, behove; —*vr* be fulfilled, come true. **por c.**, as a matter of form

cumulativo /kumula'tiβo/ *a* cumulative

cúmulo /'kumulo/ *m*, heap, pile; great many, host, mass, myriad; (cloud) cumulus, thunderhead

cuna /'kuna/ *f*, cradle; foundling hospital; birthplace; origin, genesis; *pl* cat's cradle (game)

cundir /kun'dir/ *vi* to extend, spread (gen. liquids); be diffused (news); expand, grow

cuneiforme /kunei'forme/ *a* wedge-shaped, cuneiform

cunero /ku'nero/ **(-ra)** *n* foundling, orphan

cuña /'kuna/ *f*, wedge; *Mech.* quoin. *Mil.* **practicar una c.**, to make a wedge

cuñada /ku'naða/ *f*, sister-in-law

cuñado /ku'naðo/ *m*, brother-in-law

cuño /'kuno/ *m*, die, stamp; *Fig.* impression; mark on silver, hallmark. **de viejo c.**, old-guard (e.g. socialites)

cuota /'kuota/ *f*, quota; share; subscription; fee

cupé /ku'pe/ *m*, coupé

Cupido /ku'piðo/ *m*, Cupid; philanderer

cuplé /ku'ple/ *m*, couplet; song

cupo /'kupo/ *m*, quota; share; tax rate; *Mil.* contingent

cupón /ku'pon/ *m*, coupon

cúpula /'kupula/ *f*, *Archit.* dome, cupola; *Bot.* cup

cuquería /kuke'ria/ *f*, craftiness, smartness; cuteness, prettiness

cura /'kura/ *m*, parish priest; *Inf.* Roman Catholic priest. *f*, cure (e.g. *La enfermedad tiene c.*, The illness can be cured); healing; remedy. **c. de almas**, cure of souls. **primera c.**, first aid. *Inf.* **c. de misa y olla**, ignorant priest

curable /ku'raβle/ *a* curable

curación /kura'θion; kura'sion/ *f*, cure, remedy; healing

curador /kura'ðor/ **(-ra)** *n* curer, salter. *m*, (*Scots law*) curator —*a* curing; healing

curaduría /kuraðu'ria/ *f*, *Law.* guardianship

curanderismo /kurande'rismo/ *m*, quackery, charlatanism; quack medicine

curandero /kuran'dero/ **(-ra)** *n* quack doctor; charlatan

curar /ku'rar/ *vi* to heal, cure; (*with de*) take care of; care about, mind; —*vt* cure, salt; treat medically (bandage, give medicines, etc.); cure (leather); bleach (cloth); season (timber); *Fig.* remedy (an evil)

curasao /kura'sao/ *m*, curaçao (drink)

curativo /kura'tiβo/ *a* curative

curato /ku'rato/ *m*, *Eccl.* parish, cure

Curazao /kura'θao; kura'sao/ Curaçao

cúrcuma /'kurkuma/ *f*, turmeric

curdo /'kurðo/ **(-da)** *a* Kurdish —*n* Kurd

cureña /ku'rena/ *f*, gun-carriage

curia /'kuria/ *f*, *Law.* bar; tribunal; *Eccl.* curia; care, attention

curiana /ku'riana/ *f*, cockroach

curiche /ku'ritʃe/ *m*, swamp

curiosamente /kuriosa'mente/ *adv* curiously; carefully, attentively; neatly

curiosear /kuriose'ar/ *vi* to pry; be curious (about); meddle, be a busybody

curiosidad /kuriosi'ðað/ *f*, curiosity; inquisitiveness, meddlesomeness; neatness; carefulness, conscientiousness; curio

curioso /ku'rioso/ *a* curious; inquisitive; interesting; odd; neat, clean; conscientious, careful

Curita /ku'rita/ *f*, *trademark* Band-Aid

cursado /kur'saðo/ *a* experienced, versed

cursante /kur'sante/ *m*, student

cursar /kur'sar/ *vt* to frequent, visit; do repeatedly; study, attend classes, take courses (e.g. *¿En qué escuela cursan?* At what school are you studying?); expedite (public admin.)

cursi /'kursi/ *a* *Inf.* vulgar, in bad taste; loud, crude

cursilería /kursile'ria/ *f*, *Inf.* vulgarity, bad taste

cursillo /kur'siʎo; kursiyo/ *m*, minicourse, short course; short series of lectures

cursiva /kur'siβa/ *f*, italics. **en c.**, in italics, italicized

cursivo /kur'siβo/ *a* cursive

curso /'kurso/ *m*, course, direction; duration, passage (time); progress; route; course of study; academic year; succession, series; *Com.* tender

curtido /kur'tiðo/ *m*, tanning; leather; tanned leather (gen. *pl*)

curtidor /kurti'ðor/ *m*, tanner

curtiduría /kurtiðu'ria/ *f*, tannery

curtimiento /kurti'miento/ *m*, tanning; effect of weather on the complexion; toughening-up; hardening

curtir /kur'tir/ *vt* to tan; *Fig.* bronze (complexions); make hardy, harden up; —*vr* be weatherbeaten; be hardy. *Inf.* **estar curtido en,** to be experienced in; be expert at

curul /ku'rul/ *a* **curule** *m*, seat (in parliament)

curva /'kurβa/ *f*, curve; bend. *Surv.* **c. de nivel,** contour line

curvatura, curvidad /kurβa'tura, kurβi'ðað/ *f*, curvature

curvilíneo /kurβi'lineo/ *a* curvilinear

curvo /'kurβo/ *a* curved; bent. *m*, curve

cúspide /'kuspiðe/ *f*, peak, summit; (*Geom. Archit.*) cusp

custodia /kus'toðia/ *f*, custody; guardianship, care; *Eccl.* monstrance; custodian, keeper; guardian; guard

custodiar /kusto'ðiar/ *vt* to watch, guard; look after, care for; *Naut.* convoy

custodio /kus'toðio/ *a* guardian; guarding; custodial. *m*, custodian; guard. **angel c.,** guardian angel

cutáneo /ku'taneo/ *a* cutaneous, skin

cúter /'kuter/ *m*, *Naut.* cutter

cutícula /ku'tikula/ *f*, cuticle

cutis /'kutis/ *m*, complexion; skin (sometimes *f*)

cuyo /'kuyo/ (**cuya, cuyos, cuyas**) *rel pron poss* whose, of which (e.g. *el viejo cuya barba era más blanca que la nieve,* the old man whose beard was whiter than snow) —*interr* **¿Cúyo?** Whose? (e.g. *¿Cúyos son estos lápices?* Whose pencils are these?) (gen. **de quién** or **de quiénes** is used rather than **cúyo**). *m*, beau, lover

D

dable /'daβle/ a practicable, possible

daca /'daka/ Give me!

dactilografía /daktilogra'fia/ f, typewriting

dactilógrafo /dakti'lografo/ **(-fa)** n typist

dactilología /daktilolo'hia/ f, dactylology

dádiva /'daðiβa/ f, gift, present

dadivosidad /daðiβosi'ðað/ f, generosity

dadivoso /daði'βoso/ a generous, liberal

dado /'daðo/ m, die; Archit. dado —conjunc **d. que,** given that, supposing that. **cargar los dados,** to load the dice

dador /da'ðor/ **(-ra)** n giver, donor. m, Com. bearer; Com. drawer (of a bill of exchange)

daga /'daga/ f, dagger

daguerrotipo /dagerro'tipo/ m, daguerreotype

daifa /'daifa/ f, concubine

¡dale! /'dale/ interj Stop! No more about...!

dalia /'dalia/ f, Bot. dahlia

dallar /da'ʎar; da'yar/ vt to scythe (grass)

dalle /'daʎe; 'daye/ m, scythe

dálmata /'dalmata/ a and mf Dalmatian

dalmática /dal'matika/ f, dalmatic, loose tunic or vestment

dalmático /dal'matiko/ **(-ca)** a and n Dalmatian

daltoniano /dalto'niano/ a color-blind

daltonismo /dalto'nismo/ m, color-blindness

dama /'dama/ f, lady; noblewoman; lady-in-waiting; lady-love; mistress, concubine; queen (chess); king (checkers); Theat. **d. primera,** leading lady

damajuana /dama'huana/ f, demijohn

damas /'damas/ f pl, checkers (game)

damasceno /damas'θeno; damas'seno/ **(-na)** a and n Damascene

Damasco /da'masko/ Damascus

damasco /da'masko/ m, damask

damasquino /damas'kino/ a damascened (swords, etc.)

damería /dame'ria/ f, prudery, affectation

damisela /dami'sela/ f, damsel; Inf. woman of the town

damnificar /damnifi'kar/ vt to injure

dandi /'dandi/ m, dandy

dandismo /dan'dismo/ m, dandyism

danés /da'nes/ **(-esa)** a Danish —n Dane. m, Danish (language)

danta /'danta/ f, Zool. tapir

dantesco /dan'tesko/ a Dantesque

danubiano /danu'βiano/ a Danubian

Danubio, el /da'nuβio, el/ the Danube

danza /'danθa; 'dansa/ f, dance; set (of dancers); Fig. Inf. dirty business. **d. de arcos,** dance of the arches. **d. de cintas,** maypole dance. **d. de monos,** amusing spectacle

danzador /danθa'ðor; dansa'ðor/ **(-ra)** n dancer; —a dancing

danzante /dan'θante; dan'sante/ **(-ta)** n dancer; Fig. Inf. live wire; Inf. busybody

danzar /dan'θar; dan'sar/ vt and vi to dance; —vi jump up and down, rattle; Inf. interfere, meddle

danzarín /danθa'rin; dansa'rin/ **(-ina)** n good dancer; Inf. meddler; Inf. playboy

danzón /dan'θon; dan'son/ m, Cuban dance

dañable /da'ɲaβle/ a harmful; worthy of condemnation

dañado /da'ɲaðo/ a evil, perverse; damned; spoiled, damaged

dañador /daɲa'ðor/ **(-ra)** a harmful —n injurer, offender

dañar /da'ɲar/ vt to hurt, harm; damage, spoil; —vr spoil, deteriorate

dañino /da'ɲino/ a destructive (often of animals); hurtful, harmful. **animales dañinos,** vermin, pests

daño /'daɲo/ m, hurt; damage; loss. Law. **daños y perjuicios,** damages. **hacerse d.,** to hurt oneself

dañoso /da'ɲoso/ a hurtful, harmful

dar /dar/ vt irr to give; wish, express

(congratulations, etc.); hand over; concede, grant; inspire; produce, yield; cause, create; sacrifice; propose, put forward; take (a walk); believe, consider; deliver (blows, etc.); administer (medicine); provide with; apply, coat with; occasion; perform (plays); propose (a toast); give forth, emit; set (norms), render (thanks, etc.); hold (banquets, etc.); proffer, hold out; —vi to strike (clocks); (with prep a) overlook, look on to (e.g. Su ventana da a la calle, His window looks on to the street); (with con) find, meet (things, persons); (with de) fall on, fall down (e.g. Dio de cabeza, He fell head first. Dio de espaldas, He fell on his back); (with en) fall into, incur; insist on or persist in (doing something); acquire the habit of (e.g. Dieron en no venir a vernos, They took to not coming to see us); solve, guess (riddles, etc.); strike, wound, hurt (e.g. La bala le dio en el brazo, The bullet struck him in the arm); (with por) decide on (e.g. Di por no hacerlo, I decided not to do it) —vr to yield, give in; (with prep a) engage in, devote oneself to; (with por) think or consider oneself (e.g. Me di por muerto, I gave myself up for dead). **d. alas a,** to propagate, spread (a belief). **darse a la vela,** to set sail. **darse la mano,** to shake hands. **darse por buenos,** to make up a quarrel, be friends. **darse prisa,** to hurry up, make haste. **darse uno a conocer,** to make oneself known. **darse uno por entendido,** to show that one understands; be grateful. **No se me da un bledo,** I don't care a straw. **d. abajo,** to fall down. **d. bien por mal,** to return good for evil. **d. a conocer,** to make known. **d. a entender,** to suggest, hint. **d. a luz,** to give birth; publish, issue. **d. cuenta de,** to give an account of. **d. de baja,** Mil. to muster out, discharge. **d. de comer,** to feed. **d. de sí,** to stretch, expand; produce, yield; give of itself (oneself, himself, themselves) (either in good or bad sense). **d. diente con diente,** to chatter (of teeth), shiver. **d. el pésame,** to tender condolences. **d. en cara,** Fig. Inf. to throw in one's face. **d. en el clavo,** Fig. to hit the mark. **d. en qué pensar,** to make suspicious, cause to think. **d. fe,** to certify, attest. **d. fiado,** to give on credit. **d. fianza,** to give security. **d. fin a,** to finish. **d. licencia,** to permit, allow. **d. los buenos días,** to wish good day or good morning. **d. mal,** to have bad luck at cards. **d. parte de,** to announce; issue a communiqué about (e.g. Dieron parte de la pérdida del buque, They announced the loss of the ship). **d. prestado,** to lend. **d. qué decir,** to cause a scandal. **d. qué hacer,** to cause trouble. **d. razón de,** to give an account of. **d. sobre uno,** to assault a person. **d. un abrazo,** to embrace. **d. voces,** to shriek; call out. Inf. **Donde las dan las toman,** It's only tit-for-tat. Inf. **No me da la real gana,** I darn well don't want to —Pres. Indic. **doy, das,** etc —Preterite **di, diste,** etc —Pres. Subjunc. **dé,** etc —Imperf. Subjunc. **diese,** etc.

Dardanelos, los /darða'nelos, los/ the Dardanelles

dardo /'darðo/ m, (Mil. Sports.) dart; Ichth. dace; lampoon

dares y tomares /dares i tomares/ m, pl give and take; Inf. back-chat. Generally used with andar, haber or tener

dársena /'darsena/ f, Naut. dock

darviniano /darβi'niano/ a Darwinian

darvinismo /darβi'nismo/ m, Darwinism

darvinista /darβi'nista/ a mf Darwinian

data /'data/ f, date (calendar); Com. credit

datar /'datar/ vt to date; —vi (with de) date from; —vr Com. credit

dátil /'datil/ m, Bot. date

datilado /datil'aðo/ a date-like or date-colored

datilera /datil'era/ f, Bot. date-palm

dativo /da'tiβo/ m, Gram. dative

dato /'dato/ m, datum; basis, fact

davídico /da'βiðiko/ a Davidic

de /de/ f, name of letter D —prep of (possessive) (e.g. Este cuadro es de Vd., This picture is yours); from (place and time) (e.g. Vengo de Madrid, I come from

Madrid. *de vez en cuando*, from time to time); with, of, from, as the result of (e.g. *Lloraban de miedo*, They were crying with fright. *Murió de un ataque del corazón*, He died from a heart attack); for, to (e.g. *Es hora de marchar*, It is time to leave); with (of characteristics) (e.g. *el señor de los lentes*, the gentleman with the eyeglasses. *el cuarto de la alfombra azul*, the room with the blue carpet); when, as (e.g. *De niños nos gustaban los juguetes*, When we were children we liked toys); by (e.g. *Es un ensayo del mismo autor*, It is an essay by the same author. *Fue amado de todos*, He was loved by all. *Es hidalgo de nacimiento*, He is a gentleman by birth). Indicates the material of which a thing is made (e.g. *La mesa es de mármol*, The table is marble). Indicates contents of a thing (e.g. *un vaso de leche*, a glass of milk). Shows manner in which an action is performed (e.g. *Lo hizo de prisa*, He did it hurriedly). Shows the use to which an article is put (e.g. *una mesa de escribir*, a writing-table. *una máquina de coser*, a sewing-machine. *un caballo de batalla*, a war-horse). Sometimes used for emphasis (e.g. *El tonto de tu secretario*, That fool of a secretary of yours). Used by Spanish married women before husband's family name (e.g. *Señora Martínez de Cabra*, Mrs. Cabra (née Martínez)). Used after many adverbs (generally of time or place) to form prepositional phrases (e.g. *detrás de*, behind. *enfrente de*, opposite to; in front of. *de acá para allá*, here and there. *de allí a poco*, shortly afterward. *de allí a pocos días*, a few days later. *de bamba*, by chance. *de cabo a rabo*, from cover to cover. *además de*, besides, etc.). Used at beginning of various adverbial phrases (e.g. *de noche*, at night. *de día*, by day. *de antemano*, previously, *la persona de mi derecha* the person at my right, etc.). Used partitively before nouns, pronouns, adjectives (e.g. *Estas historias tienen algo de verdad*, These stories have some truth in them. *¿Qué hay de nuevo?* What's the news?) Forms many compound words (e.g. *deponer*, *denegar*, etc.). With **"uno"** means "at" (e.g. *Lo cogió de un salto*, He caught it at one bound). **de a** is used before expressions of price, weight, etc. (e.g. *un libro de a cinco pesetas*, a five-peseta book)

dea /'dea/ *f*, *Poet.* goddess

deán /de'an/ *m*, dean

debajo /de'βaho/ *adv* underneath; below

debate /de'βate/ *m*, discussion, debate; dispute

debatible /deβa'tiβle/ *a* debatable

debatir /deβa'tir/ *vt* to discuss, debate, argue

debe /'deβe/ *m*, *Com.* debtor

debelación /deβela'θion; deβela'sion/ *f*, conquest

debelador /deβela'ðor/ **(-ra)** *a* conquering —*n* conqueror

debelar /deβe'lar/ *vt* to conquer, overthrow

deber /de'βer/ *vt* to owe (e.g. *Le debo mil pesetas*, I owe him one thousand pesetas). Used as auxiliary verb followed by infinitive, ought to, be obliged to (e.g. *Debía haberlo hecho*, I ought to have done it. *Deberá hacerlo*, He will have to do it); be destined to (e.g. *La princesa que más tarde debió ser reina*, The princess who later was destined to be queen); be essential, must (e.g. *La cuestión debe ser resuelta*, The question must be settled); (*with de* + *infin.*) be probable (indicates supposition) (e.g. *Debe de tener cincuenta años*, He is probably about fifty. *Debía de sufrir del corazón*, He probably suffered from heart trouble); (preceded by a negative *with de* + *infin.*) be impossible (e.g. *No debe de ser verdad*, It can't be true)

deber /de'βer/ *m*, duty, obligation; debt. **hacer su d.**, to do one's duty

debidamente /deβiða'mente/ *adv* justly, rightly; duly

debido /de'βiðo/ *a* correct, due. **d. a**, owing to, because of

débil /'deβil/ *a* weak; *Fig.* spineless; frail

debilidad /deβili'ðað/ *f*, weakness; feebleness

debilitación /deβilita'θion; deβilitasion/ *f*, debilitation

debilitante /deβili'tante/ *a* weakening

debilitar /deβili'tar/ *vt* to weaken; —*vr* become weak

débito /'deβito/ *m*, debit, debt; duty

debutar /deβu'tar/ *vi* to appear for the first time, make one's début

década /'dekaða/ *f*, decade

decadencia /deka'ðenθia; dekaðensia/ *f*, decadence, decline

decadente /deka'ðente/ *a* decadent, decaying

decaer /deka'er/ *vi irr* to fail (persons); decay, decline. See **caer**

decagramo /deka'gramo/ *m*, decagram

decaimiento /dekai'miento/ *m*, decadence; *Med.* prostration

decalaje /deka'lahe/ *m*, *Aer.* stagger

decalitro /deka'litro/ *m*, decaliter

decálogo /de'kalogo/ *m*, decalogue, the Ten Commandments

decámetro /de'kametro/ *m*, decameter

decampar /dekam'par/ *vi Mil.* to decamp

decanato /dekan'ato/ *m*, deanery; *Educ.* dean's rooms

decano /de'kano/ *m*, senior member; *Educ.* dean

decantación /dekanta'θion; dekantasion/ *f*, decantation

decantar /dekan'tar/ *vt* to decant (wines); praise

decapitación /dekapita'θion; dekapitasion/ *f*, decapitation

decapitar /dekapi'tar/ *vt* to decapitate, behead

decena /de'θena; de'sena/ *f*, ten; *Mus.* tenth

decenal /de'θenal; de'senal/ *a* decennial

decenario /deθe'nario; dese'nario/ *m*, decade

decencia /de'θenθia; de'sensia/ *f*, propriety, decency; decorum, modesty

decenio /de'θenio; de'senio/ *m*, decade

deceno /de'θeno; de'seno/ *a* tenth

decentar /deθen'tar; desen'tar/ *vt irr* to begin, cut (loaves, etc.); *Fig.* undermine (health, etc.); —*vr* suffer from bedsores. See **acertar**

decente /de'θente; de'sente/ *a* decent, honest; respectable; suitable; tidy

decepción /deθep'θion; desep'sion/ *f*, disillusionment, disappointment

dechado /de'tʃaðo/ *m*, model, ideal; *Sew.* sampler; exemplar, ideal

decible /de'θiβle; de'siβle/ *a* expressible

decidero /deθi'ðero; desi'ðero/ *a* that which can be safely said

decidido /deθi'ðiðo; desi'ðiðo/ *a* decided; resolute, determined

decidir /deθi'ðir; desi'ðir/ *vt* to resolve, decide; —*vr* make up one's mind

decidor /deθi'ðor; desi'ðor/ **(-ra)** *a* talkative, fluent, eloquent —*n* good talker

decigramo /deθi'gramo; desi'gramo/ *m*, decigram

décima /'deθima; 'desima/ *f*, tenth; tithe; ten-line stanza of eight-syllable verse

decimal /deθi'mal; desi'mal/ *a* decimal; pertaining to tithes. **sistema d.**, metric system

decímetro /de'θimetro; de'simetro/ *m*, decimeter

décimo /'deθimo; 'desimo/ *a* tenth. *m*, tenth part; tenth of a lottery ticket

decimoctavo /deθimok'taβo; desimok'taβo/ *a* eighteenth

decimocuarto /deθimo'kuarto; desimo'kuarto/ *a* fourteenth

decimonono /deθimo'nono; desimo'nono/ *a* nineteenth

decimoquinto /deθimo'kinto; desimo'kinto/ *a* fifteenth

decimoséptimo /deθimo'septimo; desimo'septimo/ *a* and *m*, seventeenth

decimosexto /deθimo'seksto; desimo'seksto/ *a* sixteenth

decimotercio /deθimoter'θio; desimoter'sio/ *a* thirteenth

decir /de'θir; de'sir/ *vt irr* to say; name; indicate; show; tell. **d. bien**, to go with, suit; speak the truth; be eloquent. **d. entre** (or **para**) **sí**, to say to oneself. *Inf.* **d. nones**, to refuse. **¡Diga!** Hello! (telephone). *Inf.* **el que dirán**, public opinion (what will people say!). **Es d.**, That is to say. **Se dice**, It is said, people say —*Pres. Ind.* **digo, dices**, etc —*Pres. Part.* **diciendo**. *Past Part.* **dicho**. *Fut.* **diré**, etc —*Condit.*

diría, etc —*Preterite* **dije**, etc —*Pres. Subjunc.* **diga**, etc —*Imperf. Subjunc.* **dijese**, etc.

decir /de'θir; de'sir/ *m*, saying, saw; maxim, witticism (often *pl.*)

decisión /deθi'sion; desi'sion/ *f*, decision, resolution; *Law.* judgment; firmness, strength (of character)

decisivo /deθi'siβo; desi'siβo/ *a* decisive

declamación /deklama'θion; deklama'sion/ *f*, declamation, oration; *Theat.* delivery; recitation

declamador /deklama'ðor/ **(-ra)** *a* declamatory —*n* reciter; orator

declamar /dekla'mar/ *vi* to make a speech, declaim; recite

declamatorio /deklama'torio/ *a* declamatory, rhetorical

declaración /deklara'θion; deklara'sion/ *f*, declaration; exposition, explanation; confession; statement; *Law.* deposition. **d. jurada**, affidavit, sworn statement

declaradamente /deklaraða'mente/ *adv* avowedly

declarante /dekla'rante/ *a* declaring. *mf Law.* deponent

declarar /dekla'rar/ *vt* to declare; make clear, explain; *Law.* find; —*vi Law.* give evidence; —*vr* avow, confess (one's sentiments, etc.); show, reveal itself

declarativo, **declaratorio** /deklara'tiβo, deklara'torio/ *a* explanatory, declarative.

declinación /deklina'θion; deklina'sion/ *f*, fall, descent; decadence, decay; *Astron.* declination; *Gram.* declension. *Inf.* **no saber las declinaciones**, not to know one's ABC, be very ignorant

declinante /dekli'nante/ *a* declining; sloping

declinar /dekli'nar/ *vi* to slope; diminish, fall; decline, deteriorate; *Fig.* near the end; —*vt Gram.* decline

declive, /de'kliβe,/ *m.* **declividad** *f*, slope, incline; gradient

decocción /dekok'θion; dekok'sion/ *f*, decoction

decoloración /dekolora'θion; dekolora'sion/ *f*, decoloration; decolorization

decomisar /dekomi'sar/ *vt* to confiscate, seize

decoración /dekora'θion; dekora'sion/ *f*, decoration; ornament, embellishment; *Theat.* scenery

decorado /deko'raðo/ *m*, *Theat.* scenery, décor

decorador /dekora'ðor/ *m*, decorator

decorar /deko'rar/ *vt* to adorn, ornament; *Poet.* decorate, honor

decorativo /dekora'tiβo/ *a* decorative

decoro /de'koro/ *m*, respect, reverence; prudence, circumspection; decorum, propriety; integrity, decency; *Archit.* decoration

decoroso /deko'roso/ *a* decorous, honorable, decent

decrecer /dekre'θer; dekre'ser/ *vi irr* to decrease, grow less. See **conocer**

decreciente /dekre'θiente; dekre'siente/ *a* decreasing

decrepitación /dekrepita'θion; dekrepita'sion/ *f*, *Chem.* decrepitation, crackling

decrepitar /dekrepi'tar/ *vi Chem.* to decrepitate, crackle

decrépito /de'krepito/ *a* decrepit

decrepitud /dekrepi'tuð/ *f*, decrepitude

decretar /dekre'tar/ *vt* to decree, decide; *Law.* give a judgment (in a suit)

decreto /de'kreto/ *m*, decree, order; judicial decree

decuplar, **decuplicar** /dekup'lar, dekupli'kar/ *vt* to multiply by ten

décuplo /'dekuplo/ *a* tenfold

decurso /de'kurso/ *m*, course, lapse (of time)

dedada /de'ðaða/ *f*, thimbleful, finger; pinch

dedal /de'ðal/ *m*, thimble; finger-stall

dédalo /'deðalo/ *m*, labyrinth

dedeo /de'ðeo/ *m*, *Mus.* touch

dedicación /deðika'θion; deðika'sion/ *f*, dedication (all meanings)

dedicar /deði'kar/ *vt* to dedicate; devote; consecrate; —*vr (with prep a)* dedicate oneself to, engage in

dedicatoria /deðika'toria/ *f*, dedication (of a book, etc.)

dedicatorio /deðika'torio/ *a* dedicatory

dedil /'deðil/ *m*, finger-stall

dedillo, saber al /de'ðiʎo, saβer al; de'ðiyo, saβer al/ *Fig.* to have at one's fingertips, know perfectly

dedo /'deðo/ *m*, finger; toe; finger's breadth. **d. anular**, third (ring) finger. **d. de en medio** *or* **del corazón**, middle finger. **d. índice**, forefinger. **d. meñique**, little finger. **d. pulgar**, thumb or big toe. *Fig. Inf.* **a dos dedos de**, within an inch of. *Fig. Inf.* **chuparse los dedos**, to smack one's lips over. *Inf.* **estar unidos como los dedos de la mano**, to be as thick as thieves

deducción /deðuk'θion; deðuk'sion/ *f*, inference, deduction; derivation; (*Mus. Math.*) progression

deduciente /deðu'θiente; deðu'siente/ *a* deductive

deducir /deðu'θir; deðu'sir/ *vt irr* to deduce, infer; deduct, subtract; *Law.* plead, allege in pleading. See **conducir**

deductivo /deðuk'tiβo/ *a* deductive

defecación /defeka'θion; defeka'sion/ *f*, purification; defecation

defecar /defe'kar/ *vt* to clarify, purify; defecate

defección /defek'θion; defek'sion/ *f*, defection

defectible /defek'tiβle/ *a* deficient; imperfect

defecto /de'fekto/ *m*, defect, fault; imperfection

defectuoso /defek'tuoso/ *a* imperfect, defective

defender /defen'der/ *vt irr* to defend, protect; maintain, uphold; forbid; hinder; —*vr* defend oneself. See **entender**

defendible /defen'diβle/ *a* defensible

defensa /de'fensa/ *f*, defence; protection; (hockey) pad; *Law.* defense; *Sports.* back; *pl Mil.* defenses; *Naut.* fenders. **d. química**, chemical warfare. *Mil.* **defensas costeras**, coastal defenses

defensiva /defen'siβa/ *f*, defensive

defensivo /defen'siβo/ *a* defensive. *m*, safeguard

defensor /defen'sor/ **(-ra)** *n* defender. *m*, *Law.* counsel for the defense

deferencia /defe'renθia; deferensia/ *f*, deference

deferente /defe'rente/ *a* deferential

deferir /defe'rir/ *vi irr* to defer, yield; —*vt* delegate —*Pres. Indic.* **defiero, defieres, defiere, defieren.** *Pres. Part.* **defiriendo**. *Preterite* **defirió, defirieron**. *Pres. Subjunc.* **defiera**, etc —*Imperf. Subjunc.* **defiriese**, etc.

deficiencia /defi'θienθia; defi'siensia/ *f*, defect, deficiency

deficiente /defi'θiente; defi'siente/ *a* faulty, deficient

déficit /'defiθit; 'defisit/ *m*, deficit

definible /defi'niβle/ *a* definable

definición /defini'θion; defini'sion/ *f*, definition; decision

definido /defi'niðo/ *a* definite

definir /defi'nir/ *vt* to define; decide

definitivo /defini'tiβo/ *a* definitive. **en definitiva**, definitely; in short

deflagración /deflagra'θion; deflagra'sion/ *f*, sudden blaze, deflagration

deflagrador /deflagra'ðor/ *m*, *Elec.* deflagrator

deflagrar /defla'grar/ *vi* to go up in flames

deformación /deforma'θion; deforma'sion/ *f*, deformation; *Radio.* distortion

deformado /defor'maðo/ *a* deformed; misshapen

deformador /deforma'ðor/ **(-ra)** *a* disfiguring, deforming —*n* disfigurer

deformar /defor'mar/ *vt* to deform; —*vr* become deformed or misshapen

deformidad /deformi'ðað/ *f*, deformity; gross error; vice, lapse

defraudación /defrauða'θion; defrauða'sion/ *f*, defrauding; deceit

defraudador /defrauða'ðor/ **(-ra)** *n* defrauder

defraudar /defrau'ðar/ *vt* to defraud; usurp; frustrate, disappoint; impede

defuera /de'fuera/ *adv* outwardly, externally

defunción /defun'θion; defun'sion/ *f*, decease, death

degeneración /dehenera'θion; dehenera'sion/ *f*, degeneration. **d. grasienta**, fatty degeneration

degenerado /dehene'raðo/ **(-da)** *a* and *n* degenerate

degenerar /dehene'rar/ *vi* to degenerate

deglución /deglu'θion; deglu'sion/ *f*, swallowing, deglutition

deglutir /deglu'tir/ *vi* and *vt* to swallow

degollación /degoʎa'θion; degoya'sion/ *f*, decollation, throat slitting

degolladero /deɣoʎa'ðero; degoya'ðero/ *m,* slaughterhouse; execution block

degollador /deɣoʎ'aðor; degoya'ðor/ *m,* executioner

degolladura /deɣoʎa'ðura; degoya'ðura/ *f,* slitting of the throat

degollar /deɣo'ʎar; dego'yar/ *vt irr* to behead; slit the throat; *Fig.* destroy; (*Fig. Theat.*) murder; *Inf.* annoy, bore —*Pres. Indic.* **degüello, degüellas, degüella, degüellan.** *Pres. Subjunc.* **degüelle, degüelles, degüelle, degüellen**

degollina /deɣo'ʎina; dego'yina/ *f, Inf.* massacre

degradación /deɣraða'θion; degraða'sion/ *f,* degradation; humiliation, debasement; *Art.* gradation, shading (colors, light)

degradante /deɣra'ðante/ *a* degrading, humiliating

degradar /deɣra'ðar/ *vt* to degrade; humiliate; *Art.* grade, blend; —*vr* degrade oneself

degüello /de'ɣueʎo; de'gueyo/ *m,* decollation; havoc, destruction; haft (of swords, etc.)

degustación /deɣusta'θion; degusta'sion/ *f,* act of tasting or sampling

dehesa /de'esa/ *f,* pasture, meadow

deicida /dei'θiða; dei'siða/ *mf* deicide (person)

deicidio /dei'θiðio; dei'siðio/ *m,* deicide (act)

deidad /dei'ðað/ *f,* divinity; deity, idol

deificación /deifika'θion; deifika'sion/ *f,* deification

deificar /deifi'kar/ *vt* to deify; overpraise

deífico /de'ifiko/ *a* deific, divine

deísmo /de'ismo/ *m,* Deism

deísta /de'ista/ *mf* deist —*a* deistic

dejación /deha'θion; deha'sion/ *f,* relinquishment, abandonment

dejadez /deha'ðeθ; deha'ðes/ *f,* slovenliness; neglect; laziness; carelessness

dejado /de'haðo/ *a* lazy; neglectful; slovenly; discouraged, depressed

dejamiento /deha'miento/ *m,* relinquishment; negligence; lowness of spirits; indifference

dejar /de'har/ *vt* to leave; omit, forget, allow, permit (e.g. *Déjame salir,* Let me go out); yield, produce, entrust, leave in charge; believe, consider; intend, appoint; cease, stop; forsake, desert; renounce, relinquish; bequeath; give away; —*vr* neglect oneself; engage (in); lay oneself open to, allow oneself; abandon oneself (to), fling oneself (into); *Fig.* be depressed or languid; (*with de* + *infin.*) cease to (e.g. *Se dejó de hacerlo,* He stopped doing it); —*vi* (*with de* + *adjective*) be none the less, be rather (e.g. *No deja de ser sorprendente,* It isn't any the less surprising). **d. aparte,** to omit, leave out. **d. atrás,** to overtake; *Fig.* leave behind, beat. **d. caer,** to let fall. **dejarse caer,** to let oneself fall; *Fig. Inf.* to let fall, utter; appear suddenly. **dejarse vencer,** to give way, allow oneself to be persuaded

dejo /'deho/ *m,* relinquishment; end; accent (of persons); savor, after-taste; negligence; *Fig.* touch, flavor

del /del/ contraction of **de + el,** (*def. art. m.*) of the (e.g. *del perro,* of the dog)

delación /dela'θion; dela'sion/ *f,* accusation, denunciation

delantal /delan'tal/ *m,* apron

delante /de'lante/ *adv* before, in front, in the presence (of)

delantera /delan'tera/ *f,* front, front portion; *Theat.* orchestra stall, front seat; front (of garment). **tomar la d.,** to take the lead; *Inf.* steal a march on

delantero /delan'tero/ *a* fore, front. *m,* postilion; *Sports.* forward. **d. centro,** *Sports.* centerforward

delatable /dela'taβle/ *a* impeachable; blameworthy

delatar /dela'tar/ *vt* to inform against, accuse; impeach

delator /dela'tor/ **(-ra)** *a* denunciatory, accusing —*n* denouncer, informer

delectación /delekta'θion; delekta'sion/ *f,* delectation, pleasure

delegación /deleɣa'θion; deleɣa'sion/ *f,* delegation; proxy

delegado /dele'ɣaðo/ **(-da)** *n* delegate; proxy

delegar /dele'ɣar/ *vt* to delegate

deleitable /delei'taβle/ *a* delightful

deleitar /delei'tar/ *vt* to delight, charm, please; —*vr* delight (in)

deleite /de'leite/ *m,* delight; pleasure

deleitoso /delei'toso/ *a* delightful, pleasant'

deletéreo /dele'tereo/ *a* deleterious; poisonous

deletrear /deletre'ar/ *vi* to spell; *Fig.* decipher

deletreo /dele'treo/ *m,* spelling; *Fig.* decipherment

deleznable /deleθ'naβle; deles'naβle/ *a* fragile, brittle; slippery; brief, fugitive, transitory

délfico /'delfiko/ *a* Delphic

delfín /del'fin/ *m,* (*Ichth. Astron.*) dolphin; dauphin

delfina /del'fina/ *f,* dauphiness

Delfos /'delfos/ Delphi

delgadez /delɣa'ðeθ; delɣa'ðes/ *f,* thinness; slenderness, leanness

delgado /del'ɣaðo/ *a* slim; thin; scanty; poor (of land); sharp, perspicacious

delgaducho /delɣa'ðutʃo/ *a* slenderish, somewhat thin

deliberación /deliβera'θion; deliβera'sion/ *f,* deliberation; consideration; discussion

deliberadamente /deliβeraða'mente/ *adv* deliberately

deliberante /deliβe'rante/ *a* deliberative, considering

deliberar /deliβe'rar/ *vi* to deliberate, consider; —*vt* decide after reflection; discuss

delicadez /delika'ðeθ; delika'ðes/ *f,* weakness; delicacy; hypersensitiveness; amiability

delicadeza /delika'ðeθa; delika'ðesa/ *f,* delicacy; fastidiousness; refinement, subtlety; sensitiveness; consideration, tact; scrupulosity

delicado /deli'kaðo/ *a* courteous; tactful; fastidious; weak, delicate; fragile, perishable; delicious, tasty; exquisite; difficult, embarrassing; refined, discriminating, sensitive; scrupulous; subtle; hypersensitive, suspicious. **d. de salud,** in poor health

delicia /deli'θia; deli'sia/ *f,* pleasure, delight; sensual pleasure

delicioso /deli'θioso; deli'sioso/ *a* delightful, agreeable, pleasant

delimitar /delimi'tar/ *vt* to delimit

delincuencia /delin'kuenθia; delin'kuensia/ *f,* delinquency

delincuente /delin'kuente/ *a* and *mf* delinquent

delineación /delinea'θion; delinea'sion/ *f,* delineation; diagram, design, plan

delineador /delinea'ðor/ **(-ra),** *n* **delineante** *m,* draftsman, designer

delineamiento /delinea'miento/ *m,* delineation

delinear /deline'ar/ *vt* to delineate; sketch; describe

delinquimiento /delinki'miento/ *m,* delinquency; crime

delinquir /delin'kir/ *vi irr* to commit a crime —*Pres. Indic.* **delinco.** *Pres. Subjunc.* **delinca**

deliquio /deli'kio/ *m,* faint, swoon

delirante /deli'rante/ *a* delirious

delirar /deli'rar/ *vi* to be delirious; act or speak foolishly

delirio /de'lirio/ *m,* delirium; frenzy; foolishness, nonsense. **d. de grandezas,** illusions of grandeur

delito /de'lito/ *m,* delict, offense against the law, crime

delta /'delta/ *f,* fourth letter of Greek alphabet. *m,* delta (of a river)

delusorio /delu'sorio/ *a* deceptive

demacración /demakra'θion; demakrasion/ *f,* emaciation

demacrado /dema'kraðo/ *a* emaciated

demacrarse /dema'krarse/ *vr* to become emaciated

demagogia /dema'gohia/ *f,* demagogy

demagógico /dema'gohiko/ *a* demagogic

demagogo /dema'gogo/ **(-ga)** *n* demagogue

demanda /de'manda/ *f,* petition, request; collecting (for charity); collecting box; want ad; question; search; undertaking; *Com.* order or demand; *Law.* claim

demandadero /demanda'ðero/ **(-ra)** *n* convent or prison messenger; errandboy

demandado /deman'daðo/ **(-da)** *n Law.* defendant; *Law.* respondent

demandante /deman'dante/ *mf Law.* plaintiff

demandar /deman'dar/ *vt* to ask, request; desire, yearn for; question; *Law.* claim

demarcación /demarka'θion; demarka'sion/ *f*, demarcation, limit

demarcar /demar'kar/ *vt* to fix boundaries, demarcate

demás /de'mas/ *a* other —*adv* besides. **lo d.**, the rest. **los (las) d.**, the others. **por d.**, useless; superfluous. **por lo d.**, otherwise; for the rest

demasía /dema'sia/ *f*, excess; daring; insolence; guilt, crime. **en d.**, excessively

demasiado /dema'siaðo/ *a* too; too many; too much —*adv* excessively

demencia /de'menθia; de'mensia/ *f*, madness, insanity

demencial /demen'θial; demen'sial/ *a* insane

dementar /demen'tar/ *vt* to render insane; —*vr* become insane

demente /de'mente/ *a* insane, mad. *mf* lunatic

demérito /de'merito/ *m*, demerit, fault

demeritorio /demeri'torio/ *a* undeserving, without merit

demisión /demi'sion/ *f*, submission, acquiescence

democracia /demo'kraθia; demo'krasia/ *f*, democracy

demócrata /de'mokrata/ *mf* democrat

democrático /demo'kratiko/ *a* democratic

democratizar /demokrati'θar; demokrati'sar/ *vt* to make democratic

demoledor /demole'ðor/ **(-ra)** *a* demolition —*n* demolisher

demoler /demo'ler/ *vt irr* to demolish, destroy, dismantle. See **moler**

demolición /demoli'θion; demoli'sion/ *f*, demolition, destruction, dismantling

demoníaco /demo'niako/ *a* devilish; possessed by a demon

demonio /de'monio/ *m*, devil; evil spirit —*interj* **¡Demonios!** Deuce take it! *Inf.* **tener el d. en el cuerpo**, to be always on the move, be very energetic

demontre /de'montre/ *m*, *Inf.* devil

demora /de'mora/ *f*, delay; *Naut.* bearing; *Com.* demurrage

demorar /demo'rar/ *vt* to delay; —*vi* stay, remain, tarry; *Naut.* bear

demostrable /demos'traβle/ *a* demonstrable

demostración /demostra'θion; demostra'sion/ *f*, demonstration; proof

demostrador /demostra'ðor/ **(-ra)** *a* demonstrating —*n* demonstrator

demostrar /demos'trar/ *vt irr* to demonstrate, explain; prove; teach. See **mostrar**

demostrativo /demostra'tiβo/ *a* demonstrative. *Gram.* **pronombre d.**, demonstrative pronoun

demudación /demuða'θion; demuða'sion/ *f*, change; alteration

demudar /demu'ðar/ *vt* to change, vary; alter, transform; —*vr* change suddenly (color, facial expression, etc.); grow angry

denario /de'nario/ *a* denary. *m*, denarius

denegación /denega'θion; denega'sion/ *f*, denial; refusal

denegar /dene'gar/ *vt irr* to deny, refuse. See **acertar**

dengoso /deŋ'goso/ *a* fastidious, finicky

dengue /'deŋgue/ *m*, affectation, faddiness, fastidiousness

denigrable /deni'graβle/ *a* odious

denigración /denigra'θion; denigra'sion/ *f*, slander, defamation (of character)

denigrante /deni'grante/ *a* slanderous

denigrar /deni'grar/ *vt* to slander; insult

denodado /deno'ðaðo/ *a* valiant, daring

denominación /denomina'θion; denomina'sion/ *f*, denomination

denominador /denomina'ðor/ *a* denominating *m*, *Math.* denominator

denominar /denomi'nar/ *vt* to name, designate

denostada /denos'taða/ *f*, insult

denostar /denos'tar/ *vt irr* to revile, insult. See **acordar**

denotar /deno'tar/ *vt* to denote, indicate

densidad /densi'ðað/ *f*, density; closeness, denseness; *Phys.* specific gravity; obscurity

denso /'denso/ *a* compact, close; thick, dense; crowded; dark, confused

dentado /den'taðo/ *a* toothed; pronged; dentate

dentadura /denta'ðura/ *f*, set of teeth (real or false). **d. de rumiante**, teeth like an ox. **d. postiza**, false teeth

dental /den'tal/ *a* dental

dentar /den'tar/ *vt irr* to provide with teeth, prongs, etc.; —*vi* cut teeth. See **sentar**

dentellada /dente'ʎaða; dente'yaða/ *f*, gnashing or chattering of teeth; bite; toothmark

dentellar /dente'ʎar; dente'yar/ *vt* to chatter, grind, gnash (teeth)

dentellear /denteʎe'ar; denteye'ar/ *vt* to bite, sink the teeth into

dentera /den'tera/ *f*, (**dar**) to set one's teeth on edge; *Fig. Inf.* make one's mouth water

dentición /denti'θion; denti'sion/ *f*, teething, dentition

dentífrico /den'tifriko/ *m*, toothpaste

dentista /den'tista/ *mf* dentist

dentro /'dentro/ *adv* within, inside. **d. de poco,** soon, shortly. **por d.**, from the inside; on the inside

dentudo /den'tuðo/ *a* having large teeth

denudación /denuða'θion; denuða'sion/ *f*, denudation; *Geol.* erosion

denudar /denu'ðar/ *vt* to denude

denuedo /de'nueðo/ *m*, courage, daring

denuesto /de'nuesto/ *m*, insult

denuncia /de'nunθia; de'nunsia/ *f*, denunciation, accusation

denunciante /denun'θiante; denun'siante/ *a* accusing. *mf Law.* denouncer

denunciar /denun'θiar; denun'siar/ *vt* to give notice, inform; herald, presage; declare, proclaim; denounce; *Law.* accuse

denunciatorio /denunθia'torio; denunsia'torio/ *a* denunciatory

deparar /depa'rar/ *vt* to furnish, offer, present

departamental /departamen'tal/ *a* departmental

departamento /departa'mento/ *m*, department; compartment (railway); branch, section. **d. de lactantes,** nursery (in a hospital)

departir /depar'tir/ *vi* to converse

depauperación /depaupera'θion; depaupera'sion/ *f*, impoverishment; *Med.* emaciation

depauperar /depaupe'rar/ *vt* to impoverish; —*vr Med.* grow weak, become emaciated

dependencia /depen'denθia; depen'densia/ *f*, dependence; subordination; dependency; *Com.* branch; firm, agency; business affair; kinship or affinity; *pl Archit.* offices; *Com.* staff; accessories

depender /depen'der/ *vi* (*with de*) to be subordinate to; depend on; be dependent on, need

dependiente /depen'diente/ **(-ta)** *a* and *n* dependent, subordinate. *m*, employee; shop assistant

depilación /depila'θion; depila'sion/ *f*, depilation

depilar /depi'lar/ *vt* to depilate

depilatorio /depila'torio/ *m*, depilatory

deplorar /deplo'rar/ *vt* to deplore, lament

deponente /depo'nente/ *a* deposing; affirming. *mf* deponent. *Gram.* **verbo d.**, deponent verb

deponer /depo'ner/ *vt irr* to lay aside; depose, oust; affirm, testify; remove, take from its place; *Law.* depose. See **poner**

deportación /deporta'θion; deporta'sion/ *f*, deportation

deportar /depor'tar/ *vt* to exile; deport

deporte /de'porte/ *m*, sport; *pl* games. **d. de vela,** sailing; boating

deportismo /depor'tismo/ *m*, sport

deportista /depor'tista/ *a* sporting. *mf* sportsman (sportswoman)

deportivo /depor'tiβo/ *a* sporting

deposición /deposi'θion; deposi'sion/ *f*, affirmation, statement; *Law.* deposition; degradation, removal (from office, etc.)

depositador /deposita'ðor/ **(-ra)** *a* depositing —*n* depositor

depositar /deposi'tar/ *vt* to deposit; place in safety; entrust; lay aside, put away; —*vr Chem.* settle

depositaría /deposita'ria/ f, depository; trusteeship; accounts office

depositario /deposi'tario/ **(-ia)** a pertaining to a depository —n depositary, trustee

depósito /de'posito/ m, deposit; depository; Com. depot, warehouse; Chem. deposit, sediment; tank, reservoir; Mil. depot. **d. de bencína, d. de gasolina,** gas tank; service station. **d. de municiones,** munitions dump. Com. **en d.,** in bond. **Queda hecho el d. que marca la ley,** Copyright reserved

depravación /depraβa'θion; depraβa'sion/ f, depravity

depravar /depra'βar/ vt to deprave, corrupt; —vr become depraved

deprecación /depreka'θion; depreka'sion/ f, supplication, petition; deprecation

deprecar /depre'kar/ vt to supplicate, petition; deprecate

depreciación /depreθia'θion; depresia'sion/ f, depreciation, fall in value

depreciar /depre'θiar; depre'siar/ vt to depreciate, reduce the value (of)

depredación /depreða'θion; depreða'sion/ f, depredation, robbery

depredar /depre'ðar/ vt to pillage

depresión /depre'sion/ f, depression. **d. nerviosa,** nervous breakdown

depresivo /depre'siβo/ a depressive; humiliating

deprimir /depri'mir/ vt to depress, compress, press down; depreciate, belittle; —vr be compressed

depuración /depura'θion; depura'sion/ f, cleansing, purification; Polit. purge

depurar /depu'rar/ vt to cleanse, purify; Polit. purge

derecha /de'retʃa/ f, right hand; Polit. (gen. pl) Right. Mil. **¡D.!** Right Turn! **a la d.,** on the right

derechamente /deretʃa'mente/ adv straight, directly; prudently, justly; openly, frankly

derechera /dere'tʃera/ f, direct road

derechista /dere'tʃista/ mf Polit. rightist

derecho /de'retʃo/ a straight; upright; right (not left); just, reasonable; Sports. forehand —adv straightaway. m, right; law; just claim; privilege; justice, reason; exemption; right side (cloth, etc.); pl dues, taxes; fees. **d. a la vía,** right of way. **d. de apelación,** right to appeal. **d. de visita,** (international law) right of search. **derechos de aduana,** customhouse duties. **derechos de entrada,** import duties. **según d.,** according to law. **usar de su d.,** to exercise one's right

derechura /dere'tʃura/ f, directness, straightness; uprightness

deriva /de'riβa/ f, (Naut. Aer.) drift, leeway

derivación /deriβa'θion; deriβa'sion/ f, origin, derivation; inference, consequence; Gram. derivation

derivar /deri'βar/ vi to originate; Naut. drift; —vt conduct, lead; Gram. derive; Elec. tap

derivativo /deriβa'tiβo/ a derivative

dermatitis /derma'titis/ f, dermatitis

dermatología /dermatolo'hia/ f, dermatology

dermatólogo /derma'tologo/ m, dermatologist

derogación /deroga'θion; deroga'sion/ f, repeal, annulment; deterioration

derogar /dero'gar/ vt to annul, repeal; destroy, suppress

derogatorio /deroga'torio/ a Law. repealing

derrama /de'rrama/ f, apportionment of tax

derramado /derra'maðo/ a extravagant, wasteful

derramamiento /derrama'miento/ m, pouring out; spilling; scattering

derramar /derra'mar/ vt to pour out; spill; scatter; apportion (taxes); publish abroad, spread; —vr be scattered; overflow

derrame /de'rrame/ m, spilling; leakage; overflow; scattering; slope

derredor /derre'ðor/ m, circumference. **al (or en) d.,** round about

derrelicto /derre'likto/ a, abandoned; derelict. m, Naut. derelict

derrengado /derreŋ'gaðo/ a crooked; crippled

derretimiento /derreti'miento/ m, melting; thaw; liquefaction; Inf. burning passion

derretir /derre'tir/ vt irr to melt, liquefy; waste, dissi-

pate; —vr be very much in love; Inf. be susceptible (to love); Inf. long, be impatient. See **pedir**

derribar /derri'βar/ vt to demolish; knock down; fell; throw down; Aer. shoot down; throw (in wrestling); Fig. overthrow; demolish, explode (a myth); control (emotions); —vr fall down; prostrate oneself; throw oneself down. **d. el chapeo,** humorous to doff one's hat

derribo /de'rriβo/ m, demolition; debris, rubble; throw (in wrestling)

derrocadero /derroka'ðero/ m, rocky precipice

derrocar /derro'kar/ vt to throw down from a rock; demolish (buildings); overthrow, oust

derrochador /derrotʃa'ðor/ **(-ra)** a wasteful, extravagant —n spendthrift

derrochar /derro'tʃar/ vt to waste, squander

derroche /de'rrotʃe/ m, squandering

derrota /de'rrota/ f, road; route, path; Naut. course; Mil. defeat

derrotar /derro'tar/ vt to squander; destroy, harm; Mil. defeat; —vr Naut. drift, lose course

derrotero /derro'tero/ m, Naut. course; Naut. ship's itinerary; number of sea charts; means to an end, course of action

derrotismo /derro'tismo/ m, defeatism

derrotista /derro'tista/ mf defeatist

derruir /de'rruir/ vt irr to demolish (a building). See **huir**

derrumbadero /derrumba'ðero/ m, precipice; risk, danger

derrumbamiento /derrumba'miento/ m, landslide; collapse, downfall

derrumbar /derrum'bar/ vt to precipitate; —vr throw oneself down, collapse, tumble down (buildings, etc.)

derrumbe /de'rrumbe/ m, collapse; subsidence

derviche /der'βitʃe/ m, dervish

desabarrancar /desaβarran'kar/ vt to pull out of a ditch or rut; extricate (from a difficulty)

desabillé /desaβi'ʎe; desaβi'ye/ m, deshabille

desabor /desa'βor/ m, insipidity

desabotonar /desaβoto'nar/ vt to unbutton; —vi open (flowers)

desabrido /desa'βriðo/ a insipid, poor-tasting; inclement (weather); disagreeable; unsociable; homely, plain (woman)

desabrigar /desaβri'gar/ vt to uncover; leave without shelter

desabrigo /desa'βrigo/ m, want of clothing or shelter; poverty, destitution

desabrimiento /desaβri'miento/ m, insipidity; harshness, disagreeableness; melancholy, depression

desabrir /desa'βrir/ vt to give a bad taste (to food); annoy, trouble

desabrochar /desaβro'tʃar/ vt to unbutton, untie; open; —vr Inf. confide, open up

desacatar /desaka'tar/ vt to behave disrespectfully (towards); lack reverence

desacato /desa'kato/ m, irreverence; disrespect

desacertado /desaθer'taðo; desaser'taðo/ a wrong, erroneous; imprudent

desacertar /desaθer'tar; desaser'tar/ vi irr to be wrong; act imprudently. See **acertar**

desacierto /desa'θierto; desa'sierto/ m, mistake, miscalculation; blunder

desacomodado /desakomo'ðaðo/ a lacking means of subsistence; poor; unemployed (servants); troublesome

desacomodar /desakomo'ðar/ vt to incommode, make uncomfortable, inconvenience; dismiss, discharge

desaconsejado /desakonse'haðo/ a ill-advised

desaconsejar /desakonse'har/ vt to advise against, dissuade

desacoplar /desakop'lar/ vt to disconnect

desacordar /desakor'ðar/ vt irr Mus. to put out of tune; —vr (with de) forget. See **acordar**

desacorde /desa'korðe/ a discordant, inharmonious; Mus. out of tune

desacostumbrado /desakostum'braðo/ a unaccustomed; unusual

desacostumbrar /desakostum'brar/ *vt* to break of a habit

desacotar /desako'tar/ *vt* to remove (fences); refuse, deny; —*vi* withdraw (from agreement, etc.)

desacreditar /desakreði'tar/ *vt* to discredit

desacuerdo /desa'kuerðo/ *m,* disagreement, discord; mistake; forgetfulness; swoon, loss of consciousness

desadeudar /desaðeu'ðar/ *vt* to free from debt

desadornar /desaðor'nar/ *vt* to denude of ornaments

desadorno /desa'ðorno/ *m,* lack of ornaments; bareness

desafecto /desa'fekto/ *a* disaffected; hostile. *m,* disaffection

desaferrar /desafe'rrar/ *vt irr* to untie, unfasten; *Fig.* wean from; *Naut.* weigh anchor. See **acertar**

desafiador /desafia'ðor/ **(-ra)** *a* challenging —*n* challenger. *m,* duelist

desafiar /desa'fiar/ *vt* to challenge; compete with; oppose

desafinar /desafi'nar/ *vi Mus.* to go out of tune; *Fig. Inf.* speak out of turn

desafío /desa'fio/ *m,* challenge; competition; duel

desaforado /desafo'raðo/ *a* lawless; outrageous; enormous

desaforar /desafo'rar/ *vt* to infringe (laws, etc.); —*vr* be disorderly

desaforrar /desafo'rrar/ *vt* to remove the lining of or from

desafortunado /desafortu'naðo/ *a* unfortunate

desafuero /desa'fuero/ *m,* act of injustice; outrage, excess

desagarrar /desaga'rrar/ *vt Inf.* to release, loosen; unhook

desagraciado /desagra'θiaðo; desagra'siaðo/ *a* ugly, unsightly

desagraciar /desagra'θiar; desagra'siar/ *vt* to disfigure, make ugly

desagradable /desagra'ðaβle/ *a* disagreeable; unpleasant

desagradar /desagra'ðar/ *vi* to be disagreeable, displease (e.g. *Me desagrada su voz,* I find his voice unpleasant)

desagradecer /desagraðe'θer; desagraðe'ser/ *vt irr* to be ungrateful (for). See **conocer**

desagradecido /desagraðe'θiðo; desagraðe'siðo/ *a* ungrateful

desagradecimiento /desagraðeθi'miento; desagraðe-simiento/ *m,* ingratitude

desagrado /desa'graðo/ *m,* displeasure, dislike, dissatisfaction

desagraviar /desagra'βiar/ *vt* to make amends, apologize; indemnify

desagravio /desa'graβio/ *m,* satisfaction, reparation; compensation

desagregar /desagre'gar/ **(se)** *vt* and *vr* to separate

desaguadero /desagua'ðero/ *m,* drain, waste pipe

desaguar /desa'guar/ *vt* to drain off; dissipate; —*vi* flow (into sea, etc.)

desagüe /de'sague/ *m,* drainage; outlet, drain; catchment

desaguisado /desagi'saðo/ *a* outrageous, lawless. *m,* offense, insult

desahogado /desao'gaðo/ *a* brazen, insolent; clear, unencumbered; in comfortable circumstances

desahogar /desao'gar/ *vt* to ease, relieve; —*vr* unburden oneself; recover (from illness, heat, etc.); get out of debt; speak one's mind

desahogo /desa'ogo/ *m,* relief, alleviation; ease; comfort, convenience; freedom, frankness; unburdening (of one's mind). *Inf.* **vivir con d.,** to be comfortably off

desahuciar /desau'θiar; desau'siar/ *vt* to banish all hope; give up, despair of the life of; put out (tenants). When the third syllable of this verb is stressed, it is spelled with **ú**: *Pres. Indic.* **desahúcio, desahúcias, desahúcia, desahúcian.** *Pres. Subj.* **desahúcie, desahúcies, desahúcie, desahúcien.** *Imperf.* **desahúcia, desahúcie, desahúcien**

desahúcio /desa'uθio; desa'usio/ *m,* ejection, dispossession (of tenants)

desahumar /desau'mar/ *vt* to clear of smoke

desairado /desai'raðo/ *a* unattractive, graceless, ugly; unsuccessful, crestfallen; slighted

desairar /desai'rar/ *vt* to disdain, slight, disregard; underrate (things)

desaire /des'aire/ *m,* gracelessness, ugliness; insult, slight

desalabanza /desala'βanθa; desala'βansa/ *f,* disparagement; criticism

desalabar /desala'βar/ *vt* to censure, disparage

desalación /desala'θion; desala'sion/ *f,* desalinization

desalado /desa'laðo/ *a* anxious, precipitate, hasty

desalar /desa'lar/ *vt* to remove the salt from; take off wings; —*vr* walk or run at great speed; long for, yearn

desalentar /desalen'tar/ *vt irr* to make breathing difficult (work, fatigue); discourage; —*vr* be depressed or sad. See **sentar**

desaliento /desa'liento/ *m,* depression, discouragement, dismay

desalinear /desaline'ar/ *vt* to throw out of the straight

desaliñado /desali'ɲaðo/ *a* slovenly; slipshod

desaliñar /desali'ɲar/ *vt* to disarrange, make untidy, crumple

desaliño /desa'liɲo/ *m,* untidiness, slovenliness; negligence, carelessness

desalmado /desal'maðo/ *a* soulless, conscienceless; cruel

desalmamiento /desalma'miento/ *m,* inhumanity, consciencelessness; cruelty

desalmidonar /desalmiðo'nar/ *vt* to remove starch from

desalojamiento /desaloha'miento/ *m,* dislodgement, ejection

desalojar /desalo'har/ *vt* to dislodge, remove, eject; —*vi* move out, remove

desalquilado /desalki'laðo/ *a* untenanted, vacant

desalquilar /desalki'lar/ *vt* to leave, or cause to leave, rented premises

desalterar /desalte'rar/ *vt* to soothe, calm

desamar /desa'mar/ *vt* to cease to love; hate

desamarrar /desama'rrar/ *vt* to untie; separate; *Naut.* unmoor

desamor /desa'mor/ *m,* indifference; lack of sentiment or affection; hatred

desamotinarse /desamoti'narse/ *vr* to cease from rebellion; submit

desamparar /desampa'rar/ *vt* to abandon, forsake; leave (a place)

desamparo /desam'paro/ *m,* desertion; need

desamueblado /desamue'βlaðo/ *a* unfurnished

desamueblar /desamue'βlar/ *vt* to empty of furniture

desandar lo andado /desan'dar lo an'daðo/ *vt irr* to retrace one's steps. See **andar**

desangrar /desan'grar/ *vt Med.* to bleed; drain (lake, etc.); impoverish, bleed; —*vr* lose much blood

desanidar /desani'ðar/ *vi* to leave the nest; —*vt* eject, expel

desanimado /desani'maðo/ *a* downhearted; (of places) dull, quiet

desanimar /desani'mar/ *vt* to discourage, depress

desanublar, /desanu'βlar,/ *vt* **desanublarse** *vr* to clear up (weather)

desanudar /desanu'ðar/ *vt* to untie; disentangle

desaojar /desao'har/ *vt* to cure of the evil eye

desapacibilidad /desapaθiβili'ðað; desapasiβili'ðað/ *f,* disagreeableness, unpleasantness

desapacible /desapa'θiβle; desapa'siβle/ *a* disagreeable; unpleasant; unsociable

desaparecer /desapare'θer; desapare'ser/ *vt irr* to cause to disappear; —*vi* and *vr* disappear. See **conocer**

desaparecido /desapare'θiðo; desapare'siðo/ *a* late (deceased); *Mil.* missing

desaparejar /desapare'har/ *vt* to unharness

desaparición /desapari'θion; desapari'sion/ *f,* disappearance

desapegar /desape'gar/ *vt* to unstick, undo; —*vr* be indifferent, cast off a love or affection

desapego /desa'pego/ *m,* lack of affection or interest, coolness

desapercibido /desaperθi'βiðo; desapersi'βiðo/ *a* unnoticed; unprovided, unprepared

desapercibimiento /desaperθiβi'miento; desapersiβi'miento/ *m,* unpreparedness

desapestar /desapes'tar/ *vt* to disinfect

desapiadado /desapia'ðaðo/ *a* merciless

desaplicación /desaplika'θion; desaplika'sion/ *f,* laziness, lack of application; carelessness, negligence

desaplicado /desapli'kaðo/ *a* lazy; careless

desapoderado /desapoðe'raðo/ *a* precipitate, uncontrolled; furious, violent

desapoderar /desapoðe'rar/ *vt* to dispossess, rob; remove from office

desapolillar /desapoli'ʎar; desapoli'yar/ *vt* to free from moths; —*vr Inf.* take an airing

desaposentar /desaposen'tar/ *vt* to evict; drive away

desapreciar /desapre'θiar; desapre'siar/ *vt* to scorn

desaprender /desapren'der/ *vt* to unlearn

desaprensivo /desapren'siβo/ *a* unscrupulous

desapretar /desapre'tar/ **(se)** *vt* and *vr irr* to slacken. See **acertar**

desaprisionar /desaprisio'nar/ *vt* to release from prison

desaprobación /desaproβa'θion; desaproβa'sion/ *f,* disapproval

desaprobar /desapro'βar/ *vt irr* to disapprove; disagree with. See **probar**

desapropiamiento /desapropia'miento/ *m,* renunciation or transfer of property

desapropiarse /desapropi'arse/ *vr* to renounce or transfer (property)

desaprovechado /desaproβe'tʃaðo/ *a* unprofitable; backward; unintelligent

desaprovechar /desaproβe'tʃar/ *vt* to take no advantage of, waste; —*vi Fig.* lose ground, lose what one has gained

desapuntar /desapun'tar/ *vt* to unstitch; lose one's aim

desarbolar /desarβo'lar/ *vt Naut.* to unmast

desarenar /desare'nar/ *vt* to clear of sand

desarmar /desar'mar/ *vt* to disarm; dismantle, dismount; appease

desarme /de'sarme/ *m,* disarming; disarmament

desarraigar /desarrai'gar/ *vt* to pull up by root (plants); extirpate, suppress; eradicate (opinion, etc.); exile

desarraigo /desa'rraigo/ *m,* uprooting; extirpation; eradication; exile

desarrebujar /desarreβu'har/ *vt* to disentangle, uncover; explain

desarreglado /desarre'glaðo/ *a* disarranged; untidy; intemperate, immoderate

desarreglar /desarre'glar/ *vt* to disarrange

desarreglo /desa'rreglo/ *m,* disorder; disarrangement; irregularity

desarrendar /desarren'dar/ *vt irr* to unbridle a horse; end a tenancy or lease. See **recomendar**

desarrollar /desarro'ʎar; desarro'yar/ *vt* to unroll; increase, develop, grow, unfold; explain (theory); —*vr* develop, grow

desarrollo /desa'rroʎo; des'arroyo/ *m,* unrolling; development, growth; explanation

desarropar /desarro'par/ *vt* to uncover, remove the covers, etc. from

desarrugar /desarru'gar/ *vt* to take out wrinkles or creases

desarticulación /desartikula'θion; desartikula'sion/ *f,* disarticulation

desarticular /desartiku'lar/ *vt* to disarticulate; *Mech.* disconnect

desaseado /desase'aðo/ *a* dirty; unkempt, slovenly

desaseo /desa'seo/ *m,* dirtiness; slovenliness

desasimiento /desasi'miento/ *m,* loosening; liberality; disinterestedness; indifference, coldness

desasir /desa'sir/ *vt irr* to loosen, undo —*vr* disengage oneself. See **asir**

desasnar /desas'nar/ *vt Inf.* to instruct, educate, polish

desasosegar /desasose'gar/ *vt irr* to disturb, make anxious. See **cegar**

desasosiego /desaso'siego/ *m,* uneasiness, disquiet

desastre /de'sastre/ *m,* disaster, calamity

desastroso /desas'troso/ *a* unfortunate, calamitous

desatacar /desata'kar/ *vt* to unfasten, undo, unbutton

desatadura /desata'ðura/ *f,* untying

desatar /desa'tar/ *vt* to untie; melt, dissolve; elucidate, explain; —*vr* loosen the tongue; lose self control; lose all reserve; unbosom oneself

desatascar /desatas'kar/ *vt* to pull out of the mud; free from obstruction; extricate from difficulties

desataviar /desata'βiar/ *vt* to strip of ornaments

desatavío /desata'βio/ *m,* carelessness in dress, slovenliness

desatención /desaten'θion; desaten'sion/ *f,* inattention, abstraction; incivility

desatender /desaten'der/ *vt irr* to pay no attention to; disregard, ignore. See **entender**

desatentado /desaten'taðo/ *a* imprudent, ill-advised; excessive, immoderate

desatento /desa'tento/ *a* inattentive, abstracted; discourteous

desatinado /desati'naðo/ *a* foolish, imprudent, wild

desatinar /desati'nar/ *vt* to bewilder; —*vi* behave foolishly; lose one's bearings

desatino /desa'tino/ *m,* folly, foolishness, imprudence, rashness; blunder, faux pas, mistake

desatracar /desatra'kar/ *vi Naut.* to push off

desatrancar /desatran'kar/ *vt* to unbar the door; remove obstacles

desaturdir /desatur'ðir/ *vt* to rouse (from torpor, etc.)

desautorizar /desautori'θar; desautori'sar/ *vt* to remove from authority; discredit

desavenencia /desaβe'nenθia; desaβe'nensia/ *f,* disharmony, disagreement

desavenido /desaβe'niðo/ *a* disagreeing, discordant

desavenir /desaβe'nir/ *vt irr* to upset. See **venir**

desaventajado /desaβenta'haðo/ *a* disadvantageous; unfavorable, inferior

desaviar /desa'βiar/ *vt* to lead astray; deprive of a necessity; —*vr* lose one's way

desavisado /desaβi'saðo/ *a* unaware, unprepared

desavisar /desaβi'sar/ *vt* to take back one's previous advice

desayunador /desayuna'ðor/ *m,* breakfast nook

desayunarse /desayu'narse/ *vr* to have breakfast, eat breakfast

desayuno /desa'yuno/ *m,* breakfast

desazón /desa'θon; desa'son/ *f,* insipidity, lack of flavor; poorness (soil); anxiety, trouble; vexation

desazonar /desaθo'nar; desaso'nar/ *vt* to make insipid; make anxious, worry; vex; —*vr* feel out of sorts

desbancar /desβan'kar/ *vt* to break the bank (gambling); supplant

desbandada /desβan'daða/ *f,* dispersal, rout. **a la d.,** in confusion or disorder

desbandarse /desβan'darse/ *vr* to disband, retreat in disorder; *Mil.* desert

desbaratado /desβara'taðo/ *a Inf.* corrupt, vicious

desbaratar /desβara'tar/ *vt* to spoil, destroy; dissipate, waste; foil, thwart (a plot); *Mil.* rout; —*vi* talk foolishly; —*vr* go too far, behave badly

desbarbado /desβar'βaðo/ *a* beardless

desbastar /desβas'tar/ *vt* to plane, dress; polish, refine, civilize

desbocado /desβo'kaðo/ *a* (of tools) blunt; runaway (of a horse); *Inf.* foul-tongued

desbocar /desβo'kar/ *vt* to break the spout or neck (of jars, etc.); —*vi* run (into) (of streets, etc.); —*vr* bolt (horses); curse, swear

desboquillar /desβoki'ʎar; desβoki'yar/ *vt* to remove or break a stem or mouthpiece

desbordamiento /desβorða'miento/ *m,* overflowing, flood

desbordarse /desβor'ðarse/ *vr* to overflow; lose self-control. **d. en alabanzas para,** to heap praise on

desbravar /desβra'βar/ *vt* to break in (horses, etc.); —*vi* grow less savage; lose force, decrease

desbrozar /desβro'θar; desβro'sar/ *vt* to free of rubbish, clear up

descabalgadura /deskaβalga'ðura/ *f,* alighting (from horses, etc.)

descabalgar /deskaβal'gar/ vi to alight (from horse); —vt dismantle (gun)

descabellado /deskaβe'ʎaðo; deskaβe'yaðo/ a disheveled; ridiculous, foolish

descabellar /deskaβe'ʎar; deskaβe'yar/ vt to disarrange, ruffle (hair)

descabezado /deskaβe'θaðo; deskaβe'saðo/ a headless; rash, impetuous

descabezar /deskaβe'θar; deskaβe'sar/ vt to behead; cut the top off (trees, etc.); *Fig. Inf.* break the back of (work); —vi abut, join; —vr (*with con* or *en*) rack one's brains about

descalabazarse /deskalaβa'θarse; deskalaβa'sarse/ vr *Inf.* to rack one's brains

descalabradura /deskalaβra'ðura/ f, head wound or scar

descalabrar /deskala'βrar/ vt to wound in the head; wound; harm

descalabro /deska'laβro/ m, misfortune, mishap

descalzar /deskal'θar; deskal'sar/ vt to remove the shoes and stockings; undermine; —vr remove one's shoes and stockings; lose a shoe (horses)

descalzo /des'kalθo; des'kalso/ a barefoot

descaminar /deskami'nar/ vt to lead astray; pervert, corrupt

descamisado /deskami'saðo/ (**-da**) a *Inf.* shirtless; ragged, poor —n *Inf.* down and out, outcast; vagabond

descansadero /deskansa'ðero/ m, resting place

descansado /deskan'saðo/ a rested, refreshed; tranquil

descansar /deskan'sar/ vi to rest, repose oneself; have relief (from anxiety, etc.); sleep; *Agr.* lie fallow; sleep in death; (*with en*) trust, have confidence in; (*with sobre*) lean on or upon; —vt (*with sobre*) rest (a thing) on another. ¡**Que en paz descanse!** May he rest in peace!

descanso /des'kanso/ m, rest, repose; relief (from care); landing of stairs; *Mech.* bench, support; *Mil.* stand easy

descarado /deska'raðo/ a impudent, brazen

descararse /deska'rarse/ vr to behave impudently

descarbonizar /deskarβoni'θar; deskarβoni'sar/ vt to decarbonize

descarburación /deskarβura'θion; deskarβura'sion/ f, decarbonization

descarga /des'karga/ f, unloading; *Naut.* discharge of cargo; *Elec.* discharge; *Mil.* volley. **d. cerrada**, dense volley, fusillade

descargadero /deskarga'ðero/ m, wharf

descargador /deskarga'ðor/ m, unloader, docker; *Elec.* discharger

descargar /deskar'gar/ vt to unload; *Mil.* fire; unload (fire-arms); *Elec.* discharge; rain (blows) upon; *Fig.* free, exonerate; —vi disembogue (of rivers); burst (clouds); —vr relinquish (employment); shirk responsibility; *Law.* clear oneself

descargo /des'kargo/ m, unloading; *Com.* acquittance; *Law.* answer to an impeachment

descargue /des'karge/ m, unloading

descarnado /deskar'naðo/ a fleshless; scraggy; spare, lean

descarnador /deskarna'ðor/ m, dental scraper; tanner's scraper

descarnar /deskar'nar/ vt to scrape off flesh; corrode; inspire indifference to earthly things

descaro /des'karo/ m, impudence

descarriar /deska'rriar/ vt to lead astray; —vr be lost, be separated (from others); *Fig.* go astray

descarrilamiento /deskarrila'miento/ m, derailment

descarrilar /deskarri'lar/ vi to run off the track, be derailed

descarrío /deska'rrio/ m, losing one's way

descartar /deskar'tar/ vt to put aside; —vr discard (cards); shirk, make excuses

descarte /des'karte/ m, discard (cards); excuse, pretext

descascarar /deskaska'rar/ vt to peel; shell; —vr peel off

descendencia /desθen'denθia; dessen'densia/ f, descendants, offspring; lineage, descent

descender /desθen'der; dessen'der/ vi irr to descend;

flow (liquids); (*with de*) descend from, derive from; —vt lower, let down. See **entender**

descendiente /desθen'diente; dessen'diente/ mf descendant, offspring —a descending

descendimiento /desθendi'miento; dessendi'miento/ m, descent

descenso /des'θenso; des'senso/ m, descent; lowering, letting down; degradation

descentralización /desθentraliθa'θion; dessentralisa'sion/ f, decentralization

descentralizar /desθentrali'θar; dessentrali'sar/ vt to decentralize

desceñir /desθe'ɲir; desse'ɲir/ (**se**) vt and vr irr to ungird, remove a girdle, etc. See **ceñir**

descepar /desθe'par; desse'par/ vt to tear up by the roots; *Fig.* extirpate

descercado /desθer'kaðo; desser'kaðo/ a unfenced, open

descercar /desθer'kar; desser'kar/ vt to pull down a wall or fence; *Mil.* raise a siege

descerrajar /desθerra'har; desserra'har/ vt to remove the locks (of doors, etc.)

descifrable /desθi'fraβle; dessi'fraβle/ a decipherable

descifrador /desθifra'ðor; dessifra'ðor/ m, decipherer, decoder

descifrar /desθi'frar; dessi'frar/ vt to decipher; decode

descinchar /desθin'tʃar; dessin'tʃar/ vt to loosen or remove girths (of horse)

desclavar /deskla'βar/ vt to remove nails; unnail, unfasten

descoagular /deskoagu'lar/ vt to liquefy, dissolve, melt

descobijar /deskoβi'har/ vt to uncover; undress

descocado /desko'kaðo/ a *Inf.* brazen, saucy

descoco /des'koko/ m, *Inf.* impudence

descogollar /deskogo'ʎar; deskogo'yar/ vt to prune a tree of shoots; remove hearts (of lettuces, etc.)

descolar /desko'lar/ vt irr to cut off or dock an animal's tail. See **colar**

descolgar /deskol'gar/ vt irr to unhang; lower; —vr lower oneself (by rope, etc.); come down, descend; *Inf.* come out (with), utter. See **volcar**

descollar /desko'ʎar; desko'yar/ vi irr to excel, be outstanding. See **degollar**

descoloramiento /deskolora'miento/ m, discoloration

descolorar /deskolo'rar/ vt to discolor; —vr be discolored

descolorido /deskolo'riðo/ a discolored; pale-colored; pallid

descomedido /deskome'ðiðo/ a excessive, disproportionate; rude

descomedimiento /deskomeði'miento/ m, disrespect, lack of moderation, rudeness

descomedirse /deskome'ðirse/ vr irr to be disrespectful or rude. See **pedir**

descompasarse /deskompa'sarse/ vr See **descomedirse**

descomponer /deskompo'ner/ vt irr to disorder, disarrange; *Chem.* decompose; unsettle; —vr go out of order; rot, putrefy; be ailing; lose one's temper. See **poner**

descomposición /deskomposi'θion; deskomposi'sion/ f, disorder, confusion; discomposure; *Chem.* decomposition; putrefaction

descompostura /deskompos'tura/ f, decomposition; slovenliness, dirtiness, untidiness; impudence, rudeness

descompuesto /deskom'puesto/ a rude, impudent

descomunal /deskomu'nal/ a enormous, extraordinary

desconcertar /deskonθer'tar; deskonser'tar/ vt irr to disorder, disarrange; dislocate (bones); disconcert, embarrass; —vr disagree; be impudent. See **acertar**

desconcharse /deskon'tʃarse/ vr to flake off, peel

desconcierto /deskon'θierto; deskon'sierto/ m, disorder, disarrangement; dislocation; embarrassment; disagreement; impudence

desconectar /deskonek'tar/ vt to disconnect; switch off

desconfianza /deskon'fianθa; deskon'fiansa/ f, lack of confidence

desconfiar /deskon'fiar/ vi to lack confidence

desconformidad /deskonformi'ðað/ f, See **disconformidad**

desconformismo /deskonfor'mismo/ m, nonconformism

desconocer /deskono'θer; deskono'ser/ vt irr to forget; be unaware of; deny, disown; pretend ignorance; not to understand (persons, etc.). See **conocer**

desconocido /deskono'θiðo; deskonos'iðo/ (-da) a unknown; ungrateful —n stranger; ingrate

desconocimiento /deskonoθi'miento; deskonosi'miento/ m, unawareness; ignorance; ingratitude

desconsiderado /deskonsiðe'raðo/ a inconsiderate; discourteous; rash

desconsolación /deskonsola'θion; deskonsola'sion/ f, affliction, trouble

desconsolar /deskonso'lar/ vt irr to afflict, make disconsolate; —vr grieve, despair. See **colar**

desconsuelo /deskon'suelo/ m, anguish, affliction, despair

descontar /deskon'tar/ vt irr Com. to make a discount; ignore, discount; take for granted, leave aside. See **contar**

descontentadizo /deskontenta'ðiθo; deskontenta'ðiso/ a discontented, difficult to please; fastidious, finicky

descontentar /deskonten'tar/ vt to displease; —vr be dissatisfied

descontento /deskon'tento/ m, discontent, dissatisfaction

descontextualizar /deskontekstuali'θar; deskontekstuali'sar/ vt to take out of context

descontrolarse /deskontro'larse/ vr to lose control, lose control of oneself.

desconveniencia /deskombe'nienθia; deskombe'niensia/ f, inconvenience, unsuitability, disagreement

desconvenir /deskombe'nir/ vi irr to disagree; be unsuitable, unsightly or odd (things). See **venir**

descorazonamiento /deskoraθona'miento; deskorasona'miento/ m, depression, despair

descorazonar /deskoraθo'nar; deskoraso'nar/ vt to tear out the heart; depress, discourage

descorchar /deskor'tʃar/ vt to take the cork from cork tree; draw a cork (bottles); force, break into (safes)

descorrer /desko'rrer/ vt to re-run (race, etc.); draw back (curtains, etc.); —vi run, flow (liquids)

descorrimiento /deskorri'miento/ m, overflow (liquids)

descortés /deskor'tes/ a impolite

descortesía /deskorte'sia/ f, impoliteness, discourtesy

descortezadura /deskorteθa'ðura; deskortesa'ðura/ f, peeling (of bark)

descortezar /deskorte'θar; deskorte'sar/ vt to decorticate; remove crust (bread, etc.); polish, civilize

descoser /desko'ser/ vt Sew. to unpick; —vr be unpicked; be indiscreet or tactless

descosido /desko'siðo/ a tactless, talkative; Fig. disjointed; desultory; unsewn. m, Sew. rent, hole

descoyuntamiento /deskoyunta'miento/ m, dislocation (bones); irritation, bore; ache, pain

descoyuntar /deskoyun'tar/ vt to dislocate (bones); bore, annoy; —vr be dislocated

descrédito /des'kreðito/ m, fall in value (things); discredit (persons)

descreer /deskre'er/ vt irr to disbelieve; depreciate, disparage (persons). See **creer**

descreído /deskre'iðo/ (-da) a unbelieving —n unbeliever; infidel

describir /deskri'βir/ vt to describe; outline, sketch —Past Part. **descrito**

descripción /deskrip'θion; deskrip'sion/ f, description; Law. inventory

descriptible /deskrip'tiβle/ a describable

descriptivo /deskrip'tiβo/ a descriptive

descuajar /deskua'har/ vt to liquefy; Inf. discourage; Agr. pull up by the root

descuartizar /deskuarti'θar; deskuarti'sar/ vt to quarter; joint (meat); Inf. carve, cut into pieces, break up

descubierto /desku'βierto/ a bareheaded; exposed.

m, deficit. **al d.,** openly; in the open, without shelter. **girar en d.,** to overdraw (a bank account)

descubridero /deskuβri'ðero/ m, viewpoint, lookout

descubridor /deskuβri'ðor/ (-ra) n discoverer; inventor; explorer. m, Mil. scout

descubrimiento /deskuβri'miento/ m, find; discovery; revelation; newly discovered territory

descubrir /desku'βrir/ vt to reveal; show; discover; learn; unveil (memorials, etc.); —vr remove one's hat; show oneself, reveal one's whereabouts —Past Part. **descubierto**

descuello /des'kueʎo; des'kueyo/ m, extra height; Fig. pre-eminence; arrogance

descuento /des'kuento/ m, reduction; Com. rebate, discount

descuidado /deskui'ðaðo/ a negligent; careless; untidy; unprepared

descuidar /deskui'ðar/ vt to relieve (of responsibility, etc.); distract, occupy (attention, etc.); —vi and vr be careless; —vr (with de or en) neglect

descuido /des'kuiðo/ m, carelessness, negligence; oversight, mistake; incivility; forgetfulness; shameful act

desde /'desðe/ prep since, from (time or space); after (e.g. d. hoy, from today). **d. la ventana,** from the window. **d. allá,** from the other world. **d. aquella época,** since that time

desdecir /desðe'sir/ vi irr (with de) to degenerate, be less good than; be discordant, clash; be unworthy of; —vr unsay one's words, retract. See **decir**

desdén /des'ðen/ m, indifference, coldness; disdain, scorn

desdentado /desðen'taðo/ a toothless; Zool. edentate

desdentar /desðen'tar/ vt to remove teeth

desdeñar /desðe'ɲar/ vt to scorn; —vr (with de) dislike, be reluctant

desdeñoso /desðe'ɲoso/ a disdainful, scornful

desdevanar /desðeβa'nar/ vt to unwind thread, etc.

desdibujado /desðiβu'haðo/ a badly drawn; blurred, confused

desdicha /des'ðitʃa/ f, misfortune; extreme poverty, misery. **por d.,** unfortunately

desdichado /desði'tʃaðo/ a unfortunate; Inf. timid, weak-kneed

desdicharse /desði'tʃarse/ vr to bewail one's fate

desdinerarse una fortuna /desðine'rarse 'una for'tuna/ vr to spend a fortune

desdoblar /desðo'βlar/ vt to unfold

desdorar /desðo'rar/ vt to remove the gilt; Fig. tarnish, sully

desdoro /des'ðoro/ m, discredit, dishonor

deseable /dese'aβle/ a desirable

desear /dese'ar/ vt to desire; yearn or long for

desecar /dese'kar/ vt to dry; —vr be desiccated

desechar /dese'tʃar/ vt to reject, refuse; scorn; cast out, expel; put away (thoughts, etc.); cast off (old clothes); turn (key); give up

desecho /de'setʃo/ m, residue, rest, remains; cast-off; scorn

desembalar /desemba'lar/ vt to unpack

desembanastar /desembana'star/ vt to take out of a basket; Inf. unsheath (sword); —vr break loose (animals); Inf. get out, alight

desembarazar /desembara'θar; desembara'sar/ vt to clear of obstruction; disembarrass, free; vacate; —vr Fig. rid oneself of obstacles

desembarazo /desemba'raθo; desemba'raso/ m, freedom, insouciance, naturalness

desembarcadero /desembarka'ðero/ m, landing-stage

desembarcar /desembar'kar/ vt to unload; —vi disembark; alight from vehicle

desembarco /desem'barko/ m, disembarkation, landing; staircase landing

desembargar /desembar'gar/ vt to free of obstacles or impediments; Law. remove an embargo

desembargo /desem'bargo/ m, Law. removal of an embargo

desembarque /desem'barke/ m, disembarkation, landing

desembarrancar /desembarran'kar/ vt and vi Naut. to refloat

desembaular /desembau'lar/ *vt* to unpack from a trunk; disinter, empty; *Inf.* unbosom oneself

desembocadero /desemboka'ðero/ *m,* exit, way out; mouth (rivers, etc.)

desembocadura /desemboka'ðura/ *f,* mouth (rivers, etc.); street opening

desembocar /desembo'kar/ *vi* (*with en*) to lead to, end in; flow into (rivers)

desembolsar /desembol'sar/ *vt* to take out of a purse; pay, spend

desembolso /desem'bolso/ *m,* disbursement; expenditure

desemboscarse /desembos'karse/ *vr* to get out of the wood; extricate oneself from an ambush

desembozar /desembo'θar; desembo'sar/ *vt* to unmuffle

desembozo /desem'boθo; desem'boso/ *m,* uncovering of the face

desembragar /desembra'gar/ *vt Mech.* to disengage (the clutch, etc.)

desembravecer /desembraβe'θer; desembraβe'ser/ *vt irr* to tame, domesticate. See **conocer**

desembriagar /desembria'gar/ (**se**) *vt* and *vr* to sober up (after a drinking bout)

desembrollar /desembro'ʎar; desembro'yar/ *vt Inf.* to disentangle, unravel

desemejanza /deseme'hanθa; deseme'hansa/ *f,* unlikeness

desemejar /deseme'har/ *vi* to be unlike; —*vt* disfigure, deform

desempacar /desempa'kar/ *vt* to unpack

desempapelar /desempape'lar/ *vt* to unwrap, remove the paper from; remove wallpaper

desempaquetar /desempake'tar/ *vt* to unpack

desemparejar /desempare'har/ *vt* to split (a pair); make unequal

desemparentado /desemparen'taðo/ *a* without relatives

desempedrar /desempe'ðrar/ *vt irr* to take up the flags (of a pavement). See **acertar**

desempeñar /desempe'ɲar/ *vt* to redeem (pledges); free from debt; fulfil (obligations, etc.); take out of pawn; hold, fill (an office); extricate (from difficulties, etc.); perform, carry out; *Theat.* act

desempeño /desempe'ɲo/ *m,* redemption of a pledge; fulfillment (of an obligation, etc.); performance, accomplishment; *Theat.* acting of a part

desempolvar /desempol'βar/ *vt* to free from dust, dust

desenamorar /desenamo'rar/ *vt* to kill the affection of; —*vr* fall out of love

desencadenar /desenkaðe'nar/ *vt* to unchain, unfetter; *Fig.* unleash, let loose; —*vr Fig.* break loose

desencajamiento /desenkaha'miento/ *m,* disjointedness, dislocation; ricketiness, broken-down appearance

desencajar /desenka'har/ *vt* to disconnect, disjoint; dislocate; —*vr* be out of joint; be contorted (of the face); be tired looking

desencaje /desen'kahe/ *m,* See **desencajamiento**

desencallar /desenka'ʎar; desenka'yar/ *vt Naut.* to float a grounded ship

desencantar /desenkan'tar/ *vt* to disenchant

desencanto /desen'kanto/ *m,* disenchantment; disillusionment

desencerrar /desenθe'rrar; desense'rrar/ *vt irr* to set at liberty; unlock; disclose, reveal. See **acertar**

desenchufar /desentʃu'far/ *vt* to disconnect, unplug (electric plugs, etc.)

desenclavijar /desenklaβi'har/ *vt* to remove the pegs or pins; disconnect, disjoint

desencoger /desenko'her/ *vt* to unfold, spread out; —*vr* grow bold

desencolerizar /desenkoleri'θar; desenkoleri'sar/ *vt* to placate; —*vr* lose one's anger, grow calm

desenconar /desenko'nar/ *vt* to reduce (inflammation); appease (anger, etc.); —*vr* become calm

desencono /desen'kono/ *m,* reduction of inflammation; appeasement (of anger, etc.)

desencordelar /desenkorðe'lar/ *vt* to untie the ropes (of), unstring

desencorvar /desenkor'βar/ *vt* to straighten (curves, etc.)

desenfadado /desenfa'ðaðo/ *a* expeditious; natural, at ease; gay; forward, bold; wide, spacious

desenfadar /desenfa'ðar/ *vt* to appease, make anger disappear

desenfado /desen'faðo/ *m,* freedom; ease; unconcern, frankness

desenfardar /desenfar'ðar/ *vt* to unpack bales

desenfrailar /desenfrai'lar/ *vt* to leave the cloister, become secularized; *Inf.* emancipate oneself

desenfrenar /desenfre'nar/ *vt* to unbridle (horses); —*vr* give rein to one's passions, etc.; break loose (storms, etc.)

desenfreno /desen'freno/ *m,* license, lasciviousness; complete freedom from restraint

desengalanar /desengala'nar/ *vt* to strip of ornaments

desenganchar /desengan'tʃar/ *vt* to unhook; uncouple; unfasten; unharness

desengañador /desengaɲa'ðor/ *a* undeceiving

desengañar /desenga'ɲar/ *vt* to undeceive, disillusion

desengaño /desen'gaɲo/ *m,* undeceiving, disabuse; disillusionment

desengarzar /desengar'θar; desengar'sar/ *vt* to loosen from its setting; unlink, unhook, unclasp

desengastar /desengas'tar/ *vt* to remove from its setting (jewelry, etc.)

desengrasar /desengra'sar/ *vt* to remove the grease from, clean; —*vi Inf.* grow thin

desenlace /desen'laθe; desen'lase/ *m,* loosening, untying; *Lit.* denouement, climax (of play, etc.)

desenlazar /desenla'θar; desenla'sar/ *vt* to untie, unloose; *Lit.* unravel (a plot)

desenlosar /desenlo'sar/ *vt* to remove flagstones

desenmarañar /desemara'ɲar/ *vt* to disentangle; *Fig.* straighten out

desenmascarar /desemaska'rar/ *vt* to remove the mask from; *Fig.* unmask

desenmudecer /desemuðe'θer; desemuðe'ser/ *vi irr* to be freed of a speech impediment; break silence, speak. See **conocer**

desenojar /deseno'har/ *vt* to soothe, appease; —*vr* distract oneself, amuse oneself

desenojo /dese'noho/ *m,* relenting, abatement of anger

desenredar /desenre'ðar/ *vt* to disentangle; *Fig.* set right; straighten out; —*vr* extricate oneself, get out of a difficulty

desenredo /desen'reðo/ *m,* disentanglement; *Lit.* climax

desentablar /desenta'βlar/ *vt* to tear up planks or boards; disorder, disrupt

desentenderse /desenten'derse/ *vr irr* (*with de*) to pretend to be ignorant of; take no part in. See **entender**

desenterrador /desenterra'ðor/ *m,* disinterrer, unearther

desenterramiento /desenterra'miento/ *m,* disinterment; *Fig.* unearthing, recollection

desenterrar /desente'rrar/ *vt irr* to unbury, disinter; rummage out; *Fig.* unearth, bring up, recall. See **acertar**

desentoldar /desentol'dar/ *vt* to take away an awning; *Fig.* strip of ornament

desentonar /desento'nar/ *vt* to humiliate; —*vi Mus.* be out of tune; speak rudely; —*vr* be inharmonious; raise the voice (anger, etc.), behave badly

desentono /desen'tono/ *m,* bad behavior, rudeness; *Mus.* discord; grating quality or harshness (of voice)

desentorpecer /desentorpe'θer; desentorpe'ser/ *vt irr* to restore feeling to (numbed limbs); free from torpor; —*vr* become bright and intelligent. See **conocer**

desentramparse /desentram'parse/ *vr Inf.* free oneself from debt

desentrañar /desentra'ɲar/ *vt* to disembowel; *Fig.* unravel, penetrate; —*vr* give away one's all

desentronizar /desentroni'θar; desentroni'sar/ *vt* to dethrone; dismiss from office

desentumecer /desentume'θer; desentume'ser/ *vt irr*

to free from numbness (limbs); —*vr* be restored to feeling (numb limbs). See **conocer**

desenvainar /desembai'nar/ *vt* to unsheath; *Inf.* reveal, bring into the open

desenvoltura /desembol'tura/ *f,* naturalness, ease, freedom; eloquence, facility (of speech); effrontery, audacity, shamelessness (especially in women)

desenvolver /desembol'βer/ *vt irr* to unroll; unfold; *Fig.* unravel, explain; *Fig.* develop, work out (theories, etc.); —*vr* unroll; unfold; lose one's timidity, blossom out; be over-bold; extricate oneself (from a difficulty). See **resolver**

desenvuelto /desem'buelto/ *a* natural, easy; impudent, bold

deseo /de'seo/ *m,* desire, will, wish

deseoso /dese'oso/ *a* desirous, wishful

desequilibrar /desekili'βrar/ **(se)** *vt* and *vr* to unbalance

desequilibrio /deseki'liβrio/ *m,* lack of balance; confusion, disorder; mental instability

deserción /deser'θion; deser'sion/ *f, Mil.* desertion. **d. estudiantil,** school dropout

desertar /deser'tar/ *vt Mil.* to desert; *Inf.* quit

desertor /deser'tor/ *m, Mil.* deserter; *Inf.* quitter

deservicio /deser'βiθio; deser'βisio/ *m,* disservice

desesperación /desespera'θion; desespera'sion/ *f,* desperation, despair; frenzy, violence

desesperado /desespe'raðo/ *a* desperate, hopeless; frenzied

desesperanza /desespe'ranθa; desespe'ransa/ *f,* despair; hopelessness

desesperanzar /desesperan'θar; desesperan'sar/ *vt* to render hopeless; —*vr* despair, lose hope

desesperar /desespe'rar/ *vt* to make hopeless; *Inf.* annoy, make furious; —*vr* lose hope, despair; be frenzied

desestañar /desesta'ɲar/ *vt* to unsolder

desestimación /desesti'ma'θion; desestima'sion/ *f,* disrespect, lack of esteem; rejection

desestimar /desesti'mar/ *vt* to scorn; reject

desfachatado /desfatʃa'taðo/ *a Inf.* impudent, brazen

desfachatez /desfatʃa'teθ; desfatʃa'tes/ *f, Inf.* effrontery, cheek

desfalcador /desfalka'ðor/ **(-ra)** *a* embezzling —*n* embezzler

desfalcar /desfal'kar/ *vt* to remove a part of; embezzle

desfalco /des'falko/ *m,* diminution, reduction; embezzlement

desfallecer /desfaʎe'θer; desfaye'ser/ *vt irr* to weaken; —*vi* grow weak; faint, swoon. See **conocer**

desfallecimiento /desfaʎeθi'miento; desfayesi'miento/ *m,* weakness, languor; depression, discouragement; faint, swoon

desfavorable /desfaβo'raβle/ *a* unfavorable; hostile, contrary

desfavorecer /desfaβore'θer; desfaβore'ser/ *vt irr* to withdraw one's favor, scorn; disfavor; oppose. See **conocer**

desfiguración /desfigura'θion; desfigura'sion/ *f,* deformation; disfigurement

desfigurar /desfigu'rar/ *vt* to deform, misshape; disfigure; *Fig.* disguise, mask; obscure, darken; distort, misrepresent; —*vr* be disfigured (by rage, etc.)

desfijar /desfi'har/ *vt* to unfix, pull off, remove

desfiladero /desfila'ðero/ *m,* defile, gully

desfilar /desfi'lar/ *vi* to walk in file; *Inf.* file out; *Mil.* file or march past

desfile /des'file/ *m, Mil.* march past; parade; walk past; procession

desflecarse /desfle'karse/ **(en)** *vr* to disintegrate (into)

desfloración /desflora'θion; desflora'sion/ *f,* defloration

desflorar /desflo'rar/ *vt* to tarnish, stain; deflower, violate; *Fig.* touch upon, deal lightly with

desfortalecer /desfortale'θer; desfortale'ser/ *vt irr Mil.* to dismantle a fortress. See **conocer**

desfruncir /desfrun'θir; desfrun'sir/ *vt* to unfold, shake out

desgaire /des'gaire/ *m,* untidiness, slovenliness; affectation of carelessness (in dress); scornful gesture. **al d.,** with an affectation of carelessness, negligently

desgajar /desga'har/ *vt* to tear off a tree branch; break; —*vr* break off; dissociate oneself (from)

desgalgar /desgal'gar/ *vt* to throw headlong

desgana /des'gana/ *f,* lack of appetite; lack of interest, indifference; reluctance

desganar /desga'nar/ *vt* to dissuade; —*vr* lose one's appetite; become bored or indifferent, lose interest

desgarbado /desgar'βaðo/ *a* slovenly, slatternly; gawky, graceless

desgarrado /desga'rraðo/ *a* dissolute, vicious; impudent, brazen

desgarrador /desgarra'ðor/ *a* tearing; heart-rending

desgarrar /desga'rrar/ *vt* to tear; —*vr* leave, tear oneself away

desgarro /des'garro/ *m,* tearing; rent, breach; boastfulness, impudence, effrontery

desgastar /desgas'tar/ *vt* to corrode, wear away; spoil, corrupt; —*vr* lose one's vigor, grow weak; wear away

desgaste /des'gaste/ *m,* attrition; wearing down or away; corrosion; wear and tear

desgobernado /desgoβer'naðo/ *a* uncontrolled (of persons)

desgobernar /desgoβer'nar/ *vt irr* to upset or rise against the government; dislocate (bones); *Naut.* neglect the tiller; —*vr* affect exaggerated movements in dancing. See **recomendar**

desgobierno /desgo'βierno/ *m,* misgovernment; mismanagement; maladministration; disorder, tumult

desgomar /desgo'mar/ *vt* to ungum (fabrics)

desgorrarse /desgo'rrarse/ *vr* to doff one's cap, doff one's hat

desgoznar /desgoθ'nar; desgos'nar/ *vt* to unhinge; —*vr Fig.* lose one's self-control

desgracia /des'graθia; des'grasia/ *f,* misfortune, adversity; mishap, piece of bad luck; disgrace, disfavor; disagreeableness, brusqueness; ungraciousness. **por d.,** unhappily, unfortunately

desgraciado /desgra'θiaðo; desgra'siaðo/ *a* unfortunate, unhappy; unlucky; dull, boring; disagreeable

desgraciar /desgra'θiar; desgra'siar/ *vt* to displease; spoil the development (of), destroy; maim; —*vr* fall out of friendship; be out of favor; turn out badly, fail; be destroyed or spoiled; be maimed

desgranar /desgra'nar/ *vt Agr.* to thresh, flail; —*vr* break (string of beads, etc.)

desgrasante /desgra'sante/ *m,* grease remover

desgreñar /desgre'ɲar/ *vt* to dishevel the hair; —*vr Inf.* pull each other's hair, come to blows

desguarnecer /desguarne'θer; desguarne'ser/ *vt irr* to strip of trimming; *Mil.* demilitarize; *Mil.* disarm; dismantle; unharness. See **conocer**

desguazar /desgua'θar; desgua'sar/ *vt* to break up (ships)

deshabitado /desaβi'taðo/ *a* uninhabited, empty

deshabitar /desaβi'tar/ *vt* to desert, quit, leave (a place)

deshabituar /desaβi'tuar/ *vt* to disaccustom; —*vr* lose the habit, become unaccustomed

deshacer /desa'θer; desa'ser/ *vt irr* to undo; destroy; *Mil.* rout, defeat; take to pieces; melt; pulp (paper); untie (knots, etc.); open (parcels); diminish, decrease; break in pieces, smash; *Fig.* obstruct, spoil; —*vr* be wasted or spoiled; be full of anxiety; vanish; try or work very hard; injure oneself; be emaciated, grow extremely thin; (*with de*) part with. **d. agravios,** to right wrongs. See **hacer**

desharrapado /desarra'paðo/ *a* tattered, shabby

deshebillar /deseβi'ʎar; deseβi'yar/ *vt* to unbuckle

deshebrar /dese'βrar/ *vt* to unravel; shred

deshecha /des'etʃa/ *f,* pretense, evasion; courteous farewell; obligatory departure

deshechizar /desetʃi'θar; desetʃi'sar/ *vt* to disenchant

deshelar /dese'lar/ *vt irr* to thaw, melt. See **acertar**

desherbar /deser'βar/ *vt irr* to pull up weeds. See **acertar**

desheredación /desereða'θion; desereða'sion/ *f,* disinheritance

desheredar /desere'ðar/ *vt* disinherit; —*vr Fig.* lower oneself

desherrar /dese'rrar/ vt irr to unfetter, unchain; strike off horseshoes; —vr lose a shoe (horses). See **acertar**

desherrumbrar /deserrum'brar/ vt to remove the rust from; clean off rust from

deshidratación /desiðrata'θion; desiðrata'sion/ f, dehydration

deshidratar /desiðra'tar/ vt to dehydrate

deshielo /des'ielo/ m, thaw

deshilado /desi'laðo/ a in single file. m, Sew. drawnthread work (gen. pl). **a la deshilada**, Mil. in file formation; secretly

deshiladura /desila'ðura/ f, unraveling

deshilar /desi'lar/ vt to unravel; Sew. draw threads; Cul. shred, grate

deshilvanado /desilβa'naðo/ a Fig. disjointed, disconnected

deshilvanar /desilβa'nar/ vt Sew. to remove the tacking threads

deshincar /desin'kar/ vt to pull out, remove, draw out

deshinchar /desin'tʃar/ vt to remove a swelling; deflate; lessen the anger of; —vr decrease, subside (swellings); deflate; Inf. grow humble

deshojar /deso'har/ vt to strip off leaves or petals

deshollejar /desoʎe'har; desoye'har/ vt to skin, peel (fruit); shell (peas, etc.)

deshollinador /desoʎina'ðor; desoyina'ðor/ m, chimney-sweep; wall-brush; chemical chimney cleaner

deshollinar /desoʎi'nar; desoyi'nar/ vt to sweep chimneys; clean down walls; Inf. examine closely

deshonestidad /desonesti'ðað/ f, immodesty, shamelessness; indecency

deshonesto /deso'nesto/ a shameless, immodest; dissolute, vicious; indecent

deshonor /deso'nor/ m, dishonor; disgrace, insult

deshonra /de'sonra/ f, dishonor

deshonrabuenos /desonra'βuenos/ mf Inf. slanderer; degenerate

deshonrador /desonra'ðor/ **(-ra)** a dishonorable —n dishonorer

deshonrar /deson'rar/ vt to dishonor; insult; seduce (women)

deshonroso /deson'roso/ a dishonorable, insulting, indecent

deshora /de'sora/ f, inconvenient time. **a d.**, or **a deshoras**, at an inconvenient time, unseasonably; extempore

deshuesar /desue'sar/ vt to bone, remove the bone (from meat); stone (fruit)

deshumedecer /desumeðe'θer; desumeðe'ser/ vt irr to dry; —vr become dry. See **conocer**

desidia /de'siðia/ f, negligence; laziness

desidioso /desi'ðioso/ a negligent; lazy

desierto /de'sierto/ a deserted, uninhabited, solitary. m, desert; wilderness

designación /designa'θion; designa'sion/ f, designation; appointment

designar /desig'nar/ vt to plan, intend; designate; appoint

designio /de'signio/ m, intention, idea

desigual /desi'gual/ a unequal; uneven (ground); rough; arduous, difficult; changeable

desigualar /desigua'lar/ vt to make unequal; —vr prosper

desigualdad /desigual'ðað/ f, inequality; unevenness, rockiness; Fig. changeability; variability

desilusión /desilu'sion/ f, disillusionment; disappointment

desilusionar /desilusio'nar/ vt to disillusion; —vr become disillusioned; be undeceived

desinclinar /desinkli'nar/ vt to dissuade

desinfección /desinfek'θion; desinfek'sion/ f, disinfection

desinfectante /desinfek'tante/ a and m, disinfectant

desinfectar /desinfek'tar/ vt to disinfect

desinflación /desinfla'θion; desinfla'sion/ f, deflation

desinflar /desin'flar/ vt to deflate

desinterés /desinte'res/ m, disinterestedness

desinteresado /desintere'saðo/ a disinterested; generous

desinteresarse /desintere'sarse/ vr to lose interest, grow indifferent

desistencia, /desis'tenθia,; desis'tensia,/ f, **desistimiento** m, desistance, ceasing

desistir /desis'tir/ vi to desist; cease; Law. renounce

desjuntamiento /deshunta'miento/ m, separation; division

desjuntar /deshun'tar/ **(se)** vt and vr to separate; divide

deslavado /desla'βaðo/ a brazen, impudent

deslavar /desla'βar/ vt to wash superficially; spoil by washing, take away the body of (cloth, etc.)

desleal /desle'al/ a disloyal, treacherous

deslealtad /desleal'tað/ f, disloyalty

desleír /desle'ir/ vt irr to dissolve; dilute. See **reír**

deslenguado /deslen'guaðo/ a shameless, foulmouthed

deslenguar /deslen'guar/ vt to remove the tongue; —vr Inf. be insolent

desliar /des'liar/ vt to untie, undo, unloose

desligadura /desliga'ðura/ f, untying, loosening

desligar /desli'gar/ vt to unfasten, unbind; Fig. solve, unravel; relieve of an obligation; Mus. play staccato; —vr come unfastened, grow loose. **desligarse de,** to weasel out of, wiggle out of (a promise)

deslindador /deslinda'ðor/ m, one who fixes boundaries or limits

deslindar /deslin'dar/ vt to fix the boundaries (of); limit, circumscribe

deslinde /des'linde/ m, demarcation, boundary

desliz /des'liθ; des'lis/ m, slipping, slip, slide; skid; indiscretion, slip; peccadillo, trifling fault

deslizadero /desliθa'ðero; deslisa'ðero/ m, slippery place; chute

deslizadizo /desliθa'ðiθo; deslisa'ðiso/ a slippery

deslizar /desliθar; desli'sar/ vt to slip, slide; skid; —vr commit an indiscretion; speak or act unwisely; escape, slip away; slip; skid

deslucido /des'luθiðo; des'lusiðo/ a fruitless, vain; stupid, clumsy, awkward; discolored; tarnished, dull; unsuccessful

deslucimiento /desluθi'miento; deslusi'miento/ m, clumsiness, gracelessness; failure, lack of success

deslucir /deslu'θir; deslu'sir/ vt irr to fade; discolor, stain; tarnish; spoil; sully the reputation of; —vr do a thing badly, fail at. See **lucir**

deslumbrador /deslumbra'ðor/ a dazzling

deslumbramiento /deslumbra'miento/ m, brilliant light, glare, dazzle; bewilderment, confusion

deslumbrar /deslumb'rar/ vt to dazzle; confuse, bewilder; Fig. daze (with magnificence)

deslustrar /deslus'trar/ vt to dull, dim, tarnish; frost (glass); discredit, sully (reputation)

deslustre /des'lustre/ m, dullness, tarnish; frosting (of glass); disgrace, stigma

deslustroso /deslus'troso/ a ugly, unsuitable, unbecoming

desmadejar /desmaðe'har/ vt to debilitate, enervate

desmán /des'man/ m, outrageous behavior; disaster, misfortune

desmandado /desman'daðo/ a disobedient

desmandar /desman'dar/ vt to cancel, revoke (orders); withdraw (an offer) —vr behave badly; stray

desmantelado /desmante'laðo/ a dismantled, dilapidated

desmantelamiento /desmantela'miento/ m, dismantling; dilapidation

desmantelar /desmante'lar/ vt to dismantle; abandon, forsake

desmaña /des'maɲa/ f, lack of dexterity, clumsiness, awkwardness

desmañado /desma'ɲaðo/ a clumsy, awkward, unhandy

desmayado /desma'yaðo/ a pale, faint (of colors); weak (of a voice)

desmayar /desma'yar/ vt to cause to faint; —vi grow discouraged, lose heart; —vr swoon, faint

desmayo /des'mayo/ *m,* depression, discouragement; faint, swoon

desmedido /desme'ðiðo/ *a* disproportionate; excessive

desmedirse /desme'ðirse/ *vr* to misbehave, go too far

desmedrado /desme'ðraðo/ *a* thin, emaciated; deteriorated, spoiled

desmedrar /desme'ðrar/ *vt* to spoil, ruin; —*vi* deteriorate; decline

desmedro /des''meðro/ *m,* impairment; decline, deterioration. **en d. de,** to the detriment of

desmejora /desme'hora/ *f,* deterioration

desmejorar /desmeho'rar/ *vt* to spoil, impair, cause to deteriorate; —*vr* deteriorate; —*vi* and *vr* decline in health; lose one's beauty

desmelenar /desmele'nar/ *vt* to ruffle or dishevel the hair

desmembración /desmembra'θion; desmembrasion/ *f,* dismemberment

desmembrar /desmem'brar/ *vt* to dismember; separate, divide

desmemoriarse /desmemo'riarse/ *vr* to forget, lose one's memory

desmenguar /desmeŋ'guar/ *vt* to reduce, decrease; *Fig.* diminish

desmentida /desmen'tiða/ *f,* action of giving the lie to

desmentir /desmen'tir/ *vt irr* to give the lie to; contradict, deny; lower oneself; behave unworthily; —*vi* deviate (from right direction, etc.). See **sentir**

desmenuzar /desmenu'θar; desmenu'sar/ *vt* to crumble, break into small pieces; *Fig.* examine in detail; —*vr* be broken up

desmeollar /desmeo'ʎar; desmeo'yar/ *vt* to remove the marrow of

desmerecedor /desmereθe'ðor; desmerese'ðor/ *a* unworthy

desmerecer /desmere'θer; desmere'ser/ *vt irr* to become undeserving of; —*vi* deteriorate; be inferior to. See **conocer**

desmesura /desme'sura/ *f,* insolence; disproportion; excess

desmesurado /desmesu'raðo/ *a* disproportionate; excessive, enormous; insolent, uncivil

desmesurar /desmesu'rar/ *vt* to disarrange, disorder; —*vr* be insolent

desmigajar /desmiga'har/ **(se)** *vt* and *vr* to crumble

desmigar /desmi'gar/ *vt Cul.* to make breadcrumbs

desmilitarizar /desmilitari'θar; desmilitari'sar/ *vt* to demilitarize

desmochar /desmo'tʃar/ *vt* to lop off the top; pollard (trees)

desmonetización /desmonetiθa'θion; desmonetisa'sion/ *f,* demonetization; conversion of coin into bullion

desmonetizar /desmoneti'θar; desmoneti'sar/ *vt* to convert money into bullion; demonetize; —*vr* depreciate (shares, etc.)

desmontable /desmon'taβle/ *a* movable; sectional

desmontadura /desmonta'ðura/ *f,* clearing; deforestation; leveling; demounting, dismounting

desmontar /desmon'tar/ *vt* to clear wholly or partly of trees or shrubs; clear up (rubbish); level (ground); dismantle; dismount; uncock (firearms); —*vi* and *vr* dismount (from horse, etc.)

desmonte /des'monte/ *m,* clearing of trees and shrubs; clearing, cleared ground; timber remaining

desmoralización /desmoraliθa'θion; desmoralisa'sion/ *f,* demoralization, corruption

desmoralizador /desmoraliθa'ðor; desmoralisa'ðor/ *a* demoralizing

desmoralizar /desmorali'θar; desmorali'sar/ *vt* to demoralize, corrupt

desmoronamiento /desmorona'miento/ *m,* crumbling; decay, ruin

desmoronar /desmoro'nar/ *vt* to destroy, decay; crumble; —*vr* crumble away, fall into ruin; decline, decay; wane, fade (power, etc.)

desmovilización /desmoβiliθa'θion; desmoβilisa'sion/ *f,* demobilization

desmovilizar /desmoβili'θar; desmoβili'sar/ *vt* to demobilize

desnacificación /desnaθifika'θion; desnasifika'sion/ *f,* denazification

desnatar /desna'tar/ *vt* to skim; *Fig.* take the cream or best

desnaturalización /desnaturaliθa'θion; desnaturalisa'sion/ *f,* denaturalization

desnaturalizar /desnaturali'θar; desnaturali'sar/ *vt* to denaturalize; exile; deform, disfigure, pervert; —*vr* give up one's country

desnivel /desni'βel/ *m,* unevenness; slope, drop

desnivelar /desniβe'lar/ **(se)** *vi* and *vr* to become uneven

desnudar /desnu'ðar/ *vt* to undress; *Fig.* despoil, strip, denude; —*vr* undress oneself; deprive oneself

desnudez /desnu'ðeθ; desnu'ðes/ *f,* nudity; nakedness; bareness; plainness

desnudo /des'nuðo/ *a* nude; ill-clad; bare, naked; clear, patent; *Fig.* destitute (of grace, etc.). *m, Art.* nude

desnutrición /desnutri'θion; desnutri'sion/ *f,* malnutrition

desobedecer /desoβeðe'θer; desoβeðe'ser/ *vt irr* to disobey. See **conocer**

desobediencia /desoβeðien'θia; desoβeðien'sia/ *f,* disobedience

desobediente /desoβe'ðiente/ *a* disobedient

desobligar /desoβli'gar/ *vt* to free from obligation; offend, hurt

desocupación /desokupa'θion; desokupa'sion/ *f,* lack of occupation; leisure

desocupado /desoku'paðo/ *a* idle; vacant, unoccupied

desocupar /desoku'par/ *vt* to empty; vacate; —*vr* give up an employment or occupation

desodorante /desoðo'rante/ *a* and *m,* deodorant

desoir /deso'ir/ *vt irr* to pay no attention, pretend not to hear. See **oir**

desojar /deso'har/ *vt* to break the eye of (needles, etc.); —*vr* gaze intently

desolación /desola'θion; desola'sion/ *f,* destruction, desolation; affliction

desolador /desola'ðor/ *a* desolate; grievous

desolar /deso'lar/ *vt irr* to lay waste, destroy; —*vr* grieve, be disconsolate. See **contar**

desoldar /desol'dar/ *vt* to unsolder; —*vr* become unsoldered

desolladero /desoʎa'ðero; desoya'ðero/ *m,* slaughterhouse

desollado /deso'ʎaðo; deso'yaðo/ *a Inf.* impertinent, barefaced. *m,* carcass

desolladura /desoʎa'ðura; desoya'ðura/ *f,* flaying, skinning; *Inf.* slander

desollar /deso'ʎar; deso'yar/ *vt irr* to flay, skin; harm, discredit. **d. vivo,** *Inf.* to extort an exorbitant price; slander. See **contar**

desopinado /desopi'naðo/ *a* discredited

desopinar /desopi'nar/ *vt* to discredit, defame

desorden /de'sorðen/ *m,* disorder, disarray; confusion; excess

desordenado /desorðe'naðo/ *a* disordered; vicious; licentious

desordenar /desorðe'nar/ *vt* to disorder; confuse; —*vr* go beyond the just limits; behave badly; be impertinent

desorganización /desorganiθa'θion; desorganisa'sion/ *f,* disorganization

desorganizador /desorganiθa'ðor; desorganisa'ðor/ *a* disorganizing

desorganizar /desorgani'θar; desorgani'sar/ *vt* to disorganize; disband

desorientación /desorienta'θion; desorienta'sion/ *f,* disorientation, loss of bearings; lack of method, confusion

desorientar /desorien'tar/ *vt* to disorient; perplex, confuse; —*vr* lose one's way; be disoriented

desovar /deso'βar/ *vi* to spawn

desove /de'soβe/ *m,* spawning; spawning season

desovillar /desoβi'ʎar; desoβi'yar/ *vt* to unwind; uncoil; uncurl; explain, clarify

despabiladeras /despaβila'ðeras/ *f pl,* snuffers

despabilado /despaβi'laðo/ *a* alert, wide-awake; watchful, vigilant

despabiladura /despaβila'ðura/ *f*, snuff of a candle, lamp, etc.

despabilar /despaβi'lar/ *vt* to snuff (a candle); trim (lamps); hasten, expedite; finish quickly; steal, rob; *Fig.* quicken (intelligence, etc.); *Inf.* kill; —*vr* rouse oneself, wake up

despachador /despatʃa'ðor/ **(-ra)** *n* dispatcher, sender

despachar /despa'tʃar/ *vt* to expedite; dispatch, conclude; forward, send; attend to correspondence; sell; dismiss; *Inf.* serve in a shop; *Inf.* kill; —*vi* hasten; carry letters to be signed (in offices, etc.); —*vr* get rid of

despacho /despa'tʃo/ *m*, transaction, execution; study; office, room; department; booking-office; dispatch, shipment; expedient; commission, warrant; dispatch (diplomatic); telegram; telephone message. **d. particular,** private office

despachurrar /despa'tʃurrar/ *vt Inf.* to crush, squash; recount in a muddled fashion; *Fig.* squash flat, confound

despacio /des'paθio; des'pasio/ *adv* slowly, little by little; deliberately, leisurely —*interj* Careful! Gently now!

despacito /despa'θito; despa'sito/ *adv Inf.* very slowly

despalmador /despalma'ðor/ *m*, dockyard

despalmar /despal'mar/ *vt Naut.* to careen, caulk

despampanar /despampa'nar/ *vt Agr.* to prune vines; *Inf.* amaze, stun, astound; —*vi Inf.* relieve one's feelings; —*vr Inf.* receive a serious injury (through falling)

desparpajar /desparpa'har/ *vt* to spoil; —*vi Inf.* chatter

desparpajo /despar'paho/ *m*, *Inf.* loquaciousness, pertness; disorder, muddle

desparramar /desparra'mar/ *vt* to disperse, scatter; squander, waste (money, etc.); —*vr* amuse oneself; be dissipated

despavorido /despaβo'riðo/ *a* terrified, panicstricken

despechar /despe'tʃar/ *vt* to anger; make despair; *Inf.* wean; —*vr* be angry; be in despair

despecho /des'petʃo/ *m*, rancor, malice; despair. **a d. de,** in spite of

despechugar /despetʃu'gar/ *vt* to cut off the breast (fowls); —*vr Inf.* show the bosom

despectivo /despek'tiβo/ *a* contemptuous, depreciatory

despedazar /despeða'θar; despeða'sar/ *vt* to cut or break into pieces; *Fig.* break (heart, etc.)

despedida /despe'ðiða/ *f*, dismissal, discharge; seeing off (a visitor, etc.); farewell, good-by

despedir /despe'ðir/ *vt irr* to throw out, emit, cast up; dismiss, discharge; see off (on a journey or after a visit); banish (from the mind); get rid of; —*vr* say good-by; leave (employment). See **pedir**

despedregar /despeðre'gar/ *vt* to clear of stones

despegadamente /despegaða'mente/ *adv* uninterestedly, unconcernedly, indifferently

despegado /despe'gaðo/ *a Inf.* indifferent, unconcerned, cold

despegar /despe'gar/ *vt* to unstick; unglue; separate, detach; —*vr* become estranged; come apart or unstuck; —*vi Aer.* take off. **sin d. los labios,** without saying a word

despegue /des'pege/ *m*, *Aer.* take-off

despeinar /despei'nar/ *vt* to disarrange the hair; undo the coiffure

despejado /despe'haðo/ *a* lively, sprightly; logical, clear-cut; cloudless; spacious, unobstructed, clear

despejar /despe'har/ *vt* to clear, free of obstacles; **d. el camino de,** to clear the way for; *Fig.* elucidate, solve; *Math.* find the value of; —*vr* smarten up, grow gay; amuse oneself; clear up (weather, sky, etc.); improve (a patient)

despejo /des'peho/ *m*, freeing of obstacles; smartness, gaiety; grace, elegance; perkiness; clearsightedness, intelligence

despellejar /despeʎe'har; despe'yehar/ *vt* to flay, skin; slander

despeluzar /despelu'θar; despelu'sar/ *vt* to disorder

the hair; cause the hair to stand on end; horrify; —*vr* stand on end (hair); be horrified or terrified

despeluznante /despeluθ'nante; despelus'nante/ *a* hair-raising, terrifying

despendedor /despende'ðor/ **(-ra)** *n* spendthrift, waster

despender /despen'der/ *vt* to spend; waste

despensa /des'pensa/ *f*, larder, pantry; store (of food); *Naut.* steward's room; stewardship

despensero /despen'sero/ **(-ra)** *n* steward; caterer; victualler; *Naut.* steward

despeñadero /despeɲa'ðero/ *m*, precipice, crag; dangerous undertaking, risk —*a* steep, precipitous

despeñar /despe'ɲar/ *vt* to precipitate, fling down from a height, hurl down; —*vr* fling oneself headlong; throw oneself into (vices, etc.)

despeño /des'peɲo/ *m*, precipitation; headlong fall; *Fig.* collapse, ruin

despepitar /despepi'tar/ *vt* to remove seeds or pips; —*vr* vociferate; act wildly; *Inf.* desire, long (for)

desperdiciador /desperðiθia'ðor; desperði'siaðor/ **(-ra)** *a* squandering, wasting —*n* squanderer

desperdiciar /desperðiθi'θiar; desperði'siar/ *vt* to squander; *Fig.* misspend, waste

desperdicio /desper'ðiθio; desper'ðisio/ *m*, waste; remains, leftovers (gen. *pl*)

desperdigar /desperði'gar/ *vt* to separate, sever; scatter

desperecerse /despere'θerse; despere'serse/ *vr irr* to crave, yearn (for). See **conocer**

desperezarse /despere'θarse; despere'sarse/ *vr* to stretch oneself

desperfecto /desper'fekto/ *m*, imperfection, flaw; slight deterioration

despernado /desper'naðo/ *a* weary, footsore

despertador /desperta'ðor/ **(-ra)** *a* awakening —*n* awakener. *m*, alarm clock; incentive, stimulus

despertar /desper'tar/ *vt irr* to awaken; bring to mind, recall; incite, stimulate; —*vi* waken; *Fig.* wake up, become more intelligent. See **acertar**

despiadado /despia'ðaðo/ *a* cruel, merciless

despicar /despi'kar/ *vt* to satisfy, content; —*vr* revenge oneself

despierto /des'pierto/ *a* wide-awake, clever

despilfarrado /despilfa'rraðo/ *a* ragged, shabby; wasteful; spendthrift

despilfarrar /despilfa'rrar/ *vt* to squander, waste

despilfarro /despil'farro/ *m*, slovenliness; waste, extravagance; mismanagement, maladministration

despintar /despin'tar/ *vt* to paint out; wash off the paint; efface, blot out; disfigure, deform; —*vi* be unlike or unworthy (of); —*vr* fade (colors); forget

despiojar /despio'har/ *vt* to remove lice, delouse; *Inf.* rescue from misery

despique /des'pike/ *m*, vengeance, revenge

despistar /despis'tar/ *vt* to throw off the scent; mislead

desplacer /despla'θer; despla'ser/ *vt irr* to displease. *m*, disgust, displeasure, sorrow. See **placer**

desplantar /desplan'tar/ **(se)** *vt* and *vr* to deviate from the vertical

desplazamiento /desplaθa'miento; desplasa'miento/ *m*, *Naut.* displacement

desplegadura /desplega'ðura/ *f*, unfolding

desplegar /desple'gar/ *vt irr* to unfold; spread open; *Fig.* reveal, disclose, explain; evince, display; *Mil.* deploy troops; —*vr* unfold, open (flowers, etc.); *Mil.* deploy. See **cegar**

despliegue /des'pliege/ *m*, unfolding; spreading out; evincing, demonstration; *Mil.* deployment

desplomar /desplo'mar/ *vt* to put out of the straight, cause to lean (walls, buildings); —*vr* lean, tilt (buildings); topple, fall down (walls, etc.); collapse (people); be ruined

desplome /des'plome/ *m*, collapse

desplomo /des'plomo/ *m*, tilt, cant, deviation from vertical

desplumar /desplu'mar/ *vt* to remove feathers, pluck; rob, despoil

despoblación /despoβla'θion; despoβla'sion/ *f*, depopulation. **d. forestal,** deforestation

despoblado /despo'βlaðo/ *m*, wilderness; deserted place

despoblar /despo'βlar/ *vt* to depopulate; despoil, rob; —*vr* become depopulated

despojador /despoha'ðor/ **(-ra)** *a* robbing, despoiling —*n* despoiler

despojar /despo'har/ *vt* to plunder, despoil; dispossess; —*vr* (*with de*) remove (garments, etc.); relinquish, give up

despojo /des'poho/ *m*, pillaging, spoliation; booty, plunder; butcher's offal; *pl* remains, leavings; debris, rubble; corpse

despolvorear /despolβore'ar/ *vt* to remove dust; *Fig.* shake off

desposado /despo'saðo/ *a* recently married; fettered; handcuffed. **los desposados,** the newlyweds

desposar /despo'sar/ *vt* to perform the marriage ceremony; —*vr* become betrothed; marry

desposeer /despose'er/ *vt* to dispossess; —*vr* renounce one's possessions. See **creer**

desposeimiento /desposei'miento/ *m*, dispossession

desposorio /despo'sorio/ *m*, betrothal, promise of marriage; (*gen. pl*) wedding, marriage

déspota /'despota/ *m*, despot, tyrant

despótico /des'potiko/ *a* tyrannical

despotismo /despo'tismo/ *m*, despotism

despotricarse /despotri'karse/ *vr* to rave (against), rail (against)

despreciable /despre'θiaβle; despre'siaβle/ *a* worthless, contemptible

despreciar /despre'θiar; despre'siar/ *vt* to scorn, despise; —*vr* despise oneself

despreciativo /despreθia'tiβo; despresia'tiβo/ *a* contemptuous, scornful

desprecio /des'preθio; des'presio/ *m*, contempt, scorn

desprender /despren'der/ *vt* to loosen, remove, unfix; give off (gases, etc.); —*vr* work loose, give way; deduce, infer; give away, deprive oneself (of)

desprendido /despren'diðo/ *a* disinterested; generous

desprendimiento /desprendi'miento/ *m*, loosening, removal, separation; emission; indifference, lack of interest; generosity; impartiality

despreocupación /despreokupa'θion; despreokupa'sion/ *f*, fair mindedness, impartiality; lack of interest

despreocupado /despreoku'paðo/ *a* unprejudiced, broadminded; indifferent, uninterested

despreocuparse /despreoku'parse/ *vr* to shake off prejudice; (*with de*) pay no attention to; set aside

desprestigiar /despresti'hiar/ *vt* to discredit; —*vr* lose prestige; lose caste

desprestigio /despres'tihio/ *m*, loss of prestige, discredit

desprevenido /despreβe'niðo/ *a* unprepared, improvident

desproporción /despropor'θion; despropor'sion/ *f*, disproportion

desproporcionado /desproporθio'naðo; desproporsio'naðo/ *a* disproportionate; out of proportion

despropósito /despro'posito/ *m*, nonsense, absurdity

desproveer /desproβe'er/ *vt irr* to deprive of necessities. See **creer**

despueble /des'pueβle/ *m*, depopulation

después /des'pues/ *adv* afterwards, after, next (of time and place) (e.g. *Vendrá d. de Pascua*, He will come after Easter. *Zaragoza viene d. de Madrid*, Saragossa comes after Madrid)

despuntar /despun'tar/ *vt* to blunt the point; *Naut.* double, sail round; —*vi* show green, sprout; appear (the dawn); grow clever; *Fig.* stand out, excel

desquiciamiento /deskiθia'miento; deskisia'miento/ *m*, unhinging; disconnecting; *Fig.* upsetting, throwing out of gear; downfall, fall from favor

desquiciar /deski'θiar; deski'siar/ *vt* to unhinge; disconnect; *Fig.* throw out of gear, upset; banish from favor; —*vr* become unhinged; *Fig.* be disordered; upset

desquitar /deski'tar/ **(se)** *vt* and *vr* to retrieve a loss; take revenge, retaliate

desquite /des'kite/ *m*, compensation; revenge

destacamento /destaka'mento/ *m*, *Mil.* detachment

destacar /desta'kar/ *vt Mil.* to detach; —*vr* excel; be prominent; be conspicuous; *Art.* stand out

destajador /destaha'ðor/ *m*, smith's hammer

destajar /desta'har/ *vt* to cut (cards); set forth conditions, stipulate, contract

destajista /desta'hista/ *mf* pieceworker; jobber (worker)

destajo /des'taho/ *m*, piecework; job. **a d.,** quickly and diligently. *Inf.* **hablar a d.,** to chatter, talk too much

destapar /desta'par/ *vt* to remove the cover or lid; reveal, uncover; —*vr* be uncovered; reveal oneself. **no destaparse,** to keep quiet, be mum

destartalado /destarta'laðo/ *a* tumble-down, rickety; poverty-stricken

destechado /deste'tʃaðo/ *a* roofless

destejar /deste'har/ *vt* to remove tiles or slates; leave unprotected

destejer /deste'her/ *vt* to unweave, unravel; *Fig.* undo, spoil

destello /des'teʎo; deste'yo/ *m*, gleam, sparkle, brilliance; flash, beam, ray; *Fig.* gleam (of talent)

destemplado /destem'plaðo/ *a* out of tune; inharmonious; intemperate; *Art.* inharmonious; *Inf.* out of sorts, indisposed

destemplanza /destem'planθa; destem'plansa/ *f*, inclemency, rigor (weather); intemperance, excess, abuse; *Inf.* indisposition; lack of moderation (actions, speech)

destemplar /destem'plar/ *vt* to disturb, upset, alter; *Mus.* put out of tune; put to confusion; —*vr* be unwell; *Fig.* go too far, behave badly; lose temper (metals)

destemple /des'temple/ *m*, *Mus.* being out of tune; *Med.* indisposition; uncertainty (weather); lack of temper (metals); disturbance, disorder; intemperance, excess, confusion

desternillarse de risa /desterni'ʎarse de 'rrisa; desterni'yarse de 'rrisa/ *vr* to shake with laughter

desterrado /deste'rraðo/ **(-da)** *a* exiled —*n* exile

desterrar /deste'rrar/ *vt irr* to exile; shake off the soil; *Fig.* discard, lay aside; extirpate (an error). See **recomendar**

destetar /deste'tar/ *vt* to wean

destete /des'tete/ *m*, weaning

destiempo, a /des'tiempo, a/ *adv* untimely, inopportunely

destierro /des'tierro/ *m*, banishment, exile; place of exile; remote place

destilación /destila'θion; destila'sion/ *f*, distillation

destilador /destila'ðor/ **(-ra)** *n* distiller. *m*, still

destilar /desti'lar/ *vt* to distill; filter; —*vi* to drip

destilatorio /destila'torio/ *a* distilling. *m*, distillery; still

destilería /destile'ria/ *f*, distillery

destinación /destina'θion; destina'sion/ *f*, destination

destinar /desti'nar/ *vt* to destine; appoint; assign

destino /des'tino/ *m*, fate, destiny; post, appointment; destination. **con d. a,** going to, bound for

destitución /destitu'θion; destitu'sion/ *f*, destitution; discharge, dismissal

destituir /destitu'ir/ *vt irr* (*with de*) to dismiss or discharge from (employment); deprive of. See **huir**

destorcer /destor'θer; destor'ser/ *vt irr* to untwist; straighten out; —*vr Naut.* drift. See **torcer**

destornillado /destorni'ʎaðo; destorni'yaðo/ *a* reckless; *Fig. Inf.* with a screw loose

destornillador /destorni'ʎaðor; destorni'yaðor/ *m*, screwdriver

destornillamiento /destorniʎa'miento; destorniya'miento/ *m*, unscrewing

destornillar /destorni'ʎar; destorni'yar/ *vt* to unscrew; —*vr* act rashly

destrenzar /destren'θar; destren'sar/ *vt* to unplait. **destrenzarse las cintas,** to unlace one's shoes

destreza /des'treθa; des'tresa/ *f*, dexterity; agility

destrón /des'tron/ *m*, blind person's guide

destronamiento /destrona'miento/ *m*, dethronement

destronar /destro'nar/ *vt* to dethrone; depose; oust

destroncamiento 100

destroncamiento /destronka'miento/ *m*, detruncation

destroncar /destron'kar/ *vt* to lop, detruncate (trees); dislocate, disjoint; mutilate; *Fig.* ruin, seriously harm; tire out; —*vr* be exhausted or tired

destrozar /destro'θar; destro'sar/ *vt* to destroy; break in pieces, shatter; *Mil.* wipe out, annihilate; squander, dissipate

destrozo /des'troθo; des'troso/ *m*, destruction, ruin; shattering; *Mil.* rout; dissipation, waste

destrozón /destro'θon; destro'son/ *a* hard on wearing apparel, shoes, etc.

destrucción /destruk'θion; destruk'sion/ *f*, destruction; ruin, irreparable loss

destructible /destruk'tiβle/ *a* destructible

destructivo /destruk'tiβo/ *a* destructive

destructor /destruk'tor/ (**-ra**) *a* destructive —*n* destroyer. *m*, *Nav.* destroyer

destruible /destruiβle/ *a* destructible

des'truir /destruir/ *vt irr* to destroy, ruin, annihilate; frustrate, blast, disappoint; deprive of means of subsistence; squander, waste; —*vr Math.* cancel. See **huir**

desuello /desue'ʎo; desue'yo/ *m*, flaying, skinning; forwardness, impertinence; extortion, fleecing. *Fig. Inf.* **¡Es un d.!** It's highway robbery!

desu'nión /desu'nion/ *f*, disunion, separation; *Fig.* discord, disharmony

desunir /desu'nir/ *vt* to disunite, separate; *Fig.* cause discord or disharmony

desusarse /desu'sarse/ *vr* to fall into disuse, become obsolete

desuso /de'suso/ *m*, disuse

desvaído /desβa'iðo/ *a* gaunt, lanky; pale, faded, dull (of colors)

desvainar /desβai'nar/ *vt* to shell (peas, beans)

desvalido /des'βaliðo/ *a* unprotected, helpless

desvalijar /desβali'har/ *vt* to rifle (a suitcase, etc.); swindle

desvalimiento /desβali'miento/ *m*, defenselessness, lack of protection; lack of favor; desertion, abandonment

desvalorización /desβaloriθa'θion; desβalorisa'sion/ *f*, devaluation

desván /des'βan/ *m*, garret

desvanecer /desβane'θer; desβane'ser/ *vt irr* to cause to disappear; disintegrate; make vain; remove; —*vr* evaporate; faint, swoon; grow vain or conceited. See **conocer**

desvanecimiento /desβaneθi'miento; desβanesi'miento/ *m*, faintness, loss of consciousness; vanity, conceit

desvarar /desβa'rar/ *vt* to slip, slide; *Naut.* refloat

desvariar /desβa'riar/ *vi* to be delirious; rave, talk wildly

desvarío /desβa'rio/ *m*, foolish action, absurdity; delirium; monstrosity; whim, caprice

desvedar /desβe'ðar/ *vt* to raise a ban or prohibition

desvelar /desβe'lar/ *vt* to keep awake; —*vr* be sleepless; (*with por*) take great care over

desvelo /des'βelo/ *m*, sleeplessness, vigil; care, attention, vigilance; anxiety. **con d.**, watchfully

desvencijar /desβenθi'har; desβensi'har/ *vt* to loosen, disconnect, disjoint; —*vr* work loose, become disjointed

desventaja /desβen'taha/ *f*, disadvantage. **estar en d.**, to be at a disadvantage

desventajoso /desβenta'hoso/ *a* disadvantageous

desventura /desβen'tura/ *f*, misfortune

desventurado /desβentu'raðo/ *a* unfortunate; timid, faint-hearted; miserly

desvergonzado /desβergon'θaðo; desβergonsaðo/ *a* shameless, brazen, impudent

desvergonzarse /desβergon'θarse; desβergon'sarse/ *vr irr* to be brazen, be impudent. See **avergonzar**

desvergüenza /desβer'guenθa; desβer'guensa/ *f*, insolence; shamelessness

desvestir /desβes'tir/ (**se**) *vt* and *vr irr* to undress. See **pedir**

desviación /desβia'θion; desβia'sion/ *f*, deviation, deflection

desviadero /desβia'ðero/ *m*, diversion; *Rail.* siding

desviar /des'βiar/ *vt* to divert, deflect; dissuade

desvío /des'βio/ *m*, deviation; indifference, coldness; repugnance

desvirgar /desβir'gar/ *vt* to deflower

desvirtuar /desβir'tuar/ *vt* to decrease in strength or merit

desvivirse /desβi'βirse/ *vr* (*with por*) to adore, love dearly; yearn for, be dying to; do one's best to please, (e.g. *Juan se desvive por servirme,* John does his best to help me)

detallar /deta'ʎar; deta'yar/ *vt* to tell in detail; relate

detalle /de'taʎe; de'taye/ *m*, detailed account; detail, particular

detallismo /deta'ʎismo; deta'yismo/ *m*, meticulous attention to details

detective /de'tektiβe/ *mf* detective

detector /detek'tor/ *m*, detector; *Radio.* catwhisker

detención /deten'θion; deten'sion/ *f*, stop, halt; delay; prolixity; arrest, detention. **con d.**, carefully, meticulously

detener /dete'ner/ *vt irr* to detain, stop; arrest; retain, keep; —*vr* go slowly; tarry; halt, stop; (*with en*) pause over, stop at. See **tener**

detenido /dete'niðo/ *a* timid, irresolute; miserable, mean

deterioración /deteriora'θion; deteriora'sion/ *f*, deterioration

deteriorar /deterio'rar/ (**se**) *vt* and *vr* to deteriorate

determinación /determina'θion; determina'sion/ *f*, determination; daring; decision

determinado /determi'naðo/ *a* resolute, determined

determinar /determi'nar/ *vt* to determine, limit; discern, distinguish; specify, appoint; decide, resolve; *Law.* define, judge; —*vr* make up one's mind

determinativo /determina'tiβo/ *a* determining

determinismo /determi'nismo/ *m*, determinism

determinista /determi'nista/ *mf* determinist —*a* deterministic

detersorio /deter'sorio/ *a* and *m*, detergent

detestable /detes'taβle/ *a* detestable

detestación /detesta'θion; detesta'sion/ *f*, detestation

detestar /detes'tar/ *vt* to abominate, detest

detonación /detona'θion; detona'sion/ *f*, detonation

detonador /detona'ðor/ *m*, detonator

detonar /deto'nar/ *vi* to detonate

detracción /detrak'θion; detrak'sion/ *f*, detraction

detractor /detrak'tor/ (**-ra**) *a* slandering *n* detractor, slanderer

detraer /detra'er/ *vt irr* to detract, take away; separate; slander. See **traer**

detrás /de'tras/ *adv* behind, after (place). **por d.**, in the rear; *Fig.* behind one's back

detrimento /detri'mento/ *m*, detriment; moral harm. **en d. de**, to the detriment of

deuda /'deuða/ *f*, debt; fault, offense; sin. **d. exterior**, foreign debt. **estar en d. con**, to be indebted to. **Perdónanos nuestras deudas**, Forgive us our trespasses

deudo /'deuðo/ *m*, relative, kinsman; kinship, relationship

deudor /deu'ðor/ (**-ra**) *a* indebted —*n* debtor. **d. hipotecario**, mortgagor

devanadera /deβana'ðera/ *f*, bobbin, reel, spool; winder (machine)

devanador /deβana'ðor/ (**-ra**) *n* winder (person). *m*, spool, bobbin

devanar /deβa'nar/ *vt* to reel, wind. *Inf.* **devanarse los sesos**, to rack one's brains

devanear /deβane'ar/ *vi* to rave, talk nonsense

devaneo /deβa'neo/ *m*, delirium; foolishness, nonsense; dissipation; love affair

devastación /deβasta'θion; deβasta'sion/ *f*, devastation

devastar /deβas'tar/ *vt* to devastate, lay waste; *Fig.* destroy, ruin

develador /deβela'ðor/ *m*, betrayer

devengar /deβeŋ'gar/ *vt* to have a right to, earn (salary, interest, etc.)

devoción /deβo'θion; deβo'sion/ *f*, piety; affection, love; pious custom; prayer

devocionario /deβoθio'nario; deβosio'nario/ *m,* prayer book

devolución /deβolu'θion; deβolu'sion/ *f,* restitution, return; its devolution

devolutivo /deβolu'tiβo/ *a Law.* returnable

devolver /deβol'βer/ *vt irr* to restore to original state; return, give back; repay. See **resolver**

devorador /deβora'ðor/ **(-ra)** *a* devouring —*n* devourer

devorar /deβo'rar/ *vt* to devour; destroy, consume

devoto /de'βoto/ **(-ta)** *a* devout, pious; devoted, fond —*n* devotee. *m,* object of devotion

día /dia/ *m,* day; daylight; *pl* name or saint's day; birthday (e.g. *Hoy son los días de María,* This is Mary's saint's day (or birthday)). **d. de Año Nuevo,** New Year's Day. **d. de asueto,** day off. **d. de ayuno** or **de vigilia,** fast day. **d. del cura,** *humorous* wedding day. **d. del juicio,** Day of Judgment. **d. de los difuntos,** All Souls' Day. **d. de recibo,** at home day. **d. de Reyes,** Epiphany (when Spanish children receive their Christmas presents). **d. de trabajo** or **d. laborable,** working day. **d. por medio,** every other day. **días caniculares,** dog days. **d. por d.,** day by day. **al d.,** up to date; per day. **al otro d.,** next day. **¡Buenos días!** Good morning! Good day! **de d.,** by day. **de d. en d.,** from day to day. **de un d. a otro,** any time now, very soon. **el d. de mañana,** tomorrow, the near future. **un d. sí y otro no,** every other day. **vivir al d.,** to live up to one's income

diabético /dia'βetiko/ *a* diabetic

diablillo /dia'βliʎo; dia'βliyo/ *m, dim* devilkin, imp; *Inf.* madcap

diablo /'diaβlo/ *m,* devil; Satan; *Fig.* fiend. *Inf.* **d. cojuelo,** mischievous devil; *Fig. Inf.* imp. *Inf.* **Anda el d. suelto,** The Devil's abroad, there's trouble. *Inf.* **tener el d. en el cuerpo,** to be as clever as the Devil; be mischievous

diablura /dia'βlura/ *f,* mischief, prank; devilry

diabólico /dia'βoliko/ *a* diabolical, devilish; *Inf.* fiendish, iniquitous

diaconisa /dia'konisa/ *f,* deaconess

diácono /'diakono/ *m,* deacon

diadema /dia'ðema/ *f,* diadem; crown; tiara

diafanidad /diafani'ðað/ *f,* transparency

diáfano /'diafano/ *a* transparent, diaphanous

diafragma /dia'fragma/ *m, Anat. Mech.* diaphragm; sound-box (of a phonograph)

diagnosticar /diagnosti'kar/ *vt Med.* to diagnose

diagnóstico /diag'nostiko/ *a* diagnostic. *m,* diagnosis. **d. precoz,** early diagnosis

diagonal /diago'nal/ *a* diagonal; oblique

diagrama /dia'grama/ *m,* diagram

diagramación /diagrama'θion; diagrama'sion/ *f,* layout (of a publication)

dialectal /dialek'tal/ *a* dialect

dialéctica /dia'lektika/ *f,* dialectic

dialéctico /dia'lektiko/ *a* dialectic. *m,* logician

dialecto /dia'lekto/ *m,* dialect

dialogar /dialo'gar/ *vi* to hold dialogue, converse; —*vt* write dialogue

diálogo /'dialogo/ *m,* dialogue

diamante /dia'mante/ *m,* diamond; miner's lamp; glass-cutting diamond. **d. bruto,** rough diamond

diamantífero /diaman'tifero/ *a* diamond-bearing

diamantino /diaman'tino/ *a* diamantine; *Poet.* adamant

diamantista /diaman'tista/ *mf* diamond-cutter; diamond merchant

diametral /diame'tral/ *a* diametrical

diámetro /'diametro/ *m,* diameter

diana /'diana/ *f, Mil.* reveille; bull's-eye (of a target); the moon

¡diantre! /'diantre/ *interj Inf.* the deuce!

diapasón /diapa'son/ *m, Mus.* tuning fork; diapason; neck (of violins, etc.). **d. normal,** tuning fork. **d. vocal,** pitch-pipe

diapositiva /diaposi'tiβa/ *f, Photo.* diapositive; (lantern) slide

diario /'diario/ *a* daily. *m,* diary; daily paper; daily expenses. **d. de navegación,** ship's log. **d. de viaje,** travel diary, trip journal

diarista /dia'rista/ *mf* journalist, diarist

diarrea /dia'rrea/ *f,* diarrhea

diatónico /dia'toniko/ *a Mus.* diatonic

diatriba /dia'triβa/ *f,* diatribe

diávolo /'diaβolo/ *m,* diabolo (game)

dibujante /diβu'hante/ *m,* sketcher; draftsman; designer

dibujar /diβu'har/ *vt Art.* to draw; describe, depict; —*vr* appear, be revealed; be outlined, stand out

dibujo /di'βuho/ *m,* drawing; sketch, design, pattern; depiction, description. **d. a la pluma,** pen-and-ink drawing. **d. a pulso,** freehand drawing. **d. del natural,** drawing from life

dicción /dik'θion; dik'sion/ *f,* word; diction, language, style

diccionario /dikθio'nario; diksio'nario/ *m,* dictionary

díceres /'diθeres; 'diseres/ *m pl West. Hem.* news

dicha /'ditʃa/ *f,* happiness; good fortune. **por d.,** by chance; fortunately

dicharacho /ditʃa'ratʃo/ *m, Inf.* vulgar expression, slangy expression

dicho /'ditʃo/ *m,* saying, phrase, expression; witty remark; *Law.* declaration; *Inf.* insult —*a* said, aforementioned —*past part* **decir,** "said." **D. y hecho,** No sooner said than done. **Del d. al hecho hay muy gran trecho,** There's many a slip 'twixt the cup and the lip. **Lo d. d.,** The agreement stands

dichoso /di'tʃoso/ *a* happy; lucky; *Inf.* blessed, wretched, darn

diciembre /di'θiembre; di'siembre/ *m,* December

dictado /dik'taðo/ *m,* title of honor; dictation; *pl* promptings (of heart, etc.). **escribir al d.,** to write to dictation

dictador /dikta'ðor/ *m,* dictator

dictadura /dikta'ðura/ *f,* dictatorship

dictáfono /dik'tafono/ *m,* dictaphone

dictamen /dik'tamen/ *m,* judgment, opinion

dictaminar /diktami'nar/ *vi* to give judgment or opinion

dictar /dik'tar/ *vt* to dictate; suggest, inspire. **dictar fallo,** to hand down a decision, render judgment

dictatorial, dictatorio /diktato'rial, dikta'torio/ *a* dictatorial

dicterio /dik'terio/ *m,* taunt, insult

didáctica /di'ðaktika/ *f,* didactics

didáctico /di'ðaktiko/ *a* didactic

diecinueve /dieθi'nueβe; diesi'nueβe/ *a and m,* nineteen

diecinueveavo /dieθinueβe'aβo; diesinueβe'aβo/ *a and m,* nineteenth

dieciochavo /dieθio'tʃaβo; diesio'tʃaβo/ *a and m,* eighteenth

dieciocheno /dieθio'tʃeno; diesio'tʃeno/ *a* See **décimoctavo**

dieciocho /die'θiotʃo; die'siotʃo/ *a and m,* eighteen

dieciséis /dieθi'seis; diesi'seis/ *a and m,* sixteen

dieciseisavo /dieθisei'saβo; diesisei'saβo/ *a and m,* sixteenth

dieciseiseno /dieθisei'seno; diesisei'seno/ *a* See **décimosexto**

diecisiete /dieθi'siete; diesi'siete/ *a and m,* seventeen

diecisieteavo /dieθisiete'aβo; diesisiete'aβo/ *a and m,* seventeenth

diente /diente/ *m,* tooth; tooth (of saw, etc.); tusk; cog (of wheel); prong (of fork); tongue (of a buckle). **d. de leche,** milk-tooth. *Bot.* **d. de león,** dandelion. **d. de perro,** *Sew.* feather-stitch. *Inf.* **dar d. con d.,** to chatter (teeth). *Fig. Inf.* **enseñar** (or **mostrar**) **los dientes,** to show one's teeth; threaten. *Inf.* **estar a d.,** to be famished. **hablar entre dientes,** to mutter; fume, grumble. *Inf.* **tener buen d.,** to have a good appetite. **traer a uno entre dientes,** to loathe someone; speak scandal of

Diepa /'diepa/ Dieppe

diestra /'diestra/ *f,* right hand; protection

diestro /'diestro/ *a* right (hand); skillful, dextrous; shrewd; astute, cunning; favorable, happy. *m,* expert fencer; bullfighter; halter; bridle

dieta /'dieta/ *f, Med.* diet; *Inf.* fast, abstinence; legislative assembly; travel allowance (gen. *pl*); day's journey of ten leagues; daily fee (gen. *pl*)

dietario /die'tario/ *m,* household accounts' book

dietética /die'tetika/ f, dietetics
dietético /die'tetiko/ a dietetic
dietista /die'tista/ mf dietician
diez /dieθ; dies/ a ten; tenth. m, ten; decade of rosary
diezmar /dieθ'mar; dies'mar/ vt to tithe; decimate; punish every tenth person
diezmero /dieθ'mero; dies'mero/ **(-ra)** n tax-gatherer
diezmesino /dieθme'sino; diesme'sino/ a ten months old
diezmilésimo /dieθmi'lesimo; diesmi'lesimo/ a ten-thousandth
diezmo /'dieθmo; 'diesmo/ m, ten per cent tax; tithe
difamación /difama'θion; difama'sion/ f, defamation, libel
difamador /difama'ðor/ **(-ra)** a libeling —n libeler
difamar /difa'mar/ vt to libel; denigrate
difamatorio /difama'torio/ a libelous, defamatory
diferencia /dife'renθia; dife'rensia/ f, unlikeness, dissimilarity; Math. difference; dissension, disagreement. **a d. de,** unlike; in contrast to
diferenciación /diferenθia'θion; diferensia'sion/ f, differentiation. **d. del trabajo,** division of labor
diferencial /diferen'θial; diferen'sial/ a differential
diferenciar /diferen'θiar; diferen'siar/ vt to differentiate; change the function (of); —vi dissent, disagree; —vr be different, differ; distinguish oneself
diferente /dife'rente/ a different, various
diferir /dife'rir/ vt irr to delay, retard; postpone; suspend, interrupt; —vi be different. See **discernir**
difícil /di'fiθil; di'fisil/ a difficult
dificultad /difikul'taδ/ f, difficulty; impediment, obstacle; objection
dificultar /difikul'tar/ vt to raise difficulties; put obstacles in the way; —vi think difficult (of achievements)
dificultoso /difikul'toso/ a difficult; Inf. ugly (face, figure, etc.)
difidencia /difi'ðenθia; difi'ðensia/ f, mistrust; lack of faith, doubt
difidente /difi'ðente/ a mistrustful
difracción /difrak'θion; difrak'sion/ f, diffraction
difractar /difrak'tar/ vt to diffract
difteria /dif'teria/ f, diphtheria
difundir /difun'dir/ vt to diffuse (fluids); spread, publish, divulge; Radio. broadcast
difunto /di'funto/ **(-ta)** a and n deceased. m, corpse
difusión /difu'sion/ f, diffusion; prolixity; Radio. broadcasting
difusivo /difu'siβo/ a diffusive
difuso /di'fuso/ a widespread, diffuse; prolix, wordy
digerible /dihe'riβle/ a digestible
digerir /dihe'rir/ vt irr to digest; bear patiently; consider carefully; Chem. digest. See **sentir**
digestible /dihes'tiβle/ a easily digested
digestivo /dihes'tiβo/ a digestive
digesto /di'hesto/ m, Law. digest
digitación /dihita'θion; dihita'sion/ f, Mus. fingering
digital /dihi'tal/ a digital. f, Bot. foxglove, digitalis
dígito /'dihito/ a digital. m, (Astron. Math.) digit
dignación /digna'θion; digna'sion/ f, condescension
dignarse /dig'narse/ vr to deign, condescend
dignatario /digna'tario/ m, dignitary
dignidad /digni'ðaδ/ f, dignity, stateliness; serenity, loftiness; high office or rank; high repute, honor; Eccl. dignitary
dignificar /dignifi'kar/ vt to dignify
digno /'digno/ a worthy, deserving; upright, honorable; fitting, suitable, appropriate
digresión /digre'sion/ f, digression
dije /'dihe/ m, charm; trinket, any small piece of jewelry; Inf. person of excellent qualities, jewel
dilacerar /dilaθe'rar; dilase'rar/ vt to lacerate, tear flesh; Fig. discredit
dilación /dila'θion; dila'sion/ f, delay
dilapidación /dilapiða'θion; dilapi'ðasion/ f, waste, dissipation, squandering
dilapidar /dilapi'ðar/ vt to waste, squander
dilatación /dilata'θion; dilata'sion/ f, expansion; enlargement, widening; prolongation; Surg. dilatation; respite (in trouble)

dilatador /dilata'ðor/ a dilating. m, Surg. dilater
dilatar /dila'tar/ vt to dilate, enlarge; expand; delay, postpone; spread, publish abroad; prolong; —vr expand; be prolix, spread oneself
dilatorio /dila'torio/ a procrastinating, dilatory
dilección /dilek'θion; dilek'sion/ f, affection, love
dilema /di'lema/ m, dilemma
diletantismo /diletan'tismo/ m, dilettantism
diligencia /dili'henθia; dili'hensia/ f, care, conscientiousness, industry; haste, briskness; diligence (coach); Inf. business, occupation. **hacer sus diligencias,** to try one's best
diligenciar /dilihen'θiar; dilihen'siar/ vt to set on foot, put into motion
diligente /dili'hente/ a diligent, conscientious, industrious; speedy, prompt
dilucidación /diluθiða'θion; dilusiða'sion/ f, elucidation, clarification
dilucidar /diluθi'ðar; dilusi'ðar/ vt to elucidate, clarify
dilución /dilu'θion; dilu'sion/ f, dilution
diluir /di'luir/ vt irr to dilute. See **huir**
diluviano /dilu'βiano/ a diluvian
diluviar /dilu'βiar/ vi to teem with rain
diluvio /di'luβio/ m, flood, inundation; Inf. very heavy rain, deluge; overabundance
dimanación /dimana'θion; dimana'sion/ f, emanation, source
dimanar /dima'nar/ vi (with de) to rise in (rivers); proceed from, originate in
dimensión /dimen'sion/ f, dimension; size, extent
dimes y diretes /'dimes i di'retes/ m pl, Inf. backchat
diminutivo /diminu'tiβo/ a diminutive; diminishing; Gram. diminutive
diminuto /dimi'nuto/ a defective, incomplete; minute, very small
dimisión /dimi'sion/ f, resignation (of office, etc.)
dimisorias /dimi'sorias/ f pl, Eccl. letter dimissory. Inf. **dar d. a uno,** to give a person his marching orders, dismiss
dimitente /dimi'tente/ a resigning; retiring. mf resigner (of a post)
dimitir /dimi'tir/ vt to resign (office, post, etc.)
Dinamarca /dina'marka/ Denmark
dinamarqués /dinamar'kes/ **(-esa)** a Danish —n Dane
dinámica /di'namika/ f, dynamics
dinámico /di'namiko/ a dynamic
dinamita /dina'mita/ f, dynamite
dinamo /'dinamo/ f, dynamo
dinasta /di'nasta/ mf dynast
dinastía /dinas'tia/ f, dynasty
dinástico /di'nastiko/ a dynastic
dineral /dine'ral/ m, large amount of money, fortune
dinero /di'nero/ m, money; Peruvian coin; wealth, fortune; currency. **d. contante, d. junto,** ready cash, **Poderoso caballero es Don D.,** Money talks
dinosauro /dino'sauro/ m, dinosaur
dintel /'dintel/ m, lintel
diocesano /dioθe'sano; diose'sano/ a diocesan
diocesis /di'oθesis; 'diosesis/ f, diocese
Dios /dios/ m, God; deity. **¡D. le guarde!** God keep you! **¡D. lo quiera!** God grant it! **D. mediante,** God willing (D.V.). **¡D. mío!** Good gracious! **De menos nos hizo D.,** Nothing is impossible, Never say die. Inf. **haber (or armarse) la de D. es Cristo,** to be the deuce of a row. **¡No lo quiera D.!** God forbid! **¡Plegue a D.!** Please God! **¡Por D.!** For goodness sake! Heavens! **¡Válgame D.!** Bless me! **¡Vaya Vd. con D.!** Goodbye! Off with you! Depart! **¡Vive D.!** By God!
diosa /'diosa/ f, goddess
diploma /di'ploma/ m, license, bull; diploma. **d. de suficiencia,** general diploma
diplomacia /diplo'maθia; diplo'masia/ f, diplomacy; tactfulness; Inf. astuteness
diplomático /diplo'matiko/ a diplomatic; tactful; Inf. astute. m, diplomat. **cuerpo d.,** diplomatic corps
dipsomanía /dipsoma'nia/ f, dipsomania
dipsómano /dip'somano/ **(-na)** n dipsomaniac

diptongo /dip'toŋgo/ m, diphthong

diputación /diputa'θion; diputa'sion/ f, deputation; mission

diputado /dipu'taðo/ **(-da)** n deputy, delegate. **d. a Cortes,** member of the Spanish Parliament, congressman

diputar /dipu'tar/ vt to appoint, depute; delegate; empower

dique /'dike/ m, dike; dam; dry dock; *Fig.* bulwark, check; **d. flotante,** floating dock

dirección /direk'θion; direk'sion/ f, direction; management, control, guidance; directorate; instruction; information; order, wish, command; editorial board; directorship, managership; (postal) address; managerial office. **d. cablegráfica,** cable address. **d. particular,** home address

directiva /direk'tiβa/ f, board, governing body

directivo /direk'tiβo/ a directive, control, ling, guiding, managing

directo /di'rekto/ a direct; straight

director /direk'tor/ **(-ra)** a directing, controlling —n director; manager; principal, head (schools, etc.); editor. **d. del ceremonial,** chief of protocol. **d. de escena,** stagemanager. **d. espiritual,** *Eccl.* father confessor. **d. gerente,** managing director

directorio /direk'torio/ a directory, advising. m, directory; directorate, board of directors

dirigible /diri'hiβle/ m, airship

dirigir /diri'hir/ vt to direct; regulate; govern; supervise; guide; *Mus.* conduct; address (an envelope, etc.); keep (a shop, etc.); edit; put (a question); point (a gun); cast (a glance); —vr go; wend one's way. **d. la palabra (a),** to speak to, address. **d. la vista a,** to look towards, look in the direction of, turn towards, turn in the direction of. **dirigirse a,** to go towards; make one's way to

dirimir /diri'mir/ vt to annul, make void; break, dissolve; settle (disputes, etc.)

discernidor /disθerni'ðor; disserni'ðor/ **(-ra)** n discerner —a discerning

discernimiento /disθerni'miento; disserni'miento/ m, discernment; judgment; discrimination

discernir /disθer'nir; disser'nir/ vt irr to discern, distinguish —*Pres. Indic.* **discierno, disciernes, discierne, discernimos, discernís, disciernen.** *Pres. Subjunc.* **discierna, disciernas, discierna, discernamos, discernáis, disciernan**

disciplina /disθi'plina; dissi'plina/ f, discipline; system, philosophy, education; submission, obedience; subject (arts or science); pl scourge

disciplinante /disθipli'nante; dissipli'nante/ a disciplinary. m, scourge

disciplinar /disθipli'nar; dissipli'nar/ vt to train; educate; scourge, beat; discipline; —vr scourge oneself

disciplinario /disθipli'nario; dissipli'nario/ a disciplinary

discipulado /disθipu'laðo; dissipu'laðo/ m, pupilship, studentship; education, teaching; discipleship; body of pupils (of a school, etc.)

discípulo /dis'θipulo; dis'sipulo/ **(-la)** n pupil, student; disciple, follower

disco /'disko/ m, discus; disk; phonograph record; *Astron.* disk. **d. compacto,** compact disc. **d. de señales,** railway signal. **d. giratorio,** turntable (of a phonograph)

discóbolo /dis'koβolo/ m, discus thrower

díscolo /'diskolo/ a willful, unmanageable

disconformidad /diskonformi'ðað/ f, disagreement; disconformity

discontinuo /diskon'tinuo/ a intermittent, discontinuous

discordancia /diskor'ðanθia; diskor'ðansia/ f, discord, disagreement

discordar /diskor'ðar/ vi to be discordant; disagree; *Mus.* be out of tune

discorde /dis'korðe/ a discordant; *Mus.* dissonant

discordia /dis'korðia/ f, discord, disagreement

discreción /diskre'θion; diskre'sion/ f, discretion; circumspection; prudence; good sense; shrewdness; pithy or clever saying. **a d.,** at discretion; at will; voluntarily. *Mil.* **darse (or entregarse) a d.,** to surrender unconditionally

discrecional /diskreθio'nal; diskresio'nal/ a optional, voluntary

discrepancia /diskre'panθia; diskre'pansia/ f, discrepancy; disagreement

discrepar /diskre'par/ vi to be discrepant; differ; disagree

discreto /dis'kreto/ a discreet; ingenious, witty

disculpa /dis'kulpa/ f, excuse

disculpabilidad /diskulpaβili'ðað/ f, pardonableness

disculpable /diskul'paβle/ a excusable

disculpar /diskul'par/ vt to excuse; forgive, pardon; —vr apologize; excuse oneself

discurrir /disku'rrir/ vi to wander, roam; flow, run (rivers, etc.); (with en) consider, think about; (with sobre) discourse on; —vt invent; conjecture

discursivo /diskur'siβo/ a discursive; thoughtful, reflective

discurso /dis'kurso/ m, reasoning power; oration, discourse; consideration, reflection; speech, conversation; dissertation. **d. aceptatorio,** acceptance speech

discusión /disku'sion/ f, discussion

discutible /disku'tiβle/ a debatable; disputable

discutir /disku'tir/ vt to discuss, debate, consider

disecar /dise'kar/ vt *Anat.* to dissect; stuff animals; mount plants

disección /disek'θion; disek'sion/ f, dissection

disector /disek'tor/ m, dissector, anatomist

diseminación /disemina'θion; disemina'sion/ f, dissemination

diseminar /disemi'nar/ vt to disseminate; spread

disensión /disen'sion/ f, dissension

disentería /disente'ria/ f, dysentery

disentimiento /disenti'miento/ m, dissent

disentir /disen'tir/ vi irr to dissent; disagree. See **sentir**

diseñador /diseɲa'ðor/ m, delineator, drawer

diseñar /dise'ɲar/ vt to outline, sketch

diseño /di'seɲo/ m, outline, sketch; plan; description

disertación /diserta'θion; diserta'sion/ f, dissertation

disertar /diser'tar/ vi (with sobre) to discourse on, discuss, treat of

diserto /di'serto/ a eloquent

disfavor /disfa'βor/ m, disfavor, discourtesy, slight

disforme /dis'forme/ a deformed; ugly; enormous

disfraz /dis'fraθ; dis'fras/ m, disguise; mask; fancy dress; pretense

disfrazar /disfra'θar; disfra'sar/ vt to disguise; dissemble, misrepresent; —vr disguise oneself; wear fancy dress

disfrutar /disfru'tar/ vt to enjoy (health, comfort, friendship, etc.); reap the benefit of; —vi take pleasure in, enjoy

disfrute /dis'frute/ m, enjoyment, use, benefit

disgregación /disgrega'θion; disgrega'sion/ f, separation, disjunction

disgregar /disgre'gar/ vt to separate, disjoin

disgustado /disgus'taðo/ a annoyed; discontented, dissatisfied; melancholy, depressed

disgustar /disgus'tar/ vt to displease, dissatisfy; annoy; *Fig.* depress; —vr quarrel, fall out. **Me disgusta la idea de marcharme,** I don't like the idea of going away

disgusto /dis'gusto/ m, displeasure, dissatisfaction; discontent; annoyance; affliction, sorrow, trouble; quarrel; boredom; repugnance

disidente /disi'ðente/ a dissenting. mf dissenter, nonconformist

disidir /disi'ðir/ vi to dissent

disímil /di'simil/ a dissimilar, different, unlike

disimulación /disimula'θion; disimula'sion/ f, dissimulation, pretense

disimulado /disimu'laðo/ a feigned, pretended

disimular /disimu'lar/ vt to dissemble; pretend, feign; put up with, tolerate; misrepresent, misinterpret

disimulo /di'simulo/ m, pretense, dissimulation; tolerance, patience

disipación /disipa'θion; disipa'sion/ f, dispersion; dissipation, frivolity; immorality

disipado /disi'paðo/ a spendthrift; dissipated, frivolous

disipar /disi'par/ *vt* to disperse; squander; —*vr* evaporate; vanish, fade, disappear

dislate /di'slate/ *m*, absurdity, nonsense

dislocación /disloka'θion; disloka'sion/ *f*, dislocation

dislocar /dislo'kar/ *vt* to dislocate; —*vr* dislocate; sprain

disminución /disminu'θion; disminu'sion/ *f*, diminution. **ir (una cosa) en d.**, to diminish, decrease; taper, grow to a point

disminuido físico /dismi'nuiðo 'fisiko/ *m*, physically impaired person, physically handicapped person

disminuir /dismi'nuir/ *vt* and *vi irr* to diminish, decrease. See **huir**

disociación /disoθia'θion; disosia'sion/ *f*, dissociation. **d. nuclear**, nuclear fission

disociar /diso'θiar; diso'siar/ *vt* to dissociate, separate; *Chem.* dissociate

disoluble /diso'luβle/ *a* dissoluble

disolución /disolu'θion; disolu'sion/ *f*, dissolution; immorality, laxity; disintegration; loosening, relaxation

disolutivo /disolu'tiβo/ *a* dissolvent, solvent

disoluto /diso'luto/ *a* dissolute, vicious

disolvente /disol'βente/ *m*, dissolvent, solvent

disolver /disol'βer/ *vt irr* to loosen, undo; *Chem.* dissolve; separate, disintegrate; annul. See **resolver**

disonancia /diso'nanθia; diso'nansia/ *f*, dissonance; disagreement; *Mus.* dissonance

disonante /diso'nante/ *a* dissonant; discordant, inharmonious

disonar /diso'nar/ *vi irr* to be inharmonious; disagree. See **sonar**

disono /di'sono/ *a* dissonant

dispar /dis'par/ *a* unequal; unlike, different

disparadero /dispara'ðero/ *m*, trigger of a firearm

disparador /dispara'ðor/ *m*, shooter, firer; trigger (of firearms); ratchet (of watch)

disparar /dispa'rar/ *vt* to shoot, fire; throw or discharge with violence; —*vr* run precipitately; rush (towards); bolt (horses); race (of a machine); explode, go off; *Inf.* go too far, misbehave

disparatado /dispara'taðo/ *a* foolish; absurd, unreasonable

disparatar /dispara'tar/ *vi* to act or speak foolishly

disparate /dispa'rate/ *m*, foolishness, nonsense

disparidad /dispari'ðað/ *f*, disparity, dissimilarity

disparo /dis'paro/ *m*, shooting; explosion; racing (of an engine); discharge; foolishness

dispendio /dis'pendio/ *m*, squandering, extravagance

dispendioso /dispen'dioso/ *a* costly, expensive

dispensa /dis'pensa/ *f*, dispensation; privilege

dispensable /dispen'saβle/ *a* dispensable; excusable

dispensación /dispensa'θion; dispensa'sion/ *f*, dispensation; exemption

dispensar /dispen'sar/ *vt* to grant, concede, distribute; exempt; excuse, forgive

dispensario /dispen'sario/ *m*, dispensary

dispepsia /dis'pepsia/ *f*, dyspepsia

dispéptico /dis'peptiko/ (**-ca**) *a* and *n* dyspeptic

dispersar /disper'sar/ *vt* to disperse, scatter, separate; *Mil.* rout

dispersión /disper'sion/ *f*, dispersion

disperso /dis'perso/ *a* dispersed, scattered; *Mil.* separated from regiment

displicencia /displi'θenθia; displi'sensia/ *f*, disagreeableness, coldness; hesitation, lack of enthusiasm

displicente /displi'θente; displi'sente/ *a* unpleasant, disagreeable; difficult, peevish

disponer /dispo'ner/ *vt irr* to arrange, dispose, direct, order; decide; prepare, get ready; —*vi* (*with de*) dispose of, make free with; possess; have at one's disposal; —*vr* prepare oneself to die; make one's will; get ready. See **poner**

disponible /dispo'niβle/ *a* disposable; available

disposición /disposi'θion; disposi'sion/ *f*, arrangement; order, instruction; decision; preparation; aptitude, talent; disposal; condition of health; temperament; grace of bearing; promptitude, competence; measure, step, preliminary; *Archit.* plan; proviso, stipulation; symmetry. **A la d. de Vd**, I (we, he, it, etc.) am at your disposal. **hallarse en d. de hacer**

una cosa, to be ready to do something. **última d.**, last will and testament

dispositivo /disposi'tiβo/ *a* directory, advisory

dispuesto /dis'puesto/ *a* ready, prepared; handsome, gallant; clever, wide-awake. **bien d.**, well-disposed; well, healthy. **mal d.**, ill-disposed; disinclined; out of sorts, indisposed

disputa /dis'puta/ *f*, dispute. **sin d.**, undoubtedly

disputar /dispu'tar/ *vt* to argue, debate; dispute, question; *Fig.* fight for

disquisición /diskisi'θion; diskisi'sion/ *f*, disquisition

distancia /dis'tanθia; dis'tansia/ *f*, distance; interval of time; difference, dissimilarity; unfriendliness, coolness

distanciar /distan'θiar; distan'siar/ *vt* to separate, place farther apart

distante /dis'tante/ *a* separated; distant; far off

distar /dis'tar/ *vi* to be distant (time and place); be different, unlike

distender /disten'der/ (**se**) *vt* and *vr Med.* to distend, swell

distinción /distin'θion; distin'sion/ *f*, distinction, differentiation; difference, individuality; privilege, honor; clarity, order; distinction (of bearing or mind). **a d. de**, unlike, different from

distinguible /distin'guiβle/ *a* distinguishable

distinguido /distin'guiðo/ *a* distinguished, illustrious

distinguir /distin'guir/ *vt* to distinguish, discern; differentiate; characterize; esteem, honor, respect; discriminate; see with difficulty; make out; —*vr* be different; excel, distinguish oneself

distintivo /distin'tiβo/ *a* distinguishing; distinctive. *m*, distinguishing mark

distinto /dis'tinto/ *a* different; distinct; clear

distracción /distrak'θion; distrak'sion/ *f*, distraction; abstraction, heedlessness, absentmindedness; pleasure, amusement; licentiousness

distraer /distra'er/ *vt irr* to lead astray; distract (attention); influence for bad; amuse —*vr* be absentminded; amuse oneself. See **traer**

distraído /distra'iðo/ *a* abstracted, absentminded; inattentive; licentious

distribución /distriβu'θion; distriβu'sion/ *f*, distribution; (gen. *pl*) share

distribuidor /distriβui'ðor/ (**-ra**) *a* distributing —*n* distributor

distribuir /distri'βuir/ *vt irr* to distribute; share out, divide. See **huir**

distributivo /distriβu'tiβo/ *a* distributive

distrito /dis'trito/ *m*, district

disturbio /dis'turβio/ *m*, disturbance

disuadir /disua'ðir/ *vt* to dissuade

disuasión /disua'sion/ *f*, dissuasion

disuasivo /disua'siβo/ *a* dissuasive

disyunción /disyun'θion; disyun'sion/ *f*, disjunction

ditirambo /diti'rambo/ *m*, dithyramb; excessive praise

diurético /diu'retiko/ *a* diuretic

diurno /'diurno/ *a* diurnal

diva /'diβa/ *f*, prima donna; woman singer

divagación /diβaga'θion; diβaga'sion/ *f*, wandering, roaming; digression

divagar /diβa'gar/ *vi* to wander, roam; digress

diván /di'βan/ *m*, divan (Turkish supreme council); divan, sofa; collection of Arabic, Persian or Turkish poems

divergencia /diβer'henθia; diβer'hensia/ *f*, divergence; disagreement

divergente /diβer'hente/ *a* divergent; conflicting, dissentient

divergir /diβer'hir/ *vi* to diverge; dissent

diversidad /diβersi'ðað/ *f*, diversity, unlikeness, difference; variety

diversificar /diβersifi'kar/ *vt* to differentiate; vary

diversión /diβer'sion/ *f*, pastime, amusement; *Mil.* diversion

diverso /di'βerso/ *a* diverse, unlike; *pl* various, many

divertido /diβer'tiðo/ *a* amusing, funny, entertaining

divertir /diβer'tir/ *vt irr* to lead astray, turn aside; entertain; *Mil.* create a diversion —*vr* amuse oneself. See **sentir**

dividendo /diβi'ðendo/ *m*, dividend. *Com.* **d. activo,** dividend

dividir /diβi'ðir/ *vt* to divide; distribute; stir up discord; —*vr* (*with* **de**) part company with, leave

divieso /di'βieso/ *m*, *Med.* boil

divinamente /diβina'mente/ *adv* divinely; excellently, admirably, perfectly

divinidad /diβini'ðað/ *f*, divinity, Godhead; person or thing of great beauty

divinizar /diβini'θar; diβini'sar/ *vt* to deify; sanctify; extol

divino /di'βino/ *a* divine; excellent, admirable, superb

divisa /di'βisa/ *f*, badge, emblem; *Herald.* motto

divisar /diβi'sar/ *vt* to glimpse, descry

divisibilidad /diβisiβili'ðað/ *f*, divisibility

divisible /diβi'siβle/ *a* divisible

división /diβi'sion/ *f*, division, partition; discord; (*Math. Mil.*) division; hyphen; apportionment; district, ward

divisor /diβi'sor/ **(-ra)** *a* dividing, separating. *m*, *Math.* divisor —*n* divider, separator

divisoria /diβi'soria/ *f*, dividing line

divisorio /diβi'sorio/ *a* dividing

divorciar /diβor'θiar; diβor'siar/ *vt* to divorce; separate; —*vr* be divorced, be separated

divorcio /di'βorθio; di'βorsio/ *m*, divorce

divulgación /diβulga'θion; diβulga'sion/ *f*, spreading, publication, propagation

divulgar /diβul'gar/ **(se)** *vt* and *vr* to spread abroad, publish

do /do/ *m*, *Mus.* doh, C. *Poet.* where

dobladillo /doβla'ðiʎo; doβla'ðiyo/ *m*, *Sew.* hem; turn-up (of a trouser)

doblado /do'βlaðo/ *a* stocky, thickset, sturdy; rocky, rough, uneven; dissembling. *m*, garret

dobladura /doβla'ðura/ *f*, fold, crease; crease mark

doblamiento /doβla'miento/ *m*, doubling; folding

doblar /do'βlar/ *vt* to double, multiply by two; fold, double; bend; persuade, induce; *Naut.* double, sail round; turn, walk round; —*vi Eccl.* ring the passing bell; *Theat.* double a role; —*vr* fold, double; bend; bow; stoop; allow oneself to be persuaded

doble /'doβle/ *a* double, twofold; duplicate; insincere, false; thick (cloth); *Bot.* double (flowers); hardy, robust. *m*, fold, crease; *Eccl.* passing-bell; Spanish dance step —*adv* double, twice. *Eccl.* **rito d.,** full rites

doblegar /doβle'gar/ *vt* to fold; bend; brandish; dissuade in favor of another proposition; —*vr* submit, give way, acquiesce

doblete /do'βlete/ *a* of medium thickness. *m*, imitation jewel

doblez /do'βleθ; do'βles/ *m*, fold, crease; fold mark. *mf*, double dealing, treachery

doblilla /do'βliʎa; do'βliya/ *f*, twenty-real coin

doblón /do'βlon/ *m*, doubloon

doce /'doθe; 'dose/ *a* twelve. *m*, twelve; twelfth (of the month). **las d.,** twelve o'clock

docena /do'θena; do'sena/ *f*, dozen. **la d. del fraile,** baker's dozen

docente /do'θente; do'sente/ *a* teaching

dócil /'doθil; 'dosil/ *a* docile; obedient; flexible, easily worked (metals, etc.)

docilidad /doθili'ðað; dosili'ðað/ *f*, docility; obedience; flexibility

docto /'dokto/ *a* learned, erudite

doctor /dok'tor/ **(-ra)** *n* doctor; physician; teacher. *f*, *Inf.* blue-stocking

doctorado /dokto'raðo/ *m*, doctorate

doctorarse /dokto'rarse/ *vr* to get one's doctorate

doctrina /dok'trina/ *f*, doctrine; instruction, teaching; theory, conception; *Eccl.* sermon

doctrinar /doktri'nar/ *vt* to teach, instruct

documentación /dokumenta'θion; dokumenta'sion/ *f*, documentation; collection of documents, papers

documental /dokumen'tal/ *a* documental. *m*, documentary film

documentar /dokumen'tar/ *vt* to document

Dodecaneso, el /doðeka'neso, el/ the Dodecanese

dogal /do'gal/ *m*, halter; noose; slipknot. *Fig.* **estar con el d. a la garganta,** to be in a fix

dogma /'dogma/ *m*, dogma

dogmático /dog'matiko/ *a* dogmatic

dogmatizar /dogmati'θar; dogmati'sar/ *vt* to teach heretical doctrines; dogmatize

dólar /'dolar/ *m*, dollar

dolencia /do'lenθia; do'lensia/ *f*, ailment; pain; ache

doler /do'ler/ *vi irr* to be in pain; be reluctant; —*vr* be sorry, regretful; grieve; sympathize, be compassionate; complain —*Pres. Indic.* **duelo, dueles, duele, duelen.** *Pres. Subjunc.* **duela, duelas, duela, duelan**

doliente /do'liente/ *a* suffering; ill; afflicted, sad. *mf* sufferer, ill person. *m*, chief mourner

dolo /'dolo/ *m*, fraud; deception; deceit; *Law.* premeditation

dolor /do'lor/ *m*, pain, ache; mental suffering. **d. sordo,** dull pain

dolorido /dolo'riðo/ *a* painful; afflicted, sad

doloroso /dolo'roso/ *a* sad, regrettable; mournful, sorrowful; pitiful; painful

doloso /do'loso/ *a* deceitful, fraudulent

domable /do'maβle/ *a* tamable; controllable

domador /doma'ðor/ **(-ra)** *n* subduer, controller; wild animal tamer; horsebreaker

domadura /doma'ðura/ *f*, taming, breaking in; controlling (emotions)

domar /do'mar/ *vt* to tame, break in; control, repress (emotions)

domesticable /domesti'kaβle/ *a* tamable; domesticable

domesticar /domesti'kar/ *vt* to tame; domesticate; —*vr* grow tame; become domesticated

domesticidad /domestiθi'ðað; domestisi'ðað/ *f*, domesticity

doméstico /do'mestiko/ **(-ca)** *a* domestic, domesticated; tame —*n* domestic worker

domiciliar /domiθi'liar; domisi'liar/ *vt* to domicile; —*vr* become domiciled, settle down

domiciliario /domiθi'liario; domisi'liario/ *a* domiciliary

domicilio /domi'θilio; domi'silio/ *m*, domicile; house

dominación /domina'θion; domina'sion/ *f*, domination; power, authority; command (of a military position, etc.); *Mil.* high ground; *pl* dominions, angels

dominador /domina'ðor/ *a* dominating; overbearing

dominante /domi'nante/ *a* dominating; overbearing, domineering; dominant. *f*, *Mus.* dominant

dominar /domi'nar/ *vt* to dominate; repress, subdue; *Fig.* master (branch of knowledge); —*vi* stand out; —*vr* control oneself

dómine /'domine/ *m*, *Inf.* teacher; pedant, know-all

domingo /do'miŋgo/ *m*, Sunday. **d. de Cuasimodo,** Low Sunday. **d. de Pentecostés,** Whitsuntide Sunday. **d. de Ramos,** Palm Sunday. **d. de Resurrección,** Easter Sunday

dominguero /domiŋ'guero/ *a Inf.* Sunday; special, excursion (trains)

dominicano /domini'kano/ **(-na)** *a* and *n* Dominican; native of Santo Domingo

dominio /do'minio/ *m*, authority, power; rule, sovereignty; dominion (country); domain

dominó /domi'no/ *m*, domino; game of dominoes

don /don/ *m*, gift; quality, characteristic; talent. **d. de gentes,** the human touch; charm

don /don/ *m*, title of respect equivalent to English Mr. or Esquire. Used only before given name and *not* before a family name, e.g. don *Juan Martínez, or don Juan*

donación /dona'θion; dona'sion/ *f*, donation, gift, grant

donador /dona'ðor/ **(-ra)** *a* donating —*n* donor

donaire /do'naire/ *m*, discretion; wit; witticism; gracefulness, elegance

donar /do'nar/ *vt* to bestow, give; transfer; grant

donatario /dona'tario/ *m*, recipient, grantee

donativo /dona'tiβo/ *m*, gift, present, donation

doncel /don'θel; don'sel/ *m*, squire, youth not yet armed; knight; male virgin; king's page

doncella /don'θeʎa; don'seya/ *f,* virgin, maid; maid-servant; lady's maid

doncellez /donθe'ʎeθ; donse'yes/ *f,* virginity; maid-enhood

donde /'donde/ *adv* where, wherein. Sometimes used as relative pronoun "in which" (e.g. *La casa d. estaba,* The house in which I was) —*interr* ¿**dónde?** ¿**A dónde va Vd.?** Where are you going to? ¿**De dónde viene Vd.?** Where do you come from? ¿**Por dónde se va a Madrid?** Which is the way to Madrid?

dondequiera /donde'kiera/ *adv* wherever, anywhere, everywhere

donoso /do'noso/ *a* witty; graceful

donostiarra /donos'tiarra/ *a* and *mf* of or from San Sebastian (N. Spain)

donosura /dono'sura/ *f,* wit; grace; dash, verve

doña /'doɲa/ *f,* feminine equivalent of **don** (e.g. *D. Catalina Palacios*)

dorado /do'raðo/ *a* golden, gilded; fortunate, happy. *m,* gilding

dorador /dora'ðor/ *m,* gilder

doradura /dora'ðura/ *f,* gilding

dorar /do'rar/ *vt* to gild; make golden; *Fig.* gild the pill; *Cul.* toast lightly; —*vr* become golden

dórico /'doriko/ *a* Doric

dormidero /dormi'ðero/ *a* soporiferous, narcotic

dormilón /dormi'lon/ **(-ona)** *a Inf.* sleepy —*n* sleepyhead

dormir /dor'mir/ *vi irr* to sleep; spend the night; *Fig.* grow calm; sleep (tops); (*with sobre*) sleep on, consider; —*vt* put to sleep; —*vr* go to sleep; go slow over, neglect; be dormant; go numb (limbs). **d. como un lirón,** to sleep like a top. *Inf.* **d. la mona,** to sleep oneself sober. **entre duerme y vela,** half-awake —*Pres. Indic.* **duermo, duermes, duerme, duerme, duermen.** *Pres. Part.* **durmiendo.** *Preterite* **durmió, durmieron.** *Pres. Subjunc.* **duerma, duermas, duerma, duerman**

dormitar /dormi'tar/ *vi* to doze

dormitivo /dormi'tiβo/ *a* and *m,* sedative

dormitorio /dormi'torio/ *m,* dormitory; bedroom

dorsal /dor'sal/ *a* dorsal

dorso /'dorso/ *m,* back; dorsum

dos /dos/ *a* two. *m,* two; second (of the month). **las d.,** two o'clock. **d. a d.,** two against two. **de d. en d.,** two by two. *Inf.* **en un d. por tres,** in a twinkling

doscientos /dos'θientos; dos'sientos/ *a* and *m,* two hundred; two hundredth

dosel /do'sel/ *m,* canopy; dais

dosis /'dosis/ *f,* dose; quantity

dotación /dota'θion; dota'sion/ *f,* endowment; *Naut.* crew; staff, workers; equipment

dotar /do'tar/ *vt* to give as dowry; endow, found; *Fig.* endow (with talents, etc.); equip; apportion (salary)

dote /'dote/ *mf,* dowry. *f,* (gen. *pl*) gifts, talents. **dotes de mando,** capacity for leadership

dracma /'drakma/ *f,* drachma; dram

draga /'draga/ *f,* dredger

dragado /dra'gaðo/ *m,* dredging

dragaminas /draga'minas/ *m, Nav.* minesweeper

dragar /dra'gar/ *vt* to dredge

dragón /dra'gon/ *m,* dragon; *Bot.* snapdragon; *Mil.* dragoon; *Zool.* dragon, giant lizard; *Astron.* Draco

dragona /dra'gona/ *f,* female dragon; *Mil.* shoulder-strap

drama /'drama/ *m,* play; drama. **d. lírico,** opera

dramática /dra'matika/ *f,* dramatic art

dramático /dra'matiko/ *a* dramatic; vivid, unexpected, moving

dramaturgo /drama'turgo/ *m,* dramatist, playwright

drenaje /dre'nahe/ *m,* drainage (of land and wounds)

Dresde /'dresðe/ Dresden

dril /dril/ *m,* drill, cotton cloth

droga /'droga/ *f,* drug; falsehood, deception; nuisance

droguería /droge'ria/ *f,* chemist's shop; drug trade

droguero /dro'gero/ **(-ra)** *n* chemist, druggist

dromedario /drome'ðario/ *m, Zool.* dromedary

druida /'druiða/ *m,* Druid

dualidad /duali'ðað/ *f,* duality

ducado /du'kaðo/ *m,* dukedom; duchy; ducat

ducentésimo /duθen'tesimo; dusen'tesimo/ *a* two hundredth

ducha /'dutʃa/ *f,* shower-bath; douche; stripe in cloth; furrow

ducho /'dutʃo/ *a* experienced, skillful

dúctil /'duktil/ *a* ductile (metals); adaptable, docile, flexible

ductilidad /duktili'ðað/ *f,* ductility; adaptability

duda /'duða/ *f,* doubt, hesitation; problem. **sin d.,** doubtless

dudable /du'ðaβle/ *a* doubtful

dudar /du'ðar/ *vi* to be in doubt; —*vt* doubt, disbelieve

dudoso /du'ðoso/ *a* doubtful; uncertain, not probable

duela /'duela/ *f,* hoop, stave

duelista /due'lista/ *mf* dueler; duelist

duelo /'duelo/ *m,* sorrow, grief; mourning; mourners; duel; (gen. *pl*) troubles, trials. **duelos y quebrantos,** *Cul.* fried offal. **sin d.,** in abundance

duende /'duende/ *m,* imp, elf, sprite, ghost

dueña /'dueɲa/ *f,* owner, proprietress, mistress; duenna; married lady *Obs.*

dueño /'dueɲo/ *m,* owner, proprietor; master (of servants). **d. de sí mismo,** self-controlled

Duero, el /'duero, el/ the Douro

duetista /due'tista/ *mf* duetist

dula /'dula/ *f,* common pasture ground or herds

dulce /'dulθe; dulse/ *a* sweet; fresh, pure; fresh, not salty; fragrant; melodious; pleasant, agreeable; tender, gentle; soft (metals). *m,* sweetmeat, bonbon. **d. de almíbar,** preserved fruit.

dulcedumbre /dulθe'ðumbre; dulse'ðumbre/ *f,* sweetness; softness

dulcémele /dulθe'mele; dulse'mele/ *m,* dulcimer

dulcera /dul'θera; dul'sera/ *f,* preserve dish, fruit dish

dulcería /dulθe'ria; dulse'ria/ *f,* See **confitería**

dulcificar /dulθifi'kar; dulsifi'kar/ *vt* to make sweet; alleviate, sweeten

dulcinea /dulθi'nea; dul'sinea/ *f, Inf.* sweetheart; ideal

dulzaina /dul'θaina; dul'saina/ *f, Mus.* flageolet

dulzura /dul'θura; dul'sura/ *f,* sweetness; gentleness; pleasure; meekness; agreeableness

duna /'duna/ *f,* (gen. *pl*) sand dune

Dunas, las /'dunas, las/ the Downs

Dunquerque /dun'kerke/ Dunkirk

dúo /'duo/ *m, Mus.* duet

duodécimo /duo'ðeθimo; duo'ðesimo/ *a* twelfth

duodeno /duo'ðeno/ *a* twelfth. *m, Anat.* duodenum

duplicación /duplika'θion; duplika'sion/ *f,* duplication

duplicado /dupli'kaðo/ *m,* duplicate

duplicar /dupli'kar/ *vt* to duplicate; double

duplicidad /dupliθi'ðað; duplisi'ðað/ *f,* duplicity, falseness

duplo /'duplo/ *a* double

duque /'duke/ *m,* duke

duquesa /du'kesa/ *f,* duchess

duración /dura'θion; dura'sion/ *f,* duration; durability

duradero /dura'ðero/ *a* lasting; durable

durante /du'rante/ *adv* during

durar /du'rar/ *vi* to continue; endure, last

dureza /du'reθa; du'resa/ *f,* hardness; *Med.* callosity; severity, harshness

durmiente /dur'miente/ *a* sleeping. *mf* sleeper; *m, Archit.* dormant

duro /'duro/ *a* hard; firm, unyielding; vigorous, robust; severe, inclement; exacting, cruel; *Mus.* metallic, harsh; *Art.* crude, too sharply defined; miserly, avaricious; obstinate; self-opinionated; unbearable, intolerable; merciless, hard; harsh (style). *m,* Spanish coin worth five pesetas

dux /duks/ *m,* doge

E

e /e/ *f*, letter E —*conjunc* used instead of *y* (and) before words beginning with *i* or *hi*, provided this last is not followed by a diphthong (e.g. *e invierno, e hijos, but y hierro*)

¡eal /'ea/ *interj* Well!; Come on!; Let's see! (often used with **pues**)

ebanista /eβa'nista/ *mf* cabinetmaker

ebanistería /eβaniste'ria/ *f*, cabinetmaker's shop; cabinetmaking or work

ébano /'eβano/ *m*, ebony

ebonita /eβo'nita/ *f*, ebonite, vulcanite

ebrio /'eβrio/ *a* intoxicated, inebriated

ebullición /eβuʎi'θion; eβuyi'sion/ *f*, boiling, ebullition

ebúrneo /e'βurneo/ *a* eburnine, ivory-like

echada /e'tʃaða/ *f*, throw, cast; pitch; fling; length of a man

echador /etʃa'ðor/ **(-ra)** *n* thrower. *m*, *Inf.* chucker-out

echadura /etʃa'ðura/ *f*, sitting on eggs to hatch them; (gen. *pl*) gleanings

echamiento /etʃa'miento/ *m*, throw, fling; throwing, casting; expulsion; rejection

echar /e'tʃar/ *vt* to throw, fling; eject, drive away; cast out, expel; put forth, sprout; emit, give forth; cut (teeth); dismiss, discharge; couple (animals); pour (liquids); place, apply; put into, fill; turn (keys, locks); impute; attribute; impose (penalty, taxes, etc.); play (game); try one's luck; distribute; publish, make known; perform (plays); (*with por*) go in direction of; (*with prep* a + *infin.*) begin to (**e. a andar**, to begin to walk); —*vr* throw oneself down, lie down; sit on eggs (birds); abate, calm (wind); apply oneself, concentrate on; rush (towards), fling oneself (upon). **e. abajo**, to overthrow; demolish. **e. aceite al fuego**, to add fuel to the flames. **e. a perder**, to spoil, deteriorate. *Naut.* **e. a pique**, to sink. **e. a vuelo**, to ring (bells). **e. carnes**, to put on weight, grow fat. **e. cuentas**, to reckon up. **e. de menos**, to miss; mourn absence of. **e. de ver**, to notice. *Fig.* **e. en cara**, to throw in one's face, reproach. **echarla de majo**, to play the gallant. **e. las cartas al correo**, to post the letters. **e. las cartas**, to tell fortunes. **e. el pie atrás**, *Fig.* to climb down; *Fig.* back out. **e. raíces**, to take root; **e. las bases de, e. los cimientos de**, to lay the foundation of, lay the foundation for. *Fig.* become established. **e. rayos por la boca**, to fly into a rage. **e. suertes**, to draw lots. **echarlo todo a rodar**, to spoil everything. **e. una mano**, to lend a hand

echazón /etʃa'θon; etʃa'son/ *f*, throw, cast; jetsam

eclecticismo /eklekti'θismo; eklekti'sismo/ *m*, eclecticism

ecléctico /e'klektiko/ **(-ca)** *a* and *n* eclectic

eclesiástico /ekle'siastiko/ *a* ecclesiastical. *m*, ecclesiastic, clergyman; Ecclesiasticus

eclipsar /eklip'sar/ *vt Astron.* to eclipse; surpass, outvie; —*vr Astron.* be in eclipse; disappear

eclipse /e'klipse/ *m*, *Astron.* eclipse; retirement, withdrawal

écloga /'ekloga/ *f*, eclogue

eco /'eko/ *m*, echo; verse-echo; muffled sound; slavish imitation or imitator

economato /ekono'mato/ *m*, trusteeship; cooperative store

econometría /ekonome'tria/ *f*, econometrics

economía /ekono'mia/ *f*, economy, thrift; structure, organization; poverty, shortage; saving (of time, labor, etc.); *pl* savings. **e. dirigida**, planned economy. **e. doméstica**, domestic economy. **e. política**, political economy

económico /eko'nomiko/ *a* economic; thrifty; avaricious; cheap

economista /ekono'mista/ *mf* economist

economizar /ekonomi'θar; ekonomi'sar/ *vt* to economize; save

ecónomo /e'konomo/ *m*, trustee, guardian

ecuación /ekua'θion; ekua'sion/ *f*, (*Math.* and *Astron.*) equation. **e. personal**, personal equation

ecuador /ekua'ðor/ *m*, equator

ecuánime /ekua'nime/ *a* calm, unruffled; impartial

ecuanimidad /ekuanimi'ðað/ *f*, calmness, serenity; impartiality

ecuatorial /ekuato'rial/ *a* equatorial

ecuatoriano /ekuato'riano/ **(-na)** *a* and *n* Ecuadorian

ecuestre /e'kuestre/ *a* equestrian

ecuménico /eku'meniko/ *a* ecumenical

eczema /'ekθema; 'eksema/ *m*, eczema

edad /e'ðað/ *f*, age; epoch; period. **e. de piedra**, Stone Age. **e. media**, Middle Ages. **de cierta e.**, middle-aged. **ser mayor de e.**, to have attained one's majority. **ser menor de e.**, to be a minor

edecán /eðe'kan/ *m*, aide-de-camp

edema /e'ðema/ *m*, edema

Edén /e'ðen/ *m*, Eden; *Fig.* paradise

edición /eði'θion; eði'sion/ *f*, edition. **e. diamante**, miniature edition. **e. príncipe**, first edition

edicto /e'ðikto/ *m*, edict, decree; public notice

edificación /eðifika'θion; eðifika'sion/ *f*, building, construction; edification

edificador /eðifika'ðor/ **(-ra)** *a* uplifting, edifying; building —*n* builder

edificante /eðifi'kante/ *a* building, constructing; edifying

edificar /eðifi'kar/ *vt* to build, construct; edify

edificio /eði'fiθio; eði'fisio/ *m*, building, structure, fabric

Edimburgo /eðim'burgo/ Edinburgh

editar /eði'tar/ *vt* (of a publisher) to publish; edit

editor /eði'tor/ **(-ra)** *n* publisher; editor

editorial /eðito'rial/ *a* publishing; editorial. *m*, editorial, leading article

edredón /eðre'ðon/ *m*, down of an eiderduck; eider-down, quilt

eduardiano /eðuar'ðiano/ **(-na)** *a* and *n* Edwardian

educable /eðu'kaβle/ *a* educable

educación /eðuka'θion; eðuka'sion/ *f*, upbringing; education; good breeding, good manners

educado /eðu'kaðo/ *a* educated. **ser mal e.**, to be badly brought up; be ill-mannered

educador /eðuka'ðor/ **(-ra)** *a* educating —*n* educator

educando /eðu'kando/ **(-da)** *n* pupil

educar /eðu'kar/ *vt* to educate; bring up, train, teach, develop

educativo /eðuka'tiβo/ *a* educational, educative

educción /eðuk'θion; eðuk'sion/ *f*, eduction; inference, deduction

educir /eðu'θir; eðu'sir/ *vt irr* to educe; infer, deduce. See **conducir**

efe /'efe/ *f*, name of letter F

efectismo /efek'tismo/ *m*, sensationalism; striving after effect

efectista /efek'tista/ *a* (*Art. Lit.*) striking, sensational

efectivo /efek'tiβo/ *a* effective; real. *m*, cash. **hacer e.**, to put into effect

efecto /e'fekto/ *m*, effect, result; purpose, intent; impression; *pl* assets; goods, chattels. **efectos de escritorio**, stationery. **efectos públicos**, public securities. **en e.**, in fact, actually. **llevar a e.**, to put into effect; make effective

efectuación /efektua'θion; efektua'sion/ *f*, accomplishment, execution

efectuar /efek'tuar/ *vt* to accomplish, effect; make (a payment); —*vr* be effected; happen, take place

eferente /efe'rente/ *a* efferent

efervescencia /eferβes'θenθia; eferβes'sensia/ *f*, effervescence; excitement, enthusiasm

efervescente /eferβes'θente; eferβes'sente/ *a* effervescent

Éfeso /e'feso/ Ephesus

eficacia /efi'kaθia; efi'kasia/ *f*, efficacy; effectiveness

eficaz /efi'kaθ; efi'kas/ *a* efficacious; effective

eficiencia /efi'θienθia; efi'siensia/ *f*, efficiency

eficiente /efi'θiente; efi'siente/ *a* efficient, effective

efigie /e'fihie/ *f,* effigy; image, representation, symbol

efímero /e'fimero/ *a* ephemeral; brief

eflorescencia /eflores'θenθia; eflores'sensia/ *f,* *Chem.* efflorescence

efluvio /e'fluβio/ *m,* effluvium; exhalation

efugio /e'fuhio/ *m,* subterfuge, evasion

efusión /efu'sion/ *f,* effusion; *Fig.* spate (of words, etc.)

efusivo /efu'siβo/ *a* effusive, expansive

Egeo, Mar /e'heo, mar/ Aegean Sea

égida /'ehiða/ *f,* shield; egis, protection

egipcíaco /ehip'θiako; ehip'siako/ **(-ca), egipcio (-ia)** *a* and *n* Egyptian

Egipto /e'hipto/ Egypt

egiptólogo /ehip'tologo/ **(-ga)** *n* Egyptologist

égloga /'egloga/ *f,* eclogue

egoísmo /ego'ismo/ *m,* egoism

egoísta /ego'ista/ *a* egoistic. *mf* egoist

egolatría /egola'tria/ *f,* self-love

egotismo /ego'tismo/ *m,* egotism

egotista /ego'tista/ *a* egotistical. *mf* egotist

egregio /e'grehio/ *a* distinguished, celebrated

egresado /egre'saðo/ *m,* graduate (of a certain school)

eje /'ehe/ *m,* axis; axle-tree; shaft; pivot, fundamental idea. **e. trasero,** rear-axle

ejecución /eheku'θion; eheku'sion/ *f,* accomplishment, performance; execution, technique; death penalty

ejecutable /eheku'taβle/ *a* feasible, practicable

ejecutante /eheku'tante/ *mf Mus.* executant, performer

ejecutar /eheku'tar/ *vt* to discharge, perform; put to death; *(Art. Mus.)* execute; serve (a warrant, etc.); *Law.* seize (property)

ejecutivo /eheku''tiβo/ *a* executive; urgent

ejecutor /eheku'tor/ *m,* executor

ejecutoria /eheku'toria/ *f,* letters patent of nobility; *Law.* judgment, sentence

ejecutoría /ehekuto'ria/ *f,* executorship

ejemplar /ehem'plar/ *a* exemplary. *m,* copy, specimen; precedent; example; warning

ejemplificar /ehemplifi'kar/ *vi* to exemplify

ejemplo /e'hemplo/ *m,* example, precedent; illustration, instance; specimen. **dar e.,** to set an example. **por e.,** for example

ejercer /eher'θer; eher'ser/ *vt* to practice (a profession); perform, fulfill; exercise, use

ejercicio /eher'θiθio; eher'sisio/ *m,* exercise; practice; performance; exertion, effort; *Mil.* exercises (gen. *pl*). **ejercicios espirituales,** spiritual exercises. **ejercicios físicos,** physical training

ejercitar /eherθi'tar; ehersi'tar/ *vt* to exercise; train, teach; —*vr* exercise; practice

ejército /e'herθito; e'hersito/ *m,* army

el /el/ *def art m, sing* the

él /el/ *pers pron sing m,* he; it (*f.* **ella.** *neut* **ello**) (e.g. *Lo hizo él,* He did it). Also used with prep. (e.g. *Lo hicimos por él,* We did it for him)

elaboración /elaβora'θion; elaβora'sion/ *f,* elaboration, working out

elaborado /elaβo'raðo/ *a* elaborate

elaborar /elaβo'rar/ *vt* to elaborate; produce, work out

elasticidad /elastiθi'ðað; elastisi'ðað/ *f,* elasticity; adaptability

elástico /e'lastiko/ *a* elastic; adaptable. *m,* elastic tape; elastic material

ele /'ele/ *f,* name of letter L

elección /elek'θion; elek'sion/ *f,* choice; election; selection; discrimination

electivo /elek'tiβo/ *a* elective

electo /e'lekto/ *m,* elect, candidate elect

elector /elek'tor/ **(-ra)** *n* elector, voter. *m,* German prince *Obs.*

electorado /elekto'raðo/ *m,* electorate

electoral /elekto'ral/ *a* electoral

electricidad /elektriθi'ðað; elektrisi'ðað/ *f,* electricity

electricista /elektri'θista; elektri'sista/ *mf* electrician

eléctrico /e'lektriko/ *a* electric; electrical

electrificación /elektrifika'θion; elektrifika'sion/ *f,* electrification

electrificar /elektrifi'kar/ *vt* to electrify

electrizar /elektri'θar; elektri'sar/ *vt* to electrify; startle; —*vr* be electrified

electrocución /elektroku'θion; elektroku'sion/ *f,* electrocution

electrocutar /elektroku'tar/ *vt* to electrocute

electrodinámica /elektroði'namika/ *f,* electrodynamics

electrodo /elek'troðo/ *m,* electrode

electroimán /elektroi'man/ *m,* electromagnet

electrólisis /elek'trolisis/ *f,* electrolysis

electrólito /elek'trolito/ *m,* electrolyte

electrolizar /elektroli'θar; elektroli'sar/ *vt* to electrolyze

electromagnético /elektromag'netiko/ *a* electromagnetic

electromotriz /elektro'motriθ; elektro'motris/ *a* electromotive. **fuerza e.,** electromotive force

electrón /elek'tron/ *m,* electron

electroquímica /elektro'kimika/ *f,* electrochemistry

electroscopio /elektro'skopio/ *m,* electroscope

electrotecnia /elektro'teknia/ *f,* electrical engineering

electroterapia /elektrote'rapia/ *f, Med.* electrotherapy

elefante /ele'fante/ **(-ta)** *n* elephant

elefantíasis /elefan'tiasis/ *f,* elephantiasis

elefantino /elefan'tino/ *a* elephantine

elegancia /ele'ganθia; ele'gansia/ *f,* elegance, grace; fashionableness; *Lit.* beauty of style

elegante /ele'gante/ *a* elegant; graceful, lovely; fashionable, stylish

elegía /ele'hia/ *f,* elegy

elegíaco /ele'hiako/ *a* elegiac

elegibilidad /elehiβili'ðað/ *f,* eligibility

elegible /ele'hiβle/ *a* eligible

elegir /ele'hir/ *vt irr* to select, prefer; elect —*Pres. Indic.* **elijo, eliges, elige, eligen.** *Pres. Part.* **eligiendo.** *Preterite* **eligió, eligieron.** *Pres. Subj.* **elija,** etc.

elemental /elemen'tal/ *a* elemental; fundamental; elementary

elemento /ele'mento/ *m,* element; component, constituent; *Elec.* element; *pl* rudiments; *Mil.* **elementos de choque,** shock troops

elevación /eleβa'θion; eleβa'sion/ *f,* lifting, raising; height, high ground; elevation; altitude; *Fig.* eminence; elevation, advancement; ecstasy; raising (of the voice)

elevado /ele'βaðo/ *a* sublime, lofty

elevar /ele'βar/ *vt* to raise, lift; *Fig.* exalt; —*vr* be in ecstasy, be transported. **elevarse de categoría,** to rise in status

elfo /'elfo/ *m,* elf

elidir /eli'ðir/ *vt* (phonetics) to elide

eliminación /elimina'θion; elimina'sion/ *f,* elimination

eliminador /elimina'ðor/ *a* eliminatory. *m,* eliminator

eliminar /elimi'nar/ *vt* to eliminate

elipse /e'lipse/ *f,* ellipse

elipsis /e'lipsis/ *f,* ellipsis

elíptico /e'liptiko/ *a* elliptic

elíseo /e'liseo/ *m,* Elysium —*a* Elysian. **campos elíseos,** Elysian fields

ella /'eʎa; 'eya/ *pers pron 3rd sing f* she; it. See **él**

elle /'eʎe; 'eye/ *f,* name of letter LL

ello /'eʎo; 'eyo/ *pers pron 3rd sing neut* that, the fact, it. **Ello es que...,** The fact is that... **No tengo tiempo para ello,** I have no time for that

ellos, ellas /'eʎos, 'eʎas; 'eyos, 'eyas/ *pers pron 3rd pl m* and *f,* they. See **él**

elocución /eloku'θion; eloku'sion/ *f,* elocution; style of speech

elocuencia /elo'kuenθia; elo'kuensia/ *f,* eloquence

elocuente /elo'kuente/ *a* eloquent

elogiador /elohia'ðor/ **(-ra)** *a* eulogistic —*n* eulogist

elogiar /elo'hiar/ *vt* to eulogize, praise

elogio /e'lohio/ *m,* eulogy, praise. **«Elogio de la Locura»,** "In Praise of Folly"

elucidación /eluθiða'θion; elusiða'sion/ *f,* elucidation, explanation

elucidar /eluθi'ðar; elusi'ðar/ *vt* to elucidate, clarify
eludible /elu'ðiβle/ *a* escapable, avoidable
eludir /elu'ðir/ *vt* to elude, avoid
emaciación /emaθia'θion; emasia'sion/ *f*, emaciation
emanación /emana'θion; emana'sion/ *f*, emanation; effluvium
emanar /ema'nar/ *vi* to emanate (from), originate (in)
emancipación /emanθipa'θion; emansipa'sion/ *f*, emancipation; enfranchisement
emancipador /emanθipa'ðor; emansipa'ðor/ **(-ra)** *a* emancipatory —*n* emancipator
emancipar /emanθi'par; emansi'par/ *vt* to emancipate, free; enfranchise; —*vr* emancipate oneself; become independent; free oneself
emascular /emasku'lar/ *vt* to emasculate
embadurnar /embaður'nar/ *vt* to smear, smudge, daub
embajada /emba'haða/ *f*, embassy; ambassadorship; embassy building; *Inf*. message
embajador /embaha'ðor/ *m*, ambassador; emissary
embajadora /embaha'ðora/ *f*, wife of ambassador; woman ambassador
embalador /embala'ðor/ *m*, packer
embalaje /emba'lahe/ *m*, packing; bale; wrapper; packing charge
embalar /emba'lar/ *vt* to pack
embaldosado /embaldo'saðo/ *m*, tiled pavement or floor
embaldosar /embaldo'sar/ *vt* to tile, pave with tiles
embalsamador /embalsama'ðor/ *a* embalming. *m*, embalmer
embalsamar /embalsa'mar/ *vt* to embalm; perfume
embalse /em'balse/ *m*, dam; damming, impounding (of water)
embanastar /embanas'tar/ *vt* to place in a basket; crowd, squeeze
embarazada /embara'θaða; embara'saða/ *a f*, pregnant
embarazar /embara'θar; embara'sar/ *vt* to impede, hinder, embarrass; —*vr* be hindered or embarrassed; be pregnant
embarazo /emba'raθo; emba'raso/ *m*, difficulty, impediment; pregnancy; timidity, embarrassment
embarazoso /embara'θoso; embara'soso/ *a* embarrassing, inconvenient; difficult, troublesome
embarcación /embarka'θion; embarka'sion/ *f*, ship, vessel; embarkation
embarcadero /embarka'ðero/ *m*, wharf, dock; quay; pier; jetty
embarcador /embarka'ðor/ *m*, shipper
embarcar /embar'kar/ *vt* to embark, ship; board (boat, train, etc.); —*vr* embark; board
embarco /em'barko/ *m*, embarking, embarkation
embargar /embar'gar/ *vt* to obstruct, impede; *Law*. seize; suspend, paralyse
embargo /em'bargo/ *m*, *Law*. seizure; embargo. **sin e.**, nevertheless, however
embarque /em'barke/ *m*, loading, embarkation (goods)
embarrancar /embarran'kar/ *vi Naut*. to run aground; —*vr Naut*. be stuck on a reef or in the mud
embarrilar /embarri'lar/ *vt* to barrel
embarullar /embaru'ʎar; embaru'yar/ *vt Inf*. to mix up, muddle; do hastily and badly
embasamiento /embasa'miento/ *m*, *Archit*. foundation
embastar /embas'tar/ *vt Sew*. to baste; tack
embaste /em'baste/ *m*, *Sew*. basting; tacking stitch
embate /em'bate/ *m*, beating of the waves; sudden attack; unexpected misfortune
embaucamiento /embauka'miento/ *m*, trick, deception
embaucar /embau'kar/ *vt* to deceive, hoodwink
embaular /embau'lar/ *vt* to pack in a trunk; *Inf*. stuff with food
embazar /emba'θar; emba'sar/ *vt* to dye brown; hinder; amaze; —*vr* be amazed; be tired or bored; be satiated
embebecer /embeβe'θer; embeβe'ser/ *vt irr* to enter-

tain, amuse; engross, fascinate; —*vr* be dumbfounded. See **conocer**
embebecimiento /embeβeθi'miento; embeβesi'miento/ *m*, astonishment; absorption, engrossment
embeber /embe'βer/ *vt* to absorb; contain; shrink, contract; saturate; insert, introduce; incorporate; —*vi* shrink; —*vr* be amazed; master or absorb (a subject). **embebido en sus pensamientos**, absorbed in thought
embelecar /embele'kar/ *vt* to dupe, deceive, trick
embeleco /embe'leko/ *m*, deception, fraud
embelesar /embele'sar/ *vt* to astonish; fascinate, enchant; —*vr* be astonished or fascinated
embeleso /embe'leso/ *m*, astonishment; fascination; charm
embellecer /embeʎe'θer; embeye'ser/ *vt irr* to embellish; —*vr* beautify oneself. See **conocer**
embellecimiento /embeʎeθi'miento; embeyesi'miento/ *m*, beautifying, embellishment
emberizo /embe'riθo; embe'riso/ *m*, *Ornith*. yellowhammer
embermejecer /embermehe'θer; embermehe'ser/ *vt irr* to dye red; shame, make blush; —*vi* turn red or reddish; —*vr* blush. See **conocer**
embestida /embes'tiða/ *f*, assault, attack, onrush; *Inf*. importunity
embestir /embes'tir/ *vt irr* to rush upon, assault; *Inf*. importune, be a nuisance to; —*vi Fig. Inf*. clash, be inharmonious. See **pedir**
emblema /em'blema/ *m*, emblem; symbol; badge
emblemático /emble'matiko/ *a* emblematic; symbolical
embobamiento /emboβa'miento/ *m*, stupefaction, amazement
embobar /embo'βar/ *vt* to entertain, fascinate; —*vr* be dumbfounded
embobecer /emboβe'θer; emboβe'ser/ *vt irr* to make stupid. See **conocer**
embobecimiento /emboβeθi'miento; emboβesi'miento/ *m*, stupefaction
embocadero /emboka'ðero/ *m*, narrow entrance, bottleneck; mouth of a channel
embocadura /emboka'ðura/ *f*, entrance by a narrow passage; *Mus*. mouthpiece; flavor (of wine); estuary, mouth of a river; *Theat*. proscenium
embocar /embo'kar/ *vt* to put in the mouth; go through a narrow passage; deceive; *Inf*. devour, wolf; initiate a business deal
embolia /em'bolia/ *f*, embolism
émbolo /'embolo/ *m*, *Mech*. piston, plunger
embolsar /embol'sar/ *vt* to place money in a purse; collect (a debt, etc.)
emborrachar /emborra'tʃar/ *vt* to intoxicate; daze, stupefy; —*vr* become intoxicated; run (of dyes)
emborrascarse /emborras'karse/ *vr* to be furious; become stormy (weather); *Fig*. go downhill (business concern)
emborronar /emborro'nar/ *vt* to blot; scribble, write hastily
emboscada /embos'kaða/ *f*, ambuscade, ambush; intrigue, spying
emboscar /embos'kar/ *vt Mil*. to set an ambush; —*vr* lie in ambush
embosquecer /emboske'θer; emboske'ser/ *vi irr* to become wooded. See **conocer**
embotar /embo'tar/ *vt* to blunt (cutting edge); —*vi Fig*. weaken; —*vr* become blunt
embotellado /embote'ʎaðo; embote'yaðo/ *m*, bottling; *Fig*. bottleneck
embotellador /embote'ʎaðor; embote'yaðor/ **(-ra)** *n* bottler. *f*. **embotelladora**, bottling outfit
embotellar /embote'ʎar; embote'yar/ *vt* to bottle; bottle up, prevent from escaping
embotijar /emboti'har/ *vt* to put into jars; —*vr Inf*. be enraged
embozar /embo'θar; embo'sar/ *vt Fig*. to cloak, dissemble; muffle; —*vr* muffle oneself up
embozo /em'boθo; em'boso/ *m*, anything used to cover or muffle the face; pretense, pretext; facings (gen. *pl*); yashmak
embragar /embra'gar/ *vt* to sling, lift; *Mech*. let in the clutch

embrague /em'brage/ *m*, hoisting, slinging; *Mech.* clutch

embravecer /embraβe'θer; embraβe'ser/ *vt irr* to infuriate; —*vr* be enraged; be boisterous (sea). See **conocer**

embravecimiento /embraβeθi'miento; embraβesi-'miento/ *m*, fury, rage

embrazadura /embraθa'ðura; embrasa'ðura/ *f*, grasping, clasping; handle, clasp

embreadura /embrea'ðura/ *f*, tarring

embrear /embre'ar/ *vt* to tar, paint with pitch

embriagador /embriaga'ðor/ *a* intoxicating

embriagar /embria'gar/ *vt* to intoxicate; enrapture; —*vr* become inebriated

embriaguez /embria'geθ; embria'ges/ *f*, intoxication, inebriation; rapture

embriología /embriolo'hia/ *f*, embryology

embrión /em'brion/ *m*, embryo; germ, rough idea

embrionario /embrio'nario/ *a* embryonic

embrocación /embroka'θion; embroka'sion/ *f*, *Med.* embrocation

embrollar /embro'ʎar; embro'yar/ *vt* to entangle; embroil

embrollo /em'broʎo; em'broyo/ *m*, tangle; falsehood; difficult situation

embromar /embro'mar/ *vt* to tease, chaff; trick, deceive; waste the time of; annoy; harm

embrujar /embru'har/ *vt* to bewitch

embrutecer /embrute'θer; embrute'ser/ *vt irr* to make brutish or stupid; —*vr* become brutish. See **conocer**

embudo /em'buðo/ *m*, *Chem.* funnel

embuste /em'buste/ *m*, lie, fraud; *pl* trinkets

embustero /embus'tero/ **(-ra)** *a* deceitful, knavish —*n* liar, cheat, trickster

embutido /embu'tiðo/ *m*, inlaid work; *Cul.* sausage

embutir /embu'tir/ *vt* to inlay; stuff full, cram; —*vt* and *vr Inf.* stuff with food

eme /'eme/ *f*, name of letter M

emergencia /emer'henθia; emer'hensia/ *f*, emergence; accident, emergency

emergente /emer'hente/ *a* emergent

emerger /emer'her/ *vi* to emerge; have its source (rivers, etc.)

emérito /e'merito/ *a* emeritus

emético /e'metiko/ *a* and *m*, emetic

emigración /emigra'θion; emigra'sion/ *f*, emigration; migration; number of emigrants

emigrado /emi'graðo/ *m*, emigrant, emigré

emigrante /emi'grante/ *a* and *mf* emigrant

emigrar /emi'grar/ *vi* to emigrate; migrate

emigratorio /emigra'torio/ *a* emigration

eminencia /emi'nenθia; emi'nensia/ *f*, highland; importance, prominence; outstanding personality, genius; title given to cardinals

eminente /emi'nente/ *a* high, elevated; prominent, illustrious

emirato /emi'rato/ *m*, emirate

emisario /emi'sario/ **(-ia)** *n* emissary

emisión /emi'sion/ *f*, emission; *Radio.* broadcast; *Com.* issue (bonds, etc.); floating (of a loan)

emisor /emi'sor/ *m*, *Elec.* transmitter.

emisora /emi'sora/ *f*, *Radio.* broadcasting station

emitir /emi'tir/ *vt* to emit; *Radio.* broadcast; *Com.* issue (bonds, paper money, etc.); utter, give voice to

emoción /emo'θion; emo'sion/ *f*, emotion

emocional /emo'θional; emo'sional/ *a* emotional; emotive

emocionante /emoθio'nante; emosio'nante/ *a* moving, causing emotion; thrilling

emocionar /emoθio'nar; emosio'nar/ *vt* to cause emotion, move; —*vr* be stirred by emotion; be thrilled

emoliente /emo'liente/ *a* and *m*, emollient

emolumento /emolu'mento/ *m*, emolument (gen. *pl*)

emotivo /emo'tiβo/ *a* emotive

empachado /empa'tʃaðo/ *a* awkward, clumsy

empachar /empa'tʃar/ *vt* to hinder, impede; disguise, dissemble; —*vr* overeat, stuff; be bashful

empacho /em'patʃo/ *m*, bashfulness, timidity; embarrassment, impediment; indigestion, satiety

empadronamiento /empaðrona'miento/ *m*, census

empadronar /empaðro'nar/ *vt* to take the census

empalagar /empala'gar/ *vt* to cloy (of food); tire, annoy

empalagoso /empala'goso/ *a* sickly, oversweet; cloying; *Fig.* sugary, honeyed

empalar /empa'lar/ *vt* to impale

empalizada /empali'θaða; empali'saða/ *f*, stockade, fencing

empalmar /empal'mar/ *vt* to dovetail; splice (ropes); clamp; *Fig.* combine (plans, actions, etc.); —*vi* join (railroad lines); couple (railroad trains); —*vr* palm (as in conjuring)

empalme /em'palme/ *m*, connection; splicing; *Fig.* combination (of plans, etc.); railroad junction; continuation; palming, secreting

empanada /empa'naða/ *f*, savory turnover or pie; secret negotiations, intrigue

empanar /empa'nar/ *vt* to bread; *Cul.* cover with breadcrumbs; *Agr.* sow grain

empantanar /empanta'nar/ *vt* to turn into marsh; embog; delay, embarrass

empañar /empa'ɲar/ *vt* to swaddle; tarnish, dim; blur; *Fig.* sully (fame, etc.)

empapar /empa'par/ *vt* to saturate; absorb; impregnate; —*vr* be saturated; absorb; *Fig.* be imbued

empapelado /empape'laðo/ *m*, paperhanging; wallpaper

empapelador /empapela'ðor/ *m*, paperhanger

empapelar /empape'lar/ *vt* to wrap in paper; paper (a room, etc.)

empaque /em'pake/ *m*, packing; paneling; *Inf.* mien, air; pomposity

empaquetador /empaketa'ðor/ **(-ra)** *n* packer

empaquetar /empake'tar/ *vt* to pack; make up parcels or packages; overcrowd

emparedado /empare'ðaðo/ **(-da)** *a* cloistered, reclusive —*n* recluse. *m*, *Cul.* sandwich

emparedar /empare'ðar/ *vt* to shut up, immure; —*vr* become a recluse

emparejar /empare'har/ *vt* to pair, match; equalize, make level; —*vi* come abreast (of); be equal

emparentar /emparen'tar/ *vi irr* to become related by marriage. See **acertar**

emparrado /empa'rraðo/ *m*, vine arbor; vine prop; pergola

empastadura /empasta'ðura/ *f*, filling (of teeth)

empastar /empas'tar/ *vt* to cover with glue or paste; bind in boards (books); fill (teeth). **empastado en tela,** clothbound

empaste /em'paste/ *m*, pasting, gluing; filling (teeth)

empatar /empa'tar/ *vt* to equal, tie with

empate /em'pate/ *m*, tie, draw; dead heat

empecatado /empeka'taðo/ *a* willful; evil-minded, wicked; incorrigible, impenitent; extremely unlucky

empecer /empe'θer; empe'ser/ *vt irr* to harm, damage; —*vi* hinder. See **conocer**

empedernido /empeðer'niðo/ *a* stony-hearted, cruel

empedrado /empe'ðraðo/ *a* dappled (horses); *Fig.* flecked (with clouds). *m*, paving; pavement

empedrador /empeðra'ðor/ *m*, stone paver

empedrar /empe'ðrar/ *vt irr* to pave with stones. See **acertar**

empegadura /empega'ðura/ *f*, coat of pitch

empegar /empe'gar/ *vt* to coat with pitch; mark with pitch (sheep)

empeine /em'peine/ *m*, groin; instep

empellar /empe'ʎar; empe'yar/ *vt* to push, jostle

empellón /empe'ʎon; empe'yon/ *m*, hard push. *Inf.* **a empellones,** by pushing and shoving

empenachado /empena'tʃaðo/ *a* plumed

empeñado /empe'ɲaðo/ *a* violent, heated (of disputes)

empeñar /empe'ɲar/ *vt* to pledge, leave as surety; pawn; oblige, compel; appoint as mediator; —*vr* bind oneself, be under an obligation; (*with en*) insist on; persist in; —*vr* intercede; mediate; *Mil.* begin (a battle). **empeñado en,** determined to, intent on

empeño /em'peɲo/ *m*, pledge, surety; obligation, engagement; fervent desire; purpose, intention; determination, resolve; guarantor; *Inf.* influence, favor

empeoramiento /empeora'miento/ *m*, worsening; deterioration

empeorar /empeo'rar/ *vt* to make worse; —*vi* and *vr* deteriorate, grow worse

empequeñecer /empekeɲe'θer; empekeɲe'ser/ *vt irr* to diminish, lessen; make smaller; belittle. See **conocer**

emperador /empera'ðor/ *m*, emperor

emperatriz /empera'triθ; empera'tris/ *f*, empress

emperezar /empere'θar; empere'sar/ *vt* to obstruct, hinder; —*vr* be lazy

empernar /emper'nar/ *vt* to peg, bolt

empero /em'pero/ *conjunc* but; nevertheless

empezar /empe'θar; empe'sar/ *vt irr* to begin, commence; initiate; —*vi* begin —*Pres. Indic.* **empiezo, empiezas, empieza, empiezan.** *Preterite* **empecé, empezaste,** etc —*Pres. Subjunc.* **empiece, empieces, empiece, empecemos, empecéis, empiecen**

empicotar /empiko'tar/ *vt* to pillory

empinado /empi'naðo/ *a* steep; lofty; arrogant; exalted

empinar /empi'nar/ *vt* to raise; tip, tilt (drinking vessels); —*vr* stand on tiptoe; rear, prance; tower, rise; *Aer.* zoom, climb steeply. *Inf.* **e. el codo,** to lift the elbow, tipple

empingorotado /empiŋgoro'taðo/ *a* important, prominent; *Inf.* stuck-up

empíreo /em'pireo/ *a* empyreal; heavenly, divine. *m*, empyrean

empírico /em'piriko/ **(-ca)** *a* empiric —*n* quack, charlatan

empirismo /empi'rismo/ *m*, empiricism

empizarrado /empiθa'rraðo; empisa'rraðo/ *m*, slate roof

empizarrar /empiθa'rrar; empisa'rrar/ *vt* to roof with slate

emplastar /emplas'tar/ *vt Med.* to apply plasters; make up; paint; *Inf.* hinder, obstruct; —*vr* be smeared

emplasto /em'plasto/ *m*, *Med.* plaster; poultice; *Inf.* put-up job, fraud

emplazamiento /emplaθa'miento; emplasa'miento/ *m*, placing, location; site; *Law.* summons; *Naut.* berth

emplazar /empla'θar; empla'sar/ *vt* to convene, arrange a meeting; *Law.* summon

empleado /emple'aðo/ **(-da)** *n* employee; clerk. **e. público,** civil servant

emplear /em'plear/ *vt* to employ; lay out, invest (money); use; —*vr* be employed or occupied

empleo /em'pleo/ *m*, employment; investment, laying out (of money); post, office

emplomar /emplo'mar/ *vt* to lead, solder or cover with lead; affix lead seals on or to; weight (a stick, etc.)

emplumar /emplu'mar/ *vt* to feather; decorate with feathers; tar and feather

emplumecer /emplume'θer; emplume'ser/ *vi irr* to fledge, grow feathers. See **conocer**

empobrecer /empoβre'θer; empoβre'ser/ *vt irr* to impoverish; —*vi* and *vr* become poor; decay. See **conocer**

empobrecimiento /empoβreθi'miento; empoβresi'miento/ *m*, impoverishment

empollar /empo'ʎar; empo'yar/ *vt* to hatch; —*vi* produce a brood (of bees); *Inf.* brood on, consider; *Inf.* grind, cram, swot (of studies)

empollón /empo'ʎon; empo'yon/ **(-ona)** *n Inf.* plodder, grind, swot

empolvar /empol'βar/ *vt* to cover with dust; powder

emponzoñamiento /emponθoɲa'miento; emponsoɲa'miento/ *m*, poisoning

emponzoñar /emponθo'ɲar; emponso'ɲar/ *vt* to poison; pervert, corrupt

emporio /em'porio/ *m*, emporium

empotrar /empo'trar/ *vt* to embed, implant; fix down

emprendedor /emprende'ðor/ *a* capable, efficient, enterprising

emprender /empren'der/ *vt* to undertake; (*with prep a* or *con*) *Inf.* accost, tackle, buttonhole

empresa /em'presa/ *f*, undertaking, task; motto, device; intention, design; management, firm; enterprise, deal

empresarial /empresa'rial/ *a* entrepreneurial

empresario /empre'sario/ *m*, contractor; theatrical manager

empréstito /em'prestito/ *m*, loan

empujar /empu'har/ *vt* to push; *Fig.* exert pressure, influence

empuje /em'puhe/ *m*, push; *Archit.* pressure; energy; power, influence

empujón /empu'hon/ *m*, violent thrust or push. *Inf.* **a empujones,** by pushing and shoving; intermittently

empuñadura /empuɲa'ðura/ *f*, hilt (of a sword); *Inf.* preamble

empuñar /empu'ɲar/ *vt* to grasp; grip; clutch

emu /'emu/ *m*, emu

emulación /emula'θion; emula'sion/ *f*, emulation, competition, rivalry

emulador /emula'ðor/ *a* emulative

emular /emu'lar/ *vt* to emulate, rival, compete with

émulo /'emulo/ **(-la)** *a* emulative, rival —*n* competitor, rival

emulsión /emul'sion/ *f*, emulsion

emulsivo /emul'siβo/ *a* emulsive

en /en/ *prep* in; into; on, upon; at; by. **en Madrid,** in Madrid. **en junio,** in June. **Se echó en un sillón,** He threw himself into an armchair. **Se transformó en mariposa,** It turned into a butterfly. **Hay un libro en la mesa,** There is a book on the table. **María está en casa,** Mary is at home. **en un precio muy alto,** at a very high price. **El número de candidatos ha disminuido en un treinta por ciento,** The number of candidates has decreased by thirty percent. **En** appears in a number of adverbial phrases, e.g. *en particular,* in particular, *en secreto,* in secret, *en seguida,* immediately. When it is used with a gerund, it means after, as soon as, when, e.g. *En llegando a la puerta llamó,* When he arrived at the door, he knocked. *En todas partes se cuecen habas,* That happens everywhere; It happens in the best of families

enagua /e'nagua/ *f*, slip, crinoline, petticoat

enajenación /enahena'θion; enahena'sion/ *f*, transference, alienation (property); abstraction, absentmindedness. **e. mental,** lunacy

enajenar /enahe'nar/ *vt* to transfer (property)

enaltecer /enalte'θer; enalte'ser/ *vt irr* to elevate, raise; exalt. See **conocer**

enamoradizo /enamora'ðiθo; enamora'ðiso/ *a* susceptible, easily enamored; fickle

enamorado /enamo'raðo/ *a* in love, lovesick; easily enamored

enamorar /enamo'rar/ *vt* to arouse love in; court, make love to; —*vr* fall in love; (*with de*) become fond of (things)

enano /e'nano/ **(-na)** *a* small, dwarf —*n* dwarf

enarbolar /enarβo'lar/ *vt* to hoist (flags); —*vr* prance (horses); become angry

enardecer /enarðe'θer; enarðe'ser/ *vt irr* to kindle, stimulate (passion, quarrel, etc.); —*vr* be afire (with passion); *Med.* be inflamed. See **conocer**

encabestrar /enkaβe'strar/ *vt* to halter; lead, dominate

encabezamiento /enkaβeθa'miento; enkaβesa'miento/ *m*, census taking; tax register; tax assessment; heading, inscription, running head

encabezar /enkaβe'θar; enkaβe'sar/ *vt* to take the census of; put on the tax register; open a subscription list; put a heading or title to; lead, head; —*vr* compound, settle by agreement (taxes, etc.)

encabritarse /enkaβri'tarse/ *vr* to rear, prance (horses)

encadenamiento /enkaðena'miento/ *m*, fettering, chaining; connection, link, relation

encadenar /enkaðe'nar/ *vt* to chain, fetter; *Fig.* link up, connect; *Fig.* paralyze. **encadenar el interés de,** to capture the interest of

encajar /enka'har/ *vt* to insert, fit one thing inside another; force in; fit tightly; *Inf.* be opportune, fit in (often with *bien*); —*vr* squeeze or crowd in; *Inf.* butt in, interfere

encaje /en'kahe/ *m*, fitting, insertion; socket, groove; joining; lace; inlay, mosaic

encajera /enka'hera/ f, lace maker or seller

encaladura /enkala'ðura/ f, whitewashing

encalar /enka'lar/ vt to whitewash

encalladero /enkaʎa'ðero; enkaya'ðero/ m, Naut. sandbank, reef, shoal

encallar /enka'ʎar; enka'yar/ vi Naut. to run aground; Fig. be held up (negotiations, etc.)

encalmado /enkal'maðo/ a calm; Com. dull

encalmarse /enkal'marse/ vr to become calm (wind, weather)

encalvecer /enkalβe'θer; enkalβe'ser/ vi irr to grow bald. See **conocer**

encamado /enka'maðo/ a bedridden, confined to one's bed; m, person confined to his bed

encamarse /enka'marse/ vr to go to bed (gen. illness); be laid flat (grain, etc.); crouch

encaminadura /enkamina'ðura/ f, **encaminamiento** m, directing, forwarding, routing

encaminar /enkami'nar/ vt to guide; direct; regulate; manage; promote, advance; —vr (with prep a) make for, go in the direction of

encandecer /enkande'θer; enkande'ser/ vt irr to make incandescent. See **conocer**

encandilar /enkandi'lar/ vt to dazzle; mislead; Inf. poke (the fire); —vr be bloodshot (eyes)

encanecer /enkane'θer; enkane'ser/ vi irr to grow gray- or white-haired; grow mold; grow old. See **conocer**

encanijar /enkani'har/ vt to make weak, sickly (gen. of babies); —vr be delicate or ailing

encantado /enkan'taðo/ a Inf. daydreaming, abstracted; haunted; rambling (of houses)

encantador /enkanta'ðor/ a captivating, bewitching, delightful. m, sorcerer, magician. **e. de serpientes,** snake charmer

encantamiento /enkanta'miento/ m, enchantment, spell, charm

encantar /enkan'tar/ vt to enchant, weave a spell; delight, captivate, charm

encañada /enka'ɲaða/ f, gorge, ravine

encañado /enka'ɲaðo/ m, trellis; pipeline

encañar /enka'ɲar/ vt to run water through a pipe; stake plants; wind thread on a spool

encañonar /enkaɲo'nar/ vt to run into pipes; pleat, fold

encapotarse /enkapo'tarse/ vr to muffle oneself in a cloak; scowl; be overcast; lower (sky)

encapricharse /enkapri'tʃarse/ vr to take a fancy (to); insist on having one's own way, be stubborn

encapuchar /enkapu'tʃar/ vt to cover or hide with a hood

encaramar /enkara'mar/ vt to raise, lift; climb; praise, extol. **e. al poder,** to put in power (e.g. a dictator). **encaramarse por,** to climb up

encarar /enka'rar/ vt to place face to face; aim (at); —vt and vr face; come face to face

encarcelación /enkarθela'θion; enkarsela'sion/ f, incarceration

encarcelar /enkarθe'lar; enkarse'lar/ vt to imprison, jail; clamp

encarecer /enkare'θer; enkare'ser/ vt irr to raise the price; overpraise, exaggerate; recommend strongly; —vi and vr increase in price. See **conocer**

encarecimiento /enkareθi'miento; enkaresi'miento/ m, increase (in price); enhancement; exaggeration. **con e.,** insistently, earnestly

encargado /enkar'gaðo/ m, person in charge; manager; agent, representative. **e. de negocios,** chargé d'affaires

encargar /enkar'gar/ vt to enjoin; commission; recommend; advise; Com. order

encargo /enkar'go/ m, charge, commission; order; office, employ; responsibility

encariñarse /enkari'ɲarse/ (con), vi to become fond (of)

encarnación /enkarna'θion; enkarna'sion/ f, incarnation

encarnadino /enkarna'ðino/ a incarnadine

encarnado /enkar'naðo/ a incarnate; flesh-colored; red

encarnar /enkar'nar/ vi to incarnate; pierce the flesh;

Fig. leave a strong impression; —vt symbolize, personify; —vr mingle, blend

encarnizado /enkarni'θaðo; enkarni'saðo/ a bloodshot (eyes); flesh-colored; bloody, cruel (gen. of battles)

encarnizamiento /enkarniθa'miento; enkarnisa'miento/ m, cruelty, fury

encarnizar /enkarni'θar; enkarni'sar/ vt to infuriate; —vr devour flesh (animals); persecute, ill-treat

encaro /en'karo/ m, stare, gaze; aim

encarrilar /enkarri'lar/ vt to set on the track or rails (vehicles); Fig. put right, set on the right track

encartamiento /enkarta'miento/ m, proscription; charter

encartar /enkar'tar/ vt to proscribe, outlaw; place on the tax register; Law. summon, cite

encartonar /enkarto'nar/ vt to cover with cardboard; bind in boards (books)

encasar /enka'sar/ vt Surg. to set (a bone)

encasillado /enkasi'ʎaðo; enkasi'yaðo/ m, set of pigeonholes

encasillar /enkasi'ʎar; enkasi'yar/ vt to pigeonhole; file, classify

encasquetar /enkaske'tar/ **(se)** vt and vr to pull a hat well down on the head; —vr get a fixed idea

encastillar /enkasti'ʎar; enkasti'yar/ vt to fortify with castles; —vr retire to a castle; be headstrong, obstinate

encauzamiento /enkauθa'miento; enkausa'miento/ m, channeling; Fig. direction

encauzar /enkau'θar; enkau'sar/ vt to channel; Fig. direct, guide

encefalitis /enθefa'litis; ensefa'litis/ f, encephalitis. **e. letárgica,** encephalitis lethargica, sleeping sickness.

encéfalo /en'θefalo; en'sefalo/ m, Anat. brain

encenagarse /enθena'garse; ensena'garse/ vr to wallow in mire; muddy oneself; take to vice

encendedor /enθende'ðor; ensende'ðor/ a lighting. m, lighter. **e. de bolsillo,** pocket lighter

encender /enθen'der; ensen'der/ vt irr to light; switch on; set fire to, kindle; arouse (emotions); inflame, incite; —vr blush. See **entender**

encendido /enθen'diðo; ensen'diðo/ a high-colored; inflamed; ardent. m, Auto. ignition

encerado /enθe'raðo; ense'raðo/ a wax-colored. m, oilskin; sticking plaster; blackboard; tarpaulin

enceramiento /enθera'miento; ensera'miento/ m, waxing

encerar /enθe'rar; ense'rar/ vt to wax, varnish with wax; stain with wax; inspissate (lime)

encerotar /enθero'tar; ensero'tar/ vt to wax (thread)

encerrar /enθe'rrar; ense'rrar/ vt irr to shut up, imprison; include, contain; —vr go into seclusion. See **acertar**

encerrona /enθe'rrona; ense'rrona/ f, Inf. voluntary retreat; Fig. Inf. tight corner

encespedar /enθespe'ðar; ensespe'ðar/ vt to cover with sod

enchufar /entʃu'far/ vt to connect tubes; Fig. combine (jobs, etc.); Elec. plug, connect

enchufe /en'tʃufe/ m, joint, fitting together (of tubes); Elec. wall socket, plug; part-time post; Inf. cushy job. **e. de reducción,** Elec. adapter

encía /en'θia; en'sia/ f, gum (of the mouth)

encíclica /en'θiklika; en'siklika/ f, encyclical

enciclopedia /enθiklo'peðia; ensiklo'peðia/ f, encyclopedia

enciclopédico /enθiklo'peðiko; ensiklo'peðiko/ a encyclopedic

encierro /en'θierro; en'sierro/ m, act of closing or shutting up; prison; retreat, confinement

encima /en'θima; en'sima/ adv over; above; at the top; besides; (with de) on, on top of. **por e. de esto,** over and above this, besides this

encina /en'θina; en'sina/ f, Bot. evergreen or holm oak

encinar /enθi'nar; ensi'nar/ m, grove of evergreen or holm oaks

encinta /en'θinta; en'sinta/ a f, pregnant

encintar /enθin'tar; ensin'tar/ vt to decorate with ribbons

enclavar /enkla'βar/ vt to nail; pierce; embed; Inf. deceive

enclenque /en'klenke/ a ailing, weak; puny, anemic

enclocar /enklo'kar/ vi irr to begin to brood (hens). See **contar**

encobar /enko'βar/ vi to hatch eggs

encoger /enko'her/ vt to shrink, contract, recoil; discourage; —vi shrink (wood, cloth, etc.); —vr shrink from, recoil; be discouraged; be timid or bashful

encogimiento /enkohi'miento/ m, shrinkage; contraction; depression, discouragement; timidity; bashfulness

encoladura /enkola'ðura/ f. **encolamiento** m, gluing; sizing

encolerizar /enkoleri'θar; enkoleri'sar/ vt to anger; —vr be angry

encomendar /enkomen'dar/ vt irr to charge with, entrust; recommend, commend; —vr (with prep a) put one's trust in; send greetings to. See **acertar**

encomiar /enko'miar/ vt to eulogize, praise

encomiástico /enko'miastiko/ a encomiastic

encomienda /enko'mienda/ f, commission, charge; knight commandership; insignia of knight commander; land formerly granted in America to conquistadores; recommendation, commendation; protection, defense; pl greetings, compliments, messages

encomio /en'komio/ m, eulogy; strong recommendation

enconar /enko'nar/ vt to irritate, exasperate; —vr Med. be inflamed; be exasperated; (with en) burden one's conscience with

encono /en'kono/ m, rancor, resentment, ill will

encontrado /enkon'traðo/ a facing, opposite, in front; hostile, inimical, opposed (to)

encontrar /enkon'trar/ vt irr to meet; find; —vi meet; encounter unexpectedly; (with con) run into, collide with; —vr be antagonistic; find; feel, be; differ, disagree (opinions); (with con) meet, come across. **e. eco**, to strike a responsive chord. **encontrarse con el cura de su pueblo**, to find someone who knows all about, meet someone who knows all about. **¿Cómo se encuentra Vd?** How are you? Pres. Indic. **encuentro**, etc —Pres. Subjunc. **encuentre**, etc.

encontrón /enkon'tron/ m, collision, violent impact

encopetado /enkope'taðo/ a conceited, proud; of noble descent; prominent, important

encorajar /enkora'har/ vt to encourage, inspire, hearten; —vr be angry

encordelar /enkorðe'lar/ vt to cord, rope

encorsetar /enkorse'tar/ vt to correct

encorvadura /enkorβa'ðura/ f, bending, curving

encorvar /enkor'βar/ vt to bend, curve; —vr have a leaning toward, favor

encostrar /enkos'trar/ vt to cover with a crust; —vr form a crust

encrespador /enkrespa'ðor/ m, curling irons

encrespar /enkres'par/ vt to curl (hair); enrage; —vr be curly (hair); stand on end (hair, feathers, from fright); be angry; grow rough (sea); become complicated, entangled

encrestado /enkres'taðo/ a crested; haughty, arrogant

encrestarse /enkres'tarse/ vr to stiffen the comb or crest (birds)

encrucijada /enkruθi'haða; enkrusi'haða/ f, crossroad, intersection; ambush

encrudecer /enkruðe'θer; enkruðe'ser/ vt irr to make raw-looking; annoy; —vr be annoyed. See **conocer**

encuadernación /enkuaðerna'θion; enkuaðerna'sion/ f, bookbinding; binding (of a book); bookbinder's workshop. **e. en tela**, cloth binding

encuadernador /enkuaðerna'ðor/ (-ra) n bookbinder

encuadernar /enkuaðer'nar/ vt to bind (a book)

encuadrar /enkuað'rar/ vt to frame; fit one thing into another, insert; limit; Mil. enlist

encubar /enku'βar/ vt to put into casks (wine, etc.)

encubiertamente /enkuβierta'mente/ adv secretly; deceitfully

encubierto /enku'βierto/ a concealed; secret

encubridor /enkuβri'ðor/ (-ra) a concealing, hiding —n hider; harborer; accomplice; receiver (of stolen goods); Law. accessory after the fact

encubrimiento /enkuβri'miento/ m, hiding, concealment; Law. accessory before (after) the fact; receiving (of stolen goods)

encubrir /enku'βrir/ vt to conceal; receive (stolen goods); Law. prosecute as an accessory. Past. Part. **encubierto**

encuentro /en'kuentro/ m, collision; meeting, encounter; opposition, hostility; Mil. fight, skirmish; Archit. angle. **ir al e. de**, to go in search of. **salir al e. (de)**, to go to meet; resist

encuesta /en'kuesta/ f, investigation, examination

encumbrado /enkum'braðo/ a elevated, high

encumbramiento /enkumbra'miento/ m, act of elevating; height; aggrandizement, advancement

encumbrar /enkum'brar/ vt to raise, elevate; exalt, promote; ascend, climb to the top; —vr be proud; be lofty, tower

encurtido /enkur'tiðo/ m, pickle

encurtir /enkur'tir/ vt to pickle

ende /'ende/ adv Obs. there. **por e.**, therefore

endeble /en'deβle/ a weak, frail

endeblez /ende'βleθ; ende'βles/ f, weakness

endecha /en'detʃa/ f, dirge

endémico /en'demiko/ a Med. endemic

endemoniado /endemo'niaðo/ a devil-possessed; Inf. fiendish, malevolent

endemoniar /endemo'niar/ vt to possess with a devil; Inf. enrage

endentar /enden'tar/ vt irr Mech. to cut the cogs (of a wheel); engage, interlock (gears, wheels, etc.). See **regimentar**

endentecer /endente'θer; endente'ser/ vi irr to cut teeth. See **conocer**

enderezamiento /endereθa'miento; enderesa'miento/ m, straightening; directing, guiding; putting right, correction

enderezar /endere'θar; endere'sar/ vt to straighten; direct, guide; put right, correct; —vi take the right road; —vr straighten oneself; prepare to

endeudarse /endeu'ðarse/ vr to contract debts; be under an obligation

endiablado /endia'βlaðo/ a ugly, monstrous; Inf. fiendish

endiosar /endio'sar/ vt to deify; —vr be puffed up with pride; be abstracted or lost in ecstasy

endocrino /endo'krino/ a endocrine

endocrinología /endokrinolo'hia/ f, endocrinology

endomingarse /endomiŋ'garse/ vr to put on one's Sunday best

endosante /endo'sante/ m, endorser

endosar /endo'sar/ vt Com. to endorse; transfer, pass on

endoso /en'doso/ m, Com. endorsement

endrino /en'drino/ m, sloe tree —a blue-black, sloe-colored

endulzar /endul'θar; endul'sar/ vt to sweeten; soften, mitigate

endurecer /endure'θer; endure'ser/ vt irr to harden; toughen, inure; make severe or cruel; —vr grow hard; become hardened or robust; be harsh or cruel. **endurecerse al trabajo**, to become hardened to work. See **conocer**

endurecimiento /endureθi'miento; enduresi'miento/ m, hardness; obstinacy, tenacity

ene /'ene/ f, name of letter N

enemiga /ene'miga/ f, hostility, enmity

enemigo /ene'migo/ (-ga) a hostile —n enemy; antagonist. m, devil

enemistad /enemis'taθ/ f, enmity, hostility

enemistar /enemis'tar/ vt to make enemies of; —vr (with con) become an enemy of; cease to be friendly with

energía /ener'hia/ f, energy, vigor

enérgico /e'nerhiko/ a energetic, vigorous

energúmeno /ener'gumeno/ (-na) n energumen

enero /e'nero/ m, January

enervación /enerβa'θion; enerβa'sion/ f, enervation

enervar /ener'βar/ vt to enervate, weaken; Fig. take the force out of (reasons, etc.)

enfadar /enfa'ðar/ vt to make angry; —vr become angry

enfado /en'faðo/ *m*, anger; annoyance; trouble, toil

enfadoso /enfa'ðoso/ *a* vexatious; troublesome, wearisome

enfaldada /enfal'daða/ *f*, skirtful

enfaldar /enfal'dar/ *vt* to tuck up the skirts; lop off lower branches (of trees)

enfangarse /enfaŋ'garse/ *vr* to cover oneself with mud; *Inf.* dirty one's hands, sully one's reputation; wallow in vice

enfardar /enfar'ðar/ *vt* to pack; make bales or bundles

énfasis /'enfasis/ *m*, or *f*, emphasis

enfático /en'fatiko/ *a* emphatic

enfermar /enfer'mar/ *vi* to fall ill; —*vt* cause illness; *Fig.* weaken. **Enfermó del corazón,** He fell ill with heart trouble.

enfermedad /enferme'ðað/ *f*, illness; *Fig.* malady, distemper. **e. del sueño,** sleeping sickness

enfermera /enfer'mera/ *f*, nurse

enfermería /enfer'ria/ *f*, infirmary; hospital; first-aid station

enfermero /enfer'mero/ *m*, nurse

enfermizo /enfer'miθo/ enfer''miso/ *a* ailing, delicate; unhealthy, unwholesome

enfermo /en'fermo/ **(-ma)** *a* ill; *Fig.* corrupt, diseased; delicate, sickly —*n* patient. **e. venéreo,** person with a venereal disease

enfilar /enfi'lar/ *vt* to place in line; string; *Mil.* enfilade

enflaquecer /enflake'θer; enflake'ser/ *vt irr* to make thin; weaken, enervate; —*vi* grow thin; lose heart. See **conocer**

enflaquecimiento /enflakeθi'miento; enflakesi-'miento/ *m*, loss of flesh; discouragement

enfocar /enfo'kar/ *vt* to focus; envisage

enfoque /en'foke/ *m*, focus

enfoscado /enfos'kaðo/ *a* ill-humored; immersed in business matters

enfrascar /enfras'kar/ *vt* to bottle; —*vr (with en)* plunge into, entangle oneself in (undergrowth, etc.); become engrossed or absorbed in

enfrenar /enfre'nar/ *vt* to bridle; curb (a horse); restrain, repress; check

enfrente /en'frente/ *adv* in front, opposite, facing; in opposition

enfriadero /enfria'ðero/ *m*, cooling place, cold cellar, root cellar

enfriamiento /enfria'miento/ *m*, cooling

enfriar /enf'riar/ *vt* to cool; *Fig.* chill, make indifferent; —*vr* grow cold; *Fig.* grow stormy (weather)

enfurecer /enfure'θer; enfure'ser/ *vt irr* to enrage. See **conocer**

enfurecimiento /enfureθi'miento; enfuresi'miento/ *m*, fury

enfurruñarse /enfurru'ɲarse/ *vr Inf.* to fume, be angry; be disgruntled

engalanar /engala'nar/ *vt* to decorate, embellish. **engalanado como nunca,** dressed to the nines, dressed to kill

enganchar /engan'tʃar/ *vt* to hook; couple, connect; hitch, harness, yoke; *Inf.* seduce, hook; *Mil.* bribe into army; —*vr* be hooked or caught on a hook; *Mil.* enlist

enganche /en'gantʃe/ *m*, hooking; coupling (of railroad trains, etc.); connection; yoke, harness; hook; *Inf.* enticement; *Mil.* enlistment

engañifa /enga'ɲifa/ *f*, *Inf.* swindle, fraud

engañadizo /engaɲa'ðiθo; engaɲaðiso/ *a* easily deceived, simple

engañador /engaɲa'ðor/ **(-ra)** *a* deceiving; deceptive —*n* deceiver, impostor

engañar /enga'ɲar/ *vt* to deceive; defraud, cheat; beguile, while away; hoax, humbug; —*vr* be mistaken; deceive oneself. **e. como a un chino,** *Inf.* to pull the wool over a person's eyes. **Las apariencias engañan,** Appearances are deceptive

engañifa /enga'nhook;ifa/ *f*, *Inf.* swindle, fraud

engaño /en'gaɲo/ *m*, deceit; deception, illusion; fraud; falsehood

engañoso /enga'ɲoso/ *a* deceitful, false; fraudulent; deceptive, misleading

engarabatar /engaraβa'tar/ *vt Inf.* to hook; —*vr* become hooked, curved, crooked

engarce /en'garθe; engarse/ *m*, hooking; coupling; setting (of jewels)

engarzar /engar'θar; engar'sar/ *vt* to link, couple, enchain; hook; curl; set (jewels)

engastar /engas'tar/ *vt* to set (jewels)

engaste /en'gaste/ *m*, setting (of jewels)

engatusar /engatu'sar/ *vt Inf.* to wheedle, coax, flatter

engendrador /enhendra'ðor/ **(-ra)** *a* engendering; original —*n* begetter

engendrar /enhen'drar/ *vt* to procreate; engender, produce, cause

engendro /en'hendro/ *m*, fetus; abnormal embryo; literary monstrosity

englobar /englo'βar/ *vt* to include, comprise, embrace

engolfarse /engol'farse/ *vr* to sail out to sea; *(with en) Fig.* be absorbed in

engomar /engo'mar/ *vt* to gum

engordar /engor'ðar/ *vt* to fatten; —*vi* grow fat; *Inf.* prosper, grow rich

engorde /en'gorðe/ *m*, fattening (of stock)

engorro /en'gorro/ *m*, impediment, obstacle, difficulty

engorroso /engo'rroso/ *a* difficult, troublesome

engranaje /engra'nahe/ *m*, *Mech.* gearing, gear; *Fig.* connection, link

engrandecer /engrande'θer; engrande'ser/ *vt irr* to enlarge; augment; eulogize; promote, exalt. See **conocer**

engrandecimiento /engrandeθi'miento; engrandesi-'miento/ *m*, enlargement; increase; exaggeration, eulogization; advancement, promotion

engrasado /engra'saðo/ *m*, oiling; greasing

engrasador /engrasa'ðor/ *m*, greaser, lubricator; oiler

engrasar /engra'sar/ *vt* to grease; lubricate, oil; manure; stain with grease

engreimiento /engrei'miento/ *m*, conceit, vanity

engreír /engre'ir/ *vt irr* to make conceited; —*vr* become vain or conceited. See **reír**

engrescar /engres'kar/ **(se)** *vt* and *vr* to start a quarrel

engrosar /engro'sar/ *vt irr* to fatten, thicken; *Fig.* increase, swell; manure; —*vi* put on weight, grow fat. See **contar**

engrudar /engru'ðar/ *vt* to paste, glue

engrudo /en'gruðo/ *m*, paste, glue

enguantarse /en'guantarse/ *vr* to put on one's gloves

enguijarrado /enguiha'rraðo/ *a* pebbled. *m*, pebbled path

engullir /engu'ʎir; engu'yir/ *vt* to gobble, swallow

enhebrar /ene'βrar/ *vt* to thread (needles); string

enhestar /enes'tar/ *vt irr* to erect; set upright; —*vr* rise; set up; straighten oneself up. See **acertar**

enhiesto /en'iesto/ *a* upright, erect

enhorabuena /enora'βuena/ *f*, congratulation —*adv* well and good. **dar la e.,** to congratulate

enhoramala /enora'mala/ *adv* in an evil hour. *Inf.* **¡Vete e.!** Go to the devil!

enhorquetado /enorke'taðo/ *a* in the saddle

enhuerar /enue'rar/ *vt* to addle; —*vi* become addled

enigma /e'nigma/ *m*, enigma

enigmático /enig'matiko/ *a* enigmatical

enjabonar /enhaβo'nar/ *vt* to soap; *Inf.* soap down, flatter

enjaezar /enhae'θar; enhae'sar/ *vt* to harness (a horse)

enjalbegar /enhalβe'gar/ *vt* to whitewash

enjambrar /enhamb'rar/ *vt* to hive bees; —*vi* multiply, increase

enjambre /en'hambre/ *m*, swarm (of bees); crowd

enjaretado /enhare'taðo/ *m*, latticework

enjaular /enhau'lar/ *vt* to cage; *Inf.* jail

enjoyar /enho'yar/ *vt* to adorn with jewels; beautify; set with precious stones

enjuagadura /enhuaga'ðura/ *f*, rinsing (the mouth); rinse water; mouthwash

enjuagar /enhua'gar/ *vt* to rinse; —*vr* rinse the mouth

enjuague /en'huaɣe/ *m,* rinse; rinsing; mouthwash; tooth mug; scheme, plan

enjugar /enhu'ɣar/ *vt* to dry; cancel, write off; wipe, mop (perspiration, tears, etc.); —*vr* grow lean

enjuiciar /enhui'θiar; enhui'siar/ *vt* to submit a matter to arbitration; *Law.* prosecute; *Law.* render judgment; *Law.* adjudicate (a case)

enjundia /en'hundia/ *f,* animal fat or grease; *Fig.* substance, meat; strength, vigor; constitution, temperament

enjuto /en'huto/ *a* dry; lean. *m pl,* brushwood; *Cul.* canapés, savories

enlace /en'laθe; en'lase/ *m,* connection; link; tie; *Chem.* bond; alliance, relationship; marriage

enladrillado /enladri'ʎaðo; enladri'yaðo/ *m,* brick floor or pavement

enlardar /enlar'ðar/ *vt Cul.* to baste

enlazar /enla'θar; enla'sar/ *vt* to tie, bind; join, link; lasso; —*vr* marry; be allied, related. **e. con,** to connect with (of trains); link up with

enlentecerse /enlente'θerse; enlente'serse/ *vr* to decelerate, go slow, slow down

enlodar /enlo'ðar/ *vt* to muddy; *Fig.* smirch, sully

enloquecer /enloke'θer; enloke'ser/ *vt irr* to drive insane; —*vi* go mad. See **conocer**

enlosado /enlo'saðo/ *m,* tile floor

enlosar /enlo'sar/ *vt* to pave with flags

enlucir /enlu'θir; enlu'sir/ *vt irr* to plaster (walls); polish (metals). See **lucir**

enlutar /enlu'tar/ *vt* to put in mourning, drape with crepe; darken, obscure; sadden; —*vr* go into mourning; become dark

enmaderar /emaðe'rar/ *vt* to panel in wood, board up

enmarañar /emara'ɲar/ *vt* to tangle, disorder (hair, etc.); complicate, confuse; —*vr* be tangled; be sprinkled with clouds

enmaridar /emari'ðar/ *vi* to become a wife

enmarillecerse /emariʎe'θerse; emariye'serse/ *vr irr* to grow yellow. See **conocer**

enmascarar /emaska'rar/ *vt* to mask; disguise, dissemble; —*vr* be masked

enmasillar /emasi'ʎar; emasi'yar/ *vt* to putty

enmendar /emen'dar/ *vt irr* to correct, improve; reform; compensate, indemnify; *Law.* repeal; —*vr* be improved or corrected; mend one's ways. See **acertar**

enmienda /e'mienda/ *f,* correction; reform; indemnity; compensation; amendment; *pl Agr.* fertilizers

enmohecer /emoe'θer; emoe'ser/ *vt irr* to rust; —*vr* become moldy. See **conocer**

enmudecer /emuðe'θer; emuðe'ser/ *vt irr* to silence; —*vi* become dumb; be silent. See **conocer**

enmugrecer /emugre'θer; emugre'ser/ *vt irr* to cover with grime; —*vr* be grimy, dirty. See **conocer**

ennegrecer /ennegre'θer; ennegre'ser/ *vt irr* to dye black; make black; —*vr* become black; become dark or cloudy. See **conocer**

ennoblecer /ennoβle'θer; ennoβle'ser/ *vt irr* to ennoble; enrich, embellish; adorn, befit. See **conocer**

ennoblecimiento /ennoβleθi'miento; ennoβlesi'miento/ *m,* ennoblement; enrichment

enojadizo /enoha'ðiθo; enoha'ðiso/ *a* irritable, peevish

enojar /eno'har/ *vt* to anger; annoy, irritate; —*vr* be angry; rage, be rough (wind, sea)

enojo /e'noho/ *m,* anger; resentment; vexations, troubles, trials (gen. *pl*). **con gran e. de,** much to the annoyance of

enojoso /eno'hoso/ *a* annoying; troublesome, tiresome

enorgullecer /enorguʎe'θer; enorguye'ser/ *vt irr* to make proud; —*vr* be proud. See **conocer**

enorme /e'norme/ *a* enormous, huge; monstrous, heinous

enormidad /enormi'ðað/ *f,* hugeness; enormity; wickedness

enramar /enra'mar/ *vt* to intertwine branches; embower; —*vi* branch (trees)

enramada /enrami'ðað/ *f,* bower; thick foliage

enrarecer /enrare'θer; enrare'ser/ *vt irr* to rarefy; —*vr* become rarefied; grow rare. See **conocer**

enrarecimiento /enrareθi'miento; enraresi'miento/ *m,* rarefaction

enredadera /enreða'ðera/ *f,* convolvulus —*a f,* climbing, twining (plant)

enredador /enreða'ðor/ **(-ra)** *a* mischievous, willful; intriguing, scheming; *Inf.* gossiping, meddlesome —*n* intriguer; *Inf.* meddler

enredar /enre'ðar/ *vt* to catch in a net; put down nets or snares; entangle; sow discord; compromise, involve (in difficulties); —*vi* be mischievous; —*vr* be entangled; be involved (in difficulties)

enredo /en'reðo/ *m,* tangle; mischief, prank; intrigue, malicious falsehood; difficult situation; plot

enredoso /enre'ðoso/ *a* tangled; fraught with difficulties

enrejado /enre'haðo/ *m,* railing, paling; trellis or latticework; *Sew.* openwork

enrejar /enre'har/ *vt* to fence with a railing; cover with grating

enriquecer /enrike'θer; enrike'ser/ *vt irr* to enrich; exalt, aggrandize; —*vi* grow rich; prosper, flourish. See **conocer**

enriscado /enris'kaðo/ *a* craggy, rocky

enriscar /enris'kar/ *vt* to raise; —*vr* hide among crags

enristrar /enris''trar/ *vt* to couch (a lance); string (onions, etc.); *Fig.* surmount (difficulties); go straight to (a place)

enrojecer /enrohe'θer; enrohe'ser/ *vt irr* to redden; make blush; —*vr* grow red; blush. See **conocer**

enroscar /enros'kar/ *vt* to twist, twine; —*vr* turn (screw); twist; coil

ensaimada /ensai'maða/ *f,* Spanish pastry cake

ensalada /ensa'laða/ *f,* salad; hodgepodge

ensaladera /ensala'ðera/ *f,* salad bowl

ensalmar /ensal'mar/ *vt Surg.* to set (bones); cure by spells

ensalmo /en'salmo/ *m,* spell, charm. **por e.,** as if by magic, rapidly

ensalzar /ensal'θar; ensal'sar/ *vt* to exalt, promote; praise

ensamblador /ensambla'ðor/ *m,* joiner, assembler

ensambladura /ensambla'ðura/ *f,* assemblage, joinery; joining; dovetailing

ensamblar /ensam'blar/ *vt* to assemble; join, dovetail, mortise

ensanchador /ensantʃa'ðor/ *m,* glove stretcher

ensanchar /ensan'tʃar/ *vt* to widen, enlarge, extend; *Sew.* let out, stretch; —*vr* put on airs

ensanche /en'santʃe/ *m,* dilatation, widening; stretch; extension; *Sew.* turnings, letting out; (city) extension

ensangrentar /ensaŋgren'tar/ *vt irr* to stain with blood; —*vr* be bloodstained; be overhasty. See **regimentar**

ensañar /ensa'ɲar/ *vt* to irritate, infuriate; —*vr* be merciless (with vanquished)

ensartar /ensar'tar/ *vt* to string (beads); thread (needles); spit, pierce; tell a string (of falsehoods)

ensayador /ensaia'ðor/ *m,* metal assayer

ensayar /ensa'yar/ *vt* to try out; *Chem.* test; *Theat.* rehearse; assay

ensaye /en'saye/ *m,* assaying (of metals)

ensayista /ensa'yista/ *mf* essayist

ensayo /ensa'yo/ *m,* test, trial; *Lit.* essay; assay; experiment; rehearsal. **e. general,** dress rehearsal

ensenada /ense'naða/ *f,* cove, inlet

enseña /en'seɲa/ *f,* ensign, standard

enseñanza /ense'ɲanθa; ense'ɲansa/ *f,* teaching; education; example, experience. **e. primaria,** elementary education. **e. secundaria,** secondary education. **e. superior,** higher education

enseñar /ense'ɲar/ *vt* to teach, instruct; train; point out; exhibit, show; —*vr* become accustomed. **e. la oreja,** *Fig.* to show the cloven hoof

enseñorearse /enseɲore'arse/ *vr* to take possession (of)

enseres /en'seres/ *m pl,* household goods; utensils; equipment

ensilladero /ensiʎa'ðero; ensiya'ðero/ *m,* paddock

ensillar /ensi'ʎar; ensi'yar/ *vt* to saddle

ensimismarse /ensimis'marse/ *vr* to be lost in thought

ensoberbecer /ensoβerβe'θer; ensoβerβe'ser/ *vt irr* to make haughty; —*vr* become arrogant; grow rough (sea). See **conocer**

ensordecedor /ensorðeθe'ðor; ensorðese'ðor/ *a* deafening

ensordecer /ensorðe'θer; ensorðe'ser/ *vt irr* to deafen; —*vi* become deaf; keep silent, refuse to reply. See **conocer**

ensuciar /ensu'θiar; ensu'siar/ *vt* to soil, dirty; *Fig.* sully; —*vr* be dirty; *Inf.* accept bribes

ensueño /en'sueɲo/ *m,* dream; illusion, fancy

entablado /enta'βlaðo/ *m,* stage, dais; wooden floor; planking

entablar /enta'βlar/ *vt* to plank, floor with boards; board up; *Surg.* splint; undertake, initiate (negotiations, etc.); begin (conversations, etc.); —*vr* settle (winds). **e. acción judicial,** to take legal action

entalegar /entale'gar/ *vt* to put into sacks or bags; hoard (money)

entalladura /entaʎa'ðura; entaya'ðura/ *f,* carving; sculpture; mortise, notch

entallar /enta'ʎar; enta'yar/ *vt* to carve; sculpture; engrave; notch, groove; tap (trees); fit (well or ill) at the waist

entallecer /entaʎe'θer; entaye'ser/ *vi irr* to sprout (plants). See **conocer**

entapizar /entapi'θar; entapi'sar/ *vt* to hang with tapestry; upholster; *Fig.* cover, carpet

entarimado /entari'maðo/ *m,* wooden floor; dais

ente /'ente/ *m,* entity, being; *Inf.* object, individual

enteco /en'teko/ *a* sickly, ailing, delicate

entendederas /entende'ðeras/ *f pl, Inf.* understanding

entendedor /entende'ðor/ *a* (**-ra**) understanding, comprehending —*n* one who understands. **A buen e. pocas palabras,** A word to the wise is sufficient

entender /enten'der/ *vt irr* to comprehend, understand; know; deduce, infer; intend; believe; (*with de*) be familiar with or knowledgeable about; (*with en*) have as a profession or trade; be engaged in; have authority in; —*vr* understand oneself; have a reason (for behavior); understand each other; have an amatory understanding; be meant, signify; (*with con*) have an understanding. **a mi e.,** in my opinion, as I see it —*Pres. Indic.* **entiendo, entiendes, entiende, entienden. Pres. Subjunc. entienda, entiendas, entienda, entiendan**

entendido /enten'diðo/ *a* learned, knowledgeable

entendimiento /entendi'miento/ *m,* understanding; mind, reason, intelligence

enteramente /entera'mente/ *adv* completely, entirely, wholly

enterar /ente'rar/ *vt* to inform, advise

entereza /ente'reθa; entere'sa/ *f,* entirety; completeness; impartiality, integrity; fortitude, constancy; strictness, rigor

enternecer /enterne'θer; enterne'ser/ *vt irr* to soften, make tender; move to pity; —*vr* be touched by compassion. See **conocer**

enternecimiento /enterneθi'miento; enternesi'miento/ *m,* compassion, pity; tenderness

entero /en'tero/ *a* entire; whole; robust, healthy; upright, just; constant, loyal; virgin; pure; *Inf.* strong, tough (cloth); *Math.* integral

enterrador /enterra'ðor/ *m,* gravedigger

enterrar /ente'rrar/ *vt irr* to inter; outlive; bury, forget. See **acertar**

entibiar /enti'βiar/ *vt* to make lukewarm; *Fig.* cool, temper

entidad /enti'ðað/ *f,* entity; value, importance

entierro /en'tierro/ *m,* interment, burial; grave; funeral; buried treasure

entoldar /entol'dar/ *vt* to cover with an awning; hang with tapestry, etc., drape; cover (sky, clouds)

entomología /entomolo'hia/ *f,* entomology

entomológico /entomo'lohiko/ *a* entomological

entomólogo /ento'mologo/ *m,* entomologist

entonación /entona'θion; entona'sion/ *f,* intonation; modulation (voice); conceit

entonado /ento'naðo/ *m,* haughty, conceited

entonar /ento'nar/ *vt* to modulate (voice); intone; blow (organ bellows); lead (song); *Med.* tone up;

Art. harmonize; —*vr* become conceited; *Com.* improve, harden (stock, etc.)

entonces /en'tonθes; entonses/ *adv* then, at that time; in that case, that being so

entonelar /entone'lar/ *vt* to put in barrels or casks

entontecer /entonte'θer; entonteser/ *vt irr* to make stupid or foolish; —*vr* become stupid. See **conocer**

entornar /entor'nar/ *vt* to leave ajar; half-close; upset, turn upside down

entorpecer /entorpe'θer; entorpe'ser/ *vt irr* to numb, make torpid; confuse, daze; obstruct, delay; —*vr* go numb; be confused. See **conocer**

entorpecimiento /entorpeθi'miento; entorpesi'miento/ *m,* numbness, torpidity; stupidity, dullness; delay, obstruction

entrada /en'traða/ *f,* entrance; door, gate; admission; *Cul.* entree; admission ticket; *Theat.* house; takings, gate; *Mil.* entry; beginnings (of month, etc.); intimacy; right of entry. **entradas y salidas,** comings and goings; collusion; *Com.* ingoing and outgoing

entrampar /entram'par/ *vt* to trap (animals); swindle; *Fig. Inf.* entangle (business affairs); *Inf.* load with debts; —*vr* be bogged down; *Inf.* be in debt

entrante /en'trante/ *a* incoming, entrant; next, coming (month)

entraña /en'traɲa/ *f,* entrail; *pl* heart; *Fig.* center, core; humaneness; temperament. *Inf.* **no tener entrañas,** to be heartless, be without feeling

entrañable /entra'ɲaβle/ *a* intimate; dearly loved

entrar /en'trar/ *vi* (*with en*) to enter, go into, come in; flow into; *Fig.* have access to; join, become a member; *Fig.* be taken by (fever, panic, etc.); *Mil.* enter; be an ingredient of; (*with por, en*) penetrate, pierce; (*with de*) embrace (professions, etc.); (*with prep a + infin*) begin to; (*with en + noun*) begin to be (e.g. *e. en calor,* begin to be hot) or begin to take part in (e.g. *e. en lucha,* begin to fight); —*vt* introduce, make enter; *Mil.* (*with en*) occupy; —*vr* (*with en*) squeeze in. **e. en apetito,** to work up an appetite, get an appetite. *Inf.* **no e. ni salir en,** to take no part in. *Inf.* **No me entra,** I don't understand it

entre /'entre/ *prep* between; among; to. **e. joyas,** among jewels. **E. las dos se escribió la carta,** Between them, they wrote the letter. **Dije e. mí,** I said to myself. **los días de e. semana,** weekdays. **e. tanto,** in the meanwhile.

entreabrir /entrea'βrir/ *vt* to leave ajar; half-open —*Past Part.* **entreabierto**

entreacto /entre'akto/ *m,* interval, entr'acte; small cigar

entrecano /entre'kano/ *a* going gray, grayish (hair)

entrecejo /entre'θeho; entre'seho/ *m,* space between the eyebrows; frown

entrecoger /entreko'her/ *vt* to intercept, catch; constrain, compel

entrecortado /entrekor'taðo/ *a* intermittent (sounds); faltering, broken (voice)

entrecubiertas /entreku'βiertas/ *f pl, Naut.* between decks

entredicho /entre'ðitʃo/ *m,* prohibition; *Eccl.* interdiction

entredós /en'treðos/ *m, Sew.* insertion

entrefino /entre'fino/ *a* middling, fairly fine

entrega /en'trega/ *f,* handing over; delivery; *Lit.* part, serial; installment. **por entregas,** as a serial, serial (of stories)

entregar /entre'gar/ *vt* to hand over; deliver; surrender; —*vr* give oneself up; surrender; submit; (*with prep a*) engage in, be absorbed in; (*with prep a* or *en*) give oneself over to (vice, etc.)

entreguista /entre'gista/ *mf* defeatist

entrelazar /entrela'θar; entrela'sar/ *vt* to interlace, intertwine; interweave

entrelistado /entrelis'taðo/ *a* striped

entrelucir /entrelu'θir; entrelu'sir/ *vi irr* to show through, be glimpsed. See **lucir**

entremedias /entre'meðias/ *adv* in between, halfway; in the meantime

entremés /entre'mes/ *m,* hors d'oeuvres (gen. *pl*); interlude, one-act farce

entremesista /entreme'sista/ *mf* author of, or actor in, one-act farces

entremeter /entreme'ter/ *vt* to place between or among; —*vr* intrude; meddle, pry

entremetido /entreme'tiðo/ (-da) *a* meddlesome —*n* busybody, meddler

entremetimiento /entremeti'miento/ *m,* meddlesomeness

entremezclar /entremeθ'klar; entremes'klar/ *vt* to intermingle

entrenador /entrena'ðor/ (-ra) *n* trainer; *Sports.* coach

entrenamiento /entrena'miento/ *m,* training, exercise

entrenar /entre'nar/ (se) *vt* and *vr* to train; exercise; *Sports.* coach

entreoír /entreo'ir/ *vt* to overhear; hear imperfectly

entrepaño /entre'paɲo/ *m, Archit.* panel; pier (between windows, etc.)

entrepiernas /entre'piernas/ *f pl,* crotch

entrepuente /entre'puente/ *m, Naut.* between decks; steerage quarters

entresacar /entresa'kar/ *vt* to choose or pick out; thin out (plants); thin (hair)

entresuelo /entre'suelo/ *m,* mezzanine, entresol; ground floor

entresueño /entre'sueɲo/ *m,* daydream

entretalladura /entretaʎa'ðura; entretayae'th;ura/ *f,* bas-relief

entretallar /entreta'ʎar; entreta'yar/ *vt* to carve in bas-relief; engrave; *Sew.* do openwork; intercept; —*vr* connect, dovetail

entretejer /entrete'her/ *vt* to interweave; interlace; *Lit.* insert

entretela /entre'tela/ *f, Sew.* interlining

entretener /entrete'ner/ *vt irr* to keep waiting; make more bearable; amuse, entertain; delay, postpone; maintain, upkeep; —*vr* amuse oneself. See **tener**

entretenido /entrete'niðo/ *a* amusing, entertaining

entretenimiento /entreteni'miento/ *m,* amusement; pastime, diversion; upkeep, maintenance

entretiempo /entre'tiempo/ *m,* between seasons, spring or autumn

entreventana /entreβen'tana/ *f,* space between windows

entreverado /entreβe'raðo/ *a* variegated; streaky (of bacon)

entreverar /entreβe'rar/ *vt* to intermingle

entrevía /entre'βia/ *f,* railroad gauge

entrevista /entre'βista/ *f,* meeting, interview

entristecer /entriste'θer; entriste'ser/ *vt irr* to sadden; —*vr* grieve. See **conocer**

entristecimiento /entristeθi'miento; entristesi'miento/ *m,* sadness

entrometer /entrome'ter/ *vt* See **entremeter**

entronar /entro'nar/ *vt* See **entronizar**

entroncar /entron'kar/ *vt* to prove descent; —*vi* be related, or become related (by marriage)

entronerar /entrone'rar/ *vt* to pocket (in billiards)

entronización /entroniθa'θion; entronisa'sion/ *f,* enthronement

entronizar /entroni'θar; entroni'sar/ *vt* to enthrone; exalt

entronque /entron'ke/ *m,* blood relationship, cognation; junction

entumecer /entume'θer; entume'ser/ *vt irr* to numb; —*vr* go numb; swell, rise (sea, etc.). See **conocer**

enturbiar /entur'βiar/ *vt* to make turbid or cloudy; confuse, disorder; —*vr* become turbid; be in disorder

entusiasmar /entusias'mar/ *vt* to inspire enthusiasm; —*vr* be enthusiastic

entusiasmo /entu'siasmo/ *m,* enthusiasm

entusiasta /entu'siasta/ *a* enthusiastic. *mf* enthusiast

enumeración /enumera'θion; enumera'sion/ *f,* enumeration

enumerar /enume'rar/ *vt* to enumerate

enunciación /enunθia'θion; enunsia'sion/ *f,* statement, declaration, enunciation

enunciar /enun'θiar; enun'siar/ *vt* to state clearly, enunciate

envainar /embai'nar/ *vt* to sheathe

envalentonamiento /embalentona'miento/ *m,* boldness; braggadocio, bravado

envalentonar /embalento'nar/ *vt* to make bold (gen. in a bad sense); —*vr* strut, brag; take courage

envanecer /embane'θer; embane'ser/ *vt irr* to make vain or conceited; —*vr* be vain; be conceited

envanecimiento /embaneθimiento; embanesi'miento/ *m,* conceit, vanity

envasador /embasa'ðor/ (-ra) *n* packer. *m,* funnel

envasar /emba'sar/ *vt* to bottle; barrel; sack (grain, etc.); pack in any container; pierce (with sword)

envase /em'base/ *m,* bottling; filling; container; packing

envejecer /embehe'θer; embehe'ser/ *vt irr* to make old, wear out; —*vi* grow old. See **conocer**

envenenador /embenena'ðor/ (-ra) *n* poisoner

envenenamiento /embenena'miento/ *m,* poisoning

envenenar /embene'nar/ *vt* to poison; corrupt, pervert; put a malicious interpretation on; embitter; —*vr* take poison

envergadura /emberga'ðura/ *f,* wingspan

envés /em'bes/ *m,* wrong side of anything; *Inf.* back. **al e.,** wrong side out

enviado /em'biaðo/ *m,* messenger; envoy. **e. extraordinario,** special envoy

enviar /em'biar/ *vt* to send, dispatch

enviciar /embi'θiar; embi'siar/ *vt* to corrupt, make vicious; —*vr* (*with con, en*) take to (drink, etc.)

envidia /em'biðia/ *f,* envy; emulation; desire (to possess)

envidiable /embi'ðiaβle/ *a* enviable

envidiar /embi'ðiar/ *vt* to envy, grudge; emulate

envidioso /embi'ðioso/ *a* envious

envilecer /embile'θer; embile'ser/ *vt irr* to debase; —*vr* degrade oneself. See **conocer**

envío /em'bio/ *m, Com.* remittance; consignment

envite /em'bite/ *m,* stake (at cards); offer; push, shove

enviudar /embiu'ðar/ *vi* to become a widow or widower

envoltorio /embol'torio/ *m,* bundle

envoltura /embol'tura/ *f,* swaddling clothes; covering; wrapping

envolver /embol'βer/ *vt irr* to enfold; envelop; wrap up, parcel; *Fig.* contain, enshrine; swaddle, swathe; roll into a ball; confound (in argument); *Mil.* outflank; implicate (person). See **mover**

enyesado /enye'saðo/ *m,* plastering; stucco

enyesar /enye'sar/ *vt* to plaster; *Surg.* apply a plaster bandage

enzarzar /enθar'θar; ensar'sar/ *vt* to fill or cover with brambles; —*vr* be caught on brambles; set one person against another; get in difficulties; quarrel

eñe /'eɲe/ *f,* name of letter Ñ

eón /e'on/ *m,* eon

eperlano /eper'lano/ *m,* smelt

épica /'epika/ *f,* epic

épico /'epiko/ *a* epic

epicúreo /epi'kureo/ (-ea) *a* epicurean; sensual, voluptuous —*n* epicure

epidemia /epi'ðemia/ *f,* epidemic

epidémico /epi'ðemiko/ *a* epidemic

epifanía /epifa'nia/ *f,* Epiphany, Twelfth Night

epiglotis /epi'glotis/ *f,* epiglottis

epígrafe /epi'grafe/ *m,* epigraph, inscription; title, motto

epigrafía /epigra'fia/ *f,* epigraphy

epigrama /epi'grama/ *m,* inscription; epigram

epigramático /epigra'matiko/ (-ca) *a* epigrammatic —*n* epigrammatist

epilepsia /epi'lepsia/ *f,* epilepsy

epiléptico /epi'leptiko/ (-ca) *a* and *n* epileptic

epilogar /epilo'gar/ *vt* to summarize, recapitulate

epílogo /e'pilogo/ *m,* recapitulation; summary, digest; epilogue

episcopado /episko'paðo/ *m,* episcopate; bishopric

episódico /epi'soðiko/ *a* episodic

episodio /epi'soðio/ *m,* episode, digression

epístola /e'pistola/ *f,* epistle

epistolar /episto'lar/ *a* epistolary

epitafio /epi'tafio/ *m,* epitaph

epíteto /e'piteto/ *m,* epithet

epítome /e'pitome/ *m,* epitome; summary, abstract

época /'epoka/ *f,* epoch, period; space of time. **é. de celo,** mating season. **é. de lluvias,** rainy season. **é. de secas,** dry season. **en aquella é.,** at that time

épodo /'epoðo/ *m, Poet.* epode

epopeya /epo'peya/ *f,* epic poem; *Fig.* epic

equidad /eki'ðað/ *f,* fairness; reasonableness; equity

equidistancia /ekiðis'tanθia; ekiðistansia/ *f,* equidistance

equidistante /ekiðis'tante/ *a* equidistant

equilibrar /ekili'βrar/ *vt* to balance; *Fig.* maintain in equilibrium, counterbalance

equilibrio /eki'liβrio/ *m,* equilibrium; equanimity; *Fig.* balance

equilibrista /ekili'βrista/ *mf* equilibrist, tightrope walker

equino /e'kino/ *a* equine. *m, Archit.* echinus; sea urchin

equinoccio /eki'nokθio; ekinoksio/ *m,* equinox

equipaje /eki'pahe/ *m,* luggage, baggage; *Naut.* crew

equipar /eki'par/ *vt* to equip, furnish

equipo /e'kipo/ *m,* outfitting, furnishing; equipment; team; trousseau

equis /'ekis/ *f,* name of letter X

equitación /ekita'θion; ekita'sion/ *f,* horsemanship, riding

equitativo /ekita'tiβo/ *a* equitable, just, fair

equivalencia /ekiβa'lenθia; ekiβalensia/ *f,* equivalence, equality

equivalente /ekiβa'lente/ *a* equivalent

equivaler /ekiβa'ler/ *vi irr* to be equivalent; *Geom.* be equal. See **valer**

equivocación /ekiβoka'θion; ekiβoka'sion/ *f,* error, mistake

equivocadamente /ekiβokaða'mente/ *adv* mistakenly, by mistake

equivocar /ekiβo''kar/ *vt* to mistake; —*vr* be mistaken or make a mistake. **equivocarse de medio a medio,** to be off by a long shot

equívoco /e'kiβoko/ *a* equivocal, ambiguous. *m,* equivocation

era /'era/ *f,* era; threshing floor; vegetable or flower bed

erario /e'rario/ *m,* public treasury, exchequer

erección /erek'θion; erek'sion/ *f,* raising; erection, elevation; foundation, institution

eremita /ere'mita/ *mf* hermit

ergio /'erhio/ *m,* erg

erguir /er'gir/ *vt irr* to raise; straighten; lift up; —*vr* straighten up; tower; grow proud —*Pres. Indic.* **irgo** (or **yergo), irgues, irguen.** *Pres. Part.* **irguiendo.** *Preterite* **irguió, irguieron.** *Pres. Subjunc.* **irga** or **yerga,** etc.

erial /e'rial/ *m,* uncultivated land

erigir /eri'hir/ *vt* to found, establish; promote, exalt. **erigirse contra,** to rise up against

erisipela /erisi'pela/ *f,* erysipelas

erizado /eri'θaðo; eri'saðo/ *a* a standing on end (of hair); prickly; covered with bristles or quills. **e. de espinas,** bristling with thorns; covered with bristles or quills

erizar /eri'θar; eri'sar/ *vt* to set on end (hair); beset with difficulties; —*vr* stand on end, bristle (hair, quills, etc.)

erizo /e'riθo; e'riso/ *m,* hedgehog; husk (of some fruits); *Inf.* touch-me-not, unsociable person; *Mech.* sprocket wheel. **e. de mar,** sea urchin

ermita /er'mita/ *f,* hermitage

ermitaño /ermi'taɲo/ *m,* hermit

erosión /ero'sion/ *f,* erosion

erótico /e'rotiko/ *a* erotic

errabundo /erra'βundo/ *a* wandering, errant, vagrant

erradamente /erraða'mente/ *adv* erroneously

erradicable /erraði'kaβle/ *a* eradicable

erradicación /erraðika'θion; erraðika'sion/ *f,* eradication

erradicar /erraði'kar/ *vt* to eradicate

errante /e'rrante/ *a* wandering; erring; errant

errar /e'rrar/ *vi irr* to err, fail; rove, roam; wander (attention, etc.); —*vr* be mistaken. *Auto.* **e. el encendido,** to misfire —*Pres. Indic.* **yerro, yerras, yerra, yerran.** *Pres. Subjunc.* **yerre, yerres, yerre, yerren**

errata /e'rrata/ *f,* misprint

errático /e'rratiko/ *a* wandering, vagrant; *Med.* erratic

erre /'erre/ *f,* name of letter R

erróneo /e'rroneo/ *a* erroneous, mistaken

error /e'rror/ *m,* error. **error de más,** an overestimate. **error de menos,** an underestimate

eructar /eruk'tar/ *vi* to eructate, belch

eructo /e'rukto/ *m,* eructation, belching

erudición /eruði'θion; eruði'sion/ *f,* erudition

erudito /eru'ðito/ *a* learned, erudite. *m,* scholar. **e. a la violeta,** pseudo-learned

erupción /erup'θion; erup'sion/ *f, Med.* rash; eruption

eruptivo /erup'tiβo/ *a* eruptive

es /es/ *irr 3rd pers. sing Pres. Indic.* of ser, is

esa /'esa/ *f, dem a* that. **ésa,** *f, dem. pron* that one; the former; the town in which you are (e.g. *Iré a é. mañana,* I shall come to your town tomorrow). Used generally in letters. See **ése**

esbeltez /esβel'teθ; esβel'tes/ *f,* slenderness

esbelto /es'βelto/ *a* tall and slim and graceful, willowy

esbozar /esβo'θar; esβo'sar/ *vt* to sketch, outline

esbozo /es'βoθo; es'βoso/ *m,* sketch; outline, rough plan, first draft

escabechar /eskaβe'tʃar/ *vt* to pickle; dye (the hair, etc.); *Inf.* kill in anger; *Inf.* fail (an examination)

escabeche /eska'βetʃe/ *m, Cul.* pickle; hair dye

escabechina /eskaβe'tʃina/ *f, Inf.* heavy failure (in an examination)

escabel /eska'βel/ *m,* footstool; small backless chair; *Fig.* steppingstone

escabioso /eska'βioso/ *a* scabby, scabious

escabro /es'kaβro/ *m,* scab, mange

escabroso /eska'βroso/ *a* rough; rocky; uneven; rude, unpolished, uncivil; risqué, improper

escabullirse /eskaβu'ʎirse; eskaβu'yirse/ *vr irr* to escape; run away; slip out unnoticed. See **mullir**

escafandra /eska'fandra/ *f,* diving suit, diving outfit

escala /es'kala/ *f,* ladder; (*Mus. Math.*) scale; dial (of machines); proportion, ratio; stage, stopping place; measuring rule; *Naut.* port of call. **e. de toldilla,** companion ladder. *Mus.* **e. mayor,** major scale. **e. menor,** minor scale. *Naut.* **hacer e. en un puerto,** to call at a port

escalada /eska'laða/ *f,* escalade

escalafón /eskala'fon/ *m,* salary scale; roll, list

escalamiento /eskala'miento/ *m,* scaling, climbing; storming

escalar /eska'lar/ *vt* to scale; climb, ascend; storm, assail, enter or leave violently

escaldadura /eskalda'ðura/ *f,* scalding; scald

escaldar /eskal'dar/ *vt* to scald; make red-hot; —*vr* scald or burn oneself. **Gato escaldado del agua fría huye,** Once bitten, twice shy

escalera /eska'lera/ *f,* staircase; stair. **e. abajo,** below stairs. **e. de caracol,** spiral staircase. **e. de mano,** ladder. **e. de tijera,** stepladder. **e. móvil,** escalator

escalfar /eskal'far/ *vt* to poach (eggs); burn (bread)

escalinata /eskali'nata/ *f,* outside staircase or flight of steps, perron

escalofrío /eskalo'frio/ *m,* (gen. *pl*) shiver, shudder

escalón /eska'lon/ *m,* step, stair; rung (of a ladder); *Fig.* steppingstone; grade, rank. **en escalones,** in steps

escalpar /eskal'par/ *vt* to scalp

escalpelo /eskal'pelo/ *m,* scalpel

escama /es'kama/ *f, Zool.* scale; anything scale-shaped; flake; suspicion, resentment

escamar /eska'mar/ *vt* to scale (fish); make suspicious; —*vr Inf.* be suspicious or disillusioned

escamondar /eskamon'dar/ *vt Agr.* to prune

escamoso /eska'moso/ *a* scaly

escamotear /eskamote'ar/ *vt* to make disappear; palm (in conjuring); steal

escamoteo /eskamo'teo/ *m,* disappearance; stealing

escampada /eskam'paða/ *f, Inf.* clear interval on a rainy day

escampar /eskam'par/ *vi* to cease raining; clear up (of the weather, sky); stop (work, etc.)

escamujar /eskamu'har/ *vt Agr.* to cut out superfluous wood (of trees, etc.)

escanciar /eskan'θiar; eskan'siar/ *vt* to pour out wine; —*vi* drink wine

escandalizar /eskandali'θar; eskandali'sar/ *vt* to shock, scandalize; disturb with noise; —*vr* be vexed or irritated

escandallo /eskan'daʎo; eskan'dayo/ *m, Naut.* deepsea lead; random test

escándalo /es'kandalo/ *m,* scandal; commotion, uproar; bad example; viciousness; astonishment

escandaloso /eskanda'loso/ *a* disgraceful, scandalous; turbulent

Escandinavia /eskandi'naβia/ Scandinavia

escandinavo /eskandi'naβo/ **(-va)** *a* and *n* Scandinavian

escandir /eskan'dir/ *vt* to scan (verse)

escansión /eskan'sion/ *f,* scansion

escantillón /eskanti'ʎon; eskanti'yon/ *m,* template, pattern; rule

escaño /es'kaɲo/ *m,* bench with a back

escapada /eska'paða/ *f,* escape; escapade

escapar /eska'par/ *vt* to spur on (a horse); —*vi* escape; flee; avoid, evade; —*vr* escape; leak (gas, etc.). **Se me escapó su nombre,** His name escaped me. **e. por un pelo,** to have a narrow escape

escaparate /eskapa'rate/ *m,* showcase, cabinet; shop window

escapatoria /eskapa'toria/ *f,* escape, flight; *Inf.* way out, loophole

escape /es'kape/ *m,* flight; evasion; escape (gas, etc.); *Auto.* exhaust. **a e.,** at full speed

escápula /es'kapula/ *f,* scapula

escaque /es'kake/ *m,* square (chessboard or checkerboard); *pl* chess

escaqueado /eskake'aðo/ *a* checked, worked in squares

escara /es'kara/ *f,* scar

escarabajo /eskara'βaho/ *m,* beetle, scarab; *Fig. Inf.* dwarf; *pl Inf.* scrawl

escaramuza /eskara'muθa; eskara'musa/ *f,* skirmish

escaramuzar /eskaramu'θar; eskaramu'sar/ *vi* to skirmish

escarapela /eskara'pela/ *f,* cockade, rosette; brawl

escarbadientes /eskarβa'ðientes/ *m,* toothpick

escarbar /eskar'βar/ *vt* to scratch, scrabble (fowls); root, dig; rake out (the fire); inquire into

escarcha /es'kartʃa/ *f,* hoarfrost

escarchar /eskar'tʃar/ *vt Cul.* to frost, ice; spread with frosting; —*vi* freeze lightly

escarda /es'karða/ *f,* weeding; *Fig.* weeding out

escardador /eskarða'ðor/ **(-ra)** *n* weeder

escardar /eskar'ðar/ *vt* to weed; *Fig.* separate good from bad

escarificación /eskarifika'θion; eskarifika'sion/ *f,* scarification

escarlata /eskar'lata/ *f,* scarlet; scarlet cloth

escarlatina /eskarla'tina/ *f,* scarlet fever

escarmentar /eskarmen'tar/ *vt irr* to reprehend or punish severely; —*vi* learn from experience, be warned. See **acertar**

escarmiento /eskar'miento/ *m,* disillusionment, experience; warning; punishment, fine

escarnecedor /eskarneθe'ðor; eskarneseðor/ **(-ra)** *a* mocking —*n* mocker

escarnecer /eskarne'θer; eskarne'ser/ *vt irr* to mock. See **conocer**

escarnio /es'karnio/ *m,* gibe, jeer

escarola /eska'rola/ *f,* endive; frilled ruff

escarpa /es'karpa/ *f,* steep slope, declivity; escarpment

escarpado /eskar'paðo/ *a* steep, precipitous

escarpín /eskar'pin/ *m,* pump, slipper

escasear /eskase'ar/ *vt* to dole out, give grudgingly; save, husband; —*vi* be scarce or short; grow less

escasez /eska'seθ; eska'ses/ *f,* meanness, frugality; want; shortage, scarcity

escaso /es'kaso/ *a* scarce; short; bare; parsimonious

escatimar /eskati'mar/ *vt* to cut down, curtail

escatimoso /eskati'moso/ *a* malicious, guileful

escayola /eska'yola/ *f,* plaster of Paris

escena /es'θena; es'sena/ *f, Theat.* stage; scene; scenery; theater, drama; spectacle, sight; episode, incident. **director de e.,** producer. **poner en e.,** *Theat.* to produce

escenario /esθe'nario; esse'nario/ *m, Theat.* stage; scenario

escénico /es'θeniko; es'seniko/ *a* scenic

escenografía /esθenogra'fia; essenogra'fia/ *f,* scenography

escenógrafo /esθe'nografo; esse'nografo/ **(-fa)** *n* scenographer, scene painter

escepticismo /esθepti'θismo; essepti'sismo/ *m,* scepticism

escéptico /es'θeptiko; es'septiko/ **(-ca)** *a* sceptical —*n* sceptic

escindir /esθin'dir; essin'dir/ *vt* to split

escisión /esθi'sion; essi'sion/ *f,* cleavage, split; splitting; schism; disagreement

esclarecer /esklare'θer; esklare'ser/ *vt irr* to illuminate; ennoble, make illustrious; *Fig.* enlighten; elucidate; —*vi* dawn. See **conocer**

esclarecido /esklare'θiðo; esklare'siðo/ *a* distinguished, illustrious

esclavina /eskla'βina/ *f,* short cape

esclavitud /esklaβi'tuð/ *f,* slavery; fraternity

esclavizar /esklaβi'θar; esklaβi'sar/ *vt* to enslave

esclavo /es'klaβo/ **(-va)** *n* slave; member of a brotherhood —*a* enslaved. *f,* slave bracelet; ID bracelet

esclerosis /eskle'rosis/ *f,* sclerosis

esclerótica /eskle'rotika/ *f,* sclerotic

esclusa /es'klusa/ *f,* lock; sluice gate; weir

esclusero /esklu'sero/ *m,* lock keeper

escoba /es'koβa/ *f,* broom, brush; *Bot.* yellow broom

escobada /esko'βaða/ *f,* sweep, stroke (of a broom)

escobar /esko'βar/ *vt* to sweep with a broom

escobazo /esko'βaθo; esko'βaso/ *m,* brush with a broom

escobero /esko'βero/ *m,* brush maker or seller

escobilla /esko'βiʎa; esko'βiya/ *f,* brush

escobina /esko'βina/ *f,* metal filing; woodshaving

escocer /esko'θer; esko'ser/ *vi irr* to smart; *Fig.* sear; —*vr* hurt, smart; be chafed. See **mover**

escocés /esko'θes; esko'ses/ **(-esa)** *a* Scots, Scottish —*n* Scot

Escocia /es'koθia; eskosia/ Scotland

escoda /es'koða/ *f,* claw hammer

escofina /esko'fina/ *f,* rasp, file

escoger /esko'her/ *vt* to choose, select

escogido /esko'hiðo/ *a* choice, select

escolar /esko'lar/ *a* school; pupil. *m,* pupil

escolasticismo /eskolasti'θismo; eskolasti'sismo/ *m,* scholasticism

escolástico /esko'lastiko/ *a* scholastic

escollera /esko'ʎera; esko'yera/ *f,* breakwater, sea wall, jetty

escollo /es'koʎo; es'koyo/ *m,* reef; danger, risk; difficulty, obstacle

escolopendra /eskolo'pendra/ *f,* centipede; hart's-tongue fern

escolta /es'kolta/ *f,* escort, guard

escoltar /eskol'tar/ *vt* to escort; guard, conduct

escombrar /eskom'brar/ *vt* to remove obstacles, free of rubbish; *Fig.* clean up

escombro /es'kombro/ *m,* debris, rubble, rubbish; mackerel

esconder /eskon'der/ *vt* to hide, conceal; *Fig.* contain, embrace; —*vr* hide

escondidas, a /eskon'diðas, a/ *adv* secretly

escondite, escondrijo /eskon'dite, eskon'driho/ *m,* hiding place. **jugar al escondite,** to play hide-and-seek

escopeta /esko'peta/ *f,* shotgun. **e. de aire comprimido,** air gun, popgun. **e. de pistón,** repercussion gun. **e. de viento,** air gun

escopetazo /eskope'taθo; eskope'taso/ *m,* gunshot; gunshot wound; *Fig.* bombshell

escopetear /eskopete'ar/ *vt* to shoot repeatedly

escopetero /eskope'tero/ *m,* musketeer; gunsmith; man with a gun

escoplear /eskople'ar/ *vt* to notch; chisel; gouge

escoplo /es'koplo/ *m*, chisel

escorbuto /eskor'βuto/ *m*, scurvy

escoria /es'koria/ *f*, dross, slag; scoria, volcanic ash; *Fig.* dregs

escorial /esko'rial/ *m*, slag heap

escorpión /eskor'pion/ *m*, scorpion; Scorpio

escorzo /es'korθo; es'korso/ *m*, *Art.* foreshortening

escotado /esko'taðo/ *a* low-cut (of dresses)

escotadura /eskota'ðura/ *a* low neck (of a dress); piece cut out of something; *Theat.* large trapdoor; recess

escotar /esko'tar/ *vt* to cut low in the neck (of dresses); pay one's share (of expenses)

escote /es'kote/ *m*, low neck (of a dress); shortness (of sleeves); share (of expenses); lace yoke

escotilla /esko'tiʎa; esko'tiya/ *f*, *Naut.* hatch

escozor /esko'θor; esko'sor/ *m*, smart, pricking pain; irritation, prickle; heartache

escriba /es'kriβa/ *m*, (*Jewish hist.*) scribe

escribanía /eskriβa'nia/ *f*, secretaryship; notaryship; bureau, office; writing case; inkstand

escribano /eskri'βano/ *m*, notary public; secretary

escribiente /eskri'βiente/ *mf* clerk

escribir /eskri'βir/ *vt* to write; —*vr* enlist; enroll; correspond by writing —*Past Part.* **escrito**

escrito /es'krito/ *m*, writing, manuscript; literary or scientific work; *Law.* writ. **por e.,** in writing

escritor /eskri'tor/ **(-ra)** *n* writer, author

escritorio /eskri'torio/ *m*, escritoire; office

escritura /eskri'tura/ *f*, writing; handwriting; *Law.* deed; literary work. **Sagrada E.,** Holy Scripture

escrófula /es'krofula/ *f*, scrofula

escrofuloso /eskrofu'loso/ *a* scrofulous

escroto /es'kroto/ *m*, scrotum

escrúpulo /es'krupulo/ *m*, scruple, qualm, conscientiousness; scruple (pharmacy)

escrupulosidad /eskrupulosi'ðað/ *f*, conscientiousness, scrupulousness

escrupuloso /eskrupu'loso/ *a* scrupulous; exact, accurate

escrutador /eskruta'ðor/ **(-ra)** *n* scrutinizer —*a* examining, inspecting

escrutar /eskru'tar/ *vt* to scrutinize, examine; count (votes)

escrutinio /eskru'tinio/ *m*, scrutiny, examination; count (votes)

escuadra /es'kuaðra/ *f*, carpenter's square; architect's square; *Nav.* fleet; *Aer.* squadron; *Mil.* squad. **e. de agrimensor,** *Surv.* cross-staff

escuadrar /eskuað'rar/ *vt* (and *Mas.*) to square

escuadrilla /eskuað'riʎa; eskuað'riya/ *f*, squadron (airplanes, small ships)

escuadrón /eskuað'ron/ *m*, squadron

escualidez /eskuali'ðeθ; eskuali'ðes/ *f*, squalor, sordidness

escuálido /es'kualiðo/ *a* filthy, squalid; sordid; thin

escucha /es'kutʃa/ *f*, listening; peephole; *Mil.* sentinel

escuchar /esku'tʃar/ *vt* to listen; attend to, heed; —*vr* like the sound of one's own voice

escudar /esku'ðar/ *vt* to shield, protect

escudero /esku'ðero/ *m*, squire, page; gentleman; shield maker

escudete /esku'ðete/ *m*, escutcheon; shield; gusset; white water lily

escudilla /esku'ðiʎa; esku'ðiya/ *f*, bowl

escudo /es'kuðo/ *m*, shield; escudo; escutcheon; protection, defense; ward (of a keyhole)

escudriñador /eskuðriɲa'ðor/ **(-ra)** *a* searching; curious, prying —*n* scrutinizer; pryer

escudriñar /eskuðri'ɲar/ *vt* to scrutinize; scan; investigate; pry into

escuela /es'kuela/ *f*, school; school building; style; (*Lit.* and *Art.*) school. **e. de artes y oficios,** industrial school. **e. industrial,** technical school. **e. normal,** normal school

escueto /es'kueto/ *a* dry, bare, unadorned; simple, exact; unencumbered

esculpir /eskul'pir/ *vt* to sculpture; engrave

escultor /eskul'tor/ **(-ra)** *n* sculptor

escultórico /eskul'toriko/ *a* sculptural

escultura /eskul'tura/ *f*, sculpture; carving; modeling

escupidera /eskupi'ðera/ *f*, spittoon

escupir /esku'pir/ *vi* to expectorate; —*vt Fig.* spit out; cast away, throw out

escurreplatos /eskurre'platos/ *m*, dishrack, draining rack

escurrido /esku'rriðo/ *a* narrow-hipped; skintight (of skirts)

escurridor /eskurri'ðor/ *m*, colander, sieve; dishrack; drainingboard

escurriduras /eskurri'ðuras/ *f pl*, lees, dregs

escurrir /esku'rrir/ *vt* to drain to the dregs; wring, press out, drain; —*vi* trickle, drip; slip, slide; —*vr* slip away, edge away; escape, slip out; skid

esdrújulo /es'ðru'hulo/ *a Gram.* of words where the accent falls on the antepenultimate syllable

ese /'ese/ *f*, name of letter S; S-shaped link (in a chain). *Inf.* **andar haciendo eses,** to reel about drunkenly

ese /'ese/ *m*, *dem a* (*f*, **esa**, *pl* **esos, esas**) that; those. **ése,** *m*, *dem pron* (*f*, **ésa.** *neut* **eso.** *pl* **ésos, ésas**) that one; the former (e.g. *Me gusta éste, pero ése no me gusta,* I like this one, but I do not like that one

esencia /e'senθia; e'sensia/ *f*, essence, nature, character; extract; *Chem.* essence

esencial /esen'θial; esen'sial/ *a* essential

esfera /es'fera/ *f*, *Geom.* sphere, globe, ball; sky; rank; face, dial; province, scope

esférico /es'feriko/ *a* spherical

esfinge /es'finhe/ *f*, sphinx

esforzado /esfor'θaðo; esfor'saðo/ *a* valiant, courageous; spirited

esforzador /esforθa'ðor; esforsa'ðor/ *a* encouraging

esforzar /esfor'θar; esfor'sar/ *vt irr* to encourage; invigorate; —*vr* make an effort. See **contar**

esfuerzo /es'fuerθo; es'fuerso/ *m*, effort; courage; spirit; vigor; exertion, strain; *Mech.* stress. **sin e.,** effortless

esfumar /esfu'mar/ *vt Art.* shade; *Art.* stump; dim; —*vr* disappear

esfumino /esfu'mino/ *m*, *Art.* stump

esgrima /es'grima/ *f*, (art of) fencing

esgrimidor /esgrimi'ðor/ *m*, fencer, swordsman

esgrimir /esgri'mir/ *vt* to fence; fend off

esguazar /esgua'θar; esgua'sar/ *vt* to ford (a river)

esguince /es'ginθe; es'ginse/ *m*, dodging, twist; expression or gesture of repugnance; *Med.* sprain

eslabón /esla'βon/ *m*, link (in a chain); steel for producing fire. **e. perdido,** *Fig.* missing link

eslabonar /eslaβo'nar/ *vt* to link; connect, unite

eslavo /es'laβo/ **(-va)** *a* Slavic —*n* Slav

eslora /es'lora/ *f*, *Naut.* length (of a ship)

eslovaco /eslo'βako/ **(-ca)** *a* Slovakian —*n* Slovak

esloveno /eslo'βeno/ **(-na)** *a* and *n* Slovene

esmaltador /esmalta'ðor/ **(-ra)** *n* enameler

esmaltar /esmal'tar/ *vt* to enamel; decorate, adorn

esmalte /es'malte/ *m*, enamel; enamelwork; smalt; brilliance

esmerado /esme'raðo/ *a* careful, painstaking

esmeralda /esme'ralda/ *f*, emerald

esmerar /esme'rar/ *vt* to polish; —*vr* (*with en*) take great pains with (or to)

esmeril /es'meril/ *m*, emery

esmerilar /esmeri'lar/ *vt* to polish with emery

esmero /es'mero/ *m*, great care, conscientiousness

esmoladera /esmola'ðera/ *f*, grindstone

esnob /es'noβ/ *a* snobbish. *mf* snob

eso /'eso/ *neut dem pron* that; the fact that; that idea, affair, etc.; about (of time) (e.g. *Vendrá a e. de las nueve,* He will come about nine o'clock). **Eso** refers to an abstraction, never to one definite object. **No me gusta e.,** I don't like that kind of thing. **e. es,** that's it. **por e.,** therefore, for that reason

esófago /e'sofago/ *m*, esophagus

esotérico /eso'teriko/ *a* esoteric

espaciar /espa'θiar; espa'siar/ *vt* to space; *Print.* lead; —*vr* spread oneself, enlarge (upon)

espacio /es'paθio; es'pasio/ *m*, space; capacity; interval, duration; slowness; *Print.* lead

espaciosidad /espaθiosi'ða; espasiosi'ðað/ f, spaciousness; capacity

espada /es'paða/ f, sword; matador; swordsman; (cards) spade. **entre la e. y la pared,** Fig. between a rock and a hard place; between undesirable alternatives.

espadachín /espaða'tʃin/ m, good swordsman; bully, quarrelsome fellow

espadaña /espa'ðaɲa/ f, open belfry; gladiolus

espadería /espaðe'ria/ f, sword cutler's workshop or shop

espadero /espa'ðero/ m, sword cutler

espadín /espa'ðin/ m, small dress sword

espahi /es'pai/ m, spahi

espalda /es'palda/ f, Anat. back (often pl); pl rear, back portion; Mil. rear guard. **de espaldas,** with one's (its, his, etc.) back turned; on one's (its, etc.) back

espaldar /espal'dar/ m, backpiece of a cuirass; back (of chair); garden trellis, espalier

espaldarazo /espalda'raθo; espalda'raso/ m, accolade

espaldera /espal'dera/ f, espalier, trellis

espantadizo /espanta'ðiθo; espanta'ðiso/ a easily frightened

espantapájaros /espanta'paharos/ m, scarecrow

espantar /espan'tar/ vt to frighten, terrify; chase off; —vr be amazed; be scared

espanto /es'panto/ m, terror, panic; dismay; amazement; threat

espantoso /espan'toso/ a horrible, terrifying, awesome; amazing

España /es'paɲa/ Spain

español /espa'ɲol/ **(-la)** a Spanish —n Spaniard. m, Spanish (language). **a la española,** in Spanish fashion

españolía /espaɲo'lia/ f, Spanish colony, Spanish community (outside Spain)

españolismo /espaɲo'lismo/ m, love of things Spanish; Hispanism

españolizar /espaɲoli'θar; espaɲoli'sar/ vt to hispanize; —vr adopt Spanish customs

esparadrapo /espara'ðrapo/ m, court plaster

esparavel /espara'βel/ m, casting net

esparcimiento /esparθi'miento; esparsi'miento/ m, scattering; naturalness, frankness; geniality

esparcir /espar'θir; espar'sir/ vt to scatter, sprinkle, disperse; spread, publish abroad; entertain; —vr be scattered; amuse oneself

espárrago /es'parrago/ m, asparagus

esparraguera /esparra'gera/ f, asparagus plant; asparagus bed; asparagus dish

Esparta /es'parta/ Sparta

espartano /espar'tano/ **(-na)** a and n Spartan

espartería /esparte'ria/ f, esparto industry, esparto shop

esparto /es'parto/ m, esparto grass

espasmo /es'pasmo/ m, spasm

espasmódico /espas'moðiko/ a spasmodic

espátula /es'patula/ f, spatula; palette knife

especia /es'peθia; es'pesia/ f, spice. **nuez de e.,** nutmeg

especial /espe'θial; espe'sial/ a special; particular

especialidad /espeθiali'ðað; espesiali'ðað/ f, specialty; branch (of learning)

especialista /espeθia'lista; espesia'lista/ mf specialist

especialización /espeθialiθa'θion; espesialisa'sion/ f, specialization

especializarse /espeθiali'θarse; espesiali'sarse/ vr to specialize

especie /es'peθie; es'pesie/ f, class, kind; species; affair, matter, case; idea, image; news; pretext, appearance

especiería /espeθie'ria; espesie'ria/ f, spice trade; spice shop

especiero /espe'θiero; espe'siero/ **(-ra)** n spice merchant; spice rack

especificación /espeθifika'θion; espesifika'sion/ f, specification. **e. normalizada,** standard specification

especificar /espeθifi'kar; espesifi'kar/ vt to specify, particularize

específico /espe'θifiko; espe'sifiko/ a and m, specific patent medicine

espécimen /es'peθimen; es'pesimen/ m, specimen, sample

especioso /espe'θioso; espe'sioso/ a lovely, perfect; specious

espectacular /espektaku'lar/ a spectacular

espectáculo /espek'takulo/ m, spectacle, sight; show, display

espectador /espekta'ðor/ **(-ra)** n spectator

espectral /espek'tral/ a spectral; faint, dim

espectro /es'pektro/ m, phantom, specter; Phys. spectrum

especulación /espekula'θion; espekula'sion/ f, conjecture; Com. speculation

especulador /espekula'ðor/ **(-ra)** n speculator

especular /espeku'lar/ vt to examine, look at; (with en) reflect on, consider; —vi Com. speculate

especulativo /espekula'tiβo/ a speculative; thoughtful, meditative

espejería /espehe'ria/ f, mirror shop or factory

espejero /espe'hero/ m, mirror manufacturer or seller

espejismo /espe'hismo/ m, mirage; illusion

espejo /es'peho/ m, mirror; Fig. model. **e. de cuerpo entero,** full-length mirror. **e. retrovisor,** rearview mirror

espejuelo /espe'huelo/ m, small mirror; Mineral. selenite; Mineral. sheet of talc; pl lenses, eyeglasses

espeluznante /espeluθ'nante; espelus'nante/ a hairraising

espeluznar /espeluθ'nar; espelus'nar/ vt to dishevel; untidy (hair, etc.); —vr stand on end (hair)

espera /es'pera/ f, waiting; expectation; Law. adjournment; caution, restraint; Law. respite

esperantista /esperan'tista/ mf Esperantist

esperanto /espe'ranto/ m, Esperanto

esperanza /espe'ranθa; espe'ransa/ f, hope

esperanzar /esperan'θar; esperan'sar/ vt to inspire hope in

esperar /espe'rar/ vt to hope; expect; await; (with en) have faith in. **e. sentado,** Fig. Inf. to whistle for

esperma /es'perma/ f, sperm, semen. **e. de ballena,** spermaceti

esperpento /esper'pento/ m, Inf. scarecrow, grotesque; folly, madness; fantastic dramatic composition

espesar /espe'sar/ vt to thicken; make closer; tighten (fabrics); —vr thicken; grow denser or thicker

espeso /es'peso/ a thick; dense; greasy, dirty

espesor /espe'sor/ m, thickness; density

espesura /espe'sura/ f, thickness; density; thicket; filth

espetar /espe'tar/ vt Cul. to spit, skewer; pierce; Inf. utter, give; —vr be stiff or affected; Inf. push oneself in, intrude

espetera /espe'tera/ f, kitchen or pot rack

espetón /espe'ton/ m, Cul. spit; poker; large pin

espía /es'pia/ mf spy. f, Naut. warp

espiar /es'piar/ vt to spy upon, watch; —vi Naut. warp

espiche /es'pitʃe/ m, sharp-pointed weapon or instrument; spit, spike

espiga /es'piga/ f, Bot. spike, ear; sprig; peg; tang, shank (of sword); tenon, dowel; Naut. masthead; Herald. garb

espigador /espiga'ðor/ **(-ra)** n gleaner

espigar /espi'gar/ vt to glean; tenon; —vi Bot. begin to show the ear or spike; —vr Bot. bolt; shoot up, grow (persons)

espigón /espi'gon/ m, sting; sharp point; breakwater; bearded spike (corn, etc.)

espigueo /espi'geo/ m, gleaning

espín /es'pin/ m, porcupine

espina /es'pina/ f, thorn; prickle; splinter; fish bone; Anat. spine; suspicion, doubt

espinaca /espi'naka/ f, spinach

espinal /espi'nal/ a spinal

espinar /espi'nar/ m, thorn brake; Fig. awkward position —vt to prick, wound, hurt

espinazo /espi'naθo; espi'naso/ m, backbone

espineta /espi'neta/ f, spinet; virginals

espinilla /espi'niʎa; espi'niya/ f, shinbone; blackhead

espinoso /espi'noso/ *a* thorny; difficult, intricate

espión /es'pion/ *m,* See **espía**

espionaje /espio'nahe/ *m,* espionage; spying

espira /es'pira/ *f,* (*Geom. Archit.*) helix; turn, twist (of winding stairs); whorl (of a shell)

espiración /espira'θion; espira'sion/ *f,* expiration; respiration

espiral /espi'ral/ *a* spiral. *f, Geom.* spiral; spiral watchspring

espirar /espi'rar/ *vt* to exhale, breathe out; inspire; encourage; —*vi* breathe; breathe out; *Poet.* blow (wind)

espiritisimo /espiri'tisimo/ *m,* spiritualism

espiritista /espiri'tista/ *a* spiritualist. *mf* spiritualist

espiritoso /espiri'toso/ *a* lively, active, spirited; spirituous

espíritu /es'piritu/ *m,* spirit; apparition, specter; soul; intelligence, mind; mood, temper, outlook; underlying principle, spirit; devil (*gen. pl*) vigor, ardor, vivacity; *Chem.* essence; *Chem.* spirits; turn of mind. **E. Santo,** Holy Ghost

espiritual /espiri'tual/ *a* spiritual

espiritualidad /espirituali'ðað/ *f,* spirituality

espiritualismo /espiritua'lismo/ *m, Philos.* spiritualism

espiritualizar /espirituali'θar; espirituali'sar/ *vt* to spiritualize

espita /es'pita/ *f,* spigot, tap; *Inf.* tippler

esplender /esplen'der/ *vi Poet.* to shine

esplendidez /esplendi'ðeθ; esplendi'ðes/ *f,* liberality, abundance; splendor, pomp

espléndido /es'plendiðo/ *a* magnificent; liberal; resplendent (*gen. pl*)

esplendor /esplen'dor/ *m,* splendor, brilliance; distinction, nobility

esplendoroso /esplendo'roso/ *a* splendid, brilliant, radiant

espliego /es'plieɣo/ *m,* lavender

esplín /es'plin/ *m,* spleen, melancholy

espolada /espo'laða/ *f,* prick with the spur

espolear /espole'ar/ *vt* to prick with the spur; encourage, stimulate

espoleta /espo'leta/ *f,* fuse (of explosives); breastbone (of fowls); wishbone. **e. de tiempo, e. graduada,** time fuse. **e. de seguridad,** safety fuse

espolón /espo'lon/ *m,* spur (of a bird or mountain range); *Naut.* ram; breakwater; buttress; *Naut.* fender

espolvorear /espolβore'ar/ *vt* to sprinkle with powder

espondeo /espon'deo/ *m,* (metrical foot) spondee

esponja /es'ponha/ *f,* sponge

esponjadura /esponha'ðura/ *f,* sponging

esponjar /espon'har/ *vt* to make spongy; sponge; —*vr* swell with pride; *Inf.* bloom with health

esponjera /espon'hera/ *f,* sponge holder

esponjosidad /esponhosi'ðað/ *f,* sponginess

esponjoso /espon'hoso/ *a* spongy, porous

esponsales /espon'sales/ *m pl,* betrothal; marriage contract

espontaneidad /espontanei'ðað/ *f,* spontaneity

espontáneo /espon'taneo/ *a* spontaneous

espora /es'pora/ *f,* spore

esporádico /espo'raðiko/ *a* sporadic

esportillo /espor'tiʎo; espor'tiyo/ *m,* bass, frail

esposa /es'posa/ *f,* wife; *pl* handcuffs

esposo /es'poso/ *m,* husband; *pl* husband and wife

espuela /es'puela/ *f,* spur; stimulus; (*Ornith. Bot.*) spur. **e. de caballero,** larkspur

espulgar /espul'ɣar/ *vt* to delouse; examine carefully

espuma /es'puma/ *f,* froth, foam; *Cul.* scum; *Fig.* the best of anything, flower; *Fig. Inf.* **crecer como la e.,** to flourish like weeds

espumadera /espuma'ðera/ *f,* skimming ladle

espumajear /espumahe'ar/ *vi* to foam at the mouth

espumajoso /espuma'hoso/ *a* frothy, foaming

espumar /espu'mar/ *vt* to skim (soup, etc.); —*vi* foam; increase rapidly

espumoso /espu'moso/ *a* frothy, foaming

espurio /es'purio/ *a* bastard; spurious

esputo /es'puto/ *m,* sputum

esqueje /es'kehe/ *m, Agr.* cutting

esquela /es'kela/ *f,* note; (printed) card

esqueleto /eske'leto/ *m,* skeleton; *Inf.* skinny person; framework

esquema /es'kema/ *f,* diagram, layout sketch; scheme, plan. **e. de una máquina,** drawing of a machine

esquemático /eske'matiko/ *a* schematic; diagrammatic

esquematizar /eskemati'θar; eskemati'sar/ *vt* to plan, outline

esquí /es'ki/ *m,* ski, snowshoe

esquiador /eskia'ðor/ *m,* skier

esquiar /es'kiar/ *vi* to ski

esquife /es'kife/ *m,* skiff

esquila /es'kila/ *f,* cattle bell; small bell, hand bell; sheep shearing; (*Ichth. Bot.*) squill

esquilador /eskila'ðor/ *a* shearing. *m,* sheep shearer

esquiladora /eskila'ðora/ *f,* shearing machine

esquilar /eski'lar/ *vt* to shear, clip (sheep, etc.)

esquileo /eski'leo/ *m,* shearing; shearing time or place

esquilmar /eskil'mar/ *vt* to harvest; impoverish

esquilmo /es'kilmo/ *m,* harvest

esquimal /eski'mal/ *a* and *mf* Eskimo

esquina /es'kina/ *f,* corner

esquinado /eski'naðo/ *a* having corners; *Fig.* difficult to approach (people)

esquirla /es'kirla/ *f,* splinter (of a bone); shrapnel

esquirol /eski'rol/ *m, Inf.* strikebreaker, blackleg

esquisto /es'kisto/ *m, Mineral.* slate; shale

esquivar /eski'βar/ *vt* to avoid; —*vr* slip away, disappear; excuse oneself

esquivez /eski'βeθ; eski'βes/ *f,* unsociableness; unfriendliness, aloofness

esquivo /es'kiβo/ *a* unsociable, elusive, aloof

esquizado /eski'θaðo; eskisaðo/ *a* mottled (of marble)

estabilidad /estaβili'ðað/ *f,* stability; fastness (of colors)

estabilizar /estaβili'θar; estaβili'sar/ *vt* to stabilize

estable /es'taβle/ *a* stable; fast (of colors)

establecer /estaβle'θer; estaβle'ser/ *vt irr* to establish, found, institute; decree; —*vr* take up residence; open (a business firm). See **conocer**

establecimiento /estaβleθi'miento; estaβlesi'miento/ *m,* law, statute; foundation, institution; establishment

establero /estaβ'lero/ *m,* stablegroom

establo /es'taβlo/ *m,* stable

estaca /es'taka/ *f,* stake, pole; *Agr.* cutting; cudgel

estacada /esta'kaða/ *f,* fence; *Mil.* palisade; place fixed for a duel

estacar /esta'kar/ *vt* to stake; fence; tie to a stake; —*vr Fig.* be as still as a post

estación /esta'θion; esta'sion/ *f,* position, situation; season; station (railroad, etc.); depot; time, period; stop, halt; building, headquarters; *Bot.* habitat; (*Surv. Geom. Eccl.*) station

estacional /estaθio'nal; estasio'nal/ *a* seasonal; *Astron.* stationary

estacionamiento /estaθiona'miento; estasiona'miento/ *m,* stationariness; *Auto.* parking

estacionar /estaθio'nar; estasio'nar/ *vt* to station, place; *Auto.* park (a car); —*vr* remain stationary; place oneself

estacionario /estaθio'nario; estasio'nario/ *a* motionless; *Astron.* stationary. *m,* stationer

estada /es'taða/ *f,* sojourn

estadía /esta'ðia/ *f,* stay, sojourn; *Art.* sitting (of a model)

estadio /es'taðio/ *m,* racetrack; stadium; furlong

estadista /esta'ðista/ *mf* statistician; statesman, stateswoman

estadística /esta'ðistika/ *f,* statistics

estadístico /esta'ðistiko/ *a* statistical

estadizo /esta'ðiθo; estaðiso/ *a* stagnant

estado /es'taðo/ *m,* state; condition; rank, position; *Polit.* state; profession; status; *Com.* statement. **e. de guerra,** state of war; martial law. **e. mayor central,** (*Nav. Mil.*) general staff. **e. tapón,** *Polit.* buffer state. **tomar e.,** to marry; *Eccl.* profess; be ordained a priest

Estados Unidos de América /es'taðos u'niðos de a'merika/ United States of America

estadounidense /estaðouni'ðense/ a United States

estafa /es'tafa/ f, swindle

estafador /estafa'ðor/ (-ra) n swindler

estafar /esta'far/ vt to swindle

estafeta /esta'feta/ f, courier, messenger; branch post office; diplomatic pouch

estafilococo /estafilo'koko/ m, staphylococcus

estagnación /estagna'θion; estagna'sion/ f, stagnation

estalactita /estalak'tita/ f, stalactite

estalagmita /estalag'mita/ f, stalagmite

estallar /esta'ʎar; esta'yar/ vi to explode; burst; Fig. break out

estallido /esta'ʎiðo; esta'yiðo/ m, explosion, report; crash, crack; Fig. outbreak; Auto. **e. de un neumático,** blowout (of a tire)

estambre /es'tambre/ m, woolen yarn, worsted; stamen

estameña /esta'meɲa/ f, serge

estampa /es'tampa/ f, illustration, picture; print; aspect; printing press; track, step; Metall. boss, stud

estampación /estampa'θion; estampa'sion/ f, stamping; printing; imprinting. **e. en seco,** tooling (of a book)

estampado /estam'paðo/ a printed (of textiles). m, textile printing; printed fabric

estampar /estam'par/ vt to print, stamp; leave the print (of); bestow, imprint. **e. en relieve,** to emboss. **e. en seco,** to tool (a book)

estampería /estampe'ria/ f, print or picture shop; trade in prints

estampero /estam'pero/ m, print dealer, picture dealer

estampido /estam'piðo/ m, report, bang, detonation; crash

estampilla /estam'piʎa; estam'piya/ f, rubber stamp; seal

estampillar /estampi'ʎar; estampi'yar/ vt to stamp, imprint

estancación /estanka'θion; estanka'sion/ f, stagnation

estancado /estan'kaðo/ a stagnant; blocked, held up

estancar /estan'kar/ vt to check, stem; set up a monopoly; Fig. hold up (negotiations, etc.); —vr be stagnant

estancia /es'tanθia; es'tansia/ f, stay, residence; dwelling; lounge, livingroom; stanza; West Hem. farm

estanciero /estan'θiero; estan'siero/ m, West Hem. farmer

estanco /es'tanko/ a Naut. watertight. m, monopoly; shop selling government monopoly goods; archive

estandarte /estan'darte/ m, standard, flag. **e. real,** royal standard

estanque /es'tanke/ m, tank; pool; reservoir

estanquero /estan'kero/ (-ra) n seller of government monopoly goods (tobacco, matches, etc.)

estante /es'tante/ a present; extant; permanent. m, shelf; bookcase; bin (for wine)

estantería /estante'ria/ f, shelving; shelves, bookcase

estantigua /estan'tigua/ f, hobgoblin, specter; Fig. Inf. scarecrow

estañador /estaɲa'ðor/ m, tinsmith

estañar /esta'ɲar/ vt to tin; solder

estaño /es'taɲo/ m, tin

estaquilla /esta'kiʎa; esta'kiya/ f, peg, cleat

estar /es'tar/ vi irr to be. Indicates: 1. Position or place (e.g. Está a la puerta, He is at the door). 2. State (e.g. Las flores están marchitas, The flowers are faded). 3. Used to form the continuous or progressive tense (e.g. **Siempre está (estaba) escribiendo,** He is (was) always writing). 4. In contrast to verb ser, indicates impermanency (e.g. Está enfermo, He is ill). 5. **Estar** forms an apparent passive where no action is implied (e.g. El cuadro está pintado al óleo, The picture is painted in oils). 6. Used in some impersonal expressions (e.g. ¡Bien está! All right! ¡Claro está! Of course! etc.). **e. de,** to be in, or on, or acting as (e.g. e. de prisa, to be in a hurry. e. de capitán, to be acting as a captain). **e. para,** to be on the point of; to be

nearly; to be in the mood for. **e. para llover,** to be on the point of raining. **e. por,** to remain to be done; have a mind to (e.g. La historia está por escribir, The story remains to be written). **e. bien,** to be well (healthy). Mech. **e. bajo presión,** to have the steam up. Polit. **e. en el poder,** to be in office. **e. en una cuenca,** Dominican Republic to be broke. **¿A cómo (** or **A cuántos) estamos?** What is the date? Pres. Ind. **estoy, estás, está, estamos, estáis, están.** Preterite **estuve,** etc —Pres. Subjunc. **esté, estés, esté, estén.** Imperf. Subjunc. **estuviese,** etc.

estarcir /estar'θir; estar'sir/ vt to stencil

estatal /esta'tal/ a state

estática /es'tatika/ f, Mech. statics

estático /es'tatiko/ a static

estatua /es'tatua/ f, statue

estatuaria /esta'tuaria/ f, statuary

estatuir /esta'tuir/ vt irr to establish, order. See **huir**

estatura /esta'tura/ f, stature, height (of persons)

estatuto /esta'tuto/ m, statute, law

estay /es'tai/ m, Naut. stay. **e. mayor,** Naut. mainstay

este /'este/ m, east

este /'este/ m, dem a this (f, **esta,** pl **estos, estas,** these). **éste,** m, dem pron this one; the latter. (f, **ésta,** neut **esto,** pl **éstos, éstas,** these ones; the latter) (e.g. Aquel cuadro no es tan hermoso como éste, That picture is not as beautiful as this one)

estela /es'tela/ f, wake, track (of a ship)

estenografía /estenogra'fia/ f, shorthand

estenográfico /esteno'grafiko/ a shorthand

estenógrafo /este'nografo/ (-fa) n stenographer

estenordeste /estenor'ðeste/ m, east-northeast

estentóreo /esten'toreo/ a stentorian

estepa /es'tepa/ f, steppe, arid plain

estera /es'tera/ f, matting

esterar /este'rar/ vt to cover with matting; —vi Inf. muffle oneself up

estercoladura /esterkola'ðura/ f, manuring

estercolar /esterko'lar/ vt to manure

estercolero /esterko'lero/ m, manure pile; driver of a dung cart

estereoscopio /estereo'skopio/ m, stereoscope

esterería /estere'ria/ f, matting factory, matting shop

esterero /este'rero/ (-ra) n matting maker, matting seller

estéril /es'teril/ a sterile, barren; unfruitful, unproductive

esterilidad /esterili'ðað/ f, sterility; barrenness, unfruitfulness

esterilización /esteriliθa'θion; esterilisa'sion/ f, sterilization

esterilizador /esteriliθa'ðor; esterilisa'ðor/ a sterilizing. m, sterilizer

esterilizar /esterili'θar; esterili'sar/ vt to make barren; Med. sterilize

esterilla /este'riʎa; este'riya/ f, mat, matting

esterlina /ester'lina/ a f, sterling. **libra e.,** pound sterling

esternón /ester'non/ m, sternum

estero /es'tero/ m, salt marsh

estertor /ester'tor/ m, stertorous breathing, rattle

estesudeste /estesu'ðeste/ m, east-southeast

estética /es'tetika/ f, aesthetics —a aesthete

estético /es'tetiko/ a aesthetic m, aesthete

estetoscopio /esteto'skopio/ m, stethoscope

esteva /es'teβa/ f, plow handle

estevado /este'βaðo/ a bandy-legged

estiaje /es'tiahe/ m, low water level (of rivers)

estibador /estiβa'ðor/ m, stevedore, dock worker

estibar /esti'βar/ vt Naut. to stow

estiércol /es'tierkol/ m, dung; manure

estigio /es'tihio/ a Stygian; (Fig. Poet.) infernal

estigma /es'tigma/ m, stigma

estigmatizar /estigmati'θar; estigmati'sar/ vt to brand; stigmatize; insult

estilar /esti'lar/ vi to be accustomed; —vt draw up (document)

estilete /esti'lete/ m, stiletto, dagger; needle, hand, pointer; Med. stylet

estilista /esti'lista/ mf stylist

estilística /esti'listika/ *f,* stylism, stylistics

estilizar /estili'θar; estili'sar/ *vt* to stylize

estilo /es'tilo/ *m,* (*Art. Archit. Lit.*) style, writing instrument; gnomon, pointer; manner, way; *Bot.* style. **por el e.,** in some such way, like that

estilográfico /estilo'grafiko/ *a* stylographic. **pluma estilográfica,** fountain pen

estima /es'tima/ *f,* appreciation, esteem, consideration

estimable /esti'maβle/ *a* estimable

estimación /estima'θion; estima'sion/ *f,* valuation, estimate; regard, esteem. **e. prudente,** conservative estimate

estimar /esti'mar/ *vt* to value, estimate; esteem, judge

estimulante /estimu'lante/ *m, Med.* stimulant —*a* stimulating

estimular /estimu'lar/ *vt* to stimulate, excite; goad on, encourage, incite

estímulo /es'timulo/ *m,* stimulus; incitement, encouragement

estío /es'tio/ *m,* summer

estipendiar /estipen'diar/ *vt* to pay a stipend to

estipendiario /estipen'diario/ *m,* stipendiary

estipendio /esti'pendio/ *m,* stipend, pay, remuneration

estipulación /estipula'θion; estipula'sion/ *f,* stipulation; *Law.* clause, condition

estipular /estipu'lar/ *vt* to stipulate; arrange terms; *Law.* covenant

estirado /esti'raðo/ *a* stretched out; tight, stiff; wiredrawn (metals); stiff, pompous; parsimonious

estirador /estira'ðor/ *m,* wire drawer

estirar /esti'rar/ *vt* to stretch; iron roughly (clothes); *Metall.* wire-draw; dole out (money); *Fig.* stretch, go beyond the permissible; —*vr* stretch oneself

estirpe /es'tirpe/ *f,* race, stock, lineage

estival /esti'βal/ *a* summer

esto /'esto/ *dem pron neut* this, this matter, this idea, etc. Always refers to abstractions, never to a definite object. **e. de,** the matter of. **e. es,** that's it; namely. **por e.,** for this reason. **a todo e.,** meanwhile

estocada /esto'kaða/ *f,* sword thrust

Estocolmo /esto'kolmo/ Stockholm

estofa /es'tofa/ *f, Sew.* quilting; kind, quality

estofado /esto'faðo/ *m,* stew —*a Sew.* quilted; stewed

estofar /esto'far/ *vt Sew.* to quilt; make a stew

estoicismo /estoi'θismo; estoi'sismo/ *m,* stoicism

estoico /es'toiko/ (**-ca**) *n* stoic —*a* stoical

estolidez /estoli'ðeθ; estoli'ðes/ *f,* idiocy

estólido /es'toliðo/ (**-da**) *a* idiotic —*a* idiot

estomacal /estoma'kal/ *a* stomach

estómago /es'tomago/ *m,* stomach

estomático /esto'matiko/ *a* pertaining to the mouth, oral

estomatitis /estoma'titis/ *f,* stomatitis

estonio /es'tonio/ (**-ia**) *a* and *n* Estonian. *m,* Estonian (language)

estopa /es'topa/ *f,* tow; oakum

estopilla /esto'piʎa; esto'piya/ *f,* batiste, lawn; calico, cotton cloth

estopín /esto'pin/ *m, Mil.* quick march

estoque /es'toke/ *m,* rapier; narrow sword

estoquear /estoke'ar/ *vt* to wound or kill with a rapier

estoqueo /esto''keo/ *m,* swordplay

estorbador /estorβa'ðor/ (**-ra**) *a* obstructive —*n* obstructer

estorbar /estor'βar/ *vt* to obstruct, impede; hinder

estorbo /es'torβo/ *m,* obstruction; hindrance, nuisance

estornino /estor'nino/ *m,* starling

estornudar /estornu'ðar/ *vi* to sneeze

estornudo /estor'nuðo/ *m,* sneezing; sneeze

estrabismo /estra'βismo/ *m, Med.* strabismus, squint, cast

estrada /es'traða/ *f,* road, highway

estrado /es'traðo/ *m,* dais

estrafalario /estrafa'lario/ *a Inf.* slovenly, untidy; *Inf.* eccentric, odd

estragar /estra'gar/ *vt* to corrupt, spoil, vitiate; ruin, destroy

estrago /es'trago/ *m,* devastation, destruction, ruin, havoc

estrambote /estram'bote/ *m,* refrain

estrambótico /estram'botiko/ *a Inf.* eccentric

estrangul /estraŋ'gul/ *m, Mus.* mouthpiece

estrangulación /estraŋgula'θion; estraŋgula'sion/ *f,* strangulation; *Auto.* throttling

estrangulador /estraŋgula'ðor/ (**-ra**) *a* strangling —*n* strangler. *m, Auto.* throttle

estrangular /estraŋgu'lar/ *vt* to strangle

estraperlista /estraper'lista/ *mf* black marketeer

estraperlo /estra'perlo/ *m,* black market

Estrasburgo /estras'βurgo/ Strasbourg

estratagema /estrata'hema/ *f,* stratagem, trick

estrategia /estra'tehia/ *f,* strategy

estratégico /estra'tehiko/ *a* strategic

estratego /estra'tego/ *m,* strategist

estratificación /estratifika'θion; estratifika'sion/ *f,* stratification

estrato /es'trato/ *m, Geol.* stratum

estratosfera /estratos'fera/ *f,* stratosphere

estraza /es'traθa; es'trasa/ *f,* rag. **papel de e.,** brown paper

estrechar /estre'tʃar/ *vt* to make narrower, tighten; hold tightly, clasp; compel, oblige; —*vr* tighten oneself up; reduce one's expenses; *Fig.* tighten the bonds (of friendship, etc.). **e. la mano,** to shake hands

estrechez /estre'tʃeθ; estre'tʃes/ *f,* narrowness; tightness; scantiness; poverty, want. **e. de miras,** narrowmindedness

estrecho /es'tretʃo/ *a* narrow; tight; intimate, close; austere, rigid; meanspirited. *m, Geog.* strait

estregadera /estrega'ðera/ *f,* shoe scraper; scourer

estregar /estre'gar/ *vt irr* to rub, scour, scrub, scrape, scratch. See **cegar**

estrella /es'treʎa; es'treya/ *f,* star; fortune, fate; anything star-shaped; *Fig.* star. **e. de la pantalla,** movie star. **e. de mar,** starfish. **e. de rabo,** comet. **e. fugaz,** shooting star. **tener e.,** to be born under a lucky star

estrellado /estre'ʎaðo; estre'yaðo/ *a* star-shaped; full of stars, starry; shattered, broken; fried (eggs)

estrellamar /estreʎa'mar; estreya'mar/ *f,* starfish

estrellar /estre'ʎar; estre'yar/ *vt Inf.* to shatter, break into fragments; fry (eggs); —*vr* be starry or sprinkled with stars; be dashed against; fail in, come up against

estrellón /estre'ʎon; estre'yon/ *m,* large, artificial star (painted or otherwise); star-like firework

estremecer /estreme'θer; estreme'ser/ *vt irr* to cause to tremble; perturb; —*vr* shudder, tremble. See **conocer**

estremecimiento /estremeθi'miento; estreme-si'miento/ *m,* shudder, trembling; agitation

estrenar /estre'nar/ *vt* to use or do for the first time; inaugurate; give the first performance of (plays, etc.); —*vr* do for the first time; *Com.* make the first sale of the day

estreno /es'treno/ *m,* commencement, inauguration; first appearance; *Theat.* first performance, opening night, premiere

estrenque /es'trenke/ *m,* strong esparto rope

estrenuo /es'trenuo/ *a* strong, energetic, agile

estreñimiento /estreɲi'miento/ *m,* constipation

estreñir /estre'ɲir/ *vt* to constipate

estrépito /es'trepito/ *m,* clamor, din, great noise; fuss, show

estrepitoso /estrepi'toso/ *a* noisy, clamorous

estreptococo /estrepto'koko/ *m,* streptococcus

estreptomicina /estreptomi'θina; estreptomi'sina/ *f,* streptomycin

estría /es'tria/ *f, Archit.* fluting, stria

estribadero /estriβa'ðero/ *m,* prop, support, strut

estribar /estri'βar/ *vi* (*with en*) to lean on, rest on, be supported by; *Fig.* be based on

estribillo /estri'βiʎo; estri'βiyo/ *m,* refrain

estribo /es'triβo/ *m,* stirrup; footboard, step, running board (of vehicles); *Archit.* buttress or pier; *Fig.* stay, support; *Anat.* stapes; *Mech.* stirrup piece. **perder los estribos,** to lose patience, forget oneself

estribor /estri'βor/ *m*, starboard
estricnina /estrik'nina/ *f*, strychnine
estricto /es'trikto/ *a* strict, exact; unbending, severe
estridente /estri'ðente/ *a* strident, shrill
estridor /estri'ðor/ *m*, strident or harsh sound; screech; creak
estro /'estro/ *m*, inspiration
estrofa /es'trofa/ *f*, strophe; verse, stanza
estropajo /estro'paho/ *m*, scourer, dishcloth; worthless person or thing
estropajoso /estropa'hoso/ *a Inf.* indistinct, stammering; dirty and ragged; tough (meat, etc.)
estropear /estrope'ar/ *vt* to spoil, damage; ruin, undo, spoil (plans, effects, etc.); ill-treat, maim; —*vr* hurt oneself, be maimed; spoil, deteriorate
estropicio /estro'piθio; estro'pisio/ *m*, *Inf.* crash (of china, etc.)
estructura /estruk'tura/ *f*, fabric, structure; *Fig.* construction
estructural /estruktu'ral/ *a* structural
estruendo /es'truendo/ *m*, din, clatter; clamor, noise; ostentation
estruendoso /estruen'doso/ *a* noisy
estrujar /estru'har/ *vt* to squeeze, crush (fruit); hold tightly, press, squeeze, bruise; *Fig. Inf.* squeeze dry
estrujón /estru'hon/ *m*, squeeze, pressure; final pressing (grapes)
estuario /es'tuario/ *m*, estuary
estucado /estu'kaðo/ *m*, stucco
estucar /estu'kar/ *vt* to stucco
estuche /es'tutʃe/ *m*, case; casket, box; cover; sheath
estuco /es'tuko/ *m*, stucco; plaster
estudiante /estu'ðiante/ *mf* student
estudiantil /estuðian'til/ *a Inf.* student
estudiantina /estuðian'tina/ *f*, strolling band of students playing and singing, generally in aid of charity
estudiantino /estuðian'tino/ *a Inf.* student
estudiantón /estuðian'ton/ *m*, *Inf.* grind
estudiar /estu'ðiar/ *vt* to study. **e. de**, study to be a (e.g. *e. de rabino*, study to be a rabbi); learn; *Art.* copy
estudio /es'tuðio/ *m*, study; sketch; disquisition, dissertation; studio; diligence; *Art.* study; reading room, den
estudiosidad /estuðiosi'ðað/ *f*, studiousness
estudioso /estu'ðioso/ *a* studious
estufa /es'tufa/ *f*, heating stove; hothouse; hot room (in bathhouses); drying chamber; *Elec.* heater
estufador /estufa'ðor/ *m*, stewpot or casserole
estufilla /estu'fiʎa; estu'fiya/ *f*, muff; small brazier
estufista /estu'fista/ *mf* stove maker or repairer, stove seller
estulto /es'tulto/ *a* foolish
estupefacción /estupefak'θion; estupefak'sion/ *f*, stupefaction
estupefacto /estupe'fakto/ *a* stupefied, stunned, amazed
estupendo /estu'pendo/ *a* wonderful, marvelous
estupidez /estupi'ðeθ; estupi'ðes/ *f*, stupidity
estúpido /es'tupiðo/ *a* stupid
estupor /estu'por/ *m*, *Med.* stupor; astonishment
estupro /es'tupro/ *m*, *Law.* rape
estuque /es'tuke/ *m*, stucco
estuquería /estuke'ria/ *f*, stuccowork
esturión /estu'rion/ *m*, sturgeon
esvástica /es'βastika/ *f*, swastika
etapa /e'tapa/ *f*, *Mil.* field ration; *Mil.* halt, camp; stage, juncture. **a pequeñas etapas,** by easy stages (of a journey)
etcétera /et'θetera; et'setera/ etcetera
éter /'eter/ *m*, ether; *Poet.* sky
etéreo /e'tereo/ *a* etheric; ethereal
eterizar /eteri'θar; eteri'sar/ *vt* to etherize
eternidad /eterni'ðað/ *f*, eternity
eternizar /eterni'θar; eterni'sar/ *vt* to drag out, prolong; eternize, perpetuate
eterno /e'terno/ *a* eternal, everlasting; lasting, enduring
ética /'etika/ *f*, ethics
ético /'etiko/ *a* ethical. *m*, moralist
etimología /etimolo'hia/ *f*, etymology

etimológico /etimo'lohiko/ *a* etymological
etimologista /etimolo'hista/ *mf* etymologist
etimólogo /eti'mologo/ *m*, etymologist
etiología /etiolo'hia/ *f*, etiology
etíope /e'tiope/ *a* and *mf* Ethiopian
Etiopía /etio'pia/ Ethiopia
etiqueta /eti'keta/ *f*, etiquette; label
etiquetero /etike'tero/ *a* ceremonious, stiff; prim
étnico /'etniko/ *a* ethnic; heathen
etnografía /etnogra'fia/ *f*, ethnography
etnográfico /etno'grafiko/ *a* ethnographic
etnología /etnolo'hia/ *f*, ethnology
etnólogo /et'nologo/ *m*, ethnologist
etrusco /e'trusko/ **(-ca)** *a* and *n* Etruscan
eubolia /eu'βolia/ *f*, discretion in speech
eucalipto /euka'lipto/ *m*, eucalyptus
Eucaristía /eukaris'tia/ *f*, Eucharist
euclídeo /eu'kliðeo/ *a* Euclidean
eufemismo /eufe'mismo/ *m*, euphemism
eufonía /eufo'nia/ *f*, euphony
eufónico /eu'foniko/ *a* euphonious
euforia /eu'foria/ *f*, resistance to disease; buoyancy, well-being
eufuismo /eu'fuismo/ *m*, euphuism
eugenesia /euhe'nesia/ *f*, eugenics
eugenésico /euhe'nesiko/ *a* eugenic
eunuco /eu'nuko/ *m*, eunuch
euritmia /eu'ritmia/ *f*, eurythmics
eurítmico /eu'ritmiko/ *a* eurythmic
euro /'euro/ *m*, *Poet.* east wind
Europa /eu'ropa/ Europe
europeizar /europei'θar; europei'sar/ *vt* to Europeanize
europeo /euro'peo/ **(-ea)** *a* and *n* European
éuscaro /'euskaro/ *a* Basque. *m*, Basque (language)
eutanasia /euta'nasia/ *f*, euthanasia
evacuación /eβakua'θion; eβakua'sion/ *f*, evacuation
evacuar /eβa'kuar/ *vt* to vacate; evacuate, empty; finish, conclude (a business deal, etc.)
evadir /eβa'ðir/ *vt* to avoid, elude; —*vr* escape; elope
evaluación /eβalua'θion; eβalua'sion/ *f*, valuation; estimation
evaluar /eβa'luar/ *vt* to evaluate, estimate; gauge; value
evangélico /eβan'heliko/ *a* evangelical
evangelio /eβan'helio/ *m*, Gospel; Christianity; *Inf.* indisputable truth
evangelista /eβanhe'lista/ *m*, evangelist
evangelizar /eβanheli'θar; eβanheli'sar/ *vt* to evangelize
evaporación /eβapora'θion; eβapora'sion/ *f*, evaporation
evaporar /eβapo'rar/ **(se)** *vt* and *vr* to evaporate; disappear, vanish
evasión /eβa'sion; eβa'siβa/ *f*, subterfuge; evasion; flight, escape
evasivo /eβa'siβo/ *a* evasive
evento /e'βento/ *m*, happening, event; contingency
eventual /eβen'tual/ *a* possible, fortuitous; accidental (expenses); extra (emoluments)
eventualidad /eβentuali'ðað/ *f*, eventuality
evicción /eβik'θion; eβik'sion/ *f*, *Law.* eviction
evidencia /eβi'ðenθia; eβiðensia/ *f*, proof, evidence. **ponerse en e.,** to put oneself forward
evidenciar /eβiðen'θiar; eβiðen'siar/ *vt* to show, make obvious
evidente /eβi'ðente/ *a* obvious, evident
evitable /eβi'taβle/ *a* avoidable
evitación /eβita'θion; eβita'sion/ *f*, avoidance
evitar /eβi'tar/ *vt* to avoid; shun, eschew
evocación /eβoka'θion; eβoka'sion/ *f*, evocation
evocador /eβoka'ðor/ *a* evocative
evocar /eβo'kar/ *vt* to evoke
evolución /eβolu'θion; eβolu'sion/ *f*, evolution; development; (*Mil. Nav.*) maneuver; change; *Geom.* involution
evolucionar /eβoluθio'nar; eβolusio'nar/ *vi* to evolve; change. (*Nav. Mil.*) maneuver; change, alter
evolucionismo /eβoluθio'nismo; eβolusio'nismo/ *m*, evolutionism
evolutivo /eβolu'tiβo/ *a* evolutional

ex /eks/ *prefix* out of; from; formerly
exacción /eksak'θion; eksak'sion/ *f*, exaction; tax
exacerbación /eksaθerβa'θion; eksaserβa'sion/ *f*, exacerbation
exacerbar /eksaθer'βar; eksaser'βar/ *vt* to exasperate; exacerbate
exactitud /eksakti'tuð/ *f*, exactitude; correctness; punctuality
exacto /ek'sakto/ *a* exact; correct; punctual
exactor /eksak'tor/ *m*, tax collector; tyrant, oppressor
exageración /eksahera'θion; eksahera'sion/ *f*, exaggeration
exagerador /eksahera'ðor/ **(-ra)** *a* given to exaggerating —*n* exaggerater
exagerar /eksahe'rar/ *vt* to exaggerate
exaltación /eksalta'θion; eksalta'sion/ *f*, exaltation
exaltar /eksal'tar/ *vt* to exalt, elevate; extol; —*vr* grow excited or agitated
examen /ek'samen/ *m*, inquiry; investigation, research; examination; *Geol.* survey. **e. parcial,** quiz (at school)
examinador /eksamina'ðor/ **(-ra)** *n* examiner
examinando /eksami'nando/ **(-da)** *n* candidate, examinee
examinar /eksami'nar/ *vt* to inquire into; investigate; inspect; examine; —*vr* take an examination
exangüe /ek'saŋgue/ *a* bloodless, pale; exhausted, weak; dead
exánime /eksa'nime/ *a* lifeless; spiritless, weak
exasperación /eksaspera'θion; eksaspera'sion/ *f*, exasperation
exasperador, exasperante /eksaspera'ðor, eksaspe'rante/ *a* exasperating
exasperar /eksaspe'rar/ *vt* to exasperate; irritate, annoy
excarcelar /ekskarθe'lar; ekskarse'lar/ *vt* to release from jail
excavación /ekskaβa'θion; ekskaβa'sion/ *f*, excavation
excavador /ekskaβa'ðor/ **(-ra)** *n* excavator. *f, Mech.* excavator
excavar /ekska'βar/ *vt* to hollow; excavate; *Agr.* hoe (roots of plants)
excedente /eksθe'ðente; eksse'ðente/ *a* exceeding; excessive; surplus
exceder /eksθe'ðer; eksse'ðer/ *vt* to exceed; —*vr* forget oneself, go too far
excelencia /eksθe'lenθia; eksse'lensia/ *f*, excellence, superiority; Excellency (title)
excelente /eksθe'lente; eksse'lente/ *a* excellent; *Inf.* first-rate
excelso /eks'θelso; eks'selso/ *a* lofty, high; eminent, mighty; sublime
excentricidad /eksθentriθi'ðað; ekssentrisi'ðað/ *f*, eccentricity
excéntrico /ek'θentriko; eks'sentriko/ *a* unconventional; erratic; *Geom.* eccentric
excepción /eksθep'θion; ekssep'sion/ *f*, exception
excepcional /eksθepθio'nal; ekssepsio'nal/ *a* exceptional
exceptuar /eksθep'tuar; ekssep'tuar/ *vt* to except
excerpta, excerta /eks'θerpta, eks'θerta; eks'serpta, eks'serta/ *f*, excerpt, extract
excesivo /eksθe'siβo; eksse'siβo/ *a* excessive
exceso /eks'θeso; eks'seso/ *m*, excess; *Com.* surplus; *pl* crimes, excesses. **e. de peso** *or* **e. de equipaje,** excess baggage
excipiente /eksθi'piente; ekssi'piente/ *m*, excipient
excisión /eksθi'sion; ekssi'sion/ *f*, excision
excitabilidad /eksθitaβili'ðað; ekssitaβili'ðað/ *f*, excitability
excitable /eksθi'taβle; ekssi'taβle/ *a* excitable, highstrung
excitación /eksθita'θion; ekssita'sion/ *f*, excitation; excitement
excitador /eksθita'ðor; ekssita'ðor/ *a* exciting, stimulating. *m, Phys.* exciter
excitar /eksθi'tar; ekssi'tar/ *vt* to excite, stimulate, provoke; *Elec.* energize; —*vr* become agitated or excited

exclamación /eksklama'θion; eksklama'sion/ *f*, exclamation, interjection
exclamar /ekskla'mar/ *vi* to exclaim
exclamatorio /eksklama'torio/ *a* exclamatory
excluir /eksk'luir/ *vt irr* to exclude, keep out; reject, bar. See **huir**
exclusiva /eksklu'siβa/ *f*, exclusion; special privilege, sole right
exclusive /eksklu'siβe/ *adv* exclusively; excluded
exclusivismo /eksklusi'βismo/ *m*, exclusivism
exclusivista /eksklusi'βista/ *a* exclusive. *mf* exclusivist
exclusivo /eksklu'siβo/ *a* exclusive
excomulgado /ekskomul'gaðo/ **(-da)** *a* and *n Eccl.* excommunicate; *Inf.* wicked (person)
excomulgar /ekskomul'gar/ *vt* to excommunicate
excomunión /ekskomu'nion/ *f*, excommunication
excoriar /eksko'riar/ *vt* to flay, excoriate; —*vr* graze oneself
excrecencia /ekskre'θenθia; ekskre'sensia/ *f*, excrescence
excreción /ekskre'θion; ekskre'sion/ *f*, excretion
excremento /ekskre'mento/ *m*, excrement
excretar /ekskre'tar/ *vi* to excrete
excretorio /ekskre'torio/ *a* excretory
exculpación /ekskulpa'θion; ekskulpa'sion/ *f*, exoneration
exculpar /ekskul'par/ **(se)** *vt* and *vr* to exonerate
excursión /ekskur'sion/ *f*, excursion, trip; *Mil.* incursion
excursionismo /ekskursio'nismo/ *m*, sightseeing; hiking
excursionista /ekskursio'nista/ *mf* excursionist; hiker
excusa /eks'kusa/ *f*, excuse
excusabaraja /ekskusaβa'raha/ *f*, basket with a lid
excusado /eksku'saðo/ *a* excused; exempt; unnecessary, superfluous; reserved, private. *m*, lavatory, toilet
excusar /eksku'sar/ *vt* to excuse; avoid, ward off, prevent; exempt; —*vr* excuse oneself
execración /eksekra'θion; eksekra'sion/ *f*, execration
execrar /ekse'krar/ *vt* to execrate; denounce; loathe
exención /eksen'θion; eksen'sion/ *f*, exemption
exentar /eksen'tar/ *vt* to exempt
exento /ek'sento/ *a* exempt; free, liberated; open (of buildings, etc.)
exequias /ek'sekias/ *f pl*, obsequies
exfoliar /eksfo'liar/ *vt* to strip off; —*vr* flake off
exhalación /eksala'θion; eksala'sion/ *f*, exhalation; shooting star; lightning; emanation; effluvium
exhalar /eksa'lar/ *vt* to exhale, give off; *Fig.* give vent to
exhausto /ek'sausto/ *a* exhausted
exhibición /eksiβi'θion; eksiβi'sion/ *f*, exhibition
exhibicionismo /eksiβiθio'nismo; eksiβisio'nismo/ *m*, exhibitionism
exhibicionista /eksiβiθio'nista; eksiβisio'nista/ *mf* exhibitionist
exhibir /eksi'βir/ *vt* to exhibit, show
exhortación /eksorta'θion; eksorta'sion/ *f*, exhortation
exhortar /eksor'tar/ *vt* to exhort
exhumación /eksuma'θion; eksuma'sion/ *f*, exhumation
exhumar /eksu'mar/ *vt* to exhume, disinter
exigencia /eksi'henθia; eksi'hensia/ *f*, exigency; demand
exigente /eksi'hente/ *a* exigent
exigir /eksi'hir/ *vt* to exact, collect; need, require; demand
exigüidad /eksigui'ðað/ *f*, exiguousness
exiguo /ek'siguo/ *a* exiguous, meager
eximio /ek'simio/ *a* most excellent; illustrious
eximir /eksi'mir/ *vt* to exempt
existencia /eksis'tenθia; eksis'tensia/ *f*, existence; *pl Com.* stock on hand
existir /eksis'tir/ *vi* to exist, be; live
éxito /'eksito/ *m*, success; result, conclusion
éxodo /'eksoðo/ *m*, Exodus; exodus, emigration. **é. rural,** rural depopulation
exoneración /eksonera'θion; eksonera'sion/ *f*, exoneration

exonerar /eksone'rar/ *vt* to exonerate; discharge (from employment)

exorbitancia /eksorβi'tanθia; eksorβi'tansia/ *f*, exorbitance

exorbitante /eksorβi'tante/ *a* exorbitant, excessive

exorcismo /eksor'θismo; eksor'sismo/ *m*, exorcism

exorcista /eksor'θista; eksor'sista/ *m*, exorcist

exorcizar /eksorθi'θar; eksorsi'sar/ *vt* to exorcize

exordio /ek'sorðio/ *m*, exordium, introduction

exornar /eksor'nar/ *vt* to adorn; embellish (*Lit.* style)

exótico /ek'sotiko/ *a* exotic, rare

expandir /ekspan'dir/ *vt* to expand

expansibilidad /ekspansiβili'ðað/ *f*, *Phys.* expansibility

expansión /ekspan'sion/ *f*, expansion; recreation, hobby

expansivo /ekspan'siβo/ *a* expansive; communicative, frank

expatriación /ekspatria'θion; ekspatria'sion/ *f*, expatriation

expatriarse /ekspa'triarse/ *vr* to emigrate, leave one's country

expectación /ekspekta'θion; ekspekta'sion/ *f*, expectation; expectancy

expectante /ekspek'tante/ *a* expectant

expectativa /ekspekta'tiβa/ *f*, expectancy; expectation

expectoración /ekspektora'θion; ekspektora'sion/ *f*, expectoration

expectorar /ekspekto'rar/ *vt* to expectorate

expedición /ekspeði'θion; ekspeði'sion/ *f*, expedition; speed, promptness; *Eccl.* bull, dispensation; excursion; forwarding, dispatch

expediente /ekspe'ðiente/ *m*, *Law.* proceedings; file of documents; expedient, device, means; expedition, promptness; motive, reason; provision

expedir /ekspe'ðir/ *vt irr* to expedite; forward, send, ship; issue, make out (checks, receipts, etc.); draw up (documents); dispatch, deal with. See **pedir**

expedito /ekspe'ðito/ *a* expeditious, speedy

expeler /ekspe'ler/ *vt* to expel, discharge, emit

expendedor /ekspende'ðor/ **(-ra)** *a* spending —*n* spender; agent; retailer; seller; *Law.* **e. de moneda falsa,** distributor of counterfeit money

expendeduría /ekspendeðu'ria/ *f*, shop where government monopoly goods are sold (tobacco, stamps, etc.)

expender /ekspen'der/ *vt* to spend (money); *Com.* retail; *Com.* sell on commission; *Law.* distribute counterfeit money

expensas /ek'spensas/ *f pl*, costs, charges

experiencia /ekspe'rienθia; ekspe'riensia/ *f*, experience; practice, experiment

experimentación /eksperimenta'θion; eksperimenta'sion/ *f*, experiencing

experimentar /eksperimen'tar/ *vt* to test, try; experience; feel

experimento /eksperi'mento/ *m*, experiment

experto /ek'sperto/ **(-ta)** *a* practiced, expert —*n* expert

expiación /ekspia'θion; ekspia'sion/ *f*, expiation

expiar /eks'piar/ *vt* to expiate, atone for; pay the penalty of; *Fig.* purify

expiatorio /ekspia'torio/ *a* expiatory

expiración /ekspira'θion; ekspira'sion/ *f*, expiration

expirar /ekspi'rar/ *vi* to die; *Fig.* expire; die down; exhale, expire

explanación /eksplana'θion; eksplana'sion/ *f*, leveling; explanation, elucidation

explanada /ekspla'naða/ *f*, esplanade; *Mil.* glacis

explanar /ekspla'nar/ *vt* to level; explain

explayar /ekspla'yar/ *vt* to extend, enlarge; —*vr* spread oneself, enlarge (upon); enjoy an outing; confide (in)

explicación /eksplika'θion; eksplika'sion/ *f*, explanation; elucidation

explicar /ekspli'kar/ *vt* to explain; expound; interpret; elucidate; —*vr* explain oneself

explicativo /eksplika'tiβo/ *a* explanatory

explícito /eks'pliθito; eks'plisito/ *a* explicit, clear

exploración /eksplora'θion; eksplorasion/ *f*, exploration

explorador /eksplora'ðor/ *a* exploring. *m*, explorer; prospector; boy scout; *Mil.* scout

explorar /eksplo'rar/ *vt* to explore; investigate; *Med.* probe

exploratorio /eksplora'torio/ *a* exploratory

explosión /eksplo'sion/ *f*, explosion; outburst, outbreak. **hacer falsas explosiones,** *Mech.* to misfire

explosivo /eksplo'siβo/ *a* and *m*, explosive. **e. violento,** high explosive

explotación /eksplota'θion; eksplota'sion/ *f*, development, exploitation

explotar /eksplo'tar/ *vt* to work (mines); *Fig.* exploit

expoliación /ekspolia'θion; ekspolia'sion/ *f*, spoliation

expoliar /ekspo'liar/ *vt* to despoil

exponente /ekspo'nente/ *a* and *mf* exponent. *m*, *Math.* index

exponer /ekspo'ner/ *vt irr* to show, expose; expound, interpret; risk, jeopardize; abandon (child). See **poner**

exportación /eksporta'θion; eksporta'sion/ *f*, exportation; export

exportador /eksporta'ðor/ **(-ra)** *a* export —*n* exporter

exportar /ekspor'tar/ *vt* to export

exposición /eksposi'θion; eksposi'sion/ *f*, exposition, demonstration; petition; exhibition; *Lit.* exposition; *Photo.* exposure; orientation, position

expósito /eks'posito/ **(-ta)** *a* and *n* foundling

expositor /eksposi'tor/ **(-ra)** *a* and *n* exponent —*n* exhibitor

expremijo /ekspre'miho/ *m*, cheese vat

exprés /eks'pres/ *a* express. *m*, messenger or delivery service; express train; transport office

expresar /ekspre'sar/ *vt* to express (all meanings)

expresión /ekspre'sion/ *f*, statement, utterance; phrase, wording; expression; presentation; manifestation; gift, present; squeezing; pressing (of fruits, etc.)

expresivo /ekspre'siβo/ *a* expressive; affectionate

expreso /eks'preso/ *a* express; clear, obvious. *m*, courier, messenger

exprimelimones /eksprimeli'mones/ *m*, **exprimidera,** *f*, lemon squeezer

exprimidor de la ropa /eksprimi'ðor de la 'rropa/ *m*, wringer, mangle

exprimir /ekspri'mir/ *vt* to squeeze, press (fruit); press, hold tightly; express, utter

expropiación /ekspropia'θion; ekspropia'sion/ *f*, expropriation

expropiar /ekspro'piar/ *vt* to expropriate; commandeer

expugnar /ekspug'nar/ *vt Mil.* to take by storm

expulsar /ekspul'sar/ *vt* to expel, eject, dismiss

expulsión /ekspul'sion/ *f*, expulsion

expurgar /ekspur'gar/ *vt* to cleanse, purify; expurgate

expurgatorio /ekspurga'torio/ *a* expurgatory. *m*, *Eccl.* index

exquisitez /ekskisi'teθ; ekskisi'tes/ *f*, exquisiteness

exquisito /eks'kisito/ *a* exquisite, choice; delicate, delicious

extasiarse /eksta'siarse/ *vr* to fall into ecstasy; marvel (at), delight (in)

éxtasis /'ekstasis/ *m*, ecstasy; rapture

extático /eks'tatiko/ *a* ecstatic

extemporáneo /ekstempo'raneo/ *a* untimely; inopportune, inconvenient

extender /eksten'der/ *vt irr* to spread; reach, extend; elongate; enlarge; amplify; unfold, open out, stretch; draw up (documents); make out (checks, etc.); —*vr* stretch out; lie down; spread, be generalized; extend; last (of time); record; stretch, open out. **extenderse en,** to expatiate on. See **entender**

extensión /eksten'sion/ *f*, extension; expanse; length; extent; duration; extension (logic)

extensivo /eksten'siβo/ *a* extensive, spacious; extensible

extenso /eks'tenso/ *a* extensive, vast

extensor /eksten'sor/ *a* extensor. *m*, chest expander

extenuación /ekstenua'θion; ekstenua'sion/ *f*, emaciation, weakness; extenuation

extenuar /ekste'nuar/ vt to exhaust, weaken; —vr become weak

exterior /ekste'rior/ a external; foreign (trade, etc.). m, outside, exterior; outward appearance

exterioridad /eksteriori'ðað/ f, outward appearance; outside, externality; pl ceremonies, forms; ostentation

exteriorizar /eksteriori'θar; eksteriori'sar/ vt to exteriorize, reveal

exterminador /ekstermina'ðor/ (-ra) a exterminating —n exterminator

exterminar /ekstermi'nar/ vt to exterminate; devastate

exterminio /ekster'minio/ m, extermination; devastation

externado /ekster'naðo/ m, day school

externarse /ekster'narse/ vr to stand out

externo /eks'terno/ (-na) a external —n day

extinción /ekstin'θion; ekstin'sion/ f, extinction; extinguishment; abolition, cancellation

extinguir /ekstiŋ'guir/ vt to extinguish; destroy

extintor /ekstin'tor/ m, fire extinguisher

extirpación /ekstirpa'θion; ekstirpa'sion/ f, extirpation

extirpador /ekstirpa'ðor/ (-ra) a extirpating —n extirpator

extirpar /ekstir'par/ vt to extirpate; Fig. eradicate

extorsión /ekstor'sion/ f, extortion

extorsionar /ekstorsio'nar/ vt to extort

extra /'ekstra/ prefix outside, without, beyond —prep besides —a extremely, most. m, Inf. extra

extracción /ekstrak'θion; ekstrak'sion/ f, extraction; drawing (lottery); origin, lineage; exportation

extractar /ekstrak'tar/ vt to abstract, summarize

extracto /eks'trakto/ m, abstract, summary; Chem. extract

extractor /ekstrak'tor/ a extracting. m, extractor

extradición /ekstraði'θion; ekstraði'sion/ f, extradition

extraer /ekstra'er/ vt irr to extract; draw out; export; Chem. extract. See **traer**

extranjero /ekstran'hero/ (-ra) a alien, foreign —n foreigner. m, abroad, foreign country

extrañar /ekstra'ɲar/ vt to exile; alienate, estrange; wonder at; miss, feel the loss of; —vr be exiled; be estranged; be amazed (by); refuse (to do a thing)

extrañeza /ekstra'ɲeθa; ekstra'ɲesa/ f, strangeness; estrangement; surprise

extraño /eks'traɲo/ a strange, unusual; foreign, extraneous

extraoficial /ekstraofi'θial; ekstraofi'sial/ a unofficial

extraordinario /ekstraorði'nario/ a extraordinary; special. m, Cul. extra course

extraterritorialidad /ekstraterritoriali'ðað/ f, exterritoriality

extravagancia /ekstraβa'ganθia; ekstraβa'gansia/ f, eccentricity; queerness; folly

extravagante /ekstraβa'gante/ a eccentric; queer, strange; absurd

extravertido /ekstraβer'tiðo/ m, extrovert

extraviar /ekstra'βiar/ vt to mislead; mislay; —vr lose one's way; be lost (of things); Fig. go astray

extravío /ekstra'βio/ m, deviation, divergence; error; aberration, lapse

extremado /ekstre'maðo/ a extreme

extremar /ekstre'mar/ vt to take to extremes; —vr do one's best

extremaunción /ekstremaun'θion; ekstremaun'sion/ f, extreme unction

extremeño /ekstre'meɲo/ (-ña) a and n Extremaduran

extremidad /ekstremi'ðað/ f, end; extremity; remotest part; edge; limit; pl extremities

extremista /ekstre'mista/ a and mf extremist

extremo /eks'tremo/ a last, ultimate; extreme; furthest; great, exceptional; utmost. m, end, extreme; highest degree; extreme care; pl excessive emotional display

extremoso /ekstre'moso/ a immoderate, exaggerated; very affectionate

extrínseco /ekstrin'seko/ a extrinsic

exuberancia /eksuβe'ranθia; eksuβeransia/ f, abundance; exuberance

exuberante /eksuβe'rante/ a abundant, copious; exuberant

exudar /eksu'ðar/ vi and vt to exude

exultación /eksulta'θion; eksulta'sion/ f, exultation; rejoicing

exultante /eksul'tante/ a exultant

exultar /eksul'tar/ vi to exult

exvoto /eks'βoto/ m, votive offering

eyaculación /eyakula'θion; eyakula'sion/ f, Med. ejaculation

eyacular /eyaku'lar/ vt Med. to ejaculate

F

fa /fa/ *m, Mus.* fa, F
fabada /fa'βaða/ *f,* dish of broad beans with pork, sausage or bacon
fábrica /'faβrika/ *f,* manufacture; making; factory, works; fabric, structure, building; creation; invention. **f. de papel,** paper mill. **marca de f.,** trademark
fabricación /faβrika'θion; faβrika'sion/ *f,* make; making; construction. **f. en serie,** mass production
fabricador /faβrika'ðor/ **(-ra)** *a* creative, inventive —*n* fabricator; maker
fabricante /faβri'kante/ *a* manufacturing. *m,* manufacturer; maker
fabricar /faβri'kar/ *vt* to manufacture; make; construct, build; devise; invent, create
fabril /fa'βril/ *a* manufacturing
fabriquero /faβri'kero/ *m,* manufacturer; churchwarden; charcoal burner
fábula /'faβula/ *f,* rumor, gossip; fiction; fable; story, plot; mythology; myth; laughingstock; falsehood.
fabulista /faβu'lista/ *mf* fabulist; mythologist
fabulosidad /faβulosi'ðað/ *f,* fabulousness
fabuloso /faβu'loso/ *a* fabulous; fictitious; incredible, amazing
faca /'faka/ *f,* jackknife
facción /fak'θion; fak'sion/ *f,* rebellion; faction, party, band; feature (of the face) (gen. *pl*); military exploit; any routine military duty
faccionario /fakθio'nario; faksio'nario/ *a* factional
faccioso /fak'θioso; fak'sioso/ **(-sa)** *a* factional; factious, seditious —*n* rebel
faceta /fa'θeta; fa'seta/ *f,* facet (gems); aspect, view
facha /'fatʃa/ *f, Inf.* countenance, look, face; guy, scarecrow. *Naut.* **ponerse en f.,** to lie to
fachada /fa'tʃaða/ *f,* facade, front (of a building, ship, etc.); *Inf.* build, presence (of a person); frontispiece (of a book)
fachenda /fa'tʃenda/ *f, Inf.* boastfulness, vanity
facial /fa'θial; fa'sial/ *a* facial; intuitive
fácil /'faθil; 'fasil/ *a* easy; probable; easily led; docile; of easy virtue (women) —*adv* easy
facilidad /faθili'ðað; fasili'ðað/ *f,* easiness; facility, aptitude; ready compliance; opportunity
facilitación /faθilita'θion; fasilita'sion/ *f,* facilitation
facilitar /faθili'tar; fasili'tar/ *vt* to facilitate; expedite; provide, deliver
facineroso /faθine'roso; fasine'roso/ *a* criminal, delinquent. *m,* criminal; villain
facistol /faθis'tol; fasis'tol/ *m, Eccl.* lectern; chorister's stand
facsímile /fak'simile/ *m,* facsimile
factibilidad /faktiβili'ðað/ *f,* feasibility, practicability
factible /fak'tiβle/ *a* feasible, practicable
facticio /fak'tiθio; fak'tisio/ *a* factitious, artificial
factor /fak'tor/ *m, Com.* factor, agent; *Math.* factor; element; consideration
factoría /fakto'ria/ *f,* agency; factorage; factory; merchants' trading post, especially in a foreign country
factótum /fak'totum/ *m, Inf.* factotum, handyman; *Inf.* busybody; confidential agent or deputy
factura /fak'tura/ *f, Com.* invoice, bill, account; *Art.* execution; workmanship; making
facturar /faktu'rar/ *vt Com.* to invoice; register (luggage on a railroad)
facultad /fakulta'ð/ *f,* faculty; mental or physical aptitude, capability; authority, right; science, art; *Educ.* faculty; license
facultar /fakul'tar/ *vt* to authorize, permit
facultativo /fakulta'tiβo/ *a* belonging to a faculty; optional, permissive. *m,* physician
facundia /fa'kundia/ *f,* eloquence
facundo /fa'kundo/ *a* eloquent
faena /fa'ena/ *f,* manual labor; mental work; business affairs (gen. *pl*)
faetón /fae'ton/ *m,* phaeton
fagocito /fago'θito; fago'sito/ *m,* phagocyte
fagot /fa'got/ *m,* bassoon

fagotista /fago'tista/ *mf* bassoon player
faisán /fai'san/ **(-ana)** *Ornith.* cock (hen) pheasant
faisanera /faisa'nera/ *f,* pheasantry
faja /'faha/ *f,* belt; sash, scarf; corset, girdle; *Geog.* zone; newspaper wrapper; *Archit.* fascia; swathing band
fajar /fa'har/ *vt* to swathe; swaddle (a child)
fajero /fa'hero/ *m,* swaddling band
fajín /fa'hin/ *m,* ceremonial ribbon or sash worn by generals, etc.
fajina /fa'hina/ *f,* stack; brushwood; (*fort.*) fascine
fajo /'faho/ *m,* bundle, sheaf; *pl* swaddling clothes
falacia /fa'laθia; fa'lasia/ *f,* fraud, deceit; deceitfulness; fallacy
falange /fa'lanhe/ *f, Mil.* phalanx; *Anat.* phalange; (*Spanish pol.*) Falange
falangista /falan'hista/ *a* and *mf* Falangist
falaz /fa'laθ; fa'las/ *a* deceitful; fallacious
falda /'falda/ *f,* skirt; lap, flap, panel (of a dress); slope (of a hill); the lap; loin (of beef, etc.); brim of a hat; *pl Inf.* petticoats, women. **f. escocesa,** kilt. **f.-pantalón,** divided skirt, culottes.
faldellín /falde'ʎin; falde'yin/ *m,* skirt; underskirt
faldero /fal'dero/ *a* lap (dog); fond of the company of women
faldillas /fal'diʎas; fal'diyas/ *f pl,* coattails
faldistorio /faldis'torio/ *m,* faldstool
faldón /fal'don/ *m,* long, flowing skirt; shirttail; coattail
falibilidad /faliβili'ðað/ *f,* fallibility
falible /fa'liβle/ *a* fallible
falla /'faʎa; faya/ *f,* deficiency, defect; failure; *Geol.* displacement; bonfire (Valencia); *Mineral.* slide
fallar /fa'ʎar; fa'yar/ *vt Law.* to pass sentence; —*vi* be deficient
falleba /fa'ʎeβa; fa'yeβa/ *f,* shutter bolt
fallecer /faʎe'θer; faye'ser/ *vi irr* to die; fail. See **conocer**
fallecimiento /faʎeθi'miento; fayesi'miento/ *m,* death, decease
fallido /fa'ʎiðo; fa'yiðo/ *a* frustrated; bankrupt
fallo /'faʎo; 'fayo/ *m, Law.* verdict; judgment
falsario /fal'sario/ *a* falsifying, forging, counterfeiting; deceiving, lying. *m,* falsifier, forger
falseamiento /falsea'miento/ *m,* falsifying; forging
falsear /false'ar/ *vt* to falsify; forge; counterfeit; penetrate; —*vi* weaken; *Mus.* be out of tune (strings)
falsedad /false'ðað/ *f,* falseness; falsehood
falsete /fal'sete/ *m,* spigot; *Mus.* falsetto voice
falsificación /falsifika'θion; falsifika'sion/ *f,* falsification; forgery
falsificador /falsifika'ðor/ *a* falsifying; forging. *m,* falsifier; forger
falsificar /falsifi'kar/ *vt* to forge, counterfeit; falsify
falso /'falso/ *a* false; forged, counterfeit; treacherous, untrue, deceitful; incorrect; sham; vicious (horses). **de f.,** falsely; deceitfully
falta /'falta/ *f,* lack, shortage; defect; mistake; *Sports.* fault; shortcoming; nonappearance, absence; deficiency in legal weight of coin; *Law.* offense. **f. de éxito,** failure. **hacer f.,** to be necessary. **sin f.,** without fail
faltar /fal'tar/ *vi* to be lacking; fail, die; fall short; be absent from an appointment; not to fulfill one's obligations. **f. a,** to be unfaithful to, break (e.g. *Faltó a su palabra,* He broke his promise). *Inf.* **¡No faltaba más!** I should think not!; That's the limit!
falto /'falto/ *a* lacking, wanting; defective; wretched, mean, timid. **f. de personal,** short-handed
faltriquera /faltri'kera/ *f,* pocket; hip pocket
falúa /fa'lua/ *f, Naut.* tender; longboat
falucho /fa'lutʃo/ *m,* felucca
fama /'fama/ *f,* rumor, report; reputation; fame
famélico /fa'meliko/ *a* ravenous
familia /fa'milia/ *f,* family; household; kindred. **ser de f.,** to run in the family

familiar /fami'liar/ *a* family; familiar; well known; unceremonious; plain, simple; colloquial (language). *m, Eccl.* familiar; servant; intimate friend; familiar spirit

familiaridad /familiari'ðað/ *f,* familiarity

familiarizar /familiari'θar; familiari'sar/ *vt* to familiarize; —*vr* become familiar; accustom oneself

familiarmente /familiar'mente/ *adv* familiarly

famoso /fa'moso/ *a* famous; notorious; *Inf.* excellent, perfect; *Inf.* conspicuous

fámula /'famula/ *f, Inf.* female servant

fámulo /'famulo/ *m,* servant of a college; *Inf.* servant

fanal /fa'nal/ *m,* lantern (of a lighthouse); *Naut.* poop lantern; lantern; lamp glass

fanático /fa'natiko/ **(-ca)** *a* fanatical —*n* fanatic; *Inf.* fan, enthusiast

fanatismo /fana'tismo/ *m,* fanaticism

fanatizar /fanati'θar; fanati'sar/ *vt* to make fanatical; turn into a fanatic

fandango /fan'daŋgo/ *m,* lively Andalusian dance

fanega /fa'nega/ *f,* grain measure about the weight of 1.60 bushel; land measure (about 1½ acres)

fanfarrón /fanfa'rron/ **(-ona)** *a Inf.* boastful; swaggering —*n* swashbuckler; boaster

fanfarronear /fanfarrone'ar/ *vi* to swagger; brag

fanfarronería /fanfarrone'ria/ *f,* bragging

fango /'faŋgo/ *m,* mud, mire; degradation

fangoso /faŋ'goso/ *a* muddy, miry

fantasear /fantase'ar/ *vi* to let one's fancy roam; boast

fantasía /fanta'sia/ *f,* fancy, imagination; fantasy; caprice; fiction; *Inf.* presumption; *Mus.* fantasia

fantasma /fan'tasma/ *m,* ghost, phantom; vision; image, impression; presumptuous person. *f, Inf.* scarecrow; apparition

fantasmagoría /fantasmago'ria/ *f,* phantasmagoria

fantasmagórico /fantasma'goriko/ *a* phantasmagoric

fantástico /fan'tastiko/ *a* fanciful, imaginary; fantastic, imaginative; presumptuous, conceited

fantoche /fan'totʃe/ *m,* puppet; *Inf.* yes-man, mediocrity

faquín /fa'kin/ *m,* porter, carrier

faquir /fa'kir/ *m,* fakir

faradio /fa'raðio/ *m,* farad

faralá /fara'la/ *m,* flounce, frill

farándula /fa'randula/ *f,* profession of low comedian; troupe of strolling players; cunning trick

farandulero /farandu'lero/ *m,* actor, strolling player —*a Inf.* plausible

faraón /fara'on/ *m,* pharaoh; faro (card game)

fardel /far'ðel/ *m,* bag, knapsack; bundle

fardo /far'ðo/ *m,* bundle, bale, package

farfulla /far'fuʎa/ far'fuya/ *f, Inf.* mumbling; gibbering. *mf Inf.* mumbler

farfullar /farfu'ʎar; farfu'yar/ *vt Inf.* to mumble; gibber; *Inf.* act in haste

faringe /fa'rinhe/ *f,* pharynx

faríngeo /fa'rinheo/ *a* pharyngeal

faringitis /farin'hitis/ *f,* pharyngitis

farisaico /fari'saiko/ *a* pharisaical

fariseísmo /farise'ismo/ *m,* cant, hypocrisy

fariseo /fari'seo/ *m,* Pharisee; hypocrite

farmacéutico /farma'θeutiko; farma'seutiko/ *a* pharmaceutical. *m,* pharmacist

farmacia /far'maθia; far'masia/ *f,* pharmacy

farmacología /farmakolo'hia/ *f,* pharmacology

farmacológico /farmako'lohiko/ *a* pharmacological

farmacólogo /farma'kologo/ *m,* pharmacologist

faro /'faro/ *m,* lighthouse; beacon, guide; *Auto.* headlight

farol /fa'rol/ *m,* lantern, lamp; streetlamp; cresset

farola /fa'rola/ *f,* lamppost (generally with several branches); lantern

farolero /faro'lero/ *m,* lantern maker; lamplighter; lamp tender —*a Inf.* swaggering, braggart

fárrago /'farrago/ *m,* hodgepodge

farsa /'farsa/ *f,* old name for a play; farce; theatrical company; poor, badly constructed play; sham, trick, deception

farsante /far'sante/ *m,* comedian; *Obs.* actor; *Fig. Inf.* humbug

fascinación /fasθina'θion; fassina'sion/ *f,* evil eye; enchantment, fascination

fascinador /fasθina'ðor; fassina'ðor/ **(-ra)** *a* bewitching; fascinating —*n* charmer

fascinante /fasθi'nante; fassi'nante/ *a* fascinating

fascinar /fasθi'nar; fassi'nar/ *vt* to bewitch, place under a spell; deceive, impose upon; attract, fascinate

fascismo /fas'θismo; fas'sismo/ *m,* fascism

fascista /fas'θista; fas'sista/ *a* and *mf* fascist

fase /'fase/ *f,* phase; aspect

fastidiar /fasti'ðiar/ *vt* to disgust, bore; annoy; —*vr* be bored

fastidio /fasti'ðio/ *m,* sickness, squeamishness; annoyance, boredom, dislike, repugnance

fastidioso /fasti'ðioso/ *a* disgusting, sickening; annoying; boring, tiresome

fastuoso /fas'tuoso/ *a* ostentatious; pompous

fatal /fa'tal/ *a* fatal, mortal; predetermined, inevitable; ill-fated, unhappy, disastrous; evil

fatalidad /fatali'ðað/ *f,* fatality; inevitability; disaster, ill-fatedness

fatalismo /fata'lismo/ *m,* fatalism

fatalista /fata'lista/ *a* fatalistic. *mf* fatalist

fatalmente /fatal'mente/ *adv* inevitably, unavoidably; unhappily, unfortunately; extremely badly

fatídico /fa'tiðiko/ *a* prophetic (gen. of evil)

fatiga /fa'tiga/ *f,* fatigue; toil; difficult breathing; hardship, troubles (gen. *pl*)

fatigar /fati'gar/ *vt* to tire; annoy; —*vr* be tired

fatigoso /fati'goso/ *a* tired; tiring; tiresome, annoying

fatuidad /fatui'ðað/ *f,* fatuousness, inanity, foolishness; conceit; priggishness

fatuo /fa'tuo/ *a* fatuous, foolish; conceited; priggish. *m,* self-satisfied fool. **fuego f.,** will-o'-the-wisp

fauces /'fauθes; 'fauses/ *f pl,* gullet

fauna /'fauna/ *f,* fauna

fauno /'fauno/ *m,* faun

fausto /'fausto/ *m,* pomp, magnificence, ostentation —*a* fortunate, happy

fautor /fau'tor/ *m,* protector, helper; accomplice. **f. de guerra,** warmonger

favonio /fa'βonio/ *m, Poet.* zephyr, westerly wind

favor /fa'βor/ *m,* aid, protection, support; favor, honor, service; love favor, sign of favor. **a f. de,** in favor of; on behalf of

favorable /faβo'raβle/ *a* kind, helpful; favorable

favorecedor /faβoreθe'ðor; faβorese'ðor/ **(-ra)** *a* favoring, helping —*n* helper; protector

favorecer /faβore'θer; faβore'ser/ *vt irr* to aid, protect, support; favor; do a service, grant a favor. See **conocer**

favoritismo /faβori'tismo/ *m,* favoritism

favorito /faβo'rito/ **(-ta)** *a* and *n* favorite

fayenza /fa'yenθa; fa'yensa/ *f,* faience

faz /faθ; fas/ *f,* face; external surface of a thing, side; frontage

fe /fe/ *f,* faith; confidence, trust, good opinion; belief; solemn promise; assertion; certificate, attestation; faithfulness. **f. de erratas,** *Print.* errata. **dar f.,** *Law.* to testify. **de buena f.,** in good faith. **en f.,** in proof

fealdad /feal'dað/ *f,* ugliness; base action

febo /'feβo/ *m,* Phoebus; *Poet.* sun

febrero /fe'βrero/ *m,* February

febril /fe'βril/ *a* feverish; ardent, violent; passionate

fecal /fe'kal/ *a* fecal

fecha /'fetʃa/ *f,* date. **a la f.,** at present, now. **hasta la f.,** up to the present (day)

fechar /fe'tʃar/ *vt* to date, write the date

feculento /feku'lento/ *a* starchy; dreggy

fecundación /fekunda'θion; fekunda'sion/ *f,* fecundation

fecundar /fekun'dar/ *vt* to fertilize; fecundate

fecundidad /fekundi'ðað/ *f,* fecundity; fertility, fruitfulness

fecundizar /fekundi'θar; fekundi'sar/ *vt* to fertilize; make fruitful

fecundo /fe'kundo/ *a* fertile, fecund, prolific; abundant

federación /feðera'θion; feðera'sion/ *f,* federation, league

federal /feðe'ral/ *a* federal. *mf* federalist
federalismo /feðera'lismo/ *m*, federalism
federalista /feðera'lista/ *a* federal, federalist. *mf* federalist
federativo /feðera'tiβo/ *a* federative
fehaciente /fea'θiente; fea'siente/ *a Law.* authentic, attested
feldespato /feldes'pato/ *m*, feldspar
felicidad /feliθi'ðað; felisi'ðað/ *f*, happiness; contentment, satisfaction; good fortune
felicitación /feliθita'θion; felisita'sion/ *f*, congratulation
felicitar /feliθi'tar; felisi'tar/ *vt* to congratulate; wish well; —*vr* congratulate oneself
feligrés /feli'gres/ **(-esa)** *n* parishioner
feligresía /feligre'sia/ *f*, parish
felino /fe'lino/ *a* and *m*, feline
feliz /fe'liθ; fe'lis/ *a* happy; fortunate; skillful, felicitous (of phrases, etc.)
felón /fe'lon/ **(-ona)** *n* felon
felonía /felo'nia/ *f*, felony
felpa /'felpa/ *f*, plush; *Inf.* drubbing, beating
felpilla /fel'piʎa; fel'piya/ *f*, chenille
felpudo /fel'puðo/ *a* plush
femenino /feme'nino/ *a* feminine; female; *Fig.* weak
fementido /femen'tiðo/ *a* sly, false, treacherous, unfaithful
feminismo /femi'nismo/ *m*, feminism
feminista /femi'nista/ *a* feminist. *mf* feminist
fémur /'femur/ *m*, femur, thigh bone
fenecer /fene'θer; fene'ser/ *vt irr* to conclude, finish; —*vi* die; be ended. See **conocer**
fenecimiento /feneθi'miento; fenesi'miento/ *m*, end; death
fenicio /fe'niθio; fe'nisio/ **(-ia)** *a* and *n* Phoenician
fénico /'feniko/ *a* phenic, carbolic
fénix /'feniks/ *f*, phoenix
fenomenal /fenome'nal/ *a* phenomenal; *Inf.* terrific
fenómeno /fe'nomeno/ *m*, phenomenon; *Inf.* something of great size
feo /'feo/ *a* ugly; alarming, horrid; evil. *m*, *Inf.* slight, insult
feraz /'feraθ; 'feras/ *a* fruitful, fertile
féretro /'feretro/ *m*, coffin; bier
feria /'feria/ *f*, fair, market; workday; holiday; rest
feriar /fe'riar/ *vt* to buy at a fair; bargain —*vi* cease work, take a holiday
fermentación /fermenta'θion; fermenta'sion/ *f*, fermentation
fermentar /fermen'tar/ *vi* to ferment; be agitated; —*vt* cause to ferment
fermento /fer'mento/ *m*, ferment; leaven; *Chem.* enzyme
ferocidad /feroθi'ðað; ferosi'ðað/ *f*, ferocity, cruelty
feroz /fe'roθ; fe'ros/ *a* ferocious, cruel
férreo /'ferreo/ *a* ferrous; hard, tenacious. **línea férrea,** railroad
ferrería /ferre'ria/ *f*, ironworks
ferretería /ferrete'ria/ *f*, ironworks; ironmonger's shop; ironware, hardware
férrico /'ferriko/ *a* ferric
ferrífero /fe'rrifero/ *a* iron-bearing
ferrocarril /ferroka'rril/ *m*, railroad, railway; railroad train. **f. de cremallera,** rack railroad. **f. funicular,** funicular railway
ferroso /fe'rroso/ *a* ferrous
ferroviario /ferro'βiario/ *a* railroad, railway. *m*, railroad employee
fértil /'fertil/ *a* fertile; fruitful, productive
fertilidad /fertili'ðað/ *f*, fertility
fertilización /fertiliθa'θion; fertilisa'sion/ *f*, fertilization
fertilizar /fertili'θar; fertili'sar/ *vt* to fertilize, make fruitful
férula /'ferula/ *f*, ferule; *Surg.* splint; *Fig.* yoke, rule
fervor /fer'βor/ *m*, intense heat; fervor, devotion; zeal
fervoroso /ferβo'roso/ *a* fervent, zealous, devoted
festejar /feste'har/ *vt* to feast, entertain; woo; celebrate; —*vr* amuse oneself

festejo /feste'ho/ *m*, feast, entertainment; courtship, wooing; *pl* public celebrations
festín /fes'tin/ *m*, private dinner or party; sumptuous banquet
festival /festi'βal/ *m*, musical festival; festival
festividad /festiβi'ðað/ *f*, festivity; *Eccl.* celebration, solemnity; witticism
festivo /fes'tiβo/ *a* joking, witty; happy, gay; solemn, worthy of celebration. **día f.,** holiday
festón /fes'ton/ *m*, garland, wreath; festoon; border; scalloped edging
festonear /festone'ar/ *vt* to garland, festoon; border
fetal /fe'tal/ *a* fetal
fetiche /fe'titʃe/ *m*, fetish
fetichismo /feti'tʃismo/ *m*, fetishism
fetidez /feti'ðeθ; feti'ðes/ *f*, fetidness, fetor, stink
fétido /'fetiðo/ *a* stinking, fetid
feto /'feto/ *m*, fetus
feudal /feu'ðal/ *a* feudal; despotic
feudalismo /feuða'lismo/ *m*, feudalism
feudo /'feuðo/ *m*, fief; fee. **f. franco,** freehold
fez /feθ/ *m*, fez
fiado, al /'fiaðo, al/ *adv* on credit. **en f.,** on bail
fiador /fia'ðor/ **(-ra)** *n* guarantor; bail. *m*, fastener, loop (of a coat, clock, etc.); safety catch, bolt. **salir f.,** to be surety (for); post bail
fiambre /'fiambre/ *m*, cold meat, cold dish; *Inf.* stale, out-of-date news, etc.; *Inf.* corpse
fiambrera /fiam'brera/ *f*, lunchbox, lunchpail
fianza /'fianθa; 'fiansa/ *f*, guarantee, bail; surety; security. *Law.* **dar f.,** to guarantee; post bail
fiar /fi'ar/ *vt* to go surety for, post bail; sell on credit; trust; confide; —*vr (with de)* confide in; trust
fibra /'fiβra/ *f*, fiber; filament; energy, strength; *Mineral.* vein; grain (of wood)
fibroso /fi'βroso/ *a* fibrous; fibroid
ficción /fik'θion; fik'sion/ *f*, falsehood; invention; fiction, imaginative creation; pretense
ficha /'fitʃa/ *f*, chip, counter; domino; index card, filing card. **f. antropométrica,** personal particulars card
fichar /fi'tʃar/ *vt* to record personal particulars on a filing card; file, index
fichero /fi'tʃero/ *m*, filing cabinet; card catalog
fichú /fi'tʃu/ *m*, fichu, scarf
ficticio /fik'tiθio; fik'tisio/ *a* fictitious
fidedigno /fiðe'ðigno/ *a* trustworthy, bona fide
fideicomisario /fiðeikomi'sario/ *m*, *Law.* fiduciary, trustee
fideicomiso /fiðeiko'miso/ *m*, *Law.* trust
fidelidad /fiðeli'ðað/ *f*, fidelity, honesty; loyalty; punctiliousness
fideos /fi'ðeos/ *m pl*, vermicelli. *m*, *Inf.* scraggy person
fiduciario /fiðu'θiario; fiðu'siario/ *a Law.* fiduciary. *m*, *Law.* trustee
fiebre /'fieβre/ *f*, fever; great agitation, excitement. **f. de oro,** gold fever. **f. palúdica,** malarial fever. **f. puerperal,** puerperal fever. **f. tifoidea,** typhoid fever
fiel /fiel/ *a* faithful, loyal; true, exact. *m*, axis; pointer (of a scale or balance)
fieltro /'fieltro/ *m*, felt
fiera /'fiera/ *f*, wild beast; cruel person
fiereza /fie'reθa; fie'resa/ *f*, savageness, wildness; cruelty, fierceness; deformity
fiero /'fiero/ *a* wild, savage; ugly; huge, enormous; horrible, alarming; haughty
fiesta /'fiesta/ *f*, merriment, gaiety; entertainment, feast; *Inf.* joke; festivity, celebration; public holiday; caress, cajolery (gen. *pl*); *pl* holidays. **f. fija** *Eccl.* immovable feast. *Inf.* **estar de f.,** to be making merry. **hacer f.,** to take a holiday. *Inf.* **Se acabó la f.,** It's all over and done with
figón /fi'gon/ *m*, eating house, diner
figulino /figu'lino/ *a* fictile, made of terra cotta
figura /fi'gura/ *f*, shape, form; face; *Art.* image, figure; *Law.* form; court card; *Mus.* note; *Theat.* character, role; *(Geom. Gram. Dance.)* figure. **f. de nieve,** snowman. *Naut.* **f. de proa,** figurehead. *Fig.* **f. decorativa,** figurehead. *Fig.* **hacer f.,** to cut a figure
figurado /fi'guraðo/ *a* figurative; rhetorical
figurar /figu'rar/ *vt* to shape, mold; simulate, pre-

tend; represent; —*vi* be numbered among; cut a figure; —*vr* imagine

figurativo /figura'tiβo/ *a* figurative; symbolical

figurilla /figu'riʎa; figu'riya/ *mf Inf.* ridiculous, dwarfish figure. *f, Art.* statuette

figurín /figu'rin/ *m,* fashion plate or model

fijación /fiha'θion; fiha'sion/ *f,* fixing; nailing; sticking, posting; attention, fixity; *Chem.* fixation; firmness, stability

fijador /fiha'ðor/ *m,* (*Med. Photo.*) fixative; setting lotion; *Art.* varnish —*a* fixing

fijamente /fiha'mente/ *adv* firmly; attentively

fijar /fi'har/ *vt* to fix; glue, stick; nail; make firm; settle, appoint (a date); fix, concentrate (attention, gaze); (*Photo. Med.*) fix; —*vr* decide; notice (e.g. *No me había fijado,* I hadn't noticed). **f. anuncios,** to post bills

fijeza /fi'heθa; fi'hesa/ *f,* fixedness; firmness, stability; constancy, steadfastness

fijo /'fiho/ *a* firm; fixed; stable; steadfast; permanent; exact. **de f.,** certainly, without doubt

fila /'fila/ *f,* line, row; *Mil.* rank; antipathy, hatred. **en f.,** in a line

filacteria /filak'teria/ *f,* phylactery

filamento /fila'mento/ *m,* filament

filantropía /filantro'pia/ *f,* philanthropy

filantrópico /filan'tropiko/ *a* philanthropic

filántropo /fi'lantropo/ *m,* philanthropist

filarmónico /filar'moniko/ *a* philharmonic

filatelia /fila'telia/ *f,* philately, stamp collecting

filatélico /fila'teliko/ *a* philatelic

filatelista /filate'lista/ *mf* philatelist, stamp collector

filete /fi'lete/ *m, Archit.* filet; *Cul.* small spit; filet (of meat or fish); thread of a screw; *Sew.* hem

filiación /filia'θion; filia'sion/ *f,* filiation; affiliation; relationship; *Mil.* regimental register

filial /fi'lial/ *a* filial; affiliated

filibustero /filiβus'tero/ *m,* filibuster

filiforme /fili'forme/ *a* filamentous

filigrana /fili'grana/ *f,* filigree; watermark (of paper); *Fig.* delicate creation

filípica /fili'pika/ *f,* philippic

Filipinas, las /fili'pinas, las/ the Philippines

filipino /fili'pino/ *(-na)* *a* and *n* Philippine

filisteo /filis'teo/ *(-ea)* *a* and *n* philistine

filmar /fil'mar/ *vt* to film

filme /'filme/ *m,* (cinema) film

filo /'filo/ *m,* cutting edge; dividing line

filología /filolo'hia/ *f,* philology

filológico /filo'lohiko/ *a* philological

filólogo /fi'lologo/ *m,* philologist

filomela /filo'mela/ *f, Poet.* nightingale

filón /fi'lon/ *m, Mineral.* vein, lode; *Fig.* gold mine

filosofar /filoso'far/ *vi* to philosophize

filosofía /filoso'fia/ *f,* philosophy. **f. moral,** moral philosophy. **f. natural,** natural philosophy

filosófico /filo'sofiko/ *a* philosophic

filósofo /fi'losofo/ *m,* philosopher —*a* philosophic

filoxera /filok'sera/ *f,* phylloxera

filtración /filtra'θion; filtra'sion/ *f,* filtration

filtrar /fil'trar/ *vt* to filter; —*vi* filter through, percolate; —*vr Fig.* disappear (of money, etc.)

filtro /'filtro/ *m,* filter, strainer; love potion, philter

fin /fin/ *m,* finish, end, conclusion; purpose, goal, aim; limit, extent. **a f. de,** in order to, so that. **a fines de,** toward the end of (with months, years, etc.) (e.g. *a fines de octubre,* toward the end of October). **en f.,** at last; in fine; well then! **por f.,** finally

finado /fi'naðo/ *(-da)* *n* deceased, dead person

final /fi'nal/ *a* final. *m,* end, finish; *Sports.* final (gen. pl)

finalidad /finali'ðað/ *f,* finality; purpose

finalista /fina'lista/ *mf Sports.* finalist

finalizar /finali'θar; finali'sar/ *vt* to conclude, finish; —*vi* be finished; close (stock exchange)

finalmente /final'mente/ *adv* finally

financiar /finan'θiar; finan'siar/ *vt* to finance

financiero /finan'θiero; finan'siero/ *a* financial. *m,* financier

finanzas /fi'nanθas; fi'nansas/ *f pl,* finance

finar /fi'nar/ *vi* to die; —*vr* desire, long for a thing

finca /'finka/ *f,* land, real estate; house property, country house, ranch

fineza /fi'neθa; fi'nesa/ *f,* fineness; excellence, goodness; kindness, expression of affection; good turn, friendly act; gift; beauty, delicacy

fingido /fin'hiðo/ *a* pretended; assumed; feigned; sham

fingimiento /finhi'miento/ *m,* pretense; affectation, assumption

fingir /fin'hir/ *vt* to pretend, feign; imagine

finiquitar /finiki'tar/ *vt* to close and pay up an account; *Inf.* end

finiquito /fini'kito/ *m,* closing of an account; final receipt, quittance; quietus

finito /fi'nito/ *a* finite

finlandés /finlan'des/ *(-esa)* *a* Finnish —*n* Finn. *m,* Finnish (language)

Finlandia /fin'landia/ Finland

fino /'fino/ *a* fine; excellent, good; slim, slender, thin; delicate, subtle; dainty (of people); cultured, polished; constant, loving; sagacious, shrewd; *Mineral.* refined

finta /'finta/ *f,* feint (in fencing); menace, threat

finura /fi'nura/ *f,* fineness; excellence; delicacy; courtesy

fiordo /'fiorðo/ *m,* fjord

firma /'firma/ *f,* signature; act of signing; *Com.* firm name, firm

firmamento /firma'mento/ *m,* firmament

firmante /fir'mante/ *a* signing. *mf* signatory

firmar /fir'mar/ *vt* to sign

firme /'firme/ *a* firm; hard; steady, solid; constant, resolute, loyal. *m,* foundation, base. *Mil.* **¡Firmes!** Attention! **batir de f.,** to strike hard

firmeza /fir'meθa; fir'mesa/ *f,* stability, firmness, constancy, resoluteness, loyalty

fiscal /fis'kal/ *a* fiscal. *m,* attorney general; public prosecutor; meddler. **f. de quiebras,** official receiver

fiscalizar /fiskali'θar; fiskali'sar/ *vt* to prosecute; pry into; meddle with; censure, criticize

fisco /'fisko/ *m,* national treasury, exchequer, revenue

fisgar /fis'gar/ *vt* to harpoon; pry; —*vi* mock, make fun of

fisgón /fis'gon/ *(-ona)* *a* prying; mocking —*n* pryer; mocker; eavesdropper

fisgoneo /fisgo'neo/ *m,* prying; eavesdropping

física /'fisika/ *f,* physics

físico /'fisiko/ *a* physical. *m,* physicist; physician; physique

fisiología /fisiolo'hia/ *f,* physiology

fisiológico /fisio'lohiko/ *a* physiological

fisiólogo /fisi'ologo/ *m,* physiologist

fisioterapia /fisiote'rapia/ *f,* physiotherapy

fisonomía /fisono'mia/ *f,* physiognomy

fístula /'fistula/ *f,* pipe, conduit; *Mus.* pipe; *Surg.* fistula

fisura /fi'sura/ *f,* fissure

flaccidez /flakθi'ðeθ; flaksi'ðes/ *f,* flabbiness

fláccido /'flakθiðo; 'flaksiðo/ *a* flaccid, soft, flabby

flaco /'flako/ *a* thin; weak, feeble; *Fig.* weak-minded; dispirited. *m,* failing, weakness. *Inf.* **hacer un f. servicio,** to do an ill turn. **estar f. de memoria,** to have a weak memory

flagelación /flahela'θion; flahela'sion/ *f,* flagellation

flagelante /flahe'lante/ *m,* flagellant

flagelar /flahe'lar/ *vt* to scourge; *Fig.* lash

flagelo /fla'helo/ *m,* whip, scourge

flagrante /fla'grante/ *a Poet.* refulgent; present; actual. **en f.,** in the very act, flagrante delicto

flagrar /fla'grar/ *vi Poet.* to blaze, be refulgent

flamante /fla'mante/ *a* resplendent; brand-new; fresh, spick-and-span

flamenco /fla'menko/ *(-ca)* *m, Ornith.* flamingo —*a* and *n* Flemish —*a* Andalusian; gypsy; buxom, fresh

flan /flan/ *m,* baked custard, creme caramel. **estar como un f.,** to shake like a leaf, be nervous

flanco /'flanko/ *m,* side; *Mil.* flank

Flandes /'flandes/ Flanders

flanquear /flanke'ar/ *vt Mil.* to flank

flanqueo /flan'keo/ *m, Mil.* outflanking

flaquear /flake'ar/ *vi* to grow weak; weaken; totter (buildings, etc.); be disheartened, flag

flaqueza /fla'keθa; fla'kesa/ *f*, weakness; thinness; faintness, feebleness; frailty, fault; loss of zeal

flato /'flato/ *m*, flatulence, gas

flatulento /flatu'lento/ *a* flatulent, gassy

flauta /'flauta/ *f*, flute

flautín /flau'tin/ *m*, piccolo

flautista /flau'tista/ *mf* flutist

flebitis /fle'βitis/ *f*, phlebitis

flebotomía /fleβoto'mia/ *f*, phlebotomy, bloodletting

flecha /'fletʃa/ *f*, arrow, dart

flechar /fle'tʃar/ *vt* to shoot an arrow or dart; wound or kill with arrows; *Inf.* inspire love; —*vi* bend a bow to shoot

flechazo /fle'tʃaθo; fle'tʃaso/ *m*, wound with an arrow; *Inf.* love at first sight

flechero /fle'tʃero/ *m*, archer; arrow maker

fleco /'fleko/ *m*, fringe; fringe (of hair)

fleje /'flehe/ *m*, iron hoop (for barrels, etc.)

flema /'flema/ *f*, phlegm; sluggishness

flemático /fle'matiko/ *a* phlegmatic; sluggish

flemón /fle'mon/ *m*, gumboil; abscess

flequillo /fle'kiʎo; fle'kiyo/ *m*, fringe (of hair)

fletamento /fleta'mento/ *m*, chartering (a ship)

fletar /fle'tar/ *vt* to charter a ship; embark merchandise or people

flete /'flete/ *m*, freightage; cargo, freight

flexibilidad /fleksiβili'ðað/ *f*, flexibility; suppleness, adaptability

flexible /fle'ksiβle/ *a* pliant, supple; flexible, adaptable. *m*, *Elec.* flex

flexión /fle'ksion/ *f*, flexion; bend, bending; deflection

flirtear /flirte'ar/ *vi* to flirt

flirteo /flir'teo/ *m*, flirtation

flojedad /flohe'ðað/ *f*, flabbiness; weakness, feebleness; laziness, negligence

flojo /'floho/ *a* flabby; slack, loose; weak, feeble, lazy, slothful; poor (of a literary work, etc.)

floqueado /floke'aðo/ *a* fringed

flor /flor/ *f*, flower; best (of anything); bloom (on fruit); virginity; grain (of leather); compliment (gen. *pl*); menstruation (gen. *pl*). **f. de especia,** mace. **f. de la edad,** prime, youth. **f. del cuclillo,** mayflower. **f. del estudiante,** French marigold. **flores de mano,** artificial flowers. **flores de oblón,** hops. **a f. de,** on the surface of, level with. **andarse en flores,** *Fig.* to beat about the bush. **echar flores,** to pay compliments. **en f.,** in bloom

flora /'flora/ *f*, flora

floración /flora'θion; flora'sion/ *f*, flowering

floral /flo'ral/ *a* floral. **juegos florales,** poetry contest

florear /flore'ar/ *vt* to adorn with flowers; —*vi* execute a flourish on the guitar

florecer /flore'θer; flore'ser/ *vi irr* to flower, bloom; flourish, prosper; —*vr* grow mold (of cheese, etc.). See **conocer**

floreciente /flore'θiente; flore'siente/ *a* flowering; prosperous

florecimiento /floreθi'miento; floresi'miento/ *m*, flowering; prosperity

Florencia /flo'renθia; flo'rensia/ Florence

florentino /floren'tino/ **(-na)** *a* and *n* Florentine

floreo /flo'reo/ *m*, witty conversation; flourish (on the guitar or in fencing)

florero /flo'rero/ *m*, vase; flower pot; *Art.* flower piece

florescencia /flores'θenθia; flores'sensia/ *f*, flowering; flowering season, florescence

floresta /flo'resta/ *f*, grove, wooded park, woodland; *Fig.* collector of beautiful things; anthology

florete /flo'rete/ *m*, fencing foil

floricultor /florikul'tor/ **(-ra)** *n* floriculturist

floricultura /florikul'tura/ *f*, floriculture

floridamente /floriða'mente/ *adv* elegantly, with a flourish

florido /flo'riðo/ *a* flowery; best, most select; florid, ornate

florilegio /flori'lehio/ *m*, anthology, collection

florín /flo'rin/ *m*, florin

florista /flo'rista/ *mf* artificial-flower maker; florist; flower seller

florón /flo'ron/ *m*, large flower; *Archit.* fleuron; honorable deed

flósculo /'floskulo/ *m*, *Bot.* floret

flota /'flota/ *f*, fleet of merchant ships. **f. aérea,** air force

flotación /flota'θion; flota'sion/ *f*, floating. *Naut.* **línea de f.,** water line

flotador /flota'ðor/ *a* floating. *m*, float

flotamiento /flota'miento/ *m*, floating

flotante /flo'tante/ *a* floating

flotar /flo'tar/ *vi* to float on water or in air

flote /'flote/ *m*, floating. **a f.,** afloat; independent, solvent

flotilla /flo'tiʎa; flo'tiya/ *f*, flotilla; fleet of small ships. **f. aérea,** air fleet

fluctuación /fluktua'θion; fluktua'sion/ *f*, fluctuation; hesitation, vacillation

fluctuante /fluk'tuante/ *a* fluctuating

fluctuar /fluktu'ar/ *vi* to fluctuate; be in danger (things); vacillate, hesitate; undulate; oscillate

fluidez /flui'ðeθ; flui'ðes/ *f*, fluidity

flúido /'fluiðo/ *a* fluid; fluent. *m*, fluid; *Elec.* current

fluir /flu'ir/ *vi irr* to flow. See **huir**

flujo /'fluho/ *m*, flow, flux; rising tide. **f. de sangre,** hemorrhage

fluorescencia /fluores'θenθia; fluores'sensia/ *f*, fluorescence

fluorescente /fluores'θente; fluores'sente/ *a* fluorescent

fluvial /flu'βial/ *a* fluvial

flux /fluks/ *m*, flush (in cards)

foca /'foka/ *f*, *Zool.* seal

focal /fo'kal/ *a* focal

foco /'foko/ *m*, focus; center; origin; source; *Theat.* spotlight; core (of an abscess)

fofo /'fofo/ *a* spongy, soft; flabby

fogata /fo'gata/ *f*, bonfire

fogón /fo'gon/ *m*, fire, cooking area, kitchen range, kitchen stove; furnace of a steamboiler; vent of a firearm

fogonazo /fogo'naθo; fogo'naso/ *m*, powder flash

fogonero /fogo'nero/ *m*, stoker

fogosidad /fogosi'ðað/ *f*, enthusiasm; vehemence; ardor

fogoso /fo'goso/ *a* ardent; vehement; enthusiastic

folclórico /fol'kloriko/ *a* pertaining to folklore

folclorista /folklo'rista/ *mf* folklorist

foliar /fo'liar/ *vt* to number the pages of a book

folículo /fo'likulo/ *m*, follicle

folio /'folio/ *m*, leaf of a book or manuscript, folio. **en f.,** in folio

follaje /fo'ʎahe; fo'yahe/ *m*, foliage; leafy ornamentation; crude, unnecessary decoration; verbosity

folletín /foʎe'tin; foye'tin/ *m*, feuilleton, literary article; serial story; *Inf.* dime novel, potboiler

folletinista /foʎeti'nista; foyeti'nista/ *mf* pamphleteer

folleto /fo'ʎeto; fo'yeto/ *m*, pamphlet, leaflet

follón /fo'ʎon; fo'yon/ *a* lazy; caddish; craven

fomentación /fomenta'θion; fomenta'sion/ *f*, *Med.* fomentation, poultice

fomentador /fomenta'ðor/ *a* fomenting. *m*, fomenter

fomentar /fomen'tar/ *vt* to warm, foment; incite, instigate; *Med.* apply poultices

fomento /fo'mento/ *m*, heat, shelter; fuel; protection, encouragement; *Med.* fomentation

fonda /'fonda/ *f*, inn; restaurant

fondeadero /fondea'ðero/ *m*, anchorage, anchoring ground

fondear /fonde'ar/ *vt Naut.* to sound; search a ship; examine carefully; —*vi Naut.* anchor

fondillos /fon'diʎos; fon'diyos/ *m pl*, seat (of the trousers)

fondista /fon'dista/ *mf* owner of an inn or restaurant

fondo /'fondo/ *m*, bottom (of a well, etc.); bed (of the sea, etc.); depth; rear, portion at the back; ground (of fabrics); background; *Com.* capital; *Com.* stock; *Fig.* fund (of humor, etc.); character, nature; temperament; *Fig.* substance, core, essence; *Naut.*

bottom; *pl Com.* resources, funds. **f. de amortización,** sinking fund. **f. doble** *or* **f. secreto,** false bottom. **f. muerto, f. perdido** *or* **f. vitalicio,** life annuity. *Com.* **fondos inactivos,** idle capital. **a fondo,** completely, thoroughly. **artículo de f.,** editorial, lead article. *Sports.* **carrera de f.,** long-distance race. *Naut.* **irse a f.,** to sink, founder

fonética /fo'netika/ *f,* phonetics

fonético /fo'netiko/ *a* phonetic

fonetista /fone'tista/ *mf* phonetician

fonógrafo /fo'nografo/ *m,* phonograph

fonología /fonolo'hia/ *f,* phonology

fonológico /fono'lohiko/ *a* phonological

fontanar /fonta'nar/ *m,* spring, stream

fontanería /fontane'ria/ *f,* pipe laying, plumbing

fontanero /fonta'nero/ *m,* pipe layer; plumber

forajido /fora'hiðo/ **(-da)** *a* fugitive, outlawed —*n* robber, fugitive

forastero /foras'tero/ **(-ra)** *a* strange, foreign; alien, exotic —*n* stranger

forcejear /forθehe'ar; forsehe'ar/ *vi* to struggle; try, strive; oppose, contradict

forcejo /for'θeho; for'seho/ *m,* struggle; endeavor; opposition, hostility

fórceps /'forθeps; 'forseps/ *m pl,* forceps

forense /fo'rense/ *a* forensic

forestal /fores'tal/ *a* forestal

forillo /fo'riʎo; fo'riyo/ *m, Theat.* backdrop

forja /'forha/ *f,* forge

forjador /forha'ðor/ *m,* smith, ironworker

forjar /for'har/ *vt* to forge; fabricate; create; counterfeit

forma /'forma/ *f,* shape, form; arrangement; method; style; manifestation, expression; formula, formulary; ceremonial; *Print.* form; manner; means, way; mold, matrix; style of handwriting. *Law.* **en debida f.,** in due form

formación /forma'θion; forma''sion/ *f,* formation; form, contour, shape; (*Mil. Geol.*) formation. **f. del censo,** census taking

formador /forma'ðor/ *a* forming, shaping

formal /for'mal/ *a* apparent, formal; serious, punctilious, steady; truthful, reliable; sedate; orderly, regular, methodical

formaldehído /formalde'iðo/ *m,* formaldehyde

formalidad /formali'ðað/ *f,* orderliness, propriety; formality; requirement, requisite; ceremony; seriousness, sedateness; punctiliousness

formalismo /forma'lismo/ *m,* formalism; bureaucracy, red tape

formalizar /formali'θar; formali'sar/ *vt* to put into final form; legalize; formulate, enunciate; —*vr* take seriously (a joke)

formar /for'mar/ *vt* to shape; form; educate, mold; *Mil.* form. **formarle causa a uno,** to bring charges against someone —*vr* develop, grow

formativo /forma'tiβo/ *a* formative

formato /for'mato/ *m, Print.* format; *Chem.* formate

formidable /formi'ðaβle/ *a* formidable, awe-inspiring; huge, enormous

fórmula /'formula/ *f,* formula; prescription; mode of expression. (*Math. Chem.*) **f. clásica,** standard formula

formular /formu'lar/ *vt* to formulate; prescribe

formulario /formu'lario/ *m, Law.* formulary; handbook

formulismo /formu'lismo/ *m,* formulism; bureaucracy, red tape

fornicación /fornika'θion; fornika'sion/ *f,* fornication

fornicador /fornika'ðor/ **(-ra)** *a* and *n* fornicator

fornicar /forni'kar/ *vi* to fornicate

fornido /for'niðo/ *a* stalwart, muscular, strong

foro /'foro/ *m,* forum; law courts; law, bar, legal profession; *Theat.* back scenery; leasehold

forraje /fo'rrahe/ *m,* forage, fodder; foraging

forrajeador /forrahea'ðor/ *m,* forager

forrajear /forrahe'ar/ *vt* to gather forage, go foraging

forrar /fo'rrar/ *vt Sew.* to line; cover, encase, make a cover for

forro /'forro/ *m,* lining, inner covering; cover (of a book)

fortalecedor /fortaleθe'ðor; fortalese'ðor/ *a* fortifying

fortalecer /fortale'θer; fortale'ser/ *vt irr* to fortify. See **conocer**

fortaleza /forta'leθa; forta'lesa/ *f,* vigor; fortitude; fortress; natural defense. *Aer.* **f. volante,** flying fortress

fortificable /fortifi'kaβle/ *a* fortifiable

fortificación /fortifika'θion; fortifika'sion/ *f,* fortification

fortificador /fortifika'ðor/ *a* fortifying

fortificar /fortifi'kar/ *vt* to fortify

fortísimo /for'tisimo/ *a superl* **fuerte** extremely strong

fortuito /for'tuito/ *a* fortuitous, chance

fortuna /for'tuna/ *f,* fate, destiny; fortune, capital, estate; tempest. **por f.,** fortunately. **probar f.,** to try one's luck

forzado /for'θaðo; for'saðo/ *a* forced, obliged. *m,* convict condemned to the galleys

forzador /forθa'ðor; forsa'ðor/ *m,* violator, seducer

forzar /for'θar; for'sar/ *vt irr* to force, break open; take by force; rape, ravish; oblige, compel —*Pres. Indic.* **fuerzo, fuerzas, fuerza, fuerzan.** *Preterite* **forcé, forzaste,** etc —*Pres. Subjunc.* **fuerce, fuerces, fuerce, forcemos, forcéis, fuercen**

forzoso /for'θoso; for'soso/ *a* obligatory, unavoidable, necessary

forzudo /for'θuðo; for'suðo/ *a* brawny, stalwart

fosa /'fosa/ *f,* grave; socket (of a joint). **f. común,** potter's field.

fosar /fo'sar/ *vt* to undermine; dig a trench around

fosfato /fos'fato/ *m,* phosphate

fosforecer /fosfore'θer; fosfore'ser/ *vi irr* to phosphoresce. See **conocer**

fosforera /fosfo'rera/ *f,* matchbox

fosforero /fosfo'rero/ **(-ra)** *n* match seller

fosforescencia /fosfores'θenθia; fosfores'sensia/ *f,* phosphorescence

fosforescente /fosfores'θente; fosfores'sente/ *a* phosphorescent

fósforo /'fosforo/ *m,* phosphorus; match; morning star

fósil /'fosil/ *a* and *m,* fossil; *Inf.* antique

fosilizarse /fosili'θarse; fosili'sarse/ *vr* to become fossilized

foso /'foso/ *m,* hole, hollow, pit; trench; pit (in garages); *Theat.* room under the stage.

foto /'foto/ *f,* snapshot, photo

fotocopia /foto'kopia/ *f,* photocopy

fotogénico /foto'heniko/ *a* photogenic

fotograbado /fotogra'βaðo/ *m,* photogravure

fotografía /fotogra'fia/ *f,* photography; photograph

fotografiar /fotogra'fiar/ *vt* to photograph

fotográfico /foto'grafiko/ *a* photographic

fotógrafo /fo'tografo/ *m,* photographer

fotograma /foto'grama/ *m,* (cinema) shot

fotoquímica /foto'kimika/ *f,* photochemistry

fotostato /foto'stato/ *m,* photostat

frac /frak/ *m,* tail coat

fracasar /fraka'sar/ *vi* to break, crumble, be shattered; collapse (of plans, etc.); fail; be disappointed

fracaso /fra'kaso/ *m,* shattering; collapse (of plans, etc.); disaster; failure, disappointment, downfall

fracción /frak'θion; frak'sion/ *f,* division into parts; fraction. **f. impropia,** *Math.* improper fraction

fractura /frak'tura/ *f,* fracture. **f. conminuta,** compound fracture

fracturar /fraktu'rar/ *vt* to fracture

fragancia /fra'ganθia; fra'gansia/ *f,* fragrance, perfume; renown, good name

fragante /fra'gante/ *a* fragrant; perfumed; flagrant

fragata /fra'gata/ *f,* frigate

frágil /'frahil/ *a* fragile, brittle; perishable, frail; weak, sinful

fragilidad /frahili'ðað/ *f,* fragility; frailty, sinfulness

fragmentario /fragmen'tario/ *a* fragmentary

fragmento /frag'mento/ *m,* fragment

fragor /fra'gor/ *m,* noise, crash

fragosidad /fragosi'ðað/ *f,* roughness, rockiness, unevenness

fragoso /fra'goso/ a craggy, rocky; rough; noisy, clamorous

fragua /'fragua/ f, forge

fraguado /fra'guaðo/ m, forging; Mas. setting

fraguar /fra'guar/ vt to forge, work; plot, scheme; —vi set (concrete, etc.)

fraile /'fraile/ m, friar, monk. Inf. **f. de misa y olla,** ignorant friar

frailesco /frai'lesko/ a Inf. pertaining to friars, friar-like

frambuesa /fram'buesa/ f, raspberry

francachela /franka'tʃela/ f, Inf. binge

francés /fran'θes; fran'ses/ **(-esa)** a French —n Frenchman (-woman). m, French (language). **a la francesa,** in French fashion

francesilla /franθe'siλa; franse'siya/ f, Cul. French roll

Francia /'franθia; 'fransia/ France

franciscano /franθis'kano; fransis'kano/ **(-na)** a and n Franciscan

francmasón /frankma'son/ **(-ona)** n Freemason

francmasonería /frankmasone'ria/ f, freemasonry

franco /'franko/ a generous, liberal; exempt; sincere, genuine, frank; duty-free; Frank; Franco (in compound words). m, franc (coin). **f. de porte,** post-free; prepaid

Franco-Condado /'franko-kon'daðo/ Franche-Comté

francotirador /frankotira'ðor/ m, sharpshooter, franc tireur

franela /fra'nela/ f, flannel

frangir /fran'hir/ vt to divide, quarter

frangollar /franɡo'λar; franɡo'yar/ vt to scamp, skimp (work); botch, bungle

franja /'franha/ f, fringe; border, trimming; stripe. Radio. **f. undosa,** wave band

franjar /fran'har/ vt Sew. to fringe, trim

franqueadora /frankea'ðora/ f, postage meter

franquear /franke'ar/ vt to exempt; make free, make a gift of; clear the way; stamp, prepay; free (slaves); —vr fall in easily with others' plans; make confidences

franqueo /fran'keo/ m, exemption; bestowal, making free; postage, stamping; enfranchisement (of slaves)

franqueza /fran'keθa; fran'kesa/ f, exemption, freedom; generosity, liberality; sincerity, frankness

franquicia /fran'kiθia; fran'kisia/ f, exemption from excise duties

franquista /fran'kista/ mf Franquist, supporter of Franco

frasco /'frasko/ m, bottle, flask; powder flask or horn. **f. cuentagotas,** drop bottle

frase /'frase/ f, sentence; phrase; epigram; idiom, style. **f. hecha,** cliché

frasear /frase'ar/ vt to phrase

fraseología /fraseolo'hia/ f, phraseology; wording

fratás /fra'tas/ m, plastering trowel

fraternal /frater'nal/ a brotherly

fraternidad /fraterni'ðað/ f, fraternity, brotherhood

fraternizar /fraterni'θar; fraterni'sar/ vi to fraternize

fraterno /fra'terno/ a fraternal

fratricida /fratri'θiða; fratri'siða/ a fratricidal. mf fratricide

fratricidio /fratri'θiðio; fratri'siðio/ m, fratricide (act)

fraude /'frauðe/ m, fraud, deception

fraudulento /frauðu'lento/ a fraudulent

fray /frai/ m, Abbr. **fraile.** Always followed by a proper name (e.g. F. Bartolomé, Friar Bartholomew)

frazada /fra'θaða; fra'saða/ f, blanket

frecuencia /fre'kuenθia; fre'kuensia/ f, frequency. **f. radioeléctrica,** radiofrequency

frecuentación /frekuenta'θion; frekuenta'sion/ f, frequenting, visiting

frecuentador /frekuenta'ðor/ **(-ra)** n frequenter

frecuentar /frekuen'tar/ vt to frequent

frecuente /fre'kuente/ a frequent

fregadero /frega'ðero/ m, kitchen sink

fregado /fre'gaðo/ m, scrubbing; rubbing; scouring; washing; Inf. murky business

fregador /frega'ðor/ m, kitchen sink; scrub brush; dishcloth. **f. mecánico de platos,** dishwasher

fregar /fre'gar/ vt irr to rub; scour; wash (dishes). See **cegar**

fregona /fre'gona/ f, kitchen maid

fregotear /fregote'ar/ vt Inf. to clean or scour inefficiently

freiduría /freiðu'ria/ f, fried-fish shop

freír /fre'ir/ vt irr Cul. to fry. See **reír**

fréjol /'frehol/ m, kidney bean

frenar /fre'nar/ vt to restrain, hold back; bridle, check; Mech. brake

frenesí /frene'si/ m, madness, frenzy; vehemence, exaltation

frenético /fre'netiko/ a mad, frenzied; vehement, exalted

freno /'freno/ m, bridle; Mech. brake; restraint, check. **f. de pedal,** foot brake. **f. neumático,** vacuum brake, pneumatic brake

frente /'frente/ f, brow, forehead; front portion; countenance; head; heading; beginning (of a letter, etc.). m, Mil. front. mf facade; front; obverse (of coins) —adv in front, opposite. **f. a f.,** face to face. **con la f. levantada,** with head held high; proudly; insolently. **de f.,** abreast

freo /'freo/ m, strait, narrow channel

fresa /'fresa/ f, strawberry plant and fruit (especially small or wild varieties); Mech. milling cutter, miller

fresadora /fresa'ðora/ f, milling machine

fresal /fre'sal/ m, strawberry bed

fresca /'freska/ f, cool air; fresh air; Inf. home truth

fresco /'fresko/ a cool; fresh, new; recent; buxom, fresh-colored; calm, serene; Inf. impudent, cheeky, bold; thin (cloths). m, coolness; fresh air; Art. fresco. **al f.,** in the open air. **hacer f.,** to be cool or fresh

frescote /fres'kote/ a Inf. ruddy and corpulent

frescura /fres'kura/ f, coolness; freshness; pleasant verdure and fertility; Inf. cheek, nerve; piece of insolence; unconcern, indifference; calmness, serenity

fresero /fre'sero/ **(-ra)** n strawberry seller

fresneda /fres'neða/ f, ash grove

fresno /'fresno/ m, Bot. ash

fresón /fre'son/ m, strawberry (large, cultivated varieties)

fresquera /fres'kera/ f, meat locker; cool place

fresquista /fres'kista/ mf fresco painter

friable /'friaβle/ a brittle; friable, powdery

frialdad /frial'dað/ f, coldness, chilliness; Med. frigidity; indifference, lack of interest; foolishness; negligence

friamente /fria'mente/ adv coldly; coolly, with indifference; dully, flatly

fricción /frik'θion; frik'sion/ f, friction

friccionar /frikθio'nar; friksio'nar/ vt to rub; give a massage

friega /'friega/ f, friction, massage

frigidez /frihi'ðeθ; frihi'ðes/ f, See **frialdad**

frígido /'frihiðo/ a frigid

frigio /'frihio/ a and n Phrygian

frigorífico /frigo'rifiko/ a refrigerative. m, refrigerator, cold-storage locker

frío /'frio/ a cold; Med. frigid; indifferent, uninterested; dull, uninteresting; inefficient. m, coldness, chill; cold

friolera /frio'lera/ f, bagatelle, trifle, mere nothing

friolero /frio'lero/ a sensitive to cold

frisa /'frisa/ f, frieze cloth

frisar /fri'sar/ vt to frizz, curl (cloth); scrub, rub; —vi approach, be nearly (e.g. Frisa en los setenta años, He's nearly seventy)

Frisia /'frisia/ Friesland

friso /'friso/ m, frieze; dado, border

frisón /fri'son/ **(-ona)** a and n Frisian

fritada /fri'taða/ f, Cul. fry, fried food

frito /'frito/ a fried

fritura /fri'tura/ f, frying; fried food

frivolidad /friβoli'ðað/ f, frivolity

frivolité /friβoli'te/ m, Sew. tatting

frívolo /'friβolo/ a frivolous, superficial; futile, unconvincing

fronda /'fronda/ f, Bot. leaf; frond (of ferns); pl foliage

frondosidad /frondosi'ðað/ f, luxuriance of foliage

frondoso /fron'doso/ *a* leafy

frontera /fron'tera/ *f,* frontier; facade

fronterizo /fronte'riθo; fronte'riso/ *a* frontier; facing, opposite

frontero /fron'tero/ *a* facing, opposite. *m,* (*Obs. Mil.*) frontier commander

frontispicio /frontis'piθio; frontis'pisio/ *m,* frontispiece; facade; *Fig. Inf.* face, dial

frontón /fron'ton/ *m,* pelota court; jai alai court; *Archit.* pediment

frotamiento, frote /frota'miento, 'frote/ *m,* rubbing, friction

frotar /fro'tar/ *vt* to rub

frotis /'frotis/ *m, Med.* smear

fructífero /fruk'tifero/ *a* fruitful, fructiferous

fructuoso /fruk'tuoso/ *a* fruitful, fertile; useful

frufrú /fru'fru/ *m,* rustle (of silk, etc.)

frugal /fru'gal/ *a* frugal; saving, economical

frugalidad /frugali'ðað/ *f,* frugality, abstemiousness, moderation

fruición /frui'θion; frui'sion/ *f,* enjoyment; fruition; satisfaction

fruir /fruir/ *vi irr* to enjoy what one has long desired. See **huir**

frunce /'frunθe; 'frunse/ *m, Sew.* shirring; gather; ruffling; tuck; pucker; wrinkle

fruncimiento /frunθi'miento; frunsi'miento/ *m,* wrinkling; puckering; *Sew.* shirring

fruncir /frun'θir; frun'sir/ *vt* to frown; purse (the lips); pucker; *Sew.* shirr, pleat, gather; reduce in size; conceal the truth; —*vr* pretend to be prudish. **f. el ceño,** to knit one's brow, scowl

fruslería /frusle'ria/ *f,* trifle, nothing

frustración /frustra'θion; frustra'sion/ *f,* frustration

frustrar /frus'trar/ *vt* to disappoint; frustrate, thwart

fruta /'fruta/ *f,* fruit; *Inf.* consequence, result. **f. de hueso,** stone fruit. *Cul.* **f. de sartén,** fritter

frutal /fru'tal/ *a* fruit-bearing. *m,* fruit tree

frutar /fru'tar/ *vi* to bear fruit

frutería /frute'ria/ *f,* fruit

frutero /fru'tero/ **(-ra)** *a* fruit —*n* fruit seller. *m,* fruit dish; *Art.* painting of fruit; basket of imitation fruit .

frútice /'frutiθe; frutise/ *m,* bush, shrub

fruticultura /frutikul'tura/ *f,* fruit farming

fruto /'fruto/ *m,* fruit; product, result; profit, proceeds; *Agr.* grain

fu /fu/ spitting (of cats) —*interj* expression of scorn. *Inf.* **ni f. ni fa,** neither one thing nor the other

fucilazo /fuθi'laθo; fusi'laso/ *m,* heat lightning

fucsia /'fuksia/ *f,* fuchsia

fuego /'fuego/ *m,* fire; conflagration; firing (of firearms); beacon; hearth, home; rash; ardor; heat (of an argument, etc.); —*interj* **¡F.!** *Mil.* Fire! **fuegos artificiales,** fireworks. **a sangre y f.,** by fire and sword. *Mil.* **hacer f.,** to fire (a weapon). **pegar f.,** to set on fire

fuelle /'fueʎe; 'fueye/ *m,* bellows; bag (of a bagpipe); *Sew.* pucker, wrinkle; hood (of a carriage, etc.); wind cloud; *Inf.* talebearer. **f. de pie,** foot pump

fuente /'fuente/ *f,* stream, spring; fountain; meat dish; genesis, origin; source, headwaters; tap

fuera /'fuera/ *adv* outside, out —*interj* get out! **f. de,** besides, in addition to. **f. de alcance,** out of reach. **f. de sí,** beside oneself (with rage, etc.). **de f.,** from the outside. **por f.,** on the outside, externally

fuero /'fuero/ *m,* municipal charter; jurisdiction; compilation of laws; legal right or privilege; *pl Inf.* arrogance. **los fueros de León,** the laws of León

fuerte /'fuerte/ *a* strong, resistant; robust; spirited, vigorous; hard (of diamonds, etc.); rough, uneven; impregnable; terrible, tremendous; overweight (of coins); active; efficacious, effective; expert, knowledgeable; *Gram.* strong; intense; loud; tough. *m,* fort; talent, strong point; *Mus.* forte —*adv* strongly; excessively. **tener genio f.,** to be quick-tempered

fuerza /'fuerθa; 'fuersa/ *f,* strength; power, might; force; efficacy; fortress; *Sew.* stiffening; *Mech.* power; violence; toughness, durability, solidity; potency; authority; courage; vigor; *pl Fig. Inf.* livewires; influential people. **a f. de,** by means of, by dint of. **a la f.,** forcibly. **en f. de,** because of, on account of. **por f. mayor,** by main force. **ser f.,** to be necessary

fuga /'fuga/ *f,* flight, escape, running away; leak (gas, etc.); elopement; *Mus.* fugue; ardor, strength. **f. de cerebros,** brain drain

fugarse /fu'garse/ *vr* to run away; elope; escape

fugaz /fu'gaθ; fu'gas/ *a* fugitive; fleeting, brief

fugitivo /fuhi'tiβo/ **(-va)** *a* fugitive; runaway, escaping; transient —*n* fugitive

fulano /fu'lano/ **(-na)** *n* so-and-so, such a person **f., zutano, y mengano,** *Inf.* Tom, Dick, and Harry

fulcro /'fulkro/ *m,* fulcrum

fulgente, fúlgido /ful'hente, 'fulhiðo/ *a* brilliant, shining

fulgor /ful'gor/ *m,* brilliance, brightness

fulgurar /fulgu'rar/ *vi* to shine, be resplendent, scintillate; flare

fulguroso /fulgu'roso/ *a* shining, sparkling

fúlica /'fulika/ *f, Ornith.* coot

fullería /fuʎe'ria; fuye'ria/ *f,* cheating at play; craftiness, low guile

fullero /fu'ʎero; fu'yero/ **(-ra)** *a* cheating; crafty, astute —*n* cheat, cardsharper

fulminante /fulmi'nante/ *a Med.* fulminant; fulminating; thundering. *m,* percussion cap

fulminar /fulmi'nar/ *vt* to fulminate (all meanings)

fulminato /fulmi'nato/ *m, Chem.* fulminate

fulmíneo, fulminoso /ful'mineo, fulmi'noso/ *a* fulminous, pertaining to lightning

fumadero /fuma'ðero/ *m,* smoking room

fumador /fuma'ðor/ **(-ra)** *a* smoking —*n* smoker. **«No fumadores»,** "Nonsmoking" (area)

fumar /fu'mar/ *vi* to smoke; —*vr Inf.* dissipate, waste

fumarola /fuma'rola/ *f,* fumarole

fumigación /fumiga'θion; fumiga'sion/ *f,* fumigation

fumigador /fumiga'ðor/ **(-ra)** *n* fumigator

fumigar /fumi'gar/ *vt* to fumigate

fumigatorio /fumiga'torio/ *a* fumigatory. *m,* perfume burner

fumista /fu'mista/ *m,* stove maker or seller

fumistería /fumiste'ria/ *f,* stove factory or store

funámbulo /fu'nambulo/ *n* tightrope walker, acrobat

función /fun'θion; fun'sion/ *f,* function; working, operation; *Theat.* performance; activity, duty; ceremony; celebration; *Math.* function; *Mil.* battle

funcional /funθio'nal; funsio'nal/ *a* functional

funcionamiento /funθiona'miento; funsiona'miento/ *m,* functioning

funcionar /funθio'nar; funsio'nar/ *vi* to function, work. **«No funciona»,** "Out of order"

funcionario /funθio'nario; funsio'nario/ *m,* functionary, official; civil servant

funda /'funda/ *f,* case, cover, sheath; hold-all. **f. de almohada,** pillowcase

fundación /funda'θion; funda'sion/ *f,* foundation

fundadamente /fundaða'mente/ *adv* with reason, on good evidence

fundador /funda'ðor/ **(-ra)** *n* founder, creator; originator

fundamental /funda'mental/ *a* fundamental

fundamento /funda'mento/ *m, Mas.* foundation; basis; basic principle, reason; origin, root

fundar /fun'dar/ *vt* to build, erect; base; found, institute; create, establish; —*vr* (*with en*) found, base upon. **f. una compañía,** *Com.* to float a company

fundición /fundi'θion; fundi'sion/ *f,* foundry; smelting, founding, casting; cast iron; *Print.* font

fundido fotográfico /fun'diðo foto'grafiko/ *m,* composite photograph

fundidor /fundi'ðor/ *m,* founder, smelter.

fundir /fun'dir/ *vt* to melt; found, smelt; cast (metals); —*vr* join together, unite; *Elec.* blow (fuses)

fúnebre /'funeβre/ *a* funeral; dismal, lugubrious, mournful

funeral /fune'ral/ *a* funeral

funerala /fune'rala,/ **(a la)** *adv Mil.* with reversed arms

funerales /fune'rales/ *m pl,* funeral; *Eccl.* memorial masses

funeraria /fune'raria/ *f,* funeral home, undertaker

funerario /fune'rario/ *a* funeral

funéreo /fu'nereo/ *a* funereal, mournful

funesto /fu'nesto/ *a* unlucky, unfortunate; mournful, melancholy, sad

fungoso /fuŋ'goso/ *a* spongy, fungous

funicular /funiku'lar/ *a* funicular

furgón /fur'gon/ *m,* wagon; van; guard's van, baggage car, luggage cart. **f. postal,** mail truck

furia /'furia/ *f, Myth.* fury; rage, wrath; fit of madness; raging, violence (of the elements); speed, haste

furibundo /furi'βundo/ *a* frantic, furious; raging

fúrico /'furiko/ *a* stark raving mad

furioso /fu'rioso/ *a* furious, enraged; mad, insane; violent, terrible; enormous, excessive

furor /fu'ror/ *m,* fury, rage; poetic frenzy; violence; furor

furriel /fu'rriel/ *m,* quartermaster

furtivo /fur'tiβo/ *a* furtive; covert, clandestine; pirate (editions)

fusa /'fusa/ *f,* demisemiquaver

fusco /'fusko/ *a* dark

fuselado /fuse'laðo/ *a* streamlined

fuselaje /fuse'lahe/ *m,* fuselage

fusible /fu'siβle/ *a* fusible. *m, Elec.* fuse; fuse wire

fusil /fu'sil/ *m,* rifle

fusilamiento /fusila'miento/ *m,* execution by shooting

fusilar /fusi'lar/ *vt* to execute by shooting; *Inf.* plagiarize

fusilazo /fusi'laθo; fusi'laso/ *m,* rifle shot

fusión /fu'sion/ *f,* melting, liquefying; fusion, blending; mixture, union; *Com.* merger, amalgamation

fusionar /fusio'nar/ *vt* to blend, fuse, merge; —*vr Com.* combine, form a merger

fusta /'fusta/ *f,* brushwood; whip

fuste /'fuste/ *m,* wood, timber; *Poet.* saddle; *Fig.* core, essence; importance, substance; shaft of a lance; *Archit.* shaft. **hombre de buen f.,** a man with a good (physical) constitution

fustigar /fusti'gar/ *vt* to whip, lash; rebuke harshly

fútbol /'futβol/ *m,* football; soccer

futbolista /futβo'lista/ *mf* football player; soccer player

fútil /'futil/ *a* futile, ineffectual, worthless

futilidad /futili'ðað/ *f,* futility, worthlessness

futura /fu'tura/ *f, Law.* reversion (of offices); *Inf.* fiancée

futurismo /futu'rismo/ *m,* futurism

futurista /futu'rista/ *mf* futurist

futurístico /futu'ristiko/ *a* futuristic

futuro /fu'turo/ **(-ra)** *a* future. *m,* future —*n Inf.* betrothed

G

gabacho /ga'βatʃo/ (**-cha**) *a* and *n* (*Inf.* scornful) Frenchman

gabán /ga'βan/ *m*, overcoat; cloak

gabardina /gaβar'ðina/ *f*, gabardine; weatherproof coat

gabarra /ga'βarra/ *f*, *Naut.* lighter, gabbard, barge

gabarro /ga'βarro/ *m*, flaw (in cloth); knot (in stone); snag, drawback; slip, error (in accounts)

gabela /ga'βela/ *f*, duty, tax; imposition; burden

gabinete /gaβi'nete/ *m*, study, library; sitting room; den; *Polit.* cabinet; collection, museum, gallery; laboratory; boudoir; studio; display cabinet. **g. de lectura,** reading room

gablete /ga'βlete/ *m*, *Archit.* gable

gaceta /ga'θeta; ga'seta/ *f*, bulletin, review, record; newspaper; gazette (official Spanish government organ); *Inf.* newshound

gacetero /gaθe'tero; gase'tero/ (**-ra**) *n* newsdealer. *m*, news reporter

gacetilla /gaθe'tiʎa; gase'tiya/ *f*, news in brief, miscellany column, society news; gossip column; *Inf.* newshound

gacetillero /gaθeti'ʎero; gaseti'yero/ *m*, paragrapher, penny-a-liner; reporter

gacha /'gatʃa/ *f*, unglazed crock; *pl* pap; porridge

gaché /ga'tʃe/ *m*, (among the Romany) Andalusian; *Inf.* fellow

gacho /'gatʃo/ *a* drooping, bent downward; slouch (hat); (of ears) lop

gachón /ga'tʃon/ *a Inf.* attractive, charming

gaditano /gaði'tano/ (**-na**) *a* and *n* native of, or pertaining to, Cadiz

gaélico /ga'eliko/ *a* and *m*, Gaelic

gafar /ga'far/ *vt* to claw; seize with a hook, hook; mend with a bracket (pottery)

gafas /'gafas/ *f pl*, spectacles; goggles; spectacle earhooks; grapplehooks

gafete /ga'fete/ *m*, hook and eye; clasp

gaita /'gaita/ *f*, bagpipe; hand organ; kind of clarinet; *Inf.* neck. **g. gallega,** bagpipe

gaitería /gaite'ria/ *f*, crude, gaudy garment or ornament

gaitero /gai'tero/ *a Inf.* overmerry; loud, crude. *m*, piper

gajes /'gahes/ *m pl*, salary; emoluments; perquisites

gajo /'gaho/ *m*, branch, bough (gen. cut); little cluster (of grapes); bunch (of fruit); quarter (of oranges, etc.); prong (of forks, etc.)

gala /'gala/ *f*, evening or full dress; grace, wit; flower, cream, best; gala; *pl* finery; trappings; wedding presents. **de g.,** full dress. **hacer g. de,** to glory in, boast of

galactita /galak'tita/ *f*, fuller's earth

galaico /ga'laiko/ *a* See **gallego**

galán /ga'lan/ *m*, handsome, well-made man; lover, wooer, gallant; *Theat.* leading man or one of leading male roles

galancete /galan'θete; galan'sete/ *m*, handsome little man; *Theat.* male juvenile lead

galano /ga'lano/ *a* smart, well-dressed; agreeable, pleasing; beautiful; ornamented; *Fig.* elegant (speech, style, etc.)

galante /ga'lante/ *a* gallant, courtly, attentive; flirtatious (of women); licentious

galanteador /galantea'ðor/ *a* flirtatious. *m*, philanderer; wooer

galantear /galante'ar/ *vt* to court; flirt with; make love to; *Fig.* procure assiduously

galanteo /galan'teo/ *m*, courtship; flirtation; lovemaking; wooing

galantería /galante'ria/ *f*, courtesy; attention, compliment; elegance, grace; gallantry; generosity, liberality

galanura /gala'nura/ *f*, showiness, gorgeousness; elegance, grace; prettiness

galápago /ga'lapago/ *m*, freshwater tortoise; cleat

galardón /galar'ðon/ *m*, reward, recompense; prize

galardonar /galarðo'nar/ *vt* to reward, recompense

gálata /'galata/ *a* and *mf* Galatian

galbana /gal'βana/ *f*, *Inf.* laziness, inertia

galbanoso /galβa'noso/ *a Inf.* slothful

galdrufa /gal'drufa/ *f*, top, spinning top

galeote /gale'ote/ *m*, galley slave

galera /ga'lera/ *f*, van, wagon, cart; *Naut.* galley; prison for women; *Print.* galley. **echar a galeras,** to condemn to the galleys

galerada /gale'raða/ *f*, galley proof

galería /gale'ria/ *f*, gallery; corridor, passage; collection of paintings; *Mineral.* gallery, drift; *Theat.* gallery

galerna /ga'lerna/ *f*, tempestuous northwest wind (gen. on Spanish north coast)

Gales /'gales/ Wales

galés /ga'les/ (**-esa**) *a* Welsh —*n* Welshman. *m*, Welsh (language)

galga /'galga/ *f*, boulder, rolling stone; greyhound bitch

galgo /'galgo/ *m*, greyhound. **g. ruso,** borzoi

Galia /'galia/ Gaul

gálibo /'galiβo/ *m*, *Naut.* mold; elegance

galicado /gali'kaðo/ *a* gallicized

galicismo /gali'θismo; gali'sismo/ *m*, gallicism

gálico /'galiko/ *m*, syphilis —*a* gallic

Galilea /gali'lea/ Galilee

galileo /gali'leo/ (**-ea**) *a* and *n* Galilean

galimatías /galima'tias/ *m*, *Inf.* gibberish, nonsense

gallardear /gaʎarðe'ar; gayarðe'ar/ *vi* to behave with ease and grace

gallardete /gaʎar'ðete; gayar'ðete/ *m*, pennant; bunting

gallardía /gaʎar'ðia; gayar'ðia/ *f*, grace, dignity; spirit, dash; courage; liveliness

gallardo /ga'ʎarðo; ga'yarðo/ *a* handsome, upstanding; gallant; spirited; fine, noble; lively

gallear /gaʎe'ar; gaye'ar/ *vi Inf.* to put on airs; be a bully; shout, bawl (with anger, etc.); *Fig. Inf.* stand out

gallego /ga'ʎego; ga'yego/ (**-ga**) *a* and *n* Galician. *m*, Galician (language)

galleta /ga'ʎeta; ga'yeta/ *f*, biscuit; *Inf.* slap; anthracite, lump coal; small jar or vessel

gallina /ga'ʎina; ga'yina/ *f*, hen. *mf Inf.* coward. **g. ciega,** blindman's buff. *Inf.* **acostarse con las gallinas,** to go to bed early

gallinaza /gaʎi'naθa; gayi'nasa/ *f*, hen dung

gallinero /gaʎi'nero; gayi'nero/ (**-ra**) *n* poultry dealer. *m*, henhouse; brood of hens; *Theat.* gallery; babel, noisy place

gallito /ga'ʎito; ga'yito/ *m*, small cock; cock of the walk; bully

gallo /'gaʎo; 'gayo/ *m*, *Ornith.* cock; *Inf.* false note (in singing); *Inf.* boss, chief. **g. de viento,** weathercock. *Inf.* **alzar el g.,** to put on airs, boast. **Cada g. canta en su muladar,** Every man is boss in his own house. *Inf.* **Otro g. nos cantara,** Our lot (or fate) would have been very different

gallofero /gaʎo'fero; gayo'fero/ (**-ra**) *a* mendicant, vagabond —*n* beggar

galocha /ga'lotʃa/ *f*, patten, clog; cap with earflaps

galón /ga'lon/ *m*, galloon, braid; *Mil.* stripe; gallon (measure)

galoneadura /galonea'ðura/ *f*, braiding, trimming

galonear /galone'ar/ *vt* to trim with braid

galopante /galo'pante/ *a* galloping (of consumption, etc.)

galopar /galo'par/ *vi* to gallop; *Mech.* wobble

galope /ga'lope/ *m*, gallop. **a o de g.,** at the gallop; on the run, quickly. **andar a g. corto,** to canter

galopillo /galo'piʎo; galopiyo/ *m*, scullion

galopín /galo'pin/ *m*, ragamuffin, urchin; rogue, knave; *Inf.* clever rogue; *Naut.* cabin boy

galvanización /galβaniθa'θion; galβanisa'sion/ *f*, galvanization

galvanizar /galβani'θar; galβani'sar/ *vt Elec.* to galvanize; electroplate; *Fig.* shock into life

gama /'gama/ *f, Mus.* scale; gamut, range; doe

gambito /gam'bito/ *m,* gambit (in chess)

gamella /ga'meʎa; ga'meya/ *f,* trough (for washing, feeding animals, etc.)

gamo /'gamo/ *m,* buck (of the fallow deer)

gamuza /ga'muθa; ga'musa/ *f,* chamois; chamois leather

gana /'gana/ *f,* appetite; wish, desire. **de buena g.,** willingly. **de mala g.,** reluctantly. **tener g.** (**de**), to wish, desire, want. **no tener g.,** to have no appetite, not be hungry. **No me da la g.,** I don't want (to), I won't

ganable /ga'naβle/ *a* attainable; earnable

ganadería /ganaðe'ria/ *f,* livestock; strain (of cattle); cattle raising; stock farm; cattle dealing

ganadero /gana'ðero/ *m,* cattle raiser or dealer; herdsman

ganado /ga'naðo/ *m,* livestock, herd; flock; hive (of bees); *Inf.* mob. **g. mayor,** cattle, mules, horses. **g. menor,** sheep, goats, etc. **g. moreno,** hogs, swine. **g. vacuno,** cattle

ganador /gana'ðor/ **(-ra)** *a* winning *—n* winner

ganancia /ga'nanθia; ga'nansia/ *f,* winning; gain, profit

ganancial, ganancioso /ganan'θial, ganan'θioso; ganan'sial, ganan'sioso/ *a* gainful, profitable; lucrative

ganapán /gana'pan/ *m,* laborer; porter; *Inf.* boor

ganar /ga'nar/ *vt* to gain; win; conquer; arrive at; earn; surpass, beat; achieve; acquire; *—vi* prosper

ganchero /gan'tʃero/ *m,* lumberjack

ganchillo /gan'tʃiʎo; gan'tʃiyo/ *m,* crochet hook; crochet. **hacer g.,** to crochet

gancho /'gantʃo/ *m,* hook; stump (of a branch); shepherd's crook; crochet hook; *Inf.* trickster, pimp; *Inf.* scribble

ganchoso /gan'tʃoso/ *a* hooked; bent; curved

gandujar /gandu'har/ *vt Sew.* to pleat, tuck, shirr

gandul /gan'dul/ **(-la)** *a Inf.* lazy *—n* lazybones, loafer

gandulería /gandule'ria/ *f,* loafing, idleness

ganga /'gaŋga/ *f, Mineral.* gangue, matrix; bargain, cinch

ganglio /'gaŋglio/ *m,* ganglion

gangoso /gaŋ'goso/ *a* nasal; with a twang (of speech)

gangrena /gaŋ'grena/ *f,* gangrene

gangrenarse /gaŋgre'narse/ *vr* to become gangrenous, mortify

gangrenoso /gaŋgre'noso/ *a* gangrenous

ganguear /gaŋgue'ar/ *vi* to speak nasally, or with a twang

ganoso /ga'noso/ *a* wishful, desirous, anxious

gansada /gan'saða/ *f, Inf.* impertinence, foolishness

ganso /'ganso/ **(-sa)** *n* goose, gander; slow-moving person; yokel, bumpkin

Gante /'gante/ Ghent

ganzúa /gan'θua; gan'sua/ *f,* skeleton key; *Inf.* picklock, burglar; *Inf.* pumper, inquisitive person

gañán /ga'ɲan/ *m,* farm worker; day laborer; brawny fellow

gañido /ga'ɲiðo/ *m,* yowl, yelp, howl

gañir /ga'ɲir/ *vi irr* to yowl, yelp, howl (of dogs, etc.); crow, croak; *Inf.* talk hoarsely. See **mullir**

garabatear /garaβate'ar/ *vi* to hook, catch with hooks; scribble; *Fig. Inf.* beat around the bush

garabateo /garaβa'teo/ *m,* hooking; scribbling

garabato /gara'βato/ *m,* hook; *Agr.* weed clearer; scrawl, scribble; *Inf.* charm, sex appeal; pothook; boat hook; *pl* gestures, movements (with the hands)

garaje /ga'rahe/ *m,* garage

garambaina /garam'baina/ *f,* tawdry finery gaudiness; *pl Inf.* grimaces of affectation; *Inf.* scribble, scrawl

garante /ga'rante/ *mf* guarantor; reference (person) *—a* responsible, guaranteeing

garantía /garan'tia/ *f,* guarantee; security, pledge; *Law.* warranty

garantir /garan'tir/ *vt* to guarantee; warrant, vouch for

garapiñar /garapi'ɲar/ *vt* to ice, freeze (drinks, syrups, etc.); *Cul.* candy, coat with sugar

garapiñera /garapi'ɲera/ *f,* ice-cream freezer

garbanzo /gar'βanθo; gar'βanso/ *m,* chickpea. **g. negro,** *Fig.* black sheep

garbillar /garβi'ʎar; garβi'yar/ *vt Agr.* to sift; *Mineral.* riddle

garbo /'garβo/ *m,* jaunty air; grace, elegance; frankness; generosity, liberality

garboso /gar'βoso/ *a* attractive; handsome, sprightly, gay; graceful; munificent

garduña /gar'ðuɲa/ *f,* weasel; marten

garduño /gar'ðuɲo/ **(-ña)** *n Inf.* sneak thief

garete /ga'rete/ (**ir** *or* **irse al**) *Naut.* to be adrift

garfa /'garfa/ *f,* claw (of a bird or animal)

garfear /garfe'ar/ *vi* to catch with a hook, hook

garfio /'garfio/ *m,* grappling iron, hook, drag hook; cramp; gaff

gargajear /gargahe'ar/ *vi* to expectorate

gargajo /gar'gaho/ *m,* phlegm

garganta /gar'ganta/ *f,* throat; gullet; instep; defile; neck, shaft, narrowest part

gargantear /gargante'ar/ *vi* to warble, trill

gárgara /'gargara/ *f,* gargling (gen. *pl*). **hacer gárgaras,** to gargle

gargarismo /garga'rismo/ *m,* gargling; gargle

gárgol /'gargol/ *a* rotten (eggs). *m,* groove, mortise

gárgola /'gargola/ *f, Archit.* gargoyle; linseed

garguero /gar'gero/ *m,* windpipe; esophagus

garita /ga'rita/ *f,* sentry box; porter's lodge; hut; cabin. **g. de señales,** (railroad) signal box

garitero /gari'tero/ *m,* gambling house keeper; gambler

garito /ga'rito/ *m,* gambling house; profits of a gambling house

garra /'garra/ *f,* paw with claws; talon; hand; *Mech.* clamp, claw. *Fig.* **caer en las garras de,** to fall into the clutches (of)

garrafa /ga'rrafa/ *f,* decanter, carafe; carboy

garrapata /garra'pata/ *f, Ent.* tick

garrapatear /garrapate'ar/ *vi* to scribble

garrapato /garra'pato/ *m,* scribble, scrawl

garrido /ga'rriðo/ *a* handsome; gallant; elegant; graceful

garroba /ga'rroβa/ *f,* carob bean

garrocha /ga'rrotʃa/ *f,* goad. **salto a la g.,** pole jumping

garrotazo /garro'taθo; garro'taso/ *m,* blow with a truncheon or cudgel. **dar garrotazos de ciego,** to lay about one

garrote /ga'rrote/ *m,* truncheon, club; *Med.* tourniquet; garrote. **dar g. (a),** to strangle

garrotillo /garro'tiʎo; garro'tiyo/ *m,* croup

garrucha /ga'rrutʃa/ *f,* pulley; *Mech.* gin block

garrulidad /garruli'ðað/ *f,* garrulity, loquaciousness

gárrulo /'garrulo/ *a* twittering, chirping (birds); garrulous; murmuring, babbling (wind, water, etc.)

garza /'garθa; 'garsa/ *f,* heron

garzo /'garθo; 'garso/ *a* blue (gen. of eyes)

gas /gas/ *m,* gas; fumes. **g. asfixiante,** poison gas. **cámara de g.,** gasbag, gas chamber

gasa /'gasa/ *f,* gauze. **tira de g.,** black mourning band

gascón /gas'kon/ **(-ona)** *a* and *n* Gascon

gasconada /gasko'naða/ *f,* bravado, gasconade

gaseosa /gase'osa/ *f,* aerated water

gaseoso /gase'oso/ *a* gaseous

gasista /ga'sista/ *mf* gas fitter; gasman

gasolina /gaso'lina/ *f,* gasoline, petrol

gasómetro /ga'sometro/ *m,* gas meter; gasometer

gastado /gas'taðo/ *a* worn; worn-out; exhausted

gastador /gasta'ðor/ **(-ra)** *a* extravagant, wasteful *—n* spendthrift. *m, Mil.* sapper; convict condemned to hard labor

gastar /gas'tar/ *vt* to spend (money); wear out; exhaust; ruin, destroy; display or have habitually; possess, use, wear; *—vr* wear out; run down (of a battery)

gasto /'gasto/ *m,* spending; expenditure; consumption (of gas, etc.); expense, cost, charge; wear (and tear). **g. suplementario,** extra charge

gástrico /'gastriko/ a gastric
gastritis /gas'tritis/ f, gastritis
gastronomía /gastrono'mia/ f, gastronomy
gastronómico /gastro'nomiko/ a gastronomic
gastrónomo /gas'tronomo/ **(-ma)** n gastronome
gata /'gata/ f, she-cat; wreath of mist; *Inf.* Madrilenian woman. **a gatas,** on all fours
gatada /ga'taða/ f, *Inf.* sly trick
gatear /gate'ar/ *vi* to climb like a cat; *Inf.* crawl on all fours; —*vt Inf.* scratch (of a cat); steal, pinch
gatera /ga'tera/ f, cat hole (in a door, etc.)
gatillo /ga'tiʎo; ga'tiyo/ m, *dim* small cat; dental forceps; trigger (of gun); *Inf.* juvenile petty thief
gato /'gato/ m, cat; tomcat; moneybag or its contents; *Mech.* jack; mousetrap; *Inf.* cat burglar, sneak thief; *Inf.* Madrilenian; clamp. **g. atigrado,** tiger cat. **g. de algalia,** civet cat. **g. de Angora,** Persian cat. **g. montés,** wildcat. **g. romano,** tabby cat. **dar g. por liebre,** to serve cat for hare, to deceive; misrepresent. *Inf.* **Hay g. encerrado,** There's more to this than meets the eye
gatuno /ga'tuno/ a feline
gaucho /'gautʃo/ **(-cha)** n gaucho; cowboy, rider
gaveta /ga'βeta/ f, drawer (of a desk)
gavia /'gaβia/ f, main topsail; *pl* topsails; crow's-nest
gavilán /gaβi'lan/ m, sparrow hawk; thistle flower
gavilla /ga'βiʎa; ga'βiya/ f, sheaf (of corn, etc.); gang, rabble
gaviota /ga'βiota/ f, seagull
gavota /ga'βota/ f, gavotte
gayo /'gayo/ a gay, happy; showy, attractive. **gaya ciencia,** minstrelsy, art of poetry
gazapera /gaθa'pera; gasa'pera/ f, rabbit warren; *Inf.* thieves' den; *Inf.* brawl
gazapo /ga'θapo; ga'sapo/ m, young rabbit; *Inf.* cunning fellow; fib, lie; slip, blunder
gazmoñería /gaθmoɲe'ria; gasmoɲe'ria/ f, prudery, priggish affectation
gazmoño /gaθ'moɲo; gas'moɲo/ a hypocritical, prudish, priggish
gaznápiro /gaθ'napiro; gas'napiro/ **(-ra)** n ninny, simpleton
gaznate /gaθ'nate; gas'nate/ m, windpipe
gazpacho /gaθ'patʃo; gas'patʃo/ m, cold soup containing bread, onions, vinegar, olive oil, garlic, etc.
ge /he/ f, name of the letter G
gehena /he'ena/ m, gehenna, hell
géiser /'heiser/ m, geyser
gelatina /hela'tina/ f, gelatin. **g. incendiaria,** napalm. **g. seca,** cooking gelatin
gelatinoso /helati'noso/ a gelatinous
gélido /'heliðo/ a *Poet.* icy; very cold
gema /'hema/ f, gem; *Bot.* bud
gemelo /he'melo/ **(-la)** a and n twin. m pl, field or opera glasses, binoculars; cuff links; *Astron.* Gemini
gemido /he'miðo/ m, groan, lament, moan
gemidor /hemi'ðor/ a groaning, moaning; wailing (of the wind, etc.)
gemir /he'mir/ *vi irr* to moan, groan, lament; *Fig.* wail, howl. See **pedir**
gene /'hene/ m, gene
genealogía /henealo'hia/ f, genealogy
genealógico /henea'lohiko/ a genealogical
genealogista /henealo'hista/ mf genealogist
generación /henera'θion; henera'sion/ f, generation, reproduction; species; generation
generador /henera'ðor/ a generative. m, *Mech.* generator
general /hene'ral/ a general; universal; widespread; common, usual. m, (*Mil. Eccl.*) general. **g. de división,** *Mil.* major general. **en** or **por lo g.,** generally
generalato /henera'lato/ m, generalship
generalidad /henerali'ðað/ f, majority, bulk; generality
generalísimo /henera'lisimo/ m, generalissimo, commander in chief
generalización /heneraliθa'θion; heneralisa'sion/ f, generalization
generalizar /henerali'θar; henerali'sar/ *vt* to generalize; —*vr* become widespread or general
generar /hene'rar/ *vt* to generate

genérico /he'neriko/ a generic
género /'henero/ m, kind; class; way, mode; *Com.* goods; species, genus; *Gram.* gender; cloth, material. **g. chico,** short theatrical pieces (gen. one act). **g. humano,** humankind
generosidad /henerosi'ðað/ f, hereditary nobility; generosity, magnanimity; liberality, munificence; courage
generoso /hene'roso/ a noble (by birth); magnanimous; generous (of wine); munificent; courageous; excellent
genésico /he'nesiko/ a genetic
génesis /'henesis/ m, Genesis. f, beginning, origin
genial /he'nial/ a of genius; highly talented; brilliant; characteristic, individual; pleasant; cheerful
genialidad /heniali'ðað/ f, genius; talent; brilliance; eccentricity, oddity
genio /'henio/ m, nature, individuality, temperament; temper; character; talent; genius; genie, spirit. **corto de g.,** unintelligent. **mal g.,** bad temper
genital /heni'tal/ a genital. m, testicle (gen. pl)
genitivo /heni'tiβo/ a reproductive, generative. m, *Gram.* genitive
Génova /'henoβa/ Genoa
genovés /heno'βes/ **(-esa)** a and n Genoese
gente /'hente/ f, people, a crowd; nation; army; *Inf.* family; followers, adherents. **g. baja,** rabble. **g. de bien,** honest folk; respectable people. **g. de paz,** friends (reply to sentinel's challenge). **g. fina,** nice, cultured people. **g. menuda,** children, small fry
gentecilla /hente'θiʎa; hente'siya/ f, *dim Inf.* rabble; contemptible people
gentil /hen'til/ a pagan, idolatrous; spirited, dashing, handsome; notable, extraordinary; graceful, charming
gentileza /henti'leθa; henti'lesa/ f, grace; elegance; beauty; verve, sprightliness; courtesy; show, ostentation
gentilhombre /hentil'ombre/ m, gentleman; handsome man; kind sir! **gentileshombres de cámara,** gentlemen-in-waiting
gentilicio /henti'liθio; henti'lisio/ a national; family
gentílico /hen'tiliko/ a pagan, idolatrous
gentilidad /hentili'ðað/ f, idolatry, paganism; heathendom
gentío /hen'tio/ m, crowd, throng
gentualla, gentuza /hen'tuaʎa, hen'tuθa; hen'tuaya, hen'tusa/ f, canaille, rabble
genuflexión /henuflek'sion/ f, genuflection
genuino /he'nuino/ a pure; authentic, genuine
geodesia /heo'ðesia/ f, geodesy
geodésico /heo'ðesiko/ a geodesic
geofísico /heo'fisiko/ m, geophysicist
geografía /heogra'fia/ f, geography
geográfico /heo'grafiko/ a geographical
geógrafo /he'ografo/ m, geographer
geología /heolo'hia/ f, geology
geológico /heo'lohiko/ a geological
geólogo /he'ologo/ m, geologist
geometría /heome'tria/ f, geometry. **g. del espacio,** solid geometry
geométrico /heo'metriko/ a geometrical
geranio /he'ranio/ m, geranium
gerencia /he'renθia; he'rensia/ f, *Com.* managership; manager's office; management
gerente /he'rente/ m, *Com.* manager
germanía /herma'nia/ f, thieves' slang; association of thieves; sixteenth-century political brotherhood
germánico /her'maniko/ a germanic
germanófilo /herma'nofilo/ **(-la)** a and n germanophile
germen /'hermen/ m, germ, sprout; *Bot.* embryo; genesis, origin
germinación /hermina'θion; hermina'sion/ f, germination
germinar /hermi'nar/ *vi* to germinate, sprout; develop, grow
germinativo /hermina'tiβo/ a germinative
gerundio /he'rundio/ m, *Gram.* gerund; *Inf.* pompous ass; *Inf.* tub-thumper
gesta /'hesta/ f, heroic deed. **cantar de g.,** epic or heroic poem

gestación /hesta'θion; hesta'sion/ f, gestation
gestear /heste'ar/ vi to gesture, grimace
gesticulación /hestikula'θion; hestikula'sion/ f, gesticulation; grimace
gesticular /hestiku'lar/ vi to grimace, gesticulate —a gesticulatory
gestión /hes'tion/ f, negotiation; management, conduct; effort, exertion; measure
gestionar /hestio'nar/ vt to negotiate; conduct; undertake; take steps to attain
gesto /'hesto/ m, gesture; facial expression; grimace; face, visage
gestor /hes'tor/ (**-ra**) n manager; partner; promoter —a managing
Getsemaní /hetsema'ni/ Gethsemane
giba /'hiβa/ f, hump, hunchback; Inf. nuisance, inconvenience
gibón /hi'βon/ m, gibbon
giboso /hi'βoso/ a hunchbacked
gibraltareño /hiβralta'reρo/ a Gibraltarian
giganta /hi'ganta/ f, giantess
gigante /hi'gante/ a gigantic. m, giant.
gigantesco /higan'tesko/ a giant, gigantic; Fig. outstanding
gigantez /higan'teθ; higan'tes/ f, gigantic size
gigantón /higan'ton/ (**-ona**) n enormous giant; carnival grotesque
gimnasia /him'nasia/ f, gymnastics
gimnasio /him'nasio/ m, gymnasium; school, academy
gimnasta /him'nasta/ mf gymnast
gimnástico /him'nastiko/ a gymnastic
gimotear /himote'ar/ vi Inf. to whine (often used scornfully)
gimoteo /himo'teo/ m, Inf. whining, whimpering
ginebra /hi'neβra/ f, gin (drink); confusion; babble, din
ginebrés /hine'βres/ (**-esa**), **ginebrino** (**-na**) a and n Genevan
gineceo /hine'θeo/ hine'seo/ m, (Bot. and in ancient Greece) gynaecium
ginecología /hinekolo'hia/ f, gynecology
ginecológico /hineko'lohiko/ a gynecological
ginecólogo /hine'kologo/ (**-ga**) n gynecologist
girado /hi'raðo/ m, Com. drawee
girador /hira'ðor/ m, Com. drawer
giralda /hi'ralda/ f, weathercock in the shape of a person or animal; tower at Seville
girar /hi'rar/ vi to revolve; deal (with), concern; turn, branch (streets, etc.); Com. trade; Mech. turn on, revolve; —vt and vi Com. draw, cash. **g. en descubierto,** Com. to overdraw
girasol /hira'sol/ m, sunflower
giratorio /hira'torio/ a revolving, gyrating; swiveling
giro /'hiro/ m, revolution, turn; revolving; trend; course (of affairs); style, turn (of phrase); threat; knife gash; Com. draft, drawing; Com. line of business, specialty. **g. postal,** postal order
giroscopio /hiro'skopio/ m, gyroscope
gitanería /hitane'ria/ f, cajolery, wheedling; gypsies; gypsy saying or action
gitanesco /hita'nesko/ a gypsy, gypsy-like
gitano /hi'tano/ (**-na**) a gypsy; gypsy-like; seductive, attractive; sly —m gypsy
glaciar /gla'θiar/ gla'siar/ m, glacier
gladiador /glaðia'ðor/ m, gladiator
gladiatorio /glaðia'torio/ a gladiatorial
glándula /'glandula/ f, gland
glicerina /gliθe'rina/ glise'rina/ f, glycerin, glycerol
globo /'gloβo/ m, Geom. sphere; globe, world; globe (Elec. Gas.); balloon. **g. aerostático,** air balloon. **g. terrestre,** world; geographical globe
globular /gloβu'lar/ a globular
glóbulo /'gloβulo/ m, globule
globuloso /gloβu'loso/ a globulous
gloria /'gloria/ f, heavenly bliss; fame, glory; delight, pleasure; magnificence, splendor; Art. apotheosis, glory. m, Eccl. doxology
gloriar /glo'riar/ vt to praise; —vr (with de or en) boast about; be proud of, rejoice in

glorieta /glo'rieta/ f, bower, arbor; open space in a garden; street square
glorificación /glorifika'θion; glorifika'sion/ f, glorification
glorificador /glorifika'ðor/ a glorifying
glorificar /glorifi'kar/ vt to exalt, raise up; glorify, extol; —vr (with de or en) be proud of; glory in; boast of
glorioso /glo'rioso/ a glorious; Eccl. blessed; boastful, bragging
glosa /'glosa/ f, gloss; explanation, note
glosador /glosa'ðor/ (**-ra**) n glossator; commentator —a explanatory
glosar /glo'sar/ vt Lit. to gloss
glosario /glo'sario/ m, glossary
glosopeda /gloso'peða/ f, foot-and-mouth disease
glotón /glo'ton/ (**-ona**) a greedy, gluttonous —n glutton
glotonería /glotone'ria/ f, gluttony, greed
glucosa /glu'kosa/ f, glucose
glúteo /'gluteo/ a gluteal
glutinoso /gluti'noso/ a glutinous
gn- /gn-/ For words so beginning, see spellings without **g**.
gobernación /goβerna'θion; goβerna'sion/ f, government; governor's office or building; ministry of the interior, home office (abb. for **ministerio de G.**)
gobernador /goβerna'ðor/ (**-ra**) a governing, n governor
gobernalle /goβer'naλe; goβer'naye/ m, helm
gobernante /goβer'nante/ a governing. m, Inf. self-appointed director or manager
gobernar /goβer'nar/ vt irr to govern, rule; lead, conduct; manage; steer; control; —vi govern; Naut. obey the tiller. See **recomendar**
gobierno /go'βierno/ m, government (all meanings); Naut. helm; control (of machines, business, etc.)
goce /'goθe; 'gose/ m, enjoyment; possession
godo /'goðo/ (**da**) a Gothic; aristocratic, noble —n Goth; aristocrat
gol /gol/ m, Sports. goal
gola /'gola/ f, throat; gullet; gorget; tucker, bib
goleta /go'leta/ f, schooner
golf /golf/ m, golf. **palo de g.,** golf club
golfear /golfe'ar/ vi to loaf
golfería /golfe'ria/ f, loafing; vagabondage; loafers
golfo /'golfo/ (**-fa**) m, Geog. gulf; sea, ocean —n ragamuffin, urchin. m, Inf. loafer; lounge lizard, wastrel
Golfo Pérsico /'golfo 'persiko/ Persian Gulf
golilla /go'liλa; go'liya/ f, ruff; m, Inf. magistrate
gollería /goλe'ria; goye'ria/ f, dainty, tidbit; Inf. affectation, persnicketiness
gollete /go'λete; go'yete/ m, gullet; neck (of a bottle, etc.); Mech. nozzle
golondrina /golon'drina/ f, Ornith. swallow. **g. de mar,** tern
golosina /golo'sina/ f, tidbit, delicacy; desire, caprice; pleasant useless thing
goloso /go'loso/ a fond of sweet things; greedy, desirous; appetizing
golpe /'golpe/ m, blow, knock; pull (at the oars); ring (of a bell); Mech. stroke; crowd; fall (of rain, etc.); mass, torrent; misfortune; shock, collision; spring lock; beating (of the heart); flap (of a pocket); Sew. passementerie; surprise; point, wit; bet. **g. de estado,** coup d'état. **g. de fortuna,** stroke of fortune. **g. de mano,** rising, insurrection. **g. en vago,** blow in the air; disappointment. **g. franco,** Sports. free kick. **de g.,** suddenly; quickly
golpeadura /golpea'ðura/ f. **golpeo** m, knocking, striking; beating, throbbing
golpear /golpe'ar/ vt and vi to knock, strike; beat, throb
goma /'goma/ f, gum, rubber; India rubber; rubber band
gomería /gome'ria/ f, tire store
gomero /go'mero/ a gum; rubber. m, West Hem. rubber planter
gomorresina /gomorre'sina/ f, gum resin
gomoso /go'moso/ a gummy; gum

gónada /'gonaða/ f, gonad

góndola /'gondola/ f, gondola

gondolero /gondo'lero/ m, gondolier

gongorino /goŋgo'rino/ a gongoristic, euphuistic

gonorrea /gono'rrea/ f, gonorrhea

gordo /'gorðo/ a fat, stout; greasy, oily; thick (thread, etc.). m, animal fat, suet. Inf. **ganar el g.,** to win first prize (in a lottery, etc.)

gordura /gor'ðura/ f, grease, fat; stoutness, corpulence

gorgojo /gor'goho/ m, weevil; Fig. dwarf

gorgoritear /gorgorite'ar/ vi Inf. to trill, quaver

gorgorito /gorgo'rito/ m, Inf. quaver, tremolo, trill (gen. pl)

gorgoteo /gorgo'teo/ m, gurgle

gorjear /gorhe'ar/ vi to trill, warble; twitter; —vr crow (of a baby)

gorjeo /gor'heo/ m, trill, shake; warbling, twitter; crowing, lisping (of a child)

gorra /'gorra/ f, cap; bonnet; Mil. busby; hunting cap. **vivir de g.,** Inf. to sponge

gorrión /go'rrion/ m, sparrow

gorrista /go'rrista/ mf Inf. parasite; sponger

gorro /'gorro/ m, cap; bonnet

gorrón /go'rron/ m, smooth, round pebble; Mech. pivot, gudgeon; sponger, waster —a parasitical

gota /'gota/ f, drop (of liquid); gout

gotear /gote'ar/ vi to drop, trickle, drip; leak; drizzle; give or receive in driblets

goteo /go'teo/ m, trickling, dripping

gotera /go'tera/ f, dripping; trickle; leak; leakage; valance

gótico /'gotiko/ a Gothic; noble, illustrious

gotoso /go'toso/ **(-sa)** a gouty —n sufferer from gout

goyesco /go'yesko/ a Goyesque

gozar /go'θar; go'sar/ vt to enjoy, have; take pleasure (in), delight (in); know carnally; —vi (with de) enjoy; have, possess

gozne /'goθne/ 'gosne/ m, hinge

gozo /'goθo; 'goso/ m, enjoyment, possession; gladness, joy; pl couplets in honor of the Virgin Mary or a saint. Inf. **¡Mi g. en el pozo!** I'm sunk! All is lost!

gozoso /go'θoso; go'soso/ a glad, happy —adv gladly, with pleasure

grabado /gra'βaðo/ m, engraver's art; engraving; illustration, picture. **g. al agua fuerte,** etching. **g. al agua tinta,** aquatint

grabador /graβa'ðor/ **(-ra)** n engraver

grabadura /graβa'ðura/ f, act of engraving

grabar /gra'βar/ vt to engrave; Fig. leave a deep impression

gracejo /gra'θeho; gra'seho/ m, humor, wit; cheerfulness

gracia /'graθia; 'grasia/ f, grace; attraction, grace; favor; kindness; jest, witticism; pardon, mercy; pleasant manner; obligingness, willingness; pl thanks, thank you. **gracias a,** thanks to. **¡Gracias a Dios!** Thank God! Thank goodness! **las Gracias,** the Three Graces

grácil /'graθil; 'grasil/ a slender; small

graciosidad /graθiosi'ðað; grasiosi'ðað/ f, beauty, perfection, grace

gracioso /gra'θioso; gra'sioso/ **(-sa)** a attractive, graceful, elegant; witty, humorous; free, gratis —n Theat. comic role; m, Theat. fool

grada /'graða/ f, step, stair; gradin, seat; stand, gallery; Agr. harrow; Naut. runway; pl perron, flight of stairs

gradación /graða'θion; graða'sion/ f, gradation; climax

gradería /graðe'ria/ f, flight of steps

grado /'graðo/ m, step, stair; degree (of relationship); university degree; grade, class (in schools); (Fig. Geom. Phys.) degree; will, desire. **de buen g.,** willingly. **en sumo g.,** in the highest degree

graduación /graðua'θion; graðua'sion/ f, graduation; Mil. rank; rating (of a ship's company). **g. de oficial,** Mil. commission

graduado /gra'ðuaðo/ a graded; Mil. brevet. m, graduate

gradual /gra'ðual/ a gradual

graduar /gra'ðuar/ vt to classify; Mil. grade; confer a degree on; measure; test; Com. standardize; Mech. calibrate; —vr graduate, receive a degree. **g. la vista,** to test the eyes. **graduarse de oficial,** Mil. to get one's commission

gráfica /'grafika/ f, graph

gráfico /'grafiko/ a graphic; vivid

grafito /gra'fito/ m, graphite

grafología /grafolo'hia/ f, graphology

grajear /grahe'ar/ vi to caw; gurgle, burble (of infants)

grajo /'graho/ m, Ornith. rook

gramática /gra'matika/ f, grammar. Inf. **g. parda,** horse sense

gramático /gra'matiko/ a grammatical. m, grammarian

gramo /'gramo/ m, gram

gramófono /gra'mofono/ m, phonograph

gran /gran/ a Abbr. See **grande.** Used before a singular noun. big; great; grand

grana /'grana/ f, grain, seed; seed time; cochineal; kermes; red

granada /gra'naða/ f, Mil. grenade, shell; pomegranate

granadero /grana'ðero/ m, grenadier; Inf. very tall person

granadilla /grana'ðiʎa; grana'ðiya/ f, passionflower

granadina /grana'ðina/ f, grenadine

granar /gra'nar/ vi Agr. to seed; run to seed

granate /gra'nate/ m, garnet; dark red

Gran Bretaña /gran bre'tana/ Great Britain

Gran Canaria /gran ka'naria/ Grand Canary

grande /'grande/ a big, large; great, illustrious; grand. m, great man; grandee. **en g.,** in a large size; as a whole; in style, lavishly

grandeza /gran'deθa; gran'desa/ f, largeness; greatness, magnificence; grandeeship; vastness, magnitude

grandilocuencia /grandilo'kuenθia; grandilo-'kuensia/ f, grandiloquence

grandílocuo /gran'dilokuo/ a grandiloquent

grandiosidad /grandiosi'ðað/ f, grandeur, greatness

grandioso /gran'dioso/ a grandiose, magnificent

grandor /gran'dor/ m, size

granear /grane'ar/ vt Agr. to sow; grain (of leather)

granero /gra'nero/ m, granary; grain-producing country

granito /gra'nito/ m, dim small grain; granite; small pimple

granizar /grani'θar; grani'sar/ vi to hail, sleet; —vi and vt Fig. shower down, deluge

granizo /gra'niθo; gra'niso/ m, hail, sleet; hailstorm; Fig. shower, deluge

granja /'granha/ f, farm; farmhouse; dairy farm, dairy

granjear /granhe'ar/ vt to trade, profit, earn; obtain, acquire; —vr gain, win

granjería /granhe'ria/ f, farming; agricultural profits; earnings, profits

granjero /gran'hero/ **(-ra)** n farmer

Gran Lago Salado, el /gran 'lago sa'laðo, el/ the Great Salt Lake

grano /'grano/ m, Agr. grain; seed; bean (coffee, etc.); particle; markings, grain (of wood, etc.); pimple; grain (measure). Fig. Inf. **ir al g.,** to go to the root of the matter; come to the point

granuja /gra'nuha/ f, grape pit. m, Inf. urchin, scamp; knave, rogue

granujiento /granu'hiento/ a pimply

gránulo /'granulo/ m, granule

granuloso /granu'loso/ a granulous

grapa /'grapa/ f, cramp, dowel, clamp; block hook; Elec. cleat; staple

grasa /'grasa/ f, fat; grease; oil; dripping, suet

grasiento /gra'siento/ a greasy; grubby, dirty

gratificación /gratifika'θion; gratifika'sion/ f, monetary reward; fee, remuneration; gratuity

gratificar /gratifi'kar/ vt to recompense; please, gratify

gratis /'gratis/ a and adv gratis

gratitud /grati'tuð/ f, gratitude

grato /'grato/ a pleasing, agreeable; free, gratuitous

gratuito /gra'tuito/ *a* gratuitous, free; baseless, unfounded

grava /'graβa/ *f,* gravel; stone chip, pebble; metal (of a road)

gravamen /gra'βamen/ *m,* obligation; burden; tax

gravar /gra'βar/ *vt* to burden, weigh upon; tax

grave /'graβe/ *a* heavy; important, momentous; grave; dignified, serious; sedate; tiresome; low-pitched, low; *Gram.* grave accent

gravedad /graβe'ðað/ *f, Phys.* gravity

gravitación /graβita'θion; graβita'sion/ *f, Phys.* gravitation; seriousness; sedateness; importance; enormity, gravity

gravitar /graβi'tar/ *vi* to gravitate; lean or rest (upon)

gravoso /gra'βoso/ *a* grievous, oppressive; onerous; costly

graznar /graθ'nar; gras'nar/ *vi* to caw; cackle; quack; croak; sing stridently, screech

graznido /graθ'niðo; gras'niðo/ *m,* caw; cackle; croaking; quack; screech

Grecia /'greθia; 'gresia/ Greece

greco /'greko/ **(-ca)** *a* and *n* Greek

grecorromano /grekorro'mano/ *a* Greco-Roman

gregario /gre'gario/ *a* gregarious

gregoriano /grego'riano/ *a* Gregorian

gregüescos /gre'gueskos/ *m pl,* wide breeches (sixteenth and seventeenth centuries)

gremial /gre'mial/ *a* pertaining to a guild, union, or association. *m,* member of a guild, union, or association

gremio /'gremio/ *m,* guild, corporation, union; society, association; (univ.) general council

greña /'greɲa/ *f,* tangled lock (of hair) (gen. *pl*); tangle, confused mass

gresca /'greska/ *f,* uproar, tumult; fight, row

grey /grei/ *f,* flock, drove, herd; *Eccl.* flock, company; people, nation

grial /grial/ *m,* grail

griego /'griego/ **(-ga)** *a* and *n* Greek. *m,* Greek (language); *Inf.* gibberish

grieta /'grieta/ *f,* fissure; crevice; chink; split; flaw; vein (in stone, etc.); *Mech.* leak

grietado /grie'taðo/ *a* fissured; cracked

grifo /'grifo/ *m,* griffin; tap; cock

grillo /'griʎo; 'griyo/ *m,* cricket; *Bot.* shoot; *pl* fetters, irons, chains; *Fig.* shackles

grima /'grima/ *f,* revulsion, horror

gringo /'gringo/ **(-ga)** *m* and *Inf.* foreigner (scornful)

gripe /'gripe/ *f,* influenza; grippe

gris /gris/ *a* and *m,* gray

grisú /gri'su/ *m,* firedamp

gritador /grita'ðor/ **(-ra)** *a* shouting —*n* shouter

gritar /gri'tar/ *vi* to shout, yell, scream; howl down; hoot

gritería /grite'ria/ *f,* shouting, yelling, clamor

grito /'grito/ *m,* shout, yell, shriek, scream. *Inf.* **poner el g. en el cielo,** to cry to high heaven, complain

groenlandés /groenlan'des/ **(-esa)** *a* Greenland —*n* Greenlander

Groenlandia /groen'landia/ Greenland

grog /grog/ *m,* grog

grosella /gro'seʎa; gro'seya/ *f,* currant. **g. blanca,** gooseberry

grosería /grose'ria/ *f,* rudeness; roughness (of workmanship); ignorance; rusticity

grosero /gro'sero/ *a* coarse; rough; thick; unpolished, rude

grotesco /gro'tesko/ *a* grotesque, absurd

grúa /'grua/ *f, Mech.* crane, hoist, derrick. **g. de pescante,** jib crane. **g. móvil,** traveling crane

gruesa /'gruesa/ *f,* twelve dozen, gross

grueso /'grueso/ *a* stout, corpulent; large. *m,* bulk, body; major portion, majority; thick stroke (of a letter); thickness, density. **en g.,** in bulk

grulla /'gruʎa; 'gruya/ *f, Ornith.* crane

grumete /gru'mete/ *m,* ship's boy, cabin boy

grumo /'grumo/ *m,* clot; heart (of vegetables); bunch, cluster; bud

gruñido /gru'ɲiðo/ *m,* grunt; growl

gruñidor /gruɲi'ðor/ *a* grunting; growling

gruñir /gru'ɲir/ *vi* to grunt; growl; grumble; squeak, creak (doors, etc.) —*Pres. Part.* **gruñendo.** *Pres. Indic.* **gruño, gruñes,** etc.

grupa /'grupa/ *f,* croup (of a horse); pillion (of a motorcycle)

grupera /gru'pera/ *f,* pillion (of a horse, etc.)

grupo /'grupo/ *m,* knot, cluster; band, group; *Art.* group; *Mech.* set

gruta /'gruta/ *f,* cavern, grotto

guacamayo /guaka'mayo/ *m,* macaw

guadamecí /guaðame'θi; guaðame'si/ *m,* embossed decorated leather

guadaña /gua'ðaɲa/ *f,* scythe

guagua /'guagua/, *f Caribbean* bus

gualdo /'gualdo/ *a* yellow, golden

gualdrapa /gual'drapa/ *f,* saddlecloth, trappings; *Inf.* tatter, rag

guante /'guante/ *m,* glove. **g. con puño,** gauntlet glove. **g. de boxeo,** boxing glove. **g. de cabritilla,** kid glove. **arrojar el g.,** to throw down the gauntlet; challenge, defy

guantelete /guante'lete/ *m,* gauntlet

guantería /guante'ria/ *f,* glove trade, shop, or factory

guantero /guan'tero/ **(-ra)** *n* glove maker or seller, glover

guapear /guape'ar/ *vi Inf.* to make the best of a bad job; *Inf.* pride oneself on being well dressed

guapeza /gua'peθa; gua'pesa/ *f,* prettiness; *Inf.* resolution, courage; *Inf.* smartness or showiness of dress; boastful act or behavior

guapo /'guapo/ *a* pretty; handsome; *Inf.* daring, enterprising; *Inf.* smart, well-dressed, foppish; *Inf.* handsome. *m,* braggart, brawler; beau, lover; *Inf.* fine fellow, son of a gun

guarda /'guarða/ *mf* keeper, guard. *f,* guarding, keeping, custodianship, preservation; guardianship; observance, fulfillment; flyleaf, end page (books); warder (of locks or keys); *Mech.* guard; guard (of a fan)

guardabarrera /guarðaβa'rrera/ *mf* gatekeeper at a level crossing (railroad)

guardabarro /guarða'βarro/ *m,* mudguard

guardabosque /guarða'βoske/ *mf* gamekeeper

guardabrisa /guarða'βrisa/ *m, Auto.* windshield; glass candle shield

guardacostas /guarða'kostas/ *m,* coast guard; *Naut.* revenue cutter

guardafrenos /guarða'frenos/ *m,* brakeman (railroad)

guardagujas /guarða'guhas/ *m,* pointsman (railroad)

guardainfante /guarðain'fante/ *m,* farthingale, crinoline

guardalmacén /guarðalma'θen; guarðalma'sen/ *mf* storekeeper

guardameta /guarða'meta/ *mf* goalkeeper

guardamuebles /guarða'mueβles/ *m,* furniture warehouse

guardapelo /guarða'pelo/ *m,* locket

guardapolvo /guarða'polβo/ *m,* dustcover; light overcoat; inner case of a pocket watch

guardar /guar'ðar/ *vt* to keep; preserve, retain; maintain, observe; save, put aside, lay away; defend, protect; guard; —*vr* (*with de*) avoid, guard against. **g. compás con,** to be in tune with. **guardarse mucho,** to take twice before. **g. silencio,** to keep silent. **¡Guarda!** Take care! **¡Guárdate del agua mansa!** Still waters run deep!

guardarropa /guarða'rropa/ *m,* cloakroom. *mf* cloakroom attendant; keeper of the wardrobe. *m,* wardrobe, clothes closet

guardarropía /guarðarro'pia/ *f,* theatrical wardrobe

guardavía /guarða'βia/ *m,* signalman (railroad)

guardería /guarðe'ria/ *f,* day nursery, day-care center

guardia /'guarðia/ *f,* guard, escort; protection; (*Mil. Naut.*) watch; regiment, body (of troops); guard (fencing). *m,* guardsman; policeman. **g. de asalto,** armed police. **g. de corps,** royal bodyguard. **g. civil,** civil guard. **g. marina,** midshipman. **g. municipal,** city police. *Mil.* **montar la g.,** to mount guard

guardián /guar'ðian/ **(-ana)** *n* keeper; custodian; warden. *m,* watchman; jailer

guardilla /guar'ðiʎa; guar'ðiya/ *f,* attic, garret

guarecer /guare'θer; guare'ser/ vt irr to shelter, protect, aid; preserve, keep; cure; —vr take shelter. See **conocer**

guarida /gua'riða/ f, lair, den; refuge, shelter; haunt, resort

guarismo /gua'rismo/ m, Math. figure; number, numeral

guarnecer /guarne'θer; guarne'ser/ vt irr to decorate, adorn; Sew. trim, face, border; Mil. garrison; Mas. plaster. See **conocer**

guarnecido /guarne'θiðo; guarne'siðo/ m, Mas. plastering

guarnición /guarni'θion; guarni'sion/ f, Sew. trimming, ornament, border, fringe; Mech. packing; Mil. garrison; setting (of jewels); guard (of a sword, etc.); pl harness; fittings

guarnir /guar'nir/ vt Naut. to reeve

guasa /'guasa/ f, Inf. dullness, boringness; joke. **de g.**, jokingly

guasón /gua'son/ a Inf. dull, tedious; humorous, jocose

guatemalteco /guatemal'teko/ **(-ca)** a and n Guatemalan

guau /guau/ m, bowwow, bark of a dog

guayaba /gua'yaβa/ f, guava; guava jelly

Guayana /gua'yana/ Guiana

gubernamental /guβernamen'tal/ a governmental

gubernativo /guβerna'tiβo/ a governmental; administrative

gubia /'guβia/ f, chisel; gouge

guedeja /ge'ðeha/ f, long tress or lock of hair; forelock; lion's mane

Guernesey /gerne'sei/ Guernsey

guerra /'gerra/ f, war; struggle, fight; Fig. hostility. Inf. **dar g.**, to give trouble, annoy. **en g. con**, at war with. **la g. de Cuba**, the Spanish-American War

guerrear /gerre'ar/ vi to make war, fight; oppose

guerrero /ge'rrero/ **(-ra)** a war, martial; warrior; Inf. troublesome, annoying —n fighter. m, warrior, soldier

guerrillear /gerriʎe'ar; gerriye'ar/ vi to wage guerrilla warfare; fight as a guerrilla

guerrillero /gerri'ʎero; gerri'yero/ m, guerrilla fighter

guía /'gia/ mf guide, conductor; adviser, director. f, guide, aid; guidebook; Mech. guide, slide; directory; signpost. **g. de ferrocarriles**, train schedule, railroad timetable. **g. de teléfonos**, telephone directory

guiar /giar/ vt to guide; lead, conduct; Mech. work, control; Auto. drive; pilot; teach, direct, govern

guija /'giha/ f, pebble

guijarro /gi'harro/ m, smooth, round pebble; boulder; cobblestone

guijarroso /giha'rroso/ a pebbly, cobbled

guijo /'giho/ m, gravel; granite chips; pebble

guillotina /giʎo'tina; giyo'tina/ f, guillotine; paper-cutting machine

guillotinar /giʎoti'nar; giyoti'nar/ vt to guillotine, decapitate

guinda /'ginda/ f, mazard cherry; Naut. height of masts

guinea /gi'nea/ f, guinea

guinga /'ginga/ f, gingham

guiñada /gi'ɲaða/ f, wink; blink; Naut. yaw

guiñapo /gi'ɲapo/ m, rag, tatter; sloven, ragamuffin

guiñar /gi'ɲar/ vt to wink; blink; Naut. yaw; —vr wink at each other

guiño /'giɲo/ m, wink

guión /gi'on/ m, royal standard; banner; summary; leader of a dance; Gram. hyphen; subtitle (in films). **g. mayor,** Gram. dash

guipuzcoano /gipuθ'koano; gipus'koano/ **(-na)** a and n Guipuzcoan

guirigay /giri'gai/ m, Inf. gibberish; uproar, babble

guirnalda /gir'nalda/ f, garland, wreath

guisa /'gisa/ f, way, manner; will, desire. **a g. de**, in the manner or fashion of

guisado /gi'saðo/ m, Cul. stew; cooked dish

guisante /gi'sante/ m, Agr. pea; pea plant. **g. de olor,** sweetpea

guisar /gi'sar/ vt to cook; stew; Cul. prepare, dress; adjust, arrange

guiso /'giso/ m, cooked dish

guitarra /gi'tarra/ f, guitar

guitarrista /gita'rrista/ mf guitar player

guito /'gito/ a vicious (horses, mules)

gula /'gula/ f, greed, gluttony

gusaniento /gusa'niento/ a worm-eaten; maggoty

gusano /gu'sano/ m, worm; caterpillar; maggot; meek, downtrodden person. **g. de seda,** silkworm

gusanoso /gusa'noso/ a wormy

gustar /gus'tar/ vt to taste, savor; try; —vi be pleasing, give pleasure; like. **Me gusta el libro,** I like the book. **La película no me gustó,** I didn't like the film. **g. de,** to like, is used only when a person is the subject

gusto /'gusto/ m, taste; flavor, savor; pleasure, delight; will; discrimination, taste, style, fashion; manner; whim, caprice. **a g.,** to taste; according to taste. **con mucho g.,** with great pleasure. **dar g.,** to please. **de buen g.,** in good taste

gustoso /gus'toso/ a savory, palatable; willingly, with pleasure; pleasant, agreeable

gutagamba /guta'gamba/ f, gamboge (yellow)

gutapercha /guta'pertʃa/ f, guttapercha

gutural /gutu'ral/ a guttural

H

haba /'aβa/ *f*, broad bean; bean (coffee, cocoa, etc.). **h. de las Indias,** sweetpea. **Esas son habas contadas,** That's a certainty

Habana, la /a'βana, la/ Havana

habanero /aβa'nero/ **(-ra), habano (-na)** *a* and *n* Havanese, from Havana. *m.* **habano,** Havana cigar

habar /a'βar/ *m*, bean field

haber /a'βer/ *m*, estate, property (gen. *pl*); income; *Com.* credit balance. **h. monedado,** specie

haber /a'βer/ *vt irr* to have; catch, lay hands on (e.g. *El reo fue habido,* The criminal was caught) —*v aux* (e.g. *Hemos escrito la carta,* We have written the letter) —*v impers* to happen, take place; be —*3rd pers. sing Pres. Indic.* **ha** is replaced by **hay,** meaning there is or there are (e.g. *No hay naranjas en las tiendas,* There are no oranges in the shops). In certain weather expressions, **hay** means it is (e.g. *Hay luna,* It is moonlight). Used of expressions of time, **haber** means to elapse and **ha** (*3rd pers. sing Pres. Indic.*) has adverbial force of "ago" (e.g. *muchos días ha,* many days ago). **h. de,** to be necessary (less strong than **h. que**) (e.g. *Hemos de verle mañana,* We must see him tomorrow. *He de hacer el papel de Manolo,* I am to play the part of Manolo). **h. que,** to be unavoidable, be essential. With this construction the form **hay** is used (e.g. *Hay que darse prisa,* We (or one) must hurry. **No hay que enojarse,** There's no need to get annoyed). **no h., más que pedir,** to leave nothing to be desired. **no h. tal,** to be no such thing. *Inf.* **habérselas con,** to quarrel or fall out with. **Hubo una vez...,** Once upon a time... **¡No hay de qué!,** Don't mention it!; Not at all!; You're welcome! **No hay para que...,** There's no point in.... **poco tiempo ha,** a little while ago. **¿Qué hay?** What's the matter?; What's new? **¿Qué hay de nuevo?** What's new? *Pres. Indic.* **he, has, ha, hemos, habéis, han.** *Fut.* **habré,** etc —*Condit.* **habría,** etc —*Preterite* **hube, hubiste, hubo, hubimos, hubisteis, hubieron.** *Pres. Subjunc.* **haya,** etc —*Imperf. Subjunc.* **hubiese,** etc.

habichuela /aβi'tʃuela/ *f*, kidney bean

hábil /'aβil/ *a* clever; skillful; able; lawful

habilidad /aβili'ðað/ *f*, ability; skill; accomplishment; craftsmanship, workmanship

habilidoso /aβili'ðoso/ *a* accomplished; able; skillful

habilitación /aβilita'θion; aβilita'sion/ *f*, habilitation; paymastership; equipment; furnishing

habilitado /aβili'taðo/ *m*, paymaster

habilitar /aβili'tar/ *vt* to qualify; equip; furnish; habilitate; enable; *Com.* capitalize

habitabilidad /aβitaβili'ðað/ *f*, habitability

habitable /aβi'taβle/ *a* habitable

habitación /aβita'θion; aβita'sion/ *f*, habitation, dwelling; room in a house; residence; (*Bot. Zool.*) habitat; caretaking

habitante /aβi'tante/ *m*, inhabitant

habitar /aβi'tar/ *vt* to inhabit, reside in

hábito /'aβito/ *m*, attire; *Eccl.* habit; use, custom; skill, facility; *pl* vestments; gown, robe. **tomar el h.,** to become a monk or nun

habitual /aβi'tual/ *a* habitual, usual

habituar /aβi'tuar/ *vt* to accustom; —*vr* accustom oneself; grow used (to)

habitud /aβi'tuð/ *f*, habit, custom; relationship

habla /'aβla/ *f*, speech; language; dialect; discourse

hablado /a'βlaðo/ *a* spoken. **bien h.,** well-spoken; courteous. **mal h.,** ill-spoken; rude

hablador /aβla'ðor/ **(-ra)** *a* talkative; gossipy —*n* chatterbox; gossip

habladuría /aβlaðu'ria/ *f*, gossip; impertinent chatter

hablanchín /aβlan'tʃin/ *a Inf.* chattering, gossiping

hablar /a'βlar/ *vi* to speak; converse; express oneself; arrange; (*with de*) speak about, discuss; gossip about; criticize; (*with por*) intercede on behalf of; —*vt* speak (a language); say, speak; —*vr* speak to one another. **no hablarse,** to not be on speaking terms. **h. a gritos,** to shout. **h. alto,** to speak loudly or in strong

terms. **h. bien** (*or* **mal**), to be well- (or ill-) spoken; be polite (or rude). **h. claro,** to speak frankly. **h. consigo** *or* **h. entre sí,** to talk to oneself. *Inf.* **h. cristiano, h. en cristiano,** to speak clearly or intelligibly; speak frankly. **hablarlo todo,** to talk too much. **h. por h.,** to talk for talking's sake. *Inf.* **h. por los codos,** to chatter. **h. sin ton ni son,** to speak foolishly

hablilla /a'βliʎa; a'βliya/ *f*, rumor, tittletattle, gossip

hacecillo /aθe'θiʎo; ase'siyo/ *m*, small sheaf; small bundle; *Bot.* fascicle; beam (of light)

hacedero /aθe'ðero; ase'ðero/ *a* feasible, practicable

hacedor /aθe'ðor; ase'ðor/ *m*, maker; steward, manager; Creator

hacendado /aθen'daðo; asen'daðo/ **(-da)** *a* landed —*n* landowner; *West Hem.* cattle rancher

hacendista /aθen'dista; asen'dista/ *mf* political economist

hacendoso /aθen'doso; asen'doso/ *a* diligent, hardworking

hacer /a'θer; a'ser/ *vt irr* to make; fashion, form, construct; do, perform; cause, effect; arrange, put right; contain; accustom, harden; pack (luggage); imagine, invent, create; improve, perfect; compel, oblige; deliver (speeches); compose; earn; *Math.* add up to; suppose, imagine (e.g. *Sus padres hacían a María en casa,* Her parents imagined that Mary was at home); put into practice, execute; play the part of or act like (e.g. *h. el gracioso,* to play the buffoon); shed, cast (e.g. *El roble hace sombra,* The oak casts a shadow); assemble, convoke (meetings, gatherings); give off, produce (e.g. *La chimenea hace humo,* The chimney is smoking); perform (plays); (*with el, la, lo, and some nouns*) pretend to be (e.g. *Se hizo el desconocido,* He pretended to be ignorant. (**h.** followed by infin. is sometimes translated by a past participle in English (e.g. *Lo hice h.,* I had it done).) *vi* to matter, be important, signify (e.g. *Su llegada no hace nada al caso,* His arrival makes no difference to the case. *Se me hace muy poco...,* It matters to me very little...); be fitting or suitable; concern, be pertinent; match, go with; agree, be in harmony; (*with de*) act as, discharge duties of temporarily (e.g. *h. de camarero,* to be a temporary waiter); (*with por*) try to, attempt to (e.g. *Haremos por decírselo,* We shall try to tell him) —*vi impers* Used in expressions concerning: 1. the weather. 2. lapse of time. English uses the verb "to be' in both cases, e.g.:
1. *hace buen* (*or mal*) **tiempo,** it is fine (or bad) weather. **hace mucho frío,** it is very cold. **hace sol,** it is sunny. **hace viento,** it is windy. **¿Qué tiempo hace?** What is the weather like?
2. *hace* + an expression of time is followed by **que** introducing a clause (e.g. *Hace dos horas que llegamos,* It is two hours since we arrived) or **hace** + an expression of time may be followed by **desde** + a noun (e.g. *Hace dos años desde aquel día,* It is two years since that day)
When an action or state that has begun in the past is still continuing in the present, the Spanish verb is in the Pres. Indic., whereas the English verb is in the Perfect (e.g. *Hace un mes que la veo todos los días,* I have been seeing her every day for a month). This rule holds good with other tenses. English Pluperfect, Future Perfect, Conditional Perfect become in Spanish Imperfect, Future, Conditional, respectively. *Naut.* **h. agua,** to leak. **h. aguas,** to pass water, urinate. **h. alarde de,** to boast of. **h. el amor a,** to make love to, court, woo. **h. autoridad,** to be authoritative. **h. a todo,** to have many uses; be adaptable. **h. bancarrota,** to go bankrupt. **h. un berrinche, hacerse un berrinche,** to have a fit, have a tantrum. *Fig. Inf.* **h. buena,** to justify. **h. calceta,** to knit. **h. cara** or **frente a,** to face; resist. **h. caso,** to take notice, mind (e.g. *¡No hagas caso!* Never mind!). **h. causas,** to bring charges, institute proceedings. **h. cuentas,** to reckon up. **h. daño,** to harm. *Inf.* **h. de las suyas,** to behave in his usual manner or play one of his usual

tricks. **h. diligencias por,** to endeavor to. **h. fiesta,** to take a holiday. **h. fuerza,** to struggle. **h. fuerza a,** *Fig.* to do violence to (e.g. *Hizo fuerza a sus creencias,* He did violence to his beliefs). **h. h.,** to cause to be made (e.g. *He hecho hacer un vestido,* I have had a dress made). **h. juego,** to make a set, match (e.g. *El sombrero hace juego con el traje,* The hat goes with the dress). **h. la corte (a),** to court, woo. *Fig. Inf.* **h. la vista gorda,** to turn a blind eye. **h. la vida del claustro,** to lead a cloistered existence. **h. mal,** to do wrong; be harmful (food, etc.). **h. pedazos,** to break. **h. pinos** (or **pinitos**) to totter; toddle; stagger. *Aer.* **h. rizos,** to loop the loop. **h. saber,** to make known; notify. **h. seguir,** to forward (letters). **h. señas,** to make signs (wave, beckon, etc.). *Inf.* **h. una que sea sonada,** to cause a big scandal. **¡Hágame el favor!** Please! *Pres. Indic.* **hago, haces,** etc —*Fut.* **haré,** etc —*Condit.* **haría,** etc —*Imperat.* **haz, haga, hagamos, haced, hagan.** *Preterite* **hice, hiciste, hizo, hicimos, hicisteis, hicieron.** *Pres. Subjunc.* **haga,** etc —*Imperf. Subjunc.* **hiciese,** etc.

hacerse /a'θerse; a'serse/ *vr irr* to become (e.g. *Se ha hecho muy importante,* It (or he) has become very important); grow up (e.g. *Miguel se ha hecho hombre,* Michael has grown up (become a man)); develop, mature; pass oneself off as, pretend to be; (*with prep a*) become accustomed to or used to (e.g. *Me haré a este clima,* I shall grow used to this climate); withdraw or retire to (of places); (*with de or con*) provide oneself with. **h. a la vela,** to set sail. **h. a (uno),** to seem (e.g. *Eso que me cuentas se me hace increíble,* What you tell me seems incredible). *Inf.* **h. chiquito,** to be modest. **h. tarde,** to grow late; *Fig.* be too late. See **hacer**

hacha /'atʃa/ *f,* large candle; torch; ax. **h. pequeña,** hatchet

hachazo /a'tʃaθo; a'tʃaso/ *m,* stroke of an ax

hache /'atʃe/ *f,* name of the letter H

hachero /a'tʃero/ *m,* candlestick; woodcutter, axman

hacho /'atʃo/ *m,* torch; beacon

hacia /'aθia; 'asia/ *prep* toward, near, about. **h. adelante,** forward, onward

hacienda /a'θienda; a'sienda/ *f,* country estate, land; property; *pl* domestic tasks; cattle. **h. pública,** public funds. **ministerio de h.,** national treasury, exchequer

hacina /a'θina; a'sina/ *f, Agr.* stack; heap, pile

hacinamiento /aθina'miento; asina'miento/ *m,* stacking, piling; accumulation

hacinar /aθi'nar; asi'nar/ *vt Agr.* to stack sheaves; accumulate, amass; pile up, heap

hada /'aða/ *f,* fairy

hado /'aðo/ *m,* fate; destiny

hagiografía /ahiogra'fia/ *f,* hagiography

hagiógrafo /a'hiografo/ *m,* hagiographer

Haití /ai'ti/ Haiti

haitiano /ai'tiano/ **(-na)** *a* and *n* Haitian

halagar /ala'gar/ *vt* to caress; flatter; coax; please, delight

halago /a'lago/ *m,* flattery; coaxing; caress; source of pleasure, delight

halagüeño /ala'gueɲo/ *a* flattering; pleasing; caressing; hopeful, promising

halar /a'lar/ *vt Naut.* to haul, tow

halcón /al'kon/ *m,* falcon

halconero /alko'nero/ *m,* hawker, hunter

hálito /'alito/ *m,* breath; vapor; *Poet.* breeze

hallado /a'ʎaðo; a'yaðo/ *a* and *Past Part.* found, met. **bien h.,** welcome; happy, contented. **mal h.,** unwelcome; uneasy, discontented

hallador /aʎa'ðor; aya'ðor/ **(-ra)** *n* finder

hallar /a'ʎar; a'yar/ *vt* to find; meet; observe; discover; find out; —*vr* be present; be, find oneself

hallazgo /a'ʎaθgo; a'yasgo/ *m,* finding; thing found; finder's reward

halo /'alo/ *m,* halo

halterofilia /altero'filia/ *f,* weightlifting

hamaca /a'maka/ *f,* hammock

hamadríade /ama'ðriaðe/ *f,* hamadryad

hambre /'ambre/ *f,* hunger; famine; desire, yearning. **tener h.,** to be hungry

hambriento /am'briento/ *a* hungry; famished; *Fig.* starved (of affection, etc.)

Hamburgo /am'burgo/ Hamburg

hamo /'amo/ *m,* fishhook

hampa /'ampa/ *f,* rogue's life; gang of rogues; underworld, slum

hangar /aŋ'gar/ *m,* hangar

hanseático /anse'atiko/ *a* Hanseatic

haragán /ara'gan/ **(-ana)** *a* lazy, idle —*n* idler, lazybones

harapiento /ara'piento/ *a* ragged

harapo /a'rapo/ *m,* tatter, rag

haraposo /ara'poso/ *a* ragged

harén /a'ren/ *m,* harem

harina /a'rina/ *f,* flour; powder; farina. *Inf.* **ser h. de otro costal,** to be a horse of another color

harinero /ari'nero/ *a* relating to flour. *m,* flour merchant; flour bin

harinoso /ari'noso/ *a* floury, mealy; farinaceous

harmónica /ar'monika/ *f,* (*Phys. Math.*) harmonic

harmonizar /armoni'θar; armoni'sar/ *vt* to arrange (music)

harnero /ar'nero/ *m,* sieve

harón /a'ron/ *a* slothful, slow; lazy, idle

harpillera /arpi'ʎera; arpi'yera/ *f,* sackcloth, sacking

hartar /ar'tar/ *vt* to satiate; tire, annoy; satisfy the appetite; shower (with blows, etc.)

hartazgo /ar'taθgo; ar'tasgo/ *m,* satiety

harto /'arto/ *a* satiated; tired (of), *adv* enough

hartura /ar'tura/ *f,* satiety; abundance

hasta /'asta/ *prep* until; as far as; down or up to —*conjunc* also, even. **h. la vista,** See you! Ciao! Au revoir! **h. mañana,** until tomorrow

hastial /as'tial/ *m,* gable, end wall; boor, lout

hastío /as'tio/ *m,* loathing; distaste; nausea

hato /'ato/ *m,* personal clothing; herd of cattle; gang (of suspicious characters); crowd, mob; *Inf.* group, party. *Inf.* **liar el h.,** to pack up

Hawai /'awai/ Hawaii

hay /ai/ there is; there are. See **haber**

haya /'aya/ *f,* beech tree; beechwood

Haya, La /'aya, la/ The Hague

hayal /a'yal/ *m,* wood of beech trees, beech plantation

hayuco /a'yuko/ *m,* beech mast

haz /aθ/ *as/ m,* bundle, sheaf; *Mil.* file; *pl* fasces. *f,* visage; surface, face. **h. de la tierra,** face of the earth. **h. de luz,** beam of light. *Fig.* **ser de dos haces,** to be two-faced

haz /aθ; as/ *2nd pers imperat* **hacer**

hazaña /a'θaɲa; a'saɲa/ *f,* exploit, prowess

hazañoso /aθa'ɲoso; asa'ɲoso/ *a* heroic, dauntless, courageous

hazmerreír /aθmerre'ir; asmerre'ir/ *m, Inf.* laughingstock

he /e/ *interj* and *adv* Hallo! Hist!; Behold! **¡Heme aquí!** Here I am. **he aquí,** here is...

hebilla /e'βiʎa; e'βiya/ *f,* buckle

hebra /'eβra/ *f,* thread; fiber; flesh; *Mineral.* vein, streak; filament (textiles); grain (of wood); *pl Poet.* hair. *Inf.* **pegar la h.,** to start a conversation

hebraísmo /eβra'ismo/ *m,* Hebraism

hebraísta /eβra'ista/ *m,* Hebraist

hebreo /e'βreo/ **(-ea)** *a* Hebraic, Jewish —*n* Jew. *m,* Hebrew (language)

Hébridas, las /'eβriðas, las/ the Hebrides

hecatombe /eka'tombe/ *f,* hecatomb; slaughter, massacre

hechicería /etʃiθe'ria; etʃise'ria/ *f,* sorcery; spell, enchantment

hechicero /etʃi'θero; etʃi'sero/ *a* bewitching, magic; charming, attractive

hechizar /etʃi'θar; etʃi'sar/ *vt* to bewitch; charm, attract, delight

hechizo /e'tʃiθo; e'tʃiso/ *m,* magic spell; fascination, charm; delight, pleasure

hecho /'etʃo/ *a* developed, mature; accustomed; used; perfected, finished; ready-made. **h. una furia,** like a fury, very angry. **bien h.,** well-made, well-proportioned; well or rightly done

hecho /etʃo/ *m,* deed, action; fact; happening, event. **los Hechos de los Apóstoles,** the Acts of the Apostles

hechura /e'tʃura/ f, making, make; creation; form; figure, statue; *Lit.* composition; build (of body); *Fig.* puppet, creature; *pl* price paid for work done. **de h. sastre,** a tailor-made

hectárea /ekta'rea/ f, hectare

hectógrafo /ek'tografo/ m, hectograph

hectogramo /ekto'gramo/ m, hectogram

hectolitro /ekto'litro/ m, hectoliter

heder /e'ðer/ vi irr to stink; be intolerable. See **entender**

hediondez /eðion'deθ; eðion'des/ f, stink, stench

hediondo /e'ðiondo/ a stinking; intolerable, pestilential; obscene

hedonismo /eðo'nismo/ m, hedonism

hedonista /eðo'nista/ mf hedonist

hegeliano /ehe'liano/ a Hegelian

hegemonía /ehemo'nia/ f, hegemony

helada /e'laða/ f, frost. **h. blanca,** hoarfrost

heladera /ela'ðera/ f, refrigerator

helado /e'laðo/ a frozen; ice-cold; astounded; disdainful. m, iced drink; sherbet, ice cream

helamiento /ela'miento/ m, icing; freezing

helar /e'lar/ vt irr to freeze; ice, chill; astound; discourage; —vr become iced; freeze; become ice-cold —v impers to freeze. See **acertar**

helecho /e'letʃo/ m, fern

helenismo /ele'nismo/ m, Hellenism

hélice /'eliθe; 'elise/ f, spiral, helical line; screw, propeller; *Geom.* helix; *Astron.* Ursa Major

helicóptero /eli'koptero/ m, *Aer.* helicopter

helio /'elio/ m, helium

heliógrafo /e'liografo/ m, heliograph

helioscopio /elio'skopio/ m, helioscope

helióstato /e'liostato/ m, heliostat

helioterapia /eliote'rapia/ f, heliotherapy

heliotropismo /eliotro'pismo/ m, heliotropism

heliotropo /elio'tropo/ m, heliotrope; agate

helvecio /el'βeθio; el'βesio/ (**-ia**) a and n Helvetian

hembra /'embra/ f, female; *Inf.* woman; nut of a screw; eye of a hook

hemiciclo /emi'θiklo; emi'siklo/ m, hemicycle; floor (of a legislative building)

hemisférico /emis'feriko/ a hemispherical

hemisferio /emis'ferio/ m, hemisphere

hemofilia /emo'filia/ f, hemophilia.

hemoglobina /emoglo'βina/ f, hemoglobin

hemorragia /emo'rrahia/ f, hemorrhage

hemorroides /emo'rroiðes/ f, hemorrhoids

henchido /en'tʃiðo/ a swollen

henchimiento /entʃi'miento/ m, swelling; inflation; filling

henchir /en'tʃir/ vt irr to fill; stuff; swell —*Pres. Indic.* **hincho, hinches, hinche, hinchen.** *Pres. Part.* **hinchiendo.** *Pres. Subjunc.* **hincha,** etc —*Imperf. Subjunc.* **hinchiese,** etc —*Imperat.* **hinche, hincha, hinchamos, henchid, hinchan**

hendedura /ende'ðura/ f, fissure; rift

hender /en'der/ vt irr to split, crack; *Fig.* cleave (air, water, etc.); make one's way through. See **entender**

hendidura /endi'ðura/ f, split, fissure, crack, chink

henil /e'nil/ m, hayloft

heno /'eno/ m, hay

hepático /e'patiko/ a hepatic

heráldica /e'raldika/ f, heraldry

heráldico /e'raldiko/ a heraldic

heraldo /e'raldo/ m, herald; harbinger

herbaje /er'βahe/ m, herbage; pasture, grass; thick woolen cloth

herbario /er'βario/ m, herbalist, botanist; herbarium —a herbal

herbívoro /er'βiβoro/ a herbivorous

herbolaria /erβo'laria/ f, herbal

hercúleo /er'kuleo/ a herculean

heredad /ere'ðað/ f, landed property; country estate

heredar /ere'ðar/ vt to inherit; make a deed of gift to; inherit characteristics, etc.; take as heir

heredero /ere'ðero/ (**-ra**) m, heir; inheritor. **h. aparente,** heir apparent. **presunto h.,** heir presumptive

hereditario /ereði'tario/ a hereditary

hereje /e'rehe/ mf heretic

herejía /ere'hia/ f, heresy

herencia /e'renθia; e'rensia/ f, inheritance; heredity; heritage

heresiarca /ere'siarka/ mf heresiarch

herético /e'retiko/ a heretical

herida /e'riða/ f, wound; insult; anguish. **h. contusa,** contusion. **h. penetrante,** deep wound

herir /e'rir/ vt irr to wound; strike, harm; *Fig.* pierce (of sun's rays); *Fig.* pluck (strings of a musical instrument); impress (the senses); affect (the emotions); offend (gen. of words) —*Pres. Part.* **hiriendo.** *Pres. Indic.* **hiero, hieres, hiere, hieren.** *Preterite* **hirió, hirieron.** *Pres. Subjunc.* **hiera, hieras, hiera, hiramos, hiráis, hieran.** *Imperf. Subjunc.* **hiriese,** etc.

hermafrodita /ermafro'ðita/ a and mf hermaphrodite

hermana /er'mana/ f, sister; twin, pair (of things). **h. de leche,** foster sister. **h. política,** sister-in-law

hermanar /erma'nar/ vt to join; mate; harmonize; —vt and vr be the spiritual brother of, be compatible

hermanastra /erma'nastra/ f, stepsister

hermanastro /erma'nastro/ m, stepbrother

hermandad /erman'dað/ f, brotherhood; friendship; intimacy; relationship (of one thing to another); confraternity. **Santa H.,** Spanish rural police force instituted in the fifteenth century

hermano /er'mano/ m, brother; pair, twin (of things); *Eccl.* brother. **h. de raza,** member of the same race. **h. político,** brother-in-law

hermético /er'metiko/ a hermetic

hermosear /ermose'ar/ vt to embellish, beautify, adorn

hermoso /er'moso/ a beautiful; shapely; handsome; fine, wonderful (weather, view, etc.)

hermosura /ermo'sura/ f, beauty; pleasantness, attractiveness, perfection of form; belle

hernia /'ernia/ f, hernia

héroe /'eroe/ m, hero

heroicidad /eroiθi'ðað; eroisi'ðað/ f, heroism

heroico /e'roiko/ a heroic

heroína /ero'ina/ f, heroine

heroísmo /ero'ismo/ m, heroism

herpes /'erpes/ m pl, or f pl, herpes

herrada /e'rraða/ f, pail

herradero /erra'ðero/ m, branding of livestock

herrador /erra'ðor/ m, blacksmith

herradura /erra'ðura/ f, horseshoe

herraje /e'rrahe/ m, ironwork

herramienta /erra'mienta/ f, tool; set of tools

herrar /e'rrar/ vt irr to shoe horses; brand (cattle); decorate with iron. See **acertar**

herrería /erre'ria/ f, forge; ironworks; blacksmith's shop; clamor, tumult, confusion

herrero /e'rrero/ m, smith

herrete /e'rrete/ m, ferrule, tag

herrumbre /e'rrumbre/ f, rust; taste of iron

herrumbroso /errum'broso/ a rusty

hervidero /erβi'ðero/ m, boiling, bubbling; *Fig.* ebullition; swarm, crowd

hervir /er'βir/ vi irr to boil; foam and froth (sea); seethe (emotions); surge (crowds); (*with en*) abound in, swarm with. See **sentir**

hervor /er'βor/ m, boiling; ebullition, vigor, zest; seething, agitation

hesitación /esita'θion; esita'sion/ f, hesitation, doubt, uncertainty

hesitar /esi'tar/ vi to hesitate, vacillate

heteo /e'teo/ (**-ea**) a and n Hittite

heterodina /etero'ðina/ a f, *Radio.* heterodyne

heterodoxia /etero'ðoksia/ f, heterodoxy

heterodoxo /etero'ðokso/ a heterodox

heterogeneidad /eterohenei'ðað/ f, heterogeneity

heterogéneo /etero'heneo/ a heterogeneous

hético /'etiko/ a hectic, consumptive

hexagonal /eksago'nal/ a hexagonal

hexágono /e'ksagono/ m, hexagon

hexámetro /e'ksametro/ m, hexameter

hez /eθ; es/ f, (gen. pl **heces**) lees, dregs

hiato /'iato/ m, hiatus

hibernal /'iβernal/ a wintry

hibernés /iβer'nes/ a Hibernian

hibisco /i'βisko/ m, hibiscus

hibridación /iβriða'θion; iβriða'sion/ f, hybridization

hibridismo /iβri'ðismo/ m, hybridism
híbrido /'iβriðo/ a and m, hybrid
hidalgo /i'ðalgo/ (**-ga**) n noble, aristocrat —a noble; illustrious; generous
hidalguía /iðal'gia/ f, nobility; generosity, nobility of spirit
hidra /'iðra/ f, Zool. hydra; poisonous snake; Astron. Hydra
hidratar /iðra'tar/ vt Chem. to hydrate
hidrato /i'ðrato/ m, hydrate. **h. de carbono,** carbohydrate
hidráulica /i'ðraulika/ f, hydraulics
hidráulico /i'ðrauliko/ a hydraulic
hidroavión /iðroa'βion/ m, flying boat
hidrocarburo /iðrokar'βuro/ m, hydrocarbon
hidrocéfalo /iðro'θefalo; iðro'sefalo/ a hydrocephalic
hidrodinámica /iðroði'namika/ f, hydrodynamics
hidroeléctrico /iðroe'lektriko/ a hydroelectric
hidrofobia /iðro'foβia/ f, hydrophobia; rabies
hidrógeno /i'ðroheno/ m, hydrogen
hidrografía /iðrogra'fia/ f, hydrography
hidrología /iðrolo'hia/ f, hydrology
hidropesía /iðrope'sia/ f, dropsy
hidrópico /i'ðropiko/ a dropsical
hidroplano /iðro'plano/ m, seaplane
hidroquinona /iðroki'nona/ f, hydroquinone
hidroscopio /iðro'skopio/ m, hydroscope
hidrostática /iðro'statika/ f, hydrostatics
hidroterapia /iðrote'rapia/ f, hydrotherapy
hiedra /'ieðra/ f, ivy
hiel /iel/ f, gall, bile, bitterness, affliction; pl troubles
hielo /'ielo/ m, ice, frost; freezing, icing; stupefaction; indifference, coldness. Inf. **estar hecho un h.,** to be as cold as ice
hiena /'iena/ f, hyena
hierático /ie'ratiko/ a hieratical
hierba /'ierβa/ f, grass; small plant; herb. **h. cana,** groundsel. **mala h.,** weed
hierbabuena /ierβa'βuena/ f, Bot. mint
hierofante /iero'fante/ m, hierophant
hierra /'ierra/ f, branding time
hierro /'ierro/ m, iron; brand with hot iron; iron or steel head of a lance, etc.; instrument or shape made of iron; weapon of war pl fetters. **h. colado,** cast iron. **h. dulce,** wrought iron. **h. en planchas,** sheet iron. **h. viejo,** scrap iron
hígado /'igaðo/ m, liver; courage
higiene /i'hiene/ f, hygiene; cleanliness, neatness. **h. privada,** personal hygiene. **h. pública,** public health
higiénico /i'hieniko/ a hygienic
higo /'igo/ m, fig. **h. chumbo,** prickly pear
higrómetro /i'grometro/ m, hygrometer
higuera /i'gera/ f, fig tree
hija /'iha/ f, daughter; native of a place; offspring
hijastro /i'hastro/ (**-ra**) n stepchild
hijo /'iho/ m, son; child; native of a place; offspring; shoot, sprout; pl descendants. **h. de la cuna,** foundling. **h. de leche,** foster child. **h. natural,** natural child. **h. político,** son-in-law
hijuela /i'huela/ f, little daughter; small mattress; small drain; side road; accessory, subordinate thing; piece of material for widening a garment; Law. part of an inheritance
hila /'ila/ f, row, line; gut; Surg. lint (gen. pl)
hilacha /i'latʃa/ f, thread raveled from cloth; fiber, filament. **h. de vidrio,** spun glass
hilado /i'laðo/ m, spinning; thread, yarn
hilandería /ilande'ria/ f, spinning; spinning mill; mill. **h. de algodón,** cotton mill
hilandero /ilan'dero/ (**-ra**) n spinner
hilar /i'lar/ vt to spin; reason, infer, discourse
hilaridad /ilari'ðað/ f, hilarity; quiet happiness
hilaza /i'laθa; i'lasa/ f, yarn
hilera /i'lera/ f, line, file, row; fine yarn; Mil. file, rank; Metall. wire drawer; Mas. course (of bricks)
hilo /'ilo/ m, thread; linen; wire; mesh (spiders, silkworm's web, etc.); edge (of a blade); thin stream (of liquid); thread (of discourse)
hilván /il'βan/ m, Sew. basting; tack
hilvanar /ilβa'nar/ vt Sew. to baste
himalayo /ima'layo/ a Himalayan

himen /'imen/ m, hymen
himeneo /ime'neo/ m, marriage, wedding
himnario /im'nario/ m, hymnal
himno /'imno/ m, hymn
hin /in/ m, whinny, neigh
hincapié /inka'pie/ m, foothold. **hacer h.,** to insist, make a stand
hincar /in'kar/ vt to thrust in; drive in, sink; —vr kneel. **h. el diente,** to bite. **h. la uña,** to scratch. **hincarse de rodillas,** to kneel down
hinchado /in'tʃaðo/ a puffed up, vain; pompous, high-flown, redundant (style)
hinchar /in'tʃar/ vt to inflate; puff out (the chest); swell (of a river, etc.); exaggerate (events); —vr swell; grow vain, be puffed up
hinchazón /intʃa'θon; intʃa'son/ f, swelling; vanity, presumption; pomposity, euphuism (style)
hiniesta /i'niesta/ f, Spanish broom
hinojo /i'noho/ m, Bot. fennel; knee. **de hinojos,** on bended knee
hipar /i'par/ vi to hiccup; pant (of dogs); be overanxious; be overtired; sob, cry
hipérbole /i'perβole/ f, hyperbole
hiperbólico /iper'βoliko/ a hyperbolical
hipercrítico /iper'kritiko/ m, hypercritic —a hypercritical
hipertrofiarse /ipertro'fiarse/ vr to hypertrophy
hípico /'ipiko/ a equine
hipnosis /ip'nosis/ f, hypnosis
hipnótico /ip'notiko/ a hypnotic. m, hypnotic drug
hipnotismo /ipno'tismo/ m, hypnotism
hipnotización /ipnotiθa'θion; ipnotisa'sion/ f, hypnotization
hipnotizar /ipnoti'θar; ipnoti'sar/ vt to hypnotize
hipo /'ipo/ m, hiccup; sob; longing, desire; dislike, disgust
hipocondría /ipokon'dria/ f, hypochondria
hipocondríaco /ipokon'driako/ (**-ca**) a hypochondriacal —n hypochondriac
hipocrático /ipo'kratiko/ a Hippocratic
hipocresía /ipokre'sia/ f, hypocrisy
hipócrita /i'pokrita/ a hypocritical. mf hypocrite
hipodérmico /ipo'ðermiko/ a hypodermic
hipódromo /i'poðromo/ m, hippodrome, racetrack
hipopótamo /ipo'potamo/ m, hippopotamus
hipostático /ipo'statiko/ a hypostatic
hipoteca /ipo'teka/ f, mortgage
hipotecar /ipote'kar/ vt to mortgage
hipotenusa /ipote'nusa/ f, hypotenuse
hipótesis /i'potesis/ f, hypothesis
hipotético /ipo'tetiko/ a hypothetical
hirsuto /ir'suto/ a hirsute, hairy
hirviente /ir'βiente/ a boiling
hisca /'iska/ f, birdlime
hisopear /isope'ar/ vt Eccl. to sprinkle, asperse
hisopo /i'sopo/ m, Bot. hyssop; Eccl. hyssop, sprinkler
hispánico /is'paniko/ a Spanish
hispanismo /ispa'nismo/ m, Hispanism
hispanista /ispa'nista/ mf Hispanist
hispanoamericano /ispanoameri'kano/ (**-na**) a and n Spanish-American, Hispano-American
histeria /is'teria/ f, hysteria
histérico /is'teriko/ a hysterical; hysteric
histerismo /iste'rismo/ m, Med. hysteria
histología /istolo'hia/ f, histology
histólogo /is'tologo/ m, histologist
historia /is'toria/ f, history; narrative, story; tale; Inf. gossip (gen. pl); Art. historical piece. **h. natural,** natural history. **h. sagrada,** biblical history. Fig. Inf. **dejarse de historias,** to stop beating around the bush
historiador /istoria'ðor/ (**-ra**) n historian
historiar /isto'riar/ vt to narrate, relate; record, chronicle
histórico /is'toriko/ a historical; historic
historieta /isto'rieta/ f, short story; anecdote
historiografía /istoriogra'fia/ f, historiography
historiógrafo /isto'riografo/ m, historiographer
histriónico /ist'rioniko/ a histrionic
hitlerismo /itle'rismo/ m, Hitlerism

hito /'ito/ *m*, milestone; boundary mark; *Fig*. mark, target. **de h. en h.**, from head to foot

hocico /o'θiko; o'siko/ *m*, snout; *Inf*. face, mug; *Inf*. angry gesture; *Naut*. prow. **meter el h.**, to stick one's nose into other people's business

hogaño /o'gaɲo/ *adv Inf*. during this year; at the present time

hogar /o'gar/ *m*, hearth, fireplace; home, house; family life; firebox (of a locomotive)

hoguera /o'gera/ *f*, bonfire

hoja /'oha/ *f*, *Bot*. leaf; petal; sheet (metal, paper, etc.); page (of book); blade (sharp instruments); leaf (door, window); sword. **h. de cálculo**, spreadsheet. **h. de servicios**, service or professional record. **h. de tocino**, side of bacon. **h. extraordinaria**, extra, special edition (of a newspaper). **h. volante**, handbill, supplement. **volver la h.**, to turn over (pages); change one's opinion; turn the conversation

hojalata /oha'lata/ *f*, tin plate

hojalatería /ohalate'ria/ *f*, tinware; tin shop

hojalatero /ohala'tero/ *m*, tinsmith

hojaldre /o'haldre/ *m*, or *f*, puff pastry

hojarasca /oha'raska/ *f*, withered leaves; excessive foliage; rubbish, trash

hojear /ohe'ar/ *vt* to turn the leaves of a book; skip, skim, read quickly; —*vi* exfoliate

hojuela /o'huela/ *f*, *dim* little leaf; *Bot*. leaflet; pancake

¡hola! /'ola/ *interj* Hallo! Goodness!

Holanda /o'landa/ Holland

holandés /olan'des/ **(-esa)** *a* and *n* Dutchman (-woman) *m*, Dutch (language)

holgado /ol'gaðo/ *a* leisured, free; loose, wide; comfortable; well-off, rich

holganza /ol'ganθa; ol'gansa/ *f*, repose, leisure, ease; idleness; pleasure

holgar /ol'gar/ *vi irr* to rest; be idle; be glad; be unused or unnecessary (things) —*vr* enjoy oneself, amuse oneself; be glad. See **contar**

holgazán /olga'θan; olga'san/ **(-ana)** *a* idle —*n* idler

holgazanear /olgaθane'ar; olgasane'ar/ *vi* to idle

holgazanería /olgaθane'ria; olgasane'ria/ *f*, idleness, sloth

holgorio /ol'gorio/ *m*, rejoicing, festivity, merriment

holgura /ol'gura/ *f*, enjoyment, merrymaking; width; comfort, ease; *Mech*. free play

hollar /o'ʎar; o'yar/ *vt irr* to trample under foot; humiliate. See **degollar**

hollejo /o'ʎeho; o'yeho/ *m*, peel, thin skin (of fruit); *Agr*. chaff

hollín /o'ʎin; o'yin/ *m*, soot

holocausto /olo'kausto/ *m*, holocaust

hológrafo /o'lografo/ *m*, holograph

hombradía /ombra'ðia/ *f*, manliness; courage

hombre /'ombre/ *m*, man; adult; omber (cards) —*interj* ¡h.! *Inf*. Old fellow! You don't say so! ¡**h. al agua!** Man overboard! **h. de bien**, honest, honorable man. **h. de estado**, statesman. **h. de muchos oficios**, jack-of-all-trades. **h. de negocios**, businessman; man of affairs. **h. de pro**, worthy man; famous man. **ser muy h.**, to be a real man, be very manly

hombrera /om'brera/ *f*, epaulette; shoulderpad

hombro /'ombro/ *m*, shoulder. **echar al h.**, to shoulder; undertake, take the responsibility of. **encogerse de hombros**, to shrug one's shoulders; be indifferent or uninterested

hombruno /om'bruno/ *a Inf*. mannish (of a woman)

homenaje /ome'nahe/ *m*, allegiance; homage; veneration, respect

homeópata /ome'opata/ *a* homeopathic. *mf* homeopath

homeopatía /omeopa'tia/ *f*, homeopathy

homérico /o'meriko/ *a* Homeric

homicida /omi'θiða; omi'siða/ *a* murderous, homicidal. *mf* murderer (-ess)

homicidio /omi'θiðio; omi'siðio/ *m*, homicide (act)

homilía /omi'lia/ *f*, homily

homogeneidad /omohenei'ðað/ *f*, homogeneity

homogéneo /omo'heneo/ *a* homogeneous

homólogo /o'mologo/ *a* homologous

homónimo /o'monimo/ *a* homonymous. *m*, homonym

homosexual /omose'ksual/ *a* and *mf* homosexual

honda /'onda/ *f*, sling, catapult

hondear /onde'ar/ *vt Naut*. to sound, plumb; *Naut*. unload

hondo /'ondo/ *a* deep; low; *Fig*. profound; deep, intense (emotion). *m*, depth

hondón /on'don/ *m*, depth, recess

hondonada /ondo'naða/ *f*, hollow; glen; valley

hondura /on'dura/ *f*, depth

hondureño /ondu'reɲo/ **(-ña)** *a* and *n* Honduran

honestidad /onesti'ðað/ *f*, honorableness; virtue; respectability; modesty; courtesy

honesto /o'nesto/ *a* honorable, virtuous; modest; honest, just

hongo /'oŋgo/ *m*, fungus; toadstool; bowler hat

honor /o'nor/ *m*, honor; fame; reputation (women); modesty (women); praise; *pl* rank, position; honors

honorable /ono'raβle/ *a* honorable

honorario /ono'rario/ *a* honorary. *m*, honorarium, fee

honorífico /ono'rifiko/ *a* honorary; honorable

honra /'onra/ *f*, self-respect, honor, personal dignity; reputation; chastity and modesty (women); *pl* obsequies

honradez /onra'ðeθ; onra'ðes/ *f*, honesty; honorableness, integrity; respectability

honrado /on'raðo/ *a* honest; honorable

honrar /on'rar/ *vt* to respect; honor; —*vr* to be honored

honroso /on'roso/ *a* honor-giving, honorable

hora /'ora/ *f*, hour; opportune moment; *pl* book of hours. **horas hábiles**, working hours. **horas muertas**, wee hours; wasted time. **a última h.**, at the last minute. **dar la h.**, to strike the hour. **¿Qué h. es?** What time is it?

horaciano /ora'θiano; ora'siano/ *a* Horatian

horadar /ora'ðar/ *vt* to bore, pierce

horario /o'rario/ *a* hourly. *m*, timetable; hour hand of a clock; watch

horca /'orka/ *f*, gibbet, gallows; *Agr*. pitchfork; fork; prop for trees

horcajadas /orka'haðas/ **(a)** *adv* astride

horcajadura /orkaha'ðura/ *f*, crotch

horchata /or'tʃata/ *f*, drink made of chufas or crushed almonds

horda /'orða/ *f*, horde

horizontal /oriθon'tal; orison'tal/ *a* horizontal

horizonte /ori'θonte; ori'sonte/ *m*, horizon. **nuevos horizontes**, new opportunities

horma /'orma/ *f*, mold; cobbler's last; stone wall. *Fig. Inf*. **hallar la h. de su zapato**, to find what suits one; meet one's match

hormiga /or'miga/ *f*, ant

hormigón /ormi'gon/ *m*, concrete. **h. armado**, ferroconcrete

hormiguear /ormige'ar/ *vi* to itch; crowd, swarm

hormiguero /ormi'gero/ *m*, anthill; crowd, swarm

hormona /or'mona/ *f*, hormone

hornero /or'nero/ **(-ra)** *n* baker

horno /'orno/ *m*, oven; furnace; kiln; bakery. **h. alfarero**, firing oven (for pottery). **h. de cocina**, kitchen stove. **h. de cuba**, blast furnace. **h. de ladrillo**, brick kiln. **alto h.**, iron-smelting furnace

horóscopo /o'roskopo/ *m*, horoscope

horquilla /or'kiʎa; or'kiya/ *f*, forked stick; hairpin; hatpin; *Agr*. hook. **viraje en h.**, hairpin turn

horrendo /o'rrendo/ *a* horrible, frightful

hórreo /'orreo/ *m*, granary, barn

horribilidad /orriβili'ðað/ *f*, horribleness

horribilísimo /orriβi'lisimo/ *a superl* most horrible, exceedingly horrible

horrible /o'rriβle/ *a* horrible

horrífico /o'rrifiko/ *a* horrific

horripilante /orripi'lante/ *a* hair-raising, horrifying

horrísono /o'rrisono/ *a Poet*. horrid-sounding, terrifying

horror /o'rror/ *m*, horror; horribleness; atrocity, enormity

horrorizar /orrori'θar; orrori'sar/ *vt* to horrify; —*vr* be horrified, be terrified

horroroso /orro'roso/ *a* dreadful, horrible; horrid; *Inf.* hideous, most ugly

hortaliza /orta'liθa; orta'lisa/ *f*, green vegetable, garden produce

hortelano /orte'lano/ *m*, market gardener

hortensia /or'tensia/ *f*, hydrangea

horticultor /ortikul'tor/ **(-ra)** *n* horticulturalist

horticultura /ortikul'tura/ *f*, horticulture

horticultural /ortikultu'ral/ *a* horticultural

hosanna /o'sanna/ *m*, hosanna

hosco /'osko/ *a* dark brown; unsociable, sullen; crabbed

hospedaje /ospe'ðahe/ *m*, lodging; board, payment

hospedar /ospe'ðar/ *vt* to lodge, receive as a guest; —*vr* and *vi* lodge, stay

hospedería /ospeðe'ria/ *f*, hostelry, inn; lodging

hospedero /ospe'ðero/ *n* innkeeper

hospicio /os'piθio; os'pisio/ *m*, hospice; almshouse, workhouse; lodging; orphanage

hospital /ospi'tal/ *m*, hospital; hospice. **h. de sangre,** field hospital

hospitalario /ospita'lario/ *a* hospitable

hospitalidad /ospitali'ðað/ *f*, hospitality; hospitableness; hospital

hostelero /oste'lero/ **(-ra)** *n* innkeeper

hostería /oste'ria/ *f*, hostelry; inn

hostia /'ostia/ *f*, *Eccl.* wafer, Host; sacrificial victim

hostigamiento /ostiga'miento/ *m*, harassment. **h. sexual,** sexual harassment

hostigar /osti'gar/ *vt* to chastise; harass; tease, annoy

hostil /'ostil/ *a* hostile

hostilidad /ostili'ðað/ *f*, hostility

hostilizar /ostili'θar; ostili'sar/ *vt* to commit hostile acts against; antagonize

hotel /'otel/ *m*, hotel; villa

hotelero /ote'lero/ **(-ra)** *n* hotelkeeper

hoy /oi/ *adv* today; at present. **h. día** *or* **h. en día,** today. **h. por h.,** day by day; at the present time. **de h. en adelante,** from today forward

hoya /'oya/ *f*, hole; grave; valley, glen; bed (of a river)

hoyo /'oyo/ *m*, hole; pockmark; grave; hollow

hoyuelo /o'yuelo/ *m*, *dim* little hole; dimple

hoz /oθ; os/ *f*, sickle; defile

hozar /o'θar; o'sar/ *vt* to root (pigs, etc.)

hucha /'utʃa/ *f*, large chest; strongbox; savings

hueco /'ueko/ *a* empty; hollow; vain; hollow (sound); pompous (style); spongy, soft; inflated. *m*, hollow; interval of time or place; *Inf.* vacancy; gap in a wall, etc.

huelga /'uelga/ *f*, strike; leisure; lying fallow; merrymaking. **h. de brazos caídos,** sit-down strike. **h. patronal,** lockout strike

huelguista /uel'gista/ *mf* striker

huella /'ueʎa; 'ueya/ *f*, footprint, track; footstep; tread (of stairs); *Print.* impression; vestige, trace. **h. digital,** fingerprint

huérfano /'uerfano/ **(-na)** *n* orphan —*a* unprotected, uncared for

huero /'uero/ *a* addled; empty, hollow

huerta /'uerta/ *f*, kitchen garden; orchard; irrigation land

huerto /'uerto/ *m*, orchard; kitchen garden

hueso /'ueso/ *m*, bone; stone (of fruit); kernel, core; drudgery; cheap, useless thing of poor quality. *Inf.* **no dejar un h. sano,** to tear (a person) to pieces. **tener los huesos molidos,** to be tired out; be bruised

huésped /'uespeð/ **(-da)** *n* guest; host; innkeeper

hueste /'ueste/ *f*, (gen. *pl*) army on the march; host; party, supporters

huesudo /ue'suðo/ *a* bony

hueva /'ueβa/ *f*, fish roe

huevera /ue'βera/ *f*, egg seller; eggcup

huevo /'ueβo/ *m*, egg. **h. duro,** hard-boiled egg. **h. estrellado,** fried egg. **h. pasado por agua,** soft-boiled egg. **huevos revueltos,** scrambled eggs

hugonote /ugo'note/ **(-ta)** *a* and *n* Huguenot

huida /'uiða/ *f*, flight, escape; bolting (of a horse); outlet

huir /uir/ *vi irr* to flee; fly (of time); elope; run away, bolt; (*with de*) avoid —*Pres. Part.* **huyendo.** *Pres. Indic.* **huyo, huyes, huyen.** *Preterite* **huyó, huyeron.** *Pres. Subjunc.* **huya,** etc —*Imperf. Subjunc.* **huyese,** etc.

hule /'ule/ *m*, oilcloth; rubber

hulla /'uʎa; 'uya/ *f*, coal mine, coal, soft coal

hullera /u'ʎera; u'yera/ *f*, colliery, coal mine

humanidad /umani'ðað/ *f*, humanity; human nature; human weakness; compassion; affability; *Inf.* stoutness; *pl* study of humanities

humanismo /uma'nismo/ *m*, humanism

humanista /uma'nista/ *mf* humanist —*a* humanistic

humanitario /umani'tario/ *a* humanitarian

humanizar /umani'θar; umani'sar/ *vt* to humanize

humano /u'mano/ *a* human; understanding, sympathetic. *m*, human being

humareda /uma'reða/ *f*, cloud of smoke

humeante /ume'ante/ *a* smoking; smoky

humear /ume'ar/ *vi* to give forth smoke; give oneself airs

humedad /ume'ðað/ *f*, humidity; dampness; moisture

humedecer /umeðe'θer; umeðe'ser/ *vt irr* to moisten, wet, damp; —*vr* grow moist. See **conocer**

húmedo /'umeðo/ *a* humid; damp; wet

húmero /'umero/ *m*, humerus

humildad /umil'dað/ *f*, humility; lowliness; humbleness

humilde /u'milde/ *a* meek; lowly; humble

humillación /umiʎa'θion; umiya'sion/ *f*, humiliation

humillante /umi'ʎante; umi'yante/ *a* humiliating; debasing; mortifying

humillar /umi'ʎar; umi'yar/ *vt* to humble; humiliate; —*vr* humble oneself

humo /'umo/ *m*, smoke; vapor, fume; vanity, airs

humor /u'mor/ *m*, *Med.* humor; temperament, disposition; mood. **de buen h.,** good-tempered. **de mal h.,** ill-tempered

humorada /umo'raða/ *f*, humorous saying, extravagance, witticism

humorismo /umo'rismo/ *m*, humor, comic sense; humorousness

humorista /umo'rista/ *mf* humorist

humorístico /umo'ristiko/ *a* humorous

humoso /u'moso/ *a* smoky, reeky

hundible /un'diβle/ *a* sinkable

hundido /un'diðo/ *a* sunken (of cheeks, etc.); hollow, deep-set (of eyes)

hundimiento /undi'miento/ *m*, sinking; collapse; subsidence (of earth)

hundir /un'dir/ *vt* to sink; oppress; confound; destroy, ruin; —*vr* collapse (building); sink; *Fig. Inf.* disappear

húngaro /'uŋgaro/ **(-ra)** *a* and *n* Hungarian. *m*, Hungarian (language)

Hungría /uŋ'gria/ Hungary

huno /'uno/ **(-na)** *n* Hun

huracán /ura'kan/ *m*, hurricane

huraña /ura'ɲia/ *f*, shyness, unsociableness; diffidence; wildness (of animals, etc.)

huraño /u'raɲo/ *a* shy, unsociable; diffident; wild (of animals, etc.)

hurgar /ur'gar/ *vt* to stir; poke, rake; touch; rouse, incite —*vr* pick one's nose

hurgón /ur'gon/ *m*, fire rake, poker; *Inf.* sword

hurgonada /urgo'naða/ *f*, raking (of the fire, etc.)

hurí /u'ri/ *f*, houri

hurón /u'ron/ **(-ona)** *n* ferret —*a* shy, unsociable

¡hurra! /'urra/ *interj* Hurrah!

hurtadillas /urta'ðiʎas; urta'ðiyas/ **(a)** *adv* by stealth, secretly

hurtar /ur'tar/ *vt* to steal; encroach (sea, river); plagiarize; —*vr* hide oneself

hurto /'urto/ *m*, theft. **coger con el h. en las manos,** *Fig.* to catch red-handed

husmear /usme'ar/ *vt* to sniff out; *Inf.* pry; —*vi* smell bad (of meat)

huso /'uso/ *m*, spindle; bobbin

¡huy! /'ui/ *interj* (denoting pain or surprise) Oh!

I

ibérico /i'βeriko/ *a* Iberian
ibero /i'βero/ **(-ra)** *a* and *n* Iberian
íbice /'iβiθe; 'iβise/ *m,* ibex
icnografía /iknogra'fia/ *f,* ichnography
icnográfico /ikno'grafiko/ *a* ichnographical
icono /i'kono/ *m,* icon
iconoclasta /ikono'klasta/ *a* iconoclastic. *mf* iconoclast
iconografía /ikonogra'fia/ *f,* iconography
ictericia /ikte'riθia; ikte'risia/ *f,* jaundice
ictiología /iktiolo'hia/ *f,* ichthyology
ictiólogo /ik'tiologo/ *m,* ichthyologist
ida /'iða/ *f,* setting out, departure, going; impetuous action; precipitancy; track, trail (of animals). **de i. y vuelta,** round trip (of tickets)
idea /i'ðea/ *f,* idea. *Inf.* **¡Qué ideas tienes!** What (odd) ideas you have!
ideación /iðea'θion; iðea'sion/ *f,* ideation
ideal /i'ðeal/ *a* ideal; perfect. *m,* model; ideal
idealidad /iðeali'ðað/ *f,* ideality
idealismo /iðea'lismo/ *m,* idealism
idealista /iðea'lista/ *a* idealistic. *mf* idealist
idealización /iðealiθa'θion; iðealisa'sion/ *f,* idealization
idealizar /iðeali'θar; iðeali'sar/ *vt* to idealize
idealmente /iðeal'mente/ *adv* ideally
idear /iðe'ar/ *vt* to imagine; devise; plan; design; draft, draw up
ídem /'iðem/ *adv* idem
idéntico /i'ðentiko/ *a* identical
identidad /iðenti'ðað/ *f,* identity
identificable /iðentifi'kaβle/ *a* identifiable
identificación /iðentifika'θion; iðentifika'sion/ *f,* identification
identificar /iðentifi'kar/ *vt* to identify; recognize; —*vr* (*with con*) identify oneself with
ideografía /iðeogra'fia/ *f,* ideography
ideograma /iðeo'grama/ *m,* ideogram
ideología /iðeolo'hia/ *f,* ideology. **i. racista,** racial ideology
ideológico /iðeo'lohiko/ *a* ideological
ideólogo /iðe'ologo/ **(-ga)** *n* ideologist; dreamer, planner
idílico /i'ðiliko/ *a* idyllic
idilio /i'ðilio/ *m,* idyll
idioma /i'ðioma/ *m,* language, tongue
idiomático /iðio'matiko/ *a* idiomatic
idiosincrasia /iðiosin'krasia/ *f,* idiosyncrasy
idiosincrásico /iðiosin'krasiko/ *a* idiosyncratic
idiota /i'ðiota/ *a* idiot; idiotic. *mf* idiot
idiotez /iðio'teθ; iðio'tes/ *f,* idiocy
idiotismo /iðio'tismo/ *m, Gram.* idiom; ignorance
idólatra /i'ðo'latra/ *a* idolatrous; adoring. *mf* idolater, heathen
idolatrar /iðola'trar/ *vt* to idolize; worship, love excessively
idolatría /iðola'tria/ *f,* idolatry; adoration, idolization
ídolo /'iðolo/ *m,* idol
idoneidad /iðonei'ðað/ *f,* fitness, suitability; competence; capacity
idóneo /i'ðoneo/ *a* suitable; competent, fit
idus /'iðus/ *m pl,* ides
iglesia /i'glesia/ *f,* church. **i. colegial,** collegiate church. **cumplir con la i.,** to discharge one's religious duties. **llevar a una mujer a la i.,** to lead a woman to the altar
ígneo /'igneo/ *a* igneous
ignición /igni'θion; igni'sion/ *f,* ignition
ignominia /igno'minia/ *f,* ignominy, disgrace
ignominioso /ignomi'nioso/ *a* ignominious
ignorancia /igno'ranθia; igno'ransia/ *f,* ignorance. **pretender i.,** to plead ignorance
ignorante /igno'rante/ *a* ignorant; unaware, uninformed. *mf* ignoramus
ignorar /igno'rar/ *vt* to be unaware of, not to know

ignoto /ig'noto/ *a* unknown, undiscovered
igual /i'gual/ *a* equal; level; even, smooth; very similar; alike; uniform; proportionate; unchanging; constant; indifferent; same. *mf* equal. *m, Math.* equal sign. **al i.,** equally. **sin i.,** peerless, without equal. **Me es completamente i.,** It's all the same to me
iguala /i'guala/ *f,* equalizing; leveling; agreement, arrangement; cash adjustment
igualación /iguala'θion; iguala'sion/ *f,* equalization; leveling; arrangement, agreement; matching; *Math.* equation
igualador /iguala'ðor/ *a* equalizing; leveling
igualar /igua'lar/ *vt* to equalize, make equal; match; pair; level, flatten; smooth; adjust; arrange, agree upon; weigh, consider; *Math.* equate; —*vi* be equal
igualdad /igual'dað/ *f,* equality; uniformity, harmony; evenness; smoothness; identity, sameness. **i. de ánimo,** equability, equanimity
igualitario /iguali'tario/ *a* equalizing; egalitarian
igualmente /igual'mente/ *adv* equally; the same, likewise
ijada /i'haða/ *f,* side, flank; pain in the side
ijadear /ihaðe'ar/ *vt* to pant
ijar /i'har/ *m,* See **ijada**
ilación /ila'θion; ila'sion/ *f,* connection, reference
ilegal /ile'gal/ *a* illegal
ilegalidad /ilegali'ðað/ *f,* illegality
ilegible /ile'hiβle/ *a* illegible, unreadable
ilegitimidad /ilehitimi'ðað/ *f,* illegitimacy
ilegítimo /ile'hitimo/ *a* illegitimate; false
íleon /'ileon/ *m,* ileum
ileso /i'leso/ *a* unharmed, unhurt
iletrado /ile'traðo/ *a* unlettered, uncultured
Ilíada /i'liaða/ *f,* Iliad
iliberal /iliβe'ral/ *a* illiberal; narrow-minded
iliberalidad /iliβerali'ðað/ *f,* illiberality; narrow-mindedness
ilícito /i'liθito; i'lisito/ *a* illicit
ilicitud /iliθi'tuð; ilisi'tuð/ *f,* illicitness
ilimitado /ilimi'taðo/ *a* unlimited, boundless
iliterato /ilite'rato/ *a* illiterate, uncultured
ilógico /i'lohiko/ *a* illogical
ilota /i'lota/ *mf* helot
iluminación /ilumina'θion; ilumina'sion/ *f,* illumination; lighting. **i. intensiva,** floodlighting
iluminador /ilumina'ðor/ **(-ra)** *a* lighting; illuminating —*n Art.* illuminator
iluminar /ilumi'nar/ *vt* to illuminate; light; *Art.* illuminate; enlighten
iluminativo /ilumina'tiβo/ *a* illuminating
ilusión /ilu'sion/ *f,* illusion; illusoriness; hope; dream
ilusionarse /ilusio'narse/ *vr* to harbor illusions
ilusivo /ilu'siβo/ *a* deceptive, illusive
iluso /i'luso/ *a* deceived, deluded; dreamy; visionary
ilusorio /ilu'sorio/ *a* illusory; deceptive; null
ilustración /ilustra'θion; ilustra'sion/ *f,* illustration, picture; enlightenment; explanation; illustrated newspaper or magazine; erudition, knowledge; example, illustration
ilustrado /ilu'straðo/ *a* erudite, learned; knowledgeable, well-informed
ilustrador /ilustra'ðor/ **(-ra)** *a* illustrative —*n* illustrator
ilustrar /ilus'trar/ *vt* to explain, illustrate; enlighten, instruct; illustrate (books); make illustrious; inspire with divine light
ilustrativo /ilustra'tiβo/ *a* illustrative
ilustre /i'lustre/ *a* illustrious, distinguished
ilustrísimo /ilus'trisimo/ *a superl* most illustrious (title of bishops, etc.)
imagen /i'mahen/ *f,* image; effigy, statue; idea; metaphor, simile. **i. nítida,** sharp image
imaginable /imahi'naβle/ *a* imaginable
imaginación /imahina'θion; imahina'sion/ *f,* imagination
imaginar /imahi'nar/ *vi* to imagine; —*vt* suppose,

conjecture; discover, invent; imagine. **¡Imagínese!** Just imagine!

imaginario /imahi'nario/ *a* imaginary

imaginativa /imahina'tiβa/ *f,* imagination; common sense

imaginativo /imahina'tiβo/ *a* imaginative

imaginería /imahine'ria/ *f,* imagery

imán /i'man/ *m,* magnet; attraction, charm; imam

imanación /imana'θion; imana'sion/ *f,* magnetization

imanar /ima'nar/ *vt* to magnetize

imbécil /im'beθil; im'besil/ *a* imbecile; stupid, idiotic. *mf* imbecile

imbecilidad /imbeθili'ðað; imbesili'ðað/ *f,* imbecility; folly, stupidity

imberbe /im'berβe/ *a* beardless. *Inf.* **joven i.,** stripling

imbibición /imbiβi'θion; imbiβi'sion/ *f,* imbibing, absorption

imborrable /imbo'rraβle/ *a* ineffaceable

imbuir /im'buir/ *vt irr* to imbue. See **huir**

imitable /imi'taβle/ *a* imitable

imitación /imita'θion; imita'sion/ *f,* imitation; reproduction, copy

imitado /imi'taðo/ *a* imitation; imitated

imitador /imita'ðor/ **(-ra)** *a* imitation; imitative —*n* imitator

imitar /imi'tar/ *vt* to imitate; counterfeit

imitativo /imita'tiβo/ *a* imitative

impacción /impak'θion; impak'sion/ *f,* impact

impaciencia /impa'θienθia; impa'siensia/ *f,* impatience

impacientar /impaθien'tar; impasien'tar/ *vt* to make impatient, annoy; —*vr* grow impatient

impaciente /impa'θiente; impa'siente/ *a* impatient

impacto /im'pakto/ *m,* impact. **i. de lleno,** direct hit

impalpabilidad /impalpaβili'ðað/ *f,* impalpability

impalpable /impal'paβle/ *a* impalpable

impar /im'par/ *a* odd; unpaired; single, uneven. **número impar,** odd number

imparcial /impar'θial; impar'sial/ *a* impartial

imparcialidad /imparθiali'ðað; imparsiali'ðað/ *f,* impartiality

imparisilábico /imparisi'laβiko/ *a* imparisyllabic

impartible /impar'tiβle/ *a* indivisible

impasibilidad /impasiβili'ðað/ *f,* impassivity, indifference

impasible /impa'siβle/ *a* impassive

impavidez /impaβi'ðeθ; impaβi'ðes/ *f,* dauntlessness; serenity in the face of danger

impávido /im'paβiðo/ *a* dauntless; calm, composed, imperturbable

impecabilidad /impekaβili'ðað/ *f,* impeccability, perfection

impecable /impe'kaβle/ *a* impeccable, perfect

impedido /impe'ðiðo/ *a* disabled

impedimento /impeði'mento/ *m,* obstacle; hindrance; *Law.* impediment

impedir /impe'ðir/ *vt irr* to impede; obstruct; prevent; thwart; disable; delay; *Poet.* amaze. See **pedir**

impeler /impe'ler/ *vt* to push; incite; drive; urge

impender /impen'der/ *vt* to spend money

impenetrabilidad /impenetraβili'ðað/ *f,* impenetrability; imperviousness; obscurity, difficulty

impenetrable /impene'traβle/ *a* impenetrable, dense; impervious; *Fig.* unfathomable; obscure

impenitencia /impeni'tenθia; impeni'tensia/ *f,* impenitence

impenitente /impeni'tente/ *a* impenitent

impensado /impen'saðo/ *a* unexpected, unforeseen

imperante /impe'rante/ *a* ruling, dominant

imperar /impe'rar/ *vi* to rule; command

imperativo /impera'tiβo/ *a* commanding —*a* and *m, Gram.* imperative

imperatorio /impera'torio/ *a* imperial, imperatorial

imperceptible /imperθep'tiβle; impersep'tiβle/ *a* imperceptible

imperdible /imper'ðiβle/ *m,* safety pin

imperdonable /imperðo'naβle/ *a* unpardonable, inexcusable

imperecedero /impereθe'ðero; imperese'ðero/ *a* undying, eternal, everlasting

imperfección /imperfek'θion; imperfek'sion/ *f,* imperfection, inadequacy; fault, blemish; weakness

imperfecto /imper'fekto/ *a* imperfect; inadequate; faulty —*a* and *m, Gram.* imperfect

imperial /impe'rial/ *a* imperial. *f,* upper deck of a bus or streetcar

imperialismo /imperia'lismo/ *m,* imperialism

imperialista /imperia'lista/ *a* imperialistic. *mf* imperialist

impericia /impe'riθia; impe'risia/ *f,* inexpertness; unskillfulness, unhandiness

imperio /im'perio/ *m,* empire; rule, reign; command, sway; imperial dignity; arrogance, haughtiness. *Fig. Inf.* **valer un i.,** to be priceless

imperioso /impe'rioso/ *a* imperious

imperito /impe'rito/ *a* inexpert; clumsy, unskilled

impermeabilidad /impermeaβili'ðað/ *f,* watertightness; imperviousness; impermeability

impermeabilizar /impermeaβili'θar; impermeaβili'sar/ *vt* to waterproof

impermeable /imperme'aβle/ *a* watertight, impermeable; impervious. *m,* raincoat, mackintosh

impersonal /imperso'nal/ *a* impersonal

impertérrito /imper'territo/ *a* unafraid, dauntless

impertinencia /impertinen'θia; impertinen'sia/ *f,* impertinence, insolence; peevishness; fancy, whim; overexactness, meticulousness; interference, intrusion

impertinente /imperti'nente/ *a* impertinent; irrelevant; inopportune; officious, interfering

impertinentes /imperti'nentes/ *m pl,* lorgnettes

imperturbabilidad /imperturβaβili'ðað/ *f,* imperturbability

imperturbable /impertur'βaβle/ *a* calm, imperturbable

impetrar /impe'trar/ *vt* to obtain by entreaty; implore

ímpetu /'impetu/ *m,* impetus, momentum; speed, swiftness; violence

impetuosidad /impetuosi'ðað/ *f,* impetuosity

impetuoso /impe'tuoso/ *a* impetuous; precipitate

impiedad /impie'ðað/ *f,* cruelty, harshness; irreligion

impío /im'pio/ *a* impious, wicked; irreverent, irreligious

implacabilidad /implakaβili'ðað/ *f,* implacability, relentless

implacable /impla'kaβle/ *a* implacable

implantación /implanta'θion; implanta'sion/ *f,* inculcation, implantation

implantar /implan'tar/ *vt* to inculcate, implant (ideas, etc.)

implicación /implika'θion; implika'sion/ *f,* implication; contradiction (in terms); complicity

implicar /impli'kar/ *vt* to implicate, imply, infer; involve, entangle; —*vi* imply contradiction (gen. with negatives)

implicatorio /implika'torio/ *a* contradictory; implicated (in crime)

implícito /im'pliθito; im'plisito/ *a* implicit; implied

implorante /implo'rante/ *a* imploring

implorar /implo'rar/ *vt* to implore, entreat

implume /im'plume/ *a* without feathers, unfeathered

impolítico /impo'litiko/ *a* impolitic; unwise, inexpedient; tactless

impoluto /impo'luto/ *a* unpolluted, spotless, pure

imponderabilidad /imponderaβili'ðað/ *f,* imponderability

imponderable /imponde'raβle/ *a* imponderable, immeasurable; most excellent

imponente /impo'nente/ *a* imposing; awe-inspiring

imponer /impo'ner/ *vt irr* to exact; impose; malign, accuse falsely; instruct, acquaint; *Fig.* impress (with respect, etc.); invest or deposit (money); *Print.* impose; give, bestow (a name) —*vr* assert oneself. See **poner**

imponible /impo'niβle/ *a* taxable; ratable

impopular /impopu'lar/ *a* unpopular

impopularidad /impopulari'ðað/ *f,* unpopularity

importable /impor'taβle/ *a* importable

importación /importa'θion; importa'sion/ *f, Com.* importation; import

importador /importa'ðor/ **(-ra)** *a* import, importing —*n* importer
importancia /impor'tanθia; impor'tansia/ *f*, importance; magnitude
importante /impor'tante/ *a* important
importar /impor'tar/ *vi* to matter; be important; concern, interest; —*vt* amount to; import; include, comprise. **¡No importa!** It doesn't matter! Never mind!
importe /im'porte/ *m*, amount; value, cost. **i. bruto,** gross or total amount. **i. líquido** *or* **neto,** net amount
importunación /importuna'θion; importuna'sion/ *f*, importuning; importunity
importunadamente /importunaða'mente/ *adv* importunately
importunar /importu'nar/ *vt* to importune, pester
importunidad /importuni'ðað/ (*also* **importunación**) *f*, importunity
importuno /impor'tuno/ *a* importunate, inopportune, ill-timed; persistent; tedious
imposibilidad /imposiβili'ðað/ *f*, impossibility
imposibilitado /imposiβili'taðo/ *a* disabled, crippled; incapable, unable
imposibilitar /imposiβili'tar/ *vt* to disable; render unable; make impossible
imposible /impo'siβle/ *a* impossible
imposición /imposi'θion; imposi'sion/ *f*, imposition; exaction; tax, duty, tribute; *Print.* makeup **i. de manos,** *Eccl.* laying on of hands
impostor /impos'tor/ **(-ra)** *n* impostor
impostura /impos'tura/ *f*, swindle, imposture; aspersion, slur, imputation
impotable /impo'taβle/ *a* undrinkable
impotencia /impo'tenθia; impo'tensia/ *f*, impotence
impotente /impo'tente/ *a* impotent; powerless
impracticabilidad /impraktikaβili'ðað/ *f*, impracticability; impassability (of roads, etc.)
impracticable /imprakti'kaβle/ *a* impracticable; impossible; impassable (roads, etc.)
imprecación /impreka'θion; impreka'sion/ *f*, imprecation; curse, malediction
imprecar /impre'kar/ *vt* to imprecate, curse
impregnación /impregna'θion; impregna'sion/ *f*, impregnation, permeation, saturation
impregnar /impreg'nar/ *vt* impregnate; to permeate; —*vr* become impregnated
impremeditado /impremeði'taðo/ *a* unpremeditated
imprenta /im'prenta/ *f*, printing; printing house or office; print; letterpress
impreparación /imprepara'θion; imprepara'sion/ *f*, unpreparedness
imprescindible /impresθin'diβle; impressin'diβle/ *a* indispensable, essential
impresión /impre'sion/ *f*, printing; impression; effect; influence; imprint, stamp; *Print.* impression; print. **impresión digital,** fingerprint
impresionable /impresio'naβle/ *a* impressionable, susceptible
impresionante /impresio'nante/ *a* imposing; moving, affecting
impresionar /impresio'nar/ *vt* to impress; affect; fix in the mind; *Fig.* move deeply, stir; (*Radio.* cinema) record
impresionismo /impresio'nismo/ *m*, impressionism
impresionista /impresio'nista/ *mf* impressionist —*a* impressionistic
impreso /im'preso/ *m*, (gen. *pl*) printed matter
impresor /impre'sor/ *m*, printer
imprevisión /impreβi'sion/ *f*, lack of foresight; improvidence
imprevisto /impre'βisto/ *a* unforeseen, unexpected, sudden
imprevistos /impre'βistos/ *m pl*, incidental expenses
imprimación /imprima'θion; imprima'sion/ *f*, priming (of paint, etc.)
imprimar /impri'mar/ *vt* to prime (of paint)
imprimir /impri'mir/ *vt* to print; stamp; impress upon (the mind)
improbabilidad /improβaβili'ðað/ *f*, improbability
improbable /impro'βaβle/ *a* improbable
improbo /im'proβo/ *a* vicious, corrupt, dishonest; hard, arduous

improductivo /improðuk'tiβo/ *a* unproductive; unprofitable, fruitless
impronta /im'pronta/ *f*, *Art.* cast, mold
impronunciable /impronun'θiaβle; impronun'siaβle/ *a* unpronounceable; ineffable
improperio /impro'perio/ *m*, insult, affront
impropiedad /impropie'ðað/ *f*, inappropriateness; unsuitableness; impropriety
impropio /im'propio/ *a* unsuitable; inappropriate; inadequate; improper
improporcionado /improporθio'naðo; improporsio'naðo/ *a* disproportionate, out of proportion
impróvido /im'proβiðo/ *a* improvident, heedless
improvisación /improβisa'θion; improβisa'sion/ *f*, improvisation
improvisador /improβisa'ðor/ **(-ra)** *n* improviser
improvisamente /improβisa'mente/ *adv* unexpectedly, suddenly
improvisar /improβi'sar/ *vt* to improvise
improviso, improvisto /impro'βiso, impro'βisto/ *a* unexpected, unforeseen. **al** (*or* **de**) **improviso,** unexpectedly
imprudencia /impru'ðenθia; impru'ðensia/ *f*, imprudence, rashness, indiscretion
imprudente /impru'ðente/ *a* imprudent, unwise, rash
impúbero /im'puβero/ *a* below the age of puberty
impudencia /impu'ðenθia; impu'ðensia/ *f*, impudence, impertinence
impudente /impu'ðente/ *a* brazen, impudent
impudicia /impu'ðiθia; impu'ðisia/ *f*, immodesty, brazenness
impúdico /im'puðiko/ *a* immodest, brazen
impuesto /im'puesto/ *m*, tax; duty. **i. de utilidades,** income tax. **i. sucesorio,** inheritance tax
impugnable /impug'naβle/ *a* impugnable, refutable
impugnación /impugna'θion; impugna'sion/ *f*, refutation; contradiction
impugnar /impug'nar/ *vt* to refute, contradict; oppose; criticize
impulsar /impul'sar/ *vt* to impel; prompt, cause; drive, operate, propel
impulsión /impul'sion/ *f*, impulse; impetus; *Mech.* operation, driving; propulsion
impulsivo /impul'siβo/ *a* impulsive; irreflexive, precipitate
impulso /im'pulso/ *m*, stimulus, incitement; impulse, desire; *Mech.* drive, impulse
impulsor /impul'sor/ **(-ra)** *a* driving, impelling —*n* driver, operator
impune /im'pune/ *a* unpunished
impunemente /impune'mente/ *adv* with impunity
impunidad /impuni'ðað/ *f*, impunity
impureza /impu'reθa; impu'resa/ *f*, impurity; lack of chastity; obscenity, indecency
impurificar /impurifi'kar/ *vt* to defile; make impure; adulterate
impuro /im'puro/ *a* impure; adulterated; polluted; immoral, unchaste
imputable /impu'taβle/ *a* imputable
imputación /imputa'θion; imputa'sion/ *f*, imputation
imputador /imputa'ðor/ **(-ra)** *n* imputer, attributer
imputar /impu'tar/ *vt* to impute; attribute
inacabable /inaka'βaβle/ *a* endless, interminable, ceaseless; wearisome
inaccesibilidad /inakθesiβili'ðað; inaksesiβili'ðað/ *f*, inaccessibility
inaccesible /inakθe'siβle; inakse'siβle/ *a* inaccessible; incomprehensible
inacción /inak'θion; inak'sion/ *f*, inaction
inaceptable /inaθep'taβle; inasep'taβle/ *a* unacceptable
inactividad /inaktiβi'ðað/ *f*, inactivity; quiescence; idleness
inactivo /inak'tiβo/ *a* inactive; idle; unemployed; *Naut.* laid-up
inadaptable /inaðap'taβle/ *a* inadaptable
inadecuado /inaðe'kuaðo/ *a* inadequate, insufficient
inadmisible /inaðmi'siβle/ *a* inadmissible

inadvertencia /inaðβer'tenθia; inaðβer'tensia/ *f,* inadvertence; oversight, mistake, slip

inadvertido /inaðβer'tiðo/ *a* unnoticed; inattentive; inadvertent, unintentional; negligent

inafectado /inafek'taðo/ *a* unaffected, natural

inagotable /inago'taβle/ *a* inexhaustible, unfailing; abundant

inaguantable /inaguan'taβle/ *a* unbearable, intolerable

inajenable /inahe'naβle/ *a* inalienable

inalámbrica /ina'lambrika/ *f,* radio station

inalienable /inalie'naβle/ *a* inalienable

inalterable /inalte'raβle/ *a* unalterable

inamovibilidad /inamoβiβili'ðað/ *f,* immovability

inamovible /inamo'βiβle/ *a* immovable

inanición /inani'θion; inani'sion/ *f,* inanition

inanimado /inani'maðo/ *a* inanimate

inapagable /inapa'gaβle/ *a* inextinguishable

inapelable /inape'laβle/ *a* unappealable; irremediable, inevitable

inapetencia /inape'tenθia; inape'tensia/ *f,* lack of appetite

inaplazable /inapla'θaβle; inapla'saβle/ *a* undeferable, unable to be postponed

inaplicable /inapli'kaβle/ *a* inapplicable

inaplicación /inaplika'θion; inaplika'sion/ *f,* laziness, inattention, negligence

inaplicado /inapli'kaðo/ *a* lazy; inattentive; careless

inapreciable /inapre'θiaβle; inapre'siaβle/ *a* inappreciable; invaluable

inarmónico /inar'moniko/ *a* unharmonious, discordant

inarticulado /inartiku'laðo/ *a* inarticulate

inasequible /inase'kiβle/ *a* unattainable; out of reach

inaudible /inau'ðiβle/ *a* inaudible

inaudito /inau'ðito/ *a* unheard of, unprecedented; extraordinary, strange

inauguración /inaugura'θion; inaugura'sion/ *f,* inauguration; induction; inception, commencement

inaugural /inaugu'ral/ *a* inaugural

inaugurar /inaugu'rar/ *vt* to inaugurate; induct

inaveriguable /inaβeri'guaβle/ *a* unascertainable

inca /'inka/ *mf* Inca

incaico /in'kaiko/ *a* Incan

incalculable /inkalku'laβle/ *a* incalculable; innumerable

incalificable /inkalifi'kaβle/ *a* indescribable, unclassable; vile

incandescencia /inkandes'θenθia; inkandes'sensia/ *f,* incandescence, white heat

incandescente /inkandes'θente; inkandes'sente/ *a* incandescent

incansable /inkan'saβle/ *a* indefatigable; unflagging; unwearying

incapacidad /inkapaθi'ðað; inkapasi'ðað/ *f,* incapacity; incompetence

incapacitar /inkapaθi'tar; inkapasi'tar/ *vt* to incapacitate; disable

incapaz /inka'paθ; inka'pas/ *a* incapable, incompetent; inefficient

incasable /inka'saβle/ *a* unmarriageable; antimarriage

incautarse /inkau'tarse/ *vr* to seize, take possession (of)

incauto /in'kauto/ *a* incautious; unwary

incendiar /inθen'diar; insen'diar/ *vt* to set on fire, set alight

incendiario /inθen'diario; insen'diario/ **(-ia)** *a* and *n* incendiary

incendiarismo /inθendia'rismo; insendia'rismo/ *m,* incendiarism

incendio /in'θendio; in'sendio/ *m,* conflagration, fire; consuming passion

incensar /inθen'sar; insen'sar/ *vt irr Eccl.* to cense, incense; flatter. See **acertar**

incensario /inθen'sario; insen'sario/ *m,* incense burner, incensory

incentivo /inθen'tiβo; insen'tiβo/ *m,* incentive; encouragement

incertidumbre /inθerti'ðumbre; inserti'ðumbre/ *f,* uncertainty, incertitude

incesable, incesante /inθe'saβle, inθe'sante; inse'saβle, inse'sante/ *a* incessant, continuous

incesto /in'θesto; in'sesto/ *m,* incest

incestuoso /inθes'tuoso; inses'tuoso/ *a* incestuous

incidencia /inθi'ðenθia; insi'ðensia/ *f,* incidence

incidental /inθiðen'tal; insiðen'tal/ *a* incidental

incidente /inθi'ðente; insi'ðente/ *a* incidental. *m,* incident, event, occurrence

incidir /inθi'ðir; insi'ðir/ *vi (with en)* to incur, fall into (e.g. *Incidió en el pecado,* He fell into sin)

incienso /in'θienso; in'sienso/ *m,* incense; flattery

incierto /in'θierto; in'sierto/ *a* untrue, false; uncertain; unknown

incineración /inθinera'θion; insinera'sion/ *f,* incineration

incinerador /inθinera'ðor; insinera'ðor/ *m,* incinerator

incinerar /inθine'rar; insine'rar/ *vt* incinerate, reduce to ashes

incipiente /inθi'piente; insi'piente/ *a* incipient

incircunciso /inθirkun'θiso; insirkun'siso/ *a* uncircumcised

incisión /inθi'sion; insi'sion/ *f,* incision

incisivo /inθi'siβo; insi'siβo/ *a* sharp, keen; incisive, sarcastic, caustic

inciso /in'θiso; in'siso/ *m,* clause; comma

incitación /inθita'θion; insita'sion/ *f,* incitement; *Fig.* spur, stimulus

incitar /inθi'tar; insi'tar/ *vt* to incite; stimulate, encourage

incivil /inθi'βil; insi'βil/ *a* rude, discourteous, uncivil

incivilidad /inθiβili'ðað; insiβili'ðað/ *f,* rudeness, incivility

inclasificable /inklasifi'kaβle/ *a* unclassifiable

inclemencia /inkle'menθia; inkle'mensia/ *f,* harshness, severity; inclemency (of the weather). **a la i.,** at the mercy of the elements

inclemente /inkle'mente/ *a* inclement

inclinación /inklina'θion; inklina'sion/ *f,* inclination; slope; slant; tendency, propensity; predilection, fondness; bow (in greeting); *Geom.* inclination

inclinar /inkli'nar/ *vt* to incline, tilt, slant; bow; bend; influence; persuade; —*vi* resemble; —*vr* lean; stoop; tilt; tend, incline (to), view favorably (e.g. *Me inclino a creerlo,* I am inclined to believe it)

ínclito /in'klito/ *a* famous, celebrated

incluir /in'kluir/ *vt irr* to comprise, embrace, contain; include, take into account. See **huir**

inclusa /in'klusa/ *f,* foundling home

inclusión /inklu'sion/ *f,* inclusion; relationship, intercourse, friendship

inclusive /inklu'siβe/ *adv* including

inclusivo /inklu'siβo/ *a* inclusive

incluso /in'kluso/ *adv* including, inclusive —*prep* even

incoar /inko'ar/ *vt* to begin (especially lawsuits)

incoativo /inkoa'tiβo/ *a* inceptive

incobrable /inko'βraβle/ *a* irrecoverable; irredeemable

incógnita /in'kognita/ *f, Math.* X; unknown quantity; secret motive; unknown lady

incógnito /in'kognito/ *a* unknown. *m,* incognito, assumed name, disguise

incoherencia /inkoe'renθia; inkoe'rensia/ *f,* incoherence

incoherente /inkoe'rente/ *a* incoherent, disconnected, illogical

íncola /'inkola/ *mf* resident, dweller, inhabitant

incoloro /inko'loro/ *a* colorless, uncolored

incólume /in'kolume/ *a* unharmed, unscathed; untouched, undamaged

incombustibilidad /inkombustiβili'ðað/ *f,* incombustibility

incommensurabilidad /inkommensuraβili'ðað/ *f,* incommensurability

incommutable /inkommu'taβle/ *a* unalterable, immutable, unchangeable

incomodar /inkomo'ðar/ *vt* to disturb, incommode, inconvenience; annoy; —*vr* disturb oneself, put oneself out; grow angry. **¡No se incomode!** Please don't move!; Please don't be angry!

incomodidad /inkomoðiˈðað/ *f*, discomfort; inconvenience; trouble, upset; annoyance
incómodo /inˈkomoðo/ *a* uncomfortable; inconvenient; troublesome, tiresome. *m*, discomfort; inconvenience
incomparable /inkompaˈraβle/ *a* incomparable
incompartible /inkomparˈtiβle/ *a* indivisible
incompasivo /inkompaˈsiβo/ *a* unsympathetic, hard
incompatibilidad /inkompatiβiliˈðað/ *f*, incompatibility
incompatible /inkompaˈtiβle/ *a* incompatible
incompetencia /inkompeˈtenθia; inkompeˈtensia/ *f*, incompetence
incompetente /inkompeˈtente/ *a* incompetent
incomplejo, **incomplexo** /inkomˈplexo, inkomˈplekso/ *a* noncomplex, simple
incompleto /inkomˈpleto/ *a* incomplete
incomponible /inkompoˈniβle/ *a* unrepairable, unmendable
incomprensibilidad /inkomprensiβiliˈðað/ *f*, incomprehensibility
incomprensible /inkomprenˈsiβle/ *a* incomprehensible
incomprensión /inkomprenˈsion/ *f*, incomprehension
incomunicado /inkomuniˈkaðo/ *a* in solitary confinement (of a prisoner)
incomunicar /inkomuniˈkar/ *vt* to sentence to solitary confinement; isolate, deprive of means of communication; —*vr* become a recluse
inconcebible /inkonθeˈβiβle; inkonseβiβle/ *a* inconceivable
inconciliable /inkonθiˈliaβle; inkonsiˈliaβle/ *a* irreconcilable
incondicional /inkondiθioˈnal; inkondisioˈnal/ *a* unconditional
inconexión /inkoneˈksion/ *f*, disconnectedness
inconexo /inkoneˈkso/ *a* unconnected; incoherent
inconfeso /inkonˈfeso/ *a* unconfessed
incongruencia /inkoŋgruˈenθia; inkoŋgruˈensia/ *f*, incongruity
incongruente /inkoŋgruˈente/ *a* incongruous, inappropriate
inconmovible /inkomoˈβiβle/ *a* immovable; unflinching, unshakable
inconquistable /inkonkisˈtaβle/ *a* unconquerable; *Fig.* resolute, inflexible
inconsciencia /inkonˈsθienθia; inkonssiensia/ *f*, unconsciousness; subconscious
inconsciente /inkonˈsθiente; inkonsˈsiente/ *a* unconscious, involuntary; subconscious
inconsecuencia /inkonseˈkuenθia; inkonseˈkuensia/ *f*, inconsequence; inconsistency
inconsecuente /inkonseˈkuente/ *a* inconsequential; inconsistent
inconsideración /inkonsiðeraˈθion; inkonsiðeraˈsion/ *f*, thoughtlessness
inconsiderado /inkonsiðeˈraðo/ *a* thoughtless; heedless, selfish
inconsiguiente /inkonsiˈgiente/ *a* illogical, inconsistent
inconsistencia /inkonsisˈtenθia; inkonsisˈtensia/ *f*, inconsistency
inconsistente /inkonsisˈtente/ *a* inconsistent
inconsolable /inkonsoˈlaβle/ *a* inconsolable
inconstancia /inkonsˈtanθia; inkonsˈtansia/ *f*, inconstancy, infidelity
inconstante /inkonsˈtante/ *a* inconstant, fickle
inconstitucional /inkonstituθioˈnal; inkonstitusioˈnal/ *a* unconstitutional
incontaminado /inkontamiˈnaðo/ *a* uncontaminated
incontestable /inkontesˈtaβle/ *a* undeniable, unquestionable
incontinencia /inkontiˈnenθia; inkontiˈnensia/ *f*, incontinence
incontinente /inkontiˈnente/ *a* incontinent
incontrastable /inkontrasˈtaβle/ *a* insuperable, invincible; undeniable, unanswerable; *Fig.* unshakable, inconvincible
incontrovertible /inkontroβerˈtiβle/ *a* undeniable, incontrovertible

inconvencible /inkombenˈθiβle; inkombenˈsiβle/ *a* inconvincible
inconveniencia /inkombeˈnienθia; inkombeˈniensia/ *f*, discomfort; inconvenience; unsuitability
inconveniente /inkombeˈniente/ *a* awkward, inconvenient; uncomfortable; inappropriate. *m*, inconvenience; obstacle, impediment; disadvantage
inconvertible /inkomberˈtiβle/ *a* inconvertible
incorporación /inkorporaˈθion; inkorporaˈsion/ *f*, incorporation
incorporar /inkorpoˈrar/ *vt* to incorporate; cause to sit up, lift up; —*vr* sit up, raise oneself; become a member, join (associations); be incorporated; blend, mix
incorporeidad /inkorporeiˈðað/ *f*, incorporeity
incorpóreo /inkorˈporeo/ *a* incorporeal; immaterial
incorrección /inkorrekˈθion; inkorrekˈsion/ *f*, incorrectness; indecorum, impropriety
incorrecto /inkoˈrrekto/ *a* incorrect; indecorous, unbecoming, improper
incorregible /inkorreˈxiβle/ *a* incorrigible
incorrupción /inkorrupˈθion; inkorrupˈsion/ *f*, incorruption; purity; integrity; wholesomeness
incorrupto /inkoˈrrupto/ *a* incorrupt; pure; chaste
incredibilidad /inkreðiβiliˈðað/ *f*, incredibility
incredulidad /inkreðuliˈðað/ *f*, incredulity, scepticism
incrédulo /inˈkreðulo/ **(-la)** *a* incredulous; atheistic —*n* atheist; unbeliever, sceptic
increíble /inkreˈiβle/ *a* incredible; marvelous, extraordinary
incremento /inkreˈmento/ *m*, increment, increase
increpación /inkrepaˈθion; inkrepaˈsion/ *f*, scolding, harsh rebuke
increpar /inkreˈpar/ *vt* to scold, rebuke harshly
incriminante /inkrimiˈnante/ *a* incriminating
incriminar /inkrimiˈnar/ *vt* to incriminate, accuse; exaggerate (a charge, etc.)
incruento /inkruˈento/ *a* bloodless, unstained with blood
incrustación /inkrustaˈθion; inkrustaˈsion/ *f*, incrustation; *Art.* inlay
incubación /inkuβaˈθion; inkuβaˈsion/ *f*, hatching; *Med.* incubation
incubadora /inkuβaˈðora/ *f*, incubator (for chickens)
incubar /inkuˈβar/ *vi* to sit on eggs (of hens); —*vt* hatch; *Med.* incubate
inculcación /inkulkaˈθion; inkulkaˈsion/ *f*, inculcation, instillment
inculcar /inkulˈkar/ *vt* to press one thing against another; instill, inculcate; —*vr* grow more fixed in one's views
inculpable /inkulˈpaβle/ *a* blameless, innocent
inculpar /inkulˈpar/ *vt* to blame; accuse
incultivable /inkultiˈβaβle/ *a* uncultivatable; untillable
inculto /inˈkulto/ *a* uncultivated, untilled; uncultured; uncivilized
incultura /inkulˈtura/ *f*, lack of cultivation; lack of culture
incumbencia /inkumˈbenθia; inkumbensia/ *f*, obligation, moral responsibility, duty
incumbir /inkumˈbir/ *vi* to be incumbent on; concern
incumplimiento /inkumpliˈmiento/ *m*, nonfulfilment
incurable /inkuˈraβle/ *a* incurable; inveterate, hopeless
incuria /inˈkuria/ *f*, negligence, carelessness
incurioso /inkuˈrioso/ *a* incurious
incurrir /inkuˈrrir/ *vi* (*with en*) to fall into (error, etc.); incur (dislike, etc.)
incursión /inkurˈsion/ *f*, incursion; inroad
indagación /indagaˈθion; indagaˈsion/ *f*, investigation, inquiry
indagador /indagaˈðor/ **(-ra)** *a* investigating, inquiring —*n* investigator
indagar /indaˈgar/ *vt* to investigate, examine; inquire. **i. precios**, to inquire about prices
indebido /indeˈβiðo/ *a* undue, immoderate improper; illegal, illicit
indecencia /indeˈθenθia; indeˈsensia/ *f*, indecency; obscenity; impropriety

indecente /inde'θente; inde'sente/ *a* indecent; obscene; improper

indecible /inde'θiβle; inde'siβle/ *a* unutterable, ineffable, unspeakable

indeciso /inde'θiso; inde'siso/ *a* undecided; hesitant, irresolute; vague; noncommittal

indeclinable /indekli'naβle/ *a* obligatory; unavoidable; *Gram.* indeclinable, uninflected

indecoro /inde'koro/ *m,* impropriety, indecorum

indecoroso /indeko'roso/ *a* indecorous, unbecoming; base, mean

indefectible /indefek'tiβle/ *a* unfailing; perfect

indefectiblemente /indefektiβle'mente/ *adv* invariably

indefendible /indefen'diβle/ *a* indefensible

indefenso /inde'fenso/ *a* unprotected, defenseless

indefinible /indefi'niβle/ *a* indefinable, vague; indescribable

indefinido /indefi'niðo/ *a* indefinite, vague; undefined; *Gram.* indefinite

indeleble /inde'leβle/ *a* indelible

indeliberado /indeliβe'raðo/ *a* unpremeditated; unconsidered

indemme /in'demme/ *a* unharmed, undamaged

indemnidad /indemni'ðað/ *f,* indemnity

indemnización /indemniθa'θion; indemnisa'sion/ *f,* compensation, indemnification; indemnity

indemnizar /indemni'θar; indemni'sar/ *vt* to indemnify, compensate

indemostrable /indemo'straβle/ *a* indemonstrable, incapable of demonstration

independencia /indepen'denθia; indepen'densia/ *f,* independence

independiente /indepen'diente/ *a* independent; self-contained

indescifrable /indesθi'fraβle; indessi'fraβle/ *a* undecipherable; illegible

indestructible /indestruk'tiβle/ *a* indestructible

indeterminado /indetermi'naðo/ *a* indeterminate; vague, doubtful, uncertain; hesitant, irresolute; *Math.* indeterminate

indiano /in'diano/ **(-na)** *a* and *n* Indian; East Indian; West Indian. *m,* nouveau riche, one who returns rich from the Western Hemisphere

indicación /indika'θion; indika'sion/ *f,* indication; sign, evidence; intimation, hint

indicador /indika'ðor/ *a* indicative. *m,* indicator. **i. del nivel de gasolina,** gas gauge

indicar /indi'kar/ *vt* to indicate; show; point out; simply, suggest; intimate

indicativo /indika'tiβo/ *a* indicative —*a* and *m, Gram.* indicative

índice /'indiθe; 'indise/ *m,* index; indication, sign; library catalog; catalog room; hand (of a clock); pointer, needle (of instruments); gnomon (of a sundial); *Math.* index; forefinger. **I. expurgatorio,** the Index

indicio /in'diθio; in'disio/ *m,* indication; sign; evidence. **indicios vehementes,** circumstantial evidence

índico /'indiko/ *a* Indian

indiferencia /indife'renθia; indife'rensia/ *f,* indifference

indiferente /indife'rente/ *a* indifferent

indígena /in'dihena/ *a* native, indigenous. *mf* native

indigencia /indi'henθia; indi'hensia/ *f,* destitution, indigence; impecuniosity

indigente /indi'hente/ *a* destitute, indigent; impecunious

indigestión /indihes'tion/ *f,* indigestion

indigesto /indi'hesto/ *a* indigestible; *Lit.* muddled, confused; unsociable, brusque

indignación /indigna'θion; indigna'sion/ *f,* indignation, anger

indignado /indig'naðo/ *a* indignant

indignar /indig'nar/ *vt* to anger, make indignant; —*vr* grow angry

indignidad /indigni'ðað/ *f,* unworthiness; indignity; personal affront

indigno /in'digno/ *a* unworthy; base, despicable

índigo /'indigo/ *m,* indigo

indio /'indio/ **(-ia)** *a* Indian; blue —*n* Indian. *m,* indium

indirecta /indi'rekta/ *f,* hint, covert suggestion, innuendo. *Inf.* **i. del padre Cobos,** strong hint

indirecto /indi'rekto/ *a* indirect

indisciplina /indisθi'plina; indissi'plina/ *f,* indiscipline

indisciplinado /indisθipli'naðo; indissipli'naðo/ *a* undisciplined

indiscreción /indiskre'θion; indiskre'sion/ *f,* indiscretion

indiscreto /indis'kreto/ *a* indiscreet

indiscutible /indisku'tiβle/ *a* unquestionable, undeniable

indisoluble /indiso'luβle/ *a* indissoluble

indispensable /indispen'saβle/ *a* indispensable

indisponer /indispo'ner/ *vt irr* to make unfit or incapable; indispose, make ill; (*with con* or *contra*) set against, make trouble with; —*vr* be indisposed; (*with con* or *contra*) quarrel with. See **poner**

indisposición /indisposi'θion; indisposi'sion/ *f,* reluctance, disinclination; indisposition, brief illness

indisputable /indispu'taβle/ *a* indisputable

indistinguible /indistiŋ'guiβle/ *a* undistinguishable

indistinto /indis'tinto/ *a* indistinct; indeterminate; vague

individual /indiβi'ðual/ *a* individual; peculiar, characteristic. *m,* (tennis) single

individualidad /indiβiðuali'ðað/ *f,* individuality

individualismo /indiβiðua'lismo/ *m,* individualism

individualista /indiβiðua'lista/ *a* individualistic. *mf* individualist

individuo /indi'βiðuo/ **(-ua)** *a* individual; indivisible. *m,* individual; member, associate; *Inf.* self —*n Inf.* person

indivisibilidad /indiβisiβili'ðað/ *f,* indivisibility

indivisible /indiβi'siβle/ *a* indivisible

indiviso /indi'βiso/ *a* undivided

indochino /indo'tʃino/ **(-na)** *a* and *n* Indochinese

indócil /in'doθil; in'dosil/ *a* unmanageable; disobedient; brittle, unpliable (of metals)

indocilidad /indoθili'ðað; indosili'ðað/ *f,* indocility; disobedience; brittleness (of metals)

indoeuropeo /indoeuro'peo/ *a* Indo-European

indoísmo /indo'ismo/ *m,* Hinduism

índole /'indole/ *f,* temperament, nature; kind, sort

indolencia /indo'lenθia; indo'lensia/ *f,* idleness, indolence

indolente /indo'lente/ *a* nonpainful; indifferent, insensible; idle, indolent

indoloro /indo'loro/ *a* painless

indomable /indo'maβle/ *a* untamable; invincible; indomitable; ungovernable, unmanageable

indomado /indo'maðo/ *a* untamed

indómito /in'domito/ *a* untamed; untamable; unmanageable, unruly; indomitable

indonesio /indo'nesio/ **(-ia)** *a* and *n* Indonesian

indostanés /indosta'nes/ *a* Hindustani

indostani /indos'tani/ *m,* Hindustani (language)

indubitable /induβi'taβle/ *a* unquestionable

inducción /induk'θion; induk'sion/ *f,* persuasion; *Phys.* induction

inducir /indu'θir; indu'sir/ *vt irr* to persuade, prevail upon; induce; infer, conclude. See **conducir**

inductivo, inductor /induk'tiβo, induk'tor/ *a* inductive

indudable /indu'ðaβle/ *a* indubitable

indulgencia /indul'henθia; indul'hensia/ *f,* overkindness, tenderness; *Eccl.* indulgence

indulgente /indul'hente/ *a* indulgent, tender; tolerant

indultar /indul'tar/ *vt* to pardon; exempt

indulto /in'dulto/ *m,* amnesty; exemption; forgiveness; *Eccl.* indult

indumentaria /indumen'taria/ *f,* clothing; outfit (of clothes)

industria /in'dustria/ *f,* assiduity, industriousness; pains, effort, ingenuity; industry. **i. pesada,** heavy industry. **i. cárnica,** meat industry. **i. extractivos,** mining industry

industrial /indus'trial/ *a* industrial. *m,* industrialist

industrialismo /industria'lismo/ *m,* industrialism

industrialización /industrialiθa'θion; industriali-sa'sion/ *f,* industrialization

industriar /indus'triar/ *vt* to teach, train; —*vr* find a way, manage, succeed in

industrioso /indus'trioso/ *a* industrious; diligent, assiduous

inédito /i'neðito/ *a* unpublished; unedited

inefable /ine'faβle/ *a* ineffable

ineficacia /inefi'kaθia; inefi'kasia/ *f,* inefficiency; ineffectiveness

ineficaz /inefi'kaθ; inefi'kas/ *a* ineffective; inefficient

ineludible /inelu'ðiβle/ *a* unavoidable

ineptitud /inepti'tuð/ *f,* ineptitude

inepto /i'nepto/ *a* inept, incompetent; unfit, unsuitable

inequívoco /ine'kiβoko/ *a* unequivocal

inercia /i'nerθia; i'nersia/ *f,* inertia

inerme /i'nerme/ *a* defenseless, unprotected; (*Bot. Zool.*) unarmed

inerte /i'nerte/ *a* inert

inescrutable /ineskru'taβle/ *a* inscrutable, unfathomable

inesperado /inespe'raðo/ *a* unexpected, sudden

inestabilidad /inestaβili'ðað/ *f,* instability

inestable /ines'taβle/ *a* unstable

inestimable /inesti'maβle/ *a* inestimable

inevitable /ineβi'taβle/ *a* inevitable

inexactitud /ineksakti'tuð/ *f,* inexactitude, inaccuracy; error, mistake

inexacto /ine'ksakto/ *a* inexact, inaccurate; erroneous

inexcusable /inieksku'saβle/ *a* inexcusable, unforgivable; indispensable

inexhausto /ineks'austo/ *a* inexhaustible

inexistente /ineksis'tente/ *a* nonexistent

inexorable /inekso'raβle/ *a* inexorable

inexperiencia /inekspe'rienθia; inekspe'riensia/ *f,* inexperience

inexperto /ineks'perto/ *a* inexperienced; inexpert

inexplicable /inekspli'kaβle/ *a* inexplicable

inexplorado /ineksplo'raðo/ *a* unexplored

inexplosible /ineksplo'siβle/ *a* inexplosive

inexpresivo /inekspre'siβo/ *a* inexpressive; reticent

inexpugnable /inekspug'naβle/ *a* impregnable; *Fig.* unshakable, firm; obstinate

inextinguible /inekstiŋ'guiβle/ *a* inextinguishable; everlasting, perpetual

infalibilidad /infaliβili'ðað/ *f,* infallibility

infalible /infa'liβle/ *a* infallible

infamación /infama'θion; infama'sion/ *f,* defamation

infamador /infama'ðor/ (**-ra**) *a* slandering —*n* slanderer

infamar /infa'mar/ *vt* to defame, slander

infame /in'fame/ *a* infamous, vile

infamia /in'famia/ *f,* infamy; baseness, vileness

infancia /in'fanθia; in'fansia/ *f,* infancy, babyhood; childhood

infanta /in'fanta/ *f,* female child under seven years; infanta, any Spanish royal princess; wife of a Spanish royal prince

infantado /infan'taðo/ *m,* land belonging to an *infante* or *infanta*

infante /in'fante/ *m,* male child under seven years; infante, any Spanish royal prince except an heir-apparent; infantryman. **i. de coro,** choir boy

infantería /infante'ria/ *f,* infantry

infanticida /infanti'θiða; infanti'siða/ *a* infanticidal. *mf* infanticide (person)

infanticidio /infanti'θiðio; infanti'siðio/ *m,* infanticide (act)

infantil /infan'til/ *a* infantile, babyish; innocent, candid

infatigable /infati'gaβle/ *a* unwearying, indefatigable

infatuación /infatua'θion; infatua'sion/ *f,* infatuation

infatuar /infa'tuar/ *vt* to infatuate; —*vr* become infatuated

infausto /in'fausto/ *a* unlucky, unfortunate

infección /infek'θion; infek'sion/ *f,* infection

infeccioso /infek'θioso; infek'sioso/ *a* infectious

infectar /infek'tar/ *vt* to infect; corrupt, pervert; —*vr* become infected; be corrupted

infecto /in'fekto/ *a* infected; corrupt, perverted; tainted

infecundidad /infekundi'ðað/ *f,* sterility

infecundo /infe'kundo/ *a* sterile, barren

infelice /infe'liθe; infe'lise/ *a Poet.* unhappy, unfortunate

infelicidad /infeliθi'ðað; infelisi'ðað/ *f,* unhappiness

infeliz /infe'liθ; infe'lis/ *a* unhappy; unfortunate; *Inf.* simple, good-hearted

inferencia /infe'renθia; infe'rensia/ *f,* inference, connection

inferior /infe'rior/ *a* inferior; lower; second-rate; subordinate. *mf* inferior, subordinate

inferioridad /inferiori'ðað/ *f,* inferiority

inferir /infe'rir/ *vt irr* to infer, deduce; involve, imply; occasion; inflict. See **sentir**

infernáculo /infer'nakulo/ *m,* hopscotch

infernal /infer'nal/ *a* infernal; devilish, fiendish; wicked, inhuman; *Inf.* confounded

inferno /in'ferno/ *a Poet.* infernal

infértil /in'fertil/ *a* infertile

infestación /infesta'θion; infesta'sion/ *f,* infestation

infestar /infes'tar/ *vt* to infest, swarm in; infect; injure, damage

infesto /in'festo/ *a Poet.* harmful, dangerous

inficionar /infiθio'nar; infisio'nar/ *vt* to infect; pervert, corrupt

infidelidad /infiðeli'ðað/ *f,* faithlessness, infidelity; disbelief in Christian religion; unbelievers, infidels

infidelísimo /infiðe'lisimo/, *a superl* **infiel** most disloyal; most incorrect; most incredulous, faithless

infidencia /infi'ðenθia; infi'ðensia/ *f,* disloyalty, faithlessness

infiel /in'fiel/ *a* unfaithful, disloyal; inaccurate, incorrect; infidel, unbelieving. *mf* infidel, nonbeliever

infierno /in'fierno/ *m,* hell; hades (gen. *pl*); *Fig. Inf.* inferno. **en el quinto i.,** very far off, at the end of the world. **en los quintos infiernos,** at the end of nowhere

infiltración /infiltra'θion; infiltra'sion/ *f,* infiltration; inculcation, implantation

infiltrar /infil'trar/ *vt* to infiltrate; imbue, inculcate

ínfimo /'infimo/ *a* lowest; meanest, vilest, most base; cheapest, poorest (in quality)

infinidad /infini'ðað/ *f,* infinity; infinitude; great number

infinitivo /infini'tiβo/ *a* and *m, Gram.* infinitive

infinito /infi'nito/ *a* infinite; endless; boundless; countless. *m, Math.* infinite —*adv* excessively, immensely

infinitud /infini'tuð/ *f,* See **infinidad**

inflación /infla'θion; infla'sion/ *f,* inflation; distension; pride, vanity

inflacionismo /inflaθio'nismo; inflasio'nismo/ *m,* inflationism

inflacionista /inflaθio'nista; inflasio'nista/ *mf* inflationist

inflamabilidad /inflamaβili'ðað/ *f,* inflammability

inflamable /infla'maβle/ *a* inflammable

inflamación /inflama'θion; inflama'sion/ *f,* inflammation; *Engin.* ignition

inflamador /inflama'ðor/ *a* inflammatory

inflamar /infla'mar/ *vt* to set on fire; *Fig.* inflame, excite; —*vr* take fire; *Med.* become inflamed; grow hot or excited

inflamatorio /inflama'torio/ *a Med.* inflammatory

inflar /in'flar/ *vt* to inflate; blow up, distend; throw out (one's chest); exaggerate; make haughty or vain; —*vr* be swollen or inflated; be puffed up with pride

inflexibilidad /infleksiβili'ðað/ *f,* inflexibility; rigidity; immovability, constancy

inflexible /infle'ksiβle/ *a* inflexible

inflexión /infle'ksion/ *f,* bending, flexion; diffraction (optics); inflection

infligir /infli'hir/ *vt* to impose, inflict (penalties)

influencia /influ'enθia; influ'ensia/ *f,* influence; power, authority; *Elec.* charge

influir /in'fluir/ *vt irr* to influence; affect; (*with en*) cooperate in, assist with. See **huir**

influjo /in'fluho/ *m*, influence; flux, inflow of the tide

influyente /influ'yente/ *a* influential

infolio /in'folio/ *m*, folio

información /informa'θion; informa'sion/ *f*, information; legal inquiry; report; research, investigation

informador /informa'ðor/ **(-ra)** *a* informing, acquainting —*n* informant

informal /infor'mal/ *a* informal, irregular; unreliable (of persons); unconventional

informalidad /informali'ðað/ *f*, irregularity; unconventionality; unreliability

informante /infor'mante/ *mf* informant

informar /infor'mar/ *vt* to inform, acquaint with; —*vi Law*. plead; —*vr* (*with de, en, or sobre*) find out about, investigate

informática /infor'matika/ *f*, information sciences

informativo /informa'tiβo/ *a* informative

informe /in'forme/ *a* formless, shapeless. *m*, report, statement; information; *Law*. plea; *pl* data, particulars; references

infortificable /infortifi'kaβle/ *a* unfortifiable

infortuna /infor'tuna/ *f*, *Astrol*. evil influence

infortunado /infortu'naðo/ *a* unfortunate

infortunio /infor'tunio/ *m*, misfortune; unhappiness; adversity; mischance, ill luck

infracción /infrak'θion; infrak'sion/ *f*, transgression, infringement

infracto /in'frakto/ *a* imperturbable

infractor /infrak'tor/ **(-ra)** *a* infringing —*n* transgressor, infringer

infrangible /infran'hiβle/ *a* unbreakable

infranqueable /infranke'aβle/ *a* insuperable, unsurmountable

infrarrojo /infra'rroho/ *a* infrared

infrascrito /infras'krito/ *a* undersigned; undermentioned

infrecuente /infre'kuente/ *a* infrequent

infringir /infrin'hir/ *vt* to infringe, transgress, break

infructífero /infruk'tifero/ *a* unfruitful; worthless, useless

infructuosidad /infruktuosi'ðað/ *f*, unfruitfulness; worthlessness, uselessness

infructuoso /infruk'tuoso/ *a* fruitless; useless, worthless

infumable /infu'maβle/ *a* unsmokable (of tobacco)

infundado /infun'daðo/ *a* unfounded, groundless

infundio /in'fundio/ *m*, *Inf*. nonsense, untruth

infundir /infun'dir/ *vt* to infuse, imbue with

infusión /infu'sion/ *f*, infusion

ingeniar /inhe'niar/ *vt* to devise, concoct, plan; —*vr* contrive, find a way, manage

ingeniería /inhenie'ria/ *f*, engineering

ingeniero /inhe'niero/ *m*, engineer. **i. agrónomo**, agricultural engineer. **i. de caminos, canales y puertos**, civil engineer. **i. radiotelegrafista**, radio engineer. **cuerpo de ingenieros**, royal engineers

ingenio /in'henio/ *m*, mind; inventive capacity; imaginative talent; man of genius; talent, cleverness; ingeniousness; machine; guillotine (bookbinding)

ingeniosidad /inheniosi'ðað/ *f*, ingeniousness; witticism, clever remark

ingenioso /inhe'nioso/ *a* talented, clever; ingenious

ingénito /in'henito/ *a* unengendered, unconceived; innate, inborn

ingente /in'hente/ *a* huge, enormous

ingenuidad /inhenui'ðað/ *f*, ingenuousness, naiveté

ingenuo /in'henuo/ *a* ingenuous, naive, artless, unaffected

Inglaterra /iŋgla'terra/ England

inglés /iŋ'gles/ **(-esa)** *a* English; British —*n* Englishman; Briton. *m*, English (language); *Inf*. creditor. **a la inglesa**, in English fashion. **marcharse a la inglesa**, *Inf*. to take French leave

inglesismo /iŋgle'sismo/ *m*, Anglicism

ingobernable /iŋgoβer'naβle/ *a* ungovernable, unruly

ingratitud /iŋgrati'tuð/ *f*, ingratitude

ingrato /iŋ'grato/ *a* ungrateful; irksome, thankless; disagreeable

ingrávido /iŋ'graβiðo/ *a* light weight

ingrediente /iŋgre'ðiente/ *m*, ingredient

ingresar /iŋgre'sar/ *vi* to return, come in (money); (*with en*) join, become a member of, enter

ingreso /iŋ'greso/ *m*, joining, entering, admission; *Com*. money received; opening, commencement; *pl* earnings, takings, revenue

ingurgitación /iŋgurhita'θion; iŋgurhita'sion/ *f*, *Med*. ingurgitation

ingurgitar /iŋgurhi'tar/ *vt* to ingurgitate, swallow

inhábil /in'aβil/ *a* unskillful; unpracticed; incompetent, unfit; unsuitable, ill-chosen

inhabilidad /inaβili'ðað/ *f*, unskillfulness; incompetence; unsuitability; inability

inhabilitación /inaβilita'θion; inaβilita'sion/ *f*, incapacitation; disqualification; disablement

inhabilitar /inaβili'tar/ *vt* to make ineligible; disqualify; incapacitate, make unfit; —*vr* become ineligible; be incapacitated

inhabitable /inaβi'taβle/ *a* uninhabitable

inhabitado /inaβi'taðo/ *a* uninhabited, deserted

inhalación /inala'θion; inala'sion/ *f*, inhalation

inhalador /inala'ðor/ *m*, *Med*. inhaler

inhalar /ina'lar/ *vt* to inhale

inhallable /ina'ʎaβle; ina'yaβle/ *a* nowhere to be found, unfindable

inhereditable /inereði'taβle/ *a* uninheritable

inherencia /ine'renθia; ine'rensia/ *f*, inherency

inherente /ine'rente/ *a* inherent, innate

inhestar /ines'tar/ *vt irr* to raise, lift up; erect. See **acertar**

inhibición /iniβi'θion; iniβi'sion/ *f*, inhibition

inhibir /ini'βir/ *vt Law*. to inhibit; —*vr* inhibit or restrain oneself. See **prohibir**

inhibitorio /iniβi'torio/ *a Law*. inhibitory

inhonesto /ino'nesto/ *a* indecent, obscene; immodest

inhospedable, inhospitalario /inospe'ðaβle, inospita'lario/ *a* inhospitable; bleak, uninviting; exposed

inhospitalidad /inospitali'ðað/ *f*, inhospitality

inhumación /inuma'θion; inuma'sion/ *f*, inhumation, burial

inhumadora /inuma'ðora/ *f*, crematory

inhumanidad /inumani'ðað/ *f*, inhumanity; brutality

inhumano /inu'mano/ *a* inhuman; brutal, barbarous

inhumar /inu'mar/ *vt* to bury, inter

iniciación /iniθia'θion; inisia'sion/ *f*, initiation

iniciador /iniθia'ðor; inisia'ðor/ **(-ra)** *a* initiating; —*n* initiator

inicial /ini'θial; ini'sial/ *a and f*, initial

iniciar /ini'θiar; ini'siar/ *vt* to initiate; admit, introduce; originate; —*vr* be initiated; *Eccl*. take minor or first orders

iniciativa /iniθia'tiβa; inisia'tiβa/ *f*, initiative

inicuo /ini'kuo/ *a* iniquitous, most unjust, wicked

inimaginable /inimahi'naβle/ *a* inconceivable

inimicísimo /inimi'θisimo; inimi'sisimo/ *a superl* **enemigo** most hostile

inimitable /inimi'taβle/ *a* inimitable

ininteligible /ininteli'hiβle/ *a* unintelligible

iniquidad /iniki'ðað/ *f*, iniquity, wickedness

injerir /inhe'rir/ *vt irr* to insert, place within, introduce; interpolate; —*vr* meddle. See **sentir**

injertar /inher'tar/ *vt Agr*. to graft

injerto /in'herto/ *m*, *Agr*. graft; grafting; grafted plant, briar, or tree

injuria /in'huria/ *f*, insult; slander; outrage; wrong, injustice; harm, damage

injuriador /inhuria'ðor/ **(-ra)** *a* insulting —*n* offender, persecutor

injuriar /inhu'riar/ *vt* to insult; slander; outrage; wrong, persecute; harm, damage

injurioso /inhu'rioso/ *a* insulting; slanderous; offensive, abusive; harmful

injusticia /inhus'tiθia; inhus'tisia/ *f*, injustice; lack of justice; unjust action

injustificable /inhustifi'kaβle/ *a* unjustifiable

injustificado /inhustifi'kaðo/ *a* unjustified

injusto /in'husto/ *a* unjust; unrighteous

inllevable /inʎe'βaβle; inye'βaβle/ *a* unbearable, intolerable

inmaculado /imaku'laðo/ *a* immaculate, pure

inmanejable /imane'haβle/ *a* unmanageable; uncontrollable

inmanencia /ima'nenθia; ima'nensia/ *f*, immanence

inmanente /ima'nente/ *a* immanent

inmarcesible, inmarchitable /imarθe'siβle, imartʃi'taβle; imarsesiβle, imartʃitaβle/ *a* unfading, imperishable

inmaterial /imate'rial/ *a* incorporeal; immaterial

inmaterialidad /imateriali'ðað/ *f*, incorporeity; immateriality

inmaturo /ima'turo/ *a* immature; unripe

inmediación /imeðia'θion; imeðia'sion/ *f*, nearness, proximity; contact; *pl* outskirts, neighborhood, environs

inmediatamente /imeðiata'mente/ *adv* near; immediately, at once

inmediato /ime'ðiato/ *a* adjoining, close, nearby; immediate, prompt

inmejorable /imeho'raβle/ *a* unsurpassable, unbeatable

inmemorable, inmemorial /imemo'raβle, imemo'rial/ *a* immemorial

inmensidad /imensi'ðað/ *f*, vastness, huge extent; infinity; infinite space; immensity; huge number

inmenso /i'menso/ *a* vast; infinite; immense; innumerable

inmensurable /imensu'raβle/ *a* immeasurable, incalculable

inmerecido /imere'θiðo; imere'siðo/ *a* undeserved, unmerited

inmérito /i'merito/ *a* wrongful, unjust

inmeritorio /imeri'torio/ *a* unmeritorious, unpraiseworthy

inmersión /imer'sion/ *f*, immersion; dip

inmigración /imigra'θion; imigra'sion/ *f*, immigration

inmigrante /imi'grante/ *a* and *mf* immigrant

inmigrar /imi'grar/ *vi* to immigrate

inminencia /imi'nenθia; imi'nensia/ *f*, imminence

inminente /imi'nente/ *a* imminent

inmiscuir /imis'kuir/ *vt* to mix; —*vr* meddle. May be conjugated regularly or like **huir**

inmisión /imi'sion/ *f*, inspiration

inmobiliario /imoβi'liario/ *a* concerning real estate

inmoble /i'moβle/ *a* immovable; motionless, immobile, stationary; *Fig.* unshakable, unflinching

inmoderación /imoðera'θion; imoðera'sion/ *f*, immoderateness, excess

inmoderado /imoðe'raðo/ *a* immoderate; unrestrained, excessive

inmodestia /imo'ðestia/ *f*, immodesty

inmodesto /imo'ðesto/ *a* immodest

inmolación /imola'θion; imola'sion/ *f*, immolation

inmolador /imola'ðor/ **(-ra)** *a* sacrificing —*n* immolator

inmolar /imo'lar/ *vt* to immolate; *Fig.* sacrifice, give up; —*vr Fig.* sacrifice oneself

inmoral /imo'ral/ *a* immoral

inmoralidad /imorali'ðað/ *f*, immorality

inmortal /imor'tal/ *a* immortal

inmortalidad /imortali'ðað/ *f*, immortality

inmortalizar /imortali'θar; imortali'sar/ *vt* to immortalize

inmotivado /imoti'βaðo/ *a* unfounded, without reason

inmoto /i'moto/ *a* motionless, stationary

inmóvil /i'moβil/ *a* immovable, fixed; motionless; steadfast, constant

inmovilidad /imoβili'ðað/ *f*, immovability; immobility; constancy, steadfastness

inmovilizar /imoβili'θar; imoβili'sar/ *vt* to immobilize

inmueble /i'mueβle/ *m*, *Law.* immovable estate

inmundicia /imun'diθia; imun'disia/ *f*, filth, nastiness; dirt; rubbish, refuse; obscenity, indecency

inmundo /i'mundo/ *a* dirty, filthy; obscene, indecent; unclean

inmune /i'mune/ *a* exempt; *Med.* immune

inmunidad /imuni'ðað/ *f*, exemption; immunity

inmunizar /imuni'θar; imuni'sar/ *vt* to immunize

inmutabilidad /imutaβili'ðað/ *f*, immutability, changelessness; imperturbability

inmutable /imu'taβle/ *a* immutable, unchangeable; imperturbable

inmutación /imuta'θion; imuta'sion/ *f*, change, alteration, difference

inmutar /imu'tar/ *vt* to change, alter, vary; —*vr* change one's expression (through fear, etc.)

innato /in'nato/ *a* innate; inherent; instinctive, inborn

innatural /innatu'ral/ *a* unnatural

innavegable /innaβe'gaβle/ *a* unnavigable; unseaworthy (of ships)

innecesario /inneθe'sario; innese'sario/ *a* unnecessary

innegable /inne'gaβle/ *a* undeniable; indisputable, irrefutable

innoble /in'noβle/ *a* plebeian; ignoble

innocuo /inno'kuo/ *a* harmless, innocuous

innovación /innoβa'θion; innoβa'sion/ *f*, innovation

innovador /innoβa'ðor/ **(-ra)** *a* innovatory —*n* innovator

innovar /inno'βar/ *vt* to introduce innovations

innumerabilidad /innumeraβili'ðað/ *f*, countless number, multitude

innumerable /innume'raβle/ *a* innumerable, countless

innúmero /in'numero/ *a* countless, innumerable

inobediencia /inoβe'ðienθia; inoβe'ðiensia/ *f*, disobedience

inobediente /inoβe'ðiente/ *a* disobedient

inobservable /inoβser'βaβle/ *a* unobservable

inobservancia /inoβser'βanθia; inoβser'βansia/ *f*, inobservance

inobservante /inoβser'βante/ *a* unobservant

inocencia /ino'θenθia; ino'sensia/ *f*, innocence; simplicity, candor; harmlessness

inocentada /inoθen'taða; inosen'taða/ *f*, *Inf.* naïve remark or action; fool's trap; practical joke

inocente /ino'θente; ino'sente/ *a* innocent; candid, simple; harmless; easily deceived

inocentón /inoθen'ton; inosen'ton/ *a* *Inf.* extremely credulous and easily taken in

inocuidad /inokui'ðað/ *f*, innocuousness

inoculación /inokula'θion; inokula'sion/ *f*, inoculation

inoculador /inokula'ðor/ *m*, inoculator

inocular /inoku'lar/ *vt* to inoculate; pervert, corrupt; contaminate

inodoro /ino'ðoro/ *a* odorless. *m*, toilet, lavatory

inofensivo /inofen'siβo/ *a* inoffensive, harmless

inolvidable /inolβi'ðaβle/ *a* unforgettable

inoperable /inope'raβle/ *a* inoperable

inopia /i'nopia/ *f*, poverty; scarcity

inopinable /inopi'naβle/ *a* indisputable, unquestionable

inopinado /inopi'naðo/ *a* unexpected, sudden

inoportunidad /inoportuni'ðað/ *f*, inopportuneness, unseasonableness; unsuitability

inoportuno /inopor'tuno/ *a* inopportune, untimely

inordenado /inorðe'naðo/ *a* inordinate, immoderate, excessive

inorgánico /inor'ganiko/ *a* inorganic

inoxidable /inoksi'ðaβle/ *a* rustless

inquebrantable /inkeβran'taβle/ *a* unbreakable; final, irrevocable

inquietador /inkieta'ðor/ **(-ra)** *a* disturbing —*n* disturber

inquietar /inkie'tar/ *vt* to disturb; trouble, make anxious, worry; —*vr* be disquieted, worry

inquieto /in'kieto/ *a* restless; unquiet; fidgety; disturbed, anxious, worried, uneasy

inquietud /inkie'tuð/ *f*, restlessness; uneasiness; worry; trouble, care, anxiety

inquilinato /inkili'nato/ *m*, tenancy; rent; *Law.* lease; (rental) rates

inquilino /inki'lino/ **(-na)** *n* tenant; lessee

inquina /in'kina/ *f*, dislike, grudge

inquinar /inki'nar/ *vt* to contaminate, corrupt, infect

inquiridor /inkiri'ðor/ **(-ra)** *a* inquiring, examining —*n* investigator

inquirir /inki'rir/ *vt irr* to inquire; examine, look into. See **adquirir**

inquisición /inkisi'θion; inkisi'sion/ *f*, inquiry, investigation; *Eccl.* Inquisition

inquisidor /inkisi'ðor/ **(-ra)** *a* inquiring, investigating —*n* investigator. *m*, *Eccl.* inquisitor; judge

inquisitorial /inkisito'rial/ *a* inquisitorial

insaciabilidad /insaθiaβili'ðað; insasiaβili'ðað/ *f*, insatiability

insaciable /insa'θiaβle; insa'siaβle/ *a* insatiable

insalivación /insaliβa'θion; insaliβa'sion/ *f*, insalivation

insalubre /insa'luβre/ *a* unhealthy

insanable /insa'naβle/ *a* incurable

insania /in'sania/ *f*, insanity

insano /in'sano/ *a* insane, mad

inscribir /inskri'βir/ *vt* to inscribe; record; enter (a name on a list, etc.), register, enroll; engrave; *Geom.* inscribe —*Past Part.* **inscrito**

inscripción /inskrip'θion; inskrip'sion/ *f*, inscription; record, enrollment; registration; government bond

insecable /inse'kaβle/ *a* undryable, undrying

insecticida /insekti'θiða; insekti'siða/ *a* insecticide

insectívoro /insek'tiβoro/ *a* insectivorous

insecto /in'sekto/ *m*, insect

inseguridad /inseguri'ðað/ *f*, insecurity

inseguro /inse'guro/ *a* insecure; unsafe; uncertain

insensatez /insensa'teθ; insensa'tes/ *f*, folly, foolishness

insensato /insen'sato/ *a* foolish, stupid, mad

insensibilidad /insensiβili'ðað/ *f*, insensibility; imperception; callousness, hard-heartedness

insensibilizar /insensiβili'θar; insensiβili'sar/ *vt* to make insensible (to sensations)

insensible /insen'siβle/ *a* insensible; imperceptive, insensitive; unconscious, senseless; imperceptible, inappreciable; callous

inseparabilidad /inseparaβili'ðað/ *f*, inseparability

inseparable /insepa'raβle/ *a* inseparable

insepulto /inse'pulto/ *a* unburied (of the dead)

inserción /inser'θion; inser'sion/ *f*, insertion; interpolation; grafting

insertar /inser'tar/ *vt* to insert; introduce; interpolate; —*vr* (*Bot. Zool.*) become attached

inservible /inser'βiβle/ *a* useless; unfit; unsuitable

insidia /in'siðia/ *f*, insidiousness; snare, ambush

insidiador /insiðia'ðor/ **(-ra)** *a* ensnaring —*n* schemer, ambusher

insidiar /insi'ðiar/ *vt* to waylay, ambush; set a trap for; scheme against

insidioso /insi'ðioso/ *a* insidious; treacherous; scheming, guileful

insigne /in'signe/ *a* illustrious, famous; distinguished

insignia /in'signia/ *f*, symbol; badge; token; banner, standard; *Naut.* pennant; *pl* insignia

insignificancia /insignifi'kanθia; insignifi'kansia/ *f*, meaninglessness; unimportance, triviality; insignificance, insufficiency

insignificante /insignifi'kante/ *a* meaningless; unimportant; insignificant, small

insinuación /insinua'θion; insinua'sion/ *f*, insinuation; hint; implication; suggestion

insinuador /insinua'ðor/ *a* insinuating; suggestive, implicative

insinuar /insi'nuar/ *vt* to insinuate; suggest, hint; —*vr* ingratiate oneself; creep in

insinuativo /insinua'tiβo/ *a* insinuative

insipidez /insipi'ðeθ; insipi'ðes/ *f*, tastelessness, insipidity; *Fig.* dullness

insípido /in'sipiðo/ *a* tasteless, insipid; dull, uninteresting, boring

insistencia /insis'tenθia; insis'tensia/ *f*, insistence

insistente /insis'tente/ *a* insistent

insistir /insis'tir/ *vi* (*with en or sobre*) to lay stress upon, insist on; persist in

ínsito /'insito/ *a* inherent, innate

insociabilidad /insoθiaβili'ðað; insosiaβili'ðað/ *f*, unsociability

insociable /inso'θiaβle; inso'siaβle/ *a* unsociable

insolación /insola'θion; insola'sion/ *f*, insolation, exposure to the sun; sunstroke

insolar /inso'lar/ *vt* to expose to the sun's rays; —*vr* contract sunstroke

insoldable /insol'daβle/ *a* unsolderable, unable to be soldered

insolencia /inso'lenθia; inso'lensia/ *f*, insolence; impudence, impertinence

insolentarse /insolen'tarse/ *vr* to grow insolent; be impudent

insolente /inso'lente/ *a* insolent; impudent, impertinent

insólito /in'solito/ *a* unaccustomed; infrequent; unusual; unexpected

insolubilidad /insoluβili'ðað/ *f*, insolubility

insoluble /inso'luβle/ *a* insoluble

insoluto /inso'luto/ *a* unpaid, outstanding

insolvencia /insol'βenθia; insol'βensia/ *f*, insolvency

insolvente /insol'βente/ *a* insolvent

insomne /in'somne/ *a* sleepless

insomnio /in'somnio/ *m*, insomnia

insondable /inson'daβle/ *a* unfathomable, bottomless; inscrutable, secret

insoportable /insopor'taβle/ *a* intolerable, unbearable

insostenible /insoste'niβle/ *a* indefensible; arbitrary, baseless

inspección /inspek'θion; inspek'sion/ *f*, inspection; supervision; examination; inspectorship; inspector's office

inspeccionar /inspekθio'nar; inspeksio'nar/ *vt* to inspect; survey, examine. **i. una casa,** to view a house

inspector /inspek'tor/ **(-ra)** *a* inspecting, examining —*n* supervisor. *m*, inspector; surveyor

inspiración /inspira'θion; inspira'sion/ *f*, inspiration; inhalation

inspirador /inspira'ðor/ **(-ra)** *a* inspiring —*n* inspirer

inspirar /inspi'rar/ *vt* to breathe in, inhale; blow (of the wind); inspire; —*vr* be inspired; (*with en*) find inspiration in, imitate

instabilidad /instaβili'ðað/ *f*, instability; unsteadiness; shakiness; unreliability, inconstancy

instable /ins'taβle/ *a* unstable

instalación /instala'θion; instala'sion/ *f*, plant, apparatus; erection, fitting; induction; installment, settling in

instalador /instala'ðor/ **(-ra)** *n* fitter; one who installs (electricity, etc.)

instalar /insta'lar/ *vt* to appoint, induct; erect (a plant, etc.); install, put in; lay on; *Elec.* wire; —*vr* install oneself, settle down

instancia /ins'tanθia; ins'tansia/ *f*, instance; argument; suggestion; supplication; request; formal petition. **de primera i.,** in the first instance, firstly

instantánea /instan'tanea/ *f*, *Photo.* snapshot

instantáneo /instan'taneo/ *a* instantaneous

instante /ins'tante/ *a* urgent. *m*, second; instant, moment. **a cada i.,** every minute; frequently. **al i.,** at once, immediately. **por instantes,** continually; immediately

instar /ins'tar/ *vt* to press; persuade; insist upon; —*vi* be urgent, press

instauración /instaura'θion; instaura'sion/ *f*, restoration; renewal; renovation

instaurador /instaura'ðor/ **(-ra)** *a* renovating, renewing —*n* restorer, renovator

instaurar /instau'rar/ *vt* to restore; repair; renovate, renew

instaurativo /instaura'tiβo/ *a* restorative

instigación /instiga'θion; instiga'sion/ *f*, instigation, incitement

instigador /instiga'ðor/ **(-ra)** *n* instigator

instigar /insti'gar/ *vt* to instigate, incite; induce

instilación /instila'θion; instila'sion/ *f*, instillment, pouring drop by drop; inculcation, implantation

instilar /insti'lar/ *vt* instill; implant, inculcate

instintivo /instin'tiβo/ *a* instinctive

instinto /ins'tinto/ *m*, instinct. **por i.,** by instinct, naturally

institución /institu'θion; institu'sion/ *f*, setting up, establishment; institution; teaching, instruction; *pl* institutes, digest

institucional /institu'θio'nal; institusio'nal/ a institutional

instituir /insti'tuir/ vt irr to found, establish; institute; instruct, teach. See **huir**

instituto /insti'tuto/ m, institute; secondary school. **i. de belleza,** beauty parlor, beauty salon

institutor /institu'tor/ m, founder, instituter; tutor

institutriz /institu'triθ; institu'tris/ f, governess

instrucción /instruk'θion; instruk'sion/ f, teaching, instruction; knowledge, learning; education; pl orders; rules; instruction. **i. primaria,** primary education. **i. pública,** public education

instructivo /instruk'tiβo/ a instructive

instructor /instruk'tor/ **(-ra)** a instructive —n instructor

instruido /ins'truiðo/ a cultured, well-educated; knowledgeable

instruir /ins'truir/ vt irr to teach, instruct; train; inform, acquaint with; Law. formulate. See **huir**

instrumentación /instrumenta'θion; instrumenta'sion/ f, Mus. instrumentation

instrumental /instrumen'tal/ a instrumental

instrumentar /instrumen'tar/ vt Mus. to score

instrumentista /instrumen'tista/ mf Mus. instrumentalist; instrument maker

instrumento /instru'mento/ m, tool, implement; machine, apparatus; Mus. instrument; means, medium; legal document. **i. de cuerda,** string instrument. **i. de percusión,** percussion instrument. **i. de viento,** wind instrument

insuave /in''suaβe/ a unpleasant (to the senses); rough

insubordinación /insuβorðina'θion; insuβorðina'sion/ f, insubordination, rebellion

insubordinado /insuβorði'naðo/ a insubordinate, unruly

insubordinar /insuβorði'nar/ vt to rouse to rebellion; —vr become insubordinate, rebel

insubsistencia /insuβsis'tenθia; insuβsis'tensia/ f, instability

insubsistente /insuβsis'tente/ a unstable; groundless, unfounded

insubstancial /insuβstan'θial; insuβstan'sial/ a insubstantial, unreal, illusory; pointless, worthless, superficial

insubstancialidad /insuβstanθiali'ðað; insuβstansiali'ðað/ f, superficiality, worthlessness

insuficiencia /insufi'θienθia; insufi'siensia/ f, insufficiency, shortage; incompetence, inefficiency

insuficiente /insufi'θiente; insufi'siente/ a insufficient, scarce, inadequate

insufrible /insu'friβle/ a insufferable, unbearable, intolerable

insular /insu'lar/ a insular

insulina /insu'lina/ f, insulin

insulsez /insul'seθ; insul'ses/ f, insipidity, tastelessness; dullness; tediousness

insulso /in'sulso/ a insipid, tasteless; tedious; dull

insultador /insulta'ðor/ **(-ra)** a insulting —n insulter

insultante /insul'tante/ a insulting

insultar /insul'tar/ vt to insult; call names; —vr take offense

insulto /in'sulto/ m, insult; sudden attack; sudden illness, fit

insumable /insu'maβle/ a incalculable; excessive, exorbitant

insumergible /insumer'hiβle/ a unsinkable

insumiso /insu'miso/ a rebellious

insuperable /insupe'raβle/ a insuperable

insurgente /insur'hente/ a insurgent, rebellious. m, rebel

insurrección /insurrek'θion; insurrek'sion/ f, insurrection

insurreccionar /insurrekθio'nar; insurreksio'nar/ vt to incite to rebellion; —vr rise in rebellion

insurrecto /insu'rrekto/ **(-ta)** n rebel

insustancial /insustan'θial; insustan'sial/ a See **insubstancial**

insustituible /insusti'tuiβle/ a indispensable

intachable /inta'tʃaβle/ a irreproachable; impeccable, perfect

intacto /in'takto/ a untouched; intact, uninjured; whole, entire; complete; pure

intangibilidad /intanhiβili'ðað/ f, intangibility

intangible /intan'hiβle/ a intangible

integración /integra'θion; integra'sion/ f, integration

integral /inte'gral/ a integral

integrar /inte'grar/ vt to integrate; Com. repay

integridad /integri'ðað/ f, wholeness; completeness; integrity, probity, honesty; virginity

íntegro /'integro/ a integral, whole; upright, honest

integumento /integu'mento/ m, integument; pretense, simulation

intelectiva /intelek'tiβa/ f, understanding

intelecto /inte'lekto/ m, intellect

intelectual /intelek'tual/ a intellectual

intelectualidad /intelektuali'ðað/ f, understanding, intellectuality; intelligentsia

intelectualismo /intelektua'lismo/ m, intellectualism

inteligencia /inteli'henθia; inteli'hensia/ f, intelligence; intellect; mental alertness; mind; meaning, sense; experience, skill; understanding, secret agreement; information, knowledge; Intelligence, Secret Service

inteligente /inteli'hente/ a intelligent; clever; skillful; capable, competent

inteligibilidad /intelihiβili'ðað/ f, intelligibility

inteligible /inteli'hiβle/ a intelligible; understandable; able to be heard

intemperancia /intempe'ranθia; intempe'ransia/ f, intemperance, lack of moderation

intemperante /intempe'rante/ a intemperate

intemperie /intem'perie/ f, stormy weather. **a la i.,** at the mercy of the elements; in the open air

intempestivo /intempes'tiβo/ a inopportune, illtimed

intención /inten'θion; inten'sion/ f, intention; determination, purpose; viciousness (of animals); caution. Inf. **con segunda i.,** with a double meaning, slyly

intencionado /intenθio'naðo; intensio'naðo/ a intentioned, disposed

intencional /intenθio'nal; intensio'nal/ a intentional, designed, premeditated

intendencia /inten'denθia; inten'densia/ f, management; supervision; administration; Polit. intendancy. Mil. **cuerpo de i.,** quartermaster corps, army supply corps

intendente /inten'dente/ m, director; manager; Polit. intendant. **i. de ejército,** quartermaster general

intensar /inten'sar/ vt to intensify

intensidad /intensi'ðað/ f, intensity; ardor; vehemence

intensificar /intensifi'kar/ vt to intensify

intensivo /inten'siβo/ a intensive

intenso /in'tenso/ a intense; ardent; fervent; vehement

intentar /inten'tar/ vt to intend, mean; propose; try, endeavor; initiate. **i. fortuna,** to try one's luck

intento /in'tento/ m, intention, determination; purpose. **de i.,** on purpose; knowingly

intentona /inten'tona/ f, Inf. foolhardy attempt

interacción /interak'θion; interak'sion/ f, interaction; reciprocal effect; Chem. reaction

intercalación /interkala'θion; interkala'sion/ f, interpolation; insertion

intercalar /interka'lar/ vt to intercalate; interpolate, include, insert

intercambiable /interkam'biaβle/ a interchangeable

intercambio /inter'kambio/ m, interchange

interceder /interθe'ðer; interse'ðer/ vi to intercede, plead for

interceptación /interθepta'θion; intersepta'sion/ f, interception

interceptar /interθep'tar; intersep'tar/ vt to intercept; interrupt; hinder

intercesión /interθe'sion; interse'sion/ f, intercession

intercesor /interθe'sor; interse'sor/ **(-ra)** a interceding —n intercessor

intercutáneo /interku'taneo/ a intercutaneous

interdecir /inter'ðeθir; inter'ðesir/ vt irr to forbid, prohibit. See **decir**

interdicción /inter∂ik'θion; inter∂ik'sion/ f, interdiction, prohibition

interdicto /inter'∂ikto/ m, interdict

interés /inte'res/ m, interest; yield, profit; advantage; *Com.* interest; inclination, fondness; attraction, fascination; *pl* money matters. **i. compuesto,** compound interest. **intereses creados,** bonds of interest; vested interests

interesado /intere'sa∂o/ a involved, concerned; biased; selfish

interesante /intere'sante/ a interesting

interesar /intere'sar/ **(se)** vi and vr to be interested; —vt *Com.* invest; interest

interfecto /inter'fekto/ **(-ta)** n *Law.* victim (of murder)

interferencia /interfe'renθia; interfe'rensia/ f, *Phys.* interference

interfoliar /interfo'liar/ vt to interleave (of books)

ínterin /'interin/ m, interim —adv meanwhile, in the meantime

interinamente /interina'mente/ adv in the interim; provisionally

interinar /interi'nar/ vt to discharge (duties) provisionally, act temporarily as

interino /inte'rino/ a acting, provisional, temporary

interior /inte'rior/ a interior; inner; inside; indoor; inland; internal, domestic (policies, etc.); inward, spiritual. m, interior, inside; mind, soul; *pl* entrails

interjección /interhek'θion; interhek'sion/ f, *Gram.* interjection, exclamation

interlinear /interline'ar/ vt to write between the lines; *Print.* lead

interlocución /interloku'θion; interloku'sion/ f, dialogue, conversation

interlocutorio /interloku'torio/ a *Law.* interlocutory

intérlope /in'terlope/ a interloping. mf interloper

interludio /inter'lu∂io/ m, interlude

intermediario /interme'∂iario/ **(-ia)** a and n intermediary. m, *Com.* middleman

intermedio /inter'me∂io/ a intermediate. m, interim; *Theat.* interval. **por i. de,** through, by the mediation of

intermisión /intermi'sion/ f, intermission, interval

intermitencia /intermi'tenθia; intermi'tensia/ f, intermittence

intermitente /intermi'tente/ a intermittent

intermitir /intermi'tir/ vt to interrupt, suspend, discontinue

internación /interna'θion; interna'sion/ f, going inside; penetration; taking into

internacional /internaθio'nal; internasio'nal/ a international

internacionalismo /internaθiona'lismo; internasiona'lismo/ m, internationalism

internacionalista /internaθiona'lista; internasiona'lista/ mf internationalist

internacionalización /internaθionaliθa'θion; internasionalisa'sion/ f, internationalization

internado /inter'na∂o/ m, boarding school

internamiento /interna'miento/ m, internment

internar /inter'nar/ vt to take or send inland; —vi penetrate; —vr (with en) go into the interior of (a country); get into the confidence of; study deeply (a subject)

Internet m, **el,** the Internet.

interno /in'terno/ **(-na)** a interior; internal; inner; inside; boarding (student) —n boarding school student; *Med.* intern

internodio /inter'no∂io/ m, internode

internuncio /inter'nunθio; inter'nunsio/ m, *Eccl.* internuncio; interlocutor; representative

interoceánico /interoθe'aniko; interose'aniko/ a interoceanic

interpaginar /interpahi'nar/ vt to interleave (of books)

interpelación /interpela'θion; interpela'sion/ f, *Law.* interpellation; appeal

interpelar /interpe'lar/ vt *Law.* to interpellate; appeal to, ask protection from

interpolación /interpola'θion; interpola'sion/ f, interpolation, insertion; interruption

interpolador /interpola'∂or/ **(-ra)** n interpolator; interrupter

interpolar /interpo'lar/ vt to interpolate; interject

interponer /interpo'ner/ vt irr to interpose, insert, intervene; designate as an arbitrator; —vr intervene. See **poner**

interposición /interposi'θion; interposi'sion/ f, interposition; intervention; mediation, arbitration

interpresa /inter'presa/ f, *Mil.* surprise attack

interpretación /interpreta'θion; interpreta'sion/ f, interpretation; translation

interpretador /interpreta'∂or/ **(-ra)** a interpretative —n interpreter

interpretar /interpre'tar/ vt to interpret; translate; attribute; expound, explain. **i. mal,** to misconstrue; translate wrongly

interpretativo /interpreta'ti∂o/ a interpretative

intérprete /in'terprete/ mf interpreter

interregno /inte'rregno/ m, interregnum. **i. parlamentario,** parliamentary recess

interrogación /interroga'θion; interroga'sion/ f, interrogation, question; *Gram.* question mark

interrogador /interroga'∂or/ **(-ra)** n questioner

interrogante /interro'gante/ a interrogating. m, *Print.* question mark

interrogar /interro'gar/ vt to interrogate, question

interrogativo /interroga'ti∂o/ a interrogative

interrogatorio /interroga'torio/ m, interrogatory

interrumpir /interrum'pir/ vt to interrupt; hinder, obstruct; *Elec.* break contact

interrupción /interrup'θion; interrup'sion/ f, interruption; stoppage (of work); *Elec.* break

interruptor /interrup'tor/ **(-ra)** a interrupting —n interrupter. m, *Elec.* switch, interruptor. **i. de dos direcciones,** *Elec.* two-way switch

intersecarse /interse'karse/ vr *Geom.* to intersect

intersección /intersek'θion; intersek'sion/ f, *Geom.* intersection

intersticio /inter'stiθio; inter'stisio/ m, interstice, crack, crevice; interval, intervening space

intervalo /inter'βalo/ m, interval

intervención /interβen'θion; interβen'sion/ f, intervention; mediation, intercession; auditing (of accounts)

intervenir /interβe'nir/ vi irr to take part (in); intervene, interfere; arbitrate, mediate; happen, occur; —vt *Com.* audit. See **venir**

interventor /interβen'tor/ **(-ra)** a intervening —n one who intervenes. m, auditor; inspector

intervocálico /interβo'kaliko/ a intervocalic

intestado /intes'ta∂o/ **(-da)** a and n *Law.* intestate

intestinal /intesti'nal/ a intestinal

intestino /intes'tino/ a intestinal. m, intestine

íntima, intimación /'intima, intima'θion; 'intima, intima'sion/ f, intimation, notification

intimar /inti'mar/ vt to intimate; inform, notify; —vr penetrate; —vr and vi become intimate or friendly

intimidación /intimi∂a'θion; intimi∂a'sion/ f, intimidation, terrorization

intimidad /intimi'∂a∂/ f, intimacy

intimidar /intimi'∂ar/ vt to intimidate, terrorize, cow

íntimo /'intimo/ a intimate; deep-seated, inward; private, personal

intitular /intitu'lar/ vt to give a title to, entitle, call; —vr call oneself

intolerable /intole'raβle/ a intolerable; unbearable

intolerancia /intole'ranθia; intole'ransia/ f, narrow-mindedness, intolerance, bigotry

intolerante /intole'rante/ a narrow-minded, illiberal; *Med.* intolerant

intonso /in'tonso/ a long-haired, unshorn; boorish, ignorant

intoxicación /intoksika'θion; intoksika'sion/ f, poisoning

intoxicar /intoksi'kar/ vt to poison

intraducible /intra∂u'θiβle; intra∂u'siβle/ a untranslatable

intramuros /intra'muros/ adv within the town walls, within the city

intranquilidad /intrankili'∂a∂/ f, disquiet, restlessness; anxiety

intranquilizador /intrankiliθa'ðor; intrankilisa'ðor/ *a* disquieting, perturbing

intranquilizar /intrankili'θar; intrankili'sar/ *vt* to disquiet, make uneasy, worry

intranquilo /intran'kilo/ *a* uneasy, anxious

intransferible /intransfe'riβle/ *a* untransferable, not transferable

intransigencia /intransi'henθia; intransi'hensia/ *f*, intolerance, intransigence

intransigente /intransi'hente/ *a* intolerant, intransigent

intransitable /intransi'taβle/ *a* impassable; unsurmountable

intransitivo /intransi'tiβo/ *a* intransitive

intratable /intra'taβle/ *a* intractable; impassable; rough; unsociable, difficult

intrauterino /intraute'rino/ *a* intrauterine

intravenoso /intraβe'noso/ *a* intravenous

intrepidez /intrepi'ðeθ; intrepi'ðes/ *f*, intrepidity, dauntlessness, gallantry

intrépido /in'trepiðo/ *a* intrepid, dauntless, gallant

intriga /in'triga/ *f*, scheme, intrigue; entanglement; *Lit.* plot

intrigante /intri'gante/ *mf* intriguer, schemer

intrigar /intri'gar/ *vi* to intrigue, scheme, plot

intrincación /intrinka'θion; intrinka'sion/ *f*, intricacy

intrincado /intrin'kaðo/ *a* intricate

intrincar /intrin'kar/ *vt* to complicate; obscure, confuse

intríngulis /in'triŋgulis/ *m, Inf.* ulterior motive

intrínseco /in'trinseko/ *a* intrinsic, inherent; essential

introducción /introðuk'θion; introðuk'sion/ *f*, introduction

introducir /introðu'θir; introðu'sir/ *vt irr* to introduce; insert; fit in; drive in; present, introduce; bring into use; cause, occasion; show in, bring in; —*vr* interfere, meddle; enter. See **conducir**

introductor /introðuk'tor/ **(-ra)** *n* introducer

intromisión /intromi'sion/ *f*, intromission; interference; *Geol.* intrusion

introspección /introspek'θion; introspek'sion/ *f*, introspection

introverso /intro'βerso/ *a* introvert

intruso /in'truso/ **(-sa)** *a* intruding, intrusive —*n* intruder

intuición /intui'θion; intui'sion/ *f*, intuition

intuir /in'tuir/ *vt irr* to know by intuition. See **huir**

intuitivo /intui'tiβo/ *a* intuitive

intuito /in'tuito/ *m*, glance, look, view

intumescencia /intumes'θenθia; intumes'sensia/ *f*, intumescence

inulto /i'nulto/ *a Poet.* unavenged, unpunished

inundación /inunda'θion; inunda'sion/ *f*, flood; flooding; excess, superabundance

inundar /inun'dar/ *vt* to flood; swamp; *Fig.* inundate, overwhelm

inurbanidad /inurβani'ðað/ *f*, discourtesy, impoliteness

inurbano /inur'βano/ *a* discourteous, uncivil, impolite

inusitado /inusi'taðo/ *a* unusual, unaccustomed; rare

inútil /i'nutil/ *a* useless

inutilidad /inutili'ðað/ *f*, uselessness

inutilizar /inutili'θar; inutili'sar/ *vt* to render useless; disable, incapacitate; spoil, damage

invadeable /imbaðe'aβle/ *a* impassable, unfordable

invadir /imba'ðir/ *vt* to invade

invaginación /imbahina'θion; imbahina'sion/ *f*, invagination

invalidación /imbaliða'θion; imbaliða'sion/ *f*, invalidation

invalidar /imbali'ðar/ *vt* to invalidate

invalidez /imbali'ðeθ; imbali'ðes/ *f*, invalidity; disablement; infirmity

inválido /im'baliðo/ **(-da)** *a* weak, infirm; invalid, null; disabled —*n* invalid; disabled soldier

invariabilidad /imbariaβili'ðað/ *f*, invariability

invariable /imba'riaβle/ *a* invariable

invariación /imbaria'θion; imbaria'sion/ *f*, invariableness

invariante /imba'riante/ *m*, invariant

invasión /imba'sion/ *f*, invasion, encroachment, incursion

invasor /imba'sor/ **(-ra)** *a* invading; *Med.* attacking —*n* invader

invectiva /imbek'tiβa/ *f*, invective

invencibilidad /imbenθiβili'ðað; imbensiβili'ðað/ *f*, invincibility

invencible /imben'θiβle; imben'siβle/ *a* invincible

invención /imben'θion; imben'sion/ *f*, invention, discovery; deception, fabrication, lie; creative imagination; finding (e.g. *i. de la Santa Cruz*, Invention of the Holy Cross)

invencionero /imbenθio'nero; imbensio'nero/ **(-ra)** *n* inventor; schemer, deceiver

invendible /imben'diβle/ *a* unsalable

inventar /imben'tar/ *vt* to invent; create; imagine; concoct, fabricate (lies, etc.)

inventariar /imbenta'riar/ *vt* to make an inventory of; *Com.* take stock of

inventario /imben'tario/ *m*, inventory; *Com.* stock taking

inventiva /imben'tiβa/ *f*, inventiveness, ingenuity; creativeness

inventivo /imben'tiβo/ *a* inventive

invento /im'bento/ *m*, See **invención**

inventor /imben'tor/ **(-ra)** *n* inventor, discoverer; liar, storyteller

inverecundia /imbere'kundia/ *f*, impertinence, impudence

inverecundo /imbere'kundo/ *a* shameless, brazen

inverisímil /imberi'simil/ *a* See **inverosímil**

invernáculo /imber'nakulo/ *m*, greenhouse; conservatory

invernada /imber'naða/ *f*, winter season; hibernation

invernadero /imberna'ðero/ *m*, winter quarters; greenhouse

invernal /imber'nal/ *a* wintry; winter

invernar /imber'nar/ *vi irr* to winter; hibernate; be wintertime. See **acertar**

invernizo /imber'niθo; imber'niso/ *a* wintry, winter

inverosímil /imbero'simil/ *a* unlikely, improbable

inverosimilitud /imberosimili'tuð/ *f*, improbability

inversamente /imbersa'mente/ *adv* inversely

inverso /im'berso/ *a* inverse; inverted

invertebrado /imberte'βraðo/ *a* and *m*, invertebrate

invertir /imber'tir/ *vt irr* to invert, transpose; reverse; *Com.* invest; spend (time). See **sentir**

investidura /imbesti'ðura/ *f*, investiture

investigación /imbestiga'θion; imbestiga'sion/ *f*, investigation, examination; research; inquiry

investigador /imbestiga'ðor/ **(-ra)** *a* investigating —*n* investigator; researcher

investigar /imbesti'gar/ *vt* to investigate, examine; research on

investir /imbes'tir/ *vt irr* to confer upon, decorate with; invest, appoint. See **pedir**

inveterado /imbete'raðo/ *a* inveterate

inviable /im'biaβle/ *a* unfeasible

invicto /im'bikto/ *a* invincible; unconquered

invierno /im'bierno/ *m*, winter; rainy season

inviolabilidad /imbiolaβili'ðað/ *f*, inviolability. **i. parlamentaria,** parliamentary immunity

inviolable /imbio'laβle/ *a* inviolable; infallible

inviolado /imbio'laðo/ *a* inviolate

invisibilidad /imbisiβili'ðað/ *f*, invisibility

invisible /imbi'siβle/ *a* invisible

invitación /imbita'θion; imbita'sion/ *f*, invitation

invitado /imbi'taðo/ **(-da)** *n* guest

invitar /imbi'tar/ *vt* to invite; urge, request; allure, attract

invocación /imboka'θion; imboka'sion/ *f*, invocation

invocador /imboka'ðor/ **(-ra)** *n* invoker

invocar /imbo'kar/ *vt* to invoke

involucro /imbo'lukro/ *m*, involucre

involuntariedad /imboluntarie'ðað/ *f*, involuntariness

involuntario /imbolun'tario/ *a* involuntary

invulnerabilidad /imbulneraβili'ðað/ *f*, invulnerability

invulnerable /imbulne'raβle/ *a* invulnerable

inyección /inyek'θion; inyek'sion/ *f*, injection
inyectado /inyek'taðo/ *a* bloodshot (of eyes)
inyectar /inyek'tar/ *vt* to inject
ipecacuana /ipeka'kuana/ *f*, ipecac
iperita /i'perita/ *f*, mustard gas
ir /ir/ *vi irr* to go; bet (e.g. *Van cinco pesetas que no lo hace*, I bet five pesetas he doesn't do it); be different, be changed (e.g. *¡Qué diferencia va entre esto y aquello!* What a difference there is between this and that!); suit, be becoming, fit (e.g. *El vestido no te va bien*, The dress doesn't suit you); extend; lead, go in the direction of (e.g. *Este camino va a Lérida*, This road leads to Lerida); get along, do, proceed, be (e.g. *¿Cómo te va estos días?* How are you getting along these days?); come (e.g. *Ahora voy*, I'm coming now); *Math.* carry (e.g. *siete y van cuatro*, seven, and four to carry); *Math.* leave (e.g. *De quince a seis van nueve*, Six from fifteen leaves nine). With a gerund, **ir** indicates the continuance of the action, or may mean to become or to grow (e.g. *Iremos andando hacia el mar*, We shall go on walking toward the sea, or *Entre tanto iba amaneciendo*, In the meanwhile it was growing light). With a past participle, **ir** means "to be' (e.g. *Voy encantado de lo que he visto*, I am delighted with what I have seen). With *prep a* + *infin*, **ir** means to prepare (to do) or to intend (to do) or to be on the point of doing (e.g. *Van a cantar la canción que te gusta*, They are going (or preparing) to sing the song you like). With *prep a* + *noun*, **ir** indicates destination (e.g. *Voy al cine*, I'm going to the cinema. *¿A dónde vamos?* Where are we going to?). **ir** + *con* means to go in the company of, or to do a thing in a certain manner (e.g. *Hemos de ir con cuidado*, We must go carefully). **ir** + *en* means to concern, interest (e.g. *¿Qué le va a él en este asunto?* What has this affair to do with him?). **ir** + *por* means to follow the career of, become (e.g. *Juan va por abogado*, John is going to be a lawyer). It also means to go and bring, or to go for (e.g. *Iré por agua*, I shall go and bring (or for) water) —*vr* to go away, leave, depart; die; leak (of liquids); evaporate; overbalance, slip (e.g. *Se le fueron los pies*, He slipped (and lost his balance)); be worn out, grow old, deteriorate; be incontinent; *Fig. Inf.* **írsele a uno una cosa**, not to notice or not to understand a thing. *Naut.* **irse a pique**, to founder, sink. **Se le fueron los ojos tras María**, He couldn't keep his eyes off Mary. **i. a caballo**, to ride, go on horseback. **i. adelante**, to go on ahead, lead; *Fig. Inf.* forge ahead, go ahead. **i. al cuartel**, to go into the army. **i. a una**, to cooperate in. **i. bien** *Fig. Inf.* to go on well; be well. **i. de brazo**, to walk arm in arm. **i. de compras**, to go shopping. **i. de juerga** *Inf.* to go on a binge. **i. de bicicleta** *or* **en coche**, to go by bicycle or to ride (in a car or carriage). **i. por**, to do things in order, take one thing at a time. *Fig. Inf.* **i. tirando**, to carry on, manage. **¿Cómo le va?** How are things with you? How are you getting along? *Inf.* **no irle ni venirle a uno nada en un asunto**, to be not in the least concerned in (an affair). **¡Qué va!** Rubbish! Nothing of the sort! **¿Quién va?** *Mil.* Who goes there? **Vamos**, Let's go (also used as an exclamation: Good gracious! You don't say so! Well!) **Vamos a ver...**, Let's see.... **¡Vaya!** What a...!; Come now! Never mind! **¡Vaya a paseo!** *or* **¡Vaya con su música a otra parte!** Take yourself off! Get out! **¡Vaya con Dios!** God keep you! Good-bye! *Pres. Ind.* **voy, vas, va, vamos, váis, van**. *Pres. Part.* **yendo**. *Preterite* **fui, fuiste, fue, fuimos, fuisteis, fueron**. *Imperf.* **iba**, etc —*Pres. Subjunc.* **vaya**, etc —*Imperf. Subjunc.* **fuese**, etc —*Imperat.* **vé**
ira /'ira/ *f*, wrath, anger; vengeance; raging, fury (of elements); *pl* cruelties, acts of vengeance
iracundia /ira'kundia/ *f*, irascibility, irritability; anger
iracundo /ira'kundo/ *a* irascible, irritable, choleric; angry; raging, tempestuous
Irak /i'rak/ Iraq
iranio /i'ranio/ **(-ia)** *a* and *n* Iranian
irascibilidad /irasθiβili'ðað; irassiβili'ðað/ *f*, irascibility; petulance
iridiscencia /iriðis'θenθia; iriðis'sensia/ *f*, iridescence
iridiscente /iriðis'θente; iriðis'sente/ *a* iridescent
iris /'iris/ *m*, rainbow; *Anat.* iris (of the eye)

irisación /irisa'θion; irisa'sion/ *f*, irisation
irisar /iri'sar/ *vi* to be iridescent
Irlanda /ir'landa/ Ireland
irlandés /irlan'des/ **(-esa)** *a* and *n* Irishman (woman)
ironía /iro'nia/ *f*, irony
irónico /i'roniko/ *a* ironical
iroqués /iro'kes/ **(-esa)** *a* and *n* Iroquois
irracional /irraθio'nal; irrasio'nal/ *a* irrational; illogical, unreasonable; *Math.* irrational, absurd
irracionalidad /irraθionali'ðað; irrasionali'ðað/ *f*, irrationality, unreasonableness
irradiación /irraðia'θion; irraðia'sion/ *f*, radiation, irradiation
irradiar /irra'ðiar/ *vt* to radiate, irradiate
irrazonable /irraθo'naβle; irraso'naβle/ *a* unreasonable
irreal /irre'al/ *a* unreal
irrealidad /irreali'ðað/ *f*, unreality
irrealizable /irreali'θaβle; irreali'saβle/ *a* unachievable, unattainable
irrebatible /irreβa'tiβle/ *a* irrefutable, evident
irreconciliable /irrekonθi'liaβle; irrekonsi'liaβle/ *a* irreconcilable, intransigent
irrecuperable /irrekupe'raβle/ *a* irretrievable
irredimible /irreði'miβle/ *a* irredeemable
irreemplazable /irreempla'θaβle; irreempla'saβle/ *a* irreplaceable
irreflexión /irreflek'sion/ *f*, thoughtlessness; impetuosity
irreflexivo /irreflek'siβo/ *a* thoughtless; rash, impetuous
irreformable /irrefor'maβle/ *a* unreformable
irrefragable /irrefra'gaβle/ *a* indisputable, unquestionable
irrefrenable /irrefre'naβle/ *a* unmanageable, uncontrollable
irrefutable /irrefu'taβle/ *a* irrefutable
irregular /irregu'lar/ *a* irregular; infrequent, rare
irregularidad /irregulari'ðað/ *f*, irregularity; abnormality; *Inf.* moral lapse
irreligión /irreli'hion/ *f*, irreligion
irreligiosidad /irrelihiosi'ðað/ *f*, impiety, godlessness
irreligioso /irreli'hioso/ *a* irreligious, impious
irremediable /irreme'ðiaβle/ *a* irremediable
irremediablemente /irremeðiaβle'mente/ *adv* unavoidably; hopelessly
irremisible /irremi'siβle/ *a* unpardonable, inexcusable
irremunerado /irremune'raðo/ *a* unremunerated, gratuitous
irreparable /irrepa'raβle/ *a* irreparable
irreprensible /irrepren'siβle/ *a* blameless, unexceptionable
irreprochable /irrepro't∫aβle/ *a* irreproachable
irresistible /irresis'tiβle/ *a* irresistible; ravishing
irresolución /irresolu'θion; irresolu'sion/ *f*, vacillation, indecision
irresoluto /irreso'luto/ *a* hesitant, irresolute
irrespetuoso /irrespe'tuoso/ *a* disrespectful
irresponsabilidad /irresponsaβili'ðað/ *f*, irresponsibility
irresponsable /irrespon'saβle/ *a* irresponsible
irreverencia /irreβe'renθia; irreβe'rensia/ *f*, irreverence
irreverente /irreβe'rente/ *a* irreverent
irrevocabilidad /irreβokaβili'ðað/ *f*, irrevocability, finality
irrevocable /irreβo'kaβle/ *a* irrevocable
irrigación /irriga'θion; irriga'sion/ *f*, irrigation
irrigador /irriga'ðor/ *m*, spray, sprinkler; *Med.* syringe, spray
irrigar /irri'gar/ *vt* (*Med. Agr.*) to irrigate
irrisible /irri'siβle/ *a* ridiculous, laughable, absurd
irrisión /irri'sion/ *f*, derision; laughingstock
irrisorio /irri'sorio/ *a* ridiculous; derisive
irritabilidad /irritaβili'ðað/ *f*, irritability, petulance, irascibility
irritable /irri'taβle/ *a* irritable
irritación /irrita'θion; irrita'sion/ *f*, *Med.* irritation; petulance, exasperation
irritador /irrita'ðor/ *a* irritating; exasperating. *m*, irritant

irritante /irri'tante/ *a* irritating; exasperating
irritar /irri'tar/ *vt* to exasperate, annoy; provoke, inflame; (*Med. Law.*) irritate
írrito /'irrito/ *a Law.* null, void
irrogar /irro'gar/ *vt* to occasion (damage, harm)
irrompible /irrom'piβle/ *a* unbreakable
irrumpir /irrum'pir/ *vi* to enter violently, break in
irrupción /irrup'θion; irrup'sion/ *f,* irruption, incursion, invasion
irruptor /irrup'tor/ *a* invading, attacking
isabelino /isaβe'lino/ *a* Isabelline (pertaining to Spanish Queen Isabella II (reigned 1830–68)); bay (of horses)
isla /'isla/ *f,* island; block (of houses)
islámico /is'lamiko/ *a* Islamic
islamismo /isla'mismo/ *m,* Islam
islamita /isla'mita/ *a* and *mf* Muslim
islandés /islan'des/ **(-esa), islándico (-ca)** *a* Icelandic —*n* Icelander. *m,* Icelandic (language)
Islandia /is'landia/ Iceland
isleño /is'leɲo/ **(-ña)** *a* island —*n* islander; native of the Canary Islands
isleta /is'leta/ *f,* islet
islote /is'lote/ *m,* barren islet
ismaelita /ismae'lita/ *a* and *mf* Ishmaelite
isométrico /iso'metriko/ *a* isometric
isomorfo /iso'morfo/ *a* isomorphic

isotermo /iso'termo/ *a* isothermal
isótope, isótopo /i'sotope, i'sotopo/ *m,* isotope
israelita /israe'lita/ *mf* Israelite —*a* Israeli
istmeño /ist'meɲo/ **(-ña)** *n* native of an isthmus
ístmico /'istmiko/ *a* isthmian
istmo /'istmo/ *m,* isthmus
Istmo de Suez, el /'istmo de 'sueθ, el; 'istmo de 'sues, el/ the Suez Canal
Ítaca /'itaka/ Ithaca
Italia /i'talia/ Italy
italianismo /italia'nismo/ *m,* Italianism
italianizar /italiani'θar; italiani'sar/ *vt* to italianize
italiano /ita'liano/ **(-na)** *a* and *n* Italian. *m,* Italian (language)
itálico /i'taliko/ *a* italic
iteración /itera'θion; itera'sion/ *f,* iteration, repetition
iterar /ite'rar/ *vt* to repeat, reiterate
iterativo /itera'tiβo/ *a* iterative, repetitive
itinerario /itine'rario/ *a* and *m,* itinerary
izar /i'θar; i'sar/ *vt Naut.* to hoist
izote /i'θote; i'sote/ *m,* yucca
izquierda /iθ'kierða; is'kierða/ *f,* left, left-hand side; *Polit.* left. **¡I.!** *Mil.* Left face! **a la i.,** on the left
izquierdo /iθ'kierðo; is'kierðo/ *a* left, left-hand; left-handed; bent, twisted, crooked

JK

¡ja, ja, ja! /ha, ha, ha/ *interj* Ha! ha! ha!

jabalí /haβa'li/ *m*, wild boar

jabalina /haβa'lina/ *f*, sow of wild boar; javelin

jabato /ha'βato/ *m*, young wild boar

jabón /ha'βon/ *m*, soap. **j. blando,** soft soap. **j. de olor** *or* **j. de tocador,** toilet soap. **j. de sastre,** French chalk, steatite

jabonadura /haβona'ðura/ *f*, soaping; *pl* soapsuds, lather

jabonar /haβo'nar/ *vt* to soap; wash; *Inf.* dress down, scold

jaboncillo /haβon'θiλo; haβon'siyo/ *m*, toilet soap; steatite

jabonera /haβo'nera/ *f*, soapdish or box; soapwort

jabonería /haβone'ria/ *f*, soap factory or shop

jabonoso /haβo'noso/ *a* soapy

jaca /'haka/ *f*, pony; filly

jácara /'hakara/ *f*, gay, roguish ballad; song and dance

jácena /'haθena; 'hasena/ *f*, *Archit.* beam, girder

jacinto /ha'θinto; ha'sinto/ *m*, hyacinth; jacinth. **j. de ceilán,** zircon. **j. occidental,** topaz. **j. oriental,** ruby

jaco /'hako/ *m*, short coat of mail; hack, jade

jacobinismo /hakoβi'nismo/ *m*, Jacobinism

jacobino /hako'βino/ **(-na)** *n* Jacobin

jactancia /hak'tanθia; hak'tansia/ *f*, bragging, boasting

jactancioso /haktan'θioso; haktan'sioso/ **(-sa)** *a* boastful —*n* braggart

jactarse /hak'tarse/ *vr* to brag, boast

jaculatoria /hakula'toria/ *f*, ejaculatory prayer

jaculatorio /hakula'torio/ *a* ejaculatory

jade /'haðe/ *m*, *Mineral.* jade

jadeante /haðe'ante/ *a* panting

jadear /haðe'ar/ *vi* to pant

jadeo /ha'ðeo/ *m*, pant; panting; hard breathing

jaez /ha'eθ; ha'es/ *m*, harness (gen. *pl*); kind, sort; *pl* trappings

jaguar /ha'guar/ *m*, jaguar

jalbegar /halβe'gar/ *vt* to whitewash; make up the face

jalbegue /hal'βege/ *m*, whitewash

jalde /'halde/ *a* bright yellow

jalea /ha'lea/ *f*, jelly. **j. de membrillo,** quince jelly

jalear /hale'ar/ *vt* to encourage, urge on (by shouts, etc.)

jaleo /ha'leo/ *m*, act of encouraging dancers by clapping, shouting, etc.; Andalusian song and dance, *Inf.* uproar

jalón /ha'lon/ *m*, surveying rod

jamaicano /hamai'kano/ **(-na)** *a* and *n* Jamaican

jamás /ha'mas/ *adv* never. **nunca j.,** never. **por siempre j.,** for always, forever

jamba /'hamba/ *f*, jamb (of a door or window)

jamelgo /ha'melgo/ *m*, sorry nag, miserable hack

jamón /ha'mon/ *m*, ham

jamona /ha'mona/ *f*, *Inf.* plumpish middle-aged woman

jansenismo /hanse'nismo/ *m*, Jansenism

jansenista /hanse'nista/ *mf* and *a* Jansenist

Japón /ha'pon/ Japan

japonés /hapo'nes/ **(-esa)** *a* and *n* Japanese. *m*, Japanese (language)

jaque /'hake/ *m*, check (in chess); braggart. **j. mate,** checkmate. **en j.,** at bay

jaquear /hake'ar/ *vt* to check (in chess); *Mil.* harass the enemy

jaqueca /ha'keka/ *f*, migraine, sick headache. *Inf.* **dar una j.,** to annoy

jarabe /ha'raβe/ *m*, syrup. **j. tapatío,** Mexican hat dance

jarana /ha'rana/ *f*, roundhouse; *Inf.* revelry; fight, roughhouse; trick, deception

jarcia /'harθia; 'harsia/ *f*, equipment; *Naut.* tackle,

rigging (gen. *pl*); fishing tackle; *Inf.* heap, mixture, medley

jardín /har'ðin/ *m*, garden

jardinar /harði'nar/ *vt* to landscape

jardinera /harði'nera/ *f*, plant stand, jardiniere; open streetcar

jardinería /harðine'ria/ *f*, gardening

jardinero /harði'nero/ **(-ra)** *n* gardener

jareta /ha'reta/ *f*, *Sew.* running hem; *Naut.* netting

jarra /'harra/ *f*, jar, jug. **en jarras,** arms akimbo

jarrero /ha'rrero/ *m*, jug seller or manufacturer

jarrete /ha'rrete/ *m*, calf (of the leg)

jarretera /harre'tera/ *f*, garter. **Orden de la J.,** Order of the Garter

jarro /'harro/ *m*, pitcher; jug; jar; vase

jarrón /ha'rron/ *m*, garden urn; vase

jaspe /'haspe/ *m*, jasper

jaspeado /haspe'aðo/ *a* marbled, mottled; dappled; frosted (of glass)

jauja /'hauha/ *f*, *Fig.* paradise, land of milk and honey

jaula /'haula/ *f*, cage; crate; miner's cage

jauría /hau'ria/ *f*, pack of hounds

javanés /haβa'nes/ **(-esa)** *a* and *n* Javanese

jazmín /haθ'min; has'min/ *m*, jasmine. **j. amarillo,** yellow jasmine. **j. de la India,** gardenia

jefa /'hefa/ *f*, forewoman; manager; leader, head

jefatura /hefa'tura/ *f*, chieftainship; managership; leadership. **j. de policía,** police station or headquarters

jefe /'hefe/ *m*, chief; head, leader; manager; *Mil.* commanding officer. *Mil.* **j. de estado mayor,** chief of staff. **j. del tren,** railroad guard

jengibre /hen'hiβre/ *m*, ginger

jeque /'heke/ *m*, sheik

jerarca /he'rarka/ *m*, hierarch

jerarquía /herar'kia/ *f*, hierarchy

jerárquico /he'rarkiko/ *a* hierarchical

jeremiada /here'miaða/ *f*, lamentation

jerez /he'reθ; he'res/ *m*, sherry

jerga /'herga/ *f*, thick frieze cloth; jargon

jergón /her'gon/ *m*, straw or hay mattress, pallet; misfit (garments); *Inf.* fat, lazy person

Jericó /heri'ko/ Jericho

jerigonza /heri'gonθa; heri'gonsa/ *f*, jargon; gibberish

jeringa /he'ringa/ *f*, syringe

jeringar /herin'gar/ *vt* to inject; syringe; *Inf.* annoy

jeringuilla /herin'guiλa; herin'guiya/ *f*, small syringe; mock orange

jeroglífico /hero'glifiko/ *a* hieroglyphic. *m*, hieroglyph

jersey /her'sei/ *m*, jersey, sweater

Jerusalén /herusa'len/ Jerusalem

jesuita /he'suita/ *m*, Jesuit

jesuita, jesuítico /he'suita, he'suitiko/ *a* jesuitical

Jesús /he'sus/ *m*, Jesus —*interj* Goodness!; Bless you! (said to someone after sneezing). **¡ay J.!** Alas! *Inf.* **en un decir J.,** in a trice

jeta /'heta/ *f*, hog's snout; blubber lip; *Inf.* face, mug

jibia /'hiβia/ *f*, cuttlefish

jícara /'hikara/ *f*, small cup

jifa /'hifa/ *f*, meat offal

jifia /'hifia/ *f*, swordfish

jilguero /hil'gero/ *m*, goldfinch

jinete /hi'nete/ *m*, horseman, rider; horse soldier, cavalryman

jingoísmo /hingo'ismo/ *m*, jingoism

jip /hip/ *m*, jeep

jipijapa /hipi'hapa/ *f*, very fine straw. **sombrero de j.,** panama hat

jira /'hira/ *f*, strip of cloth; picnic; tour

jirafa /hi'rafa/ *f*, giraffe

jirón /hi'ron/ *m*, rag; piece of a dress, etc.; portion of a whole

jiujitsu /hiu'hitsu/ *m*, jujitsu
jocosidad /hokosi'ðað/ *f*, pleasantry, jocularity; joke
jocoso /ho'koso/ *a* waggish; jocose, joyous
jocundidad /hokundi'ðað/ *f*, jocundity
jocundo /ho'kundo/ *a* jocund
jofaina /ho'faina/ *f*, washbowl
jónico /'honiko/ (**-ca**) *a* Ionian —*n* Ionian. *m*, (metrics) Ionic foot
Jordán /hor'ðan/ Jordan (river)
Jordania /hor'ðania/ Jordan (country)
jornada /hor'naða/ *f*, day's journey; journey, trip; *Mil.* expedition; duration of a working day; opportunity; span of life; act of a drama. **a grandes jornadas,** by forced marches, rapidly
jornal /hor'nal/ *m*, day's wages or labor
jornalear /hornale'ar/ *vi* to work by the day
jornalero /horna'lero/ (**-ra**) *n* day laborer; wage earner
joroba /ho'roβa/ *f*, hump; *Inf.* impertinence, nuisance
jorobado /horo'βaðo/ (**-da**) *a* humpbacked —*n* hunchback
jota /'hota/ *f*, name of letter J; popular Spanish dance; jot, tittle (always used negatively). **no saber j.,** to be completely ignorant
joven /'hoβen/ *a* young. *mf* young man or woman
jovenzuelo /hoβen'θuelo; hoβen'suelo/ (**-la**) *n* youngster, boy
jovialidad /hoβiali'ðað/ *f*, joviality, cheerfulness
joya /'hoia/ *f*, jewel; present; *Archit.* astragal; *Fig.* a jewel of a person
joyería /hoie'ria/ *f*, jeweler's shop or workshop
joyero /ho'iero/ *m*, jeweler; jewel box
juanete /hua'nete/ *m*, bunion; prominent cheekbone; *Naut.* topgallant sail
juanetudo /huane'tuðo/ *a* having bunions; with prominent cheekbones
jubilación /huβila'θion; huβila'sion/ *f*, retirement; pensioning off; pension
jubilado /huβi'laðo/ *a* retired
jubilar /huβi'lar/ *vt* to pension off; excuse from certain duties; *Inf.* put aside as useless (things); —*vr* rejoice; retire or be pensioned off
jubileo /huβi'leo/ *m*, jubilee
júbilo /'huβilo/ *m*, rejoicing, merriment. **j. de vivir,** joie de vivre
jubiloso /huβi'loso/ *a* jubilant, happy
jubón /hu'βon/ *m*, doublet; bodice
judaico /hu'ðaiko/ *a* Judaic
judaísmo /huða'ismo/ *m*, Judaism
judas /'huðas/ *m*, Judas; traitor
judería /huðe'ria/ *f*, Jewry
judesmo /hu'ðesmo/ *m*, Judezmo (Romance language of Jews)
judía /hu'ðia/ *f*, Jew (female); Jewish quarter, Jewish neighborhood; haricot bean. **judías verdes,** string beans
judicatura /huðika'tura/ *f*, judicature; judgeship; judiciary
judío /hu'ðio/ (**-ía**) *a* Jewish —*n* Jew. **j. errante,** wandering Jew
juego /'huego/ *m*, play, sport; gambling; hand (of cards); set; suite; *Mech.* play, working. **j. de café,** coffee set. **j. de los cientos,** piquet. **j. de manos,** sleight of hand, conjuring. **j. de naipes,** game of cards. **j. limpio,** fair play. **j. sencillo,** single (at tennis). **j. sucio,** foul play. **juegos florales,** floral games, poetry contest. **juegos malabares,** juggling. **en j.,** in operation; at stake. **entrar en j.,** to come into play. **hacer j.,** to match. **hacer juegos malabares,** to juggle
juerga /'huerga/ *f*, *Inf.* spree, binge. **ir de j.,** *Inf.* to go on a binge
jueves /'hueβes/ *m*, Thursday. **¡No es cosa del otro j.!** *Inf.* It's no great shakes! It's nothing to write home about!
juez /hueθ; hues/ *m*, judge. **j. arbitrador,** arbitrator; referee. **j. municipal,** magistrate
jugada /hu'gaða/ *f*, play; playing; move, throw; *Fig.* bad turn
jugador /huga'ðor/ (**-ra**) *a* gambling; playing —*n* gambler; player. **j. de manos,** conjurer
jugar /hu'gar/ *vi irr* to play; frolic; take part in a

game; gamble; make a move (in a game); *Mech.* work; handle (a weapon); *Com.* intervene; —*vt* play (a match); bet; handle (a weapon); risk. **j. el lance,** *Fig.* to play one's cards well. **j. limpio,** to play fair; *Fig. Inf.* be straightforward. **j. sucio,** to play foul. **jugarse el todo por el todo,** to stake everything —*Pres. Indic.* **juego, juegas, juega, juegan.** *Pres. Subjunc.* **juegue, juegues, juegue, jueguen**
jugarreta /huga'rreta/ *f*, *Inf.* bad play; dirty trick
juglar /hug'lar/ *m*, entertainer; buffoon, juggler; minstrel
juglaresco /hugla'resko/ *a* pertaining to minstrels
jugo /'hugo/ *m*, sap; juice; *Fig.* essence. **j. de muñeca,** elbow grease
jugosidad /hugosi'ðað/ *f*, juiciness, succulence; *Fig.* pithiness
jugoso /hu'goso/ *a* juicy, succulent; *Fig.* pithy
juguete /hu'gete/ *m*, toy; plaything; *Fig.* puppet
juguetear /hugete'ar/ *vi* to frolic, gambol
jugueteo /huge'teo/ *m*, gamboling; play, dalliance
juguetería /hugete'ria/ *f*, toy trade; toy shop
juguetón /huge'ton/ *a* playful
juicio /'huiθio; 'huisio/ *m*, judgment; wisdom, prudence; sanity, right mind; opinion; horoscope. **j. final,** Last Judgment. **j. sano,** right mind. **asentar el j.,** to settle down, become sensible. **estar fuera de j.,** to be insane. **pedir en j.,** to sue at law
juicioso /hui'θioso; hui'sioso/ *a* judicious; prudent
julio /'hulio/ *m*, July; *Elec.* joule
jumento /hu'mento/ *m*, ass; beast of burden
juncal /hun'kal/ *a* reedy; rushy; *Inf.* slim, lissome
juncar /hun'kar/ *m*, reedy ground
junco /'hunko/ *m*, Bot. rush, reed; *Naut.* junk
juncoso /hun'koso/ *a* reed-like; rushy; reedy
junio /'hunio/ *m*, June
junquillo /hun'kiʎo; hun'kiyo/ *m*, jonquil; *Archit.* reed molding
junta /'hunta/ *f*, joint; assembly, council; committee; union, association; session, sitting; entirety, whole; board, management. **j. de comercio,** board of trade. **j. directiva,** managerial board
juntamente /hunta'mente/ *adv* jointly; simultaneously
juntar /hun'tar/ *vt* to join, unite (*with prep a or con*); couple; assemble; amass; leave ajar (door); —*vr* (*with con*) frequent company of; meet; join; copulate
junto /'hunto/ *a* united, together —*adv* (*with prep a*) near; —*adv* together, simultaneously. **en j.,** altogether, in all
juntura /hun'tura/ *f*, joining; joint; seam; juncture
jura /'hura/ *f*, solemn oath; swearing
jurado /hu'raðo/ *m*, jury; jury
juramentar /huramen'tar/ *vt* to swear in; —*vr* take an oath
juramento /hura'mento/ *m*, oath; curse, imprecation. **j. falso, perjury, prestar j.,** to take an oath
jurar /hu'rar/ *vt* to swear an oath; swear allegiance; —*vi* curse, be profane
jurídico /hu'riðiko/ *a* juridical, legal
jurisconsulto /huriskon'sulto/ *m*, jurisconsult
jurisdicción /hurisðik'θion; hurisðik'sion/ *f*, *Law.* jurisdiction; boundary; authority
jurisprudencia /hurispru'ðenθia; hurispru'ðensia/ *f*, jurisprudence
jurista /hu'rista/ *mf* jurist
justa /'husta/ *f*, joust; tournament; contest
justar /hus'tar/ *vi* to joust
justicia /hus'tiθia; hus'tisia/ *f*, justice; equity, right; penalty, punishment; righteousness; court of justice; *Inf.* death penalty, execution. **administrar j.,** to dispense justice
justiciero /husti'θiero; husti'siero/ *a* just
justificable /hustifi'kaβle/ *a* justifiable
justificación /hustifika'θion; hustifika'sion/ *f*, justification, impartiality, fairness; convincing proof
justificar /hustifi'kar/ *vt* to justify, vindicate; adjust, regulate; prove innocent; —*vr* justify oneself; prove one's innocence
justillo /hus'tiʎo; hus'tiyo/ *m*, jerkin
justipreciar /hustipre'θiar; hustipre'siar/ *vt* to appraise, value

justiprecio /husti'preθio; husti'presio/ *m*, appraisement, valuation

justo /'husto/ *a* just; righteous, virtuous; exact, accurate; tight-fitting, close —*adv* justly; exactly; tightly

Jutlandia /hut'landia/ Jutland

juvenil /huβe'nil/ *a* young

juventud /huβen'tuð/ *f*, youthfulness, youth; younger generation

juzgado /huθ'gaðo; hus'gaðo/ *m*, court of law; jurisdiction; judgeship

juzgar /huθ'gar; hus'gar/ *vt* to judge, pass sentence on; decide, consider

ka /ka/ *f*, name of the letter K

káiser /'kaiser/ *m*, kaiser

kan /kan/ *m*, khan

kantiano /kan'tiano/ *a* Kantian

Kenia /'kenia/ Kenya

kermese /ker'mese/ *f*, kermis, festival

kerosén /kero'sen/ *m*, kerosene

kilo /'kilo/ *prefix* meaning a thousand. *m*, *Abbr.* kilogram

kilociclo /kilo'θiklo; kilo'siklo/ *m*, *Elec.* kilocycle

kilogramo /kilo'gramo/ *m*, kilogram (2.17 lb.)

kilolitro /kilo'litro/ *m*, kiloliter

kilometraje /kilome'trahe/ *m*, number of kilometers; mileage

kilométrico /kilo'metriko/ *a* kilometric. **billete k.,** tourist ticket

kilómetro /ki'lometro/ *m*, kilometer (about $\frac{5}{8}$ mile)

kilovatio /kilo'βatio/ *m*, *Elec.* kilowatt

kiosco /'kiosko/ *m*, kiosk

L

la /la/ *def art f, sing* the (e.g. *la mesa*, the table). **la** is replaced by el *m, sing* before feminine nouns beginning with stressed *a* or *ha* (e.g. *el hambre*, hunger). **la** is sometimes used before names of famous women (e.g. *la Juana de Arco, la Melba* (Joan of Arc, Melba)) and is generally not translated —*pers pron acc f sing* her; it (e.g. *La veo venir*, I see her coming) —*dem. pron* followed by *de*, or by *que* introducing relative clause, that of, that which, the one that, she who (e.g. *La casa está lejos de la en que escribo*, The house is far from the one in which I write). **la de** is used familiarly for Mrs. (e.g. *la de Jiménez*, Mrs. Jimenez). **la** means some, any, one, as substitution for noun already given (e.g. *Su hija lo haría si la tuviera*, Her daughter would do it if she had one)

lábaro /'laβaro/ *m*, labarum, standard

laberíntico /laβe'rintiko/ *a* labyrinthine

laberinto /laβe'rinto/ *m*, labyrinth; *Fig.* tangle, complication; *Anat.* labyrinth of the ear

labia /'laβia/ *f, Inf.* blarney, gab

labial /la'βial/ *a* labial

labihendido /laβien'diðo/ *a* harelipped

labio /'laβio/ *m*, lip; rim, edge. **l. leporino,** harelip. **cerrar los labios,** to close one's lips; keep silent

labor /la'βor/ *f*, work, toil; sewing; needlework; husbandry, farming; silkworm egg; *Mineral.* working; trimming; plowing, harrowing **día l.,** workday

laborar /laβo'rar/ *vt* to work; till; plow; construct; —*vi* scheme, plot, plan

laboratorio /laβora'torio/ *m*, laboratory

laborear /laβore'ar/ *vt* to work; till, cultivate; *Naut.* reeve

laboreo /laβo'reo/ *m*, tilling, cultivation; working, development (of mines, etc.)

laboriosidad /laβoriosi'ðað/ *f*, laboriousness, diligence

laborioso /laβo'rioso/ *a* industrious, diligent; laborious, tedious, hard

laborista /laβo'rista/ *a* and *mf* belonging to the Labor Party

labra /'laβra/ *f*, stonecutting; carving or working (metal, stone, or wood)

labrada /la'βraða/ *f*, fallow land ready for sowing

labradero /laβra'ðero/ *a* workable; cultivable, tillable

labrado /la'βraðo/ *a* and *past part* worked; fashioned; carved; embroidered; figured, patterned. *m*, (gen. *pl*) cultivated ground

labrador /laβra'ðor/ *m*, laborer, worker; farmer; peasant

labradora /laβra'ðora/ *f*, peasant girl; farm girl

labradoresco, labradoril /laβraðo'resko, laβraðo'ril/ *a* rustic, peasant, farming

labrandera /laβran'dera/ *f*, seamstress

labrantío /labran'βtio/ *a* tillable, cultivable. *m*, farming

labranza /la'βranθa; la'βransa/ *f*, tillage, cultivation; farm; farmland; farming; employment, work

labrar /la'βrar/ *vt* to work, do; carve; fashion, construct, make; *Agr.* cultivate, till; plow; embroider; sew; bring about, cause; —*vi Fig.* impress deeply, leave a strong impression

labriego /la'βriego/ **(-ga)** *n* agricultural laborer; peasant

laca /'laka/ *f*, lac; lacquer, varnish; *Art.* lake (pigment)

lacayo /la'kaio/ *m*, groom; lackey, footman

lacear /lase'ar; lase'ar/ *vt Sew.* to trim with bows; tie, lace; snare, trap

laceración /laθera'θion; lasera'sion/ *f*, laceration

lacerado /laθe'raðo; lase'raðo/ *a* unhappy, unfortunate; leprous

lacerar /laθe'rar; lase'rar/ *vt* to lacerate, mangle, tear; distress, wound the feelings of

lacería /laθe'ria; lase'ria/ *f*, poverty, misery; toil, drudgery; trouble, affliction

lacero /la'θero; la'sero/ *m*, cowboy, one who uses a lasso; poacher

lacio /'laθio; 'lasio/ *a* drooping, limp; withered, faded; straight (hair)

lacónico /la'koniko/ *a* laconic; concise; Laconian

lacra /'lakra/ *f*, aftereffect, trace (of illness); vice; fault

lacrar /la'krar/ *vt* to impair the health; infect with an illness; injure, prejudice (the interests, etc.); seal with sealing wax

lacre /'lakre/ *m*, sealing wax —*a* red

lacrimal /lakri'mal/ *a* lachrymal

lacrimoso /lakri'moso/ *a* tearful, lachrymose

lactancia /lak'tanθia; lak'tansia/ *f*, lactation

lactar /lak'tar/ *vt* to suckle; feed with milk; —*vi* take or drink milk

lácteo /'lakteo/ *a* lacteal; milky

lacustre /la'kustre/ *a* lacustrine, lake

ladear /laðe'ar/ *vt* to incline; tilt; turn aside, twist; skirt, pass close to; reach by a roundabout way, go indirectly to; —*vr* tilt; be in favor of, incline to; be equal to

ladeo /la'ðeo/ *m*, tilt; sloping; turning aside

ladera /la'ðera/ *f*, slope, incline; hillside

ladería /laðe'ria/ *f*, terrace on a hillside

ladero /la'ðero/ *a* lateral

ladilla /la'ðiλa; la'ðiya/ *f*, crab louse

ladino /la'ðino/ *a* eloquent; versatile linguistically; wily, crafty; *m*, Ladino (variety of Judezmo)

lado /'laðo/ *m*, side; edge, margin; slope, declivity; faction, party; side, flank; face (of a coin); *Fig.* aspect, view; line of descent; means, way; favor, protection; *pl* helpers, protectors; advisers. **al l.,** near at hand. *Inf.* **dar de l.** (**a**), to cool off, fall out with. **dejar a un l.** (**una cosa**), to omit, pass over (a thing). **mirar de l.** *or* **de medio l.,** to look upon with disapproval; steal a look at

ladrador /laðra'ðor/ *a* barking

ladrar /la'ðrar/ *vi* to bark; *Inf.* threaten without hurting

ladrido /la'ðriðo/ *m*, bark, barking; slander, gossip

ladrillado /laðri'λaðo; laðri'yaðo/ *m*, brick floor or pavement

ladrillar /laðri'λar; laðri'yar/ *vt* to floor or pave with bricks. *m*, brickyard; brickkiln

ladrillero /laðri'λero; laðri'yero/ **(-ra)** *n* brickmaker

ladrillo /la'ðriλo; la'ðriyo/ *m*, brick; tile

ladrón /la'ðron/ **(-ona)** *a* robbing, thieving —*n* thief; robber; burglar. *m*. **l. de corazones,** ladykiller

ladronera /laðro'nera/ *f*, thieves' den; thieving, pilfering; strongbox

lagar /la'gar/ *m*, wine or olive press

lagarta /la'garta/ *f*, female lizard; *Inf.* she-serpent, cunning female

lagartera /lagar'tera/ *f*, lizard hole

lagartija /lagar'tiha/ *f*, wall lizard, small lizard

lagarto /la'garto/ *m*, lizard; *Inf.* sly, artful person, fox; *Inf.* insignia of Spanish Military Order of Santiago

lago /'lago/ *m*, lake

lagotear /lagote'ar/ *vi Inf.* to wheedle, play up to

lagotería /lagote'ria/ *f*, wheedling, coaxing, flattery

lágrima /'lagrima/ *f*, tear; drop (of liquid); exudation, ozzing (from trees)

lagrimal /lagri'mal/ *a* lachrymal

lagrimear /lagrime'ar/ *vi* to shed tears

lagrimeo /lagri'meo/ *m*, weeping, crying; watering of the eyes

lagrimoso /lagri'moso/ *a* tearful; watery (of eyes); sad, tragic

laguna /la'guna/ *f*, small lake, lagoon; lacuna; gap, hiatus

lagunoso /lagu'noso/ *a* boggy, marshy

laical /lai'kal/ *a* lay, secular

laicismo /lai'θismo; lai'sismo/ *m*, secularism

laico /'laiko/ a lay, secular

lama /'lama/ f, ooze, slime. m, lama, Buddhist priest

lamaísmo /lama'ismo/ m, lamaism

lameculos /lame'kulos/ mf Inf. toady

lamedura /lame'ðura/ f, licking; lapping

lamentable /lamen'taβle/ a lamentable

lamentación /lamenta'θion; lamenta'sion/ f, lamentation; lament

lamentador /lamenta'ðor/ **(-ra)** a lamenting, wailing —n wailer, mourner

lamentar /lamen'tar/ vt to mourn, lament, bewail; —vr bemoan, bewail

lamento /la'mento/ m, lament

lamentoso /lamen'toso/ a lamenting, afflicted; lamentable

lamer /la'mer/ vt to lick; pass the tongue over; touch lightly; lap

lámina /'lamina/ f, sheet (of metal); lamina; engraving; illustration, picture; engraving plate

laminación /lamina'θion; lamina'sion/ f, lamination, rolling (of metals)

laminado /lami'naðo/ a laminate; rolled (metals). m, rolling (of metals)

laminador /lamina'ðor/ m, rolling mill (for metals)

laminar /lami'nar/ a laminate; laminated —vt to roll (metals); laminate; lick

lámpara /'lampara/ f, lamp; radiance, light, luminous body; grease spot. **l. de los mineros** or **l. de seguridad,** safety lamp. **l. de soldar,** blowpipe. **l. termiónica,** Radio. thermionic valve. **atizar la l.,** to trim the lamp; Inf. refill drinking glasses

lamparería /lampare'ria/ f, lamp factory; lamp shop

lamparero /lampa'rero/ **(-ra),** n **lamparista** mf lamplighter; lamp maker or seller

lamparilla /lampa'riʎa; lampa'riya/ f, night-light; Bot. aspen; small lamp

lamparón /lampa'ron/ m, scrofula, king's evil; tumor (disease of horses)

lampiño /lam'piɲo/ a beardless, clean-shaven; smooth-faced; Bot. nonhirsute

lampista /lam'pista/ mf See **lamparero**

lamprea /lam'prea/ f, lamprey

lana /'lana/ f, wool; fleece; woolen garments or cloth; woolen trade (gen. pl)

lanar /la'nar/ a wool; wool-bearing. **ganado l.,** sheep

lance /'lanθe; 'lanse/ m, throw, cast; casting a fishing line; catch of fish; crisis, difficult moment; Lit. episode; quarrel; move (in a game). Fig. **l. apretado,** difficult position, tight corner. **l. de fortuna,** chance, fate. **l. de honor,** affair of honor; duel

lancear /lanθe'ar; lanse'ar/ vt to wound with a lance; lance

lancero /lan'θero; lan'sero/ m, Mil. lancer; pl lancers (dance and music)

lanceta /lan'θeta; lan'seta/ f, lancet

lancha /'lantʃa/ f, Naut. launch; lighter; ship's boat; small boat; flagstone. **l. bombardera** or **l. cañonera,** gunboat. **l. de salvamento,** ship's lifeboat. **l. escampavía,** patrol boat

lancinar /lanθi'nar; lansi'nar/ vt Med. to lance

landa /'landa/ f, lande

landó /lan'do/ m, landau

lanero /la'nero/ a woolen. m, wool merchant; wool warehouse

langosta /laŋ'gosta/ f, locust; lobster. **l. migratoria,** locust

langostín /laŋgos'tin/ m, crayfish

languidecer /laŋguiðe'θer; laŋguiðe'ser/ vi irr to languish, pine. See **conocer**

languidez /laŋgui'ðeθ; laŋgui'ðes/ f, lassitude, inertia; languor

lánguido /'laŋguiðo/ a listless, weak, languid; half-hearted; languishing, languorous

lanolina /lano'lina/ f, lanolin

lanosidad /lanosi'ðað/ f, woolliness; down (on leaves, etc.)

lanoso, lanudo /la'noso, la'nuðo/ a woolly

lanza /'lanθa; 'lansa/ f, lance, spear; lancer; nozzle (of a hosepipe). **correr lanzas,** to joust (in a tournament). **estar con la l. en ristre,** to have the lance in rest; be prepared or ready. Inf. **ser una l.,** to be very clever

lanzabombas /lanθa'βombas; lansa'βombas/ m, (Aer. Nav.) bomb release

lanzada /lan'θaða; lan'saða/ f, lance or spear thrust

lanzadera /lanθa'ðera; lansa'ðera/ f, weaver's shuttle; sewing machine shuttle. Inf. **parecer una l.,** to be constantly on the go

lanzador /lanθa'ðor; lansa'ðor/ **(-ra)** m, batsman —n thrower, caster, tosser

lanzallamas /lanθa'ʎamas; lansa'yamas/ m, flame-thrower

lanzamiento /lanθa'miento; lansa'miento/ m, throwing; cast, throw; Law. dispossession; Naut. launching

lanzaminas /lanθa'minas; lansa'minas/ m, minelayer

lanzar /lan'θar; lan'sar/ vt to throw, cast, hurl; Naut. launch; vomit; Law. dispossess; Agr. take root; —vr hurl oneself, rush; take (to), embark (upon)

lanzatorpedos /lanθator'peðos; lansator'peðos/ **(tubo)** m, torpedo tube

lañar /la'ɲar/ vt to clamp; clean fish (for salting)

lapa /'lapa/ f, barnacle, limpet

lapicero /lapi'θero; lapi'sero/ m, pencil holder, pencil case; mechanical pencil

lápida /'lapiða/ f, memorial tablet; gravestone

lapidación /lapiða'θion; lapiða'sion/ f, lapidation, stoning

lapidar /lapi'ðar/ vt to stone, lapidate; throw stones at

lapidario /lapi'ðario/ a lapidary

lapislázuli /lapis'laθuli; lapis'lasuli/ m, lapis lazuli

lápiz /'lapiθ; 'lapis/ m, graphite; pencil; crayon. **l. para los labios,** lipstick

lapizar /lapi'θar; lapi'sar/ m, graphite mine —vt to pencil

lapón /la'pon/ **(-ona)** a Lappish —n Laplander. m, Sami (language)

Laponia /la'ponia/ Lapland

lapso /'lapso/ m, lapse, period, passage; slip, error, failure

laquear /lake'ar/ vt to lacquer, paint

lar /lar/ m, home; pl lares

lardear /larðe'ar/ vt Cul. to baste

lardo /'larðo/ m, lard; animal fat

lardoso /lar'ðoso/ a greasy; fat; oily

larga /'larga/ f, longest billiard cue; delay (gen. pl). **a la l.,** in the long run

largamente /larga'mente/ adv fully, at length; generously; widely, extensively; comfortably

largar /lar'gar/ vt to slacken, loosen; Naut. unfurl; set at liberty; Fig. Inf. let fly (oaths, etc.); administer (blows, etc.); —vr Inf. quit, leave (in a hurry or secretly); Naut. set sail

largo /'largo/ a long; generous, liberal; abundant, plentiful; protracted; prolonged; expeditious; pl many long (e.g. por largos años, for many long years). m, Mus. largo; length. Inf. **¡L. de aquí!** Get out! **a la larga,** in length; eventually, finally; slowly; with many digressions. **a lo l.,** lengthwise; along the length (of); in the distance, far off; along, the length (of). Fig. **ponerse de l.,** to make one's debut in society; come of age

largor /lar'gor/ m, **largura** f, length

largueza /lar'geθa; lar'gesa/ f, length; generosity, munificence

largura /lar'gura/ f, length

laringe /la'rinhe/ f, larynx

laríngeo /la'rinheo/ a laryngeal

laringitis /larin'hitis/ f, laryngitis

larva /'larβa/ f, larva; worm, grub; specter, phantom

las /las/ def art. f pl, of **la** the —pers pron acc f pl, of **la,** them

lascivia /las'θiβia; las'siβia/ f, lasciviousness

lascivo /las'θiβo; las'siβo/ a lascivious, lewd; wanton

lasitud /lasi'tuð/ f, lassitude, weariness, exhaustion

laso /'laso/ a weary, exhausted; weak; untwisted (of silk, etc.)

lástima /'lastima/ f, compassion, pity; pitiful sight; complaint, lamentation. **dar l.,** to cause pity. **Es l.,** It's a pity. **tener l.** (**a** or **de**) to be sorry for (persons)

lastimador /lastima'ðor/ *a* harmful, injurious; painful
lastimar /lasti'mar/ *vt* to hurt, harm, injure; pity; *Fig.* wound, distress; —*vr* (*with de*) be sorry for or about; complain, lament
lastimero /lasti'mero/ *a* pitiful; mournful; injurious, harmful
lastimoso /lasti'moso/ *a* pitiful, heartbreaking; mournful
lastrar /las'trar/ *vt* to ballast
lastre /'lastre/ *m*, ballast; good sense, prudence
lata /'lata/ *f*, can, tin; tin plate; can of food. **en l.**, canned, tinned (of food). *Inf.* **Es una l.**, It's a bore, It's an awful nuisance
latamente /lata'mente/ *adv* extensively, at length; broadly
latente /la'tente/ *a* latent
lateral /late'ral/ *a* lateral
látex /'lateks/ *m*, latex
latido /la'tiðo/ *m*, yelp, bark; beat; throb; palpitation
latifundios /lati'fundios/ *m pl*, latifundia (large agricultural estates)
latigazo /lati'gaθo; lati'gaso/ *m*, lash; crack of a whip; sudden blow of fate; *Inf.* draft (of wine, etc.); harsh scolding; *Naut.* jerk or flapping (of sails)
látigo /'latigo/ *m*, whip, lash; cinch, girth of a saddle
latín /la'tin/ *m*, Latin. **bajo l.**, low Latin. *Inf.* **saber l.**, to know the score; be smart
latinajo /lati'naho/ *m*, *Inf.* bad Latin
latinidad /latini'ðað/ *f*, Latinity
latinismo /lati'nismo/ *m*, Latinism
latinista /lati'nista/ *mf* Latinist
latinizar /latini'θar; latini'sar/ *vt* to latinize; —*vi Inf.* use Latin phrases
latino /la'tino/ *a* Latin; lateen sail
latinoamericano /latinoameri'kano/ **(-na)** *a and n* Latin-American
latir /la'tir/ *vi* to yelp, howl; bark; throb, palpitate, beat
latitud /lati'tuð/ *f*, latitude; area, extent; breadth
latitudinario /lati,tuði'nario/ *a* latitudinarian
lato /'lato/ *a* extensive; large; broad (of word meanings)
latón /la'ton/ *m*, brass
latonería /latone'ria/ *f*, brassworks; brass shop
latoso /la'toso/ *a* boring, troublesome, annoying
latrocinio /latro'θinio; latro'sinio/ *m*, larceny
latvio /'latβio/ **(-la)** *a and n* Latvian
laúd /la'uð/ *m*, lute
laudable /lau'ðaβle/ *a* praiseworthy, laudable
láudano /'lauðano/ *m*, laudanum
laudatorio /lauða'torio/ *a* laudatory
laurear /laure'ar/ *vt* to crown with laurel; honor, reward
laurel /lau'rel/ *m*, bay tree. **l. cerezo**, laurel. **l. rosa**, rosebay, oleander
láureo /'laureo/ *a* laurel
lauréola /lau'reola/ *f*, laurel wreath
lauro /'lauro/ *m*, bay tree; glory, triumph
Lausana /lau'sana/ Lausanne
lava /'laβa/ *f*, lava
lavable /la'βaβle/ *a* washable
lavabo /la'βaβo/ *m*, washstand; cloakroom, lavatory
lavada /la'βaða/ *f*, load of wash, load
lavadedos /laβa'ðeðos/ *m*, fingerbowl
lavadero /laβa'ðero/ *m*, washing place; laundry
lavado /la'βaðo/ *m*, washing; cleaning; wash. **l. al seco**, dry cleaning
lavadura /laβa'ðura/ *f*, washing
lavamanos /laβa'manos/ *m*, washstand; lavatory
lavamiento /laβa'miento/ *m*, washing, cleansing, ablution
lavanda /la'βanda/ *f*, lavender
lavandera /laβan'dera/ *f*, laundress; washerwoman
lavandería /laβande'ria/ *f*, laundry
lavandero /laβan'dero/ *m*, laundry; laundryman
lavaplatos /laβa'platos/ *m*, dishwasher
lavar /la'βar/ *vt* to wash; *Fig.* wipe out, purify; paint in watercolors. **l. al seco**, to dry-clean
lavativa /laβa'tiβa/ *f*, enema; syringe, clyster; *Inf.* nuisance, bore

lavatorio /laβa'torio/ *m*, washing, lavation; *Eccl.* lavabo; lavatory, washing place; *Eccl.* maundy
lavazas /la'βaθas; la'βasas/ *f pl*, dirty soapy water
laxante /lak'sante/ *a* and *m*, laxative
laxar /lak'sar/ *vt* to loosen, relax; soften
laxitud /laksi'tuð/ *f*, laxity
laxo /'lakso/ *a* lax; slack
laya /'laia/ *f*, *Agr.* spade; kind, sort, class
layar /la'iar/ *vt Agr.* to fork
lazar /la'θar; la'sar/ *vt* to lasso
lazareto /laθa'reto; lasa'reto/ *m*, leper hospital; quarantine hospital
lazarillo /laθa'riʎo; lasa'riyo/ *m*, boy who guides a blind person
lazarino /laθa'rino; lasa'rino/ *a* leprous
lázaro /'laθaro; 'lasaro/ *m*, lazar, beggar
lazo /'laθo; 'laso/ *m*, bow; knot of ribbons; tie; ornamental tree; figure (in dancing); lasso; rope, bond; lace (of a shoe); *Fig.* trap, snare; bond, obligation; slipknot. **l. corredizo**, running knot. *Fig. Inf.* **armar l.**, to set a trap. *Inf.* **caer en el l.**, to fall into the trap, be deceived
le /le/ *pers pron dat m*, or *f*, *3rd pers sing* to him, to her, to it, to you (e.g. *María le dio el perro*, Mary gave him (her, you) the dog). Clarity may require the addition of **a él, a ella, a usted** (e.g. *Le dio el perro a ella*, etc.) —*pers pron acc m*, *3rd pers sing* him (e.g. *Le mandé a casa*, I sent him home)
leal /le'al/ *a* loyal; faithful (animals)
lealtad /leal'tað/ *f*, loyalty; faithfulness; sincerity, truth
lebrel /le'βrel/ *m*, greyhound
lección /lek'θion; lek'sion/ *f*, reading; lesson; oral test; warning, example. **l. práctica**, object lesson. **dar l.**, to give a lesson. **tomar la l.**, to hear a lesson
leccionista /lekθio'nista; leksio'nista/ *mf* private teacher, coach, tutor
lechas /'letʃas/ *f pl*, soft roe; milt
leche /'letʃe/ *f*, milk; milky fluid of some plants and seeds. *Inf.* **estar con la l. en los labios**, to be young and inexperienced
lechera /le'tʃera/ *f*, milkmaid; milk can or jug
lechería /letʃe'ria/ *f*, dairy; dairy shop
lechero /le'tʃero/ **(-ra)** *a* dairy, milk; milky; milch, milk-giving —*n* milk seller. **industria lechera**, dairy farming
lecho /'letʃo/ *m*, bed; couch; animal's bed, litter; riverbed; bottom of the sea; layer; *Geol.* stratum
lechón /le'tʃon/ *m*, suckling pig; hog; *Inf.* slovenly man
lechoso /le'tʃoso/ *a* milky
lechuga /le'tʃuga/ *f*, lettuce; frill, flounce. *Inf.* **como una l.**, as fresh as a daisy
lechuguero /letʃu'gero/ **(-ra)** *n* lettuce seller
lechuguilla /letʃu'giʎa; letʃu'giya/ *f*, ruff; ruche
lechuguina /letʃu'gina/ *f*, *Inf.* affected, overdressed young woman
lechuguino /letʃu'gino/ *m*, lettuce plant; *Inf.* young blood, gallant; *Inf.* foppish young man
lechuza /le'tʃuθa; le'tʃusa/ *f*, barn owl
lector /lek'tor/ **(-ra)** *n* reader; lecturer
lectura /lek'tura/ *f*, reading; lecture; culture, knowledge
ledo /'leðo/ *a* happy, content
leer /le'er/ *vt irr* to read; explain, interpret; teach; take part in an oral test. See **creer**
lega /'lega/ *f*, *Eccl.* lay sister
legación /lega'θion; lega'sion/ *f*, *Eccl.* legateship; legation
legado /le'gaðo/ *m*, legacy; legate
legajo /le'gaho/ *m*, bundle, docket; file
legal /le'gal/ *a* legal; legitimate; upright, trustworthy
legalidad /legali'ðað/ *f*, legality
legalización /legaliθa'θion; legalisa'sion/ *f*, legalization
legalizar /legali'θar; legali'sar/ *vt* to legalize
legalmente /legal'mente/ *adv* lawfully
légamo /'legamo/ *m*, mud, slime
legamoso /lega'moso/ *a* slimy
legaña /le'gaɲa/ *f*, bleariness (of the eyes)
legañoso /lega'ɲoso/ *a* bleary-eyed

legar /le'gar/ vt to bequeath; send as a legate

legatario /lega'tario/ (-ia) n legatee, one to whom a legacy is bequeathed

legendario /lehen'dario/ a legendary

legibilidad /lehiβili'ðað/ f, legibility

legible /le'hiβle/ a legible

legión /le'hion/ f, legion

legionario /lehio'nario/ a and m, legionary

legislación /lehisla'sion; lehisla'θion/ f, legislation

legislador /lehisla'ðor/ (-ra) a legislative —n legislator

legislar /lehis'lar/ vi to legislate

legislativo /lehisla'tiβo/ a legislative

legislatura /lehisla'tura/ f, legislature

legista /le'hista/ mf jurist; student of law

legítima /le'hitima/ f, portion of a married man's estate that cannot be willed away from his wife and children

legitimación /lehitima'θion; lehitima'sion/ f, legitimation

legitimar /lehiti'mar/ vt to legitimize

legitimidad /lehitimi'ðað/ f, legitimacy

legítimo /le'hitimo/ a legitimate; real, true

lego /'lego/ a lay, secular. m, layman

legua /'legua/ f, league (approximately 5.573 meters). **a la l., de cien leguas, desde media l.,** from afar

legumbre /le'gumbre/ f, pulse; vegetable

leguminoso /legumi'noso/ a leguminous

leído /le'iðo/ a well-read

leila /'leila/ f, nocturnal Moorish merrymaking or dance

lejanía /leha'nia/ f, distance

lejano /le'hano/ a distant, remote, far off

lejía /le'hia/ f, lye; bleaching solution; Inf. dressing-down, scolding

lejos /'lehos/ adv far off, far, distant. m, perspective, view from afar; Art. background. **a lo l.,** far off, in the distance. **de** or **desde l.,** from afar, from a distance

lelo /'lelo/ a stupid; fatuous, inane

lema /'lema/ m, chapter heading; argument, summary; motto; theme, subject

lémur /'lemur/ m, lemur

lencería /lenθe'ria; lense'ria/ f, linen goods; linen merchant's shop; linen closet

lencero /len'θero; len'sero/ m, linen merchant

lene /'lene/ a smooth, soft; kind, sweet, gentle; lightweight

lengua /'lengua/ f, Anat. tongue; mother tongue, language; clapper of a bell; information. mf spokes. **l. de escorpión** or **mala l.,** scandalmonger, backbiter. **l. de fuego,** Eccl. tongue of fire, flame. **l. del agua,** waterline, tidemark. **l. de oc,** langue d'oc. **l. de oil,** langue d'oil. **l. de tierra,** neck of land, promontory. **l. viva,** modern language. Inf. **andar en lenguas,** to be on every lip, be famous. Inf. **hacerse lenguas de,** to praise to the skies. Inf. **irse (a uno) la l.,** to be indiscreet, talk too much. Inf. **poner l.** or **lenguas en,** to gossip about. Inf. **tener mucha l.,** to be very talkative. **tomar l.** or **lenguas,** to find out about, inform oneself on

lenguado /len'guaðo/ m, Ichth. sole

lenguaje /len'guahe/ m, language; style; speech, idiom. **l. vulgar,** common speech

lengüeta /len'gueta/ f, dim little tongue; Mus. tongue (of wind instruments); barb (of an arrow); needle (of a balance)

lenidad /leni'ðað/ f, lenience, indulgence, mercy

Leningrado /lenin'graðo/ Leningrad

lenitivo /leni'tiβo/ a lenitive; soothing. m, Med. lenitive; Fig. balm (of sorrow, etc.)

lente /'lente/ m, lens; pl eyeglasses. **l. de aumento,** magnifying glass

lenteja /len'teha/ f, lentil; lentil plant

lentejuela /lente'huela/ f, sequin

lentitud /lenti'tuð/ f, lentitude; slowness, deliberation

lento /'lento/ a slow, deliberate; sluggish, heavy; Med. glutinous, adhesive

leña /'leɲa/ f, firewood; Inf. beating, birching. Fig.

echar l. al fuego, to add fuel to the flame. Fig. **llevar l. al monte,** to carry coals to Newcastle

leñador /leɲa'ðor/ (-ra) n woodcutter; firewood dealer

leñera /le'ɲera/ f, woodpile; woodshed

leño /'leɲo/ m, wooden log; wood, timber; Poet. ship; Inf. blockhead

leñoso /le'ɲoso/ a woody, ligneous

león /le'on/ m, lion. Astron. Leo; valiant man. **l. marino,** sea lion

leona /le'ona/ f, lioness

leonera /leo'nera/ f, lion cage; lion's den; Inf. gambling den; Inf. lumber room

leonero /leo'nero/ (-ra) n lionkeeper; Inf. keeper of a gambling house

leonés /leo'nes/ (-esa) a and n Leonese

leonino /leo'nino/ a leonine

leopardo /leo'parðo/ m, leopard

lepra /'lepra/ f, leprosy

leproso /le'proso/ a leprous

lerdo /'lerðo/ a slow, lumbering (gen. horses); stupid, slow-witted, dull

les /les/ pers pron dat 3rd pers pl mf, to them (e.g. Les dimos las flores, We gave them flowers. Les hablé del asunto, I spoke to them about the matter)

lesbio /'lesβio/ (-ia) a and n lesbian

lesión /le'sion/ f, lesion, wound; Fig. injury

lesionar /lesio'nar/ vt to wound; Fig. injure

lesna /'lesna/ f, awl

leso /'leso/ a wounded, hurt; offensive, injurious; Fig. unbalanced, perturbed (of the mind). **crimen de lesa majestad,** crime of lèse-majesté

letal /le'tal/ a lethal; deadly

letanía /leta'nia/ f, Eccl. litany

letargia /le'tarhia/ f, Med. lethargy

letárgico /le'tarhiko/ a lethargic

letargo /le'targo/ m, lethargy; indifference, apathy

Letonia /le'tonia/ Latvia

letra /'letra/ f, letter (of alphabet); Print. type; penmanship, hand; Fig. letter, literal meaning; words (of a song); inscription; Com. bill, draft; cunning, shrewdness; pl learning, knowledge. **l. abierta,** Com. open credit. **l. de cambio,** Com. bill of exchange. **l. gótica,** Gothic characters. **l. itálica,** italics. **l. mayúscula,** capital letter. **l. paladial,** palatal. **facultad de letras,** faculty of arts. **l. con sangre entra,** Learning is acquired with pain. **primeras letras,** early education, first letters

letrado /le'traðo/ a learned, educated; Inf. presumptuous; pedantic. m, lawyer

letrero /le'trero/ m, label; inscription; poster; bill; sign, indicator. **l. luminoso,** illuminated sign

letrilla /le'triʎa; le'triya/ f, short poem, often set to music

letrina /le'trina/ f, latrine

leucocito /leuko'θito; leuko'sito/ m, leucocyte

leva /'leβa/ f, Naut. weighing anchor; Mil. levy, forced enrollment; tappet; Mech. lever; Mech. cam; Inf. **irse a l. y a monte,** to flee, beat it, quit

levadizo /leβa'ðiθo; leβa'ðiso/ a able to be raised or lowered (bridges). **puente l.,** drawbridge

levadura /leβa'ðura/ f, leaven, yeast; rising (of bread)

levantada /leβan'taða/ f, act of rising from bed

levantamiento /leβanta'miento/ m, raising, lifting; rebellion, revolt; ennoblement, elevation; settlement of accounts

levantar /leβan'tar/ vt to raise, lift; pick up; build, construct; cancel, remove; encourage, rouse; recruit, enlist; cut (cards); leave, abandon; survey; disturb (game); produce, raise (a swelling); found, institute; increase (prices); raise (the voice); Fig. ennoble, elevate; cause, occasion; libel, accuse falsely; —vr rise; get up; stand up; stand out, be prominent; rebel; leave one's bed after an illness. **l. bandera,** to rebel. **l. el campo,** to break camp. **levantarse del izquierdo,** to get out of bed on the wrong side

levante /le'βante/ m, east; Levant; east wind

levantino /leβan'tino/ (-na) a and n Levantine

levar /le'βar/ vt Naut. to weigh anchor; —vr set sail

leve /'leβe/ a light (in weight); unimportant, trifling

levedad /leβe'ðað/ *f*, lightness (in weight); unimportance, levity, flippancy
leviatán /leβia'tan/ *m*, leviathan
levita /le'βita/ *m*, Levite; deacon. *f*, frock coat
levitación /leβita'θion; leβita'sion/ *f*, levitation
levítico /le'βitiko/ *a* Levitical. *m*, Leviticus
levitón /leβi'ton/ *m*, frock coat
léxico /'leksiko/ *m*, lexicon
lexicografía /leksikogra'fia/ *f*, lexicography
lexicógrafo /leksi'kografo/ *m*, lexicographer
lexicólogo /leksi'kologo/ *m*, lexicologist
ley /lei/ *f*, law; precept; regulation, rule; doctrine; loyalty, faithfulness; affection, love; legal standard (weights, measures, quality); ratio of gold or silver in coins, jewelry; statute, ordinance; *pl* the Law. **l. de préstamo y arriendo**, Lend-Lease Act. **ley suntuaria,** sumptuary law. *Inf.* **a la l.,** with care and decorum. **a l. de caballero,** on the word of a gentleman. **de buena l.,** *a* excellent; —*adv* genuinely; in good faith. **de mala l.,** *a* disreputable, base; —*adv* in bad faith
leyenda /le'ienda/ *f*, legend; inscription; story, tale
leyente /le'iente/ *a* reading. *mf* reader
lezna /'leθna; 'lesna/ *f*, awl
lía /'lia/ *f*, plaited esparto rope; *pl* lees, dregs
liar /li'ar/ *vt* to fasten or tie up; wrap up, parcel; roll (a cigarette); *Inf.* entangle, embroil; —*vr* take a lover, enter on a liaison. *Inf.* **liarlas,** to quit, sneak off; *Inf.* kick the bucket, die
libación /liβa'θion; liβa'sion/ *f*, libation
Líbano, el /'liβano, el/ Lebanon
libar /li'βar/ *vt* to suck; perform a libation; sip, taste; sacrifice
libelista /liβe'lista/ *mf* libeler
libelo /li'βelo/ *m*, libel; *Law.* petition
libélula /li'βelula/ *f*, dragonfly
liberación /liβera'θion; liβera'sion/ *f*, liberation, freeing; receipt, quittance; *Law.* reconveyance (of mortgages)
liberador /liβera'ðor/ **(-ra)** *a* liberating, freeing —*n* liberator
liberal /liβe'ral/ *a* generous, openhanded; liberal, tolerant; learned (of professions) —*a* and *mf Polit.* liberal
liberalidad /liβerali'ðað/ *f*, generosity, magnanimity
liberalismo /liβera'lismo/ *m*, liberalism
liberalizar /liβerali'θar; liβerali'sar/ *vt* to liberalize, make liberal
liberar /liβe'rar/ *vt* to liberate
libérrimo /li'βerrimo/ *a superl* extremely free, most free
libertad /liβer'tað/ *f*, liberty, freedom; independence; privilege, right (gen. *pl*); exemption; licentiousness; forwardness, familiarity; naturalness, ease of manner; facility, capacity; immunity. **l. caucional,** freedom on bail, release on bail. **l. de cultos,** freedom of worship; religious toleration. **l. vigilada,** *Law.* probation. **poner en l.,** to set at liberty; (*with de*) *Fig.* free from
libertador /liβerta'ðor/ **(-ra)** *a* liberating, freeing —*n* liberator, deliverer
libertar /liβer'tar/ *vt* to liberate, free; save, deliver; exempt
libertario /liβer'tario/ **(-ia)** *a* anarchistic —*n* anarchist
libertinaje /liβerti'nahe/ *m*, libertinage, licentiousness
libertino /liβer'tino/ **(-na)** *a* debauched, licentious. *m*, libertine —*n* child of a freed slave
liberto /li'βerto/ **(-ta)** *n* freed slave, freedman
Libia /'liβia/ Libya
libidine /li'βiðine/ *f*, lust
libidinoso /liβiði'noso/ *a* libidinous, lustful
libio /'liβio/ **(-ia)** *a* and *n* Libyan
libra /'liβra/ *f*, pound (measure, coinage); *Astron.* Libra. **l. esterlina,** pound sterling. **l. medicinal,** pound troy
libración /liβra'θion; liβra'sion/ *f*, oscillation; *Astron.* libration
librador /liβra'ðor/ **(-ra)** *a* freeing, liberating —*n* deliverer, liberator. *m*, *Com.* drawer (of bill of exchange, etc.)
libramiento /liβra'miento/ *m*, liberation, deliverance; *Com.* delivery; order of payment

libranza /li'βranθa; li'βransa/ *f*, *Com.* draft
librar /li'βrar/ *vt* to liberate, free; protect (from misfortune); *Com.* draw (a draft); *Com.* deliver; place confidence in; issue, enact; —*vi* bring forth children; —*vr* (*with de*) escape from; get rid of
libre /'liβre/ *a* free; at liberty, disengaged; unhampered, untrammeled; independent; bold, brazen; dissolute, vicious; exempt; vacant, unoccupied; unmarried; clear, free; mutinous, rebellious; isolated, remote; innocent; unharmed. **l. cambio,** free trade
librea /li'βrea/ *f*, livery
librecambio /liβre'kambio/ *m*, free trade
librecambista /liβrekam'βista/ *a* free trade. *mf* free trader
librepensador /liβrepensa'ðor/ **(-ra)** *a* freethinking —*n* freethinker
librepensamiento /liβrepensa'miento/ *m*, free thought
librería /liβre'ria/ *f*, bookshop; book trade, bookselling; bookcase
librero /li'βrero/ *m*, bookseller. **l. anticuario,** antiquarian bookseller; rare-book dealer
libreta /li'βreta/ *f*, *Cul.* 1-lb. loaf; notebook; passbook, bankbook
libretista /liβre'tista/ *mf* librettist
libreto /li'βreto/ *m*, libretto
librillo /li'βriʎo; li'βriyo/ *m*, *dim* small book; book of cigarette papers; tub, pail; *Zool.* omasum
libro /'liβro/ *m*, book; *Mus.* libretto; *Zool.* omasum. **l. copiador,** *Com.* letter book. **l. de actas,** minute book. **l. de caja,** *Com.* cash book. **l. de cheques,** checkbook. **l. de facturas,** *Com.* invoice book. **l. de reclamaciones,** complaint book. **l. de texto,** textbook. **l. diario,** *Com.* daybook. **l. mayor,** ledger. **l. talonario,** receipt book. *Fig. Inf.* **hacer l. nuevo,** to turn over a new leaf; introduce innovations
licencia /li'θenθia; li'sensia/ *f*, permission, license; licentiousness; boldness, insolence; *Educ.* bachelor's degree, licentiate. **l. absoluta,** *Mil.* discharge
licenciado /liθen'θiaðo; lisen'siaðo/ **(-da)** *a* pedantic; free, exempt; licensed —*n Educ.* bachelor; licentiate. *m*, discharged soldier
licenciar /liθen'θiar; lisen'siar/ *vt* to allow, permit; license; dismiss, discharge; confer degree of bachelor or licentiate; *Mil.* discharge; —*vr* become licentious; receive bachelor's degree or licentiate
licenciatura /liθenθia'tura; lisensia'tura/ *f*, degree of licentiate or bachelor; graduation as such; licentiate course of study
licencioso /liθen'θioso; lisen'sioso/ *a* licentious, dissolute
liceo /li'θeo; li'seo/ *m*, lyceum
licitación /liθita'θion; lisita'sion/ *f*, bidding (at auction)
licitador /liθita'ðor; lisita'ðor/ *m*, bidder (at auction)
licitar /liθi'tar; lisi'tar/ *vt* to bid for (at auction)
lícito /'liθito; 'lisito/ *a* permissible, lawful
licor /li'kor/ *m*, liquor, alcoholic drink; liquid
licorera /liko'rera/ *f*, liqueur set; decanter
licoroso /liko'roso/ *a* aromatic, generous (of wines)
licuadora /likua'ðora/ *f*, blender
licuar /li'kuar/ *vt* to liquefy
licuefacción /likuefak'θion; likuefak'sion/ *f*, liquefaction
lid /lið/ *f*, combat, fight; dispute, controversy. **en buena l.,** in fair fight; by fair means
líder /'liðer/ *m*, leader; chief
lidia /'liðia/ *f*, fight; bullfight
lidiador /liðia'ðor/ **(-ra)** *n* combatant, fighter
lidiar /li'ðiar/ *vi* to fight; *Fig.* struggle; (*with contra or con*) oppose, fight against; —*vt* fight (a bull). **¡Cuánto tienen que l. con...!** *Fig.* What a struggle they have with...!
liebre /'lieβre/ *f*, hare
liendre /'liendre/ *f*, nit
lienza /'lienθa; liensa/ *f*, narrow strip (of cloth)
lienzo /'lienθo; 'lienso/ *m*, linen; cotton; cambric; hemp cloth; *Art.* canvas
liga /'liga/ *f*, garter; bandage; birdlime; mixture, blend; *Metall.* alloy; alliance, coalition; league (football, etc.)
ligación /liga'θion; liga'sion/ *f*, tying; binding; union

ligado /li'gaðo/ *m, Mus.* legato; *Mus.* tie
ligadura /liga'ðura/ *f,* bond, tie; binding, fastening; *Fig.* shackle, link; (*Surg. Mus.*) ligature; *Naut.* lashing
ligamento /liga'mento/ *m,* tie, bond; mixture; *Anat.* ligament
ligar /li'gar/ *vt* to tie, bind; *Metall.* alloy; join, connect; render impotent by sorcery; *Mus.* slur (notes); —*vr* ally, join together; *Fig.* bind oneself. **l. cabos,** to put two and two together
ligazón /liga'θon; liga'son/ *f,* fastening; union; bond
ligereza /lihe'reθa; lihe'resa/ *f,* lightness (of weight); swiftness, nimbleness; fickleness; tactless remark, indiscretion
ligero /li'hero/ *a* light (in weight); swift, nimble; light (sleep); unimportant, insignificant; easily digested (food); thin (fabrics, etc.); fickle, changeable. **l. de cascos,** frivolous, gay. **a la ligera,** lightly; quickly; without fuss. **de l.,** impetuously, thoughtlessly; easily, with ease
lignito /lig'nito/ *m,* lignite
lija /'liha/ *f,* dogfish; sandpaper
lijar /li'har/ *vt* to sandpaper
lila /'lila/ *f,* lilac bush and flower; lilac color —*a Inf.* foolish, vain
liliputiense /lilipu'tiense/ *a* and *mf* Lilliputian
lima /'lima/ *f,* sweet lime, citron fruit; lime tree; file (tool); filing, polishing
limadura /lima'ðura/ *f,* filing; polishing; *pl* filings
limar /li'mar/ *vt* to file, smooth with a file; *Fig.* touch up, polish
limazo /li'maθo; li'maso/ *m,* slime, viscosity (especially of snails, etc.)
limbo /'limbo/ *m,* limbo; edge, hem; (*Astron. Bot.*) limb; limb (of a quadrant, etc.). *Inf.* **estar en el l.,** to be bewildered or abstracted
limen /'limen/ *m, Poet.* threshold; *Psychol.* limen
limeño /li'meɲo/ **(-ña)** *a* and *n* native of or belonging to Lima (Peru)
limero /li'mero/ **(-ra)** *n* seller of sweet limes. *m,* sweet lime tree (citron)
limitación /limita'θion; limita'sion/ *f,* limitation; limit, extent, bound; district, area
limitado /limi'taðo/ *a* dull-witted, limited
limitáneo /limi'taneo/ *a* bordering
limitar /limi'tar/ *vt* to limit; curb, restrict; bound
límite /'limite/ *m,* limit, extent; boundary, border; end, confine
limítrofe /li'mitrofe/ *a* bordering, contiguous
limo /'limo/ *m,* mud, mire, slime
limón /li'mon/ *m,* lemon; lemon tree
limonada /limo'naða/ *f,* lemonade. **l. seca,** lemonade powder
limonar /limo'nar/ *m,* lemon grove
limonero /limo'nero/ **(-ra)** *n* lemon seller. *m,* lemon tree
limosna /li'mosna/ *f,* alms
limosnear /limosne'ar/ *vi* to beg, ask alms
limosnero /limos'nero/ *a* charitable, generous. *m,* almoner
limoso /li'moso/ *a* slimy, muddy
limpiabarros /limpia'βarros/ *m,* shoe scraper
limpiabotas /limpia'βotas/ *m,* bootblack (person)
limpiachimeneas /limpiatʃime'neas/ *m,* chimneysweep
limpiador /limpia'ðor/ **(-ra)** *a* cleaning —*n* cleaner
limpiadura /limpia'ðura/ *f,* cleaning; *pl* rubbish
limpiamente /limpia'mente/ *adv* cleanly; dexterously, neatly; sincerely, candidly; generously, charitably
limpiametales /limpiame'tales/ *m,* metal polish
limpiaparabrisas /limpiapara'βrisas/ *m,* windshield wiper
limpiapipas /limpia'pipas/ *m,* pipe cleaner
limpiar /lim'piar/ *vt* to clean; *Fig.* cleanse, clear; empty, free (from); *Agr.* thin out; *Inf.* steal, pinch; *Inf.* win (gambling); —*vr* clean oneself
limpiauñas /limpia'uɲas/ *m,* orange stick (for fingernails)
limpidez /limpi'ðeθ; limpi'ðes/ *f, Poet.* limpidity
límpido /'limpiðo/ *a Poet.* limpid
limpieza /lim'pieθa; lim'piesa/ *f,* cleanliness; cleaning; chastity; purity; altruism; uprightness, integrity; neatness, tidiness; dexterity, skill, precision; fair play
limpio /'limpio/ *a* clean; pure, unalloyed, unmixed; neat, tidy; pure-blooded; unharmed, free. **en l.,** in substance; as a fair copy; clearly; *Com.* net
linaje /li'nahe/ *m,* lineage, family; offspring; kind; sort, quality
linajudo /lina'huðo/ **(-da)** *a* highborn —*n* noble, aristocrat; one who alleges his noble descent
linar /li'nar/ *m,* field of flax
linaza /li'naθa; li'nasa/ *f,* linseed
lince /'linθe; 'linse/ *m,* lynx; fox, crafty person
linchamiento /lintʃa'miento/ *m,* lynching
linchar /lin'tʃar/ *vt* to lynch
lindar /lin'dar/ *vi* to run together, be contiguous
linde /'linde/ *mf* limit, extent; boundary
lindero /lin'dero/ *a* bordering, contiguous. *m,* boundary. *Inf.* **con linderos y arrabales,** with many digressions
lindeza /lin'deθa; lin'desa/ *f,* beauty, loveliness; witticism; *pl* (*Inf. ironical*) insults
lindo /'lindo/ *a* lovely, beautiful; perfect, exquisite. *m, Inf.* fop (gen. **lindo don Diego**)
línea /'linea/ *f,* line; kind, class; ancestry, lineage; limit, extent; *Mil.* file; equator. **l. aérea,** airline. *Naut.* **l. de flotación,** waterline. **l. de toque,** touchline (in soccer). **l. recta,** direct line (of descent)
lineal /line'al/ *a* lineal
lineamento /linea'mento/ *m,* lineament
linear /line'ar/ *a* linear —*vt* to line, mark with lines; *Art.* sketch
linfa /'linfa/ *f, Med.* lymph; vaccine; *Poet.* water
linfático /lin'fatiko/ *a* lymphatic
lingote /liŋ'gote/ *m,* ingot; bar (of iron). **l. de fundición,** pig iron
lingüista /liŋ'guista/ *mf* linguist
lingüística /liŋ'guistika/ *f,* linguistics
lingüístico /liŋ'guistiko/ *a* linguistic
linimento /lini'mento/ *m,* liniment
lino /'lino/ *m, Bot.* flax; linen; *Poet.* ship's sail, canvas
linóleo /li'noleo/ *m,* linoleum
linotipia /lino'tipia/ *f,* linotype
linterna /lin'terna/ *f,* lantern; lighthouse; lamp. **l. sorda,** dark lantern
lío /'lio/ *m,* bundle; *Inf.* muddle, imbroglio; *Inf.* liaison, amour. *Inf.* **armar un l.,** to make a muddle, cause trouble. *Inf.* **hacerse un l.,** to get in a fix; get in a muddle
liquen /'liken/ *m,* lichen
liquidable /liki'ðaβle/ *a* liquefiable
liquidación /likiða'θion; likiða'sion/ *f,* liquefaction; *Com.* clearance, sale; *Com.* settlement
liquidar /liki'ðar/ *vt* to liquefy; *Com.* settle; *Com.* liquidate; finish; —*vr* liquefy
liquidez /liki'ðeθ; liki'ðes/ *f,* liquidness
líquido /'likiðo/ *a* liquid; *Com.* net. *m,* liquid; *Com.* net profit
lira /'lira/ *f, Mus.* lyre; *Astron.* Lyra; lira (coin)
lírica /'lirika/ *f,* lyrical verse, lyric
lírico /'liriko/ *a* lyrical
lirio /'lirio/ *m,* lily. **l. cárdeno,** yellow flag (iris). **l. de los valles,** lily of the valley
lirismo /li'rismo/ *m,* lyricism
lirón /li'ron/ *m, Zool.* dormouse; *Inf.* sleepyhead
Lisboa /lis'βoa/ Lisbon
lisbonense /lisβo'nense/ *a* and *mf* **lisbonés (-esa)** *a* and *n* Lisboan
lisiado /li'siaðo/ *a* lame, crippled
lisiar /li'siar/ *vt* to cripple, lame; —*vr* be disabled; be lame
liso /'liso/ *a* smooth; sleek; unadorned, plain; unicolored
lisonja /li'sonha/ *f,* flattery, adulation
lisonjear /lisonhe'ar/ *vt* to flatter; fawn upon; *Fig.* delight (the ear). **lisonjearse de...,** to flatter oneself on...
lisonjero /lison'hero/ **(-ra)** *a* flattering; sweet, pleasant (sounds) —*n* flatterer
lista /'lista/ *f,* strip of cloth; streak; rib; stripe; catalog, list. **l. de correos,** general delivery, poste re-

stante. **l. de platos,** bill of fare. **pasar l.,** to call the roll; check the list

listado /lis'taðo/ *a* streaked; striped; ribbed

listo /'listo/ *a* clever; expeditious, diligent; ready, prepared

listón /lis'ton/ *m,* ribbon; strip (of wood)

lisura /li'sura/ *f,* smoothness; sleekness; flatness; sincerity

litera /li'tera/ *f,* litter; *Naut.* berth

literal /lite'ral/ *a* literal

literario /lite'rario/ *a* literary

literatear /literate'ar/ *vi* to write on literary subjects

literato /lite'rato/ **(-ta)** *a* literary —*n* writer, litterateur

literatura /litera'tura/ *f,* literature

litigación /litiga'θion; litiga'sion/ *f,* litigation

litigante /liti'gante/ *mf* litigant

litigar /liti'gar/ *vt* to litigate; —*vi* dispute, argue

litigio /li'tihio/ *m,* lawsuit; dispute, argument

litigioso /liti'hioso/ *a* litigious; quarrelsome, disputatious

litisexpensas /litiseks'pensas/ *f pl, Law.* costs of a suit; legal expenses

litografía /litogra'fia/ *f,* lithography

litografiar /litogra'fiar/ *vt* to lithograph

litográfico /lito'grafiko/ *a* lithographic

litoral /lito'ral/ *a* and *m,* littoral

litro /'litro/ *m,* liter

Lituania /li'tuania/ Lithuania

lituano /li'tuano/ **(-na)** *a* and *n* Lithuanian. *m,* Lithuanian (language)

liturgia /li'turhia/ *f,* liturgy

litúrgico /li'turhiko/ *a* liturgical

liviandad /liβian'dað/ *f,* lightness (of weight); fickleness; unimportance, frivolity; lewdness; act of folly, indiscretion

liviano /li'βiano/ *a* light weight; fickle; unimportant, trifling, frivolous; lascivious

lividez /liβi'ðeθ; liβi'ðes/ *f,* lividness

lívido /'liβiðo/ *a* livid

liza /'liθa; 'lisa/ *f,* list (at a tournament); arena

llaga /'ʎaga; 'yaga/ *f,* ulcer; sore; grief, affliction; *Fig.* thorn in the flesh

llagar /ʎa'gar; ya'gar/ *vt* to ulcerate; make or produce sores; *Fig.* wound; —*vr* be covered with sores

llama /'ʎama; 'yama/ *f,* flame; ardor, vehemence; marsh; *Zool.* llama

llamada /ʎa'maða; ya'maða/ *f,* call; *Mil.* call-to-arms, call. **l. molestosa,** annoyance call, nuisance call

llamado /ʎa'maðo; ya'maðo/ *a* called; so-called

llamador /ʎama'ðor; yama'ðor/ **(-ra)** *n* caller. *m,* door knocker; doorbell

llamamiento /ʎama'miento; yama'miento/ *m,* calling; call; divine summons, inspiration; invocation, appeal; summons, convocation

llamar /ʎa'mar; ya'mar/ *vt* to call; invoke, call upon; summon, convoke; name; attract; —*vi* knock (at a door); ring (a bell); —*vr* be named, be called; *Naut.* veer (wind). **Se llama Pedro,** His name is Peter

llamarada /ʎama'raða; yama'raða/ *f,* flame, flash; blaze, flare (of anger, etc.)

llamativo /ʎama'tiβo; yama'tiβo/ *a* striking, showy; provocative

llamear /ʎame'ar; yame'ar/ *vi* to throw out flames, blaze

llana /'ʎana; 'yana/ *f,* mason's trowel; plain; surface of a page

llanada /ʎa'naða; ya'naða/ *f,* plain

llanamente /ʎana'mente; yana'mente/ *adv* frankly, plainly; naturally, simply; candidly, sincerely

llanero /ʎa'nero; ya'nero/ **(-ra)** *n* plain dweller

llaneza /ʎa'neθa; ya'nesa/ *f,* naturalness; candor; familiarity; simplicity (of style)

llano /'ʎano; 'yano/ *a* flat, level; smooth, even; shallow (of receptacles); unaffected, homely, natural; plain (of dresses); manifest, evident; easy; straightforward, candid; informal; simple (of style). *m,* plain; level stretch of ground

llanta /'ʎanta; 'yanta/ *f, Auto.* tire; rim, felloe. **l. de rueda,** wheel, rim

llanto /'ʎanto; 'yanto/ *m,* weeping, flood of tears

llanura /ʎa'nura; ya'nura/ *f,* smoothness, evenness; levelness; plain

llar /ʎar; yar/ *m,* hearth

llave /'ʎaβe; 'yaβe/ **(de)** *f,* key (to); spigot (of), faucet (of), tap (of); spanner, wrench; *Elec.* switch; clock winder; *Mus.* key, clef; *Archit.* keystone; *Print.* brace; *Mech.* wrench; lock (of a gun); tuning key; piston (of musical instruments); lock (in wrestling); *Fig.* key (of a problem or a study). **l. de transmisión,** sender (telegraphy). **l. inglesa,** monkey-wrench, spanner. **l. maestra,** master key, skeleton key. **echar la l.,** to lock. **torcer la l.,** to turn the key

llavero /ʎa'βero; ya'βero/ **(-ra)** *n* keeper of the keys. *m,* key ring. **l. de cárcel,** turnkey

llavín /ʎa'βin; ya'βin/ *m,* yale key, latchkey

llegada /ʎe'gaða; ye'gaða/ *f,* arrival, advent

llegar /ʎe'gar; ye'gar/ *vi* to arrive; last, endure; reach; achieve a purpose; be sufficient, suffice; amount (to), make; —*vt* bring near, draw near; gather; —*vr* come near, approach; adhere. **l. a ser,** to become. **l. a un punto muerto,** to reach a deadlock. **l. hasta...,** to stretch as far as...

llena /'ʎena; 'yena/ *f,* spate, overflow

llenar /ʎe'nar; ye'nar/ *vt* to fill; occupy (a post); satisfy, please; fulfill; satiate; pervade; fill up (a form); —*vi* be full (of the moon); —*vr Inf.* stuff, overeat; *Fig. Inf.* be fed-up

lleno /'ʎeno; 'yeno/ *a* full; replete; abundant; complete. *m,* full moon; *Theat.* full house; *Inf.* glut, abundance; perfection. **de l., de l. en l.,** entirely, completely

llenura /ʎe'nura; ye'nura/ *f,* abundance, plenty

lleva, llevada /'ʎeβa, ʎe'βaða; 'yeβa, ye'βaða/ *f,* carrying, bearing

llevadero /ʎeβa'ðero; yeβa'ðero/ *a* tolerable, bearable

llevar /ʎe'βar; ye'βar/ *vt* to carry, transport; charge (a price); yield, produce; carry off, take away; endure, bear; persuade; guide; take; direct; wear (clothes); carry (a handbag, etc.); introduce, present; gain, achieve; manage (a horse); pass, spend (of time); (*with past part*) have (e.g. *Llevo escrita la carta,* I have written the letter); *Math.* carry; (*with prep. a*) surpass, excel. **l. a cabo,** to accomplish. **l. a cuestas,** to carry on one's back; support. **l. la correspondencia,** to look after the correspondence. **l. la delantera,** to take the lead. **l. luto,** to be in mourning. **llevarse bien,** to get on well, agree

llorar /ʎo'rar; yo'rar/ *vi* to weep, cry; drip; water (eyes); —*vt* lament, mourn; bewail one's troubles

lloriquear /ʎorike'ar; yorike'ar/ *vi* to whine, snivel

lloriqueo /ʎori'keo; yori'keo/ *m,* whining, sniveling

lloro /'ʎoro; 'yoro/ *m,* weeping, crying; flood of tears

llorón /ʎo'ron; yo'ron/ *a* weeping; sniveling, whining. *m,* long plume. **niño llorón,** crybaby

lloroso /ʎo'roso; yo'roso/ *a* tearful; grievous, sad; sorrowful

llovedizo /ʎoβe'ðiθo; yoβe'ðiso/ *a* leaky; rainy

llover /ʎo'βer; yo'βer/ *vi impers irr* to rain; come in abundance (of troubles, etc.); —*vr* leak (roofs, etc.). **l. a cántaros,** to rain in torrents, rain cats and dogs. **l. sobre mojado,** to add insult to injury. **como llovido,** unexpectedly. See **mover**

llovido /ʎo'βiðo; yo'βiðo/ *m,* stowaway

llovizna /ʎo'βiθna; yo'βisna/ *f,* drizzle, fine rain

llovizna /ʎoβiθ'nar; yoβis'nar/ *vi* to drizzle

lluvia /'ʎuβia; 'yuβia/ *f,* rain; rainwater; *Fig.* shower; rose (of watering can)

lluvioso /ʎu'βioso; yu'βioso/ *a* rainy, showery

lo /lo/ *def art. neut* the thing, part, fact, what, that which. Used before adjectives, past participles, sometimes before nouns and adverbs (e.g. *Lo barato es caro,* Cheap things are dear (in the long run).) **Lo mío es mío, pero lo tuyo es de ambos,** What's mine is mine, but what is yours belongs to both of us. **Juan siente mucho lo ocurrido,** John is very sorry for what has happened. **a lo lejos,** in the distance). **lo que,** how (e.g. *No sabes lo bueno que es,* You don't know how good he is) —*pers pron acc m,* or *neut* him, it; that, it (e.g. *Lo harán mañana,* They will do it tomorrow). Means some, any, one, as substitute for noun already mentioned (e.g. *Carecemos de azúcar.*

no lo hay, We are short of sugar; there isn't any). **Lo cortés no quita lo valiente,** One can be courteous and still insistent

loa /'loa/ *f,* praise, eulogy; *Theat.* prologue; short dramatic piece; *Obs.*; dramatic eulogy

loable /lo'aβle/ *a* praiseworthy

loador /loa'ðor/ **(-ra)** *a* eulogizing —*n* eulogist

loar /lo'ar/ *vt* to praise; commend

lobero /lo'βero/ *a* wolf; wolfish

lobezno /lo'βeθno; lo'βesno/ *m,* wolf cub

lobo /'loβo/ **(-ba)** *n* wolf. *m,* (*Bot. Anat.*) lobe; *Inf.* drinking fit. **l. marino,** *Zool.* seal. *Inf.* **pillar un l.,** to get drunk

lóbrego /'loβrego/ *a* murky, dark; dismal; mournful, lugubrious

lobreguez /loβre'geθ; loβre'ges/ *f,* obscurity, gloom, darkness

lóbulo /'loβulo/ *m,* lobe

lobuno /lo'βuno/ *a* wolf, wolfish

locación /loka'θion; loka'sion/ *f,* *Law.* lease; agreement, contract

local /lo'kal/ *a* local. *m,* premises; place, spot, scene

localidad /lokali'ðað/ *f,* location; locality; place, spot; seat (in theaters, etc.)

localización /lokaliθa'θion; lokalisa'sion/ *f,* localization, placing; place

localizar /lokali'θar; lokali'sar/ *vt* to localize

locamente /loka'mente/ *adv* insanely, madly; extraordinarily, extremely

loción /lo'θion; lo'sion/ *f,* lotion

loco /'loko/ **(-ca)** *a* insane, mad; rash, foolish, crazy; excessive, enormous; amazing; extraordinary; infatuated —*n* lunatic; rash person. *Fig. Inf.* **Es un l. de atar,** He's completely crazy!

locomoción /lokomo'θion; lokomo'sion/ *f,* locomotion

locomotor /lokomo'tor/ *a* locomotive

locomotora /lokomo'tora/ *f,* locomotive

locomóvil /loko'moβil/ *a* and *f,* locomotive

locuacidad /lokuaθi'ðað; lokuasi'ðað/ *f,* loquacity

locuaz /lo'kuaθ; lo'kuas/ *a* loquacious

locución /loku'θion; loku'sion/ *f,* style of speech; phrase, idiom; *Gram.* locution

locuelo /lo'kuelo/ **(-la)** *n* madcap

locura /lo'kura/ *f,* insanity, lunacy; madness, fury; folly, foolishness

locutor /loku'tor/ **(-ra)** *n* (radio) announcer; commentator

locutorio /loku'torio/ *m,* locutory; phone booth

lodazal, lodazar /loða'θal, loða'θar; loða'sal, loða'sar/ *m,* muddy place; quagmire

lodo /'loðo/ *m,* mud

lodoso /lo'ðoso/ *a* muddy

logarítmico /loga'ritmiko/ *a* logarithmic

logaritmo /loga'ritmo/ *m,* logarithm

logia /'lohia/ *f,* (Freemason's) lodge

lógica /'lohika/ *f,* logic. *Inf.* **l. parda,** common sense

lógico /'lohiko/ **(-ca)** *a* logical —*n* logician

logística /lo'histika/ *f,* logistics

lograr /lo'grar/ *vt* to achieve, attain, obtain; enjoy; (*with infin*) succeed in; —*vr* succeed in, achieve; reach perfection

logrear /logre'ar/ *vi* to borrow or lend at interest

logrero /lo'grero/ **(-ra)** *n* moneylender; monopolist, profiteer

logro /'logro/ *m,* achievement, attainment; profit, gain; usury, money-lending

loma /'loma/ *f,* knoll, hill

lombarda /lom'βarða/ *f,* red cabbage

Lombardía /lombar'ðia/ Lombardy

lombardo /lom'βarðo/ **(-da)** *a* of or from Lombardy —*n* native of Lombardy (Italy). *m,* mortgage bank

lombriz /lom'βriθ; lom'βris/ *f,* earthworm, common worm. **l. intestinal,** intestinal worm. **l. solitaria,** tapeworm

lomo /'lomo/ *m,* loin, back of a book; ridge between furrows; *pl* ribs; loins

lona /'lona/ *f,* canvas, sailcloth

londinense /londi'nense/ *a* London. *mf* Londoner

Londres /'londres/ London

longanimidad /loŋganimi'ðað/ *f,* longanimity, fortitude

longaniza /loŋga'niθa; loŋga'nisa/ *f,* *Cul.* pork sausage

longevidad /lonheβi'ðað/ *f,* longevity

longevo /lon'heβo/ *a* long-lived

longísimo /lon'hisimo/ *a superl* **luengo** exceedingly long

longitud /lonhi'tuð/ *f,* length; longitude. **l. de onda,** *Radio.* wavelength

lonja /'lonha/ *f,* slice, rasher; *Com.* exchange; market; grocery store; woolen warehouse

lonjista /lon'hista/ *mf* provision merchant, grocer

lontananza /lonta'nanθa; lonta'nansa/ *f,* distance (also *Art.*). **en l.,** in the distance, far off

loor /lo'or/ *m,* praise

loquear /loke'ar/ *vi* to play the fool; romp

lord /lorð/ *m,* lord; *pl* **lores,** lords

loro /'loro/ *m,* *Ornith.* parrot

los /los/ *def art m pl,* the (e.g. *l. sombreros,* the hats) —*pers pron acc 3rd pers m pl,* them. **Tus cigarrillos no están sobre la mesa; los tengo en mi bolsillo,** Your cigarettes are not on the table; I have them in my pocket. Means some, any, ones, as substitution for noun already stated (e.g. *Los cigarros están en la caja si los hay,* The cigars are in the box, if there are any). Used demonstratively followed by *de* or *que* introducing relative clause, those of; those which, those who; the ones that (who) (e.g. *Estaba leyendo algunos libros de los que tienes en tu cuarto,* I was reading some books from among those which you have in your room)

losa /'losa/ *f,* flagstone; slab; tombstone

lote /'lote/ *m,* lot, portion, share

lotería /lote'ria/ *f,* lottery; lotto (game); lottery office

lotero /lo'tero/ **(-ra)** *n* seller of lottery tickets

loto /'loto/ *m,* lotus; lotus flower or fruit

loza /'loθa; 'losa/ *f,* porcelain, china

lozanía /loθa'nia; losa'nia/ *f,* luxuriance (of vegetation); vigor, lustiness; arrogance

lozano /lo'θano; lo'sano/ *a* luxuriant, exuberant; vigorous, lusty; arrogant

lubricación /luβrika'θion; luβrika'sion/ *f,* lubrication

lubricador /luβrika'ðor/ *m,* lubricator

lubricante /luβri'kante/ *a* lubricant

lubricar /luβri'kar/ *vt* to lubricate

lúbrico /'luβriko/ *a* slippery, smooth; lascivious, lustful

lucera /lu'θera; lu'sera/ *f,* skylight

Lucerna /lu'θerna; lu'serna/ Lucerne

lucerna /lu'θerna; lu'serna/ *f,* large chandelier; skylight

lucero /lu'θero; lu'sero/ *m,* evening star; any bright star; white star (on a horse's head); brilliance, radiance; *pl Poet.* eyes, orbs. **l. del alba,** morning star

lucha /'lutʃa/ *f,* fight; struggle; wrestling match; argument, disagreement. **l. grecorromana,** wrestling. **l. igualada,** close fight. **l. libre,** catch-as-catch-can

luchador /lutʃa'ðor/ **(-ra)** *n* fighter; struggler

luchar /lu'tʃar/ *vi* to fight hand to hand; wrestle; fight; struggle; argue

lucidez /luθi'ðeθ; lusi'ðes/ *f,* brilliance, shine; lucidity, clarity

lucido /lu'θiðo; lu'siðo/ *a* splendid, brilliant; sumptuous; fine, elegant

lúcido /'luθiðo; 'lusiðo/ *a Poet.* brilliant; lucid; clear

luciente /lu'θiente; lu'siente/ *a* bright, shining

luciérnaga /lu'θiernaga; lu'siernaga/ *f,* glowworm

lucimiento /luθi'miento; lusi'miento/ *m,* brilliance, luster; success, triumph; elegance; display, ostentation

lucir /lu'θir; lu'sir/ *vi irr* to shine, scintillate; excel, outshine; be successful; —*vt* illuminate; display, show off; show; —*vr* dress elegantly; be successful; excel, be brilliant —*Pres. Indic.* **luzco, luces,** etc —*Pres. Subjunc.* **luzca,** etc

lucrativo /lukra'tiβo/ *a* lucrative

lucro /'lukro/ *m,* gain, profit

lucroso /lu'kroso/ *a* profitable

luctuoso /luk'tuoso/ *a* lugubrious, mournful

lucubración /lukuβra'θion; lukuβra'sion/ *f,* lucubration

ludibrio /lu'ðiβrio/ *m,* mockery, ridicule

luego /'luego/ *adv* immediately; afterward, later; then; soon, presently —*conjunc* therefore. **l. que,** as soon as. **desde l.,** immediately, at once; of course, naturally; in the first place. **hasta l.,** au revoir, good-by for the present

luengo /'luengo/ *a* long

lugar /lu'gar/ *m,* place; spot; village, town, city; region, locality; office, post; passage, text; opportunity, occasion; cause, motive; place on a list; room, space; seat. **l. común,** commonplace. **en l. de,** instead of. **en primer l.,** firstly, in the first place. **hacer l.,** to make room, make way. *Law.* **No ha l.,** The petition is refused. **tener l.,** to take place; have the time or opportunity (to)

lugarejo /luga'reho/ *m,* hamlet

lugareño /luga'reɲo/ **(-ña)** *a* peasant, regional —*n* villager, peasant

lugarteniente /lugarte'niente/ *m,* lieutenant; substitute, deputy

lúgubre /'luguβre/ *a* lugubrious, dismal, mournful

luis /'luis/ *m,* louis (French coin)

lujo /'luho/ *m,* luxury; abundance, profusion. **artículos de l.,** luxury goods

lujoso /lu'hoso/ *a* luxurious; abundant, profuse

lujuria /lu'huria/ *f,* lasciviousness; excess, intemperance

lujuriante /luhu'riante/ *a* luxuriant, abundant, profuse

lujurioso /luhu'rioso/ *a* lascivious, voluptuous

lumbago /lum'βago/ *m,* lumbago

lumbre /'lumbre/ *f,* fire; light; splendor, lustre; transom window, opening, skylight; *pl* tinderbox

lumbrera /lum'βrera/ *f,* luminary; skylight; dormer window; eminent authority

luminar /lumi'nar/ *m,* luminary (also *Fig.*)

luminaria /lumi'naria/ *f,* illumination; fairy lamp, small light; lamp burning before the Sacrament in Catholic churches

luminosidad /luminosi'ðað/ *f,* luminosity

luminoso /lumi'noso/ *a* luminous; bright

luna /'luna/ *f,* moon; mirror; satellite; sheet of plate glass. **l. creciente,** new or rising moon. **l. de miel,** honeymoon. **l. llena,** full moon. **l. menguante,** waning moon. **media l.,** crescent moon

lunado /lu'naðo/ *a* half-moon, crescent

lunar /lu'nar/ *m,* beauty spot; *Fig.* stain, blot (on reputation, etc.); blemish, slight imperfection —*a* lunar

lunático /lu'natiko/ **(-ca)** *a* and *n* lunatic

lunes /'lunes/ *m,* Monday

luneta /lu'neta/ *f,* lens (of eyeglasses), *Theat.* orchestra stall; (*Archit. Mil.*) lunette

lupa /'lupa/ *f,* magnifying glass

lupanar /lupa'nar/ *m,* brothel

lupino /lu'pino/ *a* wolf-like, lupine. *m, Bot.* lupine

lúpulo /'lupulo/ *m, Bot.* hop

lusitano /lusi'tano/ **(-na)** *a* and *n* Lusitanian

lustrador /lustra'ðor/ *m,* polisher. **l. de piso,** floor polisher

lustrar /lus'trar/ *vt* to lustrate, purify; polish, burnish; roam, journey

lustre /'lustre/ *m,* polish, sheen, gloss; glory, luster

lustro /'lustro/ *m,* lustrum, period of five years; chandelier

lustroso /lus'troso/ *a* shining, glossy; brilliant; glorious, noble

luteranismo /lutera'nismo/ *m,* Lutheranism

luterano /lute'rano/ **(-na)** *a* and *n* Lutheran

luto /'luto/ *m,* mourning; grief, affliction; *pl* mourning draperies. **estar de l.,** to be in mourning

luxación /luksa'θion; luksa'sion/ *f, Surg.* luxation, dislocation

Luxemburgo /luksem'βurgo/ Luxembourg

luz /luθ; lus/ *f,* light; glow; brightness, brilliance; information, news; *Fig.* luminary; day, daylight; *pl* culture, learning; windows. **luces de estacionamiento,** parking lights. **a buena l.,** in a good light; in a favorable light; after due consideration. **a primera l.,** at dawn. **dar a l.,** to publish (a book); bring forth (children); reveal. **entre dos luces,** in the dawn light; in the twilight; *Inf.* tipsy. **media l.,** half-light, twilight

M

maca /'maka/ *f*, bruise or blemish on fruit; defect, flaw; *Inf.* fraud, swindle

macabro /ma'kaβro/ *a* macabre

macadán /maka'ðan/ *m*, macadam

macagua /ma'kagua/ *f, Ornith.* macaw

macanudo /maka'nuðo/ *a* (*Inf. West. Hem.*) extraordinary; enormous; robust; fine, excellent

macareno /maka'reno/ (**-na**) *n* inhabitant of the Macarena district of Seville. *m, Inf.* braggart

macarrones /maka'rrones/ *m pl,* macaroni; *Naut.* stanchions

macarrónico /maka'rroniko/ *a* macaronic, recondite, stylized

macarse /ma'karse/ *vr* to go bad, rot (fruit)

macedón /maθe'ðon; mase'ðon/ (**-ona**), **macedonio** (**-ia**) *a* and *n* Macedonian

maceración /maθera'θion; masera'sion/ *f*, maceration; steeping, soaking; mortification of the flesh

macerar /maθe'rar; mase'rar/ *vt* to macerate; steep, soak; mortify

macero /ma'θero; ma'sero/ *m*, mace bearer

maceta /ma'θeta; ma'seta/ *f, dim* small mace; handle, haft (of tools); stonecutter's hammer; flowerpot

macetero /maθe'tero; mase'tero/ *m*, flowerpot stand

machaca /ma'tʃaka/ *f*, pestle; pulverizer. *mf Inf.* bore, tedious person

machacador /matʃaka'ðor/ (**-ra**) *a* crushing, pounding —*n* beater, crusher, pounder

machacar /matʃa'kar/ *vt* to crush, pound; —*vi* importune; harp on a subject

machacón /matʃa'kon/ *a* tiresome, prolix

machado /ma'tʃaðo/ *m*, hatchet, ax

machetero /matʃe'tero/ *m*, one who cuts sugarcane with a machete

machihembrar /matʃiem'βrar/ *vt* to dovetail

machina /ma'tʃina/ *f*, derrick, crane; pile driver

macho /'matʃo/ *m*, male; male animal (he-goat, stallion, etc.); male plant; hook (of hook and eye); screw; *Metall.* core; tap (tool); *Inf.* dunderhead, fool; *Archit.* buttress —*a* male; stupid, ignorant; vigorous, strong. **m. cabrío,** he-goat

machucadura /matʃuka'ðura/ *f,* **machucamiento** *m*, pounding, crushing; bruising

machucar /matʃu'kar/ *vt* to crush, pound; bruise

machucho /ma'tʃutʃo/ *a* prudent, sensible; adult, mature

macicez /maθi'θeθ; masi'ses/ *f*, solidity; massiveness; thickness

macilento /maθi'lento; masi'lento/ *a* thin, lean, emaciated

macillo /ma'θiʎo; ma'siyo/ *m, dim* small mace; hammer (of a piano)

macis /'maθis; 'masis/ *f, Cul.* mace

macizar /maθi'θar; masi'sar/ *vt* to block up, fill up

macizo /ma'θiθo; ma'siso/ *a* massive; compact, solid; *Fig.* well-founded, unassailable; thick; strong. *m*, solidity, compactness; bulk, volume; flowerbed; solid tire

macrocosmo /makro'kosmo/ *m*, macrocosm

mácula /'makula/ *f*, stain, spot; *Fig.* blot, blemish; *Inf.* trick, deception; *Astron.* macula

macuquero /maku'kero/ *m*, unauthorized worker of abandoned mines

madeja /ma'ðeha/ *f*, skein, hank; lock of hair; *Inf.* dummy, useless person

madera /ma'ðera/ *f*, wood; timber; *Inf.* kind, sort; *Mus.* wind instruments. **m. contrachapada,** plywood. **m. de construcción,** timber. **maderas de sierra,** lumber wood. *Inf.* **ser de mala m.,** to be a ne'er-do-well

maderada /maðe'raða/ *f*, lumber wood

maderaje /maðe'rahe/ *m*, woodwork, timber work

maderero /maðe'rero/ *m*, timber merchant; lumberjack; carpenter

madería /maðe'ria/ *f*, timber yard

madero /ma'ðero/ *m*, wooden beam; log, piece of lumber; ship, vessel; *Inf.* blockhead or insensible person

madrastra /ma'ðrastra/ *f*, stepmother; anything unpleasant

madraza /ma'ðraθa; ma'ðrasa/ *f, Inf.* overindulgent mother

madre /'maðre/ *f*, mother; matron; cause, genesis; *Inf.* dame, mother; riverbed; dam; womb; main sewer; chief irrigation channel. **m. de familia,** mother; housewife. **m. de leche,** wet nurse. **m. política,** mother-in-law; stepmother. *Inf.* **sacar de m.** (**a**), to provoke, irritate (a person)

madreperla /maðre'perla/ *f*, mother-of-pearl

madrépora /ma'ðrepora/ *f*, white coral, madrepore

madreselva /maðre'selβa/ *f*, honeysuckle

madrigado /maðri'gaðo/ *a* twice-married (women); *Inf.* experienced, wide-awake

madrigal /maðri'gal/ *m*, madrigal

madriguera /maðri'gera/ *f*, rabbit warren; burrow, den, hole, lair; haunt of thieves, etc.

madrileño /maðri'leɲo/ (**-ña**) *a* and *n* Madrilenian

madrina /ma'ðrina/ *f*, godmother; matron of honor or bridesmaid; sponsor; patroness; prop; stanchion

madroncillo /maðron'θiʎo; maðron'siyo/ *m*, strawberry

madroño /ma'ðroɲo/ *m*, strawberry tree; tuft, spot; tassel

madrugada /maðru'gaða/ *f*, dawn, daybreak; early rising. **de m.,** at dawn

madrugador /maðruga'ðor/ (**-ra**) *a* early rising —*n* early riser

madrugar /maðru'gar/ *vi* to get up early; gain time; anticipate, be beforehand

maduración /maðura'θion; maðura'sion/ *f*, ripening; mellowing; preparation; ripeness; maturity

madurador /maðura'ðor/ *a* ripening; maturing

maduramente /maðura'mente/ *adv* maturely; sensibly

madurar /maðu'rar/ *vt* to ripen; mature; think out; —*vi* ripen; grow mature, learn wisdom

madurez /maðu'reθ; maðu'res/ *f*, ripeness; maturity; mellowness; wisdom

maduro /ma'ðuro/ *a* ripe; mature; mellow; adult; wise

maestra /ma'estra/ *f*, schoolmistress; teacher, instructor; queen bee; guide, model

maestral /maes'tral/ *a* referring to the grand master of one of the Spanish military orders; teaching, pedagogic. *m*, mistral (wind); cell of a queen bee

maestrear /maestre'ar/ *vt* to direct, control, manage; prune vines; —*vi Inf.* bully, domineer

maestría /maes'tria/ *f*, mastery, skill; *Educ.* master's degree

maestril /maes'tril/ *m*, queen cell (of bees)

maestro /ma'estro/ *a* masterly; excellent; chief, main; midship. *m*, master, expert; teacher; instructor; master craftsman; *Educ.* master; *Mus.* composer; *Naut.* mainmast. **m. de armas,** fencing master. **m. de capilla,** *Eccl.* choirmaster. **m. de obras,** building contractor; master builder. **El ejercicio hace m.,** Practice makes perfect

Magallanes, Estrecho de /maga'ʎanes; es'tretʃo de; maga'yanes, es'tretʃo de/ Straits of Magellan

magdalena /magða'lena/ *f*, madeleine (cake); magdalen, penitent. *Inf.* **estar hecha una M.,** to be inconsolable

magia /'mahia/ *f*, magic

mágica /'mahika/ *f*, magic; enchantress, sorceress

mágico /'mahiko/ *a* magic; marvelous, wonderful. *m*, magician; enchanter, wizard

magín /ma'hin/ *m, Inf.* imagination; head, mind

magisterio /mahis'terio/ *m*, teaching profession; teaching diploma; teaching post; pedantry, pompousness. **ejercer su m. en,** to be employed as a teacher in

magistrado /mahis'traðo/ *m*, magistrate; magistracy

magistral /mahis'tral/ *a* magistral; authoritative, magisterial; pedantic, pompous

magistratura /mahistra'tura/ *f*, magistracy

magnanimidad /magnanimi'ðað/ *f*, magnanimity; generosity, liberality

magnánimo /mag'nanimo/ *a* magnanimous, generous, noble

magnate /mag'nate/ *m*, magnate

magnesia /mag'nesia/ *f*, magnesia

magnesio /mag'nesio/ *m*, magnesium

magnético /mag'netiko/ *a* magnetic

magnetismo /magne'tismo/ *m*, magnetism

magnetizar /magneti'θar; magneti'sar/ *vt* to magnetize; mesmerize

magneto /mag'neto/ *m*, magneto

magnificar /magnifi'kar/ *vt* to magnify, enlarge; praise, extol

magnificencia /magnifi'θenθia; magnifi'sensia/ *f*, magnificence, pomp, splendor

magnífico /mag'nifiko/ *a* magnificent; splendid, wonderful, fine; excellent

magnitud /magni'tuð/ *f*, magnitude; quantity; importance

magno /'magno/ *a* great; famous. **Alejandro M.,** Alexander the Great

magnolia /mag'nolia/ *f*, magnolia

mago /'mago/ *m*, magician; *pl* magi

magra /'magra/ *f*, rasher (of bacon, ham)

magrez, magrura /ma'greθ, ma'grura; ma'gres, ma'grura/ *f*, leanness; scragginess

magro /'magro/ *a* lean; scraggy. *m, Inf.* lean pork

magulladura /maguʎa'ðura; maguya'ðura/ *f*, **magullamiento** *m*, bruising; bruise, contusion

magullar /magu'ʎar; magu'yar/ *vt* to bruise

mahometano /maome'tano/ **(-na)** *a* and *n* Muslim

mahometismo /maome'tismo/ *m*, Islam

mahonesa /mao'nesa/ *f*, mayonnaise

maíz /ma'iθ; ma'is/ *m*, corn

maizal /mai'θal; mai'sal/ *m*, cornfield

maja /'maha/ *f*, belle

majada /ma'haða/ *f*, sheepfold; dung

majadería /mahaðe'ria/ *f*, impertinence, insolence

majadero /maha'ðero/ *a* persistent, tedious. *m*, bobbin (for lace making); pestle —*n* fool, bore

majador /maha'ðor/ *m*, pestle

majar /ma'har/ *vt* to pound, crush; *Inf.* importune, annoy

majestad /mahes'tað/ *f*, majesty (title); dignity; stateliness

majestuosidad /mahestuosi'ðað/ *f*, majesty; dignity

majestuoso /mahes'tuoso/ *a* majestic; stately; dignified

majo /'maho/ *a* arrogant, aggressive; gaudily attired, smart; dashing, handsome; attractive, pretty; elegant, well-dressed. *m*, beau, gallant, man about town

majuelo /ma'huelo/ *m*, new vine; species of white hawthorn

mal /mal/ *a Abbr.* **malo.** Used only before *m sing* nouns (e.g. *un m. cuarto de hora,* a bad quarter of an hour). *m*, evil; damage; harm; misfortune; illness, disease; trouble (e.g. *El m. es,* The trouble is). **m. de altura,** air sickness. **m. de ojo,** evil eye. **m. de piedra,** lithiasis, stone. **m. francés,** syphilis. **el m. menor,** the lesser of two evils —*interj* ¡**M. haya!** A curse upon! **echar a m.,** to scorn (things); waste, squander. **llevar a m.** (**una cosa**), to take (a thing) badly, complain. **No hay m. que por bien no venga,** It's an ill wind that blows no one any good, Every cloud has a silver lining. **parar en m.,** to come to a bad end

mal /mal/ *adv* badly; unfavorably; wrongly; wickedly; with difficulty; scarcely, barely. **m. que bien,** willingly or unwillingly; rightly or wrongly. **de m. en peor,** from bad to worse

mala /'mala/ *f*, mail, post. **m. real,** royal mail

malabarista /malaβa'rista/ *mf* juggler

malaconsejado /malakonse'haðo/ *a* ill-advised; imprudent

malacostumbrado /malakostum'βraðo/ *a* badly trained, spoiled; having bad habits

malagueña /mala'geɲa/ *f*, popular song of lament

malagueño /mala'geɲo/ *a* of or from Málaga

malandante /malan'dante/ *a* evildoing; unfortunate, miserable; poor

malandanza /malan'danθa; malan'dansa/ *f*, evildoing; misfortune, misery; poverty

malandrín /malan'drin/ *a* wicked, ill-disposed. *m*, scoundrel, miscreant

malaquita /mala'kita/ *f*, malachite

malaria /ma'laria/ *f*, malaria

malaventura /malaβen'tura/ *f*, misfortune, adversity, bad luck

malaventurado /malaβentu'raðo/ *a* unfortunate, unlucky

malayo /ma'laio/ **(-ya)** *a* Malay —*n* Malayan

malbaratador /malβarata'ðor/ **(-ra)** *a* wasteful, spendthrift —*n* squanderer, spendthrift

malbaratar /malβara'tar/ *vt* to squander, waste; sell at a loss

malcasado /malka'saðo/ *a* adulterous, unfaithful

malcasar /malka'sar/ **(se)** *vt* and *vr* to marry badly

malcomido /malko'miðo/ *a* underfed

malcontento /malkon'tento/ **(-ta)** *a* dissatisfied, discontented; rebellious —*n* malcontent, rebel

malcriado /mal'kriaðo/ *a* badly brought up; ill-bred; spoiled, peevish

maldad /mal'dað/ *f*, badness; depravity, wickedness

maldecidor /maldeθi'ðor; maldesi'ðor/ **(-ra)** *a* slanderous —*n* scandalmonger, slanderer

maldecir /malde'θir; malde'sir/ *vt irr* to curse; —*vt* and *vi* slander, backbite. See **decir**

maldiciente /maldi'θiente; maldi'siente/ *a* defamatory, slanderous; cursing, reviling. *m*, slanderer; curser

maldición /maldi'θion; maldi'sion/ *f*, malediction; curse, imprecation

maldispuesto /maldis'puesto/ *a* indisposed, ill; reluctant

maldita /mal'dita/ *f*, *Inf.* tongue. *Inf.* **soltar la m.,** to say too much, go too far

maldito /mal'dito/ *a* accursed; wicked; damned; poor (of quality); *Inf.* not a...

maleabilidad /maleaβili'ðað/ *f*, malleability, flexibility

maleable /male'aβle/ *a* malleable, flexible

maleante /male'ante/ *a* rascally, villainous. *mf* evildoer

malecón /male'kon/ *m*, breakwater

maledicencia /maleði'θenθia; maleði'sensia/ *f*, slander, abuse, backbiting; cursing

maleficencia /malefi'θenθia; malefi'sensia/ *f*, wrongdoing

maleficio /male'fiθio; male'fisio/ *m*, (magic) curse; spell; charm

maléfico /ma'lefiko/ *a* malefic, harmful. *m*, sorcerer

malestar /males'tar/ *m*, indisposition, slight illness; discomfort

maleta /ma'leta/ *f*, suitcase, valise, grip; *m, Inf.* clumsy matador; duffer (at games, etc.). **hacer la m.,** to pack a suitcase; *Inf.* prepare for a journey, get ready to leave

maletero /male'tero/ *m*, seller or maker of traveling bags; porter

maletín /male'tin/ *m*, small suitcase or valise

malevolencia /maleβo'lenθia; maleβo'lensia/ *f*, malevolence, hatred, malice

malévolo /ma'leβolo/ *a* malevolent, malicious

maleza /ma'leθa; ma'lesa/ *f*, weeds; undergrowth; thicket

malgastador /malgasta'ðor/ **(-ra)** *a* thriftless, wasteful —*n* squanderer

malgastar /malgas'tar/ *vt* to waste (time); squander, throw away (money)

malhablado /mala'βlaðo/ *a* foul-tongued, indecent

malhadado /mala'ðaðo/ *a* ill-fated, unhappy

malhecho /mal'etʃo/ *a* deformed, twisted (persons). *m*, evil deed, wrongdoing

malhechor /male'tʃor/ **(-ra)** *n* malefactor; evildoer

malhumorado /malumo'raðo/ *a* ill-humored, bad-tempered

malicia /ma'liθia; ma'lisia/ *f*, wickedness, evil; malice, maliciousness; acuteness, subtlety, shrewdness; craftiness, guile; *Inf.* suspicion

maliciar /mali'θiar; mali'siar/ *vt* to suspect; spoil, damage; hurt, harm

malicioso /mali'θioso; mali'sioso/ *a* malicious; vindictive; wicked; shrewd, clever; *Inf.* suspicious; artful

malignidad /maligni'ðað/ *f,* malignancy, spite, ill will

maligno /ma'ligno/ *a* malignant, spiteful; wicked; *Med.* malignant

malintencionado /malinten θio'naðo; malintensio-'naðo/ *a* ill-intentioned, badly disposed

malla /'maʎa; 'maya/ *f,* mesh (of a net); coat of mail; *pl Theat.* tights. **m. de alambre,** wire netting. **cota de m.,** coat of mail

Mallorca /ma'ʎorka; ma'yorka/ Majorca

mallorquín /maʎor'kin; mayor'kin/ **(-ina)** *a* and *n* Majorcan. *m,* Majorcan (variety of Catalan or Spanish)

malmandado /malman'daðo/ *a* disobedient; reluctant, unwilling

malmaridada /malmari'ðaða/ *f,* adultress, faithless wife

malo /'malo/ *a* bad; wicked; evil; injurious; harmful; illicit; licentious; ill; difficult; troublesome, annoying; *Inf.* mischievous; knavish; rotten, decaying —*interj* **¡M.!** That's bad!; You shouldn't have done that!; That's a bad sign! **de malas,** unluckily, unhappily. **el M.,** the Evil One, the Devil. **estar m.,** to be ill. **Lo m. es,** The trouble is, The worst of it is. **por malas o por buenas,** willy-nilly, willingly or unwillingly. **ser m.,** to be wicked; be evil; behave badly (children)

malograr /malo'grar/ *vt* to lose (time); waste, throw away (opportunities); —*vr* fall through, fail; wither, fade; die early, come to an untimely end

malogro /ma'logro/ *m,* loss, waste (time, opportunity); frustration; decline, fading; untimely death

malparar /malpa'rar/ *vt* to ill-treat; damage. **quedar malparado,** to get the worst of

malparir /malpa'rir/ *vt Med.* to miscarry

malparto /mal'parto/ *m,* miscarriage; abortion

malquerencia /malke'renθia; malke'rensia/ *f,* ill will, aversion, dislike

malquistar /malkis'tar/ *vt* to stir up trouble; make unpopular; estrange; —*vr* make oneself disliked

malquisto /mal'kisto/ *a* unpopular, disliked

malsano /mal'sano/ *a* unhealthy

malta /'malta/ *m,* malt

maltés /mal'tes/ **(-esa)** *a* and *n* Maltese

maltraer /maltra'er/ *vt irr* to ill-treat; insult. See **traer**

maltratamiento /maltrata'miento/ *m,* abuse, ill usage; damage, deterioration

maltratar /maltra'tar/ *vt* to ill-treat; abuse, insult; misuse, spoil, damage

maltrato /mal'trato/ *m,* maltreatment; misuse

maltrecho /mal'tretʃo/ *a* ill-treated, bruised; abused, insulted; damaged

maltusianismo /maltusia'nismo/ *m,* Malthusianism

maltusiano /maltu'siano/ *a* Malthusian

Malucas, las /ma'lukas, las/ the Moluccas

malucho /ma'lutʃo/ *a Inf.* off-color, below par, not well

malva /'malβa/ *f,* mallow. **m. real, m. rosa,** or **m. loca,** hollyhock. **ser como una m.,** *Fig. Inf.* to be a clinging vine

malvado /mal'βaðo/ *a* evil, malevolent, fiendish —*n* villain, fiend

malvasía /malβa'sia/ *f, Bot.* malvasia; malmsey (wine)

malvavisco /malβa'βisko/ *m, Bot.* marshmallow

malvender /malβen'der/ *vt* to sell at a loss

malversación /malβersa'θion; malβersa'sion/ *f,* malversation, maladministration; misappropriation (of funds)

malversador /malβersa'ðor/ **(-ra)** *n* bad or corrupt administrator

malversar /malβer'sar/ *vt* to misappropriate (funds)

mama /'mama/ *f, Inf.* mamma, mommy; breast; udder

mamá /ma'ma/ *f,* mamma

mamar /ma'mar/ *vt* to suck (the breast); *Inf.* wolf, swallow; learn from an early age; enjoy, obtain unfairly; —*vr* get drunk

mamario /ma'mario/ *a* mammary

mamarracho /mama'rratʃo/ *m, Inf.* scarecrow, dummy; anything grotesque looking

mameluco /mame'luko/ *m,* mameluke; *Inf.* ninny, fool

mamífero /ma'mifero/ *a* mammalian. *m,* mammal

mamotreto /mamo'treto/ *m,* notebook, memorandum; *Inf.* large book or bulky file of papers

mampara /mam'para/ *f,* folding screen; screen; partition

mamparo /mam'paro/ *m,* bulkhead

mampostería /mamposte'ria/ *f,* masonry, stonemasonry

mampostero /mampos'tero/ *m,* stonemason

mamut /ma'mut/ *m,* mammoth

maná /ma'na/ *m,* manna

manada /ma'naða/ *f,* handful; herd, flock; group, drove, crowd

manadero /mana'ðero/ *m,* herdsman, drover; spring, stream

manantial /manan'tial/ *m,* fountain, source, spring; head (of a river)

manar /ma'nar/ *vi* to flow, stream; be plentiful

manatí /mana'ti/ *m,* sea cow, manatee

mancar /man'kar/ *vt* to injure, maim; —*vi* grow calm (elements)

manceba /man'θeβa; man'seβa/ *f,* concubine; girl

mancebía /manθe'βia; manse'βia/ *f,* brothel; youth, young days

mancebo /man'θeβo; man'seβo/ *m,* youth, stripling; bachelor; shop assistant

mancha /'mantʃa/ *f,* spot, smear, stain; blotch; plot of ground; patch of vegetation; stigma, disgrace

manchar /man'tʃar/ *vt* to stain; smear; spot, speckle; disgrace; tarnish

manchego /man'tʃego/ **(-ga)** *a* and *n* of or from La Mancha (Spain)

manchuriano /mantʃu'riano/ **(-na)** *a* and *n* Manchurian

mancilla /man'θiʎa; man'siya/ *f,* stain; slur

mancillar /manθi'ʎar; mansi'yar/ *vt* to stain; *Fig.* smirch

manco /'manko/ **(-ca)** *a* maimed, disabled; one-handed; one-armed; armless; handless; incomplete, faulty —*n* disabled person

mancomunidad /mankomuni'ðað/ *f,* association, society; community, union; commonwealth; regional legislative assembly

manda /'manda/ *f,* offer, suggestion, proposition; legacy

mandadero /manda'ðero/ **(-ra)** *n* convent or prison messenger; errand boy (girl)

mandado /man'daðo/ *m,* order, command; errand

mandamiento /manda'miento/ *m,* order, command; *Eccl.* commandment; *Law.* writ; *pl Inf.* one's five fingers

mandar /man'dar/ *vt* to order, command; bequeath, will; send; control, drive; promise, offer; order (e.g. *Mandó hacerse un traje,* He ordered a suit to be made); —*vr* walk unaided (convalescents, etc.); lead into one another (rooms, etc.); **¿Quién manda aquí?** Who is in charge here?

mandarín /manda'rin/ *m,* mandarin; *Inf.* bureaucrat

mandarina /manda'rina/ *f,* mandarin (classical Chinese); mandarin orange

mandatario /manda'tario/ *m,* mandatary

mandato /man'dato/ *m,* mandate; command; *Eccl.* maundy. *Polit.* mandate. **cuarto m.,** fourth term (of President, Governor, etc.)

mandíbula /man'diβula/ *f,* jaw; jawbone, mandible

mandil /man'dil/ *m,* long leather apron; apron; Freemason's apron; close-meshed fishing net

mandilón /mandi'lon/ *m, Inf.* coward, nincompoop

mandioca /man'dioka/ *f,* manioc, cassava; tapioca

mando /'mando/ *m,* authority, power; (*Mil. Nav.*) command; *Engin.* regulation; controls (of a machine, etc.). **m. a distancia,** remote control. *Aer.* **m. de dos pilotos,** dual-controlled. **mandos gemelos,** dual control. **al m. de,** under the command of; under the direction of

mandolín /mando'lin/ *m.* **mandolina** *f,* mandolin

mandón /man'don/ *a* domineering, bossy

mandrágora /man'dragora/ *f,* mandrake

mandril /man'dril/ *m, Mech.* mandrel, chuck; *Zool.* mandrill

manear /mane'ar/ *vt* to hobble (a horse); manage, control

manecilla /mane'θiʎa; mane'siya/ *f, dim* little hand; hand of a clock; *Print.* fist

manejable /mane'haβle/ *a* manageable, controllable

manejar /mane'har/ *vt* to handle; use, wield; control; manage, direct; ride (horses); —*vr* manage to move around (after an accident, illness)

manejo /ma'neho/ *m,* handling; use, wielding; control; management, direction; horsemanship; intrigue

maneota /mane'ota/ *f,* hobble, shackle

manera /ma'nera/ *f,* manner, way, means; behavior, style (gen. *pl*); class (of people); *Art.* style, manner. **a la m. de,** like, in the style of. **de esa m.,** in that way; according to that, in that case. **de m. que,** so that. **en gran m.,** to a great extent. **sobre m.,** exceedingly

manga /'maŋga/ *f,* sleeve; bag; grip; handle; pipe (of a hose); strainer; waterspout; body of troops; beam, breadth of a ship; *pl* profits. **m. de viento,** whirlwind. **echar de m. a,** to make use of a person. *Inf.* **estar de m.,** to be in league. **tener m. ancha,** to be broad-minded. *Fig. Inf.* **traer (una cosa) en la m.,** to have (something) up one's sleeve

mangana /maŋ'gana/ *f,* lasso

manganeso /maŋga'neso/ *m,* manganese

manganilla /maŋga'niʎa; maŋga'niya/ *f,* sleight of hand; hoax, trick

mangle /'maŋgle/ *m,* mangrove tree

mango /'maŋgo/ *m,* handle, haft, stock; mango. **m. de cuchillo,** knife handle

mangonear /maŋgone'ar/ *vi Inf.* to loaf, roam about; interfere, meddle

mangonero /maŋgo'nero/ *a Inf.* meddlesome

mangosta /maŋ'gosta/ *f,* mongoose

mangote /maŋ'gote/ *m, Inf.* long, wide sleeve; black oversleeve

manguera /maŋ'guera/ *f,* hose; sleeve, tube; airshaft; waterspout

manguero /maŋ'guero/ *m,* fireman; hoseman

manguito /maŋ'guito/ *m,* muff; black oversleeve; wristlet, cuff; *Mech.* bush, sleeve

manía /ma'nia/ *f,* mania, obsession; whim, fancy

maníaco /ma'niako/ **(-ca)** *a* maniacal; capricious, extravagant —*n* maniac

maniatar /mania'tar/ *vt* to handcuff; hobble (a cow, etc.)

maniático /ma'niatiko/ **(-ca)** *a* maniacal; capricious; faddy, fussy —*n* crank

manicomio /mani'komio/ *m,* insane asylum, mental hospital

manicura /mani'kura/ *f,* manicure

manicuro /mani'kuro/ **(-ra)** *n* manicurist

manida /ma'niða/ *f,* lair, den; dwelling, habitation

manifestación /manifesta'θion; manifesta'sion/ *f,* declaration, statement; exhibition; demonstration; *Eccl.* exposition (of the Blessed Sacrament)

manifestante /manifes'tante/ *mf* demonstrator

manifestar /manifes'tar/ *vt irr* to declare, make known, state; exhibit, show; *Eccl.* to expose (the Blessed Sacrament). See **acertar**

manifiesto /mani'fiesto/ *a* obvious, evident. *m,* manifesto; *Naut.* manifest; *Eccl.* exposition of the Blessed Sacrament. **poner de m.,** to show; make public; reveal

manigua /ma'nigua/ *f,* thicket, jungle (in Cuba)

manija /ma'niha/ *f,* handle, stock, haft; hand lever; clamp; tether (for horses, etc.)

manileño /mani'leɲo/ **(ña)** *a* and *n* Manilan

manilla /ma'niʎa; ma'niya/ *f,* bracelet; handcuff, manacle

maniobra /ma'nioβra/ *f,* operation, process; *Mil.* maneuver; intrigue; tackle, gear; handling, management; *Naut.* working of a ship; *pl* shunting (trains)

maniobrar /manio'βrar/ *vi Mil.* to maneuver; *Naut.* handle, work (ships)

manipulación /manipula'θion; manipula'sion/ *f,* handling; manipulation; control, management

manipulador /manipula'ðor/ *a* manipulative. *m,* sending key (telegraphy)

manipular /manipu'lar/ *vt* to handle; manipulate; manage, direct

manípulo /ma'nipulo/ *m,* maniple

maniqueo /mani'keo/ **(-ea)** *a* Manichean *n* Manichee

maniquete /mani'kete/ *m,* black lace mitten

maniquí /mani'ki/ *m,* mannequin; dummy; *Inf.* puppet, weak person

manirroto /mani'rroto/ **(-ta)** *a* wasteful, extravagant —*n* spendthrift

manivela /mani'βela/ *f, Mech.* crank, lever

manjar /man'har/ *m,* dish, food; pastime, recreation, pleasure. **m. blanco,** blancmange

mano /'mano/ *f,* hand; coat, coating; quire (of paper); front paw (animals); elephant's trunk; side, hand; hand (of a clock); game (of cards, etc.); lead (at cards); way, means; ability; power; protection, favor; compassion; aid, help; scolding; *Mus.* scale; pestle; workers. *Inf.* editing, correction of a literary work (gen. by a person more skilled than the author). **m. de mortero,** pestle. **m. de obra,** (manual) labor. **manos muertas,** *Law.* mortmain. **m. sobre m.,** with folded hands; lazily, indolently. **a la m.,** at hand, nearby; within one's grasp. **a manos llenas,** in abundance, abundantly. **bajo m.,** in an underhand manner, secretly. **buenas manos,** cleverness, ability; dexterity. **de primera m.,** first-hand, new. **estar dejado de la m. de Dios,** to be very unlucky; be very foolish. **poner la m. en,** to lift; slap, buffet. **Si a m. viene...,** If by chance... **tender la m.,** to put out one's hand, shake hands. **traer entre manos,** to have on hand, be engaged in

manojo /ma'noho/ *m,* bunch, handful. **a manojos,** in handfuls; plentifully, in abundance

manolo /ma'nolo/ **(-la)** *n* inhabitant of low quarters of Madrid noted for pride, gaiety, quarrelsomeness, and wit

manopla /ma'nopla/ *f,* gauntlet

manoseado /manose'aðo/ *a* hackneyed

manosear /manose'ar/ *vt* to handle; paw, touch repeatedly; finger

manoseo /mano'seo/ *m,* handling; fingering; *Inf.* pawing, feeling

manotada /mano'taða/ *f,* slap, cuff

manotear /manote'ar/ *vt* to slap, cuff; —*vi* gesticulate, gesture with the hands

manoteo /mano'teo/ *m,* gesticulation with the hands

manquedad /manke'ðað/ *f,* disablement of hand or arm; lack of one of these; defect; incompleteness

mansalva /man'salβa/ **(a)** *adv* without danger

mansedumbre /manse'ðumbre/ *f,* meekness; kindness; gentleness

mansión /man'sion/ *f,* stay, visit; dwelling, abode; mansion

manso /'manso/ *a* soft, gentle; meek, mild; tame; peaceable, amiable; calm

manta /'manta/ *f,* blanket; horse blanket; traveling rug; *Inf.* hiding, thrashing. **m. de viaje,** traveling rug. *Inf.* **a m. de Dios,** in abundance. **dar una m.,** to toss in a blanket. *Fig. Inf.* **tirar de la m.,** to let the cat out of the bag

manteamiento /mantea'miento/ *m,* tossing in a blanket

mantear /mante'ar/ *vt* to toss in a blanket

manteca /man'teka/ *f,* lard; cooking fat; grease; *Argentina* butter. **como m.,** as mild as milk, as soft as butter

mantecada /mante'kaða/ *f,* buttered toast

mantecado /mante'kaðo/ *m,* French ice cream

mantecoso /mante'koso/ *a* greasy

mantel /man'tel/ *m,* tablecloth; altar cloth

mantelería /mantele'ria/ *f,* table linen

mantelete /mante'lete/ *m, (Eccl. Mil.)* mantlet

mantener /mante'ner/ *vt irr* to maintain; keep, feed; support; continue, persevere with; uphold, affirm; keep up; —*vr* support oneself; remain in a place; (*with* en) continue to uphold (views, etc.), persevere in. **mantenerse firme,** *Fig.* to stand one's ground. See **tener**

mantenimiento /manteni'miento/ *m,* maintenance; support; sustenance, nourishment; affirmation; upkeep; livelihood

manteo /man'teo/ *m,* tossing in a blanket; long cloak

mantequera /mante'kera/ *f,* churn; dairymaid; butter dish

mantequero /mante'kero/ *m,* dairyman; butter dish

mantequilla /mante'kiʎa; mante'kiya/ *f,* butter

mantero /man'tero/ *m,* blanket seller or maker

mantilla /man'tiʎa; man'tiya/ *f,* mantilla; saddlecloth *pl* baby's long clothes. **estar en mantillas,** to be in swaddling clothes; *Fig.* be in early infancy

manto /'manto/ *m,* cloak; cover, disguise; *Zool.* mantle; *Mineral.* layer

mantón /man'ton/ *m,* shawl. **m. de Manila,** Manila shawl

mantuano /man'tuano/ **(-na)** *a* and *n* Mantuan

manuable /ma'nuaβle/ *a* easy to handle or use, handy

manual /ma'nual/ *a* manual; handy, easy to use; docile, peaceable. *m,* manual, textbook; *Eccl.* book of ritual; notebook

manubrio /ma'nuβrio/ *m,* handle, crank

manuela /ma'nuela/ *f,* open carriage (Madrid)

manufactura /manufak'tura/ *f,* manufacture; manufactured article; factory

manufacturar /manufaktu'rar/ *vt* to manufacture

manufacturero /manufaktu'rero/ *a* manufacturing

manumisión /manumi'sion/ *f,* freeing (of a slave), manumission

manumitir /manumi'tir/ *vt Law.* to free, enfranchise (slaves)

manuscrito /manus'krito/ *a* and *m,* manuscript

manutención /manuten'θion; manuten'sion/ *f,* maintenance; upkeep; protection

manzana /man'θana; man'sana/ *f,* apple; block (of houses); city square; Adam's apple

manzanal /manθa'nal; mansa'nal/ *m,* apple orchard; apple tree

manzanar /manθa'nar; mansa'nar/ *m,* apple orchard

manzanilla /manθa'niʎa; mansa'niya/ *f,* white sherry wine; *Bot.* chamomile; chamomile tea; knob, ball (on furniture); pad (on an animal's foot)

manzano /man'θano; man'sano/ *m,* apple tree

maña /'maɲa/ *f,* skill, dexterity; craftiness, guile; vice, bad habit (gen. *pl*). **darse m. para,** to contrive to

mañana /ma'ɲana/ *f,* morning; tomorrow. *m,* future, tomorrow —*adv* tomorrow; in time to come; soon. **¡M.!** Tomorrow! Another day! Not now! (generally to beggars). **de m.,** early in the morning. **muy de m.,** very early in the morning. **pasado m.,** the day after tomorrow

mañanica /maɲa'nika/ *f,* early morning

mañear /maɲe'ar/ *vt* to arrange cleverly; —*vi* behave shrewdly

mañero /ma'ɲero/ *a* shrewd, clever; easily worked; handy

mañoso /ma'ɲoso/ *a* clever, skillful; crafty; vicious, with bad habits

mañuela /ma'ɲuela/ *f,* low guile

mapa /'mapa/ *m,* map; card. **m. en relieve,** relief map. **m. del estado mayor,** ordnance map. *Inf.* **no estar en el m.,** to be off the map; be most unusual (of things)

mapache /ma'patʃe/ *m,* raccoon

mapamundi /mapa'mundi/ *m,* map of the world

maqueta /ma'keta/ *f,* (*Art. Archit.*) model

maquiavélico /makia'βeliko/ *a* Machiavellian

maquiavelismo /makiaβe'lismo/ *m,* Machiavellism

maquillaje /maki'ʎahe; maki'yahe/ *m,* makeup, cosmetics; make up (of the face)

maquillar /maki'ʎar; maki'yar/ **(se)** *vt* and *vr* to make up (the face, etc.)

máquina /'makina/ *f,* machine, mechanism; engine; apparatus; plan, scheme; machine, puppet; *Inf.* mansion, palace; plenty; locomotive; fantasy, product of the imagination. **m. de vapor,** steam engine. **m. de arrastre,** traction engine; tractor. **m. de coser,** sewing machine. **m. de escribir,** typewriter. **m. fotográfica,** camera. **m. de impresionar,** movie camera. **m. de imprimir,** printing machine. **m. herramienta,** machine tool. **m. neumática,** air pump

maquinación /makina'θion; makina'sion/ *f,* intrigue, machination

maquinador /makina'ðor/ **(-ra)** *n* intriguer, schemer

maquinal /maki'nal/ *a* mechanical

maquinar /maki'nar/ *vt* to intrigue, scheme, plot

maquinaria /maki'naria/ *f,* machinery; applied mechanics; mechanism

maquinista /maki'nista/ *mf* driver, enginer; mechanic; machinist; locomotive driver

mar /mar/ *mf* sea; great many, abundance. **m. bonanza** *or* **m. en calma,** calm sea. **m. de fondo** *or* **m. de leva,** swell. **alta m.,** high seas. **a mares,** plentifully. **arar en el m.,** to labor in vain. *Naut.* **hacerse a la m.,** to put out to sea. **la m. de historias,** a great number of stories

maraña /ma'raɲa/ *f,* undergrowth; tangle; *Fig.* difficult position; intrigue; silk waste

marasmo /ma'rasmo/ *m, Med.* marasmus, atrophy; inactivity, paralysis

maravedí /maraβe'ði/ *m,* maravedi (old Spanish coin of fluctuating value)

maravilla /mara'βiʎa; mara'βiya/ *f,* marvel, wonder; admiration; amazement; marigold. **a m.,** wonderfully. **a las mil maravillas,** to perfection, excellently. **por m.,** by chance; occasionally

maravillar /maraβi'ʎar; maraβi'yar/ *vt* to amaze, cause admiration; —*vr* (*with de*) marvel at, admire; be amazed by

maravilloso /maraβi'ʎoso; maraβi'yoso/ *a* marvelous, wonderful

marbete /mar'βete/ *m,* label, tag; edge, border

marca /'marka/ *f,* mark, sign; brand; frontier zone, border country; standard, norm (of size); make, brand; measuring rule; *Sports.* record. **m. de fábrica,** brand, trademark. **m. de ley,** hallmark. **m. registrada,** registered name. **de m.,** excellent, of excellent quality

marcado /mar'kaðo/ *a* marked; pronounced; strong (of accents)

marcador /marka'ðor/ *a* marking. *m,* marker; scoreboard; bookmark

marcar /mar'kar/ *vt* to mark; brand; embroider initials on linen; tell the time (watches); show the amount (cash register, etc.); dial (telephone); *Sports.* score (a goal); notice, observe; set aside, earmark; —*vr Naut.* check the course. **m. el compás** to beat time

Mar Caspio /'mar 'kaspio/ Caspian Sea

marcha /'martʃa/ *f,* departure; running, working; *Mil.* march; speed (of trains, ships, etc.); *Mus.* march; progress, course (of events). **m. atrás,** backing, reversing. **m. de ensayo,** trial run. **m. forzada,** *Mil.* forced march. **a largas marchas,** with all speed. **a toda m.,** at top speed; full speed ahead; by forced marches; *Mil.* **batir la m.,** to strike up a march. **en m.,** underway; working; in operation

marchamero /martʃa'mero/ *m,* customs official who checks and marks goods

marchamo /mar'tʃamo/ *m,* customs mark on checked goods

marchar /mar'tʃar/ *vi* to run; work; function; go; leave, depart; progress, proceed; *Mil.* march; go (clocks); —*vr* leave, go away

marchitable /martʃi'taβle/ *a* perishable, fragile

marchitamiento /martʃita'miento/ *m,* withering

marchitar /martʃi'tar/ *vt* to wither, fade; blight, spoil; weaken; —*vr* wither; be blighted

marchitez /martʃi'teθ; martʃi'tes/ *f,* witheredness; fadedness

marchito /mar'tʃito/ *a* withered; faded; blighted, frustrated

marcial /mar'θial; mar'sial/ *a* martial; courageous, militant

marcialidad /marθiali'ðað; marsiali'ðað/ *f,* war-like spirit, militancy

marciano /mar'θiano; mar'siano/ *a* Martian

marco /'marko/ *m,* mark (German coin); boundary

mark; frame (of a picture, etc.). **m. de ventana,** window frame

Mar de las Indias /'mar de las 'indias/ Indian Ocean

Mar del Norte /'mar del 'norte/ North Sea

marea /ma'rea/ *f,* tide; strand; water's edge; light breeze; drizzle; dew; street dirt. **m. creciente,** flood tide. **m. menguante,** ebb tide. **m. muerta,** neap tide

mareaje /ma'reahe/ *m,* seamanship; ship's course

marear /mare'ar/ *vt* to navigate; sell; sell publicly; *Inf.* annoy; —*vr* be seasick; feel faint; feel giddy; be damaged at sea (goods)

marejada /mare'haða/ *f,* surge, swell; high sea; tidal wave; commotion, uproar

mareo /ma'reo/ *m,* seasickness; nausea, dizziness; *Inf.* irritation, tediousness

mareta /ma'reta/ *f,* movement of the waves; sound, noise (of a crowd)

marfil /mar'fil/ *m,* ivory

marfileño /marfi'leɲo/ *a* ivory; ivory-like

marfuz /mar'fuθ; mar'fus/ *a* spurned, rejected; deceitful

marga /'marga/ *f,* loam, marl

margarina /marga'rina/ *f,* margarine

margarita /marga'rita/ *f,* pearl; marguerite, oxeye daisy; daisy; periwinkle

margen /'marhen/ *mf* edge, fringe, border, verge; margin (of a book); opportunity; marginal note. **dar m. para,** to provide an opportunity for; give rise to

marginal /marhi'nal/ *a* marginal

margoso /mar'goso/ *a* marly, marly

marica /ma'rika/ *f,* magpie. *m,* (*offensive*) homosexual; milksop

maricón /mari'kon/ *m,* (*offensive*) homosexual

maridable /mari'ðaβle/ *a* marital, matrimonial

maridaje /mari'ðahe/ *m,* conjugal union and harmony; intimate relationship (between things)

maridar /mari'ðar/ *vi* to get married; mate, live as husband and wife; —*vt* unite, link, join together

marido /ma'riðo/ *m,* husband

marihuana /mari'uana/ *f,* marijuana

marimacho /mari'matʃo/ *m, Inf.* mannish woman

marina /ma'rina/ *f,* coast, seashore; *Art.* seascape; seamanship; navy, fleet. **m. de guerra,** navy. **m. mercante,** merchant navy

marinera /mari'nera/ *f,* sailor's blouse

marinería /marine'ria/ *f,* profession of a sailor; seamanship; crew of a ship; sailors (as a class)

marinero /mari'nero/ *m,* sailor, seaman. **m. de agua dulce,** freshwater sailor (a novice). **m. práctico,** able seaman. **a la marinera,** in a seaman-like fashion

marinesco /mari'nesko/ *a* seamanly

marino /ma'rino/ *a* marine, sea; seafaring; shipping. *m,* sailor, mariner

marioneta /mario'neta/ *f,* marionette, puppet

mariposa /mari'posa/ *f,* butterfly; night-light

mariposear /maripose'ar/ *vi* to flutter, flit, fly about; flirt; be fickle; follow about, dance attendance on

mariquita /mari'kita/ *f, Ent.* ladybird; parakeet.

marisabidilla /marisaβi'ðiʎa; marisaβi'ðiya/ *f, Inf.* blue-stocking, know-it-all

mariscal /maris'kal/ *m, Mil.* marshal; field marshal; blacksmith

marisco /ma'risko/ *m,* shellfish

marisma /ma'risma/ *f,* bog, morass, swamp

marital /mari'tal/ *a* marital

marítimo /ma'ritimo/ *a* maritime, sea

marjal /mar'hal/ *m,* marshland, fen

marmita /mar'mita/ *f,* stewpot; copper, boiler

marmitón /marmi'ton/ *m,* kitchen boy, scullion

mármol /'marmol/ *m,* marble; work executed in marble

marmolería /marmole'ria/ *f,* marble works; work executed in marble

marmolista /marmo'lista/ *mf* marble cutter; dealer in marble

marmóreo /mar'moreo/ *a* marble; *Poet.* marmoreal

marmota /mar'mota/ *f, Zool.* marmot; sleepyhead, dormouse

Mar Muerto /mar 'muerto/ Dead Sea

maroma /ma'roma/ *f,* rope, hawser

marqués /mar'kes/ *m,* marquis

marquesa /mar'kesa/ *f,* marchioness

marquesina /marke'sina/ *f,* marquee

marquetería /markete'ria/ *f,* marquetry

marrana /ma'rrana/ *f,* sow; *Inf.* slattern, slut

marrano /ma'rrano/ *m,* pig, hog; Marrano

marras /'marras/ (**de**) *adv* long ago, in the dim past

marrasquino /marras'kino/ *m,* maraschino liqueur

marro /'marro/ *m,* tick, tag (game)

Mar Rojo /mar 'rroho/ Red Sea

marrón /ma'rron/ *a* maroon; brown. *m,* brown color; maroon color; quoit

marroquí /marro'ki/ *a* and *mf* Moroccan. *m,* Morocco leather

marroquín /marro'kin/ (**-ina**), **marrueco (-ca)** *a* and *n* Moroccan

Marruecos /ma'rruekos/ Morocco

marrullería /marruʎe'ria; marruye'ria/ *f,* flattery, cajolery

marrullero /marru'ʎero; marru'yero/ (**-ra**) *a* wheedling, flattering —*n* wheedler, cajoler

Marsella /mar'seʎa; mar'seya/ Marseilles

marsellés /marse'ʎes; marse'yes/ (**-esa**) *a* and *n* of or from Marseilles. *f,* **la Marsellesa,** the Marseillaise

marsopa /mar'sopa/ *f,* porpoise

marta /'marta/ *f,* sable; marten

Marte /'marte/ *m,* Mars

martes /'martes/ *m,* Tuesday. **m. de carnaval,** mardi gras

martillar /marti'ʎar; marti'yar/ *vt* to hammer; oppress

martillazo /marti'ʎaθo; marti'yaso/ *m,* hammer blow

martilleo /marti'ʎeo; marti'yeo/ *m,* hammering; noise of the hammer; clink, clatter

martillo /mar'tiʎo; mar'tiyo/ *m,* hammer; oppressor, tyrant; auction rooms. **a m.,** by hammering. **de m.,** wrought (of metals)

martinete /marti'nete/ *m,* hammer (of a pianoforte); pile driver; drop hammer. **m. de báscula,** tilt hammer

Martinica /marti'nika/ Martinique

martín pescador /mar'tin peska'ðor/ *m,* kingfisher

mártir /'martir/ *mf* martyr

martirio /mar'tirio/ *m,* martyrdom

martirizar /martiri'θar; martiri'sar/ *vt* to martyr; torture, torment, martyrize; tease, annoy

martirologio /martiro'lohio/ *m,* martyrology

marxismo /mark'sismo/ *m,* Marxism

marxista /mark'sista/ *a* and *mf* Marxist

marzo /'marθo; 'marso/ *m,* March

mas /mas/ *conjunc* but; yet

más /mas/ *adv compar* more; in addition, besides; rather, preferably. *Math.* plus. **el** (**la,** etc.) **más,** *adv superl* the most, etc. **m. bien,** more; rather; preferably. **m. que,** only; but; more than; although, even if. **a lo m.,** at the most; at the worst. **a m.,** besides, in addition. **de m.,** superfluous, unnecessary, unwanted. **no... m. que,** only. **por m. que,** however; even if. **sin m. ni m.,** without further ado. **M. vale un mal arreglo que un buen pleito,** A bad peace is better than a good war

masa /'masa/ *f,* mass; dough; whole, aggregate; majority (of people); mortar. **en la m. de la sangre,** *Fig.* in the blood, in a person's nature

masada /ma'saða/ *f,* farmhouse and stock

masadero /masa'ðero/ *m,* farmer; farm laborer

masaje /ma'sahe/ *m,* massage

masajista /masa'hista/ *mf* masseur; masseuse

mascadura /maska'ðura/ *f,* chewing

mascar /mas'kar/ *vt* to chew; masticate; *Inf.* mumble, mutter

máscara /'maskara/ *f,* mask; fancy dress; pretext, excuse. *mf* masquerader, reveler; *pl* masquerade. **m. para gases,** gas mask

mascarada /maska'raða/ *f,* masquerade; company of revelers

mascarero /maska'rero/ (**-ra**) *n* theatrical costumer, fancy-dress dealer

mascarilla /maska'riʎa; maska'riya/ *f,* death mask

mascarón /maska'ron/ *m,* large mask; *Archit.* gargoyle. **m. de proa,** *Naut.* figurehead

mascota /mas'kota/ *f,* mascot

masculinidad /maskuli'niðað/ *f*, masculinity

masculino /masku'lino/ *a* masculine; male; manly, vigorous

mascullar /masku'ʎar; masku'yar/ *vt Inf.* to chew; mutter, mumble

masera /ma'sera/ *f*, kneading bowl; cloth for covering dough

masilla /ma'siʎa; ma'siya/ *f*, mastic, putty

masón /ma'son/ **(-ona)** *n* Freemason

masonería /masone'ria/ *f*, freemasonry

masónico /ma'soniko/ *a* masonic

masoquismo /maso'kismo/ *m*, masochism

mastelero /maste'lero/ *m*, *Naut.* topmast

masticación /mastika'θion; mastika'sion/ *f*, mastication

masticar /masti'kar/ *vt* to masticate, eat; *Inf.* chew upon, consider

masticatorio /mastika'torio/ *a* masticatory

mástil /'mastil/ *m*, *Naut.* mast; upright, stanchion; pole (of a tent); stem, trunk; neck (of a guitar, etc.)

mastín /mas'tin/ *m*, mastiff

mastodonte /masto'ðonte/ *m*, mastodon

mastoides /mastoi'ðes/ *a* mastoid

mastuerzo /mas'tuerθo; mas'tuerso/ *m*, watercress; fool, blockhead

masturbación /masturβa'θion; masturβa'sion/ *f*, masturbation

masturbarse /mastur'βarse/ *vr* to masturbate

mata /'mata/ *f*, plant, shrub; stalk, sprig; grove, copse. **m. de pelo,** mat of hair

matacandelas /matakan'delas/ *m*, candle snuffer

matachín /mata'tʃin/ *m*, mummer; butcher; *Inf.* swashbuckler

matadero /mata'ðero/ *m*, slaughterhouse, abattoir

matadura /mata'ðura/ *f*, sore (on animals)

matafuego /mata'fuego/ *m*, fire extinguisher; fireman

matalotaje /matalo'tahe/ *m*, ship's supplies, stores; *Inf.* hodgepodge

matamoros /mata'moros/ *a* swashbuckling, swaggering

matamoscas /mata'moskas/ *m*, fly swatter

matanza /ma'tanθa; ma'tansa/ *f*, killing, massacre, slaughter; butchery (animals); *Inf.* persistence, determination

matar /ma'tar/ *vt* to kill; quench (thirst); put out (fire, light); slake (lime); tarnish (metal); bevel (corners, etc.); pester, importune; suppress; compel; *Art.* tone down; —*vr* kill oneself; be disappointed, grieve; overwork. **estar a m.,** to be at daggers drawn. **matarse por,** to try hard to; work hard for

matasanos /mata'sanos/ *m*, *Inf.* quack (doctor); bad doctor

matasellos /mata'seʎos; mata'seyos/ *m*, cancellation, postmark

mate /'mate/ *a* matte, unpolished, dull. *m*, checkmate (chess); maté, Paraguayan tea; gourd; vessel made from gourd, coconut, etc.

maté /ma'te/ *m*, maté, Paraguayan tea

matemáticas /mate'matikas/ *f pl*, mathematics. **m. prácticas,** applied mathematics. **m. teóricas,** pure mathematics

matemático /mate'matiko/ *a* mathematical; exact. *m*, mathematician

materia /ma'teria/ *f*, matter; theme, subject matter; subject (of study); matter, stuff, substance; pus, matter; question, subject; reason, occasion. **m. colorante,** dye. **materias plásticas,** plastics. **materias primas,** raw materials. **en m. de,** concerning; in the matter of

material /mate'rial/ *a* material; dull, stupid, limited. *m*, material; ingredient; plant, factory; equipment. **m. móvil ferroviario,** rolling stock (railroads)

materialidad /materiali'ðað/ *f*, materiality; external appearance (of things)

materialismo /materia'lismo/ *m*, materialism

materialista /materia'lista/ *a* materialistic. *mf* materialist

materializar /materiali'θar; materiali'sar/ *vt* to materialize; —*vr* materialize; grow materialistic, grow less spiritual

maternidad /materni'ðað/ *f*, maternity, motherhood

materno /ma'terno/ *a* maternal

matiz /ma'tiθ; ma'tis/ *m*, combination of colors; tone, hue; shade (of meaning, etc.)

matizar /mati'θar; mati'sar/ *vt* to combine, harmonize (colors); tint, shade; tinge (words, etc.)

matojo /ma'toho/ *m*, shrub, bush

matorral /mato'rral/ *m*, thicket, bush, undergrowth

matraca /ma'traka/ *f*, rattle; *Inf.* scolding, dressing-down; insistence, importunity

matraquear /matrake'ar/ *vi* to make a noise with a rattle; *Inf.* scold

matriarcado /matriar'kaðo/ *m*, matriarchy

matricida /matri'θiða; matri'siða/ *mf* matricide (person)

matricidio /matri'θiðio; matri'siðio/ *m*, matricide (crime)

matrícula /ma'trikula/ *f*, list, register; matriculation; registration number (of a car, etc.). **m. de buques,** maritime register. **m. de mar,** mariner's register; maritime register

matriculación /matrikula'θion; matrikula'sion/ *f*, matriculation; registration

matricular /matriku'lar/ *vt* to matriculate; enrol; *Naut.* register; —*vr* matriculate; enroll, register

matrimonial /matrimo'nial/ *a* matrimonial

matrimonio /matri'monio/ *m*, marriage, matrimony; married couple. **m. a yuras,** secret marriage. **m. de la mano izquierda** *or* **m. morganático,** morganatic marriage. **contraer m.,** to get married

matritense /matri'tense/ *a* and *mf* Madrilenian

matriz /ma'triθ; ma'tris/ *f*, uterus, womb; matrix, mold; *Mineral.* matrix; nut, female screw

matrona /ma'trona/ *f*, married woman; matron; midwife; female customs officer

matusalén /matusa'len/ *m*, Methuselah, very old man

matute /ma'tute/ *m*, smuggling; contraband; gambling den

matutero /matu'tero/ **(-ra)** *n* smuggler, contrabandist

matutino /matu'tino/ *a* matutinal, morning

maula /'maula/ *f*, trash; remnant; deception, fraud, trick. *mf Inf.* good-for-nothing; lazybones. *Inf.* **ser buena m.,** to be a trickster or a fraud

maulería /maule'ria/ *f*, remnant stall; trickery

maullar /mau'ʎar; mau'yar/ *vi* to meow, mew (cats)

maullido /mau'ʎiðo; mau'yiðo/ *m*, meow, cry of the cat

Mauricio, Isla de /mau'riθio, 'isla de; mau'risio, 'isla de/ Mauritius

mauritano /mauri'tano/ **(-na)** *a* and *n* Mauritian

mausoleo /mauso'leo/ *m*, mausoleum

maxilar /maksi'lar/ *a* maxillary. *m*, jaw

máxima /'maksima/ *f*, maxim, rule, precept, principle

máxime /'maksime/ *adv* principally, chiefly

máximo /'maksimo/ *a superl* **grande** greatest, maximum, top. *m*, maximum

maya /'maya/ *f*, common daisy; May queen

mayal /ma'yal/ *m*, flail

mayo /'mayo/ *m*, May; maypole; bouquet, wreath of flowers; *pl* festivities on eve of May Day

mayólica /ma'yolika/ *f*, majolica

mayonesa /mayo'nesa/ *f*, mayonnaise

mayor /ma'yor/ *a compar* **grande** bigger; greater; elder; main, principal; older; high (mass, etc.); *Mus.* major. *mf* major (of full age) —*a superl* **grande. el, la, lo mayor, los (las) mayores,** the biggest, greatest; eldest; chief, principal. **por m.,** in short, briefly; *Com.* wholesale

mayor /ma'yor/ *m*, head, director; chief clerk; *Mil.* major; *pl* ancestors

mayoral /mayo'ral/ *m*, head shepherd; coachman, driver; foreman, overseer, supervisor, steward

mayorazgo /mayo'raθgo; mayo'rasgo/ *m*, *Law.* entail; entailed estate; heir (to an entail); eldest son; right of primogeniture

mayordoma /mayor'ðoma/ *f*, steward's wife; housekeeper; stewardess

mayordomo /mayor'ðomo/ *m*, steward, superintendent; butler; major-domo, royal chief steward

mayoría /mayo'ria/ *f*, majority

mayormente /mayor'mente/ *adv* chiefly; especially
mayúscula /ma'yuskula/ *f*, capital letter, upper-case letter
mayúsculo /ma'yuskulo/ *a* large; capital (letters). **letra mayúscula,** capital letter, upper-case letter
maza /'maθa; 'masa/ *f*, mallet; club, bludgeon; mace; bass drum stick; pile driver; bone, stick, etc., tied to dog's tail in carnival; *Inf.* pedant, bore; important person, authority. **m. de polo,** polo mallet
mazacote /maθa'kote; masa'kote/ *m*, concrete; roughhewn work of art; *Inf.* stodgy overcooked dish; bore, tedious person
mazamorra /maθa'morra; masa'morra/ *f*, dish made of cornmeal; biscuit crumbs; broken fragments, remains
mazapán /maθa'pan; masa'pan/ *m*, marzipan
mazmorra /maθ'morra; mas'morra/ *f*, dungeon
mazo /'maθo; 'maso/ *m*, mallet; bundle, bunch; importunate person; clapper (of a bell)
mazonería /maθone'ria; masone'ria/ *f*, stonemasonry
mazonero /maθo'nero; maso'nero/ *m*, stonemason
mazorca /ma'θorka; ma'sorka/ *f*, spindleful; spike, ear (of corn); cocoa berry; camarilla, group
mazurca /ma'θurka; ma'surka/ *f*, mazurka
me /me/ *pers pron acc or dat 1st sing mf* me; to me
meandro /me'andro/ *m*, meandering, twisting, winding; wandering
meato /me'ato/ *m*, meatus
Meca, la /'meka, la/ Mecca
mecánica /me'kanika/ *f*, mechanics; mechanism, machinery; *Inf.* worthless thing; mean action
mecánico /me'kaniko/ *a* mechanical; power-operated; base, ill-bred. *m*, engineer; mechanic
mecanismo /meka'nismo/ *m*, mechanism; works, machinery
mecanizar /mekani'θar; mekani'sar/ *vt* to mechanize
mecanografía /mekanogra'fia/ *f*, typewriting
mecanografiar /mekanografi'ar/ *vt* to typewrite, type
mecanográfico /mekano'grafiko/ *a* typewriting, typing; typewritten, typed
mecanografista /mekanogra'fista/ *mf* **mecanógrafo** **(-fa)** *m* typist
mecedor /meθe'ðor; mese'ðor/ *a* rocking, swaying. *m*, swing
mecedora /meθe'ðora; mese'ðora/ *f*, rocking chair
mecenas /me'θenas; me'senas/ *m*, Maecenas, patron
mecer /me'θer; me'ser/ *vt* to stir, mix; shake; rock; swing
mecha /'metʃa/ *f*, wick; bit, drill; fuse (of explosives); match (for cannon, etc.); fat bacon (for basting); lock of hair; skein, twist
mechar /me'tʃar/ *vt Cul.* to baste, lard
mechero /me'tʃero/ *m*, gas burner; pocket lighter; socket of a candlestick
mechón /me'tʃon/ *m*, tuft, skein, bundle; lock of hair; wisp
medalla /me'ðaʎa; me'ðaya/ *f*, medal; medallion; plaque, round panel; *Inf.* piece of eight (coin)
medallón /meða'ʎon; me'ðayon/ *m*, large medal; medallion; locket
médano /'meðano/ *m*, sand dune
media /'meðia/ *f*, stocking
mediación /meðia'θion; meðia'sion/ *f*, mediation, arbitration; intercession
mediado /me'ðiaðo/ *a* half-full. **a mediados (** **del** **mes,** etc.), toward the middle (of the month, etc.)
mediador /meðia'ðor/ **(-ra)** *n* mediator, arbitrator; intercessor
medianamente /meðiana'mente/ *adv* moderately; passably, fairly well
medianero /meðia'nero/ **(-ra)** *a* middle; intervening, intermediate; mediatory —*n* mediator. *m*, owner of a semidetached house or of one in a row
medianía /meðia'nia/ *f*, average; medium, mediocrity; moderate wealth or means
mediano /me'ðiano/ *a* medium, average; moderate; *Inf.* middling, passable, fair
medianoche /meðia'notʃe/ *f*, midnight
mediante /me'ðiante/ *a* mediatory —*adv* by means of, by, through

mediar /me'ðiar/ *vi* to reach the middle; get halfway; elapse half a given time; intercede, mediate; arbitrate; be in between or in the middle; intervene, take part
medicación /meðika'θion; meðika'sion/ *f*, medication
medicamento /meðika'mento/ *m*, medicament, medicine, remedy
medicar /meði'kar/ *vt* to medicate
medicastro /meði'kastro/ *m*, unskilled physician; quack, charlatan
medicina /meði'θina; meði'sina/ *f*, medicine; medicament
medicinar /meðiθi'nar; meðisi'nar/ *vt* to attend; treat (patients)
medición /meði'θion; meði'sion/ *f*, measuring; measurements; survey (land); scansion
médico /'meðiko/ **(-ca)** *a* medical —*n* doctor of medicine. **m. de cabecera,** family doctor. **m. general,** general practitioner
medida /me'ðiða/ *f*, measurement; measuring stick; measure, precaution (gen. with *tomar, adoptar,* etc.); gauge; judgment, wisdom; meter; standard. **a m. que,** while, at the same time as. **tomar las medidas (a),** *Fig.* to take a person's measure, sum him up. **tomar sus medidas,** to take his (their) measurements; take the necessary measures. **un traje hecho a m.,** a suit made to measure
medieval /meðie'βal/ *a* medieval
medio /'meðio/ *a* half; middle; intermediate; halfway. *m*, half; middle; *Art.* medium; spiritualist medium; proceeding, measure, precaution; environment, medium; middle way, mean; *Sports.* halfback. **m. galope,** canter. **m. tiempo,** *Sports.* halftime. **a medias,** by halves; half, partly. **de por m.,** by halves; in between; in the way. **estar de por m.,** to be in the way; take part in. *Inf.* **quitar de en m.,** to get rid of. *Inf.* **quitarse de en m.,** to go away, remove oneself
mediocre /me'ðiokre/ *a* mediocre
mediocridad /meðiokri'ðað/ *f*, mediocrity; insignificance
mediodía /meðio'ðia/ *m*, noon, meridian; south
medioeval /meðioe'βal/ *a* medieval
mediopelo /meðio'pelo/ *m*, lower middle class
mediquillo /meði'kiʎo; meði'kiyo/ *m*, *Inf.* quack; medicine man (in the Philippines)
medir /me'ðir/ *vt irr* to measure; (metrics) scan; survey (land); compare; —*vr* measure one's words; act with restraint. See **pedir**
meditabundo /meðita'βundo/ *a* pensive, meditative, thoughtful
meditación /meðita'θion; meðita'sion/ *f*, meditation; consideration, reflection
meditador /meðita'ðor/ *a* meditative, thoughtful
meditar /meði'tar/ *vt* to meditate, consider, muse
meditativo /meðita'tiβo/ *a* meditative
mediterráneo /meðite'rraneo/ *a* mediterranean; inland, landlocked
médium /'meðium/ *m*, *Spirit.* medium
medra /'meðra/ *f*, progress; improvement, betterment; growth; prosperity
medrar /me'ðrar/ *vi* to flourish, grow; become prosperous or improve one's position
medro /'meðro/ *m*, improvement, progress. See **medra**
medroso /me'ðroso/ *a* timid, frightened; frightful, horrible
médula /'meðula/ *f*, marrow; *Bot.* pith; *Fig.* essence, core
medusa /me'ðusa/ *f*, jellyfish
mefistofélico /mefisto'feliko/ *a* Mephistophelian
mefítico /me'fitiko/ *a* noxious, mephitic, poisonous
megáfono /me'gafono/ *m*, megaphone
megalómano /mega'lomano/ **(-na)** *n* megalomaniac
mejicano /mehi'kano/ **(-na)** *a* and *n* Mexican
Méjico /'mehiko/ Mexico
mejilla /me'hiʎa; me'hiya/ *f*, *Anat.* cheek
mejillón /mehi'ʎon; mehi'yon/ *m*, sea mussel
mejor /me'hor/ *a* **a compar bueno** better —*adv* better; rather; sooner; preferably —*a superl* **bueno. el, la, lo** **mejor; los, las mejores,** the best; most preferable. **m.** **que m.,** better and better. *Inf.* **a lo m.,** probably, in all probability. **tanto m.,** so much the better

mejora /me'hora/ f, improvement; bettering; progress; higher bid (at auctions)

mejorable /meho'raβle/ a improvable

mejoramiento /mehora'miento/ m, betterment, improvement

mejorar /meho'rar/ vt to improve; better; outbid; —vi grow better (in health); improve (weather); make progress; rally (of markets). **Mejorando lo presente,** Present company excepted

mejoría /meho'ria/ f, improvement, progress; betterment; superiority; advantage, profit

mejunje /me'hunhe/ m, Inf. brew, potion, cure-all, stuff

melado /me'laðo/ a honey-colored. m, cane syrup

melancolía /melanko'lia/ f, melancholia; sadness, depression, melancholy

melancólico /melan'koliko/ a melancholy, sad; depressing

melaza /me'laθa; me'lasa/ f, molasses

melena /me'lena/ f, long side whiskers; loose, flowing hair (in women); overlong hair (in men); lion's mane. Inf. **andar a la m.,** to start a fight or quarrel. Inf. **traer a la m.,** to drag by the hair, force

melifluidad /meliflui'ðað/ f, mellifluence, sweetness

melifluo /me'lifluo/ a mellifluous, sweet-voiced; honey-eyed

melindre /me'lindre/ m, honey fritter; affectation, scruple, fastidiousness; narrow ribbon

melindroso /melin'droso/ a overfastidious, affected, prudish

mella /'meʎa; 'meya/ f, nick, notch; dent; gap; harm, damage (to reputation, etc.). **hacer m.,** Fig. to make an impression (on the mind); Mil. breach, drive a wedge

mellar /me'ʎar; me'yar/ vt to nick, notch; dent; damage

mellizo /me'ʎiθo; me'yiso/ **(-za)** a and n twin

melocotón /meloko'ton/ m, peach; peach tree

melocotonero /melokoto'nero/ m, peach tree

melodía /melo'ðia/ f, melody, tune; melodiousness

melódico /me'loðiko/ a melodic, melodious

melodioso /melo'ðioso/ a melodious, tuneful, sweet-sounding

melodrama /melo'ðrama/ m, melodrama

melodramático /meloðra'matiko/ a melodramatic

melón /me'lon/ m, melon

melosidad /melosi'ðað/ f, sweetness

meloso /me'loso/ a honeyed; sweet; gentle; mellifluous

membrana /mem'brana/ f, membrane

membrete /mem'brete/ m, note, memorandum; note or card of invitation; superscription, heading; address (of person)

membrillo /mem'briʎo; mem'briyo/ m, quince tree; quince; quince jelly

membrudo /mem'bruðo/ a brawny, strong, muscular

memo /'memo/ a silly, stupid

memorable /memo'raβle/ a memorable

memorándum /memo'randum/ m, notebook, jotter; memorandum

memorar /memo'rar/ **(se)** vt and vr to remember, recall

memoria /me'moria/ f, memory; remembrance, recollection; monument; memorial; report; essay, article; codicil; memorandum; record, chronicle; pl regards, compliments, greetings; memoirs; memoranda. Inf. **m. de grillo,** poor memory. **de m.,** by heart. **flaco de m.,** forgetful. **hacer m.,** to remember

memorial /memo'rial/ m, notebook; memorial, petition

memorialista /memoria'lista/ mf secretary, amanuensis

memorioso /memo'rioso/ a mindful, unforgetful

mena /'mena/ f, Mineral. ore

menaje /me'nahe/ m, household or school equipment or furniture

mención /men'θion; men'sion/ f, mention. **m. honorífica,** honorable mention. **hacer m. de,** to mention

mencionar /menθio'nar; mensio'nar/ vt to mention

mendacidad /mendaθi'ðað; mendasi'ðað/ f, mendacity, untruthfulness

mendaz /men'daθ; men'das/ a mendacious, untruthful

mendelismo /mende'lismo/ m, Mendelism

mendicante /mendi'kante/ a begging; Eccl. mendicant. mf beggar

mendicidad /mendiθi'ðað; mendisi'ð/ f, mendicancy, begging

mendigar /mendi'gar/ vt to beg for alms; entreat, supplicate

mendigo /men'digo/ **(-ga)** n beggar

mendoso /men'doso/ a mendacious, untruthful; mistaken

mendrugo /men'drugo/ m, crust of bread

menear /mene'ar/ vt to sway, move; wag; shake; manage, control, direct; —vr Inf. get a move on; sway, move; wriggle

meneo /me'neo/ m, swaying movement; wagging; shaking; wriggling; management, direction; Aer. bump; Inf. spanking

menester /menes'ter/ m, lack, shortage; necessity; occupation, employment; pl physical necessities; Inf. tools, implements, equipment. **haber m.,** to need, require. **ser m.,** to be necessary or requisite

menesteroso /meneste'roso/ a indigent, poverty-stricken, needy

menestra /me'nestra/ f, vegetable soup; dried vegetable (gen. pl)

menestral /menes'tral/ **(-la)** n artisan; worker; mechanic

mengano /meŋ'gano/ **(-na)** n so-and-so (used instead of the name of the person)

mengua /'meŋgua/ f, decrease; lack, shortage; waning (of the moon, etc.); dishonor, disgrace; poverty

menguado /meŋ'guaðo/ **(-da)** a timid, cowardly; silly, stupid; mean, avaricious —n coward; fool; skinflint. m, narrowing stitch when knitting socks

menguante /meŋ'guante/ a ebb; waning; decreasing. f, ebb tide; decadence, decline. **m. de la luna,** waning of the moon

menguar /meŋ'guar/ vi to decrease; decline, decay; wane; ebb; narrow (socks); —vt diminish; disgrace, discredit

menina /me'nina/ f, child attendant (on Spanish royalty)

menino /me'nino/ m, Spanish royal page; little dandy

menjurje /men'hurhe/ m, See **mejunje**

menopausia /meno'pausia/ f, menopause

menor /me'nor/ a compar less, smaller; younger, minor; Mus. minor. m, minor. f, (logic) minor —a superl **el, la, lo m.; los, las menores,** the least; smallest; youngest. **m. de edad,** minor (in age). **por m.,** at retail; in detail

Menorca /me'norka/ Minorca

menoría /meno'ria/ f, subordination, dependence; inferiority; minority (underage); childhood, youth

menos /'menos/ adv less; minus; least; except. **m. de** or **m. que,** less than. **al m., por lo m.,** at least. **a m. que,** unless. **De m. nos hizo Dios,** Never say die, Nothing is impossible. **poco más o m.,** more or less, about

menoscabar /menoska'βar/ vt to lessen, diminish, decrease; deteriorate, damage; disgrace, discredit

menoscabo /menos'kaβo/ m, decrease, diminishment; harm, damage, loss

menospreciable /menospre'θiaβle; menospre'siaβle/ a despicable, contemptible

menospreciador /menospreθia'ðor; menospresia-'ðor/ **(-ra)** a scornful —n scorner, despiser

menospreciar /menospre'θiar; menospre'siar/ vt to despise, scorn; underestimate, have a poor opinion of

menospreciativo /menospreθia'tiβo; menospresia-'tiβo/ a scornful, slighting, derisive

menosprecio /menos'preθio; menos'presio/ m, scorn, derision; underestimation

mensaje /men'sahe/ m, message; official communication

mensajería /mensahe'ria/ f, carrier service; steamship line

mensajero /mensa'hero/ **(-ra)** n messenger; errand boy

menstruación /menstrua'θion; menstrua'sion/ f, menstruation

menstruar /menstru'ar/ vi to menstruate

mensual /men'sual/ a monthly

mensualidad /mensuali'ðað/ f, monthly salary, monthly payment

mensurable /mensu'raβle/ a measurable

mensurar /mensu'rar/ vt to measure

menta /'menta/ f, menthe, mint; peppermint

mentado /men'taðo/ a celebrated, distinguished, famous

mental /men'tal/ a mental

mentalidad /mentali'ðað/ f, mentality

mentalmente /mental'mente/ adv mentally

mentar /men'tar/ vt irr to mention. See **sentar**

mente /'mente/ f, mind; intelligence, understanding; will, intention

mentecatería /mentekate'ria/ f, folly, stupidity

mentecato /mente'kato/ (-ta) a foolish, silly; feeble-minded, simple —n fool, idiot

mentir /men'tir/ vi irr to lie, be untruthful; deceive, mislead; falsify; Poet. belie; disagree, be incompatible; —vt break a promise, disappoint. **m. como un bellaco,** to lie like a trooper See **sentir**

mentira /men'tira/ f, lie, falsehood; error (in writing); Inf. white spot (on a fingernail); cracking (of fingerjoints). **m. oficiosa,** white lie. **Parece m.,** It seems incredible

mentiroso /menti'roso/ a lying, false; full of errors (literary works); deceptive

mentís /men'tis/ m, giving the lie (literally, you lie); proof, demonstration (of error)

mentol /'mentol/ m, menthol

mentón /men'ton/ m, chin

mentonera /mento'nera/ f, chin rest

menú /me'nu/ m, menu

menudamente /menuða'mente/ adv minutely; in detail, circumstantially

menudear /menuðe'ar/ vt to do frequently; do repeatedly; —vi happen frequently; describe in detail; Com. sell by retail

menudencia /menu'ðenθia; menu'ðensia/ f, minuteness, smallness; exactness, care, accuracy; trifle, worthless object; small matter; pl offal; pork sausages

menudeo /menu'ðeo/ m, repetition; description in detail; Com. retail. **al m.,** at retail

menudillos /menu'ðiʎos; menu'ðiyos/ m pl, giblets; offal

menudo /menu'ðo/ a minute, tiny; despicable; thin; small; vulgar; meticulous, exact; small (money). m, small coal; m pl, offal, entrails; small change (money). **a m.,** often, frequently. **por m.,** in detail, carefully; Com. in small lots

meñique /me'ɲike/ a Inf. very small. m, little finger (in full, **dedo m.**)

meollo /me'oʎo; me'oyo/ m, brain; Anat. marrow; Fig. essence, core, substance; understanding; Inf. **no tener m.** (una cosa), to be worthless, unsubstantial (things)

mequetrefe /meke'trefe/ m, Inf. coxcomb, whippersnapper

meramente /mera'mente/ adv solely, simply, merely

mercachifle /merkat'ʃifle/ m, peddler; small merchant

mercadear /merkaðe'ar/ vi to trade, traffic

mercadeo /merka'ðeo/ m, marketing (study of markets)

mercader /merka'ðer/ m, dealer, merchant, trader. **m. de grueso,** wholesaler

mercadería /merkaðe'ria/ f, See **mercancía**

mercado /mer'kaðo/ m, market; marketplace

mercancía /merkan'θia; merkan'sia/ f, goods, merchandise; commerce, trade, traffic

mercante /mer'kante/ a trading; commercial. m, merchant, dealer, trader

mercantil /merkan'til/ a mercantile, commercial

mercantilismo /merkanti'lismo/ m, mercantilism

merced /mer'θeð; mer'seð/ f, salary, remuneration; favor, benefit, kindness; will, desire, pleasure; mercy, grace; courtesy title given to untitled person (e.g. *vu-estra m.*, your honor. Has now become *usted* and is universally used). **m. a,** thanks to. **estar uno a m. de,** to live at someone else's expense, be dependent on

mercenario /merθe'nario; merse'nario/ (**-ia**) n Eccl. member of the Order of la Merced. m, Mil. mercenary; day laborer —a mercenary

mercería /merθe'ria; merse'ria/ f, haberdashery, mercery

mercerizar /merθeri'θar; merseri'sar/ vt to mercerize

mercero /mer'θero; mer'sero/ m, haberdasher, mercer

mercurio /mer'kurio/ m, mercury, quicksilver; Astron. Mercury

merecedor /mereθe'ðor; merese'ðor/ a deserving, worthy

merecer /mere'θer; mere'ser/ vt irr to deserve, be worthy of; attain, achieve; be worth; —vi deserve, be deserving. **m. bien de,** to deserve well of; have a claim on the gratitude of. See **conocer**

merecido /mere'θiðo; mere'siðo/ m, due reward

merecimiento /mereθi'miento; meresi'miento/ m, desert; merit

merendar /meren'dar/ vi irr to have lunch; pry into another's affairs; —vt have (a certain food) for lunch. Inf. **merendarse** (una cosa), to obtain (a thing), have it in one's pocket. See **recomendar**

merendero /meren'dero/ m, luncheon; tearoom

merengue /me'reŋgue/ m, Cul. meringue

meretriz /mere'triθ; mere'tris/ f, prostitute

meridiana /meri'ðiana/ f, daybed, chaise longue; siesta

meridiano /meri'ðiano/ a meridian. m, meridian. **a la meridiana,** at noon

meridional /meriðio'nal/ a meridional, southern

merienda /me'rienda/ f, tea, snack; lunch; Inf. hunchback. Inf. **juntar meriendas,** to join forces, combine interests

merino /me'rino/ a merino. m, merino wool; shepherd of merino sheep

meritísimo /meri'tisimo/ a superl most worthy, most deserving

mérito /'merito/ m, merit; desert; worth, excellence. **de m.,** excellent, notable. **hacer m. de,** to mention

meritorio /meri'torio/ a meritorious. m, unpaid worker, learner

merluza /mer'luθa; mer'lusa/ f, hake; Inf. drinking bout. Inf. **pescar una m.,** to get drunk

merma /'merma/ f, decrease, drop; loss, waste, reduction; leakage

mermar /mer'mar/ vi to diminish, waste away, decrease; evaporate; leak; —vt filch, pilfer; reduce, decrease

mermelada /merme'laða/ f, conserve, preserve; jam; marmalade

mero /'mero/ a mere; simple; plain

merodeador /meroðea'ðor/ a marauding. m, marauder, raider

merodear /meroðe'ar/ vi to maraud, raid

merodeo /mero'ðeo/ m, raiding, marauding

mes /'mes/ m, month; menses, menstruation

mesa /'mesa/ f, table; board, directorate; meseta, tableland; staircase landing; flat (of a sword, etc.); game of billiards. **m. de batalla,** post office sorting table. **m. de caballete,** trestle table. **m. de noche,** bedside table. **m. de tijeras,** folding table. **m. giratoria,** turntable. **alzar** (or **levantar**) **la m.,** to clear the table. **cubrir** (or **poner**) **la m.,** to set the table

mesada /me'saða/ f, monthly wages, monthly payment

mesadura /mesa'ðura/ f, tearing of the hair or beard

mesarse /me'sarse/ vr to tear one's hair or beard

mesenterio /mesen'terio/ m, mesentery

meseta /me'seta/ f, staircase landing; plateau, tableland

mesiánico /me'sianiko/ a Messianic

Mesías /me'sias/ m, Messiah

mesilla /me'siʎa; me'siya/ f, small table; laughing admonition; landing (of a stair)

mesmerismo /mesme'rismo/ m, mesmerism

mesnada /mes'naða/ f, association, company, society

mesocracia /meso'kraθia; meso'krasia/ f, mesocracy; middle class, bourgeoisie

mesón /me'son/ m, inn, tavern

mesonero /meso'nero/ **(-ra)** n innkeeper

mesta /'mesta/ f, ancient order of sheep farmers; pl confluence, meeting (of rivers)

mester /'mester/ m, craft, occupation. **m. de clerecía,** learned poetic meter of the Spanish Middle Ages. **m. de juglaría,** popular poetry and troubadour songs

mestizo /mes'tiθo; mes'tiso/ a half-breed; hybrid; cross-breed

mesura /me'sura/ f, sedateness; dignity; courtesy; moderation

mesurado /mesu'raðo/ a sedate; dignified; moderate, restrained, temperate

meta /'meta/ f, goalpost Fig. aim, end; goal; goalkeeper

metabolismo /metaβo'lismo/ m, metabolism

metafísica /meta'fisika/ f, metaphysics

metafísico /meta'fisiko/ a metaphysical. m, metaphysician

metáfora /me'tafora/ f, metaphor

metafórico /meta'foriko/ a metaphorical

metal /me'tal/ m, metal; brass; timbre of the voice; state, condition; quality, substance; Herald. gold or silver; Mus. brass (instruments)

metalario /meta'lario/ m, metalworker

metálico /me'taliko/ a metallic. m, metalworker; coin, specie; bullion

metalistería /metaliste'ria/ f, metalwork

metalizar /metali'θar; metali'sar/ vt to metallize, make metallic; —vr become metallized; grow greedy for money

metalurgia /metalur'hia/ f, metallurgy

metalúrgico /meta'lurhiko/ a metallurgical. m, metallurgist

metamorfosis /metamor'fosis/ f, metamorphosis

metano /me'tano/ m, methane

metatarso /meta'tarso/ m, metatarsus

metátesis /me'tatesis/ f, metathesis

metedor /mete'ðor/ **(-ra)** n placer, inserter; smuggler, contrabandist

metempsicosis /metempsi'kosis/ f, metempsychosis

metemuertos /mete'muertos/ Inf. meddler, Nosy Parker

meteórico /mete'oriko/ a meteoric

meteorito /meteo'rito/ m, meteorite

meteoro /mete'oro/ m, meteor

meteorología /meteorolo'hia/ f, meteorology

meteorológico /meteoro'lohiko/ a meteorological

meteorologista /meteorolo'hista/ mf meteorologist; weather forecaster

meter /me'ter/ vt to place; put; introduce, insert; stake (gambling); smuggle; cause, occasion; place close together; persuade to take part in; Sew. take in fullness; deceive, humbug; cram in, pack tightly; Naut. take in sail; —vr interfere, butt in; meddle (with); take up, follow (occupations); be overfamiliar; disembogue, empty itself (rivers, etc.); attack with the sword; (with prep a) follow (occupations); become, turn (e.g. meterse a predicar, to turn preacher); (with con) pick a quarrel with. **meterse en precisiones,** to go into details. Inf. **meterse en todo,** to be very meddlesome

metesillas y sacamuertos /mete'siʎas i saka-'muertos; mete'siyas i saka'muertos/ m, scene shifter, stagehand

meticulosidad /metikulosi'ðað/ f, meticulosity; timorousness

meticuloso /metiku'loso/ a meticulous, fussy; timid, nervous

metido /me'tiðo/ a tight; crowded; crabbed (of handwriting). m, Sew. material for letting out (seams). **m. en años,** quite old (person)

metílico /me'tiliko/ a methylic

metimiento /meti'miento/ m, insertion, introduction; influence, sway

metódico /me'toðiko/ a methodical

metodismo /meto'ðismo/ m, Methodism

metodista /meto'ðista/ a methodistic. mf Methodist

método /'metoðo/ m, method

metodología /metoðolo'hia/ f, methodology

metralla /me'traʎa; me'traya/ f, Mil. grapeshot, shrapnel

métrica /'metrika/ f, metrics

métrico /'metriko/ a metric; metrical

metro /'metro/ m, (verse) meter; meter (measurement); subway, underground railway

metrónomo /me'tronomo/ m, metronome

metrópoli /me'tropoli/ f, metropolis, capital; see of a metropolitan bishop; mother country

metropolitano /metropoli'tano/ a metropolitan. m, metropolitan bishop

México /'mehiko/ Mexico

mezcla /'meθkla; 'meskla/ f, mixture; blend, combination; mixed cloth, tweed; mortar

mezclar /meθ'klar; mes'klar/ vt to mix, blend, combine; —vr mix, mingle; take part; interfere, meddle; intermarry

mezcolanza /meθko'lanθa; mesko'lansa/ f, Inf. hodgepodge

mezquindad /meθkin'dað; meskin'dað/ f, poverty; indigence; miserliness; paltriness; meanness, poorness

mezquino /meθ'kino; mes'kino/ a needy, impoverished; miserly, stingy; small, diminutive; unhappy; mean, paltry

mezquita /meθ'kita; mes'kita/ f, mosque

mi /'mi/ poss pron my. m, Mus. mi, E

mí /'mi/ pers pron acc gen dat 1st pers sing me. Used only after prepositions (e.g. Lo hicieron por mí, They did it for me)

miaja /'miaha/ f, See **migaja**

miasma /'miasma/ m, miasma

miasmático /mias'matiko/ a miasmatic, malarious

miau /'miau/ m, meow

mica /'mika/ f, Mineral. mica; coquette, flirt

micción /mik'θion; mik'sion/ f, micturition

micho /'mitʃo/ **(-cha)** n Inf. puss, pussycat

micología /mikolo'hia/ f, mycology

micra /'mikra/ f, micron, thousandth part of a millimeter

microbiano /mikro'βiano/ a microbial, microbic

microbio /mi'kroβio/ m, microbe

microbiología /mikroβiolo'hia/ f, microbiology

microbrigada /mikroβri'gaða/ f, team of volunteer workers (Castroist Cuba)

microcéfalo /mikro'θefalo; mikro'sefalo/ a microcephalous

microcosmo /mikro'kosmo/ m, microcosm

micrófono /mi'krofono/ m, microphone

microonda /mikro'onda/ f, microwave

microscópico /mikros'kopiko/ a microscopic

microscopio /mikros'kopio/ m, microscope

miedo /'mieðo/ m, fear, apprehension, terror. **m. al público,** stagefright. **tener m.,** to be afraid

miedoso /mie'ðoso/ a Inf. fearful, nervous

miel /miel/ f, honey. **m. de caña,** sugarcane syrup. Inf. **quedarse a media m.,** to see one's pleasure snatched away. Inf. **ser de mieles,** to be most pleasant or agreeable

mielitis /mie'litis/ f, myelitis

miembro /mi'embro/ m, Anat. limb; penis; member, associate; part, portion, section; Math. member

miente /'miente/ f, thought, imagination, mind. **parar** or **poner mientes en,** to consider, think about. **venírsele a las mientes,** to occur to one's mind

mientras /'mientras/ adv while. **m. más...,** the more.... **m. que,** while (e.g. m. que esperaba en el jardín, while he was waiting in the garden). **m. tanto,** in the meanwhile

miércoles /'mierkoles/ m, Wednesday. **m. de ceniza,** Ash Wednesday

mierda /'mierða/ f, (vulgar) shit; Inf. filth

mies /'mies/ f, cereal plant, grain; harvest time; pl grain fields

miga /'miga/ f, breadcrumb; crumb; Inf. essence, core; substance; bit, scrap; pl fried breadcrumbs. Inf. **hacer buenas (** or **malas) migas,** to get on well (or badly) together

migaja /mi'gaha/ f, breadcrumb; bit, scrap; trifle,

mere nothing; *pl* crumbs (from the table); remains, remnants

migajón /miga'hon/ *m,* crumb (of a loaf): *Fig. Inf.* essence, substance, core

migración /migra'θion; migra'sion/ *f,* migration; emigration

migraña /mi'graɲa/ *f,* migraine

migratorio /migra'torio/ *a* migratory

mijo /'miho/ *m,* millet; maize

mil /mil/ *a* thousand; thousandth; many, large number. *m,* thousand; thousandth. *Inf.* **Son las m. y quinientas,** It's extremely late (of the hour)

miladi /mi'laði/ *f,* my lady

milagrero /mila'grero/ *a Inf.* miraculous

milagro /mi'lagro/ *m,* miracle; marvel, wonder. ¡**M.**! Amazing! Just fancy!

milagroso /mila'groso/ *a* miraculous; marvelous, wonderful

milanés /mila'nes/ **(-esa)** *a* and *n* Milanese

milano /mi'lano/ *m, Ornith.* kite

mildeu /'mildeu/ *m,* mildew

milenario /mile'nario/ *a* millenary; millennial. *m,* millenary; millennium

milésimo /mi'lesimo/ *a* thousandth

milicia /mi'liθia; mi'lisia/ *f,* militia; military; art of war; military profession

miliciano /mili'θiano; mili'siano/ *a* military. *m,* militiaman

miligramo /mili'gramo/ *m,* milligram

mililitro /mili'litro/ *m,* milliliter

milímetro /mi'limetro/ *m,* millimeter

militante /mili'tante/ *a* militant

militar /mili'tar/ *a* military. *m,* soldier —*vi* to fight in the army; struggle (for a cause); *Fig.* militate (e.g. *Las circunstancias militan en favor de* (or *contra*) *sus ideas,* Circumstances militate against his ideas)

militarismo /milita'rismo/ *m,* militarism

militarista /milita'rista/ *a* militaristic. *mf* militarist

militarizar /militari'θar; militari'sar/ *vt* to militarize; make war-like

milla /'miʎa; 'miya/ *f,* mile

millar /mi'ʎar; mi'yar/ *m,* thousand; vast number (gen. *pl*)

millón /mi'ʎon; mi'yon/ *m,* million

millonario /miʎo'nario; miyo'nario/ **(-ia)** *a* and *n* millionaire

millonésimo /miʎo'nesimo; miyo'nesimo/ *a* millionth

milmillonésimo /milmiʎo'nesimo; milmiyo'nesimo/ *a* billionth

milord /mi'lorð/ *m,* my lord *pl* **milores,** my lords

mimar /mi'mar/ *vt* to spoil, overindulge; caress, fondle

mimbre /'mimbre/ *mf* osier; willow tree. *m,* wicker

mimbrear /mimbre'ar/ *vi* to sway, bend

mimbrera /mim'brera/ *f,* osier; osier bed; willow

mímica /'mimika/ *f,* mimicry; mime

mímico /'mimiko/ *a* mimic

mimo /'mimo/ *m,* mimic, buffoon; mime; caress, expression of affection, tenderness; overindulgence

mimoso /mi'moso/ *a* affectionate, demonstrative

mina /'mina/ *f,* mine; excavation, mining; underground passage; lead (in a pencil); *Mil. Nav.*) mine; *Fig.* gold mine. *Mil.* **m. terrestre,** landmine

minador /mina'ðor/ *m,* excavator; *Nav.* minelayer; *Mil.* sapper

minar /mi'nar/ *vt* to excavate, mine; *Fig.* undermine; (*Mil. Nav.*) mine; work hard for

minarete /mina'rete/ *m,* minaret

mineraje /mine'rahe/ *m,* exploitation of a mine, mining; mineral products

mineral /mine'ral/ *a* and *m,* mineral

mineralogía /mineralo'hia/ *f,* mineralogy

mineralógico /minera'lohiko/ *a* mineralogical

mineralogista /mineralo'hista/ *mf* mineralogist

minería /mine'ria/ *f,* mining, mineworking; mineworkers

minero /mi'nero/ *a* mining. *m,* miner, mineworker; source, origin

miniar /mini'ar/ *vt Art.* to illuminate

miniatura /minia'tura/ *f,* miniature

miniaturista /miniatu'rista/ *mf* miniaturist

mínima /'minima/ *f, Mus.* minim; very small thing or portion

mínimo /'minimo/ *a superl* **pequeño** smallest; minimum; meticulous, precise. *m,* minimum; (meteorological) trough

ministerial /ministe'rial/ *a* ministerial

ministerio /minis'terio/ *m,* office, post; *Polit.* cabinet; ministry; government office; government department.

ministrar /minis'trar/ *vt* and *vi* to fill; administer (an office); —*vt* minister to; give, provide

ministro /mi'nistro/ *m,* instrument, agency; minister of state, cabinet minister; clergyman, minister; minister plenipotentiary; policeman. **m. de estado,** secretary of state. **m. de gobernación,** secretary of the interior. **m. de hacienda,** treasurer. **m. de relaciones extranjeras,** foreign secretary. **primer m.** prime minister

minoración /minora'θion; minora'sion/ *f,* reduction, decrease

minorar /mino'rar/ *vt* to diminish, decrease

minoría /mino'ria/ *f,* minority, smaller number; minority (of age)

minoridad /minori'ðað/ *f,* minority (of age)

minucia /minu'θia; minu'sia/ *f,* smallness; morsel, mite; *pl* details, trifles, minutiae

minuciosidad /minuθiosi'ðað; minusiosi'ðað/ *f,* meticulousness, minuteness, precision

minucioso /minu'θioso; minu'sioso/ *a* meticulous, precise, minute

minué /mi'nue/ *m,* minuet

minúsculo /mi'nuskulo/ *a* minute, very small

minuta /mi'nuta/ *f,* memorandum, minute; note; list, catalog

minutario /minu'tario/ *m,* minute book

minutero /minu'tero/ *m,* minute hand (of a clock)

minuto /mi'nuto/ *a* minute, very small. *m,* minute

mío /'mio/ *m,* **mía,** *f,* (*m pl.* **míos,** *f pl.* **mías**) *poss pron* mine (e.g. *Las flores son mías,* The flowers are mine). **Mi** is used before nouns, *not* **mío.** Also used with article (e.g. *Este sombrero no es el mío,* This hat is not mine (my one)). **de mío,** by myself, without help. *Inf.* ¡**Esta es la mía!** This is my chance!

miope /mi'ope/ *a* myopic. *mf* myopic person

miopía /mio'pia/ *f,* shortsightedness

miosota /mio'sota/ *f,* myosotis, forget-me-not

mira /'mira/ *f,* sight (optical instruments, guns); intention, design; *Mil.* watchtower; care, precaution. **andar, estar** or **quedar a la m.,** to be vigilant, be on the lookout

mirada /mi'raða/ *f,* look; gaze. **lanzar miradas de carnero degollado** (**a**), to cast sheep's eyes at

miradero /mira'ðero/ *m,* object of attention, cynosure; observation post, lookout

mirador /mira'ðor/ **(-ra)** *n* spectator. *m, Archit.* oriel; enclosed balcony; observatory

miramiento /mira'miento/ *m,* observation, gazing; scruple, consideration; precaution, care; thoughtfulness

mirar /mi'rar/ *vt* to look at, gaze at; observe, behold; watch; consider, look after; value, appreciate; concern; believe, think; (*with prep a*) overlook, look on to; face; (*with por*) care for, protect; look after, consider. **m. contra el gobierno,** *Inf.* to be squint-eyed. **m. de hito en hito,** to look over, stare at. **mirarse en** (**una cosa,**) to consider (a matter) carefully

miríada /mi'riaða/ *f,* myriad, huge number

mirilla /mi'riʎa; mi'riya/ *f,* peephole

miriñaque /miri'ɲake/ *m,* trinket, ornament; crinoline

mirlarse /mir'larse/ *vr Inf.* to give oneself airs

mirlo /'mirlo/ *m,* blackbird; *Inf.* pompous air

mirón /mi'ron/ *a* inquisitive, curious

mirra /'mirra/ *f,* myrrh

mirto /'mirto/ *m,* myrtle

misa /'misa/ *f,* (*Eccl. Mus.*) mass. **m. de difuntos,** requiem mass. **m. del gallo,** midnight mass. **m. mayor,** high mass. **m. rezada,** low mass. **como en m.,** in profound silence. **oír m.,** to attend mass

misal /mi'sal/ *m,* missal

misantropía /misantro'pia/ *f,* misanthropy

misantrópico /misan'tropiko/ *a* misanthropic

misántropo /mi'santropo/ *m*, misanthrope

miscelánea /misθe'lanea; misse'lanea/ *f*, medley, assortment, miscellany

misceláneo /misθe'laneo; misse'laneo/ *a* assorted, miscellaneous, mixed

miscible /mis'θiβle; mis'siβle/ *a* mixable

miserable /mise'raβle/ *a* miserable, unhappy; timid, pusillanimous; miserly, mean; despicable

miseria /mi'seria/ *f*, misery; poverty, destitution; avarice, miserliness; *Inf.* poor thing, trifle

misericordia /miseri'korðia/ *f*, mercy, compassion

misericordioso /miserikor'ðioso/ *a* merciful, compassionate

mísero /'misero/ *a Inf.* fond of churchgoing

misérrimo /mi'serrimo/ *a superl* most miserable

misión /mi'sion/ *f*, mission; vocation; commission, duty, errand

misionar /misio'nar/ *vi* to missionize, act as a missionary; *Eccl.* conduct a mission

misionero /misio'nero/ *m*, missioner; missionary

Misisipi, el /misi'sipi, el/ the Mississippi

misiva /mi'siβa/ *f*, missive

mismo /'mismo/ *a* same; similar; self (e.g. *ellos mismos*, they themselves); very, same (e.g. *Ahora m. voy*, I'm going this very minute). **Me da lo m.,** It makes no difference to me. **por lo m.,** for that self-same reason

misógamo /mi'sogamo/ **(-ma)** *n* misogamist

misógino /mi'sohino/ *m*, misogynist

misterio /mis'terio/ *m*, mystery

misterioso /miste'rioso/ *a* mysterious

mística /'mistika/ *f*, **misticismo** *m*, mysticism

místico /'mistiko/ *a* mystic

mistificación /mistifika'θion; mistifika'sion/ *f*, mystification; mystery; deception

mistificar /mistifi'kar/ *vt* to mystify; deceive

Misuri, el /mi'suri, el/ the Missouri

mitad /mi'tað/ *f*, half; middle, center. *Fig. Inf.* **cara m.,** better half. *Inf.* **mentir por la m. de la barba,** to lie barefacedly

mítico /'mitiko/ *a* mythical

mitigación /mitiga'θion; mitiga'sion/ *f*, mitigation

mitigador /mitiga'ðor/ **(-ra)** *a* mitigatory —*n* mitigator

mitigar /miti'gar/ *vt* to mitigate, moderate, alleviate; appease

mitin /'mitin/ *m*, mass meeting

mito /'mito/ *m*, myth

mitología /mitolo'hia/ *f*, mythology

mitológico /mito'lohiko/ *a* mythological

mitologista, mitólogo /mitolo'hista, mi'tologo/ *m*, mythologist

mitón /mi'ton/ *m*, mitten

mitra /'mitra/ *f*, miter; bishopric; archbishopric

mitrado /mi'traðo/ *a* mitred

mixto /'miksto/ *a* mixed, blended; hybrid; composite; mongrel. *m*, mixed train (carrying freight and passengers); sulphur match

mixtura /miks'tura/ *f*, mixture, blend; compound; mixture (medicine)

¡miz, miz! /miθ, miθ; mis, mis/ puss, puss!

moabita /moa'βita/ *mf* Moabite

mobiliario /moβi'liario/ *a* movable (goods). *m*, furniture

moblaje /mo'βlahe/ *m*, household goods and furniture

mocasín /moka'sin/ *m*, moccasin

mocedad /moθe'ðað; mose'ðað/ *f*, youth, adolescence; mischief, prank. *Fig. Inf.* **correr sus mocedades,** to sow one's wild oats

mochila /mo'tʃila/ *f*, knapsack; nosebag; military rations for a march

mocho /'motʃo/ *a* blunted, topless, lopped; *Inf.* shorn, cropped. *m*, butt, butt end

mochuelo /mo'tʃuelo/ *m*, owl; *Inf.* difficult job

moción /mo'θion/ *f*, motion, movement; impulse, tendency; divine inspiration; motion (of a debate)

moco /'moko/ *m*, mucus; candle drips; snuff of a candle. *Inf.* **caérsele el m.,** to be very simple, be easily deceived

mocoso /mo'koso/ **(-sa)** *a* running of the nose, sniffling; unimportant, insignificant —*n* coxcomb, stripling

moda /'moða/ *f*, fashion. **estar** *or* **ser de m.,** to be fashionable, be in fashion. **la última m.,** the latest fashion

modales /mo'ðales/ *m pl*, manners, behavior

modalidad /moðali'ðað/ *f*, form, nature; *Mus.* modality

modelado /moðe'laðo/ *m*, *Art.* modeling

modelar /moðe'lar/ *vt Art.* to model; —*vr* model oneself (on), copy

modelo /mo'ðelo/ *m*, example, pattern; model. *mf Art.* life model

módem *m*, modem

moderación /moðera'θion; moðerasion/ *f*, moderation; restraint, temperance, equability

moderado /moðe'raðo/ *a* moderate; restrained, temperate

moderador /moðera'ðor/ **(-ra)** *a* moderating —*n* moderator

moderantismo /moðeran'tismo/ *m*, moderate opinion; moderate political party

moderar /moðe'rar/ *vt* to moderate; temper, restrain; —*vr* regain one's self-control; behave with moderation

modernidad /moðerni'ðað/ *f*, modernity

modernismo /moðer'nismo/ *m*, modernism

modernista /moðer'nista/ *a* modernistic; modern. *mf* modernist

modernización /moðerniθa'θion; moðernisa'sion/ *f*, modernization

modernizar /moðerni'θar; moðerni'sar/ *vt* to modernize

moderno /mo'ðerno/ *a* modern. *m*, modern. **a la moderna,** in modern fashion

modestia /mo'ðestia/ *f*, modesty

modesto /mo'ðesto/ *a* modest

módico /'moðiko/ *a* moderate (of prices, etc.)

modificable /moðifi'kaβle/ *a* modifiable

modificación /moðifi'kaθion; moðifi'sion/ *f*, modification

modificador, modificante /moðifi'kaðor, moðifi'kante/ *a* modifying, moderating

modificar /moðifi'kar/ *vt* to modify; moderate

modismo /mo'ðismo/ *m*, idiom, idiomatic expression

modista /mo'ðista/ *mf* dressmaker; couturier; milliner

modo /'moðo/ *m*, mode, method, style; manner, way; moderation, restraint; civility, politeness (often *pl*); *Mus.* mode; *Gram.* mood. **m. de ser,** nature, temperament. **de m. que,** so that. **de ningún m.,** not at all, by no means. **de todos modos,** in any case

modorra /mo'ðorra/ *f*, deep sleep, stupor

modorro /mo'ðorro/ *a* drowsy, heavy

modoso /mo'ðoso/ *a* demure; well-behaved

modulación /moðula'θion; moðula'sion/ *f*, modulation

modulador /moðula'ðor/ **(-ra)** *a* modulative —*n* modulator, *m*, *Mus.* modulator

modular /moðu'lar/ *vt* and *vi* to modulate

mofa /'mofa/ *f*, mockery, ridicule, jeering

mofador /mofa'ðor/ **(-ra)** *a* jeering —*n* scoffer, mocker

mofarse /mo'farse/ *vr* (*with de*) to make fun of, jeer at

mofeta /mo'feta/ *f*, noxious gas; damp (gas); *Zool.* skunk

moflete /mo'flete/ *m*, *Inf.* plump cheek

mofletudo /mofle'tuðo/ *a* plump-cheeked

mogol /'mogol/ **(-la)** *a* and *n* Mongolian.

mogote /mo'gote/ *m*, hill; pyre, stack

mohicano /moi'kano/ *a* and *n* Mohican

mohín /mo'in/ *m*, grimace

mohína /mo'ina/ *f*, grudge, rancor; sullenness; sulkiness

mohíno /mo'ino/ *a* depressed, gloomy; sulky; black or black-nosed (of animals)

moho /'moo/ *m*, mold, fungoid growth; moldiness; moss. *Inf.* **no criar m.,** to be always on the move

mohoso /mo'oso/ *a* mossy; moldy

mojada /mo'haða/ f, wetting; *Inf.* stab; sop of bread
mojador /moha'ðor/ **(-ra)** n wetter. m, stamp moistener
mojar /mo'har/ vt to wet; moisten; *Inf.* stab, wound with a dagger; —vi take part in; meddle, interfere; —vr get wet
mojicón /mohi'kon/ m, kind of spongecake; *Inf.* slap in the face
mojiganga /mohi'ganga/ f, masquerade, mummer's show; farce; funny sight, figure of fun
mojigatería /mohigate'ria/ f, hypocrisy; sanctimoniousness; prudery
mojigato /mohi'gato/ **(-ta)** a hypocritical; sanctimonious; prudish —n hypocrite; bigot; prude
mojón /mo'hon/ m, boundary marker; milestone; heap. **m. kilométrico,** milestone
molar /mo'lar/ a molar
moldavo /mol'daβo/ **(-va)** a and n Moldavian
molde /'molde/ m, mold, matrix; *Fig.* model, pattern. **de m.,** printed; suitably, conveniently; perfectly. **letra de m.,** printed letters, print
moldeador /moldea'ðor/ **(-ra)** n molder
moldear /molde'ar/ vt to mold, cast
moldura /mol'dura/ f, molding
moldurar /moldu'rar/ vt to mold
molécula /mo'lekula/ f, molecule
molecular /moleku'lar/ a molecular
moler /mo'ler/ vt irr to grind, crush; tire, exhaust; illtreat; pester, annoy. **m. a palos,** to beat black and blue —*Pres. Indic.* **muelo, mueles, muele, muelen.** *Pres. Subjunc.* **muela, muelas, muela, muelan**
molestia /mo'lestia/ f, inconvenience, trouble; annoyance; discomfort, pain; bore, nuisance. **Es una m.,** It's a nuisance
molesto /mo'lesto/ a inconvenient, troublesome; annoying; painful; uncomfortable; boring, tedious
moletón /mole'ton/ m, flannelet
molicie /mo'liθie; mo'lisie/ f, softness, smoothness; effeminacy, weakness
molienda /mo'lienda/ f, milling; grinding; mill; portion ground at one time; *Inf.* exhaustion, fatigue; *Inf.* nuisance
molificar /molifi'kar/ vt to mollify, appease
molimiento /moli'miento/ m, milling; grinding; exhaustion, fatigue
molinera /moli'nera/ f, (woman) miller; miller's wife
molinero /moli'nero/ a mill. m, miller
molinillo /moli'niʎo; moli'niyo/ m, hand mill, small grinder; mincing machine; beater. **m. de café,** coffee mill
molino /mo'lino/ m, mill; harum-scarum, rowdy; bore, tedious person; *Inf.* mouth. **m. de rueda de escalones,** treadmill. **m. de viento,** windmill
molleja /mo'ʎeha; mo'yeha/ f, gizzard
mollera /mo'ʎera; mo'yera/ f, crown of the head; brains, sense. *Inf.* **ser duro de m.,** to be obstinate; be stupid
molusco /mo'lusko/ m, mollusk
momentaneidad /momentanei'ðað/ f, momentariness
momentáneo /momen'taneo/ a momentary, brief; instantaneous, immediate
momento /mo'mento/ m, moment, minute; importance; *Mech.* moment. **al m.,** immediately. **a cada m.,** all the time; frequently. **por momentos,** continually; intermittently
momería /mome'ria/ f, mummery
momero /mo'mero/ **(-ra)** n mummer
momia /'momia/ f, mummy
momificación /momifika'θion; momifika'sion/ f, mummification
momificar /momifi'kar/ vt to mummify; —vr become mummified
mona /'mona/ f, female monkey; *Inf.* imitator; drinking bout; drunk. *Inf.* **Aunque la m. se vista de seda, m. se queda,** Breeding will tell. *Inf.* **ser la última m.,** to be of no account, be unimportant
monacal /mona'kal/ a monkish, monastic
monacillo /mona'θiʎo; mona'siyo/ m, *Eccl.* acolyte
monada /mo'naða/ f, mischievous prank; affected

gesture or grimace; small, pretty thing; childish cleverness; flattery; rash act; pl monkey shines
monaguillo /mona'giʎo; mona'giyo/ m, *Eccl.* acolyte
monarca /mo'narka/ mf monarch
monarquía /monar'kia/ f, monarchy
monárquico /mo'narkiko/ **(-ca)** a monarchic —n monarchist
monarquismo /monar'kismo/ m, monarchism
monasterio /mona'sterio/ m, monastery; convent
monástico /mo'nastiko/ a monastic
monda /'monda/ f, skinning, peeling; *Agr.* pruning; cleansing
mondadientes /monda'ðientes/ m, toothpick
mondar /mon'dar/ vt to skin, peel; *Agr.* prune; cut the hair; cleanse; free of rubbish; *Inf.* deprive of possessions; —vr pick one's teeth
mondo /'mondo/ a simple, plain; bare; unadulterated, pure
moneda /mo'neða/ f, coin, piece of money; coinage; *Inf.* wealth; cash. **m. corriente,** currency. **m. metálica,** specie. **pagar en buena m.,** to give entire satisfaction. **pagar en la misma m.,** to pay back in the same coin, return like for like. *Inf.* **ser m. corriente,** to be usual or very frequent
monedero /mone'ðero/ m, coiner, minter; handbag; purse
monería /mone'ria/ f, mischievous trick; unimportant trifle; pretty thing; childish cleverness, pretty ways
monetario /mone'tario/ a monetary. m, collection of coins and medals
monetización /monetiθa'θion; monetisa'sion/ f, monetization
monigote /moni'gote/ m, *Inf.* boor; grotesque, puppet
monitor /moni'tor/ m, monitor
monitorio /moni'torio/ a monitory
monja /'monha/ f, nun; pl sparks
monje /'monhe/ m, monk
monjil /mon'hil/ a nun-like. m, nun's habit
mono /'mono/ a *Inf.* pretty, attractive; amusing; funny. m, monkey; person given to grimacing; rash youth; coverall. *Inf.* **estar de monos,** to be on bad terms
monocromo /mono'kromo/ a monochrome; monochromatic
monóculo /mo'nokulo/ m, monocle
monogamia /mono'gamia/ f, monogamy
monógamo /mo'nogamo/ a monogamous —n monogamist
monografía /monogra'fia/ f, monograph
monograma /mono'grama/ m, monogram
monolítico /mono'litiko/ a monolithic
monolito /mono'lito/ m, monolith
monólogo /mo'nologo/ m, monologue
monomanía /monoma'nia/ f, monomania
monomaníaco /monoma'niako/ **(-ca)** n monomaniac
monopatín /monopa'tin/ m, scooter
monoplano /mono'plano/ m, monoplane
monopolio /mono'polio/ m, monopoly
monopolista /monopo'lista/ mf monopolist
monopolizar /monopoli'θar; monopoli'sar/ vt to monopolize
monosilábico /monosi'laβiko/ a monosyllabic
monosílabo /mono'silaβo/ a, monosyllable
monoteísmo /monote'ismo/ m, monotheism
monoteísta /monote'ista/ mf monotheist
monotipia /mono'tipia/ f, monotype
monotonía /monoto'nia/ f, monotony; monotone
monótono /mo'notono/ a monotonous
monroísmo /monro'ismo/ m, Monroe doctrine
monseñor /monse'nor/ m, monsignor
monserga /mon'serga/ f, *Inf.* rigmarole; jargon
monstruo /'monstruo/ m, monster; freak, monstrosity; cruel person; hideous person or thing
monstruosidad /monstruosi'ðað/ f, monstrousness, monstrosity
monstruoso /mon'struoso/ a monstrous, abnormal; enormous; extraordinary; atrocious, outrageous
monta /'monta/ f, mounting a horse; total; *Mil.* mounting signal; breeding station (horses)

montacargas /monta'kargas/ *m*, hoist, lift; freight elevator

montador /monta'ðor/ *m*, mounter; mounting block

montadura /monta'ðura/ *f*, mounting; mount, setting (of jewels)

montaje /mon'tahe/ *m*, assembling, setting up (machines); presentation (of a book); (cinema) montage

montañés /monta'ɲes/ **(-esa)** *a* mountain —*n* mountain dweller; native of Santander

montano /mon'tano/ *a* hilly, mountainous

montante /mon'tante/ *m*, upright, stanchion; tent pole

montaña /mon'taɲa/ *f*, mountain; mountainous country. **montañas rusas,** roller coaster (at an amusement park)

montañés /mon'taɲes/ **(-esa)** *a* mountain —*n* mountain dweller; native of Santander

montañoso /monta'ɲoso/ *a* mountainous; hilly

montar /mon'tar/ *vi* to ascend, climb up, get on top; mount (a horse); ride (a horse); be important; —*vt* get on top of; ride (a horse); total, amount to; set up (apparatus, machinery); *Naut.* sail around, double; set, mount (gems); cock (firearms); fine for trespassing; wind (a clock); command (a ship); *Naut.* carry, be fitted with (guns, etc.). **m. a horcajadas en,** to mount astride; straddle. **montarse en cólera,** to fly into a rage

montaraz /monta'raθ; monta'ras/ *a* mountain-dwelling; wild, savage; rude, uncivilized, uncouth. *m*, gamekeeper, forester

montazgo /mon'taθgo; mon'tasgo/ *m*, toll payable for cattle moving from one province to another

monte /'monte/ *m*, mount, hill; woodland; obstacle, impediment. **m. de piedad,** pawnshop. **m. pío,** savings fund

montenegrino /montene'grino/ **(-na)** *a* and *n* Montenegrin

montera /mon'tera/ *f*, cap; glass roof

montería /monte'ria/ *f*, hunt, chase; art of hunting

montero /mon'tero/ **(-ra)** *n* hunter, huntsman

montés /mon'tes/ *a* wild, savage, untamed

montevideano /monteβiðe'ano/ **(-na)** *a* and *n* Montevideo

montículo /mon'tikulo/ *m*, mound, hill

montón /mon'ton/ *m*, heap, pile; *Inf.* abundance, lot. *Inf.* **a, de** *or* **en m.,** all jumbled up together. **a montones,** in abundance

montuoso /mon'tuoso/ *a* mountainous

montura /mon'tura/ *f*, riding animal, mount; horse trappings; setting up, mounting (artillery, etc.)

monumental /monumen'tal/ *a* monumental

monumento /monu'mento/ *m*, monument; document, record; tomb

monzón /mon'θon; mon'son/ *mf*, monsoon

moña /'moɲa/ *f*, doll; dressmaker's model; bow for the hair; bullfighter's black bow; baby's bonnet; *Inf.* drinking bout

moño /'moɲo/ *m*, bun, chignon; topknot (birds); bunch of ribbons; *pl* tawdry trimmings

moqueta /mo'keta/ *f*, moquette

moquete /mo'kete/ *m*, slap in the face

moquillo /mo'kiʎo; mo'kiyo/ *m*, distemper (of animals)

mora /'mora/ *f*, blackberry; mulberry; bramble; Moorish girl, Moorish woman

morada /mo'raða/ *f*, dwelling, abode; sojourn, stay

morado /mo'raðo/ *a* purple

morador /mora'ðor/ **(-ra)** *n* dweller; sojourner

moral /mo'ral/ *a* moral, ethical. *f*, morality, ethics; morale. *m*, blackberry bush

moraleja /mora'leha/ *f*, moral, lesson

moralidad /morali'ðað/ *f*, morality

moralista /mora'lista/ *mf* moralist

moralización /moraliθa'θion; moralisa'sion/ *f*, moralization

moralizador /moraliθa'ðor; moralisa'ðor/ **(-ra)** *a* moralizing —*n* moralizer

moralizar /morali'θar; morali'sar/ *vt* to reform, correct; —*vi* moralize

moratoria /mora'toria/ *f*, moratorium

moravo /mo'raβo/ **(-va)** *a* and *n* Moravian

morbidez /mor'βiðeθ; mor'βiðes/ *f*, *Art.* morbidezza; softness

mórbido /'morβiðo/ *a* morbid, diseased; *Art.* delicate (of flesh tones); soft

morbo /'morβo/ *m*, illness. **m. gálico,** syphilis

morboso /mor'βoso/ *a* ill; morbid, unhealthy

morcilla /mor'θiʎa; mor'siya/ *f*, *Cul.* black pudding; (*Inf. Theat.*) gag

morcillero /morθi'ʎero; morsi'yero/ **(-ra)** *n* seller of black puddings; (*Inf. Theat.*) actor who gags

mordacidad /morðaθi'ðað; morðasi'ðað/ *f*, corrosiveness; mordacity, sarcasm; *Cul.* piquancy

mordaz /mor'ðaθ; mor'ðas/ *a* corrosive; sarcastic, caustic, mordant; *Cul.* piquant

mordaza /mor'ðaθa; mor'ðasa/ *f*, gag

mordedor /morðe'ðor/ *a* biting; scandalmongering

mordedura /morðe'ðura/ *f*, bite, biting

morder /mor'ðer/ *vt irr* to bite; nibble, nip; seize, grasp; corrode, eat away; slander; etch —*Pres. Indic.* **muerdo, muerdes, muerde, muerden.** *Pres. Subjunc.* **muerda, muerdas, muerda, muerdan**

mordiente /mor'ðiente/ *m*, fixative (for dyeing); mordant —*a* mordant (of acid)

mordiscar /morðis'kar/ *vt* to nibble, bite gently; bite

mordisco /mor'ðisko/ *m*, nibble; nibbling; bite; biting; piece bitten off

morena /mo'rena/ *f*, moraine

moreno /mo'reno/ **(-na)** *a* dark brown; swarthy complexioned; dark (of people) —*n Inf.* negro, mulatto

morera /mo'rera/ *f*, mulberry bush

morería /more'ria/ *f*, Moorish quarter

morfina /mor'fina/ *f*, morphine

morfinómano /morfi'nomano/ **(-na)** *n* morphine addict

morfología /morfolo'hia/ *f*, morphology

morfológico /morfo'lohiko/ *a* morphological

morganático /morga'natiko/ *a* morganatic

moribundo /mori'βundo/ **(-da)** *a* moribund, dying —*n* dying person

morillo /mo'riʎo; mo'riyo/ *m*, andiron, fire-dog

morir /mo'rir/ *vi irr* to die; fade, wither; decline, decay; disappear; yearn (for); long (to); go out (lights, fire); —*vr* die; go numb (limbs); (*with por*) adore, be mad about. *Inf.* **m. vestido,** to die a violent death. **¡Muera!** Down with! *Past Part.* **muerto.** For other tenses see *dormir*

morisco /mo'risko/ **(-ca)** *a* Moorish —*n* Morisco, Moor converted to Christianity

morisma /mo'risma/ *f*, Mohammedanism; multitude of Moors

mormón /mor'mon/ **(-ona)** *n* Mormon

mormónico /mor'moniko/ *a* Mormon

mormonismo /mormo'nismo/ *m*, Mormonism

moro /'moro/ **(-ra)** *a* Moorish —*n* Moor; Mohammedan. *Inf.* **haber moros y cristianos,** to be the deuce of a row. *Inf.* **Hay moros en la costa,** The coast is not clear; There's trouble in the offing

morosidad /morosi'ðað/ *f*, slowness, delay; sluggishness, sloth

moroso /mo'roso/ *a* slow, dilatory; sluggish, lazy

morra /'morra/ *f*, crown of the head

morral /mo'rral/ *m*, nose-bag; knapsack; game-bag; *Inf.* lout

morriña /mo'rriɲa/ *f*, cattle plague, murrain; *Inf.* depression, blues; homesickness

morrión /mo'rrion/ *m*, morion (helmet)

morro /'morro/ *m*, anything round; hummock, hillock; round pebble; headland, cliff

morsa /'morsa/ *f*, walrus

mortaja /mor'taha/ *f*, shroud, winding sheet

mortal /mor'tal/ *a* mortal; fatal, deadly; on the point of death; great, tremendous; certain, sure. *mf* mortal

mortalidad /mortali'ðað/ *f*, humanity, human race; mortality, death-rate

mortandad /mortan'dað/ *f*, mortality, number of deaths

mortecino /morte'θino; morte'sino/ *a* dead from natural causes (animals); weak; fading; dull, dead (of eyes); flickering; on the point of death or extinction

mortero /mor'tero/ *m*, mortar (for building); *Mil.* mortar; pounding mortar

mortífero /mor'tifero/ *a* deadly, mortal

mortificación /mortifika'θion; mortifika'sion/ *f, Med.* gangrene; humiliation, wounding; mortification (of the flesh)

mortificar /mortifi'kar/ *vt Med.* to mortify; humiliate, wound, hurt; mortify (the flesh); —*vr* become gangrenous

mortuorio /mor'tuorio/ *a* mortuary. *m,* funeral, obsequies

mosaico /mo'saiko/ *a* and *m,* mosaic

mosca /'moska/ *f,* fly; *Inf.* nuisance; bore, pest; cash; *pl* sparks. *Inf.* **m. muerta,** underhanded person. *Inf.* **papar moscas,** to gape, be dumbfounded. *Inf.* **soltar la m.,** to give or spend money unwillingly

moscardón /moskar'ðon/ *m,* gadfly

moscatel /moska'tel/ *a* muscatel. *m,* muscatel (grapes and wine); *Inf.* pest, tedious person

moscovita /mosko'βita/ *a* and *mf* Muscovite

Moscú /mos'ku/ Moscow

mosquear /moske'ar/ *vt* to drive off flies; reply crossly; whip; —*vr* be exasperated; brush aside obstacles

mosquero /mos'kero/ *m,* flypaper

mosquete /mos'kete/ *m,* musket

mosquetería /moskete'ria/ *f,* musketry; (*Obs. Theat.*) male members of the audience who stood at the back of the pit

mosquetero /moske'tero/ *m,* musketeer; (Spanish theater of the sixteenth and seventeenth centuries) male member of the audience who stood at the back of the pit

mosquitero /moski'tero/ *m,* mosquito net

mosquito /mos'kito/ *m,* mosquito; midge, gnat; *Inf.* tippler, drunkard

mostacera /mosta'θera; mosta'sera/ *f,* mustard pot

mostacho /mos'tatʃo/ *m,* mustache, whiskers; *Inf.* smudge on the face

mostaza /mos'taθa; mos'tasa/ *f,* mustard plant or seed; *Cul.* mustard

mostela /mos'tela/ *f,* sheaf (of corn, etc.)

mosto /'mosto/ *m,* must, unfermented wine

mostrador /mostra'ðor/ **(-ra)** *n* one who shows, exhibitor. *m,* shop counter; face of a watch

mostrar /mos'trar/ *vt irr* to show; indicate, point out; demonstrate, prove; manifest, reveal; —*vr* show oneself, be (e.g. *Se mostró bondadoso,* He showed himself to be kind) —*Pres. Indic.* **muestro, muestras, muestra, muestran.** *Pres. Subjunc.* **muestre, muestres, muestre, muestren**

mostrenco /mos'trenko/ *a Inf.* stray, vagrant, homeless; *Inf.* dull, ignorant; *Inf.* fat, heavy

mota /'mota/ *f,* fault in cloth; mote, defect, fault; mound, hill; thread of cotton, speck of dust, etc.; fleck (of the sun, etc.); spot

mote /'mote/ *m,* maxim, saying; motto, device; catchword, slogan; nickname

motear /mote'ar/ *vt* to speckle, dot, variegate, spot

motejar /mote'har/ *vt* to nickname, call names, dub

motete /mo'tete/ *m,* motet

motín /mo'tin/ *m,* mutiny; riot

motivar /moti'βar/ *vt* to motivate, cause; explain one's reasons

motivo /mo'tiβo/ *a* motive. *m,* cause, motive; *Mus.* motif. **con m. de,** on account of, because of. **de m. propio,** of one's own free will

motocicleta /motoθi'kleta; motosi'kleta/ *f,* motorcycle

motociclista /motoθi'klista; motosi'klista/ *mf* motorcyclist

motor /mo'tor/ **(-ra)** *a* motive, driving. *m,* motor, engine —*n* (person) mover, motive force. **m. de combustión interna,** internal combustion engine. **m. de retroacción,** jet engine

motorista /moto'rista/ *mf* motorist, driver

movedizo /moβe'ðiθo; moβe'ðiso/ *a* movable; insecure, unsteady; shaky; changeable, vacillating

mover /mo'βer/ *vt irr* to move; operate, drive; sway; wag; persuade, induce; excite; move (to pity, etc.); (*with prep a*) cause; —*vi* sprout (plants); —*vr* move —*Pres. Indic.* **muevo, mueves, mueve, mueven.** *Pres. Subjunc.* **mueva, muevas, mueva, muevan**

movible /mo'βiβle/ *a* movable; insecure, shaky. *m,* motive, cause, incentive

movilidad /moβili'ðað/ *f,* mobility; changeableness, inconstancy

movilización /moβiliθa'θion; moβilisa'sion/ *f,* mobilization

movilizar /moβili'θar; moβili'sar/ *vt* to mobilize

movimiento /moβi'miento/ *m,* movement; perturbation, excitement; *Mus.* movement; *Lit.* fire, spirit; *Mech.* motion, movement; *Mil.* **m. envolvente,** encircling movement

moza /'moθa; 'mosa/ *f,* maid; girl; waitress. **m. de partido,** party girl, prostitute. **buena m.,** fine, upstanding young woman

mozalbete /moθal'βete; mosal'βete/ *m,* lad, stripling, boy

mozárabe /mo'θaraβe; mo'saraβe/ *a* Mozarabic. *mf* Mozarab

mozo /'moθo; 'moso/ *a* young, unmarried. *m,* boy, youth; bachelor; waiter; porter. **m. de cordel** *or* **m. de esquina,** street porter, message boy. **m. de estación,** railroad porter. **buen m.,** fine, upstanding young man

muaré /mua're/ *m,* moiré silk

muceta /mu'θeta; mu'seta/ *f, Educ.* hood, short cape (of a graduate's gown)

muchacha /mu'tʃatʃa/ *f,* girl, lass; female servant

muchachada /mutʃa'tʃaða/ *f,* childish prank

muchachez /mutʃa'tʃeθ; mutʃa'tʃes/ *f,* boyhood; girlhood

muchachil /mutʃa'tʃil/ *a* boyish; girlish

muchacho /mu'tʃatʃo/ *m,* boy, youth; male servant

muchedumbre /mutʃe'ðumbre/ *f,* abundance, plenty; crowd, multitude; mass, mob

muchísimo /mu'tʃisimo/ *a superl* very much —*adv* very great deal, very much

mucho /'mutʃo/ *a* much; plenty of; very; long (time); *pl* many, numerous —*adv* a great deal; much; very much; yes, certainly; frequently, often; very (e.g. *Me alegro m.,* I am very glad); to a great extent; long (time). **con m.,** by far, easily. **ni con m.,** nor anything like it, very far from it. **ni m. menos,** and much less. **por m. que,** however much

mucílago /mu'θilago; mu'silago/ *m,* mucilage, gum

mucosa /mu'kosa/ *f,* mucous membrane

mucosidad /mukosi'ðað/ *f,* mucosity

mucoso /mu'koso/ *a* mucous

muda /'muða/ *f,* change, transformation; change of clothes; molting season; molt, sloughing of skin (snakes, etc.); change of voice (in boys)

mudable /mu'ðaβle/ *a* changeable, inconstant

mudanza /mu'ðanθa; muðansa/ *f,* change; furniture removal; step, figure (in dancing); changeability, inconstancy

mudar /mu'ðar/ *vt* to change; alter, transform; exchange; remove; dismiss (from employment); molt; slough the skin (snakes, etc.); change the voice (boys); —*vr* alter one's behavior; change one's clothes; change one's residence; change one's expression; *Inf.* go away, depart

mudéjar /mu'ðehar/ *m, Archit.* style containing Moorish and Christian elements. *mf* Moor who remained in Spain under Christian rule

mudez /mu'ðeθ; mu'ðes/ *f,* dumbness; silence, muteness

mudo /'muðo/ *a* dumb; silent, mute, quiet

mueblaje /mue'βlahe/ *m,* household goods and furniture

mueble /'mueβle/ *m,* piece of furniture; furnishing

mueblería /mueβle'ria/ *f,* furniture store or factory

mueblista /mue'βlista/ *mf* furniture maker; furniture dealer

mueca /'mueka/ *f,* grimace

muela /'muela/ *f,* grindstone; molar (tooth); millstone; flat-topped hill. **m. del juicio,** wisdom tooth. **dolor de muelas,** toothache

muellaje /mue'ʎahe; mue'yahe/ *m,* wharfage, dock dues

muelle /'mueʎe; 'mueye/ *a* soft, smooth; voluptuous, sensuous; luxurious. *m,* spring (of a watch, etc.); wharf, quay; freight platform (railroad). **m. real,** mainspring (of a watch). **m. del volante,** hairspring.

muérdago /'mwerðago/ *m,* mistletoe

muermo /'mwermo/ *m,* glanders

muerte /'mwerte/ *f,* death; destruction, annihilation; end, decline. *Inf.* **una m. chiquita,** a nervous shudder. **a m.,** to the death, with no quarter. **de m.,** implacably, inexorably (of hatred); very seriously (of being ill). **dar m.** (**a**), to kill. **estar a la m.,** to be on the point of death. **a cada m. de un obispo,** once in a blue moon

muerto /'mwerto/ **(-ta)** *a* dead; slaked (lime); *Mech.* neutral; faded, dull (colors); languid, indifferent. **m.** is used in familiar speech as *past part* **matar** (e.g. *Le ha muerto,* He has killed him) —*n* corpse. *Inf.* **desenterrar los muertos,** to speak ill of the dead. *Inf.* **echarle a uno el m.,** to pass the buck. *Inf.* **estar m. por,** to be dying, yearning for. **ser el m.,** to be dummy (at cards)

muesca /'mweska/ *f,* notch, mortise, groove

muestra /'mwestra/ *f,* shop sign; sample, specimen; pattern, model; demeanor; watch or clock face; sign, indication; poster, placard; *Mil.* muster roll. **hacer m.,** to show

muestrario /mwes'trario/ *m,* sample book, collection of samples

mufla /'mufla/ *f,* muffler (of a furnace)

mugido /mu'hiðo/ *m,* mooing or lowing (of cattle)

mugir /mu'hir/ *vi* to low or moo (cattle); bellow, shout; rage (elements)

mugre /'mugre/ *f,* grease, grime, dirt

mugriento /mu'griento/ *a* grimy, greasy

muguete /mu'gete/ *m,* lily of the valley

mujer /mu'her/ *f,* woman; wife. **m. de la vida airada** *or* **m. del partido** *or* **m. pública,** prostitute. **m. de la luna,** man in the moon. **m. de su casa,** good housewife. **tomar m.,** to take a wife

mujeriego /muhe'riego/ *a* womanly, feminine; (of men) dissolute, given to philandering. **cabalgar a mujeriegas,** to ride sidesaddle

mujeril /muhe'ril/ *a* womanly, feminine

mula /'mula/ *f,* female mule; mule (heelless slipper). *Inf.* **Se me fue la m.,** My tongue ran away with me

muladar /mula'ðar/ *m,* refuse heap, junkpile, dunghill

mular /mu'lar/ *a* mule; mulish

mulatero /mula'tero/ *m,* mule hirer; muleteer

mulato /mu'lato/ **(-ta)** *a* and *n* mulatto

muleta /mu'leta/ *f,* crutch; bullfighter's red flag; support, prop

mullir /mu'ʎir/ *vt irr* to make soft, shake out (wool, down, etc.); *Fig.* prepare the way; *Agr.* hoe the roots (of vines, etc.) —*Pres. Part.* **mullendo.** *Preterite* **mulló, mulleron.** *Imperf. Subjunc.* **mullese,** etc.

mulo /'mulo/ *m,* mule

multa /'multa/ *f,* fine

multar /mul'tar/ *vt* to impose a fine on

multicolor /multiko'lor/ *a* multicolored

multiforme /multi'forme/ *a* multiform

multilátero /multi'latero/ *a* multilateral

multimillonario /multimiʎo'nario; multimiyo'nario/ **(-ia)** *a* and *n* multimillionaire

multiplicación /multiplika'θion; multiplika'sion/ *f,* multiplication

multiplicador /multiplika'ðor/ **(-ra)** *n* multiplier. *m, Math.* multiplier

multiplicando /multipli'kando/ *m,* multiplicand

multiplicar /multipli'kar/ **((se)** *vt* and *vr* to multiply; reproduce

multiplicidad /multipliθi'ðað; multiplisi'ðað/ *f,* multiplicity

múltiplo /'multiplo/ *a* and *m,* multiple

multisecular /multiseku'lar/ *a* age-old, many centuries old

multitud /multi'tuð/ *f,* multitude, great number; crowd; rabble, masses, mob

mundanal, mundano /munda'nal, mun'dano/ *a* worldly, mundane

mundanalidad /mundanali'ðað/ *f,* worldliness

mundial /mun'dial/ *a* world, worldwide

mundo /'mundo/ *m,* world, universe; human race; earth; human society; world (of letters, science, etc.); secular life; *Eccl.* vanities of the flesh; geographical globe. **echar al m.,** to give birth to; produce, bring

forth. **el Nuevo M.,** the New World, America. *Inf.* **medio m.,** half the earth, a great crowd. *Inf.* **ponerse el m. por montera,** to treat the world as one's oyster. **ser hombre del m.,** to be a man of the world. *Inf.* **tener m.** *or* **mucho m.,** to be very experienced, know the world. **todo el m.,** everyone. **venir al m.,** to be born. **ver m.,** to travel, see the world

mundología /mundolo'hia/ *f,* worldliness, experience of the world

munición /muni'θion; muni'sion/ *f, Mil.* munition; small shot. *Mil.* **m. de boca,** fodder and food supplies

municionar /muniθio'nar; munisio'nar/ *vt* to munition, furnish with munitions

municionero /muniθio'nero; munisio'nero/ **(-ra)** *n* purveyor, supplier

municipal /muniθi'pal; munisi'pal/ *a* municipal. *m,* policeman

municipalidad /muniθipali'ðað; munisipali'ðað/ *f,* municipality

municipio /muni'θipio; muni'sipio/ *m,* municipality, town council

munificencia /munifi'θenθia; munifi'sensia/ *f,* munificence, generosity

munífico /mu'nifiko/ *a* munificent, generous

muñeca /mu'ɲeka/ *f, Anat.* wrist; doll; puppet; dressmaker's dummy; polishing pad; mannequin; boundary marker; *Inf.* flighty young woman

muñeco /mu'ɲeko/ *m,* boy doll; puppet; *Inf.* playboy

muñir /mu'ɲir/ *vt irr* to summon, convoke; arrange, dispose. See **mullir**

muñón /mu'ɲon/ *m, Surg.* stump of an amputated limb; *Mech.* gudgeon

mural /mu'ral/ *a* mural

muralla /mu'raʎa; mu'raya/ *f,* town wall; rampart, fortification

murar /mu'rar/ *vt* to surround with a wall, wall in

murciano /mur'θiano; mur'siano/ **(-na)** *a* and *n* Murcian

murciélago /mur'θielago; mur'sielago/ *m, Zool.* bat

murga /'murga/ *f,* band of street musicians

murmullo /mur'muʎo; mur'muyo/ *m,* whisper; whispering; rustling; purling, lapping, splashing; mumbling, muttering

murmuración /murmura'θion; murmura'sion/ *f,* slander, backbiting, gossip

murmurador /murmura'ðor/ **(-ra)** *a* gossiping, slanderous —*n* gossip, backbiter

murmurar /murmu'rar/ *vi* to rustle (leaves, etc.); purl, lap, splash (water); whisper; mumble, mutter; —*vi* and *vt Inf.* slander, backbite

murmurio /mur'murio/ *m,* rustling; lapping (of water); whispering; murmur; *Inf.* slander

muro /'muro/ *m,* wall; defensive wall, rampart

musa /'musa/ *f,* muse

musaraña /musa'raɲa/ *f, Zool.* shrew; any small animal; *Inf.* ridiculous effigy, guy. *Inf.* **mirar a las musarañas,** to be absent-minded

muscular /musku'lar/ *a* muscular

musculatura /muskula'tura/ *f,* musculature

músculo /'muskulo/ *m,* muscle; strength, brawn

musculoso /musku'loso/ *a* muscular; strong, brawny

muselina /muse'lina/ *f,* muslin

museo /mu'seo/ *m,* museum. **m. de pintura,** art gallery, picture gallery

musgo /'musgo/ *m,* moss

musgoso /mus'goso/ *a* mossy, moss-grown

música /'musika/ *f,* music; melody, harmony; musical performance; musical composition; group of musicians; sheet music. *Inf.* **m. celestial,** vain words, moonshine. *Inf.* **m. ratonera,** badly played music. *Inf.* **¡Vaya con su m. a otra parte!** Get out! Go to hell!

musical /musi'kal/ *a* musical

músico /'musiko/ **(-ca)** *a* music —*n* musician. **m. ambulante,** strolling musician. **m. mayor,** bandleader

musitar /musi'tar/ *vi* to mutter, mumble

muslo /'muslo/ *m,* thigh

mustio /'mustio/ *a* sad, disheartened, depressed; faded, withered

musulmán /musul'man/ **(-ana)** *a* and *n* Muslim

mutabilidad /mutaβili'ðað/ f, mutability, changeability

mutación /muta'θion; muta'sion/ f, change, mutation; sudden change in the weather; *Theat.* change of scene

mutilación /mutila'θion; mutila'sion/ f, mutilation; damage; defacement

mutilar /muti'lar/ vt to mutilate; spoil, deface, damage; cut short; reduce

mutis /'mutis/ m, *Theat.* exit. **hacer m.** *Theat.* to exit; keep quiet, say nothing

mutismo /mu'tismo/ m, mutism, dumbness; silence, speechlessness

mutualidad /mutuali'ðað/ f, reciprocity, mutuality, interdependence; principle of mutual aid; mutual aid society

mutualismo /mutua'lismo/ m, mutualism, organized mutual aid

mutualista /mutua'lista/ mf member of a mutual aid society

mutuante /mu'tuante/ mf *Com.* lender

mutuo /'mutuo/ a reciprocal, mutual, interdependent

muy /'mui/ adv very; very much; much. Used to form absolute superlative (e.g. m. *rápidamente*, very quickly). Can modify adjectives, nouns used adjectivally, adverbs, participles (e.g. *María es m. mujer*, Mary is very much a woman (very womanly)). **m. temprano**, very early. **M. señor mío**, Dear Sir (in letters)

naba /'naβa/ f, swede, turnip

nabar /na'βar/ m, turnip field

nabo /'naβo/ m, turnip; turnip root; any root stem; *Naut.* mast; stock (of a horse's tail)

nácar /'nakar/ m, mother-of-pearl

nacarado, nacáreo /naka'raðo, na'kareo/ a nacreous, mother-of-pearl

nacer /na'θer; na'ser/ vi irr to be born; rise (rivers, etc.); sprout; grow (plumage, fur, leaves, etc.); descend (lineage); appear (stars, etc.); originate; *Fig.* issue forth; appear suddenly; (*with prep a* or *para*) be destined for, have a natural leaning toward. **n. con pajitas de oro en la cuna,** to be born with a silver spoon in one's mouth —*vr* grow; sprout; *Sew.* split at the seams —*Pres. Indic.* **nazco, naces,** etc —*Pres. Subjunc.* **nazca,** etc.

nacido /na'θiðo; na'siðo/ a and *past part* born; suitable, fit. m, (gen. *pl*) the living and the dead. **bien n.,** noble, well-born; well-bred. **mal n.,** base-born; ill-bred

naciente /na'θiente; na'siente/ a growing; nascent. m, east

nacimiento /naθi'miento; nasi'miento/ m, birth; source (of rivers, etc.); birthplace; origin; lineage; *Astron.* rising; nativity crib, manger. **de n.,** from birth; by birth; born

nación /na'θion; na'sion/ f, nation; country; *Inf.* birth

nacional /naθio'nal; nasio'nal/ a national; native. mf citizen, national

nacionalidad /naθionali'ðað; nasionali'ðað/ f, nationality

nacionalismo /naθiona'lismo; nasiona'lismo/ m, nationalism

nacionalista /naθiona'lista; nasiona'lista/ a and mf nationalist

nacionalización /naθionaliθa'θion; nasionalisa'sion/ f, naturalization; nationalization; acclimatization

nacionalizar /naθionali'θar; nasionali'sar/ vt to naturalize; nationalize

nacionalsindicalismo /naθio,nalsindika'lismo; nasio,nalsindika'lismo/ m, national syndicalism

nacionalsocialismo /naθio,nalsoθia'lismo; nasio,nalsosia'lismo/ m, national socialism, nazism

nada /'naða/ f, void, nothingness —*pron indef* nothing —*adv* by no means. **casi n.,** very little, practically nothing. **¡De n.!** Not at all! Don't mention it! You're welcome! **No vale para n.,** He (it, she) is of no use

nadaderas /naða'ðeras/ f pl, water wings (for swimming)

nadador /naða'ðor/ **(-ra)** n swimmer —*a* swimming

nadar /na'ðar/ vi to swim; float; have an abundance (of); *Inf.* be too large (of garments, etc.). **n. y guardar la ropa,** *Fig.* to sit on the fence

nadería /naðe'ria/ f, trifle

nadie /'naðie/ pron indef no one. m, *Fig.* a nobody

nadir /na'ðir/ m, nadir

nado /'naðo/ a by swimming; afloat

nafta /'nafta/ f, naphtha

naftalina /nafta'lina/ f, naphthalene

naipe /'naipe/ m, playing card; pack of cards

naire /'naire/ m, elephant keeper or trainer

nalga /'nalga/ f, (gen. pl) buttock(s)

nana /'nana/ f, *Inf.* grandma; lullaby

nao /'nao/ f, ship

napoleónico /napole'oniko/ a Napoleonic

Nápoles /'napoles/ Naples

napolitano /napoli'tano/ **(-na)** a and n Neapolitan

naranja /na'ranha/ f, orange. **n. dulce,** blood orange. **n. mandarina,** tangerine. *Inf.* **media n.,** better half

naranjada /naran'haða/ f, orangeade

naranjal /naran'hal/ m, orange grove

naranjero /naran'hero/ **(-ra)** n orange seller

naranjo /na'ranho/ m, orange tree; *Inf.* lout, blockhead

narciso /nar'θiso; nar'siso/ m, narcissus; dandy, fop. **n. trompón,** daffodil

narcótico /nar'kotiko/ a and m, narcotic

narcotizar /narkoti'θar; narkoti'sar/ vt to narcotize

narcotraficante /narkotrafi'kante/ mf drug dealer

nardo /'narðo/ m, tuberose, spikenard, nard

narguile /nar'gile/ m, hookah, hubble-bubble, narghile

narigudo /nari'guðo/ a large-nosed; nose-shaped

nariz /na'riθ; na'ris/ f, nose; nostril; snout; nozzle; sense of smell; bouquet (of wine). **n. perfilada,** well-shaped nose. **n. respingona,** snub nose. *Inf.* **meter las narices,** to meddle, interfere

narración /narra'θion; narra'sion/ f, narration, account

narrador /narra'ðor/ **(-ra)** a narrative —n narrator

narrar /na'rrar/ vt to narrate, tell, relate

narrativa /narra'tiβa/ f, narrative; account; narrative skill

narrativo, narratorio /narra'tiβo, narra'torio/ a narrative

nata /'nata/ f, cream; *Fig.* the flower, elite; pl whipped cream with sugar

natación /nata'θion; nata'sion/ f, swimming. **n. a la marinera,** trudgen stroke

natal /na'tal/ a natal; native. m, birth; birthday

natalicio /nata'liθio; nata'lisio/ a natal —a and m, birthday

natalidad /natali'ðað/ f, birth rate

natatorio /nata'torio/ a swimming. m, swimming pool

natillas /na'tiʎas; na'tiyas/ f pl, custard

natividad /natiβi'ðað/ f, nativity; birth; Christmas

nativo /na'tiβo/ a indigenous; native; innate

nato /'nato/ a born; inherent; ex officio

natura /na'tura/ f, nature; *Mus.* major scale

natural /natu'ral/ a natural; native; indigenous; spontaneous; sincere, candid; physical; usual, ordinary; *Mus.* natural; unadulterated, pure; *Herald.* proper. mf native, citizen. m, temperament; disposition; instinct (of animals); natural inclination. **al n.,** naturally, without art. **del n.,** *Art.* from life

naturaleza /natura'leθa; natura'lesa/ f, nature; character; disposition; instinct; temperament; nationality; origin; naturalization; kind, class; constitution, physique. **n. humana,** humankind. **n. muerta,** *Art.* still life

naturalidad /naturali'ðað/ f, naturalness; nationality

naturalista /natura'lista/ mf naturalist

naturalización /naturaliθa'θion; naturalisa'sion/ f, naturalization; acclimatization

naturalizar /naturali'θar; naturali'sar/ vt to naturalize; acclimatize; —*vr* become naturalized; become acclimatized

naturalmente /natural'mente/ adv naturally; of course

naturismo /natu'rismo/ m, nature cure

naufragar /naufra'gar/ vi to be shipwrecked; fail, be unsuccessful

naufragio /nau'frahio/ m, shipwreck; disaster, loss

náufrago /'naufrago/ **(-ga)** n shipwrecked person. m, shark

náusea /'nausea/ f, nausea (pl more usual); repugnance

nauseabundo, nauseoso /nausea'βundo, nause'oso/ a nauseous; nauseating, repugnant

nauta /'nauta/ mf mariner

náutica /'nautika/ f, navigation; yachting; seamanship

náutico /'nautiko/ a nautical

navaja /na'βaha/ f, razor; clasp knife; boar tusk; sting; *Inf.* slanderous tongue. **n. de afeitar,** (shaving) razor

navajada /naβa'haða/ f, slash with a razor

navajero /naβa'hero/ m, razor case

naval /na'βal/ a naval

nimbo

Navarra /na'βarra/ Navarre
navarro /na'βarro/ **(-ra)** *a* and *n* Navarrese
nave /'naβe/ *f,* ship; *Archit.* nave. **n. aérea,** airship. *Archit.* **n. lateral,** aisle. **n. principal,** *Archit.* nave
navegable /naβe'gaβle/ *a* navigable
navegación /naβega'θion; naβega'sion/ *f,* navigation; sea voyage
navegante /naβe'gante/ *a* voyaging; navigating. *m,* navigator
navegar /naβe'gar/ *vi* to navigate; sail; fly
navidad /naβi'ðað/ *f,* nativity; Christmas; *pl* Christmastime
naviero /na'βiero/ *a* shipping. *m,* ship owner
navío /na'βio/ *m,* warship; ship. **n. de transporte,** transport. **n. de tres puentes,** three-decker
náyade /'naiaðe/ *f,* naiad, water nymph
nazareno /naθa'reno; nasa'reno/ **(-na)** *a* and *n* Nazarene; Christian
Nazaret /naθa'ret; nasa'ret/ Nazareth
nazismo /na'θismo; na'sismo/ *m,* nazism
neblina /ne'βlina/ *f,* fog; mist
nebulosidad /neβulosi'ðað/ *f,* nebulousness; cloudiness
nebuloso /neβu'loso/ *a* foggy; misty; cloudy; somber, melancholy; confused, nebulous
necedad /neθe'ðað; nese'ðað/ *f,* silliness
necesario /neθe'sario; nese'sario/ *a* necessary; unavoidable
neceser /neθe'ser; nese'ser/ *m,* dressing case. *Sew.* **n. de costura,** workbox
necesidad /neθesi'ðað; nesesi'ðað/ *f,* necessity; poverty, want; shortage, need; emergency. **de n.,** necessarily
necesitado /neθesi'taðo; nesesi'taðo/ **(-da)** *a* needy, poor —*n* poor person
necesitar /neθesi'tar; nesesi'tar/ *vt* to necessitate; compel, oblige; —*vi* be necessary, need
necio /'neθio; 'nesio/ *a* stupid; senseless; unreasonable
necrología /nekrolo'hia/ *f,* necrology, obituary
necromancía /nekroman'θia; nekroman'sia/ *f,* necromancy
neerlandés /neerlan'des/ *a* Dutch
nefando /ne'fando/ *a* iniquitous
nefario /ne'fario/ *a* nefarious
nefasto /ne'fasto/ *a* disastrous, ill-omened
nefrítico /ne'fritiko/ *a* nephritic
nefritis /ne'fritis/ *f,* nephritis
negable /ne'gaβle/ *a* deniable
negación /nega'θion; nega'sion/ *f,* negation; privation; negative; nay; *Gram.* negative particle; *Law.* traverse
negado /ne'gaðo/ *a* inept, unfitted; stupid
negar /ne'gar/ *vt irr* to deny; refuse; prohibit; disclaim; dissemble; disown; *Law.* traverse; —*vr* refuse, avoid; decline (to receive visitors). See **acertar**
negativa /nega'tiβa/ *f,* denial; refusal; *Photo.* negative
negativo /nega'tiβo/ *a* negative
negligencia /negli'henθia; negli'hensia/ *f,* negligence; omission; carelessness; forgetfulness
negligente /negli'hente/ *a* negligent; careless; neglectful
negociable /nego'θiaβle; nego'siaβle/ *a* negotiable
negociación /negoθia'θion; negosia'sion/ *f,* negotiation; business affair, deal
negociado /nego'θiaðo; nego'siaðo/ *m,* department, section (of a ministry, etc.); business
negociante /nego'θiante; nego'siante/ *m,* businessman —*a* negotiating; trading
negociar /nego'θiar; nego'siar/ *vi* to trade, traffic; negotiate
negocio /ne'goθio; ne'gosio/ *m,* occupation; trade; business; employment; transaction; *pl* business affairs. **hombre de negocios,** businessman
negra /'negra/ *f,* black girl, black woman; *Inf.* honey, *West Hem.* sweetheart
negrecer /negre'θer; negre'ser/ *vi irr* to become black. See **conocer**
negrero /ne'grero/ **(-ra)** *n* slave trader
negro /'negro/ *a* black; dark; melancholy; disastrous; *Herald.* sable. *m,* black; black (color). **n. de humo,** lampblack
negrura /ne'grura/ *f,* blackness
negruzco /ne'gruθko; ne'grusko/ *a* blackish
nemotécnica /nemo'teknika/ *f,* mnemonics
nene /'nene/ **(-na)** *n Inf.* baby; darling
nenúfar /ne'nufar/ *m,* white water lily
neo /'neo/ *m,* neon
neocelandés /neoθelan'des; neoselan'des/ **(-esa)** *a* New Zealand —*n* New Zealander
neófito /ne'ofito/ **(-ta)** *n* neophyte
neoguineano /neogine'ano/ *a* New Guinean
neolítico /neo'litiko/ *a* neolithic
neologismo /neolo'hismo/ *m,* neologism
neoyorquino /neoior'kino/ **(-na)** *a* New York —*n* New Yorker
nepotismo /nepo'tismo/ *m,* nepotism
Neptuno /nep'tuno/ *m, Astron.* Neptune; *Poet.* sea
nereida /ne'reiða/ *f,* nereid, sea nymph
nervio /'nerβio/ *m,* nerve; sinew; *Bot.* vein; vigor; *Mus.* string. **n. ciático,** sciatic nerve
nervioso /ner'βioso/ *a* nervous; overwrought, agitated; vigorous; neural; sinewy; jerky (of style, etc.)
nervosidad /nerβosi'ðað/ *f,* nervousness; nervosity; flexibility (metals); jerkiness (of style, etc.); force, efficacy
nervudo /ner'βuðo/ *a* strong-nerved, vigorous
nesga /'nesga/ *f, Sew.* gore
neto /'neto/ *a* neat; clean; pure; *Com.* net. *m, Archit.* dado
neumático /neu'matiko/ *a* pneumatic. *m,* rubber tire
neumococo /neumo'koko/ *m,* pneumococcus
neurálgico /neu'ralhiko/ *a* neuralgic
neurastenia /neuras'tenia/ *f,* neurasthenia
neurasténico /neuras'teniko/ **(-ca)** *a* and *n* neurasthenic
neurología /neurolo'hia/ *f,* neurology
neurólogo /neu'rologo/ *m,* neurologist
neurópata /neu'ropata/ *mf* neuropath
neurosis /neu'rosis/ *f,* neurosis. **n. de guerra,** war neurosis; shell shock
neurótico /neu'rotiko/ **(-ca)** *a* and *n* neurotic
neutral /neu'tral/ *a* neutral; indifferent
neutralidad /neutrali'ðað/ *f,* neutrality; impartiality, indifference
neutralizar /neutrali'θar; neutrali'sar/ *vt* to neutralize; counteract, mitigate
neutro /'neutro/ *a* neuter; *Chem.* neutral; *Mech.* neuter; sexless
nevada /ne'βaða/ *f,* snowfall
nevar /ne'βar/ *vi irr impers* to snow —*Pres. Indic.* **nieva.** *Pres. Subjunc.* **nieve**
nevera /ne'βera/ *f,* refrigerator; icehouse
nevero /ne'βero/ *m,* ice-cream man; iceman
nevisca /ne'βiska/ *f,* light snowfall
nevoso /ne'βoso/ *a* snowy
nexo /'nekso/ *m,* nexus; connection; union
ni /ni/ *conjunc* neither, nor. **ni bien ni mal,** neither good nor bad. **ni siquiera,** not even. **¡Ni crea!, ¡Ni creas!** Nonsense!
niara /'niara/ *f,* haystack, rick
nicaragüeño /nikara'gueɲo/ **(-ña)** *a* and *n* Nicaraguan
nicho /'nitʃo/ *m,* niche; recess (in a wall)
nicotina /niko'tina/ *f,* nicotine
nidada /ni'ðaða/ *f,* nest full of eggs; brood, clutch
nidal /ni'ðal/ *m,* nest; nest egg; haunt; cause, foundation
nido /'niðo/ *m,* nest; den; hole; dwelling; haunt. **n. de ametralladoras,** *Mil.* pillbox
niebla /'nieβla/ *f,* fog; mist; cloud; mildew; haze
nieto /'nieto/ **(-ta)** *n* grandchild; descendant
nieve /'nieβe/ *f,* snow; whiteness. **deportes de n.,** winter sports
nigromancia /nigro'manθia; nigro'mansia/ *f,* necromancy
nigromante /nigro'mante/ *m,* necromancer
nihilismo /nii'lismo/ *m,* nihilism
nihilista /nii'lista/ *mf* nihilist
Nilo, el /'nilo, el/ the Nile
nimbo /'nimbo/ *m,* halo, nimbus

nimiedad /nimie'ðað/ f, prolixity; Inf. fussiness; fastidiousness, delicacy

nimio /'nimio/ a prolix; Inf. fussy; fastidious; Inf. parsimonious

ninfa /'ninfa/ f, nymph; Ent. chrysalis

ningún /niŋ'gun/ a Abbr. of **ninguno**. Used before m, sing nouns only. **De n. modo,** In no way! Certainly not!

Nínive /'niniβe/ Nineveh

niña /'nina/ f, girl. **n. del ojo,** pupil (of the eye). **n. de los ojos,** apple of one's eye, darling

niñada /ni'naða/ f, childishness, foolish act

niñera /ni'nera/ f, nursemaid

niñería /nine'ria/ f, childish act; trifle; childishness, folly

niñez /ni'neθ; ni'nes/ f, childhood; beginning, early days; Fig. cradle

niño /'nino/ **(-ña)** a childish; young; inexperienced; imprudent —n child; young or inexperienced person. **n. de la doctrina,** charity child. **n. terrible,** enfant terrible. **desde n.,** from childhood

nipón /ni'pon/ **(-ona)** a and n Japanese

níquel /'nikel/ m, Chem. nickel

niquelar /nike'lar/ vt to chrome-plate

nirvana /nir'βana/ m, nirvana

níspero /'nispero/ m, medlar tree; medlar

níspola /'nispola/ f, medlar

nitidez /niti'ðeθ; niti'ðes/ f, brightness, neatness, cleanliness

nítido /'nitiðo/ a bright, neat, clean (often Poet.)

nitrato /ni'trato/ m, nitrate

nítrico /'nitriko/ a nitric

nitrógeno /ni'troheno/ m, nitrogen

nivel /ni'βel/ m, level; levelness. **n. de albañil,** plummet. **n. de burbuja,** spirit level. **a n.,** on the level. **estar al n. de las circunstancias,** to rise to the occasion; save the day

nivelación /niβela'θion; niβela'sion/ f, leveling

nivelador /niβela'ðor/ **(-ra)** a leveling —n leveler

nivelar /niβe'lar/ vt to level; Fig. make equal

níveo /'niβeo/ a snowy; snow-white

Niza /'niθa; 'nisa/ Nice

no /no/ adv no; not. **no bien,** no sooner. **no sea que,** unless. **no tal,** no such thing

noble /'noβle/ a noble, illustrious; generous; outstanding, excellent; aristocratic. mf nobleman (-woman)

nobleza /no'βleθa; no'βlesa/ f, nobility

noche /'notʃe/ f, night; darkness; confusion, obscurity. Inf. **n. toledana,** restless night. **¡Buenas noches!** Good night! **de n.,** by night. **esta n.,** tonight

nochebuena /notʃe'βuena/ f, Christmas Eve

nochebueno /notʃe'βueno/ m, yule log; Christmas cake

nocherniego /notʃer'niego/ a night, nocturnal

noción /no'θion; no'sion/ f, notion, idea; pl elementary knowledge

nocividad /noθiβi'ðað; nosiβi'ðað/ f, noxiousness

nocivo /no'θiβo; no'siβo/ a noxious

nocturno /nok'turno/ a nocturnal; melancholy. m, Mus. nocturne

nodriza /no'ðriθa; no'ðrisa/ f, wet nurse

nogal /no'gal/ m, walnut tree; walnut wood

nómada /'nomaða/ a nomadic

nomadismo /noma'ðismo/ m, nomadism

nombradia /nom'βraðia/ f, renown

nombramiento /nombra'miento/ m, naming; appointment; nomination

nombrar /nom'βrar/ vt to name; nominate; appoint; mention (in dispatches, etc.)

nombre /'nombre/ m, name; title; reputation; proxy; Gram. noun; Mil. password. **n. de pila,** Christian name. **por n.,** called; by name. **Su n. anda puesto en el cuerno de la Luna,** He (she) is praised to the skies

nomenclatura /nomenkla'tura/ f, nomenclature

nómina /'nomina/ f, list, register; payroll; amulet

nominación /nomina'θion; nomina'sion/ f, nomination, appointment

nominador /nomina'ðor/ **(-ra)** a nominating —n nominator

nominal /nomi'nal/ a nominal

nominalismo /nomina'lismo/ m, nominalism

nominalista /nomina'lista/ a nominalistic. mf nominalist

nomo /'nomo/ m, gnome

non /non/ a odd (of numbers)

nonada /no'naða/ f, nothing, practically nothing

nonagenario /nonahe'nario/ **(-ia)** a and n nonagenarian

nonagésimo /nona'hesimo/ a ninetieth

nones /'nones/ m, pl certainly not, definitely not, nope

nopal /no'pal/ m, nopal, prickly pear tree

noque /'noke/ m, tanner's vat

noquear /noke'ar/ vt (Boxing) to knock out, K.O.

norabuena /nora'βuena/ f, congratulation

nordeste /nor'ðeste/ m, northeast

nórdico /'norðiko/ **(-ca)** a and n Nordic

noria /'noria/ f, water well; chain pump; Inf. hard, monotonous work

norma /'norma/ f, square (used by builders, etc.); Fig. norm, standard, model

normal /nor'mal/ a normal, usual; standard, average. f, normal school, teacher's college (also **escuela n.**)

normalidad /normali'ðað/ f, normality

normalista /norma'lista/ mf student at a teacher's college

normalización /normaliθa'θion; normalisa'sion/ f, normalization; standardization

normalizar /normali'θar; normali'sar/ vt to make normal; standardize

Normandía /norman'dia/ Normandy

normando /nor'mando/ **(-da)** a Norman —n Northman; Norman

nornordeste /nornor'ðeste/ m, northnortheast

nornorueste /nornor'ueste/ m, northnorthwest

noroeste /noro'este/ m, northwest

norte /'norte/ m, north pole; north; north wind; polestar; Fig. guide

norteamericano /norteameri'kano/ **(-na)** a and n North American; (U.S.A.) American

norteño /nor'teno/ a northerly, northern

Noruega /no'ruega/ Norway

noruego /no'ruego/ **(-ga)** a and n Norwegian. m, Norwegian (language)

nos /nos/ pers pron pl mf acc and dat (direct and indirect object) of **nosotros,** us; to us (e.g. Nos lo dio, He gave it to us)

nosotros, nosotras /no'sotros, no'sotras/ pers pron pl mf we; us. Also used with preposition (e.g. Lo hicieron por nosotros, They did it for us)

nostalgia /nos'talhia/ f, nostalgia

nostálgico /nos'talhiko/ a nostalgic; melancholy; homesick

nóstico /'nostiko/ **(-ca)** a and n gnostic

nota /'nota/ f, mark, sign; annotation, comment; Mus. note; memorandum; Com. bill, account; criticism, imputation; mark (in exams); repute, renown; note (diplomatic)

notabilidad /notaβili'ðað/ f, notability

notable /no'taβle/ a notable, remarkable; outstanding, prominent; with distinction (examination mark). m pl, notabilities

notación /nota'θion; nota'sion/ f, (Mus. Math.) notation; annotation

notar /no'tar/ vt to mark, indicate; observe, notice; note down; annotate; dictate, read out; criticize, reproach; discredit

notaría /nota'ria/ f, profession of a notary; notary's office

notarial /nota'rial/ a notarial

notario /no'tario/ m, notary public

noticia /no'tiθia; no'tisia/ f, rudiment, elementary knowledge; information; news (gen. pl); pl knowledge. **atrasado de noticias,** Fig. behind the times

noticiar /noti'θiar; noti'siar/ vt to inform, give notice

noticiario /noti'θiario; noti'siario/ m, news bulletin, newsreel.

noticiero /noti'θiero; noti'siero/ m, newspaper

noticioso /noti'θioso; noti'sioso/ a informed; learned; newsy

notificación /notifika'θion; notifika'sion/ *f, Law.* notification. **n. de reclutamiento,** draft notice

notificar /notifi'kar/ *vt* to notify officially; inform; warn

noto /'noto/ *a* known. *m,* south wind

notoriedad /notorie'ðað/ *f,* notoriety, publicity; flagrancy; fame, renown

notorio /no'torio/ *a* well-known; notorious, obvious; flagrant

novatada /noβa'taða/ *f, Inf.* ragging (of a freshman); blunder

novato /no'βato/ **(-ta)** *a* new, inexperienced —*n* novice, beginner

novecientos /noβe'θientos; noβe'sientos/ *a* and *m,* nine hundred

novedad /noβe'ðað/ *f,* newness, novelty; change, alteration; latest news; surprise; *pl* novelties. **sin n.,** no change; all well (or as usual); safely, without incident

novel /no'βel/ *a* new; inexperienced

novela /no'βela/ *f,* novel; tale; falsehood. **n. caballista,** western, cowboy story. **n. por entregas,** serial (story)

novelero /noβe'lero/ **(-ra)** *a* fond of novelty and change; fond of novels; fickle —*n* newshound, gossip

novelesco /noβe'lesko/ *a* novelistic; imaginary

novelista /noβe'lista/ *mf* novelist

novelística /noβe'listika/ *f,* art of novel writing

novena /no'βena/ *f, Eccl.* novena, religious services spread over nine days

noveno /no'βeno/ *a* and *m,* ninth

noventa /no'βenta/ *a* and *m,* ninety; ninetieth

novia /'noβia/ *f,* bride; fiancée

noviazgo /no'βiaθgo; no'βiasgo/ *m,* engagement, betrothal

noviciado /noβi'θiaðo; noβi'siaðo/ *m,* novitiate; training, apprenticeship

novicio /no'βiθio; no'βisio/ **(-ia)** *n Eccl.* novice; beginner, apprentice; unassuming person

noviembre /no'βiembre/ *m,* November

novillada /noβi'ʎaða; noβi'yaða/ *f,* herd of young bulls; bullock baiting

novillo /no'βiʎo; no'βiyo/ *m,* bullock. **hacer novillos,** to play truant

novilunio /noβi'lunio/ *m,* new moon

novio /'noβio/ *m,* bridegroom; fiancé; novice, beginner

novísimo /no'βisimo/ *a superl* **nuevo** newest; latest, most recent

nubada /nu'βaða/ *f,* cloudburst, rainstorm; abundance, plenty

nubarrón /nuβa'rron/ *m,* dense, lowering cloud, storm cloud

nube /'nuβe/ *f,* cloud; *Fig.* screen, impediment. **n. de verano,** summer cloud; passing annoyance

nublado /nu'βlaðo/ *a* cloudy; overcast. *m,* storm cloud; menace, threat; multitude, crowd

nublarse /nu'βlarse/ *vr* to cloud over

nubloso /nu'βloso/ *a* cloudy; unfortunate, unhappy

nuca /'nuka/ *f,* nape

núcleo /'nukleo/ *m,* kernel; stone, pip (of fruit); nucleus; *Fig.* core, essence

nudillo /nu'ðiʎo; nu'ðiyo/ *m,* knuckle; *Mas.* plug

nudo /'nuðo/ *m,* knot; (*Bot. Med.*) node; joint; *Naut.* knot; *Fig.* bond, tie; *Fig.* crux, knotty point. **n. al revés,** granny knot. **n. de comunicaciones,** communication center. **n. de marino,** reef knot. **n. de teje-**

dor, sheet bend (knot). **n. en la garganta,** *Fig.* lump in the throat (from emotion)

nudoso /nu'ðoso/ *a* knotted, knotty; gnarled

nuera /'nuera/ *f,* daughter-in-law

nuestro, nuestra /'nuestro, 'nuestra/ *poss pron 1st pers pl mf* our; ours. **los nuestros,** our friends, supporters, party, profession, etc.

nueva /'nueβa/ *f,* news

Nueva Caledonia /'nueβa kale'ðonia/ New Caledonia

Nueva Escocia /'nueβa es'koθia; 'nueβa es'kosia/ Nova Scotia

Nueva Gales del Sur /'nueβa 'gales del sur/ New South Wales

Nueva Guinea /'nueβa gi'nea/ New Guinea

nuevamente /nueβa'mente/ *adv* again

Nueva Orleans /'nueβa orle'ans/ New Orleans

Nueva York /'nueβa york/ New York

Nueva Zelanda, Zelandia /'nueβa θe'landa, θe'landia; 'nueβa se'landa, se'landia/ New Zealand

nueve /'nueβe/ *a* nine; ninth. *m,* number nine; ninth (of the month) (e.g. *el nueve de marzo,* March 9th). **a las nueve,** at nine o'clock

nuevo /'nueβo/ *a* new; fresh; newly arrived; inexperienced; unused, scarcely worn. **de n.,** again. **¿Qué hay de n.?** What's the news? What's new?

nuez /nueθ/ nues/ *f,* walnut; *Anat.* Adam's apple. **n. moscada,** nutmeg

nulidad /nuli'ðað/ *f,* nullity; incompetence, ineptitude; worthlessness

nulo /'nulo/ *a* null, void; incapable; worthless

numen /'numen/ *m,* divinity; inspiration

numeración /numera'θion; numera'sion/ *f,* calculation; numbering

numerador /numera'ðor/ *m,* numerator

numerar /nume'rar/ *vt* to number; enumerate; calculate

numerario /nume'rario/ *a* numerary. *m,* cash

numérico /nu'meriko/ *a* numerical

número /'numero/ *m,* number; figure; numeral; size (of gloves, etc.); quantity; issue, copy; rhythm; *Gram.* number; item (of a program); *pl Eccl.* Numbers. **n. del distrito postal,** ZIP code. **n. quebrado,** *Math.* fraction. **sin n.,** numberless

numeroso /nume'roso/ *a* numerous; harmonious

numismática /numis'matika/ *f,* numismatics

nunca /'nunka/ *adv* never. **n. jamás,** nevermore. **N. digas «De esta agua no beberé!»** Never say "Never!"

nuncio /'nunθio; 'nunsio/ *m,* messenger; papal nuncio; *Fig.* harbinger

nupcial /nup'θial; nup'sial/ *a* nuptial

nupcialidad /nupθiali'ðað; nupsiali'ðað/ *f,* marriage rate

nupcias /'nupθias; 'nupsias/ *f pl,* nuptials, marriage

nutria /'nutria/ *f,* otter, nutria

nutrición /nutri'θion; nutri'sion/ *f,* nourishment; nutrition

nutrido /nu'triðo/ *a* abundant; numerous

nutrimento /nutri'mento/ *m,* nutriment; nourishment; nutrition; *Fig.* food, encouragement

nutrir /nu'trir/ *vt* to nourish; encourage; *Fig.* fill

nutritivo /nutri'tiβo/ *a* nourishing, nutritive

ñaques /'ɲakes/ *m pl,* odds and ends, rubbish

ñiquiñaque /ɲiki'ɲake/ *m, Inf.* good-for-nothing, wastrel; *Inf.* trash

ñoñería /ɲoɲe'ria/ *f, Inf.* drivel; folly, stupidity. **Déjate de ñoñerías,** *Inf.* Stop being a crybaby

ñoño /'ɲoɲo/ **(-ña)** *a Inf.* sentimental; foolish, idiotic. *n* fool.

O

o /o/ *f*, letter O —*conjunc* or, either. **o** becomes **u** before words beginning with **o** or **ho** (e.g. *gloria u honor*)

oasis /o'asis/ *m*, oasis; *Fig.* refuge, haven

obcecación /oβθeka'θion; oβseka'sion/ *f*, blindness; obstinacy; obsession

obcecar /oβθe'kar; oβse'kar/ *vt* to blind; obsess; *Fig.* dazzle; darken

obduración /oβðura'θion; oβðura'sion/ *f*, obstinacy, stubbornness, obduracy

obedecer /oβeðe'θer; oβeðe'ser/ *vt irr* to obey; *Fig.* respond; bend, yield (metals, etc.); —*vi* result (from), arise (from). See **conocer**

obedecimiento /oβeðeθi'miento; oβeðesi'miento/ *m*, **obediencia** *f*, obedience

obediente /oβe'ðiente/ *a* obedient; docile

obelisco /oβe'lisko/ *m*, obelisk

obertura /oβer'tura/ *f*, *Mus.* overture

obesidad /oβesi'ðað/ *f*, obesity

obeso /o'βeso/ *a* obese

óbice /'oβiθe; 'oβise/ *m*, obstacle, impediment

obispado /oβis'paðo/ *m*, bishopric

obispalía /oβispa'lia/ *f*, bishop's palace; bishopric

obispo /o'βispo/ *m*, bishop. **o. sufragáneo,** suffragan bishop

óbito /'oβito/ *m*, death, demise

obituario /oβi'tuario/ *m*, obituary; obituary column

objeción /oβhe'θion; oβhe'sion/ *f*, objection

objetar /oβhe'tar/ *vt* to object to, oppose

objetivar /oβheti'βar/ *vt* to view objectively

objetividad /oβhetiβi'ðað/ *f*, objectivity

objetivo /oβhe'tiβo/ *a* objective. *m*, *Opt.* eyepiece; object finder; aim, goal

objeto /oβ'heto/ *m*, object; subject, theme; purpose; aim, goal. **sin o.,** without object; aimlessly

oblea /o'βlea/ *f*, seal, wafer

oblicuidad /oβlikui'ðað/ *f*, obliqueness

oblicuo /o'βlikuo/ *a* slanting, oblique

obligación /oβliga'θion; oβliga'sion/ *f*, obligation; *Com.* bond; *Com.* debenture; *pl* responsibilities; *Com.* liabilities

obligacionista /oβligaθio'nista; oβligasio'nista/ *mf* *Com.* bond holder, debenture holder

obligado /oβli'gaðo/ *m*, contractor (to a borough, etc.); *Mus.* obbligato

obligar /oβli'gar/ *vt* to compel, oblige, constrain; lay under an obligation; *Law.* mortgage; —*vr* bind oneself, promise

obligatorio /oβliga'torio/ *a* obligatory

oblongo /o'βloŋgo/ *a* oblong

oboe /o'βoe/ *m*, oboe; oboe player, oboist

óbolo /'oβolo/ *m*, obol, ancient Greek coin

obra /'oβra/ *f*, work; anything made; literary, artistic, scientific production; structure, construction; repair, alteration (to buildings, etc.); means, influence, power; labor, or time spent; action, behavior. **o. de caridad,** charitable act. **o. maestra,** masterpiece. **obras públicas,** public works. **poner por o.,** to put into effect; to set to work on. **o. de,** about, approximately

obrar /o'βrar/ *vt* to work; make, do; execute, perform; affect; construct, build; —*vi* be, exist (things); act, behave. **o. mal,** to behave badly, do wrong

obrero /o'βrero/ **(-ra)** *a* working —*n* worker; *pl* workers

obscenidad /oβsθeni'ðað; oβsseni'ðað/ *f*, obscenity

obsceno /oβs'θeno; oβs'seno/ *a* obscene

obsequiar /oβse'kiar/ *vt* to entertain, be attentive (to); give presents (to); court, make love to. **Me obsequia con un reloj,** He is presenting me with a watch

obsequio /oβ'sekio/ *m*, attention; gift; deference. **en o. de,** as a tribute to

obsequioso /oβse'kioso/ *a* obliging, courteous, attentive

observable /oβser'βaβle/ *a* observable

observación /oβserβa'θion; oβserβa'sion/ *f*, observation; remark

observador /oβserβa'ðor/ **(-ra)** *a* observing —*n* observer

observancia /oβser'βanθia; oβser'βansia/ *f*, observance; respect, reverence

observar /oβser'βar/ *vt* to notice; inspect, examine; fulfill; remark; watch, spy upon; *Astron.* observe

observatorio /oβserβa'torio/ *m*, observatory

obsesión /oβse'sion/ *f*, obsession

obsesionar /oβsesio'nar/ *vt* to obsess

obseso /oβ'seso/ *a* obsessed

obsidiana /oβsi'ðiana/ *f*, obsidian

obsolecer /oβsole'θer; oβsole'ser/ *vi* to obsolesce, become obsolete

obsoleto /oβso'leto/ *a* obsolete

obstáculo /oβs'takulo/ *m*, impediment; obstacle

obstante, no /oβs'tante, no/ *adv* in spite of; nevertheless

obstar /oβs'tar/ *vi* to impede, hinder

obstetra /oβs'tetra/ *mf* obstetrician

obstetricia /oβste'triθia; oβste'trisia/ *f*, obstetrics

obstinación /oβstina'θion; oβstina'sion/ *f*, obstinacy

obstinado /oβsti'naðo/ *a* obstinate, stubborn

obstinarse /oβsti'narse/ *vr* (*with en*) to persist in, insist on, be stubborn about

obstinaz /oβsti'naθ; oβsti'nas/ *a* obstinate

obstrucción /oβstruk'θion; oβstruk'sion/ *f*, obstruction

obstruccionismo /oβstrukθio'nismo; oβstruksio'nismo/ *m*, obstructionism

obstruccionista /oβstrukθio'nista; oβstruksio'nista/ *mf* obstructionist

obstruir /oβs'truir/ *vt irr* to obstruct; block; hinder; —*vr* become choked or stopped up (pipes, etc.). See **huir**

obtención /oβten'θion; oβten'sion/ *f*, obtainment; attainment, realization

obtener /oβte'ner/ *vt irr* to obtain; attain; maintain, preserve. See **tener**

obturador /oβtura'ðor/ *m*, stopper; shutter (of a camera)

obturar /oβtu'rar/ *vt* to stopper, plug; block, obstruct

obtuso /oβ'tuso/ *a* blunt, dull; (*Geom.* and *Fig.*) obtuse

obús /o'βus/ *m*, howitzer; *Mil.* shell

obviar /oβ'βiar/ *vt* to obviate

obvio /'oββio/ *a* obvious, evident, apparent

oca /'oka/ *f*, goose

ocasión /oka'sion/ *f*, occasion; opportunity; motive, cause; danger, risk; *Inf.* **asir la o. por la melena,** to take time by the forelock. **de o.,** second-hand

ocasional /okasio'nal/ *a* chance, fortuitous; occasional

ocasionar /okasio'nar/ *vt* to cause, occasion; excite, provoke; risk, endanger

ocaso /o'kaso/ *m*, sunset; west; dusk; decadence, decline

occidental /okθiðen'tal; oksiðen'tal/ *a* Western

occidente /okθi'ðente; oksi'ðente/ *m*, West, Occident

occipital /okθipi'tal; oksipi'tal/ *a* *Anat.* occipital

occiso /ok'θiso; ok'siso/ *a* murdered; killed

oceánico /oθe'aniko; ose'aniko/ *a* oceanic

océano /o'θeano; o'seano/ *m*, ocean; immensity, abundance

oceanografía /oθeanogra'fia; oseanogra'fia/ *f*, oceanography

ocelote /oθe'lote; ose'lote/ *m*, ocelot

ochava /o't∫aβa/ *f*, eighth; *Eccl.* octave

ochavo /o't∫aβo/ *m*, *Obs.* small Spanish copper coin

ochenta /o't∫enta/ *a* and *m*, eighty; eightieth

ochentón /ot∫en'ton/ **(-ona)** *n* octogenarian

ocho /'ot∫o/ *a* eight; eighth. *m*, figure eight; playing card with eight pips; eight; eighth day (of the month). **las o.,** eight o'clock

ochocientos /otʃo'θientos; otʃo'sientos/ *a* and *m*, eight hundred; eight-hundredth

ocio /'oθio; 'osio/ *m*, leisure, idleness; *pl* pastimes; leisure time

ociosidad /oθiosi'ðað; osiosi'ðað/ *f*, idleness, laziness; leisure

ocioso /o'θioso; o'sioso/ **(-sa)** *a* idle; useless, worthless; unprofitable, fruitless —*n* idle fellow

ocre /'okre/ *m*, ocher

octágono /ok'tagono/ *m*, octagon

octava /ok'taβa/ *f*, octave

octaviano /okta'βiano/ *a* Octavian

octavo /ok'taβo/ *a* eighth. *m*, eighth. **en o.**, in octavo

octeto /ok'teto/ *m*, octet

octogenario /oktohe'nario/ **(-ia)** *a* and *n* octogenarian

octogésimo /okto'hesimo/ *a* eightieth

octubre /ok'tuβre/ *m*, October

óctuple /'oktuple/ *a* octuple, eightfold

ocular /oku'lar/ *a* ocular. *m*, eyepiece

oculista /oku'lista/ *mf* oculist

ocultación /okulta'θion; okulta'sion/ *f*, hiding, concealment

ocultamente /okulta'mente/ *adv* secretly

ocultar /okul'tar/ *vt* to hide, conceal; disguise; keep secret

ocultismo /okul'tismo/ *m*, occultism

oculto /o'kulto/ *a* hidden; secret; occult. **en o.**, secretly, quietly

ocupación /okupa'θion; okupa'sion/ *f*, occupancy; occupation, pursuit; employment, office, trade

ocupado /oku'paðo/ *a* occupied; busy

ocupante /oku'pante/ *m*, occupant

ocupar /oku'par/ *vt* to take possession of; obtain or hold (job); occupy, fill; inhabit; employ; hinder, embarrass; hold the attention (of); —*vr* (*with en*) be engaged in, be occupied with; (*with con*) concentrate on (a business affair, etc.)

ocurrencia /oku'rrenθia; oku'rrensia/ *f*, occurrence, incident; bright idea; witty remark

ocurrir /oku'rrir/ *vi* to anticipate; happen, take place; occur, strike (ideas)

oda /'oða/ *f*, ode

odalisca /oða'liska/ *f*, odalisk

odiar /o'ðiar/ *vt* to hate

odio /'oðio/ *m*, hatred; malevolence

odioso /o'ðioso/ *a* hateful, odious

odisea /oði'sea/ *f*, odyssey

odontología /oðontolo'hia/ *f*, odontology

odontólogo /oðon'tologo/ *m*, odontologist

odorífero /oðo'rifero/ *a* odoriferous, fragrant

odre /'oðre/ *m*, goatskin, wineskin; *Inf.* wine bibber

oesnorueste /oesno'rueste/ *m*, westnorthwest

oessudueste /oessu'ðueste/ *m*, westsouthwest

oeste /o'este/ *m*, west

ofender /ofen'der/ *vt* to ill-treat, hurt; offend, insult; anger, annoy; —*vr* be offended

ofendido /ofen'diðo/ *a* offended; resentful

ofensa /o'fensa/ *f*, injury, harm; offense, crime

ofensiva /ofen'siβa/ *f*, *Mil.* offensive. **tomar la o.**, to take the offensive

ofensivo /ofen'siβo/ *a* offensive

ofensor /ofen'sor/ **(-ra)** *n* offender

oferta /o'ferta/ *f*, offer; gift; proposal; *Com.* tender. **o. y demanda**, supply and demand

ofertorio /ofer'torio/ *m*, *Eccl.* offertory

oficial /ofi'θial; ofi'sial/ *a* official. *m*, official; officer; clerk; executioner; worker

oficiala /ofi'θiala; ofi'siala/ *f*, trained female worker

oficialidad /ofiθiali'ðað; ofisiali'ðað/ *f*, officialdom; officers

oficiar /ofi'θiar; ofi'siar/ *vt Eccl.* to celebrate or serve (mass); communicate officially, inform; *Inf.* (*with de*) act as

oficina /ofi'θina; ofi'sina/ *f*, workshop; office; pharmaceutical laboratory; *pl* cellars, basement (of a house)

oficinesco /ofiθi'nesko; ofisi'nesko/ *a* bureaucratic, red-tape

oficinista /ofiθi'nista; ofisi'nista/ *mf* clerk, office employee, office worker

oficio /o'fiθio; o'fisio/ *m*, occupation, employment; office, function, capacity; craft; operation; trade, business; official communication; office, bureau; *Eccl.* office. **Santo O.**, Holy Office. *Fig.* **buenos oficios**, good offices

oficiosidad /ofiθiosi'ðað; ofisiosi'ðað/ *f*, diligence, conscientiousness; helpfulness, friendliness; officiousness

oficioso /ofi'θioso; ofi'sioso/ *a* conscientious; helpful, useful; officious; meddlesome; unofficial, informal

ofrecer /ofre'θer; ofre'ser/ *vt irr* to offer; present; exhibit; consecrate, dedicate; —*vr* occur, suggest itself; volunteer. **¿Qué se le ofrece?** What do you require? What would you like? See **conocer**

ofrecimiento /ofreθi'miento; ofresi'miento/ *m*, offer, offering

ofrenda /o'frenda/ *f*, *Eccl.* offering; gift, present

oftalmología /oftalmolo'hia/ *f*, ophthalmology

oftalmólogo /oftal'mologo/ *m*, oculist, ophthalmologist

ofuscación /ofuska'θion; ofuska'sion/ *f*. **ofuscamiento** *m*, obfuscation, dazzle, dimness of sight; mental confusion, bewilderment

ofuscar /ofus'kar/ *vt* to dazzle, daze; dim, obfuscate; confuse, bewilder

ogro /'ogro/ *m*, ogre

ohmio /'omio/ *m*, ohm

oídas, de /o'iðas, de/ *adv* by hearsay

oído /o'iðo/ *m*, sense of hearing; ear. **de o.**, by ear. **decir al o.**, to whisper in a person's ear. *Mus.* **duro de o.**, hard of hearing; having a bad ear (for music). **estar sordo de un o.**, to be deaf in one ear

oidor /oi'ðor/ *m*, hearer; judge, *Obs.* magistrate

oír /o'ir/ *vt irr* to hear; give ear to, listen; understand —*Pres. Part.* **oyendo**. *Pres. Indic.* **oigo, oyes, oye, oyen**. *Preterite* **oyó, oyeron**. *Pres. Subjunc.* **oiga**, etc. —*Imperf. Subjunc.* **oyese**, etc.

oíslo /o'islo/ *mf Inf.* better half

ojal /o'hal/ *m*, buttonhole; slit, hole

¡ojalá! /oha'la/ *interj* If only that were so! God grant!

ojeada /ohe'aða/ *f*, glance

ojear /ohe'ar/ *vt* to look at, stare at; bewitch; scare, startle

ojera /o'hera/ *f*, dark shadow (under the eye); eye bath

ojeriza /ohe'riθa; ohe'risa/ *f*, ill-will, spite

ojeroso /ohe'roso/ *a* having dark shadows under the eyes, wan, haggard

ojete /o'hete/ *m*, eyelet

ojinegro /ohi'negro/ *a* black-eyed

ojiva /o'hiβa/ *f*, ogive

ojo /o'ho/ *m*, eye; hole; slit; socket; keyhole; eye (of a needle); span (of a bridge); core (of a corn); attention, care; mesh; spring, stream; well (of a staircase); *pl* darling. **¡Ojo!** Take care! **o. avizor**, sharp watch; lynx eye. **Ojos que no ven, corazón que no siente**, Out of sight, out of mind. **o. saltón**, prominent, bulging eye. **o. vivo**, bright eye. **a o. de buen cubero**, at a guess. **a ojos vistas**, visibly; patently

ola /'ola/ *f*, billow; wave (atmospheric)

ole /'ole/ *m*, Andalusian dance

¡olé! /o'le/ *interj* Bravo!

oleada /ole'aða/ *f*, big wave, breaker; swell (of the sea); *Fig.* surge (of a crowd)

oleaginoso /oleahi'noso/ *a* oleaginous

oleaje /ole'ahe/ *m*, swell, surge, billowing

olear /ole'ar/ *vt* to administer extreme unction

óleo /'oleo/ *m*, oil; *Eccl.* holy oil (gen. *pl*). **al ó.**, in oils

oleoducto /oleo'ðukto/ *m*, oil pipeline

oler /o'ler/ *vt irr* to smell; guess, discover; pry, smell out; —*vi* smell; (*with prep a*) smell of; smack of, be reminiscent of —*Pres. Indic.* **huelo, hueles, huele, huelen**. *Pres. Subjunc.* **huela, huelas, huela, huelan**

olfatear /olfate'ar/ *vt* to sniff, snuff, smell; *Inf.* pry into

olfativo, olfatorio /olfa'tiβo, olfa'torio/ *a* olfactory

olfato /ol'fato/ *m*, sense of smell; shrewdness

olfatorio /olfa'torio/ *a* olfactory

oliente /o'liente/ **(mal)** *a* evil-smelling

oligarquía /oligar'kia/ f, oligarchy
oligárquico /oli'garkiko/ a oligarchic
olímpico /o'limpiko/ a Olympic; Olympian
oliva /o'liβa/ f, olive tree; olive; barn owl; peace
olivar /oli'βar/ m, olive grove
olivo /o'liβo/ m, olive tree
olla /'oʎa/ 'oya/ f, stew pot; Spanish stew; whirlpool.
  o. podrida, rich Spanish stew containing bacon, fowl, meat, vegetables, ham, etc. **las ollas de Egipto,** the fleshpots of Egypt
olmeda /ol'meða/ f, **olmedo** m, elm grove
olmo /'olmo/ m, elm tree
olor /o'lor/ m, odor, scent, smell; hope, promise; suspicion, hint; reputation. **o. de santidad,** odor of sanctity
oloroso /olo'roso/ a fragrant, perfumed
olvidadizo /olβiða'ðiθo; olβiða'ðiso/ a forgetful
olvidar /olβi'ðar/ **(se)** vt and vr to forget; neglect, desert. **Se me olvidó el libro,** I forgot the book. **Me olvidé de lo pasado,** I forgot the past
olvido /ol'βiðo/ m, forgetfulness; indifference, neglect; oblivion
ombligo /om'βligo/ m, navel; Fig. core, center
ominoso /omi'noso/ a ominous
omisión /omi'sion/ f, omission; carelessness, negligence; neglect
omiso /o'miso/ a omitted; remiss; careless. **hacer caso o. de,** to set aside, ignore
omitir /omi'tir/ vt to omit
ómnibus /'omniβus/ m, bus
omnímodo /om'nimoðo/ a all-embracing
omnipotencia /omnipo'tenθia; omnipo'tensia/ f, omnipotence
omnipotente /omnipo'tente/ a omnipotent, all-powerful
omnisciencia /omnis'θienθia; omnis'siensia/ f, omniscience
omnisció /om'nisθio; om'nissio/ a omniscient
omnívoro /om'niβoro/ a omnivorous
omoplato /omo'plato/ m, scapula, shoulder blade
once /'onθe; 'onse/ a eleven; eleventh. m, eleven; eleventh (of the month). **las o.,** eleven o'clock
onceno /on'θeno; on'seno/ a eleventh
onda /'onda/ f, wave; Fig. flicker (of flames); Sew. scallop; Phys. wave; ripple; pl waves (in hair). Radio. **o. corta,** short wave. **o. etérea,** ether wave. **o. sonora,** sound wave
ondeado /onde'aðo/ a undulating; wavy; scalloped
ondeante /onde'ante/ a waving; flowing
ondear /onde'ar/ vi to wave; ripple; undulate; roll (of the sea); float, flutter, stream; Sew. scallop; —vr swing, sway
ondeo /on'deo/ m, waving; undulation
ondina /on'dina/ f, undine, water sprite
ondulación /ondula'θion; ondula'sion/ f, undulation; wave; wriggling; twisting. **o. permanente,** permanent wave, perm
ondulado /ondu'laðo/ a wavy; undulating; scalloped
ondular /ondu'lar/ vi to writhe, squirm, wriggle; twist; coil; —vt wave (in hair)
oneroso /one'roso/ a onerous, heavy; troublesome
ónice /'oniθe; 'onise/ m, onyx
onomástico /ono'mastiko/ a onomastic. **día o.,** saint's day
onomatopeya /onomato'peia/ f, onomatopoeia
onza /'onθa; 'onsa/ f, ounce. **por onzas,** by ounces; sparingly
onzavo /on'θaβo; on'saβo/ a and m, eleventh
opacidad /opaθi'ðað; opasi'ðað/ f, opacity; obscurity; gloom
opaco /o'pako/ a opaque; dark; gloomy, sad
opalescente /opales'θente; opales'sente/ a opalescent
opalino /opa'lino/ a opaline
ópalo /'opalo/ m, opal
opción /op'θion; op'sion/ f, option; choice, selection; Law. option
ópera /'opera/ f, opera
operación /opera'θion; opera'sion/ f, Surg. operation; execution, performance; Com. transaction

operar /ope'rar/ vt Surg. to operate; —vi act, have an effect; operate, control; Com. transact
operario /ope'rario/ **(-ia)** n worker, hand; operator; mechanic
opereta /ope'reta/ f, operetta, light opera
opinar /opi'nar/ vi to have or form an opinion, think; judge, consider
opinión /opi'nion/ f, opinion, view; reputation
opio /'opio/ m, opium. **fumadero de o.,** opium den
opíparo /o'piparo/ a magnificent, sumptuous (banquets, etc.)
oponer /opo'ner/ vt irr to oppose; resist, withstand; protest against; —vr oppose; be contrary or hostile (to); face, be opposite; object (to), set oneself against; compete (in public exams.). See **poner**
oporto /o'porto/ m, port (wine)
oportunidad /oportuni'ðað/ f, opportunity, occasion
oportunismo /oportu'nismo/ m, opportunism
oportunista /oportu'nista/ a and mf opportunist
oportuno /opor'tuno/ a opportune, timely
oposición /oposi'θion; oposi'sion/ f, opposition; resistance; antagonism; public competitive exam for a post; (Astron. Polit.) opposition
opositor /oposi'tor/ **(-ra)** n opponent; competitor
opresión /opre'sion/ f, oppression; hardship; pressure. **o. de pecho,** difficulty in breathing
opresor /opre'sor/ **(-ra)** a oppressive —n oppressor
oprimir /opri'mir/ vt to oppress; treat harshly; press, crush; choke
oprobio /o'proβio/ m, opprobrium
optar /op'tar/ vt to take possession of; (with por) choose
óptica /'optika/ f, Phys. optics; peepshow
óptico /'optiko/ a optic, optical. m, optician
optimismo /opti'mismo/ m, optimism
optimista /opti'mista/ mf optimist —a optimistic
óptimo /'optimo/ a superl bueno best, optimal, optimum
opugnar /opug'nar/ vt to resist violently; Mil. assault, attack; impugn, challenge
opulencia /opu'lenθia; opu'lensia/ f, opulence, riches; excess, superabundance
opulento /opu'lento/ a opulent, rich
opúsculo /o'puskulo/ m, monograph, opuscule
oquedad /oke'ðað/ f, hollow, cavity; superficiality, banality
ora /'ora/ adv now
oración /ora'θion; ora'sion/ f, oration, speech; prayer; Gram. sentence
oráculo /o'rakulo/ m, oracle
orador /ora'ðor/ **(-ra)** n orator; speech maker. m, preacher
oral /o'ral/ a oral; verbal; buccal
orangután /orangu'tan/ m, orangutan
orar /o'rar/ vi to harangue, make an oration; pray; —vt request, beg
orate /o'rate/ mf lunatic
oratoria /ora'toria/ f, oratory, eloquence
oratorio /ora'torio/ a oratorical. m, oratory, chapel; Mus. oratorio
orbe /'orβe/ m, sphere; orb; world
órbita /'orβita/ f, Astron. orbit; Fig. sphere; Anat. orbit, eye socket
Órcades, las /'orkaðes, las/ the Orkneys
ordalía /orða'lia/ f, (medieval hist.) ordeal
orden /'orðen/ mf order, mode of arrangement; succession, sequence; group; system; orderliness, neatness; coherence, plan; Eccl. order, brotherhood; (Zool. Bot.) group, class; Archit. order; Math. degree. f, precept, command; Com. order; pl Eccl. ordination. (Mil. Naut.) **o. de batalla,** battle array. **o. de caballería,** order of knighthood. **o. del día,** order of the day. Eccl. **dar órdenes,** to ordain. **en o.,** in order; with regard (to). **por su o.,** in its turn; successively
ordenación /orðena'θion; orðena'sion/ f, order, orderly arrangement, disposition; ordinance, precept; Eccl. ordination
ordenador /orðena'ðor/ m Spain computer
ordenamiento /orðena'miento/ m, ordaining; ordinance; edict

ordenancista /orðenan'θista; orðenan'sista/ *mf Mil.* martinet; disciplinarian

ordenanza /orðe'nanθa; orðe'nansa/ *f,* order, method; command, instruction; ordinance, regulation (gen. *pl*). *m, Mil.* orderly

ordenar /orðe'nar/ *vt* to put in order, arrange; command, give instructions to; decree; direct, regulate; *Eccl.* ordain; —*vr (with de) Eccl.* be ordained as

ordeñadero /orðeɲa'ðero/ *m,* milk pail

ordeñar /orðe'ɲar/ *vt* to milk

ordinal /orði'nal/ *a* ordinal. *m,* ordinal number

ordinariez /orðina'rieθ; orðina'ries/ *f,* rudeness, uncouthness; vulgarity

ordinario /orði'nario/ *a* ordinary, usual; vulgar, coarse, uncultured; rude; commonplace, average, mediocre. *m, Eccl.* ordinary; carrier; courier. **de o.,** usually, ordinarily

orear /ore'ar/ *vt* to ventilate; —*vr* dry; air; take the air

orégano /o'regano/ *m,* wild marjoram

oreja /o'reha/ *f,* external ear; lug; tab, flap; tongue (of a shoe). *Inf.* **con las orejas caídas,** down in the mouth, depressed

orejera /ore'hera/ *f,* earflap; mold board (of a plow)

orejudo /ore'huðo/ *a* large- or long-eared

oreo /o'reo/ *m,* zephyr; ventilation; airing

orfanato /orfa'nato/ *m,* orphanage, orphan asylum

orfandad /orfan'dað/ *f,* orphanhood; defenselessness, lack of protection

orfebre /or'feβre/ *mf* gold- or silversmith

orfebrería /orfeβre'ria/ *f,* gold- or silverwork

orfeón /orfe'on/ *m,* choral society

organdí /organ'di/ *m,* organdy

orgánico /or'ganiko/ *a* organic; harmonious; *Fig.* organized

organillero /organi'ʎero; organi'yero/ **(-ra)** *n* organ grinder

organillo /orga'niʎo; orga'niyo/ *m,* barrel organ

organismo /orga'nismo/ *m,* organism; organization, association

organista /orga'nista/ *mf* organist

organización /organiθa'θion; organisa'sion/ *f,* organization; order, arrangement

organizador /organiθa'ðor; organisa'ðor/ **(-ra)** *a* organizing —*n* organizer

organizar /organi'θar; organi'sar/ *vt* to organize; regulate; constitute

órgano /'organo/ *m, Mus.* organ; (*Anat. Bot.*) organ; means, agency. **o. de manubrio,** barrel organ

orgasmo /or'gasmo/ *m,* orgasm

orgía /or'hia/ *f,* orgy

orgullo /or'guʎo; or'guyo/ *m,* pride; arrogance

orgulloso /orgu'ʎoso; orgu'yoso/ *a* proud; haughty

orientación /orienta'θion; orienta'sion/ *f,* orientation; exposure, prospect; bearings

oriental /orien'tal/ *a* Oriental, Eastern. *mf* Oriental

orientalismo /orienta'lismo/ *m,* Orientalism

orientalista /orienta'lista/ *mf* Orientalist

orientar /orien'tar/ *vt* to orientate; —*vr* find one's bearings; familiarize oneself (with)

oriente /o'riente/ *m,* Orient, the East; luster (of pearls); youth, childhood; origin, source

orificio /ori'fiθio; ori'fisio/ *m,* orifice; hole

oriflama /ori'flama/ *f,* oriflamme; standard, flag

origen /o'rihen/ *m,* origin, source, root; stock, extraction; reason, genesis. **dar o. a,** to give rise to. **país de o.,** native land

original /orihi'nal/ *a* original; earliest, primitive; new, first-hand; novel, fresh; inventive, creative; eccentric; quaint. *m,* original manuscript; original; sitter (for portraits); eccentric

originalidad /orihinali'ðað/ *f,* originality

originar /orihi'nar/ *vt* to cause, originate; invent; —*vr* spring from, originate (in)

originario /orihi'nario/ *a* original, primary; primitive; native (of)

orilla /o'riʎa; o'riya/ *f,* limit, edge, hem, border; selvage; shore, margin; bank (of a river, etc.); sidewalk; brink, edge. **a la o.,** on the brink; nearly

orillar /ori'ʎar; ori'yar/ *vt* to settle, arrange, conclude;

—*vi* reach the shore or bank; *Sew.* leave a hem; *Sew.* border; leave a selvage on cloth

orillo /o'riʎo; o'riyo/ *m,* selvage (of cloth)

orín /o'rin/ *m,* rust; *pl* urine

orinal /ori'nal/ *m,* chamber pot, urinal

orinar /ori'nar/ *vi* to urinate

oriundo /o'riundo/ *a* native (of); derived (from)

orla /'orla/ *f,* border, fringe; selvage (of cloth, garments); ornamental border (on diplomas, etc.)

orlar /or'lar/ *vt* to border; edge, trim

ornamentación /ornamenta'θion; ornamenta'sion/ *f,* ornamentation

ornamental /ornamen'tal/ *a* ornamental

ornamentar /ornamen'tar/ *vt* to ornament; embellish

ornamento /orna'mento/ *m,* ornament; decoration; gift, virtue, talent; *pl Eccl.* vestments

ornar /or'nar/ *vt* to ornament, adorn, embellish

ornato /or'nato/ *m,* decoration, ornament

ornitología /ornitolo'hia/ *f,* ornithology

ornitológico /ornito'lohiko/ *a* ornithological

ornitólogo /orni'tologo/ *m,* ornithologist

oro /'oro/ *m,* gold; gold coins or jewelery; *Fig.* riches; *pl* diamonds (cards). **o. batido,** gold leaf. **o. en polvo,** gold dust. *Fig.* **como un o.,** shining with cleanliness. **el as de oros,** the ace of diamonds

orondo /o'rondo/ *a* hollow; *Inf.* pompous; *Inf.* swollen, spongy

oropel /oro'pel/ *m,* brass foil; showy, cheap thing; trinket; tinsel

oropéndola /oro'pendola/ *f,* oriole

orquesta /or'kesta/ *f,* orchestra

orquestación /orkesta'θion; orkesta'sion/ *f,* orchestration

orquestal /orkes'tal/ *a* orchestral

orquestar /orkes'tar/ *vt* to orchestrate

orquídea /or'kiðea/ *f,* orchid

ortega /or'tega/ *f, Ornith.* grouse

ortiga /or'tiga/ *f, Bot.* nettle

orto /'orto/ *m,* rising (of sun, stars)

ortodoxia /orto'ðoksia/ *f,* orthodoxy

ortodoxo /orto'ðokso/ *a* orthodox

ortografía /ortogra'fia/ *f,* orthography

ortográfico /orto'grafiko/ *a* orthographical

ortopedia /orto'peðia/ *f,* orthopedics

ortopédico /orto'peðiko/ **(-ca)** *a* orthopedic —*n* orthopedist

ortopedista /ortope'ðista/ *mf* orthopedist

oruga /o'ruga/ *f,* caterpillar

orzuelo /or'θuelo; or'suelo/ *m, Med.* sty; trap (for wild animals)

os /os/ *pers pron 2nd pl mf dat and acc of* **vos** and **vosotros** you, to you

osa /'osa/ *f,* she-bear; *Astron.* **O. mayor,** Big Bear; **O. menor,** Little Bear

osadía /osa'ðia/ *f,* boldness, audacity

osado /o'saðo/ *a* daring, bold

osamenta /osa'menta/ *f,* skeleton; bones (of a skeleton)

osar /o'sar/ *vi* to dare; risk, venture

osario /o'sario/ *m,* charnel house, ossuary

oscilación /osθila'θion; ossila'sion/ *f,* oscillation

oscilante /osθi'lante; ossi'lante/ *a* oscillating

oscilar /osθi'lar; ossi'lar/ *vi* to oscillate, sway; hesitate, vacillate

ósculo /'oskulo/ *m,* kiss, osculation

oscurantismo /oskuran'tismo/ *m,* obscurantism

oscurantista /oskuran'tista/ *a and mf* obscurantist

oscurecer /oskure'θer; oskure'ser/ *vt irr* to darken; *Fig.* tarnish, dim, sully; confuse, bewilder; express obscurely; *Art.* shade; —*vr* grow dark; —*vr* cloud over (sky); *Inf.* disappear (things, gen. by theft). See **conocer**

oscuridad /oskuri'ðað/ *f,* darkness; gloom, blackness; humbleness; obscurity, abstruseness

oscuro /os'kuro/ *a* dark; humble, unknown; abstruse, involved; obscure; uncertain, dangerous. **a oscuras,** in the dark; ignorant

óseo /'oseo/ *a* osseous

osera /o'sera/ *f,* bear's den

osezno /o'seθno; o'sesno/ *m,* bear cub

osificación /osifika'θion; osifika'sion/ *f,* ossification

osificarse /osifi'karse/ vr to ossify
ósmosis /'osmosis/ f, osmosis
oso /'oso/ m, bear. **o. blanco,** polar bear
Ostende /os'tende/ Ostend
ostensible /osten'siβle/ a ostensible; obvious
ostensión /osten'sion/ f, show, display, manifestation
ostensivo /osten'siβo/ a ostensive
ostentación /ostenta'θion; ostenta'sion/ f, manifestation; ostentation
ostentar /osten'tar/ vt to exhibit, show; boast, show off
ostentoso /osten'toso/ a magnificent, showy, ostentatious
osteología /osteolo'hia/ f, osteology
osteópata /oste'opata/ mf osteopath
osteopatía /osteopa'tia/ f, osteopathy
ostra /'ostra/ f, oyster. **vivero de ostras,** oyster bed
ostracismo /ostra'θismo; ostra'sismo/ m, ostracism
otear /ote'ar/ vt to observe; look on at
otero /o'tero/ m, hill, height, eminence
otología /otolo'hia/ f, otology
otólogo /o'tologo/ m, otologist
otomana /oto'mana/ f, ottoman, couch
otomano /oto'mano/ a Ottoman
otoñal /oto'ɲal/ a autumnal, autumn, fall
otoño /o'toɲo/ m, autumn, fall
otorgamiento /otorga'miento/ m, granting; consent, approval; license, award

otorgar /otor'gar/ vt to grant; concede, approve; *Law.* grant, stipulate, execute
otro /'otro/ **(-ra)** a other, another —n another one
otrosí /otro'si/ adv besides, moreover
ovación /oβa'θion; oβa'sion/ f, ovation, triumph; applause
ovacionar /oβaθio'nar; oβasio'nar/ vt to applaud
oval /o'βal/ a oval
óvalo /'oβalo/ m, oval
ovario /o'βario/ m, ovary
oveja /o'βeha/ f, ewe
ovejuno /oβe'huno/ a relating to ewes or sheep, sheep-like
ovillar /oβi'ʎar; oβi'yar/ vi to wind thread into a ball; —vr curl up; huddle
ovillo /o'βiʎo; o'βiyo/ m, ball, bobbin (of thread); tangled heap (of things)
ovíparo /o'βiparo/ a oviparous
OVNI /'oβni/ m, UFO
ovulación /oβula'θion; oβula'sion/ f, ovulation
óvulo /'oβulo/ m, ovule
oxidación /oksiδa'θion; oksiδa'sion/ f, oxidation
oxidar /oksi'δar/ vt oxidize; —vr become oxidized
óxido /'oksiδo/ m, oxide. **ó. de carbono,** carbon monoxide. **ó. de cinc,** zinc oxide
oxígeno /ok'siheno/ m, oxygen
oyente /o'iente/ mf hearer; pl audience
ozono /o'θono; o'sono/ m, ozone

P

pabellón /paβe'ʎon; paβe'yon/ *m*, pavilion; colors, flag; bell tent. **p. británico**, Union Jack. **p. de reposo**, rest home. **en p.**, stacked (of arms)

pábulo /'paβulo/ *m*, food; *Fig.* pabulum

pacedero /paθe'ðero; pase'ðero/ *a Agr.* grazing, meadow

pacer /pa'θer; pa'ser/ *vi irr Agr.* to graze; —*vt* nibble away; eat away. See **nacer**

paciencia /pa'θienθia; pa'siensia/ *f*, patience

paciente /pa'θiente; pa'siente/ *a* patient; long-suffering; complacent. *mf Med.* patient

pacienzudo /paθien'θuðo; pasien'suðo/ *a* extremely patient or long-suffering

pacificación /paθifika'θion; pasifika'sion/ *f*, pacification; serenity, peace of mind

pacificador /paθifika'ðor; pasifika'ðor/ **(-ra)** *a* peace making; pacifying —*n* peace maker

pacificar /paθifi'kar; pasifi'kar/ *vt* to pacify; —*vi* make peace; —*vr* grow quiet, become calm (sea, etc.)

pacífico /pa'θifiko; pa'sifiko/ *a* pacific, meek, mild; peace-loving, peaceful. **el Océano P.**, the Pacific Ocean

pacifismo /paθi'fismo; pasi'fismo/ *m*, pacifism

pacifista /paθi'fista; pasi'fista/ *a* and *mf* pacifist

pacotilla /pako'tiʎa; pako'tiya/ *f*, goods. *Inf.* **hacer su p.**, to make one's packet or fortune. **ser de p.**, to be poor stuff; be jerry-built (of houses)

pactar /pak'tar/ *vt* to stipulate, arrange; contract

pacto /'pakto/ *m*, agreement, contract; pact

padecer /paðe'θer; paðe'ser/ *vt irr* to suffer; feel keenly; experience, undergo; tolerate. **p. desnudez**, to go unclothed. **p. hambre**, to go hungry. See **conocer**

padecimiento /paðeθi'miento; paðesi'miento/ *m*, suffering

padrastro /pa'ðrastro/ *m*, stepfather; cruel father; *Fig.* impediment, obstacle; hangnail

padrazo /pa'ðraθo; pa'ðraso/ *m. Inf.* indulgent father

padre /'paðre/ *m*, father; stallion; head (of the family, etc.); *Eccl.* father; genesis, source; author, creator; *pl* parents; ancestors. **p. adoptivo**, foster father. **p. de familia**, paterfamilias. **P. Eterno**, Eternal Father. **p. nuestro**, Lord's Prayer. **P. Santo**, Holy Father, the Pope

padrear /paðre'ar/ *vi* to take after one's father; *Zool.* reproduce, breed

padrino /pa'ðrino/ *m*, godfather; sponsor; second (in duels, etc.); patron; best man

padrón /pa'ðron/ *m*, census; pattern, model; memorial stone

paella /pa'eʎa; pa'eya/ *f*, *Cul.* savory rice dish of shellfish, chicken, and meat

paga /'paga/ *f*, payment; amends, restitution; pay; payment of fine; reciprocity (in love, etc.)

pagadero /paga'ðero/ *a* payable. *m*, date and place when payment is due

pagador /paga'ðor/ **(-ra)** *n* payer. *m*, teller; wages clerk; paymaster

pagaduría /pagaðu'ria/ *f*, pay office

paganismo /paga'nismo/ *m*, paganism; heathenism

pagano /pa'gano/ **(-na)** *a* and *n* pagan; heathen

pagar /pa'gar/ *vt* to pay; make restitution, expiate; return, requite (love, etc.); —*vr* (*with de*) become fond of; be proud of. **p. adelantado**, to prepay. *Com.* **p. al contado**, to pay cash. **p. la casa**, to pay the rent (for one's residence)

pagaré /paga're/ *m*, *Com.* promissory note, I.O.U.

página /'pahina/ *f*, page (of a book); episode, occurrence

paginación /pahina'θion; pahina'sion/ *f*, pagination

paginar /pahi'nar/ *vt* to paginate

pago /'pago/ *m*, payment; recompense, reward; region of vineyards, olive groves, etc.

pagoda /pa'goða/ *f*, pagoda, temple; idol

paguro /pa'guro/ *m*, hermit crab

pailebote /paile'βote/ *m*, schooner

país /pa'is/ *m*, country, nation; region; *Art.* landscape. **del p.**, typical of the country of origin (gen. of food)

paisaje /pai'sahe/ *m*, countryside; landscape, scenery

paisajista, paisista /paisa'hista, pai'sista/ *mf* landscape painter

paisano /pai'sano/ **(-na)** *n* compatriot; peasant; civilian

Países Bajos, los /pa'ises 'bahos, los/ the Low Countries, the Netherlands

paja /'paha/ *f*, straw; chaff; trash; *Fig.* padding. **ver la p. en el ojo del vecino y no la viga en el nuestro**, to see the mote in our neighbor's eye and not the beam in our own

pajar /pa'har/ *m*, barn

pájara /'pahara/ *f*, hen (bird); kite (toy); *Inf.* jay; prostitute. **p. pinta**, game of forfeits

pajarear /pahare'ar/ *vt* to snare birds; loaf, idle about

pajarera /paha'rera/ *f*, aviary

pajarero /paha'rero/ *m*, bird catcher or seller —*a Inf.* frivolous, giddy; *Inf.* gaudy (colors)

pajarita /paha'rita/ *f*, bow tie

pájaro /'paharo/ *m*, bird. **p. bobo**, penguin. **p. carpintero**, woodpecker. *Fig. Inf.* **p. gordo**, big gun. **p. mosca**, hummingbird

pajarota /paha'rota/ *f*, *Inf.* canard, false report

paje /'pahe/ *m*, page; *Naut.* cabin boy

pajera /pa'hera/ *f*, hayloft

pajizo /pa'hiθo; pa'hiso/ *a* made of straw; covered or thatched with straw; strawcolored

pala /'pala/ *f*, paddle; blade (of an oar); shovel; spade; baker's peel (long-handled shovel); cutting edge of a spade, hoe, etc.; *Sports.* racket; vamp; upper (of a shoe); pelota or jai alai racket; tanner's knife; *Inf.* guile, cunning; cleverness, dexterity. **p. de hélice**, propeller blade. **p. para pescado**, fish server. *Inf.* **corta p.**, ignoramus; blockhead

palabra /pa'laβra/ *f*, word; power of speech; eloquence; offer, promise; *pl* magic formula, spell. **p. de clave**, code word. **p. de matrimonio**, promise of marriage. **p. de rey**, inviolable promise. **palabras cruzadas**, crossword puzzle. **bajo p. de**, under promise of. **cuatro palabras**, a few words; short conversation. **de p.**, verbally, by word of mouth. **dirigir la p. a**, to address, speak to. **faltar a su p.**, to break one's promise. **llevar la p.**, to be spokesperson. **medias palabras**, half-words; hint, insinuation. **su p. empeñada**, one's solemn word. **tener la p.**, to have the right to speak (in meetings, etc.) (e.g. *El señor Martínez tiene la p.*, Mr. Martinez has the floor)

palabrería /palaβre'ria/ *f*, verbosity, wordiness

palabrota /pala'βrota/ *f*, *Inf.* coarse language; long word

palaciego /pala'θiego; pala'siego/ **(-ga)** *a* pertaining to palaces; *Fig.* courtesan —*n* courtier

palacio /pa'laθio; pa'lasio/ *m*, palace; mansion

palada /pa'laða/ *f*, shovelful, spadeful; oar stroke

paladar /pala'ðar/ *m*, *Anat.* palate; taste; discernment, sensibility

paladear /palaðe'ar/ *vt* to taste with pleasure, savor; enjoy, relish

paladín /pala'ðin/ *m*, paladin

paladino /pala'ðino/ *a* public, clear, open

palafrén /pala'fren/ *m*, palfrey

palafrenero /palafre'nero/ *m*, groom; stablehand

palanca /pa'lanka/ *f*, *Mech.* lever; handle; bar; (high) diving board. **p. de arranque**, starting gear. **p. de cambio de velocidad**, gear-changing lever. **p. de mando**, control stick

palangana /palaŋ'gana/ *f*, washbasin

palanganero /palaŋga'nero/ *m*, washstand

palanqueta /palaŋ'keta/ *f*, *dim* small lever; jimmy

palastro /pa'lastro/ *m*, sheet iron or steel

palatinado /palati'naðo/ *m*, Palatinate

palatino /pala'tino/ *a* palatine

palatizar /palati'θar; palati'sar/ *vt* to palatilize

palazón /pala'θon; pala'son/ f, woodwork
palco /'palko/ m, Theat. box; stand, raised platform, enclosure. **p. de platea,** orchestra
palenque /pa'lenke/ m, enclosure; stand; platform; palisade
paleografía /paleogra'fia/ f, paleography
paleógrafo /pale'ografo/ m, paleographer
paleolítico /paleo'litiko/ a paleolithic
paleología /paleolo'hia/ f, paleology
paleontología /paleontolo'hia/ f, paleontology
Palestina /pales'tina/ Palestine
palestra /pa'lestra/ f, tilt yard
paleta /pa'leta/ f, dim little shovel; trowel; Art. palette; fireplace shovel; mason's trowel; Anat. shoulder blade; blade (of a propeller, ventilator, etc.); Chem. spatula
paliación /palia'θion; palia'sion/ f, palliation; excuse
paliar /pa'liar/ vt to dissemble, excuse; palliate, mitigate
paliativo /palia'tiβo/ a palliative; extenuating
palidecer /paliðe'θer; paliðe'ser/ vi irr to turn pale. See **conocer**
palidez /pali'ðeθ; pali'ðes/ f, pallor, paleness
pálido /'paliðo/ a pale, pallid
paliducho /pali'ðutʃo/ a somewhat pale, palish; sallow
palillo /pa'liʎo; pa'liyo/ m, dim small stick; toothpick; bobbin (for lacemaking); drumstick; Fig. chatter; pl castanets
palimpsesto /palimp'sesto/ m, palimpsest
palinodia /pali'noðia/ f, Lit. palinode. **cantar la p.,** to eat one's words, recant
palio /'palio/ m, Greek mantle; cape; Eccl. pallium; canopy, awning
palique /pa'like/ m, Inf. chat. **estar de p.,** to be having a chat
paliquear /palike'ar/ vi to chat
paliza /pa'liθa; pa'lisa/ f, caning, beating
palizada /pali'θaða; pali'saða/ f, paling, fence; palisade, stockade. **p. de tablas,** hoarding
palma /'palma/ f, palm tree; palm leaf; date palm; palm (of the hand); hand; triumph. **llevarse la p.,** to bear away the palm; take the cake
palmada /pal'maða/ f, slap; pl hand-clapping
palmado /pal'maðo/ a web (of feet); palmy
palmar /pal'mar/ a palmaceous; palmar; clear, obvious. m, palm grove
palmatoria /palma'toria/ f, ferule, ruler; candlestick
palmear /palme'ar/ vi to clap hands
palmera /pal'mera/ f, palm tree
palmeta /pal'meta/ f, ferrule, ruler
palmetazo /palme'taθo; palme'taso/ m, slap on the hand with a ruler; Fig. slap in the face
Palmira /pal'mira/ Palmyra
palmo /'palmo/ m, span; hand's breadth. **p. a p.,** inch by inch, piecemeal
palmotear /palmote'ar/ vt to applaud; clap
palo /'palo/ m, stick; rod; pole; timber, wood; wooden log; Naut. mast; blow with a stick; execution by hanging; suit (of playing cards); fruit stalk; Herald. pale. **p. de Campeche,** logwood. **p. de hule,** rubber tree. **p. de rosa,** tulipwood. Naut. **p. mayor,** mainmast. Naut. **a p. seco,** under bare poles. **de tal p., tal astilla,** a chip off the old block; like father like son. **estar del mismo p.,** to be of the same mind, agree
paloma /pa'loma/ f, dove; pigeon; gentle person; pl Naut. white horses. **p. buchona,** pouter pigeon. **p. mensajera,** carrier pigeon. **p. torcaz,** wood pigeon
palomar /palo'mar/ m, dovecote; pigeon loft
palomero /palo'mero/ (-ra) n pigeon fancier; pigeon dealer
palomino /palo'mino/ m, young pigeon
palomo /pa'lomo/ m, male pigeon; wood pigeon
palotes /pa'lotes/ m pl, drumsticks; pothooks (in writing)
palpabilidad /palpaβili'ðað/ f, palpability
palpable /pal'paβle/ a palpable, tangible
palpación /palpa'θion; palpa'sion/ f, Med. palpation
palpar /pal'par/ vt to palpate, examine by touch; grope, walk by touch; Fig. see clearly

palpitación /palpita'θion; palpita'sion/ f, beating (of a heart); Med. palpitation; convulsive movement
palpitante /palpi'tante/ a palpitating; quivering; beating; (of a question) burning
palpitar /palpi'tar/ vi to beat (heart); throb, palpitate; shudder, move convulsively; Fig. manifest itself (passions, etc.)
palpo /'palpo/ m, palp, feeler
palúdico /pa'luðiko/ a marshy, swampy; malarial
paludismo /palu'ðismo/ m, malaria; paludism
palurdo /pa'lurðo/ **(-da)** a Inf. gross, rude, boorish —n boor
palustre /pa'lustre/ m, mason's trowel —a marshy, swampy
pamela /pa'mela/ f, wide-brimmed straw sailor (woman's hat)
pamema /pa'mema/ f, Inf. unimportant trifle; Inf. caress
pampa /'pampa/ f, pampa, treeless plain
pámpano /'pampano/ m, young vine shoot; vine leaf
pamplina /pam'plina/ f, Inf. nonsense, rubbish
pan /pan/ m, bread; loaf; Cul. piecrust; Fig. food; wheat; gold leaf; pl cereals. **p. ázimo,** unleavened bread. **p. de oro,** gold leaf. **llamar al p. p. y al vino vino,** to call a spade a spade. **venderse como p. bendito,** to sell like hot cakes
pana /'pana/ f, velveteen, velours
panacea /pana'θea; pana'sea/ f, panacea; cure-all
panadería /panaðe'ria/ f, bakery trade or shop; bakery
panadero /pana'ðero/ **(-ra)** n baker. m pl, Spanish dance
panadizo /pana'ðiθo; pana'ðiso/ m, Med. whitlow; Inf. ailing person, crock
panal /pa'nal/ m, honeycomb; wasp's nest
Panamá /pana'ma/ Panama
panameño /pana'meɲo/ **(-ña)** a and n Panamanian
panamericanismo /panamerika'nismo/ m, pan-Americanism
panarra /pa'narra/ m, Inf. simpleton
páncreas /'pankreas/ m, pancreas
pancreático /pankre'atiko/ a pancreatic
panda /'panda/ f, gallery of a cloister. mf Zool. panda
pandémico /pan'demiko/ a pandemic
pandemónium /pande'monium/ m, pandemonium
pandereta /pande'reta/ f, tambourine
pandero /pan'dero/ m, tambourine; Inf. windbag
pandilla /pan'diʎa; pan'diya/ f, league, group; gang (of burglars, etc.); party, crowd, band
pane /'pane/ f, breakdown
panecillo /pane'θiʎo; pane'siyo/ m, dim roll (of bread)
panegírico /pane'hiriko/ a and m, panegyric
panegirista /panehi'rista/ mf panegyrist; eulogizer
panel /pa'nel/ m, panel
panetela /pane'tela/ f, panada
pánfilo /'panfilo/ **(-la)** a sluggish, phlegmatic, slow-moving —n sluggard
panfleto /pan'fleto/ m, pamphlet
paniaguado /pania'guaðo/ m, servant; favorite; protégé
pánico /'paniko/ a and m, panic
panoja /pa'noha/ f, Bot. panicle; Bot. ear, beard, awn
panoli /pa'noli/ a Inf. doltish, stupid
panoplia /pa'noplia/ f, panoply; collection of arms
panorama /pano'rama/ m, panorama; view
panorámico /pano'ramiko/ a panoramic
pantalla /pan'taʎa; pan'taya/ f, lampshade; face screen; movie screen; shade, reflector
pantalón /panta'lon/ m, pant, trouser (gen. pl); knickers. **p. de corte,** striped trousers. **pantalones bombachos,** plus fours
pantano /pan'tano/ m, marsh, swamp; impediment; artificial pool
pantanoso /panta'noso/ a marshy, swampy; Fig. awkward, full of pitfalls
panteísmo /pante'ismo/ m, pantheism
panteísta /pante'ista/ a pantheistic. mf pantheist
panteón /pante'on/ m, pantheon
pantera /pan'tera/ f, panther
pantomima /panto'mima/ f, pantomime; mime

pantoque /pan'toke/ *m*, *Naut*. bilge

pantorrilla /panto'rriʎa; panto'rriya/ *f*, calf (of the leg)

pantuflo /pan'tuflo/ *m*, house slipper

panza /'panθa; 'pansa/ *f*, paunch, stomach; belly (of jugs, etc.). *Inf*. **un cielo de p. de burra,** a dark gray sky

panzudo /pan'θuðo; pan'suðo/ *a* paunchy

pañal /pa'ɲal/ *m*, diaper; shirttail; *pl* long clothes, swaddling clothes; infancy

pañería /paɲe'ria/ *f*, drapery stores; drapery

pañero /pa'ɲero/ (**-ra**) *n* draper

paño /'paɲo/ *m*, woolen material; cloth, fabric; drapery, hanging; tapestry; linen, bandage; tarnish or other mark; *Naut*. canvas; *Sew*. breadth, width (of cloth); panel (in a dress); floor cloth, duster; livid mark on the face; *pl* garments. **p. de lágrimas,** consoler, sympathizer. **p. mortuorio,** pall (on a coffin). **paños menores,** underwear. **p. verde,** gambling table. **al p.,** *Theat*. from the wings, from without. *Inf*. **poner el p. al púlpito,** to hold forth, spread oneself

pañoleta /paɲo'leta/ *f*, kerchief, triangular scarf; fichu

pañuelo /pa'ɲuelo/ *m*, kerchief; handkerchief

papa /'papa/ *m*, pope; *Inf*. papa, daddy. *f*, *Inf*. potato; stupid rumor; nonsense; *pl* pap; *Cul*. sop; food

papá /pa'pa/ *m*, *Inf*. papa, daddy

papada /pa'paða/ *f*, double chin; dewlap

papado /pa'paðo/ *m*, papacy

papagayo /papa'gaio/ *m*, parrot

papamoscas /papa'moskas/ *m*, *Ornith*. flycatcher; *Inf*. simpleton

papanatas /papa'natas/ *m*, *Inf*. simpleton

papar /pa'par/ *vt* to sip, take soft food; *Inf*. eat; neglect, be careless about

paparrucha /papa'rrutʃa/ *f*, *Inf*. stupid rumor; nonsense

papel /pa'pel/ *m*, paper; document; manuscript; *Theat*. role, part; pamphlet; sheet of paper; paper, monograph, essay; guise, role; *Theat*. character. **p. carbón, p. carbónico,** carbon paper. **p. celofán,** cellophane. **p. cuadriculado,** graph paper, cartridge paper. **p. de calcar,** carbon paper; tracing paper. **p. de escribir,** writing paper. **p. de estaño,** tinfoil. **p. de estraza,** brown paper. **p. de fumar,** cigarette paper. **p. de lija,** emery- or sandpaper. **p. de paja de arroz,** rice paper. **p. de seda,** tissue paper. **p. de tornasol,** litmus paper. **p. del estado,** government bonds. **p. higiénico,** toilet paper. **p. moneda,** paper money. **p. pintado,** wallpaper. **p. secante,** blotting paper. **p. sellado,** official stamped paper. **hacer buen (mal) p.,** to do well (badly). **hacer el p. (de),** *Theat*. to act the part (of); feign, pretend

papelear /papele'ar/ *vi* to turn over papers, search among them; *Inf*. cut a dash

papeleo /pape'leo/ *m*, bureaucracy, red tape

papelera /pape'lera/ *f*, mass of papers; desk (for keeping papers)

papelería /papele'ria/ *f*, heap of papers; stationer's shop; stationery

papelero /pape'lero/ (**-ra**) *a* paper, stationery —*n* paper maker; stationer

papeleta /pape'leta/ *f*, slip or scrap of paper

papelista /pape'lista/ *mf* paper maker; stationer; paperhanger

papelucho /pape'lutʃo/ *m*, old or dirty piece of paper; trash, worthless writing; *Inf*. rag (newspaper)

papera /pa'pera/ *f*, mumps

papilla /pa'piʎa; pa'piya/ *f*, pap; guile, wiliness

papillote /papi'ʎote; papi'yote/ *m*, curl-paper

papiro /pa'piro/ *m*, papyrus

papista /pa'pista/ *a* and *mf* papist

papo /'papo/ *m*, dewlap; gizzard (of a bird); goiter. **p. de cardo,** thistledown

paquebote /pake'βote/ *m*, *Naut*. packet; mail boat; liner

paquete /pa'kete/ *m*, packet; parcel; package

paquidermo /paki'ðermo/ *m*, pachyderm

par /par/ *a* equal; alike; corresponding. *m*, pair, couple; team (of oxen, mules); peer (title); rafter (of a roof); *Mech*. torque, couple; *Elec*. cell. *f*, par. **a la p.,** jointly; simultaneously; *Com*. at par. **a pares,** two by

two. **de p. en p.,** wide-open (doors, etc.). **sin p.,** peerless, excellent

para /'para/ *prep* in order to; for; to; for the sake of (e.g. *Lo hice p. ella,* I did it for her sake); enough to (gen. with *bastante,* etc.); in the direction of, toward; about to, on the point of (e.g. *Está p. salir,* He is on the point of going out). Expresses:
1. *Purpose* (e.g. *La educan p. bailarina,* They are bringing her up to be a dancer. *Lo dije p. ver lo que harías,* I said it to (in order to) see what you would do)
2. *Destination* (e.g. *Salió p. Londres,* He left for London)
3. *Use* (e.g. *seda p. medias,* silk for stockings. *un vaso p. flores,* a vase for flowers)
4. *An appointed time* (e.g. *Lo pagaré p. Navidad,* I will pay it at Christmas)
p. con, toward (a person) (e.g. *Ha obrado muy bien p. con mi hermano,* He has behaved very well toward my brother)
p. coneretar, to be exact, to wit
p. que, in order to, so that (e.g. *Lo puse en la mesa p. que lo vieses,* I put it on the table so that you would see it)
¿P. qué? Why? For what reason?
p. siempre, forever. **decir p. sí,** to say to oneself. **sin qué ni p. qué,** without rhyme or reason

parábola /pa'raβola/ *f*, parable; *Geom*. parabola

parabrisas /para'βrisas/ *m*, windshield

paracaídas /paraka'iðas/ *m*, parachute

paracaidista /parakai'ðista/ *mf* parachutist

parachoques /para'tʃokes/ *m*, *Auto*. bumper; buffer (railroad)

paráclito /pa'raklito/ *m*, Paraclete

parada /pa'raða/ *f*, stopping, halting; stop; stoppage, suspension; halt; *Mil*. review; interval, pause; cattle stall; dam; gambling stakes; parry (in fencing); relay (of horses). **p. de coches,** taxi rank. **p. de tranvía,** streetcar stop. **p. discrecional,** request stop (buses, etc.)

paradero /para'ðero/ *m*, railroad station; stopping place; end, conclusion; whereabouts

paradisíaco /paraði'siako/ *a* paradisaical

parado /pa'raðo/ *a* still; indolent, lazy; unoccupied, leisured; silent, reserved; timid; unemployed

paradoja /para'ðoha/ *f*, paradox

paradójico /para'ðohiko/ *a* paradoxical

parador /para'ðor/ *m*, inn, tavern, hostelry

parafina /para'fina/ *f*, paraffin

parafinar /parafi'nar/ *vt* to paraffin

parafrasear /parafrase'ar/ *vt* to paraphrase

paráfrasis /pa'rafrasis/ *f*, paraphrase

paraguas /pa'raguas/ *m*, umbrella

paraguayo /para'guayo/ (**-ya**) *a* and *n* Paraguayan

paragüería /parague'ria/ *f*, umbrella shop

paragüero /para'guero/ (**-ra**) *n* umbrella maker, umbrella seller. *m*, umbrella stand

paraíso /para'iso/ *m*, paradise; garden of Eden; heaven; (*Inf*. *Theat*.) gallery, gods

paraje /pa'rahe/ *m*, place, locality, spot; state, condition

paralela /para'lela/ *f*, *Mil*. parallel; *pl* parallel bars (for gymnastic exercises)

paralelismo /parale'lismo/ *m*, parallelism

paralelo /para'lelo/ *a* parallel; analogous; similar. *m*, parallel, similarity; *Geog*. parallel

paralelogramo /paralelo'gramo/ *m*, parallelogram

parálisis /pa'ralisis/ *f*, paralysis

paralítico /para'litiko/ (**-ca**) *a* and *n* paralytic

paralización /paraliθa'θion; paralisa'sion/ *f*, paralysis; cessation; *Com*. dullness, quietness

paralizar /parali'θar; parali'sar/ *vt* to paralyze; stop

paramento /para'mento/ *m*, ornament; trappings (of a horse); face (of a wall); facing (of a building). **paramentos sacerdotales,** liturgical vestments or ornaments

páramo /'paramo/ *m*, paramo, treeless plain; desert, wilderness

parangón /paraŋ'gon/ *m*, comparison; similarity

parangonar /paraŋgo'nar/ *vt* to compare

paraninfo /para'ninfo/ *m*, *Archit*. paranymph, university hall; best man (weddings); messenger of good

paranoico /para'noiko/ *m,* paranoiac
parapetarse /parape'tarse/ *vr* to shelter behind a parapet; take refuge behind
parapeto /para'peto/ *m,* parapet
parapoco /para'poko/ *mf Inf.* ninny, numskull
parar /pa'rar/ *vi* to stop, halt; end, finish; lodge; come into the hands of; —*vt* stop; detain; prepare; bet, stake; point (hunting dogs); parry (fencing); —*vr* halt; be interrupted **p. mientes en,** to notice; consider. **sin p.,** immediately, at once; without stopping
pararrayos /para'rraios/ *m,* lightning conductor
parasitario, parasítico /parasi'tario, para'sitiko/ *a* parasitic
parásito /pa'rasito/ *m,* parasite; *Fig.* sponger; *pl Radio.* interference —*a* parasitic
parasitología /parasitolo'hia/ *f,* parasitology
parasol /para'sol/ *m,* sunshade; *Bot.* umbel
paratifoidea /paratifoi'ðea/ *f,* paratyphoid
parca /'parka/ *f,* Fate; *Poet.* death. **las Parcas,** the Three Fates
parcela /par'θela; par'sela/ *f,* plot, parcel (of land); atom, particle
parche /'partʃe/ *m, Med.* plaster; *Auto.* patch; drum; drumhead, parchment of drum; patch, mend
parcial /par'θial; par'sial/ *a* partial, incomplete; biased, prejudiced; factional, party; participatory
parcialidad /parθiali'ðað; parsiali'ðað/ *f,* partiality, bias, prejudice; party, faction, group; intimacy, friendship
parco /'parko/ *a* scarce, scanty; temperate, moderate; frugal
¡pardiez! /par'ðieθ par'ðies/ *interj Inf.* By god!
pardo /'parðo/ *a* brown; gray, drab, dun-colored; cloudy, dark; husky (voices). *m,* leopard
pardusco /par'ðusko/ *a* grayish; fawn-colored
parear /pare'ar/ *vt* to pair, match; put in pairs; compare
parecer /pare'θer; pare'ser/ *vi irr* to appear; look, seem; turn up (be found) —*impers* believe, think (e.g. *me parece,* it seems to me, I think, my opinion is); —*vr* look alike, resemble one another. See **conocer**
parecer /pare'θer; pare'ser/ *m,* opinion, belief; appearance, looks
parecido /pare'θiðo; pare'siðo/ *a* (*with bien or mal*) good- or bad-looking. *m,* resemblance
pared /pa'reð/ *f,* wall; partition wall; side, face. **p. maestra,** main wall. **p. medianera,** party wall. **Las paredes oyen,** The walls have ears. *Inf.* **pegado a la p.,** confused, taken aback
pareja /pa'reha/ *f,* pair; dance partner; couple. **p. desparejada,** mismatched pair. **parejas mixtas,** mixed doubles (in tennis). **correr parejas** *or* **correr a las parejas,** to be equal; go together, happen simultaneously; be on a par
parejo /pa'reho/ *a* equal; similar; smooth, flat; even, regular
parentela /paren'tela/ *f,* relatives, kindred; parentage
parentesco /paren'tesko/ *m,* kinship; relationship; affinity; *Inf.* connection, link
paréntesis /pa'rentesis/ *m,* parenthesis; digression. **entre p.,** incidentally
paresa /pa'resa/ *f,* peeress
paria /'paria/ *mf* pariah; outcast
parida /pa'riða/ *a f,* newly delivered of a child
paridad /pari'ðað/ *f,* parity; analogy, similarity
pariente /pa'riente/ **(-ta)** *n* relative, relation; *Inf.* husband (wife)
parihuela /pari'uela/ *f,* wheelbarrow; stretcher
parir /pa'rir/ *vt* to give birth to; *Fig.* bring forth; reveal, publish; —*vi* lay eggs
París /pa'ris/ Paris
parisiense /pari'siense/ *a* and *mf* Parisian
parla /'parla/ *f,* speech; loquaciousness, eloquence; verbiage
parlamentar /parlamen'tar/ *vi* to converse; discuss (contracts, etc.); *Mil.* parley
parlamentario /parlamen'tario/ *a* parliamentarian. *m,* member of parliament
parlamentarismo /parlamenta'rismo/ *m,* parliamentarianism

parlamento /parla'mento/ *m,* legislative assembly; parliament; discourse, speech; *Theat.* long speech; *Mil.* parley
parlanchín /parlan'tʃin/ *a Inf.* talkative, chattering, loquacious
parlar /par'lar/ *vt* and *vi* to speak freely or easily; chatter; reveal, speak indiscreetly; babble (of streams, etc.)
parlero /par'lero/ *a* talkative; gossiping, indiscreet; talking (birds); *Fig.* expressive (eyes, etc.); prattling, babbling (brook, etc.)
parlotear /parlote'ar/ *vi Inf.* to chatter, gossip
parloteo /parlo'teo/ *m,* chattering, gossip
parmesano /parme'sano/ **(-na)** *a* and *n* Parmesan
parnaso /par'naso/ *m,* Parnassus; anthology of verse
paro /'paro/ *m, Inf.* work stoppage; lockout; *Ornith.* tit. **p. forzoso,** unemployment
parodia /pa'roðia/ *f,* parody
parodiar /paro'ðiar/ *vt* to parody
parodista /paro'ðista/ *mf* parodist
parótida /pa'rotiða/ *f,* parotid gland; parotitis, mumps
parotiditis /paroti'ðitis/ *f,* parotitis, mumps
paroxismo /parok'sismo/ *m, Med.* paroxysm; frenzy, ecstasy, fit
parpadear /parpaðe'ar/ *vi* to blink
parpadeo /parpa'ðeo/ *m,* blinking
párpado /'parpaðo/ *m,* eyelid
parque /'parke/ *m,* park; depot, park; paddock, pen. **p. de atracciones,** pleasure ground. **p. de** (*or* **para) automóviles,** car park, parking lot
parquedad /parke'ðað/ *f,* scarcity; moderation, temperance; parsimony, frugality
parra /'parra/ *f,* vine. **hoja de p.,** *Fig.* fig leaf
párrafo /'parrafo/ *m,* paragraph; *Gram.* paragraph sign. **p. aparte,** new paragraph. **echar un p.,** to chat, gossip
parranda /pa'rranda/ *f, Inf.* binge; strolling band of musicians. **ir de p.,** to go on a binge
parricida /parri'θiða; parri'siða/ *mf* parricide (person)
parricidio /parri'θiðio; parri'siðio/ *m,* parricide (act)
parrilla /pa'rriʎa; pa'rriya/ *f, Cul.* griller, broiler; grill, gridiron; *Engin.* grate. *Cul.* **a la p.,** grilled
párroco /'parroko/ *m,* parish priest; parson
parroquia /pa'rrokia/ *f,* parish church; parish; clergy of a parish; clientele, customers
parroquial /parro'kial/ *a* parochial
parroquiano /parro'kiano/ **(-na)** *a* parochial —*n* parishioner; client, customer
parsi /'parsi/ *m,* Parsee; Parseeism
parsimonia /parsi'monia/ *f,* frugality, thrift; prudence, moderation
parsimonioso /parsimo'nioso/ *a* parsimonious
parte /'parte/ *f,* part; share; place; portion; side, faction; *Law.* party; *Theat.* part, role. *m,* communication, message; telegraph or telephone message; (*Mil. Nav.*) communiqué. *f pl,* parts, talents. **p. actora,** *Law.* prosecution. **p. de la oración,** part of speech. **partes litigantes,** *Law.* contending parties. **dar p.,** to notify; (*Mil. Naut.*) report; give a share (in a transaction). **de algún tiempo a esta p.,** for some time past. **de p. de,** in the name of, from. **en p.,** partly. **por todas partes,** on all sides, everywhere. **ser p.** *a or* **ser p. para que,** to contribute to. **tener de su p.** (*a*), to count on the favor of. **la quinta p.,** one-fifth, etc.
partear /parte'ar/ *vt* to assist in childbirth
partera /par'tera/ *f,* midwife
partero /par'tero/ *m,* accoucheur
partición /parti'θion; parti'sion/ *f,* partition, distribution; (*Aer. Naut.*) accommodation
participación /partiθipa'θion; partisipa'sion/ *f,* participation; notice, warning; announcement (of an engagement, etc.); *Com.* share
participante /partiθi'pante; partisi'pante/ *a* and *mf* participant
participar /partiθi'par; partisi'par/ *vi* to participate, take part (in), share; —*vt* inform; announce (an engagement, etc.)
partícipe /par'tiθipe; par'tisipe/ *a* sharing. *mf* participant
participio /parti'θipio; parti'sipio/ *m,* participle

partícula /par'tikula/ f, particle, grain; *Gram.* particle

particular /partiku'lar/ a private; peculiar; special, particular; unusual; individual. *mf* private individual. *m*, matter, subject. **en p.**, especially; privately

particularidad /partikulari'ðað/ f, individuality; specialty; rareness, unusualness; detail, circumstance; intimacy, friendship

particularizar /partikulari'θar; partikulari'sar/ *vt* to detail, particularize; single out, choose; —*vr (with en)* be characterized by

partida /par'tiða/ f, departure; entry, record (of birth, etc.); certificate (of marriage, etc.); *Com.* item; *Com.* lot, allowance; *Mil.* guerrilla; armed band; expedition, excursion; game (of cards, etc.); rubber (at bridge, etc.); *Inf.* conduct, behavior; place, locality; death. *Com.* **p. doble,** double entry. **Las siete Partidas,** code of Spanish laws compiled by Alfonso X (1252–84)

partidario /parti'ðario/ **(-ia)** a partisan —*n* adherent, disciple. *m*, partisan, guerrilla

partidarismo /partiða'rismo/ *m*, partisanship

partido /par'tiðo/ *m*, party, group, faction; profit; *Sports.* match; team; agreement, pact. **p. conservador,** *Polit.* conservative party. **p. obrero** or **p. laborista,** *Polit.* labor party. **buen p.,** *Fig.* good match, catch. **sacar p. de,** to take advantage of, make the most of. **tomar p.,** to enlist; join, become a supporter (of)

partidor /parti'ðor/ *m*, divider, apportioner; cleaver, chopper; hewer

partir /par'tir/ *vt* to divide; split; crack, break; separate; *Math.* divide; —*vi* go, depart; start (from). **p. como el rayo,** be off like a flash —*vr* disagree, become divided; leave, depart

partitura /parti'tura/ f, *Mus.* score

parto /'parto/ *m*, parturition, birth; newborn child; *Fig.* creation, offspring; important event

parturienta /partu'rienta/ a f, parturient

parva /'parβa/ f, light breakfast; threshed or unthreshed grain; heap, mass

parvedad /parβe'ðað/ f, smallness; scarcity; light breakfast (taken on fast days)

parvo /'parβo/ a little, small

párvulo /'parβulo/ **(-la)** *n* child —*a* small; innocent, simple; lowly, humble

pasa /'pasa/ f, raisin; *Naut.* channel; passage, flight (of birds). **p. de Corinto,** currant

pasacalle /pasa'kaʎe; pasa'kaye/ *m*, *Mus.* lively march

pasada /pa'saða/ f, passing, passage; money sufficient to live on; passage, corridor. **dar p.,** to let pass, put up with. *Inf.* **mala p.,** bad turn, dirty trick

pasadera /pasa'ðera/ f, steppingstone

pasadero /pasa'ðero/ a passable, traversable; fair (health); tolerable, passable. *m*, steppingstone

pasadizo /pasa'ðiθo; pasa'ðiso/ *m*, narrow corridor or passage; alley, narrow street; *Naut.* alleyway

pasado /pa'saðo/ *m*, past; *pl* ancestors. **Lo p., p.,** What's past is past. **p. de moda,** out of fashion, unfashionable

pasador /pasa'ðor/ *m*, bolt, fastener; *Mech.* pin, coupler; pin (of brooches, etc.); colander; *Naut.* marlin spike; shirt stud

pasajaretas /pasaha'retas/ *m*, bodkin

pasaje /pa'sahe/ *m*, passing; passage; fare; passage money; *Naut.* complement of passengers; channel, strait; (*Mus. Lit.*) passage; *Mus.* modulation, transition (of voice); voyage; passage; covered way; road

pasajero /pasa'hero/ **(-ra)** a crowded public (thoroughfare); transitory, fugitive; passing; temporary —*n* passenger

pasamanería /pasamane'ria/ f, passementerie work, industry or shop

pasamano /pasa'mano/ *m*, passementerie; banister, handrail; *Naut.* gangway

pasante /pa'sante/ a *Herald.* passant. *m*, student teacher; articled clerk; apprentice; student. **p. de pluma,** law clerk

pasaporte /pasa'porte/ *m*, passport; license, permission. **dar el p.** (**a**), *Inf.* to give the sack (to)

pasar /pa'sar/ *vt* to pass; carry, transport; cross over; send; go beyond, overstep; run through; pierce; up-set; overtake; transfer; suffer, undergo; sieve; study; dry (grapes, etc.); smuggle; surpass; omit; swallow (food); approve; dissemble; transform; spend (time); —*vi* pass; be transferred; be infectious; have enough to live on; cease; last; die; pass away; pass (at cards); be transformed; be current (money); be salable (goods); (*with prep a + infin*) begin to; (*with por*) pass as; have a reputation as; visit; (*with sin*) do without —*impers* happen, occur —*vr* end; go over to another party; forget; go stale or bad; *Fig.* go too far, overstep the mark; permeate. **p. contrato,** to draw up a contract; sign a contract. **p. la voz,** to pass the word along. **p. por alto** (**de**), to omit, overlook. **p. de largo,** to go by without stopping. **pasarse de listo,** to be too clever. **¡No pases cuidado!** Don't worry!

pasarela /pasa'rela/ f, gangplank

pasatiempo /pasa'tiempo/ *m*, pastime, hobby, amusement

pasavante /pasa'βante/ *m*, *Naut.* safe conduct; navicert

pascua /'paskua/ f, Passover; Easter; Christmas; Twelfth Night; Pentecost; *pl* twelve days of Christmas. **P. florida,** Easter Sunday. **dar las pascuas,** to wish a merry Christmas. **¡Felices pascuas!** Merry Christmas!

pascual /pas'kual/ a paschal

pase /'pase/ *m*, pass (with the hands and in football, etc.); safe conduct; free pass; thrust (in fencing)

paseante /pase'ante/ *mf* stroller, promenader, passerby

pasear /pase'ar/ *vt* to take a walk; parade up and down, display; —*vi* take a walk; go for a drive; go for a ride (on horseback, etc.); stroll up and down; —*vr* touch upon lightly, pass over; loaf, be idle; drift; float

paseo /pa'seo/ *m*, walk, stroll; drive; outing, expedition; promenade; boulevard. **p. a caballo,** ride on horseback

pasiega /pa'siega/ f, wet nurse

pasillo /pa'siʎo; pa'siyo/ *m*, gallery; corridor; lobby; railway corridor; *Sew.* basting stitch

pasión /pa'sion/ f, suffering; passivity; passion; desire; *Eccl.* passion. **con p.,** passionately

pasional /pasio'nal/ a passionate; of passion

pasionaria /pasio'naria/ f, passionflower

pasiva /pa'siβa/ f, *Gram.* passive

pasividad /pasiβi'ðað/ f, passivity

pasivo /pa'siβo/ a passive; inactive; *Com.* sleeping (partner); *Gram.* passive. *m*, *Com.* liabilities

pasmar /pas'mar/ *vt* to freeze to death (plants); dumbfound, amaze, stun; chill; —*vr* to be stunned or amazed

pasmo /'pasmo/ *m*, amazement, astonishment; wonder, marvel; *Med.* tetanus, lockjaw

pasmoso /pas'moso/ a astounding, amazing; wonderful

paso /'paso/ a dried (of fruit)

paso /'paso/ *m*, step; pace; passage, passing; way; footstep; progress; advancement; passage (in a book); *Sew.* tacking stitch; occurrence, event; *Theat.* short play; gait, walk; strait, channel; migratory flight (birds); *Mech.* pitch; event or scene from the Passion; armed combat; death; *pl* measures, steps —*adv* softly, in a low voice; gently. **p. a nivel,** level crossing. **p. a p.,** step by step. **p. doble,** quick march; Spanish dance. **p. volante,** (gymnastics) giant stride. **a cada p.,** at every step; often. **al p.,** without stopping; on the way, in passing. **ceder el p.,** to allow to pass. **de p.,** in passing; incidentally. **llevar el p.,** to keep in step. **marcar el p.,** to mark time. **salir al p.** (**a**), to waylay, confront; oppose. **seguir los pasos** (**a**), to follow; spy upon

pasquín /pas'kin/ *m*, **pasquinada** f, pasquinade, lampoon

pasta /'pasta/ f, *Cul.* dough; paste; pastry; piecrust; batter; *Cul.* noodle paste; paper pulp; board (bookbinding). **ser de buena p.,** to be good-natured

pastar /pas'tar/ *vt* to take to pasture; —*vi* graze, pasture

pastel /pas'tel/ *m*, cake; *Art.* pastel; pie; *Inf.* plot, secret understanding; cheating (at cards); *Print.* pie; *Inf.* fat, stocky person

pastelear /pastele'ar/ *vi Inf.* to indulge in shady business (especially in politics)

pastelería /pastele'ria/ *f*, cake bakery; cake shop; confectioner's art; confectionery

pastelero /paste'lero/ **(-ra)** *n* confectioner, pastry cook; *Fig. Inf.* spineless person, jellyfish

pastelillo /paste'liʎo; paste'liyo/ *m*, *Cul.* turnover

pastelista /paste'lista/ *mf* pastelist

pastelón /paste'lon/ *m*, meat or game pie

pasteurización /pasteuriθa'θion; pasteurisa'sion/ *f*, pasteurization

pasteurizar /pasteuri'θar; pasteuri'sar/ *vt* to pasteurize

pastilla /pas'tiʎa; pas'tiya/ *f*, tablet, cake; lozenge; pastille, drop; tread (of a tire)

pasto /'pasto/ *m*, grazing land, pasture; fodder; *Fig.* fuel, food; spiritual food. **a p.**, in plenty, abundantly. **de p.**, of daily use

pastor /pas'tor/ **(-ra)** *n* shepherd. *m*, *Eccl.* pastor

pastoral /pasto'ral/ *a* rustic, country; *Eccl.* pastoral, *f*, pastoral poem; *Eccl.* pastoral letter

pastorear /pastore'ar/ *vt* to graze, put to grass; *Eccl.* have charge of souls

pastorela /pasto'rela/ *f*, pastoral

pastoreo /pasto'reo/ *m*, pasturage, grazing

pastoría /pasto'ria/ *f*, pastorate

pastoril /pasto'ril/ *a* shepherd, pastoral

pastoso /pas'toso/ *a* doughy; mealy; pasty; mellow

pata /'pata/ *f*, paw and leg (animals); foot (of table, etc.); duck; *Inf.* leg. **p. de gallo**, blunder; crow's-foot, wrinkle. **meter la p.**, to interfere, put one's foot in it. *Inf.* **tener mala p.**, to be unlucky

patada /pa'taða/ *f*, kick, stamp; *Inf.* step, pace

patagón /pata'gon/ **(-ona)** *a* and *n* Patagonian

patalear /patale'ar/ *vi* to stamp (with the feet)

pataleo /pata'leo/ *m*, kicking; stamping

pataleta /pata'leta/ *f*, *Inf.* convulsion; feigned hysterics

patán /pa'tan/ *m*, *Inf.* yokel; boor, churl

patanería /patane'ria/ *f*, *Inf.* boorishness, churlishness

patarata /pata'rata/ *f*, trash, useless thing; extravagant courtesy

patata /pa'tata/ *f*, potato

patatal, patatar /pata'tal, pata'tar/ *m*, potato patch

patatús /pata'tus/ *m*, *Inf.* petty worry; mishap; *Med.* stroke, fit

patear /pate'ar/ *vt Inf.* to stamp; *Fig.* walk on, treat badly; —*vi Inf.* stamp the feet; be furiously angry; (*Golf*) putt

patena /pa'tena/ *f*, engraved medal worn by country women; *Eccl.* paten

patentar /paten'tar/ *vt* to issue a patent; take out a patent, patent

patente /pa'tente/ *a* obvious, patent; *f*, patent; warrant, commission; letters patent. **p. de invención**, patent. **p. de sanidad**, clean bill of health

patentizar /patenti'θar; patenti'sar/ *vt* to make evident

paternidad /paterni'ðað/ *f*, paternity

paterno /pa'terno/ *a* paternal

patético /pa'tetiko/ *a* pitiable; pathetic, moving

patiabierto /patia'βierto/ *a Inf.* knock-kneed

patibulario /patiβu'lario/ *a* heartrending, harrowing

patíbulo /pa'tiβulo/ *m*, scaffold

paticojo /pati'koho/ *a Inf.* lame; wobbly; unsteady

patilla /pa'tiʎa; pa'tiya/ *f*, side whisker (gen. *pl*); *pl* old Nick, the Devil

patín /pa'tin/ *m*, skate; runner (of a sled); (*Aer.* and of vehicles) skid; *Mech.* shoe. **p. del diablo**, scooter. **p. de ruedas**, roller skate

patinador /patina'ðor/ **(-ra)** *n* skater

patinaje /pati'nahe/ *m*, skating; skidding (of planes and vehicles)

patinar /pati'nar/ *vi* to skate; slip, lose one's footing; skid (vehicles and planes)

patinazo /pati'naθo; pati'naso/ *m*, skid (of a vehicle)

patinete /pati'nete/ *m*, child's scooter

patio /'patio/ *m*, courtyard; *Theat.* pit

patitieso /pati'tieso/ *a Inf.* paralyzed in the hands or feet; open-mouthed, amazed; stiff, unbending, proud

patituerto /pati'tuerto/ *a* crooked-legged; pigeon-toed; *Inf.* lopsided

patizambo /pati'θambo; pati'sambo/ *a* knock-kneed

pato /'pato/ *m*, duck; *Inf.* **pagar el p.**, to be a scapegoat

patógeno /pa'toheno/ *a* pathogenic

patojo /pa'toho/ *a* waddling

patología /patolo'hia/ *f*, pathology

patológico /pato'lohiko/ *a* pathological

patólogo /pa'tologo/ *m*, pathologist

patoso /pa'toso/ *a Fig.* heavy, pedestrian, tedious

patraña /pa'traɲa/ *f*, nonsense, rubbish, fairy tale

patria /'patria/ *f*, motherland, native country; native place. **p. chica**, native region

patriarca /pa'triarka/ *m*, patriarch

patriarcado /patriar'kaðo/ *m*, patriarchy

patriarcal /patriar'kal/ *a* patriarchal

patricio /pa'triθio; pa'trisio/ **(-ia)** *a* and *n* patrician

patrimonio /patri'monio/ *m*, patrimony

patriota /pa'triota/ *mf* patriot

patriótico /pa'triotiko/ *a* patriotic

patriotismo /patrio'tismo/ *m*, patriotism

patrocinar /patroθi'nar; patrosi'nar/ *vt* to protect, defend; favor, sponsor; patronize

patrocinio /patro'θinio; patro'sinio/ *m*, protection, defense; sponsorship; patronage

patrón /pa'tron/ **(-ona)** *n* patron, sponsor; patron saint; landlord; employer. *m*, coxswain; *Naut.* master, skipper; pattern, model; standard. **p. de oro**, gold standard

patronato /patro'nato/ *m*, patronage, protection; employers' association; charitable foundation. **p. de turismo**, tourist bureau

patronímico /patro'nimiko/ *a* and *m*, patronymic

patrono /pa'trono/ **(-na)** *n* protector; sponsor; patron; patron saint; employer

patrulla /pa'truʎa; pa'truya/ *f*, *Mil.* patrol; group, band

patrullar /patru'ʎar; patru'yar/ *vi Mil.* patrol; march about

patudo /pa'tuðo/ *a Inf.* large-footed

paulatinamente /paulatina'mente/ *adv* slowly, by degrees

pauperismo /paupe'rismo/ *m*, destitution, pauperism

paupérrimo /pau'perrimo/ *a superl* **pobre** exceedingly poor

pausa /'pausa/ *f*, pause, interruption; delay; *Mus.* rest; *Mus.* pause. **a pausas**, intermittently

pausado /pau'saðo/ *a* deliberate, slow —*adv* slowly, deliberately

pausar /pau'sar/ *vi* to pause

pauta /'pauta/ *f*, standard, norm, design; *Fig.* guide, model

pavada /pa'βaða/ *f*, flock of turkeys

pavana /pa'βana/ *f*, pavane, stately dance

pavero /pa'βero/ **(-ra)** *a* vain; strutting —*n* turkey keeper or vendor. *m*, broad-brimmed Andalusian hat

pavimentación /paβimenta'θion; paβimenta'sion/ *f*, paving, flagging

pavimento /paβi'mento/ *m*, pavement

pavo /'paβo/ **(-va)** *n* *Ornith.* turkey. **p. real**, peacock. *Inf.* **pelar la pava**, to serenade, court

pavón /pa'βon/ *m*, *Ornith.* peacock; peacock butterfly; preservative paint (for steel, etc.); gunmetal

pavonear /paβone'ar/ *vi* to strut, peacock (also *vr*); *Inf.* hoodwink, dazzle

pavor /pa'βor/ *m*, terror, panic

pavoroso /paβo'roso/ *a* fearful, awesome, dreadful

payasada /paia'saða/ *f*, clowning, practical joke; clown's patter

payaso /pa'iaso/ *m*, clown

paz /paθ/ *f*, peace; harmony, concord; peaceableness. **¡P. sea en esta casa!** Peace be upon this house! (salutation). **estar en p.**, to be at peace; be quits, be even. **poner** (*or* **meter**) **p.**, to make peace (between dissentients). **venir de p.**, to come with peaceful intentions

pazguato /paθ'guato; pas'guato/ **(-ta)** *n* simpleton, booby

pazpuerca /paθ'puerka; pas'puerka/ *f*, slattern
pe /pe/ *f*, name of the letter P. *Inf.* **de pe a pa**, from A to Z, from beginning to end
peaje /pe'ahe/ *m*, toll (on bridges, roads, etc.)
peatón /pea'ton/ *m*, pedestrian; walker; country postman
pebete /pe'βete/ *m*, joss stick; fuse; *Inf.* stench
peca /'peka/ *f*, mole, freckle
pecado /pe'kaðo/ *m*, sin; fault; excess; defect; *Inf.* the Devil. **p. capital**, mortal sin
pecador /peka'ðor/ *a* sinful. *m*, sinner. ¡**P. de mí!** Poor me!
pecadora /peka'ðora/ *f*, sinner; *Inf.* prostitute
pecaminoso /pekami'noso/ *a* sinful
pecar /pe'kar/ *vi* to sin; trespass, transgress; (*with de*) be too... (*e.g. El libro peca de largo*, The book is too long)
peceño /pe'θeɲo; pe'seɲo/ *a* pitch-black (horses, etc.); tasting of pitch
pecera /pe'θera; pe'sera/ *f*, goldfish bowl; aquarium
pechera /pe'tʃera/ *f*, shirt front; chest protector; bib, tucker; shirt frill; *Inf.* bosom
pecho /'petʃo/ *m*, *Anat.* chest; breast; bosom; mind, conscience; courage, endurance; *Mus.* quality (of voice); incline, slope. **p. arriba**, uphill. **abrir su p. a** (*or* **con**), to unbosom oneself to. **dar el p. (a)**, to suckle. **de pechos**, leaning on. **echar el p. al agua,** *Fig.* to embark courageously upon. **tomar a pechos (una cosa)**, to take (a thing) very seriously; take to heart
pechuga /pe'tʃuga/ *f*, breast (of a bird); *Inf.* breast, bosom; slope, incline
pecio /'peθio; 'pesio/ *m*, flotsam
pécora /'pekora/ *f*, sheep, head of sheep; wily woman, serpent
pecoso /pe'koso/ *a* freckled; spotted (with warts)
pecuario /pe'kuario/ *a Agr.* stock; cattle
peculiar /peku'liar/ *a* peculiar, individual
peculiaridad /pekuliari'ðað/ *f*, peculiarity
peculio /pe'kulio/ *m*, private money or property
pecunia /pe'kunia/ *f*, *Inf.* cash
pecuniario /peku'niario/ *a* pecuniary
pedagogía /peðago'hia/ *f*, education, pedagogy
pedagógico /peða'gohiko/ *a* educational, pedagogic
pedagogo /peða'gogo/ *m*, schoolmaster; educationalist; *Fig.* mentor
pedal /pe'ðal/ *m*, *Mech.* treadle, lever, *Mus.* pedal; *Mus.* sustained harmony. *Auto.* **p. de embrague,** clutch pedal
pedalear /peðale'ar/ *vi* to pedal
pedante /pe'ðante/ *a* pedantic. *mf* pedant
pedantería /peðante'ria/ *f*, pedantry
pedazo /pe'ðaθo; pe'ðaso/ *m*, bit, piece; lump; fragment, portion. *Inf.* **p. del alma, p. del corazón, p. de las entrañas**, loved one, dear one. **a pedazos** *or* **en pedazos**, in pieces, in bits. **hacer pedazos**, to break into fragments
pedernal /peðer'nal/ *m*, flint; anything very hard
pedestal /peðes'tal/ *m*, pedestal; base; stand; *Fig.* foundation
pedestre /pe'ðestre/ *a* pedestrian; dull, uninspired
pediatra /pe'ðiatra/ *mf* pediatrician
pedicuro /peði'kuro/ *m*, chiropodist
pedido /pe'ðiðo/ *m*, *Com.* order; request, petition
pedigüeño /peði'gueɲo/ *a* importunate, insistent
pedimento /peði'mento/ *m*, petition, demand; *Law.* claim; *Law.* motion
pedir /pe'ðir/ *vt irr* to ask, request; *Com.* order; demand; necessitate; desire; ask in marriage. **p. en juicio,** *Law.* to bring an action against. *Inf.* **pedírselo (a uno) el cuerpo**, to desire (something) ardently. **a p. de boca,** according to one's wish —*Pres. Part.* **pidiendo.** *Pres. Indic.* **pido, pides, pide, piden.** *Preterite* **pidió, pidieron.** *Pres. Subjunc.* **pida**, etc —*Imperf. Subjunc.* **pidiese**, etc.
pedo /'peðo/ *m*, fart
pedómetro /pe'ðometro/ *m*, pedometer
pedrada /pe'ðraða/ *f*, casting a stone; blow with a stone; innuendo
pedrea /pe'ðrea/ *f*, stone throwing; fight with stones; shower of hailstones

pedregal /peðre'gal/ *m*, stony ground
pedregoso /peðre'goso/ *a* stony
pedrera /pe'ðrera/ *f*, stone quarry
pedrería /peðre'ria/ *f*, precious stones
pedrisco /pe'ðrisko/ *m*, hailstone; shower of stones; pile of stones
pedrusco /pe'ðrusko/ *m*, *Inf.* rough, unpolished stone
pega /'pega/ *f*, sticking; cementing; joining; pitch; varnish; *Inf.* joke; beating; *Ornith.* magpie
pegadizo /pega'ðiθo; pega'ðiso/ *a* sticky, gummy, adhesive; detachable, removable; *Fig.* clinging, importunate (of people)
pegado /pe'gaðo/ *m*, sticking plaster; patch
pegajoso /pega'hoso/ *a* sticky, gluey; viscid; contagious, catching; *Inf.* oily, unctuous; *Fig. Inf.* cadging, sponging
pegar /pe'gar/ *vt* to stick; cement; join, fasten; press (against); infect with (diseases); hit, strike; give a shout, jump, etc.); patch; —*vi* spread, catch (fire, etc.); *Fig.* make an impression, have influence; be opportune; —*vr Cul.* stick, burn; meddle; become enthusiastic about; take root in the mind. **p. un tiro (a)**, to shoot
Pegaso /pe'gaso/ *m*, Pegasus
pegote /pe'gote/ *m*, sticking plaster; *Fig. Inf.* sponger; *Inf.* patch
peinado /pei'naðo/ *m*, hairdressing or style; headdress —*a Inf.* effeminate, overelegant (men); overcareful (style). **un p. al agua,** a finger wave
peinador /peina'ðor/ **(-ra)** *m*, peignoir, dressing gown —*n* hairdresser
peinadura /peina'ðura/ *f*, brushing or combing of hair; *pl* hair combings
peinar /pei'nar/ *vt* to comb, dress the hair; card (wool); cut away (rock)
peine /'peine/ *m*, comb; *Mech.* hackle, reed; instep; *Inf.* crafty person
peinería /peine'ria/ *f*, comb factory or shop
peinero /pei'nero/ *m*, comb manufacturer or seller
peineta /pei'neta/ *f*, high comb (for mantillas, etc.)
peladilla /pela'ðiʎa; pela'ðiya/ *f*, sugared almond; smooth, small pebble
pelado /pe'laðo/ *a* plucked; bare, unadorned; needy, poor; hairless; skinned; peeled; without shell; treeless
peladura /pela'ðura/ *f*, peeling; shelling; skinning; plucking (feathers)
pelafustán /pelafus'tan/ *m*, *Inf.* good-for-nothing, scamp
pelagatos /pela'gatos/ *m*, *Inf.* miserable wretch
pelágico /pe'lahiko/ *a* pelagian, oceanic
pelagra /pe'lagra/ *f*, pellagra
pelaje /pe'lahe/ *m*, fur, wool
pelamesa /pela'mesa/ *f*, brawl, fight; lock, tuft (of hair)
pelapatatas /pelapa'tatas/ *m*, potato peeler
pelar /pe'lar/ *vt* to tear out or cut the hair; pluck; skin; peel; shell; rob, fleece; —*vr* lose one's hair
peldaño /pel'daɲo/ *m*, step, stair, tread, rung
pelea /pe'lea/ *f*, battle; quarrel, dispute; fight (among animals); effort, exertion; *Fig.* struggle
peleador /pelea'ðor/ *a* fighting; quarrelsome, aggressive
pelear /pele'ar/ *vi* to fight; quarrel; struggle, strive. **p. como perro y gato**, to fight like cat and mouse —*vr* come to blows; fall out, become enemies
pelechar /pele'tʃar/ *vi* to get a new coat (of animals); grow new feathers (of birds); *Inf.* prosper, flourish; grow well
pelele /pe'lele/ *m*, effigy; *Inf.* nincompoop
peletería /pelete'ria/ *f*, furrier; fur shop
peletero /pele'tero/ *m*, furrier; skinner
peliagudo /pelia'guðo/ *a* long-haired (animals); *Inf.* complicated, difficult; wily, downy
pelícano /pe'likano/ *m*, pelican
pelicorto /peli'korto/ *a* short-haired
película /pe'likula/ *f*, film. **p. fotográfica,** roll of film. **p. sonora,** sound film
peligrar /peli'grar/ *vi* to be in danger
peligro /pe'ligro/ *m*, danger, peril. **correr p.** *or* **estar en p.,** to be in danger

peligroso /peli'groso/ *a* dangerous, perilous, risky
pelilargo /peli'largo/ *a* long-haired
pelirrojo /peli'rroho/ *a* red-haired
pelleja /pe'ʎeha; pe'yeha/ *f*, hide, skin (of animals); sheepskin
pellejo /pe'ʎeho; pe'yeho/ *m*, hide; pelt; skin; wineskin; *Inf.* drunkard; peel, skin (of fruit)
pelliza /pe'ʎiθa; pe'yisa/ *f*, fur or fur-trimmed coat
pellizcar /peʎiθ'kar; peyis'kar/ *vt* to pinch, tweak, nip; pilfer
pellizco /pe'ʎiθko; pe'yisko/ *m*, pinch, nip, tweak; pilfering, pinching; bit, pinch
pelmazo /pel'maθo; pel'maso/ *m*, squashed mass; *Inf.* idler, sluggard; *Inf.* bore
pelo /'pelo/ *m*, hair; down (on birds and fruit); fiber, filament; hair trigger (firearms); hairspring (watches); kiss (in billiards); nap (of cloth), grain (of wood); flaw (in gems); raw silk. **p. de camello,** camel's hair. **a p.,** in the nude; without a hat; opportunely. **en p.,** bareback (of horses). **hacerse el p.,** to do one's hair; have one's hair cut. *Inf.* **no tener p. de tonto,** to be smart, clever. *Inf.* **no tener pelos en la lengua,** to be outspoken. *Inf.* **tomar el p.** (**a),** to pull a person's leg. **venir a p.,** to be apposite; come opportunely
pelón /pe'lon/ *a* hairless; *Fig.* broke, fleeced
pelonería /pelone'ria/ *f*, *Inf.* poverty, misery
peloponense /pelopo'nense/ *a* and *mf* Peloponnesian
pelota /pe'lota/ *f*, ball; ball game. **p. base,** baseball. **p. vasca,** pelota. **en p.,** stark naked
pelotari /pelo'tari/ *m*, professional pelota player
pelotazo /pelo'taθo; pelo'taso/ *m*, knock or blow with a ball
pelotear /pelote'ar/ *vt* to audit accounts; —*vi* play ball; throw, cast; quarrel; argue
pelotera /pelo'tera/ *f*, *Inf.* brawl
pelotón /pelo'ton/ *m*, big ball; lump of hair; crowd, multitude; *Mil.* platoon. **p. de ejecución,** firing squad
peltre /'peltre/ *m*, pewter
peluca /pe'luka/ *f*, wig; periwig; *Inf.* scolding
peludo /pe'luðo/ *a* hairy. *m*, long-haired rug
peluquería /peluke'ria/ *f*, hairdressing establishment; hairdressing trade
peluquero /pelu'kero/ **(-ra)** *n* hairdresser; barber
peluquín /pelu'kin/ *m*, small wig
pelusa /pe'lusa/ *f*, down, soft hair; fluff, nap
pena /'pena/ *f*, punishment, penalty; grief; pain, suffering; difficulty, trouble; mourning veil; hardship; anxiety; embarrassment; tail feather. **p. capital** *or* **p. de la vida,** capital punishment. **a duras penas,** with great difficulty. **so p. de,** under penalty of. **valer** (*or* **merecer**) **la p.,** to be worth while
penable /pe'naβle/ *a* punishable
penacho /pe'natʃo/ *m*, topknot, crest (of birds); plume, panache; *Inf.* pride, arrogance
penado /pe'naðo/ **(-da)** *a* difficult, laborious; painful, troubled, afflicted —*n* convict
penal /pe'nal/ *a* penal; punitive
penalidad /penali'ðað/ *f*, trouble, labor, difficulty; *Law.* penalty
penar /pe'nar/ *vt* to penalize; punish; —*vi* suffer; undergo purgatorial pains; —*vr* suffer anguish. **p. por,** to long for
penca /'penka/ *f*, *Bot.* fleshy leaf; lash, strap, cat-o'-nine-tails
penco /'penko/ *m*, *Inf.* wretched nag
pendejo /pen'deho/ *m*, pubic hair; *Inf.* coward; jerk
pendencia /pen'denθia; pen'densia/ *f*, fight; quarrel
pendenciar /penden'θiar; penden'siar/ *vi* to fight; quarrel
pendenciero /penden'θiero; penden'siero/ *a* quarrelsome, aggressive
pender /pen'der/ *vi* to hang; depend; be pending
pendiente /pen'diente/ *a* pending; hanging; *Com.* outstanding. *m*, earring; pendant. *f*, slope, incline; gradient
péndola /'pendola/ *f*, feather, plume; quill pen; pendulum (of a clock)
pendolista /pendo'lista/ *mf* calligrapher
pendón /pen'don/ *m*, pennon, banner; *Bot.* shoot; *Inf.* lanky, slatternly woman; *pl* reins

péndulo /'pendulo/ *a* pendulous, hanging. *m*, pendulum
pene /'pene/ *m*, penis
penetrabilidad /penetraβili'ðað/ *f*, penetrability
penetración /penetra'θion; penetra'sion/ *f*, penetration; understanding, perspicuity; sagacity, shrewdness
penetrador /penetra'ðor/ *a* penetrating, perspicacious; sagacious, acute
penetrante /pene'trante/ *a* penetrating; deep; piercing (of sounds); acute, shrewd
penetrar /pene'trar/ *vt* to penetrate; permeate; master, comprehend; (*with en*) enter
penetrativo /penetra'tiβo/ *a* piercing
penicilina /peniθi'lina; penisi'lina/ *f*, penicillin
península /pe'ninsula/ *f*, peninsula. **la P.** the Iberian Peninsula
Península Ibérica, la /pe'ninsula i'βerika, la/ *m* the Iberian Peninsula
penique /pe'nike/ *m*, penny
penitencia /peni'tenθia; peni'tensia/ *f*, penitence, repentance; penance
penitencial /peniten'θial; peniten'sial/ *a* penitential
penitenciaría /penitenθia'ria; penitensia'ria/ *f*, penitentiary
penitenciario /peniten'θiario; peniten'siario/ *a* penitentiary
penitente /peni'tente/ *a* penitent, repentant. *mf* penitent
penoso /pe'noso/ *a* laborious, difficult; grievous; painful; troublesome; *Inf.* foppish
pensado /pen'saðo/ *a* premeditated, deliberate. **de p.,** intentionally. **mal p.,** malicious, evil-minded
pensador /pensa'ðor/ *a* thinking; pensive. *m*, thinker
pensamiento /pensa'miento/ *m*, mind; thought; idea; suspicion, doubt; heartsease pansy; maxim; intention, project
pensar /pen'sar/ *vt irr* to think; purpose, intend; (*with en, sobre*) reflect upon; think about; —*vt* feed (animals). **p. entre sí, p. para consigo** *or* **p. para sí,** to think to oneself. See **acertar**
pensativo /pensa'tiβo/ *a* reflective, pensive
pensil /pen'sil/ *a* hanging. *m*, hanging garden; delightful garden
pensión /pen'sion/ *f*, pension, allowance; boarding house, private hotel; scholarship grant; cost of board; trouble, drudgery
pensionado /pensio'naðo/ **(-da)** *a* pensioned; retired —*n* scholarship holder. *m*, boarding school
pensionar /pensio'nar/ *vt* to pension, grant a pension to; charge a pension on
pensionista /pensio'nista/ *mf* pensioner; boarder
pentágono /pen'tagono/ *m*, pentagon —*a* pentagonal
pentagrama /penta'grama/ *or* **pentágrama** *m*, *Mus.* pentagram, stave
pentámetro /pen'tametro/ *m*, pentameter
Pentateuco /penta'teuko/ *m*, Pentateuch
Pentecostés /pentekos'tes/ *m*, Pentecost, Whitsuntide
penúltimo /pe'nultimo/ *a* next to the last, penultimate
penuria /pe'nuria/ *f*, scarcity; want, penury
peña /'peɲa/ *f*, crag, rock; boulder; group of friends; club. **ser una p.,** to be stony-hearted
peñasco /pe'ɲasko/ *m*, craggy peak
peñascoso /peɲas'koso/ *a* craggy, rocky
peñón /pe'ɲon/ *m*, rock; cliff; peak
peón /pe'on/ *m*, pedestrian; laborer; *South America* farmhand; top (toy); piece (chess, checkers); *Mech.* axle; infantryman. **p. caminero,** road mender. **p. de ajedrez,** pawn (in chess)
peonada /peo'naða/ *f*, day's manual labor; gang of laborers
peonía /peo'nia/ *f*, peony
peonza /pe'onθa; pe'onsa/ *f*, top; teetotum
peor /pe'or/ *a compar* **malo** worse —*adv compar* **mal,** worse —*a superl* **el** (**la, lo**) **peor; los** (**las**) **peores,** the worst. **p. que p.,** worse and worse. **tanto p.,** so much the worse
pepino /pe'pino/ *m*, cucumber plant; cucumber; *Fig.* pin, straw

pepita /pe'pita/ *f, Mineral.* nugget; pip, seed (of fruit)

peplo /'peplo/ *m,* Greek tunic, peplum

péptico /'peptiko/ *a* peptic

pequeñez /peke'neθ; peke'nes/ *f,* littleness, smallness; pettiness; childhood; infancy; trifle, insignificant thing; meanness, baseness

pequeño /pe'keɲo/ *a* little, small; petty; very young; short, brief; humble, lowly

pera /'pera/ *f,* pear; goatee; *Fig.* plum, sinecure

peral /pe'ral/ *m,* pear tree; pearwood

perca /'perka/ *f, Ichth.* perch

percal /per'kal/ *m,* percale, calico

percalina /perka'lina/ *f,* percaline, binding cloth

percance /per'kanθe; per'kanse/ *m,* perquisite, attribute (gen. *pl*); disaster, mischance

percebe /per'θeβe; per'seβe/ *m,* (gen. *pl*) goose barnacle

percentaje /perθen'tahe; persen'tahe/ *m,* percentage

percepción /perθep'θion; persep'sion/ *f,* perception; idea, conception

perceptible /perθep'tiβle; persep'tiβle/ *a* perceptible

perceptivo /perθep'tiβo; persep'tiβo/ *a* perceptive

perceptor /perθep'tor; persep'tor/ **(-ra)** *a* perceptive —*n* observer

percha /'pertʃa/ *f,* stake, pole; coat hanger; perch (for birds); rack (for hay); hall stand, coat and hat stand, coatrack

perchero /per'tʃero/ *m,* hall stand; clothes rack; row of perches (for fowl, etc.)

percibir /perθi'βir; persi'βir/ *vt* to collect, draw, receive; perceive; understand, grasp

percibo /per'θiβo; per'siβo/ *m,* perceiving; collecting, drawing, receiving

percolador /perkola'ðor/ *m,* percolator (coffee)

percusión /perku'sion/ *f,* percussion; shock, vibration

percusor /perku'sor/ *m,* hammer (of a firearm)

percutir /perku'tir/ *vt* to percuss, strike

perdedor /perðe'ðor/ **(-ra)** *a* losing —*n* loser

perder /per'ðer/ *vt* to lose; throw away, squander; spoil, destroy; —*vi* fade (of colors); —*vr* lose one's way, be lost; be confused or perplexed; be shipwrecked; take to vice, become dissolute; be spoiled or destroyed; disappear; love madly. **p. la chaveta (por),** to go out of one's head (for), be wild (about). **p. la ocasión,** to let the chance slip. **p. los estribos,** to lose patience. **p. terreno,** to lose ground. **perderse de vista,** to be lost to sight. **echarse a p.,** to spoil, be damaged. See **entender**

perdición /perði'θion; perði'sion/ *f,* loss; perdition, ruin; damnation; depravity, viciousness

pérdida /'perðiða/ *f,* loss; waste. **p. cuantiosa,** heavy losses

perdidamente /perðiða'mente/ *adv* ardently, desperately; uselessly

perdigón /perði'gon/ *m,* young partridge; decoy partridge; hailstone, pellet, shot

perdigonada /perðigo'naða/ *f,* volley of hailstone; hailstone wound

perdiguero /perði'gero/ **(-ra)** *n* game dealer; setter, retriever

perdiz /per'ðiθ; per'ðis/ *f,* partridge. **p. blanca,** ptarmigan

perdón /per'ðon/ *m,* pardon, forgiveness; remission. **con p.,** with your permission; excuse me

perdonable /perðo'naβle/ *a* pardonable, excusable

perdonar /perðo'nar/ *vt* to pardon, forgive; remit, excuse; exempt; waste, lose; give up (a privilege)

perdonavidas /perðona'βiðas/ *m, Inf.* bully, braggart

perdulario /perðu'lario/ *a* careless, negligent; slovenly; vicious, depraved

perdurable /perðu'raβle/ *a* perpetual, everlasting; enduring, lasting

perdurar /perðu'rar/ *vi* to last, endure

perecedero /pereθe'ðero; perese'ðero/ *a* brief, fugitive, transient; perishable. *m, Inf.* poverty, want

perecer /pere'θer; pere'ser/ *vi irr* to end, finish; perish, die; suffer (damage, grief, etc.); be destitute; —*vr* (*with por*) long for, crave; desire ardently. See **conocer**

peregrinación /peregrina'θion; peregrina'sion/ *f,* journey, peregrination; pilgrimage

peregrinamente /peregrina'mente/ *adv* rarely, not often; beautifully, perfectly

peregrinar /peregri'nar/ *vi* to journey, travel; make a pilgrimage

peregrino /pere'grino/ **(-na)** *a* and *n* pilgrim —*a* migratory (birds); rare, unusual; extraordinary, strange; beautiful, perfect

perejil /pere'hil/ *m,* parsley; *Inf.* ornament or apparel (gen. *pl*); *pl* honors, titles

perengano /pereŋ'gano/ **(-na)** *n* so-and-so, such a one

perenne /pe'renne/ *a* incessant, constant; *Bot.* perennial

perennidad /perenni'ðað/ *f,* perpetuity

perentoriedad /perentorie'ðað/ *f,* peremptoriness; urgency

perentorio /peren'torio/ *a* peremptory; conclusive, decisive; urgent, pressing

pereza /pe'reθa; pe'resa/ *f,* laziness; languor, inertia; slowness, deliberateness

perezoso /pere'θoso; pere'soso/ *a* lazy; languid; slothful; slow, deliberate. *m, Zool.* sloth

perfección /perfek'θion; perfek'sion/ *f,* perfection; perfecting, perfect thing, virtue, grace

perfeccionamiento /perfekθiona'miento; perfeksiona'miento/ *m,* perfecting; progress, improvement

perfeccionar /perfekθio'nar; perfeksio'nar/ *vt* to perfect; complete

perfectamente /perfekta'mente/ *adv* perfectly; quite, entirely

perfecto /per'fekto/ *a* perfect; excellent, very good; complete; whole; *Gram.* perfect

perfidia /per'fiðia/ *f,* perfidy, treachery

pérfido /'perfiðo/ *a* perfidious, treacherous

perfil /per'fil/ *m,* ornament, decoration; outline, contour; profile; section (of metal); fine stroke (of letters); *pl* finishing touches; politeness, attention, courtesy. **de p.,** in profile; sideways

perfilado /perfi'laðo/ *a* long, elongated (of faces, etc.)

perfilar /perfi'lar/ *vt* to draw in profile; outline; —*vr* place oneself sideways, show one's profile; *Inf.* dress up, titivate

perforación /perfora'θion; perfora'sion/ *f,* perforation, boring; hole

perforador /perfora'ðor/ *a* perforating, boring. *m, Mech.* drill

perforar /perfo'rar/ *vt* to perforate, pierce; bore, drill, make a hole in

perfumador /perfuma'ðor/ **(-ra)** *a* perfuming —*n* perfumer. *m,* perfume burner

perfumar /perfu'mar/ *vt* to perfume; —*vi* give off perfume

perfume /per'fume/ *m,* perfume; scent, fragrance

perfumería /perfume'ria/ *f,* scent factory; perfumery; perfume shop

perfumista /perfu'mista/ *mf* perfumer

perfunctorio /perfunk'torio/ *a* perfunctory

pergamino /perga'mino/ *m,* parchment, vellum; document; diploma; *pl* aristocratic descent

pericardio /peri'karðio/ *m,* pericardium

pericia /pe'riθia; pe'risia/ *f,* expertness; skilled workmanship

pericial /peri'θial; peri'sial/ *a* expert, skillful

perico /pe'riko/ *m,* parakeet

periferia /peri'feria/ *f,* periphery

periférico /peri'feriko/ *a* peripheral

perifollos /peri'foʎos; peri'foyos/ *m pl, Inf.* frills, flounces, finery

perifrástico /peri'frastiko/ *a* periphrastic

perilla /pe'riʎa; pe'riya/ *f,* pear-shaped ornament; goatee; imperial. **p. de la oreja,** lobe of the ear. **venir de p.,** to be most opportune

perillán /peri'ʎan; peri'yan/ *m, Inf.* rascal, rogue

perímetro /pe'rimetro/ *m,* perimeter; precincts

perínclito /pe'rinklito/ *a* distinguished, illustrious; heroic

perineo /peri'neo/ *m,* perineum

perinola /peri'nola/ *f,* top, teetotum

periodicidad /perioδiθi'δaδ; perioδisi'δaδ/ f, periodicity

periódico /pe'rioδiko/ a periodic. m, newspaper; periodical publication

periodicucho /perioδi'kutʃo/ m, rag (bad newspaper)

periodismo /perio'δismo/ m, journalism

periodista /perio'δista/ mf journalist

periodístico /perio'δistiko/ a journalistic

período /pe'rioδo/ m, period; Phys. cycle; menstruation period; Gram. clause; age, era

peripatético /peripa'tetiko/ a peripatetic

peripecia /peri'peθia; peri'pesia/ f, sudden change of fortune, vicissitude

peripuesto /peri'puesto/ a Inf. overelegant, spruce, too well-dressed; smart

periquete /peri'kete/ m, Inf. jiffy, trice

periquito /peri'kito/ m, parakeet; budgerigar

periscopio /peris'kopio/ m, periscope

perito /pe'rito/ (-ta) a expert; skillful, experienced —n expert

peritoneo /perito'neo/ m, peritoneum

perjudicador /perhuδika'δor/ (-ra) a injurious, prejudicial —n injurer

perjudicar /perhuδi'kar/ vt to harm, damage, injure; prejudice

perjudicial /perhuδi'θial; perhuδi'sial/ a injurious, noxious, harmful; prejudicial

perjuicio /per'huiθio; per'huisio/ m, injury, damage; harm; Law. prejudice

perjurador /perhura'δor/ (-ra) n perjurer

perjurar /perhu'rar/ vi to perjure oneself, commit perjury; swear, curse

perjurio /per'hurio/ m, perjury

perjuro /per'huro/ (-ra) a perjured, forsworn —n perjurer

perla /'perla/ f, pearl; Archit. bead; Fig. treasure, jewel, dear. **de perlas,** excellent; exactly right

perlero /per'lero/ a pearl

perlesía /perle'sia/ f, paralysis; palsy

perlino /per'lino/ a pearly, pearl-colored

permanecer /permane'θer; permane'ser/ vi irr to stay, remain. **p. en posición de firme,** to stand at attention. See **conocer**

permanencia /perma'nenθia; perma'nensia/ f, stay, sojourn; permanence

permanente /perma'nente/ a permanent; lasting, enduring

permanganato /permanga'nato/ m, permanganate

permeabilidad /permeaβili'δaδ/ f, permeability

permisible /permi'siβle/ a permissible, allowable

permisivo /permi'siβo/ a permissive

permiso /per'miso/ m, permission, leave; permit; (Mil. etc.) pass. **¡Con p.!** Excuse me!; Allow me!

permitir /permi'tir/ vt to permit, allow

permuta /per'muta/ f, exchange

permutación /permuta'θion; permuta'sion/ f, permutation, interchange

permutar /permu'tar/ vt to exchange

pernear /perne'ar/ vi to kick; Inf. bustle; fret, be impatient

pernetas, en /per'netas, en/ adv barelegged

perniciosidad /perniθiosi'δaδ; pernisiosi'δaδ/ f, perniciousness

pernicioso /perni'θioso; perni'sioso/ a pernicious

pernil /per'nil/ m, Anat. hock; ham; leg of pork; leg (of trousers)

pernio /'pernio/ m, hinge (of doors, windows)

perniquebrar /pernike'βrar/ vt irr to break the legs of. See **quebrar**

perno /'perno/ m, bolt, pin, spike

pernoctar /pernok'tar/ vi to spend the night (away from home)

pero /'pero/ conjunc but. m, Inf. defect; difficulty, snag

perogrullada /perogru'ʎaδa; perogru'yaδa/ f, Inf. truism

perol /pe'rol/ m, Cul. pan

peroné /pero'ne/ m, fibula

peroración /perora'θion; perora'sion/ f, peroration

perorar /pero'rar/ vi to make a speech; Inf. speak pompously; ask insistently

peróxido /pe'roksiδo/ m, peroxide

perpendicular /perpendiku'lar/ a perpendicular. f, perpendicular

perpetración /perpetra'θion; perpetra'sion/ f, perpetration

perpetrar /perpe'trar/ vt to perpetrate

perpetua /per'petua/ f, Bot. immortelle, everlasting

perpetuación /perpetua'θion; perpetua'sion/ f, perpetuation

perpetuar /perpe'tuar/ vt to perpetuate; —vr last, endure

perpetuidad /perpetui'δaδ/ f, perpetuity

perpetuo /per'petuo/ a everlasting; lifelong

perplejidad /perplehi'δaδ/ f, perplexity, bewilderment, doubt

perplejo /per'pleho/ a perplexed, bewildered, doubtful

perquirir /perki'rir/ vt irr to search carefully. See **adquirir**

perra /'perra/ f, bitch; Inf. sot, drunkard; tantrums. **p. chica,** five-cent coin. **p. gorda,** ten-cent coin

perrada /pe'rraδa/ f, pack of dogs; Inf. dirty trick

perrengue /pe'rrengue/ m, Inf. short-tempered person

perrera /pe'rrera/ f, dog kennel; useless toil; Inf. tantrums

perrería /perre'ria/ f, pack of dogs; Inf. dirty trick; fit of anger

perrero /pe'rrero/ m, dog fancier; kennel worker

perro /'perro/ m, dog. **p. caliente** hot dog. **p. danés,** Great Dane. **p. de aguas,** poodle; spaniel. **p. de casta,** thoroughbred dog. **p. de lanas** poodle. **p. de muestra,** pointer. **p. de presa,** bulldog. **p. de San Bernardo,** St. Bernard (dog). **p. de Terranova,** Newfoundland (dog). **p. del hortelano,** dog in the manger. **p. dogo** bulldog. **p. esquimal** husky. **p. faldero,** lap dog. **p. lobo,** wolfhound. **p. pachón,** dachshund. **p. pastor alemán** or **p. policía,** German shepherd. **p. pequinés,** Pekingese. **p. perdiguero,** retriever. **p. pomerano,** spitz, Pomeranian (dog). **p. sabueso español,** spaniel. **p. zorrero,** foxhound. Inf. **A p. viejo no hay tus tus,** You can't fool an old dog. **vivir como perros y gatos,** Inf. to live like cat and dog

perruno /pe'rruno/ a dog, dog-like

persa /'persa/ a and mf Persian. m, Persian (language)

persecución /perseku'θion; perseku'sion/ f, pursuit; persecution; annoyance, importuning

perseguidor /persegi'δor/ (-ra) a pursuing; tormenting —n pursuer; tormentor, persecutor

perseguimiento /persegi'miento/ m, pursuit

perseguir /perse'gir/ vt irr to pursue; persecute, torment; importune. See **seguir**

perseverancia /perseβe'ranθia; perseβe'ransia/ f, perseverance

perseverante /perseβe'rante/ a persevering; constant

perseverar /perseβe'rar/ vi to persevere; last, endure

persiana /per'siana/ f, Venetian blind; flowered silk material

pérsico /'persiko/ a Persian. m, peach tree; peach

persignar /persig'nar/ vt to sign; make the sign of the cross over; —vr cross oneself

persistencia /persis'tenθia; persis'tensia/ f, persistence

persistente /persis'tente/ a persistent

persistir /persis'tir/ vi to persist

persona /per'sona/ f, person; personage; character (in a play, etc.); (Gram. Eccl.) person. **de p. a p.,** in private, face to face

personaje /perso'nahe/ m, important person, personage; character (in a play, etc.)

personal /perso'nal/ a personal. m, staff, personnel

personalidad /personali'δaδ/ f, personality

personalismo /persona'lismo/ m, personality; personal question

personalizar /personali'θar; personali'sar/ vt to become personal, be offensive

personalmente /personal'mente/ adv personally

personarse /perso'narse/ *vr* to present oneself, call, appear

personificación /personifika'θion; personifika'sion/ *f*, personification

personificar /personifi'kar/ *vt* to personify

perspectiva /perspek'tiβa/ *f*, perspective; view; outlook; aspect, appearance. **p. aérea**, bird's-eye view

perspicacia /perspi'kaθia; perspi'kasia/ *f*, perspicacity, shrewdness

perspicaz /perspi'kaθ; perspi'kas/ *a* perspicacious, clear-sighted

perspicuidad /perspikui'ðað/ *f*, perspicuity

perspicuo /pers'pikuo/ *a* lucid, clear

persuadir /persua'ðir/ *vt* to persuade

persuasible /persua'siβle/ *a* persuadable

persuasión /persua'sion/ *f*, persuasion; belief, conviction, opinion

persuasiva /persua'siβa/ *f*, persuasiveness

persuasivo /persua'siβo/ *a* persuasive

pertenecer /pertene'θer; pertene'ser/ *vi irr* to belong; relate, concern. See **conocer**

perteneciente /pertene'θiente; pertene'siente/ *a* belonging (to), pertaining (to)

pertenencia /perte'nenθia; perte'nensia/ *f*, ownership, proprietorship; property, accessory

pértiga /'pertiga/ *f*, long rod; pole. **salto de p.**, pole vaulting

pertinacia /perti'naθia; perti'nasia/ *f*, pertinacity, doggedness

pertinaz /perti'naθ; perti'nas/ *a* pertinacious, stubborn, dogged

pertinencia /perti'nenθia; perti'nensia/ *f*, relevance, appropriateness

pertinente /perti'nente/ *a* relevant, apposite; appropriate

pertrechar /pertre'tʃar/ *vt* to supply, equip; prepare, make ready

pertrechos /per'tretʃos/ *m pl, Mil.* armaments, stores; equipment, appliances

perturbación /perturβa'θion; perturβa'sion/ *f*, disturbance; agitation

perturbador /perturβa'ðor/ **(-ra)** *a* disturbing —*n* disturber; heckler

perturbar /pertur'βar/ *vt* to disturb; agitate

Perú /pe'ru/ Peru

peruano /pe'ruano/ **(-na)** *a* and *n* Peruvian

perversidad /perβersi'ðað/ *f*, wickedness, depravity

perversión /perβer'sion/ *f*, perversion; wickedness, evil

perversivo /perβer'siβo/ *a* perversive

perverso /per'βerso/ *a* wicked, iniquitous, depraved

pervertir /perβer'tir/ *vt irr* to pervert, corrupt; distort. See **sentir**

pesa /'pesa/ *f*, weight; clock weight; gymnast's weight. **pesas y medidas**, weights and measures

pesacartas /pesa'kartas/ *m*, letter scale, letter balance

pesada /pe'saða/ *f*, weighing

pesadez /pesa'ðeθ; pesa'ðes/ *f*, heaviness; obesity; tediousness, tiresomeness; slowness; fatigue

pesadilla /pesa'ðiʎa; pesa'ðiya/ *f*, nightmare

pesado /pe'saðo/ *a* heavy; obese; deep (of sleep); oppressive (of weather); slow; unwieldy; tedious; impertinent; dull, boring; offensive

pesadumbre /pesa'ðumbre/ *f*, heaviness; grief, sorrow; trouble, anxiety

pésame /'pesame/ *m*, expression of condolence. **dar el p.**, to present one's condolences

pesantez /pesan'teθ; pesan'tes/ *f*, weight, heaviness; seriousness, gravity

pesar /pe'sar/ *m*, grief, sorrow; remorse. **a p. de**, in spite of

pesar /pe'sar/ *vi* to weigh; be heavy; be important; grieve, cause regret (e.g. *Me pesa mucho,* I am very sorry); influence, affect; —*vt* weigh; consider. **Mal que me (te, etc.) pese...,** Much as I regret...

pesario /pe'sario/ *m*, pessary

pesaroso /pesa'roso/ *a* regretful, remorseful; sorrowful

pesca /'peska/ *f*, fishery; angling, fishing; catch of fish. **p. a la rastra**, trawling. **p. deportiva** sport fishing. **p. mayor**, deep-sea fishing

pescadería /peskaðe'ria/ *f*, fishery; fish store; fish market

pescadilla /peska'ðiʎa; peska'ðiya/ *f, Ichth.* whiting

pescado /pes'kaðo/ *m*, fish (out of the water); salt cod

pescador /peska'ðor/ **(-ra)** *n* fisherman; angler

pescante /pes'kante/ *m*, driving seat; coach box; jib (of a crane)

pescar /pes'kar/ *vt* to fish; *Inf.* catch in the act; acquire. **p. a la rastra**, to trawl

pescozón /pesko'θon; pesko'son/ *m*, slap on the neck or head

pescuezo /pes'kueθo; pes'kueso/ *m*, neck; throat; haughtiness, arrogance. **torcer el p.**, to wring the neck (of chickens, etc.)

pesebre /pe'seβre/ *m*, manger, stable; feeding trough

pésimamente /'pesimamente/ *adv* extremely badly

pesimismo /pesi'mismo/ *m*, pessimism

pesimista /pesi'mista/ *a* pessimistic. *mf* pessimist

pésimo /'pesimo/ *a superl* **malo** extremely bad

peso /'peso/ *m*, weighing; weight; heaviness; gravity; importance; influence; load; peso (coin); scale, balance. **p. bruto**, gross weight. **p. de joyería**, troy weight. **p. específico**, *Phys.* specific gravity. **p. pluma**, (*Boxing*) featherweight

pespunte /pes'punte/ *m*, backstitch

pesquera /pes'kera/ *f*, fishing ground, fishery

pesquería /peske'ria/ *f*, fishing, angling; fisherman's trade; fishing ground, fishery

pesquero /pes'kero/ *a* fishing (of boats, etc.)

pesquisa /pes'kisa/ *f*, investigation, examination; search

pesquisar /peski'sar/ *vt* to investigate, look into; search

pestaña /pes'tapa/ *f*, eyelash; *Sew.* edging, fringe; ear, lug; *Naut.* fluke

pestañear /pestape'ar/ *vi* to wink; blink; flutter the eyelashes

pestañeo /pesta'peo/ *m*, winking; blinking

peste /'peste/ *f*, plague, pestilence; nauseous smell; epidemic; pest; vice; *pl* oaths, curses. **p. bubónica**, bubonic plague. **p. roja** syphilis. **p. de las abejas**, foul brood. **echar pestes**, to swear; fume

pestífero /pes'tifero/ *a* noxious

pestilencia /pesti'lenθia; pesti'lensia/ *f*, plague, pestilence

pestilente /pesti'lente/ *a* pestilential

pestillo /pes'tiʎo; pes'tiyo/ *m*, latch; lock bolt. **p. de golpe**, safety latch

petaca /pe'taka/ *f*, cigarette or cigar case; tobacco pouch

pétalo /'petalo/ *m*, petal

petardista /petar'ðista/ *mf* swindler, impostor

petardo /pe'tarðo/ *m*, detonator; torpedo; firecracker; fraud

petición /peti'θion; peti'sion/ *f*, petition, request

peticionario /petiθio'nario; petisio'nario/ **(-ia)** *n* petitioner —*a* petitionary

petimetra /peti'metra/ *f*, stylish and affected young woman

petimetre /peti'metre/ *m*, fop

petirrojo /peti'rroho/ *m*, robin

petitorio /peti'torio/ *a* petitionary. *m, Inf.* importunity

peto /'peto/ *m*, breastplate; front (of a shirt); bib

pétreo /'petreo/ *a* petrous

petrificación /petrifika'θion; petrifika'sion/ *f*, petrifaction

petrificar /petrifi'kar/ *vt* to petrify; —*vr* become petrified

petrografía /petrogra'fia/ *f*, petrology

petróleo /pe'troleo/ *m*, petroleum; oil, mineral oil. **p. bruto**, crude oil. **p. de lámpara**, kerosene

petrolero /petro'lero/ **(-ra)** *a* oil, petroleum —*n* petroleum seller; incendiarist. *m*, oil tanker

petrolífero /petro'lifero/ *a* oil-bearing

petroso /pe'troso/ *a* stony, rocky

petulancia /petu'lanθia; petu'lansia/ *f*, insolence; vanity

petulante /petu'lante/ *a* insolent; vain

pez /peθ; pes/ *m*, fish; *pl* Pisces. *f*, *Chem.* pitch. **p. sierra,** swordfish

pezón /pe'θon; pe'son/ *m*, *Bot.* stalk; nipple; axle pivot; point (of land, etc.)

pezonera /peθo'nera; peso'nera/ *f*, linchpin

pezuña /pe'θuɲa; pe'suɲa/ *f*, cloven hoof (of cows, pigs, etc.)

piada /'piaða/ *f*, chirping, twittering

piadoso /pia'ðoso/ *a* compassionate; kind, pitiful; pious, religious

piafar /pia'far/ *vi* to stamp, paw the ground (horses)

piamontés /piamon'tes/ **(-esa)** *a* and *n* Piedmontese

pianista /pia'nista/ *mf* piano maker; piano dealer; pianist

piano /'piano/ *m*, pianoforte. **p. de cola,** grand piano. **p. de media cola,** baby grand. **p. vertical,** upright piano

piante /'piante/ *a* chirping, twittering

piar /piar/ *vi* to chirp, twitter

piara /'piara/ *f*, herd of swine; pack (of horses, etc.)

pica /'pika/ *f*, *Mil.* pike; bullfighter's goad; pike soldier; stonecutter's hammer. **a p. seca,** in vain. **pasar por las picas,** to suffer hardship. **poner una p. en Flandes,** to triumph over great difficulties

picacho /pi'katʃo/ *m*, peak, summit

picada /pi'kaða/ *f*, prick; bite; peck; *Aer.* dive

picadero /pika'ðero/ *m*, riding school; paddock (of a racetrack)

picado /pi'kaðo/ *a Sew.* pinked. *m*, *Cul.* hash

picador /pika'ðor/ *m*, horse trainer; meat chopper; horseman armed with a goad (bullfights)

picadura /pika'ðura/ *f*, puncture; prick; sting; *Sew.* pinking; peck (of birds); cut tobacco; black tobacco; beginning of caries in teeth

picajoso /pika'hoso/ *a* hypersensitive, touchy, peevish

picamaderos /pikama'ðeros/ *m*, woodpecker

picante /pi'kante/ *a* piquant; mordant; hot, highly seasoned. *m*, mordancy; pungency

picapleitos /pika'pleitos/ *m*, *Inf.* shady lawyer, pettifogger

picaporte /pika'porte/ *m*, latch, door catch; door knocker

picar /pi'kar/ *vt* to prick; sting; peck; bite; chop fine; mince; nibble (of fishing); irritate (the skin); *Sew.* pink; burn (the tongue); eat (grapes); goad; spur; stipple (walls); stimulate, encourage; split, cleave; *Mil.* harass; vex; *Mus.* play staccato; —*vi* burn (of the sun); smart (of cuts, etc.); eat sparingly; *Auto.* knock; (*with en*) knock at (doors, etc.); —*vr* be motheaten; go rotten (fruit, etc.); grow choppy (of the sea); be piqued; boast

pícaramente /'pikaramente/ *adv* knavishly, cunningly

picardear /pikarðe'ar/ *vi* to play the rogue; behave mischievously

picardía /pikar'ðia/ *f*, knavery, roguery; mischievousness; practical joke; wantonness

picaresco /pika'resko/ *a* roguish, picaresque, knavish

pícaro /'pikaro/ **(-ra)** *a* knavish; base, vile; astute; mischievous —*n* rogue

picatoste /pika'toste/ *m*, kind of fritter

picaza /pi'kaθa; pi'kasa/ *f*, magpie

picazo /pi'kaθo; pi'kaso/ *m*, blow with a pike or anything pointed; peck, tap with a beak (of birds); sting

picazón /pika'θon; pika'son/ *f*, itch, irritation; annoyance

pícea /'piθea; 'pisea/ *f*, *Bot.* spruce

píceo /'piθeo; 'piseo/ *a* piscine, fish-like

pichel /pi'tʃel/ *m*, tankard

pichón /pi'tʃon/ **(-ona)** *m*, male pigeon —*n Inf.* darling

pico /'piko/ *m*, beak (of birds); peak; woodpecker; odd amount (e.g. *treinta y p.,* thirty-odd); sharp point; spout (of a jug, etc.); *Inf.* mouth; blarney, gab. **p. de cigüeña,** crane's-bill. **p. de oro,** silver-tongued orator

picor /pi'kor/ *m*, burning sensation in the mouth; smarting; itching, irritation

picoso /pi'koso/ *a* pitted, marked by smallpox

picota /pi'kota/ *f*, pillory; peak; spire

picotazo /piko'taθo; piko'taso/ *m*, peck; dab; sting, bite

picoteado /pikote'aðo/ *a* peaked, having points

picotear /pikote'ar/ *vt* to peck (of a bird); —*vi* toss the head (of horses); *Inf.* chatter senselessly; —*vr Inf.* slang each other

picotero /piko'tero/ *a Inf.* chattering, talkative; indiscreet

pictografía /piktogra'fia/ *f*, picture writing

pictórico /pik'toriko/ *a* pictorial

picudo /pi'kuðo/ *a* pointed, peaked; having a spout; *Inf.* chattering

pie /pie/ *m*, foot; stand, support; stem (of a glass, etc.); standard (of a lamp); *Bot.* trunk, stem; sapling; lees, sediment; *Theat.* foot (measure); custom; (metrics) foot; motive, cause; pretext; (metrics) meter. **p. de cabra,** crowbar. **p. de imprenta,** printer's mark, printer's imprint. **p. de piña,** clubfoot. **p. de rey,** calliper. **p. palmado,** webfoot. **al p. de la letra,** punctiliously. **andar con pies de plomo,** to walk warily. **a p.,** on foot. **a p. firme,** without budging; steadfastly. *Inf.* **buscar tres pies al gato,** to look for something that isn't there; twist a person's words. **de a p.,** on foot. **en p. de guerra,** a wartime footing. *Inf.* **poner pies en polvorosa,** to quit

piedad /pie'ðað/ *f*, piety; pity, compassion; *Art.* pietà

piedra /'pieðra/ *f*, stone; tablet; *Med.* gravel. **p. de amolar,** whetstone, grindstone. **p. angular,** cornerstone (also *Fig.*). **p. caliza,** limestone. **p. clave,** keystone. **p. de construcción,** building stone; child's block. **p. de toque,** touchstone, test. **p. filosofal,** philosopher's stone. **p. fundamental,** foundation stone. **p. miliaria,** milestone. **p. mortuoria,** tombstone. *Fig. Inf.* **no dejar p. sin remover,** to leave no stone unturned. **no dejar p. sobre p.,** to demolish, destroy completely

piel /piel/ *f*, skin; fur; hide; leather; peel (of some fruits); rind (of bacon). **p. de gallina,** *Fig.* goose flesh. **p. de rata,** horse blanket. **p. de Rusia,** Russian leather.

piélago /'pielago/ *m*, high seas; sea, ocean; glut, superabundance

pienso /'pienso/ *m*, *Agr.* fodder

pierna /'pierna/ *f*, *Anat.* leg; *Mech.* shank; leg of a compass. *Inf.* **a p. suelta,** at one's ease. **en piernas,** barelegged

pietismo /pie'tismo/ *m*, pietism

pietista /pie'tista/ *a* pietistic. *mf* pietist

pieza /'pieθa; 'piesa/ *f*, portion; piece; component part; room; *Theat.* play; roll (of cloth); piece (in chess, etc.); coin; piece (of music). **p. de recambio** *or* **p. de repuesto,** spare part. **p. de recibo,** reception room. *Inf.* **quedarse en una p.,** to be struck dumb

pífano /'pifano/ *m*, fife; fife player, fifer

pigmentación /pigmenta'θion; pigmenta'sion/ *f*, pigmentation

pigmentario /pigmen'tario/ *a* pigmentary

pigmento /pig'mento/ *m*, pigment

pigmeo /pig'meo/ **(-ea)** *a* and *n* pygmy

pignoración /pignora'θion; pignora'sion/ *f*, hypothecation; pawning; mortgage

pignorar /pigno'rar/ *vt* to hypothecate; pawn; mortgage

pigre /'pigre/ *a* lazy; negligent, careless

pigricia /pi'griθia; pi'grisia/ *f*, laziness; negligence

pijama /pi'hama/ *m*, pajamas

pila /'pila/ *f*, trough, basin; heap, pile; *Elec.* battery; *Eccl.* parish; pier, pile; *Phys.* cell. **p. atómica,** atomic pile. **p. bautismal,** *Eccl.* font

pilar /pi'lar/ *m*, fountain basin; milestone; pillar

pilastra /pi'lastra/ *f*, pier, pile; pilaster

píldora /'pildora/ *f*, *Med.* pill; *Inf.* disagreeable news

pillador /piʎa'ðor; piya'ðor/ **(-ra)** *a* pillaging, plundering —*n* plunderer

pillaje /pi'ʎahe; pi'yahe/ *m*, pillaging, looting; robbery, theft

pillar /pi'ʎar; pi'yar/ *vt* to pillage; steal, rob; seize; snatch; *Inf.* surprise, find out (in a lie, etc.). **pillarse el dedo,** to get one's finger caught (in a door, etc.)

pillastre /pi'ʎastre; pi'yastre/ *m*, *Inf.* rogue, ragamuffin

pillear /piʎe'ar; piye'ar/ *vi Inf.* to lead a rogue's life

pillería /piʎe'ria; piye'ria/ *f, Inf.* gang of rogues; *Inf.* rogue's trick
pillo /'piʎo; 'piyo/ *m,* rogue, knave
pilón /pi'lon/ *m,* fountain basin; pestle; loaf sugar; pylon
pilongo /pi'loŋgo/ *a* thin, lean
píloro /'piloro/ *m,* pylorus
pilotaje /pilo'tahe/ *m,* pilotage; piling, pilework. **examen de p.,** flying test
pilotar /pilo'tar/ *vt* to pilot
pilote /pi'lote/ *m, Engin.* pile
pilotear /pilote'ar/ *vt* to pilot
piloto /pi'loto/ *m,* pilot; mate (in merchant ships). **p. de pruebas,** test pilot
pimentero /pimen'tero/ *m,* pepper plant; pepper shaker
pimentón /pimen'ton/ *m,* red pepper, cayenne
pimienta /pi'mienta/ *f,* pepper. **p. húngara,** paprika. *Inf.* **ser como una p.,** to be sharp as a needle
pimiento /pi'miento/ *m,* pimento; capsicum; red pepper; pepper plant. **p. de cornetilla,** chili pepper
pimpollo /pim'poʎo; pim'poyo/ *m,* sapling; sprout, shoot; rosebud
pina /'pina/ *f,* conical stone; felloe (of a wheel)
pinacoteca /pinako'teka/ *f,* art gallery, picture gallery
pináculo /pi'nakulo/ *m,* pinnacle, summit; climax, culmination; *Archit.* finial
pinar /pi'nar/ *m,* pinewood
pincarrasco /pinka'rrasko/ *m,* pin oak
pincel /pin'θel; pin'sel/ *m,* paintbrush; artist, painter; painting technique. **p. para las cejas,** eyebrow pencil
pincelada /pinθe'laða; pinse'laða/ *f,* brushstroke. **dar la última p.,** to add the finishing touch
pincelero /pinθe'lero; pinse'lero/ **(-ra)** *n* seller or maker of paintbrushes; brush box
pinchadura /pintʃa'ðura/ *f,* prick, puncture, piercing; sting; nipping, biting
pinchar /pin'tʃar/ *vt* to prick; puncture; pierce; sting; nip, bite. **no p. ni cortar,** to be ineffective (of persons)
pinchazo /pin'tʃaθo; pin'tʃaso/ *m,* prick; puncture; sting; incitement
pinche /'pintʃe/ *m,* scullion
pineda /pi'neða/ *f,* pinewood
pingajo /piŋ'gaho/ *m, Inf.* tatter, rag
pingajoso /piŋga'hoso/ *a Inf.* tattered, ragged
pingo /'piŋgo/ *m, Inf.* tatter, rag; *pl Inf.* cheap clothes
pingüe /'piŋgue/ *a* fat, greasy; fertile, rich
pingüino /piŋ'guino/ *m,* penguin
pino /'pino/ *a* steep. *m, Bot.* pine, deal; *Poet.* ship. **p. de tea,** pitch pine. **p. silvestre,** red fir
pinocha /pi'notʃa/ *f,* pine needle
pinta /'pinta/ *f,* spot; marking; mark; fleck; look, appearance; pint (measure); drop, drip; spot ball (in billiards)
pintamonas /pinta'monas/ *mf Inf.* dauber
pintar /pin'tar/ *vt* to paint; describe, picture; exaggerate; —*vi* show, manifest itself; —*vr* make up (one's face). *Inf.* **pintarse solo para,** to be very good at, excel at
pintiparado /pintipa'raðo/ *a* most similar, very alike; fitting, apposite
pintiparar /pintipa'rar/ *vt Inf.* to compare
pintor /pin'tor/ **(-ra)** *n* painter, artist. **p. callejero,** sidewalk artist, pavement artist. **p. de brocha gorda,** house painter
pintoresco /pinto'resko/ *a* picturesque, quaint, pretty
pintoresquismo /pintores'kismo/ *m,* picturesqueness
pintorrear /pintorre'ar/ *vt Inf.* to daub, paint badly
pintura /pin'tura/ *f,* painting; paint, pigment; picture, painting; description. **p. a la aguada,** watercolor painting. **p. al fresco,** fresco. **p. al látex,** latex paint. **p. al óleo,** oil painting. **p. al pastel,** pastel drawing
pinturería /pinture'ria/ *f,* paint store
pinturero /pintu'rero/ *a Inf.* affected, conceited; dandified, overdressed
pinza /'pinθa; 'pinsa/ *f,* clamp. **p. de la ropa,** clothes peg

pinzas /'pinθas; 'pinsas/ *f pl,* pincers; pliers; tweezers; forceps. **p. hemostáticas,** arterial forceps
pinzón /pin'θon; pin'son/ *m,* chaffinch
piña /'piɲa/ *f,* pineapple; cluster, knot (of people, etc.); pinecone
piñón /pi'ɲon/ *m,* pine nut; *Mech.* pinion, chain wheel
pío /'pio/ *a* pious; compassionate; good; piebald. *m,* chirping, cheep; *Inf.* longing
piojo /'pioho/ *m,* louse
piojoso /pio'hoso/ *a* lousy; avaricious, stingy
pionero /pio'nero/ *m,* pioneer
piorrea /pio'rrea/ *f,* pyorrhea
pipa /'pipa/ *f,* barrel, cask; tobacco pipe; pip (of fruits)
pipar /pi'par/ *vi* to smoke a pipe
pipeta /pi'peta/ *f,* pipette
pipiar /pi'piar/ *vi* to chirp, twitter
pique /'pike/ *m,* pique, resentment. **a p. de,** on the verge of, about to. **echar a p.,** *Naut.* to sink; destroy. **irse a p.,** to sink, founder
piquero /pi'kero/ *m,* pike soldier
piqueta /pi'keta/ *f,* pick, mattock; mason's hammer
piquete /pi'kete/ *m,* puncture, small wound; *Mil.* picket; pole, stake; small hole (in garments); picket (in strikes)
pira /'pira/ *f,* funeral pyre; bonfire
piragua /pi'ragua/ *f,* piragua, canoe
pirámide /pi'ramiðe/ *f,* pyramid
pirarse /pi'rarse/ *vr Inf.* to slip away
pirata /pi'rata/ *a* piratical *mf* pirate; savage, cruel person
piratear /pirate'ar/ *vi* to play the pirate
piratería /pirate'ria/ *f,* piracy; plunder, robbery
pirático /pi'ratiko/ *a* piratical
pirenaico, pirineo /pire'naiko, piri'neo/ *a* Pyrenean
pirético /pi'retiko/ *a* pyretic
piriforme /piri'forme/ *a* pear-shaped
Pirineos, los /piri'neos, los/ the Pyrenees
piromancia /piro'manθia; piro'mansia/ *f,* pyromancy
piropear /pirope'ar/ *vt Inf.* to pay compliments to
piropo /pi'ropo/ *m,* carbuncle; *Inf.* compliment. **echar piropos,** to pay compliments
pirotecnia /piro'teknia/ *f,* pyrotechnics
pirotécnico /piro'tekniko/ *a* pyrotechnical. *m,* pyrotechnist
pirrarse /pi'rrarse/ *vr Inf.* to desire ardently
pírrico /'pirriko/ *a* Pyrrhic
pirueta /pi'rueta/ *f,* pirouette, twirl
pisada /pi'saða/ *f,* treading, stepping; footprint, footstep; stepping on a person's foot. **seguir las pisadas de alguien,** *Fig.* to follow in someone's footsteps, imitate someone
pisano /pi'sano/ **(-na)** *a* and *n* Pisan
pisapapeles /pisapa'peles/ *m,* paperweight
pisar /pi'sar/ *vt* to tread upon; trample upon; crush; *Mus.* press (strings); trespass upon
pisaverde /pisa'βerðe/ *m, Inf.* fop, dandy
piscicultura /pisθikul'tura; pissikul'tura/ *f,* pisciculture, fish farming
piscina /pis'θina; pis'sina/ *f,* fishpond; swimming pool; *Eccl.* piscina
piscolabis /pisko'laβis/ *m, Inf.* snack, light meal
piso /'piso/ *m,* treading, trampling; story, floor; flooring; apartment. **p. bajo,** ground floor
pisón /pi'son/ *m,* rammer, ram
pisotear /pisote'ar/ *vt* to trample; crush under foot; tread on; step on; humiliate, treat inconsiderately
pisoteo /piso'teo/ *m,* trampling under foot; treading
pista /'pista/ *f,* track, trail (of animals); circus ring; racetrack, racecourse. **p. de patinar,** skating rink. **p. de vuelo,** *Aer.* landing field. *Inf.* **seguir la p. a,** to spy upon
pistacho /pis'tatʃo/ *m,* pistachio
pistar /pis'tar/ *vt* to pestle, pound
pistero /pis'tero/ *m,* feeding cup
pistilo /pis'tilo/ *m,* pistil
pistola /pis'tola/ *f,* pistol. **p. ametralladora,** machine gun.
pistolera /pisto'lera/ *f,* holster; pistol case
pistolero /pisto'lero/ *m,* gangster

pistoletazo /pistole'taθo; pistole'taso/ *m*, pistol shot; pistol wound

pistón /pis'ton/ *m*, *Mus.* piston; *Mil.* percussion cap; *Mech.* piston

pitada /pi'taða/ *f*, blast on a whistle, whistling; impertinence

pitagórico /pita'goriko/ **(-ca)** *a* and *n* Pythagorean

pitanza /pi'tanθa; pi'tansa/ *f*, alms, charity; *Inf.* daily food; pittance, scanty remuneration

pitar /pi'tar/ *vi* to play the whistle; —*vt* pay (debts); smoke; give alms to

pitido /pi'tiðo/ *m*, blast on a whistle; whistling (of birds)

pitillera /piti'ʎera; piti'yera/ *f*, cigarette case; female cigarette maker

pito /'pito/ *m*, whistle; *Mus.* fife. *Inf.* **Cuando pitos flautas, cuando flautas pitos,** It's always the unexpected that happens. *Inf.* **no valer un p.,** to be not worth a straw

pitoflero /pito'flero/ **(-ra)** *n* mediocre performer (gen. on a wind instrument); *Inf.* talebearer, gossip

pitón /pi'ton/ *m*, *Zool.* python; nascent horn (of goats, etc.); spout; protuberance; *Bot.* sprout

pitonisa /pito'nisa/ *f*, *Myth.* pythoness; witch, enchantress

pitorrearse /pitorre'arse/ *vr* to ridicule, mock

pituitario /pitui'tario/ *a* pituitary

pituso /pi'tuso/ *a* small and amusing (of children)

pivote /pi'βote/ *m*, pivot, swivel, gudgeon

piyama /pi'yama/ *m*, pajamas

pizarra /pi'θarra; pi'sarra/ *f*, slate; blackboard

pizarral /piθa'rral; pisa'rral/ *m*. **pizarrería,** slate quarry

pizarrero /piθa'rrero; pisa'rrero/ *m*, slater

pizarrín /piθa'rrin; pisa'rrin/ *m*, slate pencil

pizca /'piθka; 'piska/ *f*, *Inf.* atom, speck, crumb; jot, whit. **¡Ni p.!** Not a scrap!

pizpireta /piθpi'reta; pispi'reta/ *a f*, *Inf.* coquettish; smart; dressed up

placa /'plaka/ *f*, plate, disk; *Art.* plaque; *Photo.* plate; star (insignia). **p. recordatorio,** commemorative plaque

placabilidad /plakaβili'ðað/ *f*, placability, appeasability

pláceme /'plaθeme; 'plaseme/ *m*, congratulation

placentero /plaθen'tero; plasen'tero/ *a* agreeable, pleasant

placer /pla'θer; pla'ser/ *vt irr* to please, give pleasure to, gratify. *m*, *Naut.* reef, sandbank; pleasure; wish, desire; permission, consent; entertainment, diversion. **a p.,** at one's convenience; at leisure —*Pres. Indic.* **plazco, places,** etc —*Preterite* **plugo, pluguieron.** *Pres. Subjunc.* **plazca,** etc —*Imperf. Subjunc.* **pluguiese,** etc.

placibilidad /plaθiβili'ðað; plasiβili'ðað/ *f*, agreeableness, pleasantness

placible /pla'θiβle; pla'siβle/ *a* agreeable, pleasant

placidez /plaθi'ðeθ; plasi'ðes/ *f*, placidity, calmness, serenity

plácido /'plaθiðo; 'plasiðo/ *a* placid, calm, serene

placiente /pla'θiente; pla'siente/ *a* pleasing, attractive

plácito /'plaθito; 'plasito/ *m*, decision, judgment, opinion

plafón /pla'fon/ *m*, ceiling light; *Archit.* panel

plaga /'plaga/ *f*, plague; disaster, calamity; epidemic; glut; pest; grief

plagar /pla'gar/ *vt* (*with de*) to infect with; —*vr* (*with de*) be covered with; be overrun by; be infested with

plagiar /pla'hiar/ *vt* to plagiarize, copy; kidnap, hold for ransom

plagiario /pla'hiario/ **(-ia)** *n* plagiarist

plagio /'plahio/ *m*, plagiary; kidnapping

plan /plan/ *m*, plan; scheme; plane. **p. quinquenal,** five-year plan

plana /'plana/ *f*, sheet, page; mason's trowel; plain. **p. mayor,** (*Mil. Nav.*) staff

planadora /plana'ðora/ *f*, steamroller

plancha /'plantʃa/ *f*, sheet, slab, plate; flatiron; horizontal suspension (in gymnastics); *Naut.* gangway, gangplank; *Inf.* howler

planchado /plan'tʃaðo/ *m*, ironing; ironing to be done or already finished

planchador /plantʃa'ðor/ **(-ra)** *n* ironer

planchar /plan'tʃar/ *vt* to iron, press with an iron

planchear /plantʃe'ar/ *vt* to plate (with metal)

planeador /planea'ðor/ *m*, *Aer.* glider

planear /plane'ar/ *vt* to plan out; make plans for; —*vi Aer.* glide

planeo /pla'neo/ *m*, *Aer.* glide

planeta /pla'neta/ *m*, planet

planetario /plane'tario/ *a* planetary. *m*, planetarium

planicie /pla'niθie; pla'nisie/ *f*, levelness, evenness; plain

plano /'plano/ *a* flat, level; plane. *m*, *Geom.* plane; plan, map; *Aer.* aileron, wing

planta /'planta/ *f*, *Bot.* plant; sole (of the foot); plantation; layout, plan; position of the feet (in dancing, fencing); scheme, project. **p. baja,** ground floor. **p. vivaz,** perennial plant. *Inf.* **buena p.,** good appearance

plantación /planta'θion; planta'sion/ *f*, planting; plantation, nursery

plantador /planta'ðor/ **(-ra)** *n* planter. *m*, *Agr.* dibble. *f*. **plantadora,** mechanical planter

plantar /plan'tar/ *vt* to plant; erect; place; found, set up; pose (a problem); raise (a question, etc.); *Inf.* leave in the lurch; —*vr* take up one's position; jib (of horses); oppose

planteamiento /plantea'miento/ *m*, execution; putting into practice; planning; statement (of problems)

plantel /plan'tel/ *m*, nursery garden; training school, nursery

plantilla /plan'tiʎa; plan'tiya/ *f*, young plant; insole (of shoes); *Mech.* template, jig

plantío /plan'tio/ *m*, plantation, afforestation; planting —*a* planted or ready for planting (ground)

plantón /plan'ton/ *m*, plant or sapling ready for transplanting; *Bot.* cutting; doorkeeper, porter. **dar un p.,** (a), to keep (a person) waiting a long time

plañidera /plaɲi'ðera/ *f*, paid mourner

plañidero /plaɲi'ðero/ *a* mournful, piteous, anguished

plañido /pla'ɲiðo/ *m*, lament, weeping, wailing

plañir /pla'ɲir/ *vi* and *vt irr* to lament, wail, weep. See **tañer**

plasma /'plasma/ *m*, plasma

plasmar /plas'mar/ *vt* to mold, throw (pottery)

plástica /'plastika/ *f*, art of clay modeling; plastic

plasticidad /plastiθi'ðað; plastisi'ðað/ *f*, plasticity

plástico /'plastiko/ *a* plastic; flexible, malleable, soft

plata /'plata/ *f*, silver; silver (coins); money; white. **p. labrada,** silverware

plataforma /plata'forma/ *f*, platform; running board (of a train); *Rail.* turntable

plátano /'platano/ *m*, banana tree, banana; plantain; plane tree

platea /pla'tea/ *f*, *Theat.* pit. **butaca de p.,** pit stall

plateado /plate'aðo/ *a* silvered; silver-plated; silvery

plateador /platea'ðor/ *m*, plater

platear /plate'ar/ *vt* to electroplate, silver

platería /plate'ria/ *f*, silversmith's art or trade; silversmith's shop or workshop

platero /pla'tero/ *m*, silversmith; jeweler

plática /'platika/ *f*, conversation; exhortation, sermon; address, discourse

platicar /plati'kar/ *vt* and *vi* to converse (about)

platija /pla'tiha/ *f*, plaice

platillo /pla'tiʎo; pla'tiyo/ *m*, saucer; kitty (in card games); pan (of a scale); *pl* cymbals

platinado /plati'naðo/ *m*, plating

platino /pla'tino/ *m*, platinum

platívolo /pla'tiβolo/ *m*, flying saucer

plato /'plato/ *m*, plate; dish; *Cul.* course, dish; pan (of a scale). **p. sopero,** soup plate. **p. trinchero,** meat dish. *Inf.* **comer en un mismo p.,** to be on intimate terms. **nada entre dos platos,** much ado about nothing

platónico /pla'toniko/ *a* Platonic

platonismo /plato'nismo/ *m*, Platonism

plausibilidad /plausiβili'ðað/ *f*, plausibility

plausible /plau'siβle/ *a* plausible, reasonable

playa /'plaia/ *f*, beach, seashore, strand

plaza /'plaθa; 'plasa/ *f*, square (in a town, etc.); marketplace; fortified town; space; duration; employment, post.; *Com.* market. **p. de armas,** garrison town; military camp. **p. de toros,** bullring. **p. fuerte,** strong place, fortress. **sentar p.,** to enlist in the army

plazo /'plaθo; 'plaso/ *m*, term, duration; expiration of term, date of payment; installment. **a plazos,** *Com.* by installments, on the installment system

plazoleta /plaθo'leta; plaso'leta/ *f*, small square (in gardens, etc.)

pleamar /plea'mar/ *f*, *Naut.* high water

plebe /'pleβe/ *f*, common people; rabble, mob

plebeyo /ple'βeio/ **(-ya)** *a* plebeian —*n* commoner, plebeian

plebiscito /pleβis'θito; pleβis'sito/ *m*, plebiscite

plectro /'plektro/ *m*, plectrum

plegable /ple'gaβle/ *a* foldable

plegadera /plega'δera/ *f*, folder; folding knife; paper folder

plegadizo /plega'δiθo; plega'δiso/ *a* folding; collapsible; jointed

plegado /ple'gaδo/ *m*, pleating; folding

plegador /plega'δor/ *a* folding. *m*, folding machine

plegadura /plega'δura/ *f*, folding, doubling; fold, pleat

plegar /ple'gar/ *vt irr* to fold; pleat; *Sew.* gather; —*vr* submit, give in. See **acertar**

plegaria /ple'garia/ *f*, fervent prayer

pleitear /pleite'ar/ *vt* to go to court about; indulge in litigation

pleitista /plei'tista/ *a* quarrelsome, litigious

pleito /'pleito/ *m*, action, lawsuit; dispute, quarrel; litigation. **p. de familia,** family squabble. **ver el p.,** *Law.* to try a case

plenamente /plena'mente/ *adv* fully, entirely

plenario /ple'nario/ *a* full, complete; *Law.* plenary

plenilunio /pleni'lunio/ *m*, full moon

plenipotencia /plenipo'tenθia; plenipo'tensia/ *f*, full powers (diplomatic, etc.)

plenipotenciario /plenipoten'θiario; plenipoten'siario/ *a* and *m*, plenipotentiary

plenitud /pleni'tuδ/ *f*, fullness, completeness; plenitude, abundance

pleno /'pleno/ *a* full. *m*, general meeting

pleonasmo /pleo'nasmo/ *m*, *Gram.* pleonasm

pleonástico /pleo'nastiko/ *a* pleonastic

pleuresía /pleure'sia/ *f*, pleurisy

plexo /'plekso/ *m*, plexus

pléyades /'pleiaδes/ *f pl*, Pleiades

pliego /'pliego/ *m*, sheet (of paper); letter, packet of papers

pliegue /'pliege/ *m*, fold, pleat; *Sew.* gather

plinto /'plinto/ *m*, *Archit.* plinth (of a column); baseboard

plisar /pli'sar/ *vt* to pleat; fold

plomada /plo'maδa/ *f*, plummet; sounding lead; plumb, lead

plomería /plome'ria/ *f*, plumbing; plumbing business; lead roofing

plomero /plo'mero/ *m*, plumber

plomizo /plo'miθo; plo'miso/ *a* lead-like; lead-colored, gray

plomo /'plomo/ *m*, lead (metal); plummet; bullet; *Inf.* bore, tedious person

pluma /'pluma/ *f*, feather; pen; plumage; quill; penmanship; writer; writing profession. **p. estilográfica,** fountain pen. **a vuela p.,** as the pen writes, written in a hurry

plumado /plu'maδo/ *a* feathered

plumaje /plu'mahe/ *m*, plumage, feathers; plume

plúmbeo /'plumbeo/ *a* plumbeous, leaden

plúmeo /'plumeo/ *a* feathered, plumed

plumero /plu'mero/ *m*, feather duster; plume, feather; plumage

plumón /plu'mon/ *m*, down; feather bed

plumoso /plu'moso/ *a* feathered

plural /plu'ral/ *a* and *m*, plural

pluralidad /plurali'δaδ/ *f*, plurality; multitude, number

pluralizar /plurali'θar; plurali'sar/ *vt* to pluralize

plurilingüe /pluri'lingue/ *a* multilingual

pluscuamperfecto /pluskuamper'fekto/ *m*, pluperfect

plusmarquista /plusmar'kista/ *mf* *Sports.* record-holder

plutocracia /pluto'kraθia; pluto'krasia/ *f*, plutocracy

plutócrata /plu'tokrata/ *mf* plutocrat

plutocrático /pluto'kratiko/ *a* plutocratic

plutónico /plu'toniko/ *a* *Geol.* Plutonic

pluviómetro /plu'βiometro/ *m*, rain gauge

poblacho /po'βlatʃo/ *m*, miserable town or village

población /poβla'θion; poβla'sion/ *f*, peopling; population; town

poblado /po'βlaδo/ *m*, inhabited place; town; village

poblador /poβla'δor/ **(-ra)** *a* populating —*n* colonist, settler

poblar /po'βlar/ *vt irr* to colonize; people, populate; breed fast; stock, supply; —*vr* put forth leaves (of trees). See **contar**

pobre /'poβre/ *a* poor; indigent, needy; mediocre; unfortunate; humble, meek. *mf* beggar, pauper, needy person. *Inf.* **ser p. de solemnidad,** to be down and out

pobrero /po'βrero/ *m*, *Eccl.* distributor of alms

pobretería /poβrete'ria/ *f*, poverty; needy people

pobretón /poβre'ton/ *a* extremely needy

pobreza /po'βreθa; po'βresa/ *f*, poverty, need; shortage; timidity; *Mineral.* baseness; poorness (of soil, etc.)

pocero /po'θero; po'sero/ *m*, well digger

pocilga /po'θilga; po'silga/ *f*, pigsty; *Inf.* filthy place

poción /po'θion; po'sion/ *f*, potion, drink; mixture, dose

poco /'poko/ *a* little, scanty; *pl* few. *m*, small amount, a little —*adv* little; shortly, in a little while. **p. a p.,** by degrees, little by little; slowly. **p. más o menos,** more or less, approximately. **por p.,** almost, nearly (always used with the present tense, e.g. *Por p. me caigo,* I almost fell). **tener en p.** (**a),** to have a poor opinion of; undervalue

poda /'poδa/ *f*, *Agr.* pruning; pruning season

podadera /poδa'δera/ *f*, pruning knife

podar /po'δar/ *vt* *Agr.* to prune, trim

poder /po'δer/ *m*, power; authority; jurisdiction; *Law.* power of attorney; strength; ability; proxy; efficacy; possession; *pl* authority; power of attorney. **los poderes constituidos,** the established authorities; the powers that be. **p. de adquisición,** purchasing power. **casarse por poderes,** to be married by proxy

poder /po'δer/ *vt irr* to be able to (e.g. *Podemos comprar estas naranjas,* We can (are able to) buy these oranges). **Dice que la calamidad podía haberse evitado,** He says that the disaster could have been averted). **p.** also expresses possibility (e.g. *Pueden haber ido a la ciudad,* They may have gone to the city. *¡Qué distinta pudo haber sido su vida!* How different his life might have been!) —*impers* be possible. **a más no p.,** of necessity, without being able to help it; to the utmost. **no p. con,** to be unable to control or manage. **no p. hacer más,** to have no alternative, have to; be unable to do more. **no p. menos de,** to be obliged to, have no alternative but. **no p. contener su emoción,** to be overcome with emotion. **no p. ver a,** to hate (persons) —*impers* **Puede que venga esta tarde,** He may come (perhaps he will come) this afternoon —*Pres. Part.* **pudiendo.** *Pres. Indic.* **puedo, puedes, puede, pueden.** *Fut.* **podré,** etc —*Condit.* **podría,** etc —*Preterite* **pude, pudiste,** etc —*Pres. Subjunc.* **pueda, puedas, pueda, puedan.** *Imperf. Subjunc.* **pudiese,** etc.

poderío /poδe'rio/ *m*, power, authority; sway, rule; dominion; wealth

poderoso /poδe'roso/ *a* powerful; opulent; effective, efficacious; mighty, magnificent

podredumbre /poδre'δumbre/ *f*, decay; pus; *Fig.* canker, anguish

podredura, podrición /poδre'δura, poδri'θion; poδre'δura, poδri'sion/ *f*, putrefaction; decay

podrido /po'δriδo/ *a* rotten; putrid; corrupt; decayed

podrir /po'δrir/ *vt* See **pudrir**

poema /po'ema/ *m*, poem. **p. sinfónico,** tone poem

poesía /poe'sia/ *f*, poetry, verse; lyric, poem

poeta /po'eta/ *m*, poet

poetastro /poe'tastro/ *m,* poetaster
poética /po'etika/ *f,* poetics
poético /po'etiko/ *a* poetical
poetisa /poe'tisa/ *f,* poetess
poetizar /poeti'θar; poeti'sar/ *vi* to write verses; —*vt* poeticize
polaco /po'lako/ **(-ca)** *a* Polish —*n* Pole. *m,* Polish (language)
polainas /po'lainas/ *f pl,* leggings, puttees, gaiters
polar /po'lar/ *a* polar
polaridad /polari'ðað/ *f,* polarity; polarization
polarización /polariθa'θion; polarisa'sion/ *f,* polarization
polarizar /polari'θar; polari'sar/ *vt* to polarize
polca /'polka/ *f,* polka
polea /po'lea/ *f,* pulley; *Naut.* block
polémica /po'lemika/ *f,* polemic, controversy, dispute
polémico /po'lemiko/ *a* polemical
polemista /pole'mista/ *mf* disputant, controversialist
polen /'polen/ *m,* pollen
poliandria /po'liandria/ *f,* polyandry
polichinela /politʃi'nela/ *m,* Punchinello
policía /poli'θia; poli'sia/ *f,* police; government, polity, administration; civility, courtesy; cleanliness, tidiness. *m,* policeman. **p. urbana,** city police
policíaco /poli'θiako; poli'siako/ *a* police; detective
policromo /poli'kromo/ *a* polychrome
poliedro /po'lieðro/ *m,* polyhedron
polifacético /polifa'θetiko; polifa'setiko/ *a* many-sided
polifonía /polifo'nia/ *f,* polyphony
polifónico /poli'foniko/ *a* polyphonic
poligamia /poli'gamia/ *f,* polygamy
polígamo /po'ligamo/ **(-ma)** *a* polygamous —*n* polygamist
poligloto /poli'gloto/ **(-ta)** *n* polyglot. *f,* polyglot Bible
polígono /po'ligono/ *a* polygonal. *m,* polygon
polilla /po'liʎa; po'liya/ *f,* moth; moth grub; destroyer, ravager
polimorfismo /polimor'fismo/ *m, Chem.* polymorphism
polimorfo /poli'morfo/ *a* polymorphous
Polinesia /poli'nesia/ Polynesia
polinesio /poli'nesio/ **(-ia)** *a* and *n* Polynesian
polinización /poliniθa'θion; polinisa'sion/ *f,* pollination
poliomielitis /poliomie'litis/ *f,* poliomyelitis, polio
pólipo /'polipo/ *m, Zool.* polyp; octopus; *Med.* polyp
polisílabo /poli'silaβo/ *a* polysyllabic. *m,* polysyllable
polista /po'lista/ *mf* polo player
politécnico /poli'tekniko/ *a* polytechnic
politeísmo /polite'ismo/ *m,* polytheism
politeísta /polite'ista/ *a* polytheistic. *mf* polytheist
política /po'litika/ *f,* politics; civility, courtesy; diplomacy; tact; policy
politicastro /politi'kastro/ *m,* corrupt politician
político /po'litiko/ *a* political; civil, courteous; in-law, by marriage (relationships). *m,* politician
politiquear /politike'ar/ *vi Inf.* to dabble in politics, talk politics
politizarse /politi'θarse; politi'sarse/ *vr* to enter the political arena
póliza /'poliθa; 'polisa/ *f, Com.* policy; *Com.* draft; share certificate; revenue stamp; admission ticket; lampoon. **p. a prima fija,** fixed-premium policy. **p. de seguros,** insurance policy. **p. dotal,** endowment policy
polizón /poli'θon; poli'son/ *m,* loafer, tramp; stowaway; bustle (of a dress)
polla /'poʎa; 'poya/ *f,* pullet; *Inf.* flapper, young woman
pollada /po'ʎaða; po'yaða/ *f,* brood, hatch (especially of chickens)
pollastro /po'ʎastro; po'yastro/ **(-ra)** *n* pullet.
pollera /po'ʎera; po'yera/ *f,* female poultry breeder or seller; chicken coop; go-cart
pollería /poʎe'ria; poye'ria/ *f,* poultry market or shop
pollero /po'ʎero; po'yero/ *n* poultry breeder; poulterer. *m,* hen coop
pollino /po'ʎino; po'yino/ **(-na)** *n* young ass; donkey

pollo /'poʎo; 'poyo/ *m,* chicken; *Inf.* youth, stripling; *Fig. Inf.* downy bird. *Inf.* **p. pera,** young blood, lad. **sacar pollos,** to hatch chickens
polo /'polo/ *m,* pole (all meanings); *Fig.* support; popular Andalusian song; *Sports.* polo. **de p. a p.,** from pole to pole
polonés /polo'nes/ **(-esa)** *a* Polish —*n* Pole
polonesa /polo'nesa/ *f,* polonaise; short coat
Polonia /po'lonia/ Poland
poltrón /pol'tron/ *a* lazy, idle
poltronería /poltrone'ria/ *f,* idleness, laziness
polución /polu'θion; polu'sion/ *f, Med.* ejaculation
poluto /po'luto/ *a* filthy, unclean
Pólux /'poluks/ *m,* Pollux
polvareda /polβa'reða/ *f,* dust cloud; storm, agitation
polvera /pol'βera/ *f,* powder bowl; powder puff; powder compact
polvo /'polβo/ *m,* dust; powder; pinch (of snuff, etc.); *pl* face or dusting powder. **Se hizo como por polvos de la madre celestina,** It was done as if by magic. *Inf.* **limpio de p. y paja,** gratis, for nothing; net (of profit)
pólvora /'polβora/ *f,* gunpowder; bad temper. **p. de algodón,** guncotton.
polvorear /polβore'ar/ *vt* to powder, dust with powder
polvoriento /polβo'riento/ *a* dusty; powdery, covered with powder
polvorín /polβo'rin/ *m,* very fine powder; powder magazine; powder flask
polvoroso /polβo'roso/ *a* dusty; covered with powder
pomada /po'maða/ *f,* pomade; salve, ointment
pomar /po'mar/ *m,* orchard (especially an apple orchard)
pómez /'pomeθ; 'pomes/ *f,* pumice stone (**piedra p.**)
pomo /'pomo/ *m, Bot.* pome; pomander; nosegay; pommel, hilt (of a sword); handle; rose (of watering can)
pomología /pomolo'hia/ *f,* pomology, art of fruit growing
pompa /'pompa/ *f,* pomp, splendor; ceremonial procession; air bubble; peacock's outspread tail; *Naut.* pump; billowing of clothes in the wind
Pompeya /pom'peia/ Pompeii
pompeyano /pompe'iano/ *a* Pompeian
pomposidad /pomposi'ðað/ *f,* pomposity
pomposo /pom'poso/ *a* stately, ostentatious, magnificent; inflated, pompous; florid, bombastic
pómulo /'pomulo/ *m,* cheekbone
ponche /'pontʃe/ *m,* punch, toddy
ponchera /pon'tʃera/ *f,* punch bowl
poncho /'pontʃo/ *a* lazy, negligent. *m,* military cloak; poncho, cape
ponderación /pondera'θion; pondera'sion/ *f,* weighing; reflection, consideration; exaggeration
ponderador /pondera'ðor/ *a* reflective, deliberate; exaggerated
ponderar /ponde'rar/ *vt* to weigh; consider, ponder; exaggerate; overpraise
ponderosidad /ponderosi'ðað/ *f,* heaviness; ponderousness, dullness
ponderoso /ponde'roso/ *a* heavy; ponderous; circumspect
ponedero /pone'ðero/ *a* egg-laying (of hens). *m,* nest
ponencia /po'nenθia; po'nensia/ *f,* clause, section; office of referee or arbitrator; report, referendum
poner /po'ner/ *vt irr* to place, put; arrange; set (the table); bet, stake; appoint (to an office); call, name; lay (eggs); set down (in writing); calculate, count; suppose; leave to a person's judgment; risk; contribute; prepare; need, take; cause, inspire (emotions); make, cause; adapt; add; cause to become (angry, etc.); insult; praise; (*with prep a* + *infin*) begin to. **p. a contribución,** to lay under contribution, turn to account, utilize. **ponerle el cascabel al gato** *or* **el collar al gato,** to bell the cat. **p. los cuernos (a),** to cuckold. **p. al corriente,** to bring up to date, inform. **p. a prueba,** to test. **p. casa,** to set up house. *Inf.* **p. colorado a,** to make blush. **p. coto a,** to put a stop to, check. **p. en comparación,** to compare. **p. conato en,** to put a great deal of effort into. **p. en cotejo,** to

collate. **p. en limpio,** to make a fair copy (of). **p. en marcha,** to start, set in motion. **p. en práctica,** to put into effect. **p. por caso,** to take as an example (e.g. *Pongamos por caso...* For example,...). **p. por encima (de),** to prefer —*vr* to place oneself; become; put on (garments, etc.); dirty or stain oneself; set (of the sun, stars); oppose; deck oneself, dress oneself up; arrive; (*with prep a + infin*) begin to. **ponerse al corriente,** to bring oneself up to date. **ponerse bien,** to improve; get better (in health). **ponerse colorado,** to blush, flush. **p. una base racional a la fe,** to give faith a rational foundation. **p. los cimientos de,** lay the foundation of, lay the foundations for. **p. una conferencia,** to make a long-distance call —*Pres. Indic.* **pongo, pones,** etc —*Fut.* **pondré,** etc —*Condit.* **pondría,** etc —*Imperat.* **pon.** *Past Part.* **puesto.** *Preterite* **puse, pusiste,** etc —*Pres. Subjunc.* **ponga,** etc —*Imperf. Subjunc.* **pusiese,** etc.

ponientada /ponien'taða/ *f,* steady west wind
poniente /po'niente/ *m,* west; west wind
pontazgo /pon'taθgo; pon'tasgo/ *m,* bridge toll
pontear /ponte'ar/ *vt* to bridge; make bridges
pontificado /pontifi'kaðo/ *m,* pontificate, papacy
pontífice /pon'tifiθe; pon'tifise/ *m,* pontifex; pope, pontiff; archbishop; bishop
pontificial /pontifi'θial; pontifi'sial/ *a* and *m,* pontifical
pontificio /ponti'fiθio; ponti'fisio/ *a* pontifical
pontón /pon'ton/ *m, Mil.* pontoon; hulk used as a prison, hospital, store, etc.; wooden bridge
pontonero /ponto'nero/ *m,* pontonier, military engineer
ponzoña /pon'θoɲa; pon'soɲa/ *f,* poison, venom
ponzoñoso /ponθo'ɲoso; ponso'ɲoso/ *a* poisonous, venomous; noxious; harmful
popa /'popa/ *f, Naut.* stern, poop. **en p.,** abaft, astern, aft
popelina /pope'lina/ *f,* poplin
populachería /populatʃe'ria/ *f,* cheap popularity with the rabble
populachero /popula'tʃero/ *a* mob, vulgar
populacho /popu'latʃo/ *m,* mob, rabble
popular /popu'lar/ *a* popular
popularidad /populari'ðað/ *f,* popularity
popularizar /populari'θar; populari'sar/ *vt* to popularize; —*vr* grow popular
popularmente /popular'mente/ *adv* popularly
populoso /popu'loso/ *a* populous, crowded
popurrí /popu'rri/ *m, Cul.* stew; potpourri; miscellany
poquedad /poke'ðað/ *f,* paucity, scarcity; timidity, cowardice; trifle, mere nothing
poquísimo /po'kisimo/ *a superl* **poco** very little
poquito /po'kito/ *m,* very little
por /por/ *prep* for; by; through, along; during; because, as (e.g. *Lo desecharon p. viejo,* They threw it away because it was old); however (e.g. *p. bonito que sea,* however pretty it is); during; in order to (e.g. *Lo hice p. no ofenderla,* I did it in order not to offend her); toward; in favor of, for; for the sake of; on account of, by reason of (e.g. *No pudo venir p. estar enfermo,* He could not come on account of his illness); via, by (e.g. *p. correo aéreo,* by airmail); as for (e.g. *P. mí, lo rechazo,* As for me, I refuse it. *p. mi cuenta,* to my way of thinking; on my own); in exchange for (e.g. *Me vendió dos libros p. seis dólares,* He sold me two books for six dollars); in the name of; as a substitute for, instead of (e.g. *Hace mi trabajo p. mí,* He is doing my work for me); per. **Por** has several uses: 1. Introduces the agent after a passive (e.g. *La novela fue escrita p. él,* The novel was written by him). 2. Expresses movement through, along or about (e.g. *Andaban p. la calle,* They were walking along (or down) the street). 3. Denotes time at or during which an action occurs (e.g. *Ocurrió p. entonces un acontecimiento de importancia,* About that time an important event occurred). 4. Expresses rate or proportion (e.g. *seis por ciento,* six percent). 5. With certain verbs, means "to be" and expresses vague futurity (e.g. *El libro queda p. escribir,* The book remains to be written). **p. cortesía,** by courtesy, out of politeness. **p. cortesía de,** by courtesy of. **p. escrito,** in writing. **p.**

fas or p. nefas, by fair means or foul; at any cost. **p. mucho que,** however great, however much; in spite of, notwithstanding. **¿P. qué?** Why? **p. si acaso,** in case, if by chance. **estar p.,** to be about to; be inclined to. **P. un clavo se pierde la herradura,** For want of a nail, the shoe was lost.
porcelana /porθe'lana; porse'lana/ *f,* porcelain, china; chinaware
porcentaje /porθen'tahe; porsen'tahe/ *m,* percentage
porche /'portʃe/ *m,* porch, portico
porcino /por'θino; por'sino/ *a* porcine. *m,* young pig; bruise
porción /por'θion; por'sion/ *f,* portion; *Com.* share; *Inf.* crowd; allowance, pittance
porcionista /porθio'nista; porsio'nista/ *mf* shareholder; sharer; boarding school student
porcuno /por'kuno/ *a* porcine
pordiosear /porðiose'ar/ *vi* to ask alms, beg
pordioseo /porðio'seo/ *m,* asking alms, begging
pordiosero /porðio'sero/ **(-ra)** *a* begging —*n* beggar
porfía /por'fia/ *f,* obstinacy; importunity; tenacity. **a p.,** in competition
porfiadamente /porfiaða'mente/ *adv* obstinately
porfiado /por'fiaðo/ *a* obstinate, obdurate, persistent
porfiar /por'fiar/ *vi* to be obstinate, insist; persist
pórfido /'porfiðo/ *m,* porphyry
pormenor /porme'nor/ *m,* particular, detail (gen. *pl*); secondary matter
pormenorizar /pormenori'θar; pormenori'sar/ *vt* to describe in detail
pornografía /pornogra'fia/ *f,* pornography
pornográfico /porno'grafiko/ *a* pornographic, obscene
poro /'poro/ *m,* pore
porosidad /porosi'ðað/ *f,* porosity, permeability
poroso /po'roso/ *a* porous, leaky
porque /'porke/ *conjunc* because, for; in order that
porqué /por'ke/ *m,* reason, wherefore, why; *Inf.* money. **el cómo y el p.,** the why and the wherefore
porquería /porke'ria/ *f, Inf.* filth, nastiness; dirty trick; rudeness, gross act; trifle, thing of no account
porquerizo, porquero /porke'riθo, por'kero; porke'riso, por'kero/ *m,* swineherd
porra /'porra/ *f,* club, bludgeon; last player (in children's games); *Inf.* vanity, boastfulness; bore, tedious person
porrada /po'rraða/ *f,* blow with a club; buffet, knock, fall; *Inf.* folly; glut, abundance
porrazo /po'rraθo; po'rraso/ *m,* blow with a club; buffet, knock, fall
porrear /porre'ar/ *vi Inf.* to insist, harp on
porrería /porre'ria/ *f, Inf.* folly; obduracy, persistence
porreta /po'rreta/ *f,* green leaves of leeks, onions, and cereals. *Inf.* **en p.,** stark-naked
porrino /po'rrino/ *m,* seed of a leek; young leek plant
porrón /po'rron/ *m,* winebottle with a spout; earthenware jug
portaaviones /portaa'βiones/ *m,* aircraft carrier
portacartas /porta'kartas/ *m,* mailbag
portachuelo /porta'tʃuelo/ *m,* defile, narrow mountain pass
portada /por'taða/ *f,* front, facade; frontispiece; title page; portal, doorway
portado /por'taðo/ (**bien** *or* **mal**) *a* well- or ill-dressed or behaved
portador /porta'ðor/ **(-ra)** *n* carrier. *m, Com.* bearer; *Mech.* carrier
portaestandarte /ˌportaestan'darte/ *m,* standard-bearer
portafolio /porta'folio/ *m,* portfolio
portafusil /porta'fusil/ *m,* rifle sling
portal /por'tal/ *m,* entrance, porch; portico; city gate
portalámpara /porta'lampara/ *f,* lamp holder; *Elec.* socket
portalibros /porta'liβros/ *m,* bookstrap
portalón /porta'lon/ *m,* gangway
portamanteo /portaman'teo/ *m,* traveling bag
portamonedas /portamo'neðas/ *m,* pocketbook; handbag, purse

portanuevas /porta'nueβas/ *mf* bringer of news, newsmonger

portaobjetos /portaoβ'hetos/ *m*, stage (of a microscope)

portaplumas /porta'plumas/ *m*, pen holder

portar /por'tar/ *vt* to retrieve (of dogs); carry (arms); —*vr* behave (well or badly); bear oneself, act; be well, or ill (in health)

portátil /por'tatil/ *a* portable

portatostadas /portatos'taðas/ *m*, toast rack

portavoz /porta'βoθ; porta'βos/ *m*, megaphone; spokesman, mouthpiece

portazgo /por'taθgo; por'tasgo/ *m*, toll; tollbooth

portazguero /portaθ'gero; portas'gero/ *m*, toll collector

portazo /por'taθo; por'taso/ *m*, bang of the door; slamming the door in a person's face

porte /'porte/ *m*, transport; *Com.* carriage; postage; freight, transport cost; porterage; behavior, conduct; bearing, looks; capacity, volume; size, dimension; nobility (of descent); *Naut.* tonnage. **p. pagado,** charges prepaid

porteador /portea'ðor/ *m*, carrier; porter; carter

portear /porte'ar/ *vt* to carry, transport; —*vr* migrate (of birds)

portento /por'tento/ *m*, marvel, prodigy, portent

portentoso /porten'toso/ *a* marvelous, portentous

porteo /por'teo/ *m*, porterage, cartage

portería /porte'ria/ *f*, porter's lodge; porter's employment; *Sports.* goal

portero /por'tero/ **(-ra)** *n* doorman, doorkeeper; porter; concierge; janitor; *Sports.* goalkeeper. **p. eléctrico,** door buzzer

portezuela /porte'θuela; porte'suela/ *f*, *dim* small door; carriage door; pocket flap

pórtico /'portiko/ *m*, portico, piazza; porch; vestibule, hall

portillo /por'tiλo; por'tiyo/ *m*, breach, opening; defile, narrow pass; *Fig.* loophole

portón /por'ton/ *m*, hall door, inner door

portorriqueño /portorri'keɲo/ **(-ña)** *a* and *n* Puerto Rican

portuario /por'tuario/ *a* dock, port

portugués /portu'ges/ **(-esa)** *a* and *n* Portuguese. *m*, Portuguese (language)

portuguesada /portuge'saða/ *f*, exaggeration

porvenir /porβe'nir/ *m*, future time

¡porvida! /por'βiða/ *interj* By the saints! By the Almighty!

pos /pos/ *prefix* after; behind. Also *adv* **en p.,** with the same meanings

posa /'posa/ *f*, tolling bell; *pl* buttocks

posada /po'saða/ *f*, dwelling; inn, tavern; lodging; hospitality

posaderas /posa'ðeras/ *f pl*, buttocks

posadero /posa'ðero/ **(-ra)** *n* innkeeper; boarding-house keeper

posar /po'sar/ *vi* to lodge, live; rest; alight, perch; —*vt* set down (a burden); —*vr* settle (liquids); (*with en or sobre*) perch upon

posdata /pos'ðata/ *f*, P.S., postscript

pose /'pose/ *f*, *Photo.* time exposure; *Inf.* pose

poseedor /posee'ðor/ **(-ra)** *n* possessor, holder

poseer /pose'er/ *vt irr* to own, possess; know (a language, etc.); —*vr* restrain oneself. **estar poseído por,** to be possessed by (passion, etc.); be thoroughly convinced of. See **creer**

posesión /pose'sion/ *f*, ownership, occupancy; possession; property, territory (often *pl*)

posesionarse /posesio'narse/ *vr* to take possession; lay hold (of)

posesivo /pose'siβo/ *a* possessive

poseso /po'seso/ *a* possessed of an evil spirit

posesor /pose'sor/ **(-ra)** *n* owner, possessor

posfecha /pos'fetʃa/ *f*, postdate

posguerra /pos'gerra/ *f*, postwar period

posibilidad /posiβili'ðað/ *f*, possibility; probability; opportunity, means, chance; *pl* property, wealth

posibilitar /posiβili'tar/ *vt* to make possible, facilitate

posible /po'siβle/ *a* possible. *m pl*, property, personal

wealth. **hacer lo p.** *or* **hacer todo lo p.,** to do everything possible; do one's best

posición /posi'θion; posi'sion/ *f*, placing; position; situation; status

positivamente /positiβa'mente/ *adv* positively, definitely

positivismo /positi'βismo/ *m*, positivism

positivista /positi'βista/ *a* positivistic. *mf* positivist

positivo /posi'tiβo/ *a* positive; certain, definite; (*Math. Elec.*) plus; true, real

pósito /'posito/ *m*, public granary; cooperative association

posma /'posma/ *f*, *Inf.* sluggishness, sloth

posmeridiano /posmeri'ðiano/ *a* and *m*, postmeridian

poso /'poso/ *m*, sediment; lees, dregs; repose, quietness

posponer /pospo'ner/ *vt irr* (*with prep a*) to place after; make subordinate to; value less than. See **poner**

posta /'posta/ *f*, post horse; stage, post; stake (cards)

postal /pos'tal/ *a* postal. *f*, postcard, postal card

poste /'poste/ *m*, post, stake

postema /pos'tema/ *f*, tumor, abscess; bore, tedious person

postergación /posterga'θion; posterga'sion/ *f*, delay; delaying; relegation; disregard of seniority (in promotion)

postergar /poster'gar/ *vt* to delay; disregard a senior claim to promotion

posteridad /posteri'ðað/ *f*, descendants; posterity

posterior /poste'rior/ *a* back, rear; hind; subsequent

posterioridad /posteriori'ðað/ *f*, posteriority

posteriormente /posterior'mente/ *adv* later, subsequently

postigo /pos'tigo/ *m*, secret door; grating, hatch; postern; shutter (of a window)

postillón /posti'λon; posti'yon/ *m*, postilion

postizo /pos'tiθo; pos'tiso/ *a* false, artificial, not natural. *m*, switch of false hair

postor /pos'tor/ *m*, bidder (at an auction)

postración /postra'θion; postra'sion/ *f*, prostration; exhaustion; depression, distress

postrar /pos'trar/ *vt* to cast down, demolish; prostrate, exhaust; —*vr* kneel down; be prostrated or exhausted

postre /'postre/ *a* last (in order). *m*, *Cul.* dessert. **a la p.,** at last, finally

postrero /pos'trero/ *a* last (in order); rearmost, hindmost

postrimeramente /postrimera'mente/ *adv* lastly, finally

postrimería /postrime'ria/ *f*, *Eccl.* last period of life

postulación /postula'θion; postula'sion/ *f*, entreaty, request

postulado /postu'laðo/ *m*, assumption; supposition; working hypothesis; *Geom.* postulate

postulante /postu'lante/ **(-ta)** *n* *Eccl.* postulant, applicant, candidate

postular /postu'lar/ *vt* to postulate

póstumo /'postumo/ *a* posthumous

postura /pos'tura/ *f*, posture, bearing; laying (of an egg); bid (at an auction); position; agreement, pact; bet, stake; planting; transplanted tree. **p. de vida,** way of life

potable /po'taβle/ *a* drinkable. **agua p.,** drinking water

potación /pota'θion; pota'sion/ *f*, potation, drink

potaje /po'tahe/ *m*, stew, potage; dried vegetables; mixed drink; hotchpotch

potasa /po'tasa/ *f*, potash

potasio /po'tasio/ *m*, potassium

pote /'pote/ *m*, pot; jar; flowerpot; *Cul.* cauldron; *Cul.* stew

potencia /po'tenθia; po'tensia/ *f*, power; potency; *Mech.* performance, capacity; strength, force; *Math.* power; rule, dominion

potencial /poten'θial; poten'sial/ *a* potential

potentado /poten'taðo/ *m*, potentate

potente /po'tente/ *a* potent; powerful; *Inf.* enormous

potestad /potes'taθ/ *f*, authority, power; podesta,

Italian magistrate; potentate; *Math.* power; *pl* angelic powers

potestativo /potesta'tiβo/ *a Law.* facultative

potingue /po'tiŋue/ *m, Inf.* brew; mixture; lotion; medicine; filthy place, pigsty

potra /'potra/ *f,* filly

potrada /po'traða/ *f,* herd of colts

potrear /potre'ar/ *vt Inf.* to tease, annoy

potro /'potro/ *m,* colt, foal; rack (for torture); vaulting horse. **p. mesteño,** mustang

poyo /'poio/ *m,* stone seat

pozal /po'θal; po'sal/ *m,* pail, bucket

pozo /'poθo; 'poso/ *m,* well; shaft (in a mine). *Auto.* **p. colector,** crankcase

práctica /'praktika/ *f,* practice; custom, habit; method; exercise

practicabilidad /praktikaβili'ðað/ *f,* feasibility

practicable /prakti'kaβle/ *a* feasible, practicable

prácticamente /'praktikamente/ *adv* practically, in practice

practicante /prakti'kante/ *m,* medical practitioner; medical student; *Med.* intern; first-aid practitioner

practicar /prakti'kar/ *vt* to execute, perform; practice; make

práctico /'praktiko/ *a* practical; experienced, expert; workable. *m, Naut.* pilot

pradeño /pra'ðeɲo/ *a* meadow, prairie

pradera /pra'ðera/ *f,* meadow, field; lawn

pradería /praðe'ria/ *f,* meadowland, prairie

prado /'praðo/ *m,* meadow; grassland; field; lawn; walk (in cities)

Praga /'praga/ Prague

pragmatismo /pragma'tismo/ *m,* pragmatism

pragmatista /pragma'tista/ *a* pragmatic. *mf* pragmatist

pravedad /praβe'ðað/ *f,* wickedness, immorality, depravity

pravo /'praβo/ *a* wicked, immoral, depraved

pre /pre/ *m, Mil.* daily pay —*prep insep* pre-

preámbulo /pre'ambulo/ *m,* preamble, preface; importunate digression

prebenda /pre'βenda/ *f, Eccl.* prebend, benefice; *Inf.* sinecure

preboste /pre'βoste/ *m,* provost

precario /pre'kario/ *a* precarious, uncertain, insecure

precaución /prekau'θion; prekau'sion/ *f,* precaution, safeguard

precaucionarse /prekauθio'narse; prekausio'narse/ *vr* to take precautions, safeguard oneself

precautelar /prekaute'lar/ *vt* to forewarn; take precautions

precaver /preka'βer/ *vt* to prevent, avoid; —*vr* (*with de or contra*) guard against

precavido /preka'βiðo/ *a* cautious, forewarned

precedencia /preθe'ðenθia; prese'ðensia/ *f,* priority, precedence; superiority; preference, precedence

precedente /preθe'ðente; prese'ðente/ *a* preceding. *m,* antecedent; precedent

preceder /preθe'ðer; prese'ðer/ *vt* to precede; have precedence over, be superior to

preceptivo /preθep'tiβo; presep'tiβo/ *a* preceptive; didactic

precepto /pre'θepto; pre'septo/ *m,* precept; order, injunction; rule, commandment. **de p.,** obligatory

preceptor /preθep'tor; presep'tor/ **(-ra)** *n* teacher, instructor, tutor, preceptor

preces /'preθes; 'preses/ *f pl, Eccl.* prayers; entreaties

preciado /pre'θiaðo; pre'siaðo/ *a* excellent, esteemed, precious; boastful

preciar /pre'θiar; pre'siar/ *vt* to esteem, value; valuate, price; —*vr* boast

precintar /preθin'tar; presin'tar/ *vt* to seal; rope, string, tie up

precinto /pre'θinto; pre'sinto/ *m,* sealing; roping, tying up; strap

precio /'preθio; 'presio/ *m,* price, cost; recompense; reward; premium; rate; reputation, importance; esteem. **p. de tasa,** controlled price

preciosidad /preθiosi'ðað; presiosi'ðað/ *f,* preciousness; exquisiteness, fineness; richness; wittiness; *Inf.* loveliness, beauty; thing of beauty

precioso /pre'θioso; pre'sioso/ *a* precious; exquisite, fine, rare; rich; witty; *Inf.* lovely, delicious, attractive

precipicio /preθi'piθio; presi'pisio/ *m,* precipice; heavy fall; ruin, disaster

precipitación /preθipita'θion; presipita'sion/ *f,* precipitancy, haste; rashness; *Chem.* precipitation

precipitadamente /preθipitaða'mente; presipitaða'mente/ *adv* precipitately, in haste; rashly, foolishly

precipitado /preθipi'taðo; presipi'taðo/ *a* precipitate; rash, thoughtless. *m, Chem.* precipitate

precipitar /preθipi'tar; presipi'tar/ *vt* to precipitate, hurl headlong; hasten; *Chem.* precipitate; —*vr* hurl oneself headlong; hasten, rush

precipitoso /preθipi'toso; presipi'toso/ *a* precipitous; rash, heedless

precisamente /preθisa'mente; presisa'mente/ *adv* exactly, precisely, just; necessarily. **Y p. en aquel instante llegó,** And just at that moment he arrived

precisar /preθi'sar; presi'sar/ *vt* to fix, arrange; set forth, draw up, state; compel, force, oblige

precisión /preθi'sion; presi'sion/ *f,* accuracy, precision; necessity, conciseness, clarity; compulsion, obligation

preciso /pre'θiso; pre'siso/ *a* necessary, unavoidable; concise, clear; precise, exact

precitado /preθi'taðo; presi'taðo/ *a* aforementioned

preclaro /pre'klaro/ *a* illustrious, distinguished, celebrated

precocidad /prekoθi'ðað; prekosi'ðað/ *f,* precocity

precognición /prekogni'θion; prekogni'sion/ *f,* foreknowledge

preconcebido /prekonθe'βiðo; prekonse'βiðo/ *a* preconceived

preconcepto /prekon'θepto; prekon'septo/ *m,* preconceived idea, preconceived notion

preconizar /prekoni'θar; prekoni'sar/ *vt* to eulogize, praise publicly

preconocer /prekono'θer; prekono'ser/ *vt irr* to know beforehand; foresee. See **conocer**

precoz /pre'koθ; pre'kos/ *a* precocious

precursor /prekur'sor/ **(-ra)** *a* precursory; preceding, previous —*n* precursor

predecesor /preðeθe'sor; preðese'sor/ **(-ra)** *n* predecessor

predecir /preðe'θir; preðe'sir/ *vt irr* to foretell, prophesy. See **decir**

predestinación /preðestina'θion; preðestina'sion/ *f,* predestination

predestinado /preðesti'naðo; preðesti'naðo/ **(-da)** *a* predestined; foreordained —*n* one of the predestined

predestinar /preðesti'nar/ *vt* to predestine, foreordain

predeterminación /preðetermina'θion; preðetermina'sion/ *f,* predetermination

predeterminar /preðetermi'nar/ *vt* to predetermine

prédica /'preðika/ *f, Inf.* (contemptuous) sermon

predicación /preðika'θion; preðika'sion/ *f,* preaching; homily, sermon

predicadera /preðika'ðera/ *f,* pulpit; *pl Inf.* talent for preaching

predicado /preði'kaðo/ *m,* (*Gram. Philos.*) predicate

predicador /preðika'ðor/ **(-ra)** *a* preaching —*n* preacher

predicamento /preðika'mento/ *m,* predicament; reputation

predicar /preði'kar/ *vt* to publish; manifest; preach; —*vi* overpraise; *Inf.* lecture, scold. **p. en el desierto,** to preach to the wind

predicción /preðik'θion; preðik'sion/ *f,* prediction, prophecy

predilección /preðilek'θion; preðilek'sion/ *f,* predilection, preference, partiality

predilecto /preði'lekto/ *a* favorite, preferred

predisponer /preðispo'ner/ *vt irr* to predispose. See **poner**

predisposición /preðisposi'θion; preðisposi'sion/ *f,* predisposition; tendency, prejudice

predominación /preðomina'θion; preðomina'sion/ *f,* predominance

predominante /preðomi'nante/ *a* predominant; prevailing

predominar /preðomi'nar/ *vi* and *vt* to predominate; prevail; tower above; overlook

predominio /preðo'minio/ *m*, predominance, ascendancy, preponderance

preeminencia /preemi'nenθia; preemi'nensia/ *f*, preeminence

preeminente /preemi'nente/ *a* preeminent

preexistencia /preeksis'tenθia; preeksis'tensia/ *f*, preexistence

preexistente /preeksis'tente/ *a* preexistent

preexistir /preeksis'tir/ *vi* to preexist, exist before

prefacio /pre'faθio; pre'fasio/ *m*, introduction, preface, prologue; *Eccl.* preface

prefecto /pre'fekto/ *m*, prefect

prefectura /prefek'tura/ *f*, prefecture

preferencia /prefe'renθia; prefe'rensia/ *f*, preference; superiority. **de p.**, preferred, favorite; preferably

preferente /prefe'rente/ *a* preferable; preferential; preferred (of stock)

preferible /prefe'riβle/ *a* preferable

preferir /prefe'rir/ *vt irr* to prefer; excel, exceed —*Pres. Part.* **prefiriendo.** *Pres. Indic.* **prefiero, prefieres, prefiere, prefieren.** *Preterite* **prefirió, prefirieron.** *Pres. Subjunc.* **prefiera, prefieras, prefiera, prefieran.** *Imperf. Subjunc.* **prefiriese,** etc.

prefijar /prefi'har/ *vt* to prefix

prefijo /pre'fiho/ *m*, prefix

prefinir /prefi'nir/ *vt* to fix a time limit for

prefulgente /preful'hente/ *a* brilliant, shining, resplendent

pregón /pre'gon/ *m*, public proclamation; marriage banns

pregonar /prego'nar/ *vt* to proclaim publicly; cry one's wares; publish abroad; eulogize, praise; proscribe, outlaw. **p. a los cuatro vientos,** *Inf.* to shout from the rooftops

pregonería /pregone'ria/ *f*, office of the town crier

pregonero /prego'nero/ *m*, town crier

preguerra /pre'gerra/ *f*, prewar period

pregunta /pre'gunta/ *f*, question; *Com.* inquiry; questionnaire, interrogation. *Inf.* **andar** (*or* **estar) a la cuarta p.,** to be very hard up, be on the rocks. **hacer una p.,** to ask a question

preguntador /pregunta'ðor/ **(-ra)** *a* questioning; inquisitive —*n* questioner; inquisitive person

preguntar /pregun'tar/ *vt* to question, ask; (*with por*) inquire for; —*vr* ask oneself, wonder

prehistoria /preis'toria/ *f*, prehistory

prehistórico /preis'toriko/ *a* prehistoric

prejuicio /pre'huiθio; pre'huisio/ *m*, prejudice

prejuzgar /prehuθ'gar; prehus'gar/ *vt* to prejudge, judge hastily

prelacía /prela'θia; prela'sia/ *f*, prelacy

prelación /prela'θion; prela'sion/ *f*, preference

prelado /pre'laðo/ *m*, prelate

preliminar /prelimi'nar/ *a* preliminary, prefatory. *m*, preliminary

preludiar /prelu'ðiar/ *vi* and *vt Mus.* to play a prelude (to); —*vt* prepare, initiate

preludio /pre'luðio/ *m*, introduction, prologue; *Mus.* prelude; *Mus.* overture

prematuro /prema'turo/ *a* premature, untimely; unseasonable; immature, unripe

premeditación /premeðita'θion; premeðita'sion/ *f*, premeditation

premeditar /premeði'tar/ *vt* to premeditate, plan in advance

premiador /premia'ðor/ **(-ra)** *a* rewarding —*n* rewarder

premiar /pre'miar/ *vt* to reward, requite

premio /'premio/ *m*, prize; reward; premium; *Com.* interest. **p. en metálico,** cash prize. *Inf.* **p. gordo,** first prize (in a lottery)

premioso /pre'mioso/ *a* tight; troublesome, annoying; stern, strict; slow-moving; burdensome, hard; labored (of speech or style)

premisa /pre'misa/ *f*, premise; sign, indication

premonitorio /premoni'torio/ *a* premonitory

premura /pre'mura/ *f*, urgency, haste

prenda /'prenda/ *f*, pledge; token, sign; jewel; article of clothing; talent, gift; loved one; *pl* game of forfeits

prendador /prenda'ðor/ **(-ra)** *n* pledger

prendamiento /prenda'miento/ *m*, pawning

prendar /pren'dar/ *vt* to pawn; charm, delight; —*vr* (*with de*) take a liking to

prender /pren'der/ *vt* to seize; arrest; capture, catch —*vi* take root (plants); catch fire; be infectious

prendería /prende'ria/ *f*, second-hand shop

prendero /pren'dero/ **(-ra)** *n* second-hand dealer

prendimiento /prendi'miento/ *m*, seizure, capture; arrest

prenombre /pre'nombre/ *m*, given name, praenomen

prensa /'prensa/ *f*, press; printing press; newspapers, the press. **dar a la p.,** to publish

prensado /pren'saðo/ *m*, **prensadura** *f*, pressing; flattening; squeezing

prensar /pren'sar/ *vt* to press; squeeze

prensil /pren'sil/ *a* prehensile

preñado /pre'ɲaðo/ *a* pregnant; bulging, sagging (walls, etc.); swollen. *m*, pregnancy

preñez /pre'ɲeθ; pre'ɲes/ *f*, pregnancy; suspense

preocupación /preokupa'θion; preokupa'sion/ *f*, anxiety, preoccupation; prejudice

preocupadamente /preokupaða'mente/ *adv* preoccupiedly, absentmindedly; with prejudice

preocupar /preoku'par/ *vt* to preoccupy; make anxious; bias, prejudice; —*vr* be anxious; be prejudiced

preordinar /preorði'nar/ *vt Eccl.* to predestine

preparación /prepara'θion; prepara'sion/ *f*, preparation; treatment; compound, specific

preparado /prepa'raðo/ *a* ready, prepared. *m*, preparation, patent food, etc.

preparar /prepa'rar/ *vt* to prepare; —*vr* prepare oneself; qualify

preparativo /prepara'tiβo/ *a* preparatory. *m*, preparation

preparatorio /prepara'torio/ *a* preparatory

preponderancia /preponde'ranθia; preponde'ransia/ *f*, preponderance

preponderante /preponde'rante/ *a* preponderant; dominant

preponderar /preponde'rar/ *vi* to preponderate; dominate; outweigh

preponer /prepo'ner/ *vt irr* to put before. See **poner**

preposición /preposi'θion; preposi'sion/ *f*, preposition

prepósito /pre'posito/ *m*, chairman, head, president; *Eccl.* provost

prepucio /pre'puθio; pre'pusio/ *m*, prepuce

prerrafaelista /prerrafae'lista/ *a* and *mf* Pre-Raphaelite

prerrogativa /prerroga'tiβa/ *f*, prerogative

presa /'presa/ *f*, hold, grasp; seizure, capture; booty; dam; lock (on rivers, canals); weir; ditch, trench; embankment; slice, bit. **hacer p.,** to seize; take advantage of (circumstances)

presagiar /presa'hiar/ *vt* to prophesy, presage, bode

presagio /pre'sahio/ *m*, presage, sign; presentiment, foreboding

présbita /'presβita/ *a* long-sighted, farsighted

presbiterado /presβite'raðo/ *m*, priesthood; holy orders

presbiteriano /presβite'riano/ **(-na)** *a* and *n* Presbyterian

presbítero /pres'βitero/ *m*, priest

presciencia /pres'θienθia; pres'siensia/ *f*, prescience, foresight

presciente /pres'θiente; pres'siente/ *a* prescient, farsighted

prescindible /presθin'diβle; pressin'diβle/ *a* nonessential, able to be dispensed with

prescindir /presθin'dir; pressin'dir/ *vi* (*with de*) to pass over, omit; do without. **Prescindiendo de esto...,** Leaving this aside....

prescribir /preskri'βir/ *vt* to prescribe, order

prescripción /preskrip'θion; preskrip'sion/ *f*, prescription

presea /pre'sea/ *f*, jewel, object of value

presencia /pre'senθia; pre'sensia/ *f*, presence, attendance; appearance, looks; ostentation. **p. de ánimo,** presence of mind

presenciar /presen'θiar; presen'siar/ *vt* to be present at; witness, behold

presentación /presenta'θion; presenta'sion/ *f*, presentation; introduction

presentar /presen'tar/ *vt* to show; present, make a gift of; introduce (persons); —*vr* occur; present oneself; offer one's services

presente /pre'sente/ *a* present. *m*, gift; present time. *Law.* **Por estas presentes...,** By these presents.... **tener p.,** to remember

presentimiento /presenti'miento/ *m*, presentiment, apprehension

presentir /presen'tir/ *vt irr* to have a presentiment of. See **sentir**

preservación /preserβa'θion; preserβa'sion/ *f*, preservation, protection, saving

preservar /preser'βar/ *vt* to preserve, protect, save

preservativo /preserβa'tiβo/ *a* preservative. *m*, preservative, safeguard, protection

presidencia /presi'ðenθia; presi'ðensia/ *f*, presidency; chairmanship; presidential seat or residence

presidencial /presiðen'θial; presiðen'sial/ *a* presidential

presidenta /presi'ðenta/ *f*, female president; president's wife; chairwoman

presidente /presi'ðente/ *m*, president; chairman; head, director; presiding judge

presidiar /presi'ðiar/ *vt* to garrison

presidiario /presi'ðiario/ *m*, convict

presidio /pre'siðio/ *m*, garrison; garrison town; fortress; penitentiary; imprisonment; *Law.* hard labor; assistance, protection

presidir /presi'ðir/ *vt* to preside over; act as chairperson for; influence, determine

presilla /pre'siλa; pre'siya/ *f*, loop, shank, noose; press stud

presión /pre'sion/ *f*, pressure

preso /'preso/ **(-sa)** *n* prisoner, captive; convict

prestación /presta'θion; presta'sion/ *f*, lending, loan. **p. vecinal,** corvée

prestador /presta'ðor/ **(-ra)** *a* lending, loan —*n* lender

prestamente /presta'mente/ *adv* expeditiously, promptly

prestamista /presta'mista/ *mf* moneylender; pawnbroker

préstamo /'prestamo/ *m*, loan; lending. **casa de préstamos,** pawnshop

prestar /pres'tar/ *vt* to lend; assist; pay (attention); give; —*vi* be useful; give, expand; —*vr* be suitable; lend itself; offer oneself. **tomar prestado,** to borrow

prestatario /presta'tario/ **(-ia)** *n* money borrower, debtor

preste /'preste/ *m*, celebrant of high mass. **el p. Juan,** title of Prester John

presteza /pres'teθa; pres'tesa/ *f*, speed; promptness, dispatch

prestidigitación /prestiðihita'θion; prestiðihita'sion/ *f*, prestidigitation

prestidigitador /prestiðihita'ðor/ **(-ra)** *n* juggler, conjurer

prestigio /pres'tihio/ *m*, magic spell, sorcery; trick, illusion (of conjurers, etc.); influence, prestige

prestigioso /presti'hioso/ *a* illusory; influential

presto /'presto/ *a* quick, speedy; prompt, ready. *m*, pressure cooker —*adv* immediately; soon; quickly. **de p.,** speedily

presumido /presu'miðo/ *a* conceited, vain; presumptuous

presumir /presu'mir/ *vt* to suppose, presume; —*vi* be conceited

presunción /presun'θion; presun'sion/ *f*, supposition, presumption; vanity, presumptuousness

presuntivo /presun'tiβo/ *a* presumptive

presuntuosidad /presuntuosi'ðað/ *f*, presumptuousness

presuntuoso /presun'tuoso/ *a* presumptuous, vain

presuponer /presupo'ner/ *vt irr* to presuppose, assume; budget, estimate. See **poner**

presuposición /presuposi'θion; presuposi'sion/ *f*, presupposition

presupuesto /presu'puesto/ *m*, motive, reason; supposition, assumption; estimate; *Com.* tender; national budget

presuroso /presu'roso/ *a* swift, speedy

pretencioso /preten'θioso; preten'sioso/ *a* pretentious, vain

pretender /preten'der/ *vt* to seek, solicit; claim; apply for; attempt, try; woo, court

pretendiente /preten'diente/ **(-ta)** *n* pretender; candidate; petitioner; suitor

pretensión /preten'sion/ *f*, pretension; claim; *pl* ambitions

pretérito /pre'terito/ *a* past. *m*, preterite

pretextar /preteks'tar/ *vt* to allege as a pretext or excuse

pretexto /pre'teksto/ *m*, pretext, excuse

prevalecer /preβale'θer; preβale'ser/ *vi irr* to prevail; be dominant; take root (plants). See **conocer**

prevaleciente /preβale'θiente; preβale'siente/ *a* prevailing; prevalent

prevaricación /preβarika'θion; preβarika'sion/ *f*, prevarication

prevaricador /preβarika'ðor/ **(-ra)** *n* prevaricator

prevaricar /preβari'kar/ *vi* to prevaricate

prevención /preβen'θion; preβen'sion/ *f*, prevention; precaution; prejudice; police station; *Mil.* guard room; foresight, prevision; preparation. **de p.,** as a precaution

prevenido /preβe'niðo/ *a* prepared; cautious, forewarned

prevenir /preβe'nir/ *vt irr* to prepare; prevent, avoid; warn; prejudice; occur, happen; *Fig.* overcome (obstacles); —*vr* be ready; be forewarned. See **venir**

preventivo /preβen'tiβo/ *a* preventive

prever /pre'βer/ *vt irr* to foresee, forecast, anticipate. See **ver**

previamente /preβia'mente/ *adv* previously, in advance

previo /'preβio/ *a* previous, advance

previsión /preβi'sion/ *f*, forecast; foresight, prevision, prescience. **p. social,** social insurance

previsor /preβi'sor/ *a* farsighted, provident

prieto /'prieto/ *a* almost black, blackish; tight; mean, avaricious

prima /'prima/ *f*, *Eccl.* prime; *Com.* premium; female cousin

primacía /prima'θia; prima'sia/ *f*, supremacy, preeminence; primacy; primateship

primada /pri'maða/ *f*, *Inf.* act of sponging on, taking advantage of

primado /pri'maðo/ *m*, primate; primateship

primario /pri'mario/ *a* primary. *m*, professor who gives the first lecture of the day

primavera /prima'βera/ *f*, springtime; primrose; figured silk material; beautifully colored thing; youth; prime

primaveral /primaβe'ral/ *a* spring, spring-like

primeramente /primera'mente/ *adv* first; in the first place

primerizo /prime'riθo; prime'riso/ **(-za)** *n* novice; beginner; apprentice; firstborn

primero /pri'mero/ *a* first; former; excellent, first-rate —*adv* first; in the first place. **primera enseñanza,** primary education. **primera materia,** raw material. **primer plano,** *Art.* foreground. **primera cura,** first aid. **de buenas a primeras,** all at once, suddenly

primicia /pri'miθia; pri'misia/ *f*, first fruits; offering of first fruits; *pl* first effects

primitivo /primi'tiβo/ *a* original, early; primitive

primo /'primo/ **(-ma)** *a* first; excellent, fine —*n* cousin; *Inf.* simpleton; *Inf.* pigeon, dupe. **p. carnal,** first cousin. *Inf.* **hacer el p.,** to be a dupe. *Inf.* **ser prima hermana de,** to be the twin of (of things)

primogénito /primo'henito/ **(-ta)** *a* and *n* firstborn

primogenitura /primoheni'tura/ *f*, primogeniture

primor /pri'mor/ *m*, exquisite care; beauty, loveliness; thing of beauty

primoroso /primo'roso/ *a* beautiful; exquisitely done; dexterous, skillful

princesa /prin'θesa; prin'sesa/ *f*, princess

principado /prinθi'paðo; prinsi'paðo/ m, principality; princedom; superiority, preeminence

principal /prinθi'pal; prinsi'pal/ a chief, principal; illustrious; fundamental, first. m, head, principal (of a firm); *Com.* capital, principal; first floor

principalmente /prinθipal'mente; prinsipal'mente/ adv principally, chiefly

príncipe /'prinθipe; 'prinsipe/ m, leader; prince. **p. de Asturias,** prince of Asturias. **p. de la sangre,** prince of the blood royal

principesco /prinθi'pesko; prinsi'pesko/ a princely

principiante /prinθi'piante; prinsi'piante/ (**-ta**) n beginner, novice; apprentice

principiar /prinθi'piar; prinsi'piar/ vt to begin, commence

principio /prin'θipio; prin'sipio/ m, beginning; principle; genesis, origin; rudiment; axiom; constituent. **al p.,** at first. **a principios,** at the beginning of (the month, year, etc.). **en p.,** in principle

pringar /prin'gar/ vt *Cul.* to soak in fat; stain with grease; *Inf.* wound; take part in a business deal; slander; —vr *Inf.* appropriate, misuse (funds, etc.)

pringoso /prin'goso/ a greasy

pringue /'pringue/ mf, animal fat, lard; grease spot

prior /prior/ m, prior; parish priest

priora /'priora/ f, prioress

prioridad /priori'ðað/ f, priority

prisa /'prisa/ f, haste, speed; skirmish, foray. **a toda p.,** with all speed. **correr p.,** to be urgent. **dar p.,** to hasten, speed up. **darse (or estar de) p.,** to hurry

prisión /pri'sion/ f, prison, jail; seizure; captivity, imprisonment; *Fig.* bond; obstacle, shackle; pl fetters

prisma /'prisma/ m, prism

prismáticos /pris'matikos/ m pl, field glasses

prisonero /priso'nero/ (**-ra**) n prisoner; *Fig.* victim (of passion, etc.)

pristino /pris'tino/ a pristine

privación /priβa'θion; priβa'sion/ f, privation; lack, shortage; deprivation; degradation

privada /pri'βaða/ f, toilet, privy, water closet

privadamente /priβaða'mente/ adv privately; individually, separately

privado /pri'βaðo/ a private; individual, personal. m, favorite; confidant

privanza /pri'βanθa; pri'βansa/ f, court favor, intimacy of princes

privar /pri'βar/ vt to deprive; dismiss (from office); interdict, forbid; —vi prevail, be in favor; —vr swoon; deprive oneself

privilegiar /priβile'hiar/ vt to privilege; bestow a favor on

privilegio /priβi'lehio/ m, privilege; prerogative; concession; copyright; patent

pro /pro/ mf advantage, benefit. **el p. y el contra,** the pros and cons. **en p.,** in favor

proa /'proa/ f, prow, bow

probabilidad /proβaβili'ðað/ f, probability

probable /pro'βaβle/ a probable; likely; provable

probación /proβa'θion; proβa'sion/ f, proof, test; noviciate, probation

probado /pro'βaðo/ a tried, tested, proved

probar /pro'βar/ vt irr to prove; test; taste; try on (clothes); —vi suit; (with prep a + infin) try to. **p. fortuna,** to try one's luck —*Pres. Indic.* **pruebo, pruebas, prueba, prueban.** *Pres. Subjunc.* **pruebe, pruebes, prueben**

probatorio /proβa'torio/ a probationary

probidad /proβi'ðað/ f, probity, trustworthiness, honesty

problema /pro'βlema/ m, problem

problemático /proβle'matiko/ a problematical, uncertain

probo /'proβo/ a honest, trustworthy

procacidad /prokaθi'ðað; prokasi'ðað/ f, insolence, pertness

procaz /pro'kaθ; pro'kas/ a insolent, pert, brazen

procedencia /proθe'ðenθia; prose'ðensia/ f, origin, source; parentage, descent; port of sailing or call

procedente /proθe'ðente; prose'ðente/ a arriving or coming from

proceder /proθe'ðer; prose'ðer/ vi to proceed; be-

have; originate, arise; continue, go on; act. *Law.* **p. contra,** to proceed against (a person)

procedimiento /proθeði'miento; proseði'miento/ m, proceeding, advancement; procedure; legal practice; process

proceloso /proθe'loso; prose'loso/ a tempestuous

prócer /'proθer; 'proser/ a exalted, eminent; lofty. m, exalted personage

procesado /proθe'saðo; prose'saðo/ (**-da**) n defendant

procesamiento /proθesa'miento; prosesa'miento/ m, suing, suit; indictment. **p. de textos,** word processing.

procesar /proθe'sar; prose'sar/ vt *Law.* to proceed against, sue

procesión /proθe'sion; prose'sion/ f, proceeding, emanating; procession; *Inf.* train, string. **andar (or ir) por dentro la p.,** to feel keenly without betraying one's emotion

proceso /pro'θeso; pro'seso/ m, process; progress; advancement; lapse of time; lawsuit

proclama /pro'klama/ f, proclamation; announcement; publication of marriage banns

proclamación /proklama'θion; proklama'sion/ f, proclamation; acclaim, applause

proclamar /prokla'mar/ vt to proclaim; acclaim; publish abroad; reveal, show

proclividad /prokliβi'ðað/ f, proclivity, tendency

procomún /proko'mun/ m, social or public welfare

procreación /prokrea'θion; prokrea'sion/ f, procreation

procreador /prokrea'ðor/ (**-ra**) a procreative —n procreator

procrear /prokre'ar/ vt to procreate, beget, engender

procuración /prokura'θion; prokura'sion/ f, procurement; assiduity, care; *Law.* power of attorney; *Law.* attorneyship

procurador /prokura'ðor/ (**-ra**) m, proxy; *Law.* attorney; proctor —n procurer

procurar /proku'rar/ vt to try, attempt; procure, get; exercise the profession of a lawyer

prodigalidad /proðigali'ðað/ f, prodigality, lavishness; waste, extravagance

prodigar /proði'gar/ vt to waste, squander; lavish, bestow freely; —vr make oneself cheap

prodigio /pro'ðihio/ m, marvel, wonder; prodigy; monster; miracle

prodigiosidad /proðihiosi'ðað/ f, prodigiousness

prodigioso /proði'hioso/ a wonderful; prodigious; monstrous; miraculous

pródigo /'proðigo/ (**-ga**) a wasteful, extravagant; lavish, generous —n spendthrift, wastrel, prodigal

producción /proðuk'θion; proðuk'sion/ f, production; output, yield; generation (of heat, etc.); crop

producir /proðu'θir; proðu'sir/ vt irr to produce; generate; yield, give; cause, occasion; publish; —vr explain oneself; arise, appear, be produced. **p. efecto,** to have effect; take effect. See **conducir**

productividad /proðuktiβi'ðað/ f, productivity

productivo /proðuk'tiβo/ a productive; fertile; profitable

producto /pro'ðukto/ m, produce; product; profit; yield, gain; *Math.* product. *Chem.* **p. derivado,** by-product

productor /proðuk'tor/ (**-ra**) a productive —n producer

proemio /pro'emio/ m, prologue, preface, introduction

proeza /pro'eθa; pro'esa/ f, prowess, gallantry; skill

profanación /profana'θion; profana'sion/ f, profanation

profanador /profana'ðor/ (**-ra**) n profaner, transgressor

profanar /profa'nar/ vt to profane

profanidad /profani'ðað/ f, profanity

profano /pro'fano/ a profane; dissolute; pleasure-loving, worldly; immodest; lay, ignorant

profecía /profe'θia; profe'sia/ f, prophecy; *Eccl.* Book of the Prophets; opinion, view

proferir /profe'rir/ vt irr to utter, pronounce. See **herir**

profesar /profe'sar/ vt to exercise, practice (professions); *Eccl.* profess; believe in; teach

profesión /profe'sion/ f, profession; trade, occupation; avowal, admission

profesional /profesio'nal/ a professional

profesionalismo /profesiona'lismo/ m, professionalism

profeso /pro'feso/ (**-sa**) a *Eccl.* professed —n professed monk

profesor /profe'sor/ (**-ra**) n teacher; professor

profesorado /profeso'raðo/ m, teaching staff; teaching profession; professorship; professorate

profeta /pro'feta/ m, prophet; seer

profético /pro'fetiko/ a prophetic

profetisa /profe'tisa/ f, prophetess

profetizar /profeti'θar; profeti'sar/ vt to prophesy; imagine, suppose

proficiente /profi'θiente; profi'siente/ a proficient

profiláctico /profi'laktiko/ a and m, prophylactic

prófugo /'profugo/ (**-ga**) a and n fugitive from justice. m, *Mil.* one who evades military service

profundamente /profunda'mente/ adv profoundly; acutely, deeply

profundidad /profundi'ðað/ f, depth; profundity, obscurity; *Geom.* depth; concavity; intensity (of feeling); vastness (of knowledge, etc.)

profundizar /profundi'θar; profundi'sar/ vt to deepen; hollow out; *Fig.* go into deeply, fathom

profundo /pro'fundo/ a deep; low; *Fig.* intense, acute; abstruse, profound; *Fig.* vast, extensive; high. m, depth, profundity; *Poet.* ocean, the deep; *Poet.* hell

profuso /pro'fuso/ a profuse, abundant; extravagant, wasteful

progenie /pro'henie/ f, descendants

prognosis /prog'nosis/ f, prognosis; forecast

programa /pro'grama/ m, program; edict, public notice; plan, scheme; *Educ.* calendar; syllabus; timetable

progresar /progre'sar/ vt and vi to make progress; progress, advance

progresión /progre'sion/ f, progression; advancement, progress

progresista /progre'sista/ a *Polit.* progressive. mf progressive

progresivo /progre'siβo/ a progressive; advancing

progreso /pro'greso/ m, progress, advancement; growth; improvement, development

prohibente /proi'βente/ a prohibitory, prohibitive

prohibición /proiβi'θion; proiβi'sion/ f, forbidding, prohibition

prohibicionista /proiβiθio'nista; proiβisio'nista/ mf prohibitionist —a prohibitionist

prohibir /proi'βir/ vt to forbid, prohibit. «Prohibido el paso,» "No thoroughfare"

prohibitivo, prohibitorio /proiβi'tiβo, proiβi'torio/ a prohibitive

prohijador /proiha'ðor/ (**-ra**) n adopter (of a child)

prohijamiento /proiha'miento/ m, child adoption; fathering (of a bill, etc.)

prohijar /proi'har/ vt to adopt (children, ideas); *Fig.* father

prohombre /pro'ombre/ m, master of a guild; respected, wellliked man

prójimo /'prohimo/ m, fellow man, brother, neighbor.

prole /'prole/ f, progeny, young offspring

proletariado /proleta'riaðo/ m, proletariat

proletario /prole'tario/ a poor; common, vulgar. m, plebeian; pauper; proletarian

prolífico /pro'lifiko/ a prolific; abundant; fertile

prolijidad /prolihi'ðað/ f, verbosity, prolixity; nicety, scruple; importunity, tediousness

prolijo /pro'liho/ a verbose, prolix; fussy, fastidious; tedious, importunate

prologar /prolo'gar/ vt to prologue; provide with a preface

prólogo /'prologo/ m, preface; prologue; introduction

prolongación /proloŋga'θion; proloŋga'sion/ f, lengthening; prolongation, protraction; extension

prolongado /proloŋ'gaðo/ a prolonged; oblong, long

prolongar /proloŋ'gar/ vt to lengthen; *Geom.* produce; prolong, spin out

promediar /prome'ðiar/ vt to distribute or divide into two equal portions; average; —vi arbitrate; place oneself between two people; reach half-time

promedio /pro'meðio/ m, average; middle, center

promesa /pro'mesa/ f, promise; augury, favorable sign

prometedor /promete'ðor/ (**-ra**) a promising —n promiser

prometer /prome'ter/ vt to promise; attest, certify; —vi promise well, look hopeful; —vr devote oneself to service of God; anticipate confidently, expect; become engaged (marriage). *Inf.* **prometérselas muy felices,** to have high hopes

prometido /prome'tiðo/ (**-da**) n betrothed. m, promise

prometimiento /prometi'miento/ m, promise; promising

prominencia /promi'nenθia; promi'nensia/ f, prominence, protuberance; eminence, hill

prominente /promi'nente/ a prominent, protuberant; eminent, elevated

promiscuar /promis'kuar/ vi to eat meat and fish on fast days

promiscuidad /promiskui'ðað/ f, promiscuity; ambiguity

promiscuo /pro'miskuo/ a indiscriminate, haphazard, promiscuous; ambiguous

promisión /promi'sion/ f, promise

promisorio /promi'sorio/ a promissory

promoción /promo'θion; promo'sion/ f, promotion; batch, class, year (of recruits, students, etc.)

promontorio /promon'torio/ m, headland; promontory; cumbersome object

promotor /promo'tor/ (**-ra**) a promotive —n promoter; supporter

promover /promo'βer/ vt irr to promote, further, advance; promote (a person). **p. un proceso (a),** to bring a suit (against). See **mover**

promulgación /promulga'θion; promulga'sion/ f, promulgation

promulgar /promul'gar/ vt to publish officially, proclaim; promulgate. *Law.* **p. sentencia,** to pass judgment

pronombre /pro'nombre/ m, pronoun

pronosticación /pronostika'θion; pronostika'sion/ f, prognostication; presage

pronosticar /pronosti'kar/ vt to prognosticate, forecast; presage

pronóstico /pro'nostiko/ m, omen, prediction; almanac; prognosis; sign, indication. **p. del tiempo,** weather forecast

prontitud /pronti'tuð/ f, quickness, promptness; quick-wittedness; *Fig.* sharpness, liveliness; celerity, dispatch

pronto /'pronto/ a quick, speedy; prompt; ready, prepared. m, *Inf.* sudden decision —adv immediately; with all speed; soon. **de p.,** suddenly; without thinking. **por lo p.,** temporarily, provisionally

prontuario /pron'tuario/ m, compendium, handbook; summary

pronunciación /pronun'θia'θion; pronunsia'sion/ f, pronunciation

pronunciamiento /pronunθia'miento; pronunsia'miento/ m, military uprising; political manifesto; *Law.* pronouncement of sentence

pronunciar /pronun'θiar; pronun'siar/ vt to pronounce, articulate; decide, determine; *Law.* pronounce judgment; give or make (a speech)

propagación /propaga'θion; propaga'sion/ f, propagation; dissemination; transmission

propagador /propaga'ðor/ a propagative. m, propagator

propaganda /propa'ganda/ f, propaganda organization; propaganda

propagandista /propagan'dista/ mf propagandist

propagar /propa'gar/ vt to reproduce; propagate, disseminate; —vr reproduce, multiply; propagate, spread

propalar /propa'lar/ vt to disseminate, spread abroad

propasarse /propa'sarse/ vr to go too far, forget oneself; overstep one's authority

propender /propen'der/ *vi* to be inclined, have a leaning toward

propensión /propen'sion/ *f*, propensity, inclination; tendency

propenso /pro'penso/ *a* inclined, disposed; liable

propiamente /propia'mente/ *adv* properly, suitably

propiciación /propiθia'θion; propisia'sion/ *f*, propitiation

propiciador /propiθia'ðor; propisia'ðor/ **(-ra)** *a* propitiatory —*n* propitiator

propiciar /propi'θiar; propi'siar/ *vt* to propitiate, appease

propiciatorio /propiθia'torio; propisia'torio/ *a* propitiatory

propicio /pro'piθio; pro'pisio/ *a* propitious, auspicious; kind, favorable

propiedad /propie'ðað/ *f*, estate, property; ownership; landed property; attribute, quality, property; *Art.* resemblance, naturalness

propietario /propie'tario/ **(-ia)** *a* proprietary —*n* proprietor, owner

propina /pro'pina/ *f*, gratuity, tip. *Inf.* **de p.**, in addition, extra

propinar /propi'nar/ *vt* to treat to a drink; administer (medicine); *Inf.* give (slaps, etc.)

propincuidad /propinkui'ðað/ *f*, propinquity, proximity

propincuo /pro'pinkuo/ *a* near, contiguous, adjacent

propio /'propio/ *a* own, one's own; typical, characteristic; individual, peculiar; suitable, apt; natural, real; same. *m*, messenger; *pl* public lands

proponente /propo'nente/ *a* proposing. *m*, proposer; *Com.* tenderer

proponer /propo'ner/ *vt irr* to propose, suggest; make a proposition; propose (for a post, office, etc.); *Math.* state; —*vr* intend, purpose. **proponerse para un empleo**, to apply for a post. See **poner**

proporción /propor'θion; propor'sion/ *f*, proportion; chance, opportunity; size; *Math.* proportion

proporcionado /proporθio'naðo; proporsio'naðo/ *a* fit, suitable; proportionate; symmetrical

proporcional /proporθio'nal; proporsio'nal/ *a* proportional

proporcionar /proporθio'nar; proporsio'nar/ *vt* to allot, proportion; supply, provide, give; adapt

proposición /proposi'θion; proposi'sion/ *f*, proposition; motion (in a debate)

propósito /pro'posito/ *m*, proposal; intention, aim; subject, question, matter. **a p.**, suitable, apropos; by the way, incidentally. **de p.**, with the intention, proposing. **fuera de p.**, irrelevant

propuesta /pro'puesta/ *f*, proposal, tender

propugnar /propug'nar/ *vt* to defend, protect

propulsar /propul'sar/ *vt* to repulse, throw back; propel, drive

propulsión /propul'sion/ *f*, repulse; propulsion

propulsor /propul'sor/ *a* driving, propelling. *m*, propeller

prorrata /pro'rrata/ *f*, quota, share, apportionment. **a p.**, in proportion

prorratear /prorrate'ar/ *vt* to apportion, distribute proportionately, prorate

prorrogación /prorroga'θion; prorroga'sion/ *f*, prorogation, adjournment; extension (of time); renewal (of a lease, etc.)

prorrogar /prorro'gar/ *vt* to extend, prolong; defer, suspend, prorogue; renew (leases, etc.)

prorrumpir /prorrum'pir/ *vt* (*with en*) to burst out; utter, give vent to, burst into

prosa /'prosa/ *f*, prose; prosaism, prosaic style; *Inf.* dull verbosity; monotony, tediousness

prosaico /pro'saiko/ *a* prosaic; prosy; monotonous, tedious; matter-of-fact

prosapia /pro'sapia/ *f*, family, lineage, descent

proscenio /pros'θenio; pros'senio/ *m*, proscenium

proscribir /proskri'βir/ *vt* to proscribe, outlaw; forbid, prohibit —*Past Part.* **proscrito**

proscripción /proskrip'θion; proskrip'sion/ *f*, proscription

proscrito /pros'krito/ **(-ta)** *n* outlaw, exile

prosecución /proseku'θion; proseku'sion/ *f*, prosecution, performance; pursuit

proseguir /prose'gir/ *vt irr* to continue, proceed with. See **pedir**

proselitismo /proseli'tismo/ *m*, proselytism

prosélito /pro'selito/ *m*, convert, proselyte

prosificar /prosifi'kar/ *vt* to turn verse into prose

prosista /pro'sista/ *mf* prose writer

prosodia /pro'soðia/ *f*, prosody

prospecto /pros'pekto/ *m*, prospectus

prosperar /prospe'rar/ *vt* to prosper; protect; —*vi* flourish, prosper

prosperidad /prosperi'ðað/ *f*, prosperity; wealth; success

próspero /'prospero/ *a* favorable, propitious, fortunate; prosperous

próstata /'prostata/ *f*, prostate

prostitución /prostitu'θion; prostitu'sion/ *f*, prostitution

prostituir /prosti'tuir/ *vt irr* to prostitute; —*vr* become a prostitute; sell oneself, debase oneself. See **huir**

prostituta /prosti'tuta/ *f*, prostitute

protagonista /protago'nista/ *mf* hero or heroine, principal character; leading figure, protagonist

protección /protek'θion; protek'sion/ *f*, protection, defense; favor, aid

proteccionismo /protekθio'nismo; proteksio'nismo/ *m*, protectionism

proteccionista /protekθio'nista; proteksio'nista/ *mf* protectionist

protector /protek'tor/ *a* protective. *m*, protector; guard

protectorado /protekto'raðo/ *m*, protectorate

protectriz /protek'triθ; protek'tris/ *f*, protectress

proteger /prote'her/ *vt* to protect, defend; favor, assist

protegido /prote'hiðo/ **(-da)** *n* protégé

proteico /pro'teiko/ *a* protean

proteína /prote'ina/ *f*, protein

protervia /pro'terβia/ *f*, depravity, perversity

protervo /pro'terβo/ *a* depraved, perverse

protesta, protestación /pro'testa, protesta'θion; pro'testa, protesta'sion/ *f*, protest; protestation, declaration

protestante /protes'tante/ *a* and *mf* Protestant

protestantismo /protestan'tismo/ *m*, Protestantism

protestar /protes'tar/ *vt* to declare, attest; (*with contra*) protest against; (*with de*) affirm vigorously

protesto /pro'testo/ *m*, *Com.* protest; objection

protocolizar /protokoli'θar; protokoli'sar/ *vt* to protocol, draw up

protocolo /proto'kolo/ *m*, protocol

protoplasma /proto'plasma/ *m*, protoplasm

prototipo /proto'tipo/ *m*, model, prototype

protuberancia /protuβe'ranθia; protuβe'ransia/ *f*, protuberance, projection, swelling

provecho /pro'βetʃo/ *m*, gain, benefit; profit; advantage; progress, proficiency. **¡Buen p.!** Enjoy your food! Enjoy your meal! **ser de p.**, to be advantageous or useful

provechoso /proβe'tʃoso/ *a* beneficial; profitable; advantageous; useful

provecto /pro'βekto/ *a* ancient, venerable; mature, experienced

proveedor /proβee'ðor/ **(-ra)** *n* provider; purveyor, supplier

proveer /proβe'er/ *vt irr* to provide; furnish; supply; confer (an honor or office); transact, arrange. **p. de**, to furnish or supply with; fit with. See **creer**

provenir /proβe'nir/ *vi irr* (*with de*) to originate in, proceed from. See **venir**

Provenza /pro'βenθa; pro'βensa/ Provence

provenzal /proβen'θal; proβen'sal/ *a* and *mf* Provençal. *m*, Provençal (language)

proverbio /pro'βerβio/ *m*, proverb; omen; *pl* Book of Proverbs

providencia /proβi'ðenθia; proβi'ðensia/ *f*, precaution, foresight; provision, furnishing; measure, preparation. **la Divina P.**, Providence

providencial /proβiðen'θial; proβiðen'sial/ *a* providential

próvido /'proβiðo/ *a* provident, thrifty, careful; kind, favorable

provincia /pro'βinθia; pro'βinsia/ *f,* province; *Fig.* sphere

provincial /proβin'θial; proβin'sial/ *a* provincial. *m, Eccl.* provincial

provincialismo /proβinθia'lismo; proβinsia'lismo/ *m,* provincialism

provinciano /proβin'θiano; proβin'siano/ **(-na)** *a* provincial —*n* provincial, rustic, countryman; native of Biscay

provisión /proβi'sion/ *f,* stock, store; provision; supply; food supply (gen. *pl*); catering; means, way

provisional /proβisio'nal/ *a* temporary, provisional

provisor /proβi'sor/ *m,* purveyor, supplier; *Eccl.* vicar general

provocación /proβoka'θion; proβoka'sion/ *f,* provocation

provocador /proβoka'ðor/ **(-ra)** *a* provocative —*n* provoker; instigator

provocar /proβo'kar/ *vt* to provoke; incite; irritate; help, assist; *Inf.* vomit

provocativo /proβoka'tiβo/ *a* provocative

próximamente /'proksimamente/ *adv* proximately; soon; approximately

proximidad /proksimi'ðað/ *f,* nearness, proximity (in time or space)

próximo /'proksimo/ *a* near, neighboring; next; not distant (of time)

proyección /proiek'θion; proiek'sion/ *f,* projection (all meanings)

proyectante /proiek'tante/ *a* projecting, jutting

proyectar /proiek'tar/ *vt* to throw, cast; plan, contrive; design; project; —*vr* jut out; be cast (a shadow, etc.)

proyectil /proyek'til/ *m,* projectile

proyectista /proiek'tista/ *mf* planner

proyecto /pro'iekto/ *a* placed in perspective. *m,* project, plan, scheme; planning; intention, idea

proyector /proiek'tor/ **(-ra)** *n* designer, planner. *m,* searchlight; spotlight; projector

prudencia /pru'ðenθia; pru'ðensia/ *f,* prudence, sagacity, caution; moderation

prudencial /pruðen'θial; pruðen'sial/ *a* prudent, discreet; safe

prudente /pru'ðente/ *a* prudent, cautious; provident

prueba /'prueβa/ *f,* proof; test; testing; trial; fitting (of garments); sample; taste; *Law.* evidence; (*Photo. Print.*) proof. *Law.* **p. de indicios** *or* **p. indiciaria,** circumstantial evidence. *Photo.* **p. negativa,** negative. *Com.* **a p.,** on approval; on trial; up to standard, perfect. **a p. de,** proof against (water, etc.). **poner a p.,** to put to the test, try out

prurito /pru'rito/ *m,* pruritus; desire, longing

Prusia /'prusia/ Prussia

ps- /ps-/ For words so beginning (e.g. *psicología, psiquiatría*), see spellings without **p**

púa /'pua/ *f,* prong; tooth (of a comb); quill (of a porcupine); *Agr.* graft; plectrum (for playing the mandolin, etc.); anxiety, grief; pine needle; *Inf.* crafty person

púber /'puβer/ *a* pubescent

pubertad /puβer'tað/ *f,* puberty

púbico /'puβiko/ *a* pubic

publicación /puβlika'θion; puβlika'sion/ *f,* publication; announcement, proclamation; revelation; publishing of marriage banns

publicador /puβlika'ðor/ **(-ra)** *a* publishing —*n* publisher; announcer

publicar /puβli'kar/ *vt* to publish; reveal; announce, proclaim; publish (marriage banns)

publicidad /puβliθi'ðað; puβlisi'ðað/ *f,* publicity; advertising, propaganda

publicista /puβli'θista; puβli'sista/ *mf* publicist; publicity agent

público /'puβliko/ *a* well-known, universal; common, general; public. *m,* public; audience; gathering, attendance. **dar al p.** *or* **sacar al p.,** to publish

pucherazo /putʃe'raθo; putʃe'raso/ *m, Inf.* electoral fraud, vote-fixing

puchero /pu'tʃero/ *m, Cul.* kind of stew; stew pot; *Inf.* daily food; puckering of the face preceding tears

pudendo /pu'ðendo/ *a* shameful, monstrous, obscene

pudicia /pu'ðiθia; pu'ðisia/ *f,* modesty; bashfulness; chastity

púdico /'puðiko/ *a* modest; bashful; chaste

pudiente /pu'ðiente/ *a* rich, wealthy; powerful

pudín /pu'ðin/ *m,* pudding

pudor /pu'ðor/ *m,* modesty; bashfulness, shyness

pudoroso /puðo'roso/ *a* modest; shy

pudrición /puðri'θion; puðri'sion/ *f,* putrefaction

pudrir /pu'ðrir/ *vt* to rot, putrefy; irritate, worry, provoke; —*vi* rot in the grave; —*vr* rot; be consumed with anxiety

puebla /'pueβla/ *f,* town; population; gardener's seed setting

pueblo /'pueβlo/ *m,* town; village, hamlet; people, population, inhabitants; common people; working classes; nation

puente /'puente/ *mf* bridge; *Mus.* bridge (of stringed instruments); *Naut.* bridge; crossbeam, transom. **p. colgante,** suspension bridge. **p. levadizo,** drawbridge. **hacer p. de plata (a),** to remove obstacles for, make plain sailing

puerca /'puerka/ *f,* sow; *Inf.* slattern; harridan, termagant

puerco /'puerko/ *m,* pig; wild boar —*a* filthy; rough, rude; low, mean. **p. espín** *or* **p. espino,** porcupine. **p. marino,** dolphin. **p. montés** *or* **p. salvaje,** wild boar

puericultura /puerikul'tura/ *f,* child care

pueril /pue'ril/ *a* childish, puerile; foolish, silly; trivial

puerilidad /puerili'ðað/ *f,* puerility; foolishness; triviality

puerro /'puerro/ *m,* leek

puerta /'puerta/ *f,* door; gate; goal (football, soccer, hockey); means, way. **p. batiente,** swinging door. **p. caediza,** trapdoor. **p. corrediza,** sliding door. **p. de servicio,** tradesman's entrance. **p. falsa** *or* **p. secreta,** secret door; side door. **p. trasera,** back door. **a p. cerrada,** in camera; in secret. *Inf.* **dar con la p. en las narices (de),** to slam the door in a person's face; offend, insult. **llamar a la p.,** to knock at the door; be on the verge of happening. **tomar la p.,** to depart, go away

puerto /'puerto/ *m,* harbor; port; defile, narrow pass; refuge, haven. **p. fluvial,** river port. **p. franco,** free port. **tomar p.,** to put into port; take refuge

pues /pues/ *conjunc* then; since, as, for, because; well —*adv* yes, certainly —*conjunc* **p. que,** since, as

puesta /'puesta/ *f, Astron.* setting, sinking; stake (in gambling). **p. al día,** aggiornamento, updating; modernization. **p. de largo,** coming of age; coming-out party. **p. del sol,** sunset

puesto /'puesto/ *m,* post, job; booth, stall; beat, pitch; place, position; state, condition; *Mil.* encampment, barracks; office, position. **p. de los testigos,** witness box. **p. de mando,** command, position of authority.

puesto /'puesto/ *a* (*with bien* or *mal*) well-or badly dressed —*conjunc* **p. que,** since, as; although

púgil /'puhil/ *mf* pugilist, boxer

pugilato /puhi'lato/ *m,* boxing; boxing match

pugilista /puhi'lista/ *mf* boxer

pugna /'pugna/ *f,* fight, struggle; rivalry, conflict

pugnante /pug'nante/ *a* hostile, conflicting, rival

pugnar /pug'nar/ *vi* to fight; quarrel; (*with con, contra*) struggle against, oppose; (*with por, para*) strive to

pugnaz /pug'naθ; pug'nas/ *a* pugnacious

puja /'puha/ *f,* outbidding (at an auction); higher bid; push, thrust

pujador /puha'ðor/ **(-ra)** *n* bidder or outbidder (at an auction)

pujante /pu'hante/ *a* strong, powerful, vigorous

pujanza /pu'hanθa; pu'hansa/ *f,* strength, vigor

pujar /pu'har/ *vt* to push on; bid or outbid (at an auction); —*vi* stutter; hesitate; falter; *Inf.* show signs of weeping

pujo /'puho/ *m,* irresistible impulse; desire; will; purpose, intention

pulchinela /pultʃi'nela/ *m,* Punchinello

pulcritud /pulkri'tuð/ f, beauty, loveliness, delicacy; fastidiousness, subtlety

pulcro /'pulkro/ a beautiful, lovely; delicate, fine; fastidious, subtle

pulga /'pulga/ f, flea; small top (toy). **el juego de la p.**, tiddlywinks. Inf. **tener malas pulgas,** to be irritable

pulgada /pul'gaða/ f, inch

pulgar /pul'gar/ m, thumb

pulgón /pul'gon/ m, aphid, greenfly

pulgoso /pul'goso/ a full of fleas

pulidez /puli'ðeθ; puli'ðes/ f, elegance, fineness; polish, smoothness; neatness

pulido /pu'liðo/ a elegant, fine; polished, smooth; neat

pulidor /puli'ðor/ m, polisher (machine)

pulimentar /pulimen'tar/ vt to polish, burnish

pulir /pu'lir/ vt to polish, burnish; give the finishing touch to; beautify, decorate; Fig. polish up, civilize; —vr beautify oneself; become polished and polite

pulla /'puʎa/ 'puya/ f, lewd remark; strong hint; witty comment

pulmón /pul'mon/ m, lung

pulmonar /pulmo'nar/ a pulmonary

pulmonía /pulmo'nia/ f, pneumonia

pulpa /'pulpa/ f, fleshy part of fruit; Anat. pulp; wood pulp

pulpejo /pul'peho/ m, Anat. fleshy part, fat portion (of thumbs, etc.)

pulpería /pulpe'ria/ f, West Hem. grocery, grocery store, general store

púlpito /'pulpito/ m, pulpit

pulpo /'pulpo/ m, octopus. Inf. **poner como un p.,** to beat to a pulp

pulposo /pul'poso/ a pulpy, pulpous

pulquérrimo /pul'kerrimo/ a superl pulcro most lovely, most exquisite

pulsación /pulsa'θion; pulsa'sion/ f, pulsation; throb, beat

pulsar /pul'sar/ vt to touch, feel; take the pulse of; Fig. explore (a possibility); —vi beat (the heart, etc.)

pulsera /pul'sera/ f, bracelet; wrist bandage. **p. de pedida,** betrothal bracelet

pulso /'pulso/ m, pulse; steadiness of hand; tact, diplomacy, circumspection. **a p.,** freehand (drawing). **tomar a p.** (**una cosa**), to try a thing's weight. **tomar el p.** (**a**), to take a person's pulse

pulular /pulu'lar/ vi to pullulate, sprout; abound, be plentiful; swarm, teem; multiply (of insects)

pulverización /pulβeriθa'θion; pulβerisa'sion/ f, pulverization; atomization

pulverizador /pulβeriθa'ðor; pulβerisa'ðor/ m, atomizer, sprayer; scent spray

pulverizar /pulβeri'θar; pulβeri'sar/ vt to pulverize, grind, make into powder; atomize; spray

¡pum! /pum/ interj Bang! Thump!

pundonor /pundo'nor/ m, (**punto de honor**) point of honor, sense of honor

pundonoroso /pundono'roso/ a careful of one's honor; honorable, punctilious

pungir /pun'hir/ vt to prick, pierce; revive an old sorrow; Fig. wound, sting (passions)

punible /pu'niβle/ a punishable

púnico /'puniko/ a Punic

punitivo /puni'tiβo/ a punitive, punitory

punta /'punta/ f, sharp end, point; butt (of a cigarette); end, point, tip; cape, headland; trace, touch, suspicion; nib (of a pen); pointing (pointer dogs); Herald. point; pl point lace. **p. de París,** wire nail. **p. seca,** drypoint, engraving needle. **sacar p.,** to sharpen; Inf. twist (a remark)

puntación /punta'θion; punta'sion/ f, dotting, placing dots over (letters)

puntada /pun'taða/ f, Sew. stitch; innuendo, hint

puntal /pun'tal/ m, Naut. draft, depth; stanchion, prop, brace, pile; Fig. basis, foundation

puntapié /punta'pie/ m, kick

puntear /punte'aðo/ m, plucking the strings of a guitar, etc.; sewing

puntear /punte'ar/ vt to make dots; Mus. pluck the strings of; play the guitar; sew; Art. stipple; —vi Naut. tack

puntera /pun'tera/ f, mend in the toe of a stocking; toe cap; new piece on the toe of shoe; Inf. kick

puntería /punte'ria/ f, aiming (of a firearm); aim, sight (of a firearm); marksmanship

puntero /pun'tero/ a of a good aim, having a straight eye. m, pointer, wand; stonecutter's chisel

puntiagudo /puntia'guðo/ a pointed, sharp-pointed

puntilla /pun'tiʎa; pun'tiya/ f, narrow lace edging; headless nail, wire nail; brad, tack. **de puntillas,** on tiptoe

puntillismo /punti'ʎismo; punti'yismo/ m, pointillism

puntilloso /punti'ʎoso; punti'yoso/ a punctilious; overfastidious, fussy

punto /'punto/ m dot; point; pen nib; gun sight; Sew. stitch; dropped stitch, hole; weaving stitch, mesh; Gram. full stop, period; hole (in belts for adjustment); place, spot; point, mark; subject matter; Mech. cog; degree, extent; taxi stand; instant; infinitesimal amount; opportunity, chance; vacation, recess; aim, goal; point of honor. **p. de congelación,** freezing point. **p. de ebullición,** boiling point. **p. de fuga,** vanishing point. **p. de fusión,** melting point. **p. de partida,** starting point. **p. de vista,** point of view. **p. final,** Gram. period, full stop. **p. interrogante,** question mark. **p. menos,** a little less. **p. y coma,** semicolon. **p. cardinal,** cardinal point. **p. suspensivo,** Gram. ellipsis point, suspension point, leader, dot. **a p.,** in readiness; immediately. **en p.,** sharp, prompt (e.g. **a las seis en p.,** at six o'clock sharp)

puntoso /pun'toso/ a many-pointed

puntuación /puntua'θion; puntua'sion/ f, punctuation; Sports. score

puntual /pun'tual/ a punctual; punctilious; certain, indubitable; suitable, convenient

puntualidad /puntuali'ðað/ f, punctuality; punctiliousness; certainty; exactitude, accuracy

puntualizar /puntuali'θar; puntuali'sar/ vt to describe in detail; give the finishing touch to, perfect; impress on the mind

puntualmente /puntual'mente/ adv punctually; carefully, diligently; exactly

puntuar /pun'tuar/ vt to punctuate

punzada /pun'θaða; pun'saða/ f, prick, sting; puncture, piercing; sudden pain, twinge, stitch; Fig. anguish, pain

punzar /pun'θar; pun'sar/ vt to pierce, puncture; prick; punch, perforate; —vi revive, make itself felt (pain or sorrow)

punzón /pun'θon; pun'son/ m, awl; punch; die; engraver's burin

puñado /pu'ɲaðo/ m, handful; a few, some, a small quantity. **a puñados,** in handfuls; liberally, lavishly

puñal /pu'ɲal/ m, dagger

puñalada /puɲa'laða/ f, dagger thrust; stab, wound; Fig. unexpected blow (of fate). **p. por la espalda,** stab in the back

puñalero /puɲa'lero/ m, dagger maker or seller

puñetazo /puɲe'taθo; puɲe'taso/ m, blow with the fist

puño /'puɲo/ m, fist; handful; cuff (of a sleeve); wristband; handle, head, haft; hilt (of a sword); pl Inf. guts, courage. **p. de amura,** Naut. tack. **p. de manillar,** handlebar grip. Inf. **meter en un p.,** to overawe. Inf. **ser como un p.,** to be tightfisted; be small (in stature)

pupila /pu'pila/ f, female child ward; Anat. pupil; Inf. cleverness, talent

pupilaje /pupi'lahe/ m, pupilage, minority; boarding house, guesthouse; boarding school; price of board residence; dependence; bondage

pupilo /pu'pilo/ (**-la**) n ward, minor; boarder; boarding school student

pupitre /pu'pitre/ m, desk, school desk

puramente /pura'mente/ adv purely; simply, solely; Law. unconditionally, without reservation

puré /pu're/ m, purée, thick soup

pureza /pu'reθa; pu'resa/ f, purity; perfection, excellence; chastity; disinterestedness, genuineness; clearness

purga /'purga/ f, laxative, purge; waste product
purgación /purga'θion; purga'sion/ f, purging; menstruation; gonorrhea
purgante /pur'gante/ a purgative. m, purge, cathartic
purgar /pur'gar/ vt to cleanse, purify; expiate, atone for; (*Med. Law.*) purge; suffer purgatorial pains; clarify, refine; —vr rid oneself, purge oneself
purgativo /purga'tiβo/ a purgative
purgatorio /purga'torio/ m, purgatory —a purgatorial
puridad /puri'ðað/ f, purity; secrecy, privacy. **en p.**, openly, without dissembling; secretly, in private
purificación /purifika'θion; purifika'sion/ f, purification; cleansing
purificador /purifika'ðor/ (**-ra**) a purifying; cleansing —n purifier; cleanser
purificar /purifi'kar/ vt to purify; cleanse; —vr be purified
purificatorio /purifika'torio/ a purificatory
Purísima /pu'risima/ (**la**) f, the Most Blessed Virgin
purista /pu'rista/ mf purist
puritanismo /purita'nismo/ m, Puritanism
puritano /puri'tano/ (**-na**) a puritanical —n Puritan
puro /'puro/ a pure; undiluted; unalloyed; unmixed;

disinterested, honest; virgin; absolute, sheer; mere, simple. m, cigar. **de p.**, by sheer..., by dint of
púrpura /'purpura/ f, purple; *Poet.* blood; purpura; *Herald.* purpure; purple (cloth); dignity of an emperor, cardinal, consul
purpurear /purpure'ar/ vi to look like purple; be tinged with purple
purpúreo, purpurino /pur'pureo, purpu'rino/ a purple
purulencia /puru'lenθia; puru'lensia/ f, purulence
purulento /puru'lento/ a purulent
pus /pus/ m, pus, matter
pusilánime /pusi'lanime/ a pusillanimous, timid, cowardly
pusilanimidad /pusilanimi'ðað/ f, pusillanimity, timidity, cowardice
pústula /'pustula/ f, pustule
puta /'puta/ f, whore
putativo /puta'tiβo/ a putative
puto /'puto/ m, male prostitute
putrefacción /putrefak'θion; putrefak'sion/ f, putrefaction; rottenness, putrescence
putrefacto /putre'fakto/ a rotten, decayed
pútrido /'putriðo/ a putrid, rotten
puya /'puya/ f, goad
puyazo /pu'yaθo; pu'yaso/ m, prick with a goad

Q

que /ke/ *pron rel* all genders sing. and pl. who; which; that; whom; when (e.g. *Un poema en que habla de su juventud*, A poem in which he speaks of his youth. *El libro que tengo aquí*, The book (that) I have here. **No es oro todo lo que reluce**, All that glitters is not gold. **Un día que nos vimos**, One day when we met —*interr* **¿qué?** what? *interj* what a ------! what! how! (e.g. *¿Qué hay?* What's the matter? *¡Qué día más hermoso!* What a lovely day! *¿qué de...?* how many? *¿qué tal?* how? *Inf. ¿Qué tal estás hoy?* How are you today? *¿qué tanto?* how much?) **¿a qué?** why? for what reason? (e.g. *¿A qué negarlo?* Why deny it?) —*conjunc* that (e.g. *Me dijo que vendría*, He said (that) he would come). Means "so that,' "that,' "for,' in commands (e.g. *Mandó que le trajesen el libro*, He ordered that they bring him the book (He ordered them to bring him the book)). Note that the translation of **que** is often omitted in English. In compound tenses where the participle is placed first, **que** means "when' (e.g. *llegado que hube*, when I had arrived). In comparisons, **que** means "than' (e.g. *más joven que yo*, younger than I). With subjunctives and expressing commands or wishes, **que** means "let' (e.g. *¡Que venga!* Let him come!) Preceding a subjunctive, **que** is generally translated by "to' (e.g. *Quiero, que venga or que llueva*, I want him to come or I want it to rain). Also means "may' (e.g. *¡Que lo pase bien!* May you enjoy yourself! (I hope you...)). **es** (**era**) **que**, the fact is (was) that... **que... que**, whether... or...

quebrada /ke'βraða/ *f*, mountain gorge; *Com.* bankruptcy

quebradizo /keβra'ðiθo; keβra'ðiso/ *a* brittle, fragile; ailing, infirm; delicate, frail

quebrado /ke'βraðo/ **(-da)** *m*, *Math.* fraction; —*n Com.* bankrupt —*a* rough, uneven (ground); *Med.* ruptured; bankrupt; ailing, broken-down

quebradura /keβra'ðura/ *f*, snap, breaking; gap, crevice; hernia

quebraja /ke'βraha/ *f*, split, crack; flaw (in wood, metal, etc.)

quebrantahuesos /keβranta'uesos/ *m*, sea eagle, osprey; *Inf.* bore, tedious person

quebrantamiento /keβranta'miento/ *m*, crushing; splitting, cleaving; fracture, rupture; profanation, desecration; burglary; violation, breaking, infringement; fatigue; *Law.* annulment; exhaustion

quebrantanueces /keβranta'nueθes; keβranta'nueses/ *m*, nutcrackers

quebrantaolas /keβranta'olas/ *m*, breakwater

quebrantar /keβran'tar/ *vt* to break, shatter; crush, pound; transgress, infringe; break out, force; tone down, soften; moderate, lessen; bore, exhaust; move to pity; *Inf.* break in (horses); profane; overcome (difficulties); assuage, placate; *Law.* revoke (wills); —*vr* be shaken or bruised, suffer from aftereffects

quebranto /ke'βranto/ *m*, breaking, shattering; crushing, pounding; infringement; breaking out (from prison); weakness, exhaustion; compassion, pity; loss, damage; pain, suffering

quebrar /ke'βrar/ *vt irr* to break, shatter; crush; impede, hinder; make pale (color, gen. of complexion); mitigate, moderate; bend, twist; overcome (difficulties); —*vi* break off (a friendship); weaken, give way; go bankrupt; —*vr Med.* suffer from hernia; be interrupted (of mountain ranges). **quebrarse los ojos**, to strain one's eyes —*Pres. Indic.* **quiebro, quiebras, quiebra, quiebran**. *Pres. Subjunc.* **quiebre, quiebres, quiebre, quiebren**

queche /'ketʃe/ *m*, ketch

queda /'keða/ *f*, curfew; curfew bell

quedada /ke'ðaða/ *f*, stay, sojourn

quedar /ke'ðar/ *vi* to stay, sojourn; remain; be left over; (*with por* + *infin.*) remain to be (e.g. *Queda por escribir*, It remains to be written); (*with por*) be won by or be knocked down to; be, remain in a place; end, cease; (*with en*) reach an agreement (e.g.

Quedamos en no ir, We have decided not to go). **q. en esta alternativa...**, to face this alternative:... —*vr* remain; abate (wind); grow calm (sea); (*with con*) keep, retain possession of. **q. bien o mal**, to behave well or badly, come off well or badly (in business affairs, etc.). **quedarse muerto**, to be astounded

quedo /'keðo/ *a* still, motionless; quiet, tranquil —*adv* in a low voice; quietly, noiselessly. **de q.**, slowly, gradually —*interj* **¡Q.!** Quiet!

quehacer /kea'θer; kea'ser/ *m*, odd job; task; business (gen. *pl*)

queja /'keha/ *f*, lamentation, grief; complaint, grudge; quarrel

quejarse /ke'harse/ *vr* to lament; complain, grumble; *Law.* lodge an accusation (against)

quejido /ke'hiðo/ *m*, complaint, moan

quejoso /ke'hoso/ *a* querulous, complaining

quejumbre /ke'humbre/ *f*, complaint, whine; querulousness

quejumbroso /kehum'βroso/ *a* complaining, grumbling

quema /'kema/ *f*, burn; burning; fire, conflagration

quemadero /kema'ðero/ *a* burnable. *m*, stake (for burning people)

quemado /ke'maðo/ *m*, burned patch of forest; *Inf.* anything burned or burning

quemador /kema'ðor/ **(-ra)** *m*, jet, burner —*n* incendiary

quemadura /kema'ðura/ *f*, burn; scald; burning

quemajoso /kema'hoso/ *a* smarting, burning, pricking

quemar /ke'mar/ *vt* to burn; dry up, parch; scorch; tan, bronze; scald; throw away, sell at a loss; —*vi* burn, be excessively hot; —*vr* be very hot; be dried up with the heat; burn with (passions); *Inf.* be near the attainment of a desired end. **quemarse las cejas**, to burn the midnight oil, study too hard

quemazón /kema'θon; kema'son/ *f*, burning; conflagration; intense heat; *Inf.* smarting; *Inf.* hurtful remark; *Inf.* vexation, soreness

querella /ke'reʎa; ke'reya/ *f*, complaint; quarrel, fight

querellarse /kere'ʎarse; kere'yarse/ *vr* to complain; lament, bemoan; *Law.* lodge an accusation; *Law.* contest a will

querelloso /kere'ʎoso; kere'yoso/ *a* complaining, grumbling, querulous

querencia /ke'renθia; ke'rensia/ *f*, love, affection; homing instinct; lair; natural inclination or desire

querer /ke'rer/ *vt irr* to desire, wish; want, will; attempt, endeavor; (*with a*) love —*impers* be on the point of. **q. decir**, to mean. **¿Qué quiere decir esto?** What does this mean? **sin q.**, unintentionally. See **entender**

querer /ke'rer/ *m*, affection, love

querido /ke'riðo/ **(-da)** *n* lover; beloved; darling —*a* dear

querub, querube /ke'ruβ, ke'ruβe/ *Poet.* **querubín** *m*, cherub

querúbico /ke'ruβiko/ *a* cherubic

quesera /ke'sera/ *f*, dairymaid; dairy; cheese vat; cheese board; cheese dish

quesería /kese'ria/ *f*, dairy; cheese shop; season for making cheese

queso /'keso/ *m*, cheese. **q. de bola**, Dutch cheese. **q. rallado**, grated cheese

quetzal /ket'θal; ket'sal/ *m*, quetzal

quevedos /ke'βeðos/ *m pl*, glasses, eyeglasses; pince-nez

¡quia! /kia/ *interj Inf.* You don't say so!

quianti /'kianti/ *m*, chianti

quicial /ki'θial; ki'sial/ *m*, doorjamb

quicio /'kiθio; 'kisio/ *m*, threshold; hinge; *Mech.* bushing. **fuera de q.**, out of order; unhinged. **sacar de q.**, to displace (things); annoy, irritate; drive crazy

quiebra /'kieβra/ *f*, breach, crack; rut, fissure; loss; bankruptcy

quiebro /'kieβro/ *m*, twisting of the body, dodging; *Mus.* trill

quien /kien/ *rel pron mf pl* **quienes**. *interr* **quién, quiénes** who; whom; he (she, etc.) who, anyone who, whoever; which; whichever (e.g. *mis padres a quienes respeto*, my parents whom I respect. *Quien te quiere te hará llorar*, Whoever (he, those, who) love(s) you will make you weep. **¿Quién está a la puerta?** Who is at the door? **¿De quién es?** Whose is it? To whom does it belong?) —*indef pron* one (*pl* some)

quienquiera /kien'kiera/ *indef pron mf pl* **quienesquiera**, whosoever, whichever, whomsoever

quietación /kieta'θion; kieta'sion/ *f*, quieting, soothing

quietador /kieta'ðor/ **(-ra)** *a* tranquilizing, soothing —*n* soother

quietismo /kie'tismo/ *m*, quietism

quietista /kie'tista/ *mf* quietist —*a* quietistic

quieto /'kieto/ *a* quiet, still; peaceful, tranquil; virtuous, respectable

quietud /kie'tuð/ *f*, stillness, repose; peacefulness; rest, quietness

quif /kif/ *m*, hashish, marijuana

quijada /ki'haða/ *f*, jawbone, jaw; *Mech.* jaw

quijo /'kiho/ *m*, ore (gold or silver)

quijotada /kiho'taða/ *f*, quixotic action, quixotism

quijote /ki'hote/ *m*, cuisse; thigh guard; quixotic person

quijotería /kihote'ria/ *f*, **quijotismo** *m*, quixotism

quijotesco /kiho'tesko/ *a* quixotic

quilate /ki'late/ *m*, carat; degree of excellence (gen. *pl*). *Inf.* **por quilates**, in small bits, parsimoniously

quilla /'kiʎa; 'kiya/ *f*, *Naut.* keel; breastbone (of birds)

quillotrar /kiʎo'trar; kiyo'trar/ *vt Inf.* to encourage, incite; woo, make love to; consider; —*vr Inf.* fall in love; dress up; whine, complain

quillotro /ki'ʎotro; ki'yotro/ *m*, *Inf.* incentive; indication, sign; love affair; puzzle, knotty point; compliment; dressing up

quimera /ki'mera/ *f*, chimera; fancy, vision; quarrel, dispute

quimérico /ki'meriko/ *a* chimerical, fanciful

quimerista /kime'rista/ *mf* dreamer, visionary; quarreler, disputant

química /'kimika/ *f*, chemistry

químico /'kimiko/ *a* chemical. *m*, chemist. **productos químicos**, chemicals

quimono /ki'mono/ *m*, kimono

quina /'kina/ *f*, cinchona; quinine; *pl* Arms of Portugal. *Inf.* **tragar q.**, to suffer in patience, put up with

quinario /ki'nario/ *a* quinary

quincalla /kin'kaʎa; kin'kaya/ *f*, cheap jewelery; fancy goods

quincallería /kinkaʎe'ria; kinkaye'ria/ *f*, cheap jewelry shop; hardware factory or industry; cheap jewelry; fancy goods

quince /'kinθe; 'kinse/ *a* and *m*, fifteen; fifteenth

quinceañero /kinθea'ɲero; kinsea'ɲero/ *f*, sweet sixteen party, sweet sixteen (in Spanish-speaking areas, held at age fifteen)

quincena /kin'θena; kin'sena/ *f*, fortnight, two weeks; bimonthly pay; *Mus.* fifteenth

quincenal /kinθe'nal; kinse'nal/ *a* fortnightly; lasting a fortnight, lasting two weeks

quinceno /kin'θeno; kin'seno/ *a* fifteenth

quincuagenario /kinkuahe'nario/ *a* quinquagenarian

quincuagésimo /kinkua'hesimo/ *a* fiftieth

quindécimo /kin'deθimo; kin'desimo/ *a* fifteenth

quinientos /ki'nientos/ *a* five hundred; five-hundredth. *m*, five hundred

quinina /ki'nina/ *f*, quinine

quinqué /kin'ke/ *m*, oil lamp, student's lamp, table lamp; perspicuity, talent

quinquenio /kin'kenio/ *m*, period of five years, lustrum

quinta /'kinta/ *f*, country house; *Mus.* fifth; conscripting men into army by drawing lots; *Mil.* draft

quintaesencia /kintae'senθia; kintae'sensia/ *f*, quintessence

quintal /kin'tal/ *m*, hundredweight

quintar /kin'tar/ *vt* to draw one out of every five; draw lots for conscription into the army; —*vi* reach the fifth (day, etc., gen. of the moon)

quintería /kinte'ria/ *f*, farm

quintero /kin'tero/ *m*, farmer; farmworker

quinteto /kin'teto/ *m*, quintet

quintilla /kin'tiʎa; kin'tiya/ *f*, five-line stanza of eight syllables

Quintín, San. **armarse** /kin'tin, san ar'marse/ (*or* **haber**) **la de San Q.** to quarrel, make trouble; be a row

quinto /'kinto/ *a* fifth. *m*, one-fifth; *Mil.* conscript; duty of twenty percent; *Law.* fifth part of an estate. **quinta columna**, fifth column. **quinta esencia**, quintessence

quintuplicar /kintupli'kar/ *vt* to quintuplicate

quíntuplo /'kintuplo/ *a* fivefold, quintuple

quinzavo /kin'θaβo; kin'saβo/ *a* and *m*, fifteenth

quiñón /ki'ɲon/ *m*, share of land owned jointly, share of the profits

quiosco /'kiosko/ *m*, kiosk, stand; pavilion, pagoda. **q. de música**, bandstand

quiquiriquí /kikiri'ki/ *m*, cock-a-doodle-doo; *Fig. Inf.* cock of the walk

quiromancia /kiro'manθia; kiro'mansia/ *f*, chiromancy, palmistry

quiromántico /kiro'mantiko/ **(-ca)** *n* chiromancer, palmist

quirúrgico /ki'rurhiko/ *a* surgical

quirurgo /ki'rurgo/ *m*, surgeon

quisicosa /kisi'kosa/ *f*, *Inf.* riddle, puzzle, enigma

quisquilla /kis'kiʎa; kis'kiya/ *f*, trifle, quibble, scruple; prawn, shrimp

quisquilloso /kiski'ʎoso; kiski'yoso/ *a* quibbling, overscrupulous, fastidious; hypersensitive; irascible, touchy

quistarse /kis'tarse/ *vr* to make oneself well-liked or loved

quiste /'kiste/ *m*, *Med.* cyst

quita /'kita/ *f*, *Law.* discharge (of part of a debt)

quitaesmalte /kitaes'malte/ *m*, nail polish remover (for fingernails)

quitamanchas /kita'mantʃas/ *mf*, dry cleaner, clothes cleaner

quitamotas /kita'motas/ *mf Inf.* flatterer, adulator

quitanieve /kita'nieβe/ *m*, snowplow

quitanza /ki'tanθa; ki'tansa/ *f*, quittance; quietus

quitapesares /kitape'sares/ *m*, *Inf.* consolation, solace, comfort

quitar /ki'tar/ *vt* to remove; take off or away; clear (the table), rob, steal; prevent, impede; parry (in fencing); separate, redeem (pledges); forbid; annul, repeal (laws, etc.); free from (obligations); —*vr* shed, take off, remove; get rid of; leave, quit. **quitarse de encima** (**a**), to get rid of someone or something. **q. el polvo**, to dust. **de quita y pon**, detachable, removable; adjustable

quitasol /kita'sol/ *m*, parasol, sunshade

quitasueño /kita'sueɲo/ *m*, *Inf.* sleep banisher, anxiety

quite /'kite/ *m*, hindering, impeding; obstruction; parry (in fencing). **estar al q.**, to be ready to protect someone

quizá, quizás /ki'θa, ki'θas; ki'sa, ki'sas/ *adv* perhaps. **q. y sin q.**, without doubt, certainly

R

rabadán /rraβa'ðan/ *m*, head shepherd or herdsman

rabadilla /rraβa'ðiʎa; rraβa'ðiya/ *f*, rump, croup

rábano /'rraβano/ *m*, radish. **r. picante,** horseradish

rabel /rra'βel/ *m, Mus.* rebec; *Inf.* backside, seat

rabera /rra'βera/ *f*, tail-end; chaff, siftings

rabí /rra'βi/ *m*, rabbi

rabia /'rraβia/ *f*, rabies, hydrophobia; anger, fury. *Inf.* **tener r.** (**a),** to hate

rabiar /rra'βiar/ *vi* to suffer from hydrophobia; groan with pain; be furious; (*with por*) yearn for, desire. **a r.,** excessively

rabicorto /rraβi'korto/ *a* short-tailed

rabieta /rra'βieta/ *f, Inf.* tantrum

rabilargo /rraβi'largo/ *a* long-tailed

rabínico /rra'βiniko/ *a* rabbinical

rabinismo /rraβi'nismo/ *m*, rabbinism

rabino /rra'βino/ *m*, rabbi. **gran r.,** chief rabbi

rabioso /rra'βioso/ *a* rabid; furious, angry; vehement. **perro r.,** mad dog

rabo /'rraβo/ *m*, tail; *Bot.* stalk; *Inf.* train (of a dress); shank (of a button). **r. del ojo,** corner of the eye. *Fig. Inf.* **ir r. entre piernas,** to have one's tail between one's legs

rabón /rra'βon/ *a* tailless, docked; bobtailed

rabudo /rra'βuðo/ *a* big-tailed

racimo /rra'θimo; rra'simo/ *m*, bunch (of grapes or other fruits); cluster; raceme

racimoso /rraθi'moso; rrasi'moso/ *a* racemose

raciocinación /rraθioθina'θion; rrasiosina'sion/ *f*, ratiocination

raciocinar /rraθioθi'nar; rrasiosi'nar/ *vi* to reason

raciocinio /rraθio'θinio; rrasio'sinio/ *m*, reasoning; ratiocination; discourse, speech

ración /rra'θion; rra'sion/ *f*, ration; portion (in a restaurant); meal allowance; *Eccl.* prebendary. *Inf.* **r. de hambre,** starvation diet; pittance, starvation wages

racional /rraθio'nal; rrasio'nal/ *a* reasonable, logical; rational

racionalidad /rraθionali'ðað; rrasionali'ðað/ *f*, reasonableness; rationality

racionalismo /rraθiona'lismo; rrasiona'lismo/ *m*, rationalism

racionalista /rraθiona'lista; rrasiona'lista/ *a* and *mf* rationalist —*a* rationalistic

racionalización /rraθionaliθa'θion; rrasionalisa'sion/ *f*, rationalization

racionamiento /rraθiona'miento; rrasiona'miento/ *m*, rationing. *f.* **cartilla de r.,** ration book

racionar /rraθio'nar; rrasio'nar/ *vt* to ration

rada /'rraða/ *f*, bay, cove; *Naut.* road, roadstead

radar /rra'ðar/ *m*, radar

radiación /rraðia'θion; rraðia'sion/ *f*, radiation; *Radio.* broadcasting

radiactividad /rraðiaktiβi'ðað/ *f*, radioactivity

radiactivo /rraðiak'tiβo/ *a* radioactive

radiador /rraðia'ðor/ *m*, radiator (for heating); *Auto.* radiator

radial /rra'ðial/ *a* radial

radiante /rra'ðiante/ *a Phys.* radiating; brilliant, shining; *Fig.* beaming (with satisfaction)

radiar /rra'ðiar/ *vi Phys.* to radiate; —*vt* broadcast (by radio)

radical /rraði'kal/ *a* radical; fundamental; *Polit.* radical. *m, Gram.* root; (*Math. Chem.*) radical. *mf Polit.* radical

radicalismo /rraðika'lismo/ *m*, radicalism

radicar /rraði'kar/ **(se)** *vi* and *vr* to take root. **r. una solicitud,** file an application, submit an application —*vi* be (in a place)

radio /'rraðio/ *m*, (*Geom. Anat.*) radius; radium. *f*, radio

radioaficionado /rraðioafiθio'naðo; rraðioafisio-'naðo/ **(-da)** *n* radio amateur; *Inf.* ham, wireless fan or enthusiast

radioaudición /rraðioauði'θion; rraðioauði'sion/ *f*, radio broadcast

radiocomunicación /rraðiokomunika'θion; rraðioko-munika'sion/ *f*, radio transmission

radiodifundir /rraðioðifun'dir/ *vt Radio.* to broadcast

radiodifusión, radioemisión /rraðioðifu'sion, rra-ðioemi'sion/ *f, Radio.* broadcast; broadcasting

radioemisora /rraðioemi'sora/ *f*, radio station

radioescucha /rraðioes'kutʃa/ *mf* radio listener

radiofotografía /rraðiofotogra'fia/ *f*, radiophotography; x-ray photograph. **tomar una r. de,** to x-ray

radiofrecuencia /rraðiofre'kuenθia; rraðio-fre'kuensia/ *f*, radiofrequency

radiografía /rraðiogra'fia/ *f*, radiography

radiografiar /rraðiogra'fiar/ *vt* to x-ray, radiograph

radiografista /rraðiogra'fista/ *mf* radiographer

radiograma /rraðio'grama/ *m*, radiogram, cable

radiolocación /rraðioloka'θion; rraðioloka'sion/ *f*, radiolocation

radiología /rraðiolo'hia/ *f*, radiology

radiólogo /rra'ðiologo/ *mf* radiologist

radiometría /rraðiome'tria/ *f*, radiometry

radiómetro /rra'ðiometro/ *m*, radiometer

radiorreceptor /rraðiorreθep'tor; rraðiorresep'tor/ *m*, receiver, wireless set

radioscopia /rraðio'skopia/ *f*, radioscopy

radiotelefonía /rraðiotelefo'nia/ *f*, radiotelephony

radiotelefonía, radioemisión radiotelegraphy
radiotelegrafía /rraðiotelegra'fia/ *f*, radiotelegraphy

radiotelegrafiar /rraðiotelegra'fiar/ *vt* to radiotelegraph

radiotelegráfico /rraðiotele'grafiko/ *a* radiotelegraphic, wireless

radiotelegrafista /rraðiotelegra'fista/ *mf* wireless operator

radiotelegrama /rraðiotele'grama/ *m*, radiogram, radiotelegram

radioterapia /rraðiote'rapia/ *f*, radiotherapy, radiotherapeutics

radiotransmisor /rraðiotransmi'sor/ *m*, (radio) transmitter

radioyente /rraðio'yente/ *mf* radio listener

raedera /rrae'ðera/ *f*, scraper

raedor /rrae'ðor/ *a* scraping; abrasive

raedura /rrae'ðura/ *f*, scraping; rubbing; fraying

raer /rra'er/ *vt irr* to scrape; abrade; fray; *Fig.* extirpate. See **caer**

ráfaga /'rrafaga/ *f*, gust or blast of wind; light cloud; flash (of light)

rafe /'rrafe/ *m*, eaves

rafia /'rrafia/ *f*, raffia

raído /'rraiðo/ *a* frayed, threadbare; brazen, barefaced

raíz /rra'iθ; rra'is/ *f*, root. **r. amarga,** horseradish. **r. cuadrada** (**cúbica),** square (cubed) root. **r. pivotante,** tap root. **a r.,** close to the root, closely. **a r. de,** as a result of; after. **de r.,** from the root, entirely. **echar raíces,** to take root

raja /'rraha/ *f*, split, crack; chip, splinter (of wood); slice (of fruit, etc.)

rajá /rra'ha/ *m*, rajah

rajadura /rraha'ðura/ *f*, splitting; crack, split, crevice; *Geol.* break

rajar /rra'har/ *vt* to crack, split; slice; —*vi Inf.* boast; chatter; —*vr* crack, split; *Inf.* take back one's words

ralea /rra'lea/ *f*, kind, quality; (*Inf.* scornful) race, lineage

ralear /rrale'ar/ *vi* to grow thin (cloth, etc.); behave true to type (gen. in a bad sense)

rallador /rraʎa'ðor; rraya'ðor/ *m, Cul.* grater

rallar /rra'ʎar; rra'yar/ *vt Cul.* to grate; *Inf.* bother, annoy

rallo /'rraʎo; 'rrayo/ *m, Cul.* grater; rasp

ralo /'rralo/ *a* sparse, thin

rama /'rrama/ *f*, bough, branch; *Fig.* branch (of family). *Fig. Inf.* **andarse por las ramas,** to beat around the bush. **en r.,** *Com.* raw; unbound (of books)

ramaje /rra'mahe/ *m*, thickness of branches, denseness of foliage

ramal /rra'mal/ *m*, strand (of rope); halter; branch line (of a railroad); fork (of a road, etc.); ramification, division

ramalazo /rrama'laθo; rrama'laso/ *m*, blow with a rope; mark left by this; bruise

rambla /'rrambla/ *f*, bed, channel, course; avenue, boulevard (in Catalonia)

ramera /rra'mera/ *f*, whore

ramificación /rramifika'θion; rramifika'sion/ *f*, ramification; *Anat.* bifurcation

ramificarse /rramifi'karse/ *vr* to branch, fork; *Fig.* spread

ramillete /rrami'ʎete; rrami'yete/ *m*, bouquet; table centerpiece; *Bot.* cluster

ramo /'rramo/ *m*, *Bot.* branch; twig, spray; bouquet, bunch; wreath; *Fig.* branch (of learning, etc.); *Com.* line (of business); *Fig.* touch, slight attack. **Domingo de Ramos**, Palm Sunday

ramoso /rra'moso/ *a* branchy, thick with branches

rampa /'rrampa/ *f*, gradient, incline; *Mil.* ramp; launching site

ramplón /rram'plon/ *a* stout, heavy (of shoes); coarse; vulgar; bombastic

rana /'rrana/ *f*, frog. **r. de San Antonio**, tree frog

ranchero /rran'tʃero/ *m*, *Mil.* cook; small farmer; *West Hem.* rancher

rancho /'rrantʃo/ *m*, mess, rations; settlement, camp; hut, cabin; *Fig.* group, huddle; *West Hem.* ranch; *Naut.* gang. **hacer r.**, *Inf.* to make room

rancidez /rranθi'ðeθ; rransi'ðes/ *f*, rancidness; staleness; rankness; antiquity

ranciedad /rranθie'ðað; rransie'ðað/ *f*, rancidness; antiquity, oldness; mustiness

rancio /'rranθio; 'rransio/ *a* rancid, rank; mellow (of wine); ancient; traditional; musty

rango /'rrango/ *m*, grade, class; range; (*Mil. Nav.* and social) rank; file, line

ranúnculo /rra'nunkulo/ *m*, buttercup

ranura /rra'nura/ *f*, groove; rabbet; slot, notch

rapacidad /rrapaθi'ðað; rrapasi'ðað/ *f*, rapacity, avidity, greed

rapador /rrapa'ðor/ *a* scraping. *m*, *Inf.* barber

rapapolvo /rrapa'polβo/ *m*, *Inf.* severe scolding, dressing-down

rapar /rra'par/ **(se)** *vt* and *vr* to shave; —*vt* crop, cut close (hair); *Inf.* steal, pinch

rapaz /rra'paθ; rra'pas/ *a* rapacious. *m*, young boy. **ave r.**, bird of prey

rapaza /rra'paθa; rra'pasa/ *f*, young girl

rape /'rrape/ *m*, *Inf.* hasty shave or haircut. **al r.**, close-cropped

rapé /rra'pe/ *m*, snuff

rapidez /rrapi'ðeθ; rrapi'ðes/ *f*, speed, swiftness, rapidity

rápido /'rrapiðo/ *a* quick, swift; express (trains). *m*, torrent, rapid; express train

rapiña /rra'piɲa/ *f*, robbery, plundering, sacking

rapiñar /rrapi'ɲar/ *vt Inf.* to steal, pinch

raposa /rra'posa/ *f*, vixen, fox; *Inf.* wily person

raposear /rrapose'ar/ *vi* to behave like a fox

raposo /rra'poso/ *m*, (male) fox

rapsodia /rrap'soðia/ *f*, rhapsody

raptar /rrap'tar/ *vt* to abduct; rob

rapto /'rrapto/ *m*, abduction, rape; snatching, seizing; ecstasy, trance; *Med.* loss of consciousness

raptor /rrap'tor/ *m*, kidnapper, abductor

raquero /rra'kero/ *a* pirate. *m*, wrecker; pickpocket, dock rat

raqueta /rra'keta/ *f*, racket (tennis, badminton, squash rackets); croupier's rake. **r. de nieve**, snowshoe

raquianestesia /rrakianes'tesia/ *f*, spinal anesthesia

raquídeo /rra'kiðeo/ *a* spinal

raquítico /rra'kitiko/ *a Med.* rachitic; small, minute; weak, feeble; rickety

raquitismo /rraki'tismo/ *m*, rickets

rarefacción /rrarefak'θion; rrarefak'sion/ *f*, rarefaction

rarefacer /rrarefa'θer; rrarefa'ser/ **(se)** *vt* and *vr irr* to rarefy. See **satisfacer**

rareza /rra'reθa; rra'resa/ *f*, rareness, unusualness; eccentricity, whim; oddity, curio

raridad /rrari'ðað/ *f*, rarity; thinness; scarcity

raro /'rraro/ *a* rare, unusual, uncommon; notable, outstanding; odd, eccentric, queer; rarefied (gases, etc.). **rara vez**, seldom. **lo r. de**, the strange thing about (e.g. *Lo r. del caso es...*, the strange thing about the case is...)

ras /rras/ *m*, level. **a r.**, flush (with), nearly touching

rasa /'rrasa/ *f*, worn place in cloth; clearing, glade

rasar /rra'sar/ *vt* to level with a strickle; graze, brush, touch lightly; —*vr* grow clear (of the sky, etc.)

rascacielos /rraska'θielos; rraska'sielos/ *m*, skyscraper

rascador /rraska'ðor/ *m*, scraper; ornamental hairpin

rascadura /rraska'ðura/ *f*, scraping; scratching

rascar /rras'kar/ *vt* to scratch; claw; scrape; twang (a guitar, etc.). *Inf.* **¡Que se rasque!** Let him put up with it! Let him lump it!

rascatripas /rraska'tripas/ *m*, *Inf.* caterwauler, squeaker (of violinists, etc.)

rascón /rras'kon/ *a* sour, tart

rasgadura /rrasga'ðura/ *f*, tearing; tear, rip, rent

rasgar /rras'gar/ **(se)** *vt* and *vr* to tear, rip; —*vt* strum the guitar

rasgo /'rrasgo/ *m*, flourish (of the pen); felicitous expression; characteristic, quality; *pl* features (of the face)

rasgón /rras'gon/ *m*, rip, tear

rasguear /rrasge'ar/ *vt* to strum, twang (the guitar); —*vi* write with a flourish

rasgueo /rras'geo/ *m*, flourish (on a guitar); scratch (of a pen)

rasguñar /rrasgu'ɲar/ *vt* to scratch, scrape; claw; *Art.* sketch

rasguño /rras'guɲo/ *m*, scratch; *Art.* sketch, outline

raso /'rraso/ *a* flat; free of obstacles; glossy; clear (sky, etc.); plain; undistinguished; backless (chairs). *m*, satin. **al r.**, in the open air

raspa /'rraspa/ *f*, *Bot.* beard (of cereals); fishbone; bunch of grapes; *Bot.* husk; scraper

raspador /rraspa'ðor/ *m*, eraser; scraper, rasp

raspadura /rraspa'ðura/ *f*, scraping; erasing; shavings, filings

raspar /rras'par/ *vt* to scrape; erase; rob, steal; burn, bite (wine, etc.)

rastra /'rrastra/ *f*, trace, sign; sled; string of onions, etc.; anything dragging; *Agr.* harrow; *Agr.* rake. **a la r.**, dragging; reluctantly. **pescar a la r.**, to trawl

rastreador /rrastrea'ðor/ *m*, *Naut.* minesweeper —*a* dragging

rastrear /rrastre'ar/ *vt* to trace, trail; drag, trawl; surmise, conjecture, investigate; —*vi Agr.* rake; fly low

rastreo /rras'treo/ *m*, dragging (of lakes, etc.)

rastrero /rras'trero/ *a* dragging, trailing; low-flying; servile, abject; *Bot.* creeping. *m*, slaughterhouse employee

rastrillador /rrastriʎa'ðor; rrastriya'ðor/ **(-ra)** *n* raker; hackler

rastrilladora /rrastriʎa'ðora; rrastriya'ðora/ *f*, mechanical harrow

rastrillaje /rrastri'ʎahe; rrastri'yahe/ *m*, raking

rastrillar /rrastri'ʎar; rrastri'yar/ *vt* to rake; dress, comb (flax)

rastrillo /rras'triʎo; rras'triyo/ *m*, *Agr.* rake; hackle; portcullis; *Agr.* rack

rastro /'rrastro/ *m*, *Agr.* rake; track, trail; wholesale meat market; slaughterhouse; trace, vestige; secondhand market (in Madrid)

rastrojo /rras'troho/ *m*, stubble; stubble field

rasura /rra'sura/ *f*, shaving

rasurar /rrasu'rar/ **(se)** *vt* and *vr* to shave

rata /'rrata/ *f*, rat. *m*, *Inf.* pickpocket. **r. almizclera**, muskrat. *Inf.* **más pobre que las ratas**, poorer than a church mouse

rataplán /rrata'plan/ *m*, rub-a-dub-dub, beating of a drum

ratear /rrate'ar/ *vt* to rebate pro rata; apportion; thieve on a small scale, filch; —*vi* crawl, creep

ratería /rrate'ria/ *f*, filching, petty theft, picking pockets; meanness, parsimony

ratero /rra'tero/ (**-ra**) *n* pilferer, petty thief, pick-pocket

ratificación /rratifika'θion; rratifika'sion/ *f*, ratification

ratificador /rratifika'ðor/ (**-ra**) *n* ratifier

ratificar /rratifi'kar/ *vt* to ratify

ratificatorio /rratifika'torio/ *a* ratifying, confirmatory

rato /'rrato/ *m*, short interval of time, while. **buen** (**mal**) **r.,** pleasant (unpleasant) time. **r. perdido,** leisure moment. **a ratos,** sometimes, occasionally. **de r. en r.,** from time to time. **pasar el r.,** *Inf.* to while away the time

ratón /rra'ton/ (**-ona**) *n* mouse

ratonera /rrato'nera/ *f*, mousetrap; mousehole; mouse nest. *Fig.* **caer en la r.,** to fall into a trap

ratonero, ratonesco, ratonil /rrato'nero, rrato'nesko, rrato'nil/ *a* mousy

rauco /'rrauko/ *a Poet.* hoarse

raudal /rrau'ðal/ *m*, torrent, cascade; *Fig.* flood, abundance

raudo /'rrauðo/ *a* swift, rapid

ravioles /rra'βioles/ *m pl*, ravioli

raya /'rraya/ *f*, stripe, streak; limit, end; part (of the hair); boundary; *Gram.* dash; score (some games). *m*, *Ichth.* ray. **pasar de r.,** to go too far; misbehave

rayadillo /rraya'ðiʎo; rraya'ðiyo/ *m*, striped cotton

rayano /rra'yano/ *a* neighboring; border; almost identical, very similar

rayar /rra'yar/ *vt* to draw lines; streak; stripe; cross out; underline; rifle (a gun); —*vi* verge (on), border (on); appear (of dawn, daylight); excel; be similar. **Raya en los catorce años,** He is about fourteen

rayo /'rrayo/ *m*, *Phys.* beam, ray; thunderbolt; flash of lightning; spoke; quick-witted person; capable, energetic person; sudden pain; disaster, catastrophe. **r. de sol,** sunbeam. **r. catódico,** cathode ray. **r. x,** x-ray. *Fig.* **echar rayos,** to breathe forth fury

rayón /rra'yon/ *m*, rayon

raza /'rraθa; 'rrasa/ *f*, race; breed; lineage, family; kind, class; crack, crevice. **de r.,** purebred

razón /rra'θon; rra'son/ *f*, reason; reasoning; word, expression; speech, argument; motive, cause; order, method; justice, equity; right, authority; explanation; *Math.* ratio, proportion. **r. de estado,** raison d'état, reasons of state. *Com.* **r. social,** firm, trade name. **a r. de,** at a rate of. **dar la r.** (**a**), to agree with. **estar puesto en r.,** to stand to reason. **tener r.,** to be in the right

razonable /rraθo'naβle; rraso'naβle/ *a* reasonable; moderate

razonador /rraθona'ðor; rrasona'ðor/ (**-ra**) *n* reasoner

razonamiento /rraθona'miento; rrasona'miento/ *m*, reasoning

razonar /rraθo'nar; rraso'nar/ *vi* to reason; speak; —*vt* attest, confirm

razzia /'rraθθia; 'rrassia/ *f*, foray, pillaging, sacking; police raid

re /rre/ *m*, *Mus.* re, D

reabsorción /rreaβsor'θion; rreaβsor'sion/ *f*, reabsorption

reacción /rreak'θion; rreak'sion/ *f*, reaction. **r. de Bayardo,** quick reaction of someone always ready to help those in distress

reaccionar /rreakθio'nar; rreaksio'nar/ *vi* to react

reaccionario /rreakθio'nario; rreaksio'nario/ (**-ia**) *a* and *n* reactionary

reaccionarismo /rreakθiona'rismo; rreaksiona'rismo/ *m*, reactionism

reacio /rre'aθio; rre'asio/ *a* recalcitrant

reactivo /rreak'tiβo/ *m*, reagent —*a* reactive; reacting

readmisión /rreaðmi'sion/ *f*, readmission

readmitir /rreaðmi'tir/ *vt* to readmit

reajustar /rreahus'tar/ *vt* to readjust

real /rre'al/ *a* actual, real; kingly; royal; royalist; *Fig.* regal; *Inf.* fine, handsome. *m*, silver coin, real; *m pl*, encampment, camp. **alzar el r.,** *Mil.* to strike camp. **asentar el r.,** *Mil.* to encamp. **r. decreto,** royal decree. **sitio r.,** royal residence. **un r., sobre otro,** *Inf.* cash in full

realce /rre'alθe; rre'alse/ *m*, raised or embossed work; renown, glory; *Art.* high light

realeza /rrea'leθa; rrea'lesa/ *f*, royalty, royal majesty

realidad /rreali'ðað/ *f*, reality; sincerity, truth. **en r.,** in fact, actually

realismo /rrea'lismo/ *m*, realism; regalism; royalism

realista /rrea'lista/ *a* realistic; royalist. *mf* realist; royalist; regalist

realizable /rreali'θaβle; rreali'saβle/ *a* realizable; practicable

realización /rrealiθa'θion; rrealisa'sion/ *f*, realization; performance, execution

realizar /rreali'θar; rreali'sar/ *vt* to perform, execute, carry out; *Com.* realize. **r. beneficio,** to make a profit

realmente /rreal'mente/ *adv* really, truly; actually

realzar /rreal'θar; rreal'sar/ *vt* to heighten, raise; emboss; exalt; enhance; *Art.* intensify (colors, etc.)

reanimar /rreani'mar/ *vt* to reanimate; revive, restore, resuscitate; encourage

reanudación /rreanuða'θion; rreanuða'sion/ *f*, resumption, renewal

reanudar /rreanu'ðar/ *vt* to resume, continue

reaparecer /rreapare'θer; rreapare'ser/ *vi irr* to reappear. See **conocer**

reaparición /rreapari'θion; rreapari'sion/ *f*, reappearance

rearmamento /rrearma'mento/ *m*, rearmament

rearmar /rrear'mar/ *vi* to rearm

reasegurador /rreasegura'ðor/ *m*, underwriter

reasegurar /rreasegu'rar/ *vt* to reinsure, underwrite

reaseguro /rrease'guro/ *m*, reinsurance, underwriting

reasumir /rreasu'mir/ *vt* to reassume; resume

reasunción /rreasun'θion; rreasun'sion/ *f*, reassumption; resumption

reata /rre'ata/ *f*, string of horses or mules. **de r.,** in single file; *Inf.* blindly, unquestioningly; *Inf.* at once

rebaja /rre'βaha/ *f*, diminution; *Com.* discount, rebate; remission

rebajar /rreβa'har/ *vt* to lower; curtail, lessen; remit; *Com.* reduce in price; *Mech.* file; *Elec.* step down; humble, humiliate; —*vr* cringe, humble oneself

rebajo /rre'βaho/ *m*, reduction (in price, etc.); rabbet

rebanada /rreβa'naða/ *f*, slice, piece (of bread, etc.)

rebanar /rreβa'nar/ *vt* to cut into slices; split

rebaño /rre'βaɲo/ *m*, flock, drove, herd; *Eccl.* flock

rebasar /rreβa'sar/ *vt* to exceed, go beyond; *Mil.* by-pass

rebate /rre'βate/ *m*, altercation, dispute, quarrel

rebatiña /rreβa'tiɲa/ *f*, grab; scrimmage. **andar a la r.,** to scuffle

rebatir /rreβa'tir/ *vt* to repulse, repel; fight again; fight hard; oppose, resist; *Com.* deduct; refuse, reject

rebato /rre'βato/ *m*, alarm, tocsin; *Mil.* surprise attack; panic, dismay

rebeca /rre'βeka/ *f*, cardigan, jersey

rebeco /rre'βeko/ *m*, *Zool.* chamois

rebelarse /rreβe'larse/ *vr* to mutiny, rebel; oppose, resist

rebelde /rre'βelde/ *a* mutinous, rebellious; wilful, disobedient; stubborn. *mf* rebel

rebeldía /rreβel'dia/ *f*, rebelliousness; willfulness; stubbornness; *Law.* nonappearance

rebelión /rreβe'lion/ *f*, insurrection, revolt

rebién /rre'βien/ *adv* very well, extremely well

rebisabuelo /rreβisa'βuelo/ (**-la**) *n*. See **tatarabuelo**

reblandecer /rreβlande'θer; rreβlande'ser/ *vt irr* to soften; —*vr* become soft. See **conocer**

reblandecimiento /rreβlandeθi'miento; rreβlandesi'miento/ *m*, softening; *Med.* flabbiness

reborde /rre'βorðe/ *m*, rim, edge; *Mech.* flange. **r. de acera,** curb

rebordear /rreβorðe'ar/ *vt* to flange

rebosar /rreβo'sar/ *vi* to overflow, run over; *Fig.* abound in; express one's feelings

rebotar /rreβo'tar/ *vi* to rebound; clinch (nails, etc.); refuse; —*vr* change color; *Inf.* be vexed

rebote /rre'βote/ *m*, rebounding; rebound

rebotica /rreβo'tika/ *f*, back room of a pharmacy; back of a shop

rebozar /rreβo'θar; rreβo'sar/ *vt* to muffle up; coat with batter

rebozo /rre'βoθo; rre'βoso/ *m*, muffling up, hiding

the face; head shawl; pretense, excuse. *Fig.* **sin r.,** openly

rebramo /rreˈβramo/ *m*, barking of deer, stags, etc.

rebueno /rreˈβueno/ *a Inf.* extremely good, fine

rebullicio /rreβuˈʎiθio; rreβuˈyisio/ *m*, uproar, clamor

rebullir /rreβuˈʎir; rreβuˈyir/ *vi* to stir, show signs of movement; *Fig.* swarm, seethe

rebusca /rreˈβuska/ *f*, close search; gleaning; remains

rebuscado /rreβusˈkaðo/ *a* affected, unnatural (of style)

rebuscar /rreβusˈkar/ *vt* to search for; glean

rebuznar /rreβuθˈnar; rreβusˈnar/ *vi* to bray

rebuzno /rreˈβuθno; rreˈβusno/ *m*, braying

recadero /rrekaˈðero/ **(-ra)** *n* messenger, errand boy

recado /rreˈkaðo/ *m*, message; greeting, note; gift, present; daily marketing; outfit, implements; precaution, safeguard

recaer /rrekaˈer/ *vi irr* to fall again; *Med.* relapse; lapse, backslide; devolve, fall upon. See **caer**

recaída /rrekaˈiða/ *f*, falling again; *Med.* relapse; lapse

recalar /rrekaˈlar/ *vt* to impregnate; *Naut.* call at (a port), come within sight of land

recalcada /rrekalˈkaða/ *f*, pressing down, squeezing; emphasis; *Naut.* list

recalcar /rrekalˈkar/ *vt* to press down; squeeze; pack tight; stress, emphasize; —*vi Naut.* list; —*vr Inf.* say over and over, savor one's words

recalcitrante /rrekalθiˈtrante; rrekalsiˈtrante/ *a* obdurate, recalcitrant

recalentador /rrekalentaˈðor/ *m*, *Mech.* superheater

recalentar /rrekalenˈtar/ *vt irr* to overheat; superheat; reheat. See **sentar**

recamado /rrekaˈmaðo/ *m*, raised embroidery

recámara /rreˈkamara/ *f*, dressing room; explosives chamber; breech of a gun; *Inf.* caution

recambio /rreˈkambio/ *m*, spare, spare part; *Com.* reexchange

recantación /rrekantaˈθion; rrekantaˈsion/ *f*, retraction, recantation

recapacitar /rrekapaθiˈtar; rrekapasiˈtar/ *vi* to search one's memory; think over

recapitulación /rrekapitulaˈθion; rrekapitulaˈsion/ *f*, summary, résumé

recapitular /rrekapituˈlar/ *vt* to recapitulate, summarize

recargar /rrekarˈgar/ *vt* to recharge; load again; reaccuse; overcharge; overdress or overdecorate; —*vr Med.* become more feverish. **r. acumuladores,** to recharge batteries

recargo /rreˈkargo/ *m*, charge; new load; *Law.* new accusation; overcharge, extra cost; *Med.* temperature increase

recatado /rrekaˈtaðo/ *a* prudent, discreet, circumspect; modest, shy

recatar /rrekaˈtar/ *vt* to hide, conceal; —*vr* be prudent or cautious

recato /rreˈkato/ *m*, caution, prudence; modesty, shyness, reserve

recauchutar /rrekautʃuˈtar/ *vt* to retread (tires)

recaudación /rrekauðaˈθion; rrekauðaˈsion/ *f*, collecting; collection (of taxes, etc.); tax collector's office

recaudador /rrekauðaˈðor/ *m*, tax collector

recaudar /rrekauˈðar/ *vt* to collect, recover (taxes, debts, etc.); deposit, place in custody

recaudo /rreˈkauðo/ *m*, collecting; collection (of taxes, etc.); precaution, safeguard; *Law.* surety

recelar /rreθeˈlar; rreseˈlar/ *vt* to suspect, fear, mistrust; —*vr (with de)* be afraid or suspicious of

recelo /rreˈθelo; rreˈselo/ *m*, suspicion, mistrust, doubt, fear

receloso /rreθeˈloso; rreseˈloso/ *a* suspicious, distrustful, doubtful

recepción /rreθepˈθion; rresepˈsion/ *f*, receiving, reception; admission, acceptance; reception, party; *Law.* cross-examination

receptáculo /rreθepˈtakulo; rresepˈtakulo/ *m*, receptacle, container; *Fig.* refuge; *Bot.* receptacle

receptador /rreθeptaˈðor; rresseptaˈðor/ **(-ra)** *n* receiver (of stolen goods); accomplice

receptivo /rreθepˈtiβo; rresepˈtiβo/ *a* receptive

receptor /rreθepˈtor; rresepˈtor/ **(-ra)** *a* receiving —*n* recipient. *m*, *Elec.* receiver; wireless set. **r. de galena,** crystal set. **r. telefónico,** telephone receiver

receta /rreˈθeta; rreˈseta/ *f*, *Med.* prescription; *Cul.* recipe

recetar /rreθeˈtar; rreseˈtar/ *vt Med.* to prescribe; *Inf.* demand

rechapear /rretʃapeˈar/ *vt* to replate

rechazar /rretʃaˈθar; rretʃaˈsar/ *vt* to repulse; resist; refuse; oppose, deny (the truth of); contradict

rechazo /rreˈtʃaθo; rreˈtʃaso/ *m*, recoil; rebound; refusal

rechinamiento, rechino /rretʃinaˈmiento, rreˈtʃino/ *m*, squeaking, creaking; gnashing (of teeth)

rechinar /rretʃiˈnar/ *vi* to squeak, creak; gnash (teeth); chatter (teeth); do with a bad grace

rechoncho /rreˈtʃontʃo/ *a* squat, stocky

reciamente /rreθiaˈmente; rresiaˈmente/ *adv* hard; strongly, firmly, vigorously

recibí /rreθiˈβi; rresiˈβi/ *m*, *Com.* receipt

recibidor /rreθiβiˈðor; rresiβiˈðor/ **(-ra)** *a* receiving —*n* recipient. *m*, reception room

recibimiento /rreθiβiˈmiento; rresiβiˈmiento/ *m*, reception; welcome, greeting; reception room, waiting room; hall, vestibule

recibir /rreθiˈβir; rresiˈβir/ *vt* to obtain, receive; support, bear; suffer, experience (attack, injury); approve; accept, receive; entertain; stand up to (attack); —*vr (with de)* graduate as, take office as

recibo /rreˈθiβo; rreˈsiβo/ *m*, reception; *Com.* receipt; reception room, waiting room; hall, vestibule. *Com.* **acusar r.,** to acknowledge receipt

recidiva /rreθiˈðiβa; rresiˈðiβa/ *f*, *Med.* relapse

recién /rreˈθien; rreˈsien/ *adv* recently, newly. Shortened form of **reciente** before a past participle (e.g. *r. llegado,* newly arrived)

reciente /rreˈθiente; rreˈsiente/ *a* recent; new; fresh

recinto /rreˈθinto; rreˈsinto/ *m*, precincts; neighborhood; premises, place

recio /ˈrreθio; ˈrresio/ *a* strong; robust; bulky, thick; rough, uncouth; grievous, hard; severe (weather); impetuous, precipitate

recipiente /rreθiˈpiente; rresiˈpiente/ *a* receiving. *m*, receptacle, container, vessel

reciprocar /rreθiproˈkar; rresiproˈkar/ *vt* to reciprocate

reciprocidad /rreθiproθiˈðað; rresiprosiˈðað/ *f*, reciprocity; reciprocation

recíproco /rreˈθiproko; rreˈsiproko/ *a* reciprocal

recitación /rreθitaˈθion; rresitaˈsion/ *f*, recitation

recitado /rreθiˈtaðo; rresiˈtaðo/ *m*, recitative

recitador /rreθitaˈðor; rresitaˈðor/ **(-ra)** *n* elocutionist, reciter

recitar /rreθiˈtar; rresiˈtar/ *vt* to recite, declaim

reclamación /rreklamaˈθion; rreklamaˈsion/ *f*, reclamation; objection, opposition; *Com.* claim

reclamar /rreklaˈmar/ *vi* to oppose, object to; *Poet.* resound; —*vt* call repeatedly; *Com.* claim; decoy (birds)

reclamo /rreˈklamo/ *m*, decoy bird; enticement, allurement; *Law.* reclamation; advertisement. **objeto de r.,** advertising sample. **venta de r.,** bargain sale

reclinación /rreklinaˈθion; rreklinaˈsion/ *f*, reclining; leaning

reclinatorio /rreklinaˈtorio/ *m*, couch; prie-dieu

recluir /rreˈkluir/ *vt irr* to immure, shut up; detain, arrest. See **huir**

reclusión /rrekluˈsion/ *f*, confinement, seclusion; prison

recluso /rreˈkluso/ **(-sa)** *n* recluse

recluta /rreˈkluta/ *f*, recruiting. *mf Mil.* recruit

reclutador /rreklutaˈðor/ *m*, recruiting office

reclutamiento /rreklutaˈmiento/ *m*, recruiting

reclutar /rrekluˈtar/ *vt* to enlist recruits, recruit

recobrar /rrekoˈβrar/ *vt* to recover, regain; —*vr* recuperate; regain consciousness

recobro /rreˈkoβro/ *m*, recovery; *Mech.* pick-up

recocer /rrekoˈθer; rrekoˈser/ *vt irr* to reboil; recook; overboil; overcook; anneal (metals); —*vr Fig.* be tormented (by emotion), be all burned up. See **cocer**

recodo /rre'koðo/ *m*, bend, turn, loop

recogedor /rrekohe'ðor/ *a* sheltering. *m*, *Agr*. gleaner

recoger /rreko'her/ *vt* to gather, pick; pick up; retake; collect (letters from a mailbox, etc.); amass; shrink, narrow; keep; hoard; shelter; reap, pick; —*vr* withdraw, retire; go home; go to bed; retrench, economize; give oneself to meditation

recogida /rreko'hiða/ *f*, collection (of letters from a mailbox); withdrawal; retirement; harvest

recogido /rreko'hiðo/ *a* recluse; cloistered, confined

recogimiento /rrekohi'miento/ *m*, gathering, picking; collection, accumulation; seclusion; shelter; women's reformatory

recolección /rrekolek'θion; rrekolek'sion/ *f*, summary, résumé; harvest; collection (of taxes, etc.); *Eccl*. convent of a reformed order; mystic ecstasy

recoleto /rreko'leto/ *a Eccl*. reformed (of religious orders); recluse

recomendable /rrekomen'daβle/ *a* commendable, recommendable

recomendación /rrekomenda'θion; rrekomenda-'sion/ *f*, recommendation (all meanings)

recomendar /rrekomen'dar/ *vt irr* to recommend (all meanings); entrust, commend —*Pres. Indic*. **recomiendo, recomiendas, recomienda, recomiendan**. *Pres. Subjunc*. **recomiende, recomiendes, recomiende, recomienden**

recompensa /rrekom'pensa/ *f*, compensation; recompense, reward

recompensar /rrekompen'sar/ *vt* to compensate; requite; reward, recompense

recomposición /rrekomposi'θion; rrekomposi'sion/ *f*, recomposition

recomprar /rrekom'prar/ *vt* to repurchase

reconcentrar /rrekonθen'trar; rrekonsen'trar/ *vt* to concentrate; dissemble; —*vr* withdraw into oneself, meditate

reconciliable /rrekonθi'liaβle; rrekonsi'liaβle/ *a* reconcilable

reconciliación /rrekonθilia'θion; rrekonsilia'sion/ *f*, reconciliation

reconciliador /rrekonθilia'ðor; rrekonsilia'ðor/ **(-ra)** *a* reconciliatory —*n* reconciler

reconciliar /rrekonθi'liar; rrekonsi'liar/ *vt* to reconcile; *Eccl*. reconsecrate; *Eccl*. hear a short confession; —*vr* become reconciled; *Eccl*. make an additional confession

recondicionar /rrekondiθio'nar; rrekondisio'nar/ *vt* to rebuild, overhaul, recondition

recóndito /rre'kondito/ *a* recondite

reconocer /rrekono'θer; rrekono'ser/ *vt irr* to examine, inspect; recognize; admit, acknowledge; own, confess; search; *Polit*. recognize; *Mil*. reconnoiter; (with *por*) adopt as (a son, etc.); recognize as; —*vr* be seen, show; acknowledge, confess; know oneself. **Bien se reconoce que no está aquí,** It's easy to see he's not here. See **conocer**

reconocido /rrekono'θiðo; rrekono'siðo/ *a* grateful

reconocimiento /rrekonoθi'miento; rrekonosi-'miento/ *m*, examination, inspection; recognition; acknowledgement, admission; search; *Mil*. reconnoitering; adoption; gratitude

reconquista /rrekon'kista/ *f*, reconquest

reconquistar /rrekonkis'tar/ *vt* to reconquer; *Fig*. recover, win back

reconstitución /rrekonstitu'θion; rrekonstitu'sion/ *f*, reconstitution

reconstituir /rrekonsti'tuir/ *vt irr* to reconstitute. See **huir**

reconstituyente /rrekonstitu'yente/ *m*, *Med*. tonic

reconstrucción /rrekonstruk'θion; rrekonstruk'sion/ *f*, reconstruction

reconstruir /rrekons'truir/ *vt irr* to reconstruct, rebuild; recreate. See **huir**

reconvención /rrekomben'θion; rrekomben'sion/ *f*, rebuke, reproof; recrimination; *Law*. countercharge

reconversión /rrekomber'sion/ *f*, reconversion

recopilación /rrekopila'θion; rrekopila'sion/ *f*, summary, compendium; collection (of writings); digest (of laws)

recopilador /rrekopila'ðor/ *m*, compiler

recopilar /rrekopi'lar/ *vt* to compile, collect

recordar /rrekor'ðar/ *vt irr* to cause to remember, remind; remember; —*vi* remember; awake. See **acordar**

recordatorio /rrekorða'torio/ *m*, reminder —*a* commemorative (e.g. a plaque)

recorrer /rreko'rrer/ *vt* to travel over; pass through; wander around; examine, inspect; read hastily; overhaul, renovate

recorrido /rreko'rriðo/ *m*, journey, run; *Mech*. stroke; overhaul. **r. de despegue,** *Aer*. take-off run

recortado /rrekor'taðo/ *a Bot*. jagged, incised. *m*, paper cutout

recortar /rrekor'tar/ *vt* to clip, trim, pare; cut out; *Art*. outline; —*vr* stand out (against), be outlined (against)

recorte /rre'korte/ *m*, clipping, paring; cutting; cutout; *Art*. outline; *pl* snippets, clippings. **r. de periódico,** newspaper cutting, newspaper clipping

recostar /rrekos'tar/ *vt irr* (with *en* or *contra*) to lean, rest against; —*vr* (with *en* or *contra*) lean against, rest on; lean back; recline. See **contar**

recreación /rrekrea'θion; rrekrea'sion/ *f*, recreation, hobby

recrear /rrekre'ar/ *vt* to entertain, amuse; —*vr* amuse oneself; delight (in), enjoy

recreo /rre'kreo/ *m*, recreation, hobby; playtime, recess (in schools); place of amusement. **salón de r.,** recreation room

recriminación /rrekrimina'θion; rrekrimina'sion/ *f*, recrimination

recriminador /rrekrimina'ðor/ *a* recriminatory

recriminar /rrekrimi'nar/ *vt* to recriminate

recrudecer /rrekruðe'θer; rrekruðe'ser/ **(se)** *vi* and *vr irr* to recur, return. See **conocer**

recrudescencia /rrekruðes'θenθia; rrekruðes'sensia/ *f*, recrudescence, recurrence

rectángulo /rrek'taŋgulo/ *m*, rectangle —*a* rectangular

rectificable /rrektifi'kaβle/ *a* rectifiable

rectificación /rrektifika'θion; rrektifika'sion/ *f*, rectification; *Mech*. grinding

rectificador /rrektifika'ðor/ *m*, rectifier

rectificar /rrektifi'kar/ *vt* to rectify; *Mech*. grind; —*vr* mend one's ways; *Mil*. **r. el frente,** to straighten the line

rectilíneo /rrekti'lineo/ *a* rectilinear

rectitud /rrekti'tuð/ *f*, straightness; rectitude, integrity; exactness; righteousness

recto /'rrekto/ *a* straight; upright; erect; literal (meaning); just, fair; single-breasted (of coats); *m*, right angle; rectum

rector /rrek'tor/ **(-ra)** *n* director; principal, headmaster. *m*, *Eccl*. rector

rectorado /rrekto'raðo/ *m*, principalship, headmaster- (mistress-) ship; directorship; *Eccl*. rectorship

rectoría /rrekto'ria/ *f*, rectorate, rectorship

recua /'rrekua/ *f*, drove of beasts of burden; *Inf*. string or line (of things)

recubrir /rreku'βrir/ *vt* to re-cover; coat; plate —*Past Part*. **recubierto**

recuento /rre'kuento/ *m*, calculation; recount; inventory

recuerdo /rre'kuerðo/ *m*, memory, remembrance; memento; *pl* greetings, regards

reculada /rreku'laða/ *f*, drawing back; recoil

recular /rreku'lar/ *vi* to recoil, draw back; *Inf*. go back on, give up

recuperable /rrekupe'raβle/ *a* recoverable, recuperable

recuperación /rrekupera'θion; rrekupera'sion/ *f*, recovery, recuperation; *Chem*. recovery

recurrente /rreku'rrente/ *a* recurrent

recurrir /rreku'rrir/ *vi* to recur; (with prep *a*) have recourse to; appeal to

recurso /rre'kurso/ *m*, recourse, resort; choice, option; reversion; petition; *Law*. appeal; *pl* means of livelihood; *Fig*. way out, last hope

recusar /rreku'sar/ *vt* to refuse; challenge the authority (of)

red /rreð/ *f*, net; network; hairnet; railing, grating; *Fig*. snare; system (of communications, etc.); *Fig*. combination (of events, etc.); *Elec*. mains. **r. de**

arrastre, trawl net. *Fig. Inf.* **caer en la r.,** to fall into the trap

redacción /rreðak'θion; rreðak'sion/ *f,* phrasing; editorial office; editing; editorial board

redactar /rreðak'tar/ *vt* to write, phrase; draw up; edit

redactor /rreðak'tor/ **(-ra)** *a* editorial —*n* editor

redada /rre'ðaða/ *f,* cast (of a fishing net); haul, catch

redecilla /rreðe'θiʎa; rreðe'siya/ *f, dim* small net; netting; hairnet

redención /rreðen'θion; rreðen'sion/ *f,* redemption; ransom; deliverance, salvation; redeeming, paying off (a mortgage, etc.)

redentor /rreðen'tor/ **(-ra)** *a* redeeming, redemptive —*n* redeemer

redificar /rreðifi'kar/ *vt* to rebuild

redifusión /rreðifu'sion/ *f, Radio.* relay

redil /rre'ðil/ *m,* sheepfold

redimible /rreði'miβle/ *a* redeemable

redimir /rreði'mir/ *vt* to ransom; redeem, buy back; pay off (a mortgage, etc.); deliver, free; *Eccl.* redeem

reditar /rreði'tar/ *vt* to reprint, reissue

rédito /'rreðito/ *m, Com.* income, revenue, interest, profit

redoblamiento /rreðoβla'miento/ *m,* redoubling; bending back (of nails, etc.); rolling (of a drum)

redoblar /rreðo'βlar/ *vt* to redouble; repeat; bend back (nails, etc.); —*vi* roll (a drum)

redoble /rre'ðoβle/ *m,* doubling; redoubling; repetition; roll (of a drum)

redoma /rre'ðoma/ *f,* flask, vial

redomado /rreðo'maðo/ *a* astute, crafty, sly; complete, perfect

redonda /rre'ðonda/ *f,* district; pasture ground; *Naut.* square sail; *Mus.* semibreve. **a la r.,** around

redondear /rreðonde'ar/ *vt* to make round; round; free (from debt, etc.); —*vr* acquire a fortune; clear oneself (of debts, etc.)

redondel /rreðon'del/ *m,* traffic circle, rotary, roundabout

redondez /rreðon'deθ; rreðon'des/ *f,* roundness

redondo /rre'ðondo/ *a* round; circular; unequivocal, plain. *m,* round, circle; *Inf.* cash

reducción /rreðuk'θion; rreðuk'sion/ *f,* reduction; *Mil.* defeat, conquest; decrease; *Com.* rebate; (*Math. Chem.*) reduction

reducible /rreðu'θiβle; rreðu'siβle/ *a* reducible

reducir /rreðu'θir; rreðu'sir/ *vt irr* to reduce; decrease, cut down; break up; *Art.* scale down; *Elec.* step down; subdue; (*Chem. Math. Surg.*) reduce; exchange; divide into small fragments; persuade; —*vr* be obliged to, have to; live moderately. See **conducir**

reducto /rre'ðukto/ *m, Mil.* redoubt (of fortifications)

redundancia /rreðun'danθia; rreðun'dansia/ *f,* redundance

redundante /rreðun'dante/ *a* redundant

redundar /rreðun'dar/ *vi* to overflow; be excessive or superfluous; (*with en*) redound to

reduplicación /rreðuplika'θion; rreðuplika'sion/ *f,* reduplication

reduplicar /rreðupli'kar/ *vt* to reduplicate

ree /rree/ For words so beginning (e.g. *reeditar, reexportar*), see spellings with one **e**

refacción /rrefak'θion; rrefak'sion/ *f,* refection, light meal; compensation, reparation

refajo /rre'faho/ *m,* skirt, underskirt

refección /rrefek'θion; rrefek'sion/ *f,* refection, light meal

refectorio /rrefek'torio/ *m,* refectory

referencia /rrefe'renθia; rrefe'rensia/ *f,* report, account; allusion; regard, relation; *Com.* reference (gen. *pl*); consideration

referente /rrefe'rente/ *a* concerning, related (to)

referir /rrefe'rir/ *vt irr* to narrate; describe; direct, guide; relate, refer, concern; —*vr* allude (to); refer (to); concern. See **sentir**

refinación /rrefina'θion; rrefina'sion/ *f,* refining

refinado /rrefi'naðo/ *a* refined; polished, cultured; crafty

refinador /rrefina'ðor/ *m,* refiner

refinamiento /rrefina'miento/ *m,* refinement, subtlety, care

refinar /rrefi'nar/ *vt* to refine, purify; polish, perfect

refinería /rrefine'ria/ *f,* refinery

reflector /rreflek'tor/ *a* reflecting. *m,* reflector; searchlight; shade (for lamps, etc.)

reflejar /rrefle'har/ *vi Phys.* to reflect; —*vt* consider; show, mirror; —*vr Fig.* be reflected, be seen

reflejo /rre'fleho/ *m,* reflection; image; glare —*a* reflex; considered, judicious

reflexión /rreflek'sion/ *f, Phys.* reflection; consideration, thought

reflexionar /rrefleksio'nar/ *vt* (*with en or sobre*) to consider, reflect upon

reflexivo /rreflek'siβo/ *a Phys.* reflective; thoughtful

reflorecer /rreflore'θer; rreflore'ser/ *vi irr* to flower again; return to favor (ideas, etc.). See **conocer**

reflujo /rre'fluho/ *m,* reflux, refluence; ebb tide

refocilar /rrefoθi'lar; rrefosi'lar/ *vt* to warm up, brace up; give pleasure to; —*vr* enjoy oneself

reforma /rre'forma/ *f,* reform; improvement; reformation; *Hist.* Reformation

reformación /rreforma'θion; rreforma'sion/ *f,* reform, improvement

reformador /rreforma'ðor/ **(-ra)** *a* reformatory, reforming —*n* reformer

reformar /rrefor'mar/ *vt* to remake; reshape; repair, mend, restore; improve, correct; *Eccl.* reform; reorganize; —*vr* mend one's ways, improve; control oneself

reformatorio /rreforma'torio/ *m,* reformatory —*a* reforming, reformatory

reformista /rrefor'mista/ *mf* reformist, reformer —*a* reformatory

reforzador /rreforθa'ðor; rreforsa'ðor/ *m, Photo.* reinforcing bath; *Elec.* booster

reforzamiento /rreforθa'miento; rreforsa'miento/ *m,* stiffening, reinforcing

reforzar /rrefor'θar; rrefor'sar/ *vt irr* to reinforce, strengthen, stiffen; encourage, inspirit. See **forzar**

refractar /rrefrak'tar/ *vt* to refract

refractario /rrefrak'tario/ *a* stubborn; (*Phys. Chem.*) refractory; unmanageable, unruly; fireproof

refrán /rre'fran/ *m,* proverb

refranero /rrefra'nero/ *m,* collection of proverbs

refregamiento /rrefrega'miento/ *m,* rubbing; scrubbing, scouring

refregar /rrefre'gar/ *vt irr* to rub; scrub, scour; *Fig. Inf.* rub in, insist on. See **cegar**

refrenamiento /rrefrena'miento/ *m,* curbing; control, restraint

refrenar /rrefre'nar/ *vt* to curb, check (horses); control, restraint

refrendar /rrefren'dar/ *vt* to countersign, endorse, legalize

refrescante /rrefres'kante/ *a* refreshing, cooling

refrescar /rrefres'kar/ *vt* to cool, chill; repeat; *Fig.* brush up, revise; —*vi* be rested or refreshed; grow cooler; take the air; freshen (wind); take a cool drink; —*vr* grow cooler; take the air; take a cool drink

refresco /rre'fresko/ *m,* refreshment; cool drink

refriega /rre'friega/ *f,* affray, scuffle, rough-and-tumble

refrigeración /rrefrihera'θion; rrefrihera'sion/ *f,* refrigeration

refrigerador /rrefrihera'ðor/ *m,* refrigerator

refrigerante /rrefrihe'rante/ *a* refrigerative; chilling; cooling. *m,* cooling chamber, cooler

refrigerar /rrefrihe'rar/ *vt* to chill; cool; freeze, refrigerate; refresh

refrigerio /rrefri'herio/ *m,* coolness; consolation; refreshment, food

refringente /rrefrin'hente/ *a Phys.* refringent

refuerzo /rre'fuerθo; rre'fuerso/ *m,* reinforcement; strengthening; aid, help

refugiado /rrefu'hiaðo/ **(-da)** *a* and *n* refugee

refugiar /rrefu'hiar/ *vt* to protect, shelter; —*vr* take refuge

refugio /rre'fuhio/ *m,* refuge, shelter, protection; traffic island. **r. antiaéreo,** air raid shelter. **r. para peatones,** traffic island

refulgencia /rreful'henθia; rreful'hensia/ f. resplendence, splendor, brilliance

refulgente /rreful'hente/ a resplendent, refulgent, dazzling

refulgir /rreful'hir/ vi to shine, be dazzling

refundición /rrefundi'θion; rrefundi'sion/ f. recasting (of metals); adaptation; rehash, refurbishing

refundir /rrefun'dir/ vt to recast (metals); include, comprise; adapt; rehash, refurbish; —vi Fig. promote, contribute to

refunfuñador /rrefunfuɲa'ðor/ a grumbling, fuming

refunfuñar /rrefunfu'ɲar/ vi to grumble, growl, fume

refunfuño /rrefun'fuɲo/ m, grumble, fuming; snort

refutable /rrefu'taβle/ a refutable

refutación /rrefuta'θion; rrefuta'sion/ f, refutation

refutar /rrefu'tar/ vt to refute

regadera /rrega'ðera/ f, watering can; irrigation canal; sprinkler

regadío /rrega'ðio/ m, irrigated land; irrigation, watering —a irrigated

regajal, regajo /rrega'hal, rre'gaho/ m, pool, puddle; stream, brook

regalado /rrega'laðo/ a delicate, highly bred; luxurious, delightful

regalar /rrega'lar/ vt to make a gift of, give; caress, fondle; indulge, cherish; entertain, regale; —vr live in luxury

regalía /rrega'lia/ f, royal privilege; right, exemption; perquisite, emolument

regalismo /rrega'lismo/ m, regalism

regalista /rrega'lista/ a and mf regalist

regaliz /rrega'liθ; rrega'lis/ m, **regaliza** f, licorice

regalo /rre'galo/ m, gift, present; satisfaction, pleasure; entertainment, regalement; luxury, comfort

regalón /rrega'lon/ a Inf. pampered

regañadientes, a /rregaɲa'ðientes, a/ adv unwillingly, grumblingly

regañar /rrega'ɲar/ vi to snarl (dogs); crack (skin of fruits); grumble, mutter; Inf. quarrel; —vt Inf. scold

regaño /rre'gaɲo/ m, angry look or gesture; Inf. scolding

regañón /rrega'ɲon/ **(-ona)** a Inf. grumbling, complaining; scolding —n Inf. grumbler

regar /rre'gar/ vt irr to water, sprinkle with water; flow through, irrigate; spray; Fig. shower (with), strew. See **cegar**

regata /rre'gata/ f, regatta; small irrigation channel (for gardens, etc.)

regate /rre'gate/ m, twist of the body, sidestep; dribbling; (in soccer); Inf. dodging, evasion

regatear /rregate'ar/ vt to haggle over, beat down (prices); resell, retail; dribble (a ball); Fig. Inf. dodge, avoid; —vi bargain, haggle; Naut. take part in a regatta, race

regateo /rrega'teo/ m, haggling, bargaining

regatero /rrega'tero/ **(-ra)** a retail —n retailer

regatón /rrega'ton/ **(-ona)** m, ferrule, tip —a haggling, bargaining —n haggler; retailer

regatonear /rregatone'ar/ vt to resell at retail

regazo /rre'gaθo; rre'gaso/ m, lap, knees; Fig. heart, bosom

regencia /rre'henθia; rre'hensia/ f, regency

regeneración /rrehenera'θion; rrehenera'sion/ f, regeneration

regenerador /rrehenera'ðor/ **(-ra)** n regenerator —a regenerative, reforming

regenerar /rrehene'rar/ vt to regenerate, reform

regenta /rre'henta/ f, wife of the president of a court of session

regentar /rrehen'tar/ vt to fill temporarily (offices); rule, govern; manage, run (businesses)

regente /rre'hente/ a ruling. mf regent. m, president of a court of session; manager

regicida /rrehi'θiða; rrehi'siða/ mf regicide (person)

regicidio /rrehi'θiðio; rrehi'siðio/ m, regicide (act)

regidor /rrehi'ðor/ a ruling, governing. m, magistrate, alderman

régimen /'rrehimen/ m, administration, management; regime; (Med. Gram.) regimen; Mech. rating

regimentación /rrehimenta'θion; rrehimenta'sion/ f, regimentation

regimentar /rrehimen'tar/ vt irr to form into regiments; regiment —Pres. Indic. **regimiento, regimientas, regimienta, regimientan.** Pres. Subjunc. **regimiente, regimientes, regimiente, regimienten**

regimiento /rrehi'miento/ m, Mil. regiment; administration, rule

regio /'rrehio/ a royal; magnificent, regal

región /rre'hion/ f, region, country; area, tract, space. **r. industrial,** industrial area

regionalismo /rrehiona'lismo/ m, regionalism

regionalista /rrehiona'lista/ mf regionalist —a regional

regir /rre'hir/ vt irr to govern, rule; administer, conduct; Gram. govern; —vi be in force (laws, etc.); work, function; Naut. obey the helm. See **pedir**

registrador /rrehistra'ðor/ a recording. m, registrar, keeper of records; recorder. **caja (registradora),** (cash) register

registrar /rrehis'trar/ vt to examine, inspect; search; copy, record; mark the place (in a book); observe, note; (of thermometers, etc.) record, show; look on to (houses, etc.); —vr register (hotels, etc.)

registro /rre'histro/ m, search; registration, entry; record; recording; reading (of a thermometer, etc.); Mech. damper; registry; register (book); Mus. range, compass (voice); Mus. register (organ); (Mech. Print.) register; bookmark. **r. civil,** register of births, marriages, and deaths

regla /'rregla/ f, ruler, measuring stick; rule, principle, guide, precept; system, policy; Med. period; moderation; method, order. **r. de cálculo,** slide rule. **r. T,** T-square. **en r.,** in due form. **por r.,** generally, as a rule

reglamentación /rreglamenta'θion; rreglamenta'sion/ f, regulation; rules and regulations

reglamentar /rreglamen'tar/ vt to regulate

reglamento /rregla'mento/ m, bylaw; regulation, ordinance

reglar /rre'glar/ vt to rule (lines); regulate; govern; control; —vr restrain oneself, mend one's ways

regocijado /rregoθi'haðo; rregosi'haðo/ a merry, joyful, happy

regocijar /rregoθi'har; rregosi'har/ vt to cheer, delight; —vr enjoy oneself, rejoice

regocijo /rrego'θiho; rrego'siho/ m, happiness, joy; cheer, merriment

regordete /rregor'ðete/ a Inf. chubby

regresar /rregre'sar/ vi to return

regresión /rregre'sion/ f, return; retrogression; regression

regreso /rre'greso/ m, return

reguera /rre'gera/ f, irrigation channel, ditch

reguero /rre'gero/ m, trickle

regulación /rregula'θion; rregula'sion/ f, regulation; Mech. control, timing

regulador /rregula'ðor/ m, Mech. governor, regulator —a regulating, controlling

regular /rregu'lar/ vt to adjust, regulate; Mech. govern —a methodical, ordered; moderate; average, medium; (Eccl. Mil. Geom. Gram.) regular; so-so, not bad; probable. **por lo r.,** generally

regularidad /rregulari'ðað/ f, regularity

regularización /rregulariθa'θion; rregularisa'sion/ f, regularization; regulation

regularizar /rregulari'θar; rregulari'sar/ vt to regularize; regulate

regurgitar /rregurhi'tar/ vi to regurgitate

rehabilitación /rreaβilita'θion; rreaβilita'sion/ f, rehabilitation

rehabilitar /rreaβili'tar/ vt to rehabilitate; —vr rehabilitate oneself

rehacer /rrea'θer; rrea'ser/ vt irr to remake; repair, mend; —vr recover one's strength; control one's emotions; Mil. rally. See **hacer**

rehén /rre'en/ m, hostage (gen. pl); Mil. pledge, security

rehenchir /rreen'tʃir/ vt irr to restuff; refill, recharge. See **henchir**

reherir /rree'rir/ vt irr to repulse. See **herir**

rehilar /rrei'lar/ vt to spin too much or twist the yarn; —vi totter, stagger; whizz (arrows, etc.). See **prohibir**

rehuir /rre'uir/ vt irr to withdraw; avoid; reject. See **huir**

rehusar /rreu'sar/ vt to refuse, reject. See **desahuciar**

reimponer /rreimpo'ner/ vt irr to reimpose. See **poner**

reimportación /rreimporta'θion; rreimporta'sion/ f, reimportation

reimpresión /rreimpre'sion/ f, reprint

reimprimir /rreimpri'mir/ vt to reprint

reina /'rreina/ f, queen; queen (in chess); queen bee; peerless beauty, belle

reinado /rrei'naðo/ m, reign; heyday, fashion

reinante /rrei'nante/ a reigning; prevalent

reinar /rrei'nar/ vi to reign; influence; endure, prevail

reincidencia /rreinθi'ðenθia; rreinsi'ðensia/ f, relapse (into crime, etc.), recidivism

reincidente /rreinθi'ðente; rreinsi'ðente/ mf backslider

reincidir /rreinθi'ðir; rreinsi'ðir/ vi to relapse (into crime, etc.)

reincorporar /rreinkorpo'rar/ vt to reincorporate; —vr join again, become a member again

reingresar /rreiŋgre'sar/ vi to reenter

reingreso /rreiŋ'greso/ m, reentry

reino /'rreino/ m, kingdom

reinstalación /rreinstala'θion; rreinstala'sion/ f, reinstatement

reinstalar /rreinsta'lar/ vt to reinstate; —vr be reinstalled

reintegración /rreintegra'θion; rreintegra'sion/ f, reintegration

reintegrar /rreinte'grar/ vt to reintegrate; —vr be reinstated, recuperate, recover

reir /rre'ir/ vi irr to laugh; sneer, jeer; Fig. smile (nature); —vt laugh at; —vr Inf. (with de) scorn. **reírse a carcajadas,** to shout with laughter —Pres. Part. **riendo.** Pres. Indic. **río, ríes, ríe, rien.** Preterite **rió, rieron.** Pres. Subjunc. **ría,** etc —Imperf. Subjunc. **riese,** etc.

reiteración /rreitera'θion; rreitera'sion/ f, reiteration, repetition

reiteradamente /rreiteraða'mente/ adv repeatedly, reiteratively

reiterar /rreite'rar/ vt to reiterate, repeat

reiterativo /rreitera'tiβo/ a reiterative

reivindicación /rreiβindika'θion; rreiβindika'sion/ f, Law. recovery

reivindicar /rreiβindi'kar/ vt Law. to recover

reja /'rreha/ f, colter, plowshare; plowing, tilling; grating, grille

rejado /rre'haðo/ m, railing, grating

rejilla /rre'hiʎa; rre'hiya/ f, grating; grille, lattice; luggage rack (in a train); cane (for chairs, seats, etc.); wire mesh; small brazier; Elec. grid; Mech. grate

rejuntar /rrehun'tar/ vt to point (a wall)

rejuvenecer /rrehuβene'θer; rrehuβene'ser/ vt irr to rejuvenate; Fig. revive; bring up to date; —vi and vr be rejuvenated, grow young again, rejuvenesce. See **conocer**

rejuvenecimiento /rrehuβeneθi'miento; rrehuβenesi'miento/ m, rejuvenation

relación /rrela'θion; rrela'sion/ f, relation; connection (of ideas); report, statement; narrative, account; Math. ratio; Law. brief; intercourse, association, dealings (gen. pl); list; analogy, relation. **tener relaciones con,** to have dealings with; be engaged or betrothed to; woo, court

relacionar /rrelaθio'nar; rrelasio'nar/ vt to recount, narrate, report; connect, relate; —vr be connected

relajación /rrelaha'θion; rrelaha'sion/ f, relaxation; recreation; laxity, dissoluteness

relajar /rrela'har/ vt to relax; recreate, amuse; make less rigorous; Law. remit; —vr become relaxed; be dissolute, lax, or vicious

relamer /rrela'mer/ vt to lick again; —vr lick one's lips; Fig. overpaint, make up too much; ooze satisfaction, brag

relamido /rrela'miðo/ a overdressed; affected

relámpago /rre'lampago/ m, lightning; flash, gleam; streak of lightning (of quick persons or things); flash of wit, witticism

relampaguear /rrelampage'ar/ vi to lighten (of lightning); flash, gleam

relapso /rre'lapso/ a relapsed, lapsed (into error, vice)

relatar /rrela'tar/ vt to relate, narrate, report

relatividad /rrelatiβi'ðað/ f, relativeness; Phys. relativity

relativo /rrela'tiβo/ a relevant, pertinent; relative, comparative; Gram. relative

relato /rre'lato/ m, narration, account, report

relator /rrela'tor/ (-ra) a narrating —n narrator. m, Law. reporter

relavar /rrela'βar/ vt to rewash, wash again

relección /rrelek'θion; rrelek'sion/ f, reelection

releer /rrele'er/ vt irr to reread; revise. See **creer**

relegación /rrelega'θion; rrelega'sion/ f, relegation

relegar /rrele'gar/ vt to banish; relegate, set aside

relegir /rrele'hir/ vt irr to reelect. See **elegir**

relente /rre'lente/ m, night dew, dampness; Inf. cheek, impudence

relevación /rreleβa'θion; rreleβa'sion/ f, Art. relief; release; remission, exemption

relevar /rrele'βar/ vt Art. to work in relief; emboss; relieve, free; dismiss; excuse, pardon; aid, succor; Fig. aggrandize; Mil. relieve; —vi carve in relief

relevo /rre'leβo/ m, relay; Mil. relief

relicario /rreli'kario/ m, reliquary

relieve /rre'lieβe/ m, Art. relief; pl leftovers, remains (of food). **alto r.,** high relief. **bajo r.,** low relief

religar /rreli'gar/ vt to retie, fasten again; fasten more securely; solder

religión /rreli'hion/ f, religion; creed, faith, philosophy; devotion, religious practice. **r. reformada,** Protestantism. **entrar en r.,** Eccl. to profess

religionario /rrelihio'nario/ m, Protestant

religiosidad /rrelihiosi'ðað/ f, religiosity; religiousness; conscientiousness, punctiliousness

religioso /rreli'hioso/ (-sa) a religious; punctilious, conscientious; moderate —n religious

relinchar /rrelin'tʃar/ vi to whinny, neigh

relincho /rre'lintʃo/ m, neigh, whinny

reliquia /rre'likia/ f, residue (gen. pl); Eccl. relic; vestige, remnant, memento; permanent disability or ailment

rellanar /rre'ʎanar; rre'yanar/ vt to make level again; —vr stretch oneself at full length

rellano /rre'ʎano; rre'yano/ m, landing (of a staircase); level stretch (of ground)

rellenar /rreʎe'nar; rreye'nar/ vt to refill, replenish; fill up; Mas. plug, point; Cul. stuff; Inf. cram with food (gen —vr)

relleno /rre'ʎeno; rre'yeno/ m, Cul. stuffing; replenishing; filling; Fig. padding (of speeches, etc.)

reloj /rre'loh/ m, clock; watch. **r. de arena,** hourglass. **r. de bolsillo,** watch. **r. de la muerte,** death-watch beetle. **r. de péndulo,** grandfather clock. **r. de pulsera,** wristwatch. **r. de repetición,** repeater. **r. de sol** or **r. solar,** sundial

relojera /rrelo'hera/ f, clock stand; watch case

relojería /rrelohe'ria/ f, watch or clock making; jeweler, watch maker's shop

relojero /rrelo'hero/ (-ra) n watch maker, watch repairer

reluciente /rrelu'θiente; rrelu'siente/ a shining, sparkling; shiny

relucir /rrelu'θir; rrelu'sir/ vi irr to glitter, sparkle, gleam; Fig. shine, excel. See **lucir**

reluctante /rreluk'tante/ a unruly, refractory, disobedient

relumbrante /rrelum'βrante/ a resplendent, dazzling

relumbrar /rrelum'βrar/ vi to be resplendent, shine, glitter

remachar /rrema'tʃar/ vt to rivet; Fig. clinch

remache /rre'matʃe/ m, riveting; rivet

remanente /rrema'nente/ m, remains, residue

remanso /rre'manso/ m, backwater; stagnant water; sloth, dilatoriness

remar /rre'mar/ vi to row, paddle, scull; toil, strive

rematadamente /rremataða'mente/ *adv* completely, entirely, absolutely

rematado /rrema'taðo/ *a* beyond hope, extremely ill; utterly lost; *Law.* convicted

rematar /rrema'tar/ *vt* to end, finish; finish off, kill; knock down at auction; *Sew.* finish; —*vi* end; —*vr* be ruined or spoiled

remate /rre'mate/ *m*, end, conclusion; extremity; *Archit.* coping; *Archit.* terminal; highest bid; auction. **de r.,** utterly hopeless

rembarcar /rrembar'kar/ *vt* to reembark, reship

rembarque /rrem'βarke/ *m*, reembarkation, reshipment

rembolsable /rrembol'saβle/ *a* repayable

rembolsar /rrembol'sar/ *vt* to recover (money); refund, return (money)

rembolso /rrem'βolso/ *m*, repayment. **contra r.,** cash on delivery, C.O.D.

remedar /rreme'ðar/ *vt* to copy, imitate; mimic

remediador /rremeðia'ðor/ **(-ra)** *a* remedying —*n* benefactor, helper

remediar /rreme'ðiar/ *vt* to remedy; aid, help; save from danger; prevent (trouble)

remedio /rre'meðio/ *m*, remedy; emendation, correction; help; refuge, protection; *Med.* remedy. **No hay más r.,** There's nothing else to do, It's the only way open. **no tener más r.,** to be unable to help (doing something), be obliged to

remedo /rre'meðo/ *m*, imitation; poor copy

remembranza /rremem'βranθa; rremem'βransa/ *f*, remembrance, memory

rememorar /rrememo'rar/ *vt* to remember, recall to mind

remendar /rremen'dar/ *vt irr* to mend, patch; darn; repair; correct. See **recomendar**

remendón /rremen'don/ **(-ona)** *n* cobbler; mender of old clothes

remero /rre'mero/ **(-ra)** *n* oarsman, rower; sculler

remesa /rre'mesa/ *f*, remittance; consignment, shipment

remesar /rreme'sar/ **(se)** *vt* and *vr* to pluck out (hair); —*vt Com.* remit; consign

remiendo /rre'miendo/ *m*, *Sew.* patch; mend, darn; emendation; *Inf.* insignia of one of the Spanish military orders. **a remiendos,** *Inf.* piecemeal

remilgarse /rremil'garse/ *vr* to preen oneself, be overdressed

remilgo /rre'milgo/ *m*, affectation; mannerism; prudery, squeamishness

reminiscencia /rreminis'θenθia; rreminis'sensia/ *f*, reminiscence; memory, recollection

remirado /rremi'raðo/ *a* wary, cautious, prudent, circumspect

remirar /rremi'rar/ *vt* to revise, go over again; —*vr* take great care over; behold with pleasure

remisión /rremi'sion/ *f*, sending; remission; pardon, forgiveness; foregoing, relinquishment; abatement, diminution; *Lit.* reference, allusion

remiso /rre'miso/ *a* timid, spiritless; languid, slow

remitente /rremi'tente/ *mf* sender —*a* sending

remitir /rremi'tir/ *vt* to remit, send; pardon, forgive; defer, postpone; abate, diminish; relinquish, forgo; *Lit.* refer; —*vr* remit, submit, consult; refer (to), cite

remo /'rremo/ *m*, oar, scull, paddle; arm or leg (of men or animals, gen. *pl*); wing (gen. *pl*); hard, continuous toil; galleys. **al r.,** by dint of rowing; *Inf.* struggling with hardships

remojar /rremo'har/ *vt* to soak, steep; celebrate by drinking

remojo /rre'moho/ *m*, soaking, steeping

remolacha /rremo'latʃa/ *f*, beet

remolcador /rremolka'ðor/ *m*, *Naut.* tow, tug —*a Naut.* towing

remolcar /rremol'kar/ *vt* (*Naut. Auto.*) to tow; *Fig.* press into service, use

remolinar /rremoli'nar/ *vi* to spin, whirl, eddy; —*vr* throng, swarm

remolino /rremo'lino/ *m*, whirlwind; eddy, swirl; whirlpool; crowd, throng, swarm; disturbance, riot

remolonear /rremolone'ar/ *vi Inf.* to loiter, lag; avoid work; be lax or dilatory

remolque /rre'molke/ *m*, towage, towing; towline; barge; *Auto.* trailer. **a r.,** on tow

remonta /rre'monta/ *f*, resoling (of shoes); leather gusset (of riding breeches); *Mil.* remount

remontar /rremon'tar/ *vt* to scare off (game); *Mil.* supply with fresh horses; resole (shoes); *Fig.* rise to great heights (of oratory, etc.); —*vr* soar (of birds); (*with prep a*) date from, go back to; originate in

remoquete /rremo'kete/ *m*, blow with the fist; witticism; *Inf.* flirtation, courtship

rémora /'rremora/ *f*, *Ichth.* remora; delay, hindrance

remorder /rremor'ðer/ *vt irr* to bite again or repeatedly; *Fig.* gnaw, nag, cause uneasiness or remorse; —*vr* show one's feelings. See **morder**

remordimiento /rremorði'miento/ *m*, remorse

remotamente /rremota'mente/ *adv* distantly, remotely; unlikely; vaguely, confusedly

remoto /rre'moto/ *a* distant, remote; unlikely, improbable

remover /rremo'βer/ *vt irr* to remove, move; stir; turn over; dismiss, discharge. See **mover**

remozar /rremo'θar; rremo'sar/ *vt* to cause to appear young; freshen up, bring up to date; —*vr* look young

remplazar /rrempla'θar; rrempla'sar/ *vt* to replace; exchange, substitute; succeed, take the place of

remplazo /rrem'plaθo; rrem'plaso/ *m*, replacement; exchange, substitute; successor; *Mil.* replacement

remuda /rre'muða/ *f*, replacement, exchange

remudar /rremu'ðar/ *vt* to replace

remuneración /rremunera'θion; rremunera'sion/ *f*, remuneration; reward

remunerador /rremunera'ðor/ **(-ra)** *a* remunerative, recompensing —*n* remunerator

remunerar /rremune'rar/ *vt* to recompense, reward

remusgar /rremus'gar/ *vi* to suspect, imagine

renacentista /rrenaθen'tista; rrenasen'tista/ *a* renaissance

renacer /rrena'θer; rrena'ser/ *vi irr* to be reborn. See **nacer**

renacimiento /rrenaθi'miento; rrenasi'miento/ *m*, rebirth; Renaissance

renacuajo /rrena'kuaho/ *m*, tadpole; *Mech.* frog; *Inf.* twerp

renano /rre'nano/ *a* Rhenish

rencarcelar /rrenkarθe'lar; rrenkarse'lar/ *vt* to reimprison

rencarnación /rrenkarna'θion; rrenkarna'sion/ *f*, reincarnation

rencarnar /rrenkar'nar/ **(se)** *vi* and *vr* to be reincarnated

rencilla /rren'θiʎa; rren'siya/ *f*, grudge, grievance, resentment

rencilloso /rrenθi'ʎoso; rrensi'yoso/ *a* peevish, easily offended, touchy

rencor /rren'kor/ *m*, rancor, spite, old grudge. **guardar r.,** to bear malice

rencoroso /rrenko'roso/ *a* rancorous, malicious, spiteful

rencuadernar /rrenkuaðer'nar/ *vt* to rebind (books)

rencuentro /rren'kuentro/ *m*, collision; *Mil.* encounter, clash

rendición /rrendi'θion; rrendi'sion/ *f*, surrender; yield, profit

rendido /rren'diðo/ *a* submissive, obsequious

rendija /rren'diha/ *f*, crevice, cleft, crack, fissure

rendimiento /rrendi'miento/ *m*, weariness, fatigue; submissiveness, obsequiousness; yield, profit; *Mech.* efficiency

rendir /rren'dir/ *vt irr Mil.* to cause to surrender; defeat; overcome, conquer; give back, return; yield, provide; tire, exhaust; vomit; pay, render; —*vr* be exhausted, be worn out; surrender. *Mil.* **r. el puesto,** to retire from or give up a post. See **pedir**

renegado /rrene'gaðo/ **(-da)** *n* renegade, apostate; turncoat; *Inf.* malignant person —*a* renegade

renegador /rrenega'ðor/ **(-ra)** *n* blasphemer; foul-mouthed person

renegar /rrene'gar/ *vt irr* to deny, disown; loathe, hate; —*vi* (*with de*) apostatize; blaspheme; *Inf.* curse. See **cegar**

renganchar /rrengan'tʃar/ **(se)** *vt* and *vr Mil.* to reenlist

renganche /rreŋ'gantʃe/ *m*, *Mil.* reenlistment

renglón /rreŋ'glon/ *m*, *Print.* line; *pl* writing, composition

reniego /rre'niego/ *m*, blasphemy; *Inf.* foul language, cursing

renitencia /rreni'tenθia; rreni'tensia/ *f*, repugnance

reno /'rreno/ *m*, reindeer

renombrado /rrenom'βraðo/ *a* illustrious, famous

renombre /rre'nombre/ *m*, surname; renown, reputation, fame

renovable /rreno'βaβle/ *a* renewable, replaceable

renovación /rrenoβa'θion; rrenoβa'sion/ *f*, replacement; renewal; renovation; transformation, reform

renovador /rrenoβa'ðor/ **(-ra)** *n* reformer; renovator —*a* renovating; reforming

renovar /rreno'βar/ *vt irr* to renew; renovate; replace; exchange; reiterate, repeat. See **contar**

renta /'rrenta/ *f*, yield, profit; income; revenue; government securities; rent; tax

rentar /rren'tar/ *vt* to yield, produce an income

rentero /rren'tero/ **(-ra)** *n* tenant farmer. *m*, one who farms out land

rentista /rren'tista/ *mf* financier; bondholder; person who lives on a private income, rentier

rentístico /rren'tistiko/ *a* revenue, financial

renuente /rre'nuente/ *a* refractory, willful

renuevo /rre'nueβo/ *m*, *Bot.* shoot; renewal

renuncia, renunciación /rre'nunθia, rrenunθia'θion; rre'nunsia, rrenunsia'sion/ *f*, renunciation; resignation; abandonment, relinquishment

renunciar /rrenun'θiar; rrenun'siar/ *vt* to renounce; refuse; scorn; abandon, relinquish; resign; revoke (at cards). **r. a**, to give up

renuncio /rre'nunθio; rre'nunsio/ *m*, revoke (cards); *Inf.* falsehood

reñidamente /rreɲiða'mente/ *adv* strongly, stubbornly, fiercely

reñir /rre'ɲir/ *vi irr* to quarrel, dispute; fight; be on bad terms, fall out; —*vt* scold; fight (battles, etc.). See **ceñir**

reo /'rreo/ *mf* criminal; offender, guilty party; *Law.* defendant

reojo /rre'oho/ *m*, **(mirar de)** to look out of the corner of the eye; *Fig.* look askance

reorganizador /rreorganiθa'ðor; rreorganisa'ðor/ **(-ra)** *a* reorganizing —*n* reorganizer

reorganizar /rreorgani'θar; rreorgani'sar/ *vt* to reorganize

reóstato /rre'ostato/ *m*, rheostat

repantigarse /rrepanti'garse/ *vr* to stretch out one's legs, make oneself comfortable

reparable /rrepa'raβle/ *a* remediable, reparable; worthy of note

reparación /rrepara'θion; rrepara'sion/ *f*, repair, mending; reparation, satisfaction; indemnity, compensation

reparada /rrepa'raða/ *f*, shying (of horses)

reparador /rrepara'ðor/ *a* repairing, mending; faultfinding; restoring; satisfying, compensating

reparar /rrepa'rar/ *vt* to repair; restore; consider; correct, remedy; atone for, expiate; indemnify; hold up, detain; protect, guard; (*with en*) notice; —*vi* halt, be detained; —*vr* control oneself

reparo /rre'paro/ *m*, repair; restoration; remedy; note, reflection; warning; doubt, scruple; guard, protection; parry (at fencing)

repartición /rreparti'θion; rreparti'sion/ *f*, distribution

repartidero /rreparti'ðero/ *a* distributable

repartidor /rreparti'ðor/ **(-ra)** *a* distributing —*n* distributor; tax assessor

repartimiento /rreparti'miento/ *m*, distribution, allotment; assessment

repartir /rrepar'tir/ *vt* to distribute; share out; allot; deal (cards); assess; *Com.* deliver

reparto /rre'parto/ *m*, distribution; assessment; delivery (of letters, etc.); *Theat.* cast; deal (at cards)

repasar /rrepa'sar/ *vt* to pass by again; peruse, reexamine; brush up, revise; skim, glance over; mend, repair (garments); edit, revise; hone

repaso /rre'paso/ *m*, second passage through; reexamination, perusal; revision, editing; brushing up, revision; repair, mending; *Inf.* dressing-down, scolding

repatriación /rrepatria'θion; rrepatria'sion/ *f*, repatriation

repatriado /rrepa'triaðo/ **(-da)** *n* repatriate

repatriar /rrepa'triar/ *vt* to repatriate; —*vi* and *vr* return to one's own country

repecho /rre'petʃo/ *m*, steep slope. **a r.**, uphill

repelar /rrepe'lar/ *vt* to pull by the hair; put through its paces (of a horse); clip, cut; remove, diminish

repeler /rrepe'ler/ *vt* to repel, throw back; reject, refute

repelo /rre'pelo/ *m*, anything against the grain; *Inf.* skirmish; reluctance, repugnance

repente /rre'pente/ *m*, *Inf.* sudden or unexpected movement. **de r.**, suddenly

repentino /rrepen'tino/ *a* sudden, unexpected

repentizar /rrepenti'θar; rrepenti'sar/ *vi* *Mus.* to sight-read

repercusión /rreperku'sion/ *f*, repercussion; vibration

repercutir /rreperku'tir/ *vi* to recoil, rebound; —*vr* reverberate; reecho; *Fig.* have repercussions; —*vt* *Med.* repel

repertorio /rreper'torio/ *m*, repertory

repesar /rrepe'sar/ *vt* to reweigh, weigh again

repetición /rrepeti'θion; rrepeti'sion/ *f*, repetition; *Art.* replica, copy; repeater (in clocks); recital

repetidamente /rrepetiða'mente/ *adv* repeatedly

repetidor /rrepeti'ðor/ *a* repeating

repetir /rrepe'tir/ *vt irr* to repeat, do over again; reiterate; *Art.* copy, make a replica of; recite. See **pedir**

repicar /rrepi'kar/ *vt* to chop, mince; peal (of bells); prick again; —*vr* pride oneself (on), boast

repique /rre'pike/ *m*, chopping, mincing; peal, pealing (of bells); disagreement, grievance

repisa /rre'pisa/ *f*, *Archit.* bracket; ledge; shelf. **r. de chimenea**, mantelpiece

replantar /rreplan'tar/ *vt* to replant; transplant

repleción /rreple'θion; rreple'sion/ *f*, repletion, satiety

replegar /rreple'gar/ *vt irr* to refold, fold many times; —*vr* *Mil.* retreat in good order. See **cegar**

repleto /rre'pleto/ *a* replete

réplica /'rreplika/ *f*, reply, answer; replica

replicar /rrepli'kar/ *vi* to contradict, dispute; answer, reply. **¡No me repliques!** *Inf.* Don't answer back!

repliegue /rre'pliege/ *m*, double fold, crease; doubling, folding; *Mil.* withdrawal

repoblación /rrepoβla'θion; rrepoβla'sion/ *f*, repeopling, repopulation

repoblar /rrepo'βlar/ *vt* to repeople, repopulate

repollo /rre'poʎo; rre'poyo/ *m*, white cabbage; heart (of lettuce, etc.)

reponer /rrepo'ner/ *vt irr* to replace; reinstate; restore; reply; —*vr* recover, regain (possessions); grow well again; grow calm. See **poner**

reportación /rreporta'θion; rreporta'sion/ *f*, serenity, moderation

reportaje /rrepor'tahe/ *m*, journalistic report

reportar /rrepor'tar/ *vt* to restrain, moderate; achieve, obtain; carry; bring; —*vr* control oneself

reporte /rre'porte/ *m*, report, news; rumor

reporterismo /rreporte'rismo/ *m*, newspaper reporting

reportero /rrepor'tero/ **(-ra)** *a* news, report —*n* reporter

reposado /rrepo'saðo/ *a* quiet, peaceful, tranquil

reposar /rrepo'sar/ *vi* to rest, repose oneself; sleep, doze; lie in the grave; settle (liquids); rest (on)

reposición /rreposi'θion; rreposi'sion/ *f*, replacement; restoration; renewal; recovery (of health); *Theat.* revival

repositorio /rreposi'torio/ *m*, repository

reposo /rre'poso/ *m*, rest, repose; peace, tranquility; sleep

repostería /rreposte'ria/ *f*, confectioner's shop; pantry; butler's pantry

repostero /rrepos'tero/ *m*, confectioner, pastry cook

repregunta /rrepre'gunta/ *f*, cross-examination

repreguntar /rrepregun'tar/ *vt* to cross-examine

reprender /rrepren'der/ *vt* to scold, reprimand, rebuke

reprensible /rrepren'siβle/ *a* reprehensible, censurable

reprensión /rrepren'sion/ *f*, scolding, reprimand, rebuke

represa /rre'presa/ *f*, damming, holding back (water); dam, lock; restraining, controlling

represalia /rrepre'salia/ *f*, reprisal (gen. *pl*); retaliation

represar /rrepre'sar/ *vt* to dam, harness (water); *Naut.* retake, recapture; *Fig.* restrain, control

representación /rrepresenta'θion; rrepresenta'sion/ *f*, representation; *Theat.* performance; authority; dignity; *Com.* agency; portrait, image; depiction, expression; petition

representador /rrepresenta'ðor/ *a* representative

representante /rrepresen'tante/ *a* representative. *mf* representative; actor; performer

representar /rrepresen'tar/ *vt* to represent; *Theat.* perform; depict, express; describe, portray; —*vr* imagine, picture to oneself

representativo /rrepresenta'tiβo/ *a* representative

represión /rrepre'sion/ *f*, repression; recapture

represivo /rrepre'siβo/ *a* repressive

reprimenda /rrepri'menda/ *f*, rebuke, reprimand

reprimir /rrepri'mir/ *vt* to repress, restrain, control; —*vr* restrain oneself

reprobación /rreproβa'θion; rreproβa'sion/ *f*, censure; reprobation

reprobar /rrepro'βar/ *vt irr* to reprove; censure; fail (in an exam). See **probar**

réprobo /'rreproβo/ **(-ba)** *n* reprobate

reprochar /rrepro'tʃar/ *vt* to reproach

reproche /rre'protʃe/ *m*, reproaching; rebuke, reproach

reproducción /rreproðuk'θion; rreproðuk'sion/ *f*, reproduction. **r. a gran escala,** large-scale model

reproducir /rreproðu'θir; rreproðu'sir/ *vt irr* to reproduce. See **conducir**

reproductor /rreproðuk'tor/ **(-ra)** *a* reproductive —*n* breeding animal

reps /rreps/ *m*, rep (fabric)

reptil /rrep'til/ *a* reptilian; crawling. *m*, reptile

república /rre'puβlika/ *f*, republic; state, commonwealth. **la r. de las letras,** the republic of letters

República Dominicana /rre'puβlika domini'kana/ Dominican Republic

República Malgache /rre'puβlika mal'gatʃe/ Republic of Madagascar

republicanismo /rrepuβlika'nismo/ *m*, republicanism

republicano /rrepuβli'kano/ **(-na)** *a* and *n* republican

repudiación /rrepuðia'θion; rrepuðia'sion/ *f*, repudiation

repudiar /rrepu'ðiar/ *vt* to cast off (a wife); repudiate, renounce

repuesto /rre'puesto/ *a* retired, hidden. *m*, stock, provision; serving table; pantry; stake (at cards, etc.). **de r.,** spare, extra

repugnancia /rrepuɡ'nanθia; rrepuɡ'nansia/ *f*, inconsistency, contradiction; aversion, dislike; reluctance; repugnance

repugnante /rrepuɡ'nante/ *a* repugnant, loathsome

repugnar /rrepuɡ'nar/ *vt* to contradict, be inconsistent with; hate, be averse to (e.g. *La idea me repugna,* I hate the idea)

repujado /rrepu'haðo/ *m*, repoussé work

repujar /rrepu'har/ *vt* to work in repoussé

repulir /rrepu'lir/ *vt* to repolish, reburnish; —*vt* and *vr* make up too much, overdress

repulsa /rre'pulsa/ *f*, snub, rebuff; rejection; repulse

repulsar /rrepul'sar/ *vt* to decline, reject; repulse; deny, refuse; rebuff

repulsión /rrepul'sion/ *f*, repulsion; rebuff; aversion, dislike

repulsivo /rrepul'siβo/ *a* repellent

repunta /rre'punta/ *f*, headland, cape; *Fig.* first sign; *Inf.* disgust; caprice; fight

reputación /rreputa'θion; rreputa'sion/ *f*, reputation

reputar /rrepu'tar/ *vt* to believe, consider (e.g. *Le re-*

puto por honrado, I believe him to be an honorable man); appreciate, esteem

requebrar /rreke'βrar/ *vt irr* to break into smaller pieces; make love to, woo; compliment, flatter. See **quebrar**

requemado /rreke'maðo/ *a* sunburned; brown

requemar /rreke'mar/ *vt* to burn again; overcook; dry up, parch (of plants, etc.); burn (the mouth) (of spicy foods, etc.); —*vr Fig.* suffer inwardly

requerimiento /rrekeri'miento/ *m*, requirement, demand; *Law.* summons

requerir /rreke'rir/ *vt irr* to inform, notify; examine; need, necessitate; require; summon; woo; persuade. See **sentir**

requesón /rreke'son/ *m*, cream cheese; curd

requetebién /rrekete'βien/ *adv Inf.* exceedingly well

requiebro /rre'kieβro/ *m*, compliment, expression of love; wooing, flirtation

requisa /rre'kisa/ *f*, inspection, visitation; *Mil.* requisitioning

requisar /rreki'sar/ *vt Mil.* to requisition

requisito /rreki'sito/ *m*, requisite

res /rres/ *f*, animal, beast; head of cattle

resabiar /rresa'βiar/ *vt* to make vicious, cause bad habits; —*vr* contract bad habits or vices; be discontented; relish

resabio /rre'saβio/ *m*, disagreeable aftertaste; bad habit, vice

resaca /rre'saka/ *f*, surf, undertow, surge; *Com.* redraft

resalado /rresa'laðo/ *a Inf.* very witty; most attractive

resaltar /rresal'tar/ *vi* to rebound; project, jut out; grow loose, fall out; *Fig.* stand out, be prominent

resalto /rre'salto/ *m*, rebound; projection

resarcir /rresar'θir; rresar'sir/ *vt* to compensate, indemnify

resbaladizo /rresβala'ðiθo; rresβala'ðiso/ *a* slippery; difficult, delicate (of a situation)

resbalar /rresβa'lar/ *vi* to slip; slide; skid; err, fall into sin

resbalón /rresβa'lon/ *m*, slip; slide; skid; temptation, error

rescatador /rreskata'ðor/ **(-ra)** *n* ransomer; rescuer

rescatar /rreska'tar/ *vt* to ransom; redeem, buy back; barter; free, rescue; *Fig.* redeem (time, etc.)

rescate /rres'kate/ *m*, ransom; redemption; barter; amount of ransom

rescindir /rresθin'dir; rressin'dir/ *vt* to annul, repeal, rescind

rescisión /rresθi'sion; rressi'sion/ *f*, annulment, abrogation

rescoldo /rres'koldo/ *m*, ember, cinder; scruple, qualm, doubt

resentimiento /rresenti'miento/ *m*, deterioration, impairment; animosity, resentment

resentirse /rresen'tirse/ *vr irr* to deteriorate, be impaired; be hurt or offended. See **sentir**

reseña /rre'sena/ *f*, *Mil.* review; short description; review (of a book)

reseñar /rrese'nar/ *vt Mil.* to review; describe briefly, outline

reserva /rre'serβa/ *f*, store, stock; exception, qualification; reticence; restraint, moderation; (*Eccl. Law.*) reservation; (*Mil. Naut.*) reserve. **sin r.,** frankly, without reserve

reservación /rreserβa'θion; rreserβa'sion/ *f*, reservation; scruple

reservado /rreser'βaðo/ *a* reserved, reticent; prudent, moderate; kept, reserved. *m*, reserved compartment; private apartment, private garden, etc.

reservar /rreser'βar/ *vt* to keep, hold; postpone; reserve (rooms, etc.); exempt; keep secret; withhold (information); *Eccl.* reserve; —*vr* await a better opportunity; be cautious

reservista /rreser'βista/ *a* (*Mil. Nav.*) reserved. *mf* reservist

resfriado /rres'friaðo/ *m*, *Med.* cold, chill

resfriar /rres'friar/ *vt* to chill; *Fig.* cool, moderate; —*vi* grow cold; —*vr* catch a cold; *Fig.* cool off (of love, etc.)

resguardar /rresɡuar'ðar/ *vt* to protect; shelter; —*vr* take refuge; (*with de*) guard against; (*with con*) shelter by

resguardo /rres'guarðo/ *m*, protection, guard; *Com.* guarantee, security; *Com.* voucher; preservation; vigilance (to prevent smuggling, etc.); contraband guards

residencia /rresi'ðenθia; rresi'ðensia/ *f*, stay, residence; home, domicile; *Eccl.* residence

residencial /rresiðen'θial; rresiðen'sial/ *a* residential; resident, residentiary

residente /rresi'ðente/ *a* a resident. *mf* inhabitant. *m*, resident, minister resident (diplomatic)

residir /rresi'ðir/ *vi* to live, inhabit; reside officially; be found, be, exist

residuo /rre'siðuo/ *m*, residuum, remainder; *Math.* remainder; *Chem.* residue

resignación /rresigna'θion; rresigna'sion/ *f*, resignation; fortitude, submission

resignar /rresig'nar/ *vt* to resign, relinquish; —*vr* submit, resign oneself

resina /rre'sina/ *f*, resin

resinoso /rresi'noso/ *a* resinous

resistencia /rresis'tenθia; rresis'tensia/ *f*, resistance, opposition; endurance; (*Phys. Mech. Psychol.*) resistance

resistente /rresis'tente/ *a* resistant; tough; hardy (of plants)

resistir /rresis'tir/ *vi* to resist, oppose; reject; —*vt* endure, bear; resist; —*vr* fight, resist

resma /'rresma/ *f*, ream (of paper)

resollar /rreso'ʎar; rreso'yar/ *vi irr* to breathe; pant. See **degollar**

resolución /rresolu'θion; rresolu'sion/ *f*, decision; boldness, daring; determination, resolution; decree

resoluto /rreso'luto/ *a* resolute, bold; brief, concise; able, expert

resolver /rresol'ßer/ *vt irr* to determine, decide; summarize; solve; dissolve; analyze; (*Phys. Med.*) resolve; —*vr* decide, determine; be reduced to, become; *Med.* resolve —*Pres. Indic.* **resuelvo, resuelves, resuelve, resuelven.** *Past Part.* **resuelto.** *Pres. Subjunc.* **resuelva, resuelvas, resuelva, resuelvan.**

resonancia /rreso'nanθia; rreso'nansia/ *f*, resonance, sonority, ring; fame, reputation

resonante /rreso'nante/ *a* resonant; resounding

resonar /rreso'nar/ *vi irr* to resound, echo. See **tronar**

resoplido, resoplo /rreso'pliðo, rre'soplo/ *m*, heavy breathing, pant, snort

resorber /rresor'ßer/ *vt* to reabsorb

resorción /rresor'θion; rresor'sion/ *f*, reabsorption

resorte /rre'sorte/ *m*, *Mech.* spring; elasticity; *Fig.* means, instrument

respaldo /rres'paldo/ *m*, back (of chairs, etc.); reverse side (of a piece of paper)

respectivo /rrespek'tißo/ *a* respective

respecto /rres'pekto/ *m*, relation, regard, reference. **con r. a,** *or* **r. a,** with regard to, with respect to, concerning

respetabilidad /rrespetaßili'ðað/ *f*, respectability; worthiness

respetable /rrespe'taßle/ *a* worthy of respect; respectable; *Fig.* considerable, large

respetar /rrespe'tar/ *vt* to respect, revere

respeto /rres'peto/ *m*, respect, honor; consideration, reason. **de r.,** spare, extra; special, ceremonial

respetuoso /rrespe'tuoso/ *a* venerable, worthy of honor; respectful, courteous

respingar /rrespiŋ'gar/ *vi* to flinch, wince, kick; *Inf.* be uneven, rise (hem of garments); *Inf.* do (a thing) grumblingly

respingo /rres'piŋ'go/ *m*, wincing; jerk, shake; *Inf.* gesture of reluctance or dislike

respirable /rrespi'raßle/ *a* breathable

respiración /rrespira'θion; rrespira'sion/ *f*, breathing, respiration; ventilation

respiradero /rrespira'ðero/ *m*, ventilator; air hole, vent; rest, breathing space

respiratorio /rrespira'ðor/ *a* breathing; respiratory. *m*, respirator

respirar /rrespi'rar/ *vi* to breathe; exhale, give off; take courage; have a breathing space, rest; *Inf.* speak. **sin r.,** continuously, without stopping for breath

respiratorio /rrespira'torio/ *a* respiratory

respiro /rres'piro/ *m*, breathing; breathing space, respite

resplandecer /rresplande'θer; rresplande'ser/ *vi irr* to glitter, gleam; shine, excel. See **conocer**

resplandeciente /rresplande'θiente; rresplande'siente/ *a* glittering, resplendent, shining

resplandor /rresplan'dor/ *m*, radiance, brilliance; glitter, gleam; majesty, splendor

responder /rrespon'der/ *vt* to reply; satisfy, answer; —*vi* reecho; requite, return; produce, provide; *Fig.* answer, have the desired effect; *Com.* (*with de*) answer for, guarantee; *Com.* correspond

respondón /rrespon'don/ *a* *Inf.* pert, impudent, cheeky, given to answering back

responsabilidad /rresponsaßili'ðað/ *f*, responsibility

responsable /rrespon'saßle/ *a* responsible

responso /rres'ponso/ *m*, *Eccl.* response, responsory

respuesta /rres'puesta/ *f*, answer, reply; response; refutation; repartee

resquebradura /rreskeßra'ðura/ *f*, fissure, crevice, crack

resquebrajarse /rreskeßra'harse/ *vr* to crack, split

resquemar /rreske'mar/ *vt* to bite, sting (of hot dishes)

resquicio /rres'kiθio; rres'kisio/ *m*, crack, chink, slit; opportunity

resta /'rresta/ *f*, *Math.* subtraction; *Math.* remainder

restablecer /rrestaßle'θer; rrestaßle'ser/ *vt irr* to reestablish; restore; —*vr* recover one's health; reestablish oneself. See **conocer**

restablecimiento /rrestaßleθi'miento; rrestaßlesi'miento/ *m*, reestablishment; restoration

restañar /rresta'ɲar/ *vt* to re-tin; staunch

restar /rres'tar/ *vt* *Math.* to subtract; deduct; return (a ball); —*vi* remain. **No me resta más que decir adiós,** It only remains for me to say good-by

restauración /rrestaura'θion; rrestaura'sion/ *f*, restoration; renovation

restaurador /rrestaura'ðor/ **(-ra)** *a* restorative —*n* restorer

restaurante /rrestau'rante/ *m*, restaurant

restaurantero /rrestauran'tero/ *m*, restaurant operator; restaurant owner; restaurateur

restaurar /rrestau'rar/ *vt* to recover, recuperate; renovate, repair; restore

restaurativo /rrestaura'tißo/ *a* and *m*, restorative

restinga /rres'tiŋga/ *f*, sandbank, bar

restitución /rrestitu'θion; rrestitu'sion/ *f*, restitution

restituible /rresti'tuißle/ *a* returnable, replaceable

restituir /rresti'tuir/ *vt irr* to return, give back; restore; reestablish; —*vr* return to one's place of departure. See **huir**

resto /'rresto/ *m*, rest, balance; *Math.* remainder; *pl* remains

restorán /rresto'ran/ *m*, restaurant

restricción /rrestrik'θion; rrestrik'sion/ *f*, limitation, restriction

restrictivo /rrestrik'tißo/ *a* restrictive; restraining

restringir /rrestriŋ'gir/ *vt* to limit, restrict; contract

resucitar /rresuθi'tar; rresusi'tar/ *vt* to raise from the dead; *Fig. Inf.* revive; —*vi* resuscitate

resuello /rre'sueʎo; rre'sueyo/ *m*, breathing; panting, hard breathing

resuelto /rre'suelto/ *a* audacious, daring; resolute, capable

resulta /rre'sulta/ *f*, consequence, result; decision, resolution; vacant post. **de resultas de,** as the result of; in consequence of

resultado /rresul'taðo/ *m*, result, consequence, outcome

resultante /rresul'tante/ *a* resulting. *f*, *Mech.* resultant

resultar /rresul'tar/ *vi* to result, follow; turn out, happen; result (in); *Inf.* turn out well. **El vestido no me resulta,** The dress isn't a success on me

resumen /rre'sumen/ *m*, summary. **en r.,** in short

resumir /rresu'mir/ *vt* to summarize, abridge; sum up, recapitulate; —*vr* be contained, be included

resurgimiento /rresurhi'miento/ *m*, resurgence, revival

resurgir /rresur'hir/ vi to reappear, rise again, revive; resuscitate

resurrección /rresurrek'θion; rresurrek'sion/ f, resurrection

resurtir /rresur'tir/ vi to rebound

retablo /rre'taβlo/ m, Archit. altarpiece, retable; frieze; series of pictures

retaguardia /rreta'guarðia/ f, rear guard. **a r.**, in the rear. **picar la r.**, to harass the rear guard

retajar /rreta'har/ vt to cut in the round; circumcise

retal /rre'tal/ m, clipping, filing, shaving; remnant

retama /rre'tama/ f, Bot. broom. **r. común** or **r. de olor**, Spanish broom. **r. de escobas**, common broom

retar /rre'tar/ vt to challenge; Inf. reproach, accuse

retardación /rretarða'θion; rretarða'sion/ f, retardment

retardar /rretar'ðar/ vt to retard, delay

retardo /rre'tarðo/ m, delay, retardment

retazo /rre'taθo; rre'taso/ m, remnant, cutting; excerpt, fragment

retemblar /rretem'βlar/ vi to quiver, tremble constantly

retén /rre'ten/ m, stock, reserve, provision; Mil. reserve

retención /rreten'θion; rreten'sion/ f, retention

retener /rrete'ner/ vt irr to keep, retain; recollect, remember; keep back; Law. detain; deduct. See **tener**

retenidamente /rreteniða'mente/ adv retentively

retentiva /rreten'tiβa/ f, retentiveness, memory

retentivo /rreten'tiβo/ a retentive

reticencia /rreti'θenθia; rreti'sensia/ f, reticence

reticente /rreti'θente; rreti'sente/ a reticent

retículo /rre'tikulo/ m, reticulum, network; Phys. reticle

retina /rre'tina/ f, retina

retintín /rretin'tin/ m, ringing; tinkling; Inf. sarcastic tone

retiñir /rreti'ɲir/ vi to tinkle, clink; jingle

retirada /rreti'raða/ f, withdrawal; retirement; seclusion, refuge; Mil. retreat

retirado /rreti'raðo/ a remote, secluded; Mil. retired

retirar /rreti'rar/ vt to withdraw; remove; repel, throw back; hide, put aside; —vr withdraw; retire; Mil. retreat

retiro /rre'tiro/ m, withdrawal; removal; seclusion, privacy; Mil. retreat; retirement; Eccl. retreat. **dar el r. (a)**, to place on the retired list

reto /'rreto/ m, challenge; threat

retocar /rreto'kar/ vt to touch again or repeatedly; Photo. retouch; restore (pictures); Fig. put the finishing touch to

retoñar /rreto'ɲar/ vi to sprout, shoot; Fig. revive, resuscitate

retoño /rre'toɲo/ m, sprout, shoot

retoque /rre'toke/ m, frequent touching; finishing touch; touch, slight attack

retorcer /rretor'θer; rretor'ser/ vt irr to twist; contort; confound with one's own argument; misconstrue, distort; —vr contort; writhe. See **torcer**

retórica /rre'torika/ f, rhetoric; pl Inf. quibbling

retórico /rre'toriko/ (**-ca**) a rhetorical —n rhetorician

retornar /rretor'nar/ vt to return, give back; turn, twist; turn back; —vi and vr return, go back

retorno /rre'torno/ m, return, going back; recompense, repayment; exchange; return journey

retorsión /rretor'sion/ f, twisting, writhing; Fig. misconstruction

retorta /rre'torta/ f, Chem. retort

retortijón /rretorti'hon/ m, twisting, curling. **r. de tripas**, stomachache

retozar /rreto'θar; rreto'sar/ vi to skip, frisk, frolic, gambol; romp; Fig. be aroused (passions)

retozón /rreto'θon; rreto'son/ a frolicsome

retracción /rretrak'θion; rretrak'sion/ f, drawing back, retraction

retractación /rretrakta'θion; rretrakta'sion/ f, retractation, recantation

retractar /rretrak'tar/ vt to retract, recant, withdraw

retráctil /rre'traktil/ a retractile

retraer /rretra'er/ vt irr to bring back again; dissuade;

buy back, redeem; —vr take refuge; retire; withdraw; go into seclusion. See **traer**

retraído /rre'traiðo/ a fugitive, refugee; retired, solitary; timid, nervous, unsociable

retraimiento /rretrai'miento/ m, withdrawal; seclusion, privacy; refuge, asylum, sanctuary; timidity, unsociability

retrasar /rretra'sar/ vt to postpone, delay; turn back (the clock); —vi be slow (of clocks); —vr be behind time, be late; be backward (persons)

retraso /rre'traso/ m, lateness; delay, dilatoriness; loss of time (clocks); setting back (of the clock) (e.g. *El reloj lleva cinco minutos de r.*, The clock is five minutes slow)

retratar /rretra'tar/ vt to paint or draw the portrait of; portray, describe; photograph; copy, imitate

retratista /rretra'tista/ mf portrait painter; photographer; portrayer

retrato /rre'trato/ m, portrait; portrayal; Fig. image, likeness

retrechería /rretretʃe'ria/ f, Inf. craftiness, evasiveness

retreta /rre'treta/ f, Mil. retreat; tattoo

retrete /rre'trete/ m, toilet, water closet

retribución /rretriβu'θion; rretriβu'sion/ f, recompense, reward

retribuir /rretri'βuir/ vt irr to recompense, reward. See **huir**

retroactivo /rretroak'tiβo/ a retroactive

retroceder /rretroθe'ðer; rretrose'ðer/ vi to withdraw, move back, draw back; recede

retroceso /rretro'θeso; rretro'seso/ m, retrocedence, withdrawal; Med. retrogression

retrogradación /rretrograða'θion; rretrograða'sion/ f, retrogression

retrógrado /rre'trograðo/ a retrogressive, retrograde; Polit. reactionary

retronar /rretro'nar/ vi irr to bang, thunder, resound with noise. See **tronar**

retrospección /rretrospek'θion; rretrospek'sion/ f, retrospection

retrospectivo /rretrospek'tiβo/ a retrospective

retrotraer /rretrotra'er/ vt irr to antedate. See **traer**

retruécano /rre'truekano/ m, antithesis; play on words, pun

retumbante /rretum'βante/ a resounding; pompous, high-flown

retumbar /rretum'βar/ vi to resound, echo, reverberate; roll (of thunder); roar (of a cannon)

retumbo /rre'tumbo/ m, reverberation, echo; rumble; roll (of thunder); roar (of a cannon, etc.)

reuma /'rreuma/ m, rheumatism

reumático /rreu'matiko/ a rheumatic

reumatismo /rreuma'tismo/ m, rheumatism

reunión /rreu'nion/ f, reunion, union; meeting; assembly, gathering

reunir /rreu'nir/ vt to reunite; unite; join; gather, assemble; —vr meet, assemble; unite

revacunación /rreβakuna'θion; rreβakuna'sion/ f, revaccination

revacunar /rreβaku'nar/ vt to revaccinate

revalidación /rreβaliða'θion; rreβaliðasion/ f, ratification, confirmation

revalidar /rreβali'ðar/ vt to ratify, confirm; —vr pass a final examination

revejido /rreβe'hiðo/ a prematurely old

revelación /rreβela'θion; rreβela'sion/ f, revelation; Photo. developing

revelador /rreβela'ðor/ a revealing. m, Photo. developer

revelar /rreβe'lar/ vt to reveal; Photo. develop

revendedor /rreβende'ðor/ (**-ra**) a reselling, retail —n retailer

revender /rreβen'der/ vt to resell; retail (goods)

reventa /rre'βenta/ f, resale; retail

reventar /rreβen'tar/ vi irr to burst, explode; break in foam (waves); burst forth; Fig. burst (with impatience, etc.); Inf. explode (with anger, etc.); —vt break, crush; Fig. wear out, exhaust; Inf. irritate, vex; —vr burst; Fig. be exhausted. See **sentar**

reventón /rreβen'ton/ a bursting. m, explosion,

bursting; steep hill; hole, fix, difficulty; uphill work, heavy toil

rever /rre'βer/ *vt irr* to look at again, revise; *Law.* retry. See **ver**

reverberación /rreβerβera'θion; rreβerβera'sion/ *f,* reflection (of light); reverberation, resounding

reverberar /rreβerβe'rar/ *vi* to reflect; resound, reverberate

reverbero /rreβer'βero/ *m,* reverberation; reflector

reverdecer /rreβerðe'θer; rreβerðe'ser/ *vi irr* to grow green again; revive, acquire new vigor. See **conocer**

reverencia /rreβeren'θia; rreβeren'sia/ *f,* respect, veneration; bow; *Eccl.* reverence (title)

reverencial /rreβeren'θial; rreβeren'sial/ *a* reverential, respectful

reverenciar /rreβeren'θiar; rreβeren'siar/ *vt* to revere; honor; respect

reverendo /rreβe'rendo/ *a* reverend; venerable; *Inf.* overprudent

reversibilidad /rreβersiβili'ðað/ *f,* reversibility

reversión /rreβer'sion/ *f,* reversion

reverso /rre'βerso/ *m,* wrong side, back; reverse side (of coins)

reverter /rreβer'ter/ *vi irr* to overflow. See **entender**

revertir /rreβer'tir/ *vi Law.* to revert

revés /rre'βes/ *m,* wrong side, back, reverse; cuff, slap; backhand (in ballgames); check, setback, reverse; disaster, misfortune. **al r.,** on the contrary; wrong side out. **de r.,** from left to right, counterclockwise

revesado /rreβe'saðo/ *a* complicated, difficult; willful

revestimiento /rreβesti'miento/ *m, Mas.* lining, coating

revestir /rreβes'tir/ *vt irr* to dress; *Mas.* coat, line; *Fig.* cover, clothe; —*vr* be dressed or dress oneself; *Fig.* be captivated (by an idea); become haughty or full of oneself; rise to the occasion, develop qualities necessary. See **pedir**

reviejo /rre'βieho/ *a* very old. *m,* dead branch (of trees)

revisar /rreβi'sar/ *vt* to revise; examine

revisión /rreβi'sion/ *f,* revision; reexamination; *Law.* retrial

revisor /rreβi'sor/ *a* revising, examining. *m,* reviser; ticket inspector

revista /rre'βista/ *f,* reexamination, revision; review, periodical; *Theat.* revue; reinspection; review (of a book, etc.); *Law.* new trial; *Mil.* review. **pasar r.,** to inspect; review

revistero /rreβis'tero/ **(-ra)** *n* reviewer, writer of reviews

revivificación /rreβiβifika'θion; rreβiβifika'sion/ *f,* revivification

revivificar /rreβiβifi'kar/ *vt* to revivify, revive

revivir /rreβi'βir/ *vi* to resuscitate; revive

revocación /rreβoka'θion; rreβoka'sion/ *f,* revocation, cancellation, annulment

revocar /rreβo'kar/ *vt* to revoke, annul; dissuade; repel, throw back; wash (walls); *Law.* discharge

revolcadero /rreβolka'ðero/ *m,* bathing place (of animals)

revolcar /rreβol'kar/ *vt irr* to knock down, trample underfoot; lay flat (in an argument); —*vr* wallow; dig one's heels in, be obstinate. See **volcar**

revolotear /rreβolote'ar/ *vi* to flutter, fly around; twirl; —*vt* hurl, toss

revoltillo /rreβol'tiʎo; rreβol'tiyo/ *m,* jumble, hodgepodge; confusion, tangle

revoltoso /rreβol'toso/ *a* rebellious; mischievous, willful; intricate

revolución /rreβolu'θion; rreβolu'sion/ *f,* turn, revolution; rebellion, uprising; revolution

revolucionar /rreβoluθio'nar; rreβolusio'nar/ *vt* to revolutionize

revolucionario /rreβoluθio'nario; rreβolusio'nario/ **(-ia)** *a* and *n* revolutionary

revolver /rreβol'βer/ *vt irr* to turn over; turn upside down; wrap up; revolve; stir; reflect upon, consider; upset, cause disharmony; search through; disorder (papers, etc.); —*vr* move from side to side; change (in the weather). See **resolver**

revólver /rre'βolβer/ *m,* revolver

revoque /rre'βoke/ *m, Mas.* washing, whitewash; plastering

revuelco /rre'βuelko/ *m,* wallowing

revuelo /rre'βuelo/ *m,* second flight (of birds); irregular course of flight; disturbance, upset

revuelta /rre'βuelta/ *f,* second turn or revolution; revolt, rebellion; quarrel, fight; turning point; change of direction, turn; change (of opinions, posts, etc.)

revueltamente /rreβuelta'mente/ *adv* in confusion, higgledy-piggledy

revulsión /rreβul'sion/ *f,* revulsion

rexaminación /rreksamina'θion; rreksamina'sion/ *f,* reexamination

rexaminar /rreksami'nar/ *vt* to reexamine

rexpedir /rrekspe'ðir/ *vt* to forward, send on

rexportación /rreksporta'θion; rreksporta'sion/ *f,* reexport

rexportar /rrekspor'tar/ *vt Com.* to reexport

rey /rrei/ *m,* king (in cards, chess); queen bee; *Inf.* swineherd; *Fig.* king, chief. *Herald.* **r. de armas,** king-of-arms. **reyes magos,** magi. **día de Reyes,** Twelfth Night. **servir al r.,** to fight for the king

reyerta /rre'yerta/ *f,* quarrel, row, rumpus

reyezuelo /rreye'θuelo; rreye'suelo/ *m,* kinglet, petty king; golden-crested wren

rezagar /rreθa'gar; rresa'gar/ *vt* to leave behind; postpone, delay; —*vr* lag behind, straggle

rezar /rre'θar; rre'sar/ *vt* to pray, say prayers; say mass; *Inf.* state, say; —*vi* pray; *Inf.* fume, grumble. **El edicto reza así,** The edict runs like this, The edict reads like this

rezo /'rreθo; 'rreso/ *m,* prayer; devotions

rezongar /rreθoŋ'gar; rresoŋ'gar/ *vi* to grouse, grumble

rezumar /rreθu'mar; rresu'mar/ **(se)** *vr* and *vi* to percolate, ooze through; *Inf.* leak out, be known

ría /'rria/ *f,* estuary, river mouth, firth

riachuelo /rria'tʃuelo/ *m,* rivulet, stream

riada /'rriaða/ *f,* flood. *Aer.* **r. de acero,** rain of flak

ribaldería /rriβalde'ria/ *f,* ribaldry

ribaldo /rri'βaldo/ *a* ribald. *m,* knave

ribazo /rri'βaθo; rri'βaso/ *m,* slope, incline

ribera /rri'βera/ *f,* bank, margin, shore, strand

ribereño /rriβe'reɲo/ **(-ña)** *a* and *n* riparian

ribero /rri'βero/ *m,* embankment, wall

ribete /rri'βete/ *m,* binding, border, trimming; stripe; increase, addition; dramatic touch, exaggeration; *pl* indications, signs

ribetear /rriβete'ar/ *vt Sew.* to bind, trim, edge

ricacho /rri'katʃo/ **(-cha)** *n Inf.* newly rich person, nouveau riche

ricahembra /rrika'embra/ *f,* lady; daughter or wife of a Spanish noble *Obs.*

ricamente /rrika'mente/ *adv* richly, opulently; beautifully, splendidly; luxuriously

ricino /rri'θino; rri'sino/ *m,* castor oil plant

rico /'rriko/ *a* wealthy, rich; abundant; magnificent, splendid; delicious. **r. como Creso,** rich as Croesus

ricohombre /rriko'ombre/ *m,* nobleman *Obs.*

ricura /rri'kura/ *f, Inf.* richness, wealth

ridiculez /rriðiku'leθ; rriðiku'les/ *f,* absurd action or remark; ridiculousness; affectation; folly

ridiculizar /rriðikuli'θar; rriðikuli'sar/ *vt* to ridicule, poke fun at

ridículo /rri'ðikulo/ *a* ridiculous, absurd; grotesque; preposterous, outrageous. *m,* reticule

riego /'rriego/ *m,* watering, spraying; irrigation

riel /'rriel/ *m,* ingot; rail (of a train or streetcar)

rielar /rrie'lar/ *vi* to glimmer, glisten; glitter; shimmer

rienda /'rrienda/ *f,* rein (gen. *pl*); restraint; *pl* administration, government. **a r. suelta,** swiftly; without restraint

riesgo /'rriesgo/ *m,* risk, danger

rifa /'rrifa/ *f,* raffle; quarrel, disagreement

rifar /rri'far/ *vt* to raffle; —*vi* quarrel, fall out

rifle /'rrifle/ *m,* rifle

rigidez /rrihi'ðeθ; rrihi'ðes/ *f,* stiffness; rigidity; harshness

rígido /'rrihiðo/ *a* stiff; rigid; inflexible; severe, harsh

rigodón /rrigo'ðon/ *m,* rigadoon

rigor /rri'gor/ *m*, severity, sternness; rigor; hardness; inflexibility; *Med*. rigor. **en r.**, strictly speaking. **ser de r.**, to be essential, be indispensable

rigorista /rrigo'rista/ *mf* martinet

riguroso /rrigu'roso/ *a* rigorous; harsh, cruel; austere, rigid; strict, exact, scrupulous

rijoso /rri'hoso/ *a* quarrelsome; lascivious

riksha /'rriksa/ *m*, rickshaw

rima /'rrima/ *f*, rhyme, rime; heap; *pl* lyrics

rimador /rrima'ðor/ **(-ra)** *a* rhyming, rimer —*n* rhymer, rimer

rimar /rri'mar/ *vi* to compose verses; —*vi* and *vt* rhyme, rime

rimbombo /rrim'βombo/ *m*, reverberation (of a sound)

rimero /rri'mero/ *m*, heap, pile

Rin, el /rrin, el/ the Rhine

rincón /rrin'kon/ *m*, corner, angle; retreat, hiding place; *Inf*. home, nest, nook

rinconada /rrinko'naða/ *f*, corner, angle

rinconera /rrinko'nera/ *f*, corner cupboard; corner table

ringlera /rriŋ'glera/ *f*, file, line, row

ringlero /rriŋ'glero/ *m*, guiding line for writing

ringorrangos /rriŋgo'rraŋgos/ *m pl*, *Inf*. exaggerated flourishes in writing; *Inf*. unnecessary frills or ornaments

rinoceronte /rrinoθe'ronte; rrinose'ronte/ *m*, rhinoceros

riñón /rri'ɲon/ *m*, kidney; *Fig*. center, heart; *pl Anat*. back

río /'rrio/ *m*, river; *Fig*. stream, flood

rioja /'rrioha/ *m*, red wine from Rioja

ripio /'rripio/ *m*, remains, rest; debris, rubbish; *Lit*. padding; verbiage, prolixity. **no perder r.**, to lose no occasion or opportunity

riqueza /rri'keθa; rri'kesa/ *f*, riches, wealth; abundance; richness, magnificence

risa /'rrisa/ *f*, laugh; laughter; cause of amusement, joke

risco /'rrisko/ *m*, crag

riscoso /rris'koso/ *a* craggy

risible /rri'siβle/ *a* laughable

risoles /rri'soles/ *m pl*, rissoles

risotada /rriso'taða/ *f*, loud laugh

ristra /'rristra/ *f*, string (of onions, etc.); file, line, row

risueño /rri'sueɲo/ *a* smiling; cheerful; pleasant, agreeable; favorable, hopeful

rítmico /'rritmiko/ *a* rhythmic

ritmo /'rritmo/ *m*, rhythm

rito /'rrito/ *m*, rite

ritualismo /rritua'lismo/ *m*, ritualism

ritualista /rritua'lista/ *mf* ritualist

rivalidad /rriβali'ðað/ *f*, rivalry, competition; hostility

rivalizar /rriβali'θar; rriβali'sar/ *vi* to compete, rival

rizado /rri'θaðo; rri'saðo/ *m*, curling; pleating, crimping; rippling, ruffling

rizar /rri'θar; rri'sar/ *vt* to curl (hair); ripple, ruffle (of water); pleat, crimp; —*vr* be naturally wavy (of hair)

rizo /'rriθo; 'rriso/ *m*, curl, ringlet; cut velvet. *Aer*. **hacer el r.**, to loop the loop; *Naut*. to take in reefs

rizoso /rri'θoso; rri'soso/ *a* naturally curly or wavy (hair)

ro, ro /rro, rro/ *m*, hushaby!

roano /rro'ano/ *a* roan (of horses)

robador /rroβa'ðor/ **(-ra)** *a* robbing —*n* robber, thief. *m*, abductor

robar /rro'βar/ *vt* to rob; abduct; wash away, eat away (rivers, sea); remove honey from the hive; draw (in cards, dominoes); *Fig*. capture (love, etc.)

roblar /rro'βlar/ *vt* to reinforce, strengthen; clinch

roble /'rroβle/ *m*, oak tree; oak; *Fig*. bulwark, tower of strength

robledo /rro'βleðo/ *m*, oak grove

roblón /rro'βlon/ *m*, rivet

robo /'rroβo/ *m*, theft, robbery; booty

robustecer /rroβuste'θer; rroβuste'ser/ *vt irr* to strengthen. See **conocer**

robustez /rroβus'teθ; rroβus'tes/ *f*, strength, robustness

robusto /rro'βusto/ *a* vigorous, robust, hearty, strong

roca /'rroka/ *f*, rock; *Fig*. tower of strength

roce /'rroθe; 'rrose/ *m*, rubbing, brushing, touching, friction; social intercourse

rociada /rro'θiaða; rro'siaða/ *f*, dewing; sprinkling; dew-wet grass given as medicine to horses and mules; *Fig*. shower; general slander; harsh rebuke

rociar /rro'θiar; rro'siar/ *vi* to fall as dew; drizzle; —*vt* sprinkle, spray; *Fig*. shower (with)

rocín /rro'θin; rro'sin/ *m*, sorry nag; hack; *Inf*. ignoramus, boor

rocinante /rroθi'nante; rrosi'nante/ *m*, poor nag (alluding to Don Quixote's horse)

rocío /'rroθio; 'rrosio/ *m*, dew; dewdrop; drizzle, light shower; *Fig*. sprinkling, spray

rocoso /rro'koso/ *a* rocky

rodaballo /rroða'βaʎo; rroða'βayo/ *m*, turbot; *Inf*. crafty man

rodada /rro'ðaða/ *f*, wheel mark or track

rodado /rro'ðaðo/ *a* dappled (of horses)

rodaje /rro'ðahe/ *m*, wheeling; shooting (of a film)

rodante /rro'ðante/ *a* rolling

rodar /rro'ðar/ *vi* to roll; revolve, turn; run on wheels; wander, roam; be moved about; be plentiful, abound; happen successively; (*with por*) fall down, roll down

Rodas /'rroðas/ Rhodes

rodear /rroðe'ar/ *vi* to walk around; go by a roundabout way; *Fig*. beat around the bush; —*vt* encircle, surround; besiege; *West Hem*. round up (cattle)

rodela /rro'ðela/ *f*, round shield; buckler

rodeno /rro'ðeno/ *a* red (of rocks, earth, etc.)

rodeo /rro'ðeo/ *m*, encirclement; indirect and longer way; trick to evade pursuit; *West Hem*. rodeo, roundup; stockyard, cattle enclosure; *Fig*. beating around the bush; evasive reply

rodera /rro'ðera/ *f*, rail, track, line; cart rut or track

Rodesia /rro'ðesia/ Rhodesia

rodilla /rro'ðiʎa; rro'ðiya/ *f*, knee; floor cloth. **de rodillas**, on one's knees. **ponerse de rodillas**, *or* **hincar las rodillas**, to kneel down

rodillazo /rroði'ʎaθo; rroði'yaso/ *m*, push with the knee

rodillera /rroði'ʎera; rroði'yera/ *f*, kneecap, kneepad; mend at the knee of garments; bagginess of trouser knees

rodillo /rro'ðiʎo; rro'ðiyo/ *m*, roller; traction engine; *Print*. inking roller; garden roller. **r. de pastas**, *Cul*. rolling pin

rododendro /rroðo'ðendro/ *m*, rhododendron

rodrigón /rroðri'gon/ *m*, stake, prop (for plants); *Inf*. old retainer who serves as a ladies' escort

roedor /rroe'ðor/ *a* gnawing; *Fig*. nagging; biting —*a* and *m*, rodent

roedura /rroe'ðura/ *f*, biting, gnawing; corrosion

roer /rro'er/ *vt irr* to gnaw, nibble, eat; corrode, wear away; trouble, afflict —*Pres. Indic.* **roigo, roes,** etc —*Preterite* **royó, royeron.** *Imperf. Subjunc.* **royese,** etc.

rogación /rroga'θion; rroga'sion/ *f*, request, supplication, entreaty; *Eccl*. rogation

rogador /rroga'ðor/ **(-ra)** *a* requesting; beseeching —*n* suppliant

rogar /rro'gar/ *vt irr* to request; beseech, beg. See **contar**

rogativo /rroga'tiβo/ *a* supplicatory, petitioning

roído /rro'iðo/ *a* gnawed, eaten; *Inf*. miserable, stingy

rojal /rro'hal/ *a* red (of soil, etc.). *m*, red earth

rojear /rrohe'ar/ *vi* to appear red; be reddish

rojete /rro'hete/ *m*, rouge

rojez /rro'heθ; rro'hes/ *f '*, redness

rojizo /rro'hiθo; rro'hiso/ *a* reddish

rojo /'rroho/ *a* red; fair; red-gold (of hair); *Polit*. radical, red

rol /rrol/ *m*, roll, list

roldana /rrol'dana/ *f*, pulley wheel

rollizo /rro'ʎiθo; rro'yiso/ *a* round; plump, sturdy. *m*, log

rollo /'rroʎo; 'rroyo/ *m*, roll; *Cul*. rolling pin; log;

town cross or pillar; anything rolled (paper, etc.); twist (of tobacco)

Roma /'rroma/ Rome

romance /rro'manθe; rro'manse/ *a* and *m*, romance (language). *m*, Spanish; ballad; romance of chivalry; *pl Fig.* fairy tales, excuses. **en buen r.,** *Fig.* in plain words

romancear /rromanθe'ar; rromanse'ar/ *vt* to translate from Latin into the spoken language; translate into Spanish; paraphrase the Spanish to assist translation

romancero /rroman'θero; rroman'sero/ **(-ra)** *n* balladeer. *m,* collection of ballads

romancista /rroman'θista; rroman'sista/ *mf* romancist

románico /rro'maniko/ *a Archit.* Romanesque

romanista /rroma'nista/ *mf* expert in Roman law or Romance languages and literature

romanizar /rromani'θar; romani'sar/ *vt* to romanize; —*vr* become romanized

romano /rro'mano/ **(-na)** *a* and *n* Roman. **a la romana,** in the Roman way. **cabello a la romana,** *Inf.* bobbed hair

romanticismo /rromanti'θismo; rromanti'sismo/ *m,* romanticism

romántico /rro'mantiko/ **(-ca)** *a* romantic; emotional; fanciful —*n* romantic; romanticist

rombo /'rrombo/ *m,* rhombus

romería /rrome'ria/ *f,* pilgrimage; excursion, picnic (made on a saint's day)

romero /rro'mero/ **(-ra)** *m,* rosemary —*n* pilgrim

romo /'rromo/ *a* blunt, dull, unsharpened; flat (of noses)

rompecabezas /rrompeka'βeθas; rrompeka'βesas/ *m,* bludgeon; knuckleduster; *Inf.* teaser, puzzle, riddle; jigsaw puzzle

rompeimágenes /rrompei'mahenes/ *mf* iconoclast

rompeolas /rrompe'olas/ *m,* jetty, breakwater

romper /rrom'per/ *vt* to break; shatter, break into fragments; spoil, ruin; break up, plow; *Fig.* cut, divide (of water, etc.); *Fig.* end, break; interrupt; infringe, break; —*vi* break; break (of waves); sprout, flower; (*with prep a*) begin to. **Rompió a hablar,** He broke into speech —*Past Part.* **roto**

rompiente /rrom'piente/ *a* breaking. *m,* reef, shoal

rompimiento /rrompi'miento/ *m,* break, rupture; crack, split; breakage; infringement; plowing up; *Fig.* dividing (water, etc.); spoiling, ruining; opening (of buds, etc.)

ron /rron/ *m,* rum

roncar /rron'kar/ *vi* to snore; *Fig.* roar, howl (of the sea, wind, etc.); *Inf.* brag

roncear /rronθe'ar; rronse'ar/ *vi* to be dilatory or unwilling; *Inf.* flatter, cajole; *Naut.* lag behind, sail slowly

roncero /rron'θero; rron'sero/ *a* dilatory, slow; grumbling, complaining; cajoling, flattering

roncha /'rrontʃa/ *f,* wheal; bruise, bump; *Inf.* money lost through trickery; thin, round slice

ronco /'rronko/ *a* hoarse, husky

ronda /'rronda/ *f,* round, beat, patrol; serenading party; *Inf.* round (of drinks)

rondador /rronda'ðor/ *m,* watchman; roundsman; serenader; night wanderer

rondalla /rron'daʎa; rron'daya/ *f,* tale, fairy tale

rondar /rron'dar/ *vi* to patrol, police; walk the streets by night; serenade; —*vt* haunt; hover about; *Inf.* overcome (of sleep, etc.)

rondó /rron'do/ *m,* rondo

ronquear /rronke'ar/ *vi* to be hoarse

ronquera /rron'kera/ *f,* hoarseness

ronquido /rron'kiðo/ *m,* snore; hoarse sound

ronronear /rronrone'ar/ *vi* to purr (of cats)

ronzal /rron'θal; rron'sal/ *m,* halter

ronzar /rron'θar; rron'sar/ *vt* to munch, crack with the teeth

roña /'rroɲa/ *f,* mange (in sheep); grime, filth; mold; moral corruption; *Inf.* stinginess; *Inf.* trick, deception

roñería /rroɲe'ria/ *f, Inf.* meanness, stinginess

roñoso /rro'ɲoso/ *a* scabby; filthy; rusty; *Inf.* mean, stingy

ropa /'rropa/ *f,* fabric, material, stuff; clothes, wearing apparel; garment, outfit; robe (of office). **r. blanca,** underclothes; (domestic) linen. **r. hecha,** ready-made clothing. **r. talar,** long gown; cassock

ropaje /rro'pahe/ *m,* clothes, garments; vestments; drapery; *Fig.* form, outline

ropavejería /rropaβehe'ria/ *f,* old-clothes shop

ropavejero /rropaβe'hero/ **(-ra)** *n* old-clothes dealer

ropería /rrope'ria/ *f,* clothier's shop or trade; wardrobe; cloakroom

ropero /rro'pero/ **(-ra)** *n* clothier; keeper of the wardrobe. *m,* wardrobe; charitable organization

ropilla /rro'piʎa; rro'piya/ *f,* doublet

ropón /rro'pon/ *m,* a loose-fitting gown generally worn over clothes

roque /'rroke/ *m,* rook (in chess)

roqueño /rro'keɲo/ *a* rocky; hard as rock

roquete /rro'kete/ *m, Eccl.* rochet; barb of a lance

rorro /'rrorro/ *m, Inf.* infant, baby

rosa /'rrosa/ *f,* rose; anything rose-shaped; artificial rose; red spot on the body; *Archit.* rose window; *pl* rosettes. *m,* rose color. **r. de los vientos,** mariner's compass. **r. laurel,** oleander

rosado /rro'saðo/ *a* rose-colored; rose; rosé (wines)

rosal /rro'sal/ *m,* rose tree. **r. de tallo,** standard rose tree

rosaleda, rosalera /rrosa'leða, rrosa'lera/ *f,* rose garden

rosario /rro'sario/ *m,* rosary; *Fig.* string; chain pump; *Inf.* backbone

rosbif /rros'βif/ *m,* roast beef

rosca /'rroska/ *f,* screw and nut; *Cul.* twist (of bread or cake); spiral

roscado /rros'kaðo/ *a* twisted, spiral

rosear /rrose'ar/ *vi* to turn to rose, become rose-colored

Rosellón /rrose'ʎon; rrose'yon/ Rousillon

róseo /'rroseo/ *a* rose-colored

roseta /rro'seta/ *f, dim* small rose; rosette; rose of a watering can; rosette copper; *pl* toasted maize. **r. de fiebre,** rush of fever

rosetón /rrose'ton/ *m,* large rosette; *Archit.* rose window

rosicler /rrosi'kler/ *m,* rose-pink (first flush of dawn)

rosillo /rro'siʎo; rro'siyo/ *a* light red; roan (of horses)

rosmaro /rros'maro/ *m,* manatee, sea cow

roso /'rroso/ *a* bald, worn; red

rosquilla /rros'kiʎa; rros'kiya/ *f,* ring-shaped cake

rosquillero /rroski'ʎero; rroski'yero/ **(-ra)** *n* seller of rosquillas

rostrituerto /rrostri'tuerto/ *a Inf.* wry-faced (from sadness or anger)

rostro /'rrostro/ *m,* bird's beak; face, visage. **conocer de r.,** to know by sight. **dar en r.,** *Fig.* to throw in one's face

rota /'rrota/ *f, Mil.* defeat; *Eccl.* Rota; *Bot.* rattan

rotación /rrota'θion; rrota'sion/ *f,* rotation. **r. de cultivos,** rotation of crops

rotativa /rrota'tiβa/ *f,* rotary printing press

rotativo /rrota'tiβo/ *a* rotary

rotatorio /rrota'torio/ *a* rotatory

roto /'rroto/ *a* shabby, ragged; vicious, debauched

rotograbado /rrotogra'βaðo/ *m,* rotogravure

rotonda /rro'tonda/ *f,* rotunda

rótula /'rrotula/ *f,* rotula, patella

rotular /rrotu'lar/ *vt* to label; give a title or heading to

rótulo /'rrotulo/ *m,* title; poster; placard; label

rotundamente /rrotunda'mente/ *adv* tersely, roundly, plainly

rotundidad /rrotundi'ðað/ *f,* rotundity; roundness; finality (of words, etc.)

rotundo /rro'tundo/ *a* round; rotund; sonorous; final, plain (of words, etc.)

rotura /rro'tura/ *f,* breaking, shattering; plowing up; breakage; rupture

roturar /rrotu'rar/ *vt Agr.* to break up, plow up

roya /'rroya/ *f,* rust, mildew; tobacco

roza /'rroθa; 'rrosa/ *f, Agr.* clearing (of weeds, etc.);

ground ready for sowing. **de r. abierta,** open cast (of mining)

rozadura /rroθa'ðura; rrosa'ðura/ f, rubbing, friction; abrasion, chafing

rozagante /rroθa'gante; rrosa'gante/ a long and elaborate (dresses); upstanding; handsome; strapping, fine

rozamiento /rroθa'miento; rrosa'miento/ m, grazing, brushing, rubbing; discord, disharmony, disagreement; *Mech.* friction

rozar /rro'θar; rro'sar/ vt Agr. to clear of weeds; crop, nibble; scrape; brush against, touch; —vi brush, rub, touch; —vr have dealings with, know; stammer; be like, resemble

rúa /'rrua/ f, village street; highway

ruar /rru'ar/ vi to walk or ride through the streets; parade through the streets flirting with the ladies

rubeola /rruβe'ola/ f, rubella

rubí /rru'βi/ m, ruby; jewel (of a watch)

rubia /'rruβia/ f, Bot. madder; blonde (girl, woman)

rubicundez /rruβikun'deθ; rruβikun'des/ f, rubicundity, ruddiness, redness

rubicundo /rruβi'kundo/ a red-gold; ruddy-complexioned; reddish

rubio /'rruβio/ a red-gold, gold; fair, blond

rublo /'rruβlo/ m, ruble

rubor /rru'βor/ m, blush, flush; bashfulness

ruborizarse /rruβori'θarse; rruβori'sarse/ vr to blush; be shamefaced

ruboroso /rruβo'roso/ a shamefaced; blushing

rúbrica /'rruβrika/ f, rubric; personal mark, flourish added to one's signature

rubricar /rruβri'kar/ vt to sign and seal; sign with an X or other symbol; sign with a flourish

rubro /'rruβro/ a red

rucio /'rruθio; 'rrusio/ a fawn, light-gray (of animals); *Inf.* going gray, gray-haired

rudamente /rruða'mente/ adv rudely, abruptly, churlishly; roughly

rudeza /rru'ðeθa; rru'ðesa/ f, roughness; rudeness, uncouthness; stupidity

rudimentario /rruðimen'tario/ a rudimentary

rudimento /rruði'mento/ m, embryo; pl rudiments

rudo /'rruðo/ a rough; unfinished; uncouth, boorish, rude; stupid

rueca /'rrueka/ f, distaff (in spinning); spinning wheel; curve, twist

rueda /'rrueða/ f, wheel; group, circle; spread of a peacock's tail; roller, castor; round piece or slice; turn, chance; succession (of events); wheel (used for torture). **r. libre,** freewheeling. *Inf.* **hacer la r. (a),** to flatter, make a fuss of

ruedero /rrue'ðero/ m, wheelwright

ruedo /'rrueðo/ m, turning, rotation; circumference; lined hem of a cassock; circuit

ruego /'rruego/ m, request, entreaty

rufián /rru'fian/ m, ruffian; pimp

rufianesco /rrufia'nesko/ a ruffianly

rufo /'rrufo/ a fair; red-haired; curly-haired

rugido /rru'hiðo/ m, roaring, roar; creaking; gnashing; rumbling

rugir /rru'hir/ vi to roar; squeak, creak; gnash (the teeth)

ruibarbo /rrui'βarβo/ m, rhubarb

ruido /'rruiðo/ m, noise, din; disturbance; rumor. **hacer** (or **meter**) **r.,** to cause a sensation. *Inf.* **ser más el r. que las nueces,** to be much ado about nothing

ruidoso /rrui'ðoso/ a noisy; notable

ruin /rru'in/ a base, vile; despicable; mean; puny

ruina /'rruina/ f, ruin, downfall; financial ruin; fall, decline; pl ruins

ruinar /rrui'nar/ vt to ruin

ruindad /rruin'dað/ f, baseness; meanness; pettiness, unworthiness; mean trick, despicable action

ruinoso /rrui'noso/ a half-ruined; ruinous; useless, worthless

ruiseñor /rruise'ɲor/ m, nightingale

ruleta /rru'leta/ f, roulette

rumano /rru'mano/ a **(-na)** a and n Romanian. m, Romanian (language)

rumbo /'rrumbo/ m, Naut. course, way, route; direction; *Inf.* swank. **con r. a,** headed for, in the direction of. **hacer r. a,** to sail for; make for

rumboso /rrum'βoso/ a *Inf.* pompous, dignified; open-handed, generous

rumia /'rrumia/ f, rumination; cud

rumiante /rru'miante/ a and mf Zool. ruminant —a *Inf.* reflective, meditative

rumiar /rru'miar/ vt Zool. to ruminate; *Inf.* reflect upon, chew on; *Inf.* fume, rage

rumor /rru'mor/ m, noise; rumor; murmur, babble; dull sound

runa /'rruna/ f, rune

rúnico /'rruniko/ a runic

runrunearse /rrunrune'arse/ v impers to be rumored

rupia /'rrupia/ f, rupee

ruptura /rrup'tura/ f, Fig. rupture; Surg. hernia

rural /rru'ral/ a rustic, rural

ruralmente /rrural'mente/ adv rurally

Rusia /'rrusia/ Russia

rusificar /rrusifi'kar/ vt to russianize

ruso /'rruso/ **(-sa)** a and n Russian. m, Russian (language)

rusticación /rrustika'θion; rrustika'sion/ f, rustication

rusticar /rrusti'kar/ vi to rusticate

rusticidad /rrustiθi'ðað; rrustisi'ðað/ f, rusticity; boorishness, coarseness

rústico /'rrustiko/ a rustic, country; boorish, uncouth. m, countryman; yokel; peasant. **en rústica,** in paper covers (of books)

ruta /'rruta/ f, route; Fig. way. **r. de evitación,** by-pass, detour

ruteno /rru'teno/ **(-na)** a and n Ruthenian. m, Ruthenian (language)

rutilante /rruti'lante/ a Poet. sparkling, glowing

rutilar /rruti'lar/ vi Poet. to gleam, sparkle

rutina /rru'tina/ f, routine

rutinario /rruti'nario/ a routine

rutinero /rruti'nero/ **(-ra)** a routinistic —n routinist

S

sábado /'saβaðo/ *m,* Saturday; Jewish sabbath. **s. de gloria,** Easter Saturday

sábalo /'saβalo/ *m, Ichth.* shad

sabana /sa'βana/ *f,* savannah

sábana /'saβana/ *f,* bed sheet; altar cloth. *Inf.* **pegársele (a uno) las sábanas,** to be tied to the bed, get up late

sabandija /saβan'diha/ *f,* any unpleasant insect or reptile; *Fig.* vermin

sabanero /saβa'nero/ **(-ra)** *n* savannah dweller —*a* savannah

sabanilla /saβa'niʎa; saβa'niya/ *f,* small piece of linen (kerchief, towel, etc.); altar cloth

sabañón /saβa'ɲon/ *m,* chilblain

sabatario /saβa'tario/ *a* sabbatarian

sabático /sa'βatiko/ *a* sabbatical

sabatino /saβa'tino/ *a* Saturday, Sabbath

sabedor /saβe'ðor/ *a* aware; knowledgeable, knowing

sabelotodo /saβelo'toðo/ *mf Inf.* know-it-all

saber /sa'βer/ *m,* learning; wisdom

saber /sa'βer/ *vt irr* to know; be able to, know how; —*vi* know; be shrewd, be well aware of; (*with prep a*) taste of; be like or similar to. **s. al dedillo,** *Fig.* to have at one's fingertips. **a s.,** viz., namely. *Inf.* **no s. cuántas son cinco,** not to know how many beans make five. **no s. dónde meterse,** to be overcome by shame; have the jitters. **No sé cuántos,** I don't know how many. **No sé quién,** I don't know who (which person). **No sé qué,** I don't know what. **un no sé qué,** a certain something; a touch (of). **¡Quién sabe!** Who knows!; Time will tell —*Pres. Indic.* **sé, sabes,** etc —*Fut.* **sabré,** etc —*Condit.* **sabría,** etc —*Preterite* **supe,** etc —*Pres. Subjunc.* **sepa,** etc —*Imperf. Subjunc.* **supiese,** etc.

sabiamente /saβia'mente/ *adv* wisely, prudently

sabidillo /saβi'ðiʎo; saβi'ðiyo/ **(-lla)** *a* and *n Inf.* know-it-all

sabiduría /saβiðu'ria/ *f,* prudence, wisdom; erudition, learning; knowledge, awareness. **Libro de la S. de Salomón,** Book of Wisdom

sabiendas, a /sa'βiendas/, *a/ adv* knowingly, consciously

sabihondo /sa'βiondo/ **(-da)** *n Inf.* know-it-all

sabino /sa'βino/ **(-na)** *a* and *n* Sabine —*a* roan (of horses)

sabio /'saβio/ **(-ia)** *a* wise; learned, erudite; prudent, sagacious; knowing (of animals); performing (of animals) —*n* wise person; scholar, erudite person

sablazo /sa'βlaθo; sa'βlaso/ *m,* saber thrust or wound; *Inf.* sponging, taking advantage of. **dar un s.** (a), *Inf.* to sponge on; touch for money

sable /'saβle/ *m,* saber; *Herald.* sable; *Inf.* talent for sponging on people —*a Herald.* sable

sablear /saβle'ar/ *vi Inf.* to touch for invitations, loans, etc.; cadge

sablista /sa'βlista/ *mf Inf.* sponger, cadger

saboneta /saβo'neta/ *f,* hunting case watch, hunter

sabor /sa'βor/ *m,* taste, flavor; impression, effect. **a s.,** to taste; at pleasure

saboreamiento /saβorea'miento/ *m,* savoring; relishing, enjoyment

saborear /saβore'ar/ *vt* to flavor, season; relish, savor; appreciate, enjoy; —*vr* relish, savor; enjoy

saboreo /saβo'reo/ *m,* tasting; savoring; relishing

sabotaje /saβo'tahe/ *m,* sabotage

saboteador /saβotea'ðor/ *m,* saboteur

Saboya /sa'βoya/ Savoy

saboyano /saβo'yano/ **(-na)** *a* and *n* Savoyard

sabroso /sa'βroso/ *a* tasty, savory, well-seasoned; delightful, delicious; *Inf.* piquant, racy

sabueso /sa'βueso/ *m,* cocker spaniel. **s. de artois,** hound

sabuloso /saβu'loso/ *a* sandy

saburra /sa'βurra/ *f,* fur (on the tongue)

saca /'saka/ *f,* drawing out, removing; export, transport, shipping; removal, extraction; legal copy (of a document). **estar de s.,** to be on sale; *Inf.* be marriageable (of women)

sacabocados /sakaβo'kaðos/ *m,* punch (tool); *Inf.* cinch, easy matter

sacabotas /saka'βotas/ *m,* bootjack

sacabrocas /saka'βrokas/ *m,* tack puller

sacabuche /saka'βutʃe/ *m, Mus.* sackbut; sackbut player; *Inf.* insignificant little man; *Naut.* hand pump

sacacorchos /saka'kortʃos/ *m,* corkscrew

sacacuartos /saka'kuartos/ *m, Inf.* catchpenny

sacada /sa'kaða/ *f,* territory cut off from a province

sacadineros /sakaði'neros/ *m, Inf.* catchpenny

sacamanchas /saka'mantʃas/ *mf.* See **quitamanchas**

sacamantas /saka'mantas/ *m, Inf.* tax collector

sacamiento /saka'miento/ *m,* removing, taking out

sacamuelas /saka'muelas/ *mf* dentist; charlatan, quack; *Inf.* windbag

sacapotras /saka'potras/ *m, Inf.* unskilled surgeon

sacar /sa'kar/ *vt* to draw out; extract; pull out; take out; remove; dispossess, turn out; free from, relieve; examine, investigate; extort (the truth); extract (sugar, etc.); win (prizes, games); copy; discover, find out; elect by ballot; obtain, achieve; exclude; show, exhibit; quote, mention; produce, invent; manufacture; note down; put forth; unsheath (swords); bowl (in cricket); serve (in tennis). **s. a bailar,** to invite to dance. **s. a luz,** to publish, print; reveal, bring out. **s. a paseo,** to take for a walk. **s. de pila,** to be a godfather or godmother to. **s. en claro** *or* **s. en limpio,** to copy; conclude, infer, gather. **sacarse en conclusión que...,** the conclusion is that...

sacarificar /sakarifi'kar/ *vt* to saccharify

sacarina /saka'rina/ *f,* saccharin

sacasillas /saka'siʎas; saka'siyas/ *m, Inf. Theat.* stagehand

sacerdocio /saθer'ðoθio; saser'ðosio/ *m,* priesthood

sacerdotal /saθerðo'tal; saserðo'tal/ *a* priestly

sacerdote /saθer'ðote; saser'ðote/ *m,* priest

sacerdotisa /saθerðo'tisa; saserðo'tisa/ *f,* priestess. **sumo s.,** high priestess

sachar /sa'tʃar/ *vt* to weed

sacho /'satʃo/ *m,* weeder

saciable /sa'θiaβle; sa'siaβle/ *a* satiable

saciar /sa'θiar; sa'siar/ *vt* to satisfy; satiate; —*vr* be satiated

saciedad /saθie'ðað; sasie'ðað/ *f,* satiety, surfeit

saco /'sako/ *m,* handbag; sack, bag; sackful; sack coat; *Biol. sac; Mil.* sack, plundering. **s. de noche,** dressing case, weekend case. *Inf.* **no echar en s. roto,** not to forget, to remember

sacramentalmente /sakramental'mente/ *adv* sacramentally; in confession

sacramentar /sakramen'tar/ *vt* to consecrate; administer the Blessed Sacrament; hide, conceal

sacramentario /sakramen'tario/ **(-ia)** *n* sacramentalist; sacramentarian

sacramento /sakra'mento/ *m,* sacrament; *Eccl.* Host; *Eccl.* mystery. **s. del altar,** Eucharist. **con todos los sacramentos,** with all the sacraments; done in order, complete with all formalities. **recibir los sacramentos,** to receive the last sacraments

sacratísimo /sakra'tisimo/ *a* most sacred

sacrificadero /sakrifika'ðero/ *m,* place of sacrifice

sacrificador /sakrifika'ðor/ **(-ra)** *a* sacrificing —*n* sacrificer

sacrificar /sakrifi'kar/ *vt* to sacrifice; slaughter; —*vr* consecrate oneself to God; sacrifice oneself; devote or dedicate oneself (to)

sacrificio /sakri'fiθio; sakri'fisio/ *m,* sacrifice; offering, dedication; surrendering, forgoing; compliance, submission. **s. del altar,** sacrifice of the mass

sacrilegio /sakri'lehio/ *m,* sacrilege

sacrílego /sa'krilego/ *a* sacrilegious

sacristán /sakris'tan/ *m,* sacristan; sexton; hoop (for dresses). *Inf.* **s. de amén,** yes-man. *Inf.* **ser gran s.,** to be very crafty

sacristana /sakris'tana/ f, wife of a sacristan or sexton; nun in charge of a convent sacristy

sacristanía /sakrista'nia/ f, office of a sacristan or sexton

sacristía /sakris'tia/ f, sacristy; vestry; office of a sacristan or sexton

sacro /'sakro/ a sacred; *Anat.* sacral

sacrosanto /sakro'santo/ a sacrosanct

sacudida /saku'ðiða/ f, shake, shaking; jerk, jar, jolt; twitch, pull; *Aer.* bump

sacudido /saku'ðiðo/ a unsociable; difficult, wayward; determined, bold

sacudidor /sakuði'ðor/ **(-ra)** a shaking; jerking —n shaker. m, carpet beater; duster

sacudidura /sakuði'ðura/ f, shaking (especially to remove dust); jerking

sacudimiento /sakuði'miento/ m, shake, shaking; jerk; twitch, pull; jolt

sacudir /saku'ðir/ vt to shake; flap, wave; jerk, twitch; beat, bang; shake off; —vr shake off, avoid

sadismo /sa'ðismo/ m, sadism

sadista /sa'ðista/ mf sadist

sadístico /sa'ðistiko/ a sadistic

saduceo /saðu'θeo; saðu'seo/ **(-ea)** a Sadducean —n Sadducee

saeta /sa'eta/ f, arrow, dart; clock hand, watch hand; magnetic needle; short sung expression of religious ecstasy; *Astron.* Sagitta

saetada /sae'taða/ f, **saetazo** m, arrow wound

saetera /sae'tera/ f, loophole; small window

saetero /sae'tero/ a arrow, arrow-like. m, archer, bowman

sáfico /'safiko/ a Sapphic

saga /'saga/ f, saga

sagacidad /sagaθi'ðað; sagasi'ðað/ f, sagacity

sagaz /sa'gaθ; sa'gas/ a sagacious, shrewd; farseeing; quick on the scent (dogs)

sagital /sahi'tal/ a arrow-shaped

sagitario /sahi'tario/ m, archer; *Astron.* Sagittarius

sagrado /sa'graðo/ a sacred; holy; sacrosanct, venerable; accursed, detestable. m, sanctuary, refuge; haven

sagrario /sa'grario/ m, sanctuary; sacrarium

sagú /sa'gu/ m, sago

Sáhara, el /'saara, el/ the Sahara

sahornarse /saor'narse/ vr to chafe, grow sore

sahorno /sa'orno/ m, chafing, abrasion

sahumado /sau'maðo/ a improved, rendered more excellent; perfumed; fumigated

sahumador /sauma'ðor/ m, perfumer; fumigating vessel

sahumar /sau'mar/ vt to perfume; fumigate. See **desahuciar**

sahumerio /sau'merio/ m, perfuming; fumigation; fume, smoke

saín /sa'in/ m, fat, grease; sardine oil (for lamps); grease spot (on clothes)

sainar /sai'nar/ vt to fatten up (animals)

sainete /sai'nete/ m, *Cul.* sauce; *Theat.* one-act parody or burlesque; farce; delicacy, tidbit; delicate taste (of food)

sainetero /saine'tero/ m, writer of sainetes

sainetesco /saine'tesko/ a pertaining to sainetes; burlesque, satirical

sajar /sa'har/ vt *Surg.* to scarify

sajón /sa'hon/ **(-ona)** a and n Saxon

Sajonia /sa'honia/ Saxony

sal /sal/ f, salt; wit; grace, gracefulness. **s. de cocina,** common kitchen salt. **s. de la Higuera,** Epsom salts. **s. gema,** rock salt. **s. marina,** sea salt. **sales inglesas,** smelling salts. *Inf.* **estar hecho de s.,** to be full of wit. *Inf.* **hacerse s. y agua,** to melt away, disappear (of riches, etc.)

sala /'sala/ f, drawing room; large room, hall; *Law.* courtroom; *Law.* bench; **s. de apelación,** court of appeal. **s. de hospital,** hospital ward. **s. de justicia,** court of justice. **s. de lectura,** reading room. *Law.* **guardar s.,** to respect the court

salacidad /salaθi'ðað; salasi'ðað/ f, lewdness, salaciousness

saladar /sala'ðar/ m, salt marsh

saladero /sala'ðero/ m, salting or curing place; *West Hem.* meat packing factory

saladillo /sala'ðiʎo; sala'ðiyo/ m, salt pork

salado /sa'laðo/ a salty, briny; brackish; witty; attractive, amusing

salador /sala'ðor/ **(-ra)** a salting, curing —n salter, curer. m, curing place

saladura /sala'ðura/ f, salting, curing

salamandra /sala'mandra/ f, salamander; fire sprite

salar /sa'lar/ vt to salt; season with salt; oversalt; cure, pickle (meat, etc.)

salario /sa'lario/ m, salary

salaz /sa'laθ; sa'las/ a lewd, lecherous

salazón /sala'θon; sala'son/ f, salting, curing; salt meat or fish trade

salazonero /salaθo'nero; salaso'nero/ a salting, curing

salchicha /sal'tʃitʃa/ f, sausage

salchichería /saltʃitʃe'ria/ f, sausage shop

salchichero /saltʃi'tʃero/ **(-ra)** n sausage maker, sausage seller

salchichón /saltʃi'tʃon/ m, *Cul.* salami, kind of sausage

saldar /sal'dar/ vt *Com.* to settle, pay in full; sell out cheap; balance

saldista /sal'dista/ mf remnant buyer

saldo /'saldo/ m, *Com.* balance; closing of an account; bargain sale. **s. acreedor,** credit balance. **s. deudor,** debit balance. **s. líquido,** net balance

salero /sa'lero/ m, saltshaker, saltcellar; salt storage warehouse; *Inf.* wit

saleta /sa'leta/ f, *dim* small hall; royal antechamber; court of appeal

salida /sa'liða/ f, going out; leaving; departure; sailing; exit, way out; projection, protrusion; *Fig.* escape, way out; outcome, result; witty remark; *Mil.* sally; *Com.* outlay, expense; *Com.* opening, sale, salability; environs, outskirts. **s. de dólares,** dollar drain. **s. de tono,** *Inf.* an impertinent remark. **dar s.,** *Com.* to enter on the credit side

salidero /sali'ðero/ a fond of going out; m, exit, way out

salidizo /sali'ðiθo; sali'ðiso/ m, *Archit.* projection —a projecting

saliente /sa'liente/ a outgoing; salient, projecting. m, east; projection; salient. **s. continental,** continental shelf

salina /sa'lina/ f, salt mine; saltworks

salinero /sali'nero/ m, salt merchant; salter; salt worker

salino /sa'lino/ a saline. m, *Med.* saline

salir /sa'lir/ vi irr to go out; depart, leave; succeed in getting out; escape; appear (of the sun, etc.); sprout, show green; fade, come out (of stains); project, stand out; grow, develop; turn out, result; happen, take place; cost; sail; end (of seasons, time); lead off, start (some games); be published (books); do (well or badly), succeed or fail; appear, show oneself; be drawn, win (lottery tickets); balance, come out right (accounts); be elected; become; give up (posts); lead to (of streets, etc.); *Naut.* overtake; (*with prep a*) guarantee, be surety for; resemble, be like; (*with con*) utter, come out with; commit, do inopportunely; succeed in, achieve (e.g. *Salió con la suya,* He got his own way); (*with de*) originate in; break away from (traditions, conventions); get rid of; (*with por*) stand up for, protect; go surety for, guarantee —vr leak; boil over; overflow; (*with con*) achieve, get; (*with de*) *Fig.* break away from. *Theat.* **s. a la escena,** to enter, come on to the stage. **s. de,** to recover from (an illness). **no acabar de s.,** to not be completely recovered from. **s. del apuro,** to get out of trouble. **s. de estampía,** to stampede (of animals). **s. pitando,** *Inf.* to get out in a hurry. **Esta idea no salió de Juan,** This wasn't John's idea. **salga lo que saliere,** *Inf.* come what may... —*Pres. Indic.* **salgo, sales,** etc —*Fut.* **saldré,** etc —*Condit.* **saldría,** etc —*Pres. Subjunc.* **salga,** etc.

salitral /sali'tral/ a nitrous. m, saltpeter bed

salitre /sa'litre/ m, saltpeter

salitrería /salitre'ria/ f, saltpeter works

salitrero /sali'trero/ n saltpeter worker or dealer

saliva /sa'liβa/ f, saliva. Inf. **tragar s.**, to put up with; be unable to speak through emotion

salivación /saliβa'θion; saliβa'sion/ f, salivation

salival /sali'βal/ a salivary

salivar /sali'βar/ vi to salivate; spit

sallar /sa'ʎar; sa'yar/ vt to weed

salmantino /salman'tino/ **(-na)** a and n Salamanca

salmear /salme'ar/ vi to intone psalms

salmista /sal'mista/ mf psalmist; psalmodist, psalm chanter

salmo /'salmo/ m, psalm

salmodia /sal'moðia/ f, psalmody; Inf. drone; psalter

salmodiar /salmo'ðiar/ vi to chant psalms; —vt drone

salmón /sal'mon/ m, salmon

salmonado /salmo'naðo/ a salmon-like

salmonera /salmo'nera/ f, salmon net

salmonete /salmo'nete/ m, red mullet

salmuera /sal'muera/ f, brine

salobre /sa'loβre/ a salt, salty; brackish

salobridad /saloβri'ðað/ f, saltiness

salomar /salo'mar/ vi Naut. to sing chanteys

salón /sa'lon/ m, drawing room; large room or hall; reception room; salon, reception, social gathering. **s. de muestras,** showroom

saloncillo /salon'θiʎo; salon'siyo/ m, dim small room; Theat. greenroom; rest room

salpicadura /salpika'ðura/ f, sprinkling, spattering, splashing

salpicar /salpi'kar/ vt to sprinkle, scatter; bespatter, splash

salpicón /salpi'kon/ m, Cul. kind of salmagundi; Inf. hodgepodge; spattering

salpimentar /salpimen'tar/ vt irr to season with pepper and salt; sprinkle; Fig. leaven, enliven (a speech, etc.). See **regimentar**

salpresar /salpre'sar/ vt to preserve in salt, salt

salpullido /salpu'ʎiðo; salpu'yiðo/ m, rash, skin eruption

salsa /'salsa/ f, sauce; gravy. **s. mahonesa** or **s. mayonesa,** mayonnaise sauce. **s. mayordoma,** sauce maître d'hôtel

salsera /sal'sera/ f, sauce boat, gravy boat

saltabanco /salta'βanko/ m, mountebank; street entertainer, juggler

saltabarrancos /saltaβa'rrankos/ mf Inf. madcap, harum-scarum

saltable /sal'taβle/ a jumpable

saltadero /salta'ðero/ m, jumping ground; fountain, jet

saltador /salta'ðor/ **(-ra)** a jumping —n jumper; acrobat. m, jump rope, skip rope

saltamontes /salta'montes/ m, grasshopper

saltaojos /salta'ohos/ m, peony

saltaparedes /saltapa'reðes/ mf Inf. madcap, romp

saltar /sal'tar/ vi to jump, leap, spring; prance; frisk; gambol; rebound; blow up; burst, break asunder; pop (of corks); fly off, come off (buttons, etc.); gush out, shoot up (liquids); break apart, be shattered; be obvious, stand out; come to mind, suggest itself; show anger; Fig. let slip, come out with (remarks); —vt leap or jump over; poke out (eyes); cover (the female); omit, pass over; blow up, explode. **s. a la cuerda,** to jump rope, play with a skip rope. **s. a la vista,** to be obvious, leap to the eye. **s. diciendo,** Inf. to come out with, say

saltarín /salta'rin/ **(-ina)** a dancing —n dancer

saltatriz /salta'triθ; salta'tris/ f, ballet dancer, female acrobat

saltatumbas /salta'tumbas/ m, (Inf. contemptuous) cleric who makes his living off funerals

salteador /saltea'ðor/ m, highwayman

salteamiento /saltea'miento/ m, highway robbery, holdup; assault, attack

saltear /salte'ar/ vt to hold up and rob; assault, attack; jump from one thing to another, do intermittently; forestall; surprise, amaze

salterio /sal'terio/ m, psaltery

saltimbanco, saltimbanqui /saltim'βanko, saltim'βanki/ m, Inf.. See **saltabanco**

salto /'salto/ m, jump, leap, bound; leapfrog (game); precipice, ravine; waterfall; assault; important pro-motion; omission (of words). **s. de agua,** waterfall. **s. de cama,** peignoir, bathrobe. **s. de campana,** overturning. Inf. **s. de mal año,** sudden improvement in circumstances. **s. de mata,** flight, escape. **s. mortal,** leap of death; somersault. **s. de pie,** spillway. **dar un s.,** to leap. **en un s.,** at one jump; swiftly

saltón /sal'ton/ a jumping, leaping; prominent (teeth, eyes). m, grasshopper

salubérrimo /salu'βerrimo/ a superl **salubre** most healthy

salubre /sa'luβre/ a salubrious, healthful

salubridad /saluβri'ðað/ f, healthfulness

salud /sa'luð/ f, health; salvation; welfare, well-being; Eccl. state of grace; pl civilities, greetings. **¡S. y pesetas!** Here's to your good health and prosperity! (on drinking). **gastar s.,** to enjoy good health. Inf. **vender** (or **verter**) **s.,** to look full of health

saludable /salu'ðaβle/ a healthy, wholesome

saludador /saluða'ðor/ **(-ra)** a greeting, saluting —n greeter. m, charlatan, quack

saludar /salu'ðar/ vt to greet, salute; hail (as king, etc.); send greetings to; bow; Mil. fire a salute

saludo /sa'luðo/ m, greeting, salutation; bow; (Mil. Nav.) salute

salutación /saluta'θion; saluta'sion/ f, greeting, salutation; Ave Maria

salutífero /salu'tifero/ a salubrious

salva /'salβa/ f, salutation, greeting; (Mil. Nav.) salvo, volley; salute (of guns); salver; ordeal (to establish innocence); solemn assurance, oath; sampling, tasting (of food, drink). **s. de veintiún cañonazos,** twenty-one-gun salute

salvación /salβa'θion; salβa'sion/ f, liberation, deliverance; salvation

salvado /sal'βaðo/ m, bran

salvador /salβa'ðor/ **(-ra)** a saving, redeeming —n deliverer. m, redeemer

salvadoreño /salβaðore'ɲo/ **(-ña)** a and n Salvadorean

salvaguardia /salβa'guarðia/ m, guard, watch. f, safeguard; protection, defense; safe conduct, passport

salvajada /salβa'haða/ f, savagery, brutal action

salvaje /sal'βahe/ a wild (plants, animals); rough, uncultivated; uncultured, uncivilized. mf savage

salvajismo /salβa'hismo/ m, savagery

salvamano, a /salβa'mano, a/ adv safely

salvamente /salβa'mente/ adv safely, securely

salvamento /salβa'mento/ m, salvation; deliverance, security, safety; place of safety; salvage

salvante /sal'βante/ adv Inf. except, save

salvar /sal'βar/ vt to save; Eccl. redeem; avoid (difficulty, danger); exclude, except; leap, jump; pass over, clear; Law. prove innocent; Naut. salve. **s. la diferencia,** to bridge the gap —vi taste, sample (food, drink); —vr be saved from danger; Eccl. be redeemed

salvavidas /salβa'βiðas/ m, life belt; safety belt; life preserver; traffic island

¡salve! /'salβe/ interj Poet. hail!; Hail Mary, Salve Regina

salvedad /salβe'ðað/ f, qualification, reservation

salvia /'salβia/ f, Bot. sage

salvilla /sal'βiʎa; sal'βiya/ f, salver

salvo /'salβo/ a safe, unharmed; excepting, omitting —adv except. **a s.,** safely, without harm. **a su s.,** to his (her, their) satisfaction; at his (her, etc.) pleasure. **dejar a s.,** to exclude, leave aside. **en s.,** in safety

salvoconducto /salβokon'dukto/ m, safe conduct, pass

samarita /sama'rita/ a and mf **samaritano (-na)** a and n Samaritan

sambenito /sambe'nito/ m, penitent's gown (Inquisition); disgrace, dishonor

Samotracia /samo'traθia; samo'trasia/ Samothrace

samotracio /samo'traθio; samo'trasio/ **(-ia)** a and n Samothracian

samoyedo /samo'yeðo/ **(-da)** n Samoyed

san /san/ a Abbr. of **santo.** Used before masculine singular names of saints except **Santos Tomás** (or **Tomé), Domingo, Toribio**

sanable /sa'naβle/ a curable

sanador /sana'ðor/ **(-ra)** a healing, curing —n healer

sanalotodo /sanalo'toðo/ *m, Inf.* cure-all, universal remedy

sanar /sa'nar/ *vt* to cure, heal; —*vi* recover, get well; heal

sanatorio /sana'torio/ *m,* sanatorium; convalescent home

sanchopancesco /santʃopan'θesko; santʃopan'sesko/ *a* like or pertaining to Sancho Panza

sanción /san'θion; san'sion/ *f,* authorization, consent; sanction; penalty

sancionable /sanθio'naβle; sansio'naβle/ *a* sanctionable

sancionar /sanθio'nar; sansio'nar/ *vt* to authorize, approve; sanction

sancochar /sanko'tʃar/ *vt Cul.* to parboil, half-cook

sandalia /san'dalia/ *f,* sandal

sándalo /'sandalo/ *m,* sandalwood

sandez /san'deθ; san'des/ *f,* foolishness, stupidity; folly

sandía /san'dia/ *f,* watermelon

sandio /'sandio/ *a* foolish, inane

sandunga /san'duŋga/ *f, Inf.* attractiveness, winsomeness, grace

sandunguero /sanduŋ'guero/ *a Inf.* attractive, appealing, winsome

saneado /sane'aðo/ *a* unencumbered, nontaxable, free

saneamiento /sanea'miento/ *m,* guarantee, security; indemnity; stabilization (of currency); drainage

sanear /sane'ar/ *vt Com.* to guarantee, secure; indemnify; stabilize (currency); drain (land, etc.)

Sanedrín /sane'ðrin/ *m,* Sanhedrin

sangradera /saŋgra'ðera/ *f,* lancet; channel, sluice, drain

sangrador /saŋgra'ðor/ *m,* phlebotomist; outlet, drainage

sangradura /saŋgra'ðura/ *f,* inner bend of the arm; *Surg.* bleeding; draining off

sangrar /saŋ'grar/ *vt Surg.* to bleed; drain off; *Inf.* extort money, bleed; *Print.* indent; draw off resin (from pines, etc.); —*vi* bleed; —*vr* bleed; have oneself bled; run (of colors)

sangre /'saŋgre/ *f,* blood; lineage, family. **s. fría,** sang-froid. **a s. fría,** in cold blood, premeditated. **a s. y fuego,** by fire and sword, without quarter. *Inf.* **bullir la s.,** to have youthful blood in one's veins. **llevar en la s.,** *Fig.* to be in the blood. **subírsele la s. a la cabeza,** to grow excited. *Fig. Inf.* **tener s. de horchata,** to have milk and water in one's veins

sangría /saŋ'gria/ *f, Surg.* bloodletting; resin cut (on pines, etc.)

sangriento /saŋ'griento/ *a* bloody, bloodstained; bloodthirsty, cruel; mortal (insults, etc.); *Poet.* bloodcolored

sangüesa /saŋ'guesa/ *f,* raspberry

sanguijuela /saŋgi'huela/ *f,* leech; *Fig. Inf.* sponger

sanguina /saŋ'gina/ *f,* red crayon drawing, sanguine

sanguinaria /saŋgi'naria/ *f,* bloodstone

sanguinario /saŋgi'nario/ *a* vengeful, bloody, cruel

sanguíneo /saŋ'gineo/ *a* blood; sanguineous; sanguine, fresh-complexioned; blood-colored

sanguinolento /saŋgino'lento/ *a.* See **sangriento**

sanidad /sani'ðað/ *f,* safety, security; healthiness; health department. **s. interior,** Public Health. **S. militar,** army medical corps

sanitario /sani'tario/ *a* sanitary, hygienic. *m, Mil.* medical officer

sano /'sano/ *a* healthy; safe, secure; healthful, wholesome; unhurt, unharmed; upright, honest; sincere; *Inf.* entire, undamaged; sane. **s. y salvo,** safe and sound. *Inf.* **cortar por lo s.,** to cut one's losses

sánscrito /'sanskrito/ *a* and *m,* Sanscrit

santa /'santa/ *f,* female saint

santabárbara /santa'βarβara/ *f, Nav.* magazine

santamente /santa'mente/ *adv* in a saintly manner; simply

santero /san'tero/ **(-ra)** *a* given to image worship —*n* accomplice (of a burglar); caretaker (of a hermitage); beggar

¡Santiago! /san'tiago/ *interj* St. James! (Spanish war cry). *m,* attack, assault

santiamén /santia'men/ *m, Inf.* trice, twinkling

santidad /santi'ðað/ *f,* sanctity; saintliness; godliness. **Su S.,** His Holiness

santificación /santifika'θion; santifika'sion/ *f,* sanctification

santificador /santifika'ðor/ **(-ra)** *a* sanctifying —*n* sanctifier

santificar /santifi'kar/ *vt* to sanctify, make holy; consecrate; dedicate; keep (feast days)

santiguada /santi'guaða/ *f,* crossing oneself; rough treatment, harsh reproof

santiguar /santi'guar/ *vt* to make the sign of the cross over; *Inf.* beat, rain blows on; —*vr* cross oneself; *Inf.* be dumbfounded

santísimo /san'tisimo/ *a superl* most saintly, most holy

santo /'santo/ *a* holy; saintly; saint (see **san**); consecrated; inviolate, sacred; *Inf.* simple, sincere, ingenuous. *m,* saint; image of a saint; saint's day, name day (of a person); *Mil.* password. **Santa Hermandad,** Holy Brotherhood (former name of the Spanish rural police force). **S. Oficio,** Holy Office, Inquisition. **S. y bueno,** Well and good, All right! *Inf.* **alzarse con el s. y la limosna,** to take the lot, make off with everything. **llegar y besar el s.,** to do in a trice. *Inf.* **No es s. de mi devoción,** I'm not very keen on him. *Inf.* **todo el s. día,** the whole blessed day

santón /san'ton/ *m,* dervish, santon. *Inf.* hypocrite, sham saint

santoral /santo'ral/ *m,* book of saints; calendar of saints; choir book

santuario /san'tuario/ *m,* sanctuary

santurrón /santu'rron/ **(-ona)** *a* sanctimonious; hypocritical; prudish —*n* hypocrite

santurronería /santurrone'ria/ *f,* sanctimoniousness

saña /'saɲa/ *f,* fury, blind rage; lust for revenge, cruelty

sañoso, sañudo /sa'ɲoso, sa'ɲuðo/ *a* furious, blind with rage; cruel

sapidez /sapi'ðeθ; sapi'ðes/ *f,* flavor, sapidity

sápido /'sapiðo/ *a* tasty, savory

sapiencia /sa'pienθia; sa'piensia/ *f,* wisdom; knowledge; erudition

sapino /sa'pino/ *m,* fir (tree)

sapo /'sapo/ *m,* toad

saque /'sake/ *m, Sports.* serve, service; service or bowling line; *Sports.* server; *Sports.* bowler; bowling (in cricket)

saqueador /sakea'ðor/ **(-ra)** *a* looting, pillaging —*n* pillager, plunderer

saquear /sake'ar/ *vt* to pillage, plunder, sack

saqueo /sa'keo/ *m,* plundering, pillage, sacking

saquilada /saki'laða/ *f,* small sackful (especially of grain)

sarampión /saram'pion/ *m,* measles

sarao /sa'rao/ *m,* soirée, evening party

sarasa /sa'rasa/ *m,* (*Inf.* and contemptuous) pansy, faggot

sarcasmo /sar'kasmo/ *m,* sarcasm

sarcástico /sar'kastiko/ *a* sarcastic

sarcia /'sarθia; 'sarsia/ *f,* load, cargo

sarcófago /sar'kofago/ *m,* sarcophagus

sarda /'sarða/ *f,* mackerel

sardana /sar'ðana/ *f,* traditional Catalonian dance

sardina /sar'ðina/ *f,* sardine. **s. arenque,** herring. **como sardinas en banasta,** *Fig.* packed like sardines

sardinal /sarði'nal/ *m,* sardine net

sardinero /sarði'nero/ **(-ra)** *a* sardine —*n* sardine seller or dealer. *m,* famous district of Santander

sardineta /sarði'neta/ *f,* sprat; small sardine; *Mil.* chevron

sardo /'sarðo/ **(-da)** *a* and *n* Sardinian

sardónico /sar'ðoniko/ *a* sardonic

sarga /'sarga/ *f,* (silk) serge; willow

sargenta /sar'henta/ *f,* sergeant's wife; *Inf.* mannish, overbearing woman

sargentear /sarhente'ar/ *vt* to be in charge as a sergeant; command, captain; *Inf.* boss

sargento /sar'hento/ *m,* sergeant

sarmentoso /sarmen'toso/ *a* vine-like; twining

sarmiento /sar'miento/ *m,* vine shoot

sarna /'sarna/ *f*, scabies. **s. perruna,** mange. **más viejo que la s.,** *Inf.* older than the plague

sarnoso /sar'noso/ *a* itchy; mangy

sarraceno /sarra'θeno; sarra'seno/ **(-na)** *a* Saracen —*n* Saracen; Moor

sarracina /sarra'θina; sarra'sina/ *f*, scuffle

sarrillo /sa'rriʎo; sa'rriyo/ *m*, death rattle, rale; arum lily

sarro /'sarro/ *m*, furry encrustation, scale; film; tartar (on teeth)

sarta /'sarta/ *f*, string, link (of pearls, etc.); file, line

sartén /sar'ten/ *f*, frying pan. **tener la s. por el mango,** *Inf.* to be top dog

sastra /'sastra/ *f*, female tailor; tailor's wife

sastre /'sastre/ *m*, tailor. **ser buen s.,** *Inf.* to be an expert (in)

sastrería /sastre'ria/ *f*, tailoring; tailor's shop

Satanás /sata'nas/ *m*, Satan; devil

satánico /sa'taniko/ *a* satanic

satélite /sa'telite/ *m*, satellite; follower, admirer, sycophant

satén /sa'ten/ *m*, sateen

satinar /sati'nar/ *vt* to calender; glaze; satin (paper)

sátira /'satira/ *f*, satire

satírico /sa'tiriko/ *a* satiric

satirizar /satiri'θar; satiri'sar/ *vi* to write satires; —*vt* satirize

sátiro /'satiro/ *m*, satyr; *Theat.* indecent play

satisfacción /satisfak'θion; satisfak'sion/ *f*, settlement, payment; atonement, expiation; satisfaction; gratification; amends; complacency, conceit; contentment; apology. **tomar s.,** to avenge oneself

satisfacer /satisfa'θer; satisfa'ser/ *vt irr* to pay, settle; atone for, expiate; gratify; quench; fulfill, observe; compensate, indemnify; discharge, meet; convince, persuade; allay, relieve; reward; explain; answer, satisfy; —*vr* avenge oneself; satisfy oneself —*Pres. Indic.* **satisfago, satisfaces,** etc —*Fut.* **satisfaré,** etc —*Condit.* **satisfaría,** etc —*Preterite* **satisfice,** etc —*Past Part.* **satisfecho.** *Pres. Subjunc.* **satisfaga,** etc —*Imperf. Subjunc.* **satisficiese,** etc.

satisfactorio /satisfak'torio/ *a* satisfactory

satisfecho /satis'fetʃo/ *a* self-satisfied, complacent; happy, contented

sátrapa /'satrapa/ *m*, satrap; *Inf.* cunning fellow

saturación /satura'θion; satura'sion/ *f*, saturation

saturar /satu'rar/ *vt* to satiate, fill; saturate

saturnino /satur'nino/ *a* saturnine, melancholy, morose

saturnismo /satur'nismo/ *m*, saturnism, lead poisoning

Saturno /sa'turno/ *m*, Saturn

sauce /'sauθe; 'sause/ *m*, willow. **s. llorón,** weeping willow

saúco /sa'uko/ *m*, elder tree

saurio /'saurio/ *a* and *m*, saurian

savia /'saβia/ *f*, sap; energy, zest

sáxeo /'sakseo/ *a* stone, stony

saxófono /sak'sofono/ *or* **saxofón** *m*, saxophone

saya /'saya/ *f*, skirt; long tunic

sayal /sa'yal/ *m*, thick woolen material

sayo /'sayo/ *m*, loose smock; *Inf.* any garment. **cortar un s. (a),** *Inf.* to gossip behind a person's back

sayón /sa'yon/ *m*, executioner; *Inf.* hideous-looking man

sazón /sa'θon; sa'son/ *f*, ripeness, maturity; season; perfection, excellence; opportunity; taste, flavor; seasoning. **a la s.,** at that time, then. **en s.,** in season; opportunely

sazonador /saθona'ðor; sasona'ðor/ **(-ra)** *a* seasoning —*n* seasoner

sazonar /saθo'nar; saso'nar/ *vt Cul.* to season; mature; —*vr* mature, ripen

se /se/ *object pron reflexive 3rd sing* and *pl mf* 1. Used as accusative (direct object) himself, herself, yourself, themselves, yourselves (e.g. *Juan se ha cortado,* John has cut himself). 2. Used as dative or indirect object to himself, at himself, herself, themselves, etc. (e.g. *María se mira al espejo,* Mary looks at herself in the mirror). Reciprocity is also expressed by reflexive (e.g. *No se hablan,* They do not speak to one an-

other). When a direct object pron. (accusative) and an indirect object pron., both in the 3rd pers. (sing. or pl.), are used together, the indirect object pron. becomes **se** (instead of **le** or **les**) (e.g. *Se lo doy,* I give it to him). Many Spanish reflexive verbs have English equivalents that are not reflexive (e.g. *desayunarse,* to breakfast, *arrepentirse,* to repent, *quejarse,* to complain). Some intransitive (neuter) verbs have a modified meaning when used reflexively (e.g. *marcharse,* to go away, *dormirse,* to fall asleep). The passive may be formed by using **se** + 3rd pers. sing. of verb (e.g. *se dice,* it is said, people say). A number of impersonal phrases are also formed in this way (e.g. *«Se alquila,»* "To Let," *«Se vende,»* "For Sale"). The imperative is used in the same way (e.g. *Véase la página dos,* See page two)

sebáceo /se'βaθeo; se'βaseo/ *a* sebaceous

sebo /'seβo/ *m*, tallow; candle grease; fat, grease

seboso /se'βoso/ *a* tallowy; fat, greasy

seca /'seka/ *f*, drought; *Naut.* unsubmerged sandbank

secadero /seka'ðero/ *m*, drying place, drying room

secadora /seka'ðora/ *f*, dryer, drying machine, clothesdryer. **s. de cabello,** hairdryer

secafirmas /seka'firmas/ *m*, blotting pad

secamente /seka'mente/ *adv* tersely, brusquely, curtly; dryly

secamiento /seka'miento/ *m*, drying

secano /se'kano/ *m*, nonirrigated land; *Naut.* unsubmerged sandbank; anything very dry

secante /se'kante/ *a* drying —*a* and *f*, *Geom.* secant. **papel s.,** blotting paper

secar /se'kar/ *vt* to dry; desiccate; annoy, bore; —*vr* dry; dry up (of streams, etc.); wilt, fade (of plants); become parched; grow thin, become emaciated; be very thirsty; become hard-hearted

sección /sek'θion; sek'sion/ *f*, act of cutting; section, part, portion; *Geom. Mil.* section. **s. cónica,** conic section. **s. de amenidades,** entertainment section (of a newspaper). **s. de reserva,** *Mil.* reserve list

seccionar /sekθio'nar; seksio'nar/ *vt* to divide into sections, section

seccionario /sekθio'nario; seksio'nario/ *a* sectional

secesión /seθe'sion; sese'sion/ *f*, secession

secesionista /seθesio'nista; sesesio'nista/ *a* and *mf* secessionist

seco /'seko/ *a* dry; dried up, parched; faded, wilted; dead (plants); dried (fruits); thin, emaciated; unadorned; barren, arid; brusque, curt; severe, strict; indifferent, unenthusiastic; sharp (sounds); dry (wines). **a secas,** only; solely; simply, just. **en s.,** on dry land; curtly. *Inf.* **dejar s. (a),** to dumbfound, petrify

secreción /sekre'θion; sekre'sion/ *f*, segregation, separation; *Med.* secretion

secreta /se'kreta/ *f*, *Law.* secret trial or investigation; *Eccl.* secret(s); toilet, water closet

secretar /sekre'tar/ *vt Med.* to secrete

secretaría /sekreta'ria/ *f*, secretaryship; secretary's office, secretariat

secretario /sekre'tario/ **(-ia)** *n* secretary; amanuensis, clerk. *m*, actuary; registrar. **s. de asuntos exteriores** *or* **s. de asuntos extranjeros,** foreign secretary. **s. particular,** private secretary

secretear /sekrete'ar/ *vi Inf.* to whisper, have secrets

secreteo /sekre'teo/ *m*, *Inf.* whispering, exchanging of secrets

secreto /se'kreto/ *m*, secret; secrecy, silence; confidential information; mystery; secret drawer —*a* secret; private, confidential. **en s.,** in secret, confidentially. **s. a voces,** open secret

secta /'sekta/ *f*, sect

sectario /sek'tario/ **(-ia)** *a* and *n* sectarian —*n* fanatical believer

sectarismo /sekta'rismo/ *m*, sectarianism

sector /sek'tor/ *m*, sector

secuaz /se'kuaθ; se'kuas/ *mf* follower, disciple

secuela /se'kuela/ *f*, sequel, result

secuencia /se'kuenθia; se'kuensia/ *f*, *Eccl.* sequence; (cinema) sequence

secuestrador /sekuestra'ðor/ **(-ra)** *a* sequestrating —*n* sequestrator

secuestrar /sekues'trar/ *vt* to sequester; kidnap

secuestro /se'kuestro/ *m*, sequestration; kidnapping; *Surg.* sequestrum

secular /seku'lar/ *a* secular, lay; centennial; age-old, ancient; *Eccl.* secular

secularización /sekulariθa'θion/ sekularisa'sion/ *f*, secularization

secularizar /sekulari'θar/ sekulari'sar/ *vt* to secularize; —*vr* become secularized

secundar /sekun'dar/ *vt* to second, aid

secundario /sekun'dario/ *a* secondary; accessory, subordinate; *Geol.* mesozoic

sed /seð/ *f*, thirst; desire, yearning, appetite. **apagar** (*or* **matar**) **la s.**, to quench one's thirst. **tener s.**, to be thirsty

seda /'seða/ *f*, silk; bristle (boar, etc.). **s. cordelada**, twist silk. **s. ocal**, floss silk. **s. vegetal** *or* **s. artificial**, artificial silk. *Inf.* **como una s.**, as smooth as silk; sweet-tempered; achieved without any trouble

sedación /seða'θion/ seða'sion/ *f*, calming, soothing

sedal /se'ðal/ *m*, fish line

sedar /se'ðar/ *vt* to soothe, calm

sedativo /seða'tiβo/ *a* and *m*, *Med.* sedative

sede /'seðe/ *f*, *Eccl.* see; bishop's throne; *Fig.* seat (of government, etc.); Holy See (also **Santa S.**)

sedentario /seðen'tario/ *a* sedentary

sedeño /se'ðeɲo/ *a* silky; silken, made of silk

sedería /seðe'ria/ *f*, silk goods; silks; silk shop

sedero /se'ðero/ **(-ra)** *a* silk —*n* silk weaver or worker; silk merchant

sedición /seði'θion/ seði'sion/ *f*, sedition

sedicioso /seði'θioso/ seði'sioso/ *a* seditious

sediento /se'ðiento/ *a* thirsty; parched, dry (land); eager (for), desirous (of)

sedimentación /seðimenta'θion/ seðimenta'sion/ *f*, sedimentation

sedimentar /seðimen'tar/ *vt* to leave a sediment; —*vr* settle, form a sediment

sedimento /seði'mento/ *m*, sediment; dregs, lees; scale (on boilers)

sedoso /se'ðoso/ *a* silky, silk-like

seducción /seðuk'θion/ seðuk'sion/ *f*, seduction; temptation, blandishment, wile; charm, allurement

seducir /seðu'θir/ seðu'sir/ *vt irr* to seduce; tempt, lead astray; charm, attract; corrupt, bribe. See **conducir**

seductivo /seðuk'tiβo/ *a* tempting; seductive, charming

seductor /seðuk'tor/ **(-ra)** *a* tempting; charming —*n* seducer; charming person

sefardí /sefar'ði/ *mf* Iberian Jew or Jewess; *pl* Sephardim —*a* Sephardic

segadera /sega'ðera/ *f*, sickle

segadero /sega'ðero/ *a* reapable, able to be reaped

segador /sega'ðor/ *m*, reaper, harvester

segadora /sega'ðora/ *f*, mowing machine, harvester; woman harvester

segar /se'gar/ *vt irr* to scythe, cut down; reap, harvest; mow. See **cegar**

seglar /seg'lar/ *a* secular, lay. *mf* layman

segmento /seg'mento/ *m*, segment; *Geom.* segment. **s. de émbolo**, piston ring

segoviano /sego'βiano/ **(-na)** *a* and *n* Segovian

segregación /segrega'θion; segrega'sion/ *f*, segregation

segregar /segre'gar/ *vt* to segregate, separate; *Med.* secrete

seguida /se'giða/ *f*, continuation, prolongation. **de s.**, continuously; immediately. **en s.**, at once, immediately

seguidamente /segiða'mente/ *adv* continuously; immediately

seguidilla /segi'ðiʎa; segi'ðiya/ *f*, popular Spanish tune and dance and verse sung to them; *Inf.* diarrhea

seguido /se'giðo/ *a* continuous, successive; direct, straight

seguidor /segi'ðor/ **(-ra)** *a* following —*n* follower, disciple

seguimiento /segi'miento/ *m*, following, pursuit; continuation, resumption

seguir /se'gir/ *vt irr* to follow; go after, pursue; prosecute, execute; continue, go on; accompany, go with;

exercise (a profession); subscribe to, believe in; agree with; persecute; pester, annoy; imitate; *Law.* institute (a suit); handle, manage; —*vr* result, follow as a consequence; follow in order, happen by turn; originate —*Pres. Part.* **siguiendo**. *Pres. Indic.* **sigo, sigues, sigue, siguen**. *Pres. Subjunc.* **siga**, etc —*Imperf. Subjunc.* **siguiese**

según /se'gun/ *adv* according to; as. **s. parece**, as it seems. **s. y como**, as, according to

segunda /se'gunda/ *f*, *Mus.* second

segundar /segun'dar/ *vt* to repeat, do again; —*vi* be second, follow the first

segundero /segun'dero/ *a Agr.* of the second flowering or fruiting. *m*, second hand (of a watch)

segundo /se'gundo/ *a* second. *m*, second in command, deputy head; *Astron. Geom.* second. **segunda intención**, double meaning. **segunda velocidad**, *Auto.* second gear. **de segunda mano**, second-hand. **sin s.**, without peer or equal

segundogénito /segundo'henito/ **(-ta)** *a* and *n* secondborn

segundón /segun'don/ *m*, second son; any son but the eldest

segurador /segura'ðor/ *m*, surety, security (person)

seguramente /segura'mente/ *adv* securely, safely; surely, of course, naturally

seguridad /seguri'ðað/ *f*, security; safety; certainty; trustworthiness; *Com.* surety. **con toda s.**, with complete safety, surely, absolutely. **de s.**, *a* safety

seguro /se'guro/ *a* secure; safe; certain, sure; firm, fixed; reliable, trustworthy; unfailing. *m*, certainty; haven, place of safety; *Com.* insurance; permit; *Mech.* ratchet. **s. contra incendio, accidentes, robo**, fire, accident, burglary insurance. **s. sobre la vida**, life insurance. **de s.**, surely, certainly. **en s.**, in safety

seis /seis/ *a* six; sixth. *m*, six; sixth (of the month); playing card or domino with six spots. **Son las s.**, It is six o'clock

seiscientos /seis'θientos; seis'sientos/ *a* six hundred; six-hundredth. *m*, six hundred

selección /selek'θion; selek'sion/ *f*, selection, choice. **s. natural**, natural selection

seleccionar /selekθio'nar; seleksio'nar/ *vt* to select, choose

selectivo /selek'tiβo/ *a* selective

selecto /se'lekto/ *a* choice, select, excellent

sellador /seʎa'ðor; seya'ðor/ **(-ra)** *a* sealing, stamping —*n* sealer, stamper

selladura /seʎa'ðura; seya'ðura/ *f*, sealing, stamping

sellar /se'ʎar; se'yar/ *vt* to seal; stamp; end, conclude; close

sello /'seʎo; 'seyo/ *m*, seal; stamp. **s. fiscal**, stamp duty. **s. postal**, postage stamp

selva /'selβa/ *f*, forest, wood; jungle

Selva Negra, la /'selβa 'negra, la/ the Black Forest

selvático /sel'βatiko/ *a* sylvan, wood, forest; wild

selvoso /sel'βoso/ *a* wooded, sylvan

semafórico /sema'foriko/ *a* semaphoric

semáforo /se'maforo/ *m*, semaphore, traffic light.

semana /se'mana/ *f*, week; week's salary. **S. Mayor** *or* **S. Santa**, Holy Week. **entre s.**, during the week, on weekdays; weekdays

semanal /sema'nal/ *a* weekly; of a week's duration

semanario /sema'nario/ *a* weekly. *m*, weekly periodical

semanero /sema'nero/ *a* employed by the week

semántica /se'mantika/ *f*, semantics

semántico /se'mantiko/ *a* semantic

semblante /sem'βlante/ *m*, facial expression, countenance; face; appearance, look, aspect. **componer el s.**, to pull oneself together, straighten one's face. **mudar de s.**, to change color, change one's expression; alter (of circumstances)

semblanza /sem'βlanθa; sem'βlansa/ *f*, biographical sketch. **s. literaria**, short literary biography

sembradera /sembra'ðera/ *f*, sowing machine

sembradío /sembra'ðio/ *a Agr.* ready for sowing

sembrado /sem'βraðo/ *m*, sown land

sembrador /sembra'ðor/ **(-ra)** *a* sowing —*n* sower

sembradura /sembra'ðura/ *f*, *Agr.* sowing

sembrar /sem'βrar/ *vt irr Agr.* to sow; scatter, sprinkle; spread, disseminate. See **sentar**

semeja /se'meha/ f, resemblance, similarity; indication, sign (gen. pl)
semejante /seme'hante/ a like, similar; such a; Math. similar. m, similarity, imitation. mf fellow man
semejanza /seme'hanθa; seme'hansa/ f, similarity, likeness. **a s. de**, in the likeness of; like
semejar /seme'har/ (**se**) vi and vr to resemble
semen /'semen/ m, semen; Bot. seed
semental /semen'tal/ a Agr. seed; breeding (of male animals). m, stallion
sementar /semen'tar/ vt Agr. to sow
sementera /semen'tera/ f, Agr. sowing; sown land; seedbed; seedtime; Fig. hotbed, nursery, genesis
sementero /semen'tero/ m, seed bag; seed bed
semestral /semes'tral/ a biannual, half-yearly; lasting six months
semestre /se'mestre/ a biannual. m, half-year, period of six months; six months' salary; semester
semicircular /semiθirku'lar; semisirku'lar/ a semicircular
semicírculo /semi'θirkulo; semi'sirkulo/ m, semicircle
semidifunto /semiði'funto/ a half-dead
semidiós /semi'ðios/ m, demigod
semidiosa /semi'ðiosa/ f, demigoddess
semidormido /semiðor'miðo/ a half-asleep
semiesférico /semies'feriko/ a hemispherical
semilla /se'miʎa; se'miya/ f, Bot. seed; Fig. germ, genesis
semillero /semi'ʎero; semi'yero/ m, seedbed; nursery; Fig. hotbed, origin
semilunio /semi'lunio/ m, Astron. half-moon
seminario /semi'nario/ m, seedbed; nursery; genesis, origin; seminary; tutorial. **s. conciliar**, theological seminary
seminarista /semina'rista/ mf seminarist
semiótica /semi'otika/ f, Med. symptomatology; semiotics
semita /se'mita/ mf Semite —a Semitic
semítico /se'mitiko/ a Semitic
semitismo /semi'tismo/ m, Semitism
semitono /semi'tono/ m, Mus. semitone
semitransparente /semitranspa'rente/ a semitransparent
semivivo /semi'βiβo/ a half-alive
sémola /'semola/ f, semolina
sempiterna /sempi'terna/ f, everlasting flower; thick woolen material
sempiterno /sempi'terno/ a eternal
sen /sen/ m, senna
Sena, el /'sena, el/ the Seine
sena /'sena/ f, Bot. senna; six-spotted die
senado /se'naðo/ m, senate; senate house; any grave assembly
senador /sena'ðor/ m, senator
senaduría /sena'ðuria/ f, senatorship
senario /se'nario/ a senary
senatorio /sena'torio/ a senatorial
sencillez /senθi'ʎeθ; sensi'yes/ f, simplicity; naturalness; easiness; ingenuousness, candor
sencillo /sen'θiʎo; sen'siyo/ a simple; unmixed; natural; thin, light (fabric); easy; ingenuous, candid; unadorned, plain; single; sincere
senda /'senda/ f, path, footpath; way; means
senderear /sendere'ar/ vt to conduct along a path; make a pathway; —vi attain by tortuous means
sendero /sen'dero/ m, footpath, path
sendos, sendas /'sendos, 'sendas/ a m, and f pl, one each (e.g. Les dio sendos lápices, He gave them each a pencil)
senectud /senek'tuð/ f, old age
senegalés /senega'les/ (**-esa**) a and n Senegalese
senescal /senes'kal/ m, seneschal
senil /se'nil/ a senile
senilidad /senili'ðað/ f, senility
seno /'seno/ m, hollow; hole; concavity; bosom, breast; chest; uterus, womb; any internal cavity of the body; bay, cove; lap (of a woman); interior (of anything), heart; gulf; Math. sine; Anat. sinus
sensación /sensa'θion; sensa'sion/ f, sensation

sensacional /sensaθio'nal; sensasio'nal/ a sensational
sensacionalista /sensaθiona'lista; sensasiona'lista/ a sensationalist
sensatez /sensa'teθ; sensa'tes/ f, prudence, good sense
sensato /sen'sato/ a prudent, wise
sensibilidad /sensiβili'ðað/ f, sensibility
sensibilizar /sensiβili'θar; sensiβili'sar/ vt Photo. to sensitize
sensible /sen'siβle/ a sensible, sensitive; tender, feeling; perceptible; noticeable, definite; sensitive; sad, regrettable
sensiblemente /sensiβle'mente/ adv appreciably; perceptibly; painfully, sadly
sensiblería /sensiβle'ria/ f, sentimentality, sentimentalism
sensiblero /sensi'βlero/ a oversentimental
sensitiva /sensi'tiβa/ f, sensitive plant, mimosa
sensitivo /sensi'tiβo/ a sensuous; sensitive, sensible
sensorio /sen'sorio/ a sensory. m, sensorium
sensual /sen'sual/ a sensual; sensitive, sensible; carnal, voluptuous
sensualidad /sensuali'ðað/ f, sensuality; sensualism
sensualismo /sensua'lismo/ m, sensualism; Philos. sensationalism
sensualista /sensua'lista/ mf Philos. sensationalist; sensualist
sentadero /senta'ðero/ m, resting place, improvised seat
sentado /sen'taðo/ a prudent, circumspect
sentar /sen'tar/ vt ir to seat; —vi Inf. suit, agree with (e.g. No me sienta este clima (este plato), This climate (dish) doesn't suit me); fit, become; Inf. please, satisfy, be agreeable to; —vr sit down; Inf. leave a mark on the skin —Pres. Ind. **siento, sientas, sienta, sientan. Pres. Subjunc. siente, sientes, siente, sienten**
sentencia /sen'tenθia; sen'tensia/ f, opinion, belief; maxim; Law. verdict, sentence; decision, judgment. Law. **fulminar** (or **pronunciar**) **la s.**, to pass sentence
sentenciador /sentenθia'ðor; sentensia'ðor/ a Law. sentencing
sentenciar /senten'θiar; senten'siar/ vt Law. to sentence; Inf. destine, intend
sentencioso /senten'θioso; senten'sioso/ a sententious
sentidamente /sentiða'mente/ adv feelingly; sadly, regretfully
sentido /sen'tiðo/ m, sense (hearing, seeing, touch, smell, taste); understanding, sense; meaning, interpretation, signification; perception, discrimination; judgment; direction, way —a and past part felt; expressive; hypersensitive, touchy. **s. común**, common sense. **costar un s.**, Fig. Inf. to cost a fortune. **perder el s.**, to lose consciousness
sentimental /sentimen'tal/ a emotional; sentimental; romantic
sentimentalismo /sentimenta'lismo/ m, emotional quality; sentimentalism
sentimiento /senti'miento/ m, feeling, sentiment; sensation, impression; grief, sorrow. **Le acompaño a usted en su s.,** I sympathize with you in your sorrow (bereavement)
sentina /sen'tina/ f, well (of a ship); Naut. bilge; cesspool; sink of iniquity
sentir /sen'tir/ vt irr to feel, experience; hear; appreciate; grieve, regret; believe, consider; envisage, foresee; —vr complain; suffer; think or consider oneself; crack; feel, be; go rotten, decay (gen. with estar + Past Part.). m, view, opinion; feeling. **sin s.,** without feeling; without noticing —Pres. Part. **sintiendo.** Pres. Indic. **siento, sientes, siente, sienten.** Preterite **sintió, sintieron.** Pres. Subjunc. **sienta, sientas, sienta, sintamos, sintáis, sientan.** Imperf. Subjunc. **sintiese,** etc.
seña /'seña/ f, sign, mark; gesture; Mil. password; signal; pl address, domicile. **s. mortal,** definite or unmistakable sign. **dar señas,** to show signs, manifest. **hablar por señas,** to converse by signs
señal /se'ñal/ f, mark, sign; boundary stone; landmark; scar; signal; trace, vestige; indication, symp-

tom, token; symbol, sign; image, representation; prodigy, marvel; deposit, advance payment. **s. de aterrizaje,** *Aer.* landing signal. **s. de niebla,** fog signal. **señales horarias,** *Radio.* time signal. **en s.,** as a sign, in proof of. **s. luminosa de la circulación,** traffic light, traffic robot

señaladamente /seɲalaða'mente/ *adv* especially, particularly, notably

señalado /seɲa'laðo/ *a* famous, distinguished; important, notable

señalador /seɲala'ðor/ *m,* *Argentina* bookmark

señalamiento /seɲala'miento/ *m,* marking; pointing out; appointment, designation

señalar /seɲa'lar/ *vt* to mark; indicate, point out; fix, arrange; wound; signal; stamp; appoint (to office); —*vr* excel

señero /se'ɲero/ *a* solitary, isolated

señor /se'ɲor/ *a* *Inf.* gentlemanly. *m,* owner, master; mister, esquire; **(S.)** the Lord; lord, sire. **s. de horca y cuchillo,** feudal lord, lord of life and death

señora /se'ɲora/ *f,* lady; owner, mistress; madam; wife. **s. de compañía,** chaperon; lady companion. **Nuestra S.,** Our Lady

señorear /seɲore'ar/ *vt* to control, run, manage; master; domineer; appropriate, seize; dominate, overlook; restrain (emotions); —*vr* behave with dignity

señoría /seɲo'ria/ *f,* lordship (title and person); lordship, jurisdiction; area, territory; control, restraint

señoría /seɲo'ria/ *f,* dignity, sedateness; self-control

señorial /seɲo'rial/ *a* manorial; noble, dignified, lordly

señoril /seɲo'ril/ *a* lordly, noble, aristocratic

señorío /seɲo'rio/ *m,* lordship; jurisdiction, dominion

señorita /seɲo'rita/ *f,* young lady; miss; *Inf.* mistress of the house

señorito /seɲo'rito/ *m,* young gentleman; *Inf.* master of the house; master (address); *Inf.* young man about town

señuelo /se'ɲuelo/ *m,* decoy; bait; allurement, attraction. **caer en el s.,** *Fig. Inf.* to fall into the trap

sepancuantos /sepan'kuantos/ *m,* *Inf.* scolding, rebuke; spanking

separación /separa'θion; separa'sion/ *f,* separation

separado /sepa'raðo/ *a* separate

separador /separa'ðor/ **(-ra)** *a* separating —*n* separator. *m,* filter. **s. de aceite,** oil filter

separar /sepa'rar/ *vt* to separate; divide; dismiss (from a post); lay aside; —*vr* retire, resign; separate

separatismo /separa'tismo/ *m,* separatism

separatista /separa'tista/ *a* and *mf* separatist

septeno /sep'teno/ *a.* See **séptimo**

septentrión /septen'trion/ *m,* *Astron.* Great Bear; north

septentrional /septentrio'nal/ *a* north; northern

septeto /sep'teto/ *m,* septet

septicemia /septi'θemia; septi'semia/ *f,* septicemia

séptico /'septiko/ *a* septic

septiembre /sep'tiembre/ *m,* September

septillo /sep'tiʎo; sep'tiyo/ *m,* *Mus.* septuplet

séptima /'septima/ *f,* *Mus.* seventh

séptimo /'septimo/ *a* and *m,* seventh

septuagenario /septuahe'nario/ **(-ia)** *a* and *n* septuagenarian

septuagésimo /septua'hesimo/ *a* seventieth; septuagesimal. *m,* seventieth

séptuplo /'septuplo/ *a* sevenfold

sepulcral /sepul'kral/ *a* sepulchral

sepulcro /se'pulkro/ *m,* sepulcher

sepultador /sepulta'ðor/ **(-ra)** *a* burying —*n* gravedigger; burier

sepultar /sepul'tar/ *vt* to inter, bury; hide, cover up

sepultura /sepul'tura/ *f,* interment; grave; tomb

sepulturero /sepultu'rero/ *m,* gravedigger

sequedad /seke'ðað/ *f,* dryness, barrenness; acerbity, sharpness

sequía /se'kia/ *f,* drought

séquito /'sekito/ *m,* following, suite, retinue; general approval, popularity

ser /ser/ *m,* essence, nature; being; existence, life. **El S. Supremo,** The Supreme Being, God

ser /ser/ *vi irr* to be (e.g. *El sombrero es azul,* The hat

is blue). **Ser** may agree with either subject or complement, though when latter is *pl* the verb tends to be so too (e.g. *Son las once, (horas),* It is eleven o'clock. **Cien libras son poco dinero,** A hundred pounds is a small amount). If verbal complement is pers. pron., **ser** agrees with it both in number and person (e.g. *Son ellos,* It is they. *Soy yo,* It is I). In impers. phrases the pron. is not expressed (e.g. *Es difícil,* It is difficult. *Es sorprendente,* It is surprising). **ser** means to exist (e.g. *Pienso luego soy,* I think, therefore I am). **ser** (also **ser de** with nouns or obj. prons.) means to belong to, be the property of (e.g. *Este gato es mío,* This cat is mine. *El libro es de Juan,* The book belongs to John). Signifies to happen, occur (e.g. *¿Cómo fue eso?* How did that happen?). Means to be suitable or fitting (e.g. *Este vestido no es para una señora mayor,* This dress is not suitable for an elderly lady). Expresses price, to be worth (e.g. *¿A cuánto es la libra?* How much is it a pound?; How much is the pound (sterling) worth?). Means to be a member of, belong to (e.g. *Es de la Academia Española,* He is a member of the Spanish Academy). Means to be of use, be useful for (e.g. *Esta casa no es para una familia numerosa,* This house is no use for a large family). **Ser** expresses nationality (e.g. *Son francesas,* They are French. *Somos de Londres,* We are from London) —Auxiliary verb used to form passive tense (e.g. *Esta historia ha sido leída por muchos,* This story has been read by many. *Fueron mandados al Japón,* They were sent to Japan. **s. de ver,** to be worth seeing. **s. para poco,** to be of little use, amount to little. **s. testigo de,** to witness. *¿Cómo es eso!* How can that be! Surely not! *¡Cómo ha de s.!* How should it be!; One must resign oneself. *Érase una vez or que érase,* Once upon a time. *es a saber,* viz., that is to say, *un sí es no es,* a touch of, a suspicion of) —Pres. Part. **siendo.** Pres. Indic. **soy, eres, es, somos, sois, son.** Fut. **seré,** etc —Condit. **sería,** etc —Preterite **fui, fuiste, fue, fuimos, fuisteis, fueron.** Imperf. **era,** etc —Past Part. **sido.** Pres. Subjunc. **sea,** etc —Imperf. Subjunc. **fuese,** etc —Imperat. **sé**

sera /'sera/ *f,* large frail

seráfico /se'rafiko/ *a* seraphic

serafín /sera'fin/ *m,* seraphim

serbal /ser'βal/ *m,* service tree

serena /se'rena/ *f,* serenade; *Inf.* dew

serenar /sere'nar/ *vt* to soothe; clear; —*vr* grow calm; clear up (weather); clear (liquids); be soothed or pacified

serenata /sere'nata/ *f,* serenade

serenidad /sereni'ðað/ *f,* serenity, composure, tranquility; Serene Highness (title)

sereno /se'reno/ *a* cloudless, fair; composed, serene. *m,* dew; night watchman

sericultor /serikul'tor/ *m,* silk cultivator, sericulturist

sericultura /serikul'tura/ *f,* silk culture

serie /'serie/ *f,* series, sequence, succession; *Math.* progression; (*Biol. Elec.*) series; break (in billiards)

seriedad /serie'ðað/ *f,* seriousness, earnestness; gravity; austerity; sternness; importance; sincerity; solemnity

serigrafía /serigra'fia/ *f,* silkscreen printing

serio /'serio/ *a* serious, earnest; grave; austere; stern; important; sincere, genuine; solemn. **en s.,** seriously

sermón /ser'mon/ *m,* sermon; scolding. **dar un s.,** to give a sermon; scold

sermonar /sermo'nar/ *vi* to preach

sermonear /sermone'ar/ *vi* to preach sermons; —*vt* scold

sermoneo /sermo'neo/ *m,* *Inf.* scolding

seroja /se'roha/ *f,* withered leaves; brushwood

serpear /serpe'ar/ *vi* to wind, twist; wriggle, squirm; coil

serpenteado /serpente'aðo/ *a* winding

serpentear /serpente'ar/ *vi* to wind, twist, meander; stagger along; wriggle; coil; *Aer.* yaw

serpenteo /serpen'teo/ *m,* winding, twisting; wriggling; coiling; *Aer.* yaw

serpentín /serpen'tin/ *m,* *Chem.* worm; coil (in industry); *Mineral.* serpentine

serpentina /serpen'tina/ *f,* *Mineral.* serpentine; paper streamer

serpentino /serpen'tino/ a serpentine; *Poet.* winding, sinuous

serpiente /ser'piente/ f, snake, serpent; Satan, the Devil; *Astron.* Serpent. **s. de anteojos,** cobra. **s. de cascabel,** rattlesnake

serpollo /ser'poʎo; ser'poyo/ m, *Bot.* shoot, new branch; sprout; sucker

serrado /se'rraðo/ a serrate

serrallo /se'rraʎo; se'rrayo/ m, harem, seraglio; brothel

serrana, serranilla /se'rrana; serra'niʎa, serra'niya/ f, pastoral poem

serranía /serra'nia/ f, mountainous territory

serrano /se'rrano/ **(-na)** a mountain, highland —n highlander, mountain dweller

serrucho /se'rrutʃo/ m, handsaw. **s. de calar,** fretsaw

Servia /'serβia/ Serbia

servible /ser'βiβle/ a serviceable; useful

servicial /serβi'θial; serβi'sial/ a useful, serviceable; obliging, obsequious

servicio /ser'βiθio; ser'βisio/ m, service; domestic service; cult, devotion; care, attendance; military service; set, service; department, section; present of money; cover (cutlery, etc., at table); domestic staff, servants. **s. informativo,** news service. **s. nocturno permanente,** all-night service. **hacer un flaco s. (a),** *Inf.* to do someone an ill turn. **prestar servicios,** to render service, serve

servidor /serβi'ðor/ **(-ra)** n servant, domestic; name by which one refers to oneself (e.g. *Un s. lo hará con mucho gusto,* I (your servant) will do it with much pleasure). m, wooer, lover; bowler (in cricket). **los servidores de una ametralladora,** the crew (of a gun). **Quedo de Vd. atento y seguro s.,** I remain your obedient servant (in letters), Yours faithfully

servidumbre /serβi'ðumbre/ f, serfdom; servitude; servants, domestic staff; obligation, duty; enslavement (by passions); right of way; use, service

servil /ser'βil/ a servile; humble

servilismo /serβi'lismo/ m, servility; abjectness; absolutism (Spanish history)

servilleta /serβi'ʎeta; serβi'yeta/ f, table napkin. **s. higiénica,** sanitary napkin

servilletero /serβiʎe'tero; serβiye'tero/ m, napkin ring

servio /'serβio/ **(-ia)** a and n Serbian

servir /ser'βir/ vi irr to be employed (by), be in the service (of); serve (as), perform the duties (of); be of use; wait (on), be subject to. *Mil.* serve in the armed forces; wait at table; be suitable or favorable; *Sports.* serve; perform a service; follow the lead (cards); (*with de*) act as, be a deputy for; be a substitute for; —vt serve; worship; do a favor to; woo, court; serve (food, drink); —vr be pleased or willing, deign; help oneself to (food); (*with de*) make use of. **no s. para nada,** to be good for nothing, be useless. **No sirves para tales cosas,** You are no good at this sort of thing. **Para s. a Vd,** At your service. **¡Sírvase de...!** (followed by infin.), Please! **s. de,** to serve as (e.g. *s. de base a,* to serve as a basis for). See **pedir**

sésamo /'sesamo/ m, sesame

sesenta /se'senta/ a and m, sixty; sixtieth

sesentavo /sesen'taβo/ a and m, sixtieth

sesentón /sesen'ton/ **(-ona)** n *Inf.* person of sixty

sesga /'sesga/ f, *Sew.* gore

sesgadamente /sesgaða'mente/ adv on the slant; askew; obliquely

sesgado /ses'gaðo/ a oblique, slanting

sesgar /ses'gar/ vt *Sew.* to cut on the bias; slant, slope; place askew, twist to one side

sesgo /'sesgo/ a slanting, oblique; serious-faced. m, slope, slant, obliquity; compromise, middle way. **al s.,** on the slant

sesión /se'sion/ f, session, meeting; conference, consultation; *Law.* sitting; term. **abrir la s.,** to open the meeting. **levantar la s.,** to adjourn the meeting

seso /'seso/ m, brain; prudence; pl brains. **perder el s.,** to go mad; *Fig.* lose one's head

sestear /seste'ar/ vi to take an afternoon nap; rest; settle

sesudez /sesu'ðeθ; sesu'ðes/ f, prudence, shrewdness

sesudo /se'suðo/ a sensible, prudent

seta /'seta/ f, mushroom. **s. venenosa,** poisonous toadstool

setal /se'tal/ m, mushroom bed, patch, or field

setecientos /sete'θientos; sete'sientos/ a and m, seven hundred; seven-hundredth

setenta /se'tenta/ a and m, seventy; seventieth

setentavo /seten'taβo/ a and m, seventieth

setentón /seten'ton/ **(-ona)** n septuagenarian

seter /'seter/ m, setter (dog)

setiembre /se'tiembre/ m. See **septiembre**

seto /'seto/ m, fence; hedge

seudo /'seuðo/ a pseudo

seudónimo /seu'ðonimo/ m, pseudonym

severamente /seβera'mente/ adv severely, harshly

severidad /seβeri'ðað/ f, severity; harshness; strictness, rigor; austerity, seriousness

severo /se'βero/ a severe; harsh; strict, rigid, scrupulous, exact; austere, serious

sevillanas /seβi'ʎanas; seβi'yanas/ f pl, Sevillian dance and its music

sevillano /seβi'ʎano; seβi'yano/ **(-na)** a and n of or from Seville, Sevillian

sexagenario /seksahe'nario/ **(-ia)** n sexagenarian

sexagésimo /seksa'hesimo/ a sixtieth

sexo /'sekso/ m, sex; (sexual) organ

sexología /seksolo'hia/ f, sexology

sexólogo /sek'sologo/ **(-ga)** n sexologist

sexta /'seksta/ f, *Eccl.* sext; *Mus.* sixth

sextante /seks'tante/ m, *Math.* sextant

sexteto /seks'teto/ m, sextet

sexto /'seksto/ a sixth

sextuplicación /sekstuplika'θion; sekstuplika'sion/ f, multiplication by six

sextuplicar /sekstupli'kar/ vt to multiply by six, sextuple

séxtuplo /'sekstuplo/ a sixfold

sexualidad /seksuali'ðað/ f, sexuality

si /si/ m, *Mus.* B, seventh note of the scale —*conjunc* if; whether; even if, although. In conditional clause, **si,** meaning if, is followed by indicative tense unless statement be contrary to fact (e.g. *Si pierdes el tren,* *volverás a casa,* If you miss your train you will return home, *but Si hubieran venido habríamos ido al campo,* If they had come (but they didn't) we would have gone to the country). **Si** is used at the beginning of a clause to make expressions of doubt, desire, or affirmation more emphatic (e.g. *¡Si lo sabrá él, con toda su experiencia!* Of course he knows it, with all his experience. *¿Si será falsa la noticia?* Can the news be false?) **Si** also means whether (e.g. *Me preguntaron si era médico o militar,* They asked me whether I was a doctor or a soldier). Sometimes means even if, although (e.g. *Si viniesen no lo harían,* Even if they came they would not do it. *como si,* as if. *por si acaso,* in case, in the event of. *si bien,* although.

sí /si/ pers pron reflexive 3rd pers m, and f, sing and pl himself, herself, itself, themselves. Always used with prep. (e.g. *para sí,* for himself, herself, etc. *de por sí,* separately, on its own. *decir para sí,* to say to oneself)

sí /si/ adv yes. **sí** or **sí que** is frequently used to emphasize a verb generally in contrast to a previous negative (e.g. *Ellos no lo harán, pero yo sí,* They won't do it but I will). Often translated by "did" (e.g. *No lo vi todo, pero lo que sí vi,* I didn't see it all, but what I did see...). m, assent; yes; consent. **dar el sí,** to say yes; agree; accept an offer of marriage

siamés /sia'mes/ **(-esa)** a and n Siamese. m, Thai (language)

sibarita /siβa'rita/ a sybaritic. mf sybarite

sibarítico /siβa'ritiko/ a sybaritic; sensual

sibaritismo /siβari'tismo/ m, sybaritism

siberiano /siβe'riano/ **(-na)** a and n Siberian

sibila /si'βila/ f, sibyl

sibilante /siβi'lante/ a sibilant

sibilino /siβi'lino/ a sibylline

sicario /si'kario/ m, paid assassin

Sicilia /si'θilia; si'silia/ Sicily

siciliano /siθi'liano; sisi'liano/ **(-na)** a and n Sicilian

sicoanálisis /sikoa'nalisis/ m, psychoanalysis

sicoanalista /sikoana'lista/ mf psychoanalyst

sicoanalizar /sikoanali'θar; sikoanali'sar/ *vt* to psychoanalyze

sicofanta, sicofante /siko'fanta, siko'fante/ *m,* sycophant

sicología /sikolo'hia/ *f,* psychology

sicológico /siko'lohiko/ *a* psychological

sicólogo /si'kologo/ **(-ga)** *n* psychologist

sicomoro /siko'moro/ *m,* sycamore

sicopático /siko'patiko/ *a* psychopathic

sicosis /si'kosis/ *f, Med.* psychosis

sicoterapia /sikote'rapia/ *f,* psychotherapy

SIDA /'siða/ *m,* AIDS

sideral, sidéreo /siðe'ral, si'ðereo/ *a* sidereal

sidra /'siðra/ *f,* cider

siega /'siega/ *f,* reaping, harvesting; harvest time; harvest, crop

siembra /'siembra/ *f, Agr.* sowing; seedtime; sown field

siempre /'siempre/ *adv* always. **s. que,** provided that; whenever. **para s.,** forever. **por s. jamás,** for always, for ever and ever

siempreviva /siempre'βiβa/ *f, Bot.* everlasting flower. **s. mayor,** houseleek

sien /sien/ *f, Anat.* temple

sierpe /'sierpe/ *f,* serpent, snake; anything that wriggles; kite (toy); *Bot.* sucker; hideous person

sierra /'sierra/ *f,* saw; ridge of mountains; sawfish; slope; hillside. **s. de cerrojero,** hacksaw. **s. de cinta,** handsaw

siervo /'sierβo/ **(-va)** *n* slave; servant; serf

siesta /'siesta/ *f,* noonday heat; afternoon nap

siete /'siete/ *a* seven; seventh. *m,* seven; seventh (days of the month); playing card with seven spots; number seven. **las s.,** seven o'clock. *Inf.* **más que s.,** more than somewhat, extremely

sietemesino /sieteme'sino/ **(-na)** *n* seven-month-old child; *Fig. Inf.* young cock

sífilis /'sifilis/ *f,* syphilis

sifilítico /sifi'litiko/ **(-ca)** *a* and *n* syphilitic

sifón /si'fon/ *m,* siphon; siphon bottle; soda water; *Mech.* trap

sigilar /sihi'lar/ *vt* to seal; hide, conceal

sigilo /si'hilo/ *m,* seal; secrecy; concealment; silence, reserve

sigiloso /sihi'loso/ *a* secret, silent

sigla /'sigla/ *f,* acronym

siglo /'siglo/ *m,* century; long time, age; social intercourse, society, world. **s. de oro,** golden age. **en** *or* **por los siglos de los siglos,** for ever and ever

signar /sig'nar/ *vt* to sign; make the sign of the cross over; *—vr* cross oneself

signatario /signa'tario/ **(-ia)** *a* and *n* signatory

signatura /signa'tura/ *f, Print.* signature; mark, sign; *Mus.* signature

significación /signifika'θion; signifika'sion/ *f,* **significado** *m,* meaning; importance, significance

significante /signifi'kante/ *a* significant

significar /signifi'kar/ *vt* to signify, indicate; mean; publish, make known; *—vi* represent, mean; be worth

significativo /signifika'tiβo/ *a* significant

signo /'signo/ *m,* sign, indication, token; sign, character; *Math.* symbol; sign of the zodiac; *Mus.* sign; *Med.* symptom; *Eccl.* gesture of benediction; destiny, fate

siguemepollo /sigeme'poʎo; sigeme'poyo/ *m, Inf.* streamer

siguiente /si'giente/ *a* following; next, subsequent. **el día s.,** the next day

sílaba /'silaβa/ *f,* syllable

silabario /sila'βario/ *m,* speller, spelling book

silabear /silaβe'ar/ *vi* and *vt* to pronounce by syllables, syllabize

silabeo /silaβe'o/ *m,* pronouncing syllable by syllable, syllabication

silábico /si'laβiko/ *a* syllabic

sílabo /'silaβo/ *m,* syllabus, list

silba /'silβa/ *f,* hissing (as a sign of disapproval)

silbador /silβa'ðor/ **(-ra)** *a* whistling; hissing *—n* whistler; one who hisses

silbar /sil'βar/ *vi* to whistle; whizz, rush through the air; *—vi* and *vt Theat.* hiss

silbato /sil'βato/ *m,* whistle; air hole

silbido, silbo /sil'βiðo, 'silβo/ *m,* whistle, whistling; hiss, hissing

silenciador /silenθia'ðor; silensia'ðor/ *m,* (*Auto.* firearms) silencer

silenciar /silen'θiar; silen'siar/ *vt* to silence; keep secret

silenciario /silen'θiario; silen'siario/ *a* vowed to perpetual silence

silencio /si'lenθio; si'lensio/ *m,* silence; noiselessness, quietness; omission, disregard; *Mus.* rest. **en s.,** in silence; quietly; uncomplainingly. **pasar en s.** (una cosa), to pass over (something) in silence, omit. **s. de muerte,** deathly silence

silencioso /silen'θioso; silen'sioso/ *a* silent; noiseless; tranquil, quiet. *m,* (*Auto.* firearms) silencer

silesio /si'lesio/ **(-ia)** *a* and *n* Silesian

sílfide /'silfiðe/ *f,* **silfo** *m,* sylph

silicato /sili'kato/ *m, Chem.* silicate

sílice /'siliθe; 'silise/ *f, Chem.* silica

silla /'siʎa; 'siya/ *f,* chair; riding saddle; *Mech.* rest, saddle; *Eccl.* see. **s. de manos,** sedan chair. **s. de montar,** riding saddle. **s. de posta,** post chaise. **s. de ruedas,** wheelchair. **s. de tijera,** deck chair; campstool. **s. giratoria,** swivel chair. **s. poltrona,** easy chair. *Inf.* **pegársele la s.,** to overstay one's welcome

sillar /si'ʎar; si'yar/ *m,* ashlar, quarry stone; horseback

sillería /siʎe'ria; siye'ria/ *f,* set of chairs; pew; choir stalls; chair factory; shop where chairs are sold; chair making; *Mas.* ashlar masonry

sillero /si'ʎero; si'yero/ **(-ra)** *n* chair maker or seller; saddler

silleta /si'ʎeta; si'yeta/ *f,* bedpan; fireman's lift

silletero /siʎe'tero; siye'tero/ *m,* runner, sedan chair carrier

sillín /si'ʎin; si'yin/ *m,* light riding saddle; seat, saddle (of bicycles, etc.)

sillón /si'ʎon; si'yon/ *m,* armchair; sidesaddle. **s.-cama,** reclining chair. **s. de mimbres,** cane chair

silo /'silo/ *m, Agr.* silo; dark cavern, dark cave

silogismo /silo'hismo/ *m,* syllogism

silogístico /silo'histiko/ *a* syllogistic

silueta /si'lueta/ *f,* silhouette; figure

silúrico /si'luriko/ *a* silurian

siluro /si'luro/ *m,* catfish; *Nav.* self-propelling torpedo

silva /'silβa/ *f,* literary miscellany; metrical form

silvestre /sil'βestre/ *a Bot.* wild; sylvan; uncultivated; savage

silvicultor /silβikul'tor/ *m,* forester

silvicultura /silβikul'tura/ *f,* forestry

sima /'sima/ *f,* abyss, chasm

simbiosis /sim'biosis/ *f,* symbiosis

simbólico /sim'boliko/ *a* symbolical

simbolismo /simbo'lismo/ *m,* symbolism

simbolista /simbo'lista/ *mf* symbolist

simbolización /simboliθa'θion; simbolisa'sion/ *f,* symbolization

simbolizar /simboli'θar; simboli'sar/ *vt* to symbolize, represent

símbolo /'simbolo/ *m,* symbol. **s. de la fe,** *Eccl.* Creed

simetría /sime'tria/ *f,* symmetry

simétrico /si'metriko/ *a* symmetric; symmetrical

simetrizar /simetri'θar; simetri'sar/ *vt* to make symmetrical

símico /'simiko/ *a* simian

simiente /si'miente/ *f,* seed; semen; germ, genesis, origin

simiesco /si'miesko/ *a* apish, ape-like

símil /'simil/ *a* similar. *m,* comparison; simile

similar /simi'lar/ *a* similar

similitud /simili'tuð/ *f,* similarity

simio /'simio/ **(-ia)** *n* ape

simón /si'mon/ *m,* horse cab; cabdriver

simonía /simo'nia/ *f,* simony

simpatía /simpa'tia/ *f,* liking, understanding, affection; fellow feeling; sympathy

simpático /sim'patiko/ a friendly, nice, decent, congenial; sympathetic. **gran s.**, *Anat.* sympathetic

simpatizar /simpati'θar; simpati'sar/ *vi* to get on well, be congenial

simple /'simple/ a simple; single, not double; insipid; easy; plain, unadorned; stupid, silly; pure, unmixed; easily deceived, simple; naïve, ingenuous; mere; mild, meek. *mf* simpleton; fool

simpleza /sim'pleθa; sim'plesa/ f, foolishness, stupidity; simplicity

simplicidad /simpliθi'ðað; simplisi'ðað/ f, simplicity; candor, ingenuousness

simplicísimo /simpli'θisimo; simpli'sisimo/ a *superl* most simple, exceedingly simple

simplificable /simplifi'kaβle/ a simplifiable

simplificación /simplifika'θion; simplifika'sion/ f, simplification, simplifying

simplificador /simplifika'ðor/ a simplifying

simplificar /simplifi'kar/ *vt* to simplify

simplista /sim'plista/ *mf* herbalist

simulación /simula'θion; simula'sion/ f, pretense, simulation

simulacro /simu'lakro/ m, image, simulacrum; vision, fancy; *Mil.* mock battle

simuladamente /simulaða'mente/ *adv* pretendedly

simulador /simula'ðor/ **(-ra)** a feigned —*n* dissembler

simular /simu'lar/ *vt* to feign, pretend

simultanear /simultane'ar/ *vt* to perform simultaneously

simultaneidad /simultanei'ðað/ f, simultaneousness

simultáneo /simul'taneo/ a simultaneous

simún /si'mun/ m, sandstorm

sin /sin/ *prep* without (e.g. *Lo hizo s. hablar,* He did it without speaking). **s. embargo,** nevertheless. **s. fin,** endless. **s. hilos,** radio, wireless

sinagoga /sina'goga/ f, synagogue

sinapismo /sina'pismo/ m, *Med.* mustard plaster; *Inf.* pest, bore

sincerarse /sinθe'rarse; sinse'rarse/ *vr* to justify oneself; vindicate one's actions

sinceridad /sinθeri'ðað; sinseri'ðað/ f, sincerity

sincero /sin'θero; sin'sero/ a sincere

síncopa /'sinkopa/ f, *Mus.* syncopation; *Gram.* syncope

sincopar /sinko'par/ *vt* to syncopate; abbreviate

síncope /'sinkope/ m, syncope

sincrónico /sin'kroniko/ a synchronous

sincronismo /sinkro'nismo/ m, synchronism

sincronizar /sinkroni'θar; sinkroni'sar/ *vt* to synchronize; *Radio.* tune in

sindéresis /sin'deresis/ f, discretion, good sense

sindicación /sindika'θion; sindika'sion/ f, syndication

sindicado /sindi'kaðo/ m, syndicate

sindical /sindi'kal/ a syndical

sindicalismo /sindika'lismo/ m, syndicalism, trade unionism

sindicalista /sindika'lista/ *mf* syndicalist, trade unionist —a syndicalistic, trade unionist

sindicar /sindi'kar/ *vt* to accuse, charge; censure; syndicate

sindicato /sindi'kato/ m, syndicate; trade union. **s. gremial,** trade union. **S. Internacional de Trabajadoras de la Aguja,** International Ladies' Garment Workers' Union

sindicatura /sindika'tura/ f, (official) receivership

síndico /'sindiko/ m, *Com.* receiver, trustee

síndrome /'sindrome/ m, syndrome

sinecura /sine'kura/ f, sinecure

sinergia /si'nerhia/ f, synergy

sinfín /sin'fin/ m, countless number

sinfonía /sinfo'nia/ f, symphony

sinfónico /sin'foniko/ a symphonic

sinfonista /sinfo'nista/ *mf* composer of symphonies, player in a symphony orchestra

sinfonola /sinfo'nola/ f, jukebox

Singapur /singa'pur/ Singapore

singladura /singla'ðura/ f, *Naut.* day's sailing; nautical twenty-four hours (beginning at midday)

singlar /sin'glar/ *vi Naut.* to sail a given course

singular /singu'lar/ a singular, single; individual; extraordinary, remarkable —*a and m, Gram.* singular

singularidad /singulari'ðað/ f, individuality, peculiarity; strangeness, remarkableness; oddness, eccentricity

singularizar /singulari'θar; singulari'sar/ *vt* to particularize, single out; *Gram.* make singular, singularize; —*vr* distinguish oneself, stand out; be distinguished (by)

sinhueso /sin'ueso/ f, *Inf.* tongue (organ of speech)

sínico /'siniko/ a Chinese

siniestra /si'niestra/ f, left, lefthand

siniestro /si'niestro/ a left (side); vicious, perverse; sinister; unlucky. m, viciousness, depravity (gen. *pl*); shipwreck, sinking; disaster, catastrophe; *Com.* damage, loss

sinnúmero /sin'numero/ m, countless number

sino /'sino/ m, fate, destiny —*conjunct* but; except (e.g. *No lo hicieron ellos s. yo,* They didn't do it, I did. *no... s.,* not..., but); only (e.g. *No sólo lo dijo él s. ella,* Not only he said it, but she said it too)

sínodo /'sinoðo/ m, (*Eccl. Astron.*) synod; council

sinología /sinolo'hia/ f, sinology

sinólogo /si'nologo/ m, sinologist

sinonimia /sino'nimia/ f, synonymy

sinónimo /si'nonimo/ a synonymous. m, synonym

sinopsis /si'nopsis/ f, synopsis

sinóptico /si'noptiko/ a synoptic

sinrazón /sinra'θon; sinra'son/ f, injustice, wrong

sinsabor /sinsa'βor/ m, unpleasantness, trouble; grief, anxiety

sintáctico /sin'taktiko/ a syntactic

sintaxis /sin'taksis/ f, syntax

síntesis /'sintesis/ f, synthesis

sintético /sin'tetiko/ a synthetic

sintetizar /sinteti'θar; sinteti'sar/ *vt* to synthesize

sintoísmo /sinto'ismo/ m, Shintoism

síntoma /'sintoma/ m, symptom

sintomático /sinto'matiko/ a symptomatic

sintomatología /sintomatolo'hia/ f, symptomatology

sintonización /sintoniθa'θion; sintonisa'sion/ f, *Radio.* tuning in

sintonizador /sintoniθa'ðor; sintonisa'ðor/ m, *Radio.* tuner

sintonizar /sintoni'θar; sintoni'sar/ *vt Radio.* to tune in

sinuosidad /sinuosi'ðað/ f, sinuosity

sinuoso /si'nuoso/ a sinuous, winding

sinvergüenza /simber'guenθa; simber'guensa/ *mf* rascal, knave, rogue

Sión /'sion/ Zion

sionismo /sio'nismo/ m, Zionism

sionista /sio'nista/ a and *mf* Zionist

siquiatra /si'kiatra/ m, psychiatrist

siquiatría /sikia'tria/ f, psychiatry

síquico /'sikiko/ a psychic

siquiera /si'kiera/ *conjunct* although, even if. **s.... s.,** whether... or —*adv* at least; even (e.g. *Hay que pedir mucho para tener s. la mitad,* One must ask a great deal to get even half). **ni s.,** not even (e.g. *No había nadie, ni s. un perro,* There was no one, not even a dog)

Siracusa /sira'kusa/ Syracuse

siracusano /siraku'sano/ **(-na)** a and *n* Syracusan

sirena /si'rena/ f, mermaid, siren; siren; foghorn

sirga /'sirga/ f, towline

sirgar /sir'gar/ *vt Naut.* to track, tow

Siria /'siria/ Syria

siríaco /si'riako/ **(-ca)** a and *n* Syriac

sirio /'sirio/ **(-ia)** a and *n* Syrian. m, Sirius

siroco /si'roko/ m, sirocco

sirte /'sirte/ f, sandbank, submerged rock

sirvienta /sir'βienta/ f, female servant

sirviente /sir'βiente/ a serving. m, servant

sisa /'sisa/ f, pilfering; *Sew.* dart. **s. dorada,** gold lacquer

sisador /sisa'ðor/ **(-ra)** n filcher, pilferer

sisar /si'sar/ *vt* to pilfer, filch, steal; *Sew.* take in, make darts in

sisear /sise'ar/ *vi* and *vt* to hiss (disapproval); sizzle

sísmico /'sismiko/ a seismic

sismógrafo /sis'mografo/ *m*, seismograph

sismología /sismolo'hia/ *f*, seismology

sismológico /sismo'lohiko/ *a* seismological

sismómetro /sis'mometro/ *m*, seismometer

sistema /sis'tema/ *m*, system. **s. ferroviario**, railroad system. **s. métrico**, metric system

sistemático /siste'matiko/ *a* systematic

sistematización /sistemati0a'0ion; sistematisa'sion/ *f*, systematization

sistematizar /sistemati'0ar; sistemati'sar/ *vt* to systematize

sístole /'sistole/ *f*, systole

sitiador /sitia'ðor/ *a* besieging. *m*, besieger

sitial /si'tial/ *m*, ceremonial chair

sitiar /si'tiar/ *vt Mil.* to lay siege to; surround, besiege

sitio /'sitio/ *m*, place, spot; room, space; site; locality; *Mil.* siege, blockade. **No hay s.,** There's no room

sito /'sito/ *past part* situated, located

situación /situa'0ion; situa'sion/ *f*, situation; position; circumstances; condition, state; location

situado /si'tuaðo/ *past part* situated, placed. *m*, income, interest

situar /si'tuar/ *vt* to situate, locate, place; assign funds; —*vr* place oneself

smoking /'smokiŋ/ *m*, tuxedo, tux, dinner jacket

snobismo /sno'βismo/ *m*, snobbery

so /so/ *prep* under (used only with **color, pena, pretexto, capa**) (e.g. *so color de*, under the pretext of) —*interj* ¡**So!** Whoa! (to horses)

soba /'soβa/ *f*, rubbing; kneading; massaging; drubbing, beating; handling, touching

sobacal /soβa'kal/ *a* underarm, axillary

sobaco /so'βako/ *m*, armpit; *Bot.* axil

sobajar /soβa'har/ *vt* to squeeze, press

sobaquera /soβa'kera/ *f*, *Sew.* armhole; dress shield

sobar /so'βar/ *vt* to rub; knead; massage; beat, thrash; handle, touch, paw (persons); soften

soberanear /soβeranea'ar/ *vi* to tyrannize, domineer

soberanía /soβera'nia/ *f*, sovereignty; dominance, sway, rule; dignity, majesty

soberano /soβe'rano/ **(-na)** *a* sovereign; superb; regal, majestic —*n* ruler, lord. *m*, sovereign (coin)

soberbia /so'βerβia/ *f*, arrogance, haughtiness; conceit, presumption; ostentation, pomp; rage, anger

soberbio /so'βerβio/ *a* haughty, arrogant; conceited; superb, magnificent; lofty, soaring; spirited (of horses)

sobón /so'βon/ *a Inf.* overdemonstrative, mushy; *Inf.* lazy

sobordo /so'βorðo/ *m*, *Naut.* manifest, freight list

sobornación /soβorna'0ion; soβorna'sion/ *f*, bribing; bribery

sobornador /soβorna'ðor/ **(-ra)** *a* bribing —*n* briber

sobornar /soβor'nar/ *vt* to bribe

soborno /so'βorno/ *m*, bribing; bribe; inducement

sobra /'soβra/ *f*, excess, surplus; insult, outrage; *pl* leftovers (from a meal); remains, residue; rubbish, trash. **de s.,** in abundance; in excess, surplus; unnecessary, superfluous; too well

sobradamente /soβraða'mente/ *adv* abundantly; in excess

sobrado /so'βraðo/ *a* excessive; brazen, bold; wealthy, rich. *m*, garret

sobrante /so'βrante/ *a* surplus, leftover, remaining. *m*, remainder, surplus, excess

sobrar /so'βrar/ *vt* to exceed; have too much of (e.g. *Me sobran mantas*, I have too many blankets); —*vi* be superfluous; remain, be left. *Inf.* **Aquí sobro yo,** I am in the way here, My presence is superfluous

sobrasada /soβra'saða/ *f*, spicy sausage

sobre /'soβre/ *prep* upon, on; above, over; about, over (e.g. *s. las nueve*, at about nine o'clock) (indicates approximation); toward; after. *m*, envelope; address, superscription. **s. cero**, above freezing (Fahrenheit); above zero (Centigrade). **s. el nivel del mar**, above sea level. **s. manera**, excessively, extremely. **s. todo**, especially

sobreabundancia /soβreaβun'danθia; soβreaβun'dansia/ *f*, superabundance, excess

sobreabundante /soβreaβun'dante/ *a* superabundant

sobreabundar /soβreaβun'dar/ *vi* to be superabundant

sobreagudo /soβrea'guðo/ *a* and *m*, *Mus.* treble (pitch)

sobrealiento /soβrea'liento/ *m*, heavy, painful breathing

sobrealimentación /soβrealimenta'θion; soβrealimenta'sion/ *f*, overfeeding; *Auto.* supercharge

sobrealimentar /soβrealimen'tar/ *vt Auto.* to supercharge

sobreasar /soβrea'sar/ *vt* to roast or cook again

sobrecama /soβre'kama/ *f*, bedspread, quilt

sobrecarga /soβre'karga/ *f*, overload; rope, etc., for securing bales and packs; additional trouble or anxiety

sobrecargar /soβrekar'gar/ *vt* to overload; weigh down; *Sew.* oversew, fell

sobrecargo /soβre'kargo/ *m*, *Naut.* purser; flight attendant

sobrecarta /soβre'karta/ *f*, envelope (for a letter)

sobreceja /soβre'θeha; soβre'seha/ *f*, brow, lower forehead; frown

sobrecejo /soβre'θeho; soβre'seho/ *m*, frown

sobrecielo /soβre'θielo; soβre'sielo/ *m*, canopy

sobrecoger /soβreko'her/ *vt* to take by surprise; —*vr* be frightened or apprehensive

sobrecogimiento /soβrekohi'miento/ *m*, fright, apprehension

sobrecomida /soβreko'miða/ *f*, dessert

sobrecoser /soβreko'ser/ *vt Sew.* to oversew, whip

sobrecrecer /soβrekre'θer; soβrekre'ser/ *vi irr* to grow too much. See **conocer**

sobrecubierta /soβreku'βierta/ *f*, second lid or cover; dust jacket (of a book); *Naut.* upper deck

sobrecuello /soβre'kueʎo; soβre'kueyo/ *m*, overcollar; loose collar

sobredicho /soβre'ðitʃo/ *a* aforementioned, aforesaid

sobredorar /soβreðo'rar/ *vt* to gild (metals); make excuses for

sobreedificar /soβreeðifi'kar/ *vt* to build upon or above

sobreexcitar /soβreeksθi'tar; soβreekssi'tar/ *vt* to overexcite

sobrefaz /soβre'faθ; soβre'fas/ *f*, surface, exterior

sobreganar /soβrega'nar/ *vt* to make an excess profit

sobreguarda /soβre'guarða/ *m*, head guard; extra or second guard

sobreherido /soβree'riðo/ *a* lightly wounded

sobrehilar /soβrei'lar/ *vt* to oversew or overcast. See **prohibir**

sobrehumano /soβreu'mano/ *a* superhuman

sobrellenar /soβreʎe'nar; soβreye'nar/ *vt* to fill full

sobrellevar /soβreʎe'βar; soβreye'βar/ *vt* to help in the carrying of a burden; endure, bear; make excuses for, overlook; help

sobremesa /soβre'mesa/ *f*, tablecloth; after-dinner conversation. **de s.,** *Fig.* at the dinner table

sobrenadar /soβrena'ðar/ *vi* to float

sobrenatural /soβrenatu'ral/ *a* supernatural; extraordinary, singular

sobrenombre /soβre'nombre/ *m*, additional surname; nickname

sobrentender /soβrenten'der/ *vt irr* to take for granted, understand as a matter of course; —*vr* go without saying. See **entender**

sobrepaga /soβre'paga/ *f*, overpayment; extra pay

sobreparto /soβre'parto/ *m*, time after parturition; afterbirth

sobrepasar /soβrepa'sar/ *vt* to exceed; outdo, excel

sobrepelliz /soβrepe'ʎiθ; soβrepe'yis/ *f*, surplice

sobreponer /soβrepo'ner/ *vt irr* to place over; overlap; —*vr* rise above (circumstances); dominate (persons). See **poner**

sobreprecio /soβre'preθio; soβre'presio/ *m*, extra charge, rise in price

sobreproducción /soβreproðuk'θion; soβreproðuk'sion/ *f*, overproduction

sobrepuerta /soβre'puerta/ *f*, curtain pelmet; door curtain

sobrepujar /soβrepu'har/ *vt* to excel, surpass, outdo

sobrequilla /soβre'kiʎa; soβre'kiya/ *f*, keelson

sobrerrealismo /soβrerrea'lismo/ *m*, surrealism
sobrerrealista /soβrerrea'lista/ *a* and *mf* surrealist
sobresaliente /soβresa'liente/ *a* overhanging; project-ing; distinctive, outstanding; excellent, remarkable. *m*, "excellent" (mark in examinations). *mf Theat.* un-derstudy
sobresalir /soβresa'lir/ *vi irr* to overhang, project; stand out; be conspicuous or noticeable; excel; dis-tinguish oneself. See **salir**
sobresaltar /soβresal'tar/ *vt* to assail, rush upon; startle, frighten suddenly; —*vi Art.* stand out, be striking; —*vr* be startled or frightened
sobresalto /soβre'salto/ *m*, sudden attack; unex-pected shock; agitation; sudden fear. **de s.,** unexpect-edly
sobresanar /soβresa'nar/ *vi* to heal superficially but not deeply; conceal, dissemble
sobrescribir /soβreskri'βir/ *vt* to label; address, super-scribe —*Past Part.* **sobrescrito**
sobrescrito /soβres'krito/ *m*, address, superscription
sobresello /soβre'seʎo; soβre'seyo/ *m*, second seal
sobrestante /soβres'tante/ *m*, overseer; supervisor; foreman; inspector
sobresueldo /soβre'sueldo/ *m*, additional salary, bo-nus
sobresuelo /soβre'suelo/ *m*, second flooring
sobretarde /soβre'tarðe/ *f*, early evening, late after-noon
sobretodo /soβre'toðo/ *m*, overcoat
sobrevenida /soβreβe'niða/ *f*, sudden arrival
sobrevenir /soβreβe'nir/ *vi irr* occur, take place; su-pervene. See **venir**
sobrevidriera /soβreβi'ðriera/ *f*, storm window; wire-mesh window guard
sobrevienta /soβre'βienta/ *f*, gust of wind; fury, vio-lence; shock, surprise. **a s.,** suddenly
sobreviviente /soβreβi'βiente/ *a* surviving. *mf* survi-vor
sobrevivir /soβreβi'βir/ *vi* to survive
sobriedad /soβrie'ðað/ *f*, sobriety, moderation
sobrina /so'βrina/ *f*, niece
sobrino /so'βrino/ *m*, nephew
sobrio /'soβrio/ *a* sober, moderate, temperate
socaliña /soka'liɲa/ *f*, cunning, craft
socaliñero /sokali'ɲero/ **(-ra)** *a* cunning —*n* trickster
socalzar /sokal'θar; sokal'sar/ *vt Mas.* to underpin
socapa /so'kapa/ *f*, blind, pretext. **a s.,** secretly; cau-tiously
socarra /so'karra/ *f*, scorching, singeing; craftiness
socarrón /soka'rron/ *a* cunning, deceitful; malicious, sly (of humor, etc.)
socarronería /sokarrone'ria/ *f*, cunning, craftiness; slyness (of humor, etc.); knavish action
socava /so'kaβa/ *f*, undermining; *Agr.* hoeing round tree roots
socavar /soka'βar/ *vt* to undermine
sociabilidad /soθiaβili'ðað; sosiaβili'ðað/ *f*, sociabil-ity
sociable /so'θiaβle; so'siaβle/ *a* sociable; social
social /so'θial; so'sial/ *a* social
socialdemócrata /soθialde'mokrata; sosialde'mo-krata/ *a* and *mf* social democrat
socialismo /soθia'lismo; sosia'lismo/ *m*, socialism
socialista /soθia'lista; sosia'lista/ *mf* socialist —*a* socialistic
socialización /soθialiθa'θion; sosialisa'sion/ *f*, social-ization
socializar /soθiali'θar; sosiali'sar/ *vt* to socialize
sociedad /soθie'ðað; sosie'ðað/ *f*, society; associa-tion; *Com.* partnership; *Com.* company. *Com.* **s. anónima,** incorporated company, limited company. **S. de las Naciones,** League of Nations. **s. de socorros mutuos,** mutual aid society. **s. en comandita,** private company
socio /'soθio; 'sosio/ **(-ia)** *n* associate, partner; mem-ber. **s. comanditario,** *Com.* silent partner
sociología /soθiolo'hia; sosiolo'hia/ *f*, sociology
sociológico /soθio'lohiko; sosio'lohiko/ *a* sociologi-cal
sociólogo /so'θiologo; so'siologo/ **(-ga)** *n* sociologist

socollada /soko'ʎaða; soko'yaða/ *f*, *Naut.* flapping (of sails); pitching (of a ship)
socolor /soko'lor/ *m*, pretext —*adv* (also **so c.**) under pretext
socorredor /sokorre'ðor/ **(-ra)** *a* aiding, succoring —*n* helper
socorrer /soko'rrer/ *vt* to aid, succor, assist; pay on account
socorrido /soko'rriðo/ *a* helpful, generous, prompt to assist; well-equipped, well-furnished; well-supplied
socorro /so'korro/ *m*, aid, help, assistance; payment on account; *Mil.* relief (provisions or arms)
socrático /so'kratiko/ *a* socratic
sodio /'soðio/ *m*, sodium
sodomía /soðo'mia/ *f*, sodomy
sodomita /soðo'mita/ *mf* sodomite —*a* sodomitic
soez /so'eθ; so'es/ *a* base, vile; vulgar
sofá /so'fa/ *m*, sofa, couch
sofaldar /sofal'dar/ *vt* to tuck up the skirts; disclose, reveal
sofisma /so'fisma/ *m*, sophism, fallacy
sofista /so'fista/ *a* sophistic. *mf* sophist, quibbler
sofistería /sofiste'ria/ *f*, sophistry
sofístico /so'fistiko/ *a* sophistic, fallacious
soflama /so'flama/ *f*, thin flame; glow; flush, blush; specious promise, deception
soflamar /sofla'mar/ *vt* to shame, make blush; prom-ise with intent to deceive, swindle; —*vr Cul.* burn
sofocación /sofoka'θion; sofoka'sion/ *f*, suffocation, smothering; shame; anger
sofocador, sofocante /sofoka'ðor, sofo'kante/ *a* suf-focating; stifling
sofocar /sofo'kar/ *vt* to suffocate, smother; extin-guish; dominate, oppress; pester, importune; shame, make blush, make angry; agitate; —*vr* be ashamed; be angry
sofocleo /sofo'kleo/ *a* Sophoclean
sofoco /so'foko/ *m*, mortification, chagrin; shame; anger; suffocation, smothering; hot flush
sofreír /sofre'ir/ *vt irr* to fry lightly. See **reír**
sofrenada /sofre'naða/ *f*, sudden check, pulling up short (of horses); harsh scolding; moral restraint
sofrenar /sofre'nar/ *vt* to pull up, check suddenly (horses); scold harshly; restrain, repress (emotions)
soga /'soga/ *f*, rope; land measure (varies in length). *m*, *Inf.* rogue, knave
soguería /soge'ria/ *f*, rope making; rope walk; rope shop; ropes
soguero /so'gero/ *m*, rope maker or seller
soja /'soha/ *f*, soybean
sojuzgador /sohuθga'ðor; sohusga'ðor/ **(-ra)** *a* con-quering, oppressive —*n* conqueror, oppressor
sojuzgar /sohuθ'gar; sohus'gar/ *vt* to conquer, op-press, subdue
sol /sol/ *m*, sun; sunlight; day; Peruvian coin; *Mus.* G, fifth note of the scale, sol. **de s. a s.,** from sunrise to sunset. **hacer s.,** to be sunny. **morir uno sin s. sin luz y sin moscas,** *Inf.* to die abandoned by all. **no dejar a s. ni a sombra,** *Inf.* to follow everywhere; pester constantly. **tomar el s.,** to bask in the sun
solado /so'laðo/ *m*, paving; tile floor
solador /sola'ðor/ *m*, tiler
solamente /sola'mente/ *adv* only; exclusively; merely, solely. **s. que,** only that; nothing but
solana /so'lana/ *f*, sunny corner; Solarium
solanera /sola'nera/ *f*, sunburn; sunny spot
solapa /so'lapa/ *f*, lapel; excuse, pretext. **de s.,** *Inf.* secretly
solapado /sola'paðo/ *a* cunning, sly
solapar /sola'par/ *vt Sew.* to provide with lapels; *Sew.* cause to overlap; dissemble; —*vi Sew.* overlap
solapo /so'lapo/ *m*, lapel; *Inf.* slap, buffet. **a s.,** *Inf.* secretly, slyly
solar /so'lar/ *vt irr* to pave; sole (shoes). *m*, family seat, manor house; building site; lineage, family —*a* solar. See **color**
solariego /sola'riego/ *a* memorial; of an old and no-ble family
solas, a /'solas, a/ *adv* alone, in private
solaz /so'laθ; so'las/ *m*, consolation; pleasure; relief, relaxation. **a s.,** enjoyably, pleasantly

solazar /sola'θar; sola'sar/ *vt* to solace, comfort; amuse, entertain; rest; —*vr* be comforted; find pleasure (in)

soldada /sol'daða/ *f*, salary, wages, emoluments; (*Nav. Mil.*) pay

soldadesca /solda'ðeska/ *f*, soldiering, military profession; troops. **a la s.,** in a soldier-like way

soldadesco /solda'ðesko/ *a* military, soldier

soldado /sol'daðo/ *m*, soldier; defender, partisan. **s. raso,** *Mil.* private

soldador /solda'ðor/ *m*, solderer, welder; soldering iron

soldadura /solda'ðura/ *f*, welding, soldering; correction, emendation

soldar /sol'dar/ *vt irr* to weld; mend by welding; correct, put right; *Mil.* wipe out, liquidate. See **contar**

solecismo /sole'θismo; sole'sismo/ *m*, solecism

soledad /sole'ðað/ *f*, solitude; loneliness; homesickness; *pl* melancholy Andalusian song and dance (also *f pl.* **soleares**)

solemne /so'lemne/ *a* solemn; magnificent; formal; serious, grave, important; pompous; *Inf.* downright, complete

solemnidad /solemni'ðað/ *f*, solemnity; magnificence; formality; gravity, seriousness; solemn ceremony; religious ceremony; legal formality

solemnización /solemniθa'θion; solemnisa'sion/ *f*, solemnization

solemnizar /solemni'θar; solemni'sar/ *vt* to solemnize, celebrate; extol

soler /so'ler/ *vi irr defective* to be in the habit, be used; happen frequently (e.g. *Solía hacerlo los lunes,* I generally did it on Mondays. *Suele llover mucho aquí,* It rains a great deal here). See **moler**

solercia /so'lerθia; so'lersia/ *f*, shrewdness, ability, astuteness

solevantado /soleβan'taðo/ *a* agitated; restless

solevantar /soleβan'tar/ *vt* to raise, push up; incite to rebellion. **s. con gatos,** *Mech.* to jack up

solfa /'solfa/ *f*, *Mus.* sol-fa

solfear /solfe'ar/ *vt Mus.* to sing in sol-fa; *Inf.* spank, buffet; *Inf.* scold

solfeo /sol'feo/ *m*, *Mus.* sol-fa; *Inf.* spanking, drubbing

solicitación /soliθita'θion; solisita'sion/ *f*, request; application; solicitation; wooing; search (for a post); attraction, inducement

solicitador /soliθita'ðor; solisita'ðor/ **(-ra)** *a* soliciting —*n* solicitor. *m*, agent; applicant

solicitante /soliθi'tante; solisi'tante/ *mf* applicant, candidate

solicitar /soliθi'tar; solisi'tar/ *vt* to solicit; request; apply for; make love to, court; seek (posts, etc.); try to, attempt to; manage (business affairs); *Phys.* attract; appeal to

solícito /so'liθito; so'lisito/ *a* solicitous; conscientious; careful

solicitud /soliθi'tuð; solisi'tuð/ *f*, diligence, conscientiousness; solicitude; request; application; appeal, entreaty; petition; *Com.* demand. **a s.,** on request

solidaridad /soliðari'ðað/ *f*, solidarity

solidario /soli'ðario/ *a Law.* jointly responsible or liable

solideo /soli'ðeo/ *m*, *Eccl.* small skullcap

solidez /soli'ðeθ; soli'ðes/ *f*, solidity; *Fig.* force, weight (of arguments, etc.)

solidificación /soliðifika'θion; soliðifika'sion/ *f*, solidification

solidificar /soliðifi'kar/ **(se)** *vt* and *vr* to solidify

sólido /'soliðo/ *a* compact, solid; thick; fast or lasting (of colors); indisputable, convincing. *m*, (*Geom. Phys.*) solid; solidus (ancient coin)

soliloquiar /solilo'kiar/ *vi Inf.* to soliloquize, talk to oneself

soliloquio /soli'lokio/ *m*, soliloquy

solio /'solio/ *m*, throne

solista /so'lista/ *mf* soloist

solitario /soli'tario/ **(-ia)** *a* abandoned, deserted; solitary; secluded; solitude-loving —*n* recluse. *m*, solitaire diamond; hermit; solitaire (card game). **hacer solitarios,** to play solitaire (card game)

sólito /'solito/ *a* accustomed, wonted; customary, habitual

soliviantar /soliβian'tar/ *vt* to rouse, incite, excite

soliviar /soli'βiar/ *vt* to help to lift up; —*vr* half get up, raise oneself

sollastre /so'ʎastre; so'yastre/ *m*, scullion; brazen rogue

sollozante /soʎo'θante; soyo'sante/ *a* sobbing

sollozar /soʎo'θar; soyo'sar/ *vi* to sob

sollozo /so'ʎoθo; so'yoso/ *m*, sob

solo /'solo/ *a* sole, only; alone; lonely; deserted, forsaken. *m*, solo performance; (cards) solo; solitaire (card game). **a solas,** alone; without help, unaided

sólo /'solo/ *or* **solo** *adv* only; merely, solely; exclusively

solomillo /solo'miʎo; solo'miyo/ *m*, sirloin; filet (of meat)

solsticio /sols'tiθio; sols'tisio/ *m*, solstice. **s. hiemal,** winter solstice. **s. vernal,** summer solstice

soltar /sol'tar/ *vt irr* to loosen; let go; disengage; untie; release; let drop; let out (a laugh, etc.); solve; *Inf.* utter; turn on (taps); set free; —*vr* work loose; grow skillful; (*with prep. a* + *infin.*) begin to do (something). See **contar**

soltera /sol'tera/ *f*, spinster

soltería /solte'ria/ *f*, bachelorhood; spinsterhood

soltero /sol'tero/ *a* unmarried, single. *m*, bachelor

solterón /solte'ron/ *m*, confirmed bachelor

solterona /solte'rona/ *f*, confirmed old maid

soltura /sol'tura/ *f*, loosening, untying; freedom from restraint; ease, independence; impudence; immorality, viciousness; facility of speech; *Law.* release

solubilidad /soluβili'ðað/ *f*, solubility

soluble /so'luβle/ *a* soluble, dissolvable; solvable

solución /solu'θion; solu'sion/ *f*, dissolution, loosening; (*Math. Chem.*) solution; answer, solution; payment, satisfaction; *Lit.* climax; conclusion, end (of negotiations)

solucionar /soluθio'nar; solusio'nar/ *vt* to solve, find a solution for

solvencia /sol'βenθia; sol'βensia/ *f*, *Com.* solvency

solventar /solβen'tar/ *vt* to pay or settle accounts; solve (problems, difficulties)

solvente /sol'βente/ *a Com.* solvent

somático /so'matiko/ *a* somatic, corporeal

somatología /somatolo'hia/ *f*, somatology

sombra /'sombra/ *f*, shadow; shade; darkness, dimness; specter, phantom; defense, refuge, protection; resemblance, likeness; defect; *Inf.* luck; gaiety, charm; trace, vestige; *Art.* shading, shadow. **sombras chinescas,** shadow show. **a la s.,** in the shade; *Inf.* in jail. **hacer s.,** to shade; *Fig.* stand in the light, be an obstacle; protect. **ni por s.,** by no means; without warning. **no tener s. de,** to have not a trace of.... **tener buena s.,** *Inf.* to be witty or amusing and agreeable. **tener mala s.,** *Inf.* to bring bad luck, exert an evil influence upon; be dull and disagreeable

sombrear /sombre'ar/ *vt* to shadow, shade; *Art.* shade; —*vi* begin to show (of mustaches, beards)

sombrerera /sombre'rera/ *f*, milliner; hatbox

sombrerería /sombre'ria/ *f*, hat shop or trade; hat factory

sombrerero /sombre'rero/ *m*, hatter; hat manufacturer

sombrerete /sombre'rete/ *m*, *Mech.* bonnet; cap; cowl

sombrero /som'βrero/ *m*, hat; *Mech.* cap, cowl; sounding board; head (of mushrooms, toadstools). **s. calañés,** Andalusian hat. **s. chambergo,** broad-brimmed plumed hat. **s. de canal** *or* **teja,** shovel hat (worn by clergymen). **s. de copa,** top hat. **s. de jipijapa,** Panama hat. **s. de tres picos,** three-cornered hat, cocked hat. **s. flexible,** soft felt hat. **s. hongo,** bowler (hat)

sombría /som'βria/ *f*, shady spot

sombrilla /som'βriʎa; som'βriya/ *f*, sunshade

sombrío /som'βrio/ *a* dark; shadowy; overcast; *Art.* shaded; gloomy, melancholy

someramente /somera'mente/ *adv* superficially; briefly, summarily

somero /so'mero/ *a* superficial, shallow; summary, rudimentary, brief

someter /some'ter/ *vt* to put down, defeat; submit, place before; subject. **s. a votación,** to put to a vote —*vr* yield, surrender; (*with prep a*) undergo

sometimiento /someti'miento/ *m*, defeat; submission (to arbitration, etc.); subjection

somnambulismo /somnambu'lismo/ *m*, somnambulism, sleepwalking

somnámbulo /som'nambulo/ **(-la)** *a* somnambulistic —*n* somnambulist

somnífero /som'nifero/ *a* soporiferous

somnílocuo /som'nilokuo/ *a* somniloquous, sleep-talking

somnolencia /somno'lenθia; somno'lensia/ *f*, somnolence

son /son/ *m*, sound; rumor; reason, motive; means, way; guise, manner. **al s. de,** to the sound of; to the music of. **en s. de,** in the manner of, as, like, under pretext of

sonadera /sona'ðera/ *f*, nose blowing

sonado /so'naðo/ *a* famous; much admired or talked of. **hacer una que sea sonada,** *Inf.* to cause a great scandal; do something noteworthy

sonaja /so'naha/ *f*, metal jingles on a tambourine; baby's rattle

sonajero /sona'hero/ *m*, baby's rattle

sonar /so'nar/ *vi irr* to sound; be quoted, be mentioned; ring; *Inf.* be familiar, remember (e.g. *No me suena el nombre,* I don't remember the name); (*with prep a*) be reminiscent of; —*vt* sound; ring; play on; clink; —*vr* be rumored, be reported; blow one's nose —*Pres. Indic.* **sueno, suenas, suena, suenan.** *Pres. Subjunc.* **suene, suenes, suene, suenen**

sonata /so'nata/ *f*, sonata

sonda /'sonda/ *f*, *Naut.* taking of soundings, heaving the lead; sound, plummet, lead; dragrope; probe, sound

sondar /son'dar/ *vt Naut.* to take soundings; probe; *Inf.* sound, try to find out; bore, drill

sondeable /sonde'aβle/ *a* fathomable

sondeo /son'deo/ *m*, *Naut.* sounding; *Mineral.* drilling; probing

sonetear, sonetizar /sonete'ar, soneti'θar; sonete'ar, soneti'sar/ *vi* to write sonnets

sonetista /sone'tista/ *mf* sonneteer

soneto /so'neto/ *m*, sonnet

sonido /so'niðo/ *m*, sound; literal meaning; rumor, report

sonochar /sono'tʃar/ *vi* to keep watch in the early hours of the night

sonoridad /sonori'ðað/ *f*, sonorousness

sonoro /so'noro/ *a* sounding; resonant, loud; sonorous

sonreir, sonreírse /son'reir, sone'reirse/ *vi* and *vr irr* to smile; —*vi* look pleasant (landscape, etc.); look favorable (of circumstances). **sonreir tras la barba,** to laugh to oneself. See **reir**

sonriente /son'riente/ *a* smiling

sonrisa /son'risa/ *f*, smile

sonrojar /sonro'har/ *vt* to cause to blush; —*vr* blush

sonrosado /sonro'saðo/ *a* rosy, rose-colored, pink

sonrosar /sonro'sar/ *vt* to make rose-colored; —*vr* blush, flush

sonroseo /sonro'seo/ *m*, blush, flush

sonsaca /son'saka/ *f*, removal by stealth; pilfering; enticement; *Fig.* pumping (of a person for information)

sonsacar /sonsa'kar/ *vt* to remove by stealth; steal, pilfer; entice away; *Fig.* pump (a person for information), draw out

sonsonete /sonso'nete/ *m*, rhythmic tapping or drumming; monotonous sound (gen. unpleasant); sarcastic tone of voice

soñador /soɲa'ðor/ **(-ra)** *a* dreamy, sleepy —*n* dreamer

soñar /so'ɲar/ *vt* to dream; imagine, conjure up; (*with con*) dream of; (*with prep a*) fear (of persons)

soñoliento /soɲo'liento/ *a* sleepy, drowsy; soothing; slow, leisurely

¡Soo! /soo/ *interj* Whoa! (command to horses, etc.)

sopa /'sopa/ *f*, sop, piece of bread; soup. **s. boba,** beggar's portion; life of ease at others' expense. **an-**

dar a la s., to beg one's way. **hecho una s.,** *Inf.* wet through

sopapo /so'papo/ *m*, chuck under the chin; *Inf.* slap; valve

sopera /so'pera/ *f*, soup tureen

sopero /so'pero/ *m*, soup plate, soup bowl —*a* fond of soup

sopesar /sope'sar/ *vt* to try the weight of

sopetón /sope'ton/ *m*, blow, cuff. **de s.,** suddenly

soplada /so'plaða/ *f*, puff of wind

soplado /so'plaðo/ *a Inf.* overelegant; haughty, stiff. *m*, fissure, chasm

soplador /sopla'ðor/ **(-ra)** *a* instigatory. *m*, blower, fan —*n* instigator; blower

soplar /so'plar/ *vi* to blow; —*vt* blow; blow away; inflate, blow up; filch, steal; instigate, inspire; accuse; fan; prompt, help out; —*vr* eat and drink too much; *Inf.* be puffed up, grow haughty —*interj* **¡Sopla!** *Inf.* You don't say so!

soplete /so'plete/ *m*, blowpipe

soplo /'soplo/ *m*, blow; blowing; instant, trice; *Inf.* hint, tip; *Inf.* accusation; *Inf.* tale-bearer; puff, breath (of wind)

soplón /so'plon/ **(-ona)** *a Inf.* tale-bearing, backbiting —*n* tale-bearer. *m*, *Auto.* scavenger

soponcio /so'ponθio; so'ponsio/ *m*, *Inf.* fainting fit

sopor /so'por/ *m*, stupor; deep sleep

soporífero /sopo'rifero/ *a* soporiferous

soportable /sopor'taβle/ *a* bearable

soportador /soporta'ðor/ **(-ra)** *a* supporting —*n* supporter

soportal /sopor'tal/ *m*, portico

soportar /sopor'tar/ *vt* to bear; carry, support; put up with, tolerate

soporte /so'porte/ *m*, rest, support; *Mech.* bearing; *Mech.* bracket, support

sopuntar /sopun'tar/ *vt* to underline in dots

sor /sor/ *f*, *Eccl.* sister (used of nuns)

sorbedor /sorβe'ðor/ **(-ra)** *a* supping, sipping —*n* sipper

sorber /sor'βer/ *vt* to suck; imbibe; swallow; *Fig.* absorb eagerly (ideas); sip

sorbete /sor'βete/ *m*, sherbet, iced drink; French ice cream

sorbo /'sorβo/ *m*, sucking; imbibition; swallow; sip; mouthful, gulp

sordamente /sorða'mente/ *adv* secretly, quietly

sordera /sor'ðera/ *f*, deafness

sordidez /sorði'ðeθ; sorði'ðes/ *f*, sordidness

sórdido /'sorðiðo/ *a* dirty, squalid; mean, niggardly; sordid

sordina /sor'ðina/ *f*, *Mus.* sordine, mute; *Mus.* damper. **a la s.,** on the quiet, in secret

sordo /'sorðo/ *a* deaf; silent; quiet; dull, muted (of sounds); insensible, inanimate; obdurate, uncompliant. **a la sorda** *or* **a lo s.** *or* **a sordas,** in silence, quietly

sordomudez /sorðomu'ðeθ; sorðomu'ðes/ *f*, deaf-muteness, deaf-mutism

sordomudo /sorðo'muðo/ **(-da)** *a* and *n* deaf-mute

sorna /'sorna/ *f*, slowness, sluggishness; craftiness, guile, knavery; malice

sorprendente /sorpren'dente/ *a* surprising, amazing

sorprender /sorpren'der/ *vt* to surprise, amaze

sorpresa /sor'presa/ *f*, surprise; amazement; shock

sortear /sorte'ar/ *vt* to raffle; draw lots for; avoid artfully (difficulties, etc.); fight (bulls)

sorteo /sor'teo/ *m*, raffle; casting lots

sortero /sor'tero/ **(-ra)** *n* sorcerer; holder of a draw ticket

sortija /sor'tiha/ *f*, ring (for a finger); ring (for a curtain, etc.); curl

sortilegio /sorti'lehio/ *m*, sorcery, magic

sortílego /sor'tilego/ **(-ga)** *a* magic —*n* sorcerer, fortuneteller

sosa /'sosa/ *f*, sodium carbonate, soda ash. **s. cáustica,** sodiumhydroxide, caustic soda, soda

sosegado /sose'gaðo/ *a* tranquil, peaceful, calm

sosegador /sosega'ðor/ **(-ra)** *a* soothing, calming —*n* appeaser, soother

sosegar /sose'gar/ *vt irr* to soothe, quiet; reassure;

appease, moderate; —*vi* grow still; rest, sleep; —*vr* grow quiet; calm down, be appeased; grow still. See **cegar**

sosería /sose'ria/ *f,* insipidness; lack of wit, dullness; stupidity

sosia /'sosia/ *m,* double, exact likeness (of persons)

sosiego /so'siego/ *m,* calm; peace, tranquility

soslayar /sosla'yar/ *vt* to slant, place in an oblique position; *Fig.* go around (a difficulty)

soslayo /sos'layo/ *a* slanting. **al s.,** obliquely, on the slant; askance

soso /'soso/ *a* saltless, insipid; dull, uninteresting; heavy (of people)

sospecha /sos'petʃa/ *f,* suspicion

sospechar /sospe'tʃar/ *vt* and *vi* to suspect

sospechoso /sospe'tʃoso/ *a* suspicious. *m,* suspect

sostén /sos'ten/ *m,* support; *Mech.* stand, support; brassiere, bra, bustier; steadiness (of a ship)

sostenedor /sostene'ðor/ **(-ra)** *a* supporting —*n* supporter

sostener /soste'ner/ *vt irr* to support; defend, uphold; bear, tolerate; help, aid; maintain, support. **s. una conversación,** to carry on a conversation. See **tener**

sostenido /soste'niðo/ *a Mus.* sostenuto, sustained —*a* and *m, Mus.* sharp

sostenimiento /sosteni'miento/ *m,* support; defense; toleration, endurance; maintenance, sustenance

sota /'sota/ *f,* jack, knave (in cards); *Inf.* baggage, hussy. *m,* foreman, supervisor —*prep* deputy, substitute (e.g. *sotamontero,* deputy huntsman)

sotabanco /sota'βanko/ *m,* attic, garret

sotana /so'tana/ *f,* gown, cassock, robe

sótano /'sotano/ *m,* basement, cellar

sotavento /sota'βento/ *m,* leeward. **a s.,** on the lee

sotechado /sote'tʃaðo/ *m,* hut, shed

soterrar /sote'rrar/ *vt irr* to bury in the ground; hide, conceal. See **acertar**

sotileza /soti'leθa; soti'lesa/ *f,* fine cord for fishing (in Santander province)

soto /'soto/ *m,* thicket, grove, copse

soviético /so'βietiko/ *a* soviet

sovietismo /soβie'tismo/ *m,* sovietism

sovietizar /soβieti'θar; soβieti'sar/ *vt* to sovietize

sovoz, a /so'βoθ, a; so'βos, a/ *adv* in a low voice

su, sus /su, sus/ *poss pron 3rd pers mf sing* and *pl* his, her, its, one's, your, their

suasorio /sua'sorio/ *a* suasive, persuasive

suave /'suaβe/ *a* soft, smooth; sweet; pleasant; harmonious, quiet; slow, gentle; meek; delicate, subtle

suavidad /suaβi'ðað/ *f,* softness, smoothness; sweetness; pleasantness; quietness; gentleness; meekness; delicacy

suavizador /suaβiθa'ðor; suaβisa'ðor/ *a* softening, smoothing; soothing, quietening. *m,* razor strop

suavizar /suaβi'θar; suaβi'sar/ *vt* to soften; smooth; strop (a razor); moderate, temper; *Mech.* steady; quieten; ease

subalpino /suβal'pino/ *a* subalpine

subalternar /suβalter'nar/ *vt* to put down, subdue

subalterno /suβal'terno/ *a* subordinate. *m,* subordinate; *Mil.* subaltern

subarrendar /suβarren'dar/ *vt irr* to sublet. See **recomendar**

subarrendatario /suβarrenda'tario/ **(-ia)** *n* sublessee

subarriendo /suβa'rriendo/ *m,* sublease, sublet

subasta /su'βasta/ *f,* auction sale. **sacar a pública s.,** to sell by auction

subastar /suβas'tar/ *vt* to auction

subcentral /suβθen'tral; suβsen'tral/ *f,* substation

subclase /suβ'klase/ *f,* subclass

subcolector /suβkolek'tor/ *m,* assistant collector

subcomisión /suβkomi'sion/ *f,* subcommittee

subconsciencia /suβkons'θienθia; suβkons'siensia/ *f,* subconscious

subcutáneo /suβku'taneo/ *a* subcutaneous

subdelegar /suβðele'gar/ *vt* to subdelegate

subdirector /suβðirek'tor/ **(-ra)** *n* deputy, assistant director

súbdito /'suβðito/ **(-ta)** *a* dependent, subject —*n* subject (of a state)

subdividir /suβðiβi'ðir/ *vt* to subdivide

subdominante /suβðomi'nante/ *f, Mus.* subdominant

subgénero /suβ'henero/ *m,* subgenus

subgobernador /suβgoβerna'ðor/ *m,* deputy governor, lieutenant governor

subibaja /suβi'βaha/ *f,* seesaw, teetertotter

subida /su'βiða/ *f,* ascension, ascent; upgrade; rise; carrying up; raising (of a theater curtain)

subidero /suβi'ðero/ *m,* uphill road; mounting block; way up (to a higher level)

subido /su'βiðo/ *a* strong (of scents); deep (of colors); expensive, high-priced; best, finest

subidor /suβi'ðor/ *m,* porter, carrier; elevator

subintendente /suβinten'dente/ *m,* deputy or assistant intendant

subir /su'βir/ *vi* to ascend, climb, go up; mount; rise; *Com.* amount (to), reach; prosper, advance, be promoted; grow more acute (of illnesses); intensify; *Mus.* raise the pitch (of an instrument or voice); —*vt* ascend, climb; pick up, take up; raise up; place higher; build up, make taller; straighten up, place in a vertical position; increase, raise (in price or value); —*vr* ascend, climb. **s. a caballo,** to mount a horse. **subirse a la cabeza,** *Inf.* to go to one's head (of alcohol, etc.)

subitáneo /suβi'taneo/ *a* sudden

súbito /'suβito/ *a* unexpected, unforeseen; sudden; precipitate, impulsive —*adv* suddenly (also **de s.**)

subjefe /suβ'hefe/ *m,* deputy chief, second in command

subjetividad /suβhetiβi'ðað/ *f,* subjectivity

subjetivismo /suβheti'βismo/ *m,* subjectivism

subjetivo /suβhe'tiβo/ *a* subjective

subjuntivo /suβhun'tiβo/ *a* and *m,* subjunctive

sublevación /suβleβa'θion; suβleβa'sion/ *f,* **sublevamiento** *m,* rebellion, mutiny, uprising

sublevar /suβle'βar/ *vt* to rouse to rebellion; excite (indignation, etc.); —*vr* rebel

sublimación /suβlima'θion; suβlima'sion/ *f,* sublimation

sublimado /suβli'maðo/ *m, Chem.* sublimate

sublimar /suβli'mar/ *vt* to exalt, raise up; *Chem.* sublimate

sublime /su'βlime/ *a* sublime

sublimidad /suβlimi'ðað/ *f,* sublimity, majesty, nobility

submarino /suβma'rino/ *a* submarine. *m,* submarine. **s. de bolsillo** or **s. enano,** midget submarine

suboficial /suβofi'θial; suβofi'sial/ *m, Mil.* subaltern; *Nav.* petty officer

subordinación /suβorðina'θion; suβorðina'sion/ *f,* dependence, subordination

subordinado /suβorði'naðo/ **(-da)** *a* and *n* subordinate

subordinar /suβorði'nar/ *vt* to subordinate

subpolar /suβpo'lar/ *a* subpolar

subprefecto /suβpre'fekto/ *m,* subprefect

subproducto /suβpro'ðukto/ *m,* by-product

subrayar /suβra'yar/ *vt* to underline; emphasize

subrepción /suβrep'θion; suβrep'sion/ *f,* underhand dealing; *Law.* subreption

subrepticio /suβrep'tiθio; suβrep'tisio/ *a* surreptitious; clandestine

subrogación /suβroga'θion; suβroga'sion/ *f,* surrogation

subrogar /suβro'gar/ *vt Law.* to surrogate, elect as a substitute

subs /suβs/ -- For words so beginning not found here, see **sus-**

subsanar /suβsa'nar/ *vt* to make excuses for; remedy, put right; indemnify

subscriptor /suβskrip'tor/ **(-ra)** *n* subscriber

subsección /suβsek'θion; suβsek'sion/ *f,* subsection

subsecretaría /suβsekreta'ria/ *f,* assistant secretaryship; assistant secretary's office

subsecretario /suβsekre'tario/ **(-ia)** *n* assistant secretary

subsecuente /suβse'kuente/ *a* subsequent

subsidiario /suβsi'ðiario/ *a* subsidized; subsidiary

subsidio /suβ'siðio/ *m,* subsidy

subsiguiente /suβsi'giente/ *a* subsequent; next

subsistencia /suβsis'tenθia; suβsis'tensia/ f, permanence; stability; subsistence, maintenance; livelihood
subsistir /suβsis'tir/ vi to last, endure; subsist, live; make a livelihood
subsuelo /suβ'suelo/ m, subsoil, substratum
subteniente /suβte'niente/ m, Mil. second lieutenant
subterfugio /suβter'fuhio/ m, subterfuge, trick
subterráneo /suβte'rraneo/ a underground, subterranean. m, subterranean place
subtítulo /suβ'titulo/ m, subtitle; caption
subtropical /suβtropi'kal/ a subtropical
suburbano /suβur'βano/ **(-na)** a suburban —n suburbanite
suburbio /su'βurβio/ m, suburb
subvención /suββen'θion; suββen'sion/ f, subsidy, subvention, grant
subvencionar /suββenθio'nar; suββensio'nar/ vt to subsidize
subvenir /suββe'nir/ vt irr to help, succor; subsidize. See **venir**
subversivo /suββer'siβo/ a subversive
subvertir /suββer'tir/ vt irr to subvert, overturn, ruin. See **sentir**
subyugación /suβyuga'θion; suβyuga'sion/ f, subjugation
subyugador /suβyuga'ðor/ **(-ra)** a subjugating —n conqueror
subyugar /suβyu'gar/ vt to subjugate, overcome
succión /suk'θion; suk'sion/ f, suction
sucedáneo /suθe'ðaneo; suse'ðaneo/ m, Med. succedaneum
suceder /suθe'ðer; suse'ðer/ vi to follow, come after; inherit, succeed —impers happen, occur
sucedido /suθe'ðiðo; suse'ðiðo/ m, Inf. event, occurrence
sucesión /suθe'sion; suse'sion/ f, succession; series; offspring, descendants; Law. estate
sucesivo /suθe'siβo; suse'siβo/ a successive. **en lo s.,** in future
suceso /su'θeso; su'seso/ m, happening, occurrence; course (of time); outcome, result
sucesor /suθe'sor; suse'sor/ **(-ra)** a succeeding —n successor
suciedad /suθie'ðað; susie'ðað/ f, dirt; filth, nastiness; obscenity
sucinto /su'θinto; su'sinto/ a succinct, brief, concise
sucio /'suθio; 'susio/ a dirty, unclean; stained; easily soiled; Fig. sullied, spotted; obscene; dirty (of colors); Fig. tainted, infected. **jugar s.,** Sports. to play in an unsporting manner
suco /'suko/ m, juice
sucoso /su'koso/ a juicy
suculencia /suku'lenθia; suku'lensia/ f, succulence; juiciness
suculento /suku'lento/ a succulent; juicy
sucumbir /sukum'βir/ vi to yield, give in; die, succumb; lose a lawsuit
sucursal /sukur'sal/ a branch. f, Com. branch (of a firm)
sud /suð/ m, south (gen. **sur**). Used in combinations like **sudamericano**
sudadero /suða'ðero/ m, horse blanket; sudatorium, sweating bath
sudafricano /suðafri'kano/ **(-na)** a and n South African
sudamericano /suðameri'kano/ **(-na)** a and n South American
Sudán, el /su'ðan, el/ the Sudan
sudante /su'ðante/ a sweating, perspiring
sudar /su'ðar/ vi and vt to perspire, sweat; ooze; —vi Inf. toil; —vt bathe in sweat; Inf. give reluctantly. **s. frío,** to break out in a cold sweat. **s. la gota gorda,** Fig. Inf. to be in a stew
sudario /su'ðario/ m, shroud
sudeste /su'ðeste/ m, southeast; southeast wind
sudexpreso /suðeks'preso/ m, southern express
sudoeste /suðo'este/ m, southwest; southwest wind
sudor /su'ðor/ m, sweat, perspiration; toil; juice, moisture, sap, gum
sudoroso /suðo'roso/ a sweaty
sudsudeste /suðsu'ðeste/ m, southsoutheast

sudsudoeste /suðsuðo'este/ m, southsouthwest
Suecia /'sueθia; 'suesia/ Sweden
sueco /'sueko/ **(-ca)** a Swedish —n Swede. m, Swedish (language)
suegra /'suegra/ f, mother-in-law
suegro /'suegro/ m, father-in-law
suela /'suela/ f, sole (of a shoe); Ichth. sole; tanned leather; base. **no llegarle a uno a la s. del zapato,** Inf. to be not fit to hold a candle to.
sueldo /'sueldo/ m, salary, wages; Obs. Spanish coin. **a s.,** for a salary, salaried
suelo /'suelo/ m, ground, earth; soil; bottom, base; sediment, dregs; site, plot; floor; flooring; story; land, territory; hoof (of horses); earth, world; pl floor of grain. **s. natal,** native land; **besar el s.,** Inf. to fall flat. **dar consigo en el s.,** to fall down. **dar en el s. con,** to throw down; damage, spoil. Inf. **estar (una cosa) por los suelos,** to be dirt cheap
suelta /'suelta/ f, loosening, unfastening; hobble (for horses); relay of oxen. **dar s. a,** to let loose, allow to go out for a time
suelto /'suelto/ a swift; competent, efficient; odd, separate; licentious; flowing, easy (style); loose, unbound. m, single copy (of a newspaper); loose change; newspaper paragraph
sueño /'sueɲo/ m, dream; sleep; drowsiness, desire for sleep; vision, fancy. **s. pesado,** deep sleep. **conciliar el s.,** to court sleep. **echar un s.,** Inf. to take a nap. **en sueños,** in a dream; while asleep. **entre sueños,** between sleeping and waking. **¡Ni por sueño!** Inf. Certainly not! I wouldn't dream of it!
suero /'suero/ m, serum. **s. de la leche,** whey
suerte /'suerte/ f, chance, luck; good luck; destiny; fate; condition, state; kind, species, sort; way, manner; bullfighter's maneuver; parcel of land. **de s. que,** so that; as a result. **echar suertes,** to draw lots. **tener buena s.,** to be lucky
sueste /'sueste/ m, southeast; sou'wester (cap)
suéter /'sueter/ m, sweater
suevo /'sueβo/ **(-va)** a and n Swabian
suficiencia /sufi'θienθia; sufi'siensia/ f, sufficiency; talent, aptitude; pedantry. **a s.,** enough
suficiente /sufi'θiente; sufi'siente/ a sufficient, enough; suitable
sufijo /su'fiho/ m, suffix
sufismo /su'fismo/ m, Sufism
sufragar /sufra'gar/ vt to assist, aid; favor; pay, defray
sufragio /su'frahio/ m, aid, assistance; Eccl. suffragium, pious offering; vote; suffrage
sufragista /sufra'hista/ f, suffragette
sufrible /su'friβle/ a bearable, endurable
sufrido /su'friðo/ a long-suffering, resigned; complaisant (of husbands); dirt-resistant (colors)
sufrimiento /sufri'miento/ m, suffering, pain; affliction; tolerance
sufrir /su'frir/ vt to suffer, undergo, experience; bear, endure; tolerate, put up with; allow, permit; resist, oppose; expiate; —vi suffer
sugerir /suhe'rir/ vt irr to suggest. See **sentir**
sugestión /suhes'tion/ f, suggestion
sugestionable /suhestio'naβle/ a easily influenced, open to suggestion
sugestionador /suhestiona'ðor/ a suggestive
sugestionar /suhestio'nar/ vt to suggest hypnotically; dominate, influence
sugestivo /suhes'tiβo/ a suggestive, stimulating
suicida /sui'θiða; sui'siða/ a suicidal, fatal. mf suicide (person)
suicidarse /suiθi'ðarse; suisi'ðarse/ vr to commit suicide
suicidio /sui'θiðio; sui'siðio/ m, suicide (act)
Suiza /'suiθa; 'suisa/ Switzerland
suiza /'suiθa; 'suisa/ f, row, rumpus, scrap
suizo /'suiθo; 'suiso/ **(-za)** a and n Swiss
sujeción /suhe'θion; suhe'sion/ f, subjection, domination; fastening, fixture; obedience, conformity
sujetador /suheta'ðor/ m, clamp; clip
sujetar /suhe'tar/ vt to fasten, fix; hold down; grasp, clutch; subdue; —vr (with prep a) conform to, obey. **s. con alfileres,** to pin up. **s. con tornillos,** to screw down

sujeto /su'heto/ *a* liable, subject. *m*, topic, subject; person, individual; *Gram. Philos.* subject

sulfatar /sulfa'tar/ *vt* to sulphate

sulfato /sul'fato/ *m*, sulphate

sulfurar /sulfu'rar/ *vt* to sulphurate; —*vr* grow irritated, become angry

sulfúrico /sul'furiko/ *a* sulphuric

sulfuro /sul'furo/ *m*, sulphide

sulfuroso /sulfu'roso/ *a* sulphurous

sultán /sul'tan/ *m*, sultan

sultana /sul'tana/ *f*, sultana

sultanía /sulta'nia/ *f*, sultanate

suma /'suma/ *f*, total; amount, sum; *Math.* addition; summary, digest; computation. **en s.**, in brief, in short, finally

sumador /suma'ðor/ **(-ra)** *n* summarizer; computator, adder

sumamente /suma'mente/ *adv* extremely, most

sumar /su'mar/ *vt* to sum up, summarize; *Math.* add up

sumaria /su'maria/ *f*, written indictment

sumariamente /sumaria'mente/ *adv* concisely, in brief; *Law.* summarily

sumario /su'mario/ *a* brief, concise, abridged; *Law.* summary. *m*, summary, résumé, digest

sumergible /sumer'hiβle/ *a* sinkable; submergible. *m*, submarine

sumergir /sumer'hir/ *vt* to dip, immerse; sink, submerge; *Fig.* overwhelm (with grief, etc.); —*vr* sink; dive; be submerged

sumersión /sumer'sion/ *f*, immersion, dive, submersion

sumidero /sumi'ðero/ *m*, cesspool; drain; sink; pit, gully

suministración /suministra'θion; suministra'sion/ *f.* See **suministro**

suministrador /suministra'ðor/ **(-ra)** *n* purveyor

suministrar /suminis'trar/ *vt* to purvey, supply, provide

suministro /sumi'nistro/ *m*, purveyance; provision; supply

sumir /su'mir/ *vt* to sink; submerge; *Eccl.* consum-mate; *Fig.* overwhelm (with grief, etc.); —*vr* fall in, become sunken (of cheeks, etc.); sink; be submerged

sumisión /sumi'sion/ *f*, submission, obedience; *Com.* estimate, tender

sumiso /su'miso/ *a* submissive, docile

sumista /su'mista/ *mf* quick reckoner, computator. *m*, condenser, summarizer, abridger

sumo /'sumo/ *a* supreme; high; tremendous, extraordinary. **a lo s.**, at the most; even if, although. **en s. grado,** in the highest degree

suntuosidad /suntuosi'ðað/ *f*, magnificence, luxury

suntuoso /sun'tuoso/ *a* magnificent, luxurious, sumptuous

supeditación /supeðita'θion; supeðita'sion/ *f*, subjection

supeditar /supeði'tar/ *vt* to oppress; overcome, conquer; subordinate

superabundancia /superaβun'danθia; superaβun-'dansia/ *f*, superabundance, excess; glut

superabundante /superaβun'dante/ *a* superabundant, excessive

superádito /supe'raðito/ *a* superadded

superar /supe'rar/ *vt* to overcome, conquer; surpass; do better than

superávit /supe'raβit/ *m*, *Com.* balance, surplus

superchería /supertʃe'ria/ *f*, trickery, guile

superchero /super'tʃero/ *a* guileful, wily

superconsciencia /superkons'θienθia; superkons-'siensia/ *f*, higher consciousness

supereminencia /superemi'nenθia; superemi'nensia/ *f*, supereminence, greatest eminence

supereminente /superemi'nente/ *a* supereminent

superentender /superenten'der/ *vt irr* to supervise, superintend. See **entender**

supererogación /supereroga'θion; supereroga'sion/ *f*, supererogation

superestructura /superestruk'tura/ *f*, superstructure

superficial /superfi'θial; superfi'sial/ *a* surface, shallow; superficial, rudimentary; futile

superficialidad /superfiθiali'ðað; superfisiali'ðað/ *f*, superficiality; futility; shallowness

superficie /super'fiθie; super'fisie/ *f*, area; surface; outside, exterior. **s. de rodadura,** tire tread

superfino /super'fino/ *a* superfine

superfluidad /superflui'ðað/ *f*, superfluity

superfluo /su'perfluo/ *a* superfluous, redundant

superfortaleza volante /superforta'leθa bo'lante; superforta'lesa bo'lante/ *f, Aer.* superfortress

superhombre /super'ombre/ *m*, superman

superintendencia /superinten'denθia; superinten-'densia/ *f*, supervision; superintendentship; higher administration

superintendente /superinten'dente/ *mf* superintendent; supervisor

superior /supe'rior/ *a* higher, upper; excellent, fine; superior; higher (education, etc.). *m*, head, director; superior

superiora /supe'riora/ *f*, mother superior

superioridad /superiori'ðað/ *f*, superiority

superlativo /superla'tiβo/ *a* and *m*, superlative

superno /su'perno/ *a* supreme

supernumerario /supernume'rario/ **(-ia)** *a* and *n* supernumerary

superposición /superposi'θion; superposi'sion/ *f*, superposition

superproducción /superproðuk'θion; superproðuk-'sion/ *f*, overproduction; superproduction

superrealismo /superrea'lismo/ *m*, surrealism

superrealista /superrea'lista/ *a* surrealist

superstición /supersti'θion; supersti'sion/ *f*, superstition

supersticioso /supersti'θioso; supersti'sioso/ *a* superstitious

supervención /superβen'θion; superβen'sion/ *f*, *Law.* supervention

supervivencia /superβi'βenθia; superβi'βensia/ *f*, survival

superviviente /superβi'βiente/ *a* surviving. *mf* survivor

supino /su'pino/ *a* supine; foolish, stupid. *m*, *Gram.* supine

suplantación /suplanta'θion; suplanta'sion/ *f*, supplanting

suplantador /suplanta'ðor/ **(-ra)** *a* supplanting —*n* supplanter

suplantar /suplan'tar/ *vt* to forge, alter (documents); supplant

suplefaltas /suple'faltas/ *mf Inf.* scapegoat

suplementario /suplemen'tario/ *a* supplementary, additional

suplemento /suple'mento/ *m*, supplement; supply, supplying; newspaper supplement; *Geom.* supplement

suplente /su'plente/ *m*, substitute, proxy; *Fig.* makeweight

súplica /'suplika/ *f*, supplication, prayer; request

suplicación /suplika'θion; suplika'sion/ *f*, entreaty, supplication; *Law.* petition

suplicante /supli'kante/ *a* supplicatory; *Law.* petitioning. *mf* supplicator; *Law.* petitioner

suplicar /supli'kar/ *vt* to beg, supplicate; request; *Law.* appeal

suplicio /su'pliθio; su'plisio/ *m*, torment, torture; execution; place of torture or execution; affliction, anguish. **último s.**, capital punishment

suplir /su'plir/ *vt* to supply, furnish; substitute, take the place of; overlook, forgive

suponer /supo'ner/ *vt irr* to suppose, take for granted; simulate; comprise, include; —*vi* carry weight, wield authority. See **poner**

suposición /suposi'θion; suposi'sion/ *f*, supposition; conjecture, assumption; distinction, talent, importance; falsity, falsehood

supositorio /suposi'torio/ *m*, suppository

suprasensible /suprasen'siβle/ *a* supersensible

supremacía /suprema'θia; suprema'sia/ *f*, supremacy

supremo /su'premo/ *a* supreme; matchless, incomparable; last

supresión /supre'sion/ *f*, suppression; destruction, eradication; omission

suprimir /supri'mir/ *vt* to suppress; destroy, eradicate; omit, leave out. **s. una calle al tráfico,** to close a street to traffic, ban traffic from a street

supuesto /su'puesto/ *a* supposed; so-called; reputed. *m,* supposition, hypothesis. **por s.,** presumably; doubtless

supuración /supura'θion; supura'sion/ *f,* suppuration

supurar /supu'rar/ *vi* to suppurate

suputar /supu'tar/ *vt* to calculate, compute

sur /sur/ *m,* south; south wind

surcador /surka'ðor/ *m,* plowman

surcar /sur'kar/ *vt* to plow furrows; furrow, line; cut, cleave (water, etc.)

surco /'surko/ *m,* furrow; wrinkle, line; groove, channel; rut

surgidero /surhi'ðero/ *m, Naut.* road, roadstead

surgir /sur'hir/ *vi* to spout, gush, spurt; *Naut.* anchor; appear, show itself; come forth, turn up

surrealismo /surrea'lismo/ *m,* surrealism

surrealista /surrea'lista/ *a* and *mf* surrealist

surtida /sur'tiða/ *f,* hidden exit; false door; *Naut.* slipway

surtidero /surti'ðero/ *m,* outlet, drain; jet, fountain

surtido /sur'tiðo/ *a* mixed, assorted. *m,* variety, assortment; stock, range. **de s.,** in everyday use

surtidor /surti'ðor/ **(-ra)** *n* purveyor, supplier. *m,* fountain, jet. **s. de gasolina,** gasoline pump, gas pump

surtimiento /surti'miento/ *m,* assortment; stock

surtir /sur'tir/ *vt* to provide, supply, furnish; —*vi* spurt, gush

surto /'surto/ *a* calm, reposeful; *Naut.* anchored

¡sus! /sus/ *interj* Come on! Hurry up!

susceptibilidad /susθeptiβili'ðað; susseptiβili'ðað/ *f,* susceptibility

susceptible /susθep'tiβle; sussep'tiβle/ *a* susceptible, open to; touchy, oversensitive

suscitar /susθi'tar; sussi'tar/ *vt* to cause, originate; provoke, incite; —*vr* arise, take place

suscribir /suskri'βir/ *vt* to sign; agree to; —*vr* subscribe, contribute; take out a subscription (to a periodical, etc.) —*Past Part.* **suscrito**

suscripción /suskrip'θion; suskrip'sion/ *f,* subscription; agreement, accession

susodicho /suso'ðitʃo/ *a* aforesaid

suspender /suspen'der/ *vt* to suspend, hang up; postpone, defer, stop; amaze, dumbfound; suspend (from employment); fail (an exam); adjourn (meetings); —*vr* rear (of horses)

suspensión /suspen'sion/ *f,* suspension; postponement, stoppage, deferment; amazement; failure (in an exam); adjournment (of a meeting); springs (of a car). *Com.* **s. de pagos,** suspension of payments. **con mala s.,** badly sprung (of a car)

suspensivo /suspen'siβo/ *a* suspensive

suspensivos /suspen'siβos/ *m, pl* suspension points, ellipsis points

suspenso /sus'penso/ *a* amazed, bewildered. *m,* failure slip (in an exam). **en s.,** in suspense

suspicacia /suspi'kaθia; suspi'kasia/ *f,* suspiciousness; mistrust, uneasiness

suspicaz /suspi'kaθ; suspi'kas/ *a* suspicious, mistrustful

suspirado /suspi'raðo/ *a* eagerly desired, longed for

suspirar /suspi'rar/ *vt* and *vi* to sigh. **s. por,** to long for

suspiro /sus'piro/ *m,* sigh; breath; glass whistle;

Mus. brief pause, pause sign. **último s.,** *Inf.* last kick, end

suspirón /suspi'ron/ *a* given to sighing

sustancia /sus'tanθia; sus'tansia/ *f,* substance, juice, extract, essence; *Fig.* core, pith; *Fig.* meat; wealth, estate; worth, importance; nutritive part; *Inf.* common sense. *Anat.* **s. gris,** gray matter. **en s.,** in short

sustanciación /sustanθia'θion; sustansia'sion/ *f,* substantiation

sustancial /sustan'θial; sustan'sial/ *a* substantial, real; important, essential; nutritive; solid

sustanciar /sustan'θiar; sustan'siar/ *vt* to substantiate; summarize, extract, abridge

sustancioso /sustan'θioso; sustan'sioso/ *a* substantial; nutritive

sustantivo /sustan'tiβo/ *a* and *m, Gram.* substantive, noun

sustentable /susten'taβle/ *a* arguable, defensible

sustentación /sustenta'θion; sustenta'sion/ *f,* maintenance; defense

sustentar /susten'tar/ *vt* to sustain, keep; support; bear; nourish, feed; uphold, advocate. **s. un ciclo de conferencias,** to give a series of lectures

sustento /sus'tento/ *m,* maintenance, preservation; nourishment, sustenance; support

sustitución /sustitu'θion; sustitu'sion/ *f,* substitution

sustituible /sustitu'iβle/ *a* substitutive, replaceable

sustituir /sustitu'ir/ *vt irr* to substitute. See **huir**

sustitutivo /sustitu'tiβo/ *a* substitutive

sustituto /sustitu'tuto/ **(-ta)** *n* substitute

susto /'susto/ *m,* fright, shock; apprehension. **dar un s. (a),** to scare

sustracción /sustrak'θion; sustrak'sion/ *f,* subtraction

sustraendo /sustra'endo/ *m, Math.* subtrahend

sustraer /sustra'er/ *vt irr* to remove, separate; rob, steal; *Math.* subtract; —*vr* depart, remove oneself; avoid. See **traer**

sustrato /sus'trato/ *m,* substratum

susurrador /susurra'ðor/ **(-ra)** *a* whispering; murmuring; rustling —*n* whisperer

susurrante /susu'rrante/ *a* whispering; murmuring; rustling

susurrar /susu'rrar/ *vi* to whisper; murmur; rustle; babble, purl, prattle (of water); —*vi* and *vr* be whispered abroad

susurro /su'surro/ *m,* whispering, whisper; murmur; rustle; lapping

sutil /'sutil/ *a* fine, thin; penetrating, subtle, keen

sutileza, sutilidad /suti'leθa, sutili'ðað/ suti'lesa, sutili'ðað/ *f,* fineness, thinness; subtlety, penetration. **sutileza de manos,** dexterity; light-fingeredness; sleight of hand

sutilizaciones /sutiliθa'θiones; sutilisa'siones/ *f, pl* casuistry, hairsplitting, quibbling

sutilizar /sutili'θar; sutili'sar/ *vt* to make thin, refine; *Fig.* finish, perfect; *Fig.* split hairs, make subtle distinctions

sutura /su'tura/ *f,* suture

suyo, suya /'suyo, 'suya/ *m,* and *f, pl* **suyos, suyas,** *poss pron* and *a* 3rd *pers* his; hers; its; yours; theirs; of his, of hers, etc. (e.g. *Este libro es suyo,* This book is his (hers, yours, theirs). **Este libro es uno de los suyos,** This book is one of his (hers, etc.). (**suyo** is often used with def. art. **el, la,** etc.) **los suyos,** his (hers, yours, etc.) family, following, adherents, etc. **de suyo,** of its very nature, of itself; spontaneously. **salirse con la suya,** to get one's own way. *Inf.* **ver la suyo,** to see one's opportunity

tabacal /taβa'kal/ *m,* tobacco plantation

tabacalero /taβaka'lero/ **(-ra)** *a* tobacco —*n* tobacco merchant; tobacco planter

tabaco /ta'βako/ *m,* tobacco plant, tobacco leaf; tobacco; cigar. **t. de pipa,** pipe tobacco. **t. flojo,** mild tobacco. **t. rubio,** Virginia tobacco

tabalear /taβale'ar/ **(se)** *vt* and *vr* to rock, sway, swing; —*vi* drum with the fingers

tabaleo /taβa'leo/ *m,* swaying, rocking; drumming with the fingers

tabanco /ta'βanko/ *m,* market stall

tábano /'taβano/ *m, Ent.* horsefly

tabanque /ta'βanke/ *m,* potter's wheel

tabaque /ta'βake/ *m,* small osier basket (for fruit, sewing, etc.); large tack

tabaquera /taβa'kera/ *f,* tobacco jar, tobacco tin; bowl of pipe tobacco; tobacco pouch; snuffbox

tabaquería /taβake'ria/ *f,* tobacconist's shop

tabaquero /taβa'kero/ **(-ra)** *n* worker in a tobacco factory; tobacconist

tabaquismo /taβa'kismo/ *m,* nicotinism, nicotine poisoning

tabaquista /taβa'kista/ *mf* tobacco expert; heavy smoker

tabardillo /taβar'ðiʎo; taβarðiyo/ *m,* fever. **t. de tripas,** typhoid. **t. pintado,** typhus

tabardo /ta'βarðo/ *m,* tabard

taberna /ta'βerna/ *f,* public house, tavern

tabernáculo /taβer'nakulo/ *m,* tabernacle

tabernario /taβer'nario/ *a* public house, tavern; low, vulgar

tabernera /taβer'nera/ *f,* publican's wife; barmaid

tabernero /taβer'nero/ *m,* publican; barman, drawer

tabicar /taβi'kar/ *vt* to wall or board up; hide, cover up

tabique /ta'βike/ *m,* partition wall, inside wall; thin wall

tabla /'taβla/ *f,* plank of wood, board; *Metall.* plate; slab; flat side, face (of wood); *Sew.* box pleat; table (of contents, etc.); *Art.* panel; vegetable garden; butcher's slab; butcher's stall; *pl* tablets (for writing); (*Math.* etc.) tables; stalemate (chess, checkers); draw (in an election); *Theat.* boards, stage. **t. de armonía,** sounding board (of musical instruments). **t. de lavar,** washboard. **t. de materias,** table of contents. **t. de multiplicación,** multiplication table. **t. rasa,** clean sheet (of paper, etc.); complete ignorance. **T. Redonda,** Round Table (of King Arthur). **escapar** or **salvarse en una t.,** to have a narrow escape, escape in the nick of time

tablacho /ta'βlatʃo/ *m,* sluice gate. **echar el t.,** *Inf.* to interrupt the flow of someone's remarks

tablado /ta'βlaðo/ *m,* flooring; platform; *Theat.* stage; scaffold, gibbet. **sacar al t.,** to produce, put on the stage; to make known, publish

tablazón /taβla'θon; taβla'son/ *f,* planks, boards; flooring; *Naut.* deck planks or sheathing

tablear /taβle'ar/ *vt* to saw into planks; *Sew.* make box pleats in; hammer iron into sheets

tablero /ta'βlero/ *m,* board (of wood); paneling, boarding; slab; shop counter; board (checkers, chess). **t. de instrumentos,** dashboard; instrument panel

tableta /ta'βleta/ *f,* tablet; pastille, lozenge

tablilla /ta'βliʎa; ta'βliya/ *f,* small board; tablet; bulletin board, notice board

tablón /ta'βlon/ *m,* thick plank; wooden beam; *Inf.* drinking bout

tabú /ta'βu/ *m,* taboo

tabuco /ta'βuko/ *m,* miserable little room; hovel

taburete /taβu'rete/ *m,* stool; tabouret

tacañería /takaɲe'ria/ *f,* miserliness, niggardliness; craftiness

tacaño /ta'kaɲo/ *a* miserly, niggardly; crafty

tacha /'tatʃa/ *f,* imperfection, defect; spot, stain; fault; large tack. **poner t.,** to criticize, object to

tachable /ta'tʃaβle/ *a* censurable, blameworthy

tachar /ta'tʃar/ *vt* to criticize, blame; cross out, erase; charge, accuse

tacho de basura /'tatʃo de ba'sura/ *m, Argentina* garbage can

tachón /ta'tʃon/ *m,* round-headed ornamental nail; *Sew.* gold or silver studs, trimming; crossing out, erasure

tachonar /tatʃo'nar/ *vt* to stud with round-headed nails; *Sew.* trim with gold or silver studs or trimming

tachoso /ta'tʃoso/ *a* imperfect, defective, faulty; spotted, stained

tachuela /ta'tʃuela/ *f,* tack

tácito /'taθito; 'tasito/ *a* silent, unexpressed; tacit, implied

taciturnidad /taθiturni'ðað; tasiturni'ðað/ *f,* taciturnity; reserve; melancholy

taciturno /taθi'turno; tasi'turno/ *a* taciturn; reserved; dismal, gloomy, melancholy

taco /'tako/ *m,* stopper, plug; billiard cue; rammer; wad, wadding (in a gun); pop gun; taco (food); tearoff calendar; *Inf.* snack; obscenity, oath. **t. de papel,** writing tablet

tacón /ta'kon/ *m,* heel (of a shoe)

taconear /takone'ar/ *vi* to stamp with one's heels; walk heavily on one's heels; walk arrogantly

taconeo /tako'neo/ *m,* drumming or stamping of one's heels (gen. in dancing)

táctica /'taktika/ *f,* method, technique; *Mil.* tactics; policy, way, means

táctico /'taktiko/ *a* tactical. *m, Mil.* tactician

táctil /'taktil/ *a* tactile

tacto /'takto/ *m,* sense of touch; touch, feel; touching; skill; tact

tafetán /tafe'tan/ *m,* taffeta; *pl* flags, standards. **t. de heridas** or **t. inglés,** court plaster

tafilete /tafi'lete/ *m,* morocco leather

tahalí /taa'li/ *m,* sword shoulder belt

tahona /ta'ona/ *f,* horse mill; bakery; baker's shop

tahonero /tao'nero/ **(-ra)** *n* miller; baker

tahúr /ta'ur/ *m,* gambler; cardsharper

tahurería /taure'ria/ *f,* gambling den; gambling; cheating at cards

Tailandia /tai'landia/ Thailand

taimado /tai'maðo/ *a* knavish, crafty; obstinate, headstrong

taimería /taime'ria/ *f,* cunning, craftiness

taita /'taita/ *m,* daddy

taja /'taha/ *f,* cut, cutting; slice; washboard

tajada /ta'haða/ *f,* slice; steak, portion; steak, filet; *Inf.* cough; drinking bout; hoarseness

tajadera /taha'ðera/ *f,* cheese knife; chisel; *pl* sluice gate

tajado /ta'haðo/ *a* steep, sheer (of cliffs, etc.)

tajadura /taha'ðura/ *f,* cutting, dividing, dissection

tajamar /taha'mar/ *m,* cutwater; breakwater; raft

tajar /ta'har/ *vt* to cut, chop; sharpen, trim (quill pens)

tajea /ta'hea/ *f,* culvert; aqueduct; drain; watercourse

Tajo, el /'taho, el/ the Tagus

tajo /'taho/ *m,* cut, incision; task; cutting (in a mountain, etc.); cut, thrust (of sword); executioner's block; chopping board; washboard; steep cliff, precipice

tajón /ta'hon/ *m,* butcher block; chopping board

tal /tal/ *a pl* **tales,** such; said (e.g. *el t. Don Juan,* the said Don Juan). **tal** is always used before nouns and (except when meaning "the said") without def. art. **un t.,** a certain (e.g. *un t. hombre,* a certain man) —*pron* some, some people; someone; such a thing —*adv* so, thus. **t. para cual,** two of a kind, a well-matched pair; tit for tat. **con t. que,** *conjunc* on condition that, provided that. **No hay t.,** There is no such thing. *Inf.* **¿Qué t.?** How are you? What's the news? What's new?

tala /'tala/ *f*, felling or cutting down (of trees); cropping of grass (ruminants)

talabarte /tala'βarte/ *m*, sword belt

talabartería /talaβarte'ria/ *f*, saddlery

talabartero /talaβar'tero/ *m*, saddler

talador /tala'ðor/ **(-ra)** *a* felling, cutting; destructive —*n* feller, cutter; destroyer

taladrar /tala'ðrar/ *vt* to drill, bore, gouge holes; pierce, perforate; punch (a ticket); assail or hurt the ear (sounds); *Fig.* go into deeply (a subject)

taladro /ta'laðro/ *m*, drill, gimlet, gouge; drill hole, bore; puncher (for tickets, etc.)

tálamo /'talamo/ *m*, marriage bed; (*Bot. Anat.*) thalamus

talán /ta'lan/ *m*, peal, tolling (of a bell)

talanquera /talan'kera/ *f*, barricade; parapet, fence, wall; refuge, asylum; safety, security

talante /ta'lante/ *m*, mode of execution, technique; personal appearance, mien; disposition, temperament; wish, desire; aspect, appearance. **de buen (mal) t.**, willingly (unwillingly)

talar /ta'lar/ *a* full-length, long (of gowns, robes, etc.)

talar /ta'lar/ *vt* to fell, chop down (trees); ravage, lay waste; prune (gen. olive trees)

talco /'talko/ *m*, *Mineral.* talc; sequin, tinsel

talcualillo /talkua'liʎo; talkua'liyo/ *a Inf.* not too bad, fairly good; slightly better (of health)

taled /ta'leð/ *m*, prayer shawl, tales, tallit

talega /ta'lega/ *f*, sack, bag; sackful; money bag; *pl Inf.* cash wealth

talego /ta'lego/ *m*, narrow sack; *Inf.* dumpy person

talento /ta'lento/ *m*, talent (Greek coin); talent, gift, quality; intelligence, understanding; cleverness

talentoso /talen'toso/ *a* talented

tálero /'talero/ *m*, thaler (old German coin)

talión /ta'lion/ *m*, **(ley de)** law of retaliation

talismán /talis'man/ *m*, talisman

talla /'taʎa; 'taya/ *f*, carving (especially wood); cutting (of gems); reward for apprehension of a criminal; ransom; stature, height, size; height measuring rod

tallado /ta'ʎaðo; ta'yaðo/ *a* **bien** (or **mal**), well (or badly) carved; well (or badly) proportioned, of a good (or bad) figure

tallado /ta'ʎaðo; ta'yaðo/ *m*, carving

tallador /taʎa'ðor; taya'ðor/ *m*, metal engraver; die sinker

tallar /ta'ʎar; ta'yar/ *vt Art.* to carve; engrave; cut (gems); value, estimate; measure height (of persons)

tallarín /taʎa'rin; taya'rin/ *m*, (gen. *pl*) *Cul.* noodle

talle /'taʎe; 'taye/ *m*, figure, physique; waist; fit (of clothes); appearance, aspect. *Inf.* **largo de t.**, long-waisted; long drawn out, overlong. **tener buen t.**, to have a good figure

tallecer /taʎe'θer; taye'ser/ *vi irr Bot.* to sprout, shoot. See **conocer**

taller /ta'ʎer; ta'yer/ *m*, workshop; factory; mill; workroom, atelier; industrial school; school of arts and crafts; studio

tallista /ta'ʎista; ta'yista/ *mf* engraver; wood carver; sculptor

tallo /'taʎo; 'tayo/ *m*, *Bot.* stalk; shoot; slice of preserved fruit; cabbage. **t. rastrero**, *Bot.* runner

talludo /ta'ʎuðo; ta'yuðo/ *a* long-stalked; lanky, overgrown; no longer young, aging (of women); habit-ridden

talmúdico /tal'muðiko/ *a* Talmudic

talón /ta'lon/ *m*, heel; heel (of a shoe); *Com.* counterfoil; luggage receipt; *Com.* sight draft; coupon; heel (of a violin bow). *Inf.* **apretar los talones**, to take to one's heels. *Inf.* **pisarle (a uno) los talones**, to follow on a person's heels; rival successfully

talonada /talo'naða/ *f*, dig in with the spurs

talonario /talo'nario/ *m*, stub book

tamaño /ta'maɲo/ *a compar* so big; so small (e.g. *La conocí tamaña*, I knew her when she was so high) (indicating her size with a gesture)); so great, so large (e.g. *tamaña empresa*, so great an undertaking). *m*, size

tamarindo /tama'rindo/ *m*, tamarind

tambaleante /tambale'ante/ *a* tottering, rickety; staggering

tambalear /tambale'ar/ **(se)** *vi* and *vr* to totter, sway, shake; reel, stagger

tambaleo /tamba'leo/ *m*, swaying; tottering; rocking; shaking; staggering, reeling

tambarillo /tamba'riʎo; tambariyo/ *m*, chest with an arched lid

también /tam'bien/ *adv* also, too; in addition, as well

tambor /tam'bor/ *m*, *Mus.* drum; drummer; embroidery frame; *Mech.* drum, cylinder; roaster (for coffee, chestnuts, etc.). **t. mayor**, drum major. **a t. (or con t.) batiente**, with drums beating; triumphantly, with colors flying

tamborear /tambore'ar/ *vi* to totter, sway; stagger, reel

tamboreo /tambo'reo/ *m*, tottering, swaying; staggering, reeling

tamboril /tambo'ril/ *m*, tabor

tamborilada /tambori'laða/ *f*, *Inf.* slap on the back or face; *Inf.* fall on the bottom

tamborilear /tamborile'ar/ *vi* to play the tabor; —*vt* eulogize, extol

tamborilero /tambori'lero/ *m*, tabor player

tamborín /tambo'rin/ *m*, tabor

Támesis, el /'tamesis, el/ the Thames

tamiz /ta'miθ; ta'mis/ *m*, sieve

tamizar /tami'θar; tami'sar/ *vt* to sieve

tamo /'tamo/ *m*, fluff; chaff

tampoco /tam'poko/ *adv* neither, not... either, nor... either; no more (e.g. *No lo ha hecho María t.*, Mary hasn't done it either)

tampón /tam'pon/ *m*, stamp moistener; *Surg.* tampon

tan /tan/ *adv Abbr.* **tanto** so, as. Used before adjectives and adverbs, excepting **más, mejor, menos, peor**, which need **tanto. t.... como**, as... as. **t. siquiera**, even (see **siquiera**). **t. sólo**, only, solely (e.g. *No vengo t. sólo para saludarte*, I do not come merely to greet you). **qué... t.**, what a... (e.g. *¡Qué día t. hermoso!* What a lovely day!)

tanda /'tanda/ *f*, turn; opportunity; task; shift, relay; game (of billiards); bad habit; collection, batch, group; round (of a game); (*Dance.*) set

tándem /'tandem/ *m*, tandem

tandeo /tan'deo/ *m*, allowance of irrigation water, turn for using water

Tangañica /taŋga'ɲika/ Tanganyika

tangente /tan'hente/ *a* and *f*, *Geom.* tangent

Tánger /'tanher/ Tangier

tangerino /tanhe'rino/ **(-na)** *a* and *n* of or from Tangier, Tangerine

tanque /'tanke/ *m*, *Mil.* tank; cistern, tank, reservoir; ladle, dipper

tanteador /tantea'ðor/ *m*, *Sports.* scorer, marker; scoreboard

tantear /tante'ar/ *vt* to measure, compare; consider fully; test, try out; *Fig.* probe, pump (persons); estimate roughly; *Art.* sketch, block in; —*vt* and *vi Sports.* keep the score of

tanteo /tan'teo/ *m*, measurement, comparison; test; rough estimate; *Sports.* score

tanto /'tanto/ *a* so much; as much; very great; as great; *pl* **tantos**, so many; as many (e.g. *Tienen tantas flores como nosotros*, They have as many flowers as we). In comparisons **tanto** is used before **más, mejor, menos, peor**, but generally **tan** is used before adjectives and adverbs (e.g. *¡Tanto peor!* So much the worse!) —*pron dem* that (e.g. *por lo t.*, therefore, on that account). *m*, so much, a certain amount; copy of a document; man, piece (in games); point (score in games); *Com.* rate (e.g. *el t. por ciento*, the percentage, the rate); *pl* approximation, odd (e.g. *Llegaron cien hombres y tantos*, A hundred-odd men arrived) —*adv* so much; as much; so, in such a way. **t.... como**, the same as, as much as. **t.... cuanto**, as much as. **t. más, the more. t. menos**, the less (e.g. *Cuanto más (menos)* **dinero tiene t. más (menos) quiere**, The more (less) money he has, the more (less) he wants). **t. más (menos)... cuanto que**, all the more (less)... because. **algún t.**, a certain amount, somewhat. **al t. de (una cosa)**, aware of, acquainted with (a thing). **en t. or entre t.**, meanwhile. **las tantas,** *Inf.* late hour, wee hours. **No es para t.,** *Inf.* It's not as bad as that, there's no need to make such a fuss; he (she, it) isn't equal to it. **otro t.,** the same, as much; as much more. **un t.,** a bit, somewhat

tañedor /taɲe'ðor/ **(-ra)** *n Mus.* player

tañer /ta'ɲer/ *vt irr Mus.* to play; —*vi* sway, swing. **t. la occisa,** to sound the death (in hunting) —*Pres. Part.* **tañendo.** *Preterite* **tañó, tañeron.** *Imperf. Subjunc.* **tañese,** etc.

tañido /ta'ɲiðo/ *m,* tune, sound, note; toll, peal; ring

taoísmo /tao'ismo/ *m,* Taoism

taoísta /tao'ista/ *mf* Taoist

tapa /'tapa/ *f,* lid; cover; cover (of books)

tapaboca /tapa'βoka/ *m,* blow on the mouth; *f,* scarf, muffler; *Inf.* remark that silences someone

tapada /ta'paða/ *f,* veiled woman, one whose face is hidden

tapadera /tapa'ðera/ *f,* loose lid, top, cover

tapadero /tapa'ðero/ *m,* stopper

tapador /tapa'ðor/ **(-ra)** *a* covering —*n* coverer. *m,* stopper; lid; cover

tapagujeros /tapagu'heros/ *m, Inf.* unskilled mason or bricklayer; *Fig. Inf.* stopgap (person)

tapar /ta'par/ *vt* to cover; cover with a lid; muffle up, veil; hide, keep secret; close up, stop up

taparrabo /tapa'rraβo/ *m,* loincloth; swimming trunks

tapete /ta'pete/ *m,* rug; tablecover. *Inf.* **t. verde,** gaming table. *Fig.* **estar sobre el t.,** to be on the carpet, be under consideration

tapia /'tapia/ *f,* adobe; mud wall; fence. *Inf.* **más sordo que una t.,** as deaf as a post

tapiar /ta'piar/ *vt* to wall up; put a fence around, fence in

tapicería /tapiθe'ria; tapise'ria/ *f,* set of tapestries; tapestry work; art of tapestry making; upholstery; tapestry storehouse or shop

tapicero /tapi'θero; tapi'sero/ *m,* tapestry weaver or maker; upholsterer; carpet layer; furnisher

tapioca /ta'pioka/ *f,* tapioca

tapiz /ta'piθ; ta'pis/ *m,* tapestry; carpet

tapizar /tapi'θar; tapi'sar/ *vt* to cover with tapestry; cover, clothe; upholster; carpet; hang with tapestry; furnish with hangings or drapes

tapón /ta'pon/ *m,* stopper; cork (of a bottle); plug; *Surg.* tampon

taponar /tapo'nar/ *vt* to stopper, cork; plug; *Surg.* tampon; *Mil.* seal off

taponazo /tapo'naθo; tapo'naso/ *m,* pop (of a cork)

tapujarse /tapu'harse/ *vr* to wrap oneself up, muffle oneself

tapujo /ta'puho/ *m,* scarf, muffler, face covering; disguise; *Inf.* pretense, subterfuge

taquera /ta'kera/ *f,* rack (for billiard cues)

taquería /take'ria/ *f,* taco stand

taquigrafía /takigra'fia/ *f,* shorthand

taquigrafiar /takigra'fiar/ *vt* to write in shorthand

taquigráfico /taki'grafiko/ *a* shorthand

taquígrafo /ta'kigrafo/ **(-fa)** *n* shorthand writer, stenographer

taquilla /ta'kiʎa; ta'kiya/ *f,* booking office; box office; grille, window (in banks, etc.); rolltop desk, cupboard for papers; *Theat.* takings, cash

taquillero /taki'ʎero; taki'yero/ **(-ra)** *n* booking office clerk

tara /'tara/ *f,* tally stick; *Com.* tare

taracea /tara'θea; tara'sea/ *f,* inlaid work, marquetry

taracear /taraθe'ar; tarase'ar/ *vt* to inlay

tarambana /taram'bana/ *mf Inf.* madcap

tarantela /taran'tela/ *f,* tarantella

tarántula /ta'rantula/ *f,* tarantula

tararear /tarare'ar/ *vt* to hum a tune

tararreo /tara'reo/ *m,* humming, singing under one's breath

tarasca /ta'raska/ *f,* figure of a dragon (carried in Corpus Christi processions); *Inf.* hag, trollop

tarascada /taras'kaða/ *f,* bite, nip; *Inf.* insolent reply

tarascar /taras'kar/ *vt* to bite; wound with the teeth

tardanza /tar'ðanθa; tar'ðansa/ *f,* delay, tardiness; slowness

tardar /tar'ðar/ *vi* to delay; be tardy, arrive late; take a long time. **a más t.,** at the latest

tarde /'tarðe/ *f,* afternoon —*adv* late. **¡Buenas tardes!** Good afternoon! **de t. en t.,** from time to time, sometimes. **hacerse t.,** to grow late. **Más vale t. que nunca,** Better late than never

tardecer /tarðe'θer; tarðe'ser/ *vi impers irr* to grow dusk. See **conocer**

tardecica, tardecita /tarðe'θika, tarðe'θita; tarðe'sika, tarðe'sita/ *f,* dusk, late afternoon

tardíamente /tar'ðiamente/ *adv* late; too late

tardío /tar'ðio/ *a* late; backward; behind; slow, deliberate

tardo /'tarðo/ *a* slow, slothful, tardy; late; dilatory; stupid, slow-witted; badly spoken, inarticulate

tarea /ta'rea/ *f,* task, work

tarifa /ta'rifa/ *f,* price list; tariff

tarifar /tari'far/ *vt* to put a tariff on

tarima /ta'rima/ *f,* stand, raised platform

tarín barín /ta'rin ba'rin/ *adv Inf.* more or less, about

tarja /'tarha/ *f,* large shield; ancient coin; tally stick. *Inf.* **beber sobre t.,** to drink on credit

tarjar /tar'har/ *vt* to reckon by tally

tarjeta /tar'heta/ *f,* buckler, small shield; *Archit.* tablet bearing an inscription; title (of maps and charts); visiting card; invitation (card). **t. de visita,** visiting card. **t. postal,** postcard. **t. telefónica,** calling card (phone)

tarquín /tar'kin/ *m,* mud, mire

tárraga /'tarraga/ *f,* old Spanish dance

tarro /'tarro/ *m,* jar, pot

tarso /'tarso/ *m, Anat.* tarsus, ankle; *Zool.* hock; *Ornith.* shank

tarta /'tarta/ *f,* cake pan; cake; tart

tártago /'tartago/ *m,* spurge; *Inf.* misfortune, disappointment

tartajear /tartahe'ar/ *vi* to stammer; stutter

tartajeo /tarta'heo/ *m,* stammering; stutter

tartajoso /tarta'hoso/ **(-sa)** *a* stammering; stuttering —*n* stutterer

tartalear /tartale'ar/ *vi Inf.* to stagger, totter; be speechless, be dumbfounded

tartamudear /tartamuðe'ar/ *vi* to stammer, stutter

tartamudeo /tartamu'ðeo/ *m.* **tartamudez** *f,* stammering; stuttering

tartamudo /tarta'muðo/ **(-da)** *n* stammerer

tartán /tar'tan/ *m,* tartan

tartana /tar'tana/ *f, Naut.* tartan; covered two-wheeled carriage

tartáreo /tar'tareo/ *a Poet.* infernal, hellish

Tartaria /tar'taria/ *f,* Tartary

tártaro /'tartaro/ **(-ra)** *m,* cream of tartar; tartar (on teeth); *Poet.* hell, hades —*a* and *n* Tartar

tartufo /tar'tufo/ *m,* hypocrite

tarugo /ta'rugo/ *m,* thick wooden peg; stopper; wooden block

tasa /'tasa/ *f,* assessment, valuation; valuation certificate; fixed price; standard rate; measure, rule

tasación /tasa'θion; tasa'sion/ *f,* valuation; assessment

tasador /tasa'ðor/ *m,* public assessor; valuer

tasajo /ta'saho/ *m,* salt meat; piece of meat

tasar /ta'sar/ *vt* to value; price; fix remuneration; tax; regulate; rate; dole out sparingly

tasca /'taska/ *f,* gambling den; tavern

tascar /tas'kar/ *vt* to dress (hemp, etc.); graze, crop the grass

tasquera /tas'kera/ *f, Inf.* quarrel, row, rumpus

tasquil /tas'kil/ *m,* wood splinter, chip

tata /'tata/ *m, Inf. West Hem.* daddy

tatarabuela /tatara'βuela/ *f,* great-great-grandmother

tatarabuelo /tatara'βuelo/ *m,* great-great-grandfather

tataradeudo /tatara'ðeuðo/ **(-da)** *n* very old relative; ancestor

tataranieta /tatara'nieta/ *f,* great-great-granddaughter

tataranieto /tatara'nieto/ *m,* great-great-grandson

tatas, andar a /'tatas, an'dar a/ *vt* to walk on all fours

¡tate! /'tate/ *interj* Stop!; Be careful!; Go slowly!; Now I understand!, Of course!

tatuaje /ta'tuahe/ *m,* tattooing

tatuar /tatu'ar/ vt to tattoo

taumaturgia /tauma'turhia/ f, thaumaturgy, wonderworking

taumaturgo /tauma'turgo/ m, thaumaturge, magician

taurino /tau'rino/ a taurine; pertaining to bullfights

Tauro /'tauro/ m, Taurus

tauromaquia /tauro'makia/ f, bullfighting, tauromachy

tautología /tautolo'hia/ f, tautology

taxi /'taksi/ m, taxi

taxidermia /taksi'ðermia/ f, taxidermy

taxidermista /taksiðer'mista/ mf taxidermist

taxista /tak'sista/ m, taxi driver

taxonomía /taksono'mia/ f, taxonomy

taza /'taθa; 'tasa/ f, cup; cupful; basin (of a fountain)

tazar /ta'θar; ta'sar/ **(se)** vt and vr to fray (of cloth)

taz a taz /taθ a taθ; tas a tas/ adv in exchange, without payment; even

tazmía /taθ'mia; tas'mia/ f, tithe contribution; share of tithes; tithe register

tazón /ta'θon; ta'son/ m, large cup; bowl

te /te/ f, name of the letter T. mf dat. and acc. of pers pron 2nd pers sing thee; you; to thee, to you. Never used with a preposition

té /te/ m, tea

tea /tea/ f, torch; firebrand

teatral /tea'tral/ a theatrical

teatralidad /teatrali'ðað/ f, theatricality

teatro /te'atro/ m, theater; stage; dramatic works; dramatic art; drama, plays. **t. de variedades,** music hall. **t. por horas,** theater where short, one-act plays are staged hourly

tebano /te'βano/ **(-na), tebeo (-ea)** a and n Theban

Tebas /'teβas/ Thebes

teca /'teka/ f, teak

techado /te'tʃaðo/ m, ceiling; roof

techador /tetʃa'ðor/ m, roofer

techar /te'tʃar/ vt to roof

techo /'tetʃo/ m, roof; ceiling; dwelling, habitation

techumbre /te'tʃumbre/ f, ceiling; roof

tecla /'tekla/ f, key (of keyed instruments); typewriter, linotype, or calculating machine key; Fig. difficult or delicate point. Inf. **dar en la t.,** to hit on the right way of doing a thing

teclado /te'klaðo/ m, keyboard

tecleado /tekle'aðo/ m, Mus. fingering

teclear /tekle'ar/ vi to finger the keyboard; run one's fingers over the keyboard; Inf. drum or tap with the fingers; —vt tap (the keys, etc.); Inf. try out various schemes

tecleo /te'kleo/ m, fingering the keys; Inf. drumming with the fingers; scheme, means

técnica /'teknika/ f, technique

tecnicismo /tekni'θismo; tekni'sismo/ m, technical jargon; technicality, technical term

técnico /'tekniko/ a technical. m, technician

tecnicolor /tekniko'lor/ m, technicolor

tecnología /teknolo'hia/ f, technology

tecnológico /tekno'lohiko/ a technological

tecnólogo /tek'nologo/ m, technologist

tedero /te'ðero/ m, torch seller; torch holder

tedio /'teðio/ m, tedium, boredom, ennui

tedioso /te'ðioso/ a tedious, boring

tegumento /tegu'mento/ m, integument, tegument

teísmo /te'ismo/ m, theism

teísta /te'ista/ a theistic. mf theist

teja /'teha/ f, tile, slate. Inf. **de tejas abajo,** in the normal way; in the world of men. **de tejas arriba,** in a supernatural way; in heaven

tejadillo /teha'ðiʎo; teha'ðiyo/ m, roof (of a vehicle)

tejado /te'haðo/ m, roof

tejar /te'har/ m, tile works —vt to roof with tiles

tejavana /teha'βana/ f, penthouse, open shed

tejedor /tehe'ðor/ **(-ra)** a weaving; Inf. scheming —n weaver; Inf. schemer

tejedura /tehe'ðura/ f, weaving; fabric; texture

tejeduría /teheðu'ria/ f, art of weaving; weaving shed or mill

tejemaneje /tehema'nehe/ m, Inf. cleverness, knack

tejer /te'her/ vt to weave; plait; spin a cocoon; ar-

range, regulate; concoct, hatch (schemes); wind in and out (in dancing)

tejero /te'hero/ m, tile manufacturer

tejido /te'hiðo/ m, texture, weaving; textile; Anat. tissue; fabric, material

tejo /'teho/ m, quoit, discus; metal disk; yew tree

tejón /te'hon/ m, Zool. badger

tela /'tela/ f, fabric, material, cloth; membrane; film (on liquids); spiderweb, cobweb; inner skin (of fruit, vegetables); film over the eye; matter, subject; scheme, plot. **t. metálica,** wire gauze. **en t. de juicio,** under consideration, in doubt. **llegarle a uno a las telas del corazón,** to hurt deeply, cut to the quick

telar /te'lar/ m, loom, weaving machine; Theat. gridiron

telaraña /tela'raɲa/ f, cobweb; mere trifle, bagatelle. Inf. **mirar las telarañas,** to be absent-minded

telarañoso /telara'ɲoso/ a cobwebby

telecomunicación /telekomunika'θion; telekomunika'sion/ f, telecommunication

telefonear /telefone'ar/ vt to telephone, call

telefonía /telefo'nia/ f, telephony. **t. sin hilos,** wireless telephony, broadcasting

telefónico /tele'foniko/ a telephonic

telefonista /telefo'nista/ mf telephone operator

teléfono /te'lefono/ m, telephone. **t. automático,** dial telephone. **llamar por t. (a),** to telephone, call, ring up

telefundir /telefun'dir/ vt to telecast

telegrafía /telegra'fia/ f, telegraphy. **t. sin hilos,** wireless telegraphy

telegrafiar /telegra'fiar/ vt to telegraph

telegráfico /tele'grafiko/ a telegraphic

telegrafista /telegra'fista/ mf telegraph operator

telégrafo /te'legrafo/ m, telegraph. **t. sin hilos,** wireless telegraph. Inf. **hacer telégrafos,** to talk by signs

telegrama /tele'grama/ m, telegram

telemetría /teleme'tria/ f, telemetry

telémetro /te'lemetro/ m, telemeter, rangefinder

teleología /teleolo'hia/ f, teleology

telepatía /telepa'tia/ f, telepathy

telepático /tele'patiko/ a telepathic

telescópico /teles'kopiko/ a telescopic

telescopio /teles'kopio/ m, telescope

telespectador /telespekta'ðor/ m, TV viewer, member of the television audience

teletipo /tele'tipo/ m, teleprinter

televisión /teleβi'sion/ f, television

telilla /te'liʎa; te'liya/ f, film (on liquids); thin fabric

telón /te'lon/ m, Theat. curtain; drop scene. **t. contra incendios, t. de seguridad,** Theat. safety curtain. **t. de boca,** drop curtain. **t. de foro,** drop scene

tema /'tema/ m, theme, subject; Mus. motif, theme; thesis, argument, f, obstinacy; obsession, mania; hostility, grudge, rancor

temático /te'matiko/ a thematic; pigheaded, obstinate

temblador /tembla'ðor/ **(-ra)** a trembling, shaking —n Quaker

temblante /tem'blante/ a shaking; quivering. m, bracelet

temblar /tem'blar/ vi irr to tremble, shake; wave, quiver; shiver with fear. See **acertar**

temblequear, tembletear /tembleke'ar, temblete'ar/ vi Inf. tremble; shake with fear

temblón /tem'blon/ a Inf. trembling, shaking. m, Inf. aspen

temblor /tem'blor/ m, shake, trembling, shiver. **t. de tierra,** earthquake

tembloroso, tembloso /temblo'roso, tem'bloso/ a trembling, shaking, shivering, quivering

temedero /teme'ðero/ a fearsome, dread

temedor /teme'ðor/ **(-ra)** a fearful —n fearer, dreader

temer /te'mer/ vt to fear, dread; suspect, imagine; —vi be afraid

temerario /teme'rario/ a reckless, impetuous; thoughtless, hasty

temeridad /temeri'ðað/ f, recklessness, impetuosity, temerity; thoughtlessness; act of folly; rash judgment

temerón /teme'ron/ a Inf. swaggering, bombastic

temeroso /teme'roso/ *a* frightening, dread; fearful, timid; afraid, suspicious

temible /te'miβle/ *a* dread, awesome

temor /te'mor/ *m*, fear

temoso /te'moso/ *a* obstinate, headstrong

témpano /'tempano/ *m*, tabor; drumhead; block, flat piece; side of bacon. **t. de hielo,** iceberg, ice floe

temperación /tempera'θion/ tempera'sion/ *f*, tempering

temperamento /tempera'mento/ *m*, temperament, nature; compromise, agreement

temperar /tempe'rar/ *vt* to temper

temperatura /tempera'tura/ *f*, temperature

temperie /tem'perie/ *f*, weather conditions

tempestad /tempes'taθ/ *f*, storm

tempestividad /tempestiβi'θaθ/ *f*, opportuneness, seasonableness

tempestivo /tempes'tiβo/ *a* opportune, seasonable

tempestuoso /tempes'tuoso/ *a* stormy

templa /'templa/ *f*, tempera; *pl Anat.* temples

templado /tem'plaθo/ *a* moderate; temperate (of regions); lukewarm; *Mus.* in tune; restrained (of style); *Inf.* brave, long-suffering. **estar bien** (*or* **mal**) **templado,** *Inf.* to be well (or badly) tuned (of musical instruments); be in a good (or bad) temper; be good- (or ill-) natured

templador /templa'θor/ **(-ra)** *n* tuner. *m*, tuning key

templadura /templa'θura/ *f*, tuning; tempering

templanza /tem'planθa/ tem'plansa/ *f*, moderation; sobriety; mildness of climate

templar /tem'plar/ *vt* to tune; *Metall.* temper; moderate; warm; allay, appease; anneal; *Art.* harmonize, blend; *Naut.* trim the sails; —*vr* control oneself, be moderate; —*vi* grow warm

templario /tem'plario/ *m*, Knight Templar

temple /'temple/ *m*, weather conditions; temperature; temper (of metals, etc.); nature, disposition; bravery; mean, average; *Mus.* tuning. **al t.,** in tempera

templete /tem'plete/ *m*, *dim* shrine; niche (for statues); kiosk, pavilion

templo /'templo/ *m*, temple

temporada /tempo'raθa/ *f*, space of time, season, while. **de t.,** seasonal; temporary. **estar de t.,** to be out of town, on holiday

temporal /tempo'ral/ *a* temporal; temporary; secular, lay; transient, fugitive. *m*, storm, tempest; rainy period; seasonal laborer

temporalidad /temporali'θaθ/ *f*, secular character; temporality secular possession (gen. *pl*)

temporáneo, temporario /tempora'neo, tempo'rario/ *a* temporary, impermanent, fleeting

témporas /'temporas/ *f pl*, Ember days

temporejar /tempore'har/ *vt Naut.* to lie to in a storm

temporero /tempo'rero/ *a* temporary (of work)

temporizar /tempori'θar; tempori'sar/ *vi* to while away the time; temporize

tempranal /tempra'nal/ *a* early fruiting

tempranero /tempra'nero/ *a* early

temprano /tem'prano/ *a* early —*adv* in the early hours; prematurely, too soon

temulento /temu'lento/ *a* intoxicated, drunken

tenacear /tenaθe'ar; tenase'ar/ *vi* to insist, be obstinate

tenacidad /tenaθi'θaθ; tenasi'θaθ/ *f*, adhesiveness; resistance, toughness; obstinacy, tenacity

tenacillas /tena'θiʎas; tena'siyas/ *f pl*, *dim* small tongs; candle snuffers; sugar tongs; curling irons; tweezers

tenaz /te'naθ; te'nas/ *a* adhesive; hard, resistant, unyielding; tenacious, obstinate

tenaza /te'naθa; te'nasa/ *f*, claw (of a lobster, etc.); *pl* tongs; pincers; pliers; dental forceps

tenazada /tena'θaθa; tena'saθa/ *f*, seizing with tongs; strong bite, snap; rattle of tongs

tenazón /tena'θon; tena'son/ **(a** or **de)** *adv* without taking aim, wildly; unexpectedly

tenca /'tenka/ *f*, tench

tención /ten'θion; ten'sion/ *f*, retention, holding; grip

ten con ten /ten kon ten/ *m*, *Inf.* tact, diplomacy

tendal /ten'dal/ *m*, awning; sheet for catching olives

tendedero /tende'θero/ *m*, drying ground

tendedura /tende'θura/ *f*, laying out; stretching

tendencia /ten'denθia; tendensia/ *f*, tendency

tendencioso /tenden'θioso; tenden'sioso/ *a* tendentious, biased

tender /ten'der/ *vt irr* to hang out; unfold, spread out; extend, hold out; *Mas.* plaster; —*vi* tend, incline; —*vr* lie down at full length; place one's cards on the table; gallop hard (of horses). See **entender**

tendero /ten'dero/ **(-ra)** *n* shopkeeper; retailer. *m*, tent maker

tendido /ten'diðo/ *m*, row of seats in a bullfight arena; clothes hung out to dry; clear sky; *Mas.* plaster

tendón /ten'don/ *m*, tendon

tenducha /ten'dutʃa/ *f*, *Inf.* wretched little shop

tenebrosidad /teneβrosi'ðaθ/ *f*, gloom, darkness, obscurity

tenebroso /tene'βroso/ *a* dark, gloomy

tenedero /tene'ðero/ *m*, *Naut.* anchoring ground, anchorage

tenedor /tene'ðor/ *m*, table fork; possessor, retainer; *Com.* holder; payee. **t. de libros,** bookkeeper

teneduría /teneðu'ria/ *f*, employment of a bookkeeper. **t. de libros,** bookkeeping

tenencia /te'nenθia; te'nensia/ *f*, possession; tenancy, occupation; lieutenancy

tener /te'ner/ *vt irr* to have; hold; grasp; possess, own; uphold, maintain; contain; include; hold fast, grip; stop; keep (promises); lodge, accommodate; (*with en*) value, estimate (e.g. *Le tengo en poco,* I have a poor opinion of him); (*with para*) be of the opinion that (e.g. *tengo para mí,* my opinion is); (*with por*) believe, consider; —*vi* be wealthy; —*vr* steady oneself; hold on to; lean (on); rest (on); defend oneself; uphold; rely on; (*with por*) consider oneself as. **tener** is used to express: 1. *Age* (e.g. *¿Cuántos años tiene Vd?* How old are you?). 2. *Possession* (e.g. *Tenemos muchos sombreros,* We have a great many hats). 3. *Measurements* (e.g. *El cuarto tiene dieciocho metros de largo,* The room is eighteen meters long). Translated by "be" when describing some physical and mental states (e.g. *Tenemos miedo,* We are afraid. *Tengo sueño,* I am sleepy. *Tienen frío* (*calor*), They are cold (hot)). Used as *auxiliary verb* replacing **haber** in compound tenses of transitive verbs (e.g. *Tengo escritas las cartas,* I have written the letters). **t. a bien,** to think fit, please, judge convenient. **t. algo en cuenta a uno,** to hold something against someone. **t. a menos de hacer (una cosa),** to scorn to do (a thing). **t. cruda,** to have a hangover. **t. curiosidad por,** to be curious about. **t. curiosidad por que** + *subj* to be interested that. **t. en aprecio,** to appreciate, esteem, value. **t. en cuenta,** to bear in mind. **t. en menos (a),** to despise (a person). **t. gana,** to want, wish; feel disposed; have an appetite. **t. lugar,** to take place, occur. **t. muchas partes cruzadas,** to be well-traveled. **t. mucho colegio** to be well-educated. **t. muy en cuenta,** to certainly bear in mind. **t. poco colegio,** to have had little education. **t. presente,** to remember. **t. que,** to have to (e.g. *tengo que hacerlo,* I must do it). **t. que ver (con),** to have something to do (with), be related to. **no tenerlas todas consigo,** *Inf.* to have the jitters —*Pres. Ind.* **tengo, tienes, tiene, tenemos, tenéis, tienen.** *Preterite* **tuve,** etc —*Fut.* **tendré,** etc —*Condit.* **tendría,** etc —*Pres. Subjunc.* **tenga,** etc —*Imperf. Subjunc.* **tuviese,** etc.

tenguerengue, en /tengue'rengue, en/ *adv Inf.* rickety, insecure

tenia /'tenia/ *f*, tapeworm; *Archit.* fillet, narrow molding

teniente /te'niente/ *a* owning, holding; unripe (of fruit); *Inf.* slightly deaf; stingy, mean. *m*, deputy, substitute; *Mil.* first lieutenant, lieutenant. **t. coronel,** lieutenant colonel. **t. de navío,** naval lieutenant. **t. general,** *Mil.* lieutenant general. **t. general de aviación,** air marshal

tenis /'tenis/ *m*, tennis

tenor /te'nor/ *m*, import, contents (of a letter, etc.); constitution, composition; *Mus.* tenor

tenorio /te'norio/ *m*, rake, Don Juan, philanderer

tensar /ten'sar/ *vt* to tighten; tense

tensión /ten'sion/ *f*, tautness; tension; strain, stress; *Elec.* tension

tenso /'tenso/ *a* taut; tight; tense

tentación /tenta'θion; tenta'sion/ *f*, temptation; attraction, inducement

tentáculo /ten'takulo/ *m*, tentacle; feeler

tentadero /tenta'ðero/ *m*, yard for trying out young bulls for bullfighting

tentador /tenta'ðor/ **(-ra)** *a* tempting; attractive —*n* tempter. *m*, the Devil

tentalear /tentale'ar/ *vt* to examine by touch

tentar /ten'tar/ *vt irr* to touch; feel; examine by touch; incite, encourage; try, endeavor; test; tempt; *Surg.* probe. See **sentar**

tentativa /tenta'tiβa/ *f*, endeavor, attempt; preliminary exam (at some univs.)

tentativo /tenta'tiβo/ *a* tentative, experimental

tentemozo /tente'moθo; tente'moso/ *m*, support, prop; tumbler (toy)

tentempié /tentem'pie/ *m*, *Inf.* snack, bite

tenue /'tenue/ *a* thin; slender, delicate; trivial; worthless, insignificant; pale; faint

tenuidad /tenui'ðað/ *f*, slenderness; delicacy; triviality, insignificance; paleness; faintness

teñidura /teɲi'ðura/ *f*, dyeing, staining

teñir /te'ɲir/ *vt irr* to dye; *Art.* darken; color, tinge; —*vr* be dyed; be tinged or colored. See **ceñir**

teocracia /teo'kraθia; teo'krasia/ *f*, theocracy

teocrático /teo'kratiko/ *a* theocratic

teodolito /teoðo'lito/ *m*, theodolite

teologal /teolo'gal/ *a* theological

teología /teolo'hia/ *f*, theology, divinity

teológico /teo'lohiko/ *a* theological

teologizar /teolohi'θar; teolohi'sar/ *vi* to theologize

teólogo /te'ologo/ *a* theological. *m*, theologian, divine; student of theology

teorema /teo'rema/ *m*, theorem

teoría /teo'ria/ *f*, theory

teórica /te'orika/ *f*, theory

teórico /te'oriko/ *a* theoretical, speculative. *m*, theorist

teorizar /teori'θar; teori'sar/ *vt* to consider theoretically, theorize about

teoso /te'oso/ *a* resinous, gummy

teosofía /teoso'fia/ *f*, theosophy

teosófico /teo'sofiko/ *a* theosophical

teósofo /te'osofo/ *m*, theosophist

tepe /'tepe/ *m*, sod, cut turf

terapeuta /tera'peuta/ *mf* therapeutist

terapéutica /tera'peutika/ *f*, therapeutics

terapéutico /tera'peutiko/ *a* therapeutic

terapia /te'rapia/ *f*, therapy

teratología /teratolo'hia/ *f*, teratology

tercena /ter'θena; ter'sena/ *f*, warehouse for storing government monopoly goods (tobacco, etc.)

tercenista /terθe'nista; terse'nista/ *mf* person in charge of a tercena

tercer /ter'θer; ter'ser/ *a Abbr.* of **tercero** third. Used before *m*, *sing* nouns

tercera /ter'θera; ter'sera/ *f*, procuress; *Mus.* third

tercería /terθe'ria; terse'ria/ *f*, arbitration, mediation; temporary occupation of a fortress, etc.

tercero /ter'θero; ter'sero/ **(-ra)** *a* third; mediatory —*n* third; mediator. *m*, pimp; *Eccl.* tertiary; tithes collector; third person. **¡A la tercera va la vencida!** Third time lucky!

terceto /ter'θeto; ter'seto/ *m*, tercet, triplet

tercia /'terθia; 'tersia/ *f*, one-third; *Eccl.* tierce, third hour; storehouse for tithes. **tercias reales,** royal share of ecclesiastical tithes

terciana /ter'θiana; ter'siana/ *f*, tertian fever

terciar /ter'θiar; ter'siar/ *vt* to slant; sling sideways; divide into three; equalize weight (on beasts of burden); plow or dig for the third time; *Agr.* prune; —*vr* be opportune, come at the right time —*vi* mediate, arbitrate; make up a number (for cards, etc.); reach the third day (of the moon); take part, participate

terciario /ter'θiario; ter'siario/ *a* third, tertiary; *Geol.* tertiary. *m*, *Eccl.* tertiary

tercio /'terθio; 'tersio/ *a* third. *m*, one-third; *Mil.* infantry regiment; *Obs.*, body of foreign volunteers; fishermen's association; *pl* brawny limbs of a man. **hacer t.,** to take part in; make up the number of. **hacer buen** (*or* **mal**) **t. a alguien,** to do someone a good (or bad) turn

terciopelo /terθio'pelo; tersio'pelo/ *m*, velvet; velveteen

terco /'terko/ *a* pigheaded, obstinate; hard, tough

tergiversación /terhiβersa'θion; terhiβersa'sion/ *f*, tergiversation, vacillation

tergiversar /terhiβer'sar/ *vt* to tergiversate, shuffle, vacillate

termal /ter'mal/ *a* thermal

termas /'termas/ *f pl*, thermal springs, hot mineral baths; thermal

térmico /'termiko/ *a* thermic

terminable /termi'naβle/ *a* terminable

terminación /termina'θion; termina'sion/ *f*, conclusion, termination; end, finish; ending of a word; *Gram.* termination

terminador /termina'ðor/ **(-ra)** *a* concluding —*n* finisher

terminal /termi'nal/ *a* terminal; final. *m*, *Elec.* terminal. **t. de carga,** cargo terminal

terminante /termi'nante/ *a* conclusive, definite; categorical

terminar /termi'nar/ *vt* to end, conclude; complete; —*vr* and *vi* end

término /'termino/ *m*, limit, end; term, expression; boundary marker; district, suburb; space, period; state, condition; boundary; object, aim; appearance, demeanor, behavior (gen. *pl*); completion; *Mus.* tone; (*Math. Law. Logic.*) term. **t. medio,** *Math.* average; medium; compromise, middle way. **correr el t.,** to lapse (of time). **en primer t.,** *Art.* in the foreground. **medios términos,** evasions, excuses. **primer t.,** (cinema) closeup

terminología /terminolo'hia/ *f*, terminology

termita /ter'mita/ *f*, thermite. *m*, termite

termodinámica /termoði'namika/ *f*, thermodynamics

termoeléctrico /termoe'lektriko/ *a* thermoelectric

termómetro /ter'mometro/ *m*, thermometer

Termópilas /ter'mopilas/ Thermopylae

termos /'termos/ *m*, thermos, vacuum bottle

termoscopio /termos'kopio/ *m*, thermoscope

termostático /termos'tatiko/ *a* thermostatic

termóstato /ter'mostato/ *m*, thermostat

terna /'terna/ *f*, triad, trio; set of dice

ternario /ter'nario/ *a* ternal, ternary

terne /'terne/ *a Inf.* bullying, braggartly; persistent, obstinate; robust. *mf* bully

ternera /ter'nera/ *f*, female calf; veal

ternero /ter'nero/ *m*, male calf

terneza /ter'neθa; ter'nesa/ *f*, tenderness, kindness; softness; softheartedness; endearment, caress, compliment (gen. *pl*)

ternilla /ter'niʎa; ter'niya/ *f*, cartilage, gristle

ternísimo /ter'nisimo/ *a superl* **tierno** most tender

terno /'terno/ *m*, triad; suit of clothes, three-piece suit; oath, curse

ternura /ter'nura/ *f*, softness; softheartedness; tenderness, kindness, sweetness

terquedad, terquería, terqueza /terke'ðað, terke'ria, ter'keθa; ter'kesa/ *f*, obstinacy, obduracy

terracota /terra'kota/ *f*, terra cotta

terrado /te'rraðo/ *m*, flat roof

Terranova /terra'noβa/ Newfoundland

terraplén /terra'plen/ *m*, embankment; *Mil.* terreplein

terraplenar /terraple'nar/ *vt* to fill up with earth; fill in (a hollow); make into an embankment; terrace

terrateniente /terrate'niente/ *mf* landowner

terraza /te'rraθa; te'rrasa/ *f*, terrace; flat roof; flower border (of a garden)

terrazgo /te'rraθgo; te'rrasgo/ *m*, tillable land; rent for farming land

terregoso /terre'goso/ *a* lumpy, full of clods (of soil)

terremoto /terre'moto/ *m*, earthquake

terrenal /terre'nal/ *a* terrestrial

terreno /te'rreno/ *a* terrestrial. *m*, ground, land; *Fig.* sphere; region; soil; plot of land. **ganar t.,** *Fig.* to win ground, make progress. **medir el t.,** *Fig.* to feel one's way

térreo /'terreo/ *a* earthy

terrero /te'rrero/ *a* earthly; low-flying, almost touching the ground; humble. *m*, flat roof; pile or mound of earth; deposit of earth, alluvium; target; mineral refuse

terrestre /te'rrestre/ *a* terrestrial, earthly

terrezuela /terre'θuela; terre'suela/ *f*, poor soil

terribilidad /terriβili'ðað/ *f*, terribleness, horribleness; rudeness

terribilísimo /terriβi'lisimo/ *a superl* most terrible

terrible /te'rriβle/ *a* terrible, horrible; rude, unsociable, ill-humored; enormous, huge

terrífico /te'rrifiko/ *a* terrible, frightful

territorial /territo'rial/ *a* territorial

territorialidad /territoriali'ðað/ *f*, territoriality

territorio /terri'torio/ *m*, territory; jurisdiction. **t. bajo mandato,** mandated territory

terrizo /te'rriθo; te'rriso/ *a* earthen

terrón /te'rron/ *m*, clod (of earth); lump; *pl* lands, landed property. **t. de azúcar,** lump of sugar

terrorismo /terro'rismo/ *m*, terrorism

terrorista /terro'rista/ *mf* terrorist

terrosidad /terrosi'ðað/ *f*, earthiness

terroso /te'rroso/ *a* earthy; earthen

terruño /te'rruɲo/ *m*, plot of ground; native earth; country; soil

terso /'terso/ *a* smooth, shiny, glossy; *Lit.* elegant, polished (style)

tersura /ter'sura/ *f*, smoothness, glossiness; elegance (of style)

tertulia /ter'tulia/ *f*, regular social meeting (gen. in cafés); conversational group; party; part of Spanish cafés set apart for players of chess, etc. **hacer t.,** to meet for conversation

tertuliano /tertu'liano/ **(-na)** *n* **tertuliante,** *mf* **tertulio (-ia),** *n* member of a tertulia

terzuelo /ter'θuelo; ter'suelo/ *m*, third, third part

Tesalia /te'salia/ Thessaly

tesar /te'sar/ *vt Naut.* to make taut; —*vi* step backward, back (oxen)

tesela /te'sela/ *f*, tessera, square used in mosaic work

teselado /tese'laðo/ *a* tessellated

tesina /te'sina/ *f*, master's essay, thesis

tesis /'tesis/ *f*, thesis

teso /'teso/ *a* tight, taut, tense. *m*, hilltop; bulge, lump

tesón /te'son/ *m*, persistence, obstinacy, tenacity

tesonería /tesone'ria/ *f*, stubbornness, obstinacy

tesorería /tesore'ria/ *f*, treasury; treasuryship

tesorero /teso'rero/ **(-ra)** *n* treasurer

tesoro /te'soro/ *m*, treasure; public treasury; hoard; *Fig.* gem, excellent person; thesaurus. **t. de duende,** fairy gold

tespíades /tes'piaðes/ *f pl*, the muses

testa /'testa/ *f*, head; face, front; *Inf.* sense, acumen. **t. coronada,** crowned head

testación /testa'θion; testa'sion/ *f*, erasure, crossing out

testado /tes'taðo/ *a* testate

testador /testa'ðor/ **(-ra)** *n* testator

testaferro /testa'ferro/ *m*, *Fig.* figurehead, proxy

testamentar /testamen'tar/ *vt* to bequeath

testamentaria /testamen'taria/ *f*, execution of a will; *Law.* estate; executors' meeting

testamentario /testamen'tario/ *a* testamental, testamentary

testamento /testa'mento/ *m*, *Law.* will; testament. **Antiguo T.,** Old Testament. **ordenar** (*or* **otorgar) su t.,** to make one's will

testar /tes'tar/ *vi* to make a will; —*vt* erase, cross out

testarada /testa'raða/ *f*, a blow with the head; pigheadedness, stubbornness

testarrón /testa'rron/ *a Inf.* pigheaded

testarudez /testaru'ðeθ; testaru'ðes/ *f*, obstinacy, obduracy

testarudo /testa'ruðo/ *a* stubborn, obstinate

testera /tes'tera/ *f*, front, face; front seat (in a vehicle); upper half of an animal's face; tester, canopy

testículo /tes'tikulo/ *m*, testicle

testificación /testifika'θion; testifika'sion/ *f*, testification

testificar /testifi'kar/ *vt* to testify; affirm, assert; attest, prove

testigo /tes'tigo/ *mf* witness. *m*, proof, evidence. *Law.* **t. de cargo,** witness for the prosecution. *Law.* **t. de descargo,** witness for the defense. **t. de vista,** eyewitness. *Law.* **hacer testigos,** to bring forward witnesses

testimonial /testimo'nial/ *a* confirmatory, proven

testimoniar /testimo'niar/ *vt* to attest, confirm, bear witness to

testimoniero /testimo'niero/ **(-ra)** *a* slanderous; hypocritical —*n* slanderer, hypocrite

testimonio /testi'monio/ *m*, testimony, proof; slander; affidavit

testuz /tes'tuθ; tes'tus/ *m*, front of the head (of some animals); nape (of animals)

teta /'teta/ *f*, mammary gland, breast; teat, dug, udder. **dar la t.** (**a),** to suckle

tétano, tétanos /'tetano, 'tetanos/ *m*, tetanus

tetera /te'tera/ *f*, teapot; teakettle

tetilla /te'tiʎa; te'tiya/ *f*, *dim* rudimentary teat or nipple; nipple (of a nursing bottle)

tétrico /'tetriko/ *a* gloomy; somber

tetuaní /tetua'ni/ *a* and *mf* of or from Tetuan

teutón /teu'ton/ **(-ona)** *n* Teuton —*a* Teutonic

teutónico /teu'toniko/ *a* Teutonic

textil /teks'til/ *a* and *m*, textile

texto /'teksto/ *m*, text; quotation, citation; textbook

textorio /teks'torio/ *a* textile

textual /teks'tual/ *a* textual

textualista /tekstua'lista/ *mf* textualist

textura /teks'tura/ *f*, texture; weaving; structure (of a novel, etc.); animal structure

tez /teθ; tes/ *f*, complexion, skin

ti /ti/ *pers pron 2nd sing mf dat acc abl* thee, you. Always used with prep. (e.g. *por ti,* by thee (you))

tía /'tia/ *f*, aunt; *Inf.* wife, mother, dame; *Inf.* coarse creature. *Inf.* **abuela,** grandaunt, great-aunt. *Inf.* **quedarse para t.,** to be left an old maid

tiara /'tiara/ *f*, ancient Persian headdress; papal tiara; coronet; dignity and power of the papacy

tiberino /tiβe'rino/ *a* Tiberine

tibetano /tiβe'tano/ **(-na)** *a* and *n* Tibetan. *m*, Tibetan (language)

tibia /'tiβia/ *f*, flute; tibia

tibieza /ti'βieθa; ti'βiesa/ *f*, tepidity; indifference, lack of enthusiasm

tibio /'tiβio/ *a* tepid, warm; indifferent, unenthusiastic

tiburón /tiβu'ron/ *m*, shark

ticket /'tikket/ *m*, ticket; pass, membership card

tictac /tik'tak/ *m*, ticktock (of a clock)

tiempo /'tiempo/ *m*, time; season; epoch; period; chance, opportunity; leisure, free time; weather; *Mus.* tempo; *Gram.* tense; *Naut.* storm. **t. ha,** many years ago, long ago. **t. medio** *or* **medio t.,** *Sports.* halftime. **t. medio** (of the weather). **ajustar los tiempos,** to fix the date (chronology). **a largo t.,** after a long time. **andando el t.,** in the course of time. **a su t.,** in due course, at the proper time. **a t.,** in time, at the right time. **a un t.,** simultaneously, at the same time. **cargarse el t.,** to cloud over (of the sky). **con t.,** in advance, with time; in time. **correr el t.,** to pass, move on (of time). **dar t. en t.,** from time to time. **engañar** (*or* **entretener) el t.,** to kill time, while away the hours. *Inf.* **en t., de Maricastaña** *or* **del rey Perico,** long, long ago. **fuera de t.,** unseasonably, inopportunely; out of season. **ganar t.,** to gain time; *Inf.* hurry. **hacer t.,** to wait, cool one's heels; *Fig.* mark time. **perder el t.,** to waste time; misspend or lose time. **sentarse el t.,** to clear up (of the weather). **tomarse t.** (**para),** to postpone, take time for (or to)

tienda /'tienda/ *f*, tent; *Naut.* awning, canopy; shop, store. **t. de antigüedades,** antique shop. **t. de campaña,** bell tent, pavilion. **t. oxígena,** oxygen tent

tienta /'tienta/ *f*, astuteness; cleverness; *Surg.* probe;

trying out young bulls for the bullring. **a tientas,** by touch, gropingly

tientaparedes /tientapa're ðes/ *mf* one who gropes one's way

tiento /'tiento/ *m,* touching, feeling; touch, feel; blind person's cane; tightrope walker's pole; manual control, steady hand; caution, care, tact; *Mus.* preliminary flourish; *Inf.* slap buffet; tentacle. **a t.,** by touch; unsurely, gropingly

tierno /'tierno/ *a* soft; tender; kind; sweet; delicate; softhearted; fresh, recent; affectionate

tierra /'tierra/ *f,* world, planet; earth; soil; ground; cultivated ground, land; homeland, native land; region; district, territory. **t. adentro,** inland. **t. de batán,** fuller's earth. **t. de Promisión,** Promised Land. **t. de Siena,** sienna. **besar la t.,** *Inf.* to fall down. **dar en t. con,** to throw down; demolish. **echar en t.,** *Naut.* to put ashore, land. **echar por t.,** *Fig.* to overthrow, destroy. **echar t. a,** *Fig.* to bury, forget. *Inf.* **la t. de María Santísima,** Andalusia. **por t.,** overland. **saltar en t.,** to land, disembark. **venir** (*or* **venirse) a t.,** to fall down, topple over

Tierra Santa /'tierra 'santa/ Holy Land

tieso /'tieso/ *a* hard, rigid, stiff; healthy, robust; taut; spirited, courageous; obstinate, stiff-necked; distant, formal —*adv* firmly, strongly

tiesto /'tiesto/ *m,* flowerpot; broken piece of earthenware

tiesura /tie'sura/ *f,* hardness, rigidity, stiffness; physical fitness; courageousness; obstinacy; formality, stiffness

tifoidea /tifoi'ðea/ *f,* typhoid

tifón /ti'fon/ *m,* typhoon

tifus /'tifus/ *m,* typhus. **t. exantemático,** trench fever

tigre /'tigre/ *m,* tiger; ferocious person

tigresa /ti'gresa/ *f,* tigress

tigridia /ti'griðia/ *f,* tiger lily

tijera /ti'hera/ *f,* scissors (gen. *pl*); any scissor-shaped instrument; shears; drainage channel; carpenter's horse; scandalmonger, gossip

tijereta /tihe'reta/ *f,* vine tendril; earwig

tijeretada /tihere'taða/ *f,* cut or snip with scissors

tijeretear /tihere'tear/ *vt* to cut with scissors; *Inf.* interfere arbitrarily

tijereteo /tihere'teo/ *m,* scissor cut; click of the scissors

tila /'tila/ *f,* lime tree or flower; linden tree or flower; infusion made of lime flowers

tildar /til'dar/ *vt* to cross out, erase; stigmatize; place a tilde over a letter

tilde /'tilde/ *mf,* bad reputation; tilde; *f,* jot, iota

tilín /ti'lin/ *m,* tinkle, peal (of a bell)

tillar /ti'ʎar/ ti'yar/ *vt* to lay wood floors

tilo /'tilo/ *m,* lime tree

timador /tima'ðor/ **(-ra)** *n Inf.* swindler, sharper, cheat

timar /ti'mar/ *vt* to swindle, cheat, deceive; —*vr Inf.* exchange looks or winks

timba /'timba/ *f, Inf.* casino, gambling den; game of chance

timbal /tim'bal/ *m,* kettledrum

timbalero /timba'lero/ *m,* kettledrum player

timbrador /timbra'ðor/ *m,* stamper; stamping machine; rubber stamp

timbrar /tim'brar/ *vt* to stamp; place the crest over a coat of arms

timbre /'timbre/ *m,* postage stamp; heraldic crest; excise stamp; bell, push-button; *Mus.* timbre; noble deed; personal merit

timidez /timi'ðeθ/ timi'ðes/ *f,* timidity, nervousness

tímido /'timiðo/ *a* timid, nervous

timo /'timo/ *m, Inf.* swindling, trick; thymus

timón /ti'mon/ *m, Naut.* helm; rudder; management, direction; stick of a rocket. **t. de dirección,** *Aer.* tailfin

timonear /timone'ar/ *vi Naut.* to steer

timonel, timonero /timo'nel, timo'nero/ *m,* helmsman, coxswain

timorato /timo'rato/ *a* godfearing; timid, vacillating

tímpano /'timpano/ *m, Anat.* eardrum, tympanum; *Mus.* kettledrum; *Archit.* tympanum; *Print.* tympan

tina /'tina/ *f,* vat; flour bin; large earthenware jar; wooden tub; bath

tinada /ti'naða/ *f,* woodpile; cow shed

tinaja /ti'naha/ *f,* large earthenware jar; jarful

tinajero /tina'hero/ *m,* seller of earthenware jars

tinelo /ti'nelo/ *m,* servants' hall

tinerfeño /tiner'feɲo/ **(-ña)** *a* and *n* of or from Tenerife

tinglado /tiŋ'glaðo/ *m,* overhanging roof; open shed; penthouse; intrigue

tiniebla /ti'nieβla/ *f,* gloom, darkness (gen. *pl*); *pl* profound ignorance; confusion of mind; *Eccl.* tenebrae

tino /'tino/ *m,* skilled sense of touch; good eye, accurate aim; judgment, shrewdness; vat. **sacar de t.,** to bewilder, confuse; irritate, exasperate. **sin t.,** without limit, excessively

tinta /'tinta/ *f,* color, tint; ink; staining, dyeing; dye, stain; *pl* shades, colors; *Art.* mixed colors ready for painting. **t. china,** India ink. **t. simpática,** invisible ink. **recargar las tintas,** *Fig.* to overpaint, lay the colors on too thick. *Inf.* **saber de buena t.** (**una cosa),** to learn (a thing) from a reliable source

tintar /tin'tar/ *vt* to dye; color, tinge, stain

tinte /'tinte/ *m,* dyeing, staining; color; dye; stain; dye house; pretext, disguise

tintero /tin'tero/ *m,* inkwell. *Inf.* **dejar** (*or* **quedársele a uno) en el t.,** to forget, omit (to say, write)

tintín /tin'tin/ *m,* ring, peal; clink; chink

tintinar /tinti'nar/ *vi* to ring, tinkle; clink; jingle

tintineo /tinti'neo/ *m,* ringing, tinkling; clinking; jingle

tintirintín /tintirin'tin/ *m,* bray of a trumpet

tinto /'tinto/ *a* red (of wine). *m,* red wine; dark red

tintorería /tintore'ria/ *f,* dyeing industry; dyeing and dry-cleaning shop

tintorero /tinto'rero/ **(-ra)** *n* dyer; dry cleaner

tintura /tin'tura/ *f,* dyeing, staining; color, tint; dye; stain; tincture; smattering, slight knowledge

tinturar /tintu'rar/ *vt* to dye; color, tinge, stain; give a superficial notion of

tiña /'tiɲa/ *f,* ringworm; *Inf.* meanness, stinginess

tiñoso /ti'ɲoso/ *a* mangy; afflicted with ringworm; *Inf.* mean, stingy

tiñuela /ti'ɲuela/ *f,* shipworm

tío /'tio/ *m,* uncle; gaffer; fellow, chap; fool; stepfather; father-in-law. **t. abuelo,** granduncle, great-uncle

tiovivo /tio'βiβo/ *m,* merry-go-round

tipiadora /tipia'ðora/ *f,* typewriter

típico /'tipiko/ *a* typical

tiple /'tiple/ *m,* soprano or treble voice. *mf* soprano

tipo /'tipo/ *m,* model, pattern; type; print, type; species, group (of animals, etc.); *Inf.* guy, chap

tipografía /tipogra'fia/ *f,* typography

tipográfico /tipo'grafiko/ *a* typographical

tipógrafo /ti'pografo/ *m,* typographer

típula /'tipula/ *f,* daddy-longlegs

tiquismiquis /tikis'mikis/ *m pl,* ridiculous scruples; affected courtesies —*a Inf.* faddy, fussy

tira /'tira/ *f,* strip, band, ribbon; stripe, rib. **t. cómica,** comic strip

tirabotas /tira'βotas/ *m,* buttonhook

tirabuzón /tiraβu'θon/ tiraβu'son/ *m,* corkscrew; ringlet, curl; hair curler

tirada /ti'raða/ *f,* throwing; drawing, pulling; cast, throw; distance, space; *Print.* edition, issue; circulation (of a newspaper, etc.); stroke (in golf); lapse, interval (of time). **t. aparte,** reprint (of an article, etc.)

tiradero /tira'ðero/ *m,* shooting butt

tirado /ti'raðo/ *a Inf.* dirt-cheap. *m,* wire drawing

tirador /tira'ðor/ **(-ra)** *n* thrower, caster; drawer, puller; marksman. *m,* handle, knob; *Mech.* trigger; bell rope, bell pull; *Print.* pressman. **t. de bota,** boot tag. **t. de gomas,** catapult. **t. de oro,** gold wire drawer

tiralíneas /tira'lineas/ *m,* ruling pen

tiramiento /tira'miento/ *m,* pulling; stretching

tiramira /tira'mira/ *f,* long, narrow mountain range; long line of persons or things; distance

tiranía /tira'nia/ *f,* tyranny, despotism

tiranicida /tirani'θiða; tirani'siða/ *mf* tyrannicide (person)

tiranicidio /tirani'θiðio; tirani'siðio/ *m,* tyrannicide (act)

tiránico /ti'raniko/ *a* tyrannical

tiranización /tiraniθa'θion; tiranisa'sion/ *f,* tyranny, tyrannization

tiranizar /tirani'θar; tirani'sar/ *vt* to tyrannize over

tirano /ti'rano/ **(-na)** *a* tyrannous, tyrannical; *Fig.* overwhelming, dominating —*n* tyrant

tirante /ti'rante/ *a* taut; tense, strained. *m,* trace (of a harness); shoulderstrap; suspender (gen. *pl*); *Archit.* tie

tirantez /tiran'teθ/ tiran'tes/ *f,* tautness; tension, strain; straight distance between two points. **estado de t.,** *Polit.* strained relations

tiranuelo /tira'nuelo/ *m,* petty tyrant

tirar /ti'rar/ *vt* to throw, cast; fling, aim, toss; throw down, overthrow; pull; draw; discharge, shoot; stretch, pull out; rule, draw (lines); squander, waste; *Print.* print; —*vi* attract; pull; (*with prep a*) turn to, turn in the direction of; incline, tend to; incline toward, have a tinge of (colors); try, aspire to; (*with de*) wield, unsheath, draw out (firearms, arms); —*vr* cast oneself, precipitate oneself; throw oneself on. *Inf.* **ir tirando,** to carry on, get along somehow

tirilla /ti'riʎa; ti'riya/ *f, Sew.* shirt neckband

tiritaña /tiri'taɲa/ *f,* thin silk material; *Inf.* mere nothing, trifle

tiritar /tiri'tar/ *vi* to shiver with cold

tiritón /tiri'ton/ *m,* shiver, shudder

Tiro /'tiro/ Tyre

tiro /'tiro/ *m,* throwing; throw, cast; toss, fling; try (in football); shooting; piece of artillery; report, shot (of a gun); discharge (firearms); shooting range or gallery; team (of horses); range (of firearms, etc.); hoisting cable; flight (of stairs); *Mineral.* shaft; *Inf.* trick; robbery, theft; innuendo, insinuation; grave harm or injury; *pl* sword belt. **t. de pichón,** pigeon shooting. **t. par,** four-in-hand. **a t.,** within firing range; within reach. **de tiros largos,** *Inf.* in full regalia

tirocinio /tiro'θinio; tiro'sinio/ *m,* apprenticeship

tiroideo /tiroi'ðeo/ *a* thyroid

tiroides /ti'roiðes/ *f,* thyroid gland

Tirol, el /ti'rol, el/ the Tyrol

tirón /ti'ron/ *m,* novice, beginner; pull, tug, heave. **de un t.,** with one tug; at one stroke, at one blow

tiroriro /tiro'riro/ *m, Inf.* sound of a wind instrument; *pl Inf.* wind instruments

tirotearse /tirote'arse/ *vr Mil.* to exchange fire; indulge in repartee

tiroteo /tiro'teo/ *m,* shooting, exchange of shots; crackle (of rifle fire)

Tirreno, el Mar /ti'rreno, el mar/ the Tyrrhenian Sea

tirria /'tirria/ *f, Inf.* hostility, grudge, dislike

tirulato /tiru'lato/ *a* dumbfounded, stupefied

tisana /ti'sana/ *f,* tisane

tísico /'tisiko/ **(-ca)** *a* tuberculous —*n* sufferer from tuberculosis, consumptive

tisis /'tisis/ *f,* tuberculosis

tisú /ti'su/ *m,* silver or gold tissue

titánico /ti'taniko/ *a* titanesque; colossal, huge

títere /'titere/ *m,* puppet; *Fig. Inf.* gnome, grotesque; *Inf.* fool; obsession, fixed idea; *pl Inf.* circus; Punch and Judy show. *Inf.* **echar los títeres a rodar,** to upset the whole show; quarrel, fall out with. *Inf.* **no dejar t. con cabeza,** to destroy entirely, smash up completely; leave no one

titerero /tite'rero/ **(-ra),** **titiritero** **(-ra),** *n* **titerista** *mf* puppet showman; acrobat; juggler

tití /ti'ti/ *m,* marmoset

titilación /titila'θion; titila'sion/ *f,* quiver, tremor; twinkling, winking, gleam

titilador, titilante /titila'ðor, titi'lante/ *a* quivering, trembling; twinkling

titilar /titi'lar/ *vi* to quiver, tremble; twinkle

titiritaina /titiri'taina/ *f, Inf.* muffled strains of musical instruments; merrymaking, uproar

titiritar /titiri'tar/ *vi* to tremble, shiver, shudder

titiritero /titiri'tero/ **(-ra)** *n* puppet master; acrobat

titubear /tituβe'ar/ *vi* to totter, sway, rock; stutter, stammer; toddle; hesitate, vacillate

titubeo /titu'βeo/ *m,* tottering, swaying; stuttering; hesitation

titulado /titu'laðo/ *m,* titled person; one who holds an academic title

titular /titu'lar/ *a* titular —*vt* to entitle, call; —*vi* obtain a title (of nobility); —*vr* style oneself, call oneself

título /'titulo/ *m,* title; heading; inscription; pretext, excuse; diploma, certificate; claim, right; noble title and its owner; section, clause; (univ.) degree; *Com.* stock certificate, bond; *Com.* title; caption; qualification, right, merit; basis of a claim or privilege; *pl Com.* securities, stocks. **t. de la columna,** *Print.* running title. **títulos de propiedad,** title deeds. **t. del reino,** title of nobility. **a t.,** under pretext

tiza /'tiθa; 'tisa/ *f,* chalk; whiting; calcined stag's antler

tiznar /tiθ'nar; tis'nar/ *vt* to make sooty; dirty, stain, begrime; *Fig.* sully, tarnish

tizne /'tiθne; 'tisne/ *m,* (sometimes *f*) soot; charcoal; stain (on one's honor, etc.); *Agr.* blight

tizón /ti'θon; ti'son/ *m,* firebrand; *Agr.* blight; *Fig.* stain (on one's honor, etc.)

tizona /ti'θona; ti'sona/ *f, Inf.* sword (by allusion to name of that of the Cid)

tizonear /tiθone'ar; tisone'ar/ *vi* to poke or rake the fire

toalla /to'aʎa; to'aya/ *f,* towel. **t. continua,** roller towel. **t. rusa,** Turkish towel

toallero /toa'ʎero; toa'yero/ *m,* towel rail

tobillera /toβi'ʎera; toβi'yera/ *f, Inf.* girl, flapper

tobillo /to'βiʎo; to'βiyo/ *m,* ankle

tobogán /toβo'gan/ *m,* toboggan; chute (in apartment buildings or amusement parks)

toca /'toka/ *f,* headdress; toque; wimple; coif

tocable /to'kaβle/ *a* touchable

tocado /to'kaðo/ *a Fig.* touched, half-crazy. *m,* headdress; coiffure, hairdressing

tocador /toka'ðor/ **(-ra)** *n Mus.* player. *m,* dressing table; kerchief; boudoir; cloakroom; dressing room; dressing case

tocamiento /toka'miento/ *m,* touching, feeling; touch; *Fig.* inspiration

tocante /to'kante/ *a* touching. **t. a,** concerning, with regard to

tocar /to'kar/ *vt* to touch, feel; *Mus.* play; knock, rap; summon; ring, peal; brush against; discover by experience; persuade, inspire; mention, touch upon; *Naut.* touch bottom; *Art.* retouch, touch up —*vi* belong; stop (at), touch at; be one's turn; concern, interest; be one's lot; adjoin, be near to; be opportune; be allied or closely related to; find the scent (of dogs). **t. en un punto,** *Naut.* to touch at a port. **Ahora me toca a mí,** Now it's my turn. **Es un problema que me toca de cerca,** It is a problem that touches me very nearly. **a toca teja,** *Inf.* in ready cash

tocayo /to'kayo/ **(-ya)** *n* namesake

tochedad /totʃe'ðað/ *f,* boorishness, loutishness

tocho /'totʃo/ *a* boorish, loutish, countrified. *m,* iron bar

tocinería /toθine'ria; tosine'ria/ *f,* pork butcher's shop

tocinero /toθi'nero; tosi'nero/ *m,* pork butcher

tocino /to'θino; to'sino/ *m,* bacon; salt pork

tocología /tokolo'hia/ *f,* tokology, obstetrics

tocón /to'kon/ *m,* stump (of a tree or an amputated limb)

todavía /toða'βia/ *adv* still; even; nevertheless; yet. **No han venido t.,** They have not come yet. **Queda mucho que hacer t.,** There is still much to be done.

todo /'toðo/ *a* all; whole, entire; every, each. *m,* whole, entirety; whole word (in charades); all; *pl* all; everyone —*adv* wholly, entirely. **t. lo posible,** everything possible; all one can, one's best. **t. lo que,** all that which. **ante t.,** in the first place; especially, particularly. **así y t.,** nevertheless. **a t. esto,** in the meanwhile. **con t.** *or* **con t. esto** *or* **con t. y esto,** nevertheless, in spite of this. **del t.,** wholly, completely. **jugar el t. por el t.,** to risk everything on the outcome. **sobre t.,** especially. **y t.,** in addition, as well. **Todos somos hijos de Adán y Eva, sino que nos diferencia la lana y la seda,** We are all equal, but some of us are more equal than others

todopoderoso /toðopoðe'roso/ *a* all-powerful, almighty. *m,* the Almighty, God

toga /'toga/ *f,* toga; robe, gown

toisón /toi'son/ *m,* fleece. **t. de oro,** Golden Fleece

Tokio /'tokio/ Tokyo

toldadura /tolda'ðura/ *f,* awning; canopy; hanging, curtain

toldillo /tol'diʎo; tol'diyo/ *m,* covered litter or sedan chair; *West Hem.* mosquito net

toldo /'toldo/ *m,* awning; canopy; pomp, show

tole /'tole/ *m,* outcry, uproar, tumult

toledano /tole'ðano/ **(-na)** *a* and *n* Toledan

tolerable /tole'raβle/ *a* bearable, tolerable

tolerancia /tole'ranθia; tole'ransia/ *f,* tolerance, forbearance; permission

tolerante /tole'rante/ *a* tolerant, broad-minded

tolerantismo /toleran'tismo/ *m,* religious toleration

tolerar /tole'rar/ *vt* to put up with, bear, tolerate; overlook, allow, forgive

tolla /'toʎa; 'toya/ *f,* marsh, bog

tollina /to'ʎina; to'yina/ *f, Inf.* spanking, whipping

tolmo /'tolmo/ *m,* tor

tolondro /to'londro/ *a* stupid, heedless, reckless. *m,* bump, bruise

tolonés /tolo'nes/ **(-esa)** *a* and *n* of or from Toulon

Tolosa /to'losa/ Toulouse

tolva /'tolβa/ *f,* chute (for grain, etc.)

toma /'toma/ *f,* taking; receiving; conquest, capture; dose (of medicine)

tomada /to'maða/ *f,* taking; take; capture

tomadero /toma'ðero/ *m,* handle, haft

tomadura /toma'ðura/ *f,* taking; receiving; dose (of medicine). *Inf.* **t. de pelo,** leg-pull, joke

tomar /to'mar/ *vt* to take; pick up; conquer; eat; drink; adopt, employ; contract (habits); engage (employees); rent; understand; steal; remove; buy; suffer; *Fig.* overcome (by laughter, sleep, etc.); choose; possess physically; —*vi* (*with por*) go in the direction of; —*vr* grow rusty; go moldy; (*with con*) quarrel with. **t. a chacota,** to take as a joke. **t. a pechos,** to take to heart. **t. el fresco,** to take the air. **tomarla con,** to contradict, oppose; bear a grudge. **t. la delantera,** to take the lead; excel, beat. **t. las de Villadiego,** *Inf.* to quit, show one's heels. **t. por su cuenta,** to undertake, take charge of; take upon oneself. **t. su desquite con,** to get even with. **Más vale un toma que dos te daré,** A little help is worth a lot of promises. **¡Toma!** *Inf.* Fancy! You don't say!; Of course! There's nothing new about that!

tomatal /toma'tal/ *m,* tomato bed, tomato patch

tomate /to'mate/ *m,* tomato; tomato plant; *Inf.* hole, potato (in stockings, etc.)

tomatera /toma'tera/ *f,* tomato plant

tomatero /toma'tero/ **(-ra)** *n* tomato seller

tómbola /'tombola/ *f,* raffle (gen. for charity); jumble sale

tomillo /to'miʎo; to'miyo/ *m,* thyme

tomo /'tomo/ *m,* volume, book; importance, worth

ton /ton/ *m, Abbr.* **tono. sin t. ni son,** *Inf.* without rhyme or reason

tonada /to'naða/ *f,* words of a song and its tune

tonadilla /tona'ðiʎa; tona'ðiya/ *f, dim* short song; comic song; *Theat.* musical interlude *Obs.*

tonadillero /tonaði'ʎero; tonaði'yero/ **(-ra)** *n* composer or singer of tonadillas

tonal /to'nal/ *a* tonal

tonalidad /tonali'ðað/ *f,* tonality

tonar /to'nar/ *vi Poet.* to thunder or lightning

tonel /to'nel/ *m,* barrel; cask; butt

tonelada /tone'laða/ *f,* ton

tonelería /tonele'ria/ *f,* cooperage; collection or stock of casks and barrels

tonelero /tone'lero/ *m,* cooper

tonga, tongada /'toŋga, toŋ'gaða/ *f,* layer, stratum; *Inf.* task

tónica /'tonika/ *f, Mus.* keynote

tónico /'toniko/ *a* tonic. *m, Med.* tonic; pick-me-up

tonificador, tonificante /tonifika'ðor, tonifi'kante/ *a* strengthening, invigorating tonic

tonillo /to'niʎo; to'niyo/ *m, dim* monotonous singsong voice; regional accent

tonina /to'nina/ *f,* tuna; dolphin

tono /'tono/ *m,* inflection, modulation; (*Mus. Med. Art.*) tone; pitch, resonance; energy, strength; style; manner, behavior; *Mus.* key; mode of speech. **bajar el t.,** *Fig. Inf.* to change one's tune. *Inf.* **darse t.,** to put on side, give oneself airs. **de buen (mal) t.,** in good (bad) taste

tonsila /ton'sila/ *f,* tonsil

tonsilitis /tonsi'litis/ *f,* tonsillitis

tonsura /ton'sura/ *f,* shearing; hair cutting; *Eccl.* tonsure

tonsurar /tonsu'rar/ *vt* to shear, clip; cut the hair off; *Eccl.* tonsure

tontaina /ton'taina/ *mf Inf.* ninny, fool

tontear /tonte'ar/ *vi* to behave foolishly; play the fool

tontería /tonte'ria/ *f,* foolishness, stupidity; piece of folly; trifle, bagatelle

tontillo /ton'tiʎo; ton'tiyo/ *m,* dress bustle; hoop (for dresses)

tontiloco /tonti'loko/ *a Inf.* crazy, daft

tontivano /tonti'βano/ *a* vain, conceited

tonto /'tonto/ **(-ta)** *a* silly, stupid, simple; foolish, absurd —*n* fool, idiot. *m,* short coat, stroller. **t. de capirote,** *Inf.* an utter fool. **a tontas y a locas,** without rhyme or reason, topsy-turvy. **volver t.** (**a**), *Fig. Inf.* to drive crazy

topacio /to'paθio; to'pasio/ *m,* topaz

topar /to'par/ *vt* (*with con*) to run into, collide with, hit; meet unexpectedly; come across, find; —*vi* butt (of horned animals); take a bet (in cards); consist in (of obstacles); meet with (difficulties); *Inf.* be successful

tope /'tope/ *m,* projection, part that juts out; obstacle, impediment; collision, bump; crux, difficult point; quarrel, fight; *Mech.* stop; *Naut.* masthead; *Rail.* buffer. **hasta el t.,** completely full, full to the brim

topera /to'pera/ *f,* molehill

topetada /tope'taða/ *f,* butt (of horned animals); *Inf.* knock, bang

topetar /tope'tar/ *vt* and *vi* to butt (of horned animals); —*vt* meet, run into

topetón /tope'ton/ *m,* butt; collision, impact, bump; blow on the head

tópico /'topiko/ *a* topical. *m,* topic, theme

topo /'topo/ *m, Zool.* mole; *Inf.* clumsy or shortsighted person; dolt, ninny

topografía /topogra'fia/ *f,* topography

topográfico /topo'grafiko/ *a* topographical

topógrafo /to'pografo/ *m,* topographer

toque /'toke/ *m,* touch, touching; pealing, ringing (of bells); crux, essence; test, proof; touchstone; *Metall.* assay; warning; *Inf.* tap (on the shoulder, etc.); *Art.* touch. **t. de luz,** *Art.* light (in a picture). **t. de obscuro,** *Art.* shade (in a picture). **t. de queda,** curfew. **t. de tambor,** beating of a drum. **dar un t. a,** *Inf.* to put to the test; pump (for information)

toquero /to'kero/ **(-ra)** *n* manufacturer of headdresses

toquetear /tokete'ar/ *vt* to keep touching, handle repeatedly

toquilla /to'kiʎa; to'kiya/ *f,* hatband, hat trimming; kerchief; small shawl

torácico /to'raθiko; to'rasiko/ *a* thoracic

toral /to'ral/ *a* principal, chief, main

tórax /'toraks/ *m,* thorax

torbellino /torβe'ʎino; torβe'yino/ *m,* whirlwind; spate of things; *Inf.* madcap

torcedero /torθe'ðero; torse'ðero/ *a* twisted, crooked

torcedor /torθe'ðor; torse'ðor/ *a* twisting. *m,* twister; cause of continual anxiety

torcedura /torθe'ðura; torse'ðura/ *f,* twisting; sprain, wrench

torcer /tor'θer; tor'ser/ *vt irr* to twist; bend; turn, bear (of roads, etc.); slant, slope, incline; misconstrue, pervert; dissuade; wrench, sprain (muscles); corrupt (justice). **t. el gesto,** to make a wry face —*vr* turn sour (of wine, milk); *Fig.* go astray; turn out badly (of negotiations) —*Pres. Indic.* **tuerzo, tuerces,** etc —*Pres. Subjunc.* **tuerza, tuerzas, tuerza, tuerzan**

torcida /tor'θiða; tor'siða/ *f,* wick (of lamps, etc.)

torcido /tor'θiðo; tor'siðo/ *a* bent, crooked, sloping, inclined; curved; dishonest, tortuous. *m,* silk twist

torcijón /torθi'hon; torsi'hon/ *m,* stomachache

torcimiento /torθi'miento; torsi'miento/ *m,* twisting; twist, turn; circumlocution; digression

tordo /'torðo/ *a* piebald, black-and-white. *m, Ornith.* thrush. **t. de campanario** *or* **t. de Castilla,** starling

toreador /torea'ðor/ *m,* bullfighter

torear /tore'ar/ *vi* and *vt* to fight bulls; —*vt* ridicule; exasperate, provoke; *Inf.* string along, deceive

toreo /to'reo/ *m,* bullfighting

torera /to'rera/ *f,* bullfighter's jacket

torero /to'rero/ *a Inf.* bullfighting. *m,* bullfighter

torete /to'rete/ *m, dim* small bull; *inf.* problem, difficult question; engrossing topic of conversation

toril /to'ril/ *m,* pen for fighting bulls

torio /'torio/ *m,* thorium

tormenta /tor'menta/ *f,* storm; misfortune, calamity; indignation, agitation

tormento /tor'mento/ *m,* torment; torture; pain; anxiety, anguish. **dar t. (a),** to torture; inflict pain (on)

tormentoso /tormen'toso/ *a* stormy, tempestuous; *Naut.* pitching, rolling

torna /'torna/ *f,* return; restitution; backwater

tornaboda /torna'βoða/ *f,* day after a wedding; rejoicings of this day

tornada /tor'naða/ *f,* return home; return visit, revisit; *Poet.* envoy

tornadizo /torna'ðiθo; torna'ðiso/ **(-za)** *a Inf.* changeable —*n* turncoat

tornamiento /torna'miento/ *m,* return; change, transformation

tornar /tor'nar/ *vt* to return, give back; change, transform; —*vi* return, go back; continue

tornasol /torna'sol/ *m,* sunflower; sheen, changing light; *Chem.* litmus

tornasolado /tornaso'laðo/ *a* shot (of silk, etc.)

tornasolar /tornaso'lar/ *vt* to look iridescent; change the color of, cause to appear variegated

tornátil /tor'natil/ *a* turned (in a lathe); inconstant, changeable; *Poet.* spinning, revolving

tornatrás /torna'tras/ *mf* half-caste

tornaviaje /torna'βiahe/ *m,* return journey

tornavoz /torna'βoθ; torna'βos/ *m,* soundboard, sounding board

torneador /tornea'ðor/ *m,* turner; jouster, fighter in a tournament

tornear /torne'ar/ *vt Sports.* to put a spin on (balls); turn in a lathe; —*vi* turn around, spin; fight in a tournament; turn over in the mind

torneo /tor'neo/ *m,* tournament

tornería /torne'ria/ *f,* turnery

tornero /tor'nero/ *m,* turner; lathe maker; convent messenger

tornillero /torni'ʎero; torni'yero/ *m,* (*Inf. Mil.*) deserter

tornillo /tor'niʎo; tor'niyo/ *m,* screw; (*Inf. Mil.*) desertion

torniquete /torni'kete/ *m,* turnstile; tourniquet. **dar t. (a),** to pervert, misinterpret (meanings)

torniscón /tornis'kon/ *m, Inf.* slap, buffet, blow; pinch

torno /'torno/ *m,* lathe; turntable (of a convent, etc.); turn, rotation; windlass; dumbwaiter; axletree; spinning wheel; bend, loop (in a river). **en t.,** round about, around; in exchange

toro /'toro/ *m,* bull; Taurus; *pl* bullfight. *Inf.* **t. corrido,** tough nut to crack, wise guy. *Inf.* **Ciertos son los toros,** So it's true (gen. of bad news)

toronja /to'ronha/ *f,* grapefruit

toroso /to'roso/ *a* strong, vigorous, robust

torpe /'torpe/ *a* heavy, slow, encumbered; torpid; clumsy, unskilled; stupid, dull-witted; obscene, indecent; base, infamous; ugly

torpedeamiento /torpeðea'miento/ *m,* torpedoing, sinking

torpedear /torpeðe'ar/ *vt* to torpedo

torpedeo /torpe'ðeo/ *m,* torpedoing

torpedero /torpe'ðero/ *m,* torpedo boat

torpedo /tor'peðo/ *m, Ichth.* torpedo fish, electric ray; torpedo; sports car. **t. automóvil,** self-propelling torpedo

torpeza /tor'peθa; tor'pesa/ *f,* slowness, heaviness; torpidity; stupidity; lack of skill, clumsiness; indecency; ugliness; baseness, infamy

tórpido /'torpiðo/ *a* torpid

torrar /to'rrar/ *vt* to toast, brown

torre /'torre/ *f,* tower; belfry, steeple; turret; rook (in chess); *Naut.* gun turret; stack, pile (of chairs, etc.); country house with a garden. **t. del tráfico,** traffic light. **t. de viento,** castle in the air, castle in Spain

torrefacción /torrefak'θion; torrefak'sion/ *f,* toasting (of coffee, etc.)

torrencial /torren'θial; torren'sial/ *a* torrential

torrente /to'rrente/ *m,* torrent; *Fig.* spate, rush; crowd

torreón /to'rreon/ *m,* large fortified tower

torrero /to'rrero/ *m,* lighthouse keeper; gardener

torreznero /torreθ'nero; torres'nero/ **(-ra)** *n Inf.* lazybones, idler

torrezno /to'rreθno; to'rresno/ *m,* rasher of bacon

tórrido /'torriðo/ *a* torrid

torsión /tor'sion/ *f,* twisting, torsion

torta /'torta/ *f,* cake; pastry, tart; *Inf.* slap. **t. de reyes,** traditional Twelfth Night cake

tortada /tor'taða/ *f,* meat pie, game pie

tortedad /torte'ðað/ *f,* twistedness, crookedness

tortera /tor'tera/ *f,* cake pan; baking dish; whorl (of a spindle)

tortícolis /tor'tikolis/ *m,* crick (in the neck)

tortilla /tor'tiʎa; tor'tiya/ *f,* omelet. **t. a la española,** potato omelet. **hacer t.,** to smash to atoms. **Se volvió la t.,** *Inf.* The tables are turned

tórtola /'tortola/ *f,* turtledove

tórtolo /'tortolo/ *m,* male turtledove; *Inf.* devoted lover

tortuga /tor'tuga/ *f,* turtle; tortoise. **a paso de t.,** at a snail's pace

tortuosidad /tortuosi'ðað/ *f,* tortuousness; winding; indirectness; deceitfulness

tortuoso /tor'tuoso/ *a* tortuous; winding; disingenuous, deceitful

tortura /tor'tura/ *f,* twistedness; torture, torment; anguish, grief. **una t. china,** excruciating torture

torturador /tortura'ðor/ *a* torturing, tormenting

torturar /tortu'rar/ *vt* to torture

torva /'torβa/ *f,* squall of rain or snow

torzal /tor'θal; tor'sal/ *m,* sewing silk; twist, plait

tos /tos/ *f,* cough. **t. ferina,** whooping cough

Toscana /tos'kana/ Tuscany

tosco /'tosko/ *a* rough, unpolished; coarse; boorish, uncouth

toser /to'ser/ *vi* to cough

tósigo /'tosigo/ *m,* poison, venom; anguish; affliction

tosigoso /tosi'goso/ *a* poisoned, venomous

tosquedad /toske'ðað/ *f,* roughness, lack of polish; coarseness; boorishness, uncouthness

tostada /tos'taða/ *f, Cul.* toast

tostadera /tosta'ðera/ *f,* toasting fork

tostado /tos'taðo/ *a* golden brown, tanned. *m,* roasting (of coffee, etc.)

tostador /tosta'ðor/ **(-ra)** *n* toaster (of peanuts, etc.). *m,* toaster (utensil); coffee or peanut roaster

tostadura /tosta'ðura/ *f,* toasting; roasting (of coffee, etc.)

tostón /tos'ton/ *m,* buttered toast; anything overtoasted; roast pig; *Inf.* nuisance, bore

total /to'tal/ *a* total, entire, whole; general. *m,* total —*adv* in short; so, therefore

totalidad /totali'ðað/ *f,* whole; aggregate, entirety

totalitario /totali'tario/ *a* totalitarian

tótem /'totem/ *m,* totem

totemismo /tote'mismo/ *m,* totemism

toxicidad /toksiθi'ðað; toksisi'ðað/ *f,* toxicity

tóxico /'toksiko/ *a* toxic. *m,* toxic substance

toxicología /toksikolo'hia/ *f,* toxicology

toxicológico /toksiko'lohiko/ *a* toxicological

toxicólogo /toksi'kologo/ *m,* toxicologist

toxina /tok'sina/ f, toxin
tozo /'toθo; 'toso/ a dwarfish, small
tozudez /toθu'ðeθ; tosu'ðes/ f, obstinacy
tozudo /to'θuðo; to'suðo/ a obstinate, obdurate
tozuelo /to'θuelo; to'suelo/ m, scruff, fat nape (of animals)
traba /'traβa/ f, setting (of a saw's teeth); tether (for horses); difficulty, obstacle; fastening; bond, tie; shackle; Law. distraint
trabacuenta /traβa'kuenta/ f, mistake in accounts; argument, difference of opinion
trabajado /traβa'haðo/ a and past part wrought; fashioned; labored, exhausted, weary
trabajador /traβaha'ðor/ (-ra) a working; conscientious —n worker
trabajar /traβa'har/ vi to work; function; stand the strain, resist (of machines, etc.); exert oneself, strive; toil, labor; operate, work; produce, yield (the earth fruits, etc.); —vt work; till, cultivate; exercise (a horse); worry, annoy, weary; operate, drive; —vr make every effort, work hard
trabajo /tra'βaho/ m, work; toil, labor; operation, working; difficulty, obstacle; literary work; hardship, trouble; process; pl poverty; hardship. **t. a destajo,** piecework. **t. al ralenti,** go-slow tactics. **trabajos forzados** (or **forzosos**), Law. hard labor. **pasar trabajos,** to undergo hardships
trabajosamente /traβahosa'mente/ adv painstakingly
trabajoso /traβa'hoso/ a difficult, hard; ailing, delicate; needy; afflicted
trabalenguas /traβa'lenguas/ m, Inf. tongue twister, jawbreaker
trabamiento /traβa'miento/ m, joining, fastening; uniting; initiation, commencement; shackling; hobbling (of horses)
trabar /tra'βar/ vt to join, unite, fasten; grasp, seize; set the teeth (of a saw); thicken; begin, initiate; hobble (of horses); reconcile, bring together, harmonize; shackle; Law. distrain; —vr speak with an impediment; stutter, hesitate. **t. amistad,** to make friends. **t. conversación,** to get into conversation. **Se me trabó la lengua,** I began to stutter
trabazón /traβa'θon; traβa'son/ f, join, union, fastening; connection; thickness, consistency
trabilla /tra'βiʎa; tra'βiya/ f, vest strap; dropped stitch (in knitting)
trabuca /tra'βuka/ f, squib, Chinese firecracker, riprap
trabucar /traβu'kar/ vt to turn upside down, upset; confuse, bewilder; mix up, confuse (news, etc.); pronounce or write incorrectly
trabucazo /traβu'kaθo; traβu'kaso/ m, shot or report of a blunderbuss; Inf. calamity, unexpected misfortune
trabuco /tra'βuko/ m, Mil. catapult; blunderbuss
trabuquete /traβu'kete/ m, catapult
tracamundana /trakamun'dana/ f, Inf. barter, exchange of trash; hubbub, uproar
tracción /trak'θion; trak'sion/ f, pulling; traction
Tracia /'traθia; 'trasia/ Thrace
tracoma /tra'koma/ f, trachoma
tracto /'trakto/ m, tract, area, expanse; lapse of time
tractor /trak'tor/ m, tractor. **t. de orugas,** caterpillar tractor
tractorista /trakto'rista/ mf driver of a tractor, tractor driver
tradición /traði'θion; traði'sion/ f, tradition
tradicional /traðiθio'nal; traðisio'nal/ a traditional
tradicionalismo /traðiθiona'lismo; traðisiona'lismo/ m, traditionalism
tradicionalista /traðiθiona'lista; traðisiona'lista/ a traditionalistic. mf traditionalist
traducción /traðuk'θion; traðuk'sion/ f, translation; interpretation, explanation
traducible /traðu'θiβle; traðu'siβle/ a translatable
traducir /traðu'θir; traðu'sir/ vt irr to translate; interpret, explain; express. See **conducir**
traductor /traðuk'tor/ (-ra) n translator; interpreter
traedizo /trae'ðiθo; trae'ðiso/ a portable, movable
traer /tra'er/ vt irr to bring; attract; cause, occasion; wear, have on; quote, cite (as proof); compel, force; persuade; conduct, lead (persons); be engaged in; —vr dress (well or badly). **t. consigo,** to bring with it;

have or carry or bring with one. **t. entre manos,** to have on hand —Pres. Indic. **traigo, traes,** etc —Pres. Part. **trayendo.** Preterite **traje, trajiste,** etc —Pres. Subjunc. **traiga,** etc —Imperf. Subjunc. **trajese,** etc.
trafagador /trafaga'ðor/ m, dealer, trafficker, merchant
tráfago /'trafago/ m, traffic, trade; toil, drudgery
trafalmejas /trafal'mehas/ a Inf. rowdy, crazy, mf Inf. rowdy
traficante /trafi'kante/ mf dealer, merchant, trader
traficar /trafi'kar/ vi to trade; travel
tráfico /'trafiko/ m, traffic; trade, commerce
tragaderas /traga'ðeras/ f pl, throat, gullet. Inf. **tener buenas t.,** to be very credulous; be tolerant (of evil)
tragadero /traga'ðero/ m, throat, gullet; sink, drain; hole, plug
tragador /traga'ðor/ (-ra) n glutton, guzzler
tragahombres /traga'ombres/ mf Inf. braggart, bully
trágala /'tragala/ m, (**trágala tú, servilón**), title of Spanish Liberal song aimed at Absolutists; Inf. take that!
tragaleguas /traga'leguas/ mf Inf. fast walker
tragaluz /traga'luθ; traga'lus/ m, skylight; fan light
tragantón /tragan'ton/ (-ona) a Inf. guzzling, greedy —n glutton
tragantona /tragan'tona/ f, Inf. spread, large meal; swallowing with difficulty; Fig. Inf. hard pill to swallow
tragaperras /traga'perras/ m, Inf. vending machine, catchpenny
tragar /tra'gar/ vt to swallow; eat ravenously, devour; engulf, swallow up; believe, take in; tolerate, put up with; dissemble; consume, absorb
tragedia /tra'heðia/ f, tragedy
trágico /'trahiko/ (**-ca**) a tragic —n tragedian; writer of tragedies
tragicomedia /trahiko'meðia/ f, tragicomedy
tragicómico /trahi'komiko/ a tragicomic
trago /'trago/ m, swallow, gulp, draft; Fig. Inf. bitter pill. **a tragos,** Inf. little by little, slowly
tragón /tra'gon/ (**-ona**) a Inf. greedy, gluttonous —n glutton
tragonear /tragone'ar/ vt Inf. to devour, eat avidly
traición /trai'θion; trai'sion/ f, treason, treachery. **a t.,** treacherously
traicionar /traiθio'nar; traisio'nar/ vt to betray
traicionero /traiθio'nero; traisio'nero/ (**-ra**) a treacherous —n traitor
traída /tra'iða/ f, conduction. **t. de aguas,** water supply
traidor /trai'ðor/ (**-ra**) a treacherous —n traitor
traílla /tra'iʎa; tra'iya/ f, lead, leash (for animals)
traje /'trahe/ m, dress, apparel; outfit, costume; suit. **t. de americana,** lounge suit. **t. de ceremonia** or **t. de etiqueta,** full-dress uniform; evening dress (men). **t. de luces,** bullfighter's gala outfit. **t. de montar,** riding habit. **t. de noche,** evening dress (women). **t. paisano,** civilian dress; lounge suit
trajín /tra'hin/ m, carriage, transport; busyness, moving around; bustle; clatter
trajinar /trahi'nar/ vt to carry, transport; —vi be busy, go about one's business
tralla /'traʎa; 'traya/ f, rope, cord; lash (of a whip); whip
trama /'trama/ f, woof, texture (of cloth); twisted silk; intrigue, scheme; Lit. plot; olive flower
tramar /tra'mar/ vt to weave; prepare, hatch (plots); Fig. prepare the way for; —vi flower (of trees, especially olive)
tramitación /tramita'θion; tramita'sion/ f, transaction, conduct; procedure, method
tramitar /trami'tar/ vt to transact, conduct, settle
trámite /'tramite/ m, transit; negotiation, phase of a business deal; requirement, condition
tramo /'tramo/ m, plot of ground; flight of stairs, staircase; stretch, expanse, reach, tract
tramontana /tramon'tana/ f, north wind; arrogance, haughtiness
tramontano /tramon'tano/ a ultramontane, from beyond the mountains
tramontar /tramon'tar/ vi to cross the mountains;

sink behind the mountains (of the sun); —*vr* run away, escape

tramoya /tra'moya/ *f, Theat.* stage machinery; trick, deception, hoax

tramoyista /tramo'yista/ *mf* stage carpenter; stage-hand; scene-shifter; trickster, impostor, swindler

trampa /'trampa/ *f*, trap, snare; trapdoor; flap of a shop counter; trouser fly; trick, swindle; overdue debt. *Fig. Inf.* **caer en la t.**, to fall into the trap. *Inf.* **coger en la t.**, to catch in a trap; catch in the act

trampal /tram'pal/ *m*, bog, marsh

trampantojo /trampan'toho/ *m, Inf.* optical illusion, swindle

trampeador /trampea'ðor/ *a Inf.* swindling —*n* trickster, swindler

trampear /trampe'ar/ *vi Inf.* to obtain money on false pretenses; struggle on (against illness, etc.); keep oneself alive, make shift; —*vt* defraud, swindle

trampolín /trampo'lin/ *m*, springboard; diving board; *Fig.* jumping-off place

tramposo /tram'poso/ **(-sa)** *n* debtor; cardsharper; swindler

tranca /'tranka/ *f*, thick stick, cudgel; bar (of a window, etc.)

trancada /tran'kaða/ *f*, stride

trancar /tran'kar/ *vt* to bar the door; —*vi Inf.* oppose, resist

trancazo /tran'kaθo; tran'kaso/ *m*, blow with a stick; influenza, flu

trance /'tranθe; 'transe/ *m*, crisis, difficult juncture; danger, peril. **t. de armas**, armed combat. **a todo t.**, at all costs, without hesitation

tranco /'tranko/ *m*, stride; threshold. *Inf.* **en dos trancos**, in a trice

tranquera /tran'kera/ *f*, stockade, palisade

tranquilar /tranki'lar/ *vt Com.* to check off

tranquilidad /trankili'ðað/ *f*, tranquility, peace, quietness; composure, serenity

tranquilizador /trankiliθa'ðor; trankilisa'ðor/ *a* tranquilizing, soothing

tranquilizar /trankili'θar; trankili'sar/ *vt* to calm, quiet; soothe

tranquilo /tran'kilo/ *a* tranquil, quiet, peaceful; serene, composed

transacción /transak'θion; transak'sion/ *f*, compromise, arrangement; transaction, negotiation, deal

transalpino /transal'pino/ *a* transalpine

transandino /transan'dino/ *a* transandean

transatlántico /transat'lantiko/ *a* transatlantic. *m*, (transatlantic) liner

transbordar /transβor'ðar/ *vt* to transship; transfer, remove goods from one vehicle to another

transbordo /trans'βorðo/ *m*, transshipment, transshipping; transfer, removal

transcendencia /transθen'denθia; transsen'densia/ *f* See **trascendencia**

transcendental /transθenden'tal; transsenden'tal/ *a.* See **trascendental**

transcribir /transkri'βir/ *vt* to transcribe; copy —*Past Part.* **transcrito**

transcripción /transkrip'θion; transkrip'sion/ *f*, transcription; copy, transcript

transcurrir /transku'rrir/ *vi* to elapse, pass (time)

transcurso /trans'kurso/ *m*, passage, lapse, course (of time)

transepto /tran'septo/ *m*, transept

transeúnte /tran'seunte/ *a* transient, temporary. *mf* passerby; visitor, sojourner

transferencia /transfe'renθia; transfe'rensia/ *f*, transfer (from one place to another); *Law.* conveyance, transference. **t. bancaria**, bank draft

transferidor /transferi'ðor/ **(-ra)** *a* transferring —*n* transferrer; *Law.* transferor

transferir /transfe'rir/ *vt irr* to transfer, move from one place to another; *Law.* convey (property, etc.); postpone. See **sentir**

transfiguración /transfigura'θion; transfigura'sion/ *f*, transfiguration

transfigurar /transfigu'rar/ *vt* to transfigure

transfijo /trans'fiho/ *a* transfixed

transfixión /transfik'sion/ *f*, transfixion

transformable /transfor'maβle/ *a* transformable

transformación /transforma'θion; transforma'sion/ *f*, transformation

transformador /transforma'ðor/ *a* transformative. *m, Elec.* transformer

transformar /transfor'mar/ *vt* to transform; reform (persons); —*vr* be transformed; reform, mend one's ways

transfregar /transfre'gar/ *vt irr* to rub, scrub. See **cegar**

transfretar /transfre'tar/ *vt Naut.* to cross the sea; —*vi* spread

tránsfuga /'transfuga/ *mf* **tránsfugo** *m*, fugitive; political turncoat

transfundir /transfun'dir/ *vt* to transfuse, pour from one vessel to another; imbue, transmit

transfusor /transfu'sor/ *a* transfusive

transgredir /transgre'ðir/ *vt* to transgress, infringe

transgresión /transgre'sion/ *f*, infringement, violation, transgression

transgresor /transgre'sor/ **(-ra)** *a* infringing —*n* transgressor, violator

transiberiano /transiβe'riano/ *a* trans-Siberian

transición /transi'θion; transi'sion/ *f*, transition, change

transido /tran'siðo/ *a* exhausted, worn-out, spent; niggardly, mean

transigencia /transi'henθia; transi'hensia/ *f*, tolerance, forbearance, indulgence

transigente /transi'hente/ *a* tolerant, forbearing

transigir /transi'hir/ *vi* to be tolerant; be broad-minded —*vt* put up with, tolerate

transitable /transi'taβle/ *a* passable, traversable

transitar /transi'tar/ *vi* to cross, pass through; travel

transitivo /transi'tiβo/ *a* transitive

tránsito /'transito/ *m*, passage, crossing; transit; stopping place; transition, change; gallery of a cloister; *Eccl.* holy death. **de t.**, temporarily; in transit (of goods). **hacer tránsitos**, to break one's journey, stop

transitorio /transi'torio/ *a* transitory, fugitive, fleeting

translimitación /translimita'θion; translimita'sion/ *f*, trespass; bad behavior; armed intervention in a neighboring state

translimitar /translimi'tar/ *vt* to overstep the boundaries (of a state, etc.); overstep the limits (of decency, etc.)

translucidez /transluθi'ðeθ; translusi'ðes/ *f*, translucence, semitransparency

translúcido /trans'luθiðo; trans'lusiðo/ *a* translucent, semitransparent

transmarino /transma'rino/ *a* transmarine

transmigración /transmigra'θion; transmigra'sion/ *f*, transmigration

transmigrar /transmi'grar/ *vi* to migrate; transmigrate (of the soul)

transmisión /transmi'sion/ *f*, transmission. **t. del pensamiento**, thought transference

transmisor /transmi'sor/ *a* transmitting. *m, Elec.* transmitter, sender

transmitir /transmi'tir/ *vt* to transmit; *Mech.* drive

transmutable /transmu'taβle/ *a* transmutable

transmutación /transmuta'θion; transmuta'sion/ *f*, transmutation, transformation, change

transmutar /transmu'tar/ *vt* to transmute, transform, change

transmutativo /transmuta'tiβo/ *a* transmutative

transoceánico /transoθe'aniko; transose'aniko/ *a* transoceanic

transpacífico /transpa'θifiko; transpa'sifiko/ *a* transpacific

transparencia /transpa'renθia; transpa'rensia/ *f*, transparency; obviousness

transparentarse /transparen'tarse/ *vr* to be transparent; show through; *Fig.* reveal, give away (secrets)

transparente /transpa'rente/ *a* transparent; translucent; evident, obvious. *m*, windowshade, blind

transpiración /transpira'θion; transpira'sion/ *f*, transpiration; perspiration

transpirar /transpi'rar/ *vi* to perspire; transpire

transpirenaico /transpire'naiko/ *a* trans-Pyrenean

transponer /transpo'ner/ *vt irr* to move, transfer; transplant; transpose; —*vr* hide behind; sink behind the horizon (of the sun, stars); be half-asleep. See **poner**

transportable /transpor'taβle/ *a* transportable

transportación /transporta'θion; transporta'sion/ *f.* See **transporte**

transportador /transporta'ðor/ **(-ra)** *a* transport —*n* transporter. *m, Geom.* protractor

transportamiento /transporta'miento/ *m.* See **transporte**

transportar /transpor'tar/ *vt* to transport; *Mus.* transpose; carry; —*vr Fig.* be carried away by (anger, rapture)

transporte /trans'porte/ *m,* transport, carriage; cartage; *Naut.* transport; strong emotion, transport, ecstasy

transposición /transposi'θion; transposi'sion/ *f,* transposition

transpositivo /transposi'tiβo/ *a* transpositive

transubstanciación /transuβstan'θia'θion; transuβstansia'sion/ *f,* transubstantiation

transubstanciar /transuβstan'θiar; transuβstan'siar/ *vt* to transubstantiate, transmute

transversal, transverso /transβer'sal, trans'βerso/ *a* transverse

tranvía /tram'bia/ *m,* street railway; streetcar. **t. de sangre,** horse-drawn streetcar.

tranviario /tram'biario/ *a* streetcar. *m,* streetcar employee

trapacear /trapaθe'ar; trapase'ar/ *vi* to cheat, swindle

trapacete /trapa'θete; trapa'sete/ *m, Com.* daybook

trapacista /trapa'θista; trapa'sista/ *mf* trickster, swindler, knave

trapajoso /trapa'hoso/ *a* ragged, shabby, tattered

trápala /'trapala/ *f,* noise, confusion, hubbub; noise of horse's hoofs, gallop; *Inf.* trick, swindle; prattling, babbling. *mf Inf.* babbler, prattler; trickster

trapalear /trapale'ar/ *vi* to walk noisily, tramp; *Inf.* chatter, babble

trapatiesta /trapa'tiesta/ *f, Inf.* brawl, row, quarrel

trapaza /tra'paθa; tra'pasa/ *f,* hoax, swindle

trapecio /tra'peθio; tra'pesio/ *m,* trapeze; *Geom.* trapezium, trapezoid

trapería /trape'ria/ *f,* old-clothes shop; old clothes, rags, trash, frippery

trapero /tra'pero/ **(-ra)** *n* old-clothes seller; rag merchant; ragpicker

trapezoide /trape'θoiðe; trape'soiðe/ *m,* trapezium, trapezoid

trapichear /trapitʃe'ar/ *vi Inf.* to make shift, endeavor

trapiento /tra'piento/ *a* ragged, shabby

trapillo /tra'piʎo; tra'piyo/ *m, Inf.* poverty-stricken lover; nest egg, savings. *Inf.* **de t.,** in a state of undress, in négligé

trapío /tra'pio/ *m, Inf.* spirit of a fighting bull; verve, dash, independent air (of women)

trapisonda /trapi'sonda/ *f, Inf.* uproar, brawl; hubbub, bustle; snare, fix

trapisondear /trapisonde'ar/ *vi Inf.* to be given to brawling; scheme, intrigue

trapisondista /trapison'dista/ *mf* brawler; schemer, trickster

trapo /'trapo/ *m,* rag; *Naut.* canvas; bullfighter's cape; *pl* garments, bits and pieces. *Inf.* **poner como un t.** (**a),** to dress down, scold. *Inf.* **soltar el t.,** burst out crying or laughing

trapujo /tra'puho/ *m, Inf.* trick; subterfuge

traque /'trake/ *m,* report, bang (of a rocket, etc.); fuse (of a firework)

tráquea /'trakea/ *f,* trachea

traqueotomía /trakeoto'mia/ *f,* tracheotomy

traquetear /trakete'ar/ *vi* to crack, bang, go off with a report; rattle; jolt (of trains, etc.) —*vt* shake, stir; *Inf.* paw, handle too much

traqueteo /trake'teo/ *m,* banging (of fireworks); creaking; rattling; jolting (of trains, etc.)

traquido /tra'kiðo/ *m,* report (of a gun); crack (of a whip); creak

tras /tras/ *prep* after; behind; following, in pursuit of; trans- (in compounds). *m, Inf.* buttock; sound of a

blow, bang, bump. **t. t.,** knocking (at a door); banging

trasalcoba /trasal'koβa/ *f,* dressing room

trasbarrás /trasβa'rras/ *m,* bang, bump, noise

trascendencia /trasθen'denθia; trassen'densia/ *f,* transcendence, excellence; consequence, result

trascendental /trasθenden'tal; trassenden'tal/ *a* transcendental; important, farreaching

trascender /trasθen'der; trassen'der/ *vi irr* to spread to, influence; become known, leak out; exhale a scent; —*vt* investigate, discover. See **entender**

trascocina /trasko'θina; trasko'sina/ *f,* back kitchen

trascolar /trasko'lar/ *vt irr* to filter, strain; cross over, traverse. See **colar**

trascordarse /traskor'ðarse/ *vr irr* to mix up, make a muddle of, forget. See **acordar**

trasechar /trase'tʃar/ *vt* to ambush, waylay

trasegar /trase'gar/ *vt irr* to upset, turn upside down; transfer, move from one place to another; empty, pour out, upset (liquids). See **cegar**

traseñalar /traseɲa'lar/ *vt* to re-mark, mark again

trasera /tra'sera/ *f,* rear, back, rear portion

trasero /tra'sero/ *a* rear, back. *m,* hindquarters, rump; buttocks, seat; *pl Inf.* ancestors

trasgo /'trasgo/ *m,* imp, sprite, puck

trashumante /trasu'mante/ *a* nomadic (of flocks)

trashumar /trasu'mar/ *vi* to go from winter to summer pasture (or vice versa) (of flocks)

trasiego /tra'siego/ *m,* emptying, pouring out, upsetting (of liquids); decanting (of wines)

traslación /trasla'θion; trasla'sion/ *f,* removal, transfer; alteration (of the date for a meeting); metaphor

trasladable /trasla'ðaβle/ *a* removable, movable, transferable

trasladar /trasla'ðar/ *vt* to remove, transfer; move from one place to another; alter (the date of a meeting); translate; copy, transcribe; —*vr* remove (from a place)

traslado /tras'laðo/ *m,* removal; transfer; transcription

traslapar /trasla'par/ *vt* to cover, overlap

traslapo /tras'lapo/ *m,* overlap, overlapping

traslucirse /traslu'θirse; traslu'sirse/ *vr irr* to be transparent or translucent; shine through; come out (of secrets); infer, gather. See **lucir**

traslumbramiento /traslumbra'miento/ *m,* dazzle, glare, brilliance

traslumbrar /traslum'βrar/ *vt* to dazzle; —*vr* flicker, glimmer; fade quickly, disappear

trasluz /tras'luθ; tras'lus/ *m,* reflected light. **al t.,** against the light

trasmañana /trasma'ɲana/ *adv* the day after tomorrow

trasmañanar /trasmaɲa'nar/ *vt* to put off from day to day

trasminar /trasmi'nar/ *vt* to undermine, excavate; —*vi* percolate, ooze; penetrate, spread

trasnochada /trasno'tʃaða/ *f,* previous night, last night; night's vigil; sleepless night; *Mil.* night attack

trasnochado /trasno'tʃaðo/ *a* stale, old; weary; hackneyed; drawn, pinched

trasnochador /trasnotʃa'ðor/ **(-ra)** *n* one who watches by night or stays up all night; *Inf.* night owl, reveler

trasnochar /trasno'tʃar/ *vi* to stay up all night; watch through the night; spend the night; —*vt* sleep on, leave for the following day

trasnoche, trasnocho /tras'notʃe, tras'notʃo/ *m, Inf.* night out; night vigil

trasoir /traso'ir/ *vt irr* to hear incorrectly, misunderstand. See **oir**

trasojado /traso'haðo/ *a* haggard, tired-eyed

trasoñar /traso'ɲar/ *vt irr* to imagine, mistake a dream for reality. See **contar**

traspalar /traspa'lar/ *vt* to fork (grain); shovel; transfer, move

trasparencia /traspa'renθia; traspa'rensia/ *f.* See **transparencia**

traspasar /traspa'sar/ *vt* to transfer, move; cross; *Law.* convey, make over to; pierce; transgress, flout; exceed one's authority; *Fig.* go too far; reexamine, go over again; give intolerable pain (of illness, grief). **se traspasa,** to be disposed of (houses, etc.)

traspaso /tras'paso/ *m,* transport, transfer; *Law.* conveyance; property transferred; price agreed upon

traspié /tras'pie/ *m,* slip, catching of the foot, stumble; heel of the foot. **dar traspiés,** *Inf.* to blunder

trasplantación /trasplanta'θion; trasplanta'sion/ *f,* trasplante *m,* transplantation; emigration

trasplantar /trasplan'tar/ *vt Agr.* to transplant; —*vr* emigrate

trasplante /tras'plante/ *m,* planting out

traspuesta /tras'puesta/ *f,* transposition; back quarters; rear (of a house); back yard

traspunte /tras'punte/ *m, Theat.* prompter

traspuntín /traspun'tin/ *m, Auto.* folding seat

trasquilar /traski'lar/ *vt* to cut the hair unevenly; shear (sheep); *Inf.* cut down, diminish

trasquilón /traski'lon/ *m,* cropping (of hair); shearing; *Inf.* money stolen by pilfering

trastada /tras'taða/ *f, Inf.* dirty trick, mean act

traste /'traste/ *m,* fret (of stringed instruments); tasting cup. **dar al t. con,** to spoil, upset, damage. *Inf.* **sin trastes,** topsy-turvy, without method

trastear /traste'ar/ *vt* to play well (on the mandolin, etc.); *Inf.* manage tactfully; —*vi* move around, change (furniture, etc.); discuss excitedly

trastejar /traste'har/ *vt* to repair the roof; renew slates; overhaul

trastienda /tras'tienda/ *f,* back of a shop; room behind a shop; *Inf.* wariness, caution

trasto /'trasto/ *m,* piece of furniture; (household) utensil; lumber, useless furniture; *Theat.* wing or set piece; *Inf.* useless person, ne'er-do-well; oddment, thing; *pl* implements, equipment

trastornable /trastor'naβle/ *a* easily overturned or upset; easily agitated

trastornar /trastor'nar/ *vt* to turn upside down; perturb, disturb; *Fig.* overpower (of scents, etc.); disorder, upset; dissuade; make mad; derange the mind

trastorno /tras'torno/ *m,* upset, perturbation, anxiety; disorder; mental derangement; confusion (of the senses)

trastrabillar /trastraβi'ʎar; trastraβi'yar/ *vi* to stumble, slip, totter, sway; hesitate; stutter, be tongue-tied

trastrás /tras'tras/ *m, Inf.* last but one (in games)

trastrocamiento /trastroka'miento/ *m,* alteration, change; disarrangement

trastrocar /trastro'kar/ *vt irr* to alter, change, disarrange; change the order of. See **contar**

trasudar /trasu'ðar/ *vt* to perspire

trasudor /trasu'ðor/ *m,* light perspiration

trasuntar /trasun'tar/ *vt* to copy, transcribe; summarize

trasunto /tra'sunto/ *m,* copy, transcript; imitation

trasver /tras'βer/ *vt irr* to see through or between, glimpse; see incorrectly. See **ver**

trasverter /trasβer'ter/ *vi irr* to overflow. See **entender**

trata /'trata/ *f,* slave trade. **t. de blancas,** white slave traffic

tratable /tra'taβle/ *a* easily accessible, sociable, unpretentious

tratadista /trata'ðista/ *mf* writer of a treatise; expert, writer on special subjects

tratado /tra'taðo/ *m,* pact, agreement; treaty; treatise

tratador /trata'ðor/ **(-ra)** *n* arbitrator

tratamiento /trata'miento/ *m,* treatment; courtesy title; address, style; *Med.* treatment; process. **t. de textos,** word processing

tratante /tra'tante/ *m,* merchant, dealer

tratar /tra'tar/ *vt* to handle, use; conduct, manage; have dealings with, meet, know (e.g. *Yo no le trato,* I don't know him); behave well or badly toward; care for, treat; discuss, deal with (e.g. *¿De qué trata el libro?* What is the book about?); propose, suggest; *Chem.* treat; (*with de*) address as, call; —*vi* have amorous relations; (*with de*) try to, endeavor to; (*with en*) trade in; —*vr* look after oneself, treat oneself; conduct oneself

trato /'trato/ *m,* use, handling; management; conduct, behavior; manner, demeanor; appellation, title; commerce, traffic; dealings, intercourse; treatment;

agreement, arrangement. **t. colectivo,** collective bargaining

traumático /trau'matiko/ *a* traumatic

traumatismo /trauma'tismo/ *m,* traumatism

través /tra'βes/ *m,* slant, slope; mishap; (*Mil. Archit.*) traverse. **a t.** *or* **al t.,** across; through. **de t.,** athwart; through

travesaño /traβe'saɲo/ *m,* crossbar; bolster; rung (of a ladder); traverse

travesear /traβese'ar/ *vi* to run about, romp, be mischievous; lead a vicious life; speak wittily; move ceaselessly (of water, etc.)

travesía /traβe'sia/ *f,* crossing; traverse; crossroad; side road or street; distance, space; sea crossing; crosswise position; stretch of road within a town

travestido /traβes'tiðo/ *a* disguised, dressed up

travesura /traβe'sura/ *f,* romping, frolic; mischief; prank; quick-wittedness

traviesa /tra'βiesa/ *f,* sleeping car, sleeper (railroad); *Archit.* rafter; distance between two points

travieso /tra'βieso/ *a* transverse, crosswise; mischievous, willful; debauched; clever, subtle; ever-moving (of streams, etc.)

trayecto /tra'yekto/ *m,* run, distance, journey; stretch, expanse, tract; fare stage

trayectoria /trayek'toria/ *f,* trajectory; journey

traza /'traθa; 'trasa/ *f,* plan, design, draft; scheme, project; idea, proposal; aspect, appearance; means, manner. **Hombre pobre todo es trazas,** A poor man is full of schemes (for bettering himself)

trazado /tra'θaðo; tra'saðo/ *m,* designing, drawing; design, draft, model, plan; course, direction (of a canal, etc.)

trazador /traθa'ðor; trasa'ðor/ **(-ra)** *n* draftsman, designer; planner; schemer

trazar /tra'θar; tra'sar/ *vt* to plan, draft, design; make a drawing of; trace; describe; map out, arrange

trazo /'traθo; 'traso/ *m,* line, stroke; outline, contour, form, line; *Art.* fold in drapery; stroke of the pen

trebejar /treβe'har/ *vi* to frolic, skip, play

trebejo /tre'βeho/ *m,* chessman, chess piece; utensil, article (gen. *pl*); plaything

trébol /'treβol/ *m,* clover

trece /'treθe; 'trese/ *a* and *m,* thirteen, thirteenth. *m,* thirteenth (day of the month)

trecemesino /treθeme'sino; treseme'sino/ *a* thirteen months old

trecho /'tretʃo/ *m,* distance, space; interval (of time). **a trechos,** at intervals. **de t. en t.,** from time to time

trefe /'trefe/ *a* pliable, flexible; light; spurious (of coins)

tregua /'tregua/ *f,* truce, respite, rest. **dar treguas,** to afford relief, give a respite; give time

treinta /'treinta/ *a* and *m,* thirty; thirtieth. *m,* thirtieth (day of the month)

treintañal /treinta'ɲal/ *a* thirty years old

treintavo /trein'taβo/ *a* thirtieth

treintena /trein'tena/ *f,* thirtieth (part)

tremebundo /treme'βundo/ *a* fearsome, dread

tremedal /treme'ðal/ *m,* bog; quagmire

tremendo /tre'mendo/ *a* fearful, formidable; awesome; *Inf.* tremendous, enormous

trementina /tremen'tina/ *f,* turpentine

tremesino /treme'sino/ *a* three months old

tremolar /tremo'lar/ *vt* and *vi* to wave, fly (of banners); *Fig.* make a show of

tremolina /tremo'lina/ *f,* noise of the wind; *Inf.* hubbub, confusion

trémulo /'tremulo/ *a* trembling, tremulous

tren /tren/ *m,* supply, provision; outfit; equipment; pomp, show; railroad train; following, train. **t. ascendente,** up train (from coast to interior). *Inf.* **t. botijo,** excursion train. **t. con coches corridos,** corridor train. **t. correo,** mail train. **t. descendente,** down train (from interior to coast). **t. mixto,** train carrying passengers and freight. **t. ómnibus,** accommodation train, slow, stopping train. **t. rápido,** express

trencilla /tren'θiʎa; tren'siya/ *f,* braid, trimming

trencillar /trenθi'ʎar; trensi'yar/ *vt* to trim with braid, braid

treno /'treno/ *m,* threnody

Trento /'trento/ Trento

trenza /'trenθa; 'trensa/ *f*, plait, braid; plait of hair; bread twist. **en t.,** in plaits, plaited (of hair)

trenzadera /trenθa'ðera; trensa'ðera/ *f*, linen tape

trenzar /tren'θar; tren'sar/ *vt* to plait, braid; —*vi* curvet, prance

trepa /'trepa/ *f*, perforation, boring, piercing; climbing; creeping; *Inf.* half-somersault; grain, surface (of wood); craftiness, slyness; deception, fraud; beating, drubbing

trepador /trepa'ðor/ *a* climbing; crawling; *Bot.* creeping, climbing. *m*, climbing place

trepanación /trepana'θion; trepana'sion/ *f*, trepanning

trepanar /trepa'nar/ *vt* to trepan

trepante /tre'pante/ *a* creeping; *Bot.* twining, climbing

trepar /tre'par/ *vi* to climb, ascend; *Bot.* climb or creep; bore, perforate

trepatrepa /trepa'trepa/ *m*, jungle gym, monkey bars

trepidación /trepiða'θion; trepiða'sion/ *f*, trepidation, dread; vibration; jarring; shaking

trepidar /trepi'ðar/ *vi* to shiver, shudder; vibrate; shake; jar

trépido /'trepiðo/ *a* shuddering, shivering; vibrating

tres /tres/ *a* three; third. *m*, figure three; third (day of the month); three (of playing cards); trio. *Inf.* **como t. y dos son cinco,** as sure as two and two make four

trescientos /tres'θientos; tres'sientos/ *a* and *m*, three hundred; three-hundredth

tresillo /tre'siʎo; tre'siyo/ *m*, omber (card game); *Mus.* triplet

tresnal /tres'nal/ *m*, *Agr.* stook, cock, sheaf

treta /'treta/ *f*, scheme; trick, hoax; feint (in fencing)

trezavo /tre'θaβo; tre'saβo/ *a* thirteenth

tría /'tria/ *f*, selection, choice; worn place (in cloth)

triangulación /triaŋgula'θion; triaŋgula'sion/ *f*, triangulation

triángulo /tri'aŋgulo/ *a* triangular. *m*, (*Geom. Mus.*) triangle. **t. acutángulo,** acute triangle. **t. obtusángulo,** obtuse triangle. **t. rectángulo,** right-angled triangle

triar /triar/ *vt* to select, pick out; —*vi* fly in and out of the hive (of bees); —*vr* grow threadbare, become worn

tribu /'triβu/ *f*, tribe; species, family

tribulación /triβula'θion; triβula'sion/ *f*, tribulation, suffering

tribuna /tri'βuna/ *f*, tribune; platform, rostrum, pulpit; spectators' gallery; stand. **t. de la prensa,** press gallery. **t. del jurado,** jury box. **t. del órgano,** organ loft

tribunado /triβu'naðo/ *m*, tribunate

tribunal /triβu'nal/ *m*, law court; *Law.* bench; judgment seat; tribunal; board of examiners. **t. de menores,** children's court, juvenile court. *Naut.* **t. de presas,** prize court. **t. de primera instancia,** *Law.* petty sessions. **t. militar,** court-martial

tribuno /tri'βuno/ *m*, tribune; political speaker

tributar /triβu'tar/ *vt* to pay taxes; offer, render (thanks, homage, etc.)

tributario /triβu'tario/ (**-ia**) *a* tributary; tax-paying, contributive; —*n* taxpayer. *m*, tributary (of a river)

tributo /tri'βuto/ *m*, contribution; tax; tribute, homage; census

tricenal /triθe'nal; trise'nal/ *a* of thirty years' duration; occurring every thirty years

tricentésimo /triθen'tesimo; trisen'tesimo/ *a* three-hundredth

triciclo /tri'θiklo; tri'siklo/ *m*, tricycle

tricolor /triko'lor/ *a* three-colored

tricorne /tri'korne/ *a* *Poet.* three-cornered, three-horned

tricornio /tri'kornio/ *a* three-cornered. *m*, three-cornered hat

tricotomía /trikoto'mia/ *f*, trichotomy, division into three

tricromía /trikro'mia/ *f*, three-color process

tridente /tri'ðente/ *a* tridentate, three-pronged. *m*, trident

tridentino /triðen'tino/ *a* Tridentine

trienal /trie'nal/ *a* triennial

trienio /'trienio/ *m*, space of three years

trifásico /tri'fasiko/ *a* three-phase

trifolio /tri'folio/ *m*, trefoil

trigal /tri'gal/ *m*, wheat field

trigésimo /tri'hesimo/ *a* thirtieth

trigo /'trigo/ *m*, wheat plant; ear of wheat; wheat field (gen. *pl*); wealth, money. **t. sarraceno,** buckwheat. **t. tremés** *or* **t. trechel** *or* **t. tremesino** *or* **t. de marzo,** summer wheat

trigonometría /trigonome'tria/ *f*, trigonometry

trigueño /tri'geɲo/ *a* brunette, dark

triguero /tri'gero/ *a* wheat; wheat-growing. *m*, grain sieve; grain merchant

trilátero /tri'latero/ *a* three-sided, trilateral

trilingüe /tri'liŋgue/ *a* trilingual

trilla /'triʎa; 'triya/ *f*, red mullet; *Agr.* harrow; threshing; threshing season

trillado /tri'ʎaðo; tri'yaðo/ *a* frequented, trodden, worn (of paths); hackneyed

trilladora /triʎa'ðora; triya'ðora/ *f*, threshing machine

trillar /tri'ʎar; tri'yar/ *vt* to thresh; *Inf.* frequent; ill-treat

trillo /'triʎo; 'triyo/ *m*, threshing machine; harrow

trillón /tri'ʎon; tri'yon/ *m*, trillion

trilogía /trilo'hia/ *f*, trilogy

trimestral /trimes'tral/ *a* quarterly; terminal (in schools, etc.)

trimestre /tri'mestre/ *a* quarterly; terminal. *m*, quarter, three months; term (in schools, etc.); quarterly payment; quarterly rent

trinado /tri'naðo/ *m*, *Mus.* trill; twittering, shrilling (of birds)

trinar /tri'nar/ *vi Mus.* to trill; twitter, shrill; *Inf.* get in a temper, be furious

trincapiñones /trinkapi'ɲones/ *m*, *Inf.* scatterbrained youth

trincar /trin'kar/ *vt* to fasten securely; tie tightly; pinion; *Naut.* lash, make fast; cut up, chop; *Inf.* tipple; —*vi Naut.* sail close to the wind

trincha /'trintʃa/ *f*, vest strap

trinchante /trin'tʃante/ *m*, table carver; carving fork; stonecutter's hammer

trinchar /trin'tʃar/ *vt* to carve (at table); *Inf.* decide, dispose

trinchera /trin'tʃera/ *f*, *Mil.* trench; cutting (for roads, etc.); trench coat

trinchero /trin'tʃero/ *m*, platter, trencher; serving table, side table

trineo /tri'neo/ *m*, sled, sledge, sleigh

trinidad /trini'ðað/ *f*, trinity

trinitaria /trini'taria/ *f*, *Bot.* heartsease

trinitario /trini'tario/ (**-ia**) *a* and *n Eccl.* Trinitarian

trino /'trino/ *a* triune; ternary. *m*, *Mus.* trill

trinomio /tri'nomio/ *m*, trinomial

trinquete /trin'kete/ *m*, *Naut.* mainmast; mainsail; *Sports.* rackets; *Mech.* ratchet

trinquis /'trinkis/ *m*, *Inf.* draft, drink

trío /'trio/ *m*, trio

tripa /'tripa/ *f*, entrail, gut; *Inf.* belly; inside (of some fruits). **hacer de tripas corazón,** *Inf.* to take heart, buck up. **revolver las tripas (a),** *Fig. Inf.* to make one sick

tripartición /triparti'θion; triparti'sion/ *f*, tripartition

tripartir /tripar'tir/ *vt* to divide into three

tripartito /tripar'tito/ *a* tripartite

tripicallos /tripi'kaʎos; tripi'kayos/ *m pl*, *Cul.* tripe

triple /'triple/ *a* triple; three-ply (of yarn)

triplicación /triplika'θion; triplika'sion/ *f*, trebling

triplicar /tripli'kar/ *vt* to treble

trípode /'tripoðe/ *m*, (sometimes *f*) three-legged stool or table; tripod; trivet

Trípoli /'tripoli/ Tripoli

tríptico /'triptiko/ *m*, triptych

triptongo /'triptoŋgo/ *m*, triphthong

tripulación /tripula'θion; tripula'sion/ *f*, crew (ships and aircraft)

tripulante /tripu'lante/ *m*, crew member

tripular /tripu'lar/ *vt* to provide with a crew, man; equip, furnish; serve in, work as the crew of

trique /'trike/ *m*, crack, creak. *Inf.* **a cada t.**, at every moment

triquiñuela /triki'ɲuela/ *f*, *Inf.* evasion, subterfuge

triquitraque /triki'trake/ *m*, tap, rap; crack; firework

tris /tris/ *m*, crack, noise of glass, etc., cracking; *Inf.* instant, trice. **estar en un t. (de)**, to be on the verge (of), within an inch (of)

trisar /tri'sar/ *vt* to crack, break, splinter (of glass); —*vi* chirp, twitter (especially of swallows)

trisca /'triska/ *f*, cracking, crushing, crackling (of nuts, etc.); noise, tumult

triscar /tris'kar/ *vi* to make a noise with the feet; gambol, frolic; creak, crack; —*vt* blend, mingle; set the teeth of a saw

trisecar /trise'kar/ *vt* to trisect

trisección /trisek'θion; trisek'sion/ *f*, trisection

trisemanal /trisema'nal/ *a* three times weekly; every three weeks

trisílabo /tri'silaβo/ *a* trisyllabic

trismo /'trismo/ *m*, lockjaw, trismus

triste /'triste/ *a* unhappy, sorrowful; melancholy, gloomy; sad; piteous, unfortunate; useless, worthless

tristeza, tristura /tris'teθa, tris'tura; tris'tesa/ *f*, unhappiness; melancholy, gloom; sadness; piteousness

tritón /tri'ton/ *m*, merman

triturar /tritu'rar/ *vt* to crumble, crush; chew; masticate; ill-treat, bruise; refute, contradict

triunfada /triun'faða/ *f*, trumping (at cards)

triunfador /triunfa'ðor/ **(-ra)** *a* triumphant —*n* victor

triunfal /triun'fal/ *a* triumphal

triunfante /triun'fante/ *a* triumphant

triunfar /triun'far/ *vi* to triumph; be victorious, win; trump (at cards); spend ostentatiously

triunfo /'triunfo/ *m*, triumph; victory; trump card; success; booty, spoils of war; conquest

triunvirato /triumbi'rato/ *m*, triumvirate

trivial /tri'βial/ *a* well-known, hackneyed; frequented, trodden; commonplace, mediocre; trivial, unimportant

trivialidad /triβiali'ðað/ *f*, banality, triteness; mediocrity; triviality

trivio /'triβio/ *m*, road junction

triza /'triθa; 'trisa/ *f*, fragment, bit; *Naut.* rope. **hacer trizas**, to smash to bits

trizar /tri'θar; tri'sar/ *vt* to smash up, destroy

trocable /tro'kaβle/ *a* exchangeable

trocada, a la /tro'kaða, a la/ *adv* contrariwise; in exchange

trocador /troka'ðor/ **(-ra)** *n* exchanger

trocar /tro'kar/ *vt irr* to exchange; vomit; distort, misconstrue, mistake; —*vr* change, alter one's behavior; change places with another; be transferred. See **contar**

trocear /troθe'ar; trose'ar/ *vt* to divide into pieces

trocha /'trotʃa/ *f*, short cut; trail, path, track

trochemoche, a /trotʃe'motʃe, a/ *adv Inf.* without rhyme or reason, pell-mell

trofeo /tro'feo/ *m*, trophy; victory; military booty

troglodita /troglo'ðita/ *a* and *mf* troglodyte. *m*, *Fig.* savage, barbarian. *mf* glutton

troglodítico /troglo'ðitiko/ *a* troglodytic

troj /troh/ *f*, granary

trojero /tro'hero/ *m*, granary keeper

trola /'trola/ *f*, *Inf.* lie, nonsense, hoax

trole /'trole/ *m*, trolley

trolebús /trole'βus/ *m*, trolley car

trolero /tro'lero/ *a Inf.* deceiving, lying

tromba /'tromba/ *f*, waterspout

trombón /trom'bon/ *m*, trombone; trombone player. **¡Trombones y platillos!** Great Scot!

trombosis /trom'bosis/ *f*, thrombosis

trompa /'trompa/ *f*, elephant's trunk; *Mus.* horn; proboscis (of insects); waterspout; humming top. **t. de Falopio**, fallopian tube

trompada /trom'paða/ *f*, *Inf.* bang, bump; blow, buffet, slap; collision

trompazo /trom'paθo; trom'paso/ *m*, heavy blow, knock, bang

trompear /trompe'ar/ *vi* to play with a top; —*vt* knock about

trompero /trom'pero/ *m*, top maker —*a* deceiving, swindling

trompeta /trom'peta/ *f*, trumpet; bugle. *m*, trumpeter; bugler; *Inf.* ninny. **t. de amor**, sunflower

trompetada /trompe'taða/ *f*, *Inf.* stupid remark, piece of nonsense

trompetazo /trompe'taθo; trompe'taso/ *m*, bray of a trumpet; bugle blast; *Inf.* stupid remark

trompetear /trompete'ar/ *vi Inf.* to play the trumpet or bugle

trompeteo /trompe'teo/ *m*, trumpeting, trumpet call; sound of the bugle

trompetería /trompete'ria/ *f*, collection of trumpets; metal organ pipes

trompetero /trompe'tero/ *m*, trumpet or bugle maker or player

trompetilla /trompe'tiʎa; trompe'tiya/ *f*, *dim* little trumpet; ear trumpet

trompicar /trompi'kar/ *vt* to make stumble, trip —*vi* stumble, trip up

trompicón /trompi'kon/ *m*, stumble

trompo /'trompo/ *m*, humming or spinning top; *Inf.* dolt, idiot

tronada /tro'naða/ *f*, thunderstorm

tronado /tro'naðo/ *a* worn-out; threadbare, old; poor, poverty-stricken; down at the heels

tronar /tro'nar/ *v impers irr* to thunder; —*vi* growl, roar (of guns); *Inf.* go bankrupt, be ruined; *Inf.* protest against, attack; (*with con*) quarrel with —*Pres. Indic.* **trueno, truenas, truena, truenan.** *Pres. Subjunc.* **truene, truenes, truene, truenen**

troncal /tron'kal/ *a* trunk; main, principal

tronchar /tron'tʃar/ *vt* to break off, lop off (branches)

troncho /'trontʃo/ *m*, *Bot.* stem, stalk, branch

tronco /'tronko/ *m*, *Anat. Bot.* trunk; main body or line (of communications); trunk line; common origin, stock; *Inf.* blockhead, dolt; callous person. *Fig.* **estar hecho un t.**, to lie like a log; sleep like a log

tronera /tro'nera/ *f*, *Naut.* porthole; embrasure; slit window; pocket of a billiards table. *mf Inf.* madcap, harumscarum

tronido /tro'niðo/ *m*, roll of thunder

trono /'trono/ *m*, throne; *Eccl.* tabernacle; shrine; kingly might; *pl* thrones, hierarchy of angels

tronzador /tronθa'ðor; tronsa'ðor/ *m*, two-handled saw

tronzar /tron'θar; tron'sar/ *vt* to smash, break into bits; *Sew.* pleat; exhaust, overtire

tropa /'tropa/ *f*, crowd (of people); troops, military; *Mil.* call to arms; *pl* army. **t. de línea**, regiment of the line. **tropas de asalto**, storm troopers. **tropas de refresco**, fresh troops. **en t.**, in a crowd; in groups

tropel /tro'pel/ *m*, rush, surge (of crowds, etc.); bustle, confusion; crowd, multitude; heap, jumble (of things). **en t.**, in a rush; in a crowd

tropelía /trope'lia/ *f*, rush, dash; violence; outrage

tropezar /trope'θar; trope'sar/ *vi irr* to stumble, slip; (*with con*) meet unexpectedly or accidentally come up against, be faced with (difficulties); quarrel with or oppose; fall into (bad habits). See **empezar**

tropezón /trope'θon; trope'son/ *m*, stumbling, slipping; stumbling block, obstacle. **a tropezones**, *Inf.* stumblingly; by fits and starts

tropical /tropi'kal/ *a* tropical

trópicos /'tropikos/ *m pl*, tropics

tropiezo /tro'pieθo; tro'pieso/ *m*, stumble; stumbling block, obstacle; hitch; impediment; slip, peccadillo, fault; difficulty, embarrassment; fight, skirmish; quarrel

tropismo /tro'pismo/ *m*, tropism

tropo /'tropo/ *m*, trope, figure of speech

troquel /tro'kel/ *m*, die, mold

trotaconventos /trotakom'bentos/ *f*, *Inf.* go-between, procuress

trotamundos /trota'mundos/ *m*, *Inf.* globetrotter

trotar /tro'tar/ *vi* to trot; *Inf.* hurry, get a move on

trote /'trote/ *m*, trot; toil, drudgery. **t. corto**, jog-trot. **al t.**, with all speed

trotón /tro'ton/ **(-ona)** *a* trotting. *m*, horse. *f*, chaperone

trova /'troβa/ *f*, verse; song, lay, ballad; love song

trovador /troβa'ðor/ **(-ra)** *m*, troubadour, minstrel —*n* poet

trovadoresco /troβaðo'resko/ *a* pertaining to minstrels, troubadour

trovar /tro'βar/ *vi* to compose verses; write ballads; misconstrue, misinterpret

Troya /'troia/ Troy

troyano /tro'iano/ **(-na)** *a* and *n* Trojan

trozo /'troθo; 'troso/ *m*, part, fragment; piece, portion; *Lit.* selection. **t. de abordaje,** *Nav.* landing party

trucha /'trutʃa/ *f*, trout. **t. asalmonada,** salmon trout

truchuela /tru'tʃuela/ *f*, small trout; salt cod

truco /'truko/ *m*, trick, deception

truculencia /truku'lenθia; truku'lensia/ *f*, harshness, cruelty, truculence

truculento /truku'lento/ *a* fierce, harsh, truculent

trueco /'trueko/ *m*, exchange. **a t. de,** in exchange for; on condition that

trueno /'trueno/ *m*, thunder; report, noise (of firearms); *Inf.* rake, scapegrace

trueque /'trueke/ *m*, exchange. **a.** (*or* **en**) **t.,** in exchange

trufa /'trufa/ *f*, *Bot.* truffle; nonsense, idle talk

trufar /tru'far/ *vt Cul.* to stuff with truffles; —*vi Inf.* lie, tell fibs

truhán /tru'an/ **(-ana)** *a* knavish, roguish, comic —*n* knave, rogue; clown, buffoon

truhanear /truane'ar/ *vi* to be a trickster, behave like a knave; play the clown

truhanería /truane'ria/ *f*, knavery, act of a rogue; clowning, buffoonery; collection of rogues

truhanesco /trua'nesko/ *a* knavish, scoundrelly; clownish

trujal /tru'hal/ *m*, oil or grape press; oil mill; vat for soap making

trujar /tru'har/ *vt* to partition off

trulla /'truʎa; 'truya/ *f*, uproar, tumult; crowd, throng

truncar /trun'kar/ *vt* to shorten, truncate; decapitate, mutilate; omit, cut out (words, etc.); curtail, abridge; mutilate, deform (texts, etc.)

truque /'truke/ *m*, card game; kind of hopscotch

trust /trust/ *m*, *Com.* trust

tú /tu/ *pers pron 2nd sing mf* thou, you. **tratar de t. (a),** to address familiarly; be on intimate terms with

tu /tu/ *poss pron mf* thy, your. Used only before nouns

tuberculina /tuβerku'lina/ *f*, tuberculin

tubérculo /tu'βerkulo/ *m*, (*Zool. Med.*) tubercle; *Bot.* tubercle, tuber

tuberculoso /tuβerku'loso/ *a* tubercular, tuberculous

tubería /tuβe'ria/ *f*, piping, tubing; pipe system; pipe factory

tuberosa /tuβe'rosa/ *f*, tuberose

tuberoso /tuβe'roso/ *a* tuberous

tubo /'tuβo/ *m*, pipe, tube; lamp chimney; flue; *Anat.* duct, canal. **t. acústico,** speaking tube. **t. de ensayo,** test tube. **t. de escape,** exhaust pipe. **t. lanzatorpedos,** torpedo tube. **t. termiónico,** *Radio.* thermionic valve

tubular /tuβu'lar/ *a* tubular

tucán /tu'kan/ *m*, toucan

tudesco /tu'ðesko/ *a* German

tueco /'tueko/ *m*, stump (of a tree); wormhole (in wood)

tuerca /'tuerka/ *f*, nut (of a screw)

tuerto /'tuerto/ *a* one-eyed. *m*, *Law.* tort; *pl* afterpains. **a t.,** unjustly

tueste /'tueste/ *m*, toasting

tuétano /'tuetano/ *m*, marrow. *Inf.* **hasta los tuétanos,** to the depths of one's being

tufillas /tu'fiʎas; tu'fiyas/ *mf Inf.* easily irritated person

tufo /'tufo/ *m*, strong smell, poisonous vapor; *Inf.* stink; side, airs, conceit (often *pl*); lock of hair over the ears

tugurio /tu'gurio/ *m*, shepherd's hut; miserable little room; *Inf.* haunt, low dive

tul /tul/ *m*, tulle

tulipa /tu'lipa/ *f*, small tulip; lampshade

tulipán /tuli'pan/ *m*, tulip

tullido /tu'ʎiðo; tu'yiðo/ *a* partially paralyzed; maimed, crippled

tullir /tu'ʎir; tu'yir/ *vt irr* to maim, cripple; paralyze; —*vr* become paralyzed; be crippled. See **mullir**

tumba /'tumba/ *f*, tomb; tumble, overbalancing; somersault; Catherine wheel

tumbar /tum'bar/ *vt* to knock down; kill, drop; *Inf.* overpower, overcome (of odors, wine) —*vi* fall down; *Naut.* run aground; —*vr Inf.* lie down, stretch oneself out

tumbo /'tumbo/ *m*, tumble, overbalancing; undulation (of ground); rise and fall of sea waves; imminent danger; book containing deeds and privileges of monasteries and churches

tumbón /tum'bon/ *a Inf.* crafty, sly; idle, lazy. *m*, trunk with an arched lid

tumefacción /tumefak'θion; tumefak'sion/ *f*, swelling

tumefacto, túmido /tume'fakto, 'tumiðo/ *a* swollen

tumor /tu'mor/ *m*, tumor

túmulo /'tumulo/ *m*, tumulus; catafalque; mound of earth

tumulto /tu'multo/ *m*, riot, uprising; tumult, commotion, disturbance

tumultuario, tumultuoso /tumul'tuario, tumul'tuoso/ *a* noisy, tumultuous, confused

tuna /'tuna/ *f*, prickly pear tree or fruit; vagrant life; strolling student musicians (playing to raise money for charity)

tunante /tu'nante/ *a* rascally, roguish. *mf* rascal, scoundrel

tunantuelo /tunan'tuelo/ **(-la)** *n Inf.* imp, little rascal

tunda /'tunda/ *f*, shearing of cloth; *Inf.* sound beating, hiding

tundear /tunde'ar/ *vt* to beat, drub, buffet

tundidora /tundi'ðora/ *f*, woman who shears cloth; cloth-shearing machine; lawn mower

tundir /tun'dir/ *vt* to shear (cloth); mow (grass); *Inf.* beat, wallop

tunecino /tune'θino; tune'sino/ **(-na)** *a* and *n* Tunisian

túnel /'tunel/ *m*, tunnel

Túnez /'tuneθ; 'tunes/ Tunis, Tunisia

tungsteno /tuŋgs'teno/ *m*, tungsten

túnica /'tunika/ *f*, tunic, chiton; tunicle; robe

Tunicia /tu'niθia; tu'nisia/ Tunisia

tuno /'tuno/ **(-na)** *a* knavish, rascally —*n* rascal, scoundrel

tupé /tu'pe/ *m*, forelock (of a horse); toupee; *Inf.* cheek, nerve

tupido /tu'piðo/ *a* thick, dense; obtuse, dull, stupid

tupir /tu'pir/ *vt* to thicken, make dense; press tightly; —*vr* stuff oneself with food or drink

turba /'turβa/ *f*, crowd, multitude; peat

turbación /turβa'θion; turβa'sion/ *f*, disturbance; upset; perturbation; bewilderment, confusion; embarrassment

turbador /turβa'ðor/ **(-ra)** *a* disturbing, upsetting —*n* disturber, upsetter

turbamulta /turβa'multa/ *f*, *Inf.* mob, rabble

turbante /tur'βante/ *a* upsetting, perturbing. *m*, turban

turbar /tur'βar/ *vt* to disturb, upset; make turbid, muddy; bewilder, confuse; embarrass

turbera /tur'βera/ *f*, peat bog

turbiedad /turβie'ðað/ *f*, muddiness (of liquids); obscurity

turbina /tur'βina/ *f*, turbine

turbio /'turβio/ *a* turbid, muddy; troublous; turbulent, disturbed; obscure, confused (style); indistinct, blurred, *m pl*, lees, sediment (of oil)

turbión /tur'βion/ *m*, brief storm, squall; *Fig.* shower, rush

turbulencia /turβu'lenθia; turβu'lensia/ *f*, turbidity, muddiness; turbulence, commotion; disturbance, confusion

turbulento /turβu'lento/ *a* muddy, turbid; turbulent; disturbed; confused

turca /'turka/ *f*, *Inf.* drinking bout

turco /'turko/ **(-ca)** *a* Turkish —*n* Turk. *m*, Turkish (language)

turgencia /tur'henθia; tur'hensia/ f, swelling, turgidity

turgente /tur'hente/ a Med. turgescent; Poet. turgid, prominent, swollen

Turingia /tu'rinhia/ Thuringia

turismo /tu'rismo/ m, touring, tourist industry. **coche de t.,** touring car

turista /tu'rista/ mf tourist

turno /'turno/ m, turn. **por t.,** in turn

turquesa /tur'kesa/ f, turquoise

turquesco /tur'kesko/ a Turkish

Turquía /tur'kia/ Turkey

turrón /tu'rron/ m, kind of nougat; almond paste; Inf. soft job, sinecure; civil service job

turulato /turu'lato/ a Inf. dumbfounded, speechless, inarticulate

¡tus! /tus/ interj word for calling dogs. **sin decir t. ni mus,** Inf. without saying anything

tutear /tute'ar/ vt to address as tú (instead of the formal usted); treat familiarly

tutela /tu'tela/ f, guardianship; tutelage; protection, defense

tuteo /tu'teo/ m, the use in speaking to a person of the familiar tú instead of the formal usted

tutor /tu'tor/ (**-ra**) n guardian. m, stake (for plants); protector, defender

tutoría /tuto'ria/ f. See **tutela**

tuyo, tuya, tuyos, tuyas /'tuyo, 'tuya, 'tuyos, 'tuyas/ poss pron 2nd sing and pl mf thine, yours. Used sometimes with def. art. (e.g. Este sombrero es el tuyo, This hat is yours)

U

u /u/ *f,* letter U —*conjunc* Used instead of **o** or before words beginning with **o** or **ho** (e.g. *fragante u oloroso*)

ubérrimo /u'βerrimo/ *a superl* most fruitful; very abundant

ubicación /uβika'θion; uβika'sion/ *f,* situation, position, location

ubicar /uβi'kar/ *vt* to place, situate; —*vi* and *vr* be situated

ubicuidad /uβikui'ðaθ/ *f,* ubiquity

ubicuo /u'βikuo/ *a* omnipresent; ubiquitous

ubre /'uβre/ *f,* udder

ucelele /uθe'lele; use'lele/ *m,* ukulele

Ucrania /u'krania/ Ukraine

ucranio /u'kranio/ **(-ia)** *a* and *n* Ukrainian

¡uf! /uf/ *interj* ugh!

ufanarse /ufa'narse/ *vr* to pride oneself, put on airs

ufanía /ufa'nia/ *f,* pride, conceit

ufano /u'fano/ *a* conceited, vain; satisfied, pleased; expeditious, masterly

ujier /u'hier/ *m,* usher

úlcera /'ulθera; 'ulsera/ *f,* ulcer

ulceración /ulθera'θion; ulsera'sion/ *f,* ulceration

ulcerar /ulθe'rar; ulse'rar/ *vt* and *vr* to ulcerate

ulceroso /ulθe'roso; ulse'roso/ *a* ulcerous

ulterior /ulte'rior/ *a* farther, ulterior; subsequent

ulteriormente /ulterior'mente/ *adv* subsequently, later

ultimación /ultima'θion; ultima'sion/ *f,* ending, finishing

ultimar /ulti'mar/ *vt* to end, conclude

ultimátum /ulti'matum/ *m,* ultimatum

último /'ultimo/ *a* last; farthermost; ultimate; top; final, definitive; most valuable, best; latter; recent. **«Última Hora.»** "Stop Press." **a última hora,** *Fig.* at the eleventh hour. **en estos últimos años,** in recent years. **a últimos de mes,** towards the end of the month. **el ú. piso,** the top floor. **por ú.,** finally. *Inf.* **estar en las últimas,** to be at the end, be finishing

ultra /'ultra/, *adv* besides; (with words like *mar*) beyond; (as prefix) excessively

ultrajar /ultra'har/ *vt* to insult; scorn, despise

ultraje /ul'trahe/ *m,* insult, outrage

ultrajoso /ultra'hoso/ *a* offensive, insulting, abusive

ultramar /ultra'mar/ *m,* overseas, abroad

ultramarino /ultrama'rino/ *a* oversea; ultramarine. *m,* foreign produce (gen. *pl*)

ultramontano /ultramon'tano/ *a* ultramontane

ultrarrojo /ultra'rroho/ *a* infrared

ultratumba /ultra'tumba/ *adv* beyond the grave

ultravioleta /ultraβio'leta/ *a* ultraviolet

úlula /'ulula/ *f,* screech owl

ululación /ulula'θion; ulula'sion/ *f,* screech, howl; hoot of an owl

ulular /ulu'lar/ *vi* to howl, shriek, screech; hoot (of an owl)

ululato /ulu'lato/ *m,* ululation

umbilical /umbili'kal/ *a* umbilical

umbral /um'bral/ *m,* threshold; *Fig.* starting point; *Archit.* lintel. **atravesar** (*or* **pisar**) **los umbrales,** to cross the threshold

umbría /um'bria/ *f,* shady place

umbrío /um'brio/ *a* shady, dark

umbroso /um'broso/ *a* shady

un /un/ *Abbr.* of **uno,** *a,* one. Used before *m, sing f,* **una,** *indef art* a, an; a; one

unánime /u'nanime/ *a* unanimous

unanimidad /unanimi'ðaθ/ *f,* unanimity. **por u.,** unanimously

unción /un'θion; un'sion/ *f,* anointing; *Eccl.* Extreme Unction; unction, fervor

uncir /un'θir; un'sir/ *vt* to yoke

undécimo /un'deθimo; un'desimo/ *a* eleventh

undísono /un'disono/ *a Poet.* sounding, sonorous (waves, etc.)

undoso /un'doso/ *a* wavy, rippling

undulación /undula'θion; undula'sion/ *f,* undulation; *Phys.* wave

undular /undu'lar/ *vi* to undulate; wriggle; float, wave (flags, etc.)

undulatorio /undula'torio/ *a* undulatory

ungimiento /unhi'miento/ *m,* anointment

ungir /un'hir/ *vt* to anoint

ungüento /un'guento/ *m,* ointment; lotion; *Fig.* balm, unguent

unicelular /uniθelu'lar; uniselu'lar/ *a* unicellular

único /'uniko/ *a* unique; sole, solitary, only. **Lo ú. que se puede hacer es...,** The only thing one can do is...

unicolor /uniko'lor/ *a* of one color

unicornio /uni'kornio/ *m,* unicorn

unidad /uni'ðaθ/ *f,* unity; unit; (*Math. Mil.*) unit. **u. de bagaje,** piece of baggage. (of drama) **u. de lugar,** unity of place. **u. de tiempo,** unity of time

unidamente /uniða'mente/ *adv* jointly; harmoniously

unificación /unifika'θion; unifika'sion/ *f,* unification

unificar /unifi'kar/ **(se)** *vt* and *vr* to unify, unite

uniformación /uniforma'θion; uniforma'sion/ *f,* standardization

uniformar /unifor'mar/ *vt* to make uniform, standardize; put into uniform; —*vr* become uniform

uniforme /uni'forme/ *a* uniform; same, similar. *m,* uniform

uniformidad /uniformi'ðaθ/ *f,* uniformity

unigénito /uni'henito/ *a* only-begotten. *m,* Christ

unilateral /unilate'ral/ *a* one-sided, unilateral

unión /u'nion/ *f,* union; correspondence, conformity; agreement; marriage; alliance, federation; composition, mixture; combination; proximity, nearness; (mystic) union

unionista /unio'nista/ *mf Polit.* unionist

Unión Soviética /u'nion so'βietika/ Soviet Union

unir /u'nir/ *vt* to unite, join; mix, combine; bind, fasten; connect, couple; bring together; marry; *Fig.* harmonize, conciliate; —*vr* join together, unite; be combined; marry; (*with prep* a *or* con) be near to; associate with

unísono /u'nisono/ *a* unisonant. **al u.,** in unison; unanimously

unitario /uni'tario/ **(-ia)** *a* and *n* Unitarian

universal /uniβer'sal/ *a* universal; well-informed; widespread

universalidad /uniβersali'ðaθ/ *f,* universality

universalizar /uniβersali'θar; uniβersali'sar/ *vt* to make universal, generalize

universidad /uniβersi'ðaθ/ *f,* university; universality; universe

universitario /uniβersi'tario/ *a* university

universo /uni'βerso/ *a* universal. *m,* universe

uno /'uno/ (*f,* **una**) *a* a, an; single, only; same; *pl* some; about, nearly. *m,* one (number). **Tiene unos doce años,** He is about twelve. **unas pocas manzanas,** a few apples —*pron* someone; one thing, same thing; *pl* some people. **No sabe uno qué creer,** One doesn't know what to believe. **Unos dicen que no, otros que sí,** Some (people) say no, others yes. **Juan no tiene libros y le voy a dar uno,** John has no books and I am going to give him one. **Todo es uno,** It's all the same. **u. a u.,** one by one. **u. que otro,** a few. **u. y otro,** both. **unos cuantos,** a few, some. **Es la una,** It is one o'clock

untar /un'tar/ *vt* to anoint; grease, oil; *Inf.* bribe; —*vr* smear oneself with grease or similar thing; *Fig. Inf.* line one's pockets. **u. el carro,** *Fig.* to grease the wheels

unto /'unto/ *m,* grease; animal fat; *Fig.* balm

untuoso /un'tuoso/ *a* fat, greasy

uña /'uɲa/ *f,* nail (of fingers or toes); hoof, trotter, claw; stinging tail of scorpion; thorn; stump of tree branch; *Naut.* fluke; *Fig. Inf.* light fingers (gen. *pl*). **afilarse las uñas,** to sharpen one's claws, prepare for trouble. **comerse las uñas,** to bite one's nails. **caer en las uñas de,** to fall into the clutches of. **hincar la u.** (**en**), to stick the claws into; to defraud, overcharge. **ser u. y carne,** to be devoted friends

uñarada /uɲa'raða/ *f,* scratch with nails

uñero /u'ɲero/ *m,* ingrowing nail, ingrown nail

¡upa! /'upa/ *interj* Up you get! Up you go! Upsy daisy! (*gen.* to children)

Urales, los /u'rales, los/ the Urals

uranio /u'ranio/ *m,* uranium

urbanidad /urβani'ðað/ *f,* civility, good manners, urbanity

urbanismo /urβa'nismo/ *m,* town planning; housing scheme

urbanización /urβaniθa'θion; urβanisa'sion/ *f,* urbanization

urbanizar /urβani'θar; urβani'sar/ *vt* to civilize, polish; urbanize

urbano /ur'βano/ *a* urban, city; urbane

urbe /'urβe/ *f,* city, metropolis

urbícola /ur'βikola/ *mf* city dweller

urdemalas /urðe'malas/ *m,* schemer, intriguer

urdidera /urði'ðera/ *f,* warping-frame

urdimbre /ur'ðimbre/ *f,* warp; scheming, plotting

urdir /ur'ðir/ *vt* to warp; weave; scheme, intrigue

uréter /u'reter/ *m,* ureter

uretra /u'retra/ *f,* urethra

urgencia /ur'henθia; ur'hensia/ *f,* urgency; necessity; compulsion

urgente /ur'hente/ *a* urgent

urgir /ur'hir/ *vi* to be urgent; be valid, be in force (laws)

úrico /'uriko/ *a* uric

urinario /uri'nario/ *a* urinary. *m,* urinal

urna /'urna/ *f,* urn; ballot box; glass case

urraca /u'rraka/ *f,* magpie

uruguayo /uru'guayo/ (**-ya**) *a* and *n* Uruguayan

usado /u'saðo/ *a* worn out; accustomed, efficient. *Com.* **al u.,** in the usual form. **ropa usada,** second-hand clothing, worn clothing

usanza /u'sanθa; usansa/ *f,* custom, usage

usar /u'sar/ *vt* to use; wear, make use of; follow (trade, occupation); —*vi* be accustomed

uso /'uso/ *m,* use; custom; fashion; habit; wear and tear. **al u.,** according to custom. **al u. de,** in the manner of

usted /us'teð/ *mf* you *pl* **ustedes.** Often abbreviated to **Vd, V, Vds, VV** or **Ud, Uds**

usual /u'sual/ *a* usual; general, customary; sociable

usufructo /usu'frukto/ *m, Law.* usufruct; life-interest; profit

usura /u'sura/ *f,* usury; profiteering. **pagar con u.,** to pay back a thousandfold

usurario /usu'rario/ *a* usurious

usurear /usure'ar/ *vi* to lend or borrow with usury; profiteer, make excess profits

usurero /usu'rero/ (**-ra**) *n* usurer; profiteer

usurpación /usurpa'θion; usurpa'sion/ *f,* usurpation

usurpador /usurpa'ðor/ (**-ra**) *a* usurping —*n* usurper

usurpar /usur'par/ *vt* to usurp

utensilio /uten'silio/ *m,* utensil; tool, implement (*gen. pl*)

uterino /ute'rino/ *a* uterine

útero /'utero/ *m,* uterus

útil /'util/ *a* useful; profitable; *Law.* lawful (of days, etc.). *m,* usefulness, profit; *pl* **útiles,** utensils, tools

utilidad /utili'ðað/ *f,* utility; usefulness; profit

utilitario /utili'tario/ *a* utilitarian

utilitarismo /utilita'rismo/ *m,* utilitarianism

utilizable /utili'θaβle; utilisaβle/ *a* utilizable

utilización /utiliθa'θion; utilisa'sion/ *f,* utilization

utilizar /utili'θar; utili'sar/ *vt* to utilize

utillaje /uti'ʎahe; uti'yahe/ *m,* machinery

utópico /u'topiko/ *a* Utopian

uva /'uβa/ *f,* grape. **u. espina,** kind of gooseberry. **u. moscatel,** muscatel grape. *Inf.* **hecho una u.,** deaddrunk

uvero /u'βero/ (**-ra**) *a* pertaining or relating to grapes, grape —*n* grape seller

uxoricidio /uksori'θiðio; uksori'siðio/ *m,* uxoricide (act)

uxorio /uk'sorio/ *a* uxorious

V

v /be/ *f,* letter V. **v doble** *or* **doble v,** letter W. **V** *or* **Vd, VV,** *Abbr.* **vuestra (s) merced (es),** *mf sing* and *pl* you

vaca /'baka/ *f,* cow. **v. de San Antón,** *Ent.* ladybug

vacación /baka'θion; baka'sion/ *f,* vacation, holiday (gen. *pl*); vacancy; act of vacating (employment). **vacaciones retribuídas,** paid vacation

vacada /ba'kaða/ *f,* herd of cows

vacancia /ba'kanθia; ba'kansia/ *f,* vacancy

vacante /ba'kante/ *a* vacant. *f,* vacancy

vacar /ba'kar/ *vi* to be vacant; take a holiday; retire temporarily; (*with prep a*) dedicate oneself to, engage in

vaciadero /baθia'ðero; basia'ðero/ *m,* rubbish dump; sewer, drain

vaciado /ba'θiaðo; ba'siaðo/ *m,* plaster cast; *Archit.* excavation

vaciamiento /baθia'miento; basia'miento/ *m,* emptying; molding, casting; depletion

vaciar /ba'θiar; ba'siar/ *vt* to empty; drain, drink; mold, cast; *Archit.* excavate; hone; copy; —*vi* flow (into) (rivers); —*vr Inf.* blurt out

vaciedad /baθie'ðað; basie'ðað/ *f,* emptiness; foolishness, inanity

vacilación /baθila'θion; basila'sion/ *f,* swaying; tottering; staggering; hesitation, perplexity

vacilante /baθi'lante; basi'lante/ *a* swaying; tottering; staggering; hesitating, vacillating

vacilar /baθi'lar; basi'lar/ *vi* to sway; totter; stagger; flicker; hesitate

vacío /ba'θio; ba'sio/ *a* empty, void; fruitless, vain; unoccupied, vacant, deserted; imperfect; hollow, empty; conceited, immature. *m,* hollow; *Anat.* flank; vacancy; shortage; *Phys.* vacuum. **v. de aire,** airpocket. **de v.,** unloaded (carts, etc.). **en v.,** in vacuo. *Inf.* **hacer el v.** (**a),** to send to Coventry

vacuidad /bakui'ðað/ *f,* emptiness; vacuity

vacuna /ba'kuna/ *f,* cowpox; vaccine. **v. antivariolosa,** smallpox vaccine

vacunación /bakuna'θion; bakuna'sion/ *f,* vaccination

vacunar /baku'nar/ *vt* to vaccinate; inoculate

vacuno /ba'kuno/ *a* bovine

vacuo /'bakuo/ *a* empty; vacant. *m,* void; vacuum

vadeable /baðe'aβle/ *a* fordable (rivers, etc.); *Fig.* surmountable

vadear /baðe'ar/ *vt* to ford, wade; *Fig.* overcome (obstacles); *Fig.* sound, find out the opinion (of); —*vr* behave

vademécum /baðe'mekum/ *m,* vade mecum; school satchel

vado /'baðo/ *m,* ford; expedient, help

vagabundear /bagaβunde'ar/ *vi* to wander, roam, loiter

vagabundeo /bagaβun'deo/ *m,* vagabondage

vagabundo /baga'βundo/ **(-da)** *a* roving, wandering; vagrant —*n* tramp, vagabond

vagamundear /bagamunde'ar/ *vi.* See **vagabundear**

vagancia /ba'ganθia; ba'gansia/ *f,* vagrancy

vagar /ba'gar/ *m,* leisure; interval, pause —*vi* be idle or at leisure; wander, roam

vagido /ba'hiðo/ *m,* cry, wail (infants)

vagneriano /bagne'riano/ *a* Wagnerian

vago /'bago/ **(-ga)** *a* vagrant, idle; vague; *Art.* indefinite, blurred —*n* idler. *m,* tramp; loafer. **en v.,** unsuccessfully, vainly

vagón /ba'gon/ *m,* wagon; (railway) coach. **v. comedor,** dining car

vagoneta /bago'neta/ *f,* open truck (railways, mines, etc.)

vaguear /bage'ar/ *vi* to roam, wander; loaf

vaguedad /bage'ðað/ *f,* vagueness; vague remark

vaharada /baa'raða/ *f,* whiff, exhalation

vahído /ba'iðo/ *m,* vertigo

vaho /'bao/ *m,* vapor, fume

vaina /'baina/ *f,* scabbard; *Bot.* sheath, pod; case (scissors, etc.)

vainilla /bai'niʎa; bai'niya/ *f,* *Bot.* vanilla; *Sew.* drawn-thread work

vaivén /bai'βen/ *m,* swing, sway, seesaw; instability, fluctuation

vajilla /ba'hiʎa; ba'hiya/ *f,* china; dinner service

val /bal/ *m,* *Abbr.* **valle**

Valdepeñas /balde'peɲas/ *m,* red wine from Valdepeñas

vale /'bale/ *m,* *Com.* bond, I.O.U., promissory note; voucher; valediction

valedero /bale'ðero/ *a* valid, binding

valedor /bale'ðor/ **(-ra)** *n* protector, sponsor

valencia /ba'lenθia; ba'lensia/ *f,* valency

valenciano /balen'θiano; balen'siano/ **(-na)** *a* and *n* Valencian

valentía /balen'tia/ *f,* bravery; heroic deed; boast; (*Art. Lit.*) dash, imagination, fire; superhuman effort

valentón /balen'ton/ *a* boastful, blustering

valer /ba'ler/ *vt* irr to protect; defend; produce (income, etc.); cost; —*vi* be worth; deserve; have power or authority; be of importance or worth; be a protection; be current (money); be valid; —*vr* (*with de*) make use of. *m,* value, worth. **v. la pena,** to be worthwhile. **v. tanto como cualquiera,** to be as good as the next guy, be as good as the next fellow. **¡Válgame Dios!** Bless me! **Más vale así,** It's better thus. **Vale más ser cola de león que cabeza de ratón.** Better a big frog in a small puddle than a small frog in a big puddle —*Pres. Indic.* **valgo, vales,** etc —*Fut.* **valdré,** etc —*Condit.* **valdría,** etc —*Pres. Subjunc.* **valga,** etc.

valeriana /bale'riana/ *f,* valerian

valeroso /bale'roso/ *a* active, energetic; courageous; powerful

valetudinario /baletuði'nario/ *a* valetudinarian

valía /ba'lia/ *f,* value, price; influence, worth; faction, party. **a las valías,** at the highest price

validación /baliða'θion; baliða'sion/ *f,* validation; force, soundness

validar /bali'ðar/ *vt* to make strong; validate

validez /bali'ðeθ; bali'ðes/ *f,* validity

valido /ba'liðo/ *a* favorite, esteemed. *m,* court favorite; prime minister

válido /'baliðo/ *a* firm, sound, valid; strong, robust

valiente /ba'liente/ *a* strong, robust; courageous; active; excellent; excessive, enormous (gen. *iron*); boastful

valija /ba'liha/ *f,* valise, suitcase, grip; mail bag; mail

valimiento /bali'miento/ *m,* value; favor; protection, influence

valioso /ba'lioso/ *a* valuable; powerful; wealthy

valisoletano /balisole'tano/ **(-na)** *a* and *n* of or from Valladolid

valla /'baʎa; 'baya/ *f,* barricade, paling; stockade; *Fig.* obstacle. **v. publicitaria,** billboard

vallado /ba'ʎaðo; ba'yaðo/ *m,* stockade; enclosure

valle /'baʎe; 'baye/ *m,* valley; vale; river-basin

valón /ba'lon/ *a* Walloon

valona /ba'lona/ *f,* Vandyke collar

valor /ba'lor/ *m,* worth, value; price; courage; validity; power; yield, income; insolence; *pl* *Com.* securities

valoración /balora'θion; balora'sion/ *f,* valuation; appraisement

valorar /balo'rar/ *vt* to value; appraise

valorización /baloriθa'θion; balorisa'sion/ *f,* valuation

valquiria /bal'kiria/ *f,* Valkyrie

vals /bals/ *m,* waltz

valsar /bal'sar/ *vi* to waltz

valuación /balua'θion; balua'sion/ *f.* See **valoración**

valuar /balu'ar/ *vt* to value; appraise; assess

valva /'balβa/ *f,* *Zool.* valve

válvula /'balβula/ *f,* *Mech.* valve. *Auto.* **v. de cámara**

(**del neumático**), tire-valve. **v. de seguridad,** safety-valve

vampiro /bam'piro/ *m*, vampire; *Fig.* bloodsucker

vanagloria /bana'gloria/ *f*, vaingloriousness, conceit

vanagloriarse /banaglo'riarse/ *vr* to be conceited

vanaglorioso /banaglo'rioso/ **(-sa)** *a* conceited —*n* boaster

vanamente /bana'mente/ *adv* vainly; without foundation; superstitiously; arrogantly

vandálico /ban'daliko/ *a* Vandal

vandalismo /banda'lismo/ *m*, vandalism; destructiveness

vándalo /'bandalo/ **(-la)** *a* and *n* Vandal

vanguardia /baŋ'guarðia/ *f*, vanguard; *pl* outerworks. **a v.,** in the forefront

vanidad /bani'ðað/ *f*, vanity; ostentation; empty words; illusion. *Inf.* **ajar la v. de,** to take (a person) down a peg

vanidoso /bani'ðoso/ **(-sa)** *a* vain; ostentatious —*n* conceited person

vano /'bano/ *a* vain; hollow, empty; useless, ineffectual; unsubstantial, illusory. *m*, span (bridge). **v. único,** single span. **en v.,** uselessly, in vain

vapor /ba'por/ *m*, steam, vapor; fainting fit; steamboat; *pl* hysterics. **v. de ruedas, v. de paleta,** paddle steamer. **v. volandero,** tramp steamer. **al v.,** full steam ahead; *Inf.* with all speed

vaporable /bapo'raβle/ *a* vaporizable

vaporación /bapora'θion; bapora'sion/ *f*, evaporation

vaporización /baporiθa'θion; baporisa'sion/ *f*, vaporization

vaporizador /baporiθa'ðor; baporisa'ðor/ *m*, vaporizer; spray, sprayer

vaporizar /bapori'θar; bapori'sar/ *vt* to vaporize; spray

vaporoso /bapo'roso/ *a* vaporous; ethereal; gauzy

vapulación /bapula'θion; bapula'sion/ *f*, **vapulamiento** *m*, whipping

vapular /bapu'lar/ *vt* to whip

vapuleo /bapu'leo/ *m*, whipping, spanking

vaquería /bake'ria/ *f*, herd of cattle; dairy; dairy farm

vaquero /ba'kero/ **(-ra)** *n* cowboy; **vaqueros,** *m*, *pl* jeans

vaquilla /ba'kiʎa; ba'kiya/ *f*, heifer

vara /'bara/ *f*, staff; rod; wand (of authority); vara (nearly one yard); shaft (of cart). **v. de aforar,** water gauge

varada /ba'raða/ *f*, *Naut.* running aground

varadero /bara'ðero/ *m*, shipyard

varar /ba'rar/ *vi Naut.* to run aground; *Fig.* be held up (negotiations, etc.); —*vt Naut.* put in dry dock

varear /bare'ar/ *vt* to knock down (fruit from tree); beat (with a rod); measure with a rod; sell by the rod; —*vr* grow thin

variabilidad /bariaβili'ðað/ *f*, variableness

variable /ba'riaβle/ *a* variable; changeable, inconsistent

variación /baria'θion; baria'sion/ *f*, variation

variado /ba'riaðo/ *a* varied; variegated

variante /ba'riante/ *a* varying. *f*, variant; discrepancy

variar /ba'riar/ *vt* to vary; change; —*vi* change; be different

varice /ba'riθe; ba'rise/ *f*, varix

varicela /bari'θela; bari'sela/ *f*, chicken pox

varicoso /bari'koso/ *a* varicose

variedad /barie'ðað/ *f*, variety; change; inconstancy, instability; alteration; variation; *Biol.* variety

varilla /ba'riʎa; ba'riya/ *f*, *dim* rod; rib (fan, umbrella). **v. de virtudes,** conjurer's wand. *Mech.* **v. percusora,** tappet rod

vario /'bario/ *a* different, diverse; inconstant, changeable; variegated; *pl* some, a few

variopinto /bario'pinto/ *a* motley

varón /ba'ron/ *m*, male; man

varonil /baro'nil/ *a* male; manly

Varsovia /bar'soβia/ Warsaw

varsoviano /barso'βiano/ **(-na)** *a* and *n* of or from Warsaw

vasallaje /basa'ʎahe; basa'yahe/ *m*, vassalage; dependence; tribute money

vasallo /ba'saʎo; ba'sayo/ **(-lla)** *n* vassal —*a* vassal; dependent

vasco /'basko/ **(-ca), vascongado (-da)** *a* and *n* Basque

vascuence /bas'kuenθe; bas'kuense/ *m*, Basque (language); *Inf.* gibberish

vaselina /base'lina/ *f*, vaseline

vasija /ba'siha/ *f*, vessel, receptacle, jar

vaso /'baso/ *m*, receptacle; glass, tankard, mug; glassful; (*Naut. Anat. Bot.*) vessel; garden-urn; vase

vástago /'bastago/ *m*, stem, shoot; offspring, descendant; piston rod

vastedad /baste'ðað/ *f*, extensiveness, largeness, vastness

vasto /'basto/ *a* vast, extensive

vate /'bate/ *m*, bard; seer

vaticano /bati'kano/ *a* and *m*, Vatican

vaticinar /batiθi'nar; batisi'nar/ *vt* to prophesy, foretell

vaticinio /bati'θinio; bati'sinio/ *m*, prediction

vatímetro /ba'timetro/ *m*, water meter

vatio /'batio/ *m*, watt. **v. hora,** watt hour

ve /be/ *f*, name of the letter V. **v. doble** *or* **doble v.,** name of the letter W

vecinal /beθi'nal; besi'nal/ *a* neighboring

vecindad /beθin'dað; besin'dað/ *f*, neighborhood. **buena v.,** good neighborliness. **hacer mala v.,** to be a nuisance to one's neighbors

vecindario /beθin'dario; besin'dario/ *m*, neighborhood; population of a district

vecino /be'θino; be'sino/ **(-na)** *a* neighboring; near; similar —*n* neighbor; citizen; inhabitant

vector /bek'tor/ *m*, carrier (of disease)

veda /'beða/ *f*, close season; prohibition

vedamiento /beða'miento/ *m*, prohibition

vedar /be'ðar/ *vt* to forbid; prevent

vedija /be'ðiha/ *f*, tangled lock of hair; piece of matted wool; curl (of smoke)

veedor /bee'ðor/ **(-ra)** *a* prying —*n* busy-body. *m*, inspector; overseer

vega /'bega/ *f*, fertile lowland plain; meadow

vegada /be'gaða/ *f*. See **vez**

vegetable /behe'taβle/ *a* and *m*, vegetable

vegetación /beheta'θion; beheta'sion/ *f*, vegetation

vegetal /behe'tal/ *a* vegetal; plant. *m*, vegetable, plant

vegetar /behe'tar/ *vi* to flourish, grow (plants); *Fig.* vegetate

vegetarianismo /behetaria'nismo/ *m*, vegetarianism

vegetariano /beheta'riano/ **(-na)** *a* and *n* vegetarian

vegetativo /beheta'tiβo/ *a* vegetative

vehemencia /bee'menθia; bee'mensia/ *f*, vehemence

vehemente /bee'mente/ *a* vehement; vivid

vehículo /be'ikulo/ *m*, vehicle; means, instrument

veinte /'beinte/ *a* and *m*, twenty; twentieth

veintena /bein'tena/ *f*, a score

veinticinco /beinti'θinko; beinti'sinko/ *a* and *m*, twenty-five; twenty-fifth

veinticuatro /beinti'kuatro/ *a* and *m*, twenty-four; twenty-fourth

veintidós /beinti'ðos/ *a* and *m*, twenty-two; twenty-second

veintinueve /beinti'nueβe/ *a* and *m*, twenty-nine; twenty-ninth

veintiocho /bein'tiotʃo/ *a* and *m*, twenty-eight; twenty-eighth

veintiséis /beinti'seis/ *a* and *m*, twenty-six; twenty-sixth

veintisiete /beinti'siete/ *a* and *m*, twenty-seven; twenty-seventh

veintitrés /beinti'tres/ *a* and *m*, twenty-three; twenty-third

veintiuno /bein'tiuno/ *a* and *m*, twenty-one; twenty-first. Abbreviates to **veintiún** before a noun (even if one or more adjectives intervene)

vejación /beha'θion; beha'sion/ *f*, ill-treatment, persecution

vejamen /be'hamen/ *m*, irritation, provocation; taunt; lampoon

vejar /be'har/ *vt* to ill-treat, persecute; plague

vejatorio /beha'torio/ *a* vexing, annoying

vejete /be'hete/ *m*, *Inf.* silly old man

vejez /be'heθ; be'hes/ *f*, oldness; old age; platitude. **vejeces**, *pl* ailments of old age. *Inf.* **a la v., viruelas,** the older the madder

vejiga /be'higa/ *f*, bladder; blister. **v. natatoria,** float (of a fish)

vela /'bela/ *f*, vigil; watch; pilgrimage; sentinel, watchman; candle; *Naut.* sail; awning; night work, overtime. **v. de cangreja,** boom sail. **v. de mesana,** mizzen sail. **v. de trinquete,** foresail. **v. latina,** lateen sail. **a toda v.,** with all speed. **alzar velas,** to hoist sail. **en v.,** wakeful, without sleep. *Inf.* **estar entre dos velas,** to be tipsy

velación /bela'θion; bela'sion/ *f*, vigil; watch; marriage ceremony of veiling (gen. *pl*)

velada /be'laða/ *f*, vigil; watch; evening party

velado /be'laðo/ *a* veiled; dim; (of voice) thick, indistinct

velador /bela'ðor/ **(-ra)** *a* watchful; vigilant. *m*, candlestick; small round table —*n* watcher, guard

velar /be'lar/ *vi* to watch, be wakeful; work overtime or at night; *Eccl.* watch; *Fig.* (*with por*) watch over, defend; —*vt* veil; conceal; *Photo.* blur; (*with prep a*) wake (corpse); sit with (patient at night)

veleidad /belei'ðað/ *f*, velleity; fickleness

veleidoso /belei'ðoso/ *a* inconstant, changeable

velero /be'lero/ **(-ra)** *m*, sailing ship; sailmaker —*n* candlemaker

veleta /be'leta/ *f*, weathercock; float, quill (fishing). *mf* changeable person

vello /'beʎo; 'beyo/ *m*, down, soft hair

vellocino /beʎo'θino; beyo'sino/ *m*, wool; fleece

vellón /be'ʎon; be'yon/ *m*, fleece; copper and silver alloy formerly used in sense of "sterling"; *Obs.* copper coin

vellosidad /beʎosi'ðað; beyosi'ðað/ *f*, downiness, hairiness

velloso /be'ʎoso; be'yoso/ *a* downy, hairy

velludo /be'ʎuðo; be'yuðo/ *a* hairy, downy. *m*, plush, velvet

velo /'belo/ *m*, veil; curtain; *Eccl.* humeral veil; excuse, pretext; *Zool.* velum. **v. del paladar,** soft palate. **correr el v.,** to disclose a secret. **tomar el v.,** to take the veil, become a nun

velocidad /beloθi'ðað; belosi'ðað/ *f*, speed; *Mech.* velocity. *Aer.* **v. ascensional,** rate of climb. *Mech.* **v. del choque,** speed of impact. **en gran v.,** by passenger train. **en pequeña v.,** by goods train

velocípedo /belo'θipeðo; belo'sipeðo/ *m*, velocipede

velódromo /be'loðromo/ *m*, velodrome

velón /be'lon/ *m*, oil lamp

veloz /be'loθ; be'los/ *a* swift; quick-thinking or acting

vena /'bena/ *f*, (*Bot. Anat.*) vein; streak, veining (in wood or stone); *Mineral.* seam; underground spring; inspiration. **estar de v.,** to be in the mood; to be inspired

venablo /be'naβlo/ *m*, javelin

venado /be'naðo/ *m*, venison; deer

venal /be'nal/ *a* venous; saleable; venal

venalidad /benali'ðað/ *f*, saleableness; venality

vencedor /benθe'ðor; bense'ðor/ **(-ra)** *a* conquering —*n* conqueror

vencer /ben'θer; ben'ser/ *vt* to conquer; defeat; overcome, rise above; outdo, excel; restrain, control (emotions); convince, persuade; —*vi* succeed, triumph; *Com.* fall due, mature; *Com.* expire; —*vr* control oneself; twist, incline

vencible /ben'θiβle; ben'siβle/ *a* conquerable; superable

vencimiento /benθi'miento; bensi'miento/ *m*, defeat; conquest; victory; bend, twist (of things); *Com.* expiration; *Com.* maturity (of a bill)

venda /'benda/ *f*, bandage; fillet. **tener una v. en los ojos,** to be blind (to the truth)

vendaje /ben'dahe/ *m*, bandage

vendar /ben'dar/ *vt* to bandage; *Fig.* blind (generally passions)

vendaval /benda'βal/ *m*, strong wind

vendedor /bende'ðor/ **(-ra)** *a* selling —*n* seller

vender /ben'der/ *vt* to sell; betray; —*vr* sell oneself; be sold; risk all (for someone); *Fig.* give away (se-

cret); (*with por*) sell under false pretences. **v. al contado,** to sell for cash. **v. al por mayor,** to sell wholesale. **v. al por menor,** to sell retail. **venderse caro,** to be unsociable

vendí /ben'di/ *m*, *Com.* certificate of sale

vendible /ben'diβle/ *a* purchasable; saleable

vendimia /ben'dimia/ *f*, vintage; profit, fruits

vendimiador /bendimia'ðor/ **(-ra)** *n* vintager

vendimiar /bendi'miar/ *vt* to harvest the grapes; take advantage of; *Inf.* kill

Venecia /be'neθia; be'nesia/ Venice

veneciano /bene'θiano; bene'siano/ **(-na)** *a* and *n* Venetian

veneno /be'neno/ *m*, poison; venom; danger (to health or soul); evil passion

venenosidad /benenosi'ðað/ *f*, poisonousness

venenoso /bene'noso/ *a* poisonous, venomous

venera /be'nera/ *f*, scallop-shell (pilgrim's badge); badge, decoration

veneración /benera'θion; benera'sion/ *f*, respect, veneration

venerador /benera'ðor/ **(-ra)** *a* venerating —*n* venerator, respector

venerar /bene'rar/ *vt* to venerate; worship

venéreo /be'nereo/ *a* venereal

venero /be'nero/ *m*, spring of water; horary line on sundial; origin, genesis; *Mineral.* bed

venezolano /beneθo'lano; beneso'lano/ **(-na)** *a* and *n* Venezuelan

vengador /beŋga'ðor/ **(-ra)** *a* avenging —*n* avenger

venganza /beŋ'ganθa; beŋ'gansa/ *f*, revenge

vengar /beŋ'gar/ *vt* to avenge; —*vr* avenge oneself

vengativo /beŋga'tiβo/ *a* vindictive

venia /'benia/ *f*, pardon, forgiveness; permission; inclination of head (in greeting); *Law.* license issued to minors to manage their own estate

venial /be'nial/ *a* venial

venialidad /beniali'ðað/ *f*, veniality

venida /be'niða/ *f*, arrival, coming; return; attack (fencing); precipitancy

venidero /beni'ðero/ *a* future

venideros /beni'ðeros/ *m pl*, successors; posterity

venir /be'nir/ *vi irr* to come; arrive; turn up (at cards); fit, suit; consent, agree; *Agr.* grow; follow, come after, succeed; result, originate; occur (to the mind); feel, experience; (*with prep a + infin.*) happen finally, come to pass; (*with en*) decide, resolve; —*vr* ferment. **v. a menos,** to deteriorate, decline; come upon evil days. **v. a pelo,** to come opportunely, be just right. **v. a ser,** to become. **venirse abajo,** to fall, collapse. **¿A qué viene este viaje?** What is the purpose of this journey? **el mes que viene,** next month. **El vestido te viene muy ancho,** The dress is too wide for you. **Me vino la idea de marcharme,** It occurred to me to leave. **en lo por venir,** in the future —*Pres. Indic.* **vengo, vienes, viene, venimos, venís, vienen.** *Pres. Part.* **viniendo.** *Fut.* **vendré,** etc —*Condit.* **vendría,** etc —*Preterite* **vine, viniste, vino, vinimos, vinisteis, vinieron.** *Pres. Subjunc.* **venga,** etc —*Imperf. Subjunc.* **viniese,** etc.

venoso /be'noso/ *a* veined; venous

venta /'benta/ *f*, selling; sale; inn; *Inf.* wilderness; *pl* *Com.* turnover. **v. pública,** auction. **a la v.,** on sale. **la V. de la Mesilla,** the Gadsden Purchase

ventada /ben'taða/ *f*, gust of wind

ventaja /ben'taha/ *f*, advantage; profit

ventajoso /benta'hoso/ *a* advantageous

ventana /ben'tana/ *f*, window. **v. de guillotina,** sash window. **v. salediza,** bay window. **echar algo por la v.,** to waste a thing

ventanal /benta'nal/ *m*, large window

ventanilla /benta'niʎa; benta'niya/ *f*, small window (as in railway compartments); grill (ticket office, bank, etc.); nostril

ventarrón /benta'rron/ *m*, high wind

ventear /bente'ar/ *v impers* to blow (of the wind); —*vt* sniff air (animals); air, dry; investigate; —*vr* be spoiled by air (tobacco, etc.)

ventero /ben'tero/ **(-ra)** *n* innkeeper

ventilación /bentila'θion; bentila'sion/ *f*, ventilation; ventilator; current of air

ventilador /bentila'ðor/ *m*, ventilating fan; ventilator

ventilar /benti'lar/ *vt* to ventilate; shake, winnow; air; discuss

ventisca /ben'tiska/ *f*, snowstorm

ventiscar, ventisquear /bentis'kar, bentiske'ar/ *v impers* to snow with a high wind

ventisquero /bentis'kero/ *m*, glacier; snowfield, snowdrift; snowstorm

ventolera /bento'lera/ *f*, gust of wind; *Inf*. boastfulness; whim, caprice

ventor /ben'tor/ **(-ra)** *n* pointer (dog)

ventosa /ben'tosa/ *f*, vent (pipes, etc.); *Zool*. sucker; *Surg*. cupping glass

ventosidad /bentosi'ðað/ *f*, flatulence

ventoso /ben'toso/ *a* windy; flatulent

ventrículo /ben'trikulo/ *m*, ventricle

ventrílocuo /ben'trilokuo/ **(-ua)** *a* ventriloquial —*n* ventriloquist

ventriloquia /bentri'lokia/ *f*, ventriloquism

ventrudo /ben'truðo/ *a* big-bellied

ventura /ben'tura/ *f*, happiness; chance, hazard; risk, danger. **a la v.**, at a venture. **buena v.**, good luck. **por v.**, perhaps; by chance; fortunately

venturoso /bentu'roso/ *a* fortunate

Venus /'benus/ *m*, Venus. *f*, beautiful woman, beauty

ver /ber/ *vt irr* to see; witness, behold; visit; inspect, examine; consider; observe; know, understand; (*with de* + *infin*.) try to; —*vr* be seen; show oneself, appear; experience, find oneself; exchange visits; meet. **v. mundo**, to travel. **V. y creer**, Seeing is believing. **A mi v.**, In my opinion. **¡A v.!** Let's see!; Wait and see! **no tener nada que v. con**, to have no connection with, nothing to do with. **Veremos**, Time will tell. **Verse en la casa**, to be a stay-at-home. **Ya se ve**, Of course, Naturally —*Pres. Indic.* **veo**, **ves**, etc —*Imperf.* **veía**, etc —*Past Part.* **visto**. *Pres. Subjunc.* **vea**, etc —*Imperf. Subjunc.* **viese**, etc.

vera /'bera/ *f*, edge; border; shore. **a la v.**, on the edge, on the verge

veracidad /beraθi'ðað; berasi'ðað/ *f*, truthfulness, veracity

veranadero /berana'ðero/ *m*, summer pasture

veraneante /berane'ante/ *mf* summer resident, summer vacationist, holiday-maker

veranear /berane'ar/ *vi* to spend the summer

veraneo /bera'neo/ *m*, summer vacation, summer holidays, summering

veraniego /bera'niego/ *a* summer; light, unimportant

verano /be'rano/ *m*, summer; dry season *West Hem.*

veras /'beras/ *f pl*, reality, truth; fervor, earnestness. **de v.**, really; in earnest

veraz /be'raθ; be'ras/ *a* truthful, veracious

verbal /ber'βal/ *a* verbal; oral

verbena /ber'βena/ *f*, *Bot.* verbena, vervain; fair held on eve of a saint's day

verbigracia /berβi'graθia; berβi'grasia/ *adv* for instance. *m*, example

verbo /'berβo/ *m*, word; vow; *Gram.* verb. **v. activo** or **v. transitivo**, active or transitive verb. **v. auxiliar**, auxiliary verb. **v. intransitivo** or **v. neutro**, intransitive or neuter verb. **v. reflexivo** or **v. recíproco**, reflexive verb

verbosidad /berβosi'ðað/ *f*, verbosity

verboso /ber'βoso/ *a* verbose, prolix

verdad /ber'ðað/ *f*, truth, veracity; reality. **a la v.**, indeed; without doubt. **en v.**, in truth; indeed. **cantar cuatro verdades a alguien**, to tell someone a few home truths. **la pura v.**, the plain truth

verdadero /berða'ðero/ *a* true; real; sincere; truthful

verdal /ber'ðal/ *a* green. **ciruela v.**, greengage

verde /'berðe/ *a* green; unripe; fresh (vegetables); youthful; immature, undeveloped; obscene, dissolute. *m*, green (color); verdure, foliage

verdear /berðe'ar/ *vi* to look green; be greenish; grow green

verdecer /berðe'θer; berðe'ser/ *vi irr* to grow green, be verdant. See **conocer**

verdegay /berðe'gai/ *a and m*, bright green

verdemar /berðe'mar/ *a and m*, sea-green

verdín /ber'ðin/ *m*, verdure; mold; verdigris

verdinegro /berði'negro/ *a* dark green

verdor /ber'ðor/ *m*, verdure; greenness; strength; youth (also *pl*)

verdoso /ber'ðoso/ *a* greenish

verdugo /ber'ðugo/ *m*, hangman, executioner; wale, mark; shoot of tree; switch; whip; *Fig.* scourge; tyrant

verdulera /berðu'lera/ *f*, greengrocer; market woman; *Inf.* harridan

verdulería /berðule'ria/ *f*, greengrocer's shop

verdulero /berðu'lero/ *m*, greengrocer

verdura /ber'ðura/ *f*, verdure; green garden produce, vegetables (gen. *pl*); *Art.* foliage; obscenity

verecundo /bere'kundo/ *a* bashful

vereda /be'reða/ *f*, footpath; sheep track

veredicto /bere'ðikto/ *m*, *Law.* verdict; judgment, considered opinion

verga /'berga/ *f*, steel bow of crossbow; *Naut.* yard; *Inf.* penis

vergajo /ber'gaho/ *m*, rod (for punishment)

vergel /ber'hel/ *m*, orchard

vergonzoso /bergon'θoso; bergon'soso/ **(-sa)** *a* shameful; bashful, shamefaced —*n* shy person

vergüenza /ber'guenθa; ber'guensa/ *f*, shame; self-respect; bashfulness, timidity; shameful act; public punishment

vericueto /beri'kueto/ *m*, narrow, stony path

verídico /be'riðiko/ *a* veracious; true, exact

verificación /berifika'θion; berifika'sion/ *f*, verification, checking; *Law.* **v. de un testamento**, probate

verificador /berifika'ðor/ **(-ra)** *a* verifying, checking —*n* inspector, checker

verificar /berifi'kar/ *vt* to prove; verify; —*vr* take place, happen; check; come true. *Elec.* **v. las conexiones**, to check the connections

verisímil /beri'simil/ *a* credible, probable

verisimilitud /berisimili'tuð/ *f*, credibility

verismo /be'rismo/ *m*, realism; truthfulness

verja /'berha/ *f*, grating, grill; railing

vermífugo /ber'mifugo/ *a and m*, vermifuge

verminoso /bermi'noso/ *a* verminous

vermut /ber'mut/ *m*, vermouth

vernáculo /ber'nakulo/ *a* native, vernacular

vernal /ber'nal/ *a* vernal

veronés /bero'nes/ **(-esa)** *a and n* Veronese

verónica /be'ronika/ *f*, *Bot.* speedwell; veronica (bull-fighting)

verosímil /bero'simil/ *a* credible, probable

verosimilitud /berosimili'tuð/ *f*, verisimilitude, probability

verraco /be'rrako/ *m*, boar

verruga /be'rruga/ *f*, *Med.* wart; *Inf.* bore; defect

versar /ber'sar/ *vi* to revolve; (*with sobre*) concern, deal with (book, etc.); —*vr* become versed (in)

versátil /ber'satil/ *a Zool.* versatile; changeable; fickle

versatilidad /bersati'ðað/ *f*, *Zool.* versatility; changeableness; fickleness

versículo /ber'sikulo/ *m*, versicle; verse (of the Bible)

versificación /bersifika'θion; bersifika'sion/ *f*, versification

versificador /bersifika'ðor/ **(-ra)** *n* versifier

versificar /bersifi'kar/ *vi* to write verses; —*vt* put into verse, versify

versión /ber'sion/ *f*, translation; version; account

verso /'berso/ *m*, poetry, verse; stanza; line (of a poem). **v. suelto**, blank verse

vertebrado /berte'βraðo/ *a and m*, *Zool.* vertebrate

vertedor /berte'ðor/ *m*, drain, sewer; chute

verter /ber'ter/ *vt irr* to pour, spill; empty; translate; —*vi* flow. See **entender**

vertical /berti'kal/ *a and f*, vertical

verticalidad /bertikali'ðað/ *f*, verticality

vértice /'bertiθe; 'bertise/ *m*, vertex

vertiente /ber'tiente/ *a* emptying. *mf*, slope, incline; watershed

vertiginoso /bertihi'noso/ *a* giddy; vertiginous

vértigo /'bertigo/ *m*, giddiness, faintness

vesícula /be'sikula/ *f*, blister; (*Anat. Bot.*) vesicle

vespertino /besper'tino/ *a* evening

vestíbulo /bes'tiβulo/ *m*, hall, vestibule foyer

vestido /bes'tiðo/ *m*, dress; clothes

vestidura /besti'ðura/ *f*, garment; *pl* vestments

vinagre

vestigio /bes'tihio/ m, footprint; trace, mark; remains; *Fig.* vestige

vestir /bes'tir/ vt irr to clothe, dress; adorn; embellish (ideas); *Fig.* disguise (truth); simulate, pretend; —vi be dressed; —vr dress oneself; *Fig.* be covered. See **pedir**

vestuario /bes'tuario/ m, clothing, dress; *Theat.* wardrobe or dressing room; *Eccl.* vestry; *Mil.* uniform

Vesubio /be'suβio/ Vesuvius

veta /'beta/ f, vein; stripe, rib (fabric)

veterano /bete'rano/ (-na) a and n veteran

veterinaria /beteri'naria/ f, veterinary science

veterinario /beteri'nario/ a veterinary. m, veterinary surgeon

veto /'beto/ m, veto; prohibition

vetustez /betus'teθ/ betus'tes/ f, antiquity, oldness

vetusto /be'tusto/ a ancient, very old

vez /beθ/ bes/ f, time, occasion; turn; pl proxy, deputy, substitute. **a la v.**, simultaneously. **alguna v.**, sometime. **a su v.**, in its (her, his, their) turn. **a veces**, sometimes. **de una v.**, at the one time. **de v. en cuando**, from time to time. **en v. de**, instead of. **hacer las veces de**, to be a substitute for. **otra v.**, again. **Su cuarto es dos veces más grande que éste**, His room is twice as large as this one

vía /'bia/ f, way; road; railway track or gauge; *Anat.* tract; (mystic) way; route; conduct; pl procedure. **v. ancha**, broad gauge (railway). **v. angosta**, narrow gauge. **v. de agua**, *Naut.* leak. *Law.* **v. ejecutiva**, seizure, attachment. **v. férrea**, railway. **v. láctea**, Milky Way. **v. muerta**, railway siding. **v. principal**, main line. **v. pública**, public thoroughfare. **v. romana**, Roman road. **v. secundaria**, *Rail.* side line. **por v. aérea**, by air, by airplane

viabilidad /biaβili'ðað/ f, viability

viable /'biaβle/ a viable; practicable; workable; passable

viaducto /bia'ðukto/ m, viaduct

viajante /bia'hante/ mf traveling salesman, commercial traveler

viajar /bia'har/ vi to travel, journey, voyage

viaje /'biahe/ m, journey; voyage; water-supply; travel journal; *Naut.* **v. de ensayo**, trial trip. **v. redondo**, circular tour. **¡Buen v.!** Have a good trip! Bon voyage!

viajero /bia'hero/ (-ra) a traveling —n traveler; passenger

vianda /'bianda/ f, viand, victual (gen. pl); meal

viático /'biatiko/ m, *Eccl.* viaticum; provisions for a journey

víbora /'biβora/ f, viper

viborezno /biβo'reθno/ biβo'resno/ m, young viper

vibración /biβra'θion/ biβra'sion/ f, vibration; jar, jolt; thrill

vibrante /bi'βrante/ a shaking; vibrant; thrilling

vibrar /bi'βrar/ vt to shake, oscillate; —vi vibrate; jar, jolt; quiver, thrill

vibratorio /biβra'torio/ a vibratory, vibrative

vicaría /bika'ria/ f, vicarage; vestry

vicario /bi'kario/ a vicarious. m, vicar; curate; deputy

vicealmirante /biθealmi'rante/ bisealmi'rante/ m, vice-admiral

vicecanciller /biθekanθi'ʎer/ bisekansi'yer/ m, vice-chancellor

vicecónsul /biθe'konsul/ bise'konsul/ m, vice-consul

viceconsulado /biθekonsu'laðo/ bisekonsu'laðo/ m, vice-consulate

vicepresidente /biθepresi'ðente/ bisepresi'ðente/ (-ta) n vice-president

vicesecretario /biθesekre'tario/ bisesekre'tario/ (-ia) n assistant secretary

viciar /bi'θiar/ bi'siar/ vt to corrupt; adulterate; forge; annul; interpret maliciously, misconstrue; —vr become vicious

vicio /'biθio/ 'bisio/ m, vice; defect; error, fraud; bad habit; excess, exaggerated desire; viciousness (animals); overgrowth (plants); peevishness (children). **tener el v. de**, to have the bad habit of. **el v. del juego**, fondness for gambling

vicioso /bi'θioso/ bi'sioso/ a vicious, vigorous, overgrown; abundant; *Inf.* spoiled (children)

vicisitud /biθisi'tuð; bisisi'tuð/ f, vicissitude

víctima /'biktima/ f, victim

¡víctor! /'biktor/ interj Victor!; Long live!; Hurrah!

victoria /bik'toria/ f, victory, triumph; victoria

victoriano /bikto'riano/ (-na) a and n Victorian

victorioso /bikto'rioso/ a victorious

vid /bið/ f, vine

vida /'biða/ f, life; livelihood; human being; biography; vivacity. **v. airada**, dissolute life. **la v. allende la muerte**, life after death. **de por v.**, for life. **darse buena v.**, to live comfortably; enjoy one's life. **dar mala v.**, to ill-treat. **en la v.**, in life; never. **ganarse la v.**, to make one's living

vidente /bi'ðente/ m, clairvoyant; seer

videocámara /biðeo'kamara/ f, video camera, camcorder

videograbación /biðeoɣraβa'θion; biðeoɣraβa'sion/ f, videotape

vidriar /bi'ðriar/ vt to glaze (earthenware)

vidriera /bi'ðriera/ f, glass window (gen. stained or colored)

vidriero /bi'ðriero/ m, glazier —a made of glass

vidrio /'biðrio/ m, glass; anything made of glass; fragile thing; touchy person. **v. inastillable**, safety-glass. **v. jaspeado**, frosted glass. **v. pintado** or **v. de color**, stainedglass. **v. plano**, plate glass. **v. soplado**, blown glass

vidrioso /bi'ðrioso/ a brittle; slippery; fragile; hypersensitive; *Fig.* glazed (eyes)

vieja /'bieha/ f, old woman

viejo /'bieho/ a old; ancient; former; old-fashioned; worn out. m, old man

Viena /'biena/ Vienna

vienés /bie'nes/ (-esa) a and n Viennese

viento /'biento/ m, wind; scent (of game, etc.); guy (rope); upheaval; vanity. **v. en popa**, *Naut.* following wind; without a hitch, prosperously. **vientos alisios**, trade-winds. **v. terral**, land wind. **a los cuatro vientos**, in all directions. **contra v. y marea**, *Fig.* against all obstacles. **correr malos vientos**, to be unfavorable (of circumstances). **refrescar el v.**, to stiffen (of the breeze)

vientre /'bientre/ m, stomach; belly; vitals; *Law.* venter

viernes /'biernes/ m, Friday. **V. Santo**, Good Friday

viga /'biga/ f, beam, rafter; girder; joist; mill beam. **v. maestra**, main beam or girder

vigente /bi'hente/ a valid; in force (laws, customs)

vigésimo /bi'hesimo/ a twentieth

vigía /bi'hia/ f, watch tower; (gen. m) look-out, watch

vigilancia /bihi'lanθia; bihi'lansia/ f, watchfulness, vigilance; watch patrol

vigilante /bihi'lante/ a watchful. m, watcher; watchman. **v. escolar**, truant officer

vigilar /bihi'lar/ vi to watch over; supervise

vigilia /bi'hilia/ f, vigil; wakefulness; night study; *Eccl.* vigil, eve; wake; *Mil.* watch. **día de v.**, fast-day

vigor /bi'gor/ m, strength; activity; vigor, efficiency; validity

vigorizar /bigori'θar; bigori'sar/ vt to invigorate; exhilarate; encourage

vigorosidad /bigorosi'ðað/ f, vigorousness

vigoroso /bigo'roso/ a strong, vigorous

vihuela /bi'uela/ f, lute

vil /bil/ a vile, infamous; base; despicable; untrustworthy

vileza /bi'leθa; bi'lesa/ f, baseness, vileness, infamy

vilipendiar /bilipen'diar/ vt to revile

vilipendio /bili'pendio/ m, vilification; contempt

villa /'biʎa; 'biya/ f, villa; country house; town

villancico /biʎan'θiko; biyan'siko/ m, carol

villanesco /biʎa'nesko; biya'nesko/ a peasant; rustic, country

villanía /biʎa'nia; biya'nia/ f, humbleness of birth; vileness; villainy

villano /bi'ʎano; bi'yano/ (-na) n peasant —a rustic, country; boorish; base

vilo, en /'bilo, en/ adv hanging in the air; *Fig.* in suspense

vilorta /bi'lorta/ f, hoop; *Mech.* washer

vinagre /bi'nagre/ m, vinegar

vinagrera /bina'grera/ f, vinegar bottle; table cruet
vinagreta /bina'greta/ f, vinegar sauce
vinagroso /bina'groso/ a vinegary; *Inf.* bad-tempered, acid
vinatero /bina'tero/ (-ra) n wine merchant —a wine
vincapervinca /binkaper'βinka/ f, *Bot.* periwinkle
vinculación /binkula'θion; binkula'sion/ f, *Law.* entail
vincular /binku'lar/ vt *Law.* to entail; *Fig.* base; —vr perpetuate —a *Law.* entail
vínculo /'binkulo/ m, tie, bond; *Law.* entail
vindicación /bindika'θion; bindika'sion/ f, vindication; justification; excuse
vindicador /bindika'ðor/ (-ra) n vindicator —a vindicative
vindicar /bindi'kar/ vt to avenge; vindicate; justify; excuse
vindicativo /bindika'tiβo/ a avenging; vindicatory
vinícola /bi'nikola/ a wine-growing; wine
vinicultor /binikul'tor/ (-ra) n wine grower, viniculturalist
vinicultura /binikul'tura/ f, wine-growing, viniculture
vinificación /binifika'θion; binifika'sion/ f, vinification
vinillo /bi'niʎo; bi'niyo/ m, thin, weak wine
vino /'bino/ m, wine; fermented fruit juice. **v. de Oporto,** port wine. **v. generoso,** well-matured wine. **v. tinto,** red wine
vinosidad /binosi'ðað/ f, vinosity
vinoso /bi'noso/ a vinous; fond of wine
viña /'biɲa/ f, vineyard
viñador /biɲa'ðor/ m, vineyard-keeper; vine-cultivator
viñedo /bi'ɲeðo/ m, vineyard
viñeta /bi'ɲeta/ f, vignette
viola /'biola/ f, *Mus.* viola; *Bot.* viola, pansy. mf viola player
violación /biola'θion; biola'sion/ f, violation; infringement
violado /bio'laðo/ a violet
violador /biola'ðor/ (-ra) n violator. m, seducer
violar /bio'lar/ vt to violate; infringe; rape; spoil, harm
violencia /bio'lenθia; bio'lensia/ f, violence; outrage; rape
violentar /biolen'tar/ vt to force; falsify, misinterpret; force an entrance; —vr force oneself
violento /bio'lento/ a violent; repugnant; impetuous, hasty-tempered; unnatural, false; unreasonable
violeta /bio'leta/ f, *Bot.* violet. m, violet color. **v. de febrero,** snowdrop
violín /bio'lin/ m, violin
violinista /bioli'nista/ mf violinist
violón /bio'lon/ m, double-bass, bass viol; double-bass player
violoncelista /biolonθe'lista; biolonse'lista/ mf cellist
violoncelo /biolon'θelo; biolon'selo/ m, cello
viperino /bipe'rino/ a viperine; venomous, evil
vira /'bira/ f, welt (of a shoe); dart
viraje /bi'rahe/ m, *Auto.* change of direction; bend, turn
virar /bi'rar/ vt *Naut.* to put about; *Photo.* tone; —vi *Naut.* tack; *Auto.* change direction. **v. de bordo,** *Naut.* to lay off
virgen /bir'hen/ mf virgin. f, *Astron.* Virgo
virgiliano /birhi'liano/ a Virgilian
virginal /birhi'nal/ a virginal; pure, unspotted
virginidad /birhini'ðað/ f, virginity
virgulilla /birgu'liʎa; birgu'liya/ f, comma; cedilla; accent; apostrophe; fine line
viril /bi'ril/ a manly, virile. m, clear glass screen
virilidad /birili'ðað/ f, virility
virote /bi'rote/ m, arrow; shaft; *Inf.* young blood
virreina /bi'rreina/ f, vicereine
virreinato /birrei'nato/ m, viceroyship
virrey /bi'rrei/ m, viceroy
virtual /bir'tual/ a virtual; implicit
virtualidad /birtuali'ðað/ f, virtuality
virtualmente /birtual'mente/ adv virtually; tacitly

virtud /bir'tuð/ f, virtue; power; strength, courage; efficacy. **en v. de,** in virtue of
virtuosidad /birtuosi'ðað/ f, virtuosity
virtuoso /bir'tuoso/ a virtuous; powerful, efficacious. m, virtuoso, artist
viruela /bi'ruela/ f, smallpox (gen. pl)
virulencia /biru'lenθia; biru'lensia/ f, virulence
virulento /biru'lento/ a virulent
virus /'birus/ m, virus
viruta /bi'ruta/ f, wood-shaving
visaje /bi'sahe/ m, grimace
visar /bi'sar/ vt to visa; endorse
vis cómica /bis 'komika/ f, the comic spirit
viscosidad /biskosi'ðað/ f, viscosity
viscoso /bis'koso/ a viscous, sticky
visera /bi'sera/ f, visor; eye-shade; peak (of a cap)
visibilidad /bisiβili'ðað/ f, visibility
visigodo /bisi'goðo/ (-da) a Visigothic —n Visigoth
visigótico /bisi'gotiko/ a Visigothic
visillo /bi'siʎo; bi'siyo/ m, window-blind
visión /bi'sion/ f, seeing, sight; queer sight; vision; hallucination; *Inf.* scarecrow, sight
visionario /bisio'nario/ (-ia) a and n visionary
visir /bi'sir/ m, vizier. **gran v.,** grand vizier
visita /bi'sita/ f, visit; visitor; inspection. **v. de cumplido,** formal call. **v. de sanidad,** health inspection. **hacer una v.,** to pay a call
visitación /bisita'θion; bisita'sion/ f, visitation; visit
visitador /bisita'ðor/ (-ra) n regular visitor. m, inspector —a visiting; inspecting
visitar /bisi'tar/ vt to visit; inspect; *Med.* attend; *Eccl.* examine. **v. los monumentos,** to see the sights, go sightseeing
visiteo /bisi'teo/ m, receiving or paying of visits
vislumbrar /bislum'βrar/ vt to glimpse; surmise, conjecture
vislumbre /bis'lumbre/ f, glimmer, glimpse; surmise, glimmering (gen. pl); semblance, appearance
viso /'biso/ m, view point, elevation; glare; shimmer, gleam; colored slip under transparent dress; semblance. **de v.,** prominent (persons)
visón /bi'son/ m, mink
víspera /'bispera/ f, eve; *Eccl.* day before festival; prelude, preliminary pl *Eccl.* vespers. **en vísperas de,** on the eve of
vista /'bista/ f, vision, sight; view; eyes; eyesight; meeting, interview; *Law.* hearing (of a case); apparition; picture of a view; clear idea; connection (of things); proposition, intention; glance; pl window, door, skylight, opening for light. **v. corta,** short sight. **v. de lince,** sharp eyes. **a primera v.,** at first sight. **a v. de,** in sight of; in the presence of. **conocer de v.,** to know by sight. **dar una v.,** to take a look. **doble v.,** second sight; clairvoyance. **en v. de,** in view of, considering. **estar a la v.,** to be evident. *Inf.* **hacer la v. gorda,** to turn a blind eye. **¡Hasta la v.!** Good-bye! **perder de v.** (a), to lose sight of
vistazo /bis'taθo; bis'taso/ m, glance. **echar un v.,** to cast a glance
visto /'bisto/ past part irr **ver.** *Law.* whereas. **bien v.,** approved. **mal v.,** disapproved. **V. Bueno** (Vᵒ Bᵒ) Approved, Passed. **v. que,** since, inasmuch as
vistoso /bis'toso/ a showy, gaudy; beautiful
visual /bi'sual/ a visual
vital /bi'tal/ a vital; essential
vitalicio /bita'liθio; bita'lisio/ a lifelong. m, life-insurance
vitalidad /bitali'ðað/ f, vitality
vitalizar /bitali'θar; bitali'sar/ vt to vitalize
vitamina /bita'mina/ f, vitamin
vitando /bi'tando/ a odious; bad; vital
vitela /bi'tela/ f, vellum
vitícola /bi'tikola/ a viticultural. mf viticulturist
viticultura /bitikul'tura/ f, viticulture
¡vítor! /'bitor/ interj Victor!; Hurrah!; Long live!
vitorear /bitore'ar/ vt to cheer; applaud, acclaim
vítreo /'bitreo/ a glassy, vitreous
vitrificar /bitrifi'kar/ (se) vt and vr to vitrify
vitrina /bi'trina/ f, show-case; display cabinet
vitriólico /bi'trioliko/ a vitriolic
vitriolo /bi'triolo/ m, vitriol

vitualla /bi'tuaʎa; bi'tuaya/ *f,* (gen. *pl*) victuals, provisions
vituperable /bitupe'raβle/ *a* blameworthy, vituperable
vituperador /bitupera'ðor/ **(-ra)** *a* vituperative —*n* vituperator
vituperar /bitupe'rar/ *vt* to censure, blame, vituperate
vituperio /bitu'perio/ *m,* vituperation
viuda /'biuða/ *f,* widow
viudedad /biuðe'ðað/ *f,* widow's pension
viudez /biu'ðeθ; biu'ðes/ *f,* widowhood
viudita /biu'ðita/ *f,* young widow
viudo /'biuðo/ *m,* widower
¡viva! /'biβa/ *interj* Long live!; Hurrah!
vivacidad /biβaθi'ðað; biβasi'ðað/ *f,* vivacity, gaiety; ardor, warmth; brightness
vivamente /biβa'mente/ *adv* quickly, lively
vivandera /biβan'dera/ *f,* vivandiere
vivandero /biβan'dero/ *m,* sutler
vivaque /bi'βake/ *m,* bivouac
vivaquear /biβake'ar/ *vi* to bivouac
vivar /bi'βar/ *m,* warren; aquarium; breeding ground; well (of a fishing boat)
vivaracho /biβa'ratʃo/ *a* Inf. sprightly, cheery, lively
vivaz /bi'βaθ; bi'βas/ *a* vigorous; quick-witted; sprightly; *Bot.* perennial; vivid, bright
víveres /'biβeres/ *m pl,* provisions; *Mil.* stores
vivero /bi'βero/ *m,* Bot. nursery; vivarium; small marsh
viveza /bi'βeθa; bi'βesa/ *f,* quickness, briskness; vehemence; perspicuity; witticism; resemblance; brightness (eyes, colors); thoughtless word or act
vividero /biβi'ðero/ *a* habitable
vívido /bi'βiðo/ *a* Poet. vivid
vividor /biβi'ðor/ **(-ra)** *a* frugal, thrifty; dissolute —*n* liver; long-liver; libertine, rake
vivienda /bi'βienda/ *f,* dwelling
viviente /bi'βiente/ *a* living
vivificación /biβifika'θion; biβifika'sion/ *f,* vivification
vivificante /biβifi'kante/ *a* vivifying
vivificar /biβifi'kar/ *vt* to vivify; comfort
vivir /bi'βir/ *vi* to be alive, live; last, endure; (*with* en) inhabit. *m,* life. **¿Quién vive?** *Mil.* Who goes there? **v. a costillas ajenas,** to live at someone else's expense, live off someone else
vivisección /biβisek'θion; biβisek'sion/ *f,* vivisection
vivo /'biβo/ *a* alive; intense, strong; bright; *Mil.* active; subtle, ingenious; precipitate; *Fig.* lasting, enduring; diligent; hasty; persuasive, expressive. *m,* edge. **al v., a lo v.,** to the life; vividly
vizcaíno /biθ'kaino; bis'kaino/ **(-na)** *a* and *n* Biscayan
Vizcaya, el Golfo de /biθ'kaya, el 'golfo de; bis'kaya, el 'golfo de/ the Bay of Biscay
vizcondado /biθkon'daðo; biskon'daðo/ *m,* viscounty
vizconde /biθ'konde; bis'konde/ *m,* viscount
vizcondesa /biθkon'desa; biskon'desa/ *f,* viscountess
vocablo /bo'kaβlo/ *m,* word
vocabulario /bokaβu'lario/ *m,* vocabulary
vocación /boka'θion; boka'sion/ *f,* vocation; trade, profession
vocal /bo'kal/ *a* vocal; oral. *f, Gram.* vowel. *mf* voting member
vocalismo /boka'lismo/ *m,* vocalism, vowel system
vocalización /bokaliθa'θion; bokalisa'sion/ *f,* vocalization
vocalizar /bokali'θar; bokali'sar/ *vi* to vocalize
vocear /boθe'ar; bose'ar/ *vi* to cry out, shout; —*vt* proclaim; call for; acclaim
vocerío /boθe'rio; bose'rio/ *m,* shouting, clamor, outcry
vociferación /boθifera'θion; bosifera'sion/ *f,* vociferation, outcry
vociferar /boθife'rar; bosife'rar/ *vt* to boast (of); —*vi* shout, vociferate
vocinglería /boθiŋgle'ria; bosiŋgle'ria/ *f,* clamor, babble, chatter
vocinglero /boθiŋ'glero; bosiŋ'glero/ *a* vociferous; prattling, babbling

vodca /'boðka/ *m,* vodka
volada /bo'laða/ *f,* short flight. *Mech.* **v. de grúa,** jib
voladura /bola'ðura/ *f,* explosion; blasting
volandas (en), volandillas (en) /bo'landas, bo-lan'diʎas; bo'landas, bolan'diyas/ *adv* in the air, as though flying; *Inf.* in a trice
volante /bo'lante/ *a* flying; wandering, restless. *m,* frill, flounce; screen; fan (of a windmill); *Mech.* flywheel; *Mech.* balance wheel (watches); coiner's stamp mill; shuttle-cock. *Auto.* **v. de dirección,** steering-wheel
volantón /bolan'ton/ **(-ona)** *n* fledgling
volar /bo'lar/ *vi irr* to fly (birds, insects, aviation); float in the air; hurry; disappear suddenly; burst, explode; jut out (buttresses, etc.); cleave (air) (arrows, etc.); *Fig.* spread (rumors); —*vt* explode; blast; anger. See **contar**
volatería /bolate'ria/ *f,* fowling; fowls; poultry; flock of birds; *Fig.* crowd (of ideas)
volátil /bo'latil/ *a* volatile; inconstant
volatilizar /bolatili'θar; bolatili'sar/ *vt* to volatilize
volatinero /bolati'nero/ **(-ra)** *n* tight-rope walker, acrobat
volcán /bol'kan/ *m,* volcano; violent passion. **v. extinto,** extinct volcano
volcánico /bol'kaniko/ *a* volcanic
volcar /bol'kar/ *vt irr* to overturn, capsize; make dizzy; cause a change (of opinion); annoy; —*vi* overturn —*Pres. Indic.* **vuelco, vuelcas, vuelca, vuelcan.** *Preterite* **volqué, volcaste,** etc —*Pres. Subjunc.* **vuelque, vuelques, vuelque, vuelquen**
volear /bole'ar/ *vt* to strike in the air, volley; *Agr.* sow broadcast
voleo /bo'leo/ *m,* volley (tennis, etc.); high kick; straight punch
volframio /bol'framio/ *m,* wolfram, tungsten
volición /boli'θion; boli'sion/ *f,* volition
volquete /bol'kete/ *m,* tip-cart
voltaico /bol'taiko/ *a* voltaic
voltaje /bol'tahe/ *m,* voltage
voltario /bol'tario/ *a* versatile; capricious, headstrong
volteador /boltea'ðor/ **(-ra)** *n* acrobat
voltear /bolte'ar/ *vt* to whirl, turn; overturn; change place (of); *Archit.* construct an arch or vault; —*vi* revolve; tumble, twirl (acrobats)
volteo /bol'teo/ *m,* turning, revolution; whirl; overturning; twirling; *Elec.* voltage
voltereta /bolte'reta/ *f,* somersault
volteriano /bolte'riano/ *a* Voltairian
voltímetro /bol'timetro/ *m,* voltmeter
voltio /'boltio/ *m,* volt
volubilidad /boluβili'ðað/ *f,* inconstancy, fickleness
voluble /bo'luβle/ *a* easily turned; inconstant, changeable; *Bot.* twining
volumen /bo'lumen/ *m,* bulk, size; volume, book
volumétrico /bolu'metriko/ *a* volumetric
voluminoso /bolumi'noso/ *a* voluminous, bulky
voluntad /bolun'tað/ *f,* will, volition; wish; decree; free will; intention; affection; free choice; consent. **a v.,** at will; by choice. **de buena v.,** of good will; willingly, with pleasure. **de su propia v.,** of one's own free will. **mala v.,** hostility, ill-will
voluntario /bolun'tario/ **(-ia)** *a* voluntary; strong-willed —*n* volunteer
voluntarioso /bolunta'rioso/ *a* self-willed
voluptuosidad /boluptuosi'ðað/ *f,* voluptuousness
voluptuoso /bolup'tuoso/ *a* voluptuous
volver /bol'βer/ *vt irr* to turn; turn over; return; pay back; direct, aim; translate; restore; change, alter; close (doors, etc.); vomit; reflect, reverberate; —*vi* come back; continue (speech, etc.); bend, turn (roads); (*with prep a* + *infin.*) do something again (e.g. *v. a leer,* to read over again); (*with por* + *noun*) protect; —*vr* become; go sour; turn. **v. a las filas,** *Mil.* to reduce to the ranks. **v. en sí,** to regain consciousness. **v. la cabeza,** to turn one's head. **volverse atrás,** *Fig.* to back out. **volverse loco,** to go mad. See **resolver**
vomitar /bomi'tar/ *vt* to vomit; *Fig.* vomit forth; *Fig.* spit out (curses, etc.); *Inf.* burst into confidences
vomitivo /bomi'tiβo/ *a* and *m,* emetic

vómito /'bomito/ *m*, vomit
voracidad /boraθi'ðað; borasi'ðað/ *f*, voracity
vorágine /bo'rahine/ *f*, vortex, whirlpool
voraz /bo'raθ; bo'ras/ *a* voracious
vórtice /'bortiθe; 'bortise/ *m*, whirlpool; *Fig.* vortex
vortiginoso /bortihi'noso/ *a* vortical
vos /bos/ *pers pron 2nd pers sing* and *pl* you.
vosotros, vosotras /bo'sotros, bo'sotras/ *pers pron 2nd pers pl mf* you
votación /bota'θion; bota'sion/ *f*, voting
votador /bota'ðor/ **(-ra)** *n* voter; swearer
votar /bo'tar/ *vi* and *vt* to vote; make a vow; curse, swear. **v. una proposición de confianza,** to pass a vote of confidence
votivo /bo'tiβo/ *a* votive
voto /'boto/ *m*, vote; vow; voter; prayer; curse; desire; opinion. **v. de calidad,** casting vote. **v. de confianza,** vote of confidence
voz /boθ; bos/ *f*, voice; sound, noise; cry, shout (gen. *pl*); word; expression; *Mus.* singer or voice; *Gram.* mood; vote; rumor; instruction, order. **v. común,** general opinion. **a voces,** in a shout, loudly. **llevar la v. cantante,** *Inf.* to have the chief say
vuelco /'buelko/ *m*, overturning
vuelo /'buelo/ *m*, flight; wing; *Sew.* skirt-fullness; ruffle, frill; *Archit.* buttress. **v. a ciegas,** *Aer.* blind flying. **v. de distancia,** long-distance flight. **v. de patrulla,** patrol or reconnaissance flight. **v. de reconocimento,** reconnaissance flight. **v. nocturno,** *Aer.* night flying. **v. sin parar,** non-stop flight. **al v.,** on the wing; in passing; quickly. **alzar** (*or* **levantar) el v.,** to take flight

vuelta /'buelta/ *f*, revolution, turn; bend, curve; return; restitution; recompense; repetition; wrong side; beating; *Sew.* facing, cuff; change (money); conning (lessons, etc.); stroll, walk; change; vault, ceiling; *Sports.* round; *Mech.* **vueltas por minuto,** revolutions per minute. **a v. de correo,** by return mail, by return of post. **a la v.,** on returning; overleaf. **dar la v.,** to turn round, make a détour. **dar una v.,** to take a stroll. **dar vueltas,** to revolve; search (for); consider. **media v.,** half turn
vuestro, vuestra, vuestros, vuestras /'buestro, 'buestra, 'buestros, 'buestras/ *poss pron 2nd pl mf* your, yours
vulcanita /bulka'nita/ *f*, vulcanite
vulcanización /bulkaniθa'θion; bulkanisa'sion/ *f*, vulcanization
vulcanizar /bulkani'θar; bulkani'sar/ *vt* to vulcanize
vulgar /bul'gar/ *a* popular; general, common; vernacular; mediocre
vulgaridad /bulgari'ðað/ *f*, vulgarity
vulgarismo /bulga'rismo/ *m*, vulgarism
vulgarización /bulgariθa'θion; bulgarisa'sion/ *f*, vulgarization; popularization
vulgarizar /bulgari'θar; bulgari'sar/ *vt* to vulgarize; popularize; translate into the vernacular; —*vr* grow vulgar
vulgata /bul'gata/ *f*, Vulgate
vulgo /'bulgo/ *m*, mob
vulnerabilidad /bulneraβili'ðað/ *f*, vulnerability
vulnerable /bulne'raβle/ *a* vulnerable
vulpeja /bul'peha/ *f*, vixen
vulpino /bul'pino/ *a* vulpine; crafty

WXYZ

wagneriano /wagne'riano/ *a* Wagnerian

wáter /'water/ *m*, toilet, water-closet

whisky /'wiski/ *m*, whiskey

xenofobia /seno'foβia/ *f*, xenophobia, hatred of foreigners

xilófago /si'lofago/ *a* xylophagous, wood-boring. *m*, wood-borer

xilófono /si'lofono/ *m*, xylophone

xilografía /silogra'fia/ *f*, xylography

y /i/ *conjunc* and. See **e**

ya /ya/ *adv* already; formerly; soon; now; finally; immediately; well, yes, quite. Used of past, present and future time, and in various idiomatic usages. **Ha venido ya,** He has already come. **¡Ya caerá!** His time will come!, He will get his comeuppance! **Ya vendrá,** He will come soon. **¡Ya voy!** Coming! **¡Ya lo creo!** Of course!; I should think so! **¡Ya!** Quite!; I understand. **ya no,** no longer. **ya que,** since

yacente /ya'θente; ya'sente/ *a* recumbent, reclining (statues, etc.)

yacer /ya'θer; ya'ser/ *vi irr* to be lying at full length; lie (in the grave); be situated; be; lie (with), sleep (with); graze by night —*Pres. Indic.* **yazgo** *or* **yazco, yaces,** etc —*Pres. Subjunc.* **yazga** *or* **yazca,** etc.

yaciente /ya'θiente; ya'siente/ *a* recumbent

yacija /ya'θiha; ya'siha/ *f*, bed; couch; tomb

yacimiento /yaθi'miento; yasi'miento/ *m*, *Geol.* bed, deposit

yacio /'yaθio; 'yasio/ *m*, india-rubber tree

yak /yak/ *m*, yak

yámbico /'yambiko/ *a* and *m*, (metrics) iambic

yanqui /'yanki/ *a* and *mf contemptuous and offensive* North American (gen. U.S.A.)

yarda /'yarδa/ *f*, yard (English measure)

yate /'yate/ *m*, *Naut.* yacht

ye /ye/ *f*, name of the letter Y

yegua /'yegua/ *f*, mare

yelmo /'yelmo/ *m*, helmet

yema /'yema/ *f*, bud; yolk (of egg); sweetmeat; *Fig.* best of anything. **y. del dedo,** finger-tip

yermo /'yermo/ *a* uninhabited, deserted; uncultivated. *m*, wilderness, desert

yerno /'yerno/ *m*, son-in-law

yerro /'yerro/ *m*, error; mistake; fault

yerto /'yerto/ *a* stiff, rigid

yesca /'yeska/ *f*, tinder; fuel, stimulus

yeso /'yeso/ *m*, gypsum, calcium sulphate; plaster; plaster cast

yídish /'yiδis/ *n* and *a* Yiddish

yo /yo/ *pers pron 1st sing mf* I. **el yo,** the ego

yodo /'yoδo/ *m*, iodine

yuca /'yuka/ *f*, yucca

yucateco /yuka'teko/ **(-ca)** *a* and *n* from or pertaining to Yucatan

yugo /'yugo/ *m*, yoke; nuptial tie; oppression; *Naut.* transom; *Fig.* **sacudir el y.,** to throw off the yoke

Yugo /'yugo/ **(e) slavia** Yugoslavia

yugo /'yugo/ **(e) slavo (-va)** *a* and *n* Yugoslav

yugular /yugu'lar/ *a Anat.* jugular. *m*, jugular vein

Yukón, el /yu'kon, el/ the Yukon

yunque /'yunke/ *m*, anvil; patient, undaunted person; hard worker; *Anat.* incus

yunta /'yunta/ *f*, yoke (of oxen, etc.)

yute /'yute/ *m*, jute fiber or fabric

yuxtaponer /yukstapo'ner/ *vt irr* to juxtapose. See **poner**

yuxtaposición /yukstaposi'θion; yukstaposi'sion/ *f*, juxtaposition

zabarcera /θaβar'θera; saβar'sera/ *f*, vegetable seller

zaborda /θa'βorδa; sa'βorδa/ *f*, **zabordamiento** *m*, *Naut.* grounding, stranding

zabordar /θaβor'δar; saβor'δar/ *vi Naut.* to run aground, strand

zacatín /θaka'tin; saka'tin/ *m*, street or square where clothes are sold

zafar /θa'far; sa'far/ *vt* to embellish, garnish, adorn;

Naut. lighten (a ship); —*vr* escape, hide oneself; *(with de)* excuse oneself, avoid; get rid of

zafarrancho /θafa'rrantʃo; safa'rrantʃo/ *m*, *Naut.* clearing the decks; *Inf.* damage; *Inf.* scuffle

zafiedad /θafie'δaδ; safie'δaδ/ *f*, rudeness, ignorance, boorishness

zafio /'θafio; 'safio/ *a* rude, unlettered, boorish

zafiro /θa'firo; sa'firo/ *m*, sapphire

zafra /'θafra; 'safra/ *f*, olive oil container; sugar crop or factory; *Mineral.* waste

zaga /'θaga; 'saga/ *f*, rear. *m*, last player. **en z.,** behind. *Inf.* **no quedarse en z.,** not to be left behind; be not inferior

zagal /θa'gal; sa'gal/ *m*, youth; strong, handsome lad; young shepherd; full skirt

zagala /θa'gala; sa'gala/ *f*, maiden, girl; young shepherdess

zagual /θa'gual; sa'gual/ *m*, paddle

zaguán /θa'guan; sa'guan/ *m*, entrance hall; vestibule

zaguero /θa'gero; sa'gero/ *a* loitering, straggling. *m*, *Sports.* back

zahareño /θaa'reno; saa'reno/ *a* untamable, wild (birds); unsociable, disdainful

zaherimiento /θaeri'miento; saeri'miento/ *m*, upbraiding; nagging

zaherir /θae'rir; sae'rir/ *vt irr* to upbraid, reprehend; nag. See **herir**

zahina /θa'ina; sa'ina/ *f*, *Bot.* sorghum

zahón /θa'on; sa'on/ *m*, leather apron (worn by cowboys)

zahorí /θao'ri; sao'ri/ *m*, soothsayer; waterfinder; sagacious person

zahúrda /θa'urδa; sa'urδa/ *f*, pigsty

zaino /'θaino; 'saino/ *a* treacherous; vicious (horses); chestnut (horses); black (cows)

zalagarda /θala'garδa; sala'garδa/ *f*, ambush; skirmish; snare, trap; *Inf.* trick, ruse; *Inf.* mock battle

zalamería /θalame'ria; salame'ria/ *f*, adulation, flattery

zalamero /θala'mero; sala'mero/ **(-ra)** *a* wheedling, flattering —*n* flatterer

zalea /θa'lea; sa'lea/ *f*, sheepskin

zalear /θale'ar; sale'ar/ *vt* to shake; frighten away (dogs)

zalema /θa'lema; sa'lema/ *f*, salaam

zamacuco /θama'kuko; sama'kuko/ *m*, *Inf.* oaf, dolt; *Inf.* drinking bout

zamarra /θa'marra; sa'marra/ *f*, sheepskin jacket

zamarrear /θamarre'ar; samarre'ar/ *vt* to worry, shake (prey); *Fig. Inf.* beat up; *Inf.* floor, confound

zambo /'θambo; 'sambo/ *a* knock-kneed

zambomba /θam'βomba; sam'βomba/ *f*, rustic drum

zambra /'θambra; 'sambra/ *f*, Moorish festival; *Inf.* merrymaking; Moorish boat

zambuco /θam'βuko; sam'βuko/ *m*, *Inf.* concealment (especially of cards)

zambullida /θambu'ʎiδa; sambu'yiδa/ *f*, plunge, submersion; thrust (in fencing)

zambullir /θambu'ʎir; sambu'yir/ *vt* to plunge in water, submerge; —*vr* dive; hide oneself, cover oneself

zampar /θam'par; sam'par/ *vt* to conceal (one thing in another); eat greedily; *(with en)* arrive suddenly

zampatortas /θampa'tortas; sampa'tortas/ *mf Inf.* glutton

zampoña /θam'poɲa; sam'poɲa/ *f*, rustic flute; *Inf.* unimportant work

zanahoria /θana'oria; sana'oria/ *f*, carrot

zanca /'θanka; 'sanka/ *f*, long leg (birds); *Inf.* long thin leg; *Archit.* stringboard (of stairs)

zancada /θan'kaδa; san'kaδa/ *f*, swift stride

zancadilla /θanka'δiʎa; sanka'δiya/ *f*, trip (wrestling); *Inf.* trick, deceit. **echar la z.,** to trip up

zancajear /θankahe'ar; sankahe'ar/ *vi* to stride about

zancajo /θan'kaho; san'kaho/ *m*, heel-bone; torn

heel (stocking, shoe); *Inf.* ill-shaped person. *Inf.* **no llegarle al z.**, to be immensely inferior to someone

zancajoso /θanka'hoso; sanka'hoso/ *a* flatfooted; slovenly

zanco /'θanko; 'sanko/ *m*, stilt. *Fig. Inf.* **andar** (*or* **estar**) **en zancos**, to have gone up in the world

zancudo /θan'kuðo; san'kuðo/ *a* long-legged

zangandungo /θaŋgan'duŋgo; saŋgan'duŋgo/ **(-ga)** *n Inf.* loafer

zanganear /θaŋgane'ar; saŋgane'ar/ *vi Inf.* to loaf

zángano /'θaŋgano; 'saŋgano/ *m*, *Ent.* drone; *Inf.* idler, parasite

zangolotear /θaŋgolote'ar; saŋgolote'ar/ *vt Inf.* to shake violently; —*vi* fuss about, bustle; —*vr* rattle (windows, etc.)

zangoloteo /θaŋgolo'teo; saŋgolo'teo/ *m*, shaking; rattling

zanguango /θaŋ'guaŋgo; saŋ'guaŋgo/ *m*, *Inf.* lazybones

zanja /'θanha; 'sanha/ *f*, trench, ditch; drain; furrow

zanjar /θan'har; san'har/ *vt* to excavate; *Fig.* remove (obstacles)

Zanzíbar /θan'θiβar; san'siβar/ Zanzibar

zapa /'θapa; 'sapa/ *f*, shovel, spade; *Mil.* sap; sandpaper

zapador /θapa'ðor; sapa'ðor/ *m*, *Mil.* sapper

zapapico /θapa'piko; sapa'piko/ *m*, pick-ax; mattock

zapaquilda /θapa'kilda; sapa'kilda/ *f*, *Inf.* she-cat

zapar /θa'par; sa'par/ *vi Mil.* to sap

zaparrastrar /θaparras'trar; saparras'trar/ *vi Inf.* to trail along the floor (dresses)

zapata /θa'pata; sa'pata/ *f*, half-boot; piece of leather used to stop creaking of a hinge; *Archit.* lintel; (*Naut. Mech.*) shoe

zapatazo /θapa'taθo; sapa'taso/ *m*, blow with a shoe; fall, thud; stamping (horses); flap (of sail)

zapateado /θapate'aðo; sapate'aðo/ *m*, dance in which rhythmic drumming of heels plays important part

zapatear /θapate'ar; sapate'ar/ *vt* to hit with a shoe; stamp feet; drum heels (in dancing); *Inf.* ill-treat; thump ground (rabbits); —*vi* stamp (horses); *Naut.* flap (sails); —*vr Fig.* stand one's ground

zapateo /θapa'teo; sapa'teo/ *m*, stamping; rhythmic drumming of heels

zapatera /θapa'tera; sapa'tera/ *f*, cobbler's wife; woman who makes or sells shoes

zapatería /θapate'ria; sapate'ria/ *f*, shoemaking; shoe shop

zapatero /θapa'tero; sapa'tero/ *m*, shoemaker; shoe seller. **z. remendón,** cobbler

zapateta /θapa'teta; sapa'teta/ *f*, caper, leap

zapatilla /θapa'tiʎa; sapa'tiya/ *f*, slipper; trotter, hoof

zapato /θa'pato; sa'pato/ *m*, shoe

¡zape! /'θape; 'sape/ *interj Inf.* shoo! Used for frightening away cats; exclamation of surprise or warning

zapear /θape'ar; sape'ar/ *vt* to scare away cats; *Inf.* frighten off

zaque /'θake; 'sake/ *m*, leather bottle, wineskin; *Inf.* drunkard, sot

zaquizamí /θakiθa'mi; sakisa'mi/ *m*, garret; dirty little house or room

zar /θar; sar/ *m*, tsar

zarabanda /θara'βanda; sara'βanda/ *f*, saraband; *Inf.* racket, row

zaragata /θara'gata; sara'gata/ *f*, *Inf.* fight, brawl

Zaragoza /θara'goθa; sara'gosa/ Saragossa

zaragozano /θarago'θano; sarago'sano/ **(-na)** *a* and *n* Saragossan

zaragüelles /θara'gueʎes; sara'gueyes/ *m*, *pl* wide pleated breeches

zaranda /θa'randa; sa'randa/ *f*, sieve, strainer, colander

zarandajas /θaran'dahas; saran'dahas/ *f*, *pl Inf.* odds and ends

zarandar /θaran'dar; saran'dar/ *vt* to sieve (grapes, grain); strain; *Inf.* pick out the best; —*vr Inf.* move quickly

zarandillo /θaran'diʎo; saran'diyo/ *m*, small sieve, strainer; *Inf.* a live wire, energetic person; Spanish dance

zaraza /θa'raθa; sa'rasa/ *f*, chintz

zarcillo /θar'θiʎo; sar'siyo/ *m*, earring; *Bot.* tendril; *Agr.* trowel

zarco /'θarko; 'sarko/ *a* light blue (generally eyes or water)

zarina /θa'rina; sa'rina/ *f*, tsarina

zarpa /'θarpa; 'sarpa/ *f*, *Naut.* weighing anchor; paw

zarpada /θar'paða; sar'paða/ *f*, blow with a paw

zarpar /θar'par; sar'par/ *vt* and *vi Naut.* to weigh anchor, sail

zarza /'θarθa; 'sarsa/ *f*, *Bot.* bramble, blackberry bush

zarzal /θar'θal; sar'sal/ *m*, bramble patch

zarzamora /θarθa'mora; sarsa'mora/ *f*, blackberry

zarzaparrilla /θarθapa'rriʎa; sarsapa'rriya/ *f*, sarsaparilla

zarzo /'θarθo; 'sarso/ *m*, hurdle; wattle

zarzoso /θar'θoso; sar'soso/ *a* brambly

zarzuela /θar'θuela; sar'suela/ *f*, comic opera; musical comedy

zarzuelista /θarθue'lista; sarsue'lista/ *mf* writer or composer of comic operas

¡zas! /θas; sas/ *m*, sound of a bang or blow

zascandil /θaskan'dil; saskan'dil/ *m*, *Inf.* busybody

zatara /θa'tara; sa'tara/ *f*, raft

zeda /'θeða; 'seða/ *f*, name of the letter Z

zedilla /θe'ðiʎa; se'ðiya/ *f*, cedilla

zenit /'θenit; 'senit/ *m*. See **cenit**

zepelín /θepe'lin; sepe'lin/ *m*, Zeppelin

zeta /'θeta; 'seta/ *f*. See **zeda**

zigzag /θig'θag; sig'sag/ *m*, zigzag

zigzaguear /θigθage'ar; sigsage'ar/ *vi* to zigzag

zinc /θink; sink/ *m*, zinc

zipizape /θipi'θape; sipi'sape/ *m*, *Inf.* row, quarrel

zoca /'θoka; 'soka/ *f*, square

zócalo /'θokalo; 'sokalo/ *m*, *Archit.* socle

zoclo /'θoklo; 'soklo/ *m*, clog, sabot

zoco /'θoko; 'soko/ *m*, square; market; clog, sabot

zodiaco /θo'ðiako; so'ðiako/ *m*, zodiac

zona /'θona; 'sona/ *f*, girdle, band; strip (of land); zone; *Med.* shingles. **z. de depresión,** air pocket. **z. templada,** temperate zone. **z. tórrida,** torrid zone

zonal /θo'nal; so'nal/ *a* zonal

zoología /θoolo'hia; soolo'hia/ *f*, zoology

zoológico /θoo'lohiko; soo'lohiko/ *a* zoological

zoólogo /θo'ologo; so'ologo/ *m*, zoologist

zopenco /θo'penko; so'penko/ *a Inf.* oafish

zopo /'θopo; 'sopo/ *a* maimed, deformed (hands, feet)

zoquete /θo'kete; so'kete/ *m*, block; dowel; hunk of bread; *Inf.* short, ugly man; *Inf.* dunderhead

zorcico /θor'θiko; sor'siko/ *m*, Basque song and dance

zorra /'θorra; 'sorra/ *f*, vixen; fox; *Inf.* cunning person; *Inf.* prostitute; *Inf.* drinking bout; truck, dray

zorrera /θo'rrera; so'rrera/ *f*, foxhole

zorrería /θorre'ria; sorre'ria/ *f*, foxiness; *Inf.* cunning

zorro /'θorro; 'sorro/ *m*, fox; fox-skin; *Inf.* knave

zóster /'θoster; 'soster/ *f*, *Med.* shingles

zote /'θote; 'sote/ *a* dull, ignorant

zozobra /θo'θoβra; so'soβra/ *f*, *Naut.* foundering, capsizing; anxiety

zozobrar /θoθo'βrar; soso'βrar/ *vi Naut.* to founder, sink; *Naut.* plunge, shiver; be anxious, vacillate

zueco /'θueko; 'sueko/ *m*, sabot, clog

zulú /θu'lu; su'lu/ *a* and *mf* Zulu

Zululandia /θulu'landia; sulu'landia/ Zululand

zumaque /θu'make; su'make/ *m*, *Bot.* sumach tree; *Inf.* wine

zumba /'θumba; 'sumba/ *f*, cow bell; jest

zumbar /θum'βar; sum'βar/ *vi* to buzz, hum; ring (of the ears); whizz; twang (of a guitar, etc.); *Fig. Inf.* be on the brink

zumbido /θum'βiðo; sum'βiðo/ *m*, buzzing, humming; ringing (in the ears); whizz; twanging (of a guitar, etc.); *Inf.* slap, blow

zumbón /θum'βon; sum'βon/ *a* waggish, jocose

zumo /'θumo; 'sumo/ *m*, sap; juice; profit, advantage

zumoso /θu'moso; su'moso/ *a* succulent, juicy

zupia /'θupia; 'supia/ *f*, wine lees; cloudy wine; *Fig.* dregs

zurcido /θur'θiðo; sur'siðo/ *m*, *Sew.* darn; mend
zurcidor /θurθi'ðor; sursi'ðor/ **(-ra)** *n* darner, mender. **z. de voluntades,** *humorous* pimp
zurcidura /θurθi'ðura; sursi'ðura/ *f*, darning; mending; darn
zurcir /θur'θir; sur'sir/ *vt* to darn; mend, repair; join; *Fig.* concoct, weave
zurdo /'θurðo; 'surðo/ *a* left-handed
zurra /'θurra; 'surra/ *f*, *Tan.* currying; *Inf.* spanking; *Inf.* quarrel
zurrador /θurra'ðor; surra'ðor/ *m*, *Tan.* currier, dresser
zurrapa /θu'rrapa; su'rrapa/ *f*, (gen. *pl*) sediment, lees, dregs
zurrar /θu'rrar; su'rrar/ *vt* to curry (leather); *Inf.* spank; *Inf.* dress down, scold

zurriagazo /θurria'gaθo; surria'gaso/ *m*, lash with a whip; *Fig.* blow of fate
zurriago /θu'rriago; su'rriago/ *m*, whip
zurribanda /θurri'βanda; surri'βanda/ *f*, *Inf.* whipping; fight, quarrel
zurriburri /θurri'βurri; surri'βurri/ *m*, *Inf.* ragamuffin; mob; uproar
zurrido /θu'rriðo; su'rriðo/ *m*, *Inf.* blow; dull noise
zurrir /θu'rrir; su'rrir/ *vi* to have a confused sound, hum, rattle
zurrón /θu'rron; su'rron/ *m*, shepherd's pouch; leather bag; *Bot.* husk
zutano /θu'tano; su'tano/ **(-na)** *n Inf.* so-and-so, such a one
Zuyderzee, el /θuiðer'θee, el; suiðer'see, el/ the Zuider Zee

English-Spanish
Dictionary

A

a /ei/ n (letter) a, f; Mus. la, m. **symphony in A major,** sinfonía en la mayor, f. **A1,** de primera clase; de primera calidad, excelente

a, an /ə, ən; when stressed ei;, æn/ indef art. (one) un, m; una, f; (with weights, quantities) el, m; la, f; (with weeks, months, years, etc.) por, al, m; a la, f. The indef. art. is omitted in Spanish before nouns expressing nationality, profession, rank, and generally before a noun in apposition. It is omitted also before certain words such as **mil, ciento, otro, semejante, medio,** etc. Not translated in book titles, e.g., A History of Spain, Historia de España. prep a. In phrases such as to go hunting, ir a cazar. As prefix, see abed, ashore, etc. Madrid, a Spanish city, Madrid, ciudad de España. three times a month, tres veces al mes. ten dollars an hour, diez dólares por hora. thirty miles an hour, treinta millas por hora. a certain Mrs. Brown, una tal Sra. Brown. a thousand soldiers, mil soldados. half an hour later, media hora después

aback /ə'bæk/ adv Naut. en facha; Fig. sorprendido, desconcertado. **to take a.,** desconcertar, coger desprevenido (a)

abacus /'æbəkəs, ə'bækəs/ n ábaco, m

abaft /ə'bæft/ adv Naut. hacia la popa, en popa; atrás

abandon /ə'bændən/ vt abandonar; dejar; desertar, desamparar; renunciar; entregar. —n entusiasmo, fervor, m; naturalidad, f. **to a. oneself to,** (despair, vice, etc.) entregarse a

abandoned /ə'bændənd/ a entregado a los vicios, vicioso

abandonment /ə'bændənmənt/ n abandono, m; renunciación, f; deserción, f

abase /ə'beis/ vt humillar; degradar; abatir

abasement /ə'beismənt/ n humillación, degradación, f; abatimiento, m

abash /ə'bæʃ/ vt avergonzar; confundir, desconcertar

abashed /ə'bæʃt/ a avergonzado, confuso, consternado

abate /ə'beit/ vt disminuir, reducir; (a price) rebajar; (suppress) suprimir, abolir; (remit) condonar, remitir; (annul) anular; (moderate) moderar; (of pride, etc.) humillar; (of pain) aliviar. —vi disminuir; moderarse; (of the wind and Fig.) amainar; cesar; apaciguarse, calmarse

abatement /ə'beitmənt/ n disminución, f; reducción, f; mitigación, f; (of price) rebaja, f; supresión, f; remisión, f; (annulment) anulación, f; (of pride) humillación, f; (of the wind and of enthusiasm, etc.) amaine, m; (of pain, etc.) alivio, m

abattoir /'æbə,twar/ n matadero, m

abbey /'æbi/ n abadía, f

abbreviate /ə'brivi,eit/ vt abreviar; condensar, resumir

abbreviation /ə,brivi'eiʃən/ n abreviación, f; resumen, m, condensación, f; (of a word) abreviatura, f

abdicate /'æbdɪ,keit/ vt renunciar; (a throne) abdicar

abdication /,æbdɪ'keiʃən/ n renuncia,f; abdicación, f

abdomen /'æbdəmən/ n abdomen, m

abdominal /æb'dɒmənl/ a abdominal

abduct /æb'dʌkt/ vt raptar, secuestrar

abduction /æb'dʌkʃən/ n rapto, m; (Anat., Philos.) abducción, f

abductor /æb'dʌktər/ n Anat. abductor, m; raptor, m

aberration /,æbə'reiʃən/ n aberración (also Astron., Phys., Biol.), f

abet /ə'bet/ vt ayudar, apoyar, favorecer; incitar, alentar; (in bad sense) ser cómplice de

abetment /ə'betmənt/ n ayuda, f, apoyo, m; instigación, f

abettor /ə'betər/ n instigador (-ra); cómplice, mf

abeyance /ə'beiəns/ n suspensión, f; expectativa, esperanza, f. **in a.,** en suspenso; vacante; latente

abhor /æb'hɔr/ vt detestar, odiar, aborrecer; repugnar

abhorrence /æb'hɔrəns/ n detestación, f, odio, aborrecimiento, m; repugnancia, f

abhorrent /æb'hɔrənt/ a detestable, odioso, aborrecible; repugnante

abide /ə'baid/ vi morar, quedar. —vt aguardar; Inf. aguantar, sufrir. **to a. by,** atenerse a, cumplir; sostener

abiding /ə'baidɪŋ/ a permanente, constante, perenne

ability /ə'bɪlɪti/ n habilidad, facultad, f, poder, m; talento, m, capacidad, f. **to the best of my a.,** lo mejor que yo pueda

abject /'æbdʒɛkt/ a abyecto, miserable; despreciable, vil; servil

abjure /æb'dʒʊr/ vt abjurar; renunciar; retractar

ablaze /ə'bleiz/ adv en llamas, ardiendo. —a brillante; (with, of anger, etc.) dominado por

able /'eibəl/ a capaz (de); (clever) hábil; competente; en estado (de); Law. apto legalmente, capaz; bueno, excelente. **to be a. to,** poder; ser capaz de; (know how) saber. **a.-bodied,** fuerte, fornido. **a.-bodied seaman,** marinero práctico, m

abloom /ə'blum/ adv en flor

ablution /ə'bluʃən/ n ablución, f

ably /'eibli/ adv hábilmente; competentemente

abnegation /,æbnɪ'geiʃən/ n abnegación, f

abnormal /æb'nɔrməl/ a anormal; irregular

abnormality /,æbnɔr'mælɪti/ n anormalidad, f; irregularidad, f

abnormally /æb'nɔrməli/ adv anormalmente; demasiado

aboard /ə'bɔrd/ adv a bordo. —prep a bordo de. **to go a.,** embarcarse, ir a bordo. **All a.!** ¡Viajeros a bordo!; (a train) ¡Viajeros al tren!

abode /ə'boud/ n morada, habitación, f; residencia, f; (stay) estancia, f

abolish /ə'bɒlɪʃ/ vt abolir, suprimir, anular

abolition /,æbə'lɪʃən/ n abolición, supresión, f; anulación, f

abolitionism /,æbə'lɪʃə,nɪzəm/ n abolicionismo, m

abolitionist /,æbə'lɪʃənɪst/ n abolicionista, mf

abominable /ə'bɒmənəbəl/ a abominable, aborrecible; repugnante, execrable; Inf. horrible

abominably /ə'bɒmənəbli/ adv abominablemente

abominate /ə'bɒmə,neit/ vt abominar, aborrecer, detestar

abomination /ə,bɒmə'neiʃən/ n abominación, f; aborrecimiento, m; horror, m

aboriginal /,æbə'rɪdʒənl/ a aborigen; primitivo

aborigines /,æbə'rɪdʒə,niz/ n pl aborígenes, m pl

abort /ə'bɔrt/ vi abortar, malparir; Fig. malograrse

abortion /ə'bɔrʃən/ n aborto, m; Fig. fracaso, malogro, m

abortive /ə'bɔrtɪv/ a abortivo

abound /ə'baund/ vi abundar (en)

about /ə'baut/ adv (around) alrededor; (round about) a la redonda, en torno; (all over) por todas partes; (up and down) acá y acullá; por aquí, por ahí; en alguna parte; por aquí; (in circumference) en circunferencia; (almost) casi, aproximadamente; (by turns) por turnos, en rotación. —prep alrededor de; en torno; por; (near to) cerca de; (on one's person) sobre; (on the subject of) sobre; (concerning) acerca de; (over) por, a causa de; en; (of) de; (with time by the clock) a eso de, sobre; (towards) hacia; (engaged in) ocupado en; (on the point of) a punto de. **a. here,** por aquí. **a. nothing,** por nada. **a. supper time,** hacia la hora de cenar. **a. three o'clock,** a eso de las tres. **A. turn!** ¡Media vuelta! (a la izquierda or a la derecha). **He wandered a. the streets,** Vagaba por las calles. **somewhere a.,** en alguna parte. **to be a. to,** estar para, estar a punto de. **to bring a.,** ocasionar. **to come a.,** suceder. **to know a.,** saber de. **to set a.,** empezar, iniciar; (a person) acometer. **What are you thinking a.?** ¿En qué piensas?

above /ə'bʌv/ adv arriba; en lo alto; encima; (superior) superior; (earlier) antes; (higher up on a page, etc.) más arriba; (in heaven) en el cielo. —prep encima de; por encima de; sobre; (beyond) fuera de;

fuera del alcance de; (superior to) superior a; (more than) más de; (too proud to) demasiado orgulloso para; (too good to) demasiado bueno para; (in addition to) además de, en adición a; (with degrees of temperature) sobre. —*a* anterior; (with past participles) antes. **from a.,** desde arriba. **a. all,** sobre todo. **over and a.,** ademas de. **a. board,** *adv* abiertamente, con las cartas boca arriba. —*a* franco y abierto. **a. mentioned,** supradicho, susodicho, antes citado

abrasion /ə'breiʒən/ *n* abrasión, *f;* rozadura, *f; Geol.* denudación, *f*

abrasive /ə'breisiv/ *a* abrasivo. —*n* substancia abrasiva, *f,* abrasivo, *m*

abreast /ə'brɛst/ *adv* de frente, al lado uno de otro; *Naut.* por el través. **to keep a. of the times,** mantenerse al dia. **to ride six a.,** cabalgar a seis de frente. **a. with,** al nivel de, a la altura de

abridge /ə'brɪdʒ/ *vt* abreviar; resumir, condensar, compendiar; disminuir; reducir

abridgment /ə'brɪdʒmənt/ *n* abreviación, *f;* resumen, *m,* sinopsis, *f;* disminución, *f;* reducción, *f*

abroad /ə'brɔd/ *adv* (out) fuera, afuera; (gone out) salido; ausente; (everywhere) en todas partes; (in foreign lands) en el extranjero. **to go a.,** salir de casa, echarse a la calle; ir al extranjero; (of rumors, etc.) propagarse, rumorearse

abrogation /ˌæbrə'geiʃən/ *n* abrogación, anulación, *f*

abrupt /ə'brʌpt/ *a* (precipitous) escarpado, precipitado, abrupto; (unexpected) repentino, inesperado; (of persons) brusco, descortés; (of style) seco

abruptly /ə'brʌptli/ *adv* bruscamente; repentinamente

abruptness /ə'brʌptnis/ *n* precipitación, *f;* brusquedad, *f*

abscess /'æbsɛs/ *n* absceso, *m*

abscond /æb'skɒnd/ *vi* evadirse; huir, escaparse; (with money) desfalcar

absence /'æbsəns/ *n* ausencia, *f;* alejamiento, *m;* (of mind) abstracción, *f,* ensimismamiento, *m;* (lack) falta, *f.* **leave of a.,** permiso para ausentarse, *m; Mil.* licencia, *f,* permiso, *m*

absent /a 'æbsənt; *v* æb'sɛnt/ *a* ausente; alejado (de); (in mind) abstraído, ensimismado, distraído. —*vt* ausentarse; alejarse. **the a.,** los ausentes. **a.-mindedness,** ensimismamiento, *m,* abstracción, *f*

absentee /ˌæbsən'ti/ *n* ausente, *mf*

absenteeism /ˌæbsən'tiizəm/ *n* absentismo, *m*

absently /'æbsəntli/ *adv* distraídamente

absinthe /'æbsɪnθ/ *n* ajenjo, *m*

absolute /'æbsə,lut/ *a* absoluto; perfecto; puro; (unconditional) incondicional; (downright) categórico; completo; (true) verdadero; (unlimited) ilimitado. **the a.,** lo absoluto

absolutely /ˌæbsə'lutli/ *adv* absolutamente; enteramente, completamente; realmente, categóricamente

absolution /ˌæbsə'luʃən/ *n* (Eccl. Law.) absolución, *f*

absolutism /'æbsəlu,tizəm/ *n* absolutismo, despotismo, *m*

absolutist /'æbsə,lutist/ *n* absolutista, *mf*

absolve /æb'zɒlv, -'sɒlv/ *vt* absolver; (free) exentar, eximir; librar; exculpar

absorb /æb'sɔrb, -'zɔrb/ *vt* absorber; (drink) beber; (use) gastar; (of shocks) amortiguar; (Fig. digest) asimilar; (engross) ocupar (el pensamiento, etc.). **to be absorbed in,** Fig. enfrascarse en, engolfarse en, estar entregado a

absorbent /æb'sɔrbənt, -'zɔr-/ *a* and *n* absorbente, *m.* **a. cotton,** algodón hidrófilo, *m*

absorbing /æb'sɔrbɪŋ, -'zɔr-/ *a* absorbente; Fig. sumamente interesante

absorption /æb'sɔrpʃən, -'zɔrp-/ *n* absorción, *f;* (Fig. digestion) asimilación, *f;* (engrossment) enfrascamiento, *m,* preocupación, abstracción, *f*

abstain /æb'stein/ *vi* abstenerse (de); evitar

abstemious /æb'stimiəs/ *a* abstemio, abstinente; sobrio; moderado

abstention /æb'stɛnʃən/ *n* abstención, *f;* abstinencia, *f;* privación, *f*

abstinence /'æbstənəns/ *n* abstinencia, *f.* **day of a.,** día de ayuno, *m*

abstinent /'æbstənənt/ *a* abstinente; sobrio

abstract /*a, v* æb'strækt, 'æbstrækt; *n* 'æbstrækt/ *a* abstracto. —*n* extracto, resumen, *m;* abstracción, *f.* —*vt* abstraer; separar; extraer; (précis) resumir; (steal) substraer. **in the a.,** en abstracto

abstracted /æb'stræktid/ *a* distraído, desatento, absorto, ensimismado

abstraction /æb'strækʃən/ *n* abstracción, *f;* (of mind) preocupación, desatención, *f;* (stealing) substracción, *f*

abstruse /æb'strus/ *a* abstruso, ininteligible; obscuro; recóndito

absurd /æb'sɜrd/ *a* absurdo, grotesco; ridículo, disparatado; cómico

absurdity /æb'sɜrditi/ *n* absurdidad, ridiculez, *f;* disparate, *m,* tontería, *f*

abundance /ə'bʌndəns/ *n* abundancia, copia, *f;* muchedumbre (de), multitud (de), *f;* riqueza, *f;* prosperidad, *f*

abundant /ə'bʌndənt/ *a* abundante, copioso; rico. **to be a. in,** abundar en

abundantly /ə'bʌndəntli/ *adv* en abundancia, abundantemente

abuse /*n* ə'byus; *v* ə'byuz/ *n* abuso, *m;* (bad language) insulto, *m,* injuria, *f.* —*vt* (ill-use) maltratar; (misuse) abusar (de); (revile) insultar, injuriar; (deceive) engañar

abuser /ə'byuzər/ *n* abusador (-ra); injuriador (-ra); (defamer) denigrante, *mf*

abusive /ə'byusiv/ *a* abusivo; (scurrilous) insultante, injurioso, ofensivo

abusively /ə'byusivli/ *adv* insolentemente, ofensivamente

abut (on) /ə'bʌt/ *vi* lindar con; terminar en; estar adosado a

abysmal /ə'bizməl/ *a* abismal

abyss /ə'bis/ *n* abismo, *m,* sima, *f;* (hell) infierno, *m*

acacia /ə'keiʃə/ *n* acacia, *f*

academic /ˌækə'dɛmɪk/ *a* académico

academician /ˌækədə'miʃən/ *n* académico, miembro de la Academia, *m*

academy /ə'kædəmi/ *n* academia, *f;* conservatorio, *m;* (school) colegio, *m;* (of riding, etc.) escuela, *f.* **A. of Music,** Conservatorio de Música, *m*

accede /æk'sid/ *vi* (to a throne) ascender (al trono); tomar posesión (de); (join) hacerse miembro (de); aceptar; (agree) acceder (a), consentir (en), convenir (en)

accelerate /æk'sɛlə,reit/ *vt* acelerar; apresurar; (shorten) abreviar

acceleration /æk,sɛlə'reiʃən/ *n* aceleración, *f*

accelerator /æk'sɛlə,reitər/ *n* (of a vehicle) acelerador, *m*

accent /'æksɛnt/ *n* acento (all meanings), *m.* —*vt* acentuar

accentuate /æk'sɛntʃu,eit/ *vt* acentuar; dar énfasis a

accept /æk'sɛpt/ *vt* aceptar; (believe) creer; recibir; admitir; (welcome) acoger

acceptability /æk,sɛptə'biliti/ *n* aceptabilidad, *f;* mérito, *m*

acceptable /æk'sɛptəbəl/ *a* aceptable; admisible; agradable; (welcome) bien acogido

acceptably /æk'sɛptəbli/ *adv* aceptablemente; agradablemente

acceptance /æk'sɛptəns/ *n* aceptación, *f.* **a. speech** discurso aceptatorio; (approval) aprobación, *f;* (welcome) buena acogida, *f; Com.* aceptación, *f*

access /'æksɛs/ *n* acceso, *m;* entrada, *f;* (way) camino, *m; Med.* ataque, *m;* (fit) transporte, *m;* (advance) avance, *m.* **easy of a.,** accesible; fácil de encontrar

accessibility /æk,sɛsə'biliti/ *n* accesibilidad, *f*

accessible /æk'sɛsəbəl/ *a* accesible; asequible

accession /æk'sɛʃən/ *n* (to the throne, etc.) advenimiento, *m;* aumento, *m;* (acquisition) adición, *f;* adquisición, *f; Law.* accesión, *f*

accessory /æk'sɛsəri/ *a* accesorio; secundario; suplementario, adicional. —*n* accesorio, *m; Law.* cómplice, *mf.* **a. before the fact,** instigador (-ra). **a. after the fact,** encubridor (-ra)

accident /'æksidənt/ *n* accidente, *m;* (chance) casualidad, *f;* (mishap) contratiempo, *m.* **by a.,** por casualidad, accidentalmente. **a. insurance,** seguro contra accidentes, *m*

accidental /ˌæksɪ'dentl̩/ a accidental, casual, fortuito. —n Mus. accidente, m

accidentally /ˌæksɪ'dentl̩i/ adv accidentalmente; por casualidad; sin querer

acclaim /ə'kleim/ vt aclamar; proclamar; vitorear, aplaudir

acclamation /ˌæklə'meiʃən/ n aclamación, f; aplauso, vítor, m

acclimatization /ə'klaimətə,zeishən/ n aclimatación, f

acclimatize /ə'klaimə,taiz/ vt aclimatar

accolade /'ækə,leid/ n acolada, f, espaldarazo, m

accommodate /ə'kɒmə,deit/ vt acomodar; ajustar; adaptar; (reconcile) reconciliar; (provide) proveer, proporcionar; (oblige) complacer; (fit) poner, instalar; (lodge) hospedar; (lend) prestar; (hold) tener espacio para, contener; (give a seat to) dar un sitio a. **to a. oneself to,** adaptarse a

accommodating /ə'kɒmə,deitɪŋ/ a acomodadizo; (obliging) servicial

accommodation /ə,kɒmə'deiʃən/ n acomodación, f; ajuste, m; adaptación, f; (arrangement) arreglo, m; (reconciliation) reconciliación, f; (lodging) alojamiento, m; (Aer. Naut.) partición, f; (space, room or seat) sitio, m; (loan) préstamo, m. **We found the accommodations good in this hotel,** Estuvimos muy bien en este hotel. **a. ladder,** escalera real, f

accompaniment /ə'kʌmpənimənt/ n acompañamiento, m

accompanist /ə'kʌmpənist/ n acompañante (-ta)

accompany /ə'kʌmpəni/ vt acompañar

accompanying /ə'kʌmpəniɪŋ/ a anexo n acompañamiento, m

accomplice /ə'kɒmplis/ n cómplice, comparte, mf

accomplish /ə'kɒmpliʃ/ vt llevar a cabo, efectuar; terminar; (fulfil) cumplir; perfeccionar; (achieve) conseguir, lograr

accomplished /ə'kɒmpliʃt/ a consumado; perfecto; culto; (talented) talentoso

accomplishment /ə'kɒmpliʃmənt/ n efectuación, f; realización, f logro, m; (fulfilment) cumplimiento, m; (gift) prenda, f, talento, m; pl **accomplishments,** partes, dotes, f pl; conocimientos, m pl

accord /ə'kɔrd/ n acuerdo, m; unión, f; consentimiento, m; concierto, m, concordia, f; voluntad, f. —vt otorgar, conceder. —vi estar de acuerdo (con); armonizar (con). **of one's own a.,** espontáneamente. **with one a.,** unánimemente

accordance /ə'kɔrdn̩s/ n acuerdo, m, conformidad, f; arreglo, m. **in a. with,** de acuerdo con, según, con arreglo a

according /ə'kɔrdɪŋ/ adv según, conforme. **a. as,** conforme a, a medida que. **a. to,** según

accordingly /ə'kɔrdɪŋli/ adv en consecuencia, por consiguiente; pues

accordion /ə'kɔrdiən/ n acordeón, m. **to a.-pleat,** vt plisar

accost /ə'kɔst/ vt abordar, acercarse a; dirigirse a, hablar

account /ə'kaunt/ vt (judge) considerar, creer, juzgar, tener por. —vi (for) explicar; (understand) comprender; (be responsible) responder de, dar razón de; justificar

account /ə'kaunt/ n (bill) cuenta, f; factura, f; (narrative) narración, relación, f; (description) descripción, f; historia, f; versión, f; (list) enumeración, f; (reason) motivo, m, causa, f; (importance) importancia, f; (weight) peso, m; (news) noticias, f pl; (advantage) provecho, m, ventaja, f. **by all accounts,** según lo que se oye, según voz pública. **current a.,** cuenta corriente, f. **outstanding a.,** cuenta pendiente, f. **on a.,** a cuenta. **on a. of,** a causa de, por motivo de. **on no a.,** de ninguna manera. **on that a.,** por lo tanto. **to be of no a.,** ser insignificante; ser de poca importancia, Inf. ser la última mona. **to give an a.,** contar, hacer una relación (de). **to give an a. of oneself,** explicarse. **to keep a.,** llevar la cuenta. **to settle accounts,** ajustar cuentas. **to take into a.,** considerar. **to turn to a.,** sacar provecho de. **a. book,** libro de cuentas, m

accountability /ə,kauntə'bilɪti/ n responsabilidad, f

accountable /ə'kauntəbəl/ a responsable

accountancy /ə'kauntn̩si/ n contabilidad, f

accountant /ə'kauntn̩t/ n contador, m. **chartered a.,** contador autorizado, m. **accountant's office,** contaduría, f

accouterment /ə'kutərmənt/ n atavío, m; equipo, m

accredit /ə'kredit/ vt acreditar

accretion /ə'kriʃən/ n acrecentamiento, aumento, m; Law. accesión, f

accrue /ə'kru/ vi resultar (de), proceder (de); originarse (en); aumentar

accumulate /ə'kyumyə,leit/ vt acumular; amontonar, atesorar. —vi acumularse; aumentarse, crecer

accumulation /ə,kyumyə'leiʃən/ n acumulación, f; amontonamiento, m

accumulative /ə'kyumyə,leitɪv/ a acumulador; adquisitivo, ahorrador

accumulator /ə'kyumyə,leitər/ n Elec. acumulador, m

accuracy /'ækyərəsi/ n exactitud, corrección

accurate /'ækyərɪt/ a exacto, correcto, fiel; (of persons) exacto, minucioso; (of apparatus) de precisión

accurately /'ækyərɪtli/ adv con exactitud, correctamente; con precisión

accursed /ə'kɜrsɪd, ə'kɜrst/ a maldito.

accusation /ˌækyʊ'zeiʃən/ n acusación, f. **to lodge an a.,** querellarse ante el juez

accusatory /ə'kyuzə,tɔri/ a acusatorio

accuse /ə'kyuz/ vt acusar

accused /ə'kyuzd/ n Law. acusado (-da)

accuser /ə'kyuzər/ n acusador (-ra)

accustom /ə'kʌstəm/ vt acostumbrar (a), habituar (a)

accustomed /ə'kʌstəmd/ a acostumbrado, usual; general; característico

ace /eis/ n as, m; Fig. pelo, m. **to be within an ace of,** estar a dos dedos de

acerbity /ə'sɜrbɪti/ n acerbidad, f; Fig. aspereza, f; severidad, f; sequedad, f

acetate /'æsɪ,teit/ n acetato, m

acetic /ə'sitɪk/ a acético

acetylene /ə'setl̩,in/ n acetileno, m. **a. lamp,** lámpara de acetileno, f

ache /eik/ n dolor, m; pena, f. —vi doler. **My head aches,** Me duele la cabeza, Tengo dolor de cabeza

achievable /ə'tʃivəbəl/ a alcanzable, asequible; factible

achieve /ə'tʃiv/ vt conseguir, lograr; (reach) alcanzar; (obtain) obtener, ganar

achievement /ə'tʃivmənt/ n logro, m, realización, f; obtención, f; (deed) hazaña, f; (work) obra, f; (success) éxito, m; (discovery) descubrimiento, m; (victory) victoria, f

aching /'eikɪŋ/ n dolor, m; pena, angustia, f. —a doliente; afligido

achromatic /ˌeikrə'mætɪk/ a acromático

achromic /ei'kroumɪk/ a acrómico

acid /'æsɪd/ n ácido, m. **fatty a.,** ácido graso, m

acidify /ə'sɪdə,fai/ vt acidificar

acidity /ə'sɪdɪti/ n acidez, f

acidosis /ˌæsɪ'dousɪs/ n Med. acidismo, m

acidulous /ə'sɪdʒələs/ a acídulo

acknowledge /æk'nɒlɪdʒ/ vt reconocer; confesar; (reply to) contestar a; (appreciate) agradecer. **to a. receipt,** Com. acusar recibo

acknowledgment /æk'nɒlɪdʒmənt/ n reconocimiento, m; confesión, f; (appreciation) agradecimiento, m; (reward) recompensa, f; (of a letter) acuse de recibo, m

acme /'ækmi/ n cumbre, f; Fig. auge, apogeo, m

acne /'ækni/ n acné, m

acolyte /'ækə,lait/ n acólito, monacillo (male) m, acólita, monacilla f, (female)

acorn /'eikɔrn/ n bellota, f. **a. cup,** capullo de bellota, m. **a.-shaped,** en forma de bellota, abellotado

acoustic /ə'kustɪk/ a acústico

acoustics /ə'kustɪks/ n pl acústica, f

acquaint /ə'kweint/ vt dar a conocer, comunicar, informar (de), dar parte (de); familiarizar (con). **to be acquainted with,** conocer; saber. **to make oneself acquainted with,** familiarizarse con; entablar amistad con

acquaintance /ə'kweintn̩s/ n conocimiento, m; (person) conocido (-da); *pl* **acquaintances,** amistades, *f pl*. **to make their a.,** conocer (a), llegar a conocer (a)

acquiesce /ˌækwɪˈes/ *vi* asentir (en), consentir (a)

acquiescence /ˌækwɪˈesəns/ *n* acquiescencia, *f*, consentimiento, *m*

acquiescent /ˌækwɪˈesənt/ *a* conforme; resignado

acquire /əˈkwaɪər/ *vt* adquirir, obtener; (diseases, habits) contraer; ganar; (learn) aprender

Acquired Immune Deficiency Syndrome /əˈkwaɪərd/ *n* el síndrome de Inmunodeficiencia Adquirida, *m*

acquirement /əˈkwaɪərmənt/ *n* adquisición, *f*; (learning) conocimiento, *m*; (talent) talento, *m*

acquirer /əˈkwaɪərər/ *n* adquisidor (-ra)

acquisition /ˌækwəˈzɪʃən/ *n* adquisición, *f*

acquisitive /əˈkwɪzɪtɪv/ *a* adquisitivo

acquit /əˈkwɪt/ *vt* (a debt) pagar; exonerar; *Law.* absolver; (a duty) cumplir. **to a. oneself well (badly),** portarse bien (mal); salir bien (mal)

acquittal /əˈkwɪtl̩/ *n* (of a debt) pago, *m*; *Law.* absolución, *f*; (of a duty) cumplimiento, *m*

acquittance /əˈkwɪtn̩s/ *n* descargo, *m*; quitanza, *f*

acre /ˈeɪkər/ *n* (measure) acre, *m*; *pl* **acres,** terrenos, campos, *m pl*

acreage /ˈeɪkərɪdʒ/ *n* acres, *m pl*

acrid /ˈækrɪd/ *a* acre

acrimonious /ˌækrəˈmoʊniəs/ *a* acrimonioso, áspero; mordaz, sarcástico

acrimony /ˈækrəˌmoʊni/ *n* acrimonia, acritud, *f*; sarcasmo, *m*

acrobat /ˈækrəˌbæt/ *n* acróbata, *mf*

acrobatic /ˌækrəˈbætɪk/ *a* acrobático

acrobatics /ˌækrəˈbætɪks/ *n pl* acrobacia, *f*

acronym /ˈækrənɪm/ *n* sigla, *f*

acropolis /əˈkrɒpəlɪs/ *n* acrópolis, *f*

across /əˈkrɒs/ *adv* a través, de través, transversalmente; (on the other side) al otro lado; de una parte a otra; (of the arms, etc.) cruzados, *m pl*. —*prep* a través de; al otro lado de; (upon) sobre; por. **He went a. the road,** Cruzó la calle. **to run a.,** correr por; tropezar con; dar con. **a. country,** a campo travieso. **a. the way,** en frente

acrostic /əˈkrɒstɪk/ *n* (poema) acróstico, *m*, *a* acróstico

act /ækt/ *n* acción, obra, *f*, hecho, *m*; acto, *m*; *Law.* ley, *f*; *Theat.* acto, *m*. **in the act,** en el acto. **in the act (of doing),** en acto de (hacer algo). **in the very act,** en flagrante. **the Acts of the Apostles,** los Actos de los Apóstoles. **act of God,** fuerza mayor, *f*. **act of indemnity,** bill de indemnidad, *m*

act /ækt/ *vt* (a play) representar, hacer; (a part) desempeñar, hacer (un papel); (pretend) simular, fingir. —*vi* obrar, actuar; (behave) portarse, conducirse; (function) funcionar; producir su efecto; (feign) fingir; (as a profession) ser actor. **to act as,** hacer de; cumplir las funciones de. **to act as a second,** (in a duel) apadrinar. **to act for,** representar; ser el representante de. **to act upon,** obrar sobre; afectar; influir en

acting /ˈæktɪŋ/ *n* (of a play) representación (de una comedia), *f*; (of an actor) interpretación (de un papel), *f*; (as a hobby) el hacer comedia; (dramatic art) arte dramática, *f*. —*a* interino, suplente; comanditario. **He is a. captain,** Está de capitán. **a. partner,** socio (-ia) comanditario (-ia)

action /ˈækʃən/ *n* acción, *f*; función, *f*; operación, *f*; (movement) movimiento, *m*; (effect) efecto, *m*; influencia, *f*; *Law.* proceso, *m*; *Mil.* batalla, acción, *f*; *Lit.* acción, *f*. **in a.,** en actividad; en operación; *Mil.* en el campo de batalla. **man of a.,** hombre de acción, *m*. **to be killed in a.,** morir en el campo de batalla. **to bring an a. against,** pedir en juicio, entablar un pleito contra. **to put into a.,** hacer funcionar; introducir. **to take a.,** tomar medidas (para). **to take a. against,** prevenirse contra; *Law.* proceder contra

actionable /ˈækʃənəbəl/ *a* procesable, punible

active /ˈæktɪv/ *a* activo; ágil; diligente; *Mil.* vivo; enérgico; *Gram.* activo. **to make a.,** activar, estimular

activity /ækˈtɪvɪti/ *n* actividad, *f*

actor /ˈæktər/ *n* actor, *m*; (in comedy) comediante, *m*

actress /ˈæktrɪs/ *n* actriz, *f*; (in comedy) comediante, *f*

actual /ˈæktʃuəl/ *a* actual, existente; real, verdadero

actuality /ˌæktʃuˈælɪti/ *n* realidad, *f*

actually /ˈæktʃuəli/ *adv* en efecto, realmente, en realidad

actuary /ˈæktʃuˌeri/ *n* actuario de seguros, *m*

actuate /ˈæktʃuˌeit/ *vt* mover, animar, excitar

acumen /əˈkyumən/ *n* cacumen, *m*, agudeza, sagacidad, *f*

acute /əˈkyut/ *a* agudo; (shrewd) perspicaz; (of a situation) crítico. **a. accent,** acento agudo, *m*. **a.-angled,** acutángulo

acutely /əˈkyutli/ *adv* agudamente; (deeply) profundamente

acuteness /əˈkyutnɪs/ *n* agudeza, *f*; (shrewdness) perspicacia, penetración, *f*

ad /æd/ *n* anuncio, *m*. See **advertisement**

adage /ˈædɪdʒ/ *n* refrán, proverbio, decir, *m*

adagio /əˈdɑdʒoʊ/ *n* adagio, *m*

Adam /ˈædəm/ *n* Adán, *m*. **Adam's apple,** nuez de la garganta, *f*

adamant /ˈædəmənt/ *a* firme, duro, inexorable

adamantine /ˌædəˈmæntɪn/ *a* adamantino

adapt /əˈdæpt/ *vt* adaptar; ajustar, acomodar; aplicar; (a play, etc.) refundir, arreglar; *Mus.* arreglar

adaptability /əˌdæptəˈbɪlɪti/ *n* adaptabilidad, *f*

adaptable /əˈdæptəbəl/ *a* adaptable

adaptation /ˌædəpˈteɪʃən/ *n* adaptación, *f*; (of a play, etc.) refundición, *f*; (Mus. etc.) arreglo, *m*

adapter /əˈdæptər/ *n* (of a play, etc.) refundidor (-ra); *Elec.* enchufe de reducción, *m*

add /æd/ *vt* añadir; juntar; (up) sumar. **add insult to injury,** al mojado echarle agua, añadir a una ofensa otra mayor. **to add to,** añadir a; (increase) aumentar, acrecentar. **to add up,** sumar. **to add up to,** subir a; (mean) querer decir.

adder /ˈædər/ *n* víbora, serpiente, *f*

addict /ˈædɪkt/ *n* adicto (-ta).

addicted /əˈdɪktɪd/ *a* aficionado (a), amigo (de), dado (a); adicto (a)

addiction /əˈdɪkʃən/ *n* afición, propensión, *f*; adicción, *f*

addition /əˈdɪʃən/ *n* añadidura, *f*; *Math.* adición, suma, *f*. **in a. (to),** además (de), también

additional /əˈdɪʃənl̩/ *a* adicional

addled /ˈædl̩d/ *a* huero, podrido; *Fig.* confuso

address /n əˈdres, ˈædres; v əˈdres/ *n* (on a letter) sobrescrito, *m*; (of a person) dirección, *f*, señas, *f pl*; (speech) discurso, *m*; (petition) memorial, *m*, petición, *f*; (dedication) dedicatoria, *f*; (invocation) invocación, *f*; (deportment) presencia, *f*; (tact) diplomacia, habilidad, *f*; *pl* **addresses,** corte, *f*. —*vt* (a ball) golpear; (a letter) dirigir, poner el sobrescrito a; (words, prayers) dirigir (a); hablar, hacer un discurso. **to a. oneself to a task,** dedicarse a (or entregarse a or emprender) una tarea. **to deliver an a.,** pronunciar un discurso. **to pay one's addresses to,** cortejar, hacer la corte (a), galantear

addressee /ˌædreˈsi/ *n* destinatario (-ia)

adduce /əˈdus/ *vt* aducir, alegar; aportar

Aden /ˈɑdn̩/ Adén *m*

adenoids /ˈædn̩ˌɔɪdz/ *n pl* amígdalas, *f pl*

adept /a əˈdept; n ˈædept/ *a* adepto, versado, consumado. —*n* adepto, *m*

adequacy /ˈædɪkwəsi/ *n* adecuación, *f*; suficiencia, *f*; competencia, *f*

adequate /ˈædɪkwɪt/ *a* adecuado; proporcionado; suficiente; competente; a la altura (de)

adequately /ˈædɪkwɪtli/ *adv* adecuadamente

adhere /ædˈhɪər/ *vi* adherirse; pegarse; ser fiel (a); persistir (en)

adherence /ædˈhɪərəns/ *n* *Fig.* adhesión, *f*

adherent /ædˈhɪərənt/ *n* partidario (-ia)

adhesion /ædˈhiʒən/ *n* adherencia, *f*; (to a party, etc.) adhesión, *f*

adhesive /ædˈhisɪv/ *a* adhesivo; (sticky) pegajoso. **a. tape,** esparadrapo, *m*; *Elec.* cinta aisladora adherente, *f*

adipose /ˈædəˌpous/ *a* adiposo

adjacent /əˈdʒeisənt/ *a* próximo, contiguo, adyacente, vecino

adjective /ˈædʒɪktɪv/ *n* adjetivo, *m*

adjoin /ə'dʒɔin/ vt estar contiguo a, lindar con; juntar. —vi colindar

adjoining /ə'dʒɔiniŋ/ a vecino, de al lado, adyacente; cercano

adjourn /ə'dʒɜrn/ vt aplazar, diferir; (a meeting, etc.) suspender, levantar. —vi retirarse. **The debate was adjourned,** Se suspendió el debate. **to a. a meeting,** levantar la sesión

adjournment /ə'dʒɜrnmənt/ n aplazamiento, m; (of a meeting) suspensión (de la sesión), f

adjudicate /ə'dʒudɪˌkeit/ vt adjudicar; Law. declarar; juzgar. —vi ejercer las funciones del juez; fallar, dictar sentencia

adjudication /ə,dʒudɪ'keifən/ n adjudicación, f; Law. fallo, m, sentencia, f; (of bankruptcy) declaración (de quiebra), f; concesión, f, otorgamiento, m

adjudicator /ə'dʒudɪˌkeitər/ n adjudicador (-ra)

adjunct /'ædʒʌŋkt/ n atributo, m; accesorio, m; adjunto, m; Gram. adjunto, m

adjure /ə'dʒur/ vt conjurar; rogar encarecidamente

adjust /ə'dʒʌst/ vt ajustar; regular; arreglar; (correct) corregir; adaptar

adjustable /ə'dʒʌstəbəl/ a ajustable; regulable; desmontable; de quita y pon

adjustment /ə'dʒʌstmənt/ n ajuste, m; regulación, f; arreglo, m; (correction) corrección, f; adaptación, f; Com. prorrateo, m

adjutant /'ædʒətənt/ n Mil. ayudante, m

administer /æd'mɪnəstər/ vt administrar; (laws) aplicar; (blows, etc.) dar; (an office) ejercer; (govern) regir, gobernar; (provide) suministrar; (an oath) tomar; (justice) hacer; (the sacraments) administrar; (with to) contribuir a. **to a. an oath,** tomar juramento (a)

administration /æd,mɪnə'streifən/ n administración, f; (government) gobierno, m; dirección, f; (of laws) aplicación, f; distribución, f

administrative /æd'mɪnə,streitɪv/ a administrativo; gubernativo

administrator /æd'mɪnə,streitər/ n administrador, m

administratrix /æd,mɪnə'streitrɪks/ n administradora, f

admirable /'ædmərəbəl/ a admirable

admirably /'ædmərəbli/ adv admirablemente

admiral /'ædmərəl/ n almirante, m. **A. of the Fleet,** almirante supremo, m. **admiral's ship,** capitana, f

admiration /,ædmə'reifən/ n admiración, f

admire /æd'maiər/ vt sentir admiración por; (love) amar; (like) gustar; (respect) respetar

admirer /æd'maiərər/ n admirador (-ra); (amateur) aficionado (-da), apasionado (-da); (partisan) satélite, m; (lover) enamorado, amante, m

admiring /æd'maiəriŋ/ a admirativo, de admiración

admissible /æd'mɪsəbəl/ a admisible; aceptable; lícito, permitido

admission /æd'mɪfən/ n admisión, f; recepción, f; entrada, f; confesión, f; reconocimiento, m. **No a.!** Entrada prohibida. **right of a.,** derecho de entrada, m. **A. free,** Entrada libre. **a. ticket,** entrada, f

admit /æd'mɪt/ vt admitir; recibir; dejar entrar; hacer entrar, introducir; (hold) contener; (concede) conceder; (acknowledge) reconocer, confesar. **to a. of,** permitir; sufrir

admittance /æd'mɪtns/ n admisión, f; entrada, f. **No a.!** Prohibida la entrada. **to gain a.,** lograr entrar

admittedly /æd'mɪtɪdli/ adv según opinión general; sin duda

admonish /æd'mɒnɪʃ/ vt (advise) aconsejar; amonestar, advertir; (reprimand) reprender

admonition /,ædmə'nɪfən/ n amonestación, f; advertencia, f; admonición, f

admonitory /æd'mɒnɪˌtɔri/ a amonestador

ad nauseam /'æd nɔziəm/ adv hasta la saciedad

ado /ə'du/ n (noise) ruido, m; (trouble) trabajo, m, dificultad, f; (fuss) barahúnda, f. **much ado about nothing,** mucho ruido y pocas nueces, nada entre dos platos. **without more ado,** sin más ni más

adolescence /,ædl'esəns/ n adolescencia, f

adolescent /,ædl'esənt/ a and n adolescente, mf

adopt /ə'dɒpt/ vt adoptar

adopted /ə'dɒptɪd/ a adoptivo

adoption /ə'dɒpfən/ n adopción, f; (choice) elección, f

adoptive /ə'dɒptɪv/ a adoptivo

adorable /ə'dɔrəbəl/ a adorable

adoration /,ædə'reifən/ n adoración, f. **A. of the Magi,** Adoración de los Reyes, f

adore /ə'dɔr/ vt adorar

adorer /ə'dɔrər/ n adorador (-ra); amante, m

adoringly /ə'dɔriŋli/ adv con adoración

adorn /ə'dɔrn/ vt adornar, embellecer; (Fig. of persons) adornar con su presencia

adornment /ə'dɔrnmənt/ n adorno, m; ornamento, m; embellecimiento, m

adrenalin /ə'drenlɪn/ n adrenalina, f

Adriatic, the /,eidri'ætɪk/ el (Mar) Adriático, m

adrift /ə'drɪft/ a and adv a merced de las olas; a la ventura. **to turn a.,** Inf. poner de patitas en la calle

adroit /ə'drɔit/ a hábil

adulate /'ædʒə,leit/ vt adular

adulation /,ædʒə'leifən/ n adulación, f

adulatory /'ædʒə,tɔri/ a adulador

adult /ə'dʌlt/ a and n adulto (-ta)

adult education n educación de los adultos, f

adulterate /v ə'dʌltə,reit; a ə'dʌltə,reit; -tərɪt/ vt adulterar; falsificar; contaminar. —a adulterado; falsificado; impuro

adulteration /ə,dʌltə'reifən/ n adulteración, f; falsificación, f; impureza, f; contaminación, f

adulterer /ə'dʌltərər/ n adúltero, m

adulteress /ə'dʌltərɪs/ n adúltera, f

adulterous /ə'dʌltərəs/ a adúltero

adultery /ə'dʌltəri/ n adulterio, m. **to commit a.,** cometer adulterio, adulterar

advance /æd'væns/ n avance, m; (progress) progreso, adelantamiento, m; (improvement) mejora, f; (of shares) alza, f; (of price) subida, f; (loan) préstamo, m; (in rank) ascenso, m; pl **advances,** (overtures) avances, m pl; (proposals) propuestas, f pl; (of love) requerimientos amorosos, m pl. **in a.,** de antemano, con anticipación, con tiempo, previamente; (of money) por adelantado. **a. guard,** Mil. avanzada, f. **a. payment,** anticipo, m, paga por adelantado, f

advance /æd'væns/ vt avanzar; (suggest) sugerir, proponer; (encourage) fomentar; (a person) ascender; (improve) mejorar; (of events, dates) adelantar; (of prices, stocks) hacer subir; (money) anticipar; (of steps) tomar. —vi avanzar; (progress) progresar; (in rank, studies, etc.) adelantar; (of prices) subir

advanced /æd'vænst/ a avanzado; (developed) desarrollado; (mentally, of children) precoz; (course) superior. **a. research,** investigaciones superiores. **a. standing,** equivalencias, f pl. **a. views,** ideas avanzadas, f pl

advancement /æd'vænsmənt/ n adelantamiento, m; progreso, m; (encouragement) fomento, m; (in employment) promoción, f; prosperidad, f

advancing /æd'vænsiŋ/ a que avanza; (of years) que pasan

advantage /æd'væntɪdʒ/ n ventaja, f; superioridad, f; (benefit) provecho, beneficio, m; interés, m; ocasión favorable, oportunidad, f; (tennis) ventaja, f. **to have the a. of,** tener la ventaja de. **to show to a.,** embellecer, realzar; aumentar la belleza (etc.) de. **to take a. of,** sacar ventaja de, aprovecharse de; (deceive) engañar. **to take a. of the slightest pretext,** asirse de un cabello

advantageous /,ædvən'teidʒəs/ a ventajoso, provechoso. **to be a.,** ser de provecho

advent /'ædvent/ n advenimiento, m, llegada, f; Eccl. Adviento, m

adventitious /,ædvən'tɪfəs/ a adventicio (all uses)

adventure /æd'ventfər/ n aventura, f; riesgo, m; (chance) casualidad, f; Com. especulación, f, vt aventurar, arriesgar. —vi arriesgarse, osar

adventurer /æd'ventfərər/ n aventurero, m; (one living by his wits) caballero de industria, m; (in commerce) especulador, m

adventuresome /æd'ventfərsəm/ a de aventura

adventuress /æd'ventfərɪs/ n aventurera, f

adventurous /æd'ventfərəs/ a aventurero; osado, audaz; (dangerous) peligroso, arriesgado

adverb /'ædvɜrb/ n adverbio, m

adversary /'ædvər,seri/ n adversario (-ria)

adverse

adverse /ˈædˈvɜrs/ a adverso; hostil (a); malo; desfavorable; (opposite) opuesto

adversity /ædˈvɜrsɪti/ n adversidad, f

advertise /ˈædvərˌtaiz/ vt anunciar. —vi poner un anuncio; (oneself) llamar la atención

advertisement /ˌædvərˈtaizmənt, ædˈvɜrtɪsmənt/ n anuncio, m; (poster) cartel, m; (to attract attention) reclamo, m. **to put an a. in the paper,** poner un anuncio en el periódico. **a. hoarding,** cartelera, f

advertiser /ˈædvərˌtaizər/ n anunciante, mf

advertising /ˈædvərˌtaiziŋ/ n anuncios, m pl; publicidad, propaganda, f; medios publicitarios, m pl

advice /ædˈvais/ n consejo, m; (warning) advertencia, amonestación, f; (news) noticia, f, aviso, m; Com. comunicación, f; (belief) parecer, m, opinión, f. **piece of a.,** consejo, m. **to follow the a. of,** seguir los consejos de. **to give a.,** dar consejos

advisability /æd,vaizəˈbɪliti/ n conveniencia, f; prudencia, f

advisable /ædˈvaizəbəl/ a conveniente, aconsejable; prudente

advise /ædˈvaiz/ vt aconsejar; (inform) avisar, informar

advised /ædˈvaizd/ a avisado; premeditado. **ill-a.,** mal aconsejado; imprudente. **well-a.,** bien aconsejado; prudente

adviser /ædˈvaizər/ n consejero (-ra)

advisory /ædˈvaizəri/ a asesor, consultivo, consultativo

advocacy /ˈædvəkəsi/ n defensa, f; apología, f; abogacía, intercesión, f

advocate /ˈædvəkit; v -,keit/ n Law. abogado (-da); defensor (-ra); (champion) campeón, m. —vt abogar, defender; sostener, apoyar; recomendar

adze /ædz/ n azuela, f

Aegean, the /əˈdʒiən/ el (Mar) Egeo, m

aegis /ˈidʒɪs/ n égida, f; protección, f

aerated /ˈɛəˌreitɪd/ a aerado; (of lemonade, etc.) gaseoso. **a. waters,** aguas gaseosas, f pl

aeration /ˌɛəˈreiʃən/ n aeración, f

aerial /ˈɛəriəl/ a aéreo; de aire; etéreo; fantástico. —n (radio) antena, f. **indoor a.,** antena interior, f

aerobics /ɛəˈroubɪks/ n aerobismo m

aerodynamics /ˌɛəroudaiˈnæmiks/ n aerodinámica, f

aeronaut /ˈɛərəˌnɔt/ n aeronauta, mf

aeronautical /ˌɛərəˈnɔtikəl/ a aeronáutico

aeronautics /ˌɛərəˈnɔtiks/ n aeronáutica, f

afar /əˈfɑr/ adv a lo lejos, en la distancia. **from a.,** desde lejos

affability /ˌæfəˈbɪliti/ n afabilidad, condescendencia, urbanidad, f

affable /ˈæfəbəl/ a afable, condescendiente

affably /ˈæfəbli/ adv afablemente

affair /əˈfɛər/ n asunto, m, cosa, f; cuestión, f; (business) negocio, m; (Fam. applied to a machine, carriage, etc.) artefacto, m; (of the heart) amorío, m. **a. of honour,** lance de honor, m

affect /əˈfɛkt/ vt afectar; influir; Med. atacar; (move) impresionar, conmover; enternecer; (harm) perjudicar; (frequent) frecuentar; (like) gustar de; (love) amar; (wear) vestir; (use) gastar, usar; (feign) aparentar; (boast) hacer alarde de

affectation /ˌæfɛkˈteiʃən/ n afectación, f

affected /əˈfɛktɪd/ a afectado; influido; Med. atacado; (moved) conmovido, impresionado; enternecido; (inclined) dispuesto, inclinado; (artificial) artificioso; amanerado, afectado; (of style) rebuscado, artificial

affecting /əˈfɛktiŋ/ a conmovedor, emocionante

affection /əˈfɛkʃən/ n afecto, cariño, m; amor, m; apego, m; simpatía, f; (emotion) emoción, f, sentimiento, m; Med. afección, enfermedad, f

affectionate /əˈfɛkʃənɪt/ a afectuoso, cariñoso; mimoso; (tender) tierno; expresivo

affectionately /əˈfɛkʃənitli/ adv afectuosamente. **Yours a.,** tu cariñoso..., tu..., que te quiere

affective /ˈæfɛktɪv/ a afectivo

affidavit /ˌæfiˈdeivit/ n declaración jurada, declaración jurídica, f, atestiguación, f

affiliate /əˈfiliˌeit/ vt afiliar; adoptar; Law. imputar; Law. legitimar

affiliation /əˌfiliˈeiʃən/ n afiliación, f; adopción, f; legitimación de un hijo, f

affinity /əˈfiniti/ n afinidad, f

affirm /əˈfɜrm/ vt afirmar, aseverar, declarar; confirmar. —vi Law. declarar ante un juez

affirmation /ˌæfərˈmeiʃən/ n afirmación, aserción, f; confirmación, f; Law. declaración, deposición, f

affirmative /əˈfɜrmətɪv/ a afirmativo. —n afirmativa, f

affix /v əˈfiks; n ˈæfiks/ vt fijar; pegar; añadir; (seal, one's signature) poner. —n Gram. afijo, m

afflict /əˈflikt/ vt afligir, atormentar, aquejar

affliction /əˈflikʃən/ n aflicción, f; tribulación, pesadumbre, f; calamidad, f; miseria, f; (ailment) achaque, m

affluence /ˈæfluəns/ n afluencia, f; abundancia, f; riqueza, f; opulencia, f

affluent /ˈæfluənt/ a abundante; rico; opulento

afflux /ˈæflʌks/ n afluencia, f; Med. aflujo, m

afford /əˈfɔrd/ vt dar, proporcionar; producir; ofrecer; (bear) soportar; poder con; (financially) tener medios para; permitirse el lujo de; (be able) poder. **I could not a. to pay so much,** No puedo (podía) pagar tanto

afforest /əˈfɔrist/ vt convertir en bosque

afforestation /əˌfɔrəˈsteiʃən/ n conversión en bosque, f; plantación de un bosque, f

affray /əˈfrei/ n riña, refriega, f

affront /əˈfrʌnt/ n afrenta, f, insulto, agravio, m. —vt insultar, ultrajar, afrentar; (offend) ofender

Afghan /ˈæfgæn/ a and n afgano (-na)

Afghanistan /æfˈgænəˌstæn/ Afganistán, m

afield /əˈfild/ adv en el campo; lejos. **to go far a.,** ir muy lejos

afire /əˈfaiər/ adv en fuego, en llamas; Fig. ardiendo

aflame /əˈfleim/ adv en llamas; Fig. encendido

afloat /əˈflout/ adv a flote; Naut. a bordo; (solvent) solvente; en circulación; (floating) flotante; (swamped) inundado; (in full swing) en marcha, en movimiento

afoot /əˈfʊt/ adv a pie; en marcha, en movimiento; en preparación. **to set a.,** iniciar, poner en marcha

aforementioned /əˈfɔrˌmɛnʃənd/ a antedicho, ya mencionado

aforesaid /əˈfɔrˌsɛd/ a consabido, dicho, susodicho

afraid /əˈfreid/ a espantado; temeroso, miedoso. **I'm a. that...,** Me temo que.... **to be a.,** tener miedo. **to make a.,** dar miedo (a)

afresh /əˈfrɛʃ/ adv de nuevo, otra vez

African /ˈæfrikən/ a and n africano (-na)

aft /æft/ adv en popa; a popa. **fore and aft,** de proa a popa

after /ˈæftər/ prep (of place) detrás de; (of time) después de; (behind) en pos de; (following) tras; (in spite of) a pesar de; (in consequence of) después de, a consecuencia de; (in accordance with) según; (in the style of) al estilo de, en imitación de. —adv (later) después, más tarde; (subsequently) después (que); (when) cuando. —a futuro, venidero. **day a. day,** día tras día. **on the day a.,** al día siguiente. **soon a.,** poco después. **to look a.,** cuidar de. **to go a.,** ir a buscar; seguir. **the day a. tomorrow,** pasado mañana. **What are you a.?** ¿Qué buscas? **a. all,** después de todo. **a. the manner of,** a la moda de, según la moda de, al estilo de. **a.-dinner conversation,** conversación de sobremesa, f. **a. glow,** resplandor crepuscular, reflejo del sol poniente en el cielo, m. **a. life,** vida futura, f. **a. pains,** dolores de sobreparto, m pl. **a. taste,** dejo, resabio, m

afterbirth /ˈæftərˌbɜrθ/ n placenta, f

aftermath /ˈæftərˌmæθ/ n consecuencias, f pl, resultado, m

afternoon /ˌæftərˈnun/ n tarde, f. **Good a.!** ¡Buenas tardes! **a. nap,** siesta, f. **a. tea,** el té de las cinco

afterthought /ˈæftərˌθɔt/ n reflexión tardía, f; segunda intención, f. **to have an a.,** pensar en segundo lugar

afterwards /ˈæftərwərdz/ adv después; más tarde

again /əˈgɛn/ adv (once more) otra vez, de nuevo; por segunda vez, dos veces; (on the other hand) por otra parte; (moreover) además; (likewise) también; (returned) de vuelta. Sometimes translated by prefix **re** in verbs. **as much a.,** otro tanto. **never a.,** nunca más. **not a.,** no más. **now and a.,** de vez en cuando.

to do a., volver a hacer, hacer de nuevo. **a. and a.,** repetidas veces

against /ə'genst/ *prep* (facing) enfrente de; contra; (in preparation for) para; (contrary to) contrario a; (opposed to) opuesto a; (near) cerca de. **to be a.,** oponer; estar enfrente de. **a. the grain,** a contrapelo

agate /'ægɪt/ *n* ágata, *f*; heliotropo, *m*

age /eidʒ/ *n* edad, *f*; (generation) generación, *f*; (epoch) siglo, período, *m*; época, *f*; (old age) vejez, *f*; (majority) mayoría de edad, *f*, *vi* envejecer. **at any age,** a cualquier edad. **the golden age,** la edad de oro; (in literature, etc.) el siglo de oro. **from age to age,** por los siglos de los siglos. **to be of age,** ser mayor de edad. **to be under age,** ser menor de edad. **to come of age,** llegar a la mayoría de edad. **She is six years of age,** Ella tiene seis años. **age-old,** secular

aged /eidʒd/ 'eidʒɪd/ *a* de la edad de; (old) anciano, viejo. **a girl a. four,** una niña de cuatro años

ageless /'eidʒlɪs/ *a* siempre joven; eterno

agency /'eidʒənsi/ *n* órgano, *m*, fuerza, *f*; acción, *f*; influencia, *f*; intervención, *f*; mediación, *f*; *Com.* agencia, *f*. **through the a. of,** por la mediación (or influencia) de

agenda /ə'dʒendə/ *n* agenda, *f*

agent /'eidʒənt/ *n* agente, *m*; *Com.* representante, *mf*; *Law.* apoderado (-da). **business a.,** agente de negocios, *m*

agglomerate /ə'glɒmə,reit/ *vt* and *vi* aglomerar(se)

agglomeration /ə,glɒmə'reiʃən/ *n* aglomeración, *f*

agglutinate /ə'glutn̩,eit/ *vt* and *vi* aglutinar(se)

aggrandize /ə'grændaiz/ *vt* engrandecer

aggrandizement /ə'grændizmənt/ *n* engrandecimiento, *m*

aggravate /'ægrə,veit/ *vt* agravar, hacer peor; intensificar; (annoy) irritar, exasperar

aggravating /'ægrə,veitɪŋ/ *a* agravante, agravador; (tiresome) molesto; (annoying) irritante. **a. circumstance,** circunstancia agravante, *f*

aggravation /,ægrə'veiʃən/ *n* agravación, *f*, intensificación, *f*; (annoyance) irritación, *f*

aggregate /'ægrɪgət, -,geit/ *a* total. —*n* agregado, conjunto, *m*. **in the a.,** en conjunto

aggression /ə'greʃən/ *n* agresión, *f*

aggressive /ə'gresɪv/ *a* agresivo

aggressiveness /ə'gresɪvnɪs/ *n* carácter agresivo, *m*, belicosidad, *f*

aggressor /ə'gresər/ *a* and *n* agresor (-ra)

aggrieved /ə'grivd/ *a* afligido; ofendido; lastimero

aghast /ə'gæst/ *a* horrorizado, espantado; (amazed) estupefacto

agile /'ædʒəl/ *a* ágil; ligero; vivo

agility /ə'dʒɪlɪti/. *n* agilidad, *f*; ligereza, *f*

agitate /'ædʒɪ,teit/ *vt* agitar; excitar; inquietar, perturbar; discutir. **a. for,** luchar por; excitar la opinión pública en favor de

agitating /'ædʒɪ,teitɪŋ/ *a* agitador

agitation /,ædʒɪ'teiʃən/ *n* agitación, *f*; perturbación, *f*; discusión, *f*

agitator /'ædʒɪ,teitər/ *n* agitador (-ra); (apparatus) agitador, *m*

aglow /ə'glou/ *a* and *adv* brillante, fulgente; encendido

agnostic /æg'nɒstɪk/ *a* and *n* agnóstico (-ca)

agnosticism /æg'nɒstə,sizəm/ *n* agnosticismo, *m*

ago /ə'gou/ *adv* hace. **a short while ago,** hace poco. **How long ago?** ¿Cuánto tiempo hace? **long ago,** hace mucho. **many years ago,** hace muchos años. **I last saw him ten years ago,** La última vez que le vi fue hace diez años

agog /ə'gɒg/ *a* agitado; ansioso; excitado; impaciente; curioso. —*adv* con agitación; con ansia; con curiosidad

agonize /'ægə,naiz/ *vt* atormentar. —*vi* sufrir intensamente; retorcerse de dolor

agonizing /'ægə,naizɪŋ/ *a* (of pain) intenso, atormentador

agonizingly /'ægə,naizɪŋli/ *adv* dolorosamente

agony /'ægəni/ *n* agonía, *f*; angustia, *f*; paroxismo, *m*. **a. column,** columna de los suspiros, *f*

agrarian /ə'greəriən/ *a* agrario

agree /ə'gri/ *vi* estar de acuerdo. **Do you a. or disa-**

gree? ¿Coincides o discrepas?; convenir (en); acordar; ponerse de acuerdo, entenderse; (suit) sentar bien, probar; (consent) consentir (en); *Gram.* concordar, (get on well) llevarse bien; (correspond) estar conforme (con). **to a. to,** convenir en, consentir en. **to a. with,** estar de acuerdo con, apoyar; dar la razón a; (suit) sentar bien; *Gram.* concordar

agreeable /ə'griəbəl/ *a* agradable; afable, amable; (pleasant) ameno, grato; conforme; dispuesto a (hacer algo); conveniente

agreeableness /ə'griəbəlnɪs/ *n* (of persons) afabilidad, amabilidad, *f*; amenidad, *f*; deleite, *m*; conformidad, *f*

agreeably /ə'griəbli/ *adv* agradablemente; de acuerdo (con), conforme (a)

agreed /ə'grid/ *a* convenido, acordado; (approved) aprobado. —*interj* ¡convenido! ¡de acuerdo!

agreement /ə'grimənt/ *n* acuerdo, *m*; pacto, *m*; acomodamiento, concierto, *m*; contrato, *m*; *Com.* convenio, *m*; conformidad, *f*; consentimiento, *m*; *Gram.* concordancia, *f*. **in a.,** conforme. **in a. with,** de acuerdo con; según. **to reach an a.,** ponerse de acuerdo

agricultural /,ægrɪ'kʌltʃərəl/ *a* agrícola. **a. engineer,** ingeniero agrónomo, *m*. **a. laborer,** labriego, *m*. **a. show,** exposición agrícola, *f*

agriculturalist /,ægrɪ'kʌltʃərəlɪst/ *n* agrícola, *mf*

agriculture /'ægrɪ,kʌltʃər/ *n* agricultura, *f*

agronomist /ə'grɒnəmɪst/ *n* agrónomo, *m*

agronomy /ə'grɒnəmi/ *n* agronomía, *f*

aground /ə'graund/ *adv Naut.* varado, encallado. **running a.,** varada, *f*, *m*. **to run a.,** varar

ague /'eigyu/ *n* fiebre intermitente, *f*; *Fig.* escalofrío, *m*

ah! /ɑ/ *interj* ¡ah! ¡ay!

aha! /ɑ'hɑ/ *interj* ¡ajá!

ahead /ə'hed/ *adv* delante; enfrente; al frente (de); a la cabeza (de); adelante; hacia delante; *Naut.* por la proa. **Go a.!** ¡Adelante! **It is straight a.,** Está directamente enfrente. **to go straight a.,** ir hacia delante; seguir (haciendo algo)

ahoy! /ə'hɔi/ *interj* ¡ah del barco!

aid /eid/ *n* ayuda, *f*; socorro, auxilio, *m*; subsidio, *m*, *vt* ayudar; socorrer, auxiliar. **in aid of,** pro, en beneficio de. **first aid,** primera cura, *f*. **first aid post,** puesto de socorro, *m*. **to come or go to the aid of,** acudir en defensa de

aide-de-camp /'eid də 'kæmp/ *n* edecán, *m*

AIDS /eidz/ *n* el SIDA, *m*

ail /eil/ *vt* afligir, doler; pasar. —*vi* estar indispuesto (or enfermo). **What ails you?** *Inf.* ¿Qué te pasa?

ailing /'eilɪŋ/ *a* enfermizo, enclenque, achacoso

ailment /'eilmənt/ *n* enfermedad, *f*, achaque, *m*

aim /eim/ *n* (of firearms) puntería, *f*; (mark) blanco, *m*; *Fig.* objeto, fin, *m*; *Fig.* intención, *f*, propósito, *m*, *vt* (a gun) apuntar; dirigir; (throw) lanzar; (a blow) asestar. —*vi* apuntar (a); (a remark at) decir por; aspirar (a); intentar, proponerse. **Is your remark aimed at me?** ¿Lo dices por mí? **to aim high,** apuntar alto; *Inf.* picar alto. **to miss one's aim,** errar el tiro. **to take aim,** apuntar. **with the aim of,** con objeto de, a fin de

aimless /'eimlɪs/ *a* **aimlessly,** *adv* sin objeto, a la ventura

air /eər/ *n* aire, *m*, (all meanings). **by air,** en avión; (of mail) por avión; (of goods) por vía aérea. **in the air,** al aire; al aire libre; (as though flying) en volandas. **in the open air,** al aire libre, al fresco, a la intemperie. **to be on the air,** *Radio.* hablar por radio. **to give oneself airs,** darse tono, tener humos. **to take the air,** tomar el fresco; despegar. **air balloon,** globo aerostático, *m*; (toy) globo, *m*. **air-base,** base aérea, *f*. **air-bed,** colchón de viento, *m*. **air-borne (to become),** levantar el vuelo, despegar. **air-brake,** *Mech.* freno neumático, *m*. **air-chamber,** cámara de aire, *f*. **air chief marshal,** general del ejército del aire, *m*. **air-cock,** válvula de escape de aire, *f*. **air commodore,** general de brigada de aviación, *m*. **air conditioning,** purificación de aire, *f*. **air-cooled,** enfriado por aire. **air crash,** accidente de aviación, *m*. **air cur-**

rent, corriente de aire, *f.* **air-cushion,** almohadilla neumática, *f.* **air-field,** campo de aviación, *m.* **air fleet,** flotilla aérea, *f.* **air force,** fuerza aérea, flota aérea, *f.* **air-gun,** escopeta de viento, *f.* **air-hole,** respiradero, *m.* **air-hostess,** azafata, *f.* **air-lift,** puente aéreo, *m.* **air-liner,** avión de pasajeros, *m.* **airline** linea aérea, aerolínea, *f.* **airmail,** correo aéreo, *m.* **by airmail,** por ayión. **air marshal,** teniente general de aviación, *m.* **air-pocket,** bolsa (or vacío, *m*) de aire, *f.* **air pollution** contaminación atmosférica, *f.* **air pump,** bomba neumática, *f.* **air raid,** bombardeo aéreo, *m.* **air-raid shelter,** refugio antiaéreo, *m.* **air-raid warning,** alarma aérea, *f.* **air-route,** vía aérea, *f.* **air-screw,** hélice de avión, *f.* **air-shaft,** respiradero de mina, *m.* **air shuttle,** puente aéreo, *m.* **air squadron,** escuadrilla aérea, *f.* **air stream,** chorro de aire, *m.* **air taxi,** avión taxi, *m.* **air-tight,** herméticamente cerrado. **air valve,** válvula de aire, *f.* **air vice-marshal,** general de división de aviación, *m*

air /ɛər/ *vt* airear, orear; secar al aire; ventilar; *Fig.* sacar a lucir, emitir; *Fig.* ostentar

aircraft /ˈɛərˌkræft/ *n* aparato, avión, *m.* **a. barrage,** cortina de fuego de artillería, *f.* **a.-carrier,** porta-aviones, *m.* **a. factory,** fábrica de aeroplanos, *f*

airily /ˈɛərəli/ *adv* ligeramente, sin preocuparse; alegremente

airiness /ˈɛərɪnɪs/ *n* airosidad, *f;* ventilación, *f;* situación airosa, *f;* (lightness) ligereza, *f;* alegría, *f;* frivolidad, *f*

airing /ˈɛərɪŋ/ *n* aireación, *f;* ventilación, *f;* secamiento, *m;* (walk) vuelta, *f,* paseo, *m.* **to take an a.,** dar una vuelta

airless /ˈɛərlɪs/ *a* sin aire; falto de ventilación; sofocante

airman /ˈɛərmən/ *n* aviador, *m*

airplane /ˈɛərˌpleɪn/ *n* aeroplano, avión, *m.* **jet-propelled a.,** aeroplano de reacción, *m.* **model a.,** aeroplano en miniatura, *m*

airport /ˈɛərˌpɔrt/ *n* aeropuerto, *m*

airship /ˈɛərˌʃɪp/ *n* aeronave, nave aérea, *f*

airsick /ˈɛərˌsɪk/ *a* mareado en el aire, mareado

airway /ˈɛərˌweɪ/ *n* vía aérea, *f*

airwoman /ˈɛərˌwʊmən/ *n* aviadora, *f*

airy /ˈɛəri/ *a* aéreo; (breezy) airoso; ligero; vaporoso; alegre; (vain) vano; (flippant) frívolo

aisle /aɪl/ *n* nave lateral, ala, *f*

ajar /əˈdʒɑr/ *a* entreabierto, entornado. **to leave a.,** dejar entreabierto, entornar

akimbo /əˈkɪmbou/ *adv* en jarras. **with arms a.,** con los brazos en jarras

akin /əˈkɪn/ *a* consanguíneo, emparentado; análogo, relacionado; semejante

alabaster /ˈæləˌbæstər/ *n* alabastro, *m, a* alabastrino

alacrity /əˈlækrɪti/ *n* alacridad, *f*

alarm /əˈlɑrm/ *n* alarma, *f,* toque de alarma, *m;* (tocsin) rebato, *m;* sobresalto, *m,* alarma, *f.* —*vt* alarmar; *Mil.* dar la alarma (a). **to give the a.,** dar la alarma a. **bell,** timbre de alarma, *m.* **a. clock,** despertador, *m.* **a. signal,** señal de alarma, *f*

alarming /əˈlɑrmɪŋ/ *a* alarmante

alarmingly /əˈlɑrmɪŋli/ *adv* de un modo alarmante; espantosamente

alarmist /əˈlɑrmɪst/ *n* alarmista, *mf*

alas! /əˈlæs/ *interj* ¡ay!

alb /ælb/ *n* alba, *f*

Albanian /ælˈbeɪniən/ *a and n* albanés (-esa); (language) albanés, *m*

albatross /ˈælbəˌtrɔs/ *n* albatros, *m*

albeit /ɔlˈbiɪt/ *conjunc* aunque, si bien; sin embargo

albinism /ˈælbəˌnɪzəm/ *n* albinismo, *m*

albino /ælˈbaɪnou/ *a* albino

album /ˈælbəm/ *n* álbum, *m*

albumin /ælˈbyumən/ *n* albúmina, *f*

alchemist /ˈælkəmɪst/ *n* alquimista, *m*

alchemy /ˈælkəmi/ *n* alquimia, *f*

alcohol /ˈælkəˌhɔl/ *n* alcohol, *m.* **industrial a.,** alcohol desnaturalizado, *m.* **wood a.,** alcohol metílico, alcohol de madera, *m*

alcoholic /ˌælkəˈhɔlɪk/ *a* alcohólico

alcoholism /ˈælkəhɔˌlɪzəm/ *n* alcoholismo, *m*

alcove /ˈælkouv/ *n* alcoba, *f;* nicho, *m*

---

alder /ˈɔldər/ *n* (tree and wood) aliso, *m*

alderman /ˈɔldərmən/ *n* concejal, *m*

ale /eɪl/ *n* cerveza, *f.* **ale-house,** cervecería, *f*

alert /əˈlɜrt/ *a* alerto; vigilante; despierto; vivo. —*n* sirena, *f.* **to be on the a.,** estar sobre aviso; estar vigilante

alertly /əˈlɜrtli/ *adv* alertamente

alertness /əˈlɜrtnɪs/ *n* vigilancia, *f;* viveza, *f;* prontitud, *f*

Alexandria /ˌælɪgˈzændriə/ Alejandría, *f*

alga /ˈælgə/ *n* alga, *f*

algebra /ˈældʒəbrə/ *n* álgebra, *f*

algebraic /ˌældʒəˈbreɪk/ *a* algebraico

Algeria /ælˈdʒɪəriə/ Argelia, *f*

Algerian /ælˈdʒɪəriən/ *a and n* argelino (-na)

Algiers /ælˈdʒɪərz/ Argel, *m*

alias /ˈeɪliəs/ *adv* alias, por otro nombre. —*n* nombre falso, seudónimo, *m*

alibi /ˈæləˌbaɪ/ *n Law.* coartada, *f.* **to prove an a.,** probar la coartada

alien /ˈeɪliən/ *a* ajeno; (foreign) extranjero; extraño; contrario. —*n* extranjero (-ra). **a. to,** ajeno a; repugnante a. **Aliens Department,** Sección de Extranjeros, *f*

alienable /ˈeɪliənəbəl/ *a* enajenable

alienate /ˈeɪliəˌneɪt/ *vt* alejar, hacer indiferente; (property) enajenar, traspasar

alienation /ˌeɪliəˈneɪʃən/ *n* desvío, *m;* enajenación, *f;* traspaso, *m;* enajenación mental, *f*

alight /əˈlaɪt/ *vi* apearse (de), bajar (de); desmontar (de); (of birds, etc.) posarse (sobre)

alight /əˈlaɪt/ *a* encendido, iluminado; en llamas

align /əˈlaɪn/ *vt* alinear

alignment /əˈlaɪnmənt/ *n* alineación, *f*

alike /əˈlaɪk/ *a* semejante; igual. —*adv* del mismo modo; igualmente

alimentary /ˌæləˈmɛntəri/ *a* nutritivo; alimenticio. **a. canal,** tubo digestivo, *m*

alimentation /ˌæləmɛnˈteɪʃən/ *n* alimentación, *f*

alimony /ˈæləˌmouni/ *n Law.* alimentos, *m pl,* pensión alimenticia, *f*

alive /əˈlaɪv/ *a* viviente; vivo; del mundo; (busy) animado, concurrido; (aware) sensible; (alert) lleno de vida, enérgico, despierto. **He is still a.,** Aún vive. **He is the best man a.,** Es el mejor hombre que existe, Es el mejor hombre del mundo. **half-a.,** semivivo. **while a.,** en vida. **a. to,** consciente de, sensible de. **a. with,** plagado de, lleno de

alkali /ˈælkəˌlaɪ/ *n* álcali, *m*

alkaline /ˈælkəˌlaɪn/ *a* alcalino

alkaloid /ˈælkəˌlɔɪd/ *n* alcaloide, *m*

all /ɔl/ *a* todo, *m;* toda, *f;* todos, *m pl;* todas, *f pl;* (in games) iguales. —*adv* enteramente, completamente; del todo; absolutamente. **after all,** después de todo; sin embargo. **at all,** nada; de ninguna manera; en absoluto. **fifteen all,** (tennis) quince iguales. **for good and all,** para siempre. **if that's all,** si no es más que eso. **in all,** en conjunto. **It is all one to me,** Me da igual. **not at all,** de ningún modo, nada de eso; nada; (never) jamás; (as a polite formula) No hay de qué. **once for all,** una vez por todas; por última vez. **That is all,** Eso es todo. **all along,** (of time) siempre, todo el tiempo; (of place) a lo largo de, de un extremo a otro de. **all but,** (almost) casi, por poco; (except) todo menos. **all joking aside,** fuera de burla. **all of them,** todos ellos, *m pl;* todas ellas, *f pl.* **All right!** ¡Bien! ¡Está bien! ¡Entendido! **all that,** todo eso; (as much as) cuanto. **all that which,** todo lo que. **all those who,** todos los que, *m pl;* todas las que, *f pl.* **all the more,** cuanto más. **all the same,** sin embargo, a pesar de todo. **all the worse,** tanto peor

all /ɔl/ *n* todo, *m;* todas, *m pl;* todas, *f pl;* (everyone, all men) todo el mundo. **to lose one's all,** perder todo lo que se tiene. **All is lost,** Todo se ha perdido. **all told,** en conjunto

all /ɔl/ (in compounds) **all-absorbing,** que todo lo absorbe; sumamente interesante. **all-bountiful,** de suma bondad. **all-conquering,** invicto. **all-consuming,** que todo lo consume; irresistible; ardiente. **all-enduring,** resignado a todo. **All Fools' Day,** Día de los Inocentes, *m,* (December 28). **all-fours,** a cuatro patas; a gatas. **to go on all fours,** andar a gatas. **All hail!** ¡Salud! ¡Bienvenido! **all-important,** sumamente importante. **all-in insurance,** seguro contra todo riesgo, *m.* **all-in wrestling,** lucha libre, *f.* **all-loving,** de un amor infinito. **all-merciful,** de una compasión infinita, sumamente misericordioso. **all-powerful,** omnipotente, todo poderoso. **all-round,** completo, cabal; universal. **an all-round athlete,** un atleta completo. **All Souls' Day,** Día de las Ánimas, Día de los difuntos, *m.* **all-wise,** omniscio

Allah /'ælə/ *n* Alá, *m*

allay /ə'lei/ *vt* calmar; (relieve) aliviar; apaciguar

allaying /ə'leiiŋ/ *n* alivio, *m;* apaciguamiento, *m*

allegation /,ælɪ'geiʃən/ *n* alegación, *f*

allege /ə'ledʒ/ *vt* afirmar, declarar; alegar

allegiance /ə'lidʒəns/ *n* lealtad, *f;* fidelidad, *f;* obediencia, *f*

allegorical /,ælɪ'gɔrɪkəl/ *a* alegórico

allegory /'ælə,gɔri/ *n* alegoría, *f*

alleluia /,ælə'luyə/ *n* aleluya, *mf*

allergic /ə'lɜrdʒɪk/ *a* alérgico

allergist /'ælərdʒɪst/ *n* alergólogo, *m*

allergy /'ælərdʒi/ *n* alergia, *f*

alleviate /ə'livi,eit/ *vt* aliviar

alleviation /ə,livi'eiʃən/ *n* alivio, *m;* mitigación, *f*

alley /'æli/ *n* callejuela, *f,* callejón, *m;* avenida, *f;* (skittle a.) pista de bolos, *f.* **a.-way,** *Naut.* pasadizo, *m*

alliance /ə'laiəns/ *n* alianza, *f;* parentesco, *m*

allied /'ælaid/ *a* aliado; allegado

alligator /'ælɪ,geitər/ *n* caimán, *m.* **a. pear,** avocado, *m*

alliteration /ə,lɪtə'reiʃən/ *n* aliteración, *f*

allocate /'ælə,keit/ *vt* asignar, destinar; distribuir, repartir

allocation /,ælə'keiʃən/ *n* asignación, *f;* distribución, *f,* repartimiento, *m*

allotment /ə'lɔtmənt/ *n* repartimiento, *m,* distribución, *f;* porción, *f;* lote, *m;* parcela de tierra, huerta, *f*

allow /ə'lau/ *vt* permitir; autorizar; dejar; tolerar, sufrir; (provide) dar; conceder, otorgar; (acknowledge) admitir; confesar; (discount) descontar; (a pension) hacer; deducir. **to a. for,** tener en cuenta; ser indulgente con; deducir; dejar (espacio, etc.) para

allowable /ə'lauəbəl/ *a* admisible, permisible; lícito, legítimo

allowance /ə'lauəns/ *n* ración, *f;* (discount) descuento, *m;* pensión, *f;* concesión, *f;* excusa, *f;* (subsidy) subsidio, *m;* (bonus) abono, *m;* (monthly) mesada, *f.* **to make a. for,** tener presente; hacer excusas para, ser indulgente con

alloy /*n* 'æbi, *v* ə'bi/ *n* aleación, *f;* liga, *f;* mezcla, *f.* —*vt* alear, ligar; mezclar

allspice /'ɔl,spais/ *n* guindilla de Indias, *f*

all-star game /'ɔl,stɑr/ *n* juego de estrellas, *m*

allude /ə'lud/ *vi* aludir (a), referirse (a)

allure /ə'lʊr/ *vt* convidar, provocar; atraer; seducir, fascinar

allurement /ə'lʊrmənt/ *n* (snare) añagaza, *f;* atracción, *f;* tentación, seducción, *f*

alluring /ə'lʊrɪŋ/ *a* atractivo, seductor, tentador; (promising) halagüeño

allusion /ə'luʒən/ *n* alusión, referencia, *f;* insinuación, *f*

allusive /ə'lusɪv/ *a* alusivo

ally /*n* 'ælai, *v* ə'lai/ *n* aliado (-da), allegado (-da); asociado (-da); (state) aliado, *m.* —*vt* unir. **to become allies,** aliarse

almanac /'ɔlmə,næk/ *n* almanaque, *m*

almighty /ɔl'maiti/ *a* omnipotente

almond /'ɑmənd/ *n* almendra, *f;* (tree) almendro, *m.* **bitter a.,** almendra amarga, *f.* **green a.,** almendruco, *m.* **milk of almonds,** horchata de almendras, *f;* (for the hands) loción de almendras, *f.* **sugar a.,** almendra garapiñada, *f.* **a.-eyed,** con, or de, ojos rasgados. **a. paste,** pasta de almendras, *f.* **a.-shaped,** en forma de almendra, almendrado

almost /'ɔlmoust/ *adv* casi; por poco

alms /ɑmz/ *n* limosna, *f.* **to ask a.,** pedir limosna, mendigar. **to give a.,** dar limosna. **a.-box,** cepillo de limosna, *m*

almsgiving /'ɑmz,gɪvɪŋ/ *n* caridad, *f*

aloe /'ælou/ *n* áloe, *m; pl* **aloes,** *Med.* acíbar, *m*

aloft /ə'lɔft/ *adv* arriba, en alto

alone /ə'loun/ *a* solo; solitario. —*adv* a solas, sin compañía; solamente; únicamente. **to leave a.,** dejar solo; dejar en paz

along /ə'lɔŋ/ *adv* adelante; a lo largo; todo el tiempo. —*prep* a lo largo de; por; al lado (de); en compañía (de). **Come a.!** ¡Ven! **all a.,** todo el tiempo, desde el principio; a lo largo de. **a. with,** junto con; en compañía de

alongside /ə'lɔŋ'said/ *adv* al lado; *Naut.* al costado. —*prep* junto a, al lado de; *Naut.* al costado de. **to bring a.,** *Naut.* abarloar. **to come a.,** *Naut.* acostarse

aloof /ə'luf/ *adv* a distancia; lejos. —*a* altanero, esquivo; reservado. **to keep a.,** mantenerse alejado

aloofness /ə'lufnɪs/ *n* alejamiento, *m;* esquivez, *f;* reserva, *f*

aloud /ə'laud/ *adv* en alta voz, alto

alpaca /æl'pækə/ *n* alpaca, *f*

alphabet /'ælfə,bet/ *n* alfabeto, *m;* abecedario, *m*

alphabetical /,ælfə'betɪkəl/ *a* alfabético

Alpine /'ælpain/ *a* alpestre, alpino

Alps, the /ælps/ los Alpes, *m*

already /ɔl'redi/ *adv* ya; previamente

Alsace /æl'sæs, -'seis/ Alsacia, *f*

Alsatian /æl'seiʃən/ *a* and *n* alsaciano (-nat. **A. dog,** perro policía, perro pastor alemán, perro lobo, *m*

also /'ɔlsou/ *adv* también, igualmente, además

altar /'ɔltər/ *n* altar, *m.* **high a.,** altar mayor, *m.* **to lead a woman to the a.,** llevar a una mujer a la iglesia. **a.-cloth,** mantel del altar, *m.* **a.-piece,** retablo, *m.* **a.-rail,** mesa del altar, *f*

altar boy *n* acólito, monaguillo, *m*

altar girl *n* acólita, monaguilla, *f*

altar server *n* acólito, monaguillo, *m* (male), acólita, monaguilla, *f* (female)

alter /'ɔltər/ *vt* cambiar; alterar; modificar; corregir; transformar; (clothes) arreglar. —*vi* cambiar

alterable /'ɔltərəbəl/ *a* alterable

alteration /,ɔltə'reiʃən/ *n* cambio, *m,* alteración, *f;* modificación, *f;* corrección, *f;* innovación, *f;* (to buildings, etc.) reforma, *f;* renovación, *f;* arreglo, *m*

altercation /,ɔltər'keiʃən/ *n* altercación, *f*

alternate /*a* 'ɔltərnit; *v* -,neit/ *a* alternativo; (*Bot.* and of rhymes) alterno. —*vt* and *vi* alternar

alternately /'ɔltərnitli/ *adv* alternativamente; por turno

alternating /'ɔltər,neitɪŋ/ *a* alternador. **a. current,** *Elec.* corriente alterna, *f*

alternation /,ɔltər'neiʃən/ *n* alternación, *f;* (of time) transcurso, *m;* turno, *m*

alternative /ɔl'tɜrnətɪv/ *n* alternativa, *f,* a alternativo, alterno. **to have no a. but,** no poder menos de

alternatively /ɔl'tɜrnətɪvli/ *adv* alternativamente

alternative medicine /ɔl'tɜrnətɪv 'medəsɪn/ *n* medicina alternativa, *f*

alternator /'ɔltər,neitər/ *n* *Elec.* alternador, *m*

although /ɔl'ðou/ *conjunc* aunque, bien que; si bien; no obstante, a pesar de

altimeter /æl'tɪmɪtər/ *n* *Aer.* altímetro, *m*

altitude /'æltɪ,tud/ *n* altitud, elevación, *f;* altura, *f*

alto /'æltou/ *n* (voice) contralto, *m;* (singer) contralto, *mf;* viola, *f*

altogether /,ɔltə'geðər/ *adv* completamente; del todo; en conjunto

altruism /'æltru,ɪzəm/ *n* altruísmo, *m*

altruist /'æltruɪst/ *n* altruista, *mf*

aluminum /ə'lumənəm/ *n* aluminio, *m*

aluminum foil *n* hoja de aluminio, *f*

always /'ɔlweiz/ *adv* siempre

amalgam /ə'mælgəm/ *n* amalgama, *f;* mezcla, *f*

amalgamate /ə'mælgə,meit/ *vt* amalgamar; combinar, unir. —*vi* amalgamarse; combinarse, unirse

amalgamation /ə,mælgə'meiʃən/ *n* amalgamación, *f;* combinación, *f;* mezcla, *f*

amanuensis /ə,mænyu'ensɪs/ *n* amanuense, *mf;* secretario (-ia)

amass /ə'mæs/ *vt* acumular, amontonar

amateur /'æmə,tʃʊr/ *a* and *n* aficionado (-da), (sports) no profesional. **a. theatricals,** función de aficionados, *f*

amateurish /'æmə,tʃʊrɪʃ/ a no profesional; de aficionado; superficial; (clumsy) torpe

amatory /'æmə,tɔri/ a amatorio

amaze /ə'meiz/ vt asombrar, sorprender; pasmar; confundir

amazed /ə'meizd/ a asombrado; sorprendido; admirado; asustado

amazement /ə'meizmənt/ n asombro, pasmo, m; sorpresa, f; (wonderment) admiración, f; estupor, m

amazing /ə'meizɪŋ/ a asombroso, pasmoso; sorprendente

amazingly /ə'meizɪŋli/ adv asombrosamente

Amazon /'æmə,zɒn/ n amazona, f

Amazon River, the el (Río de las) Amazonas, m

ambassador /æm'bæsədər/ n embajador, m

ambassadress /æm'bæsədrɪs/ n embajadora, f

amber /'æmbər/ n ámbar, m, a ambarino

ambergris /'æmbər,gris/ n ámbar gris, m

ambidextrous /,æmbɪ'dekstrəs/ a ambidextro

ambiguity /,æmbɪ'gyuɪti/ n ambigüedad, f

ambiguous /æm'bɪgyuəs/ a ambiguo, equivoco

ambition /æm'bɪʃən/ n ambición, f

ambitious /æm'bɪʃəs/ a ambicioso. **to be a. to,** ambicionar

amble /'æmbəl/ n (of a horse) paso de andadura, m; paso lento, m. —vi (of a horse) andar a paso de andadura; andar lentamente

ambulance /'æmbyələns/ n ambulancia, f. **a. corps,** cuerpo de sanidad, m. **a. man,** sanitario, f

ambulatory /'æmbyələ,tɔri/ n paseo, m; claustro, m, a ambulante

ambush /'æmbʊʃ/ n acecho, m, asechanza, f; Mil. emboscada, f. —vt acechar, asechar; Mil. emboscar; sorprender. **to be in a.,** emboscarse, estar en acecho

ameba /ə'mibə/ n amiba, f

amelioration /ə,milyə'reiʃən/ n mejora, f

amen /'ei'mɛn, 'ɑ'mɛn/ n amén, m

amenable /ə'minəbəl/ a sujeto (a); responsable; dócil; fácil de convencer, dispuesto a ser razonable; dispuesto a escuchar. **to make a. to reason,** hacer razonable

amend /ə'mɛnd/ vt enmendar; modificar. —vi reformarse

amendment /ə'mɛndmənt/ n enmienda, f; modificación, f

amends /ə'mɛndz/ n pl reparación, f; satisfacción, f; compensación, f. **to make a.,** dar satisfacción

amenity /ə'mɛnɪti/ n amenidad, f

America /ə'mɛrɪkə/ América, f

American /ə'mɛrɪkən/ n americano (-na); (U.S.A.) norteamericano (-na). —a americano, de América; norteamericano, de los Estados Unidos. **Central A.,** a and n centroamericano (-na). **A. bar,** bar americano, m

Americanism /ə'mɛrɪkə,nɪzəm/ n americanismo, m

Americanize /ə'mɛrɪkə,naiz/ vt americanizar

amethyst /'æməθɪst/ n amatista, f

amiability /,eimiə'bɪlɪti/ n amabilidad, afabilidad, cordialidad, f

amiable /'eimiəbəl/ a amable, afable, cordial

amiably /'eimiəbli/ adv amablemente, con afabilidad

amicable /'æmɪkəbəl/ a amigable, amistoso

amicably /'æmɪkəbli/ adv amigablemente

amice /'æmɪs/ n amito, m

amid, amidst /ə'mɪd; ə'mɪdst/ prep en medio de; entre; rodeado por

amidships /ə'mɪd,ʃɪps/ adv en el centro del buque, en medio del navío

amiss /ə'mɪs/ adv mal; de más; (ill) indispuesto, enfermo; (inopportunely) inoportunamente. —a malo. **It would not come a.,** No vendría mal. **to take a.,** llevar a mal

ammeter /'æm,mitər/ n Elec. amperímetro, m

ammonia /ə'mounyə/ n amoníaco, m

ammunition /,æmyə'nɪʃən/ n munición, f. **a. box,** cajón de municiones, m

amnesia /æm'niʒə/ n amnesia, f

amnesty /'æmnəsti/ n amnistía, f. **to concede an a. to,** amnistiar

amok /ə'mʌk/ **(to run a.)** atacar a ciegas

among /ə'mʌŋ/ prep en medio de; entre; con

amoral /ei'mɔrəl/ a amoral

amorality /,eimə'rælɪti/ n amoralidad, f

amorous /'æmərəs/ a amoroso; (tender) tierno

amorousness /'æmərəsnɪs/ n erotismo, m; galantería, f

amorphous /ə'mɔrfəs/ a amorfo

amortization /,æmərtə'zeiʃən/ n amorcización, f

amortize /'æmər,taiz/ vt amortizar

amount /ə'maunt/ n importe, m, suma, f; cantidad, f, vi (to) subir a, ascender a, llegar a; valer; reducirse a. **gross a.,** importe bruto, m. **net a.,** importe líquido, importe neto, m. **It amounts to the same thing, then,** Es igual entonces, Viene a ser lo mismo pues. **What he says amounts to this,** Lo que dice se reduce a esto

amperage /'æmpərɪdʒ/ n amperaje, m

ampere /'æmpɪər/ n amper, amperio, m

amphibian /æm'fɪbiən/ n anfibio, m

amphibious /æm'fɪbiəs/ a anfibio

amphitheater /'æmfə,θiətər/ n anfiteatro, m

amphora /'æmfərə/ n ánfora, f

ample /'æmpəl/ a amplio; abundante; extenso, vasto; (sufficient) bastante, suficiente

amplification /,æmpləfɪ'keiʃən/ n amplificación, f

amplifier /'æmplə,faiər/ n amplificador, m

amplify /'æmplə,fai/ vt amplificar; aumentar, ampliar

amplitude /'æmplɪ,tud/ n amplitud, f; abundancia, f; extensión, f

amply /'æmpli/ adv ampliamente; abundantemente; suficientemente

amputate /'æmpyu,teit/ vt amputar

amputation /,æmpyu'teiʃən/ n amputación, f

amulet /'æmyəlɪt/ n amuleto, m

amuse /ə'myuz/ vt divertir, entretener, distraer. **to a. oneself,** divertirse; pasarlo bien

amusement /ə'myuzmənt/ n diversión, f, entretenimiento, m; (hobby) pasatiempo, m. **a. park,** parque de atracciones, m

amusing /ə'myuzɪŋ/ a divertido, entretenido; (of people) salado

amusingly /ə'myuzɪŋli/ adv de un modo divertido, entretenidamente

an /ən/ See a

Anabaptist /,ænə'bæptɪst/ n anabaptista, mf

anachronism /ə'nækrə,nɪzəm/ n anacronismo, m

anachronistic /ə,nækrə'nɪstɪk/ a anacrónico

anagram /'ænə,græm/ n anagrama, m

analects /'ænḷ,ɛkts/ n pl analectas, f pl

analgesia /,ænḷ'dʒiziə/ n analgesia, f

analgesic /,ænḷ'dʒizɪk/ a and n analgésico, m.

analogous /ə'næləgəs/ a análogo

analogy /ə'nælədʒi/ n analogía, f

analysis /ə'næləsɪs/ n análisis, m

analyst /'ænḷɪst/ n analista, mf

analytical /,ænḷ'ɪtɪkəl/ a analítico

analyze /'ænḷ,aiz/ vt analizar

anaphora /ə'næfərə/ n anáfora, f

anarchic /æn'ɑrkɪk/ a anárquico

anarchism /'ænər,kɪzəm/ n anarquismo, m

anarchist /'ænərkɪst/ n anarquista, mf

anarchy /'ænərki/ n anarquía, f

anastigmatic /,ænəstɪg'mætɪk/ a anastigmático

anathema /ə'næθəmə/ n anatema, mf

anathematize /ə'næθəmə,taiz/ vt anatematizar

anatomic /,ænə'tɒmɪk/ a anatómico

anatomically /,ænə'tɒmɪkli/ adv anatómicamente; físicamente

anatomist /ə'nætəmɪst/ n anatomista, mf

anatomy /ə'nætəmi/ n anatomía, f

ancestor /'ænsɛstər/ n antepasado, abuelo, m

ancestral /æn'sɛstrəl/ a de sus antepasados; de familia; hereditario. **a. home,** casa solariega, f

ancestry /'ænsɛstri/ n antepasados, m pl; linaje, abolengo, m; estirpe, f; nacimiento, m; origen, m

anchor /'æŋkər/ n ancla, f. Fig. áncora, f. —vt sujetar con el ancla. —vi anclar, echar anclas, fondear. **at a.,** al ancla. **drag a.,** ancla flotante, ancla de arrastre, f. **sheet a.,** ancla de la esperanza, f; Fig. ancla de salvación, f. **to drop a.,** anclar. **to ride at a.,** estar al ancla. **to weigh a.,** levar el ancla

anchorage /'æŋkərɪdʒ/ n anclaje, m; ancladero, fondeadero, m; derechos de anclaje, m pl

anchorite /'æŋkə,raɪt/ n anacoreta, mf

anchovy /'æntʃouvi/ n anchoa, f, boquerón, m

ancient /'einʃənt/ a anciano; antiguo. —n pl **ancients**, los antiguos. **from a. times**, de antiguo. **most a.**, antiquísimo

and /ænd, ənd/ conjunc y; (before stressed i or hi) e; (after some verbs and before infin.) de, a; que; (with) con; (often not translated before infins.). **Better and better**, Mejor que mejor. **I shall try and do it**, Trataré de hacerlo. **to come and see**, venir a ver. **We shall try and speak to him**, Procuraremos hablar con él

Andalusia /,ændļ'uʒə/ Andalucía, f

Andalusian /,ændļ'uʒən/ a andaluz. —n andaluz (-za). **A. hat**, sombrero calañés, m

Andean /'ændiən/ a andino

Andes, the /'ændiz/ los Andes, f

andiron /'ænd,aiᵊrn/ n morillo, m

Andorran /æn'dɔrən/ a and n andorrano (-na)

androgynous /æn'drɒdʒənəs/ a andrógino

anecdotal /'ænɪk,doutļ/ a anecdótico

anecdote /'ænɪk,dout/ n anécdota, f

anemia /ə'nimiə/ n anemia, f

anemic /ə'nimɪk/ a anémico

anemometer /,ænə'mɒmɪtər/ n anemómetro, m

anemone /ə'nɛmə,ni/ n anémona, anémone, f

aneroid /'ænə,rɔɪd/ a aneroide. —n barómetro aneroide, m

anesthesia /,ænəs'θiʒə/ n anestesia, f

anesthetic /,ænəs'θɛtɪk/ a and n acólito, monaguillo, m

anesthetist /ə'nɛsθɪtɪst/ n anestesiador (-ra)

anesthetize /ə'nɛsθɪ,taiz/ vt anestesiar

aneurism /'ænyə,rɪzəm/ n aneurisma, mf

angel /'eindʒəl/ n ángel, m

angelic /æn'dʒɛlɪk/ a angélico

angelica /æn'dʒɛlɪkə/ n angélica, f

angelus /'ændʒələs/ n ángelus, m

anger /'æŋgər/ n cólera, ira, f, enojo, m, vt enojar, encolerizar; hacer rabiar

angina /æn'dʒainə/ n angina, f. **a. pectoris**, angina de pecho, f

angle /'æŋgəl/ n ángulo, m; rincón, m; esquina, f; (of a roof) caballette, m; Fig. punto de vista, m, vi pescar con caña. **at an a.**, a un lado. **a.-iron**, hierro angular, m. **to a. for**, pescar; Fig. procurar obtener

Angle /'æŋgəl/ a and n anglo (-la)

angler /'æŋglər/ n pescador (-ra) de caña

Anglican /'æŋglɪkən/ a and n anglicano (-na)

Anglicanism /'æŋglɪkə,nɪzəm/ n anglicanismo, m

Anglicism /'æŋglə,sɪzəm/ n anglicismo, inglesismo, m

Anglicize /'æŋglə,saiz/ vt inglesar

angling /'æŋglɪŋ/ n pesca con caña, f

Anglo- (in compounds) anglo-. **A.-American**, a and n angloamericano (-na). **A.-Indian**, a and n angloindio (-ia). **A.-Saxon**, a and n anglosajón (-ona); (language) anglosajón, m

anglomania /,æŋglə'meiniə/ n anglomanía, f

anglophile /'æŋglə,fail/ n anglófilo (-la)

anglophobia /,æŋglə'foubiə/ n anglofobia, f

angora /æŋ'gɔrə/ n angora, f. **a. cat**, gato de angora, m. **a. rabbit**, conejo de angora, m

angrily /'æŋgrəli/ adv airadamente

angry /'æŋgri/ a (of persons) enfadado, enojado, airado; (of waves, etc.) furioso; Med. inflamado; (red) rojo; (scowling) ceñudo; (dark) obscuro. **to be a.**, estar enojado. **to grow a.**, enojarse, enfadarse; (of waves) encresparse; (of the sky) obscurecerse. **to make a.**, enojar

anguish /'æŋgwɪʃ/ n agonía, f, dolor, m; angustia, f. —vt angustiar

angular /'æŋgyələr/ a angular; (of features, etc.) anguloso

angularity /,æŋgyə'lærɪti/ n angulosidad, f

anhydrous /æn'haidrəs/ a anhidro

aniline /'ænlɪn/ n anilina, f

animal /'ænəməl/ a and n animal m. **a. fat**, grasa animal, f. **a. kingdom**, reino animal, m. **a. spirits**, Philos. espíritus animales, m pl; brío, m, energía, f

animalism /'ænəmə,lɪzəm/ n animalidad, f; sensualidad, f

animate /v 'ænə,meit/ a -mɪt/ vt animar; inspirar. —a animado; viviente

animated /'ænə,meitɪd/ a animado; vivo, lleno de vida

animation /,ænə'meiʃən/ n animación, f; vivacidad, f; calor, fuego, m

animism /'ænə,mɪzəm/ n animismo, m

animosity /,ænə'mɒsɪti/ n animosidad, hostilidad, f

aniseed /'ænə,sid/ n anís, m

anisette /,ænə'sɛt/ n (liqueur) anisete, m

ankle /'æŋkəl/ n tobillo, m. **a. bone**, hueso del tobillo, m. **a. sock**, calcetín corto, m

anklet /'æŋklɪt/ n brazalete para el tobillo, m; (support) tobillera, f

annals /'ænļz/ n pl anales, m pl

anneal /ə'nil/ vt (metals) recocer; (glass) templar; (with oil) atemperar

annex /v ə'nɛks; 'ænɛks; n 'ænɛks/ vt unir, juntar; anexar. —n anexo, m

annexation /,ænɪk'seiʃən/ n anexión, f

annihilate /ə'naiə,leit/ vt aniquilar

annihilation /ə,naiə'leiʃən/ n aniquilación, f

anniversary /,ænə'vɜrsəri/ a and n aniversario, m.

annotate /'ænə,teit/ vt anotar, acotar, comentar, hacer anotaciones a

annotation /,ænə'teiʃən/ n anotación, f; nota, f

annotator /'ænə,teitər/ n anotador (-ra), comentador (-ra)

announce /ə'nauns/ vt proclamar; declarar; publicar; anunciar

announcement /ə'naunsmənt/ n proclama, f; declaración, f; publicación, f; anuncio, m; (of a betrothal) participación, f

announcer /ə'naunsər/ n anunciador (-ra); (radio or TV) locutor (-ra)

annoy /ə'nɔi/ vt exasperar, irritar, disgustar; molestar, incomodar

annoyance /ə'nɔiəns/ n disgusto, m, exasperación, f; molestia, f, fastidio, m

annoying /ə'nɔiiŋ/ a enojoso, molesto, fastidioso

annual /'ænyuəl/ a anual. —n anuario, m; calendario, m; planta anual, f

annually /'ænyuəli/ adv anualmente, cada año

annuitant /ə'nuitnt/ n censualista, mf

annuity /ə'nuti/ n anualidad, pensión vitalicia, f

annul /ə'nʌl/ vt anular

annulment /ə'nʌlmənt/ n anulación, f

annunciation /ə,nʌnsi'eiʃən/ n anunciación, f. **the A.**, la Anunciación

anodyne /'ænə,dain/ a and n anodino, m

anoint /ə'nɔint/ vt untar; (before death) olear; (a king, etc.) ungir

anointing /ə'nɔintiŋ/ n unción, f

anomalous /ə'nɒmələs/ a anómalo

anomaly /ə'nɒməli/ n anomalía, f

anonymity /,ænə'nimiti/ n anónimo, m

anonymous /ə'nɒnəməs/ a anónimo. **a. letter**, anónimo, m

anonymously /ə'nɒnəməsli/ adv anónimamente

another /ə'nʌðər/ a otro; (different) distinto. —n otro, m; otra, f. **For one thing... and for a.**, En primer lugar... y además (y por otra cosa). **one after a.**, uno después de otro. **They love one a.**, Ellos se aman. **They sent it from one to a.**, Lo mandaron de uno a otro

answer /'ænsər, 'ɑn-/ n contestación, respuesta, f; (refutation) refutación, f; (pert reply) réplica, f; (solution) solución, f; Math. resultado, m; Law. contestación a la demanda, f

answer /'ænsər, 'ɑn-/ vt responder, contestar; (a letter, etc.) contestar a; (refute) refutar; (reply pertly) replicar; (write) escribir; (return) devolver; (suit) servir; (a bell, etc.) acudir a; (the door) abrir. —vi contestar; (succeed) tener éxito; dar resultado. **to a. by return**, contestar a vuelta de correo, **to a. back**, replicar. **to a. for**, ser responsable por; ser responsable de; (speak for) hablar por; (guarantee) garantizar, responder de

answerable /'ænsərəbəl/ a responsable; refutable;

(adequate) adecuado. **to make a. for,** hacer responsable de

answering machine n contestador telefónico, contestador, m

ant /ænt/ n hormiga, f. **ant-eater,** oso hormiguero, m. **ant-hill,** hormiguero, m

antagonism /æn'tægə,nɪzəm/ n antagonismo, m, hostilidad, oposición, f

antagonist /æn'tægənɪst/ n antagonista, mf

antagonistic /æn,tægə'nɪstɪk/ a antagónico, hostil

antagonize /æn'tægə,naiz/ vt contender; hacer hostil (a)

antarctic /ænt'ɑrktɪk/ a antártico. —n polo antártico, m

antecedent /,æntə'sidn̩t/ a and n antecedente, m.

antechamber /'ænti,tʃeimbər/ n antecámara, antesala, f

antedate /'ænti,deit/ vt antedatar; anticipar

antediluvian /,æntidɪ'luviən/ a antediluviano

antelope /'ænti,oup/ n antílope, m

antenna /æn'tɛnə/ n antena, f

anterior /æn'tɪəriər/ a anterior

anthem /'ænθəm/ n antífona, f

anthologist /æn'θɒlədʒɪst/ n antólogo, m

anthology /æn'θɒlədʒi/ n antología, floresta, f

anthracite /'ænθrə,sait/ n antracita, f, carbón mineral, m

anthrax /'ænθræks/ n ántrax, m

anthropological /,ænθrəpə'lɒdʒɪkəl/ a antropológico

anthropologist /,ænθrə'pɒlədʒɪst/ n antropólogo, m

anthropology /,ænθrə'pɒlədʒi/ n antropología, f

anti-aircraft /,ænti'ɛər,kræft, ,æntai-/ a antiaéreo. **A.A. gun,** cañon antiaéreo, m

antibody /'ænti,bɒdi/ n anticuerpo, m

antic /'æntɪk/ n travesura, f

Antichrist /'ænti,kraist/ n Anticristo, m

anticipate /æn'tɪsə,peit/ vt (foresee) prever; anticipar; adelantarse a; (hope) esperar; (frustrate) frustrar; (enjoy) disfrutar con anticipación de

anticipation /æn,tɪsə'peiʃən/ n anticipación, f; adelantamiento, m; esperanza, expectación, f. **in a. of,** en espera de

anticipatory /æn'tɪsəpə,tɔri/ a anticipador

anticlerical /'ænti'klɛrɪkəl, ,æntai-/ a anticlerical

anticlericalism /,ænti'klɛrɪkə,lɪzəm, ,æntai-/ n anticlericalismo, m

anticlimax /,ænti'klaimæks, ,æntai-/ n anticlímax, m

antidote /'ænti,dout/ n antídoto, contraveneno, m

antifreeze /'ænti,friz/ n anticongelante, m

Antilles, the /æn'tɪliz/ las Antillas, f

antimony /'æntə,mouni/ n antimonio, m

antipathetic /,æntɪpə'θɛtɪk/ a antipático

antipathy /æn'tɪpəθi/ n antipatía, f

antipode /'ænti,poud/ n pl antípodas, mf pl

antiquarian /,ænti'kwɛəriən/ a anticuario

antiquary /'ænti,kwɛri/ n anticuario, m

antiquated /'ænti,kweitid/ a anticuado

antique /æn'tik/ a antiguo. —n antigüedad, antigualla, f. **a. dealer,** anticuario, m. **a. shop,** tienda de antigüedades, f

antiquity /æn'tɪkwɪti/ n antigüedad, f; ancianidad, f

antireligious /,æntiɪr'lɪdʒəs, ,æntai-/ a antirreligioso

antirepublican /,æntiɪr'pʌblɪkən/ a antirrepublicano

anti-Semitic /,æntisə'mɪtɪk, ,æntai-/ a antisemita

anti-Semitism /,ænti'sɛmi,tɪzəm, ,æntai-/ n antisemitismo, m

antiseptic /,æntə'sɛptɪk/ a and n antiséptico, m

antisocial /,ænti'souʃəl, ,æntai-/ a antisocial

antithesis /æn'tɪθəsɪs/ n antítesis, f

antithetic /,ænti'θɛtɪk/ a antitético

antitoxin /,ænti'tɒksɪn/ n antitoxina, f

antler /'æntlər/ n asta, f

antonym /'æntənɪm/ n contrario, m

antrum /'æntrəm/ n antro, m

Antwerp /'æntwɔrp/ Amberes, m

anus /'einəs/ n ano, m

anvil /'ænvɪl/ n yunque, m, bigornia, f

anxiety /æŋ'zaiɪti/ n inquietud, intranquilidad, f; preocupación, f; ansiedad, f; curiosidad, f; impaciencia, f; (wish) deseo, afán, m

anxious /'æŋkʃəs, 'æŋʃəs/ a inquieto, intranquilo;

preocupado; ansioso; impaciente; deseoso. **to be a.,** estar inquieto; apurarse. **to be a. to,** ansiar, tener deseos de. **to make a.,** preocupar, inquietar, intranquilizar

anxiously /'æŋkʃəsli, 'æŋʃəs-/ adv con inquietud; ansiosamente; impacientemente

any /'ɛni/ a cualquiera; (before the noun only) cualquier; (some) algún, m; alguna, f; (every) todo; (expressing condition or with interrogatives or negatives, following the noun) alguno, m; alguna, f, (is often not translated in a partitive sense, e.g. *Have you any butter? ¿Tienes mantequilla?*) —pron algo; (with the relevant noun) algún, etc.; lo, m, and neut; la, f; los, m pl; las, f pl. **He hasn't any pity,** No tiene piedad alguna. **at any rate,** de todos modos; por lo menos. **If there is any,** Si lo (la, etc.) hay. **in any case,** venga lo que venga. **not any,** ninguno, m; ninguna, f. **Whether any of them...,** Si alguno de ellos... **any further,** más lejos. **any longer,** más largo; (of time) más tiempo. **any more,** nada más; nunca más

anybody /'ɛni,bɒdi/ n and pron (someone) alguien; cualquiera, mf; (everyone) todo el mundo; (with a negative) nadie; (of importance) persona de importancia, f. **hardly a.,** casi nadie

anyhow /'ɛni,hau/ adv de cualquier modo; (with a negative) de ningún modo; de cualquier manera; (at least) por lo menos, en todo caso; (carelessly) sin cuidado

anyone /'ɛni,wʌn/ n. See **anybody**

anything /'ɛni,θɪŋ/ n algo, m, alguna cosa, f; (negative) nada; cualquier cosa, f; todo (lo que). **a. but,** todo menos

anyway /'ɛni,wei/ adv de todos modos, con todo; venga lo que venga; (anyhow) de cualquier modo

anywhere /'ɛni,wɛər/ adv en todas partes, dondequiera; en cualquier parte; (after a negative) en (o a) ninguna parte

A.O.B. (any other business) asuntos varios (on an agenda)

aorta /ei'ɔrtə/ n aorta, f

apart /ə'pɑrt/ adv aparte; a un lado; separadamente; separado (de); apartado (de). **a. from,** aparte de, dejando a un lado. **to keep a.,** mantener aislado; distinguir (entre). **to take a.,** desarmar. **wide a.,** muy distante

apartment /ə'pɑrtmənt/ n cuarto, m, habitación, f; (flat) piso, m

apathetic /,æpə'θɛtɪk/ a apático; indiferente

apathy /'æpəθi/ n apatía, f; indiferencia, f

ape /eip/ n simio, m

Apennines, the /'æpə,nainz/ los Apeninos, m

aperitive /ə'pɛrɪtɪv/ a and n aperitivo, m.

aperture /'æpərtʃər/ n abertura, f; agujero, m; orificio, m

apex /'eipɛks/ n ápice, m

aphasia /ə'feiʒə/ n afasia, f

aphorism /'æfə,rɪzəm/ n aforismo, m

aphrodisiac /,æfrə'dizi,æk/ a and n afrodisíaco, m

apiary /'eipi,ɛri/ n colmenar, f

apiece /ə'pis/ adv cada uno; por persona

apish /'eipɪʃ/ a simiesco, de simio; (affected) afectado; (foolish) tonto

aplomb /ə'plɒm/ n confianza en sí, f, aplomo, m

apocalypse /ə'pɒkəlɪps/ n Apocalipsis, m

apocalyptic /ə,pɒkə'lɪptɪk/ a apocalíptico

apocopate /ə'pɒkə,peit/ vt apocopar

Apocrypha /ə'pɒkrəfə/ n libros apócrifos, m pl

apocryphal /ə'pɒkrəfəl/ a apócrifo

apogee /'æpə,dʒi/ n apogeo, m

apologetic /ə,pɒlə'dʒɛtɪk/ a apologético

apologist /ə'pɒlədʒɪst/ n apologista, mf

apologize /ə'pɒlə,dʒaiz/ vi presentar sus excusas; disculparse, excusarse; (regret) sentir

apology /ə'pɒlədʒi/ n excusa, disculpa, f; defensa, apología, f; (makeshift) substituto, m

apoplectic /,æpə'plɛktɪk/ a and n apoplético (-ca)

apoplexy /'æpə,plɛksi/ n apoplegía, f

apostasy /ə'pɒstəsi/ n apostasía, f

apostate /ə'pɒsteit/ n apóstata, mf. renegado (-da)

apostatize /ə'pɒstə,taiz/ vi apostatar, renegar

apostle /ə'pɒsəl/ n apóstol, m. **Apostles' Creed,** el Credo de los Apóstoles

apostolic /ˌæpə'stɒlɪk/ a apostólico

apostrophe /ə'pɒstrəfi/ n apóstrofe, mf; (punctuation mark) apóstrofo, m

Apothecaries' weight peso de boticario, m

apothecary /ə'pɒθə,keri/ n apotecario, m

apothegm /'æpə,θem/ n apotegma, m

apotheosis /ə,pɒθi'ousɪs/ n apoteosis, f

appall /ə'pɒl/ vt horrorizar, espantar, aterrar

appalling /ə'pɒlɪŋ/ a espantoso, horrible

apparatus /ˌæpə'rætəs/ n aparato, m; máquina, f; instrumentos, m pl

apparel /ə'pærəl/ n ropa, f; vestiduras, f pl; ornamento, m. —vt vestir

apparent /ə'pærənt/ a aparente; visible; evidente, manifiesto; (of heirs) presunto. **to become a.,** manifestarse

apparently /ə'pærəntli/ adv al parecer, aparentemente

apparition /ˌæpə'rɪʃən/ n aparición, f, fantasma, espectro, m

appeal /ə'pil/ n súplica, f; llamamiento, m; (charm) atracción, f, encanto, m; Law. apelación, alzada, f. —vi (to) suplicar (a); hacer llamamiento (a); poner por testigo (a); recurrir a; llamar la atención de; interesar (a); (attract) atraer, encantar; Law. apelar. **It doesn't a. to him,** No le atrae, No le gusta. **to allow an a.,** revocar una sentencia apelada. **without a.,** inapelable

appealing /ə'pilɪŋ/ a suplicante; atrayente

appealingly /ə'pilɪŋli/ adv de un modo suplicante

appear /ə'pɪər/ vi (of persons and things) aparecer; (seem) parecer; (before a judge) comparecer, presentarse (ante el juez); (of books) publicarse; (of lawyers) representar; (of the dawn) rayar; (of the sun, etc.) salir; (show itself) manifestarse. **to cause to a.,** hacer presentarse; (show) hacer ver; (prove) demonstrar, probar

appearance /ə'pɪərəns/ n aparición, f; (show, semblance or look, aspect) apariencia, f; presencia, f; aspecto, m; (in court of law) comparecencia, f; (of a book) publicación, f; (arrival) llegada, f; (view) perspectiva, f; (ghost) aparición, f, fantasma, m. **first a.,** (of an actor, etc.) debut, m; (of a play) estreno, m. **to all appearances,** según las apariencias. **to make one's first a.,** aparecer por primera vez; Theat. debutar. **Appearances are deceptive,** Las apariencias engañan

appease /ə'piz/ vt apaciguar, aplacar, pacificar; satisfacer

appeasement /ə'pizmənt/ n apaciguamiento, aplacamiento, m, pacificación, f; satisfacción, f

appellant /ə'pelənt/ a and n Law. apelante, mf

appellation /ˌæpə'leiʃən/ n nombre, m; título, m

append /ə'pend/ vt añadir; (a seal) poner; (enclose) incluir, anexar

appendage /ə'pendɪdʒ/ n accesorio, m; (Bot. Zool.) apéndice, m

appendicitis /ə,pendə'saitɪs/ n apendicitis, f

appendix /ə'pendɪks/ n apéndice, m

appertain /ˌæpər'tein/ vi pertenecer (a)

appetite /'æpɪ,tait/ n apetito, m; Fig. hambre, f; deseo, m. **to have a bad a.,** no tener apetito, estar desganado. **to have a good a.,** tener buen apetito. **to whet the a.,** abrir el apetito

appetizer /'æpɪ,taizər/ n aperitivo, m

appetizing /'æpɪ,taizɪŋ/ a apetitoso

applaud /ə'plɒd/ vt and vi aplaudir; aclamar, ovacionar; celebrar

applause /ə'plɒz/ n aplauso, m; ovación, f; aprobación, alabanza, f

apple /'æpəl/ n manzana, f. **the a. of one's eye,** la niña de los ojos. **a. orchard,** manzanar, m. **a. sauce,** compota de manzanas, f. **a. tart,** pastel de manzanas, m. **a. tree,** manzano, m

appliance /ə'plaiəns/ n aparato, m; instrumento, m; utensilio, m; máquina, f

applicability /ˌæplɪkə'bɪliti/ n aplicabilidad, f

applicable /'æplɪkəbəl/ a aplicable

applicant /'æplɪkənt/ n candidato, m; aspirante, m; solicitante, mf

application /ˌæplɪ'keiʃən/ n aplicación, f; solicitud, f; petición, f; empleo, m. **on a.,** a solicitar

appliqué /ˌæplɪ'kei/ a aplicado. —n aplicación, f

apply /ə'plai/ vt aplicar; (use) emplear; (place) poner; (give) dar; (the brakes) frenar; vi ser aplicable; ser a propósito; dirigirse (a); acudir (a); (for a post) proponerse para. **a. for,** solicitar, pedir; (a post) proponerse para. **a. for admission (to...),** solicitar el ingreso (en...). **a. oneself to,** ponerse a; dedicarse a, consagrarse a

appoint /ə'pɔint/ vt (prescribe) prescribir, ordenar; señalar; asignar; (furnish) amueblar; equipar; (create) ate; crear, establecer; (to a post) nombrar, designar; (manage) gobernar; organizar. **at the appointed hour,** a la hora señalada. **well-appointed,** bien amueblado; bien equipado

appointive /ə'pɔintiv/ a por nombramiento

appointment /ə'pɔintmənt/ n (assignation) cita, f; (to a post) nombramiento, m; (post, office) cargo, m; creación, f. **By Royal A.,** Proveedor de la Real Casa. **to make an a. with,** citar

apportion /ə'pɔrʃən/ vt dividir; distribuir; prorratear; (taxes) derramar

apportionment /ə'pɔrʃənmənt/ n repartimiento, m, distribución, f; división, f; prorrateo, m

apposite /'æpəzit/ a a propósito, pertinente, oportuno; justo

appositeness /'æpəzitnis/ n pertinencia, oportunidad, f

appraisal /ə'preizəl/ n valoración, valuación, f; estimación, f

appraise /ə'preiz/ vt valorar, tasar; estimar

appreciable /ə'priʃiəbəl/ a apreciable, perceptible

appreciably /ə'priʃiəbli/ adv sensiblemente

appreciate /ə'priʃi,eit/ vt (understand) darse cuenta de, comprender; estimar; apreciar; (distinguish) distinguir. —vi encarecer, aumentar en valor; (of shares) subir, estar en alza

appreciation /ə,priʃi'eiʃən/ n (understanding) comprensión, f; apreciación, f; (recognition, etc.) aprecio, reconocimiento, m; (in value) aumento (en valor), m; subida de precio, f

appreciative /ə'priʃətiv/ a apreciativo

appreciatively /ə'priʃətivli/ adv con aprecio

appreciator /ə'priʃieitər/ n apreciador (-ra)

apprehend /ˌæprɪ'hend/ vt aprehender, prender; comprender, aprehender; (fear) temer

apprehension /ˌæprɪ'henʃən/ n aprehensión, comprensión, f; (fear) aprensión, f; (seizure) aprehensión, presa, f

apprehensive /ˌæprɪ'hensiv/ a aprehensivo; (fearful) aprensivo

apprehensiveness /ˌæprɪ'hensivnis/ n aprehensión, f; (fear) aprensión, f, temor, m

apprentice /ə'prentis/ n aprendiz (-za). **to bind a.,** poner de aprendiz

apprenticeship /ə'prentisʃip/ n aprendizaje, m. **to serve an a.,** hacer el aprendizaje

apprise /ə'praiz/ vt dar parte (de), informar (de)

approach /ə'proutʃ/ vt acercarse a; aproximarse a; (pull, etc. nearer) acercar, aproximar; (resemble) parecerse a, ser semejante a; (speak to) hablar con; entablar negociaciones con. —vi acercarse, aproximarse. —n acercamiento, m; (arrival) llegada, f; aproximación, f; (of night, etc.) avance, m; (entrance) entrada, f; avenida, f; vía, f; (step) paso, m; (to a subject) punto de vista (sobre), concepto (de), m; (introduction) introducción, f; pl **approaches** (environs) alrededores, m pl, inmediaciones, f pl; (seas) mares, m pl; (overtures) avances, m pl

approachable /ə'proutʃəbəl/ a accesible

approaching /ə'proutʃɪŋ/ a venidero, próximo, cercano

approbation /ˌæprə'beiʃən/ n asentimiento, m; aprobación, f

appropriate /a ə'proupriit, v -,eit/ a apropiado, conveniente; vt adueñarse de, tomar posesión de, apropiar

appropriately /ə'proupriitli/ adv propiamente; convenientemente; justamente

appropriateness /ə'proupriitnis/ n conveniencia, f; justicia, f

appropriation /ə,prouprɪ'eiʃən/ n apropiación, f; aplicación, f; empleo, m
approval /ə'pruvəl/ n aprobación, f; consentimiento, m. **on a.,** a prueba
approve /ə'pruv/ vt aprobar; confirmar; (sanction) autorizar, sancionar; ratificar; estar contento (de); (oneself) demostrarse. —vi aprobar
approved /ə'pruvd/ a aprobado; bien visto; (on documents) Visto Bueno (V° B°)
approximate /a ə'prɒksəmɪt; v -,meit/ a aproximado. —vt acercar. —vi aproximarse (a)
approximately /ə'prɒksəmɪtli/ adv aproximadamente, poco más o menos
approximation /ə,prɒksə'meiʃən/ n aproximación, f
appurtenance /ə'pɜrtnəns/ n accesorio, m, pertenencia, f
apricot /'æprɪ,kɒt/ n albaricoque, m. **a. tree,** albaricoquero, m
April /'eiprəl/ n abril, m, a abrileño. **A. Fool's Day,** el 1° de abril; (in Spain) el Día de los Inocentes (December 28)
apron /'eiprən/ n delantal, m; (of artisans and freemasons) mandil, m. **to be tied to a mother's a.-strings,** estar cosido a las faldas de su madre. **a.-stage,** proscenio, m. **a.-string,** cinta del delantal, f
apse /æps/ n ábside, mf
apt /æpt/ a apto, listo; propenso (a), inclinado (a); expuesto (a); (suitable) apropiado, oportuno
aptitude /'æptɪ,tud/ n aptitud, disposición, facilidad, f
aptly /'æptli/ adv apropiadamente; justamente, bien
aquamarine /,ækwəmə'rin/ n aguamarina, f
aquarelle /,ækwə'rel/ n acuarela, f
aquarellist /,ækwə'relɪst/ n acuarelista, mf
aquarium /ə'kwɛəriəm/ n acuario, m
Aquarius /ə'kwɛəriəs/ n Acuario, m
aquatic /ə'kwætɪk/ a acuático
aquatint /'ækwə,tɪnt/ n acuatinta, f
aqueduct /'ækwɪ,dʌkt/ n acueducto, m
aqueous /'ækwiəs/ a ácueo, acuoso
aquiline /'ækwə,lain/ a aguileño
Arab /'ærəb/ a árabe. —n árabe, mf
arabesque /,ærə'bɛsk/ n arabesco, m
Arabian /ə'reibiən/ a árabe, arábigo. **The A. Nights,** Las Mil y Una Noches
Arabic /'ærəbɪk/ a arábigo. —n (language) arábigo, árabe, m
Arabist /'ærəbɪst/ n arabista, mf
arable /'ærəbəl/ a cultivable, labrantío
Aragonese /,ærəgə'niz/ a and n aragonés (-esa)
arbiter /'arbɪtər/ n árbitro (-ra), arbitrador (-ra)
arbitrariness /'arbɪ,trerinɪs/ n arbitrariedad, f
arbitrary /'arbɪ,treri/ a arbitrario
arbitrate /'arbɪ,treit/ vi arbitrar, juzgar como árbitro; someter al arbitraje
arbitration /,arbɪ'treiʃən/ n arbitraje, m
arbitrator /'arbɪ,treitər/ See **arbiter**
arbor /'arbər/ n glorieta, f, emparrado, m
arc /ark/ n arco, m. **arc-light,** lámpara de arco, f
arcade /ar'keid/ n arcada, f; galería, f; pasaje, m
arch /artʃ/ n arco, m; (vault) bóveda, f. —vt abovedar; arquear; encorvar
arch /artʃ/ a (roguish) socarrón; (coy) coquetón
arch- /artʃ/ prefix archi-
archaic /ar'keiɪk/ a arcaico
archaism /'arkɪ,ɪzəm/ n arcaísmo, m
archangel /'ark,eindʒəl/ n arcángel, m
archbishop /'artʃ'bɪʃəp/ n arzobispo, m
archenemy /'artʃ'ɛnəmi/ n mayor enemigo (-ga); Demonio, m
archeological /,arkiə'lɒdʒɪkəl/ a arqueológico
archeologist /,arki'ɒlədʒɪst/ n arqueólogo, m
archeology /,arki'ɒlədʒi/ n arqueología, f
archer /'artʃər/ n flechero, saetera, m; Mil. arquero, m
archery /'artʃəri/ n ballestería, f
archery range n campo de tiro con arco, m
archfiend /'artʃ'find/ n demonio, m
arching /'artʃɪŋ/ n arqueo, m
archipelago /,arkə'peləgou/ n archipiélago, m
architect /'arkɪ,tɛkt/ n arquitecto, m
architectural /,arkɪ'tɛktʃərəl/ n arquitectónico

architecturally /,arkɪ'tɛktʃərəli/ adv arquitectónicamente; desde el punto de vista arquitectónico
architecture /'arkɪ,tɛktʃər/ n arquitectura, f
archive /'arkaiv/ n archivo, m
archivist /'arkəvɪst/ n archivero, m
archness /'artʃnɪs/ n coquetería, f; malicia, f
archway /'artʃ,wei/ n arcada, f, pasaje abovedado, m; arco, m
arctic /'arktɪk, 'artɪk/ a ártico; muy frío. **A. Circle,** Círculo ártico, m
ardent /'ardnt/ a ardiente; apasionado, vehemente; fogoso
ardently /'ardntli/ adv ardientemente; con vehemencia, apasionadamente
ardor /'ardər/ n ardor, m
arduous /'ardʒuəs/ a arduo, difícil
arduousness /'ardʒuəsnɪs/ n dificultad, arduidad, f
are /ar/ pl of present indicative of **be.** See **be. There are,** Hay
area /'ɛəriə/ n área, f; superficie, f; (extent) extensión, f; espacio, m; región, f; (of a house) patio, m; (of a concert hall, etc.) sala, f
area code n característica, f, (Chile) código territorial (Spain), prefijo (Spain), código interurbano, código (Argentina), m
arena /ə'rinə/ n arena, f
argent /'ardʒənt/ n Poet. blancura, f; Herald. argén, m
Argentinian /,ardʒən'tɪniən/ a and n argentino (-na)
argonaut /'argə,nɔt/ n (Zool. and Myth.) argonauta, m
argot /'argou, -gət/ n jerga, f; (thieves') germanía, f
arguable /'argyuəbəl/ a discutible
argue /'argyu/ vt discutir; persuadir; (prove) demostrar. —vi argüir, discutir; sostener. **to a. against,** hablar en contra de, oponer
arguing /'argyuɪŋ/ n razonamiento, m; argumentación, f; discusión, f
argument /'argyəmənt/ n argumento, m
argumentative /,argyə'mɛntətɪv/ a argumentador; contencioso
arid /'ærɪd/ a árido, seco
aridity /ə'rɪdɪti/ n aridez, f
Aries /'ɛəriz/ n Aries, m
arise /ə'raiz/ vi levantarse; (appear) surgir, aparecer; ofrecerse, presentarse; (of sound) hacerse oír; provenir (de); proceder (de); (result) hacerse sentir; (rebel) sublevarse
aristocracy /,ærə'stɒkrəsi/ n aristocracia, f
aristocrat /ə'rɪstə,kræt/ n aristócrata, mf
aristocratic /ə,rɪstə'krætɪk/ a aristocrático
Aristotelian /,ærəstə'tilyən/ a aristotélico
Aristotelianism /,ærəstə'tilyənɪzəm/ n aristotelismo, m
arithmetic /ə'rɪθmətɪk/ n aritmética, f
arithmetical /,ærɪθ'mɛtɪkəl/ a aritmético
ark /ark/ n arca, f. **Noah's ark,** arca de Noé, f. **Ark of the Covenant,** arca de la alianza, f
arm /arm/ n (Anat. Geog. Mech. of a chair, a cross, and Fig.) brazo, m; (lever) palanca, f; (of a tree) rama, f, brazo, m; (sleeve) manga, f; Naut. cabo de una verga, m; (weapon) arma, f; (of army, navy, etc.) ramo, m pl. **arms,** Herald. armas, f pl, escudo, m. **in arms,** en brazos; armado; en oposición. **To arms!** ¡A las armas! **to keep at arm's length,** guardar las distancias; tratar fríamente. **to lay down arms,** rendir las armas. **to present arms,** presentar las armas. **to receive with open arms,** recibir con los brazos abiertos. **to take up arms,** alzarse en armas, empuñar las armas. **under arms,** sobre las armas. **with folded arms,** con los brazos cruzados. **arm in arm,** del bracete, de bracero. **arm of the sea,** brazo de mar, m. **arm-rest,** brazo, m
arm /arm/ vt armar; proveer (de); (Fig. fortify) fortificar. —vi armarse
armada /ar'madə/ n armada, f
armament /'arməmənt/ n armamento, m
armchair /'arm,tʃɛər/ n sillón, m, silla poltrona, f
armed /armd/ a armado
Armenian /ar'miniən/ a and n armenio (-ia); (language) armenio, m

armful /'arm,fʊl/ n brazado, m
armhole /'arm,houl/ n sobaquera, f
arming /'armɪŋ/ n armamento, m
armistice /'armǝstɪs/ n armisticio, m
armless /'armlɪs/ a sin brazos
armor /'armǝr/ n armadura, f; (for ships, etc.) blindaje, m. —vt blindar, acorazar. **(to) a.-plate,** vt blindar. —n coraza, plancha blindada, f
armored /'armǝrd/ a blindado, acorazado. **a. car,** carro blindado, m. **a. cruiser,** crucero acorazado, m
armory /'armǝri/ n armería, f
army /'armi/ n ejército, m; multitud, muchedumbre, f. **to be in the a.,** ser del ejército. **to go into the a.,** alistarse. **a. corps,** cuerpo del ejército, m. **a. estimates,** presupuesto del ejército, m. **a. list,** escalofón del ejército, m. **A. Medical Corps,** Sanidad Militar, f. **A. Supply Corps,** Cuerpo de Intendencia, m
aroma /ǝ'roumǝ/ n aroma, m
aromatic /ˌærǝ'mætɪk/ a aromático
around /ǝ'raund/ prep alrededor de; por todas partes de; cerca de; (with words like corner) a la vuelta de. —adv alrededor; a la redonda, en torno; por todas partes; de un lado para otro
arouse /ǝ'rauz/ vt despertar; excitar. **a. (someone's) suspicions,** despertar las sospechas (de fulano)
arpeggio /ɑr'pedʒi,ou/ n arpegio, m
arraign /ǝ'rein/ vt acusar; Law. procesar
arraignment /ǝ'reinmǝnt/ n acusación, f; Law. procesamiento, m
arrange /ǝ'reindʒ/ vt arreglar; acomodar; poner en orden, clasificar; (place) colocar; (order) ordenar, disponer; (contrive) agenciar; organizar; preparar; Mus. adaptar; (of differences) concertar, ajustar. —vi convenir, concertarse; arreglar; hacer preparativos
arrangement /ǝ'reindʒmǝnt/ n arreglo, m; clasificación, f; disposición, f; (agreement) acuerdo, m; Mus. adaptación, f; pl **arrangements,** preparativos, m pl
array /ǝ'rei/ n (of troops) orden de batalla, mf; formación, f; colección, f; (dress) atavío, m, vt poner en orden de batalla; formar (las tropas, etc.); ataviar, adornar
arrears /ǝ'rɪarz/ n pl atrasos, m pl. **in a.,** atrasado
arrest /ǝ'rest/ vt detener, impedir; (the attention) atraer; (capture) arrestar, prender; (judgment) suspender. —n (stop) interrupción, parada, f; (hindrance) estorbo, m; (detention) arresto, m, detención, f; (of a judgment) suspensión, f. **under a.,** bajo arresto
arresting /ǝ'restɪŋ/ a que llama la atención, notable, muy interesante; asombroso, chocador
arrival /ǝ'raivǝl/ n llegada, venida, f, advenimiento, m; Naut. arribada, f; entrada, f; el, m, (la, f), que llega. **on a.,** al llegar, a la llegada. **the new arrivals,** los recién llegados
arrive /ǝ'raiv/ vi llegar; aparecer; (happen) suceder, Naut. arribar; entrar. **to a. at,** (a place or conclusion) llegar a
arrogance /'ærǝgǝns/ n arrogancia altivez, soberbia, f
arrogant /'ærǝgǝnt/ a altivo, arrogante, soberbio
arrogate /'ærǝ,geit/ vt arrogar
arrow /'ærou/ n saeta, flecha, f. **a.-head,** punta de flecha, f. **a.-shaped,** en forma de flecha, sagital. **a. wound,** flechazo, saetazo, m
arsenal /'arsǝnl/ n arsenal, m
arsenic /'arsǝnɪk/ n arsénico, m
arson /'arsǝn/ n incendio premeditado, m
art /art/ n arte, mf; (cleverness) habilidad, f; (cunning) artificio, m. **Faculty of Arts,** Facultad de Letras, f. **fine arts,** bellas artes, f pl. **art exhibition,** exposición de pinturas, f. **art gallery,** museo de pinturas, m. **art school,** colegio de arte, m
arterial /ɑr'tɪariǝl/ a arterial; (of roads) de primera clase. **a. forceps,** pinzas hemostáticas, f pl
artery /'artǝri/ n arteria, f
artesian /ɑr'tiʒǝn/ a artesiano
artful /'artfǝl/ a habil, ingenioso; (crafty) astuto
artfully /'artfǝli/ adv ingeniosamente; con astucia
artfulness /'artfǝlnɪs/ n habilidad, ingeniosidad, f; astucia, maña, f
arthritic /ɑr'θrɪtɪk/ a artrítico
arthritis /ɑr'θraitɪs/ n artritis, f

artichoke /'artɪ,tʃouk/ n alcachofa, f. **Jerusalem a.,** aguaturma, f
article /'artɪkǝl/ n artículo, m; (object) objeto, m, cosa, f; pl **articles,** escritura, f; contrato, m; estatutos, m pl. —vt escriturar; contratar. **leading a.,** artículo de fondo, m. **articles of apprenticeship,** contrato de aprendizaje, m. **articles of association,** estatutos de asociación, m pl. **articles of war,** código militar, m
articulate /v ɑr'tɪkyǝ,leit/ a -lɪt/ vt articular; pronunciar, articular. —vi estar unido por articulación; articular. —a articulado; claro; expresivo
articulation /ɑr,tɪkyǝ'leiʃǝn/ n articulación, f, (all meanings)
artifice /'artǝfɪs/ n artificio, m; arte, m, or f, habilidad, f
artificer /ɑr'tɪfǝsǝr/ n artífice, mf
artificial /ˌartǝ'fɪʃǝl/ a artificial; falso, fingido; afectado. **a. flowers,** flores de mano, f pl. **a. silk,** seda artificial, seda vegetal, f
artificial intelligence /ˌartǝ'fɪʃǝl ɪn'tɛlɪdʒǝns/ n inteligencia artificial, f
artificiality /ˌartǝ,fɪʃi'ælɪti/ n artificialidad, f; falsedad, f; afectación, f
artificially /ˌartǝ'fɪʃǝli/ adv artificialmente; con afectación
artillery /ɑr'tɪlǝri/ n artillería, f. **field a.,** artillería volante (or ligera o montada), f. **a. practice,** ejercicio de cañón, m
artilleryman /ɑr'tɪlǝrimǝn/ n artillero, m
artisan /'artǝzǝn/ n artesano (-na)
artist /'artɪst/ n artista, mf; (painter) pintor (-ra)
artiste /ɑr'tist/ n artista, mf
artistic /ɑr'tɪstɪk/ a artístico
artistically /ɑr'tɪstɪkli/ adv artísticamente
artistry /'artɪstri/ n habilidad artística, f, arte, mf
artless /'artlɪs/ a natural; sencillo, cándido, inocente
artlessly /'artlɪsli/ adv con naturalidad; con inocencia
artlessness /'artlɪsnɪs/ n naturalidad, f; sencillez, candidez, inocencia, f
art museum n museo de arte, m
Aryan /'ɛariǝn/ a ario
as /æz/ adv conjunc rel pron como; así como; (followed by infin.) de; (in comparisons) tan... como; (while) mientras; a medida que; (when) cuando, al (followed by infin.); (since) puesto que, visto que; (because) porque; (although) aunque; por; (according to) según; en; (in order that) para (que). **as a rule,** por regla general. **Once as he was walking,** Una vez mientras andaba. **as... as,** tan... como. **as far as,** hasta; en cuanto a. **as from,** desde. **as good as,** tan bueno como. **as if,** como si. **as it were,** por decirlo así, en cierto modo. **as many,** otros tantos (e.g. six embassies in as many countries, seis embajadas en otros tantos países). **as many as,** tanto... como; todos los que. **as soon as,** en cuanto, luego que, así que. **as soon as possible,** cuanto antes. **as sure as can be,** sin duda alguna. **as to,** en cuanto a. **as usual,** como de costumbre. **as well,** también. **as well as,** (besides) además de; tan bien como. **as yet,** todavía.
asbestos /æs'bestǝs/ n asbesto, amianto, m
ascend /ǝ'send/ vt and vi subir; (on, in) subir a; ascender; (rise) elevarse; (a river) remontar. **to a. the stairs,** subir las escaleras. **to a. the pulpit,** subir al púlpito. **to a. the throne,** subir al trono
ascendancy /ǝ'sendǝnsi/ n ascendiente, influjo, m
ascendant /ǝ'sendǝnt/ n elevación, f. —a ascendente; predominante. **to be in the a.,** Fig. ir en aumento; predominar
ascending /ǝ'sendɪŋ/ a ascendente
ascension /ǝ'senʃǝn/ n subida, ascension, f; (of the throne) advenimiento (al trono), m. **The A.,** La Ascensión
ascent /ǝ'sent/ n subida, f, ascenso, m; elevación, f; (slope) cuesta, pendiente, f
ascertain /ˌæsǝr'tein/ vt averiguar, descubrir
ascertainable /ˌæsǝr'teinǝbǝl/ a averiguable, descubrible
ascertainment /ˌæsǝr'teinmǝnt/ n averiguación, f
ascetic /ǝ'setɪk/ a ascético. —n asceta, mf
asceticism /ǝ'setǝ,sɪzǝm/ n ascetismo, m
ascribable /ǝ'skraibǝbǝl/ a imputable, atribuible

ascribe /əˈskraib/ vt atribuir, adscribir, imputar

ascription /əˈskripʃən/ n atribución, adscripción, f

asepsis /əˈsepsis/ n asepsia, f

aseptic /əˈseptik/ a aséptico

asexual /eiˈsekʃuəl/ a asexual

ash /æʃ/ n ceniza, f; cenizas, f pl; (tree and wood) fresno, m; pl **ashes,** cenizas, f pl; restos mortales, m pl. **mountain ash,** serbal, m. **ash-bin,** basurero, m. **ash-coloured,** ceniciento. **ash grove,** fresneda, f. **ashtray,** cenicero, m. **Ash Wednesday,** miércoles de ceniza, m

ashamed /əˈʃeimd/ a avergonzado. **to be a. of,** avergonzarse de. **to be a. of oneself,** avergonzarse, tener vergüenza de sí mismo

ashen /ˈæʃən/ a ceniciento; (of ash wood) de fresno; pálido como un muerto

ashlar /ˈæʃlər/ n sillar, m

ashore /əˈʃɔr/ adv a tierra; en tierra. **to go** or **put a.,** desembarcar

Asia Minor /ˈeiʒə/ Asia Menor, f

Asiatic /ˌeiʒiˈætik/ a and n asiático (-ca)

aside /əˈsaid/ adv a un lado; aparte. —n Theat. aparte, m. **to set a.,** poner a un lado; (omit) dejar aparte; descontar; abandonar; (a judgment) anular. **to take a.,** llevar aparte

asinine /ˈæsəˌnain/ a asnal

ask /æsk/ vt (a question; enquire) preguntar; (request; demand) pedir; (beg) rogar; (invite) invitar. **to ask a question,** hacer una pregunta. **to ask about,** preguntar acerca de. **to ask after,** preguntar por. **to ask down,** invitar a bajar; invitar a visitar (a alguien). **to ask for,** pedir; preguntar por. **ask for the moon,** pedir cotofas en el golfo. **to ask in,** invitar (a alguien) a entrar

askance /əˈskæns/ adv al (or de) soslayo, de reojo; con recelo

askew /əˈskyu/ adv oblicuamente; al lado; a un lado; sesgadamente

aslant /əˈslænt/ prep a través de

asleep /əˈslip/ a and adv dormido. **to be a.,** estar dormido. **to fall a.,** dormirse

asparagus /əˈspærəgəs/ n espárrago, m. **a. bed,** esparraguera, f

aspect /ˈæspekt/ n aspecto, m; vista, f; apariencia, f; semblante, m. **to have a southern a.,** dar (mirar) al sur

asperity /əˈsperiti/ n aspereza, f

aspersion /əˈspɜrʒən/ n Eccl. aspersión, f; calumnia, f; insinuación, f

asphalt /ˈæsfɔlt/ n asfalto, m, vt asfaltar

asphyxia /æsˈfiksiə/ n asfixia, f

asphyxiate /æsˈfiksi,eit/ vt asfixiar

asphyxiating /æsˈfiksi,eitiŋ/ a asfixiante

aspirant /ˈæspərənt/ n aspirante, candidato, m

aspirate /v ˈæspə,reit; n -pərit/ vt aspirar. —n letra aspirada, f

aspiration /ˌæspəˈreiʃən/ n aspiración, ambición, f; deseo, anhelo, m; Gram. aspiración, f

aspire /əˈspaiər/ vi aspirar (a), pretender, ambicionar; alzarse

aspirin /ˈæspərin/ n aspirina, f

ass /æs/ n asno, m

assail /əˈseil/ vt atacar, acometer, arremeter

assailable /əˈseiləbəl/ a atacable

assailant /əˈseilənt/ n asaltador (-ra)

assassin /əˈsæsin/ n asesino, mf

assassinate /əˈsæsə,neit/ vt asesinar

assassination /əˌsæsəˈneiʃən/ n asesinato, m

assault /əˈsɔlt/ n asalto, m; acometida, embestida, f; Fig. ataque, m. —vt asaltar; acometer, embestir; atacar. **to take by a.,** tomar por asalto

assay /n ˈæsei; v æˈsei/ n ensayo, m, vt ensayar, aquilatar

assayer /æˈseiər/ n ensayador, m

assaying /æˈseiiŋ/ n ensaye, m

assemblage /əˈsemblidʒ/ n reunión, f; (of a machine) montaje, m; (of people) muchedumbre, f, concurso, m; (of things) colección, f, grupo, m

assemble /əˈsembəl/ vt (persons) reunir, convocar; (things and persons) juntar; (a machine, etc.) armar, ensamblar. —vi reunirse, congregarse; acudir

assembly /əˈsembli/ n asamblea, f; reunión, f; Eccl. concilio, m. **a. line,** cadena de montaje, línea de montaje, f. **a. room,** sala de reuniones, f; sala de baile, f

assent /əˈsent/ n asentimiento, consentimiento, m; aprobación, f; (parliamentary, Law.) sanción, f. —vi asentir (a), consentir (en); aprobar

assert /əˈsɜrt/ vt mantener, defender; declarar, afirmar; hacer valer, reclamar. **to a. oneself,** imponerse, hacerse sentir; hacer valer sus derechos

assertion /əˈsɜrʃən/ n aserción, afirmación, f; defensa, f; reclamación, f

assertive /əˈsɜrtiv/ a afirmativo; dogmático

assess /əˈses/ vt tasar, valorar; fijar, señalar; repartir (contribuciones, etc.)

assessment /əˈsesmənt/ n tasación, f; fijación, f; repartimiento, m

assessor /əˈsesər/ n Law. asesor (-ra); (of taxes) repartidor (-ra); (valuer) tasador, m. **public a.,** tasador, m

asset /ˈæset/ n ventaja, f; adquisición, f; cualidad, f; pl **assets,** fondos, m pl; Com. activo, m, créditos activos, m pl

assiduity /ˌæsiˈdyuiti/ n asiduidad, f

assiduous /əˈsidʒuəs/ a asiduo

assiduously /əˈsidʒuəsli/ adv asiduamente, con asiduidad

assign /əˈsain/ vt Law. ceder; señalar, asignar; (appoint) destinar; fijar; atribuir, imputar. —n cesionario (-ia)

assignation /ˌæsigˈneiʃən/ n asignación, f; cita, f; Law. cesión, f

assignment /əˈsainmənt/ n Law. cesión, f; escritura de cesión, f; atribución, f; parte, porción, f

assimilable /əˈsiməlabəl/ a asimilable

assimilate /əˈsimə,leit/ vt asimilar; incorporarse. —vi mezclarse

assimilation /əˌsiməˈleiʃən/ n asimilación, f; incorporación, f

assimilative /əˈsimələtiv/ a asimilativo

assist /əˈsist/ vt ayudar; auxiliar, socorrer; (uphold) apoyar; (further) promover, fomentar. —vi (be present) asistir (a)

assistance /əˈsistəns/ n ayuda, f; auxilio, socorro, m; apoyo, m; (furtherance) fomento, m. **public a.,** asistencia pública, f

assistant /əˈsistənt/ n ayudante, m; Eccl. asistente, m; (in a shop) dependiente (-ta); colaborador (-ra); (university) auxiliar, m; sub-. **a. secretary,** subsecretario (-ia). **a. secretaryship,** subsecretaría, f

associate /n əˈsousit; v -si,eit/ n asociado (-da); miembro, m; socio (-ia); compañero (-ra), amigo (-ga); colega, m; colaborador (-ra); (confederate) cómplice, mf a asociado; auxiliar. —vt asociar; unir, juntar. **to a. oneself with,** asociarse a. **to a. with,** frecuentar la compañía de, ir con

association /əˌsousiˈeiʃən/ n asociación, f; unión, f; sociedad, f; compañía, corporación, f; (connection) relación, f. **a. football,** fútbol, m

assonance /ˈæsənəns/ n asonancia, f

assort /əˈsɔrt/ vt clasificar; mezclar

assorted /əˈsɔrtid/ a surtido, mezclado. **They are a well-a. pair,** Son una pareja bien avenida

assortment /əˈsɔrtmənt/ n clasificación, f, arreglo, m; surtido, m, mezcla, f

assuage /əˈsweidʒ/ vt mitigar; suavizar; calmar; aliviar

assume /əˈsum/ vt asumir; tomar; apropiarse; (wear) revestir; (suppose) suponer; poner por caso

assumed /əˈsumd/ a fingido, falso; supuesto

assumption /əˈsʌmpʃən/ n asunción, f; apropiación, f; arrogación, f; suposición, f. **Feast of the A.,** Fiesta de la Asunción, f

assurance /əˈʃurəns/ n garantía, f; promesa, f; confianza, seguridad, f; (in a good sense) aplomo, m, naturalidad, f; (in a bad sense) presunción frescura, f, descaro, m; Com. seguro, m

assure /əˈʃur/ vt asegurar

assured /əˈʃurd/ a aseguardo; seguro

assuredly /əˈʃuridli/ adv seguramente

asterisk /ˈæstərisk/ n asterisco, m

astern /əˈstɜrn/ adv a popa; de popa; en popa; atrás

asthma /ˈæzmə/ n asma, f

asthmatic /æz'mætɪk/ *a* asmático
astigmatic /ˌæstɪg'mætɪk/ *a* astigmático
astigmatism /ə'stɪgmə,tɪzəm/ *n* astigmatismo, *m*
astir /ə'stɜr/ *adv* en movimiento; (out of bed) levantado; excitado
astonish /ə'stɒnɪʃ/ *vt* sorprender, asombrar
astonished /ə'stɒnɪʃt/ *a* atónito, estupefacto
astonishing /ə'stɒnɪʃɪŋ/ *a* sorprendente, asombroso
astonishment /ə'stɒnɪʃmənt/ *n* asombro, *m*, sorpresa, estupefacción, *f*
astound /ə'staund/ *vt* aturdir, pasmar. **to be astounded,** *Inf.* quedarse muerto
astounding /ə'staundɪŋ/ *a* asombroso
astray /ə'streɪ/ *adv* desviado, extraviado; por el mal camino. **to go a.,** errar el camino, perderse; *Fig.* descarriarse
astride /ə'straɪd/ *adv* a horcajadas. —*prep* a horcajadas sobre; a ambos lados de
astringent /ə'strɪndʒənt/ *a* astringente
astrologer /ə'strɒlədʒər/ *n* astrólogo (-ga)
astrological /ˌæstrə'lɒdʒɪkəl/ *a* astrológico
astrology /ə'strɒlədʒi/ *n* astrología, *f*
astronaut /'æstrə,nɔt/ *n* astronauta, *mf*
astronomer /ə'strɒnəmər/ *n* astrónomo, *m*
astronomical /ˌæstrə'nɒmɪkəl/ *a* astronómico
astronomy /ə'strɒnəmi/ *n* astronomía, *f*
astrophysics /ˌæstrou'fɪzɪks/ *n* astrofísica, *f*
astute /ə'stut/ *a* astuto, sagaz; (with knave, etc.) redomado, pícaro
astuteness /ə'stutnɪs/ *n* astucia, sagacidad, *f*
asunder /ə'sʌndər/ *adv* en dos; separadamente; lejos uno de otro
asylum /ə'saɪləm/ *n* asilo, *m*; (for the insane) manicomio, *m*
asymmetrical /ˌeɪsɪ'mɛtrɪkəl/ *a* asimétrico
asymmetry /ei'sɪmɪtri/ *n* asimetría, *f*
at /æt/ *prep* a; en casa de; en; de; con; por; (before) delante de. Sometimes forms part of verb, e.g. *to aim at*, apuntar. *to look at*, mirar. May be translated by using pres. part., e.g. *They were at play,* Estaban jugando. *at a bound,* de un salto. *at peace,* en paz. *at the doctor's,* en casa del médico. *at the crack of dawn,* al rayar el alba, al romper el alba. *at the head,* a la cabeza. *John is at Brighton,* Juan está en Brighton. *at first,* al principio. *at last,* por fin. *at no time,* jamás. *at once,* en seguida. *at most,* a lo más. *at all events,* en todo caso. *What is he getting at?* ¿Qué quiere saber? *at home,* en casa. *at-home day,* día de recibo, *m*
atavism /'ætə,vɪzəm/ *n* atavismo, *m*
atavistic /ˌætə'vɪstɪk/ *a* atávico
atheism /'eɪθi,ɪzəm/ *n* ateísmo, *m*
atheist /'eɪθiɪst/ *n* ateo (-ea)
atheistic /ˌeɪθi'ɪstɪk/ *a* ateo
Atheneum /ˌæθə'niəm/ *n* ateneo, *m*
Athenian /ə'θiniən/ *a* and *n* ateniense *mf*
Athens /'æθɪnz/ Atenas, *f*
athlete /'æθlit/ *n* atleta, *m*
athletic /æθ'letɪk/ *a* atlético
athletics /æθ'letɪks/ *n* atletismo, *m*
athwart /ə'θwɔrt/ *adv* de través. —*prep* al través de; contra
Atlantic /æt'læntɪk/ *a* and *n* atlántico *m*. **A. Charter,** Carta del Atlántico, *f*. **A. liner,** transatlántico, *m*
Atlantis /æt'læntɪs/ Atlántida, *f*
atlas /'ætləs/ *n* atlas, *m*
atmosphere /'ætməs,fɪər/ *n* aire, *m*; atmósfera, *f*; *Fig.* ambiente, *m*
atmospheric /ˌætməs'ferɪk/ *a* atmosférico
atmospherics /ˌætməs'ferɪks/ *n pl* perturbaciones eléctricas atmosféricas, *f pl*
atoll /'ætɒl/ *n* atolón, *m*
atom /'ætəm/ *n* átomo, *m*. **splitting of the a.,** escisión del átomo, *f*
atomic /ə'tɒmɪk/ *a* atómico. **a. bomb,** bomba atómica, *f*. **a. pile,** pila atómica, *f*. **a. theory,** teoría atómica, *f*
atomize /'ætə,maɪz/ *vt* pulverizar
atomizer /'ætə,maɪzər/ *n* pulverizador, *m*
atone /ə'toun/ *vi* (for) expiar
atonement /ə'tounmənt/ *n* expiación, *f*
atonic /ə'tɒnɪk, ei'tɒn-/ *a* átono, atónico

atrocious /ə'trouʃəs/ *a* atroz; horrible
atrocity /ə'trɒsɪti/ *n* atrocidad, *f*
atrophy /'ætrəfi/ *n* atrofia, *f*, *vi* atrofiarse
attach /ə'tætʃ/ *vt* (*Law.* of goods) embargar; (*Law.* of persons) arrestar; (fix) fijar; (tie) atar; (join) juntar; (stick) pegar; (connect) conectar; (hook) enganchar; (with a brooch, etc.) prender; (blame, etc.) imputar; (importance, etc.) dar, conceder; (assign) asignar; (attract) atraer; (enclose) adjuntar, incluir. —*vi* pertenecer (a), ser indivisible (de). **to a. oneself to,** pegarse a; adherirse a, asociarse con; acompañar; hacerse inseparable de
attaché /ˌætæ'ʃei/ *n* agregado, *m*. **a. case,** maletín, *m*
attachment /ə'tætʃmənt/ *n* (*Law.* of goods) embargo, *m*, vía ejecutiva, *f*; (*Law.* of persons) arresto, *m*; unión, *f*; conexión, *f*; (hooking) enganche, *m*; (with a brooch, etc.) prendimiento, *m*; (tying) atadura, *f*; (fixing) fijación, *f*; (affection) apego, cariño, *m*; (friendship) amistad, *f*
attack /ə'tæk/ *n* ataque, *m*; *Mil.* ofensiva, *f*; (access) acceso, *m*. —*vt* atacar
attacker /ə'tækər/ *n* atacador (-ra), asaltador (-ra)
attain /ə'tein/ *vt* alcanzar, conseguir, lograr. —*vi* llegar a; alcanzar
attainable /ə'teinəbəl/ *a* asequible, realizable; accesible
attainment /ə'teinmənt/ *n* consecución, obtención, *f*; logro, *m*; *pl* **attainments,** prendas, dotes, *f pl*
attempt /ə'tempt/ *vt* (try) procurar, tratar de, intentar; ensayar; querer; *Law.* hacer una tentativa (de), atentar. —*n* tentativa, prueba, *f*; esfuerzo, ensayo, *m*; (criminal) atentado, *m*, tentativa, *f*
attend /ə'tend/ *vi* prestar atención (a); escuchar; (look after) cuidar (de); (serve) servir; (accompany) acompañar; (await) esperar. —*vt* (be present) asistir (a); (of a doctor) visitar; (accompany) acompañar; (bring) acarrear, traer; (follow) seguir. **to be attended with,** traer consigo, acarrear
attendance /ə'tendəns/ *n* asistencia, presencia, *f*; (those present) público, *m*, concurrencia, *f*; servicio, *m*; (train) acompañamiento, *m*; *Med.* asistencia, *f*, tratamiento médico, *m*. **to be at a.,** acompañar (a)
attendant /ə'tendənt/ *a* que acompaña; que sigue; concomitante. —*n* criado (-da); (keeper) guardián (-ana); (nurse) enfermero (-ra); (in a cloakroom) guardarropa, *f*; (in a theater) acomodador (-ra); (on a train) mozo, *m*; (waiter) camarero, *m*; (at baths) bañero (-ra)
attention /ə'tenʃən/ *n* atención, *f*; cuidado, *m*. **A.!** ¡Atención!; *Mil.* ¡Firmes! **to pay a.,** prestar atención. **to stand to a.,** cuadrarse, permanecer en posición de firmes
attentive /ə'tentɪv/ *a* atento; solícito; cortés, obsequioso
attentively /ə'tentɪvli/ *adv* con atención, atentamente; solícitamente
attentiveness /ə'tentɪvnɪs/ *n* cuidado, *m*; cortesía, *f*
attenuate /ə'tenyu,eit/ *vt* atenuar
attenuating /ə'tenyu,eitɪŋ/ *a* atenuante. **a. circumstance,** circunstancia atenuante, *f*
attenuation /ə,tenyu'eiʃən/ *n* atenuación, *f*
attest /ə'test/ *vt* atestar. —*vi* atestiguar, deponer, dar fe
attestation /ˌæte'steiʃən/ *n* atestación, deposición, *f*; (certificate) certificado, *m*, fe, fe, *f*
attic /'ætɪk/ *n* buhardilla, guardilla, *f*, desván, sotabanco, *m*
Attic /'ætɪk/ *a* ático
attire /ə'taiᵊr/ *n* atavío, *m*; (dress) traje, *m*; (finery) galas, *f pl*, *vt* ataviar, vestir; engalanar
attitude /'ætɪ,tud/ *n* actitud, *f*; postura, *f*; posición, *f*
attorney /ə'tɜrni/ *n* (solicitor) abogado (-da); (agent) apoderado (-da); (public) procurador, *m*. **power of a.,** poderes, *m pl* procuración, *f*. **A.-general,** fiscal, *m*
attract /ə'trækt/ *vt* atraer; (charm) seducir, cautivar, apetecer; (invite) convidar; (goodwill, etc.) captar
attraction /ə'trækʃən/ *n* atracción, *f*; atractivo, aliciente, encanto, *m*
attractive /ə'træktɪv/ *a* atrayente; atractivo, seductivo; apetecible; encantador
attractively /ə'træktɪvli/ *adv* atractivamente
attributable /ə'trɪbyutəbəl/ *a* imputable, atribuible

attribute /v ə'trɪbyut; n 'ætrə,byut/ vt atribuir (a), achacar (a), imputar (a). —n atributo, m

attribution /,ætrə'byuʃən/ n atribución, imputación, f; atributo, m

attrition /ə'trɪʃən/ n atrición, f

auburn /'ɔbərn/ a castaño, rojizo

auction /'ɔkʃən/ n subasta, almoneda, f; venta pública, pública subasta, f, vt subastar. **to put up to a.,** sacar a pública subasta

auctioneer /,ɔkʃə'nɪər/ n subastador (-ra)

audacious /ɔ'deiʃəs/ a atrevido, audaz, osado, temerario; (shameless) descarado, impudente

audaciously /ə'deiʃəsli/ adv osadamente; descaradamente

audacity /ɔ'dæsɪti/ n audacia, osadía, temeridad, f, atrevimiento, m; (shamelessness) descaro, m, desvergüenza, f

audibility /,ɔdə'bɪlɪti/ n audibilidad, perceptibilidad, f

audible /'ɔdəbəl/ a audible, oíble

audibly /'ɔdəbli/ adv en forma audible, perceptiblemente, en alta voz

audience /'ɔdiəns/ n (interview and Law.) audiencia, f; oyentes, m pl, auditorio, público, m. **to give a.,** dar audiencia. **a. chamber,** sala de recepción, f

audiofrequency /'ɔdiou,frikwensi/ n audiofrecuencia, f

audit /'ɔdɪt/ vt intervenir, examinar (cuentas). —n intervención, f, ajuste (de cuentas), m

audition /ɔ'dɪʃən/ n audición, f

auditor /'ɔdɪtər/ n (hearer) oyente, mf; interventor, contador, m

auditorium /,ɔdi'tɔriəm/ n sala de espectáculos, f

auditory /'ɔdɪ,tɔri/ a auditivo, auditorio

Augean /ɔ'dʒiən/ a de Augeas; muy sucio

auger /'ɔgər/ n taladro, m

aught /ɔt/ n algo. **For a. I know,** Por lo que yo sepa

augment /ɔg'mɛnt/ vt aumentar, acrecentar. —vi aumentarse, acrecentarse

augmentation /,ɔgmɛn'teiʃən/ n aumento, acrecentamiento, m; añadidura, f

augmentative /ɔg'mɛntətɪv/ a aumentativo

augur /'ɔgər/ n agorero (-ra). —vt and vi presagiar, anunciar; pronosticar, agorar

augury /'ɔgyəri/ n predicción, f; agüero, presagio, pronóstico, m

August /'ɔgəst/ n agosto, m

august /'ɔgəst/ a augusto

Augustan /ɔ'gʌstən/ a (of Roman emperor) augustal. **A. Age,** siglo de Augusto, m

Augustinian /,ɔgə'stɪniən/ a and n Eccl. agustino (-na)

aunt /ænt, ɑnt/ n tía, f. **great-a.,** tía abuela, f. **A. Sally,** el pim, pam, pum

aura /'ɔrə/ n exhalación, f; influencia psíquica, f; Med. aura, f

aural /'ɔrəl/ a auricular. **a. surgeon,** otólogo, m

auricle /'ɔrɪkəl/ n (of the heart) aurícula, ala del corazón, f; oreja, f, pabellón de la oreja, m

aurora /ə'rɔrə/ n aurora, f. **a. borealis,** aurora boreal, f

auspice /'ɔspɪs/ n auspicio, m

auspicious /ɔ'spɪʃəs/ a propicio, favorable, feliz

auspiciously /ɔ'spɪʃəsli/ adv prósperamente, felizmente

auspiciousness /ɔ'spɪʃəsnɪs/ n buenos auspicios, m pl; felicidad, f

austere /ɔ'stɪər/ a severo, austero, adusto; ascético; (of style) desnudo

austerity /ɔ'stɛrɪti/ n austeridad, severidad, f; ascetismo, m; (of style) desnudez, f

Australian /ɔ'streilyən/ a and n australiano (-na)

Austrian /'ɔstriən/ a and n austríaco (-ca)

authentic /ɔ'θɛntɪk/ a auténtico

authenticate /ɔ'θɛntɪ,keit/ vt autenticar

authentication /ɔ,θɛntɪ'keiʃən/ n autenticación, f

authenticity /,ɔθɛn'tɪsɪti/ n autenticidad, f

author /'ɔθər/ n autor, m

authoress /'ɔθərɪs/ n autora, f

author index n índice de autores, m

authoritarian /ə,θɔrɪ'tɛəriən/ a autoritario

authoritative /ə'θɔrɪ,teitɪv/ a autoritario

authority /ə'θɔrɪti/ n autoridad, f; poder, m. **to have on the best a.,** tener de muy buena fuente

authorization /,ɔθərə'zeiʃən/ n autorización, f

authorize /'ɔθə,raiz/ vt autorizar

authorship /'ɔθər,ʃɪp/ n profesión de autor, f; paternidad (literaria), f; origen, m

autobiographical /,ɔtə,baiə'græfɪkəl/ a autobiográfico

autobiography /,ɔtəbai'ɒgrəfi/ n autobiografía, f

autocracy /ɔ'tɒkrəsi/ n autocracia, f

autocrat /'ɔtə,kræt/ n autócrata, mf

autocratic /,ɔtə'krætɪk/ a autocrático

autograph /'ɔtə,græf/ n autógrafo, m

autography /ɔ'tɒgrəfi/ n autografía, f

automatic /,ɔtə'mætɪk/ a automático. **a. gate,** (at level crossings, etc.) barrera de golpe, f. **a. machine,** máquina automática, f; Inf. tragaperras, m. **a. pencil,** lapicero, m

automatically /,ɔtə'mætɪkəli/ adv automáticamente

automatism /ɔ'tɒmə,tɪzəm/ n automatismo, m

automaton /ɔ'tɒmə,tɒn/ n autómata, m

automobile /,ɔtəmə'bil/ n automóvil, m

autonomous /ɔ'tɒnəməs/ a autónomo

autonomy /ɔ'tɒnəmi/ n autonomía, f

autopsy /'ɔtɒpsi/ n autopsia, f

autosuggestion /,ɔtousəg'dʒɛstʃən/ n autosugestión, f

autumn /'ɔtəm/ n otoño, m

autumnal /ɔ'tʌmnl/ a otoñal, de otoño

auxiliary /ɔg'zɪlyəri/ a auxiliar. —n auxiliador, m

avail /ə'veil/ vi servir; valer; importar. —vt aprovechar. **to a. oneself of,** valerse de, aprovecharse de. **to no a.,** en balde

availability /ə,veilə'bɪlɪti/ n utilidad, f; disponibilidad, f; provecho, m; (validity) validez, f

available /ə'veiləbəl/ a útil; disponible; aprovechable; válido

avalanche /'ævə,læntʃ/ n alud, lurte, m

avarice /'ævərɪs/ n avaricia, f

avaricious /,ævə'rɪʃəs/ a avaro, avaricioso

ave /'avei/ interj ¡ave! —n avemaría, f; despedida, f

avenge /ə'vɛndʒ/ vt vengar; vindicar. **to a. oneself for,** vengarse de

avenger /ə'vɛndʒər/ n vengador (-ra)

avenging /ə'vɛndʒɪŋ/ a vengador

avenue /'ævə,nyu/ n avenida, f

aver /ə'vɜr/ vt afirmar, asegurar

average /'ævərɪdʒ/ n promedio, término medio, m; (marine insurance) avería, f, a de promedio; típico; corriente; normal. —vt hallar el término medio (de); prorratear, proporcionar; ser por término medio. **general a.,** (marine insurance) avería gruesa, f. **on the a.,** por término medio

averse /ə'vɜrs/ a opuesto (a); desinclinado (a); enemigo (de); repugnante. **to be a. to,** no gustar de; oponerse a; estar desinclinado a; ser enemigo de; repugnar

aversion /ə'vɜrʒən/ n aversión, f; repugnancia, f

avert /ə'vɜrt/ vt apartar; (avoid) evitar

aviary /'eivi,ɛri/ n avería, pajarera, f

aviation /,eivi'eiʃən/ n aviación, f

aviator /'eivi,eitər/ n aviador (-ra)

avid /'ævɪd/ a ávido

avidity /ə'vɪdɪti/ n avidez, f

avidly /'ævɪdli/ adv ávidamente, con avidez

avocation /,ævə'keiʃən/ n pasatiempo, m, distracción, f; ocupación, f; profesión, f

avoid /ə'vɔid/ vt evitar; (pursuit) evadir, eludir; guardarse (de), rehuir; Law. anular

avoidable /ə'vɔidəbəl/ a evitable, eludible

avoidance /ə'vɔidns/ n evitación, f

avow /ə'vau/ vt confesar; declarar

avowal /ə'vauəl/ n confesión, admisión, f

avowedly /ə'vauidli/ adv por confesión propia

avuncular /ə'vʌŋkyələr/ a avuncular

await /ə'weit/ vt aguardar, esperar

awake /ə'weik/ vt despertar. —vi despertarse. —a despierto; vigilante; consciente (de); atento (a)

awakening /ə'weikənɪŋ/ n despertamiento, m

award /ə'wɔrd/ n sentencia, decisión, f; adjudicación, f; (prize) premio, m. —vt adjudicar; otorgar, con-

ceder. **She was awarded a professorship in Greek,** Ganó unas oposiciones para una cátedra de griego
aware /ə'wɛər/ a consciente, sabedor. **to be well a. of,** saber muy bien. **to make a. of,** hacer saber
awash /ə'wɒʃ/ adv a flor de agua
away /ə'wei/ adv a distancia, a lo lejos, lejos; (absent) ausente; (out) fuera; (unceasingly) sin parar, continuamente; (wholly) completamente; (visibly) a ojos vistas. In verbs of motion **a.** is rendered by the reflexive, e.g. to go a., marcharse. Sometimes not translated, e.g. to take a., quitar. —interj ¡fuera de aquí! ¡márchese Vd.!; ¡vámonos! ¡adelante! nine miles a., a nueve millas de distancia. a. in the distance, allá a lo lejos. She sang a., Ella seguía cantando
awe /ɔ/ n temor reverente, m; horror, m; respeto, m; reverencia, f, vt intimidar, aterrar; infundir respeto (a). **to stand in awe of,** tener respeto (a), reverenciar
awesome /'ɔsəm/ a pavoroso, temible, aterrador; terrible; (august) augusto; (imposing) imponente
awestruck /'ɔ,strʌk/ a espantado, aterrado
awful /'ɔfəl/ a terrible, pavoroso; horrible; temible; atroz; Inf. enorme. **How a.!** Inf. ¡Qué barbaridad!
awfully /'ɔfəli, 'ɔfli/ adv terriblemente; horriblemente; Inf. muy
awfulness /'ɔfəlnɪs/ n lo terrible; lo horrible; atrocidad, f; (of a crime, etc.) enormidad, f

awkward /'ɔkwərd/ a difícil; peligroso; delicado; embarazoso; (of time, etc.) inconveniente, inoportuno; (of things) incómodo; (clumsy) torpe, desmañado; desagradable; (ungraceful) sin gracia. **the a. age,** la edad difícil
awkwardly /'ɔkwərdli/ adv torpemente; incómodamente; mal; con dificultad; sin gracia. **He is a. placed,** Se encuentra en una situación difícil
awkwardness /'ɔkwərdnɪs/ n dificultad, f; peligro, m; delicadeza, f; inconveniencia, inoportunidad, f; (clumsiness) torpeza, desmaña, f; (ungracefulness) falta de gracia, f
awl /ɔl/ n lezna, f, punzón, m
awning /'ɔnɪŋ/ n toldo, palio, m; Naut. toldilla, f
awry /ə'rai/ adv a un lado; oblicuamente; Fig. mal. —a torcido; Fig. descarriado
ax /æks/ n hacha, f
axiom /'æksiəm/ n axioma, m
axiomatic /,æksiə'mætɪk/ a axiomático
axis /'æksɪs/ n eje, m; Zool. axis, m. **A. power,** nación del Eje
axle /'æksəl/ n eje, m; peón, árbol (de una rueda), m. **back a.,** eje trasero, m. **differential a.,** eje diferencial, m. **front a.,** eje delantero, m
aye /ai/ interj sí. —n voto afirmativo, m
azalea /ə'zeilyə/ n azalea, f
Aztec /'æztɛk/ a and n azteca, mf
azure /'æʒər/ n azul celeste, m

B

b /bi/ n (letter) be, f; Mus. si, m

baa /bɑ/ n balido, be, m, vi balar, dar balidos

babble /'bæbəl/ n (chatter) charla, f; (of a child) gorjeo, m; (confused sound) vocinglería, barbulla, f, rumor, m; (of water) murmullo, susurro, m. —vi charlar; (of children) gorjearse; (incoherently) balbucir; (water) murmurar, susurrar; (a secret) descubrir

babbler /'bæblər/ n charlatán (-ana)

babbling /'bæblɪŋ/ n garrulería, locuacidad, f; (incoherent speech) balbuceo, m. (of water) murmullo, m. —a gárrulo, locuaz; balbuciente; murmurante

babel /'bæbəl/ n babel, m

baboon /bæ'bun/ esp. Brit. bə-/ n babuino, m

baby /'beibi/ n bebé, crío, m; niño (-ña) de pecho; Fig. gran bebé, m; niño mimado, m, a infantil. **b. blue,** azul claro, m. **b. doll,** muñeca bebé, f. **b. grand piano,** piano de media cola, m

baby carriage n coche de niños, m

baby-faced /'beibi ˌfeist/ a con mejillas mofletudas

babyhood /'beibi ˌhʊd/ n infancia, niñez, f

babyish /'beibiʃ/ a infantil, aniñado, pueril

Babylon /'bæbələn, -ˌlɒn/ n babilonia, f

babysitter /'beibi ˌsitər/ n cuidaniños, mf

baccalaureate /ˌbækə'lɔriit, -'lɒr-/ n bachillerato, m

baccarat /ˌbɑkə'rɑ, ˌbækə-/ n bacará, m

bachelor /'bætʃələr/ n soltero, célibe, m; (of a university) licenciado, bachiller, m; (as a title) caballero, m. **confirmed b.,** solterón, m. **degree of b.,** licenciatura, f. **to receive the degree of b.,** licenciarse, bachillerarse

bachelorhood /'bætʃələr ˌhʊd/ n soltería, f, celibato, m

bacillus /bə'sɪləs/ n bacilo, m

back /bæk/ n Anat. espalda, f; (of an animal) lomo, espinazo, m; (reins, loins) riñones, m pl; (of chairs, sofas) respaldo, m; (of a book) lomo, m; (back, bottom) fondo, m; parte posterior, parte de atrás, f; (of a hand, brush and many other things) dorso, m; (of a coin) reverso, m; el otro lado de alguna cosa; (in football, hockey) defensa, m; Theat. foro, m; (of firearms) culata, f; (of a knife) canto, m; (upper portion) parte superior, f. —a posterior, trasero; de atrás; (remote) alejado, apartado; inferior; (overdue; past; out of date) atrasado; (earlier) anterior; Anat. dorsal. **at the b.,** detrás; en el fondo; en la última fila. **at the b. of one's mind,** por sus adentros, en el fondo del pensamiento. **behind one's b.,** a espaldas de uno, en ausencia de uno. **half-b.,** medio, m. **on one's b.,** boca arriba; a cuestas. **to see the b. of,** Inf. ver por última vez, desembarazarse de. **to turn one's b. on,** volver la espalda (a). **with one's b. to the engine,** de espaldas a la máquina. **b. to b.,** espalda con espalda

back /bæk/ vt empujar hacia atrás; (a vehicle) dar marcha atrás; hacer retroceder; (line) reforzar; (support) apoyar; (sign) endosar; (bind) forrar; (bet on) apostar a; (a sail) fachear. —vi retroceder; dar marchar atrás; (of the wind) girar; (with on to) dar sobre, dominar; (with down) abandonar (una pretensión, etc.). **to b. out,** salir, marcharse; volverse atrás; (retract) desdecirse

back /bæk/ adv detrás; atrás; otra vez, de nuevo; (returned) de vuelta; a alguna distancia; (at home) en casa. —interj ¡atrás! **A few weeks b.,** Hace unas semanas, Unas semanas atrás. **It stands b. from the road,** Está a alguna distancia del camino. **to go b. to,** (of families, etc.) remontar a. **to come b.,** regresar. **to come b. again,** regresar de nuevo, regresar por segunda vez

back axle n eje trasero, m

backbite /'bæk ˌbait/ vt cortar (a uno) un sayo, desollarle (a uno) vivo, murmurar de

backbiter /'bæk ˌbaitər/ n mala lengua, f, murmurador (-ra)

backbiting /'bæk ˌbaitɪŋ/ n murmuración, detracción, maledicencia, f, a murmurador, detractor

backbone /'bæk ˌboun/ n espinazo, m, columna vertebral, f. **to the b.,** hasta la médula

backchat /'bæk ˌtʃæt/ n dimes y diretes, m pl; insolencia, f. **to indulge in b.-c.,** andar en dimes y diretes

back door n puerta trasera, puerta de servicio, f

backed /bækt/ a (lined) forrado; (in compounds; of persons) de espalda; (of chairs) de respaldo

backer /'bækər/ n (better) apostador, m; protector (-ra, -triz)

backfire /'bæk ˌfaiər/ n contrafuego m, falsa explosión, f

backgammon /'bæk ˌgæmən/ n chaquete, m

back garden n jardín de atrás, m

background /'bæk ˌgraund/ n fondo, m; Art. último término, m. **in the b.,** en el fondo; Art. en último término; Fig. en las sombras; alejado, a distancia

backhand /'bæk ˌhænd/ n Sports. revés, m

backhanded /'bæk ˌhændɪd/ a de revés, dado con el revés de la mano; Fig. ambiguo, equívoco

backing /'bækɪŋ/ n forro, m; (lining) refuerzo, m; (of a vehicle) marcha atrás, f; retroceso, m; (betting) el apostar (a); (wagers) apuestas, f pl; (Fig. support) apoyo, m, ayuda, f; garantía, f

backlog /'bæk ˌlɔg/ n Com. rezago de pedidos, m

back number n (of a periodical) número atrasado, m

back pedal vi contrapedalear.

back premises n parte trasera (de una casa, etc.), f

backroom /'bæk ˌrum/ n cuarto interior, m, habitación trasera, f. **b. boy,** investigador ocupado en trabajos secretos para el gobierno, m

back seat n asiento trasero, m; fondo, m. **to take a b.-s.,** permanecer en el fondo, ceder el paso

back shop n trastienda, f

backside /'bæk ˌsaid/ n trasero, m, posaderas, nalgas, f pl

backslide /'bæk ˌslaid/ vi recaer, reincidir

backslider /'bæk ˌslaidər/ n (in religion or politics) apóstata, mf; reincidente, mf

backsliding /'bæk ˌslaidɪŋ/ n apostasía, f; reincidencia, f

backstage /'bæk ˌsteidʒ/ n foro, fondo del escenario, m, adv hacia el foro; detrás de bastidores

backstaircase /'bæk ˌstɛər ˌkeis/ n escalera de servicio, f; escalera secreta, f

backstairs /'bæk ˌstɛərz/ n escalera de servicio, f; Fig. vías secretas, f pl, a de cocina; Fig. secreto

backstitch /'bæk ˌstitʃ/ n Sew. pespunte, m, vt and vi pespuntar

back street n calle secundaria, callejuela, f; pl **back streets,** barrios bajos, m pl

backstroke /'bæk ˌstrouk/ n reculada, f; Sports. revés, m

back tooth n muela, f

back view n vista de detrás, f

backward /'bækwərd/ a hacia atrás; vuelto hacia atrás; (in development) atrasado, poco avanzado; lento; negligente; (shy) modesto; (late) tardío; atrasado; retrógrado; (dull) torpe; retrospectivo. —adv hacia atrás; al revés; al revés; (of falling) de espaldas; (of time) al pasado. **to go b. and forward,** ir y venir. **b. and forward,** de acá para allá

backwardness /'bækwərdnis/ n atraso, m; lentitud, f; negligencia, f; modestia, f; (lateness) tardanza, f; atraso, m; (dullness) torpeza, f; falta de progreso, f

backwards /'bækwərdz/ adv See **backward**

backwash /'bæk ˌwɒʃ/ n agua de rechazo, f

backwater /'bæk ˌwɔtər/ n remanso, m

back wheel n rueda trasera, f, vi contrapedalear

backwoods /'bæk ˌwʊdz/ n monte, m, selva, f

back yard n corral, m

bacon /'beikən/ n tocino, m

bacteria /bæk'tɪəriə/ n bacteria, f

bacterial /bæk'tɪəriəl/ a bacterial, bacteriano

bactericide /bæk'tɪərəˌsaid/ n bactericida, m

bacteriological /bæk,tɪəriə'lɒdʒɪkəl/ a bacteriológico

bacteriologist /ˌbæktɪəri'ɒlədʒist/ n bacteriólogo, m

bacteriology /ˌbæktɪəri'ɒlədʒi/ n bacteriología, f
bad /bæd/ a malo; (wicked) perverso; (ill) enfermo, malo (with estar); (naughty; undutiful) malo (with ser); (of coins) falso; (of debts) incobrable; (rotten) podrido; (harmful) nocivo; (dangerous) peligroso; (of pains, a cold) fuerte; intenso; (of a shot) errado; (mistaken) equivocado; (unfortunate) desgraciado. —n el mal, lo malo; (persons) los malos. **extremely bad,** pésimo. **from bad to worse,** de mal en peor. **It's too bad!** ¡Esto es demasiado! **to go bad,** (fruit) macarse; (food) estropearse. **bad habit,** mala costumbre, f, vicio, m. **to have the bad habit of,** tener el vicio de. **bad temper,** malhumor, mal genio, m. **bad tempered,** malhumorado. **bad turn,** flaco servicio, m, mala pasada, f
badge /bædʒ/ n insignia, f; (decoration) condecoración, f; símbolo, emblema, m; (mark) marca, f
badger /'bædʒər/ n tejón, m, vt cansar, molestar
Bad Lands (of Nebraska and South Dakota) Tierras malas f pl; (of Argentina) la Travesía, f
badly /'bædli/ adv mal. **extremely b.,** pésimamente. **to want something b.,** necesitar algo con urgencia. **b. done,** mal hecho. **b. disposed,** malintencionado
badminton /'bædmɪntn/ n el juego del volante, m
badness /'bædnɪs/ n maldad, f; mala calidad, f; lo malo
bad-smelling /'bæd ˌsmɛlɪŋ/ a maloliente
baffle /'bæfəl/ vt desconcertar; (bewilder) tener perplejo (a); contrariar, frustrar; (obstruct) impedir; (avoid) evitar. **to b. description,** no haber palabras para describir
baffling /'bæflɪŋ/ a desconcertante; difícil; confuso; perturbador; (of people) enigmático
bag /bæg/ n saco, m; talega, f; (hand) bolsa, f, saco (de mano), m; (for tools) capacho, m; (for sewing) costurero, m; (of bagpipes) fuelle, m; (saddle) alforja, f; (briefcase) cartera, f; (suitcase) maleta, f; (under the eye) ojera, f; (game shot) caza, f. —vt entalegar; coger, cazar; matar; tomar. —vi (of garments) arrugarse. **to clear out bag and baggage,** liar el petate. **a bag of bones,** (person) un manojo de huesos. **bag wig,** peluquín, m
bagatelle /ˌbægə'tɛl/ n bagatela, friolera, f; (game) billar romano, m
bagful /'bægfʊl/ n saco, m; bolsa, f
baggage /'bægɪdʒ/ n equipaje, m; Mil. bagaje, m; (madcap) pícara, f; (jade) mujerzuela, f. **b. master,** (railway) factor, m. **b. car,** furgón de equipajes, m
baggage rack n (of automobile) portaequipajes, m
baggy /'bægi/ a (creased, of trousers) con rodilleras, arrugado; (wide) bombacho
bagpipe /'bæg,paɪp/ n gaita, f
bagpiper /'bæg,paɪpər/ n gaitero, m
bah /bɑ/ interj ¡bah!
Bahamas, the /bə'hɑməz/ las Islas Bahamas, las Islas Lucayas, f
bail /beil/ n Law. fianza, caución, f; (person) fiador (-ra); (cricket) travesaño, m, barra, f. —vt Law. poner en libertad bajo fianza; salir fiador (por); (a boat) achicar. **on b.,** en fiado. **to go b.,** dar fianza, fiar.
bailiff /'beilɪf/ n Law. agente ejecutivo, m; alguacil, m; mayordomo, m; capataz, m
bait /beit/ n cebo, m; anzuelo, m; (fodder) pienso, m, vt cebar; (feed) dar pienso (a); azuzar; atormentar; (attract) atraer
baiting /'beitɪŋ/ n cebadura, f; combate, m; tormenta, f
baize /beiz/ n bayeta, f. **green b.,** tapete verde, m
bake /beik/ vt cocer; hacer (pan, etc.). **I like to bake cakes,** Me gusta hacer pasteles; Fig. endurecer. —vi cocerse
bakelite /'beiklait/ n bakelita, f
baker /'beikər/ n panadero, hornero, m. **a baker's dozen,** la docena del fraile
bakery /'beikəri, 'beikri/ n panadería, f
baking /'beikɪŋ/ n cocimiento, m, cocción, f; (batch) hornada, f; el hacer (pan, etc.) a Inf. abrasador. **b.-dish,** tortera, f. **b.-powder,** levadura química, f
balance /'bæləns/ n balanza, f; equilibrio, m; Com. balance, saldo, m; (in a bank) saldo (a favor del cuentacorrentista), m; Math. resto, m; Astron. Libra, f; (pendulum) péndola, f; (counterweight) con-

trapeso, m. **credit b.,** saldo acreedor, m. **debit b.,** saldo deudor, m. **net b.,** saldo líquido, m. **to lose one's b.,** perder el equilibrio. **to strike a b.,** hacer balance. **b. of power,** equilibrio político, m. **b. of trade,** balanza de comercio, f. **b.-sheet,** balance, avanzo, m. **b. wheel,** (of watches) volante, m
balance /'bæləns/ vt balancear, abalanzar; contrapesar; (accounts) saldar; equilibrar; comparar; considerar, examinar. —vi balancearse; ser de igual peso; equilibrarse; (accounts) saldarse
balance of trade n balanza comercial, f
balancing /'bælənsɪŋ/ n balanceo, m; Com. balance, m. **b.-pole,** balancín, m
balconied /'bælkənid/ a con balcones, que tiene balcones
balcony /'bælkəni/ n balcón, m; galería, f; Theat. anfiteatro, m
bald /bɔld/ a calvo; (of style) seco, pobre; Fig. desnudo, árido, pelado; sin adorno; (simple) sencillo. **to grow b.,** ponerse calvo, encalvecer
balderdash /'bɔldər,dæʃ/ n galimatías, m, jerigonza, f; disparate, m
baldly /'bɔldli/ adv secamente; sencillamente
baldness /'bɔldnɪs/ n calvicie, f; (of style) sequedad, pobreza, f; (bareness) desnudez, aridez, f
bale /beil/ n (bundle) fardo, m; (of cotton, paper, etc.) bala, f
Balearic /ˌbæli'ærɪk/ a baleárico
Balearic Islands, the las Islas Baleares, f
baleful /'beilfəl/ a malicioso, siniestro, maligno
balefully /'beilfəli/ adv malignamente
balk /bɔk/ n obstáculo, m; (beam) viga, f; (billiards) cabaña, f. —vt frustrar; impedir. —vi resistirse, rehusar
Balkan /'bɔlkən/ a balcánico
Balkans, the los Balcanes, m
ball /bɔl/ n globo, m, esfera, f; (plaything) pelota, f; (as in billiards, cricket, croquet) bola, f; (in football, basket-ball) balón, m; (shot) bala, f; (of wool, etc.) ovillo, m; (of the eye) globo (del ojo), m; (of the thumb) yema (del pulgar), f; (of the foot) planta (del pie), f; (dance) baile, m. —vi apelotonarse. **red b.,** (in billiards) mingo, m. **to play b.,** jugar a la pelota. **to roll oneself into a b.,** aovillarse, hacerse un ovillo. **b.-and-socket joint,** articulación esférica, f. **b.-bearing,** cojinete de bolas, m
ballad /'bæləd/ n romance, m; (song) balada, f
balladmonger /'bæləd,mʌŋgər/ n coplero (-ra)
ballast /'bæləst/ n (Naut. and Fig.) lastre, m; Rail. balasto, m. —vt lastrar; llenar de balasto
ballerina /ˌbælə'rinə/ n bailarina, f
ballet /bæ'lei/ n baile ruso, ballet, m; baile, m. **b. master,** director de ballet, m
ballistics /bə'lɪstɪks/ n balística, f
balloon /bə'lun/ n globo aerostático, m; Chem. balón, m; (toy) globo, m; Archit. bola, f. **captive b.,** globo cautivo, m. **b. barrage,** cortina de globos de intercepción, f. **b.-tyre,** neumático balón, m
balloonist /bə'lunɪst/ n aeronauta, mf
ballot /'bælət/ n votación, f; papeleta para votar, cédu&;la de votación, f. —vi votar, balotar. **b. box,** urna electoral, f
ballpoint pen /'bɔl,pɔint/ n pluma esférica, f, birome, m (Argentina), punto-bola, m (Bolivia), esfero, m (Colombia)
ballroom /'bɔl,rum/ n salón de baile, m; salón de fiestas, m
ballroom dancing n baile de salón, m
balm /bɑm/ n bálsamo, m; Fig. ungüento, m
balminess /'bɑmɪnɪs/ n fragancia, f; aroma, f; (gentleness) suavidad, f
balmy /'bɑmi/ a balsámico; fragante; aromático; (soft) suave; (soothing) calmante
balsam /'bɔlsəm/ n bálsamo, m
Baltic /'bɔltɪk/ a báltico
Baltic, the el (Mar) Báltico, m
baluster /'bæləstər/ n balaustre, m
balustrade /ˌbælə'streid/ n balaustrada, barandilla, f, antepecho, m
bamboo /bæm'bu/ n bambú, m
bamboozle /bæm'buzəl/ vt engatusar, embaucar
bamboozler /bæm'buzlər/ n embaucador (-ra)

bamboozling /bæm'buzlɪŋ/ n embaucamiento, engaño, m
ban /bæn/ n interdicción, f; prohibición, f; bando, m. —vt prohibir; proscribir
banal /bə'næl/ a banal, vulgar, trivial
banality /bə'nælɪti/ n banalidad, vulgaridad, trivialidad, f
banana /bə'nænə/ n (tree and fruit) plátano, m; (fruit) banana, f. **b. plantation,** platanar, m
band /bænd/ n lista, tira, f; zona, f; (black mourning) tira de gasa, f; (sash) faja, f; (ribbon) banda; cinta, f; (bandage) venda, f; Mech. correa, f; Archit. listón, m; Mus. banda, f; (group) pandilla, f, grupo, m. —vt congregar, reunir. —vi reunirse, asociarse. **b.-saw,** sierra de cinta, f
bandage /'bændɪdʒ/ n venda, f, vendaje, m, vt vendar, poner un vendaje en (fingers, etc. or persons)
bandaging /'bændɪdʒɪŋ/ n vendaje, m
banderol /'bændə,rol/ n banderola, f
bandit /'bændɪt/ n bandido, bandolero, m
bandmaster /'bænd,mæstər/ n músico mayor, m; director de orquesta, m
bandsman /'bændzmən/ n músico, m
bandstand /'bænd,stænd/ n quiosco de música, m
bandy /'bændi/ vt cambiar, trocar; pasar de uno a otro
bandy-legged /'bændi ,legɪd/ a estevado zanquituerto
bane /bein/ n (poison) veneno, m; perdición, ruina, f; (nuisance) plaga, f
baneful /'beinfəl/ a pernicioso, funesto; dañino; maligno
banefully /'beinfəli/ adv funestamente; malignamente
bang /bæŋ/ n golpe, golpazo, m; (of an explosive, fire-arm) estallido, m, detonación, f; (of a firework) traque, m; (of a door) portazo, m; (with the fist) puñetazo, m; (noise) ruido, m; (fringe) flequillo, m. —vt golpear; (beat) sacudir; (throw) lanzar, arrojar con violencia; (a door, etc.) cerrar de golpe, cerrar con violencia. —vi golpear; estallar; (thunder) retronar; (in the wind) cencerrear. —interj ¡pum! ¡zas!
banging /'bæŋɪŋ/ n golpeadura, f; sacudidura, f; detonación, f; ruido, m
bangle /'bæŋgəl/ n (slave b.) esclava, f; pulsera, f; brazalete, m; (for ankles) ajorca, f
banish /'bænɪʃ/ vt desterrar; apartar; (from the mind) despedir, ahuyentar; (suppress) suprimir
banishment /'bænɪʃmənt/ n destierro, m; expulsión, f; relegación, f; (suppression) supresión, f
banister /'bænəstər/ n baranda, f, pasamano, m
banjo /'bændʒou/ n banjo, m
banjoist /'bændʒouɪst/ n tocador (-ra) de banjo
bank /bæŋk/ n (of rivers, etc.) ribera, orilla, f, margen, m; (of clouds) banda, capa, f; (of sand, fog, snow) banco, m; (embankment) terraplén, m; Com. banco, m; (gaming) banca, f; (for foreign exchange) casa de cambio, f. **b. account,** cuenta corriente, f. **b. book,** libreta de banco, f. **b. clerk,** empleado del banco, m. **b. holiday,** fiesta oficial, f; **b.-note,** billete de banco, m. **b. stock,** acciones de un banco, f pl
bank /bæŋk/ vt estancar, represar; amontonar; poner (dinero) en un banco, depositar en un banco. —vi tener cuenta corriente en un banco; (gaming) tener la banca; ser banquero; Aer. inclinarse al virar
banker /'bæŋkər/ n banquero, m, (also at cards); (money-changer) cambista, mf
banking /'bæŋkɪŋ/ n Com. banca, f; Aer. vuelo inclinado, m, a Com. bancario. **b. house,** casa de banca, f
bankrupt /'bæŋkrʌpt/ a insolvente, quebrado. —n quebrado (-da). **to go b.,** declararse en quiebra, hacer bancarrota
bankruptcy /'bæŋkrʌptsi/ n bancarrota, quiebra, f; Fig. pobreza, decadencia, f. **fraudulent b.,** quiebra fraudulenta, f. **b. court,** tribunal de quiebras, m
banner /'bænər/ n bandera, f
banns /bænz/ n pl amonestaciones, f pl. **to forbid the b.,** impedir las amonestaciones. **to publish the b.,** decir las amonestaciones
banquet /'bæŋkwɪt/ n banquete, m, vt and vi banquetear

banqueting /'bæŋkwɪtɪŋ/ a de banquetes. **b. hall,** sala de banquetes, f
bantam /'bæntəm/ n gallina enana, f. **b. weight,** (Sports.) a de peso gallo. —n peso gallo, m
banter /'bæntər/ vt and vi tomar el pelo (a). —n chistes, m pl, burlas, f pl
baptism /'bæptɪzəm/ n bautismo, m; Fig. bautizo, m
baptist /'bæptɪst/ n bautista, m. **St. John the B.,** San Juan Bautista
baptistry /'bæptəstri/ n baptisterio, bautisterio, m
baptize /bæp'taiz, 'bæptaiz/ vt bautizar
baptizing /bæp'taizɪŋ/ n bautizo, m
bar /bɑr/ n barra, f; (of chocolate, soap) pastilla, f; Herald. banda, f; (on a window) reja, f; (of a door) tranca, f, (barrier) barrote, m; (bar lever) palanca, f; (of a balance) astil, m; Mus. barra, f; (in the sea, etc.) banco, alfaque, m; (barrier) barrera, f; (barrister's profession) foro, m, curia, f; Fig. tribunal, m; (in a court) barra, f; Fig. impedimento, m; (of light) rayo, m; (stripe) raya, f; (for refreshments) bar, m; mostrador del bar, m. —vt atrancar, abarrotar; impedir, obstruir; prohibir; exceptuar, excluir; (streak) rayar. **the b.,** el cuerpo de abogados. **to be called to the b.,** ser recibido como abogado en los tribunales. **b.-tender,** camarero del bar, m
bar association n colegio de abogados, m
barb /bɑrb/ n púa, f; (of an arrow, fish-hook, etc.) lengüeta, f; (of a lance) roquete, m; (of fish) barbilla, f; (of a feather) barba, f; (horse) caballo berberisco, m. —vt proveer de púas; armar de lengüetas
Barbados /bɑr'beidouz/ Isla de Barbados, f
barbarian /bɑr'bɛəriən/ a bárbaro, barbárico. —n bárbaro (-ra)
barbaric /bɑr'bærɪk/ a barbárico, salvaje
barbarism /'bɑrbə,rɪzəm/ n barbarismo, salvajismo, m; crueldad, f; (of style) barbarismo, m
barbarity /bɑr'bærɪti/ n barbaridad, ferocidad, f
barbarous /'bɑrbərəs/ a feroz, cruel, salvaje; inculto
barbarously /'bɑrbərəsli/ adv bárbaramente, cruelmente
barbarousness /'bɑrbərəsnɪs/ n barbaridad, f; crueldad, ferocidad, f
Barbary /'bɑrbəri/ Berbería, f
barbecue /'bɑrbɪ,kyu/ n barbacoa, f
barbed wire /'bɑrbd/ n alambre de púas, alambre espinoso, m
barber /'bɑrbər/ n barbero, m. **barber shop,** barbería, f
Barcelona /,bɑrsə'lounə/ (of or from) a and n barcelonés (-esa)
bard /bɑrd/ n bardo, vate, m
bare /bɛər/ a desnudo; descubierto; vacío; (mere) mero, solo; (worn) raído; pelado, raso; (unadorned) sencillo; (unsheathed) desnudo; (arid) árido; (curt) seco; (unprotected) desabrigado; pobre. —vt desnudar; descubrir; revelar. **He bared his head,** Se descubrió. **to lay b.,** dejar al desnudo; revelar
bareback /'bɛər,bæk/ a que monta en pelo. —adv en pelo
barefaced /'bɛər,feist/ a descarado, desvergonzado, cínico
barefoot /'bɛər,fut/ a descalzo
bareheaded /'bɛər,hɛdɪd/ a sin sombrero, descubierto
barelegged /'bɛər,lɛgɪd/ a en pernetas, en piernas
barely /'bɛərli/ adv apenas; escasamente; meramente, solamente
bareness /'bɛərnɪs/ n desnudez, f; desadorno, m; (aridity) aridez, f; pobreza, f
bargain /'bɑrgən/ n contrato, m; pacto, acuerdo, m; (purchase) ganga, f. —vi negociar; (haggle) regatear; (expect) esperar. **into the b.,** de añadidura, también. **It is a b.,** Es una ganga; Trato hecho. **to get the best of the b.,** salir ganando. **to strike a b.,** cerrar un trato. **b. counter,** sección de saldos, f. **b. sale,** venta de saldos, f
bargainer /'bɑrgənər/ n negociador (-ra); regatón (-ona)
bargaining /'bɑrgənɪŋ/ n negociación, gestión, f; (haggling) regateo, m
barge /bɑrdʒ/ n (for freight) barcaza, gabarra, f;

falúa, *f;* lancha, *f.* —*vi* (into) tropezar con; dar empujones

baritone /'bærɪ,toun/ *n* barítono, *m*

barium /'bɛəriəm/ *n Chem.* bario, *m*

bark /bɑrk/ *n* (of a tree) corteza, *f;* (quinine) quina, *f;* (boat, *Poet.*) barca, *f; Naut.* buque de tres palos, *m;* (of a dog) ladrido, *m;* (of a fox) aullido, *m;* (of a gun) ruido, *m.* —*vi* (of a dog) ladrar; (of a fox) aullar; (of a gun) tronar

barking /'bɑrkɪŋ/ *n* ladrido, *m;* (of stags) rebramo, *m;* (of foxes) aullidos, *m pl;* (of guns) trueno, *m*

barley /'bɑrli/ *n* cebada, *f, a* de cebada. **pearl b.**, cebada perlada, *f.* **b.-bin,** cebadera, *f.* **b. dealer,** cebadero, *m.* **b. field,** cebadal, *m.* **b.-water,** hordiate, *m*

barm /bɑrm/ *n* (froth on beer) giste, *m;* (leaven) levadura, *f*

barmaid /'bɑr,meid/ *n* moza de bar, camarera, *f*

barn /bɑrn/ *n* pajar, granero, hórreo, *m.* **b.-owl,** lechuza, *f*

barnacle /'bɑrnəkəl/ *n* lapa, *f,* barnacla, *m*

barometer /bə'rɒmɪtər/ *n* barómetro, *m*

barometric /,bærə'mɛtrɪk/ *a* barométrico

baron /'bærən/ *n* barón, *m*

baroness /'bærənɪs/ *n* baronesa, *f*

Baron Munchausen /'bærən 'mʊntʃ,hauzən/ el Baron de la Castaña

baroque /bə'rouk/ *a* barroco. **the b.,** lo barroco

barrack /'bærək/ *n Mil.* cuartel, *m,* caserna, *f, vt* acuartelar

barrage /bə'rɑʒ/ *n* presa de contención, *f; Mil.* cortina de fuego, *f;* (barrier) barrera, *f;* (of questions) lluvia, *f.* **b. balloon,** globo de intercepción, *m*

barrel /'bærəl/ *n* barril, *m;* tonel, *m,* cuba, *f;* (of a gun) cañón, *m; Mech.* cilindro, *m;* (of an animal) cuerpo, *m.* —*vt* embarrilar, entonelar. **b.-organ,** organillo, órgano de manubrio, *m*

barrelled /'bærəld/ *a* embarrilado; (of guns, generally in compounds) de... cañones. **double-b. gun,** escopeta de dos cañones, *f*

barren /'bærən/ *a* estéril; (of ground) árido; (fruitless) infructuoso

barrenness /'bærən,nɪs/ *n* esterilidad, *f;* aridez, sequedad, *f;* (fruitlessness) inutilidad, *f*

barrens /'bærənz/ *n* yermo, *m sing,* yerma, *f sing*

barricade /'bærɪ,keid/ *n* barricada, *f;* barrera, *f, vt* cerrar con barricadas; obstruir

barricading /'bærɪ,keidɪŋ/ *n* el cerrar con barricadas; la defensa con barricadas (de)

barrier /'bæriər/ *n* barrera, *f;* impedimento, *m;* (for customs duties) portazgo, *m*

barring /'bɑrɪŋ/ *prep* salvo, excepto, con la excepción de, menos

barrister /'bærəstər/ *n* abogado (-da)

barrow /'bærou/ *n* carretón, *m;* carretilla, *f;* (tumulus) túmulo, *m*

barter /'bɑrtər/ *n* cambio, trueque, *m;* tráfico, *m, vt* and *vi* cambiar, trocar; traficar

barterer /'bɑrtərər/ *n* traficante, *mf*

basal /'beisəl/ *a* básico, fundamental

basalt /bə'sɔlt/ *n* basalto, *m*

base /beis/ *a* bajo, vil, ruin; soez; indigno; impuro; (of metals) de mala ley. —*n* base, *f;* fundamento, *m;* pie, *m; Archit.* pedestal, *m; (Mil. Chem. Geom.)* base, *f;* (of a vase) asiento, *m, vt* basar; fundar. **b. action,** bajeza, *f.* **b. line,** *Sports.* línea de base, *f.* **b. metal,** metal común, *m*

baseball /'beis,bɔl/ *n* pelota base, *f*

baseless /'beislɪs/ *a* sin base; sin fundamento; insostenible

basely /'beisli/ *adv* bajamente, vilmente

basement /'beismənt/ *n* sótano, *m*

baseness /'beisnɪs/ *n* bajeza, vileza, ruindad, *f*

bashful /'bæʃfəl/ *a* vergonzoso, ruboroso; tímido, corto; (unsociable) huraño, esquivo

bashfully /'bæʃfəli/ *adv* vergonzosamente; tímidamente

bashfulness /'bæʃfəlnɪs/ *n* vergüenza, *f,* rubor, *m;* encogimiento, *m,* timidez, cortedad, *f;* (unsociableness) huraña, esquivez, *f*

basic /'beisɪk/ *a* básico; fundamental

basic commodity *n* artículo básico, producto primario, *m*

basilica /bə'sɪlɪkə/ *n* basílica, *f*

basilisk /'bæsəlɪsk/ *n* basilisco, *m*

basil (sweet) /'bæzəl, 'bei-/ *n Bot.* albahaca, *f*

basin /'beisən/ *n* vasija, *f;* (for washing) jofaina, *f;* (barber's) bacía, *f;* (of a fountain) pileta, *f; Anat.* bacinete, *m;* (of a harbor) concha, *f;* (of a river) cuenca, *f* (in the earth) hoya, *f;* (dock) dársena, *f*

basis /'beisɪs/ *n* base, *f;* fundamento, *m;* elemento principal, *m*

bask /bæsk/ *vi* calentarse; (in the sun) tomar el sol

basket /'bæskɪt/ *n* cesta, *f;* canasta, *f;* (frail) espuerta, *f.* **flat b.,** azafate, *m.* **large b.,** banasta, *f.* **b. with a lid,** excusabaraja, *f.* **b. ball,** baloncesto, *m.* **b. maker** or **dealer,** banastero, cestero, *m.* **b. work** or **shop** or **factory,** cestería, *f.* **b. work chair,** sillón de mimbres, *m*

basketful /'bæskɪt,fʊl/ *n* cesta, cestada, *f*

Basle /bɑl/ Basilea, *f*

Basque /bæsk/ *a* and *n* vasco (-ca), vascongado (-da). —*n* (language) vascuence, *m*

Basque Provinces, the las Provincias Vascongadas

bas-relief /,bɑri'lif, ,bæs-/ *n* bajo relieve, *m*

bass /beis/ *n Mus.* bajo, *m;* (for tying) esparto, *m, a Mus.* bajo. **double b.,** contrabajo, *m.* **figured b.,** bajo cifrado, *m.* **b. clef,** clave de fa, *f.* **b. string,** bordón, *m.* **b. voice,** voz baja, *f*

bassinet /,bæsə'nɛt/ *n* cochecito de niño, *m*

bassoon /bæ'sun/ *n Mus.* bajón, fagot, *m*

bassoonist /bæ'sunɪst/ *n* bajonista, fagotista, *mf*

bastard /'bæstərd/ *n* bastardo (-da), hijo (-ja) natural. —*a* bastardo, ilegítimo; espurio

baste /beist/ *vt Sew.* bastear, hilvanar, embastar; *Cul.* enlardar, lardear

basting /'beistɪŋ/ *n Sew.* embaste, *m; Cul.* lardeamiento, *m.* **b. spoon,** cacillo, *m.* **b. stitch,** pasillo, *m*

bastion /'bæstʃən/ *n* bastión, baluarte, *m.* **to fortify with bastions,** abastionar

bastioned /'bæstʃənd/ *a* abastionado, con bastiones

bat /bæt/ *n Zool.* murciélago, *m;* (in cricket) paleta, *f;* (in table tennis) pala, *f.* —*vi* (cricket) golpear con la paleta. See **without**

batch /bætʃ/ *n* (of loaves, etc.) hornada, *f;* lote, *m;* (of recruits) promoción, *f*

bath /bæθ/ *n* baño, *m;* (room) cuarto de baño, *m;* (vat) bañador, *m;* (for swimming) piscina cubierta, *f;* (in the open air) piscina al aire libre, *f; Photo.* baño, *m,* solución, *f.* —*vt* bañar, lavar. **hot mineral baths,** termas, *f pl.* **Order of the B.,** Orden del Baño, *f.* **public baths,** casa de baños, *f.* **reinforcing b.,** *Photo.* reforzador, *m.* **to take a b.,** bañarse, tomar un baño. **b.-chair,** cochecillo de inválido, *m.* **b.-robe,** bata de baño, *f,* albornoz, *m.* **b. room,** cuarto de baño, *m.* **b. towel,** toalla del baño, *f.* **b. tub,** bañera, *f,* baño, *m*

bathe /beið/ *vt* bañar, lavar; (of light, etc.) bañar, envolver. —*vi* bañarse. —*n* baño, *m.* **to go for a b.,** ir a bañarse

bather /'beiðər/ *n* bañista, *mf;* bañador (-ra)

bathing /'beiðɪŋ/ *a* de baño; balneario, *n* baño, *m.* **b. cap,** gorro de baño, *m.* **b. dress,** traje de baño, *m.* **b. gown,** albornoz, *m,* bata de baño, *f.* **b. machine,** caseta de baños, *f.* **b.-pool,** piscina, *f.* **b.-resort,** estación balnearia, *f.* **b.-shoes,** calzado de baño, *m*

bathos /'beiθɒs/ *n* paso de lo sublime a lo ridículo, *m;* anticlímax, *m*

batiste /bə'tist/ *n;* batista, *f*

baton /bə'tɒn/ *n* bastón de mando, *m; Mus.* batuta, *f;* (policeman's) porra, *f*

battalion /bə'tælyən/ *n* batallón, *m*

batten /'bætn̩/ *vi* engordar (de); medrar, prosperar. **to b. down,** cerrar las escotillas

batter /'bætər/ *n Cul.* batido, *m;* pasta, *f; Sports.* lanzador, *m.* —*vt* apalear, golpear; (demolish) derribar, demoler; (with artillery) cañonear; batir. **to coat with b.,** rebozar. **to b. down,** derribar

battering ram /'bætərɪŋ/ *n* ariete, *m*

battery /'bætəri/ *n (Mil. Nav.)* batería, *f; Elec.* pila, batería, *f; Law.* agresión, *f.* **dry b.,** batería de pilas, *f.* **storage b.,** acumulador, *m.* **b. cell,** pila de batería eléctrica, *f*

battle /'bætl̩/ *n* batalla, *f;* pelea, *f,* combate, *m;*

(struggle) lucha, *f.* —*vi* batallar, pelear; luchar. **b.-array,** orden de batalla, *f.* **b.-axe,** hacha de combate, *f.* **b.-cruiser,** acorazado, *m.* **b.-field,** campo de batalla, *m.* **b.-front,** frente de combate, *m.* **b.-piece,** *Art.* batalla, *f.* **b.-ship,** buque de guerra, *m*

battledore (and shuttlecock) /'bætɫ,dɔr/ *n* raqueta (y volante), *f*

battlement /'bætɫmənt/ *n* almenaje, *m;* muralla almenada, *f*

bauble /'bɔbəl/ *n* (trifle) chuchería, fruslería, *f;* (fool's) cetro de bufón, *m*

bauxite /'bɔksait, 'bouzait/ *n* bauxita, *f*

Bavaria /bə'vɛəriə/ Baviera, *f*

Bavarian /bə'vɛəriən/ *a* and *n* bávaro (-ra)

bawdy /'bɔdi/ *a* obsceno, indecente, escabroso

bawl /bɔl/ *vi* chillar, vocear

bawling /'bɔlɪŋ/ *n* vocerío, *m,* chillidos, *m pl*

bay /bei/ *n Geog.* bahía, *f;* (small) abra, *f; Bot.* laurel, *m;* (horse) bayo, *m;* (howl) aullido, *m; Archit.* abertura, *f; Rail.* andén, *m.* —*a* (of horses) bayo, isabelino. —*vi* aullar. **at bay,** en jaque, acorralado. **sickbay,** enfermería, *f.* **to keep at bay,** tener a distancia; tener alejado; entretener. **bay rum,** ron de malagueta, *m.* **bay window,** ventana saylediza, *f*

baying /'beiɪŋ/ *n* aullido, *m*

bayonet /'beiənɛt/ *n* bayoneta, *f, vt* herir o matar con bayoneta. **fixed b.,** bayoneta calada, *f.* **b. charge,** carga de bayoneta, *f.* **b. thrust,** bayonetazo, *m*

Bayonne /ba'yɔn/ Bayona, *f*

bazaar /bə'zɑr/ *n* bazar, *m*

be /bi/ *vi* ser; (of position, place, state, temporariness) estar; (exist) existir; (in impersonal expressions) haber; (of expressions concerning the weather and time) hacer; (remain) quedar; (leave alone) dejar; (do) hacer; (of one's health) estar; (of feeling cold, hot, afraid, etc. and of years of one's age) tener; (live) vivir; (belong) ser (de), pertenecer (a); (matter, concern) importar (a); (happen) ocurrir, suceder; (find oneself) hallarse, encontrarse, estar; (arrive) llegar (a); (cost) costar; (be worth) valer; (celebrate, hold) celebrarse, tener lugar; (forming continuous tense with present participle active or passive) estar; (with past participle forming passive) ser (this construction is often replaced by reflexive form when no ambiguity is entailed); (with infinitive expressing duty, intention) haber de; (must) tener que. **He is a soldier (doctor, etc.),** Es soldado (médico, etc.). **He is on guard,** Está de guardia. **They were at the door (in the house, etc.),** Estaban a la puerta (en la casa, etc.). **I am writing a letter,** Estoy escribiendo una carta (but this form is often replaced by a simple tense, e.g. escribo...). **It remains to be written,** Queda por escribir. **What is to be done?** ¿Qué hay que hacer? **Woe is me!** ¡Ay de mí! **to be hot (cold),** (of things) estar caliente (frío); (of weather) hacer calor (frío); (of persons) tener calor (frío). **How is John? He is well,** ¿Cómo está Juan? Está bien de salud. **It is daylight,** Es de día. **It is cloudy,** Está nublado. **She is 10,** Tiene diez años. **They are afraid,** Tienen miedo. **I am to go there tomorrow,** He de ir allí mañana. **What is to be will be,** Lo que tiene que ser será. **If John were to come we could go into the country,** Si viniera Juan podríamos ir al campo. **Be that as it may,** Sea como sea. **It is seven years since we saw him,** Hace siete años que no lo vemos. **We have been here for three years,** Hace tres años que estamos aquí, Llevamos tres años aquí. **There is** or **there are,** Hay. **There will be many people,** Habrá mucha gente. **There were many people,** Había mucha gente. **There are many people,** Hay mucha gente. **It is three miles to the next village,** Estamos a tres millas del pueblo próximo. **So be it!** Así sea. **Your pen is not to be seen,** Tu pluma no se ve. **It is to be hoped that...,** Se espera que...; ¡Ojalá que...! **The door is open,** La puerta está abierta. **The door was opened by Mary,** La puerta fue abierta por María. **He was accused of being a fascist,** Lo acusaron de fascista. **to be about to,** estar por; (of a more imminent action) estar para, estar a punto de. **to be in,** estar dentro; estar en casa. **to be off,** marcharse, irse. **Be off!** ¡Márchate! ¡Vete! ¡Fuera! **to be out,** estar fuera; haber salido; no estar en casa; (of a

light, etc.) estar apagado. **to be up,** estar levantado. **to be up to,** proyectar, traer entre manos; urdir, maquinar

beach /bitʃ/ *n* playa, *f;* costa, *f.* —*vt* (a boat) encallar en la costa. **b. shoes,** playeras, *f pl.* **b. suit,** vestido de playa, *m*

beach club *n* club de playa, *m*

beacon /'bikən/ *n* (lighthouse) faro, *m;* (buoy) baliza, *f,* fanal, *m;* (watch-tower) atalaya, *f; Fig.* guía, *f.* —*vt* iluminar. **b. fire,** almenara, *f*

bead /bid/ *n* cuenta, *f;* (of glass) abalorio, *m;* (drop) gota, *f; Archit.* perla, *f;* (bubble) burbuja, *f;* (foam) espuma, *f; pl* **beads,** rosario, *m, vt* adornar con abalorios. **to tell one's beads,** rezar el rosario. **b. work,** abalorio, *m*

beading /'bidɪŋ/ *n* abalorio, *m; Archit.* friso, listón, *m*

beadle /'bidɫ/ *n* bedel, *m*

beadleship /'bidɫ,ʃɪp/ *n* bedelía, *f*

beagle /'bigəl/ *n* perro sabueso, *m*

beak /bik/ *n* pico, *m;* punta, *f; Naut.* espolón, *m.* **to tap with the b.,** picotear

beaked /'bikt/ *a* que tiene pico; (in compounds) de... pico

beaker /'bikər/ *n* copa, *f; Chem.* vaso de precipitado, *m*

beam /bim/ *n Archit.* madero, *m,* viga, *f;* (width of a ship) manga, *f;* (of a balance) palanca, *f;* (of a plough) cama, *f;* (of light) rayo, destello, *m; Phys.* rayo, *m;* (smile) sonrisa brillante, *f; pl* **beams,** (of a building) envigado, *m;* (of a ship) baos, *m pl.* **main b.,** *Archit.* viga maestra, *f.* **on her b.-ends,** de costado; *Fig.* arruinado; en la miseria. **b. feather,** astil, *m.* **b. of light,** rayo de luz, haz de luz, *m*

beam /bim/ *vt* lanzar, emitir; difundir. —*vi* brillar, fulgurar, destellar; estar radiante, estar rebosando de alegría

beaming /'bimɪŋ/ *a* brillante; radiante

bean /bin/ *n* haba, *f;* judía, alubia, *f;* (of coffee) grano, *m.* **broad b.,** haba, *f.* **French, haricot, kidney b.,** judía, *f.* **string b.,** judía verde, *f.* **b. field,** habar, *m*

bear /bɛər/ *n Zool.* oso, *m;* (she-bear) osa, *f;* (Stock Exchange) bajista, *mf.* **Great B.,** *Astron.* Osa Mayor, *f,* Septentrión, *m.* **Little B.,** *Astron.* Osa Menor, *f.* **polar b.,** oso blanco, *m.* **b.-cub,** osezno, *m.* **bear's den,** osera, *f.* **b.-garden,** patio de osos, *m; Inf.* merienda de negros, *f.* **b.-hunting,** caza de osos, *f.* **b.-like,** osuno. **b.-pit,** recinto de los osos, *m*

bear /bɛər/ *vt* and *vi* (carry) llevar; (show) ostentar; (company, etc.) hacer; (profess) profesar; (of spite, etc. and of relation) guardar; (have) tener; (fruit) dar; (give birth to) parir; (support) sostener; (endure) aguantar; (suffer) padecer, sufrir; (tolerate) tolerar, sufrir; (a strain, an operation, etc.) resistir; (lean on) apoyarse en; (experience) experimentar; (produce) producir, dar; (enjoy) disfrutar de; (use) usar; (impel) empujar; (occupy, hold) ocupar; (go) dirigirse. **It was suddenly borne in on them that...,** De pronto vieron claro que... **I cannot b. any more,** No puedo más. **We cannot b. him,** No le aguantamos, No le sufrimos. **His language won't b. repeating,** Su lenguaje no puede repetirse. **to bring to b.,** ejercer (presión, etc.). **to b. a grudge,** guardar rencor (a), tener ojeriza (a). **to b. arms,** llevar armas; servir en el ejército o la milicia. **to b. company,** hacer compañía (a), acompañar (a). **to b. in mind,** tener en cuenta, tener presente; acordarse de. **to b. oneself,** conducirse, portarse. **to b. to the right,** ir hacia la derecha. **to b. witness,** atestiguar. **to b. false witness,** levantar falso testimonio. **to b. away,** llevarse; ganar. **to b. down,** hundir; derribar; bajar. **to b. down on,** avanzar rápidamente hacia; correr hacia; *Naut.* arribar sobre; (attack) caer sobre. **to b. in,** llevar adentro. **to b. off,** llevarse; ganar; *Naut.* apartarse de la costa. **to b. on, upon,** apoyarse en; (refer to) referirse a. **to b. out,** llevar fuera; confirmar; apoyar; justificar. **to b. up,** llevar arriba; llevar a la cumbre (de); sostener; (recover) cobrar ánimo; (against) resistir; hacer frente a. **to b. with,** soportar; sufrir; aguantar; llevar con paciencia; ser indulgente con

bearable /'bɛərəbəl/ a soportable; aguantable; tolerable

beard /bɪərd/ n barba, f; (of cereals) raspa, arista, f, vt desafiar. **thick b.,** barba bien poblada, f

bearded /'bɪərdɪd/ a con barba, barbudo

beardless /'bɪərdlɪs/ a barbilampiño, desbarbado, imberbe, lampiño

bearer /'bɛərər/ n llevador (-ra), portador (-ra); (of a bier) andero, m; Com. dador, portador, m. **good b.,** Agr. árbol fructífero, m. **to b.,** Com. al portador

bearing /'bɛərɪŋ/ n porte, m; postura, f; presencia, f; conducta, f; aspecto, m; relación, f; (meaning) significación, f; Naut. demora, orientación, f; Mech. cojinete, soporte, m; (endurance) tolerancia, f; pl **bearings,** (way) camino, m; Herald. escudo de armas, m. **to get one's bearings,** orientarse; encontrar el camino. **to lose one's bearings,** desorientarse; perderse. **to have a b. on,** tener relación con; tener que ver con; influir en

bearish /'bɛərɪʃ/ a osuno; rudo, áspero

bearskin /'bɛər,skɪn/ n piel de oso, f; birretina, f

beast /bist/ n animal, bruto, m; cuadrúpedo, m; (cattle) res, f; bestia, f. **wild b.,** fiera, f. **b. of burden,** acémila, bestia de carga, f. **b. of prey,** animal de rapiña, m

beastliness /'bistlɪnɪs/ n bestialidad, brutalidad, f; obscenidad, f

beastly /'bistli/ a bestial, brutal; obsceno; Inf. horrible

beat /bit/ n latido, m, pulsación, f; golpe, m; (of a drum) toque (de tambor), m; (of a clock) tictac, m; sonido repetido, m; vibración, f

beat /bit/ vt and vi batir; golpear; (thrash) pegar, dar una paliza (a); (to remove dust, etc.) sacudir; (shake) agitar; (the wings) aletear; (hunting) batir; (excel) exceder, superar; ganar; (defeat) vencer; (of the rain, etc.) azotar; (a drum) tocar; (of the sun) batir, dar (en); (throb) latir, palpitar, pulsar. **to b. about the bush,** andarse por las ramas. **to stop beating about the bush,** dejarse de historias. **to b. a retreat,** Mil. emprender la retirada; huir. **to b. black and blue,** moler a palos. **to b. hollow,** vencer completamente; ganar fácilmente; aventajar con mucho. **to b. it,** Inf. escaparse corriendo. **to b. time,** Mus. llevar el compás; triunfar sobre la vejez. **to b. to it,** Inf. tomar la delantera. **to b. against,** golpear contra; chocar contra. **to b. back,** rechazar; (sobs, etc.) ahogar; reprimir. **to b. down,** (prices) regatear; (of the sun) caer de plomo, caer de plano; reducir; suprimir; destruir. **to b. off,** rechazar; echar a un lado. **to b. out,** hacer salir; (metals) batir; (a tune) llevar el compás (de). **to b. up,** Cul. batir; (a mattress) mullir; asaltar; maltratar

beaten /'bitn/ a (of paths) trillado; (conquered) vencido; (of metals) batido; (dejected) deprimido; (trite) trivial, vulgar

beater /'bitər/ n batidor, f; (for carpets) sacudidor (de alfombras), m; Cul. batidor, m

beatific /,biə'tɪfɪk/ a beatífico

beatification /bi,ætəfɪ'keɪʃən/ n beatificación, f

beatify /bi'ætə,faɪ/ vt beatificar

beating /'bitɪŋ/ n batimiento, m; vencimiento, m; (thrashing) paliza, f; (of the heart, etc.) palpitación, f; latido, m; (of metals) batida, f; (of a drum) rataplán, toque de tambor, m; (of waves) embate, m; (of wings) aleteo, aletazo, m

beatitude /bi'ætɪ,tud/ n beatitud, f

beau /bou/ n galán, m; (fop) petimetre, m

beautiful /'byutəfəl/ a bello, lindo, hermoso; magnífico; excelente; exquisito; elegante; encantador, delicioso

beautifully /'byutəfəli/ adv bellamente; (richly) ricamente; admirablemente; magníficamente; elegantemente

beautify /'byutə,faɪ/ vt embellecer; hermosear; adornar. **to b. oneself,** arreglarse, ponerse elegante

beautifying /'byutə,faɪɪŋ/ n embellecimiento, m; adorno, m

beauty /'byuti/ n belleza, hermosura, lindeza, f; magnificencia, f; excelencia, f; elegancia, f; encanto, m; (belle) beldad, Venus, f. **to lose one's b.,** desmejorarse, perder su hermosura. **b. contest,** concurso de belleza, m. **b. parlor,** salón de belleza, instituto de belleza, m. **b. sleep,** el primer sueño de la noche. **b. spot,** lunar, m; lunar postizo, m; (place) sitio hermoso, m. **b. treatment,** masaje facial, m

beaver /'bivər/ n castor, m; (hat) sombrero de copa, m; (of helmet) babera, f

because /bɪ'kɔz/ conjunc porque. **b. of,** debido a, a causa de

beckon /'bɛkən/ vt and vi hacer señas (a); llamar por señas, llamar con la mano

become /bɪ'kʌm/ vi volverse; llegar a ser, venir a ser; convertirse en; ponerse; hacerse; (befit) convenir; (suit) ir bien (a), favorecer. **He became red,** Se enrojeció. **The hat becomes you,** El sombrero te va bien. **He became king,** Llegó a ser rey. **What has b. of her?** ¿Qué es de ella?; (Where is she?) ¿Qué se ha hecho de ella? **b. binding,** adquirir carácter de compromiso

becoming /bɪ'kʌmɪŋ/ a propio; correcto; decoroso; (suitable) conveniente; (of dress) que favorece, que va bien. **This dress is b. to you,** Este vestido te favorece

becomingly /bɪ'kʌmɪŋli/ adv decorosamente

bed /bɛd/ n cama, f, lecho, m; (of sea) fondo, m; (of river) cauce, m; Geol. yacimiento, m; (in a garden) cuadro, macizo (de jardín), m; (of a machine) asiento, m; (of a building) cimiento, m; Fig. fundamento, m, base, f, vt (plants) plantar; (fix) fijar, poner. **double bed,** cama de matrimonio, f. **single bed,** cama de monja, f. **in bed,** en cama. **to be gone to bed,** haber ido a la cama. **to be in bed,** estar acostado. **to get into bed,** meterse en cama. **to get out of bed,** levantarse de la cama. **to go to bed,** acostarse, ir a la cama. **to make the beds,** hacer las camas. **to put to bed,** acostar. **to stay in bed,** quedarse en cama, guardar cama. **bed-bug,** chinche, f. **bed-clothes,** ropa de cama, f. **bed-cover,** cubrecama, colcha, f. **bed-head,** cabecera, f. **bed-pan,** silleta, f. **bed-sore,** úlcera de decúbito, f

bedaub, bedazzle /bɪ'dɔb; bɪ'dæzəl/. See **daub, dazzle**

bedchamber /'bɛd,tʃeɪmbər/ n dormitorio, m, alcoba, f

bedded /'bɛdɪd/ a con... cama(s). **a double-b. room,** un cuarto con dos camas; un cuarto con cama de matrimonio

bedding /'bɛdɪŋ/ n ropa de cama, f; cama para el ganado, f

bedeck /bɪ'dɛk/ vt embellecer, adornar, engalanar

bedfellow /'bɛd,felou/ n compañero de almohada, compañero de cama

bedlam /'bɛdləm/ n belén, manicomio, m; Fig. babel, m

Bedouin /'bɛduɪn/ a and n beduino (-na)

bedraggled /bɪ'drægəld/ a mojado y sucio

bedridden /'bɛd,rɪdn/ a postrado en cama, inválido

bedrock /'bɛd,rɒk/ n lecho de roca, m; Fig. principios fundamentales, fundamentos, m pl

bedroom /'bɛd,rum/ n cuarto de dormir, dormitorio, m, habitación, f

bedside /'bɛd,saɪd/ n lado de cama, m; cabecera, f. **b. manner,** mano izquierda, diplomacia, f. **b.-table,** mesa de noche, f

bedspread /'bɛd,sprɛd/ n colcha, cubrecama, sobrecama, f

bedstead /'bɛd,stɛd/ n cama, f

bedtime /'bɛd,taɪm/ n hora de acostarse, f

bee /bi/ n abeja, f; (meeting) reunión, f. **queen bee,** rey, m, abeja maestra, f. **to have a bee in one's bonnet,** tener una manía (or idea fija). **to make a bee-line for,** ir directamente a. **bee-eater,** Ornith. abejaruco, m. **bee hive,** colmena, f; abejar, m. **bee-keeper,** apicultor (-ra), colmenero (-ra), abejero (-ra). **bee's wax,** cera de abeja, f

beech /bitʃ/ n haya, f. **plantation of b. trees,** hayal, m. **b.-nut,** hayuco, m

beef /bif/ n carne de vaca, f; (flesh) carne, f; (strength) fuerza, f. **roast b.,** rosbif, m. **b.-tea,** caldo, m

beefsteak /'bif,steik/ n biftec, bistec, m

beer /bɪər/ n cerveza, f. **b. barrel,** barril de cerveza, *m.* **b.-house,** cervecería, *f.* **b. mug,** jarro para la cerveza, *m*

beery /'bɪəri/ *a* de cerveza; (tipsy) achispado

beet /bit/ *n* remolacha, *f.* **b. sugar,** azúcar de remolacha, *m*

beetle /'bitl/ *n* escarabajo, *m.* **b.-browed,** cejijunto

beetroot /'bit,rut/ *n* remolacha, *f*

befall /bɪ'fɔl/ *vi* acontecer, suceder, ocurrir. —*vt* ocurrir (a), acontecer (a)

befeathered /bɪ'feðərd/ *a* plumado; adornado con plumas

befit /bɪ'fɪt/ *vt* convenir (a), ser digno de

befitting /bɪ'fɪtɪŋ/ *a* conveniente, apropiado; digno; oportuno

before /bɪ'fɔr/ *adv* delante; al frente; (of time), antes, anteriormente; (of order) antes; (already) ya. —*prep* delante de; en frente de; (of time, order) ante; (in presence of) ante, en presencia de; (rather than) antes de. **b. going,** antes de marcharse. **B. I did it,** Antes de que lo hiciera; Antes de hacerlo. **as never b.,** como nunca. **b. long,** en breve, dentro de poco. **b.-mentioned,** antes citado. **b. the mast,** al pie del mástil, e.g. *two years b. the mast,* dos años al pie del mástil.

beforehand /bɪ'fɔr,hænd/ *adv* previamente, de antemano

befoul /bɪ'faul/ *vt* ensuciar; *Fig.* manchar, difamar

befriend /bɪ'frɛnd/ *vt* proteger, ayudar, favorecer, amparar

beg /bɛg/ *vt* pedir, implorar, suplicar. —*vi* mendigar, pordiosear; vivir de limosna. **I beg to propose,** Me permito proponer; Tengo el gusto de proponer; (the health of) Brindo a la salud de. **I beg your pardon!** ¡Vd. dispense!; (when passing in front of anyone, etc.) Con permiso; (in conversation for repetition of a word) ¿Cómo? **to beg the question,** dar por sentado lo mismo que se trata de probar. **His conduct begs description,** No hay palabras para su comportamiento

beget /bɪ'gɛt/ *vt* procrear, engendrar; causar; suscitar

begetter /bɪ'gɛtər/ *n* procreador (-ra); creador (-ra)

begetting /bɪ'gɛtɪŋ/ *n* procreación, *f;* origen, *m,* causa, *f*

beggar /'bɛgər/ *n* mendigo (-ga), pordiosero (-ra). **beggars can't be choosers,** a falta de pan, se conforma con tortillas (Mexico); *vt* empobrecer; arruinar. **to b. description,** no haber palabras para describir

beggarliness /'bɛgərlinɪs/ *n* mendicidad, *f;* pobreza, *f*

beggarly /'bɛgərli/ *a* miserable, pobre

beggary /'bɛgəri/ *n* miseria, pobreza, *f*

begging /'bɛgɪŋ/ *a* mendicante, pordiosero. —*n* mendicidad, *f,* pordioseo, *m.* **to go b.,** andar mendigando. **b. letter,** carta pidiendo dinero, *f*

begin /bɪ'gɪn/ *vt and vi* empezar; comenzar; iniciar; (a conversation) entablar; (open) abrir; inaugurar; tener su principio; nacer. **to b. to,** empezar a; (start on) ponerse a; (with laughing, etc.) romper a. **to b. with,** empezar por; para empezar, en primer lugar

beginner /bɪ'gɪnər/ *n* principiante (-ta); (novice) novato (-ta); iniciador (-ra); autor (-ra)

beginning /bɪ'gɪnɪŋ/ *n* principio, comienzo, *m;* origen, *m.* **at the b.,** al principio; (of the month) a principios (de). **from the b. to the end,** desde el comienzo hasta el fin, *Inf.* de pe a pa. **in the b.,** al principio. **to make a b.,** comenzar, empezar

begone /bɪ'gɔn/ *interj* ¡fuera! ¡márchate! ¡vete!

begonia /bɪ'gounyə/ *n* begonia, *f*

begrudge /bɪ'grʌdʒ/ *vt* envidiar

beguile /bɪ'gail/ *vt* engañar; defraudar; (time) entretener; (charm) encantar, embelesar

beguilement /bɪ'gailmənt/ *n* engaño, *m;* (of time) entretenimiento, *m;* (charm) encanto, *m*

beguilingly /bɪ'gailɪŋli/ *adv* encantadoramente

behalf /bɪ'hæf/ *n* (preceded by on or upon) por; (from) de parte (de); a favor (de); en defensa (de)

behave /bɪ'heiv/ *vi* (oneself) conducirse, portarse; (act) obrar, proceder. **to b. badly,** portarse mal; obrar mal. **B.!** ¡Pórtate bien!

behavior /bɪ'heivyər/ *n* conducta, *f;* comportamiento, *m;* proceder, *m;* (manner) modales, *m pl; Biol.* reacción, *f*

behaviorism /bɪ'heivyə,rizəm/ *n Psychol.* behaviorismo, *m*

behead /bɪ'hɛd/ *vt* decapitar, descabezar

beheading /bɪ'hɛdɪŋ/ *n* decapitación, *f*

behest /bɪ'hɛst/ *n* precepto, mandato, *m*

behind /bɪ'haind/ *adv* detrás; por detrás; atrás; hacia atrás; en pos; (of time and order) después; (late and in arrears) con retraso; (old-fashioned) atrasado. —*prep* detrás de; por detrás de; inferior a; menos avanzado que. —*n Inf.* trasero, *m.* **from b.,** por detrás. **to be b. time,** retrasarse; llegar tarde. **b. the back of,** a espaldas de. **b. the scenes,** entre bastidores. **b. the times,** *Fig.* atrasado de noticias; pasado de moda. **the ideology b. the French Revolution,** la ideología que informó la Revolución Francesa.

behindhand /bɪ'haind,hænd/ *a* (out of date) atrasado; (late) tardío; *adv* con retraso

behold /bɪ'hould/ *vt* ver, mirar, contemplar; presenciar. —*interj* ¡he aquí! ¡mira!

beholden /bɪ'houldən/ *a* obligado, agradecido

beholder /bɪ'houldər/ *n* espectador (-ra). **the beholders,** los que lo presenciaban

beholding /bɪ'houldɪŋ/ *n* contemplación, vista, *f*

behoove /bɪ'houv/ *vt* incumbir, tocar, corresponder

beige /beiʒ/ *n* beige, color arena, *m*

being /'biɪŋ/ *n* existencia, *f;* operación, *f;* ser, *m;* (spirit) alma, *f,* espíritu, *m;* esencia, *f.* **human b.,** ser humano, *m,* alma viviente, *f.* **for the time b.,** por ahora, por el momento

bejewel /bɪ'dʒuəl/ *vt* enjoyar, adornar con joyas

belabor /bɪ'leibər/ *vt* apalear, golpear

belated /bɪ'leitid/ *a* tardío

belay /bɪ'lei/ *vt* amarrar

belch /bɛltʃ/ *n* eructo, *m;* detonación, *f;* (of a volcano) erupción, *f.* —*vi* eructar. —*vt* vomitar; (curses, etc.) escupir; despedir, arrojar

belching /'bɛltʃɪŋ/ *n* eructación, *f;* (of smoke, etc.) vómito, *m,* emisión, *f*

beleaguer /bɪ'ligər/ *vt* sitiar

belfry /'bɛlfri/ *n* campanario, *m*

Belgian /'bɛldʒən/ *a and n* belga, *mf*

Belgium /'bɛldʒəm/ Bélgica, *f*

Belgrade /'bɛlgreid/ Belgrado, *m*

belie /bɪ'lai/ *vt* desmentir, contradecir; defraudar

belief /bɪ'lif/ *n* creencia, *f;* fe, *f;* opinión, *f,* parecer, *m;* (trust) confianza, *f.* **in the b. that,** creyendo que, en la creencia de que

believable /bɪ'livəbəl/ *a* creíble

believe /bɪ'liv/ *vt and vi* creer; opinar, ser de la opinión, parecer (a uno); confiar, tener confianza. **I b. not,** Creo que no, No lo creo. **I b. so,** Creo que sí, Me parece que sí. **to make (a person) b.,** hacer (a uno) creer. **to b. in,** creer en; confiar en, tener confianza en

believer /bɪ'livər/ *n* persona que cree, *f;* creyente, *mf*

belittle /bɪ'lɪtl/ *vt* achicar; conceder poca importancia a

bell /bɛl/ *n* campana, *f;* (hand-bell) campanilla, *f;* (small, round) cascabel, *m;* (on cows, etc.) cencerro, *m,* esquila, *f;* (electric, push, or bicycle) timbre, *m;* (jester's) cascabeles, *m pl;* (cry of stag) bramido, *m.* —*vt* poner un cascabel a; (stags) bramar, roncar. **To bear away the b.,** *Fig.* llevarse la palma. **to ring the b.,** tocar el timbre; agitar la campanilla. **to ring the bells,** tocar las campanas. **to b. the cat,** ponerle el cascabel al gato, ponerle el collar al gato. **b.-boy,** botones, mozo de hotel, *m.* **b.-clapper,** badajo, *m.* **b.-flower,** campanilla, *f.* **b.-founder,** campanero, *m.* **b.-mouthed,** abocinado. **b.-pull,** tirador de campanilla, *m.* **b.-ringer,** campanero, *m.* **b.-shaped,** campanudo. **b.-tent,** pabellón, *f.* **b. tower,** campanario, *m*

belladonna /,bɛlə'dɒnə/ *n* belladona, *f*

belle /bɛl/ *n* beldad, *f*

belles-lettres /bɛl 'lɛtrə/ *n pl* bellas letras, *f pl*

bellicose /'bɛlɪ,kous/ *a* belicoso, agresivo

bellicosity /,bɛlɪ'kɒsɪti/ *n* belicosidad, *f*

belligerency /bə'lɪdʒərənsi/ *n* beligerancia, *f*

belligerent /bə'lɪdʒərənt/ *a* beligerante; belicoso, guerrero. —*n* beligerante, *mf*

bellow /'belou/ *n* (shout) grito, *m;* rugido, bramido, *m;* (of guns) trueno, *m.* —*vi* gritar, vociferar; rugir, bramar; tronar

bellowing /'belouɪŋ/ *n.* See **bellow**

bellows /'belouz/ n fuelle, m
belly /'beli/ n vientre, m, barriga, f; (of a jug, etc.) panza, f; estómago, m; (womb) seno, m. —vt hinchar. —vi hincharse
belong /bɪ'lɔŋ/ vi pertenecer (a); tocar (a), incumbir (a); (to a place) ser de; residir en
belongings /bɪ'lɔŋɪŋz/ n pl efectos, m pl; posesiones, f pl; (luggage) equipaje, m
beloved /bɪ'lʌvɪd/ a muy amado, muy querido. —n querido (-da)
below /bɪ'lou/ adv abajo; (under) debajo; (further on) más abajo; (in hell) en el infierno; (in this world) en este mundo, aquí abajo. —prep bajo; (underneath) debajo de; (after) después de; (unworthy of) indigno de; inferior a. **The valley lay b. us,** El valle se extendía a nuestros pies. **b. zero,** bajo cero
belt /belt/ n cinturón, m; (of a horse) cincha, f; (corset) faja, f; Geog. zona, f; (of a machine) correa (de transmisión), f
beltway /'belt,wei/ n anillo periférico, m
belvedere /'belvɪ,dɪər/ n mirador, m
bemoan /bɪ'moun/ vt deplorar, lamentar
bemoaning /bɪ'mounɪŋ/ n lamentación, f
bemuse /bɪ'myuz/ vt confundir, desconcertar
bench /bentʃ/ n banco, m; (with a back) escaño, m; mesa de trabajo, f; (carpenter's, shoemaker's, in a boat, in parliament) banco, m; (judges) tribunal, m
bend /bend/ n corvadura, curva, vuelta, f; (in a river, street) recodo, m; (on a road) codo viraje, m; (of the knee) corva, f; (in a pipe) codo, m; Naut. nudo, m; Herald. banda, f. **sheet b.,** (knot) nudo de tejedor, m
bend /bend/ vt encorvar; doblegar; torcer; (the head) bajar; (the body) inclinar; (steps) dirigir, encaminar; (the mind) aplicarse, dedicarse. —vi encorvarse; doblegarse; torcerse; (arch) arquear; inclinarse. **to b. the knee,** arrodillarse. **on bended knee,** de rodillas. **to b. back,** vt redoblar. —vi redoblarse; inclinarse hacia atrás. **to b. down,** agacharse; inclinarse. **to b. forward,** inclinarse hacia delante. **to b. over,** inclinarse encima de
bendable /'bendəbəl/ a que puede doblarse; plegadizo; flexible
bending /'bendɪŋ/ n doblamiento, m; flexión, f; inclinación, f. —a doblado; inclinado
beneath /bɪ'niθ/ adv abajo; debajo; (at one's feet) a los pies de uno. —prep bajo; debajo de; al pie de; (unworthy, inferior) indigno. **He married b. him,** Se casó fuera de su clase
Benedictine /,benɪ'dɪktɪn, -tin/ a benedictino. —n benedictino, m; (liqueur) benedictino, m
benediction /,benɪ'dɪkʃən/ n bendición, f; gracia divina, merced, f
benefaction /'benə,fækʃən/ n beneficiación, f; buena obra, f; beneficio, favor, m
benefactor /'benə,fæktər/ n bienhechor, m; protector, m; patrono, m; fundador, m
benefactress /'benə,fæktrɪs/ n bienhechora, f; protectora, f; patrona, f; fundadora, f
benefice /'benəfɪs/ n beneficio eclesiástico, m, prebenda, f
beneficence /bə'nefəsəns/ n beneficiencia, caridad, f, buenas obras, f pl
beneficent /bə'nefəsənt/ a benéfico, caritativo
beneficial /,benə'fɪʃəl/ a beneficioso; provechoso, útil
beneficiary /,benə'fɪʃi,eri/ n beneficiado (-da), beneficiario (-ia)
benefit /'benəfɪt/ n beneficio, bien, m; provecho, m, utilidad, f; (favor) favor, m; Theat. beneficio, m; (help) ayuda, f, servicio, m. —vt beneficiar; aprovechar; (improve) mejorar. —vi (with by) sacar provecho de; ganar. **for the b. of,** para; en pro de, a favor de. **b. society,** sociedad benéfica, f
benevolence /bə'nevələns/ n benevolencia, bondad, f; liberalidad, f; caridad, f; favor, m
benevolent /bə'nevələnt/ a benévolo; bondadoso; caritativo. **b. society,** sociedad de beneficencia, f
benevolently /bə'nevələntli/ adv benignamente, con benevolencia
Bengal /ben'gɔl/ Bengala, f
benighted /bɪ'naitɪd/ a sorprendido por la noche; Fig. ignorante
benign, benignant /bɪ'nain; bɪ'nɪgnənt/ a benigno

bent /bent/ n talento, m; inclinación, afición, f, a torcido, encorvado; resuelto
benumb /bɪ'nʌm/ See **numb**
benzine /'benzin/ n bencina, f
bequeath /bɪ'kwið/ vt legar, dejar (en el testamento); transmitir
bequest /bɪ'kwest/ n legado, m
Berber /'bɜrbər/ a and n bereber, mf
bereave /bɪ'riv/ vt privar (de), quitar; arrebatar; afligir. **the bereaved parents,** los padres afligidos
bereavement /bɪ'rivmənt/ n privación, f; (by death) pérdida, f; aflicción, f
bereft /bɪ'reft/ a privado (de); desamparado; indefenso. **utterly b.,** completamente solo
beret /bə'rei/ n boina, f
Berlin /bər'lɪn/ a and n (of or from) berlinés (-esa). —n (carriage) berlina, f
Bermudas, the /bər'myudəz/ m las Islas Bermudas
Bernard /'bɜrnərd/ n Bernardo, m. **St. B. dog,** perro de San Bernardo, m
Berne /bɜrn/ Berna, f
berry /'beri/ n baya, f; (of coffee, etc.) fruto, m, vi dar bayas; coger bayas
berth /bɜrθ/ n (bed) litera, f; (cabin) camarote, m; (anchorage) anclaje, fondeadero, m; (job) empleo, m, vt (a ship) fondear. **to give a wide b. to,** Naut. ponerse a resguardo de; apartarse mucho de; evitar
beseech /bɪ'sitʃ/ vt suplicar, rogar, implorar; (ask for) pedir con ahinco
beseeching /bɪ'sitʃɪŋ/ a suplicante, implorante. —n súplica, f; ruego, m
beseechingly /bɪ'sitʃɪŋli/ adv suplicantemente
beset /bɪ'set/ vt atacar, acosar; aquejar, acosar, perseguir. **beset by personal misfortune,** acosado por las desgracias personales; (block) obstruir; (surround) rodear, cercar
besetting /bɪ'setɪŋ/ a usual, frecuente; obsesionante
beside, besides /bɪ'said; bɪ'saidz/ prep al lado de; cerca de; (compared with) en comparación de, comparado con; (in addition) además de; aparte de; excepto. —adv además, también. **to be beside oneself,** estar fuera de sí
besiege /bɪ'sidʒ/ vt sitiar; (assail) asaltar, asediar; (surround) rodear; importunar
besieged /bɪ'sidʒd/ n sitiado (-da)
besieger /bɪ'sidʒər/ n sitiador, m
besieging /bɪ'sidʒɪŋ/ a sitiador. —n sitio, asalto, m; asedio, m, importunación, f
besmear /bɪ'smɪər/ vt embadurnar, ensuciar
besotted /bɪ'sɒtɪd/ a estúpido; embrutecido; atontado
bespangled /bɪ'spæŋgəld/ a adornado con lentejuelas; brillante (con); (studded) salpicado (de)
bespatter /bɪ'spætər/ vt manchar; derramar; salpicar
bespeak /bɪ'spik/ vt reservar; (goods) encargar; (signify) demostrar, indicar, significar; Poet. hablar
besprinkle /bɪ'sprɪŋkəl/ vt rociar
best /best/ a superl of **good** and **well,** mejor; el (la) mejor, m, f., los (las) mejores, m pl, f pl. —adv mejor; el mejor; (most) más. **as b. I can,** como mejor pueda. **at the b.,** cuando más, en el mejor caso. **He did it for the b.,** Lo hizo con la mejor intención. **the b.,** lo mejor. **to be at one's b.,** brillar; lucirse. **to do one's b.,** hacer todo lo posible. **to get the b. of,** llevar la mejor parte de; triunfar de (or sobre). **to make the b. of,** sacar el mayor provecho de. **The next b. thing to do is...,** Lo mejor que queda ahora por hacer es... **b. man,** padrino de boda, m. **to be b. man to,** apadrinar, ser padrino de. **b. seller,** libro que se vende más, libro favorito, m
bestial /'bestʃəl/ a bestial
bestiality /,bestʃi'ælɪti/ n bestialidad, f
bestir (oneself) /bɪ'stɜr/ vr menearse, moverse; preocuparse; (hurry) darse prisa
bestow /bɪ'stou/ vt (place) poner; (with upon) conferir, conceder, otorgar; (a present) regalar
bestowal /bɪ'stouəl/ n puesta, f; otorgamiento, m, concesión, f; (of a present) regalo, m, dádiva, f
bestride /bɪ'straid/ vt montar a horcajadas en; poner una pierna en cada lado de; cruzar de un tranco
bestseller /'best'selər/ n campeón de venta, éxito editorial, triunfo de librería, m

bet /bɛt/ *n* apuesta, postura, *f; vi* apostar; (gamble) jugar. **What do you bet?** ¿Qué apuesta Vd.?

betake (oneself) /bɪ'teik/ *vr* acudir (a); darse (a); marcharse

bethink (oneself) /bɪ'θɪŋk/ *vr* pensar, reflexionar; (remember) recordar, hacer memoria; ocurrirse

Bethlehem /'bɛθlɪ,hɛm/ Belén, *m*

betimes /bɪ'taimz/ *adv* pronto; de buena hora, temprano; con tiempo

betoken /bɪ'toukən/ *vt* presagiar, prometer; indicar

betray /bɪ'trei/ *vt* traicionar; revelar, descubrir; (a woman) seducir; (show) dejar ver

betrayal /bɪ'treiəl/ *n* traición, *f*; (of confidence) abuso (de confianza), *m*; (of a woman) seducción, *f*

betrayer /bɪ'treiər/ *n* traidor (-ra)

betroth /bɪ'trouð/ *vt* desposar(se) con, prometer(se). **to be betrothed to,** estar prometido con

betrothal /bɪ'trouðəl/ *n* desposorio, *m,* esponsales, *m pl;* (duration) noviazgo, *m*

betrothed /bɪ'trouðd/ *a* desposado (-da), futuro (-ra)

better /'bɛtər/ *a compar* of **good,** mejor; superior. —*adv* mejor; más. —*vt* mejorar; exceder. —*n* apostador (-ra). **He has bettered himself,** Ha mejorado su situación. **It is b. to...,** Es mejor..., Vale más... (followed by infin.). **little b.,** poco mejor; algo mejor; poco más. **much b.,** mucho mejor. **our betters,** nuestros superiores. **so much the b.,** tanto mejor. **the b. to,** para mejor. **to be b.,** ser mejor; (of health) estar mejor. **to get b.,** mejorar. **to get the b. of,** triunfar sobre, vencer. **b. half,** *Inf.* media naranja, *f.* **b. off,** mejor situado, más acomodado

betterment /'bɛtərmənt/ *n* mejora, *f,* mejoramiento, *m;* adelantamiento, avance, *m*

betting /'bɛtɪŋ/ *n* apuesta, *f*

bettor /'bɛtər/ *n* apostador (-ra)

between /bɪ'twin/ *prep* entre; en medio de; de. **the break b. Mr. X and Mrs. Y,** el rompimiento del Sr. X y la Sra. Y. —*adv* en medio; entre los dos. **far b.,** a grandes intervalos. **b. now and then,** desde ahora hasta entonces. **b. one thing and another,** entre una cosa y otra. **b. ourselves,** entre nosotros

bevel /'bɛvəl/ *n* bisel, *m, vt* abiselar

beverage /'bɛvərɪdʒ/ *n* brebaje, *m,* bebida, *f*

bevy /'bɛvi/ *n* grupo, *m;* (of birds) bandada, *f;* (of roes) manada, *f*

bewail /bɪ'weil/ *vt* lamentar, llorar

bewailing /bɪ'weilɪŋ/ *n* lamentación, *f*

beware /bɪ'wɛər/ *vi* guardarse (de); cuidar (de); desconfiar (de). —*interj* ¡cuidado! ¡atención! **B. of imitations!** ¡Desconfiad de las imitaciones!

bewilder /bɪ'wɪldər/ *vt* aturdir, abobar; dejar perplejo (a); confundir

bewildered /bɪ'wɪldərd/ *a* aturdido, abobado; perplejo; confuso

bewildering /bɪ'wɪldərɪŋ/ *a* incomprensible; complicado

bewilderment /bɪ'wɪldərmənt/ *n* aturdimiento, *m;* perplejidad, *f,* confusión, *f*

bewitch /bɪ'wɪtʃ/ *vt* hechizar; fascinar, encantar

bewitching /bɪ'wɪtʃɪŋ/ *a* encantador, hechicero, fascinante. —*n* embrujamiento, encantamiento, *m*

bewitchingly /bɪ'wɪtʃɪŋli/ *adv* de un modo encantador

bewitchment /bɪ'wɪtʃmənt/ *n.* See **bewitching**

beyond /bi'ɒnd/ *prep* más allá de; más lejos que; (behind) tras, detrás de; (of time) después de; *Fig.* fuera del alcance de; (without) fuera de; (above) encima de; (not including) aparte. —*adv* más allá; más lejos; detrás. **b. doubt,** fuera de duda. **b. question,** indiscutible. **b. the sea,** allende el mar. **That is b. me,** Eso es demasiado para mí; Eso no está en mi mano; Eso está fuera de mi alcance. **the back of b.,** donde Cristo dio las tres voces, las quimbambas. **the B.,** la otra vida

Bhutan /bu'tɑn/ Bután, *m*

bias /'baiəs/ *n* sesgo, bies, través, *m; Fig.* prejuicio, *m;* parcialidad, *f, vt* influir; predisponer. **to cut on the b.,** cortar al sesgo

biased /'baiəst/ *a* parcial; tendencioso

bib /bɪb/ *n* babero, *m;* pechera, *f, vi* beber mucho, empinar el codo

Bible /'baibəl/ *n* Biblia, *f*

biblical /'bɪblɪkəl/ *a* bíblico. **b. history,** historia sagrada, *f*

bibliographer /,bɪbli'ɒgrəfər/ *n* bibliógrafo (-fa)

bibliographical /,bɪbliə'græfɪkəl/ *a* bibliográfico

bibliography /,bɪbli'ɒgrəfi/ *n* bibliografía, *f*

bibliophile /'bɪbliə,fail/ *n* bibliófilo, *m*

bibulous /'bɪbyələs/ *a* bebedor, borrachín

bicarbonate /bai'kɑrbənɪt/ *n* bicarbonato, *m*

bicentenary /,baisɛn'tɛnəri/ *n* segundo centenario, *m*

biceps /'baisɛps/ *n* bíceps, *m*

bichloride /bai'klɔraid/ *n* bicloruro, *m*

bicker /'bɪkər/ *vi* disputar, altercar; (of stream, etc.) murmurar, susurrar; (of flame) bailar, centellear

bickering /'bɪkərɪŋ/ *n* altercado, argumento, *m*

bicycle /'baisɪkəl/ *n* bicicleta, *f, vi* andar en bicicleta, ir de bicicleta

bicycling /'baisɪklɪŋ/ *n* ciclismo, *m*

bicyclist /'baisɪklɪst/ *n* biciclista, *mf*

bid /bɪd/ *n* (at auction) postura, *f;* (bridge) puja, *f;* oferta, *f, vt* mandar, ordenar, invitar a; (at an auction) pujar, licitar. **to make a bid for,** (attempt) hacer un esfuerzo para; procurar. **to bid fair,** prometer; dar indicios de; dar esperanzas de. **to bid goodbye to,** decir adiós (a), despedirse de. **to bid welcome,** dar la bienvenida a

biddable /'bɪdəbəl/ *a* obediente, dócil; manso

bidder /'bɪdər/ *n* postor, *m,* pujador (-ra). **the highest b.,** el mejor postor

bidding /'bɪdɪŋ/ *n* (order) orden, *f;* instrucción, *f;* invitación, *f;* (at an auction) postura, licitación, *f.* **to do a person's b.,** hacer lo que se le manda

bide /baid/ *vt* aguardar, esperar. **to b. by,** (fulfil) cumplir con

bidet /bi'dei/ *n* bidé, *m*

biennial /bai'ɛniəl/ *a* bianual, bienal

bier /bɪər/ *n* andas, *f pl;* féretro, ataúd, *m*

bifocal /bai'foukəl/ *a* bifocal

bifurcate /'baifər,keit/ *vt* and *vi* bifurcar(se)

bifurcation /,baifər'keiʃən/ *n* bifurcación, *f*

big /bɪg/ *a* grande; grueso; (grown up) mayor; (tall) alto; voluminoso; (vast) extenso, vasto; (full) lleno (de); (with young) preñada; importante. **to talk big,** echarla de importante. **big-boned,** huesudo. **big-end,** *Auto.* biela, *f.* **big game,** caza mayor, *f.* **big gun,** *Inf.* pájaro gordo, *m*

bigamist /'bɪgəmɪst/ *n* bígamo (-ma)

bigamous /'bɪgəməs/ *a* bígamo

bigamy /'bɪgəmi/ *n* bigamia, *f*

bight /bait/ *n* (in a rope) vuelta (de un cabo), *f;* (bay) ensenada, *f*

bigness /'bɪgnɪs/ *n* grandor, *m;* gran tamaño, *m;* altura, *f;* (tallness of a person) gran talle, *m;* (vastness) extensión, *f;* importancia, *f*

bigot /'bɪgət/ *n* fanático (-ca)

bigoted /'bɪgətɪd/ *a* fanático, intolerante

bigotry /'bɪgətri/ *n* fanatismo, *m,* intolerancia, *f*

bikini /bɪ'kini/ *n* bikini, *m*

bilateral /bai'lætərəl/ *a* bilateral

bilberry /'bɪl,bɛri/ *n* arándano, *m*

bile /bail/ *n* bilis, hiel, *f;* mal humor, *m,* cólera, *f*

bilge /bɪldʒ/ *n Naut.* pantoque, *m,* sentina, *f.* **b. water,** agua de pantoque, *f*

bilingual /bai'lɪŋgwəl/ *a* bilingüe

bilious /'bɪlyəs/ *a* bilioso

bill /bɪl/ *n* (parliamentary) proyecto de ley, *m; Law.* escrito, *m; Com.* cuenta, *f;* (poster) cartel, *m;* (program) programa, *m;* (cast) repertorio, *m;* (bank note) billete de banco, *m;* (of a bird) pico, *m;* (for pruning) podadera, *f.* **due b.,** *Com.* abonaré, *m.* **Post no bills!** Se prohíbe fijar carteles. **b. of exchange,** letra de cambio, *f.* **b. of fare,** lista de platos, *f; Fig.* programa, *m.* **b. of health,** patente de sanidad, *f.* **b. of lading,** conocimiento de embarque, *m.* **b. of rights,** declaración de derechos, *f.* **b. of sale,** contrato de venta, *m,* carta de venta, *f.* **b.-broker,** agente de bolsa, agente de cambio, *m.* **b.-poster,** fijador de carteles, cartelero, *m*

bill /bɪl/ *vt* anunciar; publicar; poner en el programa; fijar carteles en. **to b. and coo,** (doves) arrullar; *Inf.* besuquearse

billboard /'bɪl,bɔrd/ *n* tablero publicitario, *m*

billed /bɪld/ a (in compounds) de pico
billet /'bɪlɪt/ n alojamiento, m; (of wood) pedazo (de leña), m; (job) empleo, destino, m, vt alojar (en or con)
billeting /'bɪlɪtɪŋ/ n alojamiento, m. **b. officer,** Mil. aposentador, m; oficial encargado de encontrar alojamiento, m
billiards /'bɪlyərdz/ n pl billar, m. **billiard ball,** bola de billar, f. **billiard cue,** taco, m. **billiard cushion,** baranda de la mesa de billar, f. **billiard marker,** marcador, m. **billiard match,** partida de billar, f. **billiard player,** jugador (-ra) de billar. **billiard room,** sala de billar, f. **billiard table,** mesa de billar, f
billing /'bɪlɪŋ/ n facturación, f
billion /'bɪlyən/ n billón, m; (U.S.A. and France) mil millones, m pl
billionth /'bɪlyənθ/ a billonésimo; (U.S.A. and France) milmillonésimo
bill of particulars n relación detallada, f
billow /'bɪlou/ n oleada, f; Poet. ola, f; Fig. onda, f. —vi hincharse, encresparse; ondular
billowy /'bɪloui/ a ondulante, ondeante
bimonthly /bai'mʌnθli/ a bimestral
bin /bɪn/ n hucha, f, arcón, m; recipiente, m; depósito, m; cajón, m; (for wine) estante, m
binary /'bainəri/ a binario
bind /baind/ vt atar; unir, ligar; amarrar; (in sheaves) agavillar; (bandage) vendar; sujetar; fijar; aprisionar; (a book) encuadernar; Sew. ribetear; (oblige) obligar; comprometer; (constipate) estreñir; contratar (como aprendiz). **I feel bound to,** Me siento obligado a. **to b. over,** obligar a comparecer ante el juez
binder /'baindər/ n encuadernador (-ra); Agr. agavilladora, f
binding /'baindɪŋ/ a válido, valedero; obligatorio; **become b.,** adquirir carácter de compromiso; Med. constrictivo. —n atadura, ligación, f; (of books) encuadernación, f; Sew. ribete, m
binge /bɪndʒ/ n parranda, juerga, f. **to go on the b.,** ir de parranda, ir de picos pardos, ir de juerga
binnacle /'bɪnəkəl/ n Naut. bitácora, f
binocular /bə'nokyələr/ a binocular. —n pl **binoculars,** binóculos, gemelos, m pl
binomial /bai'noumiəl/ a and n binomio m.
biochemical /,baiou'kemɪst/ n bioquímico, m
biochemistry /,baiou'keməstri/ n bioquímica, f
biodiversity /,baioudi'vərsiti/ n biodiversidad, f
biographer /bai'ogrəfər/ n biógrafo (-fa)
biographical /,baiə'græfɪkəl/ a biográfico
biography /bai'ogrəfi/ n biografía, vida, f
biological /,baiə'lodʒɪkəl/ a biológico
biologist /bai'olədʒɪst/ n biólogo, m
biology /bai'olədʒi/ n biología, f
bipartite /bai'partait/ a bipartido
biped /'baiped/ n bípedo, m, a bípedo, bípede
birch /bərtʃ/ n Bot. abedul, m; (rod) vara, f. —a de abedul. —vt pegar con una vara, dar una paliza (a)
bird /bərd/ n pájaro, m; ave, f. **Birds of a feather flock together,** Cada cual se arrima a su cada cual. **hen b.,** pájara, f. **b.-call,** voz del pájaro, f, canto del ave, m. **b. catcher or vendor,** pajarero, m. **bird's-eye view,** vista de pájaro, perspectiva aérea, f. **b.-fancier,** aficionado (-da) a las aves; criador (-ra) de pájaros. **b.-like,** como un pájaro; de pájaro. **b.-lime,** liga, f. **to go b.-nesting,** ir a coger nidos de pájaros. **b. of paradise,** ave del paraíso, f. **b. of passage,** ave de paso, f. **b. of prey,** ave rapaz, f. **b.-seed,** alpiste, m
birth /bərθ/ n nacimiento, m; (act of) parto, m; origen, m; (childhood) infancia, f; (family) linaje, m, familia, f; Fig. creación, f. **from b.,** de nacimiento. **to give b. to,** dar a luz, echar al mundo, parir. **b. certificate,** partida de nacimiento, certificación de nacimiento, f. **b. control,** anticoncepcionismo, m, regulación de la fecundidad, f. **b.-mark,** antojos, m pl. **b.-place,** lugar de nacimiento, m. **b.-rate,** natalidad, f
birthday /'bərθ,dei/ n cumpleaños, m
birthright /'bərθ,rait/ n derecho de nacimiento, m; herencia, f
Biscayan /bɪs'keiən/ a and n vizcaíno (-na)
Biscay, the Bay of /bɪs'kei/ el Golfo de Vizcaya, m

biscuit /'bɪskɪt/ n galleta, f; bizcocho, m. **b. box or maker,** galletero, m. **b.-like,** abizcochado
bisect /bai'sekt/ vt dividir en dos partes iguales; Geom. bisecar
bisexual /bai'sekʃuəl/ a bisexual
bishop /'bɪʃəp/ n obispo, m; (in chess) alfil, m. **bishop's crozier,** báculo episcopal, cayado, m
bismuth /'bɪzməθ/ n bismuto, m
bison /'baisən/ n bisonte, m
bisque /bɪsk/ n porcelana blanca, f, bizcocho, m
bistoury /'bɪstəri/ n bisturí, m
bit /bɪt/ n pedazo, m; (of grass, etc.) brizna, f; (moment) instante, m; (quantity) cantidad, f; (of a drill) mecha, f; (part) parte, f; (passage) trozo, m; (horse's) bocado, m; Inf. miga, f. **a bit,** un tanto, algo, un poco. **in bits,** en pedazos. **Not a bit!** ¡Nada!; ¡Ni pizca!; ¡Claro que no! **bit by bit,** poco a poco, gradualmente. **to give someone a bit of one's mind,** contarle cuatro verdades. **to take the bit between one's teeth,** desbocarse; Fig. rebelarse. **Wait a bit!** ¡Espera un momento!
bitch /bɪtʃ/ n (female dog) perra, f; (fox) zorra, f; (wolf) loba, f
bite /bait/ n mordedura, f; mordisco, m; (mouthful, snack) bocado, m; (of fish and insects) picada, f; (hold) asimiento, m; (sting, pain) picadura, f; (pungency) resquemor, m; (offer) oferta, f; (Fig. mordancy) mordacidad, acritud, f. —vt and vi morder; (gnaw) roer; (of fish, insects) picar; (of hot dishes) resquemar; (of acids) corroer; (deceive) engañar, defraudar; (of wheels, etc.) agarrar; (hurt, wound) herir. **to b. one's tongue,** morderse la lengua. **to b. the dust,** caer al suelo
biting /'baitɪŋ/ a (stinging) picante; (mordant) mordaz, acre; (of winds, etc.) penetrante; satírico. —n mordedura, f; roedura, f
bitter /'bɪtər/ a amargo; (sour) agrio, ácido; (of winds) penetrante; (of cold) intenso; cruel. **to the b. end,** hasta la muerte; hasta el último extremo. **b.-sweet,** agridulce
bitterly /'bɪtərli/ adv amargamente; intensamente; cruelmente
bitterness /'bɪtərnɪs/ n amargura, f; (sourness) acidez, f; (of cold) intensidad, f; crueldad, f
bitters /'bɪtərz/ n pl (drink) bíter, m, angostura, f
bitumen /bai'tumən/ n betún, m
bituminous /bai'tumənəs/ a bituminoso, abetunado
bivalve /'bai,vælv/ n bivalvo, m
bivouac /'bɪvuˌæk/ n Mil. vivaque, m, vi vivaquear
bizarre /bɪ'zar/ a raro, extravagante; grotesco
black /blæk/ a negro; obscuro; (sad) triste, melancólico; funesto; (wicked) malo, perverso; (sullen) malhumorado. —n (color) negro, m; (mourning) luto, m; (negro) negro, m; (negress) negra, f; (stain) mancha, f; (dirt) tizne, m. —vt ennegrecer; tiznar. in **b. and white,** por escrito. **to look on the b. side,** verlo todo negro. **b. art,** nigromancia, f. **b.-currant,** grosella negra, f. **b.-eyed,** ojinegro, con ojos negros. **b.-haired,** pelinegro, de pelo negro. **b.-lead,** plombagina, f. **b.-list,** lista negra, f. **b.-market,** estraperlo, mercado negro, m. **b.-marketeer,** estraperlista, mf **b.-out,** oscurecimiento, apagamiento, m. **b.-pudding,** morcilla, f. **b. sheep,** oveja negra, f; Fig. oveja descarriada, f; (of a family) garbanzo negro, m. **b.-water fever,** melanuria, f
blackberry /'blæk,beri/ n mora, zarzamora, f; (bush) zarza, f, moral, m
blackbird /'blæk,bərd/ n mirlo, m
blackboard /'blæk,bɔrd/ n encerado, m, pizarra, f
blacken /'blækən/ vt ennegrecer; tiznar; Fig. manchar, desacreditar. —vi ennegrecerse
black eye n ojo como un tomate, ojo morado, m
Black Forest, the la Selva Negra, f
blackguard /'blægard/ n tipo de cuidado, perdido, m
blackhead /'blæk,hed/ n espinilla, f
blacking /'blækɪŋ/ n betún, m
blackish /'blækɪʃ/ a negruzco
blackmail /'blæk,meil/ n chantaje, m, vt hacer víctima de un chantaje; arrancar dinero por chantaje (a)
blackmailer /'blæk,meilər/ n chantajista, m
blackness /'blæknɪs/ n negrura, f; obscuridad, f; (wickedness) maldad, perversidad, f

Black Sea, the el Mar Negro, *m*
blacksmith /'blæk,smıθ/ *n* herrero, *m*. **blacksmith's forge,** herrería, *f*
bladder /'blædər/ *n* Anat. vejiga, *f*; ampolla, *f*; (of sea-plants) vesícula, *f*; (of fish) vejiga natatoria, *f*
blade /bleid/ *n* (leaf) hoja, *f*; (of grass, etc.) brizna, *f*; (of sharp instruments) hoja, *f*; (of oar) pala, *f*; (of propeller) paleta, ala, *f*
bladed /'bleidid/ *a* de... hojas. **a two-b. knife,** un cuchillo de dos hojas
blame /bleim/ *n* culpa, *f*; responsabilidad, *f*; censura, *f*. —*vt* culpar, echar la culpa (a); tachar, censurar, criticar; acusar. **You are to b. for this,** Vd. tiene la culpa de esto
blameless /'bleimlıs/ *a* inculpable; inocente; intachable; elegante
blamelessness /'bleimlısnıs/ *n* inculpabilidad, inocencia, *f*; elegancia, *f*
blameworthy /'bleim,wɜrðı/ *a* culpable, digno de censura, vituperable
blanch /blæntʃ/ *vt* Cul. mondar; hacer palidecer. —*vi* palidecer, perder el color
blanching /'blæntʃıŋ/ *n* palidecimiento, *m;* Cul. mondadura, *f*
blancmange /blə'mɑndʒ/ *n* manjar blanco, *m*
bland /blænd/ *a* afable, cortés; dulce, agradable
blandish /'blændıʃ/ *vt* adular, halagar, acariciar
blandishment /'blændıʃmənt/ *n* adulación, *f*, halago, *m*, caricia, *f*
blandness /'blændnıs/ *n* afabilidad, urbanidad, *f*; dulzura, *f*
blank /blæŋk/ *a* en blanco; (empty) vacío; desocupado; pálido; (confused) confuso, desconcertado; (expressionless) sin expresión; (of verse) suelto; sin adorno. —*n* blanco, hueco, *m;* papel en blanco, *m;* laguna, *f*, **b. cartridge,** cartucho para salvas, cartucho de fogueo, *m*. **b. verse,** verso suelto, *m*
blanket /'blæŋkıt/ *n* manta, frazada, *f*; (of a horse) sudadero *m;* Fig. capa, *f*. —*vt* cubrir con una manta. **to toss in a b.,** mantear. **wet b.,** aguafiestas, *mf*. **b. maker or seller,** mantero, *m*. **b. vote,** voto colectivo, *m*
blanketing /'blæŋkıtıŋ/ *n* manteamiento, *m*
blankly /'blæŋklı/ *adv* con indiferencia; sin comprender; (flatly) categóricamente
blankness /'blæŋknıs/ *n* confusión, *f*, desconcierto, *m;* (emptiness) vaciedad, *f*, indiferencia, *f*; incomprensión, *f*
blare /bleər/ *n* sonido de la trompeta o del clarín, Poet. clangor, *m;* (of a car horn) ruido, *m*. —*vi* sonar
blarney /'blɑrnı/ *n* labia, *f*. —*vt* lisonjear
blaspheme /blæs'fim/ *vi* blasfemar. —*vt* renegar de, maldecir
blasphemer /blæs'fimər/ *n* blasfemador (-ra), blasfemo (-ma)
blasphemous /'blæsfəməs/ *a* blasfemo, blasfematorio
blasphemy /'blæsfəmı/ *n* blasfemia, *f*
blast /blæst/ *n* (of wind) ráfaga (de viento), *f*; (of a trumpet, etc.) trompetazo, son, *m;* (of a whistle) pitido, *m;* (draft) soplo, *m;* explosión, *f;* Fig. influencia maligna, *f*. —*vt* (rock) barrenar, hacer saltar; (wither) marchitar, secar; Fig. destruir; (curse) maldecir. **in full b.,** en plena marcha. **b.-furnace,** alto horno, horno de cuba, *m*. **b. hole,** barreno, *m*
blaster /'blæstər/ *n* barrenero, *m*
blasting /'blæstıŋ/ *n* (of rock) voladura, *f*; (withering) marchitamiento, *m;* Fig. destrucción, ruina, *f*; (cursing) maldiciones, *f pl*. **a.** destructor; Fig. funesto. **b. charge,** carga explosiva, *f*
blatant /'bleitnt/ *a* ruidoso; agresivo; llamativo; (boastful) fanfarrón
blaze /bleiz/ *n* llama, *f*; fuego, *m;* conflagración, *f*; luz brillante, *f*; (of anger, etc.) acceso, *m*. —*vi* llamear, encenderse en llamas; brillar, resplandecer. **a b. of colour,** una masa de color. **Go to blazes!** ¡Vete al infierno!
blazon /'bleizən/ *n* Herald. blasón, *m;* Fig. proclamación, *f*, *vt* blasonar; adornar; proclamar
bleach /blitʃ/ *n* lejía, *f*. —*vt* blanquear; descolorar. —*vi* ponerse blanco; descolorarse
bleaching /'blitʃıŋ/ *n* blanqueo, *m*. **b. powder,** hipoclorito de cal, *m*

bleak /blik/ *a* yermo, desierto; frío; expuesto; (sad) triste; severo
bleakness /'bliknıs/ *n* situación expuesta, *f;* desnudez, *f;* frío, *m;* (sadness) tristeza, *f;* severidad, *f*
bleary-eyed /'blıəri ,aid/ *a* legañoso, cegajoso
bleat /blit/ *n* balido, *m*, *vt* and *vi* balar, dar balidos
bleating /'blitıŋ/ *a* balador, que bala. —*n* balido, *m*
bleed /blid/ *vi* sangrar, echar sangre; sufrir. —*vt* sangrar; arrancar dinero a
bleeding /'blidıŋ/ *n* hemorragia, *f*; sangría, *f*
blemish /'blɛmıʃ/ *n* imperfección, *f*, defecto, *m;* (on fruit) maca, *f;* (stain) mancha, *f;* deshonra, *f*
blend /blend/ *n* mezcla, mixtura, *f;* combinación, *f;* fusión, *f*. —*vt* mezclar; combinar. —*vi* mezclarse; combinarse
blende /blend/ *n* Mineral. blenda, *f*
blending /'blendıŋ/ *n* mezcla, *f;* fusión, *f*
bless /bles/ *vt* bendecir; consagrar; (praise) alabar, glorificar; hacer feliz (a). **B. me!** ¡Válgame Dios!
blessed /'blesıd/ *a* bendito; Eccl. beato, bienaventurado; (dear) querido; feliz; Inf. maldito
blessedness /'blesıdnıs/ *n* felicidad, *f;* bienaventuranza, *f*
blessing /'blesıŋ/ *n* bendición, *f;* (grace) bendición de la mesa, *f;* (mercy) merced, gracia, *f;* favor, *m;* (good) bien, *m*. **He gave them his b.,** Les echó su bendición
Bless you! (to someone who has sneezed) ¡Jesús!
blight /blait/ *n* Agr. tizne, tizón, *m;* (of cereals) añublo, *m;* (mould) roña, *f;* (greenfly) pulgón, *m;* Fig. influencia maligna, *f;* (frustration) desengaño, *m;* (spoil-sport) aguafiestas, *mf vt* atizonar; anublar; (wither) marchitar, secar; Fig. frustrar, destruir; malograr
blind /blaind/ *a* ciego; (secret) secreto; (of a door, etc.) falso; (closed) cerrado, sin salida; (unaware) ignorante; sin apreciación (de). **to be b.,** ser ciego; Fig. tener una venda en los ojos. **to be b. in one eye,** ser tuerto. **to turn a b. eye,** hacer la vista gorda. **b. alley,** callejón sin salida, *m*. **b. as a bat,** más ciego que un topo. **b. flying,** Aer. vuelo a ciegas, *m*. **b. man,** ciego, hombre ciego, *m*. **b. obedience,** obediencia ciega, *f*. **b. side,** (of persons) lado débil, *m*. **b. woman,** ciega, mujer ciega, *f*
blind /blaind/ *vt* cegar; poner una venda en los ojos (de); (dazzle) deslumbrar; hacer cerrar los ojos a; hacer ignorar
blind /blaind/ *n* persiana, *f;* (Venetian) celosía, *f;* (deception) pretexto, *m;* velo, *m*
blindfold /'blaind,foʊld/ *vt* vendar los ojos (a); Fig. poner una venda en los ojos (de). —*a* and *adv* con los ojos vendados; a ciegas; con los ojos cerrados
blindly /'blaindli/ *adv* ciegamente; a ciegas; ignorantemente
blindman's buff /'blaind,mænz 'bʌf/ *n* gallina ciega, *f*
blindness /'blaindnıs/ *n* ceguedad, *f*, ofuscación, *f;* ignorancia, *f*
blink /blıŋk/ *n* parpadeo, *m*, guiñada, *f;* (of light) destello, *m;* reflejo, *m; vi* parpadear, pestañear; (of lights) destellar
blinkers /'blıŋkərz/ *n pl* anteojeras, *f pl*
bliss /blıs/ *n* felicidad, *f;* deleite, placer, *m;* Eccl. gloria, *f*
blissful /'blısfəl/ *a* feliz
blissfully /'blısfəlı/ *adv* felizmente
blissfulness /'blısfəlnıs/ *n*. See **bliss**
blister /'blıstər/ *n* Med. vesícula, *f;* ampolla, *f;* (bubble) burbuja, *f*. —*vt* ampollar; Fig. herir
blithe /blaið/ *a* alegre
blithely /'blaiðlı/ *adv* alegremente
blitheness /'blaiðnıs/ *n* alegría, *f*
blitzkrieg /'blıts,krig/ *n* blitzkrieg, *m*, guerra relámpago, *f*
blizzard /'blızərd/ *n* ventisca, nevasca, *f*
bloated /'bloutıd/ *a* abotagado, hinchado; orgulloso; indecente
bloater /'bloutər/ *n* arenque ahumado, *m*
blob /blob/ *n* masa, *f;* mancha, *f;* gota, *f*
block /blok/ *n* bloque, *m;* (log) leño, *m; Naut.* polea, *f;* (for beheading and of a butcher) tajo, *m;* (for mounting) apeadero, *m;* (of shares, etc.) lote, *m;* (of

houses) manzana, *f;* (jam) atasco, *m;* (obstruction) obstrucción, *f;* (for hats) forma, *f.* **A chip off the old b.,** De tal palo tal astilla. **b. and tackle,** *Naut.* polea con aparejo. **b.-hook,** grapa, *f.* **b.-house,** *Mil.* blocao, *m*

block /blɒk/ *vt* bloquear; cerrar (el paso); (stop up) atarugar, atascar; (a wheel) calzar; (a bill, etc.) obstruir; (hats) poner en forma. **to b. the way,** cerrar el paso.

blockade /blɒˈkeid/ *n* bloqueo, *m,* *vt* bloquear. **to run the b.,** violar el bloqueo

blockhead /ˈblɒkˌhed/ *n* leño, zoquete, imbécil, *m*

blond(e) /blɒnd/ *a* (of hair) rubio; (of complexion) de tez blanca. —*n* hombre rubio, *m;* (woman) rubia, mujer rubia, *f.* **peroxide b.,** rubia oxigenada, *f.* **b. lace,** blondina, *f*

blood /blʌd/ *n* sangre, *f;* (relationship) parentesco, *m;* (family) linaje, *m,* prosapia, *f;* (life) vida, *f;* (sap) savia, *f;* jugo, *m;* (horse) caballo de pura raza, *m;* (dandy) galán, *m.* —*vt* sangrar. **bad b.,** mala sangre, *f;* odio, *m;* mala leche, *f.* **blue b.,** sangre azul, *f.* **in cold b.,** a sangre fría, *f.* **My b. is up,** Se me enciende la sangre. **My b. runs cold,** Se me hiela la sangre. **to be in the b.,** llevar en la sangre. **b.-bank,** banco de sangre, *m.* **b.-bath,** matanza, *f.* **b.-colored,** de color de sangre, sanguíneo. **b.-feud,** venganza de sangre, *f.* **b.-guilt,** culpabilidad de homicidio, *m.* **b.-heat,** calor de sangre, *m.* **b.-letting,** sangría, *f.* **b. orange,** naranja dulce, *f.* **b.-plasma,** plasma sanguíneo, *m.* **b.-poisoning,** septicemia, *f;* infección, *f.* **b.-pressure,** presión sanguínea, *f.* **b. purity,** limpieza de sangre, *f.* **b.-red,** rojo como la sangre. **b.-relation,** pariente (-ta) consanguíneo(a). **b.-relationship,** consanguinidad, *f.* **b.-stain,** mancha de sangre, *f.* **b.-stained,** ensangrentado, manchado de sangre, *f.* **b.-stone,** sanguinaria, *f.* **b.-sucker,** sanguijuela, *f;* *Fig.* vampiro, *m;* (usurer) avaro (-ra). **b.-vessel,** vaso sanguíneo, *m*

blooded /ˈblʌdɪd/ *a* de sangre...; de casta...

bloodhound /ˈblʌdˌhaund/ *n* sabueso, *m*

bloodily /ˈblʌdəli/ *adv* sangrientamente; cruentamente; con ferocidad, cruelmente

bloodiness /ˈblʌdɪnɪs/ *n* estado sangriento, *m;* crueldad, ferocidad, *f*

bloodless /ˈblʌdlɪs/ *a* exangüe; pálido; incruento; anémico; indiferente

bloodshed /ˈblʌdˌʃed/ *n* efusión de sangre, *f;* matanza, carnicería, *f*

bloodshot /ˈblʌdˌʃɒt/ *a* (of the eye) inyectado

bloodthirstiness /ˈblʌdˌθɜrstɪnɪs/ *n* sed de sangre, *f*

bloodthirsty /ˈblʌdˌθɜrsti/ *a* sanguinario, carnicero

bloody /ˈblʌdi/ *a* sangriento; (of battles) encarnizado; (cruel) sanguinario, cruel

bloom /blum/ *n* flor, *f;* florecimiento, *m;* (on fruit) flor, *f;* (prime) lozanía, *f;* (on the cheeks) color sano, *m.* —*vi* florecer. **in b.,** en flor

blooming /ˈblumɪŋ/ *a* florido; en flor; fresco; lozano; brillante

blossom /ˈblɒsəm/ *n* flor, *f.* —*vi* florecer. **to b. out into,** hacerse, llegar a ser; (wear) lucir; (buy) comprarse

blossomed /ˈblɒsəmd/ *a* con flores, de flores

blossoming /ˈblɒsəmɪŋ/ *n* floración, *f*

blot /blɒt/ *n* borrón, *m;* mancha, *f.* —*vt* manchar; (erase) tachar; (dry) secar. **to b. out,** borrar; destruir; secar con papel secante

blotch /blɒtʃ/ *n* (on the skin, or stain) mancha, *f*

blotter /ˈblɒtər/ *n* *Com.* libro borrador, *m;* teleta, *f*

blotting paper /ˈblɒtɪŋ/ *n* papel secante, *m*

blouse /blaus/ *n* blusa, *f*

blow /blou/ *n* golpe, *m;* bofetada, *f;* (with the fist) puñetazo, *m;* (with the elbow) codazo, *m;* (with a club) porrazo, *m;* (with a whip) latigazo, *m;* (blossoming) floración, *f;* (disaster) desastre, *m,* tragedia, *f.* **to come to blows,** venirse a las manos. **at a b.,** con un solo golpe; de una vez. **We are going for a b.,** Vamos a tomar el fresco. **b. below the belt,** golpe bajo, *m.* **b. in the air,** golpe en vago, *m.* **b. of fate,** latigazo de la fortuna, *m*

blow /blou/ *vi* (of wind) soplar (el viento), hacer viento, correr aire; (pant) jadear, echar resoplidos; (of fuses) fundirse. —*vt* (wind instruments) tocar; soplar; (inflate) inflar; (swell) hinchar. **to b. a kiss,** ti-

rar un beso. **to b. one's nose,** sonarse las narices. **to b. away,** disipar; ahuyentar; llevar (el viento). **to b. down,** echar por tierra, derribar (el viento). **to b. in,** llevar adentro, hacer entrar (el viento); (windows, etc.) quebrar (el viento). **to b. off,** quitar (el viento). **to b. open,** abrir (el viento). **to b. out,** hacer salir (el viento); llevar afuera (el viento); (a light) matar de un soplo, apagar soplando. **to b. over,** pasar por (el viento); soplar por; disiparse; olvidarse. **to b. up,** (inflate) inflar; (the fire) avivar (el fuego); (explode) volar; (swell) hinchar

blowing /ˈblouɪŋ/ *n* soplo, *m;* violencia, *f;* (blossoming) florecimiento, *m.* **b. up,** voleo, *m;* explosión, *f*

blow-up /ˈblou ˌʌp/ *n* (photograph) fotografía ampliada, *f*

blowzy /ˈblauzi/ *a* desaliñado

blubber /ˈblʌbər/ *vi* gimotear; berrear. —*n* (of the whale) grasa de ballena, *f.* **b.-lip,** bezo, *m.* **b.-lipped,** bezudo

bludgeon /ˈblʌdʒən/ *n* cachiporra, porpa, *f;* garrote, *m;* estaca, *f.* —*vt* golpear con una porra, dar garrotazos (a)

blue /blu/ *a* azul; (with bruises) amoratado; (sad) deprimido, melancólico; (obscene) verde; (dark) sombrío; (traditionalist) conservador. —*n* azul, *m;* (sky) cielo, *m;* (for clothes) añil de lavandera, *m;* *pl* **blues,** melancolía, depresión, *f;* (homesickness) morriña, *f.* —*vt* (laundry) añilar. **to look b.,** parecer deprimido; (of prospects, etc.) ser poco halagüeño. **b. black,** azul negro, *m;* (of hair) azabache, *m.* **b.-bottle,** *Ent.* moscón, *m.* **b.-eyed,** con ojos azules. **b. gum,** eucalipto, *m.* **B. Peter,** bandera de salida, *f.* **b. print,** fotocopia, *f;* plan, *m*

bluebell /ˈbluˌbel/ *n* campanilla, *f*

blueness /ˈblunɪs/ *n* color azul, *m*

bluestocking /ˈbluˌstɒkɪŋ/ *n* marisabidilla, doctora, *f*

bluff /blʌf/ *a* (of cliffs, etc.) escarpado; (of persons) franco, campechano, brusco

bluffness /ˈblʌfnɪs/ *n* franqueza, brusquedad, *f*

bluish /ˈbluɪʃ/ *a* azulado

bluishness /ˈbluɪʃnɪs/ *n* color azulado, *m*

blunder /ˈblʌndər/ *n* desacierto, desatino, *m;* equivocación, *f;* (in a translation, etc.) falta, *f.* —*vi* tropezar (con); desacertar; equivocarse; *Inf.* meter la pata. —*vt* manejar mal; estropear

blunderer /ˈblʌndərər/ *n* desatinado (-da)

blundering /ˈblʌndərɪŋ/ *a* desacertado; equivocado; imprudente *n.* See **blunder**

blunt /blʌnt/ *a* romo, embotado; obtuso; (abrupt) brusco; franco; descortés; (plain) claro. —*vt* enromar, embotar; (the point) despuntar; *Fig.* hacer indiferente; (pain) mitigar

bluntly /ˈblʌntli/ *adv* sin filo; sin punta; bruscamente, francamente; claramente

bluntness /ˈblʌntnɪs/ *n* embotamiento, *m;* *Fig.* brusquedad, franqueza, *f;* claridad, *f*

blur /blɜr/ *n* borrón, *m;* mancha, *f;* imagen indistinta, *f.* —*vt* borrar; manchar; *Photo.* velar

blurred /blɜrd/ *a* borroso; indistinto; turbio

blurt (out) /blɜrt/ *vt* proferir bruscamente; revelar sin querer

blush /blʌʃ/ *n* rubor, *m;* rojo, *m.* —*vi* enrojecerse, ruborizarse, ponerse colorado; avergonzarse (por)

blushing /ˈblʌʃɪŋ/ *a* ruboroso; púdico

bluster /ˈblʌstər/ *vi* (of the wind) soplar con furia; (of waves) encresparse, embravecerse; (of persons) bravear, fanfarronear. —*n* furia, violencia, *f;* tumulto, *m;* fanfarronería, *f*

blustering /ˈblʌstərɪŋ/ *a* (of wind) violento, fuerte; (of waves) tumultuoso; (of people) fanfarrón, valentón

boar /bɔr/ *n* verraco, *m;* (wild) jabalí, *m*

board /bɔrd/ *n* tabla, *f;* (for notices) tablón, *m;* (b. residence) pensión, *f;* (table) mesa, *f;* (food) comida, *f;* (for chess, checkers) tablero, *m;* (sign) letrero, *m;* (of instruments) cuadro, *m;* (bookbinding) cartón, *m;* *Naut.* bordo, *m;* (committee) junta, dirección, *f;* tribunal, *m; pl* **boards** *Theat.* tablas, *f pl.* **above b.,** abiertamente, sin disimulo. **free on b.,** (f.o.b.) franco a bordo. **in boards,** (of books) encartonado. **managerial b.,** junta directiva, *f.* **on b.,** a bordo. **on the boards,** *Theat.* en las tablas. **to go on b.,** ir a bordo.

b. and lodging, pensión completa, casa y comida, *f.*
b. of directors, consejo de administración, *m.* **b. of examiners,** tribunal de exámenes, *m.* **b. of trade,** junta de comercio, *f;* ministerio de comercio, *m*

board /bɔrd/ *vt* entablar, enmaderar; embarcar en; (*Nav.* a ship) abordar; (lodge) alojar, tomar a pensión

boarder /'bɔrdər/ *n* huésped (-da); (at school) pensionista, *mf* alumno (-na) interno (-na)

boarding /'bɔrdɪŋ/ *n* entablado, *m;* (planking) tablazón, *f;* (of a ship) abordaje, *m;* (of a train) subida (al tren), *f.* **b.-house,** casa de huéspedes, pensión, *f.* **b.-school,** pensionado, *m*

boarding gate *n* puerta de embarque, *f*

boast /boust/ *n* jactancia, *f;* ostentación, *f;* (honor) gloria, *f.* —*vi* jactarse, vanagloriarse; alabarse; ostentar. **to b. about,** jactarse de; hacer gala de; gloriarse en

boaster /'boustər/ *n* vanaglorioso (-sa), jactancioso (-sa)

boastful /'boustfəl/ *a* vanaglorioso, jactancioso; ostentador

boastfully /'boustfəli/ *adv* con jactancia; con ostentación

boastfulness /'boustfəlnɪs/ *n* vanagloria, jactancia, *f;* fanfarronería, *f;* ostentación, *f*

boasting /'boustɪŋ/ *n* alardeo, *m;* fanfarronería, *f*

boat /bout/ *n* barco, *m;* bote, *m;* (in a fun fair) columpio, *m,* lancha, *f;* (for sauce or gravy) salsera, *f.* —*vi* ir en barco; (row) remar; navegar. **to b. down,** bajar en barco. **to b. up,** subir en barco. **b. building,** construcción de barcos, *f.* **b. club,** club náutico, *m.* **b. crew,** tripulación de un barco, *f.* **b.-hook,** bichero, garabato, *m.* **b.-house,** cobertizo de las lanchas, *m.* **b.-load,** barcada, *f.* **b.-race,** regata, *f.* **b.-scoop,** achicador, *m.* **b.-shaped,** en forma de barco. **b.-train,** tren que enlaza con un vapor, *m*

boating /'boutɪŋ/ *n* pasear en bote, *m;* manejo de un bote, *m;* (rowing) remo, *m.* **b.-pole,** botador, *m*

boatman /'boutmən/ *n* barquero, *m*

boatswain /'bousən/ *n* contramaestre, *m.* **boatswain's mate,** segundo contramaestre, *m*

bob /bɒb/ *n;* (curtsey) reverencia, *f;* (woman's hair) pelo a la romana, *m;* (of bells) toque (de campana), *m.* —*vi* saltar; moverse. —*vt* cortar corto. **bob,** (hair) melena, *f.* **to bob up,** ponerse de pie; surgir. **to bob up and down,** subir y bajar; bailar. **bob-tail,** rabo corto, *m.* **bob-tailed,** rabón

Bob /bɒb/ (pet form of *Robert*) Beto (Mexico)

bobbin /'bɒbɪn/ *n* carrete, huso, *m;* (of wool, etc.) ovillo, *m;* (of looms, sewing machines) bobina, *f;* (in lace-making) bolillo, palillo, *m*

bobsled /'bɒb,slɛd/ *n* trineo doble, *m*

bode /boud/ *vt* presagiar, prometer. **to b. ill,** prometer mal. **to b. well,** prometer bien

bodice /'bɒdɪs/ *n* corpiño, *m*

bodied /'bɒdid/ *a* (in compounds) de cuerpo-

bodiless /'bɒdilɪs/ *a* incorpóreo

bodily /'bɒdli/ *a* del cuerpo; físico; corpóreo; real; material; (of fear) de su persona. —*adv* corporalmente; en persona, personalmente; en conjunto, enteramente; en una pieza

boding /'boudɪŋ/ *a* ominoso, amenazador. —*n* presagio, *m;* agüero, *m*

body /'bɒdi/ *n Anat.* cuerpo, *m;* (trunk) tronco, *m;* (corpse) cadáver, *m;* (of a vehicle) caja, *f;* (of a motor-car) carrocería, *f;* (of a ship) casco, *m;* (of a church) nave, *f;* (centre) centro, *m;* (of a book, persons, consistency and *Astron.*) cuerpo, *m;* (person) persona, *f;* corporación, *f;* grupo, *m;* (of an army) grueso (de ejercito), *m;* organismo, *m.* **in a b.,** en masa, juntos (juntas); en corporación. **to have enough to keep b. and soul together,** tener de que vivir. **b.-snatcher,** junta cadáveres *mf* ladrón de cadáveres, *m.* **b.-snatching,** robo de cadáveres, *m*

bodyguard /'bɒdi,gard/ *n* guardia de corps, *f;* guardia, *f;* (escort) escolta, *f*

body language *n* el lenguaje del cuerpo, *m*

bog /bɒg/ *n* pantano, marjal, *m,* marisma, *f*

bogey /'bougi/ *n* duende, *m;* (to frighten children) coco, *m;* (nightmare) pesadilla, *f*

boggy /'bɒgi/ *a* pantanoso, fangoso

bogus /'bougəs/ *a* postizo, falso

Bohemian /bou'himiən/ *a* and *n* bohemio (-ia)

boil /bɔil/ *vi* bullir, hervir; (cook) cocer. —*vt* hervir; cocer. —*n* ebullición, *f; Med.* divieso, *m.* **to b. away,** consumirse hirviendo; *Chem.* evaporar a seco. **to b. over,** rebosar

boiler /'bɔilər/ *n Cul.* marmita, olla, *f;* (of a furnace) caldera, *f.* **double-b.,** baño de María, *m.* **steam-b.,** caldera de vapor, *f.* **b.-maker,** calderero, *m.* **b. room,** cámara de la caldera, *f.* **b.-suit,** mono, *m*

boiling /'bɔilɪŋ/ *n* ebullición, *f,* hervor, *m;* (cooking) cocción, *f,* a hirviente. **b. point,** punto de ebullición, *m*

boisterous /'bɔistərəs/ *a* (of persons) exuberante, impetuoso; (stormy) tempestuoso, borrascoso; violento

boisterously /'bɔistərəsli/ *adv* impetuosamente, ruidosamente; tempestuosamente; con violencia

boisterousness /'bɔistərəsnɪs/ *n* exuberancia, impetuosidad, *f;* violencia, *f;* tempestuosidad, borrascosidad, *f*

bold /bould/ *a* intrépido, audaz; (determined) resuelto; (forward) atrevido; (showy) llamativo; (clear) claro. **b.-faced,** descarado, desvergonzado. **b.-faced type,** letra negra, *f*

boldly /'bouldli/ *adv* intrépidamente; descaradamente; resueltamente; claramente

boldness /'bouldnɪs/ *n* intrepidez, valentía, *f;* resolución, *f;* (forwardness) osadia, *f,* descaro, atrevimiento, *m;* claridad, *f*

Bolivian /bou'lɪviən/ *a* and *n* boliviano (-na)

Bolognese /boulə'niz/ *a* and *n* boloñés (-esa)

Bolshevik /'boulʃəvik/ *a* and *n* bolchevique, *mf*

Bolshevism /'boulʃə,vizəm/ *n* bolchevismo, *m*

Bolshevist /'boulʃəvist/ *n* bolchevista, *mf*

bolster /'boulstər/ *n* travesaño, *m.* —*vt* apuntalar; *Fig.* apoyar

bolt /boult/ *n* pasador, cerrojo, *m;* (pin) perno, *m;* (knocker) aldaba, *f;* (roll) rollo, *m;* (flight) huida, *f;* (of a crossbow) flecha, *f;* (from the blue) rayo, *m.* —*adv* (upright) recto como una flecha; enhiesto; rígido. **b. and nut,** perno y tuerca, *m*

bolt /boult/ *vt* echar el cerrojo (a); empernar; (*Fam.* eat) zampar. —*vi* huir; (horses) desbocarse, dispararse; (plants) cerner. **to b. down,** cerrar con cerrojo. **to b. in,** entrar corriendo, entrar de repente. **to b. off,** marcharse corriendo. **to b. out,** *vi* salir de golpe. —*vt* cerrar fuera

bolus /'bouləs/ *n* bolo, *m*

bomb /bɒm/ *n* bomba, *f,* vt bombardear. **to be a b.-shell,** *Fig.* caer como una bomba. **b.-carrier,** portabombas, *m.* **b. crater,** bombazo, *m.* **b.-release,** (*Aer. Nav.*) lanzabombas, *m.* **b.-sight,** mira de avión de bombardeo, *f*

bombard /bɒm'bard/ *vt* bombardear, bombear; *Fig.* llover (preguntas, etc.) sobre

bombardier /,bɒmbər'diər/ *n* bombardero, *m*

bombardment /bɒm'bardmənt/ *n* bombardeo, *m*

bombast /'bɒmbæst/ *n* ampulosidad, pomposidad, *f*

bombastic /bɒm'bæstɪk/ *a* bombástico, altisonante, pomposo

bomber /'bɒmər/ *n* avión de bombardeo, bombardero, *m.* **dive b.,** bombardero en picado, *m.* **heavy b.,** bombardero pesado, *m.* **light b.,** bombardero ligero, *m.* **b. command,** servicio de bombardero, *m*

bombproof /'bɒm,pruf/ *a* a prueba de bomba

bonafide /'bounə,faid/ *a* fidedigno

bonbon /'bɒn,bɒn/ *n* bombón, confite, dulce, *m.* **b. box,** bombonera, *f*

bond /bɒnd/ *n* lazo, vínculo, *m; Chem.* enlace, *m;* (financial) obligación, *f;* (security) fianza, *f;* (Customs) depósito, *m; pl* **bonds,** cadenas, *f pl,* a esclavo. **in b.,** en depósito. **bonds of interest,** intereses creados, *m pl.* **b.-holder,** obligacionista, *mf*

bondage /'bɒndɪdʒ/ *n* esclavitud, *f;* servidumbre, *f;* cautiverio, *m;* prisión, *f*

bone /boun/ *n* hueso, *m;* (of fish) espina (de pez), *f;* (whale b.) ballena, *f;* *pl* **bones,** cuerpo, *m,* vt deshuesar; poner ballenas (a or en). **to be all skin and bones,** estar en los huesos. **to have a b. to pick with,** tener que arreglar las cuentas con. **b.-ash,** cendra, *f*

boned /bound/ *a* (in compounds) de huesos; deshuesado, sin hueso

boner /'bounər/ *n* gazapo, *m*, patochada, plancha, *f*

bonfire /'bɒn,faiər/ *n* fogata, hoguera, *f*

Bonn /bɒn/ Bona, *f*

bonnet /'bɒnɪt/ *n* capota, *f*; (of babies) gorra, *f*; (of men) boina, *f*; (of chimney and of machines) sombrerete, *m*

bonny /'bɒni/ *a* sano; hermoso; (fat) gordo

bonus /'bounəs/ *n* paga extraordinaria, bonificación, *f*; sobresueldo, *m*; (of food, etc.) ración extraordinaria, *f*

bon vivant /bɔ̃ vi'vɑ̃/ *n* alegre, vividor, *m*

bon voyage /bɔ̃ vwa'yaʒ/ *interj* ¡buen viaje! ¡feliz viaje!

bony /'bouni/ *a* huesudo; (of fish-bones) lleno de espinas; óseo

booby /'bubi/ *n* pazguato, bobo, *m*. **b.-prize,** último premio, *m*. **b.-trap,** trampa, *f*; *Mil.* mina, *f*

book /bʊk/ *n* libro, *m*; volumen, tomo, *m*; (of an opera) libreto, *m*. —*vt* anotar en un libro; apuntar; (seats) tomar (localidades); (tickets) sacar (billetes); (of the issuing clerk) dar; (reserve) reservar; inscribir; consignar (a suspect); (engage) contratar; (invite) comprometer. **to turn the pages of a b.,** hojear un libro. **b.-ends,** sostén para libros, sujetalibros, *m*. **b.-keeper,** tenedor de libros, *m*. **b.-keeping,** teneduría de libros, *f*. **b.-maker,** apostador de profesión, *m*. **b. of reference,** libro de consulta, *m*. **b.-plate,** exlibris, *m*. **b.-post,** tarifa de impresos, *f*. **b.-shop,** librería, *f*. **b.-trade,** venta de libros, *f*; comercio de libros, *m*

bookbinder /'bʊk,baindər/ *n* encuadernador (-ra) de libros

bookbinding /'bʊk,baindɪŋ/ *n* encuadernación de libros, *f*

bookcase /'bʊk,keis/ *n* armario de libros, *m*

booking /'bʊkɪŋ/ *n* (of rooms, etc.) reservación, *f*; (of tickets) toma, *f*; *Com.* asiento, *m*; (engagement) contratación, *f*. **b.-clerk,** vendedor (-ra) de billetes. **b.-office,** despacho de billetes, *m*; taquilla, *f*

bookish /'bʊkɪʃ/ *a* aficionado a los libros; docto, erudito

bookishness /'bʊkɪʃnɪs/ *n* afición a los libros, *f*; erudición, *f*

bookmark /'bʊk,mɑrk/ *n* marcador, *m*

bookseller /'bʊk,selər/ *n* librero, *m*

bookselling /'bʊk,selɪŋ/ *n* venta de libros, *f*; comercio de libros, *m*

bookshelf /'bʊk,ʃelf/ *n* estante para libros, *m*

bookstall /'bʊk,stɔl/ *n* puesto de libros, *m*

bookstrap /'bʊk,stræp/ *n* portalibros, *m*

bookworm /'bʊk,wɜrm/ *n* polilla que roe los libros, *f*; *Fig.* ratón de biblioteca, *m*

boom /bum/ *n Naut.* botavara, *f*; (of a crane) aguilón, *m*; (noise) ruido, *m*; (of the sea) bramido, *m*; (thunder) trueno, *m*; (in a port) cadena de puerto, *f*; *Com.* actividad, *f*; (*Fig.* peak) auge, *m*, *vi* sonar; bramar; tronar; *Com.* subir; ser famoso. **b. sail,** vela de cangreja, *f*

boomerang /'bumə,ræŋ/ *n* bumerang, *m*

boon /bun/ *n* favor, *m*, merced, *f*; bien, *m*, ventaja, *f*; don, *m*; privilegio, *m*, *a* (of friends) íntimo

boor /bʊr/ *n* monigote, patán, palurdo, *m*

boorish /'bʊrɪʃ/ *a* rudo, zafio, rústico, cerril

boorishness /'bʊrɪʃnɪs/ *n* zafiedad, patanería, tosquedad, *f*

boost /bust/ *vt Elec.* aumentar la fuerza de; *Inf.* empujar; subir; (advertise) dar bombo (a)

boot /but/ *n* bota, *f*; (of a car) compartimiento para equipaje, *m*. **button-boots,** botas de botones, *f pl*. **riding-boots,** botas de montar, *f pl*. **to b.,** además, de añadidura. **b.-maker,** zapatero, *m*. **b.-tag,** tirador de bota, *m*. **b.-tree,** horma de bota, *f*

bootblack /'but,blæk/ *n* limpiabotas, *m*

booted /'butɪd/ *a* con botas, calzado con botas; (in compounds) de botas...

bootee /bu'ti/ *n* botín, *m*

booth /buθ/ *n* puesto, *m*, barraca, *f*

bootlace /'but,leis/ *n* cordón para zapatos, *m*

bootlegger /'but,legər/ *n* contrabandista de alcohol, *m*

boots /buts/ *n* mozo de hotel, botones, *m*

booty /'buti/ *n* botín, *m*; tesoro, *m*

booze /buz/ *vi* emborracharse. —*n* alcohol, *m*; borrachera, *f*

boozer /'buzər/ *n* borracho (-cha)

boracic /bə'ræsɪk/ *a* bórico. —*n* ácido bórico, *m*

borax /'bɔræks/ *n* bórax, *m*

Bordeaux /bɔr'dou/ *a* and *n* (of or from) bordelés (-esa). —*n* (wine) vino de Burdeos, *m*

bordello /bɔr'delou/ *n* burdel, *m*

border /'bɔrdər/ *n* borde, *m*; (of a lake, etc.) orilla, *f*; (edge) margen, *m*; (of a diploma, etc.) orla, *f*; *Sew.* ribete, *m*, orla, *f*; (fringe) franja, *f*; (garden) arriate, *m*; (territory) frontera, *f*; límite, confín, *m*. —*vt Sew.* orlar, ribetear; ornar (de); (of land) lindar con. **to b. on,** (of land) tocar, lindar con; (approach) rayar en. **b. country,** región fronteriza, *f*

borderer /'bɔrdərər/ *n* habitante de una zona fronteriza, *m*; escocés (-esa) de la frontera con Inglaterra

borderland /'bɔrdər,lænd/ *n* zona fronteriza, *f*; lindes, *m pl*

borderline /'bɔrdər,lain/ *n* frontera, *f*; límite, *m*; margen, *m*, *a* fronterizo; lindero; (uncertain) dudoso, incierto

bore /bɔr/ *n* taladro, barreno, *m*; perforación, *f*; (hole) agujero, *m*; (of guns) calibre, *m*; (wave) oleada, *f*; (nuisance) fastidio, *m*; (dullness) aburrimiento, tedio, *m*; (person) pelmazo, *m*, machaca, *mf* *vt* taladrar, barrenar, horadar; perforar; hacer un agujero (en); (exhaust) aburrir; fastidiar. **It's a b.,** Es una lata. **to be bored,** aburrirse, fastidiarse

boredom /'bɔrdəm/ *n* aburrimiento, *m*; tedio, hastío, *m*

boric /'bɔrɪk/ *a* bórico

boring /'bɔrɪŋ/ *a* aburrido, pesado, tedioso; molesto; fastidioso. —*n* taladro, *m*; horadación, *f*; sondeo, *m*; perforación, *f*

born /bɔrn/ *a* nacido; (by birth) de nacimiento; (b. to be) destinado a; natural (de). **He was b. in 1870.** Nació en 1870. **to be b.,** nacer, venir al mundo. **to be b. again,** renacer, volver a nacer. **well-b.,** bien nacido. **b. with a silver spoon in one's mouth,** Nacido de pie, Nacido un domingo

-borne /-bɔrn/ trasmitido por... (e.g. *anthropod-b.*, trasmitido por los antrópodos)

borough /'bɜrou/ *n* burgo, *m*; villa, *f*; ciudad, *f*. **b. surveyor,** arquitecto municipal, *m*

borrow /'bɒrou/ *vt* pedir prestado; apropiarse, adoptar; copiar; (arithmetic) restar; (a book from a library) tomar prestado. **May I b. your pencil?** ¿Quieres prestarme tu lápiz?

borrower /'bɒrouər/ *n* el (la) que pide o toma prestado

borrowing /'bɒrouɪŋ/ *n* el pedir prestado, acto de pedir prestado, *m*

bosh /bɒʃ/ *n* patrañas, tonterías, *f pl*; palabrería, *f*

Bosnian /'bɒzniən/ *a* bosnio

bosom /'bʊzəm/ *n* pecho, *m*; (heart) corazón, *m*; (of the earth, etc.) seno, *m*. **b. friend,** amigo (-ga) del alma, amigo (-ga) íntimo (-ma)

Bosphorus, the /'bɒsfərəs/ el Bósforo, *m*

boss /bɒs/ *n* (of a shield) corcova saliente, *f*; tachón, *m*; *Archit.* pinjante, *m*. *Inf.* amo, *m*; jefe, *m*. —*vt* mandar; dominar. **political b.,** cacique, *m*

bossism /'bɒsɪzəm/ *n* caudillaje, *m*

bossy /'bɒsi/ *a* mandón, autoritario

botanical /bə'tænɪkəl/ *a* botánico. **b. garden,** jardín botánico, *m*

botanist /'bɒtənɪst/ *n* botánico (-ca)

botany /'bɒtni/ *n* botánica, *f*

botch /bɒtʃ/ *n* (clumsy work) chapucería, *f*; remiendo, *m*. —*vt* chapucear, chafallar; (patch) remendar

both /bouθ/ *a* and *pron* ambos, *m pl*; ambas, *f pl*; los dos, *m pl*; las dos, *f pl*, *adv* tan(to)... como; (and) y; a la vez, al mismo tiempo. **It appealed both to the young and the old,** Gustó tanto a los jóvenes como a los viejos. **b. of you,** ustedes dos, vosotros dos, vosotras dos. **b. pretty and useful,** bonito y útil a la vez

bother /'bɒðər/ *n* molestia, *f*, fastidio, *m*; (worry) preocupación, *f*; dificultad, *f*; (fuss) alboroto, *m*. —*vt* molestar, fastidiar; preocupar. —*vi* preocuparse

bottle /'bɒtl/ n botella, f; (smaller) frasco, m; (babies) biberón, m; (for water) cantimplora, f, vt embotellar, envasar, enfrascar. **to b. up,** (liquids, capital, armies, navies) embotellar; (feelings) refrenar. **to bring up on the b.,** criar con biberón. **b.-green,** verde botella, m. **b.-neck,** (in an industry) embotellado, m; (in traffic) atascadero, m. **b.-washer,** fregaplatos, mf; (machine) máquina para limpiar botellas, f
bottle cap n corchalata, f
bottled /'bɒtld/ a en botella; (of fruit, vegetables) conservado
bottleful /'bɒtl,fʊl/ n botella, f
bottler /'bɒtlər/ n embotellador (-ra)
bottling /'bɒtlɪŋ/ n embotellado, m; envase, m. **b. outfit,** embotelladora, f; (for fruit, etc.) aparato para conservar frutas o legumbres, m
bottom /'bɒtəm/ n base, f; (deepest part) fondo, m; (last place) último lugar, m; fundamento, m; (of a chair) asiento, m; (of a page, table, mountain, etc.) pie, m; (posterior) culo, m; (of a river) lecho, m; (of the sea) fondo, m; (of a ship) casco, m; (of a skirt) orilla, f; (truth) realidad, verdad, f; (basis) origen, m, causa, f. **at b.,** en realidad. **at the b.,** en el fondo. **false b.,** fondo doble, fondo secreto, m. **to be at the b. of,** ocupar el último lugar en; ser el causante de. **to get to the b. of,** descubrir la verdad de; profundizar en, analizar. **to sink to the b.,** (of ships) irse a pique
bottomed /'bɒtəmd/ a (in compounds) de fondo...
bottomless /'bɒtəmlɪs/ a sin fondo; (of chairs, etc.) sin asiento; (unfathomable) insondable
boudoir /'budwɑr/ n tocador, gabinete de señora, m
bough /bau/ n rama, f, brazo (de un árbol) m
boulder /'bouldər/ n roca, peña, f; canto rodado, m; bloque de roca, m
boulevard /'bulə,vɑrd/ n bulevar, m
Boulogne /bu'loun/ Boloña, f
bounce /bauns/ n bote, rebote, m; salto, m; (boasting) fanfarronería, f, vi rebotar; saltar, brincar. —vt hacer botar o saltar
bouncing /'baunsɪŋ/ a (healthy) sano, robusto; vigoroso, fuerte
bound /baund/ n límite, m; (jump) salto, brinco, m, vt limitar, confinar. —vi saltar, brincar; (bounce) botar. **within bounds,** dentro del límite. **b. for,** con destino a; (of ships) con rumbo a
boundary /'baundəri/ n límite, lindero, término, m; frontera, f; raya, f. **b. stone,** mojón, m
bounden /'baundən/ a obligatorio, forzoso; indispensable
boundless /'baundlɪs/ a sin límites, infinito; inmenso
bounteous, bountiful /'bauntiəs; 'bauntɪfəl/ a dadivoso, generoso; bondadoso
bountifulness /'bauntɪfəlnɪs/ n munificencia, dadivosidad, generosidad, f
bounty /'baunti/ n generosidad, munificencia, f; don, m; (subsidy) subvención, f
bouquet /bou'kei, bu-/ n ramo, ramillete (de flores), m; perfume, m; (of wine) nariz, f
Bourbon /'bɜrbən; 'bʊrbən/ a borbónico. —n Borbón (-ona)
bourgeois /bur'ʒwɑ/ a and n burgués (-esa)
bourgeoisie /ˌbʊrʒwɑ'zi/ n burguesía, mesocracia, f
bout /baut/ n turno, m; (in fencing, boxing, wrestling) asalto, m; (of illness, coughing) ataque, m; (fight) lucha, f, combate, m; (of drinking) borrachera, f
bovine /'bouvain/ a bovino, vacuno
bow /bou/ n (weapon) arco, m; (of a saddle) arzón (de silla), m; Mus. arco, m; (knot) lazo, m; (greeting) saludo, m; reverencia, inclinación, f; (of a boat) proa, f. **to tie a bow,** hacer un lazo. **bow and arrows,** arco y flechas, m. **bow-legged,** patizambo. **bow window,** ventana saliente, f
bow /bau/ vi inclinarse; hacer una reverencia, saludar; (remove the hat) descubrirse; Fig. inclinarse (ante); (submit) someterse (a), reconocer; agobiarse; Mus. manejar el arco. —vt (usher in) introducir en, conducir a; doblar; inclinar. **to bow down (to),** humillarse ante; obedecer; (worship) reverenciar, adorar. **to bow out,** despedir con una inclinación del cuerpo

bowel /'bauəl/ n intestino, m; pl **bowels,** Fig. seno, m, entrañas, f pl
bower /'bauər/ n (arbor) enramada, f; glorieta, f; (boudoir) tocador de señora, m
bowing /'bouɪŋ/ n Mus. arqueada, f; saludo, m, a (of acquaintance) superficial
bowl /boul/ n receptáculo, m; (of a fountain) taza, f; (of a pipe) cazoleta, f; (barber's) bacía, f; (for washing) jofaina, f; (for punch) ponchera, f; (goblet) copa, f; (for soup) escudilla, f; (for fruit) frutero, m; (of a spoon) paleta, f; (ball) boliche, m. —vt tirar; (in cricket) sacar; (a hoop) jugar con; (in ninepins) tumbar con una bola. **to b. along,** recorrer; ir en coche o carruaje (por). **to b. over,** Fig. dejar consternado (a), desconcertar
bowler /'boulər/ n (in cricket) servidor, m; (hat) sombrero hongo, m; (skittle player) jugador de bolos, m
bowling /'boulɪŋ/ n (in cricket) saque, m; (skittles) juego de bolos, m; juego de boliche, m. **b. alley,** bolera, pista de bolos, f, salón de boliche, m. **b.-green,** bolera en cesped, f
bowls /boulz/ n juego de boliche, m
bowsprit /'bausprɪt/ n bauprés, m
bowstring /'bou,strɪŋ/ n cuerda de arco, f
bow tie /bou/ n pajarita, f
bow-wow /'bau ˌwau/ n guau, m
box /bɒks/ n caja, f; (case) estuche, m; (luggage) baúl, m, maleta, f; (for a hat) sombrerera, f; Bot. boj, m; Theat. palco, m; (for a sentry, signalman, etc.) garita, casilla, f; (on a carriage) pescante, m; (blow) cachete, m, bofetada, f; (for a horse) vagón, m. **post office box,** apartado de correos, m. **box-kite,** cometa celular, f. **box-maker,** cajero, m. **box office,** taquilla, f. **box-pleat,** Sew. tabla, f
box /bɒks/ vt encajonar, meter en una caja. —vi boxear. **to box the ears of,** calentar las orejas de. **to box up,** encerrar
boxer /'bɒksər/ n Sports. boxeador, pugilista, m
boxing /'bɒksɪŋ/ n encajonamiento, m; envase, m; Sports. boxeo, pugilato, m. **B. Day,** Día de San Esteban, m, (A Spanish child receives its Christmas presents on the Día de Reyes (Twelfth Night).) **b.-gloves,** guantes de boxeo, m pl. **b.-ring,** cuadrilátero de boxeo, m
box-office success /'bɒks ˌɒfɪs/ n éxito de taquilla, m
boy /bɔi/ n muchacho, niño, rapaz, m; (older) chico, joven, m. **new boy,** nuevo alumno, m. **old boy,** (of a school) antiguo alumno, m; (Fam. address) chico. **small boy,** chiquillo, pequeño, crío, m. **b. doll,** muñeco, m. **boy scout,** muchacho explorador, m
boycott /'bɔikɒt/ vt boicotear. —n boicot, m
boyhood /'bɔihʊd/ n muchachez, mocedad, f; (childhood) niñez, f
boyish /'bɔiiʃ/ a muchachil; pueril; de niñez
brace /breis/ n (prop) puntal, barrote, m; abrazadera, f; berbiquí, m; viento, tirante, m; freno (for the teeth), m, (pair) par, m; (of beads) braces, tirantes, m pl. —vt apuntalar; asegurar; ensamblar; Naut. bracear; (trousers) tirar; Fig. fortalecer, refrescar
bracelet /'breislɪt/ n pulsera, f; brazalete, m, ajorca, f
bracing /'breisɪŋ/ a (of air, etc.) fortificante, tónico; estimulador
bracken /'brækən/ n helecho, m
bracket /'brækɪt/ n consola, f; Archit. repisa, f; soporte, m; (on furniture, etc.) cantonera, f; Print. paréntesis angular, m; (for a light) brazo (de alumbrado), m. —vt Print. poner entre paréntesis; juntar. **in brackets,** entre paréntesis. **They were bracketed equal,** Fueron juzgados iguales
brackish /'brækɪʃ/ a salobre
brag /bræg/ vi jactarse, fanfarronear. —n jactancia, f. **to b. about,** hacer alarde de
braggart /'brægərt/ a baladrón, jactancioso. —n jactancioso, fanfarrón, m
bragging /'brægɪŋ/ n jactancia, f
Brahmin /'brɑmɪn/ n brahmán, m
Brahminism /'brɑmɪ,nɪzəm/ n brahmanismo, m
braid /breid/ n trencilla, f, cordoncillo, m; (for trimming) galón, m; (plait) trenza, f. —vt (hair) trenzar; (trim) galonear; acordonar, trencillar
brain /brein/ n cerebro, m; entendimiento, m, inteli-

gencia, *f;* talento, *m;* (common sense) sentido común, *m;* *pl* **brains,** sesos, *m pl,* (animal and human); cacumen, *m.* —*vt* romper la crisma (a). **to blow one's brains out,** levantarse la tapa de los sesos. **to rack one's brains,** devanarse los sesos. **Brains Trust,** masa cefálica, *f;* consorcio de inteligencias, *m.* **b.-box,** cráneo, *m.* **b.-fever,** fiebre cerebral, *f.* **b.-storm,** crisis nerviosa, *f.* **b.-wave,** idea luminosa, *f.* **b.-work,** trabajo intelectual, *m*

brainchild /'brein,tʃaild/ *n* engendro, *m*
brain drain *n* fuga de cerebros, *f*
brained /breind/ *a* de cabeza, de cerebro
brainless /'breinlis/ *a* sin seso; tonto
brainy /'breini/ *a* sesudo, inteligente, talentudo
braise /breiz/ *vt Cul.* asar
brake /breik/ *n* (of vehicles and *Fig.*) freno, *m;* (flax and hemp) caballete, *m;* (carriage) break, *m;* (thicket) matorral, *m.* —*vt* (vehicles) frenar; (hemp, etc.) rastrillar. **foot-b.,** freno de pedal, *m.* **hand-b.,** freno de mano, *m.* **to b. hard,** frenar de repente. **to release the b.,** quitar el freno
bramble /'bræmbəl/ *n* zarza, *f.* **b. patch,** breña, *f,* zarzal, *m*
brambly /'bræmbli/ *a* zarzoso
bran /bræn/ *n* salvado, *m*
branch /bræntʃ, brantʃ/ *n* (of a tree, a family) rama, *f;* (of flowers, of learning) ramo, *m;* (of a river) tributario, afluente, *m;* (of roads, railways) ramal, *m;* (of a firm) sucursal, dependencia, *f.* —*a* sucursal, dependiente; (of roads, railways) secundario. —*vi* echar ramas; bifurcarse, dividirse; ramificarse. **to b. off,** bifurcarse, ramificarse. **to b. out,** extenderse; emprender cosas nuevas
branched /bræntʃt/ *a* con ramas; *Bot.* ramoso; (of candlesticks) de... brazos
branchiness /'bræntʃinis/ *n* ramaje, *m,* frondosidad, *f*
branching /'bræntʃiŋ/ *n* ramificación, *f;* división, *f.* **b. off,** bifurcación, *f*
brand /brænd/ *n* tizón, *m;* (torch) tea, *f;* (on cattle, etc.) hierro, *m;* (trademark) marca de fábrica, *f;* marca, *f;* (stigma) estigma, *m.* —*vt* marcar con el hierro, herrar; marcar; estigmatizar, tildar. **b.-new,** flamante
branding /'brændiŋ/ *n* (of livestock) herradero, *m;* (of slaves, criminals) estigmatización, *f;* difamación, *f.* **b.-iron,** hierro de marcar, *m*
brandish /'brændiʃ/ *vt* blandir
brandy /'brændi/ *n* coñac, *m*
brass /bræs/ *n* latón, *m; Mus.* metal, *m;* (tablet) placa conmemorativa, *f; Inf.* dinero, *m.* **the b.,** *Mus.* el metal. **b. band,** banda de instrumentos de viento, *f.* **b.-neck,** *Inf.* cara dura, *f.* **b. works** or **shop,** latonería, *f*
brassiere /brə'ziər/ *n* sostén, *m*
brat /bræt/ *n* crío, *m*
bravado /brə'vɑdou/ *n* bravata, *f*
brave /breiv/ *a* valiente, animoso, intrépido; espléndido, magnífico; bizarro. —*n* valiente, *m.* —*vt* desafiar, provocar; arrostrar
bravely /'breivli/ *adv* valientemente; espléndidamente; bizarramente
bravery /'breivəri/ *n* valentía, *f,* valor, *m,* intrepidez, *f,* coraje, *m;* esplendidez, suntuosidad, *f;* bizarría, *f*
bravo /'brɑvou/ *n* bandido, *m;* asesino pagado, *m, interj* ¡bravo! ¡ole!
bravura /brə'vyurə/ *n* bravura, *f*
brawl /brɔl/ *n* camorra, reyerta, pelotera, *f.* —*vi* alborotar; (of streams) murmurar. **to start a b.,** armar camorra
brawler /'brɔlər/ *n* camorrista, *mf*
brawling /'brɔliŋ/ *n* alboroto, *m,* vociglería, *f;* (of streams) murmullo, *m*
brawn /brɔn/ *n Cul.* embutido, *m;* músculo, *m;* (strength) fuerza, *f*
brawny /'brɔni/ *a* membrudo, musculoso, forzudo
bray /brei/ *n* rebuzno, *m;* (of trumpets) clangor, *m, vi* rebuznar; sonar
brazen /'breizən/ *a* de latón; (of voice) bronca; desvergonzado, descarado
brazier /'breizər/ *n* (fire) brasero, *m;* latonero, *m*
Brazil /brə'zil/ el Brasil, *m*
Brazilian /brə'zilyən/ *a and n* brasileño (-ña)

Brazil nut *n* nuez del Brasil, *f*
breach /britʃ/ *n* violación, contravención, *f;* (gap) abertura, *f; Mil.* brecha, *f.* —*vt Mil.* hacer brecha (en); (in a line of defence) hacer mella (en). **b. of confidence,** abuso de confianza, *f.* **b. of promise,** incumplimiento de la palabra de casamiento, *m.* **b. of the peace,** alteración del orden público, *f,* quebrantamiento de la paz, *m*
bread /bred/ *n* pan, *m.* **to earn one's b. and butter,** ganarse el pan. **brown b.,** pan moreno, *m.* **unleavened b.,** pan ázimo, *m.* **b. and butter,** pan con mantequilla, *m; Fig.* sustento diario, *m.* **b.-basket,** cesta de pan, *f; Inf.* estómago, *m.* **b.-bin,** caja del pan, *f.* **b.-crumb,** miga, *f;* migaja, *f.* **b.-knife,** cuchillo para cortar el pan, *m.* **b. poultice,** cataplasma de miga de pan, *f.* **b.-winner,** ganador (-ra) de pan, trabajador (-ra)
breadfruit tree /'bred,frut/ *n* árbol del pan, *m*
breadth /bredθ/ *n* anchura, *f;* latitud, *f;* liberalidad, *f; Sew.* ancho de una tela, *m*
breadthways /'bredθ,weiz/ *adv* a lo ancho
break /breik/ *n* rotura, *f;* (opening) abertura, *f; Geol.* rajadura, *f;* (fissure) grieta, *f;* solución de continuidad, *f;* interrupción, *f;* (billiards) serie, *f;* (change) cambio, *m;* (in a boy's voice) muda (de la voz), *f;* (blank) vacío, *m;* (in the market) baja, *f;* intervalo, *m;* descanso, *m;* pausa, *f;* (truce) tregua, *f;* (clearing) clara, *f; Mus.* quiebra (de la voz), *f;* (carriage) break, *m;* (*Fam.* folly) disparate, *m.* **with a b. in one's voice,** con voz entrecortada. **b. of day,** aurora, alba, *f.* **at the b. of day,** al despuntar el alba
break /breik/ *vt* romper; quebrar; quebrantar, fracturar; (breach) abrir brecha en; (in two) partir, dividir; (into pieces) hacer pedazos, despedazar; (into small pieces) desmenuzar; (into crumbs) desmigajar; (destroy) destrozar; (a blow) parar; (a law) infringir, violar; (the bank in gambling) quebrar; (a journey, etc.) interrumpir; (a habit) desacostumbrar, hacer perder el vicio de; (a promise) no cumplir, faltar a; (a record) superar; (plow ground) roturar; (spoil) estropear; arruinar; *Com.* ir a la quiebra; (an official) degradar; (an animal) domar, amansar; (*Fig.* crush) subyugar; (betray) traicionar; (*Fig.* of silence, a spell, a lance, peace, the ranks) romper; (cushion) amortiguar; (lessen) mitigar; (disclose) revelar; *Elec.* interrumpir. **to b. one's promise,** faltar a su palabra. **to b. the ice,** *Fig.* romper el hielo. **to b. asunder,** romper en dos (partes); dividir. **to b. down,** derribar; echar abajo; destruir; (suppress) suprimir; subyugar; abolir; disolver. **to b. in,** (animals) domar, amaestrar; (persons) disciplinar; (new shoes) ahormar, romper. **to b. in two,** partir; dividir en dos; (split) hender. **to b. off,** separar, quitar; (a branch) desgajar; *Fig.* romper; interrumpir; cesar. **to b. open,** forzar, abrir a la fuerza. **to b. up,** hacer pedazos; (scatter) poner en fuga, dispersar; hacer levantar la sesión; (the ground) roturar; (parliament) disolver; (a ship) desguazar, deshacer (un buque)
break /breik/ *vi* romperse; quebrarse; quebrantarse; (of beads) desgranarse; (burst) reventar, estallar; (of abscesses) abrirse; (of a boy's voice) mudar; (*Fig.* and of clouds, etc.) romperse; desaparecer; (of the dawn) despuntar (el alba), amanecer; (sprout) brotar; (of a ball) torcerse; (of fine weather) terminar; (change) cambiar; (of a storm) estallar. **to b. loose,** desasirse; *Fig.* desencadenarse. **to b. away,** escaparse, fugarse; (from a habit) romper con, independizarse de (another country); disparase. **to b. down,** (of machinery, cars) averiarse; (fail) frustrarse, malograrse; (weep) deshacerse en lágrimas; (lose one's grip) perder la confianza en sí; (in health) sufrir una crisis de salud. **The car broke down,** El auto tuvo una avería. **to b. in,** (of burglars) forzar la entrada; irrumpir (en), penetrar (en); exclamar. **to b. in on,** sorprender; entrar de sopetón; invadir; interrumpir; caer sobre; molestar. **to b. into,** (force) forzar; (utter) romper a, prorrumpir en; empezar (a); pasar de repente a; (of time, etc.) ocupar; hacer perder. **to b. off,** (of speech) interrumpirse; cesar; (detach) desprenderse, separarse; (of branches) desgajarse. **to b. out,** huir, escaparse; *Fig.* estallar; aparecer; declararse; (of fire) tomar fuego; derramarse; (of an eruption) salir. **to b. over,** derramarse por; bañar. **to b. down.**

through, abrirse paso (por); abrirse salida (por); atravesar; *Fig.* penetrar; (of the sun, etc.) romper (por). **to b. up,** (depart) separarse; (of meetings) levantarse la sesión; dispersarse; (smash) hacerse pedazos; disolverse; (of a school) cerrarse, empezar las vacaciones; (melt) fundir; desbandarse; (of a camp) levantar (el campo); (grow old) hacerse viejo; (be ill) estar agotado. **to b. with,** romper con; cesar; reñir con

breakable /'breikəbəl/ *a* quebradizo, frágil

breakage /'breikɪdʒ/ *n* rompimiento, quebrantamiento, *m;* cosa rota, *f;* fractura, *f*

breakdown /'breik‚daun/ *n* accidente, *m;* (of a machine) avería, *f; Auto.* pane, *f;* (failure) fracaso, *m,* falta de éxito, *f;* deterioración, *f;* (in health) crisis de salud, *f.* **b. gang,** pelotón de reparaciones, *m*

breaker /'breikər/ *n* oleada, *f*

breakfast /'brekfəst/ *n* desayuno, *m.* —*vi* desayunar(se), tomar el desayuno. **to have a good b.,** desayunar bien. **b.-cup,** tazón, *m.* **b.-time,** hora del desayuno, *f*

breaking /'breikɪŋ/ *n* rompimiento, *m;* quebrantamiento, *m;* fractura, *f;* ruptura, *f;* (in two) división, *f;* (into pieces) despedazamiento, *m;* (into small pieces) desmenuzamiento, *m;* (destruction) destrozo, *m;* (of a blow) parada, *f;* (of a law, etc.) violación, *f;* (of one's word) no cumplimiento, *m;* (of a journey, of sleep, etc.) interrupción, *f;* (escape) escape, *m,* huida, *f;* (of an animal) domadura, *f;* (of a boy's voice) muda (de la voz), *f;* (of news) revelación, *f.* **b. down,** demolición, *f;* (of negotiations) suspensión, *f.* **b. in,** irrupción, *f;* (of an animal) domadura, *f;* (training) entrenamiento, *m.* **b. open,** forzamiento, *m;* quebranto, *m.* **b. out,** huida, *f,* escape, *m; Fig.* estallido, *m;* aparición, *f;* declaración, *f;* (scattering) derramamiento, *m;* (of a rash) erupción, *f.* **b. up,** dispersión, *f;* disolución, *f;* fin, *m;* ruina, *f;* (of a school) cierre, *m;* (change in weather) cambio, *m;* (of a meeting) levantamiento (de una sesión), *m;* (of the earth) roturación, *f*

breakneck /'breik‚nek/ *a* rápido, veloz, precipitado

breakwater /'breik‚wɔtər/ *n* malecón, rompeolas, *m*

bream /brim/ *n Ichth.* sargo, *m.* **sea-b.,** besugo, *m*

breast /brest/ *n* pecho, *m;* (of birds) pechuga, *f;* (of female animals) teta, mama, *f;* (heart) corazón, *m, vt* (the waves) cortar (las olas); luchar con; *Fig.* arrostrar, hacer frente a. **b.-bone,** esternón, *m.* **b. high,** alto hasta el pecho. **b.-pin,** alfiler de pecho, *m.* **b.-pocket,** bolsillo de pecho, *m.* **b.-stroke,** estilo pecho, *m*

breast cancer *n* el cáncer del seno, *m*

breasted /'brestɪd/ *a* de pecho...; de pechuga...; de tetas... **a double-b. jacket,** una chaqueta cruzada. **a single-b. jacket,** una chaqueta

breastwork /'brest‚wɜrk/ *n Mil.* parapeto, *m*

breath /brɛθ/ *n* aliento, *m;* suspiro, *m;* (phonetics) aspiración, *f;* (breeze) soplo (de aire), *m;* (of scandal, etc.) murmurio, *m;* (fragrance) perfume, *m,* fragancia, *f;* (life) vida, *f.* **in a b.,** de un aliento. **in the same b.,** sin respirar. **out of b.,** sin aliento. **under one's b.,** por lo bajo, entre dientes. **to draw b.,** tomar aliento. **to get one's b. back,** cobrar aliento. **to hold one's b.,** contener el aliento. **to take one's b. away,** *Fig.* dejar consternado (a)

breathable /'briðəbəl/ *a* respirable

breathe /brið/ *vi* respirar; vivir; (of air, etc.) soplar; (take the air) tomar el fresco; (rest) tomar aliento. —*vt* respirar; exhalar; dar aire (a); (whisper) murmurar; (convey) expresar, revelar; (infuse) infundir. **to b. forth fury,** echar rayos. **to b. hard,** jadear. **to b. one's last,** exhalar el último suspiro. **to b. in,** inspirar

breathing /'briðɪŋ/ *n* respiración, *f;* (of the air, etc.) soplo, *m;* (phonetics) aspiración, *f.* —*a* que respira; viviente. **hard** or **heavy b.,** jadeo, resuello, resoplido, *m.* **b.-space,** *Fig.* respiro, *m*

breathless /'brɛθlɪs/ *a* jadeante, sin aliento; (dead) muerto; (sultry) sin un soplo de aire; intenso, profundo; (of haste) precipitado

breathlessly /'brɛθlɪsli/ *adv* anhelosamente; con expectación

breathlessness /'brɛθlɪsnɪs/ *n* falta de aliento, *f;* res-

piración difícil, *f;* (death) muerte, *f;* (of weather) falta de aire, *f*

bred /bred/ *a* criado. **ill (well) b.,** mal (bien) criado. **pure-b.,** de raza

breech /britʃ/ *n Anat.* trasero, *m;* (of fire-arms) recámara, *f*

breeches /'britʃɪz/ *n* calzones, *m pl;* pantalones, *m pl.* **riding-b.,** pantalones de montar, *m pl.* **to wear the b.,** *Fig.* ponerse los calzones

breed /brid/ *n* casta, raza, *f;* tipo, *m;* clase, *f, vt* procrear; engendrar, crear; (bring up) educar; criar. —*vi* reproducirse; sacar cría; multiplicarse. **to b. in-and-in,** procrear sin mezclar razas

breeder /'bridər/ *n* criador (-ra); animal reproductor, *m*

breeding /'bridɪŋ/ *n* reproducción, *f;* cría, *f;* (upbringing) crianza, *f;* educación, *f;* instrucción, *f;* producción, *f;* creación, *f,* a de cría; (of male animals) semental; prolífico. **bad b.,** mala crianza, *f.* **good b.,** buena crianza, *f.* **cross b.,** cruzamiento de razas, *m.* **B. will out,** Aunque la mona se vista de seda, mona se queda. **b. farm,** criadero, *m*

breeze /briz/ *n* brisa, *f,* vientecillo, soplo de aire, *m;* (argument) altercación, *f,* argumento, *m;* (of coke) cisco de coque, *m.* **fresh b.,** brisa fresca, *f.* **light b.,** brisa floja, *f.* **strong b.,** viento fuerte, viento muy fresco, *m*

breezy /'brizi/ *a* con brisa, fresco; expuesto a la brisa; oreado; (of manner) animado, jovial

Bremen /'bremən, 'breimən/ Brema, *f*

brethren /'brɛðrɪn/ *n pl* hermanos, *m pl*

Breton /'brɛtn̩/ *a* and *n* bretón (-ona). —*n* (language) bretón, *m*

brevet /brə'vɛt/ *n Mil.* graduación honoraria, *f;* nombramiento honorario, *m.* —*vt Mil.* graduar

breviary /'brivi‚ɛri/ *n* breviario, *m*

brevity /'brɛvɪti/ *n* brevedad, *f;* concisión, *f*

brew /bru/ *n* mezcla, *f;* brebaje, *m.* —*vt* hacer (cerveza, té, etc.); preparar, mezclar; *Fig.* urdir, tramar. —*vi* prepararse; urdirse; (storm) gestarse

brewer /'bruər/ *n* cervecero (-ra)

brewery /'bruəri/ *n* cervecería, fábrica de cerveza, *f*

brewing /'bruɪŋ/ *n* elaboración de cerveza, *f*

briar /'braiər/ *n* (wild rose) rosal silvestre, *m;* (heather) brezo, *m.* **b. pipe,** pipa de brezo, *f*

bribable /'braibəbəl/ *a* sobornable

bribe /braib/ *n* soborno, cohecho, *m, vt* sobornar, cohechar. **to take bribes,** dejarse sobornar

briber /'braibər/ *n* cohechador (-ra)

bribery /'braibəri/ *n* soborno, *m*

brick /brik/ *n* ladrillo, *m;* (for children) piedra de construcción, *f;* bloque, *m; Inf.* buen chico, *m,* joya, *f, a* de ladrillo. —*vt* enladrillar. **b.-floor,** enladrillado, *m;* **b.-kiln,** horno de ladrillo, *m.* **b.-maker,** ladrillero, *m.* **b.-yard,** ladrillar, *m*

bricklayer /'brik‚leiər/ *n* albañil, *m*

bricklaying /'brik‚leiɪŋ/ *n* albañilería, *f*

brickwork /'brik‚wɜrk/ *n* masonería, *f*

bridal /'braidl̩/ *a* nupcial; de la boda; de la novia. **b. bed,** tálamo, *m.* **b. cake,** torta de la boda, *f.* **b. shop,** tienda para novias, *f.* **b. shower,** despedida de soltera, despedida de soltería, *f.* **b. song,** epitalamio, *m.* **b. veil,** velo de la novia, velo nupcial, *m.* **b. wreath,** corona de azahar, *f*

bride /braid/ *n* novia, desposada, *f;* (after marriage) recién casada, *f*

bridegroom /'braid‚grum/ *n* novio, *m;* (after marriage) recién casado, *m*

bridesmaid /'braidz‚meid/ *n* madrina de boda, *f;* niña encargada de sostener la cola de la novia, *f*

bridge /bridʒ/ *n* (engineering, *Mus. Naut.*) puente, *m;* lomo (de la nariz), *m;* (game) bridge, *m, vt* construir un puente (sobre); pontear; (obstacles) salvar; evitar; (fill in) ocupar, llenar. **auction b.,** bridge por subasta, *m.* **contract b.,** bridge por contrato, *m.* **suspension-b.,** puente colgante, *m.* **b. toll,** portazgo, *m*

bridgehead /'bridʒ‚hed/ *n* cabeza de puente, *f*

bridle /'braidl̩/ *n* brida, *f;* freno, *m.* —*vt* embridar, enfrenar; *Fig.* reprimir. —*vi* (of horses) levantar la cabeza; (of persons) erguirse; hacer un gesto despreciativo. **snaffle b.,** bridón, *m.* **b. path,** camino de herradura, *m*

brief /brif/ *a* breve, corto; conciso; lacónico, seco; rápido; fugaz, pasajero. —*n* (papal) breve, *m; Law.* relación, *f;* escrito, *m.* —*vt* (a barrister) instruir. **to hold a b. for,** defender, abogar por. **b.-case,** portapapeles, *m;* cartera (grande), *f*

briefly /'brifli/ *adv* brevemente; en pocas palabras; sucintamente; (tersely) secamente

brier /'braiǝr/ *n* rosal silvestre, *m;* zarza, *f*

brigade /brɪ'geid/ *n Mil.* brigada, *f;* cuerpo, *m;* asociación, *f*

brigadier /ˌbrɪgǝ'diǝr/ *n* brigadier, *m*

brigand /'brɪgǝnd/ *n* bandolero, bandido, *m*

brigandage /'brɪgǝndɪdʒ/ *n* bandolerismo, *m*

bright /brait/ *a* brillante, reluciente; vivo; cristalino; subido; claro; optimista, alegre; inteligente; (quick-witted) agudo; ilustre; (smiling) risueño; (of future, etc.) halagüeño. **to be as b. as a new pin,** estar como una ascua de oro. **b. blue,** azul subido, *m.* **b.-eyed,** con ojos vivos, con ojos chispeantes, ojialegre

brighten /'braitn/ *vt* hacer brillar; (polish) pulir; (make happy) alegrar; (improve) mejorar. —*vi* (of the weather) aclarar, despejarse (el cielo); sentirse más feliz; mejorar

brightly /'braitli/ *adv* brillantemente; alegremente

brightness /'braitnis/ *n* brillo, *m;* claridad, *f;* esplendor, *m;* (of colors) brillantez, *f;* vivacidad, *f;* inteligencia, *f;* agudeza de ingenio, *f*

Bright's disease /braits/ *n* enfermedad de Bright, glomerulonefritis, *f*

brilliance /'brɪlyǝns/ *n* fulgor, brillo, *m,* refulgencia, *f;* esplendor, *m;* lustre, *m;* talento, *m;* brillantez, gloria, *f*

brilliant /'brɪlyǝnt/ *a* brillante. —*n* (gem) brillante, *m.* **to be b.,** (in conversation, etc.) brillar; (be clever) ser brillante

brilliantine /'brɪlyǝn,tin/ *n* brillantina, *f*

brim /brɪm/ *n* (of a glass, etc.) borde, *m;* (of a hat) ala, *f;* margen, *m,* orilla, *f.* **to be full to the b.,** estar lleno hasta los bordes; *Fig.* rebosar. **eyes brimming with tears,** ojos arrasados de lágrimas

brimful /'brɪm'fʊl/ *a* hasta el borde (or los bordes); *Fig.* rebosante

brimless /'brɪmlɪs/ *a* (of hats) sin ala

brimmed /brɪmd/ *a* (of hats) con ala

brimstone /'brɪm,stoun/ *n* azufre, *m*

brindled /'brɪndld/ *a* atigrado, abigarrado

brine /brain/ *n* salmuera, *f;* mar, *m;* *Poet.* lágrimas, *f pl*

bring /brɪŋ/ *vt* traer; llevar; transportar; (take a person or drive a vehicle) conducir; *Fig.* acarrear, traer; causar, ocasionar; producir; crear; (induce) persuadir; hacer (ver, etc.); (be worth) valer; (sell for) vender por; *Law.* entablar (un pleito, etc.): (before a judge) hacer comparecer (ante); (present) presentar; (attract) atraer; (place) poner. **to b. home,** llevar a casa; *Fig.* hacer ver, hacer sentir; (a crime) probar contra. **to b. near,** acercar. **to b. about,** efectuar, poner por obra; causar, ocasionar; (achieve) lograr, conseguir. **to b. again,** traer otra vez, llevar de nuevo. **to b. away,** llevarse. **to b. back,** devolver; traer; (of memories) recordar. **to b. down,** llevar abajo, bajar; (of persons) hacer bajar; (humble) humillar; hacer caer; (of prices) hacer bajar; arruinar; destruir. **to b. down the house,** *Theat.* hacer venirse el teatro abajo. **to b. forth,** (give birth to) dar a luz; producir; causar; sacar a luz. **to b. forward,** hacer adelantarse; empujar hacia adelante; *Fig.* avanzar; (allege) alegar; *Com.* llevar a nueva cuenta; presentar, producir. **brought forward,** *Com.* suma y sigue. **to b. in,** (things) llevar adentro; (persons) hacer entrar; introducir; aparecer con, presentarse con; (meals) servir; producir; declarar; (a verdict) dictar (sentencia de), fallar. **to b. into being,** poner en práctica; dar origen (a). **to b. off,** (a ship) poner a flote; (rescue) salvar, rescatar; (carry out) efectuar, poner en práctica; (achieve) conseguir, lograr. **B. me the glass off the table,** Tráeme el vaso que hay en la mesa. **to b. on,** causar, inducir; acarrear; iniciar. **He brought a book on to the stage,** Entró en escena llevando un libro (or con un libro). **to b. out,** sacar; poner afuera; (a person) hacer salir; publicar; (a play) poner en escena; sacar a luz; (an idea, jewels,

etc.) sacar a relucir; revelar; demostrar; hacer aparecer; (a girl in society) poner de largo (a). **to b. over,** llevar al otro lado; hacer venir; traer; conducir; hacer cruzar; (convert) convertir. **to b. round,** llevar; (from a swoon) sacar de un desmayo; curar; persuadir; conciliar. **to b. through,** hacer atravesar; llevar a través de; ayudar a salir (de un apuro); (an illness) curar de. **to b. to,** traer a; llevar a; (from a swoon) hacer volver en sí; *Naut.* ponerse a la capa. **He cannot b. himself to,** No puede persuadirse a. **to b. together,** reunir; (things) juntar, amontonar; reconciliar, poner en paz. **to b. under,** someter; sojuzgar; incluir. **to b. up,** llevar arriba, subir; (a person) hacer subir; hacer avanzar; (a price) hacer subir; ir (a); andar; (breed) criar; (educate) educar, criar; (in a discussion) hacer notar; vomitar. **to b. up the rear,** ir al fin (de); *Mil.* ir a la retaguardia. **well** (or **badly**) **brought up,** bien (o mal) educado. **to b. upon oneself,** buscarse, incurrir (en). **to b. up-to-date,** poner al día; refrescar; rejuvenecer

bringing /'brɪŋɪŋ/ *n* acción de llevar o traer, *f;* conducción, *f;* transporte, *m.* **b. forth,** producción, *f.* **b. in,** introducción, *f.* **b. out,** producción, *f;* publicación, *f;* (of a girl in society) puesta de largo, *f.* **b. under,** reducción, *f;* subyugación, *f.* **b. up,** educación, crianza, *f*

brink /brɪŋk/ *n* borde, margen, *m;* (of water) orilla, *f;* *Fig.* margen, *m.* **on the b.,** al margen; a la orilla. **to be on the b. of,** (doing something) estar para, estar a punto de

briny /'braini/ *a* salado

briquette /brɪ'ket/ *n* briqueta, *f,* aglomerado de carbón, *m*

brisk /brisk/ *a* activo; vivo; animado; rápido, acelerado; enérgico

brisket /'briskit/ *n* falda, *f*

briskly /'briskli/ *adv* vivamente; enérgicamente; aprisa

briskness /'brisknis/ *n* actividad, *f;* viveza, *f;* animación, *f;* rapidez, *f;* energía, *f*

brisling /'brizlɪŋ/ *n* sardina noruega

bristle /'brisǝl/ *n* cerda, seda, *f, vi* erizarse

bristly /'brisli/ *a* erizado, cerdoso; espinoso; hirsuto

Bristol board /'bristl/ *n* cartulina, *f*

British /'brɪtɪʃ/ *a* británico. **the B.,** el pueblo británico; los ingleses

British Commonwealth, the la Mancomunidad Británica, *f*

Briton /'brɪtn/ *n* inglés (-esa). **ancient B.,** britano (-na)

Brittany /'brɪtni/ Bretaña, *f*

brittle /'brɪtl/ *a* frágil, quebradizo, deleznable, friable

brittleness /'brɪtlnɪs/ *n* fragilidad, friabilidad, *f*

broach /broutʃ/ *n Cul.* espetón, asador, *m.* —*vt* espitar (un barril); abrir; *Fig.* introducir

broad /brɔd/ *a* ancho; grande; (extensive) vasto, extenso; **a b. confession,** una confesión amplia; (full) pleno; (of accents) marcado; (of words) lato; (clear) claro; (of the mind) liberal, tolerante; (of humor, etc.) grosero; (general) general, comprensivo. **in b. daylight,** en pleno día. **b.-brimmed,** de ala ancha. **b.-faced,** cariancho. **b.-minded,** tolerante, liberal, ancho de conciencia, abierto al mundo. **b.-mindedness,** tolerancia, liberalidad, *f.* **to be b.-minded,** ser tolerante, tener manga ancha. **b.-shouldered,** ancho de espaldas

broadcast /'brɔd,kæst/ *n Agr.* siembra al vuelo, *f; Radio.* radiodifusión, radiotransmisión, emisión, *f,* a radiado. —*adv* por todas partes; extensamente. —*vt Agr.* sembrar a vuelo; *Radio.* radiodifundir, radiar, transmitir por radio; (news, etc.) diseminar

broadcaster /'brɔd,kæstǝr/ *n* (lecturer) conferenciante, *mf;* radiofusor (-ra); (announcer) locutor (-ra)

broadcasting /'brɔd,kæstɪŋ/ *n* radiación, radiodifusión, *f;* radio, *f.* **b.-station,** estación de radio, emisora, *f.* **b.-studio,** estudio de emisión, *m*

broaden /'brɔdn/ *vt* ampliar, ensanchar. —*vi* ampliarse, ensancharse

broad-leaved /'brɔd,livd/ *a* frondoso

broadly /'brɔdli/ *adv* anchamente; con marcado acento dialectal; de una manera general

broadness /'brɔdnɪs/ n anchura, f; extensión, vastedad, f; tolerancia, f; liberalidad, f; grosería, f; (of accent) acento marcado, m

broadside /'brɔd,said/ n (of a ship) costado, m; (of guns) andanada, f; Fig. batería, f; Print. cara de un pliego, f. **to be b. on,** dar el costado

brocade /brou'keid/ a and n brocado m.. —vt decorar con brocado. **imitation b.,** brocatel, m

brocaded /brou'keidɪd/ a decorado con brocado; de brocado

broccoli /'brɒkəli/ n bróculi, brécol, m

brochure /brou'ʃʊr/ n folleto, m

brogue /broug/ n acento, m; acento irlandés, m; (shoe) zapato grueso, m

broil /brɔil/ vt emparrillar, asar. —vi asarse

broke /brouk/ a quebrado

broken /'broukən/ a roto; quebrado; (spiritless) abatido, desalentado; (infirm) agotado, debilitado; (ruined) arruinado; (of ground) desigual, escabroso; (of a language) chapucero; (spoilt) estropeado; imperfecto; incompleto; (loose) suelto; (of a horse, etc.) domado; (of the weather) variable; (of sleep) interrumpido; (of the heart, of shoes, etc.) roto; (of the voice, sobs, sighs) entrecortado; (of the voice through old age, etc.) cascada; (incoherent) incoherente. **b.-down,** (tired) rendido, agotado; arruinado; (not working) estropeado. **b.-hearted,** roto el corazón, angustiado. **b.-winged,** aliquebrado. **I speak broken Spanish,** Hablo el español chapuceramente

brokenly /'broukənli/ adv (of the voice) con voz entrecortada; a ratos; interrumpidamente

brokenness /'broukənnɪs/ n interrupción, f; (of the ground) desigualdad, f; (of speech) imperfección, f

broker /'broukər/ n corredor, m; (stock) corredor de bolsa, m

brokerage /'broukərɪdʒ/ n corretaje, m

bromide /'broumaid/ n bromuro, m

bromine /'broumin/ n bromo, m

bronchi /'brɒŋki/ n pl bronquios, m pl

bronchitis /brɒŋ'kaitɪs/ n bronquitis, f

broncopneumonia /'brɒŋkoʊuʊ'mounyə/ n bronconeumonia, f

Brontosaurus /,brɒntə'sɔrəs/ n brontosauro, m

bronze /brɒnz/ n bronce, m; objeto de bronce, m, a de bronce. —vt broncear. **B. Age,** Edad de Bronce, f

brooch /broutʃ/ n broche, m; alfiler de pecho, m

brood /brud/ n (of birds) nidada, f; (of chickens) pollada, f; (other animals) cría, f; prole, f, vi empollar. **to b. over,** meditar sobre, rumiar; (of mountains, etc.) dominar

broody /'brudi/ a (of hens) clueca, f

brook /brʊk/ n arroyo, riachuelo, m, vt tolerar, sufrir, permitir

broom /brum/ n escoba, f; Bot. retama, f; hiniesta, f. **common b.,** retama de escobas, f. **Spanish b.,** retama común, retama de olor, hiniesta, f. **b.-handle,** palo de escoba, m

broomstick /'brum,stɪk/ n palo de escoba, m

broth /brɔθ/ n caldo, m

brothel /'brɒθəl/ n burdel, lupanar, m, casa de trato, f

brother /'brʌðər/ n hermano, m; (colleague) colega, m; Inf. compañero, m. **foster-b.,** hermano de leche, m. **half-b.,** medio hermano, m. **step-b.,** hermanastro, m. **b.-in-law,** hermano político, cuñado, m. **b.-officer,** compañero de promoción, m

brotherhood /'brʌðər,hʊd/ n fraternidad, f; Eccl. cofradía, f; hermandad, f

brotherliness /'brʌðərlinɪs/ n fraternidad, f

brotherly /'brʌðərli/ a fraterno

brow /brau/ n frente, f; ceja, f; (of a hill) cresta, cumbre, f; (edge) borde, m. **to knit one's b.,** fruncir el ceño

browbeat /'brau,bit/ vt intimidar, amenazar

browbeating /'brau,bitɪŋ/ n intimidación, f

brown /braun/ a castaño; (gallicism often used of shoes, etc.) marrón; pardo; (of complexion, eyes, hair) moreno; (dark brown) bruno; (blackish) negruzco; (toasted) tostado; (burnt) quemado. —n color moreno, m; color pardo, m; castaño, m; (from the sun) bronce, m. —vt (toast) tostar; (a person) volver moreno, broncear; (meat) asar. —vi tostarse;

volverse moreno, broncearse; asarse. **b. bear,** oso pardo, m. **b. owl,** autillo, m. **b. paper,** papel de estraza, m. **b. study,** ensimismamiento, m, meditación, f. **b. sugar,** azúcar moreno (or quebrado), m

brownie /'brauni/ n duende benévolo, m

brownish /'braunɪʃ/ a morenucho; que tira a castaño o a bruno; parduzco; trigueño

brownness /'braunnɪs/ n color moreno, m

browse /brauz/ vi pacer; (through a publication) hojear (un libro)

browsing /'brauzɪŋ/ n apacentamiento, m; hojeo (de un libro), m; lectura, f, estudio, m

Bruges /'brudʒɪz/ Brujas, f

bruise /bruz/ n cardenal, m; abolladura, f; (in metal) bollo, m; (on fruit) maca, f. —vt acardenalar, magullar; abollar; (fruit) macar

bruising /'bruzɪŋ/ n magullamiento, m; (of metal) abolladura, f; (crushing) machacadura, f; (boxing) boxeo, pugilato, m

brunette /bru'nɛt/ n trigueña, morena, f

brunt /brʌnt/ n peso, m; golpe, m; choque, m; esfuerzo, m. **to bear the b.,** soportar el peso; sufrir el choque; Inf. pagar el pato

brush /brʌʃ/ n cepillo, m; (broom) escoba, f; (for whitewashing, etc.) brocha, f; (for painting) pincel, m; (of a fox) cola (de zorro), f; (undergrowth) breñal, matorral, m; (fight) escaramuza, f; (argument) altercación, f. **scrubbing-b.,** cepillo para fregar, m. **shoe-b.,** cepillo para limpiar los zapatos, m. **stroke of the b.,** brochada, f; pincelada, f. **whitewash-b.,** brochón, m. **b. maker** or **seller,** escobero (-ra); pincelero (-ra)

brush /brʌʃ/ vt cepillar; (sweep) barrer; frotar; (touch) rozar; (touch lightly) acariciar. **to b. against,** rozar, tocar. **to b. aside,** echar a un lado; Fig. no hacer caso de; ignorar. **to b. off,** sacudir(se); quitar(se); (sweep) barrer. **to b. up,** cepillar; (wool) cardar; (tidy) asear; (a subject) refrescar, repasar

brushing /'brʌʃɪŋ/ n acepilladura, f; (sweeping) barredura, f; (touching) roce, rozamiento, m; (of hair) peinadura, f

brushwood /'brʌʃ,wʊd/ n enjutos, m pl, chamarasca, f; matorral, m

brusque /brʌsk/ a brusco, seco

brusquely /'brʌskli/ adv secamente

brusqueness /'brʌsknɪs/ n brusquedad, f

Brussels /'brʌsəlz/ n bruselense; de Bruselas. **B. lace,** encaje de Bruselas, m

Brussels sprouts n pl bretones, m pl

brutal /'brutḷ/ a bestial, brutal; salvaje, inhumano

brutality /bru'tælɪti/ n brutalidad, bestialidad, f; barbaridad, ferocidad, f

brutalize /'brutḷ,aiz/ vt embrutecer

brutally /'brutḷi/ adv brutalmente

brute /brut/ n bruto, animal, m; salvaje, bárbaro, m. **b. force,** la fuerza bruta

brutish /'brutɪʃ/ a bruto; sensual, bestial; grosero; salvaje; estúpido; ignorante. **to become b.,** embrutecerse

bubble /'bʌbəl/ n burbuja, f; borbollón, m, vi burbujear; borbollar, bullir, hervir

bubbling /'bʌbəlɪŋ/ n burbujeo, m; hervidero, m; (of brooks) murmullo, m, a burbujeante; hirviente; (of brooks) parlero; (of wine) espumoso, efervescente

bubonic /byu'bɒnɪk/ a bubónico. **b. plague,** peste bubónica, f

buccaneer /,bʌkə'nɪər/ n corsario, m; aventurero, m

Bucharest /'bukə,rɛst/ Bucarest, m

buck /bʌk/ n Zool. gamo, m; (male) macho, m; (fop) galán, petimetre, m, vi (of a horse) caracolear; fanfarronear. **to pass the b.,** Inf. echarle en el muerto. **b.-rabbit,** conejo, m. **to b. up,** hacer de tripas corazón

bucket /'bʌkɪt/ n cubo, balde, m, cubeta, f

buckle /'bʌkəl/ n hebilla, f. —vt enhebillar, abrochar con hebilla. —vi doblarse. **to b. to,** ponerse a hacer algo con ahinco

buckled /'bʌkəld/ a con hebillas

buckler /'bʌklər/ n broquel, m, rodela, tarjeta, f

buckram /'bʌkrəm/ n bocací, m

buckshot /'bʌk,ʃɒt/ n perdigón, m

buckskin /'bʌk,skɪn/ n ante, m

buckwheat /'bʌk,wit/ n alforfón, trigo sarraceno, m

bucolic /byu'kɒlɪk/ a bucólico, pastoril

bud /bʌd/ n brote, m; botón, capullo, m; (of vines) bollón, m; (of vegetables) gema, f. —vi brotar, germinar. —vt injertar de escudete

Buddhism /'budɪzəm/ n budismo, m

Buddhist /'budɪst/ n budista, mf

budding /'bʌdɪŋ/ n brotadura, f; (of roses, etc) injerto de escudete, m; Fig. germen, m

budge /bʌdʒ/ vi moverse, menearse. —vt mover

budgerigar /'bʌdʒəri,gɑr/ n periquito, m

budget /'bʌdʒɪt/ n presupuesto, m; (of news, etc.) colección, f. —vi presuponer

Buenos Aires /'bweiˈnəs aiˈrɪz/ (of or from) a and n bonaerense, mf

buff /bʌf/ n color de ante, m; piel de ante, f. **b.-colored,** anteado

buffalo /'bʌfə,lou/ n búfalo, f

buffer /'bʌfər/ n (railway) parachoques, m; (of cars) amortiguador, m. **b. state,** estado tapón, m

buffet /bəˈfei/ n bofetón, m; bofetada, f; bar, m. —vt abofetear; golpear; luchar con las olas

buffoon /bəˈfun/ n bufón, m

buffoonery /bəˈfunəri/ n bufonería, f

bug /bʌg/ n chinche, f

bugbear /'bʌg,bɛər/ n pesadilla, f

bugle /'byugəl/ n corneta, trompeta, f; (bead) abalorio, m. **b. blast,** trompetazo, m

bugler /'byuglər/ n trompetero, m

build /bɪld/ vt edificar; (engines, ships, organs, etc.) construir; (a nest and Fig.) hacer; (have built) hacer, edificar; crear; formar; fundar. —n estructura, f; (of the body) hechura, f; talle, m. **to b. castles in Spain,** hacer castillos en el aire. **built-up area,** zona urbana, f. **to b. up,** construir; levantar; (block) tapar; (business, reputation) establecer, crear. **to b. upon,** Fig. contar con, confiar en; esperar de

builder /'bɪldər/ n constructor, m; maestro de obras, m; (laborer) albañil, m; creador (-ra), fundador (-ra); arquitecto, m

building /'bɪldɪŋ/ n edificación, f; construcción, f; edificio, m; fundación, f; creación, f. **b. contractor,** maestro de obras, m. **b. material,** material de construcción, m. **b. site,** solar, terreno, m. **b. timber,** madera de construcción, f

built-in /'bɪlt ,ɪn/ a empotrado. **b. closet,** armario empotrado, m

bulb /bʌlb/ n Bot. bulbo, m; (Elec. Phys.) bombilla, f; (of an oil lamp) cebolla, f

bulbous /'bʌlbəs/ a bulboso

Bulgarian /bʌl'gɛəriən/ a and n búlgaro (-ra)

bulge /bʌldʒ/ n bulto, m; hinchazón, f; protuberancia, f; Mil. bolsa (en el frente), f. —vi hincharse; estar lleno (de)

bulging /'bʌldʒɪŋ/ a lleno (de); con bultos; hinchado (de)

bulk /bʌlk/ n volumen, tamaño, m; bulto, m; (larger part) grueso, m; mayor parte, f; (of people) mayoría, f; (of a ship) capacidad, f. **in b.,** Com. en bruto, en grueso. **to b. large,** tener mucha importancia

bulkhead /'bʌlk,hɛd/ n Naut. mamparo, m

bulkiness /'bʌlkɪnɪs/ n abultamiento, m; volumen, tamaño, m

bulky /'bʌlki/ a voluminoso, grande, grueso

bull /bʊl/ n toro, m; Astron. Tauro, m; (of some animals) macho, m; (Stock Exchange) alcista, mf; (of the Pope) bula (del Papa), f. **a b. in a china shop,** un caballo loco en una cacharrería. **to fight bulls,** torear. **b.-calf,** ternero, m. **bull's eye,** blanco, m; acierto, m. **b. fight,** corrida de toros, f. **b. fighter's gala uniform,** traje de luces, m. **b.-ring,** plaza de toros, f

bulldog /'bʊl,dɔg/ n perro dogo, perro de presa, m

bulldozer /'bʊl,douzər/ n (excavator) tozodora, f

bullet /'bʊlɪt/ n bala, f. **spent b.,** bala fría, f. **stray b.,** bala perdida, f. **b.-proof,** a prueba de bala, blindado

bulletin /'bʊlɪtɪn/ n boletín, m

bulletin board n tablero de anuncios, tablero de avisos, tablón, m

bulletproof vest /'bʊlɪt,pruf/ n chaleco blindado, m

bullfighter /'bʊl,faitər/ n torero, m (on foot), toreador, m (on horseback)

bullfinch /'bʊl,fɪntʃ/ n pinzón real, m

bullion /'bʊlyən/ n Com. metálico, m; oro (or plata) en barras, m, f.

bullock /'bʊlək/ n becerro, m; buey, m

bullpen /'bʊl,pen/ n toril, m; (bullfighting); calentador, m (baseball)

bully /'bʊli/ n valentón, perdonavidas, gallito, m; rufián, m. —vt intimidar; tratar mal. **b. beef,** vaca en lata, f

bulrush /'bʊl,rʌʃ/ n anea, f

bulwark /'bʊlwərk/ n baluarte, m; Naut. antepecho, m

bumblebee /'bʌmbəl,bi/ n abejorro, m

bump /bʌmp/ n golpe, m; ruido, m; choque, m; (bruise) chichón, m, roncha, f; Aer. sacudida, f, meneo, m. —vi (into, against) tropezar con; (along) saltar en. —vt chocar (contra)

bumper /'bʌmpər/ n copa llena hasta los bordes, f, vaso lleno, m; (of a car) parachoques, m. **a b. harvest,** una cosecha abundante

bumpkin /'bʌmpkɪn/ n patán, villano, m

bumptious /'bʌmpʃəs/ a fatuo, presuntuoso, presumido

bumptiousness /'bʌmpʃəsnɪs/ n fatuidad, presunción, f

bumpy /'bʌmpi/ n (of surface) desigual, escabroso; (of a vehicle) incómodo, con mala suspensión

bun /bʌn/ n buñuelo, bollo, m; (hair) moño, m

bunch /bʌntʃ/ n (of fruit) racimo, m; manojo, m; (of flowers) ramo, m; (tuft) penacho, m; (gang) pandilla, f, vi arracimarse; agruparse

bundle /'bʌndl/ n atado, lío, m; (of papers) legajo, m; (of sticks) haz, m; (sheaf) fajo, m; (package) paquete, m; fardo, hatillo, m; (roll) rollo, m, vt atar, liar; envolver; empaquetar; (stuff) meter, introducir. **to b. in,** meter dentro (de). **to b. out,** despachar sin ceremonia, poner de patitas en la calle

bung /bʌŋ/ n tapón, tarugo, m, vt atarugar

bungalow /'bʌŋgə,lou/ n casa de un solo piso, f

bungle /'bʌŋgəl/ vt estropear; hacer mal. —n equivocación, f, yerro, m; cosa (o obra) mal hecha, f

bungling /'bʌŋglɪŋ/ a chapucero, torpe

bunion /'bʌnyən/ n juanete (del pie), m

bunk /bʌŋk/ n litera, f, vi Inf. poner pies en polvorosa, pirarse

bunker /'bʌŋkər/ n Naut. pañol, m; (for coal) carbonera, f; (golf) hoya de arena, f

bunkum /'bʌŋkəm/ n patrañas, f pl

bunting /'bʌntɪŋ/ n gallardete, m

buoy /'bui/ n boya, baliza, f, vt boyar; abalizar; Fig. sostener. **light b.,** boya luminosa, f

buoyancy /'bɔiənsi/ n flotación, f; Fig. optimismo, m, alegría, f

buoyant /'bɔiənt/ a boyante; ligero

burden /'bɜrdn/ n carga, f, peso, m; (of a ship) tonelaje, m, capacidad, f; (of a song) estribillo, m; (gist) esencia, f. —vt cargar. **to be a b. on,** pesar sobre

burdensome /'bɜrdnsəm/ a pesado, oneroso, gravoso; abrumador

burdensomeness /'bɜrdnsəmnɪs/ n pesadez, f; agobio, m

bureau /'byurou/ n buró, secreter, m; escritorio, m; (office) dirección, oficina, f; departamento, m

bureaucracy /byu'rɒkrəsi/ n burocracia, f

bureaucrat /'byurə,kræt/ n burócrata, mf; Inf. mandarín, m

bureaucratic /,byurə'krætɪk/ a burocrático

burgher /'bɜrgər/ n ciudadano (-na), vecino (-na)

burglar /'bɜrglər/ n ladrón de casas, escalador, m. **cat b.,** gato, m. **b. alarm,** alarma contra ladrones, f. **b. insurance,** seguro contra robo, m

burglary /'bɜrgləri/ n robo nocturno de una casa, m

burgle /'bɜrgəl/ vi robar una casa de noche. —vt robar

burgomaster /'bɜrgə,mæstər/ n burgomaestre, m

Burgundian /bər'gʌndiən/ a and n borgoñón (-ona)

burgundy /'bɜrgəndi/ n vino de Borgoña, borgoña, f

burial /'bɛriəl/ n entierro, m. **b.-ground,** campo santo, cementerio, m. **b. service,** misa de difuntos, f. **b. society,** sociedad de entierros, f

burlap /'bɜrlæp/ n arpillera, f
burlesque /bər'lesk/ a burlesco. —n parodia. f. —vt parodiar
burliness /'bɜrlinɪs/ n corpulencia, f
burly /'bɜrli/ a corpulento, fornido
Burma /'bɜrmə/ Birmania, f
Burmese /bər'miz/ a and n birmano (-na)
burn /bɜrn/ vt quemar; calcinar; (bricks) cocer; cauterizar; (the tongue) picar; (dry up) secar; (the skin by sun or wind) tostar. —vi quemar; arder; Fig. abrasarse (en). **b. at the stake,** vt quemar en la hoguera. **to b. to ashes,** reducir a cenizas. **to b. away,** consumir(se). **to b. oneself,** quemarse. **to b. up,** quemar del todo, consumir. **to b. with,** Fig. abrasarse en
burn /bɜrn/ n quemadura, f; (stream) arroyo, m
burnable /'bɜrnəbəl/ a combustible
burner /'bɜrnər/ n quemador (-ra); mechero, m
burning /'bɜrnɪŋ/ n quema, f; incendio, m; fuego, m; (inflammation) inflamación, f; (pain) quemazón, f; abrasamiento, m. —a en llamas; ardiente; intenso; (notorious) notorio, escandaloso; abrasador; palpitante. **b. question,** cuestión palpitante, f
burnish /'bɜrnɪʃ/ n bruñido, m; lustre, brillo, m, vt bruñir; pulir, pulimentar, dar brillo a; (weapons) acicalar. —vi tomar lustre
burnisher /'bɜrnɪʃər/ n bruñidor, acicalador, m
burnishing /'bɜrnɪʃɪŋ/ n bruñido, m; pulimento, m; (of weapons) acicalado, m
burnoose /bər'nus/ n albornoz, m
burr /bɜr/ n Bot. cáliz de flor con espinas, m; Mech. rebaba, f; sonido fuerte de la erre, m
burrow /'bɜrou/ n madriguera, f, vivar, m; (for rabbits) conejera, f. —vt amadrigar; minar
bursar /'bɜrsər/ n tesorero, m; becario, m
bursary /'bɜrsəri/ n tesorería, f; beca, f
burst /bɜrst/ n estallido, m, explosión, f; (in a pipe) avería, f, (fit) acceso, m; transporte, m; (effort) esfuerzo, m; (expanse) extensión, f, panorama, m. **b. of applause,** salva de aplausos, f
burst /bɜrst/ vi estallar; reventar; quebrarse; romperse; (overflow) desbordar; (of seams) nacerse; derramarse (por); (into laughter) romper a; (into tears) deshacerse en. —vt quebrar; romper; hacer estallar. **to b. upon the view,** aparecer de pronto. **to b. into,** irrumpir en; (exclamations, etc.) prorrumpir en. **to b. into tears,** romper a llorar, deshacerse en lágrimas. **to b. open,** abrir con violencia; forzar
bursting /'bɜrstɪŋ/ n estallido, m; quebrantamiento, m; (overflowing) desbordamiento, m
bury /'beri/ vt enterrar, sepultar; sumergir; (hide) esconder, ocultar; (forget) echar tierra a
bus /bʌs/ n autobús, ómnibus, m, Mexico camión, Caribbean guagua, m. **double-decker bus,** ómnibus de dos pisos, m. **to travel by bus,** ir en autobús. **bus station,** estación de autobuses, f
busby /'bʌzbi/ n birretina, gorra de húsar, f
bush /buʃ/ n arbusto, matojo, m; (undergrowth) maleza, f; tierra virgen, f; Mech. manguito, m
bushel /'buʃəl/ n medida de áridos, f, (In England 8 gallons or 36.37 liters)
bushiness /'buʃinɪs/ n espesura, f; densidad, f
bushy /'buʃi/ a lleno de arbustos; denso; espeso; grueso; (eyebrows, etc.) poblado
busily /'bɪzəli/ adv diligentemente, solícitamente; afanosamente, laboriosamente. **He was b. occupied in...,** Estaba muy ocupado en...
business /'bɪznɪs/ n ocupación, f; quehaceres, m pl; (matter) asunto, m, cosa, f; empleo, oficio, m; Com. negocio(s), m, pl; casa comercial, f; (trade) comercio, m; (clients, connection) clientela, f; (right) derecho, m; Theat. juego escénico, m, pantomima, f. **He had no b. to do that,** No tenía derecho a hacer eso. **Mind your own b.!** ¡No te metas donde no te llaman! **on b.,** por negocios. **to be in b. for oneself,** tener negocios por su propia cuenta. **to mean b.,** hacer algo en serio; estar resuelto. **to send about his b.,** mandar a paseo (a). **to set up in b.,** establecer un negocio. **b. affairs,** negocios, m pl. **b. agent,** agente de negocios, m. **b. hours,** horas de trabajo, f pl. **b.-like,** formal, práctico, sistemático. **b. man,** hombre de negocios, m; negociante, m

business administration n administración de empresas, f
bust /bʌst/ n Art. busto, bulto, m; pecho, m. **b. bodice,** sostén, m
bustard /'bʌstərd/ n avutarda, f
bustle /'bʌsəl/ n actividad, animación, f; confusión, f; (of a dress) polizón, tontillo, m. —vi menearse, darse prisa. —vt dar prisa (a)
bustling /'bʌslɪŋ/ a activo; ocupado, atareado; animado; bullicioso, ruidoso
busy /'bɪzi/ a ocupado; atareado; activo, diligente; (of places) animado, bullicioso; (of streets) de gran circulación; (officious) entrometido. **to b. oneself,** ocuparse (en, con); dedicarse (a), entregarse (a); (interfere) entrometerse (con). **to be b.,** estar ocupado; estar atareado, tener mucho que hacer. **b.-body,** bullebulle, mf. entremetido (-da), chismoso (-sa)
busyness /'bɪzinɪs/ n ocupación, f; laboriosidad, f; actividad, f
but /bʌt/ conjunc prep adv pero; sino; (only) solamente; (except) menos; excepto; (almost) casi; que no; si no; (that) que; (nevertheless) sin embargo, empero, no obstante; (without) sin, sin que; (of time recently passed) no más que, tan recientemente. —n pero, m. **He cannot choose but go,** No puede hacer otra cosa que marcharse. **to do nothing but...,** hacer únicamente..., no hacer más que... **but for,** a no ser por. **but yesterday,** solamente ayer. **but then (or but yet),** pero
butcher /'butʃər/ n carnicero, m. —vt matar reses; hacer una carnicería en. **butcher's boy,** mozo del carnicero, m. **butcher's shop,** carnicería, f
butchery /'butʃəri/ n carnicería, f; matanza, f
butler /'bʌtlər/ n mayordomo, m. **butler's pantry,** despensa, repostería, f
butt /bʌt/ n (cask) tonel, m, pipa, f; (for water) barril, m; (of a cigarette, etc.) colilla, f; (of fire-arms) culata, f; (handle) mango, cabo, m; (billiards) mocho, m; (earthwork) terrero, m; (Fig. object) objeto (de), m; (of bulls, etc.) topetada, f; pl butts, campo de tiro, m; (target) blanco, m. —vt (toss) topar, acornear; (meet) tropezar (con). **to b. in,** Inf. entrometerse, meter baza; encajarse
butter /'bʌtər/ n mantequilla, f, vt untar con mantequilla. **b.-dish,** mantequera, f. **b.-fingers,** torpe, m. **b.-knife,** cuchillo para mantequilla, m. **b.-milk,** suero de mantequilla, m. **b.-print,** molde para mantequilla, m. **b.-sauce,** mantequilla fundida, f
buttercup /'bʌtərˌkʌp/ n ranúnculo, botón de oro, m
butterfly /'bʌtərˌflai/ n mariposa, f
butterscotch /'bʌtərˌskɒtʃ/ n dulce de azúcar y mantequilla, m
buttery /'bʌtəri/ n despensa, f
buttocks /'bʌtəks/ n pl nalgas, posaderas, f pl
button /'bʌtn/ n botón, m; pl buttons, botones, paje, m. —vt abotonar, abrochar; —vi abotonarse, abrocharse. **to press the b.,** apretar el botón. **b.-hook,** abotonador, m
buttonhole /'bʌtnˌhoul/ n ojal, m; flor que se lleva en el ojal, f. —vt Sew. hacer ojales; (embroidery) hacer el festón; Inf. importunar
buttoning /'bʌtnɪŋ/ n abrochamiento, m
buttress /'bʌtrɪs/ n estribo, macho, contrafuerte, m; Fig. apoyo, sostén, m. —vt afianzar, estribar; Fig. apoyar, sostener. **flying-b.,** arbotante, m
buxom /'bʌksəm/ a (of a woman) fresca, guapetona, frescachona
buxomness /'bʌksəmnɪs/ n frescura, f
buy /bai/ vt comprar; obtener; (achieve) lograr; (bribe) sobornar. **to buy on credit,** comprar al fiado. **to buy back,** comprar de nuevo; redimir; (ransom) rescatar. **to buy for,** (a price) comprar por; (purpose or destination) comprar para. **to buy in,** (at an auction) comprar por cuenta del dueño. **to buy off,** librarse de uno con dinero. **to buy out,** (of a business) comprar la parte de un socio. **to buy up,** comprar todo, acaparar
buyable /'baiəbəl/ a comprable, que se puede comprar
buyer /'baiər/ n comprador (-ra)
buying /'baiɪŋ/ n compra, f. **b. back,** rescate, m. **b. up,** acaparamiento, m

buying power *n* capacidad de compra, *f,* valor adquisitivo, *m*

buzz /bʌz/ *n* zumbido, *m;* (whisper) susurro, murmullo, *m;* (of a bell) sonido (del timbre), *m, vi* zumbar; susurrar

buzzer /'bʌzər/ *n* zumbador, *m;* sirena, *f;* (bell) timbre, *m*

buzzing /'bʌzɪŋ/ *a* zumbador, que zumba, *n.* See **buzz**

by /bai/ *prep* por; de; en; a; con; (of place) cerca de, al lado de; (according to) según, de acuerdo con; (in front of, past) delante (de); (at the latest) antes de, al más tardar; (expressing agency) por; (by means of) mediante; (through, along) por; (upon) sobre; (for) para; (under) bajo. **He will be here by Wednesday,** Estará aquí para el miércoles; (not later than) Estará aquí antes del miércoles (or el miércoles al más tardar). **How did he come by it?** ¿Cómo llegó a su poder? **He will come by train,** Vendrá en tren. **I know her by sight,** La conozco de vista. **There are three children by the first marriage,** Hay tres niños del primer matrimonio. **He goes by the name of Pérez,** Se le conoce por (or bajo) el nombre de Pérez. **six feet by eight,** seis pies por ocho. **They called her by her name,** La llamaron por su nombre. **two by two,** dos por dos. **The picture was painted by Cézanne,** El cuadro fue pintado por Cézanne. **drop by drop,** gota a gota. **by a great deal,** con mucho. **by all means,** naturalmente; de todos modos; cueste lo que cueste. **by chance,** por ventura. **by day (night),** de día (noche). **by daylight,** a la luz del día. **by doing it,** con hacerlo. **by myself,** solo; sin ayuda. **"By Appointment"** «Cita Previa». **by chance or by mis-**chance, por ventura o por desdicha. **an hour away by car,** a una hora de automóvil. **music by Brahms,** música de Brahms. **pull by the hair,** tirar por el pelo. **take by the hand,** llevar de la mano.

by /bai/ *adv* (near) cerca; (before) delante; al lado; a un lado; aparte; (of time) pasado. **to put by,** (keep) guardar; (throw away) desechar; (accumulate) acumular; (put out of the way) arrinconar. **to pass by,** pasar; pasar delante (de). **by and by,** luego, pronto; más tarde. **by now,** ya, antes de ahora. **by the way,** entre paréntesis, a propósito; de paso; al lado del camino. **by-election,** elección parcial, *f.* **by-law,** reglamento, *m.* **by-pass,** ruta de evitación, *f,* desvío, *m; (Mech. Elec.)* derivación, *f.* —*vi* desviarse de; *Mil.* rebasar. **by-product,** derivado, *m; Chem.* producto derivado, *m; Fig.* consecuencia, *f;* resultado, *m*

bye /bai/ *n* (in cricket) meta, *f.* **by the bye,** a propósito, entre paréntesis

bygone /'bai,gɔn/ *a* pasado. **Let bygones be bygones,** Lo pasado pasado

byplay /'bai,plei/ *n* pantomima, *f,* gestos, *m pl; Theat.* juego escénico, *m,* escena muda, *f*

bystander /'bai,stændər/ *n* espectador (-ra); *pl* by-standers, los circunstantes

bystreet /'bai,strit/ *n* callejuela, *f;* calle pobre, *f*

byway /'bai,wei/ *n* camino desviado, *m; Fig.* senda indirecta, *f; pl* **byways,** andurriales, *m pl*

byword /'bai,wɜrd/ *n* proverbio, *m;* objeto de burla o escándalo, *m*

Byzantine /'bɪzən,tin/ *a* bizantino

Byzantine Empire, the el Imperio Bizantino, *m*

Byzantium /bɪ'zænʃiəm/ Bizancio, *m*

C

c /si/ *n* (letter) c, *f; Mus.* do, *m*
cab /kæb/ *n* (horse-drawn) simón, *m;* (taxi) coche de alquiler, *m;* (of a locomotive) cabina del conductor, *f.*
cab-rank, punto de coches, *m*
cabala /'kæbələ/ *n* cábala, *f*
cabaret /ˌkæbəˈrei/ *n* cabaret, *m;* taberna, *f*
cabbage /'kæbɪdʒ/ *n* col, berza, *f.* **red c.,** lombarda, *f.* **c. butterfly,** mariposa de col, *f*
cabin /'kæbɪn/ *n* cabaña, choza, *f; Naut.* camarote, *m;* (railway) garita, *f; Aer.* cabina, *f.* **c. boy,** grumete, galopín, mozo de cámara, *m.* **c. trunk,** baúl mundo, *m*
cabinet /'kæbɪnt/ *n* (piece of furniture) vitrina, *f;* colección, exposición, *f; Polit.* gabinete, *m;* (of a radio) cónsola, *f.* **c.-maker,** ebanista, *m.* **c.-making,** ebanistería, *f.* **c. meeting,** consejo de ministros, *m.* **c. minister,** ministro, *m*
cable /'keibəl/ *n* amarra, maroma, *f;* cable, *m;* cable-(grama), *m, vt* cablegrafiar. **electric c.,** cable eléctrico, *m.* **overhead c.,** cable aéreo, *m*
cabman /'kæbmən/ *n* cochero de punto, simón, *m*
caboose /kə'bus/ *n Naut.* cocina, *f*
cache /kæʃ/ *n* escondite, escondrijo, *m*
cackle /'kækəl/ *vi* (of a hen) cacarear; (of a goose) graznar; (of humans) chacharear. —*n* cacareo, *m;* graznido, *m;* cháchara, *f*
cacophony /kə'kɒfəni/ *n* cacofonía, *f*
cactus /'kæktəs/ *n* cacto, *m*
cad /kæd/ *n* sinvergüenza, *m;* tipo de cuidado, *m*
cadaverous /kə'dævərəs/ *a* cadavérico
caddish /'kædɪʃ/ *a* mal educado, grosero
caddy /'kædi/ *n* (for tea) cajita para té, *f;* (golf) cadi, *mf*
cadence /'keidns/ *n* cadencia, *f*
cadet /kə'dɛt/ *n* hermano menor, *m; Mil.* cadete, *m*
cadge /kædʒ/ *vi* sablear. —*vt* dar un sablazo (a)
cadger /'kædʒər/ *n* sablista, *mf;* mendigo, *m;* (loafer) golfo, *m*
Cadiz /'kɑdis/ Cádiz, *m*
cadmium /'kædmiəm/ *n* cadmio, *m*
café /kæ'fei/ *n* café, *m*
cafeteria /ˌkæfɪ'tɪəriə/ *n* bar automático, *m*
caffeine /kæ'fin/ *n* cafeína, *f*
cage /keidʒ/ *n* (animal's, bird's) jaula, *f;* (of a lift) camarín, *m;* (for transporting miners) jaula, *f.* —*vt* enjaular; encerrar
Cain /kein/, **to raise** armar lo de Dios es Cristo
cairn /kɛərn/ *n* montón de piedras, *m*
Cairo /'kairou/ el Cairo, *m*
cajole /kə'dʒoul/ *vt* lisonjear; engatusar, embromar; instar
cajolery /kə'dʒouləri/ *n* zalamerías, *f pl;* marrullería, *f,* engatusamiento, *m*
cake /keik/ *n Cul.* pastel, *m,* torta, *f;* (of chocolate, etc.) pastilla, *f.* —*vt* and *vi* cuajar; formar costra; (with mud) enlodar. **to sell like hot cakes,** venderse como pan bendito. **to take the c.,** llevarse la palma. **c. of soap,** pastilla de jabón, *f.* **c.-shop,** pastelería, *f*
calamine /'kælə,main/ *n* calamina, *f*
calamitous /kə'læmɪtəs/ *a* calamitoso, desastroso
calamity /kə'læmɪti/ *n* calamidad, *f;* desastre, *m*
calash /kə'læʃ/ *n* (carriage) calesa, carretela, *f;* (hood) capota, *f*
calcium /'kælsiəm/ *n* calcio, *m*
calculate /'kælkyə,leit/ *vt* calcular; adaptar. **to c. on,** contar con
calculated /'kælkyə,leitɪd/ *a* premeditado. **to be c. to,** conducir a; ser a propósito para
calculatedly /'kælkyə,leitɪdli/ *adv* calculadamente
calculating /'kælkyə,leitɪŋ/ *n* cálculo, *m, a* calculador; (of persons) interesado; (shrewd) perspicaz; atento. **c. machine,** máquina de calcular, *f,* calculador, *m*
calculation /ˌkælkyə'leiʃən/ *n* cálculo, *m;* calculación, *f*
calculus /'kælkyələs/ *n* cálculo, *m*

Calcutta /kæl'kʌtə/ Calcutta, *f*
calendar /'kæləndər/ *n* calendario, *m;* almanaque, *m;* (university, etc.) programa, *m*
calender /'kæləndər/ *n* calandria, *f, vt* calandrar, cilindrar
calf /kæf/ *n* becerro (-rra), ternero (-ra); (young of other animals) hijuelo, *m;* (of the leg) pantorrilla, *f;* (leather) cuero de becerro, *m;* piel, *f.* **calf's-foot,** pie de ternera, *m.* **c. love,** amor de muchachos, *m*
caliber /'kælɪbər/ *n* calibre, *m*
calibrate /'kælə,breit/ *vt* calibrar
calico /'kælɪ,kou/ *n* indiana, *f;* percal, *m.* **c.-printer,** fabricante de estampados, *m*
Californian /ˌkælə'fɔrnyən/ *a* californio. —*n* californio (-ia)
caliph /'keilɪf/ *n* califa, *m*
calk /kɔk/ See **caulk**
call /kɔl/ *n* llamada, *f;* (shout) grito, *m;* (of a bird) canto, *m;* (signal) señal, *f;* (visit) visita, *f;* (by a ship) escala, *f; Mil.* toque, *m;* (need) necesidad, *f;* (of religion, etc.) vocación, *f;* invitación, *f;* (demand) demanda, *f;* exigencia, *f.* **They came at my c.,** Acudieron a mi llamada. **c. to arms,** llamada, llamada a filas, *f.* **port of c.,** puerto de escala, *m.* **telephone c.,** llamada telefónica, *f.* **to pay a c.,** hacer una visita. **within c.,** al alcance de la voz. **c.-box,** cabina del teléfono, *f.* **c.-boy,** ayudante del traspunte, *m*
call /kɔl/ *vi* llamar; gritar, dar voces; (visit) visitar, hacer una visita (a); venir; (stop) parar; (of a ship) hacer escala. —*vt* llamar; (a meeting, etc.) convocar; (awaken) despertar, llamar; (say) decir; (appoint) nombrar; (at cards) declarar. **She is called Dorothy,** Se llama Dorotea. **Madrid calling!** ¡Aquí Radio Madrid! **Will you c. me at eight o'clock, please?** Haga el favor de despertarme (llamarme) a las ocho. **to c. at a port,** hacer escala en un puerto. **to c. a halt,** hacer alto. **to c. a strike,** declarar una huelga. **to c. names,** vituperar, injuriar. **to c. to account,** pedir cuentas (a). **to c. to arms,** tocar el arma; alarmar. **to c. to mind,** acordarse (de), recordar. **to c. to witness,** hacer testigo (de). **to c. back,** *vt* llamar; hacer volver; (unsay) desdecir. —*vi* (return) volver; venir a buscar; ir a buscar. **I called back for the parcel,** Volví a buscar el paquete. **to c. for,** pedir a gritos; llamar; (demand) pedir; exigir; (collect a person) pasar a buscar; (parcels, etc.) ir (or venir) a recoger. **He called for help,** Pidió socorro a gritos. **to c. forth,** producir; provocar; inspirar; revelar; (bring together) reunir. **to c. in,** hacer entrar; invitar; (a specialist, etc.) llamar; (worn coin) retirar de la circulación; recoger. **to c. in question,** poner en duda. **to c. off,** (dogs, etc.) llamar; (a strike) cancelar; parar; terminar; (a person) disuadir (de); (postpone) aplazar; suspender; (refrain) desistir (de). **to c. on,** (visit) hacer una visita (a), ir a ver, visitar; (of a doctor) visitar; (a person to do something) recurrir (a); (for a speech) invitar (a hablar); (invoke) invocar. **I shall now c. on Mr. Martínez,** Doy la palabra al señor Martínez. **to c. out,** *vt* hacer salir; provocar; inspirar; (challenge) desafiar, retar. —*vi* gritar. **to c. the roll,** pasar lista. **to c. over,** (names) pasar lista (de). **to c. up,** hacer subir; (to the army) llamar a filas (a); (telephone) llamar por teléfono (a); (memories) evocar. **to c. upon.** See **to c. on**
caller /'kɔlər/ *n* visita, *f*
calligraphist /kə'lɪgrəfɪst/ *n* calígrafo, *m*
calligraphy /kə'lɪgrəfi/ *n* caligrafía, *f*
calling /'kɔlɪŋ/ *n* llamamiento, *m;* (occupation) profesión, *m;* empleo, *m;* vocación, *f;* (of a meeting) convocación, *f*
calling card /'kɔlɪŋ ,kɑrd/ *n* (telephone) tarjeta telefónica, *f*
callipers /'kælɪpərz/ *n pl* compás de puntas, pie de rey, *m*
callisthenics /ˌkæləs'θɛnɪks/ *n pl* calistenia, *f*
callosity /kə'lɒsɪti/ *n* callosidad, *f*

callous /'kæləs/ a (of skin) calloso; *Fig.* insensible, duro, inhumano

callously /'kæləsli/ adv sin piedad

callousness /'kæləsnɪs/ n falta de piedad, inhumanidad, dureza, f

callow /'kælou/ a (of birds) implume; (inexperienced) bisoño, inexperto, novato

callus /'kæləs/ n callo, m

calm /kɑm/ n calma, f; paz, tranquilidad, f; sosiego, m; serenidad, f. —a (of the sea) en calma; tranquilo; sereno; sosegado. —vt calmar; tranquilizar; apaciguar. —vi calmarse; tranquilizarse; sosegarse. **dead c.,** calma chicha, f

calming /'kɑmɪŋ/ a calmante

calmly /'kɑmli/ adv tranquilamente, sosegadamente; con calma

calmness /'kɑmnɪs/ n calma, tranquilidad, f; ecuanimidad, serenidad, f

caloric /kə'lɔrɪk/ a calórico

calorie /'kæləri/ n caloría, f

calumniation /kə,lʌmni'eiʃən/ n calumnia, f

calumniator /kə'lʌmni,eitər/ n calumniador (-ra)

calumny /'kæləmni/ n calumnia, f

calvary /'kælvəri/ n calvario, m

calve /kæv/ vi (of a cow, etc.) parir

Calvinism /'kælvə,nɪzəm/ n calvinismo, m

Calvinist /'kælvənɪst/ n calvinista, mf

Calvinistic /,kælvə'nɪstɪk/ a calvinista

calyx /'keilɪks/ n cáliz, m

cam /kæm/ n *Mech.* leva, f. **camshaft,** árbol de levas, m

camaraderie /,kɑmə'rɑdəri/ n compañerismo, m

camber /'kæmbər/ n comba(dura), f

cambric /'keimbrɪk/ n batista, f

camcorder /'kæm,kɔrdər/ n videocámara, f, camcórder, m

camel /'kæməl/ n camello (-lla). **c.-driver,** camellero, m. **camel's hair,** pelo de camello, m

camellia /kə'milyə/ n camelia, f

cameo /'kæmi,ou/ n camafeo, m

camera /'kæmərə/ n *Photo.* máquina fotográfica, f. **folding c.,** máquina fotográfica plegable, f. **in c.,** a puerta cerrada. **c. obscura,** cámara obscura, f

Cameroons, the /,kæmə'runz/ el Camerón, los Camerones, m

camouflage /'kæmə,flɑʒ/ n camuflaje, m, vt camuflar

camp /kæmp/ n campamento, m; campo, m; *Fig.* vida de cuartel, f; (for school children, etc.) colonia, f; (party) partido, m. —vi acampar; vivir en tiendas de campaña. **to break c.,** levantar el campo. **c.-bed,** cama de campaña, f. **c.-stool,** silla de campaña, f

campaign /kæm'pein/ n campaña, f. —vi hacer una campaña

campaigner /kæm'peinər/ n veterano, m; propagandista, mf

campaigning /kæm'peinɪŋ/ n campañas, f pl

camphor /'kæmfər/ n alcanfor, m

camphorated /'kæmfə,reitid/ a alcanforado

campus /'kæmpəs/ n recinto, m (Puerto Rico), ciudad universitaria, f

can /kæn/ v aux poder; (know how to) saber. **You can go to the village when you like,** Puedes ir al pueblo cuando quieras. **I cannot allow that,** No puedo permitir eso. **What can they mean?** ¿Qué quieren decir? **If only things could have been different!** ¡Si solamente las cosas hubiesen sido distintas! **Can you come to dinner on Saturday?** ¿Puede Vd. venir a cenar el sábado? **I can come later if you like,** Puedo (or Podría) venir más tarde si Vd. quiere. **Mary can** (knows how to) **play the piano,** María sabe tocar el piano **You can't have your cake and eat it too.** No hay rosa sin espinas

can /kæn/ n lata, f; (for carrying sandwiches, etc.) fiambrera, f. —vt conservar en latas. **canopener,** abrelatas, m

Canada /'kænədə/ el Canadá, m

Canadian /kə'neidiən/ a canadiense. —n canadiense, mf

canaille /kə'nai/ n gentualla, gentuza, f

canal /kə'næl/ n canal, m

canalization /,kænḷə'zeiʃən/ n canalización, f

canalize /'kænḷ,aiz/ vt canalizar

canary /kə'neəri/ n canario (-ia); color de canario, m; vino de Canarias, m. **roller c.,** canario de raza flauta, m. **c.-seed,** alpiste, m

Canary Islands, the /kə'neəri/ las Islas Canarias, m

cancel /'kænsəl/ vt cancelar; revocar; borrar; anular. **to c. out,** *Math.* anular

cancellation /,kænsə'leiʃən/ n cancelación, f; revocación, f; anulación, f

cancer /'kænsər/ n *Med.* cáncer, m; *Astron.* Cáncer, m

cancerous /'kænsərəs/ a canceroso. **to become c.,** cancerarse

candelabrum /,kændḷ'ɑbrəm/ n candelabro, m

candescent /kæn'desənt/ a candente

candid /'kændɪd/ a franco; sincero. **If I am to be c.,** Si he de decir la verdad, Si he de ser franco

candidate /'kændɪ,deit/ n candidato (-ta); aspirante, m

candidature /'kændɪdə,tʃʊr/ n candidatura, f

candidly /'kændɪdli/ adv francamente; sinceramente

candidness /'kændɪdnɪs/ n franqueza, f; sinceridad, f

candied /'kændid/ a (of peel, etc.) almibarado, garapiñado

candle /'kændḷ/ n vela, candela, f. **wax c.,** cirio, m. **You cannot hold a c. to him,** No llegas a la suela de su zapato, Ni llegas a sus pies, Ni le llegas a los pies. **The game is not worth the c.,** La cosa no vale la pena. **to burn the c. at both ends,** consumir la vida. **c.-grease,** sebo, m. **c.-light,** luz de las velas, f; luz artificial, f. **c.-maker,** candelero, m. **c.-power,** *Elec.* potencia luminosa, bujía, f. **c.-snuffer,** apagavelas, matacandelas, m

Candlemas /'kændḷməs/ n candelaria, f

candlestick /'kændḷ,stɪk/ n candelero, m, palmatoria, f; (processional) cirial, m

candor /'kændər/ n franqueza, f; sinceridad, f; candor, m

candy /'kændi/ n caramelo, bombón, m, vt garapiñar, almibarar

candytuft /'kændi,tʌft/ n carraspique, m

cane /kein/ n *Bot.* caña, f; (for chair seats, etc.) rejilla, f; (walking stick) bastón, m; (for punishment) vara, f. —vt apalear, pegar. **sugar-c.,** caña de azúcar, f. **c.-break,** cañaveral, m. **c. chair,** sillón de mimbres, m. **c.-sugar,** azúcar de caña, m. **c.-syrup,** miel de caña, f

canine /'keinain/ a canino. —n (tooth) diente canino, m

caning /'keinin/ n paliza, f

canister /'kænəstər/ n bote, m, cajita, f

canker /'kæŋkər/ n úlcera, f; (in trees) cancro, m; *Fig.* cáncer, m, vt roer; *Fig.* corromper

canned /kænd/ a en lata

cannibal /'kænəbəl/ n caníbal, mf antropófago (-ga). —a caníbal, antropófago

cannibalism /'kænəbə,lɪzəm/ n canibalismo, m, antropofagia, f

canning /'kænɪŋ/ n conservación en latas, f. **c. factory,** fábrica de conservas alimenticias, f

cannon /'kænən/ n (fire-arm) cañón, m; (billiards) carambola, f, vi carambolear. **to c. into,** chocar con. **c.-ball,** bala de cañón, f. **c.-shot,** cañonazo, m

cannonade /,kænə'neid/ n cañoneo, m

canny /'kæni/ a cuerdo, sagaz

canoe /kə'nu/ n canoa, f; piragua, f, vi ir en canoa

canoeist /kə'nuist/ n canoero (-ra)

canon /'kænən/ n (*Eccl. Mus. Print.*) canón, m; (dignitary) canónigo, m; (criterion) criterio, m. **c. law,** derecho canónico, m

canonical /kə'nɒnɪkəl/ a canónico

canonization /,kænənə'zeiʃən/ n canonización, f

canonize /'kænə,naiz/ vt canonizar

canopy /'kænəpi/ n dosel, toldo, m; palio, m; *Fig.* capa, bóveda, f. **the c. of heaven,** la capa (or bóveda) del cielo

cant /kænt/ vt inclinar; ladear. —vi inclinarse; (be a hypocrite) camandulear. —n (slope) inclinación, f, sesgo, desplomo, m; (hypocrisy) gazmonería, f

Cantabrian /kæn'teibriən/ a cántabrico

cantankerous /kæn'tæŋkərəs/ *a* irritable, intratable, malhumorado

cantankerousness /kæn'tæŋkərəsnɪs/ *n* mal humor, *m*, irritabilidad, *f*

cantata /kən'tɑtə/ *n* cantata, *f*

canteen /kæn'tin/ *n* cantina, *f*; (water bottle) cantimplora, *f*. **c. of cutlery,** juego de cubiertos, *m*

canter /'kæntər/ *n* medio galope, *m*, *vi* andar a galope corto

Canterbury /'kæntər,beri/ Cantórbery, Cantuaria, *f*

canticle /'kæntɪkəl/ *n* cántico, *m*

canting /'kæntɪŋ/ *a* hipócrita

canto /'kæntou/ *n* canto, *m*

canton /'kæntn/ *n* (province and *Herald.*) cantón, *m*, *vt* (of soldiers) acantonar

cantonment /kæn'tɒnmənt/ *n* acantonamiento, cantón, *m*

cantor /'kæntər/ *n* *Eccl.* chantre, *m*

canvas /'kænvəs/ *n* lona, *f*; *Art.* lienzo, *m*; *Naut.* vela, *f*, paño, *m*. **under c.,** en tiendas de campaña; (of ships) a toda vela

canvass /'kænvəs/ *vt* (votes, etc.) solicitar

canvasser /'kænvəsər/ *n* solicitador (-ra) (de votos, etc.)

canvassing /'kænvəsɪŋ/ *n* solicitación (de votos, etc.), *f*

canyon /'kænyən/ *n* cañón, *m*

canzonet /,kænzə'nɛt/ *n* chanzoneta, *f*

cap /kæp/ *n* gorra, *f*; (with a peak) montera, *f*; (type of military headgear with brim at front) quépis, *m*; (cardinal's) birrete, *m*; *Educ.* bonete, *m*; (pointed) caperuza, *f*; (woman's old-fashioned) cofia, *f*; (jester's) gorro de bufón, *m*; (on a bottle) cápsula, tapa, *f*. —*vt Educ.* conferir el grado (a). **cap and bells,** gorro de bufón, *m*. **cap and gown,** birrete y muceta, toga y birrete, toga y bonete. **to throw one's cap over the windmill,** echar la capa al toro. **to cap it all,** ser el colmo

capability /,keipə'bɪlti/ *n* capacidad, *f*; aptitud, *f*

capable /'keipəbəl/ *a* capaz; competente; (of improvement) susceptible; (full of initiative) emprendedor

capably /'keipəbli/ *adv* competentemente

capacious /kə'peiʃəs/ *a* espacioso; grande; extenso

capaciousness /kə'peiʃəsnɪs/ *n* capacidad, *f*; amplitud, *f*

capacitate /kə'pæsɪ,teit/ *vt* capacitar

capacity /kə'pæsɪti/ *n* capacidad, *f*; calidad, *f*; aptitud, *f*. **in one's c. as,** en calidad de. **seating c.,** número de asientos, *m*; (in aircraft) número de plazas, *m*

caparison /kə'pærəsən/ *n* caparazón, *m*

cape /keip/ *n* (cloak) capa, *f*; (short) capotillo, *m*, capeta, *f*; (fur) cuello, *m*; *Geog.* cabo, promontorio, *m*. **c. coat,** capote, *m*

Cape Horn /'keip 'hɔrn/ Cabo de Hornos, *m*

caper /'keipər/ *vi* (gambol) brincar, saltar; cabriolar, corcovear; (play) juguetear. —*n* travesura, *f*; zapateta, *f*; cabriola, *f*; (whim) capricho, *m*; *Bot.* alcaparra, *f*. **to c. about,** dar saltos, brincar; juguetear

capillarity /,kæpə'lærɪti/ *n* capilaridad, *f*

capillary /'kæpə,leri/ *a* capilar. —*n* vaso capilar, *m*

capital /'kæpɪtl/ *a* capital; mortal; de muerte; de vida; principal; (of letters) mayúscula; (very good) excelente. —*n* (city) capital, *f*; (letter) (letra) mayúscula, *f*; *Com.* capital, *m*; *Archit.* capitel, chapitel, *m*. **floating c.,** capital fluctuante, *m*. **idle c.,** fondos inactivos, *m pl.* **c. punishment,** pena de muerte, pena capital, pena de la vida, *f.* **C.!** ¡Estupendo! ¡Excelente! **to make c. out of,** aprovecharse de, sacar ventaja de

capitalism /'kæpɪtl,izəm/ *n* capitalismo, *m*

capitalist /'kæpɪtlɪst/ *n* capitalista, *mf*

capitalistic /,kæpɪtl'ɪstɪk/ *a* capitalista

capitalization /,kæpɪtlə'zeiʃən/ *n* capitalización, *f*

capitalize /'kæpɪtl,aiz/ *vt* capitalizar

capitally /'kæpɪtli/ *adv* estupendamente

capitation /,kæpɪ'teiʃən/ *n* capitación, *f*

Capitol /'kæpɪtl/ *n* Capitolio, *m*

capitulate /kə'pɪtʃə,leit/ *vi* capitular

capitulation /kə,pɪtʃə'leiʃən/ *n* capitulación, *f*

capon /'keipɒn/ *n* capón, *m*

caprice /kə'pris/ *n* capricho, *m*

capricious /kə'prɪʃəs/ *a* caprichoso

capriciousness /kə'prɪʃəsnɪs/ *n* carácter inconstante, *m*; lo caprichoso

Capricorn /'kæprɪ,kɔrn/ *n* Capricornio, *m*

capsize /'kæpsaiz/ *vt Naut.* hacer zozobrar; volcar. —*vi Naut.* zozobrar; volcarse

capsizing /'kæp,saizɪŋ/ *n Naut.* zozobra, *f*; vuelco, *m*

capsule /'kæpsəl/ *n* (*Bot. Med. Chem. Zool.*) cápsula, *f*

captain /'kæptən/ *n* (*Mil. Nav. Aer.* and *Sports.*) capitán, *m*, *vt* capitanear. **to c. a team,** ser el capitán de un equipo. **group c.,** *Aer.* capitán de aviación, *m*

captaincy /'kæptənsi/ *n* capitanía, *f*

caption /'kæpʃən/ *n* (arrest) arresto, *m*; (heading) encabezamiento, título, pie, *m*; (cinema) subtítulo, *m*

captious /'kæpʃəs/ *a* capcioso, caviloso

captivate /'kæptə,veit/ *vt* cautivar, seducir

captivating /'kæptə,veitɪŋ/ *a* encantador, seductor

captive /'kæptɪv/ *a* cautivo, *n* cautivo (-va), prisionero (-ra), preso (-sa). **c. balloon,** globo cautivo, globo de observación, *m*

captivity /kæp'tɪvɪti/ *n* cautiverio, *m*

captor /'kæptər/ *n* el, *m*, (*f*, la) que hace prisionero (-ra)

capture /'kæptʃər/ *n* captura, *f*; presa, toma, *f*; *Law.* captura, *f*. —*vt* prender, capturar; tomar

Capuchin /'kæpyətʃɪn/ *a* capuchino. —*n* capuchino, *m*. **C. nun,** capuchina, *f*

car /kɑr/ *n* (chariot) carro, *m*; (tram) tranvía, *m*; (motor) automóvil, coche, *m*; (on a train) coche vagón, *m*. **sleeping car,** coche camas, *m*. **car park,** parque de automóviles, *m*

carabineer /,kærəbə'nɪər/ *n* carabinero, *m*

carafe /kə'ræf/ *n* garrafa, *f*

caramel /'kærəməl/ *n* caramelo, *m*; azúcar quemado, *m*

carapace /'kærə,peis/ *n* carapacho, *m*

carat /'kærət/ *n* quilate, *m*

caravan /'kærə,væn/ *n* caravana, *f*; coche de gitanos, *m*; coche habitación, *m*

caraway /'kærə,wei/ *n* alcaravea, *f*

carbarn /'kɑr,bɑrn/ *n* encierro, *m* (Mexico), cochera, cochera de tranvías, *f*, cobertizo, cobertizo para tranvías, *m*

carbide /'kɑrbaid/ *n* carburo, *m*

carbine /'kɑrbain/ *n* carabina, *f*

carbohydrate /,kɑrbou'haidreit/ *n* hidrato de carbono, *m*

carbolic /kɑr'bɒlɪk/ *a* carbólico. **c. acid,** ácido fénico, *m*

carbon /'kɑrbən/ *n* carbono, *m*. **c. copy,** copia en papel carbón, *f*. **c. dioxide,** anhídrido carbónico, *m*. **c. monoxide,** óxide de carbono, *m*. **c. paper,** papel carbón, papel de calcar, *m*

carbonate /'kɑrbə,neit/ *n* carbonato, *m*

carbonated /'kɑrbə,neitɪd/ *a* (beverage) carbónico (formal), con gas (informal)

carbonic /kɑr'bɒnɪk/ *a* carbónico

carbonization /,kɑrbənə'zeiʃən/ *n* carbonización, *f*

carbonize /'kɑrbə,naiz/ *vt* carbonizar

carboy /'kɑrbɔi/ *n* damajuana, garrafa, *f*

carbuncle /'kɑrbʌŋkəl/ *n Med.* carbunco, *m*; (stone) carbúnculo, *m*

carburetor /'kɑrbə,reitər/ *n* carburador, *m*

carcass /'kɑrkəs/ *n* (animal) res muerta, *f*; (corpse) cadáver, *m*; (body) cuerpo, *m*; (of a ship) casco, *m*

carcinoma /,kɑrsɪ'noumə/ *n* carcinoma, *m*

card /kɑrd/ *n* (playing) naipe, *m*; (pasteboard) cartulina, *f*; (visiting, postal, etc.) tarjeta, *f*; (index) ficha, *f*; (for wool, etc.) carda, *f*. —*vt* (wool, etc.) cardar. **I still have a c. up my sleeve,** Me queda todavía un recurso. **to lay one's cards on the table,** poner las cartas boca arriba. **to play one's cards well,** *Fig.* jugar el lance. **admission c.,** billete de entrada, *m*. **post c.,** tarjeta postal, *f*. **visiting c.,** tarjeta de visita, *f*. **c.-case,** tarjetero, *m*. **c.-index,** fichero, *m*. —*vt* poner en el fichero. **c.-sharper,** fullero, *m*. **c.-table,** mesa de juego, *f*. **c. trick,** juego de manos con cartas, *m*

cardboard /'kɑrd,bɔrd/ *n* cartón, *m*, *a* de cartón

cardiac /'kɑrdi,æk/ a cardíaco

cardigan /'kɑrdɪgən/ n rebeca, chaqueta de punto, f

cardinal /'kɑrdn̩l/ a cardinal. —n cardenal, m. **c. number,** número cardinal, m. **c. points,** puntos cardinales, m pl

cardinalate /'kɑrdn̩l,eit/ n cardenalato, m

carding /'kɑrdɪŋ/ n (of wool, etc.) cardadura, f. **c. machine,** carda mecánica, f

cardiogram /'kɑrdiə,græm/ n cardiograma, m

cardiograph /'kɑrdiə,græf/ n cardiógrafo, m

care /kɛər/ n cuidado, m; atención, f; inquietud, ansia, f; (charge) cargo, m. —vi preocuparse; tener interés; (suffer) sufrir. **I don't c.,** Me es igual; No me importa. **I don't c. a straw,** No se me da un bledo. **They don't c. for eggs,** No les gustan los huevos. **We don't c. what his opinion is,** Su opinión nos tiene sin cuidado (or no nos importa). **to c. for,** cuidar, mirar por; (love) querer (a); (like) gustar. **Take c.!** ¡Cuidado! ¡Ojo! **Take c. not to spoil it!** ¡Ten cuidado que no lo estropees! **Would you c. to...?** ¿Le gustaría...? ¿Tendría inconveniente en...? **c. of,** (on a letter, etc.) en casa de. **c.-free,** a libre de cuidados

careen /kə'rin/ vt carenar. —vi dar a la banda

careening /kə'riniŋ/ n carena, f

career /kə'riər/ n carrera, f; curso, m. —vi correr a carrera tendida; galopar

careful /'kɛərfəl/ a cuidadoso (de); atento (a); prudente. **Be c.!** ¡Cuidado! **to be c.,** tener cuidado

carefully /'kɛərfəli/ adv con cuidado. **drive c.,** manejar con cuidado; cuidadosamente; prudentemente; atentamente

carefulness /'kɛərfəlnɪs/ n cuidado, m; atención, f; prudencia, f

careless /'kɛərlɪs/ a sin cuidado; indiferente (a); insensible (a); negligente; (of mistakes, etc.) de (or por) negligencia

carelessly /'kɛərlɪsli/ adv indiferentemente; negligentemente; descuidadamente

carelessness /'kɛərlɪsnɪs/ n indiferencia, f; negligencia, f; descuido, m; omisión, f

caress /kə'rɛs/ n caricia, f, vt acariciar

caressing /kə'rɛsɪŋ/ a acariciador

caretaker /'kɛər,teikər/ n (of museums, etc.) guardián (-ana); (of flats, etc.) portero (-ra)

careworn /'kɛər,wɔrn/ a devorado de inquietud, ansioso

cargo /'kɑrgou/ n cargamento, m, carga, f. **c.-boat,** barco de carga, m

Caribbean /,kærə'biən, kə'rɪbi-/ a caribe

Caribbean Sea, the el Mar Caribe, m

caricature /'kærɪkətʃər/ n caricatura, f, vt caricaturizar

caricaturist /'kærɪkə,tʃʊrɪst/ n caricaturista, mf

caries /'kɛəriz/ n caries, f

carious /'kɛəriəs/ a cariado. **to become c.,** cariarse

Carmelite /'kɑrmə,lait/ a carmelita. —n carmelita, mf

carmine /'kɑrmɪn/ n carmín, m, a de carmín

carnage /'kɑrnɪdʒ/ n carnicería, f

carnal /'kɑrnl̩/ a carnal; sensual

carnality /kɑr'næliti/ n carnalidad, f

carnally /'kɑrnl̩i/ adv carnalmente

carnation /kɑr'neiʃən/ n clavel, m

carnival /'kɑrnəvəl/ n carnaval, m, a de carnaval, carnavalesco

carnivore /'kɑrnə,vɔr/ n carnívoro, m

carnivorous /kɑr'nɪvərəs/ a carnívoro

carol /'kærəl/ n villancico, m; canto, m. —vi cantar alegremente; (of birds) trinar, gorjear

Carolingian /,kærə'lɪndʒiən/ a carolingio

carotid /kə'rɒtɪd/ n carótida, f

carousal /kə'rauzəl/ n borrachera, f; holgorio, m, jarana, f

carouse /kə'rauz/ vi emborracharse. —n borrachera, orgía, f

carp /kɑrp/ n carpa, f, vi criticar, censurar

Carpathian Mountains, the /kɑr'peiθiən/ los Montes Cárpotes, m

carpel /'kɑrpəl/ n carpelo, m

carpenter /'kɑrpəntər/ n carpintero, m, vi carpintear. **carpenter's bench,** banco de carpintero, m. **carpenter's shop,** carpintería, f

carpentry /'kɑrpəntri/ n carpintería, f

carpet /'kɑrpɪt/ n alfombra, f; Fig. tapete, m. —vt cubrir de una alfombra, alfombrar; entapizar. **to be on the c.,** estar sobre el tapete. **c.-beater,** sacudidor de alfombras, m. **c. merchant,** alfombrista, m. **c. slippers,** zapatillas de fieltro, f pl. **c.-sweeper,** aspirador de polvo, m

carpeting /'kɑrpɪtɪŋ/ n alfombrado, m

carping /'kɑrpɪŋ/ a capcioso, criticón

carriage /'kærɪdʒ/ n (carrying) transporte, porte, m; (deportment) porte, continente, m, presencia, f; (vehicle) carruaje, m; carroza, f; coche, m; (railway) departamento, m; (chassis) chasis, bastidor, m; (of a typewriter, etc.) carro, m. **hackney c.,** coche de plaza, m. **c. and pair,** carroza de dos caballos, f. **c. door,** portezuela, f. **c.-forward,** porte debido. **c.-free,** franco de porte. **c.-paid,** porte pagado

carrier /'kæriər/ n el, m, (f, la) que lleva; portador (-ra); Com. mensajero, m; (on a car, bicycle) portaequipajes, m; (of a disease) vector, m; (aircraft) porta-aviones, m. **c.-pigeon,** paloma mensajera, f

carrion /'kæriən/ n carroña, f. **c.-crow,** chova, f

carrot /'kærət/ n zanahoria, f

carry /'kæri/ vt llevar; transportar; traer; conducir; (Mil. of arms) portar; (have with one) tener consigo; (an enemy position) tomar, ganar; (a motion) aprobar; (oneself) portarse; (one's point, etc.) ganar; (in the mind) retener; (conviction) convencer; (involve) implicar; (influence) influir; (send) despachar, enviar; (contain) incluir, comprender. —vi (of the voice, etc.) alcanzar, llegar. **The noise of the guns carried a long way,** El ruido de los cañones se oía desde muy lejos. **to fetch and c.,** traer y llevar. **to c. all before one,** vencer todos los obstáculos. **to c. into effect,** poner en efecto. **to c. one's audience with one,** captar (or cautivar) su auditorio. **to c. oneself well,** tener buena presencia. **to c. on one's back,** llevar a cuestas. **to c. the day,** quedar victorioso, quedar señor del campo. **to c. weight,** Fig. ser de peso. **to c. along,** llevar; (drag) arrastrar; conducir; acarrear. **to c. away,** llevar; llevarse, llevar consigo; (kidnap) robar, secuestrar; (of emotions) dominar; (by enthusiasm) entusiasmar; (inspire) inspirar. **to c. forward,** llevar a cabo; avanzar; fomentar; (bookkeeping) pasar a cuenta nueva. **to c. off,** (things) llevarse; (persons) llevar consigo (a); (abduct or steal) robar; (kill) matar; (a prize) ganar. **to c. (a thing) off well,** llevar la mejor parte, salir vencedor. **to c. on,** vt (a discussion, etc.) seguir, continuar. **to c. on a conversation,** llevar una conversación; mantener; (a business, etc.) tener; dirigir. —vi ir tirando; seguir trabajando. **to c. out,** realizar, llevar a cabo; hacer, ejecutar, efectuar; (a promise) cumplir. **to c. through,** llevar a cabo

carrying /'kæriŋ/ n transporte, m; (of a motion) adopción, f

cart /kɑrt/ n carro, m. —vt acarrear; llevar. **c.-horse,** caballo de tiro, m. **c.-load,** carretada, f, carro, m. **c.-wheel,** rueda de carro, f; (somersault) voltereta, f

cartage /'kɑrtɪdʒ/ n carreteje, transporte, porte, m

carte blanche /'kɑrt 'blɑntʃ/ n carta blanca, f

cartel /kɑr'tɛl/ n cártel, m

carter /'kɑrtər/ n carretero, m

Cartesian /kɑr'tiʒən/ a cartesiano. —n cartesiano (-na)

Carthage /'kɑrθɪdʒ/ Cartago, m

Carthaginian /,kɑrθə'dʒɪniən/ a cartaginés. —n cartaginés (-esa)

Carthusian /kɑr'θuʒən/ a cartujano. **C. monk,** cartujo, m

cartilage /'kɑrtlɪdʒ/ n cartílago, m

cartilaginous /,kɑrtl̩'ædʒənəs/ a cartilaginoso

cartographer /kɑr'tɒgrəfər/ n cartógrafo, m

cartography /kɑr'tɒgrəfi/ n cartografía, f

cartomancy /'kɑrtəmænsi/ n cartomancia, f

carton /'kɑrtn̩/ n caja de cartón, f

cartoon /kɑr'tun/ n (design for tapestry, etc.) cartón, m; caricatura, f

cartoonist /kɑr'tunɪst/ n caricaturista, mf

cartridge /'kɑrtrɪdʒ/ n cartucho, m. **blank c.,** cartucho sin bala, m. **c.-belt,** cartuchera, canana, f. **c.-case,** cápsula de proyectil, f

carve /kɑrv/ vt tallar, labrar; grabar; cortar; (meat, etc.) trinchar; (a career, etc.) hacer, forjarse

carver /'kɑrvər/ n tallador, m; (at table) trinchador, m; (implement) trinchante, m

carving /'kɑrvɪŋ/ n talla, f; (design) tallado, m. **c.-knife,** trinchante, m

cascade /kæs'keid/ n cascada, catarata, f, salto de agua, m; Fig. chorro, m. —vi chorrear

case /keis/ n caso, m; Law. proceso, m, causa, f; Gram. caso, m; Med. caso, m; enfermo (-ma); (box) caja, f; (for scissors, etc.) vaina, f; (for a cushion, etc.) funda, f; (for jewels, manicure implements, etc.) estuche, m; (of a piano, watch and Print.) caja, f; (for documents) carpeta, f; (glass) vitrina, f; (for a book) sobrecubierta, f; (dressing) neceser, m. —vt cubrir; forrar; resguardar. **packing-c.,** caja de embalaje, f. **c. of goods,** caja de mercancías, f; bulto, m. **in any c.,** en todo caso; venga lo que venga. **in c.,** por si acaso. **in c. of emergency,** en caso de urgencia. **in such a c.,** en tal caso. **in the c. of,** en el caso de; respecto a. **lower c.,** Print. caja baja, f. **upper c.,** Print. caja alta, f. **c.-hardened,** (of iron) templado; Fig. endurecido, indiferente

case closed! ¡asunto concluido!

casement window /'keismənt/ n ventana, f

cash /kæʃ/ n efectivo, metálico, m; dinero contante, m; Inf. dinero, m; Com. caja, f. —vt cobrar; pagar, hacer efectivo. **hard or ready c.,** dinero contante, m. **to pay c.,** pagar al contado. **c. on delivery,** (C.O.D.) contra reembolso. **c. on hand,** efectivo en caja, m. **c.-book,** libro de caja, m. **c.-box,** caja, f. **c.-desk,** caja, f. **c. down,** pago al contado, m. **c. prize,** premio en metálico, m. **c.-register,** caja registradora, f

cashew /'kæʃu/ n anacardo, m

cashier /kæ'ʃɪər/ n cajero (-ra). —vt degradar. **cashier's desk,** caja, f

cash machine /n cajero automático, m

cashmere /'kæʒmɪər/ n cachemira, f

casino /kə'sinou/ n casino, m

cask /kæsk/ n pipa, barrica, f, tonel, m; cuba, f

casket /'kæskɪt/ n cajita, arquilla, f, cofrecito, m

Caspian /'kæspiən/ a caspio

Caspian Sea, the el (Mar) Caspio, m

casserole /'kæsə,roul/ n cacerola, f

cassock /'kæsək/ n sotana, f

cast /kæst/ vt arrojar, tirar; (in fishing, the anchor, dice, darts, lots, a net, glances, blame, etc.) echar; (skin) mudar; (lose) perder; (a shadow, etc.) proyectar; (a vote) dar; (mold) vaciar; (accounts) echar, calcular; (a horoscope) hacer; (the parts in a play) repartir; (an actor for a part) dar el papel de; (metals) colar, fundir. **the shadow c. by the wall,** la sombra proyectada por el muro. **to c. anchor,** echar anclas, anclar. **to c. in one's lot with,** compartir la suerte de. **to c. something in a person's teeth,** echar en cara (a). **to c. lots,** echar suertes. **to c. about,** meditar, considerar; imaginar; (devise) inventar. **to c. aside,** desechar; poner a un lado; abandonar. **to c. away,** tirar lejos; desechar; (money) derrochar, malgastar. **to be c. away,** Naut. naufragar. **to c. down,** (overthrow) derribar, destruir; (eyes) bajar; (depress) desanimar, deprimir; (humiliate) humillar. **to be c. down,** estar deprimido. **c. iron,** n hierro colado, hierro fundido, m. **c.-iron,** a de hierro colado; Fig. inflexible. **to c. off,** quitarse; desechar; (a wife) repudiar; (desert) abandonar; (free oneself) librarse (de). **c.-off,** n desecho, m. **c.-off clothing,** ropa de desecho, f. **to c. out,** echar fuera, hacer salir; excluir. **to c. up,** echar; vomitar; (a sum) sumar; (something at a person) reprochar

cast /kæst/ n (of dice, fishing-line) echada, f; (of a net) redada, f; (worm) molde, m; (of a play) reparto, m; (of mind) inclinación, f; (in the eye) defecto en la mirada, m; (of colour) matiz, tinte, m. **c. of features,** facciones, f pl, fisonomía, f. **plaster c.,** vaciado, m

castanets /,kæstə'nɛts/ n pl castañuelas, f pl

castaway /'kæstə,wei/ n náufrago (-ga); Fig. perdido (-da)

caste /kæst/ n casta, f; clase social, f. **to lose c.,** desprestigiarse

castigate /'kæstɪ,geit/ vt castigar

Castile /kæ'stil/ Castilla, f

Castilian /kæ'stɪlyən/ a castellano. —n castellano (-na); (language) castellano, m

casting /'kæstɪŋ/ n lanzamiento, m; (of metals) fundición, colada, f; obra de fundición, f. **c.-net,** esparavel, m. **c.-vote,** voto de calidad, m

castle /'kæsəl/ n castillo, m; (in chess) torre, f, roque, m. **to build castles in Spain,** hacer castillos en el aire

castor /'kæstər/ n Zool. castor, m; (for sugar) azucarero, m; (cruet) convoy, m; (on chairs, etc.) ruedecilla, roldana, f. **c.-oil,** aceite de ricino, m. **c.-sugar,** azúcar en polvo, m

castrate /'kæstreit/ vt castrar, capar

castration /kæs'treiʃən/ n castración, capadura, f

casual /'kæʒuəl/ a fortuito, accidental; ligero, superficial; Inf. despreocupado. **c. worker,** jornalero, m

casually /'kæʒuəli/ adv por casualidad; de paso; negligentemente

casualness /'kæʒuəlnɪs/ n Inf. negligencia, despreocupación, f

casualty /'kæʒuəlti/ n víctima, f; herido, m; Mil. baja, f; pl **casualties,** heridos, m pl; muertos, m pl. **c.-list,** lista de víctimas, f; Mil. lista de bajas, f

casuist /'kæʒuɪst/ n casuista, mf

casuistry /'kæʒuɪstri/ n casuística, f

cat /kæt/ n gato (-ta). **She is an old cat,** Ella es una vieja chismosa. **to be like a cat on hot bricks,** estar como en brasas. **to let the cat out of the bag,** tirar de la manta. **to lead a cat-and-dog life,** vivir como perros y gatos. **cat's-cradle,** (game) cunas, f pl. **cat's paw,** (person) hombre de paja, m; Naut. bocanada de viento, f. **cat o' nine tails,** gato de siete colas, m, penca, f. **catwhisker,** Radio. detector, m

cataclysm /'kætə,klɪzəm/ n cataclismo, m

catacombs /'kætə,koumz/ n pl catacumbas, f pl

catafalque /'kætə,fɔk/ n catafalco, m

Catalan /'kætl,æn/ a catalán (-ana). —n catalán; (language) catalán, m

catalepsy /'kætl,ɛpsi/ n catalepsia, f

catalogue /'kætl,ɔg/ n catálogo, m, vt catalogar

Catalonia /,kætl'ounia/ Cataluña, f

catalysis /kə'tæləsɪs/ n catálisis, f

cat-and-mouse /'kæt ṇ 'maus/ n el juego de ratón, m

catapult /'kætə,pʌlt/ n Mil. catapulta, f; Aer. catapulta (para lanzar aviones), f; (toy) tirador de gomas, m. —vt tirar con una catapulta (con con un tirador de gomas); (throw) lanzar

cataract /'kætə,rækt/ n catarata, cascada, f, salto de agua, m; (of the eye) catarata, f

catarrh /kə'tɑr/ n catarro, m; constipado, resfriado, m

catastrophe /kə'tæstrəfi/ n catástrofe, f, desastre, m; (in drama) desenlace, m

catastrophic /,kætəs'trɒfɪk/ a catastrófico

catcall /'kæt,kɔl/ n silbido, m

catch /kætʃ/ vt coger; agarrar, asir; (capture) prender; haber; (a disease) contraer; (habit) tomar; (on a hook, etc.) enganchar; (surprise) sorprender; (understand) comprender; (hear) oír; (with blows, etc.) dar. —vi (of a lock) encajarse; (become entangled) engancharse; (of a fire) encenderse. **to c. a glimpse of,** ver por un instante (a); alcanzar a ver, entrever. **to c. at,** asir; agarrarse (a); echar mano de; procurar asir; alargar la mano hacia; (an idea, etc.) adoptar con entusiasmo. **to c. on,** (be popular) tener éxito; (understand) comprender. **to c. out,** coger en el acto; coger en un error; Sports. coger. **to c. up,** coger; interrumpir. **to c. up with,** (a person) alcanzar; (news) ponerse al corriente de

catch /kætʃ/ n presa, f; (of fish) redada, pesca, f; (of a window, etc.) cerradura, f; (latch) pestillo, m; (trick) trampa, f; Mus. canon, m. **a good c.,** (matrimonial) un buen partido. **to have a c. in one's voice,** hablar con voz entrecortada. **c.-as-c.-can,** lucha libre, f

catching /'kætʃɪŋ/ a contagioso

catchment /'kætʃmənt/ n desagüe, m

catchword /'kætʃ,wɜrd/ n reclamo, m; (theater cue) pie, apunte, m; (slogan) mote, m

catchy /'kætʃi/ a contagioso. **It's a c. tune,** Es una canción que se pega

catechism /'kætɪ,kɪzəm/ n catequismo, m

categorical /,kætɪ'gɔrɪkəl/ a categórico

category /'kætɪ,gɔri/ n categoría, f

cater /'keitər/ vi proveer, abastecer. **to c. for all tastes,** atender a todos los gustos

caterer /'keitərər/ *n* despensero (-ra)
catering /'keitəriŋ/ *n* provisión, *f*
caterpillar /'kætə,pilər/ *n* oruga, *f.* **c. tractor,** tractor de orugas, *m*
caterwaul /'kætər,wɔl/ *vi* (of a cat) maullar
caterwauler /'kætər,wɔlər/ *n* (violinist, etc.) rascatripas, *m*
caterwauling /'kætər,wɔliŋ/ *n* maullidos, *m pl*; música ratonera, *f*
catfish /'kæt,fiʃ/ *n* siluro, *m*
catgut /'kæt,gʌt/ *n Surg.* catgut, *m; Mus.* cuerda, *f*
catharsis /kə'θɑrsis/ *n Med.* purga, *f; Fig.* catarsis, *f*
cathedral /kə'θidrəl/ *n* catedral, *f*
Catherine wheel /'kæθrin/ *n Archit.* rosa, *f;* (firework) rueda de Santa Catalina, *f;* (somersault) tumba, *f*
catheter /'kæθitər/ *n* catéter, *m*
cathode /'kæθoud/ *n* cátodo, *m.* **c. rays,** rayos catódicos, *m pl.* **c. ray tube,** tubo de rayos catódicos, *m*
cathodic /kæ'θodik/ *a* catódico
catholic /'kæθəlik/ *a* católico
Catholicism /kə'θɒlə,sizəm/ *n* catolicismo, *m*
catkin /'kætkin/ *n* amento, *m.* **male c.,** amento macho, *m*
catlike /'kæt,laik/ *a* de gato; gatuno
cattle /'kætl/ *n* ganado vacuno, *m;* ganado, *m;* animales, *m pl.* **c.-dealer,** ganadero, *m.* **c.-lifter,** hurtador de ganado, *m.* **c.-pen,** corral, *m.* **c.-raiser,** criador de ganado, *m.* **c.-raising,** ganadería, *f.* **c.-ranch,** hacienda de ganado, estancia, *f.* **c.-show,** exposición de ganado, *f.* **c.-truck,** vagón de ferrocarril para ganado, *m*
cattle rustler *n* abigeo, cuatrero, ladrón de ganado, *m*
cattle rustling *n* abigeato, *m*
catty /'kæti/ *a* gatuno; malicioso, chismoso
Caucasian /kɔ'keiʒən/ *a and n* caucáseo (-ea)
Caucasus, the /'kɔkəsəs/ el Cáucaso
cauldron /'kɔldrən/ *n* caldera, *f*
cauliflower /'kɔlə,flauər/ *n* coliflor, *f*
caulk /kɔk/ *vt* calafatear
caulker /'kɔkər/ *n* calafate, *m*
caulking /'kɔkiŋ/ *n* calafateado, *m.* **c. iron,** calador, *m*
causality /kɔ'zæliti/ *n* causalidad, *f*
causative /'kɔzətiv/ *a* causante
cause /kɔz/ *n* causa, *f;* (reason) motivo, *m,* razón, *f;* (lawsuit) proceso, *m.* —*vt* causar; ocasionar, suscitar; (oblige) hacer, obligar (a). **final c.,** *Philos.* causa final, *f.* **to have good c. for,** tener buen motivo para
causeway /'kɔz,wei/ *n* dique, *m;* acera, *f*
caustic /'kɔstik/ *a* cáustico; *Fig.* mordaz. **c. soda,** sosa cáustica, *f*
caustically /'kɔstikli/ *adv* mordazmente, con sarcasmo
causticity /kɔ'stisiti/ *n* causticidad, *f*
cauterization /,kɔtərə'zeiʃən/ *n* cauterización, *f*
cauterize /'kɔtə,raiz/ *vt* cauterizar
cautery /'kɔtəri/ *n* cauterio, *f*
caution /'kɔʃən/ *n* prudencia, cautela, *f;* (warning) amonestación, *f;* aviso, *m.* —*vt* amonestar. **to proceed with c.,** ir con prudencia; ir despacio
"Caution" /'kɔʃən/ (road sign) «Precaución»
cautionary /'kɔʃə,neri/ *a* (of tales) de escarmiento
cautious /'kɔʃəs/ *a* cauteloso, cauto; prudente, circunspecto
cautiously /'kɔʃəsli/ *adv* cautamente; prudentemente. **to go c.,** *Inf.* ir con pies de plomo
cavalcade /,kævəl'keid/ *n* cabalgata, *f*
cavalier /,kævə'liər/ *n* jinete, *m;* caballero, *m;* galán, *m, a* arrogante, altanero
cavalry /'kævəlri/ *n* caballería, *f.* **c.-man,** jinete, soldado de a caballo, *m*
cave /keiv/ *n* cueva, caverna, *f.* **to c. in,** hundirse; desplomarse; *Fig.* rendirse. **c.-man,** hombre cavernícola, *m*
cavern /'kævərn/ *n* caverna, *f*
cavernous /'kævərnəs/ *a* cavernoso
caviar /'kævi,ɑr/ *n* caviar, *m*
cavil /'kævəl/ *vi* cavilar
cavity /'kæviti/ *n* cavidad, *f;* hoyo, *m;* hueco, *m;* (in a lung) caverna, *f*

cavy /'keivi/ *n* cobayo (-ya), conejillo (-lla) de las Indias
caw /kɔ/ *n* graznido, *m, vi* graznar, grajear
cawing /'kɔiŋ/ *n* graznidos, *m pl*
cayenne /kai'ɛn/ *n* pimentón, *m*
cease /sis/ *vi* cesar (de), dejar de; parar. —*vt* cesar de; parar de; (payments, etc.) suspender; discontinuar. **C. fire!** ¡Cesar fuego!
ceaseless /'sislis/ *a* incesante, continuo, sin cesar
ceaselessly /'sislisli/ *adv* sin cesar, incesantemente
ceasing /'sisiŋ/ *n* cesación, *f.* **without c.,** sin cesar
cedar /'sidər/ *n* (tree and wood) cedro, *m.* **red c.,** cedro dulce, *m*
cede /sid/ *vt* ceder, traspasar; (admit) conceder
cedilla /si'dilə/ *n* zedilla, *f*
ceiling /'siliŋ/ *n* techo, *m; Aer.* altura máxima, *f.* **c. price,** máximo precio, *m*
celebrant /'seləbrənt/ *n Eccl.* celebrante, *m*
celebrate /'selə,breit/ *vt* celebrar; solemnizar. **Their marriage was celebrated in the autumn,** Su casamiento se solemnizó en el otoño
celebrated /'selə,breitid/ *a* célebre, famoso
celebration /,selə'breiʃən/ *n* celebración, *f;* festividad, *f*
celebrity /sə'lebriti/ *n* celebridad, *f*
celerity /sə'leriti/ *n* celeridad, *f*
celery /'seləri/ *n* apio, *m*
celestial /sə'lestʃəl/ *a* celestial
celibacy /'seləbəsi/ *n* celibato, *m*
celibate /'seləbit/ *a* célibe. —*n* célibe, *mf*
cell /sel/ *n* celda, *f;* (*Bot. Biol.*) célula, *f;* (bees, wasps) celdilla, *f; Elec.* elemento, *m*
cellar /'selər/ *n* sótano, *m;* (wine) bodega, *f*
cellist /'tʃelist/ *n* violoncelista, *mf*
cello /'tʃelou/ *n* violoncelo, *m*
cellophane /'selə,fein/ *n* (papel) celofán, *m*
cellular /'selyələr/ *a* celular, celuloso
cellular phone /'selyələr 'foun/ *n* móvil, *m,* celular, *m* (WH)
cellule /'selyul/ *n* célula, *f*
celluloid /'selyə,lɔid/ *n* celuloide, *f*
cellulose /'selyə,lous/ *n* celulosa, *f*
Celt /kelt, selt/ *n* celta, *mf*
Celtiberian /,keltə'biəriən, ,sel-/ *a* celtibérico
Celtic /'keltik, 'sel-/ *a* celta
cement /si'ment/ *n* cemento, *m, vt* cementar
cemetery /'semi,teri/ *n* cementerio, *m*
cenotaph /'senə,tæf/ *n* cenotafio, *m*
cense /sens/ *vt* incensar
censer /'sensər/ *n* incensario, *m*
censor /'sensər/ *n* censor, *m, vt* censurar. **banned by the c.,** prohibido por la censura
censorious /sen'sɔriəs/ *a* severo; crítico
censoriousness /sen'sɔriəsnis/ *n* severidad, propensión a censurar, *f*
censorship /'sensər,ʃip/ *n* censura, *f*
censure /'senʃər/ *vt* censurar, culpar, criticar
census /'sensəs/ *n* censo, *m.* **to take the c.,** formar el censo, levantar el censo, tomar el censo, empadronar
census-taking /'sensəs ,teikiŋ/ *n* la formación del censo, la formación de los censos, *f,* el levantamiento del censo, el levantamientos de los censos, *m*
cent /sent/ *n* (coin) centavo, *m.* **per c.,** por ciento. **not to have a c. to one's name,** no tener donde caer muerto
centaur /'sentɔr/ *n* centauro, *m*
centenarian /,sentn'eəriən/ *a and n* centenario (-ia)
centenary /sen'teneri/ *n* centenario, *m, a* centenario
center /'sentər/ *n* centro, *m;* medio, *m.* —*a* central; centro. —*vt* centrar; concentrar (en). **nervous centers,** centros nerviosos, *m pl.* **c.-forward,** *Sports.* delantero centro, *m.* **c.-half,** *Sports.* medio centro, *m.* **c. of gravity,** centro de gravedad, *m.* **c.-piece,** centro, *m*
centerfold /'sentər,fould/ *n* páginas centrales, *f pl*
centigrade /'senti,greid/ *a* centígrado
centigram /'senti,græm/ *n* centigramo, *m*
centiliter /'sentl,itər/ *n* centilitro, *m*
centime /'sɑntim/ *n* céntimo, *m*
centimeter /'sentə,mitər/ *n* centímetro, *m.* **cubic c.,** centímetro cúbico, *m*

centipede /'sɛntə,pid/ n ciempiés, m
central /'sɛntrəl/ a central; céntrico. **The house is very c.**, La casa es muy céntrica. **C. American**, a and n centroamericano (-na). **c. depot**, central, f. **c. heating**, calefacción central, f
centralism /'sɛntrə,lɪzəm/ n centralismo, m
centralist /'sɛntrəlɪst/ n centralista, mf
centralization /,sɛntrələ'zeiʃən/ n centralización, f
centralize /'sɛntrə,laiz/ vt centralizar
centrally /'sɛntrəli/ adv centralmente; céntricamente
centric /'sɛntrɪk/ a céntrico; central
centrifugal /sɛn'trɪfyəgəl/ a centrífugo
centripetal /sɛn'trɪpɪtl̩/ a centrípeto
centumvir /'sɛntəm,vɪər/ n centunviro, m
centuple /sɛn'tupəl/ a céntuplo
centuplicate /sɛn'tupli,keit/ vt centuplicar
centurion /sɛn'tyʊriən/ n centurión, m
century /'sɛntʃəri/ n siglo, m, centuria, f
ceramic /sə'ræmɪk/ a cerámico
ceramics /sə'ræmɪks/ n cerámica, f
Cerberus /'sɜrbərəs/ n Cancerboro, m
cereal /'sɪəriəl/ a cereal. —n cereal, m
cerebellum /,sɛrə'bɛləm/ n cerebelo, m
cerebral /sə'ribrəl/ a cerebral
cerebrospinal /sə,ribrou'spainl̩/ a cerebroespinal
cerebrum /sə'ribrəm/ n cerebro, m
ceremonial /,sɛrə'mouniəl/ a ceremonial; de ceremonia. —n ceremonial, m
ceremonially /,sɛrə'mouniəli/ adv ceremonialmente; con ceremonia
ceremonious /,sɛrə'mouniəs/ a ceremonioso
ceremoniously /,sɛrə'mouniəsli/ adv ceremoniosamente
ceremoniousness /,sɛrə'mouniəsnis/ n ceremonia, formalidad, f
ceremony /'sɛrə,mouni/ n ceremonia, f. **to stand on c.**, gastar cumplidos. **without c.**, sin cumplidos
cerise /sə'ris/ a de color cereza
certain /'sɜrtn̩/ a (sure) seguro; cierto; (unerring) certero. **a c. man**, cierto hombre. **I am c. that...**, Estoy seguro de que... **to know for c.**, saber con toda seguridad, saber a ciencia cierta. **to make c. of**, asegurarse de
certainly /'sɜrtn̩li/ adv seguramente; ciertamente; (as a reply) sin duda; naturalmente. **c. not**, no, por cierto; claro que no
certainty /'sɜrtn̩ti/ n certidumbre, f; seguridad, f; convicción, f. **of a c.**, seguramente
certificate /n sər'tɪfɪkɪt; v -,keit/ n certificado, m; fe, f; partida, f; Com. bono, título, m; diploma, m. —vt certificar. **birth c.**, partida de nacimiento, f. **death c.**, partida de defunción, f. **marriage c.**, partida de casamiento, f
certificated /sər'tɪfɪ,keitid/ a (of teachers, etc.) con título
certify /'sɜrtə,fai/ vt certificar; atestiguar; declarar
certitude /'sɜrtɪ,tyud/ n certeza, certidumbre, f
cerulean /sə'ruliən/ a cerúleo
Cervantine /sər'væntin/ a cervantino
cervix /'sɜrvɪks/ n Anat. cerviz, f
Cesarean /sə'zɛəriən/ a cesáreo
cessation /sɛ'seiʃən/ n cesación, f
cession /'sɛʃən/ n cesión, f
cessionary /'sɛʃəneri/ n cesionario (-ia)
cesspool /'sɛs,pul/ n sumidero, m
cetacean /sɪ'teiʃən/ a cetáceo. —n cetáceo, m
Ceylon /sɪ'lɒn/ Ceilán, m
cf. cfr.
chafe /tʃeif/ vt (rub) frotar; (make sore) escocer, rozar. —vi raerse, desgastarse; escocerse; Fig. impacientarse; Fig. irritarse, enojarse
chaff /tʃæf/ n (of grain) ahechadura, f; (in a general sense and Fig.) paja, f; tomadura de pelo, burla, f. —vt (a person) tomar el pelo (a), burlarse de
chaffinch /'tʃæfɪntʃ/ n pinzón, m
chafing /'tʃeifɪŋ/ n frotación, f; (soreness) excoriación, f; Fig. impaciencia, f. **c.-dish**, escalfador, m
chagrin /ʃə'grɪn/ n mortificación, decepción, f, disgusto, m, vt mortificar
chain /tʃein/ n cadena, f, vt encadenar. **c. of mountains**, cadena de montañas, cordillera, f. **c.-gang**, ca-

dena de presidiarios, f. **c.-mail**, cota de malla, f. **c.-stitch**, cadeneta, f. **c.-stores**, empresa con sucursales, f. **in chains**, cargado de cadenas (e.g., prisoners in chains, prisioneros cargados de cadenas)
chair /tʃɛər/ n silla, f; Educ. cátedra, f; (of a meeting) presidencia, f. —vt llevar en hombros (a). **C.!** ¡Orden! **easy-c.**, (silla) poltrona, f. **to be in the c.**, ocupar la presidencia; presidir. **to take a c.**, sentarse, tomar asiento. **to take the c.**, presidir. **swivel-c.**, silla giratoria, f. **wheel-c.**, silla de ruedas, f. **c.-back**, respaldo de una silla, m
chairman /'tʃɛərmən/ n presidente (-ta). **to act as c.**, presidir
chairmanship /'tʃɛərmən,ʃɪp/ n presidencia, f
chaise longue /'ʃeiz 'lɒŋ/ n meridiana, tumbona, f
Chaldea /kæl'diə/ Caldea, f
Chaldean /kæl'diən/ a caldeo
chalet /ʃæ'lei/ n chalet, m
chalice /'tʃælɪs/ n cáliz, m
chalk /tʃɔk/ n creta, f; (for writing, etc.) tiza, f, yeso, m. —vt marcar con tiza; dibujar con tiza. **to c. up**, apuntar. **not by a long c.**, no con mucho
chalky /'tʃɔki/ a cretáceo; cubierto de yeso; (of the complexion) pálido
challenge /'tʃælɪndʒ/ n provocación, f; (of a sentry) quién vive, m; (to a duel, etc.) desafío, reto, m; Law. recusación, f; concurso, m. —vt (of a sentry) dar el quién vive (a); desafiar; provocar; Law. recusar
challenger /'tʃælɪndʒər/ n desafiador (-ra)
challenging /'tʃælɪndʒɪŋ/ a desafiador, provocador
chamber /'tʃeimbər/ n cuarto, m; sala, f; (bed-) dormitorio, m, alcoba, f; cámara, f; Mech. cilindro, m; (in a gun) cámara, f. **c. concert**, concierto de música de cámara, m. **c.-maid**, camarera, f. **c. music**, música de cámara, f. **c. of commerce**, cámara de comercio, f. **c.-pot**, orinal, m
chamberlain /'tʃeimbərlɪn/ n camarero, m. **court c.**, chambelán, m. **Lord C.**, camarero mayor, m
chameleon /kə'miliən/ n camaleón, m
chamfer /'tʃæmfər/ n chaflán, bisel, m
chamois /'ʃæmi/ n gamuza, f, rebeco, m. **c. leather**, piel de gamuza, f
chamomile /'kæmə,mail/ n camomila, manzanilla, f
champ /tʃæmp/ vt mascar; morder. —vi Fig. impacientarse
champagne /ʃæm'pein/ n (vino de) champaña, m
champion /'tʃæmpiən/ n campeón, m; defensor (-ra)
championship /'tʃæmpiən,ʃɪp/ n campeonato, m; (of a cause) defensa, f
chance /tʃæns/ n casualidad, f; suerte, fortuna, f; posibilidad, f; probabilidad, f; esperanza, f; (opportunity) ocasión, oportunidad, f. —a fortuito; accidental. —vi impers. suceder, acontecer. —vt Inf. arriesgar; probar. **by c.**, por casualidad; por ventura. **if by c.**, si acaso. **If it chances that...**, Si sucede que; Si a mano viene que... **The chances are that...**, Las probabilidades son que... **There is no c.**, No hay posibilidad; No hay esperanza. **to let the c. slip**, perder la ocasión. **to take a c.**, aventurarse, arriesgarse. **to c. to do**, hacer algo por casualidad. **to c. upon**, encontrar por casualidad.
chancel /'tʃænsəl/ n antealtar, entrecoro, m
chancellery /'tʃænsələri/ n cancillería, f
chancellor /'tʃænsələr/ n canciller, m; Educ. cancelario, m. **C. of the Exchequer**, Ministro de Hacienda, m
chancellorship /'tʃænsələrʃɪp/ n cancillería, f
chancery /'tʃænsəri, 'tʃɑn-/ n chancillería, f; (papal) cancelaría, f
chandelier /,ʃændl̩'iər/ n araña de luces, f
chandler /'tʃændlər/ n velero, m
change /tʃeindʒ/ vt cambiar; transformar; modificar; (clothes) mudarse (de); (one thing for another) trocar; sustituir (por). —vi cambiar; (clothes) mudarse. **All c.!** ¡Cambio de tren! **to c. a check**, cambiar un cheque. **to c. color**, cambiar de color; (of persons) mudar de color. **to c. countenance**, demudarse. **to c. front**, Fig. cambiar de frente. **to c. hands**, (of shops, etc.) cambiar de dueño. **to c. one's clothes**, cambiar de ropa, mudarse de ropa. **to c. one's mind**, cambiar de opinión. **to c. one's tune**, cambiar de tono. **to c.**

the subject, cambiar de conversación. **to c. trains,** cambiar de trenes

change /tʃeindʒ/ n cambio, m; transformación, f; modificación, f; variedad, f; (of clothes, feathers) muda, f; (Theat. of scene) mutación, f; (money) cambio, m; (small coins) suelto, m; (stock) bolsa, f; lonja, f; vicisitud, f; (of bells) toque (de campanas), m. **for a c.,** para cambiar, como un cambio; para variar. **small c.,** suelto, m, moneda suelta, f. **c. for the better,** cambio para mejor, m. **c. for the worse,** cambio para peor, m. **c. of clothes,** cambio de ropa, m; **c. of front,** Fig. cambio de frente, m. **c. of heart,** cambio de sentimientos, m; conversión, f. **c. of life,** menopausia, f. **c.-over,** cambio, m

changeability /ˌtʃeindʒəˈbɪlɪti/ n mutabilidad, f; inconstancia, volubilidad, f

changeable /ˈtʃeindʒəbəl/ a voluble; variable; cambiable

changeless /ˈtʃeindʒlɪs/ a immutable; constante

changeling /ˈtʃeindʒlɪŋ/ n niño (-ña) cambiado (-da) por otro

changing /ˈtʃeindʃɪŋ/ a cambiante. **c.-room,** vestuario, m

channel /ˈtʃænl/ n (of a river, etc.) cauce, m; canal, m; (irrigation) acequia, f; (strait) estrecho, m; Fig. conducto, m; (furrow) surco, m, estría, f; (of information, etc.) medio, m. —vt acanalar; (furrow) surcar; (conduct) encauzar

chant /tʃænt/ n canto llano, m; salmo, m. —vt salmodiar; cantar; recitar

chantey /ˈʃænti/ n saloma, f

chaos /ˈkeiɒs/ n caos, m

chaotic /keiˈɒtɪk/ a caótico, desordenado

chaotically /keiˈɒtɪkli/ adv en desorden

chap /tʃæp/ vt agrietar. —vi agrietarse. —n Inf. chico, m

chapbook /ˈtʃæp,buk/ n librito de cordel, m

chapel /ˈtʃæpəl/ n capilla, f; templo disidente, m

chaperon /ˈʃæpəˌroun/ n dama de compañía, señora de compañía, dueña, f, vt acompañar

chaplain /ˈtʃæplɪn/ n capellán, m

chaplaincy /ˈtʃæplɪnsi/ n capellanía, f

chaplet /ˈtʃæplɪt/ n guirnalda, f; rosario, m; (necklace) collar, m

chapter /ˈtʃæptər/ n (in a book) capítulo, m; Eccl. cabildo, capítulo, m. **a c. of accidents,** una serie de desgracias. **c. house,** sala capitular, f

char /tʃɑr/ vt (a house, etc.) fregar, hacer la limpieza de; (of fire) carbonizar. —n Inf. fregona, asistenta, f

character /ˈkærəktər/ n carácter, m; (of a play) personaje, m; (role) papel, m; (eccentric) tipo, m. **Gothic characters,** caracteres góticos, m pl. **in c.,** característico; apropiado. **in the c. of,** en el papel de. **out of c.,** nada característico; no apropiado. **principal c.,** protagonista, mf. **c. actor,** actor de carácter, m. **c. actress,** actriz de carácter

characteristic /ˌkærɪktəˈrɪstɪk/ a característico, típico. —n característica, peculiaridad, f, rasgo, m

characterization /ˌkærɪktərəˈzeiʃən/ n caracterización, f

characterize /ˈkærɪktə,raiz/ vt caracterizar

characterless /ˈkærɪktərlɪs/ a sin carácter; insípido, soso

charade /ʃəˈreid/ n charada, f

charcoal /ˈtʃɑr,koul/ n carbón de leña, m; (for blacking the face, etc.) tizne, m; Art. carboncillo, m. **c. burner,** carbonera, f. **c. crayon,** carboncillo, m. **c. drawing,** dibujo al carbón, m

charge /tʃɑrdʒ/ vt cargar; (enjoin) encargar; (accuse) acusar (de); (with price) cobrar; (with a mission, etc.) encomendar, confiar; Mil. acometer, atacar. —vi Mil. atacar; (a price) cobrar, pedir. **How much do you c.?** ¿Cuánto cobra Vd.? **to c. with a crime,** acusar de un crimen

charge /tʃɑrdʒ/ n (load) carga, f; (price) precio, m; gasto, m; (on an estate, etc.) derechos, m pl; (task) encargo, m; (office or responsibility) cargo, m; (guardianship) tutela, f; (care) cuidado, m; Law. exhortación, f; Law. acusación, f; Mil. ataque, m. **He is in c. of...,** Está encargado de...; Es responsable de... **The diamonds are in the c. of...,** Los diamantes están a cargo de. **depth c.,** carga de profundidad, f. **extra c.,**

gasto suplementario, m; (on a train) suplemento, m. **free of c.,** gratis. **c. for admittance,** entrada, f. **to bring a c. against,** acusar de. **to give (someone) in c.,** entregar (una persona) a la policía. **to take c. of,** encargarse de

chargé d'affaires /ʃarˈʒei dəˈfeər/ n encargado de negocios, m

charger /ˈtʃɑrdʒər/ n caballo de guerra, corcel, m

chariness /ˈtʃɛərɪnɪs/ n cautela, f

chariot /ˈtʃærɪət/ n carro, m

charioteer /ˌtʃærɪəˈtɪər/ n auriga, m

charitable /ˈtʃærɪtəbəl/ a caritativo; benéfico

charitableness /ˈtʃærɪtəbəlnɪs/ n caridad, f

charity /ˈtʃærɪti/ n caridad, f; beneficencia, f; (alms) limosna, f. **c. child,** niño (-ña) de la doctrina

charlatan /ˈʃarlətn/ n charlatán (-ana); (quack) curandero, m

charlatanism /ˈʃarlətn,izəm/ n charlatanismo, m; curanderismo, m

charm /tʃarm/ n hechizo, m; ensalmo, m; (amulet) amuleto, m; (trinket) dije, m; (general sense) encanto, atractivo, m. —vt encantar, hechizar, fascinar

charming /ˈtʃarmɪŋ/ a encantador; atractivo, seductor, fascinador

charm school n academia de buenos modales, f

chart /tʃart/ n Naut. carta de marear, f; (graph) gráfica, f. —vt poner en una carta

charter /ˈtʃartər/ n carta, f; (of a city, etc.) fuero, m; cédula, f. —vt (a ship) fletar; (hire) alquilar. **royal c.,** cédula real, f

Chartism /ˈtʃartɪzəm/ n el cartismo, m

chartist /ˈtʃartɪst/ n cartista, mf

charwoman /ˈtʃar,wumən/ n fregona, asistenta; mujer de hacer faenas, f

chary /ˈtʃɛəri/ a cauteloso; desinclinado; frugal

chase /tʃeis/ n caza, f; seguimiento, m. —vt cazar; dar caza (a); perseguir; (drive off) ahuyentar; Fig. disipar, hacer desaparecer; (engrave) cincelar. **to give c. to,** dar caza (a). **to go on a wild goose c.,** buscar pan de trastrigo

chasm /ˈkæzəm/ n sima, f, precipicio, m; Fig. abismo, m

chassis /ˈtʃæsi/ n chasis, m

chaste /tʃeist/ a casto

chasten /ˈtʃeisən/ vt castigar; corregir; humillar, mortificar

chastened /ˈtʃeisənd/ a sumiso, dócil

chastise /tʃæsˈtaiz/ vt castigar

chastisement /tʃæsˈtaizmənt/ n castigo, m

chastity /ˈtʃæstiti/ n castidad, f

chat /tʃæt/ vi charlar, conversar. —n conversación, charla, f. **They are having a c.,** Están charlando, Están de palique

chattels /ˈtʃætəlz/ n pl bienes muebles, efectos, m pl

chatter /ˈtʃætər/ vi charlar; hablar por los codos, charear; (of water) murmurar; (of birds) piar; (of monkeys, etc.) chillar; (of teeth) rechinar; (of a person's teeth) dar diente con diente. —n charla, f; cháchara, parla, f; (of water) murmurio, m; (of birds) gorjeo, m; (of monkeys, etc.) chillidos, m pl

chatterbox /ˈtʃæt,ər bɒks/ n badajo, m, cotorra, f

chatterer /ˈtʃætərər/ n hablador (-ra)

chattering /ˈtʃætərɪŋ/ n charla, cháchara, f; (of teeth) rechinamiento, m, a gárrulo, chacharero, locuaz

chauffeur /ˈʃoufər/ n chófer, m

chauvinism /ˈʃouvə,nizəm/ n chauvinismo, m

cheap /tʃip/ a barato; (of works of art) cursi. —adv barato. **dirt c.,** baratísimo. **to be dirt c.,** estar por los suelos. **to hold (something) c.,** tener en poco, estimar en poco

cheapen /ˈtʃipən/ vt disminuir el valor de; reducir el precio de

cheaply /ˈtʃipli/ adv barato; a bajo precio

cheapness /ˈtʃipnɪs/ n baratura, f; precio módico, m; mal gusto, m, vulgaridad, f

cheat /tʃit/ n engaño, fraude, m, estafa, f; (person) fullero (-ra), trampista, mf embustero (-ra). —vt engañar; defraudar; (at cards) hacer trampas. **He cheated me out of my property,** Me defraudó de mi propiedad

cheating /'tʃitɪŋ/ n engaño, m; fraude, m; (at cards) fullerías, f pl

check /tʃɛk/ n (chess) jaque, m; revés, m; impedimento, m; contratiempo, m; (of a bridle) cama, f; (control) freno, m; control, m; (checking) verificación, f; (ticket) papeleta, f; (counterfoil) talón, m; (square) cuadro, m; (bill) cuenta, f; (bank) cheque, m. —vt (chess) jaquear; (hamper) refrenar; detener; contrarrestar; (test) verificar. —vi detenerse. **to c. off,** marcar. **to c. oneself,** detenerse; contenerse. **to c. up,** comprobar. **crossed c.,** cheque cruzado, m. **c. book,** libro de cheques, m

checked /tʃɛkt/ a (cloth) a cuadros

checker /'tʃɛkər/ vt escaquear; (variegate) motear, salpicar; diversificar. **a checkered career,** una vida accidentada

checkers /'tʃɛkərz/ n. pl. damas, f.

checking /'tʃɛkɪŋ/ n represión, f; control, m; verificación, f; comprobación, f

checkmate /'tʃɛk,meit/ n mate, jaque, mate, m. —vt dar mate (a); (plans, etc.) frustrar

checks and balances n pl frenos y contrapesos, m pl

cheek /tʃik/ n mejilla, f; Inf. descaro, m; insolencia, f. **They have plenty of c.,** Tienen mucha cara dura. **c. by jowl,** cara a cara; lado a lado. **c.-bone,** pómulo, m

cheekiness /'tʃikɪnɪs/ n cara dura, insolencia, f

cheeky /'tʃiki/ a insolente, descarado; (pert) respondón

cheep /tʃip/ n pío, m, vi piar

cheer /tʃɪər/ n alegría, f, regocijo, m; vítor, m; aplauso, m. —vt animar; alegrar, regocijar; vitorear, aplaudir. **to be of good c.,** estar alegre; ser feliz. **C. up!** ¡Ánimo! **to c. up,** animarse, cobrar ánimo

cheerful /'tʃɪərfəl/ a alegre; jovial; de buen humor. **It is a c. room,** Es un cuarto alegre

cheerfully /'tʃɪərfəli/ adv alegremente; (willingly) con mucho gusto, de buena gana

cheerfulness /'tʃɪərfəlnɪs/ n alegría, f; jovialidad, f; buen humor, m

cheering /'tʃɪərɪŋ/ n vítores, m pl, aclamaciones, f pl, a animador

cheerleader /'tʃɪər,lidər/ n porro, m

cheerless /'tʃɪərlɪs/ a triste; sin alegría; (dank) obscuro, lóbrego

cheese /tʃiz/ n queso, m. **cream c.,** queso de nata, m. **grated c.,** queso rallado, m. **c.-dish,** quesera, f. **c.-mite,** cresa, f. **c.-paring,** n corteza de queso, f. —a Inf. tacaño. **c.-vat,** quesera, f

cheesy /'tʃizi/ a caseoso

chemical /'kɛmɪkəl/ a químico. **c. warfare,** defensa química, f

chemicals /'kɛmɪkəlz/ n pl productos químicos, m pl

chemise /ʃə'miz/ n camisa (de mujer), f

chemist /'kɛmɪst/ n químico, m. **chemist's shop,** farmacia, f; droguería, f

chemistry /'kɛməstri/ n química, f

chenille /ʃə'nil/ n felpilla, f

cherish /'tʃɛrɪʃ/ vt amar, querer; (a hope, etc.) abrigar, acariciar

cherry /'tʃɛri/ n (fruit) cereza, f; (tree and wood) cerezo, m. **c. brandy,** aguardiente de cerezas, m. **c. orchard,** cerezal, m

cherub /'tʃɛrəb/ n querub(e), querubín, m

cherubic /tʃə'rubɪk/ a querúbico

chess /tʃɛs/ n ajedrez, m. **c.-board,** tablero de ajedrez, m

chessman /'tʃɛs,mæn/ n pieza de ajedrez, f

chest /tʃɛst/ n arca, f, cofre, m; cajón, m; Anat. pecho, m. **to throw out one's c.,** inflar el pecho. **c.-expander,** extensor, m. **c. of drawers,** cómoda, f

chested /'tʃɛstɪd/ a (in compounds) de pecho...

chestnut /'tʃɛs,nʌt/ n (tree) castaño, m; (fruit) castaña, f; (color) castaño, color castaño, m; (horse) caballo castaño, m; (joke) chiste del tiempo de Maricastaña, m, a castaño. **horse-c. tree,** castaño de Indias, m

chevron /'ʃɛvrən/ n Herald. cabrio, m; (Mil. etc.) sardineta, f

chew /tʃu/ vt mascar, mascullar; (ponder) masticar

chewing /'tʃuɪŋ/ n masticación, f. **c.-gum,** chicle, m

chianti /ki'anti/ n (wine) quianti, m

chiaroscuro /ki,ɑrə'skyurou/ n claroscuro, m

chic /ʃik/ n chic, m, elegancia, f

chicanery /ʃɪ'keinəri/ n sofistería, f

chicken /'tʃɪkən/ n pollo, m. **c.-hearted,** medroso, cobarde, timorato. **c.-pox,** varicela, f

chickenwire /'tʃɪkən,waiər/ n alambrillo, m

chickpea /'tʃɪk,pi/ n garbanzo, m

chickweed /'tʃɪk,wid/ n pamplina, f

chicory /'tʃɪkəri/ n achicoria, f

chide /tʃaid/ vt reprender, reñir

chidingly /'tʃaidɪŋli/ adv en tono de reprensión

chief /tʃif/ n jefe, m, a principal; primero; en jefe; mayor. **c.-of-staff,** jefe de estado mayor, m

chiefly /'tʃifli/ adv principalmente; sobre todo

chieftain /'tʃiftən/ n caudillo, m; (of a clan) cabeza, jefe, m

chiffon /ʃɪ'fɒn/ n chifón, m, gasa, f

chiffonier /,ʃɪfə'nɪər/ n cómoda, f

chignon /'ʃinyɒn/ n moño, m

chilblain /'tʃɪlblein/ n sabañón, m

child /tʃaild/ n niño (-ña); hijo (-ja). **from a c.,** desde niño, desde la niñez. **with c.,** encinta, embarazada. **How many children do you have?** ¿Cuántos hijos tiene Vd.? **child's play,** juegos infantiles, m pl; Fig. niñerías, f pl. **c. welfare,** puericultura, f

childbirth /'tʃaild,bɜrθ/ n parto, m

childhood /'tʃaildhʊd/ n niñez, infancia, f. **from his c.,** desde su niñez, desde niño

childish /'tʃaildɪʃ/ a de niño; aniñado; pueril; fútil. **to grow c.,** chochear

childishly /'tʃaildɪʃli/ adv como un niño

childishness /'tʃaildɪʃnɪs/ n puerilidad, f; futilidad, f

child labor n trabajo de menores, trabajo infantil, m

childless /'tʃaildlɪs/ a sin hijos; sin niños

childlike /'tʃaild,laik/ a de niño, aniñado; pueril

children /'tʃɪldrən/ See **child**

Chilean /'tʃɪliən/ a and n chileno (-na)

chili /'tʃɪli/ n chile, pimento de cornetilla, m

chill /tʃɪl/ n frío, m; (of fear, etc.) estremecimiento, m; (illness) resfriado, m; (unfriendliness) frialdad, frigidez, f, a frío; (unfriendly) frígido. —vt enfriar; helar; (with fear, etc.) dar escalofríos (de); (discourage) desalentar. —vi tener frío; tener escalofríos. **to take the c. off,** templar, calentar un poco

chilliness /'tʃɪlinɪs/ n frío, m; (unfriendliness) frialdad, frigidez, f

chilly /'tʃɪli/ a frío; (sensitive to cold) friolero; (of politeness, etc.) glacial, frígido

chime /tʃaim/ n juego de campanas, m; repique, campaneo, m; armonía, f. —vi (of bells) repicar; Fig. armonizar. **to c. the hour,** dar la hora

chimera /kɪ'mɪərə/ n quimera, f

chimerical /kɪ'mɛrikəl/ a quimérico

chimney /'tʃɪmni/ n chimenea, f; (of a lamp) tubo (de lámpara), m. **c.-corner,** rincón de chimenea, m. **c.-pot,** sombrerete de chimenea, m. **c.-stack,** chimenea, f. **c.-sweep,** limpiador de chimeneas, deshollinador, m

chimpanzee /,tʃɪmpæn'zi, tʃɪm'pænzi/ n chimpancé, m

chin /tʃɪn/ n barbilla, barba, f, mentón, m. **c.-rest,** mentonera, f. **c.-strap,** barboquejo, m; venda para la barbilla, f

china /'tʃainə/ n china, porcelana, f; loza, f. —a de porcelana; de loza. **c. cabinet,** chinero, m

chinchilla /tʃɪn'tʃɪlə/ n (animal and fur) chinchilla, f

Chinese /tʃai'niz/ a and n chino (-na); (language) chino, m. **C. lantern,** farolillo de papel, m. **C. white,** óxido blanco de cinc, m

chink /tʃɪŋk/ n resquicio, m, grieta, hendidura, f; (clink) retintín, tintineo, m. —vi tintinar

chintz /tʃɪnts/ n zaraza, f

chip /tʃɪp/ n astilla, f; (counter) ficha, f. —vt picar; cincelar. **a c. off the old block,** de tal palo tal astilla. **c. potatoes,** patatas fritas, f

chiromancy /'kairə,mænsi/ n quiromancia, f

chiropodist /kɪ'rɒpədɪst/ n pedicuro, m, callista, f

chiropody /kɪ'rɒpədi/ n pedicura, f

chiropractor /'kairə,præktər/ n quiropráctico, m

chirp /tʃɜrp/ vi piar, gorjear. —n pío, gorjeo, m

chirping /'tʃɜrpɪŋ/ n piada, f, a gárrulo, piante

chisel /'tʃɪzəl/ n escoplo, cincel, m, vt cincelar. **cold c.,** cortafrío, m

chitchat /'tʃɪt,tʃæt/ n charla, f

chitterlings /'tʃɪtlɪnz/ n asadura, f

chivalrous /'ʃɪvəlrəs/ a caballeroso

chivalry /'ʃɪvəlri/ n caballería, f; caballerosidad, f. **novel of c.,** novela de caballería, f

chive /tʃaiv/ n Bot. cebollana, f, cebollino, m

chloral /'klɔrəl/ n cloral, m

chlorate /'klɔreit/ n clorato, m

chloride /'klɔraid/ n cloruro, m

chlorine /'klɔrin/ n cloro, m

chloroform /'klɔrə,fɔrm/ n cloroformo, m, vt cloroformizar

chlorophyll /'klɔrəfɪl/ n clorófila, f

chock-full /'tʃɒk 'fʊl/ a lleno de bote en bote

chocolate /'tʃɒkəlɪt/ n chocolate, m, a de chocolate. **thick drinking-c.,** chocolate a la española, m. **thin drinking-c.,** chocolate a la francesa, m. **c. shop,** chocolatería, f

choice /tʃɔis/ n selección, f; preferencia, f; elección, f; opción, f; alternativa, f; lo más escogido. —a escogido, selecto; excelente. **for c.,** con preferencia

choir /kwaiᵊr/ n coro, m. **c.-boy,** niño del coro, m. **c.-master,** maestro de capilla, m

choke /tʃouk/ vi ahogarse; atragantarse; obstruirse. —vt ahogar; estrangular. **to c. with laughter,** ahogarse de risa. **to c. back,** (words) tragar. **to c. off,** (a person) disuadir (de); quitarse de encima(a). **to c. up,** obstruir, cerrar, obturar; (hide) cubrir, tapar

choking /'tʃoukɪŋ/ a asfixiante, sofocante. —n ahogamiento, m, sofocación, f

cholera /'kɒlərə/ n cólera, m

choleric /'kɒlərɪk/ a colérico

cholesterol /kə'lɛstə,roul/ n colesterina, f

choline /'koulin/ n colina, f

choose /tʃuz/ vt escoger; elegir; optar por; (wish) querer, gustar. **They will do it when they c.,** Lo harán cuando les parezca bien. **If you c.,** Si Vd. quiere; Si Vd. gusta. **He was chosen as Mayor,** Fue elegido alcalde. **There is nothing to c. between them,** No hay diferencia entre ellos; Tanto vale el uno como el otro. **You cannot c. but love her,** No puedes menos de quererla

choosing /'tʃuzɪŋ/ n selección, f; (for an office, etc.) elección, f

chop /tʃɒp/ vt cortar; (mince) picar; (split) hender, partir. —n (meat) chuleta, f; (jaw) quijada, f. **to c. about, round,** (of the wind) girar, virar. **to c. down,** (trees) talar. **to c. off,** separar; cortar; tajar. **to c. up,** cortar en pedazos

chopper /'tʃɒpər/ n hacha, f

choppy /'tʃɒpi/ a picado, agitado

chopstick /'tʃɒp,stɪk/ n palillo chino, m

choragus /kə'reigəs/ n corega, corego, m

choral /'kɔrəl/ a coral

chord /kɔrd/ n cuerda, f; Mus. acorde, m; **the right c.,** Fig. la cuerda sensible

choreographer /,kɔri'ɒgrəfər/ n coreógrafo, m

choreographic /,kɔriə'græfɪk/ a coreográfico

choreography /,kɔri'ɒgrəfi, ,kour-/ n coreografía, f

chorister /'kɔrəstər/ n corista, m

chorus /'kɔrəs/ n coro, m; (in revues) comparsa, f, acompañamiento, m; (of a song) refrán, m. **to sing in c.,** cantar a coro. **c. girl,** corista, f

chosen /'tʃouzən/ a escogido; elegido. **the c.,** los elegidos

chrestomathy /krɛs'tɒməθi/ n crestomatía, f

Christ /kraist/ n Cristo, Jesucristo, m

christen /'krɪsən/ vt bautizar

Christendom /'krɪsəndəm/ n cristianismo, m, cristiandad, f

christening /'krɪsənɪŋ/ n bautizo, m, a bautismal, de bautizo

Christian /'krɪstʃən/ a cristiano. —n cristiano (-na). **C. name,** nombre de pila, m

Christianity /,krɪstʃi'æniti/ n cristianismo, m

Christmas /'krɪsməs/ n Navidad, f. **A Merry C.!** ¡Felices Pascuas (de Navidad)! **Father C.,** Padre Noel, m; (Sp. equivalent) Los Reyes Magos. **C. box,** regalo de Navidad, m. **C. card,** felicitación de Navidad, f. **C.**

carol, villancico de Navidad, m. **C. Day,** día de Navidad, m. **C. Eve,** Nochebuena, f. **C.-tide,** Navidades, f pl. **C. tree,** árbol de Navidad, m

Christopher Columbus /'krɪstəfər kə'lʌmbəs/ Cristóbal Colón, m

chromate /'kroumeit/ n cromato, m

chromatic /krou'mætɪk/ a cromático

chrome /kroum/ n cromo, m. **c. yellow,** amarillo de cromo, m

chromic /'kroumɪk/ a crómico

chromium /'kroumiəm/ n cromo, m. **c.-plated,** cromado

chromosome /'kroumə,soum/ n cromosoma, m

chronic /'krɒnɪk/ a crónico; inveterado

chronicle /'krɒnɪkəl/ n crónica, f, vt narrar

chronicler /'krɒnɪklər/ n cronista, mf

chronological /,krɒnl'ɒdʒɪkəl/ a cronológico. **in c. order,** por orden cronológico

chronology /krə'nɒlədʒi/ n cronología, f

chronometer /krə'nɒmɪtər/ n cronómetro, m

chrysalis /'krɪsəlɪs/ n crisálida, f

chrysanthemum /krɪ'sænθəməm/ n crisantemo, m

chubbiness /'tʃʌbɪnɪs/ n gordura, f

chubby /'tʃʌbi/ a regordete, gordito. **c.-cheeked,** mofletudo

chuck /tʃʌk/ vt (throw) lanzar, arrojar; (discontinue) abandonar, dejar. —n (in a lathe) mandril, m. **to c. under the chin,** acariciar la barbilla (a). **to c. away,** derrochar; malgastar, perder. **to c. out,** echar, poner en la calle

chuckle /'tʃʌkəl/ vi reír entre dientes. —n risa ahogada, f; risita, f

chum /tʃʌm/ n compinche, camarada, mf. **to c. up with,** ser camarada de

chunk /tʃʌnk/ n pedazo, trozo, m

church /tʃɜrtʃ/ n iglesia, f; (Protestant) templo, m, vt (a woman) purificar. **poor as a c. mouse,** más pobre que las ratas. **The C. of England,** la iglesia anglicana. **to go to c.,** ir a misa; ir al templo. **c. music,** música sagrada, f

churchyard /'tʃɜrtʃ,yard/ n cementerio, m

churl /tʃɜrl/ n patán, m

churlish /'tʃɜrlɪʃ/ a grosero, cazurro; (mean) tacaño, ruin

churn /tʃɜrn/ n mantequera, f. —vt (cream) batir; Fig. azotar, agitar

chute /ʃut/ n (for grain, etc.) manga de tolva, f; vertedor, m; (in flats and fun fairs) tobogán, deslizadero, m

ciborium /sɪ'bɔriəm/ n (chalice) copón, m; (tabernacle) sagrario, m; Archit. ciborio, m

cicada /sɪ'keidə/ n cigarra, f

cicatrice /'sɪkətrɪs/ n cicatriz, f

cicatrization /,sɪkətrə'zeiʃən/ n cicatrización, f

cicatrize /'sɪkə,traiz/ vt cicatrizar. —vi cicatrizarse

cider /'saidər/ n sidra, f

cigar /sɪ'gar/ n cigarro, m. **c.-box,** cigarrera, f. **c.-case,** petaca, cigarrera, f. **c.-cutter,** corta-puros, m

cigarette /,sɪgə'rɛt/ n cigarrillo, pitillo, m. **c.-butt,** colilla, f. **c.-case,** pitillera, f. **c.-holder,** boquilla, f. **c.-lighter,** encendedor de cigarrillos, m. **c.-paper,** papel de fumar, m

cinch /sɪntʃ/ n (of a saddle) cincha, f; Inf. ganga, f; Inf. seguridad, f. **c.-strap,** látigo, m

cinchona /sɪŋ'kounə/ n quina, cinchona, f

cinder /'sɪndər/ n ceniza, f; carbonilla, f. **red-hot c.,** rescoldo, m. **c.-track,** pista de ceniza, f

cinema /'sɪnəmə/ n cine, cinematógrafo, m

cinematographic /,sɪnə,mætə'græfɪk/ a cinematográfico

cinematography /,sɪnəmə'tɒgrəfi/ n cinematografía, f

cinemogul /,sɪnə'mougəl/ n magnate del cine, mf

cinnamon /'sɪnəmən/ n (spice) canela, f; (tree) canelo, m; color de canela, m

cipher /'saifər/ n Math. cero, m; Fig. nulidad, f; (code) cifra, f; monograma, m. **to be a mere c.,** ser un cero

Circassian /sər'kæʃən/ a circasiano. —n circasiano (-na)

circle /'sɜrkəl/ n círculo, m; (revolution) vuelta, f;

(group) grupo; *m;* (club, etc.) centro, *m;* (cycle) ciclo, *m.* —*vt* dar vueltas alrededor de; rodear; ceñir; (on an application, examination, etc.) encerrar en un círculo. —*vi* dar vueltas; (aircraft) volar en círculo; (of a hawk, etc.) cernerse. **dress-c.,** *Theat.* anfiteatro, *m.* **the family c.,** el círculo de la familia. **to come full c.,** dar la vuelta. **upper c.,** *Theat.* segundo piso, *m.* **vicious c.,** círculo vicioso, *m*

circlet /ˈsɜrklɪt/ *n* (of flowers, etc.) corona, *f;* (ring) anillo, *m*

circuit /ˈsɜrkɪt/ *n* circuito, *m;* (tour) gira, *f;* (revolution) vuelta, *f;* (radius) radio, *m.* **short c.,** corto circuito, *m.* **c.-breaker,** corta-circuitos, *m*

circuit court of appeals *n* tribunal colegial de circuito, *m*

circuitous /sərˈkyuɪtəs/ *a* indirecto; tortuoso

circuitously /sərˈkyuɪtəsli/ *adv* indirectamente

circular /ˈsɜrkyələr/ *a* circular; redondo. —*n* carta circular, *f;* circular, *f.* **c. tour,** viaje redondo, *m*

circularize /ˈsɜrkyələ,raiz/ *vt* enviar circulares (a)

circulate /ˈsɜrkyə,leit/ *vi* circular. —*vt* hacer circular; poner en circulación; (news, etc.) divulgar, diseminar

circulating library /ˈsɜrkyə,leitɪŋ/ *n* biblioteca por subscripción, *f*

circulation /,sɜrkyəˈleiʃən/ *n* circulación, *f;* **c. of the blood,** circulación de la sangre, *f*

circulatory /ˈsɜrkyələ,tɔri/ *a* circulatorio

circumcise /ˈsɜrkəm,saiz/ *vt* circuncidar

circumcised /ˈsɜrkəm,saizd/ *a* circunciso

circumcision /,sɜrkəmˈsɪʒən/ *n* circuncisión, *f*

circumference /sərˈkʌmfərəns/ *n* circunferencia, *f*

circumflex /ˈsɜrkəm,fleks/ *a* circunflejo. **c. accent,** acento circunflejo, *m,* (informal) capucha, *f*

circumlocution /,sɜrkəmlouˈkyuʃən/ *n* circunlocución, *f*

circumnavigate /,sɜrkəmˈnævɪ,geit/ *vt* circunnavegar

circumnavigation /ˈsɜrkəm,nævəˈgeiʃən/ *n* circunnavegación, *f*

circumscribe /ˈsɜrkəm,skraib/ *vt* circunscribir; *Fig.* limitar

circumscribed /ˈsɜrkəm,skraibd/ *a* circunscripto; *Fig.* limitado

circumscription /,sɜrkəmˈskrɪpʃən/ *n* circunscripción, *f; Fig.* limitación, restricción, *f*

circumspect /ˈsɜrkəm,spekt/ *a* circunspecto; discreto; correcto; prudente

circumspection /,sɜrkəmˈspekʃən/ *n* circunspección, *f;* prudencia, *f*

circumspectly /ˈsɜrkəm,spektli/ *adv* con circunspección; prudentemente

circumstance /ˈsɜrkəm,stæns/ *n* circunstancia, *f;* detalle, *m.* **aggravating c.,** circunstancia agravante, *f.* **attenuating c.,** circunstancia atenuante, *f.* **in the circumstances,** en las circunstancias. **in easy circumstances,** en buena posición, *m.* **Do you know what his circumstances are?** ¿Sabes cuál es su situación económica? **under the circumstances,** bajo las circunstancias

circumstantial /,sɜrkəmˈstænʃəl/ *a* circunstancial; detallado. **c. evidence,** prueba de indicios, *f*

circumvent /,sɜrkəmˈvent/ *vt* frustrar; impedir

circumvention /,sɜrkəmˈvenʃən/ *n* frustración, *f*

circumvolution /,sɜrkəmvəˈluʃən/ *n* circunvolución, *f*

circus /ˈsɜrkəs/ *n* circo, *m;* plaza redonda, *f;* (traffic) redondel, *m*

cirrhosis /sɪˈrousɪs/ *n* cirrosis, *f*

cirrus /ˈsɪrəs/ *n* (all meanings) cirro, *m*

cistern /ˈsɪstərn/ *n* tanque, *m;* cisterna, *f,* aljibe, *m*

citadel /ˈsɪtədļ/ *n* ciudadela, *f*

citation /saiˈteiʃən/ *n Law.* citación, *f;* cita, *f*

citation dictionary *n* diccionario de autoridades, *m*

cite /sait/ *vt* citar

citizen /ˈsɪtəzən/ *n* ciudadano (-na); vecino (-na); natural, *mf.* **fellow c.,** conciudadano, *m;* compatriota, *mf*

citizenship /ˈsɪtəzənˌʃip/ *n* ciudadanía, *f*

citrate /ˈsɪtreit/ *n* citrato, *m*

citric /ˈsɪtrɪk/ *a* cítrico

citrine /ˈsɪtrin/ *a* cetrino

citron /ˈsɪtrən/ *n* (fruit) cidra, *f;* (tree) cidro, *m*

city /ˈsɪti/ *n* ciudad, *f, a* municipal

city-state /ˈsɪti,steit/ *n* ciudad-estado, *f,* (plural: ciudades-estado)

civet /ˈsɪvɪt/ *n* algalia, *f*

civic /ˈsɪvɪk/ *a* cívico; municipal

civics /ˈsɪvɪks/ *n* civismo, *m*

civil /ˈsɪvəl/ *a* civil; doméstico; (polite) cortés, atento; (obliging) servicial. **C. Aeronautics Board,** Dirección general de aeronáutica civil, *f.* **c. defense,** defensa pasiva, *f.* **c. engineer,** ingeniero de caminos, canales y puertos, *m.* **C. Service,** cuerpo de empleados del Estado, *m*

civilian /sɪˈvɪlyən/ *a* civil. —*n* ciudadano (-na). **c. dress,** traje paisano, *m*

civility /sɪˈvɪliti/ *n* civilidad, cortesía, *f*

civilization /,sɪvələˈzeiʃən/ *n* civilización, *f*

civilize /ˈsɪvə,laiz/ *vt* civilizar

civilized /ˈsɪvə,laizd/ *a* civilizado

civilizing /ˈsɪvə,laizɪŋ/ *a* civilizador

civilly /ˈsɪvəli/ *adv* civilmente, cortésmente

clack /klæk/ *n* golpeo, ruido sordo, *m*

clad /klæd/ *a* vestido

claim /kleim/ *vt* reclamar; pretender exigir; *Law.* demandar; (assert) afirmar. —*vi Law.* pedir en juicio. —*n* reclamación, *f;* pretensión, *f; Law.* demanda, *f;* (in a gold-field, etc.) concesión, *f;* (right) derecho, *m.* **to lay c. to,** pretender a; exigir. **to put in a c. for,** reclamar

claimant /ˈkleimənt/ *n Law.* demandante, *mf;* pretendiente (-ta); *Com.* acreedor (-ra)

clairvoyance /klɛərˈvɔiəns/ *n* doble vista, *f*

clairvoyant /klɛərˈvɔiənt/ *n* vidente, *m*

clam /klæm/ *n* almeja, chirla, *f*

clamber /ˈklæmbər/ *vi* trepar, encaramarse. —*n* subida difícil, *f*

clamminess /ˈklæminɪs/ *n* viscosidad, humedad, *f*

clammy /ˈklæmi/ *a* viscoso; húmedo, mojado

clamor /ˈklæmər/ *n* clamor, estruendo, *m;* gritería, vocería, *f.* —*vi* gritar, vociferar. **to c. against,** protestar contra. **to c. for,** pedir a voces

clamorous /ˈklæmərəs/ *a* clamoroso, ruidoso, estrepitoso

clamp /klæmp/ *n* grapa, *f;* abrazadera, *f;* tornillo, *m;* (pile) montón, *m.* —*vt* empalmar; sujetar, lañar

clan /klæn/ *n* clan, *m;* familia, *f;* partido, grupo, *m*

clandestine /klænˈdestɪn/ *a* clandestino, furtivo

clandestinely /klænˈdestɪnli/ *adv* en secreto, clandestinamente

clang /klæŋ/ *vi* sonar; (of a gate, etc.) rechinar. —*vt* hacer sonar. —*n* sonido metálico, *m;* estruendo, *m*

clank /klæŋk/ *vi* dar un ruido metálico; crujir. —*vt* hacer sonar; (glasses) hacer chocar. —*n* ruido metálico, *m;* el crujir

clannish /ˈklænɪʃ/ *a* exclusivista

clansman /ˈklænzmən/ *n* miembro de un clan, *m*

clap /klæp/ *vt* (hands) batir; (spurs, etc.) poner rápidamente; (one's hat on) encasquetarse (el sombrero); (shut) cerrar apresuradamente. —*vi* aplaudir. —*n* (of the hands) palmada, *f;* (of thunder) trueno, *m;* (noise) ruido, *m.* **to c. eyes on,** echar la vista encima de. **to c. someone on the back,** dar una palmada en la espalda (a). **to c. the hands,** batir las palmas

clapper /ˈklæpər/ *n* (of a bell) badajo, *m*

clapping /ˈklæpɪŋ/ *n* aplausos, *m pl*

claque /klæk/ *n* claque, *f*

claret /ˈklærɪt/ *n* clarete, *m*

clarification /,klærəfəˈkeiʃən/ *n* clarificación, *f;* elucidación, *f*

clarify /ˈklærə,fai/ *vt* clarificar; elucidar, aclarar

clarinet /,klærəˈnet/ *n* clarinete, *m*

clarinettist /,klærəˈnetɪst/ *n* clarinete, *m*

clarion /ˈklæriən/ *n* clarín, *m*

clarity /ˈklærɪti/ *n* claridad, *f;* lucidez, *f*

clash /klæʃ/ *vi* chocar; encontrarse; (of events) coincidir; (of opinions, etc.) oponerse, estar en desacuerdo; (of colors) desentonar, chocar. —*n* estruendo, fragor, *m;* choque, *m; Mil.* encuentro, *m;* (of opinions, etc.) desacuerdo, *m;* disputa, *f*

clasp /klæsp/ *vt* (a brooch, etc.) abrochar, enganchar; (embrace) abrazar; (of plants, etc.) ceñir. —*n* (brooch) broche, *m;* (of a belt) hebilla, *f;* (of a necklace, handbag, book) cierre, *m;* (for the hair) pasador, *m.* **to c. someone in one's arms,** tomar en los brazos (a), abrazar. **c.-knife,** navaja, *f*

class /klæs/ *n* clase, *f;* (kind) especie, *f;* (of exhibits, etc.) categoría, *f.* —*vt* clasificar. **in a c. by itself,** único en su línea. **the lower classes,** las clases bajas. **the middle classes,** la clase media. **the upper classes,** la clase alta. **c.-mate,** condiscípulo (-la). **c.-room,** sala de clase, *f,* salón de clase, *f.* **c. war,** lucha de clases, *f*

classic /'klæsɪk/ *a* clásico. —*n* clásico, *m*

classical /'klæsɪkəl/ *a* clásico.

classicism /'klæsə,sɪzəm/ *n* clasicismo, *m*

classicist /'klæsəsɪst/ *a* and *n* clasicista, *mf*

classifiable /'klæsə,faɪəbəl/ *a* clasificable

classification /,klæsəfɪ'keɪʃən/ *n* clasificación, *f*

classified /'klæsə,faɪd/ *a* (secreto) reservado, secreto; (advertisement) por palabras

classified advertisement *n* anuncio por palabras, *m*

classify /'klæsə,faɪ/ *vt* clasificar

clatter /'klætər/ *vi* hacer ruido; (knock) golpear; (of loose horseshoes) chacolotear. —*vi* hacer ruido con; chocar (una cosa contra otra). —*n* ruido, *m;* (hammering) martilleo, *m;* (of horseshoes) chacoloteo, *m;* (of a crowd) estruendo, *m,* bulla, *f.* **John clattered along the street,** Los pasos de Juan resonaban por la calle

clause /klɔz/ *n* Gram. cláusula, *f; Law.* condición, estipulación, cláusula, *f*

claustrophobia /,klɔstrə'foubiə/ *n* claustrofobia, *f*

clavichord /'klævɪ,kɔrd/ *n* clavicordio, *m*

clavicle /'klævɪkəl/ *n* clavícula, *f*

claw /klɔ/ *n* garra, *f;* (of a lobster, etc.) tenaza, *f;* (hook) garfio, gancho, *m.* —*vt* arañar, clavar las uñas en; (tear) desgarrar. **c.-hammer,** martillo de orejas, *m*

clay /kleɪ/ *n* arcilla, *f;* barro, *m;* (pipe) pipa de barro, *f.* **c.-pit,** barrizal, *m*

clayey /'kleɪi/ *a* arcilloso

clean /klin/ *a* limpio; puro, casto. —*adv* limpio; completamente; exactamente. **to make a c. sweep (of),** no dejar títere con cabeza. **to make a c. breast of,** confesar sin tormento, no quedarse con nada en el pecho. **to show a c. pair of heels,** tomar las de Villadiego. **c. bill of health,** patente de sanidad, *m.* **c.-cut,** bien definido; claro. **c.-limbed,** bien proporcionado, gallardo. **c.-shaven,** lampiño; sin barba, bien afeitado

clean /klin/ *vt* limpiar; (streets) barrer; (a floor) fregar; (dryclean) lavar al seco. **to c. one's hands (teeth),** limpiarse las manos (los dientes). **to c. up,** limpiar; (tidy) asear; poner en orden

cleaner /'klinər/ *n* limpiador (-ra); (charwoman) fregona, *f;* (stain remover) sacamanchas, *m;* (drycleaner, person) tintorero (-ra)

cleaning /'klinɪŋ/ *n* limpieza, *f,* a de limpiar. **dry-c.,** lavado al seco, *m.* **c. rag,** trapo de limpiar, *m*

cleanliness /'klɛnlɪnɪs/ *n* limpieza, *f;* aseo, *m*

cleanness /'klinnɪs/ *n* limpieza, *f;* aseo, *m;* pureza, *f*

cleanse /klɛnz/ *vt* limpiar; lavar; purgar; purificar

cleansing /'klɛnzɪŋ/ *n* limpieza, *f;* lavamiento, *m;* purgación, *f;* purificación, *f*

clear /klɪər/ *a* claro; (of the sky) sereno, despejado; transparente; (free (from)) libre (de); (open) abierto; (of profit, etc.) neto; (of thoughts, etc.) lúcido; (apparent) evidente; explícito; (of images) distinto; absoluto; (whole) entero, completo. **c. majority,** mayoría absoluta, *f.* **c. profit,** beneficio neto, *m.* **c.-cut,** bien definido. **c.-headed,** perspicaz; inteligente. **c.-sighted,** clarividente

clear /klɪər/ *vt* aclarar; despejar; limpiar; librar (de); quitar; (one's throat) carraspear; (Com. stock) liquidar; (of a charge) absolver; (one's character) vindicar; (avoid, miss) evitar; (jump) salvar, saltar; (a court, etc.) desocupar; (a debt) satisfacer; (an account) saldar; (a mortgage) cancelar; (win) ganar; hacer un beneficio de; (through customs) despachar en la aduana. —*vi* (of sky, etc.) serenarse; escampar; (of wine, etc.) aclararse; despacharse en la aduana. **to c. the table,** levantar la mesa, levantar los manteles. **to c. the way,** abrir calle; *Fig.* abrir paso. **to c. away,** *vt* quitar; disipar. —*vi* disiparse. **to c. off,** *vi* (finish) terminar; (debts) pagar; (discharge) despedir. —*vi* (of rain) despejarse; escampar; marcharse. **to c.**

out, *vt* limpiar; (a drain, etc.) desatascar; vaciar; echar. —*vi* marcharse, escabullirse. **C. out!** ¡Fuera! **c. the decks,** hacer zafarrancho. **c. the decks for action,** hacer zafarrancho. **to c. up,** *vt* poner en orden; (a mystery, etc.) aclarar, resolver, *vi* (of weather) serenarse, escampar, despejarse

clearance /'klɪərəns/ *n* (of trees, etc.) desmonte, *m;* eliminación, *f;* expulsión, *f; Mech.* espacio muerto, *m;* despacho de aduana, *m.* **to make a c. of,** deshacerse de. **c. sale,** liquidación, venta de saldos, *f*

clearing /'klɪərɪŋ/ *n* (in a wood) claro, *m;* desmonte, *m;* (Com. of goods) liquidación, *f;* (of one's character) vindicación, *f.* **c.-house,** casa de compensación, *f*

clearly /'klɪərli/ *adv* claramente

clearness /'klɪərnɪs/ *n* claridad, *f*

cleavage /'klivɪdʒ/ *n* hendimiento, *m;* (in views, etc.) escisión, *f*

cleave /kliv/ *vt* partir; abrir; (air, water, etc.) surcar, hender. —*vi* partirse; (stick) pegarse, adherirse

cleaver /'klivər/ *n* partidor, *m;* hacha, *f*

clef /klɛf/ *n* clave, *f.* **treble c.,** clave de sol, *f*

cleft /klɛft/ *n* hendedura, fisura, rendija, abertura, *f.* **c.-palate,** paladar hendido, *m*

clematis /'klɛmətɪs/ *n* clemátide, *f*

clemency /'klɛmənsi/ *n* (of weather) benignidad, *f;* (of character, etc.) clemencia, *f*

clement /'klɛmənt/ *a* (of weather) benigno; (of character, etc.) clemente, benévolo

clench /klɛntʃ/ *vt* agarrar; (teeth, etc.) apretar; (a bargain) cerrar, concluir

clergy /'klɜrdʒi/ *n* clero, *m,* clérigos, *m pl*

clergyman /'klɜrdʒimən/ *n* clérigo, *m*

cleric /'klɛrɪk/ *n* eclesiástico, *m*

clerical /'klɛrɪkəl/ *a* clerical; de oficina. **c. error,** error de oficina, *m.* **c. work,** trabajo de oficina, *m*

clericalism /'klɛrɪkə,lɪzəm/ *n* clericalismo, *m*

clerk /klɜrk/ *n* (clergyman) clérigo, *m;* (in an office) oficinista, escribiente, *m;* oficial, *m;* secretario, *m*

clerkship /'klɜrkʃɪp/ *n* puesto de oficinista, *m;* escribanía, *f;* secretaría, *f*

clever /'klɛvər/ *a* listo, inteligente; ingenioso; hábil; (dexterous) diestro

cleverly /'klɛvərli/ *adv* hábilmente; diestramente, con destreza

cleverness /'klɛvərnɪs/ *n* talento, *m;* inteligencia, *f;* habilidad, *f;* (dexterity) destreza, *f*

cliché /kli'ʃeɪ/ *n* frase hecha, frase de cajón, *f*

click /klɪk/ *vi* (of the tongue) dar un chasquido; (of a bolt, etc.) cerrarse a golpe; hacer tictac. —*vt* (one's tongue) chascar; (a bolt, etc.) cerrar a golpe. —*n* golpe seco, *m;* tictac, *m;* (of the tongue) chasquido, *m.* **to c. one's heels together,** hacer chocar los talones

client /'klaɪənt/ *n* cliente, *mf;* (customer) parroquiano (-na)

clientele /,klaɪən'tɛl/ *n* clientela, *f*

cliff /klɪf/ *n* acantilado, *m,* roca, escarpa, *f*

cliff dweller *n* hombre de la roca, hombre de las rocas, *m,* mujer de la roca, mujer de las rocas, *f*

climate /'klaɪmɪt/ *n* clima, *m*

climatic /klaɪ'mætɪk/ *a* climático

climatology /,klaɪmə'tɒlədʒi/ *n* climatología, *f*

climax /'klaɪmæks/ *n* culminación, *f;* (rhetoric) clímax, *m;* gradación, *f;* punto más alto, apogeo, cenit, *m;* (of a play, etc.) desenlace, *m*

climb /klaɪm/ *vt* and *vi* trepar; escalar; montar; subir; ascender. **rate of c.,** *Aer.* velocidad ascensional, *f.* **to c. down,** bajar; *Fig.* echar el pie atrás. **to c. over,** (obstacles) salvar. **to c. up,** encaramarse por; subir por; montar

climber /'klaɪmər/ *n* alpinista, *mf;* (plant) trepadora, enredadera, *f;* (social) arribista, *mf*

clime /klaɪm/ *n* clima, *m*

clinch /klɪntʃ/ *vt* (nails, etc.) remachar, rebotar; (a bargain, etc.) cerrar; (an argument, etc.) remachar. —*n* (wrestling) cuerpo a cuerpo, *m*

cling /klɪŋ/ *vi* pegarse (a); agarrarse (a); (of scents) pegarse; (follow) seguir. **They clung together for an instant,** Quedaron abrazados un instante

clinging /'klɪŋɪŋ/ *a* tenaz; (of plants, etc.) trepador; (of persons) manso, dócil. **to be a c. vine,** *Inf.* ser una malva

clinic /'klɪnɪk/ n clínica, f
clinical /'klɪnɪkəl/ a clínico. **c. thermometer,** termómetro clínico, m
clink /klɪŋk/ vi retiñir; (of glasses) chocarse. —vt hacer sonar; (glasses) chocar. —n retintín, m; (of a hammer) martilleo, m; sonido metálico, m; (of glasses) choque, m
clip /klɪp/ vt (grasp) agarrar; (sheep, etc.) esquilar; (trim) recortar, cercenar; (prune) podar; (a ticket) taladrar. —n pinza, f; (paper-clip) sujetapapeles, m; Mech. grapa, escarpia, f; (for ornament) sujetador, m. **to c. a person's wings,** Fig. cortar (or quebrar) las alas (a)
clipper /'klɪpər/ n (person) esquilador (-ra); (Naut. and Aer.) clíper, m; pl **clippers,** tenazas de cortar, f pl; (for pruning) podaderas, f pl; (punch) taladro, m
clipping /'klɪpɪŋ/ n (of sheep, etc.) esquileo, m; (of a newspaper, etc.) recorte, m
clique /klik/ n camarilla, f
cliquish /'klikɪʃ/ a exclusivista
cloak /klouk/ n capa, f; manto, m; Fig. velo, m. —vt encapotar; embozar; (conceal) ocultar, encubrir. **c. and sword play,** comedia de capa y espada, f. **c.-room,** guardarropa, m; (ladies') tocador, m; (on a station) consigna, f
clock /klɒk/ n reloj, m; (of a stocking) cuadrado, m. **It is six o'clock,** Son las seis. **c.-face,** esfera de reloj, f. **c.-maker,** relojero, m. **c.-making,** relojería, f. **c.-work,** aparato de relojería, m. **to go like c.-work,** ir como un reloj. **c.-work train,** tren de cuerda, m
clockwise /'klɒk,waɪz/ a and adv en el sentido de las agujas del reloj; de derecha a izquierda
clod /klɒd/ n (of earth) terrón, m; (corpse) tierra, f; (person) zoquete, m. **c.-hopper,** patán, m
clog /klɒg/ n (shoe) zueco, zoclo, m; (obstacle) estorbo, obstáculo, m. —vt embarazar; estorbar, impedir; (block) obturar, cerrar; Fig. paralizar
cloister /'klɔɪstər/ n claustro, m; convento, m. —vt enclaustrar
cloistered /'klɔɪstərd/ a enclaustrado; retirado, aislado
cloistered nun n monja de claustro, f
close /klous/ a estrecho; (of a prisoner) incomunicado; (reticent) reservado; (niggardly) tacaño, avaro; (scarce) escaso; (of friends) íntimo; (equal) igual; (lacking space) apretado; (dense) denso; (thick) tupido; compacto; (of a copy, etc.) fiel, exacto; (thorough) concienzudo; (careful) cuidadoso; (attentive) atento; (to the roots) a raíz; (of shaving) bueno; (of weather) pesado, sofocante; (of rooms) mal ventilado. **at c. quarters,** de cerca. **It is c. to eight o'clock,** Son casi las ocho. **to press c.,** perseguir de cerca; fatigar. **c. at hand, c. by,** cerca; al lado; a mano. **c.-cropped,** (of hair) al rape. **c. fight,** lucha igualada, f. **c.-fisted,** tacaño, apretado. **c.-fitting,** ajustado, ceñido al cuerpo; pequeño. **c. season,** veda, f. **c.-up,** n (cinema) primer plano, m
close /klouz/ n (end) fin, m, conclusión, f; (of day) caída, f; Mus. cadencia, f; (enclosure) cercado, m; (square) plazoleta, f; (alley) callejón, m; (of a cathedral) patio, m. **at the c. of day,** a la caída de la tarde. **to bring to a c.,** terminar; llevar a cabo. **to draw to a c.,** tocar a su fin; estar terminando
close /klouz/ vt cerrar; (end) concluir, terminar; poner fin a. —vi cerrar(se); (of a wound) cicatrizarse, cerrarse; (end) terminar(se), acabar, concluir. **to c. the ranks,** cerrar filas. **to c. about,** (surround) rodear, cercar; (envelop) envolver. **to c. down,** vt cerrar. —vi cerrar. Radio. cerrarse. **to c. in,** (surround) cercar; (of night) cerrar; caer; (envelop) envolver; (of length of days) acortarse. **to c. on, c. up,** vt cerrar; (of water) tragar. **to c. up,** vt cerrar; cerrar completamente; obstruir. —vi (of persons) acercarse; (of a wound) cicatrizarse; cerrar
closed /klouzd/ a cerrado. **"Road C.,"** Paso Cerrado. **to have a c. mind,** ser cerrado de mollera; sufrir de estrechez de miras
closely /'klousli/ adv estrechamente; de cerca; (carefully) cuidadosamente; (exactly) exactamente; (attentively) con atención, atentamente
closeness /'klousnɪs/ n estrechez, f; densidad, f; (nearness) proximidad, f; (of a copy, etc.) fidelidad,

exactitud, f; (stuffiness), falta de aire, f; (of friendship) intimidad, f; (stinginess) tacañería, f; (reserve) reserva
closet /'klɒzɪt/ n camarín, m; (cupboard) alacena, f; (water) excusado, m
closing /'klouzɪŋ/ n cerramiento, m; (of an account) saldo, m. **c. time,** cierre, m, hora de cerrar, f
closure /'klouʒər/ n conclusión, f; Polit. clausura, f
clot /klɒt/ n coágulo, grumo, m. —vt coagular. —vi coagularse, cuajarse
cloth /klɔθ/ n tela, f; paño, m; (table) mantel, m; (clergy) clero, m. **She cleaned the books with a c.,** Ella limpió los libros con un paño. **in c.,** (of books) en tela
clothe /klouð/ vt vestir; cubrir; (with authority, etc.) revestir. **to c. oneself,** vestirse
clothes /klouz/ n pl vestidos, m pl, ropa, f. **a suit of c.,** un traje. **old c. shop,** ropavejería, f. **c.-basket,** cesta de la colada, f. **c.-brush,** cepillo para ropa, m. **c.-hanger,** percha, f. **c.-horse,** enjugador, m. **c.-line,** cuerda de la ropa, f. **c.-peg,** pinza de la ropa, f. **c.-prop,** palo para sostener la cuerda de la colada, m
clothier /'klouðiər/ n ropero, m. **clothier's shop,** ropería, f
clothing /'klouðɪŋ/ n vestidos, m pl, ropa, f. **article of c.,** prenda de vestir, f
clotted /'klɒtɪd/ a grumoso
cloud /klaud/ n nube, f. —vt anublar, oscurecer; empañar; (blot out) borrar. —vi anublarse. **to be under a c.,** estar bajo sospecha. **summer c.,** nube de verano, f. **storm-c.,** nubarrón, m. **c.-burst,** nubada, f, chaparrón, m. **c.-capped,** coronado de nubes
cloudiness /'klaudinɪs/ n nebulosidad, f; obscuridad, f; (of liquids) turbiedad, f
cloudless /'klaudlɪs/ a sin nubes, despejado; sereno, claro
cloudy /'klaudi/ a nublado, nubloso; obscuro; (of liquids) turbio
clove /klouv/ n clavo de especia, m; (of garlic) diente de ajo, m. **c.-tree,** clavero, m
cloven /'klouvən/ a hendido. **to show the c. hoof,** enseñar la oreja. **c. hoof,** pezuña, f
clover /'klouvər/ n trébol, m. **to be in c.,** nadar en la abundancia
clown /klaun/ n patán, m; bufón, tonto, m; (in a circus) payaso, m. —vi hacer el tonto, hacer el payaso
clowning /'klaunɪŋ/ n payasada, f
clownish /'klaunɪʃ/ a grosero; palurdo, zafio; bufón
cloy /klɔɪ/ vt empalagar
cloying /'klɔɪɪŋ/ a empalagoso
club /klʌb/ n porra, cachiporra, clava, f; (gymnastic) maza, f; (hockey) bastón de hockey, m; (golf) palo de golf, m; (in cards) basto, m; (social) club, m. —vt golpear. **to c. together,** asociarse, unirse. **We clubbed together to buy him a present,** Entre todos le compramos un regalo. **c.-house,** club, m
clubfoot /'klʌb,fʊt/ n pie calcáneo, pie contrahecho, pie de piña, pie equino, pie talo, pie zambo, m
clubman /'klʌb,mæn/ n miembro de un club, m
cluck /klʌk/ vi cloquear. —n cloqueo, m
clucking /'klʌkɪŋ/ n cloqueo, m
clue /klu/ n indicio, m; (to a problem) clave, f; (of a crossword) indicación, f; idea, f
clump /klʌmp/ n bloque, pedazo, m; (of trees) grupo, m; (of feet) ruido, m
clumsily /'klʌmzəli/ adv torpemente; pesadamente
clumsiness /'klʌmzɪnɪs/ n torpeza, f; falta de maña, f; pesadez, f
clumsy /'klʌmzi/ a torpe; desmañado; chapucero, sin arte; (lumbering) pesado; (in shape) disforme
cluster /'klʌstər/ n (of currants, etc.) racimo, m; (of flowers) ramillete, m; grupo, m. —vi arracimarse; agruparse. **They clustered round him,** Se agrupaban a su alrededor
clutch /klʌtʃ/ vt agarrar; sujetar, apretar. —n Mech. embrague, m; (of eggs) nidada, f; Fig. garras, f pl. **to fall into the clutches of,** caer en las garras de. **to make a c. at,** procurar agarrar. **to throw in the c.,** Mech. embragar. **to throw out the c.,** Mech. desembragar. **c. pedal,** pedal de embrague, m
clutter /'klʌtər/ n desorden, m, confusión, f, vt desordenar

coach /koutʃ/ n carroza, f; charabán, m; Rail. vagón, coche, m; (hackney) coche de alquiler, m; Sports. entrenador, m; (tutor) profesor particular, m. —vt Sports. entrenar; (teach) preparar, dar lecciones particulares (a). **through c.,** coche directo, m. **c.-box,** pescante, m. **c.-house,** cochera, f
coaching /'koutʃɪŋ/ n Sports. entrenamiento, m; le cciones particulares, f pl
coachman /'koutʃmən/ n cochero, m
coagulate /kou'ægyə,leit/ vi coagularse. —vt coagular, cuajar
coagulation /kou,ægyə'leiʃən/ n coagulación, f
coal /koul/ n carbón, m; pedazo de carbón, m; (burning) brasa, f. —vi carbonear, hacer carbón. —vt proveer de carbón; carbonear. **to carry coals to Newcastle,** llevar leña al monte, elevar aqua al mar. **to haul a person over the coals,** reprender a alguien. **c.-barge,** (barco) carbonero, m. **c.-black,** negro como el azabache, m. **c.-cellar, house,** carbonera, f. **c.-dust,** cisco, m. **c.-field,** yacimiento de carbón, m. **c.-gas,** gas de hulla, m. **c.-heaver,** cargador de carbón, m. **c.-merchant,** carbonero, m. **c.-mine,** mina de carbón, f. **c.-miner,** minero de carbón, m. **c.-scuttle,** carbonera, f. **c.-tar,** alquitrán mineral, m
coalesce /,kouə'les/ vi fundirse; unirse; incorporarse
coalescence /,kouə'lesəns/ n fusión, f; unión, f; incorporación, f
coalition /,kouə'lɪʃən/ n coalición, f
coarse /kɔrs/ a (in texture) basto, burdo; tosco; (gross) grosero; vulgar. **c.-grained,** de fibra gruesa; (of persons) vulgar, poco fino
coarsen /'kɔrsən/ vt (of persons) embrutecer. —vi embrutecerse; (of the skin) curtirse
coarseness /'kɔrsnɪs/ n basteza, f; tosquedad, f; (of persons) grosería, indelicadeza, f; vulgaridad, f
coast /koust/ n costa, f; litoral, m. —vi costear; deslizarse en un tobogán; dejar muerto el motor. **The c. is not clear,** Hay moros en la costa. **c.-guard,** guardacostas, m. **c.-line,** litoral, m
coastal /'koustl/ a costanero, costero. **c. defences,** defensas costeras, f pl
coaster /'koustər/ n Naut. barco costanero, barco de cabotaje, m
coasting /'koustɪŋ/ n Naut. cabotaje, m
coat /kout/ n abrigo, m; gabán, m; chaqueta, f; (animal's) capa, f; (of paint) mano, f. —vt recubrir; (with paint, etc.) dar una mano de. **fur c.,** abrigo de pieles, m. **sports c.,** Americana sport, f. **c. of arms,** escudo de armas, m. **c. of mail,** cota de malla, f. **c.-hanger,** percha, f
coating /'koutɪŋ/ n (of paint, etc.) capa, mano, f
co-author /,kou'ɔθər/ n coautor, m
coax /kouks/ vt instar; halagar; persuadir (a)
coaxing /'kouksɪŋ/ n ruegos, m pl; mimos, m pl, caricias, f pl; persuasión, f. —a mimoso, zalamero; persuasivo
cob /kɒb/ n (horse) jaca, f; (lump) pedazo, m; (swan) cisne macho, m
cobalt /'koubɔlt/ n cobalto, m. **c. blue,** azul cobalto, m
cobble /'kɒbəl/ n (stone) guijarro, m, vt (with stones) empedrar con guijarros; (shoes) remendar
cobbler /'kɒblər/ n zapatero remendón, m. **cobbler's last,** horma, f. **cobbler's wax,** cerote, m
cobblestone /'kɒbəl,stoun/ n guijarro, m, piedra, f
cobelligerent /,koubə'lɪdʒərənt/ n cobeligerante, mf
cobra /'koubrə/ n cobra, serpiente de anteojos, f
cobweb /'kɒb,wɛb/ n telaraña, f
cobwebby /'kɒb,wɛbi/ a cubierto de telarañas; transparente; de gasa
cocaine /kou'kein/ n cocaína, f
coccyx /'kɒksɪks/ n cóccix, m, Inf. rabadilla, f
cochlea /'kɒkliə/ n caracol (del oído), m
cock /kɒk/ n gallo, m; (male) macho, m; (tap) grifo, m, espita, f; (of a gun) martillo, m; (weather-vane) veleta, f; (of hay) montón, m. —vt (a gun) amartillar; (a hat) ladear; (raise) erguir, enderezar. **a cocked hat,** un sombrero de tres picos. **at half c.,** (of a gun) desamartillada f. **He cocked his head,** Erguió la cabeza. **The dog cocked its ears,** El perro aguzó las orejas. **to c. one's eye at,** lanzar una mirada (a). **c.-a-doodle-doo,** quiquiriquí, m. **c.-a-hoop,** triunfante,

jubiloso; arrogante. **c.-crow,** canto del gallo, m. **c.-fight,** riña de gallos, f. **c.-of-the-walk,** gallito, m. **c.-sure,** pagado de sí mismo; completamente convencido
cockerel /'kɒkərəl/ n gallo joven, gallito, m
cocker spaniel /,kɒkər 'spænyəl/ n cóquer, m
cockle /'kɒkəl/ n (bivalve) bucarda, f. —vi arrugarse; (warp) torcerse; doblarse. **c.-shell,** (pilgrims') concha, f
cockpit /'kɒk,pɪt/ n galliería, f; Aer. casilla del piloto, f; Fig. arena, f
cockroach /'kɒk,routʃ/ n cucaracha, f
cockscomb /'kɒks,koum/ n cresta de gallo, f
cocktail /'kɒk,teil/ n (drink) cótel, coctel, m. **to shake a c.,** mezclar un coctel. **c. party,** coctel m. **c. shaker,** cotelera, f
cocky /'kɒki/ a fatuo, presuntuoso
cocoa /'koukou/ n cacao, m
coconut /'kouka,nʌt/ n coco, m; Inf. cabeza, f. **c. milk,** agua de coco, f. **c. shy,** pim, pam, pum, m. **c. tree,** cocotero, m
cocoon /kə'kun/ n capullo, m
cod /kɒd/ n bacalao, m. **cod-liver oil,** aceite de hígado de bacalao, m
coddle /'kɒdl/ vt criar con mimo, mimar, consentir
code /koud/ n código, m; clave, f; (secret) cifra, f. —vt poner en cifra. **signal c.,** Naut. código de señales, m. **c. word,** palabra de clave, f
codeine /'koudin/ n codeína, f
codex /'koudɛks/ n códice, m
codicil /'kɒdəsəl/ n codicilio, m
codification /,kɒdəfɪ'keiʃən/ n codificación, f
codify /'kɒdə,fai/ vt codificar
coeducation /,kouɛdʒu'keiʃən/ n coeducación, f
coefficient /,kouə'fɪʃənt/ n coeficiente, m
coequality /,kour'kwɒlɪti/ n coigualdad, f
coerce /kou'ɜrs/ vt forzar, obligar; constreñir
coercion /kou'ɜrʃən/ n coerción, coacción, f
coercive /kou'ɜrsɪv/ a coercitivo, coactivo
coeval /kou'ivəl/ a coevo
coexist /,kouɪg'zɪst/ vi coexistir
coexistence /,kouɪg'zɪstəns/ n coexistencia, f
coffee /'kɔfi/ n café, m. **black c.,** café solo, m. **white c.,** café con leche, m. **c.-bean,** grano de café, m. **c.-cup,** taza para café, f. **c.-house,** café, m. **c.-mill,** molinillo de café, m. **c.-plantation,** cafetal, m. **c.-pot,** cafetera, f. **c.-set,** juego de café, m. **c.-tree,** cafeto, m
coffer /'kɔfər/ n cofre, m; arca, caja, f
coffin /'kɔfɪn/ n ataúd, féretro, m; caja, f
cog /kɒg/ n Mech. diente (de rueda), m
cogency /'koudʒənsi/ n fuerza, f
cogent /'koudʒənt/ a convincente, fuerte; urgente
cogitate /'kɒdʒɪ,teit/ vi pensar, considerar, meditar
cogitation /,kɒdʒɪ'teiʃən/ n reflexión, meditación, consideración, f
cognac /'kounyæk/ n coñac, m
cognate /'kɒgneit/ a (of stock) consanguíneo; afín; análogo; semejante
cognition /kɒg'nɪʃən/ n cognición, f
cognitive /'kɒgnɪtɪv/ a cognoscitivo
cognizance /'kɒgnəzəns/ n conocimiento, m; jurisdicción, f
cogwheel /'kɒg,wil/ n rueda dentada, f
cohabit /kou'hæbɪt/ vi cohabitar
cohabitation /kou,hæbɪ'teiʃən/ n cohabitación, f
coheir /kou'ɛər/ n coheredero, m
coheiress /kou'ɛərɪs/ n coheredera, f
cohere /kou'hɪər/ vi pegarse, adherirse; unirse
coherent /kou'hɪərənt/ a coherente; consecuente
cohesion /kou'hiʒən/ n cohesión, f; coherencia, f
cohort /'kouhɔrt/ n cohorte, f
coif /kwɑf/ n cofia, f; toca, f
coiffure /kwɑ'fyʊr/ n peinado, m; tocado, m
coil /kɔil/ vt arrollar (Naut. of ropes) adujar. —vi arrollarse; enroscarse; serpentear. —n rollo, m; (of a serpent and ropes) anillo, m; (of hair) trenza, f; Elec. carrete, m. **coil of smoke,** nube de humo, f. **to c. up,** hacerse un ovillo
coiling /'kɔilɪŋ/ n arrollamiento, m; serpenteo, m
coin /kɔin/ n moneda, f; Inf. dinero, m. —vt acuñar;

(a new word) inventar. **to pay back in the same c.,** pagar en la misma moneda

coinage /'kɔinidʒ/ n acuñación, f; moneda, f; sistema monetario, m; invención, f; (new word) neologismo, m

coincide /,kouin'said/ vi coincidir (con); estar conforme, estar de acuerdo

coincidence /kou'insidəns/ n coincidencia, f; (chance) casualidad, f

coiner /'kɔinər/ n acuñador de moneda, m; monedero falso, m; (of phrases, etc.) inventor, m

coitus /'kouitəs/ n coito, m

coke /kouk/ n (carbón de) coque, m

colander /'kɔləndər/ n colador, m

cold /kould/ a frío. —n frío, m; Med. catarro, constipado, m. **I am c.,** Tengo frío. **It is c.,** Está frío; (weather) Hace frío. **to catch a c.,** acatarrarse, resfriarse. **to grow c.,** enfriarse; (of the weather) empezar a hacer frío. **in c. blood,** a sangre fría. **c.-blooded,** (fishes, etc.) de sangre fría; (chilly, of persons) friolero; (pitiless) insensible, sin piedad; (of actions) a sangre fría, premeditado. **c.-chisel,** cortafrío, m. **c. cream,** crema (para el cutis), f. **c.-hearted,** seco, insensible. **c.-shoulder,** n frialdad, f. —vt tratar con frialdad (a). **c.-storage,** conservación refrigerada, f

coldly /'kouldli/ adv fríamente

coldness /'kouldnis/ n frío, m; (of one's reception, etc.) frialdad, f; (of heart) inhumanidad, f

coleopterous /,kouli'ɒptərəs/ a coleóptero

colic /'kɒlik/ n cólico, m

coliseum /,kɒli'siəm/ n coliseo, m

colitis /kə'laitis/ n colitis, f

collaborate /kə'læbə,reit/ vi colaborar (con)

collaboration /kə,læbə'reiʃən/ n colaboración, f

collaborationist /kə,læbə'reiʃənist/ n colaboracionista, mf

collaborator /kə'læbə,reitər/ n colaborador (-ra); (quisling) colaboracionista, mf

collapse /kə'læps/ n derrumbamiento, m; desplome, m; Med. colapso, m; (of buildings and Fig.) hundimiento, m; (of plans) frustración, f; (failure) fracaso, m. —vi derrumbarse; (of buildings, etc.) hundirse, venirse abajo; (of persons, fall) desplomarse; Med. sufrir colapso; (of plans, etc.) frustrarse, venirse abajo. **George came to us after the c. of France,** Jorge vino a quedarse con nosotros después del hundimiento de Francia

collapsible /kə'læpsəbəl/ a plegable

collar /'kɒlər/ n (of a garment and of fur) cuello, m; (of a dog, etc., and necklace) collar, m. —vt (seize) agarrar. **detachable c.,** cuello suelto, m. **high c.,** alzacuello, m. **c.-bone,** clavícula, f

collate /kou'leit/ vt cotejar; (to a benefice) colacionar

collateral /kə'lætərəl/ a colateral

collation /kə'leiʃən/ n colación, f

colleague /'kɒlig/ n colega, m; compañero (-ra)

collect /kə'lɛkt/ vt (assemble) reunir; (catch) coger; acumular; (call for) pasar a buscar, ir (or venir) a buscar; (pick up) recoger; (taxes, etc.) recaudar; cobrar; (one's strength, etc. and debts, etc.) cobrar; (letters) recoger. —vi reunirse, congregarse; acumularse. —n Eccl. colecta, f. **to c. oneself,** reponerse

collected /kə'lɛktid/ a (of persons) seguro de sí.

collection /kə'lɛkʃən/ n reunión, f; (of data, etc.) acumulación, f; (of pictures, stamps, etc.) colección, f; (of a debt, etc.) cobranza, f; (of taxes, etc.) recaudación, f; (from a mail box) recogida, f; (of laws, etc.) compilación, f; Eccl. ofertorio, m; (of donations) colecta, f

collection agency n agencia de cobros de cuentas, f

collective /kə'lɛktiv/ a colectivo. **c. bargaining,** regateo colectivo, trato colectiva, m

collectivism /kə'lɛktə,vizəm/ n colectivismo, m

collector /kə'lɛktər/ n (of pictures, etc.) coleccionador (-ra), coleccionista, mf; cobrador, m; Elec. colector, m

college /'kɒlidʒ/ n colegio, m; escuela, f; universidad, f. **C. of Cardinals,** Colegio de Cardenales, m

collegiate /kə'lidʒiit/ a colegial, colegiado. **c. church,** iglesia colegial, f

collide /kə'laid/ vi chocar (contra), topar (con); estar en conflicto (con). **c. head-on,** chocar frontalmente

collie /'kɒli/ n perro de pastor escocés, m

collier /'kɒlyər/ n minero de carbón, m; (barco) carbonero, m

collision /kə'liʒən/ n choque, m, colisión, f; (of interests, etc.) antagonismo, conflicto, m. **to come into c. with,** chocar con

colloid /'kɒlɔid/ a coloide. —n coloide, m

colloquial /kə'loukwiəl/ a familiar

colloquialism /kə'loukwiə,lizəm/ n expresión familiar, f

colloquially /kə'loukwiəli/ adv en lenguaje familiar; familiarmente

colloquy /'kɒləkwi/ n coloquio, m

collusion /kə'luʒən/ n colusión, f. **to be in c.,** Law. coludir; conspirar, estar de manga

Cologne /kə'loun/ Colonia, f

Colombia /kə'lʌmbiə/ Colombia, f

Colombian /kə'lʌmbiən/ a colombiano. —n colombiano (-na)

colon /'koulən/ n Anat. colon, m; (punctuation) dos puntos, m pl

colonel /'kɜrnḷ/ n coronel, m

colonial /kə'lounial/ a colonial. —n habitante de las colonias, m. **C. Office,** Ministerio de Asuntos Coloniales, m

colonist /'kɒlənist/ n colono, m; colonizador (-ra)

colonization /,kɒlənə'zeiʃən/ n colonización, f

colonize /'kɒlə,naiz/ vt colonizar. —vi establecerse en una colonia

colonizer /'kɒlə,naizər/ n colonizador (-ra)

colonizing /'kɒlə,naiziŋ/ n colonización, f, a colonizador

colonnade /,kɒlə'neid/ n columnata, f

colony /'kɒləni/ n colonia, f

color /'kʌlər/ n color, m; colorido, m; tinta, f; materia colorante, f; pl **colors,** insignia, f; bandera, f, estandarte, m; Naut. pabellón, m. —vt colorar; pintar; iluminar; (influence) influir, afectar. —vi colorarse; ruborizarse; encenderse. **fast c.,** color estable, color sólido, m. **regimental colors,** bandera del regimiento, f. **with colors flying,** con tambor batiente, a banderas desplegadas. **to be off c.,** estar malucho, estar indispuesto. **to change c.,** (of persons) mudar de color, mudar de semblante. **to give c. to,** (a story, etc.) hacer verosímil. **to lay the colors on too thick,** recargar las tintas. **to pass with flying colors,** salir triunfante. **under c. of,** so color de, a pretexto de. **c.-blind,** daltoniano. **c.-blindness,** daltonismo, m

Colorado beetle /,kɒlə'radou/ n escarabajo de la patata, m

colored /'kʌlərd/ a colorado; de color

colorimeter /,kʌlə'rimitər/ n colorímetro, m

coloring /'kʌləriŋ/ n (substance) colorante, m; (act of) coloración, f; Art. colorido, m; (of complexion) colores, m pl

colorist /'kʌlərist/ n colorista, mf

colorless /'kʌlərlis/ a sin color, incoloro; Fig. insípido

colossal /kə'lɒsəl/ a colosal, gigantesco; enorme; Inf. estupendo

colossus /kə'lɒsəs/ n coloso, m

colt /koult/ n potro, m; (boy) muchacho alegre, m

colter /'koultər/ n reja, reja del arado, f

colt's-foot n Bot. fárfara, f

columbine /'kɒləm,bain/ n Bot. aguileña, f; (in pantomime) Colombina, f

column /'kɒləm/ n columna, f. **Fifth c.,** quinta columna, f

columned /'kɒləmd/ a con columnas

columnist /'kɒləmnist/ n periodista, m

coma /'koumə/ n coma, m

comatose /'kɒmə,tous/ a comatoso

comb /koum/ n peine, m; (for flax) carda, f; (curry) almohaza, f; (of cock) cresta, carúncula, f; (of a wave) cima, cresta, f; (honey) panal, m, vt (hair) peinar; (flax) rastrillar, cardar. **c. and brush,** cepillo y peine. **high c.,** peineta, f. **to c. one's hair,** peinarse

combat /v kəm'bæt; n 'kɒmbæt/ vt luchar contra, combatir, resistir. —vi combatir, pelear. —n combate, m; lucha, batalla, f. **in single c.,** cuerpo a cuerpo

combatant /kəm'bætn̩t/ n combatiente, m, a combatiente

combative /kəm'bætɪv/ a belicoso, pugnaz

combination /ˌkɒmbə'neɪʃən/ n combinación, f; mezcla, f; unión, f; asociación, f; pl **combinations.** camisa pantalón, f. **c. lock,** cerradura de combinación, f

combine / v kəm'bain; n 'kɒmbain/ vt combinar; reunir, juntar; Chem. combinar. —vi combinarse; asociarse (con); Com. fusionarse. —n asociación, f; Com. monopolio, m

combings /'koumɪŋz/ n pl peinaduras, f pl

combustible /kəm'bʌstəbəl/ a combustible. —n combustible, m

combustion /kəm'bʌstʃən/ n combustión, f. **rapid c.,** combustión rápida, f. **spontaneous c.,** combustión espontánea, f

come /kʌm/ vi venir; llegar; avanzar; acercarse; (happen) suceder, acontecer; (result) resultar; (find oneself) encontrarse, hallarse; (become) llegar a ser; (begin to) ponerse (a), empezar (a). **Coming!** ¡Voy! ¡Allá voy! **C., c.!** ¡Vamos! ¡No es para tanto! ¡Ánimo! **I am ready whatever comes,** Estoy preparado venga lo que venga. **He comes of a good family,** Es (Viene) de buena familia. **I came to know him well,** Llegué a conocerle bien. **I don't know what came over me,** No sé lo que me pasó. **When I came to consider it,** Cuando me puse a considerarlo. **The bill comes to six thousand pesetas,** La cuenta sale a seis mil pesetas. **He comes up before the judge tomorrow,** Ha de comparecer ante el juez mañana. **What you say comes to this,** Lo que dice Vd. se reduce a esto. **What is the world coming to?** ¿A dónde va parar el mundo? **It does not c. within my scope,** No está dentro de mi alcance. **to c. apart,** deshacerse; romperse; dividirse. **to c. home to,** Fig. impresionar mucho, tocar en lo más íntimo; hacer comprender (a). **to c. into bloom,** empezar a tener flores, florecer. **to c. into one's head,** venir a las mientes. **to c. into the world,** venir al mundo. **to c. near,** acercarse; aproximarse, estar próximo. **to c. next,** venir después; suceder luego. **to c. to an end,** terminar, acabarse. **to c. to blows,** venir a las manos. **to c. to grief,** salir mal parado; (of schemes, etc.) malograrse. **to c. to hand,** venir a mano; (of letters) llegar a las manos (de). **to c. to life,** despertar; animarse; resucitarse. **to c. to nothing,** frustrarse; no quedar en nada. **to c. to pass,** suceder; realizarse. **to c. to terms,** ponerse de acuerdo. **to c. true,** cumplirse, verificarse. **to c. about,** suceder, acontecer, tener lugar; (of the wind) girar. **to c. across,** dar con, encontrar por casualidad; tropezar con. **to c. after,** (a situation) solicitar; (follow) seguir (a); venir más tarde (que); (succeed) suceder. **to c. again,** volver. **to c. along,** caminar (por); andar (por); (arrive) llegar. **C. along!** ¡Ven! ¡Vamos! ¡Andamos! **to c. at,** alcanzar; (attack) embestir, atacar; (gain) obtener, adquirir. **to c. away,** irse, marcharse; (break) deshacerse. **to c. back,** volver. **c.-back,** n Inf. respuesta, f; contraataque, m. **to c. before,** llegar antes; preceder (a). **to c. between,** interponerse (entre); intervenir. **to c. by,** pasar por, pasar junto a; (acquire) obtener, adquirir; (achieve) conseguir. **to c. down,** bajar, descender; (in the world) venir a menos; (be demolished) demolerse; (collapse) derrumbarse, hundirse; (of prices) bajar; (of traditions, etc.) llegar e.g. This work has c. down to us in two fifteenth-century manuscripts Esta obra nos ha llegado en dos manuscritos del siglo quince; (fall) caer. **c.-down,** n caída, f; frustración, f; desengaño, m; desprestigio, m; pérdida de posición, f. **to c. down on a person,** cantar la cartilla (a). **to c. forward,** avanzar, adelantarse; (offer) ofrecerse; presentarse. **to c. in,** entrar; (of money) ingresar; (of trains, etc.) llegar; (of the tide) crecer; (of the new year) empezar; (of fashion) ponerse de moda; (be useful) servir (para). **C. in!** ¡Adelante! ¡Pase Vd.! **to c. into,** (a scheme) asociarse con; (property) heredar; (the mind) presentarse a la imaginación, ocurrirse (a). **to c. off,** (happen) tener lugar; realizarse, efectuarse; (be successful) tener éxito; (break off) separarse (de); romperse. **c. off well,** tener éxito; (of persons) salir bien. **c. off the press,** salir de prensas (a). **to c. on,** avanzar; (of actors) salir a

la escena; (progress) hacer progresos; (develop) desarrollarse; (of pain, etc.) acometer (a); (arrive) llegar; (of a lawsuit) verse. **C. on!** ¡Vamos! ¡En marcha! **to c. out,** salir; (of stars) nacer; (of buds, etc.) brotar; (of the moon, etc.) asomarse; (of stains) borrarse, salir; (of a book) ver la luz, publicarse; (of secrets) divulgarse, saberse; (of a girl, in society) ponerse de largo; (on strike) declararse en huelga; (of fashions, etc.) aparecer. **to c. out with,** (a remark) soltar; (oaths, etc.) prorrumpir (en); (disclose) revelar, hacer público. **to c. round,** (to see someone) venir a ver (a); (coax) engatusar; (after a faint, etc.) volver en sí; (after illness) reponerse; (to another's point of view) aceptar, compartir. **to c. through,** pasar por; (trials, etc.) subir; salir de; (of liquids) salirse. **to c. to,** volver en sí. **to c. together,** reunirse, juntarse; venir juntos; unirse. **to c. under,** venir (or estar) bajo la jurisdicción de; (the influence of) estar dominado por; (figure among) figurar entre, estar comprendido en. **to c. up,** subir; (of sun, moon) salir; (of plants) brotar; (of problems, etc.) surgir; (in conversation) discutirse; (before a court) comparecer. **to c. up to,** (equal) igualar, ser igual (a); rivalizar con; (in height) llegar hasta. **He came up to them in the street,** Les abordó (or se les acercó) en la calle. **We have c. up against many difficulties,** Hemos tropezado con muchas dificultades. **This novel does not c. up to his last,** Esta última novela no es tan buena como la anterior. **The party did not c. up to their expectations,** La reunión no fue tan divertida como esperaban. **to c. up with,** (a person) alcanzar (a). **to c. upon,** encontrar, hallar; tropezar con; encontrar por casualidad. **to c. upon evil days,** venir a menos

comedian /kə'midiən/ n actor cómico, comediante, m

comedy /'kɒmɪdi/ n comedia, f. **c. of manners,** comedia de costumbres, f

comeliness /'kʌmlinɪs/ n hermosura, f

comely /'kʌmli/ a hermoso

comer /'kʌmər/ n el, m, (f, la) que viene. **all comers,** todo el mundo. **first c.,** primer (-ra) venido (-da)

comet /'kɒmɪt/ n cometa, m

comfort /'kʌmfərt/ vt consolar, confortar; (encourage) animar; (reassure) alegrar. —n consuelo, m; satisfacción, f; comodidad, f; bienestar, m. **He lives in great c.,** Vive con mucha comodidad. **c.-loving,** comodón

comfortable /'kʌmftəbəl/ a cómodo; (with income) suficiente; (consoling) consolador. **to make oneself c.,** ponerse cómodo

comfortably /'kʌmftəbli/ adv cómodamente; suficientemente; fácilmente; con facilidad; (well) bien. **He is c. off,** Está bien de dinero

comforter /'kʌmfərtər/ n consolador (-ra), f; (baby's) chupador, m; (scarf) bufanda, f

comforting /'kʌmfərtɪŋ/ a consolador

comfortless /'kʌmfərtlɪs/ a incómodo, sin comodidad; desconsolador; (of persons) inconsolable, desconsolado

comic /'kɒmɪk/ a cómico; bufo; satírico. —n cómico, m; pl **comics,** (printed) historietas cómicas, f pl. **c. opera,** ópera cómicas, f. **c. paper,** periódico satírico, m

comical /'kɒmɪkəl/ a cómico; divertido, gracioso

coming /'kʌmɪŋ/ a (with year, etc.) próximo, que viene; (promising) de porvenir; (approaching) que se acerca. —n venida, f; llegada, f; advenimiento, m. **c.-out party,** puesta de largo, f. **comings and goings,** entradas y salidas, f pl

comma /'kɒmə/ n coma, f. **inverted commas,** comillas, f pl

command /kə'mænd/ vt mandar, ordenar; (silence, respect, etc.) imponer; (an army, fleet, etc.) comandar; capitanear; (one's emotions) dominar; (have at one's disposal) disponer de; (a military position, view) dominar; (sympathy, etc.) despertar, merecer; (of price) venderse por. —vi mandar. —n orden, f; (Mil. Nav.) mando, m; (of an army, etc.) comandancia, f; (of one's emotions, etc.) dominio, m; (of a military position, etc.) dominación, f; disposición, f. **By Royal C.,** Por Real Orden. (of shops, etc.) Proveedor de la Real Casa. **The house commands lovely views of the mountains,** La casa tiene hermosas vistas de las montañas. **word of c.,** orden, *f.* **Yours to c.,** A la disposición de Vd.

commandant /ˌkɒmənˈdænt/ *n* comandante, *m*

commandeer /ˌkɒmənˈdɪər/ *vt* (conscript) reclutar; *Mil.* requisar; expropiar

commander /kəˈmændər/ *n Mil.* comandante, *m; Nav.* capitán de fragata, *m;* (of order of Knighthood) comendador, *m.* **c.-in-chief,** generalísimo, *m.* **C. of the Faithful,** Comendador de los creyentes, *m*

commanding /kəˈmændɪŋ/ *a Mil.* comandante; imponente; (of manner) imperioso; dominante. **c. officer,** comandante en jefe, *m*

commandment /kəˈmændmənt/ *n* precepto, mandamiento, *m.* **the Ten Commandments,** los diez mandamientos

commando /kəˈmændou/ *n Mil.* comando, *m*

commemorate /kəˈmɛməˌreit/ *vt* conmemorar

commemoration /kəˌmɛməˈreiʃən/ *n* conmemoración, *f*

commemorative /kəˈmɛməˌreitɪv/ *a* conmemorativo

commence /kəˈmɛns/ *vt* comenzar, empezar, principiar. —*vi* comenzar. **He commenced to eat,** Empezó a comer

commencement /kəˈmɛnsmənt/ *n* principio, comienzo, *m*

commend /kəˈmɛnd/ *vt* (entrust) encomendar; recomendar; alabar

commendable /kəˈmɛndəbəl/ *a* loable; recomendable

commendation /ˌkɒmənˈdeiʃən/ *n* aprobación, alabanza, *f,* aplauso, *m*

commendatory /kəˈmɛndəˌtɔri/ *a* (of letters) comendatorio

commensurable /kəˈmɛnsərəbəl/ *a* conmensurable

commensurate /kəˈmɛnsərɪt/ *a* proporcionado (a); conforme (a)

comment /ˈkɒmɛnt/ *n* observación, *f;* (on a work) comento, *m;* explicación, nota, *f.* —*vi* hacer una observación (sobre); (a work) comentar, anotar. **to c. unfavorably on,** criticar

commentary /ˈkɒmənˌtɛri/ *n* comentario, *m;* (on a person, etc.) comentos, *m pl,* observaciones, *f pl*

commentator /ˈkɒmənˌteitər/ *n* comentador (-ra); (of a work) comentarista, *mf*

commerce /ˈkɒmərs/ *n* comercio, *m;* negocios, *m pl;* (social) trato, *m*

commercial /kəˈmərʃəl/ *a* comercial; mercantil. **c. traveler,** viajante, *mf*

commercialism /kəˈmərʃəˌlizəm/ *n* mercantilismo, *m*

commercialize /kəˈmərʃəˌlaiz/ *vt* hacer objeto de comercio

commercially /kəˈmərʃəli/ *adv* comercialmente

commingle /kəˈmɪŋɡəl/ *vt* mezclar. —*vi* mezclarse

commiserate /kəˈmɪzəˌreit/ *vi* compadecerse (de), apiadarse (de)

commiseration /kəˌmɪzəˈreiʃən/ *n* conmiseración, compasión, *f*

commissariat /ˌkɒməˈsɛəriət/ *n* comisaría, *f; Inf.* despensa, *f*

commissary /ˈkɒməˌsɛri/ *n* comisario, *m*

commission /kəˈmɪʃən/ *n* comisión, *f; Mil.* graduación de oficial, *f.* —*vt* comisionar; (a ship) poner en servicio activo, armar; (appoint) nombrar. **in c.,** en servicio, activo. **out of c.,** (of ships) inutilizado; inservible. **c. agent,** comisionista, *mf* **to gain one's c.,** *Mil.* graduarse de oficial. **to put out of c.,** retirar del servicio; poner fuera de combate; estropear

commissionaire /kəˌmɪʃəˈnɛər/ *n* portero, *m*

commissioned /kəˈmɪʃənd/ *a* comisionado. **c. officer,** oficial, *m*

commissioner /kəˈmɪʃənər/ *n* comisario, *m.* **High C.,** alto comisario, *m.* **c. for oaths,** notario, *m.* **c. of police,** jefe de policía, *m*

commit /kəˈmɪt/ *vt* entregar (a); (a crime) cometer; (to prison) encarcelar; (for trial) remitir. **to c. oneself,** comprometerse. **to c. to memory,** aprender de memoria. **to c. to writing,** poner por escrito

commitment /kəˈmɪtmənt/ *n* (financial, etc.) obligación, responsabilidad, *f;* compromiso, *m*

committal /kəˈmɪtl̩/ *n* (of an offence) comisión, *f;*

(placing, entrusting) entrega, *f;* (to prison) encarcelamiento, *m;* (legal procedure) auto de prisión, *m*

committee /kəˈmɪti/ *n* comité, *m;* comisión, junta, *f;* consejo, *m.* **They decided in c.,** Tomaron la resolución en comité. **c. of management,** consejo de administración, *m*

commodious /kəˈmoudiəs/ *a* espacioso, grande

commodiousness /kəˈmoudiəsnɪs/ *n* espaciosidad, *f*

commodity /kəˈmɒdɪti/ *n* artículo, *m,* mercancía, *f*

commodore /ˈkɒməˌdɔr/ *n Nav.* jefe de escuadra, *m;* comodoro, *m*

common /ˈkɒmən/ *a* común; general, corriente; universal; vulgar; (disparaging) cursi; (elementary) elemental. —*n* pastos comunes, *m pl.* **He is not a c. man,** No es un hombre cualquiera; No es un hombre vulgar. **in c.,** en común. **the c. man,** el hombre medio. **the c. people,** el pueblo, *m.* **c. sense,** sentido común, *m.* **c. soldier,** soldado raso, *m.* **c. speech,** lenguaje vulgar, *m.* **c. usage,** uso corriente, *m*

commoner /ˈkɒmənər/ *n* plebeyo (-ya)

commonly /ˈkɒmənli/ *adv* comúnmente, por lo general

commonness /ˈkɒmənnɪs/ *n* frecuencia, *f;* vulgaridad, *f*

commonplace /ˈkɒmənˌpleis/ *n* lugar común, *m;* trivialidad, *f.* —*a* trivial

commons /ˈkɒmənz/ *n* el pueblo; (House of) Cámara de los Comunes, *f;* (food) provisiones, *f pl.* **to be on short c.,** comer mal, estar mal alimentado

Commonwealth /ˈkɒmənˌwɛlθ/ *n* estado, *m;* república, *f;* comunidad (de naciones), *f;* mancomunidad, *f.* **the Commonwealth of Puerto Rico,** el Estado Libre Asociado de Puerto Rico, *m*

commotion /kəˈmouʃən/ *n* confusión, *f;* conmoción, perturbación, *f;* tumulto, *m*

communal /kəˈmyunl̩/ *a* comunal

commune /ˈkɒmyun/ *n* comuna, *f;* comunión, *f, vi* conversar (con). **to c. with oneself,** hablar consigo

communicable /kəˈmyunɪkəbəl/ *a* comunicable

communicant /kəˈmyunɪkənt/ *n Eccl.* comulgante, *mf;* (of information) informante, *mf*

communicate /kəˈmyunɪˌkeit/ *vt* comunicar; (diseases) transmitir. —*vi* comunicarse (con); *Eccl.* comulgar

communication /kəˌmyunɪˈkeiʃən/ *n* comunicación, *f.* **lines of c.,** comunicaciones, *f pl.* **to get into c. with,** ponerse en comunicación con. **c.-cord,** (in a railway carriage) timbre de alarma, *m*

communicative /kəˈmyunɪˌkeitɪv/ *a* comunicativo; expansivo

communicativeness /kəˈmyunɪˌkeitɪvnɪs/ *n* carácter expansivo, *m;* locuacidad, *f*

communion /kəˈmyunyən/ *n* comunión, *f.* **Holy c.,** comunión, *f.* **to take c.,** comulgar. **c. card,** cédula de comunión, *f.* **c. cup,** cáliz, *f.* **c. table,** sagrada mesa, *f;* altar, *m*

communiqué /kəˌmyunɪˈkei/ *n* comunicación, parte, *f.* **to issue a c.,** dar parte

communism /ˈkɒmyəˌnizəm/ *n* comunismo, *m*

communist /ˈkɒmyənɪst/ *n* comunista, *mf a* comunista

community /kəˈmyunɪti/ *n* comunidad, *f.* **the c.,** la nación; el público. **c. center,** centro social, *m*

commutation /ˌkɒmyəˈteiʃən/ *n* conmutación, *f;* reducción, *f*

commute /kəˈmyut/ *vt* conmutar; reducir

compact / *n* ˈkɒmpækt; *v* kəmˈpækt/ *n* (pact) acuerdo, pacto, *m;* (powder) polvorera, *f.* —*a* compacto; firme; sólido; apretado, cerrado; (of persons) bien hecho; (of style) conciso, sucinto

compact disc /ˈkɒmpækt ˈdɪsk/ *n* disco compacto, *m*

compactness /kəmˈpæktnɪs/ *n* compacidad, *f;* (of style) concisión, *f*

companion /kəmˈpænyən/ *n* compañero (-ra); camarada, *mf;* (of an Order) compañero, *m;* (or dama, *f).* —*vt* acompañar. **lady c.,** señora de compañía, *f.* **c.-hatch,** cubierta de escotilla, *f.* **c.-ladder,** escala de toldilla, *f*

companionable /kəmˈpænyənəbəl/ *a* sociable, amistoso

companionably /kəmˈpænyənəbli/ *adv* sociablemente, amistosamente

companionship /kəm'pænyən‚ʃɪp/ n compañía, f; compañerismo, m

company /'kʌmpəni/ n (*Com. Mil.* etc.) compañía, f; (ship's) tripulación, f. **I will keep you c.,** Te haré compañía. **to part c. with,** separarse de. **Present c. excepted!** ¡Mejorando lo presente! **They are not very good c.,** No son muy divertidos

company store n tienda de raya, f (Mexico)

comparable /'kɒmpərəbəl/ a comparable

comparably /'kɒmpərəbli/ adv comparablemente

comparative /kəm'pærətɪv/ a comparativo; relativo

comparatively /kəm'pærətɪvli/ adv comparativamente; relativamente

compare /kəm'pɛər/ vt comparar. —vi compararse; poder compararse. ser comparable. **beyond c.,** sin comparación; sin igual. **to c. favorably with,** no perder por comparación con. **to c. notes,** cambiar impresiones

comparison /kəm'pærəsən/ n comparación, f. **in c. with,** comparado con

compartment /kəm'pɑrtmənt/ n compartimiento, m; *Rail.* departamento, m

compass /'kʌmpəs/ n circuito, m; límites, m pl; alcance, m; (of a voice) gama, f; *Naut.* brújula, f; pl **compasses,** compás, m. —vt (achieve) conseguir; (plan) idear, **mariner's c.,** compás de mar. m, rosa de los vientos, f. **pocket c.,** brújula de bolsillo, f. **to c. about,** cercar, rodear

compassion /kəm'pæʃən/ n compasión, f. **to have c. on,** apiadarse de, compadecerse de

compassionate /kəm'pæʃənɪt/ a compasivo, piadoso. **c. leave,** permiso, m

compassionately /kəm'pæʃənɪtli/ adv compasivamente, con piedad

compatibility /kəm‚pætə'bɪlɪti/ n compatibilidad, f

compatible /kəm'pætəbəl/ a compatible, conciliable

compatriot /kəm'peitriət/ n compatriota, mf

compel /kəm'pɛl/ vt obligar (a), forzar (a); exigir; imponer. **His attitude compels respect,** Su actitud impone el respeto

compelling /kəm'pɛlɪŋ/ a compulsivo

compendious /kəm'pɛndiəs/ a compendioso, sucinto

compendium /kəm'pɛndiəm/ n compendio, m; resumen, m

compensate /'kɒmpən‚seit/ vt compensar; (reward) recompensar; (for loss, etc.) indemnizar. **to c. for,** compensar; indemnizar contra

compensation /‚kɒmpən'seiʃən/ n compensación, f; (reward) recompensa, f; (for loss, etc.) indemnización, f

compensatory /kəm'pɛnsə‚təri/ a compensatorio

compete /kəm'pit/ vi competir (con); rivalizar; ser rivales; (in a competition) concurrir

competence /'kɒmpɪtəns/ n aptitud, f; capacidad, f; competencia, f

competent /'kɒmpɪtənt/ a competente; capaz

competently /'kɒmpɪtəntli/ adv competentemente

competition /‚kɒmpɪ'tɪʃən/ n competencia, competición, rivalidad, f; emulación, f; (contest, etc.) concurso, m. **spirit of c.,** espíritu de competencia, m

competitive /kəm'pɛtɪtɪv/ a competidor; de competición. **c. examination,** oposición, f

competitor /kəm'pɛtɪtər/ n competidor (-ra)

compilation /‚kɒmpə'leiʃən/ n compilación, f

compile /kəm'pail/ vt compilar

compiler /kəm'pailər/ n compilador (-ra)

complacence /kəm'pleisəns/ n complacencia, satisfacción, f; contento de sí mismo, m

complacent /kəm'pleisənt/ a satisfecho; pagado de sí mismo

complacently /kəm'pleisəntli/ adv con satisfacción

complain /kəm'plein/ vi quejarse; lamentarse; *Law.* querellarse. **He complains about everything,** Se queja de todo

complainant /kəm'pleinənt/ n *Law.* demandante, mf

complaint /kəm'pleint/ n queja, f; lamento, m; *Law.* demanda, f; (illness) enfermedad, f. **to lodge a c. (against),** quejarse (de)

complaisance /kəm'pleisəns/ n afabilidad, cortesía, f

complaisant /kəm'pleisənt/ a complaciente, cortés, afable; (of husbands) consentido, sufrido

complement / n 'kɒmpləmənt; v -‚mɛnt/ n complemento, m; total, número completo, m. —vt completar

complementary /‚kɒmplə'mɛntəri/ a complementario

complete /kəm'plit/ a entero; completo; perfecto; acabado. —vt completar; acabar; (happiness, etc.) coronar, poner el último toque (a); (years) cumplir; (forms) llenar

completely /kəm'plitli/ adv completamente, enteramente

completeness /kəm'plitnɪs/ n entereza, f; totalidad, f

completion /kəm'pliʃən/ n terminación, f, fin, m

complex / a kəm'plɛks; n 'kɒmplɛks/ a complejo. —n complejo, m. **inferiority c.,** complejo de inferioridad, m

complexion /kəm'plɛkʃən/ n tez, f, cutis, m; *Fig.* carácter, m

complexity /kəm'plɛksɪti/ n complejidad, f

compliance /kəm'plaiəns/ n condescendencia, f; (subservience) sumisión, f; obediencia, f. **in c. with,** de acuerdo con, en conformidad con

compliant /kəm'plaiənt/ a condescendiente; sumiso, dócil; obediente

complicate /'kɒmplɪ‚keit/ vt complicar

complicated /'kɒmplɪ‚keitɪd/ a complejo; complicado; enredado

complication /‚kɒmplɪ'keiʃən/ n complicación, f

complicity /kəm'plɪsɪti/ n complicidad, f. **c. in a crime,** complicidad en un crimen

compliment / n 'kɒmpləmənt; v -‚mɛnt/ n cumplido, m, cortesía, f; requiebro, *Inf.* piropo, m; favor, m; honor, m; (greeting) saludo, m; (congratulation) felicitación, f. —vt cumplimentar; requebrar; (flatter) adular, lisonjear; (congratulate) felicitar. **They did him the c. of reading his book,** Le hicieron el honor de leer su libro. **to pay compliments,** hacer cumplidos, *Inf.* echar piropos

complimentary /‚kɒmplə'mɛntəri/ a lisonjero; galante. **c. ticket,** billete gratuito, m

comply /kəm'plai/ vi (with) cumplir, obedecer; conformarse (con); consentir

component /kəm'pounənt/ a componente. —n componente, m

comport /kəm'pɔrt/ vt (oneself), comportarse

comportment /kəm'pɔrtmənt/ n comportamiento, m, conducta, f

compose /kəm'pouz/ vt (all meanings) componer. **to c. oneself,** serenarse, calmarse. **to c. one's features,** componer el semblante

composed /kəm'pouzd/ a sereno, tranquilo, sosegado

composer /kəm'pouzər/ n compositor (-ra)

composite /kəm'pɒzɪt/ a compuesto; mixto. —n compuesto, m; *Bot.* planta compuesta, f

composition /‚kɒmpə'zɪʃən/ n (all meanings) composición, f

compositor /kəm'pɒzɪtər/ n *Print.* cajista, mf

composure /kəm'pouʒər/ n tranquilidad, serenidad, calma, f; sangre fría, f, aplomo, m

compote /'kɒmpout/ n compota, f

compound /'kɒmpaund/ vt mezclar, componer; concertar. —a compuesto. —n compuesto, m; mixtura, f. **c. interest,** interés compuesto, m

comprehend /‚kɒmprɪ'hɛnd/ vt comprender

comprehensible /‚kɒmprɪ'hɛnsəbəl/ a comprensible

comprehensibly /‚kɒmprɪ'hɛnsəbli/ adv comprensiblemente

comprehension /‚kɒmprɪ'hɛnʃən/ n comprensión, f

comprehensive /‚kɒmprɪ'hɛnsɪv/ a comprensivo

comprehensiveness /‚kɒmprɪ'hɛnsɪvnɪs/ n alcance, m, extensión, f

compress / v kəm'prɛs; n 'kɒmprɛs/ vt comprimir; condensar; reducir, abreviar. —n compresa, f

compression /kəm'prɛʃən/ n compresión, f

compressor /kəm'prɛsər/ n compresor, m

comprise /kəm'praiz/ vt comprender, abarcar, incluir

compromise /'kɒmprə‚maiz/ n compromiso, m, transacción, f; componenda, f. —vt (settle) componer, arreglar; (jeopardize) arriesgar; comprometer. —vi transigir. **to c. oneself,** comprometerse

compromising /'kɒmprə‚maizɪŋ/ a comprometedor

compulsion /kəm'pʌlʃən/ n compulsión, fuerza, f. **under c.,** a la fuerza

compulsory /kəm'pʌlsəri/ a obligatorio. **c. measures,** medidas obligatorias, f pl. **c. powers,** poderes absolutos, m pl

compunction /kəm'pʌŋkʃən/ n compunción, f, remordimiento, m; escrúpulo, m. **without c.,** sin escrúpulo

computable /kəm'pyutəbəl/ a calculable

computation /ˌkɒmpyu'teiʃən/ n computación, f, cómputo, m

compute /kəm'pyut/ vt computar, calcular.

computer /kəm'pyutər/ m computador, m (Western Hemisphere), ordenador, m (Spain)

computer center n centro calculador, centro de computación, m

comrade /'kɒmræd/ n camarada, mf compañero (-ra)

comradeship /'kɒmrædˌʃɪp/ n compañerismo, m

con /kɒn/ vt estudiar; leer con atención; Naut. gobernar (el buque)

concatenation /kɒnˌkætŋ'eiʃən/ n concatenación, f

concave /kɒn'keiv/ a cóncavo

conceal /kən'sil/ vt esconder, ocultar; (the truth, etc.) encubrir, callar; disimular

concealed /kən'sild/ a oculto; escondido; disimulado. **c. lighting,** iluminación indirecta, f. **c. turning,** (on a road) viraje oculto, m

concealment /kən'silmənt/ n ocultación, f; encubrimiento, m; (place of) escondite, m; secreto, m

concede /kən'sid/ vt conceder

conceit /kən'sit/ n presunción, vanidad, fatuidad, f, envanecimiento, m. **to have a good c. of oneself,** estar pagado de sí mismo

conceited /kən'sitɪd/ a presumido, fatuo, vanidoso

conceivable /kən'sivəbəl/ a concebible, imaginable

conceivably /kən'sivəbli/ adv posiblemente

conceive /kən'siv/ vt concebir; (affection, etc.) tomar; (an idea, etc.) formar; (plan) formular, idear. —vi concebir; (understand) comprender; (suppose) imaginar, suponer

concentrate /'kɒnsənˌtreit/ vt concentrar. —vi concentrarse; (on, upon) dedicarse (a), entregarse (a); prestar atención (a), concentrar atención (en)

concentrated /'kɒnsənˌtreitɪd/ a concentrado

concentration /ˌkɒnsən'treiʃən/ n concentración, f. **c. camp,** campo de concentración, m

concentric /kən'sentrɪk/ a concéntrico

concept /'kɒnsept/ n concepto, m

conception /kən'sepʃən/ n concepción, f; conocimiento, m; idea, f, concepto, m. **to have not the remotest c. of,** no tener la menor idea de

conceptualism /kən'septʃuəˌlɪzəm/ n conceptualismo, m

concern /kən'sɜrn/ vt tocar, tener que vercon, importar, concernir; interesar; referirse (a); tratar (de); (trouble) preocupar, inquietar; (take part in) ocuparse (de or con). —n asunto, m, cosa, f; (share) interés, m; (anxiety) inquietud, f; solicitud, f; (business) casa comercial, firma, f. **as concerns...,** en cuanto a..., respecto a... **It concerns the date of the next meeting,** Es cuestión de la fecha de la próxima reunión. **It is no c. of yours,** No tiene nada que ver contigo. **The book is concerned with the adventures of two boys,** El libro trata de las aventuras de dos muchachos

concerned /kən'sɜrnd/ a ocupado (en); afectado; (in a crime) implicado (en); (troubled) preocupado; inquieto, agitado

concerning /kən'sɜrnɪŋ/ prep tocante a, con respecto a, referente a, sobre

concert /'kɒnsərt/ n acuerdo, concierto, m, armonía, f; Mus. concierto, m, vt concertar, acordar. **in c. with,** de acuerdo con. **c. hall,** sala de conciertos, f

concerted /kən'sɜrtɪd/ a concertado

concertina /ˌkɒnsər'tinə/ n concertina, f

concerto /kən'tʃɛrtou/ n concierto, m

concession /kən'sɛʃən/ n concesión, f; privilegio, m

concessionaire /kənˌsɛʃə'nɛər/ n concesionario, m

concierge /ˌkɒnsi'ɛərʒ/ n conserje, m

conciliate /kən'sɪliˌeit/ vt conciliar

conciliation /kənˌsɪli'eiʃən/ n conciliación, f

conciliatory /kən'sɪliəˌtɔri/ a conciliador

concise /kən'sais/ a conciso, breve, sucinto

concisely /kən'saisli/ adv concisamente

concision /kən'sɪʒən/ n concisión, f

conclave /'kɒnkleiv/ n conciliábulo, m; (of cardinals) conclave, m

conclude /kən'klud/ vt concluir. —vi concluirse

conclusion /kən'kluʒən/ n conclusión, f. **in c.,** en conclusión, para terminar. **to come to the c. that...,** concluir que...

conclusive /kən'klusɪv/ a conclusivo, concluyente, decisivo

conclusively /kən'klusɪvli/ adv concluyentemente

conclusiveness /kən'klusɪvnɪs/ n carácter decisivo, m, lo concluyente

concoct /kɒn'kɒkt/ vt confeccionar; inventar

concoction /kɒn'kɒkʃən/ n confección, f; mezcla, f; invención, f; (of a plot) maquinación, f

concomitant /kɒn'kɒmɪtənt/ a concomitante. —n concomitante, m

concord /'kɒnkɔrd/ n concordia, buena inteligencia, armonía, f; (Mus. Gram.) concordancia, f; (of sounds) armonía, f

concordance /kɒn'kɔrdns/ n concordia, armonía, f; (book) concordancias, f pl

concordat /kɒn'kɔrdæt/ n concordato, m

concourse /'kɒnkɔrs/ n concurrencia, muchedumbre, f

concrete /'kɒnkrit/ a concreto; de hormigón. —n hormigón, m. —vt concretar; cubrir de hormigón. **reinforced c.,** hormigón armado, m

concretion /kɒn'kriʃən/ n concreción, f

concubine /'kɒŋkyəˌbain/ n concubina, manceba, f

concur /kən'kɜr/ vi coincidir, concurrir; estar de acuerdo, convenir (en)

concurrence /kən'kɜrəns/ n (agreement) acuerdo, consentimiento, m, aprobación, f

concurrent /kən'kɜrənt/ a concurrente; unánime; coincidente

concurrently /kən'kɜrəntli/ adv concurrentemente

concussion /kən'kʌʃən/ n concusión, f; Med. concusión cerebral, f

condemn /kən'dem/ vt condenar; censurar, culpar; (forfeit) confiscar. **condemned cell,** celda de los condenados a muerte, f

condemnation /ˌkɒndem'neiʃən/ n condenación, f; censura, f

condensation /ˌkɒnden'seiʃən/ n condensación, f

condense /kən'dens/ vt condensar. —vi condensarse

condenser /kən'densər/ n (Elec. Mech. Chem.) condensador, m

condescend /ˌkɒndə'send/ vi dignarse; (in a bad sense) consentir (en); (with affability) condescender

condescending /ˌkɒndə'sendɪŋ/ a condescendiente

condescendingly /ˌkɒndə'sendɪŋli/ adv con condescendencia

condescension /ˌkɒndə'senʃən/ n condescendencia, f; afabilidad, f

condign /kən'dain/ a condigno

condiment /'kɒndəmənt/ n condimento, m

condition /kən'dɪʃən/ n condición, f; estado, m; pl **conditions,** condiciones, f pl; circunstancias, f pl. on **c. that,** con tal que; siempre que, dado que. **to be in no c. to,** no estar en condiciones de. **to change one's c.,** cambiar de estado. **to keep oneself in c.,** mantenerse en buena forma

conditional /kən'dɪʃənl/ a condicional. **to be c. on,** depender de

conditionally /kən'dɪʃənli/ adv condicionalmente

conditioned /kən'dɪʃənd/ a acondicionado. **c. reflex,** reflejo acondicionado, m

condole /kən'doul/ vi condolerse (de); (on a bereavement) dar el pésame

condolence /kən'douləns/ n condolencia, f. **to present one's condolences,** dar el pésame

condom /'kɒndəm/ n condón, m

condone /kən'doun/ vt condonar, perdonar

conduce /kən'dus/ vi contribuir, conducir

conducive /kən'dusɪv/ a que contribuye, conducente; favorable

conduct /n 'kɒndʌkt; v kən'dʌkt/ n conducta, f. —vt conducir; guiar; Mus. dirigir; (oneself) portarse, con-

ducirse; *Phys.* conducir. —*vi Mus.* dirigir (una orquesta, etc.); *Phys.* ser conductor. **conducted tour,** excursión acompañada, *f;* viaje acompañado, *m*
conduction /kən'dʌkʃən/ *n* conducción, *f*
conductive /kən'dʌktɪv/ *a* conductivo
conductivity /ˌkɒndʌk'tɪvɪti/ *n* conductibilidad, *f*
conductor /kən'dʌktər/ *n* (guide) guía, *mf;* (of an orchestra) director, *m;* (on a tram, etc.) cobrador, *m; Phys.* conductor, *m*
conduit /'kɒnduɪt/ *n* conducto, *m;* cañería, *f;* canal, *m*
cone /koun/ *n* (*Bot. Geom.* etc.) cono, *m*
confabulation /kənˌfæbyə'leɪʃən/ *n* confabulación, *f*
confection /kən'fɛkʃən/ *n* confección, *f, vt* confeccionar
confectioner /kən'fɛkʃənər/ *n* confitero (-ra); pastelero (-ra)
confectionery /kən'fɛkʃəˌnɛri/ *n* confitería, pastelería, repostería, *f*
confederate / *a, n* kən'fɛdərɪt; *v* -'fɛdəˌreit/ *a* confederado; aliado. —*n* confederado, *m;* (in crime) cómplice, *mf.* —*vt* confederar. —*vi* confederarse; aliarse
confederation /kənˌfɛdə'reɪʃən/ *n* confederación, *f*
confer /kən'fɜr/ *vt* conceder, conferir; (an honor, etc.) otorgar, investir (con). —*vi* consultar (con); deliberar, considerar
conference /'kɒnfərəns/ *n* conferencia, consulta, *f;* conversación, *f*
conferment /kən'fɜrmənt/ *n* otorgamiento, *m;* concesión, *f*
confess /kən'fɛs/ *vt* confesar, reconocer; *Inf.* admitir; (of a priest) confesar; (of a penitent) confesarse. —*vi* hacer una confesión; (one's sins) confesarse. **I c. that I was surprised,** No puedo negar que me sorprendió
confessed /kən'fɛst/ *a* confesado, declarado
confession /kən'fɛʃən/ *n* confesión, *f;* reconocimiento, *m;* declaración, *f;* religión, *f;* (creed) credo, *m.* **to go to c.,** confesarse. **to hear a c.,** confesar (a)
confessional /kən'fɛʃənl/ *n* confesionario, *m*
confessor /kən'fɛsər/ *n* confesor, *m*
confetti /kən'fɛti/ *n pl* confeti, papel picado *m,* serpentina, *f*
confidant /'kɒnfɪˌdænt/ *n* confidente, *m*
confidante /ˌkɒnfɪ'dænt/ *n* confidente, *m*
confide /kən'faɪd/ *vi* confiar (a or en). —*vt* confiar
confidence /'kɒnfɪdəns/ *n* confianza, *f;* seguridad, *f;* (revelation) confidencia, *f.* **in c.,** en confianza. **over-c.,** presunción, *f.* **to have c. in,** tener confianza en. **c. man,** caballero de industria, estafador, *m.* **c. trick,** timo, *m*
confident /'kɒnfɪdənt/ *a* confiado; seguro; (conceited) presumido
confidential /ˌkɒnfɪ'dɛnʃəl/ *a* confidencial; de confianza. **c. clerk,** empleado (-da) de confianza. **c. letter,** carta confidencial
confidentially /ˌkɒnfɪ'dɛnʃəli/ *adv* en confianza, confidencialmente
confidently /'kɒnfɪdəntli/ *adv* confiadamente
confiding /kən'faɪdɪŋ/ *a* confiado
confidingly /kən'faɪdɪŋli/ *adv* con confianza
configuration /kənˌfɪgyə'reɪʃən/ *n* configuración, *f*
confine /kən'faɪn/ *vt* limitar; (imprison) encerrar. **confined space,** espacio limitado, *m.* **to be confined,** (of a woman) estar de parto, parir. **to be confined to one's room,** no poder dejar su cuarto. **to c. oneself to,** limitarse a
confinement /kən'faɪnmənt/ *n* encierro, *m,* prisión, *f;* reclusión, *f;* (of a woman) parto, *m.* **to suffer solitary c.,** estar incomunicado
confines /'kɒnfaɪnz/ *n pl* límites, *m pl;* confines, *m pl;* fronteras, *f pl*
confirm /kən'fɜrm/ *vt* confirmar; corroborar; *Eccl.* confirmar
confirmation /ˌkɒnfər'meɪʃən/ *n* confirmación, *f;* (of a treaty) ratificación, *f; Eccl.* confirmación, *f*
confirmatory /kən'fɜrməˌtɔri/ *a* confirmatorio
confirmed /kən'fɜrmd/ *a* inveterado
confiscate /'kɒnfəˌskeit/ *vt* confiscar
confiscation /ˌkɒnfə'skeiʃən/ *n* confiscación, *f*

conflagration /ˌkɒnflə'greiʃən/ *n* conflagración, *f,* incendio, *m*
conflict / *n* 'kɒnflɪkt; *v* kən'flɪkt/ *n* conflicto, *m;* lucha, *f.* —*vi* estar opuesto (a), estar en contradicción (con)
conflicting /kən'flɪktɪŋ/ *a* opuesto; incompatible; (of evidence) contradictorio
confluence /'kɒnfluəns/ *n* confluencia, *f*
conform /kən'fɔrm/ *vt* ajustar, conformar. —*vi* ajustarse (a), amoldarse (a); conformarse (a); adaptarse (a)
conformation /ˌkɒnfɔr'meiʃən/ *n* conformación, *f*
conformity /kən'fɔrmɪti/ *n* conformidad, *f.* **in c. with,** en conformidad con, con arreglo a
confound /kɒn'faund/ *vt* confundir. **C. it!** ¡Demonio!
confounded /kɒn'faundɪd/ *a* perplejo; *Inf.* maldito
confraternity /ˌkɒnfrə'tɜrnɪti/ *n* cofradía, hermandad, *f*
confront /kən'frʌnt/ *vt* hacer frente (a), afrontar; salir al paso; confrontar
Confucianism /kən'fyuʃəˌnɪzəm/ *n* el confucianismo, *m*
confuse /kən'fyuz/ *vt* turbar, aturdir; confundir (con); (the issue) obscurecer; (disconcert) desconcertar, dejar confuso (a); dejar perplejo (a). **You have confused one thing with another,** Has confundido una cosa con otra. **My mind was confused,** Mis ideas eran confusas; Tenía la cabeza trastornada
confused /kən'fyuzd/ *a* confuso
confusing /kən'fyuzɪŋ/ *a* turbador; desconcertante. **It is all very c.,** Todo ello es muy difícil de comprender
confusion /kən'fyuʒən/ *n* confusión, *f.* **covered with c.,** confuso, avergonzado. **to be in c.,** estar confuso; estar en desorden
confute /kən'fyut/ *vt* (a person) confundir; (by evidence) refutar, confutar
congeal /kən'dʒil/ *vt* congelar; (blood) coagular. —*vi* congelarse, helarse; coagularse
congealment /kən'dʒilmənt/ *n* congelación, *f;* (of blood) coagulación, *f*
congenial /kən'dʒinyəl/ *a* (of persons) simpático; propicio, favorable; agradable
congenital /kən'dʒɛnɪtl/ *a* congénito
congest /kən'dʒɛst/ *vt* atestar; amontonar; *Med.* congestionar
congested /kən'dʒɛstɪd/ *a Med.* congestionado; (of places) atestado de gente; de mayor población, concurrido. **c. area,** área de mayor densidad de población, *f*
congestion /kən'dʒɛstʃən/ *n Med.* congestión, *f;* densidad del tráfico, *f;* mayor densidad de población, *f*
conglomerate /kən'glɒmərɪt/ *a* conglomerado. —*n* conglomerado, *m*
conglomeration /kənˌglɒmə'reiʃən/ *n* conglomeración, *f*
congratulate /kən'grætʃəˌleit/ *vt* felicitar, dar la enhorabuena (a); congratular
congratulation /kənˌgrætʃə'leiʃən/ *n* felicitación, enhorabuena, *f;* congratulación, *f*
congratulatory /kən'grætʃələˌtɔri/ *a* de felicitación, congratulatorio
congregate /'kɒŋgrɪˌgeit/ *vi* congregarse, reunirse, juntarse
congregation /ˌkɒŋgrɪ'geiʃən/ *n* congregación, *f;* asamblea, reunión, *f;* (in a church) fieles, *m pl;* (parishioners) feligreses, *m pl*
congress /'kɒŋgrɪs/ *n* congreso, *m.* **C.-man,** miembro del Congreso, *m*
conical /'kɒnɪkəl/ *a* cónico
conifer /'kounəfər/ *n* conífera, *f*
coniferous /kou'nɪfərəs/ *a* conífero
conjectural /kən'dʒɛktʃərəl/ *a* conjetural
conjecture /kən'dʒɛktʃər/ *n* conjetura, *f, vt* conjeturar
conjoint /kən'dʒɔɪnt/ *a* asociado, conjunto
conjointly /kən'dʒɔɪntli/ *adv* juntamente, en común
conjugal /'kɒndʒəgəl/ *a* conyugal
conjugate /'kɒndʒəˌgeit/ *vt* conjugar. —*vi* conjugarse
conjugation /ˌkɒndʒə'geiʃən/ *n* conjugación, *f*
conjunction /kən'dʒʌŋkʃən/ *n* conjunción, *f.* **in c. with,** de acuerdo con

conjunctive /kən'dʒʌŋktɪv/ a conjuntivo. —n conjunción, f

conjunctivitis /kən,dʒʌŋktə'vaitɪs/ n conjuntivitis, f

conjure /'kɒndʒər/ vt (implore) rogar, suplicar. —vi (juggle) hacer juegos de manos. **a name to c. with,** un nombre todopoderoso. **to c. up,** (spirits) conjurar; Fig. evocar

conjurer, conjuror /'kɒndʒərər/ n (magician) nigromante, m; prestidigitador, m. **conjuror's wand,** varilla de virtudes, f

conjuring /'kɒndʒərɪŋ/ n prestidigitación, f, juegos de manos, m pl. **c. trick,** juego de manos, m. **c. up,** evocación, f

connect /kə'nɛkt/ vt juntar, unir; (relate) relacionar; asociar; (Elec. and Mech.) conectar. —vi juntarse, unirse; relacionarse; asociarse; (of events) encadenarse; (of trains) enlazar. **This train connects with the Madrid express,** Este tren enlaza con el expreso de Madrid. **They are connected with the Borgia family,** Están emparentados con los Borgia, Son parientes de los Borgia

connected /kə'nɛktɪd/ a conexo; (coherent) coherente; relacionado; asociado; (in a crime) implicado; (by marriage, etc.) emparentado

connectedly /kə'nɛktɪdli/ adv coherentemente

connecting /kə'nɛktɪŋ/ a que une; (Mech. and Elec.) conectivo; (of doors, etc.) comunicante. **c.-link,** Mech. varilla de conexión, f; Fig. lazo, m. **c.-rod,** biela, f

connection /kə'nɛkʃən/ n conexión, f; unión, f; (of ideas) relación, f; (junction) empalme, m; (of trains, boats) enlace, m; (intimacy) intimidad, f; (relative) pariente, m; (of a firm, etc.) clientela, f; Elec. conexión, f. **in c. with,** con referencia a; en asociación con. **in this c.,** respecto a esto

conning tower /'kɒnɪŋ/ n torre de mando, f

connivance /kə'naivəns/ n consentimiento, m; complicidad, f

connive (at) /kə'naiv/ vi hacer la vista gorda, ser cómplice (en)

connotation /,kɒnə'teiʃən/ n connotación, f

connote /kə'nout/ vt connotar

connubial /kə'nubiəl/ a conyugal

conquer /'kɒŋkər/ vt conquistar; vencer. —vi triunfar

conquering /'kɒŋkərɪŋ/ a conquistador, vencedor; triunfante, victorioso

conqueror /'kɒŋkərər/ n conquistador, m; vencedor, m

conquest /'kɒnkwɛst/ n conquista, f. **to make a c. of,** conquistar

consanguineous /,kɒnsæŋ'gwɪniəs/ a consanguíneo

consanguinity /,kɒnsæŋ'gwɪniti/ n consanguinidad, f

conscience /'kɒnʃəns/ n conciencia, f. **in all c.,** en verdad. **with a clear c.,** con la conciencia limpia. **c.-stricken,** lleno de remordimientos

conscienceless /'kɒnʃənslɪs/ a desalmado, falto de conciencia

conscientious /,kɒnʃi'enʃəs/ a concienzudo; diligente. **c. objector,** objetor de conciencia, m

conscientiously /,kɒnʃi'enʃəsli/ adv concienzudamente

conscientiousness /,kɒnʃi'enʃəsnɪs/ n conciencia, diligencia, f; rectitud, f

conscious /'kɒnʃəs/ a consciente. —n Psychol. consciente, m. **to become c.,** (after unconsciousness) volver en sí. **to become c. of,** darse cuenta de

consciously /'kɒnʃəsli/ adv conscientemente, a sabiendas

consciousness /'kɒnʃəsnɪs/ n conciencia, f; conocimiento, sentido, m. **to lose c.,** perder el conocimiento, perder el sentido. **to recover c.,** recobrar el sentido, volver en sí

conscript / n 'kɒnskrɪpt; v kən'skrɪpt/ n conscripto, m, a conscripto. —vt reclutar

conscription /kən'skrɪpʃən/ n conscripción, f

consecrate /'kɒnsɪ,kreit/ vt consagrar; bendecir

consecration /,kɒnsɪ'kreiʃən/ n consagración, f; dedicación, f

consecutive /kən'sɛkyətɪv/ a consecutivo

consecutively /kən'sɛkyətɪvli/ adv consecutivamente

consensus /kən'sɛnsəs/ n consenso, m, unanimidad, f. **c. of opinion,** opinión general, f

consent /kən'sɛnt/ vi consentir. —n consentimiento,

m; permiso, m, aquiescencia, f. **by common c.,** de común acuerdo

consequence /'kɒnsɪ,kwɛns/ n consecuencia, f; resultado, m; importancia, f, **in c.,** por consiguiente. **in c. of,** de resultas de. **of no c.,** sin importancia

consequences /'kɒnsɪ,kwɛnsɪz/ n (game) cartas rusas, f pl

consequent /'kɒnsɪ,kwɛnt/ a consecuente, consiguiente

consequential /,kɒnsɪ'kwɛnʃəl/ a consecuente; (of persons) fatuo, engreído

consequently /'kɒnsɪ,kwɛntli/ adv por consiguiente, en consecuencia

conservation /,kɒnsər'veiʃən/ n conservación, f. **c. of energy,** conservación de energía, f

conservatism /kən'sɜrvə,tɪzəm/ n conservadurismo, m

conservative /kən'sɜrvətɪv/ a preservativo; conservador. —n conservador (-ra). **c. party,** partido conservador, m

conservatoire /kən,sɜrvə'twɑr/ n conservatorio de música, m

conservatory /kən'sɜrvə,tɔri/ n invernáculo, invernadero, m

conserve /kən'sɜrv/ vt conservar

consider /kən'sɪdər/ vt considerar, pensar meditar; tomar en cuenta; examinar; (deem) juzgar; (believe) creer, estar convencido de (que); (of persons) considerar. **all things considered,** considerando todos los puntos, después de considerarlo todo

considerable /kən'sɪdərəbəl/ a considerable

considerably /kən'sɪdərəbli/ adv considerablemente

considerate /kən'sɪdərɪt/ a considerado, solícito

considerately /kən'sɪdərɪtli/ adv con consideración, solícitamente

consideration /kən,sɪdə'reiʃən/ n consideración, f; reflexión, deliberación, f; remuneración, f. **out of c. for,** en consideración de; por consideración a. **to take into c.,** tomar en cuenta, tomar en consideración

considered /kən'sɪdərd/ a considerado

considering /kən'sɪdərɪŋ/ prep en consideración de, considerando, en vista de

consign /kən'sain/ vt consignar; Fig. enviar. **to c. to oblivion,** sepultar en el olvido

consignee /,kɒnsai'ni/ n consignatario, m

consignment /kən'sainmənt/ n consignación, f; envío, m

consignor /kən'sainər/ n consignador, m

consist /kən'sɪst/ vi consistir (en); ser compatible (con). **to c. of,** componerse de, consistir de

consistence, consistency /kən'sɪstəns; kən'sɪstənsi/ n consistencia, f; compatibilidad, f; lógica, f; (of persons) consecuencia, f

consistent /kən'sɪstənt/ a compatible; lógico; (of persons) consecuente

consistently /kən'sɪstəntli/ adv conformemente (a); consecuentemente

consolation /,kɒnsə'leiʃən/ n consuelo, m, consolación, f

console /'kɒnsoul/ vt consolar; confortar. —n Archit. cartela, f. **c. table,** consola, f

consolidate /kən'sɒlɪ,deit/ vt consolidar. —vi consolidarse

consolidation /kən,sɒlɪ'deiʃən/ n consolidación, f

consoling /kən'soulɪŋ/ a consolador; confortador

consols /'kɒnsɒlz, kən'sɒlz/ n pl (títulos) consolidados, m pl

consonance /'kɒnsənəns/ n consonancia, f

consonant /'kɒnsənənt/ a consonante

consort / n 'kɒnsɔrt, v kən'sɔrt/ n consorte, mf. **to c. with,** frecuentar la compañía de; ir con; acompañar (a). **prince c.,** príncipe consorte, m

conspicuous /kən'spɪkyuəs/ a conspicuo; prominente; notable. **to be c.,** destacarse; llamar la atención. **to make oneself c.,** ponerse en evidencia, llamar la atención

conspicuously /kən'spɪkyuəsli/ adv visiblemente; muy en evidencia

conspiracy /kən'spɪrəsi/ n conspiración, f; complot, m

conspirator /kən'spɪrətər/ n conspirador (-ra)

conspire /kən'spaiər/ vi conspirar

constable /'kɒnstəbəl/ n agente de policía, m; (historical) condestable, m. **chief c.,** jefe de policía, m
constabulary /kən'stæbyə,lɛri/ n policía, f
constancy /'kɒnstənsi/ n constancia, f
constant /'kɒnstənt/ a constante; incesante. —n constante, m
Constantinople /,kɒnstæntn̩'oupəl/ Constantinopla, f
constantly /'kɒnstəntli/ adv constantemente
constellation /,kɒnstə'leiʃən/ n constelación, f
consternation /,kɒnstər'neiʃən/ n consternación, f; espanto, terror, m
constipate /'kɒnstə,peit/ vt estreñir
constipation /,kɒnstə'peiʃən/ n estreñimiento, m, constipación de vientre, f
constituency /kən'stɪtʃuənsi/ n distrito electoral, m
constituent /kən'stɪtʃuənt/ a constituyente. —n constituyente, m; componente, m; elector (-ra)
constitute /'kɒnstɪ,tut/ vt constituir; nombrar; autorizar
constitution /,kɒnstɪ'tuʃən/ n constitución, f
constitutional /,kɒnstɪ'tuʃən/ a constitucional
constitutionally /,kɒnstɪ'tuʃənl̩i/ adv constitucionalmente
constrain /kən'strein/ vt obligar, forzar. **I felt constrained to help them,** Me sentí obligado a ayudarles
constrained /kən'streind/ a (of smiles, etc.) forzado; (of silences) violento; (of persons) avergonzado
constraint /kən'streint/ n fuerza, compulsión, f; (of atmosphere) tensión, f; (reserve) reserva, f; vergüenza, f
constrict /kən'strɪkt/ vt apretar, estrechar
constriction /kən'strɪkʃən/ n constricción, f
construct /kən'strʌkt/ vt edificar; construir
construction /kən'strʌkʃən/ n construcción, f; interpretación, f. **to put a wrong c. on,** interpretar mal
constructional /kən'strʌkʃənl/ a construccional
constructive /kən'strʌktɪv/ a constructor
constructor /kən'strʌktər/ n constructor, m
construe /kən'stru/ vt construir; (translate) traducir; Fig. interpretar
consul /'kɒnsəl/ n cónsul, m
consular /'kɒnsələr/ a consular
consular fees n pl derechos consulares, m pl
consulate /'kɒnsəlɪt/ n consulado, m. **c. general,** consulado general, m
consult /kən'sʌlt/ vt consultar. —vi consultar (con), aconsejarse (con)
consultant /kən'sʌltənt/ n (Med. and other uses) especialista, m
consultation /,kɒnsəl'teiʃən/ n consulta, f
consultative /kən'sʌltətɪv/ a consultativo
consulting /kən'sʌltɪŋ/ a consultor. **c. hours,** horas de consulta, f pl. **c. rooms,** consultorio, m
consume /kən'sum/ vt consumir; (eat) comerse, tragarse. —vi consumirse. **to be consumed by envy,** estar consumido por la envidia. **to be consumed by thirst,** estar muerto de sed
consumer /kən'sumər/ n consumidor (-ra)
consummate / a 'kɒnsəmɪt; v -,meit/ a consumido, perfecto. —vt consumar
consummation /,kɒnsə'meiʃən/ n consumación, f
consumption /kən'sʌmpʃən/ n consumo, m; gasto, m; Med. tuberculosis, f. **fuel c.,** consumo de combustible, m
consumptive /kən'sʌmptɪv/ a destructivo; Med. tísico, hético. —n tísico (-ca)
contact /'kɒntækt/ n contacto, m, vt ponerse en contacto con. **to be in c. with,** estar en contacto con
contagion /kən'teidʒən/ n contagio, m
contagious /kən'teidʒəs/ a contagioso
contain /kən'tein/ vt contener; incluir; Geom. encerrar; (arithmetic) ser divisible por; (oneself) dominarse. **I could not c. myself,** No pude dominarme
container /kən'teinər/ n recipiente, m; envase, m; (box) caja, f
contaminate /kən'tæmə,neit/ vt contaminar; corromper
contamination /kən,tæmə'neiʃən/ n contaminación, f
contemplate /'kɒntəm,pleit/ vt contemplar; meditar, considerar; (plan) tener intención de, pensar, proponerse

contemplation /,kɒntəm'pleiʃən/ n contemplación, f; meditación, f; expectación, esperanza, f; (plan) proyecto, m. **to have something in c.,** proyectar algo
contemplative /kən'templətɪv/ a contemplativo
contemplatively adv contemplativamente; atentamente
contemporaneous /kən,tɛmpə'reiniəs/ a contemporáneo
contemporary /kən'tɛmpə,rɛri/ a contemporáneo; (of persons) coetáneo; (of events, etc.) actual. —n contemporáneo (-ea)
contempt /kən'tɛmpt/ n desprecio, menosprecio, m; desdén, m. **c. of court,** falta de respeto a la sala, f
contemptible /kən'tɛmptəbəl/ a menospreciable, despreciable; vil
contemptibly /kən'tɛmptəbli/ adv vilmente
contempt of court n rebeldía a la corte, f
contempt of law n rebeldía a la ley, f
contemptuous /kən'tɛmptʃuəs/ a desdeñoso; despectivo; de desprecio. **to be c. of,** desdeñar; menospreciar, tener en poco (a)
contemptuously /kən'tɛmptʃuəsli/ adv con desprecio, desdeñosamente
contend /kən'tɛnd/ vi contender; (affirm) sostener, mantener. **He contended that...,** Sostuvo que...; **contending party,** Law. parte litigante, f
content / n 'kɒntɛnt; a, v kən'tɛnt/ n contenido, m; capacidad, f; (emotion) contento, m; satisfacción, f. —a contento; satisfecho (de). —vt contentar; satisfacer. **to one's heart's c.,** a pedir de boca; a gusto de uno; cuanto quisiera
contented /kən'tɛntɪd/ a satisfecho, contento
contentedly /kən'tɛntɪdli/ adv con satisfacción, contentamente
contention /kən'tɛnʃən/ n disputa, controversia, discusión, f; argumento, m, opinión, f
contentious /kən'tɛnʃəs/ a contencioso
contentment /kən'tɛntmənt/ n contentamiento, m; contento, m
contest / v kən'tɛst; n 'kɒntɛst/ vt disputar; (a suit) defender; (a match, an election, etc.) disputar. —n disputa, f; combate, m, lucha, f; (competition) concurso, m
contestant /kən'tɛstənt/ n contendiente, mf
context /'kɒntɛkst/ n contexto, m
contiguity /,kɒntɪ'gyuɪti/ n contigüidad, f
contiguous /kən'tɪgyuəs/ a contiguo, lindero, adyacente
continence /'kɒntn̩əns/ n continencia, f
continent /'kɒntn̩ənt/ a continente. —n continente, m
continental /,kɒntn̩'ɛntl/ a continental
continental shelf n plataforma continental, f
contingency /kən'tɪndʒənsi/ n contingencia, f
contingent /kən'tɪndʒənt/ a contingente. —n Mil. contingente, m. **to be c. on,** (of events) depender de
continual /kən'tɪnyuəl/ a continuo
continually /kən'tɪnyuəli/ adv continuamente
continuance /kən'tɪnyuəns/ n continuación, f
continuation /kən,tɪnyu'eiʃən/ n continuación, f; prolongación, f
continue /kən'tɪnyu/ vi continuar; seguir; prolongarse; durar. —vi continuar; seguir; proseguir; perpetuar; (in an office) retener. **to be continued,** se continuará, continuará, seguirá
continuer /kən'tɪnyuər/ n continuador (-ra)
continuity /,kɒntn̩'yuɪti/ n continuidad, f
continuous /kən'tɪnyuəs/ a continuo. **c. performance,** sesión continua, f
continuously /kən'tɪnyuəsli/ adv de continuo, continuamente
contort /kən'tɔrt/ vt retorcer
contortion /kən'tɔrʃən/ n contorsión, f
contortionist /kən'tɔrʃənɪst/ n contorsionista, m
contour /'kɒntʊr/ n contorno, m; curva de nivel, f. **c. map,** mapa con curvas de nivel, m
contraband /'kɒntrə,bænd/ n contrabando, m
contrabandist /'kɒntrə,bændɪst/ n contrabandista, mf
contrabass /'kɒntrə,beis/ n contrabajo, m
contraception /,kɒntrə'sɛpʃən/ n anticoncepción, f
contraceptive /,kɒntrə'sɛptɪv/ n anticonceptivo, m

contract /n 'kɒntrækt; v kən'trækt/ n pacto, m; (Com. and Law.) contrato, m; (betrothal) esponsales, m pl; (marriage) capitulaciones, f pl; (cards) "Bridge," m. —vt contraer; (acquire) adquirir, contraer; (a marriage, etc.) contraer; (be betrothed to) desposarse con; (by formal contract) contratar; pactar. —vi (shrink) contraerse, encogerse; comprometerse por contrato. **breach of c.,** no cumplimiento de contrato, m. **c. party,** (of matrimony) contrayente, mf

contractile /kən'træktl/ a contráctil

contraction /kən'trækʃən/ n contracción, f (act or process); forma contracta, f (like isn't or can't)

contractor /'kɒntræktər/ n contratista, mf

contradict /ˌkɒntrə'dɪkt/ vt contradecir; desmentir

contradiction /ˌkɒntrə'dɪkʃən/ n contradicción, f; negación, f

contradictory /ˌkɒntrə'dɪktəri/ a contradictorio; opuesto (a), contrario (a)

contralto /kən'træltou/ n (voice) contralto, m; (woman) contralto, f

contraption /kən'træpʃən/ n Inf. artefacto, m

contrapuntal /ˌkɒntrə'pʌntl/ a Mus. de contrapunto

contrariness /'kɒntrerinɪs/ n Inf. testarudez, terquedad, f

contrariwise /'kɒntreri,waiz/ adv al contrario; al revés

contrary /'kɒntreri/ a contrario; opuesto (a); desfavorable, poco propicio; (of persons) difícil, terco. —n contraria, f; (logic) contrario, m, adv en contra, contrariamente. **on the c.,** al contrario. **to be c.,** (of persons) llevar la contraria

contrast /n 'kɒntræst; v kən'træst/ n contraste, m. —vt contrastar (con). —vi contrastar (con), hacer contraste (con)

contravene /ˌkɒntrə'vin/ vt contravenir; atacar, oponerse (a)

contravention /ˌkɒntrə'vɛnʃən/ n contravención, f

contribute /kən'trɪbyut/ vt contribuir; (an article) escribir

contribution /ˌkɒntrə'byuʃən/ n contribución, f; (to a review, etc.) artículo, m

contributor /kən'trɪbyətər/ n contribuyente, mf; (to a journal) colaborador (-ra)

contributory /kən'trɪbyə,tɔri/ a contribuyente

contrite /kən'trait/ a penitente, arrepentido, contrito

contritely /kən'traitli/ adv contritamente

contrition /kən'trɪʃən/ n contrición, penitencia, f, arrepentimiento, m

contrivance /kən'traivəns/ n invención, f; (scheme) treta, idea, estratagema, f; (machine) aparato, mecanismo, artefacto, m

contrive /kən'traiv/ vt inventar; idear, proyectar. —vi (succeed in) lograr, conseguir; (manage) arreglárselas

control /kən'troul/ n autoridad, f; dominio, m; gobierno, m; dirección, f; regulación, f; (restraint) freno, m; (Biol. and Spirit.) control, m; (of a vehicle) conducción, f; manejo, m, manipulación, f; pl **controls,** Mech. mando, m. —vt dirigir, regir; regular; usar, manejar, manipular; controlar; (dominate) dominar; (curb) refrenar, reprimir; (command) mandar. **He lost c. of the car,** Perdió el mando (or control) del automóvil. **out of c.,** fuera de mando, fuera de control. **remote c.,** mando a distancia, m. **to c. oneself,** dominarse, contenerse. **to lose c. of oneself,** no lograr dominarse, perder el control. **c. stick,** Aer. palanca de mando, f. **c. tower,** Aer. torre de mando, f

controller /kən'troulər/ n interventor, m; (device) regulador, m

controlling /kən'troulɪŋ/ n See **control.** a regulador

controversial /ˌkɒntrə'vərʃəl/ a debatible, discutible

controversy /'kɒntrə,vərsi/ n controversia, f; argumento, m; altercación, disputa, f

contumacious /ˌkɒntu'meiʃəs/ a contumaz

contumacy /'kɒntuməsi/ n contumacia, f

contumely /'kɒntuməli/ n contumelia, f

contusion /kən'tuʒən/ n herida contusa, f

conundrum /kə'nʌndrəm/ n acertijo, rompecabezas, m; problema, m

convalesce /ˌkɒnvə'lɛs/ vi convalecer, estar convaleciente

convalescence /ˌkɒnvə'lɛsəns/ n convalecencia, f

convalescent /ˌkɒnvə'lɛsənt/ a convaleciente. —n convaleciente, mf. **c. home,** casa de convalecencia, f

convene /kən'vin/ vt (a meeting) convocar; (person) citar. —vi reunirse

convenience /kən'vinyəns/ n conveniencia, f; (comfort) comodidad, f; utilidad, f; (advantage) ventaja, f; (public) retretes, m pl. **at one's c.,** cuando le sea conveniente a uno. **to make a c. of,** abusar de. **with all modern conveniences,** con todo el confort moderno

convenient /kən'vinyənt/ a conveniente; apropiado; cómodo. **I shall make it c. to see him at 6 p.m.,** Arreglaré mis asuntos para verle a las seis

conveniently /kən'vinyəntli/ adv cómodamente; oportunamente; sin inconveniente

convent /'kɒnvent/ n convento, m

convention /kən'vɛnʃən/ n convención, f

conventional /kən'vɛnʃənl/ a convencional

conventual /kən'vɛntʃuəl/ a conventual. —n conventual, m

converge /kən'vərdʒ/ vi convergir

convergence /kən'vərdʒəns/ n convergencia, f

convergent /kən'vərdʒənt/ a convergente

conversance /kən'vərsəns/ n familiaridad, f, conocimiento, m

conversant /kən'vərsənt/ a familiar, versado, conocedor. **c. with,** versado en

conversation /ˌkɒnvər'seiʃən/ n conversación, f. **to engage in c. with,** entablar conversación con

conversational /ˌkɒnvər'seiʃənl/ a de conversación; (talkative) locuaz

conversationally /ˌkɒnvər'seiʃənli/ adv en tono familiar; familiarmente; en conversación

converse /kən'vərs/ vi conversar. **to c. by signs,** hablar por señas

conversely /kən'vərsli/ adv recíprocamente

conversion /kən'vərʒən/ n conversión, f

convert /v kən'vərt; n 'kɒnvərt/ vt convertir; transformar. —n converso (-sa). **to become a c.,** convertirse

convertible /kən'vərtəbəl/ a convertible; transformable

convex /a kɒn'vɛks; n 'kɒnvɛks/ a convexo

convey /kən'vei/ vt transportar; conducir, llevar; (a meaning, etc.) comunicar, dar a entender; expresar; Law. traspasar

conveyance /kən'veiəns/ n transporte, m; conducción, f; medio de transporte, m; vehículo, m; carruaje, m; (of property) traspaso, m; (document) escritura de traspaso, f. **public c.,** coche de alquiler, m; ómnibus, m

convict /n 'kɒnvɪkt; v kən'vɪkt/ n convicto, m; presidiario, m. —vt Law. condenar; culpar. **c. settlement,** colonia penal, f

conviction /kən'vɪkʃən/ n (of a prisoner) condenación, f; (belief) convencimiento, m, convicción, f

convince /kən'vɪns/ vt convencer

convincing /kən'vɪnsɪŋ/ a convincente

convivial /kən'vɪviəl/ a convivial

conviviality /kən,vɪvi'æliti/ n jovialidad, f

convocation /ˌkɒnvə'keiʃən/ n convocación, f

convoke /kən'vouk/ vt convocar

convolution /ˌkɒnvə'luʃən/ n circunvolución, f; espira, f

convoy /'kɒnvɔi/ vt convoyar, escoltar. —n convoy, m. **to sail in a c.,** navegar en convoy

convulse /kən'vʌls/ vt agitar; sacudir; estremecer. **to be convulsed with laughter,** desternillarse de risa, morirse de risa

convulsion /kən'vʌlʃən/ n convulsión, f; conmoción, f

convulsive /kən'vʌlsɪv/ a convulsivo

coo /ku/ vi arrullar; (of infants) gorjearse. —n arrullo, m

cooing /'kuɪŋ/ n arrullo, m

cook /kʊk/ n cocinero (-ra). —vt guisar, cocer, cocinar; (falsify) falsear

cooker /'kʊkər/ n cocina, f. **gas c.,** cocina de gas, f

cookery /'kʊkəri/ n cocina, f. **c.-book,** libro de cocina, m

cooking /'kʊkɪŋ/ n arte de guisar, m, or f; cocina, f;

(of accounts, etc.) falsificación, *f.* **c. range,** cocina económica, *f.* **c.-stove,** cocina, *f.* **c. utensils,** batería de cocina, *f*

cool /kul/ *a* fresco; bastante frío; (not ardent and of receptions, etc.) frío; (calm) sereno, imperturbable. —*n* fresco, *m.* —*vi* enfriarse; (of love, etc.) resfriarse; (of the weather) refrescar; (of persons) refrescarse. —*vt* refrescar; enfriar. **to grow cooler,** (of weather) refrescarse; (of persons) tener menos calor. **It is c.,** Hace fresco. **to be as c. as a cucumber,** tener sangre fría. **c. drink,** bebida fría, *f.* **c.-headed,** sereno, imperturbable

coolie /'kuli/ *n* culí, *m*

cooling /'kulɪŋ/ *n* enfriamiento, *m, a* refrescante

coolly /'kuli/ *adv* frescamente; fríamente, con frialdad; imperturbablemente; (impudently) descaradamente

coolness /'kulnɪs/ *n* frescura, *f;* (of a welcome, etc.) frialdad, *f;* (sangfroid) sangre fría, serenidad, *f;* aplomo, *m*

coop /kup/ *n* gallinero, *m;* caponera, *f, vt* enjaular; encerrar. **to keep** (someone) **cooped up,** tener encerrado (a)

cooper /'kupər/ *n* tonelero, barrilero, *m, vt* hacer barriles

cooperate /kou'ppə,reit/ *vi* cooperar; colaborar

cooperation /kou,ppə'reifən/ *n* cooperación, *f*

cooperative /kou'ppərətɪv/ *a* cooperativo. **c. society,** cooperativa, *f*

coopt /kou'ppt/ *vt* elegir por votación

coordinate /*v* kou'ɔrdn̩,eit; *n, a* kou'ɔrdn̩ɪt/ *vt* coordinar. —*n Math.* coordenada, *f.* —*a* coordenado

coordination /kou,ɔrdn̩'eifən/ *n* coordinación, *f*

coot /kut/ *n* fúlica, *f*

cop /kɒp/ *n* (police officer) chapa (Ecuador), polizonte, *mf*

copartner /kou'pɑrtnər/ *n* copartícipe, *mf;* socio (-ia)

cope /koup/ *n Eccl.* capa, *f;* (of heaven) dosel, *m,* bóveda, *f.* **to c. with,** contender con; (a difficulty) hacer cara a, arrostrar

copeck /'koupɛk/ *n* copec, *m*

Copenhagen /,koupən'heigən, -'hagən/ Copenhague, *m*

Copernican /kou'pɜrnɪkən/ *a* copernicano

copier /'kɒpiər/ *n* copiador (-ra)

coping /'koupɪŋ/ *n Archit.* albardilla, *f.* **c.-stone,** teja cumbrera, *f; Fig.* coronamiento, *m*

copious /'koupiəs/ *a* copioso, abundante

copiously /'koupiəsli/ *adv* en abundancia

copiousness /'koupiəsnɪs/ *n* abundancia, *f*

copper /'kɒpər/ *n* cobre, *m;* (coin) calderilla, *f;* (vessel) caldera, *f.* —*a* de color. **c.-colored,** cobrizo. **c.-smith,** calderero, *m.* **c.-sulphate,** sulfato de cobre, *m*

copperplate /'kɒpər,pleit/ *n* lámina de cobre, *f;* grabado en cobre, *m*

coppery /'kɒpəri/ *a* cobrizo

coppice /'kɒpɪs/ *n* soto, bosquecillo, *m.* **c. with standards,** monte medio, *m*

coproprietor /,kouprə'praitər/ *n* copropietario, *m*

copse /kɒps/ *n* arboleda, *f,* bosquecillo, *m*

Coptic /'kɒptɪk/ *a* cóptico, copto. —*n* (language) copto, cóptico, *m*

copulate /'kɒpyə,leit/ *vi* copularse

copulation /,kɒpyə'leifən/ *n* cópula, *f*

copy /'kɒpi/ *n* copia, *f;* (of a book) ejemplar, *m;* (of a paper) número, *m;* manuscrito, *m;* (subject-matter) material, *m.* —*vt* copiar; imitar; tomar como modelo (a). **rough c.,** borrador, *m.* **c.-book,** cuaderno de escritura, *m*

copy editor *n* redactor de textos, *m*

copying /'kɒpiɪŋ/ *n* imitación, *f;* transcripción, *f.* **c. ink,** tinta de copiar, *f*

copyist /'kɒpiɪst/ *n* copiador (-ra); (plagiarist) copiante, *mf*

copyright /'kɒpi,rait/ *n* derechos de autor, *m pl;* propiedad literaria, *f.* **c.** protegido por los derechos de autor. —*vt* registrar como propiedad literaria. **C. reserved,** Derechos reservados, Queda hecho el depósito que marca la ley

copywriter /'kɒpi,raitər/ *n* escritor de anuncios, *m*

coquet /kou'kɛt/ *vi* coquetear; *Fig.* jugar (con)

coquetry /'koukɪtri/ *n* coquetería, *f*

coquette /kou'kɛt/ *n* coqueta, *f*

coquettish /kou'kɛtɪʃ/ *a* coquetón; atractivo

coral /'kɒrəl/ *n* coral, *m;* (polyp) coralina, *f.* —*a* de coral, coralino. **white c.,** madrépora, *f.* **c. beads,** corales, *m pl.* **c.-island,** atolón, *m.* **c.-reef,** escollo de coral, *m.* **c. snake,** coral, *f*

corbel /'kɔrbəl/ *n Archit.* ménsula, *f*

cord /kɔrd/ *n* cuerda, *f;* cordel, *m;* cordón, *m.* —*vt* encordelar. **spinal c.,** médula espinal, *f.* **umbilical c.,** cordón umbilical, *m*

cordial /'kɔrdʒəl/ *a* cordial; sincero, fervoroso. —*n* cordial, *m*

cordiality /kɔr'dʒælɪti/ *n* cordialidad, *f*

cordon /'kɔrdn̩/ *n* cordón, *m;* cinto, *m.* **to c. off,** acordonar

Cordova /'kɔrdəvə/ Córdoba, *f*

cordovan /'kɔrdəvən/ *a* cordobés. —*n* (leather) cordobán, *m*

corduroy /'kɔrdə,rɔi/ *n* pana de cordoncillo, *f*

core /kɔr/ *n* (of a fruit) corazón, *m;* (of a rope) alma, *f,* centro, *m;* (of an abscess) foco, *m;* (of a corn) ojo, *m; Fig.* núcleo, *m;* esencia, *f;* lo esencial

coreligionist /,kourɪ'lɪdʒənɪst/ *n* correligionario (-ia)

corespondent /,kourɪ'spɒndənt/ *n* cómplice en un caso de divorcio, *mf*

Corinth /'kɔrɪnθ/ Corinto, *m*

Corinthian /kə'rɪnθiən/ *a* corintio. —*n* corintio (-ia)

cork /kɔrk/ *n* corcho, *m;* (of a bottle) tapón, *m, a* de corcho. —*vt* tapar con corcho, taponar; (wine) encorchar; (the face) tiznar con corcho quemado. **pop of a c.,** taponazo, *m.* **to draw a c.,** descorchar. **c.-jacket,** chaleco salvavidas, *m.* **c. tree,** alcornoque, *m*

corkscrew /'kɔrk,skru/ *n* sacacorchos, *m*

cormorant /'kɔrmərənt/ *n* cormorán, *m*

corn /kɔrn/ *n* grano, cereal, *m;* (wheat) trigo, *m;* (maize) maíz, *m;* (single seed) grano, *m;* (on the foot, etc.) callo, *m.* **Indian c.,** maíz, *m.* **c. cure,** callicida, *m.* **c.-exchange,** bolsa de granos, *f.* **c.-field,** campo de trigo, *m*

cornea /'kɔrniə/ *n* córnea, *f*

corner /'kɔrnər/ *n* ángulo, *m;* (of a street or building) esquina, *f;* (of a room) rincón, *m; Auto.* viraje, *m; Com.* monopolio, *m;* (of the eye) rabo, *m;* (Assoc. football) "corner," *m.* —*vt* arrinconar; acorralar; *Com.* acaparar. **the four corners of the earth,** las cinco partes del mundo. **a tight c.,** un lance apretado, un apuro. **to drive into a c.,** *Fig.* poner entre la espada y la pared. **to look out of the c. of the eye,** mirar de reojo. **to turn ̦the c.,** doblar la esquina; *Fig.* pasar la crisis. **c.-cupboard,** rinconera, *f.* **c. seat,** asiento del rincón, *m.* **c.-stone,** piedra angular, *f*

cornered /'kɔrnərd/ *a* (of a person) acorralado, en aprieto; (of hats) de... picos. **three-c. hat,** sombrero de tres picos, *m*

cornet /kɔr'nɛt/ *n* (musical instrument) corneta, *f; Mil.* corneta, *m;* (paper) cucurucho, *m.* **c. player,** cornetín, *m*

cornflour /'kɔrn,flauər/ *n* harina de maíz, *f*

cornice /'kɔrnɪs/ *n* cornisa, *f*

Cornish /'kɔrnɪʃ/ *a* de Cornualles

cornucopia /,kɔrnə'koupiə/ *n* cornucopia, *f*

corollary /'kɔrə,lɛri/ *n* corolario, *m*

corona /kə'rounə/ *n* (*Astron. Archit.*) corona, *f*

coronation /,kɔrə'neifən/ *n* coronación, *f*

coroner /'kɔrənər/ *n* juez de guardia, *mf,* médico forense, *m*

coronet /,kɔrə'nɛt/ *n* (of a peer, etc.) corona, *f;* tiara, *f;* guirnalda, *f*

corporal /'kɔrpərəl/ *a* corporal, *n Mil.* cabo, *m;* (altar-cloth) corporal, *m.* **c. punishment,** castigo corporal, *m*

corporate /'kɔrpərɪt/ *a* corporativo

corporation /,kɔrpə'reifən/ *n* corporación, *f;* concejo, cabildo municipal, *m;* (*Com.* U.S.A.) sociedad anónima, *f*

corporeal /kɔr'pɔriəl/ *a* corpóreo

corps /kɔr/ *n* cuerpo, *m*

corpse /kɔrps/ *n* cadáver, *m*

corpulence /'kɔrpyələns/ *n* gordura, obesidad, *f*

corpulent /'kɔrpyələnt/ *a* corpulento, grueso, gordo

corpus /'kɔrpəs/ *n* cuerpo, *m*. **C. Christi,** Corpus, *m*. **c. delicti,** cuerpo del delito, *m*

corpuscle /'kɔrpəsəl/ *n* corpúsculo, *m*

correct /kə'rekt/ *a* correcto; exacto, justo. —*vt* corregir; rectificar; amonestar, reprender

correction /kə'rekʃən/ *n* corrección, *f*; rectificación, *f*

corrective /kə'rektɪv/ *a* correctivo. —*n* correctivo, *m*

correctness /kə'rektnɪs/ *n* corrección, *f*; exactitud, *f*; justicia, *f*

correlate /'kɔrə,leit/ *vt* poner en correlación. —*vi* tener correlación

correlation /,kɔrə'leiʃən/ *n* correlación, *f*

correspond /,kɔrə'spɒnd/ *vi* corresponder (a); (by letter) escribirse, corresponderse

correspondence /,kɔrə'spɒndəns/ *n* correspondencia, *f*; *Com.* correo, *m*. **c. course,** curso por correspondencia, *m*

correspondent /,kɔrə'spɒndənt/ *n* correspondiente, *mf*; (*Com.* and journalist) corresponsal, *mf.* **special c.,** corresponsal extraordinario, *m*

corresponding /,kɔrə'spɒndɪŋ/ *a* correspondiente. **c. member,** miembro correspondiente, *m*

corridor /'kɔridər/ *n* corredor, pasillo, *m*; (railway) pasillo, *m*; *Polit.* corredór, *m*. **c. train,** tren con coches corridos, *m*

corroborate /kə'rɒbə,reit/ *vt* corroborar, confirmar

corroboration /kə,rɒbə'reiʃən/ *n* corroboración, confirmación, *f*

corroborative /kə'rɒbə,reitɪv/ *a* corroborativo, confirmatorio

corrode /kə'roud/ *vt* corroer, morder; *Fig.* roer

corrosion /kə'rouʒən/ *n* corrosión, *f*

corrosive /kə'rousɪv/ *a* corrosivo; mordaz

corrugate /'kɔrə,geit/ *vt* arrugar. —*vi* arrugarse

corrugated /'kɔrə,geitɪd/ *a* arrugado; ondulado. **c. iron,** chapa canaleta, *f*

corrugation /,kɔrə'geiʃən/ *n* corrugación, *f,* arrugamiento, *m*

corrupt /kə'rʌpt/ *a* corrompido; vicioso, desmoralizado. —*vt* corromper. —*vi* corromperse

corrupter /kə'rʌptər/ *n* corruptor (-ra)

corruption /kə'rʌpʃən/ *n* corrupción, *f*

corsage /kɔr'sɑʒ/ *n* corpiño, *m*

corset /'kɔrsɪt/ *n* corsé, *m, vt* encorsetar. **c. shop,** corsetería, *f*

Corsica /'kɔrsɪkə/ Córcega, *f*

Corsican /'kɔrsɪkən/ *a* corso. —*n* corso (-sa)

cortege /kɔr'tɛʒ/ *n* séquito, acompañamiento, *m;* desfile, *m*

cortex /'kɔrteks/ *n* *Bot. Anat.* corteza, *f*

cortisone /'kɔrtə,zoun/ *n* (drug) cortisona, *f*

Corunna /kə'runyə/ La Coruña, *f*

coruscation /,kɔrə'skeiʃən/ *n* brillo, *m*

corvette /kɔr'vet/ *n* corbeta, *f*

cosignatory /kou'sɪgnə,tɔri/ *n* cosignatario (-ia)

cosine /'kousain/ *n* coseno, *m*

cosiness /'kouzinɪs/ *n* comodidad, *f*

cosmetic /kɒz'metɪk/ *a* cosmético. —*n* afeite, cosmético, *m*

cosmic /'kɒzmɪk/ *a* cósmico

cosmographer /kɒz'mɒgrəfər/ *n* cosmógrafo, *m*

cosmography /kɒz'mɒgrəfi/ *n* cosmografía, *f*

cosmopolitan /,kɒzmə'pɒlitn/ *a* cosmopolita. —*n* cosmopolita, *mf*

cosmopolitanism /,kɒzmə'pɒlitn,izəm/ *n* cosmopolitismo, *m*

cosmos /'kɒzməs/ *n* cosmos, universo, *m*

Cossack /'kɒsæk/ *a* cosaco. —*n* cosaco (-ca)

cosset /'kɒsit/ *vt* mimar, consentir

cost /kɔst/ *vi* costar. —*n* costa, *f,* coste, precio, *m*; *Fig.* costa, *f*; *pl* **costs,** *Law.* costas, *f pl*. **at all costs,** cueste lo que cueste, a toda costa. **to my c.,** a mi costa. **c. of living,** coste de la vida, *m*. **to c. a fortune,** costar un sentido

Costa Rican /'kɒstə'rikən/ *a* costarriqueño. —*n* costarriqueño (-ña)

coster /'kɒstər/ *n* vendedor (-ra) ambulante

costliness /'kɒstlinɪs/ *n* alto precio, *m*; suntuosidad, *f*

costly /'kɒstli/ *a* costoso; suntuoso, magnífico

costume /'kɒstum/ *n* traje, *m*; (fancy-dress) disfraz,

m; (tailored) traje sastre, *m*; **"Costume,"** (among credits in films and plays) «Vestuario»

costumier /,kɒstu'miər/ *n* modista, *mf*; sastre, *m*

cot /kɒt/ *n* (hut) choza, cabaña, *f*; (child's) camita, *f*

coterie /'koutəri/ *n* círculo, grupo, *m*; (clique) camarilla, *f*

cotillion /kə'tilyən/ *n* cotillón, *m*

cottage /'kɒtidʒ/ *n* cabaña, choza, *f*; casita, *f*; hotelito, *m*; torre, villa, *f*

cotter /'kɒtər/ *n* chaveta, llave, *f*

cotton /'kɒtn/ *n* algodón, *m, a* de algodón. **I don't c. to the idea at all,** No me gusta nada la idea; La idea no me seduce. **sewing-c.,** hilo de coser, *m*. **c. goods,** géneros de algodón, *m pl*. **c. mill,** hilandería de algodón, algodonería, *f*. **c. plantation,** algodonal, *m*. **c.-seed oil,** aceite de semilla de algodón, *m*. **c.-spinner,** hilandero (-ra) de algodón. **c.-wool,** algodón en rama, *m*. **c.-yarn,** hilo de algodón, *m*

cottony /'kɒtni/ *a* algodonoso

couch /kautʃ/ *n* sofá, canapé, *m*; (bed) lecho, *m*; (lair) cama, *f*. —*vt* (lay down) acostar, echar; (a lance) enristrar; (express) expresar, redactar. —*vi* acostarse; (crouch) agacharse; estar en acecho

cough /kɔf/ *vi* toser. —*n* tos, *f*. **to c. up,** escupir, expectorar. **c.-drop,** pastilla para la tos, *f*

coughing /'kɔfɪŋ/ *n* tos, *f*

could /kud/. See **can**

council /'kaunsəl/ *n* consejo, *m*; junta, *f*; *Eccl.* concilio, *m*. **Privy C.,** consejo privado, *m*. **C. of the Realm,** Concejo del Reino, *m*. **to hold c.,** celebrar un consejo; aconsejarse (con); consultarse. **town c.,** ayuntamiento, *m*. **c. chamber,** sala consistorial, *f*; sala de actos, *f*. **c. houses,** casas baratas, *f pl*. **c. of war,** consejo de guerra, *m*

councilor /'kaunsələr/ *n* concejal, *m*; miembro de la junta, *m*

counsel /'kaunsəl/ *n* consultación, *f*; deliberación, *f*; consejo, *m*; *Law.* abogado, *m*. —*vt* aconsejar. **a c. of perfection,** un ideal imposible. **to keep one's own c.,** no decir nada, callarse, guardar silencio. **to take c. with,** consultar (a), aconsejarse con

counselor /'kaunsələr/ *n* consejero, *m*. **c. of state,** consejero de estado, *m*

count /kaunt/ *vt* contar; calcular; (consider) creer, considerar. —*vi* contar. —*n* cuenta, *f*; (of votes) escrutinio, *m*; *Law.* capítulo, *m*. **John simply doesn't c.,** Juan no cuenta para nada. **Erudition alone counts for very little,** La mera erudición sirve para muy poco. **to keep c. of,** tener cuenta de. **to lose c. of,** perder cuenta de. **to c. on,** contar con; (doing something) esperar. **to c. up,** contar

count /kaunt/ *n* (title) conde, *m*

countenance /'kauntnəns/ *n* semblante, *m*; expresión de la cara, *f*; aspecto, *m*; (favor) apoyo, *m,* ayuda, *f*. —*vt* autorizar, aprobar; apoyar, ayudar. **to put (a person) out of c.,** desconcertar (a)

counter /'kauntər/ *n* (in a bank) contador, *m*; (in a shop) mostrador, *m*; (in games) ficha, *f, adv* contra, al contrario (a). —*a* opuesto (a), contrario (a). —*vt* parar; contestar. **to run c. to my inclinations,** oponerse a mis deseos. **to c. with the left,** (boxing) contestar con la izquierda. **c.-attack,** contraataque, *m*. **c.-attraction,** atracción contraria, *f*. **c.-offensive,** contraofensiva, *f*. **c.-reformation,** contrarreforma, *f*. **c.-revolution,** contrarrevolución, *f*

counteract /,kauntər'ækt/ *vt* neutralizar; frustrar

counterbalance /'kauntər,bæləns/ *n* contrapeso, *m, vt* contrabalancear; compensar, igualar

counterblast /'kauntər,blæst/ *n* denunciación, *f*; respuesta, *f*

countercharge /'kauntər,tʃardʒ/ *n* recriminación, *f*. —*vt* recriminar; *Law.* reconvenir

counterfeit /'kauntər,fit/ *a* falso, espurio; fingido. —*n* falsificación, *f*; imitación, *f*; moneda falsa, *f*; (person) impostor (-ra). —*vt* imitar; (pretend) fingir; (coins, handwriting, etc.) falsificar

counterfeiter /'kauntər,fitər/ *n* falsario (-ia)

counterfoil /'kauntər,fɔil/ *n* talón, *m*

countermand /v ,kauntər'mænd; n 'kauntər,mænd/ *vt* contramandar; (an order) revocar, cancelar. —*n* contraorden, *f*; revocación, *f*

countermarch /'kauntər,mɑrtʃ/ *n* contramarcha, *f*

countermeasure /'kauntər‚mɛʒər/ n contramedida, f
counterpane /'kauntər‚pein/ n sobrecama, colcha, f
counterpart /'kauntər‚part/ n contraparte, f; (of a document) duplicado, m
counterplot /'kauntər‚plɒt/ n contratreta, f
counterpoint /'kauntər‚pɔint/ n Mus. contrapunto, m
counterpoise /'kauntər‚pɔiz/ n contrapeso, m; equilibrio, m, vt contrabalancear, contrapesar
countersign /'kauntər‚sain/ n contraseña, f, vt refrendar
countess /'kauntɪs/ n condesa, f
counting /'kauntɪŋ/ n cuenta, f; numeración, f; (of votes) escrutinio, m. **c.-house,** contaduría, f
countless /'kauntlɪs/ a innumerable. **a c. number,** un sinfín, un sinnúmero
countrified /'kʌntrə‚faid/ a rústico, campesino
country /'kʌntri/ n país, m; (fatherland) patria, f; región, campiña, tierra, f; (as opposed to town) campo, m. —a del campo; campesino, campestre, rústico. **He lives in the c.,** Vive en el campo. **c. club,** club campestre, m. **c. cousin,** provinciano (-na). **c.-dance,** baile campestre, m. **c. gentleman,** hacendado, m. **c. girl,** campesina, f; aldeana, f. **c.-house,** finca, f; casa de campo, f. **c. life,** vida del campo, f. **c.-seat,** finca, f
countryman /'kʌntrimən/ n campesino, m; hombre del campo, m; compatriota, m
countryside /'kʌntri‚said/ n campo, m; campiña, f
countrywoman /'kʌntri‚wumən/ n campesina, f; compatriota, f
county /'kaunti/ n condado, m; provincia, f. **c. council,** diputación provincial, f. **c. town,** cabeza de partido, f; ciudad provincial, f
county seat n cabecera municipal, cabeza de partido, m
coup /ku/ n golpe, m. **c. d'état,** golpe de estado, m
coupe /kup/ n cupé, m
couple /'kʌpəl/ n par, m; (in a dance, etc.) pareja, f. —vt enganchar, acoplar; (in marriage) casar; (animals) aparear; (ideas) asociar; (names) juntar. **the young (married) c.,** el matrimonio joven
couplet /'kʌplɪt/ n copla, f
coupling /'kʌplɪŋ/ n enganche, acoplamiento, m; (of railway carriages) enganche, m; (of ideas) asociación, f
coupon /'kupɒn/ n talón, m; cupón, m
courage /'kɜrɪdʒ/ n valor, m. **C.!** ¡Ánimo! **to muster up c.,** cobrar ánimo
courageous /kə'reidʒəs/ a valiente
courageously /kə'reidʒəsli/ adv valientemente
courier /'kʌriər/ n correo, m, estafeta, f; (guide) guía, m; (newspaper) estafeta, f
course /kɔrs/ n curso, m; (of time) transcurso, m; (of events) marcha, f; (of a river, etc.) cauce, m; (of stars) carrera, f, curso, m; (of a ship) derrota, f, rumbo, m; (way) camino, m, ruta, f; (of conduct) línea de conducta, f; actitud, f; (of study) curso, m; (of a meal) plato, m; (of an illness) desarrollo, m; Med. tratamiento, m. **He took it as a matter of c.,** Lo tomó sin darle importancia. **in due c.,** a su tiempo debido. **in the c. of time,** andando el tiempo, en el transcurso de los años. **of c.,** claro está; naturalmente. **Are you coming tomorrow? Of c.!** ¿Vienes mañana? ¡Ya lo creo! **the best c. to take,** lo mejor que se puede hacer, el mejor plantamiento, m
course /kɔrs/ vt cazar, perseguir; Poet. correr por, cruzar. —vi (of blood, etc.) correr; cazar
court /kɔrt/ n (yard) patio, m; (tennis) campo de tenis, m; (fives, racquets) cancha, f; (royal) corte, f; (of justice) tribunal, m; (following) séquito, acompañamiento, m. —vt hacer la corte (a); cortejar, pretender; solicitar; (sleep) conciliar. **to pay c. to,** (a woman) galantear, pretender; (a person) hacer la rueda (a). **to respect the c.,** guardar sala a. **c. of appeal,** sala de apelación, f. **c. of justice,** sala de justicia, f; tribunal de justicia, m. **supreme c.,** tribunal supremo, m. **c.-card,** figura, f. **c.-dress,** traje de corte, m. **c. house,** palacio de justicia, m. **c. jester,** bufón, m. **c.-martial,** tribunal militar, m. **c.-plaster,** tafetán inglés, tafetán de heridas, m. **c.-room,** sala de justicia, f
courteous /'kɜrtiəs/ a cortés

courteousness /'kɜrtiəsnɪs/ n cortesía, f
courtesan /'kɔrtəzən/ n cortesana, f
courtesy /'kɜrtəsi/ n cortesía, f; favor, m, merced, f; permiso, m
courtier /'kɔrtiər/ n cortesano, palaciego, m
courtliness /'kɔrtlinɪs/ n cortesía, urbanidad, f; dignidad, f; elegancia, f
courtly /'kɔrtli/ a cortés, galante; digno; elegante
courtship /'kɔrtʃɪp/ n noviazgo, m; galanteo, m
courtyard /'kɔrt‚yard/ n patio, m
cousin /'kʌzən/ n primo (-ma). **first c.,** primo (-ma) carnal. **second c.,** primo (-ma) segundo (-da)
cove /kouv/ n cala, abra, ensenada, f
covenant /'kʌvənənt/ n contrato, m; estipulación, f; pacto, m; alianza, f. —vt prometer; estipular
Coventry, to send to, /'kʌvəntri/ hacer el vacío (a)
cover /'kʌvər/ vt cubrir; abrigar; (dissemble) disimular; (a distance) recorrer; (comprise) comprender, abarcar; (with confusion, etc.) llenar (de); (with a revolver, etc.) amenazar (con); (an overdraft, etc.) garantizar; (of stallions) cubrir; (of a hen and eggs) empollar; (a story, journalism) investigar. —n cubierta, f; (for a chair, umbrella, etc.) funda, f; (of a saucepan, jar, etc.) tapa, f; (dish-cover) tapadera, f; (of a book) cubierta, tapa, f; (of a letter) sobre, m; (shelter) abrigo, m; protección, f; (undergrowth) maleza, f; Fig. velo, manto, m; (pretence) pretexto, m; Com. garantía, f. **outer c.,** (of tire) cubierta de neumático, f. **to c. oneself with glory,** cubrirse de gloria. **to c. up,** cubrir completamente; (with clothes) arropar; (wrap up) envolver. **to c. with a revolver,** amenazar con un revólver. **to read a book from c. to c.,** leer un libro del principio al fin. **to take c.,** refugiarse, tomar abrigo. **under c.,** bajo tejado; al abrigo
cover charge n consumo mínimo, precio del cubierto, m
covering /'kʌvərɪŋ/ n cubrimiento, m; cubierta, f; envoltura, f; capa, f, abrigo, m. **c. letter,** carta adjunta, f
coverlet /'kʌvərlɪt/ n colcha, sobrecama, f
covert /a 'kouvərt; n 'kʌvərt/ a oculto; furtivo. —n guarida, f
covertly /'kouvərtli/ adv secretamente, furtivamente
covet /'kʌvɪt/ vt codiciar; ambicionar, suspirar por
covetous /'kʌvɪtəs/ a codicioso; ávido; ambicioso
covetously /'kʌvɪtəsli/ adv codiciosamente; ávidamente
covetousness /'kʌvɪtəsnɪs/ n codicia, avaricia, f; avidez, f; ambición, f
cow /kau/ vt intimidar, acobardar
cow /kau/ n vaca, f; (of other animals) hembra, f. **c.-bell,** cencerro, m, zumba, f. **c.-catcher,** Auto. salvavidas, m. **c.-hide,** cuero, cuero de vaca, zurriago, m; penca, f. **c.-house,** establo, m, boyera, f. **c.-pox,** vacuna, f
coward /'kauərd/ n cobarde, m, a cobarde
cowardice /'kauərdɪs/ n cobardía, f
cowardly /'kauərdli/ a cobarde
cowboy /'kau‚bɔi/ n vaquero, m; gaucho, "cowboy," m
cower /'kauər/ vi no saber dónde meterse; temblar, acobardarse
cowherd /'kau‚hɜrd/ n vaquero, boyero, m
cowl /kaul/ n capucha, f; (of a chimney) sombrerete, m
cowlike /'kau‚laik/ a de vaca; bovino
coworker /'kou‚wɜrkər, kou'wɜr-/ n colaborador (-ra)
cowshed /'kau‚ʃed/ n establo, m
cowslip /'kauslɪp/ n prímula, f
cox /kɒks/ n timonel, m
coxcomb /'kɒks‚koum/ n (of a jester) gorra de bufón, f; mequetrefe, m
coxswain /'kɒksən/ n patrón, m; (of a rowboat) timonel, m
coy /kɔi/ a modoso, tímido; coquetón
coyly /'kɔili/ adv tímidamente; con coquetería
coyness n timidez, modestia, f; coquetería, f
cozy /'kouzi/ a cómodo; agradable; caliente. **You are very c. here,** Estás muy bien aquí
crab /kræb/ n (sea) cangrejo de mar, cámbaro, m; (river) cangrejo, m; Astron. Cáncer, m. —vt (thwart)

frustrar. **hermit c.,** cangrejo ermitaño, *m.* **c.-apple,** manzana silvestre, *f.* **c.-louse,** ladilla, *f*

crabbed /'kræbɪd/ *a* áspero, hosco, desabrido, arisco; (of handwriting) apretado, metido

crack /kræk/ *vt* hender; quebrantar, romper; (nuts) cascar; (a whip and fingers) chasquear; (a bottle of wine) abrir. —*vi* (of earth, skin, etc.) agrietarse; romperse, quebrarse; (of the voice) romper; (of the male voice) mudar. —*n* hendedura, rendija, *f;* quebraja, *f;* (of a whip) chasquido, *m;* (of a rifle) estallido, *m;* (blow) golpe, garrotazo, *m, a* excelente, de primera categoría; estupendo. **to c. a joke,** decir un chiste. **to c. up,** *vt* dar bombo (a), alabar. —*vi* (in health) quebrantarse; (airplane) cuartearse, estrellarse. **c.-brained,** chiflado; estúpido, loco

cracked /krækt/ *a* grietado; (of a bell, etc.) hendido; (of the voice) cascada; (of a person) chiflado

cracker /'krækər/ *n* (firework) petardo, *m;* buscapiés, *m*

crackle /'krækəl/ *vi* (of burning wood, etc.) crepitar; (rustle) crujir; (of rifle fire) tirotear. —*n* crepitación, *f;* crujido, *m;* (of rifle fire) tiroteo, *m*

crackling /'kræklɪŋ/ *n.* See crackle; *Cul.* chicharrón, *m*

Cracow /'krækau/ Cracovia, *f*

cradle /'kreidl/ *n* cuna, *f;* Fig. niñez, infancia, *f;* (for a limb) arco de protección, *m;* (for winebottle) cesta, *f.* —*vt* mecer. **c.-song,** canción de cuna, *f*

craft /kræft/ *n* (guile) astucia, *f;* (skill) habilidad, *f;* arte, *mf;* (occupation) oficio manual, *m;* profesión, *f;* (guild) gremio, *m;* (boat) barco, *m,* embarcación, *f*

craftily /'kræftli/ *adv* astutamente

craftiness /'kræftinɪs/ *n* astucia, *f*

craftsman /'kræftsmən/ *n* artífice, *m;* arte sano, *m;* artista, *m*

craftsmanship /'kræftsmənˌʃɪp/ *n* arte, *m,* or *f;* habilidad, *f;* artificio, *m*

crafty /'kræfti/ *a* astuto, taimado

crag /kræg/ *n* peña, *f,* risco, despeñadero, *m*

cragginess /'kræginɪs/ *n* escabrosidad, aspereza, fragosidad, *f*

craggy /'krægi/ *a* escabroso, escarpado, peñascoso, riscoso

cram /kræm/ *vt* henchir; atestar; (one's mouth) llenar (de); (poultry) cebar; (a pupil) preparar para un examen; (a subject) empollar. —*vi* (with food) atracarse. **The room was crammed with people,** La sala estaba atestada de gente

cramp /kræmp/ *n* Med. calambre, *m;* (numbness) entumecimiento, *m;* (rivet) grapa, *f.* —*vt* dar calambre (a); (numb) entumecer; (fasten) lañar; (Fig. hamper) estorbar. **to c. someone's style,** cortar los vuelos (a). **writer's c.,** calambre del escribiente, *m*

cramped /kræmpt/ *a* (of space) apretado, estrecho; (of writing) menuda

cranberry /'kræn,beri/ *n* arándano, *m*

crane /krein/ *n* Ornith. grulla, *f;* (machine) grúa. *f.* **jib c.,** grúa de pescante, *f.* **travelling c.,** grúa móvil, *f.* **to c. one's neck,** estirar el cuello. **crane's bill,** pico de cigüeña, *m*

cranium /'kreiniəm/ *n* cráneo, *m*

crank /kræŋk/ *n* (handle) manivela, *f;* (person) maniático (-ca). —*vt* poner en marcha (un motor) con la manivela

crankiness /'kræŋkinɪs/ *n* (crossness) irritabilidad, *f,* mal humor, *m;* (eccentricity) excentricidad, *f*

cranky /'kræŋki/ *a* (cross) irritable, malhumorado; (eccentric) chiflado, maniático, excéntrico

cranny /'kræni/ *n* hendedura, grieta, *f*

crape /kreip/ *n* crespón, *m*

crash /kræʃ/ *vi* caer estrepitosamente; romperse; estallarse; (of aircraft, cars) estrellarse; Fig. hundirse, arruinarse. —*n* estrépito, estruendo, *m;* estallido, *m;* (of aircraft) accidente de aviación, *m;* (car) accidente, *m,* (or choque, *m)* de automóviles; (financial) ruina, *f; Fig.* hundimiento, *m.* **to c. into,** estrellarse contra, chocar con. **c. helmet,** casco, *m.* **c.-landing,** aterrizaje violento, *m*

crass /kræs/ *a* craso

crassness /'kræsnɪs/ *n* estupidez, *f*

crate /kreit/ *n* (box) caja de embalaje, *f;* (basket) canasto, *m,* banasta, *f*

crater /'kreitər/ *n* cráter, *m*

cravat /krə'væt/ *n* corbata, *f*

crave /kreiv/ *vt* suplicar, implorar. **to c. for,** perecer por, suspirar por, anhelar

craven /'kreivən/ *a* cobarde, pusilánime. —*n* poltrón, cobarde, *m*

craving /'kreivɪŋ/ *n* deseo vehemente, *m,* sed, *f*

crawfish /'krɔ,fiʃ/ *n* cangrejo de río, *m;* cigala, *f*

crawl /krɔl/ *vi* arrastrarse; andar a gatas; andar a paso de tortuga; (abase oneself) humillarse; (be full of) abundar (en). —*n* paso de tortuga, *m;* (swimming) arrastne *m*

crayfish /'krei,fiʃ/ *n* cangrejo de río, *m;* cigala, *f*

crayon /'kreion/ *n* carbón, *m;* pastel, *m;* (pencil) lápiz de color, *m.* —*vt* dibujar con pastel, etc. **c. drawing,** dibujo al carbón, *m*

craze /kreiz/ *vt* enloquecer, volver loco (a). —*n* manía, *f,* capricho, entusiasmo, *m;* (fashion) moda, *f*

crazily /'kreizəli/ *adv* locamente

craziness /'kreizinɪs/ *n* locura, *f*

crazy /'kreizi/ *a* loco; chiflado; (of structure) dilapidado. **He is c. about music,** Está loco por la música. **to be completely c.,** (of persons) ser un loco de atar; ser completamente loco. **to drive c.,** volver loco (a)

creak /krik/ *vi* (of shoes, chairs, etc.) crujir; (of gates, etc.) rechinar, chirriar. —*n* crujido, *m;* chirrido, *m*

creaking /'krikɪŋ/ *n.* See **creak**

creaky /'kriki/ *a* crujiente, que cruje; chirriador

cream /krim/ *n* crema, *f;* nata, *f; Fig.* flor, nata, *f.* —*a* de nata. **whipped c.,** nata batida, *f.* **c. cake,** pastel de nata, *m.* **c.-cheese,** queso de nata, *m.* **c.-colored,** de color crema. **c.-jug,** jarro para crema, *m.* **c. of tartar,** cremor, tártaro, *m*

creamery /'kriməri/ *n* lechería, *f*

creamy /'krimi/ *a* cremoso

crease /kris/ *n* (wrinkle) arruga, *f;* (fold) pliegue, *m;* (in trousers) raya, *f;* (in cricket) línea de la meta, *f.* —*vt* (wrinkle) arrugar; (fold) plegar; (trousers) poner la raya en. —*vi* arrugarse

create /kri'eit/ *vt* crear; (appoint) nombrar; (produce) suscitar, producir

creation /kri'eiʃən/ *n* creación, *f;* establecimiento, *m;* (appointment) nombramiento, *m*

creative /kri'eitɪv/ *a* creador; de la creación

creativeness /kri'eitɪvnɪs/ *n* facultad creativa, inventiva, *f*

creator /kri'eitər/ *n* creador (-ra)

creature /'kritʃər/ *n* criatura, *f;* animal, *m.* **c. comforts,** bienestar material, *m*

crèche /krɛʃ/ *n* casa cuna, *f*

credence /'kridns/ *n* crédito, *m,* fe, creencia, *f; Eccl.* credencia, *f.* **to give c. to,** dar crédito (a), creer

credentials /krɪ'dɛnʃəlz/ *n pl* credenciales, *f pl*

credibility /ˌkrɛdə'bɪlɪti/ *n* credibilidad, verosimilitud, *f*

credible /'krɛdəbəl/ *a* creíble, verosímil; (of persons) digno de confianza

credibly /'krɛdəbli/ *adv* creíblemente

credit /'krɛdɪt/ *n* crédito, *m;* reputación, *f;* honor, *m;* (Com. and banking) crédito, *m;* (in bookkeeping) data, *f.* —*vt* dar fe (a), dar crédito (a); creer; atribuir; (bookkeeping) acreditar. **It does them c.,** Les hace honor. **on c.,** a crédito, al fiado. **open c.,** Com. letra abierta, *f.* **to give on c.,** dar fiado. **c. balance,** haber, *m*

creditable /'krɛdɪtəbəl/ *a* loable, honroso, digno de alabanza

creditably /'krɛdɪtəbli/ *adv* honrosamente

creditor /'krɛdɪtər/ *n* acreedor (-ra); (bookkeeping) haber, *m*

credulity /krə'dulɪti/ *n* credulidad, *f*

credulous /'krɛdʒələs/ *a* crédulo

credulously /'krɛdʒələsli/ *adv* con credulidad, crédulamente

creed /krid/ *n* credo, *m*

creek /krik/ *n* caleta, abra, *f.*

creel /kril/ *n* (for fish) cesta de pescador, *f*

creep /krip/ *vi* arrastrarse; (of plants and birds) trepar; (of infants) andar a gatas; (totter) hacer pinitos; (slip) deslizarse; (cringe) lisonjear, rebajarse; (of one's flesh) sentir hormigueo. **to c. about on tiptoe,**

andar de puntillas. **to c. into a person's favor,** insinuarse en el favor de. **to c. in,** entrar sin ser notado (en); deslizarse en. **to c. on,** (of time) avanzar lentamente; (of old age, etc.) acercarse insensiblemente. **to c. out,** salir sin hacer ruido; escurrirse. **to c. up,** trepar por; subir a gatas

creeper /ˈkripər/ n *Bot.* enredadera, f; *Ornith.* trepador, m; *Zool.* reptil, m

creeping /ˈkripɪŋ/ a *Bot.* trepante; *Zool.* trepador; (servile) rastrero

cremate /ˈkrimeit/ vt incinerar

cremation /krɪˈmeiʃən/ n cremación, f

crematorium /ˌkriməˈtɔriəm/ n crematorio, m; horno de incineración, m, inhumadora, f

creole /ˈkrioul/ a criollo. —n criollo (-lla)

creolize /ˈkriəˌlaiz/ vt acriollar

crescent /ˈkresənt/ n media luna, f; *Herald.* creciente, m; calle en forma de semicírculo, f. —a en forma de media luna; *Poet.* creciente

cress /kres/ n *Bot.* berro, m

crest /krest/ n (of a cock, etc.) cresta, f; (plume) penacho, m; (of a helmet) cimera, f; (of a hill) cumbre, cima, f; (of a wave) cresta, f. **family c.,** blasón, escudo, m

crestfallen /ˈkrestˌfɔlən/ a cabizbajo, cariacontecido

cretan /ˈkritn̩/ a cretense. —n cretense, mf

Crete /krit/ Creta, f

cretin /ˈkritn̩/ n cretino (-na)

cretinism /ˈkritn̩ˌizəm/ n cretinismo, m

crevasse /krəˈvæs/ n grieta en un ventisquero, f

crevice /ˈkrevis/ n intersticio, m, rendija, grieta, f

crew /kru/ n (of ships, boats, aircraft) tripulación, f; (of a gun) servidores de una ametralladora, m pl; (gang) pandilla, cuadrilla, f

crib /krib/ n pesebre, m; (child's) camita de niño, f; (plagiary) plagio, m. —vt (plagiarize) plagiar; (steal) hurtar

crick /krik/ n (in the neck) tortícolis, m

cricket /ˈkrikit/ n *Ent.* grillo, m; (game) cricquet, m. **c. ball,** pelota de cricquet, f. **c. bat,** paleta de cricquet, f. **c. ground,** campo de cricquet, m. **c. match,** partido de cricquet, m

cricketer /ˈkrikitər/ n jugador de cricquet, m

crier /ˈkraiər/ n (town) pregonero, m

crime /kraim/ n crimen, m; ofensa, f, delito, m

Crimean War, the /kraiˈmiən/ la guerra de Crimea, la guerra de Oriente, f

Crimea, the /kraiˈmiə/ la Crimea, f

criminal /ˈkrimənl/ a criminal. —n criminal, m; reo, mf **C. Investigation Department,** (nearest equivalent) policía secreta, f. **c. laws,** código penal, m

criminally /ˈkrimənli/ adv criminalmente

criminologist /ˌkriməˈnɒlədʒist/ n criminalista, m

criminology /ˌkriməˈnɒlədʒi/ n criminología, f

crimp /krimp/ vt (hair) rizar

crimson /ˈkrimzən, -sən/ n carmesí, m. —a de carmesí. —vt teñir de carmesí. —vi enrojecerse

cringe /krindʒ/ vi temblar; asustarse, acobardarse; inclinarse (ante)

cringing /ˈkrindʒɪŋ/ a servil, humilde; adulador

crinkle /ˈkrɪŋkəl/ vi arrugarse; rizarse. —vt arrugar. —n arruga, f

crinoline /ˈkrɪnl̩ɪn/ n crinolina, f, miriñaque, guardainfante, m

cripple /ˈkripəl/ n tullido (-da); cojo (-ja). —vt lisiar, tullir, estropear; *Fig.* paralizar

crisis /ˈkraisis/ n crisis, f

crisp /krisp/ a (of hair and of leaves) crespo; (fresh) fresco; (stiff) tieso; (of style) nervioso, vigoroso; (of manner) decidido; (of repartee) chispeante; (of tone) incisivo

crisscross /ˈkris,krɔs/ vt (a body of water or land) surcar

criterion /kraiˈtiəriən/ n criterio, m

critic /ˈkritik/ n crítico, m; censor, m

critical /ˈkritikəl/ a crítico

criticism /ˈkritəˌsizəm/ n crítica, f

criticize /ˈkritəˌsaiz/ vt criticar; censurar

critique /krɪˈtik/ n crítica, f

croak /krouk/ vi (of frogs) croar; (of ravens) graznar; (of persons) lamentarse, gruñir

croaking /ˈkroukɪŋ/ n canto de la rana, m; graznido, m

Croat /ˈkrouæt/ a croata. —n croata, mf

Croatia /krouˈeiʃə/ Crocia, f

crochet /ˈkrouˈʃei/ n ganchillo, m, vi hacer ganchillo. —vt hacer (algo) de ganchillo. **c. hook,** aguja de gancho, f, ganchillo, m. **c. work,** croché, ganchillo, m

crockery /ˈkrɒkəri/ n loza, f, cacharros, m pl. **c. store,** cacharrería, f

crocodile /ˈkrɒkəˌdail/ n cocodrilo, m. **c. tears,** lágrimas de cocodrilo, f pl

crocus /ˈkroukəs/ n azafrán, m

croft /krɒft/ n campillo, m; (farm) heredad, f

crofter /ˈkrɒftər/ n colono, m

crone /kroun/ n bruja, f

crony /ˈkrouni/ n compinche, mf

crook /kruk/ n curva, f; (staff) cayado, m; (swindler) caballero de industria, estafador, m; vt doblar, encorvar

crooked /ˈkrukid/ a curvo; encorvado; torcido; ladeado; (deformed) contrahecho; (of paths, etc.) tortuoso; (dishonest) torcido, tortuoso

crookedly /ˈkrukidli/ adv torcidamente; de través

crookedness /ˈkrukidnis/ n encorvadura, f; tortuosidad, f; sinuosidad, f

croon /krun/ vt and vi canturrear; cantar

crooner /ˈkrunər/ n cantante, mf

crop /krɒp/ n (of birds) buche, m; (whip) látigo, m, fusta, f; (handle) mango, m; (harvest) cosecha, f; (of the hair) cortadura, f. —vt cortar; (nibble) rozar; (hair) rapar. **Eton c.,** pelo a la garçonne, m. **to c. up,** aparecer, surgir

crop rotation n la rotación de cultivos, f

croquet /krouˈkei/ n juego de la argolla, juego de croquet, m

croquette /krouˈket/ n *Cul.* croqueta, f

crosier /ˈkrouʒər/ n báculo, cayado del obispo, m

cross /krɔs/ n cruz, f; *Biol.* cruzamiento, m; (*Sew.* bias) bies, m. **in the shape of a c.,** en cruz. **the Red C.,** la Cruz Roja. **c.-bearer,** *Eccl.* crucero, m

cross /krɔs/ vt cruzar; atravesar; pasar por; (a check and animals) cruzar; (thwart) contrariar. **It did not c. my mind,** No se me ocurrió. **Our letters must have crossed,** Nuestras cartas deben haberse cruzado. **to c. oneself,** *Eccl.* persignarse. **to c. out,** tachar, rayar. **to c. over,** vt atravesar, cruzar. —vi ir al otro lado

cross /krɔs/ a transversal; cruzado; oblicuo; (contrary) opuesto (a); (bad-tempered) malhumorado. **c.-breed,** a mestizo, atravesado. **c.-country,** a campo travieso. **c.-examination,** *Law.* repregunta, f, contrainterrogatorio, m. **c.-examine,** vt *Law.* repreguntar; interrogar. **c.-eyed,** bizco. **c.-fire,** *Mil.* fuego cruzado, m sing fuegos cruzados, m pl; *Fig.* tiroteo, m. **c.-grained,** (of wood) vetiseagado; (of persons) áspero, intratable, desabrido. **c.-legged,** con las piernas cruzadas. **c.-purpose,** despropósito, m. **at c.-purposes,** a despropósito. **c.-question,** vt *Law.* repreguntar; interrogar. **c. reference,** contrarreferencia, f. **c. section,** sección transversal, f. **c.-stitch,** punto cruzado, m. **c.-word puzzle,** crucigrama, m

crossbar /ˈkrɔs,bɑr/ n travesaño, m

crossbeam /ˈkrɔs,bim/ n viga transversal, f

crossbench /ˈkrɔs,bentʃ/ a atravesado

crossbred /ˈkrɔs,bred/ a cruzado, mestizo; híbrido

crossbreed /ˈkrɔs,brid/ n mestizo (-za); híbrido, m

crossing /ˈkrɔsiŋ/ n cruzamiento, m; (of the sea) travesía, f; (intersection) cruce, m; paso, m. **level c.,** paso a nivel, m. **pedestrian c.,** paso para peatones, m. **c.-sweeper,** barrendero, m

crossly /ˈkrɔsli/ adv con mal humor, con displicencia, irritablemente

crossness /ˈkrɔsnis/ n irritabilidad, f, mal humor, m

crossroad /ˈkrɔs,roud/ n travesía, f; cruce, m; pl **crossroads,** cruce, cruce de caminos, m sing encrucijada, f sing

crosswise /ˈkrɔs,waiz/ adv en cruz; a través

crotch /krɒtʃ/ n (of a tree) bifurcación, f; *Anat.* horcajadura, f; (of breeches) entrepiernas, f pl

crotchet /ˈkrɒtʃit/ n *Mus.* semínima, f; (fad) capricho, m; extravagancia, excentricidad, f

crotchety /ˈkrɒtʃiti/ a caprichoso; raro, excéntrico; difícil

crouch /krautʃ/ vi acurrucarse, agacharse, acuclillarse
croup /krup/ n (disease) crup, garrotillo, m; (of a horse) grupa, anca, f
croupier /'krupiər/ n coime, crupié, m
crow /krou/ n Ornith. cuervo, m; Ornith. grajo, m; (of a cock) canto del gallo, cacareo, m; (of an infant) gorjeo, m. —vi (of a cock) cantar, cacarear; (of an infant) gorjearse. **as the c. flies,** en línea recta. **to c. over,** gallear, cantar victoria. **crow's-foot,** pata de gallo, f. **crow's-nest,** Naut. gavias, f pl
crowbar /'krou,bar/ n alzaprima, palanca, f
crowd /kraud/ n multitud, muchedumbre, f; concurso, m; vulgo, m; (majority) mayoría, f; Theat. acompañamiento, m. —vi reunirse, congregarse; agolparse, remolinarse, apiñarse. —vt (fill) llenar; atestar. **in a c.,** en tropel. **So many ideas crowded in on me,** Se me ocurrieron tantas ideas a la vez. **to follow the c.,** seguir la multitud; Fig. ir con la mayoría. **to c. in,** entrar en tropel. **to c. round,** cercar, agruparse alrededor de. **to c. together,** apiñarse. **to c. up,** subir en masa, subir en tropel
crowded /'kraudıd/ a lleno; atestado, apiñado; (weighed down) agobiado; (of hours, etc.) lleno
crowing /'krouɪŋ/ n cacareo, canto del gallo, m; (of an infant) gorjeos, m pl; (boasting) jactancia, f
crown /kraun/ n corona, f; (of the head) coronilla, corona, f; (of a hat) copa, f; Archit. coronamiento, m. —vt coronar. **c. prince,** príncipe heredero, m
crowning /'kraunɪŋ/ n coronamiento, m; Archit. remate, m, a final; supremo
crozier /'krouʒər/ n. See **crosier**
crucial /'kruʃəl/ a decisivo, crítico; difícil
crucible /'krusəbəl/ n crisol, m
crucifix /'krusəfıks/ n crucifijo, m
crucifixion /,krusə'fıkʃən/ n crucifixión, f
cruciform /'krusə,fɔrm/ a cruciforme
crucify /'krusə,faı/ vt crucificar
crude /krud/ a crudo; (of colors) chillón, llamativo; (uncivilized) cerril, inculto; (vulgar) cursi; (of truth, etc.) desnudo
crudity /'krudıti/ n crudeza, f
cruel /'kruəl/ a cruel
cruelty /'kruəlti/ n crueldad, f
cruet /'kruıt/ n ánfora, vinagrera, f; (stand) angarillas, f pl, convoy, m
cruise /kruz/ vi cruzar, navegar; (of cars) correr. —n viaje por mar, m
cruiser /'kruzər/ n crucero, m
crumb /krʌm/ n miga, f; (spongy part of bread) migaja, f. —vt (bread) desmigajar; desmenuzar. **c. brush,** recogemigas, m
crumble /'krʌmbəl/ vt desmigajar, desmenuzar. —vi desmoronarse, desmigajarse; Fig. hundirse, derrumbarse; Fig. desaparecer
crumbling /'krʌmblıŋ/ n (of buildings, etc.) desmoronamiento, m; Fig. destrucción, f
crumple /'krʌmpəl/ vt arrugar, ajar. —vi arrugarse. **to c. up,** vt (crush) estrujar; (persons) dejar aplastado. —vi (collapse) hundirse, derrumbarse; (of persons) desplomarse; (despair) desalentarse
crunch /krʌntʃ/ vt mascar; hacer crujir. —vi crujir
crupper /'krʌpər/ n baticola, f
crusade /kru'seid/ n cruzada, f
crusader /kru'seidər/ n cruzado, m
crush /krʌʃ/ vt aplastar; (to powder) moler, triturar; (grapes, etc.) exprimir; (crease) arrugar; (opposition, etc.) vencer; (annihilate) aniquilar, destruir; (abash) humillar, confundir; (hope, etc.) matar; (of sorrow, etc.) agobiar. **We all crushed into his diningroom,** Fuimos en tropel a su comedor. **to c. up,** machacar, moler; (paper, etc.) estrujar
crushing /'krʌʃıŋ/ a (of defeats and replies) aplastante; (of sorrow, etc.) abrumador
crust /krʌst/ n (of bread, pie) corteza, f; (scab) costra, f; (of the earth, snow) capa, f. —vt encostrar. —vi encostrarse. **c. of bread,** mendrugo de pan, m
crustacean /krʌ'steiʃən/ a crustáceo. —n crustáceo, m
crustily /'krʌstli/ adv irritablemente, malhumoradamente
crustiness /'krʌstınıs/ n mal humor, m, aspereza, f

crusty /'krʌsti/ a costroso; (of persons) malhumorado, irritable; áspero
crutch /krʌtʃ/ n muleta, f; (fork) horquilla, f; (crotch) horcajadura, f
crux /krʌks/ n problema, m; (knotty point) nudo, m
cry /krai/ vi (weep) llorar; (shout) gritar; (exclaim) exclamar. —vt (one's wares) pregonar. —n grito, m. **to cry for help,** pedir socorro a voces. **to cry to high heaven,** poner el grito en el cielo. **to cry one's eyes out,** llorar a mares. **to cry down,** desacreditar. **to cry off,** desdecirse; volverse atrás. **to cry out,** vt gritar. —vi dar gritos; gritar; Fig. clamar. **cry-baby,** niño (-ña) llorón (-ona)
crying /'kraiɪŋ/ a urgente; notorio. —n gritos, m pl; (weeping) llanto, m, lamentaciones, f pl; (tears) lágrimas, f pl
crypt /kript/ n cripta, f
cryptic /'kriptık/ a secreto, oculto
cryptography /krip'togrəfi/ n criptografía, f
crystal /'kristl/ n cristal, m. **c. set,** Radio. receptor de galena, m
crystal ball n bola de cristal, esfera de cristal, f
crystalline /'kristlın/ a cristalino
crystallization /,kristlə'zeifən/ n cristalización, f
crystallize /'kristl,aiz/ vt and vi cristalizar
crystallography /,kristl'ogrəfi/ n cristalografía, f
cub /kʌb/ n cachorro (-rra)
Cuban /'kyubən/ a cubano. —n cubano (-na)
cubbyhole /'kʌbi,houl/ n refugio, m; garita, f; cuarto pequeño, m; chiribitil, m
cube /kyub/ n cubo, m; (of sugar) terrón, m. —vt cubicar. **c. root,** raíz cúbica, f
cubic /'kyubık/ a cúbico
cubicle /'kyubıkəl/ n cubículo, m
cubism /'kyubızəm/ n cubismo, m
cubist /'kyubıst/ n cubista, mf
cubit /'kyubıt/ n codo, m
cuckold /'kʌkəld/ n cornudo, m
cuckoo /'kuku/ n cuclillo, m; (cry) cucú, m. **c.-clock,** reloj de cuclillo, m
cucumber /'kyukʌmbər/ n cohombro m
cud /kʌd/ n rumia, f. **to chew the cud,** rumiar
cuddle /'kʌdl/ vt abrazar. —n abrazo, m. **to c. up together,** estar abrazados
cudgel /'kʌdʒəl/ n porra, estaca, tranca, f, vt aporrear, apalear. **to c. one's brains,** devanarse los sesos. **to take up the cudgels for,** salir en defensa de
cue /kyu/ n Theat. pie, m; (lead) táctica, f; (hint) indicación, f; (of hair) coleta, f; (billiard) taco (de billar), m. **to take one's cue from,** tomar como modelo (a); seguir el ejemplo de
cuff /kʌf/ vt abofetear. —n (blow) bofetón, m; (of sleeve) puño, m, bocamanga, valenciana, f. **c.-links,** gemelos, m pl
cuisine /kwı'zin/ n cocina, f
cul-de-sac /'kʌldə,sæk/ n callejón sin salida, m
culinary /'kyulə,neri/ a culinario
cullender /'kʌləndər/ n colador, m
culminate /'kʌlmə,neit/ vi culminar (en), terminar (en). **culminating point,** punto culminante, m
culmination /,kʌlmə'neifən/ n culminación, f; Fig. apogeo, punto culminante, m
culpability /,kʌlpə'bılıti/ n culpabilidad, f
culpable /'kʌlpəbəl/ a culpable
culpably /'kʌlpəbli/ adv culpablemente
culprit /'kʌlprıt/ n culpado (-da)
cult /kʌlt/ n culto, m
cultivable /'kʌltəvəbəl/ a cultivable, labradero
cultivate /'kʌltə,veit/ vt cultivar
cultivated /'kʌltə,veitıd/ a cultivado; (of persons) culto, fino
cultivation /,kʌltə'veifən/ n cultivación, f; (of the land) cultivo, m; (of persons, etc.) cultura, f
cultivator /'kʌltə,veitər/ n cultivador (-ra); (machine) cultivador, m
cultural /'kʌltʃərəl/ a cultural
culture /'kʌltʃər/ n cultura, f; (bacteriology) cultivo, m, vt (bacteriology) cultivar
cultured /'kʌltʃərd/ a culto
culvert /'kʌlvərt/ n alcantarilla, f
cumbersome /'kʌmbərsəm/ a pesado; incómodo

cumulative /'kyumyələtɪv/ a cumulativo
cumulus /'kyumyələs/ n cúmulo, m
cuneiform /kyu'niə,fɔrm/ a cuneiforme
cunning /'kʌnɪŋ/ a astuto, taimado. —n (skill) habilidad, f; astucia, f
cup /kʌp/ n taza, f; (Eccl. and Bot.) cáliz, m; Sports. copa, f; (hollow) hoyo, m, hondonada, f. **c.-final,** Sports. final de la copa, m. **c.-tie,** Sports. partido eliminatorio, m
cup-and-ball /'kʌpən'bɔl/ n boliche, m
cupboard /'kʌbərd/ n armario, m; (in the wall) alacena, f. **c. love,** amor interesado, m
cupful /'kʌpful/ n taza, f
cupidity /kyu'pɪdɪti/ n avaricia, codicia, f
cup of sorrow n ramito de amargura, m
cupola /'kyupələ/ n cúpula, f
cur /kɜr/ n perro mestizo, m; canalla, m
curable /'kyurəbəl/ a curable
curableness /'kyurəbəlnɪs/ n curabilidad, f
curative /'kyurətɪv/ a curativo, terapéutico
curator /kyu'reitər/ n (of a museum) director, m; (Scots law) curador, m
curb /kɜrb/ n (of a bridle) barbada, f; Fig. freno, m; (stone) bordillo, m, guarnición, f. —vt (a horse) enfrenar; Fig. refrenar, reprimir; (limit) limitar
curd /kɜrd/ n requesón, m; cuajada, f
curdle /'kɜrdl/ vi coagularse; (of blood) helarse. —vt coagular; (blood) helar
cure /kyur/ n cura, f; Eccl. curato, m. —vt curar; (salt) salar; Fig. remediar. **to take a c.,** tomar una cura. **c.-all,** panacea, f. **c. of souls,** cura de almas, f
curer /'kyurər/ n (of fish, etc.) salador, m; (of evils, etc.) remediador, m
curfew /'kɜrfyu/ n toque de queda, m
curia /'kyuriə/ n Eccl. curia, f
curing /'kyurɪŋ/ n curación, f; (salting) saladura, f
curio /'kyuri,ou/ n curiosidad, antigüedad, f
curiosity /,kyuri'ɒsɪti/ n curiosidad, f
curious /'kyuriəs/ a (all meanings) curioso
curiously /'kyuriəsli/ adv curiosamente
curl /kɜrl/ n (of hair) rizo, bucle, m; (of smoke) penacho, m. —vt rizar. —vi rizarse; Sports. jugar al curling. **in c.,** rizado. **to c. one's lip,** hacer una mueca de desdén. **to c. up,** vt arrollar; Fig. dejar fuera de combate (a). —vi hacerse un ovillo, enroscarse; (of leaves) abarquillarse; Fig. desplomarse, desanimarse. **c.-paper,** papillote, m
curlew /'kɜrlu/ n Ornith. zarapito, m
curling /'kɜrlɪŋ/ n (game) curling, m, a rizado. **c.-tongs,** encrespador, m
curly /'kɜrli/ a rizado, crespo
curmudgeon /kər'mʌdʒən/ n erizo, misántropo, cara de viernes, m
currant /'kɜrənt/ n (dry) pasa de Corinto, f; (fresh) grosella, f. **black c.,** grosella negra, f; (bush) groselliero negro, m. **c.-bush,** grosellero, m
currency /'kɜrənsi/ n uso corriente, m; moneda corriente, f, dinero, m; dinero en circulación, m; valor corriente, m; estimación, f
current /'kɜrənt/ a corriente; presente, de actualidad; (of money) en circulación. —n (of water, etc., f, Fig. Elec.) corriente, f. **alternating c.,** Elec. corriente alterna, f. **direct c.,** Elec. corriente continua, f. **the c. number of a magazine,** el último número de una revista. **c. events,** actualidades, f pl
currently /'kɜrəntli/ adv corrientemente, generalmente
curricle /'kʌrɪkəl/ n carriola, f
curriculum /kə'rɪkyələm/ n plan de estudios, m; curso, m
curriculum vitae /'vaiti/ n hoja de vida, f
curry /'kɜri/ vt (leather) zurrar; (a horse) almohazar; Cul. condimentar con cari. **to c. favor with,** insinuarse en el favor de. **c.-comb,** almohaza, f
curse /kɜrs/ n maldición, f; blasfemia, f; (ruin) azote, castigo, m. —vt maldecir; (afflict) castigar. —vi blasfemar, echar pestes
cursed /'kɜrsɪd, kɜrst/ a maldito; abominable, odioso
cursing /'kɜrsɪŋ/ n maldición, f; blasfemias, f pl
cursive /'kɜrsɪv/ a cursivo

cursorily /'kɜrsərəli/ adv rápidamente; de prisa; superficialmente
cursory /'kɜrsəri/ a rápido; apresurado; superficial
curt /kɜrt/ a seco, brusco; corto
curtail /kər'teil/ vt abreviar; reducir; disminuir
curtailment /kər'teilmənt/ n abreviación, f; reducción, f; disminución, f
curtain /'kɜrtn/ n cortina, f; Theat. telón, m. —vt poner cortinas (a) **drop c.,** telón de boca, m. **iron c.,** Polit. telón de acero, m. **to c. off,** separar por cortinas. **c.-lecture,** reprimenda conyugal, f. **c.-raiser,** entremés, m. **c.-ring,** anilla, f
curtly /'kɜrtli/ adv secamente, bruscamente
curtness /'kɜrtnɪs/ n brusquedad, sequedad, f
curtsey /'kɜrtsi/ n reverencia, cortesía, f, vi hacer una reverencia
curvature /'kɜrvətʃər/ n curvatura, f
curve /kɜrv/ n curva, f; Mech. codo, m; (Auto. of a road) viraje, m. —vt encorvar, torcer. —vi encorvarse, torcerse; (of a road) hacer un viraje.
curved /kɜrvd/ a curvo
curvet /'kɜrvɪt/ n corveta, cabriola, f, vi corvetear, corcovear, cabriolar
curvilinear /,kɜrvə'lɪniər/ a curvilíneo
cushion /'kuʃən/ n almohada, f; cojín, m; (billiards) banda, f; (of fingers, etc.) pulpejo, m. —vt proveer de almohadas; (a shock) amortiguar; suavizar
custard /'kʌstərd/ n flan, m, natillas, f pl
custodian /kʌ'stoudiən/ n custodio, m; guardián, m; (of a museum, etc.) director, m
custody /'kʌstədi/ n custodia, f; guarda, f; prisión, f. **in safe c.,** en lugar seguro. **to take** (a person) **into c.,** arrestar
custom /'kʌstəm/ n costumbre, f; uso, m; Com. parroquia, clientela, f; (sales) ventas, f pl; pl **Customs,** aduana, f. **to go through the Customs,** pasar por la aduana. **Customs duty,** derechos de aduana, m pl. **Customs officer,** aduanero, m. **C.-house,** aduana, f
customarily /,kʌstə'merəli/ adv habitualmente, por lo general
customary /'kʌstə,meri/ a acostumbrado, usual, habitual
customer /'kʌstəmər/ n cliente, mf parroquiano (-na). **He is a queer c.,** Es un tipo raro
customs barrier n barrera aduanera, barrera arancelaria, f
cut /kʌt/ vt cortar; (diamonds) tallar; (hay, etc.) segar; (carve) labrar, tallar; (engrave) grabar; (a lecture, etc.) no asistir a; (cards) destajar, cortar; (Fig. wound) herir; (reduce) reducir; abreviar; (teeth) echar; (of lines) cruzar. —vi cortar; cortar bien; (Fam. go) marcharse a prisa y corriendo. **I must get my hair cut,** He de hacerme cortar el pelo. **That cuts both ways,** Es una arma de dos filos. **His opinion cuts no ice,** Su opinión no cuenta. **Mary cut him dead,** María hizo como si no le reconociera. **to cut a caper,** dar saltos; hacer cabriolas. **to cut a person short,** echar el tablacho (a). **to cut and run,** poner los pies en polvorosa. **to cut for deal,** (cards) cortar para ver quién da las cartas. **to cut short,** (a career) terminar. **to cut to the quick,** herir en lo más vivo. **to cut across,** cortar al través; (fields, etc.) atravesar; tomar por un atajo. **to cut away,** vt quitar. —vi Inf. poner pies en polvorosa. **to cut down,** derribar; (by the sword) acuchillar; (by death, etc.) segar, malograr; (expenses, etc.) reducir; (abbreviate) cortar, abreviar. **to cut off,** cortar, separar; amputar; (on a telephone) cortar la comunicación; (gas, water, etc.) cortar; (supply of food, etc.) interrumpir; (of death) llevarse. **to cut off with a shilling,** desheredar (a). **to cut out,** (dresses, etc.) cortar; (oust) suplantar. **He is not cut out for medicine,** No tiene la disposición para la medicina. **to cut up,** trinchar, cortar en pequeños trozos; (afflict) entristecer, afligir. **to cut up rough,** Inf. ponerse furioso
cut /kʌt/ a cortado. **well-cut features,** facciones regulares, f pl. **cut and dried opinion,** opinión hecha, idea fija, f; ideas cerradas, f pl. **cut glass,** cristal tallado, m
cut /kʌt/ n corte, m; (with a whip) latigazo, m; (with a sword) cuchillada, f; (with a sharp instrument) tajo, m; cortadura, f; (in prices, etc.) reducción, f; (en-

graving) grabado, *m;* clisé, *m;* (of cards) corte, *m.*
short cut, atajo, *m.* **the cut of a coat,** el corte de un
abrigo. **to give** (someone) **the cut direct,** pasar cerca
de (una persona) sin saludarle. **cut-out,** *n* (paper) recortado, *m; Elec.* cortacircuitos, *m.* **cut-throat,** *n* asesino, *m*
cutaneous /kyu'teiniəs/ *a* cutáneo
cute /kyut/ *a* cuco, listo; mono
cuteness /'kyutnıs/ *n* cuquería, inteligencia, *f;*
monería, *f*
cuticle /'kyutıkəl/ *n* cutícula, *f*
cutler /'kʌtlər/ *n* cuchillero, *m*
cutlery /'kʌtləri/ *n* cuchillería, *f*
cutlet /'kʌtlıt/ *n* chuleta, *f*
cutter /'kʌtər/ *n* cortador, *m; Naut.* cúter, *m;* escampavía, *f*
cutting /'kʌtıŋ/ *n* corte, *m;* (of diamonds) talla, *f;* (in
a mountain, etc.) tajo, *m; Agr.* plantón, *m;* (of cloth)
retazo, *m;* (newspaper) recorte, *m.* —*a* cortante; (of
remarks) mordaz. **newspaper c.,** recorte de periódico. **c. down,** (of trees) tala, *f;* reducción, *f*
cuttingly /'kʌtıŋli/ *adv* mordazmente, con malicia.
cuttlefish /'kʌtl̩ˌfıʃ/ *n* jibia, *f*
cyanide /'saiəˌnaid/ *n* cianuro, *m*
cyberspace /'saibərˌspeis/ *n* ciberespacio, *m*
cycle /'saikəl/ *n* ciclo, *m;* período, *m;* (bicycle) bicicleta, *f.* —*vi* ir en bicicleta
cyclic /'saiklık/ *a* cíclico

cycling /'saiklıŋ/ *n* ciclismo, *m*
cyclist /'saiklıst/ *n* ciclista, *mf*
cyclone /'saikloun/ *n* ciclón, *m*
Cyclopean /ˌsaiklə'piən/ *a* ciclópeo
Cyclopean task *n* obra ciclopéa, *f*
cygnet /'sıgnıt/ *n* pollo del cisne, *m*
cylinder /'sılındər/ *n* cilindro, *m; Mech.* tambor, *m.* **c.
head,** culata, *f*
cylindrical /sı'lındrıkəl/ *a* cilíndrico
cymbal /'sımbəl/ *n* címbalo, platillo, *m*
cymbalist /'sımbəlıst/ *n* cimbalero (-ra)·
cynic /'sınık/ *n* cínico, *m*
cynical /'sınıkəl/ *a* cínico
cynicism /'sınəˌsızəm/ *n* cinismo, *m*
cynosure /'sainəˌʃʊr/ *n Astron.* Osa Menor, *f;* blanco,
m
cypress /'saiprəs/ *n* (tree and wood) ciprés, *m.* **c.
grove,** cipresal, *m*
Cypriot /'sıpriət/ *a* chipriota. —*n* chipriota, *mf*
Cyprus /'saiprəs/ Isla de Chipre, *f*
cyst /sıst/ *n* quiste, *m*
cystic /'sıstık/ *a* cístico
Czech /tʃɛk/ *a* checo. —*n* checo (-ca); (language)
checo, *m*
Czechoslovak /'tʃɛkə'slouvæk/ *n* checoslovaco (-ca)
Czechoslovakia /ˌtʃɛkəslə'vakiə/ Czechoslovaquia, *f*
Czechoslovakian /ˌtʃɛkəslə'vakiən/ *a* checoslovaco

D

d /di/ *n* (letter) de, *f; Mus.* re, *m*
dab /dæb/ *vt* golpear suavemente, tocar; (sponge) esponjar; (moisten) mojar. —*n* golpecito, golpe blando, *m;* (small piece) pedazo pequeño, *m;* (blob) borrón, *m;* (peck) picotazo, *m; Inf.* experto (-ta). **to dab at one's eyes,** secarse los ojos
dabble /'dæbəl/ *vt* mojar (en). —*vi* chapotear; (engage in) entretenerse en; (meddle in) meterse en; (speculate in) especular en. **to d. in politics,** meterse en política
dabbler /'dæblər/ *n* aficionado (-da)
dace /deis/ *n* dardo, albur, *m*
dachshund /'dɑks,hʊnt/ *n* perro pachón, *m*
daddy /'dædi/ *n* papaíto, *m.* **d.-longlegs,** típula, *f*
dado /'deidou/ *n Archit.* dado, neto, *m;* friso, *m*
daffodil /'dæfədɪl/ *n* narciso trompón, *m*
daft /dæft/ *a* bobo, tonto, chiflado; loco
dagger /'dægər/ *n* daga, *f,* puñal, *m; Print.* cruz, *f.* **to be at daggers drawn,** estar a matar. **to look daggers (at),** lanzar miradas de odio (hacia), mirar echando chispas. **d. thrust,** puñalada, *f*
daguerreotype /də'gεərə,taip/ *n* daguerrotipo, *m*
dahlia /'dælyə/ *n* dalia, *f*
daily /'deili/ *a* diario, de todos los días; cotidiano. —*adv* diariamente, cada día, todos los días; cotidianamente. —*n* (paper) diario, *m.* **d. bread,** pan cotidiano, pan de cada día, *m.* **d. help,** (person) asistenta, *f.* **d. pay,** jornal, *m; Mil.* pre, *m*
daintily /'deintli/ *adv* delicadamente; elegantemente; con primor
daintiness /'deintinɪs/ *n* delicadeza, *f;* elegancia, *f;* (beauty) primor, *m*
dainty /'deinti/ *a* delicado; elegante; primoroso, exquisito; (fastidious) melindroso, difícil. —*n* bocado exquisito, *m,* golosina, *f*
dairy /'dεəri/ *n* lechería, *f.* **d. cattle,** vacas lecheras, *f pl.* **d.-farm,** granja, *f.* **d.-farmer,** granjero (-ra). **d.-farming,** industria lechera, *f*
dairymaid /'dεəri,meid/ *n* lechera, *f*
dairyman /'dεərimən/ *n* lechero, *m*
dais /'deiis/ *n* estrado, *m*
daisy /'deizi/ *n* margarita, *f*
dale /deil/ *n* valle, *m*
dalliance /'dæliəns/ *n* (delay) tardanza, *f;* (play) jugueteo, *m;* diversiones, *f pl;* (caresses) caricias, *f pl,* abrazos, *m pl*
dally /'dæli/ *vi* tardar, perder el tiempo; entretenerse, divertirse; (make love) holgar (con); (with an idea) entretenerse con, jugar con
Dalmatian /dæl'meiʃən/ *a* dalmático, dálmata. —*n* dálmata, *mf.* **D. dog,** perro dálmata, *m*
dalmatic /dæl'mætɪk/ *n* dalmática, *f*
daltonism /'dɔltn,ɪzəm/ *n* daltonismo, *m*
dam /dæm/ *n* (of animals) madre, *f;* (of a river, etc.) presa, *f,* embalse, *m;* (mole) dique, *m;* pared de retención, *f.* —*vt* represar, embalsar; cerrar; (restrain) contener, reprimir
damage /'dæmɪdʒ/ *n* daño, perjuicio, *m;* mal, *m;* avería, *f;* pérdida, *f;* (Fam. price) precio, *m; pl* **damages,** *Law.* daños y perjuicios, *m pl.* —*vt* dañar, perjudicar; estropear; deteriorar; (reputation, etc.) comprometer
damageable /'dæmɪdʒəbəl/ *a* que puede ser dañado; frágil
damaging /'dæmɪdʒɪŋ/ *a* perjudicial; comprometedor
damascene /'dæməsin/ *vt* damasquinar
Damascus /də'mæskəs/ Damasio, *m*
damask /'dæməsk/ *n* (cloth) damasco, *m;* (steel) acero damasquino, *m.* —*a* de damasco; damasquino. —*vt* (metals) damasquinar; (cloth) adamascar. **d.-like,** adamascado. **d. rose,** rosa de Damasco, *f*
dame /deim/ *n* dama, señora, *f; Inf.* madre, *f;* (schoolmistress) amiga, *f.* **to attend a d. school,** ir a la amiga
damming /'dæmɪŋ/ *n* embalse, *m,* represa, *f;* retención, *f;* represión, *f*

damn /dæm/ *vt* condenar al infierno; maldecir; vituperar. **D. it!** ¡Maldito sea!
damnable /'dæmnəbəl/ *a* detestable, infame; *Inf.* horrible
damnably /'dæmnəbli/ *adv* abominablemente; *Inf.* horriblemente
damnation /dæm'neiʃən/ *n* condenación, perdición, *f;* maldición, *f;* vituperación, *f*
damned /dæmd/ *a* condenado; maldito; detestable, odioso
damning /'dæmɪŋ/ *a* que condena; irresistible
damp /dæmp/ *a* húmedo. —*n* humedad, *f;* (mist) niebla, *f;* exhalación, *f;* (gas) mofeta, *f; Fig.* tristeza, depresión, *f.* —*vt* humedecer, mojar; apagar, amortiguar; (depress) deprimir, entristecer; (stifle) ahogar; (lessen) moderar; (trouble) turbar. **d.-proof,** impermeable
damper /'dæmpər/ *n* (of a chimney) registro de humos, *m;* (of a piano) batiente, *m;* (for stamps) mojador, *m;* (gloom) depresión, tristeza, *f;* (restraint) freno, *m*
dampish /'dæmpɪʃ/ *a* algo húmedo
dampness /'dæmpnɪs/ *n* humedad, *f*
damsel /'dæmzəl/ *n* chica, muchacha, *f;* damisela, *f*
damson /'dæmzən/ *n* ciruela damascena, *f.* **d. tree,** ciruelo damasceno, *m*
dance /dæns/ *n* danza, *f;* baile, *m.* —*vi* bailar, danzar; saltar, brincar. —*vt* bailar; hacer saltar. **to d. attendance on,** servir humildemente; hacer la rueda (a). **to lead someone a d.,** hacer bailar. **d. band,** orquestina, *f;* orquesta de jazz, *f.* **d. floor,** pista de baile, *f.* **d. hall,** salón de baile, *m.* **d. music,** música bailable, *f.* **d.-number,** (in a theater) bailable, *m.* **d. of death,** danza de la muerte, *f*
dancer /'dænsər/ *n* bailarín (-ina); danzador (-ra), bailador (-ra); *pl* **dancers,** (partners) parejas de baile, *f pl*
dancing /'dænsɪŋ/ *n* baile, *m,* danza, *f.* **d.-girl,** bailarina, *f;* (Indian) bayadera, *f.* **d.-master,** maestro de baile, *m.* **d. school,** academia de baile, *f.* **d. slipper,** zapatilla de baile, *f*
dandelion /'dændl,aiən/ *n* diente de león, *m*
dandle /'dændl/ *vt* mecer, hacer saltar sobre las rodillas, hacer bailar
dandruff /'dændrəf/ *n* caspa, *f*
dandy /'dændi/ *n* dandi, petimetre, barbilindo, *m*
Dane /dein/ *n* danés (-esa). **Great D.,** perro danés, *m*
danger /'deindʒər/ *n* peligro, *m;* riesgo, *m.* **out of d.,** fuera de peligro. **to be in d.,** correr peligro, peligrar, estar en peligro
dangerous /'deindʒərəs/ *a* peligroso; arriesgado; nocivo
dangerously /'deindʒərəsli/ *adv* peligrosamente
dangerousness /'deindʒərəsnɪs/ *n* peligro, *m*
dangle /'dæŋgəl/ *vi* colgar, pender. —*vt* dejar colgar; oscilar; (show) mostrar
Danish /'deinɪʃ/ *a* danés, de Dinamarca. —*n* (language) danés, *m*
dank /dæŋk/ *a* húmedo
dankness /'dæŋknɪs/ *n* humedad, *f*
Danube, the /'dænyub/ el (Río) Danubio, *m*
dapper /'dæpər/ *a* apuesto, aseado; activo, vivaz
dapple /'dæpəl/ *vt* motear, salpicar, manchar. **d.-grey,** *a* rucio
dappled /'dæpəld/ *a* (of horses) rodado, empedrado
Dardanelles, the /,dɑrdn'elz/ los Dardanelos, *m*
dare /dεər/ *vi* atreverse, osar. —*vt* arriesgar; desafiar, provocar; hacer frente a, arrostrar. —*n* reto, *m.* **I d. say!** ¡Ya lo creo! ¡No lo dudo! **I d. say that...,** No me sorprendería que...; Supongo que... **d.-devil,** calavera, *m;* atrevido (-da), valeroso (-sa)
daring /'dεərɪŋ/ *a* intrépido, audaz; atrevido; (dangerous) arriesgado, peligroso. —*n* audacia, osadía, *f,* atrevimiento, *m;* peligro, *m*
daringly /'dεərɪŋli/ *adv* atrevidamente
dark /dɑrk/ *a* oscuro; (of complexion, etc.) moreno;

negro; lóbrego; (of colours) oscuro; misterioso; enigmático; secreto, escondido; (sad) funesto, triste; (evil) malo, malévolo; (ignorant) ignorante, supersticioso. —*n* oscuridad, *f;* (shade) sombra, *f;* ignorancia, *f.* **after d.,** *a* nocturno. —*adv* después del anochecer. **in the d.,** a oscuras; de noche; *Fig.* be in the **d.,** quedarse en la luna. **to become d.,** oscurecerse; (cloud over) anublarse; (become night) anochecer. **to keep d.,** *vt* tener secreto. —*vi* esconderse. **d. ages,** los siglos de la ignorancia y de la superstición. **d.-eyed,** de ojos negros, ojinegro. **d. horse,** caballo desconocido, *m; Polit.* batacazo, *m.* **d. lantern,** linterna sorda, *f.* **d. room,** cuarto oscuro, *m; Photo.* laboratorio fotográfico, *m;* (optics) cámara oscura, *f*

darken /'darkən/ *vt* obscurecer; sombrear; (of color) hacer más oscuro; (sadden) entristecer. —*vi* obscurecerse; (of the sky) anublarse; (of the face with emotion) inmutarse

darkening /'darkənɪŋ/ *n* oscurecimiento, *m*

darkly /'darkli/ *adv* oscuramente; misteriosamente; con malevolencia; secretamente; (archaic) indistintamente

darkness /'darknɪs/ *n* oscuridad, *f,* tinieblas, *f pl;* sombra, *f;* (of color) oscuro, *m;* (of the complexion) color moreno, *m;* (of eyes, hair) negrura, *f;* (night) noche, *f;* (ignorance) ignorancia, *f;* (privacy) secreto, *m.* **Prince of d.,** el príncipe de las tinieblas

darling /'darlɪŋ/ *a* querido, amado; (greatest) mayor. —*n* querido (-da); (favorite) el predilecto, la predilecta, el favorito, la favorita. **My d.!** ¡Amor mío! ¡Vida mía! ¡Pichoncito mío!

darn /darn/ *vt* zurcir, remendar. —*n* zurcido, remiendo, *m*

darner /'darnər/ *n* zurcidor (-ra); (implement) huevo de zurcir, *m*

darning /'darnɪŋ/ *n* zurcidura, *f;* zurcido, recosido, *m.* **d.-needle,** aguja de zurcir, *f.* **d. wool,** lana de zurcir, *f*

dart /dart/ *n* dardo, *m;* movimiento rápido, *m;* avance rápido, *m; Sew.* sisa, *f.* —*vi* lanzarse, abalanzarse (sobre); volar; correr, avanzar rápidamente. —*vt* lanzar, arrojar; dirigir. **to make darts in,** *Sew.* sisar

Darwinian /dar'wɪniən/ *a* darviniano. —*n* darvinista, *mf*

Darwinism /'darwə,nɪzəm/ *n* darvinismo, *m*

dash /dæʃ/ *n* (spirit) fogosidad, *f,* brío, *m;* energía, *f;* (impact) choque, golpe, *m;* (mixture) mezcla, *f;* (of a liquid) gota, *f;* (of the pen) rasgo, *m;* (attack) ataque, *m;* avance rápido, *m;* (a little) algo, un poco (de); *Gram.* raya, *f;* (show) ostentación, *f.* **He made a d. for the door,** Se precipitó a la puerta, Corrió hacia la puerta. **to cut a d.,** hacer gran papel. **d.-board,** tablero de instrumentos, *m*

dash /dæʃ/ *vt* arrojar con violencia; (break) quebrar, estrellar; (sprinkle) rociar (con), salpicar (con); (mix) mezclar; (knock) golpear; (disappoint) frustrar, destruir; (confound) confundir; (depress) desanimar. —*vi* (rush) precipitarse; quebrarse, estrellarse; chocar (contra); (of waves) romperse. **to d. to pieces,** hacer añicos, estrellar. **to d. along,** avanzar rápidamente; correr. **to d. away,** *vi* marcharse apresuradamente. —*vt* apartar bruscamente. **to d. down,** *vi* bajar aprisa. —*vt* derribar; (overturn) volcar; (throw) tirar. **to d. off,** *vi* marcharse rápidamente. —*vt* hacer apresuradamente; (a letter, etc.) escribir de prisa; (sketch) bosquejar rápidamente. **to d. out,** *vi* salir precipitadamente; lanzarse a la calle. —*vt* (erase) borrar; hacer saltar. **to d. through,** atravesar rápidamente; hacer de prisa. **to d. up,** llegar a prisa; (sprout) saltar

dashing /'dæʃɪŋ/ *a* valiente; (spirited) fogoso, gallardo; majo, brillante. —*n* choque, *m;* (breaking) quebrantamiento, *m;* (of the waves) embate, *m*

dastardly /'dæstardli/ *a* cobarde

data /'deitə/ *n pl* datos, *m pl*

database /'deitə,beis/ *n* base de datos, *f*

data processing *n* elaboración electrónica de datos, *f,* recuento de datos, *m*

date /deit/ *n* fecha, *f;* (period) época, *f;* (term) plazo, *m;* (duration) duración, *f;* (appointment) cita, *f; Bot.* dátil, *m.* —*vt* fechar, datar; poner fecha a; asignar. —*vi* datar (de), remontar (a). **out of d.,** anticuado;

pasado de moda; (of persons) atrasado de noticias. **to be up to d.,** ser nuevo; ser de última moda; (of persons) estar al día. **to bring up to d.,** renovar; (of persons) poner al corriente. **to fix the d.,** señalar el día; (chronologically) ajustar los tiempos. **to d.,** hasta la fecha. **under d. (of),** con fecha (de). **up to d.,** hasta hoy, hasta ahora. **What is the d.?** ¿Qué fecha es? ¿A cómo estamos hoy? ¿A cuántos estamos hoy? **d. palm,** datilera, *f*

date of expiry *n* fecha de caducidad, *f*

daub /dɔb/ *vt* barrar, embadurnar; manchar, ensuciar; untar; (paint) pintorrear. —*n* embadurnamiento, *m;* (paint) aleluya, *f*

dauber /'dɔbər/ *n* chafalmejas, pintamonas, *mf* pintor (-ra) de brocha gorda

daughter /'dɔtər/ *n* hija, *f.* **adopted d.,** hija adoptiva, *f.* **little d.,** hijuela, *f.* **d.-in-law,** nuera, *f*

daughterly /'dɔtərli/ *a* de hija

daunt /dɔnt, dant/ *vt* intimidar, acobardar; dar miedo (a), espantar; (dishearten) desanimar

dauntless /'dɔntlɪs/ *a* impávido, intrépido

dauphin /'dɔfɪn/ *n* delfín, *m*

dawdle /'dɔdl/ *vi* perder el tiempo; haraganear, gandulear

dawdler /'dɔdlər/ *n* gandul (-la)

dawdling /'dɔdlɪŋ/ *a* perezoso, lento

dawn /dɔn/ *n* alba, madrugada, primera luz, *f; Fig.* aurora, *f.* —*vi* amanecer, alborear, romper el día; (appear) mostrarse, asomar. **at d.,** a primera luz, al amanecer, de madrugada, al alba. **It had not dawned on me,** No me había ocurrido

day /dei/ *n* día, *m;* luz del día, *f;* (day's work) jornada, *f;* (battle) batalla, *f;* (victory) victoria, *f; pl* **days,** (time) tiempos, *m pl,* época, *f;* (life) vida, *f;* (years) años, *m pl, a* diario. **all day long,** durante todo el día. **any day,** cualquier día. **by day,** de día. **by the day,** al día. **every day,** todos los días, cada día. **every other day,** un día sí y otro no, cada dos días. **from this day forward,** desde hoy en adelante. **from day to day,** de día en día. **Good day!** ¡Buenos días! **in these days,** en estos días. **in olden days,** en la antigüedad; *Inf.* en tiempos de Maricastaña. **in the days of,** en los tiempos de; durante los años de; durante la vida de uno. **next day,** el día siguiente. **(on) the next day,** al día siguiente, al otro día. **one of these days,** un día de éstos. **some fine day,** el mejor día, de un día a otro. **the day after tomorrow,** pasado mañana. **the day before yesterday,** anteayer. **the day before,** la víspera. **to win the day,** ganar el día, salir victorioso. **day after day,** cada día, día tras día. **day by day,** día a día. **day in, day out,** sin cesar, día tras día. **day-book,** *Com.* libro diario, *m.* **day's holiday,** día de asueto, *m;* día libre, *m.* **day laborer,** jornalero, *m.* **day nursery,** guardería de niños, *f.* **day-pupil,** alumno (-na) externo (-na). **day-school,** externado, *m.* **day shift,** turno de día, *m.* **day-star,** lucero del alba, *m.* **day ticket,** billete de excursión, *m*

daybreak /'dei,breik/ *n* alba, *f,* amanecer, *m.* **at d.,** al romper el día, al amanecer

daydream /'dei,drim/ *n* ensueño, *m;* ilusión, *f;* fantasía, visión, *f.* —*vi Lit.* soñar despierto, dejar volar sus pensamientos; *Fig.* hacerse ilusiones

daydreamer /'dei,drimər/ *n* soñador (-ra); visionario (-ia)

daylight /'dei,lait/ *n* luz del día, *f,* día, *m;* (contrasted with artificial light) luz natural, *f.* **in broad d.,** a plena calle, a plena luz, en plena luz del día. **It's d. robbery!** ¡Es un desuello! **d.-saving,** hora de verano, *f*

daytime /'dei,taim/ *n* día, *m.* **in the d.,** durante el día

daze /deiz/ *vt* aturdir, confundir; (dazzle) deslumbrar. —*n* aturdimiento, *m,* confusión, *f;* perplejidad, *f*

dazzle /'dæzəl/ *vt* (camouflage) disfrazar; deslumbrar, ofuscar. —*n* deslumbramiento, *m;* brillo, *m,* refulgencia, *f*

dazzling /'dæzlɪŋ/ *a* deslumbrador; brillante

deacon /'dikən/ *n* diácono, *m*

deaconess /'dikənɪs/ *n* diaconisa, *f*

dead /dɛd/ *a* and *past part* muerto; inanimado; (withered) marchito; (deep) profundo; (unconscious) inerte; inmóvil; insensible; (numb) entumecido;

(complete) absoluto, completo; (sure) certero, excelente; (useless) inútil; (of color and human character) apagado; sin espíritu; inactivo; (of eyes) mortecino; (of sound) sordo, opaco; (of villages, etc.) desierto, despoblado; (quiet) silencioso; (empty) vacío; (monotonous) monótono; (of fire) apagado; (with weight, language) muerto; *Elec.* interrumpido; *Law.* muerto civilmente. —*adv* completamente, enteramente; del todo; directamente; exactamente; profundamente. **the d.,** los muertos. **in the d. of night,** en las altas horas de la noche. **to be d.,** estar muerto; haber muerto. **to be d. against,** estar completamente opuesto a. **to drop d.,** caer muerto; morir de repente. **to go d. slow,** ir muy lentamente. **to rise from the d.,** resucitar. **to sham d.,** hacer la mortecina, fingirse muerto. **to speak ill of the d.,** hablar mal de los muertos; *Inf.* desenterrar los muertos. **d. ball,** pelota fuera de juego, *f.* **d.-beat,** muerto de cansancio. **d. body,** cadáver, cuerpo muerto, *m.* **d. calm,** calma profunda, *f; Naut.* calma chicha, *f.* **d. certainty,** seguridad completa, *f.* **d.-drunk,** hecho una uva. **d. end,** callejón sin salida, *m.* **d. heat,** empate, *m.* **d. language,** lengua muerta, *f.* **d.-letter,** letra muerta, *f;* carta devuelta o no reclamada, *f.* **d.-lock,** punto muerto, *m.* **to reach a d.-lock,** llegar a un punto muerto. **d. march,** marcha fúnebre, *f.* **d. season,** temporada de calma, *f.* **d. set,** empeñado (en). **d. shot,** (person) tirador (-ra) certero (-ra) (shot) tiro certero, *m.* **d. silence,** silencio profundo, *m.* **d. stop,** parada en seco, *f.* **d. tired,** rendido. **d. weight,** peso muerto, *m.* **d. wood,** leña seca, *f;* material inútil, *m*

deaden /'dɛdn̩/ *vt* amortiguar; (of pain) calmar; (remove) quitar; (of colours) apagar

deadening /'dɛdnɪŋ/ *n* amortiguamiento, *m*

deadliness /'dɛdlɪnɪs/ *n* carácter mortal, *m;* implacabilidad, *f*

deadly /'dɛdli/ *a* mortal; implacable; *Inf.* insoportable. —*adv* mortalmente. **He was d. pale,** Estaba pálido como un muerto. **the seven d. sins,** los siete pecados mortales. **d. nightshade,** belladona, *f*

deadness /'dɛdnɪs/ *n* falta de vida, *f;* inercia, *f;* marchitez, *f;* (numbness) entumecimiento, *m;* desanimación, *f;* parálisis, *f*

Dead Sea Scrolls, the los rollos del mar Muerto, *m pl*

Dead Sea, the el mar Muerto, *m*

deaf /dɛf/ *a* sordo. **d. people,** los sordos. **to be d.,** ser sordo; padecer sordera. **to be as d. as a post,** ser más sordo que una tapia. **to become d.,** ensordecer, volverse sordo. **to fall on d. ears,** caer en saco roto. **to turn a d. ear,** hacerse el sordo. **d. aid,** audífono, *m.* **d.-and-dumb,** sordomudo. **d.-and-dumb alphabet,** alfabeto manual, abecedario manual, *m.* **d.-mute,** sordomudo (-da). **d.-mutism,** sordomudez, *f*

deafen /'dɛfən/ *vt* asordar, ensordecer

deafening /'dɛfənɪŋ/ *a* ensordecedor

deafly /'dɛfli/ *adv* sordamente

deafness /'dɛfnɪs/ *n* sordera, *f*

deal /dil/ *n* (transaction) negocio, trato, *m;* (at cards) reparto, *m;* (wood) pino, *m;* (plank) tablón de pino, *m.* **a d., a great d.,** mucho. **a very great d.,** muchísimo. **to conclude a d.,** cerrar un trato

deal /dil/ *vt* repartir; (a blow) asestar, dar; (cards) dar; (justice) dispensar. **to d. a blow at,** asestar un golpe; *Fig.* herir (en); *Fig.* destruir de un golpe. **to d. in,** comerciar en, traficar en; ocuparse en; meterse en. **to d. out,** dispensar. **to d. with,** (buy from) comprar de; tener relaciones con, tratar con; entenderse con; portarse con; (of affairs) ocuparse en, arreglar, dirigir; (contend) luchar con; (discuss) discutir, tratar de; (of books) versar sobre

dealer /'dilər/ *n* traficante, *mf* mercader, *m;* (at cards) el que da las cartas

dealing /'dilɪŋ/ *n* conducta, *f;* proceder, *m;* trato, *m;* tráfico, *m; pl* **dealings,** relaciones, *f pl;* transacciones, *f pl*

dean /din/ *n Eccl.* deán, *m; Educ.* decano, *m*

dear /dɪər/ *a* (beloved) querido, amado; (charming) encantador, simpático; (in letters) estimado, querido; (favorite) predilecto; (expensive) caro. —*n* querido (-da); persona querida, *f,* bien amado (-da). —*adv* caro. **Oh d.!** ¡Dios mío! ¡Ay!

dearly /'dɪərli/ *adv* tiernamente, entrañablemente; caro

dearness /'dɪərnɪs/ *n* cariño, afecto, *m,* ternura, *f;* (of price) precio alto, *m*

dearth /dɜrθ/ *n* carestía, *f;* (of news, etc.) escasez, *f*

death /dɛθ/ *n* muerte, *f;* (*Law.* and in announcements) fallecimiento, *m,* defunción, *f.* **to be at death's door,** estar a la muerte. **to put to d.,** ajusticiar. **to the d.,** a muerte. **untimely d.,** muerte repentina, *f;* malogro, *m.* **death's head,** calavera, *f.* **d. certificate,** partida de defunción, *f.* **d.-duties,** derechos de herencia, *m pl.* **d.-like,** cadavérico. **d.-mask,** mascarilla, *f.* **d. penalty,** pena de muerte, *f.* **d.-rate,** mortalidad, *f.* **d.-rattle,** sarrillo, *m.* **d.-trap,** lugar peligroso, *m; Fig.* trampa, *f.* **d.-warrant,** sentencia de muerte, *f.* **d.-watch bettle,** reloj de la muerte, *m*

deathbed /'dɛθ,bɛd/ *n* lecho mortuorio, lecho de muerte, *m.* **on one's d.,** en su lecho de muerte

deathblow /'dɛθ,blou/ *n* golpe mortal, *m*

deathless /'dɛθlɪs/ *a* inmortal, eterno

deathly /'dɛθli/ *a* mortal

death toll *n* (of a bell) doble, toque de difuntos, *m;* (casualties) número de muertos, saldo de muertos, *m*

debacle /də'bɑkəl/ *n Fig.* ruina, *f*

debar /dɪ'bɑr/ *vt* excluir, privar

debase /dɪ'beis/ *vt* degradar, humillar, envilecer; (the coinage) alterar (la moneda)

debasement /dɪ'beismənt/ *n* degradación, humillación, *f,* envilecimiento, *m;* (of the coinage) alteración (de la moneda), *f*

debasing /dɪ'beisɪŋ/ *a* degradante, humillante

debatable /dɪ'beitəbəl/ *a* discutible

debate /dɪ'beit/ *n* debate, *m;* discusión, *f;* disputa, *f.* —*vt* and *vi* debatir; discutir; disputar; considerar

debater /dɪ'beitər/ *n* discutidor (-ra); orador (-ra).

debating /dɪ'beitɪŋ/ *n* discusión, *f;* argumentación, *f*

debauch /dɪ'bɔtʃ/ *vt* corromper, pervertir; (a woman) seducir, violar. —*n* libertinaje, *m;* borrachera, *f*

debauched /dɪ'bɔtʃt/ *a* vicioso, licencioso

debauchee /,dɛbɔ'tʃi, -'ʃi/ *n* libertino, vicioso, *m*

debauchery /dɪ'bɔtʃəri/ *n* libertinaje, mal vivir, *m,* viciosidad, licencia, *f*

debenture /dɪ'bɛntʃər/ *n* obligación, *f.* **d. holder,** obligacionista, *mf*

debilitate /dɪ'bɪlɪ,teit/ *vt* debilitar

debilitating /dɪ'bɪlɪ,teitɪŋ/ *a* debilitante

debilitation /dɪ,bɪlɪ'teifən/ *n* debilitación, *f*

debility /dɪ'bɪliti/ *n* debilidad, *f*

debit /'dɛbɪt/ *n* débito, cargo, *m;* saldo deudor, *m;* "debe" de una cuenta, *m.* —*vt* adeudar. **d. and credit,** el cargo y la data. **d. balance,** saldo deudor, *m*

debonair /,dɛbə'nɛər/ *a* gallardo, gentil, donairoso; alegre

debonairly /,dɛbə'nɛərli/ *adv* gallardamente; alegremente

débris /dei'bri/ *n* escombros, desechos, *m pl;* ruinas, *f pl; Geol.* despojos, *m pl*

debt /dɛt/ *n* deuda, *f.* **a bad d.,** una deuda incobrable. **to be in the d. of,** ser en cargo a; deber dinero a; *Fig.* sentirse bajo una obligación. **to get into d.,** adeudarse, contraer deudas

debtor /'dɛtər/ *n* deudor (-ra); *Com.* debe, *m*

debunk /dɪ'bʌŋk/ *vt* demoler

debut /dei'byu/ *n* (of a debutante) puesta de largo, *f;* (of a play, etc.) estreno, *m.* **to make one's d.,** ponerse de largo, presentarse en sociedad

debutante /'dɛbyu,tɑnt/ *n* debutante, *f*

decade /'dɛkeid/ *n* década, *f;* decenio, *m;* (of the rosary) decena, *f*

decadence /'dɛkədəns/ *n* decadencia, *f*

decadent /'dɛkədənt/ *a* decadente

decagram /'dɛkə,græm/ *n* decagramo, *m*

decaliter /'dɛkə,litər/ *n* decalitro, *m*

decalogue /'dɛkə,lɔg/ *n* decálogo, *m*

decameter /'dɛkə,mitər/ *n* decámetro, *m*

decamp /dɪ'kæmp/ *vi Mil.* decampar; escaparse, fugarse

decant /dɪ'kænt/ *vt* decantar

decanter /dɪ'kæntər/ *n* garrafa, *f*

decapitate /dɪ'kæpɪ,teit/ *vt* decapitar, descabezar

decapitation /dɪ,kæpɪ'teɪʃən/ n decapitación, f
decarbonization /dɪ,kɑrbənə'zeɪʃən/ n descarburación, f
decarbonize /di'kɑrbə,naiz/ vt descarbonizar
decay /dɪ'kei/ vi (rot) pudrirse; degenerar; marchitarse; (of teeth) cariarse; (crumble) desmoronarse, caer en ruinas; decaer, declinar; (come down in the world) venir a menos, arruinarse. —n pudrición, putrefacción, f; (of teeth) caries, f; (withering) marchitez, f; degeneración, f; desmoronamiento, m; ruina, f; (oldness) vejez, f; decadencia, declinación, f; (fall) caída, f
decease /dɪ'sis/ n fallecimiento, m, defunción, f, vi fallecer
deceased /dɪ'sist/ n finado (-da), difunto (-ta). —a difunto
deceit /dɪ'sit/ n engaño, fraude, m; duplicidad, f
deceitful /dɪ'sitfəl/ a engañoso, falso; embustero, mentiroso; ilusorio
deceitfully /dɪ'sitfəli/ adv engañosamente
deceitfulness /dɪ'sitfəlnɪs/ n falsedad, duplicidad, f
deceivable /dɪ'sivəbəl/ a fácil a engañar, engañadizo
deceive /dɪ'siv/ vt engañar; (disappoint) decepcionar, desilusionar; frustrar. **If my memory does not d. me,** Si la memoria no me engaña, Si mal no me acuerdo
deceiver /dɪ'sivər/ n engañador (-ra); seductor, m
deceiving /dɪ'sivɪŋ/ a engañador
December /dɪ'sɛmbər/ n diciembre, m
decency /'disənsi/ n decoro, m, decencia, f; pudor, m, modestia, f; conveniencias, f pl; Inf. bondad, f; (manners) cortesía, f, buenos modales, m pl
decennial /dɪ'sɛniəl/ a decenal
decent /'disənt/ a decente; decoroso, honesto; púdico; (likable) simpático; (of things) bastante bueno; (honorable) honrado
decently /'disəntli/ adv decentemente
decentralization /di,sɛntrələ'zeɪʃən/ n descentralización, f
decentralize /di'sɛntrə,laiz/ vt descentralizar
deception /dɪ'sɛpʃən/ n engaño, m; ilusión, f
deceptive /dɪ'sɛptɪv/ a engañoso, mentiroso, ilusorio
deceptively /dɪ'sɛptɪvli/ adv engañosamente
decide /dɪ'said/ vt decidir; Law. determinar. —vi decidir, resolver; acordar, quedar en; juzgar; Law. dictar sentencia, fallar
decided /dɪ'saidɪd/ a decidido; (downright) categórico, inequívoco; resuelto; positivo; definitivo
decidedly /dɪ'saidɪdli/ adv decididamente; categóricamente; definitivamente
deciduous /dɪ'sɪdʒuəs/ a Bot. caedizo
decigram /'dɛsɪ,græm/ n decigramo, m
decimal /'dɛsəməl/ a decimal. **d. fraction,** fracción decimal, f. **d. point,** punto decimal, m. **d. system,** sistema métrico, m
decimate /'dɛsə,meit/ vt diezmar
decimation /,dɛsə'meiʃən/ n gran mortandad, f; matanza, f
decimeter /'dɛsə,mitər/ n decímetro, m
decipher /dɪ'saifər/ vt descifrar; deletrear
decipherable /dɪ'saifərəbəl/ a descifrable
decipherer /dɪ'saifərər/ n descifrador, m
decipherment /dɪ'saifərmənt/ n el descifrar; deletreo, m
decision /dɪ'sɪʒən/ n decisión, determinación, f; Law. sentencia, f, fallo, m; (agreement) acuerdo, m; (of character) firmeza, resolución, f
decisive /dɪ'saisɪv/ a decisivo; terminante, conclusivo; crítico
decisively /dɪ'saisɪvli/ adv decisivamente
decisiveness /dɪ'saisɪvnɪs/ n carácter decisivo, m; firmeza, resolución, f; decisión, f
deck /dɛk/ n cubierta, f; (of cards) baraja (de naipes), f. —vt adornar, ataviar; decorar. **between decks,** entrecubiertas, f pl. **lower d.,** cubierta, f. **promenade d.,** cubierta de paseo, f. **upper d.,** cubierta superior, f. **d.-cabin,** camarote de cubierta, m. **d.-chair,** silla de cubierta, silla de tijera, silla extensible, f. **d.-hand,** marinero, estibador, m
decked /dɛkt/ a ornado, ataviado; engalanado; Naut. de... puentes

declaim /dɪ'kleim/ vt recitar. —vi perorar, declamar
declamation /,dɛklə'meiʃən/ n declamación, f
declamatory /dɪ'klæmə,tɔri/ a declamatorio
declaration /,dɛklə'reiʃən/ n declaración, f; manifiesto, m; proclamación, f
declarative /dɪ'klærətɪv/ a declaratorio, declarativo
declare /dɪ'klɛər/ vt declarar; proclamar; afirmar; manifestar; confesar. —vi declarar; Law. deponer, testificar. **to d. war (on)** declarar la guerra (a)
declaredly /dɪ'klɛərɪdli/ adv declaradamente, explícitamente, abiertamente
declension /dɪ'klɛnʃən/ n declinación, f
declination /,dɛklə'neiʃən/ n declinación, f
decline /dɪ'klain/ n declinación, decadencia, f; disminución, f; debilitación, f; (of the day) caída, f; (of stocks, shares) depresión, f; (illness) consunción, f; (Fig. setting) ocaso, m, vi declinar; inclinarse; decaer; disminuir; debilitarse; (refuse) negarse (a). —vt (refuse) rechazar, rehusar; Gram. declinar; (avoid) evitar
declining /dɪ'klainɪŋ/ a declinante. **in one's d. years,** en sus últimos años
declivity /dɪ'klɪvɪti/ n cuesta, pendiente, f, declive, m
declutch /di'klʌtʃ/ vi desembragar
decoction /dɪ'kɒkʃən/ n decocción, f
decode /di'koud/ vt descifrar
decoder /di'koudər/ n descifrador, m
décolletee /,deikɒlə'tei/ a escotado
decoloration /di,kʌlə'reiʃən/ n decoloración, f
decompose /,dikəm'pouz/ vt descomponer. —vi descomponerse
decomposition /di,kɒmpə'zɪʃən/ n descomposición, f
decompressor /,dikəm'prɛsər/ n decompresor, m
decontaminate /,dikən'tæmə,neit/ vt descontaminar
decontamination /,dikən,tæmə'neiʃən/ n descontaminación, f
decontrol /,dikən'troul/ vt suprimir las restricciones sobre
decorate /'dɛkə,reit/ vt adornar (con), embellecer; (by painting, etc.) decorar, pintar; (honor) investir (con), condecorar
decoration /,dɛkə'reiʃən/ n decoración, f; Theat. decorado, m; (honor) condecoración, f; ornamento, m
decorative /'dɛkərətɪv/ a decorativo
decorator /'dɛkə,reitər/ n decorador, m; (interior) adornista, m
decorous /'dɛkərəs/ a decoroso, decente; correcto
decorum /dɪ'kɔrəm/ n decoro, m; corrección, f
decoy /n 'dikɔi; v dɪ'kɔi/ n señuelo, m; añagaza, f; (trap) lazo, m, trampa, f; Fig. añagaza, f. —vt (birds) reclamar, atraer con señuelo; Fig. tentar (con), seducir (con). **d. bird,** pájaro de reclamo, m
decrease /'dikris; v dɪ'kris/ n disminución, f; baja, f; reducción, f; (of the moon, waters) mengua, f, vi decrecer, disminuir; bajar; menguar. —vt disminuir; reducir
decreasingly /dɪ'krisɪŋli/ adv de menos en menos
decree /dɪ'kri/ n decreto, m; edicto, m. —vi and vt decretar, mandar
decrepit /dɪ'krɛpɪt/ a decrépito
decry /dɪ'krai/ vt desacreditar, rebajar
dedicate /v 'dɛdɪ,keit; a -kɪt/ vt dedicar; consagrar; destinar; aplicar; (a book, etc.) dedicar. **to d. oneself to,** dedicarse a, consagrarse a, entregarse a
dedication /,dɛdɪ'keiʃən/ n dedicación, f; consagración, f; (of a book, etc.) dedicatoria, f
dedicatory /'dɛdɪkə,tɔri/ a dedicatorio
deduce /dɪ'dus/ vt derivar; deducir, inferir
deduct /dɪ'dʌkt/ vt deducir, descontar
deduction /dɪ'dʌkʃən/ n deducción, f; descuento, m
deductive /dɪ'dʌktɪv/ a deductivo
deed /did/ n acción, f; hecho, acto, m; hazaña, f; (reality) realidad, f; Law. escritura, f; Law. contrato, m. **d. of gift,** escritura de donación, f
deem /dim/ vt juzgar, creer, estimar
deep /dip/ a profundo; (wide) ancho; (low) bajo; (thick) espeso; (of colours) subido; (of sounds) grave, profundo; (immersed in) absorto (en); (of the mind) penetrante; (secret) secreto; (intense) intenso, hondo; (cunning) astuto, artero; (dark) oscuro; (of mourning) riguroso. —n Poet. piélago, mar, m;

profundidad, *f;* abismo, *m, adv* profundamente; a una gran profundidad. **to be in d. waters,** *Fig.* estar con el agua al cuello. **to be three feet d.,** tener tres pies de profundidad. **to be d. in,** estar absorto en; (of debt) estar cargado de. **three d.,** tres de fondo. **d. into the night,** hasta las altas horas de la noche. **d.-felt,** hondamente sentido. **d. mourning,** luto riguroso, *m.* **d.-rooted,** arraigado. **d.-sea fishing,** pesca mayor, *f.* **d.-sea lead,** escandallo, *m.* **d.-seated,** íntimo, profundo; arraigado. **d.-set,** hundido

deepen /'dipən/ *vt* profundizar, ahondar; (broaden) ensanchar; (intensify) intensificar; (increase) aumentar; (of colors) aumentar el tono de, intensificar. —*vi* hacerse más profundo, hacerse más hondo; intensificarse; aumentarse; (of sound) hacerse más grave

deeply /'dipli/ *adv* profundamente; intensamente, fuertemente

deepness /'dipnɪs/ *n* (cunning) astucia, *f;* see **depth**

deer /dɪər/ *n* ciervo (-va), venado, *m, a* cervuno. **d.-hound,** galgo de cazar venados, *m.* **d.-skin,** piel de venado, *f.* **d.-stalking,** caza del ciervo, *f*

deface /dɪ'feɪs/ *vt* desfigurar, mutilar; estropear; (erase) borrar

defacement /dɪ'feɪsmənt/ *n* desfiguración, mutilación, *f;* afeamiento, *m;* borradura, *f*

defamation /ˌdɛfə'meɪʃən/ *n* difamación, denigración, *f*

defamatory /dɪ'fæmə,tɔri/ *a* difamatorio, denigrante

defame /dɪ'feɪm/ *vt* difamar, denigrar, calumniar

default /dɪ'fɔlt/ *n* omisión, *f,* descuido, *m;* falta, *f;* ausencia, *f; Law.* rebeldía, *f.* —*vi* dejar de cumplir; faltar; no pagar. —*vt Law.* condenar en rebeldía. **in d. of,** en la ausencia de

defaulter /dɪ'fɔltər/ *n* el, *m,* (*f,* la) que no cumple sus obligaciones; delincuente, *mf;* desfalcador (-ra); *Law.* rebelde, *mf*

defeat /dɪ'fit/ *vt* vencer, derrotar; frustrar; (reject) rechazar; (elude) evitar; *Fig.* vencer, triunfar sobre. —*n* derrota, *f;* vencimiento, *m;* frustración, *f;* rechazamiento, *m.* **to d. one's own ends,** defraudar sus intenciones

defeatism /dɪ'fitɪzəm/ *n* derrotismo, *m*

defeatist /dɪ'fitɪst/ *n* derrotista, *mf*

defecate /'dɛfɪ,keɪt/ *vi* defecar

defecation /ˌdɛfɪ'keɪʃən/ *n* defecación, *f*

defect /*n* 'difɛkt, dɪ'fɛkt; *v* dɪ'fɛkt/ *n* defecto, *m;* imperfección, *f;* falta, *f*

defection /dɪ'fɛkʃən/ *n* defección, *f;* deserción, *f;* (from a religion) apostasía, *f*

defective /dɪ'fɛktɪv/ *a* defectuoso; *Gram.* defectivo; falto; imperfecto; (mentally) anormal. —*n* persona anormal, *f,* anormal, *m*

defectiveness /dɪ'fɛktɪvnɪs/ *n* imperfección, *f;* deficiencia, *f;* defecto, *m*

defend /dɪ'fɛnd/ *vt* defender; proteger; preservar; sostener; (a thesis) sustentar

defendant /dɪ'fɛndənt/ *n Law.* acusado (-da), procesado (-da), demandado (-da)

defender /dɪ'fɛndər/ *n* defensor (-ra); (of a thesis) sustentante, *mf*

defense /dɪ'fɛns/ *n* defensa, *f;* justificación, *f; pl* **defenses,** defensas, *f pl;* obras de fortificación, *f pl.* **for the d.,** (of witnesses) de descargo; (of counsel) para la defensa. **in d. of,** en defensa de. **in one's own d.,** en su propia defensa. **d. in depth,** *Mil.* defensa en fondo, *f*

defenseless /dɪ'fɛnslɪs/ *a* indefenso, sin defensa

defenselessness /dɪ'fɛnslɪsnɪs/ *n* incapacidad de defenderse, *f;* debilidad, *f,* desvalimiento, *m*

defensible /dɪ'fɛnsəbəl/ *a* defendible; justificable

defensive /dɪ'fɛnsɪv/ *a* defensivo. —*n* defensiva, *f.* **to be on the d.,** estar a la defensiva

defensively /dɪ'fɛnsɪvli/ *adv* defensivamente

defer /dɪ'fɜr/ *vt* (postpone) diferir, aplazar; suspender. —*vi* (yield) deferir, ceder; (delay) tardar, aguardar. **deferred payment,** pago a plazos, *m*

deference /'dɛfərəns/ *n* deferencia, *f,* respeto, *m;* consideración, *f*

deferential /ˌdɛfə'rɛnʃəl/ *a* deferente, respetuoso

deferment /dɪ'fɜrmənt/ *n* aplazamiento, *m;* suspensión, *f*

defiance /dɪ'faɪəns/ *n* desafío, *m;* provocación, *f;* oposición, *f;* insolencia, *f.* **in d. of,** en contra de

defiant /dɪ'faɪənt/ *a* provocativo; insolente

defiantly /dɪ'faɪəntli/ *adv* de un aire provocativo; insolentemente

deficiency /dɪ'fɪʃənsi/ *n* falta, deficiencia, *f;* imperfección, *f;* defecto, *m;* omisión, *f;* (scarcity) carestía, *f;* (in accounts) déficit, *m*

deficient /dɪ'fɪʃənt/ *a* deficiente; falto, incompleto; imperfecto; pobre; defectuoso; (not clever at) débil (en); (mentally) anormal. **to be d. in,** carecer de; ser pobre en

deficit /'dɛfəsɪt/ *n* déficit, *m;* descubierto, *m*

defile /dɪ'faɪl/ *n* desfiladero, *m.* —*vt* contaminar; profanar; manchar; deshonrar. —*vi Mil.* desfilar

defilement /dɪ'faɪlmənt/ *n* contaminación, *f;* corrupción, *f;* profanación, *f*

definable /dɪ'faɪnəbəl/ *a* definible

define /dɪ'faɪn/ *vt* definir; (throw into relief) destacar; fijar; *Law.* determinar

definite /'dɛfənɪt/ *a* definido; positivo; categórico; exacto; concreto. **d. article,** artículo definido, *m*

definitely /'dɛfənɪtli/ *adv* positivamente; claramente. **definitely not!** ¡definitivamente no!

definiteness /'dɛfənɪtnɪs/ *n* carácter definido, *m;* exactitud, *f;* lo categórico

definition /ˌdɛfə'nɪʃən/ *n* definición, *f*

definitive /dɪ'fɪnɪtɪv/ *a* definitivo

deflate /dɪ'fleɪt/ *vt* desinflar. —*vi* desinflarse, deshincharse

deflation /dɪ'fleɪʃən/ *n* desinflación, *f*

deflect /dɪ'flɛkt/ *vt* desviar; apartar. —*vi* desviarse; apartarse

deflection /dɪ'flɛkʃən/ *n* desviación, *f;* apartamiento, *m*

defloration /ˌdɛflə'reɪʃən/ *n* desfloración, *f*

deflower /dɪ'flaʊər/ *vt* desflorar

deforestation /dɪˌfɔrɪ'steɪʃən/ *n* desforestación, desmontadura, despoblación forestal, *f*

deform /dɪ'fɔrm/ *vt* deformar, desfigurar; afear

deformation /ˌdifɔr'meɪʃən/ *n* deformación, *f*

deformed /dɪ'fɔrmd/ *a* deformado; contrahecho

deformity /dɪ'fɔrmɪti/ *n* deformidad, *f*

defraud /dɪ'frɔd/ *vt* defraudar

defrauder /dɪ'frɔdər/ *n* defraudador (-ra)

defrauding /dɪ'frɔdɪŋ/ *n* defraudación, *f*

defray /dɪ'freɪ/ *vt* sufragar, costear, pagar

defrayal /dɪ'freɪəl/ *n* pago, *m*

defrost /dɪ'frɔst/ *vt* deshelar

deft /dɛft/ *a* diestro; hábil

deftly /'dɛftli/ *adv* con destreza; hábilmente

deftness /'dɛftnɪs/ *n* destreza, *f;* habilidad, *f*

defunct /dɪ'fʌŋkt/ *a* and *n* difunto (-ta)

defy /dɪ'faɪ/ *vt* desafiar; (face) arrostrar; (violate) contravenir

degeneracy /dɪ'dʒɛnərəsi/ *n* degeneración, *f;* depravación, degradación, *f*

degenerate /*a,* *n* dɪ'dʒɛnərɪt; *v* -ˌreɪt/ *a* and *n* degenerado (-da). —*vi* degenerar

degeneration /dɪˌdʒɛnə'reɪʃən/ *n* degeneración, *f*

degradation /ˌdɛgrɪ'deɪʃən/ *n* degradación, *f;* abyección, *f*

degrade /dɪ'greɪd/ *vt* degradar; envilecer, deshonrar

degrading /dɪ'greɪdɪŋ/ *a* degradante

degree /dɪ'gri/ *n* grado, *m;* punto, *m;* clase social, *f.* **by degrees,** poco a poco, gradualmente, **five degrees below zero,** cinco grados bajo cero. **in the highest d.,** en sumo grado, en grado superlativo. **to a certain d.,** hasta cierto punto. **to receive a d.,** graduarse

degree-granting institution /dɪ'gri ˌgræntɪŋ/ *n* plantel habilitado para expedir títulos, *m*

dehydrate /di'haɪdreɪt/ *vt* deshidratar

dehydration /ˌdihaɪ'dreɪʃən/ *n* deshidratación, *f*

de-ice /di'aɪs/ *vt* deshelar

deicide /'diəˌsaɪd/ *n* (act) deicidio, *m;* (person) deicida, *mf*

deification /ˌdiəfɪ'keɪʃən/ *n* deificación, *f*

deify /'diəˌfaɪ/ *vt* deificar, endiosar

deign /deɪn/ *vi* dignarse. —*vt* conceder

deism /'diɪzəm/ *n* deísmo, *m*

deist /'diɪst/ *n* deísta, *mf*

deity /'diːti/ *n* deidad, divinidad, *f*; dios, *m*

dejected /dɪ'dʒɛktɪd/ *a* abatido, desanimado, deprimido

dejectedly /dɪ'dʒɛktɪdli/ *adv* tristemente, abatidamente

dejection /dɪ'dʒɛkʃən/ *n* abatimiento, desaliento, *m*, melancolía, *f*

delay /dɪ'lei/ *n* retraso, *m*, dilación, tardanza, demora, *f*. —*vt* retrasar, demorar; (a person) entretener; (postpone) aplazar; (obstruct) impedir. —*vi* tardar; entretenerse. **without more d.,** sin más tardar

delectable /dɪ'lɛktəbəl/ *a* deleitoso, delicioso

delectably /dɪ'lɛktəbli/ *adv* deliciosamente

delectation /ˌdilɛk'teifən/ *n* delectación, *f*, deleite, *m*

delegacy /'dɛligəsi/ *n* delegación, *f*

delegate /*n* 'dɛlɪgɪt; *v* -ˌgeit/ *n* delegado (-da). —*vt* delegar, diputar

delegation /ˌdɛli'geifən/ *n* delegación, *f*

delete /dɪ'lit/ *vt* suprimir, borrar

deleterious /ˌdɛlɪ'tɪriəs/ *a* deletéreo

deletion /dɪ'lifən/ *n* supresión, borradura, *f*

deliberate /*a* dɪ'lɪbərɪt; *v* -əˌreit/ *a* premeditado, intencionado; (slow) pausado, lento. —*vi* and *vt* deliberar, discurrir, considerar

deliberately /dɪ'lɪbərɪtli/ *adv* (intentionally) con premeditación, a sabiendas; (slowly) pausadamente, lentamente

deliberation /dɪˌlɪbə'reifən/ *n* reflexión, deliberación, consideración, *f*; (slowness) lentitud, pausa, *f*

deliberative /dɪ'lɪbərətɪv/ *a* deliberativo, de liberante

delicacy /'dɛlɪkəsi/ *n* delicadeza, *f*; fragilidad, *f*; suavidad, *f*; sensibilidad, *f*; escrupulosidad, *f*; (of health) debilidad, delicadez, *f*; (difficulty) dificultad, *f*; (food) manjar exquisito, *m*, golosina, *f*

delicate /'dɛlɪkɪt/ *a* delicado; fino; frágil; suave; exquisito; delicado (de salud); (of situations) difícil

delicatessen /ˌdɛlɪkə'tɛsən/ *n* (store) fiambrería, *f*

delicious /dɪ'lɪfəs/ *a* delicioso

deliciously /dɪ'lɪfəsli/ *adv* deliciosamente

deliciousness /dɪ'lɪfəsnɪs/ *n* deleite, *m*, lo delicioso; excelencia, *f*; delicias, *f pl*

delict /dɪ'lɪkt/ *n* delito, *m*

delictive /dɪ'lɪktɪv/ *a* delictivo

delight /dɪ'lait/ *n* deleite, regocijo, *m*; encanto, *m*, delicia, *f*; placer, gozo, *m*. —*vt* deleitar, encantar; halagar. —*vi* deleitarse, complacerse. **to be delighted with,** estar encantado con. **to d. in,** deleitarse en, complacerse en; tomar placer en

delightful /dɪ'laitfəl/ *a* delicioso, precioso, encantador

delightfully /dɪ'laitfəli/ *adv* deliciosamente

delimit /dɪ'lɪmɪt/ *vt* delimitar

delimitation /dɪˌlɪmɪ'teifən/ *n* delimitación, *f*

delineate /dɪ'lɪni,eit/ *vt* delinear, diseñar; *Fig.* pintar, describir

delineation /dɪˌlɪni'eifən/ *n* delineación, *f*; retrato, *m*; *Fig.* descripción, *f*

delineator /dɪ'lɪnieitər/ *n* diseñador, *m*

delinquency /dɪ'lɪŋkwənsi/ *n* delincuencia, *f*; criminalidad, *f*; culpa, *f*; delito, *m*

delinquent /dɪ'lɪŋkwənt/ *a* delincuente. —*n* delincuente, *mf*

deliquescence /ˌdɛlɪ'kwɛsəns/ *n* delicuescencia, *f*

deliquescent /ˌdɛlɪ'kwɛsənt/ *a* delicuescente

delirious /dɪ'lɪəriəs/ *a* delirante; desvariado; *Inf.* loco. **to be d.,** delirar, desvariar

delirium /dɪ'lɪəriəm/ *n* delirio, desvarío, *m*. **d. tremens,** delírium tremens, *m*

deliver /dɪ'lɪvər/ *vt* librar (de); salvar (de); (distribute) repartir; (hand over) entregar; (recite) recitar, decir; (a speech) pronunciar; comunicar; (send) despachar, expedir; (a blow) asestar; (give) dar; (bring) traer; (battle, a lecture) dar; (a woman, of a doctor) asistir en el parto (a); (a child) traer al mundo; (a judgment) pronunciar. **to be delivered (of a child),** dar a luz. **to d. oneself up,** entregarse. **delivered free,** porte pagado.

deliverance /dɪ'lɪvərəns/ *n* libramiento, rescate, *m*; redención, salvación, *f*; (of a judgment) pronuncia, *f*

deliverer /dɪ'lɪvərər/ *n* libertador (-ra); salvador (-ra); (distributor) repartidor (-ra); entregador (-ra)

delivery /dɪ'lɪvəri/ *n* (distribution) reparto, *m*, distri-

bución, *f*; entrega, *f*; *Law.* cesión, *f*; (of a judgment) pronuncia, *f*; (of a speech) pronunciación, *f*; (manner of speaking) declamación, *f*; dicción, *f*; (of a child) parto, *m*. **on d.,** al entregarse. **The letter came by the first d.,** La carta llegó en el primer reparto. **d. man,** mozo de reparto, *m*. **d. note,** nota de entrega, *f*. **d. van,** camión de reparto, *m*

delivery truck *n* camioneta de reparto, furgoneta, *f*, sedán de reparto, *m*

dell /dɛl/ *n* hondonada, *f*; pequeño valle, *m*

delouse /di'laus/ *vt* despiojar, espulgar

Delphi /'dɛlfai/ Delfos, *m*

delta /'dɛltə/ *n* (Greek letter) delta, *f*; (of a river) delta, *m*

delude /dɪ'lud/ *vt* engañar; ilusionar. **to d. oneself,** engañarse

deluded /dɪ'ludɪd/ *a* iluso, engañado, ciego

deluge /'dɛlyudʒ/ *n* diluvio, *m*. —*vt* diluviar; inundar (con)

delusion /dɪ'luʒən/ *n* engaño, *m*, ceguedad, *f*; error, *m*; ilusión, *f*

delve /dɛlv/ *vt* and *vi* cavar; *Fig.* ahondar (en), penetrar (en), investigar

demagogic /ˌdɛmə'gɒdʒɪk/ *a* demagógico

demagogue /'dɛməˌgɒg/ *n* demagogo (-ga)

demagogy /'dɛmə,goudʒi/ *n* demagogia, *f*

demand /dɪ'mænd/ *n* exigencia, *f*; *Com.* demanda, *f*; petición, *f*; *Polit. Econ.* consumo, *m*. —*vt* exigir; requerir; pedir; (claim) reclamar. **in d.,** en demanda. **on d.,** al solicitarse. **to be in d.,** ser popular. **d. note,** apremio, *m*

demanding /dɪ'mændɪŋ/ *a* exigente

demarcate /dɪ'markeit/ *vt* demarcar

demarcation /ˌdimar'keifən/ *n* demarcación, *f*

demean (oneself) /dɪ'min/ *vr* degradarse, rebajarse

demeanor /dɪ'minər/ *n* conducta, *f*; continente, porte, aire, *m*; (manners) modales, *m pl*

demented /dɪ'mɛntɪd/ *a* demente, loco

demerit /dɪ'mɛrɪt/ *n* demérito, *m*

demi- *prefix* semi; casi. **d.-tasse,** taza cafetera, jícara, *f*

demigod /'dɛmi,gɒd/ *n* semidios, *m*

demigoddess /'dɛmi,gɒdɪs/ *n* semidiosa, *f*

demijohn /'dɛmi,dʒɒn/ *n* damajuana, *f*

demilitarize /di'mɪlitə,raiz/ *vt* desmilitarizar

demise /dɪ'maiz/ *n* *Law.* traslación de dominio, *f*; sucesión de la corona, *f*; (death) óbito, fallecimiento, *m*

demisemiquaver /ˌdɛmi'sɛmi,kweivər/ *n* fusa, *f*

demobilization /di,moubələ'zeifən/ *n* desmovilización, *f*

demobilize /di'moubə,laiz/ *vt* desmovilizar

democracy /dɪ'mɒkrəsi/ *n* democracia, *f*

democrat /'dɛmə,kræt/ *n* demócrata, *mf*

democratic /ˌdɛmə'krætɪk/ *a* democrático. **to make d.,** democratizar

demolish /dɪ'mɒlɪʃ/ *vt* demoler, derribar; *Fig.* destruir; (eat) engullir, devorar

demolisher /dɪ'mɒlɪʃər/ *n* demoledor, *m*; *Fig.* destructor (-ra)

demolition /ˌdɛmə'lɪʃən/ *n* demolición, *f*; derribo, *m*, *a* demoledor; de demolición. **d. squad,** pelotón de demolición, *m*

demon /'dimən/ *n* demonio, diablo, *m*

demonetization /di,mɒnɪtə'zeifən/ *n* desmonetización, *f*

demonetize /di'mɒnɪ,taiz/ *vt* desmonetizar

demoniacal /ˌdimə'naiikəl/ *a* demoníaco

demonology /ˌdimə'nɒlədʒi/ *n* demonología, *f*

demonstrable /dɪ'mɒnstrəbəl, 'dɛmən-/ *a* demostrable

demonstrably /dɪ'mɒnstrəbli/ *adv* demostrablemente

demonstrate /'dɛmən,streit/ *vt* demostrar; mostrar, probar. —*vi* hacer una demostración

demonstration /ˌdɛmən'streifən/ *n* demostración, *f*; manifestación, *f*

demonstrative /də'mɒnstrətɪv/ *a* demostrativo; (of persons) expresivo, mimoso. **d. pronoun,** pronombre demostrativo, *m*

demonstrator /'dɛmən,streitər/ *n* demostrador (-ra)

demoralization /dɪˌmɔrələ'zeiʃən/ n desmoralización, f

demoralize /dɪ'mɔrəˌlaiz, -'mɒr-/ vt desmoralizar

demoralizing /dɪ'mɔrəˌlaizɪŋ/ a desmoralizador

demur /dɪ'mɜr/ vi dudar, vacilar; objetar, protestar; poner dificultades. —n objeción, protesta, f

demure /dɪ'myʊr/ a serio, modoso recatado; púdico; de una coquetería disimulada

demurely /dɪ'myʊrli/ adv modestamente; con recato; con coquetería disimulada

demureness /dɪ'myʊrnɪs/ n seriedad, f, recato, m; modestia fingida, coquetería disimulada, f

demy /də'mai/ n papel marquilla, m; becario de Magdalen College, Oxford, m

den /dɛn/ n madriguera, guardia, f; (of thieves) cueva, f; (in a zoo) cercado, recinto, m; (study) gabinete, m; (squalid room) cuartucho, m

denaturalization /diˌnætʃərələ'zeiʃən/ n desnaturalización, f

denaturalize /di'nætʃərəˌlaiz/ vt desnaturalizar

denial /dɪ'naiəl/ n negación, f; rechazo, m; contradicción, f; negativa, f

denizen /'dɛnəzən/ n habitante, m; ciudadano (-na)

Denmark /'dɛnmɑrk/ Dinamarca, f

denominate /dɪ'nɒməˌneit/ vt denominar, nombrar

denomination /dɪˌnɒmə'neiʃən/ n denominación, f; secta, f; clase, f

denominational /dɪˌnɒmə'neiʃənl/ a sectario

denominator /dɪ'nɒməˌneitər/ n Math. denominador, m

denote /dɪ'nout/ vt denotar, indicar; significar

dénouement /ˌdeinu'mɑ̃/ n desenlace, desenredo, m; solución, f

denounce /dɪ'nauns/ vt denunciar; delatar, acusar

denouncer /dɪ'naunsər/ n denunciante, mf delator (-ra)

dense /dɛns/ a denso; espeso, compacto; tupido; impenetrable; Inf. estúpido

densely /'dɛnsli/ adv densamente; espesamente. **d. populated,** con gran densidad de población

density /'dɛnsɪti/ n densidad, f; espesor, m; consistencia, f; Inf. estupidez, f

dent /dɛnt/ n mella, f; (in metal) abolladura, f, vt mellar; abollar

dental /'dɛntl/ a dental. —n letra dental, f. **d. forceps,** gatillo, m. **d. mechanic,** mecánico dentista, m. **d. surgeon,** odontólogo, m

dental floss n seda dental, f

dentifrice /'dɛntəfrɪs/ n dentífrico, m

dentist /'dɛntɪst/ n dentista, mf; odontólogo, m

dentistry /'dɛntəstri/ n odontología, f

dentition /dɛn'tɪʃən/ n dentición, f

denture /'dɛntʃər/ n dentadura, f

denudation /ˌdinu'deiʃən/ n denudación, f

denude /dɪ'nud/ vt denudar, despojar, privar (de)

denunciation /dɪˌnʌnsi'eiʃən/ n denuncia, f; acusación, delación, f

denunciatory /dɪ'nʌnsiəˌtɔri/ a denunciatorio

Denver boot /'dɛnvər/ n cepo, m

deny /dɪ'nai/ vt negar; desmentir; rehusar; rechazar; renegar (de); (give up) renunciar, sacrificar. **to d. oneself,** privarse (de); sacrificar; negarse

deodorant /di'oudərənt/ a and n desodorante m.

deodorize /di'oudəˌraiz/ vt desinfectar, destruir el olor de

depart /dɪ'pɑrt/ vi marcharse, irse, partir; (of trains, etc., and meaning go out) salir; (deviate) desviarse (de), apartarse (de); (go away) alejarse; (leave) dejar; (disappear) desaparecer; (alter) cambiar; (die) morir

departed /dɪ'pɑrtɪd/ a (past) pasado; desaparecido; (dead) difunto, muerto. —n difunto (-ta)

department /dɪ'pɑrtmənt/ n departamento, m; sección, f; (of learning) ramo, m; (in France) distrito administrativo, m. **d. store,** grandes tiendas, f pl, (Argentina), grandes almacenes, m pl

departmental /dɪˌpɑrt'mɛntl/ a departamental

departure /dɪ'pɑrtʃər/ n partida, ida, f; (going out, and of trains, etc.) salida, f; (deviation) desviación, el apartarse. **d. from the rules,** el apartarse de las reglas), f; (disappearance) desaparición, f; (change)

cambio, m; (giving up) renuncia, f; (death) muerte, f. **to take one's d.,** marcharse

depend /dɪ'pɛnd/ vi depender. **to d. on,** depender de; (rest on) apoyarse en; (count on) contar con; (trust) fiarse de; tener confianza en, estar seguro de. **That depends!** ¡Eso depende!

dependable /dɪ'pɛndəbəl/ a digno de confianza; seguro

dependence, dependency /dɪ'pɛndəns/ dɪ'pɛndənsi/ n dependencia, f; subordinación, f; (trust) confianza, f

dependent /dɪ'pɛndənt/ a dependiente; subordinado; condicional. —n dependiente, m. **to be d. on,** depender de

depict /dɪ'pɪkt/ vt representar; pintar; dibujar; Fig. describir, retratar

depiction /dɪ'pɪkʃən/ n representación, f; pintura, f; dibujo, m; Fig. descripción, f

depilate /'dɛpəˌleit/ vt depilar

depilation /ˌdɛpə'leiʃən/ n depilación, f

depilatory /dɪ'pɪləˌtɔri, -ˌtouri/ a and n depilatorio m.

deplete /dɪ'plit/ vt agotar; disipar

depletion /dɪ'pliʃən/ n agotamiento, m

deplorable /dɪ'plɔrəbəl/ a lamentable, deplorable

deplorably /dɪ'plɔrəbli/ adv lamentablemente

deplore /dɪ'plɔr/ vt deplorar, lamentar

deploy /dɪ'plɔi/ vt desplegar. —vi desplegarse. —n despliegue, m

deployment /dɪ'plɔimənt/ n despliegue, m

deponent /dɪ'pounənt/ a Law. declarante, deponente, mf a deponente. **d. verb,** verbo deponente, m

depopulate /di'pɒpyəˌleit/ vt despoblar

depopulation /diˌpɒpyə'leiʃən/ n despoblación, f

deport /dɪ'pɔrt/ vt deportar

deportation /ˌdipɔr'teiʃən/ n deportación, f

deportment /dɪ'pɔrtmənt/ n comportamiento, m; porte, aire, m; conducta, f

depose /dɪ'pouz/ vt destronar; (give evidence) testificar, declarar

deposit /dɪ'pɒzɪt/ n depósito, m; Geol. yacimiento, filón, m; sedimento, m. —vt depositar. **to leave a d.,** dejar un depósito. **d. account,** cuenta corriente, f

deposition /ˌdɛpə'zɪʃən/ n deposición, f; Law. testimonio, m, declaración, f; (from the Cross) descendimiento, m, (de la Cruz)

depositor /dɪ'pɒzɪtər/ n depositador (-ra)

depository /dɪ'pɒziˌtɔri/ n depositaría, f, almacén, m; (of knowledge, etc.) pozo, m

depot /'dipou/ n almacén, m; (military headquarters) depósito, m; (for army vehicles, etc.) parque, m; (for buses, etc.) estación, f

depravation /ˌdɛprə'veiʃən/ n depravación, f

depraved /dɪ'preivd/ a depravado, perverso, vicioso

depravity /dɪ'prævɪti/ n corrupción, maldad, perversión, f

deprecate /'dɛprɪˌkeit/ vt desaprobar, criticar; lamentar, deplorar

deprecatingly /'dɛprɪˌkeitɪŋli/ adv con desaprobación, críticamente

deprecation /ˌdɛprɪ'keiʃən/ n deprecación, f; desaprobación, crítica, f

deprecatory /'dɛprɪkəˌtɔri/ a deprecativo; de desaprobación, de crítica

depreciate /dɪ'priʃiˌeit/ vt depreciar, rebajar; Fig. tener en poco, menospreciar. —vi depreciarse, deteriorarse; bajar de precio

depreciatingly /dɪ'priʃiˌeitɪŋli/ adv con desprecio

depreciation /dɪˌpriʃi'eiʃən/ n (in value) amortización, depreciación, f; Fig. desprecio, m

depreciatory /dɪ'priʃiəˌtɔri/ a Fig. despectivo, despreciativo

depredation /ˌdɛprə'deiʃən/ n depredación, f

depress /dɪ'prɛs/ vt deprimir; (weaken) debilitar; (humble) humillar; (dispirit) abatir, entristecer; (trade) desanimar, paralizar

depressed /dɪ'prɛst/ a deprimido, desalentado, melancólico, triste; (of an area) necesitado

depressing /dɪ'prɛsɪŋ/ a melancólico, triste; pesimista

depressingly /dɪ'prɛsɪŋli/ adv con tristeza; con pesimismo

depression /dɪ'prɛʃən/ n depresión, f; (hollow) hoyo, m; (sadness) desaliento, abatimiento, m, melancolía, f; (in prices) baja, f; (in trade) desanimación, parálisis, f; Astron. depresión, f

deprivation /ˌdɛprə'veɪʃən/ n privación, f; pérdida, f

deprive /dɪ'praɪv/ vt privar (de), despojar (de); defraudar (de); Eccl. destituir (de)

depth /dɛpθ/ n profundidad, f; (thickness) espesor, m; fondo, m; (of night, winter, the country) medio, m; (of sound) gravedad, f; (of colour, feeling) intensidad, f; (abstruseness) dificultad, f; (sagacity) sagacidad, f; pl **depths**, profundidades, f pl; abismo, m; lo más hondo; lo más íntimo. **to be 4 feet in d.**, tener cuatro pies de profundidad. **to the depths of one's being**, hasta lo más íntimo de su ser; hasta los tuétanos. **d. charge**, carga de profundidad, f

deputation /ˌdɛpyə'teɪʃən/ n deputación, delegación, f

deputize (for) /'dɛpyəˌtaɪz/ vi desempeñar las funciones de, substituir

deputy /'dɛpyəti/ n (substitute) lugarteniente, m; (agent) representante, m; apoderado, m; (parliamentary) diputado, m; (in compounds) sub, vice. **d.-governor**, subgobernador, m. **d.-head**, subjefe, m; (of a school) subdirector (-ra)

derail /dɪ'reɪl/ vt (hacer) descarrilar

derailment /dɪ'reɪlmənt/ n descarrilamiento, m

derange /dɪ'reɪndʒ/ vt desordenar; desorganizar; turbar; (mentally) trastornar, hacer perder el juicio (a)

derangement /dɪ'reɪndʒmənt/ n desorden, m; turbación, f; (mental) trastorno, m, locura, f

derby /'dɜrbi/ n carrera del Derby, f; (hat) sombrero hongo, m

deregulate /di'rɛgyəˌleɪt/ vt desregular

deregulation /diˌrɛgyə'leɪʃən/ n desregulación, f

derelict /'dɛrəlɪkt/ a abandonado, derrelicto. —n derrelicto, m

dereliction /ˌdɛrə'lɪkʃən/ n abandono, m; omisión, negligencia, f; descuido, m

deride /dɪ'raɪd/ vt burlarse de, mofarse de; ridiculizar

derision /dɪ'rɪʒən/ n irrisión, f, menosprecio, m

derisive /dɪ'raɪsɪv/ a irrisorio; irónico

derisively /dɪ'raɪsɪvli/ adv irrisoriamente; con ironía, irónicamente

derivation /ˌdɛrə'veɪʃən/ n derivación, f

derivative /dɪ'rɪvətɪv/ a derivativo. —n derivado, m

derive /dɪ'raɪv/ vt derivar; obtener; extraer; Fig. sacar, hallar. —vi (from) derivar de; proceder de; remontar a

dermatitis /ˌdɜrmə'taɪtɪs/ n dermatitis, f

dermatologist /ˌdɜrmə'tɒlədʒɪst/ n dermatólogo, m

dermatology /ˌdɜrmə'tɒlədʒi/ n dermatología, f

derogatory /dɪ'rɒgəˌtɔri/ a despectivo, despreciativo; deshonroso

derrick /'dɛrɪk/ n grúa, machina, f; abanico, m

descant /n 'dɛskænt; v dɛs'kænt/ n Mus. discante, m. —vi Mus. discantar; discurrir (sobre), disertar (sobre)

descend /dɪ'sɛnd/ vi descender, bajar; (be inherited) pasar a; (fall) caer; (of the sun) ponerse. —vt bajar. **to d. from**, descender de. **to d. to**, (lower oneself) rebajarse; (consider) venir a, considerar. **to d. upon**, caer sobre; (arrive unexpectedly) llegar inesperadamente, invadir

descendant /dɪ'sɛndənt/ n descendiente, mf; pl **descendants**, descendencia, f

descent /dɪ'sɛnt/ n descenso, m; bajada, f; (slope) pendiente, cuesta, f; (attack) invasión, f, ataque, m; (lineage) descendencia, alcurnia, procedencia, f; (inheritance) herencia, f; transmisión, f. **D. from the Cross**, Descendimiento de la Cruz, m

describable /dɪ'skraɪbəbəl/ a descriptible

describe /dɪ'skraɪb/ vt describir; pintar

description /dɪ'skrɪpʃən/ n descripción, f

descriptive /dɪ'skrɪptɪv/ a descriptivo

descry /dɪ'skraɪ/ vt divisar, descubrir; Poet. ver

Desdemona /ˌdɛzdə'mounə/ Desdémona, f

desecrate /'dɛsɪˌkreɪt/ vt profanar

desecration /ˌdɛsɪ'kreɪʃən/ n profanación, f

desert /dɪ'zɜrt/ vt abandonar; dejar; (Mil. etc.) desertar. —vi desertar

desert /'dɛzərt/ n desierto, m

desert /dɪ'zɜrt/ n (merit) mérito, m **to receive one's deserts**, llevar su merecido

deserted /dɪ'zɜrtɪd/ a abandonado; desierto; solitario; inhabitado, despoblado

deserter /dɪ'zɜrtər/ n desertor, m

desertion /dɪ'zɜrʃən/ n abandono, m, deserción, f; (Mil. etc.) deserción, f

deserve /dɪ'zɜrv/ vt and vi merecer

deservedly /dɪ'zɜrvɪdli/ adv merecidamente

deserving /dɪ'zɜrvɪŋ/ a merecedor; meritorio. **to be d. of**, merecer

desiccate /'dɛsɪˌkeɪt/ vt desecar. —vi desecarse

design /dɪ'zaɪn/ n proyecto, m; plan, m; intención, f, propósito, m; objeto, m; modelo, m; (pattern) diseño, dibujo, m; arte del dibujo, mf vt idear; proyectar; (destine) destinar, dedicar; diseñar, dibujar, delinear; planear. **by d.**, expresamente, intencionalmente

designate /v 'dɛzɪgˌneɪt; n -nɪt/ vt señalar; designar; (appoint) nombrar. —a electo

designation /ˌdɛzɪg'neɪʃən/ n designación, f; nombramiento, m

designedly /dɪ'zaɪnɪdli/ adv de propósito

designer /dɪ'zaɪnər/ n inventor (-ra), autor (-ra); delineador (-ra); dibujante, mf; (of public works, etc.) proyectista, mf

designing /dɪ'zaɪnɪŋ/ a intrigante, astuto

desirability /dɪˌzaɪərə'bɪliti/ n lo deseable; conveniencia, f; ventaja, f

desirable /dɪ'zaɪərəbəl/ a deseable; conveniente; ventajoso; agradable; apetecible

desire /dɪ'zaɪər/ vt desear; querer; ansiar, ambicionar; (request) rogar, pedir; (order) mandar. —n deseo, m; ansia, aspiración, f; ambición, f; impulso, m; (will) voluntad, f. **to d. ardently**, perecerse por; suspirar por

desirous /dɪ'zaɪərəs/ a deseoso (de); ambicioso (de); ansioso (de); impaciente (a); curioso (de)

desist /dɪ'sɪst/ vi desistir; dejar (de)

desk /dɛsk/ n pupitre, m; escritorio, buró, m; mesa de trabajo, f; (cashier's) caja, f; (teacher's, lecturer's; pulpit) cátedra, f

desolate /a 'dɛsəlɪt; v -ˌleɪt/ a solitario; desierto; deshabitado; abandonado; arruinado; árido; (afflicted) desolado, angustiado. —vt desolar; despoblar

desolation /ˌdɛsə'leɪʃən/ n desolación, f; aflicción, angustia, f, desconsuelo, m

despair /dɪ'spɛər/ n desesperación, f, vi perder toda esperanza. **His life is despaired of**, Se ha perdido la esperanza de salvarle (la vida). **to be in d.**, estar desesperado

despairing /dɪ'spɛərɪŋ/ a desesperado

despairingly /dɪ'spɛərɪŋli/ adv sin esperanza

desperate /'dɛspərɪt/ a desesperado; sin esperanza; irremediable; furioso; violento; (dangerous) arriesgado, peligroso; terrible

desperately /'dɛspərɪtli/ adv desesperadamente; furiosamente; terriblemente

desperation /ˌdɛspə'reɪʃən/ n desesperación, f; furia, violencia, f

despicable /'dɛspɪkəbəl/ a vil, despreciable; insignificante

despise /dɪ'spaɪz/ vt despreciar; desdeñar

despiser /dɪ'spaɪzər/ n menospreciador (-ra)

despite /dɪ'spaɪt/ prep a pesar de

despoil /dɪ'spɔɪl/ vt despojar, desnudar

despoiler /dɪ'spɔɪlər/ n despojador (-ra)

despoliation /dɪˌspouli'eɪʃən/ n despojo, m

despondency /dɪ'spɒndənsi/ n abatimiento, desaliento, m, desesperación, f

despondent /dɪ'spɒndənt/ a abatido, desanimado, deprimido

despondently /dɪ'spɒndəntli/ adv con desaliento

despot /'dɛspət/ n déspota, m

despotic /dɛs'pɒtɪk/ a despótico

despotism /'dɛspəˌtɪzəm/ n despotismo, m

dessert /dɪ'zɜrt/ n postre, m, a de postre. **d. plate**, plato para postre, m. **d.-spoon**, cuchara de postre, f

destination /ˌdɛstə'neɪʃən/ n destinación, f

destine /'dɛstɪn/ vt destinar; dedicar; predestinar

destiny /'dɛstəni/ n destino, m

destitute /'dɛstɪˌtut/ a indigente, menesteroso; desnudo (de); privado (de); desprovisto (de), falto (de); desamparado

destitution /,dɛstɪ'tuʃən/ n destitución, indigencia, miseria, f; privación, falta, f; desamparo, m

destroy /dɪ'strɔɪ/ vt destruir; demoler; deshacer; (kill) matar; exterminar; (finish) acabar con

destroyer /dɪ'strɔɪər/ n destructor (-ra); Nav. destructor, cazatorpedero, m

destructible /dɪ'strʌktəbəl/ a destructible, destruible

destruction /dɪ'strʌkʃən/ n destrucción, f; demolición, f; ruina, f; pérdida, f; muerte, f; exterminio, m; perdición, f

destructive /dɪ'strʌktɪv/ a destructivo, destructor; (of animals) dañino. **d. animal,** animal dañino, m, alimaña, f

destructiveness /dɪ'strʌktɪvnɪs/ n destructividad, f; instinto destructor, m

desultory /'dɛsəl,tɔri/ a inconexo; sin método, descosido; irregular

detach /dɪ'tætʃ/ vt separar, desprender; (unstick) despegar; Mil. destacar

detachable /dɪ'tætʃəbəl/ a separable, de quita y pon

detached /dɪ'tætʃt/ a suelto, separado; (Fig. with outlook, etc.) imparcial; indiferente, despegado. **d. house,** hotelito, m

detachment /dɪ'tætʃmənt/ n separación, f; Mil. destacamento, m; (Fig. of mind) imparcialidad, f; independencia (de espíritu, etc.), f; indiferencia, f

detail /dɪ'teil/ n detalle, m; pormenor, m, particularidad, f; circunstancia, f; Mil. destacamento, m. —vt detallar; particularizar; referir con pormenores; Mil. destacar. **in d.,** detalladamente; al por menor; Inf. ce por be. **to go into details,** entrar en detalles

detain /dɪ'tein/ vt detener; (arrest) arrestar, prender; (withhold) retener; (prevent) impedir

detect /dɪ'tɛkt/ vt descubrir; averiguar; (discern) discernir, percibir; Elec. detectar

detectable /dɪ'tɛktəbəl/ a perceptible

detection /dɪ'tɛkʃən/ n descubrimiento, m; averiguación, f; percepción, f

detective /dɪ'tɛktɪv/ n detective, m, a de detectives, policíaco. **d. novel,** novela policíaca, f

detector /dɪ'tɛktər/ n descubridor, m; Elec. detector, m; Mech. indicador, m

detention /dɪ'tɛnʃən/ n detención, f; (arrest) arresto, m; (confinement) encierro, m

deter /dɪ'tɜr/ vt desanimar, desalentar; acobardar; (dissuade) disuadir; (prevent) impedir

detergent /dɪ'tɜrdʒənt/ a detersorio. —n detersorio, m

deteriorate /dɪ'tɪriə,reit/ vt deteriorar. —vi deteriorarse; empeorar

deterioration /dɪ,tɪriə'reiʃən/ n deterioración, f; empeoramiento, m

determinable /dɪ'tɜrmənəbəl/ a determinable

determination /dɪ,tɜrmə'neiʃən/ n determinación, f; definición, f; resolución, decisión, f; Law. fallo, m; Med. congestión, f

determine /dɪ'tɜrmɪn/ vt determinar; definir; decidir, resolver; concluir; (fix) señalar; Law. sentenciar. —vi resolverse, decidirse; (insist (on)) empeñarse en, insistir en

determined /dɪ'tɜrmɪnd/ a determinado; resuelto, decidido; (of price) fijo

determining /dɪ'tɜrmənɪŋ/ a determinante

determinism /dɪ'tɜrmə,nɪzəm/ n determinismo, m

deterministic /dɪ,tɜrmə'nɪstɪk/ a determinista

deterrent /dɪ'tɜrənt/ a disuasivo. —n freno, m. **to act as a d.,** servir como un freno

deterrent capability n poder de disuasión, m

detest /dɪ'tɛst/ vt detestar, abominar, aborrecer

detestable /dɪ'tɛstəbəl/ a detestable, aborrecible, abominable

detestation /,ditɛ'steiʃən/ n detestación, abominación, f, aborrecimiento, m

dethrone /di'θroun/ vt destronar

detonate /'dɛtn̩,eit/ vt hacer detonar. —vi detonar, estallar

detonation /,dɛtn̩'eiʃən/ n detonación, f

detonator /'dɛtn̩,eitər/ n detonador, m; señal detonante, f

detour /'ditʊr/ n rodeo, m; desvío, m, desviación, f

detract /dɪ'trækt/ vt quitar; (diminish) disminuir; (slander) detraer, denigrar

detraction /dɪ'trækʃən/ n detracción, denigración, f

detractor /dɪ'træktər/ n detractor (-ra); infamador (-ra)

detriment /'dɛtrəmənt/ n detrimento, m; perjuicio, m; daño, m

detrimental /,dɛtrə'mɛntl̩/ a perjudicial

deuce /dus/ n (dice, cards) dos, m; (tennis) "dos," m. **The d.!** ¡Diantre! **to be the d. of a row,** haber moros y cristianos. **D. take it!** ¡Demonios!

Deuteronomy /,dutə'rɒnəmi/ n Deuteronomio, m

devaluation /di,vælyu'eiʃən/ n desvalorización, f

devalue /di'vælyu/ vt rebajar el valor de

devastate /'dɛvə,steit/ vt devastar, asolar

devastation /,dɛvə'steiʃən/ n devastación, f

develop /dɪ'vɛləp/ vt desarrollar; (make progress) avanzar, fomentar; perfeccionar; Photo. revelar. —vi desarrollarse; crecer; avanzar, progresar; evolucionar

developer /dɪ'vɛləpər/ n Photo. revelador, m

development /dɪ'vɛləpmənt/ n desarrollo, m; evolución, f; progreso, avance, m; (encouragement) fomento, m; (event) acontecimiento, suceso, m; (product) producto, m; (working) explotación, f; Photo. revelación, f

deviate /'divi,eit/ vi desviarse (de); (disagree) disentir (de)

deviation /,divi'eiʃən/ n desviación, f

device /dɪ'vais/ n (contrivance) aparato, artefacto, mecanismo, m; (invention) invento, m; (trick) expediente, artificio, m; (scheme) proyecto, m; (design) dibujo, emblema, m; (motto) divisa, leyenda, f; pl **devices,** placeres, caprichos, m pl

devil /'dɛvəl/ n diablo, Satanás, m; demonio, m; (printer's) aprendiz de impresor, m. **Go to the d.!** ¡Vete enhoramala! **He is a poor d.,** Es un pobre diablo. **little d.,** diablillo, m. **The devil's abroad,** Anda el diablo suelto. **The d. take it!** ¡Lléveselo el diablo! **to play the d. with,** arruinar por completo. **What the d.!** ¡Qué diablos! **d.-possessed,** endemoniado

devilish /'dɛvəlɪʃ/ a diabólico, demoníaco; infernal

devilry /'dɛvəlri/ n diablura, f; magia, f; demonología, f; (wickedness) maldad, f; crueldad, f

devious /'diviəs/ a desviado; tortuoso

deviousness /'diviəsnɪs/ n tortuosidad, f

devise /dɪ'vaiz/ vt idear, inventar; fabricar; Law. legar

deviser /dɪ'vaizər/ n inventor (-ra)

devitalize /di'vaitl̩,aiz/ vt restar vitalidad, privar de vitalidad

devoid /dɪ'vɔid/ a desprovisto (de), privado (de); libre (de), exento (de)

devolve /dɪ'vɒlv/ vt traspasar, transmitir. —vi (on, upon) incumbir (a), corresponder (a), tocar (a)

devote /dɪ'vout/ vt dedicar; consagrar. **to d. oneself to,** darse a, dedicarse a; consagrarse a

devoted /dɪ'voutɪd/ a fervoroso, apasionado; (faithful) fiel, leal

devotedly /dɪ'deva'ti/ adv con devoción

devotee /,dɛvə'ti/ n devoto (-ta), admirador (-ra); aficionado (-da)

devotion /dɪ'vouʃən/ n devoción, f; dedicación, f; (zeal) celo, m; afición, f; (loyalty) lealtad, f; pl **devotions,** rezos, m pl, oraciones, f pl

devotional /dɪ'vouʃənl̩/ a devoto, religioso, de devoción. **devotional literature,** literatura de devoción, f

devour /dɪ'vaur/ vt devorar; consumir

devourer /dɪ'vaurər/ n devorador (-ra)

devouring /dɪ'vaurɪŋ/ a devorador; absorbente

devout /dɪ'vaut/ a devoto, piadoso, practicante (e.g., a d. Catholic, un católico practicante)

devoutly /dɪ'vautli/ adv piadosamente

devoutness /dɪ'vautnɪs/ n piedad, devoción, f

dew /du/ n rocío, sereno, relente, m; Fig. rocío, m, vt rociar; humedecer; (refresh) refrescar. **d.-drop,** aljófar, m, gota de rocío, f

dewlap /'du,læp/ n papada, f, papo, m

dewy /'dui/ a rociado, lleno de rocío; húmedo; (of eyes) lustroso

dexterity /dɛk'stɛrɪti/ n destreza, f

dextrine /'dɛkstrɪn/ n dextrina, f
dextrose /'dɛkstrous/ n dextrosa, glucosa, f
dextrous /'dɛkstrəs/ a diestro; hábil, listo
diabetes /,daiə'bitis/ n diabetes, f
diabetic /,daiə'bɛtɪk/ a diabético
diabolical /,daiə'bɒlɪkəl/ a diabólico
diadem /'daiə,dɛm/ n diadema, f
diagnose /'daiəg,nous/ vt diagnosticar
diagnosis /,daiəg'nousɪs/ n diagnóstico, m, diagnosis, f
diagnostician /,daiəgnɒ'stɪʃən/ n diagnóstico, m
diagonal /dai'ægənl/ n diagonal, f
diagram /'daiə,græm/ n diagrama, m; esquema, f; gráfico, m
diagrammatic /,daiəgrə'mætɪk/ a esquemático
dial /'daiəl/ n (sundial) reloj de sol, m; (of clocks, gas-meter) esfera, f; (of machines) indicador, m; (of a wireless set) cuadrante graduado, m; (of a telephone) marcador, disco, m. —vt (a telephone number) marcar. **d. telephone**, teléfono automático, m
dialect /'daiə,lɛkt/ n dialecto, m, habla, f, a dialectal
dialectic /,daiə'lɛktɪk/ a dialéctico
dialectics /,daiə'lɛktɪks/ n dialéctica, f
dialogue /'daiə,lɔg/ n diálogo, m. **to hold a d.,** dialogar
dialysis /dai'æləsɪs/ n diálisis, f
diameter /dai'æmɪtər/ n diámetro, m
diametrical /,daiə'mɛtrɪkəl/ a diametral
diamond /'daimənd/ n diamante, m; brillante, m; (tool) cortavidrios, m; (cards) oros (de baraja), m pl. **rough d.,** diamante bruto, m. **d.-bearing,** diamantífero. **d. cutter,** diamantista, mf **d. cutting,** talla de diamantes, f. **d. edition,** edición diamante, f. **d.-like,** adiamantado. **d. wedding,** bodas de diamante, f pl
diapason /,daiə'peizən/ n diapasón, m
diaper /'daipər/ n lienzo adamascado, m; (baby's) pañal, m; (woman's) servilleta higiénica, f
diaphanous /dai'æfənəs/ a diáfano, transparente
diaphragm /'daiə,fræm/ n diafragma, m
diarist /'daiərɪst/ n diarista, mf
diarrhea /,daiə'riə/ n diarrea, f
diary /'daiəri/ n diario, m
diastase /'daiə,steis/ n diastasa, f
diastole /dai'æstl/ n diástole, f
diatribe /'daiə,traib/ n diatriba, denunciación violenta, f
dibble /'dɪbəl/ n plantador, m, vt and vi plantar con plantador
dice /dais/ n pl dados, m pl. **to load the d.,** cargar los dados
dicky /'dɪki/ n (front) pechera postiza, f; (seat) trasera, f; (apron) delantal, m. **d. seat,** Inf. ahí te pudras, m
dictaphone /'dɪktə,foun/ n dictáfono, m
dictate /'dɪkteit/ vt dictar; mandar. —n (order) dictamen, m; Fig. dictado, m
dictation /dɪk'teiʃən/ n dictado, m. **to write from d.,** escribir al dictado
dictator /'dɪkteitər/ n dictador, m
dictatorial /,dɪktə'tɔriəl/ a dictatorial, dictatorio, imperioso
dictatorship /dɪk'teitər,ʃɪp/ n dictadura, f
diction /'dɪkʃən/ n dicción, f
dictionary /'dɪkʃə,nɛri/ n diccionario, m
dictum /'dɪktəm/ n dictamen, m; (saying) sentencia, f; Law. fallo, m
didactic /dai'dæktɪk/ a didáctico
die /dai/ vi morir; fallecer, finar; (wither) marchitarse; (disappear) desvanecerse, desaparecer; (of light) palidecer; extinguirse; (end) cesar; (desire) ansiar, perecerse (por). **Never say die!** ¡Mientras hay vida, hay esperanza! **to die early,** morir temprano; malograrse. **to die a violent death,** tener una muerte violenta, Inf. morir vestido. **to die from natural causes,** morir por causas naturales; Inf. morir en la cama. **to die hard,** luchar contra la muerte; tardar en morir; tardar en desaparecer. **to die of a broken heart,** morir con el corazón destrozado, morir de pena. **to die away,** desaparecer gradualmente; extinguirse poco a poco; dejar de oírse poco a poco; cesar; pasar. **to die down,** extinguirse gradualmente;

palidecer; dejar de oírse; desaparecer; (of the wind) amainar; perder su fuerza. **to die out,** desaparecer; olvidarse; dejar de existir; pasarse de moda
die /dai/ n dado, m; Fig. suerte, f; (stamp) cuño, troquel, m; Archit. cubo, m. **The die is cast,** La suerte está echada. **die-sinker,** grabador en hueco, m
diehard /'dai,hard/ n valiente, m; tradicionalista empedernido, m; partidario (-ia) entusiasta
Dieppe /di'ɛp/ Diepa, f
dieresis /dai'ɛrəsɪs/ n diéresis, crema, f
diesel /'dizəl, -səl/ a Diesel. **d. engine,** motor Diesel, m
diet /'daiit/ n dieta, f, régimen dietario, m; (assembly) dieta, f. —vi estar a dieta, hacer régimen
dietetic /,daii'tɛtɪk/ a dietético
dietetics /,daii'tɛtɪks/ n dietética, f
dietician /,daii'tɪʃən/ n dietista, mf
differ /'dɪfər/ vi diferenciarse; (contradict) contradecir; (disagree) no estar de acuerdo; disentir
difference /'dɪfərəns/ n diferencia, f; disparidad, f; contraste, m; (of opinion) disensión, f; controversia, disputa, f. **to make no d.,** no hacer diferencia alguna; no afectar; dar lo mismo, no importar
different /'dɪfərənt/ a distinto; diferente; vario, diverso
differential /,dɪfə'rɛnʃəl/ a diferencial. **d. calculus,** cálculo diferencial, m
differentiate /,dɪfə'rɛnʃi,eit/ vt diferenciar, distinguir. —vi diferenciarse, distinguirse
differentiation /,dɪfə,rɛnʃi'eiʃən/ n diferenciación, f
differently /'dɪfərəntli/ adv diferentemente
difficult /'dɪfɪ,kʌlt/ a difícil. **to make d.,** dificultar
difficulty /'dɪfɪ,kʌlti/ n dificultad, f. **d. in breathing,** opresión de pecho, f
diffidence /'dɪfɪdəns/ n modestia, timidez, f; huranía, f; falta de confianza en sí mismo, f
diffident /'dɪfɪdənt/ a modesto, tímido; huraño; sin confianza en sí mismo
diffidently /'dɪfɪdəntli/ adv tímidamente; vergonzosamente
diffract /dɪ'frækt/ vt difractar
diffraction /dɪ'frækʃən/ n difracción, f
diffractive /dɪ'fræktɪv/ a difrangente
diffuse /v dɪ'fyuz; a -'fyus/ vt difundir. —a difuso; (long-winded) prolijo
diffuseness /dɪ'fyusnɪs/ n difusión, f; prolijidad, f
diffusion /dɪ'fyuʒən/ n difusión, f; esparcimiento, m; diseminación, f
diffusive /dɪ'fyusɪv/ a difusivo
dig /dɪg/ vt and vi cavar; excavar; (of animals) escarbar; (mine) zapar, minar; (into a subject) ahondar (en); (with the spurs) aguijonear, dar con las espuelas; (poke) clavar. **to dig in,** enterrarse; Mil. abrir trincheras; Inf. arreglarse las cosas. **to dig out,** excavar; sacar cavando, sacar con azadón; extraer. **to dig up,** desenterrar; descubrir
digest /v dɪ'dʒɛst, dai-; n 'daidʒɛst/ vt clasificar; codificar; (food, also chem. and Fig. tolerate and think over) digerir; (of knowledge and territory) asimilar. —vi digerir. —n compendio, resumen, m; Law. digesto, m; recopilación, f. **This food is easy to d.,** Este alimento es fácil de digerir; Este alimento es muy ligero
digestibility /dɪ,dʒɛstə'bɪlɪti, dai-/ n digestibilidad, f
digestible /dɪ'dʒɛstəbəl, dai-/ a digerible, digestible
digestion /dɪ'dʒɛstʃən, dai-/ n digestión, f; (of ideas) asimilación, f; Chem. digestión, f
digestive /dɪ'dʒɛstɪv, dai-/ a digestivo
digger /'dɪgər/ n cavador (-ra)
digging /'dɪgɪŋ/ n cavadura, f; excavación, f; pl **diggings,** minas, f pl; excavaciones, f pl; Inf. alojamiento, m, posada, f
digit /'dɪdʒɪt/ n dígito, m
digital /'dɪdʒɪtl/ a digital, dígito
digitalin /,dɪdʒɪ'tælɪn/ n digitalina, f
digitalis /,dɪdʒɪ'tælɪs/ n digital, f
dignified /'dɪgnə,faid/ a serio, grave; majestuoso; (worthy) digno; solemne; altivo; noble
dignify /'dɪgnə,fai/ vt dignificar, honrar; exaltar; dar dignidad (a); ennoblecer
dignitary /'dɪgnɪ,tɛri/ n dignatario, m; dignidad, f

dignity /'dɪgnɪti/ *n* dignidad, *f;* (rank) rango, *m;* (post) cargo, puesto, *m;* (honor) honra, *f;* (stateliness) majestad, *f;* mesura, seriedad, *f;* (haughtiness) altivez, *f;* (nobility) nobleza, *f.* **to stand on one's d.,** darse importancia

digress /dɪ'grɛs, daɪ-/ *vi* divagar

digression /dɪ'grɛʃən, daɪ-/ *n* digresión, divagación, *f*

dike /daɪk/ *n* dique, *m;* (ditch) acequia, *f;* canal, *m;* (embankment) zanja, *f, vt* represar

dilapidated /dɪ'læpɪˌdeɪtɪd/ *a* arruinado, destartalado; (of fortune) dilapidado; (of persons, families) venido a menos; (shabby) raído

dilapidation /dɪˌlæpə'deɪʃən/ *n* deterioración, *f;* ruina, *f,* estado ruinoso, *m*

dilatation /ˌdɪlə'teɪʃən/ *n* dilatación, *f;* ensanche, *m*

dilate /daɪ'leɪt/ *vt* dilatar; ensanchar. —*vi* dilatarse. **to d. upon,** extenderse sobre, dilatarse en

dilator /daɪ'leɪtər/ *n* dilatador, *m*

dilatoriness /'dɪlətɔrɪnɪs/ *n* tardanza, *f;* (slowness) lentitud, *f*

dilatory /'dɪləˌtɔri/ *a* dilatorio, tardo; (slow) lento

dilemma /dɪ'lemə/ *n* dilema, *m*

dilettante /ˌdɪlɪˌtɑnt/ *n* diletante, *m;* aficionado (-da)

dilettantism /'dɪlɪtɑnˌtɪzəm/ *n* diletantismo, *m*

diligence /'dɪlɪdʒəns/ *n* diligencia, *f;* asiduidad, *f;* (care) cuidado, *m;* (coach) diligencia, *f*

diligent /'dɪlɪdʒənt/ *a* diligente, asiduo, aplicado, industrioso; (painstaking) concienzudo

dilute /dɪ'lut, daɪ-/ *vt* diluir; *Fig.* adulterar. —*a* diluido

dilution /dɪ'luʃən, daɪ-/ *n* dilución, *f; Fig.* adulteración, *f*

diluvian /dɪ'luviən/ *a* diluviano

dim /dɪm/ *a* (of light) apagado, débil, tenue; (of sight) turbio; (dark) sombrío, oscuro; (blurred, etc.) empañado; indistinto, confuso. —*vt* obscurecer; empañar; (dazzle) ofuscar; (eclipse) eclipsar; reducir la intensidad (de una luz); (of memories) borrar. **dim intelligence,** de brumoso seso

dimension /dɪ'menʃən/ *n* dimensión, *f;* (size) tamaño, *m;* (scope) extensión, *f,* alcance, *m*

dimensional /dɪ'menʃənl/ *a* dimensional

diminish /dɪ'mɪnɪʃ/ *vt* disminuir; reducir; debilitar, atenuar. —*vi* disminuir; reducirse; debilitarse, atenuarse

diminishing /dɪ'mɪnɪʃɪŋ/ *a* menguante

diminution /ˌdɪmə'nuʃən/ *n* disminución, *f;* reducción, *f,* atenuación, *f*

diminutive /dɪ'mɪnyətɪv/ *a* diminutivo. —*n* diminutivo, *m*

diminutiveness /dɪ'mɪnyətɪvnɪs/ *n* pequeñez, *f*

dimly /'dɪmli/ *adv* obscuramente; vagamente; indistintamente. **dimly lit,** apenas alumbrado

dimness /'dɪmnɪs/ *n* oscuridad, *f;* deslustre, *m;* (of light) tenuidad (de la luz), *f;* confusión, *f*

dimple /'dɪmpəl/ *n* hoyuelo, *m*

dimpled /'dɪmpəld/ *a* con hoyuelos, que tiene hoyuelos

din /dɪn/ *n* estrépito, estruendo, ruido, *m;* algarabía, barahúnda, *f, vt* ensordecer

dine /daɪn/ *vi* (in the evening) cenar; (at midday) comer. —*vt* convidar a cenar o a comer. **to d. out,** cenar o comer fuera

diner /'daɪnər/ *n* (on a train) coche comedor, coche restaurante, *m;* cenador, *m;* comedor, *m*

ding-dong /'dɪŋˌdɔŋ/ *n* tintín, *m*

dinghy /'dɪŋgi/ *n* lancha, *f;* canoa, *f,* bote, *m.* **rubber d.,** canoa de goma, *f*

dinginess /'dɪndʒɪnɪs/ *n* deslustre, *m;* suciedad, *f;* oscuridad, *f;* (of a person) desaseo, *m*

dingy /'dɪndʒi/ *a* deslucido, empañado; sucio; oscuro; (of persons) desaseado

dining car /'daɪnɪŋ/ *n* coche comedor, vagón restaurante, *m*

dining room *n* comedor, *m;* refectorio, *m*

dining table *n* mesa del comedor, *f*

dinner /'dɪnər/ *n* (in the evening) cena, *f;* (at midday) comida, *f.* **over the d. table,** de sobremesa. **d.-jacket,** smoking, *m.* **d. party,** cena, *f.* **d. plate,** plato, *m.* **d. roll,** panecillo, *m.* **d. service,** vajilla, *f*

dinosaur /'daɪnəˌsɔr/ *n* dinosauro, *m*

dint /dɪnt/ **(by d. of)** a fuerza de, a costa de

diocesan /daɪ'ɒsəsən/ *a* diocesano

diocese /'daɪəsɪs/ *n* diócesis, *f*

Dionysus Thrax /ˌdaɪə'naɪsəs 'θræks/ Dionisio el Tracio, *m*

dioxide /daɪ'ɒksaɪd, -sɪd/ *n* dióxido, *m*

dip /dɪp/ *n* inmersión, *f;* baño, *m;* (in the ground) declive, *m;* (in the road) columpio, *m,* depresión, *f;* (slope) pendiente, *f;* (candle) vela de sebo, *f;* (of the horizon) depresión (del horizonte), *f;* (of the needle) inclinación (de la aguja), *f.* —*vt* sumergir; bañar; (put) poner. —*vi* inclinarse hacia abajo. **to dip into a book,** hojear un libro. **to dip the colors,** saludar con la bandera. **to dip the headlights,** bajar los faros

diphtheria /dɪf'θɪriə/ *n* difteria, *f*

diphthong /'dɪfθɒŋ/ *n* diptongo, *m*

diploma /dɪ'ploumə/ *n* diploma, *m*

diplomacy /dɪ'plouməsi/ *n* diplomacia, *f;* tacto, *m*

diploma mill *n* fábrica de títulos académicos, *f*

diplomat /'dɪpləˌmæt/ *n* diplomático, *m*

diplomatic /ˌdɪplə'mætɪk/ *a* diplomático. **d. bag,** valija diplomática, *f.* **d. corps,** cuerpo diplomático, *m*

diplomatically /ˌdɪplə'mætɪkəli/ *adv* diplomáticamente

dipper /'dɪpər/ *n* (ladle) cazo, *m; Astron.* Osa Mayor, *f*

dipsomania /ˌdɪpsə'meɪniə/ *n* dipsomanía, *f*

dipsomaniac /ˌdɪpsə'meɪniæk/ *n* dipsómano (-na)

diptych /'dɪptɪk/ *n* díptica, *f*

dire /daɪ°r/ *a* espantoso, horrible; cruel; funesto

direct /dɪ'rekt, daɪ-/ *a* directo; claro, inequívoco; (of descent) recto; (of electric current) continuo; exacto. —*adv* directamente. —*vt* dirigir; (command) ordenar, encargar; dar instrucciones. **d. action,** acción directa, *f.* **d. current,** corriente continua, *f.* **d. line,** línea directa, *f;* (of descent) línea recta, *f.* **d. object,** acusativo, *m.* **d. speech,** oración directa, *f*

direct dialing *n* discado directo, *m*

direction /dɪ'rekʃən, 'daɪ-/ *n* dirección, *f;* rumbo, *m;* instrucción, *f;* (on a letter) sobrescrito, *m;* señas, *f pl.* **in the d. of,** en la dirección de; hacia; *Naut.* con rumbo a. **in all directions,** por todas partes; a los cuatro vientos. **to go in the d. of,** ir en la dirección de; tomar por. **Directions for use,** Direcciones para el uso. **d. indicator, d. signal,** (on car) indicador de dirección, *m*

directive /dɪ'rektɪv, daɪ-/ *a* directivo, director

directly /dɪ'rektli, daɪ-/ *adv* directamente; inmediatamente, en seguida

directness /dɪ'rektnɪs, daɪ-/ *n* derechura, *f*

director /dɪ'rektər, daɪ-/ *n* director (-triz, -ora), **managing d.,** director gerente, *m*

directorate /dɪ'rektərɪt, daɪ-/ *n* directorio, *m,* junta directiva, *f;* cargo de director, *m*

directory /dɪ'rektəri, daɪ-/ *n* directorio, *m,* guía, *f.* **telephone d.,** guía de teléfonos, *f*

dirge /dɜrdʒ/ *n* endecha, *f,* lamento, *m;* canto fúnebre, *m*

dirigible /'dɪrɪdʒəbəl/ *n* dirigible, *m*

dirt /dɜrt/ *n* mugre, suciedad, *f;* (mud) lodo, *m;* (earth) tierra, *f;* (dust) polvo, *m; Fig.* inmundicia, *f.* **d.-cheap,** sumamente barato. **to be d. cheap,** (of goods) estar por los suelos. **d.-track,** pista de ceniza, *f.* **d.-track racing,** carreras en pista de ceniza, *f pl*

dirtiness /'dɜrtinɪs/ *n* suciedad, *f;* (untidiness) desaseo, *m;* sordidez, *f;* (meanness) bajeza, *f*

dirty /'dɜrti/ *a* sucio; (untidy) desaseado; (muddy) enlodado; (dusty) polvoriento; (of weather) borrascoso; (sordid) sórdido; (base, mean) vil; (indecent) indecente, verde, obsceno. —*vt* ensuciar. **d. trick,** mala pasada, *f*

disability /ˌdɪsə'bɪlti/ *n* incapacidad, *f;* impotencia, *f;* desventaja, *f*

disable /dɪs'eɪbəl/ *vt* (cripple) estropear, tullir; hacer incapaz (de), incapacitar; imposibilitar; (destroy) destruir; *Law.* incapacitar legalmente

disabled /dɪs'eɪbəld/ *a* inválido; impedido, lisiado; (in the hand) manco; incapacitado; (of ships, etc.) fuera de servicio, estropeado. **d. soldier,** inválido, *m*

disablement /dɪs'eɪbəlmənt/ *n* (physical) invalidez, *f;* inhabilitación, *f; Law.* impedimento, *m*

disabuse /ˌdɪsə'byuz/ vt desengañar, sacar de un error

disadvantage /ˌdɪsəd'væntɪdʒ/ n desventaja, f. **to be under the d. of,** sufrir la desventaja de

disadvantaged /ˌdɪsəd'væntɪdʒd/ a (financially) de escasos recursos

disadvantageous /dɪsˌædvən'teɪdʒəs/ a desventajoso

disaffected /ˌdɪsə'fɛktɪd/ a desafecto

disaffection /ˌdɪsə'fɛkʃən/ n desafecto, descontento, m

disagree /ˌdɪsə'gri/ vi no estar de acuerdo; diferir; (quarrel) reñir; (not share the opinion of) no estar de la opinión (de); (of food, etc.) sentar mal; no probar. **The meat disagreed with me,** La carne me sentó mal

disagreeable /ˌdɪsə'griəbəl/ a desagradable; repugnante; (of persons) antipático, displicente

disagreeableness /ˌdɪsə'griəbəlnɪs/ n lo desagradable; (of persons) displicencia, f

disagreeably /ˌdɪsə'griəbli/ adv desagradablemente; con displicencia

disagreement /ˌdɪsə'grimənt/ n desacuerdo, m; diferencia, f; desavenencia, f; discordia, f; (quarrel) riña, disputa, f; discrepancia, f

disallow /ˌdɪsə'lau/ vt negar; rechazar

disappear /ˌdɪsə'pɪər/ vi desaparecer. **to cause to d.,** hacer desaparecer

disappearance /ˌdɪsə'pɪərəns/ n desaparición, f

disappoint /ˌdɪsə'pɔɪnt/ vt desilusionar; frustrar; (hopes) defraudar; (deprive) privar de; (annoy) contrariar; (break a promise) faltar (a la palabra)

disappointedly /ˌdɪsə'pɔɪntɪdli/ adv con desilusión, con desengaño

disappointing /ˌdɪsə'pɔɪntɪŋ/ a desengañador; pobre; triste; poco halagüeño

disappointment /ˌdɪsə'pɔɪntmənt/ n desengaño, m, decepción, f; frustración, f; desilusión, f; (vexation) contrariedad, f; contratiempo, m. **to suffer a d.,** sufrir un desengaño; Inf. llevarse un chasco

disapproval /ˌdɪsə'pruvəl/ n desaprobación, f

disapprove /ˌdɪsə'pruv/ vt desaprobar

disapproving /ˌdɪsə'pruvɪŋ/ a de desaprobación, severo

disapprovingly /ˌdɪsə'pruvɪŋli/ adv con desaprobación

disarm /dɪs'ɑrm/ vt desarmar. —vi desarmarse; deponer las armas

disarmament /dɪs'ɑrməmənt/ n desarme, m

disarrange /ˌdɪsə'reɪndʒ/ vt desarreglar; descomponer, desajustar; (hair) despeinar

disarrangement /ˌdɪsə'reɪndʒmənt/ n desarreglo, m; desajuste, m; desorden, m

disarray /ˌdɪsə'reɪ/ n desorden, desarreglo, m; confusión, f. —vt desordenar, desarreglar

disarticulate /ˌdɪsɑr'tɪkyə,leɪt/ vt desarticular

disarticulation /ˌdɪsɑr,tɪkyə'leɪʃən/ n desarticulación, f

disaster /dɪ'zæstər/ n desastre, m; catástrofe, m; infortunio, m

disastrous /dɪ'zæstrəs/ a desastroso; funesto, trágico

disastrously /dɪ'zæstrəsli/ adv desastrosamente

disastrousness /dɪ'zæstrəsnɪs/ n carácter desastroso, m

disavow /ˌdɪsə'vau/ vt repudiar; retractar

disavowal /ˌdɪsə'vauəl/ n repudiación, f

disband /dɪs'bænd/ vt licenciar. —vi desbandarse, dispersarse

disbelief /ˌdɪsbɪ'lif/ n incredulidad, f; desconfianza, f

disbelieve /ˌdɪsbɪ'liv/ vt and vi descreer, no creer; desconfiar (de)

disburse /dɪs'bərs/ vt desembolsar, pagar

disbursement /dɪs'bərsmənt/ n desembolso, m

disc /dɪsk/ n disco, m

discard /v dɪ'skɑrd; n 'dɪskɑrd/ vt desechar, arrinconar; despedir; (at cards) descartar. —n (at cards) descarte, m

discern /dɪ'sərn/ vt discernir, distinguir, percibir

discerner /dɪ'sərnər/ n discernidor (-ra)

discernible /dɪ'sərnəbəl/ a distinguible, perceptible

discerning /dɪ'sərnɪŋ/ a perspicaz, discernidor

discernment /dɪ'sərnmənt/ n discernimiento, m

discharge /v dɪs'tʃɑrdʒ/ vt descargar; (a gun) disparar, tirar; (an arrow) lanzar; Elec. descargar; emitir; (dismiss) destituir, despedir; arrojar; Mil. licenciar; (exempt) dispensar (de); (exonerate) absolver, exonerar; (free) dar libertad (a); (from hospital) dar de baja (a); Law. revocar; (perform) cumplir, ejecutar; (pay) pagar, saldar; (of an abscess, etc.) supurar.

discharge /n 'dɪstʃɑrdʒ/ n (of firearms) disparo, tiro, m; (of artillery) descarga, f; (of goods, cargo) descargue, m; Elec. descarga, f; (from a wound, etc.) pus, m, supuración, f; (from the intestine) flujo, m; (of a debt) pago, m.; Com. descargo, m; (receipt) carta de pago, quitanza, f; Mil. licencia absoluta, f; (dismissal) despedida, destitución, f; (exoneration) exoneración, f; (freeing) liberación, f; (from hospital) baja, f; (performance) cumplimiento, m; ejecución, f

disciple /dɪ'saɪpəl/ n discípulo (-la)

disciplinarian /ˌdɪsəplə'nɛəriən/ n disciplinario (-ia)

disciplinary /'dɪsəplə,nɛri/ a disciplinario

discipline /'dɪsəplɪn/ n disciplina, f, vt disciplinar

disclaim /dɪs'kleɪm/ vt renunciar (a); (repudiate) rechazar, repudiar

disclaimer /dɪs'kleɪmər/ n Law. renunciación, f; repudiación, f

disclose /dɪ'sklouz/ vt descubrir, revelar

disclosure /dɪ'sklouʒər/ n descubrimiento, m, revelación, f

discolor /dɪs'kʌlər/ vt descolorar. —vi descolorarse

discoloration /dɪs,kʌlə'reɪʃən/ n descoloramiento, m

discomfit /dɪs'kʌmfɪt/ vt desconcertar

discomfiture /dɪs'kʌmfɪtʃər/ n desconcierto, m

discomfort /dɪs'kʌmfərt/ n falta de comodidades, f; incomodidad, f; malestar, m; molestia, f; inquietud, f; dolor, m

discomposure /ˌdɪskəm'pouʒər/ n confusión, agitación, inquietud, f

disconcert /ˌdɪskən'sərt/ vt desconcertar, turbar; (of plans, etc.) frustrar

disconnect /ˌdɪskə'nɛkt/ vt separar; (of railway engines, etc.) desacoplar; desconectar; (of electric plugs) desenchufar

disconnected /ˌdɪskə'nɛktɪd/ a inconexo; incoherente, deshilvanado

disconnectedness /ˌdɪskə'nɛktɪdnɪs/ n inconexión, f; incoherencia, f

disconsolate /dɪs'kɒnsəlɪt/ a desconsolado, triste

disconsolately /dɪs'kɒnsəlɪtli/ adv desconsoladamente, tristemente

disconsolateness /dɪs'kɒnsəlɪtnɪs/ n desconsuelo, m

discontent /ˌdɪskən'tɛnt/ n descontento, disgusto, m, vt descontentar, desagradar

discontented /ˌdɪskən'tɛntɪd/ a descontentadizo, descontento, disgustado

discontinuance /ˌdɪskən'tɪnyuəns/ n descontinuación, cesación, f; interrupción, f

discontinue /ˌdɪskən'tɪnyu/ vt descontinuar; cesar; interrumpir; (of payments, etc.) suspender. —vi cesar

discontinuous /ˌdɪskən'tɪnyuəs/ a descontinuo; interrumpido; intermitente

discord /'dɪskɔrd/ n discordia, f; Mus. disonancia, f, desentono, m

discordant /dɪs'kɔrdənt/ a discorde, poco armonioso; incongruo; Mus. disonante, desentonado. **to be d.,** discordar; ser incongruo; Mus. disonar

discount /'dɪskaunt/ v also dɪs'kaunt/ n descuento, m; rebaja, f. —vt descontar; rebajar; balancear; (disconsider) desechar. **at a d.,** al descuento; bajo la par; fácil de obtener; superfluo; Fig. en desfavor, en descrédito. **rate of d.,** tipo de descuento, m. **d. for cash,** descuento por venta al contado, m

discourage /dɪ'skərɪdʒ/ vt desalentar, desanimar; oponerse a; disuadir; frustrar

discouragement /dɪ'skərɪdʒmənt/ n desaliento, m; desaprobación, oposición, f; disuasión, f; (obstacle) estorbo, m

discouraging /dɪ'skərɪdʒɪŋ/ a poco animador, que ofrece pocas esperanzas; (with prospect, etc.) nada halagüeño

discourse /n 'dɪskɔrs; v dɪs'kɔrs/ n discurso, m; plática, f; (treatise) disertación, f. —vi (converse) platicar, conversar; (with on, upon) disertar sobre, discurrir sobre; tratar de

discourteous /dɪs'kɜrtɪəs/ *a* descortés, desconsiderado

discourtesy /dɪs'kɜrtəsi/ *n* descortesía, *f*

discover /dɪ'skʌvər/ *vt* descubrir; (see) ver; (realize) darse cuenta de; (show) manifestar; revelar

discoverable /dɪ'skʌvərəbəl/ *a* que se puede descubrir; averiguable; distinguible, perceptible

discoverer /dɪ'skʌvərər/ *n* descubridor (-ra); revelador (-ra)

discovery /dɪ'skʌvəri/ *n* descubrimiento, *m;* revelación, *f*

discredit /dɪs'krɛdɪt/ *n* descrédito, *m;* des honra, *f;* duda, *f.* —*vt* dudar (de), no creer (en); desacreditar; deshonrar

discreditable /dɪs'krɛdɪtəbəl/ *a* deshonroso, ignominioso, vergonzoso

discreet /dɪ'skrit/ *a* discreto; prudente, circunspecto

discreetly /dɪ'skritli/ *adv* discretamente; prudentemente

discrepancy /dɪ'skrɛpənsi/ *n* discrepancia, diferencia, *f;* contradicción, *f*

discrepant /dɪ'skrɛpənt/ *a* discrepante; contradictorio, inconsistente

discretion /dɪ'skrɛʃən/ *n* discreción, *f;* prudencia, circunspección, *f;* juicio, *m;* voluntad, *f.* **at d.,** a discreción. **at one's own d.,** a voluntad (de uno). **years of d.,** edad de discreción, *f*

discriminate /dɪ'skrɪm,əneit/ *vi* distinguir (entre); hacer una distinción (en favor de or en perjuicio de). —*vt* distinguir

discriminating /dɪ'skrɪmə,neitɪŋ/ *a* discerniente, que sabe distinguir, juicioso; culto; diferencial

discrimination /dɪ,skrɪmə'neiʃən/ *n* discernimiento, *m;* gusto, *m;* distinción, *f;* discriminación, *f*

discursive /dɪ'skɜrsɪv/ *a* discursivo; digresivo

discus /'dɪskəs/ *n* disco, *m.* **d. thrower,** discóbolo, *m*

discuss /dɪ'skʌs/ *vt* discutir; hablar de; debatir; (deal with) tratar; (*Fam.* a dish) probar; (a bottle of wine) vaciar

discussion /dɪ'skʌʃən/ *n* discusión, *f;* debate, *m*

disdain /dɪs'dein/ *n* desdén, *m;* altivez, *f.* —*vt* desdeñar, desairar; despreciar. **to d. to,** desdeñarse de

disdainful /dɪs'deinfəl/ *a* desdeñoso; altivo

disdainfully /dɪs'deinfəli/ *adv* desdeñosamente

disease /dɪ'ziz/ *n* enfermedad, *f;* Fig. mal, *m.* **infectious d.,** enfermedad contagiosa, *f*

diseased /dɪ'zizd/ *a* enfermo; (of fruit, etc.) malo

disembark /,dɪsɛm'bark/ *vt* and *vi* desembarcar

disembarkation /dɪs,ɛmbɑr'keiʃən/ *n* desembarque, *m;* Mil. desembarco (de tropas), *m*

disembodied /,dɪsɛm'bɒdid/ *a* incorpóreo

disembowel /,dɪsɛm'bauəl/ *vt* desentrañar, destripar

disenchant /,dɪsɛn'tʃænt/ *vt* desencantar; deschechizar; desilusionar

disenchantment /,dɪsɛn'tʃæntmənt/ *n* desencanto, *m;* desilusión, *f*

disengage /,dɪsɛn'geidʒ/ *vt* desasir; soltar; (gears) desembragar; (uncouple) desacoplar; (free) librar

disengaged /,dɪsɛn'geidʒd/ *a* (free) libre

disentangle /,dɪsɛn'tæŋgəl/ *vt* (undo) desatar, desanudar; separar; (of threads, etc., and *Fig.*) desenredar, desenmarañar. —*vi* desenredarse

disentanglement /,dɪsɛn'tæŋgəlmənt/ *n* desatadura, *f;* separación, *f;* desenredo, *m*

disestablish /,dɪsɪ'stæblɪʃ/ *vt* separar (la Iglesia del Estado)

disestablishment /,dɪsɪ'stæblɪʃmənt/ *n* separación (de la Iglesia del Estado), *f*

disfavor /dɪs'feivər/ *n* disfavor, *m;* (disapproval) desaprobación, *f.* —*vt* desaprobar

disfigure /dɪs'fɪgyər/ *vt* desfigurar, afear; deformar; (mar) estropear

disfigurement /dɪs'fɪgyərmənt/ *n* desfiguración, *f;* deformidad, *f;* defecto, *m*

disfranchise /dɪs'fræntʃaiz/ *vt* privar de los derechos civiles (a)

disfranchisement /dɪs'fræntʃaizmənt/ *n* privación de los derechos civiles, privación del derecho de votar, *f*

disgorge /dɪs'gɔrdʒ/ *vt* and *vi* vomitar; (of a river) desembocar (en); hacer restitución (de lo robado)

disgrace /dɪs'greis/ *n* vergüenza, ignominia, *f;* des-honra, *f;* (insult) afrenta, *f;* (scandal) escándalo, *m;* disfavor, *m.* —*vt* deshonrar; despedir con ignominia. **in d.,** fuera de favor; desacreditado; (of children and animals) castigado

disgraceful /dɪs'greisfəl/ *a* deshonroso; ignominioso; escandaloso

disgracefully /dɪs'greisfəli/ *adv* escandalosamente

disgracefulness /dɪs'greisfəlnɪs/ *n* ignominia, vergüenza, *f;* deshonra, *f*

disgruntled /dɪs'grʌntl̩d/ *a* refunfuñador, enfurruñado, malhumorado

disguise /dɪs'gaiz/ *n* disfraz, *m;* (mask) máscara, *f.* —*vt* disfrazar; cubrir, tapar; (*Fig.* conceal) ocultar. **in d.,** disfrazado

disgust /dɪs'gʌst/ *n* repugnancia, aversión, *f;* aborrecimiento, *m;* asco, *m.* —*vt* repugnar, inspirar aversión; disgustar; dar asco (a)

disgusted /dɪs'gʌstɪd/ *a* asqueado; disgustado; furioso; (bored) aburrido

disgusting /dɪs'gʌstɪŋ/ *a* repugnante; odioso, horrible; asqueroso

dish /dɪʃ/ *n* (for meat, vegetables, fruit, etc.) fuente, *f;* (food) plato, *m; pl* **dishes,** platos, *m pl,* vajilla, *f.* —*vt* servir; Inf. frustrar. **cooked d.,** guiso, *m.* **special d. for today,** plato del día, *m.* **to wash the dishes,** fregar los platos. **d.-cloth,** (for washing) fregador, *m;* (for drying) paño de los platos, *m.* **d.-cover,** cubre-platos, *m.* **d.-rack,** escurre-platos, *m.* **d.-washer,** lavaplatos, lavavajillas, *m.* **d.-water,** agua de lavar los platos, *f*

disharmony /dɪs'harməni/ *n* falta de armonía, *f;* (disagreement) discordia, desavenencia, *f;* incongruencia, *f;* Mus. disonancia, *f*

dishearten /dɪs'hartn̩/ *vt* desalentar, desanimar; desesperar; disuadir (de)

disheveled /dɪ'ʃɛvəld/ *a* despeinado, desgreñado; (untidy) desaseado

dishonest /dɪs'ɒnɪst/ *a* falto de honradez, tramposo; fraudulento; falso, desleal

dishonestly /dɪs'ɒnɪstli/ *adv* de mala fe, sin honradez; fraudulentamente; deslealmente

dishonesty /dɪs'ɒnɪsti/ *n* falta de honradez, falta de integridad, *f;* fraude, *m;* falsedad, deslealtad, *f*

dishonor /dɪs'ɒnər/ *n* deshonra, *f, vt* deshonrar; Com. no pagar, no aceptar, un giro

dishonorable /dɪs'ɒnərəbəl/ *a* deshonroso

dishonorer /dɪs'ɒnərər/ *n* deshonrador (-ra); profanador (-ra)

disillusion /,dɪsɪ'luʒən/ *vt* desengañar, desilusionar

disillusionment /,dɪsɪ'luʒənmənt/ *n* desilusión, *f,* desengaño, desencanto, *m*

disinclination /dɪs,ɪnklə'neiʃən/ *n* aversión, *f*

disincline /,dɪsɪn'klain/ *vt* desinclinar

disinfect /,dɪsɪn'fɛkt/ *vt* desinfectar

disinfectant /,dɪsɪn'fɛktənt/ *a* and *n* desinfectante *m.*

disinfection /,dɪsɪn'fɛkʃən/ *n* desinfección, *f*

disingenuous /,dɪsɪn'dʒɛnyuəs/ *a* tortuoso, doble, falso, insincero

disinherit /,dɪsɪn'hɛrɪt/ *vt* desheredar

disinheritance /,dɪsɪn'hɛrɪtəns/ *n* desheredación, *f*

disintegrate /dɪs'ɪntə,greit/ *vt* despedazar, disgregar. —*vi* disgregarse; desmoronarse

disintegration /dɪs,ɪntə'greiʃən/ *n* disgregación, *f;* disolución, *f;* desmoronamiento, *m*

disinter /,dɪsɪn'tɜr/ *vt* desenterrar

disinterested /dɪs'ɪntə,rɛstɪd, -trɪstɪd/ *a* desinteresado

disinterestedness /dɪs'ɪntə,rɛstɪdnɪs, -trɪstɪd-/ *n* desinterés, *m*

disinterment /,dɪsɪn'tɜrmənt/ *n* desenterramiento, *m*

disjointed /dɪs'dʒɔintɪd/ *a* dislocado; desarticulado; incoherente, inconexo; (of a speech, etc.) descosido

disjointedness /dɪs'dʒɔintɪdnɪs/ *n* descoyuntamiento, desencajamiento, *m;* incoherencia, *f*

disk /dɪsk/ *n* disco, *m*

dislike /dɪs'laik/ *n* aversión, *f;* antipatía, *f;* (hostility) animosidad, *f.* —*vt* desagradar; no gustar; repugnar. **I d. the house,** No me gusta la casa. **I d. them,** No me gustan

dislocate /'dɪslou,keit/ *vt* dislocar, descoyuntar; *Fig.* interrumpir

dislocation /,dɪslou'keiʃən/ *n* dislocación, *f,* descoyuntamiento, *m;* Fig. interrupción, *f*

dislodge /dɪs'lɒdʒ/ vt desalojar

dislodgement /dɪs'lɒdʒmənt/ n desalojamiento, m

disloyal /dɪs'lɔiəl/ a desleal, infiel, falso

disloyalty /dɪs'lɔiəlti/ n deslealtad, infidelidad, falsedad, f

dismal /'dɪzməl/ a lóbrego, sombrío; lúgubre; funesto; triste

dismantle /dɪs'mæntl/ vt (a ship or fort) desmantelar; (a machine) desmontar; (a house, etc.) desamueblar

dismantling /dɪs'mæntlɪŋ/ n desmantelamiento, m

dismay /dɪs'mei/ n desmayo, desaliento, m; consternación, f; espanto, terror, m. —vt desanimar; consternar; espantar, horrorizar

dismember /dɪs'mɛmbər/ vt desmembrar

dismemberment /dɪs'mɛmbərmənt/ n desmembración, f

dismiss /dɪs'mɪs/ vt (from a job) despedir (de); (from an official position) destituir (de); (bid good-bye to) despedirse de; (after military parade) dar la orden de romper filas; (thoughts) apartar de sí; ahuyentar; (discard) desechar, descartar; (omit) pasar por alto de; (disregard) rechazar; (a parliament, etc.) disolver; (a law case) absolver de la instancia. **to d. in a few words**, tratar someramente; hablar brevemente de

dismissal /dɪs'mɪsəl/ n despedida, f; (from an official post) destitución, f; apartamiento, m; (discard) descarte, m; (of a parliament, etc.) disolución, f

dismount /v dɪs'maunt; n also 'dɪs,maunt/ vi apearse, desmontar, echar pie a tierra; bajar. —vt desmontar; (dismantle) desarmar

disobedience /ˌdɪsə'bidiəns/ n desobediencia, f

disobedient /ˌdɪsə'bidiənt/ a desobediente

disobey /ˌdɪsə'bei/ vt and vi desobedecer

disobliging /ˌdɪsə'blaidʒɪŋ/ a poco servicial

disobligingly /ˌdɪsə'blaidʒɪŋli/ adv descortésmente

disorder /dɪs'ɔrdər/ n desorden, m; confusión, f; (unrest) perturbación del orden público, f, motín, m; (disease) enfermedad, f; (mental) enajenación mental, f; trastorno, m. —vt desordenar, desarreglar; (of health) perjudicar; (the mind) trastornar. **in d.**, en desorden, desarreglado; (helter-skelter) atropelladamente

disordered /dɪs'ɔrdərd/ a en desorden; irregular, desordenado; (of the mind and bodily organs) trastornado; (ill) enfermo; (confused) confuso

disorganization /dɪs,ɔrgənə'zeiʃən/ n desorganización, f

disorganize /dɪs'ɔrgə,naiz/ vt desorganizar

disorganizing /dɪs'ɔrgə,naizɪŋ/ a desorganizador

disorientate /dɪs'ɔriən,teit/ vt desorientar

disorientation /dɪs,ɔriən'teiʃən/ n desorientación, f

disown /dɪs'oun/ vt repudiar; negar; renegar de

disparage /dɪ'spærɪdʒ/ vt menospreciar; desacreditar; denigrar; (spoil) perjudicar; (scorn) despreciar

disparagement /dɪ'spærɪdʒmənt/ n menosprecio, m; denigración, f; desprecio, m

disparagingly /dɪ'spærɪdʒɪŋli/ adv con desprecio

disparity /dɪ'spærɪti/ n disparidad, f

dispassionate /dɪs'pæʃənɪt/ a desapasionado, sereno; imparcial; moderado

dispassionately /dɪs'pæʃənɪtli/ adv con imparcialidad; serenamente; con moderación

dispatch /dɪ'spætʃ/ n despacho, m; Com. envío, m; (message) mensaje, m; (communiqué) parte, f; (cable) telegrama, m; (promptness) prontitud, presteza, f; (execution) ejecución, muerte, f. —vt despachar; enviar, remitir; (Fam. kill) despachar. **d.-case**, cartera, f. **d.-rider**, mensajero motociclista, m

dispel /dɪ'spel/ vt disipar

dispensable /dɪ'spensəbəl/ a dispensable

dispensary /dɪ'spensəri/ n dispensario, m

dispensation /ˌdɪspən'seiʃən/ n dispensación, f; (of the Pope, etc.) dispensa, f; (decree) ley, f, decreto, m; (of justice) administración, f

dispense /dɪ'spens/ vt dispensar; (of justice) administrar. **to d. with**, pasar sin, prescindir de

dispenser /dɪ'spensər/ n dispensador (-ra); administrador (-ra)

dispersal /dɪ'spɜrsəl/ n dispersión, f; disipación, f; esparcimiento, m

disperse /dɪ'spɜrs/ vt dispersar; disipar; esparcir. —vi dispersarse disiparse

dispirited /dɪ'spɪrɪtɪd/ a abatido, desanimado, deprimido; lánguido

dispiritedly /dɪ'spɪrɪtli/ adv desanimadamente, con desaliento; lánguidamente

displace /dɪs'pleis/ vt desalojar; cambiar de situación; (of liquids) desplazar; (oust) quitar el puesto (a), destituir

displacement /dɪs'pleismənt/ n desalojamiento, m; cambio de situación, m; (of liquid) desplazamiento, m; (from a post) destitución, f

display /dɪ'splei/ n exhibición, f; ostentación, f; presentación, f; (development) desarrollo, m; manifestación, f; (naval or military) maniobras, f pl; espectáculo, m; (pomp) pompa, f; fausto, m. —vt exhibir; mostrar, manifestar; ostentar; (unfold) desplegar, extender; (develop) desarrollar. **d. cabinet**, vitrina, f

displease /dɪs'pliz/ vt desagradar; ofender; enojar

displeasing /dɪs'plizɪŋ/ a desagradable

displeasure /dɪs'plɛʒər/ n desagrado, m; disgusto, m; disfavor, m; indignación, f; enojo, m; (grief) angustia, f

disport /dɪ'spɔrt/ vi (**oneself**), divertirse, entretenerse, recrearse; retozar, jugar

disposal /dɪ'spouzəl/ n disposición, f; (transfer) cesión, enajenación, f; (sale) venta, f; (gift) donación, f. **I am at your d.**, Estoy a la disposición de Vd. **the d. of the troops**, la disposición de las tropas

dispose /dɪ'spouz/ vt disponer; inclinar. —vi disponer. **to d. of**, disponer de; (finish) terminar, concluir; (get rid of) deshacerse de; (give away) regalar; (sell) vender; (transfer) ceder; (of houses, etc.) traspasar; (kill) matar; (send) enviar; (use) servirse de; (refute) refutar. **"To be disposed of,"** (a business, etc.) «Se traspasa»

disposed /dɪ'spouzd/ a (in compounds) intencionado, dispuesto. **well-d.**, bien intencionado

disposition /ˌdɪspə'zɪʃən/ n disposición, f; (temperament) naturaleza, índole, f, temperamento, carácter, m; (humor) humor, m

dispossess /ˌdɪspə'zɛs/ vt desposeer (de); privar (de); desahuciar

dispossession /ˌdɪspə'zɛʃən/ n desposeimiento, m; desahúcio, m

disproportion /ˌdɪsprə'pɔrʃən/ n desproporción, f

disproportionate /ˌdɪsprə'pɔrʃənɪt/ a desproporcionado

disproportionately /ˌdɪsprə'pɔrʃənɪtli/ adv desproporcionadamente

disprovable /dɪs'pruvəbəl/ a refutable

disprove /dɪs'pruv/ vt refutar

disputable /dɪ'spyutəbəl/ a disputable; discutible

disputant /dɪ'spyutənt/ n disputador (-ra)

dispute /dɪ'spyut/ n disputa, controversia, f; altercación, f; discusión, f; debate, m. —vt and vi disputar. **beyond d.**, a incontestable. —adv incontestablemente; fuera de duda

disqualification /dɪs,kwɒləfɪ'keiʃən/ n incapacidad, f; inhabilitación, f; impedimento, m; Sports. descalificación, f

disqualify /dɪs'kwɒlə,fai/ vt incapacitar; inhabilitar; Sports. descalificar

disquiet /dɪs'kwaiət/ n desasosiego, m; intranquilidad, inquietud, agitación, f. —vt desasosegar, intranquilizar, perturbar, agitar

disquieting /dɪs'kwaiətɪŋ/ a intranquilizador, perturbador

disquisition /ˌdɪskwə'zɪʃən/ n disquisición, f

disregard /ˌdɪsrɪ'gard/ n indiferencia, f; omisión, f; descuido, m; (scorn) desdén, m. —vt no hacer caso de, desatender; omitir; desconocer; descuidar; despreciar

disregardful /ˌdɪsrɪ'gardfəl/ a indiferente; negligente; desatento; desdeñoso

disrepair /ˌdɪsrɪ'pɛər/ n deterioro, mal estado, m

disreputable /dɪs'rɛpyətəbəl/ a de mala fama; (shameful) vergonzoso, vil; (compromising) comprometedor; de mal aspecto, horrible; ruin

disreputably /dɪs'rɛpyətəbli/ adv ruinmente; vergonzosamente

disrepute /ˌdɪsrɪ'pyut/ n disfavor, m; mala fama, f; deshonra, f; descrédito, m. **to come into d.**, caer en disfavor; perder su reputación

disrespect /ˌdɪsrɪ'spɛkt/ n falta de respeto, f; irreverencia, f

disrespectful /ˌdɪsrɪ'spɛktfəl/ a irrespetuoso, irreverente

disrobe /dɪs'roub/ vt desnudar. —vi desnudarse

disrupt /dɪs'rʌpt/ vt quebrar; desorganizar; interrumpir; separar

disruption /dɪs'rʌpʃən/ n quebrantamiento, m; desorganización, f; interrupción, f; separación, f

dissatisfaction /ˌdɪssætɪs'fækʃən/ n descontento, desagrado, disgusto, m

dissatisfied /dɪs'sætɪs,faid/ a descontentado, malcontento, no satisfecho

dissect /dɪ'sɛkt/ vt disecar; Fig. analizar

dissecting table n mesa de disección, f

dissection /dɪ'sɛkʃən/ n disección, f; análisis, m

dissector /dɪ'sɛktər/ n disector, m; Fig. analizador (-ra)

dissemble /dɪ'sɛmbəl/ vt and vi disimular, fingir

dissembler /dɪ'sɛmblər/ n hipócrita, mf; disimulador (-ra)

disseminate /dɪ'sɛmə,neit/ vt diseminar; propagar, sembrar

dissemination /dɪ,sɛmə'neiʃən/ n diseminación, f; propagación, f

dissension /dɪ'sɛnʃən/ n disensión, f; disidencia, f

dissent /dɪ'sɛnt/ n disentimiento, m, vi disentir, disidir

dissenter /dɪ'sɛntər/ n disidente, mf

dissentient /dɪ'sɛnʃənt/ a disidente, divergente. **without one d. voice,** unánimemente

dissertation /ˌdɪsər'teiʃən/ n disertación, f

disservice /dɪs'sɜrvɪs/ n deservicio, m

dissimilar /dɪ'sɪmələr/ a disímil, desemejante, diferente

dissimilarity /dɪ,sɪmə'lærɪti/ n desemejanza, diferencia, disparidad, f

dissimulation /dɪ,sɪmyə'leiʃən/ n disimulación, f, disimulo, m

dissipate /'dɪsə,peit/ vt disipar; dispersar; (waste) derrochar, desperdiciar. —vi disiparse; dispersarse; (vanish) desvanecerse; (of persons) ser disoluto

dissipated /'dɪsə,peitɪd/ a (of persons) disipado, disoluto, vicioso

dissipation /ˌdɪsə'peiʃən/ n disipación, f; (waste) derroche, m; libertinaje, m

dissociate /dɪ'souʃi,eit/ vt disociar

dissociation /dɪ,sousi'eiʃən/ n disociación, f

dissoluble /dɪ'sɒlyəbəl/ a disoluble

dissolute /'dɪsə,lut/ a disoluto, vicioso, licencioso

dissoluteness /'dɪsə,lutnɪs/ n disolución, inmoralidad, f

dissolution /ˌdɪsə'luʃən/ n disolución, f; separación, f; muerte, f

dissolvable /dɪ'zɒlvəbəl/ a soluble

dissolve /dɪ'zɒlv/ vt disolver; derretir; (of parliament) prorrogar; (a marriage, etc.) anular; Fig. disipar. —vi disolverse; derretirse; (vanish) desvanecerse, disiparse, evaporarse. **to d. into tears,** deshacerse en lágrimas

dissolvent /dɪ'zɒlvənt/ a disolutivo. —n disolvente, m

dissonance /'dɪsənəns/ n disonancia, f; Fig. discordia, falta de armonía, f

dissonant /'dɪsənənt/ n disonancia, f, a disonante

dissuade /dɪ'sweid/ vt disuadir (de), apartar (de)

dissuasion /dɪ'sweiʒən/ n disuasión, f

distaff /'dɪstæf/ n rueca, f

distance /'dɪstəns/ n distancia, f; lontananza, f; lejanía, f; trecho, m; (of time) intervalo, m; (difference) diferencia, f. **at a d.,** a alguna distancia; lejos; (from afar) desde lejos. **from a d.,** desde (or de) lejos. **in the d.,** a lo lejos, en lontananza. **to keep at a d.,** mantener lejos; guardar las distancias (con). **to keep one's d.,** mantenerse a distancia; no intimarse, guardar las distancias. **What is the d. from London to Madrid?** ¿Qué distancia hay desde Londres a Madrid?

distant /'dɪstənt/ a distante; lejano; remoto; (of manner) frío, reservado; (slight) ligero; (of references, etc.) indirecto. **He is a d. relation,** Es un pariente le-

jano. **They are always rather d. with her,** La tratan siempre con bastante frialdad

distantly /'dɪstəntli/ adv a distancia; a lo lejos; desde lejos; remotamente; (of manner) con frialdad; (slightly) ligeramente

distaste /dɪs'teist/ n aversión, repugnancia, f; disgusto, hastío, m

distasteful /dɪs'teistfəl/ a desagradable

distemper /dɪs'tɛmpər/ n enfermedad, f; (in animals) moquillo, m; Fig. mal, m; (for walls) pintura al temple, f. —vt desordenar, perturbar; (walls) pintar al temple

distend /dɪ'stɛnd/ vt ensanchar; dilatar; inflar, henchir; Med. distender. —vi ensancharse, etc.

distension /dɪs'tɛnʃən/ n dilatación, f; inflación, f; henchimiento, m; Med. distensión, f

distill /dɪ'stɪl/ vt destilar; extraer. —vi destilar; exudar

distillation /ˌdɪstl'eiʃən/ n destilación, f; extracción, f; exudación, f

distiller /dɪ'stɪlər/ n destilador (-ra)

distillery /dɪ'stɪləri/ n destilería, f, destilatorio, m

distinct /dɪ'stɪŋkt/ a distinto; diferente; claro; notable, evidente

distinction /dɪ'stɪŋkʃən/ n distinción, f

distinctive /dɪ'stɪŋktɪv/ a distintivo; característico

distinctive feature n Ling. rasgo pertinente, m

distinctly /dɪ'stɪŋktli/ adv claramente; distintamente

distinctness /dɪ'stɪŋktnɪs/ n claridad, f; distinción, f; carácter distintivo, m

distinguish /dɪ'stɪŋgwɪʃ/ vt distinguir; discernir; caracterizar; (honor) honrar. —vi distinguir, diferenciar

distinguishable /dɪ'stɪŋgwɪʃəbəl/ a distinguible; perceptible, discernible

distinguished /dɪ'stɪŋgwɪʃt/ a distinguido; eminente, famoso, ilustre, egregio

distinguishing /dɪ'stɪŋgwɪʃɪŋ/ a distintivo

distort /dɪ'stɔrt/ vt (twist) torcer; deformar; falsear; pervertir

distorting mirror n (at fairs) espejo de la risa, m; espejo deformador, m

distortion /dɪ'stɔrʃən/ n deformación, f; torcimiento, m; contorsión, f; perversión, f; Radio. deformación, f

distract /dɪ'strækt/ vt distraer; interrumpir; perturbar; (turn aside) desviar, apartar; (madden) enloquecer, volver loco (a)

distracted /dɪ'stræktɪd/ a aturdido; demente, loco

distractedly /dɪ'stræktɪdli/ adv locamente; perdidamente

distraction /dɪ'strækʃən/ n distracción, f; (amusement) diversion, f, pasatiempo, m; (bewilderment) confusión, f, aturdimiento, m; (madness) locura, f; frenesí, m. **to drive to d.,** trastornar, sacar de quicio.

distrain /dɪ'strein/ vi embargar

distraint /dɪ'streint/ n embargo, m

distraught /dɪ'strɔt/ a aturdido; desesperado; enloquecido

distress /dɪ'strɛs/ n dolor, m, aflicción, f; pena, f; miseria, penuria, f; (exhaustion) fatiga, f, cansancio, m; (pain) dolor, m; (misfortune) desdicha, f; apuro, m; (danger) peligro, m; Law. embargo, m. —vt afligir, dar pena (a), llenar de angustia; cansar, fatigar; (pain) doler

distressed /dɪ'strɛst/ a afligido; necesitado, pobre

distressing /dɪ'strɛsɪŋ/ a congojoso, doloroso, penoso

distributable /dɪ'strɪbyʊtəbəl/ a repartible

distribute /dɪ'strɪbyut/ vt (of justice, etc.) administrar; distribuir; repartir

distribution /ˌdɪstrə'byuʃən/ n (of justice) administración, f; distribución, f; reparto, m

distributive /dɪ'strɪbyətɪv/ a distributivo

distributor /dɪ'strɪbyətər/ n distribuidor (-ra); repartidor (-ra). **d. of false money,** expendedor (-ra) de moneda falsa

district /'dɪstrɪkt/ n distrito, m; comarca, f; (of a town) barrio, m; (judicial) partido judicial, m; jurisdicción, f; región, zona, f

distrust /dɪs'trʌst/ n desconfianza, f; recelo, m, sospecha, f. —vt desconfiar de, sospechar

distrustful /dɪs'trʌstfəl/ a desconfiado, receloso, suspicaz

distrustfully /dɪs'trʌstfəli/ *adv* desconfiadamente, con recelo

disturb /dɪ'stɜrb/ *vt* perturbar; interrumpir; incomodar; (make anxious) inquietar; (alter) cambiar; (disarrange) desordenar, desarreglar. **to d. the peace,** perturbar el orden público

disturbance /dɪ'stɜrbəns/ *n* perturbación, *f;* disturbio, *m,* conmoción, *f;* incomodidad, *f;* agitación, *f;* confusión, *f;* tumulto, *m;* desorden, *m; Radio.* parásitos, *m pl*

disturber /dɪ'stɜrbər/ *n* perturbador (-ra)

disturbing /dɪ'stɜrbɪŋ/ *a* perturbador; inquietador; conmovedor, impresionante, emocionante

disunion /dɪs'yunyən/ *n* desunión, *f;* discordia, *f*

disunite /ˌdɪsyu'naɪt/ *vt* desunir; separar, dividir. —*vi* separarse

disuse /*n* dɪs'yus; *v* -'yuz/ *n* desuso, *m.* —*vt* desusar; desacostumbrar. **to fall into d.,** caer en desuso

ditch /dɪtʃ/ *n* zanja, *f;* (for defense, etc.) foso, *m;* (irrigation) acequia, *f.* —*vt* zanjar; abarrancar. **to die in the last d.,** morir en la brecha

ditto /'dɪtou/ *adv* ídem; también

ditty /'dɪti/ *n* canción, cantinela, *f*

diuretic /ˌdaɪə'rɛtɪk/ *a* diurético

divan /dɪ'væn/ *n* diván, *m*

dive /daɪv/ *n* buceo, *m; Aer.* picada, *f, vi* bucear; sumergirse (en); *Aer.* volar en picado; penetrar (en); (into a book) enfrascarse en. **to d. out,** salir precipitadamente. **to d.-bomb,** bombardear en picado. **d.-bomber,** avión en picado, *m.* **d.-bombing,** bombardeo en picado, *m*

diver /'daɪvər/ *n* buceador, *m;* buzo, *m;* (bird) somorgujo, *m*

diverge /dɪ'vɜrdʒ/ *vi* divergir

divergence /dɪ'vɜrdʒəns/ *n* divergencia, *f*

divergent /dɪ'vɜrdʒənt/ *a* divergente

diverse /dɪ'vɜrs/ *a* diverso, vario

diversify /dɪ'vɜrsəˌfaɪ/ *vt* diversificar

diversion /dɪ'vɜrʒən/ *n* diversión, *f;* entretenimiento, *m,* recreación, *f;* pasatiempo, *m;* placer, *m; Mil.* diversión, *f*

diversity /dɪ'vɜrsɪti/ *n* diversidad, variedad, *f*

divert /dɪ'vɜrt/ *vt* desviar; (amuse) divertir, entretener

diverting /dɪ'vɜrtɪŋ/ *a* divertido, entretenido

divide /dɪ'vaɪd/ *vt* dividir; partir; separar; (cut) cortar; (share) repartir, distribuir; (hair) hacer la raya (del pelo); (of voting) provocar una votación. —*vi* dividirse; separarse; (of roads, etc.) bifurcarse; (of voting) votar. **divided skirt,** *n* falda pantalón, *f*

dividend /'dɪvɪˌdɛnd/ *n* dividendo, *m.* **d. warrant,** cupón de dividendo, *m*

dividers /dɪ'vaɪdərz/ *n pl* compás de puntas, *m*

dividing /dɪ'vaɪdɪŋ/ *a* divisorio, divisor

divination /ˌdɪvə'neɪʃən/ *n* adivinación, *f*

divine /dɪ'vaɪn/ *a* divino; sublime. *Inf.* estupendo. —*n* teólogo, *m.* —*vt* (foretell) vaticinar, pronosticar; presentir; (guess) adivinar

diving /'daɪvɪŋ/ *n* buceo, *m; Aer.* picado, *m.* **d.-bell,** campana de bucear, *f.* **d.-board,** (low) trampolín, *m;* (high) palanca, *f.* **d.-suit,** escafandra, *f*

divining rod /dɪ'vaɪnɪŋ/ *n* vara divinatoria, *f*

divinity /dɪ'vɪnɪti/ *n* divinidad, *f;* teología, *f*

divisibility /dɪˌvɪzə'bɪlɪti/ *n* divisibilidad, *f*

divisible /dɪ'vɪzəbəl/ *a* divisible

division /dɪ'vɪʒən/ *n* división, *f;* separación, *f;* (distribution) repartimiento, *m;* (*Mil. Math.*) división, *f;* sección, *f;* grupo, *m;* (voting) votación, *f;* (discord) discordia, desunión, *f.* **without a d.,** por unanimidad, sin votar

divisor /dɪ'vaɪzər/ *n Math.* divisor, *m*

divorce /dɪ'vɔrs/ *n* divorcio, *m.* —*vt* divorciarse de; *Fig.* divorciar, separar. **to file a petition of d.,** poner una petición de divorcio

divorcee /dɪvɔr'seɪ/ *n* (wife) divorciada, *f;* (husband) divorciado, *m*

divulge /dɪ'vʌldʒ/ *vt* divulgar, revelar

dizzily /'dɪzəli/ *adv* vertiginosamente

dizziness /'dɪzɪnɪs/ *n* vértigo, *m;* mareo, *m;* (bewilderment) aturdimiento, *m,* confusión, *f*

dizzy /'dɪzi/ *a* vertiginoso; mareado; confuso, perplejo, aturdido

do /du/ *vt* hacer; ejecutar; (one's duty, etc.) cumplir con; concluir; (cause) causar; (homage) rendir; (commit) cometer; (arrange) arreglar; (cook) cocer, guisar; (roast) asar; (*Fam.* cheat) engañar; (suit) convenir; (suffice) bastar; (act) hacer el papel (de); (*Fam.* treat) tratar (bien o mal); (learn) aprender; (exhaust) agotar; (walk) andar; (travel, journey) recorrer; (translate) traducir; (prepare) preparar. —*vi* hacer; (behave) conducirse; (of health) estar (bien o mal); (act) obrar; (get on) ir; (be suitable, such) convenir; (suffice) bastar; (of plants) florecer; (cook) cocerse; (last) durar. **Don't!** ¡No lo hagas! ¡Quieto! ¡Calla! **How do you do?** ¿Cómo está Vd.? ¡Buenos días! **Have done!** ¡Acaba de una vez! **It will do you good,** Te conviene; Te hará bien; Te sentará bien. **It will do you no harm,** No te perjudicará; No te hará daño. **I could do with one,** Me gustaría (tener) uno; (of drinks) Me bebería uno con mucho gusto. **That will do,** Eso basta; Se puede servirse de eso; Está bien así; (leave it alone) ¡Déjate de eso! (be quiet!) ¡No digas más! ¡Cállate! **That won't do,** Eso no es bastante; Eso no sirve; Eso no se hace así; Eso no se hace. **That will never do,** Eso no servirá; Eso no puede ser. **This will do,** (when buying an article) Me quedaré con éste; Me serviré de éste; Esto basta; Esto será suficiente; (is all right) Está bien así. **Thy will be done!** ¡Hágase tu voluntad! **to be doing,** estar haciendo; estar ocupado en (or con) hacer; (of food) estar cocinando. **to be done for,** estar perdido; estar muerto. **to do better,** hacer mejor (que); (mend one's ways) enmendarse, corregirse; (improve) mejorar, hacer progresos; (in health) encontrarse mejor. **to do nothing,** no hacer nada. **to do reverence,** rendir homenaje; inclinarse. **to do to death,** matar; asesinar; ejecutar. **to do violence to,** *Fig.* hacer fuerza a. **to do well,** hacer bien; obrar bien; (be successful) tener éxito; hacer buena impresión; (prosperous) tener una buena posición. **to do wonders,** hacer maravillas. **to have done with,** renunciar (a); dejar de usar; dejar de hacer, cesar; concluir, terminar; no tener más que ver con; (forsake) abandonar; (a person) romper con. **to have nothing to do,** no tener nada que hacer. **to have nothing to do with,** no tener nada que ver con; (of people) no tratar; (end a friendship) romper su amistad con, dejar de ver. **well done,** bien hecho; (of food) bien guisado; (of meat) bien asado. **What is to be done?** ¿Qué hay que hacer? ¿Qué se puede hacer? **What is to do?** ¿Qué pasa? ¿Qué hay? **When he had done speaking,** Cuando hubo terminado de hablar. **to do again,** hacer de nuevo, volver a hacer, rehacer; repetir. **He will not do it again,** No lo hará más. **to do away with,** quitar; eliminar; suprimir; hacer desaparecer; poner fin a; hacer cesar; destruir; matar. **to do by,** tratar (a), portarse con. **to do for,** arruinar; matar; (suffice) bastar para; ser a propósito para, servir para; (look after) cuidar; (as a housekeeper) dirigir la casa para. **to do out,** (a room) limpiar. **to do out of,** quitar; privar de; (steal) robar. **to do up,** (tie) atar; (fold) enrollar, plegar; envolver; (parcel) empaquetar; (arrange) arreglar; decorar; poner en orden; poner como nuevo; (iron) planchar; (launder) lavar y planchar; (tire) fatigar. **to do with,** (of people) tratar; (of things) tener que ver con; (put up with) poder con; poder sufrir. **to do without,** prescindir de; pasarse sin

do /du/ *vi* as an auxiliary verb not translated in Spanish, e.g. *I do believe,* creo. *Do not do that,* no hagas eso. *I did not know,* no sabía. When it is used for emphasis, *do* is translated by *sí, ciertamente, claro* and similar words, e.g.: *She did not know, but he did,* Ella no lo sabía pero él sí. *You do paint well,* Pintas muy bien por cierto. *Do come this time,* No dejes de venir esta vez.

docile /'dɒsəl/ *a* dócil

docility /dɒ'sɪlti/ *n* docilidad, *f*

dock /dɒk/ *n* dique, *m,* dársena, *f;* (wharf) muelle, *m;* (in a law court) banquillo de los acusados, *m; Bot.* romaza, *f.* —*vt* (a tail) descolar; cortar, cercenar; reducir; (money) descontar; (a ship) poner en dique. —*vi* entrar en dársena, entrar en dique, entrar en muelle. **dry-d.**, dique seco, *m.* **floating-d.**, dique flotante, *m.* **d.-dues**, muellaje, *m.* **d. rat**, (thief) raquero, *m*

docker /'dɒkər/ *n* estibador, descargador del muelle, *m*

docket /'dɒkɪt/ *n* (bundle) legajo, *m;* extracto, *m;* minuta, *f;* (label) etiqueta, *f,* marbete, *m*

dockyard /'dɒk,yɑrd/ *n* arsenal, astillero, *m*

doctor /'dɒktər/ *n* doctor (-ra); (medical practitioner) médico (-ca), asistir; (repair) reparar, componer; adulterar; mezclar drogas con; falsificar. —*vi* ejercer la medicina. **family d.**, médico de cabecera, *m.* **to graduate as a d.**, doctorarse. **d. of divinity, laws, medicine,** doctor (-ra) en teología, en derecho, en medicina, *m*

doctoral /'dɒktərəl/ *a* doctoral

doctorate /'dɒktərɪt/ *n* doctorado, *m*

doctrinaire /'dɒktrə'nɛər/ *a* and *n* doctrinario (-ia)

doctrinal /'dɒktrənḷ/ *a* doctrinal

doctrine /'dɒktrɪn/ *n* doctrina, *f*

document /n 'dɒkyəmənt; *v* -,mɛnt/ *n* documento, *m.* —*vt* documentar; probar con documentos. **d.-case,** carpeta, *f*

documentary /,dɒkyə'mɛntəri/ *a* documental; escrito, auténtico. **d. film,** película documental, *f*

documentation /,dɒkyəmən'teɪʃən/ *n* documentación, *f*

Dodecanese, the /,dɒdɪkə'niz/ el Dodecaneso, *m*

dodge /dɒdʒ/ *n* esguince, regate, *m;* evasiva, *f;* (trick) estratagema, *m,* maniobra, *f;* artefacto, *m.* —*vt* esquivar, evadir

doe /dou/ *n* gama, *f.* **doe rabbit,** coneja, *f*

doer /'duər/ *n* hacedor (-ra); autor (-ra)

doeskin /'dou,skɪn/ *n* ante, *m,* piel de gama, *f*

doff /dɒf/ *vt* quitar; (of hats, etc.) quitarse; desnudarse de

dog /dɔg/ *n* perro, *m;* (male) macho, *m;* (andiron) morillo, *m; Astron.* Can Mayor (or Menor), Sirio, *m.* —*vt* perseguir; seguir los pasos de; espiar. **You can't deceive an old dog,** A perro viejo no hay tus tus. **to go to the dogs,** ir a las carreras de galgos; *Fig.* ir cuesta abajo. **mongrel dog,** perro mestizo, *m.* **thoroughbred dog,** perro de raza pura, *m.* **dog-collar,** collar de perro, *m; Eccl.* alzacuello, *m.* **dog-days,** días caniculares, *m pl,* canícula, *f.* **dog-eared** (of books) con las puntas de las hojas dobladas. **dog-fight,** lucha de perros, *f;* combate aéreo, *m.* **dog-fish,** lija, *f,* cazón, *m.* **dog in the manger,** el perro del hortelano. **dog-kennel,** perrera, *f.* **dog-latin,** bajo latín, *m.* **dog license,** matrícula de perros, *f.* **dog-racing,** carrera de galgos, *f.* **dog-rose,** escaramujo, *m.* **dog show,** exposición canina, *f.* **dog-tooth,** *Archit.* diente de perro, *m.* **dog-vane,** *Naut.* cataviento, *m*

doge /doudʒ/ *n* dux, *m*

dogged /'dɔgɪd/ *a* persistente, tenaz, pertinaz, obstinado

doggedly /'dɔgɪdli/ *adv* tenazmente

doggedness /'dɔgɪdnɪs/ *n* pertinacia, tenacidad, terquedad, persistencia, *f*

doggerel /'dɔgərəl/ *n* malos versos, *m pl;* aleluyas, coplas de ciego, *f pl,* a malo, irregular

dogma /'dɔgmə/ *n* dogma, *m*

dogmatic /dɔg'mætɪk/ *a* dogmático

dogmatize /'dɔgmə,taiz/ *vt* and *vi* dogmatizar; mostrarse dogmático

doh /dou/ *n Mus.* do, *m*

doily /'dɔili/ *n* carpeta, *f,* pañito de adorno, *m*

doings /'duɪŋz/ *n pl* acciones, *f pl;* (deeds) hechos, *m pl;* (behavior) conducta, *f;* (happenings) acontecimientos, *m pl;* (works) obras, *f pl;* (things) cosas, *f pl*

doldrums /'douldrəmz/ *n pl* calmas ecuatoriales, *f pl*

dole /doul/ *n* limosna, *f;* porción, *f,* ración, *f.* **to d. out,** repartir; distribuir en porciones pequeñas; racionar; dar contra la voluntad de uno.

doleful /'doulfəl/ *a* triste, lúgubre, melancólico; doloroso

dolefulness /'doulfʌlnɪs/ *n* tristeza, melancolía, *f;* dolor, *m*

doll /dɒl/ *n* muñeca, *f*

dollar /'dɒlər/ *n* dólar, *m*

dolly /'dɒli/ *n* muñeca, *f;* (for clothes) moza, *f.* **d.-tub,** cubo para la colada, *m*

dolman /'doulmən/ *n* dormán, *m*

dolphin /'dɒlfɪn/ *n* delfín, *m*

dolt /doult/ *n* cabeza de alcornoque, *mf,* zamacuco, *m*

domain /dou'mein/ *n* territorio, *m;* heredad, posesión, propiedad, *f;* (empire) dominio, *m*

dome /doum/ *n* cúpula, *f;* bóveda, *f;* (palace) palacio, *m*

domestic /də'mɛstɪk/ *a* doméstico; familiar; (home-loving) casero; (of animals) doméstico; (national) interior, nacional. —*n* doméstico, sirviente, *m;* criada, *f.* **d. economy,** economía doméstica, *f*

domesticate /də'mɛstɪ,keit/ *vt* domesticar

domesticated /də'mɛstɪ,keitɪd/ *a* (of animals) domesticado; (of persons) casero

domestication /də,mɛstɪ'keiʃən/ *n* domesticación, *f*

domesticity /,doumɛ'stɪsɪti/ *n* domesticidad, *f*

domicile /'dɒmə,sail/ *n* domicilio, *m, vt* domiciliar

domiciliary /,dɒmə'sɪli,ɛri/ *a* domiciliario

dominant /'dɒmənənt/ *a* dominante; imperante. —*n Mus.* dominante, *f.* **to be d.,** prevalecer

dominate /'dɒmə,neit/ *vt* and *vi* dominar

domination /,dɒmə'neiʃən/ *n* dominación, *f*

domineer /,dɒmə'nɪər/ *vi* dominar, tiranizar. **to d. over,** mandar en

domineering /,dɒmə'nɪərɪŋ/ *a* dominante, mandón, tiránico

Dominican /də'mɪnɪkən/ *a* dominicano. —*n* dominicano, *m*

Dominican Republic, the la República Dominicana, *f*

dominion /də'mɪnyən/ *n* dominio, *m;* autoridad, soberanía, *f;* imperio, *m;* *pl* **dominions,** *Eccl.* dominaciones, *f pl*

Dominions, the /də'mɪnyənz/ los Dominios, *m*

domino /'dɒmə,nou/ *n* dominó, *m.* **to go d.,** nacer domino

don /dɒn/ *n* (Spanish and Italian title) don, *m;* señor, *m.* —*vt* ponerse, vestirse

donation /dou'neiʃən/ *n* donación, dádiva, *f;* contribución, *f*

done /dʌn/ *a* and *past part* hecho; (of food) cocido; (roasted) asado; (tired) rendido; (*Fam.* deceived) engañado. **Well d.!** ¡Bien hecho! **d. for,** arruinado; muerto; perdido; vencido; (spoilt) estropeado

donkey /'dɒŋki/ *n* borrico (-ca), burro (-rra). **d.-engine,** máquina auxiliar, *f*

donor /'dounər/ *n* donador (-ra); dador (-ra)

doodle /'dudḷ/ *v* borrajear, garabatear, hacer garabatos

doom /dum/ *n* condena, *f;* (fate) suerte, *f;* (judgment) destino, *m;* ruina, *f;* juicio, *m.* —*vt* sentenciar; condenar

doomsday /'dumz,dei/ *n* día del juicio final, *m*

door /dɔr/ *n* puerta, *f;* entrada, *f.* **front d.,** puerta de entrada, *f.* **next d.,** la casa vecina; la puerta de al lado, la puerta vecina. **next d. neighbor,** vecino (-na) de al lado. **out of doors,** al aire libre; en la calle. **to knock at the d.,** llamar a la puerta. **to slam the d. in a person's face,** dar con la puerta en las narices de alguien. **d.-bell,** timbre (non-electric, campanilla, *f*) de llamada, *m.* **d.-jamb,** quicial, *m.* **d. keeper,** portero, *m.* **d.-knob,** tirador, *m.* **d.-knocker,** manija, *f;* picaporte, *m,* aldaba, *f.* **d.-plate,** placa, *f.* **d.-shutter,** cierre metálico, *m.* **d.-step,** peldaño de la puerta, *m;* umbral, *m.* **d.-way,** portal, *m*

dope /doup/ *n* drogas, *f pl,* narcóticos, *m pl;* (news) información, *f.* **d. fiend,** morfinómano (-na)

dope-pusher /'doup ,puʃər/ *n* narcotraficante, *mf*

Doric /'dɒrɪk/ *a* dórico

dormant /'dɔrmənt/ *a* durmiente; latente; secreto; inactivo. **to go d.,** dormirse

dormer window /'dɔrmər/ *n* lumbrera, *f*

dormitory /'dɔrmɪ,tɔri/ *n* dormitorio, *m*

dormouse /'dɔr,maus/ *n* lirón, *m*

dorsal /'dɔrsəl/ *a* dorsal

dorsum /'dɔrsəm/ *n* dorso, *m*

dory /'dɔri/ *n* (fish) dorado, *m*

dose, dosage /dous; 'dousɪdʒ/ *n;* dosis, *f*

dossier /'dɒsi,ei/ *n* documentación, *f*

dot /dɒt/ *n* punto, *m; Mus.* puntillo, *m; pl* **dots,** *Gram.* puntos suspensivos, *m pl.* —*vt* poner punto (a una letra); (scatter) salpicar. **on the dot,** (of time) en punto. **to dot one's i's,** poner los puntos sobre las íes

dotage /'doutɪdʒ/ n senectud, chochera, f

dotard /'doutərd/ n viejo chocho, m; vieja chocha, f; Inf. carcamal, m

dote /dout/ vi chochear. **to d. on,** adorar en, idolatrar

doting /'doutɪŋ/ a chocho

double /'dʌbəl/ a and adv doble; dos veces; (in a pair) en par; en dos; doblemente; (deceitful) doble, de dos caras, falso; ambiguo. —n doble, m; duplicado, m; Theat. contrafigura, f; pl **doubles,** (tennis) dobles, m pl, juego doble, m. —vt doblar; duplicar; (fold) doblegar; (the fist) cerrar (el puño); (Theat. and Naut.) doblar. —vi doblarse; (dodge) volverse atrás, hacer un rodeo, dar una vuelta; esquivarse. **to d. up,** vt envolver; arrollar; (a person) doblar. —vi doblegarse; arrollarse; (collapse) desplomarse. **at the d.,** corriendo. **He was doubled up with pain,** El dolor le hacía retorcerse. **mixed doubles,** parejas mixtas, f pl; dobles mixtos, m pl. **double two,** (telephone) dos dos. **with a d. meaning,** con segunda intención. **d.-barrelled,** de dos cañones. **d.-bass,** contrabajo, m. **d. bed,** cama de matrimonio, f. **d.-bedded,** con cama de matrimonio; con dos camas. **d.-breasted,** cruzado. **d.-chin,** papada, f. **d.-dealing,** duplicidad, f. **d.-edged,** de doble filo. **d.-entry,** Com. partida doble, f. **d.-faced,** de dos caras. **d.-jointed,** con articulaciones flexibles

double-spaced /'dʌbəl 'speist/ a doble espacio, a dos espacios

doublet /'dʌblɪt/ n (garment) jubón, justillo, m; pareja, f, par, m

doubling /'dʌblɪŋ/ n doblamiento, m; doblez, plegadura, f; duplicación, f; (dodging) evasiva, f, esguince, m

doubloon /dʌ'blun/ n doblón, m

doubly /'dʌbli/ adv doblemente; con duplicidad

doubt /daut/ n duda, f; incertidumbre, f; sospecha, f. —vt and vi dudar; sospechar; titubear, hesitar; temer. **beyond all d.,** fuera de duda. **no d.,** sin duda. **There is no d. that,** No hay duda de que, No cabe duda de que. **When in d....,** En caso de duda...

doubter /'dautər/ n incrédulo (-la)

doubtful /'dautfəl/ a dudoso; incierto; perplejo; ambiguo; (of places) sospechoso

doubtfully /'dautfəli/ adv dudosamente; inciertamente; irresolutamente; ambiguamente

doubtfulness /'dautfəlnɪs/ n duda, incertidumbre, f; ambigüedad, f

doubtless /'dautlɪs/ adv sin duda, por supuesto; probablemente

douche /duʃ/ n ducha, f, vt duchar

dough /dou/ n pasta, masa, f; (money) lana, f

dour /dʊr/ a huraño, adusto, austero

dourly /'dʊrli/ adv severamente

douse /daus/ vt zambullir; (a sail) recoger; Inf. apagar

dove /duv/ n paloma, f. **d.-cote,** palomar, m

Dover /'douvər/ Dóver, m

dovetail /'dʌv,teil/ n cola de milano, f, vt machihembrar, empalmar; Fig. encajar

dowager /'dauədʒər/ n viuda, f; matrona, f. **d. countess,** condesa viuda, f

dowager empress n emperatriz viuda, f

dowdiness /'daudinɪs/ n desaliño, desaseo, m; falta de elegancia, f

dowdy /'daudi/ a desaliñado, desaseado; poco elegante. —n mujer poco elegante, f

dowel /'dauəl/ n espiga, clavija, f, zoquete, m, vt enclavijar

down /daun/ n (of a bird) plumón, m; (on a peach, etc.) pelusilla, f; (hair) vello, m; (before the beard) bozo, m; (of a thistle, etc.) vilano, m. **ups and downs,** vicisitudes, f pl

down /daun/ a pendiente; (of trains, etc.) descendente. —adv abajo; hacia abajo; (lowered) bajado; (of the eyes) bajos; (on the ground) en tierra, por tierra; (stretched out) tendido a lo largo; (depressed) triste, abatido; (ill) enfermo; (fallen) caído; (of the wind) cesado; (closed) cerrado; (exhausted) agotado; Com. al contado; (of temperature) más bajo. —prep abajo de; abajo; en la dirección de; (along) a lo largo de; por. **"Down"** (on elevators) «Para bajar». —interj ¡Abajo!; ¡A tierra! **He went d. the hill,** Bajaba la colina. **He is d. now,** Ha bajado ahora; Está abajo ahora; Está derribado ahora. **The sun has gone d.,** Se ha puesto el sol. **His stock has gone d.,** Fig. Inf. Ha caído en disfavor. **Prices have come d.,** Los precios han bajado. **Their numbers have gone d.,** Sus números han disminuido. **to be d. and out,** estar completamente arruinado, ser pobre de solemnidad. **to boil d.,** reducir hirviendo. **to come d. in the world,** venir a menos. **while I was going d. the river,** mientras iba río abajo, mientras bajaba al río. **d. below,** allá abajo; abajo; en el piso de abajo. **D. on your knees!** ¡De rodillas! **d. to,** hasta. **d. spout,** tubo de bajada, m. **D. with!** ¡Abajo! ¡Muera! **d.-stream,** agua abajo. **d. train,** tren descendente, m

down /daun/ vt derribar; vencer. **to d. tools,** declararse en huelga

downcast /'daun,kæst/ a bajo; cabizbajo, deprimido, abatido

downfall /'daun,fɔl/ n caída, f; derrumbamiento, m; (failure) fracaso, m; (Fig. ruin) decadencia, ruina, f

downhearted /'daun'hɑrtɪd/ a descorazonado, alicaído, desalentado

downhill / adv 'daun'hɪl; a 'daun,hɪl/ adv cuesta abajo, hacia abajo. —a en declive, inclinado. **to go d.,** ir cuesta abajo

downiness /'dauninɪs/ n vellosidad, f

downpour /'daun,pɔr/ n chubasco (Mexico), aguacero, chaparrón, m

downright /'daun,rait/ a franco, sincero; categórico, terminante; absoluto. —adv muy; completamente

downstairs /'daun'stɛrz/ adv escalera abajo; al piso de abajo; en el piso bajo; abajo. —a del piso de abajo. —n planta baja, f; piso de abajo, m. **to go d.,** bajar la escalera; ir al piso de abajo

downtrodden /'daun,trodn̩/ a oprimido, esclavizado

downward /'daunwərd/ a descendente; inclinado. —adv hacia abajo

downy /'dauni/ a velloso; (Fam. of persons) con más conchas que un galápago

dowry /'dauri/ n dote, mf. **to give as a d.,** dotar

dowse /dauz/ vt. See **douse**

doze /douz/ vi dormitar. —n sueño ligero, m

dozen /'dʌzən/ n docena, f

drab /dræb/ a pardo, parduzco, grisáceo; Fig. gris, monótono. —n (slut) pazpuerca, f; (prostitute) ramera, f

drachma /'drækmə/ n dracma, f

draft /dræft/ n (act of drawing) tiro, m; (of liquid) trago, m; (of a ship) calado, m; (of air) corriente de aire, f; Com. giro, m, letra de cambio, f; (for the army, navy) conscripción, leva, f; (outline) bosquejo, m; proyecto, m; borrador, m. —vt (recruit) reclutar; proyectar, m; (outline) bosquejar, delinear; (draw up) redactar. **on d.,** (of beer, etc.) por vaso. **d. horse,** caballo de tiro, m

draft card n cartilla (Mexico), libreta de enrolamiento (Argentina), m

draft dodger n emboscado, prófugo, m

drafting /'dræftɪŋ/ n (Mil. Nav.) reclutamiento, m; (of a bill, etc.) redacción, f; (wording) términos, m pl

draftsman /'dræftsmən/ n dibujante, m; delineante, m; redactor, m

drag /dræg/ n (for dredging) draga, f; (harrow) rastrillo, m; (break) freno, m; (obstacle) estorbo, m; Aer. sonda, f. —vt arrastrar; (fishing nets) rastrear; (harrow) rastrillar. —vi (of the anchor) garrar; arrastrarse por el suelo; (of time) pasar lentamente; ir más despacio (que); (of interest) decaer, disminuir. **d.-hook,** garfio, m. **d.-net,** brancada, f

dragging /'drægɪŋ/ n arrastre, m; (of lakes, etc.) rastreo, m, a rastrero; cansado

draggled /'drægəld/ a mojado y sucio

dragon /'drægən/ n dragón, m. **d.-fly,** libélula, f, caballito del diablo, m

dragoon /drə'gun/ n Mil. dragón, m, vt someter a una disciplina rigurosa; obligar a la fuerza (a)

drain /drein/ n desaguadero, m; (sewer) cloaca, alcantarilla, f; sumidero, m; Agr. acequia, f. —vt desaguar; sanear; (lakes, etc.) desangrar; secar;

(bail) achicar; (empty and drink) vaciar; (swallow) tragar; (*Fig.* of sorrow, etc.) apurar; (despoil) despojar; (deprive) privar (de); (impoverish) empobrecer; (exhaust) agotar. —*vi* desaguarse; vaciarse; (with off) escurrirse. **to d. be well drained,** tener buen drenaje. **to d. the sump,** vaciar la culata. **to d. away,** vaciar. **d.-pipe,** tubo de desagüe, *m*

drainage /'dreɪnɪdʒ/ *n* (of land) drenaje, *m;* desagüe, *m;* (of wounds) drenaje, *m;* (sewage) aguas del alcantarillado, *f pl.* **main d.,** drenaje municipal, *m*

draining /'dreɪnɪŋ/ *a* de desagüe; de drenaje. **d.-board,** escurridor, *m*

drake /dreɪk/ *n* ánade macho, *m*

dram /dræm/ *n* dracma, *f;* (of liquor) trago, *m*

drama /'drɑmə, 'dræmə/ *n* drama, *m*

dramatic /drə'mætɪk/ *a* dramático

dramatically /drə'mætɪkli/ *adv* dramáticamente

dramatis personae /'dræmətɪs pər'souni/ *n pl* personajes, *m pl*

dramatist /'dræmətɪst, 'drɑmə-/ *n* dramaturgo, *m*

dramatization /ˌdræmətə'zeɪʃən, ˌdrɑmə-/ *n* versión escénica, *f;* descripción dramática, *f;* (of emotions) dramatización, *f*

dramatize /'dræmə,taɪz, 'drɑmə-/ *vt* dramatizar

drape /dreɪp/ *vt* colgar, cubrir; vestir

draper /'dreɪpər/ *n* pañero (-ra)

drapery /'dreɪpəri/ *n* colgaduras, *f pl;* ropaje, *m,* ropas, *f pl;* pañería, *f*

drastic /'dræstɪk/ *a* drástico; enérgico, fuerte; **a drastic measure,** una medida avanzada, *f*

draw /drɔ/ *vt* tirar; arrastrar; traer; (pluck) arrancar; (attract) atraer; (extract) extraer; sacar; hacer salir; (unsheath) desenvainar; (a bow-string) tender; (cards, dominoes) tomar, robar; (threads) deshilar; (disembowel) destripar; (a check, etc.) girar, librar; (of a ship) calar; (of lines) hacer (rayas); (curtains) correr; (to draw curtains back) descorrer; (salary, money) cobrar, percibir; (obtain) obtener; (persuade) persuadir, inducir; (inhale) respirar; (a sigh) dar; (win) ganar; (a conclusion) deducir, inferir; (a distinction) hacer formular; *Sports.* empatar; (a number, etc.) sortear; (suck) chupar; (tighten) estirar; (lengthen) alargar; (comfort, etc.) tomar; (inspiration) inspirarse en; (obtain money) procurarse (recursos); (withdraw funds) retirar; (write) escribir; (draw) dibujar; (trace) trazar; (provoke) provocar. **to be drawn,** (of tickets in a lottery and cards) salir. **to d. lots,** echar suertes. **to d. water,** sacar agua. **to d. along,** arrastrar; conducir. **to d. aside,** tomar a un lado, tomar aparte; quitar de en medio, poner a un lado; (curtains) descorrer. **to d. away,** (remove) quitar; (a person) llevarse (a); apartar. **to d. back,** hacer recular; hacer retirarse; hacer volverse atrás; (curtains) descorrer. **to d. down,** hacer bajar; tirar a lo largo de (or por); bajar; (attract) atraer. **to d. forth,** hacer salir; hacer avanzar; tirar hacia adelante; conducir; (develop) desarrollar; sacar; hacer aparecer; (comment, etc.) suscitar. **to d. in,** tirar hacia adentro; sacar; acercar; atraer. **to d. off,** sacar; retirar; quitar; (water from pipes, etc.) vaciar; *Print.* tirar; (turn aside) desviar. **to d. on,** (of apparel) ponerse; (boots) calzarse; (occasion) ocasionar. **to d. out,** sacar fuera; hacer salir; tirar (de); (extract) extraer; (trace) trazar; (a person) hacer hablar. **to d. over,** poner encima de; arrastrar por; hacer acercarse (a), tirar hacia; atraer; persuadir. **d. prestige (from),** cobrar prestigio (de). **to d. round,** poner alrededor de. **to d. together,** reunir; acercar. **to d. up,** tirar hacia arriba; subir; sacar; extraer; (raise) levantar; alzar; (bring) traer; (bring near) acercar; (order) ordenar; *Mil.* formar; (a document) redactar; formular. **to d. oneself up,** erguirse

draw /drɔ/ *vi* (shrink) encogerse; (wrinkle) arrugarse; (of chimneys, etc.) tirar; (a picture) dibujar; *Sports.* empatar; (move) moverse; avanzar, adelantarse; (of a ship) calar; (a sword) desnudar (la espada); (lots) echar suertes; (attract people) atraer gente; *Com.* girar. **to d. aside,** ponerse a un lado; retirarse. **to d. back,** retroceder, recular; retirarse; vacilar. **to d. in,** retirarse; (of days) hacerse corto; (of dusk) caer. **to d. off,** alejarse; apartarse, retirarse. **to d. on,** (approach) acercarse; avanzar; *Com.* girar con-

tra; inspirarse en. **to d. out,** hacerse largo; (of a vehicle) ponerse en marcha, empezar a andar. **to d. round,** ponerse alrededor; reunirse alrededor. **to d. together,** reunirse. **to d. up,** parar.

draw /drɔ/ *n* tirada, *f;* (of lotteries) sorteo, *m; Sports.* empate, *m;* atracción, *f;* (*Fig.* feeler) tanteo, *m.* **to be a big d.,** ser una gran atracción

drawback /'drɔˌbæk/ *n* desventaja, *f,* inconveniente, *m*

drawbridge /'drɔˌbrɪdʒ/ *n* puente levadizo, *m*

drawee /drɔ'i/ *n Com.* girado, *m*

drawer /'drɔər for / drɔr for / *n* tirador (-ra); (of water) aguador (-ra); extractor (-ra); (in a public-house) mozo de taberna; (designer) diseñador, *m;* (sketcher) dibujante, *mf; Com.* girador, *m;* (receptacle) cajón, *m; pl* **drawers,** (men's) calzoncillos, *m pl;* (women's) pantalones, *m pl*

drawing /'drɔɪŋ/ *n* (pulling) tiro, *m;* atracción, *f;* (extraction) extracción, *f;* saca, *f;* (in raffles, etc. and of lots) sorteo, *m;* (of money) percibo, *m; Com.* giro, *m;* (sketch) dibujo, *m;* (plan) esquema, *f.* **free-hand d.,** dibujo a pulso, *m.* **d. from life,** dibujo del natural, *m.* **d.-board,** tablero de dibujo, *m.* **d.-paper,** papel para dibujar, *m.* **d.-pin,** chinche, *f.* **d.-room,** salón, *m*

drawl /drɔl/ *vi* hablar arrastrando las palabras

drawn /drɔn/ *past part* See **draw.** *a* (tired) ojeroso, con ojeras, con un aspecto de cansancio; (with pain) desencajado. **long d. out,** demasiado largo. **d. sword,** espada desnuda, *f.* **d.-thread work,** deshilados, *m pl*

dray /dreɪ/ *n* carro, *m.* **d.-horse,** caballo de tiro, *m*

dread /drɛd/ *n* pavor, temor, terror, espanto, *m;* trepidación, *f,* miedo, *m.* —*a* temible, espantoso, terrible; augusto. —*vt* temer. —*vi* tener miedo, temer. **in d. of,** con miedo de, con terror de

dreader /'drɛdər/ *n* el, *m,* (*f,* la) que teme, temedor (-ra)

dreadful /'drɛdfəl/ *a* terrible, pavoroso, espantoso, horroroso; formidable; augusto

dreadfully /'drɛdfəli/ *adv* terriblemente, horriblemente

dreadfulness /'drɛdfəlnɪs/ *n* horror, *m*

dreadnought /'drɛdˌnɔt/ *n* acorazado de línea, *m*

dream /drim/ *n* sueño, *m;* ilusión, *f;* ensueño, *m;* fantasía, *f.* —*vt* and *vi* soñar; imaginar. **He dreamed away the hours,** Pasaba las horas soñando. **I wouldn't d. of it!** ¡Ni por sueño! **in a d.,** en sueños; (waking) como en sueños; mecánicamente. **Sweet dreams!** ¡Duerme bien! **to d. of,** soñar con

dreamer /'drimər/ *n* soñador (-ra); visionario (-ia)

dreamily /'driməli/ *adv* como en sueños; soñolientamente; vagamente

dreaming /'drimɪŋ/ *n* sueños, *m pl*

dreamland /'drimˌlænd/ *n* reino de los sueños, *m*

dreamy /'drimi/ *a* soñador; soñoliento; fantástico; (empty) vacío

dreariness /'drɪərinɪs/ *n* tristeza, *f;* melancolía, *f;* lobreguez, *f*

dreary /'drɪəri/ *a* triste; melancólico; lóbrego

dredge /drɛdʒ/ *vt* dragar; (with sugar, etc.) espolvorear

dredger /'drɛdʒər/ *n* draga, *f;* (for sugar) azucarera, *f;* (for flour) harinero, *m*

dredging /'drɛdʒɪŋ/ *n* dragado, *m;* (sprinkling) salpicadura, *f.* **d. bucket,** cangilón, *m*

dregs /drɛgz/ *n pl* heces, *f pl,* posos, *m pl.* **to drain to the d.,** vaciar hasta las heces

drench /drɛntʃ/ *vt* mojar, calar. **He is drenched to the skin,** Está calado hasta los huesos

Dresden /'drɛzdən/ *n* Dresde, *f.* **D. china,** loza de Dresde, *f*

dress /drɛs/ *vt* (with clothes) vestir; (arrange) arreglar; (the hair) peinar(se); (a wound) curar; (dishes) adobar; (cloth) aprestar; (flax) rastrillar; (stone) labrar; (wood) desbastar; (prune) podar; (a garden) cultivar; (manure) abonar; *Cul.* aderezar; preparar; (season) condimentar; (a table) poner; (adorn) ataviar, adornar; revestir; (a dead body) amortajar. —*vi* vestirse; ataviarse; (of troops) alinearse. **all dressed up and nowhere to go,** compuesta y sin novio. **dressed up to the nines,** vestido de veinticinco alfileres. **Left (Right) d.!** ¡A la izquierda (A la derecha) alinearse! **to d. down,** (scold) poner como un trapo (a), dar una calada (a). **to d. up,** *vt* ataviar; (disguise) disfrazar. —*vi* ponerse muy elegante; disfrazarse

dress /drɛs/ *n* (in general) el vestir; (clothes) ropa, *f;* (frock) vestido, traje, *m;* (uniform) uniforme, *m;* (Fig. covering) hábitos, *m pl;* (appearance) aspecto, *m;* forma, *f.* **full d.,** (uniform) uniforme de gala, *m;* (civilian, man's) traje de etiqueta, *m;* (woman's) traje de gala, *m.* **morning d.,** (man's) traje de paisano, *m;* (woman's) vestido de todos los dias, *m;* (man's formal dress) chaqué, *m.* **ready-made d.,** traje hecho, *m.* **d. allowance,** alfileres, *m pl.* **d.-circle,** anfiteatro, *m.* **d.-coat,** frac, *m.* **d. protector,** sobaquera, *f.* **d. rehearsal,** ensayo general, *m.* **d. shirt,** camisa de pechera dura, *f.* **d. suit,** (with white tie) traje de frac, *m;* (with black tie) smoking, *m.* **d. sword,** espada de gala, *f.* **d. tie,** corbata de smoking (or de frac), *f*

dresser /'drɛsər/ *n* el que adereza; (of wounds) practicante (de hospital), *m;* (valet) ayuda de cámara, *m;* (maid) doncella, *f;* (of skins) adobador de pieles, *m;* (furniture) aparador, *m;* (in the kitchen) armario de la cocina, *m*

dressing /'drɛsɪŋ/ *n* el vestir(se); aderezamiento, *m;* (for cloth) apresto, *m;* (of leather) adobo, *m;* (of wood) desbaste, *m;* (of stone) labrado, *m;* (manuring) estercoladura, *f;* (sauce) salsa, *f;* (seasoning) condimentación, *f;* (of a wound) cura, *f;* (bandage) apósito, *m,* vendaje, *m.* **d.-case,** neceser, saco de noche, *m.* **d.-down,** *Inf.* rapapolvo, *m.* **d.-gown,** (woman's) salto de cama, quimono, *m;* (man's) batín, *m.* **d.-jacket,** chambra, *f,* peinador, *m.* **d.-room,** *Theat.* camarín, *m;* (in a house) trasalcoba, recámara, *f.* **d.-station,** puesto de socorro, *m.* **d.-table,** tocador, *m,* mesa de tocador, *f*

dressmaker /'drɛs,meikər/ *n* modista, *mf*

dressmaking /'drɛs,meikɪŋ/ *n* confección de vestidos, *f;* arte de la modista, *mf*

dribble /'drɪbəl/ *vi* gotear; (slaver) babear. —*vt* (in football) regatear. —*n* (in football) regate, *m*

dried /draid/ *a* seco; (of fruit) paso. **d. up,** (withered) marchito; (of people) enjuto. **d. fish,** cecial, *m.* **d. meat,** cecina, *f*

drift /drɪft/ *n* (in a ship or airplane's course) deriva, *f;* (of a current) velocidad, *f;* (tendency) tendencia, *f;* (meaning) significación, *f;* (heap) montón, *m;* (aim) objeto, propósito, fin, *m; Mineral.* galería, *f* (of dust, etc.) nube, *f;* (shower) lluvia, *f;* (impulsion) impulso, *m;* violencia, *f.* —*vi* flotar, ir arrastrado por la corriente; amontonarse; *Naut.* derivar; *Aer.* abatir. —*vt* llevar; amontonar. **drifts of sand,** arena movediza, *f.* **to d. into,** (war, etc.) entrar sin querer en; (habits) dar en la flor de; (a room, etc.) deslizarse en. **d.-wood,** madera de deriva, *f*

drill /drɪl/ *n* (instrument) taladro, perforador, *m,* barrena, *f;* ejercicio, *m,* educación física, *f; Mil.* instrucción militar, *f;* (cloth) dril, *m; Agr.* sembradora mecánica, *f;* (for seeds) hilera, *f;* (discipline) disciplina, *f;* (teaching) instrucción, *f.* —*vt* taladrar, barrenar; enseñar el ejercicio (a); enseñar la instrucción; disciplinar; (seed) sembrar en hileras. —*vi* hacer el ejercicio; hacer la instrucción militar. **d. ground,** (in a barracks) patio de un cuartel, *m;* (in a school) patio de recreo, *m.* **d.-sergeant,** sargento instructor, *m*

drilling /'drɪlɪŋ/ *n* (boring) perforación, *f,* barrenamiento, *m;* (of seeds) sembradura en hileras, *f;* ejercicios, *m pl;* (maneuvers) maniobras, *f pl*

drink /drɪŋk/ *n* bebida, *f;* (glass of wine, etc.) copita, *f;* (of water, etc.) vaso, *m.* —*vt* beber; tomar; (empty) vaciar. —*vi* beber. **to d. the health of,** beber a la salud de, brindar por. **to give someone a d.,** dar a beber. **Would you like a d.?** ¿Quieres tomar algo? **to d. in,** absorber. **to d. off, up,** beber de un trago

drinkable /'drɪŋkəbəl/ *a* potable, bebedero

drinker /'drɪŋkər/ *n* bebedor (-ra)

drinking /'drɪŋkɪŋ/ *n* acción de beber, *f;* el beber, *m;* (alcoholism) bebida, *f.* —*a* que bebe; aficionado a la bebida; (of things) para beber; (drinkable) potable; (tavern) de taberna. **d.-fountain,** fuente pública para beber agua, *f.* **d. place,** bebedero, *m;* bar, *m.* **d.-**

song, canción de taberna, *f.* **d.-trough,** abrevadero, *m;* **d.-water,** agua potable, *f*

drip /drɪp/ *vi* and *vt* chorrear, gotear; caer gota a gota; escurrir; destilar; chorrear. —*n* goteo, *m;* gota, *f; Archit.* goterón, *m*

dripping /'drɪpɪŋ/ *n* goteo, *m;* chorreo, *m;* (fat) grasa, *f;* (of a wet gotea; mojado; que chorrea agua. **d.-pan,** grasera, *f*

drive /draiv/ *vt* empujar; arrojar; conducir; (grouse, etc.) batir; (a ball) golpear; (a nail, etc.) clavar; (oblige) compeler, forzar a; (a horse, plough, etc.) manejar; (*Mech.* work) mover; (cause to work, of machines) hacer funcionar; (a tunnel, etc.) abrir, construir; (a bargain, etc.) hacer; (cause) impulsar, hacer; (mad, etc.) volver. —*vi* lanzarse; (of rain) azotar; (a vehicle) conducir; (in a vehicle) ir en (coche, etc.). **to let d. at,** (aim) asestar. **to d. a wedge,** hacer mella. **to d. home an argument,** convencer; hacer convincente. **What is he driving at?** ¿Qué se propone?; ¿Qué quiere?; ¿Qué quiere decir con sus indirectas? ¿A dónde quiere llegar con esto? **to d. along,** ir en coche o carruaje por; pasearse en coche o carruaje; conducir un auto, etc., por. **to d. away,** *vt* echar; (chase) cazar; (flies, etc.) sacudirse, espantar; (care, etc.) ahuyentar; (of persons) apartar, alejar. —*vi* (depart) marcharse (en coche, etc.). **to d. back,** *vt* rechazar; (a ball) devolver. —*vi* volver (en auto, etc.); (arrive) llegar. **to d. down,** hacer bajar; arrojar hacia abajo; (in a vehicle) bajar (por). **to d. in, into,** *vt* hacer entrar; (of teeth, etc.) hincar; (nails) clavar; *Fig.* introducir. —*vt* entrar (en coche, carruaje); llegar (en coche, etc.). **to d. off,** See **away. to d. off the stage,** hacer dejar la escena, silbar. **to d. on,** *vt* empujar; hacer avanzar; (attack) atacar. —*vi* seguir su marcha; seguir avanzando; emprender la marcha. **to d. out,** *vt* expulsar; hacer salir; (chase) cazar. —*vi* salir en coche, etc. **to d. up,** *vi* llegar (en coche, etc.); parar. **to d. up to,** avanzar hasta, llegar hasta; conducir (el coche, etc.) hasta

drive /draiv/ *n* paseo (en coche, etc.), *m;* (avenue) avenida, *f;* (distance) trayecto, *m;* (journey) viaje, *m; Mech.* acción, *f,* conducción, *f; Mech. Mil.* ataque, *m;* (of a person) energía, *f,* campaña vigorosa, *f;* impulso, *m.* **left (right) hand d.,** conducción a la izquierda (derecha). **to take a d.,** dar un paseo en (auto, etc.). **to take for a d.,** llevar a paseo en (auto, etc.)

drive-in /'draiv,ɪn/ *n* autocine, autocinema, *m*

drivel /'drɪvəl/ *n* vaciedades, patrañas, *f pl,* disparates, *m pl,* *vi* decir disparates, chochear

driver /'draivər/ *n* conductor (-ra); chófer, *m;* (of an engine) maquinista, *m;* (of a cart) carretero, *m;* (of a coach, carriage) cochero, *m;* (of cattle, etc.) ganadero, *m;* (golf) conductor, *m*

"Driveway" «Vado Permante», «Paso de Carruajes»

driving /'draivɪŋ/ *n* conducción, *f;* modo de conducir, *m;* paseo (en coche, etc.), *m;* impulsión, *f.* —*a* de conducir; de chófer; para choferes; motor; propulsor; impulsor; de transmisión; *Fig.* impulsor; (violent) violento, impetuoso. **to go d.,** ir de paseo (en auto o carruaje). **d. license,** carnet de chófer, *m.* **d. mirror,** espejo retrovisor, *m.* **d. seat,** asiento del conductor, *m;* (of an old-fashioned coach, etc.) pescante, *m.* **d.-shaft,** *Mech.* árbol motor, *m.* **d. test,** examen para choferes, *m.* **d.-wheel,** volante, *m;* rueda motriz, *f.* **d.-whip,** látigo, *m*

drizzle /'drɪzəl/ *n* llovizna, *f,* *vi* lloviznar

droll /droul/ *a* chusco, gracioso. —*n* bufón, *m*

dromedary /'drɒmɪˌdɛri/ *n* dromedario, *m*

drone /droun/ *n* abejón, *m; Fig.* zángano, *m;* (hum) zumbido, *m;* (of a song, voice) salmodia, *f,* *vt* and *vi* (hum) zumbar; (of a song, voice) salmodiar; (idle) zanganear

droning /'drounɪŋ/ *a* zumbador; confuso

droop /drup/ *vi* inclinarse; colgar; caer; (wither) marchitarse; (fade) consumirse; (pine) desanimarse. —*vt* bajar; dejar caer. —*n* caída, *f,* inclinación, *f*

drooping /'drupɪŋ/ *a* caído; debilitado; lánguido; (of ears) gacho; (depressed) alicaído, deprimido

drop /drɒp/ *n* gota, *f;* (tear) lágrima, *f;* (for the ear) pendiente, *m;* (sweet) pastilla, *f;* (of a chandelier) almendra, *f;* (fall) caída, *f;* (in price, etc.) baja, *f;*

(slope) pendiente, cuesta, *f.* **by drops,** a gotas. **d. bottle,** frasco cuentagotas, *m.* **d.-curtain,** telón de boca, *m.* **d.-hammer,** martinete, *m.* **d.-head coupé,** cupé descapotable, *m.* **d.-scene,** telón de foro, *m*

drop /drɒp/ *vt* verter a gotas; destilar; (sprinkle) salpicar, rociar; dejar caer; soltar; (lower) bajar; (of clothes, etc.) desprenderse de, quitar; (lose) perder; (a letter in a mailbox) echar; (leave) dejar; (give up) renunciar (a); desistir (de); abandonar; (kill) tumbar; (a hint) soltar; (a curtsey) hacer. —*vi* gotear, caer en gotas, destilar; (descend) bajar, descender; caer muerto; caer desmayado; (sleep) dormirse; (fall) caer; (of the wind) amainar; (of prices, temperature) bajar. **to let the matter d.,** poner fin a una cuestión. **to d. a line,** poner unas líneas. **to d. anchor,** anclar. **to d. behind,** quedarse atrás. **to d. down,** caer (a tierra). **to d. in,** entrar al pasar. **d. in on somebody,** pasarse por casa de fulano, pasarse por el despacho de (etc.). **to d. off,** separarse (de); disminuir; (sleep) quedar dormido; (die) morir de repente. **to d. out,** separarse; (from a race, etc.) retirarse (de); quedarse atrás; desaparecer; ausentarse, apartarse; (decrease) disminuir; decaer. **He has dropped out of my life,** Le he perdido de vista. **to d. through,** caer por; frustrarse; no dar resultado

dropping /'drɒpɪŋ/ *n* gotera, *f;* gotas, *f pl;* (fall) caída, *f; pl* **droppings** (of a candle) moco, *m;* (dung) cagadas, *f pl.* **Constant d. wears away the stone,** La gotera cava la piedra

dropsy /'drɒpsi/ *n* hidropesía, *f*

dross /drɔs/ *n* escoria, *f;* (rubbish) basura, *f*

drought /draut/ *n* aridez, *f;* (thirst) sed, *f;* (dry season) sequía, *f*

drove /drouv/ *n* manada, *f,* hato, *m;* (of sheep) rebaño, *m;* (crowd) muchedumbre, *f*

drown /draun/ *vi* ahogarse. —*vt* ahogar; sumergir; inundar; (*Fig.* of cries, sorrow, etc.) ahogar

drowning /'draunɪŋ/ *n* ahogamiento, *m;* sumersión, *f;* inundación, *f.* —*a* que se ahoga

drowse /drauz/ *vi* adormecerse

drowsily /'drauzəli/ *adv* soñolientamente

drowsiness /'drauzɪnɪs/ *n* somnolencia, *f;* sueño, *m;* (laziness) indolencia, pereza, *f*

drowsy /'drauzi/ *a* soñoliento; adormecedor, soporífero; (heavy) amodorrado. **to grow d.,** adormecerse. **to make d.,** adormecer

drubbing /'drʌbɪŋ/ *n* tunda, zurra, felpa, *f*

drudgery /'drʌdʒəri/ *n* trabajo arduo, *m,* faena monótona, *f*

drug /drʌg/ *n* droga, *f;* medicamento, *m;* narcótico, *m.* —*vt* mezclar con drogas; administrar drogas (a); narcotizar. —*vi* tomar drogas. **d. trade,** comercio de drogas, *m.* **d. traffic,** contrabando de drogas, narcotráfico *m*

drug addict *n* toxicómano, *m*

drug addiction *n* toxicomanía, *f*

druggist /'drʌgɪst/ *n* droguero (-ra)

druid /'druɪd/ *n* druida, *m*

drum /drʌm/ *n* tambor, *m;* (of the ear) tímpano (del oído), *m;* (cylinder) cilindro, *m;* (box) caja, *f; Archit.* cuerpo de columna, *m.* **bass d.,** bombo, *m.* **with drums beating,** con tambor batiente. **d.-head,** parche (del tambor), *m.* **d.-head service,** misa de campaña, *f.* **d.-major,** tambor mayor, *m*

drum /drʌm/ *vt and vi* tocar el tambor; (with the fingers) tabalear, teclear; (with the heels) zapatear; (into a person's head) machacar. **to d. out,** *Mil.* expulsar a tambor batiente

drummer /'drʌmər/ *n* tambor, *m*

drumming /'drʌmɪŋ/ *n* ruido del tambor, *m;* (of the heels) taconeo, *m;* (of the fingers) tabaleo, tecleo, *m*

drumstick /'drʌmˌstɪk/ *n* palillo (de tambor), *m*

drunk /drʌŋk/ *a* borracho, ebrio. —*n* borracho, *m.* **to be d.,** estar borracho. **to get d.,** emborracharse. *Inf.* pillar un lobo. **to make d.,** emborrachar

drunkard /'drʌŋkərd/ *n* borracho (-cha)

drunken /'drʌŋkən/ *a* borracho, ebrio

drunkenness /'drʌŋkənnɪs/ *n* embriaguez, borrachera, ebriedad, *f*

dry /drai/ *vi* secarse. —*vt* secar; desaguar; (wipe) enjugar. **to dry one's tears,** enjugarse las lágrimas; *Fig.* secarse las lágrimas. **to dry up,** secarse; (of persons)

acecinarse; (with old age) apergaminarse; (of ideas, etc.) agotarse; (be quiet) callarse

dry /drai/ *a* seco; árido; estéril; (thirsty) sediento; (of wine) seco; (U.S.A.) prohibicionista; (squeezed) exprimido; (of toast) sin mantequilla; (*Fig.* chilly) aburrido; (sarcastic) sarcástico; (of humour) agudo. **on dry land,** en seco. **dry battery,** pila seca, *f.* **to dry-clean,** lavar al seco. **dry-cleaner,** tintorero (-ra). **dry-cleaning,** lavado al seco, *m.* **dry-cleaning shop,** tintorería, *f.* **dry goods,** lencería, *f.* **dry land,** tierra firme, *f.* **dry measure,** medida para áridos, *f.* **dry-nurse,** ama seca, *f.* **dry-point,** punta seca, *f.* **dry-rot,** carcoma, *f.* **dry-shod,** con los pies secos

drying /'draiɪŋ/ *n* secamiento, *m;* desecación, *f, a* secante; seco; para secar. **d. ground,** tendedero, *m.* **d. machine,** secadora, *f;* (for the hair) secadora de cabello, *f.* **d. room,** secadero, *m*

dryly /'draili/ *adv* secamente

dryness /'drainɪs/ *n* sequedad, *f;* aridez, *f;* (of humour) agudeza, *f*

dual /'duəl/ *a* doble; *Gram.* dual. **d. control,** mandos gemelos, *m pl.* **d. personality,** conciencia doble, *f*

dualism /'duəˌlɪzəm/ *n* dualismo, *m*

duality /du'ælɪti/ *n* dualidad, *f*

dub /dʌb/ *vt* (a knight) armar caballero; (call) apellidar; (nickname) motejar, apodar

dubbing /'dʌbɪŋ/ *n* (of films) doblaje, *m*

dubious /'dubiəs/ *a* dudoso, incierto; indeciso; problemático; ambiguo

dubiously /'dubiəsli/ *adv* dudosamente

dubiousness /'dubiəsnɪs/ *n* carácter dudoso, *m;* incertidumbre, *f;* ambigüedad, *f*

Dublin /'dʌblɪn/ Dublín, *f*

Dubliner /'dʌblənər/ *n* dublinés (-esa)

ducat /'dʌkət/ *n* ducado, *m*

duchess /'dʌtʃɪs/ *n* duquesa, *f*

duchy /'dʌtʃi/ *n* ducado, *m*

duck /dʌk/ *n* pato (-ta), ánade, *mf; Sports.* cero, *m;* (darling) vida mía, querida, *f;* (jerk) agachada, *f;* (under the water) chapuz, *m;* (material) dril, *m; Mil.* auto anfibio, *m; pl* **ducks,** pantalones de dril, *m pl.* —*vi* agacharse; (under water) chapuzarse. —*vt* zabullir, sumergir; bajar, inclinar

ducking /'dʌkɪŋ/ *n* chapuz, *m.* **d.-stool,** silla de chapuzar, *f*

duckling /'dʌklɪŋ/ *n* anadino (-na)

duct /dʌkt/ *n* conducto, canal, *m; Bot.* tubo, *m*

ductile /'dʌktl/ *a* dúctil

ductility /dʌk'tɪlɪti/ *n* ductilidad, *f*

ductless /'dʌktlɪs/ *a* sin tubos

due /du/ *a* debido; (payable) pagadero; (fallen due) vencido; (fitting) propio; (expected) esperado. —*n* impuesto, *m;* derecho, *m.* **in due form,** en regla. **in its due time,** a su tiempo debido. **to fall due,** vencerse. **due bill,** *Com.* abonaré, *m.* **due west,** poniente derecho, *m*

duel /'duəl/ *n* duelo, lance de honor, *m; Fig.* lucha, *f.* **to fight a d.,** batirse en duelo

dueling /'duəlɪŋ/ *n* el (batirse en) duelo

duelist /'duəlɪst/ *n* duelista, *m*

duenna /du'ɛnə/ *n* dueña, *f*

duet /du'ɛt/ *n* dúo, *m*

duettist /du'ɛtɪst/ *n* duetista, *mf*

duffer /'dʌfər/ *n* estúpido (-da); ganso, *m;* (at games, etc.) maleta, *m*

dug /dʌg/ *n* teta, *f*

dugout /'dʌgˌaut/ *n* trinchera, *f*

duke /duk/ *n* duque, *m*

dukedom /'dukdəm/ *n* ducado, *m*

dulcet /'dʌlsɪt/ *a* dulce

dulcimer /'dʌlsəmər/ *n* dulcémele, *m*

dull /dʌl/ *a* (stupid) lerdo, estúpido, obtuso; (boring, tedious) aburrido; (of pain, sounds) sordo; (of colors and eyes) apagado; (of light, beams, etc.) sombrío; (not polished) mate; (pale) pálido; (insipid) insípido, insulso; (of people) soso, poco interesante; (dreary, sad) triste; (gray) gris; (of mirrors, etc.) empañado; (of weather) anublado; (of hearing) duro; (slow) lento; lánguido; insensible; (blunt) romo; *Com.* encalmado, inactivo. **to find life d.,** encontrar la vida aburrida. **d. of hearing,** duro de oído, algo sordo. **d.**

pain, dolor sordo, *m.* **d. season,** temporada de calma, *f.* **d.-eyed,** con ojos apagados. **d.-witted,** lerdo

dull /dʌl/ *vt* (make stupid) entontecer; (lessen) mitigar; (weaken) debilitar; (pain) calmar, aliviar; (sadden) entristecer; (blunt) embotar; (spoil) estropear; (a mirror, etc.) empañar; (a polished surface) hacer mate, deslustrar; (of enthusiasm, etc.) enfriar; (tire) fatigar; (obstruct) impedir

dullness /'dʌlnɪs/ *n* (stupidity) estupidez, *f;* (boredom) aburrimiento, *m;* (heaviness) pesadez, *f;* (drowsiness) somnolencia, *f;* (insipidity) insipidez, insulsez, *f;* (of literary style) prosaísmo, *m;* (of persons) sosería, *f;* (of a surface) deslustre, *m;* (laziness) pereza, languidez, *f;* (slowness) lentitud, *f;* (tiredness) cansancio, *m;* (sadness) tristeza, *f;* (bluntness) embotamiento, *m;* (of hearing) dureza, *f; Com.* desanimación, *f*

dully /'dʌli/ *adv* (stupidly) estúpidamente; sin comprender; (insipidly) insípidamente; (not brightly) sin brillo; (slowly) lentamente; (sadly) tristemente; (tiredly) con cansancio; (of sound) sordamente

duly /'duli/ *adv* debidamente; puntualmente

dumb /dʌm/ *a* mudo; callado; silencioso; *Inf.* tonto, estúpido. **to become d.,** enmudecer. **to strike d.,** dejar sin habla. **d.-bell,** barra con pesas, *f.* **d. show,** pantomima, *f.* **d. waiter,** bufete, *m*

dumbfound /dʌm'faund/ *vt* dejar sin habla; confundir; pasmar

dumbness /'dʌmnɪs/ *n* mudez, *f,* mutismo, *m;* silencio, *m*

dummy /'dʌmi/ *n* (tailor's, etc.) maniquí, *m;* (puppet) títere, *m;* cabeza para pelucas, *f;* (figurehead) hombre de paja, testaferro, *m;* (baby's) chupador, *m;* (at cards) el muerto. —*a* fingido. **to be d.,** (at cards) ser el muerto

dump /dʌmp/ *n* depósito, *m;* vaciadero, *m.* —*vt* depositar; (goods on a market) inundar (con)

dumping /'dʌmpɪŋ/ *n* depósito, *m;* vaciamiento, *m;* (of goods on a market) inundación, *f.* **"D. prohibited,"** «Se prohíbe arrojar la basura»

dumps /dʌmps/ *n* murria, *f*

dun /dʌn/ *vt* apremiar, importunar

dunce /dʌns/ *n* asno, bobo, zoquete, *m.* **dunce's cap,*** coroza, *f*

dun-colored /'dʌn,kʌlərd/ *a* pardo

dunderhead /'dʌndər,hɛd/ *n* cabeza de alcornoque, zoquete, *m*

dune /dun/ *n* duna, *f*

dung /dʌŋ/ *n* estiércol, *m;* (of rabbits, mice, deer, sheep, goats) cagarruta, *f;* (of cows) boñiga, *f;* (of hens) gallinaza, *f.* **d.-cart,** carro de basura, *m*

dungarees /,dʌŋgə'riz/ *n* mono, *m,* pantalones-vaquero, *m pl*

dungeon /'dʌndʒən/ *n* mazmorra, *f,* calabozo, *m*

dunghill /'dʌŋ,hɪl/ *n* muladar, *m*

Dunkirk /'dʌnkɑrk/ Dunquerque, *m*

duodenum /,duə'dinəm/ *n* duodeno, *m*

dupe /dup/ *n* víctima, *f;* tonto (-ta). —*vt* embelecar, engañar. **to be a d.,** *Inf.* hacer el primo

duplicate /*a, n* 'duplɪkɪt, 'dyu-; *v* -,keit/ *a* duplicado, doble. —*n* duplicado, *m;* copia, *f.* —*vt* duplicar

duplication /,duplɪ'keifən/ *n* duplicación, *f*

duplicator /'duplɪ,keitər/ *n* copiador, *m*

duplicity /du'plɪsɪti/ *n* duplicidad, *f*

durability /,dʊrə'bɪlɪti/ *n* duración, *f.* **This is a cloth of great d.,** Este es un paño que dura mucho, Este es un paño muy duradero

durable /'dʊrəbəl/ *a* duradero

duration /dʊ'reifən/ *n* duración, *f*

duress /dʊ'rɛs/ *n* compulsión, *f;* (prison) prisión, *f*

during /'dʊrɪŋ/ *prep* durante

dusk /dʌsk/ *n* atardecer, anochecer, *m;* (twilight) crepúsculo, *m;* (darkness) oscuridad, *f.* **at d.,** al atardecer, a la caída de la tarde

dusky /'dʌski/ *a* (swarthy) moreno; (black) negro; (dim, dark) oscuro; (of colors) sucio

dust /dʌst/ *n* polvo, *m;* (cloud of dust) polvareda, *f;* (ashes) cenizas, *f pl;* (of coal) cisco, *m;* (sweepings) barreduras, *f pl;* (of grain) tamo, *m.* —*vt* desempolvar, quitar (or sacudir) el polvo de; (cover

with dust) polvorear; (scatter) salpicar; (sweep) barrer; (clean) limpiar. **d.-bin,** basurero, *m.* **d.-cart,** carro de la basura, *m.* **d. cloud,** polvareda, *f.* **d. jacket,** (books) sobrecubierta, *f.* **d.-pan,** recogedor de basura, *m.* **d.-sheet,** guardapolvo, *m.* **d. storm,** vendaval de polvo, *m*

duster /'dʌstər/ *n* el, *m,* que quita el polvo; paño (para quitar el polvo), *m;* (of feathers) plumero, *m*

dustiness /'dʌstɪnɪs/ *n* empolvoramiento, *m;* estado polvoriento, *m*

dusting /'dʌstɪŋ/ *n* limpieza, *f;* (sweeping) barredura, *f;* (powder) polvos antisépticos, *m pl*

dusty /'dʌsti/ *a* polvoriento, polvoroso, empolvado; del color del polvo; (of colours) sucio. **It is very d.,** Hay mucho polvo. **to get d.,** llenarse (or cubrirse) de polvo

Dutch /dʌtʃ/ *a* holandés. **the D.,** los holandeses. **double D.,** griego, galimatías, *m.* **D. cheese,** queso de bola, *m.* **D. courage,** coraje falso, *m.* **D. woman,** holandesa, *f*

Dutchman /'dʌtʃmən/ *n* holandés, *m*

dutiable /'dutiəbəl/ *a* sujeto a derechos de aduana

dutiful /'dutəfəl/ *a* que cumple con sus deberes; obediente, sumiso; respetuoso; excelente, muy bueno

dutifully /'dutəfəli/ *adv* obedientemente; respetuosamente

dutifulness /'dutəfəlnɪs/ *n* obediencia, docilidad, *f;* respeto, *m*

duty /'duti/ *n* deber, *m;* obligación, *f;* (greetings) respetos, *m pl;* (charge, burden) carga, *f;* (tax) derecho, impuesto, *m; Mil.* servicio, *m;* (guard) guardia, *f.* **off d.,** libre. **on d.,** de servicio. **to be on sentry d.,** estar de guardia. **to do d. as,** servir como. **to do one's d.,** hacer (or cumplir con) su deber. **to pay d. on,** pagar derechos de aduana sobre. **d.-free,** franco de derechos

dwarf /dwɔrf/ *a* enano. —*n* enano (-na). —*vt* impedir el crecimiento de; empequeñecer

dwarfish /'dwɔrfɪʃ/ *a* enano

dwell /dwɛl/ *vi* vivir, habitar; (with on, upon) (think about) meditar sobre, pensar en; (deal with) tratar de; hablar largamente de; (insist on) insister en; apoyarse en, hacer hincapié en; (pause over) detenerse en

dweller /'dwɛlər/ *n* habitante, *mf;* (more poetic) morador (-ra)

dwelling /'dwɛlɪŋ/ *n* vivienda, *f;* (abode) morada, habitación, *f;* residencia, *f;* casa, *f;* (domicile) domicilio, *m.* **d.-house,** casa, *f*

dwindle /'dwɪndl/ *vi* disminuirse; consumirse; (decay) decaer; (degenerate) degenerar. **to d. to,** reducirse a

dwindling /'dwɪndlɪŋ/ *n* disminución, *f*

dye /dai/ *vt* teñir, colorar. —*vi* teñirse. —*n* tinte, *m;* (colour) color, *m.* **fast dye,** tinte estable, *m.* **dye-house,** tintorería, *f.* **dye-stuff,** materia colorante, *f.* **dye-works,** tintorería, *f*

dyed-in-the-wool /'daid ən ðə 'wʊl/ *a* de pies a cabeza

dyeing /'daiɪŋ/ *n* teñidura, tintura, *f;* (as a trade) tintorería, *f.* **d. and dry-cleaning shop,** tintorería, *f*

dyer /'daiər/ *n* tintorero (-ra)

dyestuff /'dai,stʌf/ *n* materia colorante, materia de tinte, materia tintórea, *f*

dying /'daiɪŋ/ *a* moribundo, agonizante; de la muerte; (of light) mortecino; (last) último; supremo; (languishing) lánguido; (deathbed) hecho en su lecho mortuorio. **to be d.,** estar agonizando; (of light) fenecer. **to be d. for,** estar muerto por

dynamic /dai'næmɪk/ *a* dinámico

dynamics /dai'næmɪks/ *n* dinámica, *f*

dynamite /'dainə,mait/ *n* dinamita, *f*

dynamo /'dainə,mou/ *n* dínamo, *f*

dynastic /dai'næstɪk/ *a* dinástico

dynasty /'dainəsti/ *n* dinastía, *f*

dysentery /'dɪsən,tɛri/ *n* disentería, *f*

dyspepsia /dɪs'pɛpʃə/ *n* dispepsia, *f*

dyspeptic /dɪs'pɛptɪk/ *a* dispéptico. —*n* dispéptico (-ca)

E

e /i/ *n* (letter) e, *f*; *Mus.* mi, *m*
each /itʃ/ *a* cada (invariable), todo. —*pron* cada uno, *m*; cada una, *f*. **e. of them**, cada uno de ellos. **They help e. other**, Se ayudan mutuamente, Se ayudan entre sí. **to love e. other**, amarse
eager /ˈigər/ *a* impaciente; ansioso, deseoso; ambicioso
eagerly /ˈigərli/ *adv* con impaciencia; con ansia; ambiciosamente
eagerness /ˈigərnɪs/ *n* impaciencia, *f*; ansia, *f*, deseo, *m*; (promptness) alacridad, *f*; (zeal) fervor, *m*
eagle /ˈigəl/ *n* águila, *f*. **royal e.**, águila caudal, águila real, *f*. **e.-eyed**, con ojos de lince, de ojo avizor. **have the eyes of an e.**, tener ojos de lince, tener vista de lince
ear /ɪər/ *n* (outer ear) oreja, *f*; (inner ear and sense of hearing) oído, *m*; *Bot.* espiga, panoja, *f*. **to begin to show the ear**, (grain) espigar. **to be all ears**, ser todo oídos. **to give ear**, dar oído. **to have a good ear**, tener buen oído. **to play by ear**, tocar de oído. **to turn a deaf ear**, hacerse el sordo. **ear-ache**, dolor de oídos, *m*. **ear-drum**, tímpano (del oído), *m*. **ear-flap**, orejera, *f*. **ear-phone, ear-piece**, auricular, *m*. **ear-piercing**, penetrante, agudo. **ear-shot**, alcance del oído, *m*. **to be within ear-shot**, estar al alcance del oído. **ear-trumpet**, trompetilla, *f*. **ear wax**, cerilla, *f*
eared /ɪərd/ *a* con orejas; de orejas; *Bot.* con espigas
earl /ɜrl/ *n* conde, *m*
earldom /ˈɜrldəm/ *n* condado, *m*
earlier, earliest /ˈɜrliər; ˈɜrliɪst/ *a compar* and *superl* más temprano; más primitivo; más antiguo; (first, of time) primero. —*adv* más temprano; más pronto; antes
earliness /ˈɜrlinɪs/ *n* lo temprano; antigüedad, *f*, lo primitivo; (precocity) precocidad, *f*. **The e. of his arrival**, Su llegada de buena hora
early /ˈɜrli/ *a* temprano; primitivo; (of fruit, etc.) temprano, adelantado; (movement) primero (e.g. *early Romanticism*, el primer romanticismo); (person) de la primera época (e.g. *the early Cervantes*, Cervantes de la primera época); (work) un primer (e.g. *an early work of Unamuno's*, una primera obra de Unamuno); (advanced) avanzado; (precocious) precoz; (first, of time) primero; (in the morning) matutino; (near) próximo; cercano; (premature) prematuro; (of child's age) tierno; joven. **in the e. hours**, en las primeras horas; en las altas horas (de la noche). **e. age**, edad temprana, tierna edad, *f*. **e.-fruiting**, *Agr.* tempranal. **e. riser**, madrugador (-ra). **e.-rising**, *a* madrugador. **e. years**, primeros años, años de la niñez, *m pl*
early /ˈɜrli/ *adv* temprano; al principio (de); en los primeros días (de); desde los primeros días (de); (in the month, year) a principios (de); (in time) a tiempo; (in the day) de buena hora; (soon) pronto; (among the first) entre los primeros (de). **as e. as possible**, lo más temprano posible; lo más pronto posible. **to be e.**, llegar antes de tiempo; llegar de buena hora. **to get up e.**, madrugar. **to go to bed e.**, acostarse temprano. **too e.**, demasiado temprano. **e. in the morning**, de madrugada
earmark /ˈɪər,mɑrk/ *vt* marcar; *Fig.* destinar, reservar
earn /ɜrn/ *vt* ganar; obtener, adquirir; (deserve) merecer
earnable /ˈɜrnəbəl/ *a* ganable
earnest /ˈɜrnɪst/ *a* serio; fervoroso; diligente; sincero. **to be in e. about something**, tomarlo en serio; ser sincero (en). **e. money**, arras, *f pl*
earnestly /ˈɜrnɪstli/ *adv* seriamente; fervorosamente; con diligencia; sinceramente, de buena fe
earnestness /ˈɜrnɪstnɪs/ *n* seriedad, *f*; fervor, celo, *m*; diligencia, *f*; sinceridad, buena fe, *f*
earnings /ˈɜrnɪŋz/ *n pl Com.* ingresos, *m pl*; (salary) salario, *m*; estipendio, *m*; (of a workman) jornal, *m*
earring /ˈɪər,rɪŋ/ *n* pendiente, arete, *m*
earth /ɜrθ/ *n* tierra, *f*; (of a badger, etc.) madriguera,

f; *Radio.* tierra, *f*. —*vt* cubrir con tierra; *Radio.* conectar con tierra. **clod of e.**, terrón, *m*. **half the e.**, *Inf.* medio mundo, *m*. **on e.**, en este mundo, sobre la tierra
earthen /ˈɜrθən/ *a* terrizo, terroso; (of mud) de barro
earthenware /ˈɜrθən,wɛər/ *n* alfar, *m*, —*a* de loza, de barro
earthiness /ˈɜrθinɪs/ *n* terrosidad, *f*
earthly /ˈɜrθli/ *a* terrestre, terrenal; de la tierra; (fleshly) carnal; (worldly) mundano; material. **There is not an e. chance**, No hay la más mínima posibilidad
earthquake /ˈɜrθ,kweik/ *n* terremoto, temblor de tierra, *m*
earth tremor movimiento sísmico, *m*
earthwork /ˈɜrθ,wɜrk/ *n* terraplén, *m*
earthworm /ˈɜrθ,wɜrm/ *n* gusano de tierra, *m*
earthy /ˈɜrθi/ *a* térreo, terroso
earwig /ˈɪər,wɪg/ *n* tijereta, *f*
ease /iz/ *n* bienestar, *m*; tranquilidad, *f*; descanso, *m*; (leisure) ocio, *m*; (comfortableness) comodidad, *f*; (freedom from embarrassment) naturalidad, *f*, desembarazo, desenfado, *m*; (from pain) alivio, *m*; (simplicity) facilidad, *f*. —*vt* (widen) ensanchar; aflojar; (pain) aliviar; (lighten) aligerar; (moderate) moderar; (soften) suavizar; (free) librar; (one's mind) tranquilizar. **in my moments of e.**, en mis ocios, en mis momentos de ocio. **Stand at e.!** *Mil.* ¡En su lugar descansen! **to be at e.**, estar a sus anchas; encontrarse bien; comportarse con toda naturalidad. **with e.**, fácilmente. **to e. off**, *vt* (*Naut.* cables, sails) arriar. —*vi* sentirse menos, cesar
easel /ˈizəl/ *n* caballete (de pintor) *m*
easily /ˈizəli/ *adv* fácilmente. **The engine runs e.**, El motor marcha bien
easiness /ˈizinɪs/ *n* facilidad, *f*; sencillez, *f*; (of manner) desembarazo, *m*, naturalidad, *f*
east /ist/ *n* este, *m*; oriente, *m*, (of countries) Oriente, *m*; Levante, *m*. —*a* del este; del oriente; (of countries) de Oriente, oriental; levantino. **e. North e.**, estenordeste, *m*. **e. South e.**, estesudeste, *m*. **e. wind**, viento del este, *m*
Easter /ˈistər/ *n* Pascua de Resurrección, *f*. **E. egg**, huevo de Pascua, *m*. **E. Saturday**, sábado de gloria, *m*. **E. Sunday**, domingo de Pascua, *m*
easterly /ˈistərli/ *a* del este; al este. —*adv* hacia el este
eastern /ˈistərn/ *a* del este; de Oriente; oriental. —*n* oriental, *mf*
easternmost /ˈistərn,moust/ *a* situado más al este
East Indies Indias Orientales, *f pl*
eastward /ˈistwərd/ *adv* hacia el este, hacia oriente
easy /ˈizi/ *a* fácil; sencillo; (comfortable) cómodo; (free from pain) aliviado; *Com.* flojo; (well-off) acomodado, holgado; (calm) tranquilo; tolerante; natural; afable, condescendiente; (of virtue, women) fácil. —*adv* con calma; despacio. **I must make myself e. about**, he de tranquilizarme sobre. **Stand e.!** ¡En su lugar descansen! **to take it e.**, tomarlo con calma. **e.-chair**, (silla) poltrona, *f*. **easy come, easy go**, lo que por agua, agua (Mexico and Colombia), los dineros del sacristán cantando vienen y cantando se van (Spain). **e.-going**, acomodadizo; indolente; (morally) de manga ancha; (casual) descuidado
eat /it/ *vt* comer; (meals, soup, refreshments) tomar; (with a good, bad appetite) hacer; consumir; (corrode) corroer; desgastar. —*vi* comer; (*Fam.* of food) ser de buen (or mal) comer. **to eat one's breakfast (lunch)**, tomar el desayuno, desayunar (almorzar). **to eat one's words**, retractarse. **to eat away**, comer; consumir; corroer. **to eat into**, (of chemicals) morder; (a fortune) consumir; gastar. **eat out of s. b.'s hand**, comer de la mano de fulano, comer en la mano de fulano. **to eat up**, devorar (also *Fig.*)
eatable /ˈitəbəl/ *a* comestible, comedero. —*n pl* **eatables**, comestibles, *m pl*

eater /'itər/ n el, m, (f, la) que come

eating /'itɪŋ/ n el comer; comida, f. **e. and drinking,** el comer y beber. **e.-house,** casa de comidas, f

eau de cologne /'ou də kə'loun/ n agua de Colonia, f

eaves /ivz/ n rafe, alero, m. **under the e.,** debajo del alero

eavesdrop /'ivz,drɒp/ vi escuchar a las puertas; fisgonear, espiar

eavesdropper /'ivz,drɒpər/ n fisgón (-ona)

eavesdropping /'ivz,drɒpɪŋ/ n fisgoneo, m

ebb /ɛb/ n (of the tide) reflujo, m; menguante, f; Fig. declinación, f; Fig. decadencia, f; (of life) vejez, f. —vi (of tide) menguar; declinar; decaer. **to ebb and flow,** fluir y refluir. **to ebb away from,** dejar; dejar aislado. **ebb-tide,** marea menguante, f

ebonite /'ɛbə,nait/ n ebonita, f

ebony /'ɛbəni/ n ébano, m

ebullience /ɪ'bʌlyəns/ n efervescencia, exuberancia, f

ebullient /ɪ'bʌlyənt/ a efervescente, exuberante

ebullition /,ɛbə'lɪʃən/ n (boiling) ebullición, f, hervor, m; Fig. efervescencia, f, estallido, m

eccentric /ɪk'sɛntrɪk/ a Geom. excéntrico; raro, original; extravagante, excéntrico. —n persona excéntrica, f, original, m

eccentrically /ɪk'sɛntrɪkəli/ adv excéntricamente

eccentricity /,ɛksən'trɪsɪti/ n Geom. excentricidad, f; rareza, extravagancia, excentricidad, f

Ecclesiastes /ɪ,klizi'æstiz/ n Eclesiastés, m

ecclesiastic /ɪ,klizi'æstɪk/ a eclesiástico. —n eclesiástico, clérigo, m

ecclesiastically /ɪ,klizi'æstɪkəli/ adv eclesiásticamente

echo /'ɛkou/ n eco, m; reverberación, resonancia, f. —vt repercutir; Fig. repetir. —vi resonar, retumbar, reverberar

echoing /'ɛkouɪŋ/ a retumbante. —n eco, m

eclectic /ɪ'klɛktɪk/ a and n ecléctico (-ca)

eclecticism /ɪ'klɛktə,sɪzəm/ n eclecticismo, m

eclipse /ɪ'klɪps/ n Astron. eclipse, m, vt eclipsar, hacer eclipse a. **to be in e.,** estar en eclipse

ecliptic /ɪ'klɪptɪk/ n Astron. eclíptica, f, a eclíptico

eclogue /'ɛklɔg/ n égloga, f

economic /,ɛkə'nɒmɪk, ,ikə-/ a económico

economical /,ɛkə'nɒmɪkəl, ,ikə-/ a económico

economics /,ɛkə'nɒmɪks, ,ikə-/ n economía política, f

economist /ɪ'kɒnəmɪst/ n economista, mf

economize /ɪ'kɒnə,maiz/ vt economizar, ahorrar. —vi hacer economías

economy /ɪ'kɒnəmi/ n economía, f. **domestic e.,** economía doméstica, f. **political e.,** economía política, f

ecstasy /'ɛkstəsi/ n éxtasis, arrebato, m; transporte, m. **to be in e.,** estar en éxtasis

ecstatic /ɛk'stætɪk/ a extático

Ecuador /'ɛkwə,dɔr/ el Ecuador

Ecuadorian /,ɛkwə'dɔriən/ a and n ecuatoriano (-na)

ecumenical /'ɛkyu'mɛnɪkəl/ a ecuménico

eczema /'ɛksəmə/ n eczema, f

eddy /'ɛdi/ n remolino, m, vi remolinar; Fig. remolinear

edelweiss /'eidl,wais/ n inmortal de las nieves, f

edema /ɪ'dimə/ n Med. edema, m

Eden /'idn/ n Edén, m

edge /ɛdʒ/ n (of sharp instruments) filo, m; (of a skate) cuchilla, f; margen, mf; (shore) orilla, f; (of two surfaces) arista, f; (of books) borde, m; (of a coin) canto, m; (of a chair, a precipice, a forest, a curb, etc.) borde, m; (extreme) extremidad, f. **on e.,** de canto, f. Fig. ansioso. **to be on e.,** Fig. tener los nervios en punta. **to set on e.,** poner de canto; (of teeth) dar dentera

edge /ɛdʒ/ vt (sharpen) afilar; Sew. ribetear; orlar; poner un borde (a); (cut) cortar. **to e. away,** escurrirse. **to e. into,** vt insinuarse. —vi deslizarse en. **to e. out,** salir poco a poco

edged /ɛdʒd/ a afilado, cortante; (in compounds) de... filos; (bordered) bordeado; (of books) de bordes...

edgeways /'ɛdʒweiz/ adv de lado; de canto. **He couldn't get a word in e.,** No pudo meter baza en la conversación

edging /'ɛdʒɪŋ/ n borde, m; ribete, m

edibility /,ɛdə'bɪlɪti/ n el ser comestible

edible /'ɛdəbəl/ a comestible

edict /'idɪkt/ n edicto, m

edification /,ɛdəfɪ'keiʃən/ n edificación, f

edifice /'ɛdəfɪs/ n edificio, m

edify /'ɛdə,fai/ vt edificar

edifying /'ɛdə,faiɪŋ/ a edificante, edificador, de edificación

Edinburgh /'ɛdn,bərə/ Edinburgo, m

edit /'ɛdɪt/ vt editar; (a newspaper, journal) ser director de; (prepare for press) redactar; (correct) corregir

editing /'ɛdɪtɪŋ/ n trabajo editorial, m; redacción, f; dirección, f; corrección, f

edition /ɪ'dɪʃən/ n edición, f; Print. tirada, f. **first e.,** edición príncipe, f. **miniature e.,** edición diamante, f

editor /'ɛdɪtər/ n (of a book) editor (-ra); (of a newspaper, journal) director (-ra)

editorial /,ɛdɪ'tɔriəl/ a de redacción; editorial. —n editorial, artículo de fondo, m. **e. staff,** redacción, f

editorial board consejo de redacción, m

editorship /'ɛdɪtər,ʃɪp/ n dirección (de un periódico, de una revista), f

educability /,ɛdʒəkə'bɪlɪti/ n educabilidad, f

educable /'ɛdʒʊkəbəl/ a educable

educate /'ɛdʒʊ,keit/ vt educar; formar; (accustom) acostumbrar

educated /'ɛdʒʊ,keitɪd/ a culto

education /,ɛdʒʊ'keiʃən/ n educación, f; enseñanza, f; pedagogía, f. **chair of e.,** cátedra de pedagogía, f. **early e.,** primeras letras, f pl. **higher e.,** enseñanza superior, f

educational /,ɛdʒʊ'keiʃənl/ a educativo; pedagógico; instructivo

educationalist /,ɛdʒʊ'keiʃənl,ɪst/ n pedagogo, m

educative /'ɛdʒʊ,keitɪv/ a educativo

educator /'ɛdʒʊ,keitər/ n educador (-ra)

educe /ɪ'dus/ vt educir; deducir; Chem. extraer

eduction /ɪ'dʌkʃən/ n educción, f

Edwardian /ɛd'wɔrdiən/ a and n eduardiano (-na)

eel /il/ n anguila, f. **electric eel,** gimnoto, m. **eel-basket,** nasa para anguilas, f

eerie /'ɪəri/ a misterioso, fantástico; sobrenatural; lúgubre

eerily /'ɪərəli/ adv fantásticamente; de modo sobrenatural

eeriness /'ɪərɪnɪs/ n ambiente de misterio, m; efecto misterioso, m

efface /ɪ'feis/ vt borrar, destruir; quitar. **to e. oneself,** retirarse; permanecer en el fondo

effacement /ɪ'feismənt/ n borradura, f

effect /ɪ'fɛkt/ n efecto, m; impresión, f; (result) resultado, m, consecuencia, f, (meaning) substancia, f, significado, m; pl. **effects,** efectos, bienes, m pl. —vt efectuar; producir. **in e.,** en efecto, efectivamente. **of no e.,** inútil. **striving after e.,** efectismo, m. **to feel the effects of,** sentir los efectos de; padecer las consecuencias de. **to put into e.,** poner en práctica; hacer efectivo. **to take e.,** producir efecto; ponerse en vigor

effective /ɪ'fɛktɪv/ a eficaz; (striking) de mucho efecto, poderoso, vistoso. **to make e.,** llevar a efecto

effectively /ɪ'fɛktɪvli/ adv eficazmente; (strikingly) con gran efecto; efectivamente, en efecto

effectiveness /ɪ'fɛktɪvnɪs/ n eficacia, f; efecto, m

effectuate /ɪ'fɛktʃu,eit/ vt efectuar

effeminacy /ɪ'fɛmənəsi/ n afeminación, f

effeminate /ɪ'fɛmənɪt/ a afeminado, adamado. **to make e.,** afeminar

efferent /'ɛfərənt/ a eferente

effervesce /,ɛfər'vɛs/ vi estar efervescente, hervir

effervescence /,ɛfər'vɛsəns/ n efervescencia, f

effervescent /,ɛfər'vɛsənt/ a efervescente

effete /ɪ'fit/ a gastado; estéril; decadente

effeteness /ɪ'fitnɪs/ n decadencia, f; esterilidad, f

efficacious /,ɛfɪ'keiʃəs/ a eficaz

efficacy /'ɛfɪkəsi/ n eficacia, f

efficiency /ɪ'fɪʃənsi/ n eficiencia, f; buen estado, m; habilidad, f; Mech. rendimiento, m

efficient /ɪ'fɪʃənt/ a (e.g. medicine) eficaz; eficiente; (person) competente, capaz

efficiently /ɪˈfɪʃəntli/ *adv* eficientemente; eficazmente; competentemente
effigy /ˈɛfɪdʒi/ *n* efigie, imagen, *f*
efflorescence /ˌɛfləˈrɛsəns/ *n Chem.* eflorescencia, *f; Bot.* florescencia, *f*
effluvium /ɪˈfluviəm/ *n* efluvio, *m*
effort /ˈɛfərt/ *n* esfuerzo, *m.* **to make an e.,** hacer un esfuerzo. **make every effort to,** hacer lo posible por + *Inf.*; empeñar sus máximos esfuerzos en el sentido de + *Inf.*
effortless /ˈɛfərtlɪs/ *a* sin esfuerzo
effrontery /ɪˈfrʌntəri/ *n* descaro, *m,* insolencia, *f*
effulgence /ɪˈfʌldʒəns/ *n* esplendor, fulgor, *m*
effulgent /ɪˈfʌldʒənt/ *a* fulgente, resplandeciente
effusion /ɪˈfyuʒən/ *n* efusión, *f*
effusive /ɪˈfyusɪv/ *a* efusivo, expansivo
egg /ɛg/ *n* huevo, *m.* **to egg on,** incitar (a). **boiled egg,** huevo cocido, *m.* **fried egg,** huevo frito, *m.* **hard egg,** huevo duro, *m.* **poached egg,** huevo escalfado, *m.* **scrambled egg,** huevos revueltos, *m pl.* **soft egg,** huevo pasado por agua, *m.* **to lay eggs,** poner huevos. **to put all one's eggs in one basket,** *Fig.* poner toda la carne en el asador. **egg-cup,** huevera, *f.* **egg dealer,** vendedor (-ra) de huevos. **egg flip,** huevo batido con ron, *m.* **eggplant,** berenjena, *f.* **egg-shaped,** aovado. **egg-shell,** cascarón, *m,* cáscara de huevo, *f.* **egg-shell china,** loza muy fina, *f.* **egg-spoon,** cucharita para comer huevos, *f.* **egg-whisk,** batidor de huevos, *m*
ego /ˈigou/ *n* yo
egoism /ˈigou,ɪzəm/ *n* egoísmo, *m*
egoist /ˈigouɪst/ *n* egoísta, *mf*
egoistic /ˌigouˈɪstɪk/ *a* egoísta
egoistically /ˌigouˈɪstɪkəli/ *adv* egoístamente
egotism /ˈigə,tɪzəm/ *n* egotismo, *m,* egolatría, *f*
egotist /ˈigətɪst/ *n* egotista, *mf*
egotistic /ˌigəˈtɪstɪk/ *a* egotista
egregious /ɪˈgridʒəs/ *a* notorio
egress /ˈigrɛs/ *n* salida, *f*
Egypt /ˈidʒɪpt/ *Egipto, m*
Egyptian /ɪˈdʒɪpʃən/ *a* egipcio. —*n* egipcio (-ia); cigarrillo egipcio; *m*
Egyptologist /ˌidʒɪpˈtɒlədʒɪst/ *n* egiptólogo (-ga)
Egyptology /ˌidʒɪpˈtɒlədʒi/ *n* egiptología, *f*
eh? /ei/ *interj* ¿eh? ¿qué?
eider /ˈaidər/ *n Ornith.* pato de flojel, *m*
eiderdown /ˈaidər,daun/ edredón, *m*
eight /eit/ *a* and *n* ocho *m.* **He is e. years old,** Tiene ocho años. **It is e. o'clock,** Son las ocho. **e.-day clock,** reloj con cuerda para ocho días, *m.* **e. hundred,** *a* and *n* ochocientos *m..* **e.-syllabled,** octosilábico
eighteen /ˈeiˈtin/ *a* and *n* diez y ocho, *m.*
eighteenth /ˈeiˈtinθ/ *a* décimoctavo; (of the month) (el) diez y ocho, dieciocho; (of monarchs) diez y ocho. —*n* décimoctava parte, *f.* **Louis the E.,** Luis diez y ocho
eightfold /ˈeit,fould/ *a* óctuple
eighth /eitθ/ *a* and *n* octavo, *m;* (of the month) (el) ocho; (of monarchs) octavo. —*n* octavo, *m*
eighthly /ˈeitθli/ *adv* en octavo lugar
eightieth /ˈeitiəθ/ *a* octogésimo
eighty /ˈeiti/ *a* and *n* ochenta, *m.*
either /ˈiðər/ *a* and *pron* uno u otro, cualquiera de los dos; ambos (-as). —*conjunc* o (becomes **u** before words beginning with **o** or **ho**). **I do not like e.,** No me gusta ni el uno ni el otro (ni la una ni la otra). **e.... or,** o.... o
ejaculate /ɪˈdʒækyə,leit/ *vt* exclamar, lanzar; *Med.* eyacular
ejaculation /ɪˌdʒækyəˈleiʃən/ *n* exclamación, *f; Med.* eyaculación, *f*
ejaculatory /ɪˈdʒækyələ,tɔri/ *a* jaculatorio
eject /ɪˈdʒɛkt/ *vt* echar, expulsar; *Law.* desahuciar; (emit) despedir, emitir
ejection /ɪˈdʒɛkʃən/ *n* echamiento, *m,* expulsión, *f; Law.* desahúcio, *m;* (emission) emisión, *f*
eke /ik/ (out) *vt* aumentar, añadir *m*
elaborate /*a* ɪˈlæbərɪt; *v* -ə,reit/ *a* elaborado; primoroso; elegante; complicado; (detailed) detallado;

(of meals) de muchos platos; (of courtesy, etc.) estudiado. —*vt* elaborar; amplificar
elaborately /ɪˈlæbərɪtli/ *adv* primorosamente; elegantemente; complicadamente; con muchos detalles
elaborateness /ɪˈlæbərɪtnɪs/ *n* primor, *m;* elegancia, *f;* complicación, *f;* (care) cuidado, *m;* minuciosidad, *f*
elaboration /ɪˌlæbəˈreiʃən/ *n* elaboración, *f*
elapse /ɪˈlæps/ *vi* transcurrir, andar, pasar
elastic /ɪˈlæstɪk/ *a* elástico. —*n* elástico, *m.* **e. band,** anillo de goma, *m;* cinta de goma, *f.* **e. girdle,** faja elástica, *f*
elasticity /ɪlæˈstɪsɪti/ *n* elasticidad, *f*
elate /ɪˈleit/ *vt* alegrar; animar
elatedly /ɪˈleitɪdli/ *adv* alegremente; triunfalmente
elation /ɪˈleiʃən/ *n* alegría, *f,* júbilo, *m;* triunfo, *m*
elbow /ˈɛlbou/ *n* codo, *m;* ángulo, *m;* (of a chair) brazo, *m.* —*vt* codear, dar codazos (a). **at one's e.,** a la mano. **nudge with the e.,** codazo, *m.* **to be out at e.,** enseñar los codos, tener los codos raídos; ser harapiento. **to e. one's way,** abrirse paso a codazos. **e.-chair,** silla de brazos, *f.* **e.-grease,** jugo de muñeca, *m.* **e.-piece** or **patch,** codera, *f.* **e. room,** libertad de movimiento, *f*
elder /ˈɛldər/ *a compar* mayor. —*n* persona mayor, *f;* señor mayor, *m;* (among Jews and in early Christian Church) anciano, *m; Bot.* saúco, *m*
elderly /ˈɛldərli/ *a* mayor
eldest /ˈɛldɪst/ *a superl* old (el, la, etc.) mayor. **e. daughter,** hija mayor, *f.* **e. son,** hijo mayor, *m*
elect /ɪˈlɛkt/ *vt* elegir. —*a* elegido; predestinado. —*n* electo, *m;* elegido, *m*
election /ɪˈlɛkʃən/ *n Theol.* predestinación, *f;* elección, *f.* **by-e.,** elección parcial, *f*
electioneer /ɪˌlɛkʃəˈnɪər/ *vi* solicitar votos; distribuir propaganda electoral
electioneering /ɪˌlɛkʃəˈnɪərɪŋ/ *n* solicitación de votos, *f;* propaganda electoral, *f*
elective /ɪˈlɛktɪv/ *a* electivo. —*n* (subject at school) materia optativa, *f*
elector /ɪˈlɛktər/ *n* elector (-ra); (prince) elector, *m*
electoral /ɪˈlɛktərəl/ *a* electoral. **e. register,** lista electoral, *f*
electoral college colegio de compromisarios, *m*
electorate /ɪˈlɛktərɪt/ *n* electorado, *m*
electric, electrical /ɪˈlɛktrɪk; ɪˈlɛktrɪkəl/ *a* eléctrico; *Fig.* vivo, instantáneo. **e. arc,** arco voltaico, *m.* **e. engineer,** ingeniero electricista, *m.* **electric fan,** (Spain) ventilador, (Western Hemisphere) ventilador eléctrico, *m.* **e. fire,** estufa eléctrica, *f.* **e. immersion heater,** calentador de agua eléctrico, *m.* **e. light,** luz eléctrica, *f.* **e. pad,** alfombrilla eléctrica, *f.* **e. shock,** conmoción eléctrica, *f.* **e. washing-machine,** lavadora eléctrica, *f.* **e. wire** or **cable,** conductor eléctrico, *m*
electrically /ɪˈlɛktrɪkəli/ *adv* por electricidad
electrician /ɪlɛkˈtrɪʃən/ *n* electricista, *mf*
electricity /ɪlɛkˈtrɪsɪti/ *n* electricidad, *f*
electrification /ɪˌlɛktrəfɪˈkeiʃən/ *n* electrificación, *f*
electrify /ɪˈlɛktrə,fai/ *vt* electrificar; *Fig.* electrizar
electro- *prefix* (in compounds) electro. **e.-chemistry,** electroquímica, *f.* **e.-dynamics,** electrodinámica, *f.* **e.-magnet,** electroimán, *m.* **e.-magnetic,** electromagnético. **e.-plate,** *vt* galvanizar, platear. —*n* artículo galvanizado, *m.* **e.-therapy,** electroterapia, *f*
electrocute /ɪˈlɛktrə,kyut/ *vt* electrocutar
electrocution /ɪˌlɛktrəˈkyuʃən/ *n* electrocución, *f*
electrode /ɪˈlɛktroud/ *n* electrodo, *m*
electrolysis /ɪlɛkˈtrɒləsɪs/ *n* electrólisis, *f*
electrolyte /ɪˈlɛktrə,lait/ *n* electrólito, *m*
electrolyze /ɪˈlɛktrə,laiz/ *vt* electrolizar
electrometer /ɪlɛkˈtrɒmɪtər/ *n* electrómetro, *m*
electromotive /ɪˌlɛktrəˈmoutɪv/ *a* electromotriz. **e. force,** fuerza electromotriz, *f*
electron /ɪˈlɛktrɒn/ *n* electrón, *m*
electroscope /ɪˈlɛktrə,skoup/ *n* electroscopio, *m*
elegance /ˈɛlɪgəns/ *n* elegancia, *f*
elegant /ˈɛlɪgənt/ *a* elegante; bello
elegantly /ˈɛlɪgəntli/ *adv* elegantemente, con elegancia
elegiac /ɛlɪˈdʒaiək/ *a* elegíaco
elegy /ˈɛlɪdʒi/ *n* elegía, *f*
element /ˈɛləmənt/ *n* elemento, *m;* factor, *m;* in-

grediente, *m; Elec.* par, elemento, *m; Chem. Phys.* cuerpo simple, *m; pl* **elements,** rudimentos, *m pl,* nociones, *f pl;* (weather) intemperie, *f;* (Eucharist) el pan y el vino. **to be in one's e.,** estar en su elemento

elemental /ˌɛləˈmɛntl/ *a* elemental; rudimentario, lo elemental

elementariness /ˌɛləˈmɛntərɪnɪs/ *n* el carácter, elemental

elementary /ˌɛləˈmɛntəri/ *a* elemental; rudimentario; primario. **e. education,** enseñanza primaria, *f*

elephant /ˈɛləfənt/ *n* elefante (-ta). **e. keeper** or **trainer,** naire, *m*

elephantiasis /ˌɛləfənˈtaiəsɪs/ *n* elefantíasis, *f*

elephantine /ˌɛləˈfæntin/ *a* elefantino

elevate /ˈɛləˌveit/ *vt* (the Host) alzar; elevar; (the eyes, the voice) levantar; (honor) enaltecer

elevated /ˈɛləˌveitɪd/ *a* noble, elevado, sublime; edificante; (drunk) achispado

elevation /ˌɛləˈveiʃən/ *n* elevación, *f;* enaltecimiento, *m;* (of style, thought) nobleza, sublimidad, *f;* (hill) eminencia, altura, *f*

elevator /ˈɛləˌveitər/ *n* (lift) ascensor, *m;* (for grain, etc.) montacargas, *m*

elevator shaft caja, *f,* hueco pozo, *m*

eleven /ɪˈlɛvən/ *a* once. —*n* once, *m.* **It is e. o'clock,** Son las once

eleventh /ɪˈlɛvənθ/ *a* onceno, undécimo; (of month) (el) once; (of monarchs) once. —*n* onzavo, *m;* undécima parte, *f.* **at the e. hour,** *Fig.* a última hora. **Louis the E.,** Luis once (XI)

elf /ɛlf/ *n* elfo, duende, *m;* (child) trasgo, *m;* (dwarf) enano, *m*

elfin /ˈɛlfɪn/ *a* de duendes; de hada

elicit /ɪˈlɪsɪt/ *vt* sacar; hacer contestar; hacer confesar; descubrir

elicitation /ɪˌlɪsɪˈteiʃən/ *n* descubrimiento, *m*

elide /ɪˈlaid/ *vt* elidir

eligibility /ˌɛlɪdʒəˈbɪlɪti/ *n* elegibilidad, *f*

eligible /ˈɛlɪdʒəbəl/ *a* elegible; deseable

eliminate /ɪˈlɪməˌneit/ *vt* eliminar; quitar

elimination /ɪˌlɪməˈneiʃən/ *n* eliminación, *f*

eliminatory /ɪˈlɪmənəˌtɔri/ *a* eliminador

elision /ɪˈlɪʒən/ *n* elisión, *f*

elite /ɪˈlit/ *n* nata, flor, *f*

elixir /ɪˈlɪksər/ *n* elixir, *m*

Elizabethan /ɪˌlɪzəˈbiθən/ *a* de la época de la Reina Isabel I de Inglaterra

elk /ɛlk/ *n* ante, *m*

ell /ɛl/ *n* (measure) ana, *f*

ellipse /ɪˈlɪps/ *n Geom.* elipse, *f;* óvalo, *m*

ellipsis /ɪˈlɪpsɪs/ *n Gram.* elipsis, *f*

elliptic /ɪˈlɪptɪk/ *a Geom. Gram.* elíptico

elm /ɛlm/ *n* olmo, *m.* **e. grove,** olmeda, *f*

elocution /ˌɛləˈkyuʃən/ *n* elocución, *f;* (art of elocution) declamación, *f*

elocutionist /ˌɛləˈkyuʃənɪst/ *n* recitador (-ra), declamador (-ra)

elongate /ɪˈlɔŋgeit/ *vt* alargar; extender. —*vi* alargarse; extenderse. —*a* alargado; (of face) perfilado

elongation /ɪlɔŋˈgeiʃən/ *n* alargamiento, *m;* prolongación, *f;* extensión, *f*

elope /ɪˈloup/ *vi* evadirse, huir; fugarse (con un amante)

elopement /ɪˈloupmənt/ *n* fuga, *f*

eloquence /ˈɛləkwəns/ *n* elocuencia, *f*

eloquent /ˈɛləkwənt/ *a* elocuente

eloquently /ˈɛləkwəntli/ *adv* elocuentemente

else /ɛls/ *adv* (besides) más; (instead) otra cosa, más; (otherwise) si no, de otro modo. **anyone e.,** (cualquier) otra persona; alguien más. **Anything e.?** ¿Algo más? **everyone e.,** todos los demás. **everything e.,** todo lo demás. **nobody e.,** ningún otro, nadie más. **nothing e.,** nada más. **or e.,** o bien, de otro modo; si no. **someone e.,** otra persona, otro. **somewhere e.,** en otra parte. **There's nothing e. to do,** No hay nada más que hacer; No hay más remedio

elsewhere /ˈɛlsˌwɛər/ *adv* a, or en, otra parte

elucidate /ɪˈlusɪˌdeit/ *vt* elucidar, aclarar

elucidation /ɪˌlusɪˈdeiʃən/ *n* elucidación, aclaración, *f*

elucidatory /ɪˈlusɪdəˌtɔri/ *a* aclaratorio

elude /ɪˈlud/ *vt* eludir, evitar

elusive /ɪˈlusɪv/ *a* (of persons) esquivo; fugaz; difícil de comprender

elusiveness /ɪˈlusɪvnɪs/ *n* esquivez, *f;* fugacidad, *f*

Elysian /ɪˈlɪʒən/ *a* elíseo. **E. Fields,** campos elíseos, *m pl*

Elysium /ɪˈlɪʒiəm/ *n* elíseo, *m*

emaciate /ɪˈmeiʃiˌeit/ *vt* extenuar, demacrar, enflaquecer

emaciated /ɪˈmeiʃiˌeitɪd/ *a* extenuado, demacrado. **to become e.,** demacrarse

emaciation /ɪˌmeiʃiˈeiʃən/ *n* demacración, emaciación, *f; Med.* depauperación, *f*

e-mail /ˈiˌmeil/ *n* correo electrónico, *m*

emanate /ˈɛməˌneit/ *vi* emanar (de), proceder (de)

emanation /ˌɛməˈneiʃən/ *n* emanación, *f;* exhalación, *f*

emancipate /ɪˈmænsəˌpeit/ *vt* emancipar

emancipated /ɪˈmænsəˌpeitɪd/ *a* emancipado

emancipation /ɪˌmænsəˈpeiʃən/ *n* emancipación, *f*

emancipator /ɪˈmænsəˌpeitər/ *n* emancipador (-ra), libertador (-ra)

emancipatory /ɪˈmænsəpəˌtɔri/ *a* emancipador

emasculate /*a* ɪˈmæskyəlɪt; *v* -ˌleit/ *a* afeminado. —*vt* emascular; *Fig.* afeminar; mutilar

emasculation /ɪˌmæskyəˈleiʃən/ *n* emasculación, *f*

embalm /ɛmˈbam/ *vt* embalsamar; *Fig.* conservar el recuerdo de; perfumar

embalmer /ɛmˈbamər/ *n* embalsamador, *m*

embalmment /ɛmˈbammənt/ *n* embalsamamiento, *m*

embankment /ɛmˈbæŋkmənt/ *n* declive, *m;* ribera, *f;* terraplén, *m;* dique, *m;* (quay) muelle, *m*

embargo /ɛmˈbargou/ *n* embargo, *m,* *vt* embargar. **to put an e. on,** embargar. **to remove an e.,** sacar de embargo

embark /ɛmˈbark/ *vi* embarcarse; lanzarse (a). —*vt* embarcar

embarkation /ˌɛmbarˈkeiʃən/ *n* (of persons) embarcación, *f;* (of goods) embarque, *m*

embarrass /ɛmˈbærəs/ *vt* impedir; (financially) apurar; (perplex) tener perplejo; (worry) preocupar; (confuse) desconcertar, turbar; (annoy) molestar

embarrassed /ɛmˈbærəst/ *a* turbado

embarrassing /ɛmˈbærəsɪŋ/ *a* embarazoso; desconcertante; molesto

embarrassingly /ɛmˈbærəsɪŋli/ *adv* de un modo desconcertante; demasiado

embarrassment /ɛmˈbærəsmənt/ *n* impedimento, *m;* (financial) apuro, *m;* (obligation) compromiso, *m;* (perplexity) perplejidad, *f;* (worry) preocupación, *f;* (confusion) turbación, *f*

embassy /ˈɛmbəsi/ *n* embajada, *f*

embattled /ɛmˈbætld/ *a* en orden de batalla; *Herald.* almenado

embed /ɛmˈbɛd/ *vt* empotrar, enclavar; fijar

embellish /ɛmˈbɛlɪʃ/ *vt* embellecer; adornar

embellishment /ɛmˈbɛlɪʃmənt/ *n* embellecimiento, *m;* adorno, *m*

ember /ˈɛmbər/ *n* rescoldo, *m.* **E. days,** témporas, *f pl*

embezzle /ɛmˈbɛzəl/ *vt* desfalcar

embezzlement /ɛmˈbɛzəlmənt/ *n* desfalco, *m*

embezzler /ɛmˈbɛzlər/ *n* desfalcador (-ra)

embitter /ɛmˈbɪtər/ *vt Fig.* amargar; envenenar

embittering /ɛmˈbɪtərɪŋ/ *a* amargo

embitterment /ɛmˈbɪtərmənt/ *n* amargura, *f*

emblazon /ɛmˈbleizən/ *vt* blasonar; *Fig.* ensalzar

emblem /ˈɛmbləm/ *n* emblema, *f*

emblematic /ˌɛmbləˈmætɪk/ *a* emblemático

embodiment /ɛmˈbɒdimənt/ *n* incarnación, *f;* expresión, *f;* personificación, *f;* símbolo, *m;* síntesis, *f*

embody /ɛmˈbɒdi/ *vt* encarnar; expresar; personificar; incorporar; contener; formular; sintetizar. **to be embodied in,** quedar plasmado en

embolden /ɛmˈbouldən/ *vt* animar, dar valor (a)

embolism /ˈɛmbəˌlɪzəm/ *n Med.* embolia, *f*

emboss /ɛmˈbɔs/ *vt* repujar, abollonar; estampar en relieve

embossment /ɛmˈbɔsmənt/ *n* abolladura, *f;* relieve, *m*

embrace /ɛmˈbreis/ *n* abrazo, *m.* —*vt* abrazar, dar un abrazo (a); (*Fig.*. seize) aprovechar; (accept) aceptar; adoptar; (engage in) dedicarse a; (comprise) incluir, abarcar; (comprehend) comprender. **They embraced,** Se abrazaron

embroider /ɛm'brɔɪdər/ *vt* bordar; embellecer; (a tale, etc.) exagerar; *vi* hacer bordado

embroiderer /ɛm'brɔɪdərər/ *n* bordador (-ra)

embroidery /ɛm'brɔɪdəri, -dri/ *n* bordado, *m;* labor, *f.* **e.-frame,** bastidor, *m.* **e. silk,** hilo de bordar, *m*

embroil /ɛm'brɔɪl/ *vt* enredar, embrollar; desordenar

embryo /'ɛmbri,ou/ *n* embrión, *m; Fig.* germen, *m.* —*a* embrionario

embryology /,ɛmbri'ɒlədʒi/ *n* embriología, *f*

embryonic /,ɛmbri'ɒnɪk/ *a* embrionario

emend /ɪ'mɛnd/ *vt* enmendar; corregir

emendation /,imən'deɪʃən/ *n* enmienda, *f;* corrección, *f*

emerald /'ɛmərəld/ *n* esmeralda, *f, a* de color de esmeralda. **e. green,** verde esmeralda, *m*

emerge /ɪ'mɜrdʒ/ *vt* emerger; surgir; *Fig.* salir; aparecer

emergence /ɪ'mɜrdʒəns/ *n* emergencia, *f;* salida, *f;* aparición, *f*

emergency /ɪ'mɜrdʒənsi/ *n* urgencia, *f;* necesidad, *f;* emergencia, *f;* aprieto, *m.* **e. exit,** salida de urgencia, *f.* **e. port,** *Naut.* puerto de arribada, *m*

emergent /ɪ'mɜrdʒənt/ *a* emergente; que sale; naciente

emery /'ɛməri/ *n* esmeril, *m.* **to polish with e.,** esmerilar. **e.-paper,** papel de lija, *m*

emetic /ɪ'mɛtɪk/ *a* and *n* emético, vomitivo, *m*.

emigrant /'ɛmɪɡrənt/ *a* emigrante. —*n* emigrante, *mf* emigrado, *m*

emigrate /'ɛmɪ,ɡreɪt/ *vi* emigrar; *Inf.* trasladarse

emigration /,ɛmə'ɡreɪʃən/ *n* emigración, *f.* **e. officer,** oficial de emigración, *m*

eminence /'ɛmənəns/ *n* (hill) elevación, prominencia, *f;* eminencia (also as title), *f;* distinción, *f*

eminent /'ɛmənənt/ *a* distinguido, eminente; famoso, ilustre; notable; conspicuo

eminently /'ɛmənəntli/ *adv* eminentemente

emir /ə'mɪər/ *n* amir, *m*

emissary /'ɛmə,sɛri/ *n* emisario (-ia); embajador (-ra); agente, *m*

emission /ɪ'mɪʃən/ *n* emisión, *f*

emit /ɪ'mɪt/ *vt* despedir; exhalar; emitir

emollient /ɪ'mɒlyənt/ *a* emoliente, lenitivo. —*n* emoliente, *m*

emolument /ɪ'mɒlyəmənt/ *n* emolumento, *m*

emotion /ɪ'mouʃən/ *n* emoción, *f.* **to cause e.,** emocionar

emotional /ɪ'mouʃənl/ *a* emocional, sentimental; emocionante

emotionalism /ɪ'mouʃənl̩,ɪzəm/ *n* sentimentalismo, *m*

emotionalize /ɪ'mouʃənl̩,aɪz/ *vt* considerar bajo un punto de vista sentimental

emotionally /ɪ'mouʃənl̩i/ *adv* con emoción, sentimentalmente

emotionless /ɪ'mouʃənlɪs/ *a* sin emoción

emotive /ɪ'moutɪv/ *a* emotivo

emperor /'ɛmpərər/ *n* emperador, *m*

emphasis (on) /'ɛmfəsɪs/ *n* énfasis (en), *mf;* insistencia especial (en), especial atención (a), *f;* accentuación, *f*

emphasize /'ɛmfə,saɪz/ *vt* subrayar, dar énfasis a, poner de relieve, hacer resaltar, dar importancia a; acentuar; insistir en, hacer hincapié (en)

emphatic /ɛm'fætɪk/ *a* enfático

emphatically /ɛm'fætɪkəli/ *adv* con énfasis

empire /'ɛmpaɪər/ *n* imperio, *m*

empiric /ɛm'pɪrɪk/ *a* empírico

empiricism /ɛm'pɪrə,sɪzəm/ *n* empirismo, *m*

employ /ɛm'plɔɪ/ *n* empleo, *m;* servicio, *m.* —*vt* emplear; ocupar; tomar; servirse de, usar. **How do you e. yourself?** ¿Cómo te ocupas? ¿Cómo pasas el tiempo?

employable /ɛm'plɔɪəbəl/ *a* empleable; utilizable

employee /ɛm'plɔii/ *n* empleado (-da)

employer /ɛm'plɔɪər/ *n* el, *m,* (*f,* la) que emplea; dueño (-ña), amo (-a); patrón (-ona)

employment /ɛm'plɔɪmənt/ *n* empleo, *m;* uso, *m;* ocupación, *f;* aprovechamiento, *m;* (post) puesto, cargo, *m;* (situation) colocación, *f.* **e. exchange,** bolsa de trabajo, *f*

emporium /ɛm'pɔriəm/ *n* emporio, *m;* (store) almacén, *m*

empower /ɛm'pauər/ *vt* autorizar; permitir; ayudar (a); dar el poder (para)

empress /'ɛmprɪs/ *n* emperatriz, *f*

emptiness /'ɛmptinɪs/ *n* vaciedad, *f;* futilidad, *f;* vacuidad, *f;* (verbosity) palabrería, *f*

empty /'ɛmpti/ *a* vacío; (of a house, etc.) deshabitado, desocupado; (deserted) desierto; (vain) vano, inútil; frívolo; (hungry) hambriento. —*n* envase vacío, *m.* —*vt* vaciar; descargar. —*vi* vaciarse; (river, etc.) desembocar, venir a morir en. **e.-handed,** con las manos vacías. **e.-headed,** casquivano

emptying /'ɛmptiɪŋ/ *n* vaciamiento, *m;* abandono, *m; pl* **emptyings,** heces de la cerveza, *f pl*

emu /'imyu/ *n* emu, *m*

emulate /'ɛmyə,leɪt/ *vt* emular

emulation /,ɛmyə'leɪʃən/ *n* emulación, *f*

emulative /'ɛmyə,leɪtɪv/ *a* emulador

emulsify /ɪ'mʌlsɪfaɪ/ *vt* emulsionar

emulsion /ɪ'mʌlʃən/ *n* emulsión, *f*

emulsive /ɪ'mʌlsɪv/ *a* emulsivo

enable /ɛn'eibəl/ *vt* (to) hacer capaz (de); ayudar (a); autorizar (para); permitir (de)

enact /ɛn'ækt/ *vt Law.* promulgar; decretar; (a part) hacer, desempeñar (un papel); (a play) representar; (happen) ocurrir, tener lugar

enaction /ɛn'ækʃən/ *n Law.* promulgación, *f*

enamel /ɪ'næməl/ *n* esmalte, *m, vt* esmaltar

enameler /ɪ'næmələr/ *n* esmaltador (-ra)

enameling /ɪ'næməlɪŋ/ *n* esmaltadura, *f*

enamor /ɛ'næmər/ *vt* enamorar. **to be enamored of,** estar enamorado de; estar aficionado a

encamp /ɛn'kæmp/ *vt* and *vi* acampar

encampment /ɛn'kæmpmənt/ *n* campamento, *m*

encase /ɛn'keis/ *vt* encajar; encerrar; (line) forrar

encasement /ɛn'keismənt/ *n* encaje, *m;* encierro, *m*

encephalitis /ɛn,sɛfə'laitɪs/ *n* encefalitis, *f.* **e. lethargica,** encefalitis letárgica, *f*

enchant /ɛn'tʃænt/ *vt* encantar, hechizar; fascinar, embelesar, deleitar

enchanter /ɛn'tʃæntər/ *n* encantador, *m*

enchanting /ɛn'tʃæntɪŋ/ *a* encantador, fascinador

enchantment /ɛn'tʃæntmənt/ *n* encantamiento, *m;* fascinación, *f,* encanto, deleite, *m*

enchantress /ɛn'tʃæntrɪs/ *n* bruja, *f; Fig.* mujer seductora, *f*

encircle /ɛn'sɜrkəl/ *vt* cercar; rodear; dar la vuelta (a)

enclose /ɛn'klouz/ *vt* cercar; meter dentro de; encerrar; (with a letter, etc.) incluir, adjuntar

enclosed /ɛn'klouzd/ *a* (of letters) adjunto

enclosure /ɛn'klouʒər/ *n* cercamiento, *m;* cercado, *m;* recinto, *m;* (wall) tapia, cerca, *f;* (with a letter) contenido adjunto, *m*

encomium /ɛn'koumiəm/ *n* encomio, *m*

encompass /ɛn'kʌmpəs/ *vt* cercar, rodear

encore /'aŋkɔr/ *n* repetición, *f, interj* ¡bis!

encounter /ɛn'kauntər/ *n* encuentro, *m;* combate, *m;* conflicto, *m;* lucha, *f.* —*vt* encontrar; atacar; tropezar con

encourage /ɛn'kɜrɪdʒ/ *vt* animar; alentar; estimular; incitar; ayudar; (approve) aprobar; (foster) fomentar

encouragement /ɛn'kɜrɪdʒmənt/ *n* ánimos, *m pl;* estímulo, incentivo, *m;* ayuda, *f;* (approval) aprobación, *f;* (promotion) fomento, *m*

encourager /ɛn'kɜrɪdʒər/ *n* instigador (-ra); ayudador (-ra); aprobador (-ra); fomentador (-ra)

encouraging /ɛn'kɜrɪdʒɪŋ/ *a* alentador; estimulante; fomentador; (favorable) halagüeño, favorable

encouragingly /ɛn'kɜrɪdʒɪŋli/ *adv* de un modo alentador; con aprobación

encroach /ɛn'kroutʃ/ *vi* usurpar; abusar (de); invadir; robar; (of sea, river) hurtar

encroaching /ɛn'kroutʃɪŋ/ *a* usurpador; invadiente

encroachment /ɛn'kroutʃmənt/ *n* usurpación, *f;* abuso, *m;* invasión, *f*

encrust /ɛn'krʌst/ *vt* encostrar; incrustar

encumber /ɛn'kʌmbər/ vt impedir, estorbar; llenar; (burden) cargar; (mortgage) hipotecar; (overwhelm) agobiar

encumbrance /ɛn'kʌmbrəns/ n impedimento, estorbo, m; gravamen, m; carga, f; (mortgage) hipoteca, f

encyclical /ɛn'sɪklɪkəl/ n encíclica, f

encyclopedia /ɛn,saiklə'pidiə/ n enciclopedia, f

encyclopedic /ɛn,saiklə'pidik/ a enciclopédico

encyclopedist /ɛn,saiklə'pidist/ n enciclopedista, m

end /ɛnd/ n fin, m; extremidad, f; extremo, m; conclusión, f; (point) punta, f; cabo, m; (district) barrio, m; cabeza, f; (death) muerte, f; (aim) objeto, intento, m; (purpose) propósito, m; (issue) resultado, m; (bit) fragmento, pedazo, m; (of a word) terminación, f. —vi terminar; acabar; concluir; cesar; (in) terminar en; resultar en; (with) terminar con. —vt terminar; acabar, dar fin a. **at an end,** terminado. **at the end,** al cabo (de); al extremo (de). **end of quotation,** fin de cita, final de la cita, m. **from end to end,** de un extremo a otro; de un cabo a otro. **in the end,** por fin, finalmente. **on end,** de pie, de cabeza, derecho; de punta; (of hair) erizado. **no end of,** un sinnúmero de. **to make both ends meet,** pasar con lo que se tiene. **to make an end of,** acabar con. **to put an end to,** poner fin a. **to the end that,** a fin de que, para que; con objeto de. **toward the end of,** (months, years, etc.) a fines de, a últimos de; hacia el fin de. **two hours on end,** dos horas seguidas. **end-paper,** guarda, f

endanger /ɛn'deindʒər/ vt arriesgar, poner en peligro

endear /ɛn'dɪr/ vt hacer querer

endearing /ɛn'dɪrɪŋ/ a que inspira cariño; atrayente; cariñoso

endearment /ɛn'dɪrmənt/ n cariño, amor, m; caricia, terneza, f; palabra de cariño, f

endeavor /ɛn'dɛvər/ vi procurar, intentar, hacer un esfuerzo. —n esfuerzo, m, tentativa, f

endemic /ɛn'dɛmɪk/ a Med. endémico

ending /'ɛndɪŋ/ n fin, m; conclusión, f; Gram. terminación, f; cesación, f; (climax) desenlace, m

endive /'ɛndaiv/ n Bot. escarola, f

endless /'ɛndlɪs/ a eterno; inacabable; infinito; sin fin; interminable; incesante

endlessly /'ɛndlisli/ adv sin fin; incesantemente; sin parar

endlessness /'ɛndlisnɪs/ n eternidad, f; infinidad, f; continuidad, f

endocrine /'ɛndəkrɪn/ a endocrino. —n secreción interna, f

endocrinology /,ɛndoukrə'nɒlədʒi/ n endocrinología, f

end-of-season /'ɛnd əv 'sizən/ a por final de temporada (e.g., end-of-season reductions, rebajos por final de temporada, m pl. end-of-season sale, liquidación por final de temporada, f)

endogenous /ɛn'dɒdʒənəs/ a endógeno

endorse /ɛn'dɔrs/ vt Com. endosar; garantizar; (uphold) apoyar; confirmar

endorsee /ɛndɔr'si/ n endosatario (-ia)

endorsement /ɛn'dɔrsmənt/ n Com. endoso, m; aval, m, garantía, f; corroboración, confirmación, f

endorser /ɛn'dɔrsər/ n Com. endosante, m

endow /ɛn'dau/ vt dotar; fundar; crear

endowment /ɛn'daumənt/ n dotación, f; fundación, f; creación, f; (mental) inteligencia, f; cualidad, f; don, m. **e. policy,** póliza dotal, f

endurable /ɛn'dʊrəbəl/ a sufrible, soportable; tolerable

endurance /ɛn'dʊrəns/ n aguante, m; resistencia, f; sufrimiento, m; tolerancia, f; paciencia, f; (lastingness) duración, continuación, f. **beyond e.,** intolerable, inaguantable. **e. test,** prueba de resistencia, f

endure /ɛn'dʊr/ vt soportar; tolerar, aguantar; sufrir; resistir. —vi sufrir; (last) durar, continuar

enduring /ɛn'dʊrɪŋ/ a permanente, perdurable; continuo; constante

enduringness /ɛn'dʊrɪŋnɪs/ n (lastingness) permanencia, f; paciencia, f; aguante, m

enema /'ɛnəmə/ n lavativa, enema, f

enemy /'ɛnəmi/ n enemigo (-ga); adversario (-ia); (in war) enemigo, m. —a del enemigo, enemigo. **to be**

one's own e., ser enemigo de sí mismo. **to become an e. of,** enemistarse con; hacerse enemigo de, volverse hostil a

energetic /,ɛnər'dʒɛtɪk/ a enérgico

energy /'ɛnərdʒi/ n energía, fuerza, f, vigor, m

enervate / v 'ɛnər,veit/ a 'ɪnɜrvɪt/ vt enervar; debilitar. —a enervado

enervation /,ɛnər'veiʃən/ n enervación, f; debilitación, f

enfeeble /ɛn'fibəl/ vt debilitar

enfeeblement /ɛn'fibəlmənt/ n debilitación, f, desfallecimiento, m

enfold /ɛn'fould/ vt envolver; abrazar

enforce /ɛn'fɔrs/ vt (a law) poner en vigor; (impose) imponer a la fuerza; hacer cumplir; conseguir por fuerza; (demonstrate) demostrar

enforcement /ɛn'fɔrsmənt/ n (of a law) ejecución (de una ley), f; imposición a la fuerza, f; observación forzosa, f

enfranchise /ɛn'fræntʃaiz/ vt emancipar; conceder derechos civiles (a)

enfranchisement /ɛn'fræntʃaizmənt/ n emancipación, f; concesión de derechos civiles, f

engage /ɛn'geidʒ/ vt empeñar; contratar; tomar en alquiler; tomar a su servicio; (seats, etc.) reservar; (occupy) ocupar; (attention) atraer; (in) aplicarse a, dedicarse a; Mil. combatir con, librar batalla con; atacar; (of wheels) endentar con. —vi obligarse; dedicarse (a); tomar parte (en); (bet) apostar; Mil. librar batalla; (fight) venir a las manos. **to be engaged in,** traer entre manos, ocuparse en. **to become engaged,** prometerse. **Number engaged!** (telephone) ¡Están comunicando!

engaged /ɛn'geidʒd/ a ocupado; (betrothed) prometido; reservado

engagement /ɛn'geidʒmənt/ n obligación, f; compromiso, m; (date) cita, f; (betrothal) palabra de casamiento, f; (battle) combate, m, batalla, f. **I have an e. at two o'clock.** Tengo una cita a las dos

engagement gift regalo de esponsales, m

engaging /ɛn'geidʒɪŋ/ a simpático, atractivo

engagingly /ɛn'geidʒɪŋli/ adv de un modo encantador

engender /ɛn'dʒɛndər/ vt Fig. engendrar; excitar

engine /'ɛndʒən/ n máquina, f; motor, m; (locomotive) locomotora, f; (pump) bomba, f. **to sit with one's back to the e.,** estar sentado de espaldas a la máquina (or locomotora). **e. builder,** constructor de máquinas, m. **e. driver,** maquinista, mf. **e. room,** cuarto de máquinas, m. **e. works,** taller de maquinaria, m

engineer /,ɛndʒə'nɪr/ n ingeniero, m; mecánico, m. —vt Fig. gestionar, arreglar. **civil e.,** ingeniero de caminos, canales y puertos, m. **Royal Engineers,** Cuerpo de Ingenieros, m

engineering /,ɛndʒə'nɪrɪŋ/ n ingeniería, f; Fig. manejo, m. —a de ingeniería

England /'ɪŋglənd/ Inglaterra, f

English /'ɪŋglɪʃ/ a inglés. —n (language) inglés, m. **in E. fashion,** a la inglesa. **to speak E.,** hablar inglés. **to speak plain E.,** hablar sin rodeos; hablar en cristiano. **E. Church,** iglesia anglicana, f. **E.-teacher,** maestro (-ra) de inglés. **English-translator,** traductor al inglés, m

English Channel, the el Canal de la Mancha

Englishman /'ɪŋglɪʃmən/ n inglés, m

Englishwoman /'ɪŋglɪʃ,wumən/ n inglesa, f

engrain /ɛn'grein/ vt inculcar

engrave /ɛn'greiv/ vt grabar; esculpir, cincelar; Fig. grabar

engraver /ɛn'greivər/ n grabador (-ra); (tool) cincel, m

engraving /ɛn'greivɪŋ/ n grabadura, f; (picture) grabado, m. **e. needle,** punta seca, f

engross /ɛn'grous/ vt (a document) poner en limpio; redactar; (absorb) absorber

engrossing /ɛn'grousɪŋ/ a absorbente

engulf /ɛn'gʌlf/ vt hundir, sumir, sumergir

enhance /ɛn'hæns/ vt realzar; intensificar; aumentar; mejorar

enhancement /ɛn'hænsmənt/ n realce, m; intensificación, f; aumento, m; mejoría, f

enigma /ə'nıgmə/ n enigma, m
enigmatic /ˌenıg'mætık/ a enigmático
enjoin /en'dʒɔin/ vt imponer; ordenar, mandar; encargar
enjoy /en'dʒɔi/ vt disfrutar; gustar de; gozar de; poseer, tener. **to e. oneself,** recrearse, regocijarse; (amuse oneself) divertirse; entretenerse; pasarlo bien. **Did you e. yourself?** ¿Lo pasaste bien?
enjoyable /en'dʒɔiəbəl/ a agradable; divertido, entretenido
enjoyableness /en'dʒɔiəbəlnıs/ n lo agradable; lo divertido
enjoyably /en'dʒɔiəbli/ adv de un modo muy agradable
enjoyer /en'dʒɔiər/ n el, m, (f, la) que disfruta; poseedor (-ra); (amateur) aficionado (-da)
enjoyment /en'dʒɔimənt/ n posesión, f; goce, disfruto, m; (pleasure) placer, m; aprovechamiento, m; utilización, f; (satisfaction) satisfacción, f
enlarge /en'lɑrdʒ/ vt agrandar; aumentar; ensanchar; extender; Photo. ampliar; dilatar; (the mind, etc.) ensanchar. —vi agrandarse; ensancharse; aumentarse; extenderse. **an enlarged heart,** dilatación del corazón, f. **to e. upon,** tratar detalladamente, explayarse en
enlargement /en'lɑrdʒmənt/ n engrandecimiento, m; ensanchamiento, m; Photo. ampliación, f; Med. dilatación, f; aumento, m; amplificación, f; (of a town, etc.) ensanche, m
enlarger /en'lɑrdʒər/ n Photo. ampliadora, f
enlighten /en'laitn̩/ vt iluminar; aclarar; informar
enlightened /en'laitn̩d/ a culto; ilustrado; inteligente
enlightening /en'laitn̩ıŋ/ a instructivo
enlightenment /en'laitn̩mənt/ n ilustración, f; cultura, civilización, f
enlist /en'lıst/ vt Mil. reclutar; alistar; obtener, conseguir. —vi Mil. sentar plaza, sentar plaza de soldado; engancharse; alistarse
enlistment /en'lıstmənt/ n Mil. enganche, m; reclutamiento, m; alistamiento, m
enliven /en'laivən/ vt animar; avivar; alegrar
enmity /'enmıti/ n enemistad, enemiga, hostilidad, f
ennoble /en'noubəl/ vt ennoblecer; ilustrar
ennui /ɑn'wi/ n tedio, m; aburrimiento, m
enormity /ı'nɔrmıti/ n enormidad, f; gravedad, f; atrocidad, f
enormous /ı'nɔrməs/ a enorme, colosal
enormously /ı'nɔrməsli/ adv enormemente
enormousness /ı'nɔrməsnıs/ n enormidad, f
enough /ı'nʌf/ a bastante, suficiente. —n lo bastante, lo suficiente. —adv bastante; suficientemente. —interj ¡bastante! ¡basta! **to be e.,** ser suficiente; bastar. **two are enough,** con dos tenemos bastante, con dos tengo bastante
enquire /en'kwaiᵊr/. See **inquire**
enrage /en'reidʒ/ vt enfurecer; hacer furioso; Inf. hacer rabiar
enraged /en'reidʒd/ a furioso
enrapture /en'ræptʃər/ vt entusiasmar, extasiar; (intoxicate) embriagar; (charm) encantar, deleitar
enrich /en'rıtʃ/ vt enriquecer; (adorn) adornar, embellecer; (the land) fertilizar
enrichment /en'rıtʃmənt/ n enriquecimiento, m; embellecimiento, m; (of the land) abono, m
enroll /en'roul/ vt alistar; matricular; inscribir; (perpetuate) inmortalizar
enrollment /en'roulmənt/ n alistamiento, m; inscripción, f
ensconce /en'skɒns/ vt acomodar, colocar; ocultar
ensemble /ɑn'sɑmbəl/ n conjunto, m
enshrine /en'ʃrain/ vt poner en sagrario; guardar con cuidado; Fig. guardar como una reliquia
enshroud /en'ʃraud/ vt amortajar; envolver; esconder
ensign /'ensən/ n (badge) insignia, f; (flag) enseña, bandera, f; pabellón, m; bandera de popa, f; Mil. alférez, m; (U.S.A. navy) subteniente, m
enslave /en'sleiv/ vt esclavizar; Fig. dominar
enslavement /en'sleivmənt/ n esclavitud, f
ensue /en'su/ vt conseguir. —vi resultar; suceder, sobrevenir

ensuing /en'suıŋ/ a (next) próximo; (resulting) resultante
ensure /en'ʃʊr/ vt asegurar; estar seguro de que; garantizar
entail /en'teil/ vt traer consigo, acarrear; Law. vincular; n Law. vinculación, f; herencia, f
entangle /en'tæŋgəl/ vt enredar; coger; Fig. embrollar
entanglement /en'tæŋgəlmənt/ n enredo, m; complicación, f; intriga, f; (Mil. of wire) alambrada, f
entangling /en'tæŋglıŋ/ a enmarañador (e.g., entangling alliances, alianzas enmarañadoras, f pl)
enter /'entər/ vt entrar en; penetrar; (of thoughts) ocurrirse; (join) ingresar en; entrar en; (become a member of) hacerse miembro de; (enroll) alistarse; (a university) matricularse; (inscribe) inscribir, poner en la lista; (note) anotar, apuntar; (a protest) hacer constar; (make) hacer; formular. —vi entrar; Theat. salir (a la escena); entrar; Com. anotarse. **to e. for,** vt inscribir. —vi inscribirse, tomar parte en. **to e. into,** entrar en; formar parte de; (conversation) entablar (conversación); (negotiations) iniciar; considerar; (another's emotion) acompañar en; (an agreement, etc.) hacer; (sign) firmar; (bind oneself) obligarse a, comprometerse a; tomar parte en; (undertake) emprender; empezar; adoptar. **to e. up,** anotar; poner en la lista; registrar. **to e. upon,** comenzar, emprender; tomar posesión de; encargarse de, asumir; inaugurar, dar principio a
enteric /en'terık/ a entérico
enteritis /ˌentə'raitıs/ n enteritis, f
enterprise /'entər,praiz/ n empresa, f; aventura, f; (spirit) iniciativa, f, empuje, m
enterprising /'entər,praizıŋ/ a emprendedor, acometedor; de mucha iniciativa
entertain /ˌentər'tein/ vt (an idea, etc.) acariciar, abrigar; considerar; (as a guest) agasajar, obsequiar; recibir en casa; (amuse) divertir, entretener. —vi ser hospitalario; tener invitados en casa; dar fiestas
entertaining /ˌentər'teinıŋ/ a entretenido, divertido
entertainingly /ˌentər'teinıŋli/ adv entretenidamente; (witty) graciosamente
entertainment /ˌentər'teinmənt/ n convite, m; fiesta, f; reunión, f; banquete, m; (hospitality) hospitalidad, f; (amusement) diversión, f, entretenimiento, m; espectáculo, m; función, f; concierto, m
enthrall /en'θrɔl/ vt seducir, atraer, encantar; absorber, captar la atención
enthralling /en'θrɔlıŋ/ a absorbente; atrayente, halagüeño
enthrallment /en'θrɔlmənt/ n absorción, f; atracción, f
enthrone /en'θroun/ vt entronizar
enthronement /en'θrounmənt/ n entronización, f
enthusiasm /en'θuzi,æzəm/ n entusiasmo, m
enthusiast /en'θuzi,æst, -ıst/ n entusiasta, mf
enthusiastic /en,θuzi'æstık/ a entusiasta. **to make e.,** entusiasmar. **to be e.,** entusiasmarse
enthusiastically /en,θuzi'æstıkəli/ adv con entusiasmo
entice /en'tais/ vt tentar, inducir; atraer, seducir
enticement /en'taismənt/ n tentación, f; atractivo, m
enticing /en'taisıŋ/ a seducente, atrayente; halagüeño
entire /en'taiᵊr/ a entero; completo; intacto; absoluto; perfecto; íntegro; total
entirely /en'taiᵊrli/ adv enteramente; completamente; integralmente; totalmente
entirety /en'taiᵊrti/ n totalidad, f; integridad, f; todo, m
entitle /en'taitl̩/ vt (designate) intitular; dar derecho (a); autorizar. **to be entitled to,** tener derecho a
entity /'entıti/ n entidad, f; ente, ser, m
entombment /en'tummənt/ n sepultura, f, entierro, m
entomological /ˌentəmə'lɒdʒıkəl/ a entomológico
entomologist /ˌentə'mɒlədʒıst/ n entomólogo, m
entomology /ˌentə'mɒlədʒi/ n entomología, f
entourage /ˌɑntu'rɑʒ/ n séquito, m; (environment) medio ambiente, m
entr'acte /ɑn'trækt/ n entreacto, m

entrails

406

entrails /'ɛntreilz/ n entrañas, tripas, f pl, intestinos, m pl

entrain /ɛn'trein/ vi tomar el tren, subir al tren

entrance /ɛn'trɑns/ n entrada, f; *Theat.* salida (a la escena), f; (into a profession, etc.) ingreso, m; alistamiento, m; (beginning) principio, m; (door) puerta, f; (porch) portal, m; (of a cave) boca, f. **e. fee,** cuota de entrada, f. **e. hall,** zaguán, m. **e. money,** entrada, f

entrance /ɛn'træns/ vt *Fig.* encantar, fascinar; ecstasiar

entrancing /ɛn'trænsɪŋ/ a encantador

entreat /ɛn'trit/ vt suplicar, implorar, rogar

entreating /ɛn'tritɪŋ/ a suplicante, implorante

entreatingly /ɛn'tritɪŋli/ adv de un modo suplicante; insistentemente

entreaty /ɛn'triti/ n súplica, instancia, f, ruego, m

entree /'ɑntrei/ n entrada, f

entrench /ɛn'trɛntʃ/ vt atrincherar

entrenchment /ɛn'trɛntʃmənt/ n atrincheramiento, m; *Mil.* parapeto, m; (encroachment) invasión, f

entresol /'ɛntər,sɒl/ n entresuelo, m

entrust /ɛn'trʌst/ vt confiar a (or en), encomendar a; encargar

entry /'ɛntri/ n entrada, f; (passage) callejuela, f; (note) inscripción, apuntación, f; *Com.* partida, f; (registration) registro, m. **double e.,** *Com.* partida doble, f. **single e.,** *Com.* partida simple, f

entwine /ɛn'twain/ vt entrelazar, entretejer

enumerate /ɪ'numə,reit/ vt enumerar

enumeration /ɪ,numə'reiʃən/ n enumeración, f

enumerative /ɪ'numə,reitɪv/ a enumerativo

enunciate /ɪ'nʌnsi,eit/ vt enunciar; articular

enunciation /ɪ,nʌnsi'eiʃən/ n enunciación, f; articulación, f

envelop /ɛn'vɛləp/ vt envolver, cubrir

envelope /'ɛnvə,loup/ n sobre, m

envelopment /ɛn'vɛləpmənt/ n envolvimiento, m; cubierta, f

enviable /'ɛnviəbəl/ a envidiable

envious /'ɛnviəs/ a envidioso. **an e. look,** una mirada de envidia

enviously /'ɛnviəsli/ adv con envidia

environment /ɛn'vairənmənt/ n medio ambiente, m

environs /ɛn'vairənz/ n inmediaciones, f pl, alrededores, m pl

envisage /ɛn'vɪzɪdʒ/ vt hacer frente a; contemplar; imaginar

envoy /'ɛnvɔi/ n enviado, m; mensajero (-ra)

envy /'ɛnvi/ n envidia, f, vt envidiar

enzyme /'ɛnzaim/ n fermento, m, enzima, f

eon /'iən/ n eón, m

epaulette /'ɛpə,lɛt/ n hombrera, f

ephemeral /ɪ'fɛmərəl/ a efímero; *Fig.* fugaz, pasajero

Ephesus /'ɛfəsəs/ Efiso, m

Ephraim /'ifriəm/ Efraín, m

Ephraimite /'ifriə,mait/ n and a efraíta, mf

epic /'ɛpɪk/ a épico. —n epopeya, f

epicenter /'ɛpə,sɛntər/ n epicentro, m

epicure /'ɛpɪ,kyur/ n epicúreo (-ea)

epicurean /,ɛpɪkyu'riən/ a epicúreo

Epicureanism /,ɛpɪkyu'riə,nɪzəm/ n epicureísmo, m

epidemic /,ɛpɪ'dɛmɪk/ n epidemia, f; plaga, f, a epidémico

epidermis /,ɛpɪ'dɜrmɪs/ n epidermis, f

epiglottis /,ɛpɪ'glɒtɪs/ n epiglotis, f

epigram /'ɛpɪ,græm/ n epigrama, m

epigrammatic /,ɛpɪgrə'mætɪk/ a epigramático

epigraph /'ɛpɪ,græf/ n epígrafe, m

epigraphy /ɪ'pɪgrəfi/ n epigrafía, f

epilepsy /'ɛpə,lɛpsi/ n epilepsia, alferecía, f

epileptic /,ɛpə'lɛptɪk/ a and n epiléptico (-ca). **e. fit,** ataque epiléptico, m. **e. aura,** aura epiléptica, f

epilogue /'ɛpə,lɔg/ n epílogo, m

epiphany /ɪ'pɪfəni/ n epifanía, f

Epirus /ɪ'pairəs/ Epiro, m

episcopacy /ɪ'pɪskəpəsi/ n episcopado, m

episcopal /ɪ'pɪskəpəl/ a episcopal

episcopalianism /ɪ,pɪskə'peilyə,nɪzəm/ n episcopalismo, m

episode /'ɛpə,soud/ n suceso, incidente, m; *Lit.* episodio, m

episodic /,ɛpə'sɒdɪk/ a episódico

epistle /ɪ'pɪsəl/ n epístola, f

epistolary /ɪ'pɪstl,ɛri/ a epistolar

epitaph /'ɛpɪ,tæf/ n epitafio, m

epithet /'ɛpə,θɛt/ n epíteto, m

epitome /ɪ'pɪtəmi/ n epítome, m

epitomize /ɪ'pɪtə,maiz/ vt resumir, abreviar

epoch /'ɛpək/ n época, edad, f

epode /'ɛpoud/ n épodo, m

Epsom salts /'ɛpsəm/ n sal de la Higuera, f

equability /,ɛkwə'bɪlɪti/ n igualdad (de ánimo), ecuanimidad, f; uniformidad, f

equable /'ɛkwəbəl/ a igual, ecuánime; uniforme

equably /'ɛkwəbli/ adv con ecuanimidad; igualmente; uniformemente

equal /'ikwəl/ a igual; uniforme; imparcial; equitativo, justo. —n igual, mf. —vt ser igual a; equivaler a; igualar; *Sports.* empatar. **to be e. to,** (of persons) ser capaz de; servir para; atreverse a; (circumstances) estar al nivel de; sentirse con fuerzas para. **without e.,** sin igual; (of beauty, etc.) sin par. **e. sign,** *Math.* igual, m

equality /ɪ'kwɒlɪti/ n igualdad, f; uniformidad, f

equalization /,ikwələ'zeiʃən/ n igualación, f

equalize /'ikwə,laiz/ vt igualar

equalizing /'ikwə,laizɪŋ/ a igualador; compensador

equally /'ikwəli/ adv igualmente; imparcialmente

equanimity /,ikwə'nɪmɪti/ n ecuanimidad, f

equation /ɪ'kweiʒən/ n ecuación, f

equator /ɪ'kweitər/ n ecuador, m

equatorial /,ikwə'tɔriəl/ a ecuatorial

equerry /'ɛkwəri/ n caballerizo del rey, m

equestrian /ɪ'kwɛstriən/ a ecuestre

equiangular /,ikwi'æŋgyələr/ a equiángulo

equidistance /,ikwi'dɪstəns/ n equidistancia, f

equidistant /,ikwi'dɪstənt/ a equidistante

equilateral /,ikwə'lætərəl/ a equilátero

equilibrist /ɪ'kwɪləbrɪst/ n equilibrista, mf

equilibrium /,ikwə'lɪbriəm/ n equilibrio, m

equine /'ikwain/ a equino; hípico; de caballo

equinoctial /,ikwə'nɒkʃəl/ a equinoccial. **e. gale,** tempestad equinoccial, f

equinox /'ikwə,nɒks/ n equinoccio, m

equip /ɪ'kwɪp/ vt proveer; pertrechar; equipar

equipage /'ɛkwəpɪdʒ/ n (train) séquito, tren, m; (carriage) carruaje, m

equipment /ɪ'kwɪpmənt/ n habilitación, f; equipo, m; pertrechos, m pl; material, m; aparatos, m pl; armamento, m

equitable /'ɛkwɪtəbəl/ a equitativo, justo

equitableness /'ɛkwɪtəbəlnɪs/ n equidad, justicia, f

equitably /'ɛkwɪtəbli/ adv equitativamente, con justicia

equity /'ɛkwɪti/ n equidad, f; imparcialidad, justicia, f

equivalence /ɪ'kwɪvələns/ n equivalencia, f

equivalent /ɪ'kwɪvələnt/ a and n equivalente, m. **to be e. to,** equivaler a

equivocal /ɪ'kwɪvəkəl/ a equívoco, ambiguo

equivocally /ɪ'kwɪvəkəli/ adv equivocadamente

equivocate /ɪ'kwɪvə,keit/ vi usar frases equívocas, emplear equívocos, tergiversar

equivocation /ɪ,kwɪvə'keiʃən/ n equívoco, m

era /'ɪərə, 'ɛrə/ n época, era, f

eradiation /ɪ,reidi'eiʃən/ n irradiación, f

eradicable /ɪ'rædɪkəbəl/ a erradicable

eradicate /ɪ'rædɪ,keit/ vt erradicar; destruir, extirpar; suprimir

eradication /ɪ,rædɪ'keiʃən/ n erradicación, f; destrucción, f; supresión, f

erasable /ɪ'reisəbəl/ a borrable

erase /ɪ'reis/ vt borrar; tachar

eraser /ɪ'reisər/ n goma de borrar, f. **ink e.,** goma para tinta, f

erasure /ɪ'reiʃər/ n borradura, f; tachón, m

ere /ɛər/ conjunc antes de (que), antes de. —prep antes de

erect /ɪ'rɛkt/ a (upright) derecho; erguido; vertical; (uplifted) levantado; (standing) de pie; (firm) firme, resuelto; (alert) vigilante. —*vt* (build) edificar, construir; instalar; (raise) alzar; convertir

erectile /ɪˈrɛktl̩/ *a* eréctil

erection /ɪˈrɛkʃən/ *n* erección, *f;* construcción, edificación, *f;* (building) edificio, *m;* (structure) estructura, *f;* instalación, *f;* (assembling) montaje, *m*

erectly /ɪˈrɛktli/ *adv* derecho

erectness /ɪˈrɛktnɪs/ *n* derechura, *f*

erg /ɜrg/ *n Phys.* ergio, *m*

ermine /ˈɜrmɪn/ *n* armiño, *m, a* de armiño

erode /ɪˈroud/ *vt* corroer; comer; *Geol.* denudar

erosion /ɪˈrouʒən/ *n* erosión, *f*

erotic /ɪˈrɒtɪk/ *a* erótico

err /ɜr, ɛr/ *vi* desviarse; errar; desacertar; pecar

errand /ˈɛrənd/ *n* mensaje, recado, *m;* encargo, *m;* misión, *f.* **e.-boy,** mandadero, mensajero, motril, mozo, recadero, *m*

errant /ˈɛrənt/ *a* errante; (of knights) andante

erratic /ɪˈrætɪk/ *a* (of conduct) excéntrico, irresponsable; (of thoughts, etc.) errante; *Med.* errático

erratum /ɪˈrɑtəm/ *n* errata, *f*

erring /ˈɛrɪŋ/ *a* extraviado; pecaminoso

erroneous /əˈrouniəs/ *a* erróneo; falso; injusto

erroneously /əˈrouniəsli/ *adv* erróneamente; falsamente; injustamente

erroneousness /əˈrouniəsnɪs/ *n* falsedad, *f*

error /ˈɛrər/ *n* error, *m;* equivocación, *f,* desacierto, *m;* (sin) pecado, *m.* **in e.,** por equivocación

erudite /ˈɛryuˌdaɪt/ *a* erudito; sabio

erudition /ˌɛryʊˈdɪʃən/ *n* erudición, *f*

erupt /ɪˈrʌpt/ *vi* entrar en erupción, estar en erupción; *Fig.* salir con fuerza

eruption /ɪˈrʌpʃən/ *n* erupción, *f*

erysipelas /ˌɛrəˈsɪpələs/ *n* erisipela, *f*

escalade /ˌɛskəˈleɪd/ *n* escalada, *f, vt* escalar

escalator /ˈɛskəˌleɪtər/ *n* escalera automática, escalera eléctrica, escalera mecánica, escalera móvil, escalera rodante, *f*

escapable /ɪˈskeipəbəl/ *a* evitable, eludible

escapade /ˈɛskəˌpeɪd/ *n* escapada, *f;* aventura, *f*

escape /ɪˈskeɪp/ *n* huida, fuga, *f;* evasión, evitación, *f;* (leak) escape, *m; Fig.* salida, *f.* —*vt* eludir, evitar; (of cries, groans, etc.) dar, salir de. —*vi* huir, fugarse, escapar; (slip away) escurrirse; librarse; salvarse; (leak) escape, *m.* **His name escapes me,** Se me escapa (o se me olvida) su nombre. **to e. notice,** pasar inadvertido. **to have a narrow e.,** salvarse en una tabla. **to e. from,** escaparse de; librarse de; huir de

escape clause *n* cláusula de salvaguardia, *f*

escaping /ɪˈskeɪpɪŋ/ *a* fugitivo

escarpment /ɪˈskɑrpmənt/ *n* escarpa, *f*

eschew /ɛsˈtʃu/ *vt* evitar

eschewal /ɛsˈtʃuəl/ *n* evitación, *f*

escort /*n* ˈɛskɔrt; *v* ɪˈskɔrt/ *n Mil.* escolta, *f;* (of ships) convoy, *m;* acompañamiento, *m;* acompañante, *m.* —*vt Mil.* escoltar; (of ships) convoyar; acompañar

escritoire /ˌɛskrɪˈtwɑr/ *n* escritorio, *m*

escudo /ɛˈskudou/ *n* escudo, *m*

escutcheon /ɪˈskʌtʃən/ *n* escudo, blasón, *m*

Eskimo /ˈɛskəˌmou/ *a* and *n* esquimal *mf*

esoteric /ˌɛsəˈtɛrɪk/ *a* esotérico

esparto /ɪˈspɑrtou/ *n* esparto, *m*

especial /ɪˈspɛʃəl/ *a* especial; particular

especially /ɪˈspɛʃəli/ *adv* especialmente; ante todo; en particular

Esperantist /ˌɛspəˈrɑntɪst/ *n* esperantista, *mf*

Esperanto /ˌɛspəˈrɑntou/ *n* esperanto, *m*

espionage /ˈɛspiəˌnɑʒ/ *n* espionaje, *m*

esplanade /ˈɛspləˌnɑd/ *n Mil.* explanada, *f;* bulevar, paseo, *m*

espousal /ɪˈspauzəl/ *n* desposorio, *m; Fig.* adhesión (a una causa), *f*

espouse /ɪˈspauz/ *vt* desposar; (a cause) abrazar; defender

espy /ɪˈspai/ *vt* divisar, ver, observar

esquire /ˈɛskwaɪᵊr/ *n* escudero, *m;* (landowner) hacendado, *m;* (as a title) don (before given name)

essay /ˈɛsei; *v* ɛˈsei/ *n* tentativa, *f; Lit.* ensayo, *m, vt* probar; procurar; (on an examination) tema, *m.* **essay question,** tema, *m*

essayist /ˈɛseiɪst/ *n* ensayista, *mf*

essence /ˈɛsəns/ *n* esencia, *f*

essential /əˈsɛntʃəl/ *a* esencial; indispensable, imprescindible; intrínseco. —*n* artículo de primera necesidad, *m;* elemento necesario, *m*

essentially /əˈsɛntʃəli/ *adv* esencialmente

establish /ɪˈstæblɪʃ/ *vt* establecer; fundar; crear; erigir; (constitute) constituir; (order) disponer; (prove) demostrar, probar; (take root, settle) arraigarse

established /ɪˈstæblɪʃt/ *a* establecido; arraigado; (proved) demostrado; bien conocido; (author) consagrado; (of churches) oficial

establishment /ɪˈstæblɪʃmənt/ *n* establecimiento, *m;* fundación, *f;* creación, *f;* institución, *f;* (building) erección, *f;* arraigo, *m;* (house) casa, *f;* (church) iglesia oficial, *f;* demostración, *f;* reconocimiento, *m*

estate /ɪˈsteit/ *n* estado, *m;* clase, *f;* condición, *f;* (land) propiedad, finca, *f;* fortuna, *f;* (inheritance) heredad, *f,* patrimonio, *m; Law.* bienes, *m pl.* **personal e.,** bienes muebles, *m pl;* fortuna personal, *f.* **third e.,** estado llano, *m.* **e. agent,** agente de fincas, *m;* agente de casas, *m*

esteem /ɪˈstim/ *n* estima, *f,* aprecio, *m;* consideración, *f, vt* estimar, apreciar; creer, juzgar

ester /ˈɛstər/ *n Chem.* éster, *m*

esthete /ˈɛsθit/ *n* estético, *m*

esthetic /ɛsˈθɛtɪk/ *a* estético

esthetically /ɛsˈθɛtɪkli/ *adv* estéticamente

esthetics /ɛsˈθɛtɪks/ *n* estética, *f*

estimable /ˈɛstəməbəl/ *a* apreciable, estimable

estimableness /ˈɛstəməbəlnɪs/ *n* estimabilidad, *f*

estimate /*n* ˈɛstəˌmɪt; *v* -ˌmeit/ *n* estimación, tasa, *f;* cálculos, *m pl;* apreciación, *f;* opinión, *f; pl* **estimates,** presupuesto, *m.* —*vt* (value) avalorar, tasar; calcular, computar; considerar. —*vi* hacer un presupuesto

estimation /ˌɛstəˈmeifən/ *n* opinión, *f;* cálculo, cómputo, *m;* (esteem) aprecio, *m,* estima, *f*

Estonian /ɛˈstounian/ *a* and *n* estonio (-ia); (language) estonio, *m*

estrange /ɪˈstreindʒ/ *vt* enajenar; ofender

estrangement /ɪˈstreindʒmənt/ *n* enajenación, alienación, *f*

estuary /ˈɛstʃuˌɛri/ *n* estuario, *m,* ría, *f*

etcetera /ɛtˈsɛtərə/ *n* etcétera. (Used as noun, *f*)

etch /ɛtʃ/ *vt* grabar al agua fuerte

etcher /ˈɛtʃər/ *n* grabador (-ra) al agua fuerte

etching /ˈɛtʃɪŋ/ *n* aguafuerte, *f;* grabado al agua fuerte, *m.* **e. needle,** punta seca, aguja de grabador, *f*

eternal /ɪˈtɜrnl̩/ *a* eterno; incesante. —*n* (E.) el Eterno

eternally /ɪˈtɜrnl̩i/ *adv* eternamente

eternity /ɪˈtɜrnɪti/ *n* eternidad, *f*

eternize /ɪˈtɜrnaiz/ *vt* eternizar

ether /ˈiθər/ *n* éter, *m*

ethereal /ɪˈθɪriəl/ *a* etéreo; vaporoso, aéreo

etheric /ɪˈθɛrɪk/ *a* etéreo

etherize /ˈiθəˌraiz/ *vt* eterizar

ethical /ˈɛθɪkəl/ *a* ético, moral; *n* droga de ordenanza, *f*

ethics /ˈɛθɪks/ *n* ética, *f;* (filosofía) moral, *f*

Ethiopia /ˌiθiˈoupiə/ Etiopia, *f*

ethnic /ˈɛθnɪk/ *a* étnico

ethnographic /ˌɛθnouˈgræfɪk/ *a* etnográfico

ethnography /ɛθˈnɒgrəfi/ *n* etnografía, *f*

ethnologist /ɛθˈnɒlədʒɪst/ *n* etnólogo, *m*

ethnology /ɛθˈnɒlədʒi/ *n* etnología, *f*

ethyl /ˈɛθəl/ *n Chem.* etilo, *m*

ethylene /ˈɛθəˌlin/ *n Chem.* etileno, *m*

etiquette /ˈɛtɪkɪt/ *n* etiqueta, *f*

Etna, Mount /ˈɛtnə/ el Etna

Eton coat /ˈitn̩/ *n* chaquetilla, *f*

Eton collar *n* cuello de colegial, *m*

Eton crop *n* pelo a la garçonne, *m*

Etruscan /ɪˈtrʌskən/ *a* and *n* etrusco (-ca)

etymological /ˌɛtəməˈlɒdʒɪkəl/ *a* etimológico

etymologist /ˌɛtəˈmɒlədʒɪst/ *n* etimólogo, *m,* etimologista, *m*

etymology /ˌɛtəˈmɒlədʒi/ *n* etimología, *f*

eucalyptus /ˌyukəˈlɪptəs/ *n* eucalipto, *m*

Eucharist /ˈyukərɪst/ *n* Eucaristía, *f*

eucharistic /ˌyukəˈrɪstɪk/ *a* eucarístico
Euclidean /yuˈklɪdiən/ *a* euclídeo
eugenic /yuˈdʒɛnɪk/ *a* eugenésico
eugenics /yuˈdʒɛnɪks/ *n* eugenesia, *f*
eulogist /ˈyulədʒɪst/ *n* elogiador (-ra), loador (-ra)
eulogistic /ˌyuləˈdʒɪstɪk/ *a* elogiador
eulogize /ˈyuləˌdʒaɪz/ *vt* elogiar, alabar, encomiar
eulogy /ˈyulədʒi/ *n* elogio, encomio, *m;* alabanza, *f;* panegírico, *m*
eunuch /ˈyunək/ *n* eunuco, *m*
euphemism /ˈyufəˌmɪzəm/ *n* eufemismo, *m*
euphonious /yuˈfouniəs/ *a* eufónico
euphony /ˈyufəni/ *n* eufonía, *f*
euphuistic /ˌyufyuˈɪstɪk/ *a* alambicado, gongorino
Eurasian /yuˈreiʒən/ *a* and *n* eurasio (-ia)
eurhythmic /yuˈrɪðmɪk/ *a* eurítmico
eurhythmics /yuˈrɪðmɪks/ *n* euritmia, *f*
European /ˌyurəˈpiən/ *a* and *n* europeo (-ea)
europeanize /ˌyurəˈpiəˌnaiz/ *vt* europeanizar
euthanasia /ˌyuθəˈneiʒə, -ʒiə, -ziə/ *n* eutanasia, *f*
evacuate /ɪˈvækyuˌeit/ *vt* evacuar
evacuation /ɪˌvækyuˈeiʃən/ *n* evacuación, *f*
evade /ɪˈveid/ *vt* evadir, eludir; evitar, esquivar; rehuir
evaluate /ɪˈvælyuˌeit/ *vt* evaluar, estimar; calcular
evaluation /ɪˌvælyuˈeiʃən/ *n* evaluación, estimación, *f*
evanescent /ˌɛvəˈnɛsənt/ *a* transitorio, fugaz, pasajero
evangelical /ˌivænˈdʒɛlɪkəl/ *a* evangélico
evangelicalism /ˌivænˈdʒɛlɪkəˌlɪzəm/ *n* evangelismo, *m*
evangelist /ɪˈvændʒəlɪst/ *n* evangelista, *m*
evangelize /ɪˈvændʒəˌlaiz/ *vt* evangelizar
evaporate /ɪˈvæpəˌreit/ *vi* evaporarse; desvanecerse. **—***vt* evaporar
evaporation /ɪˌvæpəˈreiʃən/ *n* evaporación, *f;* desvanecimiento, *m*
evaporative /ɪˈvæpəˌreitɪv/ *a* evaporatorio
evasion /ɪˈveiʒən/ *n* (escape) fuga, *f;* evasión, *f;* evasiva, *f,* efugio, *m*
evasive /ɪˈveisɪv/ *a* evasivo, ambiguo
evasively /ɪˈveisɪvli/ *adv* evasivamente
evasiveness /ɪˈveisɪvnɪs/ *n* carácter evasivo, *m*
eve /iv/ *n* víspera, *f;* *Eccl.* vigilia, *f.* **on the eve of,** la víspera de; *Fig.* en vísperas de
even /ˈivən/ *a* (flat) llano; (smooth) liso; igual; (level with) al mismo nivel (de); uniforme; (of numbers) par; (approximate, of sums) redondo; rítmico; invariable, constante; (of temper) apacible; (just) imparcial; (monotonous) monótono, igual; (paid) pagado; (*Com.* of date) mismo. **to get e. with,** pagar en la misma moneda, vengarse de
even /ˈivən/ *adv* siquiera; aun; hasta; (also) también. **not e.,** ni siquiera. **e. as,** así como, del mismo modo que. **e. if,** aun cuando, si bien. **e. now,** aun ahora; ahora mismo. **e. so,** aun así; (nevertheless) sin embargo. **e. though,** aunque; suponiendo que
even /ˈivən/ *vt* igualar; (level) allanar, nivelar; (accounts) desquitar; compensar; hacer uniforme
evening /ˈivnɪŋ/ *n* tarde, *f,* atardecer, *m;* noche, *f; Fig.* fin, *m, a* vespertino, de la tarde. **Good e.!** ¡Buenas tardes! ¡Buenas noches! **in the e.,** al atardecer. **tomorrow e.,** mañana por la tarde. **yesterday e.,** ayer por la tarde. **e. class,** clase nocturna, *f.* **e. dress,** (women) traje de noche, *m;* (men) traje de etiqueta, *m.* **e. meal,** cena, *f.* **e. paper,** periódico (or diario) de la noche, *m.* **evening primrose,** hierba del asno, onagra, *f.* **e. star,** estrella vespertina, estrella de la tarde, *f;* (Venus) lucero de la tarde, *m*
evenly /ˈivənli/ *adv* igualmente; (on a level) a nivel; uniformemente; imparcialmente; (of speech) con suavidad
evenness /ˈivənnɪs/ *n* igualdad, *f;* (smoothness) lisura, *f;* uniformidad, *f;* imparcialidad, *f;* (of temper) ecuanimidad, serenidad, *f*
evensong /ˈivənˌsɔŋ/ *n* vísperas, *f pl*
event /ɪˈvɛnt/ *n* incidente, suceso, acontecimiento, *f;* (result) consecuencia, *f;* resultado, *m;* caso, *m;* (athletics) prueba, *f;* (race) carrera, *f.* **at all events,** de todas maneras. **in such an e.,** en tal caso. **in the e. of,** en el caso de

eventful /ɪˈvɛntfəl/ *a* lleno de acontecimientos; accidentado; memorable
eventual /ɪˈvɛntʃuəl/ *a* eventual; final, último
eventuality /ɪˌvɛntʃuˈælɪti/ *n* eventualidad, *f*
eventually /ɪˈvɛntʃuəli/ *adv* a la larga, al fin
ever /ˈɛvər/ *adv* siempre; (at any time) jamás; alguna vez; nunca; (even) siquiera; (very) muy; (in any way) en modo alguno. **As fast as e. he can,** Lo más aprisa que pueda. **Be it e. so big,** Por grande que sea. **Did you e.!** ¡Habráse visto! ¡Qué cosa! **for e.,** para siempre. **for e. and e.,** para siempre jamás; (mostly ecclesiastical) por los siglos de los siglos; eternamente. **He is e. so nice,** Es muy simpático. **Hardly e.,** casi nunca. **I don't think I have e. been there,** No creo que haya estado nunca allí. **if e.,** si alguna vez; (rarely) raramente. **nor... e.,** ni nunca. **not... e.,** nunca. **e. after,** desde entonces; (afterward) después. **e. and anon,** de vez en cuando. **e. so little,** siquiera un poco; muy poco
evergreen /ˈɛvərˌɡrin/ *a* siempre verde. **—***n* planta vivaz, *f.* **e. oak,** encina, *f*
everlasting /ˌɛvərˈlæstɪŋ/ *a* eterno, perpetuo; (of colors) estable; incesante. **e. flower,** perpetua, *f*
evermore /ˌɛvərˈmɔr/ *adv* eternamente
every /ˈɛvri/ *a* todo; cada (invariable); todos los, *m pl;* todas las, *f pl.* **e. day,** todos los días, cada día. **e. now and then,** de cuando en cuando. **e. other day,** cada dos días
everybody /ˈɛvriˌbɑdi/ *n* todo el mundo, *m;* todos, *m pl;* todas, *f pl;* cada uno, *m;* cada una, *f*
everyday /ˈɛvriˌdei/ *a* diario, cotidiano; corriente, de cada día, usual
everything /ˈɛvriˌθɪŋ/ *n* todo, *m;* (e. that, which) todo lo (que). **e. possible,** todo lo posible
everywhere /ˈɛvriˌwɛr/ *adv* por todas partes
evict /ɪˈvɪkt/ *vt* desahuciar; expulsar
eviction /ɪˈvɪkʃən/ *n* evicción, *f,* desahúcio, *m;* expulsión, *f*
evidence /ˈɛvidəns/ *n* *Law.* testimonio, *m,* deposición, *f;* indicios, *m pl;* evidencia, *f;* prueba, *f;* hecho, *m, vt* patentizar, probar. **to give e.,** dar testimonio, deponer
evident /ˈɛvidənt/ *a* evidente, patente, manifiesto; claro. **to be e.,** ser patente, estar a la vista
evidently /ˈɛvidəntli/ *adv* evidentemente; claramente
evil /ˈivəl/ *a* malo; malvado, perverso; de maldad; (unfortunate) aciago; de infortunio; (of spirits) diabólico, malo. **—***n* mal, *m;* maldad, perversidad, *f;* (misfortune) desgracia, *f.* **the E. one,** el Malo. **e.-doer,** malhechor (-ra). **e. eye,** mal de ojo, aojo, *m.* **e.-minded,** mal pensado; malintencionado. **e.-speaking,** maledicencia, calumnia, *f.* **e. spirit,** demonio, espíritu malo, *m*
evince /ɪˈvɪns/ *vt* evidenciar; mostrar
eviscerate /ɪˈvɪsəˌreit/ *vt* destripar, desentrañar
evocation /ˌɛvəˈkeiʃən/ *n* evocación, *f*
evocative /ɪˈvɑkətɪv/ *a* evocador
evoke /ɪˈvouk/ *vt* evocar
evolution /ˌɛvəˈluʃən/ *n* evolución, *f;* desarrollo, *m;* (*Nav. Mil.*) maniobra, *f;* *Math.* extracción de una raíz, *f;* (revolution) revolución, vuelta, *f*
evolutionism /ˌɛvəˈluʃəˌnɪzəm/ *n* evolucionismo, *m*
evolutive /ˌɛvəˈlutɪv/ *a* evolutivo
evolve /ɪˈvɑlv/ *vi* evolucionar; desarrollarse. **—***vt* producir por evolución; desarrollar; pensar
ewe /yu/ *n* oveja, *f.* **ewe lamb,** cordera, *f*
ewer /ˈyuər/ *n* aguamanil, *m*
exacerbate /ɪɡˈzæsərˌbeit/ *vt* exacerbar; agravar, empeorar
exacerbation /ɪɡˌzæsərˈbeiʃən/ *n* exacerbación, *f;* agravación, *f*
exact /ɪɡˈzækt/ *a* exacto; fiel; metódico; estricto. **—***vt* exigir
exacting /ɪɡˈzæktɪŋ/ *a* exigente, severo, estricto; (hard) agotador, arduo
exaction /ɪɡˈzækʃən/ *n* exigencia, *f;* extorsión, exacción, *f*
exactly /ɪɡˈzæktli/ *adv* exactamente; precisamente
exactness /ɪɡˈzæktnɪs/ *n* exactitud, *f*
exaggerate /ɪɡˈzædʒəˌreit/ *vt* exagerar; acentuar. **—***vi* exagerar
exaggerated /ɪɡˈzædʒəˌreitɪd/ *a* exagerado

exaggeration /ɪgˌzædʒə'reiʃən/ n exageración, f
exaggerator /ɪg'zædʒəˌreitər/ n exagerador (-ra)
exalt /ɪg'zɔlt/ vt exaltar; enaltecer, elevar; (praise) glorificar, magnificar; (intensify) realzar; intensificar
exaltation /ˌɛgzɔl'teiʃən/ n exaltación, elevación, f; alegría, f, júbilo, m; (ecstasy) éxtasis, arrobamiento, m; (of the Cross) exaltación, f
exalted /ɪg'zɔltɪd/ a exaltado, eminente
exaltedness /ɪg'zɔltɪdnɪs/ n exaltación, f
examination /ɪgˌzæmə'neiʃən/ n examen, m; inspección, f; investigación, f; Law. interrogatorio, m; prueba, f. **to sit an e.,** examinarse. **written e.,** prueba escrita, f
examine /ɪg'zæmɪn/ vt examinar; inspeccionar; investigar; Law. interrogar; (search) reconocer; (by touch) tentar; observar; analizar. **to e. into,** examinar; considerar detenidamente; ahondar en
examinee /ɪgˌzæmə'ni/ n examinando (-da)
examiner /ɪg'zæmɪnər/ n examinador (-ra); inspector (-ra)
examinership /ɪg'zæmɪnərˌʃɪp/ n cargo de examinador, m
examining /ɪg'zæmɪnɪŋ/ a que examina; de examen; Law. interrogante
example /ɪg'zæmpəl/ n ejemplo, m; ilustración, f; (parallel) ejemplar, m; (warning) escarmiento, m. **for e.,** por ejemplo. **to set an e.,** dar ejemplo, dar el ejemplo.
exasperate /ɪg'zæspəˌreit/ vt exasperar, irritar; (increase) aumentar; (worsen) agravar
exasperating /ɪg'zæspəˌreitɪŋ/ a exasperante, irritante, provocador
exasperation /ɪgˌzæspə'reiʃən/ n exasperación, irritación, f; (worsening) agravación, f; enojo, m
excavate /'ɛkskəˌveit/ vt excavar; (hollow) vaciar
excavation /ˌɛkskə'veiʃən/ n excavación, f; Archit. vaciado, m
excavator /'ɛkskəˌveitər/ n excavador (-ra); (machine) excavadora, f
exceed /ɪk'sid/ vt exceder; (excel) superar, aventajar; (one's hopes, etc.) sobrepujar. —vi excederse. **e. all expectations,** exceder a toda ponderación. **to e. one's rights,** abusar de sus derechos, ir demasiado lejos
exceedingly /ɪk'sidɪŋli/ adv sumamente, extremadamente; sobre manera
excel /ɪk'sɛl/ vt aventajar, superar; vencer. —vi sobresalir; distinguirse, señalarse; ser superior
excellence /'ɛksələns/ n excelencia, f; superioridad, f; perfección, f; mérito, m; buena calidad, f
excellency /'ɛksələnsi/ n (title) Excelencia, f. **Your E.,** Su Excelencia
excellent /'ɛksələnt/ a excelente; superior; perfecto; magnífico; (in examinations) sobresaliente
excellently /'ɛksələntli/ adv excelentemente; perfectamente; magníficamente
except /ɪk'sɛpt/ vt exceptuar; omitir
except, excepting /ɪk'sɛpt/ /ɪk'sɛptɪŋ/ prep excepto, con excepción de; exceptuando; menos; salvo; fuera de. —conjunc a menos que. **except for,** si no fuese por; con excepción de; fuera de
exception /ɪk'sɛpʃən/ n excepción, f; objeción, protesta, f. **to make an e.,** hacer una excepción. **to take e. to,** protestar contra; tachar, criticar; desaprobar
exceptional /ɪk'sɛpʃənl̩/ a excepcional
excerpt /n 'ɛksɜrpt; v ɪk'sɜrpt/ n excerpta, f, extracto, m. —vt extraer
excess /n 'ɛksɛs, 'ɛksɛs/ n exceso, m; superabundancia, f; demasía, f; Com. superávit, m. **in e.,** en exceso, de sobra. **in e. of,** en exceso de; arriba de. **to e.,** excesivamente, demasiado. **e. fare,** suplemento, m. **e. luggage,** exceso de equipaje, m; (overweight) exceso de peso, m
excessive /ɪk'sɛsɪv/ a excesivo; superabundante; inmoderado, desmesurado; exagerado
excessively /ɪk'sɛsɪvli/ adv excesivamente; exageradamente
excessiveness /ɪk'sɛsɪvnɪs/ n exceso, m; superabundancia, f; exageración, f
exchange /ɪks'tʃeindʒ/ n cambio, trueque, m; (of prisoners) canje, m; (financial) cambio, m; (building) bolsa, lonja, f; (telephone) oficina central de telé-

fonos, f. —vt cambiar (for, por); trocar; (replace) reemplazar; (prisoners) canjear; (of blows) darse; (pass from, into) pasar de... a. —vi hacer un cambio. **in e. for,** en cambio de, a trueque de; por. **to e. greetings,** saludarse; cambiar saludos. **They exchanged looks,** Se miraron. **What is the rate of e.?** ¿Cuál es el tipo de cambio? **e. of prisoners,** canje de prisioneros, m
exchangeable /ɪks'tʃeindʒəbəl/ a cambiable; trocable
exchequer /'ɛkstʃɛkər/ n (public finance) Hacienda pública, f; tesorería, f; (funds) fondos, m pl. **Chancellor of the E.,** Ministro de Hacienda, m
excise /n 'ɛksaiz; v ɪk'saiz/ n contribución indirecta, f; (customs and e.) Aduana, f. —vt (cut) cortar, extirpar; imponer una contribución indirecta. **e. duty,** derecho de aduana, m
excise tax arbitrios, m pl
excision /ɛk'sɪʒən/ n excisión, f; extirpación, f
excitability /ɪkˌsaitə'bɪlɪti/ n excitabilidad, f
excitable /ɪk'saitəbəl/ a excitable
excitation /ˌɛksai'teiʃən/ n excitación, f
excite /ɪk'sait/ vt emocionar; conmover; agitar; excitar; suscitar, provocar; incitar, instigar; (attention, interest) despertar; estimular. **to become excited,** emocionarse; exaltarse; (annoyed) acalorarse; (upset) agitarse
excitedly /ɪk'saitɪdli/ adv con emoción; acaloradamente; agitadamente
excitement /ɪk'saitmənt/ n conmoción, f; agitación, f; (annoyance) acaloramiento, m; emoción, f; estímulo, m; instigación, f, fomento, m; (amusement) placer, m
exciting /ɪk'saitɪŋ/ a emocionante; conmovedor; agitador; muy interesante
exclaim /ɪk'skleim/ vt and vi exclamar. **to e. against,** clamar contra
exclamation /ˌɛkskla'meiʃən/ n exclamación, f. **e. mark,** punto de exclamación, m
exclamatory /ɪk'sklæməˌtɔri/ a exclamatorio
exclude /ɪk'sklud/ vt excluir; exceptuar; evitar; (refuse) rechazar
exclusion /ɪk'skluʒən/ n exclusión, f; exceptuación, f; eliminación, f
exclusive /ɪk'sklusɪv/ a exclusivo; (snobbish) exclusivista. **e. of,** no incluido; aparte de
exclusively /ɪk'sklusɪvli/ adv exclusivamente; únicamente
exclusiveness /ɪk'sklusɪvnɪs/ n carácter exclusivo, m
exclusivism /ɪk'sklusɪˌvizəm/ n exclusivismo, m
exclusivist /ɪk'sklusəvɪst/ n exclusivista, mf
excommunicate /v ˌɛkskə'myunɪˌkeit/ -kɪt/ vt excomulgar. —a excomulgado
excommunication /ˌɛkskəˌmyunɪ'keiʃən/ n excomunión, f
excrement /'ɛkskrəmənt/ n excremento, m
excrescence /ɪk'skrɛsəns/ n excrecencia, f
excrescent /ɪk'skrɛsənt/ a que forma excrecencia; superfluo
excrete /ɪk'skrit/ vt excretar
excretion /ɪk'skriʃən/ n excreción, f
excretory /'ɛkskrɪˌtɔri/ a excretorio
excruciating /ɪk'skruʃiˌeitɪŋ/ a atormentador, angustioso; (of pain) agudísimo
excursion /ɪk'skɜrʒən/ n excursión, f; expedición, f; (digression) digresión, f. **e. ticket,** billete de excursión, m. **e. train,** tren de excursionistas, m
excursionist /ɪk'skɜrʒənɪst/ n excursionista, mf; turista, mf
excusable /ɪk'skyuzəbəl/ a disculpable, excusable
excusably /ɪk'skyuzəbli/ adv excusablemente
excuse /ɪk'skyus/ n excusa, f; disculpa, f; pretexto, m; justificación, defensa, f. **to give as an e.,** pretextar
excuse /ɪk'skyuz/ vt disculpar, excusar; dispensar (de); librar (de); (forgive) perdonar; (defend) justificar, defender; (minimize) paiar; (oneself) disculparse. **E. me!** ¡Con permiso!; ¡Perdone Vd.!; ¡Dispense Vd.!
execrable /'ɛksɪkrəbəl/ a execrable, abominable
execrate /'ɛksɪˌkreit/ vt execrar, abominar. —vi maldecir
execration /ˌɛksɪ'kreiʃən/ n execración, abominación, f; maldición, f
execute /'ɛksɪˌkyut/ vt (perform) ejecutar, poner en

efecto, realizar; (*Art. Mus.*) ejecutar; (part in a play) hacer, desempeñar; (fulfil) cumplir; *Law.* otorgar (un documento); (kill) ajusticiar

execution /ˌɛksɪ'kyuʃən/ *n* efectuación, realización, *f;* (*Art., Mus.*) ejecución, *f;* (of part in a play) desempeño (de un papel), *m;* (fulfilment) cumplimiento, *m; Law.* otorgamiento (de un documento), *m;* (killing) suplicio, *m,* ejecución de la pena de muerte, *f;* (*Law.* seizure) ejecución, *f*

executioner /ˌɛksɪ'kyuʃənər/ *n* verdugo, *m*

executive /ɪg'zɛkyətɪv/ *a* ejecutivo; administrativo. —*n* poder ejecutivo, *m*

executor /ɪg'zɛkyətər/ *n* administrador testamentario, *m*

executorship /ɪg'zɛkyətərˌʃɪp/ *n* ejecutoría, *f*

executrix /ɪg'zɛkyətrɪks/ *n* administradora testamentaria, *f*

exegesis /ˌɛksɪ'dʒɪsɪs/ *n* exégesis, *f*

exegetical /ˌɛksɪ'dʒɛtɪkəl/ *a* exegético

exemplary /ɪg'zɛmpləri/ *a* ejemplar

exemplification /ɪgˌzɛmpləfɪ'keiʃən/ *n* ejemplificación, ilustración, demostración, *f*

exemplify /ɪg'zɛmpləˌfai/ *vt* ejemplificar; ilustrar, demostrar

exempt /ɪg'zɛmpt/ *vt* exentar, eximir; librar; dispensar, excusar. —*a* exento; libre; excusado; inmune

exemption /ɪg'zɛmpʃən/ *n* exención, *f;* libertad, *f;* inmunidad, *f*

exercise /'ɛksərˌsaiz/ *n* ejercicio, *m;* uso, *m;* (essay) ensayo, *m;* (of muscles, etc.) **exercises,** (on land or sea) maniobras, *f pl.* —*vt* ejercer; usar, emplear; (train) ejercitar, entrenar; adiestrar; pasear, dar un paseo; (worry) preocupar. —*vi* hacer ejercicio; ejercitarse; adiestrarse. **spiritual exercises,** ejercicios espirituales, *m pl.* **to take e. in the open air,** tomar ejercicio al aire libre. **to write an e.,** escribir un ejercicio. **e. book,** cuaderno de ejercicios, *m*

exert /ɪg'zɜrt/ *vt* hacer uso de, emplear, ejercer, poner en juego; (deploy) desplegar. **to e. oneself,** hacer un esfuerzo (para); esforzarse (de); trabajar mucho; tratar (de); apurarse, tomarse mucha molestia; preocuparse

exertion /ɪg'zɜrʃən/ *n* esfuerzo, *m;* uso, *m;* (exercise) ejercicio, *m;* (good offices) diligencias, gestiones, *f pl;* buenos oficios, *m pl*

exhalation /ˌɛkshə'leiʃən/ *n* exhalación, *f;* efluvio, *m;* vapor, *m;* humo, *m*

exhale /ɛks'heil/ *vt* exhalar; emitir, despedir. —*vi* evaporarse; disiparse

exhaust /ɪg'zɔst/ *vt* agotar; (empty) vaciar; (end) acabar; apurar; consumir; (tire) rendir, cansar mucho; (weaken) debilitar; (a subject) tratar detalladamente. —*n Mech.* escape, *m;* emisión de vapor, *f;* vapor de escape, *m.* **e. pipe,** tubo de escape, *m*

exhaustible /ɪg'zɔstəbəl/ *a* agotable

exhausting /ɪg'zɔstɪŋ/ *a* cansado, agotador

exhaustion /ɪg'zɔstʃən/ *n* agotamiento, *m;* rendimiento, cansancio, *m;* lasitud, *f;* postración, *f*

exhaustive /ɪg'zɔstɪv/ *a* completo; minucioso

exhaustively /ɪg'zɔstɪvli/ *adv* detenidamente; detalladamente; minuciosamente

exhaustiveness /ɪg'zɔstɪvnɪs/ *n* lo completo; minuciosidad, *f*

exhibit /ɪg'zɪbɪt/ *vt* exhibir; manifestar, ostentar; revelar, descubrir; presentar. —*vi* exhibir, ser expositor. —*n* objeto exhibido, *m; Law.* prueba, *f*

exhibition /ˌɛksə'bɪʃən/ *n* exposición, *f;* (performance) función, *f;* espectáculo, *m;* exhibición, *f;* (showing) manifestación, *f;* (grant) bolsa de estudio, beca, *f*

exhibitionism /ˌɛksə'bɪʃəˌnɪzəm/ *n* exhibicionismo, *m*

exhibitionist /ˌɛksə'bɪʃənɪst/ *n* exhibicionista, *mf*

exhibitor /ɪg'zɪbɪtər/ *n* expositor (-ra)

exhilarate /ɪg'zɪləˌreit/ *vt* alegrar, alborozar

exhilarating /ɪg'zɪləˌreitɪŋ/ *a* alegre; estimulador, vigorizador, tonificante

exhilaration /ɪgˌzɪlə'reiʃən/ *n* alegría, *f,* alborozo, regocijo, *m*

exhort /ɪg'zɔrt/ *vt and vi* exhortar

exhortation /ˌɛgzɔr'teiʃən/ *n* exhortación, *f*

exhumation /ˌɛkshyu'meiʃən/ *n* exhumación, *f*

exhume /ɪg'zum/ *vt* exhumar

exigence /'ɛksɪdʒəns/ *n* exigencia, *f;* urgencia, *f;* (need) necesidad, *f*

exigent /'ɛksɪdʒənt/ *a* exigente; urgente

exiguous /ɪg'zɪgyuəs/ *a* exiguo

exiguousness /ɪg'zɪgyuəsnɪs/ *n* exigüidad, *f*

exile /'ɛgzail/ *n* destierro, *m;* (person) desterrado (-da). —*vt* desterrar

exist /ɪg'zɪst/ *vi* existir

existence /ɪg'zɪstəns/ *n* existencia, *f;* (being) ser, *m;* (life) vida, *f.* **to bring into e.,** causar; producir

existentialism /ˌɛgzɪ'stɛnʃəˌlɪzəm/ *n* existencialismo, *m*

existing /ɪg'zɪstɪŋ/ *a* existente

exit /'ɛgzɪt, 'ɛksɪt/ *n* salida, *f;* partida, *f;* (death) muerte, *f; Theat.* mutis, *m.* —*vi Theat.* hacer mutis. **to make one's e.,** salir; marcharse; irse; morir; *Theat.* hacer mutis

exodus /'ɛksədəs/ *n* éxodo, *m;* salida, *f;* emigración, *f;* (Old Testament) Éxodo, *m*

exonerate /ɪg'zɒnəˌreit/ *vt* exonerar

exoneration /ɪgˌzɒnə'reiʃən/ *n* exoneración, *f*

exorbitance /ɪg'zɔrbɪtəns/ *n* exorbitancia, *f*

exorbitant /ɪg'zɔrbɪtənt/ *a* exorbitante

exorcism /'ɛksɔrˌsɪzəm/ *n* exorcismo, *m*

exorcist /'ɛksɔrsɪst/ *n* exorcista, *m*

exorcize /'ɛksɔrˌsaiz/ *vt* exorcizar, conjurar

exotic /ɪg'zɒtɪk/ *a* exótico. —*n* planta exótica, *f; Fig.* flor de estufa, *f*

expand /ɪk'spænd/ *vt* extender; abrir; (wings, etc.) desplegar; (the chest, etc.) expandir; dilatar; (amplify) ampliar; (an edition) ampliar, aumentar; (develop) desarrollar; *Fig.* ensanchar; (increase) aumentar. —*vi* dilatarse; hincharse; abrirse; extenderse; *Fig.* ensancharse; (increase) aumentarse

expanse /ɪk'spæns/ *n* extensión, *f*

expansibility /ɪkˌspænsə'bɪliti/ *n Phys.* expansibilidad, *f;* dilatabilidad, *f*

expansible /ɪk'spænsəbəl/ *a Phys.* expansible; dilatable

expansion /ɪk'spænʃən/ *n* expansión, *f;* extensión, *f;* dilatación, *f;* (amplification) ampliación, *f;* (development) desarrollo, *m; Fig.* ensanchamiento, *m;* (increase) aumento, *m*

expansionism /ɪk'spænʃəˌnɪzəm/ *n* expansionismo, *m*

expansive /ɪk'spænsɪv/ *a* expansivo; (of persons) efusivo, expresivo, comunicativo, afable

expansiveness /ɪk'spænsɪvnɪs/ *n* expansibilidad, *f;* (of persons) afabilidad, *f*

expatiate /ɪk'speiʃiˌeit/ **(upon)** *vi* extenderse en

expatiation /ɪkˌspeiʃi'eiʃən/ *n* discurso, *m;* digresión, *f*

expatriation /ɛksˌpeitri'eiʃən/ *n* expatriación, *f*

expect /ɪk'spɛkt/ *vt* esperar; (await) aguardar; (suppose) suponer; (demand) exigir; (count on) contar con. —*vi* creer

expectance /ɪk'spɛktəns/ *n* expectación, *f;* esperanza, *f*

expectant /ɪk'spɛktənt/ *a* expectante; (hopeful) esperanzudo; (pregnant) embarazada

expectantly /ɪk'spɛktəntli/ *adv* con expectación

expectation /ˌɛkspɛk'teiʃən/ *n* expectación, *f;* (hope) esperanza, expectativa, *f;* probabilidad, *f*

expectorate /ɪk'spɛktəˌreit/ *vt* expectorar. —*vi* escupir

expectoration /ɪkˌspɛktə'reiʃən/ *n* expectoración, *f*

expedience /ɪk'spidiəns/ *n* conveniencia, *f;* oportunidad, *f;* aptitud, *f;* (self-interest) egoísmo, *m*

expedient /ɪk'spidiənt/ *a* conveniente; oportuno; apto; prudente; político. —*n* expediente, recurso, medio, *m*

expedite /'ɛkspɪˌdait/ *vt* acelerar; facilitar; (send off) despachar

expedition /ˌɛkspɪ'dɪʃən/ *n* expedición, *f;* (haste) celeridad, diligencia, *f*

expeditionary /ˌɛkspɪ'dɪʃəˌnɛri/ *a* expedicionario. **e. force,** fuerza expedicionaria, *f*

expeditious /ˌɛkspɪ'dɪʃəs/ *a* expedito, pronto

expeditiously /ˌɛkspɪ'dɪʃəsli/ *adv* expeditamente, prontamente

expeditiousness /ˌɛkspɪ'dɪʃəsnɪs/ *n* prontitud, *f*

expel /ɪk'spɛl/ vt expeler, expulsar; echar, arrojar; despedir

expend /ɪk'spɛnd/ vt gastar, expender; (time) perder

expenditure /ɪk'spɛndɪtʃər/ n gasto, desembolso, m; (of time) pérdida, f

expense /ɪk'spɛns/ n gasto, m; pérdida, f; costa, f; pl **expenses,** expensas, f pl, gastos, m pl. **at the e. of,** a costa de. **to be put to great e.,** tener que gastar mucho. **to pay one's expenses,** pagar sus gastos

expensive /ɪk'spɛnsɪv/ a costoso; caro

expensively /ɪk'spɛnsɪvli/ adv costosamente

expensiveness /ɪk'spɛnsɪvnɪs/ n lo costoso; costa, f

experience /ɪk'spɪəriəns/ n experiencia, f. —vt experimentar; sentir; sufrir. **by e.,** por experiencia

experienced /ɪk'spɪəriənst/ a experimentado; experto; hábil; (lived) vivido

experiment /n ɪk'spɛrəmənt; v -ˌmɛnt/ n experimento, m; prueba, f; ensayo, m, tentativa, f. —vi experimentar; hacer una prueba

experimental /ɪk,spɛrə'mɛntl/ a experimental; tentativo

experimentally /ɪk,spɛrə'mɛntli/ adv experimentalmente; por experiencia

expert /'ɛkspɜrt/ a experto; perito; hábil; (finished) acabado. —n experto, m, especialista, mf

expertly /'ɛkspɜrtli/ adv expertamente; hábilmente

expertness /'ɛkspɜrtnɪs/ n pericia, f; maestría, f; habilidad, f; (knowledge) conocimiento, m

expiable /'ɛkspiəbəl/ a que se puede expiar

expiate /'ɛkspiˌeit/ vt expiar; reparar

expiation /ˌɛkspi'eiʃən/ n expiación, f

expiatory /'ɛkspiəˌtɔri/ a expiatorio

expiration /ˌɛkspə'reiʃən/ n (breathing out) espiración, f; (ending) expiración, f; terminación, f; Com. vencimiento, m; (death) muerte, f

expiration date fecha de caducidad, f

expire /ɪk'spaiər/ vi (exhale) espirar; (die) morir, dar el último suspiro; (of fire, light) extinguirse; (end) expirar; terminar; Com. vencer

expiry /ɪk'spaiəri/ n terminación, f; expiración, f; Com. vencimiento, m

explain /ɪk'splein/ vt explicar; aclarar; demostrar; exponer; (justify) justificar, defender. —vi explicarse. **to e. away,** explicar; justificar

explainable /ɪk'spleinəbəl/ a explicable

explanation /ˌɛksplə'neiʃən/ n explicación, f; aclaración, f

explanatory /ɪk'splænəˌtɔri/ a explicativo; aclaratorio

expletive /'ɛksplɪtɪv/ a expletivo. —n interjección, f

explicable /'ɛksplɪkəbəl/ a explicable

explicit /ɪk'splɪsɪt/ a explícito

explode /ɪk'sploud/ vi estallar; detonar; reventar. —vt hacer estallar; (a mine) hacer saltar; (a belief, etc.) hacer abandonar; desechar

exploit /ɪk'splɔit/ n hazaña, proeza, f; aventura, f. —vt explotar

exploitation /ˌɛksplɔi'teiʃən/ n explotación, f

exploiter /ɪk'splɔitər/ n explotador (-ra)

exploration /ˌɛksplə'reiʃən/ n exploración, f

exploratory /ɪk'splɔrəˌtɔri/ a exploratorio

explore /ɪk'splɔr/ vt explorar; examinar; averiguar; investigar; (Med. Surg.) explorar

explorer /ɪk'splɔrər/ n explorador (-ra)

explosion /ɪk'splouʒən/ n explosión, f; estallido, m, detonación, f

explosive /ɪk'splousɪv/ a and n explosivo, m. **high e.,** explosivo violento, m. **explosives chamber,** recámara, f

explosiveness /ɪk'splousɪvnɪs/ n propiedad explosiva, f; lo explosivo; violencia, f

exponent /ɪk'spounənt/ a and n exponente, mf

export /n 'ɛkspɔrt; v ɪk'spɔrt/ n exportación, f. —vt exportar. **e. license,** permiso de exportación, m. **e. trade,** comercio de exportación, m

exportation /ˌɛkspɔr'teiʃən/ n exportación, f

exporter /ɪk'spɔrtər/ n exportador (-ra)

expose /ɪk'spouz/ vt exponer; arriesgar; (exhibit) exhibir; (unmask) desenmascarar; descubrir; revelar; Photo. exponer; (ridicule) ridiculizar

exposed /ɪk'spouzd/ a descubierto; no abrigado; expuesto, peligroso

exposition /ˌɛkspə'zɪʃən/ n explicación, interpretación, f; declaración, f; (exhibition) exposición, f

expostulate /ɪk'spɒstʃəˌleit/ vi protestar, **to e. with,** reprochar; reconvenir

expostulation /ɪk,spɒstʃə'leiʃən/ n protesta, f; reconvención, f

exposure /ɪk'spouʒər/ n exposición, f; (aspect) orientación, f; (scandal) revelación, f, escándalo, m; peligro, m; exposición al frío or al calor, f

expound /ɪk'spaund/ vt exponer, explicar; comentar

expounder /ɪk'spaundər/ n intérprete, mf; comentador (-ra)

express /ɪk'sprɛs/ a (clear) categórico, explícito, claro; expreso; (exact) exacto; (quick) rápido. —n (messenger, post) expreso, m; (train) (tren) expreso, (tren) rápido, m; (goods) exprés, m. —vt expresar; (a letter, etc.) mandar por expreso

expressible /ɪk'sprɛsəbəl/ a decible

expression /ɪk'sprɛʃən/ n expresión, f

expressionless /ɪk'sprɛʃənlɪs/ a sin expresión

expressive /ɪk'sprɛsɪv/ a expresivo; que expresa

expropriate /ɛks'prouprɪˌeit/ vt expropiar

expropriation /ɛks,prouprɪ'eiʃən/ n expropiación, f

expulsion /ɪk'spʌlʃən/ n expulsión, f

expunge /ɪk'spʌndʒ/ vt borrar; testar; omitir

expunging /ɪk'spʌndʒɪŋ/ n borradura, f; testación, f; omisión, f

expurgate /'ɛkspərˌgeit/ vt expurgar

expurgation /ˌɛkspər'geiʃən/ n expurgación, f

expurgator /'ɛkspərˌgeitər/ n expurgador, m

expurgatory /ɪk'spɜrgəˌtɔri/ a expurgatorio

exquisite /ɪk'skwɪzɪt/ a exquisito, precioso, primoroso; excelente; (acute) agudo, intenso; (keen) vivo. —n elegante, petimetre, m

exquisitely /ɪk'skwɪzɪtli/ adv primorosamente, pulcramente; a la perfección

exquisiteness /ɪk'skwɪzɪtnɪs/ n primor, m; pulcritud, perfección, f; excelencia, f; (of pain) intensidad, f; (keenness) viveza, f

ex-serviceman /'ɛks'sɜrvɪsmən/ n excombatiente, antiguo soldado, m

extant /'ɛkstənt/ a estante; existente; viviente

extempore /ɪk'stɛmpəri/ a improvisado

extemporize /ɪk'stɛmpəˌraiz/ vt and vi improvisar

extend /ɪk'stɛnd/ vt extender; (hold out) tender, alargar; (lengthen) prolongar; (a period of time) prorrogar, diferir; (make larger) ensanchar; (increase) aumentar; dilatar; ampliar; (offer) ofrecer; vi extenderse; dilatarse; continuar; (give) dar de sí, estirarse; (last) prolongarse, durar; (become known) propagarse

extensible /ɪk'stɛnsəbəl/ a extensible

extension /ɪk'stɛnʃən/ n extensión, f; expansión, f; (increase) aumento, m; prolongación, f; ampliación, f; Com. prórroga, f; (telephone number) extensión, f, interno, m

extension cord n cordón de extensión, m; ladrón m, (Mexico; slang)

extensive /ɪk'stɛnsɪv/ a extenso, ancho, vasto, grande, considerable; (comprehensive) comprensivo

extensively /ɪk'stɛnsɪvli/ adv extensamente; generalmente

extensiveness /ɪk'stɛnsɪvnɪs/ n extensión, f; amplitud, f

extensor /ɪk'stɛnsər, -sɔr/ n Anat. extensor, m

extent /ɪk'stɛnt/ n extensión, f; (degree) punto, m; (limit) límite, m. **to a great e.,** en gran parte; considerablemente. **to some e.,** hasta cierto punto. **to the full e.,** en toda su extensión; completamente. **to what e.?** ¿hasta qué punto?

extenuate /ɪk'stɛnyuˌeit/ vt atenuar, desminuir, mitigar, paliar

extenuating /ɪk'stɛnyuˌeitɪŋ/ a atenuante

extenuation /ɪk,stɛnyu'eiʃən/ n atenuación, mitigación, f

exterior /ɪk'stɪəriər/ a exterior, externo; de fuera; (foreign) extranjero. —n exterior, m; aspecto, m; forma, f

exterminate /ɪk'stɜrməˌneit/ vt exterminar

extermination /ɪk,stɜrmə'neiʃən/ n exterminio, m

exterminator /ɪk'stɜrməˌneitər/ n exterminador (-ra)

exterminatory /ɪk'stɜrmənə,tɔri/ *a* exterminador
external /ɪk'stɜrnl/ *a* externo, exterior; (foreign) extranjero. —*n pl* **externals**, apariencias, *f pl*; aspecto exterior, *m*; comportamiento, *m*
externally /ɪk'stɜrnli/ *adv* exteriormente
exterritorial /ˌɛkstɛrɪ'tɔriəl/ *a* extraterritorial
exterritoriality /ˌɛkstɛrɪtɔri'ælɪti/ *n* extraterritorialidad, *f*
extinct /ɪk'stɪŋkt/ *a* extinto; (of light, fire) extinguido; suprimido
extinction /ɪk'stɪŋkʃən/ *n* extinción, *f*
extinguish /ɪk'stɪŋgwɪʃ/ *vt* extinguir; apagar; *Fig.* eclipsar
extinguishable /ɪk'stɪŋgwɪʃəbəl/ *a* apagable
extinguisher /ɪk'stɪŋgwɪʃər/ *n* apagador (-ra); (for fires) extintor, *m*; (snuffer) matacandelas, *m*
extinguishment /ɪk'stɪŋgwɪʃmənt/ *n* apagamiento, *m*; extinción, *f*; abolición, *f*; (destruction) aniquilamiento, *m*
extirpate /'ɛkstər,peit/ *vt* extirpar
extirpation /ˌɛkstər'peiʃən/ *n* extirpación, *f*
extol /ɪk'stoul/ *vt* elogiar, encomiar, alabar; cantar
extoller /ɪk'stoulər/ *n* alabador (-ra)
extort /ɪk'stɔrt/ *vt* arrancar, sacar por fuerza; exigir por amenazas
extortion /ɪk'stɔrʃən/ *n* extorsión, *f*; exacción, *f*
extortionate /ɪk'stɔrʃənɪt/ *a* injusto; opresivo; (of price) exorbitante, excesivo
extra /'ɛkstrə/ *a* and *adv* adicional; extraordinario; suplementario; (spare) de repuesto. —*prefix* (in compounds) extra. —*n* extra, *m*; suplemento, *m*; (of a paper) hoja extraordinaria, *f*; (actor) supernumerario (-ia). **e. charge**, gasto suplementario, *m*; (on the railway, etc.) suplemento, *m*. **e.-mural**, *a* de extramuros.
extract /*v* ɪk'strækt; *n* 'ɛkstrækt/ *vt* sacar; (*Chem. Math.*) extraer; extractar; (obtain) obtener. —*n Chem.* extracto, *m*; (excerpt) cita, *f*
extraction /ɪk'strækʃən/ *n* saca, *f*; extracción, *f*; obtención, *f*
extradite /'ɛkstrə,dait/ *vt* entregar por extradición
extradition /ˌɛkstrə'dɪʃən/ *n* extradición, *f*
extraneous /ɪk'streiniəs/ *a* extraño; (irrelevant) ajeno (a)
extraordinarily /ɪk,strɔrdn̩'ɛrəli/ *adv* extraordinariamente, singularmente
extraordinariness /ɪk'strɔrdn̩,ɛrinɪs/ *n* lo extraordinario; singularidad, *f*; (queerness) rareza, *f*
extraordinary /ɪk'strɔrdn̩,ɛri/ *a* extraordinario; singular; (queer) raro, excéntrico; (incredible) increíble
extravagance /ɪk'strævəgəns/ *n* (in spending) prodigalidad, *f*, derroche, *m*; (of dress, speech) extravagancia, *f*; (foolishness) disparate, *m*; (luxury) lujo, *m*
extravagant /ɪk'strævəgənt/ *a* extravagante; (queer) extraño, raro; (wasteful) pródigo; (of persons) gastador, manirroto; (of price) exorbitante; excesivo
extravagantly /ɪk'strævəgəntli/ *adv* extravagantemente; de un modo extraño; pródigamente; profusamente; excesivamente
extreme /ɪk'strim/ *a* extremo. —*n* extremo, *m*. **in e.**, extremamente, en extremo, en sumo grado. **to carry**

to extremes, llevar a extremos; **E. Unction,** Extremaunción, *f*
extremely /ɪk'strimli/ *adv* sumamente; *Inf.* muy
extremism /ɪk'stri,mɪzəm/ *n* extremismo, *m*
extremist /ɪk'strimɪst/ *a* and *n* extremista, *mf*
extremity /ɪk'stremɪti/ *n* extremidad, *f*; (point) punta, *f*; necesidad, *f*; *pl* **extremities,** *Anat.* extremidades, *f pl*; (measures) medidas extremas, *f pl*
extricate /'ɛkstrɪ,keit/ *vt* desenredar; librar; sacar
extrication /ˌɛkstrɪ'keiʃən/ *n* liberación, *f*
extrinsic /ɪk'strɪnsɪk/ *a* extrínseco
extrovert /'ɛkstrə,vɜrt/ *n Psychol.* extravertido, *m*
exuberance /ɪg'zubərəns/ *n* exuberancia, *f*
exuberant /ɪg'zubərənt/ *a* exuberante
exudation /ˌɛksyu'deiʃən/ *n* exudación, *f*
exude /ɪg'zud/ *vt* exudar; rezumar; sudar. —*vi* exudar; rezumarse
exult /ɪg'zʌlt/ *vi* exultar; alegrarse
exultant /ɪg'zʌltn̩t/ *a* exultante, triunfante
exultantly /ɪg'zʌltn̩tli/ *adv* con exultación; triunfalmente
exultation /ˌɛgzʌl'teiʃən/ *n* exultación, *f*; triunfo, *m*
eye /ai/ *n* ojo, *m*; (sight) vista, *f*; (look) mirada, *f*; atención, *f*; (opinion) opinión, *f*, juicio, *m*; (of a needle, of cheese) ojo, *m*; (of a hook) corcheta, *f*; *Bot.* yema, *f*; (of a potato) grillo, *m*. —*vt* ojear; fijar los ojos en; examinar, mirar detenidamente. **bright eyes,** ojos vivos, *m pl.* **prominent eyes,** ojos saltones, *m pl.* **He couldn't keep his eyes off Mary,** Se le fueron los ojos tras María. **as far as the eye can reach,** hasta donde alcanza la vista. **before one's eyes,** a la vista de uno, ante los ojos de uno. **in my (etc.) eyes,** *Fig.* según creo yo, en mi opinión. **in the twinkling of an eye,** en un abrir y cerrar de ojos. **with an eye to,** pensando en. **with my own eyes,** con mis propios ojos. **with the naked eye,** con la simple vista. **to keep an eye on,** vigilar. **to make eyes at,** guiñar el ojo; mirar con ojos de enamorado. **to have one's eyes opened,** *Fig.* caérsele la venda. **eye-bath,** ojera, *f.* **eye-opener,** revelación, sorpresa, *f.* **eye-pencil,** pincel para las cejas, *m.* **eye-piece,** objetivo, ocular, *m.* **eye-shade,** visera, *f.* **eye-tooth,** colmillo, *m.* **eye-witness,** testigo ocular, testigo de vista, testigo presencial, *mf*
eyeball /'ai,bɔl/ *n* globo ocular, *m*
eyebrow /'ai,brau/ *n* ceja, *f*
eye care atención de la vista, *f*
eyed /aid/ *a* que tiene ojos; (in compounds) de ojos..., con ojos...; con los ojos; (of a needle) con el ojo... **She is a blue-eyed child,** Es una niña de ojos azules
eyeglass /'ai,glæs/ *n* lente, *m*
eyelash /'ai,læʃ/ *n* pestaña, *f*
eyeless /'ailɪs/ *a* sin ojos
eyelet /'ailɪt/ *n* ojete, *m*
eyelid /'ai,lɪd/ *n* párpado, *m*
eyesight /'ai,sait/ *n* vista, *f*
eyewash /'ai,wɒʃ/ *n* colirio, *m*; *Inf.* camelo, *m.* **That's all e.!** ¡Eso es un camelo!
eyrie /'ɛəri/ *n* nido (of any bird of prey), nido de águila (eagle's) *m*

F

f /ɛf/ n (letter) efe, f; Mus. fa, m. **f sharp,** fa sostenido, m

fa /fɑ/ n Mus. fa, m

fable /'feibəl/ n fábula, leyenda, historia, f, apólogo, cuento, m; (untruth) invención, mentira, f

fabled /'feibəld/ a celebrado, famoso

fabric /'fæbrɪk/ n obra, fábrica, f; estructura, construcción, f; (making) manufactura, f; (cloth) tejido, paño, m; textura, f

fabricate /'fæbrɪ,keit/ vt fabricar, construir; (invent) fingir, inventar

fabrication /,fæbrɪ'keiʃən/ n fabricación, manufactura, f; construcción, f; (lie) invención, ficción, f

fabulist /'fæbyəlɪst/ n fabulista, mf

fabulous /'fæbyələs/ a fabuloso

fabulousness /'fæbyələsnɪs/ n fabulosidad, f

façade /fə'sɑd/ n fachada, frente, f

face /feis/ n superficie, f; (of persons) cara, f, rostro, m; (look) semblante, aire, m; (of coins) anverso, m; (grimace) mueca, f, gesto, m; (dial) esfera, f; (of gems) faceta, f; (of a wall) paramento, m; (front) fachada, frente, f; (effrontery) cara dura, f, descaro, m. **in the f. of,** ante; en presencia de. Mil. **Left f.!** ¡Izquierda! **on the f. of it,** juzgando por las apariencias. **to bring f. to f.,** confrontar (con). **to laugh in a person's f.,** reírse a la cara (de). **to make a f.,** hacer muecas. **to my f.,** en mi cara, en mis barbas. **to put a good f. on,** Fig. poner (or hacer) buena cara a. **to set one's f. against,** oponerse resueltamente a. **to straighten one's f.,** componer el semblante. **to throw in one's f.,** Fig. dar en rostro, dar en cara. **to wash one's f.,** lavarse la cara. **f. card,** figura (de la baraja), f. **f.-cloth,** paño para lavar la cara, m. **f. downward,** boca abajo. **f. lift,** operación estética facial, f. **f. of the waters,** faz de las aguas, f. **f. powder,** polvos de arroz, m pl. **f. to f.,** cara a cara, de persona a persona; frente a frente. **f. value,** significado literal, m; Com. valor nominal, m

face /feis/ vt mirar hacia; confrontar, hacer cara (a); (of buildings, etc.) mirar a, caer a (or hacia); Fig. arrostrar, enfrentarse con; Sew. guarnecer, aforrar. —vi estar orientado. **to f. the facts,** enfrentarse con la realidad. **to f. the music,** Fig. arrostrar las consecuencias. **to f. about,** volver la espalda; Mil. dar una vuelta, cambiar de frente. **to f. up to,** Fig. hacer cara a

faced /feist/ a con cara..., de cara...; Sew. forrado (de). **to be two-f.,** Fig. ser de dos haces

facer /'feisər/ n puñetazo en la cara, m; Fig. dificultad insuperable, f, problema muy grande, m

facet /'fæsɪt/ n faceta, f

facetious /fə'siʃəs/ a chancero, chistoso, jocoso

facetiousness /fə'siʃəsnɪs/ n jocosidad, festividad, f

facial /'feiʃəl/ a facial. **f. expression,** expresión de la cara, f, semblante, m

facile /'fæsɪl/ a (frivolous) ligero (e.g., a deduction or inference)

facilitate /fə'sɪlɪ,teit/ vt facilitar

facilitation /fə,sɪlɪ'teiʃən/ n facilitación, f

facility /fə'sɪlɪti/ n facilidad, f; habilidad, destreza, f

facing /'feisɪŋ/ n Sew. vuelta, f; (of a building) paramento, m; (of lumber) chapa f; encaramiento, m

facsimile /fæk'sɪməli/ n facsímile, m

fact /fækt/ n (event) hecho, suceso, m; (datum) dato, m; realidad, verdad, f. **as a matter of f.,** en realidad. **in f.,** en efecto, en realidad. **I know as a f.,** Tengo por cierto. **The f. is...,** La verdad es (que)... **the f. that,** el hecho de que

fact-finding /'fækt ,faindɪŋ/ informador (e.g. send s.b. on a fact-finding mission, enviar a fulano en misión informadora)

faction /'fækʃən/ n facción, f, partido, bando, m; (tumult) alboroto, m

factional /'fækʃənļ/ a partidario

factious /'fækʃəs/ a faccioso, sedicioso

factiousness /'fækʃəsnɪs/ n espíritu de facción, m; rebeldía, f

factitious /fæk'tɪʃəs/ a falso; artificial

factor /'fæktər/ n (fact) factor, elemento, m; consideración, f; Math. factor, m; Com. agente, factor, m

factory /'fæktəri/ n fábrica, manufactura, f; taller, m. **F. Act,** ley de trabajadores industriales, f. **f. hand,** operario (-ia)

factotum /fæk'toutəm/ n factótum, m

factual /'fæktʃuəl/ a basado en hechos, objetivo

faculty /'fækəlti/ n facultad, f; (talent) habilidad, f, talento, m; (university division) facultad, f; (teachers as a group) claustro de profesores, claustro, profesorado, m; (authorization) privilegio, m, autoridad, f

fad /fæd/ n capricho, m, chifladura, f, dengue, m

faddiness /'fædinɪs/ n manías, f pl, excentricidad, f

faddist /'fædɪst/ n chiflado (-da)

faddy /'fædi/ a caprichoso, dengoso, difícil, excéntrico

fade /feid/ vi (of plants) marchitarse, secarse; (of color) palidecer, descolorarse; (vanish) disiparse, desaparecer; (of persons) desmejorarse; (of stains) salir. —vt descolorar. **to f. away,** desvanecer; (of persons) consumirse. **f.-out,** n (cinema) desaparecimiento gradual, m

faded /'feidɪd/ a (of plants) seco, marchito, mustio; (of colors) descolorado, pálido; (of people) desmejorado

fadeless /'feidlɪs/ a de colores resistentes; eterno, no olvidado; siempre joven

fading /'feidɪŋ/ a que palidece; (of flowers) medio marchito; (of light) mortecino, pálido; decadente. —n desaparecimiento, m, marchitez, f; decadencia, f

fag /fæg/ n Inf. pitillo, m. **f.-end,** fin, m; restos, m pl, sobras, f pl; (of a cigarette) colilla, f; (offensive) maricón. —vi trabajar mucho. —vt fatigar mucho; hacer trabajar

faggot /'fægət/ n haz (or gavilla) de leña, f

faience /fai'ɑns/ n fayenza, f

fail /feil/ vi faltar; fracasar, malograrse; no tener éxito, salir mal; (of strength) decaer, acabarse; (be short of) carecer (de); Com. hacer bancarrota, suspender pagos. —vt abandonar; (disappoint) decepcionar, engañar; (in exams) suspender. **Do not f. to see her,** No dejes de verla. **He failed to do his duty,** Faltó a su deber

fail /feil/ n **without f.,** sin falta

failing /'feilɪŋ/ n falta, f; (shortcoming) vicio, flaco, m, debilidad, f; malogro, fracaso, m; decadencia, f

failure /'feilyər/ n fracaso, m; falta de éxito, f; (in exams) suspensión, f; (of power) no funcionamiento, m; omisión, f, descuido, m; Com. quiebra, bancarrota, f; (decay) decadencia, f. **on f. of,** al fracasar; bajo pena de

fain /fein/ a deseoso, muy contento. **He was f. to...,** Se sintió obligado a...; Quería

faint /feint/ a débil; (dim) indistinto, vago, borroso; (of colors) pálido, desmayado; (weak) lánguido, desfallecido; (slight) superficial, rudimentario. —vi perder el sentido, desmayarse. —n desmayo, m. **to be f. with hunger,** estar muerto de hambre. **to cause to f.,** hacer desmayar. **f.-hearted,** pusilánime, medroso. **f.-heartedness,** pusilanimidad, f

faintly /'feintli/ adv débilmente; en voz débil; indistintamente

faintness /'feintnɪs/ n languidez, debilidad, f; (swoon) desmayo, m; lo indistinto; lo borroso

fair /fɛər/ n feria, f; (sale) mercado, m; (exhibition) exposición, f

fair /fɛər/ a (beautiful) hermoso, lindo, bello; (of hair) rubio; (of skin) blanco; (clear, fresh) limpio, claro; (good) bueno; (favorable) favorable, propicio, próspero; (of weather) despejado, sereno; (just) imparcial; (straightforward) honrado, recto, justo; (passable) regular, mediano; (of writing) legible; (proper) conveniente. —adv honradamente; (politely) cortésmente; exactamente. **by f. means,** por medios honrados. **It's not f.!** ¡No hay derecho! **to become f.,** (of weather) serenarse. **to give a f. trial,** juzgar imparcialmente; dar una buena oportunidad; *Law.* procesar imparcialmente. **to make a f. copy,** poner en limpio. **f.-haired,** de pelo rubio, rubio. **f. one,** una beldad, *f.* **f. play,** *Sports.* juego limpio, *m;* proceder leal, *m.* **f.-skinned,** de tez blanca, rubio. **f.-weather,** buen tiempo, *m,* bonanza, *f.* **f.-weather friends,** amigos de los días prósperos, *m pl*

fairing /'fɛərɪŋ/ *n Brit* regalo de feria, *m.* **to give fairings,** feriar

fairly /'fɛərli/ *adv* (justly) con imparcialidad; (moderately) bastante; totalmente, enteramente. **f. good,** bastante bueno; regular

fairness /'fɛərnɪs/ *n* belleza, hermosura, *f;* (of skin) blancura, *f;* (justness) imparcialidad, *f;* (reasonableness) justicia, equidad, *f;* (of hair) color rubio, oro, *m*

fairway /'fɛər,wei/ *n Naut.* canalizo, paso, *m;* (golf) terreno sin obstáculos, *m*

fairy /'fɛəri/ *n* hada, *f,* duende, *m.* —*a* de hada, de duendes; *Fig.* delicado. **f.-gold,** tesoro de duendes, *m;* **f.-light,** lucecillo, *m;* luminaria, *f.* **f.-like,** aduendado, como una hada. **f.-ring,** círculo mágico, *m.* **f.-tale,** cuento de hadas, *m;* patraña, *f,* cuento de viejas, *m*

fairyland /'fɛəri,lænd/ *n* país de las hadas, *m*

faith /feiθ/ *n* fe, *f;* confianza, *f;* (doctrine) creencia, religión, filosofía, *f;* (honor) palabra, *f.* **in good f.,** de buena fe. **to break f.,** faltar a la palabra dada. **f.-healing,** curanderismo, *m*

faithful /'feiθfəl/ *a* fiel, leal; (accurate) exacto; (trustworthy) veraz. **the f.,** los creyentes

faithfully /'feiθfəli/ *adv* fielmente, lealmente; (accurately) con exactitud. **Yours f.,** Queda de Vd. su att. s.s.

faithfulness /'feiθfəlnɪs/ *n* fidelidad, lealtad, *f;* (accuracy) exactitud, *f*

faithless /'feiθlɪs/ *a* infiel, desleal, pérfido.

faithlessness /'feiθlɪsnɪs/ *n* infidelidad, deslealtad, traición, *f*

fake /feik/ *vt* imitar, falsificar. —*n* imitación, falsificación, *f.* **to f. up,** inventar

Falangist /fei'lɑndʒɪst/ *a and n* falangista *mf*

falcon /'fɔlkən/ *n* halcón, *m.* **f. gentle,** *Ornith.* neblí, *m*

falconer /'fɔlkənər/ *n* halconero, *m*

falconry /'fɔlkənri/ *n* cetrería, *f*

fall /fɔl/ *n* caída, *f;* (of temperature, mercury) baja, *f;* (of water) salto de agua, *m,* catarata, cascada, *f;* (in value) depreciación, *f;* (in price and Stock Exchange) baja, *f;* (descent) bajada, *f;* (autumn) otoño, *m;* (declivity) declinación, *f,* declive, desnivel, *m;* (ruin) ruina, *f;* destrucción, *f;* (of night, etc.) caída (de la noche), *f;* (of snow) nevada, *f;* (of rain) golpe, *m;* (*Theat.* of curtain) caída, bajada, *f;* (surrender) capitulación, rendición, *f;* (of earth) desprendimiento de tierras, *m;* (of the tide) reflujo, *m*

fall /fɔl/ *vi* caer; (of mercury, temperature) bajar; (collapse) desplomarse, hundirse, derrumbarse; (die) caer muerto; (descend) descender; (*Theat.* of the curtain) bajar, caer; (of a river into the sea, etc.) desembocar, desaguar; (of hair, draperies) caer; (decrease) disminuir; (of spirits) ponerse triste, sentirse deprimido; (sin) caer; (come upon) sobrevenir; (of dusk, etc.) caer, llegar; (strike, touch) tocar; (as a share) tocar en suerte; (as a duty, responsibility) tocar, corresponder; (of seasons) caer en; (of words from the lips) caer de (los labios); (say) decir, pronunciar palabras; (of exclamations) escaparse; (become) venir a ser; (happen) suceder; (be) caer. **fallen upon evil days,** venido a menos. **His face fell,** Puso una cara de desengaño. **Christmas falls on a Thursday this year,** Navidad cae en jueves este año. **to let f.,** dejar caer. **to f. a-** (followed by verb) empezar a. **He fell a-crying,** Empezó a llorar. **to f. again,** volver a caer, recaer. **to f. among,** caer entre. **to f. astern,** quedarse atrás. **to f. away,** (leave) abandonar, dejar; (grow thin) enflaquecer; marchitarse; (crumble) desmoronarse. **to f. back,** retroceder, volver hacia atrás. **to f. back upon,** recurrir a; *Mil.* replegarse hacia. **to f. backward,** caer de espaldas,

caer hacia atrás. **to f. behind,** quedarse atrás. **to f. down,** venirse a tierra; venirse abajo, dar consigo en el suelo, caer. **to f. due,** vencer. **to f. flat,** caer de bruces; (be unsuccessful) no tener éxito. **to f. in,** caer en; (collapse) desplomarse; *Mil.* alinearse; (expire) vencer. **to f. into,** caer en. **to f. in with,** tropezar con; reunirse con, juntarse con; (agree) convenir en; **to f. off,** caer de; (of leaves, etc.) desprenderse de, separarse de; (abandon) abandonar; (diminish) disminuir. **to f. on,** caer de (e.g. *to f. on one's back,* caer de espaldas); (of seasons) caer en; (attack) echarse encima de, atacar. **to f. out,** (of a window, etc.) caer por; (happen) acontecer, suceder; (quarrel) pelearse, reñir; *Mil.* romper filas. **to f. out with,** reñir con. **to f. over,** volcar, caer; (stumble) tropezar con. **to f. short,** faltar; carecer, ser deficiente; (fail) malograrse, no llegar a sus expectaciones; (of shooting) errar el tiro. **to f. through,** caer por; (fail) malograrse, fracasar. **to f. to,** empezar a, ponerse a; (be incumbent on) tocar a, corresponder a; (attack) atacar. **to f. under,** caer debajo; caer bajo; sucumbir, perecer; (incur) incurrir en, merecer. **to f. upon,** (attack) caer sobre, acometer; acaecer, tener lugar; (be incumbent) tocar a

fallacious /fə'leiʃəs/ *a* falaz, engañoso, ilusorio

fallaciousness /fə'leiʃəsnɪs/ *n* falacia, *f,* engaño, *m*

fallacy /'fæləsi/ *n* error, *m,* ilusión, *f*

fallen /'fɔlən/ *a* caído; arruinado; degradado. **f. angel,** ángel caído, *m.* **f. woman,** perdida, mujer caída, *f*

fallibility /,fælə'bɪlɪti/ *n* falibilidad, *f*

fallible /'fæləbəl/ *a* falible

falling /'fɔlɪŋ/ *a* que cae, cayente. —*n* caída, *f;* (of mercury, temperature) baja, *f;* (crumbling) desmoronamiento, *m;* (collapse) hundimiento, derrumbamiento, *m;* (of tide) reflujo, *m;* (of waterlevel) bajada, *f;* (in value) depreciación, *f;* (of prices and Stock Exchange) baja, *f;* (diminishment) disminución, *f;* (in level of earth) declinación, *f; (Com.* expiry) vencimiento, *m; (Theat.* of curtain) bajada, caída, *f.* **f. away,** (crumbling) desmoronamiento, *m;* desprendimiento de tierras, *m;* (desertion) deserción, *f,* abandono, *m.* **f. back,** retirada, *f,* retroceso, *m.* **f. down,** caída, *f;* derrumbamiento, *m.* **f. due,** vencimiento, *m.* **f. in,** hundimiento, *m;* (crumbling) desmoronamiento, *m.* **f. off,** caída de, *f;* (disappearance) desaparición, *f;* (diminution) disminución, *f;* (deterioration) deterioración, *f.* **f. out,** caída por, *f;* disensión, *f.* **f. short,** falta, *f;* carácter inferior, *m;* frustración, *f.* **f. star,** estrella fugaz, *f*

fallout /'fɔl,aut/ caída radiactiva, llovizna radiactiva, precipitación radiactiva, *f*

fallow /'fælou/ *a* (of color) leonado; *Agr.* barbechado; descuidado. —*n* barbecho, *m.* —*vt* barbechar. **to leave f.,** dejar en barbecho. **f. deer,** corzo (-za)

false /fɔls/ *a* incorrecto, erróneo, equivocado; falso; (unfounded) infundado; (disloyal) infiel, traidor, desleal; (not real) postizo; artificial; de imitación; *Mus.* desafinado; (pretended) fingido; engañoso, mentiroso. **to play a person f.,** traicionar (a). **f. bottom,** fondo doble, *m;* **f. claim,** pretensión infundada, *f.* **f. door,** surtida, *f.* **f.-hearted,** pérfido, desleal. **f. teeth,** dientes postizos, *m pl,* dentadura postiza, *f*

falsehood /'fɔlshʊd/ *n* mentira, *f*

falseness /'fɔlsnɪs/ *n* falsedad, *f;* (disloyalty) duplicidad, perfidia, traición, *f*

falsetto /fɔl'sɛtou/ *n* falsete, *m,* voz de cabeza, *f*

falsification /,fɔlsəfɪ'keiʃən/ *n* falsificación, *f;* (of texts) corrupción, *f*

falsifier /'fɔlsəfaiər/ *n* falsificador (-ra)

falsify /'fɔlsəfai/ *vt* falsear, falsificar; (disappoint) defraudar, frustrar, contrariar

falter /'fɔltər/ *vi* (physically) titubear; (of speech) balbucir, tartamudear; (of action) vacilar. **to f. out,** balbucir; hablar con voz entrecortada; decir con vacilación

faltering /'fɔltərɪŋ/ *a* titubeante; (of speech) entrecortado; vacilante. —*n* temblor, *m;* vacilación, *f*

falteringly /'fɔltərɪŋli/ *adv* (of speech) balbuciente, en una voz temblorosa; con dificultad, vacilantemente

fame /feim/ n fama, f; reputación, f; (renown) celebridad, f, renombre, m. **of ill f.,** de mala fama

famed /feimd/ a reputado; renombrado, célebre, famoso

familiar /fə'mɪlyər/ a íntimo, familiar; afable, amistoso; (ill-bred) insolente, demasiado familiar; (usual) corriente, usual, común; conocido. —n amigo (-ga) íntimo (-ma); Eccl. familiar, m; demonio familiar, m. **to be f. with,** (a subject) estar versado en, conocer muy bien; (a person) tratar con familiaridad. **to become f. with,** acostumbrarse a; familiarizarse con; (a person) hacerse íntimo de

familiarity /fə,mɪli'æriti/ n intimidad, familiaridad, confianza, f; (friendliness) afabilidad, f; (overfamiliarity) insolencia, demasiada familiaridad, f; (with a subject) conocimiento (de), m, experiencia (de), f

familiarize /fə'mɪlyə,raiz/ vt familiarizar, acostumbrar, habituar. —vr familiarizarse

familiarly /fə'mɪlyərli/ adv familiarmente; amistosamente

family /'fæməli/ n familia, f; (lineage) linaje, abolengo, m; (Bot. Zool.) familia, f; (of languages) grupo, m. —a de familia; familiar; casero. **f. doctor,** médico de cabecera, m. **f. life,** vida de familia, f; hogar, m. **f. man,** padre de familia, m. **f. name,** apellido, m. **f. seat,** casa solar, f. **f. tree,** árbol genealógico, m

family quarrel disputa de familia, f

famine /'fæmɪn/ n hambre, f; carestía, escasez, f

famish /'fæmɪʃ/ vt matar de hambre. —vi morirse de hambre

famished /'fæmɪʃt/ a hambriento

famous /'feiməs/ a famoso, célebre, renombrado; insigne, distinguido; Inf. excelente

famously /'feiməsli/ adv Inf. muy bien, excelentemente

fan /fæn/ n abanico, m; Agr. aventador, m; Mech. ventilador, m; (on a windmill) volante, m; (amateur) aficionado (-da); (admirer) admirador (-ra); Archit. abanico, m. —vt abanicar; Agr. aventar; ventilar. **fan oneself,** hacerse viento. **tap with a f.,** abanicazo, golpecito con el abanico, m. **f.-belt,** Mech. correa de transmisión del ventilador, f. **f.-light,** tragaluz, m. **f. maker** or **seller,** abaniquero (-ra). **f.-shaped,** en abanico, abanicado, en forma de abanico

fanatic /fə'nætɪk/ a and n fanático (-ca)

fanaticism /fə'nætə,sɪzəm/ n fanatismo, m

fanaticize /fə'nætə,saiz/ vt fanatizar

fancied /'fænsid/ a imaginario

fancier /'fænsiər/ n aficionado (-da); (of animals) criador (-ra)

fanciful /'fænsɪfəl/ a romántico, caprichoso; fantástico

fancifulness /'fænsɪfəlnɪs/ n extravagancia, f; romanticismo, m

fancy /'fænsi/ n fantasía, imaginación, f; (idea) idea, f, ensueño, m; (caprice) capricho, antojo, m; (liking) afecto, cariño, m; gusto, m, afición, f; (wish) deseo, m; (fantasy) quimera, f, a imaginario; elegante, ornado; Com. de capricho, de fantasía; fantástico, extravagante. —vt imaginar, figurarse; (like) gustar de; aficionarse a; antojarse. **I have a f. for...,** Se me antoja.... **Just f.!** ¡Toma! ¡Quia! ¡Parece mentira! **to take a f. to,** (things) tomar afición a; (people) tomar cariño (a). **f.-dress,** disfraz, m. **f.-dress ball,** baile de trajes, m

fancy goods n pl artículos suntuarios m pl

fane /fein/ n templo, m

fanfare /'fænfeər/ n tocata de trompetas, f

fang /fæŋ/ n colmillo, m; raíz de un diente, f

fanged /fæŋd/ a que tiene colmillos; (of teeth) acolmillado

fangless /'fæŋlɪs/ a sin colmillos

fanner /'fænər/ n abanicador (-ra); Agr. aventador, m

fanning /'fænɪŋ/ n abaniqueo, m; Agr. avienta, f

fantastic /fæn'tæstɪk/ a fantástico; extravagante

fantastically /fæn'tæstɪkəli/ adv fantásticamente; extravagantemente

fantasy /'fæntəsi/ n imaginación, f; fantasía, quimera, visión, f; creación imaginativa, f

far /fɑr/ adv lejos; a lo lejos; (much, greatly) mucho,

en alto grado; (very) muy; (mostly) en gran parte. —a lejano, distante; (farther) ulterior. **as far as,** tan lejos como; (up to, until) hasta; en cuanto, por lo que, según que. (e.g. As far as we know, Por lo que nosotros sepamos. As far as we are concerned, En cuanto a nosotros toca). **by far,** con mucho. **from far and near,** de todas partes. **from far off,** desde lejos. **He read far into the night,** Leyó hasta las altas horas de la noche. **how far?** ¿a qué distancia?; (to what extent) ¿hasta qué punto? ¿hasta dónde? **How far is it to...?** ¿Qué distancia hay a...? **in so far as,** en tanto que. **on the far side,** al lado opuesto; al otro extremo. **so far,** tan lejos; (till now) hasta ahora. **to go far,** ir lejos. **far away,** a distante, remoto, lejano; Fig. abstraído. —adv muy lejos. **far beyond,** mucho más allá. **far-fetched,** increíble, improbable. **far-off,** a distante. —adv a lo lejos, en lontananza. **far-reaching,** de gran alcance. **far-sighted,** sagaz, presciente, previsor. **far-sightedness,** sagacidad, previsión, f

farce /fɑrs/ n farsa, f. —vt Cul. embutir, rellenar

farcical /'fɑrsɪkəl/ a burlesco, cómico, sainetesco; absurdo, grotesco, ridículo

fare /feər/ n (price) pasaje, precio del billete, m; (traveler) viajero (-ra), pasajero (-ra); (food) comida, f. —vi pasarlo (e.g. to f. well, pasarlo bien). **bill of f.,** menú, m. **full f.,** billete entero, m. **f. stage,** trayecto, m

farewell /,feər'wel/ n despedida, f, adiós, m. —a de despedida. —interj ¡adiós! ¡quede Vd. con Dios! **to bid f. to,** despedirse de

farewell address n discurso de despedida m

farflung /'fɑr'flʌŋ/ de gran alcance, extenso, vasto; (empire) dilatado

farina /fə'rinə/ n harina (de cereales), f; Chem. fécula, f, almidón, m; Bot. polen, m

farm /fɑrm/ n granja, hacienda, quintería, finca, chacra, f, cortijo, m. —vt cultivar, labrar (la tierra); (taxes) arrendar. —vi ser granjero. **to f. out,** (taxes) dar en arriendo. **f. girl,** labradora, f. **f. house,** alquería, casa de labranza, granja, f. **f. laborer,** labriego, peón, m. **f. yard,** corral de una granja, m

farmer /'fɑrmər/ n granjero, hacendado, quintero, m, agrícola, mf; (small) colono, labrador, m; (of taxes) arrendatario, m

farmhand /'fɑrm,hænd/ gañán, mozo, mozo de granja, peón m

farming /'fɑrmɪŋ/ n labranza, f, cultivo, m; agricultura, labor agrícola, f; (of taxes) arriendo, m. —a de labranza, labradoril; agrícola

faro /'feərou/ n (card game) faraón, m

farouche /fə'ruʃ/ a huraño, esquivo

farrago /fə'rɑgou/ n fárrago, m, mezcla, f

farrier /'færiər/ n herrador, m

farther /'fɑrðər/ adv más lejos; (beyond) más adelante; (besides) además. —a ulterior; más distante. **at the f. end,** al otro extremo; en el fondo. **f. on,** más adelante; más allá

farthest /'fɑrðɪst/ adv más lejos. —a más lejano, más distante; extremo

farthing /'fɑrðɪŋ/ n cuarto, m; Fig. ardite, maravedí, m. **He hasn't a brass f.,** No tiene dos maravedís

fasces /'fæsiz/ n pl fasces, f pl

fascicle /'fæsɪkəl/ n Bot. hacecillo, m

fascinate /'fæsə,neit/ vt fascinar; encantar, hechizar, seducir

fascinating /'fæsə,neitɪŋ/ a fascinador; encantador, seduciente

fascination /,fæsə'neiʃən/ n fascinación, f; encanto, hechizo, m

Fascism /'fæʃ,ɪzəm/ n fascismo, m

Fascist /'fæʃɪst/ a and n fascista mf

fashion /'fæʃən/ n (form) forma, hechura, f; (way) modo, m; (custom) costumbre, f, uso, m; (vogue) moda, f; (high life) alta sociedad, f; (tone) buen tono, m. —vt hacer, labrar; inventar. **in Spanish f.,** a la española, al uso de España. **the latest f.,** la última moda. **to be in f.,** estar de moda. **to go out of f.,** dejar de ser de moda, perder la popularidad. **f. book,** revista de modas, f. **f. plate,** figurín, m

fashionable /'fæʃənəbəl/ a de moda; elegante; de

buen tono. **to be f.**, estar en boga, ser de moda. **f. world,** mundo elegante, mundo de sociedad, *m*

fashionableness /'fæʃənəbəlnıs/ *n* buen tono, *m;* elegancia, *f*

fashionably /'fæʃənəbli/ *adv* a la moda, elegantemente

fashion show desfile de modas, *m,* exhibición de modas, *f*

fast /fæst/ *a* (firm) firme; (secure) seguro; (strong) fuerte; (fixed) fijo; (closed) cerrado; (of boats) amarrado; (tight) apretado; (of colors) estable; (of trains) rápido; (of sleep) profundo; (of friends) leal, seguro; (quick) rápido, veloz; (of a watch) adelantado; (dissipated) disoluto. —*adv* firmemente, seguramente; (quickly) rápidamente; (of sleep) profundamente; (tightly) estrechamente, apretadamente; (of rain) (llover) a cántaros; (ceaselessly) continuamente; (often) frecuentemente; (entirely) completamente. **to be f.**, (clocks) adelantar. **to make f.**, *Naut.* amarrar, trincar. **f. asleep**, profundamente dormido. **f. color,** color estable, color sólido, *m*

fast /fæst/ *n* ayuno, *m, vi* ayunar. **to break one's f.,** romper el ayuno. **f.-day,** día de ayuno, día de vigilia, *m*

fasten /'fæsən/ *vt* (tie) atar; (fix) fijar; sujetar; (stick) pegar; (a door) cerrar; (bolt) echar el cerrojo; *Naut.* trincar; (together) juntar, unir; (with buttons, hooks, etc.) abrochar; (on, upon) fijar en; *Fig.* imputar (a). —*vi* fijarse; pegarse; (upon) agarrarse a, asir. **to f. one's eyes on,** fijar los ojos en. **to f. up,** cerrar; atar; (nail) clavar

fastener /'fæsənər/ *n* (bolt) pasador, *m;* (for bags, jewelery, etc.) cierre, *m;* (buckle) hebilla, *f;* (of a coat, etc.) tiador, *m;* (of a book, file) sujetador, *m;* (lock) cerrojo, *m.* **paper-f.,** sujetador de papeles, *m.* **patent-f.,** botón automático, *m*

fastening /'fæsənıŋ/ *n* atadura, *f;* sujeción, *f,* afianzamiento, *m;* (together) union, *f;* (of a garment) brochadura, *f;* (of a handbag) cierre, *m*

fastidious /fæ'stıdiəs/ *a* dengoso, melindroso, desdeñoso; (sensitive) sensitivo, delicado; (critical) discerniente, crítico

fastidiously /fæs'tıdiəsli/ *adv* melindrosamente

fastidiousness /fæs'tıdiəsnıs/ *n* dengues, melindres, *m pl,* nimiedad, *f,* desdén, *m;* sensibilidad, delicadeza, *f;* sentido crítico, *m*

fasting /'fæstıŋ/ *n* ayuno, *m.* —*a and part* de ayuno; en ayunas

fastness /'fæstnıs/ *n* firmeza, solidez, *f;* (stronghold) fortaleza, *f;* (retreat) refugio, *m;* (speed) velocidad, rapidez, *f;* (dissipation) disipación, *f,* libertinaje, *m*

fat /fæt/ *a* (stout) gordo, grueso; mantecoso, graso, seboso; (greasy) grasiento; (rich) fértil, pingüe; (productive) lucrativo. —*n* (stoutness) gordura, *f;* (for cooking) manteca, *f;* (lard) lardo, *m;* (of animal or meat) grasa, *f;* sebo, saín, *m; Fig.* riqueza, *f; Fig.* fertilidad, *f.* **to grow fat,** engordarse, ponerse grueso

fatal /'feıtl/ *a* fatal, mortal; funesto

fatalism /'feıtl̩ˌızəm/ *n* fatalismo, *m*

fatalist /'feıtlıst/ *n* fatalista, *mf*

fatalistic /ˌfeıtl'ıstık/ *a* fatalista

fatality /feı'tælıti/ *n* fatalidad, *f;* infortunio, *m,* calamidad, *f;* muerte, *f*

fatally /'feıtl̩i/ *adv* mortalmente, fatalmente; inevitablemente

fate /feıt/ *n* destino, sino, hado, *m,* providencia, *f;* fortuna, suerte, *f;* destrucción, ruina, *f;* muerte, *f.* **the Three Fates,** las Parcas

fated /'feıtıd/ *a* fatal, destinado; predestinado

fateful /'feıtfəl/ *a* decisivo, fatal; aciago, ominoso

father /'faðər/ *n* padre, *m.* —*vt* prohijar, adoptar; (on or upon) atribuir (a), imputar (a). **Eternal F.,** Padre Eterno, *m.* **Holy F.,** Padre Santo, *m.* **indulgent f.,** padre indulgente, padrazo, *m.* **Like f. like son,** De tal palo tal astilla. **f. confessor,** *Eccl.* director espiritual, *m.* **f.-in-law,** suegro, *m*

fatherhood /'faðərˌhʊd/ *n* paternidad, *f*

fatherland /'faðərˌlænd/ *n* patria, madre patria, *f*

fatherless /'faðərlıs/ *a* sin padre, huérfano de padre

fatherliness /'faðərlinıs/ *n* amor paternal, *m;* sentimiento paternal, *m*

fatherly /'faðərli/ *a* paternal, de padre

fathom /'fæðəm/ *n Naut.* braza, *f.* —*vt* sondear; *Fig.* profundizar, tantear; (a mystery) desentrañar

fathomless /'fæðəmlıs/ *a* insondable; *Fig.* incomprensible, impenetrable

fatigue /fə'tig/ *n* fatiga, *f,* cansancio, *m; Mil.* faena, *f; Mech.* pérdida de resistencia, *f.* —*vt* fatigar, cansar. **to be fatigued,** estar cansado, cansarse, fatigarse. **f. party,** *Mil.* pelotón de castigo, *m*

fatiguing /fə'tigıŋ/ *a* fatigoso

fatness /'fætnıs/ *n* (stoutness) gordura, carnosidad, *f;* grasa, *f,* gordo, *m;* (richness) fertilidad, *f;* lo lucrativo

fatten /'fætn̩/ *vt* engordar; (animals) cebar, sainar; (land) abonar, fertilizar. —*vi* ponerse grueso, echar carnes

fatty /'fæti/ *a* untoso, grasiento; *Chem.* graso. **f. acid,** ácido graso, *m.* **f. degeneration,** degeneración grasienta, *f*

fatuity /fə'tuıti/ *n* fatuidad, necedad, *f*

fatuous /'fætʃuəs/ *a* fatuo, necio, lelo

faucet /'fɔsıt/ *n* canilla, llave, *f,* grifo, *m*

fault /fɔlt/ *n* defecto, *m,* imperfección, *f;* (blame) culpa, *f;* (mistake) falta, *f,* error, *m;* (in cloth) canilla, barra, *f; Geol.* falla, quiebra, *f; Elec.* avería, *f; Sports.* falta, *f,* in *Sports.* cometer una falta. **to a f.,** excesivamente. **to be at f.,** (to blame) tener la culpa; (mistaken) estar equivocado; (puzzled) estar perplejo; (of dogs) perder el rastro. **to find f.,** tachar, culpar, criticar. **Whose f. is it?** ¿Quién tiene la culpa?

faultfinder /'fɔltˌfaındər/ *n* criticón (-ona)

faultiness /'fɔltınıs/ *n* defectuosidad, imperfección, *f*

faultless /'fɔltlıs/ *a* sin faltas; perfecto, sin tacha; impecable

faulty /'fɔlti/ *a* defectuoso, imperfecto

faun /fɔn/ *n* fauno, *m*

fauna /'fɔnə/ *n* fauna, *f*

favor /'feıvər/ *n* favor, *m;* (protection) amistad, protección, *f,* amparo, *m;* (permission) permiso, *m,* licencia, *f;* (kindness) merced, gracia, *f;* (gift) obsequio, *m;* (favoritism) favoritismo, *m,* preferencia, *f;* (benefit) beneficio, *m;* (badge) colores, *m pl; Com.* grata, atenta, *f.* —*vt* favorecer, apoyar; mirar con favor, mostrar parcialidad (hacia); (suit) favorecer; (be advantageous) ser propicio (a); (contribute to) contribuir a, ayudar; (resemble) parecerse (a). **Circumstances f. the idea,** Las circunstancias son propicias a la idea, Las circunstancias militan en pro de la idea: **I f. the teaching of modern languages,** Soy partidario de la enseñanza de lenguas vivas. **in f. of,** a favor de, en pro de. **in the f. of,** en el favor de. **out of f.,** fuera de favor; (not fashionable) fuera de moda. **to count on the f. of,** tener de su parte (a), contar con el apoyo de. **to do a f.,** hacer un favor. **to enjoy the f. of,** gozar del favor de. **to fall out of f.,** caer en desgracia; (go out of fashion) pasar de moda. **to grow in f.,** aumentar en favor

favorable /'feıvərəbəl/ *a* favorable; propicio, próspero

favorableness /'feıvərəbəlnıs/ *n* lo favorable; lo propicio; benignidad, benevolencia, *f*

favorably /'feıvərəbli/ *adv* favorablemente

favored /'feıvərd/ *a* favorecido; predilecto; (in compounds) parecido, encarado

favoring /'feıvərıŋ/ *a* favorecedor, propicio

favorite /'feıvərıt/ *a* favorito; predilecto, preferido. —*n* favorito (-ta). **court f.,** valido, privado, *m;* (mistress) querida (de un rey), *f;* (lover) amante (de una reina), *m.* **to be a f.,** ser favorito

favoritism /'feıvərˌtızəm/ *n* favoritismo, *m*

fawn /fɔn/ *n Zool.* cervato, *m;* (color) color de cervato, color de ante, *m.* —*a* de color de cervato, anteado, pardo; (of animals) rucio, pardo. —*vt* and *vi* parir la cierva. —*vi* acariciar; (on, upon) adular, lisonjear

fawning /'fɔnıŋ/ *n* adulación, *f,* a adulador, lisonjero

fear /fıər/ *n* miedo, temor, *m;* (apprehension) ansiedad, aprensión, *f,* recelo, *m;* (respect) veneración, *f.* —*vt* temer; (respect) reverenciar. —*vi* tener miedo; estar receloso, estar con cuidado. **for f. of,** por miedo de. **for f. that,** por temor de que, por miedo de que. **from f.,** por miedo. **There is no f. of...,** No hay miedo de (que)...

fearer /'fıərər/ *n* temedor (-ra), el (la) que teme

fearful /'fɪərfəl/ a miedoso, aprensivo, receloso; (cowardly) tímido, pusilánime; (terrible) horrible, espantoso, pavoroso; Inf. tremendo, enorme

fearfully /'fɪərfəli/ adv con miedo; tímidamente; (terribly) horriblemente; Inf. enormemente

fearfulness /'fɪərfəlnɪs/ n temor, miedo, m; (horribleness) lo horrible

fearless /'fɪərlɪs/ a sin miedo, intrépido, audaz

fearlessness /'fɪərlɪsnɪs/ n intrepidez, valentía, f

fearsome /'fɪərsəm/ a temible, horrible, espantoso

feasibility /ˌfizəˈbɪlɪti/ n practicabilidad, posibilidad, f

feasible /'fizəbəl/ a factible, hacedero, practicable, ejecutable

feast /fist/ n Eccl. fiesta, f; banquete, m; Fig. abundancia, f, vi regalarse. —vt festejar, agasajar; (delight) recrear, deleitar. **immovable f.,** Eccl. fiesta fija, f. **movable f.,** fiesta movible, f. **f. day,** día de fiesta, m, festividad f

feasting /'fistɪŋ/ n banquetes, m pl; fiestas, f pl

feat /fit/ n hazaña, proeza, f, hecho, m

feather /'fɛðər/ n pluma, f; (of the tail) pena, f; pl **feathers,** plumaje, m; plumas, f pl. —vt emplumar; adornar con plumas; (rowing) poner casi horizontal la pala del remo. **to f. one's nest,** Inf. hacer su agosto. **f.-bed,** plumón, colchón de plumas, m. **f.-brained,** casquivano, alocado, aturdido. **f.-duster,** plumero, m. **f.-stitch,** Sew. diente de perro, m. **f. weight,** (boxing) peso pluma, m

feathered /'fɛðərd/ a plumado, plumoso; adornado con plumas; (winged) alado

feathery /'fɛðəri/ a plumoso; como plumas

feature /'fitʃər/ n rasgo, m, característica, f; (cinema) número de programa, m; pl **features** (of the face) facciones, f pl. —vt dar importancia (a); (cinema) presentar. **f. film,** documentaria, f

febrile /'fibrəl/ a febril

February /'februˌɛri, 'febyu-/ n febrero, m

fecal /'fikəl/ a fecal

feces /'fisiz/ n heces, f pl; excremento, m

fecund /'fikʌnd/ a fecundo, fértil

fecundate /'fikənˌdeit/ vt fecundar

fecundity /fɪ'kʌndɪti/ n fecundidad, fertilidad, f

federal /'fedərəl/ a federal, federalista

federalism /'fedərəˌlɪzəm/ n federalismo, m

federalist /'fedərəlɪst/ n federalista, federal, mf

federate /v 'fedəˌreit; -ərɪt/ vt confederar. —vi confederarse. —a confederado

federation /ˌfedəˈreiʃən/ n confederación, federación, f; liga, unión, asociación, f

federative /'fedəˌreitɪv/ a federativo

fee /fi/ n (feudal law) feudo, m; (homage) homenaje, m; (duty) derecho, m; (professional) honorario, estipendio, m; (to a servant) gratificación, f; (entrance, university, etc.) cuota, f; (payment) paga, f

feeble /'fibəl/ a débil; lánguido; enfermizo; (of light, etc.) tenue; Fig. flojo. **to grow f.,** debilitarse; disminuir. **f.-minded,** anormal

feebleness /'fibəlnɪs/ n debilidad, f; Fig. flojedad, f

feebly /'fibli/ adv débilmente; lánguidamente

feed /fid/ n alimento, m; (meal) comida, f; (of animals) pienso, forraje, m; Mech. alimentación, f. —vt alimentar; dar de comer (a); (animals) cebar; Mech. alimentar; mantener; Fig. nutrir. —vi comer, alimentarse; (graze) pastar. **to be fed up,** Inf. estar hasta la coronilla, estar harto. **to f. on,** alimentarse de; Fig. nutrirse de. **f. pipe,** tubo de alimentación, m

feedback /'fidˌbæk/ n retrocomunicación, f

feeder /'fidər/ n el, m, (f, la) que da de comer a; (eater) comedor (-ra); (of a river) tributario, afluente, m; (bib) babero, m; Mech. alimentador, m; (cup for invalids) pistero, m

feeding /'fidɪŋ/ n alimentación, f, a alimenticio, de alimentación. **f.-bottle,** biberón, m. **f.-cup,** pistero, m. **f.-trough,** pesebre, m

feel /fil/ n (touch) tacto, m; (feeling) sensación, f; (instinct) instinto, m, percepción innata, f

feel /fil/ vt (touch) tocar, tentar, palpar; (experience) sentir, experimentar; (understand) comprender; (believe) creer; (be conscious of) estar consciente de; (the pulse) tomar; examinar. —vi sentir, ser sensible; sentirse, encontrarse; (to the touch) ser... al tacto, estar. **How do you f.?** ¿Cómo se siente Vd.? **I f. cold,**

Tengo frío. **I f. for you,** Lo siento en el alma; Estoy muy consciente de ello. **I f. strongly that...,** Estoy convencido de que... **I f. that it is a difficult question,** Me parece una cuestión difícil. **It feels like rain,** Creo que va a llover. **to f. at home,** sentirse a sus anchas, sentirse como en su casa. **to f. hungry (thirsty),** tener hambre (sed). **to f. one's way,** andar a tientas, Fig. medir el terreno. **to f. soft,** ser blando al tacto. **to make itself felt,** hacerse sentir. **Your hands f. cold,** Tus manos están frías

feeler /'filər/ n (of insects) palpo, m, antena, f; tentáculo, m; Fig. tentativa, f, balón de ensayo, m

feeling /'filɪŋ/ n (touch) tacto, m; (sensation) sensación, f; (sentiment) sentimiento, m; emoción, f; (premonition) corazonada, intuición, premonición, f; (tenderness) ternura, f; (perception) sensibilidad, percepción, f; (passion) pasión, f; (belief) opinión, f, sentir, m. —a sensible; tierno; (compassionate) compasivo; apasionado; (moving) conmovedor

feelingly /'filɪŋli/ adv con emoción; (strongly) enérgicamente, vivamente; (understandingly) comprensivamente

feign /fein/ vt fingir; (invent) inventar, imaginar; simular; (allege) pretextar; (dissemble) disimular. —vi disimular

feint /feint/ n artificio, engaño, m; (in fencing) treta, finta, f. —vi hacer finta

feldspar /'feldˌspar/ n Mineral. feldespato, m

felicitate /fɪ'lɪsɪˌteit/ vt felicitar, congratular, dar el parabién (a)

felicitation /fɪˌlɪsɪˈteiʃən/ n felicitación, f, parabién, m

felicitous /fɪ'lɪsɪtəs/ a feliz, dichoso, afortunado; (of phrases, etc.) feliz, acertado; oportuno

felicity /fɪ'lɪsɪti/ n felicidad, dicha, f

feline /'filain/ a felino, gatuno, de gato. —n felino, m

fell /fel/ n (skin) piel, f; (upland) altura, cuesta de montaña, f. —a cruel, feroz; (unhappy) aciago, funesto. —vt talar, cortar; (knock down) derribar; Sew. sobrecoser

feller /'felər/ n talador, leñador, m

felling /'felɪŋ/ n corta, tala, f

fellow /'felou/ n compañero (-ra); (equal) igual, mf; (in crime) cómplice, mf; (man) hombre, m; (boy, youth) chico, m; (colleague) colega, m; (of a society) miembro, m; (of a pair of objects) pareja, f; Inf. tipo, chico, m. **He's a good f.,** Es un buen chico. **How are you, old f.?** ¡Hombre! ¿Cómo estás? **f.-citizen,** conciudadano (-na). **f.-countryman,** compatriota, m; paisano (-na). **f.-creature,** semejante, mf **f.-feeling,** simpatía, comprensión mutua, f. **f.-member,** compañero (-ra); colega, m. **f.-passenger,** compañero (-ra) de viaje. **f.-prisoner,** compañero (-ra) de prisión. **f.-student,** condiscípulo (-la). **f.-worker,** compañero (-ra) de trabajo; (collaborator) colaborador (-ra); (colleague) colega, m

fellowship /'felouˌʃɪp/ n coparticipación, f; (companionship) compañerismo, m; (brotherhood) comunidad, confraternidad, f; (society) asociación, f; (grant) beca, f; (of a university) colegiatura, f

felon /'felən/ n reo, criminal, mf; felón (-ona); malvado (-da); (swelling) panadizo, m

felonious /fə'louniəs/ a criminal; pérfido, traidor

felony /'feləni/ n felonía, f

felt /felt/ n fieltro, m. **a f. hat,** un sombrero de fieltro

female /'fimeil/ n hembra, f, a femenino. (f. is often rendered in Sp. by the feminine ending of the noun, e.g. a f. cat, una gata; a f. friend, una amiga.) **This is a f. animal,** Este animal es una hembra. **f. screw,** hembra de tornillo, tuerca, f

feminine /'femənɪn/ a femenino; mujeril, afeminado. **in the f. gender,** en el género femenino

feminism /'feməˌnɪzəm/ n feminismo, m

feminist /'femənɪst/ n feminista, mf

feministic /ˌfemə'nɪstɪk/ a feminista

femur /'fimər/ n Anat. fémur, m

fen /fen/ n marjal, pantano, m

fence /fens/ n cerca, f; (of stakes) estacada, palizada, f; (hedge) seto, m; (fencing) esgrima, f; Mech. guía, f; Inf. comprador (-ra) de efectos robados. —vi esgrimir; Fig. defenderse; Inf. recibir efectos robados. —vt cercar; estacar; Fig. defender; proteger. **to sit on the f.,** Fig. estar a ver venir

fencer /'fɛnsər/ n esgrimidor, m

fencesitter /'fɛns,sɪtər/ bailarín de la cuerda flaja, m

fencing /'fɛnsɪŋ/ n esgrima, f; palizada, empalizada, f. **f. mask,** careta, f. **f. master,** maestro de esgrima, maestro de armas, m. **f. match,** asalto de esgrima, m

fend /fɛnd/ **(off)** vt parar; defenderse de, guardarse de. —vi (for) mantener, cuidar de. **to f. for oneself,** ganarse la vida; defenderse

fender /'fɛndər/ n (round hearth) guardafuegos, m; Naut. espolón, m, defensas, f pl; Auto. parachoques, m

fennel /'fɛnl/ n Bot. hinojo, m

ferment /n 'fɑrmɛnt; v fər'mɛnt/ n fermento, m; fermentación, f; Fig. agitación, conmoción, efervescencia f. —vt hacer fermentar; Fig. agitar, excitar. —vi fermentar, estar en fermentación; Fig. hervirse, agitarse, excitarse

fermentation /,fɑrmɛn'teiʃən/ n fermentación, f

fern /fɑrn/ n helecho, m

ferny /'fɑrni/ a cubierto de helechos

ferocious /fə'rouʃəs/ a feroz, bravo, salvaje

ferocity /fə'rɒsɪti/ n ferocidad, braveza, fiereza, f

ferreous /'fɛrəs/ a férreo

ferret /'fɛrɪt/ n Zool. hurón (-ona); **to f. out,** cazar con hurones; (discover) husmear, descubrir

Ferris wheel /'fɛrɪs/ n estrella giratoria, gran rueda, novia, rueda de feria, f

ferroconcrete /,fɛrou'kɒnkrit/ n hormigón armado, m

ferrous /'fɛrəs/ a ferroso

ferruginous /fə'rudʒənəs/ a ferruginoso; aherrumbrado, rojizo

ferrule /'fɛrəl/ n herrete, regatón, m, contera, f; garrucha de tornillos, f

ferry /'fɛri/ n barca de transporte, f; barca de pasaje, f, transbordador, m. —vt transportar de una a otra orilla, llevar en barca. —vi cruzar un río en barca. **ferry across** vt transbordar. **F.-Command,** servicio de entrega y transporte de aeroplanos, m

ferryman /'fɛrimæn/ n barquero, m

fertile /'fɑrtl/ a fértil, fecundo; (rich) pingüe; Fig. prolífico, abundante

Fertile Crescent, the el Creciente Fértil m

fertility /fər'tɪlɪti/ n fertilidad, fecundidad, f

fertilization /,fɑrtlə'zeiʃən/ n Biol. fecundación, f; Agr. fertilización, f, abono, m

fertilize /'fɑrtl,aiz/ vt Biol. fecundar; Agr. fertilizar, abonar

fertilizer /'fɑrtl,aizər/ n abono, m

ferule /'fɛrəl/ n palmatoria, palmeta, férula, f

fervent /'fɑrvənt/ a ardiente; fervoroso, intenso; (enthusiastic) entusiasta, apasionado

fervently /'fɑrvəntli/ adv con fervor, con vehemencia

fervor /'fɑrvər/ n ardor, fervor, m, pasión, f; (enthusiasm) entusiasmo, celo, m; vehemencia, f

festal /'fɛstl/ a de fiesta; alegre, festivo, regocijado

fester /'fɛstər/ vi ulcerarse, enconarse; Fig. inflamarse, amargarse. —vt ulcerar

festival /'fɛstəvəl/ a de fiesta. —n festividad, f; Eccl. fiesta, f; (musical, etc.) festival, m

festive /'fɛstɪv/ a de fiesta; festivo, alegre

festivity /fɛ'stɪvɪti/ n festividad, fiesta, f; (merriment) alegría, f, júbilo, m

festoon /fɛ'stun/ n festón, m, guirnalda, f. —vt festonear

festschrift /'fɛst,ʃrift/ n libro de homenaje, libro jubilar, m

fetal /'fitl/ a fetal

fetch /fɛtʃ/ vt traer; ir a buscar; ir por; llevar; (conduct) conducir; (of tears) hacer derramar lágrimas, hacer saltársele las lágrimas; (blood) hacer correr la sangre; (produce, draw) sacar; (a blow, a sigh) dar; (acquire) conseguir; (charm) fascinar; (of price) venderse por. **to go and f.,** ir a buscar. **to f. and carry,** vt (news) divulgar, publicar. —vi estar ocupado en oficios humildes, trajinar. **to f. away,** llevarse; ir a buscar; venir a buscar. **to f. back,** devolver; (of persons) traer (a casa, etc.); traer otra vez. **to f. down,** bajar, llevar abajo; hacer bajar. **to f. in,** hacer entrar; (place inside) poner adentro; (persons and things) llevar adentro. **to f. out,** hacer salir; (bring out things) sacar; (put out) poner afuera; (an idea,

etc.) sacar a relucir. **to f. up,** (a parcel, etc.) subir; (a person) hacer subir; llevar arriba

fete /feit/ n fiesta, f

fetid /'fɛtɪd/ a fétido, hediondo

fetidness /'fɛtɪdnɪs/ n fetidez, f, hedor, m

fetish /'fɛtɪʃ/ n fetiche, m

fetishism /'fɛtɪ,ʃɪzəm/ n fetichismo, m

fetter /'fɛtər/ n grillete, m; pl **fetters,** grillos, m pl, cadenas, f pl; prisión, cárcel, f. —vt encadenar, atar

fettle /'fɛtl/ n condición, f, estado, m

fetus /'fitəs/ n feto, m

feud /fyud/ n enemistad, riña, f; (feudal law) feudo, m

feudal /'fyudl/ a feudal. **f. lord,** señor feudal, señor de horca y cuchillo, m

feudalism /'fyudl,ɪzəm/ n feudalismo, m

feudatory /'fyudə,tɔri/ a and n feudatario (-ia)

fever /'fivər/ n fiebre, f; calentura, f; (enthusiasm) pasión, afición, f. **to be in a f.,** tener fiebre; (agitated) estar muy agitado. **to be in a f. to,** estar muy impaciente de. **puerperal f.,** fiebre puerperal, f. **tertian f.,** fiebre terciana, f. **yellow f.,** fiebre amarilla, f

feverish /'fivərɪʃ/ a febril; Fig. ardiente, febril, vehemente. **to grow f.,** empezar a tener fiebre, acalenturarse

feverishness /'fivərɪʃnɪs/ n calentura, f; (impatience) impaciencia, f

few /fyu/ a and n pocos, m pl; pocas, f pl; algunos, m pl; algunas, f pl; (few in number) número pequeño (de), m. **a good f.,** bastantes, mf pl. **not a f.,** no pocos, m pl, (pocas, f pl). **the f.,** la minoría, f. **f. and far between,** raramente, en raras ocasiones; pocos y contados

fewer /'fyuər/ a compar menos. **The f. the better,** Cuantos menos mejor

fewest /'fyuist/ a superl (el) menos, m; el menor número (de), m; (el) menos posible de, m

fewness /'fyunɪs/ n corto número, m

fez /fɛz/ n fez, m

fiancé(e) /,fiɑn'sei/ n novio (-ia); desposado (-da), prometido (-da)

fiasco /fi'æskou/ n fiasco, mal éxito, fracaso, malogro, m

fiat /'fiɑt/ n fiat, mandato, m, orden, f

fib /fɪb/ n mentirilla, f, vt decir mentirillas, mentir

fibber /'fɪbər/ n embustero (-ra), mentiroso (-sa)

fiber /'faibər/ n fibra, f; filamento, m, hebra, f; (of grass, etc.) brizna, f; Fig. naturaleza, f

fibroid /'faibrɔid/ a fibroso. —n fibroma, m

fibrous /'faibrəs/ a fibroso

fibula /'fɪbyələ/ n Anat. peroné, m

fichu /'fɪʃu/ n pañoleta, f, fichú, m

fickle /'fɪkəl/ a inconstante; mudable; (of persons) liviano, ligero, voluble

fickleness /'fɪkəlnɪs/ n inconstancia, f; mudanza, f; liviandad, ligereza, veleidad, volubilidad, f

fiction /'fɪkʃən/ n ficción, f; invención, f; literatura narrativa, f; novelas, f pl. **legal f.,** ficción legal, ficción de derecho, f

fictitious /fɪk'tɪʃəs/ a ficticio; imaginario; fingido

fictitiousness /fɪk'tɪʃəsnɪs/ n carácter ficticio, m; falsedad, f

fiddle /'fɪdl/ n violín, m. —vt tocar... en el violín. —vi tocar el violín; (fidget) jugar; perder el tiempo. **to play second f.,** tocar el segundo violín; Fig. ser plato de segunda mesa

fiddler /'fɪdlər/ n violinista, mf

fiddling /'fɪdlɪŋ/ a insignificante, trivial, frívolo

fidelity /fɪ'dɛlɪti/ n fidelidad, f

fidget /'fɪdʒɪt/ vi estar nervioso, estar inquieto; impacientarse; trajinar; (with) jugar con. —vt molestar; impacientar

fidgetiness /'fɪdʒɪtinɪs/ n inquietud, nerviosidad, f

fidgety /'fɪdʒɪti/ a inquieto, nervioso. **to be f.,** tener hormiguillo

fiduciary /fɪ'duʃi,ɛri/ a fiduciario. —n fideicomisario (-ia)

fief /fif/ n feudo, m

field /fild/ n campo, m; (meadow) prado, m, pradera, f; (sown field) sembrado, m; (Phys. Herald.) campo, m; (of ice) banco, m; Mineral. yacimiento, m;

(background) fondo, *m;* (campaign) campaña, *f;* (battle) batalla, lucha, *f;* (space) espacio, *m;* (of knowledge, etc.) especialidad, esfera, *f;* (hunting) caza, *f; Sports.* campo, *m;* (competitors) todos los competidores en una carrera, etc.; (horses in a race) el campo. **—a** campal, pradeño; de campo; de los campos. **—**vt *Sports.* parar y devolver la pelota. **in the f.,** *Mil.* en el campo de batalla, en campaña. **magnetic f.,** campo magnético, *m.* **to take the f.,** entrar en campaña. **f.-artillery,** artillería ligera, artillería montada, *f.* **f.-day,** (holiday) día de asueto, *m;* (day out) día en el campo, *m; Mil.* día de maniobras, *m.* **f.-glasses,** anteojos, gemelos, *m pl.* **f.-hospital,** hospital de sangre, *m;* ambulancia fija, *f.* **f.-kitchen,** cocina de campaña, *f.* **f.-marshal,** capitán general de ejército, *m.* **f.-mouse,** ratón silvestre, *m.* **f. of battle,** campo de batalla, *m.* **f. of vision,** campo visual, *m.* **f.-telegraph,** telégrafo de campaña, *m*

fielder /'fildər/ *n* (baseball) jardinero (-ra)

field work prácticas de campo, *f pl*

fiend /find/ *n* diablo, demonio, *m;* malvado (-da); (addict) adicto (-ta). **morphia f.,** morfinómano (-ma)

fiendish /'findɪʃ/ *a* diabólico, infernal; malvado, cruel, malévolo

fiendishness /'findɪʃnɪs/ *n* perversidad, crueldad, *f*

fierce /fɪərs/ *a* salvaje, feroz, cruel; (of the elements) violento, furioso; (intense) intenso, vehemente

fiercely /'fɪərsli/ *adv* ferozmente; violentamente, con furia; intensamente, con vehemencia

fierceness /'fɪərsnɪs/ *n* ferocidad, fiereza, *f;* violencia, furia, *f;* intensidad, vehemencia, *f*

fieriness /'faiərɪnɪs/ *n* ardor, *m;* (flames) las llamas, *f pl;* (redness) rojez, *f;* (irritability) ferocidad, irritabilidad, *f;* (vehemence) pasión, vehemencia, *f;* (of horses) fogosidad, *f*

fiery /'faiəri/ *a* ardiente; (red) rojo; (irritable) feroz, colérico, irritable; (vehement) apasionado, vehemente; (of horses) fogoso

fife /faif/ *n Mus.* pífano, pito, *m*

fifteen /'fɪf'tin/ *a* and *n* quince *m.;* (of age) quince años, *m pl*

fifteenth /'fɪf'tinθ/ *a* and *n* décimoquinto *m.;* (part) quinzavo, *m,* décimoquinta parte, *f;* (of the month) (el) quince, *m;* (of monarchs) quince; *Mus.* quincena, *f*

fifth /fɪfθ/ *a* quinto; (of monarchs) quinto; (of the month) (el) cinco. **—**n quinto, *m;* (part) quinto, *m,* quinta parte, *f; Mus.* quinta, *f,* **Charles V,** Carlos quinto. **f. column,** quinta columna, *f*

fifthly /'fɪfθli/ *adv* en quinto lugar

fiftieth /'fɪftiɪθ/ *a* quincuagésimo; (part) quincuagésima parte, *f,* cincuentavo, *m*

fifty /'fɪfti/ *a* and *n* cincuenta *m.;* (of age) cincuenta años, *m pl*

fiftyfold /'fɪfti,fould/ *a* and *adv* cincuenta veces

fig /fɪg/ *n* higo, *m;* (tree) higuera, *f; Fig.* bledo, ardite, *m.* **green fig,** higo, *m,* breva, *f.* **I don't care a fig,** No se me da un higo. **to be not worth a fig,** no valer un ardite. **fig-leaf,** hoja de higuera, *f; Fig.* hoja de parra, *f*

fight /fait/ *n* lucha, pelea, *f,* combate, *m;* batalla, *f;* (struggle) lucha, *f;* (quarrel) riña, pelea, *f;* (conflict) conflicto, *m;* (valor) coraje, brío, *m.* **hand-to-hand f.,** cachetina, *f.* **in fair f.,** en buena lid. **to have a f.,** tener una pelea. **to show f.,** mostrarse agresivo

fight /fait/ *vt* luchar contra, batirse con; (a battle) dar (batalla); (oppose) oponer; (defend) defender, pelear por; hacer batirse. **—**vi luchar, batirse, pelear; (with words) disputar; (struggle) luchar; (make war) hacer la guerra; (in a tournament) tornear. **to f. one's way,** abrirse paso con las armas. **to f. against,** luchar contra. **to f. off,** librarse de; sacudirse. **to f. with,** luchar con; pelear con; reñir con

fighter /'faitər/ *n* luchador (-ra); combatiente, *m;* guerrero, *m;* duelista, *m;* (boxer) boxeador, *m; Aer.* (avión de) caza, *m.* **night f.,** *Aer.* (avión de) caza nocturno, *m.* **f.-bomber,** *Aer.* caza bombardero, *m.* **Command,** *Aer.* servicio de aviones de caza, *m*

fighting /'faitɪŋ/ *n* lucha, *f,* combate, *m;* el pelear; (boxing) boxeo, *m,* a combatiente; (bellicose) agresivo, belicoso. **f.-man,** combatiente, guerrero, *m*

figment /'fɪgmənt/ *n* ficción, invención, *f*

figurative /'fɪgyərətɪv/ *a* figurado, metafórico; figurativo; simbólico

figuratively /'fɪgyərətɪvli/ *adv* en sentido figurativo; metafóricamente

figure /'fɪgyər/ *n* figura, *f;* forma, *f;* (statue) estatua, figura, *f;* (of a person) silueta, *f;* talle, *m;* (number) cifra, *f,* número, *m;* (quantity) cantidad, *f;* (price) precio, *m; Geom. Gram. Dance.* (skating) figura, *f;* (appearance) presencia, *f,* aire, *m;* (picture) imagen, *m;* (on fabric) diseño, *m; Mus.* cifra, *f; pl* **figures,** aritmética, *f,* matemáticas, *f pl.* **—**vt figurar; (imagine) figurarse, imaginar; *Mus.* cifrar. **—**vi figurar, hacer un papel; (calculate) calcular, hacer cuentas. **to f. out,** calcular; (a problem, etc.) resolver. **a fine f. of a woman,** *Inf.* una real hembra. **lay f.,** maniquí, *m.* **to be good at figures,** estar fuerte en matemáticas. **to cut a f.,** *Fig.* hacer figura. **to have a good f.,** tener buen talle. **f. of speech,** figura retórica, figura de dicción *f;* (manner of speaking) metáfora *f.* **f. dance,** baile de figuras, *m,* contradanza, *f.* **f.-head,** *Naut.* mascarón, *m,* (or figura, *f)* de proa; *Fig.* figura decorativa, *f*

figured /'fɪgyərd/ *a* estampado, con diseños, labrado

figurine /,fɪgyə'rin/ *n* figurilla, *f*

filament /'fɪləmənt/ *n* filamento, *m;* hebra, *f*

filamentous /,fɪlə'mentəs/ *a* filamentoso, fibroso

filbert /'fɪlbərt/ *n* avellana, *f;* (tree) avellano, *m*

filch /fɪltʃ/ *vt* sisar, ratear

filching /'fɪltʃɪŋ/ *n* sisa, *f*

file /fail/ *n* (line) fila, hilera, sarta, línea, *f; Mil.* fila, *f;* (tool) lima, *f;* (rasp) escofina, *f;* (list) lista, *f,* catálogo, *m;* (for documents) carpeta, *f,* cartapacio, *m;* (bundle of papers) legajo, *m;* (for bills, letters, etc.) clasificador, *m;* archivo, *m;* (in an archives) expediente *m.* **in a f.,** en fila; en cola

file /fail/ *vt* hacer marchar en fila; (smooth) limar; (literary work) pulir; (classify) clasificar; (note particulars) fichar; (a petition, etc.) presentar, registrar. **—**vi marchar en fila. **to f. in,** entrar en fila. **to f. off,** desfilar. **to file a brief,** presentar un escrito. **to f. letters,** clasificar correspondencia. **to f. past,** *Mil.* desfilar

filial /'fɪliəl/ *a* filial

filiation /,fɪli'eiʃən/ *n* filiación, *f*

filibuster /'fɪlə,bʌstər/ *n* filibustero, pirata, *m*

filigree /'fɪlə,gri/ *n* filigrana, *f,* a afiligranado

filing /'failɪŋ/ *n* (with a tool) limadura, *f;* clasificación, *f;* (of a petition, etc.) presentación, *f,* registro, *m; pl* **filings,** limaduras, *f pl,* retales, *m pl.* **f.-cabinet,** fichero, *m.* **f.-card,** ficha, *f*

fill /fɪl/ *vt* llenar; (stuff) rellenar; (appoint to a post) proveer; (occupy a post) desempeñar; (imbue) henchir; (saturate) saturar; (occupy) ocupar; (a tooth) empastar; (fulfil) cumplir; (charge, fuel) cargar; (with food) hartar. **—**vi llenarse. **fill an order,** servir un pedido. **fill a prescription,** surtir una receta. **to f. the chair,** ocupar la presidencia; (university) ocupar la cátedra. **to f. the place of,** ocupar el lugar de; substituir; suplir. **It will be difficult to find someone to f. his place,** Será difícil de encontrar uno que haga lo que hizo él. **to f. to the brim,** llenar hasta los bordes. **to f. in, f. out,** (a form) llenar (or completar) (una hoja); (insert) insertar, añadir; (a hollow) terraplenar. **to f. out,** vt hinchar. **—**vi hincharse; echar carnes; (of the face) redondearse. **to f. up,** colmar, llenar hasta los bordes; (an office) proveer; (block) macizar; (a form) completar, llenar

fillet /'fɪlɪt/ *n* venda, cinta, *f;* (of meat or fish) filete, *m;* (of meat) solomillo, *m; Archit.* filete, *m.* **—**vt atar con una venda o cinta; *Cul.* cortar en filetes

filling /'fɪlɪŋ/ *n* envase, *m;* (swelling) henchimiento, *m;* (of a tooth) empastadura, *f;* (in or up, of forms, etc.) llenar, *m.* **f. station,** depósito de gasolina, *m*

fillip /'fɪləp/ *n* capirotazo, *m;* (stimulus) estímulo, *m;* (trifle) bagatela, *f.* **—**vt and vi dar un capirotazo (a); vt estimular, incitar

filly /'fɪli/ *n* jaca, potra, *f*

film /fɪlm/ *n* (on liquids) tela, *f;* membrana, *f;* (coating) capa ligera, *f;* (on eyes) tela, *f;* (cinema) película, cinta, *f; Photo.* película, *f; Fig.* velo, *m;* nube, *f,* vi cubrirse de un velo, etc. **—**vt cubrir de un velo, etc.; filmar, fotografiar para el cine. **roll f.,**

película fotográfica, f. **silent f.**, película muda, f. **talking f.**, película sonora, f. **to shoot a f.**, hacer una película. **to take part in a f.**, actuar, or tomar parte, en una película. **f. pack**, película en paquetes f. **f. star**, estrella de la pantalla (or del cine), f

film industry industria fílmica, f

filminess /'fɪlmɪnɪs/ n transparencia, diafanidad, f

filmy /'fɪlmi/ a transparente, diáfano

filter /'fɪltər/ n filtro, m. —vt filtrar. —vi infiltrarse; (Fig. of news) trascender, divulgarse. **f.-bed**, filtro, m. **f.-paper**, papel filtro, m

filth /fɪlθ/ n inmundicia, suciedad, f; Fig. corrupción, f; Fig. obscenidad, f

filthiness /'fɪlθɪnɪs/ n suciedad, f; escualidez, f; Fig. asquerosidad, f; Fig. obscenidad, f

filthy /'fɪlθi/ a inmundo, sucio; escuálido; Fig. asqueroso; Fig. obsceno

filtrate /'fɪltreɪt/ n filtrado, m, vt filtrar

filtration /fɪl'treɪʃən/ n filtración, f

fin /fɪn/ n (of fish) aleta, ala, f; (of whale) barba, f; Aer. aleta, f

final /'faɪnl̩/ a último, final; (conclusive) conclusivo, decisivo, terminante. —n Sports. finales, m pl; Educ. último examen, m. **f. blow,** Fig. golpe decisivo, m. **f. cause,** Philos. causa final, f

finale /fɪ'næli/ n final, m

finalist /'faɪnl̩ɪst/ n Sports. finalista, mf

finality /faɪ'næltti/ n finalidad, f; (decision) determinación, resolución, decisión, f

finally /'faɪnli/ adv por fin, finalmente, por último, a la postre; (irrevocably) irrevocablemente

finance /'faɪnæns/ n hacienda pública, f, asuntos económicos, m pl; finanzas, f pl. —vt financiar

financial /fɪ'nænʃəl/ a financiero, monetario. **f. year,** año económico, m

financially /fɪ'nænʃəli/ adv del punto de vista financiero

financier /ˌfɪnən'sɪər, ˌfaɪnən-/ n financiero, m

find /faɪnd/ vt encontrar, hallar; (discover) descubrir, dar con; (invent) inventar, crear; (supply) facilitar, proporcionar; (provide) proveer; (instruct) instruir; Law. declarar. —vi Law. fallar, dar sentencia. —n hallazgo, m; descubrimiento, m. **I found him out a long time ago,** Fig. Hace tiempo que me di cuenta de cómo era él. **I found it possible to go out,** Me fue posible salir. **The judge found them guilty,** El juez les declaró culpables. **to f. a verdict,** Law. dar sentencia, fallar. **to f. one's way,** encontrar el camino. **to f. oneself,** hallarse, verse, encontrarse. **to f. out,** averiguar, descubrir. **to f. out about,** informarse sobre (or de)

finder /'faɪndər/ n hallador (-ra); (inventor) inventor (-ra), descubridor (-ra); (telescope, camera) buscador, m

finding /'faɪndɪŋ/ n hallazgo, m; (discovery) descubrimiento, m; Law. fallo, m, sentencia, f

fine /faɪn/ n multa, f; (end) fin, m. **in f.,** en fin, en resumen

fine /faɪn/ vt multar, cargar una multa de

fine /faɪn/ a (thin) delgado; (sharp) agudo; (delicate) fino, delicado; (minute) menudo; (refined) refinado, puro; (healthy) saludable; (of weather) bueno; magnífico; (beautiful) hermoso, lindo, excelente; (perfect) perfecto; (good) bueno, elegante; (showy) ostentoso, vistoso; (handsome) guapo; (subtle) sutil; (acute) agudo; (noble) noble; (eminent, accomplished) distinguido, eminente; (polished) pulido; (affected) afectado; (clear) claro; (transparent) transparente, diáfano. —adv muy bien. **a f. upstanding young man,** un buen mozo. **a f. upstanding young woman,** una real moza. **He's a f. fellow,** (ironically) Es una buena pieza. **That is all very f. but...,** Todo eso está muy bien pero.... **to become f.,** (weather) mejorar

finely /'faɪnli/ adv finamente; menudamente; elegantemente; (ironically) lindamente

fineness /'faɪnnɪs/ n (thinness) delgadez, f; (excellence) excelencia, f; delicadeza, f; (softness) suavidad, f; elegancia, f; (subtlety) sutileza, f; (acuteness) agudeza, f; (perfection) perfección, f; (nobility) nobleza, f; (beauty) hermosura, f

finery /'faɪnəri/ n galas, f pl, atavíos magníficos, m pl; adornos, m pl; primor, m, belleza, f

finesse /fɪ'nes/ n sutileza, diplomacia, f; estratagema, artificio, m; (cunning) astucia, f, vi valerse de estratagemas y artificios

finger /'fɪŋgər/ n dedo, m; (of a clock, etc.) manecilla, f; (measurement) dedada, f; Fig. mano, f. —vt manosear, tocar; (soil) ensuciar con los dedos; (steal) sisar; (Mus. a keyed instrument) teclear, (a stringed instrument) tocar. **first f.,** dedo índice, m. **fourth f.,** dedo anular, m. **little f.,** dedo meñique, m. **second f.,** dedo de en medio, dedo del corazón, m. **to burn one's fingers,** quemarse los dedos; Fig. cogerse los dedos. **to have at one's f.-tips,** Fig. saber al dedillo. **f.-board,** (of piano) teclado, m; (of stringed instruments) diapasón, m. **f.-bowl,** lavadedos, lavafrutas, m. **finger's breadth,** dedo, m. **f.-mark,** huella digital, f. **f.-nail,** uña del dedo, f. **f.-print,** impresión digital, f. **f.-stall,** dedil, m. **f.-tip,** punta del dedo, yema del dedo, f. **f.-wave,** peinado al agua, m

fingered /'fɪŋgərd/ a (in compounds) con dedos, que tiene los dedos...

fingering /'fɪŋgərɪŋ/ n (touching) manoseo, m; Mus. digitación, f; (Mus. the keys) tecleo, m; (wool) estambre, m

finial /'fɪniəl/ n pináculo, m

finicky /'fɪnɪki/ a (of persons) dengoso, remilgado; (of things) nimio

finish /'fɪnɪʃ/ n fin, m, conclusión, terminación, f; (final touch) última mano, f; perfección, f; (of an article) acabado, m; Sports. llegada, (horse race) meta, f. —vt terminar, acabar, concluir; llevar a cabo, poner fin a; (perfect) perfeccionar; (put finishing touch to) dar la última mano a; (kill) matar; (exhaust) agotar, rendir; (overcome) vencer. —vi acabar; concluirse. **to f. off,** acabar, terminar; (kill) matar, acabar con; (destroy) destruir. **to f. up,** acabar; (eat) comer; (drink) beber

finishable /'fɪnɪʃəbəl/ a acabable

finished /'fɪnɪʃt/ a acabado, terminado, completo; perfecto; (careful) cuidadoso

finished goods n pl bienes terminados, m pl

finisher /'fɪnɪʃər/ n terminador (-ra), acabador (-ra); pulidor (-ra); (final blow) golpe de gracia, m

finishing /'fɪnɪʃɪŋ/ a concluyente. —n terminación, f, fin, m; perfección, f; (last touch) última mano, f. **to put the f. touch,** dar la última pincelada

finite /'faɪnaɪt/ a finito

Finland /'fɪnlənd/ Finlandia, f

Finn /fɪn/ n finlandés (-esa)

Finnish /'fɪnɪʃ/ a finlandés. —n (language) finlandés, m

fir /fɜr/ n abeto, sapino, pino, m. **red fir,** pino silvestre, m. **fir-cone,** piña de abeto, f. **fir grove,** abetal, m

fire /faɪər/ n fuego, m; (conflagration) incendio, m; (on the hearth) lumbre, f, fuego, m; Fig. ardor, m, pasión, f; (shooting) fuego, tiro, m. **by f. and sword,** a sangre y fuego. **by the f.,** cerca del fuego; (in a house) al lado de la chimenea. **long-range f.,** Mil. fuego de largo alcance, m. **short-range f.,** Mil. fuego de corto alcance, m. **on f.,** en fuego, ardiendo, en llamas; Fig. impaciente; Fig. lleno de pasión. **to be between two fires,** Fig. estar entre dos aguas. **to make a f.,** encender un fuego. **to miss f.,** no dar en el blanco, errar el tiro. **to open f.,** Mil. hacer una descarga. **to set on f.,** prender fuego a, incendiar. **to take f.,** encenderse. **under f.,** bajo fuego. **f.-alarm,** alarma de incendios, f. **f.-arm,** arma de fuego, f. **f.-box,** hogar, m. **f.-brand,** tea, f. **f.-brigade,** cuerpo de bomberos, m. **f.-damp,** aire detonante, grisú, m, mofeta, f. **f.-dog,** morillo, m. **f.-drill,** (firefighters') instrucción de bomberos, f, (others') simulacro de incendio, m. **f.-engine,** autobomba, bomba, de incendios, f. **f.-escape,** escalera de incendios, f. **f.-extinguisher,** apagador de incendio, extintor, matafuego, m. **f.-guard,** vigilante de incendios, m; alambrera, f. **f.-hose,** manguera de incendios, f. **f.-insurance,** seguro contra incendios, m. **f.-irons,** badil m. y tenazas f pl. **f.-lighter,** encendedor, m. **f.-screen,** pantalla, f. **f.-ship,** brulote, m. **f.-shovel,** badil, m, paleta, f. **f.-spotter,** vigilante de incendios, m. **f.-sprite,** salamandra, f. **f.-watching,** servicio de vigilancia de incendios, m

fire /faiᵊr/ vt incendiar, prender (or pegar) fuego a; quemar; (bricks) cocer; (fire-arms) disparar; (cauterize) cauterizar; (Fig. stimulate) estimular, excitar; (inspire) inspirar; (Inf. of questions) disparar; (Inf. sack) despedir. —vi encenderse; (shoot) hacer fuego, disparar (un tiro); (Inf. away) disparar; (up) enojarse. **to f. a salute,** disparar un saludo. Mil. **F.I** ¡Fuego!

fire department n parque de bomberos, servicis de bomberos, servicio de incendios, parque de bombas (Puerto Rico), m

firefly /'faiᵊr,flai/ n cocuyo, m

fireman /'faiᵊrmən/ n bombero, m; (of an engine, etc.) fogonero, m. **fireman's lift,** silleta, f

fireplace /'faiᵊr,pleis/ n chimenea francesa, chimenea, f; (hearth) hogar, m

fireproof /'faiᵊr,pruf/ a a prueba de incendios; incombustible

firer /'faiᵊrər/ n disparador, m

firewood /'faiᵊr,wud/ n leña, f. **f. dealer,** leñador (-ra), vendedor (-ra) de leña

firework /'faiᵊr,wərk/ n fuego artificial, m

firing /'faiᵊriŋ/ n (of fire-arms) disparo, m; (burning) incendio, m, quema, f; (of bricks, etc.) cocimiento, m; (of pottery) cocción, f; (cauterization) cauterización, f; (fuel) combustible, m; (Inf. sacking) despedida, f. **within f. range,** a tiro. **f.-line,** línea de fuego, f. **f.-oven,** (pottery) horno alfarero, m. **f.-squad,** pelotón de ejecución, m

firm /fərm/ a firme; (strong) fuerte; (secure) seguro; sólido; (resolute) inflexible, resoluto; severo; (steady) constante; (persistent) tenaz. —n Com. casa (de comercio), empresa, f; razón social, f

firmament /'fərməmənt/ n firmamento, m

firmly /'fərmli/ adv firmemente; inflexiblemente; constantemente

firmness /'fərmnɪs/ n firmeza, f; solidez, f; inflexibilidad, resolución, f; severidad, f; constancia, f; tenacidad, f

first /fərst/ a primero (primer before m sing nouns); (of monarchs) primero; (of dates) (el) primero. —n primero, m; (beginning) principio, m. —adv primero, en primer lugar; (before, of time) antes; (for the first time) por primera vez; (at the beginning) al principio; (ahead) adelante. **at f.,** al principio. **to appear for the f. time,** aparecer (or presentarse) por primera vez; Theat. debutar. **to go f.,** ir delante de todos, ir a la cabeza; ir adelante. **f. and foremost,** en primer lugar; ante todo. **f.-aid,** primera cura, f. **f.-aid post,** casa de socorro, f. **f.-aider,** practicante, m. **f.-born,** a and n primogénito (-ta). **f.-class,** a de primera clase; Fig. excelente. **f.-cousin,** primo (-ma) carnal, primo (-ma) hermano (-na). **f. edition,** edición príncipe, f. **f. floor,** primer piso, m. **f. fruits,** frutos primerizos, m pl; Fig. primicias, f pl. **f.-hand,** a original, de primera mano. **f. letters,** primeras letras, f pl. **f. night,** Theat. estreno, m. **f. of all,** primero, ante todo. **f.-rate,** a de primera clase

firstly /'fərstli/ adv en primer lugar, primero

firth /fərθ/ n ría, f

fiscal /'fɪskəl/ a and n fiscal m.. **f. year,** año económico, m

fish /fɪʃ/ n pez, m; (out of the water) pescado, m; Inf. tipo, indivíduo, m. —vt pescar; (out) sacar. —vi pescar; Fig. buscar. **fried f.,** pescado frito, m. **He is a queer f.,** Es un tipo muy raro. **to be neither f. nor fowl,** no ser ni carne ni pescado. **to feel like a f. out of water,** sentirse fuera de su ambiente. **to f. in troubled waters,** no hay revuelto ganancia de pescadores. **f.-eating,** a ictiófago. **f.-fork,** tenedor de pescado, m. **f.-glue,** cola de pescado, f. **f.-hook,** anzuelo, m. **f.-knife,** cuchillo de pescado, m. **f.-like,** de pez; como un pez, parecido a un pez. **f. roe,** hueva, f. **f.-server,** pala para pescado, f

fishbone /'fɪʃ,boun/ n espina de pescado, raspa de pescado, f

fisherman /'fɪʃərmən/ n pescador, m

fishery /'fɪʃəri/ n pesquería, f

fishing /'fɪʃiŋ/ n pesca, f, a de pescar. **to go f.,** ir de pesca. **f.-boat,** bote de pesca, m. **f.-floats,** levas, f pl. **f.-line,** sedal, m. **f.-net,** red de pesca, f. **f.-reel,** carrete, carrete, m. **f.-rod,** caña de pescar, f. **f.-tackle,**

aparejo de pesca, m. **f. village,** pueblo de pescadores, m

fishmeal /'fɪʃ,mil/ n harina de pescado, f

fishmonger /'fɪʃ,mʌŋgər/ n pescadero (-ra).

fishmonger's shop pescadería, f

fishpond /'fɪʃ,pɒnd/ n vivero, m, piscina, f

fishwife /'fɪʃ,waif/ n pescadora, f

fishy /'fɪʃi/ a de pescado; (of eyes, etc.) de pez, como un pez; (in smell) que huele a pescado; Inf. sospechoso; (of stories) inverosímil

fissure /'fɪʃər/ n grieta, hendidura, rendija, f; (Anat. Geol.) fisura, f

fissured /'fɪʃərd/ a hendido

fist /fɪst/ n puño, m; Print. manecilla, f; (handwriting) letra, f. **with clenched fists,** a puño cerrado

fisticuff /'fɪstɪ,kʌf/ n puñetazo, m; pl **fisticuffs,** agarrada, riña, f

fit /fɪt/ n espasmo, paroxismo, m; ataque, m; (impulse) acceso, arranque, m; (whim) capricho, m; (of a garment) corte, m; (adjustment) ajuste, encaje, m. **by fits and starts,** a tropezones, espasmódicamente

fit /fɪt/ a a propósito (para), bueno (para); (opportune) oportuno; (proper) conveniente; apto; (decent) decente; (worthy) digno; (ready) preparado, listo; (adequate) adecuado; (capable) capaz, en estado (de); (appropriate) apropiado; (just) justo. **It is not in a fit state to be used,** No está en condiciones para usarse. **to be not fit for,** no servir para; (through ill-health) no tener bastante salud para. **to think fit,** creer (or juzgar) conveniente. **fit for use,** usable. **fit to eat,** comestible

fit /fɪt/ vt ajustar, acomodar, encajar; adaptar (a); (furnish) proveer (de), surtir (con); (of tailor, dressmaker) entallar, probar; (of shoemaker) calzar; (of garments, shoes) ir (bien o mal); (prepare) preparar; (go with) ser apropiado (a); (adapt itself to) adaptarse a. —vi ajustarse, acomodarse, encajarse; adaptarse; (clothes) ir (bien o mal). **to fit in,** vt encajar; incluir. —vi encajarse; caber; adaptarse. **to fit out,** equipar, proveer (de); preparar. **to fit up,** montar, instalar; proveer (de). **to fit with,** proveer de

fitful /'fɪtfəl/ a intermitente, espasmódico; caprichoso

fitfully /'fɪtfəli/ adv por intervalos, a ratos; caprichosamente

fitly /'fɪtli/ adv adecuadamente; justamente; apropiadamente

fitment /'fɪtmənt/ n equipo, m; instalación, f; (of bookcase, etc.) sección, f; (furniture) pieza, f, mueble, m

fitness /'fɪtnɪs/ n conveniencia, f; aptitud, capacidad, f; oportunidad, f; salud, f; (good health) vigor, m

fitted /'fɪtɪd/ a (of clothes) ajustado

fitter /'fɪtər/ n ajustador, m; (mechanic) armador, mecánico, m; (tailoring) cortador, m; (dressmaking) probador (-ra)

fitting /'fɪtiŋ/ n encaje, ajuste, m; adaptación, f; (of a garment) prueba, f; (size) medida, f; (installation) instalación, f; pl. **fittings,** guarniciones, f pl; instalaciones, f pl; accesorios, m pl. —a conveniente, justo; apropiado; adecuado; (worthy) digno; (of coats, etc.) ajustado. **f. room,** cuarto de pruebas, m. **f. in,** encaje, m. **f. out,** equipo, m. **f. up,** arreglo, m; (of machines) montaje, m; (of a house) mueblaje, m

five /faiv/ a and n cinco m.; (of the clock) las cinco, f pl; (of age) cinco años, m pl. **to be f.,** tener cinco años. **f. feet deep,** de cinco pies de profundidad. **f. feet high,** cinco pies de altura. **f.-finger exercises,** ejercicios de piano, m pl. **F.-Year Plan,** Plan Quinquenal, m

fivefold /'faiv,fould/ a quíntuplo

fix /fɪks/ n aprieto, apuro, m; callejón sin salida, m. —vt fijar; sujetar; afianzar; (bayonets) calar; (with nails) clavar; (Photo., Chem., Med.) fijar; (decide) establecer; (a date) señalar; (eyes, attention) clavar; (on the mind) grabar, estampar; (one's hopes) poner; (base) basar, fundar; (Inf. put right) arreglar, componer. —vi fijarse; establecerse; determinarse. **to get in a fix,** hacerse un lío. **to fix a price,** fijar un precio. **to fix on, upon,** elegir, escoger; decidir, determinar. **to fix up,** arreglar; decidir; organizar; (differences) olvidar (sus disensiones)

fixation /fɪk'seiʃən/ n obsesión, idea fija, f; (scientific) fijación, f

fixative /'fɪksətɪv/ n (Med., Photo.) fijador, m; (dyeing) mordiente, m. —a que fija

fixed /fɪkst/ a fijo; inmóvil; permanente; (of ideas) inflexible. **f. bayonet,** bayoneta calada, f. **f. price,** precio fijo, m. **f. star,** estrella fija, f

fixedly /'fɪksɪdli/ adv fijamente; resueltamente; firmemente

fixing /'fɪksɪŋ/ n fijación, f; afianzamiento, m; arreglo, m; (of a date) señalamiento, m. **f. bath,** Photo. baño fijador, m

fixity /'fɪksɪti/ n permanencia, f; inmovilidad, f; invariabilidad, f; firmeza, f

fixture /'fɪkstʃər/ n instalación, f; accesorio fijo, m; Sports. partido, m; Inf. permanencia, f. **f. card,** Sports. calendario deportivo, m

fizz /fɪz/ n espuma, f; chisporroteo, m. Inf. champaña, m. —vi (liquids) espumear; (sputter) chisporrotear

fizzle /'fɪzəl/ n (failure) fiasco, fracaso, m. —vi chisporrotear; (out) apagarse; (fail) fracasar, no tener éxito

fjord /fyɔrd/ n fiordo, m

flabbergast /'flæbər,gæst/ vt dejar con la boca abierta, dejar de una pieza

flabbiness, flaccidity /'flæbɪnɪs; flæk'sɪdɪti/ n flaccidez, flojedad, f; Med. reblandecimiento, m; (of character) debilidad, flaqueza del ánimo, f

flabby, flaccid /'flæbi; 'flæksɪd/ a fláccido, flojo; Fig. débil

flag /flæg/ n bandera, f; pabellón, estandarte, m; (small) banderola, f; (iris) (yellow) cala, f, (purple) lirio cárdeno, m; (stone) losa, f. **to dip the f.,** saludar con la bandera. **to hoist the f.,** izar la bandera. **to strike the f.,** bajar la bandera; (in defeat) rendir la bandera. **f. bearer,** portaestandarte, abanderado, m. **f.-day,** día de la banderita, m; (in U.S.A.) día de la bandera, m. **f.-officer,** almirante, m; vicealmirante, m; jefe de escuadra, m. **f. of truce,** bandera blanca, bandera de paz, f

flag /flæg/ vi flaquear, debilitarse; languidecer; (wither) marchitarse; decaer, disminuir. —vt adornar con banderas; (signal) hacer señales con una bandera; (for a race, etc.) marcar con banderas; (with stones) enlosar, embaldosar

flagellant /'flædʒələnt/ n flagelante, m

flagellate /'flædʒə,leit/ vt flagelar

flagellation /,flædʒə'leiʃən/ n flagelación, f

flageolet /,flædʒə'let/ n Mus. caramillo, m, chirimía, f. **f. player,** chirimía, m

flagging /'flægɪŋ/ n pavimentación, f; (floor) enlosado, m. —a lánguido, flojo

flagon /'flægən/ n frasco, m; botella, f

flagrancy /'fleigrənsi/ n escándalo, m, notoriedad, f

flagrant /'fleigrənt/ a escandaloso, notorio

flagship /'flæg,ʃɪp/ n capitana, f

flagstaff /'flæg,stæf/ n asta de bandera, f

flagstone /'flæg,stoun/ n losa, lancha, f

flail /fleil/ n mayal, m

flair /fleər/ n instinto natural, m, comprensión innata, f; habilidad natural, f

flak /flæk/ n cortina (or barrera) antiaérea, f

flake /fleik/ n escama, f; laminilla, hojuela, f; (of snow) copo, m; (of fire) chispa, f. —vi cubrir con escamas, etc.; exfoliar; (crumble) hacer migas de, desmigajar. —vi escamarse; (off) exfoliarse; caer en copos

flaky /'fleiki/ a escamoso; en laminillas; (of pastry) hojaldrado. **f. pastry,** hojaldre, f

flamboyance /flæm'bɔiəns/ n extravagancia, f, Lit. ampulosidad, f

flamboyant /flæm'bɔiənt/ a Archit. flamígero; extravagante, llamativo, rimbombante; (of style) ampuloso. **f. gothic,** gótico florido, m

flame /fleim/ n llama, f; Fig. fuego, m. Inf. amorío, m, vi flamear, llamear; arder, abrasarse; (shine) brillar; (up, Fig.) inflamarse; acalorarse. **f.-colored,** de color de llama, anaranjado. **f.-thrower,** lanzallamas, m

flaming /'fleimɪŋ/ a llameante; abrasador; (of colors)

llamativo, chillón; (of feelings) ardiente, fervoroso, apasionado

flamingo /flə'mɪŋgou/ n Ornith. flamenco, m

Flanders /'flændərz/ flandes, m

flange /flændʒ/ n Mech. reborde, m, vt rebordear

flank /flæŋk/ n (of animal) ijada, f; (human) costado, m; (of hill, etc.) lado, m, falda, f; Mil. flanco, m. —a (Mil. Nav.) por el flanco. —vt lindar con, estar contiguo a; (Mil., Nav.) flanquear. —vi estar al lado de; tocar a, lindar con.

flannel /'flænl/ n franela, f, a de franela

flannelette /,flænl'et/ n moletón, m

flap /flæp/ n golpe, m; (of a sail) zapatazo, m, sacudida, f; (of a pocket) cartera, tapa, f; (of skin) colgajo, m; (of a shoe, etc.) oreja, f; (of a shirt, etc.) falda, f; (of a hat) ala, f; (of trousers) bragueta, f; (rever) solapa, f; (of a counter) trampa, f; (of a table) hoja plegadiza, f; (of the wings) aletazo, m; (of w.c.) tapa, f. —vt sacudir, golpear, batir; agitar; (the tail) menear. —vi agitarse; (of wings) aletear; (of sails) zapatear, sacudirse; colgar. **f.-eared,** de orejas grandes y gachas

flapjack /'flæp,dʒæk/ n Cul. torta de sartén, f; (for powder) polvorera, f

flapper /'flæpər/ n Inf. polla, tobillera, chica "topolino," f

flapping /'flæpɪŋ/ n batimiento, m; (waving) ondulación, f; (of sails) zapatazo, m; (of wings) aleteo, m

flare /fleər/ n fulgor, m, llama, f; hacha, f; Aer. cohete de señales, m; Sew. vuelo, m. —vi relampaguear, fulgurar; brillar; (of a lamp) llamear; (up) encolerizarse, salirse de tino; (of epidemic) declararse; (war, etc.) desencadenarse

flash /flæʃ/ n relámpago, centelleo, m, ráfaga de luz, f; brillo, m; (from a gun) fuego, fogonazo, m; (of wit, genius) rasgo, m; (of joy, etc.) acceso, m. —vi relampaguear, fulgurar, centellear; brillar; cruzar rápidamente, pasar como un relámpago. —vt hacer relampaguear; hacer brillar; (a look, etc.) dar; lanzar; (light) encender; (powder) quemar; transmitir señales por heliógrafo; Inf. sacar a relucir, enseñar. **shoulder-f.,** Mil. emblema, m. **to be gone like a f.,** desaparecer como un relámpago. **to f. out,** brillar, centellear. **f. of lightning,** relámpago, rayo, m. **f. of wit,** agudeza, f, rasgo de ingenio, m

flashback /'flæʃ,bæk/ n episodio intercalado, m, retrospección, f

flashily /'flæʃəli/ adv llamativamente, con mal gusto

flashing /'flæʃɪŋ/ n centelleo, m, llamarada, f. —a centellador, relampagueante; brillante; chispeante

flashlight /'flæʃ,lait/ n luz de magnesio, f; (torch) lamparilla eléctrica, f, rayo, m (Mexico); **f. photograph,** magnesio, m

flashy /'flæʃi/ a llamativo, de mal gusto, charro; frívolo, superficial

flask /flæsk/ n frasco, m, redoma, botella, f; (for powder) frasco, m; (vacuum) termos, m

flat /flæt/ a llano; (smooth) liso; (lying) tendido, tumbado; (flattened) aplastado; (destroyed) arrasado; (stretched out) extendido; (of nose, face) chato, romo; (of tire) desinflado; (uniform) uniforme; (depressed) desanimado; (uninteresting) monótono; (boring) aburrido; Com. paralizado; (downright) categórico; absoluto; (net) neto; Mus. bemol; (of boats) de fondo plano. —adv See **flatly.** n planicie, f; (of a sword) hoja, f; (of the hand) palma, f; (land) llanura, f; (apartment) piso, m; Mus. bemol, m. **to fall f.,** caer de bruces; Fig. no tener éxito. **to make f.,** allanar. **to sing f.,** desafinar. **f. boat,** barco de fondo plano, m. **f.-footed,** de pies achatados; Fig. pedestre. **f.-iron,** plancha, f. **f. roof,** azotea, f

flatly /'flætli/ adv de plano; a nivel; (plainly) llanamente, netamente; (dully) indiferentemente; (categorically) categóricamente

flatness /'flætnɪs/ n planicie, f; llanura, f; (smoothness) lisura, f; (evenness) igualdad, f; (uninteresting-ness) insulsez, insipidez, f; aburrimiento, m; (depression) desaliento, abatimiento, m

flatten /'flætn/ vt aplanar, allanar; aplastar; (smooth) alisar; (even) igualar; (destroy) derribar, arrasar, destruir; (dismay) desconcertar; (out) extender. —vi aplanarse, allanarse; aplastarse

flattening /'flætnɪŋ/ n achatamiento, m, allanamiento, m; aplastamiento, m; igualación, f
flatter /'flætər/ vt adular, lisonjear, halagar; (of a dress, photograph, etc.) favorecer, (please the senses) regalar, deleitar; (oneself) felicitarse
flatterer /'flætərər/ n adulador (-ra), lisonjero (-ra)
flattering /'flætərɪŋ/ a adulador, lisonjero; (promising) halagüeño; favoreciente; deleitoso
flattery /'flætəri/ n adulación, f
flat tire llanta desinflada, f
flatulence /'flætʃələns/ n flatulencia, f
flatulent /'flætʃələnt/ a flatulento
flaunt /flɔnt/ vi (flutter) ondear; pavonearse. —vt desplegar; ostentar, sacar a relucir; enseñar
flaunting /'flɔntɪŋ/ n ostentación, f; alarde, m. —a ostentoso; magnífico; (fluttering) ondeante
flautist /'flɔtɪst/ n flautista, mf
flavor /'fleivər/ n sabor, gusto, m; Cul. condimento, m; Fig. dejo, m. —vt Cul. sazonar, condimentar; dar un gusto (de), hacer saborear (a); Fig. dar un dejo (de)
flavored /'fleivərd/ a (in compounds) de sabor...; sazonado; que tiene sabor de...
flavoring /'fleivərɪŋ/ n Cul. condimento, m; Fig. sabor, dejo, m
flavorless /'fleivərlɪs/ a insípido, soso, sin sabor
flaw /flɔ/ n desperfecto, m, imperfección, f; (crack) grieta, hendedura, f; (in wood, metals) quebraja, f; (in gems) pelo, m; (in fruit) maca, f; (in cloth) gabarro, m; Fig. defecto, error, m; (wind) ráfaga de viento, f
flawless /'flɔlɪs/ a sin defecto; perfecto; impecable
flawlessness /'flɔlɪsnɪs/ n perfección, f; impecabilidad, f
flax /flæks/ n lino, m. **to dress f.**, rastrillar lino. **f.-comb**, rastrillo, m. **f. field**, linar, m
flaxen /'flæksən/ a de lino; (fair) rubio, blondo. **f.-haired**, de pelo rubio
flay /flei/ vt desollar; (criticize) despellejar
flaying /'fleiɪŋ/ n desuello, m, desolladura, f
flea /fli/ n pulga, f. **f. bite**, picada de pulga, f
fleck /flɛk/ n pinta, mancha, f, lunar, m; (of sun) mota, f; (speck) partícula, f; (freckle) peca, f. —vt abigarrar; manchar; (dapple) salpicar, motear
fledged /flɛdʒd/ a emplumecido, plumado; alado; Fig. maduro
fledgling /'flɛdʒlɪŋ/ n volantón, m; Fig. niño (-ña); Fig. novato (-ta)
flee /fli/ vi huir, fugarse, escapar; (vanish) desaparecer; (avoid) evitar, huir de. —vt abandonar
fleece /flis/ n vellón, f; lana, f; toisón, m. —vt esquilar; Fig. Inf. pelar. **Order of the Golden F.**, Orden del Toisón de Oro, f
fleecy /'flisi/ a lanudo, lanar; (white) blanquecino; (of clouds) borreguero. **f. clouds**, borregos, m pl
fleet /flit/ n (navy) armada, f; escuadra, flota, f; Fig. serie, f, a alado, rápido, veloz. **F. Air Arm**, Aviación Naval, f. **f.-footed**, ligero de pies
fleeting /'flitɪŋ/ a fugaz, momentáneo, efímero, pasajero
Flemish /'flɛmɪʃ/ a flamenco. —n (language) flamenco, m
flesh /flɛʃ/ n carne, f; (mankind) género humano, m, humanidad, f; (of fruit) pulpa, f. **a man of f. and blood**, un hombre de carne y hueso. **of one's own f. and blood**, de la misma sangre de uno. **to make one's f. creep**, dar carne de gallina (a). **f.-coloured**, encarnado, de color de carne. **f.-eating**, carnívoro. **f. wound**, herida superficial, f
fleshiness /'flɛʃɪnɪs/ n carnosidad, gordura, f
fleshpot /'flɛʃˌpɒt/ n marmita, f; Fig. olla, f. **the fleshpots of Egypt**, las ollas de Egipto
fleshy /'flɛʃi/ a carnoso, grueso; (of fruit) pulposo; suculento
fleur-de-lis /ˌflɜrdl̩'i/ n flor de lis, f
flex /flɛks/ n Elec. flexible, m, vt doblar. —vi doblarse
flexibility /ˌflɛksə'bɪlɪti/ n flexibilidad, f; (of style) plasticidad, f; docilidad, f
flexible /'flɛksəbəl/ a flexible; dúctil, maleable; (of style) plástico; of) voice) quebradizo; adaptable; dócil

flexion /'flɛkʃən/ n flexión, f; Gram. inflexión, f; Gram. flexión, f
flexor /'flɛksər/ n Anat. músculo flexor, m
flick /flɪk/ n golpecito, toque, m; (of the finger) capirotazo, m; Inf. cine, m, vt dar un golpecito a; dar ligeramente con un látigo; sacudir. **flick one's wrist** hacer girar la muñeca a **to f. over the pages of,** hojear
flicker /'flɪkər/ n estremecimiento, temblor, m; fluctuación, f; (of bird) aleteo, m; (of flame) onda (de una llama), f; (of eyelashes) pestañeo, m; (of a smile) indicio, f, vi agitarse; (of flags) ondear; vacilar
flickering /'flɪkərɪŋ/ a tenue; vacilante
flier /'flaiər/ n volador (-ra); aviador (-ra); piloto, m; fugitivo (-va)
flight /flait/ n vuelo, m; (of bird of prey) colada, f; (flock of birds) bandada, f; (migration) migración, f; (of time) transcurso, m; (of imagination, etc.) arranque, m; (volley) lluvia, f; (of aeroplanes) escuadrilla (de aviones), f; (of stairs) tramo, tiro, m; (staircase) escalera, f; (of locks on canal, etc.) ramal, m; (escape) huida, fuga, f. **long-distance f.,** Aer. vuelo de distancia, m. **non-stop f.,** Aer. vuelo sin parar, m. **reconnaissance f.,** Aer. vuelo de reconocimiento, vuelo de patrulla, m. **test f.,** Aer. vuelo de pruebas, m. **to put to f.,** ahuyentar, poner en fuga. **to take f.,** alzar el vuelo. **f.-lieutenant,** teniente aviador, m. **f.-sergeant,** sargento aviador, m
flight attendant sobrecarbo mf
flightiness /'flaitinɪs/ n frivolidad, veleidad, ligereza, f
flighty /'flaiti/ a frívolo, inconstante, veleidoso
flimsiness /'flɪmzinɪs/ n falta de solidez, endeblez, f; fragilidad, f; (of arguments) futilidad, f
flimsy /'flɪmzi/ a endeble; frágil; fútil, insubstancial
flinch /flɪntʃ/ vi echarse atrás, retirarse (ante); vacilar, titubear. **without flinching,** sin vacilar; sin quejarse
fling /flɪŋ/ vt arrojar, echar, tirar; lanzar; (scatter) derramar; (oneself) echarse; (oneself upon) echarse encima; Fig. confiar en. —vi lanzarse; marcharse precipitadamente; saltar. —n tiro, m; (of dice, etc.) echada, f; (gibe) sarcasmo, m, burla, chufleta, f; (of horse) respingo, brinco, m; baile escocés, m. **in full f.,** en plena operación; en progreso. **to have one's f.,** darse un verde, correrla. **to f. away,** vt desechar; (waste) desperdiciar, malgastar, perder. —vi marcharse enfadado; marcharse rápidamente. **to f. back,** (a ball) devolver; (the head) echar atrás. **to f. down,** tirar al suelo; arrojar; derribar. **to f. off,** vt rechazar; apartar; (a garment, etc.) quitar. —vi marcharse sin más ni más. **to f. oneself down,** tumbarse, echarse; despeñarse (por). **to f. oneself headlong,** despeñarse. **to f. open,** abrir violentamente, abrir de repente. **to f. out,** echar a la fuerza; (a hand) alargar, extender. —vi salir apresuradamente. **to f. over,** (upset) volcar; arrojar por; abandonar. **to f. up,** lanzar al aire; levantar, erguir; renunciar (a), abandonar; dejar
flint /flɪnt/ n pedernal, m; (for producing fire) piedra de encender, f
flinty /'flɪnti/ a pedernalino; Fig. endurecido
flippancy /'flɪpənsi/ n levedad, ligereza, f; frivolidad, f; impertinencia, f
flippant /'flɪpənt/ a poco serio, ligero; frívolo; impertinente
flipper /'flɪpər/ n aleta, f
flirt /flɜrt/ n (man) coquetón, castigador, m; (woman) coqueta, castigadora, f. —vt (shake) sacudir; (move) agitar; (wave) menear. —vi flirtear, coquetear; (toy with) jugar con; divertirse con
flirtation /flɜr'teiʃən/ n flirteo, amorío, m
flirtatious /flɜr'teiʃəs/ a (of men) galanteador, castigador; (of women) coqueta
flit /flɪt/ vi revolotear, mariposear; (move silently) deslizarse, pasar silenciosamente; (depart) irse, marcharse; mudarse por los aires. **to f. about,** ir y venir silenciosamente. **to f. past,** pasar como una sombra
flitch /flɪtʃ/ n (of bacon) hoja de tocino, f
float /flout/ n masa flotante, f; (raft) balsa, f; Mech. flotador, m; (of fishing rod or net) corcho, m; (of fish) vejiga natatoria, f; (for swimming) nadadera, calabaza, f; (for tableaux) carroza, f; pl **floats,** Theat.

candilejas, f pl. —vi flotar; (flags, hair, etc.) ondear; (wander) vagar; Naut. boyar. —vt poner a flote; hacer flotar; (a grounded ship) desencallar; (Com. a company) fundar; (a loan, etc.) emitir, poner en circulación; (launch a ship) botar; (flood) inundar

floating /'floutɪŋ/ n flotación, f, flote, m; Com. fundación (de una compañía), f; (of a loan) emisión, f; (of a ship) botadura, f. —a flotante; boyante; Com. en circulación, flotante; fluctuante, variable. **f. capital**, capital fluctuante, m. **f. debt,** deuda flotante, f. **f. dock,** dique flotante, m. **f. light,** buque faro, m. **f. population,** población flotante, f. **f. rib,** costilla flotante, f

flock /flɒk/ n rebaño, m, manada, f; (of birds) bandada, f; Fig. grey, f; (crowd) multitud, muchedumbre, f; (parishioners) congregación, f; (of wool or cotton) vedija (de lana or de algodón), f; pl **flocks,** (for stuffing) borra, f. —vi concurrirse, reunirse, congregarse; ir en tropel, acudir; (birds) volar en bandada. **f.-bed,** colchón de borra, m

floe /flou/ n banco de hielo, m

flog /flɒg/ vt azotar; castigar

flogging /'flɒgɪŋ/ n azotamiento, vapuleo, m

flood /flʌd/ n inundación, f; (Bible) diluvio, m; (of the tide) flujo, m; Fig. torrente, m; (abundance) copia, abundancia, f; (fit) paroxismo, m. —vt inundar; sumergir; (of tears) mojar. —vi desbordar. **f. lighting,** iluminación intensiva, f

floodgate /'flʌd,geit/ n compuerta (de esclusa), f

flooding /'flʌdɪŋ/ n inundación, f; desbordamiento, m; Med. hemorragia uterina, f

floodtide /'flʌd,taid/ n marea creciente, f

floor /flɔr/ n suelo, piso, m; (wooden) entarimado, m; (story) piso, m; (of a cart) cama, f; Agr. era, f. —vt entablar; echar al suelo, derribar; Fig. desconcertar, confundir. **on the f.,** en el suelo. **on the ground f.,** en el piso bajo. **to take the f.,** Fig. tener la palabra. **f.-polisher,** lustrador de piso, m

flooring /'flɔrɪŋ/ n tablado, m, tablazón, f; piso, m

flop /flɒp/ n golpe, m; ruido sordo, m; (splash) chapoteo, m; Inf. fiasco, m. —vi dejarse caer

flora /'flɔrə/ n flora, f

floral /'flɔrəl/ a floral. **f. games,** juegos florales, m pl

Florence /'flɔrəns/ Florencia, f

Florentine /'flɔrən,tin/ a and n florentino (-na)

florescence /flɔ'rɛsəns/ n florescencia, f

florid /'flɔrɪd/ a florido; demasiado ornado, cursi, llamativo; (of complexion) rubicundo

floridness /'flɔrɪdnɪs/ n floridez, f, estilo florido, f; demasiada ornamentación, vulgaridad, f, mal gusto, m; (of complexion) rubicundez, f

florin /'flɔrɪn/ n florín, m

florist /'flɔrɪst/ n florista, mf

floss /flɔs/ n seda floja, filoseda, f; (of maize) penacho, m; (of a cocoon) cadarzo, m. **f. silk,** seda floja, f

flotilla /flou'tɪlə/ n flotilla, f

flotsam /'flɒtsəm/ n pecio, m

flounce /flauns/ n volante, m, vi saltar de impaciencia. **to f. out,** salir airadamente

flounder /'flaundər/ n (nearest equivalent) Ichth. platija, f; tumbo, m. —vi tropezar; revolcarse; andar dificultosamente

flour /flauᵊr/ n harina, f, vt enharinar. **f.-bin,** tina, f, harinero, m. **f. merchant,** harinero, m

flourish /'flɜrɪʃ/ n movimiento, m; gesto, saludo, m; (of a pen) plumada, f; (on the guitar, in fencing) floreo, m; preludio, m; (fanfare) tocata (de trompetas), f; (of a signature) rúbrica, f; (in rhetoric) floreo, m. —vi (of plants) vegetar; (prosper) prosperar, medrar; florecer; (of the guitar, in fencing) florear; Mus. preludiar; (with a pen) hacer plumadas (or rasgos de pluma); (of a signature) firmar con rúbrica; (sound a fanfare) hacer una tocata (de trompetas). —vt agitar en el aire, blandir

flourishing /'flɜrɪʃɪŋ/ a (of plants) lozano; floreciente; (prosperous) próspero; (happy) feliz

flourmill /'flauᵊr,mɪl/ n molino de harina, m, fábrica de harina, f, molina harinero, m

floury /'flauri, 'flauəri/ a harinoso

flout /flaut/ vt burlarse de; despreciar, no hacer caso de

flow /flou/ n flujo, m; corriente, f; chorro, m; (of water) caudal, m; (output) producción total, cantidad, f; (of the tide) flujo (de la marea), m; (of words) facilidad, f. —vi fluir, manar; correr; (of the tide) crecer (la marea); (pass) pasar, correr; (result) resultar (de), provenir (de); (of hair, drapery) caer, ondular; (abound) abundar (en). **to f. away,** escaparse, salir. **to f. back,** refluir. **to f. down,** descender, fluir hacia abajo; (of tears) correr por. **to f. from,** dimanar de; manar de; Fig. provenir de. **to f. in,** llegar en abundancia. **to f. into,** (rivers) desaguar en, desembocar en. **to f. over,** derramarse por. **to f. through,** fluir por; atravesar; (water) regar. **to f. together,** (rivers) confluir

flower /'flauər/ n flor, f; (best) flor y nata, crema, f. —vi florecer. **in f.,** en flor. **No flowers by request,** (for a funeral) No flores por deseo del finado. **f.-bud,** capullo, m. **f.-garden,** jardín, m. **f. girl,** florista, vendedora de flores, f. **f. market,** mercado de flores, m. **f.-piece,** florero, m. **f. pot,** tiesto, m, maceta, f. **f. show,** exposición de flores, f. **f. vase,** florero, m

flowerbed /'flauər,bɛd/ n cuadro, macizo, m

flower car coche portacoronas, m

flowered /'flauərd/ a (in compounds) con flores; con dibujos de flores

floweriness /'flauərɪnɪs/ n abundancia de flores, f; (of style) floridez, f, estilo florido, m

flowering /'flauərɪŋ/ n florecimiento, m. —a floreciente; con flores; (of shrubs) de adorno. **f. season,** época de la floración, f

flowery /'flauəri/ a florido

flowing /'flouɪŋ/ n flujo, m; derrame, m. —a fluente, corriente, f; (of tide) creciente; (waving) ondeante; suelto; (of style) flúido

flow of capital corriente de capital, f

fluctuate /'flʌktʃu,eit/ vi fluctuar, vacilar; variar

fluctuating /'flʌktʃu,eitɪŋ/ a fluctuante, vacilante; variable; (hesitating) irresoluto, dudoso

fluctuation /,flʌktʃu'eiʃən/ n fluctuación, f; cambio, m, variación, f; (hesitancy) indecisión, vacilación, f

flue /flu/ n (of a chimney) cañón, m; (of a boiler) tubo, m

fluency /'fluənsi/ n fluidez, f

fluent /'fluənt/ a flúido; fácil

fluently /'fluəntli/ adv corrientemente, con facilidad, de corrido

fluff /flʌf/ n borra, pelusa, f, tamo, m

fluffy /'flʌfi/ a velloso; (feathered) plumoso; (woolly) lanudo; (of hair) encrespado

fluid /'fluːd/ n flúido, líquido, m, a flúido

fluidity /flu'ɪdɪti/ n fluidez, f

fluke /fluk/ n (in billiards) chiripa, f; Naut. uña, f; Inf. carambola, chiripa, chambonada, f. **by a f.,** de carambola, por suerte. **f.-worm,** duela del hígado, f

flunkey /'flʌŋki/ n lacayo, m; Fig. adulador, m

fluorescence /flu'rɛsəns/ n fluorescencia, f

fluorescent /flu'rɛsənt/ a fluorescente

fluorine /'flurin/ n Chem. flúor, m

fluorite /'flurait/ n fluorita, f

flurry /'flʌri/ n (of wind) ráfaga, f; (squall) chubasco, m; agitación, f; conmoción, f. —vt agitar

flush /flʌʃ/ n rubor, m; (in the sky) arrebol, rojo, color de rosa, m; emoción, f; acceso, m; sensación, f; (at cards) flux, m; vigor, m; (flowering) floración, f; abundancia, f; (of youth, etc.) frescura, f. —a (level) igual, parejo; abundante; (generous) pródigo, liberal; (rich) adinerado. —vi ruborizarse, enrojecerse, ponerse colorado; (flood) inundarse, llenarse (de agua, etc.); (of sky) arrebolarse. —vt inundar, limpiar con un chorro de agua, etc., lavar; (of blood) circular por; (redden) enrojecer; (make blush) hacer ruborizarse; (exhilarate) excitar, animar; (inflame) inflamar, encender; (make level) igualar, nivelar. **f. with,** a ras de

flushing /'flʌʃɪŋ/ n rojez, f; (cleansing) limpieza, lavadura, f; (flooding) inundación, f

fluster /'flʌstər/ n agitación, confusión, f, aturdimiento, m. —vt agitar, poner nervioso (a); aturdir; (oneself) preocuparse. —vi agitarse; estar nervioso, estar perplejo; (with drink) estar entre dos velas

flute /flut/ n flauta, f; Archit. estría, f; (organ-stop) flautado, m. —vi tocar la flauta, flautear; tener la voz flauteada. —*vt* tocar (una pieza) en la flauta; (groove) encanutar, acanalar, estriar. **f. player,** flautista, *mf*

fluted /'flutɪd/ *a* (grooved) acanalado

fluting /'flutɪŋ/ *n Mus.* son de la flauta, *m;* (of birds) trinado, *m; Archit.* estría, *f; Sew.* rizado, *m*

flutter /'flʌtər/ *n* (of wings) aleteo, *m;* (of leaves, etc.) murmureo, *m;* (of eyelashes) pestañeo, *m;* (of flags, etc.) ondeo, *m,* ondulación, *f;* (excitement) agitación, *f;* (stir) sensación, *f;* (gamble) jugada, *f.* —*vi* (of birds) aletear; revolotear; (of butterflies) mariposear; (of flags) ondear; palpitar; (of persons) estar agitado. —*vt* agitar; (the eyelashes) pestañear; (agitate) agitar, alarmar

fluttering /'flʌtərɪŋ/ *n* mariposeo, *m;* revoloteo, *m;* (of birds) aleteo, *m;* (of leaves, etc.) murmureo, *m;* (of flags, etc.) ondeo, *m,* ondulación, *f;* (of eyelashes) pestañeo, *m*

fluvial /'fluviəl/ *a* fluvial

flux /flʌks/ *n* flujo, *m*

fly /flaɪ/ *n* (insect) mosca, *f;* (on a fishhook) mosca artificial, *f;* (carriage) calesín, *m;* (of breeches) bragueta, *f; Theat.* bambalina, *f;* (of a tent) toldo, *m;* (flight) vuelo, *m;* (of a flag) vuelo, *m.* **fly-blown,** manchado por las moscas. **fly-by-night,** trasnochador (-ra). **fly-catcher,** *Ornith.* papamoscas, *m;* matamoscas, *m.* **fly-fishing,** pesca con moscas artificiales, *f.* **fly-leaf,** guarda (de un libro), *f.* **fly-paper,** papel matamoscas, *m.* **fly-swatter,** matamoscas, *m.* **fly-wheel,** *Mech.* volante, *m*

fly /flaɪ/ *vi* volar; (flutter) ondear; (jump) saltar; (rush) lanzarse, precipitarse; (pass away) pasar volando, volar; (run off) marcharse a todo correr; (escape) huir, escapar; (seek refuge) refugiarse; (to the head, of intoxicants) subirse; (vanish) desaparecer. —*vt* hacer volar; hacer ondear, enarbolar; (an airplane) pilotar, dirigir; (flee from) huir de; evitar. **to let fly (at),** descargar, tirar; *Fig.* saltar la sinhueso. **to fly about,** volar en torno de; revolotear. **to fly at,** lanzarse sobre; acometer, asaltar. **to fly away,** emprender el vuelo. **to fly back,** volar hacia el punto de partida; (of doors, etc.) abrir, o cerrar, de repente. **to fly down,** volar abajo. **to fly in,** volar dentro de; volar adentro; (of airplanes) llegar (el avión). **to fly in pieces,** hacerse pedazos. **to fly into a rage,** montarse en cólera. **to fly low,** rastrear; *Aer.* volar a poca altura. **to fly off,** emprender el vuelo; (hasten) marcharse volando; (of buttons, etc.) saltar (de), separarse (de). **to fly open,** abrirse de repente. **to fly over,** volar por, volar por encima de. **to fly upwards,** volar hacia arriba; subir

flying /'flaɪɪŋ/ *n* vuelo, *m.* —*a* volante, volador; que vuela; de volar; volátil; (hasty) rápido; (flowing) ondeante, ondulante. **to shoot f.,** tirar al vuelo. **with f. colors,** con banderas desplegadas, triunfante. **f.-boat,** hidroavión, *m.* **f.-buttress,** botarel, arbotante, *m.* **f.-column,** columna volante, *m.* **f.-fish,** (pez) volador, *m.* **f.-fortress,** *Aer.* fortaleza volante, *f.* **f.-officer,** oficial de aviación, *m.* **f.-sickness,** mal de altura, *m.* **f.-squad,** escuadra ligera, *f.* **f.-test,** *Aer.* examen de pilotaje, *m*

foal /foul/ *n* potro (-ra). —*vi* and *vt* parir una yegua

foam /foum/ *n* espuma, *f.* —*vi* espumar; (of horses, etc.) echar espumarajos. **to f. and froth,** (of the sea) hervir. **f. at the mouth,** echar espuma por la boca.

foam rubber *n* caucho esponjoso, *m,* espuma de caucho, *f,* espuma sintética, *f*

foamy /'foumi/ *a* espumoso

fob /fɒb/ *n* bolsillo del reloj, *m;* faltriquera pequeña, *f.* —*vt* (off) engañar con

focal /'foukəl/ *a* focal

focus /'foukəs/ *n* foco, *m;* centro, *m.* —*vt* enfocar; concentrar. —*vi* convergir. **in f.,** en foco

fodder /'fɒdər/ *n Agr.* pienso, forraje, *m.* —*vt* dar forraje (a)

foe /fou/ *n* enemigo, *m*

fog /fɒg/ *n* neblina, niebla, *f; Fig.* confusión, *f; Fig.* perplejidad, *f, vt* obscurecer; *Photo.* velar; *Fig.* ofuscar. —*vi* hacerse nebuloso; *Photo.* velarse. **fog-signal,** señal de niebla, *f*

fogbound /'fɒg,baund/ *a* rodeado de niebla; detenido por la niebla

fogey /'fougi/ *n* obscurantista, *m.* **He is an old f.,** Es un señor chapado a la antigua

fogginess /'fɒgɪnɪs/ *n* oscuridad, neblina, *f*

foggy /'fɒgi/ *a* nebuloso; *Photo.* velado. **It is f.,** Hay niebla

foghorn /'fɒg,hɔrn/ *n* sirena, *f;* bocina, *f*

foible /'fɔɪbəl/ *n* flaco, *m,* debilidad, *f*

foil /fɔɪl/ *n* (sword) florete, *m;* (coat) hoja, *f;* (of a mirror) azogado, *m.* —*vt* frustrar. **f. a plot,** desbaratar un complot. **She makes a good f. for her sister's beauty,** Hace resaltar la belleza de su hermana

foiling /'fɔɪlɪŋ/ *n* frustración, *f*

foist /fɔɪst/ *vt* imponer; insertar, incluir; engañar (con)

fold /fould/ *n* doblez, *f,* pliegue, *m;* arruga, *f; Sew.* cogido, *m;* (for sheep) redil, aprisco, *m; Fig.* iglesia, congregación de los fieles, *f;* (in compounds) vez, *f.* —*vt* doblar, plegar, doblegar; (the arms) cruzar (los brazos); (embrace) abrazar; (wrap) envolver; (clasp) entrelazar; (sheep) meter en redil, encerrar. —*vi* doblarse, plegarse; cerrarse

folder /'fouldər/ *n* doblador (-ra); plegadera, *f*

folding /'fouldɪŋ/ *n* plegadura, *f,* doblamiento, *m;* (of sheep) encerramiento, *m, a* plegadizo. **f.-door,** puerta plegadiza, *f.* **f.-machine,** plegador, *m.* **f.-seat,** *Auto.* traspuntín, *m.* **f.-table,** mesa de tijeras, *f;* mesa plegadiza, *f*

foliage /'fouliɪdʒ/ *n* follaje, *m,* frondas, *f pl.* **thick f.,** frondosidad, *f*

folio /'fouli,ou/ *n* folio, *m;* (a volume) infolio, *m.* —*a* de infolio. —*vt* foliar

folk /fouk/ *n* (nation) pueblo, *m,* nación, *f;* gente, *f; pl* **folks,** *Inf.* familia, *f;* parientes, *m pl.* **f.-dance,** danza popular, *f*

folklore /'fouk,lɔr/ *n* folclore, *m,* tradiciones folclóricas, *f pl*

folklorist /'fouk,lɔrɪst/ *n* folclorista, *mf*

folksong /'fouk,sɔŋ/ *n* canción popular, *f;* romance, *m;* copla, *f*

folktale /'fouk,teil/ *n* conseja, *f,* cuento popular, *m*

follicle /'fɒlɪkəl/ *n* (Anat., Bot.) folículo, *m*

follow /'fɒlou/ *vt* seguir; (pursue) perseguir; (hunt) cazar; (adopt) adoptar; (understand) comprender; (notice) observar. —*vi* ir, or venir, detrás; (of time) venir después; (gen. impers.) seguir, resultar; seguirse. **as follows,** como sigue. **I shall f. your advice,** Seguiré tus consejos. **to f. on the heels of,** *Fig.* pisar los talones (a). **to f. suit,** (at cards) asistir, jugar el mismo palo; *Fig.* imitar. **to f. up,** proseguir; continuar; (pursue) perseguir; (enhance) reforzar. **f.-me-lads,** *Inf.* siguemepollo, *m*

follower /'fɒlouər/ *n* seguidor (-ra); adherente, secuaz, *mf;* (imitator) imitador (-ra); (lover) novio, *m; pl* **followers,** acompañamiento, séquito, *m*

following /'fɒlouɪŋ/ *n* séquito, acompañamiento, *m,* comitiva, *f;* partidarios, *m pl,* adherentes, *mf pl.* —*a* siguiente; próximo. **f. wind,** viento en popa, *m*

folly /'fɒli/ *n* locura, extravagancia, absurdidad, tontería, *f,* disparate, *m*

foment /fou'ment/ *vt* (poultice) fomentar, provocar, incitar, instigar; (assist) fomentar, proteger, promover

fomentation /,foumen'teiʃən/ *n Med.* fomentación, *f;* provocación, instigación, *f;* fomento, *m,* protección, *f*

fomenter /'foumentər/ *n* fomentador (-ra), instigador (-ra)

fond /fɒnd/ *a* (credulous) vano, crédulo, vacío; (doting) demasiado indulgente; (loving) cariñoso, tierno, afectuoso; (addicted to) aficionado a, adicto a, amigo de. **to be f. of,** (things) tener afición a, estar aficionado de; (people) tener cariño (a). **to grow f. of,** (things) aficionarse a; (people) tomar cariño (a)

fondle /'fɒndl/ *vt* mimar, acariciar; jugar (con.)

fondly /'fɒndli/ *adv* (vainly) vanamente, sin razón; cariñosamente, tiernamente

fondness /'fɒndnɪs/ *n* cariño, afecto, *m;* (for things) afición, inclinación, *f;* gusto, *m*

font /fɒnt/ *n* pila bautismal, *f; Poet.* fuente, *f; Print.* fundición, *f*

food /fud/ *n* alimento, *m;* comida, *f,* el comer; (of animals) pasto, *m; Fig.* pábulo, *m;* materia, *f.* **She gave him f.** Le dio de comer. **You have given me f. for thought,** Me has dado en qué pensar. **f.-card,**

cartilla de racionamiento, **food, clothing, and shelter** comida, abrigo y vivienda, *f.* **F. Ministry,** Ministerio de Alimentación, *m.* **f. value,** valor nutritivo, *m.*

food poisoning, intoxicación alimenticia, *f*

foodstuffs /'fud,stʌfs/ *n pl* comestibles, víveres, *m pl*

fool /ful/ *n* tonto (-ta), mentecato (-ta), majadero (ra) necio (-ia); (jester) bufón, *m;* (butt of jest) hazmerreír, *m;* víctima, *f; Cul.* compota de frutas con crema, *f, vt* tontear, hacer tonterías. —*vt* poner en ridículo (a); (deceive) engañar, embaucar; (with) jugar con. **to make a f. of** oneself, ponerse en ridículo. **to f. about,** *vi* perder el tiempo, vagabundear. **to f. away,** malgastar, malbaratar. **fool's bauble,** cetro de bufón, *m.* **fool's cap,** gorra de bufón, *m*

foolhardiness /'ful,hardinɪs/ *n* temeridad, *f*

foolhardy /'ful,hardi/ *a* temerario, atrevido

fooling /'fulɪŋ/ *n* payasada, bufonada, *f;* (deceiving) engaño, *m,* burla, *f*

foolish /'fulɪʃ/ *a* imprudente; estúpido, tonto; ridículo, absurdo; imbécil

foolishly /'fulɪʃli/ *adv* imprudentemente; tontamente; imbécilmente

foolishness *n* /'fulɪʃnɪs/ imprudencia, *f;* estupidez, tontería, *f,* disparate, *m;* ridiculez, *f;* imbecilidad, *f*

foolproof /'ful,pruf/ *a* (of utensils, etc.) con garantía absoluta

foolscap /'fulz,kæp/ *n* (nearest equivalent) papel de barba, *m*

fool's gold *n* pirita amarilla, *f,* sulfuro de hierro *m*

foot /fut/ *n* pie, *m;* (of animals, furniture) pata, *f;* (of bed, sofa, grave, ladder, page, etc.) pie, *m;* (hoof) pezuña, *f;* (metric unit and measure) pie, *m; Mil.* infantería, *f;* (base) base, *f;* (step) paso, *m.* —*a Mil.* de a pie; a pie. —*vi* ir a pie; venir a pie; bailar. —*vt* hollar; (account) pagar (una cuenta); (stockings) poner pie (a). **on f.,** a pie; (of soldiers) de a pie; (in progress) en marcha. **to go on f.,** ir a pie, andar. **to put one's best f. forward,** apretar el paso; *Fig.* hacer de su mejor. **to put one's f. down,** poner pies en pared, pararle fulano el alto. **To put one's f. in it,** meter la pata. **to rise to one's feet,** ponerse de pie. **to set f. on,** pisar, hollar. **to set on f.,** poner en pie; *Fig.* poner en marcha. **to trample under f.,** pisotear. **f.-and-mouth disease,** glosopeda, *f.* **f.-brake,** freno de pedal, *m.* **f.-pump,** fuelle de pie, *m.* **f.-rule,** (nearest equivalent) doble decímetro, *m.* **f.-soldier,** soldado de a pie, infante, *m*

football /'fut,bɔl/ *n* (game) fútbol, *m;* (ball) pelota de fútbol, *f.* **f. field,** campo de fútbol, *m.* **f. match,** partida de fútbol, *f.* **f. pools,** apuestas de fútbol, *f pl;* (in Spain) apuestas benéficas de fútbol, *f pl*

footballer /'fut,bɔlər/ *n* futbolista, *m*

footbath /'fut,bæθ/ *n* baño de pies, *m*

footbridge /'fut,brɪdʒ/ *n* puente para peatones, *m*

footed /'futɪd/ *a* con pies; de pies...; de patas...

footfall /'fut,fɔl/ *n* pisada, *f,* paso, *m*

foothills /'fut,hɪlz/ *n pl* faldas de la montaña, *f pl*

foothold /'fut,hould/ *n* hincapié, *m;* posición establecida, *f*

footing /'futɪŋ/ *n* hincapié, *m;* posición firme, *f;* condiciones, *f pl;* relaciones, *f pl.* **on a peacetime f.,** en pie de paz. **to be on an equal f.,** estar en pie de igualdad, estar en iguales condiciones. **to miss one's f.,** resbalar

footlights /'fut,laits/ *n pl* candilejas, candilejas, *f pl.* **to get across the f.,** hacer contacto con el público

footman /'futmən/ *n* lacayo, *m*

footnote /'fut,nout/ *n* llamada a pie de página, nota a pie de página, *f*

footpath /'fut,pæθ/ *n* senda, vereda, *f,* sendero, *m*

footprint /'fut,prɪnt/ *n* huella, pisada, *f,* vestigio, *m*

footsore /'fut,sɔr/ *a* con los pies lastimados

footstep /'fut,stɛp/ *n* paso, *m;* (trace) pisada, huella, *f.* **to follow in the footsteps of,** *Fig.* seguir las pisadas de

footstool /'fut,stul/ *n* escabel, banquito, *m*

footwarmer /'fut,wɔrmər/ *n* calientapiés, *m*

footwear /'fut,wɛər/ *n* calzado, *m*

fop /fɒp/ *n* petimetre, *m*

foppery /'fɒpəri/ *n* afectación en el vestir, *f;* vanidad, *f*

foppish /'fɒpɪʃ/ *a* presumido, afectado; elegante

for /fɔr; *unstressed* fər/ *prep* (expressing exchange, price or penalty of, instead of, in support or favor of, on account of) por; (expressing destination, purpose, result) para; (during) durante, por; (for the sake of) para; (because of) a causa de; (in spite of) a pesar de; (as) como; (with) de; (in favor of) en favor de; (in election campaign) con (e.g., "Ecuadorians for Martínez!" ¡Ecuatorianos con Martínez!) (toward) hacia; (that) que, para que (with *subjunc*); a, (before) antes de; (searching for) en busca de; (bound for) con rumbo a; (regarding) en cuanto a; (until) hasta. What's for dinner? ¿Qué hay de comida? **center for...** centro de... (e.g., *Center for Applied Linguistics,* Centro de Lingüística Aplicada). **He is in business for himself,** Tiene negocios por su propia cuenta. **It is raining too hard for you to go there,** Llueve demasiado para que vayas allí. **It is not for him to decide,** No le toca a él decidirlo. **Were it not for...,** Si no fuese por... **She has not been to see me for a week,** Hace una semana que no viene a verme. **It is impossible for them to go out,** Les es imposible salir. **but for all that,** pero con todo. **for ever,** por (or para) siempre. **for fear that,** por miedo de que. **for myself,** en cuanto a mí, personalmente. **for the present,** por ahora. **for what reason?** ¿para qué? ¿por cuál motivo? **for brevity's sake, for the sake of brevity,** por causa de la brevedad

for /fɔr; *unstressed* fər/ *conjunc* porque; visto que, pues, puesto que, en efecto, ya que

forage /'fɔrɪdʒ/ *n* forraje, *m.* —*vt* and *vi* forrajear. **to f. for,** buscar. **f. cap,** gorra de cuartel, *f*

forager /'fɔrɪdʒər/ *n* forrajeador, *m*

foraging /'fɔrɪdʒɪŋ/ *n* forraje, *m*

forasmuch as /,fɔrəz'mʌtʃ ,æz/ *conjunc* puesto que, como que, ya que

foray /'fɔrei/ *n* correría, cabalgada, *f;* saqueo, *m*

forbear /'fɔr,bɛər/ *vt* and *vi* dejar (de), guardarse (de); abstenerse de; evitar; reprimirse (de); rehusarse (de); (cease) cesar (de); (be patient) ser paciente; ser tolerante

forbearance /fɔr'bɛərəns/ *n* abstención, *f;* tolerancia, transigencia, *f;* indulgencia, *f;* paciencia, *f*

forbearing /fɔr'bɛərɪŋ/ *a* tolerante, transigente; generoso, magnánimo; paciente

forbid /fər'bɪd/ *vt* prohibir, defender (de); impedir. **I f. you to do it,** Te prohíbo hacerlo. **The game is forbidden,** El juego está prohibido. **They have forbidden me to...,** Me han defendido de... **Heaven f.!** ¡Dios no lo quiera!

forbidden /fər'bɪdn/ *a* prohibido; ilícito. **f. fruit,** fruto prohibido, *m*

forbidding /fər'bɪdɪŋ/ *a* repugnante, horrible; antipático, desagradable; (dismal) lúgubre; (threatening) amenazador. —*n* prohibición, *f*

force /fɔrs/ *n* fuerza, *f;* violencia, *f;* vigor, *m;* (efficacy) eficacia, *f;* (validity) validez, *f;* (power) poder, *m;* (motive) motivo, *m,* razón, *f;* (weight) peso, *m,* importancia, *f;* (police) policía, *f;* *pl* **forces,** *Mil.* fuerzas, tropas, *f pl.* **by main f.,** por fuerza mayor. **in f.,** vigente, en vigor. **to be in f.,** estar vigente

force /fɔrs/ *vt* forzar; (compel) obligar, constreñir, precisar; (ravish) violar; *Cul.* rellenar; (impose) imponer; (plants) forzar; (the pace) apresurar; (cause) hacer; (a lock, etc.) forzar. **to f. oneself into,** entrar a la fuerza en; (a garment) ponerse con dificultad; imponerse a la fuerza. **to f. oneself to,** esforzarse a. **to f. the pace,** forzar el paso. **to f. away,** ahuyentar. **to f. back,** hacer retroceder; rechazar; (a sigh, etc.) ahogar. **to f. down,** hacer bajar, obligar a bajar; (make swallow) hacer tragar; (of airplanes) hacer tomar tierra. **to f. in,** introducir a la fuerza; obligar a entrar. **to f. into,** meter a la fuerza; obligar a entrar (en). **to f. on, upon,** imponer. **to f. open,** abrir a la fuerza; (a lock) romper, forzar. **to f. out,** hacer salir; empujar hacia fuera; (words) pronunciar con dificultad. **to f. up,** obligar a subir; hacer subir; hacer vomitar

forced /fɔrst/ *a* forzado; forzoso; afectado. **f. landing,** *Aer.* aterrizaje forzoso, *m.* **f. march,** *Mil.* marcha forzada, *f*

forceful /'fɔrsfəl/ *a* See **forcible**

forcemeat /ˈfɔrsˌmiːt/ n picadillo, m; relleno, m. **f. ball,** albóndiga, f

forceps /ˈfɔrsəps/ n pl fórceps, m pl; pinzas, f pl. **arterial f.,** pinzas hemostáticas, f pl

forcible /ˈfɔrsəbəl/ a fuerte; a la fuerza; violento; enérgico, vigoroso; poderoso; Lit. vívido, gráfico, vehemente. **f. feeding,** alimentación forzosa, f

forcibleness /ˈfɔrsəbəlnɪs/ n fuerza, f; vigor, m, energía, f; vehemencia, f

forcibly /ˈfɔrsəbli/ adv a la fuerza

forcing /ˈfɔrsɪŋ/ n forzamiento, m; compulsión, f. **f. frame,** semillero, m, especie de invernadero, f

ford /fɔrd/ n esguazo, vado, m. —vt esguazar, vadear

fordable /ˈfɔrdəbəl/ a esguazable, vadeable

fore /fɔr/ a delantero; Naut. de proa. —adv delante; Naut. de proa. **f.-and-aft,** Naut. de popa a proa.

forearm /fɔrˈɑrm/ n antebrazo, m. —vt armar de antemano; preparar

forebear /ˈfɔrˌbɛər/ n antecesor, m, ascendiente, mf

forebode /fɔrˈboud/ vt presagiar, augurar, anunciar; presentir

foreboding /fɔrˈboudɪŋ/ n presagio, augurio, m; presentimiento, m, corazonada, f

forecast /ˈfɔrˌkæst/ n pronóstico, m; proyecto, plan, m, vt pronosticar; proyectar. **weather f.,** pronóstico del tiempo, m

forecastle /ˈfouksəl/ n Naut. castillo de proa, m

foreclose /fɔrˈklouz/ vt excluir; impedir; vender por orden judicial; anticipar el resultado de; decidir de antemano

foreclosure /fɔrˈklouʒər/ n venta por orden judicial, f; juicio hipotecario, m

foredoom /fɔrˈdum/ vt predestinar

forefather /ˈfɔrˌfɑðər/ n antepasado, antecesor, m

forefinger /ˈfɔrˌfɪŋɡər/ n índice, dedo índice, m

forefoot /ˈfɔrˌfʊt/ n pata delantera, f

forefront /ˈfɔrˌfrʌnt/ n delantera, primera línea, f; frente, m; vanguardia, f. **in the f.,** en la vanguardia; en el frente

foregoing /fɔrˈɡouɪŋ/ a precedente, anterior

foregone /fɔrˈɡɔn/ a decidido de antemano; previsto

foreground /ˈfɔrˌɡraund/ n primer plano, primer término, m, frente, m. **in the f.,** Art. en primer término

forehand /ˈfɔrˌhænd/ a derecho. **f. stroke,** golpe derecho, m

forehead /ˈfɔrɪd/ n frente, f

foreign /ˈfɔrɪn/ a extranjero; extraño; exótico; exterior; (alien) ajeno. **f. affairs,** asuntos extranjeros, m pl. **f. body,** cuerpo extraño, m. **f. debt,** deuda exterior, f. **F. Legion,** tercio extranjero, m. **F. Office,** Ministerio de Relaciones Extranjeras, m. **f. parts,** extranjero, m. **f. policy,** política internacional, f. **F. Secretary,** Secretario de Asuntos Extranjeros, Secretario de Asuntos Exteriores, Ministro de Relaciones Extranjeras, m. **f. trade,** comercio con el extranjero, m

foreigner /ˈfɔrənər/ n extranjero (-ra)

foreignness /ˈfɔrənnɪs/ n extranjerismo, m; (strangeness) extrañeza, f; lo exótico

foreknowledge /fɔrˌnɒlɪdʒ/ n presciencia, precognición, f

foreland /ˈfɔrˌlænd/ n promontorio, cabo, m

foreleg /ˈfɔrˌlɛɡ/ n pata delantera, f

forelock /ˈfɔrˌlɒk/ n guedeja, vedeja, f; (of a horse) copete, tupé, m. **to take time by the f.,** asir la ocasión por la melena

foreman /ˈfɔrmən/ n (of jury) presidente (del jurado), m; (of a farm) mayoral, m; (in a works) capataz, m

foremost /ˈfɔrˌmoust/ a delantero; de primera fila; más importante. —adv en primer lugar; en primera fila

forensic /fəˈrɛnsɪk/ a forense, legal. **f. medicine,** medicina legal, f

foreordained /ˌfɔrɔrˈdeind/ a predestinado

forerunner /ˈfɔrˌrʌnər/ n precursor (-ra), predecessor (-ra); (presage) anuncio, presagio, m

foresee /fɔrˈsi/ vt prever, anticipar

foreseeing /fɔrˈsiɪŋ/ a presciente, sagaz

foreseer /fɔrˈsiər/ n previsor (-ra)

foreshadow /fɔrˈʃædou/ vt anunciar, prefigurar; simbolizar; hacer sentir

foreshorten /fɔrˈʃɔrtn/ vt Art. escorzar

foreshortening /fɔrˈʃɔrtnɪŋ/ n Art. escorzo, m

foresight /ˈfɔrˌsait/ n presciencia, f; previsión, prudencia, f; (of gun) punto de mira, m; (optical) croquis de nivel, m

forest /ˈfɔrɪst/ n bosque, m, selva, f. —vt arbolar

forestall /fɔrˈstɔl/ vt anticipar, saltear; prevenir; Com. acaparar

forestalling /fɔrˈstɔlɪŋ/ n anticipación, f

forestation /ˌfɔrəˈsteiʃən/ n repoblación forestal, f

forester /ˈfɔrəstər/ n silvicultor, guardamonte, ingeniero forestal, m; habitante de los bosques, m

forest fire incendio forestal, m

forestry /ˈfɔrəstri/ n silvicultura, f

foresworn /fɔrˈswɔrn/ a perjuro

foretaste /n ˈfɔrˌteist/ v fɔrˈteist/ n muestra, f; presagio, m. —vt gustar con anticipación

foretell /fɔrˈtɛl/ vt predecir, profetizar; anunciar, presagiar

foreteller /fɔrˈtɛlər/ n profeta, m; presagio, m

foretelling /fɔrˈtɛlɪŋ/ n profecía, predicción, f

forethought /ˈfɔrˌθɔt/ n presciencia, previsión, f; prevención, f

forewarn /fɔrˈwɔrn/ vt prevenir

forewarning /fɔrˈwɔrnɪŋ/ n presagio, m

forewoman /ˈfɔrˌwumən/ n encargada, f; primera oficiala, f

foreword /ˈfɔrˌwərd/ n prefacio, m, introducción, f

forfeit /ˈfɔrfɪt/ n pérdida, f; (fine) multa, f; (in games) prenda, f; (of rights, goods, etc.) confiscación, f. —a confiscado. —vt perder; perder el derecho o el título de

forfeiture /ˈfɔrfɪtʃər/ n pérdida, f; confiscación, f; secuestro, m

forge /fɔrdʒ/ n fragua, f; (smithy) herrería, f. —vt and vi fraguar, forjar; (fabricate) inventar, fabricar; falsificar; (advance) avanzar lentamente. **to f. ahead,** abrirse camino; avanzar

forged /fɔrdʒd/ a (of iron) forjado; (of checks, etc.) falso, falsificado

forger /ˈfɔrdʒər/ n falsificador (-ra), falsario (-ia); (creator) artífice, mf

forgery /ˈfɔrdʒəri/ n falsificación, f

forget /fərˈɡɛt/ vt olvidar; descuidar. —vi olvidarse. **to f. about,** olvidarse de, desacordarse de. **to f. oneself,** olvidarse de sí mismo; propasarse; (in anger) perder los estribos

forgetful /fərˈɡɛtfəl/ a olvidadizo; descuidado, negligente

forgetfulness /fərˈɡɛtfəlnɪs/ n olvido, m; descuido, m; falta de memoria, f

forget-me-not /fərˈɡɛtmiˌnɒt/ n Bot. miosota nomeolvides, f

forging /ˈfɔrdʒɪŋ/ n fraguado, m; falsificación, f

forgivable /fərˈɡɪvəbəl/ a perdonable, excusable

forgive /fərˈɡɪv/ vt perdonar, disculpar, condonar; (debts) remitir

forgiveness /fərˈɡɪvnɪs/ n perdón, m; condonación, f; (remission) remisión, f

forgiving /fərˈɡɪvɪŋ/ a misericordioso, clemente, dispuesto a perdonar

forgo /fɔrˈɡou/ vt renunciar, sacrificar, privarse de; abandonar, ceder

forgoing /fɔrˈɡouɪŋ/ n renunciación, f, sacrificio, m; cesión, f

"For Immediate Occupancy" «De Ocupación Inmediata»

fork /fɔrk/ n Agr. horca, horquilla, f; (table fork) tenedor, m; bifurcación, f; (of rivers) confluencia, f; (of branches) horcadura, f; (of legs) horcajadura, f; (for supporting trees, etc.) horca, f; Mus. diapasón normal, m. —vt hacinar con horca. —vi bifurcarse; ramificarse

forked /fɔrkt/ a bifurcado, hendido, ahorquillado. **f. lightning,** relámpago, m. **f. tail,** cola hendida, f

forlorn /fɔrˈlɔrn/ a abandonado, desamparado, desesperado. **f. hope,** aventura desesperada, f

forlornness /fɔrˈlɔrnnɪs/ n desamparo, m, miseria, f; desolación, f, desconsuelo, m

form /fɔrm/ n forma, f; figura, f; (shadowy) bulto, m; (formality) formalidad, f; ceremonia, f; Eccl. rito, *m;* método, *m;* regla, *f;* (in a school) clase, *f;* (lair) cama, *f;* (seat) banco, *m;* (system) sistema, *m;* (ghost) espectro, *m;* aparición, *f;* (to fill up) documento, *m;* hoja, *f;* (state) condición, *f; Lit.* construcción, forma, *f.* **It is a matter of f.,** Es una pura formalidad. **in due f.,** en debida forma, en regla. **in the usual f.,** *Com.* al usado. **It is not good f.,** No es de buena educación

form /fɔrm/ *vt* formar; (a habit) contraer; (an idea) hacerse (una idea). —*vi* formarse. **to f. fours,** *Mil.* formar a cuatro

formal /'fɔrməl/ *a* esencial; formal; ceremonioso, solemne; (of person) etiquetero, formalista. **f. call,** visita de cumplido, *f*

formaldehyde /fɔr'mældə,haid/ *n* formaldehído. *m*

formalism /'fɔrmə,lizəm/ *n* formalismo, *m*

formality /fɔr'mæliti/ *n* formalidad, *f;* ceremonia, solemnidad, *f*

formally /'fɔrməli/ *adv* formalmente

format /'fɔrmæt/ *n* formato, *m*

formation /fɔr'meiʃən/ *n* formación, *f;* disposición, *f,* arreglo, *m;* organización, *f;* (*Mil., Geol.*) formación, *f*

formative /'fɔrmətɪv/ *a* formativo

former /'fɔrmər/ *a* primero; antiguo; anterior; pasado. **in f. times,** antes, antiguamente. **the f.,** ése, aquél, *m;* ésa, aquélla, *f;* aquéllos, *m pl;* aquéllas, *f pl*

former /'fɔrmər/ *n* formador (-ra); creador (-ra), autor (-ra)

formerly /'fɔrmərli/ *adv* antiguamente, antes

formidable /'fɔrmidəbəl/ *a* formidable; terrible, espantoso

formless /'fɔrmlɪs/ *a* informe

formlessness /'fɔrmlɪsnɪs/ *n* falta de forma, *f*

formula /'fɔrmyələ/ *n* fórmula, *f.* **standard f.,** (*Math. ,Chem.*) fórmula clásica, *f*

formulate /'fɔrmyə,leit/ *vt* formular

fornicate /'fɔrni,keit/ *vi* fornicar

fornication /,fɔrni'keiʃən/ *n* fornicación, *f*

fornicator /'fɔrni,keitər/ *n* fornicador (-ra)

forsake /fɔr'seik/ *vt* dejar, desertar; abandonar, desamparar; separarse de; (of birds, the nest) aborrecer;• (one's faith) renegar de

forsaker /fɔr'seikər/ *n* el, *m,* (la, *f*) que abandona; desertor, *m;* renegado (-da)

"For Sale" «Se Vende»

forsooth /fɔr'suθ/ *adv* ciertamente, claro está

forswear /fɔr'swɛər/ *vt* abjurar; renunciar a. **to f. oneself,** perjurarse

forswearing /fɔr'swɛərɪŋ/ *n* abjuración, *f;* renuncia, *f;* perjurio, *m*

fort /fɔrt/ *n* fortaleza, *f,* fuerte, *m*

forte /'fɔrtei/ *n* fuerte, *m.* —*a Mus.* fuerte

forth /fɔrθ/ *adv* (on) adelante, hacia adelante; (out) fuera; (in time) en adelante, en lo consecutivo; (show) a la vista. **and so f.,** y así en lo sucesivo; etcétera

forthcoming /'fɔrθ'kʌmɪŋ/ *a* próximo; futuro; en preparación

forthwith /,fɔrθ'wiθ/ *adv* en seguida, sin tardanza

fortieth /'fɔrtiiθ/ *a* cuadragésimo; cuarenta. —*n* cuarentavo, *m*

fortifiable /'fɔrtə,faiəbəl/ *a* fortificable

fortification /,fɔrtəfɪ'keiʃən/ *n* fortificación, *f*

fortify /'fɔrtə,fai/ *vt* fortificar; fortalecer; confirmar; *Fig.* proveer de

fortitude /'fɔrti,tud/ *n* aguante, *m,* fortaleza, *f,* estoicismo, *m*

fortnight /'fɔrt,nait/ *n* quince días, *m pl,* dos semanas, *f pl;* quincena, *f.* **a f. ago,** hace quince días. **a f. tomorrow,** mañana en quince. **in a f.,** dentro de quince días; al cabo de quince días. **once a f.,** cada quince días

fortnightly /'fɔrt,naitli/ *a* quincenal. —*adv* cada dos semanas, dos veces al mes. —*n* revista quincenal, *f*

fortress /'fɔrtrɪs/ *n* fortaleza, plaza fuerte, *f*

fortuitous /fɔr'tuitəs/ *a* fortuito, accidental

fortuitously /fɔr'tuitəsli/ *adv* accidentalmente

fortuity /fɔr'tuiti/ *n* casualidad, *f;* accidente, *m*

fortunate /'fɔrtʃənit/ *a* dichoso, feliz; afortunado; próspero. **to be f.,** (of persons) tener suerte

fortunately /'fɔrtʃənitli/ *adv* afortunadamente, por dicha, felizmente

fortune /'fɔrtʃən/ *n* suerte, fortuna, *f,* destino, *m;* (money) caudal, *m,* fortuna, *f;* bienes, *m pl;* buena ventura, *f.* **good f.,** buena fortuna, dicha, *f.* **ill f.,** mala suerte, *f.* **to cost a f.,** costar un sentido. **to make one's f.,** enriquecerse; *Inf.* hacer su pacotilla. **to tell fortunes,** echar las cartas. **f. hunter,** buscador de dotes, cazador de dotes, cazador de fortunas, aventurero, *m.* **f.-teller,** adivinadora, *f;* echadora de cartas, *f.* **f.-telling,** buenaventura, *f*

forty /'fɔrti/ *a* and *n* cuarenta, *m.* **He is turned f.,** Ha cumplido los cuarenta. **person of f.,** cuarentón (-ona). **She is f.,** Tiene cuarenta años

forum /'fɔrəm/ *n* foro, tribuna *f,* (e.g., *to serve as a forum for discussion,* servir de tribuna de discusión)

forward /'fɔrwərd/ *a* avanzado; adelantado; (of position) delantero; (ready) preparado; (eager) pronto, listo, impaciente; activo, emprendedor; (of persons, fruit, etc.) precoz; (pert) insolente, desenvuelto, atrevido. —*adv* adelante; hacia adelante; (of time) en adelante; (farther on) más allá; hacia el frente; en primera línea. —*vt* ayudar, promover; adelantar; (letters) hacer seguir; *Com.* expedir, remitir; (a parcel) despachar; (hasten) apresurar; (plants) hacer crecer. —*n Sports.* delantero, *m.* **center-f.,** *Sports.* delantero centro, *m.* **from this time f.,** de hoy en adelante. **Please f.,** ¡Haga seguir! **putting f. of the clock,** el adelanto de la hora. **to carry f.,** *Com.* pasar a cuenta nueva. **to go f.,** adelantarse; estar en marcha, estar en preparación. **f. line,** *Sports.* delantera, *f.* **F.! ¡Adelante!**

forwarder /'fɔrwərdər/ *n* promotor (-ra); *Com.* remitente, *m*

forwarding /'fɔrwərdɪŋ/ *n* fomento, *m,* promoción, *f; Com.* expedición, *f,* envío, *m*

forwardness /'fɔrwərdnɪs/ *n* progreso, adelantamiento, *m;* (haste) apresuramiento, *m;* (of persons, fruit, etc.) precocidad, *f;* (pertness) desenvoltura, insolencia, frescura, *f,* descaro, *m;* (eagerness) impaciencia, *f*

fosse /fɔs/·*n* foso, *m*

fossil /'fɔsəl/ *a* and *n* fósil, *m.*

fossilization /,fɔsələ'zeiʃən/ *n* fosilización, *f*

fossilize /'fɔsə,laiz/ *vt* fosilizar; petrificar. —*vi* fosilizarse

foster /'fɔstər/ *vt* provocar, promover, suscitar; (favor) favorecer, ser propicio a. **f.-brother,** hermano de leche, *m.* **f.-child,** hijo (-ja) de leche. **f.-father,** padre adoptivo, *m.* **f.-mother,** ama de leche, *f.* **f.-sister,** hermana de leche, *f*

foul /faul/ *a* sucio, asqueroso, puerco; (evil-smelling) hediondo, fétido; (of air) viciado; impuro; (language) ofensivo; (coarse) indecente, obsceno; (harmful) nocivo, dañino; (wicked) malvado, infame; vil; (unfair) injusto; *Sports.* sucio; (ugly) feo; (entangled) enredado; (with corrections) lleno de erratas; (choked) atascado; (of weather) borrascoso, tempestuoso; malo, desagradable; (repulsive) repugnante. —*n Sports.* juego sucio, *m.* —*vt* ensuciar; *Naut.* chocar, abordar; (block) atascar; (the anchor) enredar; (dishonor) deshonrar. —*vi* atascarse; (anchor) enredarse; *Naut.* chocar. **to fall f. of,** *Naut.* abordar (un buque); *Fig.* habérselas con. **by fair means or f.,** a las buenas o a las malas. **f. breath,** aliento fétido, aliento corrompido, *m.* **f. brood,** peste de las abejas, *f.* **f. language,** palabras ofensivas, *f pl;* lenguaje obsceno, *m.* **f. play,** juego sucio, *m.* **f. weather,** mal tiempo, tiempo borrascoso, *m*

found /faund/ *vt* fundar; (metal, glass) fundir; (create, etc.) establecer

foundation /faun'deiʃən/ *n* fundación, *f;* establecimiento, *m;* creación, *f; Archit.* cimiento, embasamiento, *m;* (basis) base, *f;* (cause) causa, *f,* origen, principio, *m;* (endowment) dotación, *f; Sew.* refuerzo, *m.* **to lay the f.,** poner las fundaciones. **f. stone,** piedra angular, *f; Fig.* primera piedra, *f.* **to lay the f. stone,** poner la piedra angular

founder /'faundər/ *n* fundador (-ra); (of metals) fundidor, *m.* —*vi* (a ship) hacer zozobrar. —*vi* zozobrar, irse a pique; *Fig.* fracasar

foundering /'faundərɪŋ/ *n Naut.* zozobra, *f*

founding /'faundɪŋ/ n fundación, f; establecimiento, m; (of metals) fundición, f

foundling /'faundlɪŋ/ n hijo (-ja) de la cuna, expósito (-ta). **f. hospital** or **home,** casa de cuna, casa de expósitos, inclusa, f

foundry /'faundri/ n fundición, f

fountain /'fauntn/ n fuente, f; (spring) manantial, m; (jet) chorro, m; (artificial) fuente, f, surtidero, m; (source) origen, principio, m. **f.-head,** fuente, f. **Fountain of Youth,** Fuente de la juventud, Fuente de Juvencio, f. **f. pen,** pluma estilográfica, f

four /fɔr/ a and n cuatro, m. **It is f. o'clock,** Son las cuatro. **She is f.,** Tiene cuatro años. **on all fours,** a gatas. **f.-course,** (of meals) de cuatro platos. **f.-engined,** cuadrimotor. **f.-engined plane,** cuadrimotor, m. **f.-footed,** cuadrúpedo. **f.-horse,** de cuatro caballos. **f. hundred,** cuatrocientos. **f.-inhand,** tiro par, m. **f.-part,** (of a song) a cuatro voces. **f.-wheel brakes,** freno en las cuatro ruedas, m

fourfold /'fɔr,fould/ a cuádruple

fourposter /'fɔr'poustər/ n cama de matrimonio, f

fourscore /'fɔr'skɔr/ a and n ochenta, m.

foursome /'fɔrsəm/ n partido de cuatro personas, m

fourteen /'fɔr'tin/ a and n catorce, m. **He is f.,** Tiene catorce años

fourteenth /'fɔr'tinθ/ a and n décimocuarto m.; (of the month) (el) catorce, m; (of monarchs) catorce. **April f.,** El 14 (catorce) de abril

fourth /fɔrθ/ a cuarto; (of the month) el cuatro; (of monarchs) cuarto. —n (fourth part) cuarta parte, f; Mus. cuarta, f. **f. dimension,** cuarta dimensión, f. **f. term,** (U.S.A. Polit.) cuarto mandato, m

fourthly /'fɔrθli/ adv en cuarto lugar

fowl /faul/ n gallo, m; gallina, f; (chicken) pollo, m; (bird) ave, f; (barndoor f.) ave de corral, f. —vi cazar aves. **f.-house** or **run,** gallinero, m

fox /fɒks/ n zorro, m; (vixen) zorra, raposa, f; Fig. zorro, taimado, m. —vi disimular. —vt (books) descolorar. **f.-brush,** cola de raposa, f. **f.-earth,** zorrera, f. **f.-hunting,** caza de zorras, f. **f. terrier,** fox-térrier, m

foxglove /'fɒks,glʌv/ n digital, dedalera, f

foxhound /'fɒks,haund/ n perro zorrero, m

foxiness /'fɒksɪnɪs/ n zorrería, astucia, f

foxtrot /'fɒks,trɒt/ n foxtrot, m

foxy /'fɒksi/ a de zorro; zorrero, astuto

foyer /'fɔiər/ n foyer, salón de descanso, m

fraction /'frækʃən/ n Math. fracción, f, número quebrado, m; pequeña parte, f; fragmento, m. **improper f.,** Math. fracción impropia, f. **proper f.,** Math. fracción propia, f.

fractional /'frækʃənl̩/ a fraccionario

fractious /'frækʃəs/ a malhumorado, enojadizo

fractiousness /'frækʃəsnɪs/ n mal humor, m

fracture /'fræktʃər/ n Surg. fractura, f. —vt fracturar. **compound f.,** fractura conminuta, f

fragile /'frædʒəl/ a frágil, quebradizo; (of persons) delicado

fragility /frə'dʒɪlɪti/ n fragilidad, f

fragment /'frægmənt/ n fragmento, m; trozo, pedazo, m. **to break into fragments,** hacer pedazos, hacer añicos

fragmentary /'frægmən,tɛri/ a fragmentario

fragrance /'freigrəns/ n fragancia, f, buen olor, perfume, aroma, m

fragrant /'freigrənt/ a fragante, oloroso. **to make f.,** perfumar

frail /freil/ a frágil, quebradizo; débil, endeble. —n capacho, m, espuerta, f

frailty /'freilti/ n fragilidad, f; debilidad, f

frame /freim/ n constitución, f; sistema, m; organización, f; (of the body) figura, f, talle, m; (of window, picture) marco, m; (of machine, building) armadura, f; (of a bicycle) cuadro (de bicicleta), m; Agr. cajonera, f; (embroidery) bastidor (para bordar), m; (skeleton) esqueleto, m; Lit. composición, creación, construcción, f; (of spectacles) armadura, f; (of mind) disposición (de ánimo), f; humor, m. —vt formar; construir; arreglar; ajustar; (a picture) enmarcar; componer, hacer; (draw up) redactar; (think up) idear, inventar; (words) articular, pronunciar. **f. a constitution,** elaborar una constitución

framer /'freimər/ n fabricante de marcos, m; autor (-ra), creador (-ra), inventor (-ra)

framework /'freim,wɜrk/ n armadura, armazón, f, esqueleto, m; organización, f; (basis) base, f

franc /fræŋk/ n (coin) franco, m

France /fræns/ Francia, f

Franche-Comté /frɑʃ kɔ'tei/ Franco-Condado, m

franchise /'fræntʃaiz/ n (exemption) franquicia, f; privilegio, m; (vote) derecho de sufragio, m; (citizenship) derecho político, m

Franciscan /fræn'sɪskən/ a and n franciscano (-na)

Franco- (in compounds) franco-... —a (referring to General Franco) franquista

Francophile /'fræŋkə,fail/ a and n afrancesado (-da)

Frank /fræŋk/ n franco (-ca), galo (-la)

frank /fræŋk/ a franco, cándido, sincero; abierto. —vt franquear

frankincense /'fræŋkɪn,sɛns/ n incienso, m

frankly /'fræŋkli/ adv francamente; sinceramente; cara a cara; sin rodeos, claramente; abiertamente. **to speak f.,** hablar claro, hablar sin rodeos

frankness /'fræŋknɪs/ n franqueza, f; sinceridad, f, candor, m

frantic /'fræntɪk/ a frenético, furioso, loco. **He drives me f.,** Me vuelve loco

fraternal /frə'tɜrnl̩/ a fraterno, fraternal

fraternity /frə'tɜrnɪti/ n fraternidad, hermandad, f

fraternization /,frætɜrnə'zeiʃən/ n fraternización, f

fraternize /'frætər,naiz/ vi fraternizar

fratricidal /,frætrɪ'said/ a fratricida

fratricide /'frætrɪ,said/ n (person) fratricida, mf; (action) fratricidio, m

fraud /frɔd/ n fraude, m; engaño, embuste, m; (person) farsante, m, embustero (-ra)

fraudulence /'frɔdʒələns/ n fraudulencia, fraude, f

fraudulent /'frɔdʒələnt/ a fraudulento

fraught /frɔt/ a (with) cargado de; lleno de, preñado de

fray /frei/ n refriega, riña, f; combate, m, batalla, f; (rubbing) raedura, f. —vt raer, tazar. —vi tazarse, deshilarse

frayed /freid/ a raído

fraying /'freiɪŋ/ n raedura, deshiladura, f

freak /frik/ n monstruo, m; fenómeno, m; (whim) capricho, m

freakish /'frikɪʃ/ a monstruoso; caprichoso; extravagante; raro, singular

freakishness /'frikɪʃnɪs/ n carácter caprichoso, m; extravagancia, f; rareza, extrañeza, f

freckle /'frɛkəl/ n peca, f. —vi tener pecas; salir pecas (a la cara, etc.)

freckled /'frɛkəld/ a pecoso, con pecas

free /fri/ a (in most senses) libre; independiente; emancipado; desembarazado; abierto; limpio (de); franco; (voluntary) voluntario; (self-governing) autónomo, independiente; accesible; (disengaged) desocupado; (vacant) vacío; (exempt) exento (de); (immune) immune (de); ajeno; gratuito; (loose) suelto; (generous) generoso, liberal; (vicious) disoluto, licencioso; (bold) atrevido; (impudent) insolente, demasiado familiar. —adv gratis, gratuitamente. **There are two f. seats in the train,** Hay dos asientos libres en el tren. **to get f.,** libertarse. **to make f. with,** tomarse libertades con; usar como si fuera suyo. **to set f.,** poner en libertad. **f. agent,** libre albedrío, m. **f. and easy,** familiar, sin ceremonia. **f. gift,** Com. objeto de reclamo, m. **f.-hand drawing,** dibujo a pulso, m. **f. kick,** Sports. golpe franco, m. **f. love,** amor libre, m. **f. play,** rienda suelta, f; Mech. holgura, f. **f. port,** puerto franco, m. **f. speech,** libertad de palabra, f. **f. thought,** libre pensamiento, m. **f. ticket,** Theat. billete de favor, m. **f. trade,** a librecambista. —n librecambio, m. **f. trader,** librecambista, mf. **f. verse,** verso libre, verso suelto, m. **f.-wheeling,** desenfrenado, libre. **f. will,** propia voluntad, f; (theology) libre albedrío, m

free /fri/ vt libertar, poner en libertad (a); librar (de); (slave) salvar; emancipar; exentar; (of obstacles, difficulties) desembarazar; liberar de; librar de; (clean) limpiar de. **to f. from,** libertar de; librar de; (clean) limpiar de

freebooter /'fri,butər/ n pirata, filibustero, m

freeborn /'fri,bɔrn/ a nacido libre, libre por herencia

freedman /'fridmən/ n liberto, m

freedom /'fridəm/ n libertad, f; independencia, f; exención, f; inmunidad, f; soltura, facilidad, f, franqueza, f; (over-familiarity) insolencia, f; (boldness) audacia, intrepidez, f; (of customs) licencia, f. **to receive the f. of a city,** ser recibido como ciudadano de honor. **f. of speech,** libertad de palabra, f. **f. of the press,** libertad de la prensa, f. **f. of worship,** libertad de cultos, f

freehold /'fri,hould/ n feudo franco, m

freeing /'friɪŋ/ n liberación, f; emancipación, f; salvación, f; (from obstruction) desembarazo, m; limpieza, f

freelance /'fri,læns/ n Mil. soldado libre, m; Polit. independiente, m; aventurero (-ra). **f. journalist,** periodista libre, m

freely /'frili/ adv libremente; francamente; generosamente; sin reserva

freeman /'frimən/ n hombre libre, m; (of a city) ciudadano de honor, m

freemason /'fri,meisən/ n francmasón, m. **freemason's lodge,** logia masónica, f

freemasonry /'fri,meisənri/ n francmasonería, masonería, f

freethinker /'fri'θɪŋkər/ n librepensador (-ra)

freeze /friz/ vt helar; (meat, etc.) congelar; Fig. helar. —vi helarse; congelarse; (impers. of the weather) helar. **to f. to death,** morir de frío

freezing /'frizɪŋ/ n hielo, m; congelación, f. —a glacial; congelante, frigorífico. **f. mixture,** mezcla frigorífica, f. **f. of assets,** bloqueo de los depósitos bancarios, m. **f.-point,** punto de congelación, m. **above f.-point,** sobre cero. **below f.-point,** bajo cero

freight /freit/ n flete, m; porte, m. —vt fletar

freighter /'freitər/ n fletador, m; (ship) buque de carga, m

French /frentʃ/ a francés. —n (language) francés, m; (people) los franceses, m pl. **in F. fashion,** a la francesa. **to take F. leave,** despedirse a la inglesa. **What is the F. for "hat"?** ¿Cómo se dice «sombrero» en francés? **F. spoken,** Se habla francés. **F. bean,** judía, f. **F. chalk,** jabón de sastre, m. **F. horn,** trompa, f. **F. lesson,** lección de francés, f. **F. marigold,** flor del estudiante, f. **F. polish,** barniz de muebles, m. **F. poodle,** perro (-rra) de aguas. **F. roll,** panecillo, m. **F. window,** puerta ventana, f

Frenchify /'frentʃə,fai/ vt afrancesar

Frenchman /'frentʃmən/ n francés, m. **a young F.,** un joven francés

Frenchwoman /'frentʃ,wumən/ n francesa, mujer francesa, f. **a young F.,** una joven francesa, una muchacha francesa, f

frenzied /'frenzid/ a frenético

frenzy /'frenzi/ n frenesí, delirio, paroxismo, m

frequency /'frikwənsi/ n frecuencia, f. **high f.,** alta frecuencia, f. **low f.,** baja frecuencia, f

frequent /'frikwənt/ v frɪ'kwɛnt/ a frecuente; (usual) común, corriente. —vt frecuentar

frequentation /,frikwən'teiʃən/ n frecuentación, f

frequenter /'frikwəntər/ n frecuentador (-ra)

frequently /'frikwəntli/ adv frecuentemente, con frecuencia, muchas veces; comúnmente

fresco /'freskou/ n Art. fresco, m, pintura al fresco, f. —vt pintar al fresco

fresh /freʃ/ a fresco; nuevo; reciente; (newly arrived) recién llegado; (inexperienced) inexperto, bisoño; (of water, not salt) dulce; puro; (healthy) sano; (brisk) vigoroso, enérgico; (vivid) vivo, vívido; (bright) brillante; (cheeky) fresco. —adv nuevamente, recién (with past participle). **He came to us f. from school,** Vino a nosotros recién salido de su colegio. **We are going to take the f. air,** Vamos a tomar el fresco. **The milk is not f.,** La leche no está fresca. **f.-complexioned,** de buenos colores. **f. news,** noticias nuevas, f pl. **f. troops,** tropas nuevas, f pl, (reinforcements) tropas de refuerzo, f pl. **f. water,** agua fresca, f; (not salt) agua dulce, f. **f. wind,** viento fresco, m

freshen /'freʃən/ vt refrescar; (remove salt) desalar. —vi (wind) refrescar. **to f. up,** renovar; refrescar; (of dress, etc.) arreglar

freshly /'freʃli/ adv nuevamente; recientemente

freshness /'freʃnɪs/ n frescura, f; (newness) novedad, f; (vividness, brightness) intensidad, f; pureza, f; (beauty) lozanía, hermosura, f; (cheek) frescura, f, descaro, m

freshwater /'freʃ,wɔtər/ n agua dulce, f. **f. sailor,** marinero de agua dulce, m

fret /fret/ n agitación, f; ansiedad, preocupación, f; Archit. greca, f; (of stringed instrument) traste, m. —vt roer; (of a horse) bocezar; (corrode) desgastar, corroer; (of the wind, etc.) rizar; (worry) tener preocupado (a); irritar, enojar; (lose) perder; (oneself) apurarse, consumirse; Archit. calar. —vi torturarse, preocuparse, inquietarse; (complain) quejarse; (mourn) lamentarse, estar triste

fretful /'fretfəl/ a mal humorado, mohíno, quejoso, irritable

fretfully /'fretfəli/ adv irritablemente, con mal humor

fretwork /'fret,wɜrk/ n calado, m

Freudian /'frɔidiən/ a freudiano

friar /'fraiər/ n fraile, m. **Black f.,** dominicano, m. **Gray f.,** franciscano, m. **White f.,** carmelita, m. **f.-like,** frailesco

friction /'frɪkʃən/ n frote, frotamiento, roce, m; Phys. rozamiento, m; fricción, f. **to give a f.,** friccionar, dar fricciones (a). **f. gearing,** engranaje de fricción, m. **f. glove,** guante de fricciones, m

Friday /'fraidei/ n viernes, m. **Good F.,** Viernes Santo, m

fried /fraid/ a frito. **f. egg,** huevo frito, m

friend /frend/ n amigo (-ga); (acquaintance) conocido (-da); (Quaker) cuáquero (-ra); (follower) adherente, m; partidario (-ia); (ally) aliado (-da); pl **friends,** amistades, f pl; amigos, m pl. **a f. of yours,** un amigo tuyo, uno de tus amigos. **to make friends,** hacer amigos; (become friends) hacerse amigos; (after a quarrel) hacer las paces. **Friends!** (to sentinel) ¡Gente de paz!

friendless /'frendlɪs/ a sin amigos; desamparado

friendliness /'frendlinɪs/ n amabilidad, afabilidad, cordialidad, amigabilidad, f

friendly /'frendli/ a amistoso, amigable, amigo; afable, acogedor, simpático; propicio, favorable. **to be f. with,** ser amigo de. **f. society,** sociedad de socorros, f

friendship /'frendʃip/ n amistad, intimidad, f

Friesland /'frizlənd/ n Frisia, f

frieze /friz/ n friso, m; (cloth) frisa, jerga, f

frigate /'frɪgɪt/ n Nav. fragata, f

fright /frait/ n terror, susto, m; (guy) espantajo, m. —vt asustar. **to have a f.,** tener un susto. **to take f.,** asustarse

frighten /'fraitn/ vt espantar, dar un susto (a), alarmar, asustar; horrorizar; (overawe) acobardar. **to be frightened out of one's wits,** estar muerto de miedo. **to f. away,** ahuyentar, espantar

frightened /'fraitnd/ a miedoso, tímido, medroso, nervioso

frightening /'fraitnɪŋ/ a que da miedo; alarmante, amedrentador; horrible

frightful /'fraitfəl/ a horrible, espantoso, horroroso; Inf. tremendo, enorme

frightfully /'fraitfəli/ adv horrorosamente; Inf. enormemente

frigid /'frɪdʒɪd/ a frío; helado; Med. impotente

frigidity /frɪ'dʒɪdɪti/ n frialdad, frigidez, f; Med. impotencia, f

frigidly /'frɪdʒɪdli/ adv fríamente

frill /frɪl/ n Sew. volante, m; (jabot) chorrera, f; (round a bird's neck) collarín de plumas, m; (of paper) frunce, m. —vt alechugar; fruncir

fringe /frɪndʒ/ n fleco, m, franja, f; (of hair) flequillo, m; (edge) borde, m, margen, mf. —vt guarnecer con fleco, franjar; adornar; (grow by) crecer al margen (de)

Frisian /'frɪʒən/ a and n frisón (-ona); (language) frisón, m

frisk /frɪsk/ vi retozar, brincar

friskiness /'frɪskinɪs/ n viveza, agilidad, f

frisky /'frɪski/ a retozón, juguetón

fritter /'frɪtər/ n Cul. fruta de sartén, f. —vt (away) malgastar, desperdiciar; perder

frivolity /frɪ'vɒlɪti/ n frivolidad, ligereza, f; futilidad, f

frivolous /'frɪvələs/ a frívolo, ligero, liviano; (futile) trivial, fútil

frizz /frɪz/ vt (cloth) frisar; (hair) rizar

frizzy /'frɪzi/ a (of hair) crespo, rizado

fro /frou/ adv hacia atrás. **movement to and fro,** vaivén, m. **to and fro,** de un lado a otro. **to go to and fro,** ir y venir

frock /frɒk/ n vestido, m; (of a monk) hábito, m; (of priest) sotana, f. **f.-coat,** levita, f

frog /frɒg/ n rana, f. **to have a f. in the throat,** padecer carraspera

frolic /'frɒlɪk/ n (play) juego, m; (mischief) travesura, f; (folly) locura, extravagancia, f; (joke) chanza, f; (amusement) diversión, f; (wild party) holgorio, m, parranda, f. —vi retozar, juguetear; divertirse

frolicsome /'frɒlɪksəm/ a retozón, juguetón

from /frʌm, frɒm; unstressed frəm/ prep de; desde; (according to) según; (in the name of, on behalf of) de parte de; (through, by) por; (beginning on) a contar de; (with) con; **F.** (on envelope) Remite, Remitente. **He is coming here f. the dentist's,** Vendrá aquí desde casa del dentista. **Give him this message f. me,** Dale este recado de mi parte. **Judging f. his appearance,** Juzgando por su apariencia. **prices f. five hundred pesetas upward,** precios desde quinientos pesetas en adelante. **f. what I hear,** según mi información, según lo que oigo. **f. above,** desde arriba. **f. among,** de entre. **f. afar,** de lejos, desde lejos. **f. time to time,** de cuando en cuando, de vez en cuando

frond /frɒnd/ n Bot. fronda, f

front /frʌnt/ n frente, f; cara, f; Mil. frente, m; (battle line) línea de combate, f; (of a building) fachada, f; (of shirt) pechera, f; (at the seaside) playa, f; (promenade) paseo de la playa, m; (forefront) primera línea, f; (forepart) parte delantera, f; Theat. auditorio, m; (organization) organización de fachada, f; (impudence) descaro, m, a delantero; anterior; de frente; primero. —adv hacia delante. —vi mirar a, dar a; hacer frente a. **in f.,** en frente. **in f. of,** en frente de; (in the presence of) delante de, en la presencia de. **to face f.,** hacer frente. **to put on a bold f.,** hacer de tripas corazón. **f. door,** puerta de entrada, puerta principal, f. **f. line,** Mil. línea del frente, f; primera línea, f. **f. seat,** (at an entertainment, etc.) delantera, f. **f. organization** organización de fachada f. **f. tooth,** diente incisivo, m. **f. view,** vista de frente, f; vista de cerca, f

frontage /'frʌntɪdʒ/ n (of a building) fachada, f; (site) terreno de... metros de fachada, m

frontal /'frʌntl/ a Mil. de frente; Anat. frontal

frontier /frʌn'tɪər/ n frontera, f; Fig. límite, m. —a fronterizo

frontispiece /'frʌntɪsˌpis/ n (of a building) frontispicio, m, fachada, f; (of a book) portada, f

frontless /'frʌntlɪs/ a sin frente

frost /frɒst/ n escarcha, f; helada, f. —vt helar; Cul. escarchar; (glass) deslustrar; Fig. escarchar. —vi helar. **f.-bitten,** helado

frostbite /'frɒstˌbait/ n efectos del frío, m pl

frosted /'frɒstɪd/ a escarchado; helado; (of glass) deslustrado, opaco; Cul. escarchado

frostily /'frɒstəli/ adv Fig. glacialmente, con frialdad.

frostiness /'frɒstinɪs/ n; frío glacial, m

frosting /'frɒstɪŋ/ n escarcha, f; (of glass) deslustre, m; Cul. cobertura, escarcha, f

frosty /'frɒsti/ a helado; de hielo; (of hair) canoso; Fig. glacial, frío. **It was f. last night,** Anoche heló

froth /frɒθ/ n espuma, f; Fig. frivolidad, vanidad, f, vi espumar, hacer espuma; echar espuma. —vt hacer espumar; hacer echar espuma

frothiness /'frɒθinɪs/ n espumosidad, f; Fig. frivolidad, superficialidad, vaciedad, f

frothy /'frɒθi/ a espumoso, espumajoso; Fig. frívolo, superficial

frown /fraun/ n ceño, m; cara de juez, expresión severa, f; desaprobación, f; (of fortune) revés, golpe, m. —vi fruncir el ceño. **to f. at, on, upon,** mirar con desaprobación, ver con malos ojos; ser enemigo de; desaprobar

frowning /'fraunɪŋ/ a ceñudo; severo; amenazador

frowningly /'frauniŋli/ adv severamente

frowsiness /'frauzinɪs/ n mal olor, m; (dirtiness) suciedad, f; (untidiness) desaliño, desaseo, m

frowsy /'frauzi/ a fétido, mal oliente; mal ventilado; (dirty) sucio; (untidy) desaliñado, desaseado

frozen /'frouzən/ a helado; cubierto de hielo; congelado; (Geog. and Fig.) glacial. **to be f. up,** estar helado. **f. meat,** carne congelada, f

frugal /'frugəl/ a económico; frugal; sobrio

frugality /fru'gælɪti/ n economía, f; frugalidad, sobriedad, f

fruit /frut/ n (in general sense) fruto, m; (off a tree or bush) fruta, f; Fig. fruto, m; resultado, m, consecuencia, f. —vi frutar, dar fruto. **bottled f.,** fruta en almíbar, f. **candied f.,** fruta azucarada, f. **dried f.,** fruta seca, f. **first fruits,** primicias, f pl. **soft f.,** frutas blandas, f pl. **stone f.,** fruta de hueso, f. **f.-bearing,** frutal. **f.-cake,** pastel de fruta, m. **f.-dish,** frutero, m. **f. farming,** fruticultura, f. **f.-knife,** cuchillo de postres, m. **f. shop,** frutería, f. **f. tree,** frutal, m

fruiterer /'frutərər/ n frutero (-ra)

fruitful /'frutfəl/ a fructuoso, fértil; prolífico, fecundo; provechoso

fruitfulness /'frutfəlnɪs/ n fertilidad, f; fecundidad, f; provecho, m

fruition /fru'ɪʃən/ n fruición, f

fruitless /'frutlɪs/ a infructuoso, estéril; inútil

fruitlessness /'frutlɪsnɪs/ n infructuosidad, esterilidad, f; inutilidad, f

fruity /'fruti/ a de fruta; (wines) vinoso; (of voice) melodioso

frump /frʌmp/ n estantigua, f

frumpish /'frʌmpɪʃ/ a estrafalario; fuera de moda

frustrate /'frʌstreit/ vt frustrar; defraudar; malograr; destruir; anular

frustration /frʌ'streiʃən/ n frustración, f; defraudación, f; malogro, m; destrucción, f; desengaño, m

fry /frai/ n Cul. fritada, f, vt freír. —vi freírse. **small fry,** Inf. gente menuda, f

frying /'fraiɪŋ/ n fritura, f, el freír. **to fall out of the f.-pan into the fire,** ir de mal en peor, andar de zocos en colodros, ir de Guatemala en Guatapeor. **f.-pan,** sartén, f

fuchsia /'fyuʃə/ n Bot. fuscia, f

fuddle /'fʌdl/ vt atontar, aturdir; embriagar, emborrachar

fudge /fʌdʒ/ n patraña, tontería, f, disparate, m. —interj ¡qué disparate! ¡qué va!

fuel /'fyuəl/ n combustible, m; Fig. cebo, pábulo, m. —vt cebar, echar combustible en. —vi tomar combustible. **to add f. to the flame,** echar leña al fuego. **f. consumption,** consumo de combustible, m. **f.-oil,** aceite combustible, aceite de quemar, m. **f.-tank,** depósito de combustible, m

fueling /'fyuəlɪŋ/ n aprovisionamiento de combustible, m

fugitive /'fyudʒɪtɪv/ a fugitivo; pasajero, perecedero; transitorio, efímero, fugaz. —n fugitivo (-va); (from justice) prófugo (-ga); Mil. desertor, m; (refugee) refugiado (-da)

fugue /fyug/ n Mus. fuga, f

fulcrum /'fʊlkrəm/ n Mech. fulcro, m

fulfill /fʊl'fɪl/ vt cumplir; (satisfy) satisfacer; (observe) observar; guardar. **to be fulfilled,** cumplirse, realizarse

fulfillment /fʊl'fɪlmənt/ n cumplimiento, m; desempeño, ejercicio, m; (satisfaction) satisfacción, realización, f; (observance) observancia, f

full /fʊl/ a lleno; colmado; todo; pleno; (crowded) atestado; (replete) harto; abundante; (intent on) preocupado con, pensando en; (loose) amplio; (plentiful) copioso; (occupied) ocupado; completo; (resonant) sonoro; (mature) maduro; puro; perfecto; (satiated) saciado (de); (of the moon, sails) lleno; (weighed down) agobiado, abrumado; (detailed) detallado; (with uniform, etc.) de gala; (with years, etc.) cumplido. —n colmo, m; totalidad, f. —adv muy; completamente, totalmente. **f. many a flower,** muchas flores. **at f. gallop,** a galope tendido. **at f. speed,** a todo correr; a toda velocidad. **His hands are f.,** Sus manos están llenas. **The moon was at the f.,** La luna estaba llena. **in f.,** por completo; sin abreviaciones; integralmente. **in f. swing,** en plena actividad. **in f.**

vigor, en pleno vigor. **to the f.,** completamente; hasta la últi.na gota; a la perfección. **to be f. to the brim,** estar lleno hasta el tope. **f.-blooded,** sanguíneo; de pura raza; *Fig.* viril, vigoroso; *Fig.* apasionado. **f.-blown,** en plena flor, abierto. **f. dress,** a de gala. —*n* traje de etiqueta, traje de ceremonia, *m.* **f.-face,** de cara. **f.-flavored,** (wine) abocado. **f.-grown,** adulto; completamente desarrollado. **f.-length,** de cuerpo entero. **f. moon,** luna llena, *f;* plenilunio, *m.* **f. name,** nombre y apellidos, *m.* **f. powers,** plenos poderes, *m pl.* **f. scale,** tamaño natural, *m.* **f. scope,** carta blanca, *f;* toda clase de facilidades. **f. steam ahead,** a todo vapor. **f. stop,** *Gram.* punto final, *m*

full /fʊl/ *vt* (cloth) abatanar
full-color /'fʊl 'kʌlər/ *a* a todo color. **full-color plates,** láminas a todo color
fuller /'fʊlər/ *n* batanero, *m.* **fuller's earth,** tierra de batán, galactita, *f*
fulling /'fʊlɪŋ/ *n* abatanadura, *f.* **f.-mill,** batán, *m*
fullness /'fʊlnɪs/ *n* abundancia, *f;* plenitud, *f;* (repletion) hartura, *f;* (of clothes) amplitud, *f;* (stoutness) gordura, *f;* (swelling) hinchazón, *f.* **She wrote with great f. of all that she had seen,** Describía muy detalladamente todo lo que había visto. **in the f. of time,** andando el tiempo
full-page /'fʊl 'peidʒ/ *a* a toda plana. **full-page advertisement,** anuncio a toda plana.
full-time /'fʊl 'taim/ *a* de tiempo completo
fully /'fʊli/ *adv* plenamente; enteramente. **It is f. six years since...,** Hace seis años bien cumplidos que... **It is f. 9 o'clock,** Son las nueve bien sonadas. **f. dressed,** completamente vestido
fulminant /'fʌlmənənt/ *a Med.* fulminante
fulminate /'fʌlmə,neit/ *n Chem.* fulminato, *m.* —*vi* estallar; fulminar. —*vt* volar; fulminar
fulminous /'fʌlmənəs/ *a* fulmíneo, fulminoso
fulsome /'fʊlsəm/ *a* servil; insincero, hipócrita; asqueroso, repugnante
fumble /'fʌmbəl/ *vi* (grope) ir a tientas; procurar hacer algo; chapucear (con); (for a word) titubear
fumbling /'fʌmblɪŋ/ *n* hesitación, *f;* tacto incierto, *m.* —*a* incierto; vacilante
fumblingly /'fʌmblɪŋli/ *adv* de manera incierta; a tientas
fume /fyum/ *n* vaho, humo, gas, *m;* emanación, *f;* mal olor, *m,* fetidez, *f; Fig.* vapor, *m;* (state of mind) agitación, *f;* frenesí, *m.* —*vi* humear; refunfuñar, echar pestes
fumigate /'fyumɪ,geit/ *vt* fumigar; sahumar, perfumar; desinfectar
fumigation /,fyumə'geiʃən/ *n* fumigación, *f;* sahumerio, *m*
fumigator /'fyumɪ,geitər/ *n* fumigador (-ra); (apparatus) fumigador, *m*
fumigatory /'fyuməgə,tɔri/ *a* fumigatorio
fuming /'fyumɪŋ/ *n* refunfuño, *m.* —*a* refunfuñador
fumy /'fyumi/ *a* humoso
fun /fʌn/ *n* diversión, *f,* entretenimiento, *m;* (joke) chanza, broma, *f.* **for fun,** para divertirse; en chanza. **in fun,** de burlas. **to have fun,** divertirse. **to poke fun at,** burlarse de, mofarse de, ridiculizar
funambulist /fyu'næmbyəlɪst/ *n* funámbulo (-la)
function /'fʌŋkʃən/ *n* función, *f.* —*vi* funcionar
functional /'fʌŋkʃənl/ *a* funcional
functionary /'fʌŋkʃə,neri/ *n* funcionario, *m.* —*a* funcional
functioning /'fʌŋkʃənɪŋ/ *n* funcionamiento, *m*
fund /fʌnd/ *n* fondo, *m; pl* **funds,** fondos, *m pl; Inf.* dinero, *m.* **public funds,** fondos públicos, *m pl.* **sinking f.,** fondo de amortización, *m*
fundamental /,fʌndə'mɛntl/ *a* fundamental, básico; esencial. —*n* fundamento, *m*
fundamentally /,fʌndə'mɛntli/ *adv* fundamentalmente, básicamente; esencialmente
funeral /'fyunərəl/ *a* funeral, fúnebre, funerario. —*n* funerales, *m pl;* entierro, *m.* **to attend the f. (of),** asistir a los funerales (de). **f. feast,** banquetes fúnebres, *m pl.* **f. director,** **f. furnisher,** director de pompas fúnebres, *m.* **f. procession,** cortejo fúnebre, *m.* **f. pyre,** pira funeraria, *f.* **f. service,** misa de difuntos, *f*
funereal /fyu'nɪəriəl/ *a* fúnebre, lúgubre

fungicide /'fʌndʒə,said/ *n* anticriptógamo, *m*
fungous /'fʌŋgəs/ *a* fungoso
fungus /'fʌŋgəs/ *n* hongo, *m*
funicular /fyu'nɪkyələr/ *a* funicular. **f. railway,** ferrocarril funicular, *m*
funnel /'fʌnl/ *n Chem.* embudo, *m; Naut.* chimenea, *f;* (of a chimney) cañón (de chimenea), *m.* **f.-shaped,** en forma de embudo
funnily /'fʌnli/ *adv* de un modo raro
funniness /'fʌnɪnɪs/ *n* lo divertido; rareza, extrañeza, *f*
funny /'fʌni/ *a* cómico, gracioso; divertido; (strange) extraño, raro; (mysterious) misterioso. **It struck me as f.,** (amused me) Me hizo gracia; (seemed strange) Me pareció raro. **f.-bone,** hueso de la alegría, *m*
fur /fɜr/ *n* piel, *f;* depósito, sarro, *m;* (on tongue) saburra, *f.* —*a* hecho de pieles. —*vt* forrar, or adornar, or cubrir, con pieles; depositar sarro sobre; (the tongue) ensuciarse la lengua. —*vi* estar forrado, or adornado, or cubierto, con pieles; formarse incrustaciones; (of the tongue) tener la lengua sucia. **fur cap,** gorra de pieles, *f.* **fur cape,** cuello de piel, *m;* capa de pieles, *f.* **fur trade,** peletería, *f*
furbish /'fɜrbɪʃ/ *vt* pulir; renovar; limpiar
furious /'fyʊriəs/ *a* furioso. **to become f.,** ponerse furioso, enfurecerse
furiously /'fyʊriəsli/ *adv* furiosamente, con furia
furiousness /'fyʊriəsnɪs/ *n* furia, *f*
furl /fɜrl/ *vt* plegar; enrollar; *Naut.* aferrar
furlong /'fɜrlɔŋ/ *n* estadio, *m*
furlough /'fɜrlou/ *n Mil.* permiso, *m.* —*vt* conceder un permiso (a). **on f.,** de permiso
furnace /'fɜrnɪs/ *n* horno, *m;* (of steam boiler) fogón, *m;* (for central heating) caldera de calefacción central, *f;* (for smelting) cubilote, *m*
furnish /'fɜrnɪʃ/ *vt* proveer (de), equipar (de), suplir (de); amueblar; (an opportunity) proporcionar; producir
furnished /'fɜrnɪʃt/ *a* amueblado, con muebles. **f. house,** casa amueblada, *f*
furnisher /'fɜrnɪʃər/ *n* decorador, *m;* proveedor (-ra)
furnishing /'fɜrnɪʃɪŋ/ *n* provisión, *f,* equipo, *m; pl* **furnishings,** accesorios, *m pl;* mobiliario, mueblaje, *m*
furniture /'fɜrnɪtʃər/ *n* mobiliario, mueblaje, *m;* ajuar, equipo, *m;* avíos, *m pl; Naut.* aparejo, *m.* **a piece of f.,** un mueble. **to empty of f.,** desamueblar, quitar los muebles (de). **f. dealer** or **maker,** mueblista, *mf.* **f. factory,** mueblería, *f.* **f. polish,** crema para muebles, *f.* **f. mover,** transportador de muebles, *m;* (packer) embalador, *m.* **f. repository,** guardamuebles, *m.* **f. van,** carro de mudanzas, *m*
furor /'fyʊrɔr/ *n* furor, *m*
furred /fɜrd/ *a* forrado or cubierto or adornado de piel; (of the tongue) sucia
furrier /'fɜriər/ *n* peletero, *m.* **furrier's shop,** peletería, *f*
furrow /'fɜrou/ *n* surco, *m;* muesca, estría, *f;* (wrinkle) arruga, *f.* —*vt* surcar
furry /'fɜri/ *a* cubierto de piel; parecido a una piel; hecho de pieles
further /'fɜrðər/ *a* ulterior, más distante; (other) otro; opuesto; adicional, más. —*adv* más lejos; más allá; además; también; por añadidura. —*vt* promover, fomentar; ayudar. **on the f. side,** al otro lado. **till f. orders,** hasta nueva orden. **f. on,** más adelante; más allá
furtherance /'fɜrðərəns/ *n* fomento, *m,* promoción, *f;* progreso, avance, *m*
furthermore /'fɜrðər,mɔr/ *adv* además, por añadidura
furthest /'fɜrðɪst/ *a* (el, la, lo) más lejano or más distante; extremo. —*adv* más lejos
furtive /'fɜrtɪv/ *a* furtivo
furtively /'fɜrtɪvli/ *adv* furtivamente, a hurtadillas. **to look at f.,** mirar de reojo
fury /'fyʊri/ *n* furor, enfurecimiento, *m,* rabia, *f;* violencia, *f;* frenesí, arrebato, *m;* furia, *f.* **like a f.,** hecho una furia. **to breathe forth f.,** echar rayos
fuse /fyuz/ *n* (of explosives) espoleta, mecha, *f; Elec.* fusible, *m.* —*vt* (metals) fundir; fusionar, mezclar. —*vi* (metals) fundirse; mezclarse. **safety-f.,** espoleta de seguridad, *f.* **time-f.,** espoleta de tiempo, *f.* **to**

blow a f., fundir un fusible. **f. box,** caja de fusibles, *f.* **f. wire,** fusible, *m*

fuselage /'fyusə,laʒ/ *n Aer.* fuselaje, *m*

fusible /'fyuzəbəl/ *a* fusible

fusillade /'fyusə,lad/ *n* descarga cerrada, *f*

fusion /'fyuʒən/ *n* fusión, *f;* unión, *f;* (melting) fundición, *f*

fuss /fʌs/ *n* agitación, *f;* (bustle) conmoción, bulla, *f;* bullicio, *m.* —*vi* agitarse, preocuparse. —*vt* poner nervioso. **There's no need to make such a f.,** No es para tanto. **to make a f. of,** (a person) hacer la rueda (a), ser muy atento (a); (spoil) mimar mucho (a). **to f. about,** andar de acá para allá

fussily /'fʌsəli/ *adv* nerviosamente; de un aire importante

fussy /'fʌsi/ *a* meticuloso, nimio; nervioso; (of style) florido, hinchado; (of dress) demasiado adornado

fustigate /'fʌsti,geit/ *vt* fustigar

fusty /'fʌsti/ *a* (moldy) mohoso; mal ventilado; mal oliente; (of views, etc.) pasado de moda

futile /'fyutl/ *a* fútil, superficial, frívolo; inútil

futility /fyu'tɪlɪti/ *n* futilidad, superficialidad, frivolidad, *f;* (action) tontería, estupidez, *f*

future /'fyutʃər/ *a* futuro, venidero. —*n* futuro, porvenir, *m.* **in the f.,** en adelante, en lo venidero, en lo sucesivo. **for f. reference,** para información futura. **f. perfect tense,** *Gram.* futuro perfecto, *m.* **f. tense,** *Gram.* futuro, *m*

futurism /'fyutʃə,rɪzəm/ *n* futurismo, *m*

futurist /'fyutʃərɪst/ *n* futurista, *mf*

futuristic /,fyutʃə'rɪstɪk/ *a* futurístico

fuzz /fʌz/ *n* tamo, *m,* pelusa, *f.* **f.-ball,** *Bot.* bejín, *m*

fuzzy /'fʌzi/ *a* crespo rizado; velloso

G

g /dʒi/ n (letter) ge, f; Mus. sol, m. **G clef,** clave de sol, f

gab /gæb/ n Inf. labia, f. **to have the gift of the gab,** tener mucha labia

gabardine /ˈgæbərˌdin/ n gabardina, f

gabble /ˈgæbəl/ vi chacharear, garlar; hablar indistintamente; (of goose and some birds) graznar. —vt decir indistintamente; decir rápidamente; (a language) chapurrear; mascullar. —n cháchara, f; vocerío, m; (of goose and some birds) graznido, m

gabber /ˈgæblər/ n charlatán (-ana), chacharero (-ra)

gabbling /ˈgæblɪŋ/ n See **gabble**

gable /ˈgeibəl/ n Archit. gablete, hastial, m. **g.-end,** alero, m

gad /gæd/ vi corretear, callejear. **to gad about,** correr por todos lados; divertirse.

gadabout /ˈgædəˌbaut/ n azotacalles, mf; gandul (-la), vagabundo (-da)

gadding /ˈgædɪŋ/ a callejero; vagabundo. —n vagancia, f; vida errante, f; gandulería, f

gadfly /ˈgædˌflai/ n Ent. tábano, m; Inf. moscardón, m

gadget /ˈgædʒɪt/ n accesorio, m; aparato, m; chuchería, f

Gadsden Purchase /ˈgædzdən/ la Venta de la Meseta, f

Gael /geil/ n escocés (-esa) del norte; celta, mf

Gaelic /ˈgeilɪk/ a gaélico. —n gaélico, m

gaff /gæf/ n (hook) garfio, m; Naut. pico de cangrejo, m; Theat. teatrucho, m

gaffer /ˈgæfər/ n viejo, tío, abuelo, m

gag /gæg/ n mordaza, f; Theat. morcilla, f. —vt amordazar; Fig. hacer callar. —vi Theat. meter morcillas

gage /geidʒ/ n prenda, fianza, f; (symbol of challenge) guante, m; (challenge) desafío, m. See **gauge**

gagging /ˈgægɪŋ/ n amordazamiento, m

gaggle /ˈgægəl/ n (cry) graznido, m; (of geese) manada (de ocas), f. —vi graznar; cacarear

gaiety /ˈgeiti/ n alegría, f; animación, vivacidad, f; (entertainment) diversión, festividad, f

gaily /ˈgeili/ adv alegremente

gain /gein/ n ganancia, f; provecho, beneficio, m; (increase) aumento, m; (riches) riqueza, f. —vt ganar; (acquire) conseguir; adquirir; obtener; conquistar, captar; (friends) hacerse; (reach) llegar a, alcanzar. —vi ganar; (improve) mejorar; (of a watch) adelantarse. **What have they gained by going to Canada?** ¿Qué han logrado con marcharse al Canadá? **to g. ground,** Fig. ganar terreno. **to g. momentum** adquirir velocidad **to g. time,** ganar tiempo. **to g. on, upon,** acercarse a; (overtake) alcanzar; (outstrip) dejar atrás, pasar; (of sea) invadir; (of habits) imponerse

gainful /ˈgeinfəl/ a ganancioso, lucrativo; ventajoso

gainfully /ˈgeinfəli/ adv ventajosamente; lucrativamente

gainsay /ˈgeinˌsei/ vt contradecir; oponer; negar

gainsaying /ˈgeinˌseiɪŋ/ n contradicción, f; oposición, f; negación, f

gait /geit/ n porte, andar, m; paso, m, andadura, f

gaiter /ˈgeitər/ n polaina, f; (spat) botín, m

gala /ˈgeilə/ n gala, fiesta, f. **g.-day,** día de fiesta, m. **g.-dress,** traje de gala, m

galaxy /ˈgæləksi/ n Astron. vía láctea, f; Fig. constelación, f; grupo brillante, m

gale /geil/ n vendaval, ventarrón, m; (storm) temporal, m; tempestad, f

Galician /gəˈliʃən/ a n gallego (-ga).

Galilean /ˌgæləˈleiən/ a and n galileo (-ea)

Galilee /ˈgæləˌli/ Galilea, f

gall /gɔl/ n (on horses) matadura, f; (abrasion) rozadura, f; hiel, bilis, f; Fig. hiel, amargura, f; rencor, m; (American slang) descaro, m, impertinencia, f; Bot. agalla, f. —vt rozar; Fig. mortificar, herir. **g.-apple,**

agalla, f. **g.-bladder,** vejiga de la hiel, f. **g.-stone,** cálculo hepático, m

gallant /ˈgælənt/ a (brave) valiente, -'lɑnt/ a hermoso; (imposing) imponente, majestuoso; (brave) valiente, gallardo, valeroso, intrépido; (chivalrous) caballeroso; noble; (attentive to ladies, or amorous) galante. —n galán, m. —vt galantear, cortejar

gallantly /ˈgæləntli/ adv (bravely) valientemente; caballerosamente; cortésmente; galantemente

gallantry /ˈgæləntri/ n (bravery) valentía, f, valor, m; heroísmo, m, proeza, f; (chivalry) caballerosidad, f; (toward women, or amorousness) galantería, f

galleon /ˈgæliən/ n galeón, m

gallery /ˈgæləri/ n galería, f; pasillo, m; (of a cloister) tránsito, m; (cloister) claustro, m; (for spectators) tribuna, f; Theat. paraíso, gallinero, m; (theater audience) galería, f; (of portraits, etc.) galería, colección, f; (Mineral., Mil.) galería, f; (building) museo, m. **art g.,** museo de pinturas, m

galley /ˈgæli/ n (Naut., Print.) galera, f; (kitchen) cocina, f; (rowboat) falúa de capitán, f. **to condemn to the galleys,** echar a galeras. **wooden g.,** Print. galerín, m. **g.-proof,** galerada, f. **g.-slave,** galeote, m

Gallic /ˈgælɪk/ a gálico, galicano; francés

gallicism /ˈgælɪsɪzəm/ n galicismo, m

galling /ˈgɔlɪŋ/ a Fig. irritante; mortificante

gallivant /ˈgæləˌvænt/ vi callejear, corretear; divertirse; ir de parranda

gallon /ˈgælən/ n galón, m

galloon /gəˈlun/ n galón, m, trencilla, f

gallop /ˈgæləp/ n galope, m. —vi galopar; ir aprisa. —vt hacer galopar, **at full g.,** a rienda suelta, a galope tendido. **to g. back,** volver a galope. **to g. down,** bajar a galope. **to g. off,** marcharse galopando; alejarse corriendo. **to g. past,** desfilar a galope ante. **to g. through,** cruzar a galope. **to g. up,** vt subir a galope. —vi llegar a galope

gallopade /ˌgæləˈpeid/ n (dance) galop, m

galloping /ˈgæləpɪŋ/ n galope, m; galopada, f. —a que va a galope; Med. galopante. **g. consumption,** tisis galopante, f

gallows /ˈgæloʊz/ n patíbulo, m, horca, f; (framework) montante, m. **g.-bird,** criminal digno de la horca, m

galop /ˈgæləp/ n galop, m

galore /gəˈlɔr/ adv a granel, en abundancia (e.g. sunshine galore, sol a granel)

galosh /gəˈlɒʃ/ n chanclo, m

galvanic /gælˈvænɪk/ a Elec. galvánico; espasmódico

galvanism /ˈgælvəˌnɪzəm/ n Elec. galvanismo, m

galvanize /ˈgælvəˌnaiz/ vt galvanizar

gambit /ˈgæmbɪt/ n (chess) gambito, m; Fig. táctica, f

gamble /ˈgæmbəl/ n juego de azar, m; jugada, f; aventura, f; Com. especulación, f. —vi jugar por dinero; especular; (with) Fig. aventurar, arriesgar. **to g. on the Stock Exchange,** jugar en la bolsa. **to g. away,** perder al juego

gambler /ˈgæmblər/ n jugador (-ra)

gambling /ˈgæmblɪŋ/ n juego, m. —a jugador; de juego. **g.-den,** casa de juego, f, garito, m

gambol /ˈgæmbəl/ n salto, brinco, retozo, m; cabriola, f; juego, m. —vi saltar, brincar, retozar; juguetear

game /geim/ n juego, m; (match) partido, m; (jest) chanza, f; (trick) trampa, f; (birds, hares, etc.) caza menor, f; (tigers, lions, etc.) caza mayor, f; (flesh of game) caza, f; pl **games,** deportes, m pl. —a de caza; (courageous) valiente, animoso, brioso; resuelto. —vi jugar por dinero. **He is g. for anything,** Se atreve a todo. **big g. hunting,** caza mayor, f. **head of g.,** pieza de caza, f. **It is a g. at which two can play,** Donde las dan las toman. **The g. is not worth the candle,** La cosa no vale la pena. **The g. is up,** Fig. El proyecto se ha frustrado. **to make g. of,** (things) burlarse de; (persons) tomar el pelo a; mofarse de. **to**

play the g., *Fig.* jugar limpio. **to g. away,** perder al juego. **g. of cards,** juego de naipes, *m.* **g. of chance,** juego de azar, *m.* **g.-bag,** morral, *m.* **g. drive,** batida de caza, *f.* **g.-laws,** leyes de caza, *f pl.* **g.-licence,** licencia de caza, *f.* **g.-pie,** tortada, *f.* **g. preserve,** coto de caza, *m*

gamekeeper /'geim,kipər/ *n* guardabosque, *m*

gamely /'geimli/ *adv* valientemente

gameness /'geimnis/ *n* valentía, resolución, fortaleza, *f*

gamete /'gæmit/ *n* gameto, *m*

gaming /'geimiŋ/ *n* juego, *m*, *a* de juego. **g.-house,** garito, *m.* **g.-table,** mesa de juego, *f; Fig.* juego, *m*

gammon /'gæmən/ *n* (of bacon) jamón, *m.* —*vt* curar (jamón)

gamut /'gæmət/ *n* gama, *f*

gander /'gændər/ *n* ganso, *m*

gang /gæŋ/ *n* cuadrilla, pandilla, *f;* (squad) pelotón, *m;* (of workers) brigada, cuadrilla, *f;* group, *m.* **g.-plank,** plancha, *f*

ganglion /'gæŋgliən/ *n* ganglio, *m; Fig.* centro, *m*

gangrene /'gæŋgrin/ *n* gangrena, *f.* —*vt* gangrenar. —*vi* gangrenarse

gangrenous /'gæŋgrɪnəs/ *a* gangrenoso

gangster /'gæŋstər/ *n* pistolero, gángster, *m*

gangway /'gæŋ,wei/ *n* pasillo, *m; Naut.* plancha, *f,* pasamano, *m;* (opening in ship's side) portalón, *m.* **midship g.,** crujía, *f*

gap /gæp/ *n* brecha, *f;* abertura, *f;* (hole) boquete, *m;* (pass) desfiladero, paso, *m;* (ravine) hondonada, barranca, *f;* (blank) laguna, *f,* vacío, *m;* (crack) intersticio, *m,* hendedura, *f,* resquicio, *m.* **to fill a gap,** llenar un boquete; llenar un vacío

gape /geip/ *vi* estar con la boca abierta, papar moscas. **to g. at,** mirar con la boca abierta

gaping /'geipiŋ/ *n* huelgo, *m;* abertura, *f, a* que bosteza; boquiabierto; abierto

garage /gə'raʒ/ *n* garaje, *m.* —*vt* poner (un coche, etc.) en un garaje. **g. owner,** garajista, *mf*

garb /garb/ *n* traje, vestido, *m;* uniforme, *m; Herald.* espiga, *f.* —*vt* vestir, ataviar

garbage /'garbidʒ/ *n* basura, inmundicia, *f*

garbage can basurero, tarro de la basura, *m*

garble /'garbəl/ *vt* falsear, mutilar, pervertir

garden /'gardn/ *n* jardín, *m;* huerto, *m;* (fertile region) huerta, *f.* —*a* de jardín. —*vi* trabajar en el jardín, cultivar un huerto. **g. city,** ciudad jardín, *f.* **g.-frame,** semillero, *m.* **g. mold,** tierra vegetal, *f.* **g.-party,** fiesta de jardín, *f.* **g.-plot,** parterre, *m.* **g. produce,** hortalizas, legumbres, *f pl.* **g. roller,** rodillo, *f.* **g.-seat,** banco de jardín, *m.* **g. urn,** jarrón, *m*

gardener /'gardnər/ *n* jardinero, *m*

gardenia /gar'dinyə/ *n* gardenia, *f,* jazmín de la India, *m*

gardening /'gardnɪŋ/ *n* jardinería, *f;* horticultura, *f.* —*a* de jardinería

gargantuan /gar'gæntʃuən/ *a* gargantuesco; tremendo, enorme

gargle /'gargəl/ *n* (liquid) gargarismo, *m;* gárgaras, *f pl.* —*vi* hacer gárgaras, gargarizar

gargling /'garglɪŋ/ *n* gargarismo, *m*

gargoyle /'gargɔil/ *n* gárgola, *f*

garish /'geərɪʃ/ *a* cursi, llamativo, charro, chillón

garishness /'geərɪʃnɪs/ *n* curseria, ostentación, *f,* lo llamativo

garland /'garlənd/ *n* guirnalda, *f;* corona, *f;* (anthology) florilegio, *m; Archit.* festón, *m.* —*vt* enguirnaldar

garlic /'garlɪk/ *n* ajo, *m*

garment /'garmənt/ *n* prenda de vestir, *f;* traje, vestido, *m; Fig.* vestidura, *f;* (Fig. cloak) capa, *f*

garner /'garnər/ *n* granero, *m;* tesoro, *f,* colección, *f.* —*vt* atesorar, guardar

garnet /'garnit/ *n* granate, *m*

garnish /'garnɪʃ/ *n Cul.* aderezo, *m;* adorno, *m.* —*vt Cul.* aderezar; embellecer, adornar

garnishing /'garnɪʃɪŋ/ *n.* See **garnish**

garret /'gærit/ *n* guardilla, buhardilla, *f,* desván, *m*

garrison /'gærəsən/ *n* guarnición, *f,* presidio, *m.* —*vt* guarnecer, presidiar. **g. town,** plaza de armas, *f*

garrote /gə'rɒt/ *n* garrote, *m.* —*vt* agarrotar, dar garrote (a)

garrulity /gə'rulɪti/ *n* garrulidad, locuacidad, charlatanería, *f*

garrulous /'gærələs/ *a* gárrulo, locuaz, charlatán

garter /'gartər/ *n* liga, *f;* (G.) Jarretera, *f, vt* atar con liga; investir con la Jarretera. **Order of the G.,** Orden de la Jarretera, *f*

gas /gæs/ *n* gas, *m; Fig. Inf.* palabrería, *f;* (petrol) bencina, *f, a* de gas; con gas; para gases. —*vt* asfixiar con gas; *Mil.* atacar con gas; saturar de gas. **gas attack,** ataque con gases asfixiantes, *m.* **gas-bag,** bolsa de gas, *f; Inf.* charlatán (-ana). **gas-burner,** mechero de gas, *m.* **gas-chamber,** cámara de gas, *f.* **gas detector,** detector de gases, *m.* **gas-fire,** estufa de gas, *f.* **gas-fitter,** gasista, *m.* **gas-fittings,** lámparas de gas, *f pl.* **gas-light,** luz de gas, *f;* mechero de gas, *m.* **gas-main,** cañería maestra de gas, *f.* **gas-man,** gasista, *m.* **gas-mantle,** camiseta incandescente, *f.* **gas-mask,** máscara para gases, *f.* **gas-meter,** contador de gas, *m.* **gas-pipes,** cañerías (or tuberías) de gas, *f pl.* **gas-ring,** fogón de gas, *m.* **gas-shell,** obús de gases asfixiantes, *m.* **gas-stove,** cocina de gas, *f.* **gas warfare,** guerra química, *f.* **gas-works,** fábrica de gas, *f*

Gascon /'gæskən/ *a* and *n* gascón (-ona)

Gascony /'gæskəni/ *n* Gascuña, *f*

gaseous /'gæsiəs/ *a* gaseoso

gash /gæʃ/ *n* cuchillada, *f;* herida extensa, *f.* —*vt* acuchillar; herir extensamente

gasket /'gæskit/ *n* aro de empaquetadura, *m*

gasoline /,gæsə'lin/ *n* gasolina, *f*

gasp /gæsp/ *n* boqueada, *f.* —*vi* boquear. **to be at the last g.,** estar agonizando. **to g. for breath,** luchar por respirar. **to g. out,** decir anhelante, decir con voz entrecortada

gastric /'gæstrɪk/ *a* gástrico

gastritis /gæ'straitis/ *n* gastritis, *f*

gastronome /'gæstrə,noum/ *n* gastrónomo (-ma)

gastronomic /,gæstrə'nɑmɪk/ *a* gastronómico

gastronomy /gæ'stronəmi/ *n* gastronomía, *f*

gate /geit/ *n* puerta, *f;* cancela, verja, *f;* entrada, *f;* (of a lock, etc.) compuerta, *f;* (across a road, etc.) barrera, *f;* (money) entrada, *f; Fig.* puerta, *f.* **automatic g.,** (at level crossings, etc.) barrera de golpe, *f.* **to g.-crash,** asistir sin invitación. **g.-keeper,** portero, *m;* guardabarrera, *mf* **g.-money,** entrada, *f.* **g.-post,** soporte de la puerta, *m*

gateway /'geit,wei/ *n* entrada, *f;* puerta, *f;* paso, *m;* vestíbulo, *m; Fig.* puerta, *f*

gather /'gæðər/ *vt* (assemble) reunir; (amass) acumular, amontonar; (acquire) obtener, adquirir; hacer una colección (de); cobrar; (harvest) cosechar, recolectar; (pick up) recoger; (pluck) coger; (infer) sacar en limpio, aprender; *Sew.* fruncir; (the brows) fruncir (el ceño). —*vi* reunirse, congregarse; amontonarse; (threaten) amenazar; (sadden) amargar; (Fig. hover over) cernerse (sobre); (increase) aumentar, crecer; (be covered) cubrirse; (fester) supurar. —*n Sew.* frunce, pliegue, *m.* **to g. breath,** tomar aliento. **to g. speed,** ganar velocidad. **to g. strength,** cobrar fuerzas. **I g. from Mary that they are going abroad,** Según lo que me ha dicho María, van al extranjero. **to g. in,** juntar; recoger; (harvest) cosechar; coger. **to g. together,** *vt* reunir. —*vi* reunirse. **to g. up,** recoger; coger; tomar; (one's limbs) encoger. **to g. up the threads,** *Fig.* recoger los hilos.

gatherer /'gæðərər/ *n* cogedor, colector, *m;* (harvester) segador, *m;* (of grapes) vendimiador (-ra) *f;* (of taxes) recaudador, *m*

gathering /'gæðərɪŋ/ *n* cogedura, *f;* (fruit, etc.) recolección, *f;* (of taxes) recaudación, *f;* amontonamiento, *m;* colección, *f; Med.* absceso, *m; Sew.* fruncimiento, *m;* (assembly) reunión, asamblea, *f;* (crowd) concurrencia, muchedumbre, *f*

gathers /'gæðərz/ *n Sew.* fruncidos, pliegues, *m pl*

gauche /gouʃ/ *a* torpe, huraño

gaudily /'gɔdəli/ *adv* ostentosamente; brillantemente

gaudiness /'gɔdinɪs/ *n* ostentación, *f;* brillantez, *f*

gaudy /'gɔdi/ *a* llamativo, vistoso, brillante, ostentoso

gauge /geidʒ/ *n* (of gun) calibre, *m;* (railway) entrevía, *f;* (for measuring) indicator, *m;* regla de medir, *f; Naut.* calado, *m; Fig.* medida, *f;* (test) indicación, *f;* (model) norma, *f.* —*vt* calibrar; medir; estimar; (ship's capacity) arquear; (judge) juzgar; (size up) tomar la medida (de); *Fig.* interpretar; *Sew.* fruncir; (liquor) aforar. **broad (narrow) g. railway,** ferrocarril de vía ancha (estrecha), *m.* **pressure g.,** manómetro, *m.* **water g.,** indicador del nivel de agua, *m*

gauging /'geidʒɪŋ/ *n* medida, *f;* (of ship's capacity) arqueo, *m;* (of liquor) aforamiento, *m; Fig.* apreciación, *f;* interpretación, *f*

Gaul /gɔl/ Galia, *f*

gaunt /gɔnt/ *a* anguloso, huesudo, desvaído; (of houses, etc.) lúgubre

gauntlet /'gɔntlɪt/ *n* guante de manopla, *m;* (part of armor) manopla, *f,* guantelete, *m.* **to throw down the g.,** echar el guante, desafiar

gauntness /'gɔntnɪs/ *n* angulosidad, flaqueza, *f*

gauze /gɔz/ *n* gasa, *f;* (mist) bruma, *f.* **wire-g.,** tela metálica, *f*

gauziness /'gɔzɪnɪs/ *n* diafanidad, *f*

gauzy /'gɔzi/ *a* diáfano; de gasa

gavotte /gə'vɒt/ *n* gavota, *f*

gawkiness /'gɔkɪnɪs/ *n* torpeza, desmaña, *f*

gawky /'gɔki/ *a* anguloso, desgarbado, torpe

gay /gei/ *a* alegre; festivo, animado; ligero de cascos, disipado; homosexual; (of colors) brillante, llamativo

Gaza Strip /'gɑzə/ la franja de Gaza, *f*

gaze /geiz/ *n* mirada, *f;* mirada fija, *f.* —*vi* mirar; mirar fijamente, contemplar

gazelle /gə'zɛl/ *n* gacel (-la)

gazer /'geizər/ *n* espectador (-ra)

gazette /gə'zɛt/ *n* gaceta, *f.* —*vt* publicar en la gaceta.

gazing /'geizɪŋ/ *n* contemplación, *f, a* contemplador; que presencia, que asiste a

gear /gɪər/ *n* (apparel) atavíos, *m pl;* (harness) guarniciones, *f pl,* arneses, *m pl;* (tackle) utensilios, *m pl,* herramientas, *f pl; Naut.* aparejo, *m; Mech.* engranaje, *m;* juego, *m,* marcha, *f.* —*vt* aparejar, enjaezar; *Mech.* poner en marcha, hacer funcionar. —*vi Mech.* engranar, endentar. **low g.,** pimera velocidad, *f.* **neutral g.,** punto muerto, *m.* **reverse g.,** marcha atrás, *f.* **second g.,** segunda velocidad, *f.* **three-speed g.,** cambio de marchas de tres velocidades, *m.* **top g.,** tercera (or cuarta--according to gear-box) velocidad, *f.* **to change g.,** cambiar de marcha, cambiar de velocidad. **to throw out of g.,** *Fig.* desquiciar. **g.-box,** caja de velocidades, *f.* **g.-changing,** cambio de velocidad, *m.* **g.-changing lever,** palanca de cambio de velocidad, palanca de cambio de marchas, *f*

gearing /'gɪərɪŋ/ *n* engranaje, *m*

gee up /dʒi/ *interj* ¡arre!

gehenna /gɪ'hɛnə/ *n* gehena, *m*

geisha /'geiʃə/ *n* geisha, *f*

gelatin /'dʒɛlətɪn/ *n* gelatina, *f.* **cooking g.,** gelatina seca, *f*

gelatinous /dʒə'lætnəs/ *a* gelatinoso

geld /gɛld/ *vt* capar, castrar

gelder /'gɛldər/ *n* castrador, *m*

gelding /'gɛldɪŋ/ *n* castración, capadura, *f;* caballo castrado, *m;* animal castrado, *m*

gelid /'dʒɛlɪd/ *a* gélido, helado; *Fig.* frío, frígido

gem /dʒɛm/ *n* piedra preciosa, *f;* joya, alhaja, *f; Fig.* joya, *f.* —*vt* adornar con piedras preciosos; enjoyar

Gemini /'dʒɛmə,nai/ *n* (los) Gemelos

gender /'dʒɛndər/ *n Gram.* género, *m;* sexo, *m*

gene /dʒin/ *n Biol.* gene, *m*

genealogical /,dʒiniə'lɒdʒɪkəl/ *a* genealógico. **g. tree,** árbol genealógico, *m*

genealogist /,dʒini'ɒlədʒɪst/ *n* genealogista, *mf*

genealogy /,dʒini'ɒlədʒi/ *n* genealogía, *f*

general /'dʒɛnərəl/ *a* general; universal; común; corriente; (usual) acostumbrado, usual; del público, público. —*n* lo general; (*Mil., Eccl.*) general, *m; Inf.* criada para todo, *f.* **in g.,** por lo general, en general, generalmente. **to become g.,** generalizarse. **to make g.,** generalizar, hacer general. **g. average,** (marine insurance) avería gruesa, *f.* **g. election,** elección general, *f.* **g. meeting,** pleno, mitin general, *m.* **g. opinion,** voz común, opinión general, *f.* **G. Post Office,** Oficina Central de Correos, *f.* **g. practitioner,** médico (-ca) general. **g. public,** público, *m.* **the general reader** el lector de tipo general *m*

generalissimo /,dʒɛnərə'lɪsə,mou/ *n* generalísimo, *m*

generality /,dʒɛnə'rælɪti/ *n* generalidad, *f*

generalization /,dʒɛnərələ'zeiʃən/ *n* generalización, *f*

generalize /'dʒɛnərə,laiz/ *vt* and *vi* generalizar

generally /'dʒɛnərəli/ *adv* en general, por regla general, por lo general, generalmente; comúnmente, por lo común

generalship /'dʒɛnərəl,ʃɪp/ *n Mil.* generalato, *m;* (strategy) táctica, estrategia, *f;* dirección, jefatura, *f*

generate /'dʒɛnə,reit/ *vt* (beget) engendrar, procrear; (*Phys., Chem.*) generar; *Fig.* producir, crear

generation /,dʒɛnə'reiʃən/ *n* procreación, *f;* generación, *f; Fig.* producción, creación, *f.* **the younger g.,** los jóvenes

generative /'dʒɛnərətɪv/ *a* generador

generator /'dʒɛnə,reitər/ *n Mech.* generador, *m;* dínamo, *f*

generic /dʒə'nɛrɪk/ *a* genérico

generosity /,dʒɛnə'rɒsɪti/ *n* generosidad, *f;* liberalidad, *f*

generous /'dʒɛnərəs/ *a* generoso; liberal, dadivoso; magnánimo; (plentiful) abundante; (of wines) generoso

generously /'dʒɛnərəsli/ *adv* generosamente; abundantemente

genesis /'dʒɛnəsɪs/ *n* principio, origen, *m;* (G.) Génesis, *m*

genetic /dʒə'nɛtɪk/ *a* genético

genetics /dʒə'nɛtɪks/ *n* genética, *f*

Geneva /dʒə'nivə/ Ginebra *f*

Genevan /dʒə'nivən/ *a* and *n* ginebrés (-esa), ginebrino (-na)

genial /'dʒinyəl/ *a* (of climate) agradable, bueno; (of persons) afable, bondadoso; de buen humor, bonachón

geniality /,dʒini'ælɪti/ *n* afabilidad, bondad, *f;* buen humor, *m*

genially /'dʒinyəli/ *adv* afablemente

genie /'dʒini/ *n* genio, *m*

genital /'dʒɛnɪtl/ *a* genital, sexual. —*n pl* **genitals,** genitales, *m pl*

genitive /'dʒɛnɪtɪv/ *a* and *n Gram.* genitivo *m.*

genius /'dʒinyəs/ *n* genio, *m;* carácter, *m,* índole, *f;* ingenio, *m; Inf.* talento, *m*

Genoa /'dʒɛnouə/ Genova, *f*

Genoese /,dʒɛnou'iz/ *a* and *n* genovés (-esa)

genre /'ʒɑnrə/ *n* género, *m.* **g. painting,** cuadro de género, *m*

genteel /dʒɛn'til/ *a* fino; (affected) remilgado, melindroso; de buen tono; de buena educación

gentile /'dʒɛntail/ *a* and *n* gentil *mf*

gentility /dʒɛn'tɪlɪti/ *n* aristocracia, *f;* respetabilidad, *f*

gentle /'dʒɛntl/ *a* noble, bien nacido, de buena familia; amable; suave; ligero; dulce; (docile) manso, dócil; (affectionate) cariñoso; bondadoso; sufrido, paciente; cortés; pacífico, tolerante. **He was a man of g. birth,** Era un hombre bien nacido. **"G. reader,"** «Querido lector»

gentlefolk /'dʒɛntl,fouk/ *n pl* gente de bien, gente fina, *f;* gente de buena familia, *f*

gentleman /'dʒɛntlmən/ *n* caballero, señor, *m;* gentilhombre, *m.* **Ladies and gentlemen,** Señoras y caballeros, Señores. **young g.,** señorito, *m.* **to be a perfect g.,** ser un caballero perfecto. **g.-inwaiting,** gentilhombre de la cámara, *m*

gentlemanliness /'dʒɛntlmənlinɪs/ *n* caballerosidad, *f*

gentlemanly /'dʒɛntlmənli/ *a* caballeroso

gentleness /'dʒɛntlnɪs/ *n* amabilidad, *f;* suavidad, *f;* dulzura, *f;* mansedumbre, docilidad, *f;* bondad, *f;* paciencia, *f;* cortesía, *f;* tolerancia, *f*

gentlewoman /'dʒɛntl,wʊmən/ *n* dama, *f;* dama de servicio, *f*

gently /'dʒɛntli/ *adv* suavemente; dulcemente; silenciosamente, sin ruido; (slowly) despacio, poco a poco. **g. born,** bien nacido

gentry /'dʒɛntri/ *n* pequeña aristocracia, alta clase media, *f;* (disparaging) gentle, *f*

genuflect /'dʒɛnyu,flɛkt/ *vi* doblar la rodilla

genuflection /,dʒɛnyə'flɛkʃən/ *n* genuflexión, *f*

genuine /'dʒɛnyuɪn/ *a* puro; genuino; verdadero; real; sincero; auténtico

genuinely /'dʒɛnyuɪnli/ *adv* genuinamente; verdaderamente; realmente; sinceramente
genuineness /'dʒɛnyuɪnɪs/ *n* pureza, *f;* autenticidad, *f;* verdad, *f;* sinceridad, *f*
genus /'dʒinəs/ *n* género, *m*
geodesic /ˌdʒiə'dɛsɪk/ *a* geodésico
geodesy /dʒi'ɒdəsi/ *n* geodesia, *f*
geographer /dʒi'ɒɡrəfər/ *n* geógrafo, *m*
geographical /ˌdʒiə'ɡræfɪkəl/ *a* geográfico
geographically /ˌdʒiə'ɡræfɪkəli/ *adv* geográficamente; desde el punto de vista geográfico
geography /dʒi'ɒɡrəfi/ *n* geografía, *f*
geological /ˌdʒiə'lɒdʒɪkəl/ *a* geológico
geologically /ˌdʒiə'lɒdʒɪkəli/ *adv* geológicamente; desde el punto de vista geológico
geologist /dʒi'ɒlədʒɪst/ *n* geólogo, *m*
geologize /dʒi'ɒlə,dʒaiz/ *vi* estudiar la geología. —*vt* estudiar desde un punto de vista geológico
geology /dʒi'ɒlədʒi/ *n* geología, *f*
geometric /ˌdʒiə'mɛtrɪk/ *a* geométrico
geometry /dʒi'ɒmɪtri/ *n* geometría, *f*
geophysics /ˌdʒiou'fɪzɪks/ *n* geofísica, *f*
Georgian /'dʒɔrdʒən/ *a Geog.* georgiano; del principio del siglo diez y nueve
georgic /'dʒɔrdʒɪk/ *n* geórgica, *f*
geotropism /dʒi'ɒtrə,pɪzəm/ *n* geotropismo, *m*
geranium /dʒə'reiniəm/ *n* geranio, *m*
germ /dʒɜrm/ *n* embrión, germen, *m;* microbio, bacilo, *m; Fig.* germen, *m.* **g.-cell,** célula germinal, *f*
German /'dʒɜrmən/ *a* alemán; germánico. —*n* alemán (-ana); (language) alemán, *m;* germano (-na), germánico (-ca). **Sudeten G.,** alemán (-ana) sudete. **G. measles,** rubeola, *f.* **G. silver** alpaca, *f,* melchor *m,* plata alemana *f*
germander /dʒər'mændər/ *n Bot.* camedrio, *m*
germane /dʒər'mein/ *a* pertinente (a), a propósito (a)
Germanic /dʒər'mænɪk/ *a* germánico. —*n* (language) germánico, *m*
Germanization /ˌdʒɜrmənɪ'zeiʃən/ *n* germanización, *f*
Germanize /'dʒɜrmə,naiz/ *vt* germanizar. —*vi* germanizarse
Germanophile /dʒər'mænə,fail/ *n* germanófilo (-la)
Germany /'dʒɜrməni/ *n* Alemania, *f*
germicidal /ˌdʒɜrmə'saidl/ *a* bactericida
germicide /'dʒɜrmə,said/ *n* desinfectante, *m*
germinal /'dʒɜrmənl/ *a* germinal. —*n* (G.) germinal, *m*
germinate /'dʒɜrmə,neit/ *vi* germinar, brotar. —*vt* hacer germinar
germination /ˌdʒɜrmə'neiʃən/ *n* germinación, *f*
germinative /'dʒɜrmə,neitɪv/ *a* germinativo
gerund /'dʒɛrənd/ *n* gerundio, *m*
gerundive /dʒə'rʌndɪv/ *n* gerundio adjetivado, *m*
Gestapo /ɡə'stɑpou/ *n* Gestapo, *f*
gestation /dʒɛ'steiʃən/ *n* gestación, *f*
gesticulate /dʒɛ'stɪkyə,leit/ *vi* gesticular, hacer gestos; accionar. —*vt* expresar por gestos
gesticulation /dʒɛ,stɪkyə'leiʃən/ *n* gesticulación, *f*
gesticulatory /dʒɛ'stɪkyələ,tɔri/ *a* gesticular
gesture /'dʒɛstʃər/ *n* movimiento, *m;* gesticulación, *f;* (of the face) gesto, *m,* mueca, *f;* ademán, *m,* acción, *f.* —*vi* gesticular. —*vt* decir por gestos; acompañar con gestos
get /ɡɛt/ *vt* (obtain) obtener; (acquire) adquirir; (buy) comprar; (take) tomar; (receive) recibir; (gain, win) ganar; (hit) acertar, dar; (place) poner; (achieve) alcanzar, lograr; (make) hacer; (call) llamar; (understand) comprender; (catch) coger; (procreate) procrear, engendrar; (induce) persuadir; (invite) convidar, invitar; (cause) hacer; (with have and past part.) tener; (with have and past part. followed by infin.) tener que; (followed by noun and past part.) hacer; (fetch) buscar, ir a buscar; (order) mandar, disponer; (procure) procurar; (bring) traer; (money) hacer; (a reputation, etc.) hacerse; (a prize, an advantage) llevar; (learn) aprender; (be) ser. —*vi* (become) hacerse; ponerse; venir a ser; (old) envejecerse; (angry) montar (en cólera), enojarse; (arrive) llegar a; (attain) alcanzar; (accomplish) conseguir, lograr; (drunk) emborracharse; (hurt) hacerse daño;

(wet) mojarse; (cool) enfriarse; (money) hacer (dinero); (of health) ponerse; (find oneself) hallarse, encontrarse; (late) hacerse (tarde); (dark) empezar a caer (la noche), empezar a caer (la noche), empezar a oscurecer; (put oneself) meterse; (grow, be) estar; (on to or on top of) montar sobre, subir a. **He has got run over,** Ha sido atropellado. **It gets on my nerves,** Se me pone los nervios en punta. **Let's get it over!** ¡Vamos a concluir de una vez! **How do you get on with her?** ¿Cómo te va con ella? **She must be getting on for twenty,** Tendrá alrededor de veinte años. **to get a suit made,** mandar hacerse un traje. **to get better,** (in health) mejorar de salud; hacer progresos adelantar. **to get dark,** obscurecer. **to get into conversation with,** trabar conversación con. **to get into bad company,** frecuentar malas compañías. **to get into the habit of,** acostumbrarse a. **to get married,** casarse. **to get near,** acercarse. **to get one's own way,** salir con la suya. **to get oneself up as,** disfrazarse de. **to get out in a hurry,** salir apresuradamente; marcharse rápidamente, *Inf.* salir pitando. **to get out of the way,** quitarse de en medio, apartarse. **to get rid of,** desembarazarse de, librarse de; salir de; perder. **to have got,** poseer; tener; padecer. **Get on!** ¡Adelante!; (to a horse) ¡Arre!; (continue) ¡Sigue! **Get out!** ¡Fuera! ¡Largo de aquí! ¡Sal! **Get up!** ¡Levántate!; (to a horse) ¡Arre! **to get about,** moverse mucho; andar mucho; (attend to business affairs) ir a sus negocios; (travel) viajar; (get up from sick bed) levantarse; (go out) salir; (be known) saberse, divulgarse, hacerse público. **to get above,** subir a un nivel más alto (de). **to get across,** *vi* cruzar, atravesar. —*vt* hacer cruzar. **to get along,** *vi* (depart) marcharse; (continue) seguir, vivir; (manage) ir, ir tirando. —*vt* llevar; tener; hacer andar por. **How are you getting along?** ¿Cómo le va? **I am getting along all right, thank you,** Voy tirando, gracias. **to get along without,** pasarse sin. **to get at,** (remove) sacar; (find) encontrar; (reach) llegar a; alcanzar; (discover) descubrir; (allude to) aludir a; (understand) comprender. **to get away,** *vi* dejar (un lugar); marcharse, irse; (escape) escaparse. —*vt* ayudar a marcharse; ayudar a escaparse. **to get away with,** llevarse, marcharse con; *Inf.* salir con la suya. **to get back,** *vi* regresar, volver; (get home) volver a casa; (be back) estar de vuelta. —*vt* (recover) recobrar; (receive) recibir; (find again) hallar de nuevo. **to get down,** *vi* bajar, descender. —*vt* bajar; (take off a hook) descolgar; (swallow) tragar; (note) anotar; escribir. **to get down on all fours,** ponerse en cuatro patas. **to get down to,** ponerse a (estudiar, trabajar, etc.). **to get in,** *vi* entrar en; lograr entrar en; (slip in) colarse en; (of political party) entrar en el poder; (of a club) hacerse socio de; (return) regresar; (home) volver a casa; (find oneself) hallarse, estar; (a habit) adquirir. —*vt* hacer entrar en; (a club, etc.) hacer socio de; (a word) decir. **to get into.** See **to get in. to get off,** *vt* apearse de; bajar de; (send) enviar; (from punishment) librar; (bid goodbye) despedirse de; (remove) quitar, sacar. —*vi* apearse; bajar; (from punishment) librarse; (leave) ponerse en camino, marcharse. **to get on,** *vi* (wear) tener puesto; (progress) hacer progresos, adelantar; (prosper) medrar, prosperar; (succeed) tener éxito; avanzar; seguir el camino; (agree) avenirse. —*vt* (push) empujar; (place) poner; (cause) hacer; (clothes) ponerse; (mount) subir a. **to get open,** abrir. **to get out,** *vt* hacer salir; sacar; (publish) publicar; divulgar. —*vi* salir; escapar; **to get out of a jam,** salir de un paso; (descend) bajar (de). **to get over,** (cross) atravesar, cruzar; (an illness, grief, etc.) reponerse, reponerse de; (excuse) perdonar; (surmount) superar; (ground) recorrer. **to get round,** (a person) persuadir; (surround) rodear; (avoid) evitar; (difficulties) superar, vencer. **to get through,** pasar por; (time) pasar, entretener; (money) gastar; (finish) terminar, acabar; (pierce or enter) penetrar; (communicate) comunicar (con); (difficulties) vencer; (an exam) aprobar. **to get to,** llegar a; encontrar; (begin) empezar a. **to get together,** *vt* reunir, juntar. —*vi* reunirse, juntarse. **to get under,** ponerse debajo de; (control) dominar. **to get up,** *vt* (raise) alzar, levantar; (carry up things) subir; hacer subir; organizar;

preparar; (learn) aprender; (linen) blanquear, colar; (ascend) subir; hacer; (dress) ataviar; (steam) generar; (a play) ensayar, poner en escena. —*vi* levantarse; (on a horse) montar a caballo; (of the wind) refrescarse; (of the fire) avivarse; (of the sea) embravecerse. **to get up to,** llegar a; alcanzar

get-at-able /'gɛt ˌæt əbəl/ *a* accesible

getting /'gɛtɪŋ/ *n* adquisición, *f;* (of money) ganancia, *f.* **g. up,** preparación, *f;* organización, *f;* (of a play) representación (de una comedia), puesta en escena, *f*

get-up /'gɛt ˌʌp/ *n* atavío, *m;* (of a book, etc.) aspecto, *m*

gewgaw /'gyugɔ/ *n* chuchería, *f*

geyser /'gaizər/ *n* géiser, *m;* (for heating water) calentador (de agua), *m*

ghastliness /'gæstlinis/ *n* horror, *m;* palidez mortal, *f;* aspecto miserable, *m;* (boringness) tedio, aburrimiento, *m;* lo desagradable

ghastly /'gæstli/ *a* horrible; de una palidez mortal; cadavérico; (boring) aburrido; muy desagradable

gherkin /'gɜrkin/ *n* cohombrillo, *m*

ghetto /'gɛtou/ *n* gueto *m*

ghost /goust/ *n* fantasma, espectro, aparecido, *m;* (spirit) alma, *f,* espíritu, *m;* (shadow) sombra, *f;* (writer) mercenario, *m.* **Holy G.,** Espíritu Santo, *m.* **to give up the g.,** entregar el alma; perder la esperanza, desesperarse. **to look like a g.,** parecer un fantasma

ghostliness /'goustlinis/ *n* espiritualidad, *f;* lo misterioso; palidez, *f;* tenuidad, *f*

ghostly /'goustli/ *a* espiritual; espectral; misterioso; pálido; vaporoso, tenue; indistinto

ghost town *n* pueblo-fantasma, *m*

ghost word *n* palabra-fantasma, *f*

ghoul /gul/ *n* vampiro, *m*

ghoulish /'gulɪʃ/ *a* insano; cruel; sádico

giant /'dʒaiənt/ *n* gigante, *m;* Fig. coloso, *m,* a gigantesco; de gigantes; de los gigantes. **g.-killer,** matador de gigantes, *m.* **g.-stride,** (gymnastics) paso volante, *m*

giantess /'dʒaiəntɪs/ *n* giganta, *f*

gibber /'dʒɪbər/ *vi* hablar incoherentemente, hablar entre dientes; farfullar, hablar atropelladamente; decir disparates

gibberish /'dʒɪbərɪʃ/ *n* galimatías, *m;* jerigonza, *f,* griego, *m*

gibbet /'dʒɪbɪt/ *n* horca, *f,* patíbulo, *m.* **to die on the g.,** morir ahorcado

gibbon /'gɪbən/ *n* Zool. gibón, *m*

gibe /dʒaib/ *n* improperio, escarnio, *m,* burla, mofa, *f.* —*vi* criticar. **to g. at,** burlarse de, ridiculizar, mofarse de

gibing /'dʒaibɪŋ/ *a* burlón, mofador. —*n* mofas, burlas, *f pl*

gibingly /'dʒaibɪŋli/ *adv* burlonamente, con sorna

giblets /'dʒɪblɪts/ *n* menudillos, *m pl*

giddily /'gɪdli/ *adv* vertiginosamente; frívolamente, atolondradamente

giddiness /'gɪdinɪs/ *n* vértigo, *m;* atolondramiento, *m;* inconstancia, *f;* frivolidad, ligereza de cascos, *f*

giddy /'gɪdi/ *a* vertiginoso; mareado; atolondrado, casquivano, frívolo; inconstante. **She felt very g.,** Se sintió muy mareada. **to make g.,** dar vértigo (a), marear

gift /gɪft/ *n* regalo, *m,* dádiva, *f;* (quality) don, talento, *m;* prenda, *f;* poder, *m;* Law. donación, *f;* (offering) ofrenda, oblación, *f.* —*vt* dotar. **deed of g.,** Law. escritura de donación, *f.* **in the g. of,** el poder de, en las manos de. **I wouldn't have it as a g.,** No lo tomaría ni regalado. **Never look a g. horse in the mouth,** A caballo regalado no se le mira el diente. **g. of tongues,** don de las lenguas, genio de las lenguas, *m*

gifted /'gɪftɪd/ *a* talentoso

gig /gɪg/ *n* (carriage) carrocín, *m;* (boat) falúa, lancha, *f;* (for wool) máquina de cardar paño, *f;* (harpoon) arpón, *m*

gigantic /dʒai'gæntɪk/ *a* gigantesco; colosal, enorme

giggle /'gɪgəl/ *vi* reírse sin motivo; reírse disimuladamente. —*n* risa disimulada, *f*

giggling /'gɪglɪŋ/ *n* risa estúpida, *f;* risa nerviosa, *f*

gigolo /'dʒɪgəˌlou/ *n* gigolo, mantenido, jinetero (Cuba), *m*

gild /gɪld/ *vt* dorar; (metals) sobredorar; embellecer. **to g. the pill,** dorar la píldora

gilder /'gɪldər/ *n* dorador, *m*

gilding /'gɪldɪŋ/ *n* dorado, *m,* doradura, *f;* embellecimiento, *m*

Gileadite /'gɪliəˌdait/ *n* and *a* galaadita, *mf*

gill /gɪl/ *n* (of fish) agalla, branquia, *f;* (ravine) barranco, *m;*

gill /dʒɪl/ *n* (measure) cierta medida de líquidos, *f,* ($\frac{1}{8}$ litro)

gilt /gɪlt/ *n* dorado, *m;* pan de oro, *m;* relumbrón, *m;* Fig. encanto, *m,* a dorado, áureo. **g.-edged,** (of books) con los bordes dorados. **g.-edged security,** papel del Estado, *m;* valores de toda confianza, *m pl*

gimcrack /'dʒɪmˌkræk/ *n* chuchería, *f.* —*a* de baratillo, cursi; mal hecho

gimlet /'gɪmlɪt/ *n* barrena, *f,* taladro, *m*

gin /dʒɪn/ *n* (drink) ginebra, *f;* (snare) trampa, *f.* —*vt* (snare) coger con trampa. **g. block,** Mech. garrucha, *f*

ginger /'dʒɪndʒər/ *n* jengibre, *m;* Inf. energía, *f,* brío, *m,* a rojo. —*vt* sazonar con jengibre; Inf. animar, estimular. **g.-beer,** gaseosa, *f*

gingerly /'dʒɪndʒərli/ *adv* con gran cuidado; delicadamente

gingham /'gɪŋəm/ *n* guinga, *f*

gingivitis /ˌdʒɪndʒə'vaitɪs/ *n* gingivitis, *f*

gipsy /'dʒɪpsi/ *n.* See **gypsy**

giraffe /dʒə'ræf/ *n* jirafa, *f*

gird /gɜrd/ *vt* ceñir; (invest) investir; (surround) cercar, rodear; (put on) revestir. **to g. oneself for the fray,** prepararse para la lucha

girder /'gɜrdər/ *n* viga, jácena, *f.* **main g.,** viga maestra, *f*

girdle /'gɜrdl̩/ *n* (belt) cinturón, *m;* (corset) faja, *f;* circunferencia, *f;* zona, *f.* —*vt* ceñir; Fig. cercar, rodear

girl /gɜrl/ *n* niña, *f;* chica, muchacha, *f;* (maidservant) criada, muchacha, *f;* (young lady) señorita, *f.* **a young g.,** una jovencita; (a little older) una joven. **old g.,** (of a school) antigua alumna, *f;* Inf. vieja, *f;* (Inf. affectionate) chica, *f.* **g. friend,** amiguita, *f.* **g. guide, girl scout,** exploradora, *f.* **girls' school,** colegio de niñas, colegio de señoritas, *m*

girlhood /'gɜrlhʊd/ *n* niñez, *f;* juventud, *f*

girlish /'gɜrlɪʃ/ *a* de niña, de muchacha; (of boys) afeminado; joven

girth /gɜrθ/ *n* (of horse, etc.) cincha, *f;* circunferencia, *f;* (of person) talle, *m;* (obesity) corpulencia, obesidad, *f*

gist /dʒɪst/ *n* esencia, substancia, *f,* importe, *m*

give /gɪv/ *vt* dar; (a present) regalar; (infect) contagiar; (impart) comunicar; (grant) otorgar; (allow, concede) conceder; (assign) asignar, señalar; (appoint) nombrar; (a toast) brindar (a la salud de); (a party, ball, etc.) dar; (a bill) presentar; (wish) desear; (punish) castigar; (pay) pagar; (hand over) entregar; (names at baptism) imponer; (produce) producir; dar; (cause) causar; (of judicial sentences) condenar a; (evoke) proporcionar; (provoke) provocar; (devote) dedicar, consagrar; (sacrifice) sacrificar; (evidence, an account, orders, a lesson, a performance, a concert) dar; (a cry, shout) lanzar, proferir; (a laugh) soltar; (describe) describir; (paint) pintar; (write) escribir; (offer) ofrecer; (show) mostrar; (transmit) transmitir; (heed, pain) hacer; (a speech) pronunciar, hacer; (award, adjudge) adjudicar; (ear) prestar (oído (a)). —*vi* dar; ser dadivoso, mostrarse generoso; (give in) ceder; (be elastic) dar de sí; ablandarse; (collapse) hundirse. **G. them my best wishes!** ¡Dales mis mejores recuerdos! **G. us a song!** ¡Cántanos algo! **I can g. him a lift in my car,** Puedo ofrecerle un asiento en mi auto. **I g. you my word,** Os doy mi palabra. **to g. a good account of oneself,** defenderse bien; hacer bien; salir bien. **to g. a person a piece of one's mind,** contarle cuatro verdades. **to g. chase,** dar caza (a). **to g. it to a person,** poner a uno como nuevo; reprender; (beat) pegar, dar de palos. **to g. of itself,** dar de sí. **to g. rise to,** dar lugar a, ocasionar, causar. **to g. way,** no poder resistir; (break) romperse;

(yield) ceder; (collapse) hundirse; (retreat) retroceder. **to g. way to,** (retreat before) retirarse ante; (abandon oneself to) entregarse a, abandonarse a. **to g. away,** enajenar; dar; regalar; (sell cheaply) vender a un precio muy bajo; (get rid of) deshacerse de; (sacrifice) sacrificar; (a secret) revelar; (betray) traicionar; (expose) descubrir; (tell) contar; (a bride) conducir al altar. **He gave himself away,** Reveló su pensamiento sin querer. **to g. back,** vt devolver; restituir. —vi retirarse, cejar. **to g. forth,** divulgar, publicar; (scatter) derramar; (emit) emitir, despedir; (smoke, rays) echar. **to g. in,** vt entregar; presentar. —vi darse por vencido. **to g. in to,** (agree with) asentir en, consentir en; rendirse ante. **Mary always gives in to George,** María hace siempre lo que Jorge quiere. **to g. off,** (of odors, etc.) emitir, exhalar, despedir. **to g. out,** vt (distribute) distribuir, repartir; (allocate) asignar; (publish) publicar; (announce) anunciar; (reveal) divulgar; (allege) afirmar, hacer saber; (emit) emitir. —vi (be exhausted) agotarse; (end) acabarse; (be lacking) faltar. **to g. over,** vt entregar; (transfer) traspasar; cesar de. —vi cesar de. **to g. up,** entregar; ceder; (renounce) renunciar (a); (sacrifice) sacrificar; (abandon) abandonar; (cease) dejar de; (as lost) dar por perdido; (of a patient) desahuciar; (a post) dimitir de; (return) devolver, restituir; (a problem) renunciar (a resolver un problema); (lose hope) perder la esperanza; (give in) darse por vencido. **I had given you up,** (didn't expect you), Creí que no ibas a venir. **to g. oneself up to,** entregarse a; dedicarse a; Mil. rendirse a. **to g. up one's seat,** ceder su sitio (or asiento). **to g. upon,** (overlook) dar sobre

give /gɪv/ n elasticidad, f; el dar de sí; (concession) concesión, f. **g. and take,** concesiones mutuas, f pl. **g. away,** Inf. revelación indiscreta, f

given /'gɪvən/ a dado; especificado; convenido; (with to) dado a, adicto a. **in a g. time,** en un tiempo dado. **g. that,** dado que

giver /'gɪvər/ n dador (-ra); donador (-ra)

gizzard /'gɪzərd/ n molleja, f. **It sticks in my g.,** Inf. No lo puedo tragar

glacial /'gleɪʃəl/ a glacial

glacier /'gleɪʃər/ n glaciar, m

glad /glæd/ a feliz, alegre; contento, satisfecho; Inf. elegante. **to be g.,** alegrarse, estar contento; estar satisfecho. **to give the g. eye,** hacer ojos

gladden /'glædn/ vt alegrar, regocijar

glade /gleɪd/ n claro, m; rasa, f

gladiator /'glædi,eɪtər/ n gladiador, m

gladiatorial /ˌglædiə'tɔriəl/ a gladiatorio

gladiolus /ˌglædi'oʊləs/ n Bot. gladíolo, gladio, m; espadaña, f

gladly /'glædli/ adv alegremente; con mucho gusto, gustoso, de buena gana

gladness /'glædnɪs/ n alegría, felicidad, f, contento, m; placer, m

glamorous /'glæmərəs/ a exótico; garboso

glamour /'glæmər/ n encanto, m, fascinación, f; garbo, m. **g. girl,** belleza exótica, f

glance /glæns/ n (of a projectile) desviación, f; (of light) vislumbre, m; relumbrón, centelleo, m; (look) vistazo, m, ojeada, f; mirada, f, vi desviarse; relumbrar, centellear, brillar; (with at) ojear, echar un vistazo a, lanzar miradas a; (a book) hojear; mirar; mirar de reojo; Fig. indicar brevemente. **at a g.,** con un vistazo; en seguida. **at the first g.,** a primera vista. **to g. off,** desviarse (al chocar). **to g. over,** repasar, echar un vistazo a; (a book) hojear

glancing /'glænsɪŋ/ a (of a blow) que roza

gland /glænd/ n (Anat., Bot.) glándula, f; (in the neck) ganglio, m. **to have swollen glands,** tener inflamación de los ganglios

glandular /'glændʒələr/ a glandular

glare /glɛər/ n brillo, fulgor, m; luminosidad, f; reflejo, m; (look) mirada feroz, f. —vi relumbrar, centellear; (stare) mirar con ferocidad, mirar fijamente

glaring /'glɛərɪŋ/ a deslumbrante, brillante; (of colors) chillón, llamativo; (of looks) de mirada feroz; (flagrant) notorio, evidente

glaringly /'glɛərɪŋli/ adv brillantemente; con mirada feroz; notoriamente

glass /glæs/ n vidrio, m; cristal, m; (glassware) artículos de vidrio, m pl; cristalería, f; (for drinking) vaso, m, copa, f; (pane) cristal, m; (mirror) espejo, m; (telescope) telescopio, m; catalejo, m; (barometer) barómetro, m; (hour-glass) reloj de arena, m; (of a watch) vidrio (de reloj), m; pl **glasses,** (binoculars) anteojos, m pl; (spectacles) gafas, lentes, m pl; (opera glasses) gemelos de teatro, m pl, a de vidrio; de cristal. —vt vidriar. **John wears glasses,** Juan lleva gafas. **The g. is falling (rising),** El barómetro baja (sube). **to clink glasses,** trincar las copas. **to look in the g.,** mirarse en el espejo. **clear g.,** vidrio transparente, m. **cut g.,** cristal tallado, m. **frosted g.,** vidrio jaspeado, m. **plate-g.,** vidrio plano, m; **safety g.,** vidrio inastillable, m. **stained g.,** vidrio de color, vidrio pintado, m. **under g.,** bajo vidrio; en invernáculo. **g. bead,** abalorio, m; cuenta de vidrio, f. **g.-blower,** soplador de vidrio, m. **g.-blowing,** el soplar de vidrio. **g. case,** escaparate, m. **g.-cloth,** paño para vasos, m. **g. eye,** ojo de cristal, m. **g. paper,** papel de vidrio, m. **g. roof,** techo de cristal, m. **g. window,** vidriera, f

glasscutter /'glæs,kʌtər/ n cortador de vidrio, m

glassful /'glæsfʊl/ n contenido de un vaso, m; vaso, vaso lleno, m, copa, f

glasshouse /'glæs,haʊs/ n fábrica de vidrio, f; vidriería, f; invernáculo, invernadero, m, estufa, f

glassware /'glæs,wɛər/ n cristalería, f

glassy /'glæsi/ a vitreo; (of eyes) vidrioso; Fig. cristalino; (smooth) liso, raso

glaucous /'glɔkəs/ a de color verdemar; Bot. glauco

glaze /gleɪz/ n barniz, m; lustre, brillo, m. —vt poner vidrios (a); vidriar; barnizar; (paper, leather, etc.) estinar. —vi (of eyes) vidriarse, ponerse vidrioso

glazier /'gleɪʒər/ n vidriero, m

glazing /'gleɪzɪŋ/ n vidriado, m; barnizado, m; satinado, m; (material) barniz, m

gleam /glim/ n rayo, destello, m; (of color) viso, m, mancha, f; Fig. rayo, m; (in the eye) chispa, f. —vi relucir, centellear, resplandecer; brillar; reflejar la luz; Fig. brillar. **g. of hope,** rayo de esperanza, m

gleaming /'glimɪŋ/ a reluciente, centelleante; brillante. —n see **gleam**

glean /glin/ vt espigar, rebuscar; recoger. —vi espigar

gleaner /'glinər/ n espigador, m; recogedor (-ra)

gleaning /'glinɪŋ/ n espigueo, m; rebusca, recolección, f; pl **gleanings,** fragmentos, m pl

glee /gli/ n alegría, f, júbilo, alborozo, m; Mus. canción para voces solas, f

gleeful /'glifəl/ a alegre, jubiloso, gozoso

gleefully /'glifəli/ adv alegremente, con júbilo

glen /glɛn/ n cañada, f, cañón, m, hondonada, f

glib /glɪb/ a locuaz, voluble; (easy) fácil

glibness /'glɪbnɪs/ n locuacidad, volubilidad, f; (easiness) facilidad, f

glide /glaɪd/ n deslizamiento, m; Aer. planeo, m. —vi deslizarse; resbalar; Aer. planear. **to g. away,** escurrirse; desaparecer silenciosamente

glider /'glaɪdər/ n Aer. deslizador, planeador, m

gliding /'glaɪdɪŋ/ n Aer. vuelo sin motor, m

glimmer /'glɪmər/ n luz trémula, luz débil, f, tenue resplandor, m; vislumbre, m. —vi brillar con luz trémula, rielar Fig.; tener vislumbres (de)

glimpse /glɪmps/ n vistazo, m; vislumbre, m; indicio, m; impresión, f; vista, f. —vt entrever, divisar; tener una vista (de); ver por un instante; vislumbrar

glint /glɪnt/ n tenue resplandor, m; lustre, m; centelleo, m; reflejo, m; (in the eye) chispa, f. —vi relucir, destellar, rutilar; reflejar

glisten /'glɪsən/ vi brillar, relucir

glistening /'glɪsənɪŋ/ a coruscante; brillante, reluciente

glitter /'glɪtər/ n brillo, resplandor, m, rutilación, f. —vi brillar, resplandecer, relucir; rutilar. **All that glitters is not gold,** Todo lo que reluce no es oro

glittering /'glɪtərɪŋ/ a reluciente, resplandeciente; Fig. brillante

gloat (over) /gloʊt/ vi recrearse en, gozarse en, deleitarse en

globe /gloʊb/ n globo, m; esfera, f; (for fish) pecera, f; (for gas, electric light) globo, m. **geographical g.,** globo terrestre, m. **g.-trotter,** trotamundos, m

globular /'glɒbyələr/ a globular, esférico

globule /'glɒbyul/ n glóbulo, m

globulous /'glɒbyələs/ a globuloso

gloom /glum/ n obscuridad, f; lobreguez, f, tinieblas, f pl; Fig. melancolía, tristeza, f; taciturnidad, f. —vi Fig. ponerse melancólico; ser taciturno

gloomily /'gluməli/ adv obscuramente; Fig. tristemente; taciturnamente

gloomy /'glumi/ a obscuro; sombrío, lóbrego; melancólico, triste; taciturno; (of prospects, etc.) poco halagüeño, nada atrayente

glorification /ˌglɔrəfiˈkeɪʃən/ n glorificación, f

glorify /'glɔrəˌfaɪ/ vt glorificar; exaltar; alabar

glorious /'glɔriəs/ a glorioso; espléndido, magnífico; insigne; Inf. estupendo

glory /'glɔri/ n gloria, f; esplendor, m, magnificencia, f; Art. gloria, f. —vi recrearse, gozarse; glorificarse, jactarse. **to be in one's g.**, estar en la gloria. **to g. in,** hacer gala de, glorificarse en

gloss /glɒs/ n (sheen) lustre, brillo, m; Fig. apariencia, f; (note) glose, m; (excuse) disculpa, f. —vt pulir; glosar. **to g. over,** (faults) disculpar, excusar

glossary /'glɒsəri/ n glosario, m

glossiness /'glɒsinɪs/ n lustre, m, tersura, f; brillo, m

glossy /'glɒsi/ a lustroso, terso; brillante; (of hair) liso

glottal stop /'glɒtḷ/ n choque glótica, golpe de glotis, m

glottis /'glɒtɪs/ n Anat. glotis, f

glove /glʌv/ n guante. **evening gloves,** guantes largos, m pl. **to be hand in g. with,** juntar diestra con diestra. **to fit like a g.,** sentar como un guante. **to put on one's gloves,** ponerse los guantes. **g. shop,** guantería, f. **g.-stretcher,** ensanchador (or abridor) de guantes, m

glove compartment gaveta, guantera, f, guantero, portaguantes m

glove-compartment light luz de portaguantes, f

glover /'glʌvər/ n guantero (-ra)

glow /glou/ n incandescencia, f; claridad, f; luz difusa, f; (heat) calor, m; (of color) intensidad, f; color vivo, m; (enthusiasm) ardor, entusiasmo, m; (redness) rojez, f; (in the sky) arrebol, m; (of pleasure, etc.) sentimiento de placer, m; sensación de bienestar, f. —vi estar incandescente; arder; abrasarse; sentir entusiasmo; mostrarse rojo; experimentar un sentimiento de placer o una sensación de bienestar. **to g. with health,** estar rebosando de salud. **g.-worm,** luciérnaga, f

glower /'glauər/ n ceño, m; mirada amenazadora, f. —vi poner cara de pocos amigos, mirar airadamente; tener los ojos puestos (en)

glowing /'glouɪŋ/ a candente, incandescente; ardiente; entusiasta; satisfecho; intenso; (bright) vivo; (red) encendido; (with health) rebosante de salud. —n see **glow**

glowingly /'glouɪŋli/ adv encendidamente; Fig. con entusiasmo

glucose /'glukous/ n glucosa, f

glue /glu/ n engrudo, m, cola, f. —vt encolar, engrudar; pegar; Fig. fijar, poner. **He kept his eyes glued on them,** Tenía los ojos fijados (or pegados) en ellos. **g.-pot,** pote de cola, m

gluey /'glui/ a gomoso; pegajoso, viscoso

glueyness /'gluinɪs/ n viscosidad, f

gluing /'gluɪŋ/ n encoladura, f

glum /glʌm/ a deprimido, taciturno, sombrío

glumly /'glʌmli/ adv taciturnamente

glut /glʌt/ n superabundancia, f, exceso, m. —vt (satiate) hartar; Fig. saciar; (the market) inundar

gluteal /'glutiəl/ a glúteo

glutinous /'glutnəs/ a glutinoso, pegajoso, viscoso

glutton /'glʌtn/ n glotón (-ona); Fig. ávido (-da)

gluttonous /'glʌtnəs/ a glotón, comilón

gluttony /'glʌtni/ n glotonería, gula, f

glycerin /'glɪsərɪn/ n glicerina, f

gnarled /nɑrld/ a nudoso; (of human beings) curtido

gnash /næʃ/ vt rechinar, crujir (los dientes)

gnashing /'næʃɪŋ/ n rechinamiento (de dientes), m

gnat /næt/ n mosquito, m

gnaw /nɔ/ vt roer; morder; (of wood by worms) carcomer; Fig. roer

gnawing /'nɔɪŋ/ n roedura, f; mordedura, f, a roedor; mordedor

gnome /noum/ n nomo, m

gnostic /'nɒstɪk/ a and n nóstico (-ca)

gnosticism /'nɒstɪsɪzəm/ n nosticismo, m

go /gou/ vi ir; (depart) irse, marcharse; (go toward) dirigirse a, encaminarse a; (lead to, of roads, etc.) conducir a, ir a; (vanish) desaparecer; (leave) dejar, salir de; (lose) perder; (pass) pasar; (of time) transcurrir, pasar; (be removed) quitarse; (be prohibited) prohibirse; (fall) caer; (collapse) hundirse; (be torn off) desprenderse; desgajarse; Mech. funcionar, trabajar, andar; (sound) sonar; (of the heart) palpitar, latir; (follow) seguir; (gesture) hacer un gesto; (be stated) decirse, afirmarse; (live) vivir; (wear) llevar; (turn out) salir, resultar; (improve) mejorar; (prosper) prosperar; (turn, become) ponerse; volverse; (to sleep) dormirse; (into a faint) desmayarse; (decay) echarse a perder, estropearse; (turn sour) agriarse; (become, adopt views, etc.) hacerse; (be sold) venderse; (be decided) decidirse, ser decidido; (have) tener; (by will) pasar; (belong) pertenecer; (receive) recibir; (have its place) estar; (put) ponerse; (going plus infin.) ir a; (die) morir, irse; (do a journey, a given distance) hacer; (a pace, step) dar; (take) tomar; (escape) escaparse, (contribute) contribuir (a); (harmonize) armonizar (con); (be current) ser válido; (be) ser; (of a document, etc., run) rezar, decir; (attend) asistir a; (be broken) estar roto; (be worn) estar raído; (be granted) darse, otorgarse. **It's gone five,** Ya dieron las cinco. **It's time to be going,** Es hora de marcharse. **Let's go!** ¡Vamos! **These two colours go well together,** Estos colores armonizan bien. **Well, how goes it?** Bueno, ¿qué tal? ¿Cómo te va? **Who goes there?** Mil. ¿Quién va? **to go and fetch,** ir a buscar. **to let go,** soltar; dejar ir. **to go one's way,** seguir su camino. **to go wrong,** salir mal, fracasar; (sin) descarriarse. **"Go!"** (traffic sign) «¡Siga!» **Go on!** ¡Adelante!; (continue) ¡Siga!; Inf. ¡Qué va! **to go about,** dar la vuelta a; rodear; recorrer; (undertake) emprender, hacer; intentar; (of news, etc.) circular; Naut. virar de bordo. **Go about your business!** ¡Métete en lo que te importa! **to go abroad,** ir al extranjero; salir a la calle; publicarse, divulgarse. **to go across,** cruzar, atravesar; pasar. **to go after,** andar tras; seguir; (seek) ir a buscar; (persecute) perseguir. **to go again,** ir de nuevo; (be present) asistir otra vez; volver. **to go against,** ir contra; militar contra; oponerse a; ser desfavorable a. **to go ahead,** adelantar, avanzar; progresar; prosperar; (lead) ir a la cabeza (de), conducir; Naut. marchar hacia adelante. **to go along,** andar por; recorrer; (depart) irse, marcharse. **go apartment-hunting,** ir en busca de piso. **to go along with,** acompañar (a). **to go aside,** quitarse de en medio; apartarse, retirarse. **to go astray,** perderse; extraviarse, descarriarse. **to go at,** atacar, acometer; (undertake) emprender; empezar a. **to go at it again,** Inf. volver a la carga. **to go away,** irse, marcharse; ausentarse; alejarse; desaparecer. **to go away with,** marcharse con; (an object) llevarse. **to go back,** volver; (retreat) retroceder, volverse atrás; (in history) remontarse a. **to go back on,** (a promise, etc.) faltar a; (retract) retractarse; (betray) traicionar. **to go backwards,** retroceder, cejar; desandar lo andado; Fig. deteriorar, empeorar. **to go backwards and forwards,** ir y venir; oscilar. **to go before,** (lead) ir a la cabeza de, conducir; anteceder; proceder; (a judge, etc.) comparecer ante. **to go behind,** ir detrás de; esconderse detrás de; seguir; (evidence, etc.) mirar más allá de. **to go between,** ponerse entre; interponerse; (as a mediator) mediar; (insert) intercalarse; (travel) ir entre; llevar cartas entre, ser mensajero de. **to go beyond,** ir más allá; exceder. **to go by,** pasar por; pasar cerca de, pasar junto a; ir por; (of time) transcurrir, pasar; (follow) seguir; guiarse por, atenerse a; (judge by) juzgar por; (a name) pasar por; tomar el nombre de. **to go down,** bajar, descender; (of the sun) ponerse; (sink) hundirse; sumergirse; (fall) caer; (be remembered) ser recordado; (believe) tragar; ser creído. **to go down again,** bajar de nuevo; volver a caer. **go Dutch,** ir a escote, ir a la gringa, ir a la par, ir a limón. **to go far,** ir lejos; influir mucho (en); impresionar mucho; (contribute) contribuir (a). **to go for,** (seek) ir en busca de; procurar tener; (attack) echarse encima de, atacar. **to go for a ride (by car, bicycle, on horseback),** dar un paseo (en coche, en bicicleta, a caballo). **to go forth,** salir; publicarse. **to go forward,** adelantar, avanzar; progresar; continuar; (happen) tener lugar. **to go from,** dejar, abandonar; separarse de, apartarse de; marcharse de. **to go in,** entrar en; (a railway carriage, etc.) subir a; (compete) concurrir. **to go in again,** volver a entrar en, entrar de nuevo en. **to go in and out,** entrar y salir; ir y venir. **to go in for,** entrar a buscar; dedicarse a, entregarse a; (buy) comprarse; tomar parte en; (an examination) tomar (un examen); (for a competition) entrar en (un concurso); (try) ensayar; arriesgar. **to go into,** entrar en; examinar; investigar; ocuparse con. **to go near,** acercarse a. **to go off,** marcharse; (explode) estallar; (of fire-arms) dispararse; (of the voice, etc.) perder (la voz, etc.); (run away) huir, fugarse. **to go off badly,** salir mal, fracasar, no tener éxito. **to go off well,** salir bien, tener éxito. **to go on,** subirse a; continuar; durar; avanzar; proseguir su marcha; progresar; prosperar; *Theat.* entrar en escena; (of clothes) ponerse; (rely on) apoyarse en. **Don't go on like that,** No seas así, No te pongas así. **This glove will not go on me,** No puedo ponerme este guante. **to be gone on a person,** *Inf.* estar loco por. **I went on to say...,** Después dije; Continuando mi discurso dije... **It was going on for six o'clock when...** Serían alrededor de las seis cuando... **He is going on for fifty,** Raya en los cincuenta años. **to go on foot,** ir a pie. **to go on with,** continuar con; empezar. **to go out,** salir; (descend) bajar; (of fires, lights) extinguirse, apagarse; (of fashion, etc.) pasar (de); (the tide) menguar; (retire) retirarse; (in society) frecuentar la alta sociedad; (die) morir; (arouse) excitar. **to go out of fashion,** pasar de moda. **to go out of one's way (to),** dejar su camino (para); (lose oneself) perder el camino, extraviarse; (take trouble) desvivirse (por), tomarse molestia (para). **to go over,** cruzar; pasar por encima; (to another party or to the other side) pasarse a; (read) repasar; examinar. **to go past,** pasar; pasar en frente de. **to go round,** dar la vuelta a; (revolve) girar; (surround) rodear; (of news, etc.) divulgarse; (be enough) ser suficiente para todos. **to go through,** ir por, pasar por; recorrer; (pierce) penetrar, atravesar; (examine) examinar; (suffer) padecer, sufrir; (experience) experimentar; (live) vivir; (of time) pasar; (of money) malgastar, derrochar. **to go through with,** llevar a cabo; terminar. **to go to,** ir a, encaminarse a; (a person) acercarse a, dirigirse a; (help, be useful) servir para; (be meant for) destinarse a; (rise of price) subir a; (find) encontrar; (of a bid) subir una apuesta hasta. **to go to war,** declarar la guerra. **to go together,** ir juntos (juntas). **to go toward,** encaminarse hacia; ir hacia; (help) ayudar a. **to go under,** pasar por debajo de; (sink) hundirse; (fail) fracasar; (be bankrupt) arruinarse, declarare en quiebra; (the name of) hacerse pasar por. **to go up,** subir; ir arriba; (a tree) trepar; (a ladder, etc.) subir; (a river) ir río arriba; (to town) ir a; (explode) estallar. **to go up and down,** subir y bajar; oscilar; ir de una parte a otra. **to go upon,** subirse a; (rely on) apoyarse en; obrar según; emprender. **to go upstairs,** ir arriba; (to another story, as in a flat) subir al otro piso; subir la escalera. **to go up to,** acercarse a; (of a bid) subir una apuesta hasta. **to go with,** acompañar; (agree with) estar de acuerdo con; (of principles) seguir, ser fiel a; (harmonize) armonizar con; (be suitable to) ir bien con; convenir a; (*Inf.* get along) ir. **to go without,** marcharse sin; (lack) pasarse sin. **It goes without saying that...,** Huelga decir que **Where are you going with this?** (What do you mean?) ¿A dónde quieres llegar con esto?

go /gou/ *n* (fashion) moda, boga, *f;* (happening) suceso, *m;* (fix) apuro, *m;* (energy) energía, *f,* empuje, brío, *m;* (turn) turno, *m;* (attempt) tentativa, *f;* (action) movimiento, *m,* acción, *f;* (bargain) acuerdo, *m.* **It's a go!** (agreed) ¡Trato hecho! ¡Acordado! ¡Entendidos! ¡Entendidas! **It is all the go,** Hace furor, Es

la gran moda. **It is no go,** No puede ser, Es imposible. **Now it's my go,** Ahora me toca a mí, Ahora es mi turno. **on the go,** en movimiento; entre manos; ocupado. **to have a go,** probar suerte; procurar, tratar de; tener un turno
goad /goud/ *n* garrocha, aguijada, *f,* aguijón, *m; Fig.* acicate, estímulo, *m.* —*vt* aguijar, picar; *Fig.* incitar, estimular, empujar. **prick with a g.,** aguijonazo, *m*
go-ahead /ˈgou əˌhed/ *a* emprendedor: progresivo
goal /goul/ *n* (posts in football, etc.) meta, portería, *f;* (score) gol, *m;* (in racing) meta, *f;* (destination) destinación, *f; Fig.* ambición, *f;* (purpose, objective) fin, objeto, *m.* **to score a g.,** marcar un gol. **g.-keeper,** guardameta, *m,* portero (-ra). **g.-post,** palo de la portería, *m*
goat /gout/ *n* cabra, *f; Astron.* capricornio, *m.* **he-g.,** cabrón, *m.* **young g.,** cabrito, *m,* chivo (-va). **g.-herd,** cabrero, *m.* **g. skin,** piel de cabra, *f;* (wineskin) odre, *m*
goatee /gouˈti/ *n* pera, perilla, *f*
goatish /ˈgoutiʃ/ *a* cabruno; de cabra; lascivo
gobble /ˈgɒbəl/ *vt* and *vi* engullir, tragar. —*vi* (of turkey) gluglutear. —*n* glugluteo, *m,* voz del pavo, *f*
gobbler /ˈgɒblər/ *n* engullidor (-ra), tragón (-ona); *Inf.* pavo, *m*
go-between /ˈgou bɪˌtwin/ *n* trotaconventos, *f;* alcahuete, *m;* (mediator) medianero (-ra)
goblet /ˈgɒblɪt/ *n* copa, *f*
goblin /ˈgɒblɪn/ *n* trasgo, duende, *m*
go-by, to give the /ˈgou ˌbai/ evitar; pasar por alto de; omitir
go-cart /ˈgou ˌkart/ *n* andaderas, *f pl;* pollera, *f,* cochecito de niño, *m*
god /gɒd/ *n* dios, *m; pl* **gods,** dioses, *m pl;* (in a theater) público del paraíso, *m;* paraíso, *m.* **By God!** ¡Vive Dios! **For God's sake,** ¡Por el amor de Dios!; ¡Por Dios! **Please God,** ¡Plegue a Dios! **Thank God!** ¡Gracias a Dios! **God Bless You!** (to someone who has sneezed) ¡Jesús! **God forbid!** ¡No lo quiera Dios! **God grant it!** ¡Dios lo quiera! **God keep you!** ¡Dios te guarde! ¡Vaya Vd. con Dios! **God willing,** Dios mediante. **My father, God rest his soul, was...,** Mi padre, que Dios perdone, era...
godchild /ˈgɒd.tʃaild/ *n* ahijado (-da)
goddaughter /ˈgɒd.dɔtər/ *n* ahijada, *f*
goddess /ˈgɒdɪs/ *n* diosa, *f; Poet.* dea, *f*
godfather /ˈgɒd.faðər/ *n* padrino, *m.* **to be a g. to,** ser padrino de, sacar de pila (a)
godfearing /ˈgɒd.fiərɪŋ/ *a* timorato, temeroso de Dios; religioso
godforsaken /ˈgɒdfər.seikən/ *a* dejado de la mano de Dios; (of places) remoto, solitario
Godhead /ˈgɒd.hed/ *n* divinidad, *f*
godless /ˈgɒdlɪs/ *a* impío, irreligioso; sin Dios
godlessness /ˈgɒdlɪsnɪs/ *n* impiedad, irreligiosidad, *f*
godlike /ˈgɒd.laik/ *a* divino
godliness /ˈgɒdlɪnɪs/ *n* piedad, *f;* santidad, *f*
godling /ˈgɒdlɪŋ/ *n* diosecillo, *m*
godly /ˈgɒdli/ *a* devoto, piadoso, religioso
godmother /ˈgɒd.mʌðər/ *n* madrina, *f.* **fairy g.,** hada madrina, *f.* **to be a g. to,** ser madrina de
godparent /ˈgɒd.peərənt/ *n* padrino, *m;* madrina, *f pl.* **godparents,** padrinos, *m pl*
godsend /ˈgɒd.send/ *n* bien, *m;* buena suerte, *f;* fortuna, *f*
go-getter /ˈgou ˌgetər/ *n* buscavidas, *mf*
goggle /ˈgɒgəl/ *n* mirada fija, *f; pl* **goggles,** anteojos, *m pl,* gafas, *f pl;* (of a horse) anteojeras, *f pl.* —*vi* mirar fijamente; salirse a uno los ojos de la cabeza. **g.-eyed,** de ojos saltones. **g.-eyes,** ojos saltones, *m pl*
going /ˈgouɪŋ/ *n* ida, *f;* (departure) partida, marcha, *f;* salida, *f;* (pace) paso, *m;* (speed) velocidad, *f.* **It was heavy g.,** El avance era lento; El progreso era lento; (of parties, etc.) Era aburrido. **The g. was difficult on those mountainous roads,** El conducir (or el ir or el andar) era difícil en aquellos caminos de montaña. **g. back,** vuelta, *f,* regreso, *m.* **g. down,** bajada, *f,* descenso, *m;* (of the sun, etc.) puesta, *f.* **g. forward,** avance, *m;* progreso, *m.* **g. in,** entrada, *f.* **g. in and out,** idas y venidas, *f pl.* **g. out,** salida, *f;* (of a fire, light) apagamiento, *m*
going /ˈgouɪŋ/ *a* and *pres part* que va, yendo; que

funciona. **G., g., gone** (at an auction) A la una, a las dos, a las tres. **goings-on,** (tricks) trapujos, *m pl;* (conduct) conducta, *f.* **g. concern,** empresa próspera, *f.* **g. to,** con destino a

going-away present /'gouɪŋ ə,wei/ *n* regalo de despedida, *f*

goiter /'gɔitər/ *n* bocio, *m*

gold /gould/ *n* oro, *m;* color de oro, *m.* —*a* de oro; áureo. **All that glitters is not g.,** No es oro todo lo que reluce. **cloth of g.,** tela de oro, *f.* **dull g.,** oro mate, *m.* **light g.,** oro pálido, *m.* **old g.,** oro viejo, *m.* **g.-beater,** batidor de oro, *m.* **g.-digger,** minero de oro, *m;* (woman) aventurera, *f.* **g. dust,** oro en polvo, *m.* **g.-fever,** fiebre de oro, *f.* **g. lace,** galón de oro, *m.* **g. lacquer,** sisa dorada, *f.* **g. leaf,** pan de oro, oro batido, *m.* **g.-mine,** mina de oro, *f.* **g. piece,** moneda de oro, *f.* **g. plate,** vajilla de oro, *f.* **g. standard,** patrón oro, *m.* **g.-thread,** hilo de oro, *m.* **g.-yielding,** *a* aurífero

golden /'gouldən/ *a* de oro; dorado; áureo; amarillo; *Fig.* feliz; excelente. **to become g.,** dorarse. **g. age,** edad de oro, *f.* **g.-crested wren,** abadejo, *m.* **g. hair,** cabellos dorados (or de oro), *m pl.* **G. Legend,** leyenda áurea, *f.* **g. mean,** justo medio, *m.* **g. rose,** rosa de oro, *f.* **g. rule,** regla áurea, *f.* **g. syrup,** jarabe de arce, *m.* **g. voice,** voz de oro, *f.* **g. wedding,** bodas de oro, *f pl*

goldfinch /'gould,fɪntʃ/ *n* jilguero, *m*

goldfish /'gould,fɪʃ/ *n* carpa dorada, *f.* **g. bowl,** pecera, *f*

goldrush /'gould,rʌʃ/ *n* carrera de oro, *f*

goldsmith /'gould,smiθ/ *n* orfebre, oribe, orífice, *m*

golf /gɒlf/ *n* golf, *m.* **g.-club,** (stick) palo de golf, *m;* (organization) club de golf, *m.* **g.-course,** campo de golf, *m*

golfer /'gɒlfər/ *n* jugador (-ra) de golf

gonad /'gounæd/ *n* gonada, *f*

gondola /'gɒndlə/ *n* góndola, *f*

gondolier /,gɒndl'iər/ *n* gondolero, *m*

gone /gɒn/ *a and past part* ido; (lost) perdido; (ruined) arruinado; (dead) muerto; (past) pasado; (disappeared) desaparecido; (fainted) desmayado; (suppressed) suprimido; (pregnant) encinta; (drunk) borracho; (ended) terminado; (exhausted) agotado; (ill) enfermo. **far g.,** avanzado; (in years) de edad avanzada; (of illness) cerca de la muerte, muy enfermo; (in love) loco de amor; (drunk) muy borracho. **It is all g.,** No hay más. **It is g. seven o'clock,** Son las siete y pico, Son las siete ya

gong /gɒŋ/ *n* gong, *m;* (Chinese) batintín, *m*

gonorrhea /,gɒnə'riə/ *n* gonorrea, *f*

good /gʊd/ *a* bueno (before *m sing* nouns) buen; agradable; afortunado; provechoso; apropiado, oportuno; (beneficial) provechoso, ventajoso; (wholesome) sano, saludable; (suitable) apto; (useful) útil; (kind) bondadoso; (much) mucho; (obliging) amable; (virtuous) virtuoso; (skilled) experto; (fresh) fresco; (genuine) genuino, legítimo; verdadero. —*adv* bien. —*interj* ¡bueno! ¡bien! **a g. deal,** mucho. **a g. many,** bastantes. **a g. turn,** un favor. **a g. way,** (distance) un buen trecho; mucho. **a g. while,** un buen rato. **as g. as,** tan bueno como. **Be so g. as to...!** Haga el favor de, Tenga Vd. la bondad de (followed by infin.). **fairly g.,** *a* bastante bueno. —*adv* bastante bien. **I'm g. for another five miles,** Tengo fuerzas para cinco millas más. **It was g. of you to do it,** Vd. fue muy amable de hacerlo, Vd. tuvo mucha bondad de hacerlo. **to be no g. at this sort of thing,** no servir para tales cosas. **to have a g. time,** pasarlo bien. **to make g.,** reparar; indemnizar; (accomplish) llevar a cabo, poner en práctica; justificar; (a promise) cumplir. **very g.,** *a* muy bueno. —*adv* muy bien. **g.-feeling,** buena voluntad, *f.* **g.-fellowship,** compañerismo, *m;* buena compañía, *f.* **g.-for-nothing,** *n* papanatas, badulaque, *m.* **to be g.-for-nothing,** no servir para nada. **g. luck,** buena suerte, *f.* **g. manners,** buenos modales, *m pl;* buena crianza, educación, *f.* **g. nature,** buen natural, *m;* buen humor, *m.* **g.-natured,** de buen natural; de buen humor, bonachón. **g. offices,** buenos oficios, *m pl.* **g.-tempered,** de buen humor

good /gʊd/ *n* bien, *m;* provecho, *m;* utilidad, *f; pl*

goods. See separate entry. **I am saying this for your g.,** Lo digo para tu bien. **Much g. may it do you!** ¡Buen provecho te haga! **for g. and all,** para siempre jamás. **It is no g.,** Es inútil; No vale la pena. **the g.,** el bien; (people) los buenos. **They have gone for g.,** Se han marchado para no volver. **to do one g.,** hacer bien a uno; mejorar; ser provechoso (a uno); (suit) sentar bien (a uno). **What is the g. of...?** ¡Para qué sirve...?; ¿Qué vale...? **g. and evil,** el bien y el mal

good-bye /,gʊd 'bai/ *interj* ¡adiós! —*n* adiós, *m,* despedida, *f.* **to bid g.-b.,** decir adiós. **G.-b. for the present!** ¡Hasta la vista! ¡Hasta luego! **G.-b. until to-morrow, then,** Hasta mañana pues, adiós, Hasta mañana entonces

goodness /'gʊdnɪs/ *n* bondad, *f;* (of quality) buena calidad, *f;* (of persons) amabilidad, benevolencia, *f;* (essence) esencia, substancia, *f;* bien, *m:* excelencia, *f; interj* ¡Jesús! ¡Dios mío! **For g. sake!** ¡Por Dios! **I wish to g. that,** ¡Ojalá que...!

goods /gʊdz/ *n pl* bienes, efectos, *m pl;* artículos, *m pl;* Com. mercancías, *f pl,* géneros, *m pl.* **by g.-train,** en pequeña velocidad. **stolen g.,** objetos robados, *m pl.* **g. lift,** montacargas, *m.* **g. office,** depósito de mercancías, *m.* **g. station,** estación de carga, *f.* **g.-train,** tren de mercancías, *m.* **g. van,** furgón, *m.* **g. wagon,** vagon de mercancías, *m*

good-smelling /'gʊd ,smelɪŋ/ *a* oloroso

goodwill /'gʊd'wɪl/ *n* benevolencia, *f;* buena voluntad, *f;* (of a business) clientela, *f*

goose /gus/ *n* oca, *f,* ganso (-sa); plancha de sastre, *f.* —*a* de oca. **g.-flesh,** *Fig.* carne de gallina, *f.* **g. girl,** ansarera, *f.* **g.-step,** paso de oca, *m*

gooseberry /'gus,beri/ *n* uva espina, *f*

Gordian /'gɔrdiən/ *a* gordiano. **G. knot,** nudo gordiano, *m*

gore /gɔr/ *n* sangre, *f; Sew.* sesga, nesga, *f.* —*vt* acornear; desgarrar; herir (con arma blanca)

gorge /gɔrdʒ/ *n* (valley) cañón, barranco, *m;* (heavy meal) comilona, *f,* atracón, *m.* —*vt* engullir, tragar. —*vi* hartarse, atracarse

gorgeous /'gɔrdʒəs/ *a* magnífico; espléndido, suntuoso; *Inf.* maravilloso, estupendo

gorgeously /'gɔrdʒəsli/ *adv* magníficamente

gorgeousness /'gɔrdʒəsnɪs/ *n* magnificencia, *f;* suntuosidad, *f,* esplendor, *m*

gorilla /gə'rɪlə/ *n* gorila, *m*

gormandize /'gɔrmən,daiz/ *vi* glotonear

gormandizer /'gɔrmən,daizər/ *n* glotón (-ona)

gorse /gɔrs/ *n* tojo, *m,* aulaga, *f*

gory /'gɔri/ *a* ensangrentado; sangriento

gosh /gɒʃ/ *interj* ¡caray! ¡caramba!

goshawk /'gɒs,hɔk/ *n Ornith.* azor, *m*

gosling /'gɒzlɪŋ/ *n* ansarino, *m*

gospel /'gɒspəl/ *n* evangelio, *m;* doctrina, *f.* **The G. according to St. Mark,** El Evangelio según San Marcos. **to believe as g. truth,** creer como si fuese el evangelio. **to preach the G.,** predicar el evangelio

gossamer /'gɒsəmər/ *n* hilo de araña, *m,* red de araña, telaraña, *f;* (filmy material) gasa, *f;* hilo finísimo, *m,* de gasa; sutil, delgado, fino

gossip /'gɒsəp/ *n* murmurador (-ra), chismoso (-sa), hablador (-ra); (scandal) chisme, *m;* habladuría, murmuración, *f;* (obsolete, of a woman) comadre, *f;* (talk) charla, *f.* —*vi* charlar, conversar; (in bad sense) murmurar, chismear; criticar. **to g. about,** charlar de; poner lenguas en, cortar un sayo (a); hablar mal de. **g. column,** gacetilla, *f*

gossiping /'gɒsəpɪŋ/ *a* charlatán, hablador; chismoso, murmurador. —*n* See **gossip**

Goth /gɒθ/ *n* godo (-da); bárbaro (-ra)

Gothic /'gɒθɪk/ *a Art.* gótico; (of race) godo; bárbaro. —*n* (language) gótico, *m;* arquitectura gótica, *f.* **G. characters,** letra gótica, *f*

gouge /gaudʒ/ *n* gubia, *f.* —*vt* escoplear. **to g. out,** vaciar; sacar

gourd /gɔrd/ *n* calabaza, *f*

gourmand /gʊr'mɒnd/ *n* glotón, *m*

gourmet /gʊr'mei/ *n* gastrónomo, *m*

gout /gaut/ *n Med.* gota, *f*

gouty /'gauti/ *a* gotoso

govern /'gʌvərn/ *vt* gobernar; regir; (guide) guiar;

dominar; domar, refrenar; *Gram.* regir; (regulate) regular

governable /'gʌvərnəbəl/ *a* gobernable; manejable; dócil

governess /'gʌvərnɪs/ *n* institutriz, *f;* (in a school) maestra, *f*

governing /'gʌvərnɪŋ/ *a* gubernante; director; (with principle, etc.) directivo. —*n* See **government**

government /'gʌvərnmənt, -ərmənt/ *n* gobierno, *m;* dirección, *f;* autoridad, *f.* **g. bond,** bono del gobierno, *m.* **g. house,** palacio del gobernador, *m.* **g. office,** oficina del gobierno, *f.* **g. stock,** papel del Estado, *m*

governmental /ˌgʌvərn'mentḷ, ˌgʌvər-/ *a* gubernamental, gubernativo

Government Printing Office Talleres Gráficos de la Nación, *m pl*

governor /'gʌvərnər/ *n* gobernador (-ra); vocal de la junta de gobierno, *mf;* (of a prison) director (-ra) (de una prisión); *Mech.* regulador, *m.* **g.-general,** gobernador general, *m*

governorship /'gʌvərnərˌʃɪp/ *n* gobierno, *m;* dirección, *f*

gown /gaun/ *n* toga, *f;* (cassock) sotana, *f;* (dressing-g.) bata, *f;* (for sleeping) camisa de noche, *f;* (bathing-wrap) albornoz, *m;* (dress) vestido, traje, *m*

Goyesque /gɔi'esk/ *a* goyesco

grab /græb/ *n* asimiento, *m,* presa, *f; Mech.* gancho, *m.* —*vt* arrebatar, asir, agarrar; *Fig.* alzarse con, tomar

grabber /'græbər/ *n* cogedor (-ra); codicioso (-sa)

grace /greis/ *n* elegancia, *f;* simetría, armonía, *f;* gracia, gentileza, *f;* donaire, *m;* encanto, *m;* (goodness) bondad, *f;* gracia, *f;* merced, *f,* favor, *m;* (period of time) plazo, *m;* (privilege) privilegio, *m; Theol.* gracia divina, *f;* (at table) bendición de la mesa, *f;* (as a title) excelentísimo, (to an archbishop) ilustrísimo. —*vt* adornar; favorecer; honrar. **airs and graces,** humos, *m pl.* **the Three Graces,** las Gracias. **three days' g.,** plazo de tres días, *m.* **to get into a person's good graces,** congraciarse con; caer en gracia con. **to say g.,** bendecir la mesa. **with a bad g.,** a regañadientes. **with a good g.,** de buena gana. **g.-note,** *Mus.* nota de adorno, *f*

graceful /'greisfəl/ *a* airoso, gentil, gracioso; elegante; bonito

gracefully /'greisfəli/ *adv* airosamente, gentilmente; con gracia; elegantemente

gracefulness /'greisfəlnɪs/. See **grace**

graceless /'greislɪs/ *a* réprobo; dejado de la mano de Dios; sin gracia

gracious /'greiʃəs/ *a* (merciful) piadoso, clemente; (urbane) afable, condescendiente, agradable. **Good g.!** ¡Vamos!, ¡Dios mío!

graciously /'greiʃəsli/ *adv* afablemente; con benevolencia. **to be g. pleased,** tener a bien

graciousness /'greiʃəsnɪs/ *n* amabilidad, afabilidad, condescendencia, *f*

gradate /'greideit/ *vt* graduar; *Art.* degradar

gradation /grei'deiʃən/ *n* graduación, *f; Mus.* gradación, *f;* paso gradual, *m;* serie, *f*

grade /greid/ *n* grado, *m;* (quality) calidad, clase, *f;* (in a school) clase, *f;* (gradient) pendiente, *f,* declive, *m.* —*vt* graduar, clasificar; (cattle breeding) cruzar. **down g.,** cuesta abajo. **up g.,** cuesta arriba. **highest g.,** *n* primera clase, *f.* —*a* de primera clase; de calidad excelente

gradient /'greidiənt/ *n* declive, *m.* cuesta, pendiente, *f*

gradual /'grædʒuəl/ *a* gradual. —*n Eccl.* gradual, *m*

gradually /'grædʒuəli/ *adv* gradualmente; poco a poco

graduate / *n,* a 'grædʒuɪt; *v* -ˌeit/ *n* licenciado (-da). —*a* graduado. —*vt* graduar. —*vi* graduarse; (as a doctor) doctorarse. **to g. as,** recibirse de

graduation /ˌgrædʒu'eiʃən/ *n* graduación, *f*

graft /græft/ *n Bot.* injerto, *m;* (swindle) estafa, *f;* (bribery) soborno, *m.* —*vt Bot.* injertar; *Surg.* injertar un trozo de piel; *Fig.* injerir

grafting /'græftɪŋ/ *n Bot.* injerto, *m; Surg.* injerto de piel, *m; Fig.* inserción, *f*

grain /grein/ *n* (corn) grano, *m;* (cereal) cereal, *m,* or *f;* (seed, weight) grano, *m;* (trace) pizca, *f;* (of wood,

etc.) hila, *m,* fibra, hebra, veta, *f;* (of leather) flor, *f;* (texture) textura, *f.* —*vt* granear; granular; (wood, marble, etc.) vetear. **against the g.,** a contrapelo. **g. lands,** mieses, *f pl*

gram /græm/ *n* gramo, *m*

grammar /'græmər/ *n* gramática, *f.* **g. school,** instituto de segunda enseñanza, *m*

grammarian /grə'meəriən/ *n* gramático, *m*

grammatical /grə'mætɪkəl/ *a* gramático

grammatically /grə'mætɪkəli/ *adv* gramaticalmente, como la gramática lo quiere. (e.g., *She now speaks Catalan g.,* Ahora habla el catalán como la gramática lo quiere)

grammaticalness /grə'mætɪkəlnɪs/ *n* corrección gramatical, *f*

gramophone /'græməˌfoun/ *n* gramófono, *m.*

granary /'greinəri/ *n* granero, hórreo, *m,* troj, *f.* **g. keeper,** trojero, *m*

grand /grænd/ *a* magnífico, soberbio; imponente; (of dress) espléndido, vistoso; (of people) distinguido, importante; aristocrático; (proud) orgulloso; (of style) elevado, sublime; (morally) noble; augusto; (main) principal; (full) completo; *Inf.* estupendo, magnífico; (with duke, etc.) gran. —*n* piano de cola, *m.* **g.-aunt,** tía abuela, *f.* **g. cross,** gran cruz, *f.* **g. duchess,** gran duquesa, *f.* **g. duke,** gran duque, *m.* **g. lodge,** (of freemasons) Gran Oriente, *m.* **g. master,** gran maestre, *m.* **g.-nephew,** resobrino, *m.* **g.-niece,** resobrina, *f.* **g. opera,** ópera, *f.* **g. piano,** piano de cola, *m.* **g.-stand,** tribuna, *f.* **g.-uncle,** tío abuelo, *m.* **g. vizier,** gran visir, *m*

grandchild /'græn,tʃaild/ *n* nieto (-ta). **great-g.,** bisnieto (-ta). **great-great-g.,** tataranieto (-ta)

granddaughter /'græn,dɔtər/ *n* nieta, *f.* **great-g.,** bisnieta, *f.* **great-great-g.,** tataranieta, *f*

grandee /græn'di/ *n* grande (de España, grande de Portugal), *m*

grandeur /'grændʒər/ *n* magnificencia, *f;* grandiosidad, *f;* magnitud, grandeza, *f;* (pomp) pompa, *f,* fausto, *m*

grandfather /'græn,fɑðər/ *n* abuelo, *m.* **great-great-g.,** bisabuelo, *m.* **great-great-g.,** tatarabuelo, *m*

grandfatherly /'græn,fɑðərli/ *a* de abuelo

grandfather's clock reloj de péndulo, *m*

grandiloquence /græn'dɪləkwəns/ *n* grandilocuencia, *f*

grandiloquent /græn'dɪləkwənt/ *a* grandílocuo

grandiose /'grændi,ous/ *a* grandioso, sublime; impresionante; imponente; (in a bad sense) extravagante; (of style) bombástico, hinchado

grand jury *n* jurado de acusación, jurado de jucio, *m*

grandmother /'græn,mʌðər/ *n* abuela, *f.* **great-g.,** bisabuela, *f.* **great-great-g.,** tatarabuela, *f*

grandness /'grændnɪs/ *n* magnificencia, *f;* aristocracia, *f;* (pride) orgullo, *m;* grandiosidad, *f;* (of style) sublimidad, *f;* (of character) nobleza, *f*

grandparent /'græn,peərənt/ *n* abuelo, *m;* abuela, *f; pl* **grandparents,** abuelos, *m pl.* **great-great-grandparents,** bisabuelos, *m pl.* **great-great-grandparents,** tatarabuelos, *m pl*

grandson /'græn,sʌn/ *n* nieto, *m.* **great-g.,** bisnieto, *m.* **great-great-g.,** tataranieto, *m*

grange /greindʒ/ *n* granja, *f;* casa de campo, *f*

granite /'grænɪt/ *n* granito, *m*

granny /'græni/ *n* abuelita, nana, *f;* abuela, *f.* **g. knot,** nudo al revés, *m*

grant /grænt/ *n* concesión, *f;* otorgamiento, *m;* donación, *f;* privilegio, *m;* (for study) beca, bolsa de estudio, *f;* (transfer) traspaso, *m,* cesión, *f.* —*vt* conceder; (bestow) otorgar, dar; donar; (agree to) acceder a, asentir en; permitir; (transfer) traspasar; (assume) suponer. **to g. a degree,** expedir un título. **to g. a motion,** dar por entrada a una moción. **to take for granted,** descontar; dar por hecho, dar por sentado. **God g. it!** ¡Dios lo quiera! **granted that,** dado que

grantee /græn'ti/ *n* cesionario (-ia), adjudicatorio (-ia)

grantor /'græntər/ *n* cesionista, *mf;* otorgador (-ra)

granulated /'grænyə,leitid/ *a* granulado

granule /'grænyul/ *n* gránulo, *m*

granulous /'grænyələs/ *a* granuloso

grape /greip/ *n* uva, *f.* **bunch of grapes,** racimo de

graph 444

uvas, *m.* **muscatel g.,** uva moscatel, *f.* **sour grapes,** uvas agrias, *f pl;* (phrase) ¡están verdes! **g.-fruit,** toronja, *f.* **g. gatherer,** vendimiador (-ra). **g. harvest,** vendimia, *f.* **g. juice,** mosto, *m.* **g.-shot,** metralla, *f.* **g. stone,** granuja, *f.* **g.-sugar,** glucosa, *f.* **g.-vine,** vid, parra, *f*

graph /græf/ *n* gráfica, *f;* diagrama, *m*

graphic /'græfɪk/ *a* gráfico

graphite /'græfait/ *n* grafito, *m*

graphology /græ'fɒlədʒi/ *n* grafología, *f*

grapple /'græpəl/ *n Naut.* rezón, arpeo, *m;* lucha a brazo partido, *f.* —*vt Naut.* aferrar; asir, agarrar. —*vi Naut.* aferrarse. **to g. with,** luchar a brazo partido (con); *Fig.* luchar con

grappling /'græplɪŋ/ *n Naut.* aferramiento, *m;* lucha cuerpo a cuerpo, *f;* (with a problem) lucha con, *f*

grasp /græsp/ *n* agarro, *m;* (reach) alcance, *m;* (of a hand) apretón, *m;* (power) garras, *f pl,* poder, *m;* (understanding) comprensión, *f;* inteligencia, capacidad intelectual, *f.* —*vt* agarrar, asir; empuñar; abrazar; *Fig.* comprender, alcanzar; (a hand) estrechar. —*vi* agarrarse. **within one's g.,** al alcance de uno. **to g. at,** asirse de

grasping /'græspɪŋ/ *n* asimiento, *m;* (understanding) comprensión, *f, a* codicioso, tacaño, mezquino

graspingness /'græspɪŋnɪs/ *n* codicia, *f*

grass /græs/ *n* hierba, *f;* (pasture) pasto, herbaje, *m;* (sward) césped, *m.* —*vt* cubrir de hierba; sembrar de hierba; apacentar. **to hear the g. grow,** sentir crecer la hierba. **to let the g. grow,** *Fig.* dejar crecer la hierba. **to turn out to g.,** echar al pasto. **g.-blade,** brizna de hierba, *f.* **g.-green,** *a* and *n* verde como la hierba *m..* **g.-grown,** cubierto de hierba. **g.-land,** pradera, *f.* **g.-snake,** culebra *f.* **g. widow,** mujer cuyo marido está ausente

grasshopper /'græs,hɒpər/ *n* saltamontes, *m.* **grasshopper's chirp,** chirrido (del saltamontes), *f*

grassy /'græsi/ *a* parecido a la hierba, como la hierba; cubierto de hierba; de hierba

grate /greit/ *n* parrilla, *f;* (grating) reja, *f.* —*vt* raspar, raer; *Cul.* rallar; (make a noise) hacer rechinar. —*vi* rozar; rechinar, chirriar. **to g. on, upon,** (of sounds) irritar, molestar; chocar con. **to g. on the ear,** herir el oído

grateful /'greitfəl/ *a* agradecido, reconocido; (pleasant) agradable, grato

gratefully /'greitfəli/ *adv* agradecidamente; gratamente

gratefulness /'greitfəlnɪs/ *n* agradecimiento, *m,* gratitud, *f;* (pleasantness) agrado, *m*

grater /'greitər/ *n Cul.* rallador, *m*

gratification /,grætəfɪ'keiʃən/ *n* satisfacción, *f;* (pleasure) placer, gusto, *m*

gratified /'grætə,faid/ *a* satisfecho, contento

gratify /'grætə,fai/ *vt* satisfacer; (please) gratificar, agradar

gratifying /'grætə,faiɪŋ/ *a* satisfactorio, agradable

grating /'greitɪŋ/ *n* reja, *f;* rejilla, *f; Naut.* jareta, *f;* (optics) retículo, *m;* (sound) rechinamiento, chirrido, *m.* —*a* rechinante, chirriador; áspero

gratis /'grætɪs/ *a* and *adv* gratis

gratitude /'grætɪ,tud/ *n* agradecimiento, *m,* gratitud, *f*

gratuitous /grə'tuɪtəs/ *a* gratuito

gratuitousness /grə'tuɪtəsnɪs/ *n* gratuidad, *f*

gratuity /grə'tuɪti/ *n* gratificación, propina, *f*

grave /greiv/ *n* (hole) sepultura, fosa, *f;* (monument) tumba, *f,* sepulcro, *m; Fig.* muerte, *m.* **g.-digger,** enterrador, sepulturero, *m*

grave /a greiv/ *n* grɒv/ *a* grave; importante; serio; sobrio; (anxious) preocupado; (of accent) grave. —*n* (grave accent) acento grave, *m*

gravel /'grævəl/ *n* grava, *f;* cascajo, casquijo, *m; Med.* arenillas, *f pl,* cálculo, *m*

gravely /'greivli/ *adv* gravemente; seriamente

Graves' disease /greivz/ *n* bocio exoftálmico, *m*

gravestone /'greiv,stoun/ *n* lápida mortuoria, *f*

graveyard /'greiv,yɑrd/ *n* camposanto, cementerio, *m*

gravitate /'grævɪ,teit/ *vi* gravitar; tender

gravitation /,grævɪ'teiʃən/ *n* gravitación, *f;* tendencia, *f*

gravitational /,grævɪ'teiʃn̩l/ *a* de gravitación, gravitacional, gravitatorio

gravitational pull *n* atracción gravitatoria, *f*

gravity /'grævɪti/ *n Phys.* gravedad, *f;* seriedad, *f;* solemnidad, *f;* gravedad, *f;* (weight) peso, *m;* importancia, *f;* (enormity) enormidad, *f;* (danger) peligro, *m.* **center of g.,** centro de gravedad, *m.* **law of g.,** ley de la gravedad, *f.* **specific g.,** peso específico, *m*

gravy /'greivi/ *n* salsa, *f;* jugo (de la carne), *m.* **g.-boat,** salsera, *f*

gray /grei/ *a* gris; (of animals) rucio. —*n* color gris, gris, *m;* caballo gris, *m.* **His hair is turning g.,** El pelo se le vuelve gris. **g.-haired,** de pelo gris. **g. matter,** materia gris, *f;* cacumen, *m.* **g. mullet,** *Ichth.* mújol, *m.* **g. squirrel,** gris, *m.* **g. wolf,** lobo gris, *m*

grayish /'greiɪʃ/ *a* grisáceo, agrisado; (of hair) entrecano

grayness /'greinɪs/ *n* color gris, gris, *m; Fig.* monotonía, *f*

graze /greiz/ *n* abrasión, *f;* (brush) roce, *m, vi* pacer, apacentarse. —*vt* pastorear, apacentar; (brush) rozar

grazing /'greizɪŋ/ *n Agr.* apacentamiento, pastoreo, *m;* (brushing) rozadura, *f.* —*a* que pace, herbívoro; (of land) pacedero. **g. land,** pasto, *m*

grease /gris/ *n* grasa, *f;* (dirt) mugre, *f;* (of a candle) sebo, *m,* cera, *f.* —*vt* engrasar; manchar con grasa; *Fig. Inf.* untar. **to g. the wheels,** *Fig.* untar el carro. **g.-box,** *Mech.* caja de sebo, *f.* **g.-gun,** engrasador de compresión, *m.* **g.-paint,** afeites de actor (or de actriz), *m pl.* **g.-proof paper,** papel impermeable, *m.* **g. spot,** lámpara, mancha de grasa, *f,* saín, *m*

greaser /'grisər/ *n* engrasador, *m*

greasiness /'grisinɪs/ *n* graseza, *f;* lo aceitoso; untuosidad, *f*

greasing /'grisɪŋ/ *n* engrasado, *m*

greasy /'grisi/ *a* grasiento; (oily) aceitoso; (grubby) mugriento, bisunto; *Fig.* lisonjero. **g. pole,** cucaña, *f*

great /greit/ *a* gran; grande; enorme; vasto; (much) mucho; (famous) famoso, ilustre; noble, sublime; (intimate) íntimo; importante; principal; poderoso; magnífico, impresionante; *Inf.* famoso, estupendo; (of time) largo; (clever) fuerte. **Alexander the G.,** Alejandro Magno. **the G. Mogul,** el Gran Mogul. **a g. deal,** mucho. **a g. man,** un grande hombre, un hombre famoso. **a g. many,** muchos (muchas). **He lived to a g. age,** Vivió hasta una edad avanzada. **so g.,** tan grande, tamaño. **the g.,** los grandes hombres. **g. on,** aficionado a. **g.-aunt,** tía abuela, *f.* **g.-grandchild,** etc. See **grandchild,** etc. **g.-hearted,** valeroso; magnánimo, generoso. **g. power,** gran poder, *m.* **G. War,** Gran Guerra, *f.* **the Great Schism,** el Gran Cisma, *m*

greater /'greitər/ *a* comp. of **great,** mayor; más grande. **to make g.,** agrandar. **G. London,** el Gran Londres, *m*

greatest /'greitɪst/ *a* sup. of **great,** más grande; mayor; máximo; más famoso; sumo

greatly /'greitli/ *adv* mucho; con mucho; (very) muy; noblemente

greatness /'greitnɪs/ *n* grandeza, *f;* grandiosidad, *f;* extensión, vastedad, *f;* importancia, *f;* poder, *m;* majestad, *f;* esplendor, *m;* (intensity) intensidad, *f;* (enormity) enormidad, *f*

Grecian /'griʃən/ *a* griego

Greco- *prefix* (in compounds) greco-, greco

Greece /gris/ *Grecia, f*

greed /grid/ *n* (cupidity) codicia, rapacidad, avaricia, *f;* avidez, ansia, *f;* (of food) gula, glotonería, *f*

greedily /'gridəli/ *adv* codiciosamente; con avidez; (of eating) vorazmente

greedy /'gridi/ *a* (for food) glotón; codicioso, ambicioso; ávido; deseoso

Greek /grik/ *a* and *n* griego (-ga) (language) griego, *m.* **It's all G. to me,** Para mí es como si fuese en latín, Me es chino. **G. tunic,** peplo, *m*

green /grin/ *a* verde; (inexpert) inexperto, bisoño; (recent) nuevo, reciente; (fresh) fresco; (of complexion) pálido, descolorido; (flowery) floreciente; (vigorous) lozano; (young) joven; (unripe) verde; (credulous) crédulo; (raw) crudo; (of wood, vegetables) verde. —*n* verde, color verde, *m;* (vegetables) verdura, *f;* (meadow) prado, *m;* (turf) césped, *m;* (grass) hierba, *f;* (bowling) campo de juego, *m.* —*vt* teñir (or pintar) de verde. **bright g.,** *n* verdegay, verde claro, *m*. **dark g.**, *n* verdinegro, *m*. **light g.**, *n* verde pálido, *m*. **to grow** or **look g.**, verdear. **g.-eyed**, de ojos verdes. **g. peas**, guisantes, *m pl*. **g. table**, tapete verde, *m*

greenery /'grinəri/ *n* follaje, *m*; verdura, *f*

greengrocer /'grin,grousər/ *n* verdulero (-ra)

greengrocery /'grin,grousəri/ *n* verdulería, *f*

greenhorn /'grin,hɔrn/ *n* bisoño (-ña); papanatas, *m*

greenhouse /'grin,haus/ *n* invernáculo, invernadero, *m*

greenish /'grinɪʃ/ *a* verdoso. **g.-yellow**, cetrino

Greenland /'grinlənd/ Groenlandia, *f*

Greenlander /'grinləndər/ *n* groenlandés (-esa)

greenness /'grinnɪs/ *a* lo verde; verdor, *m*, verdura, *f*; (inexperience) falta de experiencia, *f*; (vigor) vigor, *m*, lozanía, *f*; (newness) novedad, *f*; (of wood, fruit) falta de madurez, *f*

greenroom /'grin,rum/ *n* Theat. saloncillo, *m*

greenstuff /'grin,stʌf/ *n* hortalizas, legumbres, *f pl*

greet /grit/ *vt* saludar; recibir; (express pleasure) dar la bienvenida (a)

greeting /'gritɪŋ/ *n* salutación, *f*, saludo, *m*; recepción, *f*; (welcome) bienvenida, *f*; *pl* **greetings**, recuerdos, *m pl*

gregarious /grɪ'gɛəriəs/ *a* gregario

gregariousness /grɪ'gɛəriəsnɪs/ *n* gregarismo, *m*

Gregorian /grɪ'gɔriən/ *a* gregoriano

grenade /grɪ'neid/ *n* granada, bomba, *f*. **hand-g.**, bomba de mano, *f*

grey /grei/ See **gray**

greyhound /'grei,haund/ *n* galgo, lebrel, *m*. **g. bitch**, galga, *f*; **g. racing**, carreras de galgos, *f pl*

grid /grid/ *n* (of electric power) red, *f*; rejilla, *f*; (for water, etc.) alcantarilla, *f*

gridiron /'grid,aiərn/ *n* Cul. parrilla, *f*; (of electric power) red, *f*; Theat. telar, *m*

grief /grif/ *n* angustia, pena, aflicción, *f*; dolor, suplicio, *m*. **to come to g.**, pasarlo mal, tener un desastre

grievance /'grivəns/ *n* injusticia, *f*; motivo de queja, *m*

grieve /griv/ *vt* entristecer, afligir, angustiar; atormentar. —*vi* entristecerse, afligirse, acongojarse. **to g. for**, lamentar: echar de menos

grievous /'grivəs/ *a* (heavy) oneroso, gravoso; opresivo; doloroso, penoso; lamentable; cruel. **g. error**, error lamentable

grievousness /'grivəsnɪs/ *n* (weight) peso, *m*; carácter opresivo, *m*; dolor, *m*, aflicción, *f*; enormidad, *f*; crueldad, *f*

griffin /'grifin/ *n* grifo, *m*; (Fig. chaperon) carabina, *f*; (dog) grifón, *m*

grill /gril/ *n* Cul. parrilla, *f*; (grating) rejilla, *f*; (before a window) reja, *f*; (food) asado a la parrilla, *m*. —*vt* Cul. asar a la parrilla; (burn) quemar; (question) interrogar; (torture) torturar. —*vi* Cul. asarse a la parrilla; (be burnt) quemarse. **g.-room**, parrilla, *f*

grille /gril/ *n* reja, *f*; rejilla, *f*; (screen) verja, *f*

grilled /grild/ *a* Cul. a la parrilla; con rejilla

griller /'grilər/ *n* Cul. parrilla, *f*

grim /grim/ *a* (fierce) feroz, salvaje; (severe) severo, ceñudo, adusto; inflexible; (frightful) horrible

grimace /'griməs/ *n* mueca, *f*, gesto, mohín, visaje, *m*, *vi* hacer muecas

grime /graim/ *n* mugre, *f*; suciedad, *f*. **to cover with g.**, enmugrecer

grimly /'grimli/ *adv* severamente; sin sonreír; inflexiblemente; (without retreating) sin cejar; (frightfully) horriblemente; de un modo espantoso

grimness /'grimnɪs/ *n* (ferocity) ferocidad, *f*; (severity) severidad, *f*; inflexibilidad, *f*; (frightfulness) horror, *m*, lo espantoso

grimy /'graimi/ *a* mugriento, sucio

grin /grin/ *n* sonrisa grande, *f*; sonrisa burlona, *f*; (grimace) mueca, *f*. —*vi* sonreír mostrando los dientes; sonreír bonachonamente; sonreír de un modo burlón

grind /graind/ *vt* (to powder) pulverizar; moler; (break up) quebrantar; (oppress) agobiar, oprimir; (sharpen) afilar, amolar; (a barrel-organ) tocar (un manubrio); (the teeth) crujir, rechinar (los dientes); (into) reducir a; (Inf. teach) empollar. —*vi* moler;

Fig. Inf. trabajar laboriosamente. —*n Fig. Inf.* trabajo pesado, *m*; *n Fig. Inf.* estudiantón, *m*

grinder /'graindər/ *n* (of scissors, etc.) afilador, *m*; (of an organ) organillero; (mill-stone) piedra de moler, *f*; (molar) muela, *f*

grinding /'graindɪŋ/ *a* (tedious) cansado, aburrido; opresivo; (of pain) incesante. —*n* pulverización, *f*; amoladura, *f*; (of grain) molienda, *f*; (polishing) pulimento, bruñido, *m*; (oppression) opresión, *f*; (of teeth) rechinamiento, *m*

grindstone /'graind,stoun/ *n* amoladera, afiladera, piedra de amolar, *f*. **to have one's nose to the g.**, batir el yunque

grinning /'grinɪŋ/ *a* sonriente; riente; (mocking) burlón

grip /grip/ *n* asimiento, agarro, *m*; (claws, clutches) garras, *f pl*; (hand) mano, *f*; (of shaking hands) apretón de manos, *m*; (of a weapon, etc.) empuñadura, *f*; (reach) alcance, *m*; (understanding) comprensión, *f*; (control) dominio, *m*; (bag) portamanteo, *m*; maleta, *f*. —*vt* asir, agarrar; (of wheels) agarrarse; Mech. morder; (a sword, etc.) empuñar; (pinch) pellizcar; (surround) cercar; (understand) comprender; (press; to grip the hand and Fig. the heart) apretar; (fill) llenar; (the attention) atraer, llamar; (sway, hold) dominar

gripe /graip/ *n* (Inf. pain) retortijón (de tripas), *m*

grisly /'grizli/ *a* espantoso; repugnante

grist /grist/ *n* molienda, *f*. **Everything is g. to their mill**, Sacan partido de todo

gristle /'grisəl/ *n* cartílago, *m*, ternilla, *f*

gristly /'grisli/ *a* cartilaginoso

grit /grit/ *n* cascajo, *m*; polvo, *m*; Fig. firmeza (de carácter), *f*; (courage) valor, *m*; (endurance) aguante, *m*

gritty /'griti/ *a* arenoso, arenisco

grizzled /'grizəld/ *a* (of hair, etc.) gris; canoso; grisáceo

grizzly bear /'grizli/ *n* oso (-sa) pardo (-da)

groan /groun/ *n* gemido, *m*. —*vi* gemir; (creak) crujir. **to g. out**, decir (or contar) entre gemidos. **to g. under**, sufrir bajo, gemir bajo; (of weight) crujir bajo

groaning /'grounɪŋ/ *n* gemidos, *m pl*. —*a* que gime, gemidor; (under a weight) crujiente

grocer /'grousər/ *n* abacero (-ra) vendedor (-ra) de comestibles. **grocer's shop**, tienda de comestibles, bodega, *f*

grocery /'grousəri/ *n* tienda de comestibles, tienda de ultramarinos, abarrotería, lonja, bodega, *f*, negocio de comestibles, *m*; *pl* **groceries**, provisiones, *f pl*, comestibles, *m pl*

grog /grog/ *n* grog, *m*

groin /groin/ *n* Anat. ingle, *f*

groom /grum/ *n* (in a royal household) gentilhombre, *m*; lacayo, *m*; mozo de caballos, *m*; (of a bride) novio, *m*. —*vt* (a horse) cuidar; (oneself) arreglarse. **She is always well groomed**, Está siempre muy bien arreglada

groomsman /'grumzmən/ *n* padrino de boda, *m*

groove /gruv/ *n* ranura, muesca, *f*; estría, *f*; surco, *m*; Fig. rutina, *f*. —*vt* entallar; estriar

grooved /gruvd/ *a* con ranura; estriado

grope /group/ *vi* andar a tientas; (with for) buscar a tientas; procurar, encontrar, buscar. **to g. one's way toward**, avanzar a tientas hacia; Fig. avanzar poco a poco hacia

gropingly /'groupɪŋli/ *adv* a tientas; irresolutamente

gross /grous/ *n* Com. gruesa, *f*; totalidad, *f*, a grueso; denso, espeso; (unrefined) grosero; (great) grande; (crass) craso; total; Com. bruto; (tremendous) enorme. **in g.**, en grueso. **g. amount**, total, *m*; Com. importe bruto, *m*. **g. weight**, peso bruto, *m*

grossly /'grousli/ *adv* groseramente; (much) enormemente

grossness /'grousnɪs/ *n* gordura, *f*; (vulgarity) grosería, *f*; obscenidad, *f*; (enormity) enormidad, *f*

grotesque /grou'tɛsk/ *a* grotesco; extravagante, estrambótico; ridículo. —*n* grotesco, *m*

grotesqueness /grou'tɛsknɪs/ *n* lo grotesco; ridiculez, *f*

grotto /'grotou/ *n* gruta, *f*

ground /graund/ *n* suelo, *m*; (of water and Naut.)

fondo, *m;* (earth) tierra, *f; Fig.* terreno, *m;* (strata) capa, *f; Sports.* campo, *m;* (parade) plaza (de armas), *f;* (background) fondo, *m;* (basis) base, *f,* fundamento, *m;* (reason) causa, *f;* motivo, *m;* (excuse) pretexto, *m; pl* **grounds,** jardines, *m pl,* parque, *m;* (sediment) sedimento, *m,* heces, *f pl;* (reason) causa, *f.* —*vi Naut.* varar, encallar. —*vt* poner en tierra; *Naut.* hacer varar; *Elec.* conectar con tierra; (base) fundar (en), basar (en); (teach) enseñar los rudimentos (de). —*a* molido; en polvo; (of floors, stories) bajo; (of glass) deslustrado; *Bot.* terrestre. **common g.,** tierra comunal, *f; Fig.* tierra común, *f.* **He is on his own g.,** Está en terreno propio. **It fell to the g.,** Cayó al suelo; *Fig.* Fracasó. **It is on the g.,** Está en el suelo. **It suits me to the g.,** Me viene de perilla. **to break fresh g.,** *Fig.* tratar problemas nuevos. **to be well grounded in,** conocer bien los elementos (or rudimentos) de. **to cover g.,** cubrir terreno; recorrer; (in discussion) tocar muchos puntos. **to cut the g. from beneath one's feet,** hacer perder la iniciativa (a). **to give g.,** retroceder; perder terreno. **to raze to the g.,** echar por tierra, arrasar. **to stand one's g.,** resistir el ataque; no darse por vencido; *Fig.* mantenerse firme, mantenerse en sus trece. **to win g.,** ganar terreno. **g. coffee,** café molido, *m.* **g.-color,** (of paint) primera capa, *f;* (color de) fondo, *m;* **g.-floor,** piso bajo, *m.* **g. glass,** vidrio deslustrado, *m.* **g.-ivy,** hiedra terrestre, *f.* **g. nut,** cacahuete, *m.* **g.-plan,** *Archit.* planta, *f.* **g.-rent,** censo, *m.* **g.-sheet,** tela impermeable, *f;* **g. staff,** *Aer.* personal del aeropuerto, *m.* **g.-swell,** mar de fondo, *m*

grounded /'graundɪd/ *a* fundado. **The airplanes are g.,** Los aviones están sin volar. **His suspicions are well g.,** Tiene motivos para sus sospechas

grounding /'graundɪŋ/ *n Naut.* encalladura, *f;* (teaching) instrucción en los rudimentos, *f*

groundless /'graundlɪs/ *a* sin fundamento, inmotivado, sin causa, sin motivo

groundwork /'graund,wɜrk/ *n* fundamento, *m;* base, *f;* principio, *m*

group /grup/ *n* grupo, *m.* —*vt* agrupar. —*vi* agruparse. **g. captain,** coronel de aviación, *m*

grouping /'grupɪŋ/ *n* agrupación, *f*

grouse /graus/ *n Ornith.* ortega, *f.* —*vi* rezongar, refunfuñar

grove /grouv/ *n* soto, boscaje, *m;* arboleda, *f*

grovel /'grɒvəl/ *vi* arrastrarse; *Fig.* humillarse

groveling /'grɒvəlɪŋ/ *a Fig.* servil; ruin

grow /grou/ *vi* crecer; (increase) aumentar; (become) hacerse; empezar a; llegar a; (turn) volverse, ponerse; (flourish) progresar, adelantar; (develop) desarrollarse; (extend) extenderse. —*vt* cultivar; dejar crecer. **I grew to fear it,** Llegué a temerlo. **to g. cold,** ponerse frío; enfriarse; (of weather) empezar a hacer frío. **to g. fat,** engordar. **to g. hard,** ponerse duro; *Fig.* endurecerse. **to g. hot,** ponerse caliente; calentarse; (of weather) empezar a hacer calor. **to g. like Topsy,** crecer a la buena de Dios. **to g. old,** envejecer. **to g. tall,** crecer mucho; ser alto. **to g. again,** crecer de nuevo. **to g. into,** hacerse, llegar a ser; venir a ser. **to g. out of,** brotar de; originarse en; (a habit) desacostumbrarse poco a poco. **He is growing out of his clothes,** La ropa se le hace pequeña. **to g. up,** (of persons) hacerse hombre (mujer); desarrollarse; (of a custom, etc.) imponerse. **to g. on,** upon, crecer sobre; llegar a dominar; (make think) hacer creer, empezar a pensar; (of a habit) arraigar en

grower /'grouər/ *n* cultivador (-ra)

growing /'grouɪŋ/ *n* crecimiento, *m;* desarrollo, *m;* (increase) aumento, *m;* (of flowers, etc.) cultivación, *f,* a creciente

growing pains *n pl* crisis de desarrollo, *f*

growl /graul/ *n* gruñido, *m;* reverberación, *f;* trueno, *m.* —*vi* gruñir; (of guns) tronar; (of thunder) reverberar. **to g. out,** decir gruñendo

grown /groun/ *a* crecido; maduro; adulto. **a g. up,** una persona mayor. **to be full-g.,** estar completamente desarrollado; haber llegado a la madurez. **g. over with,** cubierto de

growth /grouθ/ *n* crecimiento, *m;* (development) desarrollo, *m;* (progress) progreso, adelanto, *m;* (in-

crease) aumento, *m;* (cultivation) cultivo, *m;* (vegetation) vegetación, *f; Med.* tumor, *m.* **He has a week's g. on his chin,** Tiene una barba de una semana

grub /grʌb/ *n* larva, *f,* gusano, *m.* —*vt* (with up, out) desarraigar; cavar; desmalezar; *Fig. Inf.* buscar

grubbiness /'grʌbinɪs/ *n* suciedad, *f;* (untidiness) desaliño, *m*

grubby /'grʌbi/ *a* lleno de gusanos; sucio; bisunto; desaliñado

grudge /grʌdʒ/ *n* motivo de rencor, *m;* rencor, resentimiento, *m,* ojeriza, *f;* mala voluntad, *f;* aversión, *f.* —*vt* envidiar. **to bear a g.,** tener ojeriza

grudging /'grʌdʒɪŋ/ *a* (niggardly) mezquino; envidioso; poco generoso; de mala gana; nada afable

grudgingly /'grʌdʒɪŋli/ *adv* de mala gana, contra su voluntad; con rencor; a regañadientes

gruel /'gruəl/ *n* gachas, *f pl*

gruesome /'grusəm/ *a* pavoroso, horrible; macabro

gruff /grʌf/ *a* (of the voice) bronco, grave, áspero; (of manner) brusco, malhumorado

gruffly /'grʌfli/ *adv* en una voz bronca (or áspera); bruscamente, con impaciencia, malhumoradamente

gruffness /'grʌfnɪs/ *n* aspereza, bronquedad, *f;* brusquedad, sequedad, impaciencia, *f,* mal humor, *m*

grumble /'grʌmbəl/ *n* ruido sordo, trueno, *m;* estruendo, *m;* (complaint) refunfuño, rezongo, *m.* —*vi* tronar; refunfuñar, rezongar; hablar entre dientes; quejarse; protestar (contra). —*vt* decir refunfuñando

grumbler /'grʌmblər/ *n* murmurador (-ra), refunfuñador (-ra)

grumbling /'grʌmblɪŋ/ *a* gruñón, refunfuñador; regañón; descontento. —*n* See **grumble**

grumblingly /'grʌmblɪŋli/ *adv* a regañadientes, refunfuñando

grumpiness /'grʌmpinɪs/ *n* mal humor, *m,* irritabilidad, *f*

grumpy /'grʌmpi/ *a* malhumorado, irritable

grunt /grʌnt/ *n* gruñido, *m.* —*vi* gruñir

grunting /'grʌntɪŋ/ *a* gruñidor

guarantee /ˌgærən'ti/ *n Law.* persona de quien otra sale fiadora, *f;* garantía, *f;* abono, *m.* —*vt* garantizar; responder de; abonar; (assure) asegurar, acreditar

guarantor /'gærən,tɔr/ *n* garante, *mf*

guard /gɑrd/ *n* (watchfulness) vigilancia, *f;* (in fencing) guardia, *f;* (of a sword) guarnición, *f;* (sentry) centinela, *m;* (soldier) guardia, *m;* (body of soldiers) guardia, *f;* (escort) escolta, *f;* (keeper) guardián, *m;* (protection) protección, defensa, *f;* (of a train) jefe de tren, *m.* —*vt* guardar; proteger, defender; vigilar; (escort) escoltar. **to g. against,** guardarse de. **the changing of the g.,** el relevo de la guardia. **to be on g.,** *Mil.* estar de guardia; (in fencing) estar en guardia. **to be on one's g.,** estar prevenido, estar alerta. **to be off one's g.,** estar desprevenido. **to mount g.,** *Mil.* montar la guardia; vigilar. **guard's van,** furgón de equipajes, *m.* **g.-house,** cuerpo de guardia, *m;* prisión militar, *f*

guarded /'gɑrdɪd/ *a* (reticent) reservado, circunspecto, prudente, discreto

guardedly /'gɑrdɪdli/ *adv* prudentemente, con circunspección, discretamente

guardian /'gɑrdiən/ *n* protector (-ra); guardián (-ana); *Law.* tutor, *m.* —*a* que guarda; tutelar. **g. angel,** ángel de la guarda, ángel custodio, *m;* deidad tutelar, *f*

guardianship /'gɑrdiən,ʃɪp/ *n* protección, *f;* patronato, *m;* *Law.* curaduría, tutela, *f*

guardsman /'gɑrdzmən/ *n* guardia, *m*

Guatemalan /ˌgwɑtə'mɑlən/ *a* and *n* guatemalteco (-ca)

guava /'gwɑvə/ *n Bot.* guayaba, *f*

Guernsey /'gɜrnzi/ Guenesy, *m*

guerrilla /gə'rɪlə/ *n* guerrilla, *f;* (soldier) guerrillero, *m.* —*a* de guerrilla. **g. warfare,** guerra de guerrillas, *f*

guess /gɛs/ *n* adivinación, *f;* estimación, *f;* conjetura, *f;* sospecha, *f.* —*vt* and *vi* adivinar; conjeturar; sospechar; imaginar; (suppose) suponer, creer; calcular. **to g. at,** formar una opinión sobre; imaginar. **a rough g.,** estimación aproximada, *f.* **at a g.,** a poco más o menos, a ojo de buen cubero. **g.-work,** conjeturas, suposiciones, *f pl*

guest /gɛst/ *n* (at a meal) convidado (-da), invitado

(-da); (at a hotel, etc.) cliente (-da); *Biol.* parásito, *m.*
g.-room, alcoba de respeto, alcoba de honor, alcoba de huéspedes, *f.* cuarto de amigos, cuarto para invitados, *m*

guffaw /gʌ'fɔ/ *n* carcajada, *f.* —*vi* reírse a carcajadas, soltar el trapo

Guiana /gi'ænə/ Guayana, *f*

guidance /'gaidn̩s/ *n* dirección, *f;* gobierno, *m;* (advice) consejos, *m pl;* inspiración, *f*

guide /gaid/ *n* (person) guía, *mf;* (girl g.) exploradora, *f;* (book and *Fig.*) guía, *f;* mentor, *m;* modelo, *m;* (inspiration) norte, *m; Mech.* guía, *f.* —*vt* guiar; conducir; encaminar; dirigir; (govern) gobernar. **g.-book,** guía (de turistas), *f.* **g.-post,** poste indicador, *m*

guided tour /'gaidid/ *n* visita explicada, visita programada, *f*

guideline /'gaid,lain/ *Lit.* falsarregla, falsilla, *f; Fig.* pauta, *f*

guiding /'gaidiŋ/ *a* que guía; directivo; decisivo. —*n* See **guidance**

guild /gild/ *n* gremio, *m.* —*a* gremial. **g. member,** gremial, *m*

guilder /'gildər/ *n* (coin) florín holandés, *m*

guile /gail/ *n* astucia, superchería, maña, *f*

guileful /'gailfəl/ *a* astuto

guileless /'gaillis/ *a* cándido, sin malicia, inocente

guilelessly /'gaillisli/ *adv* inocentemente

guilelessness /'gaillisnis/ *n* inocencia, candidez, *f*

guillotine /'gilə,tin/ *n* guillotina, *f.* —*vt* guillotinar

guilt /gilt/ *n* culpabilidad, *f;* crimen, *m;* (sin) pecado, *m*

guilt complex complejo de culpa, *m*

guiltily /'giltəli/ *adv* culpablemente; como si fuese culpable

guiltless /'giltlis/ *a* libre de culpa, inocente; puro; ignorante

guilty /'gilti/ *a* culpable; delincuente; criminal. **to find g.,** encontrar culpable. **to plead g.,** confesarse culpable. **g. party,** culpable, *m*

Guinea /'gini/ Guinea, *f*

guinea /'gini/ *n* guinea, *f.* **g.-fowl,** gallina de Guinea, *f.* **g.-pig,** conejillo de Indias, cobayo, *m*

guise /gaiz/ *n* manera, guisa, *f;* (garb) traje, *m;* máscara, *f; Fig.* pretexto, *m.* **under the g. of,** bajo el pretexto de; bajo la apariencia de

guitar /gi'tɑr/ *n* guitarra, *f*

guitarist /gi'tɑrist/ *n* guitarrista, *mf*

gulf /gʌlf/ *n* golfo, *m;* abismo, *m*

Gulf Stream, the la Corriente del Golfo

gull /gʌl/ *n Ornith.* gaviota, *f;* (dupe) primo, *m.* —*vt* engañar, timar, defraudar

gullet /'gʌlit/ *n* esófago, *m;* garganta, *f*

gullibility /,gʌlə'biliti/ *n* credulidad, *f*

gullible /'gʌləbəl/ *a* crédulo

gully /'gʌli/ *n* hondonada, barranca, *f;* (gutter) arroyo, *m*

gulp /gʌlp/ *n* trago, sorbo, *m.* —*vt* engullir, tragar; (repress) ahogar; (believe) tragar. **to g. up,** vomitar

gum /gʌm/ *n* (of the mouth) encía, *f;* goma, *f.* —*vt* engomar; pegar con goma. **gum arabic,** goma arábiga, *f.* **gum boots,** botas de goma, *f.* **gum-resin,** gomorresina, *f.* **gum starch,** aderezo, *m.* **gum tree,** eucalipto, *m*

gumminess /'gʌminis/ *n* gomosidad, *f*

gummy /'gʌmi/ *a* gomoso

gumption /'gʌmpʃən/ *n* sentido común, seso, *m*

gun /gʌn/ *n* arma de fuego, *f;* (handgun) fusil, *m;* (sporting g.) escopeta, *f;* (pistol) pistola, *f,* revólver, *m;* (cannon) cañón, *m;* (firing) cañonazo, *m.* **big gun,** *Inf.* pájaro gordo, *m.* **heavy gun,** cañón de grueso calibre, *m.* **gun-barrel,** cañón de escopeta, *m.* **gun-carriage,** cureña, *f.* **gun-cotton,** pólvora de algo-

dón, *f.* **gun-fire,** cañonazos, *m pl,* fuego, *m.* **gun-metal,** bronce de cañón, *m;* pavón, *m.* **gun-room,** armería, *f;* (on a ship) polvorín, *m.* **gun-running,** contrabanda de armas, *f.* **gun-turret,** torre, *f.* **gun wound,** balazo, *m*

gunboat /'gʌn,bout/ *n* cañonero, *m,* lancha bombardera, *f*

gunflint /'gʌn,flint/ *n* piedra de escopeta, *f*

gunman /'gʌnmən/ *n* escopetero, armero, *m;* bandido armado, *m;* gángster, apache, *m*

gunner /'gʌnər/ *n* artillero, *m;* escopetero, *m*

gun permit *n* licencia de armas, *f,* permiso de armas, *m*

gunpowder /'gʌn,paudər/ *n* pólvora, *f*

gunshot /'gʌn,ʃɒt/ *n* escopetazo, *m;* tiro de fusil, *m*

gunsmith /'gʌn,smiθ/ *n* escopetero, armero, *m*

gunwale /'gʌnl/ *n Naut.* regala, borda, *f*

gurgle /'gərgəl/ *n* murmullo, murmurio, gorgoteo, *m;* gluglú, *m;* (of a baby) gorjeo, *m.* —*vi* murmurar; hacer gluglú; (of babies) gorjear

gurgling /'gərgliŋ/ *a* murmurante; (of babies) gorjeador. —*n* See **gurgle**

gush /gʌʃ/ *n* chorro, *m;* (of words) torrente, *m;* (of emotion) efusión, *f.* —*vi* chorrear, borbotar; surtir, surgir. **to g. out,** saltar, brotar a borbotones, salir a borbollones, salira borbotones. **to g. over,** *Fig.* hablar con efusión de

gushing /'gʌʃiŋ/ *a* hirviente; (of people) efusivo, extremoso, empalagoso

gusset /'gʌsit/ *n Sew.* escudete, *m*

gust /gʌst/ *n* (of wind) ráfaga, bocanada (de aire), *f; Fig.* arrebato, acceso, *m*

gusto /'gʌstou/ *n* brío, *m;* entusiasmo, *m*

gusty /'gʌsti/ *a* borrascoso

gut /gʌt/ *n* intestino, *m,* tripa, *f;* (catgut) cuerda de tripa, *f; Naut.* estrecho, *m;* *pl* **guts,** tripas, *f pl;* (content) meollo, *m,* substancia, *f;* (stamina) aguante, espíritu, *m.* —*vt* (of fish, etc.) destripar; (plunder) saquear; destruir por completo; quemar completamente

gutta-percha /'gʌtə 'pərtʃə/ *n* gutapercha, *f*

gutter /'gʌtər/ *n* canal, *m;* (of a street) arroyo (de la calle), *m;* (ditch) zanja, *f; Fig.* hampa, *f.* —*vt* surcar. —*vi* gotear; (of a candle) cerotear, gotear la cera. **g. spout,** canalón, *m*

guttersnipe /'gʌtər,snaip/ *n* golfillo, *m,* niño (-ña) del hampa

guttural /'gʌtərəl/ *a* gutural. —*n* letra gutural, *f*

guy /gai/ *n* (rope) viento, *m; Naut.* guía, *f;* (effigy) mamarracho, *m;* (scarecrow) espantajo, *m, vt* sujetar con vientos o guías; burlarse de

guzzle /'gʌzəl/ *vt* tragar, engullir. —*vi* atracarse, engullir; emborracharse. —*n* comilón, *m;* borrachera, *f*

guzzler /'gʌzlər/ *n* tragador (-ra); borracho (-cha)

gymnasium /dʒim'nɑziəm/ *n* gimnasio, *m*

gymnast /'dʒimnæst/ *n* gimnasta, *mf*

gymnastic /dʒim'næstik/ *a* gimnástico. **g. rings,** anillas, *f pl*

gymnastics /dʒim'næstiks/ *n* gimnasia, *f*

gynecological /,gainikə'lɒdʒikəl/ *a* ginecológico

gynecologist /,gaini'kɒlədʒist/ *n* ginecólogo (-ga)

gynecology /,gaini'kɒlədʒi/ *n* ginecología, *f*

gypsum /'dʒipsəm/ *n* yeso, *f*

gypsy /'dʒipsi/ *n* gitano (-na). —*a* gitano, gitanesco; (music) flamenco

gyrate /'dʒaireit/ *vi* girar, rodar

gyration /dʒai'reiʃən/ *n* giro, *m,* vuelta, *f*

gyratory /'dʒairə,tɔri/ *a* giratorio

gyro-compass /'dʒairou ,kʌmpəs/ *n* brújula giroscópica, *f*

gyroscope /'dʒairə,skoup/ *n Phys.* giroscopio, *m*

H

h /eitʃ/ *n* (letter) hache, *f*
ha /hɑ/ *interj* ¡ah!
haberdasher /'hæbər,dæʃər/ *n* mercero, *m*
haberdashery /'hæbər,dæʃəri/ *n* mercería, *f*
habiliment /hə'bɪləmənt/ *n* vestidura, *f; pl* **habiliments**, indumentaria, *f*
habilitate /hə'bɪlɪ,teit/ *vt* habilitar
habilitation /hə,bɪlɪ'teiʃən/ *n* habilitación, *f*
habit /'hæbɪt/ *n* costumbre, *f*, hábito, *m;* (temperament) temperamento, carácter, *m;* (use) uso, *m;* (of body) complexión, constitución, *f; Eccl.* hábito, *m.* **to be in the h. of,** soler, acostumbrar, estar acostumbrado a. **to have bad habits,** estar malacostumbrado. **to have the bad h. of,** tener el vicio (or la mala costumbre) de. **to contract the h. of,** contraer la costumbre de. **h. maker,** sastre de trajes de montar, *m*
habitable /'hæbɪtəbəl/ *a* habitable, vividero
habitat /'hæbɪ,tæt/ *n* (*Bot., Zool.*) medio, *m*, habitación, *f*
habitation /,hæbɪ'teiʃən/ *n* habitación, *f*
habit-forming /'hæbɪt,fɔrmɪŋ/ *a* enviciador, que crea vicio
habitual /hə'bɪtʃuəl/ *a* habitual, acostumbrado, usual; constante; común
habitually /hə'bɪtʃuəli/ *adv* habitualmente; constantemente; comúnmente
habituate /hə'bɪtʃu,eit/ *vt* habituar, acostumbrar
habituation /hə,bɪtʃu'eiʃən/ *n* habituación, *f*
habitué /hə'bɪtʃu,ei/ *n* parroquiano (-na); veterano (-na)
hack /hæk/ *n* caballo de alquiler, *m;* rocín, jaco, *m;* (writer) escritor mercenario, *m.* —*vt* acuchillar; tajar, cortar. —*vi* cortar. **to h. to pieces,** cortar en pedazos; pasar a cuchillo
hacking /'hækɪŋ/ *a* (of coughs) seco
hackle /'hækəl/ *n* (for flax, hemp) rastrillo, *m*
hackney carriage /'hækni/ *n* coche de plaza, coche de alquiler, *m*
hackneyed /'hæknid/ *a* gastado, trillado, muy usado, repetido, resobado
hacksaw /'hæk,sɔ/ *n* sierra de cerrajero, sierra para metal, *f*
hackwork /'hæk,wɜrk/ *n* trabajo de rutina, *m*
haddock /'hædək/ *n* merlango, *m*, pescadilla, *f*
Hades /'heidiz/ *n* Hades, *m; Inf.* el infierno, *m*
haft /hæft/ *n* mango, tomadero, *m*, manija, *f;* puño, *m*
hag /hæg/ *n* bruja, *f*
haggard /'hægərd/ *a* ojeroso, trasnochado, trasojado
haggardly /'hægərdli/ *adv* ansiosamente
haggardness /'hægərdnɪs/ *n* aspecto ojeroso, *m*
haggle /'hægəl/ *vi* regatear; vacilar
haggling /'hæglɪŋ/ *n* regateo, *m*, a regatón
hagiographer /,hægi'ɒgrəfər/ *n* hagiógrafo, *m*
hagiography /,hægi'ɒgrəfi/ *n* hagiografía, *f*
Hague, The /heig/ La Haya
ha, ha! /'hɑ 'hɑ/ *interj* ¡ja, ja!
hail /heil/ *n* (salutation) saludo, *m;* (shout) grito, *m;* aclamación, *f;* (frozen rain) granizo, *m;* (of blows) lluvia, *f.* —*interj* ¡salve! —*vt* saludar; llamar; aclamar; *Fig.* lanzar, echar. —*vi* (hailstones) granizar; (blows, etc.) llover. **to h. from,** proceder de, ser natural de. **within h.,** al habla. **H. Mary,** Salve Regina, Avemaría, *f*
hailstone /'heil,stoun/ *n* granizo, pedrisco, *m*
hailstorm /'heil,stɔrm/ *n* granizada, *f*
hair /hɛər/ *n* (single h.) cabello, *m;* (*Zool. Bot.*) pelo, *m;* (of horse's mane) crin, *f;* (head of h.) cabellera, mata de pelo, *f*, pelo, *m;* (superfluous) vello, *m;* (fiber) fibra, *f*, filamento, *m;* (on the pen) raspa, *f*, pelo, *m; Fig.* pelo, *m.* **lock of h.,** bucle, rizo, *m;* mecha, *f.* **to dress one's h.,** peinarse. **to have one's h. cut,** hacerse cortar el pelo. **to part the h.,** hacer(se) la raya del pelo. **to put up one's h.,** hacerse el moño; (to "come out") ponerse de largo. **to tear one's h.,** mesarse los cabellos. **h. combings,** peinaduras, *f pl.*

h.-curler, tirabuzón, *m.* **h. dryer,** secadora de cabello, *f.* **h. dye,** tinte para el pelo, *m.* **h.-net,** redecilla, *f.* **h.-oil,** brillantina, *f.* **h.-raising,** horripilante, espeluznante. **h.-ribbon,** cinta para el pelo, *f.* **h.-shirt,** cilicio, *m.* **h. slide,** pasador, *m.* **h.-splitting,** sofistería, argucia, *f;* mez quinas argucias, quis quillas, *f pl.* **h.-spring,** muelle del volante, *m.* **h.-switch,** añadido, *m.* **h.-trigger,** pelo de una pistola, *m*
hairbrush /'hɛər,brʌʃ/ *n* cepillo para el cabello, *m*
hairdresser /'hɛər,drɛsər/ *n* peluquero (-ra), peinadora, *f*
hairdressing /'hɛər,drɛsɪŋ/ *n* peinado, *m.* **h. establishment or trade,** peluquería, *f*
haired /hɛərd/ *a* peludo, con pelo; (in compounds) de pelo...
hairiness /'hɛərinɪs/ *n* vellosidad, *f*
hairless /'hɛərlɪs/ *a* sin pelo; calvo
hairlike /'hɛər,laik/ *a* filiforme
hairpin /'hɛər,pɪn/ *n* horquilla, *f.* **h. bend,** viraje en horquilla, *m*
hairsbreadth /'hɛərz,brɛdθ/ *n* pelo, *m.* **to have a h. escape,** escapar por un pelo.
hairy /'hɛəri/ *a* peludo; velloso; *Bot.* hirsuto
Haiti /'heiti/ Haití, *m*
Haitian /'heiʃən/ *a and n* haitiano (-na)
hake /heik/ *n* merluza, *f*
halcyon /'hælsiən/ *n* alción, martín pescador, *m.* —*a Fig.* feliz, sereno, tranquilo
hale /heil/ *a* fuerte, sano, robusto. —*vt* hacer comparecer
half /hæf/ *n* mitad, *f;* (school term) trimestre, *m.* —*a* medio; semi. —*adv* a medias; mitad; (almost) casi; insuficientemente; imperfectamente. **I don't k. like it,** No me gusta nada. **It is h.-past two,** Son las dos y media. **an hour and a h.,** una hora y media. **better h.,** *Inf.* media naranja, cara mitad, *f.* **by halves,** a medias. **in h.,** en dos mitades. **one h.,** la mitad. **to go halves,** ir a medias. **to h. close,** entornar. **to h. open,** entreabrir. **h. a bottle,** media botella, *f.* **h. a crown,** media corona, *f.* **h.-alive,** semivivo. **h. an hour,** media hora, *f.* **h.-and-h.,** mitad y mitad; en partes iguales. **h.-asleep,** semidormido, medio dormido. **h.-awake,** medio despierto, entre duerme y vela. **h.-back,** *Sports,* medio, *m.* **h.-baked,** medio cocido, crudo; *Fig.* poco maduro. **h.-binding,** encuadernación en media pasta, *f.* **h.-breed,** a mestizo. —*n* cruce, *m.* **h.-brother,** hermanastro, hermano de padre, hermano de madre, *m.* **h.-caste,** mestizo. **h. circle,** semicírculo, *m.* **h.-closed,** entreabierto; medio cerrado. **h.-dead,** medio muerto; más muerto que vivo. **h.-done,** hecho a medias, sin acabar. **h.-dozen,** media docena, *f.* **h.-dressed,** medio desnudo. **h. fare,** medio billete, *m.* **h.-full,** medio lleno. **h.-hearted,** débil, poco eficaz, lánguido; indiferente, sin entusiasmo. **h.-heartedness,** debilidad, *f;* indiferencia, *f.* **h.-holiday,** media fiesta, *f.* **h.-hourly,** cada media hora. **h.-length,** (portrait) de medio cuerpo. **h.-length coat,** abrigo de tres cuartos, *m.* **h.-light,** media luz, *f.* **h.-mast,** a media asta. **h.-measure,** medida poco eficaz, *f.* **h.-moon,** *n* media luna, *f; Astron.* semilunio, *m;* (of a nail) blanco (de la uña), *m.* **h.-mourning,** medio luto, *m.* **h.-pay,** media paga, *f.* **h.-price,** a mitad de precio. **h.-seas-over,** *Inf.* entre dos velas. **h.-sister,** hermanastra, hermana de padre, hermana de madre, *f.* **h.-time,** *Sports,* media parte, *f*, medio tiempo, *m.* **h.-tone,** de medio tono. **h.-tone illustration,** fotograbado a media tinta, *f.* **h.-truth,** verdad a medias, *f.* **h.-turn,** media vuelta, *f.* **h.-way,** a medio camino; medio. **h.-witted,** medio loco, tonto, imbécil. **h.-year,** medio año, *m.* **h.-yearly,** semestral
halfpenny /'heipəni/ *n* medio penique, *m; Inf.* perra gorda, *f*
half title anteportada, falsa portada, portadilla, preportada, *f*
halibut /'hæləbət/ *n* halibut, *m;* (genus) hipogloso, *m*
halitosis /,hælɪ'tousɪs/ *n* halitosis, *f*
hall /hɔl/ *n* (mansion) mansión, casa de campo, *f,*

caserón, *m;* (public building) edificio, *m,* casa (de); (town h.) casa del ayuntamiento, *f;* (room) sala, *f;* (entrance) vestíbulo, *m;* (dining room) comedor, *m;* (of residence for students) residencia, *f.* **h. door,** portón, *m,* puerta del vestíbulo, *f.* **h. porter,** conserje, *m.* **h.-stand,** perchero, *m*

hallelujah /ˌhælə'luyə/ *n* aleluya, *f*

hallmark /'hɔl,mɑrk/ *n* marca de ley, *f; Fig.* señal, *f;* indicio, *m.* —*vt* poner la marca de ley sobre; *Fig.* sellar

halloo /hə'lu/ *vt* (hounds) azuzar; perseguir dando voces; (call) llamar

hallow /'hælou/ *vt* santificar; reverenciar; (consecrate) consagrar

Halloween /ˌhælə'win/ *n* la víspera de Todos los Santos, *f*

hallucination /həˌlusə'neiʃən/ *n* alucinación, ilusión, *f;* visión, *f;* fantasma, *m*

hallucinatory /hə'lusənəˌtɔri/ *a* alucinador

halo /'heilou/ *n* halo, nimbo, *m*

halogen /'hælədʒən/ *n Chem.* halógeno, *m*

halt /hɔlt/ *n Mil.* alto, *m;* cesación, *f;* interrupción, *f;* (on a railway) apeadero, *m;* (for trams, buses) parada, *f.* —*vt* parar, detener. —*vi* pararse, detenerse; *Mil.* hacer alto; cesar; interrumpirse; (in speech) titubear; (of verse) estar cojo; (doubt) dudar; (limp) cojear. **H.!** *Mil.* ¡Alto!

halter /'hɔltər/ *n* ronzal, cabestro, *m;* (for hanging) dogal, *m.* —*vt* encabestrar, cabestrar

halting /'hɔltɪŋ/ *n* parada, *f;* interrupción, *f.* —*a* (of gait) cojo; incierto; vacilante; (of speech) titubeante

halve /hæv/ *vt* partir (or dividir) en dos mitades

ham /hæm/ *n* jamón, *m; Anat.* pernil, *m;* (radio-operator) radioaficionado, *m*

Hamburg /'hæmbɜrg/ Hamburgo, *m*

hamlet /'hæmlɪt/ *n* aldea, *f,* pueblecito, *m*

hammer /'hæmər/ *n* martillo, *m;* (stone cutter's) maceta, *f;* (mason's) piqueta, *f;* (of fire-arms) percusor, *m;* (of piano) macillo, *m.* —*vt* amartillar, martillar, batir. **to throw the h.,** lanzar el martillo. **under the h.,** en subasta, al remate. **h. blow,** martillazo, *m*

hammering /'hæmərɪŋ/ *n* martilleo, martillazo, *m.* **by h.,** a martillo

hammock /'hæmək/ *n* hamaca, *f; Naut.* coy, *m*

hamper /'hæmpər/ *n* banasta, canasta, *f,* cesto grande, *m.* —*vt* estorbar, dificultar, impedir; *Fig.* embarazar

hamster /'hæmstər/ *n Zool.* hámster, *m,* marmota de Alemania, rata del trigo, *f*

hand /hænd/ *n* mano, *f;* (of animal) pata, mano, *f;* (worker) operario (-ia); obrero (-ra); (skill) habilidad, *f;* (side) mano, *f,* lado, *m;* (measure) palmo, *m;* (of a clock) manecilla, *f;* (of instruments) aguja, *f;* (applause) aplauso, *m;* (power) poder, *m;* las manos; (at cards) mano, *f;* (card player) jugador, *m;* (signature) firma, *f;* (handwriting) letra, escritura, *f;* (influence) influencia, parte, mano, *f.* **old h.,** veterano; perro viejo. **at h.,** a mano, al lado, cerca. **have at hand,** tener a la mano. **at the hands of,** de manos de. **by h.,** a mano; (on the bottle) con biberón. **from h. to h.,** de mano a mano. **in h.,** entre manos; (of money) de contado. **in the hands of,** *Fig.* en el poder de. **"Hands wanted,"** «Se desean trabajadores.» **h. over h.,** mano sobre mano. **hand's breadth,** palmo, *m.* **Hands off!** ¡Fuera las manos! **Hands up!** ¡Manos arriba! **lost with all hands,** (of a ship) perdido con toda su tripulación. **off one's hands,** despachado; (of a daughter) casada. **on all hands,** por todas partes. **on h.,** entre manos; (of goods) existente; (present) presente. **on one's hands,** a cargo de uno. **on the one h.,** por un lado; a un lado. **on the other h.,** por otra parte; en cambio. **out of h.,** luego, inmediatamente; revoltoso. **to come to h.,** venir a mano; (of letters) llegar a las manos (de). **to get one's h. in,** ejercitarse. **to have a h. in,** tener parte en; intervenir en. **to have no h. in,** no tener arte ni parte en. **to have on h.,** traer entre manos. **to have the upper h.,** tener la sartén por el mango, llevar la ventaja. **to hold one's h.,** abstenerse; detenerse. **to hold hands,** cogerse de las manos. **to lay hands on,** tocar; poner mano en; echar manos a. **to set one's h. to,** emprender; (sign) firmar. **to shake hands,** estrechar la

mano. **to stretch out one's hands,** tender las manos. **to take one's hands off,** no tocar. **with folded hands,** mano sobre mano. **with his hands behind his back,** con las manos en la espalda. **h.-in-h.,** cogidos (cogidas) de las manos. **h.-lever,** manija, *f.* **h.-loom,** telar de mano, *m.* **h. luggage,** equipaje de mano, *m.* **h.-made,** hecho a mano. **h.-mill,** molinillo, *m.* **h.-pump,** *n Naut.* sacabuche, *m.* **h. rail,** pasamano, *m,* baranda, balustrada, *f.* **h.-sewn,** cosido a mano. **h.-to-h.,** de mano en mano; (of a fight) a brazo partido, cuerpo a cuerpo. **h.-to-h. fight,** cachetina, *f.* **h.-to-mouth,** precario, *m.* **to live from h.-to-mouth,** vivir de día en día

hand /hænd/ *vt* dar; entregar; alargar. **to h. down,** bajar; (a person) ayudar a bajar; transmitir. **to h. in,** entregar; (a person) ayudar a entrar; (one's resignation) dimitir; (send) mandar, enviar. **to h. on,** transmitir. **to h. out,** *vt* distribuir; (a person) ayudar a salir; (from a vehicle) ayudar a bajar. —*vi Inf.* pagar. **to h. over,** *vt* entregar. —*vi Mil.* traspasar los poderes (a). **to h. round,** pasar de mano en mano; pasar; ofrecer. **to h. up,** subir; (a person) ayudar a subir

handbag /'hænd,bæg/ *n* bolso, saco, monedero, *m*

handbill /'hænd,bɪl/ *n* anuncio, *m*

handbook /'hænd,bʊk/ *n* manual, compendio, tratado, *m;* anuario, *m;* (guide) guía, *f*

handcart /'hænd,kɑrt/ *n* carretilla de mano, *f,* carretón, *m*

handcuff /'hænd,kʌf/ *n* esposa, *f,* grillo, *m,* (gen. —*pl*). —*vt* poner las esposas (a), maniatar

handed /'hændɪd/ *a* (in compounds) que tiene manos; de manos...; con las manos... **four-h.,** *Sports.* de cuatro personas. **one-h.,** manco

handful /'hændful/ *n* puño, puñado, manojo, *m.* **to be a h.,** *Inf.* tener el diablo en el cuerpo. **in handfuls,** a manojos

handgrip /'hænd,grɪp/ *n* apretón de manos, *m*

handicap /'hændiˌkæp/ *n* desventaja, *f;* obstáculo, *m; Sports.* handicap, *m;* ventaja, *f.* —*vt Fig.* perjudicar, impedir, dificultar. **the handicapped,** los lisiados, *m pl*

handicraft /'hændiˌkræft/ *n* mano de obra, *f;* (skill) destreza manual, *f,*

handiwork /'hændiˌwɜrk/ *n* mano de obra, *f;* trabajo manual, *m;* obra, *f;* (deed) acción, *f,* hecho, *m*

handkerchief /'hæŋkərtʃɪf/ *n* pañuelo, *m*

handle /'hændl/ *n* mango, puño, *m;* (lever) palanca, *f;* (of baskets, dishes, jugs) asa, *f;* (of doors, windows, drawers) pomo, *m,* (of a car door) picaporte *m;* (to one's name) designación, *f;* título, *m;* (excuse) pretexto, *m.* —*vt* (touch) tocar; manejar, manipular; (treat) tratar; **h. with kid gloves,** tratar con guantes de seda; (deal in) comerciar en; tomar; (paw) manosear; (direct) dirigir; (control) gobernar; (pilot) pilotar; (a theme) explicar, tratar de. **h.-bar,** manillar, *m.* **h.-bar grip,** puño de un manillar, *m*

handless /'hændlɪs/ *a* sin manos; manco; *Fig.* torpe

handling /'hændlɪŋ/ *n* manejo, *m;* manipulación, *f;* (treatment) trato, *m,* relaciones (con), *f pl;* (thumbing) manoseo, *m;* interpretación, *f; Art.* tratamiento, *m,* técnica, *f*

handmaid /'hænd,meid/ *n* sirvienta, criada, *f; Fig.* mayordomo, *m*

handsaw /'hænd,sɔ/ *n* sierra de mano, *f,* serrucho, *m*

handsbreadth /'hændz,bredθ/ *n* palmo, *m*

handshake /'hænd,ʃeik/ *n* apretón de manos, *m*

handsome /'hænsəm/ *a* (generous) generoso; magnánimo; considerable; hermoso, bello; elegante; (of people) guapo, distinguido; excelente; (flattering) halagüeño. **He was a very h. man,** Era un hombre muy guapo

handsomely /'hænsəmli/ *adv* generosamente; con magnanimidad; elegantemente; bien

handsomeness /'hænsəmnɪs/ *n* generosidad, *f;* magnanimidad, *f;* hermosura, *f;* elegancia, *f;* distinción, *f*

handspring /'hænd,sprɪŋ/ *n* voltereta sobre las manos, *f*

handwork /'hænd,wɜrk/ *n* obra hecha a mano, *f,* trabajo a mano, *m;* (needlework) labor de aguja, *f*

handworked /'hænd,wɜrkt/ *a* hecho a mano; (embroidered) bordado

handwriting /'hænd,raitɪŋ/ *n* caligrafía, letra, escritura, *f.* **the h. on the wall,** la mano que escribía en la pared, *f*

handy /'hændɪ/ *a* (of persons) diestro, mañoso, hábil; (of things) conveniente; útil; (near) cercano, a mano. —*adv* cerca. **h.-man,** hombre de muchos oficios, *m;* factótum, *m*

hang /hæŋ/ *vt* colgar; suspender; (execute) ahorcar; (the head) bajar; dejar caer; (upholster) entapizar; (with wallpaper) empapelar; (drape) poner colgaduras en; (place) poner; (cover) cubrir. —*vi* colgar, pender; estar suspendido; (be executed) ser ahorcado; (of garments) caer. —*n* (of garments) caída, *f;* (of a machine) mecanismo, *m;* (meaning) sentido, *m,* significación, *f.* **to h. by a thread,** pender de un hilo. **to h. in the balance,** estar en la balanza. **to h. fire,** estar (una cosa) en suspenso. **to h. loose,** caer suelto; (clothes) venir ancho. **to h. about,** (surround) rodear, pegarse a; (frequent) frecuentar; (haunt) rondar; (be imminent) ser inminente, amenazar; (embrace) abrazar. **to h. back,** retroceder; quedarse atrás; *Fig.* vacilar, titubear. **to h. down,** colgar, pender; estar caído; caerse. **to h. on,** seguir agarrado (a); apoyarse en; *Fig.* persistir; (a person's words) estar pendiente de, beber; (remain) quedarse. **to h. out,** *vt* tender. —*vi* (lean out) asomarse (por); (*Inf.* live) habitar. **to h. over,** colgar por encima; (brood) cernerse sobre; (lean over) inclinarse sobre; quedarse cerca de; (overhang) sobresalir; (overarch) abovedar; (threaten) amenazar. **to h. together,** (of persons) permanecer unidos; (of things) tener cohesión; (be consistent) ser lógico, ser consistente. **to h. up,** colgar; suspender; *Fig.* dejar pendiente, interrumpir. **to h. upon,** apoyarse en; (a person's words) beber las palabras de uno

hangar /'hæŋər/ *n* cobertizo; *Aer.* hangar, *m*

hanger /'hæŋər/ *n* colgadero, *m;* percha *f.* **h.-on,** parásito, *m;* dependiente, *m*

hanging /'hæŋɪŋ/ *n* colgamiento, *m;* (killing) ahorcamiento, *m; pl* **hangings,** colgaduras, *f pl,* cortinajes, *m pl.* —*a* pendiente colgante; (péndulo; (of gardens) pensil. **It's not a h. matter,** No es una cuestión de vida y muerte. **h. bridge,** puente colgante, *m.* **h. committee,** junta (de una exposición,) *f.* **h. lamp,** lámpara de techo, *f*

hangman /'hæŋmən/ *n* verdugo, *m*

hangnail /'hæŋ,neɪl/ *n* padrastro, *m*

hangover /'hæŋ,ouvər/ *n* (after drinking) resaca, cruda (Mexico), *f*

hank /hæŋk/ *n* madeja, *f*

hanker /'hæŋkər/ *vi* (with after) ansiar, ambicionar; (with for) anhelar, suspirar por, desear con vehemencia

hankering /'hæŋkərɪŋ/ *n* ambición, *f;* deseo vehemente, *m*

hanky-panky /'hæŋki 'pæŋki/ *n* superchería, *f;* engaño, *m*

hap /hæp/ *n* casualidad, suerte, *f;* suceso fortuito, *m*

haphazard /*n* 'hæp,hæzərd/ *a* hæp'hæzərd/ *n* casualidad, *f.* —*a* fortuito, casual

hapless /'hæplɪs/ *a* desgraciado, desdichado

haplessness /'hæplɪsnɪs/ *n* desgracia, desdicha, *f*

happen /'hæpən/ *vi* suceder, acontecer, ocurrir, pasar; (to be found, be) hallarse por casualidad; (take place) tener lugar, verificarse; (arise) sobrevenir. **Do you know what has happened to...?** ¿Sabes qué se ha hecho de...? **as if nothing had happened,** como si no hubiese pasado nada. **He turned up as if nothing had happened,** Se presentó como si tal cosa. **How did it h.?** ¿Cómo fue esto? **If they h. to see you,** Si acaso te vean. **I happened to be in London,** Me hallaba por casualidad en Londres. **It won't h. again,** No volverá a suceder. **whatever happens,** venga lo que venga

happening /'hæpənɪŋ/ *n* suceso, acontecimiento, hecho, *m,* ocurrencia, *f*

happily /'hæpəli/ *adv* felizmente; por suerte

happiness /'hæpɪnɪs/ *n* felicidad, dicha, *f;* alegría, *f,* regocijo, *m*

happy /'hæpi/ *a* (lucky) afortunado; (felicitous) feliz, oportuno; feliz, dichoso; alegre, regocijado. **to be h.,** estar contento, ser feliz. **to be h. about,** alegrarse de.

to make h., hacer feliz, alegrar. **h.-go-lucky,** irresponsable, descuidado

harangue /hə'ræŋ/ *n* arenga, *f.* —*vt* arengar. —*vi* pronunciar una arenga

harass /hə'ræs/ *vt* hostigar, acosar; atormentar; preocupar; *Mil.* picar. **to h. the rear-guard,** picar la retaguardia

harbinger /'harbɪndʒər/ *n Fig.* precursor, heraldo, *m;* presagio, anuncio, *m.* —*vt* anunciar, presagiar

harbor /'harbər/ *n* puerto, *m;* (bay) bahía, *f;* (haven) asilo, refugio, *m.* —*vt* dar refugio (a), albergar, acoger; (cherish) abrigar, acariciar; (conceal) esconder. **inner h.,** puerto, *m.* **outer h.,** rada del puerto, *f.* **to put into h.,** entrar en el puerto. **h. bar,** barra del puerto, *f.* **h.-dues,** derechos de puerto, *m pl.* **h.-master,** capitán de puerto, contramaestre de puerto, *m*

harborer /'harbərər/ *n* amparador (-ra), protector (-ra); (criminal) encubridor (-ra)

hard /hard/ *a* duro; (firm) firme; difícil; laborioso, agotador; violento; poderoso; arduo; fuerte, recio; vigoroso, robusto; insensible, inflexible; cruel; (of weather) inclemente, severo; (unjust) injusto, opresivo; (stiff) tieso; (of water) cruda; (of wood) brava. —*adv* duro; duramente; con ahínco; con fuerza; de firme; difícilmente; (of gazing) fijamente; severamente; (firmly) firmemente; vigorosamente; (of raining) a cántaros, mucho; (quickly) rápidamente; (of bearing misfortune) a pechos; (attentively) atentamente; (heavily) pesadamente; (badly) mal; (closely) de cerca, inmediatamente. **It was a h. blow,** Fue un golpe recio. **to be h. put to,** encontrar difícil. **to go h.,** endurecerse. **to go h. with,** irle mal a uno. **to have a h. time,** pasar apuros, pasarlo mal. **to look h. at,** mirar atentamente, examinar detenidamente; mirar fijamente. **to be a h. drinker,** ser un bebedor empedernido. **h. and fast rule,** regla inalterable, *f.* **h.-bitten,** de carácter duro. **a h.-boiled egg,** un huevo duro. **h. breathing,** resuello, *m.* **h. by,** muy cerca. **h. cash,** efectivo, *m.* **h.-earned,** difícilmente conseguido; ganado con el sudor de la frente. **h.-featured,** de facciones duras. **h.-fisted,** tacaño. **h.-fought,** arduo, reñido. **h.-headed,** práctico, perspicaz. **h.-hearted,** duro de corazón, insensible. **h.-heartedness,** insensibilidad, *f.* **h. labor,** *Law.* trabajos forzados, *m pl,* presidio, *m.* **h.-mouthed,** (of horses) boquiduro. **h. of hearing,** duro de oído. **h.-up,** apurado. **to be very h.-up,** ser muy pobre; *Inf.* estar a la cuarta pregunta. **h.-wearing,** duradero; sufrido. **h.-won,** See **h.-earned. h.-working,** trabajador, hacendoso, diligente

harden /'hardn/ *vt* endurecer; (metal) templar; robustecer; (to war) aguerrir; (make callous) hacer insensible. —*vi* endurecerse; hacerse duro; templarse; robustecerse; (of shares) entonarse

hardening /'hardnɪŋ/ *n* endurecimiento, *m;* (of metal) temple, *m.* **h. of the arteries,** arteriosclerosis, *f*

hardiness /'hardɪnɪs/ *n* vigor, *m,* fuerza, robustez, *f;* audacia, *f*

hardly /'hardli/ *adv* duramente; difícilmente; (badly) mal; severamente; (scarcely) apenas, casi. **h. ever,** casi nunca

hardness /'hardnɪs/ *n* dureza, *f;* severidad, *f;* inhumanidad, insensibilidad, *f;* (stiffness) tiesura, *f;* (difficulty) dificultad, *f;* (of water) crudeza, *f;* (of hearing) dureza de oído, *f*

hardship /'hardʃɪp/ *n* penas, *f pl,* trabajos, *m pl;* infortunio, *m,* desdicha, *f;* (suffering) sufrimiento, *m;* (affliction) aflicción, *f;* (privation) privación, *f.* **to undergo h.,** pasar trabajos

hardware /'hard,wɛər/ *n* ferretería, *f*

hardwood /'hard,wʊd/ *n* madera brava, *f*

hardy /'hardi/ *a* audaz, intrépido; (strong) fuerte, robusto; *Bot.* resistente

hare /hɛər/ *n* liebre, *f.* **young h.,** lebrato, *m.* **h. and hounds,** rally paper, *m,* caza de papelitos, *f.* **h.-brained,** casquivano, atronado, con cabeza de chorlito. **hare's foot,** mano de gato, *f.* **h.-lip,** labio leporino, *m.* **h.-lipped,** labihendido

harebell /'hɛər,bɛl/ *n* campanilla, campánula, *f*

harem /'hɛərəm/ *n* harén, serrallo, *m*

haricot /'hærə‚kou/ n (green bean) judía, f; (dried bean) alubia, f

hark /hɑrk/ vt escuchar; oír. **to h. back,** volver al punto de partida; volver a la misma canción

harlequin /'hɑrləkwɪn/ n arlequín, m

harlequinade /‚hɑrləkwɪ'neid/ n arlequinada, f

harlot /'hɑrlət/ n ramera, prostituta, meretriz, f

harlotry /'hɑrlətri/ n prostitución, f

harm /hɑrm/ n mal, m; daño, m; perjuicio, m; (danger) peligro, m; (detriment) menoscabo, m; (misfortune) desgracia, f, vt hacer mal (a); dañar, hacer daño (a); perjudicar. **And there's no h. in that,** Y en eso no hay mal. **to keep out of harm's way,** evitar el peligro; guardarse del mal

harmful /'hɑrmfəl/ a malo; dañino, perjudicial, nocivo; (dangerous) peligroso. **to be h.,** (of food, etc.) hacer mal (a); (of pests) ser dañino; (of behavior, etc.) perjudicar

harmfulness /'hɑrmfəlnɪs/ n lo malo; perniciosidad, f; daño, m; peligro, m

harmless /'hɑrmlɪs/ a innocuo; inofensivo; inocente

harmlessness /'hɑrmlɪsnɪs/ n innocuidad, f; inocencia, f

harmonic /hɑr'mɒnɪk/ n (Phys. Math.) harmónica, f; Mus. armónico, m, a Mus. armónico

harmonica /hɑr'mɒnɪkə/ n armónica, f

harmonics /hɑr'mɒnɪks/ n armonía, f; (tones) armónicos, m pl

harmonious /hɑr'mouniəs/ a armonioso

harmoniously /hɑr'mouniəsli/ adv armoniosamente; Fig. en armonía

harmoniousness /hɑr'mouniəsnɪs/ n armonía, f

harmonium /hɑr'mouniəm/ n armonio, m

harmonization /‚hɑrmənɪ'zeifən/ n armonización, f

harmonize /'hɑrmə‚naiz/ vt armonizar. —vi armonizarse, estar en armonía

harmony /'hɑrməni/ n armonía, f; Fig. paz, f, buenas relaciones, f pl; música, f. **to live in h.,** vivir en paz

harness /'hɑrnɪs/ n guarniciones, f pl, jaeces, m pl; (armor) arnés, m. —vt enjaezar; (yoke) enganchar; (water) represar. **to die in h.,** Fig. morir en la brecha. **h. maker,** guarnicionero, m. **h. room,** guadarnés, m

harp /hɑrp/ n arpa, f. **to h. on,** volver a la misma canción, volver a repetir

harpist /'hɑrpɪst/ n arpista, mf

harpoon /hɑr'pun/ n arpón, m. —vt arponear

harpooner /hɑr'punər/ n arponero, m

harpsichord /'hɑrpsɪ‚kɔrd/ n arpicordio, m

harpy /'hɑrpi/ n arpía, f

harridan /'hærədɪn/ n bruja, f

harrow /'hærou/ n Agr. rastra, f, escarificador, m. —vt Agr. escarificar; Fig. lastimar, atormentar

harrowing /'hærouɪŋ/ a patibulario, conmovedor, atormentador, angustioso

harry /'hæri/ vt devastar, asolar; (persons) robar; perseguir; (worry) atormentar; (annoy) molestar

harsh /hɑrʃ/ a áspero; (of voice) ronco; (of sound) discordante; (of colors) áspero; duro; chillón; severo, duro; (of features) duro; (of taste) ácido, acerbo

harshly /'hɑrʃli/ adv severamente

harshness /'hɑrʃnɪs/ n (roughness) aspereza, f; (of voice) ronquedad, aspereza, f; (of sound) disonancia, f; (of colors) aspereza, f; severidad, f; dureza, f; (of taste) acidez, f

hart /hɑrt/ n ciervo, m

harum-scarum /'hɛərəm 'skɛərəm/ n tronera, saltabarrancos, mf molino, m, a irresponsable

harvest /'hɑrvɪst/ n cosecha, siega, f; recolección, f; Fig. producto, fruto, m. —vt cosechar; recoger. **h. festival,** fiesta de la cosecha, f

harvester /'hɑrvəstər/ n segador, m, cosechero (-ra); (machine) segadora, f

hash /hæʃ/ n Cul. picado, m. —vt Cul. picar

hashish /'hæʃɪʃ/ n hachich, hachís, quif, m

hasp /hæsp/ n pasador, m; sujetador, m

hassock /'hæsək/ n cojín, m

haste /heist/ n prisa, rapidez, f; precipitación, f; urgencia, f. —vt dar prisa (a); acelerar; precipitar. —vi darse prisa; acelerarse; precipitarse. **in h.,** de prisa, aprisa. **to be in h.,** estar de prisa, llevar prisa. **in**

great h., muy aprisa, aprisa y corriendo, precipitadamente; con mucha prisa. **More h. less speed,** (Spanish equivalent. Words said by Charles III of Spain to his valet) ¡Vísteme despacio que voy de prisa!

hasten /'heisən/ vt acelerar, apresurar; precipitar. —vi darse prisa, apresurarse; moverse con rapidez; correr. **to h. one's steps,** apretar el paso. **to h. away,** marcharse rápidamente. **to h. back,** regresar apresuradamente. **to h. down,** bajar rápidamente. **to h. on,** seguir el camino sin descansar; seguir rápidamente. **to h. out,** salir rápidamente. **to h. towards,** ir rápidamente hacia; correr hacia. **to h. up,** subir aprisa, correr hacia arriba; darse prisa

hastily /'heistli/ adv de prisa, rápidamente; con precipitación, precipitadamente; (angrily) impacientemente, airadamente; (thoughtlessly) sin reflexión

hastiness /'heistinɪs/ n rapidez, f; precipitación, f; (anger) impaciencia, irritación, f

hasty /'heisti/ a rápido, apresurado; precipitado; (superficial) superficial, ligero; (ill-considered) desconsiderado, imprudente; (angry) impaciente, irritable; violento, apasionado

hat /hæt/ n sombrero, m. **to pass round the h.,** pasar el platillo. **Andalusian h.,** sombrero calañés, m. **bowler h.,** sombrero hongo, m. **broad-brimmed h.,** sombrero chambergo, m. **Panama h.,** sombrero de jipijapa, m. **picture h.,** pamela, f. **shovel h.,** sombrero de teja, m. **soft felt h.,** sombrero flexible, m. **straw h.,** sombrero de paja, m. **three-cornered h.,** sombrero de tres picos, m. **top-h.,** sombrero de copa, m. **h. shop** or **trade,** sombrerería, f

hatband /'hæt‚bænd/ n cinta de sombrero, f, cintillo, m

hatblock /'hæt‚blɒk/ n formillón, f

hatbox /'hæt‚bɒks/ n sombrerera, f

hatbrush /'hæt‚brʌʃ/ n cepillo para sombreros, m

hatch /hætʃ/ n (wicket) compuerta, f; (trap-door) puerta caediza, f; Naut. escotilla, f; compuerta de esclusa, f; (of chickens) pollada, f; (of birds) nidada, f. —vt (birds) empollar; incubar, encobar; Fig. tramar, urdir. —vi empollarse, salir del cascarón; incubarse; Fig. madurarse. **to h. a plot,** urdir un complot, conspirar. **to h. chickens,** sacar pollos

hatchet /'hætʃɪt/ n hacha pequeña, f, machado, m. **to bury the h.,** hacer la paz. **h.-faced,** de cara de cuchillo

hatching /'hætʃɪŋ/ n incubación, f; (of a plot) maquinación, f

hatchway /'hætʃ‚wei/ n Naut. escotilla, f

hate /heit/ n odio, aborrecimiento, m, aversión, f; abominación, f. —vt odiar, aborrecer, detestar; repugnar; saber mal, sentir. **I h. to trouble you,** Me sabe mal molestarle, Siento mucho molestarle. **to h. the sight of,** Inf. no poder ver (a)

hateful /'heitfəl/ a odioso, aborrecible; repugnante

hatefulness /'heitfəlnɪs/ n odiosidad, f, lo odioso; maldad, f

hater /'heitər/ n aborrecedor (-ra). **to be a good h.,** saber odiar

hatful /'hætfəl/ n un sombrero lleno (de)

hatless /'hætlɪs/ a sin sombrero, descubierto

hatpin /'hæt‚pɪn/ n horquilla de sombrero, f

hatred /'heitrɪd/ n odio, aborrecimiento, m, detestación, f; aversión, enemistad, f

hatstand /'hæt‚stænd/ n perchera, f

hatter /'hætər/ n sombrerero, m. **as mad as a h.,** loco como una cabra

haughtiness /'hɔtinɪs/ n altanería, arrogancia, altivez, soberbia, f, orgullo, m

haughty /'hɔti/ a altanero, arrogante, altivo, orgulloso

haul /hɔl/ n (pull) tirón, m; (of fish) redada, f; (booty) botín, m. —vt arrastrar, tirar de; Naut. halar. **to h. at, upon,** (ropes, etc.) aflojar, soltar, arriar. **to h. down,** (flags, sails) arriar

haulage /'hɔlɪdʒ/ n transporte, acarreo, m; coste de transporte, m. **h. contractor,** contratista de transporte, m

haunch /hɔntʃ/ n anca, culata, f; (of meat) pierna, f. **h.-bone,** hueso ilíaco, m

haunt /hɔnt/ n punto de reunión, lugar frecuentado (por), m; (lair) cubil, nido, m, guarida, f. —vt frecuentar; rondar; (of ideas) perseguir; (of ghosts) aparecer, visitar. **It is a h. of thieves,** Es una cueva de ladronés

haunted /'hɔntɪd/ a (by spirits) encantado

haunter /'hɔntər/ n frecuentador (-ra); (ghost) fantasma, espectro, m

haunting /'hɔntɪŋ/ n frecuentación, f; aparición de un espectro, f. —a persistente

hautboy /'houbɔɪ, 'oubɔɪ/ n oboe, m

hauteur /hou'tɜr/ n altivez, f

Havana /hə'vænə/ la Habana, f. —n (cigar) habano, m. (native) habanero (-ra), habano (-na)

have /hæv; unstressed həv, əv/ vt tener; poseer; (suffer) padecer; (spend) pasar; (eat or drink) tomar; (eat) comer; (a cigarette) fumar; (a bath, etc.) tomar; (a walk, a ride) dar; (cause to be done) mandar (hacer), hacer (hacer); (deceive) engañar; (defeat) vencer; (catch) coger; (say) decir; (allow) permitir; (tolerate) tolerar, sufrir; (obtain) lograr, conseguir; (wish) querer; (know) saber; (realize) realizar, (buy) comprar; (acquire) adquirir. As an auxiliary verb, haber (e.g. **I h. done it,** Lo he hecho, etc.). **As fate would h. it,** Según quiso la suerte. **Do you h. to go?** ¿Tiene Vd. que marcharse? **H. him come here,** Hazle venir aquí. **I h. been had,** Me han engañado. **I h. a good mind to...,** Tengo ganas de... **I had all my books stolen,** Me robaron todos los libros. **You had better go,** Es mejor que te vayas. **I had rather,** Preferiría, Me gustaría más bien. **I h. had a suit made,** Mandé hacerme un traje, Hice hacerme un traje. **I would not h. had it otherwise,** No lo hubiese querido de otra manera. **I will not h. it,** No lo quiero; No quiero tomarlo; (object) No lo permitiré. **If we had known,** Si lo hubiésemos sabido. **It has to do with the sun,** Está relacionado con el sol, Tiene que ver con el sol. **Have a good trip!** ¡Buen viaje!, ¡Feliz viaje! **What are you going to h.?** ¿Qué quiere Vd. tomar? **Will you h. some jam?** ¿Quiere Vd. mermelada? **to h. breakfast,** desayunar. **to h. dinner, supper,** cenar. **to h. lunch,** almorzar. **to h. for tea,** invitar a tomar el té; (of food) merendar. **to h. tea,** tomar el té. **to h. it out with,** habérselas con. **to h. just,** acabar de. **I h. just done it,** Acabo de hacerlo. **to h. on hand,** traer entre manos. **to h. one's eye on,** no perder de vista (a), vigilar. **to h. one's tail between one's legs,** ir rabo entre piernas. **to h. to,** tener que; deber. **It has to be so,** Tiene que ser así. **to h. too much of,** sobrar, tener demasiado de. **He has too much time,** Le sobra tiempo. **to h. about one,** tener (or llevar) consigo. **to h. back,** aceptar; recibir. **to h. down,** hacer bajar. **She had her hair down,** El pelo le caía por las espaldas. **to h. in,** hacer entrar. **to h. on,** vestir, llevar puesto; (engagements) tener (compromisos). **to h. out,** hacer salir; llevar a paseo; llevar fuera; (have removed) hacerse sacar; quitar. **to h. up,** (persons) hacer subir; (things) subir; Law. llevar a (ante) los tribunales. **to h. with one,** tener consigo. **I h. her with me,** La tengo conmigo, Ella me acompaña

haven /'heivən/ n puerto, m, abra, f; Fig. oasis, abrigo, refugio, m

haversack /'hævər,sæk/ n mochila, f, morral, m

havoc /'hævək/ n destrucción, ruina, f; Fig. estrago, m. **to wreak h. among,** destruir; Fig. hacer estragos entre (or en)

Hawaii /hə'waii/ Hawai, m

Hawaiian /hə'waiən/ a and n hawaiano; n (language) hawaiano, m

hawk /hɔk/ n halcón, m; gavilán, milano, m. —vi cazar con halcón. —vt vender mercancías por las calles; Fig. difundir. **h.-eyed,** de ojos de lince. **h.-nosed,** de nariz aguileña

hawker /'hɔkər/ n halconero, m; (vendor) buhonero, m, vendedor (-ra) ambulante

hawking /'hɔkɪŋ/ n caza con halcones, cetrería, f; (expectorating) gargajeo, m; (selling) buhonería, f

hawser /'hɔzər/ n maroma, f, calabrote, m

hawthorn /'hɔ,θɔrn/ n espino, m. **white h.,** espino blanco, m

hay /hei/ n heno, m. **to make hay while the sun shines,** hacer su agosto. **hay fever,** fiebre del heno, f. **hay-fork,** horca, f

hayloft /'hei,lɔft/ n henil, m

haymaker /'hei,meikər/ n segador (-ra); (machine) segadora, f

haymaking /'hei,meikɪŋ/ n recolección del heno, f

haystack /'hei,stæk/ n almiar, m, niara, f

hazard /'hæzərd/ n azar, m, suerte, f; riesgo, peligro, m; (game) juego de azar, m. —vt arriesgar, aventurar. **at all hazards,** a todo riesgo

hazardous /'hæzərdəs/ a azaroso, arriesgado, peligroso

haze /heiz/ n bruma, f; confusión, f

hazel /'heizəl/ n avellano, m. **h.-nut,** avellana, f

hazy /'heizi/ a brumoso, calinoso; confuso

he /hi/ pers pron él. —n (of humans) varón, m; (of animals) macho, m. **he who,** el que, quien. **he-goat,** macho cabrío, m. **he-man,** todo un hombre, hombre cabal, m

head /hɛd/ vt golpear con la cabeza; encabezar; (lead) capitanear; (direct) dirigir, guiar; (wine) cabecear. —vi estar a la cabeza de; dirigirse a. **headed for,** con rumbo a, en dirección a. **to h. off,** interceptar; desviar; Fig. distraer

head /hɛd/ n Anat. cabeza, f; (upper portion) parte superior, f; (of a coin) cara, f; (hair) cabellera, f; (individual) persona, f; (of cattle) res, f; (of a mountain) cumbre, f; (of a ladder) último peldaño, m; (of toadstools) sombrero, m; (of trees) copa, f; (of a stick) puño, m; (of a cylinder) culata, f; (of a river, etc.) manantial, origen, m; (of a bed) cabecera, f; (of nails, pins) cabeza, f; (froth) espuma, f; (flower) flor, f; (leaves) hojas, f pl; (first place) primer puesto, m; (of game, fish) pieza, f; (of a page, column) cabeza, f; (cape) cabo, m; (of an arrow, dart, lance) punta, f; (front) frente, m; (leader) jefe, cabeza, m; (chief) director (-ra), superior (-ra); presidente (-ta); (of a school) director (-ra); (of a cask) fondo, m; Mech. cabezal, m; (of an ax) filo, m; (of a bridge) cabeza, f; (of a jetty, pier) punta, f; (of a ship) proa, f; (of a flower) cabezuela, f; (of asparagus) punta, f; (of a table) cabeza, f; (of the family) jefe, cabeza, m; (seat of honor) cabecera, f; (title) título, m; (aspect) punto de vista, m; (division) capítulo, m; (management, direction) dirección, f; (talent) talento, m, cabeza, f; (intelligence) inteligencia, f. —a principal; primero; en jefe. **at the h. of,** a la cabeza de. **crowned h.,** testa coronada, f. **from h. to foot,** de pies a cabeza; de hito en hito; de arriba abajo. **He took it into his h. to...,** Se le ocurrió de... **This story has neither h. nor tail,** Este cuento no tiene pies ni cabeza. **with h. held high,** con la frente levantada. **to come to a h.,** llegar a una crisis; llegar al punto decisivo. **to get an idea out of a person's h.,** quitar una idea a uno de la cabeza. **to keep one's h.,** Fig. conservar la sangre fría, no perder la cabeza. **to lose one's h.,** Fig. perder la cabeza. **to put into a person's h.,** Fig. meter (a uno) en la cabeza. **to run one's h. against,** golpear la cabeza contra. **h. first,** de cabeza. **h. of cattle,** res, f. **h. office,** central, f. **h. of hair,** cabellera, f; mata de pelo, f. **h.-on,** de cabeza. **h.-on collision,** choque de frente, m. **h. opening,** (of a garment) cabezón, m. **heads or tails,** cara o cruz, águila o sol (Mexico). **h. over heels,** de patas arriba. **h. over heels in love,** calado hasta los huesos. **h.-dress,** tocado, m; peinado, m; sombrero, m. **h. voice,** voz de cabeza, f. **h. waiter,** encargado de comedor, jefe de camareros, m

headache /'hɛd,eik/ n dolor de cabeza, m; Fig. quebradero de cabeza, m

headboard /'hɛd,bɔrd/ n cabecera de una cama, f

headed /'hɛdɪd/ a con cabeza...; que tiene la cabeza...; de cabeza...; (of an article) intitulado. **large h.,** cabezudo

header /'hɛdər/ n caída de cabeza, f; salto de cabeza, m

headgear /'hɛd,gɪər/ n tocado, m; sombrero, gorro, m

head-hunting /'hɛd,hʌntɪŋ/ n la caza de cabezas, f

heading /'hɛdɪŋ/ n Naut. el poner la proa en dirección (a); el guiar en dirección (a); (of a book, etc.) título, encabezamiento, m; (soccer) golpe de cabeza, m. **to come under the h. of,** estar incluido entre; clasificarse bajo

headland /'hɛdlənd/ n cabo, promontorio, m
headless /'hɛdlɪs/ a sin cabeza
headlight /'hɛd,laɪt/ n Auto. faro, m; (Rail. Naut.) farol, m. **to dip the headlights,** bajar los faros. **to switch on the headlights,** encender los faros (or los faroles)
headline /'hɛd,laɪn/ n (of a newspaper) titular, m; (to a chapter) título de la columna, m
headlong /'hɛd,lɔŋ/ a precipitado; despeñado. —adv de cabeza; precipitadamente. **to fall h.,** caer de cabeza
headman /'hɛd'mæn/ n cacique, cabecilla, m; (foreman) capataz, contramaestre, m
headmaster /'hɛd'mæstər/ n director de colegio, rector, m
headmistress /'hɛd'mɪstrɪs/ n directora de colegio, rectora, f
head nurse enfermero-jefe, m
head-on collision /'hɛd ,ɒn/ n choque frontal, m
headphones /'hɛd,founz/ n pl auriculares, m pl
headquarters /'hɛd,kwɔrtərz/ n Mil. cuartel general, m; oficina central, f; jefatura, f; centro, m
headrest /'hɛd,rɛst/ n respaldo, m; apoyo para la cabeza, m
headstone /'hɛd,stoun/ n piedra mortuoria, f
headstrong /'hɛd,strɔŋ/ a impetuoso, terco, testarudo
headway /'hɛd,weɪ/ n marcha, f; Fig. progreso, avance, m. **to make h.,** avanzar; Fig. hacer progresos; Fig. prosperar
headwind /'hɛd,wɪnd/ n viento en contra, m
heady /'hɛdi/ a apasionado, violento; impetuoso, precipitado; (obstinate) terco; (of alcohol) encabezado; Fig. embriagador
heal /hil/ vt curar, sanar; (flesh) cicatrizar. —vi curar, sanar; cicatrizarse; (superficially) sobresanar
healable /'hiləbəl/ a curable
healer /'hilər/ n sanador (-ra), curador (-ra); curandero, m
healing /'hilɪŋ/ a curador, sanador; médico. —n curación, f; cura, f, remedio, m
health /hɛlθ/ n salud, f; higiene, sanidad, f. **Here's to your very good h.!** ¡Salud y pesetas! **He is in good h.,** Disfruta de buena salud. **to drink a person's h.,** beber a la salud de. **to enjoy good h.,** gozar de buena salud. **to look full of h.,** vender salud. **h.-giving,** saludable. **h. inspection,** visita de sanidad, f. **h. officer,** inspector de sanidad, m. **h. resort,** balneario, m
healthiness /'hɛlθɪnɪs/ n buena salud, f; sanidad, salubridad, f
healthy /'hɛlθi/ a sano; con buena salud; (healthful) saludable. **to be h.,** tener buena salud
heap /hip/ n montón, m; rima, pila, f, acervo, m; (of people) muchedumbre, f, tropel, m. —vt amontonar; apilar; colmar. **in heaps,** a montones. **We have heaps of time,** Nos sobra tiempo, Tenemos tiempo de sobra. **to h. together,** juntar, mezclar. **to h. up, upon,** colmar; amontonar; Agr. hacinar; Fig. acumular
hear /hɪər/ vt oír; (listen) escuchar; (attend) asistir a; (give audience) dar audiencia (a); (a lawsuit) ver (un pleito); (speak) hablar; (be aware of, feel) sentir. —vi oír; tener noticias; (learn) enterarse de; (allow) permitir. **H.! H.!** ¡Muy bien! ¡Bravo! **I have heard it said that...** He oído decir que... **Let me h. from you!** ¡Mándame noticias tuyas! **They were never heard of again,** No se volvió a saber de ellos, No se supo más de ellos. **to h. about,** oír de; (know) saber de, tener noticias de; recibir información sobre. **to h. from,** ser informado por; tener noticias de: recibir carta de. **to h. of,** enterarse de, saber; recibir información sobre; (allow) permitir
hearer /'hɪərər/ n oyente, mf
hearing /'hɪərɪŋ/ n (sense of) oído, m; alcance del oído, m; presencia, f; audición, f; Law. vista (de una causa) f. **It was said in my h.,** Fue dicho en mi presencia. **out of h.,** fuera del alcance del oído. **within h.,** al alcance del oído. **have a h. problem,** ser parcialmente sordo
hearing aid acústica, aparato auditivo, aparato acústico, audífono, m

hearsay /'hɪər,seɪ/ n fama, f, rumor, m. **by h.,** de oídas
hearse /hɜrs/ n coche fúnebre, m
heart /hɑrt/ n corazón, m; (feelings) entrañas, f pl; (of the earth, etc.) seno, corazón, m; (of lettuce, etc.) cogollo, repollo, m; (suit in cards) copas, f pl; Bot. médula, f; (soul) alma, f; (courage) valor, m; ánimo, m. **at h.,** en el fondo, esencialmente. **by h.,** de memoria. **from the h.,** con toda sinceridad, de todo corazón. **He is a man after my own h.,** Es un hombre de los que me gustan. **I have no h. to do it,** No tengo valor de hacerlo. **in the h. of the country,** en medio del campo. **to break one's h.,** partirse el corazón. **to have one's h. in one's mouth,** tener el alma en un hilo, estar muerto de miedo. **to have no h.,** Fig. no tener entrañas. **to lose h.,** desanimarse, descorazonarse. **to set one's h. on,** poner el corazón en. **to take h.,** cobrar ánimo; Inf. hacer de tripas corazón. **to take to h.,** tomar a pechos. **to wear one's h. on one's sleeve,** tener el corazón en la mano. **with all my h.,** con toda el alma. **h.-ache,** angustia, pena, f; **h.-beat,** latido del corazón, m. **h.-breaker,** (woman) coqueta, f; (man) ladrón de corazones, m. **h. disease,** enfermedad del corazón, enfermedad cardíaca, f. **h. failure,** colapso cardíaco, m. **h.-rending,** desgarrador, angustioso. **h.-searching,** examen de conciencia, m. **h.-shaped,** acorazonado, en forma de corazón. **h.-strings,** fibras del corazón, f pl. **h.-to-h. talk,** conversación íntima, f. **h.-whole,** libre de afectos
heartbreaking /'hɑrt,breɪkɪŋ/ a desgarrador, angustioso, doloroso, lastimoso
heartbroken /'hɑrt,broukən/ a acongojado, afligido, transido de dolor
heartburn /'hɑrt,bɜrn/ n acidez del estómago, acedia, pirosis, rescoldera, f
heartburning /'hɑrt,bɜrnɪŋ/ n rencor, m, animosidad, envidia, f
hearted /'hɑrtɪd/ a de corazón... que tiene el corazón... **kind-h.,** de buen corazón, bondadoso
hearten /'hɑrtn/ vt alentar, animar
heartfelt /'hɑrt,fɛlt/ a hondo; de todo corazón, sincero; más expresivo
hearth /hɑrθ/ n hogar, m; chimenea, f; Fig. hogar, m
heartily /'hɑrtli/ adv cordialmente; sinceramente; enérgicamente; con entusiasmo; (of eating) con buen apetito; (very) muy, completamente. **I am h. sick of it all,** Inf. Estoy harto hasta los dientes
heartiness /'hɑrtɪnɪs/ n cordialidad, f; sinceridad, f; energía, f, vigor, m; vehemencia, f; entusiasmo, m; (of appetite) buen diente, buen apetito, m
heartless /'hɑrtlɪs/ a sin corazón, sin piedad, despiadado, inhumano, cruel
heartlessness /'hɑrtlɪsnɪs/ n falta de corazón, inhumanidad, crueldad, f
hearty /'hɑrti/ a cordial; sincero; enérgico; vigoroso; robusto; (frank) campechano; (of appetite) voraz; bueno; (big) grande
heat /hit/ n calor, m; (in animals) celo, m; (of an action) calor, m; Fig. vehemencia, fogosidad, f; Fig. fuego, m; (passion) ardor, m, pasión, f; (of a race) carrera eliminatoria, f. —vt calentar; (excite) conmover, acalorar, excitar; (annoy) irritar. —vi calentarse; acalorarse; exaltarse. **dead h.,** empate, m. **in h.,** en celo. **in the h. of the moment,** en el calor del momento. **to become heated,** Fig. acalorarse, exaltarse. **white h.,** candencia, incandescencia, f. **h. lightning,** fucilazo, m. **h. spot,** pápula, f; terminación sensible, f. **h. stroke,** insolación, f. **h. wave,** onda de calor, f
heated /'hitɪd/ a calentado; caliente; excitado; apasionado
heatedly /'hitɪdli/ adv con vehemencia, con pasión
heater /'hitər/ n calentador, m; calorífero, m; (stove) estufa, f; (for plates) calientaplatos, m. **water-h.,** calentador de agua, m
heath /hiθ/ n brezal, m; yermo, páramo, m; Bot. brezo, m
heathen /'hiðən/ n pagano (-na); idólatra, mf; ateo (-ea), descreído (-da). —a pagano; ateo; bárbaro
heathenism /'hiðə,nɪzəm/ n paganismo, m; idolatría, f; ateísmo, m
heather /'hɛðər/ n brezo, m

heating /'hitɪŋ/ n calefacción, f, a calentador; (of drinks) fortificante. **central h.,** calefacción central, f
heave /hiv/ vt alzar, levantar; Naut. izar; (the anchor, etc.) virar; (throw) arrojar, lanzar; elevar; (extract) extraer; (emit) dar, exhalar. —vi subir y bajar; palpitar; agitarse. —n tirón, m; (of the sea) vaivén, m. **to h. in sight,** aparecer, surgir. **to h. out sail,** Naut. desenvergar. **to h. the lead,** Naut. escandallar. **to h. to,** Naut. estarse a la capa
heaven /'hɛvən/ n cielo, m; firmamento, m; paraíso, m. **Heavens!** ¡Cielos! ¡Por Dios! **Thank H.!** ¡Gracias a Dios! **h.-born,** celeste. **h.-sent,** Fig. providencial
heavenliness /'hɛvənlɪnɪs/ n carácter celestial, m; delicia, f
heavenly /'hɛvənli/ a celeste, celestial; divino; Fig. delicioso. **h. body,** astro, m
heavily /'hɛvəli/ adv pesadamente; torpemente; penosamente; (slowly) lentamente; severamente; excesivamente; (of sighing) hondamente; (sadly) tristemente; (of rain, etc.) reciamente, fuertemente; (of wind) con violencia. **He fell h.,** Cayó de plomo. **to lie h. upon,** pesar mucho sobre. **to rain h.,** llover mucho, diluviar
heaviness /'hɛvɪnɪs/ n peso, m; (lethargy) torpor, letargo, m; sueño, m, languidez, f; (clumsiness) torpeza, f; (severity) severidad, f; importancia, responsabilidad, f; dificultad, f; (gravity) gravedad, f; tristeza, melancolía, f; (boredom) sosería, insulsez, f; (of style) monotonía, ponderosidad, f
heaving /'hivɪŋ/ n levantamiento, m; (of the anchor, etc.) virada, f; (of the sea) vaivén, m; (of the breast) palpitación, f
heavy /'hɛvi/ a pesado; torpe; sin gracia; (slow) lento; (thick) grueso; (strong) fuerte; (hard) duro; grave; difícil; oneroso, responsable, importante; (oppresive) opresivo; penoso; grande; (sad) triste, melancólico; (of the sky) anublado; (of food) indigesto; (tedious) aburrido, soso; (pompous) pomposo; (of roads) malo; (of scents) fuerte, penetrante; (of sleep, weather) pesado; (weary) rendido; (charged with) cargado de; (of a meal) grande, abundante; (violent) violento; (of a cold, etc.) malo; (drowsy) soñoliento; (torpid) tórpido; (of rain, snow, hail) fuerte, recio; (of firing) intenso; (of soil) grasiento, profundo; (of soil) recio, de mucha miga; (Phys. Chem.) pesado. **to be h.,** pesar mucho. **How h. are you?** ¿Cuánto pesa Vd.? **h.-armed,** pesado; armado hasta los dientes. **h.-eyed,** con ojeras. **h. guns,** artillería pesada, f. **h.-handed,** de manos torpes; Fig. tiránico, opresivo. **h.-hearted,** triste, apesadumbrado. **h. industry,** la gran industria, la industria pesada, f. **h.-laden,** muy cargado. **h. losses,** Mil. pérdidas cuantiosas, f pl. **h.weight,** Sports. peso pesado, m
Hebraic /hɪ'breɪɪk/ a hebraico, hebreo, judaico
Hebraism /'hibrei,ɪzəm/ n judaísmo, hebraísmo, m
Hebraist /'hibreiɪst/ n hebraísta, m
Hebrew /'hibru/ n hebreo (-ea), judío (-ía): (language) hebreo, m
Hebrides, the /'hɛbrɪdiz/ las Hébridas
hecatomb /'hɛkə,toum/ n hecatombe, f
heckle /'hɛkəl/ vt Fig. interrumpir, importunar con preguntas
heckler /'hɛklər/ n perturbador (-ra)
heckling /'hɛklɪŋ/ n interrupción, f
hectare /'hɛktɛər/ n hectárea, f
hectic /'hɛktɪk/ a (consumptive) hético; (feverish) febril; Fig. Inf. agitado
hectogram /'hɛktə,græm/ n hectogramo, m
hectoliter /'hɛktə,litər/ n hectolitro, m
hector /'hɛktər/ vt intimidar, amenazar
hectoring /'hɛktərɪŋ/ a imperioso; amenazador
hectowatt /'hɛktə,wɑt/ n Elec. hectovatio, m
hedge /hɛdʒ/ n seto, m; barrera, f. —vt cercar con un seto; rodear. —vi Fig. titubear, vacilar. **h.-hopping,** Aer. vuelo a ras de tierra, m. **h.-sparrow,** acentor de bosque, m
hedgehog /'hɛdʒ,hɒg/ n erizo, m. **h. position,** Mil. puesto fuerte, m
hedonism /'hidn,ɪzəm/ n hedonismo, m
hedonist /'hidnɪst/ n hedonista, mf
heed /hid/ n atención, f, cuidado, m. —vt atender; observar, considerar; escuchar. —vi hacer caso

heedful /'hidfəl/ a atento; cuidadoso
heedless /'hidlɪs/ a desatento; descuidado, negligente; distraído
heedlessly /'hidlɪsli/ adv sin hacer caso; negligentemente; distraídamente
heedlessness /'hidlɪsnɪs/ n desatención, distracción, f; descuido, m; negligencia, f; inconsideración, f
heel /hil/ n Anat. talón, calcañar, m; (of shoe) tacón, m; (of a violin, etc., bow) talón, m; (remains) restos, m pl. —vt poner tacón a; poner talón a; Naut. hacer zozobrar. —vi Naut. zozobrar. **rubber h.,** tacón de goma, m. **She let him cool his heels for half an hour,** le dio un plantón de media hora. **to follow on a person's heels,** pisarle (a uno) los talones. **to be down at h.,** (of shoes) estar gastados los tacones; estar desaseado. **to take to one's heels,** apretar a correr, poner pies en polvorosa. **to turn on one's h.,** dar media vuelta. **h.-bone,** zancajo, m. **h.-piece,** talón, m
heeltap /'hil,tæp/ n tapa de tacón, f; escurridura, f
heft /hɛft/ vt sopesar, tomar al peso
hegemony /hɪ'dʒɛməni/ n hegemonía, f
heifer /'hɛfər/ n ternera, vaquilla, f
heigh /hei/ interj (calling attention) ¡oye! ¡oiga! **h. -ho!** ¡ay!
height /hait/ n altura, f; elevación, f; altitud, f; (stature) estatura, f; (high ground) cerro, m, colina, f; (sublimity) sublimidad, excelencia, f; colmo, m; (zenith) auge, m, cumbre, f
heighten /'haitn/ vt hacer más alto; (enhance) realzar; (exaggerate) exagerar; (perfect) perfeccionar; (intensify) intensificar
heightening /'haitnɪŋ/ n elevación, f; (enhancement) realce, m; (exaggeration) exageración, f; (perfection) perfección, f; (intensification) intensificación, f
heinous /'heinəs/ a atroz, nefando, horrible.
heinousness /'heinəsnɪs/ n atrocidad, enormidad, f
heir /ɛər/ n heredero, m. **h. apparent,** heredero aparente, m. **h.-at-law,** heredero forzoso, m. **h. presumptive,** presunto heredero, m
heiress /'ɛərɪs/ n heredera, f
heirloom /'ɛər,lum/ n reliquia de familia, f; Fig. herencia, f
helicopter /'hɛlɪ,kɒptər/ n helicóptero, m
helium /'hiliəm/ n Chem. helio, m
helix /'hilɪks/ n Geom. hélice, m; (Archit. Geom.) espira, f
hell /hɛl/ n infierno, m. **h.-fire,** fuego del infierno, m, llamas del infierno, f pl
Hellenic /hɛ'lɛnɪk/ a helénico
Hellenism /'hɛlə,nɪzəm/ n helenismo, m
Hellenist /'hɛlənɪst/ n helenista, mf
Hellenistic /,hɛlə'nɪstɪk/ a helenístico
Hellenize /'hɛlə,naiz/ vt helenizar
hellish /'hɛlɪʃ/ a infernal; Inf. horrible, detestable
hello /hɛ'lou/ interj ¡hola!; (on telephoning someone) ¡oiga! ¡alo!; (answering telephone) ¡diga! ¡alo!
helm /hɛlm/ n caña del timón, f; timón, gobernalle, m. **to obey the h.,** obedecer el timón. **to take the h.,** gobernar el timón; ponerse a pilotar
helmet /'hɛlmɪt/ n casco, m; (in olden days) yelmo, capacete, m; (sun) casco colonial, m
helminthic /hɛl'mɪnθɪk/ a helmíntico, vermífugo
helmsman /'hɛlmzmən/ n timonero, m
help /hɛlp/ n ayuda, f; auxilio, socorro, m; (protection) favor, m, protección, f; (remedy) remedio, m; (cooperation) cooperación, f, concurso, m; (domestic) criada, f. **A little h. is worth a lot of sympathy,** Más vale un toma que dos te daré. **There's no h. for it,** No hay más remedio. **to call for h.,** pedir socorro a gritos. **without h.,** a solas, sin la ayuda de nadie
help /hɛlp/ vt ayudar; socorrer, auxiliar; (favor) favorecer; (mitigate) aliviar; (contribute to) contribuir a, facilitar; (avoid) evitar. —vi ayudar. **He cannot h. worrying,** No puede menos de preocuparse. **God h. you!** ¡Dios te ampare! **So h. me God!** ¡Así Dios me salve! **to h. one another,** ayudarse mutuamente, ayudarse los unos a los otros. **to h. oneself,** (to food) servirse. **to h. down, off,** ayudar a bajar; ayudar a apearse. **to h. in,** ayudar a entrar. **to h. along, forward, on,** avanzar, fomentar, promover; contribuir a. **Shall I h. you on with the dress?** ¿Quieres que te

ayude a ponerte el vestido? **to h. out,** ayudar a salir; (from a vehicle) ayudar a bajar; (of a difficulty, etc.) sacar; suplir la falta de; ayudar. **to h. over,** ayudar a cruzar; (a difficulty) ayudar a salir (de un apuro); ayudar a vencer (un obstáculo, etc.); (a period) ayudar a pasar. **to h. to,** contribuir a, ayudar en; (food) servir. **to h. up,** ayudar a subir; ayudar a levantarse, levantar

helper /'hɛlpər/ *n* auxiliador (-ra); asistente (-ta); (protector) favorecedor (-ra); bienhechor (-ra); (colleague) colega, *m;* (co-worker) colaborador (-ra). **He thanked all his helpers,** Dio las gracias a todos los que le habían ayudado

helpful /'hɛlpfəl/ *a* útil, provechoso; (obliging) servicial, atento; (favorable) favorable; (healthy) saludable

helpfulness /'hɛlpfəlnɪs/ *n* utilidad, *f;* bondad, *f*

helping /'hɛlpɪŋ/ *n* ayuda, *f;* (of food) porción, ración, *f,* plato, *m.* **Won't you have a second h.?** ¿No quiere usted servirse más (or otra vez)? ¿No quiere usted repetir? **to lend a h. hand (to),** prestar ayuda (a)

helpless /'hɛlplɪs/ *a* desamparado, abandonado; (through infirmity) imposibilitado; impotente, sin fuerzas (para); (shiftless) incompetente, inútil

helplessness /'hɛlplɪsnɪs/ *n* desamparo, *m;* invalidez, debilidad, *f;* impotencia, *f;* incompetencia, *f*

helpmeet /'hɛlp,mit/ *n* compañero (-ra) perfecto (-ta); esposa, *f*

helter-skelter /'hɛltər 'skɛltər/ *adv* atropelladamente; en desorden. —*n* barahunda, *f*

hem /hɛm/ *n* Sew. dobladillo, filete, *m,* bastilla, *f;* (edge) orilla, *f.* —*interj* ¡ejem! —*vt* hacer dobladillo en, dobladillar. —*vi* (cough) fingir toser. **false hem,** Sew. dobladillo falso, *m.* **running hem,** Sew. jareta, *f.* **to hem and haw,** tartamudear; vacilar. **to hem in,** cercar, sitiar

hemisphere /'hɛmɪ,sfɪər/ *n* hemisferio, *m*

hemispherical /,hɛmɪ'sfɛrɪkəl/ *a* hemisférico, semiesférico

hemlock /'hɛm,lɒk/ *n* Bot. cicuta, *f*

hemoglobin /'himə,gloubɪn/ *n* Chem. hemoglobina, *f*

hemophilia /,himə'fɪliə/ *n* Med. hemofilia, *f*

hemorrhage /'hɛmərɪdʒ/ *n* hemorragia, *f,* flujo de sangre, *m*

hemorrhoids /'hɛmə,rɔɪdz/ *n pl* Med. hemorroides, *f*

hemp /hɛmp/ *n* cáñamo, *m.* **h. cloth,** lienzo, *m.* **h.-seed,** cañamón, *m*

hemstitch /'hɛm,stɪtʃ/ *n* vainica, *f.* —*vt* hacer vainica en

hen /hɛn/ *n* gallina, *f;* (female bird) hembra, *f.* **the hen pheasant,** la hembra del faisán. **hen bird,** pájara, *f.* **hen-coop** or **house,** gallinero, *m.* **hen party,** Inf. reunión de mujeres, *f.* **hen-roost,** nidal, *m.* ponedero, *m*

hence /hɛns/ *adv* (of place) de aquí; (of time) de ahora, de aquí a, al cabo de, en; (therefore) por eso, por lo tanto, por consiguiente. —*interj* ¡fuera! ¡fuera de aquí! **I shall come to see you a month h.,** Vendré a verte en un mes (or al cabo de un mes). **ten years h.,** de aquí a diez años. **h. the fact that...,** de aquí que.... **H. it happens that...,** Por eso sucede que...

henceforth /,hɛns'fɔrθ/ *adv* desde aquí en adelante, de hoy en adelante

henchman /'hɛntʃmən/ *n* escudero, *m;* satélite, secuaz, *m*

henna /'hɛnə/ *n* alheña, *f*

henpecked /'hɛn,pɛkt/ *a* gobernado por su mujer, que se deja mandar por su mujer

her /hɜr/ *unstressed* hər, ər/ *pers pron direct object* la; (with prepositions) ella. —*pers pron indirect object* le, a ella. —*poss a* su, *mf;* sus, *mf pl,* de ella. **I saw her on Wednesday,** La vi el miércoles. **The message is for her,** El recado es para ella. **It is her book,** Es su libro, Es el libro de ella

herald /'hɛrəld/ *n* heraldo, *m;* presagio, anuncio, *m.* —*vt* proclamar, anunciar, presagiar

heraldic /hɛ'rældɪk/ *a* heráldico

heraldry /'hɛrəldri/ *n* heráldica, *f*

herb /ɜrb/ *esp. Brit.* hɜrb/ *n* hierba, *f*

herbaceous /hɜr'beɪʃəs, ɜr-/ *a* herbáceo

herbage /'ɜrbɪdʒ, 'hɜr-/ *n* herbaje, *m;* pasto, *m*

herbal /'ɜrbəl, 'hɜr-/ *a* herbario. —*n* herbolaria, *f*

herbalist /'hɜrbəlɪst, 'ɜr-/ *n* herbario, *m,* simplista, *mf*

herbarium /hɜr'bɛəriəm, ɜr-/ *n* herbario, *m*

herbivorous /hɜr'bɪvərəs, ɜr-/ *a* herbívoro

herby /'ɜrbi, 'hɜr-/ *a* herbáceo

Herculean /,hɜrkyə'liən/ *a* hercúleo

herd /hɜrd/ *n* manada, *f;* (of cattle) hato, *m;* (race) raza, *f;* (Fig. contemptuous) populacho, *m,* masa, *f.* —*vt* reunir en manadas; reunir en hatos; (sheep) reunir en rebaños; guiar las manadas, etc. —*vi* ir en manadas, hatos o rebaños; asociarse, reunirse. **h. instinct,** instinto gregario, *m;* instinto de las masas, *m*

herdsman /'hɜrdzmən/ *n* ganadero, pastor, manadero, *m;* (head herdsman) rabadán, *m*

here /hɪər/ *adv* aquí; (at roll-call) ¡presente!; acá; an este punto; ahora. —*n* presente, *m.* **And h. he looked at me,** Y a este punto me miró. **Come h.!** ¡Ven acá! **in h.,** aquí dentro. **h. below,** aquí abajo, en la tierra. **h. and there,** aquí y allá. **h., there and everywhere,** en todas partes. **H. I am,** Heme aquí. **h. is...,** he aquí.... **H. they are,** Aquí los tienes, Aquí están. **Here's to you!** (on drinking) ¡Salud y pesetas! ¡A tu salud!

hereabouts /'hɪərə,bauts/ *adv* por aquí cerca

hereafter /hɪər'æftər/ *adv* en lo futuro; desde ahora; en adelante. —*n* futuro, *m.* **the H.,** la otra vida

hereat /hɪər'æt/ *adv* en esto

hereby /hɪər'baɪ/ *adv* por esto, por las presentes

hereditarily /hə,rɛdɪ'tɛrəli/ *adv* hereditariamente, por herencia

hereditary /hə'rɛdɪ,tɛri/ *a* hereditario

heredity /hə'rɛdɪti/ *n* herencia, *f*

herein /hɪər'ɪn/ *adv* en esto; aquí dentro; incluso

hereinafter /,hɪərɪn'æftər/ *adv* después, más abajo, más adelante, en adelante, en lo sucesivo

hereinbefore /,hɪərɪnbɪ'fɔr/ *adv* en la anterior, en lo arriba citado, en lo antes mencionado, en lo precedente

hereof /hɪər'ʌv/ *adv* de esto

heresy /'hɛrəsi/ *n* herejía, *f*

heretic /'hɛrɪtɪk/ *n* hereje, *mf*

heretical /hə'rɛtɪkəl/ *a* herético

hereunder /hɪər'ʌndər/ *adv* abajo

hereupon /,hɪərə'pɒn/ *adv* en esto, en seguida

herewith /hɪər'wɪθ/ *adv* junto con esto, con esto; ahora, en esta ocasión

heritage /'hɛrɪtɪdʒ/ *n* herencia, *f*

hermaphrodite /hɜr'mæfrə,daɪt/ *a and n* hermafrodita, *mf*

hermetic /hɜr'mɛtɪk/ *a* hermético

hermit /'hɜrmɪt/ *n* ermitaño, *m.* **h. crab,** paguro, cangrejo ermitaño, *m*

hernia /'hɜrniə/ *n* hernia, *f*

hero /'hɪərou/ *n* héroe, *m.* **h.-worship,** culto a los héroes, *m*

heroic /hɪ'rouɪk/ *a* heroico, épico

heroin /'hɛrouɪn/ *n* Chem. heroína, *f*

heroine /'hɛrouɪn/ *n* heroína, *f*

heroism /'hɛrou,ɪzəm/ *n* heroísmo, *m*

heron /'hɛrən/ *n* garza, *f*

herpes /'hɜrpiz/ *n pl* herpes, *mf pl*

herring /'hɛrɪŋ/ *n* arenque, *m*

hers /hɜrz/ *poss pron 3rd sing* (el) suyo, *m;* (la) suya, *f;* (los) suyos, *m pl;* (las) suyas, *f pl;* de ella. **This book is h.,** Este libro es suyo, Este libro es de ella. **This book is h., not mine,** Este libro es el suyo no el mío. **a sister of h.,** una de sus hermanas, una hermana suya

herself /hər'sɛlf/ *pron* sí misma, sí; ella misma; (with reflexive verb) se. **She has done it by h.,** Lo ha hecho por sí misma. **She h. told me so,** Ella misma me lo dijo. **She is by h.,** Está a solas, Está sola

hesitancy /'hɛzɪtənsi/ *n.* See **hesitation**

hesitant /'hɛzɪtənt/ *a* indeciso, vacilante, irresoluto. **to be h.,** mostrarse irresoluto

hesitate /'hɛzɪ,teit/ *vi* vacilar, dudar; titubear. **I do not h. to say...,** No vacilo en decir... **He hesitated over his reply,** Tardaba en dar su respuesta

hesitatingly /'hɛzɪ,teitɪŋli/ *adv* irresolutamente; titubeando

hesitation /,hɛzɪ'teiʃən/ *n* vacilación, hesitación, *f;*

irresolución, indecisión, *f;* (reluctance) aversión, repugnancia, *f;* titubeo, *m*

heterodox /'hetərə,dɒks/ *a* heterodoxo

heterodoxy /'hetərə,dɒksi/ *n* heterodoxia, *f*

heterogeneity /,hetəroudʒə'niiti/ *n* heterogeneidad, *f*

heterogeneous /,hetərə'dʒiniəs/ *a* heterogéneo

hew /hyu/ *vt* cortar, tajar; (trees) talar; (a career, etc.) hacerse

hewer /'hyuər/ *n* partidor, talador, *m*

hexagon /'heksə,gɒn/ *n* hexágono, *m*

hey /hei/ *interj* ¡he! ¡oye!

heyday /'hei,dei/ *n* apogeo, colmo, *m;* buenos tiempos, *m pl;* reinado, *m;* pleno vigor, *m*

hi /hai/ *interj* ¡oye! ¡hola!

hiatus /hai'eitəs/ *n* hiato, *m;* laguna, *f,* vacío, *m*

hibernate /'haibər,neit/ *vi* invernar

hibernation /,haibər'neiʃən/ *n* invernada, *f*

hibiscus /hai'biskəs/ *n Bot.* hibisco, *m*

hiccup /'hikʌp/ *n* hipo, *m.* —*vi* hipar. —*vt* decir con hipo

hidden /'hidn/ *a* escondido, secreto, oculto

hide /haid/ *n* piel, *f;* pellejo, cuero, *m*

hide /haid/ *vt* esconder, ocultar; (cover) cubrir, tapar; (dissemble) disimular; (meaning) obscurecer. —*vi* esconderse; ocultarse; refugiarse. **to h. from each other,** esconderse el uno del otro. **h.-and-seek,** escondite, dormirlas, *m*

hidebound /'haid,baund/ *a Fig.* muy conservador, reaccionario, de ideas muy tradicionales

hideous /'hidiəs/ *a* horrible, repulsivo, horroroso; repugnante, odioso

hideously /'hidiəsli/ *adv* horriblemente. **to be h. ugly,** (of people) ser más feo que Picio

hideousness /'hidiəsnis/ *n* fealdad, horribilidad, *f;* repugnancia, *f*

hiding /'haidiŋ/ *n* ocultación, *f;* encubrimiento, *m;* refugio, *m; Inf.* paliza, tunda, *f.* **h.-place,** escondite, escondrijo, *m*

hie /hai/ *vi* apresurarse, ir a prisa

hierarch /'haiə,rɑrk/ *n* jerarca, *m*

hierarchical /,haiə'rɑrkikəl/ *a* jerárquico

hierarchy /'haiə,rɑrki/ *n* jerarquía, *f*

hieroglyph /'haiərə,glif/ *n* jeroglífico, *m*

higgledy-piggledy /'higəldi 'pigəldi/ *adv* revueltamente, en confusión; en montón, en desorden

high /hai/ *a* alto; elevado; (with altar, Mass, street, festival) mayor; grande; eminente; aristocrático; (of shooting) fijante; (of quality) superior; excelente; (haughty) orgulloso; (solemn) solemne; (good) bueno; noble; supremo; sumo; (of price) subido; *Mus.* agudo; (of the sea) tempestuoso, borrascoso; (of wind and explosives) violento, fuerte; (of polish) brillante; (with speed) grande; (with tension, frequency) alto; (with number, etc.) importante, grande; (with colors) subido; (of food) pasado; (angry) enojado, airado; (of cheek bones) saliente, prominente; (well-seasoned) picante; (flattering) lisonjero. —*adv* alto; hacia altura; arriba; (deeply) profundamente; fuertemente; con violencia; (of price) a un precio elevado; (luxuriously) lujosamente; *Mus.* agudo. **a room 12 ft. h.,** un cuarto de doce pies de altura. **I knew her when she was so h.,** La conocí tamaña. **It is h. time he came,** Ya es hora de que viniese. **on h.,** en alto, arriba; en los cielos. **h. altar,** altar mayor, *m.* **h. and dry,** en la playa, varado; *Fig.* en seco. **h. and low,** de arriba abajo; por todas partes. **h.-born,** aristocrático, de alta alcurnia. **h.-bred,** (of people) de buena familia; (of animals) de buena raza. **h.-class,** de buena clase; de alta calidad. **h. collar,** alzacuello, *m.* **h. colored,** de colores vivos; *Fig.* exagerado. **h. command,** (*Mil. Nav.*) alto mando, *m.* **h. court,** tribunal supremo, *m.* **h. day,** día festivo, *m.* **h. explosive,** explosivo violento, *m.* **h.-flown,** hinchado, retumbante, altisonante. **h. frequency,** alta frecuencia, *f.* **h.-handed,** arbitrario, dominador, despótico. **h.-heeled,** *a* de tacón alto. **h. jump,** salto de altura, *m.* **h. land,** tierras altas, *f pl;* eminencia, *f.* **h. light,** *Art.* realce, *m;* acontecimiento de más interés, *m;* momento culminante, *m.* **h. mass,** misa mayor, *f.* **h.-minded,** de nobles pensamientos; arrogante. **h.-necked,** con cuello alto. **h.-pitched,** de tono alto, agudo. **h.-powered,** de alta potencia. **h.-powered car,** coche de

muchos caballos, *m.* **h. precision,** suma precisión, *f.* **h. pressure,** *n* alta presión, *f; Fig.* urgencia, *f; n* de alta presión, *Fig.* urgente. **h.-priced,** caro. **h. priest,** sumo pontífice, sumo sacerdote, alto sacerdote, *m.* **h. relief,** alto relieve, *m.* **h. road,** carretera mayor, *f.* **h. school,** instituto de segunda enseñanza, instituto, colegio, liceo, *m;* colegio, liceo, instituto, *m,* escuela secundaria, secundaria, *f.* **h. sea,** marejada, *f.* **h. seas,** alta mar, *f.* **h.-seasoned,** picante. **h. society,** alta sociedad, *f.* **h.-sounding,** altisonante, bombástico. **h.-speed,** de alta velocidad. **h.-spirited,** brioso; alegre. **h.-strung,** nervioso, excitable, sensitivo. **h. tension,** alta tensión, *f.* **h. tide,** marea alta, *f.* **h.-toned,** *Mus.* agudo; *Inf.* de alto copete; aristocrático. **h. treason,** alta traición, *f.* **h. water,** marea alta, pleamar, *f.* **h.-water mark,** límite de la marea, *m; Fig.* colmo, *m;* apogeo, *m*

highbrow /'hai,brau/ *a* and *n* intelectual, *mf*

high-ceilinged /'hai 'siliŋd/ *a* alto de techo

higher /'haiər/ *a* compar of **high,** más alto; más elevado; superior. **on a h. plane,** en un nivel más alto. **h. education,** enseñanza superior, *f.* **h. mathematics,** la alta matemática, *f.* **h. criticism,** la alta crítica, *f.* **h. up,** más arriba. **h. up the river,** río arriba

highest /'haiist/ *a superl* of **high,** el más alto; la más alta; los más altos; las más altas; sumo, supremo; excelente. **h. common factor,** *Math.* máximo común divisor, *m.* **h. references,** (of cook, gardener, etc.) informes inmejorables, *m pl; Com.* referencias excelentes, *f pl*

highland /'hailənd/ *n* altiplanicie, *f;* montañas, *f pl,* distrito montañoso, *m.* —*a* montañoso

highlander /'hailəndər/ *n* montañés (-esa); esocés (-esa) del norte

highlight /'hai,lait/ *vt* dar relieve a, destacar

highly /'haili/ *adv* altamente; mucho; muy; extremadamente; grandemente; bien; favorablemente; con lisonja, lisonjeramente. **h. seasoned,** picante. **h. strung,** nervioso, excitable

highness /'hainis/ *n* altura, *f;* elevación, *f;* excelencia, *f;* nobleza, *f;* (title) Alteza, *f.* **His Royal H., Her Royal Highness,** Su Alteza Real

high-ranking /'hai 'ræŋkiŋ/ *a* de alta jerarquía, de alto rango

highway /'hai,wei/ *n* camino real, *m,* carretera, *f.* **h. code,** código de la vía pública (or de la circulación), *m.* **h. robbery,** salteamiento de caminos, atraco, *m*

highwayman /'hai,weimən/ *n* salteador de caminos, *m*

highways and byways /'hai,weiz ən 'bai,weiz/ caminos y veredas

hike /haik/ *vi* ir de excursión. —*n* marcha con equipo, *f*

hiker /'haikər/ *n* excursionista, *mf*

hiking /'haikiŋ/ *n* excursionismo, *m;* marcha con equipo, *f*

hilarious /hi'leəriəs/ *a* alegre

hilarity /hi'læriti/ *n* hilaridad, *f*

hill /hil/ *n* colina, *f,* cerro, otero, *m;* monte, *m,* montaña, *f;* (pile) montón, *f.* **h.-side,** falda de montaña, ladera de una colina, *f.* **h.-top,** cumbre de una colina, *f*

hilliness /'hilinis/ *n* montuosidad, *f,* lo montañoso

hillman /'hil,mæn/ *n* montañés, *m*

hillock /'hilək/ *n* altozano, montículo, collado, *m*

hilly /'hili/ *a* montañoso

hilt /hilt/ *n* puño, *m,* empuñadura, *f*

him /him/ *pron 3rd sing direct object* le, lo; (with prep.) él; *indirect object* le, a él; (with a direct obj. in 3rd person) se. **I gave him the magazine,** Le di la revista. **I gave it to him,** Se lo di a él. **This is for him,** Esto es para él

Himalayan /,himə'leiən/ *a* himalayo

Himalayas, the /,himə'leiəz/ los Himalayas, *m pl*

himself /him'self/ *pron* sí, sí mismo; él mismo; (reflexive) se. **He did it by h.,** Lo hizo por sí mismo. For more examples see **herself**

hind /haind/ *n* corza, cierva, *f.* —*a* trasero, posterior. **h.-quarters,** cuarto trasero, *m;* (of a horse) ancas, *f pl*

hinder /'hindər/ *a* trasero, posterior

hinder /'hindər/ *vt* impedir, estorbar; embarazar, dificultar; interrumpir. —*vi* ser un obstáculo; formar un obstáculo

hinderer /'hɪndərər/ *n* estorbador (-ra); interruptor (-ra)

hindmost /'haind,moust/ *a* posterior, postrero, último

hindrance /'hɪndrəns/ *n* obstáculo, estorbo, impedimento, *m*; perjuicio, *m*; interrupción, *f*

Hindu /'hɪndu/ *a* hindú, *mf*

Hinduism /'hɪndu,ɪzəm/ *n* indoísmo, *m*

Hindustani /,hɪndu'stɑni/ *a* indostanés. —*n* (language) indostani, *m*

hinge /hɪndʒ/ *n* gozne, pernio, *m*, bisagra, *f*; articulación, *f*; *Fig.* eje, *m*. —*vi* moverse (or abrirse) sobre goznes; *Fig.* depender (de). —*vt* engoznar

hinged /hɪndʒd/ *a* con goznes

hint /hɪnt/ *n* indirecta, insinuación, sugestión, *f*; (advice) consejo, *m*. —*vt* dar a entender, decir con medias palabras, insinuar, sugerir. —*vi* insinuar. **to take the h.,** darse por aludido

hinterland /'hɪntər,lænd/ *n* interior (de un país), *m*

hip /hɪp/ *n* *Anat.* cadera, *f*; *Bot.* fruto del rosal silvestre, *m*. **h.-bath,** baño de asiento, *m*. **h.-bone,** hueso ilíaco, *m*. **h.-joint,** articulación de la cadera, *f*. **h.-pocket,** faltriquera, *f*

hipped /hɪpt/ *a* de caderas

hippodrome /'hɪpə,droum/ *n* hipódromo, *m*

hippopotamus /,hɪpə'pɒtəməs/ *n* hipopótamo, *m*

hire /haɪᵊr/ *n* alquiler, arriendo, *m*; salario, *m*. —*vt* alquilar, arrendar; tomar en arriendo; (person) contratar; tomar a su servicio. **to h. out,** alquilar. **for** or **on h.,** de alquiler. **h.-purchase,** compra a plazos, *f*

hireling /'haɪᵊrlɪŋ/ *n* mercenario, *m*

hirer /'haɪᵊrər/ *n* alquilador (-ra), arrendador (-ra)

hirsute /'hɜrsut/ *a* hirsuto. **non-h.** *Bot.* lampiño

his /hɪz/ *unstressed* ɪz/ *poss pron 3rd sing* (el) suyo, *m*; (la) suya, *f*; (los) suyos, *m pl*; (las) suyas, *f pl*; de él. —*poss a* su, *mf*; sus, *mf pl*; de él. **his handkerchiefs,** sus pañuelos. **his mother,** su madre, la madre de él. **a sister of his,** una de sus hermanas, una hermana suya. See **hers** for more examples.

Hispanism /'hɪspə,nɪzəm/ *n* hispanismo, *m*

Hispanist /'hɪspənɪst/ *n* hispanista, *mf*

hispanize /'hɪspə,naɪz/ *vt* españolizar

Hispano-American /hɪs'pænou ə'merɪkən/ *a* hispano-americano

hiss /hɪs/ *n* silbido, *m*; (sputter) chisporroteo, *m*. —*vi* silbar

hissing /'hɪsɪŋ/ *n* silbido, *m*; chisporroteo, *m*. —*a* silbante

hist /hɪst/ *interj* ¡chist!

histologist /hɪs'tɒlədʒɪst/ *n* histólogo, *m*

histology /hɪ'stɒlədʒi/ *n* histología, *f*

historian /hɪ'stɔriən/ *n* historiador (-ra)

historic /hɪ'stɔrɪk/ *a* histórico

historical /hɪ'stɔrɪkəl/ *a* histórico. **h. truth,** verdad histórica, *f*

historically /hɪs'tɔrɪkəli/ *adv* históricamente

historiographer /hɪ,stɔri'ɒgrəfər/ *n* historiógrafo, *m*

historiography /hɪ,stɔri'ɒgrəfi/ *n* historiografía, *f*

history /'hɪstəri/ *n* historia, *f*. **Biblical h.,** historia sagrada, *f*. **natural h.,** historia natural, *f*

histrionic /,hɪstri'ɒnɪk/ *a* histriónico

hit /hɪt/ *n* golpe, *m*; *Aer.* impacto, *m*; (success) éxito, *m*; (piece of luck) buena suerte, *f*; (satire) sátira, *f*. —*vt* golpear; (buffet) abofetear, pegar; (find) dar con, tropezar con; (attain) acertar; (guess) adivinar; (attract) atraer; (deal) lanzar, dar; (wound) herir, hacer daño (a). **The sun hits me right in the eyes,** El sol me da en la cabeza. **direct hit,** *Aer.* impacto de lleno, *m*. **lucky hit,** acierto, *m*. **to hit a straight left,** (boxing) lanzar un directo con la izquierda. **to hit the mark,** dar en el blanco; *Fig.* dar en el clavo. **hit or miss,** acierto o error. **to hit against,** dar contra, estrellar contra. **to hit back,** defenderse; devolver golpe por golpe. **to hit off,** imitar; (a likeness) coger. **to hit out,** abofetear; *Fig.* atacar; golpear (la pelota) fuera. **to hit upon,** dar con; tropezar con; encontrar por casualidad; (remember) acordarse de

hitch /hɪtʃ/ *n* (jerk) sacudida, *f*; nudo fácil de soltar, *m*; *Fig.* obstáculo, *m*; *Fig.* dificultad, *f*. **give s.b. a hitch,** levantar a fulano. —*vt* sacudir; (a chair, etc.)

arrastrar, empujar; amarrar, enganchar; atar. —*vi* (along a seat, etc.) correrse (en); (get entangled) enredarse, cogerse; (rub) rascarse. **without a h.,** sin dificultad alguna, viento en popa; (smoothly) a pedir de boca. **to h. up,** sacudir, dar una sacudida (a)

hitchhike /'hɪtʃ,haik/ *vi* ir a dedo (Argentina), pedir aventón (Mexico), pedir botella (Cuba), hacer autostop, ir por autostop (Spain)

hither /'hɪðər/ *adv* acá, hacia acá; *a* citerior, más cercano. **h. and thither,** acá y aculla allá

hitherto /'hɪðər,tu/ *adv* hasta ahora, hasta el presente

Hitlerian /hɪt'lɪəriən/ *a* hitleriano, nacista

Hitlerism /'hɪtlə,rɪzəm/ *n* hitlerismo, nacismo, *m*

Hittite /'hɪtait/ *a* and *n* heteo (-ea)

hive /haiv/ *n* (for bees) colmena, *f*; (swarm) enjambre, *m*; *Fig.* centro, *m*. —*vt* (bees) enjambrar. **h. of industry,** centro de industria

hoard /hɔrd/ *n* acumulación, *f*; provisión, *f*; tesoro, *m*. —*vt* acumular, amasar, amontonar; guardar

hoarder /'hɔrdər/ *n* acaparador (-ra)

hoarding /'hɔrdɪŋ/ *n* amontonamiento, *m*; acaparamiento, *m*; (fence) empalizada, cerca, *f*; palizada de tablas, *f*

hoarfrost /'hɔr,frɔst/ *n* escarcha, helada blanca, *f*

hoariness /'hɔrinɪs/ *n* (of the hair) canicie, *f*; blancura, *f*; (antiquity) vejez, vetustez, *f*

hoarse /hɔrs/ *a* ronco; discordante. **to be h.,** tener la voz ronca. **to grow h.,** enronquecerse

hoarsely /'hɔrsli/ *adv* roncamente

hoarseness /'hɔrsnɪs/ *n* ronquera, *f*; *Inf.* carraspera, *f*

hoary /'hɔri/ *a* (of the hair) canoso; blanco; (old) vetusto, antiguo, viejo

hoax /houks/ *n* estafa, *f*, engaño, *m*; broma pesada, *f*; burla, *f*. —*vt* estafar, engañar; burlar

hoaxer /'houksər/ *n* burlador (-ra); estafador (-ra)

hob /hɒb/ *n* repisa interior del hogar, *f*

hobble /'hɒbəl/ *n* (gait) cojera, *f*; traba, maniota, *f*. —*vi* cojear. —*vt* manear. **h. skirt,** falda muy estrecha, *f*

hobby /'hɒbi/ *n* pasatiempo, *m*, recreación, *f*; manía, afición, *f*. **h.-horse,** caballo de cartón, *m*; *Fig.* caballo de batalla, *m*

hobgoblin /'hɒb,gɒblɪn/ *n* trasgo, duende, *m*

hobnail /'hɒb,neil/ *n* clavo de herradura, clavo de botas, *m*

hobnailed /'hɒb,neild/ *a* (of boots) con clavos

hobnob /'hɒb,nɒb/ *vi* codearse, tratar con familiaridad

hock /hɒk/ *n* *Anat.* pernil, *m*; (wine) vino del Rin, *m*

hockey /'hɒki/ *n* chueca, *m*. **h. ball,** bola, pelota de chueca, *f*. **h. stick,** bastón de chueca, *m*

hocus-pocus /'houkəs 'poukəs/ *n* juego de pasa pasa, *m*; engaño, *m*, treta, *f*

hod /hɒd/ *n* cuezo, *m*

hodgepodge /'hɒdʒ,pɒdʒ/ See **hotchpotch**

hoe /hou/ *n* azadón, *m*. —*vt* azadonar; sachar

hoeing /'houɪŋ/ *n* cavadura con azadón, *f*; sachadura, *f*

hoer /'houər/ *n* azadonero, *m*

hog /hɒg/ *n* cerdo, puerco, *m*. **to go the whole hog,** ir al extremo. **hogskin,** piel de cerdo, *f*

hoggish /'hɔgɪʃ/ *a* porcuno; (greedy) comilón, tragón; (selfish) egoísta

hoist /hɔist/ *n* levantamiento, *m*; (lift) montacargas, *m*; (winch) cabria, *f*; (crane) grúa, *f*. —*vt* levantar, alzar; (flags) enarbolar; suspender; *Naut.* izar

hoity-toity /'hɔiti 'tɔiti/ *a* picajoso, quisquilloso; presuntuoso

hold /hould/ *n* asimiento, agarro, *m*, presa, *f*; asidero, *m*; *Fig.* autoridad, *f*, poder, *m*; *Fig.* comprensión, *f*; (of a ship) cala, bodega, *f*. **to loose one's h.,** aflojar su presa. **to lose one's h.,** perder su presa. **to seize h. of,** asirse de, echar mano de. **h.-all,** funda, *f*. **h.-up,** (robbery) atraco, robo a mano armada, *m*; (in traffic) atasco (or obstáculo) en el tráfico, *m*; (in work) parada, paración (de trabajo), *f*

hold /hould/ *vt* tener; asir, agarrar; coger; retener; (embrace) abrazar; (a post) ocupar; (a meeting, etc.) celebrar; (bear weight of) aguantar, soportar; (own) poseer; *Mil.* ocupar, defender; (contain) contener; (have in store) reservar; tener capacidad para; (retain) retener; (believe) creer, sostener; (consider) opinar, tener para (mí, etc.); juzgar; (restrain) detener; contener; (of attention, etc.) mantener; (maneuvers) hacer; (observe) guardar. —*vi* resistir, aguantar; (be valid) ser válido; regir; (apply) aplicarse; (last) continuar, seguir. —*interj* ¡tente! ¡para! **The room won't h. more,** En este cuarto no caben más. **They h. him in great respect,** Le tienen mucho respeto. **The theory does not h. water,** La teoría es falsa, La teoría no es lógica. **to h. one's own,** defenderse, mantenerse en sus trece. **to h. one's breath,** contener la respiración. **to h. one's tongue,** callarse. **to h. sway,** mandar; reinar. **to h. tightly,** agarrar fuertemente; (clasp) estrechar. **H. the line!** (telephone) ¡Aguarde un momento! **to h. back,** *vt* detener; contener; retener; esconder; abstenerse de entregar. —*vi* quedarse atrás; vacilar, dudar; tardar en. **to h. by,** seguir; basarse en, apoyarse en. **to h. down,** sujetar; (oppress) oprimir. **to h. fast,** *vt* sujetar fuertemente. —*vi* mantenerse firme; *Fig.* estar agarrado (a). **to h. forth,** *vt* ofrecer; expresar. —*vi* hacer un discurso, perorar. **to h. in,** *vt* contener; retener. —*vi* contenerse. **to h. off,** *vt* apartar, alejar. —*vi* apartarse, alejarse, mantenerse alejado. **to h. on,** seguir, persistir en; aguantar. **to h. out,** *vt* alargar, extender; ofrecer. —*vi* aguantar; durar, resistir. **to h. over,** tener suspendido sobre; (postpone) aplazar; *Fig.* amenazar con. **to h. to,** agarrarse a; atenerse a. **to h. together,** *vt* unir; juntar. —*vi* mantenerse juntos. **to h. up,** *vt* (display) mostrar, enseñar; levantar; sostener, soportar; (rob) atracar, saltear; (delay) atrasar; (stop) interrumpir, parar. —*vi* mantenerse en pie; (of weather) seguir bueno. **The train has been held up by fog,** El tren viene con retraso a causa de la niebla

holder /'houldər/ *n* el m, (f, la) que tiene; poseedor (-ra); *Com.* tenedor (-ra); inquilino (-na); propietario (-ia); (support) soporte, m; mango, m; asa, f; (in compounds) porta...

holding /'houldɪŋ/ *n* tención, f; posesión, f; propiedad, f; (leasing) arrendamiento, m; (celebration) solemnización, f; (of a meeting) el celebrar, el tener; *pl* **holdings,** *Com.* valores habidos, m pl

holding company *n* compañía de cartera, f

hole /houl/ *n* hoyo, m; boquete, m; agujero, m; cavidad, f; (hollow) depresión, f, hueco, m; orificio, m; (tear) roto, desgarro, m; (eyelet) punto, m; (in cheese) ojo, m; (in stocking) rotura, f, punto, m; (lair) madriguera, f; (nest) nido, m; (golf) hoyo, m; (fix) aprieto, m. —*vt* agujerear; excavar; (bore) taladrar; *Sports.* meter la pelota (en). **to h. out,** (golf) meter la pelota en el hoyo. **h.-and-corner,** *a Inf.* bajo mano, secreto

hole-puncher /'houl ˌpʌntʃər/ *n* agujereadora, f

holiday /'hɒlɪˌdei/ *n* día feriado, m; día de fiesta, día festivo, m; vacación, f. —*a* festivo, alegre; de vacación; de excursión; (summer) veraniego. **day's h.,** día de asueto, m. **to take a h.,** tomar una vacación; hacer fiesta. **h. camp,** colonia veraniega, f. **h.-maker,** excursionista, turista, mf; (in the summer) veraneante, mf **holidays with pay,** vacaciones retribuidas, f pl

holiness /'houlinɪs/ *n* santidad, f

Holland /'hɒlənd/ Holanda, f

holland /'hɒlənd/ *n* lienzo crudo. —*a* holandés. **H. gin,** ginebra holandesa, f

hollow /'hɒlou/ *a* hueco; cóncavo; (empty) vacío; (of eyes, etc.) hundido; (of sound) sordo; (of a cough) cavernoso; (echoing) retumbante; (*Fig.* unreal) vacío, falso; insincero. —*adv* vacío, *Inf.* completamente. —*n* hueco, m; concavidad, f; (hole) hoyo, m; cavidad, f; (valley) hondanada, f, barranco, m; (groove) ranura, f; (depression) depresión, f; (in the back) curvadura, f. —*vt* excavar, ahuecar; vaciar. **h.-cheeked,** con las mejillas hundidas. **h.-eyed,** con los ojos hundidos, de ojos hundidos

hollowness /'hɒlounɪs/ *n* concavidad, f; (falseness) falsedad, f; insinceridad, f

holly /'hɒli/ *n* acebo, agrifolio, m

holocaust /'hɒləˌkɔst/ *n* holocausto, m

holograph /'hɒləˌgræf/ *n* hológrafo, m

holster /'houlstər/ *n* pistolera, f

holy /'houli/ *a* santo; sagrado; (blessed) bendito.

most h., *a* santísimo. **to make h.,** santificar. **H. Father,** Padre Santo, el Papa, m. **H. Ghost,** Espíritu Santo, m. **H. Office,** Santo Oficio, m, Inquisición, f. **H. Orders,** órdenes sagradas, f pl. **H. places,** santos lugares, m pl. **H. Scripture,** Sagrada Escritura, f. **H. See,** Cátedra de San Pedro, f. **h. water,** agua bendita, f. **H. Souls,** las Ánimas Benditas. **h. water stoup,** acetre, m. **H. Week,** Semana Santa, f

Holy Land, the la Tierra Santa, f

homage /'hɒmɪdʒ/ *n* homenaje, m; culto, m; reverencia, f. **to pay h.,** rendir homenaje

home /houm/ *n* casa, f; hogar, m; domicilio, m, residencia, f; (institution) asilo, m; (haven) refugio, m; (habitation) morada, f; (country of origin) país de origen, m; (native land) patria, f; (environment) ambiente natural, m; *Sports.* meta, f. —*a* casero, doméstico; nativo; nacional, del país; indígena. —*adv* a casa, hacia casa; (in one's country) en su patria; (returned) de vuelta; (of the feelings) al corazón, al alma; (to the limit) al límite. **at h.,** en casa; *Fig.* en su elemento; (of games) en campo propio; de recibo. **at-h. day,** día de recibo, m. **He shot the bolt h.,** Echó el cerrojo. **one's long h.,** su última morada. **to be at h.,** estar en casa; estar de recibo. **to be away from h.,** estar fuera de casa; estar ausente. **to bring h.,** traer (o llevar) a casa; hacer ver; convencer; llegar al alma; (a crime) probar (contra). **to go h.,** volver a casa; volver a la patria; (be effective) hacer su efecto; (move) herir en lo más vivo. **to make oneself at h.,** ponerse a sus anchas, sentirse como en casa de uno. **Please make yourself at home!** ¡Ha tomado posesión de su casa! **to strike h.,** dar en el blanco; herir; (hit) golpear; herir en lo más vivo; hacerse sentir. **h. affairs,** asuntos domésticos, m pl, (Ministry of) Gobernación, f. **h.-bred,** criado en el país. **h.-brewed,** fermentado en el país; fermentado en casa. **h.-coming,** regreso al hogar, m. **h. counties,** condados alrededor de Londres, m pl. **H. Defense,** defensa nacional, f. **h. farm,** residencia del propietario de una finca, f. **h. for the aged,** asilo de ancianos, m. **h. front,** frente doméstico, m. **H. Guard,** milicia nacional, f. **h. life,** vida de familia, f. **h.-made,** casero, de fabricación casera, hecho en casa. **H. Office,** Ministerio de Gobernación, m. **H. Rule,** autonomía, f. **H. Secretary,** Ministro de Gobernación, m. **h. stretch,** último trecho (de una carrera), m. **h. truth,** verdad, *Inf.* fresca, f. **to tell someone a few h. truths,** contarle cuatro verdades

homeless /'houmlɪs/ *a* sin casa; sin hogar. **the h.,** los sin techo

homeliness /'houmlinɪs/ *n* comodidad, f; sencillez, f; (ugliness) fealdad, f

homely /'houmli/ *a* doméstico; familiar; (unpretentious) sencillo; llano; (ugly) feo; desabrido

homemaker /'houmˌmeikər/ *n* ama de casa, f

homeopath /'houmiəˌpæθ/ *n* homeópata, mf

homeopathic /ˌhoumiəˈpæθɪk/ *a* homeópata

homeopathy /ˌhoumiˈɒpəθi/ *n* homeopatía, f

Homeric /houˈmɛrɪk/ *a* homérico

homesick /'houmˌsɪk/ *a* nostálgico. **to be h.,** tener morriña

homesickness /'houmˌsɪknɪs/ *n* nostalgia, añoranza, morriña, f

homespun /'houmˌspʌn/ *n* tejido en casa; hecho en casa; basto, grueso

homestead /'houmstɛd/ *n* hacienda, f; casa solariega, f; casa, f

homeward /'houmwərd/ *adv* hacia casa, en dirección al hogar; de vuelta; hacia la patria. **h.-bound,** en dirección a casa; (of ships) con rumbo al puerto de origen; (of other traffic) de vuelta

homicidal /ˌhɒməˈsaidl/ *a* homicida

homicide /'hɒməˌsaid/ *n* (act) homicidio, m; (person) homicida, mf

homily /'hɒməli/ *n* Eccl. homilía, f; sermón, m

homing pigeon /'houmɪŋ/ *n* palomo (-ma) mensajero (-ra)

homogeneity /ˌhoumədʒəˈniiti/ *n* homogeneidad, f

homogeneous /ˌhoumæˈdʒiniəs/ *a* homogéneo

homologous /həˈmɒləgəs/ *a* homólogo

homonym /'hɒmənɪm/ *n* homónimo, m

homonymous /həˈmɒnəməs/ *a* homónimo

homosexual /ˌhoumə'sɛkʃuəl/ *a and n* homosexual, *mf*

Honduran /hɒn'durən/ *a and n* hondureño (-ña)

hone /houn/ *n* piedra de afilar, *f.* —*vt* afilar, vaciar

honest /'ɒnɪst/ *a* honrado; decente, honesto; (chaste) casto; (loyal) sincero, leal; (frank) franco; imparcial. **an h. man**, un hombre de buena fe, un hombre honrado, un hombre decente

honesty /'ɒnəsti/ *n* honradez, *f;* honestidad, *f;* (chastity) castidad, *f;* sinceridad, *f;* rectitud, imparcialidad, *f*

honey /'hʌni/ *n* miel, *f.* **h.-bee,** abeja obrera, *f.* **h.-colored,** melado. **h.-pot,** jarro de miel, *m.* **h.-tongued,** melifluo; de pico de oro

honeycomb /'hʌni,koum/ *n* panal, *m*

honeycombed /'hʌni,koumd/ *a* apanalado

honeydew /'hʌni,du/ *n* mielada, *f; Fig.* ambrosia, *f*

honeyed /'hʌnid/ *a* de miel; *Fig.* meloso, adulador

honeymoon /'hʌni,mun/ *n* luna de miel, *f;* viaje de novios, viaje nupcial, *m.* —*vi* hacer un viaje nupcial

honeysuckle /'hʌni,sʌkəl/ *n* madreselva, *f*

honor /'ɒnər/ *n* honor, *m;* honra, *f;* honradez, rectitud, integridad, *f; pl* **honors,** honores, *m pl;* condecoraciones, *f pl;* (last h.) honras, pompas fúnebres, *f pl.* —*vt* honrar; (God) glorificar; (decorate) condecorar, laurear; (respect) respetar; reverenciar; *Com.* aceptar; (a toast) beber. **On my h.,** A fe mía. **point of h.,** punto de honor, pundonor, *m.* **word of h.,** palabra de honor, *f.* **Your H.,** (to a judge) Excelentísimo Señor Juez

honorable /'ɒnərəbəl/ *a* honorable; glorioso; digno; ilustre; (sensitive of honor) pundonoroso

honorable mention *n* accésit, *m*

honorableness /'ɒnərəbəlnɪs/ *n* honradez, *f*

honorably /'ɒnərəbli/ *adv* honorablemente; dignamente

honorarium /ˌɒnə'rɛəriəm/ *n* honorario, *m*

honorary /'ɒnə,rɛri/ *a* honorario, honorífico. **h. member,** socio (-ia) honorario (-ia). **h. mention,** mención honorífica, *f*

hood /hʊd/ *n* capucha, caperuza, *f;* (folding, of vehicles) capota, cubierta, *f;* (of a carriage) caparazón, fuelle, *m;* (of a car) capó, *m,* (university) muceta, *f;* (of a fireplace) campana (de hogar), *f;* (cowl of chimney) sombrerete (de chimenea), *m.* —*vt* cubrir con capucha; cubrir; (the eyes) ocultar, cubrir, velar

hooded /'hʊdɪd/ *a* con capucha

hoodwink /'hʊd,wɪŋk/ *vt* vendar (los ojos); *Fig.* engañar, embaucar, burlar

hoof /hʊf/ *n* casco, *m;* (cloven) pezuña, *f*

hoofed /hʊft/ *a* ungulado

hoof it ir a golpe de calcetín

hook /hʊk/ *n* gancho, garfio, *m;* (boat-) bichero, *m;* (fish-) anzuelo, *m;* (on a dress) corchete, *m;* (hanger) colgadero, *m;* (claw) garra, *f.* —*vt* enganchar; (a dress) abrochar; (fish) pescar, coger; (nab) atrapar, pescar. **by h. or by crook,** a tuertas o a derechas. **left h.,** (boxing) izquierdo, *m.* **right h.,** (boxing) derecho, *m.* **to catch oneself on a h.,** engancharse. **h. and eye,** los corchetes, *m pl.* **h.-nosed,** con nariz de gancho, con nariz aguileña. **h.-up,** *Radio.* circuito, *m;* transmisión en circuito, *f*

hooked /hʊkt/ *a* con ganchos; corvo, ganchoso

hooking /'hʊkɪŋ/ *n* enganche, *m;* (of a dress) abrochamiento, *m;* (of fish and *Inf.*) pesca, *f*

hookworm /'hʊk,wɜrm/ *n* anquilostoma, *m*

hooligan /'hʊlɪgən/ *n* rufián, *m*

hooliganism /'hʊlɪgə,nɪzəm/ *n* rufianería, *f*

hoop /hup/ *n* aro, arco, *m;* (of a skirt) miriñaque, *m;* (croquet) argolla, *f;* (toy) aro, *m;* círculo, *m.* —*vt* poner aros a; *Fig.* rodear

hoot /hut/ *n* (of owls) ululación, *f,* grito, *m;* (whistle) silbido, *m;* ruido, clamor, *m.* —*vi* (of owls) ulular, gritar; silbar; *Auto.* avisar con la bocina. **to h. off the stage,** hacer abandonar la escena. **to h. down,** silbar

hooter /'hʊtər/ *n* sirena, *f; Auto.* bocina, *f;* (whistle) pito, *m*

hooting /'hutɪŋ/ *n* See **hoot**

hop /hɒp/ *n* salto, brinco, *m; Bot.* lúpulo, *m; Bot.* flores de oblón, *f pl;* (dance) baile, *m.* —*vi* saltar con un

pie; andar dando brincos; saltar; (limp) cojear; (of plant) dar lúpulo. —*vt* saltar. **hop-garden,** huerto de lúpulo, *m.* **hop-kiln,** horno para secar lúpulo, *m.* **hop-picker,** recolector (-ra) de lúpulo. **hop-picking,** recolección de lúpulos, *f*

hope /houp/ *n* esperanza, *f;* (faith) confianza, *f;* (expectation) anticipación, expectación, *f;* (probability) probabilidad, *f;* (illusion) ilusión, *f;* sueño, *m.* —*vi* esperar. **to live in h. that,** vivir con la esperanza de que. **to lose h.,** desesperarse. **to h. against h.,** esperar sin motivo, esperar lo imposible. **to h. for,** desear. **to h. in,** confiar en

hopeful /'houpfəl/ *a* lleno de esperanzas, confiado; optimista; *(Fig.)* risueño. —*n Inf.* la esperanza de la casa. **to look h.,** *Fig.* prometer bien

hopefully /'houpfəli/ *adv* con esperanza

hopefulness /'houpfəlnɪs/ *n* optimismo, *m; Fig.* aspecto prometedor, *m*

hopeless /'houplɪs/ *a* desesperado, sin esperanza; irremediable; (of situations) imposible; (of disease) incurable. **to be h.,** (lose hope) desesperarse; (have no remedy) ser irremediable; (of disease) no tener cura. **to make h.,** hacer perder la esperanza, desesperar; dejar sin remedio; (a situation) hacer imposible; (an illness) hacer imposible de curar

hopelessly /'houplɪsli/ *adv* sin esperanza; sin remedio; imposiblemente; incurablemente

hopelessness /'houplɪsnɪs/ *n* desesperación, *f;* (of an illness) imposibilidad de curar, *f;* lo irremediable; imposibilidad, *f*

hopscotch /'hɒp,skɒtʃ/ *n* infernáculo, *m,* rayuela, *f*

horal, horary /'hɔrəl; 'hɔrəri/ *a* horario

horde /hɔrd/ *n* horda, *f*

horizon /hə'raizən/ *n* horizonte, *m*

horizontal /ˌhɔrə'zɒntḷ/ *a* horizontal. **h. suspension,** (gymnastics) plancha, *f*

horizontality /ˌhɔrəzɒn'tælti/ *n* horizontalidad, *f*

horizontally /ˌhɔrə'zɒntḷi/ *adv* horizontalmente

hormone /'hɔrmoun/ *n* hormona, *f*

horn /hɔrn/ *n* (of bull, etc.) cuerno, *m;* (antler) asta, *f;* (of an insect) antena, *f;* (of a snail) tentáculo, *m; Mus.* cuerno, *m;* trompa, *f;* (of motor and phonograph) bocina, *f;* (of moon) cuerno (de la luna), *m.* **article made of h.,** objeto de cuerno, *m.* **on the horns of a dilemma,** entre la espada y la pared. **h. of plenty,** cuerno de abundancia, *m;* cornucopia, *f.* **h.-rimmed spectacles,** anteojos de concha, *m pl.* **h. thrust,** cornada, *f*

horned /hɔrnd/ *a* cornudo; (antlered) enastado

hornet /'hɔrnɪt/ *n* avispón, abejón, *m*

horny /'hɔrni/ *a* córneo; calloso; duro. **h.-handed,** con manos callosas

horoscope /'hɔrə,skoup/ *n* horóscopo, *m*

horrible /'hɔrəbəl/ *a* horrible, repugnante, espantoso; (of price) enorme; *Inf.* horrible

horribleness /'hɔrəbəlnɪs/ *n* horribilidad, *f,* horror, *m,* lo espantoso

horribly /'hɔrəbli/ *adv* horriblemente

horrid /'hɔrɪd/ *a* horroroso; desagradable

horridness /'hɔrɪdnɪs/ *n* horror, *m;* lo desagradable

horrific /hə'rɪfɪk/ *a* horrífico, horrendo

horrify /'hɔrə,fai/ *vt* horrorizar; escandalizar

horrifying /'hɔrə,faiɪŋ/ *a* horroroso, horripilante

horror /'hɔrər/ *n* horror, *m.* **h.-stricken,** horrorizado

hors d'oeuvres /ɔr'dɜrvz/ *n pl* entremeses, *m pl*

horse /hɔrs/ *n* caballo, *m;* (cavalry) caballería, *f;* (frame) caballete, *m;* (gymnastics and as punishment) potro, *m.* —*a* caballar, caballuno. —*vt* montar a caballo. **pack of horses,** caballada, *f.* **to ride a h.,** cabalgar, montar a caballo. **H. Artillery,** artillería montada, *f.* **h. blanket,** manta para caballos, *f;* sudadero, *m.* **h.-block,** montador, *m.* **h.-box,** vagón para caballos, *m.* **h.-breaker,** domador de caballos, *m.* **h.-cab,** simón, *m.* **h.-chestnut,** castaña pilonga, *f.* **h.-chestnut flower,** candela, *f.* **h.-collar,** collera, *f.* **h.-dealer,** chalán, *m.* **h.-doctor,** veterinario, *m.* **h.-flesh,** carne de caballo, *f.* **h.-fly,** tábano, *m.* **H. Guards,** guardias montadas, *f pl.* **h.-latitudes,** calmas de Cáncer, *f pl.* **h.-laugh,** carcajada, *f.* **h.-master,** maestro de equitación, *m.* **h. meat,** carne de caballo, *f.* **h. pistol,** pistola de arzón, *f.* **h.-play,** payasada, *f.* **h.-power,** caballo de vapor, *m;* potencia, *f.* **a twelve-**

h.p. car, un coche de doce caballos. **h.-race,** carrera de caballos, *f.* **h.-radish,** rábano picante, raíz amarga, *m.* **h.-sense,** sentido común, *m,* gramática parda, *f.* **h. show,** exposición de caballos, feria equina *f;* concurso de caballos, *m.* **h.-trainer,** entrenador de caballos, *m.* **h. tram,** tranvía de sangre. *m.* **h. trappings,** monturas, *f pl*

horseback /'hɔrs,bæk/ *n* lomo de caballo, *m.* **on h.,** a caballo. **to ride on h.,** ir a caballo

horseman /'hɔrsmən/ *n* jinete, cabalgador, *m*

horsemanship /'hɔrsmən,ʃɪp/ *n* equitación, *f,* manejo del caballo, *m*

horseshoe /'hɔrs,ʃu/ *n* herradura, *f.* **h. arch,** arco de herradura, arco morisco, *m*

horsewhip /'hɔrs,wɪp/ *n* látigo, *m.* —*vt* zurriagar, pegar con látigo

horsewoman /'hɔrs,wʊmən/ *n* amazona, *f*

horsey /'hɔrsi/ *a* de caballo; aficionado a caballos; grosero

horticultural /,hɔrtɪ'kʌltʃərəl/ *a* horticultural. **h. show,** exposición de flores, *f*

horticulturalist /,hɔrtɪ'kʌltʃərɪst/ *n* horticultor (-ra)

horticulture /'hɔrtɪ,kʌltʃər/ *n* horticultura, *f*

hosanna /hou'zænə/ *n* hosanna, *m*

hose /houz/ *n* (tube) manga, *f;* (breeches) calzón, *m;* (stockings) medias, *f pl;* (socks) calcetines, *m pl.* **h. man,** manguero, *m.* **h.-pipe,** manga de riego, manguera, *f*

hosier /'houʒər/ *n* calcetero (-ra)

hosiery /'houʒəri/ *n* calcetería, *f.* **h. trade,** calcetería, *f*

hospice /'hɒspɪs/ *n* hospicio, *m;* asilo, refugio, *m*

hospitable /'hɒspɪtəbəl/ *a* hospitalario

hospitableness /'hɒspɪtəbəlnɪs/ *n* hospitalidad, *f*

hospitably /'hɒspɪtəbəli/ *adv* hospitalariamente

hospital /'hɒspɪtl/ *n* hospital, *m;* (school) colegio, *m.* **h. nurse,** enfermera, *f.* **h. ship,** buque hospital, *m*

hospital bed cama hospitalaria, *f*

hospitality /,hɒspɪ'tælɪti/ *n* hospitalidad, *f*

host /houst/ *n* huésped, convidador, (of radio or tv program) presentador, *m;* (at an inn) patrón, mesonero, *m;* (army) ejército, *m;* (crowd) multitud, muchedumbre, *f; Eccl.* hostia, *f; pl* **hosts,** huestes, *f pl.* **h.-plant,** planta huésped, *f*

hostage /'hɒstɪdʒ/ *n* rehén, *m; Fig.* prenda, *f*

host country *n* (of an organization) país-sede, *m*

hostel /'hɒstl/ *n* hostería, *f;* club, *m;* residencia de estudiantes, *f*

hostelry /'hɒstlri/ *n* hospedería, *f;* parador, mesón, *m*

hostess /'houstɪs/ *n* ama de la casa, *f;* la que recibe a los invitados; la que convida; (of an inn) patrona, mesonera, *f*

hostile /'hɒstl/ *a* enemigo; hostil, contrario (a); (of circumstances, etc.) desfavorable

hostility /hɒ'stɪlɪti/ *n* enemistad, *f,* antagonismo, *m,* mala voluntad, *f;* hostilidad, guerra, *f.* **suspension of hostilities,** suspensión de hostilidades, *f*

hot /hɒt/ *a* caliente; (of a day, etc.) caluroso; (piquant) picante; ardiente, vehemente, impetuoso; violento; impaciente; colérico; entusiasta; lleno de deseo; *Art.* intenso; (great) grande, mucho; (vigorous) enérgico. **You are getting very hot now,** *Inf.* (in a game, etc.) Te estás quemando. **It is hot,** Está caliente; (of weather) Hace calor. **to grow hot,** calentarse; *Fig.* acalorarse; (of weather) empezar a hacer calor. **to make hot,** calentar; dar calor (a); *Inf.* dar vergüenza. **hot-blooded,** de sangre caliente; apasionado; colérico. **hot-foot,** aprisa, apresuradamente. **hot-headed,** impetuoso. **hot-plate,** *Elec.* calientaplatos, *m.* **hot springs,** termas, *f pl.* **hot-tempered,** colérico, irascible. **hot water,** agua caliente, *f.* **hot-water bottle,** bolsa de goma, *f.* **hot-water pipes,** las cañerías del agua caliente

hotbed /'hɒt,bed/ *n* semillero, vivero, *m; Fig.* semillero, foco, *m*

hotchpotch /'hɒtʃ,pɒtʃ/ *n* potaje, *m; Fig.* mezcolanza, *f,* fárrago, *m*

hotel /hou'tel/ *n* hotel, *m.* **h.-keeper,** hotelero (-ra)

hothead /'hɒt,hed/ *n* exaltado (-da), fanático (-ca)

hothouse /'hɒt,haus/ *n* invernáculo, *m,* estufa, *f.* **h. plant,** *Fig.* planta de estufa, *f*

hotly /'hɒtli/ *adv* calurosamente; con vehemencia; coléricamente

hough /hɒk/ *n Zool.* pernil, *m;* (in man) corva, *f*

hound /haund/ *n* perro de caza, sabueso de artois, *m;* perro, *m; Inf.* canalla, *m.* —*vt* cazar con perros; *Fig.* perseguir; *Fig.* incitar. **master of hounds,** montero, *m.* **pack of hounds,** jauría, *f*

hour /auər/ *n* hora, *f;* momento, *m;* ocasión, oportunidad, *f pl.* **hours,** horas, *f pl.* **after hours,** fuera de horas. **at the eleventh h.,** en el último minuto. **by the h.,** por horas; horas enteras. **small hours,** altas horas de la noche, *Inf.* las tantas, *f pl.* **to keep late hours,** acostarse tarde. **to strike the h.,** dar la hora. **h.-glass,** reloj de arena, *m.* **h.-hand,** horario, *m.* **h. of death,** hora suprema, hora de la muerte, *f*

hourly /'auərli/ *a* cada hora; por hora; continuo. —*adv* a cada hora; de un momento a otro

house /n haus; *v* hauz/ *n* casa, *f;* (home) hogar, *m;* (lineage) familia, *f,* abolengo, *m; (Theat.)* sala, *f,* teatro, *m; Com.* casa comercial, *f;* (takings) entrada, *f;* (audience) público, *m;* (of Lords, Commons) cámara, *f;* (college) colegio, *m;* (parliament) parlamento, *m;* (building) edificio, *m.* —*a* de casa; de la casa; doméstico. —*vt* dar vivienda (a); alojar, recibir (or tener) en casa de uno; (store) poner, guardar.∴ **The cottage will not h. them all,** No habrá bastante lugar para todos ellos en la cabaña, No cabrán todos en la cabaña. **country-h.,** finca, *f;* casa de campo, *f.* **full h.,** casa llena, *f; Theat.* lleno, *m.* **to bring down the h.,** *Theat.* hacer venirse el teatro abajo. **to keep h.,** llevar la casa; ser ama de casa. **to keep open h.,** tener mesa puesta, ser hospitalario. **to set up h.,** poner casa. **h. of cards,** castillo de naipes, *m.* **H. of Commons,** Cámara de los Comunes, *f.* **H. of Lords,** Cámara de los Lores, *f.* **h.-agent,** agente de casas, *m.* **h.-boat,** barco-habitación, *m,* casa flotante, *f.* **h.-dog,** perro de guardia, *m;* perro de casa, *m.* **h.-fly,** mosca doméstica, *f.* **h. furnisher,** mueblista, *mf.* **h. painter,** pintor de brocha gorda, *m.* **h. party,** reunión en una casa de campo, *f.* **h.-physician,** médico (-ca) interno (-na). **h. porter,** portero, *m.* **h. property,** propiedad inmueble, *f.* **h.-room,** capacidad de una casa, *f.* **h. slipper,** zapatilla, *f,* pantuflo, *m.* **h.-surgeon,** cirujano interno, *m.* **h.-to-h.,** de casa en casa. **h.-warming,** reunión para colgar la cremallera, *f*

housebreaker /'haus,breikər/ *n* ladrón de casas, *m*

housebreaking /'haus,breikɪŋ/ *n* robo de una casa, *f*

houseful /'hausfʊl/ *n* casa, *f*

house furnishings *n pl* artefactos para el hogar, accesorios caseros, aparatos electrodomésticos, *m pl*

household /'haus,hould/ *n* casa, *f;* familia, *f;* hogar, *m.* —*a* de la casa; doméstico; del hogar. **to be a h. word,** andar en lenguas. **h. accounts,** cuentas de la casa, *f pl.* **h. duties,** labores de la casa, *f pl.* **h. gods,** penates, *m pl.* **h. goods,** ajuar, mobiliario, *m.* **h. management,** gobierno de la casa, *m*

householder /'haus,houldər/ *n* padre de familia, *m;* dueño (-ña) (or inquilino (-na)) de una casa

housekeeper /'haus,kipər/ *n* ama de llaves, *f;* mujer de su casa, *f*

housekeeping /'haus,kipɪŋ/ *n* gobierno de la casa, *m;* economía doméstica, *f.* —*a* doméstico. **to set up h.,** poner casa

housemaid /'haus,meid/ *n* camarera, sirvienta, *f.* **housemaid's knee,** rodilla de fregona, *f*

house of ill repute *n* burdel, *m,* casa de citas, casa de zorras, casa pública, *f;* lupanar, *m*

housetops /'haus,tɒps/ *n* tejado, *m;* (flat roof) azotea, *f.* **to shout from the h.,** pregonar a los cuatro vientos

housewife /'haus,waif/ *n* madre de familia, mujer de su casa, *f;* (sewing-bag) neceser de costura, *m*

housewifely /'haus,waifli/ *a* propio de una mujer de su casa; doméstico; (of a woman) hacendosa

housewifery /'haus,waifəri/ *n* economía doméstica, *f*

housing /'hauzɪŋ/ *n* provisión de vivienda, *f;* (storage) almacenaje, *m;* alojamiento, *m; Inf.* casa, vivienda, *f.* **h. scheme,** urbanización, *f.* **h. shortage,** crisis de vivienda, *f,* déficit habitacional, *m*

hovel /'hʌvəl/ *n* casucha, *f*

hover /'hʌvər/ *vi* revolotear; (of hawks, etc.)

cernerse; estar suspendido; rondar; seguir de cerca,
estar al lado (de); *Fig.* vacilar, dudar

hovering /'hʌvərɪŋ/ *n* revoloteo, *m;* (of birds of
prey) calada, *f; Fig.* vacilación, *f.* —*a* revolante, que
revolotea; que se cierne (sobre); (menacing) que
amenaza, inminente

how /hau/ *adv* cómo; (by what means, in what manner) de qué modo; (at what price) a qué precio; qué;
cuánto. —*n* el cómo. **to know how,** saber. **For how
long?** ¿Por cuánto tiempo? **How are you?** ¿Cómo está
Vd.? *Inf.* ¿Qué tal? **How do you do!** ¡Mucho gusto
(en conocerlo/conocerla/conocerlos/conocerlas)! **How
old are you?** ¿Qué edad tiene Vd.? **How beautiful!**
¡Qué hermoso! **How big!** ¡Cuán grande! **How early?**
¿Cuán temprano?; ¿Cuándo a más tardar? **How far?**
¿A qué distancia? ¡Hasta qué punto? ¿Hasta dónde?
How fast? ¿A qué velocidad? **How few!** ¡Qué pocos!
How little! ¡Qué pequeño!; ¡Qué poco! **How long?**
¿Cuánto tiempo? **How many?** ¿Cuántos? *m pl;*
¿Cuántas? *f pl.* **How much is it?** ¿Cuánto vale? **How
much cloth do you want?** ¿Cuánta tela quieres? **How
often?** ¿Cuán a menudo? ¿Cuántas veces? **How
would you like to go for a walk?** ¿Te gustaría pase-
arte? **How are you going to Lisbon?** ¿En qué vas a
Lisboa?

however /hau'evər/ *adv* como quiera (que) (followed
by subjunctive); por más que (followed by subjunctive); por... que (followed by subjunctive). —*conjunc*
(nevertheless) sin embargo, no obstante. **h. good it
is,** por bueno que sea. **h. he does it,** como quiera
que lo haga. **h. it may be,** sea como sea. **h. much,**
por mucho que

howl /haul/ *n* aullido, *m;* (groan) gemido, *m;* (cry)
grito, *m;* (roar) rugido, bramido, *m;* lamento, *m.* —*vi*
aullar; gemir; gritar; rugir, bramar. —*vt* chillar. **Each
time he opened his mouth he was howled down,**
Cada vez que abrió la boca se armó una bronca

howler /'haulər/ *n* aullador (-ra); *Zool.* mono (-na)
chillón (-ona); (blunder) coladura, plancha, *f*

howling /'haulɪŋ/ *a* aullante; gemidor; (crying) que
llora; bramante, rugiente. —*n* los aullidos; (groaning)
el gemir, los gemidos; (crying) los gritos; (weeping)
el lloro; (roaring) los bramidos, el rugir; los lamentos

hub /hʌb/ *n* (of a wheel) cubo (de rueda) *m; Fig.*
centro, *m.* **hub cap,** tapa de cubo, *f*

hubbub /'hʌbʌb/ *n* algarada, barahúnda, *f*

huckster /'hʌkstər/ *n* revendedor (-ra). —*vi* revender;
(haggle) regatear

huddle /'hʌdl/ *n* (heap) montón, *m;* colección, *f;*
(group) corrillo, grupo, *m;* (mixture) mezcla, *f.* —*vt*
arrebujar, amontonar; acurrucar, arrebujar; (throw
on) echarse. —*vi* amontonarse; apiñarse; acurrucarse,
arrebujarse

hue /hyu/ *n* color, *m;* matiz, tono, *m;* (of opinion)
matiz, *m;* (clamor) clamor, *m,* gritería, *f.* **hue and
cry,** alarma, *f*

huff /hʌf/ *n* acceso de cólera, *m*

huffily /'hʌfəli/ *adv* malhumoradamente; petulante-
mente

huffiness /'hʌfinɪs/ *n* mal humor, *m;* petulancia, *f;*
arrogancia, *f*

hug /hʌg/ *n* abrazo, *m.* —*vt* abrazar, apretujar; *Fig.*
acariciar; *Naut.* navegar muy cerca de. **to hug oneself,** *Fig.* congratularse

huge /hyudʒ/ *a* enorme, inmenso; gigante; vasto

hugely /'hyudʒli/ *adv* inmensamente, enormemente

hugeness /'hyudʒnɪs/ *n* inmensidad, enormidad, *f;*
vastedad, *f*

Huguenot /'hyugə,nɒt/ *a and n* hugonote (-ta)

hulk /hʌlk/ *n* barco viejo, *m;* pontón, *m*

hulking /'hʌlkɪŋ/ *a* pesado, desgarbado

hull /hʌl/ *n Naut.* casco (de un buque), *m;* (shell)
cáscara, *f;* (pod) vaina, *f, vt* mondar

hullabaloo /'hʌləbə,lu/ *n* alboroto, tumulto, *m;*
vocerío, *m*

hullo /hə'lou/ *interj* See **hallo**

hum /hʌm/ *n* zumbido, *m;* ruido confuso, *m.* —*vi*
(sing) canturrear; zumbar; (confused sound) zurrir;
(hesitate) vacilar. —*vt* (a tune) tararear

human /'hyumən/ *a* humano. **the h. touch,** el don
de gentes. **h. being,** ser humano, hombre, *m*

humane /hyu'mein/ *a* humanitario, humano

humanely /hyu'meinli/ *adv* humanitariamente

humaneness /hyu'meinnɪs/ *n* humanidad, *f*

humanism /'hyumə,nɪzəm/ *n* humanismo, *m*

humanist /'hyumənɪst/ *n* humanista, *mf*

humanistic /,hyumə'nɪstɪk/ *a* humanista

humanitarian /hyu,mænɪ'teəriən/ *a* humanitario

humanitarianism /hyu,mænɪ'teəriə,nɪzəm/ *n* hu-
manitarismo, *m*

humanity /hyu'mænɪti/ *n* humanidad, *f;* raza humana, *f.* **the humanities,** las humanidades

humanize /'hyumə,naiz/ *vt* humanizar; (milk) ma-
ternizar. —*vi* humanizarse

humanly /'hyumənli/ *adv* humanamente

humble /'hʌmbəl/ *a* humilde; modesto; (cringing)
servil; sumiso; pobre. —*vt* humillar; mortificar. **to h.
oneself,** humillarse

humbleness /'hʌmbəlnɪs/ *n* humildad, *f;* modestia, *f;*
(abjectness) servilismo, *m;* sumisión, *f;* pobreza, *f;*
(of birth, etc.) obscuridad, *f*

humbling /'hʌmblɪŋ/ *n* humillación, *f;* mortificación,
f

humbly /'hʌmbli/ *adv* humildemente; modestamente;
servilmente

humbug /'hʌm,bʌg/ *n* (fraud) embuste, engaño, *m;*
(nonsense) disparate, *m,* tontería, *f;* mentira, *f;* (person) farsante, charlatán, *m;* (sweetmeat) caramelo de
menta, *m.* —*vt* engañar, embaucar; burlarse de

humdrum /'hʌm,drʌm/ *a* monótono; aburrido

humeral /'hyumərəl/ *a* humeral. —*n Eccl.* velo humeral, *m*

humerus /'hyumərəs/ *n Anat.* húmero, *m*

humid /'hyumɪd/ *a* húmedo

humidity /hyu'mɪdɪti/ *n* humedad, *f*

humiliate /hyu'mɪli,eit/ *vt* humillar, mortificar. **to h.
oneself,** humillarse

humiliating /hyu'mɪli,eitɪŋ/ *a* humillante; degradante

humiliation /hyu,mɪli'eiʃən/ *n* humillación, mortificación, *f;* degradación, *f*

humility /hyu'mɪlɪti/ *n* humildad, *f;* modestia, *f*

humming /'hʌmɪŋ/ *n* zumbido, *m;* (of a tune) ta-
rareo, *m.* —*a* zumbador. **h.-bird,** pájaro mosca,
colibrí, *m.* **h.-top,** trompa, *f*

humor /'hyumər/ *n* humor, *m;* humorismo, *m;* (temperament) disposición, *f,* carácter, *m;* (whim) capricho, *m.* —*vt* seguir el humor (a), complacer; satisfacer, consentir en; (a lock, etc.) manejar. **in a good
(bad) h.,** de buen (mal) humor. **I am not in the h.
to...** no estoy de humor para... **sense of h.,** sentido
de humor, *m*

humored /'hyumərd/ *a* (in compounds) de humor...
good-h., de buen humor. **ill-h.,** malhumorado, de mal
humor

humoresque /,hyumə'rɛsk/ *n Mus.* capricho musical,
m

humorist /'hyumərɪst/ *n* humorista, *mf*

humorless /'hyumərlɪs/ *a* sin sentido humorístico, sin
sentido de humor

humorous /'hyumərəs/ *a* humorístico; cómico, risible

humorously /'hyumərəsli/ *adv* humorísticamente;
cómicamente

humorousness /'hyumərəsnɪs/ *n* humorismo, *m;* lo
cómico

hump /hʌmp/ *n* joroba, giba, *f;* (hillock) montecillo,
m; Inf. depresión, *f*

humpback /'hʌmp,bæk/ *n* giba, joroba, *f;* (person)
jorobado (-da), giboso (-sa)

humpbacked /'hʌmp,bækt/ *a* jorobado, giboso, corcovado

humph /*an inarticulate expression resembling a snort
or grunt; spelling pron.* hʌmf/ *interj* ¡qué va!; ¡patrañas!

humus /'hyuməs/ *n* humus, mantillo, *m*

hunchback /'hʌntʃ,bæk/ *n* joroba, giba, *f;* (person)
jorobado (-da), corcovado (-da), giboso (-sa)

hunchbacked /'hʌntʃ,bækt/ *a* jorobado, giboso, corcovado

hundred /'hʌndrɪd/ *n* ciento, *m;* centenar, *m,* centena, *f.* —*a* ciento; (before nouns and adjectives, excluding numerals, with the exception of mil and millón) cien. **a h. thousand,** cien mil. **one h. and one,**
ciento uno. **by the h.,** a centenares. **hundreds of
people,** centenares de personas, *m pl.* **h.-millionth,** *a*

and *n* cienmillonésimo *m*. **h.-thousandth,** *a* and *n* cienmilésimo *m*.

hundredfold /'hʌndrɪd,fould/ *adv* cien veces. —*n* céntuplo, *m*

hundredth /'hʌndrɪdθ/ *a* centésimo, céntimo. —*n* centésimo, *m*, centésima parte, *f*

hundredweight /'hʌndrɪd,weit/ *n* quintal, *m*

Hungarian /hʌŋ'gɛəriən/ *a* and *n* húngaro (-ra); (language) húngaro, *m*

Hungary /'hʌŋgəri/ Hungría, *f*

hunger /'hʌŋgər/ *n* hambre, *f*; apetito, *m*; (craving) deseo, *m*, ansia, *f*. —*vi* estar hambriento, tener hambre. **to h. for,** desear, ansiar. **h.-strike,** huelga de hambre, *f*

hungrily /'hʌŋgrəli/ *adv* hambrientamente, con hambre; ansiosamente

hungry /'hʌŋgri/ *a* hambriento; (of land) pobre; (anxious) deseoso. **to be h.,** tener hambre. **to make h.,** dar hambre

hunk /hʌŋk/ *n* rebanada, *f*, pedazo, *m*

hunt /hʌnt/ *n* caza, cacería, montería, *f*; grupo de cazadores, *m*; (search) busca, *f*; (pursuit) persecución, *f*. —*vt* cazar; cazar a caballo; (search) buscar; rebuscar, explorar; (pursue) perseguir. **to h. down,** perseguir. **to h. for,** buscar. **to h. out,** buscar; descubrir, desenterrar

hunter /'hʌntər/ *n* cazador, *m*; caballo de caza, *m*; (watch) saboneta, *f*

hunting /'hʌntɪŋ/ *n* caza, *f*; caza a caballo, *f*; persecución, *f*. —*a* cazador, de caza. **to go h.,** ir a cazar. **h.-box,** pabellón de caza, *m*. **h.-cap,** gorra de montar, *f*. **h.-crop,** látigo para cazar, *m*. **h.-ground,** coto de caza, terreno de caza, *m*. **h.-horn,** cuerno de caza, *m*, corneta de monte, *f*. **h. party,** partido de caza, *m*, cacería, *f*

hunting lodge *n* pabellón *m*

huntress /'hʌntrɪs/ *n* cazadora, *f*

huntsman /'hʌntsmən/ *n* cazador, montero, *m*

huntsmanship /'hʌntsmən,ʃɪp/ *n* montería, arte de cazar, *f*

hurdle /'hɜrdl/ *n* valla, *f*; zarzo, *m*. **h.-race,** carrera de obstáculos, *f*; carrera de vallas, *f*

hurdy-gurdy /'hɜrdi'gɜrdi/ *n* organillo, *m*

hurl /hɜrl/ *vt* lanzar, tirar, arrojar, echar. **to h. oneself,** lanzarse. **to h. oneself against,** arrojarse a (or contra). **to h. oneself upon,** abalanzarse sobre

hurly-burly /'hɜrli'bɜrli/ *n* alboroto, tumulto, *m*

hurrah /hə'rɑ/ *interj* ¡hurra! ¡viva! —*n* vítor, *m*. **H. for...!** ¡Viva...!, ¡Vivan...! **to shout h.,** vitorear

hurricane /'hɜrɪ,kein/ *n* huracán, *m*. **h.-lamp,** lámpara sorda, *f*

hurried /'hɜrid/ *a* apresurado, precipitado; hecho a prisa; superficial

hurriedly /'hɜridli/ *adv* apresuradamente, precipitadamente, con prisa; superficialmente; (of writing) a vuela pluma

hurry /'hɜri/ *n* prisa, *f*; precipitación, *f*; urgencia, *f*; confusión, *f*; alboroto, *m*. **in a h.,** aprisa. **in a great h.,** aprisa y corriendo. **to be in a h.,** llevar prisa, estar de prisa. **There is no h.,** No corre prisa, No hay prisa

hurry /'hɜri/ *vt* apresurar, dar prisa (a); llevar aprisa; hacer andar aprisa; enviar apresuradamente; precipitar; acelerar. —*vi* darse prisa; apresurarse. **to h. after,** correr detrás de, seguir apresuradamente. **to h. away,** *vi* marcharse aprisa, marcharse corriendo; huir; salir precipitadamente. —*vt* hacer marcharse aprisa; llevar con prisa. **to h. back,** *vi* volver aprisa, apresurarse a volver. —*vt* hacer volver aprisa. **to h. in,** *vi* entrar aprisa, entrar corriendo. —*vt* hacer entrar aprisa. **to h. off. See to h. away. to h. on,** *vi* apresurarse. —*vt* apresurar, precipitar. **to h. out,** salir rápidamente. **to h. over,** hacer rápidamente; concluir aprisa; despachar rápidamente; (travel over) atravesar aprisa; pasar rápidamente por. **to h. toward,** llevar rápidamente hacia; arrastrar hacia; impeler hacia. **to h. up,** *vi* darse prisa. —*vt* apresurar, precipitar; estimular

hurt /hɜrt/ *n* herida, *f*; (harm) daño, mal, *m*; perjuicio, *m*. —*vt* (wound) herir; (cause pain) doler; hacer daño (a); hacer mal (a); (damage) perjudicar, estropear; (offend) ofender; (the feelings) mortificar, lasti-

mar, herir. —*vi* doler; hacer mal; perjudicarse, estropearse. **I haven't h. myself,** No me he hecho daño. **Does it still h. you?** ¿Te duele todavía? **to h. deeply,** *Fig.* herir en el alma. **to h. a person's feelings,** herirle (a uno) el amor propio, lastimar, ofender

hurtful /'hɜrtfəl/ *a* nocivo, dañino; injurioso, pernicioso

hurtfulness /'hɜrtfəlnɪs/ *n* nocividad, *f*; perniciosidad, *f*

hurtle /'hɜrtl/ *vt* lanzar. —*vi* lanzarse; volar; caer

husband /'hʌzbənd/ *n* esposo, marido, *m*. —*vt* economizar, ahorrar. **h. and wife,** los esposos, los cónyuges

husbandry /'hʌzbəndri/ *n* labor de los campos, agricultura, *f*; (thrift) frugalidad, parsimonia, *f*

hush /hʌʃ/ *n* silencio, *m*, tranquilidad, *f*. —*interj* ¡chitón! ¡calla! ¡silencio! —*vt* silenciar, hacer callar, imponer silencio (a); (a baby) adormecer; *Fig.* sosegar, calmar. —*vi* callarse, enmudecer. **to h. up,** mantener secreto, ocultar. **h.-h.,** secreto. **h. money,** soborno, chantaje, *m*

hushaby /'hʌʃə,bai/ *interj* ¡duerme!

husk /hʌsk/ *n* (of grain) cascabillo, *m*; zurrón, *m*; cáscara, *f*; (of chestnut) erizo, *m*

huskily /'hʌskəli/ *adv* roncamente

huskiness /'hʌskɪnɪs/ *n* ronquera, *f*; *Inf.* robustez, *f*

husky /'hʌski/ *a* (of voice) ronco; *Bot.* cascarudo; (Eskimo) esquimal; *Inf.* robusto, fuerte. —*n* perro esquimal, *m*

hussy /'hʌsi/ *n* pícara, bribona, *f*

hustle /'hʌsəl/ *vt* empujar, codear; *Fig.* precipitar; *Inf.* acelerar. —*vi* codearse; andarse de prisa

hut /hʌt/ *n* choza, cabaña, barraca, *f*

hutch /hʌtʃ/ *n* (chest) arca, *f*, cofre, *m*; (cage) jaula, *f*; (for rabbits) conejera, *f*; (for rats) ratonera, *f*; *Inf.* choza, *f*

hutment /'hʌtmənt/ *n* campamento de chozas, *m*

hyacinth /'haiəsɪnθ/ *n* jacinto, *m*

hybrid /'haibrɪd/ *a* híbrido; mestizo, mixto. —*n* híbrido, *m*

hybridism /'haibri,dɪzəm/ *n* hibridismo, *m*

hybridization /,haibrɪdə'zeiʃən/ *n* hibridación, *f*

hybridize /'haibri,daiz/ *vt* cruzar. —*vi* producir (or generar) híbridos

hydrangea /hai'dreindʒə/ *n* *Bot.* hortensia, *f*

hydrant /'haidrənt/ *n* boca de riego, *f*

hydrate /'haidreit/ *n* *Chem.* hidrato, *m*. —*vt* hidratar

hydration /hai'dreiʃən/ *n* hidratación, *f*

hydraulic /hai'drɔlɪk/ *a* hidráulico. **h. engineering,** hidrotecnia, *f*

hydraulics /hai'drɔlɪks/ *n* hidráulica, *f*

hydrocarbon /,haidrə'karbən/ *n* *Chem.* hidrocarburo, *m*

hydrochloric /,haidrə'klɔrɪk/ *a* clorhídrico. **h. acid,** ácido clorhídrico, *m*

hydrogen /'haidrədʒən/ *n* hidrógeno, *m*. **h. peroxide,** agua oxigenada, *f*

hydrogenation /,haidrədʒə'neiʃən/ *n* hidrogenación, *f*

hydrogenize /'haidrədʒə,naiz/ *vt* hidrogenizar

hydrolysis /hai'drɒləsɪs/ *n* hidrólisis, *f*

hydromel /'haidrə,mɛl/ *n* aguamiel, *f*, hidromel, *m*

hydropathic /,haidrə'pæθɪk/ *a* hidropático. **h. establishment,** balneario, *m*

hydrophobia /,haidrə'foubiə/ *n* hidrofobia, rabia, *f*

hydrophobic /,haidrə'foubɪk/ *a* hidrofóbico, rabioso

hydroplane /'haidrə,plein/ *n* hidroplano, *m*

hydrotherapic /,haidrouθə'ræpɪk/ *a* hidroterápico

hydrotherapy /,haidrə'θɛrəpi/ *n* hidroterapia, *f*

hyena /hai'inə/ *n* hiena, *f*

hygiene /'haidʒin/ *n* higiene, *f*. **personal h.,** higiene privada, *f*

hygienic /,haidʒi'ɛnɪk/ *a* higiénico

hymen /'haimən/ *n* *Anat.* himen, *m*; himeneo, *m*

hymeneal /,haimə'niəl/ *a* nupcial

hymn /hɪm/ *n* himno, *m*. **h.-book,** himnario, *m*

hyperbole /hai'pɜrbəli/ *n* hipérbole, *f*

hyperbolical /,haipər'bɒlɪkəl/ *a* hiperbólico

hypercorrection /,haipərkə'rɛkʃən/ *n* seudocultismo, supercultismo, *m*, ultracorrección, *f*

hypercritic /ˌhaipər'krɪtɪk/ n hipercrítico, m
hypercritical /ˌhaipər'krɪtɪkəl/ a hipercrítico, criticón
hypersensitive /ˌhaipər'sɛnsɪtɪv/ a vidrioso, quisquilloso
hypertrophy /hai'pɜrtrəfi/ n hipertrofia, f. —vi hipertrofiarse
hyphen /'haifən/ n guión, m
hypnosis /hɪp'nousɪs/ n hipnosis, f
hypnotic /hɪp'nɒtɪk/ a hipnótico. —n (person) hipnótico (-ca); (drug) hipnótico, narcótico, m
hypnotism /'hɪpnə,tɪzəm/ n hipnotismo, m
hypnotist /'hɪpnətɪst/ n hipnotizador (-ra)
hypnotization /ˌhɪpnətə'zeifən/ n hipnotización, f
hypnotize /'hɪpnə,taiz/ vt hipnotizar
hypo /'haipou/ n (sodium hyposulphite) hiposulfito sólido, m
hypochondria /ˌhaipə'kɒndriə/ n hipocondria, f
hypochondriac /ˌhaipə'kɒndri,æk/ n hipocondríaco (-ca)

hypochondriacal /ˌhaipoukən'draiəkəl/ a hipocondríaco
hypocrisy /hɪ'pɒkrəsi/ n hipocresía, f; mojigatería, gazmoñería, f
hypocrite /'hɪpəkrɪt/ n hipócrita, mf; mojigato (-ta). **to be a h.,** ser hipócrita
hypocritical /ˌhɪpə'krɪtɪkəl/ a hipócrita; mojigato, gazmoño
hypocritically /ˌhɪpə'krɪtɪkəli/ adv hipócritamente, con hipocresía
hypodermic /ˌhaipə'dɜrmɪk/ a hipodérmico. **h. syringe,** jeringa de inyecciones, f
hypotenuse /hai'pɒtṇ,us/ n Geom. hipotenusa, f
hypothesis /hai'pɒθəsɪs/ n hipótesis, f
hypothetical /ˌhaipə'θɛtɪkəl/ a hipotético
hysterectomy /ˌhɪstə'rɛktəmi/ n Surg. histerectomía, f
hysteria /hɪ'stɛriə/ n Med. histerismo, m; histeria, f, ataque de nervios, m
hysterical /hɪ'stɛrɪkəl/ a histérico. **to become h.,** tener un ataque de nervios. **hysterics,** n pl ataque de nervios, m

I

i /ai/ *n* (letter) i. —*1st pers pron* yo. **It is I,** Soy yo. Normally omitted, the verb alone being used except when **yo** is needed for emphasis, e.g. *Hablo a María,* I speak to Mary, but *Yo toco el violín, pero Juan toca el piano,* I play the violin, but *John* plays the piano
Iago /i'ɑgou/ Yago, *m*
Iberian /ai'bɪəriən/ *a* ibero, ibérico. —*n* ibero (-ra)
Iberian Peninsula, the la Península Ibérica
ibex /'aibɛks/ *n Zool.* íbice, *m*
ice /ais/ *n* hielo, *m;* (ice cream) helado, *m.* —*vt* helar; cubrir de hielo; congelar, cuajar; (a cake, etc.) garapiñar, escarchar, alcorzar. **to ice up,** (*Aer., Auto.*) helarse. **to be as cold as ice,** *Inf.* estar hecho un hielo. **His words cut no ice,** Sus palabras ni pinchan ni cortan. **ice-age,** edad del hielo, *f.* **ice-ax,** piolet, *m.* **ice-box,** nevera, *f.* **ice-cream,** helado, mantecado, *m.* **ice-cream cone,** cucurucho de helado, *m.* **ice-cream freezer,** heladora, *f.* **ice-cream vendor,** mantequero (-ra). **ice-field,** campo de hielo, *m.* **ice-floe,** témpano de hielo flotante, *m.* **ice hockey,** hockey sobre patines, *m.* **ice-pack,** bolsa para hielo, *f.* **ice-skates,** patines de cuchilla, *m pl.* **ice water,** agua helada, *f*
iceberg /'aisbɜrg/ *n* iceberg, témpano de hielo, banco de hielo, *m*
icebound /'ais,baund/ *a* aprisionado por el hielo; atascado en el hielo; (of roads, etc.) helado
iced /aist/ *a* helado; congelado, cuajado; (cakes) garapiñado, escarchado; (of drinks) con hielo. **i. drink,** sorbete, *m*
Iceland /'aislənd/ Islandia, *f*
Icelander /'ais,lændər/ *n* islandés (-esa)
icelandic /'ais'lændɪk/ *a* islandes, islándico. —*n* (language) islandés, *m*
icicle /'aisɪkəl/ *n* carámbano, canelón, cerrión, *m*
icily /'aisəli/ *adv* fríamente; *Fig.* frígidamente, con indiferencia, con frialdad
iciness /'aisinɪs/ *n* frialdad, frigidez, *f; Fig.* indiferencia, frigidez, *f*
icing /'aisɪŋ/ *n* helada, *f,* hielo, *m;* (on a cake, etc.) alcorza, capa de azúcar, *f*
icon /'aikɒn/ *n* icono, *m*
iconoclast /ai'kɒnə,klæst/ *n* iconoclasta, *mf*
iconoclastic /ai,kɒnə'klæstɪk/ *a* iconoclasta
iconography /,aikə'nɒgrəfi/ *n* iconografía, *f*
iconology /,aikə'nɒlədʒi/ *n* iconología, *f*
icy /'aisi/ *a* helado; glacial, frío; *Med.* álgido; *Fig.* indiferente, desabrido; *Poet.* frígido, gélido
idea /ai'diə/ *n* idea, *f,* concepto, *m;* (opinion) juicio, *m,* opinión, *f;* (notion) impresión, noción, *f;* (plan) proyecto, plan, designio, *m.* **to form an i. of,** hacerse una idea de, formar un concepto de. **to have an i. of,** tener una idea de; tener nociones de. **An i. struck me,** Se me ocurrió una idea. **full of ideas,** preñado (or lleno) de ideas. **I had no i. that...** No tenía la menor idea de que... No sabía que... **What an i.!** ¡Qué idea!
ideal /ai'diəl/ *a* ideal; excelente, perfecto; (utopian) utópico; (imaginary) imaginario, irreal, ficticio. —*n* ideal, *m;* modelo, prototipo, *m*
idealism /ai'diə,lɪzəm/ *n* idealismo, *m*
idealist /ai'diəlɪst/ *n* idealista, *mf*
idealistic /ai,diə'lɪstɪk/ *a* idealista
idealization /ai,diəlɪ'zeiʃən/ *n* idealización, *f*
idealize /ai'diə,laiz/ *vt* idealizar
ideally /ai'diəli/ *adv* idealmente
ideation /,aidi'eiʃən/ *n Philos.* ideación, *f*
idem /'aidɛm/ *pron* ídem
identical /ai'dɛntɪkəl/ *a* idéntico, mismo, igual; muy parecido, semejante
identically /ai'dɛntɪkəli/ *adv* idénticamente
identifiable /ai,dɛntɪ'faiəbəl/ *a* identificable
identification /ai,dɛntəfɪ'keiʃən/ *n* identificación, *f.* **i. number,** placa de identidad, *f*
identify /ai'dɛntə,fai/ *vt* identificar. **to i. oneself with,** identificarse con
identity /ai'dɛntɪti/ *n* identidad, *f.* **i. card,** cédula per-

sonal, *f;* carnet de identidad, *m.* **i. disc,** disco de identidad, *m*
ideogram /'ɪdiə,græm/ *n* ideograma, *m*
ideography /,ɪdi'ɒgrəfi/ *n* ideografía, *f*
ideological /,aidiə'lɒdʒɪkəl/ *a* ideológico
ideologist /,aidi'ɒlədʒɪst/ *n* ideólogo (-ga)
ideology /,aidi'ɒlədʒi/ *n* ideología, *f*
Ides /aidz/ *n pl* idus, *m pl*
idiocy /'ɪdiəsi/ *n* idiotez, imbecilidad, *f;* (foolishness) necedad, tontería, sandez, *f*
idiom /'ɪdiəm/ *n* idiotismo, *m;* modismo, *m,* locución, *f;* (language) habla, *f;* lenguaje, *m*
idiomatic /,ɪdiə'mætɪk/ *a* idiomático
idiopathy /,ɪdi'ɒpəθi/ *n Med.* idiopatía, *f*
idiosyncrasy /,ɪdiə'sɪŋkrəsi/ *n* idiosincrasia, *f*
idiosyncratic /,ɪdiousɪn'krætɪk/ *a* idiosincrásico
idiot /'ɪdiət/ *n* idiota, imbécil, *mf;* (fool) necio (-ia), tonto (-ta), mentecato (-ta)
idiotic /,ɪdi'ɒtɪk/ *a* idiota, imbécil; (foolish) necio, tonto, sandío
idle /'aidl/ *a* desocupado; indolente, ocioso; (unemployed) cesante, sin empleo; (lazy) perezoso, holgazán; (of machines) parado, inactivo; (useless) vano, inútil, sin efecto; (false) falso, mentiroso, infundado; (stupid) fútil, frívolo. —*vi* holgar, estar ocioso; holgazanear, haraganear, gandulear. **to i. away,** malgastar, perder. **to i. away the time,** pasar el rato, matar el tiempo. **i. efforts,** vanos esfuerzos, *m pl.* **i. fancies,** ilusiones, fantasías, *f pl,* sueños, *m pl.* **i. hours,** horas desocupadas, *f pl,* ratos perdidos, *m pl.* **i. question,** pregunta ociosa, *f.* **i. tale,** cuento de viejas, *m.* **i. threat,** reto vacuo, *m*
idleness /'aidlnɪs/ *n* ociosidad, indolencia, inacción, *f;* pereza, holgazanería, gandulería, *f;* (uselessness) inutilidad, futilidad, *f*
idler /'aidlər/ *n* ocioso (-sa); haragán (-ana); perezoso (-sa), holgazán (-ana), gandul (-la)
idly /'aidli/ *adv* ociosamente, perezosamente; (uselessly) vanamente
idol /'aidl/ *n* ídolo, *m.* **a popular i.,** el ídolo de las masas, *m*
idolater /ai'dɒlətər/ *n* idólatra, *mf;* (admirer) amante, *mf* esclavo (-va), admirador (-ra)
idolatrous /ai'dɒlətrəs/ *a* idólatra, idolátrico
idolatrously /ai'dɒlətrəsli/ *adv* idolatradamente, con idolatría
idolatry /ai'dɒlətri/ *n* idolatría, *f;* (devotion) adoración, pasión, *f*
idolization /,aidlə'zeiʃən/ *n* idolatría, *f*
idolize /'aidl,aiz/ *vt* idolatrar, adorar
idyll /'aidl/ *n* idilio, *m*
idyllic /ai'dɪlɪk/ *a* idílico
if /ɪf/ *conjunc* si; (even if) aunque, aun cuando; (whenever) cuando, en caso de que; (whether) si. **as if,** como si (foll. by subjunc.). **If he comes, we shall tell him,** Si viene se lo diremos. **If he had not killed the tiger, she would be dead,** Si él no hubiera matado al tigre, ella estaría muerta. **If ever there was one,** Si alguna vez lo hubiera. **if necessary,** si fuese necesario. **if not,** si no, si no es que (e.g., *Poet and philosopher are twins, if not one and the same,* Poeta y filósofo son hermanos gemelos, si no es que la misma cosa). **If only!** ¡Ojalá que! (foll. by subjunc.)
igloo /'ɪglu/ *n* iglú, *m*
igneous /'ɪgniəs/ *a* ígneo
ignite /ɪg'nait/ *vt* encender, pegar fuego (a), incendiar. —*vi* prender fuego, incen&diarse; arder
ignition /ɪg'nɪʃən/ *n* ignición, *f; Auto.* encendido, *m.* **i. coil,** *Auto.* carrete de inducción del encendido, *m.* **i. key,** *Auto.* llave del contacto, *f*
ignoble /ɪg'noubəl/ *a* innoble, vil, indigno
ignobly /ɪg'noubli/ *adv* bajamente, vilmente
ignominious /,ɪgnə'mɪniəs/ *a* ignominioso
ignominiously /,ɪgnə'mɪniəsli/ *adv* ignominiosamente
ignominy /'ɪgnə,mɪni/ *n* ignominia, deshonra, afrenta, *f*

ignoramus /ˌɪgnə'reɪməs/ n ignorante, mf
ignorance /'ɪgnərəns/ n ignorancia, f; (unawareness) desconocimiento, m. **to plead i.,** pretender ignorancia
ignorant /'ɪgnərənt/ a ignorante; inculto. **He is an i. fellow,** Es un ignorante. **to be i. of,** no saber, ignorar. **to be very i.,** ser muy ignorante, Inf. ser muy burro
ignorantly /'ɪgnərəntli/ adv ignorantemente, por ignorancia; neciamente
ignore /ɪg'nɔr/ vt no hacer caso de, desatender; (omit) pasar por alto de; Law. rechazar; (pretend not to recognize) hacer semblante de no reconocer; (not recognize) no reconocer
iguana /ɪ'gwɑnə/ n Zool. iguana, f
ileac /'ɪliæk/ a Anat. ilíaco
ileum /'ɪliəm/ n Anat. íleon, m
Iliad /'ɪliəd/ n Ilíada, f
ilium /'ɪliəm/ n Anat. ilion, m
ill /ɪl/ n mal, m. —a (sick) enfermo, malo; (bad) malo; (unfortunate) desdichado, funesto. —adv mal. **to be ill,** estar malo. **to be taken ill,** caer enfermo. **ill-advised,** mal aconsejado; desacertado, imprudente. **ill-advisedly,** imprudentemente. **ill at ease,** incómodo. **ill-bred,** mal criado, mal educado, mal nacido. **ill-breeding,** mala crianza, mala educación, f. **ill-disposed,** malintencionado. **ill fame,** mala fama, f. **ill-fated,** malhadado, malaventurado, aciago, fatal. **ill-favored,** mal parecido, feúcho. **ill-feeling,** hostilidad, f, rencor, m. **ill-gotten,** maladquirido. **ill-humor,** mal humor, m. **ill-humored,** de mal humor, malhumorado. **ill-luck,** desdicha, mala suerte, malaventura, f; infortunio, m. **ill-mannered,** mal educado. **ill-natured,** malévolo, perverso. **ill-naturedly,** malignamente. **ill-omened,** nefasto. **ill-spent,** malgastado, perdido. **ill-spoken,** mal hablado. **ill-suited,** malavenido. **ill-timed,** inoportuno, intempestivo. **ill-treat,** maltratar, malparar, tratar mal. **ill-treated,** que ha sido tratado mal; maltrecho. **ill-treatment,** maltratamiento, m, crueldad, f. **ill-turn,** mala jugada, f. **to do an ill-turn,** hacer un flaco servicio. **ill will,** mala voluntad, f; rencor, m, ojeriza, f. **to bear a person ill will,** guardarle rencor
illegal /ɪ'ligəl/ a ilegal; indebido, ilícito
illegality /ˌɪli'gælɪti/ n ilegalidad, f
illegally /ɪ'ligəli/ adv ilegalmente
illegibility /ˌɪˌledʒə'bɪlɪti/ n ilegibilidad, f
illegible /ɪ'ledʒəbəl/ a ilegible, indescifrable
illegibly /ɪ'ledʒəbli/ adv de un modo ilegible
illegitimacy /ˌɪlɪ'dʒɪtəməsi/ n ilegitimidad, f; falsedad, f
illegitimate /ˌɪlɪ'dʒɪtəmɪt/ a ilegítimo, bastardo; falso; ilícito, desautorizado
illegitimately /ˌɪlɪ'dʒɪtəmɪtli/ adv ilegítimamente
illiberal /ɪ'lɪbərəl/ a iliberal; intolerante, estrecho de miras; (mean) avaro, tacaño, ruin
illiberality /ˌɪlɪbə'rælɪti/ n iliberalidad, f; intolerancia, f; (avarice) tacañería, avaricia, ruindad, f
illiberally /ɪ'lɪbərəli/ adv avariciosamente, ruinmente
illicit /ɪ'lɪsɪt/ a ilícito, indebido, ilegal
illicitly /ɪ'lɪsɪtli/ adv ilícitamente, ilegalmente
illicitness /ɪ'lɪsɪtnɪs/ n ilicitud, ilegalidad, f
illimitable /ɪ'lɪmɪtəbəl/ a ilimitado, sin límites, infinito
illiteracy /ɪ'lɪtərəsi/ n analfabetismo, m
illiterate /ɪ'lɪtərɪt/ a and n analfabeto (-ta), iliterato (-ta)
illness /'ɪlnɪs/ n enfermedad, dolencia, f, mal, m
illogical /ɪ'lɒdʒɪkəl/ a ilógico; absurdo, irracional
illogicality /ɪˌlɒdʒɪ'kælɪti/ n falta de lógica, f; absurdo, m, irracionalidad, f
illuminant /ɪ'lumənənt/ a iluminador, alumbrador
illuminate /ɪ'lumə,neit/ vt iluminar, alumbrar; Art. iluminar; (explain) aclarar, ilustrar
illuminated /ɪ'lumə,neitɪd/ a iluminado, encendido; Art. iluminado. **i. sign,** letrero luminoso, m
illuminati /ɪˌlumə'nɑti/ n pl secta de los alumbrados, f
illuminating /ɪ'lumə,neitɪŋ/ a iluminador; (explanatory) aclaratorio. —n Art. iluminación, f
illumination /ɪˌlumə'neɪʃən/ n iluminación, f, alumbrado, m; (for decoration) luminaria, f; Art. iluminación, f; Fig. inspiración, f

illuminator /ɪ'lumə,neɪtər/ n Art. iluminador (-ra)
illumine /ɪ'lumɪn/ vt encender, alumbrar; Fig. inspirar
illusion /ɪ'luʒən/ n ilusión, f, engaño, m; (dream) esperanza, ilusión, f, ensueño, m. **to harbor illusions,** tener ilusiones
illusive /ɪ'lusɪv/ a ilusivo, engañoso, falso
illusively /ɪ'lusɪvli/ adv falsamente, aparentemente
illusoriness /ɪ'lusərinɪs/ n ilusión, falsedad, f, engaño, m
illusory /ɪ'lusəri/ a ilusorio, deceptivo, falso, irreal
illustrate /'ɪlə,streit/ vt ilustrar, aclarar, explicar, elucidar; Art. ilustrar; (prove) probar, demostrar
illustration /ˌɪlə'streiʃən/ n ejemplo, m; ilustración, f; Art. grabado, m; estampa, f; (explanation) elucidación, aclaración, f
illustrative /ɪ'lʌstrətɪv/ a ilustrativo, ilustrador, explicativo, aclaratorio
illustrator /'ɪlə,streitər/ n ilustrador (-ra), grabador (-ra)
illustrious /ɪ'lʌstriəs/ a ilustre, famoso, renombrado, distinguido
illustriously /ɪ'lʌstriəsli/ adv ilustremente, noblemente
illustriousness /ɪ'lʌstriəsnɪs/ n eminencia, f, renombre, m, grandeza, f
image /'ɪmɪdʒ/ n (optics) imagen, f; efigie, imagen, f; (religious) imagen, estatua, f; Art. figura, f; (metaphor) metáfora, expresión, f; (of a person) retrato, m. **to be the i. of,** ser el retrato de. **sharp i.,** imagen nítida, f. **i. breaker,** iconoclasta, mf. **i. vendor,** vendedor (-ra) de imágenes
imagery /'ɪmɪdʒri/ n Art. imaginería, f; (style) metáforas, f pl
imaginable /ɪ'mædʒənəbəl/ a imaginable
imaginary /ɪ'mædʒə,nɛri/ a imaginario; fantástico, de ensueño
imagination /ɪˌmædʒə'neɪʃən/ n imaginación, f; imaginativa, fantasía, inventiva, f, ingenio, m
imaginative /ɪ'mædʒənətɪv/ a imaginativo; fantástico
imagine /ɪ'mædʒɪn/ vt imaginar, concebir; idear, proyectar, inventar; figurarse, suponer. **Just i.!** ¡Imagínese usted!
imam /ɪ'mɑm/ n imán, m
imbecile /'ɪmbəsɪl/ a imbécil; (foolish) necio, estúpido, tonto. —n imbécil, mf; (fool) necio (-ia), tonto (-ta), estúpido (-da)
imbecility /ˌɪmbə'sɪlɪti/ n imbecilidad, f; (folly) necedad, sandez, f
imbibe /ɪm'baib/ vt embeber, absorber; (drink) sorber, chupar; emparparse de
imbibing /ɪm'baibɪŋ/ n imbibición, absorción, f
imbricate /'ɪmbrɪkɪt/ a (Zool. Bot.) imbricado
imbroglio /ɪm'broulyou/ n embrollo, lío, m
imbue /ɪm'byu/ vt imbuir, calar, empapar; teñir. **to i. with,** infundir de
imitable /'ɪmɪtəbəl/ a imitable
imitate /'ɪmɪ,teit/ vt imitar; copiar, reproducir; (counterfeit) contrahacer
imitation /ˌɪmɪ'teiʃən/ n imitación, f; copia, f; remedo, traslado, m. —a imitado; falso, artificial
imitative /'ɪmɪ,teitɪv/ a imitativo; imitador
imitativeness /'ɪmɪ,teitɪvnɪs/ n facultad imitativa (or de imitacion), f
imitator /'ɪmɪ,teitər/ n imitador (-ra); contrahacedor (-ra), falsificador (-ra)
immaculate /ɪ'mækyəlɪt/ a inmaculado, puro; (of dress) elegante. **I. Conception,** la Purísima Concepción
immaculately /ɪ'mækyəlɪtli/ adv inmaculadamente; elegantemente
immaculateness /ɪ'mækyəlɪtnɪs/ n pureza, f; (of dress) elegancia, f
immanence /'ɪmənəns/ n inmanencia, inherencia, f
immanent /'ɪmənənt/ a inmanente; inherente
immaterial /ˌɪmə'tɪəriəl/ a inmaterial, incorpóreo; sin importancia. **It is i. to me,** Me es indiferente, No me importa, Me da lo mismo, Me da igual
immateriality /ˌɪmə,tɪəri'ælɪti/ n inmaterialidad, f
immature /ˌɪmə'tʃur/ a inmaturo; precoz; (of fruit) verde

immaturity /ˌɪmə'tʃʊrɪti/ n falta de madurez, f; precocidad, f

immeasurability /ˌɪ,mɛʒərə'bɪlɪti/ n inmensurabilidad, inmensidad, f

immeasurable /ɪ'mɛʒərəbəl/ a inmensurable, inmenso, imponderable

immeasurably /ɪ'mɛʒərəbli/ adv inmensamente, enormemente

immediate /ɪ'midiɪt/ a (of place) inmediato, cercano, contiguo; (of time) próximo, inmediato, directo; (of action) inmediato, perentorio; (on letters) urgente. **to take i. action,** tomar acción inmediata

immediately /ɪ'miditli/ adv (of place) próximamente, contiguamente; (of time) luego, seguidamente, en el acto, ahora mismo, enseguida; directamente; (as soon as) así que

immemorial /ˌɪmə'mɔriəl/ a inmemorial, inmemorable

immemorially /ˌɪmə'mɔriəli/ adv desde tiempo inmemorial

immense /ɪ'mɛns/ a inmenso, enorme; vasto, extenso; infinito

immensely /ɪ'mɛnsli/ adv inmensamente, enormemente

immensity /ɪ'mɛnsɪti/ n inmensidad, f; extensión, vastedad, f

immerse /ɪ'mɜrs/ vt sumergir, hundir en, zambullir; bautizar por sumersión. Fig. **to be immersed in,** estar absorto en

immersion /ɪ'mɜrʒən/ n sumersion, f, hundimiento, m; Astron. inmersión, f

immigrant /'ɪmɪgrənt/ a and n inmigrante, mf

immigrate /'ɪmɪ,greit/ vi inmigrar

immigration /ˌɪmɪ'greiʃən/ n inmigración, f

imminence /'ɪmənəns/ n inminencia, f

imminent /'ɪmənənt/ a inminente

immobile /ɪ'moubəl/ a inmóvil, inmoble; impasible, imperturbable

immobility /ˌɪmou'bɪlɪti/ n inmovilidad, f; impasibilidad, imperturbabilidad, f

immobilization /ɪ,moubələ'zeiʃən/ n inmovilización, f

immobilize /ɪ'moubə,laiz/ vt inmovilizar

immoderate /ɪ'mɒdərɪt/ a inmoderado, excesivo, indebido

immoderately /ɪ'mɒdərɪtli/ adv inmoderadamente, excesivamente

immoderateness /ɪ'mɒdərɪtnɪs/ n inmoderación, f, exceso, m

immodest /ɪ'mɒdɪst/ a inmodesto; indecente, deshonesto; (pert) atrevido, descarado

immodestly /ɪ'mɒdɪstli/ adv impúdicamente, inmodestamente

immodesty /ɪ'mɒdɪsti/ n inmodestia, impudicia, f; deshonestidad, licencia, f; (forwardness) descaro, atrevimiento, m

immolate /'ɪmə,leit/ vt inmolar, sacrificar

immolation /ˌɪmə'leiʃən/ n inmolación, f, sacrificio, m

immolator /'ɪmə,leitər/ n inmolador (-ra)

immoral /ɪ'mɔrəl/ a inmoral; licencioso, vicioso; incontinente

immorality /ˌɪmə'rælɪti/ n inmoralidad, f

immortal /ɪ'mɔrtl/ a inmortal; perenne, eterno, imperecedero. —n inmortal, mf

immortality /ˌɪmɔr'tælɪti/ n inmortalidad, f; fama inmortal, f

immortalize /ɪ'mɔrtl,aiz/ vt inmortalizar, perpetuar

immortally /ɪ'mɔrtli/ adv inmortalmente, eternamente, para siempre

immovability /ɪ,muvə'bɪlɪti/ n inamovilidad, inmovilidad, f; (of purpose) inflexibilidad, tenacidad, constancia, f

immovable /ɪ'muvəbəl/ a inmoble, fijo, inmóvil; (of purpose) inconmovible, inalterable, constante. —n pl. **immovables** Law. bienes inmuebles, m pl. Eccl. **i. feast,** fiesta fija, f

immovably /ɪ'muvəbli/ adv inmóvilmente, fijamente

immune /ɪ'myun/ a inmune, libre; Med. inmune. **i. from,** exento de; libre de

immunity /ɪ'myunɪti/ n inmunidad, libertad, f; exención, f; Med. inmunidad, f

immunization /ˌɪ,myunə'zeiʃən/ n Med. inmunización, f

immunize /'ɪmyə,naiz/ vt inmunizar

immure /ɪ'myʊr/ vt emparedar, recluir, encerrar

immutability /ˌɪ,myutə'bɪlɪti/ n inmutabilidad, inalterabilidad, f

immutable /ɪ'myutəbəl/ a inmutable, inalterable, constante

immutably /ɪ'myutəbli/ adv inmutablemente

imp /ɪmp/ n trasgo, diablillo, duende, m; (child) picaruelo (-la)

impact /'ɪmpækt/ n impacto, m, impacción, f; choque, m, colisión, f

impair /ɪm'pɛər/ vt perjudicar, echar a perder, deteriorar, empeorar, desmejorar. **to be impaired,** deteriorarse, perjudicarse

impairment /ɪm'pɛərmənt/ n deterioración, perjuicio, empeoramiento, m

impale /ɪm'peil/ vt (punishment) empalar; (with a sword) atravesar, espetar

impalement /ɪm'peilmənt/ n (punishment) empalamiento, m; atravesamiento, m, transfixión, f

impalpability /ɪm,pælpə'bɪlɪti/ n impalpabilidad, intangibilidad, f

impalpable /ɪm'pælpəbəl/ a impalpable, intangible; incorpóreo

impart /ɪm'part/ vt comunicar, dar parte (de); conferir

impartial /ɪm'parʃəl/ a imparcial, ecuánime

impartiality /ɪm,parʃi'ælɪti/ n imparcialidad, ecuanimidad, entereza, f, desinterés, m

impartially /ɪm'parʃəli/ adv imparcialmente, con desinterés

impassability /ɪm,pæsə'bɪlɪti/ n impracticabilidad, f

impassable /ɪm'pæsəbəl/ a intransitable, impracticable; (of water) invadeable

impasse /'ɪmpæs/ n callejón sin salida, m

impassibility /ɪm,pæsə'bɪlɪti/ n impasibilidad, imperturbabilidad, indiferencia, f

impassible /ɪm'pæsəbəl/ a impasible, insensible; indiferente, imperturbable

impassion /ɪm'pæʃən/ vt apasionar, conmover

impassioned /ɪm'pæʃənd/ a apasionado, vehemente, ardiente

impassive /ɪm'pæsɪv/ a impasible, insensible; indiferente, imperturbable; apático

impassively /ɪm'pæsɪvli/ adv indiferentemente

impassivity /ˌɪmpæ'sɪvɪti/ n impasibilidad, f; indiferencia, f; apatía, f

impatience /ɪm'peiʃəns/ n impaciencia, f

impatient /ɪm'peiʃənt/ a impaciente; intolerante. **to make i.,** impacientar. **to grow i.,** impacientarse, perder la paciencia. **to grow i. at,** impacientarse ante. **to grow i. to,** impacientarse a or por. **to grow i. under,** impacientarse bajo

impatiently /ɪm'peiʃəntli/ adv con impaciencia, impacientemente

impeach /ɪm'pitʃ/ vt Law. denunciar, delatar, acusar, hacer juicio político (Argentina); censurar, criticar, tachar

impeachable /ɪm'pitʃəbəl/ a Law. delatable, denunciable, acusable; censurable

impeacher /ɪm'pitʃər/ n acusador (-ra), denunciador (-ra), delator (-ra)

impeachment /ɪm'pitʃmənt/ n Law. acusación, denuncia, f; reproche, m, queja, f

impeccability /ɪm,pekə'bɪlɪti/ n (perfection) impecabilidad, perfección, f; elegancia, f

impeccable /ɪm'pekəbəl/ a impecable, intachable, perfecto; elegante

impeccably /ɪm'pekəbli/ adv perfectamente; elegantemente

impecuniosity /ˌɪmpə,kyuni'ɒsɪti/ n indigencia, pobreza, f

impecunious /ˌɪmpə'kyuniəs/ a indigente, pobre

impede /ɪm'pid/ vt impedir, obstruir, estorbar; Fig. dificultar, embarazar

impediment /ɪm'pɛdəmənt/ n obstáculo, estorbo, m; Fig. dificultad, f; Law. impedimento, m. **to have an i. in one's speech,** tener una dificultad en el hablar

impel /ɪm'pɛl/ vt impulsar, impeler; Fig. estimular,

obligar, mover, constreñir. **I felt impelled (to),** Me sentí obligado (a)

impend /ɪm'pɛnd/ *vi* ser inminente, amenazar

impending /ɪm'pɛndɪŋ/ *a* inminente, pendiente

impenetrability /ɪm,pɛnɪtrə'bɪlɪti/ *n* impenetrabilidad, *f; Fig.* enigma, secreto, misterio, *m*

impenetrable /ɪm'pɛnɪtrəbəl/ *a* impenetrable; intransitable; denso, espeso; *Fig.* enigmático, insondable, secreto

impenetrably /ɪm,pɛnɪtrə'bɪlɪti/ *adv* impenetrablemente, densamente

impenitence /ɪm'pɛnɪtəns/ *n* impenitencia, *f*

impenitent /ɪm'pɛnɪtənt/ *a* impenitente, incorregible

impenitently /ɪm'pɛnɪtəntli/ *adv* sin penitencia

imperative /ɪm'pɛrətɪv/ *a* imperioso, perentorio; *Gram.* imperativo; (necessary) esencial, urgente. —*n* mandato, *m*, orden, *f; Gram.* imperativo, *m.* **in the i.,** en el imperativo

imperatively /ɪm'pɛrətɪvli/ *adv* imperativamente

imperativeness /ɪm'pɛrətɪvnɪs/ *n* perentoriedad, *f;* urgencia, importancia, *f*

imperceptible /,ɪmpər'sɛptəbəl/ *a* imperceptible, insensible

imperceptibly /,ɪmpər'sɛptəbli/ *adv* imperceptiblemente

imperceptive /,ɪmpər'sɛptɪv/ *a* insensible

imperfect /ɪm'pɜrfɪkt/ *a* imperfecto; incompleto, defectuoso. —*a* and *n Gram.* imperfecto *m*

imperfection /,ɪmpər'fɛkʃən/ *n* imperfección, *f;* defecto, desperfecto, *m;* falta, tacha, *f*

imperfectly /ɪm'pɜrfɪktli/ *adv* imperfectamente

imperial /ɪm'pɪəriəl/ *a* imperial, imperatorio. —*n* (beard) pera, *f.* **i. preference,** preferencia dentro del Imperio, *f*

imperial /ɪm'pɪəriəl/ *vt* arriesgar, poner en peligro, aventurar

imperialism /ɪm'pɪəriə,lɪzəm/ *n* imperialismo, *m*

imperialist /ɪm'pɪəriəlɪst/ *n* imperialista, *mf*

imperialistic /ɪm,pɪəriə'lɪstɪk/ *a* imperialista

imperious /ɪm'pɪəriəs/ *a* imperioso, altivo, arrogante; (pressing) urgente, apremiante

imperiously /ɪm'pɪəriəsli/ *adv* imperiosamente, con arrogancia

imperiousness /ɪm'pɪəriəsnɪs/ *n* autoridad, arrogancia, altivez, *f;* necesidad, urgencia, *f,* apremio, *m*

imperishability /ɪm,pɛrɪʃə'bɪlɪti/ *n* (immortality) inmortalidad, perennidad, *f*

imperishable /ɪm'pɛrɪʃəbəl/ *a* imperecedero, inmarchitable, perenne, eterno

impermanence /ɪm'pɜrmənəns/ *n* inestabilidad, interinidad, *f;* brevedad, fugacidad, *f*

impermanent /ɪm'pɜrmənənt/ *a* interino, no permanente

impermeability /ɪm,pɜrmiə'bɪlɪti/ *n* impermeabilidad, *f*

impermeable /ɪm'pɜrmiəbəl/ *a* impermeable

impersonal /ɪm'pɜrsənḷ/ *a* impersonal, objetivo; *Gram.* impersonal

impersonality /ɪm,pɜrsə'nælɪti/ *n* objetividad, *f*

impersonally /ɪm'pɜrsənḷi/ *adv* impersonalmente

impersonate /ɪm'pɜrsə,neit/ *vt* personificar, simbolizar; *Theat.* representar

impersonation /ɪm,pɜrsə'neiʃən/ *n* personificación, simbolización, *f; Theat.* representación, *f*

impertinence /ɪm'pɜrtṇəns/ *n* impertinencia, majadería, insolencia, *f;* inoportunidad, *f;* despropósito, *m*

impertinent /ɪm'pɜrtṇənt/ *a* impertinente, insolente; (unseasonable) intempestivo, inoportuno; (irrelevant) fuera de propósito

impertinently /ɪm'pɜrtṇəntli/ *adv* con insolencia, impertinentemente

imperturbability /,ɪmpərtɜrbə'bɪlɪti/ *n* imperturbabilidad, serenidad, impasibilidad, *f;* impavidez, *f*

imperturbable /,ɪmpər'tɜrbəbəl/ *a* imperturbable, impasible, sereno; impávido

imperturbably /,ɪmpər'tɜrbəbli/ *adv* con serenidad, imperturbablemente

impervious /ɪm'pɜrviəs/ *a* impermeable, impenetrable; *Fig.* insensible. **He is i. to arguments,** No hace caso de argumentos

imperviousness /ɪm'pɜrviəsnɪs/ *n* impermeabilidad, impenetrabilidad, *f; Fig.* insensibilidad, *f*

impetigo /,ɪmpɪ'taigou/ *n Med.* impétigo, *m*

impetuosity /ɪm,pɛtʃu'ɒsɪti/ *n* impetuosidad, temeridad, irreflexión, *f*

impetuous /ɪm'pɛtʃuəs/ *a* impetuoso, temerario, irreflexivo; violento, vehemente

impetuously /ɪm'pɛtʃuəsli/ *adv* impetuosamente; con vehemencia

impetus /'ɪmpɪtəs/ *n Mech.* ímpetu, *m,* impulsión, *f; Fig.* incentivo, estímulo, impulso, *m*

impiety /ɪm'paiɪti/ *n* impiedad, irreligión, irreligiosidad, *f*

impinge (upon) /ɪm'pɪndʒ/ *vi* chocar con, tropezar con

impious /'ɪmpiəs/ *a* impío, irreligioso, sacrílego; (wicked) malvado, perverso, malo

impish /'ɪmpɪʃ/ *a* travieso, revoltoso, enredador

implacability /ɪm,plækə'bɪlɪti/ *n* implacabilidad, *f*

implacable /ɪm'plækəbəl/ *a* implacable, inexorable, inflexible, riguroso

implacably /ɪm'plækəbli/ *adv* implacablemente

implant /ɪm'plænt/ *vt Fig.* implantar, inculcar, instilar

implantation /,ɪmplæn'teiʃən/ *n Fig.* implantación, instilación, inculcación, *f*

implement /*n* 'ɪmpləmənt/ *v also* -,mɛnt/ *n* instrumento, utensilio, *m,* herramienta, *f;* (of war) elemento, *m.* —*vt* cumplir, hacer efectivo; llevar a cabo

implicate /'ɪmplɪ,keit/ *vt* enredar, envolver; (imply) implicar, contener, llevar en sí; (in a crime) comprometer. **to be implicated in a crime,** estar implicado en un crimen.

implication /,ɪmplɪ'keiʃən/ *n* implicación, inferencia, repercusión, sugestión, *f;* (in a crime) complicidad, *f*

implicit /ɪm'plɪsɪt/ *a* implícito, virtual, tácito; (absolute) ciego, absoluto, implícito. **with i. faith,** con fe ciega

implicitness /ɪm'plɪsɪtnɪs/ *n* carácter implícito, *m,* lo implícito

implied /ɪm'plaid/ *a* tácito, implícito

implore /ɪm'plɔr/ *vt* implorar, suplicar

imploring /ɪm'plɔrɪŋ/ *a* suplicante, implorante

imploringly /ɪm'plɔrɪŋli/ *adv* con encarecimiento, a súplica, de un modo suplicante

imply /ɪm'plai/ *vt* implicar, indicar, presuponer; (mean) querer decir, significar; (hint) insinuar, sugerir

impolicy /ɪm'pɒləsi/ *n* indiscreción, imprudencia, impolítica, *f*

impolite /,ɪmpə'lait/ *a* descortés, mal educado

impolitely /,ɪmpə'laitli/ *adv* con descortesía

impoliteness /,ɪmpə'laitnɪs/ *n* descortesía, falta de urbanidad, *f*

impolitic /ɪm'pɒlɪtɪk/ *a* impolítico

imponderability /ɪm,pɒndərə'bɪlɪti/ *n* imponderabilidad, *f*

imponderable /ɪm'pɒndərəbəl/ *a* imponderable

import /*v* ɪm'pɔrt; *a, n* 'ɪmpɔrt/ *v Com.* importar; (mean) significar, querer decir. —*a Com.* importado, de importación. —*n Com.* importación, *f;* (meaning) significado, sentido, *m;* (value) importe, valor, *m;* (contents) contenido, tenor, *m;* importancia, *f.* **i. duty,** derechos de importación derechos de entrada, *m pl,* gravamen a la importación, *m.* **i. licence,** permiso de importación, *m.* **i. trade,** negocios de importación, *m pl*

importable /ɪm'pɔrtəbəl/ *a* importable, que se puede importar

importance /ɪm'pɔrtṇs/ *n* importancia, *f;* valor, alcance, *m,* magnitud, *f;* consideración, eminencia, *f.* **to be fully conscious of one's i.,** tener plena conciencia de su importancia

important /ɪm'pɔrtṇt/ *a* importante; distinguido; presuntuoso, vanidoso. **to be i.,** importar, ser importante. **i. person,** personaje, *m,* persona importante, *f*

importantly /ɪm'pɔrtṇtli/ *adv* importantemente, con importancia

importation /,ɪmpɔr'teiʃən/ *n* importación, *f; Com.* introducción (or importación) de géneros extranjeros, *f*

importer /ɪm'pɔrtər/ *n* importador (-ra)

importunate /ɪm'pɔrtʃənɪt/ *a* (of a demand) insistente, importuno; (of persons) impertinente, pesado

importunately /ɪm'pɔrtʃənɪtli/ *adv* importunadamente

importune /,ɪmpɔr'tun/ *vt* importunar, asediar, perseguir

importuning /,ɪmpɔr'tunɪŋ/ *n* persecución, importunación, *f*

importunity /,ɪmpɔr'tunɪti/ *n* importunidad, insistencia, impertinencia, *f*

impose /ɪm'pouz/ *vt* (on, upon) imponer, infligir, cargar; *Print.* imponer. —*vi* (on, upon) (deceive) engañar, embaucar

imposing /ɪm'pouzɪŋ/ *a* imponente, impresionante; (of persons) majestuoso, importante

imposition /,ɪmpə'zɪʃən/ *n* imposición, *f;* (burden) impuesto, tributo, *m,* carga, *f;* (*Print., etc.*) imposición, *f;* (trick) fraude, engaño, *m,* decepción, *f*

impossibility /ɪm,pɒsə'bɪlɪti/ *n* imposibilidad, *f*

impossible /ɪm'pɒsəbəl/ *a* imposible. **Nothing is i.,** No hay nada imposible, *Inf.* De menos nos hizo Dios. **to do the i.,** hacer lo imposible

impost /'ɪmpoust/ *n* impuesto, *m,* contribución, gabela, *f*

impostor /ɪm'pɒstər/ *n* impostor (-ra), bribón (-ona), embustero (-ra)

imposture /ɪm'pɒstʃər/ *n* impostura, *f,* engaño, fraude, *m*

impotence /'ɪmpətəns/ *n* impotencia, *f*

impotent /'ɪmpətənt/ *a* impotente

impound /ɪm'paund/ *vt* acorralar; (water) embalsar; (goods) confiscar

impoverish /ɪm'pɒvərɪʃ/ *vt* empobrecer, depauperar, arruinar; (health) debilitar; (land) agotar

impoverished /ɪm'pɒvərɪʃt/ *a* indigente, necesitado; (of land) agotado

impoverishment /ɪm'pɒvərɪʃmənt/ *n* empobrecimiento, *m,* ruina, *f;* (of land) agotamiento, *m*

impracticability /ɪm,præktɪkə'bɪlɪti/ *n* impracticabilidad, imposibilidad, *f*

impracticable /ɪm'præktɪkəbəl/ *a* impracticable, no factible, imposible

imprecation /,ɪmprɪ'keɪʃən/ *n* imprecación, maldición, *f*

imprecatory /'ɪmprɪkə,tɔri/ *a* imprecatorio, maldiciente

impregnable /ɪm'pregnəbəl/ *a* inexpugnable, inconquistable

impregnate /ɪm'pregneit/ *vt* impregnar, empapar; *Biol.* fecundar. **to become impregnated,** impregnarse

impregnation /,ɪmpreg'neiʃən/ *n* impregnación, *f; Biol.* fecundación, fertilización, *f; Fig.* inculcación, *f*

impresario /,ɪmprə'sɑri,ou/ *n* empresario, *m*

imprescriptible /,ɪmprə'skrɪptəbəl/ *a* imprescriptible, inalienable

impress /*v* ɪm'prɛs; *n* 'ɪmprɛs/ *vt* imprimir; (on the mind) impresionar; inculcar, imbuir; (with respect) imponer; *Mil.* reclutar; (of goods) confiscar. —*n* impresión, marca, señal, huella, *f*

impression /ɪm'prɛʃən/ *n* impresión, *f;* marca, señal, huella, *f; Print.* impresión, *f;* efecto, *m;* idea, noción, *f.* **He has the i. that they do not like him,** Sospecha que no les es simpático. **to be under the i.,** tener la impresión

impressionability /ɪm,prɛʃənə'bɪlɪti/ *n* susceptibilidad, sensibilidad, *f*

impressionable /ɪm'prɛʃənəbəl/ *a* susceptible, impresionable, sensitivo

impressionism /ɪm'prɛʃə,nɪzəm/ *n* impresionismo, *m*

impressionist /ɪm'prɛʃənɪst/ *n* impresionista, *mf*

impressionistic /ɪm,prɛʃə'nɪstɪk/ *a* impresionista

impressive /ɪm'prɛsɪv/ *a* impresionante; emocionante; imponente, majestuoso; enfático

impressively /ɪm'prɛsɪvli/ *adv* solemnemente, de modo impresionante; enfáticamente

impressiveness /ɪm'prɛsɪvnɪs/ *n* efecto impresionante, *m;* grandiosidad, pompa, *f;* majestuosidad, *f;* fuerza, *f*

imprint /*n* 'ɪmprɪnt; *v* ɪm'prɪnt/ *n* impresión, señal, marca, huella, *f; Print.* pie de imprenta, *m.* —*vt* imprimir; (on the mind) grabar, fijar

imprison /ɪm'prɪzən/ *vt* encerrar, encarcelar, aprisionar

imprisonment /ɪm'prɪzənmənt/ *n* encarcelación, prisión, *f,* encierro, *m*

improbability /ɪm,prɒbə'bɪlɪti/ *n* improbabilidad, *f;* inverosimilitud, *f*

improbable /ɪm'prɒbəbəl/ *a* improbable; inverosímil

improbity /ɪm'proubɪti/ *n* improbidad, *f*

impromptu /ɪm'prɒmptu/ *a* indeliberado, impremeditado, espontáneo. —*adv* de improviso, in promptu. —*n* improvisación, *f*

improper /ɪm'prɒpər/ *a* impropio, inadecuado; incorrecto; indebido; indecente, indecoroso. **i. fraction,** *Math.* quebrado impropio, *m*

improperly /ɪm'prɒpərli/ *adv* impropiamente, incorrectamente; indecorosamente

impropriety /,ɪmprə'praiɪti/ *n* inconveniencia, *f;* incorrección, *f;* (style) impropiedad, *f;* falta de decoro, *f*

improvable /ɪm'pruvəbəl/ *a* mejorable, perfectible

improve /ɪm'pruv/ *vt* mejorar; perfeccionar; (beautify) embellecer, hermosear; (land) bonificar; *Lit.* corregir, enmendar; (cultivate) cultivar; (increase) aumentar; (an opportunity) aprovechar; (strengthen) fortificar; (business) sacar provecho de, explotar. —*vi* mejorar; perfeccionarse; (progress) hacer progresos, progresar, adelantarse; *Com.* subir; (become beautiful) hacerse hermoso, embellecerse; (increase) aumentarse. **to i. upon,** mejorar, perfeccionar; pulir

improvement /ɪm'pruvmənt/ *n* mejora, *f;* perfeccionamiento, *m;* aumento, *m;* adelantamiento, progreso, *m;* (in health) mejoría, *f;* embellecimiento, *m;* cultivación, *f;* (of land) abono, *m*

improver /ɪm'pruvər/ *n* aprendiz (-za)

improvidence /ɪm'prɒvɪdəns/ *n* imprevisión, *f;* improvidencia, *f*

improvident /ɪm'prɒvɪdənt/ *a* impróvido, desprevenido

improvidently /ɪm'prɒvɪdəntli/ *adv* impróvidamente

improvisation /ɪm,prɒvə'zeiʃən/ *n* improvisación, *f*

improvise /'ɪmprə,vaiz/ *vt* improvisar

improviser /'ɪmprə,vaizər/ *n* improvisador (-ra)

imprudence /ɪm'prudns/ *n* imprudencia, *f;* desacierto, *m,* indiscreción, *f*

imprudent /ɪm'prudnt/ *a* imprudente; desacertado, indiscreto, mal avisado, irreflexivo

imprudently /ɪm'prudntli/ *adv* imprudentemente; sin pensar

impudence /'ɪmpyədəns/ *n* impudencia, *f,* descaro, *m,* insolencia, desvergüenza, *f,* atrevimiento, *m*

impudent /'ɪmpyədənt/ *a* impudente, descarado, insolente, desvergonzado, atrevido

impudently /'ɪmpyədntli/ *adv* descaradamente, con insolencia

impugn /ɪm'pyun/ *vt* impugnar, contradecir, atacar

impugnable /ɪm'pyunəbəl/ *a* impugnable, atacable

impugnment /ɪm'pyunmənt/ *n* impugnación, *f*

impulse /'ɪmpʌls/ *n* ímpetu, *m,* impulsión, *f;* impulso, estímulo, *m;* incitación, instigación, *f;* motivo, *m;* (fit) arranque, arrebato, acceso, *m*

impulsion /ɪm'pʌlʃən/ *n* ímpetu, *m,* impulsión, *f;* empuje, *m,* arranque, *m*

impulsive /ɪm'pʌlsɪv/ *a* impelente; irreflexivo, impulsivo

impulsively /ɪm'pʌlsɪvli/ *adv* por impulso

impulsiveness /ɪm'pʌlsɪvnɪs/ *n* irreflexión, *f;* carácter impulsivo, *m*

impunity /ɪm'pyunɪti/ *n* impunidad, *f.* **with i.,** impunemente

impure /ɪm'pyur/ *a* impuro; adulterado, mezclado; (indecent) deshonesto, indecente; (dirty) turbio, sucio

impurity /ɪm'pyurɪti/ *n* impureza, *f;* adulteración, mezcla, *f;* deshonestidad, liviandad, *f;* suciedad, turbiedad, *f*

imputable /ɪm'pyutəbəl/ *a* imputable, atribuible

imputation /,ɪmpyu'teiʃən/ *n* imputación, atribución, *f;* (in a bad sense) acusación, *f,* reproche, *m*

impute /ɪm'pyut/ *vt* imputar, achacar, atribuir; acusar, reprochar

imputer /ɪm'pyutər/ *n* imputador (-ra); recriminador (-ra), acusador (-ra)

in /ɪn/ *prep* en; a; (of duration) durante, mientras; (with) con; (through) por; dentro de; (under) bajo;

(following a superlative) de; (of specified time) dentro de, de aquí a; (with afternoon, etc.) por; (out of) sobre. **course in medieval Catalan literature,** curso de literatura catalana medioeval. **dressed in black,** vestido de negro. **in London,** en Londres. **in the morning,** por la mañana; (in the course of) durante la mañana. **in time,** a tiempo; dentro de algún tiempo. **in a week,** dentro de una semana. **in the best way,** del mejor modo. **in writing,** por escrito. **in anger,** con enojo. **in one's hand,** en la mano. **in addition to,** además de, a más de. **in case,** por si acaso, en caso de que. **in order to,** a fin de, para (foll. by infin.). **in order that,** para que (foll. by subjunc.). **in so far as,** en cuanto. **in spite of,** a pesar de. **in the distance,** a lo lejos, en lontananza. **in the meantime,** entre tanto. **in the middle of,** en el medio de; a la mitad de. **in the style of,** al modo de; a la manera de, a la (francesa, etc.)

in /ın/ *adv* adentro, dentro; (at home) en casa; (of sun) escondido; (of fire) alumbrado; (in power) en el poder; (of harvest) cosechado; (of boats) entrado (with haber); (of trains) llegado (with haber). **to be in,** estar dentro; haber llegado; estar en casa. **to be in for,** estar expuesto a, correr el riesgo de. **to be in with a person,** ser muy amigo de, estar muy metido con. **Come in!** ¡Adelante!; ¡Pase usted! **ins and outs,** sinuosidades, *f pl*; (of river) meandros, *m pl*; (of an affair) pormenores, detalles, *m pl*. **in less time than you can say Jack Robinson,** en menos de Jesús, en un credo, en menos que canta un gallo, en menos que se persigna un cura loco. **in the middle of nowhere,** donde Cristo dio las tres voces, (Western Hemisphere) donde el diablo perdió el poncho.

in /ın/ *a* interno. **in-law** (of relations) político. **in-patient,** enfermo (-ma) de hospital

inability /,ınə'bılıti/ *n* incapacidad, inhabilidad, ineptitud, incompetencia, *f*; impotencia, *f*

inaccessibility /,ınæk,sesə'bılıti/ *n* inaccesibilidad, *f*

inaccessible /,ınæk'sesəbəl/ *a* inaccesible

inaccuracy /ın'ækyərəsi/ *n* inexactitud, incorrección, *f*

inaccurate /ın'ækyərıt/ *a* inexacto, incorrecto

inaccurately /ın'ækyərıtli/ *adv* inexactamente, erróneamente

inaction /ın'ækʃən/ *n* inacción, *f*

inactive /ın'æktıv/ *a* inactivo, pasivo; (of things) inerte; (lazy) perezoso, indolente; (machinery) parado; (motionless) inmóvil; (at leisure) desocupado, sin empleo

inactivity /,ınæk'tıvıti/ *n* inactividad, pasividad, *f*; (of things) inercia, *f*; pereza, indolencia, *f*; (of machinery) paro, *m*; inmovilidad, *f*; (leisure) desocupación, *f*

inadaptable /,ınə'dæptəbəl/ *a* inadaptable, no adaptable

inadequacy /ın'ædıkwəsi/ *n* insuficiencia, escasez, *f*; imperfección, *f*, defecto, *m*

inadequate /ın'ædıkwıt/ *a* inadecuado, insuficiente, escaso; imperfecto, defectuoso

inadequately /ın'ædıkwıtli/ *adv* inadecuadamente

inadmissible /,ınəd'mısəbəl/ *a* inadmisible, no admisible

inadvertence /,ınəd'vɜrtns/ *n* inadvertencia, *f*; equivocación, *f*, descuido, *m*

inadvertent /,ınəd'vɜrtnt/ *a* inadvertido, accidental, casual; negligente

inadvertently /,ınəd'vɜrtntli/ *adv* inadvertidamente, sin querer

inalienability /ın,eilyənə'bılıti/ *n* inalienabilidad, *f*

inalienable /ın'eilyənəbəl/ *a* inajenable, inalienable

inalterability /ın,ɔltərə'bılıti/ *n* inalterabilidad, *f*

inalterable /ın'ɔltərəbəl/ *a* inalterable

inalterably /ın'ɔltərəbli/ *adv* inalterablemente, sin alteración

inane /ı'nein/ *a* lelo, fatuo, vacío, necio

inanimate /ın'ænəmıt/ *a* (of matter) inanimado; sin vida, exánime, muerto

inanition /,ınə'nıʃən/ *n* inanición, *f*

inanity /ı'nænıti/ *n* vacuidad, fatuidad, necedad, *f*

inappeasable /,ınə'pizəbəl/ *a* implacable, riguroso

inapplicability /ın,æplıkə'bılıti/ *n* no aplicabilidad, *f*

inapplicable /ın'æplıkəbəl/ *a* inaplicable

inapposite /ın'æpəzıt/ *a* fuera de propósito, no pertinente, inoportuno

inappreciable /,ınə'priʃəbəl/ *a* inapreciable, imperceptible

inappreciation /,ınəpriʃi'eiʃən/ *n* falta de apreciación, *f*

inappreciative /,ınə'priʃıtıv/ *a* desagradecido, ingrato. **i. of,** insensible a, indiferente a

inapproachable /,ınə'proutʃəbəl/ *a* inaccesible, huraño, adusto

inappropriate /,ınə'proupriıt/ *a* impropio, inconveniente, inadecuado, incongruente; inoportuno

inappropriately /,ınə'proupriıtli/ *adv* impropiamente; inoportunamente

inappropriateness /,ınə'proupriıtnıs/ *n* impropiedad, inconveniencia, incongruencia, *f*; inoportunidad, *f*

inapt /ın'æpt/ *a* inepto, inhábil; impropio

inaptitude /ın'æptı,tud/ *n* ineptitud, inhabilidad, *f*; impropiedad, *f*

inarticulate /,ınɑr'tıkyəlıt/ *a* (of speech) inarticulado; (reticent) inexpresivo, reservado; indistinto; *Anat.* inarticulado

inarticulately /,ınɑr'tıkyəlıtli/ *adv* indistintamente, de un modo inarticulado

inarticulateness /,ınɑr'tıkyəlıtnıs/ *n* tartamudez, *f*; inexpresión, reserva, *f*; silencio, *m*

inartistic /,ınɑr'tıstık/ *a* antiartístico, antiestético

inartistically /,ınɑr'tıstıkli/ *adv* sin gusto (estético)

inasmuch (as) /,ınəz'mʌtʃ/ *adv* puesto que, visto que, dado que

inattention /,ınə'tenʃən/ *n* desatención, inaplicación, abstracción, *f*; falta de solicitud, *f*

inattentive /,ınə'tentıv/ *a* desatento, distraído; poco solícito, no atento

inattentively /,ınə'tentıvli/ *adv* sin atención, distraídamente

inaudibility /ın,ɔdə'bılıti/ *n* imposibilidad de oír, *f*

inaudible /ın'ɔdəbəl/ *a* inaudible, no audible, ininteligible

inaudibly /ın'ɔdəbli/ *adv* indistintamente, de modo inaudible

inaugurate /ın'ɔgyə,reit/ *vt* inaugurar; (open) estrenar, abrir, dedicar; (install) investir, instalar; (initiate) originar, iniciar, dar lugar (a)

inauguration /ın,ɔgyə'reiʃən/ *n* inauguración, *f*; (opening) estreno, *m*, apertura, *f*; (investiture) instalación, investidura, *f*

inauspicious /,ınɔ'spıʃəs/ *a* poco propicio, desfavorable; ominoso, triste, infeliz

inauspiciously /,ınɔ'spıʃəsli/ *adv* en condiciones desfavorables, desfavorablemente; infelizmente, bajo malos auspicios

inauspiciousness /,ınɔ'spıʃəsnıs/ *n* condiciones desfavorables, *f pl*; infelicidad, *f*; malos auspicios, *m pl*

inborn /'ın'bɔrn/ *a* innato, instintivo, inherente

inbred /'ın'bred/ *a* innato, inherente, instintivo

Inca /'ıŋkə/ *a* incaico, de los incas. —*n* inca, *m*

incalculability /ın,kælkyələ'bılıti/ *n* imposibilidad de calcular, *f*; (of persons) volubilidad, veleidad, *f*; infinidad, immensidad, *f*

incalculable /ın'kælkyələbəl/ *a* incalculable, innumerable; (of persons) voluble, veleidoso, caprichoso; infinito, immenso

incalculably /ın'kælkyələbli/ *adv* enormemente, infinitamente; caprichosamente

incandescence /,ınkən'desəns/ *n* incandescencia, candencia, *f*

incandescent /,ınkən'desənt/ *a* incandescente, candente. **i. light,** luz incandescente, *f*. **to make i.,** candecer

incantation /,ınkæn'teiʃən/ *n* hechizo, *m*, encantación, *f*, ensalmo, *m*

incapability /ın,keipə'bılıti/ *n* incapacidad, *f*; inhabilidad, ineptitud, incompetencia, *f*

incapable /ın'keipəbəl/ *a* incapaz; inhábil, incompetente; (physically) imposibilitado

incapacitate /,ınkə'pæsı,teit/ *vt* imposibilitar, incapacitar, inutilizar; (disqualify) inhabilitar, incapacitar

incapacitation /,ınkə,pæsı'teiʃən/ *n* inhabilitación, *f*

incapacity /,ınkə'pæsıti/ *n* incapacidad, inhabilidad, *f*

incarcerate /ın'kɑrsə,reit/ *vt* encarcelar

incarceration /ın,kɑrsə'reiʃən/ *n* encarcelación, prisión, *f*

incarnate /a ɪnˈkɑrnɪt/ v -neit/ a encarnado. —vt encarnar

incarnation /ˌɪnkɑrˈneiʃən/ n encarnación, f

incautious /ɪnˈkɔʃəs/ a incauto, imprudente

incautiously /ɪnˈkɔʃəsli/ adv incautamente

incautiousness /ɪnˈkɔʃəsnɪs/ n imprudencia, negligencia, falta de cautela, f

incendiary /ɪnˈsɛndiˌɛri/ a incendiario. **i. bomb,** incendiaria, f

incense /ɪnˈsens/ n incienso, m; Fig. adulación, f. —vt Eccl. incensar; (annoy) irritar, exasperar, enojar. **i. burner,** incensario, m

incentive /ɪnˈsentɪv/ n incentivo, estímulo, motivo, m. —a estimulador, incitativo

inception /ɪnˈsepʃən/ n comienzo, principio, m; inauguración, f

incertitude /ɪnˈsɜrtɪˌtud/ n incertidumbre, f

incessant /ɪnˈsɛsənt/ a incesante, continuo, constante

incessantly /ɪnˈsɛsəntli/ adv incesantemente, sin cesar

incest /ˈɪnsɛst/ n incesto, m

incestuous /ɪnˈsɛstʃuəs/ a incestuoso

inch /ɪntʃ/ n pulgada, f. **every i. a man,** hombre hecho y derecho. **Not an i.!** ¡Ni pizca! **within an i. of,** a dos dedos de. **i. by i.,** palmo a palmo, paso a paso. **i. tape,** cinta métrica, f

inchoate /ɪnˈkouɪt/ a rudimentario; imperfecto, incompleto

incidence /ˈɪnsɪdəns/ n incidencia, f

incident /ˈɪnsɪdənt/ a propio, característico, incidental. —n incidente, acontecimiento, m, ocurrencia, f

incidental /ˌɪnsɪˈdɛntl/ a incidente, incidental; accidental, accesorio, no esencial. **i. expense,** gasto imprevisto, m

incidentally /ˌɪnsɪˈdɛntli/ adv (secondarily) incidentalmente; (by the way) de propósito

incident of navigation n accidente de navegación, m

incinerate /ɪnˈsɪnəˌreit/ vt incinerar

incineration /ɪnˌsɪnəˈreiʃən/ n incineración, cremación, f

incinerator /ɪnˈsɪnəˌreitər/ n incinerador, m

incipient /ɪnˈsɪpiənt/ a incipiente, naciente, rudimentario

incise /ɪnˈsaiz/ vt cortar; Art. grabar, tajar

incision /ɪnˈsɪʒən/ n incisión, f; corte, tajo, m; Med. abscisión, f

incisive /ɪnˈsaisɪv/ a (of mind) agudo, penetrante; (of words) mordaz, incisivo, punzante

incisively /ɪnˈsaisɪvli/ adv en pocas palabras; mordazmente, incisivamente

incisiveness /ɪnˈsaisɪvnɪs/ n (of mind) agudeza, penetración, f; (of words) mordacidad, f, sarcasmo, m

incisor /ɪnˈsaizər/ n diente incisivo, m

incite /ɪnˈsait/ vt incitar, estimular, animar; provocar, tentar. **to i. to,** mover a, incitar a

incitement /ɪnˈsaitmənt/ n incitación, instigación, f; estímulo, m; tentación, f; aliciente, m

incivility /ˌɪnsəˈvɪlɪti/ n incivilidad, descortesía, f

inclemency /ɪnˈklɛmənsi/ n inclemencia, f, rigor, m

inclement /ɪnˈklɛmənt/ a inclemente, riguroso, borrascoso

inclination /ˌɪnkləˈneiʃən/ n inclinación, f; (slope) declive, m, pendiente, cuesta, f; (tendency) propensión, tendencia, f; (liking) afición, f; amor, m; (bow) reverencia, f; Geom. inclinación, f

incline /v ɪnˈklain; n ˈɪnklain/ vt inclinar, torcer; doblar; (cause) inclinar (a), hacer. —vi inclinarse, torcerse; (tend) tender, propender, inclinarse; (colors) tirar (a). —n declive, m, pendiente, cuesta, inclinación, f. **I am inclined to believe it,** Me inclino a creerlo. **I am inclined to do it,** Estoy por hacerlo, Creo que lo haré

inclined /ɪnˈklaind/ a torcido, inclinado, doblado; Fig. propenso, adicto. **i. plane,** plano inclinado, m

include /ɪnˈklud/ vt incluir, contener, encerrar; comprender, abrazar

including /ɪnˈkludɪŋ/ present part incluso, inclusive. **not i.,** no comprendido

inclusion /ɪnˈkluʒən/ n inclusión, f

inclusive /ɪnˈklusɪv/ a inclusivo. **January 2 to January 12 i.,** del 2 al 12 de enero, ambos inclusivos. **not**

i. of, sin contar, exclusivo de. **i. of,** que incluye. **i. terms,** todo incluido, todos los gastos incluidos

incognito /ɪnˈkɒgnitou/ a and adv and n incógnito, m.

incoherence /ˌɪnkouˈhiərəns/ n incoherencia, inconsecuencia, f

incoherent /ˌɪnkouˈhiərənt/ a incoherente, inconexo, inconsecuente. **an i. piece of writing,** un escrito sin pies ni cabeza

incoherently /ˌɪnkouˈhiərəntli/ adv con incoherencia

incombustibility /ˌɪnkəmˌbʌstəˈbɪliti/ n incombustibilidad, f

incombustible /ˌɪnkəmˈbʌstəbəl/ a incombustible

income /ˈɪnkʌm/ n renta, f, ingreso, m; Com. rédito, m. **i.-tax,** impuesto de utilidades, m. **i.-tax commissioners,** inspectores de impuestos de utilidades, m pl. **i.-tax return,** declaración de utilidades, f

incoming /ˈɪnˌkʌmɪŋ/ a entrante; nuevo. —n entrada, llegada, f. —n pl **incomings,** ingresos, m pl

incommensurability /ˌɪnkəˌmɛnsərəˈbɪliti/ n inconmensurabilidad, f

incommensurable /ˌɪnkəˈmɛnsərəbəl/ a inconmensurable, no conmensurable

incommensurate /ˌɪnkəˈmɛnsərɪt/ a desproporcionado, desmedido

incommode /ˌɪnkəˈmoud/ vt incomodar, molestar, fastidiar

incommodious /ˌɪnkəˈmoudiəs/ a estrecho; incómodo, inconveniente

incommodiousness /ˌɪnkəˈmoudiəsnɪs/ n estrechez, f; incomodidad, f

incommunicable /ˌɪnkəˈmyunɪkəbəl/ a incommunicable, indecible, inexplicable

incommunicative /ˌɪnkəˈmyunɪkətɪv/ a insociable, intratable, adusto, huraño

incomparable /ɪnˈkɒmpərəbəl/ a incomparable; sin par, sin igual, excelente

incomparableness /ɪnˈkɒmpərəbəlnɪs/ n excelencia, perfección, f

incomparably /ɪnˈkɒmpərəbli/ adv incomparablemente, con mucho

incompatibility /ˌɪnkəmˌpætəˈbɪliti/ n incompatibilidad, f

incompatible /ˌɪnkəmˈpætəbəl/ a incompatible

incompetence /ɪnˈkɒmpɪtəns/ n incompetencia, ineptitud, inhabilidad, f; Law. incapacidad, f

incompetent /ɪnˈkɒmpɪtənt/ a incompetente, incapaz, inepto, inhábil; Law. incapaz

incompetently /ɪnˈkɒmpɪtəntli/ adv inhábilmente

incomplete /ˌɪnkəmˈplit/ a incompleto; imperfecto, defectuoso; (unfinished) sin terminar, inacabado, inconcluso. **incomplete sentence,** frase que queda colgando, f

incompletely /ˌɪnkəmˈplitli/ adv incompletamente; imperfectamente

incompleteness /ˌɪnkəmˈplitnɪs/ n estado incompleto, m; imperfección, f; inconclusión, f

incomprehensibility /ˌɪnkɒmprɪˌhɛnsəˈbɪliti/ n incomprensibilidad, f

incomprehensible /ˌɪnkɒmprɪˈhɛnsəbəl/ a incomprensible

incomprehension /ˌɪnkɒmprɪˈhɛnʃən/ n incomprensión, falta de comprensión, f

inconceivable /ˌɪnkənˈsivəbəl/ a inconcebible, inimaginable

inconclusive /ˌɪnkənˈklusɪv/ a inconcluyente, cuestionable, dudoso, no convincente

inconclusiveness /ˌɪnkənˈklusɪvnɪs/ n carácter inconcluso, m, falta de conclusiones, f

incongruity /ˌɪnkənˈgruiti/ n incongruencia, desproporción, disonancia, f

incongruous /ɪnˈkɒŋgruəs/ a incongruente, incongruo; chocante, desproporcionado, disonante

incongruously /ɪnˈkɒŋgruəsli/ adv incongruentemente, incongruamente

inconsequence /ɪnˈkɒnsɪˌkwɛns/ n inconsecuencia, f

inconsequent, inconsequential /ɪnˈkɒnsɪˌkwɛnt; ɪnˌkɒnsɪˈkwɛnʃəl/ a inconsecuente, ilógico; inconsistente

inconsiderable /ˌɪnkənˈsɪdərəbəl/ a insignificante

inconsiderate /ˌɪnkənˈsɪdərɪt/ a desconsiderado, irreflexivo, irrespetuoso

inconsiderately /ˌɪnkən'sɪdərɪtli/ *adv* sin consideración, desconsideradamente

inconsiderateness /ˌɪnkən'sɪdərɪtnɪs/ *n* desconsideración, falta de respeto, *f*

inconsistency /ˌɪnkən'sɪstənsi/ *n* inconsistencia, inconsecuencia, incompatibilidad, contradicción, anomalía, *f*

inconsistent /ˌɪnkən'sɪstənt/ *a* inconsistente, inconsiguiente, incompatible, contradictorio, anómalo

inconsistently /ˌɪnkən'sɪstəntli/ *adv* contradictoriamente

inconsolable /ˌɪnkən'soʊləbəl/ *a* inconsolable, desconsolado. **to be i.,** estar inconsolable, (*Inf.* of a woman) estar hecha una Magdalena

inconsolably /ˌɪnkən'soʊləbli/ *adv* desconsoladamente

inconspicuous /ˌɪnkən'spɪkyuəs/ *a* que no llama la atención; insignificante, humilde, modesto

inconspicuously /ˌɪnkən'spɪkyuəsli/ *adv* humildemente, modestamente

inconspicuousness /ˌɪnkən'spɪkyuəsnɪs/ *n* modestia, humildad, *f*

inconstancy /ɪn'kɒnstənsi/ *n* inconstancia, movilidad, *f;* mudanza, veleidad, *f*

inconstant /ɪn'kɒnstənt/ *a* inconstante, mudable, variable; veleidoso, volátil, voluble

incontestable /ˌɪnkən'testəbəl/ *a* incontestable, evidente, indisputable

incontinence /ɪn'kɒntṇəns/ *n* incontinencia, *f*

incontinent /ɪn'kɒntṇənt/ *a* incontinente

incontrollable /ˌɪnkən'troʊləbəl/ *a* ingobernable, indomable

incontrovertible /ˌɪnkɒntrə'vɜrtəbəl/ *a* incontrovertible, incontrastable

inconvenience /ˌɪnkən'vinyəns/ *n* incomodidad, inconveniencia, *f;* (of time) inoportunidad, *f.* —*vt* incomodar, causar inconvenientes (a)

inconvenient /ˌɪnkən'vinyənt/ *a* incómodo, inconveniente, molesto, embarazoso; (of time) inoportuno. **at an i. time,** a deshora

inconveniently /ˌɪnkən'vinyəntli/ *adv* incómodamente; (of time) inoportunamente

incorporate /*v* ɪn'kɔrpəˌreit; *a* -pərɪt/ *vt* incorporar, agregar; comprender, incluir, encerrar. —*vi* asociarse, incorporarse. —*a* incorpóreo, inmaterial; incorporado, asociado

incorporation /ɪnˌkɔrpə'reiʃən/ *n* incorporación, agregación, *f;* asociación, *f*

incorporeal /ˌɪnkɔr'pɔriəl/ *a* incorpóreo, inmaterial

incorporeity /ɪnˌkɔrpə'riɪti/ *n* incorporeidad, inmaterialidad, *f*

incorrect /ˌɪnkə'rekt/ *a* incorrecto; inexacto, erróneo, falso

incorrectness /ˌɪnkə'rektnɪs/ *n* incorrección, *f*

incorrigibility /ɪnˌkɔrɪdʒə'bɪlɪti/ *n* incorregibilidad, *f*

incorrigible /ɪn'kɔrɪdʒəbəl/ *a* incorregible, empecatado

incorrigibly /ɪn'kɔrɪdʒəbli/ *adv* incorregiblemente, obstinadamente

incorrupt /ˌɪnkə'rʌpt/ *a* incorrupto; recto, honrado

incorruptibility /ˌɪnkəˌrʌptə'bɪlɪti/ *n* incorruptibilidad, *f;* honradez, probidad, *f*

incorruptible /ˌɪnkə'rʌptəbəl/ *a* incorrupto; honrado, incorruptible

incorruption /ˌɪnkə'rʌpʃən/ *n* incorrupción, *f*

increase /*v* ɪn'kris; *n* 'ɪnkris/ *vt* aumentar, acrecentar; (in numbers) multiplicar; (extend) ampliar, extender; (of price) encarecer, aumentar. —*vi* aumentar, crecer; multiplicarse; extenderse; encarecerse, aumentar. —*n* aumento, crecimiento, *m;* multiplicación, *f;* (in price) encarecimiento, *m*, alza, *f;* (of water) crecida, *f;* (of moon) creciente, *f.* **It is on the i.,** Va en aumento. **to i. and multiply,** crecer y multiplicar

increasingly /ɪn'krisɪŋli/ *adv* más y más; en creciente, en aumento

incredibility /ɪnˌkredə'bɪlɪti/ *n* incredibilidad, *f*

incredible /ɪn'kredəbəl/ *a* increíble; fabuloso, extraordinario. **It seems i.,** Es increíble, *Inf.* Parece mentira

incredibly /ɪn'kredəbli/ *adv* increíblemente

incredulity /ˌɪnkrɪ'dulɪti/ *n* incredulidad, *f*, escepticismo, *m*

incredulous /ɪn'kredʒələs/ *a* incrédulo, escéptico

incredulously /ɪn'kredʒələsli/ *adv* con incredulidad, escépticamente

increment /'ɪnkrəmənt/ *n* aumento, incremento, *m;* adición, añadidura, *f; Math.* incremento, *m.* **unearned i.,** plusvalía, mayor valía, *f*

incriminate /ɪn'krɪməˌneit/ *vt* incriminar

incriminating /ɪn'krɪməˌneitɪŋ/ *a* incriminante, acriminador

incrust /ɪn'krʌst/ *vt* incrustar, encostrar

incrustation /ˌɪnkrʌ'steiʃən/ *n* incrustación, *f;* (scab) costra, *f*

incubate /'ɪnkyəˌbeit/ *vt* empollar; *Med.* incubar

incubation /ˌɪnkyə'beiʃən/ *n* empolladura, incubación, *f; Med.* incubación, *f*

incubator /'ɪnkyəˌbeitər/ *n* incubadora, *f*

incubus /'ɪnkyəbəs/ *n* íncubo, *m;* (burden) carga, *f*

inculcate /ɪn'kʌlkeit/ *vt* inculcar, implantar, instilar

inculcation /ˌɪnkʌl'keiʃən/ *n* inculcación, implantación, instilación, *f*

incumbency /ɪn'kʌmbənsi/ *n* posesión, duración de, posesión, duración (de cualquier puesto), *f*

incumbent /ɪn'kʌmbənt/ *a* obligatorio. —*n Eccl.* beneficiado, *m.* **to be i. on,** incumbir a, ser de su obligación

incur /ɪn'kɜr/ *vi* incurrir (en), incidir (en). **to i. an obligation,** contraer una obligación

incurability /ɪnˌkyʊrə'bɪlɪti/ *n* incurabilidad, *f*

incurable /ɪn'kyʊrəbəl/ *a* incurable, insanable; *Fig.* sin solución, irremediable. —*n* incurable, *mf*

incurably /ɪn'kyʊrəbli/ *adv* incurablemente, irremediablemente

incurious /ɪn'kyʊriəs/ *a* indiferente, sin interés; incurioso, negligente, descuidado

incursion /ɪn'kɜrʒən/ *n* incursión, invasión, irrupción, *f*, acometimiento, *m*

indebted /ɪn'detɪd/ *a* empeñado, adeudado; (obliged) reconocido

indebtedness /ɪn'detɪdnɪs/ *n* deuda, *f;* (gratitude) obligación, *f;* agradecimiento, *m*

indecency /ɪn'disənsi/ *n* indecencia, *f*

indecent /ɪn'disənt/ *a* indecente; obsceno, deshonesto

indecently /ɪn'disəntli/ *adv* torpemente, indecentemente

indecision /ˌɪndɪ'sɪʒən/ *n* indecisión, vacilación, irresolución, *f*

indecisive /ˌɪndɪ'saisɪv/ *a* indeciso, irresoluto, vacilante

indeclinable /ˌɪndɪ'klainəbəl/ *a* indeclinable

indecorous /ɪn'dekərəs/ *a* indecoroso, indecente, indigno

indecorum /ˌɪndɪ'kɔrəm/ *n* indecoro, *m*, indecencia, *f;* incorrección, *f*

indeed /ɪn'did/ *adv* en efecto, de veras, a la verdad, realmente, por cierto, claro está. —*interr* ¿de veras? ¿es posible? **I shall be very glad i.,** Estaré contento de veras. **It is i. an excellent book,** Es en efecto un libro excelente. **There are differences i. between this house and the other,** Hay diferencias, claro está, entre esta casa y la otra

indefatigability /ˌɪndɪˌfætɪgə'bɪlɪti/ *n* resistencia, *f*, aguante, *m*, tenacidad, *f*

indefatigable /ˌɪndɪ'fætɪgəbəl/ *a* incansable, infatigable, resistente

indefatigably /ˌɪndɪ'fætɪgəbli/ *adv* infatigablemente

indefensible /ˌɪndɪ'fensəbəl/ *a* indefendible, insostenible

indefinable /ˌɪndɪ'fainəbəl/ *a* indefinible

indefinite /ɪn'defənɪt/ *a* indefinido, incierto; (delicate) sutil, delicado; *Gram.* indefinido; (vague) vago. *Gram.* **i. article,** artículo indefinido, *m*

indefinitely /ɪn'defənɪtli/ *adv* indefinidamente

indefiniteness /ɪn'defənɪtnɪs/ *n* lo indefinido, el carácter indefinido, *m;* vaguedad, *f*

indelibility /ɪnˌdelə'bɪlɪti/ *n* resistencia, *f*, lo indeleble; *Fig.* duración, tenacidad, *f*

indelible /ɪn'deləbəl/ *a* indeleble, imborrable; *Fig.* inolvidable

indelibly /ɪn'deləbli/ *adv* indeleblemente

indelicacy /ɪn'delɪkəsɪ/ n falta de buen gusto, grosería, f; (tactlessness) indiscreción, falta de tacto, f
indelicate /ɪn'delɪkɪt/ a grosero, descortés; indecoroso, inmodesto; (tactless) inoportuno, indiscreto
indemnification /ɪn,demnəfɪ'keɪʃən/ n indemnización, compensación, f
indemnify /ɪn'demnɪˌfaɪ/ vt indemnizar, compensar
indemnity /ɪn'demnɪtɪ/ n indemnización, reparación, f
indent /ɪn'dent/ vt endentar, mellar; *Print.* sangrar
indentation /ˌɪnden'teɪʃən/ n impresión, depresión, f; corte, m, mella, f; línea quebrada, f, zigzag, m
indenture /ɪn'dentʃər/ n escritura, f, instrumento, m. —vt escriturar
independence /ˌɪndɪ'pendəns/ n independencia, libertad, f; (autonomy) autonomía, f. **I. Day,** Fiesta de la Independencia, f. **i. movement,** movimiento en favor de la independencia, m
independent /ˌɪndɪ'pendənt/ a independiente; libre; (autonomous) autónomo; **i. of,** libre de; aparte de. **a person of i. means,** una persona acomodada
independently /ˌɪndɪ'pendəntlɪ/ adv independientemente
indescribability /ˌɪndɪˌskraɪbə'bɪlɪtɪ/ n imposibilidad de describir, f, lo indescriptible
indescribable /ˌɪndɪ'skraɪbəbəl/ a indescriptible; indefinible, indecible, inexplicable; incalificable
indestructibility /ˌɪndɪˌstrʌktə'bɪlɪtɪ/ n indestructibilidad, f
indestructible /ˌɪndɪ'strʌktəbəl/ a indestructible
indeterminable /ˌɪndɪ'tɜrmənəbəl/ a indeterminable
indeterminate /ˌɪndɪ'tɜrmənɪt/ a indeterminado, indefinido, vago; *Math.* indeterminado
indetermination /ˌɪndɪˌtɜrmə'neɪʃən/ n irresolución, indecisión, duda, vacilación, f
index /'ɪndeks/ n (forefinger) dedo índice, m; (of book) tabla de materias, f, índice, m; (on instruments) manecilla, aguja, f; *Math.* índice, m; (sign) señal, indicación, f. —vt poner índice (a); poner en el índice. **i. card,** ficha, f. **I. expurgatorius,** Índice expurgatorio, m
India /'ɪndɪə/ n la India, f. **I. paper,** papel de China, m. **i.-rubber,** *Bot.* caucho, m; (eraser) goma de borrar, f. **i.-rubber tree,** yacio, m
Indian /'ɪndɪən/ a y n indio (-ia). **I. chief,** cacique, m. **I. club,** maza, f. **I. corn,** maíz, m. **I. ink,** tinta china, f. **I. summer,** veranillo, veranillo de San Martín, m
Indian Ocean, the el Océano Indico, m
indicate /'ɪndɪˌkeɪt/ vt indicar, señalar; (show) denotar, mostrar, anunciar
indication /ˌɪndɪ'keɪʃən/ n indicación, f; señal, f, indicio, síntoma, m; prueba, f
indicative /ɪn'dɪkətɪv/ a indicador, indicativo, demostrativo; *Gram.* indicativo. —n *Gram.* indicativo, m. **to be i. of,** indicar, señalar
indicator /'ɪndɪˌkeɪtər/ n indicador, señalador, m
indict /ɪn'daɪt/ vt acusar; *Law.* demandar, enjuiciar
indictable /ɪn'daɪtəbəl/ a procesable, denunciable, enjuiciable
indictment /ɪn'daɪtmənt/ n acusación, f; *Law.* procesamiento, m
indifference /ɪn'dɪfərəns/ n indiferencia, apatía, f, desinterés, desapego, m; imparcialidad, neutralidad, f; (coldness) frialdad, tibieza, f
indifferent /ɪn'dɪfərənt/ a indiferente, apático; imparcial, neutral; frío; (ordinary) regular, ordinario, ni bien ni mal
indifferently /ɪn'dɪfərəntlɪ/ adv con indiferencia; imparcialmente; framente
indigence /'ɪndɪdʒəns/ n indigencia, necesidad, penuria, f
indigenous /ɪn'dɪdʒənəs/ a indígena, nativo, natural
indigent /'ɪndɪdʒənt/ a indigente, necesitado, menesteroso
indigestible /ˌɪndɪ'dʒestəbəl/ a indigesto
indigestion /ˌɪndɪ'dʒestʃən/ n indigestión, f; *Fig.* empacho, ahíto, m
indignant /ɪn'dɪɡnənt/ a indignado. **to make i.,** indignar
indignantly /ɪn'dɪɡnəntlɪ/ adv con indignación
indignation /ˌɪndɪɡ'neɪʃən/ n indignación, cólera, f

indignity /ɪn'dɪɡnɪtɪ/ n indignidad, f; ultraje, m
indigo /'ɪndɪˌɡoʊ/ n añil, índigo, m
indirect /ˌɪndə'rekt/ a indirecto; oblicuo; tortuoso; *Gram.* **i. case,** caso oblicuo, m
indirectness /ˌɪndə'rektnɪs/ n (of route) rodeo, m, desviación, f; oblicuidad, f; (falsity) tortuosidad, f
indiscernible /ˌɪndɪ'sɜrnəbəl/ a imperceptible
indiscipline /ɪn'dɪsəplɪn/ n indisciplina, falta de disciplina, f
indiscreet /ˌɪndɪ'skrit/ a indiscreto, imprudente, impolítico
indiscreetly /ˌɪndɪ'skritlɪ/ adv indiscretamente
indiscretion /ˌɪndɪ'skreʃən/ n indiscreción, imprudencia, f; (slip) desliz, m
indiscriminate /ˌɪndɪ'skrɪmənɪt/ a general, universal; indistinto, promiscuo
indiscriminately /ˌɪndɪ'skrɪmənɪtlɪ/ adv promiscuamente
indiscrimination /ˌɪndɪˌskrɪmə'neɪʃən/ n universalidad, indistinción, f
indispensability /ˌɪndɪˌspensə'bɪlɪtɪ/ n indispensabilidad, precisión, necesidad, f
indispensable /ˌɪndɪ'spensəbəl/ a imprescindible, indispensable, insustituible
indispensably /ˌɪndɪ'spensəblɪ/ adv forzosamente, indispensablemente
indispose /ˌɪndɪ'spoʊz/ vt indisponer. **to be indisposed,** estar indispuesto, indisponerse
indisposed /ˌɪndɪ'spoʊzd/ a indispuesto, enfermo, destemplado; (reluctant) maldispuesto
indisposition /ˌɪndɪspə'zɪʃən/ n indisposición, enfermedad, f
indisputability /ˌɪndɪˌspyutə'bɪlɪtɪ/ n verdad manifiesta, certeza, evidencia, f
indisputable /ˌɪndɪ'spyutəbəl/ a innegable, incontestable; irrefutable, evidente
indisputably /ˌɪndɪ'spyutəblɪ/ adv indisputablemente
indissolubility /ˌɪndɪˌsɒlyə'bɪlɪtɪ/ n indisolubilidad, f
indissoluble /ˌɪndɪ'sɒlyəbəl/ a indisoluble
indistinct /ˌɪndɪ'stɪŋkt/ a indistinto; indeterminado, confuso, vago
indistinctly /ˌɪndɪ'stɪŋktlɪ/ adv indistintamente; confusamente, vagamente
indistinctness /ˌɪndɪ'stɪŋktnɪs/ n incertidumbre, vaguedad, indistinción, indeterminación, f
indistinguishable /ˌɪndɪ'stɪŋɡwɪʃəbəl/ a indistinguible
individual /ˌɪndə'vɪdʒuəl/ a (single) solo, único; individual, individuo, particular, propio; personal. —n individuo, m, particular, mf
individualism /ˌɪndə'vɪdʒuəˌlɪzəm/ n individualismo, m
individualist /ˌɪndə'vɪdʒuəlɪst/ n individualist, mf
individualistic /ˌɪndəˌvɪdʒuə'lɪstɪk/ a individualista
individuality /ˌɪndəˌvɪdʒu'ælɪtɪ/ n individualidad, personalidad, f; carácter, m, naturaleza, f
individualize /ˌɪndə'vɪdʒuəˌlaɪz/ vt particularizar, individuar
individually /ˌɪndə'vɪdʒuəlɪ/ adv individualmente, particularmente
indivisibility /ˌɪndəˌvɪzə'bɪlɪtɪ/ n indivisibilidad, f
indivisible /ˌɪndə'vɪzəbəl/ a incompartible, impartible, indivisible
indivisibly /ˌɪndə'vɪzəblɪ/ adv indivisiblemente
Indo (in compounds) indo. **I.-Chinese,** a and n indochino (-na). **I.-European,** indoeuropeo. **I.-Germanic,** indogermánico
indocile /ɪn'dɒsɪl/ a indócil, desobediente, rebelde
indocility /ɪndɒ'sɪlɪtɪ/ n indocilidad, desobediencia, falta de docilidad, f
indolence /'ɪndləns/ n indolencia, pereza, desidia, f
indolent /'ɪndlənt/ a indolente, perezoso, holgazán; *Med.* indoloro
indolently /'ɪndləntlɪ/ adv perezosamente
indomitable /ɪn'dɒmɪtəbəl/ a indomable, indómito
indoor /'ɪnˌdɔr/ a de casa; de puertas adentro, interno. **i. swimming pool,** piscina bajo techo, f. **i. tennis,** tenis en pistas cubiertas, tenis bajo techo, m
indoors /ɪn'dɔrz/ adv en casa; adentro, bajo techo
indorsee /ɪndɔr'si/ n endosatario (-ia)
indubitable /ɪn'dubɪtəbəl/ a indudable

indubitably /ɪn'dubɪtəbli/ *adv* indudablemente, sin duda

induce /ɪn'dus/ *vt* inducir, mover; instigar, incitar; producir, ocasionar; *Elec.* inducir. **Nothing would i. me to do it,** Nada me induciría a hacerlo

inducement /ɪn'dusmənt/ *n* incitamiento, *m;* estímulo, *m;* aliciente, atractivo, *m;* tentación, *f*

induct /ɪn'dʌkt/ *vt* instalar; introducir, iniciar

induction /ɪn'dʌkʃən/ *n* instalación, *f;* iniciación, introducción, *f; Phys.* inducción, *f.* **i. coil,** carrete de inducción, *m*

inductive /ɪn'dʌktɪv/ *a* (of reasoning) inductivo; *Phys.* inductor

indulge /ɪn'dʌldʒ/ *vt* (children) consentir, mimar; (a desire) satisfacer, dar rienda suelta a; (with a gift) agasajar (con), dar gusto (con). **to i. in,** *vt* consentir en. —*vi* entregarse a, permitirse, gustar de

indulgence /ɪn'dʌldʒəns/ *n* (of children) mimo, cariño excesivo, *m;* (of a desire) propensión (a), afición (a), *f;* (toward others) tolerancia, transigencia, *f; Eccl.* indulgencia, *f*

indulgent /ɪn'dʌldʒənt/ *a* indulgente; tolerante, transigente

indult /ɪn'dʌlt/ *n Eccl.* indulto, *m*

industrial /ɪn'dʌstriəl/ *a* industrial. **i. alcohol,** alcohol desnaturalizado, *m.* **i. school,** escuela de artes y oficios, *f, Com.* **i. shares,** valores industriales, *m pl*

industrialism /ɪn'dʌstriə,lɪzəm/ *n* industrialismo, *m*

industrialist /ɪn'dʌstriəlɪst/ *n* industrial, *m*

industrialization /ɪn,dʌstriəlɪ'zeɪʃən/ *n* industrialización, *f*

industrialize /ɪn'dʌstriə,laɪz/ *vt* industrializar

industrious /ɪn'dʌstriəs/ *a* industrioso, aplicado, diligente

industriously /ɪn'dʌstriəsli/ *adv* industriosamente, diligentemente

industriousness /ɪn'dʌstriəsnɪs/ *n* industria, laboriosidad, *f*

industry /'ɪndəstri/ *n* diligencia, aplicación, *f;* (work) trabajo, *m,* labor, *f; Com.* industria, *f*

inebriate /a, ɪ'nibriɪt/ *v* -bri,eɪt/ *a* borracho, ebrio. —*n* borracho (-cha). —*vt* embriagar, emborrachar

inebriation /ɪ,nibri'eɪʃən/ *n* embriaguez, borrachera, *f*

inedible /ɪn'edəbəl/ *a* incomible, no comestible

inedited /ɪn'edɪtɪd/ *a* inédito

ineffable /ɪn'efəbəl/ *a* indecible, inefable

ineffaceable /,ɪnɪ'feɪsəbəl/ *a* imborrable, indeleble

ineffective /,ɪnɪ'fektɪv/ *a* ineficaz; vano, fútil. **to be i.,** (of persons) no pinchar ni cortar. **to prove i.,** quedar sin efecto; no tener influencia

ineffectiveness /,ɪnɪ'fektɪvnɪs/ *n* ineficacia, *f;* futilidad, *f*

inefficiency /,ɪnɪ'fɪʃənsi/ *n* ineficacia, incompetencia, ineptitud, *f*

inefficient /,ɪnɪ'fɪʃənt/ *a* ineficaz, incapaz

inefficiently /,ɪnɪ'fɪʃəntli/ *adv* ineficazmente

inelastic /,ɪnɪ'læstɪk/ *a* inelástico

inelegance /ɪn'elɪgəns/ *n* inelegancia, fealdad, vulgaridad, *f*

inelegant /ɪn'elɪgənt/ *a* inelegante, ordinario, de mal gusto

inelegantly /ɪn'elɪgəntli/ *adv* sin elegancia

ineligibility /ɪn,elɪdʒə'bɪlɪti/ *n* ineligibilidad, *f*

ineligible /ɪn'elɪdʒəbəl/ *a* inelegible

inept /ɪn'ept/ *a* inepto, inoportuno; absurdo, ridículo; (of persons) incompetente, ineficaz

ineptitude /ɪn'eptɪ,tud/ *n* ineptitud, *f;* necedad, *f;* (of persons) incapacidad, incompetencia, *f*

ineptly /ɪn'eptli/ *adv* ineptamente, neciamente

inequality /,ɪnɪ'kwɒlɪti/ *n* desigualdad, desemejanza, disparidad, *f;* (of surface) escabrosidad, aspereza, *f; Fig.* injusticia, *f;* (of opportunity) diferencia, *f*

inequitable /ɪn'ekwɪtəbəl/ *a* desigual, injusto

inequity /ɪn'ekwɪti/ *n* injusticia, desigualdad, *f*

ineradicable /,ɪnɪ'rædɪkəbəl/ *a* indeleble, imborrable

ineradicably /,ɪnɪ'rædɪkəbli/ *adv* indeleblemente

inert /ɪn'ɜrt/ *a* inerte, inactivo, pasivo; ocioso, flojo, perezoso

inertia /ɪn'ɜrʃə/ *n* inercia, inacción, *f;* abulia, pereza, *f; Phys.* inercia, *f*

inertly /ɪn'ɜrtli/ *adv* indolentemente, sin mover, pasivamente

inescapable /,ɪnə'skeɪpəbəl/ *a* ineludible, inevitable

inessential /,ɪnɪ'senʃəl/ *a* no esencial

inestimable /ɪn'estəməbəl/ *a* inestimable

inevitability /ɪn,evɪtə'bɪlɪti/ *n* fatalidad, necesidad, *f;* lo inevitable

inevitable /ɪn'evɪtəbəl/ *a* inevitable, necesario, fatal, forzoso, ineludible

inevitably /ɪn'evɪtəbli/ *adv* inevitablemente, necesariamente, forzosamente

inexact /,ɪnɪg'zækt/ *a* inexacto, incorrecto

inexactitude /,ɪnɪg'zæktɪ,tud/ *n* inexactitud, *f*

inexcusable /,ɪnɪk'skyuzəbəl/ *a* imperdonable, inexcusable, irremisible

inexcusableness /,ɪnɪk'skyuzəbəlnɪs/ *n* enormidad, *f;* lo inexcusable

inexcusably /,ɪnɪk'skyuzəbli/ *adv* inexcusablemente

inexhaustible /,ɪnɪg'zɔstəbəl/ *a* inagotable, inexhausto

inexorability /ɪn,eksərə'bɪlɪti/ *n* inflexibilidad, inexorabilidad, *f*

inexorable /ɪn'eksərəbəl/ *a* inexorable, inflexible, duro

inexorably /ɪn'eksərəbli/ *adv* inexorablemente, implacablemente

inexpediency /,ɪnɪk'spidiənsi/ *n* inoportunidad, inconveniencia, imprudencia, *f*

inexpedient /,ɪnɪk'spidiənt/ *a* inoportuno; inconveniente; impolítico, imprudente. **to deem i.,** creer inoportuno

inexpensive /,ɪnɪk'spensɪv/ *a* poco costoso, barato

inexpensiveness /,ɪnɪk'spensɪvnɪs/ *n* baratura, *f,* bajo precio, *m*

inexperience /,ɪnɪk'spɪəriəns/ *n* inexperiencia, falta de experiencia, *f*

inexperienced /,ɪnɪk'spɪəriənst/ *a* inexperto, novato

inexpert /ɪn'ekspɜrt/ *a* inexperto, imperito

inexpertly /ɪn'ekspɜrtli/ *adv* sin habilidad

inexpertness /ɪn'ekspɜrtnɪs/ *n* impericia, torpeza, *f*

inexpiable /ɪn'ekspiəbəl/ *a* inexpiable

inexplicable /ɪn'eksplɪkəbəl/ *a* inexplicable

inexplicit /,ɪnɪk'splɪsɪt/ *a* no explícito

inexplosive /,ɪnɪk'sploʊsɪv/ *a* inexplosible

inexpressible /,ɪnɪk'spresəbəl/ *a* inexplicable, indecible, inefable

inexpressive /,ɪnɪk'spresɪv/ *a* inexpresivo; (of persons) reservado, callado, poco expresivo, retraído

inexpressiveness /,ɪnɪk'spresɪvnɪs/ *n* falta de expresión, *f;* (of persons) reserva, *f,* silencio, retraimiento, *m*

inexpugnable /,ɪnɪk'spʌgnəbəl/ *a* inexpugnable

inextinguishable /,ɪnɪk'stɪŋgwɪʃəbəl/ *a* inapagable, inextinguible

inextricable /ɪn'ekstrɪkəbəl/ *a* inextricable, intrincado, enmarañado

inextricably /ɪn'ekstrɪkəbli/ *adv* intrincadamente

infallibility /ɪn,fælə'bɪlɪti/ *n* infalibilidad, *f*

infallible /ɪn'fæləbəl/ *a* infalible

infamous /'ɪnfəməs/ *a* infame, torpe, vil, ignominioso; odioso, repugnante

infamously /'ɪnfəməsli/ *adv* infamemente

infamy /'ɪnfəmi/ *n* infamia, torpeza, vileza, ignominia, *f;* deshonra, *f*

infancy /'ɪnfənsi/ *n* infancia, niñez, *f; Law.* minoridad, *f*

infant /'ɪnfənt/ *n* criatura, *f;* crío (-ía), niño (-ña), *f; Law.* menor, *mf* **i. school,** escuela de párvulos, *f*

infanticidal /ɪn,fæntə'saɪdl/ *a* infanticida

infanticide /ɪn'fæntə,saɪd/ *n* (act) infanticidio, *m;* (person) infanticida, *mf*

infantile /'ɪnfən,taɪl/ *a* infantil. **i. paralysis,** parálisis infantil, *f*

infantry /'ɪnfəntri/ *n Mil.* infantería, *f*

infantryman /'ɪnfəntrimən/ *n Mil.* infante, peón, *m*

infatuate /ɪn'fætʃu,eɪt/ *vt* infatuar, embobar

infatuation /ɪn,fætʃu'eɪʃən/ *n* infatuación, *f,* encaprichamiento, *m*

infect /ɪn'fekt/ *vt* infectar, contagiar; *Fig.* pegar, influir; (*Fig.* in a bad sense) corromper, pervertir, inficionar. **to become infected,** infectarse

infected /ɪn'fɛktɪd/ *a* infecto

infection /ɪn'fɛkʃən/ *n* infección, *f*, contagio, *m; Fig.* influencia, *f; (Fig.* in a bad sense) corrupción, perversión, *f*

infectious /ɪn'fɛkʃəs/ *a* infeccioso, contagioso; (*Fig.* in a bad sense) corruptor; *Fig.* contagioso

infectiousness /ɪn'fɛkʃəsnɪs/ *n* contagiosidad, *f*

infelicitous /ˌɪnfə'lɪsɪtəs/ *a* poco apropiado, desacertado

infelicity /ˌɪnfə'lɪsɪti/ *n* infelicidad, desdicha, *f*, infortunio, *m;* desacierto, *m*, inoportunidad, *f*

infer /ɪn'fɜr/ *vt* inferir, concluir, educir, deducir, implicar

inferable /ɪn'fɜrəbəl/ *a* deducible, demostrable

inference /'ɪnfərəns/ *n* inferencia, deducción, conclusión, *f*

inferential /ˌɪnfə'rɛnʃəl/ *a* ilativo, deductivo

inferior /ɪn'fɪəriər/ *a* inferior; (in rank) subordinado, subalterno; (of position) secundario. —*n* inferior, *mf* subordinado (-da). **to be not i.,** no ser inferior, *Inf.* no quedarse en zaga

inferiority /ɪnˌfɪəri'ɒrɪti/ *n* inferioridad, *f.* **i. complex,** complejo de inferioridad, *m*

infernal /ɪn'fɜrnl/ *a* infernal; *Poet.* inferno, tartáreo

infernally /ɪn'fɜrnli/ *adv* infernalmente

inferno /ɪn'fɜrnou/ *n* infierno, *m*

infertile /ɪn'fɜrtl/ *a* infértil, infecundo, estéril

infertility /ˌɪnfər'tɪlɪti/ *n* infertilidad, infecundidad, esterilidad, *f*

infest /ɪn'fɛst/ *vt* infestar. **to be infested with,** plagarse de

infestation /ˌɪnfɛs'teɪʃən/ *n* infestación, *f*

infidel /'ɪnfɪdl/ *n* infiel, gentil, *mf* pagano (-na); (atheist) descreído (-da), ateo (-ea). —*a* pagano; infiel, descreído, ateo

infidelity /ˌɪnfɪ'dɛlɪti/ *n* infidelidad, alevosía, perfidia, *f*

infiltrate /ɪn'fɪltreɪt/ *vt* infiltrar. —*vi* infiltrarse

infiltration /ˌɪnfɪl'treɪʃən/ *n* infiltración, *f*

infinite /'ɪnfənɪt/ *a* infinito, ilimitado; inmenso, enorme; (of number) innumerable, infinito. —*n* infinito, *m*

infinitely /'ɪnfənɪtli/ *adv* infinitamente

infinitesimal /ˌɪnfɪnɪ'tɛsəməl/ *a* infinitesimal. **i. calculus,** cálculo infinitesimal, *m*

infinitive /ɪn'fɪnɪtɪv/ *a* and *n Gram.* infinitivo, *m.*

infinitude, infinity /ɪn'fɪnɪtud; ɪn'fɪnɪti/ *n* infinidad, infinitud, *f;* (extent) inmensidad, *f;* (of number) sinfín, *m; Math.* infinito, *m*

infirm /ɪn'fɜrm/ *a* achacoso, enfermizo, enclenque; (shaky) inestable, inseguro; (of purpose) irresoluto, vacilante

infirmary /ɪn'fɜrməri/ *n* enfermería, *f*, hospital, *m*

infirmity /ɪn'fɜrmɪti/ *n* achaque, *m*, enfermedad, dolencia, *f;* (fault) flaqueza, falta, *f*

inflame /ɪn'fleɪm/ *vt* encender; (excite) acalorar, irritar, provocar; *Med.* inflamar. —*vi* encenderse, arder; acalorarse, irritarse; *Med.* inflamarse

inflammability /ɪnˌflæmə'bɪlɪti/ *n* inflamabilidad, *f*

inflammable /ɪn'flæməbəl/ *a* inflamable

inflammation /ˌɪnflə'meɪʃən/ *n* inflamación, *f*

inflammatory /ɪn'flæmə,tɔri/ *a* inflamador; *Med.* inflamatorio

inflate /ɪn'fleɪt/ *vt* inflar, hinchar; (with pride) engreír, ensoberbecer

inflation /ɪn'fleɪʃən/ *n* inflación, hinchazón, *f; Com.* inflación, *f*

inflationism /ɪn'fleɪʃə,nɪzəm/ *n* inflacionismo, *m*

inflator /ɪn'fleɪtər/ *n Mech.* bomba para inflar, *f*

inflect /ɪn'flɛkt/ *vt* torcer; (voice) modular; *Gram.* conjugar, declinar

inflection /ɪn'flɛkʃən/ *n* dobladura, *f;* (of voice) tono, acento, *m*, modulación, *f; Gram.* conjugación, declinación, *f*

inflexibility /ɪnˌflɛksə'bɪlɪti/ *n* inflexibilidad, dureza, rigidez, *f*

inflexible /ɪn'flɛksəbəl/ *a* inflexible, rígido; *Fig.* inexorable, inalterable

inflexibly /ɪn'flɛksəbli/ *adv* inflexiblemente

inflict /ɪn'flɪkt/ *vt* infligir, imponer

infliction /ɪn'flɪkʃən/ *n* imposición, *f;* castigo, *m*

inflorescence /ˌɪnflɔ'rɛsəns/ *n Bot.* inflorescencia, *f*

inflow /'ɪn,flou/ *n* afluencia, *f*, flujo, *m*

influence /'ɪnfluəns/ *n* influencia, *f*, influjo, *m;* ascendiente, *m;* (importance) influencia, importancia, *f.* —*vt* influir, afectar; persuadir, inducir. **to have i. over,** (a person) tener ascendiente sobre. *Law.* **undue i.,** influencia indebida, *f*

influential /ˌɪnflu'ɛnʃəl/ *a* influyente; (of person) prestigioso, importante

influenza /ˌɪnflu'ɛnzə/ *n Med.* gripe, *f*, trancazo, *m*

influx /'ɪn,flʌks/ *n* influjo, *m;* (of rivers) desembocadura, afluencia, *f*

inform /ɪn'fɔrm/ *vt* (fill) infundir, llenar; (tell) informar, enterar, advertir; instruir; (with about) poner al corriente de, participar. —*vi* (with against) delatar (a), denunciar. **to i. oneself,** informarse, enterarse. **to be informed about,** estar al corriente de

informal /ɪn'fɔrməl/ *a* irregular; sin ceremonia, de confianza; (meeting) no oficial, extraoficial

informality /ˌɪnfɔr'mælɪti/ *n* irregularidad, *f;* falta de ceremonia, sencillez, *f;* intimidad, *f*

informally /ɪn'fɔrməli/ *adv* sin ceremonia

informant /ɪn'fɔrmənt/ *n* informante, *mf;* informador (-ra)

information /ˌɪnfər'meɪʃən/ *n* información, instrucción, *f;* noticia, *f*, aviso, *m; Law.* denuncia, delación, *f.* **piece of i.,** información, *f.* **i. bureau,** oficina de información, *f*

informative /ɪn'fɔrmətɪv/ *a* informativo

informer /ɪn'fɔrmər/ *n* delator (-ra), denunciador (-ra)

infraction /ɪn'frækʃən/ *n* contravención, infracción, transgresión, *f*

infrared /ˌɪnfrə'rɛd/ *a Phys.* infrarrojo, ultrarrojo

infrequency /ɪn'frikwənsi/ *n* infrecuencia, rareza, irregularidad, *f*

infrequent /ɪn'frikwənt/ *a* infrecuente, raro, irregular

infrequently /ɪn'frikwəntli/ *adv* rara vez, infrecuentemente

infringe /ɪn'frɪndʒ/ *vt* infringir, violar, contravenir, quebrantar

infringement /ɪn'frɪndʒmənt/ *n* contravención, violación, infracción, *f*

infringer /ɪn'frɪndʒər/ *n* infractor (-ra), contraventor (-ra), violador (-ra), transgresor (-ra)

infuriate /ɪn'fyuri,eit/ *vt* enfurecer, enloquecer, enojar. **to be infuriated,** estar furioso

infuse /ɪn'fyuz/ *vt* vaciar, infiltrar; *Fig.* infundir, inculcar, instilar

infusible /ɪn'fyuzəbəl/ *a* infundible

infusion /ɪn'fyuʒən/ *n* infusión, *f; Fig.* instilación, inculcación, *f*

ingathering /ɪn'gæðərɪŋ/ *n* cosecha, recolección, *f*

ingenious /ɪn'dʒinyəs/ *a* ingenioso; mañoso, hábil

ingeniously /ɪn'dʒinyəsli/ *adv* ingeniosamente, hábilmente

ingenuity /ˌɪndʒə'nuɪti/ *n* ingeniosidad, inventiva, listeza, habilidad, *f*

ingenuous /ɪn'dʒɛnyuəs/ *a* ingenuo, franco, sincero, cándido, sencillo, inocente

ingenuousness /ɪn'dʒɛnyuəsnɪs/ *n* ingenuidad, franqueza, sinceridad, *f;* candor, *m*

ingest /ɪn'dʒɛst/ *vt* ingerir

ingestion /ɪn'dʒɛstʃən/ *n* ingestión, *f*

inglorious /ɪn'glɔriəs/ *a* vergonzoso, ignominioso, deshonroso; desconocido, obscuro

ingloriously /ɪn'glɔriəsli/ *adv* vergonzosamente, ignominiosamente; obscuramente

ingloriousness /ɪn'glɔriəsnɪs/ *n* deshonra, ignominia, *f;* obscuridad, *f*

ingoing /'ɪn,gouɪŋ/ *a* entrante, que entra. —*n* ingreso, *m*, entrada, *f; Com.* **i. and outgoing,** entradas y salidas, *f pl*

ingot /'ɪŋgət/ *n* pepita, *f*, lingote, *m;* (of any metal) barra, *f*

ingrained /ɪn'greind, 'ɪn,greind/ *a* innato, natural

ingratiate /ɪn'greiʃi,eit/ *vt* (oneself with) congraciarse con, captarse la buena voluntad de, insinuarse en el favor de

ingratiating /ɪn'greiʃi,eitɪŋ/ *a* obsequioso

ingratitude /ɪnˈgrætɪˌtud/ n ingratitud, f, desagradecimiento, m

ingredient /ɪnˈgridiənt/ n ingrediente, m

ingress /ˈɪngres/ n ingreso, m; derecho de entrada, m

ingrowing /ˈɪnˌgrouɪŋ/ a que crece hacia adentro. **i. nail,** uñero, m

inhabit /ɪnˈhæbɪt/ vt habitar, ocupar, vivir en, residir en

inhabitable /ɪnˈhæbɪtəbəl/ a habitable, vividero

inhabitant /ɪnˈhæbɪtənt/ n habitante, residente, m; vecino (-na)

inhabited /ɪnˈhæbɪtɪd/ a habitado, poblado

inhalation /ˌɪnhəˈleɪʃən/ n inspiración, f; Med. inhalación, f

inhale /ɪnˈheɪl/ vt aspirar; Med. inhalar

inharmonious /ˌɪnhɑrˈmouniəs/ a Mus. disonante, inarmónico; desavenido, discorde, desconforme. **to be i.,** disonar; (of people) llevarse mal

inhere /ɪnˈhɪər/ vi ser inherente; pertenecer (a), residir (en)

inherence /ɪnˈhɪərəns/ n inherencia, f

inherent /ɪnˈhɪərənt/ a inherente; innato, intrínseco, natural

inherently /ɪnˈhɪərəntli/ adv intrínsecamente

inherit /ɪnˈherɪt/ vt heredar

inheritance /ɪnˈherɪtəns/ n herencia, f; patrimonio, abolengo, m

inheritor /ɪnˈherɪtər/ n heredero (-ra)

inhibit /ɪnˈhɪbɪt/ vt inhibir, impedir; Eccl., prohibir. **be inhibited, became inhibited,** cohibirse

inhibition /ˌɪnɪˈbɪʃən/ n inhibición, f

inhibitory /ɪnˈhɪbɪˌtɔri/ a inhibitorio

inhospitable /ɪnˈhɒspɪtəbəl/ a inhospitalario

inhospitably /ɪnˈhɒspɪtəbli/ adv desabridamente

inhospitality /ˌɪnhɒspɪˈtælɪti/ n inhospitalidad, f

inhuman /ɪnˈhyumən/ a inhumano; cruel, bárbaro

inhumanity /ˌɪnhyuˈmænɪti/ n inhumanidad, crueldad, f

inhumanly /ɪnˈhyumənli/ adv inhumanamente, cruelmente

inhume /ɪnˈhyum/ vt inhumar, sepultar

inimical /ɪˈnɪmɪkəl/ a enemigo, hostil, opuesto, contrario

inimically /ɪˈnɪmɪkəli/ adv hostilmente

inimitable /ɪˈnɪmɪtəbəl/ a inimitable

inimitably /ɪˈnɪmɪtəbli/ adv inimitablemente

iniquitous /ɪˈnɪkwɪtəs/ a inicuo, malvado, perverso, nefando; Inf. diabólico

iniquity /ɪˈnɪkwɪti/ n iniquidad, maldad, injusticia, f

initial /ɪˈnɪʃəl/ a inicial. —n inicial, letra inicial, f. —vt firmar con las iniciales

initially /ɪˈnɪʃəli/ adv al principio, en primer lugar

initiate /a ɪˈnɪʃiɪt; v ɪˈnɪʃiˌeɪt/ a iniciado. —vt iniciar, poner en pie, empezar, entablar; (a person) admitir

initiation /ɪˌnɪʃiˈeɪʃən/ n principio, m; (of a person) iniciación, admisión, f

initiative /ɪˈnɪʃiətɪv/ n iniciativa, f. **to take the i.,** tomar la iniciativa

initiator /ɪˈnɪʃiˌeɪtər/ n iniciador (-ra)

inject /ɪnˈdʒekt/ vt inyectar

injection /ɪnˈdʒekʃən/ n inyección, f. **i. syringe,** jeringa de inyecciones, f

injudicious /ˌɪndʒuˈdɪʃəs/ a imprudente, indiscreto

injudiciously /ˌɪndʒuˈdɪʃəsli/ adv imprudentemente

injudiciousness /ˌɪndʒuˈdɪʃəsnɪs/ n imprudencia, indiscreción, f

injunction /ɪnˈdʒʌŋkʃən/ n precepto, mandato, m; Law. embargo, m

injure /ˈɪndʒər/ vt perjudicar, dañar; menoscabar, deteriorar; (hurt) lastimar, lisiar. **to i. oneself,** hacerse daño

injured /ˈɪndʒərd/ a (physically) lisiado; (morally) ofendido

injurer /ˈɪndʒərər/ n perjudicador (-ra)

injurious /ɪnˈdʒʊriəs/ a dañoso, perjudicial, malo; ofensivo, injurioso

injuriously /ɪnˈdʒʊriəsli/ adv perjudicialmente

injury /ˈɪndʒəri/ n perjuicio, daño, m; (physical) lesión, f; (insult) agravio, insulto, m

injustice /ɪnˈdʒʌstɪs/ n injusticia, desigualdad, f. **You do him an i.,** Le juzgas mal

ink /ɪŋk/ n tinta, f. —vt entintar. **copying-ink,** tinta de copiar, f. **marking-ink,** tinta indeleble, f. **printer's ink,** tinta de imprenta, f. **ink-stand** or **ink-well,** tintero, m

inker /ˈɪŋkər/ n Print. rodillo, m

inkling /ˈɪŋklɪŋ/ n sospecha, noción, f

inky /ˈɪŋki/ a manchado de tinta. **i. black,** negro como el betún

inland /ˈɪnlænd/ n el interior de un país, a interior, mediterráneo; del país, regional. —adv tierra adentro. **to go i.,** internarse en un país. **I. Revenue,** delegación de contribuciones, f. **i. town,** ciudad del interior, f

inlay /ˈɪnˌleɪ/ vt taracear, ataracear, embutir; incrustar. —n taracea, f, embutido, m

inlet /ˈɪnlet/ n entrada, admisión, f; Geog. ensenada, f. **i. valve,** válvula de admisión, f

inmate /ˈɪnˌmeɪt/ n residente, habitante, m; (of hospital) paciente, mf; enfermo (-ma); (of prison) prisionero

inmost /ˈɪnmoust/. See **innermost**

inn /ɪn/ n posada, fonda, venta, f, mesón, m. **Inns of Court,** Colegio de Abogados, m

innate /ɪˈneɪt/ a innato, inherente, instintivo, nativo

innately /ɪˈneɪtli/ adv naturalmente, instintivamente

innavigable /ɪˈnævɪgəbəl/ a innavegable

inner /ˈɪnər/ a interior, interno. **i. tube** Auto. cámara de neumatico, cámara de aire, f

innermost /ˈɪnərˌmoust/ a más adentro; Fig. más íntimo, más hondo

innings /ˈɪnɪŋz/ n (sport) turno, m

innkeeper /ˈɪnˌkipər/ n fondista, mf; tabernero (-ra), mesonero (-ra), posadero (-ra)

innocence /ˈɪnəsəns/ n inocencia, f; pureza, f; (guilelessness) simplicidad, f, candor, m

innocent /ˈɪnəsənt/ a inocente, puro; (guiltless) inocente, inculpable; (foolish) simple, tonto, candoroso, inocentón; (harmless) innocuo. —n inocente, mf **Holy Innocents,** Santos Inocentes, m pl

innocuous /ɪˈnɒkyuəs/ a innocuo, inofensivo

innocuousness /ɪˈnɒkyuəsnɪs/ n inocuidad, f

innovate /ˈɪnəˌveɪt/ vt innovar

innovation /ˌɪnəˈveɪʃən/ n innovación, f

innovator /ˈɪnəˌveɪtər/ n innovador (-ra)

innuendo /ˌɪnyuˈendou/ n indirecta, insinuación, f

innumerable /ɪˈnumərəbəl/ a innumerable, incalculable. **i. things,** un sinfín de cosas

inobservance /ˌɪnəbˈzɜrvəns/ n inobservancia, f, incumplimiento, m

inoculate /ɪˈnɒkyəˌleɪt/ vt inocular

inoculation /ɪˌnɒkyəˈleɪʃən/ n inoculación, f

inoculator /ɪˈnɒkyəˌleɪtər/ n inoculador, m

inodorous /ɪnˈoudərəs/ a inodoro

inoffensive /ˌɪnəˈfensɪv/ a inofensivo, innocuo; (of people) pacífico, apacible, manso

inoffensively /ˌɪnəˈfensɪvli/ adv inofensivamente

inoffensiveness /ˌɪnəˈfensɪvnɪs/ n inocuidad, f; (of people) mansedumbre, f

inoperable /ɪnˈɒpərəbəl/ a inoperable

inoperative /ɪnˈɒpərətɪv/ a ineficaz, impracticable, inútil

inopportune /ɪnˌɒpərˈtun/ a inoportuno, intempestivo, inconveniente

inopportunely /ɪnˌɒpərˈtunli/ adv inoportunamente, a destiempo

inopportuneness /ɪnˌɒpərˈtunnɪs/ n inoportunidad, inconveniencia, f

inordinate /ɪnˈɔrdnɪt/ a desordenado, excesivo

inordinately /ɪnˈɔrdnɪtli/ adv desmedidamente

inorganic /ˌɪnɔrˈgænɪk/ a inorgánico

inoxidizable /ɪnˈɒksɪˌdaɪzəbəl/ a inoxidable

input /ˈɪnˌpʊt/ n capacidad instalada, f, insumo, m

inquest /ˈɪnkwest/ n Law. indagación, investigación, f

inquietude /ɪnˈkwaɪɪˌtud/ n inquietud, f, desasosiego, m, agitación, preocupación, f

inquire /ɪnˈkwaɪər/ vt and vi preguntar, averiguar, indagar. **to i. about,** (persons) preguntar por; (things) hacer preguntas sobre. **to i. into,** investigar, examinar, averiguar. **to i. of,** preguntar a. **"I. within,"** «Se dan informaciones»

inquirer /ɪn'kwaiᵊrər/ n indagador (-ra), inquiridor (-ra)

inquiring /ɪn'kwaiᵊrɪŋ/ a indagador, inquiridor

inquiringly /ɪn'kwaiᵊrɪŋli/ adv interrogativamente

inquiry /ɪn'kwaiᵊri/ n interrogación, pregunta, f; indagación, pesquisa, investigación, f; examen, m. **i. office,** oficina de informaciones, f. **on i.,** al preguntar

inquisition /ˌɪnkwə'zɪʃən/ n investigación, indagación, f; inquisición, f. **Holy I.,** Santo Oficio, m, Inquisición, f

inquisitive /ɪn'kwɪzɪtɪv/ a curioso, inquiridor; preguntador, impertinente, mirón

inquisitively /ɪn'kwɪzɪtɪvli/ adv con curiosidad, impertinentemente

inquisitiveness /ɪn'kwɪzɪtɪvnɪs/ n curiosidad, f; impertinencia, f

Inquisitor /ɪn'kwɪzɪtər/ n Eccl. inquisidor, m

inquisitorial /ɪnˌkwɪzɪ'tɔriəl/ a inquisitorial, inquisidor

inroad /'ɪnˌroud/ n incursión, f

insalubrious /ˌɪnsə'lubriəs/ a malsano, insalubre

insane /ɪn'sein/ a loco, demente, insano; (senseless) insensato, ridículo. **to become i.,** enloquecer, volverse loco, perder la razón. **to drive i.,** volver a uno el juicio, enloquecer, trastornar. **i. person,** demente, mf. loco (-ca)

insanely /ɪn'seinli/ adv locamente

insanitary /ɪn'sænɪˌteri/ a antihigiénico, malsano

insanity /ɪn'sænɪti/ n demencia, locura, f; enloquecimiento, m; (folly) insensatez, ridiculez, f

insatiability /ɪnˌseiʃə'bɪlɪti/ n insaciabilidad, f

insatiable /ɪn'seiʃəbəl/ a insaciable

insatiably /ɪn'seiʃəbli/ adv insaciablemente

inscribe /ɪn'skraib/ vt inscribir

inscription /ɪn'skrɪpʃən/ n inscripción, f; letrero, m; (of a book) dedicatoria, f; Com. inscripción, anotación, f, asiento, m

inscrutability /ɪnˌskrutə'bɪlɪti/ n enigma, misterio, m; incomprensibilidad, f

inscrutable /ɪn'skrutəbəl/ a enigmático, insondable, incomprensible, inescrutable

inscrutably /ɪn'skrutəbli/ adv incomprensiblemente, enigmáticamente

insect /'ɪnsekt/ n insecto, m. **i. powder,** polvos insecticidas, m pl

insecticide /ɪn'sektəˌsaid/ a and n insecticida m.

insecure /ˌɪnsɪ'kyʊr/ a inseguro, precario

insecurely /ˌɪnsɪ'kyʊrli/ adv inseguramente

insecurity /ˌɪnsɪ'kyʊrɪti/ n inseguridad, f; incertidumbre, inestabilidad, f

inseminate /ɪn'seməˌneit/ vt Fig. implantar; Med. fecundar

insemination /ɪnˌsemə'neiʃən/ n Fig. implantación, f; Med. fecundación, f

insensate /ɪn'senseit/ a (unfeeling) insensible, insensitivo; (stupid) insensato, sin sentido, necio

insensibility /ɪnˌsensə'bɪlɪti/ n insensibilidad, inconsciencia, f; (stupor) sopor, letargo, m; impasibilidad, indiferencia, f

insensible /ɪn'sensəbəl/ a insensible, inconsciente, indiferente, impasible, duro de corazón; (scarcely noticeable) imperceptible. **to make i.,** (to sensations) hacer indiferente (a); insensibilizar

insensibly /ɪn'sensəbli/ adv insensiblemente, imperceptiblemente

insensitive /ɪn'sensɪtɪv/ a insensible, insensitivo; (person) hecho un tronco, hecho un leño

insensitiveness /ɪn'sensɪtɪvnɪs/ n insensibilidad, f

insentient /ɪn'senʃənt/ a insensible

inseparability /ɪnˌsepərə'bɪlɪti/ n inseparabilidad, f

inseparable /ɪn'sepərəbəl/ a inseparable

inseparably /ɪn'sepərəbli/ adv inseparablemente

insert /ɪn'sɜrt/ vt insertar, intercalar; (introduce) meter dentro, introducir, encajar; (in a newspaper) publicar

insertion /ɪn'sɜrʃən/ n inserción, intercalación, f; (introduction) introducción, f; metimiento, encaje, m; Sew. entredós, m; (in a newspaper) publicación, f

inshore /'ɪn'ʃɔr/ a cercano a la orilla. —adv cerca de la orilla. **i. fishing,** pesca de arrastre, f

inside /ˌɪn'said/ a interior, interno. —adv adentro,

dentro. —n interior, m; (contents) contenido, m; (lining) forro, m; (Inf. stomach) entrañas, f pl. **to turn i. out,** volver al revés. **to walk on the i. of the pavement,** andar a la derecha de la acera. **from the i.,** desde el interior; por dentro. **on the i.,** por dentro, en el interior. **i. information,** información confidencial, f. **i. out,** al revés, de dentro afuera

insidious /ɪn'sɪdiəs/ a insidioso, enganoso, traidor

insidiously /ɪn'sɪdiəsli/ adv insidiosamente

insidiousness /ɪn'sɪdiəsnɪs/ n insidia, f; engaño, m, traición, f

insight /'ɪnˌsait/ n percepción, perspicacia, intuición, f. atisbo, m

insignia /ɪn'sɪgniə/ n pl insignias, f pl

insignificance /ˌɪnsɪg'nɪfɪkəns/ n insignificancia, futilidad, pequeñez, f

insignificant /ˌɪnsɪg'nɪfɪkənt/ a insignificante; fútil, trivial

insincere /ˌɪnsɪn'sɪər/ a insincero, hipócrita, falso

insincerely /ˌɪnsɪn'sɪərli/ adv falsamente, hipócritamente

insincerity /ˌɪnsɪn'serɪti/ n insinceridad, hipocresía, falsedad, falta de sinceridad, doblez, f

insinuate /ɪn'sɪnyuˌeit/ vt insinuar, introducir; (hint) soltar una indirecta, sugerir; (oneself) insinuarse, introducirse con habilidad

insinuation /ɪnˌsɪnyu'eiʃən/ n insinuación, introducción, f; (hint) indirecta, f

insipid /ɪn'sɪpɪd/ a insípido, insulso; (dull) soso

insipidity /ˌɪnsə'pɪdɪti/ n insipidez, insulsez, f, desabor, m; (dullness) sosería, f

insist /ɪn'sɪst/ vi insistir; persistir, obstinarse. **to i. on,** insistir en; obstinarse en, hacer hincapié en, aferrarse en (or a)

insistence /ɪn'sɪstəns/ n insistencia, f; obstinación, pertinacia, f

insistent /ɪn'sɪstənt/ a insistente; porfiado, obstinaz

insistently /ɪn'sɪstəntli/ adv con insistencia; porfiadamente

insobriety /ˌɪnsə'braiɪti/ n falta de sobriedad, f; embriaguez, ebriedad, f

insole /'ɪnˌsoul/ n (of shoes) plantilla, f

insolence /'ɪnsələns/ n insolencia, altanería, majadería, frescura, f, atrevimiento, descaro, m

insolent /'ɪnsələnt/ a insolente, arrogante, atrevido, descarado, desmesurado, fresco

insolently /'ɪnsələntli/ adv insolentemente, con descaro

insolubility /ɪnˌsɒljə'bɪlɪti/ n insolubilidad, f

insoluble /ɪn'sɒljəbəl/ a insoluble

insolvency /ɪn'sɒlvənsi/ n in volencia, f

insolvent /ɪn'sɒlvənt/ a insolvente

insomnia /ɪn'sɒmniə/ n insomnio, m

insomuch /ˌɪnsə'mʌtʃ/ adv (gen. with as or that) de modo (que), así (que), de suerte (que)

inspect /ɪn'spekt/ vt examinar, investigar, inspeccionar; (officially) registrar, reconocer

inspection /ɪn'spekʃən/ n inspección, investigación, f; examen, m; (official) reconocimiento, registro, m

inspector /ɪn'spektər/ n inspector, m, veedor, interventor, m

inspectorate /ɪn'spektərɪt/ n inspectorado, m; cargo de inspector, m

inspiration /ˌɪnspə'reiʃən/ n (of breath) inspiración, aspiración, f; numen, m, inspiración, vena, f. **to find i. in,** inspirarse en

inspire /ɪn'spaiᵊr/ vt (inhale) aspirar, inspirar; (stimulate) animar, alentar, iluminar; (suggest) sugerir, inspirar; infundir. **to i. enthusiasm,** entusiasmar. **to i. hope,** dar esperanza, esperanzar

inspired /ɪn'spaiᵊrd/ a inspirado, intuitivo, iluminado; (of genius) genial

inspirer /ɪn'spaiᵊrər/ n inspirador (-ra)

inspiring /ɪn'spaiᵊrɪŋ/ a alentador, animador; inspirador

inspirit /ɪn'spɪrɪt/ vt alentar, inspirar, estimular, animar

inspiriting /ɪn'spɪrɪtɪŋ/ a alentador, estimulador

instability /ˌɪnstə'bɪlɪti/ n inestabilidad, mutabilidad, inconstancia, f

install /ɪn'stɔl/ *vt* (all meanings) instalar. **to i. one-self**, instalarse, establecerse

installation /,ɪnstə'leiʃən/ *n* (all meanings) instalación, *f*

installment /ɪn'stɔlmənt/ *n* (of a story) entrega, *f*; *Com.* plazo, *m*, cuota, *f*. **by installments,** *Com.* a plazos. **i. plan,** pago a plazos, pago por cuotas, *m*

instance /'ɪnstəns/ *n* ejemplo, caso, *m*; (request) solicitación, *f*, ruego, *m*; *Law.* instancia, *f*. —*vt* citar como ejemplo, mencionar; demostrar, probar. **for i.,** por ejemplo, verbigracia. **in that i....**, en el caso... **in the first i.,** en primer lugar, primero

instant /'ɪnstənt/ *a* immediato, urgente; *Com.* corriente, actual. —*n* instante, momento, *m*; *Inf.* tris, santiamén, *m*. *Com.* **the 2nd i.,** el 2° (segundo) del corriente. **this i.,** (immediately) en seguida

instantaneous /,ɪnstən'teiniəs/ *a* instantáneo. *Photo.* **i. exposure**, instantánea, *f*

instantaneously /,ɪnstən'teiniəsli/ *adv* instantáneamente

instantaneousness /,ɪnstən'teiniəsnɪs/ *n* instantaneidad, *f*

instantly /'ɪnstəntli/ *adv* en seguida, al instante, inmediatamente

instead /ɪn'sted/ *adv* en cambio; (with of) en vez de, en lugar de

instep /'ɪn,stɛp/ *n* empeine, *m*

instigate /'ɪnstɪ,geit/ *vt* instigar, incitar, aguijar, animar, provocar; fomentar

instigating /'ɪnstɪ,geitɪŋ/ *a* instigador, provocador, fomentador

instigation /,ɪnstɪ'geiʃən/ *n* instigación, incitación, *f*; estímulo, *m*

instigator /'ɪnstɪ,geitər/ *n* instigador (-ra), provocador (-ra), fomentador (-ra)

instill /ɪn'stɪl/ *vt* instilar; (ideas) inculcar, infundir

instillment /ɪn'stɪlmənt/ *n* inculcación, implantación, insinuación, *f*

instinct /'ɪnstɪŋkt/ *n* instinto, *m*. **i. with**, imbuido de, lleno de. **by i.,** por instinto, movido por instinto

instinctive /ɪn'stɪŋktɪv/ *a* instintivo, espontáneo

instinctively /ɪn'stɪŋktɪvli/ *adv* por instinto

institute /'ɪnstɪ,tut/ *vt* instituir, fundar, establecer; (an inquiry) iniciar, empezar. —*n* instituto, *m*; *pl* **institutes,** *Law.* instituta, *f*

institution /,ɪnstɪ'tuʃən/ *n* (creation) fundación, creación, *f*; institución, *f*, instituto, *m*; (beginning) comienzo, *m*, iniciación, *f*; (charitable) asilo, *m*; (custom) uso, *m*, costumbre, tradición, *f*

institutional /,ɪnstɪ'tuʃənl/ *a* institucional

instruct /ɪn'strʌkt/ *vt* (teach) instruir, enseñar; (order) mandar, dar orden (a)

instruction /ɪn'strʌkʃən/ *n* (teaching) instrucción, enseñanza, *f*; *pl* **instructions,** (orders) instrucciones, *f pl* orden, *f*, mandato, *m*

instructive /ɪn'strʌktɪv/ *a* instructivo, instructor, informativo

instructively /ɪn'strʌktɪvli/ *adv* instructivamente

instructiveness /ɪn'strʌktɪvnɪs/ *n* el carácter informativo, lo instructivo

instructor /ɪn'strʌktər/ *n* instructor, preceptor, *m*

instrument /'ɪnstrəmənt/ *n* instrumento, *m*; (tool) herramienta, *f*, utensilio, aparato, *m*; (agent) órgano, agente, medio, *m*; *Law.* instrumento, *m*, escritura, *f*. —*vt Mus.* instrumentar. **percussion i.,** instrumento de percusión, *m*. **scientific i.,** instrumento científico, *m*. **stringed i.,** instrumento de cuerda, *m*. **wind i.,** instrumento de viento, *m*

instrumental /,ɪnstrə'mɛntl/ *a* instrumental; influyente. **to be i. in,** contribuir a

instrumentalist /,ɪnstrə'mɛntlɪst/ *n Mus.* instrumentista, *m*

instrumentality /,ɪnstrəmən'tælɪti/ *n* mediación, intervención, agencia, *f*, buenos oficios, *m pl*

instrumentation /,ɪnstrəmən'teiʃən/ *n Mus.* instrumentación, *f*; mediación, *f*

insubordinate /,ɪnsə'bɔrdn̩ɪt/ *a* insubordinado, rebelde, desobediente, refractario

insubordination /,ɪnsə,bɔrdn̩'eiʃən/ *n* insubordinación, rebeldía, desobediencia, *f*

insubstantial /,ɪnsəb'stænʃəl/ *a* irreal; insubstancial

insubstantiality /,ɪnsəb,stænʃi'ælɪti/ *n* irrealidad, *f*; insubstancialidad, *f*

insufferable /ɪn'sʌfərəbəl/. See **intolerable**

insufficiency /,ɪnsə'fɪʃənsi/ *n* insuficiencia, falta, carestía, *f*

insufficient /,ɪnsə'fɪʃənt/ *a* insuficiente, falto. **"I. Postage,"** «Falta de franqueo»

insufficiently /,ɪnsə'fɪʃəntli/ *adv* insuficientemente

insular /'ɪnsələr/ *a* isleño, insular; (narrow-minded) intolerante, iliberal

insularity /,ɪnsə'lɛərɪti/ *n* carácter isleño, *m*; (narrow-mindedness) iliberalidad, intolerancia, *f*

insulate /'ɪnsə,leit/ *vt* aislar

insulating /'ɪnsə,leitɪŋ/ *a* aislador. **i. tape,** *Elec.* cinta aisladora, *f*

insulation /,ɪnsə'leiʃən/ *n* aislamiento, *m*

insulator /'ɪnsə,leitər/ *n Elec.* aislador, *m*

insulin /'ɪnsəlɪn/ *n Med.* insulina, *f*

insult /*n.* 'ɪnsʌlt; *v.* ɪn'sʌlt/ *n* insulto, agravio, ultraje, *m*, afrenta, ofensa, *f*. —*vt* insultar, ofender, afrentar. **He was insulted,** Fue insultado; Se mostró ofendido

insulter /ɪn'sʌltər/ *n* insultador (-ra)

insulting /ɪn'sʌltɪŋ/ *a* insultante, injurioso, ofensivo. **He was very i. to them,** Les insultó, Les trató con menosprecio

insultingly /ɪn'sʌltɪŋli/ *adv* con insolencia, ofensivamente

insuperability /ɪn,supərə'bɪlɪti/ *n* dificultades insuperables, *f pl*, imposibilidad, *f*, lo insuperable

insuperable /ɪn'supərəbəl/ *a* insuperable, invencible

insuperably /ɪn'supərəbli/ *adv* invenciblemente

insupportable /,ɪnsə'pɔrtəbəl/ *a* insoportable, inaguantable, intolerable, insufrible

insupportably /,ɪnsə'pɔrtəbli/ *adv* insufriblemente, insoportablemente

insurable /ɪn'ʃurəbəl/ *a* asegurable

insurance /ɪn'ʃurəns/ *n* aseguramiento, *m*; *Com.* seguro, *m*; aseguración, *f*. **accident i.,** seguro contra accidentes, *m*. **fire-i.,** seguro contra incendio, *m*. **life i.,** seguro sobre la vida, *m*. **maritime i.,** seguro marítimo, *m*. **National I. Act,** Ley del Seguro Nacional Obligatorio, *f*. **i. broker,** corredor de seguros, *m*. **i. company,** compañía de seguros, *f*. **i. policy,** póliza de seguros, *f*. **i. premium,** prima de seguros, *f*

insure /ɪn'ʃur, -'ʃər/ *vt Com.* asegurar. **to i. oneself,** asegurarse. **the insured,** (person) el asegurado

insurer /ɪn'ʃurər/ *n* asegurador (-ra)

insurgent /ɪn'sɜrdʒənt/ *a* insurgente, rebelde; (of sea) invasor. —*n* rebelde, *mf* insurrecto (-ta)

insurmountable /,ɪnsər'mauntəbəl/ *a* insalvable, insuperable, invencible, intransitable

insurrection /,ɪnsə'rɛkʃən/ *n* insurrección, sublevación, *f*, levantamiento, *m*

insurrectionary /,ɪnsə'rɛkʃə,nɛri/ *a* rebelde, amotinado, insurgente

insusceptible /,ɪnsə'sɛptəbəl/ *a* no susceptible, indiferente, insensible

intact /ɪn'tækt/ *a* intacto, íntegro, indemne

intake /'ɪn,teik/ *n* (of a stocking) menguado, *m*; *Mech.* aspiración, *f*; válvula de admisión, *f*; *Aer.* admisión, toma, *f*; orificio de entrada, *m*

intangibility /ɪn,tændʒə'bɪlɪti/ *n* intangibilidad, *f*

intangible /ɪn'tændʒəbəl/ *a* intangible; incomprensible

integer /'ɪntɪdʒər/ *n Math.* número entero, *m*

integral /'ɪntɪgrəl/ *a* íntegro, intrínseco, inherente; *Math.* entero. —*n Math.* integral, *f*. **i. calculus,** cálculo integral, *m*

integrate /'ɪntɪ,greit/ *vt* integrar, completar; formar en un todo; *Math.* integrar

integrity /ɪn'tɛgrɪti/ *n* integridad, honradez, rectitud, entereza, *f*

intellect /'ɪntl̩,ɛkt/ *n* intelecto, entendimiento, *m*

intellectual /,ɪntl̩'ɛktʃuəl/ *a* intelectual, mental. —*n* intelectual

intellectualism /,ɪntl̩'ɛktʃuə,lɪzəm/ *n* intelectualismo, *m*, intelectualidad, *f*

intellectually /,ɪntl̩'ɛktʃuəli/ *adv* intelectualmente, mentalmente

intelligence /ɪn'tɛlɪdʒəns/ *n* inteligencia, comprensión, mente, *f*; (quickness of mind) agudeza, perspi-

cacia, *f;* (news) noticia, *f,* conocimiento, informe, *m.*
the latest i., las últimas noticias. **i. quotient,** cociente de inteligencia, *m.* **I. Service,** Inteligencia, *f;*
policía secreta, *f.* **i. test,** prueba de inteligencia, *f*
intelligent /ɪn'telɪdʒənt/ *a* inteligente
intelligentsia /ɪn,telɪ'dʒentsiə/ *n* clase intelectual, intelectualidad, *f, Inf.* masa cefálica, *f*
intelligibility /ɪn,telɪdʒə'bɪlɪti/ *n* comprensibilidad, inteligibilidad, *f*
intelligible /ɪn'telɪdʒəbəl/ *a* inteligible, comprensible
intelligibly /ɪn'telɪdʒəbəl/ *adv* inteligiblemente
intemperance /ɪn'tempərəns/ *n* intemperancia, inmoderación, *f;* exceso en la bebida, *m*
intemperate /ɪn'tempərɪt/ *a* intemperante, destemplado, descomedido; inmoderado; bebedor en exceso
intemperately /ɪn'tempərɪtli/ *adv* inmoderadamente
intend /ɪn'tend/ *vt* intentar, proponerse, pensar; destinar, dedicar; (mean) querer decir. **to be intended,**
estar destinado; tener por fin; querer decir
intendant /ɪn'tendənt/ *n* intendente, *m*
intended /ɪn'tendɪd/ *a* pensado, deseado. —*n Inf.*
novio (-ia), futuro (-ra), prometido (-da)
intense /ɪn'tens/ *a* intenso, vivo, fuerte; (of emotions) profundo, hondo, vehemente; (of colors) subido, intenso; (great) extremado, sumo, muy grande
intensification /ɪn,tensəfɪ'keɪʃən/ *n* intensificación, *f;*
aumento, *m*
intensify /ɪn'tensə,faɪ/ *vt* intensar, intensificar; aumentar
intensity /ɪn'tensɪti/ *n* intensidad, fuerza, *f;* (of emotions) profundidad, vehemencia, violencia, *f;* (of
colors) intensidad, *f*
intensive /ɪn'tensɪv/ *a* intensivo
intensive-care unit /ɪn'tensɪv'keər/ *n* sala de terapia
intensiva, unidad de cuidados intensivos, unidad de
vigilancia intensiva, *f*
intent /ɪn'tent/ *n* intento, propósito, deseo, *m.* —*a*
atento; (absorbed) absorto, interesado; (on doing) resuelto a, decidido a. **to all intents and purposes,** en
efecto, en realidad. **to be i. on,** (reading, etc.) estar
absorto en, entregarse a. **with i. to defraud,** con el
propósito deliberado de defraudar
intention /ɪn'tenʃən/ *n* intención, voluntad, *f,* propósito, pensamiento, proyecto, *m*
intentional /ɪn'tenʃənl/ *a* intencional, deliberado,
premeditado
intentionally /ɪn'tenʃənļi/ *adv* a propósito, intencionalmente, de pensado
intentioned /ɪn'tenʃənd/ *a* intencionado
intently /ɪn'tentli/ *adv* atentamente
inter /ɪn'tɜr/ *vt* enterrar, sepultar
inter- *prefix* inter, entre. **i.-allied,** interaliado, de los
aliados. **i.-denominational,** intersectario. **i.-
university,** interuniversitario. **i.-urban,** interurbano
interaction /ɪntər'ækʃən/ *n* interacción, acción recí-
proca, acción mutua, *f*
intercalate /ɪn'tɜrkə,leɪt/ *vt* intercalar, interpolar
intercede /ɪntər'sid/ *vi* interceder, mediar. **to i. for,**
hablar por
intercept /ɪntər'sept/ *vt* interceptar, detener; entrecoger, atajar
interception /ɪntər'sepʃən/ *n* interceptación, detención, *f*
intercession /ɪntər'seʃən/ *n* mediación, intercesión, *f*
intercessor /ɪntər'sesər/ *n* intercesor (-ra), mediador
(-ra)
interchange /*n.* 'ɪntər,tʃeɪndʒ; *v.* ,ɪntər'tʃeɪndʒ/ *n* intercambio, *m;* (of goods) comercio, tráfico, *m.* —*vt*
cambiar, trocar; alternar
interchangeable /ɪntər'tʃeɪndʒəbəl/ *a* intercambiable
intercom /'ɪntər,kɒm/ *n* teléfono interior, *m*
intercommunicate /ɪntərkə'myunɪ,keɪt/ *vi* comunicarse
intercommunication /ɪntərkə,myunɪ'keɪʃən/ *n*
comunicación mutua, *f;* comercio, *m*
intercostal /ɪntər'kɒstļ/ *a Anat.* intercostal
intercourse /'ɪntər,kɔrs/ *n* (social) trato, *m,* relaciones, *f pl; Com.* comercio, tráfico, *m;* (of ideas) intercambio, *m;* (sexual) coito, trato sexual, *m*
interdependence /ɪntərdɪ'pendəns/ *n* dependencia
mutua, mutualidad, *f*
interdependent /ɪntərdɪ'pendənt/ *a* mutuo

interdict /*n* 'ɪntər,dɪkt; *v* ,ɪntər'dɪkt/ *n* interdicto,
veto, *m,* prohibición, *f; Eccl.* entredicho, *m.* —*vt*
interdecir, prohibir, privar; *Eccl.* poner entredicho
interdiction /,ɪntər'dɪkʃən/ *n* interdicción, prohibición, *f*
interest /'ɪntərɪst/ *n* interés, *m;* provecho, *m; Com.*
premio, rédito, interés, *m;* (in a firm) participación, *f;*
(curiosity) interés, *m;* curiosidad, *f;* simpatía, *f;* (influence) influencia, *f.* —*n pl* **interests,** (commercial
undertakings) empresas, *f pl,* intereses, negocios, *m
pl.* —*vt* interesar. **to be interested in,** interesarse en,
(on behalf of) por. **to be in one's own i.,** ser en provecho de uno, ser en su propio interés. **to bear eight
per cent. i.,** dar interés del ocho por ciento. **to pay
with i.,** pagar con creces. **to put out at i.,** dar a interés. **in the interests of,** en interés de. **compound
i.,** interés compuesto, *m.* **simple i.,** interés sencillo,
m. **vested interests,** intereses creados, *m pl*
interesting /'ɪntərəstɪŋ/ *a* interesante, curioso, atractivo
interestingly /'ɪntərəstɪŋli/ *adv* amenamente, de
modo interesante
interfere /,ɪntər'fɪər/ *vi* intervenir, meterse, entremeterse, mezclarse; *Inf.* mangonear, meter las narices; (with) meterse con; (impede) estorbar, impedir
interference /,ɪntər'fɪərəns/ *n* intervención, *f,* entrometimiento, *m;* (obstacle) estorbo, obstáculo, *m;
Phys.* interferencia, *f; Radio.* parásitos, *m pl*
interfering /,ɪntər'fɪərɪŋ/ *a* entremetido, oficioso; *Inf.*
mangoneador
interim /'ɪntərəm/ *n* ínterin, intermedio, *m.* —*a*
interino, provisional. **in the i.,** entre tanto, en el ínterin. *Com.* **i. dividend,** dividendo interino, *m*
interior /ɪn'tɪəriər/ *a* interior, interno; doméstico. —*n*
interior, *m*
interject /,ɪntər'dʒekt/ *vt* interponer
interjection /,ɪntər'dʒekʃən/ *n* exclamación, interjección, *f;* interposición, *f*
interlace /,ɪntər'leɪs/ *vt* entrelazar, entretejer
interleave /,ɪntər'liv/ *vt* interfoliar, interpaginar
interline /'ɪntər,laɪn/ *vt* entrerrenglonar, interlinear
interlinear /,ɪntər'lɪniər/ *a* interlineal
interlineation /,ɪntər,lɪni'eɪʃən/ *n* interlineación, *f*
interlining /'ɪntər,laɪnɪŋ/ *n* entretela, *f*
interlock /,ɪntər'lɒk/ *vt* (of wheels, etc.). endentar;
trabar; cerrar. —*vi* endentarse; entrelazarse, unirse;
cerrar
interlocutor /,ɪntər'lɒkyətər/ *n* interlocutor (-ra)
interloper /'ɪntər,loupər/ *n* intruso (-sa); *Com.* intérlope, *m*
interloping /,ɪntər'loupɪŋ/ *a* intérlope
interlude /'ɪntər,lud/ *n* intervalo, intermedio, *m;
Mus.* interludio, *m; Theat.* entremés, *m*
intermarriage /,ɪntər'mærɪdʒ/ *n* casamiento entre
parientes próximos, entre razas distintas, o entre
grupos étnicos distintos, *m*
intermarry /,ɪntər'mæri/ *vi* contraer matrimonio entre
parientes próximos, entre personas de razas distintas,
o entre grupos étnicos distintos
intermediary /,ɪntər'midi,eri/ *a and n* intermediario
(-ia)
intermediate /,ɪntər'midi,eit/ *a* intermedio, medio,
medianero. —*n* sustancia intermedia, *f.* —*vi*
intervenir, mediar
interment /ɪn'tɜrmənt/ *n* entierro, *m*
intermezzo /,ɪntər'metsou/ *n Theat.* intermedio, *m;
Mus.* intermezzo, *m*
interminable /ɪn'tɜrmənəbəl/ *a* interminable, inacabable
interminably /ɪn'tɜrmənəbli/ *adv* interminablemente,
sin fin, sin cesar
intermingle /,ɪntər'mɪŋgəl/ *vt* entremezclar, entreverar. —*vi* mezclarse
intermission /,ɪntər'mɪʃən/ *n* intermisión, interrupción, pausa, *f; Theat.* entreacto, *m.* **without i.,** sin
pausa, sin tregua
intermittence /,ɪntər'mɪtņs/ *n* intermitencia, alternación, *f*
intermittent /,ɪntər'mɪtņt/ *a* intermitente, discontinuo; (of fever) intermitente
intermittently /,ɪntər'mɪtņtli/ *adv* a intervalos, a ratos, a pausas

intern /ɪn'tɜrn/ n Med. practicante de hospital m, interno (-na), interno de hospital, alumno interno, m. —vt confinar, encerrar

internal /ɪn'tɜrnl/ a interno, interior; (of affairs) doméstico, civil; intrínseco; íntimo. **i.-combustion engine,** motor de combustión interna, m

internally /ɪn'tɜrnli/ adv interiormente

international /ˌɪntər'næʃənl/ a internacional. —n Sports. un partido internacional. **i. law,** derecho internacional, m

internationalism /ˌɪntər'næʃənlˌɪzəm/ n internacionalismo, m

internationalist /ˌɪntər'næʃənlˌɪst/ n internacionalista, mf

internationalization /ˌɪntər,næʃənləˈzeɪʃən/ n internacionalización, f

internationalize /ˌɪntər'næʃənlˌaɪz/ vt hacer internacional, poner bajo un control internacional

internecine /ˌɪntər'nisin/ a sanguinario, feroz

internee /ˌɪntər'ni/ n internado (-da)

Internet, the /'ɪntər,nɛt/ n el Internet, m

internment /ɪn'tɜrnmənt/ n internamiento, m. **i. camp,** campo de internamiento, m

interoceanic /ˌɪntər,ouʃi'ænɪk/ a interoceánico

interpolate /ɪn'tɜrpə,leɪt/ vt interpolar, intercalar, interponer

interpolation /ɪn,tɜrpə'leɪʃən/ n interpolación, inserción, añadidura, f

interpolator /ɪn'tɜrpə,leɪtər/ n interpolador (-ra)

interpose /ˌɪntər'pouz/ vt interponer; (a remark) interpolar. —vi interponerse, intervenir; (interfere) entrometerse; interrumpir

interposition /ˌɪntərpə'zɪʃən/ n interposición, f; entrometimiento, m

interpret /ɪn'tɜrprɪt/ vt interpretar; (translate) traducir; (explain) explicar, descifrar. —vi interpretar.

interpretation /ɪn,tɜrprɪ'teɪʃən/ n interpretación, f; (translation) traducción, f; (explanation) explicación, f

interpretative /ɪn'tɜrprɪ,teɪtɪv/ a interpretativo, interpretador

interpreter /ɪn'tɜrprɪtər/ n intérprete, mf

interregnum /ˌɪntər'rɛgnəm/ n interregno, m

interrelation /ˌɪntərɪ'leɪʃən/ n relación mutua, f

interrogate /ɪn'tɛrə,geɪt/ vt interrogar, examinar, preguntar

interrogating /ɪn'tɛrə,geɪtɪŋ/ a interrogante

interrogation /ɪn,tɛrə'geɪʃən/ n interrogación, f, examen, m; pregunta, f. **mark of i.,** punto de interrogación, m

interrogative /ˌɪntə'rɒgətɪv/ a interrogativo. —n palabra interrogativa, f

interrogatively /ˌɪntə'rɒgətɪvli/ adv interrogativamente

interrogator /ɪn'tɛrə'geɪtər/ n examinador (-ra), interrogador (-ra)

interrogatory /ˌɪntə'rɒgə,tɔri/ a interrogatorio. —n interrogatorio, m

interrupt /ˌɪntə'rʌpt/ vt interrumpir

interruptedly /ˌɪntə'rʌptɪdli/ adv interrumpidamente

interrupter /ˌɪntə'rʌptər/ n interruptor (-ra); Elec. interruptor, m

interruption /ˌɪntə'rʌpʃən/ n interrupción, f

intersect /ˌɪntər'sɛkt/ vt cruzar. —vi cruzarse, intersecarse

intersection /ˌɪntər'sɛkʃən/ n intersección, f; cruce, m, (of streets) bocacalle, f

intersperse /ˌɪntər'spɜrs/ vt diseminar, esparcir; interpolar, entremezclar

interstice /ɪn'tɜrstɪs/ n intervalo, intermedio, m; (chink) intersticio, m, hendedura, f

intertwine /ˌɪntər'twaɪn/ vt entretejer, entrelazar. —vi entrelazarse

interval /'ɪntərvəl/ n intervalo, intermedio, m, pausa, f; Theat. entreacto, m, intermisión, f; (in schools) recreo, m. **at intervals,** a trechos, de vez en cuando. **lucid i.,** intervalo claro, intervalo lúcido, m

intervene /ˌɪntər'vin/ vi intervenir, tomar parte (en), mediar; (occur) sobrevenir, acaecer; Law. interponerse

intervening /ˌɪntər'vinɪŋ/ a intermedio; interventor

intervention /ˌɪntər'vɛnʃən/ n intervención, mediación, f

interventionist /ˌɪntər'vɛnʃənɪst/ n Polit. partidario (-ia) de la intervención

interview /'ɪntər,vyu/ n entrevista, f, interviev, m. —vt entrevistarse con

interviewer /'ɪntər,vyuər/ n interrogador (-ra); (reporter) reportero, periodista, m

interweave /ˌɪntər'wiv/ vt entretejer, entrelazar

interweaving /ˌɪntər'wivɪŋ/ n entretejimiento, m

intestacy /ɪn'tɛstəsi/ n ausencia de un testamento, f

intestate /ɪn'tɛsteɪt/ a and n intestado (-da)

intestinal /ɪn'tɛstənl/ a intestinal, intestino. **i. worm,** lombriz intestinal, f

intestine /ɪn'tɛstɪn/ n intestino, m. **large i.,** intestino grueso, m. **small i.,** intestino delgado, m

intimacy /'ɪntəməsi/ n intimidad, f, familiaridad, f; (of nobility and others) privanza, f

intimate /'ɪntəmɪt/ a íntimo; (of relations) entrañable, estrecho; intrínseco, esencial; (of knowledge) profundo, completo, detallado. —n amigo (-ga) de confianza. —vt intimar, dar a entender, indicar. **to become i.,** intimarse. **to be on i. terms with,** tratar de tú (a), ser amigo íntimo de

intimately /'ɪntəmɪtli/ adv íntimamente, al fondo

intimation /ˌɪntə'meɪʃən/ n intimación, indicación, f; (hint) insinuación, indirecta, f

intimidate /ɪn'tɪmɪ,deɪt/ vt intimidar, aterrar, infundir miedo (a), espantar, acobardar, amedrentar

intimidation /ɪn,tɪmɪ'deɪʃən/ n intimidación, f

intimidatory /ɪn'tɪmɪdə,tɔri/ a aterrador, amenazador

into /'ɪntu; unstressed -tu, -tə/ prep en; a, al, a la; dentro, adentro; (of transforming, forming, etc.) en. **Throw it i. the fire,** Échalo al (or en el) fuego. **She went i. the house,** Entró en la casa. **to look i.,** mirar dentro de; mirar hacia el interior (de); investigar

intolerable /ɪn'tɒlərəbəl/ a intolerable, insufrible, inaguantable, insoportable, inllevable

intolerableness /ɪn'tɒlərəbəlnɪs/ n intolerabilidad, f

intolerably /ɪn'tɒlərəbli/ adv intolerablemente, insufriblemente

intolerance /ɪn'tɒlərəns/ n intolerancia, intransigencia, f

intolerant /ɪn'tɒlərənt/ a intolerante, intransigente; Med. intolerante

intonation /ˌɪntou'neɪʃən/ n entonación, f

intone /ɪn'toun/ vt entonar; Eccl. salmodiar

intoxicant /ɪn'tɒksɪkənt/ a embriagador. —n bebida alcohólica, f

intoxicate /ɪn'tɒksɪ,keɪt/ vt emborrachar, embriagar; Med. intoxicar, envenenar; (excite) embriagar, embelesar

intoxicated /ɪn'tɒksɪ,keɪtɪd/ a borracho; (excited) ebrio, embriagado; Med. intoxicado

intoxicating /ɪn'tɒksɪ,keɪtɪŋ/ a embriagador

intoxication /ɪn,tɒksɪ'keɪʃən/ n borrachera, embriaguez, f; Med. intoxicación, f, envenenamiento, m; (excitement) entusiasmo, m, ebriedad, f

intractability /ɪn,træktə'bɪlɪti/ n insociabilidad, hurañería, f

intractable /ɪn'træktəbəl/ a intratable, insociable, huraño

intramural /ˌɪntrə'myurəl/ adv intramuros

intransigence /ɪn'trænsɪdʒəns/ n intransigencia, intolerancia, f

intransigent /ɪn'trænsɪdʒənt/ a intransigente, intolerante

intransitive /ɪn'trænsɪtɪv/ a intransitivo, neutro

intrauterine /ˌɪntrə'yutərɪn/ a Med. intrauterino

intravenous /ˌɪntrə'vinəs/ a Med. intravenoso

intrepid /ɪn'trɛpɪd/ a intrépido, osado, audaz

intrepidity /ˌɪntrə'pɪdɪti/ n intrepidez, osadía, audacia, f

intrepidly /ɪn'trɛpɪdli/ adv intrépidamente, audazmente

intricacy /'ɪntrɪkəsi/ n intrincación, complejidad, f

intricate /'ɪntrɪkɪt/ a intrincado, complejo

intricately /'ɪntrɪkɪtli/ adv intrincadamente

intrigue /ɪn'trig/ n. also 'ɪntrig/ n intriga, maquinación, f, enredo, m; (amorous) lío, m. —vi intrigar, enredar; (amorous) tener un lío. —*vt* (interest) atraer, interesar; (with) intrigar con

intriguer /ɪn'trigər/ *n* intrigante, *mf*. urdemalas, *m*, enredador (-ra)

intriguing /ɪn'trigɪŋ/ *a* enredador; (attractive) atrayente, interesante, seductor

intrinsic /ɪn'trɪnsɪk/ *a* intrínseco, innato, inherente, esencial

intrinsically /ɪn'trɪnsɪkli/ *adv* intrínsecamente, esencialmente

introduce /ˌɪntrə'dus/ *vt* introducir; hacer entrar; insertar, injerir; (a person) presentar; poner de moda, introducir; (a bill) presentar; (a person to a thing) llamar la atención sobre. **Permit me to i. my friend,** Permítame le presente mi amigo

introduction /ˌɪntrə'dʌkʃən/ *n* introducción, *f*; (of a book) prefacio, prólogo, *m*, advertencia, *f*; (of a person) presentación, *f*; inserción, *f*

introductory /ˌɪntrə'dʌktəri/ *a* introductor, preliminar, preparatorio

intromission /ˌɪntrə'mɪʃən/ *n* intromisión, *f*

introspection /ˌɪntrə'spɛkʃən/ *n* introspección, *f*

introspective /ˌɪntrə'spɛktɪv/ *a* introspectivo

introversion /ˌɪntrə'vɜrʒən/ *n* Psychol. introversión *f*

introvert /'ɪntrəˌvɜrt/ *a* and *n* Psychol. introverso (-sa)

intrude /ɪn'trud/ *vt* introducir, imponer. —*vi* entremeterse, inmiscuirse. **Do I i.?** ¿Estorbo?

intruder /ɪn'trudər/ *n* intruso (-sa)

intrusion /ɪn'truʒən/ *n* intrusión, *f*; Geol. intromisión, *f*

intrusive /ɪn'trusɪv/ *a* intruso

intuition /ˌɪntu'ɪʃən/ *n* intuición, *f*. **to know by i.,** intuir, saber por intuición

intuitive /ɪn'tuɪtɪv/ *a* intuitivo

inundate /'ɪnənˌdeit/ *vt* inundar, anegar; Fig. abrumar

inundation /ˌɪnən'deiʃən/ *n* inundación, anegación, *f*; Fig. diluvio, *m*, abundancia, *f*

inure /ɪn'yʊr/ *vt* endurecer, habituar

inurement /ɪn'yʊrmənt/ *n* habituación, *f*

invade /ɪn'veid/ *vt* invadir, irrumpir, asaltar; Med. invadir

invader /ɪn'veidər/ *n* invasor (-ra), acometedor (-ra), agresor (-ra)

invading /ɪn'veidɪŋ/ *a* invasor, irruptor

invalid /ɪn'vælɪd/ *a* inválido, nulo. **to become i.,** caducar

invalid /'ɪnvəlɪd/ *n* inválido (-da), enfermo (-ma). **to become an i.,** quedarse inválido. **to i. out of the army,** licenciar por invalidez. **i. carriage,** cochecillo de inválido, *m*

invalidate /ɪn'vælɪˌdeit/ *vt* invalidar, anular

invalidation /ɪnˌvælɪ'deiʃən/ *n* invalidación, *f*

invalidity /ˌɪnvə'lɪdɪti/ *n* invalidez, nulidad, *f*

invaluable /ɪn'vælyuəbəl/ *n* inestimable

invariability /ɪnˌvɛəriə'bɪlɪti/ *n* invariabilidad, invariación, inalterabilidad, inmutabilidad, *f*

invariable /ɪn'vɛəriəbəl/ *a* invariable, inmutable, inalterable

invariably /ɪn'vɛəriəbli/ *adv* invariablemente, inmutablemente

invariant /ɪn'vɛəriənt/ *n* Math. invariante, *m*

invasion /ɪn'veiʒən/ *n* invasión, irrupción, *f*; Med. invasión, *f*

invective /ɪn'vɛktɪv/ *n* invectiva, diatriba, *f*

inveigh (against) /ɪn'vei/ *vi* desencadenarse (contra), prorrumpir en invectivas (contra)

inveigle /ɪn'veigəl/ *vt* seducir, engatusar, persuadir

inveiglement /ɪn'veigəlmənt/ *n* seducción, persuasión, *f*

invent /ɪn'vɛnt/ *vt* inventar, descubrir, originar; (a falsehood) fingir; (create) idear, componer

invention /ɪn'vɛnʃən/ *n* invención, *f*, invento, descubrimiento, *m*; (imagination) ingeniosidad, inventiva, *f*; (falsehood) ficción, mentira, *f*; (finding) invención, *f*, hallazgo, *m*

inventive /ɪn'vɛntɪv/ *a* inventor, inventivo; ingenioso, despejado

inventiveness /ɪn'vɛntɪvnɪs/ *n* inventiva, *f*

inventor /ɪn'vɛntər/ *n* inventor (-ra), autor (-ra)

inventory /'ɪnvənˌtɔri/ *n* inventario, *m*; descripción, *f*. —*vt* inventariar

inverse /ɪn'vɜrs/ *a* inverso. **i. proportion,** razón inversa, *f*

inversely /ɪn'vɜrsli/ *adv* inversamente, a la inversa

inversion /ɪn'vɜrʒən/ *n* inversión, *f*, trastrocamiento, *m*; Gram. hipérbaton, *m*

invert /ɪn'vɜrt/ *vt* invertir, trastornar, trastrocar. **inverted commas,** comilla, *f*

invertebrate /ɪn'vɜrtəbrɪt/ *a* and *n* invertebrado *m*.

invest /ɪn'vɛst/ *vt* Com. invertir; Mil. sitiar, cercar; (foll. by with) poner, cubrir con; (of qualities) conferir, otorgar, dar. —*vi* (with in) poner dinero en, echar caudal en; Inf. comprar

investigable /ɪn'vɛstɪgəbəl/ *a* averiguable

investigate /ɪn'vɛstɪˌgeit/ *vt* investigar, estudiar; examinar, averiguar; explorar

investigation /ɪnˌvɛstɪ'geiʃən/ *n* investigación, *f*, estudio, *m*; examen, *m*, averiguación, *f*; encuesta, pesquisa, *f*

investigator /ɪn'vɛstɪˌgeitər/ *n* investigador (-ra); averiguador (-ra)

investigatory /ɪn'vɛtɪgəˌtɔri/ *a* investigador

investiture /ɪn'vɛstɪtʃər/ *n* investidura, instalación, *f*

investment /ɪn'vɛstmənt/ *n* (Com. of money) inversión, *f*, empleo, *m*; Mil. cerco, *m*; (investiture) instalación, *f*; *pl* **investments,** Com. acciones, *f pl*, fondos, *m pl*

investor /ɪn'vɛstər/ *n* inversionista, *m*; accionista, *mf*

inveteracy /ɪn'vɛtərəsi/ *n* antigüedad, *f*, lo arraigado

inveterate /ɪn'vɛtərɪt/ *a* inveterado, antiguo, arraigado, incurable

invidious /ɪn'vɪdiəs/ *a* odioso, repugnante, injusto

invidiousness /ɪn'vɪdiəsnɪs/ *n* injusticia, *f*, lo odioso

invigorate /ɪn'vɪgəˌreit/ *vt* vigorizar, dar fuerza (a), avivar

invigorating /ɪn'vɪgəˌreitɪŋ/ *a* fortaleciente, fortificador, vigorizador

invincibility /ɪnˌvɪnsə'bɪlɪti/ *n* invencibilidad, *f*

invincible /ɪn'vɪnsəbəl/ *a* invencible, indomable; Fig. insuperable

inviolability /ɪnˌvaiələ'bɪlɪti/ *n* inviolabilidad, *f*

inviolable /ɪn'vaiələbəl/ *a* inviolable

inviolate /ɪn'vaiəlɪt/ *a* inviolado

invisibility /ɪnˌvɪzə'bɪlɪti/ *n* invisibilidad, *f*

invisible /ɪn'vɪzəbəl/ *a* invisible. **i. ink,** tinta simpática, *f*. **i. mending,** zurcido invisible, *m*

invitation /ˌɪnvɪ'teiʃən/ *n* invitación, *f*; convite, *m*; (card) tarjeta de invitación, *f*

invite /ɪn'vait/ *vt* invitar, convidar; (request) pedir, rogar; (of things) incitar, tentar.

inviting /ɪn'vaitɪŋ/ *a* atrayente, incitante; (of food) apetitoso; (of looks) provocativo

invocation /ˌɪnvə'keiʃən/ *n* invocación, *f*

invocatory /ɪn'vɒkətɔri/ *a* invocatorio, invocador

invoice /'ɪnvɔis/ *n* Com. factura, *f*. —*vt* facturar. **proforma i.,** factura simulada, *f*. **shipping i.,** factura de expedición, *f*. **i. book,** libro de facturas, *m*

invoke /ɪn'vouk/ *vt* invocar; suplicar, implorar; (laws) acogerse (a)

involuntarily /ɪnˌvɒlən'tɛərəli/ *adv* sin querer, involuntariamente

involuntariness /ɪn'vɒlənˌtɛrɪnɪs/ *n* involuntariedad, *f*

involuntary /ɪn'vɒlənˌtɛri/ *a* involuntario; instintivo, inconsciente

involve /ɪn'vɒlv/ *vt* (entangle) enredar, embrollar, enmarañar; (implicate) comprometer; (imply) implicar, ocasionar, suponer, traer consigo

involved /ɪn'vɒlvd/ *a* complejo, intrincado; (of style) confuso, obscuro

invulnerability /ɪnˌvʌlnərə'bɪlɪti/ *n* invulnerabilidad, *f*

invulnerable /ɪn'vʌlnərəbəl/ *a* invulnerable

inward /'ɪnwərd/ *a* interior, interno; íntimo, espiritual. —*adv* adentro

inwardly /'ɪnwərdli/ *adv* interiormente; para sí, entre sí

inwards /'ɪnwərdz/ *adv* hacia dentro; adentro

iodine /'aiəˌdain/ *n* yodo, *m*. **i. poisoning,** yodismo, *m*

ion /'aiən/ n *Chem.* ion, m
Ionian /ai'ouniən/ a and n jónico (-ca)
Ionic /ai'ɒnɪk/ a jónico. **i. foot** *Poet.* jónico, m
iota /ai'outə/ n (letter) iota, f; jota, pizca, f, ápice, m.
  not an i., ni pizca
I.O.U. n *Com.* abonaré, m
ipecacuanha /ˌɪpɪˌkækyə'wany'ə/ n ipecacuana, f
Iranian /ɪ'reiniən/ a and n iranio (-ia)
Iraq /ɪ'ræk/ Irak, m
irascibility /ɪˌræsə'bɪlɪti/ n irascibilidad, iracundia,
  irritabilidad, f
irascible /ɪ'ræsəbəl/ a irascible, iracundo, irritable
irate /ai'reit/ a airado, colérico, enojado
ire /aiᵊr/ n ira, cólera, furia, f
Ireland /'aiᵊrlənd/ Irlanda, f
iridescence /ˌɪrɪ'desəns/ n iridiscencia, f
iridescent /ˌɪrɪ'desənt/ a iridiscente. **to look i.,** irisar,
  tornasolarse
iridium /ɪ'rɪdiəm/ n *Chem.* iridio, m
iris /'airɪs/ n *Anat.* iris, m; *Bot.* irídea, f
Irish /'airɪʃ/ a and n irlandés (-esa). **the I.,** los ir-
  landeses
Irish Sea Mar de Irlanda, f
irksome /'ɜrksəm/ a fastidioso, tedioso, aburrido
irksomeness /'ɜrksəmnɪs/ n tedio, fastidio, aburrimiento, m
iron /'aiərn/ n hierro, m; (for clothes) plancha, f;
  (tool) utensilio, m, herramienta, f; (golf) hierro, m; pl
  irons, grillos, m pl, cadenas, f pl. —a de hierro, férreo; *Fig.* duro, severo. —vt (linen) planchar; (with
  out) allanar. **to have too many irons in the fire,**
  tener demasiados asuntos entre manos. **to put in**
  irons, echar grillos (a). **to strike while the i. is hot,**
  A hierro caliente batir de repente. **cast-i.,** hierro
  colado, m. **scrap i.,** hierro viejo, m. **sheet i.,** hierro
  en planchas, m. **wrought i.,** hierro dulce, m. **i. age,**
  edad de hierro, f. **i.-foundry,** fundición de hierro, f. **i.**
  lung, *Med.* pulmón de hierro, pulmón de acero, m. **i.-**
  mold, mancha de orín, f. **i. smelting furnace,** alto
  horno, m. **i. tonic,** *Med.* reconstituyente ferruginoso,
  m. **i. will,** voluntad de hierro, f
ironclad /a 'aiərn'klæd; n -,klæd/ a blindado, acorazado. —n buque de guerra blindado, acorazado, m
ironer /'aiərnər/ n planchador (-ra)
ironical /ai'rɒnɪkəl/ a irónico
ironically /ai'rɒnɪkli/ adv con ironía, irónicamente
ironing /'aiərnɪŋ/ n planchado, m; ropa por planchar,
  f. —a de planchar. **i. board,** tabla de planchar, f
ironist /'airənɪst/ n ironista, mf
ironmonger /'aiərnˌmʌŋgər/ n ferretero (-ra). **iron-**
  monger's shop, ferretería, f
ironmongery /'aiərnˌmʌŋgəri/ n ferretería, quincallería, f
iron sulphide sulfuro de hierro, m
ironwork /'aiərnˌwɜrk/ n herraje, m; obra de hierro, f
ironworks /'aiərnˌwɜrks/ n herrería, f
irony /'airəni/ n ironía, f. —a (like iron) ferruginoso
Iroquois /'ɪrəˌkwɔi/ a and n iroqués (-esa)
irradiate /ɪ'reidiˌeit/ vt irradiar; *Fig.* iluminar, aclarar
irradiation /ɪˌreidi'eiʃən/ n irradiación, f; *Fig.* iluminación, f
irrational /ɪ'ræʃənl/ a ilógico, ridículo, irracional
irrationality /ɪˌræʃə'nælɪti/ n irracionalidad, f
irreclaimable /ˌɪrɪ'kleiməbəl/ a irrecuperable, irredimible; (of land) inservible, improductivo; irreformable
irreconcilable /ɪ'rekənˌsailəbəl/ a irreconciliable
irreconcilably /ɪ'rekənˌsailəbli/ adv irremediablemente
irrecoverable /ˌɪrɪ'kʌvərəbəl/ a irrecuperable, incobrable
irredeemable /ˌɪrɪ'diməbəl/ a irredimible, perdido. **i.**
  government loan, deuda perpetua, f
irredeemably /ˌɪrɪ'diməbli/ adv perdidamente
irreducible /ˌɪrɪ'dusəbəl/ a irreducible
irrefutability /ɪˌrefyətə'bɪlɪti/ n verdad, f
irrefutable /ɪ'refyətəbəl/ a irrefutable, indisputable,
  innegable, irrebatible
irregular /ɪ'regyələr/ a irregular; anormal; (of shape)
  disforme; desordenado; *Gram.* irregular; (of surface)
  desigual, escabroso

irregularity /ɪˌregyə'lærɪti/ n irregularidad, f; anormalidad, f; (of shape) desproporción, irregularidad, f;
  (of surface) escabrosidad, desigualdad, f; exceso, m,
  demasía, f
irrelevance /ɪ'reləvəns/ n inconexión, f; inoportunidad, f; futilidad, poca importancia, f; (stupidity) desatino, m, impertinencia, f
irrelevant /ɪ'reləvənt/ a inaplicable, fuera de propósito; inoportuno; sin importancia, fútil; (stupid) impertinente
irreligion /ˌɪrɪ'lɪdʒən/ n irreligión, impiedad, f
irreligious /ˌɪrɪ'lɪdʒəs/ a irreligioso, impío
irremediable /ˌɪrɪ'midiəbəl/ a irremediable, irreparable
irremediably /ˌɪrɪ'midiəbli/ adv sin remedio, irremediablemente
irreparable /ɪ'repərəbəl/ a irreparable
irreplaceable /ˌɪrɪ'pleisəbəl/ a irreemplazable
irrepressible /ˌɪrɪ'presəbəl/ a incontrolable, indomable
irreproachable /ˌɪrɪ'proutʃəbəl/ a irreprochable, intachable
irresistible /ˌɪrɪ'zɪstəbəl/ a irresistible
irresistibleness /ˌɪrɪ'zɪstəbəlnɪs/ n superioridad, f
irresolute /ɪ'rezəˌlut/ a irresoluto, indeciso, vacilante
irresoluteness /ɪ'rezəˌlutnɪs/ n irresolución, indecisión, f
irrespective /ˌɪrɪ'spektɪv/ a (with of) independiente
  de, aparte de, sin distinción de
irresponsibility /ˌɪrɪˌspɒnsə'bɪlɪti;/ n irresponsabilidad, f
irresponsible /ˌɪrɪ'spɒnsəbəl/ a irresponsable
irretrievable /ˌɪrɪ'trivəbəl/ a irrecuperable
irretrievably /ˌɪrɪ'trivəbli/ adv irreparablemente, sin
  remedio
irreverence /ɪ'revərəns/ n irreverencia, f
irreverent /ɪ'revərənt/ a irreverente, irrespetuoso
irrevocability /ɪˌrevəkə'bɪlɪti/ n irrevocabilidad, f
irrevocable /ɪ'revəkəbəl/ a irrevocable; inquebrantable
irrigable /'ɪrɪgəbəl/ a regadío
irrigate /'ɪrɪˌgeit/ vt *Agr.* poner en regadío, regar;
  Med. irrigar
irrigation /ˌɪrɪ'geiʃən/ n *Agr.* riego, m; *Med.* irrigación, f. **i. channel,** cacera, acequia, f, canal de riego,
  m
irritability /ˌɪrɪtə'bɪlɪti/ n irritabilidad, iracundia, f
irritable /'ɪrɪtəbəl/ a irritable, irascible, iracundo
irritably /'ɪrɪtəbli/ adv con irritación, airadamente
irritant /'ɪrɪtnt/ a irritante, irritador. —n irritador, m;
  Med. medicamento irritante, m
irritate /'ɪrɪˌteit/ vt provocar, estimular; irritar, molestar, exasperar; *Med.* irritar
irritating /'ɪrɪˌteitɪŋ/ a irritador, irritante
irritatingly /'ɪrɪˌteitɪŋli/ adv de un modo irritante
irritation /ˌɪrɪ'teiʃən/ n irritación, f, enojo, m; *Physiol.*
  picazón, f, desazón, m
irruption /ɪ'rʌpʃən/ n irrupción, invasión, f
isinglass /'aizənˌglæs/ n cola de pescado, f
Islamic /ɪs'læmɪk/ a islámico
Islamism /ɪs'lɑmɪzəm/ n islamismo, m
Islamite /ɪs'læmait/ a and n islamita mf
island /'ailənd/ n isla, f, a isleño
islander /'ailəndər/ n isleño (-ña)
islet /'ailɪt/ n isleta, f; isolote, m
isobaric /ˌaisə'bærɪk/ a isobárico
isolate /v. 'aisəˌleit/ vt aislar, apartar
isolated /'aisəˌleitɪd/ a aislado, apartado, solitario;
  único, solo
isolation /ˌaisə'leiʃən/ n aislamiento, apartamiento,
  m, soledad, f
isolationism /ˌaisə'leiʃəˌnɪzəm/ n *Polit.* aislacionismo,
  aislamientismo, m
isolationist /ˌaisə'leiʃənɪst/ a and n *Polit.* aislacionista, aislamientista, mf
isomerism /ai'sɒməˌrɪzəm/ n *Chem.* isomería, f
isometric /ˌaisə'metrɪk/ a isométrico
isosceles /ai'sɒsəˌliz/ a isósceles
isotope /'aisəˌtoup/ n *Chem.* isótopo, isotopo, m
Israelite /'ɪzriəˌlait/ a and n israelita mf
issue /'ɪʃu/ n salida, f; (result) resultado, m, consecuencia, f; (of a periodical) número, m; *Print.* edi-

ción, tirada, *f;* (offspring) prole, sucesión, *f;* (of notes, bonds) emisión, *f; Med.* flujo, *m;* cuestión, *f,* problema, *m.* —*vi* salir, fluir, manar; nacer, originarse; resultar, terminarse. —*vt* (an order) expedir, emitir, dictar; publicar, dar a luz; (of notes, bonds) poner en circulación, librar. **at i.,** en disputa, en cuestión. **to join i.,** llevar la contraria, oponer

isthmian /'ısmıən/ *a* ístmico

isthmus /'ısməs/ *n* istmo, *m*

it /ıt/ *pron* (as subject) él, *m;* ella, *f;* (gen. omitted with all verbs in Sp.); (as object) lo, *m;* la, *f;* (as indirect object) le (se with an object in 3rd pers.); (meaning that thing, that affair) eso, ello. Sometimes omitted in other cases, e.g. *He has thought it necessary to stay at home,* Ha creído necesario de quedarse en casa. *We heard it said that...,* Oímos decir que... *to make it perfectly clear that...,* dejar bien claro que... —*n* (slang) garbo, aquél, *m;* atractivos, *m pl.* **Is it not so?** ¿No es así? **That is it,** Eso es. **It's me,** Soy yo

Italian /ı'tælyən/ *a* and *n* italiano (-na) (language) italiano, *m. Art.* **I. School,** escuela italiana, *f*

italic /ı'tælık/ *a* (of Italy) itálico; *Print.* itálico, bastardilla. —*n* letra bastardilla, bastardilla, letra itálica, *f.* **italics mine,** el subrayado es mío, los subrayados son míos

italicize /ı'tælə‚saiz/ *vt* imprimir en bastardilla; dar énfasis (a)

Italy /'ıtli/ Italia, *f*

itch /ıtʃ/ *n* sarna, *f; Fig.* picazón, *f;* prurito, capricho, *m.* —*vi* picar; *Fig.* sentir picazón; (with to) rabiar por, suspirar por.

itching /'ıtʃıŋ/ *n* picazón, *f,* picor, *m.* —*a* sarnoso, picante; *Med.* pruriginoso. **to have an i. palm,** *Fig.* ser de la virgen del puño

item /*n* 'aitəm; *adv* 'aitɛm/ *n* ítem, artículo, *m; Com.* partida, *f;* punto, detalle, *m;* (of a program) número, *m;* asunto, *m.* —*adv* ítem

iterative /'ıtə‚reitıv/ *a* iterativo

Ithaca /'ıθəkə/ Ítaca, *f*

itinerant /ai'tınərənt/ *a* nómada, errante

itinerary /ai'tınə'reri/ *n* itinerario, *m,* ruta, *f*

its /ıts/ *poss a* su (with pl. obj.) sus. **a book and its pages,** un libro y sus páginas.

itself /ıt'sɛlf/ *pron* él mismo, *m;* ella misma, *f;* (with prep.) sí; (with reflex. verb) se; (with noun) el mismo, la misma; (meaning alone) solo. **in i.,** en sí

ivied /'aivid/ *a* cubierto de hiedra

ivory /'aivəri/ *n* marfil, *m.* —*a* ebúrneo, de marfil, marfileño. **vegetable i.,** marfil vegetal, *m.* **i. carving,** talla de marfil, *f*

ivory tower *n* torre de marfil, *f*

ivory-tower /'aivəri 'tauər/ *a* de torre de marfil

ivy /'aivi/ *n* hiedra, *f*

J

j /dʒei/ n (letter) jota, f
jab /dʒæb/ vt (with a hypodermic needle, etc.) pinchar; introducir (en); clavar (con); (scrape) hurgar; (place) poner. —n pinchazo, m; golpe, m. **He jabbed his pistol in my ribs,** Me puso la pistola en las costillas
jabber /'dʒæbər/ vt and vi chapurrear; (of monkeys) chillar
jabbering /'dʒæbərɪŋ/ n chapurreo, m; (of monkeys) chillidos, m pl
Jack /dʒæk/ n Juan, m; (man) hombre, m; (sailor) marinero, m; (in cards) sota, f; (for raising weights) gato, m; (of a spit) torno, m; (of some animals) macho, m; (bowls) boliche, m. —vt (with up) solevantar con gatos. **Union J.,** pabellón británico, m. **j.-boot,** bota de montar, f. **J.-in-office,** mandarín, funcionario impertinente, m. **J.-in-the-box,** faca, f. **j.-knife,** navaja, f. **J. of all trades,** hombre de muchos oficios, m. **jack of all trades, master of none,** aprendiz de todo, oficial de nada. **j.-rabbit,** liebre americana, f. **J.-tar,** marinero, m
jackal /'dʒækəl/ n chacal, adive, m
jackanapes /'dʒækəˌneips/ n impertinente, m; mequetrefe, m
jackass /'dʒæk,æs/ n asno, m; (fool) tonto, asno, m. **laughing j.,** martín pescador, m
jacket /'dʒækɪt/ n chaqueta, f; americana, f; (for boilers, etc.) camisa, f; (of a book) forro, m, sobrecubierta, f. **strait j.,** camisa de fuerza, f
jacks /dʒæks/ n (game) matatenas, f pl, cantillos, m pl
jade /dʒeid/ n Mineral. jade, m; (horse) rocín, m; (woman) mala pécora, f; (saucy wench) mozuela, picaruela, f
jaded /'dʒeidɪd/ a fatigado, agotado, rendido; (of the palate) saciado
jagged /dʒægɪd/ a dentado
jaguar /'dʒægwɑr/ n jaguar, m
jail /dʒeil/ cárcel, prisión, f; encierro, m. —vt encarcelar. —a carcelario, carcelero.
jailbird /'dʒeil,bɜrd/ malhechor; presidiario, m
jailer /'dʒeilər/ n carcelero (-ra)
jalopy /dʒə'lɒpi/ carcacho, m, (Mexico), cafetera rusa, f, (Spain)
jalousie /'dʒælə,si/ n celosía, f
jam /dʒæm/ vt (ram) apretar; apiñar; estrujar; (a machine) atascar; (radio) causar interferencia (a); (preserve) hacer confitura de. —vi atascarse. —n (of people) agolpamiento, m; (traffic) atasco, m; (preserve) confitura, mermelada, compota, f. **He jammed his hat on,** Se encasquetó el sombrero. **She suddenly jammed down on the brakes,** Frenó de repente. **jam-dish,** compotera, f. **jam-jar,** pote para confitura, m
Jamaican /dʒə'meikən/ a jamaicano, n jamaicano (-na)
jamboree /ˌdʒæmbə'ri/ campamento, m
jamming /'dʒæmɪŋ/ n Radio. interferencias, f pl
jangle /'dʒæŋgəl/ vi cencerrear; chocar; rechinar. —n cencerreo, m; choque, m; rechinamiento, m
janissary /'dʒænəˌseri/ n jenízaro, m
janitor /'dʒænɪtər/ n portero, m; (in a university, etc.) bedel, m
Jansenist /'dʒænsənɪst/ a and n jansenista, mf
January /'dʒænyuˌɛri/ n enero, m
Japan /dʒə'pæn/ el Japón, m
japan /dʒə'pæn/ n charol, m. —vt charolar
Japanese /ˌdʒæpə'niz/ a japonés. —n japonés (-esa); (language) japonés, m
jar /dʒɑr/ n chirrido, m; choque, m; sacudida, f; vibración, trepidación, f; (quarrel) riña, f; (receptacle) jarra, f; (for tobacco, honey, cosmetics, etc.) pote, m, (Leyden) botella (de Leyden), f. —vi chirriar; vibrar, trepidar; chocar; (of sounds) ser discorde; (of colors) chillar. —vt sacudir; hacer vibrar. **It jarred on my nerves,** Me atacaba los nervios. **It gave me a nasty**

jar, Fig. Me hizo una impresión desagradable. **on the jar,** entreabierto
jardiniere /ˌdʒɑrdn̩'iər/ n jardinera, f
jargon /'dʒɑrgən/ n jerga, jerigonza, f; monserga, f; (technical) lenguaje especial, m
jarring /'dʒɑrɪŋ/ a discorde, disonante; en conflicto, opuesto; (to the nerves) que ataca a los nervios
jasmine /'dʒæzmɪn/ n jazmín, m. **yellow j.,** jazmín amarillo, m
jasper /'dʒæspər/ n Mineral. jaspe, m
jaundice /'dʒɔndɪs/ n ictericia, f
jaundiced /'dʒɔndɪst/ a envidioso; desengañado, desilusionado
jaunt /dʒɔnt/ n excursión, f, vi ir de excursión
jauntily /'dʒɔntli/ adv airosamente, con garbo
jauntiness /'dʒɔntinɪs/ n garbo, m, gentileza, ligereza, f
jaunty /'dʒɔnti/ a garboso, airoso
Javanese /ˌdʒævə'niz/ a javanés. —n javanés (-esa)
javelin /'dʒævlɪn/ n jabalina, f. **j. throwing,** lanzamiento de la jabalina, m
jaw /dʒɔ/ n quijada, f; maxilar, m; pl **jaws,** boca, f; (of death, etc.) garras, f pl; Mech. quijada, f; (narrow entrance) boca, abertura, f. **jaw-bone,** mandíbula, f; Anat. hueso maxilar, m
jay /dʒei/ n arrendajo, m
jazz /dʒæz/ n jazz, m. —vi bailar el jazz. **j. band,** orquesta de jazz, f
jealous /'dʒeləs/ a celoso; envidioso. **to be j. of,** tener celos de. **to make j.,** dar celos (a)
jealously /'dʒeləsli/ adv celosamente
jealousy /'dʒeləsi/ n celos, m pl
jeans /dʒinz/ n vaqueros, m pl
jeep /dʒip/ n Mil. yip, m
jeer /dʒɪər/ n burla, mofa, f; insulto, m, vi burlarse; (with at) mofarse de
jeerer /'dʒɪərər/ n mofador (-ra)
jeering /'dʒɪərɪŋ/ a mofador. —n burlas, f pl; insultos, m pl
jeeringly /'dʒɪərɪŋli/ adv burlonamente
jellied /'dʒelid/ a en gelatina
jelly /'dʒeli/ n jalea, f; gelatina, f, vi solidificarse. **j.-bag,** manga, f. **j.-fish,** aguamala, aguaviva, malagna, medusa, f
jeopardize /'dʒepərˌdaiz/ vt arriesgar, poner en juego; comprometer
jeopardy /'dʒepərdi/ n peligro, m
jeremiad /ˌdʒerə'maiəd/ n jeremiada, f
jerk /dʒɜrk/ n sacudida, f. —vt sacudir, dar una sacudida (a); lanzar bruscamente; (pull) tirar de; (push) empujar. —vi moverse a sacudidas. **I jerked myself free,** Me libré de una sacudida
jerkily /'dʒɜrkəli/ adv con sacudidas; espasmódicamente; nerviosamente
jerkin /'dʒɜrkɪn/ n justillo, m
jerky /'dʒɜrki/ a espasmódico; nervioso (also of style)
jerry-built /'dʒɛri,bɪlt/ a mal construido, de pacotilla
jersey /'dʒɜrzi/ n jersey, m. —a de jersey; de Jersey. **football j.,** camiseta de fútbol, f, jersey de fútbol, m. **J. cow,** vaca jerseysa, f
Jerusalem /dʒɪ'rusələm/ Jerusalén, m
jest /dʒest/ n broma, chanza, f; (joke) chiste, m; (laughingstock) hazmerreír, m. —vi bromear; burlarse (de). **in j.,** en broma, de guasa
jester /'dʒestər/ n burlón (-ona); (practical joker, etc.) bromista, mf; (at a royal court) bufón, m
jesting /'dʒestɪŋ/ n bromas, f pl; chistes, m pl; burlas, f pl. —a de broma; burlón
jestingly /'dʒestɪŋli/ adv en broma
Jesuit /'dʒeʒuɪt/ n Jesuita, m
Jesuitical /ˌdʒeʒu'ɪtɪkəl/ a jesuítico
jet /dʒet/ n Mineral. azabache, m; (stream) chorro, m; (pipe) surtidero, m; (burner) mechero, m, vi chorrear. **jet-black,** negro como el azabache, de azabache. **jet-propelled engine,** motor de retroacción, m. **jet-propelled plane,** aeroplano de reacción, m

jetsam /'dʒɛtsəm/ n echazón, f; Fig. víctima, f
jettison /'dʒɛtəsən/ n echazón, f. —vt echar (mercancías) al mar; Fig. librarse de, abandonar
jetty /'dʒɛti/ n dique, malecón, m; (landing pier) embarcadero, muelle, m
Jew /dʒu/ n judío, m. **Jew's harp,** birimbao, m
jewel /'dʒuəl/ n joya, alhaja, f; (of a watch) rubí, m; Fig. alhaja, f. —vt enjoyar, adornar con piedras preciosas. **j.-box, -case,** joyero, m
jeweled /'dʒuəld/ a adornado con piedras preciosas, enjoyado; (of a watch) con rubíes
jeweler /'dʒuələr/ n joyero (-ra). **jeweler's shop,** joyería, f
jewelry /'dʒuəlri/ n joyas, f pl; artículos de joyería, m pl
Jewess /'dʒuɪs/ n judía, f
Jewish /'dʒuɪʃ/ a judío
Jewry /'dʒuri/ n judería, f
jib /dʒɪb/ n Naut. foque, m. —vi (of a horse) plantarse; (refuse) rehusar. **to jib at,** vacilar en; mostrarse desinclinado. **jib-boom,** Naut. botalón de foque, m
jiffy /'dʒɪfi/ n instante, credo, m. **in a j.,** en un decir Jesús, en un credo, en un santiamén
jig /dʒɪg/ n (dance) jiga, f. —vi bailar una jiga; bailar, agitarse, sacudirse. —vt agitar, sacudir; (sieve) cribar
jigger /'dʒɪgər/ n Naut. cangreja de mesana, f; aparejo de mano, m; jigger, m
jigsaw puzzle /'dʒɪg,sɔ/ n rompecabezas, m
jilt /dʒɪlt/ vt dar calabazas (a)
jingle /'dʒɪŋgəl/ n tintineo, m; ruido, m; verso, m; estribillo, m. —vi tintinar; sonar; rimar
jingoism /'dʒɪŋgoʊ,ɪzəm/ n jingoísmo, m
jitters, to have the /'dʒɪtərz/ no tenerlas todas consigo, no saber dónde meterse
job /dʒɒb/ n tarea, f; trabajo, m; empleo, m; (affair) asunto, m; (thing) cosa, f; (unscrupulous transaction) intriga, f. **It is a good (bad) job that...,** Es una buena (mala) cosa que... **He has done a good job,** Ha hecho un buen trabajo. **He has lost his job,** Ha perdido su empleo, Le han declarado cesante. **odd-job man,** factótum, m. **job-lot,** colección miscelánea, f; Com. saldo de mercancías, m
jobber /'dʒɒbər/ n (workman) destajista, m; (in stocks) agiotista, m; Com. corredor, m
jobless /'dʒɒblɪs/ a sin trabajo
jockey /'dʒɒki/ n jockey, m. —vt engañar; (with into) persuadir, hacer; (with out of) quitar, robar. **j. cap,** gorra de jockey, f. **J. Club,** jockey-club, m
jocose /dʒoʊ'koʊs/ a jocoso, gracioso, guasón
jocosity /dʒoʊ'kɒsɪti/ n jocosidad, f
jocular /'dʒɒkyələr/ a gracioso, alegre; chistoso, zumbón
jocularity /,dʒɒkyə'lærɪti/ n alegría, jocosidad, f
jocularly /'dʒɒkyələrli/ adv en broma; alegremente
jocund /'dʒɒkənd/ a alegre, jovial; jocundo
jocundity /dʒoʊ'kʌndɪti/ n alegría, f; jocundidad, f
jog /dʒɒg/ vt empujar; (the memory) refrescar. —vi ir despacio; andar a trote corto. —n empujón, m. **He jogged me with his elbow,** Me dio con el codo. **jog-trot,** trote corto, m
joie de vivre /ʒwad²'vivr²/ n goce de vivir, arregosto de vivir, m
join /dʒɔin/ vt juntar; unir; añadir; (railway lines) empalmar; juntarse con; (meet) encontrarse (con); reunirse (con); (a club, etc.) hacerse miembro (de); (share) acompañar; (regiments, ships) volver (a). —vi juntarse; unirse; asociarse. —n unión, f; (railway) empalme, m; (roads) bifurcación, f. **At what time will you j. me?** ¿A qué hora me vendrás a buscar? **He has joined his ship,** Ha vuelto a su buque. **Will you j. me in a drink?** ¿Me quieres acompañar en una bebida? **to j. battle,** librar batalla. **to j. forces,** combinar, Inf. juntar meriendas. **to j. in,** tomar parte en, participar en. **to j. together,** vt unir, juntar. —vi juntarse; asociarse. **to j. up,** alistarse
joiner /'dʒɔinər/ n carpintero, ensamblador, m
joinery /'dʒɔinəri/ n ensambladuría, f; carpintería, f
joining /'dʒɔiniŋ/ n juntura, conjunción, f; (etc.) ensambladura, f; Fig. unión, f
joint /dʒɔint/ n juntura, junta, f; Anat. coyuntura, articulación, f; (knuckle) nudillo, m; (of meat) cuarto,

m; (hinge) bisagra, f; Bot. nudo, m, a unido; combinado; colectivo; mixto; mutuo; (in compounds) co. —vt juntar; (meat) descuartizar. **out of j.,** dislocado; (of the times) fuera de compás. **j. account,** cuenta corriente mutua, f. **j.-heir,** coheredero, m. **j. stock company,** compañía por acciones, sociedad anónima, f
jointed /'dʒɔintɪd/ a articulado; (foldable) plegadizo
jointly /'dʒɔintli/ adv juntamente, en común, colectivamente
joist /dʒɔist/ n sopanda, viga, f
joke /dʒoʊk/ n chiste, m; burla, broma, f. —vi bromear, chancearse. —vt burlarse (de). **Can he take a j.?** ¿Sabe aguantar una broma? **practical j.,** broma pesada, f. **to play a j.,** gastar una broma, hacer una burla
joker /'dʒoʊkər/ n bromista, mf; (in cards) comodín, m
joking /'dʒoʊkɪŋ/ n chistes, m pl, bromas, f pl. —a chistoso; cómico
jokingly /'dʒoʊkɪŋli/ adv en broma, de guasa
jollification /,dʒɒləfɪ'keɪʃən/ n regocijo, m; festividades, fiestas, f pl
jollity /'dʒɒlɪti/ n alegría, f; regocijo, m
jolly /'dʒɒli/ a alegre, jovial; (tipsy) achispado; (amusing) divertido; (nice) agradable. —adv muy. **He is a j. good fellow,** Es un hombre estupendo. **I am j. glad,** Estoy contentísimo, Me alegro mucho
jolt /dʒoʊlt/ n sacudida, f. —vt sacudir. —vi (of a vehicle) traquetear
jolting /'dʒoʊltɪŋ/ n sacudidas, f pl, sacudimiento, m; (of a vehicle) traqueteo, m
jongleur /dʒoʊ'nglər/ n juglar, m
jonquil /'dʒɒŋkwɪl/ n Bot. junquillo, m
Jordan /'dʒɔrdn/ Jordania, f
joss /dʒɒs/ n ídolo chino, m. **j.-stick,** pebete, m
jostle /'dʒɒsəl/ vt empujar, empellar. —vi dar empujones, codear
jot /dʒɒt/ n jota, pizca, f. —vt (down) apuntar. **not a jot,** ni jota, ni pizca. **to be not worth a jot,** no valer un comino
jotter /'dʒɒtər/ n taco para notas, m; (exercise book) cuaderno, m
jotting /'dʒɒtɪŋ/ n apunte, m; observación, f
journal /'dʒɜrnl/ n (diary) diario, m; (ship's) diario de navegación, m; (newspaper) periódico, m; (review) revista, f
journalese /,dʒɜrnl'iz/ n lenguaje periodístico, m
journalism /'dʒɜrnl,ɪzəm/ n periodismo, m
journalist /'dʒɜrnlɪst/ n periodista, mf
journalistic /,dʒɜrnl'ɪstɪk/ a periodístico
journey /'dʒɜrni/ n viaje, m; expedición, f; trayecto, m; camino, m. —vi viajar. **j. by sea,** viaje por mar. **Pleasant j.!** ¡Buen viaje! ¡Feliz viaje! **outward j.,** viaje de ida, m. **return j.,** viaje de regreso, m
Jove /dʒoʊv/ n Júpiter, m. **By J.!** ¡Pardiez! ¡Caramba!
jovial /'dʒoʊviəl/ a jovial
joviality /,dʒoʊvi'ælɪti/ n jovialidad, f
jowl /dʒaʊl/ n (cheek) carrillo, m; (of cattle, etc.) papada, f; (jaw) quijada, f
joy /dʒɔi/ n alegría, f; felicidad, f; deleite, placer, m, vi alegrarse. **I wish you joy,** Te deseo la felicidad. **joy-ride,** excursión en coche, f; vuelo en avión, m. **joy-stick,** (of an airplane) palanca de gobierno, f
joyful /'dʒɔifəl/ a alegre
joyfulness /'dʒɔifəlnɪs/ n alegría, f
joyless /'dʒɔilɪs/ a sin alegría, triste
joylessness /'dʒɔilɪsnɪs/ n falta de alegría, tristeza, f
joyous /'dʒɔiəs/. See **joyful**
jubilant /'dʒubələnt/ a jubiloso; triunfante
jubilantly /'dʒubələntli/ adv con júbilo, alegremente; triunfalmente
jubilation /,dʒubə'leɪʃən/ n júbilo, m, alegría, f; ruido triunfal, m
jubilee /'dʒubə,li/ n jubileo, m
jubilee volume n libro de homenaje, libro jubilar, m
Judaic /dʒu'deɪɪk/ a judaico
Judaism /'dʒudi,ɪzəm/ n judaísmo, m
Judas /'dʒudəs/ n (traitor and hole) judas, m
Judezmo /dʒu'dezmoʊ/ el judesmo, m
judge /dʒʌdʒ/ n juez, m; (connoisseur) conocedor

(-ra) (de); (umpire) arbitrio, *m.* —*vt* juzgar; considerar, tener por. —*vi* servir como juez; juzgar. **judging by,** a juzgar por. **to be a good j. of,** ser buen juez de. **to j. for oneself,** formar su propia opinión

judgment /'dʒʌdʒmənt/ *n Law.* fallo, *m;* sentencia, *f;* juicio, *m;* (understanding) entendimiento, discernimiento, *m;* (opinion) opinión, *f,* parecer, *m.* **In my j...,** Según mi parecer,... Según creo yo... **Last J.,** Juicio Final, *m.* **to pass j. on,** *Law.* pronunciar sentencia (en or sobre); dictaminar sobre; juzgar. **to sit in j. on,** ser juez de; juzgar. **j.-day,** Día del Juicio, *m.* **j.-seat,** tribunal, *m*

judicature /'dʒudɪ,keitʃər/ *n* judicatura, *f;* (court) juzgado, *m*

judicial /dʒu'dɪʃəl/ *a* judicial; legal; (of the mind) juicioso. **j. inquiry,** investigación judicial, *f.* **j. separation,** separación legal, *f*

judiciary /dʒu'dɪʃɪ,ɛri/ *a* judicial. —*n* judicatura, *f*

judicious /dʒu'dɪʃəs/ *a* juicioso, prudente.

judiciously /dʒu'dɪʃəsli/ *adv* prudentemente, juiciosamente

judiciousness /dʒu'dɪʃəsnɪs/ *n* juicio, *m,* prudencia, sensatez, *f*

judo /'dʒudou/ *n* yudo, *m*

judoka /'dʒudou,ka/ *n* yudoca, *mf*

jug /dʒʌg/ *n* jarro, *m;* cántaro, *m;* pote, *m.* —*vt Cul.* estofar. —*vi* (of nightingale) trinar, cantar. **jugged hare,** *n* liebre en estofado, *f*

juggle /'dʒʌgəl/ *vi* hacer juegos malabares. **to j. out of,** (money, etc.) quitar con engaño, estafar. **to j. with,** *Fig.* (facts, etc.) tergiversar, falsificar; (person) engañar

juggler /'dʒʌglər/ *n* malabarista, *mf;* (deceiver) estafador (-ra)

jugglery /'dʒʌgləri/ *n* prestidigitación, *f;* juegos malabares, *m pl;* (imposture) engaño, *m,* estafa, *f;* trampas, *f pl*

jugular /'dʒʌgyələr/ *a Anat.* yugular. **j. vein,** yugular, *m*

juice /dʒus/ *n* jugo, *m;* *Fig.* zumo, *m.* **digestive j.,** jugo digestivo, *m*

juiciness /'dʒusɪnɪs/ *n* jugosidad, *f;* suculencia, *f*

juicy /'dʒusi/ *a* jugoso; suculento

jujube /'dʒudʒub/ *n* pastilla, *f*

jukebox /'dʒuk,bɒks/ *n* tocadiscos, vitrola, sinfonola, *f*

July /dʒu'lai/ *n* julio, *m*

jumble /'dʒʌmbəl/ *vt* mezclar, confundir. —*n* mezcla confusa, colección miscelánea, confusión, *f.* **j. sale,** tómbola, *f*

jump /dʒʌmp/ *n* salto, *m;* (in prices, etc.) aumento, *m.* **at one j.,** de un salto. **high j.,** salto de altura, *m.* **long j.,** salto de longitud, *m.* **to be on the j.,** *Inf.* estar nervioso, tener los nervios en punta

jump /dʒʌmp/ *vi* saltar; dar un salto; brincar; (of tea-cups, etc.) bailar; (throb) pulsar. —*vt* saltar; hacer saltar; (a child) brincar; (omit) pasar por alto de, omitir. **The train jumped the rails,** El tren se descarriló. **to j. out of bed,** saltar de la cama. **to j. to the conclusion that...,** darse prisa a concluir que... **to j. about,** dar saltos, brincar; revolverse, moverse de un lado para otro. **to j. at,** saltar sobre; precipitarse sobre, abalanzarse hacia; (an offer) apresurarse a aceptar; (seize) coger con entusiasmo. **to j. down,** bajar de un salto. **to j. over,** saltar; saltar por encima de. **to j. up,** saltar; (on to a horse, etc.) montar rápidamente; levantarse apresuradamente. **to j. with,** (agree) convenir en, estar conforme con

jumper /'dʒʌmpər/ *n* saltador (-ra); (sailor's) blusa, *f* jersey, sweater, *m*

jumpiness /'dʒʌmpinɪs/ *n* nerviosidad, *f*

jumping /'dʒʌmpiŋ/ *n* saltos, *m pl.* —*a* saltador. **j.-off place,** base avanzada, *f;* *Fig.* trampolín, *m.* **j.-pole,** pértiga, *f*

jumpy /'dʒʌmpi/ *a* nervioso, agitado

junction /'dʒʌŋkʃən/ *n* unión, *f;* (of roads) bifurcación, *f;* (railway) empalme, *m;* (connection) conexión, *f*

juncture /'dʒʌŋktʃər/ *n* coyuntura, *f;* momento, *m;* crisis, *f,* momento crítico, *m;* (joint) junta, *f*

June /dʒun/ *n* junio, *m*

jungle /'dʒʌŋgəl/ *n* selva, *f.* **j.-fever,** fiebre de los grandes bosques, *f*

junior /'dʒunyər/ *a* joven; hijo; más joven; menos antiguo; subordinado, segundo. —*n* joven, *mf* **Carmen is my j. by three years,** Carmen es tres años más joven que yo. **James Thomson, Jr.,** James Thomson, hijo. **the j. school,** los pequeños. **j. partner,** socio menor, *m*

juniper /'dʒunəpər/ *n Bot.* enebro, *m*

junk /dʒʌŋk/ *n* trastos viejos, *m pl;* (nonsense) patrañas, *f pl;* *Naut.* junco, *m;* (salt meat) tasajo, *m.* **j.-shop,** tienda de trastos viejos, *f*

junk bond bono-basura, *m*

junketing /'dʒʌŋkitɪŋ/ *n* festividades, *f pl*

juridical /dʒu'rɪdɪkəl/ *a* jurídico

jurisconsult /,dʒʊrɪskən'sʌlt/ *n* jurisconsulto, *m*

jurisdiction /,dʒʊrɪs'dɪkʃən/ *n* jurisdicción, *f;* competencia, *f*

jurisprudence /,dʒʊrɪs'prudns/ *n* jurisprudencia, *f*

jurist /'dʒʊrɪst/ *n* jurista, legista, *mf*

juror /'dʒʊrər/ *n* (miembro del) jurado, *m*

jury /'dʒʊri/ *n* jurado, *m.* **to be on the j.,** formar parte del jurado. **j.-box,** tribuna del jurado, *f*

juryman /'dʒʊrimən/ *n* miembro del jurado, *m*

just /dʒʌst/ *a* justo; justiciero; exacto; fiel. **Peter the J.,** Pedro el justiciero

just /dʒʌst/ *adv* justamente, exactamente; precisamente; (scarcely) apenas; (almost) casi; (entirely) completamente; (simply) meramente, solamente, tan sólo; (newly) recién (followed by past part.), recientemente. **He only j. missed being run over,** Por poco le atropellan. **It is j. near,** Está muy cerca. **It is j. the same to me,** Me es completamente igual. **J. as he was leaving,** Cuando estaba a punto de marcharse, En el momento de marcharse. **Just as you arrive in Spain, you must...** Nada más llegar a España, tienes que... **That's j. it!** ¡Eso es! ¡Exactamente! **to have j.,** acabar de. **They have j. dined,** Acaban de cenar. **J. as you wish,** Como Vd. quiera. **j. at that moment,** precisamente en aquel momento. **j. by,** muy cerca; al lado. **j. now,** ahora mismo; hace poco; pronto, dentro de poco. **j. yet,** todavía. **They will not come j. yet,** No vendrán todavía. **Just looking** (browser to shopkeeper) Estoy viendo, Estamos viendo

justice /'dʒʌstɪs/ *n* justicia, *f;* (judge) juez, *m;* (magistrate) juez municipal, *m.* **to bring to j.,** llevar ante el juez (a). **to do j. to,** (a person) hacer justicia (a); (a meal) hacer honor (a). **to do oneself j.,** quedar bien

justifiable /'dʒʌstə,faiəbəl/ *a* justificable

justifiably /'dʒʌstə,faiəbli/ *adv* con justicia, justificadamente

justification /,dʒʌstəfɪ'keiʃən/ *n* justificación, *f*

justify /'dʒʌstə,fai/ *vt* justificar, vindicar; (excuse) disculpar; *Print.* justificar. **to be justified (in),** tener derecho (a), tener motivo (para), tener razón (en)

justly /'dʒʌstli/ *adv* justamente; con justicia; con derecho; con razón; exactamente; debidamente

justness /'dʒʌstnɪs/ *n* justicia, *f;* exactitud, *f*

jute /dʒut/ *n* yute, *m*

jut (out) /dʒʌt/ *vi* salir, proyectar; sobresalir

juvenile /'dʒuvənl/ *a* juvenil; de la juventud; para la juventud; joven; de niños; para niños. —*n* joven, *mf.* **j. court,** tribunal de menores, *m.* **j. lead,** *Theat.* galancete, galán joven, *m.* **j. offender,** delincuente infantil, *m*

juxtapose /'dʒʌkstə,pouz/ *vt* yuxtaponer

juxtaposition /,dʒʌkstəpə'zɪʃən/ *n* yuxtaposición, *f*

K

k /kei/ n (letter) ka, f
kaiser /'kaizər/ n káiser, emperador, m. **the K.** el emperador alemán, m
kaleidoscope /kə'laidə,skoup/ n calidoscopio, m
kaleidoscopic /kə,laidə'skɒpɪk/ a calidoscópico
kangaroo /,kæŋgə'ru/ n canguro, m
kaolin /'keiəlɪn/ n caolín, m
kapok /'keipɒk/ n miraguano, m
keel /kil/ n quilla, f. —vt carenar. **to k. over,** volcar; caer; Naut. zozobrar
keelson /'kɛlsən/ n sobrequilla, f
keen /kin/ a (of edges) afilado; agudo; penetrante; vivo; sutil; ardiente; celoso, entusiasta; mordaz; (desirous) ansioso; (of appetite) grande, bueno. **He is a k. tennis player,** Es tenista entusiasta. **Joan has a very k. ear,** Juana tiene un oído muy agudo. **I'm not very k. on apples,** No me gustan mucho las manzanas
keenly /'kinli/ adv agudamente; vivamente; (of feeling) hondamente; (of looking) atentamente
keenness /'kinnɪs/ n (of a blade) afiladura, f; agudeza, f; viveza, f; sutileza, f; perspicacia, f; (enthusiasm) entusiasmo, m, afición, f; (desire) ansia, f
keep /kip/ vt guardar; tener; que darse con; retener; conservar; mantener; (a shop, hotel, etc.) dirigir, tener; (a school) ser director de; (a promise, etc.) cumplir; (the law, etc.) observar, guardar; (celebrate) solemnizar; (a secret) guardar; (books, accounts, a house, in step) llevar; (sheep, etc., one's bed) guardar; (a city, etc.) defender; (domestic animals, cars, etc.) tener; (lodge) alojar; (detain) detener; (reserve) reservar; (cause) hacer. **They had kept this room for me,** Me habían reservado este cuarto. **Dorothy has kept the blue dress,** Dorotea se ha quedado con el vestido azul. **The government could not k. order,** El gobierno no sabía mantener el orden. **I did not know how to k. their attention,** No sabía retener su atención. **Carmen kept quiet,** Carmen guardó silencio, Carmen se calló. **Can you k. a secret?** ¿Sabes guardar un secreto? **to k. an appointment,** acudir a una cita. **to k. in repair,** conservar en buen estado. **to k. someone from doing something,** evitar que uno haga algo. **to k. someone waiting,** hacer que espere uno. **to k. something from someone,** ocultar algo de uno. **We were kept at it night and day,** Nos hacían trabajar día y noche. **I always k. it by me,** Lo tengo siempre a mi lado (or conmigo). **to k. away,** alejar; mantener a distancia; no dejar venir. **to k. back,** (a crowd, etc.) detener; cortar el paso (a); no dejar avanzar; (retain) guardar, retener; reservar; (tears, words) reprimir, contener; (evidence, etc.) callar, suprimir. **to k. down,** no dejar subir (a); sujetar; (a nation, etc.) oprimir, subyugar; (emotions) dominar; (prices, expenses) mantener bajo; (check) moderar, reprimir. **to k. in,** (feelings) contener; reprimir; (the house) hacer quedarse en casa, no dejar salir; (imprison) encerrar; (school) hacer quedar en la escuela (a). **to k. off,** alejar; tener a distancia (a); cerrar el paso (a), no dejar avanzar; no andar sobre; no tocar; (a subject) no tratar de, no discutir, no tocar. **K. your hands off!** ¡No toques! **to k. on,** guardar; retener; (eyes) fijar en, poner en. **to k. out,** no dejar entrar; excluir. **It is difficult to k. him out of trouble,** Es difícil de evitar que se meta en líos. **to k. to,** seguir; limitarse a; adherirse a; **K. to the Left,** «Tome su izquierda», **K. to the right,** «Tome su derecha»; (a path, etc.) seguir por; (one's bed) guardar; (fulfil) cumplir; (oblige) hacer, obligar. **to k. under,** subyugar, oprimir; dominar; controlar. **to k. up,** mantener; (appearances) guardar; conservar; persistir en; (prices) sostener; (in good repair) conservar en buen estado; (go on doing) continuar. **He kept me up late last night,** Anoche me entretuvo hasta muy tarde; Ayer me hizo trasnochar; Anoche me hizo velar. **to k. one's end up,** volver por sí, hacerse fuerte. **to k. up one's spirits,** no desanimarse
keep /kip/ vi quedar; (be) estar; (continue) seguir,

continuar; mantenerse; (at home, etc.) quedarse, permanecer; (be accustomed) acostumbrar, soler; (persist) perseverar; (of food) conservarse fresco. **How is he keeping?** ¿Cómo está? **to k. in with someone,** cultivar a alguien. **to k. up with the times,** mantenerse al corriente. **to k. at,** seguir; persistir; perseverar; (pester) importunar. **John keeps at it,** Juan trabaja sin descansar. **to k. away,** mantenerse apartado; mantenerse a distancia; no acudir. **to k. back,** hacerse a un lado, apartarse, alejarse. **to k. down,** quedarse tumbado; seguir acurrucado; no levantarse; esconderse. **to k. from,** (doing something) guardarse de. **to k. off,** mantenerse a distancia. **If the storm keeps off,** Si no estalla una tempestad. **If the rain keeps off,** Si no empieza a llover, Si no hay lluvia. **to k. on,** continuar; seguir. **to k. straight on,** seguir derecho. **I'm tired, but I still k. on,** Estoy cansado, pero sigo trabajando. **to k. out,** quedarse fuera. **to k. out of,** (quarrels, trouble, etc.) no meterse en, evitar. **to k. out of sight,** no dejarse ver, no mostrarse, mantenerse oculto. **to k. together,** quedarse juntos; reunirse
keep /kip/ n (of a castle) mazmorra, f; (maintenance) subsistencia, f; comida, f. **for keeps,** para siempre jamás
keeper /'kipər/ n guarda, mf; (in a park, zoo, of a lunatic) guardián, m; (of a museum, etc.) director, m; (of animals) criador (-ra); (gamekeeper) guardabosque, m; (of a boardinghouse, shop, etc.) dueño (-ña); (of accounts, books) tenedor, m. **Am I my brother's k.?** ¿Soy yo responsable por mi hermano?
keeping /'kipɪŋ/ n guarda, f; conservación, f; protección, f; (of a rule) observación, f; (of an anniversary, etc.) celebración, f; (of a person) mantenimiento, m. **in k. with,** en armonía con; de acuerdo con. **out of k. with,** en desacuerdo con. **to be in safe k.,** estar en buenas manos; estar en un lugar seguro. **k. back,** retención, f
keepsake /'kip,seik/ n recuerdo, m
keg /kɛg/ n barrilete, m
ken /kɛn/ n alcance de la vista, m; vista, f; comprensión, f
Kennedy Round /'kɛnɪdi/ **, the** la serie Kénnedy, f
kennel /'kɛnl/ n (of a dog) perrera, f; (of hounds) jauría, f; (dwelling) cuchitril, m; (gutter) arroyo, m. **k. man,** perrero, m
kepi /'keipi/ n quepis, m
Kepler /'kɛplər/ Keplero
kerchief /'kɜrtʃɪf/ n pañuelo, m; pañoleta, f. **brightly-colored k.,** pañuelo de hierbas, m
kernel /'kɜrnl/ n almendra, semilla, f; Fig. meollo, m, esencia, f
kerosene /'kɛrə,sin/ n petróleo de lámpara, m; kerosén, m
ketchup /'kɛtʃəp/ n salsa de tomate y setas, f
kettle /'kɛtl/ n caldero, m. **pretty k. of fish,** olla de grillos, f. **k.-drum,** timbal, m. **k.-drum player,** timbalero, m
key /ki/ n llave, f; (Fig. Archit. Mus.) clave, f; (tone) tono, m; (of a piano, typewriter, etc.) tecla, f; Mech. chaveta, f; (of a wind instrument) pistón, m; (winged fruit) sámara, f; Elec. conmutador, m. **major (minor) key,** tono mayor (menor), m. **latch-key,** llave de la puerta, f; (Yale) llavín, m. **master key,** llave maestra, f. **skeleton key,** ganzúa, f. **He is all keyed up,** Tiene los nervios en punta. **key industry,** industria clave, f. **key man,** hombre indispensable, m. **key point,** punto estratégico, m. **key-ring,** llavero, m. **key signature,** Mus. clave, f. **key word,** palabra clave, f
keyboard /'ki,bɔrd/ n teclado, m
keyhole /'ki,houl/ n ojo de la cerradura, m. **through the k.,** por el ojo de la cerradura
keynote /'ki,nout/ n Mus. tónica, f; Fig. piedra clave, idea fundamental, f
keystone /'ki,stoun/ n piedra clave, f
khaki /'kæki/ n caqui, m

kick /kɪk/ *vt* dar un puntapié (a); golpear; (a goal) chutar. —*vi* (of horses, etc.) dar coces, cocear; (of guns) recular. **to k. one's heels,** hacer tiempo. **to kick the bucket,** palmarla. **to k. up a row,** hacer un ruido de mil diablos; (quarrel) armar camorra. **to k. about,** dar patadas (a). **to k. away,** quitar con el pie; lanzar con el pie. **to k. off,** quitar con el pie; lanzar; sacudirse. **k.-off,** *n* golpe de salida, puntapié inicial, saque, *m.* **to k. out,** echar a puntapiés

kick /kɪk/ *n* puntapié, *m;* golpe, *m;* coz, *f;* (of guns) culatazo, *m.* **free k.,** golpe franco, *m*

kicking /'kɪkɪŋ/ *n* coces, *f pl;* acoceamiento, *m;* pataleo, *m;* golpeamiento, *m*

kid /kɪd/ *n* cabrito, *m,* chivo (-va); carne de cabrito, *f;* (leather) cabritilla, *f; Inf.* crío, *m.* **kid gloves,** guantes de cabritilla, *m pl*

kidnap /'kɪdnæp/ *vt* secuestrar

kidnapper /'kɪdnæpər/ *n* secuestrador (-ra); ladrón (-ona) de niños

kidnapping /'kɪdnæpɪŋ/ *n* secuestro, *m*

kidney /'kɪdni/ *n* riñón, *m; Fig.* especie, índole, *f.* **k.-bean,** (plant) judía, *f;* (fruit) habichuela, judía, *f,* fréjol, *m*

Kidron /'kɪdrən/ Cedrón, *m*

kill /kɪl/ *vt* matar; destruir; suprimir. **to k. off,** exterminar. **to k. time,** entretener el tiempo, pasarse las horas muertas. **to k. two birds with one stone,** matar dos pájaros de un tiro. **k.-joy,** aguafiestas, *mf*

killer /'kɪlər/ *n* matador (-ra); (murderer) asesino, *mf*

killing /'kɪlɪŋ/ *n* matanza, *f;* (murder) asesinato, *m.* —*a* matador; destructivo; (comic) cómico; ridículo, absurdo; (ravishing) irresistible

kiln /kɪl/ *n* horno de cerámica, horno, *m*

kilo /'kilou/ *n* kilo, *m*

kilocycle /'kɪlə,saikəl/ *n Elec.* kilociclo, *m*

kilogram /'kɪlə,græm/ *n* kilogramo, *m*

kiloliter /'kɪlə,litər/ *n* kilolitro, *m*

kilometer /kɪ'lɒmɪtər/ *n* kilómetro, *m*

kilometric /,kɪlə'mɛtrɪk/ *a* kilométrico

kilowatt /'kɪlə,wɒt/ *n Elec.* kilovatio, *m*

kilt /kɪlt/ *n* enagüillas, *f pl*

kimono /kə'mounə/ *n* quimono, *m*

kin /kɪn/ *n* parientes, *m pl;* familia, *f;* clase, especie, *f.* **the next of kin,** los parientes próximos, la familia

kind /kaɪnd/ *n* género, *m,* clase, *f;* especie, *f; Inf.* tipo, *m.* **He is a queer k. of person,** Es un tipo muy raro. **What k. of cloth is it?** ¡Qué clase de tela es? **Nothing of the k!** ¡Nada de eso! **payment in k.,** pago en especie, *m*

kind /kaɪnd/ *a* bondadoso, bueno; cariñoso, tierno; amable; favorable; propicio. **Will you be so k. as to...** Tenga Vd. la bondad de... **With k. regards,** Con un saludo afectuoso. **You have been very k. to her,** Vd. ha sido muy bueno para ella. **k.-hearted,** bondadoso. **k.-heartedness,** bondad, benevolencia, *f*

kindergarten /'kɪndər,gɑrtn/ *n* jardín de la infancia, kindergarten, *m*

kindle /'kɪndl/ *vt* encender; hacer arder; *Fig.* avivar. —*vi* prender, empezar a arder; encenderse; *Fig.* inflamarse

kindliness /'kaɪndlɪnɪs/ *n* bondad, *f*

kindling /'kɪndlɪŋ/ *n* encendimiento (del fuego), *m;* (wood) leña menuda, *f*

kindly /'kaɪndli/ *a* bondadoso; bueno; benévolo; propicio, favorable; (of climate) benigno. —*adv* con bondad, bondadosamente; fácilmente. **K. sit down,** Haga el favor de sentarse

kindness /'kaɪndnɪs/ *n* bondad, *f;* benevolencia, *f;* amabilidad, *f;* cariño, *m;* favor, *m,* atención, *f*

kindred /'kɪndrɪd/ *n* parentesco, *m;* parientes, *m pl;* familia, *f;* afinidad, *f,* a emparentado; hermano

king /kɪŋ/ *n* (ruler, important person, chess, cards) rey, *m;* (in draughts) dama, *f.* **king's evil,** escrófula, *f.* **k.-bolt,** perno real, *m.* **k.-craft,** arte de reinar, *m,* or *f.* **k.-cup,** *Bot.* botón de oro, *m.* **K.-of-Arms,** rey de armas, *m.* **k.-post,** pendolón, *m*

kingdom /'kɪŋdəm/ *n* reino, *m.* **animal k.,** reino animal, *m*

kingfisher /'kɪŋ,fɪʃər/ *n* martín pescador, alción, *m*

kink /kɪŋk/ *n* nudo, *m;* pliegue, *m;* (curl) rizo, *m; Fig.* peculiaridad, *f*

kinsfolk /'kɪnz,fouk/ *n* parientes, *m pl,* familia, *f*

kinship /'kɪnʃɪp/ *n* parentesco, *m;* afinidad, *f*

kinsman /'kɪnzmən/ *n* pariente, deudo, *m*

kinswoman /'kɪnz,wʊmən/ *n* parienta, *f*

kiosk /'kiɒsk/ *n* quiosco, *m*

kipper /'kɪpər/ *n* arenque ahumado, *m.* —*vt* ahumar

kiss /kɪs/ *n* beso, *m;* (in billiards) pelo, *m.* —*vt* besar; dar un beso (a); (of billiard balls) tocar. **to k. each other,** besarse. **k.-curl,** rizo de la sien, *m,* sortijilla, *f*

kit /kɪt/ *n* (tub) cubo, *m;* (for tools, etc.) cajita, caja, *f;* (soldier's) equipo, *m.* **kit-bag,** mochila, *f*

kitchen /'kɪtʃən/ *n* cocina, *f.* **k.-boy,** pinche (de cocina), *m.* **k.-garden,** huerta, *f.* **k.-maid,** fregona, *f.* **k.-range,** cocina económica, *f.* **k.-sink,** fregadero, *m.* **k.-stove,** horno de cocina, *m.* **k. utensils,** batería de cocina, *f*

kitchenette /,kɪtʃə'nɛt/ *n* cocinilla, *f*

kite /kaɪt/ *n Ornith.* milano, *m;* cometa, pájara, *f.* **to fly a k.,** hacer volar una cometa. **box-k.,** cometa celular, *f*

kith and kin /kɪθ/ *n pl* parientes y amigos, *m pl*

kitten /'kɪtn/ *n* gatito (-ta). —*vi* (of a cat) parir

kittenish /'kɪtnɪʃ/ *a* de gatito; juguetón

kitty /'kɪti/ *n* michito, *m;* (in card games) platillo, *m*

kleptomania /,klɛptə'meiniə/ *n* cleptomanía, *f*

kleptomaniac /,klɛptə'meiniæk/ *a* cleptómano. —*n* cleptómano (-na)

knack /næk/ *n* destreza, *f;* talento, *m;* (trick) truco, *m*

knapsack /'næp,sæk/ *n* mochila, *f; Mil.* alforja, *f*

knave /neiv/ *n* bellaco, truhán, tunante, *m;* (at cards) sota, *f*

knavery /'neivəri/ *n* bellaquería, truhanería, *f*

knavish /'neivɪʃ/ *a* de bribón; taimado, truhanesco

knead /nid/ *vt* amasar; (massage) sobar; *Fig.* formar

kneading /'nidɪŋ/ *n* amasijo, *m;* (massaging) soba, *f.* **k.-trough,** amasadera artesa *f*

knee /ni/ *n* rodilla, *f; Fig.* ángulo, codillo, *m.* **on bended k.,** de hinojos. **on one's knees,** de rodillas, arrodillado. **to go down on one's knees,** arrodillarse, ponerse de rodillas. **k.-breeches,** calzón corto, *m;* calzón ceñido, *m;* (Elizabethan) gregüescos, *m pl.* **k.-cap,** rótula, *f.* **k.-deep,** hasta las rodillas. **k.-joint,** articulación de la rodilla, *f; Mech.* junta de codillo, *f.* **k.-pad,** rodillera, *f*

kneel (down) /nil/ *vi* arrodillarse, hincarse de rodillas, ponerse de rodillas

kneeling /'nilɪŋ/ *a* arrodillado, de rodillas

knell /nɛl/ *n* toque de difuntos, tañido fúnebre, *m;* toque de campanas, *m; Fig.* muerte, *f.* —*vi* tocar a muerto. —*vt Fig.* anunciar, presagiar

knickerbockers /'nɪkər,bɒkərz/ *n pl* bragas, *f pl;* calzón corto, *m;* (women's) pantalones, *m pl*

knickknack /'nɪk,næk/ *n* chuchería, *f*

knife /naif/ *n* cuchillo, *m.* **to have one's k. in someone,** tener enemiga (a), querer mal (a). **war to the k.,** guerra a muerte, *f.* **k.-edge,** filo de cuchillo, *m;* fiel de soporte, *m.* **k. grinder,** amolador, *m.* **k.-handle,** mango de cuchillo, *m.* **k. thrust,** cuchillada, *f*

knife, fork, and spoon cuchara, tenedor, y cuchillo

knight /nait/ *n* caballero, *m;* (chess) caballo, *m.* —*vt* armar caballero, calzar la espuela; (in modern usage) dar el título de caballero. **untried k.,** caballero novel, *m.* **k. commander,** comendador, *m.* **k.-errant,** caballero andante, *m.* **k.-errantry,** caballería andante, *f.* **Knight of Labor,** Caballero del Trabajo *m.* **k. of the rueful countenance,** el caballero de la triste figura

knighthood /'naithʊd/ *n* caballería, *f;* (in modern usage) título de caballero

knightly /'naitli/ *a* caballeresco; de caballero; de caballería

knit /nɪt/ *vt* and *vi* hacer calceta, hacer media; juntar; ligar; unir. **Isabel is knitting me a jumper,** Isabel me hace un jersey de punto de media. **to k. one's brows,** fruncir el ceño

knitted /'nɪtɪd/ *a* de punto. **k. goods,** géneros de punto, *m pl*

knitter /'nɪtər/ *n* calcetero (-ra); (machine) máquina de hacer calceta, *f*

knitting /'nɪtɪŋ/ *n* acción de hacer calceta, *f;* trabajo de punto, *m,* labor de calceta, *f;* unión, *f.* **k.-machine,** máquina de hacer calceta, *f.* **k.-needle,** aguja de media, aguja de hacer calceta, *f*

knob /nɒb/ n protuberancia, f; (of a door, etc.) perilla, borlita, f; (ornamental) bellota, f; (of sugar) terrón, m; (of a stick) puño, m

knock /nɒk/ n golpe, m; choque, m; (with a knocker) aldabada, f

knock /nɒk/ vt golpear; chocar (contra). —vi llamar a la puerta; (of an engine) picar. **to k. one's head against,** chocar con la cabeza contra, dar con la cabeza contra. **to k. about,** vt pegar; aporrear. —vi viajar; vagar, rodar; callejear. **to k. against,** golpear contra; chocar contra. **to k. down,** derribar; (of vehicles) atropellar; (houses, etc.) demoler; (an argument, etc.) destruir; (a tender, etc.) rebajar; (of an auctioneer) rematar al mejor postor. **to k. in,** (nails, etc.) clavar. **to k. into one another,** toparse. **to k. off,** hacer caer; sacudir; quitar; (from price) descontar; (from speed, etc.) reducir; (finish) terminar pronto; (runs in cricket) hacer. **to k. out,** (remove) quitar; (boxing) dejar fuera de combate, noquear; (Fig. stun) atontar; (an idea, etc.) bosquejar. **to k. over,** volcar. **to k. up,** hacer saltar; (call) llamar; (runs at cricket) hacer; (tire) agotar, rendir; (building) construir toscamente. **to k. up against,** chocar contra; tropezar con. **k.-kneed,** a patiabierto. **k.-out,** "knock-out," m

knocker /'nɒkər/ n (on a door) aldaba, f. **k.-up,** despertador, m

knocking /'nɒkɪŋ/ n golpes, m pl, golpeo, m; (with a knocker) aldabeo, m. **k. over,** vuelco, m; (by a vehicle) atropello, m

knoll /noul/ n altillo, otero, m

knot /nɒt/ n nudo, m; (bow) lazo, m; (of hair) moño, m; Naut. nudo, m, milla náutica, f; (of people) corrillo, grupo, m; (on timber) nudo, m. —vt anudar. —vi hacer nudos; enmarañarse. **to tie a k.,** hacer un nudo

knotted /'nɒtɪd/ a nudoso

knotty /'nɒti/ a nudoso; Fig. intrincado, difícil, complicado. **a k. problem,** problema espinoso

know /nou/ vt conocer; saber; (understand) comprender; (recognize) reconocer. **I k. her very well by sight,** La conozco muy bien de vista. **John knows Latin,** Juan sabe latín. **How can I k.?** ¿Cómo lo voy a saber yo? **I knew you at once,** Te reconocí en seguida. **They always k. best,** Siempre tienen razón. **Did you k. about Philip?** ¿Has oído lo de Felipe? **to be in the k.,** estar bien informado, saber de buena tinta. **to get to k.,** (a person) llegar a conocer, trabar amistad con. **to make known,** dar a conocer; manifestar. **Who knows?** ¿Quién sabe? **to k. by heart,** saber de coro. **to k. how,** (to do something) saber. **to k. oneself,** conocerse a sí mismo. **k.-it-all,** sabelotodo, mf, marisabidilla, f

knowing /'nouɪŋ/ a inteligente; malicioso; (of animals) sabio. **There is no k.,** No hay modo de saberlo. **worth k.,** digno de saberse

knowingly /'nouɪŋli/ adv a sabiendas, de intento; conscientemente; (cleverly) hábilmente; (with look, etc.) de un aire malicioso

knowledge /'nɒlɪdʒ/ n conocimiento, m. **To the best of my k. the book does not exist,** El libro no existe que yo sepa. **He has a thorough k. of...,** Conoce a fondo... **lack of k.,** ignorancia, f. **He did it without my k.,** Lo hizo sin que lo supiera yo. **It is a matter of common k. that...** Es notorio que...

knowledgeable /'nɒlɪdʒəbəl/ a sabedor

known /noun/ a conocido

knuckle /'nʌkəl/ n (of a finger) nudillo, m, articulación del dedo, f; (of meat) jarrete, m. **He knuckled down to his work,** Se puso a trabajar con ahínco. **to k. under,** someterse. **k.-duster,** rompecabezas, m

Koran /kə'ran/ n Corán, Alcorán, m

Korea /kə'riə/ n Corea, f

kosher /'kouʃər/ a cosher; (slang) genuino

kowtow /'kau'tau/ vi saludar humildemente; Fig. bajar la cerviz

Kremlin /'krɛmlɪn/ n Kremlín, m

kudos /'kudouz/ n prestigio, m, gloria, f

Kurdish /'kərdɪʃ/ a curdo

kyrie eleison /'kɪəri,ei ɛ'leiə,sɔn/ n kirieleisón, m

L

l /ɛl/ n (letter) ele, f
la /lɑ/ n Mus. la, m
label /'leibəl/ n etiqueta, (on a garment), rótula, m, (on a can), f; (on a museum specimen, etc.) letrero, m; Fig. calificación, f. —vt poner etiqueta en; marcar, rotular; Fig. calificar, designar, clasificar
labial /'leibiəl/ a labial. —n letra labial, f
labor /'leibər/ n trabajo, m; labor, f; fatiga, pena, f; clase obrera, f; (manual workers) mano de obra, f; (effort) esfuerzo, m; (of childbirth) dolores de parto, m pl. —vi trabajar; (strive) esforzarse, afanarse; (struggle) forcejar; luchar; (try) procurar, tratar de; avanzar con dificultad; (in childbirth) estar de parto. —vt elaborar; pulir, perfeccionar. **to l. under**, sufrir; tener que luchar contra. **hard l.,** trabajo arduo, m; Law. trabajos forzosos, m pl, presidio, m. **Ministry of L.,** Ministerio de Trabajo, m. **to be in l.,** estar de parto. **to l. in vain,** trabajar en balde, arar en el mar. **to l. under a delusion,** estar en el error, estar equivocado. **L. Exchange,** Bolsa de Trabajo, f. **l. leader,** dirigente sindical, m. **l. party,** partido laborista, partido obrero, m. **l. question,** cuestión obrera, f; (domestic) problema del servicio, m. **l.-saving,** a que ahorra trabajo. **l. union,** sindicato, m
laboratory /'læbrə,tɔri/ n laboratorio, m
labored /'leibərd/ a (of style) premioso, artificial; forzado; (of breathing) fatigoso; (slow) torpe, lento
laborer /'leibərər/ n obrero, m; (on the land) labrador, labriego, m; (on the roads, etc.) peón, m; (by the day) jornalero, m
laborious /lə'bɔriəs/ a laborioso; arduo, difícil, penoso
laboriously /lə'bɔriəsli/ adv laboriosamente; con dificultad, penosamente
laboriousness /lə'bɔriəsnɪs/ n laboriosidad, f; dificultad, f
Labrador dog /'læbrə,dɔr/ n perro de Labrador, m
labyrinth /'læbərɪnθ/ n laberinto, m
labyrinthine /,læbə'rɪnθɪn/ a laberíntico; intrincado
lace /leis/ n (of shoes, corsets, etc.) cordón, m; (tape) cinta, f; encaje, m; (narrow, for trimming) puntilla, f; (of gold or silver) galón, m. —vt and vi (shoes, etc.) atarse los cordones, (trim) guarnecer con encajes, etc.; Fig. ornar; (a drink) echar (coñac, etc.) en. **blond l.,** blonda, f. **gold l.,** galón de oro, m. **point l.,** encaje de aguja, m. **l. curtain,** cortina de encaje, f; (of net) visillo, m. **l. maker** or **seller,** encajera, f. **l. making,** obra de encaje, f. **l.-pillow,** almohadilla para encajes, f. **l. shoes,** zapatos con cordones, m pl
lacerate /'læsə,reit/ vt lacerar
laceration /,læsə'reifən/ n laceración, f
lachrymal /'lækrəməl/ a lagrimal, lacrimal
lachrymose /'lækrə,mous/ a lacrimoso
lack /læk/ n falta, f. **l. of evidence,** falta de pruebas, f; carestía, escasez, f; (absence) ausencia, f; (need) necesidad, f. —vt carecer de; no tener; necesitar. —vi hacer falta; necesitarse. **l. of confidence in oneself,** no tener confianza en sí mismo, carecer de confianza en sí mismo. **l.-luster,** (of eyes) apagado, mortecino. **l. of evidence,** falta de pruebas, f
lackadaisical /,lækə'deizikəl/ a lánguido; indiferente; (dreamy) ensimismado, distraído
lackey /'læki/ n lacayo, m
laconic /lə'kɒnɪk/ a lacónico
lacquer /'lækər/ n laca, f; vt dar laca (a), barnizar con laca. **gold l.,** sisa dorada, f. **l. work,** laca, f
lacquering /'lækərɪŋ/ n barnizado de laca, m; laca, capa de barniz de laca, f
lactate /'lækteit/ n lactato, m, vi lactar
lactation /læk'teifən/ n lactancia, f
lacteal /'læktiəl/ a lácteo
lactic /'læktɪk/ a láctico
lactose /'læktous/ n lactosa, f
lacuna /lə'kyunə/ n laguna, f
lacy /'leisi/ a de encaje; parecido a encaje; Fig. transparente, etéreo

lad /læd/ n muchacho, joven, mozalbete, m; zagal, m; (stable, etc.) mozo, m. **He's some l.!** ¡Qué tío que es! **l. of the village,** chulo, m
ladder /'lædər/ n escalera de mano, f; Naut. escala, f; (in a stocking, etc.) carrera, f. **companion l.,** escala de toldilla, f. **to l. one's stocking,** escurrirse un punto de las medias
Ladies and gentlemen /'leidiz/ n pl Señoras y señores, Señoras y caballeros. **ladies' man,** hombre de salón, Perico entre ellas, mujeriego, m
lading /'leidɪŋ/ n flete, m, carga, f
ladle /'leidl/ n cucharón, cazo, m. —vt servir con cucharón; (a boat) achicar; Inf. distribuir, repartir
lady /'leidi/ n dama, f; señora, f; (English title) milady, f; (woman) mujer, f. **to be a l.,** ser una señora. **leading l.,** Theat. dama primera, f. **Our L.,** Nuestra Señora. **young l.,** señorita, f; Inf. novia, f. **lady's maid,** doncella, f. **l. of the house,** señora de la casa, f. **l. bug,** Ent. catalina mariquita, vaca de San Antonio, f. **L. Chapel,** capilla de la Virgen, f. **L. Day,** día de la Anunciación (de Nuestra Señora), m. **l.-help,** asistenta, f. **l.-in-waiting,** dama de servicio, f. **l.-killer,** ladrón de corazones, castigador, tenorio, m. **l.-love,** querida, amada, f. **l. mayoress,** alcaldesa, f
ladylike /'leidi,laik/ a de dama; elegante; distinguido; bien educado; delicado; (of men) afeminado
ladyship /'leidi,ʃɪp/ n señoría, f. **Your L.,** Su Señoría
lag /læg/ vt recubrir; aislar. —vi retrasarse; quedarse atrás; ir (or andar) despacio; rezagarse; Naut. roncear. —n retraso, m; Mech. retardación de movimiento, f
laggard /'lægərd/ n holgazán (-ana), haragán (-ana)
lagoon /lə'gun/ n laguna, f
laid /leid/ past part of verb **to lay. l. up,** (ill) enfermo; Naut. inactivo; (of cars, etc.) fuera de circulación
lair /lɛr/ n cubil, m; guarida, madriguera, f
laity /'leiti/ n legos, m pl
lake /leik/ n lago, m; (pigment) laca, f. **small l.,** laguna, f. **l. dwelling,** vivienda palustre, f
lama /'lɑmə/ n lama, m
lamb /læm/ n cordero (-ra). —vi parir corderos. **lamb's wool,** lana de cordero. f
lambent /'læmbənt/ a ondulante, vacilante; centelleante
lamblike /'læm,laik/ a manso como un cordero; inocente
lambskin /'læm,skɪn/ n corderina, piel de cordero, f
lame /leim/ a estropeado, lisiado; (in the feet) cojo; (of meter) que cojea, malo; (of arguments) poco convincente; frívolo, flojo. —vt lisiar; hacer cojo. **l. excuse,** pretexto frívolo. **to be l.,** (in the feet) (permanently) ser cojo; (temporarily) estar cojo
lamely /'leimli/ adv cojeando, con cojera; Fig. sin convicción; mal
lameness /'leimnɪs/ n cojera, f; falta de convicción, f
lament /lə'mɛnt/ n lamento, m; queja, lamentación, f. —vi lamentarse; quejarse. —vt lamentar, deplorar, llorar
lamentable /lə'mɛntəbəl/ a lamentable, deplorable; lastimero
lamentation /,læmən'teifən/ n lamentación, f, lamento, m. **Book of Lamentations,** Libro de los lamentos, m
lamenting /lə'mɛntɪŋ/ n lamentación, f
lamina /'læmənə/ n lámina, f
laminate /'læmə,neit/ a laminado, laminar. —vt laminar
lamp /læmp/ n lámpara, f; (on vehicles, trains, ships and in the street) farol, m; luz, f; (oil) candil, m, lámpara de aceite, f. **safety-l.,** lámpara de seguridad, lámpara de los mineros, f. **street l.,** farol (de las calles), m. **l.-black,** negro de humo, m. **l.-chimney,** tubo de una lámpara, m. **l. factory** or **shop,** lamparería, f. **l.-holder,** portalámpara, f. **l.-lighter,**

farolero, lamparero, *m.* **l.-post,** farola, *f.* **l.-shade,** pantalla (de lámpara,) *f.* **l. stand,** pie de lámpara, *m*
lamplight /'læmp,lait/ *n* luz de la lámpara, *f;* luz artificial, *f.* **in the l.,** a la luz de la lámpara; en luz artificial
lampoon /læm'pun/ *n* pasquinada, *f,* pasquín, *m, vt* pasquinar, satirizar
lampooner /læm'punər/ *n* escritor (-ra) de pasquinadas, libelista, *m*
lamprey /'læmpri/ *n* lamprea, *f*
lance /læns/ *n* lanza, *f;* (soldier) lancero, *m.* —*vt* alancear; *Med.* lancinar. **l. in rest,** lanza en ristre, *f.* **l. thrust,** lanzada, *f.* **l.-corporal,** soldado de primera clase, *m*
lancer /'lænsər/ *n Mil.* lancero, *m; pl* lancers, (dance and music) lanceros, *m pl*
lancet /'lænsɪt/ *n* apostemero, *m,* lanceta, *f.* **l. arch,** arco puntiagudo, *m*
land /lænd/ *n* tierra, *f;* terreno, *m;* (country) país, *m;* (region) región, *f;* territorio, *m;* (estate) bienes raíces, *m pl,* tierras, fincas, *f pl.* —*vt* desembarcar; echar en tierra; (*Fig.* place) poner; *Inf.* dejar plantado (con); (obtain) obtener; (a fish) sacar del agua; (a blow) dar (un golpe); (leave) dejar. —*vi* desembarcar; saltar en tierra; (of a plane) aterrizar; (arrive) llegar; (fall) caer. **cultivated l.,** tierras cultivadas, *f pl.* **dry l.,** (not sea) tierra firme, *f.* **native l.,** patria, *f;* suelo natal, *m.* **on l.,** en tierra. **to see how the l. lies,** *Fig.* tantear el terreno. **l. of milk and honey,** jauja, *f,* paraíso, *m.* **l. of promise,** tierra de promisión, *f.* **l. agent,** procurador de fincas, *m.* **l. breeze,** brisa de tierra, *f.* **l. forces,** fuerzas terrestres, *f pl.* **l. law,** leyes agrarias, *f pl.* **l.-locked,** cercado de tierra, mediterráneo **l.-lubber,** marinero de agua dulce, *m.* **l. mine,** mina terrestre, *f.* **l. surveying,** agrimensura, *f.* **l. surveyor,** agrimensor, *m.* **l. tax,** contribución territorial, *f*
landau /'lændɔ/ *n* landó, *m*
landed /'lændɪd/ *a* hacendado. **l. gentry,** hacendados, terratenientes, *m pl.* **l. property,** bienes raíces, *m pl*
landfall /'lænd,fɔl/ *n* derrumbamiento de tierras, *m*
landing /'lændɪŋ/ *n* desembarque, desembarco, *m;* (landing place) desembarcadero, *m;* *Aer.* aterrizaje, *m;* (of steps) descanso, rellano, *m,* mesa, mesilla, *f.* **forced l.,** aterrizaje forzoso, *m.* **l. certificate,** *Com.* tornaguía, *f.* **l. craft,** barcaza de desembarco, *f.* **l. field,** campo de aterrizaje, *m,* pista de vuelo, *f.* **l.-net,** salabardo, *m.* **l. party,** trozo de abordaje, *m.* **l. signal,** *Aer.* señal de aterrizaje, *f.* **l.-stage,** desembarcadero, *m;* (jetty) atracadero, *m*
landlady /'lænd,leidi/ *n* patrona, huéspeda, *f*
landlord /'lænd,lɔrd/ *n* (of houses, land) propietario, *m;* hotelero, patrón, *m*
landmark /'lænd,mɑrk/ *n* (of a hill or mountain) punto destacado, *m;* lugar conocido, *m;* característica, *f;* *Fig.* monumento, *m*
landmass /'lænd,mæs/ *n* unidad territorial, *f*
landowner /'lænd,ounər/ *n* hacendado, terrateniente, *m*
landscape /'lænd,skeip/ *n* paisaje, *m;* perspectiva, *f.* **l. gardener,** arquitecto de jardines, *m.* **l. painter,** paisajista, *mf*
landslide /'lænd,slaid/ *n* desprendimiento de tierras, *m;* *Fig.* cambio brusco de la opinión pública, *m*
landward /'lændwərd/ *adv* hacia tierra
lane /lein/ *n* vereda, senda, *f;* (of traffic) carril, *m,* (Argentina, Spain), línea, *f*
language /'læŋgwɪdʒ/ *n* lenguaje, *m;* lengua, *f,* idioma, *m.* **modern l.,** lengua viva, *f.* **strong l.,** palabras mayores, *f pl*
languid /'læŋgwid/ *a* lánguido
languidness /'læŋgwidnɪs/ *n* languidez, *f*
languish /'læŋgwiʃ/ *vi* languidecer
languishing /'læŋgwiʃiŋ/ *a* lánguido; amoroso, sentimental
languishingly /'læŋgwiʃiŋli/ *adv* lánguidamente; amorosamente
languor /'læŋgər/ *n* languidez, *f*
languorous /'læŋgərəs/ *a* lánguido
languorously /'læŋgərəsli/ *adv* con langor
lank /læŋk/ *a* flaco, descarnado, alto y delgado; (of hair) lacio

lankiness /'læŋkinɪs/ *n* flacura, *f*
lanky /'læŋki/ *a* larguirucho, descarnado
lanolin /'lænlɪn/ *n* lanolina, *f*
lantern /'læntərn/ *n* linterna, *f;* (*Naut.* and of a lighthouse) farol, *m;* *Archit.* linterna, *f;* (small) farolillo, *m.* **dark l.,** linterna sorda, *f.* **magic l.,** linterna mágica, *f.* **l.-jawed,** carilargo. **l. maker,** farolero, *m.* **l. slide,** diapositiva, *f*
lap /læp/ *n* regazo, *m;* falda, *f;* (knees) rodillas, *f pl;* (lick) lamedura, *f;* (of water) murmurio, susurro, *m;* (in a race) vuelta, *f;* (stage) etapa, *f.* —*vt* (wrap) envolver; (cover) cubrir; (fold) plegar; (lick) lamer; (swallow) tragar. —*vi* (overlap) traslaparse; estar replegado; (lick) lamer; (of water) murmurar, susurrar, besar. **l.-dog,** perro de faldas, perro faldero, *m*
lapel /lə'pɛl/ *n* solapa, *f*
lapidary /'læpɪ,deri/ *a* lapidario
lapidate /'læpɪ,deit/ *vt* lapidar
lapis lazuli /'læp'ɪs læzuli/ *n* lapislázuli, *m*
Lapland /'læp,lænd/ Laponia, *f*
Laplander /'læp,lændər/ *n* lapón (-ona)
lapping /'læpɪŋ/ *n* (licking) lamedura, *f;* (of water) murmurio, susurro, chapaleteo, *m*
lapse /læps/ *n* lapso, *m;* (fault) desliz, *m,* falta, *f;* (of time) transcurso, intervalo, *m;* (fall) caída, *f;* (*Law.* termination) caducidad, *f.* **lapse (into),** *vi* caer (en), recaer (en), reincidir (en); volver a, caer de nuevo (en); (*Law.* cease) caducar; (*Law.* pass to) pasar (a); dejar de existir, desaparecer. **after the l. of three days,** después de tres días, al cabo de tres días. **with the l. of years,** en el transcurso de los años
larboard /'lɑr,bɔrd/ *n* babor, *m,* a de babor
larceny /'lɑrsəni/ *n* latrocinio, *m*
lard /lɑrd/ *n* manteca, *f;* lardo, *m.* —*vt Cul.* lardear, mechar; *Fig.* sembrar (con), adornar (con)
larder /'lɑrdər/ *n* despensa, *f*
large /lɑrdʒ/ *a* grande; grueso; amplio; vasto, extenso; (wide) ancho; considerable; (in number) numeroso; (main, chief) principal; liberal; magnánimo. **at l.,** en libertad, suelto. **on the l. side,** algo grande. **l.-headed,** cabezudo. **l.-hearted,** que tiene un gran corazón, magnánimo. **l. mouth,** boca grande, boca rasgada, *f.* **l.-nosed,** nariguado. **l. scale,** en gran escala. **l.-sized,** de gran tamaño. **l.-toothed,** dentudo, que tiene dientes grandes. **l. type,** letras grandes, *f pl*
largely /'lɑrdʒli/ *adv* grandemente; en gran manera; en so mayor parte, considerablemente; muy; ampliamente; liberalmente; extensamente
largeness /'lɑrdʒnɪs/ *n* gran tamaño, *m;* (of persons) gran talle, *m;* amplitud, *f;* vastedad, extensión, *f;* (width) anchura, *f;* liberalidad, *f;* (generosity) magnanimidad, *f;* grandeza de ánimo, *f*
larger /'lɑrdʒər/ *a compar* más grande, etc. See **large.** **to grow l.,** crecer, aumentarse. **to make l.,** hacer más grande; aumentar
largesse /lɑr'dʒɛs/ *n* liberalidad, *f*
largo /'lɑrgou/ *n* and *adv Mus.* largo, *m*
lariat /'læriət/ *n* lazo, *m*
lark /lɑrk/ *n* alondra, *f;* (spree) juerga, *f;* (joke) risa, *f.* **to rise with the l.,** levantarse con las gallinas
larva /'lɑrvə/ *n* larva, *f*
laryngeal /lə'rɪndʒiəl/ *a* laríngeo
laryngitis /,lærən'dʒaitɪs/ *n* laringitis, *f*
larynx /'lærɪŋks/ *n* laringe, *f*
lascivious /lə'sɪviəs/ *a* lascivo, lujurioso
lasciviousness /lə'sɪviəsnɪs/ *n* lujuria, lascivia, lascivia, *f*
lash /læʃ/ *n* (thong) tralla, *f;* (whip) látigo, *m;* (blow) latigazo, *m;* azote, *m;* (of the eye) pestaña, *f.* —*vt* dar latigazos (a); azotar; (of waves) romper contra; (of hail, rain) azotar; (excite) provocar; (the tail) agitar (la cola); (scold) fustigar; (fasten) sujetar, atar; *Naut.* trincar. **to l. out,** (of horses, etc.) dar coces; (in words) prorrumpir (en)
lashing /'læʃɪŋ/ *n* (whipping) azotamiento, *m;* (tying) ligadura, atadura, *f;* amarradura, *f*
lass /læs/ *n* muchacha, chica, mozuela, *f;* zagala, *f;* niña, *f*
lassitude /'læsɪ,tud/ *n* lasitud, *f*
lasso /'læsou/ *n* lazo, *m,* mangana, *f, vt* lazar, manganear
last /læst/ *vi* durar; subsistir, conservarse; continuar
last /læst/ *a* último; (with month, week, etc.) pasado;

(supreme) extremo, (el) mayor. —*adv* al fin; finalmente; por último; después de todos; por última vez; la última vez. —*n* el, *m*, (*f*, la) último (-ma); los últimos, *m pl*, (*f pl*, las últimas); (end) fin, *m*; (for shoes) horma, *f*. **at l.**, en fin; por fin, a la postre. **at the l. moment**, a última hora. **I have not been there these l. five years**, Hace cinco años que no voy allá. **John spoke l.**, Juan habló el último. **She came at l.**, Por fin llegó. **to the l.**, hasta el fin. **l. but one**, penúltimo (-ma). **l. hope**, última esperanza, *f*; último recurso, *m*. **l. kick**, *Inf.* último suspiro, *m*. **l. night**, anoche. **l. week**, la semana pasada

lasting /'læstɪŋ/ *a* permanente, perdurable; duradero; constante; (of colours) sólido

lastingness /'læstɪŋnɪs/ *n* permanencia, *f*; duración, *f*

lastly /'læstli/ *adv* en conclusión, por fin, finalmente, por último

latch /lætʃ/ *n* pestillo, *m*, *vt* cerrar con pestillo. **l.-key**, llave de la puerta, *f*; (Yale) llavín, *m*

late /leit/ *a* tarde; tardío; (advanced) avanzado; (last) último; reciente; (dead) difunto; (former) antiguo, ex...; (new) nuevo. —*adv* tarde. **Better l. than never**, Más vale tarde que nunca. **Helen arrived l.**, Elena llegó tarde. **The train arrived five minutes l.**, El tren llegó con cinco minutos de retraso. **He keeps l. hours**, Se acuesta muy tarde, Se acuesta a las altas horas de la noche (*Inf.* a las tantas). **of l.**, últimamente. **to grow l.**, hacerse tarde. **l.-eighteenth-century poetry**, la poesía de fines del siglo diez y ocho; llorado, malogrado (e.g. *the l. Mrs. Smith*, la llorada Sra. Smith, la malograda Sra. Smith)

lateen /læ'tin/ *a* latino. **l. sail**, vela latina, *f*

lately /'leitli/ *adv* recientemente; últimamente, hace poco

latency /'leitn̩si/ *n* estado latente, *m*

lateness /'leitnɪs/ *n* lo tarde; lo avanzado; retraso, *m*. **the l. of the hour**, la hora avanzada

latent /'leitn̩t/ *a* latente

later /'leitər/ *a* más tarde; posterior; más reciente. —*adv* más tarde; (afterwards) luego, después; posteriormente. **sooner or l.**, tarde o temprano. **l. on**, más tarde

lateral /'lætərəl/ *a* lateral, ladero

late registration *n* matrícula tardía, *f*

latest /'leitɪst/ *a* and *adv superl* último; más reciente, etc. See **late. at the l.**, a lo más tarde, a más tardar. **l. fashion**, última moda, *f*. **l. news**, últimas noticias, *f pl*; novedad, *f*

latex /'leiteks/ *n* (*Bot. Chem.*) látex, *m*

lath /læθ/ *n* listón, *m*. **to be as thin as a l.**, no tener más que el pellejo, estar en los huesos

lathe /leið/ *n* torno, *m*

lather /'læðər/ *n* espuma de jabón, *f*, jabonaduras, *f pl*; (of sweat) espuma, *f*. —*vt* enjabonar; *Inf.* zurrar. —*vi* hacer espuma

lathering /'læðərɪŋ/ *n* jabonadura, *f*; *Inf.* tunda, zurra, *f*

Latin /'lætn̩/ *n* latín, *m*, *a* latino. **Low L.**, bajo latín, *m*. **L.-American**, *a* latinoamericano. —*n* latinoamericano (-na)

Latinism /'lætn̩ˌɪzəm/ *n* latinismo, *m*

Latinist /'lætn̩ɪst/ *n* latinista, *mf*

latitude /'lætɪˌtud/ *n* latitud, *f*; libertad, *f*

latitudinal /ˌlætɪ'tudn̩l/ *a* latitudinal

latrine /lə'trin/ *n* letrina, *f*

latter /'lætər/ *a* más reciente; último, posterior; moderno. **the l.**, éste, *m*; ésta, *f*; esto, *neut*; éstos, *m pl*; éstas, *f pl*. **the l. half**, la segunda mitad. **toward the l. end of the year**, hacia fines del año. **L.-Day Saint**, santo de los últimos días *m*, santa de los últimos días, *f*

latterly /'lætərli/ *adv* recientemente, últimamente; en los últimos tiempos; hacia el fin

lattice /'lætɪs/ *n* rejilla, *f*; celosía, reja, *f*. —*vt* poner celosía (a); entrelazar. **l.-work**, enrejado, *m*

latticed /'lætɪst/ *a* (of windows, etc.) con reja

Latvia /'lætviə/ Latvia, Letonia, *f*

Latvian /'lætviən/ *a* latvio. —*n* latvio (-ia)

laud /lɔd/ *n* alabanza, *f*; *pl* **lauds**, *Eccl.* laudes, *f pl*. —*vt* alabar, elogiar

laudability /ˌlɔdə'bɪlɪti/ *n* mérito, *m*, lo meritorio

laudable /'lɔdəbəl/ *a* loable, meritorio

laudably /'lɔdəbli/ *adv* laudablemente

laudatory /'lɔdəˌtɔri/ *a* laudatorio

laugh /læf/ *n* risa, *f*; carcajada, *f*. —*vi* reír; (smile) sonreír; reírse. **loud l.**, risa estrepitosa, *f*. **to l. in a person's face**, reírsele a uno en las barbas. **to l. loudly**, reírse a carcajadas. **to l. to oneself**, reírse interiormente. **to l. to scorn**, poner en ridículo. **to l. at**, reírse de; burlarse de, ridiculizar

laughable /'læfəbəl/ *a* risible, irrisible, ridículo, absurdo

laughing /'læfɪŋ/ *a* risueño, alegre; (absurd) risible, *n* risa, *f*. **to burst out l.**, reírse a carcajadas. **l.-gas**, gas hilarante, *m*. **l.-stock**, hazmerreír, *m*

laughingly /'læfɪŋli/ *adv* riendo

laughter /'læftər/ *n* risa, *f*; (in a report) risas, *f pl*. **burst of l.**, carcajada, *f*. **to burst into l.**, soltar el trapo, reírse a carcajadas, desternillarse de risa

launch /lɔntʃ/ *n* botadura (de un buque), *f*; lancha, *f*; bote, *m*; canoa, *f*. —*vt* (throw) lanzar; (a blow) asestar; (a vessel) botar, echar al agua; (begin) iniciar, dar principio a; (make) hacer. **to l. an offensive**, *Mil.* emprender una ofensiva. **to l. into**, arrojarse en; entregarse a. **motor l.**, canoa automóvil, *f.* **steam l.**, bote de vapor, *m*

launching /'lɔntʃɪŋ/ *n* botadura (de un buque), *f*; (throwing) lanzamiento, *m*; (beginning) iniciación, *f*; inauguración, *f*; (of a loan, etc.) emisión, *f*. **l. site**, rampa, *f*

launder /'lɔndər/ *vt* lavar y planchar (ropa)

laundress /'lɔndrɪs/ *n* lavandera, *f*

laundromat /'lɔndrəˌmæt/ *n* lavandería automática, *f*

laundry /'lɔndri/ *n* lavadero, *m*, lavandería, *f*; (washing) colada, *f*; *Inf.* ropa lavada o ropa para lavar, *f*. **l.-man**, lavandero, *m*

laureate /'lɔriɪt/ *a* laureado. —*n* poeta laureado, *m*

laurel /'lɔrəl/ *n* laurel, cerezo, *m*, a láureo. **to crown with l.**, laurear. **l. wreath**, lauréola, *f*

Lausanne /lou'zæn/ Lausana, Losana, *f*

lava /'lɑvə/ *n* lava, *f*

lavabo /lə'veibou/ *n* lavabo, *m*; *Eccl.* lavatorio, *m*

lavatory /'lævəˌtɔri/ *n* lavabo, *m*; retrete, excusado, *m*

lave /leiv/ *vt* bañar

lavender /'lævəndər/ *n* espliego, *m*, lavanda, *f*. **l.-water**, agua de lavanda, *f*

lavish /'lævɪʃ/ *a* pródigo; profuso, abundante. —*vt* prodigar

lavishly /'lævɪʃli/ *adv* pródigamente; en profusión

lavishness /'lævɪʃnɪs/ *n* prodigalidad, *f*; profusión, abundancia, *f*

law /lɔ/ *n* ley, *f*; derecho, *m*; jurisprudencia, *f*; código de leyes, *m*. **according to law**, según derecho. **canon law**, derecho civil, *m*. **constitutional law**, derecho político, *m*. **criminal law**, derecho penal, *m*. **in law**, por derecho, de acuerdo con la ley; desde el punto de vista legal. **international law**, derecho internacional, *m*. **maritime law**, código marítimo, *m*. **sumptuary law**, ley suntuaria, *f*. **to be the law**, ser la ley. **to go to law**, pleitear (sobre). **to sue at law**, pedir en juicio, poner pleito. **to take the law into one's own hands**, tomar la ley por su propia mano. **law-abiding**, observante de la ley; amigo del orden. **law-breaker**, transgresor (-ra). **law court**, tribunal de justicia, *m*; palacio de justicia, *m*. **law of nature**, ley natural, *f*. **law report**, revista de tribunales, *f*. **law school**, escuela de derecho, *f*. **law student**, estudiante de derecho, *mf*

lawful /'lɔfəl/ *a* legítimo; legal; lícito; válido

lawfully /'lɔfəli/ *adv* legalmente; legítimamente, lícitamente

lawfulness /'lɔfəlnɪs/ *n* legalidad, *f*; legitimidad, *f*

lawgiver /'lɔˌgɪvər/ *n* legislador (-ra)

lawless /'lɔlɪs/ *a* ilegal; desordenado; ingobernable, rebelde

lawlessness /'lɔlɪsnɪs/ *n* ilegalidad, *f*; desorden, *m*; rebeldía, *f*

lawn /lɔn/ *n* césped, prado, *f*; (cloth) estopilla, *f*. **l.-mower**, cortacésped *m*, tundidora de césped, *f*, máquina segadora del césped, *f*. **l.-tennis**, tenis (en pista de hierba), *m*

lawsuit /'lɔˌsut/ *n* pleito, litigio, *m*, causa, acción, *f*

lawyer /'lɔyər/ n abogado (-da). **lawyer's office** or **practice,** bufete, m

lax /læks/ a laxo; indisciplinado; vago; descuidado

laxative /'læksətɪv/ n laxante, m, purga, f, a laxativo

laxity /'læksɪti/ n laxitud, f; descuido, m; indiferencia, f

lay /lei/ a laico, seglar, lego; profano. —n poema, m, trova, f; romance, m; (song) canción, f. **the lay of the land,** la configuración del terreno. **lay brother,** confeso, monigote, m. **lay figure,** maniquí, m. **lay sister,** (hermana) lega, f

lay /lei/ vt and vi poner; colocar; dejar; (strike) tumbar; (demolish) derribar; (the dust) matar; (pipes, etc.) instalar; (hands on) asentar (la mano en); (deposit) depositar; (beat down corn, etc.) encamar, abatir; (eggs, keel) poner; (the table) cubrir, poner; (stretch) extender(se); (bury) depositar en el sepulcro; (a bet) hacer; (wager) apostar; (an accusation) acusar; (the wind, etc.) sosegar, amainar; (a ghost) exorcizar; (impute) atribuir, imputar; (impose) imponer; (prepare) prepara; (make) hacer; (open) abrir; (blame, etc.) echar; (claim) reclamar; (reveal) revelar. **Don't lay the blame on me!** ¡No me eches la culpa! **We laid our plans,** Hicimos nuestros planes; Hicimos nuestros preparativos. **to lay siege to,** asediar. **to lay the colors on too thick,** Fig. recargar las tintas. **to lay the foundations,** abrir los cimientos; Fig. crear, establecer; fundar. **to lay about one,** dar garrotazos de ciego. **to lay aside,** poner a un lado; arrinconar; (save) ahorrar; (cast away) desechar; abandonar; (reserve) reservar; (a person) apartar de sí; (incapacitate) incapacitar. **lay something at somebody's feet,** embutir algo en el guante de fulano. **to lay before,** mostrar; presentar; poner a la vista; revelar. **to lay by,** See **to lay aside. to lay down,** acostar; depositar; (a burden) posar; (arms) rendir; (one's life); entregar; (give up) renunciar (a); (sketchout) trazar, dibujar; (plan) proyectar; (keep) guardar; (as a principle) establecer, sentar; (the law) dictar. **to lay oneself down,** echarse, tumbarse. **to lay in,** (a stock) proveerse de, hacer provisión de; (hoard) ahorrar; (buy) comprara. **to lay off,** Naut. virar de bordo; Inf. quitarse de encima. **to lay on,** vt colocar sobre; (thrash) pegar; (blows) descargar; (paint, etc.) dar; (water, etc.) instalar; (impose) imponer; (exaggerate) exagerar. —vi atacar. **to lay open,** abrir; descubrir, revelar; manifestar; exponer. **to lay oneself open to attack,** exponerse a ser atacado. **to lay out,** poner; arreglar; (the dead) amortajar; (one's money) invertir, emplear; (at interest) poner a rédito; (plan) planear; (knock down) derribar. **to lay oneself out to,** esforzarse a; tomarse la molestia de. **to lay over,** cubrir; sobreponer; extender sobre. **to lay to,** vi Naut. estar a la capa. **to lay up,** guardar, acumular, atesorar; poner a un lado; (a ship) desarmar; (a car) poner fuera de circulación; (a person) obligar a guardar cama, incapacitar

layer /'leiər/ n capa, f; Geol. estrato, m; Mineral. manto, m; (bird) gallina (pata, etc.) ponedera, f; (one who bets) apostador (-ra); Agr. acodo, m. —vt (of plants) acodar

layette /lei'ɛt/ n canastilla, f

laying /'leiɪŋ/ n colocación, f; puesta, f; (of an egg) postura, f. **l. down,** depósito, m; conservación, f; (explanation) exposición, f. **l. on of hands,** imposición de manos, f. **l. out,** tendedura, f; (of money) empleo, m; inversión, f; (arrangement) arreglo, m

layman /'leimən/ n seglar, mf; profano (-na)

layout /'lei,aut/ n plan, m; diagramación, disposición, f; distribución, f; esquema, m

laze /leiz/ vi holgazanear, gandulear, no hacer nada; encontrarse a sus anchas

lazily /'leizəli/ adv perezosamente; indolentemente; lentamente

laziness /'leizinɪs/ n pereza, holgazanería, f; indolencia, f; lentitud, f

lazy /'leizi/ a perezoso, holgazán; indolente. **l.-bones,** gandul (m)

lead /led/ n (metal) plomo, m; (in a pencil) mina, f; (plummet) sonda, f; Print. interlínea, f; pl **leads,** (roofs) tejados, m pl. —vt emplomar; guarnecer con plomo; Print. interlinear. **black-l.,** grafito, m. **deep-**

sea l., Naut. escandallo, m. **white l.,** albayalde, m. **to heave the l.,** echar el escandallo, sondar. **l.-colored,** de color de plomo, plomizo. **l. mine,** mina de plomo, f. **l. poisoning,** saturnismo, m

lead /lid/ n delantera, f; primer lugar, m; dirección, f; mando, m; (suggestion) indicación, f; (influence) influencia, f; (dog's) traílla, f; Theat. protagonista, mf; Theat. papel principal, m; (at cards) mano, f

lead /lid/ vt and vi (conduct) conducir, llevar; guiar; (induce) mover, persuadir, inducir; inclinar; (cause) hacer, causar; (captain) capitanear, encabezar; dirigir; (channel) encauzar; (with life) llevar; (give) dar; (head) ir a la cabeza de; Mil. mandar; (at cards) salir; (at games) jugar en primer lugar; tomar la delantera; Fig. superar a los demás; (of roads) conducir. **to take the l.,** ir delante; ir a la cabeza, tomar la delantera; tomar la iniciativa. **to l. one to think,** hacer pensar. **to l. the way,** mostrar el camino; ir adelante. **to l. along,** llevar (por la mano, etc.), conducir; conducir por; guiar. **to l. astray,** descarriar; desviar (de), seducir (a). **to l. away,** conducir (a otra parte); llevarse (a). **to l. back,** conducir de nuevo; hacer volver. **This path leads back to the village,** Por esta senda se vuelve al pueblo. **to l. in, into,** conducir a (or ante); introducir en, hacer entrar en; invitar a entrar en; (of rooms) comunicarse con; (sin, etc.) inducir a. **to l. off,** vi ir adelante; (begin) empezar; (of rooms) comunicarse con. —vt hacer marcharse, llevarse (a). **to l. on,** vt conducir; guiar; hacer pensar en; (make talk) dar cuerda (a). —vi ir a la cabeza; tomar la delantera. **to l. out,** conducir afuera; (to dance) sacar. **to l. to,** conducir a; desembocar en, salir a; (cause) dar lugar a, causar; (make) hacer; (incline) inclinar. **This street leads to the square,** Por esta calle se va a la plaza, Esta calle conduce a la plaza. **to l. up to,** conducir a; (in conversation, etc.) preparar el terreno para; preparar; tener lugar antes de, ocurrir antes de

leaden /'lɛdn/ a hecho de plomo, plúmbeo; (of skies, etc.) plomizo, de color de plomo, aplomado. **l.-footed,** pesado; lento

leader /'lidər/ n conductor (-ra); guía, mf; jefe (-fa); general, m; director (-ra); (in a journal) artículo de fondo, m; (of an orchestra) primer violín, m. **follow-the-l.,** (game) juego de seguir la fila, m

leadership /'lidər,ʃɪp/ n dirección, f; jefatura, f; Mil. mando, m

lead-in /'lid ,ɪn/ a Radio. de entrada. —n Radio. conductor de entrada, m

leading /'lɛdɪŋ/ n (leadwork) emplomadura, f

leading /'lidɪŋ/ n (guidance) dirección, f. —a principal; primero; importante; eminente. **l. article,** artículo de fondo, m; editorial, m. **l. card,** primer naipe, m. **l. counsel,** abogado (-da) principal. **l. lady,** Theat. dama primera, primera actriz, f; (cinema) estrella (de la pantalla), f. **l. man,** Theat. primer galán, m. **l. question,** pregunta que sugiere la respuesta, f. **l. strings,** andadores, m pl; Fig. tutelaje, m

leaf /lif/ n (Bot. and of a page, door, window, table, screen, etc.) hoja, f; (petal) pétalo, m, vi echar hojas. **gold l.,** pan de oro, m. **to turn over a new l.,** volver la hoja, hacer libro nuevo, hacer vida nueva. **to turn over the leaves of a book,** hojear (un libro). **l.-bud,** yema, f; **l.-mold,** abono verde, m. **l. tobacco,** tabaco en hoja, m

leafiness /'lifinɪs/ n frondosidad, f

leafless /'liflɪs/ a sin hojas

leaflet /'liflɪt/ n hojuela, f; (pamphlet) folleto, m

leafy /'lifi/ a frondoso

league /lig/ n (measure) legua, f; liga, federación, sociedad, f; (football) liga, f. —vt aliar; asociar. —vi aliarse; asociarse, confederarse. **to be in l.,** Inf. estar de manga. **L. of Nations,** Sociedad de las Naciones, f

leak /lik/ n (hole) agujero, m; grieta, f; Naut. vía de agua, f; (of gas, liquids, etc.) escape, m; (in a roof, etc.) gotera, f; Elec. resistencia de escape, f. —vi Naut. hacer agua; (of liquids, etc.) escaparse, salirse; (drip) gotear. **to l. out,** (of news, etc.) trascender, saberse. **to spring a l.,** aparecer una vía de agua, hacer agua

leakage /'likɪdʒ/ n (of gas, liquids) escape, m, fuga, f; derrame, m; pérdida, f; (of information) revelación, f

leaky /'liki/ a Naut. que hace agua; agujereado; poroso; que tiene goteras

lean /lin/ a magro, seco, enjuto, delgado; (of meat) magro; Fig. pobre, estéril. —n carne magra, f, magro, m. **to grow l.,** enflaquecer

lean /lin/ vi inclinarse; apoyarse (en). —vt apoyar (en); dejar arrimado (en). **to l. out of the window,** asomarse a la ventana. **to l. against,** apoyarse en, recostarse en (or contra). **to l. back,** echarse hacia atrás; recostarse. **to l. over,** inclinarse. **to l. upon,** apoyarse en; descansar sobre

leaning /'linɪŋ/ n inclinación, tendencia, f; predilección, afición, f

leanness /'linnɪs/ n magrura, flaqueza, f; (of meat) magrez, f; Fig. pobreza, f

leap /lip/ n salto, m; brinco, m; (caper) zapateta, f; Fig. salto, m. —vi saltar, dar un salto; brincar. —vt saltar; hacer saltar. **at one l.,** en un salto. **by leaps and bounds,** en saltos. **My heart leaped,** Mi corazón dio un salto. **to l. to the conclusion that...,** saltar a la conclusión de que... **to l. to the eye,** saltar a la vista. **l. frog,** salto, salto de la muerte, m, pídola f. **l. year,** año bisiesto, m, salta cabrillas, f pl

leaping /'lipɪŋ/ a saltador. —n saltos, m pl

learn /lɜrn/ vt and vi aprender; instruirse; enterarse de. **to l. by heart,** aprender de memoria. **to l. from a reliable source,** saber de buena tinta. **to l. from experience,** aprender por experiencia

learned /'lɜrnɪd/ a sabio, docto; erudito; (of professions) liberal; versado (en), entendido (en). **a l. society,** una sociedad erudita

learner /'lɜrnər/ n aprendedor (-ra)

learning /'lɜrnɪŋ/ n saber, m; conocimientos, m pl; erudición, f; estudio, m; (literature) literatura, f

lease /lis/ n arrendamiento, arriendo, m; contrato de arrendamiento, m. —vt dar en arriendo, arrendar. **on l.,** en arriendo. **to take a new l. on life,** recobrar su vigor. **Lend L. Act,** ley de préstamo y arriendo, f

leasehold /'lis,hould/ n censo, m, a censatario

leaseholder /'lis,houldər/ n concesionario, m; arrendatario (-ia)

leash /liʃ/ n (of a dog) traílla, f

least /list/ a superl little, mínimo; el (la, etc.) menor; más pequeño. —adv menos. —n lo menos. **at l.,** siquiera; por lo menos, al menos. **at the very l.,** a lo menos. **not in the l.,** de ninguna manera, nada. **to say the l. of,** sin exagerar, para no decir más

leather /'lɛðər/ n cuero, m; piel, f, a de cuero; de piel. **patent l.,** charol, m. **Spanish l.,** cordobán, m. **tanned l.,** curtido, m. **l. apron,** mandil, m. **l. bag,** saco de cuero, m. **l. bottle,** bota, f. **l. breeches,** pantalón de montar, m. **l. jerkin,** coleto, m. **l. shield,** adarga, f. **l. strap,** correa, f. **l. trade,** comercio en cueros, m

leatherette /,lɛðə'rɛt/ n cartón cuero, m

leathery /'lɛðəri/ a de cuero; (of the skin) curtido por la intemperie; (tough) correoso

leave /liv/ n (permission) permiso, m; (Mil. etc.) licencia, f; (farewell) despedida, f. —vt and vi dejar; abandonar; salir (de), quitar, marcharse (de); (as surety) empeñar; (by will) legar, mandar; (an employment) darse de baja (de), dejar; (give into the keeping of) entregar; (bid farewell) despedirse (de). **By your l.,** Con permiso de Vd. (Vds.). Con la venia de Vd. (Vds.) **on l.,** de permiso. **l.-taking,** despedidas, f pl. **to be left,** quedar. **to be left over,** quedar; sobrar. **Two from four leaves two,** De cuatro a dos van dos. **to take French l.,** despedirse a la inglesa. **to take l. of,** despedirse de. **to take one's l.,** marcharse; despedirse. **to l. a deep impression,** Fig. impresionar mucho; quedar grabado (en). **to l. undone,** dejar de hacer, no hacer; dejar sin terminar. **to l. about,** vt dejar por todas partes. —vi (of time) marcharse a eso de... **to l. ajar,** entreabrir, entornar. **to l. alone,** dejar a solas; dejar en paz; no molestar, no meterse con. **to l. aside,** omitir; prescindir de; olvidar. **to l. behind,** dejar atrás; olvidar. **l. much to be desired,** tener mucho que desear. **to l. off,** vt dejar de; abandonar; (garments) no ponerse, quitarse. —vi terminar. **to l. out,** dejar fuera; dejar a un lado, des-

contar; omitir; pasar por; (be silent about) callar; suprimir. **to l. to,** dejar para; dejar hacer

leaven /'lɛvən/ n levadura, f, fermento, m, vt fermentar; (Fig. permeate) penetrar (en), infiltrar en, imbuir; (a speech) salpimentar (con)

leaving /'livɪŋ/ n salida, partida, marcha, f; pl **leavings,** sobras, f pl; desechos, m pl

Lebanon /'lɛbənən/ el Líbano, m

lecherous /'lɛtʃərəs/ a lascivo, lujurioso

lechery /'lɛtʃəri/ n lascivia, lujuria, f

lectern /'lɛktərn/ n atril, m; (in a church) facistol, m

lecture /'lɛktʃər/ n conferencia, f; (in a university) lección, clase, f; discurso, m; (Inf. scolding) sermoneo, m. —vi dar una conferencia; (in a university) dar clase. —vt (Inf. scold) predicar, sermonear. **l. room,** sala de conferencias, f; (in a university) sala de clase, aula, f

lecturer /'lɛktʃərər/ n conferenciante, mf; (in a university) auxiliar, m; (professor) catedrático (-ca), profesor (-ra)

lectureship /'lɛktʃərʃɪp/ n auxiliaría, f

ledge /lɛdʒ/ n borde, m; capa, f; (of a window) alféizar, m; (shelf) anaquel, m

ledger /'lɛdʒər/ n libro mayor, m

lee /li/ n Naut. sotavento, m, a a sotavento

leech /litʃ/ n sanguijuela, f

leek /lik/ n puerro, m

leer /lɪər/ vi mirar de soslayo; guiñar el ojo; mirar con los ojos llenos de deseo. —n mirada de soslayo, f; mirada de lascivia, f

lees /liz/ n pl heces, f pl; sedimento, m

leeward /'liwərd/ n sotavento, m. **on the l. side,** a sotavento

leeway /'li,wei/ n Naut. deriva, f; Fig. amplitud, margen de holgura, márgenes de maniobra, f pl

left /lɛft/ past part dejado, etc. See **leave.** a izquierdo. —adv a la izquierda; hacia la izquierda. —n izquierda, f. **on the l.,** a la izquierda. **the L.,** Polit. las izquierdas. **the Left Bank** (of Paris) la Ribera izquierda, la Orilla izquierda **L. face!** ¡Izquierda! **l.-hand,** mano izquierda, f; izquierda, f. **l.-hand drive,** conducción a la izquierda, f. **l.-handed,** zurdo. **l. luggage office,** consigna, f. **l.-overs,** sobras, f pl, desperdicios, m pl

leg /lɛg/ n pierna, f; (of animals, birds, furniture) pata, f; (of a triangle) cateto, m; (of a pair of compasses, trousers, lamb, veal) pierna, f; (of boots, stockings) caña, f; (of pork) pernil, m; (support) pie, m; (stage) etapa, f. **to be on one's last legs,** estar en las últimas; estar acabándose; estar sin recursos. **to pull a person's leg,** tomar el pelo (a). **leg-pull,** tomadura de pelo, f. **leg-of-mutton sleeve,** manga de pernil, f

legacy /'lɛgəsi/ n legado, m, manda, f; herencia, f

legal /'ligəl/ a legal; de derecho; jurídico; (lawful, permissible) legítimo, lícito; (of a lawyer) de abogado. **l. expenses,** litisexpensas, f pl. **l. inquiry,** investigación jurídica, f

legality /li'gæliti/ n legalidad, f

legalization /,ligələ'zeifən/ n legalización, f

legalize /'ligə,laiz/ vt legalizar; autorizar, legitimar

legally /'ligəli/ adv según la ley; según derecho; legalmente

legal tender n moneda de curso liberatorio, f

legate /'lɛgɪt/ n legado, m. **papal l.,** legado papal, m

legatee /,lɛgə'ti/ n legatario (-ia)

legation /lɪ'geifən/ n legación, f

legend /'lɛdʒənd/ n leyenda, f

legendary /'lɛdʒən,dɛri/ a legendario

legerdemain /,lɛdʒərdə'mein/ n juegos de manos, m pl

legged /'lɛgɪd/ a con piernas; de piernas...; de patas... **a three-l. stool,** un taburete de tres patas. **long l.,** zancudo

leggings /'lɛgɪŋz/ n pl polainas, f pl

legibility /,lɛdʒə'bɪlɪti/ n legibilidad, f

legible /'lɛdʒəbl/ a legible

legion /'lidʒən/ n legión, f. **L. of Honor,** Legión de Honor, f

legionary /'lidʒə,nɛri/ a legionario. —n legionario, m

legislate /'lɛdʒɪs,leit/ vt legislar

legislation /,lɛdʒɪs'leifən/ n legislación, f

legislative /'lɛdʒɪs,leitɪv/ a legislativo, legislador
legislator /'lɛdʒɪs,leitər/ n legislador (-ra)
legislature /'lɛdʒɪs,leitʃər/ n legislatura, f
legitimacy /lɪ'dʒɪtəməsi/ n legitimidad, f; justicia, f
legitimate /lɪ'dʒɪtəmɪt/ a legítimo; justo
legitimation /lɪ,dʒɪtə'meiʃən/ n legitimación, f
leguminous /lɪ'gyumənəs/ a leguminoso
leisure /'liʒər/ n ocio, m, desocupación, f; tiempo libre, m. **at one's l.,** con sosiego, despacio. **You can do it at your l.,** Puedes hacerlo cuando tengas tiempo. **to be at l.,** estar desocupado, no tener nada que hacer. **l. moments,** ratos perdidos, momentos de ocio, m pl
leisured /'liʒərd/ a desocupado, libre; sin ocupación; (wealthy) acomodado
leisurely /'liʒərli/ a pausado, lento, deliberado; tardo
lemon /'lɛmən/ n limón, m; (tree) limonero, m, a limonado, de color de limón; hecho o sazonado con limón. **l. drop,** pastilla de limón, f. **l.-grove,** limonar, m. **l.-squash,** limonada natural, f. **l.-squeezer,** exprime limones, m, exprimidera, f
lemonade /,lɛmə'neid/ n limonada, f. **l. powder,** limonada seca, f
lemur /'limər/ n lemur, m
lend /lɛnd/ vt prestar. **to l. an ear to,** prestar atención a. **It does not l. itself to...,** No se presta a... **to l. a hand,** echar una mano, dar una mano
lender /'lɛndər/ n el, m, (f, la) que presta; prestador (-ra); (of money) prestamista, mf; Com. mutuante, mf
lending /'lɛndɪŋ/ n prestación, f, préstamo, m. **l.-library,** biblioteca circulante, f
length /lɛŋkθ/ n largo, m; longitud, f; (of fabric) corte, m; (of a ship) eslora, f; (in racing) largo, m; distancia, f; (in time) duración, f; alcance, m. **at l.,** por fin, finalmente; (in full) extensamente, largamente. **by a l.,** por un largo. **full-l.,** de cuerpo entero. **three feet in l.,** tres pies de largo. **to go the l. of...,** llegar al extremo de...
lengthen /'lɛŋkθən/ vt alargar; prolongar; extender. —vi alargarse; prolongarse; extenderse; (of days) crecer
lengthening /'lɛŋkθənɪŋ/ n alargamiento, m; prolongación, f; crecimiento, m
lengthily /'lɛŋkθəli/ adv largamente
lengthiness /'lɛŋkθɪnɪs/ n largueza, f; prolijidad, f
lengthy /'lɛŋkθi/ a largo; demasiado largo, larguísimo; (of speech) prolijo; verboso
leniency /'liniənsi/ n lenidad, f; indulgencia, f
lenient /'liniənt/ a indulgente; poco severo
leniently /'liniəntli/ adv con indulgencia
Leningrad /'lɛnɪn,græd/ Leningrado, m
lenitive /'lɛnɪtɪv/ a lenitivo. n lenitivo, m
lens /lɛnz/ n lente, m; (of the eye) cristalino, m
Lent /lɛnt/ n Cuaresma, f
Lenten /'lɛntn/ a de Cuaresma, cuaresmal
lentil /'lɛntɪl/ n lenteja, f
lentitude /'lɛnti,tud/ n lentitud, f
Leo /'liou/ n León, m
leonine /'liə,nain/ a leonino
leopard /'lɛpərd/ n leopardo, m
leper /'lɛpər/ n leproso (-sa). **l. colony,** colonia de leprosos, f
leprosy /'lɛprəsi/ n lepra, f
leprous /'lɛprəs/ a leproso
lesbian /'lɛzbiən/ a and n lesbiana
lesion /'liʒən/ n lesión, f
less /lɛs/ a menor; más pequeño; menos; inferior. —adv menos; sin. **l. than,** menos de (que). **more or l.,** poco más o menos. **no l.,** nada menos. **none the l.,** sin embargo. **to grow l.,** disminuir. **l. and l.,** cada vez menos
lessee /lɛ'si/ n arrendatario (-ia); inquilino (-na)
lessen /'lɛsən/ vi disminuir; reducirse. —vt disminuir; reducir; (lower) rebajar; (disparage) menospreciar
lessening /'lɛsənɪŋ/ n disminución, f; reducción, f
lesser /'lɛsər/ a compar menor; más pequeño. See **little**
lesson /'lɛsən/ n lección, f. **to give a l.,** dar lección, dar clase; Fig. dar una lección (a). **to hear a l.,** tomar la lección
lessor /'lɛsɔr/ n arrendador (-ra)

lest /lɛst/ conjunc para que no; por miedo de (que), no sea que. **I did not do it l. they should not like it,** No lo hice por miedo de que no les gustase
let /lɛt/ vt dejar, permitir; (lease) arrendar. —vi alquilarse, ser alquilado. **Let** as an expression of the imperative is rendered in Spanish by the subjunctive or the imperative, e.g. Let them go! ¡Que se vayan! ¡Déjalos marchar! He let them go, Les dejó marchar. to let fall, dejar caer. to let go, dejar marchar; soltar; poner en libertad (a). **to let loose,** dar suelta a; Fig. desencadenar. **to let one know,** hacer saber, comunicar. **to let the cat out of the bag,** tirar de la manta. **to let th chance slip,** perder la ocasión. **to let alone,** (a thing) no tocar; (a person) dejar en paz, dejar tranquilo; (an affair) no meterse (en o con); (omit) no mencionar, omitir toda mención de. **to let down,** bajar; (by a rope) descolgar; (hair, etc.) dejar caer; (a dress, etc.) alargar; Naut. calar; (disappoint) dejar plantado. **to let in,** dejar entrar; hacer entrar; invitar a entrar; recibir; (insert) insertar. **to let into,** (initiate) iniciar en, admitir en; (a secret) revelar. Other meanings, see **to let in.** **to let off,** dejar salir; dejar en libertad; exonerar; perdonar; (a gun) disparar; (fireworks, etc.) hacer estallar. **to let out,** dejar salir; poner en libertad; (from a house) acompañar a la puerta; abrir la puerta; Sew. ensanchar; (hire) alquilar; (the fire, etc.) dejar extinguirse. **to let up,** dejar subir; (decrease) disminuir; (end) terminar
let /lɛt/ n estorbo, impedimento, obstáculo, m. **without let or hindrance,** sin estorbo ni obstáculo
lethal /'liθəl/ a letal. **l. weapon,** instrumento de muerte, m
lethargic /lə'θɑrdʒɪk/ a aletargado; letárgico
lethargy /'lɛθərdʒi/ n letargo, m; Med. letargía, f
letter /'lɛtər/ n (of the alphabet) letra, f; (epistle) carta, f; Print. carácter, m; (lessor) arrendador (-ra); pl **letters,** letras, f pl; (correspondence) correo, m; correspondencia, f. —vt inscribir; imprimir. **capital l.,** letra mayúscula, f. **first letters,** Fig. primeras letras, f pl. **registered l.,** carta certificada, f, certificado, m. **small l.,** letra minúscula, f. **the l. of the law,** la ley escrita. **to be l.-perfect,** saber de memoria. **to the l.,** Fig. a la letra. **letters patent,** patente, f; título de privilegio, m. **l.-balance,** pesacartas, m. **l.-book,** Com. libro copiador, m. **l.-box,** buzón de correos, m. **l.-card,** tarjeta postal del gobierno, f. **l. of credit,** carta de crédito, f. **l. of introduction,** carta de presentación, f. **l.-writer,** escritor (-ra) de cartas
lettered /'lɛtərd/ a culto, instruido; (printed) impreso
lettering /'lɛtərɪŋ/ n inscripción, f; letrero, rótulo, m
letterpress /'lɛtər,prɛs/ n imprenta, f; (not illustrations) texto, m
letting /'lɛtɪŋ/ n (hiring) arrendamiento, m
lettuce /'lɛtɪs/ n lechuga, f. **l. plant,** lechuguino, m. **l. seller,** lechuguero (-ra)
Leuven /'luvən/ Lovaina, f
Levantine /'lɛvən,tain/ a and n levantino (-na)
Levant, the /lɪ'vænt/ el Levante, m
levee /'lɛvi/ n besamanos, m, recepción, f
level /'lɛvəl/ n nivel, m; ras, m, flor, f; llano, m; (plain) llanura, f; (instrument) nivel, m, a llano; igual; al nivel (de); uniforme; imparcial. —adv a nivel; igualmente. —vt nivelar; igualar; allanar; (a blow) asestar; (a gun) apuntar; (raze) arrasar, derribar; adaptar; hacer uniforme. **on the l.,** a nivel; Fig. de buena fe. **spirit l.,** nivel de burbuja, m. **to make l. again,** rellanar. **l. country,** campaña, llanura, f. **l. with the ground,** a ras de la tierra. **l. with the water,** a flor de agua. **l. crossing,** paso a nivel, m. **l.-headed,** sensato, cuerdo. **l. stretch,** rellano, m; llanura, f
leveler /'lɛvələr/ n nivelador (-ra)
leveling /'lɛvəlɪŋ/ a nivelador; de nivelación; igualador. —n nivelación, f; allanamiento, m; (to the ground) arrasamiento, m; igualación, f
levelness /'lɛvəlnɪs/ n nivel, m; planicie, f; igualdad,
lever /'lɛvər/ n palanca, f; (handle) manivela, f; escape de reloj, m; (excuse) pretexto, m; (means) modo, m. —vt sopalancar. **control l.,** Aer. palanca de mando, f. **hand-l.,** palanca de mano, f

leverage /'levərɪdʒ/ n sistema de palancas, m; acción de palanca, f; Fig. influencia, fuerza, f, poder, m
Leviathan /lɪ'vaɪəθən/ n leviatán, m
levitation /ˌlevɪ'teɪʃən/ n levitación, f
Levite /'liːvaɪt/ n levita, m
Levitical /lɪ'vɪtɪkəl/ a levítico
Leviticus /lɪ'vɪtɪkəs/ n Levítico, m
levity /'levɪti/ n levedad, frivolidad, ligereza, f
levy /'leviː/ n exacción (de tributos), f; impuesto, m; (of a fine) imposición, f; Mil. leva, f. —vt (taxes) exigir; (a fine) imponer; (troops) reclutar, enganchar
levying /'leviːɪŋ/ n (of a tax) exacción (de tributos), f; (of a fine) imposición, f; (of troops) leva, f
lewd /luːd/ a lascivo, lujurioso, impúdico
lewdness /'luːdnɪs/ n lascivia, lujuria, impudicia, f
lexicographer /ˌleksɪ'kɒgrəfər/ n lexicógrafo, m
lexicography /ˌleksɪ'kɒgrəfi/ n lexicografía, f
lexicon /'leksɪˌkɒn/ n léxico, m
liability /ˌlaɪə'bɪlɪti/ n responsabilidad, obligación, f; tendencia, f; riesgo, m; pl **liabilities,** obligaciones, f pl; Com. pasivo, m
liable /'laɪəbəl/ a responsable; propenso (a); expuesto (a); sujeto (a)
liaison /li'eɪzən/ n lío, m; coordinación, f. **l. officer,** oficial de coordinación, m
liar /'laɪər/ n mentiroso (-sa)
libation /laɪ'beɪʃən/ n libación, f
libel /'laɪbəl/ n libelo, m; difamación, f, vt difamar, calumniar
libeler /'laɪbələr/ n libelista, mf difamador (-ra)
libelous /'laɪbələs/ a difamatorio
liberal /'lɪbərəl/ a liberal; generoso; abundante. —n liberal, mf **l. profession,** carrera liberal, f. **l.-minded,** tolerante. **l.-mindedness,** tolerancia, f
liberalism /'lɪbərəˌlɪzəm/ n liberalismo, m
liberality /ˌlɪbə'rælɪti/ n liberalidad, f; generosidad, f
liberalize /'lɪbərəˌlaɪz/ vt liberalizar
liberate /'lɪbəˌreɪt/ vt (a prisoner) poner en libertad; librar (de); (a gas, etc.) dejar escapar
liberation /ˌlɪbə'reɪʃən/ n liberación, f; (of a captive) redención, f; (of a slave) manumisión, f
liberator /'lɪbəˌreɪtər/ n libertador (-ra)
libertinage /'lɪbərˌtɪnɪdʒ/ n libertinaje, m
libertine /'lɪbərˌtin/ n libertino, m
libertinism /'lɪbərtɪˌnɪzəm/ n libertinaje, m
liberty /'lɪbərti/ n libertad, f; (familiarity) familiaridad, f; (right) privilegio, m, prerrogativa, f; (leave) permiso, m. **at l.,** en libertad; desocupado, libre. **I have taken the l. of giving them your name,** Me he tomado la libertad de darles su nombre. **to set at l.,** poner en libertad (a). **to take liberties with,** tratar con familiaridad; (a text) tergiversar. **l. of speech,** libertad de palabra, libertad de expresión, f. **l. of thought,** libertad de pensamiento, f
libidinous /lɪ'bɪdnəs/ a libidinoso
Libra /'liːbrə/ n Libra, f
librarian /laɪ'breəriən/ n bibliotecario (-ia)
librarianship /laɪ'breəriənˌʃɪp/ n carrera f, or empleo m, de bibliotecario
library /'laɪˌbreri/ n biblioteca, f; (book shop) librería, f. **l. catalog,** catálogo de la biblioteca, m
librettist /lɪ'bretɪst/ n libretista, mf
libretto /lɪ'bretoʊ/ n libreto, m
Libya /'lɪbiə/ n Libia, f
Libyan /'lɪbiən/ a and n libio (-ia)
license /'laɪsəns/ n licencia, f, permiso, m; autorización, f; (driving) carnet de chófer, permiso de conducción, m; (of a car) permiso de circulación, m; (for a wireless, etc.) licencia, f; (marriage) licencia de casamiento, f; (excess) libertinaje, desenfreno, m. **import l.,** permiso de importación, m. **poetic l.,** licencia poética, f. **l. number,** (of a car) número de matriculación, m. —vt licenciar; autorizar; (a car) sacar la licencia del automóvil
licensee /ˌlaɪsən'si/ n concesionario (-ia)
licentiate /laɪ'senʃɪt/ n licenciado (-da)
licentious /laɪ'senʃəs/ a licencioso, disoluto
licentiousness /laɪ'senʃəsnɪs/ n libertinaje, m, disipación, f
lichen /'laɪkən/ n liquen, m
licit /'lɪsɪt/ a lícito

lick /lɪk/ vt lamer; (of waves) besar; (of flames) bailar; (thrash) azotar; (defeat) vencer. **to l. one's lips,** relamerse los labios, chuparse los dedos. **to l. the dust,** morder el polvo
licking /'lɪkɪŋ/ n lamedura, f; (beating) paliza, tunda, f; (defeat) derrota, f
licorice /'lɪkərɪʃ, 'lɪkrɪʃ, 'lɪkərɪs/ n regaliz, m
lid /lɪd/ n cobertera, f; tapa, f; (of the eye) párpado, m
lie /laɪ/ n mentira, f; invención, falsedad, f; mentís, m, vi mentir. **to give the lie to,** desmentir, dar el mentís. **to lie barefacedly,** mentir por la mitad de la barba. **white lie,** mentira oficiosa, f
lie /laɪ/ vi estar tumbado, estar echado; estar recostado; descansar, reposar; (in the grave) yacer; (be) estar; (be situated) hallarse, estar situado; (stretch) extenderse; (sleep) dormir; (depend) depender; (consist) consistir, estribar; (as an obligation) incumbir. **Here lies...,** Aquí descansa..., Aquí yace... **It does not lie in my power,** No depende de mí. **to let lie,** dejar; dejar en paz. **to lie at anchor,** estar anclado. **to lie fallow,** estar en barbecho; Fig. descansar. **to lie about,** estar esparcido por todas partes; estar en desorden. **to lie along,** estar tendido a lo largo de; Naut. dar a la banda. **to lie back,** recostarse; apoyarse (en). **to lie by,** estar acostado al lado de; (of things, places) estar cerca (de); descansar. **to lie down,** tenderse, tumbarse, echarse, acostarse; reposar. **Lie down!** (to a dog) ¡Echate! **to lie down under,** tenderse bajo; (an insult) tragar, sufrir. **to lie in,** consistir en; depender de; (of childbirth) estar de parto. **to lie open,** estar abierto; estar expuesto (a); estar al descubierto, estar a la vista. **to lie over,** (be postponed) quedar aplazado. **to lie to,** Naut. estarse a la capa, ponerse en facha. **to lie under,** estar bajo, hallarse bajo; estar bajo el peso de; (be exposed to) estar expuesto a. **to lie with,** dormir con; (concern) tocar (a); corresponder (a)
lie /laɪ/ n configuración, f; disposición, f; posición, f. **the lie of the land,** la configuración del terreno
lieu /luː/ n lugar, m. **in l. of,** en lugar de, en vez de
lieutenant /luː'tenənt/ n teniente, lugarteniente, m; (naval) alférez, m. **first l.,** (in the army) primer teniente, teniente, m; (in the navy) alférez de navío, m. **naval l.,** teniente de navío, m. **second l.,** (in the army) segundo teniente, m; (in the navy) alférez de fragata, m. **l.-colonel,** teniente coronel, m. **l.-commander,** capitán de fragata, m. **l.-general,** teniente general, m. **l.-governor,** subgobernador, m
life /laɪf/ n vida, f; (being) ser, m; (society) mundo, m, sociedad, f; (vitality) vitalidad, f, vigor, m, a de vida; (of annuities, etc.) vitalicio; (life-saving) de salvamento. **for l.,** de por vida. **from l.,** del natural. **high l.,** gran mundo, m, alta sociedad, f. **low l.,** vida del hampa, vida de los barrios bajos, f. **to the l.,** al vivo. **to lay down one's l.,** entregar la vida. **to take one's l. in one's hands,** jugarse la vida. **l. annuity,** fondo vitalicio, m. **l.-belt,** (cinturón) salvavidas, m. **l.-blood,** sangre vital, f; Fig. nervio, m; vigor, m. **l.-boat,** (on a ship) bote salvavidas, m; (on the coast) lancha de salvamento, f. **l.-boat station,** estación de salvamento, f. **l.-giving,** vivificante, que da vida; tonificante, m. **l.-guard,** (soldier) guardia militar, f; Guardia de Corps, f. (at beach or swimming pool) guardavivas, mf. **l.-insurance,** seguro sobre la vida, m. **l.-interest,** usufructo, m. **l.-jacket,** chaleco salvavidas, m. **l.-like,** natural. **l.-line,** cable de salvamento, m. **l.-saving,** a de salvamento; curativo. **l.-saving apparatus,** aparato salvavidas, m. **l.-sized,** de tamaño natural
life cycle n ciclo vital, m
life imprisonment n reclusión perpetua, f
life jacket n chaleco salvavidas, f
lifeless /'laɪflɪs/ a sin vida, muerto; inanimado; Fig. desanimado
lifelong /'laɪfˌlɒŋ/ a de toda la vida
lifetime /'laɪfˌtaɪm/ n vida, f
lift /lɪft/ n esfuerzo para levantar, m; acción de levantar, f; alza, f; (blow) golpe, m; (help) ayuda, f; (elevator) ascensor, m; (for goods) montacargas, m; pl **lifts,** Naut. balancines, m pl. **to give a l. to,** (help)

ayudar; (hitchhiker etc.) dar un aventón. **l. attend-ant,** ascensorista, *mf*

lift /lɪft/ *vt* levantar; alzar, elevar; (pick up) coger; (one's hat) quitarse; (steal) hurtar; exaltar. —*vi* (of mist) disiparse; desaparecer. **to l. the elbow,** empinar el codo. **to l. down,** quitar (de); (a person) bajar en brazos. **to l. up,** alzar; erguir, levantar; levantar en brazos

lifting /'lɪftɪŋ/ *n* acción de levantar, *f;* levantamiento, alzamiento, *m*

ligament /'lɪgəmənt/ *n* ligamento, *m*

ligature /'lɪgətʃər/ *n* (*Surg. Mus.*) ligadura, *f*

light /laɪt/ *a* (not dark) claro, con mucha luz, bañado de luz; (of colors) claro; (not heavy, and of sleep, food, troops, movements) ligero; (of reading) de entretenimiento; (irresponsible) frívolo; (easy) fácil; (slight) leve; (of hair) rubio; (happy) alegre; (fickle) inconstante, liviano; (of complexion) blanco. —*adv* ligero. **to be l.,** no pesar mucho; estar de día. **to grow l.,** (dawn) clarear; iluminarse. **to make l. of,** no tomar en serio; no preocuparse de; (suffering) sufrir sin quejarse. **l.-colored,** (de color) claro. **l.-fingeredness,** sutileza de manos, *f.* **l.-footed,** ligero de pies. **l.-haired,** de pelo rubio. **l.-headed,** casquivano, ligero de cascos; delirante. **l.-headedness,** ligereza de cascos, frivolidad, *f;* delirio, *m.* **l.-hearted,** alegre (de corazón). **l.-heartedness,** alegría, *f.* **l. horse,** *Mil.* caballería ligera, *f.* **l. troops,** tropas ligeras, *f pl.* **l.-weight,** *n* (boxing) peso ligero, *m, a* de peso ligero

light /laɪt/ *n* luz., *f;* (day) día, *m;* (match) cerilla, *f;* (of a cigarette, etc.) fuego, *m;* (of a window) cristal, vidrio, *m;* (point of view) punto de vista, *m;* (in a picture) toque de luz, *m; pl* **lights,** (offal) bofes, *m pl.* **against the l.,** al trasluz. **by the l. of,** a la luz de; según. **half-l.,** media luz, *f.* **high light (s),** *Art.* claros, *m pl; Fig.* momento culminante, *m;* acontecimiento de más interés, *m.* **to come to l.,** descubrirse. **to put a l. to the fire,** encender el fuego. **l.-year,** año de luz, *m*

light /laɪt/ *vt* (a lamp, fire, etc.) encender; iluminar. —*vi* encenderse; iluminarse; *Fig.* animarse; brillar. **to l. upon,** encontrar por casualidad; tropezar con

lighten /'laɪtn/ *vt* (illuminate) iluminar; (of weight) aligerar; (cheer) alegrar; (mitigate) aliviar. —*vi* (grow light) clarear; (of lightning) relampaguear; (become less heavy) disminuir de peso, aligerarse; volverse más alegre

lightening /'laɪtnɪŋ/ *n* aligeramiento, *m;* (easing) alivio, *m;* luz, *f*

lighter /'laɪtər/ *n* (boat) lancha, barcaza, gabarra, *f;* (device) encendedor, *m.* **pocket l.,** encendedor de bolsillo, *m.* **l. man,** gabarrero, *m*

light-fingered *a* ligero de manos

lighthouse /'laɪt,haʊs/ *n* faro, *m.* **l.-keeper,** guardafaro, *m*

lighting /'laɪtɪŋ/ *n* iluminación, *f;* alumbrado, *m.* **flood l.,** iluminación intensiva, *f.* **l.-up time,** hora de encender los faros, *f*

lightly /'laɪtli/ *adv* ligeramente; fácilmente; (slightly) levemente; ágilmente; sin seriedad. **l. wounded,** levemente herido

lightness /'laɪtnɪs/ *n* ligereza, *f;* poco peso, *m;* agilidad, *f;* (brightness) claridad, *f;* (inconstancy) liviandad, inconstancia, *f;* frivolidad, *f*

lightning /'laɪtnɪŋ/ *n* relámpago, rayo, *m.* **as quick as l.,** como un relámpago. **to be struck by l.,** ser herido por un relámpago. **l.-rod,** pararrayos, *m*

lightship /'laɪt,ʃɪp/ *n* buque faro, *m*

ligneous /'lɪgniəs/ *a* leñoso

lignite /'lɪgnaɪt/ *n* lignito, *m*

likable /'laɪkəbəl/ *a* simpático

like /laɪk/ *a* semejante; parecido; igual, mismo; (characteristic) típico, característico; (likely) probable; (equivalent) equivalente. —*adv* como; igual (que); del mismo modo (que). —*n* semejante, igual, *mf;* tal cosa, *f;* cosas semejantes, *f pl.* **Don't speak to me l. that,** No me hables así. **He was l. a fury,** Estaba hecho una furia. **They are very l. each other,** Se parecen mucho. **to be l.,** parecerse (a), semejar. **to look l.,** parecer ser (que); tener el aspecto de; (of

persons) parecerse (a). **to return l. for l.,** pagar en la misma moneda

like /laɪk/ *vt* gustar, agradar; estar aficionado (a), gustar de; (wish) querer. **As you l.,** Como te parezca bien, Como quieras. **If you l.,** Si quieres. **James likes painting,** Jaime está aficionado a la pintura. **Judith does not l. the north of England,** A Judit no le gusta el norte de Inglaterra. **I don't l. to do it,** No me gusta hacerlo. **I should l. him to go to Madrid,** Me gustaría que fuese a Madrid

likelihood /'laɪkli,hʊd/ *n* posibilidad, *f;* probabilidad, *f*

likely /'laɪkli/ *a* probable; verosímil, creíble, plausible; posible; (suitable) satisfactorio, apropiado; (handsome) bien parecido. —*adv* probablemente. **They are not l. to come,** No es probable que vengan

liken /'laɪkən/ *vt* comparar

likeness /'laɪknɪs/ *n* parecido, *m,* semejanza, *f;* (portrait) retrato, *m*

likewise /'laɪk,waɪz/ *adv* igualmente, asimismo, también. —*conjunc* además

liking /'laɪkɪŋ/ *n* (for persons) simpatía, *f,* cariño, *m;* (for things) gusto, *m,* afición, *f;* (appreciation) aprecio, *m.* **I have a l. for old cities,** Me gustan (or me atraen) las viejas ciudades. **to take a l. to,** (things) aficionarse a; (persons) prendarse de, tomar cariño (a)

lilac /'laɪlək/ *n* lila, *f.* **l. color,** color de lila, *m*

Lilliputian /,lɪlɪ'pyuʃən/ *a* liliputiense. —*n* liliputiense, *mf*

lilt /lɪlt/ *n* canción, *f;* ritmo, *m;* armonía, *f*

lily /'lɪli/ *n* lirio, *m,* azucena, *f;* (of France) flor de lis, *f.* **l. of the valley,** lirio de los valles, muguete, *m.* **l.-white,** blanco como la azucena

limb /lɪm/ *n Anat.* miembro, *m;* (of a tree) rama, *f*

limbless /'lɪmlɪs/ *a* mutilado

limbo /'lɪmboʊ/ *n* limbo, *m*

lime /laɪm/ *n Chem.* cal, *f;* (for catching birds) liga, hisca, *f;* (linden tree) tilo, *m;* (tree like a lemon) limero, *m;* (fruit) lima, *f.* —*vt* (whiten) encalar; *Agr.* abonar con cal. **slaked l.,** cal muerta, *f.* **l.-flower,** flor del tilo, tila, *f;* flor del limero, *f.* **l.-juice,** jugo de lima, *m.* **l.-kiln,** calera, *f.* **l.-pit,** pozo de cal, *m*

limelight /'laɪm,laɪt/ *n* luz de calcio, *f; Fig.* centro de atención, *m;* publicidad, *f.* **to be in the l.,** ser el centro de atención, estar a la vista de (público)

limestone /'laɪm,stoʊn/ *n* piedra caliza, *f.* **l. deposit,** calar, *m*

limit /'lɪmɪt/ *n* límite, *m;* confín, *m;* linde, *m, or f;* limitación, *f, vt* limitar; fijar; (restrict) restringir. **This is the l.!** ¡Este es el colmo! ¡No faltaba más!

limitation /,lɪmɪ'teɪʃən/ *n* limitación, *f;* restricción, *f*

limitative /'lɪmɪ,teɪtɪv/ *a* restrictivo, limitativo

limited /'lɪmɪtɪd/ *a* limitado; restringido; escaso; (of persons) de cortos alcances; *Com.* anónimo. **l. company,** sociedad anónima, *f*

limited monarchy *n* monarquía moderada, *f*

limiting adjective /'lɪmɪtɪŋ/ *n* adjetivo determinativo, *m*

limitless /'lɪmɪtlɪs/ *a* sin límites; ilimitado, inmenso

limousine /'lɪmə,zin/ *n* limousina, *f,* coche cerrado, *m*

limp /lɪmp/ *a* flojo; débil; fláccido; lánguido. —*n* cojera, *f.* —*vi* cojear. **to l. off,** marcharse cojeando. **to l. up,** acercarse cojeando; subir cojeando

limpid /'lɪmpɪd/ *a* límpido, cristalino, puro

limpidity /lɪm'pɪdɪti/ *n* limpidez, *f*

limping /'lɪmpɪŋ/ *a* cojo

limply /'lɪmpli/ *adv* flojamente; débilmente; lánguidamente

limpness /'lɪmpnɪs/ *n* flojedad, *f;* debilidad, *f;* languidez, *f*

linchpin /'lɪntʃ,pɪn/ *n* pezonera, *f*

linden /'lɪndən/ *n* tilo, *m*

line /laɪn/ *vt* (furrow) surcar; (troops, etc.) poner en fila; alinear; (clothes, nests, etc.) forrar; (building) revestir; (one's pocket) llenar. —*vi* estar en línea, alinearse

line /laɪn/ *n* (most meanings) línea, *f;* (cord) cuerda, *f; Naut.* cordel, *m;* (fishing) sedal, *m;* (railway) vía, *f;* (wrinkle) surco, *m;* arruga, *f;* (row) hilera, ringlera, fila, *f;* (of verse) verso, *m; Print.* renglón, *m;* (of business) ramo, *m;* profesión, *f;* (interest) especialidad, *f.* **bowling** or **serving l.,** línea de saque, *f;* **hard lines,** mala suerte, *f;* apuro, *m,* situación difícil, *f.* **in a l.,** en fila; en cola. **in direct l.,** (of descent) en línea recta. **It is not in my l.,** No es una especialidad mía; No es uno de mis intereses. **on the lines of,** conforme a; parecido a. **to cross the l.,** (equator) pasar la línea; (railway) cruzar la vía. **to drop a l.,** escribir unas líneas, poner unas líneas. **to read between the lines,** leer entre líneas. **l.-drawing,** dibujo de líneas, *m.* **l. of battle,** línea de batalla, *f*

lineage /'lɪnɪdʒ/ *n* linaje, *m,* familia, raza, *f*

lineal /'lɪniəl/ *a* lineal

lineament /'lɪnɪəmənt/ *n* lineamento, *m;* (of the face) facciones, *f pl*

linear /'lɪniər/ *a* lineal. **l. equation,** ecuación de primer grado, *f*

lined /laind/ *a* rayado, con líneas; (of the face) surcado, arrugado; (of gloves, etc.) forrado. **lined paper,** papel rayado, *m*

linen /'lɪnən/ *n* lino, *m; Inf.* ropa blanca, *f; a* de lino. **clean l.,** ropa limpia, *f.* **dirty l.,** ropa sucia, *f;* ropa para lavar, *f.* **table-l.,** mantelería, *f.* **l. cupboard,** armario para ropa blanca, *m.* **l. draper,** lencero (-ra). **l.-draper's shop,** lencería, *f.* **l. room,** lencería, *f.* **l. tape,** trenzadera, *f.* **l. thread,** hilo de lino, *m*

liner /'lainər/ *n* (ship) transatlántico, *m;* buque de vapor, *m; Aer.* avión de pasaje, *m*

linesman /'lainzmən/ *n* soldado de línea, *m; Sports.* juez de línea, *m*

ling /lɪŋ/ *n Bot.* brezo, *m; Ichth.* especie de abadejo, *m*

linger /'lɪŋgər/ *vi* (remain) quedarse; tardar en marcharse; ir lentamente; hacer algo despacio

lingerie /,lɑnʒə'rei/ *n* ropa blanca, *f*

lingering /'lɪŋgərɪŋ/ *a* lento; largo; prolongado; melancólico, triste

lingeringly /'lɪŋgərɪŋli/ *adv* lentamente; largamente; melancólicamente

linguist /'lɪŋgwɪst/ *n* lingüista, *mf*

linguistic /lɪŋ'gwɪstɪk/ *a* lingüístico

linguistics /lɪŋ'gwɪstɪks/ *n* lingüística, *f*

liniment /'lɪnəmənt/ *n* linimento, *m*

lining /'lainɪŋ/ *n* (of a garment, etc.) forro, *m;* (building) revestimiento, *m*

link /lɪŋk/ *n* (in a chain) eslabón, *m;* (of beads) sarta, *f; Fig.* enlace, *m,* cadena, *f;* conexión, *f; Mech.* corredera, *f;* (torch) hacha de viento, *f.* —*vt* enlazar, unir; *Fig.* encadenar. **missing l.,** *Fig.* eslabón perdido, *m.* **to l. arms,** cogerse del brazo

linking /'lɪŋkɪŋ/ *n* encadenamiento, *m; Fig.* conexión, *f*

links /lɪŋks/ *n pl* campo de golf, *m*

linoleum /lɪ'nouliəm/ *n* linóleo, *m*

linotype /'lainəˌtaip/ *n* linotipia, *f*

linseed /'lɪnˌsid/ *n* linaza, *f.* **l. cake,** bagazo, *m.* **l.-oil,** aceite de linaza, *m*

lint /lɪnt/ *n Med.* hilas, *f pl;* (fluff) borra, *f*

lintel /'lɪntl/ *n* dintel, *m;* (threshold) umbral, *m*

lion /'laiən/ *n* león, *m; Fig.* celebridad, *f.* **l. cage** or **den,** leonera, *f.* **l.-hearted,** valeroso. **l.-hunter,** cazador (-ra) de leones. **l.-keeper,** leonero (-ra). **lion's mane,** melena, *f.* **l.-tamer,** domador (-ra) de leones

lioness /'laiənɪs/ *n* leona, *f*

lionize /'laiəˌnaiz/ *vt* dar bombo (a), hacer la rueda (a), tratar como a una celebridad (a)

lion's share *n* parte del león, tajada del león, *f*

lip /lɪp/ *n* labio, *m;* (of a vessel) pico, *m;* (of a crater) borde, *m; Fig.* boca, *f.* **to open one's lips,** abrir la boca. **to smack one's lips,** chuparse los dedos. **lip reading,** lectura labial, *f.* **lip-service,** amor fingido, *m;* promesas hipócritas, *f pl.* **lip stick,** lápiz para los labios, *m*

lipped /lɪpt/ *a* (in compounds) con labios..., que tiene labios; (of vessels in compounds) con... picos

liquefaction /,lɪkwə'fækʃən/ *n* licuefacción, *f*

liquefiable /'lɪkwəˌfaiəbəl/ *a* liquidable

liquefy /'lɪkwəˌfai/ *vt* liquidar; —*vi* liquidarse

liqueur /lɪ'kɜr/ *n* licor, *m.* **l.-glass,** copita de licor, *f.* **l.-set,** licorera, *f*

liquid /'lɪkwɪd/ *n* líquido, *m, a* líquido; límpido, *f.* **l.**

air, aire líquido, *m.* **l. measure,** medida para líquidos, *f*

liquidate /'lɪkwɪˌdeit/ *vt* liquidar; saldar (cuentas); *Mil.* soldar

liquidation /,lɪkwɪ'deiʃən/ *n* liquidación, *f*

liquidness /'lɪkwɪdnɪs/ *n* liquidez, *f;* fluidez, *f*

liquor /'lɪkər/ *n* licor, *m.* **l. shop,** aguardentería, *f.* **l. traffic,** negocio de vinos y licores, *m;* contrabando, *m*

lira /'lɪərə/ *n* lira, *f*

Lisbon /'lɪzbən/ Lisboa, *f*

lisp /lɪsp/ *n* ceceo, *m;* balbuceo, *m, vi* cecear; balbucir

lisping /'lɪspɪŋ/ *a* ceceoso; balbuciente. —*n* ceceo, *m;* (of a child, etc.) balbuceo, *m*

lissome /'lɪsəm/ *a* flexible; ágil

list /lɪst/ *n* lista, *f;* catálogo, *m;* matrícula, *f; Naut.* recalcada, *f;* inclinación, *f;* (tournament) liza, *f.* —*vt* hacer una lista de; catalogar; matricular, inscribir. —*vi Naut.* recalcar; inclinarse a un lado. **to enter the lists,** entrar en liza. **l. of wines,** lista de vinos, *f*

listen /'lɪsən/ *vi* escuchar; (attend) attender. **Don't you want to l. to the music?** ¿No quieres escuchar la música? **to l. in,** (to the radio) escuchar la radio; (eavesdrop) escuchar a hurtadillas

listener /'lɪsənər/ *n* oyente, *mf;* (to radio) radiooyente, *mf*

listless /'lɪstlɪs/ *a* lánguido, apático, indiferente

listlessly /'lɪstlɪsli/ *adv* lánguidamente, indiferentemente

listlessness /'lɪstlɪsnɪs/ *n* apatía, languidez, indiferencia, inercia, *f*

litany /'lɪtn̩i/ *n* letanía, *f*

liter /'lɪtər/ *n* litro, *m*

literal /'lɪtərəl/ *a* literal. **l.-minded,** sin imaginación

literalness /'lɪtərəlnɪs/ *n* literalidad, *f*

literary /'lɪtəˌreri/ *a* literario. **l. executor** *n* depositario de la obra literaria, *m*

literate /'lɪtərɪt/ *a and n* literato (-ta)

literature /'lɪtərətʃər/ *n* literatura, *f*

lithe /laið/ *a* flexible; sinuoso y delgado; ágil

litheness /'laiðnɪs/ *n* flexibilidad, *f;* sinuosidad, *f;* delgadez, *f;* agilidad, *f*

lithograph /'lɪθəˌgræf/ *n* litografía, *f, vt* litografiar

lithographer /lɪ'θɒgrəfər/ *n* litógrafo, *m*

lithographic /,lɪθə'græfɪk/ *a* litográfico

lithography /lɪ'θɒgrəfi/ *n* litografía, *f*

Lithuania /,lɪθu'einiə/ Lituania, *f*

Lithuanian /,lɪθu'einiən/ *a* lituano, *m* lituano (-na); (language) lituano, *m*

litigant /'lɪtɪgənt/ *n* litigante, *mf*

litigate /'lɪtɪˌgeit/ *vi and vt* litigar, pleitear

litigation /,lɪtɪ'geiʃən/ *n* litigación, *f*

litigious /lɪ'tɪdʒəs/ *a* litigioso

litmus /'lɪtməs/ *n* tornasol, *m.* **l. paper,** papel de tornasol, *m*

litter /'lɪtər/ *n* litera, *f;* (stretcher) camilla, *f;* (bed) lecho, *m;* cama de paja, *f;* (brood) camada, cría, *f;* (rubbish) cosas en desorden, *f pl;* (papers) papeletas, *f pl;* (untidiness) desarreglo, desorden, *m,* confusión, *f, vt* poner en desorden

little /'lɪtl̩/ *a* pequeño; poco; (scanty) escaso; insignificante; bajo, mezquino. —*adv* poco. **a l.,** un poco (de); un tanto. **in l.,** en pequeño. **not a l.,** no poco; bastante. **l. by l.,** poco a poco. **l. or no,** poco o nada. **however l.,** por pequeño que. **as l. as possible,** lo menos posible. **to make l. of,** no dar importancia a; sacar poco en claro de, no comprender bien; no hacer caso de; (persons) acoger mal. **l. by l.,** poco a poco. **l. finger,** dedo meñique, *m.* **l. one,** pequeñuela, *f,* pequeñito, *m*

littleness /'lɪtl̩nɪs/ *n* pequeñez, *f;* poquedad, *f;* mezquindad, *f;* trivialidad, *f*

littoral /'lɪtərəl/ *a and n* litoral, *m*

liturgical /lɪ'tɜrdʒɪkəl/ *a* litúrgico. **l. calendar,** calendario litúrgico, *m*

liturgical vestment *n* paramento litúrgico, *m*

liturgy /'lɪtərdʒi/ *n* liturgia, *f*

live /laiv/ *a* vivo, viviente; (alight) encendido; (of a wire, etc.) cargado de electricidad. **l. cartridge,** cartucho con bala, *m.* **l. coal,** ascua, *f.* **l.-stock,**

ganadería, f. **l. wire,** conductor eléctrico, m; Fig. fuerza viva, f

live /laɪv/ vi vivir; residir, habitar; (of ships) mantenerse a flote; salvarse; subsistir. —vt (one's life) llevar, pasar. **Long l.!** ¡Viva! **to have enough to l. on,** tener de que vivir. **to l. together,** convivir. **to l. again,** volver a vivir. **to l. at,** vivir en, habitar. **to l. down,** sobrevivir a; (a fault) lograr borrar. **to l. on,** vivir de. **to l. up to,** vivir con arreglo a, vivir en conformidad con; estar al nivel de, merecer. **to l. up to one's income,** vivir al día, gastarse toda la renta

live broadcast n emisión en directo, f

livelihood /'laɪvli,hʊd/ n vida, subsistencia, f. **to make a l.,** ganarse la vida

liveliness /'laɪvlɪnɪs/ n vivacidad, vida, f; animación, f; alegría, f

livelong /'lɪv,lɔŋ/ a entero, todo; eterno. **all the l. day,** todo el santo día

lively /'laɪvli/ a vivo; vivaracho; brioso, enérgico; alegre; bullicioso; animado; (fresh) fresco; (of colors) brilliante; intenso

liver /'lɪvər/ n vividor (-ra), el, m, (f, la) que vive; habitante, m; Anat. hígado, m. **l. cancer,** cáncer del hígado, m. **l. complaint,** mal de hígado, m. **l. extract,** extracto de hígado, m

livery /'lɪvəri/ n librea, f; uniforme, m; Poet. vestiduras, f pl. **l. stables,** pensión de caballos, f; cochería de alquiler, f

livid /'lɪvɪd/ a lívido; cárdeno, amoratado

lividness /'lɪvɪdnɪs/ n lividez, f

living /'lɪvɪŋ/ a viviente; vivo, vital. —n vida, f; modo de vivir, m; beneficio eclesiástico, m. **the l.,** los vivos. **to make one's l.,** ganarse la vida. **l. memory,** memoria de personas vivientes, memoria de los que aún viven, f. **l.-room,** sala de estar, f. **l. soul,** ser viviente; Inf. bicho viviente, m. **l. wage,** jornal básico, m

lizard /'lɪzərd/ n lagarto (-ta). **giant l.,** dragón, m. **wall l.,** lagartija, f. **l. hole,** lagartera, f

llama /'lɑmə/ n llama, f

load /loud/ n carga, f; peso, m; (cart) carretada, f; Elec. carga, f; (quantity) cantidad, f. —vt cargar (con); (with honors) llenar (de); (Fig. weigh down) agobiar (con); (a stick with lead) emplomar; (Elec. and of dice) cargar; (wine) mezclar vino con un narcótico. **to be loaded with fruit,** estar cargado de fruta. **to l. oneself with,** cargarse de. **to l. the dice,** cargar los dados. **to l. again,** recargar

loader /'loudər/ n cargador, m

loading /'loudɪŋ/ n carga, f. **l. depot,** cargadero, m

loaf /louf/ n pan, m; (French) barra de pan, f. —vi golfear, vagabundear, gandulear. **l. sugar,** azúcar de pilón, m

loafer /'loufər/ n vago (-ga); azotacalles, mf; gandul (-la); golfo (-fa)

loafing /'loufɪŋ/ n gandulería, f, vagabundeo, m

loam /loum/ n marga, f

loamy /'loumi/ a margoso

loan /loun/ n empréstito, m; (lending) prestación, f; préstamo, m. —vt prestar. **l. fund,** caja de empréstitos, f. **l. company office,** casa de préstamos, f

loath /louθ/ a desinclinado, poco dispuesto

loathe /louð/ vt abominar, detestar, odiar, aborrecer; repugnar

loather /'louðər/ n el, m, (f, la) que odia; aborrecedor (-ra)

loathing /'louðɪŋ/ n aborrecimiento, odio, m; repugnancia, aversión, f

loathsome /'louðsəm/ a odioso, aborrecible; asqueroso; repugnante

loathsomeness /'louðsəmnɪs/ n carácter repugnante, m; asquerosidad, f

lobby /'lɒbi/ n pasillo, m; antecámara, f; (in a hotel, house) vestíbulo, recibidor, m; (waiting-room) sala de espera, f. —vt and vi cabildear

lobe /loub/ n Bot. lobo, m; (Anat. Archit.) lóbulo, m

lobster /'lɒbstər/ n langosta, f; bogavante, m. **l.-pot,** cambín, m, nasa, f

local /'loukəl/ a local; de la localidad. **l. anesthetic,** anestésico local, m. **l. color,** color local, m

locale /lou'kæl/ n local, m

locality /lou'kælɪti/ n localidad, f; situación, f

localization /,loukələ'zeɪʃən/ n localización, f

localize /'loukə,laɪz/ vt localizar

locate /'loukeɪt/ vt situar; colocar; localizar. **to be located,** situarse; hallarse

location /lou'keɪʃən/ n colocación, f; emplazamiento, m; localidad, f; situación, posición, f

loch /lɒk/ n lago, m

lock /lɒk/ n cerradura (of a door, including a vehicle) f; (of a gun) cerrojo, m; (in wrestling) llave, f; (on rivers, canals) presa, f; (at a dock) esclusa, f; (of hair) mechón, m, guedeja, f; (ringlet) bucle, m; pl **locks,** (hair) cabellos, m pl, pelo, m. **spring l.,** cerradura de golpe, f. **to put a l. on,** poner cerradura a. **under l. and key,** bajo cuatro llaves. **l.-jaw,** trismo, m. **l. keeper,** esclusero, m. **l.-out strike,** huelga patronal, f

lock /lɒk/ vt cerrar con llave; Fig. encerrar; (embrace) abrazar estrechamente; (of wheels, etc.) trabar; (twine) entrelazar. —vi cerrarse con llave. **to l. in,** cerrar con llave; encerrar. **to l. out,** cerrar la puerta (a); dejar en la calle (a). **to l. up,** encerrar; (imprison) encarcelar

locker /'lɒkər/ n (drawer) cajón, m; (cupboard) armario, m; Naut. cajonada, f

locket /'lɒkɪt/ n guardapelo, m; medallón, m

locksmith /'lɒk,smɪθ/ n cerrajero, m. **locksmith's trade,** cerrajería, f

locomotion /,loukə'mouʃən/ n locomoción, f

locomotive /,loukə'moutɪv/ a locomotor. —n locomotora, f

locum tenens /'loukəm 'tinɛnz/ n interino (-na)

locust /'loukəst/ n langosta migratoria, f

locution /lou'kyuʃən/ n locución, f

lode /loud/ n filón, m

lodestar /'loud,stɑr/ n estrella polar, f; Fig. norte, m

lodge /lɒdʒ/ n casita, garita, f; casa de guarda, f; (freemason's) logia, f; (porter's) portería, f, vi hospedarse, alojarse, vivir, parar; penetrar; entrar (en); fijarse (en). —vt hospedar, alojar; albergar; (a blow) asestar; (a complaint) hacer, dar; (money, etc.) depositar. **to l. an accusation against,** querellarse contra, quejarse de. **l.-keeper,** conserje, m

lodger /'lɒdʒər/ n huésped (-eda)

lodging /'lɒdʒɪŋ/ n hospedaje, alojamiento, m; (inn) posada, f; residencia, f; casa, f. **l.-house,** casa de huéspedes, f

loft /lɔft/ n desván, sotabanco, m; pajar, m

loftily /'lɔftɪli/ adv en alto; (proudly) con arrogancia, con altanería

loftiness /'lɔftɪnɪs/ n altura, f; sublimidad, f; nobleza, f; dignidad, f; (haughtiness) altanería, soberbia, f

lofty /'lɔfti/ a alto; sublime; noble; eminente; (haughty) altanero, soberbio

log /lɔg/ n madero, tronco, m; palo, m; leño, m; Naut., diario de a bordo m, barquilla, f. **to lie like a log,** estar hecho un tronco. **log-book,** Naut. cuaderno de bitácora, m. **log-cabin,** cabañas de troncos, m. **log-wood,** palo campeche, m

logarithm /'lɔgə,rɪðəm/ n logaritmo, m

logarithmic /,lɔgə'rɪðmɪk/ a logarítmico

logic /'lɒdʒɪk/ n lógica, f

logical /'lɒdʒɪkəl/ a lógico

logician /lou'dʒɪʃən/ n lógico (-ca)

loin /lɔɪn/ n ijar, m; (of meat) falda, f; pl **loins,** lomos, riñones m pl. **to gird up one's loins,** Fig. arremangarse los faldones. **l.-cloth,** taparrabo, m

loiter /'lɔɪtər/ vi vagabundear, vagar, errar; haraganear; rezagarse

loiterer /'lɔɪtərər/ n haragán (-ana); vago (-ga); rezagado (-da)

loll /lɒl/ vi recostarse (en), apoyarse (en). —vt (the tongue) sacar

Lombardy-Venetia /'lɒmbərdi və'niʃə/ Lombardo-Véneto, m

London /'lʌndən/ Londres, m

Londoner /'lʌndənər/ n londinense, mf

lone /loun/. See **lonely**

loneliness /'lounlinɪs/ n soledad, f; aislamiento, m

lonely /'lounli/ a solitario; solo; aislado, remoto; desierto

lonesome /'lounsəm/ a solo, solitario

long /lɒŋ/ *a* largo; prolongado; de largo; (extensive) extenso; (big) grande; (much) mucho. **a l. time**, mucho tiempo. **It is five feet l.**, Tiene cinco pies de largo. **l.-armed**, que tiene los brazos largos. **l.-boat**, falúa, *f.* **l. clothes**, (infant's) mantillas, *f pl.* **l.-distance call**, conferencia telefónica, *f.* **l.-distance race**, carrera de fondo, *f.* **l.-eared**, de orejas largas. **l.-faced**, de cara larga, carilargo. **l.-forgotten**, olvidado hace mucho tiempo. **l.-haired**, que tiene el pelo largo. **l.-headed**, dolicocéfalo; *Fig.* astuto, sagaz. **l.-legged**, zanquilargo, zancudo. **l.-lived**, que vive hasta una edad avanzada; longevo; duradero. **l.-lost**, perdido hace mucho tiempo. **l.-sighted**, présbita; previsor; sagaz. **l.-standing**, viejo, de muchos años. **l.-suffering**, sufrido, paciente. **l.-tailed**, de cola larga. **l.-waisted**, de talle largo. **l.-winded**, prolijo

long *long adv* mucho tiempo; mucho; durante mucho tiempo. **as l. as**, mientras (que). **before l.**, dentro de poco. **the l. and the short of it**, en resumidas cuentas. **How l. has she been here?** ¿Cuánto tiempo hace que está aquí? **not l. before**, poco tiempo antes. **l. ago**, tiempo ha, muchos años ha

long /lɒŋ/ *vi* anhelar, suspirar (por), desear con vehemencia

longanimity /ˌlɒŋɡəˈnɪmɪti/ *n* longanimidad, *f*

longer /ˈlɒŋɡər/ *a compar* más largo. —*adv compar* más tiempo. **How much l. must we wait?** ¿Cuánto tiempo más hemos de esperar? **He can no l. walk as he used**, Ya no puede andar como antes

longevity /lɒnˈdʒɛvɪti/ *n* longevidad, *f*

longing /ˈlɒŋɪŋ/ *a* anheloso, ansioso; de envidia. —*n* anhelo, *m*, ansia, *f*; deseo vehemente, *m*; envidia, *f*

longingly /ˈlɒŋɪŋli/ *adv* con ansia; impacientemente; con envidia

longish /ˈlɒŋɪʃ/ *a* algo largo

longitude /ˈlɒndʒɪˌtud/ *n* longitud, *f*

longitudinal /ˌlɒndʒɪˈtudn̩l/ *a* longitudinal

long take *n Cinema*. toma larga, *f*

loofah /ˈlufə/ *n* esponja vegetal, *f*

look /lʊk/ *n* mirada, *f*; (glance) vistazo, *m*, ojeada, *f*; (air) semblante, aire, porte, *m*; (appearance) aspecto, *m*; apariencia, *f*. **good looks**, buen parecer, *m*; guapeza, *f*. **the new l.**, la nueva línea, la nueva silueta, la nueva moda. **to be on the l.-out**, andar a la mira

look /lʊk/ *vi and vt* mirar; considerar, contemplar; (appear, seem) parecer; tener aire (de); tener aspecto (de); hacer el efecto (de); (show oneself) mostrarse; (of buildings, etc.) caer (a), dar (a); mirar (a).; (seem to be) revelar (e.g., You don't l. thirty, No revelas treinta años) **to l. alike**, parecerse. **to l. hopeful**, *Fig.* prometer bien. **to l. out of the corner of the eye**, mirar de reojo. **to l.** (a person) **up and down**, mirar de hito en hito. **to l. about one**, mirar a su alrededor; observar. **to l. after**, tener la mirada puesta en, mirar; (care for) cuidar; (watch) vigilar; mirar por. **to l. at**, mirar; considerar; examinar. **He looked at his watch**, Miró su reloj. **He looked at her**, La miró. **to l. away**, desviar los ojos, apartar la mirada. **to l. back**, mirar hacia atrás, volver la cabeza; (in thought) pensar en el pasado. **to l. down**, bajar los ojos; mirar el suelo; mirar hacia abajo. **to l. down upon**, dominar, mirar a; (scorn) despreciar; mirar de arriba para abajo. **to l. for**, buscar; buscar con los ojos; (await) aguardar; (expect) esperar. **to l. forward**, mirar hacia el porvenir; pensar en el futuro; esperar con ilusión. **to l. in**, entrar por un instante, hacer una visita corta. **to l. into**, mirar dentro de; mirar hacia el interior de; estudiar, investigar. **to l. on**, *vt* mirar; considerar; (of buildings, etc.) dar a. —*vi* ser espectador. **to l. on to**, dar a, mirar a. **to l. out**, *vi* (be careful) tener cuidado; (look through) mirar por; asomarse a. —*vt* (search) buscar; (find) hallar; (choose) escoger, elegir. **L. out!** ¡Atención! ¡Ojo! **to l. out for**, buscar; (await) aguardar, esperar; (be careful) tener cuidado con. **to l. out of**, mirar por; asomarse a. **to l. over**, mirar bien; (persons) mirar de hito en hito; examinar; visitar; (a house) inspeccionar; (a book) hojear; mirar superficialmente. **to l. round**, *vt* (a place) visitar. —*vi* volver la cabeza, volverse; mirar hacia atrás. **to l. round for**, buscar con los ojos; buscar por todas partes. **to l. through**, mirar por; mirar a través de; examinar;

(search) registrar; (understand) registrar. **to l. to**, (be careful of) tener cuidado de; (attend to) atender a; (care for) cuidar de; (count on) contar con; (resort to) acudir a; (await) esperar. **to l. toward**, mirar hacia, mirar en la dirección de; caer a. **to l. up**, *vi* mirar hacia arriba; (aspire) aspirar; (improve) mejorar. —*vt* visitar, ir (or venir) a ver; (turn up) buscar; averiguar. **to l. upon**, mirar. Other meanings see to l. on. **They l. upon her as their daughter**, La miran como una hija suya. **to l. up to**, *Fig.* respetar

looked-for /ˈlʊkt ˌfɔr/ *a* esperado; deseado

looking /ˈlʊkɪŋ/ *a* (in compounds) de... aspecto, de... apariencia. **dirty-l.**, de aspecto sucio. **l.-glass**, espejo, *m*

lookout /ˈlʊkˌaʊt/ *n* vigilancia, observación, *f*; (view) vista, *f*, panorama, *m*; (viewpoint) miradero, *m*; *Mil.* atalaya, *m*; *Naut.* gaviero, *m*; (Fig. prospect) perspectiva, *f*

loom /lum/ *n* telar, *m*, *vi* asomar, aparecer

loop /lup/ *n* (turn) vuelta, *f*; (in rivers, etc.) recodo, *m*, curva, *f*; (fold) pliegue, *m*; bucle, *m*; (fastening) fiador, *m*, presilla, *f*; *Aer.* rizo, *m*; (knot) nudo corredizo, *m*. **to l. the l.**, *Aer.* hacer el rizo, hacer rizos. **l.-line**, empalme de ferrocarril, *m*

loophole /ˈlupˌhoʊl/ *n* saetera, aspillera, *f*; *Fig.* escapatoria, *f*; pretexto, *m*, excusa, *f*

loose /lus/ *a* suelto; (free) libre; (slack) flojo; (of garments) holgado; (untied) desatado; (unfastened) desprendido; movible; (unchained) desencadenado; en libertad; (of the bowels) suelto (de vientre); (pendulous) colgante; (of a nail, tooth, etc.) inseguro; poco firme; que se mueve; (of knots, etc.) flojo; (of the mind, etc.) incoherente, ilógico; poco exacto; (of style, etc.) vago, impreciso; (of conduct) disoluto, vicioso; (careless) negligente, descuidado. —*vt* (untie) desatar; desprender; soltar; aflojar; (of a priest) absolver; *Fig.* desencadenar. **to break l.**, desprenderse; soltarse; libertarse; escapar; *Fig.* desencadenarse. **to let l.**, desatar; aflojar; poner en libertad; soltar; *Fig.* desencadenar; (interject) lanzar. **to turn l.**, poner en libertad; dar salida (a); echar de casa, poner en la calle. **to work l.**, desprenderse; aflojarse; desvenciarse. **l.-box**, caballeriza, *f.* **l. change**, suelto, *m.* **l.-leaf notebook**, libreta de hojas sueltas, *f*

loosely /ˈlusli/ *adv* flojamente; sueltamente; (vaguely) vagamente; incorrectamente; incoherentemente; (carelessly) negligentemente; (viciously) disolutamente

loosen /ˈlusən/ *vt* (untie) desatar; aflojar; soltar; desasir; (the tongue) desatar; *Fig.* hacer menos riguroso, ablandar

looseness /ˈlusnɪs/ *n* flojedad, *f*; (of clothing) holgura, *f*; soltura, *f*; relajación, *f*; (of the bowels) diarrea, *f*; (viciousness) licencia, *f*, libertinaje, *m*; (vagueness) vaguedad, *f*; incoherencia, *f*

loosening /ˈlusənɪŋ/ *n* desprendimiento, *m*; desasimiento, *m*; aflojamiento, *m*

loot /lut/ *n* botín, *m*, *vt* saquear

looter /ˈlutər/ *n* saqueador (-ra)

looting /ˈlutɪŋ/ *n* saqueo, pillaje, *m*, *a* saqueador

lop /lɒp/ *vt* mochar; podar; destroncar; cortar de un golpe. —*a* (of ears) gacho. **to lop off the ends**, cercenar. **to lop off the top**, desmochar. **lop-sided**, desproporcionado; desequilibrado

lopping /ˈlɒpɪŋ/ *n* desmoche, *m*; poda, *f*

loquacious /loʊˈkweɪʃəs/ *a* locuaz, garrulo

loquacity /loʊˈkwæsɪti/ *n* locuacidad, garrulidad, *f*

lord /lɔrd/ *n* señor, *m*; (husband) esposo, *m*; (English title) lord, *m*, (pl lores) (Christ) Señor, *m.* **feudal l.**, señor de horca y cuchillo, *m.* **my l.**, milord. **my lords**, milores. **Our L.**, Nuestro Señor. **the Lord's Prayer**, el Padrenuestro. **to l. it over**, mandar como señor, mandar a la baqueta. **L. Chamberlain**, camarero mayor, *m.* **L. Chancellor**, gran canciller, *m.* **L. Chief Justice**, presidente del tribunal supremo, *m.* **L.-Lieutenant**, virrey, *m.* **L. Mayor**, alcalde, *m.* **L. Privy Seal**, guardasellos del rey, *m*

lordliness /ˈlɔrdlɪnɪs/ *n* suntuosidad, *f*; liberalidad, munificencia, *f*; dignidad, *f*; (haughtiness) altivez, arrogancia, *f*

lordly /ˈlɔrdli/ *a* señorial, señoril; altivo, arrogante

lordship /'lɔrdʃɪp/ n señoría, f; señorío, poder, m. **his l.,** su señoría

lore /lɔr/ n saber, m; erudición, f; tradiciones, f pl

lorgnette /lɔrn'yet/ n impertinentes, m pl

lorry /'lɔri/ n camión, m; carro, m

lose /luz/ vt perder; hacer perder, quitar; (forget) olvidar. —vi perder; (of clocks) atrasar. **to be lost in thought,** estar ensimismado, estar absorto. **to l. one-self (in)** perderse (en); abstraerse (en); entregarse (a). **to l. one's footing,** resbalar. **to l. one's way,** extraviarse, perder el camino. **to l. one's self-control,** perder el tino. **to l. one's head,** perder la cabeza. **to l. ground,** perder terreno. **to l. one's voice,** perder la voz. **to l. patience,** perder la paciencia, perder los estribos

loser /'luzər/ n perdedor (-ra)

losing /'luzɪŋ/ a perdedor. —n pérdida, f

loss /lɔs/ n pérdida, f. **at a l.,** Com. con pérdida; perplejo, dudoso. **heavy losses,** Mil. pérdidas cuantiosas, f pl. **We are at a l. for words...,** No tenemos palabras para...

lot /lɒt/ n suerte, f; fortuna, f; lote, m; parte, porción, cuota, f; (for building) solar, m. **a lot of people,** muchas personas. **Our lot would have been very different,** Nuestra suerte hubiera sido muy distinta, Otro gallo nos cantara. **to draw lots,** echar suertes, sortear. **to take the lot,** Inf. alzarse con el santo y la limosna

lotion /'louʃən/ n loción, f

lottery /'lɒtəri/ n lotería, f. **l. ticket,** billete de la lotería, m

lotus /'loutəs/ n loto, m. **l.-eating,** lotofagía, f; Fig. indolencia, pereza, f

loud /laud/ a fuerte; (noisy) ruidoso, estrepitoso; alto; (gaudy) chillón, llamativo, cursi. —adv ruidosamente. **l.-speaker,** Radio. altavoz, altoparlante, m

loudly /'laudli/ adv en alta voz; fuertemente; ruidosamente, con estrépito

loudness /'laudnɪs/ n (noise) ruido, m; sonoridad, f; (force) fuerza, f; (of colors, etc.) mal gusto, m, vulgaridad, f

lounge /laundʒ/ n sala de estar, f; salón, m, vi reclinarse, ponerse a sus anchas; apoyarse (en); gandulear; vagar. **l. chair,** poltrona, f. **l.-lizard,** Inf. pollo pera, m. **l.-suit,** traje americano, m

lounger /'laundʒər/ n holgazán (-ana); golfo (-fa), azotacalles, mf

louse /laus/ n piojo, m

lousy /'lauzi/ a piojoso

lout /laut/ n patán, zamacuco, m

loutish /'lautɪʃ/ a rústico

lovable /'lʌvəbəl/ a amable; simpático

lovableness /'lʌvəbəlnɪs/ n amabilidad, f

love /lʌv/ n amor, m; (friendship) amistad, f; (enthusiasm, liking) afición, f; (in tennis) cero, m, vt querer, amar; gustar mucho; tener afición (a). —vi estar enamorado. **I should l. to dine with you,** Me gustaría mucho cenar con Vds. **to be in l. with,** estar enamorado de. **to fall in l. with,** enamorarse de. **They l. each other,** Se quieren. **to make l. to,** hacer el amor (a), galantear. **l. affair,** amorío, lance de amor, m. **l.-bird,** periquito, m. **l.-letter,** carta amatoria, carta de amor, f. **l.-making,** galanteo, m. **l.-philtre,** filtro, m. **l.-song,** canción de amor, f. **l.-story,** historia de amor, f. **l.-token,** prenda de amor, f

loveless /'lʌvlɪs/ a sin amor

loveliness /'lʌvlinɪs/ n hermosura, belleza, f; encanto, m; amabilidad, f

lovely /'lʌvli/ a hermoso, bello; delicioso; amable; Inf. estupendo

lover /'lʌvər/ n amante, mf; aficionado (-da)

lovesick /'lʌv,sɪk/ a enfermo de amor, enamorado

loving /'lʌvɪŋ/ a amoroso, cariñoso; (friendly) amistoso; de amor

low /lou/ a bajo; de poca altura; (of dresses, etc.) escotado; (of musical notes) grave; (soft) suave; (feeble) débil; (depressed) deprimido, triste, abatido; (plain) sencillo; (of a fever) lento; (of a bow) profundo; pequeño; inferior; humilde; (ill) enfermo; (vile) vil, ruin; obsceno, escabroso. —adv bajo; cerca de la tierra; en voz baja; (cheaply) barato, a bajo pre-

cio. **in a low voice,** en voz baja, paso. **to lay low,** (kill) tumbar; (knock down) derribar; incapacitar. **to lie low,** descansar; estar muerto; esconderse, agacharse; callar. **to run low,** escasear. **low-born,** de humilde cuna. **low-brow,** nada intelectual. **low comedy,** farsa, f. **low flying,** n bajo vuelo, m, a que vuela bajo; terrero, rastrero; que vuela a ras de tierra. **low frequency,** baja frecuencia, f. **low Latin,** bajo latín, m. **Low Mass,** misa rezada, f. **low neck,** escote, m. **low-necked,** escotado. **low-pitched,** grave. **low-spirited,** deprimido. **Low Sunday,** domingo de Cuasimodo, m. **low tension,** baja tensión, f. **low trick,** mala pasada, f. **low water,** marea baja, bajamar, f; (of rivers) estiaje, m

low /lou/ vi berrear, mugir. —n berrido, mugido, m

low-ceiling /'lou 'silɪŋ/ a bajo de techo.

Low Countries, the Los Países Bajos, m

lower /'louər/ vt bajar; descolgar; disminuir; (price) rebajar; (a boat, sails) arriar. —vi (of persons) fruncir el ceño, mostrarse malhumorado; (of the sky) encapotarse, cargarse; (menace) amenazar. **to l. a boat,** arriar un bote. **to l. oneself,** (by a rope, etc.) descolgarse. **to l. the flag,** abatir la bandera

lower /'louər/ a comparative más bajo; menos alto; bajo; inferior. **l. classes,** clase obrera, f, clases bajas, f pl. **l. down,** más abajo. **L. House,** Cámara de los Comunes, f; cámara baja, f. **l. jaw,** mandíbula inferior, f. **l. storey,** piso bajo, m; piso de abajo, m

lowering /'louərɪŋ/ n abajamiento, m; descenso, m; (of prices) baja, f; (of a boat) arriada, f; (of the flag) abatimiento, m, a (of persons) ceñudo; (of the sky) anublado, encapotado; (threatening) amenazador

lowest /'louɪst/ a superl el (la, etc.) más bajo; el (la, etc.) más profundo; ínfimo

lowing /'louɪŋ/ n berrido, mugido, m

lowland /'loulənd/ n tierra baja, f. **the Lowlands,** las tierras bajas de Escocia

lowliness /'loulɪnɪs/ n humildad, f; modestia, f

lowly /'louli/ a humilde

lowness /'lounɪs/ n poca altura, f; situación poco elevada, f; pequeñez, f; (of musical notes) gravedad, f; (softness) suavidad, f; (feebleness) debilidad, f; (sadness) tristeza, f, abatimiento, m; (of price) baratura, f; inferioridad, f; humildad, f; (vileness) bajeza, f; obscenidad, f

loyal /'lɔiəl/ a leal, fiel

loyalist /'lɔiəlɪst/ n realista, mf; defensor (-ra) del gobierno legítimo

loyalty /'lɔiəlti/ n lealtad, fidelidad, f

loyalty oath n (approximate equivalent) certificado de adhesión, m

lozenge /'lɒzɪndʒ/ n pastilla, f

lubricant /'lubrɪkənt/ a and n lubricante m

lubricate /'lubrɪ,keit/ vt lubricar, engrasar

lubricating oil n aceite lubricante, m

lubrication /,lubrɪ'keiʃən/ n lubricación, f, engrasado, m

lubricator /'lubrɪ,keitər/ n lubricador, m; engrasador, m

Lucerne /lu'sɜrn/ Lucerna, f

lucid /'lusɪd/ a lúcido; claro

lucidity /lu'sɪdɪti/ n lucidez, f; claridad, f

lucidly /'lusɪdli/ adv claramente

luck /lʌk/ n destino, azar, m; (good) buenaventura, suerte, f. **to bring bad l.,** traer mala suerte. **to try one's l.,** probar fortuna

luckily /'lʌkəli/ adv por fortuna, afortunadamente, felizmente

luckless /'lʌklɪs/ a desdichado

lucky /'lʌki/ a afortunado; dichoso, venturoso; feliz. **to be l.,** tener buena suerte

lucrative /'lukrətɪv/ a lucrativo

lucre /'lukər/ n lucro, m

lucubration /,lukyu'breiʃən/ n lucubración, f

ludicrous /'ludɪkrəs/ a absurdo, risible, ridículo

ludicrousness /'ludɪkrəsnɪs/ n ridiculez, f

lug /lʌg/ n tirón, m; (ear and projection) oreja, f, vt tirar de; arrastrar. **to lug about,** arrastrar (por); llevar con dificultad. **to lug in,** arrastrar adentro; introducir; hacer entrar. **to lug out,** arrastrar afuera; hacer salir

luggage /'lʌgɪdʒ/ n equipaje, m. **excess l.,** exceso de equipaje, *m.* **piece of I.,** bulto, *m.* **to register one's I.,** facturar el equipaje. **I. carrier,** (on buses, etc.) baca, *f;* (on a car) portaequipajes, *m.* **I. porter,** mozo de equipajes, *m.* **I. rack,** (on a car) portaequipajes, *m;* (in a train) rejilla para el equipaje, *f.* **I. receipt,** talón de equipaje, *m.* **I. room,** consigna, *f.* **I. van,** furgón de equipajes, *m*

lugubrious /lu'gubriəs/ *a* lúgubre

lukewarm /'luk'wɔrm/ *a* tibio, templado; *Fig.* indiferente, frío

lukewarmness /'luk'wɔrmnɪs/ *n* tibieza, *f; Fig.* indiferencia, frialdad, *f*

lull /lʌl/ *n* momento de calma, *m;* tregua, *f;* silencio, *m, vt* (a child) arrullar, adormecer; (soothe) sosegar, calmar; disminuir, mitigar

lullaby /'lʌlə,bai/ *n* canción de cuna, *f*

lumbago /lʌm'beigou/ *n* lumbago, *m*

lumbar /'lʌmbər/ *a* lumbar

lumber /'lʌmbər/ *n* (wood) maderas de sierra, *f pl;* (rubbish) trastos viejos, *m pl.* —*vt* amontonar trastos viejos; obstruir. —*vi* andar pesadamente; avanzar ruidosamente, avanzar con ruido sordo. **I.-jack,** maderero, ganchero, *m.* **I.-room,** leonera, *f.* **I.-yard,** maderería, *f,* depósito de maderas, *m*

lumbering /'lʌmbəriŋ/ *a* pesado

luminary /'lumə,nɛri/ *n* lumbrera, *f*

luminosity /,lumə'nɒsɪti/ *n* luminosidad, *f*

luminous /'lumənəs/ *a* luminoso

lump /lʌmp/ *n* masa, *f;* bulto, *m;* pedazo, *m;* (of sugar) terrón *m;* (swelling) hinchazón, *f;* protuberancia, *f.* —*vt* amontonar. **to I. together,** mezclar; incluir. **in the I.,** en la masa; en grueso. **Let him I. it!** ¡Que se rasque! **I. in one's throat,** nudo en la garganta, *m.* **I. of sugar,** terrón de azúcar, *m.* **I. sum,** cantidad gruesa, *f*

lumpishness /'lʌmpɪʃnɪs/ *n* hobachonería, *f*

lunacy /'lunəsi/ *n* locura, *f*

lunar /'lunər/ *a* lunar

lunatic /'lunətɪk/ *n* loco (-ca); demente, *mf a* de locos; loco. **I. asylum,** manicomio, *m*

lunch, luncheon /lʌntʃ; 'lʌntʃən;/ *n* almuerzo, *m;* (snack) merienda, *f.* —*vi* almorzar. **I. basket** or **pail,** fiambrera, *f*

lunette /lu'nɛt/ *n* (*Archit. Mil.*) luneta, *f*

lung /lʌŋ/ *n* pulmón, *m*

lunge /lʌndʒ/ *n* (fencing) estocada, *f;* embestida, *f, vi* dar una estocada; abalanzarse sobre

lurch /lɜrtʃ/ *n* sacudida, *f; Naut.* guiñada, *f;* tambaleo, *m;* movimiento brusco, *m.* —*vi* *Naut.* guiñar; tambalearse; andar haciendo eses. **to leave in the I.,** dejar plantado

lure /lur/ *n* añagaza, *f;* reclamo, *m;* aliciente, atractivo, *m;* seducción, *f.* —*vt* atraer, tentar

lurid /'lurɪd/ *a* misterioso, fantástico; cárdeno; ominoso; funesto, triste; (orange) anaranjado; (vicissitudinous) accidentado

lurk /lɜrk/ *vi* acechar, espiar; esconderse

lurking /'lɜrkɪŋ/ *a* (in ambush) en acecho; (of fear, etc.) vago

luscious /'lʌʃəs/ *a* delicioso; suculento; meloso; atractivo, apetitoso; sensual

lusciousness /'lʌʃəsnɪs/ *n* suculencia, *f;* melosidad, *f;* atractivo, *m;* sensualidad, *f*

lush /lʌʃ/ *a* jugoso; fresco y lozano; maduro

lust /lʌst/ *n* lujuria, lascivia, *f;* codicia, *f;* deseo, *m.* **I. for revenge,** deseo de venganza, *m*

luster /'lʌstər/ *n* lustre, brillo, *m;* brillantez, *f*

lusterless /'lʌstərlɪs/ *a* sin brillo; mate, deslustrado; (of eyes) apagado

lustful /'lʌstfəl/ *a* lujurioso, lúbrico, lascivo

lustrous /'lʌstrəs/ *a* lustroso

lusty /'lʌsti/ *a* vigoroso, fuerte, lozano

lute /lut/ *n* laúd, *m,* vihuela, *f.* **I.-player,** vihuelista, *mf*

Lutheran /'luθərən/ *a* luterano. —*n* luterano (-na)

Lutheranism /'luθərə,nɪzəm/ *n* luteranismo, *m*

luxation /lʌk'seiʃən/ *n* luxación, *f*

Luxembourg /'lʌksəm,bɔrg/ Luxemburgo, *m*

luxuriance /lʌg'ʒuriəns/ *n* lozanía, *f;* exuberancia, superabundancia, *f*

luxuriant /lʌg'ʒuriənt/ *a* lozano; fértil; exuberante

luxuriate /lʌg'ʒuri,eit/ *vi* crecer con exuberancia; complacerse (en); disfrutar (de), gozar (de)

luxurious /lʌg'ʒuriəs/ *a* lujoso

luxuriously /lʌg'ʒuriəsli/ *adv* lujosamente, con lujo

luxury /'lʌkʃəri/ *n* lujo, *m.* **I. goods,** artículos de lujo, *m pl*

lyceum /lai'siəm/ *n* liceo, *m*

lye /lai/ *n* lejía, *f*

lying /'laiiŋ/ *a* (recumbent) recostado; (untrue) mentiroso, falso. —*n* mentiras, *f pl.* **I.-in,** parto, *m*

lymph /lɪmf/ *n* linfa, *f;* vacuna, *f*

lymphatic /lɪm'fætɪk/ *a* linfático; flemático

lynch /lɪntʃ/ *vt* linchar

lynching /'lɪntʃɪŋ/ *n* linchamiento, *m*

lynx /lɪŋks/ *n* lince, *m.* **I.-eyed,** de ojos de lince

lyre /'laiᵊr/ *n* lira, *f.* **I.-bird,** pájaro lira, *m*

lyric /'lɪrɪk/ *n* poesía lírica, *f;* poema lírico *m;* letra (de una canción,) *f*

lyrical /'lɪrɪkəl/ *a* lírico

lyricism /'lɪrə,sɪzəm/ *n* lirismo, *m*

M

m /ɛm/ n (letter) eme, f
ma'am /mæm/ n señora, f
macabre /məˈkɑbrə/ a macabro
macadam /məˈkædəm/ n macadán, m, a de macadán
macadamize /məˈkædəˌmaiz/ vt macadanizar
macaroni /ˌmækəˈrouni/ n macarrones, m pl
macaronic /ˌmækəˈrɒnɪk/ a macarrónico
macaroon /ˌmækəˈrun/ n macarrón de almendras, m
Macassar oil /məˈkæsər/ n aceite de Macasar, m
macaw /məˈkɔ/ n macagua, f, guacamayo, m
mace /meis/ n maza, f; Cul. macis, f. m.-bearer, macero, m
Macedonian /ˌmæsɪˈdouniən/ a macedón, macedonio. —n macedonio (-ia)
macerate /ˈmæsəˌreit/ vt macerar. —vi macerarse
Machiavellian /ˌmækiəˈveliən/ a maquiavélico
Machiavellism /ˌmækiəˈvelɪzəm/ n maquiavelismo, m
machination /ˌmækəˈneiʃən/ n maquinación, f
machine /məˈʃin/ n máquina, f; mecanismo, m; aparato, m; instrumento, m; organización, f, vt trabajar a máquina; Sew. coser a máquina. m.-gun, n ametralladora, f. —vt ametrallar. m.-gun carrier, portametralladoras, m. m.-gunner, ametrallador, m. m.-made, hecho a máquina. m. needle, brújula, f m.-shop, taller de maquinaria, m. m.-tool, máquina herramienta, f
machinery /məˈʃinəri/ n maquinaria, f; mecanismo, m; organización, f; sistema, m
machinist /məˈʃinɪst/ n maquinista, mf; Sew. costurera a máquina, f
mackerel /ˈmækərəl/ n caballa, f. m. sky, cielo aborregado, m
mackintosh /ˈmækɪnˌtɒʃ/ n impermeable, m
macrocosm /ˈmækrəˌkɒzəm/ n macrocosmo, m
mad /mæd/ a loco; fuera de sí; (of a dog, etc.) rabioso; furioso. as mad as a hatter, loco como una cabra. to drive mad, volver loco (a). to go mad, volverse loco, enloquecer, perder el seso. mad with joy (pain), loco de alegría (dolor). mad dog, perro rabioso, m
madam /ˈmædəm/ n señora, f; (French form) madama, f. Yes, m., Sí señora
madcap /ˈmædˌkæp/ n locuelo (-la), f, botarate, m; tarambana, mf
madden /ˈmædn/ vt enloquecer; enfurecer, exasperar
maddening /ˈmædnɪŋ/ a exasperante, irritador
madder /ˈmædər/ n Bot. rubia, f
made /meid/ past part and a hecho; formado. self-m. man, un hombre hecho y derecho. m.-to-measure, hecho a la medida. m.-up, compuesto; (of clothes) confeccionado, ya hecho; (of the face) pintado; (fictitious) inventado, ficticio; artificial
Madeira /məˈdɪərə/ n vino de Madera, m, a de Madera
madhouse /ˈmædˌhaus/ n casa de locos, f, manicomio, m
madly /ˈmædli/ adv locamente; furiosamente
madman /ˈmædˌmæn/ n loco, m
madness /ˈmædnɪs/ n locura, f; (of a dog, etc.) rabia, f; furia, f
Madonna /məˈdɒnə/ n Madona, f
madrigal /ˈmædrɪgəl/ n madrigal, m
Madrilenian /ˌmædrəˈliniən/ a madrileño, matritense. —n madrileño (-ña)
madwoman /ˈmædˌwʊmən/ n loca, f
Maecenas /miˈsinəs/ n mecenas, m
maelstrom /ˈmeilstrəm/ n remolino, vórtice, m
magazine /ˌmægəˈzin/ n (store) almacén, m; (for explosives) polvorín, m, santabárbara, f; (periodical) revista, f. m. rifle, rifle de repetición, m
Magdalene /ˈmægdəˌlin/ n magdalena, f
magenta /məˈdʒɛntə/ n color magenta, m
maggot /ˈmægət/ n gusano, m, cresa, f; Fig. manía, f, capricho, m
maggoty /ˈmægəti/ a gusanoso
magic /ˈmædʒɪk/ n magia, f; mágica, f; Fig. encanto, m,

m, a mágico. as if by m., por ensalmo. m. lantern, linterna mágica, f
magically /ˈmædʒɪkli/ adv por encanto
magician /məˈdʒɪʃən/ n mago, mágico, brujo, m; (conjurer) jugador de manos, m
magisterial /ˌmædʒəˈstɪəriəl/ a magistral
magistracy /ˈmædʒəstrəsi/ n magistratura, f
magistrate /ˈmædʒəˌstreit/ n magistrado, m; juez municipal, m
Magi, the /ˈmeidʒai/ n pl los reyes magos
Magna Carta /ˈmægnə ˈkartə/ n Carta Magna, f
magnanimity /ˌmægnəˈnɪmɪti/ n magnanimidad, generosidad, f
magnanimous /mægˈnænəməs/ a magnánimo, generoso
magnanimously /mægˈnænəməsli/ adv magnánimamente
magnate /ˈmægneit/ n magnate, m
magnesia /mægˈniʒə/ n magnesia, f
magnesium /mægˈniziəm/ n magnesio, m. m. light, luz de magnesio, f
magnet /ˈmægnɪt/ n imán, m
magnetic /mægˈnɛtɪk/ a magnético; Fig. atractivo. m. field, campo magnético, m. m. needle, brújula, f
magnetics /mægˈnɛtɪks/ n la ciencia del magnetismo, f
magnetism /ˈmægnɪˌtɪzəm/ n magnetismo, m
magnetization /ˌmægnɪtɪˈzeiʃən/ n imanación, magnetización, f
magnetize /ˈmægnɪˌtaiz/ vt magnetizar, imanar; (hypnotize) magnetizar; Fig. atraer
magnification /ˌmægnəfɪˈkeiʃən/ n (by a lens, etc.) aumento, m; exageración, f
magnificence /mægˈnɪfəsəns/ n magnificencia, f
magnificent /mægˈnɪfəsənt/ a magnífico
magnify /ˈmægnəˌfai/ vt (by lens) aumentar; exagerar; (praise) magnificar
magnifying /ˈmægnəˌfaiɪŋ/ a de aumento, vidrio de aumento. m. glass, lente de aumento, m
magniloquence /mægˈnɪləkwəns/ n grandilocuencia, f
magniloquent /mægˈnɪləkwənt/ a grandílocuo
magnitude /ˈmægnɪˌtud/ n magnitud, f
magnolia /mægˈnoulyə/ n magnolia, f
magnum /ˈmægnəm/ n botella de dos litros, f
magpie /ˈmægˌpai/ n marica, picaza, f
maharajah /ˌmɑhəˈradʒə/ n maharajá, m
mahogany /məˈhɒgəni/ n caoba, f, a de caoba
maid /meid/ n doncella, muchacha, f; virgen, f; soltera, f; (servant) criada, f; (daily) asistenta, f. old m., solterona, f. m.-of-all-work, criada para todo, f. m.-of-honor, dama de honor, f
maiden /ˈmeidn/ n doncella, joven, soltera, f; virgen, f; zagala, f. —a de soltera; soltera f; virginal; (of speeches, voyages, etc.) primero. m. lady, dama soltera, f. m.-name, apellido de soltera, m. m. speech, primer discurso, m
maidenhood /ˈmeidnˌhʊd/ n doncellez, virginidad, f
maidenly /ˈmeidnli/ a virginal; modesto, modoso; tímido
maidservant /ˈmeidˌsərvənt/ n criada, sirvienta, f
mail /meil/ n mala, f; (bag) valija, f; correo, m; correspondencia, f; (armour) cota de malla, f. —vt mandar por correo; armar con cota de malla. coat of m., cota de malla, f. m. royal m., malla real, f. m.-bag, valija de correo, f; portacartas, m. m.-boat, buque correo, m. m.-cart, ambulancia de correos, f. m.-clad, vestido de cota de malla; armado. m.-coach, coche correo, m; diligencia, f. m.-order, pedido postal, m. m.-order business, negocio de ventas por correo, m. m.-plane, avión postal, m. m. service, servicio de correos, m. m. steamer, vapor correo, m. m. train, tren correo, m. m. van, (on a train) furgón postal, m
mailed /meild/ a de malla; armado. m. fist, Fig. puño de hierro, m
maim /meim/ vt mancar; mutilar, tullir; estropear

maimed /meimd/ a manco; tullido, mutilado
main /mein/ a mayor; principal; más importante,
esencial; maestro. —n (mainland) continente, m;
(sea) océano, m; (pipe) cañería maestra, f. **by m.
force,** por fuerza mayor. **in the m.,** en general, generalmente; en su mayoría. **m. beam,** viga maestra, f.
m. body, (of a building) ala principal, f; (of a
church) cuerpo (de iglesia), m; (of an army) cuerpo
(del ejército), m; mayor parte, mayoría, f. **m. line,**
línea principal, f. **m. mast,** palo mayor, m. **m. thing,**
cosa principal, f, lo más importante. **m. wall,** pared
maestra, f
mainland /'mein,lænd/ n continente, m; tierra firme,
f
mainly /'meinli/ adv principalmente; en su mayoría;
generalmente
mainsail /'mein,seil/ n vela mayor, f
mainspring /'mein,sprɪŋ/ n (of a watch) muelle real,
m; motivo principal, m; origen, m
mainstay /'mein,stei/ n estay mayor, m; Fig. sostén
principal, m
maintain /mein'tein/ vt mantener; sostener; tener;
guardar; afirmar
maintainable /mein'teinəbəl/ a sostenible; defendible
maintenance /'meintənəns/ n mantenimiento, m;
manutención, f, sustento, m; conservación, f, subsistencia, f
maize /meiz/ n maíz, m. **m. field,** maizal, m
majestic /mə'dʒɛstɪk/ a majestuoso
majesty /'mædʒəsti/ n majestad, f; majestuosidad, f.
His or **Her M.,** Su Majestad
majolica /mə'dʒɒlɪkə/ n mayólica, f
major /'meidʒər/ a mayor; principal. —n mayor de
edad, m; Mil. comandante. **anthropology major,**
alumno con la especialidad en antropología m. **m.-
domo,** mayordomo, m. **m.-general,** general de división, m. **m. road,** carretera, f; ruta de prioridad, f. **m.
scale,** escala mayor, f
Majorca /mə'dʒɔrkə/ Mallorca, f
majority /mə'dʒɒrɪti/ n mayoría, f; mayor número,
m; generalidad, f. **to have attained one's m.,** ser
mayor de edad
make /meik/ vt hacer; crear, formar; (manufacture)
fabricar, confeccionar; construir; (produce) producir;
causar; (prepare) preparar; (a bed, a fire, a remark,
poetry, friends, enemies, war, a curtsey) hacer; (earn,
win) ganar; (a speech) pronunciar; (compel) obligar
(a), forzar (a); inclinar (a); (arrive at) alcanzar, llegar
(a); (calculate) calcular; (arrange) arreglar; deducir;
(be) ser; (equal) ser igual a; (think) creer; (appoint
as) constituir (en), hacer; (behave) portarse (como).
—vi (begin) ir (a), empezar (a); (make as though)
hacer (como si); (of the tide) crecer; contribuir (a);
tender (a). **He made as if to go,** Hizo como si de
marcharse. **to m. as though...,** aparentar, fingir. **It
made me ill,** Me hizo sentir mal. **They have made it
up,** Han hecho las paces. **They m. a great deal of
money,** Hacen (or ganan) mucho dinero. **You cannot
m. me believe it,** No puedes hacerme creerlo. **He is
making himself ridiculous,** Se está poniendo en
ridículo. **to m. ready,** preparar. **to m. the tea,** hacer
el té; preparar el té. **Two and two m. four,** Dos y
dos son cuatro. **to m. oneself known,** darse a conocer. **to m. one of...,** ser uno de... **to m. after,**
seguir; correr detrás de. **to m. again,** hacer de
nuevo, rehacer. **to m. away with,** quitar; suprimir;
destruir; (kill) matar; (squander) derrochar; (steal)
llevarse; hurtar. **to m. away with oneself,** quitarse
la vida, suicidarse. **to m. for,** encaminarse a, dirigirse
a; (attack) abalanzarse sobre, atacar; (tend to) contribuir a, tender a. **to m. off,** marcharse corriendo, largarse; huir, escaparse. **to m. out,** (discern) distinguir;
descifrar; (understand) comprender; (prove) probar,
justificar; (draw up) redactar; (fill in a form) completar, llenar; (a check, etc.) extender; (an account)
hacer; (get on, succeed or otherwise) ir (with bien or
mal); (convey) dar la impresión de que; sugerir. **I
cannot m. it out,** No lo puedo comprender. **How did
you m. out** (get on)**?** ¿Cómo te fue? **to m. over,**
hacer de nuevo, rehacer; (transfer) ceder, traspasar.
to m. up, hacer; acabar; concluir; (clothes) confec-

cionar; fabricar; (the face) pintarse, maquillarse; (the
fire) echar carbón, etc. a; Print. compaginar; (invent)
inventar; (lies) fabricar; (compose) formar; (package)
empaquetar; reparar; indemnizar; compensar; (an account) ajustar; preparar; arreglar; (conciliate) conciliar; enumerar; Theat. caracterizarse. **to m. up for,**
reemplazar; compensar; (lost time, etc.) recobrar. **to
m. up to,** compensar; indemnizar; (flatter) adular,
halagar; procurar congraciarse con, procurar obtener
el favor de; (court) galantear (con). **m. an impression (on),** dejar(le a fulano) una impresión
make /meik/ n forma, f; hechura, f; estructura, f;
confección, f; manufactura, f; producto, m; (trade
name) marca, f; (character) carácter, temperamento,
m. **m.-believe,** n artificio, pretexto, m, a fingido, vi
fingir. **land of m.-believe,** reino de los sueños, m. **m.
-up,** (for the face, etc.) maquillaje, m; Theat. caracterización, f; Print. imposición, f; (whole) conjunto, m;
(character) carácter, modo de ser, m
maker /'meikər/ n creador, m; autor (-ra); artífice,
mf; (manufacturer) fabricante, m; constructor, m; (of
clothes, etc.) confeccionador (-ra); (worker) obrero
(-ra)
makeshift /'meik,ʃɪft/ n expediente, m, a provisional
makeweight /'meik,weit/ n añadidura (de peso), f,
contrapeso, m; Fig. suplente, m
making /'meikɪŋ/ n creación, f; hechura, f; (manufacture) fabricación, f; construcción, f; (of clothes,
etc.) confección, f; formación, f; preparación, f; estructura, f; composición, f; pl **makings,** (profits) ganancias, f pl; (elements) elementos, m pl; germen, m;
rasgos esenciales, m pl, características, f. —pl **m.-up,**
(of clothes) confección, f; Print. ajuste, m; (of the
face) maquillaje, m; (invention) invención, f; fabricación, f
Malachite /'mælə,kait/ n malaquita, f
maladjustment /,mælə'dʒʌstmənt/ n mal ajuste, m;
inadaptación, f
maladministration /,mæləd,mɪnə'streiʃən/ n desgobierno, m, mala administración, f; (of funds) malversación, f
maladroit /,mælə'drɔit/ a torpe
maladroitness /,mælə'drɔitnɪs/ n torpeza, f
malady /'mælədi/ n enfermedad, f; mal, m
Malaga /'mæləgə/ n vino de Málaga, m
malaria /mə'lɛəriə/ n paludismo, m
malarial /mə'lɛəriəl/ a palúdico. **m. fever,** fiebre
palúdica, f
Malaya /mə'leiə/ Malasia, f, Archipiélago Malayo, m
Malayan /mə'leiən/ a malayo. —n malayo (-ya)
malcontent /,mælkən'tɛnt/ n malcontento (-ta). —a
descontento
Maldives /'mɔldivz/ Maldivas, f pl
male /meil/ a macho; masculino. —n macho, m;
varón, m. **m. child,** niño, m; niño varón, m; (son)
hijo varón, m. **m. flower,** flor masculina, f. **m. issue,**
sucesión masculina, f. **m. nurse,** enfermero, m. **m.
sex,** sexo masculino, m
malediction /,mælɪ'dɪkʃən/ n maldición, f
malefactor /'mælə,fæktər/ n malhechor (-ra)
malefic /mə'lɛfɪk/ a maléfico
malevolence /mə'lɛvələns/ n malevolencia, f
malevolent /mə'lɛvələnt/ a malévolo, maligno
malformation /,mælfɔr'meiʃən/ n formación anormal, deformidad, deformación congénita, f
malice /'mælɪs/ n malicia, f; Law. alevosía, f. **to bear
m.,** guardar rencor
malicious /mə'lɪʃəs/ a malicioso; maligno, rencoroso
maliciousness /mə'lɪʃəsnɪs/ n malicia, mala intención,
f
malign /mə'lain/ vt calumniar, difamar. —a maligno;
malévolo
malignancy /mə'lɪgnənsi/ n malignidad, f;
malevolencia, f
malignant /mə'lɪgnənt/ a maligno; malévolo; Med.
maligno
malinger /mə'lɪŋgər/ vi fingirse enfermo
malingerer /mə'lɪŋgərər/ n enfermo (-ma) fingido
(-da)
malingering /mə'lɪŋgərɪŋ/ n enfermedad fingida, f
mallard /'mælərd/ n pato (-ta), silvestre
malleability /,mæliə'bɪlɪti/ n maleabilidad, f

malleable /'mæliəbəl/ a maleable

mallet /'mælɪt/ n mazo, m; (in croquet) pala, f, mazo, m; (in polo) maza (de polo), f

mallow /'mælou/ n malva, f

malmsey /'mɑmzi/ n (wine) malvasía, f

malnutrition /,mælnu'trɪʃən/ n desnutrición, alimentación deficiente, f

malodorous /mæl'oudərəs/ a de mal olor, hediondo, fétido

malpractice /mæl'præktɪs/ n (wrongdoing) maleficencia, f; (by a doctor) tratamiento equivocado, perjudicial o ilegal, m; (malversation) malversación, f; inmoralidad, f

malt /mɔlt/ n malta, m. —vt preparar el malta. **m.-house,** fábrica de malta, f. **m. vinegar,** vinagre de malta, m

malted milk /'mɔltɪd/ n leche malteada, f

Maltese /mɔl'tiz/ a maltés. —n maltés (-esa). **M. cat,** gato maltés, m. **M. cross,** cruz de Malta, f. **M. dog,** perro maltés, m

Malthusian /mæl'θuʒən/ a maltusiano

Malthusianism /mæl'θuʒə,nɪzəm/ n maltusianismo, m

maltose /'mɔltous/ n maltosa, f

maltreat /mæl'trit/ vt maltratar

maltreatment /mæl'tritmənt/ n maltrato, m,

malt shop n café-nevería, m

mamma /'mæmə for 1; 'mamə for 2/ n Anat. mama, f; (mother) mamá, f

mammal /'mæməl/ n mamífero, m

mammalian /mə'meiliən/ a mamífero

mammary /'mæməri/ a mamario. **m. gland,** mama, teta, f

mammon /'mæmən/ n becerro de oro, m

mammoth /'mæməθ/ n mamut, m, a gigantesco, enorme

man /mæn/ n hombre, m; varón, m; persona, f; (servant) criado, m; (workman) obrero, m; (soldier) soldado, m; (sailor) marinero, m; (humanity) raza humana, f; (husband) marido, m; (chess) peón, m; (checkers) dama, f; (a ship) buque, m. **no man,** nadie; ningún hombre. **young man,** joven, m. **to a man,** como un solo hombre. **to come to man's estate,** llegar a la edad viril. **Man overboard!** ¡Hombre al agua! **man and wife,** marido y mujer, m, cónyuges, esposos, m pl. **man about town,** hombre de mundo, señorito, m. **man-at-arms,** hombre de armas, m. **man-eater,** caníbal, mf; tigre, m. **man-eating,** a antropófago. **man hater,** misántropo, m; mujer que odia a los hombres, f. **man-hole,** pozo, m. **man-hunter,** caníbal, mf; (woman) castigadora, f. **man in charge,** encargado, m. **man in the moon,** mujer de la luna, f. **man in the street,** hombre de la calle, hombre medio, m. **man of letters,** hombre de letras, literato, m; **man of straw,** bausán, m; (figure-head) testaferro, m. **man of the world,** hombre del mundo, m. **man of war,** buque de guerra, m. **man-power,** mano de obra, f, brazos, m pl, (e.g. lack of man-power, falta de brazos, f). **man servant,** criado, m

man /mæn/ vt armar; Mil. poner guarnición (a); ocupar; Naut. tripular; dirigir; Fig. fortificar

manacle /'mænəkəl/ n manilla, f; pl **manacles,** esposas, f pl; grillos, m pl. —vt poner esposas (a)

manage /'mænɪdʒ/ vt manejar; (animals) domar; dirigir; gobernar; administrar; (arrange) agenciar, arreglar; (work) explotar; (do) hacer; (eat) comer. —vi arreglárselas (para); (get along) ir tirando; (know how) saber hacer; (succeed in) lograr; (do) hacer

manageability /,mænɪdʒə'bɪlɪti/ n lo manejable; flexibilidad, f; (of animals, persons) docilidad, mansedumbre, f

manageable /'mænɪdʒəbəl/ a manejable; flexible; (of persons, animals) dócil

management /'mænɪdʒmənt/ n manejo, m; dirección, f; gobierno, m; administración, f; arreglo, m; (working) explotación, f; Com. gerencia, f; Theat. empresa, f; conducta, f; (economy) economía, f; (skill) habilidad, f; prudencia, f. **the m.,** la dirección, el cuerpo de directores. **domestic m.,** economía doméstica, f

manager /'mænɪdʒər/ n director, m; administrador, m; jefe, m; Theat. empresario, m; Com. gerente, m;

regente, m. **She is not much of a m.,** No es muy mujer de su casa. **manager's office,** dirección, f

managerial /,mænɪ'dʒɪəriəl/ a directivo; administrativo. **m. board,** junta directiva, f

managership /'mænɪdʒər,ʃɪp/ n puesto de director, m; jefatura, f

managing /'mænɪdʒɪŋ/ a directivo; (officious) mandón, dominante; (niggardly) tacaño

manatee /'mænə,ti/ n manatí, m

Manchurian /mæn'tʃuriən/ a manchuriano. —n manchuriano (-na)

mandarin /'mændərɪn/ n mandarín, m; (language) mandarina, f. **m. orange,** mandarina, f

mandate /'mændeit/ n mandato, m. **mandated territory,** territorios bajo mandato, m pl

mandatory /'mændə,tɔri/ a obligatorio

mandible /'mændəbəl/ n mandíbula, f

mandolin /'mændlɪn/ n bandolín, m, bandurria, f

mandrake /'mændreik, -drɪk/ n mandrágora, f

mandrill /'mændrɪl/ n mandril, m

mane /mein/ n melena, f; (of a horse) crines, f pl

maned /meind/ a (in compounds) con melena...; con crines...

maneuver /mə'nuvər/ n maniobra, f. —vi maniobrar, hacer maniobras. —vt hacer maniobrar; manipular

maneuvering /mə'nuvərɪŋ/ n maniobras, f pl; maquinaciones, intrigas, f pl

manfully /'mænfəli/ adv valientemente; vigorosamente

manganate /'mæŋgəneit/ n manganato, m

manganese /'mæŋgə,nis, -,niz/ n manganeso, m

mange /meindʒ/ n sarna, f; (in sheep) roña, f

manger /'meindʒər/ n pesebre, m

manginess /'meindʒinɪs/ n estado sarnoso, m

mangle /'mæŋgəl/ n (for clothes) exprimidor de la ropa, m. —vt pasar por el exprimidor; (mutilate) mutilar, lacerar, magullar; (a text) mutilar

mangling /'mæŋglɪŋ/ n (mutilation) mutilación, laceración, f

mango /'mæŋgou/ n mango, m

mangy /'meindʒi/ a sarnoso

manhandle /'mæn,hændl/ vt maltratar

manhood /'mænhʊd/ n virilidad, f; edad viril, f; masculinidad, f; los hombres; (manliness) hombradía, f, valor, m

mania /'meiniə/ n manía, f; obsesión, f; capricho, m, chifladura, f

maniac /'meini,æk/ n maníaco (-ca). —a maníaco, maniático

manicure /'mænɪ,kyʊr/ n manicura, f. —vt arreglar las uñas. **m.-set,** estuche de manicura, m

manicurist /'mænɪ,kyʊrɪst/ n manicuro (-ra)

manifest /'mænə,fest/ n Naut. manifiesto, m. —vt mostrar; hacer patente, probar; manifestarse. —vi publicar un manifiesto; (of spirits) manifestarse. —a manifiesto, evidente, claro, patente. **to make m.,** poner de manifiesto

manifestation /,mænəfə'steiʃən/ n manifestación, f

manifestly /'mænə,festli/ adv evidentemente, manifiestamente

manifesto /,mænə'festou/ n manifiesto, m

manifold /'mænə,fould/ a múltiple; numeroso; diverso, vario

manikin /'mænɪkɪn/ n enano, m; muñeco, m; Art. maniquí, m

Manilla /mə'nɪlə/ n Manila, f; cigarro filipino, m. **M. hemp,** cáñamo de Manila, m

maniple /'mænəpəl/ n manípulo, m

manipulate /mə'nɪpyə,leit/ vt manipular

manipulation /mə,nɪpyə'leiʃən/ n manipulación, f

manipulative /mə'nɪpyə,leitɪv/ a manipulador

mankind /'mæn'kaind/ n humanidad, raza humana, f, género humano, m

manlike /'mæn,laik/ a de hombre, masculino; varonil; (of a woman) hombruno

manliness /'mænlinɪs/ n masculinidad, hombradía, f; virilidad, f; valor, m; (of a woman) aire hombruno, m

manly /'mænli/ a masculino, de hombre; varonil, viril; valiente; fuerte. **to be very m.,** ser muy hombre, ser todo un hombre

manna /'mænə/ n maná, m

mannequin /'mænıkın/ n manequín, modelo, f. **m. parade,** exposición de modelos, f

manner /'mænər/ n manera, f, modo, m; aire, porte, m; conducta, f; (style) estilo, m; (sort) clase, f; Gram. modo, m; pl **manners,** modales, m pl, crianza, educación, f; (customs) costumbres, f pl. **after the m. of,** en (or según) el estilo de. **in a m. of speaking,** en cierto modo, para decirlo así. **in this m.,** de este modo. **to have bad (good) manners,** tener malos (buenos) modales, ser mal (bien) criado. **the novel of manners,** la novela de costumbres

mannered /'mænərd/ a amanerado; (in compounds)... educado, de... modales; de costumbres... **well-m.,** bien educado, de buenos modales

mannerism /'mænə,rızəm/ n amaneramiento, m; afectación, f; Theat. latiguillo, m. **to acquire mannerisms,** amanerarse

mannerliness /'mænərlinıs/ n cortesía, buena educación, urbanidad, f

mannerly /'mænərli/ a cortés, bien educado, atento

mannish /'mænıʃ/ a (of a woman) hombruno; de hombre, masculino

manor /'mænər/ n feudo, m; finca, hacienda, f; casa solariega, f; señorío, m

manorial /mə'nɔriəl/ a señorial

mansion /'mænʃən/ n mansión, f; casa solariega, f; hotel, m. **m.-house,** casa solariega, f; residencia del alcalde de Londres, f

manslaughter /'mæn,slɔtər/ n homicidio, m; Law. homicidio sin premeditación, m

mantelpiece /'mæntḷ,pis/ n repisa de chimenea, f

mantilla /mæn'tılə/ n mantilla, f

mantle /'mæntḷ/ n capa, f, manto, m; Fig. cobertura, f; (gas) camiseta, f, manguito, mf; Zool. manto, m. —vt cubrir; envolver; ocultar. —vi extenderse; (of blushes) inundar, subirse (a las mejillas)

Mantuan /'mæntʃuən/ a mantuano

manual /'mænyuəl/ a manual. —n manual, m; Mus. teclado de órgano, m. **m. work,** trabajo manual, m

manufactory /,mænyə'fæktəri/ n fábrica, f, taller, m

manufacture /,mænyə'fæktʃər/ n fabricación, f; manufactura, f. —vt manufacturar, fabricar

manufacturer /,mænyə'fæktʃərər/ n fabricante, industrial, m. **manufacturer's price,** precio de fábrica, m

manufacturing /,mænyə'fæktʃərıŋ/ a manufacturero, fabril. —n fabricación, f

manure /mə'nʊr/ n estiércol, abono, m. —vt estercolar, abonar. **m. heap,** estercolero, m

manuring /mə'nʊrıŋ/ n estercoladura, f

manuscript /'mænyə,skrıpt/ n manuscrito, m, a manuscrito

Manx /mæŋks/ a manés

many /'meni/ a muchos (-as); numeroso; diversos (-as); varios (-as). —n muchos (-as); la mayoría; las masas; muchedumbre, multitud, f. **a great m.,** muchísimos, m pl, muchísimas, f pl; un gran número. **as m. as...,** tantos como... **How m. are there?** ¿Cuántos hay? ¿Cuántas hay? **m. a time,** muchas veces. **three too m.,** tres de más. **for m. long years,** por largos años. **m.-colored,** multicolor. **m.-headed,** con muchas cabezas. **m.-sided,** multilátero; polifacético; complicado

Maori /'mauri/ n maorí, m, (pl maoríes)

map /mæp/ n mapa, m; plano, m; (chart) carta, f. —vt hacer un mapa (or plano) de. **to map out,** Surv. apear; trazar; (plan) proyectar. **ordnance map,** mapa del estado mayor, m. **map of the world,** mapamundi, mapa del mundo, m. **map-making,** cartografía, f

maple /'meipəl/ n (tree) arce, m; (wood) madera de arce, f. **m.-syrup,** jarabe de arce, m

mapping /'mæpıŋ/ n cartografía, f

mar /mɑr/ vt estropear; desfigurar; (happiness) destruir, aguar; frustrar

marabou /'mærə,bu/ n marabú, m

maraschino /,mærə'skinou/ n marrasquino, m. **m. cherry,** cerezas en marrasquino, f pl

maraud /mə'rɔd/ vi merodear

marauder /mə'rɔdər/ n merodeador, m

marauding /mə'rɔdıŋ/ a merodeador, n merodeo, m

marble /'mɑrbəl/ n mármol, m; (for playing with) canica, f, a de marmol, marmóreo; Fig. insensible; (of paper, etc.) jaspeado. —vt jaspear. **m. cutter,** marmolista, m. **m. works,** marmolería, f

marbled /'mɑrbəld/ a jaspeado

March /mɑrtʃ/ n marzo, m. **as mad as a M. hare,** loco como una cabra, loco de atar

march /mɑrtʃ/ n marcha, f; (step) paso, m; Fig. marcha, f, progreso, m. **forced m.,** marcha forzada, f. **quick m.,** paso doble, m. **to steal a m. on,** tomar la delantera (a), ganar por la mano (a). **to strike up a m.,** batir la marcha. **m.-past,** desfile, m

march /mɑrtʃ/ vi marchar; (of properties) lindar (con). —vt hacer marchar, poner en marcha (a). **to m. back,** vi regresar (or volver) a pie. —vt hacer volver a pie. **to m. in,** entrar (a pie) en. **to m. off,** marcharse. **to m. on,** seguir marchando; seguir adelante; avanzar. **to m. past,** desfilar ante

marching /'mɑrtʃıŋ/ n marcha, f. —a en marcha; de marcha. **to receive one's m. orders,** recibir la orden de marchar; Inf. ser despedido. **m. order,** orden de marcha, m. **m. song,** canción de marcha, f

marchioness /'mɑrʃənıs/ n marquesa, f

mardi gras /'mɑrdi ,grɑ/ n martes de carnaval, m

mare /mɛər/ n yegua, f

margarine /'mɑrdʒərın/ n margarina, f

margin /'mɑrdʒın/ n borde, lado, m, orilla, f; (of a page) margen, mf; reserva, f; sobrante, m. **in the m.,** al margen

marginal /'mɑrdʒənḷ/ a marginal. **m. note,** acotación, nota marginal, f

marigold /'mærı,gould/ n caléndula, maravilla, f

marine /mə'rin/ a marino, de mar; marítimo; naval. —n (fleet) marina, f; (soldier) soldado de marina, m. **Tell that to the marines!** ¡Cuéntaselo a tu tía! **mercantile m.,** marina mercante, f. **m. forces,** infantería de marina, f. **m. insurance,** seguro marítimo, m

mariner /'mærənər/ n marinero, marino, m. **mariner's compass,** aguja de marear, brújula, f

marionette /,mæriə'nɛt/ n marioneta, f, títere, m

marital /'mærıtḷ/ a marital

maritime /'mærı,taım/ a marítimo

mark /mɑrk/ n marca, f; señal, f; mancha, f; impresión, f; (target) blanco, m; (standard) norma, f; (level) nivel, m; (distinction) importancia, distinción, f; (in examinations) nota, f; calificación, f; (signature) cruz, f; (coin) marco, m. —vt marcar; señalar; (price) poner precio (a); (notice) observar, darse cuenta (de); (characterize) caracterizar. **trade-m.,** marca de fábrica, f. **to be beside the m.,** no dar en el blanco; errar el tiro; Fig. no tener nada que ver con; equivocarse. **to hit the m.,** dar en el blanco; Fig. dar en el clavo. **to make one's m.,** firmar con una cruz; distinguirse. **to m. time,** marcar el paso; Fig. hacer tiempo. **to m. down,** (a person) señalar; escoger; (in price) rebajar. **to m. out,** marcar; trazar; definir; (erase) borrar; (a person) escoger; destinar. **m. somebody absent,** ponerle a fulano su ausencia. **m. somebody present,** ponerle a fulano su asistencia.

Mark /mɑrk/ n Marcos. **the Gospel according to St. M.,** el Evangelio de San Marcos

marked /mɑrkt/ a marcado; señalado; notable; acentuado; particular, especial. **He speaks with a m. Galician accent,** Habla con marcado acento gallego

markedly /'mɑrkıdli/ adv marcadamente; notablemente; especialmente, particularmente

marker /'mɑrkər/ n (billiards) marcador, m; (football, etc.) tanteador, m

market /'mɑrkıt/ n mercado, m; tráfico, m; venta, f; (price) precio, m; (shop) bazar, emporio, m. —vt and vi comprar en un mercado; vender en un mercado. **black m.,** mercado negro, estraperlo, m. **open m.,** mercado al aire libre, m; Fig. mercado libre, m. **m. day,** día de mercado, m. **m. garden,** huerto, m, huerta, f. **m. gardener,** hortelano, m. **m.-place,** plaza de mercado, f; Fig. mercado, m. **m. price,** precio corriente, m. **m. stall,** tabanco, puesto de mercado, m. **m.-woman,** verdulera, f

marketable /'mɑrkıtəbəl/ a comerciable, vendible; corriente

marketing /'mɑrkıtıŋ/ n venta, f; compra en un mercado, f; mercado, m. **to go m.,** ir al mercado

marking /'mɑrkɪŋ/ n marca, f; (spot on animals, etc.) pinta, f. **m.-ink,** tinta de marcar, f. **m.-iron,** ferrete, hierro de marcar, m

marksman /'mɑrksmən/ n tirador (-ra)

marksmanship /'mɑrksmənˌʃɪp/ n puntería, f

marl /mɑrl/ n marga, f

marlinespike /'mɑrlɪnˌspaik/ n pasador, m

marmalade /'mɑrməˌleɪd/ n mermelada de naranjas amargas, f

marmoset /'mɑrməˌzɛt/ n tití, m

marmot /'mɑrmət/ n Zool. marmota, f

maroon /mə'run/ n (color) marrón, m; (slave) cimarrón (-ona); (firework) petardo, m. **—a** de marrón. **—vt** abandonar, dejar

marquee /mɑr'ki/ n marquesina, f

marquetrie /'mɑrkɪtri/ n marquetería, f

marquis /'mɑrkwɪs/ n marqués, m

marriage /'mærɪdʒ/ n matrimonio, m; unión, f; (wedding) boda, f, casamiento, m. **by m.,** (of relationship) político. **She is an aunt by m.,** tía política. **m. articles,** capitulaciones (matrimoniales), f pl. **m. contract,** contrato matrimonial, m. **m. license,** licencia de casamiento, f. **m.** rappone, dote, mf. **m. rate,** nupcialidad, f. **m. register,** acta matrimonial, f. **m. song,** epitalamio, m

marriageable /'mærɪdʒəbəl/ a casadero

married /'mærɪd/ past part and a casado; matrimonial, conyugal. **newly-m. couple,** los recién casados. **to get m. to,** casarse con. **m. couple,** matrimonio, m, cónyuges, m pl. **m. life,** vida conyugal, f

married name n nombre de casada, f

marrow /'mærou/ n tuétano, m, médula, f; Fig. meollo, m. **to the m. of one's bones,** hasta los tuétanos.

marrowbone /'mærouˌboun/ n hueso medular, m. **on one's marrowbones,** de rodillas

marry /'mæri/ vt casarse con, contraer matrimonio con; casar; (of a priest) unir en matrimonio; Fig. juntar, unir. **—vi** casarse. **to m. again,** volver a casarse

Marseillaise /ˌmɑrseɪ'ez/ n marsellesa, f

Marseilles /mɑr'seɪ/ Marsella, f

marsh /mɑrʃ/ n marjal, pantano, m. **m.-mallow,** Bot. malvavisco, m. **m. marigold,** calta, f

marshal /'mɑrʃəl/ n mariscal, m, vt poner en orden, arreglar; dirigir. **field-m.,** capitán general de ejército, m

marshaling /'mɑrʃəlɪŋ/ n ordenación, f; dirección, f. **m.-yard,** (railway) apartadero ferroviario, m

marshy /'mɑrʃi/ a pantanoso

mart /mɑrt/ n Poet. plaza de mercado, f; mercado, m; emporio, m; (auction rooms) martillo, m

marten /'mɑrtn/ n marta, f

martial /'mɑrʃəl/ a militar; marcial, belicoso. **m. array,** orden de batalla, m. **m. law,** derecho militar, m; estado de guerra, m. **m. spirit,** marcialidad, f, espíritu belicoso, m

martially /'mɑrʃəli/ adv militarmente; marcialmente

Martian /'mɑrʃən/ a marciano

martinet /ˌmɑrtn'et/ n Mil. ordenancista, m; rigorista, mf

Martinique /ˌmɑrtn'ik/ Martinica, f

Martinmas /'mɑrtnməs/ n día de San Martín, m

martyr /'mɑrtər/ n mártir, mf vt martirizar

martyrdom /'mɑrtərdəm/ n martirio, m

martyrize /'mɑrtəˌraɪz/ vt martirizar

marvel /'mɑrvəl/ n maravilla, f. **to m. at,** maravillarse de, admirarse de

marvelous /'mɑrvələs/ a maravilloso

marvelousness /'mɑrvələsnɪs/ n maravilla, f, carácter maravilloso, m, lo maravilloso

Marxism /'mɑrksɪzəm/ n marxismo, m

Marxist /'mɑrksɪst/ a and n marxista, mf

marzipan /'mɑrzəˌpæn/ n mazapán, m

mascot /'mæskɒt/ n mascota, f

masculine /'mæskyəlɪn/ a masculino; varonil, macho; de hombre; (of a woman) hombruno. **—n** masculino, m

masculinity /ˌmæskyə'lɪnɪti/ n masculinidad, f

mash /mæʃ/ n mezcla, f; amasijo, m; pasta, f, puré, m. **—vt** mezclar; amasar. **mashed potatoes,** puré de patatas (de papas), m

mask /mæsk/ n máscara, f; antifaz, m; (death) mascarilla, f; (person) máscara, mf. **—vt** enmascarar; Fig. encubrir, disimular. **—vi** ponerse una máscara; disfrazarse. **masked ball,** n baile de máscaras, m

masker /'mæskər/ n máscara, mf

masochism /'mæsəˌkɪzəm/ n masoquismo, m

mason /'meisən/ n albañil, m; (freemason) francmasón, masón, m

masonic /mə'sɒnɪk/ a masónico. **m. lodge,** logia de francmasones, f

masonry /'meisənri/ n (trade) albañilería, f; (mampostería, f

masque /mæsk/ n mascarada, f

masquerade /ˌmæskə'reid/ n mascarada, f

masquerader /ˌmæskə'reidər/ n máscara, mf

mass /mæs/ n misa, f. **to hear m.,** oír misa. **to say m.,** celebrar misa. **high m.,** misa mayor, f. **low m.,** misa rezada, f. **m. book,** libro de misa, m

mass /mæs/ n masa, f; (shape) bulto, m; (heap) montón, m; (great number) muchedumbre, f; (cloud of steam, etc.) nube, f. **—vt** amasar; Mil. concentrar. **—vi** congregarse en masa. **in a m.,** en masa; en conjunto. **the m.** (of)..., la mayoría (de)... **the masses,** las masas, el vulgo, el pueblo. **m. formation,** columna cerrada, f. **m.-meeting,** mitin, mitin popular, m. **m.-production,** fabricación en serie, f

massacre /'mæsəkər/ n matanza, carnicería, f, vt hacer una carnicería (de)

massage /mə'sɑʒ/ n masaje, m; (friction) fricción, f. **—vt** dar un masaje (a)

masseur, masseuse /mə'sɜr; mə'sus/ n masajista, mf

massive /'mæsɪv/ a macizo; sólido

massively /'mæsɪvli/ adv macizamente; sólidamente

massiveness /'mæsɪvnɪs/ n macicez, f; solidez, f

mast /mæst/ n Naut. palo, árbol, m; (for wireless) mástil, m; poste, m; (beech) hayuco, m; (oak) bellota, f. **—vt** Naut. arbolar. **at half-m.,** a media asta. **m.-head,** calcés, tope, m

masted /'mæstɪd/ a arbolado; (in compounds) de... palos

master /'mæstər/ n (of the house, etc.) señor, amo, m; maestro, m; Naut. patrón, m; (owner) dueño, m; (teacher) profesor, maestro, m; (young master and as address) señorito, m; director, m; jefe, m; (expert) perito, m; (of a military order) maestre, m, a maestro; superior. **—vt** dominar; ser maestro en; dominar, conocer a fondo. **This picture is by an old m.,** Este cuadro es de un gran maestro antiguo. **to be m. of oneself,** ser dueño de sí. **to be one's own m.,** ser dueño de sí mismo; trabajar por su propia cuenta; ser independiente; estar libre. **m. builder,** maestro de obras, m. **m. hand,** mano maestra, f. **M. of Arts,** maestro (-tra) en artes. **M. of Ceremonies,** maestro de ceremonias, m. **M. of Foxhounds,** cazador mayor, m. **M. of the Horse,** caballerizo mayor del rey, m. **M. of the Rolls,** archivero mayor, m. **m.-key,** llave maestra, f. **m. mind,** águila, f, ingenio, m. **m. stroke,** golpe maestro, m

masterful /'mæstərfəl/ a imperioso, dominante; autoritario, arbitrario

masterfulness /'mæstərfəlnɪs/ n imperiosidad, f; arbitrariedad, f

masterless /'mæstərlɪs/ a sin amo

masterliness /'mæstərlɪnɪs/ n maestría, f; excelencia, f; perfección, f

masterly /'mæstərli/ a maestro; excelente; perfecto. **m. performance,** obra maestra, f; Theat. representación perfecta, f; ejecución excelente, f

masterpiece /'mæstərˌpis/ n obra maestra, f

master plan n plan regulador, m

masterstroke /'mæstərˌstrouk/ n golpe magistral, golpe de maestro, m

mastery /'mæstəri/ n dominio, m; autoridad, f; poder, m; ventaja, f; superioridad, maestría, f; conocimiento profundo, m. **to gain the m. of,** hacerse el señor de; llegar a dominar

mastic /'mæstɪk/ n masilla, almáciga, f

masticate /'mæstɪˌkeit/ vt masticar, mascar

mastication /ˌmæstɪ'keiʃən/ n masticación, f

mastiff /'mæstɪf/ n mastín, alano, m

mastodon /'mæstəˌdɒn/ n mastodonte, m

mastoid /'mæstɔid/ a mastoides. —n apófisis mastoides, f

masturbate /'mæstər,beit/ vi masturbarse

masturbation /,mæstər'beiʃən/ n masturbación, f

mat /mæt/ n esterilla, f; alfombrilla, f; (on the table) tapete individual, m. —vt (tangle) enmarañar, desgreñar. —vi enmarañarse

match /mætʃ/ n Sports. partido, m; (wrestling, boxing) lucha, f; (fencing) asalto, m; (race) carrera, f; (contest) concurso, m; (equal) igual, mf; (pair) pareja, f; compañero (-ra); (marriage) boda, f, casamiento, m; (for lighting) cerilla, f, fósforo, m; (for guns) mecha, f. —vt competir con; (equal) igualar; ser igual (a); hacer juego con; emparejar, aparear; armonizar. —vi ser igual; hacer juego; armonizarse. **good m.,** Inf. buen partido, m. **as thin as a m.,** más delgado que una cerilla. **to meet one's m.,** dar con la horma de su zapato. **to play a m.,** jugar un partido. **m.-box,** cajita de cerillas, fosforera, f. **m.-seller,** fosforero (-ra)

matchless /'mætʃlis/ a incomparable, sin igual, sin par

matchwood /'mætʃ,wʊd/ n madera para cerillas, f

mate /meit/ n compañero, camarada, m; (spouse) compañero (-ra); pareja, f; (on merchant ships) piloto, m; (assistant) ayudante, m; (at chess) mate, m. —vt (marry) casar, desposar; (animals, birds) aparear, acoplar; (chess) dar jaque mate (a). —vi casarse; aparearse, acoplarse

maté /'mɑtei/ maté, té del Paraguay, m

materfamilias /,meitərfə'miliəs/ n madre de familia, f

material /mə'tiəriəl/ a material; importante, esencial; considerable; sensible, notable; grave. —n material, m; materia, f; (fabric) tela, f; tejido, m. **raw materials,** materias primas, f pl. **writing materials,** utensilios de escritorio, m pl; papel de escribir, m

materialism /mə'tiəriə,lizəm/ n materialismo, m

materialist /mə'tiəriəlist/ n materialista, mf

materialistic /mə,tiəriə'listik/ a materialista

materiality /mə,tiəri'æliti/ n materialidad, f; importancia, f

materialization /mə,tiəriəli'zeiʃən/ n materialización, f

materialize /mə'tiəriə,laiz/ vt materializar

maternal /mə'tərnl/ a materno, maternal. **m. grandparents,** abuelos maternos, m pl

maternity /mə'tərniti/ n maternidad, f. **m. center,** centro de maternidad, m. **m. hospital,** casa de maternidad, f

mathematical /,mæθə'mætikəl/ a matemático

mathematician /,mæθəmə'tiʃən/ n matemático, m

mathematics /,mæθə'mætiks/ n pl matemáticas, f pl. **applied m.,** matemáticas prácticas, f pl. **higher m.,** matemáticas superiores, f pl. **pure m.,** matemáticas teóricas, f pl

matinee /,mætn'ei/ n función de tarde, f

mating /'meitiŋ/ n (of animals) apareamiento, acoplamiento, m; unión, f; casamiento, m

matins /'mætnz/ n pl Eccl. maitines, m pl

matriarch /'meitri,ɑrk/ n matriarca, f

matriarchal /,meitri'ɑrkəl/ a matriarcal

matriarchy /'meitri,ɑrki/ n matriarcado, m

matricide /'mætri,said/ n (crime) matricidio, m; (person) matricida, mf

matriculate /mə'trikyə,leit/ vt matricular. —vi matricularse

matriculation /mə,trikyə'leiʃən/ n matriculación, f

matrimonial /,mætrə'mouniəl/ a matrimonial, de matrimonio; marital. **m. agency,** agencia de matrimonios, f

matrimony /'mætrə,mouni/ n matrimonio, m

matrix /'meitriks/ n matriz, f

matron /'meitrən/ n matrona, mujer casada, madre de familia, f; (of a hospital) matrona, f; (of a school) ama de llaves, f; directora, f. **m. of honor,** (at a wedding) madrina, f

matronly /'meitrənli/ a de matrona, matronal; respetable; serio

matte /mæt/ a mate

matted /'mætid/ a enmarañado, enredado

matter /'mætər/ n materia, f; substancia, f; caso, m; cuestión, f; asunto, m; causa, f; (distance) distancia, f; (amount) cantidad, f; (duration) espacio de tiempo, m; (importance) importancia, f; Med. pus, m; pl **matters,** asuntos, m pl, etc.; situación, f. **as if nothing were the m.,** como si no hubiese pasado nada. **for that m.,** en cuanto a eso. **grey m.,** substancia gris, f. **in the m. of,** en el caso de. **It is a m. of taste,** Es cuestión de gusto. **printed m.,** impresos, m pl. **What is the m.?** ¿Qué pasa? ¿Qué hay? **What is the m. with him?** ¿Qué tiene? ¿Qué le pasa? **m.-of-course,** cosa natural, f. **m.-of-fact,** práctico; sin imaginación; positivista. **m. of fact,** n hecho positivo, m, realidad, f. **As a m. of fact...,** En realidad..., El caso es que... **m. of form,** cuestión de fórmula, f; pura formalidad, f

matter /'mætər/ vi importar; (discharge) supurar. **What does it m.?** ¿Qué importa? **It doesn't m.,** Es igual, No importa, Da lo mismo

Matterhorn /'mætər,hɔrn/, **the** el Matterhorn, m

matting /'mætiŋ/ n estera, f

mattress /'mætris/ n colchón, m. **spring-m.,** colchón de muelles, m. **m.-maker,** colchonero, m

mature /mə'tʃʊr/ a maduro; Com. vencido. —vt madurar. —vi madurarse; Com. vencer

maturity /mə'tʃʊriti/ n madurez, f; edad madura, f; (Com. of a bill) vencimiento, m

matutinal /mə'tutnl/ a matutino

maudlin /'mɔdlin/ a sensiblero; lacrimoso; (tipsy) calamocano

maul /mɔl/ vt maltratar; herir

maundy /'mɔndi/ n lavatorio, m. **M. Thursday,** Jueves Santo, m

Mauritius /mɔ'riʃəs/ Mauricio, m, Isla de Francia, f

mausoleum /,mɔsə'liəm/ n mausoleo, m

mauve /mouv/ n color purpúreo delicado, color de malva, m, a de color de malva

maw /mɔ/ n (of a ruminant) cuajar, m; (of a bird) buche, m; Fig. abismo, m

mawkish /'mɔkiʃ/ a insípido, insulso; sensiblero; asqueroso

mawkishness /'mɔkiʃnis/ n insipidez, insulsez, f; sensiblería, f; asquerosidad, f

maxilla /mæk'silə/ n hueso maxilar, maxilar, m

maxillary /'mæksə,leri/ a maxilar

maxim /'mæksim/ n máxima, f

maximum /'mæksəməm/ a máximo. —n máximo, m

may /mei/ v aux poder; ser posible; (expressing wish, hope) ojalá que..., Dios quiera que..., or the present subjunctive may be used, e.g. May you live many years! ¡(qué) Viva Vd. muchos años! (to denote uncertainty, the future tense of the verb is often used, e.g. You may perhaps remember the date, Vd. quizás se acordará de la fecha. Who may he be? ¿Quién será? **May God grant it!** ¡(que) Dios lo quiera! **It may be that...,** Puede ser que..., Es posible que..., Quizás... **He may come on Saturday,** Es posible que venga el sábado; Puede venir el sábado. **May I come in?** ¿Puedo entrar? ¿Se puede entrar? **May I come and see you?** ¿Me das permiso para hacerte una visita? ¿Me dejas venir a verte? **May I go then?** ¿Puedo irme pues? ¿Tengo permiso para marcharme entonces?

May /mei/ n mayo, m; Fig. abril, m; Bot. espina blanca, f. **May Day,** primero de mayo, m. **mayflower,** flor del cuclillo, f. **mayfly,** cachipolla, f. **May queen,** maya, f

maybe /'meibi/ adv quizás, tal vez

mayonnaise /,meiə'neiz/ n mayonesa, f. **m. sauce,** salsa mayonesa, f

mayor /'meiər/ n alcalde, m

mayoral /'meiərəl/ a de alcalde

mayoress /'meiəris/ n alcaldesa, f

maypole /'mei,poul/ n mayo, m. **m. dance,** danza de cintas, f

maze /meiz/ n laberinto, m; Fig. perplejidad, f. —vt dejar perplejo, aturdir

mazurka /mə'zɜrkə/ n mazurca, f

me /mi/ pron me; (after a preposition only) mí. **They sent it for me,** Lo mandaron para mí. **Dear me!** ¡Ay de mí!

meadow /'mɛdou/ n prado, m, pradera, f. **m.-sweet,** reina de los prados, f

meager /'migər/ a magro, enjuto, flaco; (scanty) exiguo, escaso, insuficiente; pobre; *Fig.* árido

meagerly /'migərli/ adv pobremente

meagerness /'migərnɪs/ n exigüidad, escasez, f; pobreza, f; *Fig.* aridez, f

meal /mil/ n comida, f; (flour) harina, f. **to have a good m.,** comer bien. **test m.,** *Med.* comida de prueba, f. **m.-time,** hora de comida, f

mealy /'mili/ a harinoso; (of the complexion) pastoso

mean /min/ a (middle) medianero; (average) mediano; (humble) humilde; pobre; inferior; bajo, vil, ruin; (avaricious) tacaño, mezquino. **m.-spirited,** vil, de alma ruin

mean /min/ n medio, m; medianía, f; pl **means,** medio, m; expediente, m; medios, m pl; (financial) recursos, m pl; modo, m, manera, f. **by all means,** por todos los medios; (certainly) ¡ya lo creo! ¡no faltaba más! ¡naturalmente! **by means of,** mediante, por medio de; con la ayuda de. **by no means,** de ningún modo; nada. **by some means,** de algún modo, de alguna manera

mean /min/ vt destinar (para); pretender, proponerse; intentar, pensar; querer decir, significar; importar; (wish) querer; (concern, speak about) tratarse (de). —vi tener el propósito, tener la intención. **I did not m. to do it,** Lo hice sin querer. **What does this word m.?** ¿Qué significa esta palabra? **What do you m. by that?** ¿Qué quieres decir con eso? **This portrait is meant to be Joan,** Este retrato quiere ser Juana. **What do they m. to do?** ¿Qué piensan (or se proponen) hacer? **Do you really m. it?** ¿Lo dices en serio? **Charles always means well,** Carlos siempre tiene buenas intenciones

meander /mi'ændər/ n meandro, serpenteo, m; camino tortuoso, m, vi serpentear; errar, vagar; (in talk) divagar

meandering /mi'ændərɪŋ/ n meandros, m pl, serpenteo, m; (in talk) divagaciones, f pl, a serpentino, tortuoso

meaning /'minɪŋ/ n intención, voluntad, f; significación, f; significado, m; (of words) acepción, f; (sense) sentido, m; (thought) pensamiento, m. —a significante. **double m.,** doble intención, f. **He gave me a m. look,** Me miró con intención. **What is the m. of it?** ¿Qué significa? ¿Qué quiere decir?

meaningful /'minɪŋfəl/ a significante

meaningless /'minɪŋlɪs/ a sin sentido; insensato; insignificante

meaningly /'minɪŋli/ adv significativamente; con intención

meanness /'minnɪs/ n pobreza, f; inferioridad, f; mediocridad, f; bajeza, ruindad, f; (stinginess) mezquindad, tacañería, f

meantime, meanwhile /'min,taim; 'min,wail/ n ínterin, m, adv entre tanto, mientras tanto, a todo esto. **in the m.,** mientras tanto, en el ínterin

measles /'mizəlz/ n sarampión, m. **German m.,** rubéola, f

measurable /'mɛʒərəbəl/ a mensurable

measure /'mɛʒər/ n medida, f; capacidad, f; (for measuring) regla, f; número, m; proporción, f; (limit) límite, m; (*Fig.* step) medida, f; (metre) metro, m; *Mus.* compás, m; (degree) grado, m; manera, f; (parliamentary) proyecto (de ley), m. —vt medir; proporcionar, distribuir; (water) aforar; (land) apear; (height of persons) tallar; (for clothes) tomar las medidas (a); (judge) juzgar; (test) probar; (*Poet.* traverse) recorrer. **a suit made to m.,** un traje hecho a medida. **in great m.,** en gran manera, en alto grado. **in some m.,** hasta cierto punto. **to m. one's length,** caer tendido. **to take a person's m.,** *Fig.* tomar las medidas (a). **to m. up to,** *Fig.* estar al nivel de, ser igual a

measured /'mɛʒərd/ a mesurado, moderado; uniforme; limitado. **to walk with m. tread,** andar a pasos contados

measurement /'mɛʒərmənt/ n medición, f; medida, f; dimensión, f

meat /mit/ n carne, f; (food) alimento, m; (meal) comida, f; *Fig.* substancia, f. **to sit at m.,** estar a la mesa. **cold meats,** fiambres, m pl. **m.-ball,** albóndiga, f. **m.-chopper,** picador, m. **m.-dish,** fuente, f. **m.-eater,** comedor (-ra) de carne. **m. extract,** carne concentrada, f. **m.-market,** carnicería, f. **m.-pie,** pastel de carne, m. **m.-safe,** fresquera, f

meaty /'miti/ a carnoso; *Fig.* substancial

Mecca /'mɛkə/ la Meca, f

mechanic /mə'kænɪk/ n mecánico, m

mechanical /mə'kænɪkəl/ a mecánico; maquinal

mechanically /mə'kænɪkli/ adv mecánicamente; maquinalmente

mechanical pencil n lapicero, m

mechanics /mə'kænɪks/ n mecánica, f

mechanism /'mɛkə,nɪzəm/ n mecanismo, m; (philosophy) mecanicismo, m

mechanize /'mɛkə,naiz/ vt convertir en máquina; (gen. *Mil.*) mecanizar; motorizar

medal /'mɛdl/ n medalla, f

medallion /mə'dælyən/ n medallón, m

medallist /'mɛdlɪst/ n grabador de medallas, m; el, m, (f, la) que recibe una medalla

meddle /'mɛdl/ vi tocar; meterse (con or en); entremeterse, inmiscuirse; intrigar

meddler /'mɛdlər/ n entremetido (-da); intrigante, mf

meddlesome /'mɛdlsəm/ a entremetido; oficioso; impertinente; enredador, intrigante. **to be very m.,** meterse en todo

meddlesomeness /'mɛdlsəmnɪs/ n entremetimiento, m; oficiosidad, f; impertinencia, f; intrigas, f pl

median /'midiən/ a del medio

mediate /v 'midi,eit; a -ɪt/ vi intervenir, mediar, arbitrar; abogar (por). —a medio; interpuesto

media /'midiə/, the los medios informativos, m pl

mediation /,midi'eiʃən/ n mediación, intervención, f; intercesión, f; interposición, f

mediator /'midi,eitər/ n mediador (-ra); arbitrador, m; intercesor (-ra)

mediatory /'midiə,tɔri/ a de mediador; intercesor

medical /'mɛdɪkəl/ a médico; de medicina; de médico. —n *Inf.* estudiante de medicina, m. **Army M. Service,** Servicio de Sanidad Militar, m. **m. books,** libros de medicina, m pl. **m. examination,** examen médico, m, exploración médica, f. **m. jurisprudence,** medicina legal, f. **m. knowledge,** conocimientos médicos, m pl. **m. practitioner,** médico (-ca). **m. school,** escuela de medicina, f

medicament /mə'dɪkəmənt/ n medicamento, m

medicate /'mɛdɪ,keit/ vt medicar; medicinar

medicated /'mɛdɪ,keitɪd/ a medicado

medication /,mɛdɪ'keiʃən/ n medicación, f

medicinal /mə'dɪsənl/ a medicinal

medicine /'mɛdəsɪn/ n medicina, f; medicamento, m; (charm) ensalmo, hechizo, m. **patent m.,** específico farmacéutico, m. **m. ball,** balón medical, m. **m. chest,** botiquín, m. **m. man,** hechizador, m

medico- prefix médico-. **m.-legal,** médicolegal

medieval /,midi'ivəl/ a medieval

medievalism /,midi'ivə,lɪzəm/ n afición a la edad media, f; espíritu medieval, m

mediocre /,midi'oukər/ a mediocre

mediocrity /,midi'ɒkrɪti/ n mediocridad, f; medianía, f

meditate /'mɛdɪ,teit/ vt idear, proyectar, meditar. —vi meditar, reflexionar; pensar, intentar

meditation /,mɛdɪ'teiʃən/ n meditación, f

meditative /'mɛdɪ,teitɪv/ a meditabundo, contemplativo; de meditación

meditatively /'mɛdɪ,teitɪvli/ adv reflexivamente

Mediterranean /,mɛdɪtə'reiniən/ a mediterráneo. —n Mar Mediterráneo, m

medium /'midiəm/ n medio, m; (cooking) término medio, a medio cocer, a medio asar, m; (environment) medio ambiente, m; (agency) intermediario, m; (spiritualism) médium, m; *Art.* medio, m, a mediano; regular; mediocre. **through the m. of,** por medio de. **m.-sized,** de tamaño regular

medlar /'mɛdlər/ n (fruit) níspola, f; (tree) níspero, m

medley /'mɛdli/ n mezcla, f; miscelánea, f, a mezclado, mixto

medulla /mə'dʌlə/ n medula, f

meek /mik/ a dulce, manso; humilde; modesto; pacífico

meekly /'mikli/ *adv* mansamente; humildemente; modestamente

meekness /'miknıs/ *n* mansedumbre, *f*; humildad, *f*; modestia, *f*

meet /mit/ *vt* encontrar; encontrarse con; tropezar con; (by arrangement) reunirse con; (make the acquaintance of) conocer (a); (satisfy) satisfacer; cumplir (con); (a bill) pagar, saldar; (refute) refutar; (fight) batirse (con); (confront) hacer frente (a). —*vi* juntarse; encontrarse; reunirse; verse; (of rivers) confluir. —*n* montería, *f*, *a* conveniente. **I shall m. you at the station,** Te esperaré en la estación. **Until we m. again!** ¡Hasta la vista! **to go to m.,** ir al encuentro de. **to m. half-way,** encontrar a la mitad del camino; partir la diferencia (con); hacer concesiones (a). **to m. the eye,** saltar a la vista. **to m. with,** encontrar; experimentar; sufrir

meeting /'mitıŋ/ *n* encuentro, *m*; reunión, *f*; (interview) entrevista, *f*; (of rivers, etc.) confluencia, *f*; (public, etc.) mitin, *m*; (council) concilio, *m*; concurso, *m*; (race) concurso de carreras de caballos, *m*. **creditors' m.,** concurso de acreedores, *m*. **m.-house,** templo de los Cuáqueros, *m*. **m.-place,** lugar de reunión, *m*; lugar de cita, *m*; centro, *m*. **to adjourn the m.,** levantar la sesión. **to call a m.,** convocar una sesión. **to open the m.,** abrir la sesión

megalomania /ˌmɛgəlou'meiniə/ *n* megalomanía, *f*, monomanía de grandezas, *f*

megalomaniac /ˌmɛgəlou'meiniæk/ *n* megalómano (-na)

megaphone /'mɛgəˌfoun/ *n* megáfono, portavoz, *m*

Meknès /mɛk'nɛs/ Mequínez, *f*

melancholia /ˌmɛlən'kouliə/ *n* melancolía, *f*

melancholy /'mɛlən,kɒli/ *a* melancólico. —*n* melancolía, *f*

mellifluence /mə'lıfluəns/ *n* melifluidad, *f*

mellifluous /mə'lıfluəs/ *a* melifluo; dulce

mellow /'mɛlou/ *a* maduro; dulce; (of wine) rancio; blando; suave; (of sound) melodioso; (slang) alegre; (tipsy) entre dos luces. —*vt* madurar; ablandar; suavizar. —*vi* madurarse

mellowing /'mɛlouıŋ/ *n* maduración, *f*

mellowness /'mɛlounıs/ *n* madurez, *f*; dulzura, *f*; (of wine) ranciedad, *f*; blandura, *f*; suavidad, *f*; melodía, *f*

melodic /mə'lɒdık/ *a* melódico

melodious /mə'loudiəs/ *a* melodioso

melodiously /mə'loudiəsli/ *adv* melodiosamente

melodiousness /mə'loudiəsnıs/ *n* melodía, *f*

melodrama /'mɛlə,dramə/ *n* melodrama, *m*

melodramatic /ˌmɛlədrə'mætık/ *a* melodramático

melody /'mɛlədi/ *n* melodía, *f*

melon /'mɛlən/ *n* melón, *m*; sandía, *f*. **slice of m.,** raja de melón, *f*. **m. bed,** sandiar, *m*. **m.-shaped,** amelonado

melt /mɛlt/ *vi* derretirse; deshacerse; disolverse; evaporarse; desaparecer; (of money, etc.) hacerse sal y agua; (relent) enternecerse, ablandarse. —*vt* fundir; (snow, etc.) derretir; (*Fig.* soften) ablandar. **He melted away,** *Inf.* Se escurrió. **to m. into tears,** deshacerse en lágrimas. **to m. down,** fundir

melting /'mɛltıŋ/ *a* fundente; (forgiving) indulgente; (tender) de ternura; lánguido; dulce. —*n* fusión, *f*; derretimiento, *m*. **m. point,** punto de fusión, *m*. **m. pot,** *Metall.* crisol, *m*; *Fig.* caldera de razas, *f*, *m*

member /'mɛmbər/ *n* miembro, *m*; (of a club, etc.) socio (-ia). **M. of Parliament,** diputado a Cortes, *m*

membership /'mɛmbərˌʃıp/ *n* calidad de miembro, socio(-ia); número de miembros (*or* socios), *m*, composición, integración, *f*

membrane /'mɛmbrein/ *n* membrana, *f*

membranous /'mɛmbrənəs/ *a* membranoso

memento /mə'mɛntou/ *n* recuerdo, *m*

memoir /'mɛmwar/ *n* memoria, *f*

memorable /'mɛmərəbəl/ *a* memorable

memorably /'mɛmərəbli/ *adv* memorablemente

memorandum /ˌmɛmə'rændəm/ *n* memorándum, *m*

memorial /mə'mɔriəl/ *a* conmemorativo. —*n* monumento conmemorativo, *m*; memorial, *m*

memorize /'mɛmə,raiz/ *vt* aprender de memoria

memory /'mɛməri/ *n* memoria, *f*; recuerdo, *m*. **from m.,** de memoria. **If my m. does not deceive me,** Si

mal no me acuerdo. **in m. of,** en conmemoración de; en recuerdo de

memory span *n* retentiva memorística, *f*

menace /'mɛnıs/ *n* amenaza, *f*, *vt* amenazar

menacing /'mɛnəsıŋ/ *a* amenazador

menacingly /'mɛnəsıŋli/ *adv* con amenazas

menagerie /mə'nædʒəri/ *n* colección de fieras, *f*; casa de fieras, *f*

mend /mɛnd/ *vt* remendar; componer; reparar; (darn) zurcir; (rectify) remediar; reformar; enmendar; (a fire) echar carbón (or leña, etc.) a; (one's pace) avivar. —*vi* (in health and of the weather) mejorar. —*n* remiendo, *m*; (darn) zurcido, *m*. **to be on the m.,** ir mejorando. **to m. one's ways,** reformarse, enmendarse

mendacious /mɛn'deiʃəs/ *a* mendaz

mendacity /mɛn'dæsıti/ *n* mendacidad, *f*

Mendelism /'mɛndl,ızəm/ *n* mendelismo, *m*

mender /'mɛndər/ *n* componedor (-ra); (darner) zurcidor (-ra); reparador (-ra); (cobbler and tailor) remendón, *m*

mendicancy /'mɛndıkənsi/ *n* mendicidad, *f*

mendicant /'mɛndıkənt/ *a* mendicante. —*n* mendicante, *mf*. **m. friar,** fraile mendicante, *m*

mending /'mɛndıŋ/ *n* compostura, *f*; reparación, *f*; (darning) zurcidura, *f*; ropa por zurcir, *f*

menial /'miniəl/ *a* doméstico; servil; bajo, ruin. —*n* criado (-da); lacayo, *m*

meningeal /ˌmɛnın'dʒiəl/ *a* meníngeo

meningitis /ˌmɛnın'dʒaitıs/ *n* meningitis, *f*

menopause /'mɛnə,pɔz/ *n* menopausia, *f*

menses /'mɛnsiz/ *n* menstruación, *f*

menstrual /'mɛnstruəl/ *a* menstrual

menstruate /'mɛnstru,eit/ *vi* menstruar

menstruation /ˌmɛnstru'eiʃən/ *n* menstruación, *f*,

mental /'mɛntl̩/ *a* mental; intelectual. **m. derangement,** enajenación mental, *f*. **m. hospital,** manicomio, *m*

mentality /mɛn'tælıti/ *n* mentalidad, *f*

mentally /'mɛntl̩i/ *adv* mentalmente. **m. deficient,** anormal

menthol /'mɛnθɔl/ *n* mentol, *m*

mention /'mɛnʃən/ *n* mención, *f*; alusión, *f*. —*vt* hacer mención (de), mencionar, mentar, hablar (de); aludir (a); (quote) citar; (in dispatches) nombrar. **Don't m. it!** (keep silent) ¡No digas nada!; (you're welcome) ¡No hay de que!

mentor /'mɛntɔr/ *n* mentor, *m*

menu /'mɛnyu/ *n* menú, *m*; lista de platos, *f*

meow /mi'au/ *vi* maullar. —*n* maullido, *m*

Mephistophelean /ˌmɛfəstə'filiən/ *a* mefistofélico

mephitic /mə'fitık/ *a* mefítico

mercantile /'mɜrkən,til/ *a* mercantil; mercante. **m. law,** derecho mercantil, *m*. **m. marine,** marina mercante, *f*

mercantilism /'mɜrkəntı,lızəm/ *n* mercantilismo, *m*

mercenariness /'mɜrsə,nerinıs/ *n* lo mercenario

mercenary /'mɜrsə,neri/ *a* mercenario. —*n* (soldier) mercenario, *m*

mercer /'mɜrsər/ *n* mercero, *m*

mercerize /'mɜrsə,raiz/ *vt* mercerizar

mercery /'mɜrsəri/ *n* mercería, *f*

merchandise /'mɜrtʃən,daiz/ *n* mercancía, *f*

merchant /'mɜrtʃənt/ *n* traficante (en), *mf*, negociante (en), *m*; comerciante, *mf* mercader, *m*. —*a* mercante. **The M. of Venice,** El Mercader de Venecia. **m. navy, service,** marina mercante, *f*. **m. ship,** buque mercante, *m*

merchantman /'mɜrtʃəntmən/ *n* buque mercante, *m*

merciful /'mɜrsıfəl/ *a* misericordioso, piadoso; compasivo; clemente; indulgente

mercifully /'mɜrsıfəli/ *adv* misericordiosamente; compasivamente; con indulgencia

mercifulness /'mɜrsıfəlnıs/ *n* misericordia, *f*; compasión, *f*; indulgencia, *f*

merciless /'mɜrsılıs/ *a* despiadado, inhumano

mercilessly /'mɜrsılısli/ *adv* sin piedad

mercilessness /'mɜrsılısnıs/ *n* inhumanidad, *f*; falta de compasión, *f*

mercurial /mər'kyuriəl/ *a* mercurial; (changeable) volátil; (lively) vivo

mercury /'mɜrkyəri/ n mercurio, m; (Astron. and Myth.) Mercurio, m. **Mercury's wand,** caduceo, m

mercy /'mɜrsi/ n misericordia, f; compasión, f; clemencia, f; indulgencia, f; merced, f. **at the m. of the elements,** a la intemperie. **to be at the m. of,** estar a la merced de

mere /mɪər/ a mero; simple; no más que, solo. —n lago, m

merely /'mɪərli/ adv meramente, solamente; simplemente, sencillamente

meretricious /ˌmɛrɪ'trɪʃəs/ a (archaic) meretricio; (flashy) de oropel; llamativo, charro

meretriciousness /ˌmɛrɪ'trɪʃəsnɪs/ n mal gusto, m

merge /mɜrdʒ/ vt fundir; Com. fusionar; mezclar. —vi fundirse; Com. fusionarse; mezclarse

merger /'mɜrdʒər/ n combinación, f; Com. fusión, f

meridian /mə'rɪdiən/ n (Geog. Astron.) meridiano, m; (noon) mediodía, m; (peak) apogeo, m

meringue /mə'ræŋ/ n merengue, m

merino /mə'rinou/ a de merino; merino. —n (fabric and sheep) merino, m

merit /'mɛrɪt/ n mérito, m, vt merecer, ser digno de

meritorious /ˌmɛrɪ'tɔriəs/ a meritorio

meritoriously /ˌmɛrɪ'tɔriəsli/ adv merecidamente

meritoriousness /ˌmɛrɪ'tɔriəsnɪs/ n mérito, m

merlon /'mɜrlən/ n merlón, m, almena, f

mermaid /'mɜr,meid/ n sirena, f

merrily /'mɛrɪli/ adv alegremente

merriment /'mɛrɪmənt/ n alegría, f; júbilo, m; regocijo, m; diversión, f; juego, m

merriness /'mɛrinɪs/ n alegría, f; regocijo, m; Inf. ebriedad, f

merry /'mɛri/ a alegre; jovial; feliz; regocijado, divertido; (tipsy) calamocano. **to make m.,** divertirse. **to make m. over,** reírse de. **M. Christmas!** ¡Felices Navidades! **m.-andrew,** bufón, m. **m.-go-round,** caballitos, m pl, tiovivo, m. **m.-making,** festividades, fiestas, f pl

meseta /mesa/ n meseta, f

mesh /mɛʃ/ n malla, f; Mech. engranaje, m; (network) red, f; (snare) lazo, m. —vt coger con red; Mech. endentar

mesmerism /'mɛzmə,rɪzəm/ n mesmerismo, m

mesmerize /'mɛzmə,raiz/ vt hipnotizar

mess /mɛs/ n (of food) plato de comida, m; porción, ración, f; rancho, m; (mixture) mezcla, f; (disorder) desorden, m; suciedad, f; (failure) fracaso, m. —vt (dirty) ensuciar; desordenar; (mismanage) echar a perder. **to be in a m.,** Inf. estar aviado. **to get in a m.,** Inf. hacerse un lío. **to make a m. of,** ensuciar; desordenar; (spoil) echarlo todo a rodar

message /'mɛsɪdʒ/ n mensaje, m; recado, m; (telegraphic) parte, m. **I have to take a m.,** Tengo que hacer un recado

messenger /'mɛsəndʒər/ n mensajero (-ra); (of telegrams) repartidor, m; heraldo, m; anuncio, m

Messiah /mɪ'saiə/ n Mesías, m

Messianic /ˌmɛsi'ænɪk/ a mesiánico

messrs. /'mɛsərz/ n pl (abbreviation) sres. (from señores), m pl

metabolism /mə'tæbə,lɪzəm/ n metabolismo, m

metabolize /mə'tæbə,laiz/ vt metabolizar

metal /'mɛtl/ n metal, m; vidrio en fusión, m; (road) grava, f; Herald. metal, m; (mettle) temple, temperamento, m; brío, fuego, m; pl metals, (of a railway) rieles, m pl. **m. engraver,** grabador en metal, m. **m. polish,** limpiametales, m. **m. shavings,** cizallas, f pl. **m. work,** metalistería, f. **m. worker,** metalario, m

metallic /mə'tælɪk/ a metálico

metalliferous /ˌmɛtl'ɪfərəs/ a metalífero

metalloid /'mɛtl,ɔid/ n metaloide, m

metallurgic /ˌmɛtl'ɜrdʒɪk/ a metalúrgico

metallurgist /'mɛtl,ɜrdʒɪst/ n metalúrgico, m

metallurgy /'mɛtl,ɜrdʒi/ n metalurgia, f

metamorphosis /ˌmɛtə'mɔrfəsɪs/ n metamorfosis, f

metaphor /'mɛtə,fɔr/ n metáfora, f

metaphorical /ˌmɛtə'fɔrɪkəl/ a metafórico

metaphysical /ˌmɛtə'fɪzɪkəl/ a metafísico

metaphysician /ˌmɛtəfə'zɪʃən/ n metafísico, m

metaphysics /ˌmɛtə'fɪzɪks/ n metafísica, f

metathesis /mə'tæθəsɪs/ n metátesis, f

mete /mit/ vt repartir, distribuir

metempsychosis /mə,tɛmsə'kousɪs/ n metempsicosis, f

meteor /'mitiər/ n meteoro, m

meteoric /ˌmiti'ɔrɪk/ a meteórico

meteorite /'mitiə,rait/ n meteorito, m

meteorological /ˌmitiərə'lɒdʒɪkəl/ a meteorológico

meteorologist /ˌmitiə'rɒlədʒɪst/ n meteorologista, mf

meteorology /ˌmitiə'rɒlədʒi/ n meteorología, f

meter /'mitər/ n (for gas, etc.) contador, m; (verse and measure) metro, m

methane /'mɛθein/ n metano, m

method /'mɛθəd/ n método, m; técnica, f; táctica, f

methodical /mə'θɒdɪkəl/ a metódico; ordenado, sistemático

Methodism /'mɛθə,dɪzəm/ n metodismo, m

Methodist /'mɛθədɪst/ n metodista, mf

methyl /'mɛθəl/ n metilo, m. **m. alcohol,** alcohol metílico, m

methylated spirit /'mɛθə,leitɪd/ n alcohol desnaturalizado, m

meticulous /mə'tɪkyələs/ a meticuloso; minucioso

meticulously /mə'tɪkyələsli/ adv con meticulosidad

meticulousness /mə'tɪkyələsnɪs/ n meticulosidad, f; minuciosidad, f

metric /'mɛtrɪk/ a métrico. **m. system,** sistema métrico, m

metrics /'mɛtrɪks/ n métrica, f

metronome /'mɛtrə,noum/ n metrónomo, m

metropolis /mɪ'trɒpəlɪs/ n metrópoli, f; capital, f

metropolitan /ˌmɛtrə'pɒlɪtn/ a metropolitano; de la capital. —n Eccl. metropolitano, m

mettle /'mɛtl/ n temple, temperamento, m; fuego, brío, m; valor, m. **You have put him on his m.,** Le has picado en el amor propio

mew /myu/ n (gull) gaviota, f; (of a cat) maullido, m; (of sea-birds) alarido, m. —vi (of a cat) maullar; (of sea-birds) dar alaridos. **to mew up,** encerrar

mews /myuz/ n establos, m pl, caballeriza, f

Mexican /'mɛksɪkən/ a mejicano. —n mejicano (-na)

Mexico /'mɛksɪ,kou/ Méjico, m

mezzanine /'mɛzə,nin/ n entresuelo, m

mezzo soprano /'mɛtsou sə'prænou/ n mezzosoprano

mi /mi/ n Mus. mi, m

miaow /mi'au/ n miau, m, vi maullar

miasma /mai'æzmə/ n miasma, m

miasmatic /ˌmaiəz'mætɪk/ a miasmático

mica /'maikə/ n mica, f

microbe /'maikroub/ n microbio, m

microbial /mai'kroubiəl/ a microbiano

microbiologist /ˌmaikroubai'ɒlədʒɪst/ n microbiólogo, m

microbiology /ˌmaikroubai'ɒlədʒi/ n microbiología, f

microcosm /'maikrə,kɒzəm/ n microcosmo, m

microphone /'maikrə,foun/ n micrófono, m

microscope /'maikrə,skoup/ n microscopio, m

microscopic /ˌmaikrə'skɒpɪk/ a microscópico

microwave /'maikrou,weiv/ n microonda, f

mid /mɪd/ a medio. —prep entre; en medio de; a mediados de. **from mid May to August,** desde mediados de mayo hasta agosto. **a mid-fourteenth century castle,** un castillo de mediados del siglo catorce. **in mid air,** en medio del aire. **in mid channel,** en medio del canal. **in mid winter,** en medio del invierno

midday /'mɪd'dei/ n mediodía, m, a del mediodía, meridional. **at m.,** a mediodía

midden /'mɪdn/ n muladar, m

middle /'mɪdl/ a medio; en medio de; del centro; intermedio; (average) mediano. —n medio, m; mitad, f; centro, m; (waist) cintura, f. **in the m. of,** en medio de. **in the m. of nowhere,** donde Cristo dio las tres voces. **toward the m. of the month,** a mediados del mes. **m. age,** edad madura, f. **m.-aged,** de edad madura, de cierta edad. **M. Ages,** edad media, f. **m. class,** clase media, burguesía, f, a de la clase media, burgués. **m. distance,** término medio, m. **m. ear,** oído medio, m. **m. finger,** dedo de en medio (or del corazón), m. **m. way,** Fig. término medio, m. **m. weight,** peso medio, m

Middle East, the el Oriente Medio, el Levante, *m*
middleman /'mɪdl̩,mæn/ *n* agente de negocios, *m;* (retailer) revendedor, *m;* intermediario, *m*
middling /'mɪdlɪŋ/ *a* mediano; mediocre; regular, así, así
midge /mɪdʒ/ *n* mosquito, *m*, mosca de agua, *f*
midget /'mɪdʒɪt/ *n* enano (-na). **m. submarine,** submarino de bolsillo, *m*
midnight /'mɪd,naɪt/ *n* medianoche, *f.* —*a* de medianoche; nocturno. **at m.,** a medianoche. **to burn the m. oil,** quemarse las cejas. **m. mass,** misa del gallo, *f*
midriff /'mɪdrɪf/ *n* diafragma, *m*
midship /'mɪd,ʃɪp/ *a* maestro. —*n* medio del buque, *m.* **m. beam,** bao maestro, *m.* **m. gangway,** crujía, *f*
midshipman /'mɪd,ʃɪpmən/ *n* guardiamarina, *m*
midst /mɪdst/ *n* medio, *m;* seno, *m, prep* entre. **in the m. of,** en medio de. **There is a traitor in our m.,** Hay un traidor entre nosotros (or en nuestra compañía)
midstream, /'mɪd'strim/ *n* **in m.** *m.* en medio de la corriente
midsummer /'mɪd'sʌmər/ *n* pleno verano, *m;* solsticio estival, *m;* fiesta de San Juan, *f.* **A M. Night's Dream,** El Sueño de la Noche de San Juan
midway / *adv, a* 'mɪd'weɪ; *n* -,weɪ/ *a* and *adv* situado a medio camino; a medio camino, a la mitad del camino; entre. —*n* mitad del camino, *f;* medio, *m.* **m. between...,** equidistante de..., entre
midwife /'mɪd,waɪf/ *n* comadrona, partera, *f*
midwifery /mɪd'wɪfəri/ *n* obstetricia, *f*
midwinter /*n.* 'mɪd'wɪntər, -,wɪn-; *a* -,wɪn-/ *n* medio del invierno, *f*
mien /min/ *n* aire, *m;* porte, semblante, *m*
might /maɪt/ *vi* poder. **It m. or m. not be true,** Podría o no podría ser verdad. **How happy Mary m. have been!** ¡Qué feliz pudo haber sido María! **I thought that you m. have seen him in the theater,** Creí que pudieras haberle visto en el teatro. **That I m....!** ¡Que yo pudiese...! **This m. have been avoided if...,** Esto podía haberse evitado si...
might /maɪt/ *n* fuerza, *f;* poder, *m.* **with m. and main,** con todas sus fuerzas
mightily /'maɪtl̩i/ *adv* fuertemente; poderosamente; *Inf.* muchísimo, sumamente
mightiness /'maɪtinɪs/ *n* fuerza, *f;* poder, *m;* grandeza, *f*
mighty /'maɪti/ *a* fuerte, vigoroso; poderoso; grande; *Inf.* enorme; (proud) arrogante. —*adv Inf.* enormemente, muy
migraine /'maɪgreɪn/ *n* migraña, jaqueca, *f*
migrant /'maɪgrənt/ *a* migratorio, de paso. —*n* ave migratoria, ave de paso, *f*
migrate /'maɪgreɪt/ *vi* emigrar
migration /maɪ'greɪʃən/ *n* migración, *f*
migratory /'maɪgrə,tɔri/ *a* migratorio, de paso; (of people) nómada, pasajero
migratory worker *n* trabajador golondrino, *m*
Milanese /,mɪlə'niz/ *a* milanés. —*n* milanés (-esa)
milch /mɪltʃ/ *a f,* (of cows) lechera
mild /maɪld/ *a* apacible, pacífico; manso; dulce; suave; (of the weather) blando; *Med.* benigno; (light) leve; (of drinks) ligero; (weak) débil
mildew /'mɪl,du/ *n* mildiu, añublo, *m;* moho, *m.* —*vt* anublar; enmohecer. —*vi* anublarse; enmohecerse
mildly /'maɪldli/ *adv* suavemente; dulcemente; con indulgencia
mildness /'maɪldnɪs/ *n* apacibilidad, *f;* mansedumbre, *f;* suavidad, *f;* (of weather) blandura, *f;* dulzura, *f;* indulgencia, *f;* (weakness) debilidad, *f*
mile /maɪl/ *n* milla, *f*
mileage /'maɪlɪdʒ/ *n* distancia en millas, *f;* kilometraje, *m*
milestone /'maɪl,stoun/ *n* hito, *m*, piedra miliaria, *f;* mojón kilométrico, *m*
milfoil /'mɪl,fɔɪl/ *n* milenrama, *f*
militancy /'mɪlɪtənsi/ *n* carácter militante, *m;* belicosidad, *f*
militant /'mɪlɪtənt/ *a* militante, combatiente; belicoso; agresivo. —*n* combatiente, *mf*
militarily /,mɪlɪ'tɛrəli/ *adv* militarmente

militariness /'mɪlɪ,tɛrinɪs/ *n* lo militar, el carácter militar
militarism /'mɪlɪtə,rɪzəm/ *n* militarismo, *m*
militarist /'mɪlɪtərɪst/ *n* militarista, *mf*
militaristic /,mɪlɪtə'rɪstɪk/ *a* militarista
militarization /,mɪlɪtərɪ'zeɪʃən/ *n* militarización, *f*
militarize /'mɪlɪtə,raɪz/ *vt* militarizar
military /'mɪlɪ,tɛri/ *a* militar; de guerra. **the m.,** los militares. **m. academy,** colegio militar, *m.* **m. camp,** campo militar, *m.* **m. law,** código militar, *m.* **m. man,** militar, *m.* **m. police,** policía militar, *f.* **m. service,** servicio militar, *m*
militate /'mɪlɪ,teɪt/ **(against)** *vi* militar contra
militia /mɪ'lɪʃə/ *n* milicia, *f*
militiaman /mɪ'lɪʃəmən/ *n* miliciano, *m*
milk /mɪlk/ *n* leche, *f.* —*a* de leche; lácteo. —*vt* ordeñar. —*vi* dar leche. **to have m. and water in one's veins,** tener sangre de horchata. **condensed m.,** leche condensada, leche en lata, *f.* **m.-can,** lechera, *f.* **m.-cart,** carro de la leche, *m.* **m. chocolate,** chocolate con leche, *m.* **m. of magnesia,** leche de magnesia, *f.* **m.-pail,** ordeñadero, *m.* **m.-tooth,** diente de leche, *m.* **m.-white,** blanco como la leche
milkiness /'mɪlkinɪs/ *n* lactescencia, *f;* carácter lechoso, *m;* (whiteness) blancura, *f*
milking /'mɪlkɪŋ/ *n* ordeño, *m.* **m.-machine,** máquina ordeñadora, *f.* **m.-stool,** taburete, banquillo, *m*
milkmaid /'mɪlk,meɪd/ *n* lechera, *f*
milkman /'mɪlk,mæn/ *n* lechero, *m*
milksop /'mɪlk,sɒp/ *n* marica, *m*
milky /'mɪlki/ *a* lechoso; de leche; lechoso, como leche; *Astron.* lácteo. **the Milky Way** la Vía láctea *f*
mill /mɪl/ *n* molino, *m;* (for coffee, etc.) molinillo, *m;* (factory) fábrica, *f;* taller, *m;* (textile) fábrica, *f;* fábrica de tejidos, *f;* (fight) riña a puñetazos, *f;* pugilato, *m.* —*vt* (grind) moler; (coins) acordonar; (cloth) abatanar; (chocolate) batir. **cotton m.,** hilandería de algodón, *f.* **hand-m.,** molinillo, *m.* **paper-m.,** fábrica de papel, *f.* **saw-m.,** serrería, *f.* **spinning m.,** hilandería, *f.* **water m.,** molino de agua, *m.* **m.-course,** saetín, canal de molino, *m.* **m.-dam,** esclusa de molino, *f.* **m.-hand,** obrero (-ra). **m.-pond,** cubo, *m.* **m.-race,** caz, *m.* **m.-wheel,** rueda de molino, *f*
millennial /mɪ'lɛniəl/ *a* milenario
millennium /mɪ'lɛniəm/ *n* milenario, *m*
miller /'mɪlər/ *n* molinero, *m.* **miller's wife,** molinera
millet /'mɪlɪt/ *n* mijo, *m*
milligram /'mɪlɪ,græm/ *n* miligramo, *m*
milliliter /'mɪlə,litər/ *n* mililitro, *m*
millimeter /'mɪlə,mitər/ *n* milímetro, *m*
milliner /'mɪlənər/ *n* sombrerero (-ra), modista, *mf* **milliner's shop,** sombrerería, tienda de modista, *f*
millinery /'mɪlə,nɛri/ *n* sombreros, *m pl;* modas, *f pl;* tienda de modista, *f*
milling /'mɪlɪŋ/ *n* molienda, *f;* acuñación, *f;* (edge of coin) cordoncillo, *m.* **m. machine,** fresadora, *f*
million /'mɪlyən/ *n* millón, *m.* **the m.,** las masas
millionaire /,mɪlyə'nɛər/ *a* millonario. —*n* millonario, *m*
millionairess /,mɪlyə'nɛərɪs/ *n* millonaria, *f*
millionth /'mɪlyənθ/ *a* millonésimo
millstone /'mɪl,stoun/ *n* piedra de moler, muela, *f*
mime /maɪm/ *n* (Greek farce and actor) mimo, *m;* (mimicry) mímica, *f;* pantomima, *f.* —*vi* hacer en pantomima
mimetic /mɪ'mɛtɪk/ *a* mímico, imitativo
mimic /'mɪmɪk/ *a* mímico; (pretended) fingido. —*n* imitador (-ra). —*vt* imitar, contrahacer; *Biol.* imitar, adaptarse a
mimicry /'mɪmɪkri/ *n* mímica, imitación, *f; Biol.* mimetismo, *m*
minaret /,mɪnə'rɛt/ *n* minarete, *m;* (of a mosque) alminar, *m*
minatory /'mɪnə,tɔri, -,touri/ *a* amenazador
mince /mɪns/ *vt* desmenuzar; (meat) picar; (words) medir (las palabras). —*vi* andar con pasos menuditos; andar o moverse con afectación; hacer remilgos. **m.-meat,** carne picada, *f;* (sweet) conserva de fruta y especias, *f*
mincing /'mɪnsɪŋ/ *a* afectado. —*n* acción de picar carne, *f.* **m. machine,** máquina de picar carne, *f*

mincingly /'mɪnsɪŋli/ adv con afectación; con pasos menuditos

mind /maind/ n inteligencia, f; espíritu ánimo, m; imaginación, f; alma, f; (memory) memoria, f, recuerdo, m; (understanding) entendimiento, m; (genius) ingenio, m; (cast of mind) mentalidad, f; (opinion) opinión, f; (liking) gusto, m; (thoughts) pensamiento, m; (intention) propósito, m, intención, f; (tendency) propensión, inclinación, f. **I have a good m. to go away,** Por poco me marcho; Tengo ganas de marcharme. **I have changed my m.,** He cambiado de opinión. **out of m.,** olvidado. **I shall give him a piece of my m.,** Le diré cuatro verdades. **It had quite gone out of my m.,** Lo había olvidado completamente. **I can see it in my mind's eye,** Está presente a mi imaginación. **I shall bear it in m.,** Lo tendré en cuenta. **I thought in my own m. that...,** Pensé por mis adentros que... **We are both of the same m.,** Ambos somos de la misma opinión. **to be out of one's m.,** estar fuera de juicio. **to call to m.,** acordarse de. **to have something on one's m.,** estar preocupado. **to make up one's m.** (to), resolverse (a), decidirse (a), determinar; animarse (a). **m.-reader,** adivinador (-ra) del pensamiento

mind /maind/ vt (remember) recordar, no olvidar; (heed) atender a; hacer caso de; tener cuidado de; (fear) tener miedo de; (obey) obedecer; preocuparse de; (object to) molestar; importar; (care for) cuidar. —vi tener cuidado; molestar; (feel) sentir; (fear) tener miedo; (be the same thing) ser igual. **Do you m. being quiet a moment?** ¿Quieres hacer el favor de callarte un momento? **Do you m. if I smoke?** ¡Le molesta si fumo? **They don't m.,** No les importa, Les da igual. **Never m.!** ¡No se moleste!; ¡No se preocupe!; ¡No importa! ¡Vaya! **M. what you are doing!** ¡Cuidado con lo que haces! **M. your own business!** ¡No te metas donde no te llaman!

minded /'maindɪd/ a dispuesto, inclinado; de... pensamientos; de... disposición

mindful /'maindfəl/ a atento (a), cuidadoso (de); que se acuerda (de)

mine /main/ a poss mío, m, (mía, f; míos, m pl; mías, f pl); el mío, m, (la mía, f; lo mío, neut; los míos, m pl; las mías, f pl); mi (pl mis). **a friend of m.,** un amigo mío; uno de mis amigos

mine /main/ n mina, f. —vt minar; extraer; sembrar minas en, colocar minas en. —vi minar; hacer una mina; dedicarse a la minería. **drifting m.,** mina a la deriva, f. **land m.,** mina terrestre, f. **magnetic m.,** mina magnética, f. **to lay mines,** colocar (or sembrar) minas. **m.-sweeper,** dragaminas, buque barreminas, m

minefield /'main,fild/ n campo de minas, m; barrera de minas, f

minelayer /'main,leiər/ n barca plantaminas, f, barco siembraminas, lanzaminas, m

miner /'mainər/ n minero, m; Mil. zapador minador, m

mineral /'mɪnərəl/ n mineral, m, a mineral. **m. baths,** baños, m pl. **m. water,** agua mineral, f; gaseosa, f

mineralogical /,mɪnərə'lɒdʒɪkəl/ a mineralógico

mineralogist /,mɪnə'blædʒɪst/ n mineralogista, m

mineralogy /,mɪnə'rɒlədʒi/ n mineralogía, f

mingle /'mɪŋgəl/ vt mezclar; confundir. —vi mezclarse; confundirse

mingling /'mɪŋglɪŋ/ n mezcla, f

miniature /'mɪniətʃər/ n miniatura, f. —a en miniatura. **m. edition,** edición diamante, f

miniature golf n minigolf, m

miniaturist /'mɪniətʃərɪst/ n miniaturista, mf

minimize /'mɪnə,maiz/ vt aminorar, reducir al mínimo; mitigar; (underrate) tener en menos, despreciar

minimum /'mɪnəməm/ n mínimo, m, a mínimo

mining /'mainɪŋ/ n minería, f, a minero; de mina; de minas; de minero. **m. engineer,** ingeniero de minas, m

minion /'mɪnyən/ n favorito (-ta); satélite, m; Print. miñona, f

minister /'mɪnəstər/ n ministro, m. —vi servir; suministrar, proveer de; (contribute) contribuir (a).

m. of health, ministro de sanidad, m. **m. of war,** ministro de la guerra, m

ministerial /,mɪnə'stɪəriəl/ a ministerial

ministration /,mɪnə'streiʃən/ n Eccl. ministerio, m; servicio, m; agencia, f

ministry /'mɪnəstri/ n ministerio, m. **m. of food,** Ministerio de Abastecimientos, m

mink /mɪŋk/ n visón, m

minnow /'mɪnou/ n pez pequeño de agua dulce, m

minor /'mainər/ a menor. —n menor de edad, m; (logic) menor, f; Mus. tono menor, m; Eccl. menor, m. **to be a m.,** ser menor de edad. **m. key,** tono menor, m. **m. orders,** Eccl. órdenes menores, f pl. **m. scale,** escala menor, f

Minorca /mɪ'nɔrkə/ Menorca, f

minority /mɪ'nɔrɪti/ n minoría, f; (of age) minoridad, f. **in the m.,** en la minoría

minster /'mɪnstər/ n catedral, f; monasterio, m

minstrel /'mɪnstrəl/ n trovador, juglar, m; músico, m; cantante, m

minstrelsy /'mɪnstrəlsi/ n música, f; canto, m; arte del trovador, m, or f; gaya ciencia, f

mint /mɪnt/ n Bot. menta, hierbabuena, f; casa de moneda, casa de la moneda, ceca, f; Fig. mina, f; (source) origen, m. —vt (money) acuñar; Fig. inventar, a (postage stamp) en estado nuevo

minter /'mɪntər/ n acuñador, m; Fig. inventor (-ra)

minting /'mɪntɪŋ/ n (of coins) acuñación, f; Fig. invención, f

minuet /,mɪnyu'et/ n minué, m

minus /'mainəs/ a menos; negativo; desprovisto de; sin. —n signo menos, m; cantidad negativa, f

minute /mai'nut/ a menudo, diminuto; insignificante; minucioso

minute /'mɪnɪt/ n minuto, m; momento, m; instante, m; (note) minuta, f; pl **minutes,** actas, f pl. **in a m.,** en un instante. **m.-book,** libro de actas, minutario, m. **m.-hand,** minutero, m

minutely /mai'nutli/ adv minuciosamente; en detalle; exactamente

minuteness /mai'nutnɪs/ n suma pequeñez, f; minuciosidad, f

minx /mɪŋks/ n picaruela, f; coqueta, f

miracle /'mɪrəkəl/ n milagro, m. **m. m.-monger,** milagrero (-ra). **m. play,** milagro, m

miraculous /mɪ'rækyələs/ a milagroso

miraculously /mɪ'rækyələsli/ adv milagrosamente, por milagro

miraculousness /mɪ'rækyələsnɪs/ n carácter milagroso, m, lo milagroso

mirage /mɪ'rɑʒ/ n espejismo, m

mire /maiər/ n fango, lodo, m; (miry place) lodazal, m

mirror /'mɪrər/ n espejo, m. —vt reflejar. **to look in the m.,** mirarse al espejo. **full-length m.,** espejo de cuerpo entero, m. **small m.,** espejuelo, m

mirth /mɜrθ/ n alegría, f, júbilo, m; risa, f; hilaridad, f

mirthful /'mɜrθfəl/ a alegre

mirthless /'mɜrθlɪs/ a sin alegría, triste

miry /'maiəri/ a lodoso, fangoso, cenagoso

misadventure /,mɪsəd'ventʃər/ n desgracia, f; accidente, m

misanthrope /'mɪsən,θroup/ n misántropo, m

misanthropic /,mɪsən'θrɒpɪk/ a misantrópico

misanthropy /mɪs'ænθrəpi/ n misantropía, f

misapplication /,mɪsæplɪ'keiʃən/ n mala aplicación, f; mal uso, m; abuso, m

misapply /,mɪsə'plai/ vt aplicar mal; hacer mal uso de; abusar de

misapprehend /,mɪsæprɪ'hɛnd/ vt comprender mal; equivocarse sobre

misapprehension /,mɪsæprə'hɛnʃən/ n concepto erróneo, m; equivocación, f, error, m

misappropriate /,mɪsə'proupri,eit/ vt malversar

misappropriation /,mɪsəproupri'eiʃən/ n malversación, f

misbehave /,mɪsbɪ'heiv/ vi portarse mal; (of a child) ser malo

misbehavior /,mɪsbɪ'heivyər/ n mala conducta, f

mistake

miscalculate /mɪsˈkælkyəleit/ *vt* calcular mal; engañarse (sobre)

miscalculation /ˌmɪskælkyəˈleiʃən/ *n* mal cálculo, error, *m;* desacierto, *m*

miscall /mɪsˈkɔl/ *vt* mal nombrar; llamar equivocadamente; (abuse) insultar

miscarriage /mɪsˈkærɪdʒ/ *n Med.* aborto, *m;* (failure) malogro, fracaso, *m;* (of goods) extravío, *m*

miscarriage of justice *n* yerro en la administración de la justicia, *m*

miscarry /mɪsˈkæri/ *vi Med.* abortar, malparir; (fail) malograrse, frustrarse; (of goods) extraviarse

miscellaneous /ˌmɪsəˈleiniəs/ *a* misceláneo; vario, diverso

miscellany /ˈmɪsəˌleini/ *n* miscelánea, *f*

mischance /mɪsˈtʃæns/ *n* mala suerte, *f;* infortunio, *m,* desgracia, *f;* accidente, *m*

mischief /ˈmɪstʃif/ *n* daño, *m;* mal, *m;* (wilfulness) travesura, *f;* (person) diablillo, *m.* **m.-maker,** enredador (-ra), chismoso (-sa); alborotador, *m;* malicioso (-sa). **m.-making,** *a* enredador; chismoso; malicioso; alborotador

mischievous /ˈmɪstʃəvəs/ *a* dañino, perjudicial, malo; malicioso; chismoso; (wilful) travieso; juguetón; (of glances, etc.) malicioso

mischievously /ˈmɪstʃəvəsli/ *adv* maliciosamente; con (or por) travesura

mischievousness /ˈmɪstʃəvəsnɪs/ *n* mal, *m;* malicia, *f;* maleficencia, *f;* travesura, *f*

misconceive /ˌmɪskənˈsiv/ *vt* formar un concepto erróneo de; concebir mal, juzgar mal

misconception /ˌmɪskənˈsepʃən/ *n* concepto erróneo, *m,* idea falsa, *f;* error, *m,* equivocación, *f;* engaño, *m*

misconduct / *n* mɪsˈkɒndʌkt; *v* ˌmɪskənˈdʌkt/ *n* mala conducta, *f.* **to m. oneself,** portarse mal

misconstruction /ˌmɪskənˈstrʌkʃən/ *n* mala interpretación, *f;* falsa interpretación, *f;* tergiversación, *f;* mala traducción, *f*

misconstrue /ˌmɪskənˈstru/ *vt* interpretar mal; entender mal; tergiversar; traducir mal

miscount / *v* mɪsˈkaunt; *n* ˈmɪsˌkaunt/ *vt* contar mal, equivocarse en la cuenta de; calcular mal. —*n* error, *m;* yerro de cuenta, *m*

miscreant /ˈmɪskriənt/ *n* malandrín, *m;* bribón, *m, a* vil, malandrín

misdeed /mɪsˈdid/ *n* delito, malhecho, crimen, *m*

misdemeanor /ˌmɪsdɪˈminər/ *n* mala conducta, *f; Law.* delito, *m;* ofensa, *f,* malhecho, *m*

misdirect /ˌmɪsdɪˈrekt/ *vt* informar mal (acerca del camino); (a letter) dirigir mal, poner unas señas incorrectas a

miser /ˈmaizər/ *n* avaro (-ra)

miserable /ˈmɪzərəbəl/ *a* infeliz, desgraciado; miserable; despreciable; sin valor

miserably /ˈmɪzərəbli/ *adv* miserablemente

miserliness /ˈmaizərlɪnɪs/ *n* avaricia, tacañería, *f*

miserly /ˈmaizərli/ *a* avaro, tacaño

misery /ˈmɪzəri/ *n* miseria, *f;* sufrimiento, *m;* dolor, tormento, *m*

misfire /mɪsˈfiʳr/ *vi* no dar fuego; (of a motor-car, etc.) hacer falsas explosiones, errar el encendido

misfit /mɪsˈfit; ˈmɪsˌfit *for person*/ *n* traje que no cae bien, *m;* zapato que no va bien, *m;* (person) inadaptado, *m*

misfortune /mɪsˈfɔrtʃən/ *n* infortunio, *m,* mala suerte, adversidad, *f;* desdicha, desgracia, *f;* mal, *m*

misgive /mɪsˈgɪv/ *vt* hacer temer; llenar de duda; hacer recelar; hacer presentir

misgiving /mɪsˈgɪvɪŋ/ *n* temor, *m;* duda, *f;* recelo, *m;* presentimiento, *m*

misgovern /mɪsˈgʌvərn/ *vt* gobernar mal; administrar mal; dirigir mal

misgovernment /mɪsˈgʌvərnmənt/ *n* desgobierno, *m;* mala administración, *f*

misguided /mɪsˈgaidid/ *a* mal dirigido; extraviado; engañado; (blind) ciego

misguidedly /mɪsˈgaididli/ *adv* equivocadamente

mishap /ˈmɪshæp/ *n* desgracia, *f;* contratiempo, accidente, *m.* **to have a m.,** sufrir una desgracia; tener un accidente

misinform /ˌmɪsɪnˈfɔrm/ *vt* informar mal; dar informes erróneos (a)

misinformation /ˌmɪsɪnfərˈmeiʃən/ *n* noticia falsa, *f;* información errónea, *f*

misinterpret /ˌmɪsɪnˈtɜrprɪt/ *vt* interpretar mal; entender mal; torcer; tergiversar; traducir mal

misinterpretation /ˌmɪsɪnˌtɜrprɪˈteiʃən/ *n* mala interpretación, *f;* interpretación falsa, *f;* tergiversación, *f;* mala traducción, *f*

misjudge /mɪsˈdʒʌdʒ/ *vt* juzgar mal; equivocarse (en or sobre); tener una idea falsa de

misjudgment /mɪsˈdʒʌdʒmənt/ *n* juicio errado, *m;* idea falsa, *f;* juicio injusto, *m*

mislay /mɪsˈlei/ *vt* extraviar, perder

mislead /mɪsˈlid/ *vt* extraviar; llevar a conclusiones erróneas, despistar; engañar

misleading /mɪsˈlidɪŋ/ *a* de falsas apariencias; erróneo, falso; engañoso

mismanage /mɪsˈmænɪdʒ/ *vt* administrar mal; dirigir mal; echar a perder

mismanagement /mɪsˈmænɪdʒmənt/ *n* mala administración, *f;* desgobierno, *m*

misname /mɪsˈneim/ *vt* mal nombrar; llamar equivocadamente

misnomer /mɪsˈnoumər/ *n* nombre equivocado, *m;* nombre inapropiado, *m*

misogynist /mɪsˈɒdʒənɪst/ *n* misógino, *m*

misogyny /mɪˈsɒdʒəni/ *n* misoginia, *f*

misplace /mɪsˈpleis/ *vt* colocar mal; poner fuera de lugar

misplaced /mɪsˈpleist/ *a* mal puesto; inoportuno; equivocado

misprint /*n* ˈmɪsˌprɪnt; *v* mɪsˈprɪnt/ *n* error de imprenta, *m,* errata, *f, vt* imprimir con erratas

mispronounce /ˌmɪsprəˈnauns/ *vt* pronunciar mal

mispronunciation /ˌmɪsprənʌnsiˈeiʃən/ *n* mala pronunciación, *f*

misquotation *n* cita errónea, *f*

misquote /mɪsˈkwout/ *vt* citar mal, citar erróneamente

misrepresent /ˌmɪsreprɪˈzent/ *vt* desfigurar; tergiversar; falsificar

misrepresentation /ˌmɪsˌreprɪzenˈteiʃən/ *n* desfiguración, *f;* tergiversación, *f;* falsificación, *f*

misrule /mɪsˈrul/ *vt* gobernar mal. —*n* mal gobierno, desgobierno, *m;* confusión, *f*

miss /mɪs/ *n* señorita, *f*

miss /mɪs/ *vt* (one's aim) errar (el tiro, etc.); no acertar (a); (let fall) dejar caer; (lose a train, the post, etc., one's footing, an opportunity, etc.) perder; (fall short of) dejar de; no ver; no notar; pasar por alto de; omitir; echar de menos; notar la falta de; no encontrar. —*vi* errar; (fail) salir mal, fracasar. **I m. you,** Te echo de menos. **to be missing,** faltar; estar ausente; haberse marchado; haber desaparecido. **to m. one's mark,** errar el blanco. **to m. out,** omitir, pasar por alto de. **She doesn't miss a beat,** (fig.) No se le escapa nada

missal /ˈmɪsəl/ *n* misal, *m*

misshapen /mɪsˈʃeipən/ *a* deforme

missile /ˈmɪsəl/ *n* arma arrojadiza, *f;* proyectil, *m*

missing /ˈmɪsɪŋ/ *a* que falta; perdido; ausente; *Mil.* desaparecido

mission /ˈmɪʃən/ *n* misión, *f*

missionary /ˈmɪʃəˌneri/ *n* misionero, *m*

missionize /ˈmɪʃəˌnaiz/ *vi* misionar

missis /ˈmɪsəz/ *n* señora, *f; Inf.* mujer, *f*

Mississippi /ˌmɪsəˈsɪpi/ el Misisipí, *m*

missive /ˈmɪsɪv/ *n* misiva, *f*

Missouri /mɪˈzuri/ el Misuri, *m*

misspend /mɪsˈspend/ *vt* malgastar; desperdiciar; perder

mist /mɪst/ *n* bruma, neblina, *f;* vapor, *m;* (drizzle) llovizna, *f; Fig.* nube, *f.* —*vt* anublar, empañar. —*vi* lloviznar

mistakable /mɪˈsteikəbəl/ *a* confundible

mistake /mɪˈsteik/ *vt* comprender mal; equivocarse sobre; errar; (with for) confundir con, equivocarse con. —*n* equivocación, *f;* error, *m;* inadvertencia, *f;* (in an exercise, etc.) falta, *f.* **And no m.!** *Inf.* Sin duda alguna. **by m.,** por equivocación; (involuntarily) sin querer. **If I am not mistaken,** Si no me engaño, Si no estoy equivocado. **to make a m.,** equivocarse

mistaken /mɪ'steikən/ a (of persons and things) equivocado; (of things) erróneo; incorrecto
mistakenly adv equivocadamente; injustamente, falsamente
mister /'mɪstər/ n señor, m
mistily /'mɪstəli/ adv a través de la neblina; obscuramente; indistintamente, vagamente
mistimed /mɪs'taimd/ a intempestivo; inoportuno
mistiness /'mɪstɪnɪs/ n neblina, bruma, f; vaporosidad, f; obscuridad, f
mistletoe /'mɪsəl,tou/ n muérdago, m
mistranslate /,mɪstrænz'leit/ vt traducir mal; interpretar mal
mistranslation /,mɪstrænz'leiʃən/ n mala traducción, f; traducción inexacta, f
mistress /'mɪstrɪs/ n señora, f; maestra, f; (fiancée) prometida, f; (beloved) amada, dulce dueña, f; (concubine) amiga, querida, f. **M. (Mrs.) Gómez**, Sra Gómez. **m. of the robes**, camarera mayor, f
mistrust /mɪs'trʌst/ vt desconfiar de, no tener confianza en; dudar de. —n desconfianza, f; recelo, m, suspicacia, f; aprensión, f
mistrustful /mɪs'trʌstfəl/ a desconfiado; receloso, suspicaz. **to be m. of**, recelarse de
misty /'mɪsti/ a brumoso, nebuloso; vaporoso; (of the eyes) anublado; (of windows, etc.) empañado
misunderstand /,mɪsʌndər'stænd/ vt comprender mal; tomar en sentido erróneo; interpretar mal
misunderstanding /,mɪsʌndər'stændɪŋ/ n concepto erróneo, error, m; equivocación, f; (disagreement) desavenencia, f
misuse /n mɪs'yus; v -'yuz/ vt emplear mal; abusar de; (funds) malversar; (ill-treat) tratar mal. —n abuso, m; (of funds) malversación, f
mite /mait/ n (coin) ardite, m; (trifle) pizca, f; óbolo, m; Ent. ácaro, m
miter /'maitər/ n mitra, f; inglete, m, vt cortar ingletes en
mitigate /'mɪtɪ,geit/ vt (pain) aliviar; mitigar; suavizar
mitigation /,mɪtɪ'geiʃən/ n (of pain) alivio, m; mitigación, f
mitten /'mɪtn̩/ n mitón, m
mix /mɪks/ vt mezclar; (salad) aderezar; (concrete, etc.) amasar; combinar, unir; (sociably) alternar (con); (confuse) confundir. —vi mezclarse; frecuentar la compañía (de); frecuentar; (get on well) llevarse bien
mixed /mɪkst/ a mezclado; vario, surtido; mixto; (confused) confuso. **m. doubles**, parejas mixtas, f pl. **m. up**, (in disorder) revuelto; confuso. **m. up with**, implicado en; asociado con
mixer /'mɪksər/ n mezclador, m; (person) mezclador (-ra); Inf. persona sociable, f. **electric m.**, mezclador eléctrico, m
mixture /'mɪkstʃər/ n mezcla, f; (medicine) poción, medicina, f
mizzen /'mɪzən/ n mesana, f. **m.-mast**, palo de mesana, m. **m.-sail**, vela de mesana, f. **m.-topsail**, sobremesana, f
mnemonics /nɪ'mɒnɪks/ n mnemotecnia, f
Moabite /'mouə,bait/ n moabita, mf
moan /moun/ vt lamentar; llorar. —vi gemir; quejarse, lamentarse. —n gemido, m; lamento, m; quejido, m
moaning /'mounɪŋ/ n gemidos, m pl
moat /mout/ n foso, m
mob /mɒb/ n (crowd) muchedumbre, multitud, f; (rabble) populacho, m, gentuza, f. —vt atropellar; atacar. **mob-cap**, cofia, f
mobile /'moubil/ a móvil; ambulante; (fickle) voluble. **m. canteen**, cantina ambulante, f
mobility /mou'bɪliti/ n movilidad, f
mobilization /,moubələ'zeiʃən/ n movilización, f
mobilize /'moubə,laiz/ vt movilizar. —vi movilizarse
moccasin /'mɒkəsɪn, -zən/ n mocasín, m
mocha /'moukə/ n café de Moca, m
mock /mɒk/ vt ridiculizar; burlarse (de), mofarse (de); (cause to fail) frustrar; (mimic) imitar; (delude) engañar. —vi mofarse, burlarse, reírse. —a cómico, burlesco; falso; fingido; imitado. **to make a m. of**, poner en ridículo; hacer absurdo; burlarse de. **m.-**

heroic, heroico-cómico. **m.-orange,** Bot. jeringuilla, f.
m.-turtle soup, sopa hecha con cabeza de ternera a imitación de tortuga, f
mocker n mofador (-ra); el, m, (f, la) que se burla de
mockery /'mɒkəri/ n mofa, burla, f; ridículo, m; ilusión, apariencia, f. **to make a m. of,** mofarse de; hacer ridículo
mocking /'mɒkɪŋ/ a burlón. **m. bird,** pájaro burlón, m
mockingly /'mɒkɪŋli/ adv burlonamente
modality /mou'dæliti/ n modalidad, f
mode /moud/ n modo, m; manera, f; (fashion) moda, f; uso, m, costumbre, f
model /'mɒdl/ n modelo, m; (artist's) modelo vivo, m, a modelo; en miniatura. —vt modelar; moldear; formar; hacer; planear. **m. display,** (hats, etc.) exposición de modelos, f. **m. railway,** ferrocarril en miniatura, m
modeler /'mɒdlər/ n modelador (-ra); disenador, m
modeling /'mɒdlɪŋ/ n modelado, m; modelo, m. **m. wax,** cera para moldear, f
modem /'moudəm, -dem/ n módem, m
moderate /a, n. 'mɒdərɪt v. -ə,reit/ a moderado; (of prices, etc.) módico; (fair, medium) regular, mediano; razonable; mediocre. —n moderado, m. —vt moderar; modificar; calmar. —vi moderarse; calmarse
moderately /'mɒdərɪtli/ adv moderadamente; módicamente; medianamente; bastante; razonablemente; mediocremente
moderation /,mɒdə'reiʃən/ n moderación, f. **in m.,** en moderación
moderator /'mɒdə,reitər/ n moderador, m; (Church of Scotland) presidente, m; Educ. examinador, m; Educ. inspector de exámenes, m. **m. lamp,** lámpara de regulador, f
modern /'mɒdərn/ a moderno. —n modernista, mf. **in the m. way,** a la moderna. **m. language,** lengua viva, f
modernism /'mɒdər,nɪzəm/ n modernismo, m
modernist /'mɒdərnɪst/ n modernista, mf
modernistic /,mɒdər'nɪstɪk/ a modernista
modernity /mɒ'dərnɪti/ n modernidad, f
modernization /,mɒdərnə'zeiʃən/ n modernización, f
modernize /'mɒdər,naiz/ vt modernizar
modernness /'mɒdərnnɪs/ n modernidad, f
modest /'mɒdɪst/ a modesto; (of a woman) púdico
modesty /'mɒdəsti/ n modestia, f; (of a woman) pudor, m
modicum /'mɒdɪkəm/ n porción pequeña, f; poco, m
modifiable a modificable
modification /,mɒdəfɪ'keiʃən/ n modificación, f
modify /'mɒdə,fai/ vt modificar. **It has been much modified,** Se ha modificado mucho; Se han hecho muchas modificaciones
modifying a modificante, modificador
modish /'moudɪʃ/ a de moda en boga; elegante
modishness /'moudɪʃnɪs/ n elegancia, f
modiste /mou'dist/ n modista, mf
modulate /'mɒdʒə,leit/ vt and vi modular
modulation /,mɒdʒə'leiʃən/ n modulación, f
modus vivendi /'moudəs vɪ'vɛndi, -dai/ n modo de conveniencia, m
Mogul /'mougəl/ a mogol. —n mogol (-la). **the Great M.,** el Gran Mogol
Mohammedan /mu'hæmɪdn̩, mou-/ a mahometano, agareno
Mohammedanism /mu'hæmɪdn̩,ɪzəm, mou-/ n mahometismo, m
Mohican /mou'hikən/ n mohican, m
moiety /'mɔiti/ n mitad, f
moiré /mwɑ'rei, mɔ-/ n muaré, m
moist /mɔist/ a húmedo
moisten /'mɔisən/ vt humedecer, mojar
moisture /'mɔistʃər/ n humedad, f
molar /'moulər/ n muela, f, a molar
molasses /mə'læsɪz/ n pl melaza, f
mold /mould/ n (fungus) moho, m; (humus) mantillo, m; (iron-mould) mancha de orín, f; (matrix) molde, m, matriz, f; Cul. cubilete, m; Naut. gálibo, m; (for jelly, etc.) molde, m; Archit. moldura, f;

(temperament) temple, *m*, disposición, *f*. —*vt* moldear; (cast) vaciar; moldurar; *Naut.* galibar; *Fig.* amoldar, formar; *Agr.* cubrir con mantillo. **to m. oneself on,** modelarse sobre. **m.-board,** (of a plough) orejera, *f*

Moldavian /moul'deiviən/ *a* moldavo. —*n* moldavo (-va)

molder /'mouldər/ *n* moldeador, *m; Fig.* amolador (-ra); creador (-ra). —*vi* desmoronarse, convertirse en polvo; *Fig.* decaer, desmoronarse; vegetar

moldiness /'mouldinis/ *n* moho, *m*

molding /'mouldiŋ/ *n* amoldamiento, *m;* vaciado, *m; Archit.* moldura, *f; Fig.* formación,

moldy /'mouldi/ *a* mohoso, enmohecido; *Fig.* anticuado

mole /'moulei/ *n* (animal) topo, *m;* (spot) lunar, *m;* (breakwater) dique, malecón, *m;* muelle, *m*

molecular /mə'lɛkyələr/ *a* molecular

molecule /'mɒlɪˌkyul/ *n* molécula, *f*

molehill /'moulˌhil/ *n* topera, *f*

moleskin /'moulˌskin/ *n* piel de topo, *f*

molest /mə'lɛst/ *vt* molestar; perseguir, importunar; faltar al respeto (a)

molestation /ˌmoulə'steiʃən/ *n* importunidad, persecución, *f;* molestia, incomodidad, *f*

mollification /ˌmɒləfɪ'keiʃən/ *n* apaciguamiento, *m;* mitigación, *f*

mollify /'mɒləˌfai/ *vt* apaciguar, calmar; mitigar

mollusk /'mɒləsk/ *n* molusco, *m*

mollycoddle /'mɒliˌkɒdl/ *n* alfeñique, mírame y no me toques, *m;* niño (-ña), mimado (-da)

Moloch /'moulɒk/ *n* Moloc, *m*

molt /moult/ *vi* mudar, *n* muda, *f*

molten /'moultn/ *a* fundido; derretido

Moluccas, the /mə'lukəz/ las Malucas, *f pl*

moment /'moumənt/ *n* momento, *m;* instante *m;* (importance) importancia, *f.* **at this m.,** en este momento. **Do it this m.!** ¡Hazlo al instante (or en seguida)!

momentarily /ˌmoumən'tɛərəli, 'moumənˌtɛr-/ *adv* momentáneamente; cada momento

momentariness /'moumənˌtɛrinɪs/ *n* momentaneidad, *f*

momentary /'moumənˌtɛri/ *a* momentáneo

momentous /mou'mɛntəs/ *a* de suma importancia; crítico; grave

momentousness /mou'mɛntəsnɪs/ *n* importancia, *f;* gravedad, *f*

momentum /mou'mɛntəm/ *n* momento, *m,* velocidad adquirida *f; Fig.* ímpetu, *m.* **to gather m.,** cobrar velocidad, acelerar

monarch /'mɒnərk/ *n* monarca, *m*

monarchic /mə'narkik/ *a* monárquico

monarchism /'mɒnərˌkizəm/ *n* monarquismo, *m*

monarchist *n* monárquico (-ca)

monarchy /'mɒnərki/ *n* monarquía, *f*

monastery /'mɒnəˌstɛri/ *n* monasterio, *m*

monastic /mə'næstik/ *a* monástico. **m. life,** vida de clausura, *f*

monasticism *n* vida monástica, *f*

Monday /'mʌndei, -di/ *n* lunes, *m*

monetary /'mɒniˌtɛri/ *a* monetario

monetization *n* monetización, *f*

money /'mʌni/ *n* dinero, *m;* (coin) moneda, *f;* sistema monetario, *m.* **paper m.,** papel moneda, *m.* **ready m.,** dinero contante, *m.* **to make m.,** ganar (or hacer) dinero; enriquecerse. **M. talks,** Poderoso caballero es Don Dinero. **m.-bag,** talega, *f;* (person) ricacho (-cha). **m.-bags,** riqueza, *f.* **m.-box,** alcancía, hucha, *f.* **m.-changer,** cambista, *mf* **m.-lender,** prestamista, *mf* **m.-making,** *n* el hacer dinero; prosperidad, ganancia, *f.* —*a* lucrativo. **m.-order,** giro postal, *m*

moneyed /'mʌnid/ *a* adinerado; acomodado

Mongolian /mɒŋ'gouliən/ *a* mogol. —*n* mogol (-la); (language) mogol, *m*

mongoose /'mɒŋˌgus/ *n* mangosta, *f*

mongrel /'mʌŋgrəl/ *a* mestizo, atravesado. —*n* perro mestizo, *m;* (in contempt) mestizo, *m*

monitor /'mɒnitər/ *n* monitor, *m*

monitory /'mɒniˌtɔri/ *a* monitorio. —*n Eccl.* monitorio, *m*

monk /mʌŋk/ *n* monje, *m.* **to become a m.,** hacerse monje, tomar el hábito. **monk's-hood,** acónito, *m*

monkey /'mʌŋki/ *n* mono (-na); (imp) diablillo, *m;* (of a pile-driver) pilón de martinete, *m;* (in glassmaking) crisol, *m.* **to m. with,** meterse con; entremeterse. **m. nut,** cacahuete, *m.* **m.-puzzle,** (tree) araucaria, *f.* **m. tricks,** monadas, travesuras, diabluras, *f pl.* **m.-wrench,** llave inglesa, *f*

monkish /'mʌŋkiʃ/ *a* monacal, de monje; monástico

monochromatic /ˌmɒnəkrou'mætik/ *a* monocromo

monochrome /'mɒnəˌkroum/ *n* monocromo, *m*

monocle /'mɒnəkəl/ *n* monóculo, *m*

monogamist /mə'nɒgəmist/ *n* monógamo (-ma)

monogamous /mə'nɒgəməs/ *a* monógamo

monogamy /mə'nɒgəmi/ *n* monogamia, *f*

monogram /'mɒnəˌgræm/ *n* monograma, *m*

monograph /'mɒnəˌgræf/ *n* monografía, *f,* opúsculo, *m*

monolith /'mɒnəliθ/ *n* monolito, *m*

monolithic /ˌmɒnə'liθik/ *a* monolítico

monologue /'mɒnəˌlɔg/ *n* monólogo, *m*

monomania /ˌmɒnə'meiniə/ *n* monomanía, *f*

monomaniac /ˌmɒnə'meiniˌæk/ *n* monomaníaco (-ca)

monomial /mou'noumiəl/ *n* monomio, *m, a* de un solo término

monoplane /'mɒnəˌplein/ *n* monoplano, *m*

monopolist /mə'nɒpəlist/ *n* monopolista, *mf;* acaparador (-ra)

monopolization /məˌnɒpələ'zeiʃən/ *n* monopolio, *m*

monopolize /mə'nɒpəˌlaiz/ *vt* monopolizar

monopoly /mə'nɒpəli/ *n* monopolio, *m*

monotheism /'mɒnəθiˌizəm/ *n* monoteísmo, *m*

monotheist /'mɒnəˌθiist/ *n* monoteísta, *mf*

monotone /'mɒnəˌtoun/ *n* monotonía, *f*

monotonous /mə'nɒtnəs/ *a* monótono

monotony /mə'nɒtni/ *n* monotonía, *f*

monoxide /mɒn'ɒksaid/ *n* monóxido, *m*

Monroe doctrine /mən'rou/ *n* monroísmo, *m*

monsignor /mɒn'sinyər/ *n* monseñor, *m*

monsoon /mɒn'sun/ *n* monzón, *mf*

monster /'mɒnstər/ *n* monstruo, *m*

monstrance /'mɒnstrəns/ *n* custodia, *f*

monstrosity /mɒn'strɒsiti/ *n* monstruosidad, *f*

monstrous /'mɒnstrəs/ *a* monstruoso; horrible, atroz; enorme

montage /mɒn'taʒ/ *n* montaje, *m*

month /mʌnθ/ *n* mes, *m.* **He arrived a m. ago,** Llegó hace un mes

monthly /'mʌnθli/ *a* mensual. —*adv* mensualmente, cada mes. —*n* revista (or publicación) mensual, *f; pl* **monthlies,** menstruación, regla, *f.* **m. salary or payment,** mensualidad, *f*

monument /'mɒnyəmənt/ *n* monumento, *m*

monumental /ˌmɒnyə'mɛntl/ *a* monumental

moo /mu/ *vi* (of cattle) mugir. —*n* mugido, *m*

mood /mud/ *n* humor, *m;* espíritu, *m; Gram.* modo, *m*

moodily /'mudļi/ *adv* taciturnamente; tristemente, pensativamente

moodiness /'mudinis/ *n* mal humor, *m,* taciturnidad, *f;* melancolía, tristeza, *f*

moody /'mudi/ *a* taciturno, de mal humor; triste, melancólico, pensativo

mooing /'muiŋ/ *n* (of cattle) mugido, *m*

moon /mun/ *n* luna, *f;* satélite, *m;* mes lunar, *m;* luz de la luna, *f.* **full m.,** plenilunio, *m;* luna llena, *f.* **new m.,** novilunio, *m,* luna nueva, *f*

moonbeam /'munˌbim/ *n* rayo de luna, *m*

moonless /'munlis/ *a* sin luna

moonlight /'munˌlait/ *n* luz de la luna, *f.* **in the m.,** a la luz de la luna. **to do a m. flit,** *Inf.* mudarse por el aire

moonlighting /'munˌlaitiŋ/ *n* el pluriempleo, *m*

moonlit /'munˌlit/ *a* iluminado por la luna. **moonlit night,** noche de luna, *f*

moonshine /'munˌʃain/ *n* claridad de la luna, *f; Fig.* música celestial, ilusión, *f*

moonstone /'munˌstoun/ *n* adularia, *f*

moonstruck /'mun,strʌk/ a lunático
Moor /mur/ n moro (-ra)
moor /mur/ n páramo, brezal, m; (marsh) pantano, m; (for game) coto, m. —vt amarrar, aferrar; afirmar con anclas o cables. **m.-hen,** polla de agua, f
mooring /'murɪŋ/ n amarre, m. **m.-mast,** Aer. poste de amarre, m
moorings /'murɪŋz/ n pl amarradero, m
Moorish /'murɪʃ/ a moro; árabe. **M. architecture,** arquitectura árabe, f. **M. girl,** mora, f
moorland /'murlənd/ n páramo, brezal, m
moose /mus/ n anta, m
moot /mut/ n junta, f; ayuntamiento, m. —a discutible. —vt (bring up) suscitar; (discuss) discutir, debatir
mop /mɒp/ n (implement) trapeador, m (Ecuador), escoba con fleco, f; (of hair) mata (de pelo), f. —vt trapear (Ecuador); (dry) enjugar, secar. **to mop up,** Inf. limpiar; Mil. acabar con (el enemigo)
mope /moup/ vi replace by tristear. **to m. about,** vagar tristemente
moquette /mou'kɛt/ n moqueta, f
moraine /mə'rein/ n morena, f
moral /'mɔrəl/ a moral; (chaste) casto, virtuoso; honrado. —n (maxim) moraleja, f; pl **morals,** moralidad, f; ética, f; moral, f; (conduct) costumbres, f pl. **m. philosophy,** filosofía moral, f. **m. support,** apoyo moral, m. **m. tale,** apólogo, m
morale /mə'ræl/ n moral, f
moralist /'mɔrəlɪst/ n moralista, m
morality /mə'ræliti/ n moralidad, f; virtud, f; castidad, f. **m. play,** moralidad, f, drama alegórico, m
moralization /,mɔrələ'zeiʃən/ n moralización, f
moralize /'mɔrə,laiz/ vt and vi moralizar
moralizer /'mɔrə,laizər/ n moralizador (-ra)
moralizing /'mɔrə,laizɪŋ/ a moralizador
morally /'mɔrəli/ adv moralmente
morals /'mɔrəlz/. See **moral**
morass /mə'ræs/ n marisma, ciénaga, f
moratorium /,mɔrə'tɔriəm/ n moratoria, f
Moravian /mɔ'reiviən/ a moravo. —n moravo (-va)
morbid /'mɔrbɪd/ a mórbido, mórboso; (of the mind, etc.) insano
morbidezza /,mɔrbɪ'dɛtsə/ n (Art. and Lit.) morbidez, f
morbidity /mɔr'bɪdɪti/ n morbidez, f
mordacity /mɔr'dæsɪti/ n mordacidad, f
mordant /'mɔrdṇt/ a mordaz; (of acid) mordiente. —n mordiente, m
more /mɔr/ a and adv más. **The m. he earns, the less he saves,** Cuanto más gana, menos ahorra. **the m. the better,** cuanto más, tanto mejor. **without m. ado,** sin más ni más; sin decir nada. **Would you like some m.?** ¿Quiere Vd. más? (of food) ¿Quiere Vd. repetir? **no m.,** no más; (never) nunca más; (finished) se acabó. **once m.,** otra vez, una vez más. **m. and m.,** cada vez más, más y más. **m. or less,** más o menos; (about) poco más o menos
moreover /mɔr'ouvər/ adv además, también; por otra parte
morganatic /,mɔrgə'nætɪk/ a morganático
morgue /mɔrg/ n depósito de cadáveres, m
moribund /'mɔrə,bʌnd/ a moribundo
Mormon /'mɔrmən/ a mormónico. —n mormón (-ona)
Mormonism /'mɔrmə,nɪzəm/ n mormonismo, m
morning /'mɔrnɪŋ/ n mañana, f, a matutino, de la mañana. **Good m.!** ¡Buenos días! **the next m.,** la mañana siguiente. **very early in the m.,** muy de mañana. **m. coat,** chaqué, m. **m. dew,** rocío de la mañana, m. **m. paper,** periódico de la mañana, m. **m. star,** lucero del alba, m. **m. suit,** chaqué, m
Moroccan /mə'rɒkən/ a marroquí, marrueco. —n marrueco (-ca), marroquí, mf
Morocco /mə'rɒkou/ Marruecos, m
morocco /mə'rɒkou/ n (leather) marroquí, tafilete, m
morose /mə'rous/ a sombrío, taciturno, malhumorado
morosely /mə'rousli/ adv taciturnamente
moroseness /mə'rousnɪs/ n taciturnidad, f; mal humor, m

morphine /'mɔrfin/ n morfina, f. **m. addict,** morfinómano (-na)
morrow /'mɔrou/ n mañana, f; día siguiente, m
Morse code /mɔrs/ n la clave telegráfica de Morse, f, el alfabeto de Morse, m
morsel /'mɔrsəl/ n pedazo, m; (mouthful) bocado, m
mortal /'mɔrtḷ/ a mortal. —n mortal, mf. **m. sin,** pecado mortal, pecado capital, m
mortality /mɔr'tælɪti/ n mortalidad, f
mortally wounded /'mɔrtḷi/ adv herido de muerte
mortar /'mɔrtər/ n (for building) argamasa, f; (for mixing and Mil.) mortero, m. **m. and pestle,** mortero y majador, m. **m.-board,** (in building) cuezo, m; (academic cap) birrete, m
mortgage /'mɔrgɪdʒ/ n hipoteca, f. —vt hipotecar. —a hipotecario. **to pay off a m.,** redimir una hipoteca
mortgageable /'mɔrgɪdʒəbəl/ a hipotecable
mortgaged debt /'mɔrgɪdʒd/ n deuda garantizada con una hipoteca, f
mortgagee /,mɔrgə'dʒi/ n acreedor (-ra) hipotecario (-ia)
mortgagor /'mɔrgədʒər/ n deudor (-ra) hipotecario (-ia)
mortification /,mɔrtəfɪ'keiʃən/ n mortificación, f; humillación, f; Med. gangrena, f
mortify /'mɔrtə,fai/ vt mortificar; humillar. —vi Med. gangrenarse
mortifying /'mɔrtə,faiɪŋ/ a humillante
mortise /'mɔrtɪs/ n muesca, f. —vt hacer muescas (en); ensamblar
mortuary /'mɔrtʃu,ɛri/ a mortuorio. —n depósito de cadáveres, m
Mosaic /mou'zeiɪk/ a mosaico
mosaic /mou'zeiɪk/ n mosaico, m
Moscow /'mɒskou,-kau/ Moscú, m
mosque /mɒsk/ n mezquita, f
mosquito /mə'skitou/ n mosquito, m. **m. net,** mosquitero, m
moss /mɔs/ n musgo, m; moho, m; (swamp) marjal, m
mossgrown /'mɔs,groun/ a musgoso, cubierto de musgo; Fig. anticuado
mossiness /'mɔsinɪs/ n estado musgoso, m
mossy /'mɔsi/ a musgoso
most /moust/ a el (la, los, etc.) más; la mayor parte de; la mayoría de; (el, etc.) mayor. —adv más; el (la, etc.) más; (extremely) sumamente; (very) muy; (before adjectives sometimes expressed by superlative, e.g. m. reverend, reverendísimo, m. holy, santísimo, etc.). —n (highest price) el mayor precio; la mayor parte; el mayor número; lo más. **m. of all,** sobre todo. **m. people,** la mayoría de la gente. **at the m.,** a lo más, a lo sumo. **for the m. part,** en su mayor parte; casi todos; generalmente, casi siempre. **to make the m. of,** sacar el mayor partido posible de; aprovechar bien; exagerar
mostly /'moustli/ adv principalmente; en su mayoría; en su mayor parte; casi siempre; en general, generalmente
mote /mout/ n átomo, m; mota, f. **to see the m. in our neighbor's eye and not the beam in our own,** ver la paja en el ojo del vecino y no la viga en el nuestro
motet /mou'tɛt/ n motete m
moth /mɔθ/ n mariposa nocturna, f; polilla, f. **m.ball,** bola de naftalina, f. **m.-eaten,** apolillado
mother /'mʌðər/ n madre, f; madre de familia, f; (of alcoholic beverages) madre, f. —vt cuidar como una madre (a); servir de madre (a); (animals) ahijar. **M. Church,** madre iglesia, f; iglesia metropolitana, f. **m.-in-law,** suegra, f. **m. land,** (madre) patria, f. **m.-of-pearl,** madreperla, f, nácar, m. —a nacarado, nacáreo. **M. Superior,** (madre) superiora, f. **m. tongue,** lengua materna, f
motherhood /'mʌðər,hud/ n maternidad, f
motherless /'mʌðərlɪs/ a huérfano de madre, sin madre
motherlike a de madre, como una madre
motherliness /'mʌðərlinɪs/ n cariño maternal, m
motherly /'mʌðərli/ a maternal

motif /mou'tif/ n motivo, m; tema, m; Sew. adorno, m

motion /'mouʃən/ n movimiento, m; Mech. marcha, operación, f; mecanismo, m; (sign) seña, señal, f; (gesture) ademán, gesto, m; (carriage) aire, porte, m; (of the bowels) movimiento del vientre, m, deyección, f; (will) voluntad, f, deseo, m; (proposal in an assembly or debate) proposición, moción, f; Law. pedimento, m. —vt hacer una señal (a). —vi hacer señas. **to set in m.,** poner en marcha. **m. picture,** fotografía cinematográfica, película, f. **m.-picture theater,** cine, m

motionless /'mouʃənlɪs/ a inmóvil

motivate /'moutə,veit/ vt motivar

motive /'moutɪv/ n motivo, m. —a motor motivo. **with no m.,** sin motivo. **m. power,** fuerza motriz, f

motley /'mɒtli/ a abigarrado, multicolor; (mixed) diverso, vario. —n traje de colores, m, botarga, f

motor /'moutər/ n motor, m; automóvil, m, a motor; movido por motor; con motor; (traveling) de viaje. —vi ir en automóvil. —vt llevar en automóvil (a). **m. boat,** lancha automóvil, f. **m.bus,** autobús, ómnibus, m. **m.car,** automóvil, m. **m.-coach,** autobús, m. **m. cycle,** motocicleta, f. **m.cyclist,** motociclista, mf **m.-launch,** canoa automóvil, f. **m.oil,** aceite para motores, m. **m.-road,** autopista, f. **m.-rug,** manta de viaje, f. **m.-scooter,** bicicleta con motor, f. **m.-spirit,** bencina, f

motoring /'moutərɪŋ/ n automovilismo, m

motorist /'moutərɪst/ n automovilista, motorista, mf

mottled /'mɒtld/ a abigarrado; (of marble, etc.) jaspeado, esquizado; manchado (con), con manchas (de); pintado (con)

motto /'mɒtou/ n Herald. divisa, f; mote, m; (in a book, etc.) lema, m

mound /maund/ n montón, m; (knoll) altozano, m; (for defence) baluarte, m; (for burial) túmulo, m

mount /maunt/ n (hill, and in palmistry) monte, m; (for riding) caballería, f; montadura, f; (for a picture) borde, m. —vt subir; (machines, etc.) montar; (jewels) engastar; (a picture) poner un borde a; (a play) poner en escena; poner a caballo; proveer de caballo. —vi montar; subir; (increase) aumentar. **to m. a horse,** subir a caballo, montar. **to m. guard,** Mil. montar la guardia. **to m. the throne,** subir al trono

mountain /'mauntṇ/ n montaña, f; (mound) montón, m. —a de montaña(s); montañés; alpino, alpestre. **to make a m. out of a molehill,** convertir un grano de arena en una montaña. hacer de una pulga un camello, hacer de una pulga un elefante. **m.-chain,** cadena de montañas, f. **m. dweller,** montañés (-esa). **m. railway,** ferrocarríl de cremallera, m. **m.-side,** falda de una montaña, f

mountaineer /,mauntṇ'ɪər/ n (inhabitant) montañés (-esa); (climber) alpinista, mf. —vi hacer alpinismo

mountaineering /,mauntṇ'ɪərɪŋ/ n alpinismo, m

mountainous /'mauntṇəs/ a montañoso; (huge) enorme

mountebank /'mauntə,bæŋk/ n saltabanco, m; charlatán, m

mounting /'mauntɪŋ/ n (ascent) subida, f; ascensión, f; (of machinery, etc.) armadura, f; montadura, f; (of a precious stone) engaste, m. **m.-block,** subidero, m

mourn /mɔrn/ vi afligirse, lamentarse; (wear mourning) estar de luto. —vt llorar; lamentar; llevar luto por

mourner /'mɔrnər/ n lamentador (-ra); (paid) plañidera, f; el, m, (f, la) que acompaña al féretro

mournful /'mɔrnfəl/ a triste, acongojado; funesto, lúgubre; fúnebre; lamentable

mournfully /'mɔrnfəli/ adv tristemente

mournfulness /'mɔrnfəlnɪs/ n tristeza, f; melancolía, aflicción, f, pesar, m

mourning /'mɔrnɪŋ/ n aflicción, f; lamentación, f; luto, m. **deep m.,** luto riguroso, m. **half m.,** medio luto, m. **to be in m.,** estar de luto. **to be in m. for,** llevar luto por. **to come out of m.,** dejar el luto. **m.-band,** (on the hat) tira de gasa, f; (on the arm) brazal de luto, m. **m.-coach,** coche fúnebre, m

mouse /n. maus; v. mauz/ n ratón (-na); Naut. barri-

lete, m. —vi cazar ratones. **m.-coloured,** de color de rata. **m.-hole, m.-trap,** ratonera, f

mouser /'mauzər/ n gato ratonero, m

mousing /'mausɪŋ/ n caza de ratones, f

moustache /'mʌstæʃ, mə'stæʃ/ n bigote, mostacho, m

mousy /'mausi/ a ratonesco, ratonil

mouth /n. mauθ; v. mauð/ n (Anat. human being, of a bottle, cave) boca, f; entrada, f; (of a river) desembocadura, f; (of a channel) embocadero, m; (of a wind-instrument) boquilla, f. —vt pronunciar con afectación; (chew) mascar. —vi clamar a gritos, vociferar. **down in the m.,** Inf. con las orejas caídas. **It makes my m. water,** Se me hace la boca agua. **large m.,** boca rasgada, f. **m.-gag,** abrebocas, m. **m.-organ,** armónica, f. **m.-wash,** antiséptico bucal, m (Argentina), enjuague, m

mouthed /mauðd, mauθt/ a que tiene boca...; de boca... **open-m.,** boquiabierto

mouthful /'mauθ,ful/ n bocado, m; (of smoke, air) bocanada, f

mouthpiece /'mauθ,pis/ n (of wind-instruments), tobacco-pipe, waterpipe) boquilla, f; (of a wineskin) brocal, m; (spokesman) portavoz, m; intérprete, mf

movable /'muvəbəl/ a movible; (of goods) mobiliario. **m. feast,** fiesta movible, f

movables /'muvəbəlz/ n pl bienes muebles, efectos, m pl

movable type n tipos sueltos, m pl

move /muv/ n movimiento, m; (of household effects) mudanza, f; (motion) marcha, f; (in a game) jugada, f; (Fig. step) paso, m; (device) maniobra, f. **Whose m. is it?** ¿A quién le toca jugar? **to be on the m.,** estar en movimiento; estar de viaje. **to be always on the m.,** Inf. parecer una lanzadera

move /muv/ vt mover; poner en marcha; (furniture) trasladar; cambiar de lugar; (stir) remover; (shake) agitar, hacer temblar; (transport) transportar; (a piece in chess, etc.) jugar; (pull) arrancar; (impel) impulsar; (incline) inclinar, disponer; (affect emotionally) conmover, emocionar, enternecer; impresionar. —vi moverse; ponerse en marcha; (walk) andar; ir; avanzar; (a step forward, etc.) dar; (move house) trasladarse; (act) entrar en acción; (in games) hacer una jugada; (progress) progresar; (shake) agitarse, temblar; removerse; (propose in an assembly) hacer una proposición; (in a court of law) hacer un pedimento; (grow) crecer. **to m. about,** pasearse; ir y venir; (of traffic) circular; (remove) trasladarse; (stir, tremble) agitarse. **to m. along,** caminar por; avanzar por. **to m. aside,** vt apartar; poner a un lado; (curtains) descorrer. —vi ponerse a un lado; quitarse de en medio. **to m. away,** vt alejar. —vi alejarse; marcharse; trasladarse; mudar de casa. **to m. back,** retroceder; volver hacia atrás. **to m. down,** bajar, descender. **to m. forward,** adelantarse; avanzar; progresar. **to m. in,** entrar (en); tomar posesión de una casa. **to m. off,** vt quitar. —vi marcharse; ponerse en marcha; alejarse, apartarse. **to m. on,** avanzar; ponerse en marcha; circular; (of time) pasar, correr. **to m. out,** vt sacar, quitar. —vi salir; (from a house) mudarse, abandonar (una casa, etc.). **to m. round,** dar vueltas, girar; (turn round) volverse. **to m. to,** (make) animar (a); causar. **to m. up,** vt montar, subir. —vi montar; avanzar

movement /'muvmənt/ n movimiento, m; Mech. mecanismo, m; (Stock Exchange) actividad, f. **encircling m.,** Mil. movimiento envolvente, m

mover /'muvər/ n motor, m; móvil, m; promotor (-ra); (of a motion, proposer) autor (-ra) de una moción

movie /'muvi/ n Inf. cine, m. **m. camera,** máquina de impresionar, f. **m. star,** estrella de la pantalla, f

moving /'muvɪŋ/ a móvil; motor; (affecting) emocionante, conmovedor; impresionante; patético. —n movimiento, m; traslado, m; cambio de domicilio, m. **m. picture,** fotografía cinematográfica, f. **m. staircase,** escalera móvil, f

movingly /'muvɪŋli/ adv con emoción; patéticamente

mow /mou/ vt segar.

mowing /'mouɪŋ/ n siega, f. **m.-machine,** segadora, f

Mr. /'mɪstər/ See **mister**

Mrs. /'mɪsəz/ See **mistress**

much

much /mʌtʃ/ a mucho. —adv mucho; (by far) con mucho; (with past part.) muy; (pretty nearly) casi, más o menos. **m. of a size,** más o menos del mismo tamaño. **I was m. angered,** Estuve muy enfadado. **as m. as,** tanto como. **as m. more,** otro tanto. **How m. is it?** ¿Cuánto es? ¿Cuánto cuesta? **however m....,** por mucho que... **not m.,** no mucho. **not to think m. of,** tener en poco (a). **so m. so that,** tanto que. **too m.,** demasiado. **to make m. of,** dar grande importancia a; (a person) apreciar, querer; agasajar; (a child) mimar, acariciar

mucilage /ˈmyusəlɪdʒ/ n mucílago, m

muck /mʌk/ n (dung) estiércol, m; (filth) porquería, inmundicia, f; suciedad, f; (rubbish, of a literary work, etc.) porquería, n. **to m. up,** ensuciar; (spoil) estropear por completo

mucky /ˈmʌki/ a muy sucio; puerco; asqueroso, repugnante

mucosity /muˈkɒsɪti/ n mucosidad, f

mucous /ˈmyukəs/ a mucoso. **m. membrane,** mucosa, f

mucus /ˈmyukəs/ n mucosidad, f; (from the nose) moco, m

mud /mʌd/ n lodo, barro, fango, m. **to stick in the mud,** (of a ship, etc.) embarrancarse. **mudbath,** baño de barro, m. **mud wall,** tapia, f

muddiness /ˈmʌdɪnɪs/ n estado fangoso, m; (of liquids) turbiedad, f; suciedad, f

muddle /ˈmʌdl̩/ vt (bewilder) dejar perplejo, aturdir; (intoxicate) emborrachar; (stupefy) entontecer; (spoil) estropear; embarullar, dejar en desorden; hacer un lío de. —n desorden, m; confusión, f; lío, embrollo, m. **in a m.,** en desorden; en confusión. **to make a m.,** armar un lío. **to m. away,** derrochar sin ton ni son

muddled /ˈmʌdl̩d/ a desordenado; confuso; estúpido; torpe; (drunk) borracho

muddy /ˈmʌdi/ a fangoso, lodoso, barroso; cubierto de lodo; (of liquids, etc.) turbio; (of the complexion) cetrino. —vt enlodar, cubrir de lodo; ensuciar; (liquids) enturbiar

mudguard /ˈmʌd.gɑrd/ n guardabarro, m

muezzin /myuˈɛzɪn, mu-/ n almuecín, almuédano, m

muff /mʌf/ n manguito, m; (for a car radiator) cubierta para radiador, f; (Inf. at games, etc.) maleta, m. —vt dejar escapar (una pelota); (an opportunity) perder

muffin /ˈmʌfɪn/ n mollete, m

muffle /ˈmʌfəl/ vt embozar, arrebozar; envolver; encubrir, ocultar, tapar; (stifle sound of) apagar; (oars, bells) envolver con tela para no hacer ruido; Fig. ahogar. **to m. oneself up,** embozarse

muffled /ˈmʌfəld/ a (of sound) sordo; confuso; apagado. **m. drum,** tambor enlutado, m

muffler /ˈmʌflər/ n bufanda, tapaboca, f; (furnace) mufla, f; (of a car radiator) cubierta para radiador, f; (silencer) silencioso, m

mufti /ˈmʌfti/ n mufti, m

mug /mʌg/ n vaso, m; (tankard) pichel, tarro, m; (face) jeta, f; (dupe) primo, m; (at games, etc.) maleta, m

mulatto /məˈlætou/ a mulato. —n mulato (-ta). **m.-like,** amulatado

mulberry /ˈmʌl.beri/ n (fruit) mora, f; (bush) morera, f. **m. plantation,** moreral, m

mule /myul/ n mulo (-la); (slipper) mula, chinela, f; (spinning-jenny) huso mecánico, m

mulish /ˈmyulɪʃ/ a mular; (pers.) terco como una mula

mulishness /ˈmyulɪʃnɪs/ n terquedad de mula, f

mullet /ˈmʌlɪt/ n (red) salmonete, m, trilla, f; (grey) mújol, m

multicolored /ˈmʌlti.kʌlərd/ a multicolor

multifarious /ˌmʌltəˈfɛriəs/ a numeroso, mucho; diverso, vario

multiform /ˈmʌltə.fɔrm/ a multiforme

multilateral /ˌmʌltɪˈlætərəl/ a multilátero

multimillionaire /ˌmʌltɪˈmɪlyəˌnɛər/ a archimillonario, multimillonario, n multimillonario, m

multiple /ˈmʌltəpəl/ a múltiple, múltiplo. —n múltiplo, m

multiple-choice question n pregunta optativa, f

multiplicand /ˌmʌltəplɪˈkænd/ n multiplicando, m

multiplication /ˌmʌltəplɪˈkeɪʃən/ n multiplicación, f. **m. table,** tabla de multiplicación, f

multiplicity /ˌmʌltəˈplɪsɪti/ n multiplicidad, f

multiplier /ˈmʌltəˌplaɪər/ n Math. multiplicador, m; máquina de multiplicar, f

multiply /ˈmʌltəpli/ vt multiplicar. —vi multiplicarse

multitude /ˈmʌltɪˌtud/ n multitud, f. **the m.,** las masas

multitudinous /ˌmʌltɪˈtudnəs/ a muy numeroso

mumble /ˈmʌmbl̩/ vi and vt musitar, hablar entre dientes; refunfuñar; (chew) masticar

mummer /ˈmʌmər/ n momero (-ra); máscara, mf

mummery /ˈmʌməri/ n momería, f; mascarada, f

mummification /ˌmʌməfɪˈkeɪʃən/ n momificación, f

mummify /ˈmʌməˌfaɪ/ vt momificar. —vi momificarse

mummy /ˈmʌmi/ n momia, f; carne de momia, f; (Inf. mother) mama, f. **m. case,** sarcófago, m

mumps /mʌmps/ n pl parotiditis, papera, f

munch /mʌntʃ/ vt masticar, mascullar, mascar

mundane /mʌnˈdeɪn/ a mundano

municipal /myuˈnɪsəpəl/ a municipal. **m. charter,** fuero municipal, m. **m. government,** gobierno municipal, m

municipality /myuˌnɪsəˈpælɪti/ n municipio, m

munificence /myuˈnɪfəsəns/ n munificencia, f

munificent /myuˈnɪfəsənt/ a munífico, generoso

munition /myuˈnɪʃən/ n munición, f. —vt municionar. **m. dump,** depósito de municiones, m. **m. factory,** fábrica de municiones, f. **m. worker,** obrero (-ra) de una fábrica de municiones

mural /ˈmyʊrəl/ a mural. —n pintura mural, f

murder /ˈmɜrdər/ n asesinato, m. —vt asesinar; dar muerte (a), matar; (a work, etc.) degollar. **He was murdered,** Fue asesinado. **willful m.,** homicidio premeditado, m

murderer /ˈmɜrdərər/ n asesino, m

murderess /ˈmɜrdərɪs/ n asesina, f

murderous /ˈmɜrdərəs/ a homicida; cruel, sanguinario; fatal; imposible, intolerable

murderously /ˈmɜrdərəsli/ adv con intento de asesinar; (with look) con ojos asesinos; cruelmente

murkiness /ˈmɜrkinɪs/ n obscuridad, lobreguez, f, tinieblas, f pl

murky /ˈmɜrki/ a lóbrego, negro, obscuro; (of one's past, etc.) negro, accidentado

murmur /ˈmɜrmər/ n murmullo, m; rumor, m; susurro, m; (grumble) murmurio, m. —vi murmurar, susurrar; (complain) murmurar, quejarse. —vt murmurar, decir en voz baja

murmuring /ˈmɜrmərɪŋ/ n murmurio, m, a que murmura, susurrante

muscatel /ˌmʌskəˈtɛl/ a moscatel. —n moscatel, m. **m. grape,** uva moscatel, f

muscle /ˈmʌsəl/ n músculo, m

Muscovite /ˈmʌskəˌvaɪt/ a moscovita. —n moscovita, mf

muscular /ˈmʌskyələr/ a muscular, musculoso; (brawny) membrudo, fornido. **m. pains,** (in the legs, etc.) agujetas, f pl

muscularity /ˌmʌskyəˈlærɪti/ n fuerza muscular, f

musculature /ˈmʌskyələtʃər/ n musculatura, f

Muse /myuz/ n musa, f

muse /myuz/ n meditación, f. —vi meditar, reflexionar, rumiar; mirar las musarañas, estar distraído. **to m. on,** meditar en (o sobre)

museum /myuˈziəm/ n museo, m

museum of arms n museo de armas, m, apoteca, f

mushroom /ˈmʌʃrum/ n seta, f. —a de setas; de forma de seta; (upstart) advenedizo; (ephemeral) efímero, de un día. **m.-bed,** setal, m. **m.-spawn,** esporas de setas, f pl

music /ˈmyuzɪk/ n música, f; armonía, f; melodía, f. —a de música. **to set to m.,** poner en música. **m.-hall,** teatro de variedades, m; salón de conciertos, m. **m. master,** profesor de música, m. **m. publisher,** editor de obras musicales, m. **m. stand,** atril, m; tablado para una orquesta, m. **m. stool,** taburete de piano, m

musical /ˈmyuzɪkəl/ a musical; de música; armonioso, melodioso. **She is very m.,** Es muy aficionada a la música; Tiene mucho talento para la mú-

sica. **m.-box,** caja de música, *f.* **m. comedy,**
zarzuela, *f.* **m. instrument,** instrumento de música, *m*
musical chairs *n* escobas, *f pl,* el juego de sillas, *m*
sing
musically /'myuzɪkli/ *adv* musicalmente; melodiosamente
musician /myu'zɪʃən/ *n* músico (-ca)
musing /'myuzɪŋ/ *n* meditación, *f;* ensueños, *m pl, a*
pensativo, meditabundo
musingly /'myuzɪŋli/ *adv* reflexivamente
musk /mʌsk/ *n* (substance) almizcle, *m;* perfume de
almizcle, *m.* —*a* de almizcle; almizclero; (of scents)
almizcleño. **m.-deer,** almizclero, *m.* **m.-rat,** rata almizclera, *f*
musket /'mʌskɪt/ *n* mosquete, *m*
musketeer /,mʌskɪ'tɪər/ *n* mosquetero, *m*
Muslim /'mʌzlɪm/ *a* musulmán, mahometano. —*n*
musulmán (-ana)
muslin /'mʌzlɪn/ *n* muselina, *f, a* de muselina
mussel /'mʌsəl/ *n* mejillón, *m.* **m.-bed,** criadero de
mejillones, *m*
must /mʌst/ *vi* haber de; tener que; deber; (expressing probability) deber de, ser. **This question m. be
settled without delay,** Esta cuestión debe ser resuelta sin demora. **You m. do it at once,** Tienes que
hacerlo en seguida. **I m. have seen him in the street
sometime,** Debo haberle visto en la calle alguna vez.
One m. eat to live, Se ha de comer para vivir. **Well,
go if you m.,** Bueno, vete si no hay más remedio. **It
m. be a difficult decision for him,** Debe ser una decisión difícil para él. **It m. have been about twelve
o'clock when...,** Serían las doce cuando...
must /mʌst/ *n* mosto, zumo de la uva, *m;* (mould)
moho, *m*
mustang /'mʌstæŋ/ *n* potro mesteño, *m*
mustard /'mʌstərd/ *n* mostaza, *f.* **m. gas,** iperita, *f.*
m. plaster, sinapismo, *m.* **m. pot,** mostacera, *f.* **m.
spoon,** cucharita para la mostaza, *f*
muster /'mʌstər/ *n* lista, *f,* rol, *m;* revista, *f;* reunión,
f, vt pasar lista (de); pasar revista (a); reunir. —*vi*
juntarse, reunirse. **to m. out,** (from the army) dar de
baja (a). **to m. up sufficient courage,** cobrar ánimos
suficientes. **to pass m.,** pasar revista; ser aceptado.
m.-roll, *Mil.* muestra, *f; Naut.* rol de la tripulación, *m*
mustiness /'mʌstɪnɪs/ *n* moho, *m;* ranciedad, *f;* (of a
room, etc.) olor de humedad, *m*
musty /'mʌsti/ *a* mohoso; rancio; que huele a humedad. **to go m.,** enmohecerse
mutability /,myutə'bɪlɪti/ *n* mutabilidad, *f;* inconstancia, inestabilidad, *f*
mutable /'myutəbəl/ *a* mudable; inconstante, inestable
mutation /myu'teiʃən/ *n* mutación, *f*
mute /myut/ *a* mudo; silencioso. —*n* mudo (-da);
Mus. sordina, *f;* (phonetics) letra muda, *f.* **deaf m.,**
sordomudo (-da)
muted /'myutɪd/ *a* (of sounds) sordo, apagado
mutely /'myutli/ *adv* mudamente; en silencio

muteness /'myutnɪs/ *n* mudez, *f;* silencio, *m*
mutilate /'myutḷ,eit/ *vt* mutilar; estropear
mutilation /,myutḷ'eiʃən/ *n* mutilación, *f*
mutineer /,myutṇ'ɪər/ *n* amotinador, rebelde, *m*
mutinous /'myutṇəs/ *a* amotinado; rebelde, sedicioso; turbulento
mutiny /'myutṇi/ *n* motín, *m;* sublevación, insurrección, *f, vi* amotinarse, sublevarse
mutt /mʌt/ *n* chucho, *m*
mutter /'mʌtər/ *vt* and *vi* murmurar, musitar;
mascullar, decir (or hablar) entre dientes; gruñir, refunfuñar; (of thunder, etc.) tronar, retumbar. —*n*
murmurio, *m;* rumor, *m;* retumbo, *m*
mutton /'mʌtṇ/ *n* carnero, *m, a* de carnero. **m.-chop,**
chuleta, *f*
mutual /'myutʃuəl/ *a* mutuo, recíproco; común. **by
m. consent,** de común acuerdo. **m. aid society,** sociedad de socorros mutuos, *f.* **m. insurance company,** sociedad de seguros mutuos, *f*
mutual fund *n* fondo de inversiones rentables, *m*
mutualism /'myutʃuə,lɪzəm/ *n* mutualismo, *m*
mutuality /,myutʃu'ælɪti/ *n* mutualidad, *f*
mutually /'myutʃuəli/ *adv* mutuamente, recíprocamente
muzzle /'mʌzəl/ *n* (snout) hocico, *m;* (for a dog) bozal, *m;* (of a gun) boca, *f.* —*vt* abozalar, poner un
bozal (a); (*Fig.* gag) amordazar, imponer silencio (a)
muzzling /'mʌzlɪŋ/ *n* acción de abozalar, *f;* (*Fig.* gagging) amordazamiento, *m*
my /mai/ *a poss* mi, *mf;* mis, *mf pl* **my relatives,** mis
parientes. **My goodness!** ¡Dios mío!
myelitis /,maiə'laitɪs/ *n* mielitis, *f*
myopia /mai'oupiə/ *n* miopía, *f*
myopic /mai'ɒpɪk/ *a* miope
myriad /'mɪriəd/ *n* miríada, *f*
myrmidon /'mɜrmɪ,dɒn/ *n* rufián, *m;* asesino, *m;*
secuaz, *m*
myrrh /mɜr/ *n* mirra, *f*
myrtle /'mɜrtḷ/ *n* mirto, arrayán, *m*
myself /mai'self/ *pron* yo mismo; (as a reflexive with
a preposition) mí; (with a reflexive verb) me. **I m.
sent it,** yo mismo (-ma) lo mandé
mysterious /mɪ'stɪəriəs/ *a* misterioso
mysteriousness /mɪ'stɪəriəsnɪs/ *n* misterio, *m,* lo misterioso
mystery /'mɪstəri/ *n* misterio, *m.* **m. play,** (religious)
misterio, drama litúrgico, *m;* (thriller) comedia de detectives, *f.* **m. story,** novela policíaca, *f;* novela de
aventuras, *f*
mystic /'mɪstɪk/ *a* místico
mysticism /'mɪstə,sɪzəm/ *n* misticismo, *m*
mystification /,mɪstəfɪ'keiʃən/ *n* mistificación, *f*
mystify /'mɪstə,fai/ *vt* mistificar
myth /mɪθ/ *n* mito, *m*
mythical /'mɪθɪkəl/ *a* mítico
mythologist /mɪ'θɒlədʒɪst/ *n* mitólogo, *m*
mythology /mɪ'θɒlədʒi/ *n* mitología, *f*

N

n /ɛn/ n (letter) ene, f
nab /næb/ vt Inf. atrapar, apresar, agazapar
nabob /'neibɒb/ n nabab, m; ricacho, m
nacre /'neikər/ n nácar, m, madreperla, f
nadir /'neidər/ n nadir, m
nag /næg/ n jaca, f; (wretched hack) rocín, jamelgo, penco, m. —vt zaherir, echar en cara, regañar; (of one's conscience) remorder. —vi criticar, regañar
nagging /'nægɪŋ/ n zaherimiento, m. —a zaheridor, criticón; (pain) continuo, incesante, constante
naiad /'neiæd/ n Myth. náyade, f
nail /neil/ vt clavar, enclavar; (for ornament) clavetear, tachonar, adornar con clavos. —n uña, f; Mech. clavo, m; (animal's) garra, f. **to n. down,** sujetar (or cerrar) con clavos. **to n. to (on to),** clavar en. **to n. together,** fijar con clavos. Inf. **on the n.,** en el acto, en seguida. Inf. **to hit the n. on the head,** dar en el clavo. **brass-headed n.,** tachón, m. **French n.,** punta de París, f. **headless n.,** puntilla, f. **hob-n.,** clavo de herradura, m. **hook n.,** gancho, m. **round-headed n.,** bellota, f. **n.-brush,** cepillo para las (or de) uñas, m. **n.-file,** lima para las uñas, f. **n. head,** cabeza de un clavo, f. **n.-puller,** sacaclavos, arrancaclavos, botador, m. **n.-scissors,** tijeras para las uñas, f pl. **n. trade,** ferretería, f. **n. varnish,** barniz para las uñas, m
nailed /neild/ a adornado con clavos, claveteado
nailer /'neilər/ n fabricante de clavos, chapucero, m
nailing /'neilɪŋ/ n enclavación, f
naive /nɑ'iv/ a ingenuo, candoroso, espontáneo
naively /nɑ'ivli/ adv ingenuamente, espontáneamente
naiveté /nɑiv'tei, -,ivə'tei, -'ivtei, -'ivə-/ n ingenuidad, naturalidad, franqueza, f; candor, m
naked /'neikɪd/ a desnudo, nudo; desabrigado, indefenso, desamparado; (birds) implume; calvo; (truth) simple, sencillo, puro; evidente, patente. **stark n.,** en cueros vivos, tal como le parió su madre. **with the n. sword,** con la espada desnuda. **n. eye,** simple vista, f. **n. light,** llama descubierta, f
nakedly /'neikɪdli/ adv nudamente; desabrigadamente; abiertamente, claramente
nakedness /'neikɪdnɪs/ n desnudez, f; Fig. desabrigo, m, aridez, f; Fig. claridad, f. **the truth in all its n.,** la verdad desnuda
namby-pamby /'næmbi'pæmbi/ a soso, insípido, ñoño
name /neim/ n nombre, m; título, m; fama, opinión, f; renombre, crédito, m; autoridad, f; apodo, mal nombre, m. —vt nombrar, llamar, imponer el nombre de, apellidar; mencionar, señalar; (appoint) designar, elegir; (ships) bautizar. **by n.,** por nombre. **Christian n.,** nombre de pila, m. **in his n.,** en nombre de él, en nombre suyo; de parte de él. **in n. only,** nada más que en nombre. **to be named,** llamarse. **to call (a person) names,** poner como un trapo (a). **to go under the n. of,** vivir bajo el nombre de. **to have a good n.,** tener buena fama. **What is her n.?** ¿Cómo se llama? **n. day,** santo, m. **n. plate,** (machinery) placa de fábrica, f; (streets) rótulo, m; (professional) placa profesional, f
nameless /'neimlɪs/ a anónimo; desconocido; (inexpressible) vago, indecible
namely /'neimli/ adv a saber, es decir
namesake /'neim,seik/ n tocayo (-ya)
naming /'neimɪŋ/ n bautizo, m; nombramiento, m; designación, f
nannygoat /'næni,gout/ n cabra, f
nap /næp/ n (cloth) pelusa, f, pelo, tamo, m; (plants) vello, m, pelusilla, f; (sleep) siesta, f, sueño, m; (cards) napolitana, f. **to take a nap,** vi dormitar, echar un sueño, echar una siesta. **to take an afternoon nap,** dormir la siesta. **to be caught napping,** estar desprevenido
nape /neip/ n nuca, f, cogote, m; (animal's) testuz, m,
naphtha /'næfθə, 'næp-/ n Chem. nafta, f. **wood n.,** alcohol metílico, m

naphthalene /'næfθə,lin, 'næp-/ n Chem. naftalina, f
napkin /'næpkɪn/ n (table) servilleta, f; (babies') pañal, m. **n.-ring,** servilletero, m
Naples /'neipəlz/ Nápoles, m
Napoleonic /nə,pouli'ɒnɪk/ a napoleónico
narcissism /'nɑrsə,sɪzəm/ n narcisismo, m
narcissus /nɑr'sɪsəs/ n narciso, m
narcosis /nɑr'kousɪs/ n Med. narcosis, f
narcotic /nɑr'kɒtɪk/ a Med. narcótico, calmante, soporífero. —n Med. narcótico, m, opiata, f
nard /nɑrd/ n Bot. nardo, m, tuberosa, f
narrate /'næreit/ vt narrar, contar; referir, relatar
narration /næ'reiʃən/ n narración, narrativa; relación, descripción, f, relato, m
narrative /'nærətɪv/ a narrador, narrativo, narratorio. —n narrativa, f; descripción, f
narrator /'næreitər/ n narrador (-ra), relator (-ra), descriptor (-ra)
narrow /'nærou/ vt estrechar, angostar; reducir, limitar. —vi reducirse, hacerse más estrecho; (eyes) entornarse; (knitting) menguar. —a estrecho, angosto; limitado, restringido, reducido, corto; (avaricious) ruin, avaro, mezquino; (ideas) intolerante, intransigente. **"Narrow Road,"** «Camino Estrecho». —n pl **narrows,** Naut. estrecho, m; desfiladero, paso estrecho, m. **to have a n. escape,** escapar en una tabla. **n.-brimmed** (hats), de ala estrecha. **n. circumstances,** estrechez, escasez de medios, f. **n.-gauge railway,** ferrocarril de vía estrecha (or de vía angosta), m. **n. life,** vida de horizontes estrechos, f. **n. majority,** escasa mayoría, f. **n.-minded,** cerrado al mundo, intolerante, intransigente. **n.-mindedness,** intolerancia, intransigencia, estrechez de miras, f
narrowing /'nærouɪŋ/ n estrechez, f; estrechamiento, m; reducción, limitación, f; (in knitting) menguado, m
narrowly /'nærouli/ adv estrechamente; por poco, con dificultad; atentamente, cuidadosamente. **I n. escaped being run over,** Por poco me atropellan
narrowness /'nærounɪs/ n estrechez, angostura, f; (of means) pobreza, miseria, f; (of ideas) intolerancia, intransigencia, f
nasal /'neizəl/ a nasal, gangoso. —n letra nasal, f
nasalize /'neizə,laiz/ vt nasalizar
nasally /'neizəli/ adv nasalmente. **to speak n.,** hablar por las narices, ganguear
nascent /'næsənt, 'neisənt/ a naciente
nastily /'næstəli/ adv suciamente; ofensivamente, de un modo insultante; maliciosamente, con malignidad
nastiness /'næstɪnɪs/ n suciedad, inmundicia, porquería, f; (indecency) obscenidad, indecencia, f; (rudeness) insolencia, impertinencia, grosería, f; (difficulty) dificultad, f, lo malo
nasturtium /nə'stɜrʃəm/ n mastuerzo, m, capuchina, f
nasty /'næsti/ a nauseabundo, repugnante; asqueroso, inmundo, sucio; (obscene) indecente, obsceno; desagradable, malo; (malicious) rencoroso, malicioso; violento; malévolo, amenazador; peligroso; difícil. Fig. **to be in a n. mess,** tener el agua al cuello. **to turn n.,** Inf. ponerse desagradable
natal /'neitl̩/ a natal, natalicio, de nacimiento, nativo
nation /'neiʃən/ n nación, f, estado, país, m; (people) pueblo, m
national /'næʃənl̩/ a nacional; público; patriótico. —n nacional, mf. **n. anthem,** himno nacional, m. **n. debt,** deuda pública, f. **n. schools,** escuelas públicas, f pl. **n. socialism,** nacionalsocialismo, m. **n. socialist,** a and n nacionalsocialista mf. **n. syndicalism,** Polit. nacionalsindicalismo, m. **n. syndicalist,** a and n Polit. nacionalsindicalista, mf
nationalism /'næʃənl̩,ɪzəm/ n nacionalismo, patriotismo, m
nationalist /'næʃənlɪst/ a and n nacionalista, mf
nationality /,næʃ ə'nælɪti/ n nacionalidad, f; nación, f

nationalization /ˌnæʃənl‚ə'zeiʃən/ n nacionalización, f
nationalize /'næʃənl‚aiz, 'næʃnə‚laiz/ vt nacionalizar
National Labor Relations Board n Junta Nacional de Relaciones Laborales
nationally /'næʃənl‚i/ adv nacionalmente, como nación; del punto de vista nacional
native /'neitɪv/ a (of a place) nativo, natal, oriundo; indígena; nacional, típico, del país; (vocabulary) patrimonial (as opposed to borrowed vocabulary); (of genius) natural, innato, instintivo; Mineral. nativo; (language) vernáculo. —n nacional, mf; natural, mf; ciudadano (-na) indígena, aborigen (gen. pl.), mf; producto nacional, m. **He is a n. of Madrid,** Nació en Madrid, Es natural de Madrid, Es madrileño. **native informant,** sujeto, m. **n. land,** patria, tierra, f. **n. place,** lugar natal, m. **n. region,** patria chica, f. **n. soil,** terruño, m. **n. tongue,** lengua materna, f
nativity /nə'tɪvɪti/ n navidad, natividad, f; (manger) nacimiento, m
natty /'næti/ a Inf. chulo, majo; coquetón
natural /'nætʃərəl/ a natural; (wild) virgen, salvaje; nativo; (of products) crudo; normal; (usual) acostumbrado, corriente, natural; (of likeness) fiel, verdadero; (illegitimate) ilegítimo, bastardo; (of qualities) innato, instintivo; físico; característico, propio; (of people) inafectado, sencillo, genuino; Mus. natural. —n Mus. becuadro, m; Mus. nota natural, f; imbécil, mf n pl. **features,** geografía física, f. **n. history,** historia natural, f. **n. philosophy,** filosofía natural, f. **n. science,** ciencias naturales, f pl. **n. selection,** selección natural, f. **n. state,** estado virgen, m
natural child n hijo ilegítimo, m
natural daughter n hija ilegítima, f
naturalism /'nætʃərə‚lɪzəm/ n naturalismo, m
naturalist /'nætʃərəlɪst/ n (Lit. and Science.) naturalista, mf
naturalistic /ˌnætʃərə'lɪstɪk/ a naturalista
naturalization /ˌnætʃərələ'zeiʃən/ n naturalización, f; aclimatación, f. **n. papers,** carta de naturaleza, f
naturalize /'nætʃərə‚laiz/ vt naturalizar; aclimatar. **to become naturalized,** naturalizarse
naturally /'nætʃərəli/ adv naturalmente, por naturaleza; normalmente; sin afectación; instintivamente, por instinto; (without art) al natural
naturalness /ˌnætʃərəlnɪs/ n naturalidad, f; sencillez, desenvoltura, f; desembarazo, m
nature /'neitʃər/ n naturaleza, f; (of people) carácter, fondo, temperamento, genio, natural, modo de ser, m; (kind) género, m, especie, f; (essence) condición, esencia, cualidad, f, Art. **from n.,** del natural. **good n.,** bondad natural, afabilidad, f. **ill n.,** mala índole, f. **nature cure,** naturismo, m. **n. curist,** naturista, mf. **n. study,** historia natural, f. **n. worship,** panteísmo, culto de la naturaleza, m
natured /'neitʃərd/ a de carácter, de índole, con un modo de ser, de condición
naught /nɔt/ n nada, f; cero, m. —a inútil, sin valor. **all for n.,** todo en balde. **to come to n.,** malograrse. **to set at n.,** tener en menos; despreciar
naughtily /'nɔtli/ adv traviesamente; con picardía, con malicia
naughtiness /'nɔtinɪs/ n travesura, picardía, mala conducta, f; malicia, f
naughty /'nɔti/ a travieso, pícaro, revoltoso, malo; salado, escabroso, verde (stories, etc.). **to be n.,** (children) ser malo
nausea /'nɔziə, -ʒə/ n náusea, f; bascas, f pl, mareo, m; Fig. asco, m; repugnancia, f
nauseate /'nɔzi‚eit, -ʒi-/ vt dar náuseas; Fig. repugnar, dar asco
nauseating /'nɔzi‚eitɪŋ, -ʒi-/ a repugnante, horrible; asqueroso
nauseous /'nɔʃəs/ a nauseabundo, asqueroso; Fig. repugnante
nauseousness /'nɔʃəsnɪs/ n náusea, asquerosidad, f; Fig. repugnancia, f, asco, m
nautical /'nɔtɪkəl/ a náutico, marítimo. **n. day, twenty-four hours,** singladura, f
nautilus /'nɔtləs/ n Zool. argonauta, nautilo, m
naval /'neivəl/ a naval; de marina, marítimo. **n. base,** base naval, f. **n. engagement,** batalla naval, f. **n. hospital,** hospital de marina, m. **n. law,** código na-

val, m. **n. officer,** oficial de marina, m. **n. power,** poder marítimo, m. **n. reservist,** marinero de reserva, m. **n. yard,** arsenal, m
Navarre /nə'vɑr/ Navarra, f
Navarrese /ˌnævə'riz/ a and n navarro (-rra)
nave /neiv/ n Archit. nave, f; (of wheels) cubo, m
navel /'neivəl/ n ombligo, m. **n. string,** cordón umbilical, m
navigability /ˌnævɪgə'bɪliti/ n navegación, practicabilidad de navegar, f
navigable /'nævɪgəbəl/ a navegable, practicable
navigate /'nævɪ‚geit/ vt navegar, marear, dirigir (unbuque); Fig. conducir, guiar. —vi navegar
navigation /ˌnævɪ'geiʃən/ n navegación, f; (science of) náutica, marina, f. **n. company,** empresa naviera, f. **n. laws,** derecho marítimo, m. **n. lights,** luces de navegación, f pl
navigator /'nævɪ‚geitər/ n navegador, navegante, m; piloto, m
navvy /'nævi/ n peón, bracero, jornalero, m; Mech. máquina, excavadora, f. **road n.,** peón caminero, m. **to work like a n.,** estar hecho un azacán, sudar la gota gorda
navy /'neivi/ n marina, f; armada, f; (color) azul marino, m. **n. board,** consejo de la armada, m. **n. department** ministerio de marina, m. **n. estimates,** presupuesto de marina, m. **n. list,** escalafón de marina, m
nay /nei/ adv no; al contrario, más bien, mejor dicho. —n negativa, f, voto contrario, m
Nazarene /ˌnæzə'rin/ a and n nazareno (-na)
Nazareth /'næzərəθ/ Nazaret, m
Nazi /'nɑtsi/ a and n nacionalsocialista, naci, mf
Nazism /'nɑtsizəm/ n nacismo, m
n.d. (no date) s.f. (sin fecha)
Neapolitan /ˌniə'pɒlɪtn/ a and n neapolitano (-na)
near /nɪər/ vi acercarse, aproximarse. —a cercano, immediato, contiguo; (of time) inminente, próximo; (relationship) cercano, consanguíneo; (of friends) íntimo, entrañable; (mean) tacaño, avariento
near /nɪər/ prep cerca de, junto a; hacia, en la dirección de; (of time) cerca de, casi. —adv cerca; (time) cerca, próximamente. **to be n. to,** estar cerca de. **to bring n.,** acercar, aproximar. **It was a n. thing,** Escapamos por un pelo. **n. at hand,** a la mano; (time) cerca, inminente. **n.-by,** a cercano, inmediato. —adv cerca. **n. side,** (of vehicles) lado de la acera, m. **n.-sighted,** corto de vista, miope. **n.-sightedness,** miopía, cortedad de vista, f
nearest /'nɪərɪst/ a comparar and superl más cercano, más cerca; más corto. **the n. way,** el camino más corto, el camino más directo
nearly /'nɪərli/ adv casi; cerca de, aproximadamente; estrechamente; íntimamente. **It touches me n.,** Me toca de cerca, Es de sumo interés para mí. **They n. killed me,** Por poco me matan. **to be n.,** (of age) frisar en, rayar en
nearness /'nɪərnɪs/ n (of place) cercanía, proximidad, contigüidad, f; (of time) inminencia, proximidad, f; (relationship) consanguinidad, f; (avarice) avaricia, tacañería, f; (dearness) intimidad, amistad estrecha, f
neat /nit/ a Zool. vacuno; elegante, sencillo, de buen gusto; (of the body) bien hecho, airoso, esbelto; (clean) limpio, aseado; (of handwriting) legible, bien proporcionado; pulido, esmerado, acabado; hábil, astuto, diestro; (of liquor, spirits) puro, solo. **to make a n. job of,** hacer (algo) bien
neatly /'nitli/ adv sencillamente, con elegancia, con primor; con aseo, limpiamente; bien (proporcionado); diestramente, hábilmente
neatness /'nitnɪs/ n aseo, m, limpieza, f; elegancia, sencillez, f; buen gusto, m; destreza, habilidad, f; (aptness) pertinencia, f
nebula /'nɛbyələ/ n Astron. nebulosa, f
nebulosity /ˌnɛbyə'lɒsɪti/ n nebulosidad, f; Astron. nebulosa, f; vaguedad, imprecisión, f
nebulous /'nɛbyələs/ a nebuloso; vago, impreciso, confuso
necessarily /ˌnɛsə'sɛərəli/ adv necesariamente; inevitablemente, sin duda
necessary /'nɛsə‚sɛri/ a necesario, inevitable; imprescindible, preciso, indispensable, esencial; obligatorio,

debido, forzoso. —*n* requisito esencial, *m*. **if n.,** en caso de necesidad; si fuera necesario. **to be n.,** hacer falta; necesitarse

necessitate /nə'sɛsɪ,teit/ *vt* necesitar, exigir, requerir, obligar

necessitous /nə'sɛsɪtəs/ *a* pobre, indigente, miserable, necesitado

necessity /nə'sɛsɪti/ *n* necesidad, *f;* menester, *m*, (e.g., *an indispensable n.,* un menester imprescindible); consecuencia, *f*, resultado, efecto, *m;* inevitabilidad, fatalidad, *f;* (poverty) indigencia, pobreza, *f*. *Fire and clothing are necessities,* El fuego y el vestir son cosas necesarias. **from n.,** por necesidad. **in case of n.,** si fuese necesario, en caso de necesidad. **of n.,** de necesidad, sin remedio. **physical necessities,** menesteres físicos, *m pl*. **prime n.,** artículo de primera necesidad, *m*. **to be under the n. of,** tener que, tener la necesidad de

Necessity is the mother of invention La necesidad es una gran inventora, La necesidad aguza el ingenio

neck /nɛk/ *n* cuello, *m*, garganta, *f;* (of bottles) gollete, cuello, *m;* (of animals) pescuezo, *m; Geog.* istmo, *m*, lengua de tierra, *f;* (of musical instruments) clavijero, mástil, *m; Sew.* escote, *m.* **low-necked,** (of dresses) escotado. **She fell on his n.,** Se colgó de su cuello. **He won by a n.,** Ganó por un cuello; *Fig.* Ganó por un tris. **to break anyone's n.,** romperle el pescuezo. **to wring the n. of,** torcer el pescuezo (a). **n. and n.,** parejos. **n. or nothing,** todo o nada, perdiz o no comerla. **in stock,** alzacuello, *m*

neckband /'nɛk,bænd/ *n* tirilla de camisa, *f*

necklace /'nɛklɪs/ *n* collar, *m*

necklet /'nɛklɪt/ *n* collar, *m;* (of fur) cuello, *m*

necktie /'nɛk,tai/ *n* corbata, *f*

necrological /,nɛkrə'lɒdʒɪkəl/ *a* necrológico

necrology /nə'krɒlədʒi/ *n* necrología, *f*

necropolis /nə'krɒpəlɪs/ *n* necrópolis, *f*

nectar /'nɛktər/ *n* néctar, *m*

nectarine /,nɛktə'rin/ *n Bot.* variedad de melocotón, *f*

need /nid/ *vt* necesitar, haber menester, requerir, exigir. —*vi* ser necesario, hacer falta; carecer; haber (de). **N. I obey?** ¿He de obedecer? **You need to write carefully,** Hay que escribir con cuidado. **The work n. not be done for tomorrow,** No es preciso hacer el trabajo para mañana

need /nid/ *n* necesidad, *f;* cosa necesaria, *f;* falta; (poverty) indigencia, pobreza, *f;* urgencia, *f;* (shortage) escasez, carestía, *f.* **in case of n.,** en caso de necesidad, en caso de urgencia. **I have n. of two more books,** Me hacen falta dos libros más

needful /'nidfəl/ *a* necesario, preciso; indispensable, esencial. **the n.,** lo necesario

needfulness /'nidfəlnɪs/ *n* necesidad, falta, *f*

neediness /'nidinɪs/ *n* pobreza, penuria, miseria, estrechez, *f*

needle /'nidḷ/ *n Sew.* aguja, *f;* (of compass) brújula, aguja imanada, *f;* (monument) obelisco, *m;* (of scales) field, *m*, lengüeta, *f;* (of phonograph) pría, *f*, (of measuring instruments) índice, *m; Med.* aguja de inyecciones, *f. Inf.* **to be as sharp as a n.,** no tener pelo de tonto. **pack n.,** aguja espartera, *f.* **n.-case,** alfiletero, agujero, *m.* **n. maker,** fabricante de agujas, *m.* **n.-shaped,** en forma de aguja, acicular

needle and thread hilo y aguja

needless /'nidlɪs/ *a* innecesario, superfluo. **n. to say,** claro está que..., huelga decir que...

needlessly /'nidlɪsli/ *adv* innecesariamente, inútilmente; en vano, de balde

needlessness /'nidlɪsnɪs/ *n* superfluidad, *f*, lo innecesario

needlewoman /'nidḷ,wʊmən/ *n* (professional) cosedora, *f;* costurera, *f*. **She is a good n.,** Cose bien (or es una buena cosedora)

needlework /'nidḷ,wɜrk/ *n* labor de aguja, labor blanca, costura, *f;* bordado, *m*. **to do n.,** hacer costura

needs /nidz/ *adv* necesariamente, sin remedio *n pl* necesidades, *f pl*. **if n. must,** si hace falta. **N. must when the devil drives,** A la fuerza ahorcan

needy /'nidi/ *a* necesitado, menesteroso, corto de medios, pobre, apurado

ne'er-do-well /'nɛərdu,wɛl/ *n* calavera, perdido, *m*. **to be a n.,** ser de mala madera

nefarious /nɪ'fɛəriəs/ *a* nefario, vil, nefando

nefariously /nɪ'fɛəriəsli/ *adv* vilmente, nefariamente

negation /nɪ'geiʃən/ *n* negación, *f*

negative /'nɛgətɪv/ *vt* negar, denegar; votar en contra (de), oponerse (a); (prevent) impedir, imposibilitar. —*a* negativo. —*n* negativa, negación, *f;* repulsa, denegación, *f; Photo.* negativo, *m*, prueba negativa, *f; Elec.* electricidad negativa, *f.* **to reply in the n.,** dar una respuesta negativa

negativeness /'nɛgətɪvnɪs/ *n* el carácter negativo, *m*

neglect /nɪ'glɛkt/ *vt* descuidar, desatender; abandonar, dejar; (ignore) despreciar, no hacer caso (de); omitir, olvidar. —*n* descuido, *m*, desatención, *f;* inobservancia, *f;* abandono, olvido, *m;* desdén, *m*, frialdad, *f.* **to fall into n.,** caer en desuso. **to n. one's obligations,** descuidar sus obligaciones

neglectful /nɪ'glɛktfəl/ *a* negligente, descuidado, omiso

negligee /,nɛglɪ'ʒei/ *n* salto de cama, quimono, *m*, bata, *f*

negligence /'nɛglɪdʒəns/ *n* negligencia, *f*, descuido, *m;* flojedad, pereza, *f;* (of dress) desaliño, *m*

negligent /'nɛglɪdʒənt/ *a* negligente, descuidado; remiso, flojo, perezoso

negligently /'nɛglɪdʒəntli/ *adv* negligentemente; con indiferencia

negligible /'nɛglɪdʒəbəl/ *a* insignificante, escaso, insuficiente; sin importancia, desdeñable

negotiable /nɪ'gouʃiəbəl, -ʃəbəl/ *a* negociable; (of a road) practicable, transitable

negotiate /nɪ'gouʃi,eit/ *vt* gestionar, agenciar, tratar; (a bend) tomar; (an obstacle) salvar, franquear; *vi* negociar. **to n. a bill of exchange,** descontar una letra de cambio. **to n. for a contract,** tratar un contrato

negotiation /nɪ,gouʃi'eiʃən/ *n* negociación, *f; Com.* gestión, transacción, *f;* (of a bend) toma, *f;* (of an obstacle) salto, *m*

negotiator /nɪ'gouʃi,eitər/ *n* negociador (-ra)

neigh /nei/ *vi* relinchar. —*n* relincho, relinchido, *m*

neighbor /'neibər/ *n* vecino (-na); (biblical) prójimo (-ma)

neighborhood /'neibər,hʊd/ *n* vecindad, *f*, vecindario, *m;* cercanía, *f*, afueras, *f pl*, alrededores, *m pl;* *a* de barrio (e.g. *neighborhood moviehouse,* cine del barrio)

neighboring /'neibərɪŋ/ *a* vecino; cercano, inmediato, adyacente

neighborliness /'neibərlinɪs/ *n* buena vecindad, *f*

neighborly /'neibərli/ *a* amistoso, sociable, bondadoso. **to be n.,** ser de buena vecindad

neither /'niðər, 'nai-/ *a* ningún; ninguno de los dos, e.g. *N. explanation is right,* Ninguna de las dos explicaciones es correcta. —*conjunc* ni, tampoco, e.g. *N. Mary nor John,* Ni María ni Juan. *N. will he give it to her,* Tampoco se lo dará. —*pron* ni uno ni otro, ninguno, e.g. *N. of them heard it,* Ni uno ni otro lo oyó.

nemesis /'nɛməsɪs/ *n* némesis, *f;* justicia, *f*

neo- *prefix* neo. **neo-Catholic,** *a* and *n* neo-católico (-ca). **neo-Platonic,** neoplatónico. **neo-Platonism,** neoplatonismo, *m*

neolithic /,niə'lɪθɪk/ *a* neolítico

neologism /ni'ɒlə,dʒɪzəm/ *n* neologismo, *m*

neon /'niɒn/ *n Chem.* neón, *m*

neon sign anuncio luminoso, *m*

neophyte /'niə,fait/ *n* neófito (-ta); aspirante, *mf*

nephew /'nɛfyu/ *n* sobrino, *m*

nephritis /nə'fraitɪs/ *n Med.* nefritis, *f*

nepotism /'nɛpə,tɪzəm/ *n* nepotismo, *m*

nerve /nɜrv/ *n* (*Anat. Bot.*) nervio, *m;* valor, ánimo, *m;* vitalidad, *f; Inf.* descaro, *m*, desvergüenza, frescura, *f.* —*vt* animar, alentar, envalentonar; esforzar; dar fuerza (a). —*vi* animarse, esforzarse (a). **My nerves are all on edge,** Se me crispan los nervios. **n.-cell,** neurona, *f.* **to lose one's n.,** perder la cabeza; perder los nervios. **to strain every n.,** hacer un esfuerzo supremo. **n. center,** centro nervioso, *m.* **n.-racking,** espantoso, horripilante. **n. strain,** tensión nerviosa, *f*

nerveless /'nɜrvlɪs/ *a* sin nervio; enervado

nerviness /'nɜrvɪnɪs/ *n* nervosidad, *f*

nervous /'nɜrvəs/ *a* nervioso, asustadizo, tímido; agitado, excitado; (of style) vigoroso. **n. breakdown,** crisis nerviosa, *f.* **n. system,** sistema nervioso, *m*

nervously /'nɜrvəsli/ *adv* nerviosamente; tímidamente

nervousness /'nɜrvəsnɪs/ *n* nervosidad, timidez, *f;* agitación, *f;* (of style) vigor, *m;* energía, *f*

nervy /'nɜrvi/ *a* nervioso

nest /nɛst/ *vi* anidar, hacerse un nido. —*n* (bird's) nido, *m;* (animal's) madriguera, *f;* (of drawers) juego, *m,* serie, *f;* (of thieves) cueva, guarida, *f; Inf.* casita, *f,* hogar, *m.* **to feather one's n.,** hacer su agosto. **n.-egg,** *Fig.* nidal, *m.* **n. of eggs,** nidada de huevos, *f*

nestle /'nɛsəl/ *vt* apoyar. —*vi* apiñarse, hacerse un ovillo. **to n. up to a person,** apretarse contra

nestling /'nɛstlɪŋ/ *n* pichón, pollo, *m;* pajarito, *m*

net /nɛt/ *vt* coger con redes; obtener, coger; cubrir con redes. —*vi* hacer redes. —*n* red, *f;* (mesh) malla, *f;* (fabric) tul, *m.* **net making,** manufactura de redes, *f*

net /nɛt/ *a Com.* líquido, neto, limpio; (of fabric) de tul. **net amount,** importe líquido, importe neto, *m.* **net balance,** saldo líquido, *m.* **net cost,** precio neto, *m.* **net profit,** beneficio neto (or líquido), *m*

nether /'nɛðər/ *a* inferior, bajero, más bajo. **n. regions,** infierno, *m*

Netherland /'nɛðərlənd/ *a* neerlandés, holandés

Netherlander /'nɛðərˌlændər/ *n* neerlandés (-esa), holandés (-esa)

Netherlands, the /'nɛðərləndz/ los Países Bajos *m pl*

nethermost /'nɛðərˌmoust/ *a* lo más bajo, ínfimo, más hondo

netting /'nɛtɪŋ/ *n* red, (obra de) malla, *f; Naut.* jareta, *f;* manufactura de redes, *f;* pesca con redes, *f.* **wire-n.,** tela metálica, malla de alambre, *f*

nettle /'nɛtl/ *vt* picar; *Fig.* irritar, picar, fastidiar, disgustar. —*n* ortiga, *f.* **n.-rash,** urticaria, *f*

network /'nɛtˌwɜrk/ *n* red, malla, randa, *f;* (of communications) sistema, *m,* red, *f*

neuralgia /nʊ'rældʒə/ *n* neuralgia, *f*

neuralgic /nʊ'rældʒɪk/ *a* neurálgico

neurasthenia /ˌnʊrəs'θiniə/ *n* neurastenia, *f*

neurasthenic /ˌnʊrəs'θɛnɪk/ *a and n* neurasténico (-ca)

neuritis /nʊ'raitɪs/ *n* neuritis, *f*

neurologist /nʊ'rɒlədʒɪst/ *n* neurólogo, *m*

neurology /nʊ'rɒlədʒi/ *n* neurología, *f*

neuropath /'nʊrəˌpæθ/ *n* neurópata, *m*

neuropathic /ˌnʊrə'pæθɪk/ *a* neuropático

neurosis /nʊ'rousɪs/ *n* neurosis, *f*

neurosurgeon /'nʊrouˌsɜrdʒən/ *n* neurocirujano, *m*

neurotic /nʊ'rɒtɪk/ *a and n* neurótico (-ca)

neuter /'nʊtər/ *a* neutro; (of verbs) intransitivo; (*Zool. Bot.*) sin sexo

neutral /'nʊtrəl/ *a* neutral; (*Chem. Mech.*) neutro; (of colors) indeciso, indeterminado; (of persons) imparcial, indiferente. —*n* neutral, *mf Mech.* **to go into n.,** pasar a marcha neutra

neutrality /nʊ'trælɪti/ *n* neutralidad, *f;* indiferencia, *f;* imparcialidad, *f*

neutralization /'nʊtrələ'zeɪʃən/ *n* neutralización, *f*

neutralize /'nʊtrəˌlaiz/ *vt* neutralizar

never /'nɛvər/ *adv* nunca, jamás; de ningún modo, no; ni aun, ni siquiera. **Better late than n.,** Más vale tarde que nunca. **Never look a gift horse in the mouth,** A caballo regalado no se le mira el diente. **Were the hour n. so late,** Por más tarde que fuese la hora. **n. again,** nunca jamás. **n. a one,** ni siquiera uno. **n. a whit,** ni pizca. **N. mind!** ¡No importa! ¡No te preocupes! ¡No hagas caso! **n.-ceasing,** continuo, incesante. **n.-ending,** inacabable, eterno, sin fin. **n.-failing,** infalible. **n.-to-be-forgotten,** inolvidable

nevermore /ˌnɛvər'mɔr/ *adv* nunca jamás

nevertheless /ˌnɛvərðə'lɛs/ *adv* sin embargo, no obstante, con todo

new /nu/ *a* nuevo; novel, fresco; distinto, diferente; moderno; (inexperienced) novato, no habituado; reciente. —*adv* (in compounds) recién. **as good as new,** como nuevo. **brand-new,** flamante, nuevecito. **new-born,** recién nacido. **new-comer,** recién llegado

(-da). **new-fashioned,** de última moda. **new-found,** recién hallado. **new-laid egg,** huevo fresco, *m.* **new moon,** luna nueva, *f,* novilunio, *m.* **new rich,** ricacho (-cha); indio, *m.* **new student,** alumno de nuevo ingreso. **New Testament,** Nuevo Testamento, *m.* **New World,** Nuevo Mundo, *m.* **New York (er),** *a and n* neoyorquino (-na). **New Zealand (er),** *a and n* neozelandés (-esa)

newel /'nuəl/ *n* (of stair) alma, *f,* árbol, nabo, *m.* **n.-post,** pilarote (de escalera), *m*

newest /'nuɪst/ *a superl* novísimo; más reciente

Newfoundland /'nufənlənd/ Terranova, *f.* **N. dog,** perro de Terranova, *m*

New Guinea /'gɪni/ Nueva Guinea, *f*

newish /'nuɪʃ/ *a* bastante nuevo

newly /'nuli/ *adv* nuevamente; hace poco, recientemente. The abb. form **recién** is used only with past part, e.g. *the n. painted door,* la puerta recién pintada. *the n.-weds,* los desposados, los recién casados

newness /'nunɪs/ *n* novedad, *f;* inexperiencia, falta de práctica, *f;* innovación, *f*

New Orleans /'ɔrliənz, ɔr'linz/ Nueva Orleans, *f*

news /nuz/ *n, pl* noticias, *f pl;* nueva, *f;* reporte, aviso, *m;* novedad, *f.* **No n. is good n.,** Falta de noticias, buena señal. **piece of n.,** noticia, *f.* **What's the n.?** ¿Qué hay de nuevo? **n. agency,** agencia de noticias, agencia periodística, *f.* **n.-agent,** agente de la prensa, *m;* vendedor (-ra) de periódicos. **n. bulletin,** *Radio.* boletín de noticias, *m. Inf.* **n.-hound,** gacetillero (-ra). **n. item,** noticia de actualidad, *f.* **n.-print,** papel para periódicos, *m.* **n.-room,** gabinete de lectura, *m.* **n. reel,** película noticiera, revista cinematográfica, *f,* noticiario cinematográfico, noticiero *m,* actualidades, *f pl.* **n.-stand,** puesto de periódicos, quiosco de periódicos, *m.* **n. theater,** cine de actualidades, *m*

newscast /'nuzˌkæst/ *n* noticiario, *m*

newsletter circular /'nuzˌlɛtər/ noticiario, relación de sucesos, *f*

New South Wales La Nueva Gales del Sur, *f*

newspaper /'nuzˌpeɪpər/ *n* periódico, diario, noticiero, *m.* **n. clipping, n. cutting,** recorte de periódico, *m.* **n. paragraph,** suelto, *m.* **n. reporter,** reportero (-ra); reportista, *mf n.* **reporting,** reporterismo, *m.* **n. serial,** folletín, *m,* novela por entregas, *f.* **n. vendor,** vendedor (-ra) de periódicos, *n*

news report *n* reportaje, *m*

newsy /'nuzi/ *a Inf.* lleno de noticias, noticioso

newt /nut/ *n* tritón, *m*

Newtonian /nu'tounian/ *a* neutoniano

New York /yɔrk/ Nueva York, *f*

New Zealand /'ziland/ Nueva Zelandia, *f*

next /nɛkst/ *a* (of place) siguiente, vecino, contiguo; (of time) próximo, siguiente. **on the n. page,** en la página siguiente. **the n. day,** el día siguiente. **the n.-door house,** la casa vecina. **the n. life,** la otra vida. **n. month (year),** el mes (año) próximo (or que viene). **n. time,** otra vez, la próxima vez

next /nɛkst/ *adv* (of time) luego, en seguida, *f;* (of place) inmediatamente después. **I come n.,** Ahora me toca a mí. **It is n. to a certainty that...,** Es casi seguro que... **the n. best,** el segundo mejor. **the n. of kin,** los pariente más cercarro, *m,* parientes más cercanos, *m pl.* **to wear n. to the skin,** llevar sobre la piel. **n. to,** al lado de, junto a; primero después de; casi. **n. to nothing,** casi nada, muy poco. **What n.?** ¿Qué más?; ¿Y ahora qué?

nib /nɪb/ *n* punto, tajo (de una pluma), *m*

nibble /'nɪbəl/ *vt* mordiscar, mordisquear, roer; (horses) rozar; (fish) picar; *Fig.* considerar, tantear; *vi* picar. —*n* mordisco, *m;* roedura, *f*

Nicaraguan /ˌnɪkə'ragwən/ *a and n* nicaragüeño (-ña)

Nice /nis/ Niza, *f*

nice /nais/ *a* escrupuloso, minucioso, exacto; (of persons) simpático, afable, amable; fino; (of things) agradable, bonito; bueno; sutil, delicado; (*Inf. Ironic.*) bonito. **a n. point,** un punto delicado. **a n. view,** una vista agradable (or bonita). **n.-looking,** guapo. **n. people,** gente fina, *f;* gente simpática, *f*

nicely /'naisli/ *adv* muy bien; con elegancia; primorosamente; con amabilidad, gentilmente; agradablemente

Nicene /nai'sin/ *a* niceno

niceness /'naisnɪs/ *n* exactitud, minuciosidad, *f;* (of persons) bondad, amabilidad, *f;* amenidad, hermosura, *f;* lo bonito; sutileza, *f;* refinamiento, *m*

nicety /'naisɪti/ *n* exactitud, *f;* sutileza, *f,* refinamiento, *m.* **niceties,** *n pl* detalles, *m pl.* **to a n.,** con la mayor precisión; a la perfección

niche /nɪtʃ/ *n* nicho, templete, *m;* (vaulted) hornacina, *f, Fig.* **to find a n. for oneself,** encontrarse una buena posición; situarse

nick /nɪk/ *vt* cortar en muescas, mellar, tarjar. —*n* mella, muesca, *f.* **in the n. of time,** en el momento oportuno, a tiempo

nickel /'nɪkəl/ *n* níquel, *m; Com.* moneda de níquel, *f.* **n.-plated,** niquelado

nickname /'nɪk,neim/ *vt* apodar, motejar, apellidar. —*n* apodo, sobrenombre, mote, mal nombre, *m*

nicotine /'nɪkə,tin/ *n* nicotina, *f*

nicotinism /'nɪkəti,nɪzəm/ *n* nicotismo, *m*

nictitating membrane /'nɪktɪ,teitɪŋ/ *n Anat.* membrana nictitante, *f*

niece /nis/ *n* sobrina, *f*

niggardliness /'nɪgərdlinɪs/ *n* tacañería, avaricia, parsimonia, mezquindad, *f*

niggardly /'nɪgərdli/ *a* tacaño, avaricioso, mezquino, ruin, miserable

niggling /'nɪglɪŋ/ *a* nimio, meticuloso; escrupuloso, minucioso

nigh. /nai/ See **near**

night /nait/ *n* noche, *f; Fig.* oscuridad, *f,* tinieblas, *f pl.* **all n.,** toda la noche, la noche entera. **all n. service,** servicio nocturno permanente, *m.* **at** or **by n.,** de noche. **every n.,** todas las noches, cada noche. **Good n.!** ¡Buenas noches! **last n.,** ayer por la noche, anoche, la noche pasada. **restless n.,** noche mala, noche toledana, *f.* **the n. before last,** anteayer por la noche, *m.* **to-n.,** esta noche. **tomorrow n.,** mañana por la noche. **to be n.,** ser de noche. **to spend the n.,** pernoctar, pasar la noche. **n.-bird,** pájaro nocturno, *m; Inf.* trasnochador (-ra). **n.-blindness,** nictalopia, *f.* **n.-cap,** gorro de dormir, *m.* **n.-clothes,** traje de dormir, *m.* **n. club,** cabaret *m.* **n. dew,** relente, sereno, *m.* **n. flying,** vuelo nocturno, *m.* **n.-jar,** *Ornith.* chotacabras, *m.* **n.-light,** mariposa, lamparilla, *f.* **n. mail,** último correo, *m;* tren correo de la noche, *m.* **n. school,** escuela nocturna, *f.* **n. shift,** turno de noche, *m.* **n. watch,** ronda de noche, *f; Naut.* sonochada, *f.* **n. watchman,** (in the street) sereno, *m;* (of a building) vigilante nocturno, *m*

nightfall /'nait,fɔl/ *n* anochecer, crepúsculo, atardecer, *m*

nightgown /'nait,gaun/ *n* camisa de noche, *f*

nightingale /'naitn̩,geil, 'naitɪŋ-/ *n* ruiseñor, *m*

nightly /'naitli/ *a* de noche; nocturno, nocturnal. —*adv* todas las noches, cada noche

nightmare /'nait,mɛər/ *n* pesadilla, *f*

nightmarish /'nait,mɛərɪʃ/ *a* de pesadilla, horrible

nightshade /'nait,ʃeid/ *n Bot.* hierba mora, *f,* solano, *m*

nihilism /'naiə,lɪzəm/ 'ni-/ *n* nihilismo, *m*

nihilist /'naiəlɪst, 'ni-/ *n* nihilista, *mf*

Nile, the /nail/ el Nilo, *m*

nimble /'nɪmbəl/ *a* ágil, activo; vivo, listo. **n.-fingered,** ligero de dedos. **n.-witted,** despierto, vivo

nimbleness /'nɪmbəlnɪs/ *n* agilidad, actividad, *f;* viveza, habilidad, *f*

nimbly /'nɪmbli/ *adv* ágilmente, ligeramente

nimbus /'nɪmbəs/ *n* nimbo, *m,* aureola, *f*

nincompoop /'nɪnkəm,pup, 'nɪŋ-/ *n* papirote, *m,* papanatas, *mf* tonto (-ta)

nine /nain/ *a and n* nueve, *m.* **He is n.,** Tiene nueve años. **the N.,** las nueve Musas. **n. o'clock,** las nueve. **to be dressed up to the nines,** estar hecho un brazo de mar

ninefold /*a* 'nain,fould; *adv.* 'nain'fould/ *a and adv* nueve veces

ninepins /'nain,pɪnz/ *n* juego de bolos, *m*

nineteen /'nain'tin/ *a and n* diez y nueve, diecinueve *m*

nineteenth /'nain'tinθ/ *a* décimonono. —*n* (of month) el diez y nueve; (of monarchs) diez y nueve. **the n. century,** el siglo diez y nueve

ninetieth /'naintiəθ/ *a* nonagésimo, noventa

ninety /'nainti/ *a and n* noventa *m.* **n.-one,** noventa y uno. **n.-two,** noventa y dos. **the n.-first chapter,** el capítulo noventa y uno

ninny /'nɪni/ *n* parapoco, chancleta, *mf;* mentecato (-ta)

ninth /nainθ/ *a* noveno, nono. —*n* nueve, *m;* (of the month) el nueve (of sovereigns) nono. **one n.,** un noveno

ninthly /'nainθli/ *adv* en noveno (or nono) lugar

nip /nɪp/ *vt* pellizcar, pinchar; mordiscar, morder; (wither) marchitar; (freeze) helar; (run) correr. —*vi* pinchar; picar (el viento). —*n* pellizco, pinchazo, *m;* mordisco, *m;* (of spirits) trago, *m;* copita, *f;* (in the air) viento frío, hielo, *m.* **to nip in,** colarse dentro, deslizarse en. **to nip off,** pirarse, mudarse. *Fig.* **to nip in the bud,** cortar en flor

nippers /'nɪpərz/ *pl* alicates, *m pl;* tenacillas, pinzas, *f pl*

nipping /'nɪpɪŋ/ *n* pinchadura, *f;* mordedura, *f.* —*a* punzante; helado, glacial, mordiente. **n. off,** (of a point) despuntadura, *f*

nipple /'nɪpəl/ *n* pezón, *m;* pezón artificial, *m*

nit /nɪt/ *n Ent.* liendre, *f*

niter /'naitər/ *n* salitre, *m*

nitrate /'naitreit/ *n Chem.* nitrato, *m*

nitric /'naitrɪk/ *a* nítrico

nitrite /'naitrait/ *n Chem.* nitrito, *m*

nitro- prefix *Chem.* nitro. **n.-cellulose,** algodón pólvora, *m.* **n.-glycerine,** nitroglicerina, *f*

nitrogen /'naitrədʒən/ *n Chem.* nitrógeno, *m*

nitrous /'naitrəs/ *a* nitroso, salitrar

no /nou/ *a* ningún, ninguno, ninguna, e.g. *by no means,* de ningún modo. *No* is often not translated in Sp., e.g. *I have no time,* No tengo tiempo. —*adv* no. —*n* voto negativo, no, *m.* *to be of no account,* no tener importancia, no significar nada. *to be no good for,* no servir para. *to be of no use,* ser inútil. *to have no connection with,* no tener nada que ver con. *for no reason,* sin motivo alguno. *"No Admittance,"* «Entrada Prohibida.» *no, indeed,* Cierto que no. *no-man's land,* tierra de nadie, *f. no more,* no más. *No more of this!* ¡No hablemos más de eso! *no one,* nadie, ninguno. *no sooner,* no bien, tan pronto (como). *no such thing,* no tal. **"No Thoroughfare,"** «Prohibido el Paso.» *whether or not,* sea o no sea

Noah's Ark /'nouəz/ *n* arca de Noé, *f*

nobility /nou'bɪlɪti/ *n* nobleza, *f;* (of rank) aristocracia, nobleza, *f;* (of conduct) caballerosidad, hidalguía, generosidad, bondad, *f;* (grandeur) grandeza, sublimidad, *f.* **the higher n.,** los nobles de primera clase

noble /'noubəl/ *a* noble; (in rank) aristocrático, noble, linajudo; (of conduct) caballeroso, generoso; (of buildings) sublime, magnífico. —*n* noble, *m,* aristócrata, *mf* **to make n.,** ennoblecer. **n.-mindedness,** generosidad, grandeza de alma, *f.* **n. title,** título del reino, *m*

noblewoman /'noubəl,wumən/ *n* dama noble, mujer noble, aristócrata, *f*

nobly /'noubli/ *adv* noblemente, generosamente. **n. born,** noble de nacimiento

nobody /'nou,bɒdi/ *n* nadie, ninguno. **There was n. there,** No había nadie allí. *Inf.* **a n.,** un (una) cualquiera, una persona insignificante. **n. else,** nadie más, ningún otro

nocturnal /nɒk'tɜrnl̩/ *a* nocturno, nocherniego, nocturnal

nocturne /'nɒktɜrn/ *n Mus.* nocturno, *m*

nod /nɒd/ *vt* inclinar la cabeza; hacer una señal (or señas) con la cabeza; *vi* dar cabezadas; cabecear; (of trees) mecerse, inclinarse; inclinar la cabeza. —*n* señal (or seña) con la cabeza, *f;* inclinación de la cabeza, *f;* cabeceo, *m,* cabezada, *f.* **A nod is as good as a wink,** A buen entendedor pocas palabras. **He nodded to me as he passed,** Me saludó con la cabeza al pasar. **He signed to me with a nod,** Me hizo una señal con la cabeza

nodding /'nɒdɪŋ/ *a* que cabecea; *Bot.* colgante, inclinado; temblante. —*n* cabeceo, *m;* saludo con la cabeza, *m*

noddle /'nɒdl̩/ *n* mollera, *f*

node /noud/ *n* (Bot. Med.) nudo, *m*

nodule /'nɒdʒul/ *n* nódulo, *m;* nudillo, *m*

noise /nɔiz/ n ruido, son, m; tumulto, clamor, estruendo, alboroto, m. **to make a n.,** hacer ruido. **to n. abroad,** divulgar, publicar
noiseless /'nɔizlɪs/ a silencioso, callado, sin ruido
noiselessness /'nɔizlɪsnɪs/ n silencio, m, falta de ruido, f
noisily /'nɔizəli/ adv ruidosamente
noisiness /'nɔizɪnɪs/ n ruido, estrépito, tumulto, clamor, m; (of voices) gritería, f
noisome /'nɔisəm/ a ofensivo; fétido, apestoso
noisy /'nɔizi/ a ruidoso; estruendoso; estrepitoso, clamoroso
nomad /'noumæd/ a nómada, errante; (of flocks) trashumante. —n nómada, mf
nomadism /'noumædizəm/ n nomadismo, m
nomenclature /'noumən,kleitʃər/ n nomenclatura, f
nominal /'nomənl/ a nominal; titular; insignificante, de poca importancia. **the n. head,** el director en nombre
nominalism /'nomənl,izəm/ n nominalismo, m
nominalist /'nomənlist/ a and n nominalista mf
nominally /'nomənli/ adv nominalmente, en nombre
nominate /'nomə,neit/ vt nombrar, designar, elegir; fijar, señalar
nominating /'nomə,neitiŋ/ a nominador
nomination /,nomə'neiʃən/ n nombramiento, m, nominación, f; señalamiento, m
nominator /'nomə,neitər/ n nominador (-ra)
nominee /,nomə'ni/ n nómino propuesto, m
non /non/ adv non; des-; in-; falta de. **non-acceptance,** rechazo, m. **non-acquaintance,** ignorancia, f. **non-admission,** no admisión, f; denegación, f, rechazo, m. **non-aggression,** no agresión, f. **non-alcoholic,** no alcohólico. **non-appearance,** ausencia, f; Law. no comparecencia, contumacia, f. **non-arrival,** ausencia, f; falta de recibo, f. **non-attendance,** falta de asistencia, ausencia, f. **non-carbonated,** sin gas. **non-combatant,** no combatiente. **non-commissioned officer,** oficial subalterno, m. **non-committal,** evasivo, equívoco, ambiguo. **non-compliance,** falta de obediencia, f. **non-concurrence,** falta de acuerdo, f. **non-conducting,** no conductivo. **non-conductor,** mal conductor, m; Elec. aislador, m. **non-contagious,** no contagioso. **non-cooperation,** Polit. resistencia pasiva, f; no cooperación, f. **non-delivery,** falta de entrega, f. **non-essential,** no esencial, prescindible. **non-execution,** no cumplimiento, m. **non-existence,** no existencia, f. **non-existent,** inexistente, no existente. **non-intervention,** no intervención, f. **non-manufacturing,** no industrial. **non-member,** visitante, mf **non-observance,** incumplimiento, m; violación, f. **non-payment,** falta de pago, f. **non-performance,** falta de ejecución, f. **non-poisonous,** no venenoso, innocuo. **non-resistance,** falta de resistencia, f; obediencia pasiva, f. **non-skid,** antideslizante, antirresbaladizo. **non-smoking,** que no fuma; (of a railway compartment, etc.) para no fumadores. **non-stop,** continuo, incesante; directo, sin parar; Aer. sin escalas
nonagenarian /,nonədʒə'nεəriən/ a and n nonagenario (-ia)
non-aligned /,non ə'laind/ a no abanderado
non-alignment /,non ə'lainmənt/ n no abanderamiento m
nonce word /nons/ n palabra ocasional, f
nonchalance /,nonʃə'lɑns/ n aplomo, m, indiferencia, frialdad, calma, f
nonchalant /,nonʃə'lɑnt/ a indiferente, frío, impasible
nonchalantly /,nonʃə'lɑntli/ adv con indiferencia
nonconformist /,nonkən'fɔrmist/ a and n disidente mf; a inconforme, n, inconformista, mf
nonconformity /,nonkən'fɔrmiti/ n disidencia, f
nondescript /,nondi'skript/ a indeterminado, indefinido, indeciso, mediocre
none /nʌn/ pron nadie, ninguno; nada. —a and n ninguno (-na). —adv no; de ningún modo, de ninguna manera. **I have n.,** No lo tengo, No tengo ninguno. **We have n. of your things,** No tenemos ninguna de tus cosas. **I was n. the worse,** No me hallaba peor. **N. can read his account with pleasure,**

Nadie puede leer su narración con gusto. **n. the less,** no menos; sin embargo
nonentity /non'entiti/ n persona sin importancia, medianía, f, cero, m
nones /nounz/ n pl Eccl. nona, f; (Roman Calendar) nonas, f pl.
nonplussed /non'plʌst/ a cortado, perplejo, confuso
non-profit /non 'profit/ a sin fines de lucro, sin fines lucrativos
non-self-governing /'non sεlf'gʌvərniŋ/ a no autónomo
nonsense /'nonsεns/ n disparate, despropósito, desatino, m, absurdidad, f; Inf. galimatías, m; pamplina, patraña, f. **to talk n.,** hablar sin ton ni son. **N.!** ¡A otro perro con este hueso! ¡Patrañas!
nonsensical /non'sεnsikəl/ a absurdo, ridículo, disparatado
noodle /'nudl/ n Cul. tallarín, m; Inf. mentecato (-ta), bobo (-ba)
nook /nʊk/ n escondrijo, lugar retirado, rincón, m
noon /nun/ n mediodía, m; Fig. punto culminante, apogeo, m, a de mediodía, meridional. **at n.,** a mediodía
noose /nus/ vt coger con lazos. —n lazo corredizo, dogal, m
nopal /'noupəl/ n Bot. nopal, m
No Parking «Se Prohibe Estacionar,» «Se Prohibe Estacionarse»
nor /nɔr/ unstressed nər/ conjunc ni, no, tampoco. **He removed neither his coat nor his hat,** No se quitó ni el gabán ni el sombrero. **Nor was this the first time,** Y no fue ésta la primera vez. **Nor I,** Ni yo tampoco
Nordic /'nɔrdik/ a and n nórdico (-ca)
norm /nɔrm/ n modelo, m, norma, regla, pauta, f; (of size) marca, f; (Bot. Zool.) tipo, m
normal /'nɔrməl/ a normal; común, natural, corriente, regular; Math. perpendicular, normal. —n condición normal, f, estado normal, m; Math. normal, f. **to become n.,** normalizarse, hacerse normal. **to make n.,** normalizar. **n. school,** escuela normal, f
normality /nɔr'mæliti/ n normalidad, f
normalization /,nɔrmələ'zeiʃən/ n normalización, f
normalize /'nɔrmə,laiz/ vt normalizar
normally /'nɔrməli/ adv normalmente
Norman /'nɔrmən/ a and n normando (-da)
Normandy /'nɔrməndi/ Normandía, f
Norse /nɔrs/ n noruego (language), m, a escandinavo
Norseman /'nɔrsmən/ n normando, viking (pl -os), hombre del norte, m
north /nɔrθ/ n norte, m. —a del norte, septentrional. **n. by west,** norte, cuarta noroeste. **n. of the city,** al norte de la ciudad. **N.-American** a and n norteamericano (-na). **n.-east,** a and n nordeste m. **n.-easter,** viento del nordeste, m. **n.-easterly,** del nordeste (winds). **n.-eastern,** del nordeste (places). **n.-eastward,** hacia el nordeste. **n.-n.-east,** nornordeste, m. **n.-n.-west,** nornoroeste, m. **n.-polar,** ártico. **N. Star,** estrella del norte, estrella polar, f. **n.-west,** noroeste, m. **n.-wester,** viento del noroeste, m. **n.-westerly,** del noroeste (winds). **n.-westerly gale,** temporal del noroeste, m. **n.-western,** del noroeste; situado al noroeste. **n.-westwards,** hacia el noroeste. **n. wind,** el viento del norte, el cierzo
North America, Norteamérica, América del Norte, f
northern /'nɔrðərn/ a del norte, septentrional, norteño; (of cars) nórdico. **N. Cross,** crucero, m. **n. lights,** aurora boreal, f
northerner /'nɔrðərnər/ n hombre del norte, m, habitante del norte, f
northernmost /'nɔrðərn,moust/ a superl al extremo norte, más septentrional
northwards /'nɔrθwərdz/ adv hacia el norte
Norway /'nɔrwei/ Noruega, f
Norwegian /nɔr'widʒən/ a and n noruego (-ga) (language) noruego, m
nose /nouz/ n nariz, f; (of animals) hocico, m; (sense of smell) olfato, m; (of ships) proa, f; (of jug) pico, m, boca, f; (projecting piece) cuerno, m, nariz, f; (of airplane) cabeza, f, vt acariciar con la nariz; avanzar lentamente. —vi husmear, olfatear. **to n. into,** Inf. meter las narices, poner baza. **to n. out,** descubrir, averiguar. **to bleed at the n.,** echar sangre

por las narices. **to blow one's n.**, sonar (or limpiarse) las narices. **to keep one's n. to the grindstone,** estar sobre el yunque, batir el cobre. *Fig.* **to lead by the n.**, tener a uno agarrado por las narices. **to pay through the n.**, costar un ojo de la cara. **to speak through the n.**, ganguear. **to turn up one's n.**, *Fig.* hacer gestos (a), volver la cara. **flat n.**, nariz chata, *f.* **snub n.**, nariz respingona, *f.* **well-shaped n.**, nariz perfilada, *f.* **under one's n.**, bajo las narices de uno. **n.-bag**, cebadera, mochila, *f;* morral, *m.* **n.-bleeding,** *Med.* epistaxis, *f;* hemorragia de las narices, *f.* **n.-dive**, *Aer.* descenso de cabeza, picado, *m.* —*vi* picar. **n.-piece**, (of microscope) ocular, *m.* **n.-ring**, (of a bull, etc.) narigón, *m*

-nosed *a* de nariz..., con la nariz...

nosegay /'nouz,gei/ *n* ramillete, *m*

nosey Parker /'nouzi 'parkər/ *n Inf.* mequetrefe, *m;* cócora, *mf*

No Smoking «Prohibido Fumar», Se Prohibe Fumar

nostalgia /nɒ'stældʒə/ *n* nostalgia, añoranza, *f*

nostalgic /nɒ'stældʒɪk/ *a* nostálgico

nostril /'nɒstrəl/ *n* ventana de la nariz, *f*, *n pl* **nostrils,** narices, *f pl*

nostrum /'nɒstrəm/ *n* panacea, *f,* curalotodo, *m;* medicina patentada, *f*

not /nɒt/ *adv* no; sin; ni, ni siquiera. **Is it not true? We think not,** ¿No es verdad? No lo creemos. **You have seen Mary, have you not?** Vd. ha visto a María, ¿verdad? **not caring whether he came or not,** sin preocuparse de que viniese o no. **not that he will come,** no es decir que venga. **not at all,** de ningún modo; (courtesy) ¡de nada! **not even,** ni siquiera. **not guilty,** no culpable. **not one,** ni uno. **not so much as,** no tanto como; ni siquiera. **It is not so much that, as it is...** No es tanto eso, cuanto que... **not to say,** por no decir

notability /,noutə'bɪliti/ *n* notabilidad, *f;* (person) notable, *mf* persona de importancia, *f*

notable /'noutəbəl/ *a* notable, señalado, memorable; digno de atención. —*n* persona eminente, *f,* notable, *mf*

notably /'noutəbli/ *adv* notablemente, señaladamente

notary /'noutəri/ *n* notario, escribano, *m*

notation /nou'teifən/ *n* notación, *f*

notch /nɒtʃ/ *vt* cortar muescas (en); mellar, ranurar, entallar. —*n* muesca, mella, ranura, entalladura, *f*

note /nout/ *vt* notar, observar; anotar, apuntar; advertir, hacerse cuenta de. —*n Mus.* nota, *f;* son, acento, *m;* (letter) recado, billete, *m;* anotación, glosa, *f;* apuntación, *f,* apunte, *m,* nota, *f;* (importance) importancia, distinción, *f; Com.* vale, abonaré, *m;* (sign) marca, señal, *f.* **to n. down,** anotar. **worthy of note,** digno de atención. **n.-book,** libro de apuntes, cuaderno, *m,* libreta, *f.* **n.-case,** cartera, *f, Com.* **n.-of hand,** pagaré, *m.* **n.-paper,** papel de escribir, *m.* **n.-taker,** apuntador (-ra)

noted /'noutid/ *a* célebre, famoso, ilustre, eminente, insigne

noteworthy /'nout,wɜrði/ *a* digno de nota, notable, digno de atención

nothing /'nʌθɪŋ/ *n* nada, *f;* la nada; cero, *m.* —*adv* en nada. **to come to n.**, anonadarse, fracasar. **to do n.**, no hacer nada. **to do n. but,** no hacer más que. **to have n. to do with,** no tener nada que ver con; *Inf.* no tener arte ni parte en. **There is n. else to do,** No hay nada más que hacer; No hay más remedio. **There is n. to fear,** no hay más que tener miedo. **We could make n. of the book,** No llegamos a comprender el libro. **for n.,** de balde, en vano; gratis. **next to n.,** casi nada. **n. else or more,** nada más. **n. like,** ni con mucho. **n. much,** poca cosa. **n. new,** nada nuevo. **n. similar,** nada semejante. **n. to speak of,** poca cosa

nothingness /'nʌθɪŋnɪs/ *n* nada, *f*

notice /'noutis/ *vt* observar, reparar en, darse cuenta (de), marcar, caer en la cuenta (de), fijarse (en). —*n* observación, atención, *f;* aviso, *m,* notificación, *f;* anuncio, *m;* (term) plazo, *m;* (review) crítica, *f.* **at short n.**, a corto aviso. **until further n.**, hasta nuevo aviso (or orden). **to attract n.**, atraer la atención. **I hadn't noticed,** No me había fijado. **to be beneath one's n.**, no merecer su atención. **to be under n.**, es-

tar dimitido. **to bring to the n. of,** dar noticia de. **to escape n.**, pasar desapercibido. **to give n.**, hacer saber, informar; (of employer) despedir (a); (of employee) dimitir, dar la dimisión. **to take n. of,** notar, darse cuenta de; hacer caso, atender (a). **n. board,** letrero, tablero de anuncios, *m.* **n. to quit,** desahúcio, *m*

noticeable /'noutisəbəl/ *a* perceptible, evidente; digno de observación, notable

noticeably /'noutisəbli/ *adv* perceptiblemente; notablemente

notifiable /,noutə'faiəbəl/ *a* declarable, notificable

notification /,noutəfɪ'keifən/ *n* notificación, intimación, advertencia, *f,* aviso, *m*

notify /'noutə,fai/ *vt* notificar, comunicar, avisar, intimar, hacer saber

notion /'noufən/ *n* noción, idea, *f,* concepto, *m;* (view) opinión, *f,* parecer, *m;* (novelty) novedad, *f;* artículo de fantasía, *m.* **I have a n. that...,** Tengo la idea de que..., Sospecho que... **I haven't a n.,** No tengo idea

No Tipping «No Se Admiten Propinas»

notoriety /,noutə'raiiti/ *n* notoriedad, publicidad, *f;* escándalo, *m;* persona notoria, *f*

notorious /nou'tɔriəs/ *a* notorio, famoso, conocido; escandaloso, sensacional

notoriously /nou'tɔriəsli/ *adv* notoriamente

notwithstanding /,nɒtwɪð'stændɪŋ/ *prep* a pesar de. —*adv* sin embargo, no obstante. —*conjunc* aunque, bien que, por más que

nougat /'nugət/ *n* turrón, *m*

nought /nɔt/ *n Math.* cero, *m;* nada, *f*

noun /naun/ *n* substantivo, nombre, *m*

nourish /'nʌrɪʃ/ *vt* sustentar, alimentar, nutrir; *Fig.* fomentar, favorecer

nourishing /'nʌrɪʃɪŋ/ *a* nutritivo, alimenticio, nutricio

nourishment /'nʌrɪʃmənt/ *n* nutrición, *f;* sustento, *m;* alimento, *m; Fig.* fomento, pasto, *m*

Nova Scotia /'nouvə 'skouʃə/ Nueva Escocia, *f*

novel /'nɒvəl/ *a* nuevo, original, inacostumbrado. —*n* novela, *f.* **n. of roguery,** novela picaresca, *f*

novelette /,nɒvə'let/ *n* novela corta, *f*

novelist /'nɒvəlɪst/ *n* novelista, *mf*

novelty /'nɒvəlti/ *n* novedad, *f;* innovación, *f;* cambio, *m*

November /nou'vɛmbər/ *n* noviembre, *m*

novice /'nɒvɪs/ *n Eccl.* novicio (-ia); comenzante, principiante, *mf,* aspirante, *m*

novocain /'nɒvə,kein/ *n Med.* novocaína, *f*

now /nau/ *adv* ahora, actualmente, al presente, a la fecha; en seguida, ahora, inmediatamente; poco ha, hace poco; pues bien. —*interj* ¡A ver! ¡Vamos! —*conjunc* pero, mas. —*n* presente, *m,* actualidad, *f.* **before now,** antes, en otras ocasiones, ya, previamente. **just now,** ahora mismo, hace poco. **now...,** now, ya... ya; sucesivamente, en turno. **now and then,** de vez en cuando, de tarde en tarde. **now that,** ya que, ahora que, dado que. **until now,** hasta el presente, hasta aquí, hasta ahora

nowadays /'nauə,deiz/ *adv* hoy en día, actualmente, en nuestros días

nowhere /'nou,wɛər/ *adv* en ninguna parte. **in the middle of n.**, donde Cristo dio las tres voces. **n. else,** en ninguna otra parte. *Inf.* **n. near,** ni con mucho; muy lejos (de)

nowise /'nou,waiz/ *adv* de ningún modo, en modo alguno, de ninguna manera

noxious /'nɒkʃəs/ *a* dañoso, nocivo; pestífero

noxiousness /'nɒkʃəsnɪs/ *n* nocividad, *f*

nozzle /'nɒzəl/ *n* (of a hose-pipe) boquilla, *f; Mech.* gollete, *m;* tubo de salida, *m,* tobera, *f;* inyector, *m*

n.p. (no place) s.l. (sin lugar)

nuance /'nuans/ *n* matiz, *m,* gradación, sombra, *f*

nubile /'nubil, -bail/ *a* núbil

nuclear /'nukliər/ *a* nuclear

nucleus /'nukliəs/ *n* núcleo, *m;* centro, foco, *m*

nude /nud/ *a* desnudo, nudo

nudge /nʌdʒ/ *vt* dar un codazo (a). —*n* codazo, *m*

nudism /'nudɪzəm/ *n* nudismo, *m*

nudist /'nudɪst/ *n* nudista, *mf*

nudity /'nuditi/ *n* desnudez, *f*

nugget /'nʌgɪt/ n Mineral. pepita, f

nuisance /'nusəns/ n molestia, incomodidad, f, fastidio, m; Inf. tostón, m, lata, f. **to make a n. of one-self**, meterse donde no le llaman, ser un pelmazo. **What a n.!** ¡Qué lata! ¡Qué fastidio!

null /nʌl/ a nulo, inválido, sin fuerza legal. **n. and void**, nulo, írrito

nullification /ˌnʌləfɪ'keɪʃən/ n anulación, invalidación, f

nullity /'nʌlɪti/ n nulidad, f

numb /nʌm/ vt entumecer, entorpecer. —a entumecido; torpe, dormido; paralizado; Fig. insensible, pasmado. **n. with cold**, entumecido de frío

number /'nʌmbər/ vt numerar, contar; poner número (a); (pages of a book) foliar; ascender a. —n número, m; (figure) cifra, f; (crowd) multitud, muchedumbre, f; cantidad, f; (of a periodical) ejemplar, m; Gram. número, m; pl versos, m pl. **Numbers**, (Bible) Números, m pl; **to be numbered among**, figurar entre. **among the n. of**, entre la muchedumbre de. **a n. of**, varios, muchos, una cantidad de. **in great n.**, en gran número; en su mayoría. **6 Peace Street**, Calle de la Paz Nº (número) 6. **one of their n.**, uno entre ellos. **n. board**, (racing) indicador, m. **n. plate**, Auto. chapa de identidad, placa de número, f

numbering /'nʌmbərɪŋ/ n numeración, f

numberless /'nʌmbərlɪs/ a innumerable, sin número, sin fin, infinito

numbness /'nʌmnɪs/ n entumecimiento, entorpecimiento, m; Fig. insensibilidad, f

numeral /'numərəl/ a numeral. —n número, m, cifra, f; Gram. nombre o adjetivo numeral, m

numerator /'numəˌreɪtər/ n numerador, m

numerical /nu'mɛrɪkəl/ a numérico

numerous /'numərəs/ a numeroso; nutrido, grande; muchos (-as)

numerousness /'numərəsnɪs/ n numerosidad, multitud, muchedumbre, f

numismatic /ˌnumɪz'mætɪk/ a numismático. —n pl **numismatics**, numismática, f

numismatist /nu'mɪzmətɪst/ n numismático, m

numskull /'nʌmˌskʌl/ n zote, topo, m

nun /nun/ n monja, religiosa, f. **to become a nun**, profesar, tomar el hábito, meterse monja

nuncio /'nʌnʃiˌoʊ/ n nuncio, m. **acting n.**, pronuncio, m

nunnery /'nʌnəri/ n convento de monjas, m

nuptial /'nʌpʃəl/ a nupcial. —n pl **nuptials**, nupcias, f pl, enlace, m. **n. mass**, Eccl. misa de velaciones, f. **n. song**, epitalamio, m

nurse /nɜrs/ vt criar; dar de mamar (a), amamantar; (the sick) cuidar, asistir; (fondle) acariciar, mecer; Fig. fomentar, promover. —vi trabajar como enfermera. —n (of the sick) enfermera, f; (wet) nodriza, ama de leche, f; (children's) niñera, f; Fig. fomentador, m. **male n.**, enfermero, m

nursery /'nɜrsəri/ n Agr. plantel, vivero semillero, criadero, m; (children's room) cuarto de los niños, m; Fig. sementera, f; semillero, m. **n. governess**, aya, f. **n. rhyme**, canción infantil, f

nurseryman /'nɜrsərimən/ n horticultor, m; jardinero, m

nursing /'nɜrsɪŋ/ n lactancia, crianza, f; (of the sick) asistencia, f, cuido, m. **n. home**, clínica, f. **n. mother**, madre lactante, f

nurture /'nɜrtʃər/ vt alimentar; criar, educar. —n nutrición, alimentación, f; crianza, educación, f

nut /nʌt/ vi coger nueces. —n Bot. nuez, f; Mech. tuerca, hembra de tornillo, f, Inf. to crack, cascar nueces. **to go nutting**, coger nueces. **cashew nut**, anacardo, m. **loose nut**, Mech. tuerca aflojada, f. **nut-brown**, castaño. **nut tree**, nogal, m

nutcrackers /'nʌtˌkrækərz/ n pl cascanueces, quebrantanueces, m

nutmeg /'nʌtmɛg/ n nuez moscada, nuez de especia, f

nutria /'nutriə/ n Zool. nutria, f

nutriment /'nutrəmənt/ n nutrimento, alimento, m

nutrition /nu'trɪʃən/ n nutrición, alimentación, f

nutritious, nutritive /nu'trɪʃəs; 'nutrɪtɪv/ a nutritivo, alimenticio, alible

nutshell /'nʌtˌʃɛl/ n cáscara de nuez, f. **to put in a n.**, decir en resumidas cuentas, decir en forma apastillada

nutty /'nʌti/ a de nuez

nuzzle /'nʌzəl/ vt acariciar con la nariz

nylon /'naɪlɒn/ n nilón, nylon, m. **n. stockings**, medias de cristal (or de nilón), f pl

nymph /nɪmf/ n ninfa, f; Ent. crisálida, f. **n.-like**, como una ninfa; de ninfa

nymphomania /ˌnɪmfə'meɪniə/ n ninfomanía, f, furor uterino, m

O

o /ou/ n (letter) o, f, interj ¡o! **O that...!** ¡Ojalá que!
oaf /ouf/ n zoquete, zamacuco, m
oafish /'oufiʃ/ a lerdo, torpe
oafishness /'oufiʃnɪs/ n torpeza, estupidez, f
oak /ouk/ n (tree and wood) roble, m, a de roble. **carved oak,** roble tallado, m. **holm-oak,** encina, f. **oak-apple,** agalla, f. **oak grove,** robledo, m
oakum /'oukəm/ n estopa, f
oar /ɔr/ n remo, m. **to lie on the oars,** cesar de remar. **to pull at the oars,** bogar, remar. **to put in one's oar,** Inf. meter baza. **to ship the oars,** armar los remos. **to unship the oars,** desarmar los remos. **oar-stroke,** palada, f
oarsman /'ɔrzmən/ n remero, bogador, m
oarsmanship /'ɔrzmənˌʃɪp/ n arte de remar, m, or f
oasis /ou'eisɪs/ n oasis, m
OAS (Organization of American States) OEA (Organización de los Estados Americanos)
oast /oust/ n horno para secar el lúpulo, m
oat /out/ n Bot. avena, f. **wild oat,** avena silvestre, f. **to sow one's wild oats,** correrla, andarse a la flor del berro. **oat field,** avenal, m
oath /ouθ/ n juramento, m; (curse) blasfemia, f, reniego, m. **on o.,** bajo juramento. **to break an o.,** violar el juramento. **to put on o.,** tomar juramento, hacer prestar juramento. **to take an o.,** prestar (or hacer) juramento. **to take the o. of allegiance,** jurar la bandera
oatmeal /'outˌmil/ n harina de avena, f
obduracy /'ɒbdʊrəsi/ n obduración, obstinación, terquedad, f
obdurate /'ɒbdʊrɪt/ a obstinado, terco, porfiado. **He is o. to our requests,** Es sordo a nuestros ruegos
obedience /ou'bidiəns/ n obediencia, sumisión, docilidad, f. **blind o.,** obediencia ciega, f. **in o. to,** conforme a, de acuerdo con
obedient /ou'bidiənt/ a obediente, sumiso, dócil. **to be o. to,** ser obediente (a), obedecer (a)
obediently /ou'bidiəntli/ adv obedientemente, dócilmente. **Yours o.,** Su atento servidor (su att. s.)
obeisance /ou'beisəns, ou'bi-/ n reverencia, cortesía, f, saludo, m; (homage) homenaje, m
obelisk /'ɒbəlɪsk/ n obelisco, f
obese /ou'bis/ a obeso, corpulento, grueso, gordo
obesity /ou'bisɪti/ n obesidad, gordura, corpulencia, f
obey /ou'bei/ vt and vi obedecer. —vt (carry out) cumplir, observar. **to be obeyed,** ser obedecido
obfuscate /'ɒbfəˌskeit/ vt ofuscar, cegar
obfuscation /ˌɒbfə'skeiʃən/ n ofuscamiento, m, confusión, f
obituary /ou'bɪtʃuˌɛri/ a mortuorio, necrológico. —n obituario, m, necrología, f. **o. column,** (in newspaper) sección necrológica, f. **o. notice,** esquela de defunción, f
object /n. 'ɒbdʒɪkt; v. əb'dʒɛkt/ n objeto, artículo, m, cosa, f; (purpose) propósito, intento, m; (aim) fin, término, m; Gram. complemento, m; Inf. individuo, m. —vt objetar, poner reparos (a). —vi oponerse, poner objeciones. **I o. to that remark,** Protesto contra esa observación. **If you don't o.,** Si Vd. no tiene inconveniente. **o. finder,** objetivo, m. **o. lesson,** lección de cosas, f; lección práctica, f
objection /əb'dʒɛkʃən/ n objeción, protesta, f, reparo, m; (obstacle) dificultad, f, inconveniente, m. **to have no o.,** no tener inconveniente. **to raise an o.,** hacer constar una protesta, poner una objeción
objectionable /əb'dʒɛkʃənəbəl/ a censurable, reprensible; desagradable, molesto
objective /əb'dʒɛktɪv/ a objetivo; Gram. acusativo. —n objeto, propósito, m; destinación, f; Mil. objetivo, m, Gram. **o. case,** caso acusativo, m,
objectivism /əb'dʒɛktəˌvɪzəm/ n Philos. objetivismo, m
objectivity /ˌɒbdʒɪk'tɪvɪti/ n objetividad, f
objector /əb'dʒɛktər/ n objetante, mf, impugnador

(-ra). **conscientious o.,** (dissident) el, m, (f, la) que protesta contra; (pacifist) pacifista, mf
oblation /ɒ'bleiʃən/ n oblación, ofrenda, f
obligation /ˌɒblɪ'geiʃən/ n obligación, f; deber, m, precisión, f; compromiso, m. **of o.,** de deber; de precepto. **to be under an o.,** estar bajo una obligación; deber un favor. **to place under an o.,** poner bajo una obligación
obligatory /ə'blɪgəˌtɔri/ a obligatorio, forzoso
oblige /ə'blaidʒ/ vt (insist on) obligar, hacer, forzar; (gratify) hacer un favor (a), complacer. **He obliged me with a match,** Me hizo el favor de una cerilla. **They are much obliged to you,** Le están muy reconocidos. **Much obliged!** ¡Se agradece!
obliging /ə'blaidʒɪŋ/ a atento, condescendiente, complaciente, servicial
obligingly /ə'blaidʒɪŋli/ adv cortésmente
obligingness /ə'blaidʒɪŋnɪs/ n cortesía, amabilidad, bondad, f
oblique /ə'blik/ a oblicuo, sesgado; (indirect) indirecto, evasivo; Gram. oblicuo
obliquely /ə'blikli/ adv oblicuamente, al sesgo, sesgadamente; indirectamente. **to place o.,** poner al sesgo
obliquity /ə'blɪkwɪti/ n oblicuidad, f, sesgo, m; (of conduct, etc.) tortuosidad, f
obliterate /ə'blɪtəˌreit/ vt borrar; destruir, aniquilar. **to be obliterated,** borrarse; quedar destruido
obliteration /əˌblɪtə'reiʃən/ n testación, f; destrucción, f. **o. raid,** bombardeo de saturación, m
oblivion /ə'blɪviən/ n olvido, m. **to cast into o.,** echar al olvido
oblivious /ə'blɪviəs/ a olvidadizo, descuidago
oblong /'ɒbˌlɔŋ/ a oblongo, cuadrilongo, rectangular. —n rectángulo, cuadrilongo, m
obloquy /'ɒbləkwi/ n infamia, maledicencia, deshonra, f
obnoxious /əb'nɒkʃəs/ a odioso, ofensivo, aborrecible
obnoxiously /əb'nɒkʃəsli/ adv odiosamente
obnoxiousness /əb'nɒkʃəsnɪs/ n odiosidad, f
oboe /'oubou/ n Mus. oboe, m. **o. player,** oboe, m
obol /'ɒbəl/ n óbolo, m
obscene /əb'sin/ a indecente, obsceno, escabroso
obscenely /əb'sinli/ adv obscenamente, escabrosamente
obscenity /əb'sɛniti/ n indecencia, obscenidad, f
obscurantism /əb'skyʊrənˌtɪzəm/ n obscurantismo, m
obscurantist /əb'skyʊrəntɪst/ a and n obscurantista, mf
obscure /əb'skyʊr/ a (indistinct) obscuro, indistinto; (dark) lóbrego, tenebroso; (remote) retirado, apartado; (puzzling) confuso; (unknown) desconocido; humilde; (difficult to understand) abstruso, obscuro; (vague) vago. —vt obscurecer; (hide) esconder; (eclipse) eclipsar. **to o. the issue,** hacer perder de vista el problema
obscurely /əb'skyʊrli/ adv obscuramente; humildemente, retiradamente; confusamente; vagamente
obscurity /əb'skyʊriti/ n (darkness) obscuridad, lobreguez, f; (difficulty of meaning) ambigüedad, confusión, vaguedad, f; humildad, f
obsequies /'ɒbsɪkwiz/ n pl exequias, f pl, ritos fúnebres, m pl
obsequious /əb'sikwiəs/ a servil, empalagoso, zalamero
obsequiously /əb'sikwiəsli/ adv servilmente
obsequiousness /əb'sikwiəsnɪs/ n servilismo, m, sumisión, f
observable /əb'zɜrvəbəl/ a observable, perceptible, visible; notable
observably /əb'zɜrvəbli/ adv notablemente
observance /əb'zɜrvəns/ n observancia, f, cumplimiento, m; práctica, costumbre, f; (religious) rito, m
observant /əb'zɜrvənt/ a observador; obediente, atento. **o. of,** observador de; atento a
observation /ˌɒbzɜr'veiʃən/ n observación, f, exa-

men, escrutinio, *m;* (experience) experiencia, *f;* (remark) advertencia, *f,* comento, *m.* **to escape o.,** no ser advertido. **o. car.,** vagón-mirador, *m,* **o. post,** puesto de observación, *m*

observatory /əb'zɜrvə,tɔri/ *n* observatorio, *m*

observe /əb'zɜrv/ *vt* (laws) cumplir; (holy days, etc.) guardar; (notice) observar, mirar, notar, ver, reparar en; (remark) decir, advertir; (examine) vigilar, atisbar, examinar; *Astron.* observar. —*vi* ser observador. **to o. silence,** guardar silencio

observer /əb'zɜrvər/ *n* observador (-ra)

obsess /əb'sɛs/ *vt* obsesionar, obcecar

obsessed /əb'sɛst/ *a* obseso

obsession /əb'sɛʃən/ *n* obsesión, obcecación, idea fija, manía, *f*

obsidian /əb'sɪdiən/ *n Mineral.* obsidiana, *f*

obsolescent /ˌɒbsə'lɛsənt/ *a* que se hace antiguo, que cae en desuso

obsolete /ˌɒbsə'lit/ *a* obsoleto, anticuado; *Biol.* rudimentario, atrofiado

obstacle /'ɒbstəkəl/ *n* obstáculo, impedimento, *m;* dificultad, *f,* inconveniente, *m.* **to put obstacles in the way of,** *Fig.* dificultar, hacer difícil. **o. race,** carrera de obstáculos, *f*

obstetric /əb'stɛtrɪk/ *a* obstétrico

obstetrician /ˌɒbstɪ'trɪʃən/ *n* obstétrico (-ea), médico (-ca) partero (-ra)

obstetrics /əb'stɛtrɪks/ *n* obstetricia, tocología, *f*

obstinacy /'ɒbstənəsi/ *n* obstinación, terquedad, tenacidad, porfía, *f,* tesón, *m;* persistencia, *f*

obstinate /'ɒbstənɪt/ *a* terco, porfiado, obstinado, tenaz; refractario; persistente, pertinaz. **to be o.,** ser terco; porfiar. **to be o. about,** obstinarse en.

obstinately /'ɒbstənɪtli/ *adv* tercamente

obstreperous /əb'strɛpərəs/ *a* turbulento, ruidoso

obstruct /əb'strʌkt/ *vt* obstruir; impedir; cerrar; (thwart) estorbar; (hinder) dificultar, embarazar; (the traffic) obstruir, atascar. —*vi* estorbar. **to become obstructed,** obstruirse, cerrarse

obstruction /əb'strʌkʃən/ *n* obstrucción, *f;* estorbo, obstáculo, *m.* **to cause a street o.,** obstruir el tráfico

obstructionism /əb'strʌkʃə,nɪzəm/ *n* obstruccionismo, *m*

obstructionist /əb'strʌkʃənɪst/ *n* obstruccionista, *mf*

obstructive /əb'strʌktɪv/ *a* estorbador, obstructor

obtain /əb'tein/ *vt* obtener, conseguir, lograr; recibir; (by threats) arrancar. —*vi* estar en boga, estar en vigor, predominar. **to o. on false pretences,** conseguir por engaño

obtainable /əb'teinəbəl/ *a* asequible, alcanzable. **easily o.,** fácil a obtener

obtainer /əb'teinər/ *n* conseguidor (-ra), adquisidor (-ra)

obtainment /əb'teinmənt/ *n* obtención, *f,* logro, *m*

obtrude /əb'trud/ *vt* imponer

obtrusion /əb'truʒən/ *n* imposición, *f;* importunidad, *f*

obtrusive /əb'trusɪv/ *a* importuno; entremetido; pretencioso

obtrusiveness /əb'trusɪvnɪs/ *n* importunidad, *f;* entremetimiento, *m*

obtuse /əb'tus/ *a* (blunt) obtuso, romo; (stupid) estúpido, torpe, lerdo. **o. angle,** obtusángulo, *m*

obtuseness /əb'tusnɪs/ *n* (bluntness) embotamiento, *m;* (stupidity) estupidez, torpeza, *f*

obverse / *a.* ɒb'vɜrs; *n.* 'ɒbvɜrs/ *a* del anverso. —*n* anverso, *m*

obviate /'ɒbvi,eit/ *vt* obviar, evitar

obvious /'ɒbviəs/ *a* evidente, manifiesto, patente, obvio, aparente, transparente; poco sutil

obviously /'ɒbviəsli/ *adv* evidentemente, patentemente

obviousness /'ɒbviəsnɪs/ *n* evidencia, transparencia, *f*

occasion /ə'keiʒən/ *n* ocasión, *f;* oportunidad, *f,* momento oportuno, tiempo propicio, *m;* (reason) motivo, origen, *m,* causa, razón, *f;* (need) necesidad, *f.* —*vt* ocasionar, causar, producir. **as o. demands,** cuando las circunstancias lo exigen, en caso necesario. **for the o.,** para la ocasión. **on an o.,** una vez. **on the o. of,** en la ocasión de. **on that o.,** en tal ocasión, en aquella ocasión. **He has given me no o. to say so,** No me ha dado motivos de decirlo.

There is no o. for it, No hay necesidad para ello. **to have o. to,** haber de, tener que, necesitar. **to lose no o.,** no perder ripio (or oportunidad). **to rise to the o.,** estar al nivel de las circunstancias. **to take this o.,** aprovechar esta oportunidad

occasional /ə'keiʒənl/ *a* (occurring at times) de vez en cuando, intermitente; poco frecuente, infrecuente; (of verse) de ocasión. **o. table,** mesilla, *f*

occasionally /ə'keiʒənli/ *adv* de vez en cuando

occiput /'ɒksə,pʌt/ *n Anat.* occipucio, *m*

occlude /ə'klud/ *vt* obstruir, cerrar; *Med.* ocluir; *Chem.* absorber

occlusion /ə'kluʒən/ *n* cerramiento, *m; Med.* oclusión, *f; Chem.* absorción de gases, *f*

occlusive /ə'klusɪv/ *a* oclusivo

occult /ə'kʌlt/ *a* oculto, escondido, misterioso; mágico. **o. sciences,** creencias ocultas, *f pl*

occultation /ˌɒkʌl'teiʃən/ *n Astron.* ocultación, *f,* eclipse, *m*

occultism /ə'kʌltɪzəm/ *n* ocultismo, *m*

occultist /ə'kʌltɪst/ *n* ocultista, *mf*

occupancy /'ɒkyəpənsi/ *n* ocupación, posesión, *f;* (tenancy) tenencia, *f*

occupant /'ɒkyəpənt/ *n* habitante, *mf;* ocupante, *mf;* (tenant) inquilino (-na)

occupation /ˌɒkyə'peiʃən/ *n* ocupación *f;* (tenure) inquilinato, *m,* tenencia, *f;* (work) trabajo, quehacer, *m,* labor, *f;* (employment) empleo, oficio, *m;* profesión, *f*

occupational /ˌɒkyə'peiʃənl/ *a* de oficio. **o. disease,** enfermedad profesional, *f*

occupier /'ɒkyə,paiər/ *n* ocupante, *mf,* inquilino (-na)

occupy /'ɒkyə,pai/ *vt* ocupar; (live in) vivir en, habitar; (time) emplear, pasar; (take over) apoderarse de, ocupar. **to o. oneself in** or **with,** ocuparse en, ocuparse con. **to be occupied in** or **with,** estar ocupado con, ocuparse en

occur /ə'kɜr/ *vi* (happen) suceder, tener lugar, acaecer; (exist) encontrarse, existir; (of ideas) ocurrirse, venirse. **to o. to one's mind,** venírsele a las mientes. **to o. again,** volver a suceder, ocurrir de nuevo. **An idea occurred to her,** Se le ocurrió una idea

occurrence /ə'kɜrəns/ *n* ocurrencia, *f;* incidente, suceso, acontecimiento, *m.* **to be of frequent o.,** ocurrir con frecuencia, acontecer a menudo

ocean /'ouʃən/ *n* océano, *m; Fig.* mar, abundancia, *f.* **o.-going vessel,** buque de alta mar, *m*

Oceania /ˌouʃi'æniə/ el Mundo Novísimo, *m*

oceanic /ˌouʃi'ænɪk/ *a* oceánico

oceanography /ˌouʃə'nɒgrəfi/ *n* oceanografía, *f*

ocelot /'ɒsə,lɒt/ *n Zool.* ocelote, *m*

ocher /'oukər/ *n* ocre, *m*

octagon /'ɒktə,gɒn/ *n* octágono, *m*

octagonal /ɒk'tægənl/ *a* octagonal

octave /'ɒktɪv/ *n* (*Eccl.* metrics, *Mus.*) octava, *f*

octavo /ɒk'teivou, -'ta-/ *n Print.* libro, etc. en octavo (8°), *m.* **in o.,** en octavo. **large o.,** octavo mayor, *m.* **small o.,** octavo menor, *m*

octet /ɒk'tɛt/ *n Mus.* octeto, *m*

October /ɒk'toubər/ *n* octubre, *m,* 2 October 1996; el segundo (2°) de octubre de mil novecientos noventa y seis

octogenarian /ˌɒktədʒə'nɛəriən/ *a* and *n* octogenario (-ia)

octopus /'ɒktəpəs/ *n* pulpo, *m*

ocular /'ɒkyələr/ *a* ocular, visual. —*n* ocular, *m*

oculist /'ɒkyəlɪst/ *n* oculista, *mf*

odd /ɒd/ *a* (of numbers) impar (of volumes, etc.) suelto; (strange) raro, curioso, extraño, extravagante; (casual) casual, accidental; (extra) y pico, y tantos, sobrante; (of gloves, etc.) sin pareja. **at odd moments,** en momentos de ocio. **at odd times,** de vez en cuando. **thirty odd,** treinta y pico. **odd number,** número impare, *m.* **odd or even,** pares o impares. **odd trick,** (at cards) una baza más

oddity /'ɒditi/ *n* excentricidad, rareza, extravagancia, *f;* (person) ente singular, *m;* (curio) objeto curioso, *m,* antigüedad, *f*

oddly /'ɒdli/ *adv* singularmente

oddment /'ɒdmənt/ *n* bagatela, baratija, *f*

oddness /'ɒdnɪs/ *n* singularidad, rareza, extravagancia, *f*

odds /ɒdz/ n pl diferencia, desigualdad, f; (superiority) ventaja, superioridad, f; (quarrel) disputa, riña, f. **The o. are that...,** Lo más probable es que... **to fight against dreadful o.,** luchar contra fuerzas muy superiores. **o. and ends,** (remains) sobras y picos, f pl; (trifles) ñaques, m pl, chucherías, f pl

Odessa /ou'desə/ Odesa, f

odious /'oudiəs/ a odioso, detestable, aborrecible, repugnante

odiousness /'oudiəsnɪs/ n odiosidad, f

odium /'oudiəm/ n odio, m

odor /'oudər/ n olor, m; (fragrance) perfume, aroma, m, fragancia, f; Fig. sospecha, f. **in bad o.,** Fig. en disfavor. **o. of sanctity,** olor de santidad, m

odoriferous /,oudə'rɪfərəs/ a odorífero; (perfumed) oloroso, perfumado

odorless /'oudərlɪs/ a inodoro

odorous /'oudərəs/ a fragante, oloroso

odyssey /'ɒdəsi/ n odisea, f

Oedipus complex /'ɛdəpəs/ n complejo de Edipo, m

of /əv/ prep de. of has many idiomatic translations which are given as far as possible under the heading of the word concerned. It is also not translated. **I robbed him of his reward,** Le robé su recompensa. **I was thinking of you,** Pensaba en tí. **It was very good of you to...,** Vd. ha tenido mucha bondad de... **Your naming of the child Mary,** El que Vd. haya dado el nombre de María al niño. **29th of Sept., 1936,** el 29 de septiembre de 1936. **Of course!** ¡Claro está! ¡Ya lo creo! ¡Naturalmente! **of late,** últimamente. **of the** (before m, sing) del; (before f, sing) de la; (before m pl) de los; (before f pl) de las. **to dream of,** soñar con. **to smell of,** oler a tener olor de. **to taste of, etc.,** saber a, tener gusto de.

off /ɔf/ prep de; fuera de; cerca de; desde; Naut. a la altura de. **from off,** de. **Take your gloves off the table!** ¡Quítate los guantes de la mesa! **The wheel was off the car,** La rueda se había desprendido del coche. **to be off duty,** no estar de servicio; Mil. no estar de guardia. **to lunch off cold meat,** almorzar de carne fría. **off one's head,** chiflado

off /ɔf/ a (contrasted with near) de la derecha, derecho; (unlikely) improbable, remoto. —adv (with intransitive verbs of motion) se (e.g. He has gone off, Se ha marchado); (contrasted with on) de (e.g. He has fallen off the horse, Ha caído del caballo); (of place at a distance) lejos, a distancia de; (of time) generally a verb is used (e.g. The wedding is three months off, Faltan tres meses para la boda); (completely) enteramente. Off is often not translated in Sp. (e.g. to put off, aplazar, to cut off, cortar). **day off,** día libre, día de asueto, m. **How far off is the house from here? The house is five miles off.** ¿Cuántas millas está la casa de aquí? La casa está a cinco millas de aquí. **His hat is off,** Está sin sombrero, Se ha quitado el sombrero. **The cover is off,** La cubierta está quitada. **The party is off,** Se ha anulado la reunión. **6% off,** un descuento de seis por ciento. —interj Off with you! ¡Márchate! ¡Fuera! **off and on,** de vez en cuando, espasmódicamente. **off color,** (ill) malucho; (of jokes) verde. **off season,** estación muerta, f. **off-shore,** a vista de tierra. **off-stage,** entre bastidores

offal /'ɔfəl/ n (butchers') menudencias, f pl, asadura, f, menudos, despojos, m pl; desperdicio, m

offend /ə'fɛnd/ vt ofender; agraviar, insultar; herir; desagradar, disgustar; vi ofender, pecar. **to be offended,** resentirse, insultarse. **This offends my sense of justice,** Ofende mi sentimiento de justicia. **to o. against,** pecar contra; violar

offender /ə'fɛndər/ n delincuente, mf; agraviador (-ra), pecador (-ra), transgresor (-ra). **old o.,** Law. criminal inveterado, m

offense /ə'fɛns/ n ofensa, transgresión, violación, f; pecado, m; Law. delito, crimen, m; (insult) agravio, m, afrenta, f. **the first o.,** el primer delito, m. **fresh o.,** nuevo delito, m. **political o.,** crimen político, m. **technical o.,** Law. cuasidelito, m. **to commit an o. against,** ofender contra. **to take o.,** resentirse, darse por ofendido

offensive /ə'fɛnsɪv/ a ofensivo, desagradable, repugnante; (insulting) injurioso, agraviador, agresivo. —n Mil. ofensiva, f. **to take the o.,** tomar la ofensiva

offensiveness /ə'fɛnsɪvnɪs/ n lo desagradable; (insult) ofensa, f; lo injurioso

offer /'ɔfər/ n oferta, f; ofrecimiento, m; (of help) promesa, f; proposición, f; Com. oferta, f. —vt ofrecer; prometer; (opportunities, etc.) deparar, brindar; tributar. —vi ofrecerse, ocurrir, surgir. **to o. up,** ofrecer; inmolar, sacrificar. **He did not offer to go,** No hizo ademán de marcharse. **to o. resistance,** oponer resistencia. **o. of marriage,** oferta de matrimonio, f

offerer /'ɔfərər/ n ofrecedor (-ra)

offering /'ɔfərɪŋ/ n ofrecimiento, m; Eccl. ofrenda, oblación, f; sacrificio, m; regalo, don, m, dádiva, f

offhand /'ɔf'hænd/ a sin preparación, de repente; (casual) casual, despreocupado; (discourteous) brusco, descortés

offhandedly /'ɔf'hændɪdli/ adv sin preparación, espontáneamente; negligentemente; bruscamente

office /'ɔfɪs/ n oficina, m; (post) cargo, puesto, destino, m; (state department) ministerio, m; (of a Cabinet minister) cartera, f; (room) oficina, f; despacho, escritorio, m; (of a newspaper) redacción, f; (lawyer's) bufete, m; departamento, m; Eccl. oficio, m pl. **offices,** negocio, m; oficinas, f pl; (prayers) rezos, m pl; Eccl. oficios, m pl. **domestic offices,** dependencias, f pl. **good offices,** Fig. buenos oficios, m pl. **head o.,** casa central, oficina principal, f. **private o.,** despacho particular, m. **to be in o.,** estar en el poder. **o.-bearer,** miembro de la junta, m; funcionario, m. **o.-boy,** mozo de oficina, m. **o. employee,** oficinista, mf. **o. hours,** horas de oficina, f pl; (professions) horas de consulta, f pl. **o.-seeker,** aspirante, m; pretendiente, m. **o. work,** trabajo de oficina, m

officer /'ɔfəsər/ n oficial, funcionario, m; (police) agente de policía, m; (of the Church) dignatario, m; (Mil. Nav. Aer.) oficial, m. vt mandar. **commissioned o.,** oficial, m. **non-commissioned o.,** oficial subalterno, m. **to be well officered,** tener buena oficialidad. **Officers' Training Corps,** Escuela de Oficiales, f

office worker n oficinista, mf

official /ə'fɪʃəl/ a oficial; autorizado; ceremonioso, grave. —n funcionario, m; oficial público, m. **high o.,** funcionario importante, m. **o. mourning,** duelo oficial, m. **o. receiver,** fiscal de quiebras, m

officialdom /ə'fɪʃəldəm/ n funcionarismo, m; círculos oficiales, m pl

officiant /ə'fɪʃənt/ n oficiante, m

officiate /ə'fɪʃi,eit/ vi celebrar; oficiar, funcionar

officiating /ə'fɪʃi,eitɪŋ/ a oficiante; celebrante. **o. priest,** sacerdote oficiante, celebrante, m

officious /ə'fɪʃəs/ a oficioso, entremetido

officiousness /ə'fɪʃəsnɪs/ n oficiosidad, f

offing /'ɔfɪŋ/ n Naut. mar afuera, m. **in the o.,** cerca

off season fuera de temporada

offset /'ɔf,sɛt/ v. 'ɔf'sɛt/ n compensación, f, vt compensar, neutralizar

offshoot /'ɔf,ʃut/ n renuevo, vástago, m

offside /'ɔf'said/ a (of a car) del lado derecho (or izquierda); Sports. fuera de juego

offspring /'ɔf,sprɪŋ/ n vástago, m; descendiente, mf; prole, f; hijos, m pl

often /'ɔfən/ adv a menudo, mucho, con frecuencia, frecuentemente, muchas veces. **as o. as,** tan a menudo como, siempre que. **as o. as not,** no pocas veces. **How o.?** ¿Cuántas veces? **It is not so that...,** No ocurre con frecuencia que... **so o.,** tantas veces, con frecuencia. **Do you go there o.?** ¿Va Vd. allí con frecuencia (or frecuentemente)? **Not o.,** Voy rara vez allá

ogival /'oudʒaivəl/ a Archit. ojival

ogive /'oudʒaiv/ n Archit. ojiva, f

ogle /'ougəl/ vt and vi comer(se) con los ojos (a), ojear, guiñar el ojo (a). —n ojeada, f, guiño, m

ogling /'ouglɪŋ/ n guiño, m, ojeada, f

ogre /'ougər/ n ogro, m

oh! /ou/ interj ¡o! **O no!** ¡Ca! ¡Claro que no!

ohm /oum/ n Elec. ohmio, m

oil /ɔil/ n aceite, m; petróleo, m; óleo, m. —vt aceitar, engrasar; olear, ungir, untar; (bribe) sobornar, untar la mano; Fig. suavizar. —a aceitero; petrolero. **to pour oil on troubled waters,** echar

aceite sobre aguas turbulentas. **to strike oil,** encontrar un pozo de petróleo; *Fig.* encontrar un filón.
crude oil, petróleo bruto, *m.* **heavy oil,** aceite pesado, *m.* **thin oil,** aceite ligero, *m. Art.* **in oils,** al óleo. **oil-bearing,** petrolífero. **oil-box,** engrasador, *m.* **oil-burner,** quemador de petróleo, *m.* **oil-can,** aceitera, *f.* **oil-colors,** pinturas al óleo, *f pl.* **oil field,** yacimiento petrolífero, campo de petróleo, *m.* **oil-filter,** separador de aceite, *m.* **oil-gauge,** nivel de aceite, *m.* **oil lamp,** velón, candil, quinqué, *m.* **oil of turpentine,** aceite de trementina, aguarrás, *m.* esencia de trementina, *A.* **oil-painting,** pintura al óleo, *f.* **oil pipeline,** oleoducto, *m.* **oil shop,** aceitería, *f.* **oil-silk,** encerado, *m.* **oil stove,** estufa de petróleo, *f.* **oil tanker,** *Naut.* petrolero, *m.* **oil-well,** pozo de petróleo, *m*

oilcake /'ɔil,keik/ *n* bagazo, *m*
oilcloth /'ɔil,klɔθ/ *n* hule, *m*; linóleo, *m*
oiler /'ɔilər/ *n* (can) aceitera, *f; Naut.* petrolero, *m;* lubricador, *m*
oiliness /'ɔilinɪs/ *n* oleaginosidad, untuosidad, *f*
oiling /'ɔiliŋ/ *n* engrasado, *m*
oil seed *n* semilla oleaginosa, *f*
oilskin /'ɔil,skɪn/ *n* encerado, *m*
oily /'ɔili/ *a* aceitoso, grasiento
ointment /'ɔintmənt/ *n* ungüento, *m,* pomada, *f*
old /ould/ *a* viejo; antiguo, anciano; (of wines, etc.) añejo; (worn out) usado, gastado; (inveterate) arraigado, inveterado. **How old are you?** ¿Cuántos años tiene usted? **to be sixteen years old,** tener dieciséis años. **He is old enough to know his own mind,** Tiene bastante edad para saber lo que quiere. **to grow old,** envejecer. **to remain an old maid,** quedar soltera, *Inf.* quedarse para vestir imágenes. **of old,** antiguamente. **prematurely old,** revejido averiado. **old age,** vejez, senectud, *f.* **old bachelor,** solterón, *m.* **old clothes,** ropa vieja (or usada), ropa de segunda mano, *f.* **old-clothes dealer,** ropavejero (-ra). **old-clothes shop,** ropavejería, *f.* **old-established,** viejo. **old-fashioned,** pasado de moda, viejo; (of people) chapado a la antigua. **old lady,** anciana, dama vieja, *f.* **old-looking,** de aspecto viejo, avejentado. **old maid,** solterona, *f.* **old-maidish,** remilgado. **old man,** viejo, *m; Theat.* barba, *m.* **old salt,** lobo de mar, *m.* **Old Testament,** Antiguo Testamento, *m.* **old wives' tale,** cuento de viejas, *m.* **old woman,** vieja, *f.* **Old World,** Viejo Mundo, mundo antiguo, *m*
old-age home /'ould 'eidʒ/ *n* asilo de ancianos, *m*
olden /'ouldən/ *a* antiguo. **o. days,** días pasados, *m pl*
older /'ouldər/ *a compar* más viejo, mayor. **The older the madder,** A la vejez viruelas
old hat *n* viejo conocido
oldish /'ouldiʃ/ *a* bastante viejo, de cierta edad
oldness /'ouldnɪs/ *n* antigüedad, ancianidad, edad, *f*
oleaginous /,ouli'ædʒənəs/ *a* oleaginoso
oleander /'ouli,ændər/ *n Bot.* adelfa, *f,* baladre, *m*
olfactory /ɒl'fæktəri/ *a* olfatorio, olfativo
oligarchic /,ɒlɪ'gɑrkɪk/ *a* oligárquico
oligarchy /'ɒlɪ,gɑrki/ *n* oligarquía, *f*
olive /'ɒlɪv/ *n* (tree) olivo, *m;* (fruit) aceituna, oliva, *f, a* aceitunado. **wild o. tree,** acebuche, *m.* **o.-complexioned,** de tez aceitunada. **o. green,** verde oliva, *m.* **o. grove,** olivar, *m.* **o. oil,** aceite de oliva, *m*
olympiad /ə'lɪmpi,æd/ *n* olimpíada, *f*
olympian /ə'lɪmpiən/ *a* olímpico
olympic /ə'lɪmpɪk/ *a* olímpico. **o. games,** juegos olímpicos, *m pl*
olympus /ə'lɪmpəs/ *n* olimpo, *m*
omasum /ou'meisəm/ *n Zool.* librillo, libro, *m*
omber /'ɒmbər/ *n* tresillo, hombre, *m*
omega /ou'migə, ou'mei–/ *n* omega, *f*
omelet /'ɒmlɪt/ *n* tortilla, *f.* **sweet o.,** tortilla dulce, *f*
omen /'oumən/ *n* pronóstico, presagio, agüero, *m, vt* agorar, anunciar
ominous /'ɒmənəs/ *a* ominoso, azaroso, siniestro, amenazante
ominously /'ɒmənəsli/ *adv* ominosamente, con amenazas

omission /ou'mɪʃən/ *n* omisión, *f;* olvido, descuido, *m;* supresión, *f*
omit /ou'mɪt/ *vt* omitir; olvidar, descuidar; (suppress) suprimir, excluir, callar, dejar a un lado
omitting /ou'mɪtɪŋ/ *pres part* salvo, excepto
omnibus /'ɒmnɪ,bʌs/ *n* ómnibus, autobús, *m.* **o. conductor,** cobrador de autobús, *m.* **o. driver,** conductor de autobús, *m.* **o. route,** trayecto de autobús, *m.* **o. service,** servicio de autobuses, *m.* **o. volume,** volumen de obras coleccionadas, *m*
omnipotence /ɒm'nɪpətəns/ *n* omnipotencia, *f*
omnipotent /ɒm'nɪpətənt/ *a* omnipotente, todopoderoso
omnipresence /,ɒmnə'prɛzəns/ *n* omnipresencia, ubicuidad, *f*
omnipresent /,ɒmnə'prɛzənt/ *a* ubicuo
omniscience /ɒm'nɪʃəns/ *n* omnisciencia, *f*
omniscient /ɒm'nɪʃənt/ *a* omniscio, omnisciente
omnivorous /ɒm'nɪvərəs/ *a* omnívoro
on /ɒn/ *prep* (upon) sobre, en, encima de; (concerning) de, acerca de, sobre; (against) contra; (after) después; (according to) según; (with gerund) en; (with infin.) al; (at) a; (connected with, employed in) de; (by means of) por, mediante; (near to) cerca de, sobre; (into) en. Untranslated before days of week, dates of month or time of day (e.g. *on Monday,* el lunes. *on Friday afternoons,* los viernes por la tarde). **She has a bracelet on her wrist,** Tiene una pulsera en la muñeca. **He will retire on a good income,** Se jubilará con una buena renta. **on my uncle's death,** después de la muerte de mi tío, al morir. **On seeing them, he stopped,** Al verles se paró. **on leave,** con licencia, en uso de licencia. **on the next page,** en la página siguiente. **on this occasion,** en esta ocasión. **on the other hand,** en cambio. **on second thoughts,** luego de pensarlo bien. **on the way,** en camino. **on one side,** a un lado. **on the left,** a la izquierda. **on time,** a tiempo. **on my honor,** bajo palabra de honor. **on pain of death,** so pena de muerte, bajo pena de muerte. **on an average,** por término medio. **on his part,** por su parte. **on and after,** desde, a partir de. **on credit,** de fiado. **on fire,** ardiendo, en llamas. **on foot,** a pie. **on purpose,** a propósito; con intención. **on,** *adv* puesto (e.g. *She has her gloves on,* Tiene los guantes puestos); (forward) adelante, hacia adelante; (continue, with a verb) seguir, continuar (e.g. *He went on talking,* Siguió hablando). Often *on* is included in Sp. verb (e.g. *The new play is on,* Se ha estrenado la nueva comedia. *The fight is on,* Ya ha empezado la lucha). **On!** *interj* ¡Adelante! **and so on,** y así sucesivamente. **to have on,** llevar puesto. **on and off,** de vez en cuando. **on and on,** sin cesar
onanism /'ounə,nɪzəm/ *n* onanismo, *m*
once /wʌns/ *adv* una vez; (formerly) en otro tiempo, antiguamente; *conjunc* si (e.g. *O. you give him the opportunity,* Si le das la oportunidad). **all at o.,** todo junto, a un mismo tiempo; simultáneamente; (suddenly) súbitamente, de repente. **at o.,** en seguida, inmediatamente. **for o.,** por una vez. **more than o.,** más de una vez. **not o.,** ni siquiera una vez. **o. before,** una vez antes. **o. and for all,** una vez para siempre; por última vez. **o. in a while,** de vez en cuando. **o. more,** otra vez. **o. or twice,** una vez o dos, algunas veces. **o. too often,** una vez demasiado. **O. upon a time,** En tiempos pasados, En tiempos de Maricastaña; (as beginning of a story) Érase una vez, Había una vez, Hubo una vez
once in a blue moon a cada muerte de un obispo
one /wʌn/ *a* un, uno, una; (first) primero; (single) único, solo; (indifferent) igual, indiferente; (some, certain) algún, cierto, un (e.g. *one day,* cierto día). —*n* uno; (hour) la una; (of age) un año. Often not translated in Sp. (e.g. *I shall take the blue one,* Tomaré el azul). —*pron* se; uno. **one's,** su, de uno (e.g. *one's work,* el trabajo de uno). **I for one do not think so,** Yo por uno no lo creo. **It is all one,** Es igual, No hace diferencia alguna. **only one,** un solo. **that one,** ése, *m,* ésa, *f,* eso, *neut.* **this one,** éste, *m,* ésta, *f,* esto, *neut.* **these ones,** éstos, etc. **those ones,** ésos, etc. **the one,** el (que), *m,* la (que), *f.* **with one accord,** unánimemente. **one and all,** todos. **one an-**

other, se, uno a otro, mutuamente. **one by one,** uno a uno. **one day,** un día; un día de éstos, algún día. **one-eyed,** tuerto. **one-handed,** manco. **one-sided,** parcial. **one-way street,** calle de dirección única, *f.* **one-way traffic,** tráfico en una sola dirección, *m*

oneiric /ou'nairik/ *a* onírico

oneness /'wʌnnis/ *n* unidad, *f*

onerous /'ɒnərəs/ *a* oneroso, pesado, molesto, gravoso

onerousness /'ɒnərəsnis/ *n* pesadez, molestia, dificultad, inconveniencia, *f*

one-seater /wʌn 'sitər/ *n* avión de una plaza, *m*

oneself /wʌn'sɛlf/ *pron* se, uno mismo (una misma); (after prep.) sí mismo, sí. **It must be done by o.,** Uno mismo ha de hacerlo

onion /'ʌnyən/ *n* cebolla, *f.* **string of onions,** ristra de cebollas, *f.* **young o.,** babosa, *f.* **o. bed,** cebollar, *m.* **o. seed,** cebollino, *m.* **o. seller,** cebollero (-ra)

on-line /'ɒn,lain, 'ɔn-/ *a* conectado, en línea

onlooker /'ɒn,lʊkər/ *n* espectador (-ra), observador (-ra); testigo, *mf*

only /'ounli/ *a* único, solo. —*adv* únicamente, sólo; no... más (que), tan sólo; con la excepción de, salvo. —*conjunc* pero, salvo (que), si no fuera (que). **I shall o. give you three,** No te daré más de tres. **The o. thing one can do,** Lo único que se puede hacer. **I o.** **wished to see her,** Quería verla nada más. **if o.,** ¡ojalá (que)! **not o.....,** no sólo... **o.-begotten,** *a* unigénito. **o. child,** hijo (-ja) único (-ca)

onomatopoeia /,ɒnə,mætə'piə/ *n* onomatopeya, *f*

onomatopoeic /,ɒnə,mætə'piik/ *a* onomatopéyico

onrush /'ɒn,rʌʃ/ *n* asalto, ataque, acometimiento, *m*, acometida, embestida, *f*; (of water, etc.) acceso, *m*; torrente, *m*, corriente, *f*

onset /'ɒn,sɛt/ *n* ataque, *m*, acometida, *f*; (beginning) principio, *m.* **at the first o.,** Al primer ímpetu

onslaught /'ɒn,slɔt/ *n* asalto, ataque, *m*

ontology /ɒn'tɒlədʒi/ *n Philos.* ontología, *f*

onus /'ounəs/ *n* responsabilidad, *f.* **o. of proof,** obligación de probar, *f*

onward /'ɒnwərd/ *a* progresivo. —*adv* adelante, hacia adelante; (as a command) ¡Adelante!

onyx /'ɒniks/ *n Mineral.* ónice, *m*

ooze /uz/ *n* légamo, limo, fango, *m*, lama, *f.* —*vi* exudar, rezumarse; manar; *vt* sudar. **to o. satisfaction,** caérsele (a uno) la baba. **to o. away,** (of money, etc.) desaparecer, volar. **to o. out,** (news) divulgarse

oozing /'uzɪŋ/ *a* fangoso, legamoso, lamoso

opacity /ou'pæsiti/ *n* opacidad, *f*

opal /'oupəl/ *n* ópalo, *f*

opalescence /,oupə'lɛsəns/ *n* opalescencia, *f*

opalescent /,oupə'lɛsənt/ *a* opalescente, iridiscente

opaline /'oupəlin/ *a* opalino

opaque /ou'peik/ *a* opaco

opaqueness /ou'peiknis/ *n* opacidad, *f*

op. cit. /'ɒp' sit/ (opere citato) obra cit. (obra citada)

open /'oupən/ *vt* abrir; (a package) desempaquetar, desenvolver; (remove lid) destapar; (unfold) desplegar; (inaugurate) inaugurar; iniciar, empezar; establecer; (an abscess) cortar; (with arms, heart, eyes) abrir; (with mind, thought) descubrir, revelar; (make accessible) franquear, hacer accesible; (tear) romper; *vi* abrirse; empezar, comenzar; (of a view, etc.) aparecer, extenderse; inaugurarse; (of a career, etc.) prepararse. **to o. fire against,** abrir el fuego contra. **to o. into,** comunicar con, salir a. **to o. into each other,** (of rooms) comunicarse. **to o. on,** mirar a, dar a, caer a. **to o. out,** *vt* abrir; desplegar; revelar. —*vi* extenderse; revelarse. **to o. the eyes of,** *Fig.* desengañar, desilusionar. **to o. up,** abrir; explorar, hacer accesible; revelar; *Fig. Inf.* desabrocharse. **to o. with** or **by,** empezar con

open /'oupən/ *a* abierto; descubierto; expuesto; (unfenced) descercado; (not private) público; libre; (unfolded) desplegado, extendido; (persuasible) receptivo; no resuelto, pendiente; (frank) franco, candoroso; (with sea) alto; (liberal) generoso, hospitalario; sin prejuicios; *Com.* abierto, pendiente; sin defensa; (of weather) despejado; (of a letter) sin sellar; (without a lid) destapado; (well-known) manifiesto, bien conocido. —*n* aire libre, *m.* **in the o.,** al

descubierto. **in the o. air,** al aire libre, al raso, a cielo abierto. **to break o.,** forzar. **to cut o.,** abrir de un tajo, cortar. **to leave o.,** dejar abierto. **wide o.,** muy abierto; (of doors) de par en par. **o. boat,** barco descubierto, *m.* **o. car,** coche abierto, *m.* **o. carriage,** carruaje descubierto, *m.* **o. cast,** *Mineral.* roza abierta, *f.* **o.-eyed,** con los ojos abiertos. **o.-handed,** generoso, dadivoso. **o. letter,** carta abierta, *f.* **o.-minded,** imparcial. **o.-mouthed,** con la boca abierta, boquiabierto. **o. question,** cuestión por decidir, cuestión discutible, *f.* **o. secret,** secreto a voces, *m.* **o. sea,** alta mar, *f.* **o. town,** ciudad abierta, *f.* **o. tram-car,** jardinera, *f.* **o. truck,** vagoneta, *f.* **o.-work,** *Sew.* calado, enrejado, *m*

opener /'oupənər/ *n* abridor, *m*

opening /'oupənɪŋ/ *n* abertura, brecha, *f*; orificio, *m*; inauguración, apertura, *f*; principio, *m*; (chance) oportunidad, *f*; (employment) puesto, *m.* **o. price,** *Com.* (on Exchange) precio de apertura, *m*, primer curso *m*

openly /'oupənli/ *adv* abiertamente, francamente; públicamente

openness /'oupənnis/ *n* situación expuesta, *f*; espaciosidad, *f*; franqueza, *f*, candor, *m*; imparcialidad, *f*

opera /'ɒpərə/ *n* ópera, *f.* **comic o.,** zarzuela, *f.* **o.-cloak,** abrigo de noche, *m.* **o.-glasses,** gemelos de teatro, *m pl.* **o.-hat,** clac, *m.* **o.-house,** teatro de la ópera, *m.* **o. singer,** cantante de ópera, operista, *mf*

operate /'ɒpə,reit/ *vi* funcionar, trabajar; obrar; (with on, upon) producir efecto sobre; influir; *Surg.* operar; (on Exchange) especular, jugar a la bolsa; *vt* hacer funcionar, manejar; mover, impulsar; dirigir

operatic /,ɒpə'rætik/ *a* de ópera, operístico

operating /'ɒpə,reitɪŋ/ *a* (of surgeons) operante; de operación. **o. table,** mesa de operaciones, *f.* **o. theater,** anfiteatro, *m*; sala de operaciones, *f*

operation /,ɒpə'reiʃən/ *n* funcionamiento, *m*, acción, *f*; *Surg.* intervención quirúrgica, operación, *f*; (*Mil. Naut.*) maniobra, *f*; manipulación, *f.* **to come into o.,** (laws) seguir en vigor. **to perform an o.,** *Surg.* operar, praticar una intervención quirúrgica; hacer una maniobra. **to put into o.,** poner en práctica

operative /'ɒpərətiv/ *a* operativo, activo. —*n* operario (-ia), obrero (-ra). **to become o.,** tener efecto

operator /'ɒpə,reitər/ *n* operario (-ia); (telephone) telefonista, *mf*; (machines, engines) maquinista, *mf*; *Surg.* operador, *m*

operetta /,ɒpə'rɛtə/ *n* opereta, *f*

ophthalmologist /,ɒfθəl'mɒlədʒist/ *n* oftalmólogo, *m*

ophthalmology /,ɒfθəl'mɒlədʒi/ *n* oftalmología, *f*

opiate /'oupiit/ *n* opiata, *f*, narcótico, *m*, *a* opiado

opine /ə'pain/ *vi* and *vt* opinar, creer

opinion /ə'pinyən/ *n* opinión, *f*, parecer, juicio, *m*; concepto, *m*, idea, *f.* **in my o.,** según mi parecer. **to be of the o. that,** ser de la opinión que, opinar que. **to be of the same o.,** estar de acuerdo, concurrir. **public o.,** opinión (or voz) pública, *f*

opinionated /ə'pinyə,neitid/ *a* terco, obstinado

opium /'oupiəm/ *n* opio, *m.* **o. addict,** opiónamo (-ma). **o. den,** fumadero de opio, *m.* **o. eater,** mascador de opio, opiófago, *m.* **o. smoker,** fumador (-ra) de opio

Oporto /ou'pɔrtou/ Oporto, Porto, *m*

opponent /ə'pounənt/ *n* antagonista, *mf*, enemigo (-ga); contrario (-ia), adversario (-ia), competidor (-ra)

opportune /,ɒpər'tun/ *a* oportuno, tempestivo, conveniente, a propósito. **to be o.,** venir al caso. **o. moment,** momento oportuno, *m*; hora propicia, *f*

opportunely /,ɒpər'tunli/ *adv* oportunamente. **to come o.,** venir a pelo

opportuneness /,ɒpər'tunnis/ *n* oportunidad, tempestividad, conveniencia, *f*

opportunism /,ɒpər'tunizəm/ *n* oportunismo, *m*

opportunist /,ɒpər'tunist/ *n* oportunista, *mf*

opportunity /,ɒpər'tuniti/ *n* oportunidad, ocasión, posibilidad, *f.* **to give an o. for,** dar margen para. **to open new opportunities,** abrir nuevos horizontes. **to take the o.,** tomar la oportunidad

opposable /ə'pouzəbəl/ *a* oponible

oppose /ə'pouz/ *vt* (counterbalance) oponer, contrarrestar; combatir; hacer frente (a), contrariar, pugnar contra, oponerse (a)

opposed (to) /ə'pouzd/ *a* opuesto a, enemigo de, contra

opposing /ə'pouziŋ/ *a* opuesto; enemigo, contrario

opposite /'ɒpəzit/ *a* (facing) de cara a, frente a, del otro lado de; opuesto; (antagonistic) contrario, antagónico; otro, diferente. —*n* contraria, *f,* lo opuesto; antagonista, *mf;* adversario (-ia). **the o. sex,** el otro sexo. **o. leaves,** *Bot.* hojas opuestas, *f pl.* **o. to,** frente a; distinto de

opposition /ˌɒpə'ziʃən/ *n* oposición, *f;* (obstacle) estorbo, impedimento, *m,* dificultad, *f;* resistencia, hostilidad, *f;* (*Astron. Polit.*) oposición, *f;* (difference) contraste, *m,* diferencia, *f.* —*a* de la oposición. **in o.,** en oposición; *Polit.* en la oposición. **to be in o.,** estar en oposición; *Polit.* ser de la oposición, estar en la oposición

oppress /ə'pres/ *vt* oprimir, tiranizar, sojuzgar, apremiar; (of moral causes) abrumar, agobiar, desanimar; (of heat, etc.) ahogar

oppression /ə'preʃən/ *n* opresión, tiranía, crueldad, *f;* (moral) agobio, sufrimiento, *m,* ansia, *f;* (difficulty in breathing) sofocación, *f,* ahogo, *m*

oppressive /ə'presiv/ *a* opresivo, tiránico, cruel; (taxes, etc.) gravoso; (of heat) sofocante, asfixiante; agobiador, abrumador

oppressor /ə'presər/ *n* opresor (-ra), sojuzgador (-ra), tirano (-na)

opprobrious /ə'proubriəs/ *a* oprobioso, vituperioso; infame

opprobrium /ə'proubriəm/ *n* oprobio, *m,* ignominia, *f*

opt /ɒpt/ *vi* optar, escoger, elegir

optic, optical *a* óptico. **o. illusion,** ilusión óptica, *f;* engaño a la vista, trampantojo, *m.* **o. nerve,** nervio óptico, *m*

optician /ɒp'tiʃən/ *n* óptico, *m*

optics /'ɒptiks/ *n* óptica, *f*

optimism /'ɒptəˌmizəm/ *n* optimismo, *m*

optimist /'ɒptəmist/ *n* optimista, *mf*

optimistic /ˌɒptə'mistik/ *a* optimista

optimum /'ɒptəməm/ *n* lo óptimo; (used as adjective) óptimo

option /'ɒpʃən/ *n* opción, *f,* (all meanings)

optional /'ɒpʃənl/ *a* discrecional, facultativo

opulence /'ɒpyələns/ *n* opulencia, riqueza, magnificencia, *f;* (abundance) abundancia, copia, *f*

opulent /'ɒpyələnt/ *a* opulento, rico, acaudalado; abundante

opus /'oupəs/ *n* obra, composición, *f*

opuscule /ou'pʌskyul/ *n* opúsculo, *m*

or /ɔr/ *conjunc* o; (before a word beginning with o or ho) u; (negative) ni. —*n Herald.* oro, *m.* **an hour or so,** una hora más o menos, alrededor de una hora. **either... or,** o... o. **or else,** o bien. **whether... or,** que... que, siquiera... siquiera, ya... ya. **without... or,** sin... ni

oracle /'ɔrəkəl/ *n* oráculo, *m*

oracular /ɔ'rækyələr/ *a* profético, vatídico; ambiguo, misterioso, sibilino; dogmático, magistral

oral /'ɔrəl/ *a* verbal, hablado; *Anat.* oral, bucal

oral cavity *n* cavidad bucal, *f*

orange /'ɒrindʒ/ *n* (tree) naranjo, *m;* (fruit) naranja, *f;* **bitter o.,** naranja amarga, *f.* **blood o.,** naranja dulce, *f.* **tangerine o.,** naranja mandarina, *f.* **o. blossom,** azahar, *m.* **o. color,** color de naranja, *m.* **o.-colored,** de color de naranja, anaranjado. **o.-flower water,** agua de azahar, *f.* **o. grove,** naranjal, *m.* **o. grower** (or **seller**), naranjero (-ra). **o. peel,** piel de naranja, *f.* **o.-stick,** (for nails) limpiauñas, *m*

orangeade /ˌɒrindʒ'eid/ *n* naranjada, *f;* (mineral water) gaseosa, *f*

orangery /'ɒrindʒri/ *n* naranjal, *m*

orangutan /ɔ'ræŋu̩tæn/ *n Zool.* orangután, *m*

oration /ɔ'reiʃən/ *n* oración, declamación, *f,* discurso, *m*

orator /'ɔrətər/ *n* orador (-ra), declamador (-ra)

oratorical /ˌɔrə'tɔrikəl/ *a* oratorio, declamatorio, retórico

oratorio /ˌɔrə'tɔri̩ou/ *n Mus.* oratorio, *m*

oratory /'ɔrəˌtɔri/ *n* oratoria, elocuencia, *f; Eccl.* oratorio, *m,* capilla, *f*

orb /ɔrb/ *n* orbe, *m;* esfera, *f,* globo, *m;* astro, *m; Poet.* ojo, *m*

orbit /'ɔrbit/ *n Astron.* órbita, *f; Anat.* órbita, cuenca del ojo, *f*

orbital /'ɔrbit/ *a Anat.* orbital

orchard /'ɔrtʃərd/ *n* huerto, vergel, *m;* (especially of apples) pomar, *m*

orchestra /'ɔrkəstrə/ *n* orquesta, *f.* **with full o.,** con gran orquesta. *Theat.* **o. seat, o. stall,** butaca de platea, *f*

orchestral /ɔr'kestrəl/ *a* orquestal, instrumental

orchestrate /'ɔrkə̩streit/ *vt* orquestar, instrumentar

orchestration /ˌɔrkə'streiʃən/ *n* orquestración, instrumentación, *f*

orchid /'ɔrkid/ *n* orquídea, *f*

orchitis /ɔr'kaitis/ *n Med.* orquitis, *f*

ordain /ɔr'dein/ *vt* mandar, disponer, decretar; *Eccl.* ordenar. **to be ordained as,** *Eccl.* ordenarse de

ordeal /ɔr'dil/ *n Hist.* ordalías, *f pl;* prueba severa, *f*

order /'ɔrdər/ *n* (most meanings) orden, *m;* (command) precepto, mandamiento, decreto, *m;* orden, *f;* (rule) regla, *f;* (for money) libranza postal, *f;* (for goods) pedido, encargo, *m;* (arrangement) método, arreglo, *m,* clasificación, *f;* (condition) estado, *m; Archit.* estilo, *m;* (*Zool. Bot.*) orden, *m;* (sort) clase, especie, *f;* (rank) clase social, *f; Eccl.* orden, *f;* (badge) condecoración, insignia, *f;* (association) sociedad, asociación, compañía, *f;* (to view a house, etc.) permiso, *m;* (series) serie, *f.* **in good o.,** en buen estado; arreglado. **in o.,** (alphabetical, etc.) en orden; arreglado; (parliamentary) en regla. **in o. that,** para que, a fin de que. **in o. to,** a fin de, para. **out of o.,** estropeado, descompuesto; (on a notice) No funciona; (parliamentary) fuera del orden del día. **till further o.,** hasta nueva orden. **to o.,** *Com.* por encargo especial. **to give an o.,** dar una orden; *Com.* poner un pedido. **to go out of o.,** descomponerse. **to keep in o.,** mantener en orden. **to put in o.,** poner en orden, ordenar. **O.!** ¡Orden! orden real, *f.* **o. of knighthood,** orden de caballería, *f.* **o. of the day,** orden del día, *f;* reglamento, *m*

order /'ɔrdər/ *vt* disponer; arreglar; (command) mandar, ordenar; (request) rogar, pedir; (direct) dirigir, gobernar; *Com.* encargar, cometer; (a meal, a taxi) encargar. **I ordered them to do it,** Les mandé hacerlo. **to o. about,** mandar. **to o. back,** hacer volver, mandar que vuelva. **to o. down,** hacer bajar, pedir (a uno) que baje. **to o. in,** mandar entrar. **to o. off,** despedir, decir (a uno) que se vaya. **to o. out,** mandar salir; (the troops) hacer salir la tropa; echar. **to o. up,** mandar subir, hacer subir

orderliness /'ɔrdərlinis/ *n* orden, aseo, método, *m;* limpieza, *f;* buena conducta, formalidad, *f;* buena administración, *f*

orderly /'ɔrdərli/ *a* bien arreglado, metódico; aseado, en orden; (of behaviour) formal, bien disciplinado. —*n Mil.* ordenanza, *m;* ayudante de hospital *m*

ordinal /'ɔrdnəl/ *a* and *n* ordinal *m*

ordinance /'ɔrdnəns/ *n* ordenanza, *f,* reglamento, *m; Archit.* ordenación, *f; Eccl.* rito, *m*

ordinarily /ˌɔrdn'ɛərəli/ *adv* de ordinario, ordinariamente, comúnmente

ordinary /'ɔrdn̩ɛri/ *a* (usual) corriente, común, usual, ordinario, normal; (average) mediano, mediocre; (somewhat vulgar) ordinario, vulgar. —*n Eccl.* ordinario, *m.* **out of the o.,** excepcional; poco común. **o. seaman,** marinero, *m.* **o. share,** *Com.* acción ordinaria, *f*

ordination /ˌɔrdn'eiʃən/ *n Eccl.* ordenación, *f*

ordnance /'ɔrdnəns/ *n* artillería, *f,* cañones, *m pl;* pertrechos de guerra, *m pl.* **o. survey map,** mapa del estado mayor, *m.* **o. survey number,** acotación, *f*

ore /ɔr/ *n Mineral.* mena, *f,* quijo, *m*

organ /'ɔrgən/ *n* (all meanings) órgano, *m.* **barrel-o.,** organillo, órgano de manubrio, *m.* **o.-blower,** entonador (-a). **o.-grinder,** organillero (-ra). **o.-loft,** tribuna del órgano, *f.* **o.-pipe,** cañón de órgano, *m.* **o.-stop,** registro de órgano, *m*

organdy *n* organdí, *f*

organic /ɔr'gænɪk/ a orgánico. **o. chemistry,** química orgánica, f

organism /'ɔrgə,nɪzəm/ n organismo, m

organist /'ɔrgənɪst/ n organista, mf

organization /,ɔrgənə'zeɪʃən/ n organización, f; grupo, m, asociación, sociedad, f; organismo, m

organize /'ɔrgə,naɪz/ vt organizar; arreglar. —vi organizarse; asociarse, constituirse

organizer /'ɔrgə,naɪzər/ n organizador (-ra)

organizing /'ɔrgə,naɪzɪŋ/ a organizador

orgasm /'ɔrgæzəm/ n Med. orgasmo, m

orgiastic /,ɔrdʒi'æstɪk/ a orgiástico

orgy /'ɔrdʒi/ n orgía, f

oriel /'ɔriəl/ n Archit. mirador, m

orient /'ɔriənt/ a Poet. naciente, oriental. —n Oriente, Este, m. **pearl of fine o.,** perla de hermoso oriente, f

oriental /,ɔri'ɛntl/ a and n oriental, mf

orientalism /,ɔri'ɛntlɪzəm/ n orientalismo, m

orientalist /,ɔri'ɛntlɪst/ n orientalista, mf

orientate /'ɔriən,teɪt/ vt orientar; dirigir, guiar. —vi mirar (or caer) hacia el este; orientarse

orientation /,ɔriən'teɪʃən/ n orientación, f

orifice /'ɔrəfɪs/ n orificio, m; abertura, boca, f

origin /'ɔrɪdʒɪn/ n origen, génesis, m; raíz, causa, f; principio, comienzo, m; (extraction) descendencia, procedencia, familia, f, nacimiento, m

original /ə'rɪdʒənl/ a original; primitivo, primero; ingenioso. —n original, m; prototipo, modelo, m. **o. sin,** pecado original, m

originality /ə,rɪdʒə'nælɪti/ n originalidad, f

originally /ə'rɪdʒənļi/ adv originalmente; al principio; antiguamente

originate /ə'rɪdʒə,neɪt/ vt (produce) ocasionar, producir, suscitar, iniciar, engendrar; (create) inventar, crear. —vi originarse, surgir, nacer. **to o. in,** tener su origen en, surgir de, emanar de, venir de

origination /ə,rɪdʒə'neɪʃən/ n origen, principio, génesis, m

originator /ə'rɪdʒə,neɪtər/ n iniciador (-ra), fundador (-ra); autor (-ra), creador (-ra)

oriole /'ɔri,oul/ n Ornith. oropéndola, f

Orion /ə'raɪən/ n Astron. Orión, m

Orkneys, the /'ɔrkniz/ las Orcades, f pl

ornament /n. 'ɔrnəmənt/ v. -,mɛnt/ n adorno, m; decoración, f; Fig. ornamento, m; (trinket) chuchería, f, n pl. **ornaments,** Eccl. ornamentos, m pl. —vt ornar, adornar, decorar, embellecer

ornamental /,ɔrnə'mɛntl/ a ornamental, decorativo

ornamentation /,ɔrnəmɛn'teɪʃən/ n ornamentación, f decoración, f

ornate /ɔr'neɪt/ a vistoso, ornado en demasía, barroco

ornateness /ɔr'neɪtnɪs/ n elegancia, vistosidad, magnificencia, f

ornithological /,ɔrnəθə'lɒdʒɪkəl/ a ornitológico

ornithologist /,ɔrnə'θɒlədʒɪst/ n ornitólogo, m

ornithology /,ɔrnə'θɒlədʒi/ n ornitología, f

orphan /'ɔrfən/ a and n huérfano (-na)

orphanage /'ɔrfənɪdʒ/ n orfanato, hospicio, m

orphanhood /'ɔrfən,hʊd/ n orfandad, f

Orphean /ɔr'fiən/ a órfico

orthodox /'ɔrθə,dɒks/ a ortodoxo

orthodoxy /'ɔrθə,dɒksi/ n ortodoxia, f

orthographic /,ɔrθə'græfɪk/ a ortográfico

orthography /ɔr'θɒgrəfi/ n ortografía, f

orthopedic /,ɔrθə'pidɪk/ a ortopédico

orthopedics /,ɔrθə'pidɪks/ n ortopedia, f

orthopedist /,ɔrθə'pidɪst/ n ortopedista, mf ortopédico (-ca)

oscillate /'ɒsə,leɪt/ vi oscilar, fluctuar; (hesitate) dudar, vacilar. —vt hacer oscilar

oscillation /,ɒsə'leɪʃən/ n oscilación, fluctuación, vibración, f; Elec. oscilación, f

oscillator /'ɒsə,leɪtər/ n oscilador, m

oscillatory /'ɒsələ,tɔri/ a oscilatorio, m

osculation /,ɒskyə'leɪʃən/ n ósculo, m

osier /'ouʒər/ n Bot. mimbre, m, or f. **o. bed,** mimbrera, f

osmic /'ɒzmɪk/ a Chem. ósmico

osmosis /ɒz'mousɪs/ n (Phys. Chem.) ósmosis, f

osprey /'ɒspri, -prei/ n Ornith. quebrantahuesos, m

osseous /'ɒsiəs/ a óseo

ossification /,ɒsəfɪ'keɪʃən/ n osificación, f

ossify /'ɒsə,faɪ/ vt osificar; vi osificarse

ossuary /'ɒʃu,ɛri/ n osario, m

osteitis /,ɒsti'aɪtɪs/ n Med. osteítis, f

Ostend /ɒs'tɛnd/ Ostende, m

ostensible /ɒ'stɛnsəbəl/ a ostensible; aparente, engañoso, ilusorio

ostensibly /ɒ'stɛnsəbli/ adv en apariencia, ostensiblemente

ostentation /,ɒstɛn'teɪʃən/ n ostentación, f; aparato, fausto, boato, alarde, m, soberbia, f

ostentatious /,ɒstɛn'teɪʃəs/ a ostentoso; aparatoso, fastuoso, rumboso

ostentatiously /,ɒstɛn'teɪʃəsli/ adv con ostentación

osteology /,ɒsti'ɒlədʒi/ n osteología, f

osteomyelitis /,ɒstiou,maɪə'laɪtɪs/ n Med. osteomielitis, f

osteopath /'ɒstiə,pæθ/ n osteópata, m

osteopathy /,ɒsti'ɒpəθi/ n osteopatía, f

osteoplasty /'ɒstiə,plæsti/ n Surg. osteoplastia, f

ostler /'ɒslər/ n mozo de cuadras, establero, m

ostracism /'ɒstrə,sɪzəm/ n ostracismo, m

ostracize /'ɒstrə,saɪz/ vt desterrar; excluir del trato, echar de la sociedad

ostrich /'ɔstrɪtʃ/ n avestruz, m.

otalgia /ou'tældʒiə/ n Med. otalgia, f, dolor de oídos, m

other /'ʌðər/ a otro. —pron el otro, m; la otra, f; lo otro, neut adv (with than) de otra manera que, de otro modo que; otra cosa que. **this hand, not the o.,** esta mano, no la otra. **every o. day,** un día sí y otro no, cada dos días. **no o.,** ningún otro, m; otra ninguna, f. **someone or o.,** alguien. **the others,** los (las) demás, m, f pl; los otros, m pl; las otras, f pl. **o. people,** otros, m pl, los demás

otherwise /'ʌðər,waiz/ adv de otra manera, de otro modo, otramente; (in other respects) por lo demás, por otra parte; (if not) si no

otitis /ou'taitɪs/ n Med. otitis, f

otologist /ou'tɒlədʒɪst/ n otólogo, m

otology /ou'tɒlədʒi/ n otología, f

otter /'ɒtər/ n Zool. nutria, f. **o. hound,** perro para cazar la nutria

ottoman /'ɒtəmən/ a otomano, turco. —n otomana, f

ouch! /autʃ/ interj ¡ax!, ¡huy!

ought /ɔt/ v aux deber, tener la obligación (de); ser conveniente, convenir; ser necesario (que), tener que. **I o. to have done it yesterday,** Debía haberlo hecho ayer. **She o. not to come,** No debe (debiera, debería) venir. **He o. to see them tomorrow,** (should) Conviene que les vea mañana; Tiene la obligación de verles mañana; (must) Es necesario que les vea mañana, Tiene que verles mañana.

ounce /auns/ n (animal and weight) onza, f. **He hasn't an o. of common sense,** No tiene pizca de sentido común

our /auᵊr aɪr/ a unstressed nuestro

ours /auᵊrz/ pron nuestro, m; nuestra, f; nuestros, m pl; nuestras, f pl; de nosotros, m pl; de nosotras, f pl; el nuestro, m; la nuestra, f; lo nuestro, neut; los nuestros, m pl; las nuestras, f pl. **This book is ours,** Este libro es nuestro (or el nuestro)

ourselves /ar'sɛlvz/ pron pl nosotros mismos, m pl; nosotras mismas, f pl

oust /aust/ vt despedir, desahuciar, expulsar, echar

out /aut/ adv afuera; hacia fuera; (gone out) fuera, salido, ausente; (invested) puesto; (published) publicado, salido; (discovered) conocido, descubierto; (on strike) en huelga; (mistaken) en error, equivocado; (of journeys) de ida, (on ships) de navegación (e.g. on the second day out, al segundo día de navegación); (of fire, etc.) extinguido; (at sea) en el mar; (of girls in society) puesta de largo, que ha entrado en sociedad; (of fashion) fuera de moda; (of office) fuera del poder; (in holes) roto, agujereado, andrajoso; (exhausted) agotado; (expired) vencido; (of a watch) llevar... minutos (horas) de atraso o de adelanto; (unfriendly) reñido; (way out) salida, f; (sport) fuera de juego; (of flowers) abierto; (of chickens) empollado. **a scene out of one of Shakespeare's plays,** una escena de una de las comedias de Shakespeare. **I am**

out $6, He perdido seis dólares. **I am out of tea,** Se me ha acabado el té. **to drink out of a glass,** beber de un vaso. **to read out of a book,** leer en un libro. **to speak out,** hablar claro. **Murder will out,** El asesinato se descubrirá. **out-and-out,** completo; (with rogue, etc.) redomado. **out of,** fuera de; (beyond) más allá de; (through, by) por; (with) con; (without) sin; (from among) entre; (in) en; (with a negative sense) no. **out of breath,** jadeante, sin aliento. **out of character,** impropio. **out of commission,** fuera de servicio. **out of danger,** fuera de peligro. **out of date,** anticuado. **out of hand,** en seguida; indisciplinado. **out of money,** sin dinero. **out of necessity,** por necesidad. **out of one's mind,** loco, demente. **out of order.** See **order. out of print,** agotado. **out of reach,** fuera de alcance, inasequible. **out of season,** fuera de temporada. **out of sight,** fuera del alcance de la vista; invisible. **Out of sight, out of mind,** Ojos que no ven, corazón que no siente. **out of sorts,** indispuesto. **out of temper,** de mal genio. **out of the question,** imposible. **out of the way,** *adv* (of work) terminado, hecho; (remote) fuera del camino; (put aside) arrinconado; donde no estorbe. **out-of-the-way,** *a* remoto, aislado; (unusual) extraordinario, singular. **out of this world,** lo máximo, lo último. **out of touch with,** alejado de; sin relaciones con; sin simpatía con. **out of work,** sin empleo, sin trabajo, en paro forzoso. **out-patient,** enfermo (-ma) de un dispensario. **Out!** *interj* ¡Fuera! ¡Fuera de aquí! ¡Márchate! **Out with it!** ¡Hable Vd.! ¡sin rodeos! ¡Hablen claro!

outbalance /ˌautˈbæləns/ *vt* exceder, sobrepujar

outbid /ˌautˈbɪd/ *vt* pujar, mejorar

outbidding /ˌautˈbɪdɪŋ/ *n* puja, mejora, *f*

outbreak /ˈautˌbreik/ *n* (of war) declaración, *f*; comienzo, *m*; (of disease) epidemia, *f*; (of crimes, etc.) serie, *f*

outbuilding /ˈautˌbɪldɪŋ/ *n* dependencia, *f*, edificio accesorio, anexo, *m*

outburst /ˈautˌbɜrst/ *n* acceso, arranque, *m*, explosión, *f*

outcast /ˈautˌkæst/ *n* paria, *mf*; desterrado (-da), proscripto (-ta)

outclass /ˌautˈklæs/ *vt* aventajar, ser superior (a), exceder

outcome /ˈautˌkʌm/ *n* consecuencia, *f*, resultado, *m*

outcry /ˈautˌkrai/ *n* clamor, grito, *m*; protesta, *f*

outdistance /ˌautˈdɪstəns/ *vt* dejar atrás

outdo /ˌautˈdu/ *vt* eclipsar, aventajar, sobrepujar

outdoor /ˈautˌdɔr/ *a* externo; (of activities) al aire libre; fuera de casa

outdoors /ˌautˈdɔrz/ *adv* fuera de casa; al aire libre

outer /ˈautər/ *a* externo, exterior

outermost /ˈautərˌmoust/ *a superl* (el, etc.) más externo, más exterior; extremo, de más allá

outer space espacio extraatmosférico, espacio extraterreste, espacio exterior, espacio sideral, espacio sidéreo, espacio ultraterrestre, *m*

outfit /ˈautˌfit/ *n* equipo, *m*; (of clothes) traje, *m*; (of furniture or trousseau) ajuar, *m*; (gear) pertrechos, avíos, *m pl*. —*vt* aviar equipar

outfitter /ˈautˌfitər/ *n* proveedor (-ra), abastecedor (-ra)

outflank /ˌautˈflæŋk/ *vt* Mil. flanquear; ser más listo (que)

outgoing /ˈautˌgouɪŋ/ *a* saliente, que sale; cesante. **outgoings,** *n pl* gastos, *m pl*

outgrow /ˌautˈgrou/ *vt* hacerse demasiado grande para; crecer más que; (ideas) perder; (illness) curarse de, curarse con la edad; pasar de la edad de, ser ya viejo para. **to o. one's clothes,** quedársele a uno chica la ropa.

outgrowth /ˈautˌgrouθ/ *n* excrecencia, *f*; resultado, fruto, *m*, consecuencia, *f*

outhouse /ˈautˌhaus/ *n* edificio accesorio, *m*

outing /ˈautɪŋ/ *n* excursión, vuelta, *f*, paseo, *m*

outlandish /autˈlændɪʃ/ *a* extraño, singular, raro; absurdo, ridículo

outlast /ˌautˈlæst/ *vt* durar más que; (outlive) sobrevivir a

outlaw /ˈautˌlɔ/ *n* bandido, proscrito, *m*, *vt* proscribir

outlay /ˈautˌlei/ *n* gasto, desembolso, *m*

outlet /ˈautlet/ *n* salida, *f*; orificio de salida, *m*; (of drains, etc.) desagüe, *m*; (of streets, rivers) desembocadura, *f*; Fig. escape, *m*, válvula de seguridad, *f*

outline /ˈautˌlain/ *n* perfil, contorno, *m*; (drawing) esbozo, bosquejo, *m*; idea general, *f*; plan general, *m*, *vt* esbozar, bosquejar. **in o.,** en esbozo; en perfil. **to be outlined** (against), dibujarse (contra), destacarse (contra)

outlive /ˌautˈlɪv/ *vt* sobrevivir (a); (live down) hacer olvidar

outlook /ˈautˌluk/ *n* (view) perspectiva, vista, *f*; (opinion) actitud, *f*, punto de vista, *m*; aspecto, *m*, apariencia, *f*; (for trade, etc.) perspectiva, *f*, posibilidades, *f pl*. **o. tower,** atalaya, *f*

outlying /ˈautˌlaiɪŋ/ *a* remoto, lejano, distante

outmaneuver /ˌautməˈnuvər/ *vt* superar en estrategia

outmatch /ˌautˈmætʃ/ *vt* aventajar, superar

outmoded /ˌautˈmoudɪd/ *a* anticuado, pasado de moda

outnumber /ˌautˈnʌmbər/ *vt* ser más numerosos que, exceder en número

out-of-court settlement /ˈaut əv ˌkɔrt/ *n* arreglo pacífico, *m*

out-of-town *a* de las provincias

outpost /ˈautˌpoust/ *n* Mil. avanzada, *f*, puesto avanzado, *m*

outpouring /ˈautˌpɔrɪŋ/ *n* derramamiento, *m*; efusión, *f*

output /ˈautˌput/ *n* producción, *f*. **o. capacity,** capacidad de producción, *f*

outrage /ˈautreidʒ/ *n* barbaridad infamia, atrocidad, *f*; rapto, *m*, violación, *f*. —*vt* ultrajar; violar;

outrageous /autˈreidʒəs/ *a* atroz, terrible; desaforado, monstruoso; injurioso; ridículo

outrageousness /autˈreidʒəsnɪs/ *n* lo atroz; violencia, furia, *f*; escándalo, *m*; enormidad, *f*; lo excesivo; lo horrible

outré /uˈtrei/ *a* cursi, extravagante

outride /ˌautˈraid/ *vt* cabalgar más a prisa que

outright /*adv.* ˈautˈrait; *a.* ˈautˌrait/ *adv* (frankly) de plano (e.g. *to reject outright,* rechazar de plano), francamente, sin reserva; (immediately) en seguida, immediatamente. —*a* categórico; completo; franco

outrival /ˌautˈraivəl/ *vt* vencer, superar

outrun /ˌautˈrʌn/ *vt* correr más que

outset /ˈautˌset/ *n* principio, comienzo, *m*

outshine /ˌautˈʃain/ *vt* brillar más que, eclipsar en brillantez; superar, eclipsar

outside /*adv., prep., a.* ˌautˈsaid; *n.* ˈautˌsaid/ *adv* afuera, fuera. —*prep* fuera de, al otro lado de, al exterior de; (besides) aparte de, fuera de. —*a* externo, exterior; (of labor, etc.) desde fuera; máximo; ajeno. —*n* exterior, *m*; superficie, *f*; aspecto, *m*, apariencia, *f*. **at the o.,** a lo sumo, cuando más. **from the o.,** de (o desde) fuera. **on the o.,** (externally) por fuera. **o. the door,** a la puerta

outsider /ˌautˈsaidər/ *n* forastero (-ra); desconocido (-da); caballo desconocido, *m*; persona poco deseable, *f*

outsize /ˈautˌsaiz/ *n* artículo de talla mayor que las corrientes, *m*

outskirts /ˈautˌskɜrts/ *n pl* alrededores, *m pl*, afueras, immediaciones, cercanías, *f pl*

outspoken /ˈautˈspoukən/ *a* franco. **to be o.,** decir lo que se piensa, no tener pelos en la lengua

outspokenness /ˈautˈspoukənnɪs/ *n* franqueza, *f*,

outspread /ˈautˌspred/ *a* extendido; (of wings) desplegadas

outstanding /ˌautˈstændɪŋ/ *a* excelente; sobresaliente, conspicuo; Com. pendiente, sin pagar. **to be o.,** Com. estar pendiente; Fig. sobresalir. **o. account,** Com. cuenta pendiente, *f*

outstay /ˌautˈstei/ *vt* quedarse más tiempo que. **to o. one's welcome,** pegársele la silla

outstretched /ˈautˈstretʃt/ *a* extendido

outstrip /ˌautˈstrip/ *vt* dejar atrás, pasar; aventajar, superar

outvote /ˌautˈvout/ *vt* emitir más votos que; rechazar por votación

outward /ˈautwərd/ *a* exterior, externo; aparente, visible. —*adv* exteriormente; hacia fuera; superficialmente. **o. bound,** con rumbo a... **o. voyage,** el viaje de ida

outwardly /'autwərdli/ adv exteriormente; hacia fuera; en apariencia

outwear /ˌaut'weər/ vt durar más que; gastar

outweigh /ˌaut'wei/ vt exceder, valer más que

outwit /aut'wɪt/ vt ser más listo que; vencer

outworn /'aut'wɔrn/ a anticuado, ya viejo

oval /'ouvəl/ n óvalo, m, a oval, ovalado, aovado

ovarian /ou'veəriən/ a (Bot. Zool.) ovárico

ovary /'ouvəri/ n ovario, m

ovation /ou'veiʃən/ n ovación, recepción entusiasta, f

oven /'ʌvən/ n horno, m. **o. peel,** pala de horno, f. **o. rake,** hurgón, m

over /'ouvər/ prep (above, upon, over) sobre, encima de; (on the other side) al otro lado de; (across) allende, a través de; (more than) más de; (beyond) más allá de; (of rank) superior a; (during) durante; (in addition) además de; (through) por. —n en; por encima; al otro lado; de un lado a otro; enfrente; al lado contrario; de un extremo a otro; (finished) terminado; (ruined) arruinado, perdido; (more) más; (excessively) demasiado, excesivamente; (covered) cubierto (de); (extra) en exceso; (completely) enteramente; (from head to foot) de pies a cabeza, de hito en hito; (of time) pasado. **over** is also used as a prefix. Indicating excess, it is generally translated by demasiado or excesivamente. In other meanings, it is either not translated or its meaning forms part of the verb, being translated as re-, super-, trans-, ultra. Very often a less literal translation is more successful than the employment of the above prefixes. **all o.,** (everywhere) en todas partes; (finished) todo acabado; (covered) cubierto (de); (up and down) de pies a cabeza. **all the world o.,** en todo el mundo. **He is o. in Germany,** Está en Alemania. **He trembled all o.,** Estaba todo tembloroso. **that which is o.,** el exceso, lo que queda. **to read o.,** leer, repasar. **o. again,** de nuevo. **o. and above,** por encima de, fuera de, en exceso de. **o. and o.,** repetidamente, muchas veces. **o. my signature,** bajo mi firma. **o. six months since...,** más de seis meses desde que...

overabundance /ˌouvərə'bʌndəns/ n sobreabundancia, f

overabundant /ˌouvərə'bʌndənt/ a sobreabundante

overact /ˌouvər'ækt/ vt exagerar (un papel)

overall /'ouvər,ɔl/ n bata, f; guardapolvo, m; a de conjunto (e.g., overall assessment, evaluación de conjunto); pl **overalls,** mono, m

overanxious /ˌouvər'æŋkʃəs/ a demasiado ansioso; demasiado inquieto. **to be o.-a.,** preocuparse demasiado

overarch /ˌouvər'ɑrtʃ/ vt abovedar

overawe /ˌouvər'ɔ/ vt intimidar, acobardar

overbalance /ˌouvər'bæləns/ vt hacer perder el equilibrio. hacer caer; preponderar. —vi perder el equilibrio, caer

overbalancing /'ouvər,bælənsɪŋ/ n pérdida del equilibrio, caída, f; preponderancia, f

overbearing /ˌouvər'beərɪŋ/ a dominante, autoritario, imperioso

overboard /'ouvər,bɔrd/ adv al agua, al mar.

overburden /ˌouvər'bɜrdn/ vt sobrecargar, agobiar

overcast /a. 'ouvər'kæst; v. ˌouvər'kæst/ a anublado, cerrado, encapotado. —vt Sew. sobrehilar. **to become o.,** anublarse

overcharge /n. 'ouvər,tʃɑrdʒ; v. ˌouvər'tʃɑrdʒ/ n recargo, m; (price) recargo de precio, precio excesivo, m. —vt recargar, cobrar un precio excesivo; Elec. sobrecargar. —vi cobrar demasiado

overcloud /ˌouvər'klaud/ vt anublar; Fig. entristecer

overcoat /'ouvər,kout/ n abrigo, sobretodo, gabán, m

overcome /ˌouvər'kʌm/ vt vencer, rendir, subyugar; (difficulties) triunfar de, allanar, dominar. —vi saber vencer. —a (by sleep, etc.) rendido; (at a loss) turbado, confundido; (by kindness) agradecidísimo

overconfidence /ˌouvər'kɒnfɪdəns/ n confianza excesiva, f

overcooked /'ouvər,kʊkt/ a recocido, demasiado cocido

overcrowd /ˌouvər'kraud/ vt atestar, llenar de bote en bote; (over-populate) sobrepoblar

overcrowding /ˌouvər,kraudɪŋ/ n sobrepoblación, f

overdo /ˌouvər'du/ vt exagerar; ir demasiado lejos, hacer demasiado; Cul. recocer; (overtire) fatigarse demasiado

overdose /'ouvər,dous/ n dosis excesiva, f

overdraft /'ouvər,dræft/ n Com. giro en descubierto, m

overdraw /ˌouvər'drɔ/ vt and vi Com. girar en descubierto

over-dressed /'ouvər 'drest/ a que viste demasiado; cursi

overdue /ˌouvər'du/ a atrasado; Com. vencido y no pagado

overeat /ˌouvər'it/ vi comer demasiado, atracarse

overestimate /ˌouvər'estə,meit/ vt estimar en valor excesivo; exagerar, sobreestimar, n presupuesto excesivo, m; estimación excesiva, f

overexcite /ˌouvərɪk'sait/ vt sobreexcitar

overexposure /ˌouvərɪk'spouʒər/ n Photo. exceso de exposición, m

overfatigue /ˌouvərfə'tig/ vt fatigar demasiado. —n cansancio excesivo, m

overfeeding /ˌouvər,fidɪŋ/ n sobrealimentación, f

overflow /v. ˌouvər'flou; n. 'ouvər,flou/ vt inundar, derramarse por; Fig. cubrir, llenar; desbordarse. —vi (with) rebosar de. —n inundación, f, desbordamiento, derrame, m; Fig. residuo, resto, exceso, m; (plumbing) sumidero, vertedero, m, descarga, f. **The river overflowed its banks,** El río se desbordó, El río salió de cauce

overflowing /ˌouvər'flouɪŋ/ a rebosante; superabundante. **filled to o.,** lleno hasta los bordes.

overgrown /ˌouvər'groun/ a (gawky) talludo; (plants) exuberante, vicioso; frondoso, cubierto de verdura

overhang /ˌouvər'hæŋ/ vt caer a, mirar a; colgar; Fig. amenazar. —vi colgar, sobresalir; Fig. amenazar

overhanging /'ouvər,hæŋɪŋ/ a saledizo, sobresaliente; colgante, pendiente

overhaul /v. ˌouvər'hɔl; n. 'ouvər,hɔl/ vt examinar, investigar; componer, hacer una inspección general de; (of boats overtaking) alcanzar. —n examen, m, investigación, f; Med. exploración general, f

overhead /'ouvər'hed/ adv arriba, en lo alto, encima de la cabeza. —a aéreo, elevado; general, fijo. **o. cable,** cable eléctrico, m. **o. expenses,** gastos generales, m pl. **o. railway,** ferrocarril aéreo (or elevado), m

overhear /ˌouvər'hɪər/ vt (accidentally) oír por casualidad, oír sin querer; (on purpose) alcanzar a oír, lograr oír

overheat /ˌouvər'hit/ vt acalorar, hacer demasiado caliente, recalentar. —vi (in argument) acalorarse; hacerse demasiado caliente

overheating /ˌouvər'hitɪŋ/ n recalentamiento, m

overindulge /ˌouvərɪn'dʌldʒ/ vt mimar demasiado; dedicarse a algo con exceso; tomar algo con exceso. —vi darse demasiada buena vida

overjoyed /'ouvər,dʒɔid/ a contentísimo, lleno de alegría, encantado

overland /'ouvər,lænd/ adv por tierra. —a terrestre, trascontinental

overlap /v. ˌouvər'læp; n. 'ouvər,læp/ vi traslaparse; coincidir. —n traslapo, m

overlay /ˌouvər'lei/ vt cubrir, dar una capa; (with silver) platear; (with gold) dorar. —n capa, f; cubierta,

overleaf /'ouvər,lif/ adv a la vuelta

overload /v. ˌouvər'loud; n. 'ouvər,loud/ vt sobrecargar, recargar. —n sobrecarga, f

overlook /ˌouvər'lʊk/ vt (face) dar a, mirar a, dominar; (supervise) vigilar, examinar, inspeccionar; (not notice) no notar, pasar por alto, no hacer, caso de, no fijarse en; (neglect) desdeñar; (ignore) no darse cuenta de, ignorar; (excuse) perdonar, tolerar, hacer la vista gorda

overlord /'ouvər,lɔrd/ n señor de horca y cuchillo, señor, jefe, m

overmuch /'ouvər'mʌtʃ/ adv demasiado, en exceso

overnight /adv. 'ouvər'nait; a. 'ouvər,nait/ adv la noche pasada, durante la noche; toda la noche. —a de la víspera, nocturno. **to stay o. with,** pasar la noche con

overpass /'ouvər,pæs/ n pasaje elevado, viaducto, m
overpay /,ouvər'pei/ vt pagar demasiado
overpayment /'ouvər,peimənt/ n pago excesivo, m
overpopulate /,ouvər'pɒpyə,leit/ vt sobrepoblar, become overpopulated recargarse de habitantes (with people), recargarse de animales (with animals)
overpower /,ouvər'pauər/ vt vencer, subyugar; (of scents, etc.) trastornar; rendir, dominar
overpowering /,ouvər'pauəriŋ/ a irresistible
overpraise /,ouvər'preiz/ vt encarecer, alabar mucho
overproduce /,ouvərprə'dus/ vt and vi sobreproducir
overproduction /,ouvərprə'dʌkʃən/ n sobreproducción, f
overrate /,ouvər'reit/ vt exagerar el valor de; (of property) sobrevalorar
overreach /,ouvər'ritʃ/ vt sobrealcanzar. **to o. oneself,** sobrepasarse, ir demasiado lejos
override /,ouvər'raid/ vt (trample) pasar por encima (de); Fig. rechazar, poner a un lado; (bully) dominar; (a horse) fatigar, reventar
overripe /'ouvər'raip/ a demasiado maduro
overrule /,ouvər'rul/ vt Law. denegar, no admitir; vencer
overrun /,ouvər'rʌn/ vt (flood) inundar; (ravage) invadir; (infest) plagar, infestar; desbordarse, derramarse
overseas /a. 'ouvər'siz; adv. ,ouvər'siz/ a ultramarino, de ultramar. —adv en ultramar, allende los mares
oversee /,ouvər'si/ vt vigilar, inspeccionar
overseer /'ouvər,siər/ n capataz, mayoral, sobrestante, contramaestre, m; inspector (-ra), veedor (-ra)
oversell /,ouvər'sɛl/ vt and vi vender en exceso
oversensitive /,ouvər'sɛnsɪtɪv/ a demasiado sensitivo; vidrioso; susceptible
oversew /'ouvər,sou/ vt sobrecoser
overshadow /,ouvər'ʃædou/ vt sombrear; Fig. eclipsar, obscurecer; (sadden) entristecer
overshoe /'ouvər,ʃu/ n chanclo, m; (for snow) galocha, f
overshoot /,ouvər'ʃut/ vt tirar más allá del blanco; Fig. exceder, rebasar el límite conveniente, **overshoot the target** (fig.) ir más allá del blanco, ir más allá de lo razonable. **to o. oneself,** exagerar; propasarse, descomedirse
oversight /'ouvər,sait/ n inadvertencia, omisión, equivocación, f; descuido, m
oversimplify /,ouvər'simplə,fai/ vt simplificar en exceso
oversleep /,ouvər'slip/ vi dormir demasiado; Inf. pegársele a uno las sábanas, levantarse demasiado tarde
overspend /,ouvər'spɛnd/ vt and vi gastar demasiado
overspread /,ouvər'sprɛd/ vt desparramar, salpicar, esparcir, sembrar; cubrir
overstate /,ouvər'steit/ vt exagerar, encarecer, ponderar
overstatement /,ouvər'steitmənt/ n exageración, ponderación, f
overstep /,ouvər'stɛp/ vt exceder, violar, rebasar, pasar más allá (de)
overstrain /,ouvər'strein/ vt fatigar demasiado, agotar. —n fatiga, f. **to o. oneself,** esforzarse demasiado, cansarse demasiado
overstrung /,ouvər'strʌŋ/ a nervioso, excitable; (piano) de cuerdas cruzadas
oversubscribe /,ouvərsəb'skraib/ vt subscribir en exceso
overt /ou'vɜrt/ a abierto, público; manifiesto, evidente
overtake /,ouvər'teik/ vt alcanzar, pasar, dejar atrás; adelantarse (a); (surprise) coger, sorprender; (overwhelm) vencer, dominar
overtax /,ouvər'tæks/ vt oprimir de tributos; agobiar, cansar demasiado
overthrow /v. ,ouvər'θrou; n. 'ouvər,θrou/ vt volcar, echar por tierra, derribar; Fig. vencer, destruir, destronar. —n vuelco, derribo, m; Fig. destrucción, ruina, f
overtime /'ouvər,taim/ adv fuera de las horas estipuladas. —n horas extraordinarias de trabajo, f pl. **to work o.,** trabajar horas extraordinarias
overtone /'ouvər,toun/ n Mus. armónico, m

overtop /,ouvər'tɒp/ vt dominar, sobresalir, elevarse encima de
overture /'ouvərtʃər/ n Mus. obertura, f
overturn /,ouvər'tɜrn/ vt volcar, derribar, echar a rodar, echar abajo; (upset) revolver, desordenar. —vi volcar, venirse abajo, allanarse; estar revuelto
overturning /,ouvər'tɜrnɪŋ/ n vuelco, salto de campana, m
overweening /'ouvər'winɪŋ/ a arrogante, insolente, altivo
overweight /'ouvər,weit/ n sobrepeso, exceso en el peso, m. **to be o.,** pesar más de lo debido
overwhelm /,ouvər'wɛlm/ vt (conquer) vencer, aplastar, derrotar; (of waves, etc.) sumergir, hundir, inundar, engolfar; (in argument) confundir, dejar confuso, avergonzar; (of grief, etc.) vencer, postrar, dominar; (of work) inundar
overwhelming /,ouvər'wɛlmɪŋ/ a irresistible, invencible, abrumador, apabullante
overwind /,ouvər'waind/ vt (a watch) dar demasiada cuerda a; romper la cuerda de
overwork /v. ,ouvər'wɜrk; n. 'ouvər,wɜrk/ vt hacer trabajar demasiado (or con exceso); esclavizar. —vi trabajar demasiado. —n exceso de trabajo, demasiado trabajo, m
overwrought /'ouvər'rɔt/ a (overworked) agotado por el trabajo, rendido, muy cansado; nerviosísimo, sobreexcitado, exaltado, muy agitado
ovine /'ouvain/ a ovejuno
ovoid /'ouvɔid/ a ovoide
ovulation /,ɒvyə'leiʃən/ n Med. ovulación, f
owe /ou/ vt deber, tener deudas (de); deber, estar agradecido (por), estar obligado (a). —vi estar en deuda, estar endeudado, tener deudas. **He owes his tailor $30,** Le debe treinta dólares a su sastre. **I owe him thanks for his help,** Le estoy agradecido por su ayuda (or Le debo las gracias por...). **He owes his success to good fortune,** Su éxito se debe a la suerte
owing /'ouɪŋ/ a sin pagar. **o. to,** debido a, a causa de, por. **We had to stay in o. to the rain,** Tuvimos que quedarnos en casa a causa de la lluvia. **What is o. to you now?** ¿Cuánto se le debe ahora?
owl /aul/ n búho, mochuelo, m. **barn** or **screech owl,** lechuza, f. **brown owl,** autillo, m
owlish /'aulɪʃ/ a parecido a un búho, de búho
own /oun/ a propio. —n (dearest) bien, m. —vt poseer, tener, ser dueño de; (recognize) reconocer; (admit) confesar. —vi confesar. **my (thy, his, our, your) own,** mi (tu, su, nuestro, vuestro) propio, m, (f, propia); mis (tus, sus, nuestros, vuestros) propios, m pl, (f pl, propias); (when not placed before a noun) el mío (tuyo, suyo, nuestro, vuestro), la mía (tuya, etc.), los míos (tuyos, etc.), las mías (tuyas, etc.); (relations) los suyos. **in his own house,** en su propia casa. **my (thy, his, etc.) own self,** yo (tú, él) mismo, m, (f, misma, m pl, mismos, f pl, mismas). **a room of one's own,** un cuarto para sí (or para uno mismo). **to be on one's own,** ser independiente; estar a solas. **to hold one's own,** mantenerse en sus trece. **to own up,** confesar
owner /'ounər/ n dueño (-ña), propietario (-ia), posesor (-ra)
ownerless /'ounərlɪs/ a sin dueño, sin amo
ownership /'ounərʃɪp/ n posesión, f, dominio, m; propiedad, f
ox /ɒks/ n buey (pl bueyes), m. **oxeye daisy,** margarita, f. **oxstall,** boyera, f
oxidation /,ɒksɪ'deiʃən/ n Chem. oxidación, f
oxide /'ɒksaid/ n Chem. óxido, m
oxidization /,ɒksədɪ'zeiʃən, -,dai-/ n oxidación, f
oxidize /'ɒksɪ,daiz/ vt Chem. oxidar; vi oxidarse
oxygen /'ɒksɪdʒən/ n oxígeno, m. **o. mask,** máscara de oxígeno, f. **o. tent,** tienda de oxígeno, f
oxygenate /'ɒksɪdʒə,neit/ vt Chem. oxigenar
oxygenation /,ɒksɪdʒə'neiʃən/ n Chem. oxigenación, f
oyez, oyez! /'ouyei, 'ouyes, 'ouɛz/ interj ¡oíd!
oyster /'ɔistər/ n ostra, f. **o. bed,** pescadero (or criadero) de ostras, m. **o. culture,** ostricultura, f
ozone /'ouzoun/ n ozono, m

P

p /pi/ n (letter) pe, f. **to mind one's p's and q's,** poner los puntos sobre las íes; ir con pies de plomo

pabulum /'pæbyələm/ n pábulo, m; sustento, m

pace /peis/ n paso, m; (gait) andar, m, marcha, f; (of a horse) andadura, f; (speed) velocidad, f. —vi pasear(se), andar; (of a horse) amblar. —vt recorrer, andar por; marcar el paso para; (with out) medir a pasos. **at a good p.,** a un buen paso. **to keep p. with,** ajustarse al paso de, ir al mismo paso que; andar al paso de; (events) mantenerse al corriente de. **to p. up and down,** pasearse, dar vueltas. **p.-maker,** el que marca el paso

paced /peist/ a de andar...; (of a horse) de andadura...; de paso...

pachyderm /'pækɪˌdɜrm/ n paquidermo, m

pacific /pə'sɪfɪk/ a Geog. pacífico; sosegado, tranquilo, pacífico. **He is of a p. disposition,** Es amigo de la paz

pacification /ˌpæsəfɪ'keɪʃən/ n pacificación, f

pacificatory /pə'sɪfɪkəˌtɔri/ a pacificador

Pacific, the el (Océano) Pacífico, m

pacifier /'pæsəˌfaɪər/ n pacificador (-ra)

pacifism /'pæsəˌfɪzəm/ n pacifismo, m

pacifist /'pæsəfɪst/ a pacifista. —n pacifista, mf

pacify /'pæsəˌfaɪ/ vt pacificar; calmar, tranquilizar; aplacar, conciliar

pack /pæk/ n (bundle) fardo, lío, m; paquete, m; (load) carga, f; (of hounds) jauría, f; (herd) hato, m; (of seals) manada, f; (of cards) baraja (de naipes), f; (of rogues) cuadrilla, f; (of lies, etc.) colección, f; masa, f; (of ice) témpanos flotantes, m pl; (Rugby football) delanteros, m pl; (for the face) compresa, f. **p.-horse,** caballo de carga, m. **p.-needle,** aguja espartera, f. **p.-saddle,** albarda, f. **p.-thread,** bramante, m

pack /pæk/ vt embalar; empaquetar; envasar; encajonar; (a suit-case, etc.) hacer; (cram) apretar; (crowd) atestar, llenar; (a pipe joint, etc.) empaquetar; (an animal) cargar. —vi llenar; (one's luggage) hacer el equipaje, hacer el baúl, arreglar el equipaje. **packed like sardines,** como sardinas en banasta. **The train was packed,** El tren estaba lleno de bote en bote. **to p. off,** (a person) despachar; poner de partidas en la calle. **to p. up,** hacer el equipaje; empaquetar; embalar; Inf. liar el hato

package /'pækɪdʒ/ n paquete, m; bulto, m; (bundle) fardo, m

packer /'pækər/ n embalador, m; envasador (-ra)

packet /'pækɪt/ n paquete, m; (of cigarettes, etc.) cajetilla, f; (boat) paquebote, m. **to make one's p.,** Inf. hacer su pacotilla

packing /'pækɪŋ/ n embalaje, m; envoltura, f; envase, m; (on a pipe, etc.) guarnición, f. **I must do my p.,** Tengo que hacer las maletas. **p.-case,** caja de embalaje, f. **p.-needle,** aguja espartera, f

pact /pækt/ n pacto, convenio, m. **to make a p.,** pactar

pad /pæd/ n almohadilla, f; cojinete, m; (on a bed, chair) colchoneta, f; (on a wound) cabezal, m; (for polishing) muñeca, f; (hockey) defensa, f; (cricket) espinillera, f; (writing) bloque, m; (of a calendar) taco, m; (blotting) secafirmas, m; (of a quadruped's foot) pulpejo, m; (of fox, hare) pata, f; (leaf) hoja grande, f, vt almohadillar; acolchar; rellenar, forrar; (out, a book, etc.) meter paja en. **inking-pad,** almohadilla de entintar, f. **padded cell,** celda acolchonada, f. **shoulder-pad,** (in a garment) hombrera, f

padding /'pædɪŋ/ n relleno, m, almohadilla, f; (material) borra, f, algodón, m; Fig. paja, f, ripio, m,

paddle /'pædl/ n (oar) canalete, zagual, m; paleta, f; (flipper) aleta, f, vt and vi remar con canalete; (dabble) chapotear. **double p.,** remo doble, m. **p.-steamer,** vapor de ruedas, vapor de paleta, m. **p.-wheel,** rueda de paletas, f

paddler /'pædlər/ n remero (-ra); el, m, (f, la) que chapotea

paddling n chapoteo, chapaleo, m

paddock /'pædək/ n prado, m, dehesa, f; parque, m; (near a racecourse) en silla dero, picadero, m; (toad) sapo, m

padlock /'pæd,lɒk/ n candado, m, vt cerrar con candado, acerrojar

Paduan /'pædʒuən/ a and n paduano (-na)

paean /'piən/ n himno de alegría, m

pagan /'peigən/ a and n pagano (-na)

paganism /'peigənɪzəm/ n paganismo, m

page /peidʒ/ n (boy) paje m; (squire) escudero, m; (of a book, action) página, f; Fig. hoja, f. —vt compaginar; (a person) vocear. **on p. nine,** en la página nueve. **to turn the p.,** Fig. volver la hoja

pageant /'pædʒənt/ n espectáculo, m; (procession) desfile, m; representación teatral, f; fiesta, f; Fig. pompa, f, aparato, m

pageantry /'pædʒəntri/ n pompa, f, aparato, m, magnificencia, f

pager /'peidʒər/ n buscapersonas, m, bip, m (Mexico)

paginate /'pædʒə,neit/ vt paginar

pagination /,pædʒə'neiʃən/ n paginación, f

pagoda /pə'goudə/ n pagoda, f

paid /peid/ a pagado; (on a parcel) porte pagado. **p. mourner,** plañidera, f. **p.-up share,** acción liberada, f

pail /peil/ n cubo, pozal, m, cubeta, f

pailful /'peil,ful/ n cubo (de agua, etc.), m

pain /pein/ n dolor, m; sufrimiento, m; (mental) tormento, m, angustia, f; Law. pena, f; pl **pains,** (effort) trabajo, esfuerzo, m. —vt dolor; atormentar, afligir. **dull p.,** dolor sordo, m. **I have a p. in my head,** Me duele la cabeza. **on p. of death,** so pena de muerte. **to be in great p.,** sufrir mucho. **to take pains,** tomarse trabajo, esforzarse, esmerarse

pained /peind/ a dolorido; afligido; de angustia

painful /'peinfəl/ a doloroso; angustioso; fatigoso; (troublesome) molesto; (embarrassing) embarazoso; difícil; (laborious) arduo

painfully /'peinfəli/ adv dolorosamente; penosamente; fatigosamente; con angustia; laboriosamente

painfulness /'peinfəlnɪs/ n dolor, m; angustia, aflicción, f; tormento, m; dificultad, f

painless /'peinlɪs/ a sin dolor, indoloro

painlessly /'peinlɪsli/ adv sin dolor; sin sufrir

painlessness /'peinlɪsnɪs/ n falta de dolor, f

painstaking /'peinz,teikɪŋ, 'pein,stei-/ a concienzudo; diligente, industrioso; cuidadoso. —n trabajo, m; diligencia, industria, f; cuidado, m

paint /peint/ n pintura, f; (for preserving metal) pavón, m; (rouge) colorete, m. —vt pintar. —vi pintar; pintarse. **The door is painted blue,** La puerta está pintada de azul. **p.-box,** caja de pinturas, f. **p.-brush,** pincel, m; (for house painting) brocha, f

painter /'peintər/ n pintor (-ra); (house) pintor de brocha gorda, pintor de casas, m; (of a boat) boza, f. **sign-p.,** pintor de muestras, m

painting /'peintɪŋ/ n pintura, f; (picture) cuadro, m, pintura, f

pair /pɛər/ n par, m; (of people) pareja, f; (of oxen) yunta, f. —vt parear, emparejar; (persons) unir, casar; (animals) aparear. —vi parearse; casarse; aparearse. **a carriage and p.,** un landó con dos caballos. **a p. of steps,** una escalera de mano. **a p. of pants a p. of trousers,** unos pantalones. **in pairs,** de dos en dos; por parejas. **to p. off,** vi formar pareja, m; Inf. casarse

pal /pæl/ n camarada, compinche, mf; amigote, m

palace /'pælɪs/ n palacio, m

paladin /'pælədɪn/ n paladín, m

palatable /'pælətəbəl/ a sabroso, apetitoso; Fig. agradable, aceptable

palatableness /'pælɪtəbəlnɪs/ n buen sabor, gusto agradable, m; Fig. lo agradable

palatably /'pælɪtəbli/ adv agradablemente

palatal /'pælətl/ a paladial. —n letra paladial, f

palatalize /'pælətl,aiz/ vt palatizar

palate /'pælɪt/ n paladar, m. **hard p.,** paladar, m. **soft p.,** velo del paladar, m

palatial /pə'leɪʃəl/ a (of a palace) palaciego; (sumptuous) magnífico, suntuoso

pale /peɪl/ n (stake) estaca, f; límite, m; Herald. palo, m, a pálido; (wan) descolorido; (of colours) claro, desmayado; (of light) tenue, mortecino; (lustreless) sin brillo, muerto. —vi palidecer, perder el color; Fig. eclipsarse

palely /'peɪlli/ adv pálidamente; vagamente, indistintamente

paleness /'peɪlnɪs/ n palidez, f; (wanness) descoloramiento, m, amarillez, f; (of light) tenuidad, f

paleographer /ˌpeɪli'ɒɡrəfər/ n paleógrafo, m

paleography /ˌpeɪli'ɒɡrəfi; esp. Brit. ˌpæli-/ n paleografía, f

paleolithic /ˌpeɪliə'lɪθɪk/ a paleolítico

paleology /ˌpeɪli'ɒlədʒi/ n paleología, f

paleontology /ˌpeɪliən'tɒlədʒi; esp. Brit. ˌpæli-/ n paleontología, f

Palestine /'pælə,staɪn/ Palestina, f

palette /'pælɪt/ n paleta, f. **p.-knife,** espátula, f

palimpsest /'pælɪmp,sest/ n palimpsesto, m

palindrome /'pælɪn,droum/ n capicúa f, (of numbers), palíndromo m

paling /'peɪlɪŋ/ n palizada, estacada, valla, f

palisade /ˌpælə'seɪd/ n palenque, m, tranquera, palizada, f; Mil. estacada, f

palish /'peɪlɪʃ/ a algo pálido; paliducho

pall /pɔl/ n (on a coffin) paño mortuorio, m; (Fig. covering) manto, m, capa, f; Eccl. palio, m; (over a chalice) palia, f. —vi perder el sabor, hacerse insípido; saciarse (de); aburrirse (de), cansarse (de). **The music of Bach never palls on me,** No me canso nunca de la música de Bach

palladium /pə'leɪdiəm/ n Mineral. paladio, m; (safeguard) paladión, m

pallet /'pælɪt/ n jergón, m; camilla, f; Mech. fiador de rueda, m; torno de alfarero, m

palliate /'pæli,eɪt/ vt (pain) paliar, aliviar; mitigar; (excuse) disculpar, excusar

palliation /ˌpæli'eɪʃən/ n paliación, f; mitigación, f; disculpa, f

palliative /'pæli,eɪtɪv, -iətɪv/ a paliativo; (extenuating) atenuante. —n paliativo, m

pallid /'pælɪd/ a pálido

pallidness /'pælɪdnɪs/ n palidez, f

pallor /'pælər/ n palidez, f

palm /pɑm/ n (of the hand, and Fig., victory) palma, f; (measurement) ancho de la mano, m; (tree) palmera, f. —vt (a card, etc.) empalmar; (with off) defraudar (con); dar gato por liebre (a). **to bear away the p.,** llevar la palma. **p. branch,** palma, f. **p. grove,** palmar, m. **p.-oil,** aceite de palma, m; (bribe) soborno, m. **P. Sunday,** Domingo de Ramos, m. **p. tree,** palmera, f

palmate /'pælmeɪt, -mɪt, 'pɑl-, 'pɑmeɪt/ a palmeado

palmer /'pɑmər, 'pɑl-/ n peregrino, m; (caterpillar) oruga velluda, f

palming /'pɑmɪŋ/ n (in conjuring, etc.) empalme, m

palmist /'pɑmɪst/ n quiromántico (-ca)

palmistry /'pɑməstri/ n quiromancia, f

palmy /'pɑmi/ a palmar; (flourishing) floreciente; (happy) dichoso, feliz; (prosperous) próspero; triunfante

Palmyra /pæl'maɪrə/ Palmira, f

palp /pælp/ n palpo, m

palpability /ˌpælpə'bɪlɪti/ n palpabilidad, f

palpable /'pælpəbəl/ a palpable

palpate /'pælpeɪt/ vt palpar

palpation /pæl'peɪʃən/ n palpación, f

palpitate /'pælpɪ,teɪt/ vi palpitar

palpitating /'pælpɪ,teɪtɪŋ/ a palpitante

palpitation /ˌpælpɪ'teɪʃən/ n palpitación, f

palsied /'pɔlzid/ a paralítico

palsy /'pɔlzi/ n parálisis, f, vt paralizar

paltriness /'pɔltrinɪs/ n mezquindad, f; pequeñez, f

paltry /'pɔltri/ a mezquino, insignificante, pobre

paludism /'pælyə,dɪzəm/ n Med. paludismo, m

pampas /'pæmpəz/ attributively 'pæmpəs/ n pampa, f

pamper /'pæmpər/ vt mimar, consentir demasiado; criar con mimos, regalar; alimentar demasiado bien

pampered /'pæmpərd/ a mimado, consentido; demasiado bien alimentado

pamphlet /'pæmflɪt/ n folleto, m

pamphleteer /ˌpæmflɪ'tɪər/ n folletinista, mf

pan /pæn/ n (vessel) cazuela, f; cacerola, f; (brain) cráneo, m; (of a balance) platillo, m; (of a firelock) cazoleta, f, Cinema. toma panorámica f, prefix pan-. **to pan off,** separar el oro en una gamella. **to pan out,** dar oro; Fig. suceder. **Pan-Americanism,** panamericanismo, m

Pan /pæn/ n Pan, m. **pipes of Pan,** flauta de Pan, f

panacea /ˌpænə'siə/ n panacea, f

panache /pə'næʃ/ n penacho, m

panada /pənə'da/ n Cul. panetela, f

Panama /'pænə,mɑ/ el Panamá, m

Panama /'pænə,mɑ/ a panameño. (-ña). **P. hat,** sombrero de jipijapa, panamá m

pancake /'pæn,keɪk/ n fruta de sartén, hojuela, f. **p. landing,** Aer. aterrizaje brusco, m. **P. Tuesday,** martes de Carnaval, m

panchromatic /ˌpænkrou'mætɪk, -krə-/ a pancromático

pancreas /'pænkriəs, 'pæn-/ n páncreas, m

pancreatic /ˌpænkri'ætɪk/ a pancreático

panda /'pændə/ n Zool. panda, mf

pandemic /pæn'demɪk/ a pandémico

pandemonium /ˌpændə'mouniəm/ n pandemonio

pander /'pændər/ n alcahuete, m, vi alcahuetear. **to p. to,** prestarse a; favorecer, ayudar

pandore /pæn'dɔr/ n Mus. bandola, f

pane /peɪn/ n hoja de vidrio, hoja de cristal, f; cuadro, m

panegyric /ˌpænɪ'dʒɪrɪk/ a panegírico. —n panegírico, m

panegyrist /ˌpænɪ'dʒɪrɪst/ n panegirista, mf

panel /'pænl/ n panel, entrepaño, m; Art. tabla, f; (in a dress) paño, m; (list) lista, f, registro, m; (jury) jurado, m; lista de jurados, f; n labrar a entrepaños; artesonar. **p. doctor,** médico (-ca) de seguros

paneled /'pænld/ a entrepañado; (of ceilings) artesonado. **p. ceiling,** artesonado, m

paneling /'pænlɪŋ/ n entrepaños, m pl; artesonado, m

panful /'pæn,fʊl/ n cazolada, f

pang /pæŋ/ n punzada (de dolor), f, dolor agudo, m; dolor, m; (anguish of mind) angustia, f, tormento, m; (of conscience) remordimiento, m

panic /'pænɪk/ n pánico, m; pavor, espanto, m; terror súbito, m, a pánico. —vi espantarse. **p.-monger,** alarmista, mf **p.-stricken,** aterrorizado, despavorido

panicky /'pænɪki/ a lleno de pánico; nervioso

panicle /'pænɪkəl/ n Bot. panoja, f

pannier /'pænyər/ n (basket) alforja, f; cesto, m; (bustle) caderillas, f pl

panoply /'pænəpli/ n panoplia, f

panorama /ˌpænə'ræmə, -'rɑmə/ n panorama, m

panoramic /ˌpænə'ræmɪk/ a panorámico

pansy /'pænzi/ n pensamiento, m, trinitaria, f

pant /pænt/ vi jadear; (of dogs) hipar; resollar; (of the heart) palpitar. —n jadeo, m; palpitación, f. **to p. after,** suspirar por

pantaloon /ˌpæntḷ'un/ n (trouser) pantalón, m; (Pantaloon) Pantalón, m

pantechnicon /pæn'teknɪ,kɒn/ n almacén de muebles, m; (van) carro de mudanzas, m

pantheism /'pænθi,ɪzəm/ n panteísmo, m

pantheist /'pænθiɪst/ n panteísta, mf

pantheistic /ˌpænθi'ɪstɪk/ a panteísta

pantheon /'pænθi,ɒn, -ən or, esp. Brit. pæn'θiən/ n panteón, m

panther /'pænθər/ n pantera, f

panties /'pæntiz/ n pl pantalones, m pl

panting /'pæntɪŋ/ a jadeante, sin aliento. —n jadeo, m; resuello, m; respiración difícil, f; palpitación, f

pantograph /'pæntə,græf/ n pantógrafo, m

pantomime /'pæntə,maɪm/ n pantomima, f; revista, f. **in p.,** en pantomima; por gestos

pantry /'pæntri/ n despensa, f

pants /pænts/ *n pl* calzoncillos, *m pl*; (trousers) pantalones, *m pl*

panzer division /'pænzər/ *n* división motorizada, *f*

pap /pæp/ *n* (nipple) pezón, *m*; (soft food) papilla, *f*

papa /'pɑpə, pə'pɑ/ *n* papá, *m*

papacy /'peipəsi/ *n* papado, pontificado, *m*

papal /'peipəl/ *a* papal, pontificio. **p. bull,** bula pontificia, *f*. **p. nuncio,** nuncio del Papa, nuncio apostólico, *m*. **p. see,** sede apostólica, *f*

paper /'peipər/ *n* papel, *m*; hoja de papel, *f*; documento, *m*; (lecture) comunicación, *f*; (newspaper) periódico, *m*; (journal) revista, *f*; (exam.) examen escrito, trabajo, *m*; ejercicio, *m*; *pl* **papers,** (credentials) documentación, *f*, credenciales, *f pl*; *Com.* valores negociables, *m pl*; (packet) paquete, *m*, *a* de papel; para papeles; parecido al papel. —*vt* (a room) empapelar; (a parcel) envolver. **daily p.,** diario, *m*. **in p. covers,** (of books) en rústica. **slip of p.,** papeleta. *f*. **to send in one's papers,** entregar su dimisión. **p. bag,** saco de papel, *m*. **p.-chase,** rally-paper, *m*. **p. clip,** prendedero de oficina, "sujeta papels," *m*. **p.-cutting machine,** guillotina, *f*. **p. folder,** plegadera, *f*. **p.-hanger,** empapelador, *m*. **p.-hanging,** empapelado, *m*. **p.-knife,** cortapapel, *m*. **p.-maker,** fabricante de papel, *m*. **p.-making,** manufactura de papel, *f*. **p.-mill,** fábrica de papel, *f*. **p.-money,** papel moneda, *m*. **p.-pulp,** pasta, *f*. **p.-streamer,** serpentina, *f*. **p.-weight,** pisapapeles, *m*

papering /'peipəriŋ/ *n* (of a room) empapelado, *m*

papery /'peipəri/ *a* semejante al papel

papier-mâché /,peipərmə'ʃei, pɑ,pyei-/ *n* cartón piedra, *m*

papillary /'pæpə,lɛri/ *a* papilar

papist /'peipist/ *n* papista, *mf*; católico (-ca)

papoose /pæ'pus/ *n* niño indio, *m*

paprika /pæ'prikə, pə-, pɑ-, 'pæprikə/ *n* pimienta húngara, *f*

papyrus /pə'pairəs/ *n* papiro, *m*

par /pɑr/ *n* par, *f*. **at par,** *Com.* a la par. **above (below) par,** *Com.* por encima (or debajo) de la par. **He is a little below par,** No está muy bien de salud. **to be on par with,** ser el equivalente de; ser igual a. **par excellence,** por excelencia

parable /'pærəbəl/ *n* parábola, *f*

parabola /pə'ræbələ/ *n Geom.* parábola, *f*

parachute /'pærə,ʃut/ *n* paracaídas, *m*; *Bot.* vilano, *m* **to p. down,** lanzarse en paracaídas. **p. troops,** cuerpo de paracaidistas, *m*

parachutist /'pærə,ʃutist/ *n* paracaidista, *mf*

parade /pə'reid/ *n* alarde, *m*; *Mil.* parada, revista, *f*; (procession) desfile, *m*, procesión, *f*; (promenade) paseo, *m*. —*vt* (display) hacer alarde de, hacer gala de, ostentar; (troops) formar en parada; pasar revista (a); (patrol) recorrer. —*vi Mil.* tomar parte en una parada; desfilar. **to p. up and down,** pasearse. **p.-ground,** campo de instrucción, *m*; plaza de armas, *f*

paradigm /'pærə,daim/ *n* paradigma, *m*

paradise /'pærə,dais/ *n* paraíso, edén, *m*; *Fig.* jauja, *f*. **bird of p.,** ave del paraíso, *f*

paradisiac /,pærə'dizi,æk/ *a* paradisíaco

paradox /'pærə,dɒks/ *n* paradoja, *f*

paradoxical /,pærə'dɒksikəl/ *a* paradójico

paradoxicality /,pærə,dɒksi'kæliti/ *n* lo paradójico

paraffin /'pærəfin/ *n* parafina, *f*. —*vt* parafinar. **p. oil,** parafina líquida, *f*

paragon /'pærə,gɒn/ *n* modelo perfecto, dechado, *m*

paragraph /'pærə,græf/ *n* párrafo, *m*; (in a newspaper) suelto, *m*, *vt* dividir en párrafos; escribir un suelto sobre. **new p.,** párrafo aparte, *m*

Paraguay /'pærə,gwai, -,gwei/ el Paraguay, *m*

Paraguayan /,pærə'gwaiən/ *a* and *n* paraguayo (-ya)

parakeet /'pærə,kit/ *n Ornith.* perico, *m*

parallel /'pærə,lɛl/ *a* paralelo; igual; semejante, análogo. —*n* línea paralela, *f*; paralelo, *m*; *Mil.* paralela, *f*; *Geog.* paralelo, *m*; *Print.* pleca, *f*. —*vt* poner en paralelo; cotejar, comparar; igualar. **to run p. to,** ser paralelo a; ser conforme a. **p. bars,** paralelas, *f pl*

parallelism /'pærələ,lizəm/ *n* paralelismo, *m*

parallelogram /,pærə'lɛlə,græm/ *n* paralelogramo, *m*

paralysis /pə'ræləsis/ *n* parálisis, *f*

paralytic /,pærə'litik/ *a* and *n* paralítico (-ca)

paralyzation *n* paralización, *f*

paralyze *vt* paralizar

paramount /'pærə,maunt/ *a* supremo, sumo

paramour /'pærə,mur/ *n* amante, querido, *m*; querida, amiga, *f*

paranoia /,pærə'nɔiə/ *n* paranoia, *f*

paranoiac /,pærə'nɔiæk/ *n* paranoico, *m*

parapet /'pærəpit/ *n* (*Archit.* and *Mil.*) parapeto, *m*

paraphernalia /,pærəfər'neilyə, -fə'neil-/ *n Law.* bienes parafernales, *m*, *pl*; (finery) atavíos, adornos, *m pl*; equipo, *m*; arreos, *m pl*; insignias, *f pl*

paraphrase /'pærə,freiz/ *n* paráfrasis, *f*, *vt* parafrasear

parasite /'pærə,sait/ *n* parásito, *m*; *Inf.* zángano, *m*, gorrista, *mf*

parasitic /,pærə'sitik/ *a* parásito, parasitario; *Med.* parasítico

parasitology /,pærəsai'tɒlədʒi, -si-/ *n* parasitología, *f*

parasol /'pærə,sɔl, -,sɒl/ *n* parasol, quitasol, *m*

parathyroid /,pærə'θairɔid/ *a* paratiroides. —*n* paratiroides, *f pl*

paratroops /'pærə,trups/ *n pl* paracaidistas, *m pl*

paratyphoid /,pærə'taifɔid/ *n* paratifoidea, *f*

parboil /'pɑr,bɔil/ *vt* sancochar

parcel /'pɑrsəl/ *n* paquete, *m*; fardo, *m*; (of land) parcela, *f*. **to p. out,** repartir, distribuir; dividir. **to p. up,** envolver, empaquetar. **p. post,** servicio de paquetes, *m*

parceling /'pɑrsəliŋ/ *n* empaque, *m*; (out) reparto, *m*, distribución, *f*; división, *f*

parch /pɑrtʃ/ *vt* secar; abrasar, quemar; (roast) tostar. —*vi* secarse; quemarse, abrasarse

parched /pɑrtʃt/ *a* seco, sediento. **p. with thirst,** muerto de sed

parchedness /'pɑrtʃidnis/ *n* sequedad, aridez, *f*

parchment /'pɑrtʃmənt/ *n* pergamino, *m*; (of a drum) parche, *m*. **p.-like,** apergaminado

pardon /'pɑrdn/ *n* perdón, *m*; *Eccl.* indulgencia, *f*. —*vt* perdonar; indultar, amnistiar. **a general p.,** una amnistía. **I beg your p.!** ¡Vd. dispense!; ¡Perdone Vd.! **to beg p.,** pedir perdón; disculparse. **P.?** ¿Cómo?

pardonable /'pɑrdṇəbəl/ *a* perdonable, disculpable, excusable

pardonableness /'pɑrdṇəbəlnis/ *n* disculpabilidad, *f*

pardonably /'pɑrdṇəbli/ *adv* disculpablemente, excusablemente

pardoner /'pɑrdnər/ *n* vendedor de indulgencias, *m*; perdonador (-ra)

pardoning /'pɑrdnɪŋ/ *n* perdón, *m*; remisión, *f*

pare /pɛər/ *vt* (one's nails) cortar; (fruit) mondar; (potatoes, etc.) pelar; (remove) quitar; (reduce) reducir

parent /'pɛərənt, 'pær-/ *n* padre, *m*; madre, *f*; (ancestor) antepasado, *m*; (origin) origen, *m*, fuente, *f*; (cause) causa, *f*; (author) autor, *m*; autora, *f*; *pl* **parents,** padres, *m pl*. —*a* madre, materno; principal

parentage /'pɛərəntidʒ, 'pær-/ *n* parentela, *f*; linaje, *m*, familia, alcurnia, *f*; procedencia, *f*, nacimiento, origen, *m*

parental /pə'rɛntl/ *a* paternal; maternal, de madre

parentally /pə'rɛntli/ *adv* como un padre; como una madre

parenthesis /pə'rɛnθəsis/ *n* paréntesis, *m*

parenthetical /,pɛərən'θɛtikəl/ *a* entre paréntesis; de paréntesis

parenthood /'pɛərənt,hʊd, 'pær-/ *n* paternidad, *f*; maternidad, *f*

pariah /pə'raiə/ *n* paria, *mf*

parietal /pə'raiitl/ *a* parietal

paring /'pɛəriŋ/ *n* (act) raedura, *f*; peladura, mondadura, *f*; (shred) brizna, *f*; (refuse) desecho, desperdicio, *m*. **p.-knife,** trinchete, *m*

Paris /'pæris/ París, *m*

parish /'pæriʃ/ *n* parroquia, *f*; feligresía, *f*, a parroquial. **p. church,** parroquia, *f*. **p. clerk,** sacristán de parroquia, *m*. **p. priest,** párroco, *m*. **p. register,** registro de la parroquia, *m*

parishioner /pə'riʃənər/ *n* parroquiano (-na); feligrés (-esa)

Parisian /pə'riʒən, -'riʒən, -'riziən/ *a* parisiense. —*n* parisiense, *mf*

parity /'pæriti/ *n* paridad, *f*

park /pɑrk/ n parque, m; jardín, m. —vt (vehicles) estacionar; (dump) depositar. **car p.,** parque de automóviles, m. **p.-keeper,** guardián del parque, m

parking /'pɑrkɪŋ/ n (of vehicles) estacionamiento, m; (dumping) depósito, m. **p. lights,** Auto. luces de estacionamiento, f pl. **p. place,** parque de estacionamiento, m

parking meter n parquímetro, m (Argentina)

parlance /'pɑrləns/ n lenguaje, m. **in common p.,** en lenguaje vulgar

parley /'pɑrli/ n plática, conversación, f; discusión, f; Mil. parlamento, m. —vi Mil. parlamentar; discutir; conversar. —vt hablar

parliament /'pɑrləmənt/ n parlamento, m; cortes, f pl; cuerpo legislativo, m

parliamentarian /,pɑrləmɛn'tɛəriən/ a and n parlamentario; (of an academy) censor, m

parliamentarianism /,pɑrləmɛn'tɛəriənɪzəm/ n parlamentarismo, m

parliamentary /,pɑrlə'mɛntəri, -tri; sometimes ,pɑrlyə-/ a parlamentario. **p. immunity,** inviolabilidad parlamentaria, f

parlor /'pɑrlər/ n salón, gabinete, m; sala de recibo, f; (in a convent) locutorio, m. **p. games,** diversión de salón, f, juego de sociedad, m. **p.-maid,** camarera, f

parlous /'pɑrləs/ a crítico, malo. —adv sumamente, muy

Parmesan /'pɑrmə,zæn, ,pɑrmə'zæn/ a parmesano, de Parma. —n parmesano (-na). **P. cheese,** queso de Parma, m

Parnassian /pɑr'næsiən/ a del parnaso; parnasiano. —n parnasiano, m

Parnassus /pɑr'næsəs/ n Parnaso, m

parochial /pə'roukiəl/ a parroquial, parroquiano; Fig. provincial

parochialism /pə'roukiə,lɪzəm/ n provincialismo, m

parochially /pə'roukiəli/ adv por parroquias

parodist /'pærədɪst/ n parodista, mf

parody /'pærədi/ n parodia, f, vt parodiar

parole /pə'roul/ n (of convict) libertad vigilada, f

paroxysm /'pærək,sɪzəm/ n paroxismo, m; ataque, acceso, m

parquet /pɑr'kei/ (floor) entarimado m; (of theater) platea, f

parricide /'pærə,said/ n (act) parricidio, m; (person) parricida, mf

parrot /'pærət/ n papagayo, loro, m

parry /'pæri/ vt (a blow, and in fencing) parar; rechazar; evitar. —n parada, f; (in fencing) quite, m, parada, f

parse /pɑrs, pɑrz/ vt analizar

Parsee /'pɑrsi, pɑr'si/ n parsi, m

parsimonious /,pɑrsə'mouniəs/ a parsimonioso

parsimoniously /,pɑrsə'mouniəsli/ adv con parsimonia

parsimony /'pɑrsə,mouni/ n parsimonia, f

parsley /'pɑrsli/ n perejil, m

parsnip /'pɑrsnɪp/ n chirivía, f

parson /'pɑrsən/ n párroco, cura, m; (clergyman) clérigo, m

parsonage /'pɑrsənɪdʒ/ n rectoría, f

part /pɑrt/ n parte, f; porción, f; trozo, m; Mech. pieza, f; (Gram. and of a literary work) parte, f; (of a living organism) miembro, m; (duty) deber, m, obligación, f; Theat. papel, m; Mus. voz, f; pl parts, (region) partes, f pl, lugar, m; (talents) partes, dotes, f pl. **foreign parts,** países extranjeros, m pl, el extranjero. **For my p....,** Por lo que a mí toca, Por mi parte. **for the most p.,** en su mayoría. **from all parts,** de todas partes. **in p.,** en parte; parcialmente. **spare p.,** pieza de recambio, f. **The funny p. of it is...,** Lo cómico del asunto es... **the latter p. of the month,** los últimos días del mes, la segunda quincena del mes. **to form p. of,** formar parte de. **to play a p.,** hacer un papel. **to take a person's p.,** apoyar a alguien, ser partidario de alguien. **to take in good p.,** tomar bien. **to take p. in,** tomar parte en, participar en. **p. of speech,** parte de la oración, f. **p.-owner,** copropietario (-ia). **p.-time job,** trabajo de unas cuantas horas, m

part /pɑrt/ vt distribuir, repartir; dividir; separar (de); (open) abrir. —vi partir, marcharse; despedirse; (of roads, etc.) bifurcarse; dividirse; (open) abrirse. **to p. one's hair,** hacerse la raya. **to p. from,** (things) separarse de; (people) despedirse de. **to p. with,** separarse de; deshacerse de; perder; (dismiss) despedir (a)

partake /pɑr'teik/ vt participar de, compartir; tomar parte en. —vi tomar algo (de comer, de beber). **to p. of,** comer (beber) de; tener rasgos de

partaker /pɑr'teikər/ n partícipe, mf

Parthian /'pɑrθiən/ a parto. —n parto (-ta). **P. shot,** la flecha del parto

partial /'pɑrʃəl/ a parcial; (fond of) aficionado (a). **p. eclipse,** eclipse parcial, m

partiality /,pɑrʃi'ælɪti, pɑr'ʃæl-/ n parcialidad, f; preferencia, predilección, f

partially /'pɑrʃəli/ adv en parte, parcialmente; (with bias) con parcialidad

participant /pɑr'tɪsəpənt/ a participante. —n partícipe, mf

participate /pɑr'tɪsə,peit/ vi participar (de), compartir; tomar parte (en)

participation /pɑr,tɪsə'peiʃən/ n participación, f

participial /,pɑrtə'sɪpiəl/ a Gram. participial

participle /'pɑrtə,sɪpəl, -səpəl/ n Gram. participio, m. **past p.,** participio pasado (or pretérito or pasivo), m. **present p.,** participio activo (or presente), m

particle /'pɑrtɪkəl/ n partícula, f; Fig. átomo, grano, m, pizca, f; Gram. partícula, f

parti-colored /'pɑrti,kʌlərd/ a bicolor

particular /pər'tɪkyələr/ a particular; especial; individual; singular; cierto; exacto; escrupuloso; difícil, exigente. —n detalle, pormenor, m; circunstancia, f; caso particular, m; pl **particulars,** informes, detalles, m pl. **further particulars,** más detalles. **in p.,** en particular; sobre todo. **He is very p. about...,** Es muy exigente en cuanto a...; **Le es muy importante...,** Le importa mucho...

particularize /pər'tɪkyələ,raiz/ vt particularizar, detallar; especificar

particularly /pər'tɪkyələrli/ adv en particular; particularmente; sobre todo

parting /'pɑrtɪŋ/ n despedida, f; partida, f; separación, f; (of the hair) raya, crencha, f; (cross roads) bifurcación, f. —a de despedida. **at p.,** al despedirse. **to reach the p. of the ways,** Fig. llegar al punto decisivo

partisan /'pɑrtəzən, -sən/ n partidario (-ia); (fighter) guerrillero, m, a partidario; de guerrilleros

partisanship /'pɑrtə,zənʃɪp/ n partidarismo, m

partition /pɑr'tɪʃən, pər-/ n partición, f; división, f; (wall) pared, f, tabique, m. **the p. of Ireland,** la división de Irlanda

partly /'pɑrtli/ adv en parte

partner /'pɑrtnər/ n asociado (-da); Com. socio (-ia); (dancing) pareja, f; (in games, and companion) compañero (-ra); (spouse) consorte, mf; (in crime) codelincuente, mf **sleeping p.,** socio comanditario, m. **working p.,** socio industrial, m

partnership /'pɑrtnər,ʃɪp/ n asociación, f; Com. sociedad, compañía, f. **deed of p.,** artículos de sociedad, m pl. **to take into p.,** tomar como socio (a). **to form a p.,** asociarse

partridge /'pɑrtrɪdʒ/ n Ornith. perdiz, f. **young p.,** perdigón, m

parturient /pɑr'turiənt/ a f, parturienta. —n parturienta, f

parturition /,pɑrtu'rɪʃən, -tʃu-/ n parto, m

party /'pɑrti/ n partido, m; grupo, m; (of pleasure, etc.) partida, f; reunión, fiesta, f; Mil. pelotón, destacamento, m; Law. parte, f; (person) interesado (-da); (accessory) cómplice, mf. **rescue p.,** pelotón de salvamento, m. **to be a p. to,** prestarse a; ser cómplice en. **to give a p.,** dar una fiesta, dar una reunión. **p.-spirit,** espíritu del partido, m. **p.-wall,** pared medianera, f

parvenu /'pɑrvə,nu/ n advenedizo (-za)

parvis /'pɑrvɪs/ n Archit. atrio, m

Paschal /'pæs'kæl/ a pascual

pass /pæs/ n (in an exam.) aprobación, f; (crisis) crisis, situación crítica, f; estado, m; (with the hands) pase, m; (permit) permiso, m; Mil. licencia, f; (safeconduct) salvoconducto, m; (in football, etc.) pase, *m;* (membership card) carnet, *m;* (defile) desfiladero, paso, puerto, *m; Naut.* rebasadero, *m;* (fencing) estocada, *f.* **free p.,** billete de favor, *m.* **p.-book,** libreta de banco, *f.* **p. certificate,** (in exams.) aprobado, *m.* **p.-key,** llave maestra, *f*

pass /pæs/ *vi* pasar; (of time) correr, pasar, transcurrir; (happen) occurrir, tomar lugar; (end) cesar, desaparecer; (die) morir. —*vt* pasar; hacer pasar; (the butter, etc.) dar, alargar; (in football, hockey) pasar; (excel) aventajar, exceder; (a bill, an examination) aprobar; (sentence) fallar, pronunciar; (a remark) hacer; (transfer) traspasar; (tolerate) sufrir, tolerar; evacuar. **He passed in psychology,** Aprobó sicología. **to allow to p.,** ceder el paso (a). **to bring to p.,** ocasionar. **to come to p.,** suceder. **to let p.,** (put up with) dejar pasar; no hacer caso de; (forgive) perdonar. **to p. a vote of confidence,** votar una proposición de confianza. **to p. the buck,** *Inf.* echarle a uno el muerto. **pass the hat, pass the plate,** pasar la gorra. **to p. along,** pasar por; pasar. **to p. away,** pasar; desaparecer; (die) morir, fallecer; (of time) transcurrir. **to p. by,** pasar por, pasar delante de, pasar al lado de; (omit) pasar por alto de, omitir; (ignore) pasar sin hacer caso de. **to p. for,** pasar por. **to p. in,** entrar. **to p. in and out,** entrar y salir. **to p. off,** *vi* pasar; cesar, acabarse; desaparecer; evaporarse, disiparse; (of events) tener lugar. —*vt* (oneself) darse por; dar por, hacer pasar por. **to p. a cat off as hare,** dar gato por liebre. **to p. on,** *vi* pasar; seguir su camino, continuar su marcha. —*vt* pasar algo de uno a otro. **to p. out,** salir. **to p. over,** pasar por encima de; pasar; cruzar, atravesar; (transfer) traspasar; (disregard) pasar por alto de, dejar a un lado; omitir. **to p. over in silence,** pasar en silencio (por). **to p. round,** circular. **to p. through,** cruzar, atravesar, pasar por; (pierce) traspasar; *Fig.* experimentar

passable /'pæsəbəl/ *a* transitable, pasadero; (fairly good) regular, mediano; tolerable

passably /'pæsəbli/ *adv* medianamente, pasaderamente, tolerablemente

passage /'pæsɪdʒ/ *n* pasaje, *m;* paso, tránsito, *m;* (voyage) viaje, *m,* travesía, *f;* (corridor) pasillo, *m;* (entrance) entrada, *f;* (way) camino, *m;* (alley) callejón, *m;* (in a mine) galería, *f;* (of time) transcurso, *m;* (of birds) pasa, *f;* (in a book, and *Mus.*) pasaje, *m;* (occurrence) episodio, incidente, *m;* (of a bill) aprobación, *f.* **p. money,** pasaje, *m.* **p. of arms,** lucha, *f,* combate, *m;* disputa, *f*

passementerie /pæs'mɛntri/ *n* pasamanería, *f*

passenger /'pæsəndʒər/ *n* viajero (-ra); (on foot) peatón, *m.* **by p. train,** en gran velocidad

passerby /'pæsər'bai/ *n* transeúnte, paseante, *mf*

passing /'pæsɪŋ/ *a* pasajero; fugitivo; momentáneo. —*adv* sumamente, extremadamente. —*n* pasada, *f;* paso, *m;* (death) muerte, *f;* (disappearance) desaparición, *f;* (of a law) aprobación, *f.* **in p.,** de paso. **p.-bell,** toque de difuntos, *m*

passing grade *n* mínima calificación aprobatoria, *f*

passion /'pæʃən/ *n* pasión, *f;* (Christ's) Pasión, *f;* (anger) cólera, *f.* **to fly into a p.,** montar en cólera. **p.-flower,** pasionaria, granadilla, *f.* **P. play,** drama de la Pasión, *m.* **P. Sunday,** Domingo de Pasión, *m.* **P. Week,** Semana Santa, *f*

passionate /'pæʃənɪt/ *a* apasionado; (quick-tempered) irascible, colérico; (fervid) vehemente, intenso, ardiente

passionately /'pæʃənɪtli/ *adv* con pasión, apasionadamente; (irascibly) coléricamente; (fervidly) con vehemencia, ardientemente

passionless /'pæʃənlɪs/ *a* sin pasión, frío; impasible; imparcial

passive /'pæsɪv/ *a* pasivo. —*n Gram.* pasiva, *f.* **p. resistance,** resistencia pasiva, *f*

passivity /pæ'sɪvɪti/ *n* pasividad, *f*

Passover /'pæs,ouvər/ *n* Pascua de los judíos, *f*

passport /'pæspɔrt/ *n* pasaporte, *m*

password /'pæs,wɜrd/ *n* contraseña, *f*

past /pæst/ *a* pasado; último; (expert) consumado; (former) antiguo, ex-. —*n* pasado, *m;* historia, *f,* antecedentes, *m pl, prep* después de; (in front of) delante de; (next to) al lado de; (beyond) más allá de; (without) sin; fuera de; (of age) más de; (no longer

able to) incapaz de. —*adv* más allá. (The translation of **past** as an adverb is often either omitted, or included in the verb, e.g. *The years flew p.,* Los años transcurrieron. *for centuries p.,* durante siglos.) **I am p. caring,** Nada me importa ya. **It is a quarter p. ten,** Son las diez y cuarto. **It is p. four o'clock,** Son las siete pasadas, Son después de las cuatro. **what's p. is p.,** lo pasado, pasado. **p. doubt,** fuera de duda. **p. endurance,** insoportable. **p. help,** sin remedio, irremediable. **p. hope,** sin esperanza. **p.-master,** maestro, consumado, experto, *m.* **p. participle,** participio pasado, *m.* **p. president,** ex-presidente, *m.* **p. tense,** (tiempo) pasado, *m*

paste /peist/ *n* pasta, *f;* (gloy) engrudo, *m.* —*vt* (affix) pegar; (glue) engomar, engrudar

pasteboard /'peist,bɔrd/ *n* cartón, *m,* cartulina, *f,* a de cartón, de cartulina

pastel /pæ'stɛl/ *n Art.* pastel, *m.* **p. drawing,** pintura al pastel, *f*

pastelist /'pæ'stɛlɪst/ *n* pastelista, *mf*

pasteurization /,pæstʃərə'zeiʃən/ *n* pasteurización, *f*

pasteurize /'pæstʃə,raiz/ *vt* pasteurizar

pastille /pæ'stil/ *n* pastilla, *f*

pastime /'pæs,taim/ *n* pasatiempo, entretenimiento, *m,* diversión, recreación, *f*

pastor /'pæstər/ *n* pastor, *m*

pastoral /'pæstərəl/ *a* pastoril; *Eccl.* pastoral. —*n Eccl.* pastoral, *f;* (*Poet. Mus.*) pastorela, *f*

pastorate /'pæstərɪt/ *n* pastoría, *f*

pastry /'peistri/ *n* (dough) pasta, *f;* pastel, *m,* torta, *f;* pastelería, *f.* **p.-cook,** repostero, *m,* pastelero (-ra)

pasturage /'pæstʃərɪdʒ/ *n* (grass, etc.) pasto, *m;* pasturaje, *m;* pastoreo, *m*

pasture /'pæstʃər/ *n* (grass, etc.) pasto, herbaje, *m;* pasturaje, *m;* (field) prado, *m,* pradera, dehesa, *f.* —*vi* pacer; pastar. —*vt* apacentar, pastar

pasty /'pæsti/ *a* pastoso; (pale) pálido. —*n* empanada, *f*

pat /pæt/ *n* toque, *m;* caricia, *f;* (for butter) molde (de mantequilla), *m.* —*vt* tocar; acariciar, pasar la mano (sobre). —*adv* a propósito; oportunamente; fácilmente. **pat of butter,** pedacito de mantequilla, *m.* **pat on the back,** golpe en la espalda, *m; Fig.* elogio, *m*

Patagonian /,pætə'gounian/ *a* and *n* patagón (-ona)

patch /pætʃ/ *n* (mend) remiendo, *m;* (piece) pedazo, *m;* (plaster and *Auto.,* etc.) parche, *m;* (beauty spot) lunar postizo, *m;* (of ground) parcela, *f;* (of flowers, etc.) masa, *f;* (stain, and *Fig.*) mancha, *f.* —*vt* (mend) remendar; poner remiendo (a); pegar; (roughly) chafallar; (the face) ponerse lunares postizos. **p. of blue sky,** pedazo de cielo azul. **patch of green grass,** mancha de hierba verde. **to be not a p. on,** no ser de la misma clase que; (of persons) no llegarle a los zancajos de. **to p. up a quarrel,** hacer las paces

patchwork /'pætʃ,wɜrk/ *n* labor de retazos, obra de retacitos, *f; Fig.* mezcla, mezcolanza, *f.* **p. quilt,** centón, *m*

patchy /'pætʃi/ *a* desigual; manchado

patella /pə'tɛlə/ *n Anat.* rótula, *f*

patency /'peitnsi/ *n* evidencia, claridad, *f*

patent /'pætnt/ *a* evidente, patente; patentado. —*n* patente, *f.* —*vt* patentar. **p. of nobility,** carta de hidalguía, ejecutoria, *f.* **"P. Applied For,"** «Patente Solicitada.» **Patent Pending** marca en trámite. **p. leather,** *n* charol, *m.* —*a* de charol. **p. medicine,** específico farmacéutico, *m*

patentee /,pætn'ti/ *n* el, *m,* (f, la) que obtiene una patente; inventor (-ra)

patently /'pætntli/ *adv* evidentemente, claramente

paterfamilias /,peitərfə'miliəs, ,pɑ-, ,pætər-/ *n* padre de familia, *m*

paternal /pə'tɜrnl/ *a* paterno, paternal

paternally /pə'tɜrnli/ *adv* paternalmente

paternity /pə'tɜrnɪti/ *n* paternidad, *f*

path /pæθ/ *n* senda, vereda, *f,* sendero, *m;* camino, *m;* (track) pista, *f;* (traject) trayectoria, *f.* **the beaten p.,** el camino trillado

pathetic /pə'θɛtɪk/ *a* patético

pathless /'pæθlɪs/ *a* sin senda

pathogenic /,pæθə'dʒɛnɪk/ *a Med.* patógeno

pathological /,pæθə'lɒdʒɪkəl/ *a* patológico

pathologist /pə'θɒlədʒɪst/ n patólogo, m
pathology /pə'θɒlədʒi/ n patología, f
pathos /'peɪθɒs/ n lo patético
patience /'peɪʃəns/ n paciencia, f. **He tries my p. very much,** Me cuesta mucho no impacientarme con él. **to lose p.,** perder la paciencia; (grow angry) perder los estribos. **to play p.,** hacer solitarios
patient /'peɪʃənt/ a paciente. —n paciente, mf; (ill person) enfermo (-ma); (of a physician) cliente, mf
patiently /'peɪʃəntli/ adv con paciencia, pacientemente
patina /'pætnə, pə'tinə/ n pátina, f
patriarch /'peɪtri,ɑrk/ n patriarca, m
patriarchal /,peɪtri'ɑrkəl/ a patriarcal
patriarchy /'peɪtri,ɑrki/ n patriarcado, m
patrician /pə'trɪʃən/ a and n patricio (-ia)
patrimonial /,pætrə'mouniəl/ a patrimonial
patrimony /'pætrə,mouni/ n patrimonio, m
patriot /'peɪtriət/ n patriota, mf
patriotic /,peɪtri'ɒtɪk/ a patriótico
patriotism /'peɪtriə,tɪzəm/ n patriotismo, m
patrol /pə'troul/ n patrulla, f; ronda, f, vi and vt patrullar; rondar; recorrer. **p. boat,** lancha escampavía, f. **p. flight,** vuelo de patrulla, m
patron /'peɪtrən/ n (of a freed slave) patrono, m; (of the arts, etc.) mecenas, protector, m; (customer) parroquiano (-na), cliente, mf. **p. saint,** santo (-ta) de patrón (-ona)
patronage /'peɪtrənɪdʒ/ n (protection) patrocinio, m; protección, f; Eccl. patronato, m; (regular custom) clientela, f; (of manner) superioridad, f
patroness /'peɪtrənɪs/ n patrona, f; protectora, f; (of a charity, etc.) patrocinadora, f; (of a regiment, etc.) madrina, f
patronize /'peɪtrə,naɪz/ vt patrocinar; proteger, favorecer; (a shop) ser parroquiano de; (treat arrogantly) tratar con superioridad
patronizing /'peɪtrə,naɪzɪŋ/ a (with air, behavior, etc.) de superioridad, de altivez
patten /'pætn/ n zueco, chanclo, m
patter /'pætər/ n (jargon) jerga, f; charla, f; (of rain) azotes, m pl; (of feet) son, m; golpecitos, m pl. —vt (repeat) decir mecánicamente. —vi (chatter) charlar; (of rain) azotar, bailar; correr ligeramente
pattern /'pætərn/ n modelo, m; (Sew. and dressmaking) patrón, m; (in founding) molde, m; (template) escantillón, m; (of cloth, etc.) muestra, f; (design) dibujo, diseño, m; (example) ejemplar, m. —vt diseñar; estampar. **p. book,** libro de muestras, m
patty /'pæti/ n empanada, f, pastelillo, m
paucity /'pɔsɪti/ n poquedad, f; corto número, m; insuficiencia, escasez, f
paunch /pɔntʃ/ n panza, barriga, f
pauper /'pɔpər/ n pobre, mf
pauperism /'pɔpə,rɪzəm/ n pauperismo, m
pauperization /,pɔpərə'zeɪʃən/ n empobrecimiento, m
pauperize /'pɔpə,raɪz/ vt empobrecer, reducir a la miseria
pause /pɔz/ n pausa, f; intervalo, m; silencio, m; interrupción, f; Mus. pausa, f. —vi pausar, hacer una pausa; detenerse, interrumpirse; vacilar. **to give p. to,** hacer vacilar (a)
pavan /'pævən/ n (dance) pavana, f
pave /peɪv/ vt empedrar, enlosar. **to p. the way for,** facilitar el paso de, preparar el terreno para, abrir el camino de
pavement /'peɪvmənt/ n pavimento, m; (sidewalk) acera, f. **p.-artist,** pintor callejero, m
pavilion /pə'vɪlyən/ n pabellón, m; (for a band, etc.) quiosco, m; (tent) tienda de campaña, f
paving /'peɪvɪŋ/ n pavimentación, f; empedrado, m; see **pavement. p.-stone,** losa, f
paw /pɔ/ n pata, f; (with claws) garra, f; Inf. manaza, f. —vt tocar con la pata; (scratch) arañar; (handle) manosear. —vi (of a horse) piafar
pawing /'pɔɪŋ/ n (of a horse) el piafar; (handling) manoseo, m
pawn /pɔn/ n (chess) peón (de ajedrez), m; empeño, m; Fig. prenda, f. —vt empeñar, pignorar; dar en prenda. **p.-ticket,** papeleta de empeño, f
pawnbroker /'pɔn,broukər/ n prestamista, mf

pawning /'pɔnɪŋ/ n empeño, m, pignoración, f
pawnshop /'pɔn,ʃɒp/ n casa de préstamos, casa de empeño, f, monte de piedad, m
pay /peɪ/ n paga, f; (Mil. Nav.) soldada, f; salario, m; (of a workman) jornal, m; (reward) recompensa, compensación, f; (profit) beneficio, provecho, m. **pay-day,** día de paga, m. **pay-office,** pagaduría, f. **pay-sheet,** nómina, f
pay /peɪ/ vt pagar; (a debt) satisfacer; (spend) gastar; (recompense) remunerar, recompensar; (hand over) entregar; (yield) producir; (a visit) hacer; (attention) prestar; (homage) rendir; (one's respects) presentar. —vi pagar; producir ganancia; sacar provecho; ser una ventaja, ser provechoso. **It would not pay him to do it,** No le saldría a cuenta hacerlo. **This job doesn't pay,** Este trabajo no da dinero. **to pay a compliment (to),** cumplimentar, decir alabanzas (a), echar una flor (a). **to pay attention,** prestar atención; hacer caso. **to pay cash,** pagar al contado. **to pay in advance,** pagar adelantado. **to pay in full,** saldar. **to pay off old scores,** ajustar cuentas viejas. **to pay one's addresses to,** hacer la corte (a), pretender en matrimonio (a). **to pay the penalty,** sufrir el castigo, hacer penitencia. **to pay with interest,** Fig. pagar con creces. **to pay again,** volver a pagar, pagar de nuevo. **to pay back,** devolver, restituir; (money only) reembolsar; Fig. pagar en la misma moneda, vengarse (de). **to pay down,** pagar al contado. **to pay for,** pagar, costear; satisfacer. **to pay in,** ingresar. **to pay off,** (persons) despedir; (a debt) saldar; (a mortgage) cancelar, redimir. **to pay out,** (persons) vengarse de; (money) pagar; (ropes, etc.) arriar. **to pay up,** pagar; pagar por completo; (shares, etc.) redimir
payable /'peɪəbəl/ a pagadero; a pagar; que puede ser pagado
payee /peɪ'i/ n tenedor, m
payer /'peɪər/ n pagador (-ra)
paying /'peɪɪŋ/ n. See **payment**
paymaster /'peɪ,mæstər/ n pagador, m; tesorero, m. **P.-General,** ordenador general de pagos, m
payment /'peɪmənt/ n pago, m, paga, f; remuneración, f; Fig. recompensa, satisfacción, f; Fig. premio, m. **in p. of,** en pago de. **on p. of,** mediante el pago de. **p. in advance,** pago adelantado, anticipo, m
pea /pi/ n guisante, m. **dry or split pea,** guisante seco, m. **sweet pea,** guisante de olor, m. **pea-flour,** harina de guisantes, f. **pea-green,** verde claro, m. **pea-jacket,** chaquetón de piloto, m. **pea-shooter,** cerbatana, f
peace /pis/ n paz, f; tranquilidad, quietud, f, sosiego, m; Law. orden público, m. **P.!** ¡Silencio! **to hold one's p.,** callarse, guardar silencio. **to make p.,** hacer las paces. **P. be upon this house!** ¡Paz sea en esta casa! **p.-footing,** pie de paz, m. **p.-loving,** pacífico. **p.-offering,** sacrificio propiciatorio, m; satisfacción, oferta de paz, f
peaceable /'pisəbəl/ a pacífico; apacible; tranquilo, sosegado
peaceableness /'pisəbəlnɪs/ n paz, f; apacibilidad, f; tranquilidad, quietud, f, sosiego, m
peaceably /'pisəbli/ adv pacíficamente; tranquilamente
peaceful /'pisfəl/ a pacífico; tranquilo; silencioso. **to come with p. intentions,** venir de paz
peacefully /'pisfəli/ adv en paz; pacíficamente; tranquilamente
peacefulness /'pisfəlnɪs/ n paz, f; tranquilidad, calma, quietud, f; silencio, m; carácter pacífico, m
peacemaker /'pis,meɪkər/ n pacificador (-ra); conciliador (-ra)
peach /pitʃ/ n (fruit) melocotón, m; (tree) melocotonero, melocotón, m; (girl) breva, f. **p.-colour,** color de melocotón, m
peacock /'pi,kɒk/ n pavo real, pavón, m. —vi pavonearse; darse humos. **The p. spread its tail,** El pavo real hizo la rueda
peahen /'pi,hɛn/ n pava real, f
peak /pik/ n punta, f; (of a cap) visera, f; (of a mountain) peñasco, m, cumbre, cima, f; (mountain itself) pico, m; (Naut. of a hull) pico, m; Fig. auge,

apogeo, *m;* punto más alto, *m.* —*vi* consumirse, enflaquecer. **p. hours,** horas de mayor tráfico, *f pl*

peaked /'pikɪd/ *a* en punta; puntiagudo; pícudo; (of a cap) con visera; (wan) ojeroso; (thin) delgaducho, macilento, consumido

peal /pil/ *n* toque (or repique) de campanas, *m;* campanillazo, *m;* carillón, *m;* (noise) estruendo, ruido, *m;* (of thunder) trueno, *m;* (of an organ) sonido, *m.* —*vi* repicar; sonar. —*vt* tañer, echar a vuelo (las campanas); (of a bell that one presses) hacer sonar, tocar. **a p. of laughter,** una carcajada

peanut /'pi,nʌt/ *n* cacahuete, *m.* **p. butter,** mantequilla de cacahuete, *f*

pear /pɛər/ *n* pera, *f.* **p.-shaped,** piriforme, de figura de pera. **p. tree,** peral, *m*

pearl /pɜrl/ *n* perla, *f;* (mother-of-pearl) nácar, *m, a* de perla; perlero. —*vt* (dew) rociar, aljofarar. —*vi* pescar perlas; formar perlas. **seed p.,** aljófar, *m.* **p.-ash,** carbonato potásico, *m.* **p.-barley,** cebada perlada, *f.* **p.-button,** botón de nácar, *m.* **p.-fisher,** pescador de perlas, *m.* **p.-fishery,** pescaduría de perlas, *f.* **p.-grey,** gris de perla, *m*

pearly /'pɜrli/ *a* perlino; de perla; nacarado; (dewy) aljofarado

peasant /'pɛzənt/ *n* campesino (-na), labrador (-ra). —*a* campesino

peasantry /'pɛzəntri/ *n* campesinos, *m pl,* gente del campo, *f*

peat /pit/ *n* turba, *f.* **p.-bog,** turbera, *f*

pebble /'pɛbəl/ *n* guijarro, *m,* pedrezuela, guija, *f;* (gravel) guijo, *m;* cristal de roca, *m;* lente de cristal de roca, *m*

pebbled, pebbly /'pɛbəld; 'pɛbli/ *a* guijarroso, enguijarrado

peccadillo /,pɛkə'dɪloʊ/ *n* pecadillo, *m*

peck /pɛk/ *n* (of a bird) picotazo, *m,* picada, *f;* (kiss) besito, *m;* (large amount) montón, *m;* multitud, *f.* —*vt* (of a bird) picotear; sacar (or coger) con el pico; (kiss) besar rápidamente. —*vi* (with at) picotear; picar

pectoral /'pɛktərəl/ *a* pectoral

peculiar /pɪ'kyulyər/ *a* particular, peculiar, individual; propio, característico; (marked) especial; (unusual) extraño, raro, extraordinario

peculiarity /pɪ,kyuli'ærɪti/ *n* peculiaridad, particularidad, *f;* singularidad, *f;* (eccentricity) excentricidad, rareza, *f*

peculiarly /pɪ'kyulyərli/ *adv* particularmente, peculiarmente; especialmente; extrañamente

pecuniarily /pɪ,kyuni'ɛərəli/ *adv* pecuniariamente

pecuniary /pɪ'kyuni,ɛri/ *a* pecuniario

pedagogic /,pɛdə'gɒdʒɪk/ *a* pedagógico

pedagogue /'pɛdə,gɒg/ *n* pedagogo, *m*

pedagogy /'pɛdə,goudʒi, -,gɒdʒi/ *n* pedagogía, *f*

pedal /'pɛdl/ *n* pedal, *m.* —*vi* pedalear

pedant /'pɛdnt/ *n* pedante, *mf*

pedantic /pə'dæntɪk/ *a* pedante

pedantically /pə'dæntɪkli/ *adv* con pedantería, pedantescamente

pedantry /'pɛdntri/ *n* pedantería, *f*

peddle /'pɛdl/ *vi* ser buhonero. —*vt* revender

peddling /'pɛdlɪŋ/ *n* buhonería, *f.* —*a* trivial, insignificante; mezquino

pedestal /'pɛdəstl/ *n* pedestal, *m;* Fig. fundamento, *m,* base, *f.* **to put on a p.,** *Fig.* poner sobre un pedestal

pedestrian /pə'dɛstriən/ *n* peatón, peón, *m, a* pedestre; *Fig.* patoso. **p. traffic,** circulación de los peatones, *f*

pedestrian crosswalk, cruce peatonal (Argentina), cruce de peatones, *m*

pediatrician /,pidiə'trɪʃən/ *n* pediatra, *mf*

pedigree /'pɛdɪ,gri/ *n* genealogía, *f;* raza, *f;* (of words) etimología, *f.* —*a* (of animals) de raza, de casta. **p. dog,** perro de casta, *m*

pediment /'pɛdəmənt/ *n Archit.* frontón, *m*

pedlar /'pɛdlər/ *n* buhonero, *m*

pedometer /pə'dɒmɪtər/ *n* pedómetro, cuentapasos, *m*

peel /pil/ *n* (baker's) pala, *f;* (of fruit, etc.) piel, *f,* hollejo, *m.* —*vt* pelar, mondar; (bark) descortezar.

—*vi* descascararse, desconcharse; (of the bark of a tree) descortezarse

peeling /'pilɪŋ/ *n* (of fruit, etc.) peladura, monda, *f;* (of bark) descortezadura, *f;* (of paint, etc.) desconchadura, *f*

peep /pip/ *vi* (of birds) piar; (of mice) chillar; (peer) atisbar, mirar a hurtadillas; (appear) asomar; mostrarse; (of the dawn) despuntar. —*n* (of birds) pío, *m;* (of mice) chillido, *m;* (glimpse) vista, *f;* (glance) ojeada, mirada furtiva, *f;* **at the p. of day,** al despuntar el día. **p.-hole,** mirilla, *f,* atisbadero, *m;* escucha, *f.* **p.-show,** óptica, *f*

peeper /'pipər/ (eye) avizón *m*

peer /pɪər/ *n* par, *m;* igual, *m.* —*vi* atisbar; escudriñar; *Fig.* asomar, aparecer

peerage /'pɪərɪdʒ/ *n* nobleza, aristocracia, *f;* dignidad de par, *f*

peeress /'pɪərɪs/ *n* paresa, *f*

peerless /'pɪərlɪs/ *a* sin par, incomparable, sin igual

peevish /'pivɪʃ/ *a* displicente, malhumorado; picajoso, vidrioso, enojadizo

peevishness /'pivɪʃnɪs/ *n* displicencia, *f,* mal humor, *m;* impaciencia, *f*

peg /pɛg/ *n* clavija, *f;* (of a tent) estaca, *f;* (of a barrel) estaquilla, *f;* (of a violin, etc.) clavija, *f;* (for coats, etc.) colgadero, *m;* (of whisky, etc.) trago, *m;* *Fig.* pretexto, *m.* —*vt* clavar, enclavijar, empernar. **to take down a peg,** bajar los humos (a). **to peg away,** batirse el cobre. **to peg down,** fijar con clavijas; (a tent) sujetar con estacas; (prices) fijar

Pegasus /'pɛgəsəs/ *n* Pegaso, *m*

peignoir /pein'wɑr/ *n* peinador, salto de cama, *m,* bata, *f*

pekinese /,pikə'niz/ *n* perro (-rra) pequinés (-esa)

pelican /'pɛlɪkən/ *n* pelícano, *m*

pellagra /pə'lægrə/ *n Med.* pelagra, *f*

pellet /'pɛlɪt/ *n* bolita, *f;* (pill) píldora, *f;* (shot) perdigón, *m*

pellmell /'pɛl'mɛl/ *adv* a trochemoche; atropelladamente

pellucid /pə'lusɪd/ *a* diáfano

Peloponnesian /,pɛləpə'niʒən/ *a and n* peloponense, *mf*

pelota /pə'loutə/ *n* pelota vasca, *f.* **p. player,** pelotari, *m*

pelt /pɛlt/ *n* pellejo, *m;* cuero, *m;* (fur) piel, *f;* (blow) golpe, *m.* —*vt* llover (piedras, etc.) sobre, arrojar... sobre; (questions) disparar; (throw) tirar. —*vi* (of rrain) azotar, diluviar

pelvic /'pɛlvɪk/ *a* pélvico, pelviano

pelvis /'pɛlvɪs/ *n* pelvis, *f*

pen /pɛn/ *n* (for sheep, etc.) aprisco, *m;* corral, *m;* (paddock) parque, *m;* (for hens) pollera, *f;* (for writing and *Fig.,* author, etc.) pluma, *f.* —*vt* (shut up) acorralar; encerrar; (write) escribir (con pluma). **pen-and-ink drawing,** dibujo a la pluma, *m.* **pen-holder,** portaplumas, *m.* **pen-name,** seudónimo, *m.* **pen-wiper,** limpiaplumas, *m*

penal /'pinl/ *a* penal. **p. code,** código penal, *m.* **p. colony,** colonia penal, *f.* **p. servitude,** trabajos forzados (or forzosos), *m pl.* **p. servitude for life,** cadena perpetua, *f*

penalization /,pinlə'zeiʃən/ *n* castigo, *m*

penalize /'pinl,aiz/ *vt* penar, imponer pena (a); castigar

penalty /'pɛnlti/ *n Law.* penalidad, *f;* castigo, *m;* (fine) multa, *f;* (risk) riesgo, *m;* *Sports.* sanción, *m.* **the p. of,** la desventaja de. **under p. of,** so pena de. **p. kick,** (football) penalty, *m*

penance /'pɛnəns/ *n* penitencia, *f.* **to do p.,** hacer penitencia

penchant /'pɛntʃənt;/ *n* tendencia, *f;* inclinación, *f*

pencil /'pɛnsəl/ *n* lápiz, *m;* (automatic) lapicero, *m.* —*vt* escribir (or dibujar or marcar) con lápiz. **p.-case,** estuche para lápices, *m.* **p.-holder,** lapicero, *m.* **p.-sharpener,** cortalápices, afilalápices, *m*

pendant /'pɛndənt/ *n* (jewel) pendiente, *m;* *Archit.* culo de lámpara, *m;* (Naut. rope) amantillo, *m;* (flag) gallardete, *m*

pending /'pɛndɪŋ/ *a* pendiente. —*prep* durante. **to be p.,** pender; amenazar

pendulous /'pɛndʒələs/ *a* péndulo; colgante; oscilante

pendulum /'pɛndʒələm/ *n* péndola, *f*, péndulo, *m*

penetrability /,pɛnɪtrə'bɪlɪti/ *n* penetrabilidad, *f*

penetrable /'pɛnɪtrəbəl/ *a* penetrable

penetrate /'pɛnɪ,treit/ *vt and vi* penetrar

penetrating /'pɛnɪ,treitɪŋ/ *a* penetrante

penetration /,pɛnɪ'treiʃən/ *n* penetración, *f*

penguin /'pɛŋgwɪn/ *n* pingüino, pájaro bobo, *m*

penicillin /,pɛnə'sɪlɪn/ *n* penicilina, *f*

peninsula /pə'nɪnsələ, -'nɪnsyələ/ *n* península, *f*

peninsular /pə'nɪnsələr, -'nɪnsyələr/ *a* peninsular. **P. War,** Guerra de la Independencia, *f*

penis /'pinɪs/ *n* pene, *m*

penitence /'pɛnɪtəns/ *n* penitencia, *f*

penitent /'pɛnɪtənt/ *a* penitente. —*n* penitente, *mf*

penitential /,pɛnɪ'tɛnʃəl/ *a* penitencial

penitentiary /,pɛnɪ'tɛnʃəri/ *n Eccl.* penitenciaria, *f*; casa de corrección, *f*; penitenciaria, *f*, presidio, *m*; cárcel modelo, *f*, *a* penitenciario

penknife /'pɛn,naif/ *n* cortaplumas, *m*

penmanship /'pɛnmən,ʃɪp/ *n* caligrafía, *f*

pennant /'pɛnənt/ *n Naut.* gallardete, *m*; banderola, *f*; (ensign) insignia, bandera, *f*

penniless /'pɛnɪlɪs/ *a* sin un penique, sin blanca; indigente, pobre de solemnidad. **to leave p.,** dejar en la miseria; *Inf.* dejar sin camisa

pennilessness /'pɛnɪlɪsnɪs/ *n* falta de dinero, extrema pobreza, *f*

penning /'pɛnɪŋ/ *n* escritura, *f*; (drawing up) redacción, *f*; (of bulls, etc.) acorralamiento, *m*

pennon /'pɛnən/ *n* pendón, *m*, banderola, *f*; (ensign) bandera, insignia, *f*

Pennsylvanian /,pɛnsəl'veinyən/ *a and n* pensilvano (-na)

penny /'pɛni/ *n* de un centavo, penique, *m*; perra gorda, *f*. —*a* de un penique. **p.-a-liner,** gacetillero, *m*. **p. dreadful,** folletín, *m*, novela por entregas, *f*. **p.-in-the-slot machine,** tragaperras, *m*

pennyworth /'pɛni,wɜrθ/ *n* penique, valor de un penique, *m*

pension /'pɛnʃən/ *n* pensión, *f*; *Mil.* retiro, *m*; (grant) beca, *f*; (boardinghouse) pensión de familia, *f*. —*vt* pensionar, dar una pensión (a); (with off) jubilar. **old age p.,** pensión para la vejez, *f*. **retirement p.,** pensión vitalicia, *f*

pensioner /'pɛnʃənər/ *n* pensionista, *mf*; (*Mil.* and *Nav.*) inválido, *m*

pensive /'pɛnsɪv/ *a* pensativo, meditabundo; cabizbajo, triste

pensively /'pɛnsɪvli/ *adv* pensativamente; tristemente

pensiveness /'pɛnsɪvnɪs/ *n* reflexión, meditación profunda, *f*; tristeza, melancolía, *f*

pentagon /'pɛntə,gɒn/ *n* pentágono, *m*

Pentateuch /'pɛntə,tuk/ *n* pentateuco, *m*

Pentecost /'pɛntɪ,kɒst/ *n* Pentecostés, *m*, Pascua, *f*

pentecostal /,pɛntɪ'kɒstḷ/ *a* de Pentecostés, pascual

penthouse /'pɛnt,haus/ *n* cobertizo, tinglado, *m*, tejavana, *f*

pent-up /pɛnt 'ʌp/ *a* encerrado; enjaulado; (of emotion) reprimido

penultimate /pɪ'nʌltəmɪt/ *a* penúltimo. —*n* penúltimo, *m*

penurious /pə'nʊriəs/ *a* pobre; escaso; (stingy) tacaño, avaro

penury /'pɛnyəri/ *n* penuria, *f*

peony /'piəni/ *n* peonía, *f*, saltaojos, *m*, rosa albardera, rosa montés, *f*

people /'pipəl/ *n* pueblo, *m*; nación, *f*; gente, *f*; personas, *f pl*; (used disparagingly, mob) populacho, vulgo, *m*; (inhabitants) habitantes, *m pl*; (subjects) súbditos, *m pl*; (relations) parientes, *m pl*; familia, *f*. —*vt* poblar. **little p.,** (children) gente menuda, *f*. **respectable p.,** gente de bien, *f*. **the p. of Burgos,** los habitantes de Burgos. **P. say,** Se dice, La gente dice. **Very few p. think as you do,** Hay muy pocas personas que opinan como Vd. **How are your p.** (family)? ¿Cómo están los de tu casa? ¿Cómo está tu familia? **"People Working"** «Trabajadores»

peopling /'piplɪŋ/ *n* población, *f*; colonización, *f*

pep /pɛp/ *n Inf.* energía, *f*, ánimo, *m*. **p. talk,** discurso estimulante, *m*. **p. up,** animar

Pepin the Short /'pɛpɪn/ Pipino el Breve

peplum /'pɛpləm/ *n* peplo, *m*

pepper /'pɛpər/ *n* pimienta, *f*; (plant) pimentero, pimiento, *m*, *vt* sazonar con pimienta; (pelt) acribillar; (with questions) disparar; (a literary work with quotations, etc.) salpimentar. **black p.,** pimienta negra, *f*. **red p.,** pimiento, *m*; (cayenne) pimentón, *m*. **p.-castor,** pimentero, *m*

peppercorn /'pɛpər,kɔrn/ *n* grano de pimienta, *m*

peppermint /'pɛpər,mɪnt/ *n* menta, *f*. **p. drop,** pastilla de menta, *f*

peppery /'pɛpəri/ *a* picante; (irascible) colérico, irascible

pepsin /'pɛpsɪn/ *n Chem.* pepsina, *f*

peptic /'pɛptɪk/ *a* péptico

per /pər/ *unstressed* pər/ *prep* por. **ninety miles per hour,** noventa millas por hora. **ten pesetas per dozen,** diez pesetas la docena. **$60 per annum,** sesenta dólares al año. **per cent.,** por ciento

perambulate /pər'æmbyə,leit/ *vt* recorrer

perambulator /pər'æmbyə,leitər/ *n* cochecito para niños, *m*

percale /pər'keil/ *n* percal, *m*

percaline /,pɔrkə'lin/ *n* percalina, *f*

perceive /pər'siv/ *vt* percibir, comprender, darse cuenta de; percibir, discernir

percentage /pər'sɛntɪdʒ/ *n* tanto por ciento, *m*; porcentaje, *m*

perceptible /pər'sɛptəbəl/ *a* perceptible, visible; sensible

perceptibly /pər'sɛptəbli/ *adv* visiblemente; sensiblemente

perception /pər'sɛpʃən/ *n* percepción, *f*; sensibilidad, *f*

perceptive /pər'sɛptɪv/ *a* perceptivo

perch /pɔrtʃ/ *n Ichth.* perca, *f*; (for birds) percha, *f*; (measure) pértiga, *f*. —*vi* posarse (en o sobre). —*vt* posar (en o sobre)

percolate /'pɔrkə,leit/ *vi* filtrar; *Fig.* penetrar. —*vt* filtrar, colar

percolation /,pɔrkə'leiʃən/ *n* filtración, *f*

percolator /'pɔrkə,leitər/ *n* filtro, *m*. **coffee p.,** colador de café, *m*

percussion /pər'kʌʃən/ *n* percusión, *f*; choque, *m*. **p. cap,** fulminante, *m*. **p. instrument,** instrumento de percusión, *m*

perdition /pər'dɪʃən/ *n* perdición, *f*; ruina, *f*

peregrination /,pɛrɪgrə'neiʃən/ *n* peregrinación, *f*

peremptorily /pə'rɛmptərəli/ *adv* perentoriamente

peremptoriness /pə'rɛmptərɪnɪs/ *n* perentoriedad, *f*

peremptory /pə'rɛmptəri/ *a* perentorio; (of manner, etc.) imperioso, autoritario

perennial /pə'rɛniəl/ *a Bot.* vivaz; perenne; eterno, perpetuo. —*n* planta vivaz, *f*

perennially /pə'rɛniəli/ *adv* perennemente

perfect /*a.*, *n.* 'pɔrfɪkt; *v.* pər'fɛkt/ *a* perfecto; (of a work) acabado; completo. —*n Gram.* (tiempo) perfecto, *m*. —*vt* perfeccionar; (oneself) perfeccionarse. **to have a p. knowledge of...,** conocer a fondo... **They are p. strangers to me,** Me son completamente desconocidos

perfectible /pər'fɛktəbəl/ *a* perfectible

perfecting /pər'fɛktɪŋ/ *n* perfeccionamiento, *m*; terminación, *f*

perfection /pər'fɛkʃən/ *n* perfección, *f*; excelencia, *f*. **to p.,** a la perfección, a las mil maravillas

perfectionist /pər'fɛkʃənɪst/ *n* perfeccionista, *mf*

perfidious /pər'fɪdiəs/ *a* pérfido

perfidy /'pɔrfɪdi/ *n* perfidia, *f*

perforate /'pɔrfə,reit/ *vt* perforar, agujerear

perforating /'pɔrfə,reitɪŋ/ *a* perforador

perforation /,pɔrfə'reiʃən/ *n* perforación, *f*; agujero, *m*

perforce /pər'fɔrs/ *adv* a la fuerza, forzosamente

perform /pər'fɔrm/ *vt* hacer; poner por obra, llevar a cabo; desempeñar, cumplir; ejercer; (a piece of music, etc.) ejecutar; realizar; (a play) representar, dar; (a part in a play) desempeñar (el papel de...); (Divine Service) oficiar. —*vi Theat.* trabajar, representar un papel; (a musical instrument) tocar; (sing) cantar; (of animals) hacer trucos

performable /pər'fɔrməbəl/ a hacedero, practicable, ejecutable; *Theat.* que puede representarse; *Mus.* tocable

performance /pər'fɔrməns/ n ejecución, realización, f; desempeño, ejercicio, m; cumplimiento, m; acción, f; hazaña, f; (work) obra, f; *Theat.* función, representación, f; (*Theat.* acting of a part) interpretación, f; *Mus.* ejecución, f; *Mech.* potencia, f. **first p.,** *Theat.* estreno, m

performer /pər'fɔrmər/ n *Mus.* ejecutante, mf, músico, m; *Theat.* actor (-triz), representante, mf; artista, mf

performing /pər'fɔrmɪŋ/ a (of animals) sabio. **p. dog,** perro sabio, m

perfume /n. 'pɜrfyum; v. pər'fyum/ n perfume, m; fragancia, f; aroma, m. —vt perfumar; embalsamar, aromatizar, llenar con fragancia. **p. burner,** perfumador, m

perfumer /pər'fyumər/ n perfumista, mf

perfumery /pər'fyuməri/ n perfumería, f

perfuming /'pɜrfyumɪŋ/ n acción de perfumar, f, a que perfuma

perfunctorily /pər'fʌŋktərəli/ adv perfunctoriamente, sin cuidado; superficialmente

perfunctoriness /pər'fʌŋktərɪnɪs/ n descuido, m, negligencia, f; superficialidad, f

perfunctory /pər'fʌŋktəri/ a perfunctorio, negligente; superficial; ligero, de cumplido

pergola /'pɜrgələ/ n emparrado, cenador, m

perhaps /pər'hæps/ adv quizá, quizás(s), tal vez

peril /'perəl/ n peligro, m; riesgo, m. —vt poner en peligro; arriesgar. **at one's p.,** a su riesgo. **in p.,** en peligro

perilous /'perələs/ a peligroso, arriesgado

perimeter /pə'rɪmɪtər/ n perímetro, m

perineum /,perə'niəm/ n *Anat.* perineo, m

period /'pɪəriəd/ n período, m; época, f; edad, f; tiempo, m; duración, f; término, plazo, m; *Gram.* período, m; (full stop) punto final, m; *Med.* menstruación, regla, f. **p. furniture,** muebles de época, m pl

periodic /,pɪəri'ɒdɪk/ a periódico

periodical /,pɪəri'ɒdɪkəl/ a periódico. —n publicación periódica, revista, f

periodicity /,pɪəriə'dɪsɪti/ n periodicidad, f

peripatetic /,perəpə'tetɪk/ a peripatético

peripheral /pə'rɪfərəl/ a periférico

periphery /pə'rɪfəri/ n periferia, f

periphrastic /,perə'fræstɪk/ a perifrástico

periscope /'perə,skoup/ n periscopio, m

perish /'perɪʃ/ vi perecer; marchitarse; desaparecer, acabar. **to be perished with cold,** estar muerto de frío

perishable /'perɪʃəbəl/ a perecedero, frágil

peritoneum /,perɪtṇ'iəm/ n peritoneo, m

peritonitis /,perɪtṇ'aitɪs/ n peritonitis, f

periwig /'peri,wɪg/ n peluca, f

periwinkle /'peri,wɪŋkəl/ n *Zool.* caracol marino, m; *Bot.* vincapervinca, f

perjure /'pɜrdʒər/ vt perjurar. **to p. oneself,** perjurarse

perjurer /'pɜrdʒərər/ n perjuro (-ra); perjurador (-ra)

perjury /'pɜrdʒəri/ n perjurio, m. **to commit p.,** jurar en falso, perjurar

perkiness /'pɜrkinɪs/ n desenvoltura, gallardía, f, despejo, m

perk (up) /pɜrk/ vi levantar la cabeza; recobrar sus bríos, alzar la cabeza; sacar la cabeza

perky /'pɜrki/ a desenvuelto, gallardo; coquetón; atrevido; (gay) alegre

permanence /'pɜrmənəns/ n permanencia, f; estabilidad, f

permanent /'pɜrmənənt/ a permanente; estable; (of posts, etc.) fijo. **p. wave,** ondulación permanente, f. **p. way,** *Rail.* vía, f

permanganate /pər'mæŋgə,neit/ n permanganato, m

permeability /,pɜrmiə'bɪlɪti/ n permeabilidad, f

permeable /'pɜrmiəbəl/ a permeable

permeate /'pɜrmi,eit/ vt penetrar; impregnar; *Fig.* infiltrar (en)

permeation /,pɜrmi'eiʃən/ n penetración, f; impregnación, f; *Fig.* infiltración, f

permissible /pər'mɪsəbəl/ a permisible, admisible; lícito

permission /pər'mɪʃən/ n permiso, m, licencia, f

permissive /pər'mɪsɪv/ a permisivo, tolerado; (optional) facultativo

permit /v / pər'mɪt; n 'pɜrmɪt/ vt permitir; dar permiso (a), dejar; tolerar, sufrir; admitir. —n permiso, m; licencia, f; pase, m. **Will you p. me to smoke?** ¿Me permites fumar?

permutation /,pɜrmyu'teiʃən/ n permutación, f

permute /pər'myut/ vt permutar

pernicious /pər'nɪʃəs/ a pernicioso. **p. anemia,** anemia perniciosa, f

perniciousness /pər'nɪʃəsnɪs/ n perniciosidad, f

pernickety /pər'nɪkɪti/ a tiquismiquis

peroration /,perə'reiʃən/ n peroración, f

peroxide /pə'rɒksaid/ n peróxido, m

perpendicular /,pɜrpən'dɪkyələr/ a perpendicular. —n perpendicular, f

perpendicularity /,pɜrpən,dɪkyə'lærɪti/ n perpendicularidad, f

perpendicularly /,pɜrpən'dɪkyələrli/ adv perpendicularmente

perpetrate /'pɜrpɪ,treit/ vt *Law.* perpetrar; cometer

perpetration /,pɜrpɪ'treiʃən/ n *Law.* perpetración, f; comisión, f

perpetrator /'pɜrpɪ,treitər/ n el, m, (f, la) que comete; *Law.* autor (-ra); perpetrador (-ra)

perpetual /pər'petʃuəl/ a perpetuo, perdurable, eterno; incesante, constante; (life-long) perpetuo

perpetually /pər'petʃuəli/ adv perpetuamente; sin cesar; continuamente; constantemente

perpetuate /pər'petʃu,eit/ vt perpetuar, eternizar; inmortalizar

perpetuation /pər,petʃu'eiʃən/ n perpetuación, f

perpetuity /,pɜrpɪ'tuiti/ n perpetuidad, f. **in p.,** para siempre

perplex /pər'pleks/ vt dejar perplejo, aturdir, confundir; embrollar

perplexed /pər'plekst/ a perplejo, irresoluto; confuso; (of questions, etc.) complicado, intrincado

perplexedly /pər'pleksɪdli/ adv perplejamente

perplexing /pər'pleksɪŋ/ a difícil; complicado; confuso

perplexity /pər'pleksɪti/ n perplejidad, f; confusión, f

perquisites /'pɜrkwəzɪts/ n pl emolumentos, m pl; gajes, percances, m pl; (tips) propinas, f pl

persecute /'pɜrsɪ,kyut/ vt perseguir; importunar, molestar

persecution /,pɜrsɪ'kyuʃən/ n persecución, f

persecutor /'pɜrsɪ,kyutər/ n perseguidor (-ra)

perseverance /,pɜrsə'vɪərəns/ n perseverancia, f

persevere /,pɜrsə'vɪər/ vi perseverar

persevering /,pɜrsə'vɪərɪŋ/ a perseverante

perseveringly /,pɜrsə'vɪərɪŋli/ adv con perseverancia, perseverantemente

Persia /'pɜrʒə/ (la) Persia, f

Persian /'pɜrʒən/ a persa; de Persia; pérsico. —n persa, mf; (language) persa, m. **P. blinds,** persianas, f pl. **P. cat,** gato (-ta) de Angora

persiennes /,pɜrsi'enz/ n pl persianas, f pl

persist /pər'sɪst/ vi persistir; persistir (en), empeñarse (en), obstinarse (en)

persistence /pər'sɪstəns/ n persistencia, f

persistent /pər'sɪstənt/ a persistente

persistently /pər'sɪstəntli/ adv con persistencia, persistentemente

person /'pɜrsən/ n persona, f. **first p.,** *Gram.* primera persona, f. **in p.,** en persona. **no p.,** nadie

personable /'pɜrsənəbəl/ a bien parecido

personage /'pɜrsənɪdʒ/ n personaje, m

personal /'pɜrsənəl/ a personal; íntimo; particular; en persona; (movable) mueble. **He is to make a p. appearance,** Va a estar presente en persona. **p. column,** (in a newspaper) columna de los suspiros, f. **p. equation,** ecuación personal, f. **p. estate,** (goods) bienes muebles, m pl

personality /ˌpɜrsə'næləti/ n personalidad, f; (insult) personalismo, m. **dual p.,** conciencia doble, f

personate /'pɜrsə,neit/ vt (in a play) hacer el papel de; (impersonate) hacerse pasar por

personification /pər,sɒnəfɪ'keiʃən/ n personificación, f

personify /pər'sɒnə,fai/ vt personificar

personnel /ˌpɜrsə'nɛl/ n personal, m

perspective /pər'spɛktɪv/ n perspectiva, f, a en perspectiva

perspicacious /ˌpɜrspɪ'keiʃəs/ a perspicaz, clarividente, sagaz

perspicacity /ˌpɜrspɪ'kæsɪti/ n perspicacia, clarividencia, sagacidad, f

perspicuity /ˌpɜrspɪ'kyuɪti/ n perspicuidad, claridad, lucidez, f

perspicuous /pər'spɪkyuəs/ a perspicuo, claro

perspiration /ˌpɜrspə'reiʃən/ n sudor, m

perspire /pər'spaiᵊr/ vi sudar, transpirar

persuadable /pər'sweidəbəl/ a persuasible

persuade /pər'sweid/ vt persuadir; inducir (a), instar (a), mover (a), inclinar (a)

persuasion /pər'sweiʒən/ n persuasión, f; persuasiva, f; opinión, f; creencia, f; religión, f; secta, f

persuasive /pər'sweisɪv/ a persuasivo. —n persuasión, f; aliciente, atractivo, m

persuasively /pər'sweisɪvli/ adv de un modo persuasivo, persuasivamente

persuasiveness /pər'sweisɪvnɪs/ n persuasiva, f

pert /pɜrt/ a petulante; respondón, desparpajado

pertain /pər'tein/ vi pertenecer (a); tocar (a), incumbir (a), convenir (a); estar relacionado (con)

pertinacious /ˌpɜrtṇ'eiʃəs/ a pertinaz

pertinaciously /ˌpɜrtṇ'eiʃəsli/ adv con pertinacia

pertinacity /ˌpɜrtṇ'æsɪti/ n pertinacia, f

pertinence /'pɜrtṇəns/ n pertinencia, f

pertinent /'pɜrtṇənt/ a pertinente, atinado

pertinently /'pɜrtṇəntli/ adv atinadamente

pertly /'pɜrtli/ adv con petulancia; con descaro

pertness /'pɜrtnɪs/ n petulancia, f; desparpajo, descaro, m

perturb /pər'tɜrb/ vt perturbar, agitar, turbar, inquietar

perturbation /ˌpɜrtər'beiʃən/ n perturbación, agitación, inquietud, f; confusión, f; desorden, m

perturbed /pər'tɜrbd/ a perturbado, agitado, ansioso, intranquilo

perturbing /pər'tɜrbɪŋ/ a perturbador, inquietador

Peru /pə'ru/ el Perú

peruke /pə'ruk/ n peluca, f

perusal /pə'ruzəl/ n lectura, f; examen, m

peruse /pə'ruz/ vt leer con cuidado, estudiar, examinar

Peruvian /pə'ruvi ən/ a and n peruano (-na)

pervade /pər'veid/ vt penetrar; llenar, saturar; difundirse por; reinar en

pervasion /pər'veiʒən/ n penetración, f

pervasive /pər'veisɪv/ a penetrante

perverse /pər'vɜrs/ a (wicked) perverso, depravado; obstinado; travieso; intratable

perversion /pər'vɜrʒən/ n perversión, f

perversity /pər'vɜrsɪti/ n (wickedness) perversidad, f; obstinacia, f; travesura, f

perversive /pər'vɜrsɪv/ a perversivo

pervert /pər'vɜrt/ vt pervertir; (words, etc.) torcer, tergiversar

pervious /'pɜrviəs/ a penetrable; permeable

pessary /'pɛsəri/ n Surg. pesario, m

pessimism /'pɛsə,mɪzəm/ n pesimismo, m

pessimist /'pɛsəmɪst/ n pesimista, mf

pessimistic /ˌpɛsə'mɪstɪk/ a pesimista

pessimistically /ˌpɛsə'mɪstɪkli/ adv con pesimismo

pest /pɛst/ n insecto nocivo, m; animal dañino, m; parásito, m; (pestilence) peste, f; Fig. plaga, f; (person) mosca, f

pester /'pɛstər/ vt importunar, molestar, incomodar.
to p. constantly, Inf. no dejar a sol ni a sombra

pestering /'pɛstərɪŋ/ n importunaciones, f pl

pestilence /'pɛstḷəns/ n pestilencia, peste, f; plaga, f

pestilential /ˌpɛstḷ'ɛnʃəl/ a pestilente, pestífero; pernicioso

pestle /'pɛsəl/ n mano de mortero, f, vt pistar, machacar, majar

pet /pɛt/ n animal doméstico, m; niño (-ña) mimado (-da); favorito (-ta); (dear) querido (-da); (peevishness) despecho, malhumor, m. —vt acariciar; (spoil) mimar. **to be a great pet,** ser un gran favorito

petal /'pɛtḷ/ n pétalo, m, hoja, f

Peter /'pitər/ n Pedro, m. **blue P.,** bandera de salida, f. **Peter's pence,** los diezmos de San Pedro

peter (out) /'pitər/ vi desaparecer; agotarse

petition /pə'tɪʃən/ n petición, f; súplica, f; instancia, solicitud, f; memorial, m. —vt suplicar; pedir, demandar; dirigir un memorial (a). **to file a p.,** elevar una instancia

petitioner /pə'tɪʃənər/ n peticionario (-ia)

Petrarchan /pɪ'trɑrkən/ a petrarquista

petrel /'pɛtrəl/ n petrel, m

petrifaction /ˌpɛtrə'fækʃən/ n petrificación, f

petrify /'pɛtrə,fai/ vt petrificar; Inf. dejar seco. **to become petrified,** petrificarse

petrol /'pɛtrəl/ n bencina, gasolina, f. —a de gasolina, de bencina. **to run out of p.,** tener una pana de bencina. **p. gauge,** indicador del nivel de gasolina, m. **p. pump,** surtidor de gasolina, m. **p. station,** puesto de bencina, m, estación de servicio, f. **p. tank,** depósito de bencina, m

petroleum /pə'trouliəm/ n petróleo, m. —a petrolero; de petróleo. **p. works,** refinería de petróleo, f

petrology /pɪ'trɒlədʒi/ n petrografía, f

petrous /'pɛtrəs/ a pétreo

petticoat /'pɛti,kout/ n enagua, f; pl **petticoats,** (slang) faldas, f pl. —a de faldas, de mujeres; de mujer

pettifogger /'pɛti,fɒgər/ n (lawyer) picapleitos, m, rábula, mf; (quibbler) sofista, mf

pettifogging /'pɛti,fɒgɪŋ/ a charlatán, mezquino, trivial

pettiness /'pɛtinɪs/ n trivialidad, insignificancia, f; pequeñez, f; mezquindad, f; ruindad, bajeza, f

petty /'pɛti/ a trivial, sin importancia, insignificante; inferior; pequeño; mezquino; ruin; bajo. **p. cash,** gastos menores de caja, m pl. **p. expense,** gasto menudo, m. **p. officer,** suboficial, m. **p. thief,** ratero (-ra)

petulance /'pɛtʃələns/ n mal humor, m, displicencia, irritabilidad, f

petulant /'pɛtʃələnt/ a malhumorado, displicente, enojadizo, irritable

petulantly /'pɛtʃələntli/ adv displicentemente, con mal humor

petunia /pɪ'tunyə/ n petunia, f

pew /pyu/ n banco (de iglesia), m. **p.-opener,** sacristán, m

pewter /'pyutər/ n peltre, m, a de peltre

phalange /'fæləndʒ/ n falange, f

phalanx /'feilæŋks/ n falange, f

phallic /'fælɪk/ a fálico

phallus /'fæləs/ n falo, m

phantasmagoria /fæn,tæzmə'gɔriə/ n fantasmagoría, f

phantasmagoric /fæn,tæzmə'gɔrɪk/ a fantasmagórico

phantom /'fæntəm/ n fantasma, espectro, m; sombra, ficción, f; visión, f

Pharisaical /ˌfærə'seiikəl/ a farisaico

Pharisee /'færə,si/ n fariseo, m

pharmaceutical /ˌfɑrmə'sutɪkəl/ a farmacéutico; n producto farmacéutico, m

pharmacist /'fɑrməsɪst/ n farmacéutico, m

pharmacological /ˌfɑrməkə'lɒdʒəkəl/ a farmacológico

pharmacologist /ˌfɑrmə'kɒlədʒɪst/ n farmacólogo, m

pharmacology /ˌfɑrmə'kɒlədʒi/ n farmacología, f

pharmacopeia /ˌfɑrmə'koupiə/ n farmacopea, f

pharmacy /'fɑrməsi/ n farmacia, f

pharyngeal /fə'rɪndʒiəl/ a faríngeo

pharyngitis /ˌfærɪn'dʒaitɪs/ n faringitis, f

pharynx /'færɪŋks/ n faringe, f

phase /feiz/ n fase, f; aspecto, m; Astron. fase, f

pheasant /'fɛzənt/ n faisán, m. **hen p.,** faisana, f. **p. shooting,** caza de faisanes, f

phenic /'finɪk/ a fénico

phenol /'finɔl/ n fenol, m
phenomenal /fɪ'nɒmənl/ a fenomenal
phenomenon /fɪ'nɒmə,nɒn/ n fenómeno, m
phial /'faiəl/ n redoma, f
philander /fɪ'lændər/ vi galantear
philanderer /fɪ'lændərər/ n Tenorio, galanteador, m
philandering /fɪ'lændərɪŋ/ n galanteo, m
philanthropic /,fɪlən'θrɒpɪk/ a filantrópico
philanthropist /fɪ'lænθrəpɪst/ n filántropo, m
philanthropy /fɪ'lænθrəpi/ n filantropía, f
philatelic /,fɪlə'tɛlɪk/ a filatélico
philatelist /fɪ'lætlɪst/ n filatelista, mf
philately /fɪ'lætli/ n filatelia, f
philharmonic /,fɪlhɑr'mɒnɪk/ a filarmónico
philippic /fɪ'lɪpɪk/ n filípica, f
Philippine /'fɪlə,pin/ a and n filipino (-na)
Philippines, the /'fɪlə,pinz/ las (Islas) Filipinas, f pl
Philistine /'fɪlə,stin/ a and n filisteo (-ea)
philological /,fɪlə'lɒdʒɪkəl/ a filológico
philologist /fɪ'lɒlədʒɪst/ n filólogo, m
philology /fɪ'lɒlədʒi/ n filología, f
philosopher /fɪ'lɒsəfər/ n filósofo, m. **philosopher's stone,** piedra filosofal, f
philosophical /,fɪlə'sɒfɪkəl/ a filosófico
philosophize /fɪ'lɒsə,faiz/ vi filosofar
philosophy /fɪ'lɒsəfi/ n filosofía, f. **moral p.,** filosofía moral, f. **natural p.,** filosofía natural, f
philter /'fɪltər/ n filtro, m
phlebitis /flə'baitis/ n flebitis, f
phlebotomist /flə'bɒtəmɪst/ n sangrador, flebotomiano, m
phlebotomy /flə'bɒtəmi/ n flebotomía, f
phlegm /flɛm/ n flema, f
phlegmatic /flɛg'mætɪk/ a flemático
phlox /flɒks/ n flox, m
Phoenician /fɪ'nɪʃən/ a and n fenicio (-ia)
phoenix /'finɪks/ n fénix, f
phonetic /fə'nɛtɪk/ a fonético
phoneticist /fe'nɛtəsɪst/ n fonetista, mf
phonetics /fə'nɛtɪks, fou-/ n fonética, f
phonograph /'founə,græf/ n fonógrafo, m
phonological /,fɒn|ɒdʒɪkəl/ a fonológico
phonology /fə'nɒlədʒi/ n fonología, f
phony /'founi/ a falso; espurio. **p. war,** guerra tonta, guerra falsa, f
phosphate /'fɒsfeit/ n fosfato, m
phosphoresce /,fɒsfə'rɛs/ vi fosforecer, ser fosforescente
phosphorescence /,fɒsfə'rɛsəns/ n fosforescencia, f
phosphorescent /,fɒsfə'rɛsənt/ a fosforescente
phosphoric /fɒs'fɔrɪk/ a fosfórico
phosphorus /'fɒsfərəs/ n fósforo, m
photo /'foutou/ n foto, f
photochemistry /,foutou'kɛməstri/ n fotoquímica, f
photogenic /,foutə'dʒɛnɪk/ a fotogénico
photograph /'foutə,græf/ n fotografía, f. —vt fotografiar, retratar. **to have one's p. taken,** hacerse retratar
photographer /fə'tɒgrəfər/ n fotógrafo, m
photographic /,foutə'græfɪk/ a fotográfico
photography /fə'tɒgrəfi/ n fotografía, f
photogravure /,foutəgrə'vyʊr/ n fotograbado, m
photostat /'foutə,stæt/ n fotostato, m
photosynthesis /,foutə'sɪnθəsɪs/ n fotosíntesis, f
phrase /freiz/ n frase, f; Mus. frase musical, f. —vt expresar, frasear; redactar. **p.-book,** libro de frases, m
phraseology /,freizi'ɒlədʒi/ n fraseología, f
phrasing /'freizɪŋ/ n (drawing up) redacción, f; (style) estilo, m; Mus. frases, f pl
phrenetic /frɪ'nɛtɪk/ a frenético
Phrygian /'frɪdʒiən/ a and n frigio (-ia)
Phrygian cap n gorro frigio, m
phthisis /'θaisɪs/ n tisis, f
phylactery /fɪ'læktəri/ n filactria, f
phylloxera /fɪ'lɒksərə/ n filoxera, f
physical /'fɪzɪkəl/ a físico. **p. fitness,** buen estado físico, m. **p. geography,** geografía física, f. **p. jerks,** ejercicios físicos, m pl. **p. sciences,** ciencias físicas, f pl. **p. training,** educación física, f
physician /fɪ'zɪʃən/ n médico (-ca)

physicist /'fɪzəsɪst/ n físico, m
physics /'fɪzɪks/ n física, f
physiognomist /,fɪzi'ɒgnəmɪst/ n fisonomista, mf
physiognomy /,fɪzi'ɒgnəmi/ n fisonomía, f
physiological /,fɪziə'lɒdʒɪkəl/ a fisiológico
physiologist /,fɪzi'ɒlədʒɪst/ n fisiólogo, m
physiology /,fɪzi'ɒlədʒi/ n fisiología, f
physiotherapy /,fɪziou'θɛrəpi/ n fisioterapia, f
physique /fɪ'zik/ n físico, m
pianist /pi'ænɪst, 'piənɪst/ n pianista, mf
pianola /,piə'noulə/ n piano mecánico, m
piano, pianoforte /pi'ænou; pi'ænə,fɔrt/ n piano, m. **baby grand p.,** piano de media cola, m. **grand p.,** piano de cola, m. **upright p.,** piano vertical, m. **p. maker,** fabricante de pianos, m. **p. stool,** taburete de piano, m. **p. tuner,** afinador de pianos, m
picaresque /,pɪkə'rɛsk/ a picaresco
piccolo /'pɪkə,lou/ n flautín, m
pick /pɪk/ n (tool) pico, zapapico, m; (mattock) piqueta, f; (choice) selección, f; derecho de elección, m; (best) lo mejor, lo más escogido; (Fig. cream) flor, nata, f. **tooth-p.,** mondadientes, m. **p.-a-back,** sobre los hombros, a cuestas. **p.-ax,** zapapico, m, alcotana, f. **p.-me-up,** tónico, m; trago, m
pick /pɪk/ vt (with a pick-ax, make a hole) picar; (pluck, pick up) coger; (remove) sacar; (clean) limpiar; (one's teeth) mondarse (los dientes); (one's nose) hurgarse (las narices); (a bone) roer; (a lock) abrir con ganzúa; (a pocket) bolsear, robar del bolsillo; (peck) picotear; (choose) escoger; (a quarrel) buscar. —vi (steal) hurtar, robar; (nibble) picar. **I have a bone to p. with you,** Tengo que ajustar unas cuentas contigo. **Take your p.!** ¡Escoja! **to p. and choose,** mostrarse difícil. **to p. to pieces,** Fig. criticar severamente. **to p. one's way through,** abrirse camino entre; andar con precaución por; andar a tientas por. **to p. off,** coger; arrancar; quitar; (shoot) disparar; fusilar. **to p. out,** entresacar; escoger; (recognize) reconocer; (understand) llegar a comprender; (a tune) tocar de oídas; (a song) cantar de oídas; (of colours) contrastar, resaltar. **to p. up,** vt (ground, etc.) romper con pico; coger; tomar; recoger; (raise) levantar, alzar; (information, etc.) cobrar, adquirir; (a living) ganar; (make friends with) trabar amistad con; (recover) recobrar; (find) encontrar, hallar; (buy) comprar; (learn) aprender; (a wireless message) interceptar; (a radio station) oír, tener. —vi recobrar la salud; reponerse; mejorar. —n Mech. recobro, m
picket /'pɪkɪt/ n estaca, f; (Mil. and during strikes) piquete, m. —vt cercar con estacas; poner piquetes ante (or alrededor de); poner de guardia; estacionar
picking /'pɪkɪŋ/ n (gathering) recolección, f; (choosing) selección, f; (pilfering) robo, m; pl pickings, desperdicios, m pl; (perquisites) gajes, m pl; ganancias, f pl
pickle /'pɪkəl/ n (solution) escabeche, m; (vegetable, etc.) encurtido, m; (plight) apuro, m; (child) diablillo, m. —vt encurtir, escabechar
picklock /'pɪk,lɒk/ n (thief and instrument) ganzúa, f
pickpocket /'pɪk,pɒkɪt/ n carterista, mf ratero (-ra)
picnic /'pɪknɪk/ n partida de campo, jira, f, picnic, m. —vi llevar la merienda al campo, hacer un picnic
picnicker /'pɪknɪkər/ n excursionista, mf
pictorial /pɪk'tɔriəl/ a pictórico; ilustrado. —n revista ilustrada, f
pictorially /pɪk'tɔriəli/ adv pictóricamente; en grabados; por imágenes
picture /'pɪktʃər/ n cuadro, m; (of a person) retrato, m; imagen, f; (illustration) grabado, m, lámina, f; fotografía, f; (outlook) perspectiva, f; idea, f. —vt pintar; describir; imaginar. **to go to the pictures,** ir al cine. **motion p.,** película, f. **talking p.,** película sonora, f. **p. book,** libro con láminas, m. **p. frame,** marco, m. **p. gallery,** museo de pinturas, m; galería de pinturas, f. **p. hat,** pamela, f. **p. palace,** cine, m. **p. postcard,** tarjeta postal, f. **p. restorer,** restaurador de cuadros, m. **p. writing,** pictografía, f
picturesque /,pɪktʃə'rɛsk/ a pintoresco
picturesqueness /,pɪktʃə'rɛsknɪs/ n carácter pintoresco, m, lo pintoresco; pintoresquismo, m
pie /pai/ n (savoury) empanada, f; (sweet) pastel, m, torta, f; (of meat) pastelón, m; Print. pastel, m. **apple**

pie, torta de manzanas, *f.* **to eat humble pie,** bajar las orejas. **to have a finger in the pie,** meter baza

piebald /'paɪˌbɔld/ *a* pío; tordo

piece /pis/ *n* pedazo, *m;* trozo, *m;* parte, porción, *f;* (literary, artistic work, coin, of fabric, at chess, etc. and slang) pieza, *f;* (of luggage) bulto, *m;* (of paper) hoja, *f;* (of ground) parcela, *f;* (of money) moneda, *f, vt* remendar; unir, juntar. **a p. of advice,** un consejo. **a p. of bread,** un pedazo de pan; una rebanada de pan. **a p. of folly,** un acto de locura. **a p. of furniture,** un mueble. **a p. of insolence,** una insolencia. **a p. of news,** una noticia. **a p. of paper,** un papel, una hoja de papel, una cuartilla. **a p. of poetry,** una poesía. **Peter has a five-shilling p.,** Pedro tiene una moneda de cinco chelines. **to break in pieces,** *vt* hacer pedazos, romper. —*vi* hacerse pedazos, romperse. **to come or fall to pieces,** deshacerse; (of machines) desarmarse. **to cut in pieces,** cortar en pedazos; (an army) destrozar. **to give a p. of one's mind (to),** decir cuatro verdades (a), decir cuántas son cinco (a). **to go to pieces,** (of persons) hacerse pedazos. **to take to pieces,** (a machine) desmontar; deshacer. **to tear or pull to pieces,** hacer pedazos, despedazar; desgarrar. **p. goods,** géneros en piezas, *m pl.* **p.-work,** trabajo a destajo, *m.* **to do p.-work,** trabajar a destajo. **p.-worker,** destajista, *mf*

piecemeal /'pisˌmil/ *adv* en pedazos; a remiendos; en detalle; poco a poco

piecrust /'paɪˌkrʌst/ *n* pasta, *f*

pied /paɪd/ *a* bicolor; abigarrado, de varios colores

pier /pɪər/ *n* (jetty) dique, *m;* embarcadero, *m;* malecón, *m;* (of a bridge) pila, *f;* (pillar) columna, *f;* (between windows, etc.) entrepaño, *m.* **p.-glass,** espejo de cuerpo entero, *m.* **p. head,** punta del dique, *f.* **p. table,** consola, *f*

pierce /pɪərs/ *vt* penetrar; (of sorrow, etc.) traspasar, herir; (bore) agujerear, taladrar. —*vi* penetrar

pierced ear /pɪərst/ *n* oreja perforada, *f*

piercing /'pɪərsɪŋ/ *a* penetrante; (of the wind, etc.) cortante; (of the voice, etc.) agudo. —*n* penetración, *f*

piercingly /'pɪərsɪŋli/ *adv* de un modo penetrante; agudamente

pietism /'paɪɪˌtɪzəm/ *n* pietismo, *m*

pietist /'paɪɪtɪst/ *n* pietista, *mf*

pietistic /ˌpaɪɪ'tɪstɪk/ *a* pietista

piety /'paɪɪti/ *n* piedad, devoción, *f*

piezometer /ˌpaɪə'zɒmɪtər/ *n Phys.* piezómetro, *m*

piffle /'pɪfəl/ *n* patrañas, tonterías, *f pl*

pig /pɪg/ *n* puerco, cerdo, *m;* *Inf.* cochino, *m;* (metal) lingote, *m.* **to buy a p. in a poke,** cerrar un trato a ciegas. **p.-eyed,** de ojos de cerdo. **p.-iron,** arrabio, hierro colado en barras, lingote de fundición, *m*

pigeon /'pɪdʒən/ *n* paloma, *f,* palomo, *m;* *Inf.* primo, *m.* —*vt* embaucar, engañar. **carrier p.,** paloma mensajera, *f.* **clay p.,** pichón de barro, platillo de arcilla, *m.* **male p.,** pichón, *m.* **pouter p.,** paloma buchona, *f.* **young p.,** palomino, *m.* **p. fancier,** palomero, *m.* **p.-hole,** casilla, *f.* —*vt* encasillar. **set of p.-holes,** encasillado, *m.* **p.-shooting,** tiro de pichón, *m.* **p.-toed,** patituerto

piggy bank /'pɪgi/ *n* alcancía, *f*

pigheaded /'pɪgˌhɛdɪd/ *a* terco, testarudo

pigheadedness /'pɪgˌhɛdɪdnɪs/ *n* terquedad, testarudez, *f*

piglet /'pɪglɪt/ *n* cerdito, *m*

pigment /'pɪgmənt/ *n* pigmento, *m*

pigmentary /'pɪgmənˌtɛri/ *a* pigmentario

pigmentation /ˌpɪgmən'teɪʃən/ *n* pigmentación, *f*

pigskin /'pɪgˌskɪn/ *n* piel de cerdo, *f*

pigsty /'pɪgˌstaɪ/ *n* pocilga, *f*

pigtail /'pɪgˌteɪl/ *n* coleta, *f*

pike /paɪk/ *n Mil.* pica, *f,* chuzo, *m;* (peak) pico, *m*

pilaster /pɪ'læstər/ *n* pilastra, *f*

pile /paɪl/ *n* estaca, *f;* poste, *m;* (engineering) pilote, *m;* (heap) pila, *f,* montón, *m;* (pyre) pira, *f;* (building) edificio grande, *m;* *Elec.* pila, *f;* (hair) pelo, *m;* (nap) pelusa, *f;* *pl* **piles,** *Med.* almorranas, *f pl.* —*vt* clavar pilotes en; apoyar con pilotes; (heap) amontonar; (load) cargar. **to make one's p.,** *Inf.* hacer su pacotilla. **to p. arms,** poner los fusiles en pabellón. **to p. on,** (coal, etc.) echar; (increase) aumentar. **to p. it on,** exagerar, intensificar; (a table) cargar. **to p.**

up, amontonarse; acumularse; (of a ship) encallar. **p.-driver,** machina, *f;* martinete, *m.* **p. dwelling,** vivienda palustre, sostenida por pilares, *f*

pilfer /'pɪlfər/ *vt* sisar, sonsacar, hurtar, ratear

pilferer /'pɪlfərər/ *n* sisador (-ra), ratero (-ra)

pilfering /'pɪlfərɪŋ/ *n* sisa, ratería, *f*

pilgrim /'pɪlgrɪm/ *n* peregrino (-na). **pilgrim's staff,** bordón, *m*

pilgrimage /'pɪlgrəmɪdʒ/ *n* peregrinación, *f;* romería, *f.* **to make a p.,** hacer una peregrinación, peregrinar; ir en romería

piling /'paɪlɪŋ/ *n* amontonamiento, *m;* (of buildings) pilotaje, *m*

pill /pɪl/ *n* píldora, *f.* **to gild the p.,** *Fig.* dorar la píldora. **p.-box,** caja de píldoras, *f;* casamata, *f, Mil.* nido de ametralladoras, *m*

pillage /'pɪlɪdʒ/ *vt* pillar, saquear. —*n* saqueo, *m*

pillager /'pɪlɪdʒər/ *n* saqueador (-ra)

pillaging /'pɪlɪdʒɪŋ/ *n* pillaje, *m, a* pillador, saqueador

pillar /'pɪlər/ *n* pilar, *m,* columna, *f;* (person) sostén, soporte, *m.* **from p. to post,** de Ceca en Meca. **p. of salt,** estatua de sal, *f.* **the Pillars of Hercules,** las Columnas de Hércules. **to be a p. of strength,** *Inf.* ser una roca. **p.-box,** buzón, *m*

pillared /'pɪlərd/ *a* con columnas, sostenido por columnas; en columnas

pillion /'pɪlyən/ *n* (on a horse, etc.) grupera, *f;* (on a motor-cycle) grupa, *f.* **to ride p.,** ir a la grupa

pillory /'pɪləri/ *n* picota, argolla, *f.* —*vt* empicotar; *Fig.* poner en ridículo; censurar duramente

pillow /'pɪloʊ/ *n* almohada, *f;* (for lace-making) cojín, *m;* (of a machine) cojinete, *m.* —*vt* apoyar; reposar; servir como almohada. **to take counsel of one's p.,** consultar con la almohada. **p.-case,** funda de almohada, *f*

pilot /'paɪlət/ *n* piloto, *m;* *Naut.* práctico, piloto (de puerto), *m.* —*vt* guiar, conducir; (*Naut. Aer.*) pilotar, pilotear. **p. boat,** vaporcito del práctico, *m.* **p. jacket,** chaquetón de piloto, *m.* **p. officer,** oficial de aviación, *m*

pilotage /'paɪlətɪdʒ/ *n* pilotaje, *m;* *Naut.* practicaje, *m*

pilotless /'paɪlətlɪs/ *a* sin piloto

pimento /pɪ'mɛntoʊ/ *n* pimiento, *m*

pimp /pɪmp/ *n* rufián, alcahuete, *m, vi* alcahuetear

pimple /'pɪmpəl/ *n* grano, *m*

pimply /'pɪmpli/ *a* con granos

pin /pɪn/ *n* alfiler, *m;* prendedor, *m;* clavija, *f;* clavo, *m,* chaveta, *f;* (bolt) perno, *m.* —*vt* prender con alfileres; (with a peg) enclavijar; fijar; sujetar. **to pin up,** sujetar con alfileres; (the hair) sujetar con horquillas. **I don't care a pin,** No me importa un bledo. **to be on pins,** estar en ascuas. **to suffer from pins and needles,** tener aguijones. **pin-head,** cabeza de alfiler, *f.* **pin-money,** alfileres, *m pl.* **pin-oak,** *Bot.* pincarrasco, *m,* carrasca, *f.* **pin point,** punta de alfiler, *f.* **pin-prick,** alfilerazo, *m*

pinafore /'pɪnəˌfɔr/ *n* delantal de niño, *m*

pince-nez /'pæns,neɪ/ *n* quevedos, *m pl*

pincers /'pɪnsərz/ *n pl* pinzas, tenazas, *f pl,* alicates, *m pl;* (of crustaceans) pinzas, *f pl.* **p. movement,** movimiento de pinzas, *m*

pinch /pɪntʃ/ *vt* pellizcar; (crush) estrujar; aplastar; apretar; (of the cold) helar; (steal) hurtar, birlar; (arrest) coger, prender. —*n* pellizco, torniscón, *m;* pulgarada, *f;* (of snuff) polvo, *m;* (distress) miseria, *f;* (pain) dolor, *m,* angustia. *f.* **at a p.,** en caso de apuro. **to know where the shoe pinches,** saber dónde le aprieta el zapato

pinched /pɪntʃt/ *a* (by the cold) helado; (wan) marchito, descolorido

pincushion /'pɪnˌkuʃən/ *n* acerico, *m*

Pindaric /pɪn'dærɪk/ *a* pindárico

pine /paɪn/ *n Bot.* pino, *m.* —*vi* languidecer, marchitarse, consumirse. **to p. for,** anhelar, suspirar por, perecer por. **pitch-p.,** pino de tea, *m.* **p.-apple,** piña de las Indias, *f,* ananás, *m.* **p. cone,** piña, *f.* **p. kernel,** piñón, *m.* **p. needle,** pinocha, *f.* **p. wood,** pinar, *m,* pineda, *f*

pineal /'pɪniəl/ *a* en figura de piña; *Anat.* pineal

ping /pɪŋ/ n silbido de una bala, m; zumbido, m. **p. pong,** tenis de mesa, pingpong, m

pinion /'pɪnyən/ n (wing) ala, f; (small feather) piñón, m; (in carving) alón, m; (wheel) piñón, m. —vt atar las alas de; cortar un piñón de; (a person) atar; (the arms of) trincar, asegurar

pink /pɪŋk/ n Bot. clavel, m; color de rosa, m; (perfection) modelo, m; colmo, m; (hunting) color rojo, m; levitín rojo de caza, m. —a de color de rosa, rosado. —vt Sew. picar; (pierce) penecrar, atravesar. —vi (of an engine) picar

pinking /'pɪŋkɪŋ/ n Sew. picadura, f

pinkish /'pɪŋkɪʃ/ a rosáceo

pinnacle /'pɪnəkəl/ n Naut. pinaza, f

pinnacle /'pɪnəkəl/ n pináculo, m

pinpoint /'pɪn,pɔɪnt/ vt precisar

pint /paɪnt/ n (measure) pinta, f

pintle /'pɪntl/ n (pin) perno, m

piolet /,piə'lei/ n piolet, m

pioneer /,paiə'nɪər/ n pionero, explorador, m; introductor, m. **to be a p. in...,** ser el primero en (or a)...

pioneering role, papel de iniciador (e.g. *She played a pioneering role,* jugó un papel de iniciadora)

pious /'paiəs/ a pío, devoto, piadoso

piously /'paiəsli/ adv piadosamente, devotamente

pip /pɪp/ n (of fruit) pepita, f; (on cards, dice) punto, m; (disease) moquillo, m; (of an army, etc., officer) insignia, f

pipe /paip/ n (for tobacco) pipa de fumar, f; Mus. caramillo, m; (boatswain's) pito, m; (of a bird) trino, m; (voice) voz aguda, f; tubo, m; (for water, etc.) cañería, f; (of a hose) manga, f; (of an organ) cañón, m; (of wine) pipa, f; pl **pipes,** Mus. gaita, f. —vi tocar el caramillo (or la gaita); empezar a cantar; silbar; (of birds) trinar. —vt (a tune) tocar; (sing) cantar; (whistle) llamar con pito; conducir con cañerías; instalar cañerías en. **He smokes a p.,** Fuma una pipa. **I smoked a p.** (of tobacco) **before I went to bed,** Fumé una pipa antes de acostarme. **Put that in your p. and smoke it!** ¡Chúpate eso! **p. clay,** blanquizal, m. **p. cleaner,** limpiapipas, m. **p. layer,** cañero, fontanero, m. **p. laying,** instalación de cañerías, f. **p.-line,** cañería, f; (oil) oleoducto, m. **p. tobacco,** tabaco de pipa, m

pipeful /'paipfʊl/ n pipa, f

piper /'paipər/ n (bagpiper) gaitero, m; flautista, mf

pipette /pai'pɛt/ n Chem. pipeta, f

piping /'paipɪŋ/ n sonido del caramillo, m; música de la flauta, etc., f; (of birds) trinos, m pl; voz aguda, f; (for water, etc.) cañería, tubería, f; Sew. cordoncillo, m. **p.-hot,** hirviente

pipkin /'pɪpkɪn/ n ollita de barro, f

pippin /'pɪpɪn/ n (apple) camuesa, f

piquancy /'pikənsi/ n picante, m

piquant /'pikənt/ a picante

pique /pik/ n (resentment, and score in game) pique, m. **to p. oneself upon,** preciarse de, jactarse de. **to be piqued,** estar enojado; Inf. amoscarse

piquet /pɪ'kei/ n juego de los cientos, m

piracy /'pairəsi/ n piratería, f

pirate /'pairət/ n pirata, mf. —vi piratear. —vt publicar una edición furtiva de. **p. edition,** edición furtiva, f

piratical /pɪ'rætɪkəl/ a pirata, pirático; de pirata, de piratas

pirouette /,pɪru'ɛt/ n pirueta, f

Pisces /'paisiz/ n pl peces, m pl

pisciculture /'pɪsɪ,kʌltʃər/ n piscicultura, f

Pisgah /'pɪzgə/ Fasga, f

pistachio /pɪ'stæʃɪ,ou/ n pistacho, f

pistil /'pɪstl/ n Bot. pistilo, m

pistol /'pɪstl/ n pistola, f. **p. belt,** charpa, f, cinto de pistolas, m. **p. case,** pistolera, f. **p. shot,** pistoletazo, m

piston /'pɪstən/ n Mech. émbolo, pistón, m; Mus. pistón, m, llave, f. **p. ring,** anillo de émbolo, segmento de émbolo, m. **p. rod,** biela, f. **p. stroke,** carrera del émbolo, f

pit /pɪt/ n hoyo, m; foso, m; (in a garage) foso de reparación, m; Theat. platea, f; (trap) trampa, f; (scar) hoyo, m; precipicio, m; (hell) infierno, m. —vt (with smallpox) marcar con viruelas; (against) competir

con. **pithead,** boca de mina, f. **pit of the stomach,** boca del estómago, f. **pit stall,** butaca de platea, f

pitch /pɪtʃ/ n Chem. pez, brea, f, alquitrán, m; (place) puesto, m; (throwing) lanzamiento, m; (distance thrown) alcance, m; (for cricket) cancha, f; (bowling) saque, m; (slope) pendiente, inclinación, f; (height) elevación, f; Mus. tono, m; (Fig. degree) grado, extremo, m; (Naut. Aer.) cabeceo, m; (of threads of a screw, etc.) paso, m. —vt (camp) asentar; (a tent, etc.) colocar, poner; (throw) lanzar, arrojar, tirar; (cricket, etc.) lanzar; (fix in) clavar; Mus. graduar el tono de; (tell) narrar. —vi (fall) caer; Naut. cabecear, zozobrar; Aer. cabecear. **to paint with p.,** embrear. **to p. into,** (attack) acometer, atacar; (scold) desatarse contra; (food) engullir. **p.-black,** negro como la pez; oscuro como boca de lobo. **p.-pine,** pino de tea, m. **p.-pipe,** diapasón vocal, m

pitched battle /pɪtʃt/ n batalla campal, f

pitcher /'pɪtʃər/ n jarro, cántaro, m; (in baseball) lanzador de pelota, m

pitcherful /'pɪtʃər,fʌl/ n jarro (de), m

pitchfork /'pɪtʃ,fɔrk/ n horquilla, f, aventador, m. —vt levantar con horquilla; Fig. lanzar

pitching /'pɪtʃɪŋ/ n (pavement) adoquinado, m; (of a ship) socollada, f; cabeceo, m

piteous /'pɪtiəs/ a lastimero; triste; plañidero; compasivo, tierno

piteousness /'pɪtiəsnɪs/ n estado lastimero, m; tristeza, f; compasión, ternura, f

pitfall /'pɪt,fɔl/ n trampa, f; Fig. añagaza, f, lazo, peligro, m

pith /pɪθ/ n Bot. médula, f; médula espinal, f; Fig. meollo, m; fuerza, f, vigor, m; substancia, f; quinta esencia, f; importancia, f

pithiness /'pɪθɪnɪs/ n jugosidad, f; fuerza, f, vigor, m

pithy /'pɪθi/ a meduloso; Fig. jugoso; enérgico, vigoroso

pitiable /'pɪtiəbəl/ a lastimoso, digno de compasión; (paltry) despreciable

pitiful /'pɪtɪfəl/ a piadoso, compasivo; conmovedor, doloroso, lastimero; (contemptible) miserable

pitifully /'pɪtɪfəli/ adv lastimosamente

pitiless /'pɪtɪlɪs/ a sin piedad, despiadado

pitilessness /'pɪtɪlɪsnɪs/ n crueldad, inhumanidad, f

pitman /'pɪtmən/ n minero, m; aserrador de foso, m

pittance /'pɪtns/ n pitanza, f; pequeña porción, f; ración de hambre, f

pitted /'pɪtɪd/ a picoso

pituitary /pɪ'tui,tɛri/ a pituitario

pity /'pɪti/ n piedad, compasión, f; lástima, f. —vt compadecerse de, tener lástima (a); compadecer. **It is a p. that...,** Es lástima que... **Have p.!** ¡Ten piedad! **to take p. on,** tener lástima (de). **to move to p.,** dar lástima (a), enternecer

pityingly /'pɪtiɪŋli/ adv con lástima

pivot /'pɪvət/ n pivote, m; eje, m; Fig. punto de partida, m, vi girar sobre un pivote o eje

pivotal /'pɪvətl/ a Fig. cardinal, principal, fundamental

pixy /'pɪksi/ n duende, m. **p. hood,** caperuza, f

pizzicato /,pɪtsɪ'katou/ a pichigato

placability /,plækə'bɪlɪti/ n placabilidad, f

placable /'plækəbəl/ a aplacable, placable

placard /'plækard/ n cartel, m. —vt fijar carteles (en); publicar por carteles

placate /'pleikeit/ vt aplacar, ablandar, apaciguar

placatory /'pleikə,tɔri/ a placativo

place /pleis/ n lugar, m; sitio, m; (position) puesto, m; (seat) asiento, m; (laid at table) cubierto, m; (square) plaza, f; (house) residencia, f; (in the country) casa de campo, finca, f; (in a book) pasaje, m; (in an examination) calificación, f; (rank) posición, f, rango, m; situación, f; (employment) empleo, m, colocación, f. —vt—poner; colocar; (in employment) dar empleo (a); (appoint) nombrar; (an order) dar; (money) invertir; (remember) recordar, traer a la memoria; (size up) fijar; (confidence) poner. **in p.,** en su lugar; apropiado. **in p. of,** en vez de, en lugar de. **in the first p.,** en primer lugar, primero. **in the next p.,** luego, después. **out of p.,** fuera de lugar; inoportuno. **It is not my p. to...,** No me toca a mí de... **to give p. to,** ceder el paso (a); ceder (a). **to**

take p., verificarse, tener lugar, ocurrir. **p. of business,** establecimiento, local de negocios, *m*. **p. of worship,** edificio de culto, *m*

placenta /plə'sentə/ *n* placenta, *f*

placid /'plæsɪd/ *a* plácido, apacible; calmoso; sereno, sosegado; dulce

placidity /plə'sɪdɪti/ *n* placidez, *f*; serenidad, tranquilidad, *f*, sosiego, *m*

placidly /'plæsɪdli/ *adv* plácidamente

placing /'pleɪsɪŋ/ *n* colocación, *f*; posición, *f*; localización, *f*

placket /'plækɪt/ *n* abertura (en una falda), *f*

plagiarism /'pleɪdʒə,rɪzəm/ *n* plagio, *m*

plagiarist /'pleɪdʒərɪst/ *n* plagiario (-ia)

plagiarize /'pleɪdʒə,raɪz/ *vt* plagiar, hurtar

plague /pleɪg/ *n* plaga, *f*; peste, pestilencia, *f*. —*vt* importunar, atormentar; plagar

plaice /pleɪs/ *n* (nearest equivalent) platija, *f*

plaid /plæd/ *n* manta escocesa, *f*; género de cuadros, *m*, *a* a cuadros

plain /pleɪn/ *a* claro; evidente; (simple) sencillo; llano; sin adorno; (flat) liso, igual; (candid) franco; (with truth, etc.) desnudo; (flat) liso, igual; (candid) franco; (with truth, etc.) desnudo; mero; puro, sin mezcla; (of words) redondo; (ugly) feo. —*adv* claramente; llanamente; sencillamente; francamente. —*n* llanura, *f*, llano, *m*. **the p. truth,** la pura verdad. **p. clothes,** traje de paisano, *m*. **p. clothes man,** detective, *m*. **p. cooking,** cocina sencilla, cocina casera, *f*. **p. dealing,** buena fe, sinceridad, *f*. **p. dweller,** llanero (-ra). **p. living,** vida sencilla, *f*. **p. people,** gente sencilla, *f*. **p. sailing,** *Fig.* camino fácil, *m*. **p. sewing,** costura, *f*. **p.-song,** canto llano, *m*. **p. speaking,** franqueza, *f*. **p.-spoken,** franco. **in p. English,** sin rodeos, en cristiano (e.g. *Speak in p. English!* Habla sin rodeos! Habla en cristiano!)

plainly /'pleɪnli/ *adv* claramente; sencillamente; llanamente; francamente; rotundamente

plainness /'pleɪnnɪs/ *n* claridad, *f*; sencillez, *f*; llaneza, *f*; franqueza, *f*; (ugliness) fealdad, *f*

plainsman /'pleɪnzmən/ *n* hombre de las llanuras, *m*

plaint /pleɪnt/ *n* queja, *f*, lamento, *m*; *Law.* demanda, querella, *f*

plaintiff /'pleɪntɪf/ *n* demandante, *mf*, actor, *m*, parte actora, actora, *f*

plaintive /'pleɪntɪv/ *a* quejumbroso, dolorido; patético

plaintively /'pleɪntɪvli/ *adv* quejumbrosamente

plaintiveness /'pleɪntɪvnɪs/ *n* melancolía, tristeza, *f*; voz quejumbrosa, *f*

plait /pleɪt/ *n* trenza, *f*. —*vt* trenzar; tejer. **in plaits,** (of hair) en trenzas

plan /plæn/ *n* plan, *m*; (map) plano, *m*; proyecto, *m*. —*vt* planear; proyectar; proponerse. **the Marshall P.,** el Plan Marshall. **to make a p. of,** trazar un plano de. **to make plans,** hacer planes

planchette /plæn'ʃɛt/ *n* mesa giratoria, *f*

plane /pleɪn/ *n* (tree) plátano, *m*; (tool) cepillo, *m*; *Geom.* plano, *m*; (level) nivel, *m*; *Aer.* avión, *m*, plano. —*vt* acepillar, alisar. —*vi Aer.* planear

planet /'plænɪt/ *n* planeta, *m*

planetarium /,plænɪ'teəriəm/ *n* planetario, *m*

planetary /'plænɪ,teri/ *a* planetario

planing /'pleɪnɪŋ/ *n* acepilladura, alisadura, *f*,

plank /plæŋk/ *n* tabla, *f*; *Fig.* fundamento, principio, *m*; *pl* **planks,** tablazón, *f*. —*vt* entablar, enmaderar

planking /'plæŋkɪŋ/ *n* entablado, *m*, tablazón, *f*

plankton /'plæŋktən/ *n* plancton, *m*

planned /plænd/ *a* proyectado, planeado; dirigido. **p. economy,** economía dirigida, *f*

planner /'plænər/ *n* proyectista, *mf*; autor (-ra) de un plan

planning /'plænɪŋ/ *n* proyecto, *m*; concepción, *f*

plant /plænt/ *n Bot.* planta, *f*; instalación, *f*, material, *m*. —*vt* plantar; (place) colocar; fijar; (a blow) asestar; (people) establecer; (instil) inculcar, imbuir (con); (conceal) esconder. **p. pot,** florero, *m*. **p. stand,** jardinera, *f*

plantain /'plæntɪn/ *n Bot.* llantén, *m*

plantation /plæn'teɪʃən/ *n* plantación, *f*; plantío, *m*; *Fig.* colonia, *f*; introducción, *f*, establecimiento, *m*

planter /'plæntər/ *n* plantador, cultivador, *m*

planting /'plæntɪŋ/ *n* plantación, *f*; *Fig.* colonia, *f*; introducción, *f*. **p. out,** trasplante, *m*

plantlike /'plænt,laɪk/ *a* como una planta; de planta

plaque /plæk/ *n* placa, *f*; medalla, *f*

plash /plæʃ/ *n* (puddle) charco, *m*; (sound) chapaleteo, *m*. —*vt* and *vi* chapotear, chapalear

plasma /'plæzmə/ *n* plasma, *m*

plaster /'plæstər/ *n* (for walls, etc.) argamasa, *f*; yeso, *m*; *Med.* parche, emplasto, *m*. —*vt* (walls, etc.) enlucir, enyesar; poner emplastos (a or en); (daub) embadurnar manchar; (cover) cubrir. **p. cast,** vaciado, yeso, *m*. **p. of Paris,** escayola, *f*

plasterer /'plæstərər/ *n* yesero, *m*

plastering /'plæstərɪŋ/ *n* revoque, enyesado, guarnecido, *m*. **p. trowel,** fratás, *m*.

plastic /'plæstɪk/ *a* plástico. —*n* plástica, *f*; *pl* **plastics,** materias plásticas, *f pl.* **p. surgery,** cirugía plástica, cirugía estética, *f*

plasticine /'plæstə,sin/ *n* plasticina, *f*

plasticity /plæ'stɪsɪti/ *n* plasticidad, *f*

plate /pleɪt/ *n* plancha, chapa, *f*; (engraving and *Photo.*, of a doctor, etc.) placa, *f*; (illustration) lámina, *f*; (cutlery, etc.) vajilla, *f*; (for eating) plato, *m*; (for money) platillo, *m*; electrotipo, *m*; (dental) dentadura postiza, *f*. —*vt* (with armor) blindar; (with metal) planchear; (silver) platear; (electro-plate) niquelar. **silver p.,** vajilla de plata, plata, *f*. **p.-armor,** armadura, *f*; (of a ship) blindaje, *m*. **p.-draining rack,** escurreplatos, *m*. **p.-glass,** vidrio plano, *m*. **p.-rack,** escurridero para platos, *m*. **p. warmer,** calientaplatos, *m*

plateau /plæ'tou/ *n* meseta, altiplanicie, *f*

plateful /'pleɪt,fʌl/ *n* plato (de), *m*

plater /'pleɪtər/ *n* plateador, *m*; platero, *m*

plateresque /,plætə'rɛsk/ *a Archit.* plateresco

platform /'plætfɔrm/ *n* plataforma, *f*; (railway) andén, *m*. **p. ticket,** billete de andén, *m*

plating /'pleɪtɪŋ/ *n* niquelado, *m*; electrogalvanización, *f*; (with armor) blindaje, *m*

platinum /'plætnəm/ *n* platino, *m*. **p. blonde,** rubia platino, *f*

platitude /'plætɪ,tud/ *n* perogrullada, *f*, lugar común, *m*; trivialidad, vulgaridad, *f*

platitudinous /,plætɪ'tudnəs/ *a* lleno de perogrulladas; trivial

platonic /plə'tɒnɪk/ *a* platónico

Platonism /'pleɪtn,ɪzəm/ *n* platonismo, *f*

Platonist /'pleɪtnɪst/ *n* platonista, *mf*

platoon /plə'tun/ *n Mil.* pelotón, *m*

platter /'plætər/ *n* fuente, *f*, trinchero, *m*; plato, *m*

plaudit /'plɔdɪt/ *n* aplauso, *m*, aclamación, *f*; (praise) elogio, *m*, alabanza, *f*

plausibility /,plɔzə'bɪlɪti/ *n* plausibilidad, *f*

plausible /'plɔzəbəl/ *a* plausible

plausibly /'plɔzəbli/ *adv* plausiblemente

play /pleɪ/ *vi* jugar; (frolic) juguetear, retozar; recrearse, divertirse; *Mech.* moverse; (on a musical instrument) tocar; (wave) ondear, flotar; *Theat.* representar; (behave) conducirse. —*vt* jugar; (of a searchlight, etc.) enfocar; (direct) dirigir; (a fish) agotar; (a joke, etc.) hacer; (a piece in a game) mover; (a musical instrument or music) tocar; (a string instrument) tañer; (a character in a play) hacer el papel de; (a drama, etc.) representar, poner en escena. **to p. a joke,** gastar una broma, hacer una burla. **to p. fair,** jugar limpio. **to p. false,** jugar sucio, engañar. **to p. the fool,** hacerse el tonto, hacerse el payaso. **to p. at,** jugar a; (pretend) fingir; hacer sin entusiasmo. **to p. off,** confrontar, contraponer. **to p. on.** See **to p. upon. to p. on the...,** (of musical instruments) tocar. **to p. to,** (a person) tocar para. **to p. upon,** tocar; (a person's fears, etc.) explotar. **to p. up to,** (a person) adular, hacer la rueda (a). **to p. with,** jugar con; burlarse de; (an idea) acariciar play, *n* juego, *m*; diversión, *f*, recreo, *m*; (reflection) reflejo, *m*; movimiento libre, *m*; (to the imagination, etc.) rienda suelta, *f*; *Mech.* holgura, *f*; *Lit.* pieza dramática, comedia, *f*; (performance) función, representación, *f*; (*Theater.*) teatro, *m*. **fair p.,** juego limpio, *m*. **foul p.,** juego sucio, *m*; traición, perfidia, *f*. **to bring into p.,** poner en juego. **to come into p.,** entrar en juego. **to give**

p. to, dar rienda a. **p. on words,** juego de palabras, *m.* **p.-pen,** cuadro enrejado, *m*

playact /'plei,ækt/ *vi* hacer la comedia

playbill /'plei,bil/ *n* cartel, *m;* programa, *m*

played-out /,pleid 'aut/ *a* agotado; viejo

player /'pleiər/ *n* jugador (-ra); *Theat.* actor (-triz), representante, *mf; Mus.* músico (-ca), tocador (-ra)

playfellow /'plei,felou/ *n* camarada, *mf;* compañero (-ra) de juego, compañero de juegos

playful /'pleifəl/ *a* juguetón; travieso; alegre

playfully /'pleifəli/ *adv* en juego, de broma; alegremente

playfulness /'pleifəlnis/ *n* carácter juguetón, *m;* travesuras, *f pl;* alegría, *f*

playgoer /'plei,gouər/ *n* persona que frecuenta los teatros, *f;* espectador de comedias, *m*

playground /'plei,graund/ *n* patio de recreo, *m*

playing /'pleiiŋ/ *n* juego, *m.* **p.-cards,** naipes, *m pl,* cartas, *f pl.* **p.-field,** campo de deportes, *m*

playlet /'pleilit/ *n* comedia corta, *f*

playmate /'plei,meit/. See **playfellow**

plaything /'plei,θiŋ/ *n* juguete, *m*

playtime /'plei,taim/ *n* recreación, *f;* (in schools) hora de recreo, *f,* recreo, *m*

playwright /'plei,rait/ *n* dramaturgo, *m,* autor (-ra) de comedias

plea /pli/ *n Law.* informe, *m;* declaración, *f; Law.* acción, *f,* proceso, *m;* (excuse) pretexto, *m,* excusa, *f;* (entreaty) súplica, *f.* **under p. of,** bajo pretexto de, con excusa de

plead /plid/ *vi Law.* pleitear; *Law.* declarar; suplicar; (of counsel, etc.) abogar (por); interceder (por). —*vt* defender en juicio; aducir, alegar; pretender. **to p. guilty,** confesarse culpable. **to p. not guilty,** negar la acusación. **to p. ignorance,** pretender ignorancia

pleading /'plidiŋ/ *n* súplicas, *f pl; Law.* defensa, *f; pl* **pleadings,** alegatos, *m pl, a* implorante

pleasant /'plɛzənt/ *a* agradable; placentero; ameno; encantador; dulce; alegre; (of persons) simpático, amable; bueno; divertido

pleasantly /'plɛzəntli/ *adv* agradablemente; de un modo muy amable; alegremente

pleasantness /'plɛzəntnis/ *n* agrado, *m;* placer, *m;* amabilidad, *f;* alegría, *f*

pleasantry /'plɛzəntri/ *n* jocosidad, *f;* broma, chanza, *f*

please /pliz/ *vi* dar placer, gustar, dar gusto, agradar; parecer bien, querer, servirse; tener a bien, placer. —*vt* deleitar, agradar, gustar; halagar; contentar, satisfacer. **I will do what I p.,** Haré lo que me parezca bien. **If you p.,** Si te parece bien; Con tu permiso. **She is very easy to p.,** Es muy fácil de darle placer. **When you p.,** Cuando Vd. quiera, Cuando a Vd. le venga bien Cuando Vd. guste. **"Please Do Not Disturb,"** «No Molesten.» **P. sit down!** ¡Haga el favor de sentarse! ¡Sírvase de sentarse! **P. God!** ¡Plegue a Dios!

pleased /plizd/ *a* contento (de or con); encantado (de); alegre (de); satisfecho (de or con). **I am p. with my new house,** Estoy contento con mi nueva casa. **I'm p. to meet you,** Mucho gusto (en conocerle), Mucho gusto (en conocerla). **to be p.,** estar contento, complacerse en

pleasing /'pliziŋ/ *a* agradable, grato; placentero; halagüeño

pleasurable /'plɛʒərəbəl/ *a* agradable; divertido, entretenido

pleasure /'plɛʒər/ *n* placer, *m;* gusto, *m;* satisfacción, *f;* (will) voluntad, *f;* recreo, *m;* diversión, distracción, *f.* **to give p. (to),** dar placer (a); deleitar, agradar; complacer. **to take p. in,** gustar de, disfrutar de; complacerse en. **I shall do it with great p.,** Lo haré con mucho gusto, Lo haré con mucho placer. **p.-boat,** barco de recreo, *m.* **p.-ground,** parque de atracciones, *m.* **p.-seeking,** amigo de placeres, frívolo. **p. trip,** viaje de recreo, *m;* excursión, *f*

pleasure craft *n* barco de recreo, *m,* (one vessel); barcas de recreo (collectively), *m pl*

pleat /plit/ *n* pliegue, *m, vt* plegar, hacer pliegues en

pleating /'plitiŋ/ *n* plegado, *m*

plebeian /pli'biən/ *a* plebeyo. —*n* plebeyo (-ya)

plebiscite /'plɛbə,sait/ *n* plebiscito, *m.* **to take a p.,** hacer un plebiscito

plectrum /'plɛktrəm/ *n* plectro, *m*

pledge /plɛdʒ/ *n* prenda, *f;* empeño, *m;* garantía, *f;* (hostage) rehén, *m;* (toast) brindis, *m.* —*vt* empeñar, dar en prenda; garantizar; brindar por; prometer. **to p. oneself,** comprometerse. **to p. support for,** prometer apoyo para

Pleiades /'pliə,diz/ *n pl* pléyades, *f pl*

plenary /'plinəri/ *a* pleno; plenario. **p. indulgence,** indulgencia plenaria, *f.* **p. session,** sesión plenaria, *f*

plenipotentiary /,plɛnəpə'tɛnʃi,ɛri/ *a* plenipotenciario. —*n* plenipotenciario, *m*

plenitude /'plɛni,tud/ *n* plenitud, *f*

plentiful /'plɛntəfəl/ *a* copioso, abundante. **to be p.,** abundar

plentifully /'plɛntəfəli/ *adv* en abundancia

plenty /'plɛnti/ *n* abundancia, *f;* en abundancia; de sobra; mucho. —*adv Inf.* bastante. **There is p. of food,** Hay comida en abundancia. **We have p. of time,** Tenemos tiempo de sobra

pleonasm /'pliə,næzəm/ *n* pleonasmo, *m*

plethora /'plɛθərə/ *n* plétora, *f*

pleurisy /'plurəsi/ *n* pleuresía, *f*

plexus /'plɛksəs/ *n* plexo, *m*

pliability /,plaiə'biliti/ *n* flexibilidad, *f;* docilidad, *f*

pliable, pliant /'plaiəbəl; 'plaiənt/ *a* flexible; dócil

pliers /'plaiərz/ *n pl* pinzas, *f pl,* alicates, *m pl,* tenazas, *f pl*

plight /plait/ *vt* (one's word) empeñar, dar; prometer en matrimonio. —*n* (fix) aprieto, apuro, *m.* **to p. one's troth,** dar palabra de matrimonio

plinth /plinθ/ *n Archit.* plinto, *m*

Pliny the Elder /'plini/ Plinio el Antiguo, Plinio el Mayor

Pliny the Younger Plinio el Menor

plod /plod/ *vi* andar despacio, caminar con trabajo; *Fig.* trabajar con ahínco

plodder /'plodər/ *n* trabajador lento y concienzudo, *m;* (student) empollón (-ona)

plot /plot/ *n* (of land) parcela, *f;* terreno, solar, *m;* (plan) proyecto, *m;* estratagema, *m;* (literary) intriga, trama, *f;* (story) argumento, *m;* (conspiracy) conjuración, *f,* complot, *m.* —*vt* trazar (un plano, etc.); urdir, tramar. —*vi* conspirar, intrigar

plotter /'plotər/ *n* conspirador (-ra conjurado (-da)

plotting /'plotiŋ/ *n* trazado (de un plano, una gráfica), *m;* (conspiracy) conspiración, *f;* maquinaciones, *f pl;* (hatching) trama, *f*

plover /'plʌvər, 'plouvər/ *n* ave fría, *f,* chorlito, *m*

plow /plau/ *n* arado, *m; Astron.* el Carro, la Osa Mayor; (in an examination) escabechina, *f.* —*vt* and *vi* arar; *Fig.* surcar; (in examinations) escabechar, dar calabazas (a), suspender. **plow the sands,** arar en el mar. **p. handle,** esteva, *f.* **to p. up,** roturar

plowman /'plaumən/ *n* arador, surcador, *m;* (peasant) labrador, *m*

plowshare /'plau,ʃeər/ *n* reja de arado, *f*

pluck /plʌk/ *vt* (pick) coger; (a bird) desplumar; *Mus.* puntear; (in an examination) calabacear escabechar. —*vi* tirar (de). —*n* (tug) tirón, *m;* (of an animal) asadura, *f;* (courage) coraje, *m.* **to p. up courage,** tomar coraje, sacar ánimos. **to p. off,** quitar. **to p. out,** arrancar; quitar

pluckily /'plʌkili/ *adv* valientemente

pluckiness /'plʌkinis/ *n* coraje, valor, *m*

plucky /'plʌki/ *a* valiente, esforzado, resuelto, animoso

plug /plʌg/ *n* tapón, tarugo, *m;* (in building) nudillo, *m;* (of a switchboard) clave, *f; Elec.* enchufe, *m;* (of a w.c.) tirador, *m;* (of a bath, etc.) tapón, *m;* (of tobacco) rollo, *m.* —*vt* atarugar, taponar, obturar; (in building) rellenar. —*vi* (with away) batirse el cobre, sudar la gota gorda. **to p. in,** enchufar

plum /plʌm/ *n* (tree) ciruelo, *m;* (fruit) ciruela, *f;* (raisin) pasa, *f; (Inf.* prize) breva, golosina, *f.* **p. cake,** pastel de fruta, *m*

plumage /'plumidʒ/ *n* plumaje, *m*

plumb /plʌm/ *n* plomada, *f;* (sounding-lead) escandallo, *m.* —*a* perpendículo; recto; completo. —*adv* a plomo, verticalmente; exactamente. —*vt* aplomar; *Naut.* sondar; (*Fig.* pierce) penetrar; (understand) comprender. —*vi* trabajar como plomero. **p.-line,** plomada, *f*

plumbago /plʌmˈbeigou/ *n* plombagina, *f*

plumber /ˈplʌmər/ *n* plomero, fontanero, *m;* instalador de cañerías, *m*

plumbic /ˈplʌmbɪk/ *a Chem.* plúmbico

plumbing /ˈplʌmɪŋ/ *n* plomería, fontanería, *f;* instalación de cañerías, *f*

plumbless /ˈplʌmlɪs/ *a Poet.* insondable

plume /plum/ *n* pluma, *f;* penacho, *m.* —*vt* adornar con plumas; desplumar; **to p. itself,** (of a bird) limpiarse las plumas. **to p. oneself on,** echárselas de, hacer alarde de; jactarse de

plumed /plumd/ *a* plumado; con plumas; empenachado

plumelet /ˈplumlɪt/ *n* agujas, *f pl*

plummet /ˈplʌmɪt/ *n* plomada, *f;* (weight) plomo, *m;* (sounding-lead) sonda, *f*

plump /plʌmp/ *a* gordo, llenito; rollizo; hinchado. —*adv* de golpe; claramente. —*vt* (swell) hinchar, rellenar; (make fall) hacer (or dejar) caer. —*vi* (swell) hincharse; engordar; (fall) caer a plomo; dejarse caer. **to p. for,** escoger, dar apoyo (a); votar por. **p.-cheeked,** mofletudo

plumpness /ˈplʌmpnɪs/ *n* gordura, *f;* lo rollizo

plumy /ˈplumi/ *a* como una pluma; plumado

plunder /ˈplʌndər/ *vt* saquear; pillar; despojar. —*n* saqueo, pillaje, *m;* (booty) botín, despojo, *m*

plunderer /ˈplʌndərər/ *n* saqueador (-ra); ladrón (-ona)

plundering /ˈplʌndərɪŋ/ *n* saqueo, *m;* despojo, *m.* —*a* saqueador

plunge /plʌndʒ/ *vt* chapuzar; sumergir; hundir; meter. —*vi* sumergirse; (into water) zambullirse; (rush) precipitarse, lanzarse; *Naut.* zozobrar; (of a horse) encabritarse; (gamble) jugarse el todo. —*n* sumersión, *f;* zambullida, *f;* chapuz, *m;* (rush) salto, *m;* (Fig. step) paso, *m*

plunger /ˈplʌndʒər/ *n Mech.* émbolo, *m*

plunging /ˈplʌndʒɪŋ/ *n* (of a ship) zozobra, *f;* (of a horse) cabriolas, *f pl;* saltos, *m pl,* For other meanings, see **plunge**

plural /ˈplʊrəl/ *a* plural. —*n* plural, *m.* **in the p.,** en el plural. **to make p.,** poner en plural

plurality /plʊˈrælɪti/ *n* pluralidad, *f*

pluralize /ˈplʊrə,laiz/ *vt* pluralizar

plus /plʌs/ *prep and a* más; (Math. Elec.) positivo. —*n* signo más, *m;* Math. cantidad positiva, *f.* **p. fours,** pantalones de golf, *m pl*

plush /plʌʃ/ *n* felpa, *f;* velludo, *m*

plushy /ˈplʌʃi/ *a* felpudo; de felpa

Pluto /ˈplutou/ *n* Plutón, *m;* (pipe-line) oleoducto, *m*

plutocracy /pluˈtɒkrəsi/ *n* plutocracia, *f*

plutocrat /ˈplutə,kræt/ *n* plutócrata, *mf*

plutocratic /,plutəˈkrætɪk/ *a* plutocrático

pluviometer /,pluviˈɒmɪtər/ *n* pluviómetro, *m*

ply /plai/ *n* cabo, *m.* —*vt* emplear, usar; manejar; ejercer; ofrecer, servir (con); importunar (con). —*vi* hacer el trayecto; hacer el servicio; ir y venir; hacer viajes. **to ply for hire,** tomar viajeros; ofrecerse para ser alquilado

plywood /ˈplai,wʊd/ *n* madera contrachapada, *f*

pneumatic /nʊˈmætɪk/ *a* neumático. —*n* (tire) neumático, *m.* **p. drill,** barreno neumático, *m*

pneumococcus /,numəˈkɒkəs/ *n* neumococo, *m*

pneumonia /nʊˈmounyə/ *n* pulmonía, *f.* **double p.,** pulmonía doble, *f*

poach /poutʃ/ *vi* cazar (or pescar) en vedado. —*vt* robar caza de un vedado; *Fig.* invadir; (Fig. steal) hurtar; (eggs) escalfar. **to p. upon another's preserves,** meterse en los asuntos de otro

poacher /ˈpoutʃər/ *n* cazador furtivo, *m*

poaching /ˈpoutʃɪŋ/ *n* caza (or pesca) furtiva, *f*

pock /pɒk/ *n* pústula, *f.* **p.-mark,** hoyo, *m.* **p.-marked,** picado de viruelas

pocket /ˈpɒkɪt/ *n* bolsillo, *m;* bolsillo del reloj, *m;* faltriquera, *f;* Mineral. bolsa, *f,* depósito, *m;* Fig. bolsa, *f;* (in billiards) tronera, *f.* —*vt* meter (or poner) en el bolsillo; (an insult) tragarse; (in billiards) entronerar; (a profit) ganar; apropiarse. **air-p.,** bolsa de aire, *f.* **to be out of p.,** haber perdido, tener una pérdida. **to have a person in one's p.,** calzarse a una

persona. **to p. one's pride,** olvidarse de su orgullo. **p. battleship,** acorazado de bolsillo, *m.* **p.-book,** cartera, *f.* **p. dictionary,** diccionario de bolsillo, *m.* **p.-flap,** portezuela, *f.* **p.-handkerchief,** pañuelo (de bolsillo), *m.* **p.-knife,** cortaplumas, *m.* **p.-lighter,** encendedor de bolsillo, *m.* **p.-money,** alfileres, *m pl,* dinero del bolsillo, *m.* **p. picking,** ratería de carteriza, *f*

pocketful /ˈpɒkɪt,fʊl/ *n* bolsillo lleno (de), *m;* lo que cabe en un bolsillo

pocket of resistance *n* foco de resistencia, *m*

pod /pɒd/ *n Bot.* vaina, *f;* (of a silkworm) capullo, *m.* —*vt* desvainar; mondar. —*vi* hincharse, llenarse

podgy /ˈpɒdʒi/ *a* gordo, grueso

poem /ˈpouəm/ *n* poema, *m;* *pl* **poems,** poesías, *f pl,* versos, *m pl*

poet /ˈpouɪt/ *n* poeta, *m.* **p. laureate,** poeta laureado, *m*

poetaster /ˈpouɪt,æstər/ *n* poetastro, *m*

poetess /ˈpouɪtɪs/ *n* poetisa, *f*

poetic /pouˈɛtɪk/ *a* poético. **p. licence,** licencia poética, *f*

poeticize /pouˈɛtə,saiz/ *vt* poetizar; hacer un poema (de)

poetics /pouˈɛtɪks/ *n* poética, *f*

poetry /ˈpouɪtri/ *n* poesía, *f;* versos, poemas, *m pl*

pogrom /pəˈgrʌm/ *n* pogrom, *m*

poignancy /ˈpɔinyənsi/ *n* (of emotions) profundidad, violencia, *f,* lo patético; (of a retort, etc.) mordacidad, acerbidad, *f*

poignant /ˈpɔinyənt/ *a* (moving) conmovedor, hondo, agudo; patético; (mordant) mordaz, agudo

poignantly /ˈpɔinyəntli/ *adv* de un modo conmovedor, patéticamente; mordazmente

poinsettia /pɔinˈsetiə/ *n* flor de nochebuena, *f*

point /pɔint/ *n* (usual meanings and Astrol., Math., in cards, in a speech, etc.) punto, *m;* característica, *f;* cualidad, *f;* (purpose) motivo, fin, *m;* (question) cuestión, *f;* asunto, *m;* (wit) agudeza, *f;* (significance) significación, *f;* (detail) detalle, *m;* (in rationing) cupón, *m;* (sharp end) punta, *f;* (of a shawl, etc.) pico, *m;* (of land) promontorio, cabo, *m;* (engraving) buril, *m;* (railway) aguja, *f;* (of horses) cabo, *m.* **Mary has many good points,** María tiene muchas cualidades buenas. **There is no p. in being angry,** No hay para que enfadarse. **in p.,** en cuestión; a propósito. **in p. of fact,** en efecto, en verdad. **on the p. of,** a punto de. **to be to the p.,** venir al caso; ser apropiado. **to carry one's p.,** salir con la suya. **to come to the p.,** ir al grano, ir al caso, ir al mollo del asunto. **to make a p. of,** insistir en; tener por principio. **to win on points,** (boxing) ganar por puntos. **p. at issue,** cuestión bajo consideración, *f,* punto en cuestión, *f.* **p.-blank,** a boca de jarro, *f.* **p.-duty,** regulación de tráfico, *f.* **p. lace,** encaje de aguja, *m.* **p. of honor,** punto de honor, *m;* cuestión de honor, *f.* **p. or order,** cuestión de orden, *f.* **p. of view,** punto de vista, *m.* **What's your p.?** ¿A dónde quieres llegar con esto?

point /pɔint/ *vt* sacar punta (a), afilar; (a moral, etc.) inculcar; (in building) rejuntar; *Gram.* puntuar; (of dogs) mostrar la caza. **He pointed his gun at them,** Les apuntó con su fusil. **The hands of the clock pointed to seven o'clock,** Las agujas del reloj marcaban las siete. **to p. with the finger,** señalar con el dedo. **to p. at,** señalar, indicar; (with a gun) apuntar; dirigir. **to p. out,** señalar, indicar; enseñar, mostrar; advertir

pointed /ˈpɔintɪd/ *a* (sharpened) afilado; (in shape) puntiagudo; picudo; *Archit.* ojival; *Fig.* mordaz; satírico; (of a remark, etc.) directo; personal; aparente, evidente

pointedly /ˈpɔintɪdli/ *adv* explícitamente, categóricamente; mordazmente; directamente; satíricamente

pointedness /ˈpɔintɪdnɪs/ *n* forma puntiaguda, *f;* (incisiveness) mordacidad, aspereza, *f;* claridad, *f*

pointer /ˈpɔintər/ *n* (of a clock, weighing-machine, etc.) aguja, *f;* (of a balance) fiel, *m;* (wand) puntero, *m;* *Fig.* índice, *m;* (dog) perro de muestra, *m*

pointillism *n Art.* puntillismo, *m*

pointillisme /ˈpwantḷ,izem/ *n Art.* puntillismo, *m*

pointing /'pɔɪntɪŋ/ n (in building) rejuntado, m; (of a gun) puntería, f

pointless /'pɔɪntlɪs/ a sin motivo, innecesario; fútil; sin importancia

pointlessly /'pɔɪntlɪsli/ adv sin motivo, sin necesidad; fútilmente

pointsman /'pɔɪntsmən/ n (railway) guardagujas, m; (policeman) guardia del tráfico, m

poise /pɔɪz/ vt balancear; pesar. —vi balancearse; posar, estar suspendido. —n equilibrio, m; (of mind) serenidad de ánimo, sangre fría, f; aplomo, m; (bearing) porte, aire, m

poison /'pɔɪzən/ n veneno, m; Fig. ponzoña, f, veneno, m. —vt envenenar; intoxicar; Fig. emponzoñar. **p. gas,** gas asfixiante, m

poisoner /'pɔɪzənər/ n envenenador (-ra); Fig. corruptor (-ra)

poisoning /'pɔɪzənɪŋ/ n envenenamiento, m; intoxicación, f

poisonous /'pɔɪzənəs/ a venenoso; tóxico; Fig. ponzoñoso, pernicioso. **p. snake,** serpiente venenosa

poisonousness /'pɔɪzənəsnɪs/ n venenosidad, f; toxicidad, f; Fig. veneno, m, ponzoña, f

poke /pouk/ vt (thrust) clavar; (make) hacer; (the fire) atizar; hurgar; (push) empujar; (put away) arrinconar. —vi andar a tientas; meterse. **Don't p. your nose into other people's business!** ¡No te metas donde no te llaman! **They poked his eyes out,** Le saltaron los ojos. **to p. fun at,** burlarse de, mofarse de. **to p. the fire,** atizar la lumbre (or el fuego). **to p. about for,** buscar a tientas. **p.-bonnet,** capelina, f

poker /'poukər/ n (game) póker, m; (for the fire) hurgón, atizador, m. **p. work,** pirograbado, m

poky /'pouki/ a estrecho, ahogado, pequeño; miserable

Poland /'poulənd/ Polonia, f

polar /'poulər/ a polar. **p. bear,** oso (-sa) blanco (-ca). **p. lights,** aurora boreal, f

polarimeter /,poulə'rɪmɪtər/ n polarímetro, m

polarity /pou'lærɪti/ n polaridad, f

polarization /,poulərə'zeɪʃən/ n polarización, f

polarize /'poulə,raɪz/ vt polarizar

pole /poul/ n palo largo, m; poste, m; (of a tent) mástil, m; (of a cart) pértiga, f; Sports. pértiga, garrocha, f; (measurement) percha, f; (Astron. Geog. Biol. Math. Elec.) polo, m. —vt (a punt) impeler con pértiga. **from p. to p.,** de polo a polo. **greasy p.,** cucaña, f. **under bare poles,** Naut. a palo seco. **p.-ax,** hachuela de mano, f; hacha de marinero, f; (butcher's) mazo, m. **p. jumping,** salto de pértiga, salto a la garrocha, m. **p.-star,** estrella polar, f

Pole /poul/ n polaco (-ca)

polemic /pə'lemɪk/ n polémica, f

polemical /pə'lemɪkəl/ a polémico

police /pə'lis/ n policía, f. —vt mantener servicio de policía en; mantener el orden público en; administrar, regular. **mounted p.,** policía montada, f. **p. constable,** (agente de) policía, guardia urbano, m. **p. court,** tribunal de la policía, m. **p. dog,** perro de policía, m. **p. force,** cuerpo de policía, m, policía, f. **p. magistrate,** juez municipal, m. **p. station,** comisaría de policía, f. **p. trap,** puesto oculto de la policía del tráfico, m. **p. woman,** policía, f

policeman /pə'lismən/ n policía, guardia, m

policy /'pɔlɪsi/ n política, f; táctica, f; sistema, m; norma de conducta, f; ideas, f pl, principios, m pl; prudencia, f; (insurance) póliza, f. **fixed premium p.,** póliza a prima fija, f. **p.-holder,** asegurado (-da), tenedor (de una póliza), m

poliomyelitis /,pouliou,maɪə'laɪtɪs/ n poliomielitis, f

polish /'pɔlɪʃ/ vt (metals and wood) pulir; (furniture and shoes) dar brillo (a); (Lit. works) pulir, limar; (persons) descortezar, civilizar. —n (shine) brillo, m; (furniture) cera para los muebles, f; (metal, silver) líquido para limpiar metales, m; (for shoes) betún para zapatos, m; (varnish) barniz, m; (of Lit. works) pulidez, elegancia, f; (of persons) urbanidad, cultura, f. **to p. off,** terminar a prisa; (a person) acabar con; (food) engullir

Polish /'poulɪʃ/ a polaco, polonés. —n (language) polaco, m

polished /'pɔlɪʃt/ a (of verses, etc.) pulido, elegante;

(of person) culto, distinguido; (of manners) fino, cortés

polisher /'pɔlɪʃər/ n (machine) pulidor, m; lustrador, m. **floor-p.,** lustrador de piso, m. **French p.,** barnizador, m

polite /pə'laɪt/ a cortés, bien educado; atento; elegante

politely /pə'laɪtli/ adv cortésmente; atentamente

politeness /pə'laɪtnɪs/ n cortesía, f. **for p. sake,** por cortesía

politic /'pɔlɪtɪk/ a político

political /pə'lɪtɪkəl/ a político. **p. agent,** agente político, m. **p. economist,** hacendista, mf **p. economy,** economía política, f

politically /pə'lɪtɪkli/ adv políticamente

politician /,pɔlɪ'tɪʃən/ n político (-ca)

politics /'pɔlɪtɪks/ n política, f. **to dabble in p.,** meterse en política

polity /'pɔlɪti/ n forma de gobierno, constitución política, f

polka /'poulkə/ n polca, f

polka-dot /'poukə,dɒt/ a con puntos

poll /poul/ n (head of person) cabeza, f; (voters' register) lista electoral, f; (voting) votación, f; (polling booth) colegio electoral, m; (counting of votes) escrutinio, m. —vt (trees) desmochar; (vote) votar, dar su voto (a); (obtain votes) obtener, recibir; (count votes) escrutar. **p.-tax,** capitación, f

pollard /'pɔlərd/ vt desmochar. —n (tree) árbol desmochado, m

pollen /'pɔlən/ n polen, m

pollinate /'pɔlə,neit/ vt fecundar con polen

pollination /,pɔlə'neiʃən/ n polinización, f

polling /'poulɪŋ/ n votación, f. **p. booth,** colegio electoral, m

pollute /pə'lut/ vt contaminar; ensuciar; profanar; (corrupt morally) corromper

polluter /pə'lutər/ n profanador (-ra), corruptor (-ra)

pollution /pə'luʃən/ n contaminación, f; profanación, f; corrupción, f

polo /'poulou/ n polo, m. **p. mallet,** maza de polo, f. **p. player,** jugador de polo, m, polista, mf

polonaise /,pɔlə'neiz/ n polonesa, f

poltroon /pɒl'trun/ n cobarde, m

polychrome /'pɔli,kroum/ a policromo

polygamist /pə'lɪgəmɪst/ n polígamo (-ma)

polygamous /pə'lɪgəməs/ a polígamo

polygamy /pə'lɪgəmi/ n poligamia, f

polygenesis /,pɔli'dʒenəsɪs/ n poligenismo, m

polyglot /'pɔli,glɒt/ n poligloto (-ta). **p. Bible,** poliglota, f

polygon /'pɔli,gɒn/ n polígono, m

Polynesia /,pɔlə'niʒə/ Polinesia, f

Polynesian /,pɔlə'niʒən/ n polinesio (-ia)

polyp /'pɔlɪp/ n pólipo, m

polyphonic /,pɔli'fɒnɪk/ a polifónico

polyphony /pə'lɪfəni/ n polifonía, f

polytechnic /,pɔli'teknɪk/ n politécnico

polytheism /'pɔliθi,ɪzəm/ n politeísmo, m

polytheistic /,pɔliθi'ɪstɪk/ a politeísta

pomade /pɒ'meid/ n pomada, f

pomegranate /'pɒm,grænɪt/ n granada, f

Pomeranian /,pɒmə'reiniən/ a pomerano. **P. dog,** perro pomerano, m

pommel /'pʌməl/ n pomo, m, vt aporrear

pomp /pɒmp/ n pompa, magnificencia, f, fausto, aparato, m; ostentación, f

Pompeian /pɒm'peiən/ a pompeyano

Pompeii /pɒm'pei/ Pompeya, f

pompom /'pɒm,pɒm/ n pompón, m

pomposity /pɒm'pɒsɪti/ n pomposidad, presunción, f; (of language) ampulosidad, f

pompous /'pɒmpəs/ a pomposo, ostentoso; (of style) ampuloso, hinchado; importante. **to be p.,** (of persons) darse tono

pompously /'pɒmpəsli/ adv pomposamente

pond /pɒnd/ n charca, f, estanque, m

ponder /'pɒndər/ vt ponderar, estudiar, considerar. —vi meditar (sobre), reflexionar (sobre)

ponderable /'pɒndərəbəl/ a ponderable

ponderous /'pɒndərəs/ a pesado; macizo, abultado; grave; (dull) pesado, aburrido

ponderously /'pɒndərəsli/ adv pesadamente; gravemente

ponderousness /'pɒndərəsnɪs/ n pesadez, f; gravedad, importancia, f

poniard /'pɒnyərd/ n puñal, m, vt apuñalar

pontiff /'pɒntif/ n pontífice, m

pontifical /pɒn'tifikəl/ a pontificio

pontificate /pɒn'tifi,kit/ n pontificado, m

pontonier /,pɒntnɪər/ n pontonero, m

pontoon /pɒn'tun/ n pontón, m. **p. bridge,** puente de pontones, m

pony /'pouni/ n jaca, f

poodle /'pudḷ/ n perro (-rra) de aguas, perro de lanas, perro lanudo

pooh-pooh /'pu'pu/ vt despreciar, desdeñar. **Pooh!** ¡Bah!

pool /pul/ n (in a river) rebalsa, f; charca, f, estanque, m; (of blood, etc.) charco, m; (in cards) baceta, f; Com. asociación, f; Fig. fuente, f; pl **pools,** (football) apuestas benéficas de fútbol, f pl. —vt (resources, etc.) combinar; juntar

poop /pup/ n popa, f. **p. lantern,** fanal, m

poor /pʊr/ a pobre; (insignificant or unfortunate) infeliz, desgraciado. **the p.,** los pobres. **to be in p. health,** estar mal de salud. **to be p. stuff,** ser de pacotilla. **to be poorer than a church mouse,** ser más pobre que las ratas. **to have a p. opinion of,** tener en poco (a). **P. me!** ¡Ay de mí! ¡Pecador de mí! **p.-box,** cepillo, m. **p.-law,** ley de asistencia pública, f. **p.-spirited,** apocado

poorhouse /'pʊr,haus/ n asilo, m

poorly /'pʊrli/ adv pobremente; mal. —a indispuesto, malo

poorness /'pʊrnɪs/ n pobreza, f; mala calidad, f; (lack) carestía, f; (of soil) infertilidad, f; (of character) mezquindad, f

pop /pɒp/ n (of a cork) taponazo, m; (of a gun) detonación, f; (drink) gaseosa, f, adv ¡pum! —vi (of a cork) saltar; (of guns) detonar. —vt (corks) hacer saltar; (a gun, a question, etc.) disparar. **popgun,** escopeta de aire comprimido, f. **to pop down,** bajar a presuradamente. **to pop in,** (visit) dejarse caer; entrar rápidamente. **to pop off,** marcharse a prisa; (die) estirar la pata. **to pop up,** subir corriendo; aparecer de pronto

pope /poup/ n Papa, m

popinjay /'pɒpɪn,dʒei/ n (fop) pisaverde, m

popish /'poupɪʃ/ a papista

poplar /'pɒplər/ n (black) chopo, álamo, m; (white) álamo blanco, m. **p. grove,** alameda, f

poplin /'pɒplɪn/ n popelina, f

poppy /'pɒpi/ n amapola, adormidera, f

populace /'pɒpyələs/ n pueblo, m; (scornful) populacho, m

popular /'pɒpyələr/ a popular; en boga, de moda; común. **He is a p. hero,** Es un héroe popular

popularity /,pɒpyə'læriti/ n popularidad, f

popularization /,pɒpyələrə'zeiʃən/ n vulgarización, f

popularize /'pɒpyələ,raiz/ vt popularizar, vulgarizar

popularly /'pɒpyələrli/ adv popularmente

populate /'pɒpyə,leit/ vt poblar

population /,pɒpyə'leiʃən/ n población, f

populous /'pɒpyələs/ a populoso; muy poblado

porcelain /'pɒrsəlɪn/ n porcelana, f

porch /pɒrtʃ/ n pórtico, m; (of a house) portal, m

porcine /'pɒrsain/ a porcino, porcuno

porcupine /'pɔrkyə,pain/ n puerco espín, m

pore /pɔr/ n poro, m. **to p. over,** estar absorto en; examinar cuidadosamente

pork /pɔrk/ n carne de cerdo, f. **salt p.,** tocino, m. **p. butcher,** tocinero, m. **p. pie,** pastel de carne de cerdo, m

pornographic /,pɔrnə'græfik/ a pornográfico

pornography /pɔr'nɒgrəfi/ n pornografía, f

porosity /pɔ'rɒsiti/ n porosidad, f

porous /'pɔrəs/ a poroso

porphyry /'pɔrfəri/ n pórfido, m

porpoise /'pɔrpəs/ n marsopa, f, puerco marino, m

porridge /'pɒridʒ/ n gachas, f pl, m

port /pɔrt/ n puerto, m; (in a ship) porta, f; (larboard) babor, m; (wine) vino de Oporto, m; (mien) porte, m, presencia, f. —vt (the helm) poner a babor; Mil. llevar un fusil terciado. **to put into p.,** tomar puerto. **to stop at a p.,** hacer escala en un puerto. **p. dues,** derechos de puerto, m pl

portable /'pɔrtəbəl/ a portátil; móvil. **p. typewriter,** máquina de escribir portátil (or de viaje), f. **p. wireless,** radio portátil, f

portal /'pɔrtḷ/ n portal, m

portcullis /pɔrt'kʌlɪs/ n rastrillo, m

portend /pɔr'tend/ vt presagiar, anunciar

portent /'pɔrtent/ n augurio, presagio, m; portento, m

portentous /pɔr'tentəs/ a ominoso; portentoso; importante

porter /'pɔrtər/ n (messenger) mozo de cordel, m; (of a university, hotel) portero, m; (of a block of flats) conserje, m; (railway) mozo de estación, m; (drink) cerveza negra, f. **porter's lodge,** portería, f; conserjería, f

porterage /'pɔrtərɪdʒ/ n porte, m

portfolio /pɔrt'fouli,ou/ n carpeta, f; (Polit. of a minister) cartera, f; (Polit. ministry) ministerio, m

porthole /'pɔrt,houl/ n tronera, f

portico /'pɔrti,kou/ n pórtico, m

portiere /pɔr'tyɛər/ n antepuerta, f

portion /'pɔrʃən/ n porción, f; parte, f; (marriage) dote, mf; (piece) pedazo, m; (in a restaurant) ración, f; (in life) fortuna, f. —vt dividir; repartir; (dower) dotar

portliness /'pɔrtlinɪs/ n corpulencia, f

portly /'pɔrtli/ a corpulento, grueso

portmanteau /pɔrt'mæntou/ n maleta, f

portmanteau word n palabra de acarreo, f

portrait /'pɔrtrɪt/ n retrato, m. **p. painter,** pintor (-ra) de retratos

portraiture /'pɔrtrɪtʃər/ n retratos, m pl; descripción, pintura, f

portray /pɔr'trei/ vt retratar; pintar, representar; (in words) describir, pintar

portrayal /pɔr'treial/ n pintura, f; retrato, m; (in words) descripción, f

portrayer /pɔr'treiər/ n retratista, mf, pintor (-ra)

portress /'pɔrtrɪs/ n portera, f; (in a convent) tornera, f

Portuguese /,pɔrtʃə'giz/ a portugués. —n portugués (-esa); (language) portugués, m

pose /pouz/ vt colocar; (a problem, etc.) plantear; (a question) hacer; vi colocarse; (with as) echárselas de, dárselas de, fingir ser; hacerse pasar por. —n actitud, postura, f; (affected) pose, f; (deception) engaño, m

poser /'pouzər/ n problema difícil, m; (in an examination) pega, f; pregunta embarazosa, f

position /pə'zɪʃən/ n posición, f; situación, f; actitud, postura, f; condición, f, estado, m; (post) puesto, empleo, m. **He is not in a p. to...,** No está en condiciones de..., No está para... **to place in p.,** poner en posición, colocar

positive /'pɒzɪtɪv/ a positivo; absoluto; (convinced) convencido, seguro; (downright) categórico; Inf. completo. —n realidad, f; Photo. (prueba) positiva, f

positively /'pɒzɪtɪvli/ adv positivamente; categóricamente

positiveness /'pɒzɪtɪvnɪs/ n certitud, seguridad, f; terquedad, obstinacia, f

positivism /'pɒzɪtə,vizəm/ n positivismo, m

positivist /'pɒzɪtɪvɪst/ n positivista, mf

positivistic /,pɒzɪtɪ'vɪstɪk/ a positivista

posse /'pɒsi/ n pelotón, m; multitud, muchedumbre, f

possess /pə'zɛs/ vt poseer; gozar (de); (of ideas, etc.) dominar. **to p. oneself of,** apoderarse de, apropiarse. **What possessed you to do it?** ¿Qué te hizo hacerlo?

possession /pə'zɛʃən/ n posesión, f. **to take p. of,** tomar posesión de; hacerse dueño de, apoderarse de; (a house, etc.) entrar en, ocupar

possessive /pə'zɛsɪv/ a posesivo. —n posesivo, m

possessor /pə'zɛsər/ n poseedor (-ra); dueño (-ña); propietario (-ia)

possibility /,pɒsə'bɪliti/ n posibilidad, f

possible /'pɒsəbəl/ a posible. **as soon as p.,** cuanto antes, lo más pronto posible. **to make p.,** hacer posible, posibilitar

possibly /'pɒsəbli/ *adv* posiblemente; (perhaps) quizás. **I shall come as soon as I p. can,** Vendré lo más pronto posible

post /poust/ *n* (pole) poste, *m;* (of a sentry, etc.) puesto, *m;* (employment) empleo, *m;* (mail) correo, *m; Mil.* toque, *m.* —*vt* (a notice) fijar; anunciar; (to an appointment) destinar; (letters, etc.) echar al correo; *Com.* pasar al libro mayor; (inform) tener al corriente. —*vi* viajar en posta. **"P. no bills!"** «Se prohibe fijar carteles.» **registered p.,** correo certificado, *m.* **p. card,** postal, *f.* **p.-chaise,** silla de posta, *f.* **p.-date,** posfecha, *f.* **p.-free,** franco de porte. **p.-haste,** con gran celeridad. **p.-horse,** caballo de posta, *m.* **p.-impressionism,** post-impresionismo, *m.* **p.-mortem,** *n* autopsia, *f.* **p.-natal,** post-natal. **p.-nuptial,** postnupcial. **p. office,** correo, *m,* correos, *m pl;* (on a train) ambulancia de correos, *f.* **p. office box,** apartado de correos, *m.* **p. office savings bank,** caja postal de ahorros, *f.* **p.-paid,** porte pagado; franco. **p.-war,** *n* postguerra, *f.* —*a* de la postguerra

postage /'poustɪdʒ/ *n* porte de correos, franqueo, *m.* **p. stamp,** sello postal, *m*

postage meter *n* franqueadora, *f*

postal /'poustḷ/ *a* postal. **p. order,** orden postal de pago, *f.* **p. packet,** paquete postal, *m*

poster /'poustər/ *n* cartel, *m.* —*vt* fijar carteles (a or en); anunciar por carteles. **bill-p.,** fijador de carteles, *m*

poste restante /,poust rɛ'stɑnt/ *n* lista de correos, *f*

posterior /pɒ'stɪəriər/ *a* posterior. —*n* trasero, *m,* asentaderas, *f pl*

posteriority /pɒ,stɪəri'ɒriti/ *n* posterioridad, *f*

posterity /pɒ'stɛriti/ *n* posteridad, *f*

postern /'poustərn/ *n* postigo, *m; Mil.* poterna, *f*

postgraduate /'poust'grædʒuɪt/ *n* estudiante graduado que hace estudios avanzados, *m.* —*a* avanzado; para estudiantes graduados

posthumous /'pɒstʃəməs/ *a* póstumo

posthumously /'pɒstʃəməsli/ *adv* después de la muerte

postman /'poustmən/ *n* cartero, *m*

postmark /'poust,mɑrk/ *n* matasellos, *m,* *vt* poner matasellos (a)

postmaster /'poust,mæstər/ *n* administrador de correos, *m*

postmeridian /,poustmə'rɪdiən/ *a* postmeridiano

postmistress /'poust,mɪstrɪs/ *n* administradora de correos, *f*

postpone /poust'poun/ *vt* aplazar, diferir; retrasar; (subordinate) postergar

postponement /poust'pounmənt/ *n* aplazamiento, *m;* tardanza, *f*

postscript /'poust,skrɪpt/ *n* posdata, *f*

postulate /*n.* 'pɒstʃəlɪt; *v.* -,leɪt/ *n* postulado, *m,* *vt* postular

posture /'pɒstʃər/ *n* postura, actitud, *f;* (of affairs) estado, *m,* situación, *f.* —*vi* tomar una postura

posy /'pouzi/ *n* (nosegay) ramillete de flores, *m;* flor, *f;* (motto) mote, *m*

pot /pɒt/ *n* pote, *m;* tarro, *m;* (flower-) tiesto, *m;* (for cooking) olla marmita, *f;* jarro, *m.* —*vt* plantar en tiestos; conservar en potes. **pot-bellied,** panzudo. **pot-boiler,** obra literaria escrita con el sólo propósito de ganar dinero, *f.* **pot-herb,** hierba que se emplea para sazonar, hortaliza, *f.* **pot-hole,** bache, **pot-luck,** comida ordinaria, *f.* **pot-shot,** tiro fácil, *m;* tiro al azar, *m*

potable /'poutəbəl/ *a* potable

potage /pou'tɑʒ/ *n* potaje, *m*

potash /'pɒt,æʃ/ *n* potasa, *f.* **caustic p.,** potasa cáustica, *f*

potassium /pə'tæsiəm/ *n* potasio, *m*

potato /pə'teitou/ *n* patata, *f,* **sweet p.,** batata, *f.* **p. beetle,** coleóptero de la patata, *m.* **p. omelet,** tortilla a la española, *f.* **p. patch,** patatal, *m.* **p. peeler,** pelapatatas, *m*

potency /'poutṇsi/ *n* potencia, *f;* fuerza, eficacia, *f*

potent /'poutṇt/ *a* potente, fuerte; eficaz

potentate /'poutṇ,teit/ *n* potentado, *m*

potential /pə'tɛnʃəl/ *a* potencial; virtual; (*Phys.* *Gram.*) potencial, *n* poder, *m; Gram.* modo potencial, *m; Phys.* energía potencial, *f; Elec.* tensión potencial, *f*

potentiality /pə,tɛnʃi'æliti/ *n* potencialidad, *f*

pothook /'pɒt,hʊk/ *n* garabato de cocina, *m;* palote, *m;* (scrawl) garabato, *m*

potion /'pouʃən/ *n* poción, *f,*

potpourri /,poupu'ri/ *n* popurrí, *m*

potter /'pɒtər/ *n* alfarero, *m.* —*vi* gandulear. —*vt* perder. **potter's clay,** barro de alfarero, *m.* **potter's wheel,** tabanque, *m.* **potter's workshop,** alfar, *m*

pottery /'pɒtəri/ *n* alfarería, *f;* (china) loza, porcelana, *f*

pouch /pautʃ/ *n* bolsa, *f; Zool.* bolsa marsupial, *f;* (for tobacco) tabaquera, *f;* (for cartridges) cartuchera, *f.* —*vt* embolsar. —*vi* bolsear

poulterer /'poultərər/ *n* pollero (-ra)

poultice /'poultɪs/ *n* apósito, emplasto, *m,* *vt* poner emplastos (a or en)

poultry /'poultri/ *n* volatería, *f.* **p. dealer,** gallinero (-ra) vendedor (-ra) de volatería. **p. yard,** gallinero, *m*

poultry farming *n* avicultura, *f*

pounce /pauns/ *n* (swoop) calada, *f.* —*vi* (swoop) calarse; saltar (sobre); agarrar, hacer presa (en); *Fig.* atacar; descubrir, hacer patente

pound /paund/ *n* (weight and currency) libra, *f;* (for cattle) corral de concejo, *m;* (thump) golpe, *m.* —*vt* (break up) machacar, pistar; (beat) batir; (thump) golpear, aporrear. **p. sterling,** libra esterlina, *f.* **p. troy,** libra medicinal, *f*

pounding /'paundɪŋ/ *n* machucamiento, *m;* batimiento, *m*

pour /pɔr/ *vt* vaciar, verter; derramar. —*vi* correr; (of rain) diluviar, llover a cántaros; (fill) llenar; (of crowds, words, etc.) derramarse. **to p. out the tea,** servir el té. **The crowd poured in,** La multitud entró en tropel

pouring /'pɔrɪŋ/ *a* (of rain) torrencial

pout /paut/ *vi* torcer el gesto; hacer pucheritos

poverty /'pɒvərti/ *n* pobreza, *f.* **p.-stricken,** menesteroso, indigente, necesitado

powder /'paudər/ *n* polvo, *m;* (face) polvos de arroz, *m pl;* (gun) pólvora, *f.* —*vt* polvorear; (crush) reducir a polvo, pulverizar. —*vi* ponerse polvos. **p.-flash,** fogonazo, *m.* **p.-flask,** polvorín, *m.* **p.-magazine,** santabárbara, *f.* **p.-mill,** fábrica de pólvora, *f.* **p.-puff,** polvera, borla de empolvarse, *f*

powdered /'paudərd/ *a* en polvo

powdery /'paudəri/ *a* polvoriento; friable

power /'pauər/ *n* poder, *m;* facultad, capacidad, *f;* vigor, *m,* fuerza, *f;* (*Polit.* and *Math.*) potencia, *f; Mech.* fuerza, *f;* influencia, *f.* **as far as lies within my p.,** en cuanto me sea posible. **It does not lie within my p.,** No está dentro de mis posibilidades, No está en mi poder. **the Great Powers,** las grandes potencias. **the powers that be,** los que mandan. **to be in p.,** estar en el poder. **p.-house,** *n* central eléctrica, *f.* **p. of attorney,** poderes, *m pl,* procuración, *f.* **to grant p. of attorney (to),** dar poderes (a)

powerful /'pauərfəl/ *a* poderoso; fuerte; eficaz; potente; (of arguments, etc.) convincente

powerfully /'pauərfəli/ *adv* poderosamente; fuertemente

powerless /'pauərlɪs/ *a* impotente

power steering *n* dirección asistida *f* (Spain), servo dirección *f*

powwow /'pau,wau/ *n* conferencia, *f;* conversación, *f*

pox /pɒks/ *n* sífilis, *f;* (smallpox) viruelas, *f pl;* (chicken-pox) viruelas falsas, *f pl*

practicability /,præktikə'biliti/ *n* factibilidad, *f*

practicable /'præktikəbəl/ *a* practicable, factible, posible; viable, transitable

practical /'præktikəl/ *a* (doable) factible; práctico; virtual. **p. joke,** burla de consecuencias

practically /'præktikli/ *adv* prácticamente; en práctica; virtualmente; (in fact) en efecto. **p. nothing,** casi nada

practicalness /'præktikəlnis/ *n* carácter práctico, *m*

practice /'præktis/ *n* (custom) costumbre, *f;* práctica, *f;* ejercicio, *m;* (of a doctor, etc.) clientela, *f;* profesión, f; (religious) rito, m, ceremonias, f pl; (experience) experiencia, f. **It is not his p. to...,** No es su costumbre de... **to be out of p.,** estar desentrenado. **to put into p.,** poner en práctica. **P. makes perfect,** El ejercicio hace maestro. —vt tener la costumbre de; practicar; (a profession) ejercer; (a game) entrenarse en; (work at) estudiar; (a musical instrument) tocar; (accustom) acostumbrar. **to p. what one preaches,** predicar con el ejemplo

practiced /'præktɪst/ a experimentado; experto

practitioner /præk'tɪʃənər/ n médico (-ca). **general p.,** médico (-ca) general

pragmatic /præg'mætɪk/ a pragmatista; (historical) pragmático; práctico

pragmatism /'prægmə,tɪzəm/ n pragmatismo, m

pragmatist /'prægmətɪst/ n pragmatista, mf

Prague /prɑg/ Praga, f

prairie /'prɛəri/ n pradera, sabana, pampa, f. a de la pradera, etc.

praise /preɪz/ vt alabar; ensalzar, glorificar; elogiar. —n alabanza, f; elogio, m; glorificación, f, ensalzamiento, m. **to p. to the skies,** poner en los cuernos de la luna poner por las nubes, poner sobre las estrellas hacerse lenguas de

praiseworthiness /'preɪz,wɜrðɪnɪs/ n mérito, m

praiseworthy /'preɪz,wɜrði/ a digno de alabanza, laudable

prance /præns/ vi (of a horse) caracolear, encabritarse, cabriolar; saltar; andar airosamente. —n corveta, cabriola, f; salto, m

prank /præŋk/ n travesura, diablura, f. **to play pranks,** hacer diabluras

prate, prattle /preɪt; 'prætl/ vi charlar, chacharear; (lisp) balbucir; (of brooks, etc.) murmurar, susurrar. —vt divulgar. —n charla, cháchara, f; balbuceo, m

prattler /'prætlər/ n parlanchín (-ina); (gossip) chismoso (-sa); (child) niño (-ña)

prattling /'prætlɪŋ/ n charla, f; (lisping) balbuceo, m; (of brooks, etc.) murmullo, susurro, ruido armonioso, m. —a charlatán, gárrulo; balbuciente; (of brooks, etc.) parlero

prawn /prɔn/ n camarón, m

pray /preɪ/ vt and vi suplicar; implorar; rezar, orar. **P. be seated,** Haga el favor de sentarse

prayer /'preɪər/ n rezo, m, plegaria, oración, f; súplica, f; Law. petición, f. **p. book,** libro de devociones, devocionario, m. **p.-meeting,** reunión para rezar, f. **p.-rug,** alfombra de rezo, f

praying /'preɪɪŋ/ n rezo, m; suplicación, f

pre- prefix de antes de (e.g. pre-World-War-1 publications, publicaciones de antes de la Primera Guerra Mundial)

preach /pritʃ/ vt and vi predicar

preacher /'pritʃər/ n predicador (-ra). **to turn p.,** meterse a predicar

preaching /'pritʃɪŋ/ n predicación, f, a predicador

preamble /'pri,æmbəl/ n preámbulo, m

prearrange /,priə'reɪndʒ/ vt preparar de antemano, predisponer

precarious /prɪ'kɛəriəs/ a precario; inseguro; incierto, arriesgado

precariousness /prɪ'kɛəriəsnɪs/ n condición precaria, f; inseguridad, f; incertidumbre, f

precaution /prɪ'kɔʃən/ n precaución, f. **to take precautions,** tomar precauciones

precautionary /prɪ'kɔʃə,nɛri/ a de precaución; preventivo

precede /prɪ'sid/ vt preceder (a), anteceder (a); tomar precedencia (a), exceder en importancia (a). —vi ir delante; tener la precedencia

precedence /'prɛsɪdəns/ n precedencia, f; prioridad, f; superioridad, f. **to take p. over,** tomar precedencia (a), preceder (a)

precedent /n. 'prɛsɪdənt; a. prɪ'sidnt/ n precedente, m, a precedente. **without p.,** sin precedente

preceding /prɪ'sidɪŋ/ a anterior, precedente

precept /'prisɛpt/ n precepto, m

preceptor /prɪ'sɛptər/ n preceptor, m

precinct /'prisɪŋkt/ n (police station) comisaría de sección (Argentina), delegación (Mexico), f

precincts /'prisɪŋkts/ n pl recinto, m; ámbito, m; distrito, barrio, m

preciosity /,prɛʃi'ɒsɪti/ n afectación, f

precious /'prɛʃəs/ a precioso; de gran valor; hermoso; amado; muy querido; (with rogue, etc.) redomado; completo. **p. little,** muy poco. **p. nearly,** casi, por poco... **p. stone,** piedra preciosa, f

preciousness /'prɛʃəsnɪs/ n preciosidad, f; gran valor, m

precipice /'prɛsəpɪs/ n precipicio, m

precipitancy /prɪ'sɪpɪtənsi/ n precipitación, f

precipitant /prɪ'sɪpɪtənt/ a precipitado

precipitate /v. prɪ'sɪpɪ,teɪt; n., a. -tɪt/ vt precipitar, despeñar, arrojar; acelerar; Chem. precipitar. —vi precipitarse. —n precipitado, m. —a precipitado, súbito. **to p. oneself,** tirarse, lanzarse

precipitately /prɪ'sɪpɪtɪtli/ adv precipitadamente

precipitation /prɪ,sɪpɪ'teɪʃən/ n Chem. precipitación, f; Chem. precipitado, m; (rain, etc.) precipitación pluvial, f

precipitous /prɪ'sɪpɪtəs/ a precipitoso, escarpado, acantilado

precipitously /prɪ'sɪpɪtəsli/ adv en precipicio

precise /prɪ'saɪs/ a preciso; exacto; justo; puntual; escrupuloso; formal; claro; pedante, afectado; ceremonioso

precisely /prɪ'saɪsli/ adv precisamente; exactamente; puntualmente; escrupulosamente; claramente; con afectación; ceremoniosamente. **at six o'clock p.,** a las seis en punto

precision /prɪ'sɪʒən/ n precisión, f; exactitud, f; puntualidad, f; escrupulosidad, f; claridad, f; afectación, f; ceremonia, f

preclude /prɪ'klud/ vt excluir; impedir, hacer imposible

preclusion /prɪ'kluʒən/ n exclusión, f; imposibilidad, f

precocious /prɪ'koʊʃəs/ a precoz

precocity /prɪ'kɒsɪti/ n precocidad, f

preconceived /,prikən'sivd/ a preconcebido

preconception /,prikən'sɛpʃən/ n idea preconcebida, f; (prejudice) prejuicio, m

preconcerted /,prikən'sɜrtɪd/ a concertado de antemano

precursor /prɪ'kɜrsər/ n precursor (-ra)

precursory /prɪ'kɜrsəri/ a precursor

predatory /'prɛdə,tɔri/ a rapaz; de rapiña; voraz

predecease /,pridɪ'sis/ vt morir antes (de or que); Law. premorir. —n Law. premuerto, m

predecessor /'prɛdə,sɛsər/ n predecesor (-ra); (ancestor) antepasado, m

predestination /prɪ,dɛstə'neɪʃən/ n predestinación, f

predestine /prɪ'dɛstɪn/ vt predestinar

predetermination /,pridɪ,tɜrmɪ'neɪʃən/ n predeterminación, f

predetermine /,pridɪ'tɜrmɪn/ vt predeterminar

predicament /prɪ'dɪkəmənt/ n /'prɛdɪkəmənt/ (logic) predicamento, m; situación, f; (fix) apuro, m; pl **predicaments,** categorías, f pl

predicate /v. 'prɛdɪ,keɪt; n. -kɪt/ vt afirmar. —n (logic, Gram.) predicado, m

predict /prɪ'dɪkt/ vt predecir, pronosticar, profetizar

prediction /prɪ'dɪkʃən/ n predicción, f; pronóstico, vaticinio, m, profecía, f

predilection /,prɛdl'ɛkʃən/ n predilección, f

predispose /,pridɪ'spouz/ vt predisponer

predisposition /,pridɪspə'zɪʃən/ n predisposición, f

predominance /prɪ'dɒmənəns/ n predominio, m

predominant /prɪ'dɒmənənt/ a predominante

predominate /prɪ'dɒmə,neɪt/ vi predominar

preeminence /pri'ɛmənəns/ n preeminencia, f; primacia, superioridad, f

preeminent /pri'ɛmənənt/ a preeminente; superior; extraordinario

preeminently /pri'ɛmənəntli/ adv preeminentemente; extraordinariamente; por excelencia; entre todos

preen /prin/ vt (of birds) limpiarse; (of people) darse humos, jactarse

preexist /,priɪg'zɪst/ vi preexistir

preexistence /,priɪg'zɪstəns/ n preexistencia, f

prefabricated /pri'fæbrɪ,keɪtɪd/ a prefabricado

preface /'prɛfɪs/ n prólogo, m; Eccl. prefacio, m; introducción, f. —vt dar principio (a), empezar. **He**

prefaced his remarks by..., Dijo a modo de introducción

prefatory /'prefə,tɔri/ a preliminar, introductorio; a manera de prólogo

prefect /'prifɛkt/ n prefecto, m

prefecture /'prifɛktʃər/ n prefectura, f

prefer /prɪ'fɜr/ vt preferir, gustar más (a); (promote) ascender, elevar; (a charge, etc.) presentar. **to p. a charge against,** pedir en juicio (a). **I p. oranges to apples,** Me gustan más las naranjas que las manzanas, Prefiero las naranjas a las manzanas

preferability /,prefərə'bɪlɪti/ n preferencia, ventaja, f

preferable /'prefərəbəl/ a preferible

preferably /'prefərəbli/ adv preferiblemente, con preferencia

preference /'prefərəns/ n preferencia, f; privilegio, m. **p. share,** acción privilegiada, acción preferente, f

preferential /,prefə'rɛnʃəl/ a preferente

preferment /prɪ'fɜrmənt/ n promoción, f, ascenso, m; puesto eminente, m

preferred /prɪ'fɜrd/ a preferente; favorito, predilecto. **p. share,** acción preferente, f

prefix /'prifɪks/ vt anteponer, prefijar; (to a word) poner prefijo (a). —n prefijo, m

pregnancy /'prɛgnənsi/ n embarazo, m, preñez, f

pregnant /'prɛgnənt/ a embarazada, encinta, preñada, f; Fig. fértil; Fig. preñado

prehensile /prɪ'hɛnsɪl/ a prensil

prehistoric /,prihɪ'stɔrɪk/ a prehistórico

prehistory /pri'hɪstəri/ n prehistoria, f

prejudge /pri'dʒʌdʒ/ vt prejuzgar

prejudice /'prɛdʒədɪs/ n prejuicio, m; Law. perjuicio, m. —vt influir, predisponer; (damage) perjudicar. **without p.,** sin perjuicio

prejudiced /'prɛdʒədɪst/ a parcial; con prejuicios

prejudicial /,prɛdʒə'dɪʃəl/ a perjudicial

prelacy /'prɛləsi/ n prelacía, f; episcopado, m

prelate /'prɛlɪt/ n prelado, m

preliminarily /prɪ,lɪmə'nɛərəli/ adv preliminarmente

preliminary /prɪ'lɪmə,nɛri/ a preliminar. —n preliminar, m

prelude (to) /'prɛlyud/ n preludio (de) m; presagio (de) m, vt and vi preludiar

premature /,primə'tʃʊr/ a prematuro

prematurely /,primə'tʃʊrli/ adv prematuramente

prematureness /,primə'tʃʊrnɪs/ n lo prematuro

premeditate /pri'mɛdɪ,teit/ vt premeditar

premeditatedly /prɪ'mɛdɪ,teitɪdli/ adv premeditadamente, con premeditación

premeditation /prɪ,mɛdɪ'teiʃən/ n premeditación, f

premier /prɪ'mɪər/ a primero, principal. —n primer minístro, m; (in Spain) presidente del Consejo de Ministros, m

premiere /prɪ'mɪər/ n estreno, m

premiership /prɪ'mɪərʃɪp/ n puesto de primer ministro, m; (in Spain) presidencia del Consejo de Ministros, f

premise /'prɛmɪs/ n (logic) premisa, f; pl **premises,** local, m; recinto, m; establecimiento, m; propiedad, f; tierras, f pl. **on the premises,** en el local; en el establecimiento

premium /'primiəm/ n (prize) premio, m, recompensa, f; Com. prima, f; precio, m. **at a p.,** a premio; a una prima; (of shares) sobre la par; Fig. en boga, muy solicitado, en gran demanda

premonition /,primə'nɪʃən/ n presentimiento, presagio, m

premonitory /prɪ'mɒnɪ,tɔri/ a premonitorio

prenatal /pri'neitl/ a prenatal, antenatal

preoccupation /pri,ɒkyə'peiʃən/ n preocupación, f

preoccupied /pri'ɒkyə,paid/ a preocupado; abstraído, absorto

preoccupy /pri'ɒkyə,pai/ vt preocupar

prepaid /pri'peid/ a porte pagado, franco de porte

preparation /,prɛpə'reiʃən/ n preparación, f; preparativo, m, disposición, f; (patent food) preparado, m. **I have made all my preparations,** He hecho todos mis preparativos. **The book is in p.,** El libro está en preparación

preparative /prɪ'pærətɪv/ a preparativo. —n preparativo, m

preparatory /prɪ'pærə,tɔri/ a preparatorio, preparativo; preliminar. **p. school,** escuela preparatoria, f, m. **p. to,** como preparación para; antes de

prepare /prɪ'pɛər/ vt preparar; aparejar, aviar; equipar; (cloth) aprestar. —vi prepararse; hacer preparativos

preparedness /prɪ'pɛərdnɪs/ n estado de preparación, m; preparación, f, apercibimiento, m

prepay /prɪ'pei/ vt pagar adelantado; (a letter, etc.) franquear

prepayment /pri'peimənt/ n pago adelantado, m; (of a letter, etc.) franqueo, m

preponderance /prɪ'pɒndərəns/ n preponderancia, f

preponderant /prɪ'pɒndərənt/ a preponderante, predominante

preponderantly /prɪ'pɒndərəntli/ adv predominantemente; en su mayoría

preponderate /prɪ'pɒndə,reit/ vi preponderar; prevalecer (sobre), predominar (sobre)

preposition /,prɛpə'zɪʃən/ n preposición, f

prepossess /,prɪpə'zɛs/ vt predisponer; causar buena impresión (a)

prepossessing /,prɪpə'zɛsɪŋ/ a atractivo

preposterous /prɪ'pɒstərəs/ a ridículo, absurdo

preposterously /prɪ'pɒstərəsli/ adv absurdamente

preposterousness /prɪ'pɒstərəsnɪs/ n ridiculez, f

Prep School /prɛp/ n preparatoria, f

prepuce /'pripyus/ n prepucio, m

Pre-Raphaelite /pri'ræfiə,lait/ a and n prerrafaelista, mf

prerequisite /prɪ'rɛkwəzɪt/ n requisito necesario, esencial, m, a previamente necesario, esencial

prerogative /prɪ'rɒgətɪv/ n prerrogativa, f

presage /'prɛsɪdʒ/ n presagio, m; anuncio, m. —vt presagiar; anunciar

Presbyterian /,prɛzbɪ'tɪəriən/ a and n presbiteriano (-na)

prescience /'prɛʃəns/ n presciencia, previsión, f

prescient /'prɛʃənt/ a presciente

prescind /prɪ'sɪnd/ vt prescindir (de); separar (de). —vi separarse

prescribe /prɪ'skraib/ vt and vi prescribir; Med. recetar; dar leyes; Law. prescribir

prescription /prɪ'skrɪpʃən/ n prescripción, f; Med. receta, f

presence /'prɛzəns/ n presencia, f; (ghost) aparición, f. **in the p. of,** en presencia de, delante; a vista de. **p. of mind,** presencia de ánimo, serenidad de ánimo, f

present /'prɛzənt/ a presente; actual; (with month) corriente; Gram. presente. **at p.,** al presente, actualmente. **at the p. day,** a la fecha, en la actualidad, hoy día. **P. company excepted!** ¡Mejorando lo presente! **the present writer,** el que suscribe, el que esto escribe, el que estas líneas traza. **to be p. at,** presenciar, ser testigo de; asistir a, acudir a; hallarse en. **p.-day,** de hoy, actual. **p. tense,** Gram. tiempo presente, m

present /'prɛzənt/ n (time) presente, m; actualidad, f; Gram. tiempo presente, m; (gift) regalo, m, dádiva, f. **By these presents...,** Law. Por estas presentes... **to make a p. of,** regalar. **Jane made me a p. of a watch,** Juana me regaló un reloj

present /prɪ'zɛnt/ vt presentar; ofrecer; manifestar; (a gift) regalar, dar; (Eccl. Mil.) presentar. **New problems presented themselves,** Nuevos problemas surgieron. **to p. arms,** presentar las armas. **He presented himself in the office,** Se presentó en la oficina. **He presented his friend Mr. Moreno to me,** Me presentó a su amigo el Sr. Moreno

presentable /prɪ'zɛntəbəl/ a presentable

presentation /,prɛzən'teiʃən/ n presentación, f; homenaje, m; (exhibition) exposición, f. **on p.,** Com. a presentación

presentiment /prɪ'zɛntəmənt/ n presentimiento, m, corazonada, f. **I had a p. that...,** Tuve el presentimiento de que..., Tuve una corazonada que... **to have a p. about,** presentir

presently /'prɛzəntli/ adv pronto; en seguida; dentro de poco

preservation /,prɛzər'veiʃən/ n conservación, f; (from harm) preservación, f

preservative /prɪ'zɜrvətɪv/ *a* preservativo. —*n* preservativo, *m*

preserve /prɪ'zɜrv/ *vt* preservar (de); guardar; proteger; conservar; *Cul.* hacer conservas de; (in syrup) almibarar. —*n Cul.* conserva, *f;* (of fruit) compota, confitura, *f;* (covert) coto, *m.* **preserved fruit,** dulce de almibar, *m.* **p. dish,** compotera, *f*

preserver /prɪ'zɜrvər/ *n* conservador (-ra); (saviour) salvador (-ra); (benefactor) bienhechor (-ra)

preserving /prɪ'zɜrvɪŋ/ *n* (from harm) preservación, *f;* conservación, *f.* **p. pan,** cazuela para conservas, *f*

preside /prɪ'zaid/ *vi* (over) presidir; dirigir, gobernar. **He presided at the meeting,** Presidio la reunión

presidency /'prezɪdənsi/ *n* presidencia, *f*

president /'prezɪdənt/ *n* presidente, *m;* (of a college) rector, *m.* **lady p.,** presidenta, *f*

presidential /,prezɪ'dɛnʃəl/ *a* presidencial

presidentship /'prezɪdənt,ʃɪp/ *n* presidencia, *f*

press /pres/ *vt* prensar; (juice out of) exprimir; (clothes) planchar; (a bell, a hand, and of a shoe, etc.) apretar; (embrace) dar un abrazo (a); (a stamp, a kiss, etc.) imprimir; (an enemy) hostigar, acosar; (in a game) apretar; (crowd upon) oprimir; (emphasize) insistir en; (urge) instar, instigar; (compel) obligar; apremiar; (oppress) abrumar, agobiar; (paper) satinar; (an advantage) aprovecharse de. **Lola pressed his hand,** Lola le apretó la mano. **Time presses,** El tiempo es breve. **I did not p. the point,** No insistí. **to p. against,** pegar(se) contra. **to p. down,** comprimir; *Fig.* agobiar. **to p. for,** exigir, reclamar. **to p. forward, on,** avanzar; seguir el camino, continuar la marcha; (hurry) apretar el paso

press /pres/ *n* (pressure) apretón, *m;* (push) golpe, *m;* (throng) muchedumbre, *f;* (of business, etc.) urgencia, *f;* (apparatus) prensa, *f;* (printing press and publishing firm) imprenta, *f;* (cupboard) armario, *m.* **Associated P.,** Prensa Asociada, *f.* **freedom of the p.,** libertad de la prensa, *f.* **in p., in the p.,** en prensa. **in the p. of battle,** en lo más reñido de la batalla. **to go to p.,** entrar en prensa. **p.-agent,** agente de publicidad, *m.* **p.-box,** tribuna de la prensa, *f.* **p. clipping, p.-cutting,** recorte de prensa, *m.* **p.-gallery,** tribuna de la prensa, *f.* **p.-gang,** ronda de enganche, *f.* **p.-mark,** número de catálogo, *m.* **p. proof,** prueba de imprenta, *f.* **p.-room,** taller de imprenta, *m.* **p.-stud,** botón automático, *m.* **p. conference,** rueda de prensa, entrevista de prensa, conferencia de pensa, *f*

pressing /'presɪŋ/ *a* urgente, apremiante; importuno. —*n* prensado, *m,* prensadura, *f;* expresión, *f;* (of a garment) planchado, *m*

pressingly /'presɪŋli/ *adv* urgentemente, con urgencia; importunamente

pressman /'presmən/ *n* tirador, *m;* (journalist) periodista, *m*

pressure /'preʃər/ *n* presión, *f;* (of the hand) apretón, *m;* apremio, *m;* opresión, *f;* (weight) peso, *m;* (force) fuerza, *f;* urgencia, *f.* **p.-cooker,** cazuela de presión, olla de presión, *f,* presto, *m.* **p.-gauge,** manómetro, *m*

prestidigitation /,prestɪ,dɪdʒɪ'teiʃən/ *n* prestidigitación, *f,* juegos de manos, *m pl*

prestige /pre'stiʒ/ *n* prestigio, *m*

prestigious /pre'stɪdʒəs/ *a* prestigiado

presumable /prɪ'zuməbəl/ *a* presumible

presume /prɪ'zum/ *vt* presumir; suponer, sospechar; (attempt) pretender. —*vi* presumir; tomarse libertades; abusar (de)

presumption /prɪ'zʌmpʃən/ *n* presunción, *f;* suposición, *f;* (effrontery) atrevimiento, *m;* insolencia, *f*

presumptive /prɪ'zʌmptɪv/ *a* presuntivo; (with heir, etc.) presunto

presumptuous /prɪ'zʌmptʃuəs/ *a* presumido, insolente, presuntuoso; atrevido

presumptuously /prɪ'zʌmptʃuəsli/ *adv* presuntuosamente

presumptuousness /prɪ'zʌmptʃuəsnɪs/ *n* presunción, presuntuosidad, *f;* atrevimiento, *m*

presuppose /,prisə'pouz/ *vt* presuponer

presupposition /,prisʌpə'zɪʃən/ *n* presuposición, *f*

pretence /prɪ'tɛns/ *n* (claim) pretensión, *f;* afectación, *f;* (simulation) fingimiento, *m;* pretexto, *m.* **false pretences,** apariencias fingidas, *f pl;* engaño, *m,*

estafa, *f.* **to make a p. of,** fingir. **under p. of,** bajo pretexto de

pretend /prɪ'tɛnd/ *vt* dar como pretexto de; aparentar, fingir, simular, hacer el papel (de). —*vi* pretender (a); tener pretensiones (de); ser pretendiente (a); fingir

pretended /prɪ'tɛndɪd/ *a* supuesto, fingido; falso

pretender /prɪ'tɛndər/ *n* pretendiente, *m;* hipócrita, *mf*

pretension /prɪ'tɛnʃən/ *n* pretensión, *f;* afectación, simulación, *f*

pretentious /prɪ'tɛnʃəs/ *a* pretencioso; (of persons) presumido

pretentiousness /prɪ'tɛnʃəsnɪs/ *n* pretensiones, *f pl,* lo pretencioso

preterite /'pretərɪt/ *n* (tiempo) pretérito, *m, a* pretérito, pasado

pretext /'pritɛkst/ *n* pretexto, *m.* —*vt* pretextar. **under p. of,** bajo pretexto de, so color de

prettily /'prɪtli/ *adv* lindamente; con gracia; agradablemente

prettiness /'prɪtinɪs/ *n* lo bonito; elegancia, *f;* gracia, *f*

pretty /'prɪti/ *a* bonito; (of women, children) guapo, mono; (of men) lindo; elegante; excelente; *Ironic.* bueno. —*adv* bastante; medianamente; (very) muy; (almost) casi. **p. good,** bastante bueno. **p.-p.,** de muñeca; mono. —*n* chuchería, *f,* guapos, *m pl.* **p. ways,** monerías, *f pl*

prevail /prɪ'veil/ *vi* prevalecer, predominar; ser la costumbre. **to p. against or over,** triunfar de, vencer (a). **to p. on, upon,** inducir, convencer, persuadir. **to be prevailed upon to,** dejarse persuadir a

prevailing /prɪ'veilɪŋ/ *a* prevaleciente; dominante; predominante, reinante; general; común; (fashionable) en boga

prevalence /'prevələns/ *n* predominio, *m;* existencia, *f;* (habit) costumbre, *f;* (fashion) boga, *f*

prevalent /'prevələnt/ *a* prevaleciente; predominante; general; común; corriente; (fashionable) en boga

prevaricate /prɪ'væri,keit/ *vi* tergiversar; *Law.* prevaricar

prevarication /prɪ,væri'keiʃən/ *n* tergiversación, *f,* equívoco, *m*

prevaricator /prɪ'væri,keitər/ *n* tergiversador (-ra)

prevent /prɪ'vɛnt/ *vt* evitar; (hinder) impedir (a)

preventable /prɪ'vɛntəbəl/ *a* evitable

prevention /prɪ'vɛnʃən/ *n* prevención, *f;* (preventive) estorbo, obstáculo, *m*

preventive /prɪ'vɛntɪv/ *a* preventivo. —*n* preservativo, *m*

preview /'pri,vyu/ *n* vista de antemano, *f;* (of a film) avances, *m pl* (Cuba, Mexico), colas, *f pl* (Argentina), cortos *m pl* (Venezuela), sinopsis, *f* (Uruguay), tráiler, *m* (Spain)

previous /'priviəs/ *a* previo, anterior. **p. to,** antes de

previously /'priviəsli/ *adv* anteriormente, antes, previamente

previousness /'priviəsnɪs/ *n* anterioridad, *f;* inoportunidad, *f*

prevision /prɪ'vɪʒən/ *n* previsión, *f*

prewar /'pri'wɔr/ *a* de antes de la guerra

prey /prei/ *n* presa, *f; Fig.* víctima, *f;* (booty) botín, *m.* —*vi* (of animals) devorar; (plunder) robar, pillar; (of sorrow, etc.) hacer presa (de); agobiar, consumir; (sponge on) vivir a costa de. **to fall a p. to,** ser víctima de

price /prais/ *n* precio, *m;* valor, *m;* costa, *f.* —*vt* evaluar, tasar; poner precio a; preguntar el precio de; fijar el precio de. **at any p.,** a cualquier precio; (whatever the cost) cueste lo que cueste. **at a reduced p.,** a precio reducido. **fixed p.,** precio fijo, *m.* **p. ceiling,** precio máximo, precio tope, *m.* **p. control,** control de precios, *m.* **price list,** lista de precios, *f;* tarifa, *f;* (of shares, etc.) boletín de cotización, *m.* **Prices are subject to change without notice,** Los precios están sujetos a variación sin previo aviso.

priceless /'praislɪs/ *a* sin precio; (amusing) divertidísimo. **These jewels are p.,** Estas joyas no tienen precio

prick /prɪk/ *n* pinchazo, *m;* picadura, *f;* punzada, *f;* (prickle) espina, *f;* (with a goad) aguijonazo, *m;*

(with a pin) alfilerazo, *m;* (with a spur) espolada, *f;* (of conscience) remordimiento, escrúpulo, *m.* —*vt* pinchar, punzar; picar; (with remorse) atormentar, causar remordimiento (a); (urge on) incitar. **to p. the ears,** aguzar las orejas

pricking /'prɪkɪŋ/ *n* picadura, *f;* punzada, *f.* **prickings of conscience,** remordimientos, *m pl*

prickle /'prɪkəl/ *n* espina, *f;* (irritation) escozor, *m*

prickly /'prɪkli/ *a* espinoso; erizado. **p. heat,** salpullido causado por exceso de calor, *m.* **p. pear,** higo chumbo, *m,* chumbera, *f*

pride /praid/ *n* orgullo, *m;* arrogancia, *f;* (splendour) pompa, *f,* fausto, aparato, *m;* belleza, *f;* vigor, *m;* (of lions) manada, *f.* **to take p. in,** estar orgulloso de. **to p. oneself,** sentirse orgulloso, ufanarse. **to p. oneself upon,** jactarse de, preciarse de

prie-dieu /'pri'dyu/ *n* reclinatorio, *m*

prier /'praiər/ *n* espía, *mf;* curioso (-sa)

priest /prist/ *n* sacerdote, *m;* cura, *m.* **high-p.,** sumo sacerdote, *m.* **p.-ridden,** dominado por el clero

priestess /'pristɪs/ *n* sacerdotisa, *f*

priesthood /'pristhʊd/ *n* sacerdocio, *m*

priestly /'pristli/ *a* sacerdotal

prig /prɪg/ *n* fatuo (-ua), mojigato (-ta)

priggish /'prɪgɪʃ/ *a* fatuo, gazmoño

priggishness /'prɪgɪʃnɪs/ *n* gazmoñería, fatuidad, *f*

prim /prɪm/ *a* almidonado, etiquetero; peripuesto; afectado

primacy /'praiməsi/ *n* primacía, *f*

prima donna /ˌprimə 'dɒnə/ *n* cantatriz, *f*

primarily /prai'mɛərəli/ *adv* en primer lugar principalmente

primary /'praimɛri/ *a* primario; primitivo; principal. **p. education,** enseñanza primaria, *f.* **p. color,** color primario, *m.* **p. school,** escuela primaria, *f.* **p. election,** elección interna (dentro de un partido), *f*

primate /'praimeit/ *n* primado, *m*

prime /praim/ *a* primero; principal; excelente; de primera calidad; de primera clase. —*n* (spring) primavera, *f;* (of life, etc.) flor, *f,* vigor, *m;* (best) nata, crema, *f; Eccl.* prima, *f;* (number) número primo, *m.* —*vt* preparar, aprestar; (fire-arms) cebar. **p. the pump,** cebar la bomba; (with paint, etc.) imprimar; (instruct) dar instrucciones (a), informar. **in his p.,** en la flor de su edad. **of p. quality,** de primera calidad. **P. Minister,** Primer Ministro, *m.* **p. necessity,** artículo de primera necesidad, *m*

primer /'praimər/ *n* cartilla, *f,* abecedario, *m;* libro de lectura, *m;* (prayer book) devocionario, *m*

primeval /prai'mivəl/ *a* primevo, primitivo

priming /'praimɪŋ/ *n* preparación, *f;* (of fire-arms) cebo, *m;* (of paint, etc.) imprimación, *f;* instrución, *f*

primitive /'prɪmɪtɪv/ *a* primitivo; anticuado. —*n* primitivo, *m*

primitiveness /'prɪmɪtɪvnɪs/ *n* lo primitivo; carácter primitivo, *m*

primly /'prɪmli/ *adv* afectadamente, con afectación; gravemente

primness /'prɪmnɪs/ *n* afectación, *f;* gravedad, *f*

primogeniture /ˌpraimə'dʒɛnɪtʃər/ *n* primogenitura, *f*

primordial /prai'mɔrdiəl/ *a* primordial

primrose /'prɪmˌrouz/ *n* primavera, *f;* color amarillo pálido, *m*

prince /prɪns/ *n* príncipe, *m.* **P. Consort,** príncipe consorte, *m.* **P. of Wales,** (Britain) príncipe heredero, *m;* (Spanish equivalent) Príncipe de Asturias, *m.* **p. regent,** príncipe regente, *m.* **P. Charming,** el Príncipe Azul, *m*

princeliness /'prɪnslinɪs/ *n* magnificencia, *f;* nobleza, *f*

princely /'prɪnsli/ *a* principesco; magnífico; noble

princess /'prɪnsɪs/ *n* princesa, *f*

principal /'prɪnsəpəl/ *a* principal; fundamental; mayor. —*n* principal, jefe, *m;* (of a university) rector, *m;* (of a school) director (-ra); *Law.* causante, *m; Com.* capital, *m*

principality /ˌprɪnsə'pælɪti/ *n* principado, *m*

principally /'prɪnsəpli/ *adv* principalmente

principle /'prɪnsəpəl/ *n* principio, *m.* **in p.,** en principio

principled /'prɪnsəpəld/ *a* de principios...

print /prɪnt/ *n* (mark) impresión, marca, *f;* (type)

letra de molde, *f,* tipo, *m;* (of books) imprenta, *f;* (fabric) estampado, *m;* (picture) grabado, *m;* (photograph) positiva impresa, *f;* (mold) molde, *m.* —*vt* marcar; imprimir; (on the mind) grabar; *Print.* tirar, hacer una tirada (de); (in photography) tirar una prueba (de); (publish) sacar a luz, publicar; (fabrics) estampar. **in p.,** impreso; publicado; **He likes to see his name in print,** Le gusta ver su nombre en letras de molde; (available) existente. **to be out of p.,** estar agotado. **p. dress,** vestido estampado, *m*

printed /'prɪntɪd/ *a* impreso. **p. fabric,** estampado, *m.* **p. matter,** impresos, *m pl*

printer /'prɪntər/ *n* impresor, *m;* tipógrafo, *m.* **printer's devil,** aprendiz de impresor, *m.* **printer's ink,** tinta de imprenta, tinta tipográfica, *f.* **printer's mark,** pie de imprenta, *m*

printing /'prɪntɪŋ/ *n* imprenta, *f;* impresión, *f;* (of fabrics) estampación, *f;* (art of) tipografía, *f.* **p. house,** imprenta, *f.* **p. machine,** máquina de imprimir, *f.* **p. press,** prensa tipográfica, *f.* **p. types,** caracteres de imprenta, *m pl*

prior /'praiər/ *n* prior, *m, a* anterior, previo. **p. to,** anterior a, antes de

prioress /'praiərɪs/ *n* priora, *f*

priority /prai'ɔrɪti/ *n* prioridad, *f*

prism /'prɪzəm/ *n* prisma, *m;* espectro solar, *m*

prismatic /prɪz'mætɪk/ *a* prismático

prison /'prɪzən/ *n* prisión, cárcel, *f.* **p.-breaking,** huida de la prisión, *f.* **p. camp,** campo de prisioneros, *m.* **p. van,** coche celular, *m.* **p. yard,** patio de la prisión, *m*

prisoner /'prɪzənər/ *n* prisionero (-ra), preso (-sa). **to take p.,** prender, hacer prisionero (a)

pristine /'prɪstin/ *a* pristino, original

privacy /'praivəsi/ *n* soledad, *f,* aislamiento, retiro, *m;* intimidad, *f;* secreto, *m*

private /'praivɪt/ *a* particular; privado; secreto; confidencial; reservado; íntimo; personal; doméstico; (of hearings, etc.) a puertas cerradas, secreto; (own) propio. —*n* (soldier) soldado raso, *m.* **in p.,** en secreto; confidencialmente, de persona a persona. **They wish to be p.,** Quieren estar a solas. **p. company,** sociedad en comandita, *f.* **p. hotel,** pensión, *f.* **p. house,** casa particular, *f.* **p. individual,** particular, *mf.* **p. interview,** entrevista privada, *f.* **p. life,** vida privada, *f.* **p. office,** despacho particular, *m.* **p. secretary,** secretario (-ia) particular. **p. viewing, (of a film)** función privada, *f;* **(of an exhibition)** día de inauguración, *m*

privateer /ˌpraivə'tɪər/ *n* corsario, *m*

privately /'praivɪtli/ *adv* privadamente; en secreto; personalmente; confidencialmente; (of hearings) a puertas cerradas

privation /prai'veiʃən/ *n* privación, *f;* carencia, escasez, *f*

privet /'prɪvɪt/ *n* alheña, *f*

privilege /'prɪvəlɪdʒ/ *n* privilegio, *m;* derecho, *m;* inmunidad, *f.* —*vt* privilegiar

privileged /'prɪvəlɪdʒd/ *a* privilegiado; confidencial

privy /'prɪvi/ *a* privado; cómplice; enterado; personal, particular. —*n* (latrine) retrete, *m.* **p. council,** consejo privado, *m*

prize /praiz/ *n* premio, *m;* recompensa, *f,* galardón, *m;* (capture) presa, *f.* —*a* que ha ganado un premio; premiado; (huge) enorme; (complete) de primer orden. —*vt* estimar, apreciar. **to p. open,** abrir con una palanca. **to carry off the p.,** ganar el premio. **cash p.,** premio en metálico, *m.* **first p.,** primer premio, *m;* (in a lottery) premio gordo, *m.* **p. court,** tribunal de presas, *m.* **p. fight,** partido de boxeo, *m.* **p. fighter,** boxeador, *m.* **p. giving,** distribución de premios, *f.* **p. money,** premio en metálico, *m;* (boxing) bolsa, *f*

pro /prou/ *prep* pro. **pro forma invoice,** factura simulada, *f*

probability /ˌprɒbə'bɪlɪti/ *n* probabilidad, *f*

probable /'prɒbəbəl/ *a* probable

probably /'prɒbəbli/ *adv* probablemente

probate /'proubeit/ *n* verificación de un testamento, *f*

probation /prou'beiʃən/ *n* probación, *f; Law.* libertad vigilada, *f*

probationary /prou'beiʃəˌnɛri/ *a* de probación; de prueba

probationer /prou'beɪʃənər/ n novicio, m; estudiante de enfermera, f; candidato, m; aspirante, m

probe /proub/ n Surg. sonda, cala, tienta, f. —vt Surg. tentar; escudriñar

probing /'proubɪŋ/ n sondeo, m

probity /'proubɪtɪ/ n probidad, integridad, f

problem /'probləm/ n problema, m; cuestión, f. **p. play,** drama de tesis, m

problematic /,problə'mætɪk/ a problemático

problem child n niño problemático, m (male), niña problemática, f (female)

proboscis /prou'bosɪs/ n (of an elephant) trompa, f; (of an insect) trompetilla, f

Probus /'proubəs/ Probo, m

procedure /prə'sidʒər/ n procedimiento, m

proceed /prə'sid/ vi seguir el camino, continuar la marcha; avanzar, seguir adelante; ir; proceder; ponerse (a); empezar (a); (say) proseguir; (come to) llegar a, ir a; (of a play, etc.) desarrollarse. **Before we p. any further...** Antes de ir más lejos... **to p. to blows,** llegar a las manos. **to p. against,** proceder contra, procesar. **to p. from,** venir de. **to p. with,** proseguir; poner por obra; usar

proceeding /prə'sidɪŋ/ n modo de obrar, m; conducta, f; procedimiento, m; transacción, f; pl **proceedings,** (measures) medidas, f pl, actos, m pl; (of a learned society or a conference) actas, f pl. **to take proceedings against,** Law. procesar

proceeds /'prousidz/ n pl producto, m; ganancias, f pl; beneficios, m pl. **net p.,** producto neto, m

process /'proses/ n proceso, m; (method) procedimiento, m; (course) curso, m; marcha, f; (Law. Zool.) proceso, m. —vt beneficiar (ore), trasformar, elaborar. **in p. of,** en curso de. **in the p. of time,** con el tiempo marchando el tiempo

processing industry /'prosesɪŋ/ n industria de trasformación, industria de elaboración, f

procession /prə'seʃən/ n desfile, m; cortejo, m; (religious) procesión, f. **funeral p.,** cortejo fúnebre, m. **to walk in p.,** desfilar

processional /prə'seʃənl/ a procesional

proclaim /prou'kleɪm/ vt proclamar; publicar, pregonar; anunciar; (reveal) revelar; (outlaw) denunciar

proclamation /,proklə'meɪʃən/ n proclamación, f; proclama, f, anuncio, m; declaración, f

proclivity /prou'klɪvɪtɪ/ n proclividad, propensión, f

procrastinate /prou'kræstə,neɪt/ vi tardar (en decidirse), aplazar su decisión; vacilar; perder el tiempo

procrastination /prou,kræstə'neɪʃən/ n dilación, tardanza, f; vacilación, f; pereza, f

procrastinator /prou'kræstə,neɪtər/ n perezoso (-sa)

procreate /'proukri,eɪt/ vt procrear

procreation /,proukri'eɪʃən/ n procreación, f

procreator /'proukri,eɪtər/ n procreador (-ra)

proctor /'proktər/ n procurador, m; Educ. censor, m

procurable /prou'kyurəbəl/ a procurable; asequible

procure /prou'kyur/ vt obtener, conseguir, lograr

procurement /prou'kyurmənt/ n obtención, f, logro, m

procurer /prou'kyurər/ n alcahuete, m

procuress /prou'kyurɪs/ n alcahueta, celestina, trotaconventos, f

prod /prod/ n (with a bayonet, etc.) punzada, f; Fig. pinchazo, m. —vt punzar; (in the ribs, etc.) clavar; Fig. pinchar

prodigal /'prodɪgəl/ a and n pródigo (-ga)

prodigality /,prodɪ'gælɪtɪ/ n prodigalidad, f

prodigally /'prodɪgəlɪ/ adv pródigamente

prodigious /prə'dɪdʒəs/ a prodigioso

prodigiousness /prə'dɪdʒəsnɪs/ n prodigiosidad, f; enormidad, f

prodigy /'prodɪdʒɪ/ n prodigio, m; portento, m. **child p.,** niño prodigio

produce /v. prə'dus; n. 'produs, 'proudus/ vt producir; dar frutos; (show) mostrar, presentar; (take out) sacar; (occasion) causar, traer consigo, ocasionar; (goods) fabricar, manufacturar; (of shares, etc.) rendir; Geom. prolongar; (a play) poner en escena. —n producto, m; víveres, comestibles, m pl

producer /prə'dusər/ n productor (-ra); Theat. director de escena, m

product /'prodəkt/ n producto, m; (result) fruto, resultado, m, consecuencia, f; Math. producto, m

production /prə'dʌkʃən/ n producción, f; producto, m; Geom. prolongación, f; (of a play) dirección escénica, f; (performance) producción, f. **p. cost,** coste de producción, m

productive /prə'dʌktɪv/ a productivo

productivity /,proudʌk'tɪvɪtɪ/ n productividad, f

profanation /,profə'neɪʃən/ n profanación, f

profane /prə'feɪn/ a profano; sacrílego, blasfemo. —vt profanar

profaner /prə'feɪnər/ n profanador (-ra)

profanity /prə'fænɪtɪ/ n profanidad, f; blasfemia, f

profess /prə'fes/ vt (assert) afirmar, manifestar; declarar; (a faith, a profession, teach) profesar; (feign) fingir; (pretend) tener pretensiones de. —vi (as a monk or nun) tomar estado, entrar en religión. **He professed himself surprised,** Se declaró sorprendido

professed /prə'fest/ a declarado; Eccl. profeso; ostensible, fingido

profession /prə'feʃən/ n profesión, f; carrera, f; declaración, f. **p. of faith,** profesión de fe, f. **the learned professions,** las carreras liberales

professional /prə'feʃənl/ a profesional; de la profesión; de profesión; de carrera. **p. diplomat,** diplomático (-ca) de carrera. **p. etiquette,** etiqueta profesional, f. **p. man,** hombre profesional, m; hombre de carrera liberal, m

professor /prə'fesər/ n catedrático (-ca), profesor (-ra)

professorate /prə'fesərɪt/ n profesorado, m

professorial /,proufə'sorɪəl/ a de catedrático; de profesor

professorship /prə'fesər,ʃɪp/ n cátedra, f

proffer /'profər/ vt proponer; ofrecer. —n oferta, f

proficiency /prə'fɪʃənsɪ/ n pericia, habilidad, f

proficient /prə'fɪʃənt/ a proficiente, experto, adepto, perito

profile /'proufaɪl/ n perfil, m. —vt perfilar. **in p.,** de perfil

profit /'profɪt/ n provecho, m; utilidad, f; ventaja, f; Com. ganancia, f, vt aprovechar. —vi ganar; Com. sacar ganancia. **to p. by,** aprovechar. **gross p.,** ganancia total, f. **p. and loss,** ganancias y pérdidas, f pl. **p. sharing,** participación en las ganancias, participación de utilidades, f

profitable /'profɪtəbəl/ a provechoso, útil, ventajoso; lucrativo. **p. use,** aprovechamiento, m

profitably /'profɪtəblɪ/ adv con provecho, provechosamente; lucrativamente

profiteer /,profɪ'tɪər/ n estraperlista, mf

profit incentive n acicate del lucro, m

profitless /'profɪtlɪs/ a sin provecho, infructuoso, inútil

profligacy /'proflɪgəsɪ/ n libertinaje, m

profligate /'proflɪgɪt/ a licencioso, disoluto. —n libertino, m

profound /prə'faund/ a profundo

profundity /prə'fʌndɪtɪ/ n profundidad, f

profuse /prə'fyus/ a profuso; pródigo; lujoso

profusely /prə'fyuslɪ/ adv profusamente; pródigamente; lujosamente

profusion /prə'fyuʒən/ n profusión, abundancia, f; prodigalidad, f; exceso, m

progenitor /prou'dʒenɪtər/ n progenitor, m; (ancestor) antepasado, m

progeny /'prodʒənɪ/ n prole, f

prognosis /prog'nousɪs/ n prognosis, f; presagio, m; Med. pronóstico, m

prognosticate /prog'nostɪ,keɪt/ vt pronosticar, presagiar

prognostication /prog,nostɪ'keɪʃən/ n pronosticación, f; pronóstico, presagio, augurio, m

program /'prougræm/ n programa, m

progress /n. 'progres; v. prə'gres/ n progreso, m; avance, m; (betterment) mejora, f; (of events) marcha, f. —vi avanzar, marchar; (improve) progresar, adelantar; mejorar. **to make p.,** adelantarse; hacer progresos

progression /prə'greʃən/ n progresión, f

progressive /prə'gresɪv/ a progresivo; avanzado; Polit. progresista. —n Polit. progresista, mf

progressiveness /prə'grɛsɪvnɪs/ n carácter progresivo, m

prohibit /prou'hɪbɪt/ vt prohibir; defender; (prevent) impedir, privar. **His health prohibited him from doing it,** Su salud le impidió hacerlo

prohibition /,prouə'bɪʃən/ n prohibición, f; interdicción, f; (of alcohol) prohibicionismo, m

prohibitionist /,prouə'bɪʃənɪst/ n prohibicionista, mf

prohibitive /prou'hɪbɪtɪv/ a prohibitivo, prohibitorio

project /v. prə'dʒɛkt; n. 'prɒdʒɛkt/ vt (all meanings) proyectar. —vi sobresalir; destacarse. —n proyectil, plan, m

projectile /prə'dʒɛktɪl/ n proyectil, m, a arrojadizo

projecting /prə'dʒɛktɪŋ/ a saliente; (of teeth) saltón

projection /prə'dʒɛkʃən/ n (hurling) lanzamiento, m; prominencia, protuberancia, f; (other meanings) proyección, f

projector /prə'dʒɛktər/ n proyectista, mf; proyector, m

proletarian /,proulɪ'tɛəriən/ a proletario

proletariate /,proulɪ'tɛərɪt/ n proletariado, m

prolific /prə'lɪfɪk/ a prolífico; fecundo, fértil

prolix /prou'lɪks/ a prolijo

prolixity /prou'lɪksɪti/ n prolijidad, f

prolog /'prou,lɒg/ n prólogo, m, vt prologar

prolong /prə'lɔŋ/ vt prolongar

prolongation /,proulɔŋ'geɪʃən/ n prolongación, f

promenade /,prɒmə'neid, -'nɑd/ n paseo, m; bulevar, m; avenida, f. —vi pasearse. —vt recorrer, andar por, pasearse por. **p. deck,** cubierta de paseo, f

Promethean /prə'miθiən/ a de Prometeo

prominence /'prɒmənəns/ n prominencia, f; protuberancia, f; eminencia, f; importancia, f

prominent /'prɒmənənt/ a prominente, saliente; (of eyes, teeth) saltón; (distinguished) eminente, distinguido. **They placed the vase in a p. position,** Pusieron el florero muy a la vista. **to play a p. part,** desempeñar un papel importante. **p. eyes, ojos** saltones, m pl

promiscuous /prə'mɪskyuəs/ a promiscuo

promiscuousness /prə'mɪskyuəsnɪs/ n promiscuidad, f

promise /'prɒmɪs/ n promesa, f; (hope) esperanza, f; (word) palabra, f; (future) porvenir, m. —vt and vi prometer. **a young man of p.,** un joven de porvenir. **to break one's p.,** faltar a su palabra; no cumplir una promesa. **to keep one's p.,** guardar su palabra; cumplir su promesa. **to p. and do nothing,** apuntar y no dar. **under p. of,** bajo palabra de. **p. of marriage,** palabra de matrimonio, f

promised /'prɒmɪst/ a prometido. **P. Land,** Tierra de promisión, f

promising /'prɒməsɪŋ/ a que promete bien, que promete mucho; prometedor; (of the future, etc.) halagüeño; (of persons) que llegará

promissory /'prɒmə,sɔri/ a promisorio. **p. note,** pagaré, abonaré, m

promontory /'prɒmən,tɔri/ n promontorio, m

promote /prə'mout/ vt fomentar, promover; provocar; (aid) favorecer, proteger; avanzar; estimular; (to a post) ascender; (an act bill) promover; Com. negociar

promoter /prə'moutər/ n promotor (-ra); instigador (-ra); (Theat. etc.) empresario, m

promotion /prə'mouʃən/ n (encouragement) fomento, m; (furtherance) adelanto, m; protección, f; favorecimiento, m; (in employment, etc.) promoción, f, ascenso, m; (of a company, etc.) creación, f

prompt /prɒmpt/ a pronto; diligente; presuroso; puntual; rápido; Com. inmediato. —vt impulsar, incitar, mover; dictar; insinuar; Theat. apuntar; (remind) recordar. **He came at five o'clock p.,** Vino a las cinco en punto. **p. book,** libro del traspunte, m. **p. box,** concha (del apuntador), f

prompter /'prɒmptər/ n Theat. apuntador, (in the wings) traspunte, m

prompting /'prɒmptɪŋ/ n sugestión, f; instigación, f; pl **promptings,** impulso, m; (of the heart, etc.) dictados, m pl

promptitude /'prɒmptɪ,tud/ n prontitud, presteza, f; prisa, expedición, f; puntualidad, f

promptly /'prɒmptli/ adv inmediatamente, en seguida; con prontitud, con celeridad; puntualmente

promptness /'prɒmptnɪs/ n See **promptitude**

promulgate /'prɒməl,geit/ vt promulgar; divulgar, diseminar

promulgation /'prɒməl'geiʃən/ n promulgación, f; divulgación, diseminación, f

prone /proun/ a postrado; inclinado, propenso

proneness /'prounɪs/ n postración, f; inclinación, tendencia, propensión, f

prong /prɔŋ/ n (pitchfork) horquilla, f; (of a fork) diente, m, púa, f

pronged /prɔŋd/ a dentado, con púas

pronoun /'prou,naun/ n pronombre, m

pronounce /prə'nauns/ vt pronunciar; declarar; articular

pronounced /prə'naunst/ a marcado; perceptible; bien definido

pronouncement /prə'naunsmənt/ n pronunciamiento, m

pronunciation /prə,nʌnsi'eiʃən/ n pronunciación, f; articulación, f

proof /pruf/ n prueba, f; demostración, f; ensayo, m; Law. testimonio, m; (Photo. Print.) prueba, f; Math. comprobación, f, a hecho a prueba (de); impenetrable (a); Fig. insensible (a). —vt (raincoats, etc.) impermeabilizar. **in p. whereof,** en fe de lo cual. **p. against bombs,** a prueba de bombas. **p. reading,** corrección de pruebas, f

prop /prɒp/ n apoyo, puntal, estribadero, m; (for a tree) horca, f, rodrigón, m; Naut. escora, f; Fig. báculo, m, columna, f, apoyo, m. —vt apoyar; apuntalar; (a tree) ahorquillar; (a building) acodalar; Naut. escorar; Fig. sostener. **He propped himself against the wall,** Se apoyó en el muro, Se arrimó al muro

propaganda /,prɒpə'gændə/ n propaganda, f

propagandist /,prɒpə'gændɪst/ n propagandista, mf

propagate /'prɒpə,geit/ vt propagar. —vi propagarse

propagation /,prɒpə'geiʃən/ n propagación, f

propagator /'prɒpə,geitər/ n propagador (-ra)

propel /prə'pɛl/ vt propulsar, empujar, mover

propeller /prə'pɛlər/ n propulsor, m; Mech. hélice, f

propelling /prə'pɛlɪŋ/ n propulsión, f. **p. pencil,** lapicero, m

propensity /prə'pɛnsɪti/ n propensión, tendencia, inclinación, f

proper /'prɒpər/ a propio; apropiado; correcto; decente; (prim) afectado; serio, formal; (exact) justo, exacto; (suitable (for)) bueno (para), apto (para); (true) verdadero; (characteristic) peculiar; Herald. natural; (with rascal, etc.) redomado; (handsome) guapo. **If you think it p.,** Si te parece bien. **p. noun,** nombre propio, m

properly /'prɒpərli/ adv decentemente; correctamente; propiamente; bien. **to do (a thing) p.,** hacer algo bien. **p. speaking,** propiamente dicho, hablando con propiedad

propertied /'prɒpərtid/ a propietario, hacendado; (rich) pudiente, adinerado

property /'prɒpərti/ n propiedad, f; (belongings) bienes, m pl; posesiones, f pl; (estate) hacienda, f; (quality) cualidad, f; pl **properties,** Theat. accesorios, m pl. **personal p.,** bienes muebles, m pl; cosas personales, f pl. **real p.,** bienes raíces, m pl. **p. man,** Theat. encargado de los accesorios, m. **p. owner,** propietario (-ia). **p. tax,** contribución sobre la propiedad, f

prophecy /'prɒfəsi/ n profecía, f; predicción, f

prophesier /'prɒfə,siər/ n See **prophet**

prophesy /'prɒfə,sai/ vt profetizar; presagiar, predecir. —vi hacer profecías

prophet /'prɒfɪt/ n profeta, m

prophetess /'prɒfɪtɪs/ n profetisa, f

prophetic /prə'fɛtɪk/ a profético

prophylactic /,proufə'læktɪk/ a and n profiláctico, m

propinquity /prou'pɪŋkwɪti/ n propincuidad, proximidad, f; (relationship) parentesco, f

propitiate /prə'pɪʃi,eit/ vt propiciar; apaciguar, conciliar

propitiation /prə,pɪʃi'eiʃən/ n propiciación, f

propitiator /prə'pɪʃi,eitər/ n propiciador (-ra)

propitiatory /prə'pɪʃɪə,tɔri/ a propiciador
propitious /prə'pɪʃəs/ a propicio, favorable
propitiousness /prə'pɪʃəsnɪs/ n lo propicio
proportion /prə'pɔrʃən/ n proporción, f; parte, f; porción, f; pl **proportions,** proporciones, f pl; dimensiones, f pl. —vt proporcionar; repartir, distribuir. **in p.,** en proporción; conforme (a), según; Com. a prorrata. **in p. as,** a medida que. **out of p.,** desproporcionado. **He has lost all sense of p.,** Ha perdido su equilibrio (mental)
proportional /prə'pɔrʃənl/ a proporcional; en proporción (a); proporcionado (a). **p. representation,** representación proporcional
proportionally /prə'pɔrʃənli/ adv proporcionalmente, en proporción
proportionate /a. prə'pɔrʃənɪt; v. -,neit/ a proporcionado; proporcional. —vt proporcionar
proportionately /prə'pɔrʃənɪtli/ adv See **proportionally**
proposal /prə'pouzəl/ n proposición, f; oferta, f; (plan) propósito, proyecto, m. **p. of marriage,** oferta de matrimonio, f
propose /prə'pouz/ vt proponer; ofrecer; (a toast) dar, brindar. —vi pretender, intentar, tener la intención de; pensar; (marriage) declararse
proposer /prə'pouzər/ n proponente, m; (of a motion) autor (-ra) de una proposición
proposition /,prɒpə'zɪʃən/ n proposición, f; (plan) proyecto, propósito, m
propound /prə'paund/ vt proponer; plantear, presentar
proprietary /prə'praɪɪ,teri/ a propietario; de propiedad
proprietor /prə'praɪɪtər/ n propietario, m; dueño, m
proprietorship /prə'praɪɪtər,ʃɪp/ n propiedad, pertenencia, f
proprietress /prə'praɪɪtrɪs/ n propietaria, f; dueña, f
propriety /prə'praɪɪti/ n decoro, m; conveniencia, f; corrección, f
propulsion /prə'pʌlʃən/ n propulsión, f
propulsive /prə'pʌlsɪv/ a propulsor
prorogation /,prourou'geiʃən/ n prorrogación, f
prorogue /prou'roug/ vt prorrogar, suspender (la sesión de una asamblea legislativa)
prosaic /prou'zeiɪk/ a prosaico
pros and cons /'prouz ən 'kɒnz/ el pro y el contra
proscenium /prou'siniəm/ n proscenio, m
proscribe /prou'skraib/ vt proscribir
proscription /prou'skrɪpʃən/ n proscripción, f
prose /prouz/ n prosa, f. **p. writer,** prosista, mf
prosecute /'prɒsɪ,kyut/ vt proseguir, llevar adelante; (Law. a person) procesar; (Law. a claim) pedir en juicio
prosecution /,prɒsɪ'kyuʃən/ n prosecución, f; cumplimiento, m; Law. acusación, f; (Law. party) parte actora, f. **in the p. of his duty,** en el cumplimiento de su deber
prosecutor /'prɒsɪ,kyutər/ n demandante, actor, m. **public p.,** fiscal, m
proselyte /'prɒsə,lait/ n prosélito, m
proselytism /'prɒsəlɪ,tɪzəm/ n proselitismo, m
prose writer n prosador, m
prosody /'prɒsədi/ n prosodia, f
prospect /'prɒspɛkt/ n perspectiva, f; esperanza, f; probabilidad, f; (in mining) indicio de filón, m; criadero (de oro, etc.), m. —vi explorar; (of a mine) prometer (bien), dar buenas esperanzas. —vt explorar, inspeccionar; examinar. **He is a man with good prospects,** Es un hombre de porvenir
prospecting /'prɒspɛktɪŋ/ n la prospección, f
prospective /prə'spɛktɪv/ a en expectativa, futuro; previsor
prospector /'prɒspɛktər/ n explorador, operador, m
prospectus /prə'spɛktəs/ n prospecto, programa, m
prosper /'prɒspər/ vi prosperar. —vt favorecer, prosperar
prosperity /prɒ'spɛriti/ n prosperidad, f
prosperous /'prɒspərəs/ a próspero; favorable
prostate /'prɒsteit/ n próstata, f
prostitute /'prɒstɪ,tut/ n prostituta, f, vt prostituir
prostitution /,prɒstɪ'tuʃən/ n prostitución, f

prostrate /'prɒstreit/ a tendido; postrado; abatido. —vt derribar; arruinar; (by grief, etc.) postrar; (oneself) postrarse
prostration /prɒ'streiʃən/ n postración, f; abatimiento, m. **nervous p.,** neurastenia, f
prosy /'prouzi/ a aburrido, árido; pedestre, prosaico; verboso, prolijo
protagonist /prou'tægənɪst/ n protagonista, mf
protean /'proutiən/ a proteico
protect /prə'tɛkt/ vt proteger
protection /prə'tɛkʃən/ n protección, f; defensa, f; garantía, f; abrigo, m; refugio, m; (passport) salvoconducto, m; Polit. proteccionismo, m
protectionism /prə'tɛkʃə,nɪzəm/ n proteccionismo, m
protectionist /prə'tɛkʃənɪst/ n proteccionista, mf
protective /prə'tɛktɪv/ a protector; Polit. proteccionista
protector /prə'tɛktər/ n protector, m
protectorate /prə'tɛktərɪt/ n protectorado, m
protectress /prou'tɛktrɪs/ n protectriz, f
protein /'proutin/ n proteína, f
protest /v. prə'tɛst, 'proutɛst; n. 'proutɛst/ vt protestar; Law. hacer el protesto de una letra de cambio. —vi declarar; insistir (en); hacer una protesta. —n protesta, f; Law. protesto, m. **under p.,** bajo protesta. **to p. against,** protestar contra
Protestant /'prɒtəstənt/ a and n protestante, mf
Protestantism /'prɒtəstən,tɪzəm/ n protestantismo, m
protestation /,prɒtə'steiʃən/ n protestación, f
protester /'proutɛstər/ n el, m, (f, la) que protesta
protest literature n literatura de denuncia, f
protocol /'proutə,kɒl/ n protocolo, m, vt protocolizar
protoplasm /'proutə,plæzəm/ n protoplasma, m
prototype /'proutə,taip/ n prototipo, m
protract /prou'trækt/ vt prolongar; dilatar
protracted /prou'træktɪd/ a prolongado; largo
protraction /prou'trækʃən/ n prolongación, f
protractor /prou'træktər/ n (Geom. and Surv.) transportador, m. **p. muscle,** músculo extensor, m
protrude /prou'trud/ vt sacar fuera. —vi salir fuera; sobresalir
protuberance /prou'tubərəns/ n protuberancia, f
protuberant /prou'tubərənt/ a protuberante, prominente
proud /praud/ a orgulloso; arrogante; noble; glorioso; magnífico; soberbio. **to be p.,** enorgullecerse. **to make p.,** enorgullecer; hacer orgulloso. **to be p. of,** ser orgulloso de, pagarse de, gloriarse en. **p. flesh,** carnosidad, f, bezo, m
proudly /'praudli/ adv con orgullo, orgullosamente
provable /'pruvəbəl/ a demostrable
prove /pruv/ vt probar; demostrar; (experience) experimentar, sufrir; poner a prueba; (a will) verificar; (show) mostrar; confirmar. —vi resultar, salir (bien or mal)
provenance /'prɒvənəns/ n origen, m
Provençal /,prouvɛn'sɑl, ,prɒvɑ̃-/ a provenzal. —n provenzal, mf; (language) provenzal, m
Provence /prə'vɑns/ Provenza, f
provender /'prɒvəndər/ n forraje, m; Inf. provisiones, f pl
proverb /'prɒvərb/ n refrán, m; proverbio, m. **collection of proverbs,** refranero, m. **Book of Proverbs,** Proverbios, m pl
proverbial /prə'vərbiəl/ a proverbial
proverbially /prə'vərbiəli/ adv proverbialmente
provide /prə'vaid/ vt proporcionar, dar; proveer, surtir, suplir; (stipulate) estipular; preparar (por); tomar precauciones (contra); sufragar los gastos (de); proporcionar medios de vida (a); señalar una pensión (a). **to p. oneself with,** proveerse de
provided (that) /prə'vaidɪd/ conjunc si; a condición de que, siempre que, con tal que
providence /'prɒvɪdəns/ n providencia, f
provident /'prɒvɪdənt/ a próvido, previsor, prudente; económico
providential /,prɒvɪ'dɛnʃəl/ a providencial
providentially /,prɒvɪ'dɛnʃəli/ adv providencialmente
providently /'prɒvɪdəntli/ adv próvidamente, prudentemente
provider /prə'vaidər/ n proveedor (-ra)

province /'prɒvɪns/ n provincia, f; esfera, f; función, incumbencia, f
provincial /prə'vɪnʃəl/ a provincial, de provincia; provinciano. —n provinciano (-na); *Eccl.* provincial, m
provincialism /prə'vɪnʃə,lɪzəm/ n provincialismo, m
provision /prə'vɪʒən/ n provisión, f; (stipulation) estipulación, f; pl **provisions**, provisiones, f pl; víveres, comestibles, m pl. —vt abastecer, aprovisionar. **to make p. for,** hacer provisión para, proveer de. **to make p. for one's family,** asegurar el porvenir de su familia. **p. merchant,** vendedor (-ra) de comestibles
provisional /prə'vɪʒənl/ a provisional, interino
provisioning /prə'vɪʒənɪŋ/ n aprovisionamiento, abastecimiento, m
proviso /prə'vaizou/ n condición, estipulación, disposición, f
provisory /prə'vaizəri/ a provisional; condicional
provocation /,prɒvə'keiʃən/ n provocación, f
provocative /prə'vɒkətɪv/ a provocativo, provocador
provocatively /prə'vɒkətɪvli/ adv de un modo provocativo
provoke /prə'vouk/ vt provocar; suscitar; incitar, excitar; (irritate) sacar de madre (a), indignar
provoker /prə'voukər/ n provocador (-ra); instigador (-ra)
provoking /prə'voukɪŋ/ a provocativo; (irritating) enojoso, irritante
provost /'prouvoust or, esp. in military usage,* 'prouvou/ n preboste, m; (of a college) director, m; (in Scotland) alcalde, m. **p.-marshal,** capitán preboste, m
prow /prau/ n proa, f
prowess /'prauɪs/ n valor, m, destreza, f; proeza, f
prowl /praul/ vi and vt rondar; cazar al acecho
prowler /'praulər/ n rondador (-ra); ladrón (-ona)
proximity /prɒk'sɪmɪti/ n proximidad, f
proximo /'prɒksə,mou/ adv en (or del) mes próximo
proxy /'prɒksi/ n poder, m; delegación, f; apoderado, m; delegado (-da); substituto (-ta). **to be married by p.,** casarse por poderes
prude /prud/ n mojigata, beata, f
prudence /'prudns/ n prudencia, f
prudent /'prudnt/ a prudente
prudently /'prudntli/ adv con prudencia
prudery /'prudəri/ n mojigatería, beatería, damería, gazmoñería, f
prudish /'prudɪʃ/ a mojigato, gazmoño, remilgado
prune /prun/ n ciruela pasa, f; color de ciruela, m, vt podar; (cut) cortar; reducir
pruning /'prunɪŋ/ n poda, f; reducción, f. **p. knife,** podadera, f
prurient /'pruriənt/ a lascivo, lujurioso, salaz
Prussia /'prʌʃə/ Prusia, f
Prussian /'prʌʃən/ a and n prusiano (-na). **P. blue,** azul de Prusia, m
prussic acid /'prʌsɪk/ n ácido prúsico, m
pry /prai/ vi escudriñar; acechar, espiar, fisgonear; (meddle) entremeterse, meterse donde no le llaman. —vt See **prize**
prying /'praiɪŋ/ n fisgoneo, m; curiosidad, f, a fisgón, curioso
psalm /sɑm/ n salmo, m. **to sing psalms,** salmodiar
psalmist /'sɑmɪst/ n salmista, m
psaltery /'sɔltəri/ n salterio, m
pseudo- a seudo. **p.-learned,** erudito a la violeta
pseudonym /'sudnɪm/ n seudónimo, m
psychiatrist /sɪ'kaiətrɪst, sai-/ n siquiatra, m
psychiatry /sɪ'kaiətri, sai-/ n siquiatría, f
psychic /'saikɪk/ a síquico
psychoanalysis /,saikouə'næləsɪs/ n sicoanálisis, mf
psychoanalyst /,saikou'ænlɪst/ n sicoanalista, mf
psychoanalyze /,saikou'ænl,aiz/ vt sicoanalizar
psychological /,saikə'lɒdʒəkəl/ a sicológico
psychologist /sai'kɒlədʒɪst/ n sicólogo (-ga)
psychology /sai'kɒlədʒi/ n sicología, f
psychopathic /,saikə'pæθɪk/ a sicopático
psychosis /sai'kousɪs/ n sicosis, f
psychotherapy /,saikou'θɛrəpi/ n sicoterapia, f
ptomaine poisoning /'toumein/ n intoxicación por tomaínas, f
puberty /'pyubərti/ n pubertad, f

pubescent /pyu'besənt/ a púber
pubic /'pyubɪk/ a púbico
pubis /'pyubɪs/ n pubis, m
public /'pʌblɪk/ a and n público m. **in p.,** en público. **p. assistance,** asistencia pública, f. **p. funds,** hacienda pública, f. **p. health,** higiene pública, f. **p.-house,** taberna, f. **p. opinion,** opinión pública, f. *Inf.* el qué dirán. **p.-spirited,** patriótico. **p. thoroughfare,** vía pública, f. **p. works,** obras públicas, f pl
publican /'pʌblɪkən/ n tabernero, m
publication /,pʌblɪ'keiʃən/ n publicación, f
publicist /'pʌbləsɪst/ n publicista, mf
publicity /pʌ'blɪsɪti/ n publicidad, f
publicity agent n publicista, mf
publish /'pʌblɪʃ/ vt publicar, divulgar, difundir; (a book, etc.) dar a luz, dar a la prensa, publicar; (of a publisher) editar. **to p. abroad,** pregonar a los cuatro vientos. **to p. banns of marriage,** correr las amonestaciones
publisher /'pʌblɪʃər/ n publicador (-ra); (of books) editor (-ra)
publishing /'pʌblɪʃɪŋ/ n publicación, f. **p. house,** casa editorial, f. **the p. world,** el mundo de la edición, m
puck /pʌk/ n trasgo, m; diablillo, picaruelo, m
pucker /'pʌkər/ vt (one's brow, etc.) fruncir; (crease) arrugar. —vi arrugarse. —n frunce, m; arruga, f; (fold) bolsa, f
puckering /'pʌkərɪŋ/ n fruncido, m; arrugas, f pl
puckish /'pʌkɪʃ/ a travieso
pudding /'pudɪŋ/ n pudín, budín, m. **black p.,** morcilla, f
puddle /'pʌdl/ n charco, m
puerile /'pyuəril/ a pueril
puerility /pyuə'rɪliti/ n puerilidad, f
puerperal /pyu'ɜrpərəl/ a puerperal. **p. fever,** fiebre puerperal, f
Puerto Rican /'pwɛrtə 'rikən, 'pɔr-/ a and n puertorriqueño (-ña)
puff /pʌf/ vt and vi (blow) soplar; (at a pipe, etc.) chupar; (smoke) lanzar bocanadas de humo; (make pant) hacer jadear; (advertise) dar bombo (a); (distend) hinchar; (make conceited) envanecerse; (of a train, etc.) bufar; resoplar. —n soplo, m; (of smoke, etc.) bocanada, f; (of an engine, etc.) resoplido, bufido, m; (for powder) borla (para polvos), f; (pastry) bollo, m; (advertisement) bombo, m. **to be puffed up,** *Fig.* hincharse, inflarse. **p. of wind,** ráfaga de aire, f. **p.-ball,** bejín, m. **p.-pastry,** hojaldre, m, or f. **p.-sleeve,** manga de bullón, f
puffiness /'pʌfinɪs/ n hinchazón, f
puffy /'pʌfi/ a (of the wind) a ráfagas; (panting) jadeante; (swollen) hinchado
pug /pʌg/ n (dog) doguino, m. **p.-nosed,** de nariz respingona
pugilism /'pyudʒə,lɪzəm/ n boxeo, pugilato, m
pugilist /'pyudʒəlɪst/ n pugilista, mf, boxeador, m
pugnacious /pʌg'neiʃəs/ a pugnaz, belicoso
pugnacity /pʌg'næsɪti/ n pugnacidad, belicosidad, f
pull /pul/ n tirón, m; sacudida, f; golpe, m; (row) paseo en barco, m; (with the oars) golpe (de remos), m; (at a bell) tirón, m; (bell-rope) tirador, m; (at a bottle) trago, m; (strain) fuerza, f; atracción, f; (struggle) lucha, f; (advantage) ventaja, f; (influence) influencia, f. **to give a p.,** tirar (de), dar un tirón (a). **to have plenty of p.,** *Inf.* tener buenas aldabas
pull /pul/ vt tirar (de); (drag) arrastrar; (extract) sacar; (a boat) remar; (gather) coger; *Print.* imprimir. **He pulled the trigger (of his gun),** Apretó el gatillo. **He was sitting by the fire pulling at his pipe,** Estaba sentado cerca del fuego fumando su pipa. **to p. a hat well down on the head,** calarse el sombrero. **to p. a person's leg,** tomar el pelo (a). **to p. oneself together,** componer el semblante, serenarse; recobrar el aplomo; (tidy oneself) arreglarse. **to p. apart,** vt separar; romper en dos. —vi separarse; romperse en dos. **to p. away,** vt arrancar; quitar. —vi con esfuerzo. **to p. back,** tirar hacia atrás; hacer retroceder (a); retener. **to p. down,** hacer bajar, obligar a bajar; (objects) bajar; (buildings) derribar, demoler; (humble) humillar; degradar; (weaken) debilitar. **to p. in,** tirar hacia dentro; hacer entrar; (a horse) enfrenar;

(expenditure) reducir. **to p. off,** arrancar; (clothes) quitarse; (a deal) cerrar (un trato), concluir con éxito; (win) ganar. **to p. on,** *vt* (gloves, etc.) meterse, ponerse. —*vi* seguir remando. **to p. open,** abrir; abrir rápidamente. **to p. out,** hacer salir; obligar a salir; (teeth, daggers, etc.) sacar; (hair) arrancar. **to p. round, through,** *vt* ayudar a reponerse (a); sacar de un aprieto. —*vi* restablecerse; reponerse, cobrar la salud, sanar. **to p. together,** obrar de acuerdo; (get on) llevarse (bien or mal). **He pulled himself together very quickly,** Se repuso muy pronto. **to p. up,** *vt* montar, subir; (a horse) sofrenar; (stop) parar; (by the root) desarraigar, extirpar; (interrupt) interrumpir; (scold) reñir. —*vi* parar(se); (restrain oneself) re- primirse, contenerse

pullet /'pʊlɪt/ *n* polla, *f*

pulley /'pʊli/ *n* polea, *f; Naut.* garrucha, *f.* **p. wheel,** roldana, *f*

pulling /'pʊlɪŋ/ *n* tracción, *f;* tirada, *f;* arranque, *m*

pullover /'pʊl,oʊvər/ *n* jersey, *m*

pullulate /'pʌlyə,leɪt/ *vi* pulular

pulmonary /'pʌlmə,neri/ *a* pulmonar

pulp /pʌlp/ *n* pulpa, *f;* (of fruit) carne, *f;* (paper) pasta, *f;* (of teeth) bulbo dentario, *m.* —*vt* reducir a pulpa; deshacer (el papel). **to beat to a p.,** *Inf.* poner como un pulpo

pulpit /'pʊlpɪt, 'pʌl-/ *n* púlpito, *m*

pulpy /'pʌlpi/ *a* pulposo; *Bot.* carnoso

pulsate /'pʌlseɪt/ *vi* pulsar, latir

pulsation /pʌl'seɪʃən/ *n* pulsación, *f,* latido, *m*

pulsatory /'pʊlsə,tɔri/ *a* pulsante, pulsativo, latiente

pulse /pʌls/ *n* pulso, *m;* pulsación, *f,* latido, *m;* vi- bración, *f;* (vegetable) legumbre, *f,* vi pulsar, latir; vi- brar. **to take a person's p.,** tomar el pulso (a)

pulverization /,pʌlvərə'zeɪʃən/ *n* pulverización, *f*

pulverize /'pʌlvə,raɪz/ *vt* pulverizar

puma /'pyumə, 'pu-/ *n* puma, *f*

pumice /'pʌmɪs/ *n* piedra pómez, *f*

pummel /'pʌməl/ *vt* aporrear

pump /pʌmp/ *n Mech.* bomba, *f;* (for water, etc.) aguatocha, *f; Naut.* pompa, *f;* (slipper) escarpín, *m, vt* bombear, extraer por medio de una bomba; (in- flate) inflar; (for information) sondear, sonsacar. **hand-p.,** bomba de mano, *f.* **to work a p.,** darle a la bomba

pumpkin /'pʌmpkɪn/ *n* calabaza, *f,* (Chile) zapallo *m;* (plant) calabacera, *f*

pun /pʌn/ *n* retruécano, *m*

punch /pʌntʃ/ *n* (drink) ponche, *m;* (blow) puñetazo, golpe, *m; Mech.* punzón, *m;* (for tickets, etc.) taladro, *m; Inf.* fuerza, *f.* —*vt* (perforate) taladrar, punzar; es- tampar; (hit) dar un puñetazo (a). **p.-ball,** pelota de boxeo, *f.* **p.-bowl,** ponchera, *f*

Punchinello /,pʌntʃə'nɛloʊ/ *n* Polichinela, *m.* **Punch and Judy show,** títeres, *m pl*

punctilious /pʌŋk'tɪliəs/ *a* formal, puntual, puntilloso

punctiliousness /pʌŋk'tɪliəsnɪs/ *n* formalidad, punc- tualidad, *f*

punctual /'pʌŋktʃuəl/ *a* puntual

punctually /'pʌŋktʃuəli/ *adv* puntualmente

punctuate /'pʌŋktʃu,eɪt/ *vt* puntuar

punctuation /,pʌŋktʃu'eɪʃən/ *n* puntuación, *f*

puncture /'pʌŋktʃər/ *n* pinchazo, *m;* perforación, *f; Surg.* punción, *f.* —*vt* pinchar; perforar; punzar. **We have a p. in the right tire,** Tenemos un pinchazo en el neumático derecho

pungency /'pʌndʒənsi/ *n* picante, *m;* acerbidad, mordacidad, *f*

pungent /'pʌndʒənt/ *a* picante; acerbo, mordaz

Punic /'pyunɪk/ *a* púnico, cartaginés

punish /'pʌnɪʃ/ *vt* castigar; maltratar

punishable /'pʌnɪʃəbəl/ *a* punible

punishment /'pʌnɪʃmənt/ *n* castigo, *m;* pena, *f;* maltrato, *m*

punitive /'pyunɪtɪv/ *a* punitivo

punt /pʌnt/ *n* batea, *f.* —*vt* impeler una batea con una pértiga; ir en batea; (a ball) golpear, dar un pun- tapié (a)

puny /'pyuni/ *a* débil, encanijado; insignificante; pe- queño

pup /pʌp/ *n* cachorro (-rra). —*vi* parir la perra

pupa /'pyupə/ *n* crisálida, *f*

pupil /'pyupəl/ *n* alumno (-na), discípulo (-la); (of the eye) pupila, niña (del ojo), *f; Law.* pupilo (-la). —*a* escolar. **day p.,** alumno (-na) externo (-na). **p. teacher,** maestro (-tra) alumno (-na)

puppet /'pʌpɪt/ *n* títere, *m,* marioneta, *f;* muñeca, *f;* (person) maniquí, *m.* **p. show,** función de títeres, *f.* **p. showman,** titiritero, titerero, *m*

puppy /'pʌpi/ *n* perrito (-ta), cachorro (-rra)

purblind /'pɜr,blaɪnd/ *a* ciego; (short-sighted and *Fig.*) miope

purchasable /'pɜrtʃəsəbəl/ *a* comprable, que puede comprarse; *Fig.* sobornable

purchase /'pɜrtʃəs/ *vt* comprar; adquirir; *Fig.* lograr, conseguir. —*n* compra, *f;* adquisición, *f; Mech.* apa- lancamiento, *m;* fuerza, *f;* (lever) palanca, *f,* aparejo, *m; Fig.* influencia, *f.* **p. tax,** impuesto de lujo, *m*

purchaser /'pɜrtʃəsər/ *n* comprador (-ra)

purchasing /'pɜrtʃəsɪŋ/ *n* See **purchase. p. power,** poder de adquisición, *m*

pure /pyʊr/ *a* puro. **p.-bred,** de raza

pureness /'pyʊrnɪs/ *n* pureza, *f*

purgation /pɜr'geɪʃən/ *n* purgación, *f*

purgative /'pɜrgətɪv/ *a* purgativo. —*n* purga, *f*

purgatorial /,pɜrgə'tɔriəl/ *a* del purgatorio; (expia- tory) purgatorio

purgatory /'pɜrgə,tɔri/ *n* purgatorio, *m*

purge /pɜrdʒ/ *n* purgación, *f;* (laxative) purga, *f; Polit.* depuración, *f;* purificación, *f.* —*vt* purgar; *Polit.* depurar; purificar; expurgar

purging /'pɜrdʒɪŋ/ *n* purgación, *f; Polit.* depuración, *f; Fig.* purificación, *f*

purification /,pyʊrəfɪ'keɪʃən/ *n* purificación, *f*

purificatory /pyʊ'rɪfɪkə,tɔri/ *a* purificador, purifica- torio, que purifica

purifier /'pyʊrə,faɪər/ *n* purificador (-ra)

purify /'pyʊrə,faɪ/ *vt* purificar; (metals) acrisolar; re- finar; depurar; (purge) purgar

purist /'pyʊrɪst/ *n* purista, *mf*

puritan /'pyʊrɪtn/ *a* and *n* puritano (-na)

Puritanism /'pyʊrɪtn,ɪzəm/ *n* puritanismo, *m*

purity /'pyʊrɪti/ *n* pureza, *f*

purl /pɜrl/ *vi* (of a stream, etc.) murmurar, susurrar. —*n* (of a stream, etc.) susurro, murmullo, *m*

purlieu /'pɜrlu/ *n* límite, *m; pl* **purlieus,** alrededores, *m pl,* inmediaciones, *f pl;* (slums) barrios bajos, *m pl*

purling /'pɜrlɪŋ/ *a* murmurante, que susurra, parlero. —*n* murmullo, susurro, *m*

purloin /pər'lɔɪn/ *vt* hurtar, robar

purple /'pɜrpəl/ *n* púrpura, *f, a* purpúreo. —*vt* purpurar, teñir de púrpura. —*vi* purpurear

purplish /'pɜrplɪʃ/ *a* purpurino, algo purpúreo

purport /v. pər'pɔrt; n. 'pɜrpɔrt/ *vt* dar a entender, querer decir; significar; indicar; parecer; tener el ob- jeto de; pretender. —*n* importe, *m;* sentido, signifi- cado, *m;* objeto, *m*

purpose /'pɜrpəs/ *n* objeto, *m;* propósito, fin, *m;* in- tención, *f;* proyecto, *m;* designio, *m;* determinación, voluntad, *f;* efecto, *m;* ventaja, utilidad, *f, vi* and *vt* proponerse; pensar, tener el propósito (de), intentar. **It will serve my p.,** Servirá para lo que yo quiero. **for the p. of...,** con el propósito de..., con el fin de... **for purposes of...** para efectos de... **on p.,** de propósito, expresamente. **to no p.,** inútilmente; en vano

purposeful /'pɜrpəsfəl/ *a* resuelto; de substancia

purposeless /'pɜrpəslɪs/ *a* irresoluto, vacilante, vago; sin objeto; inútil

purposely /'pɜrpəsli/ *adv* expresamente, de intento

purr /pɜr/ *vi* ronronear. —*n* ronroneo, *m*

purse /pɜrs/ *n* bolsa, *f;* monedero, portamonedas, *m.* **to p. one's lips,** apretar los labios

purser /'pɜrsər/ *n Naut.* contador, sobrecargo, *m.* **purser's office,** contaduría, *f*

pursuance /pər'suəns/ *n* cumplimiento, desempeño, *m,* prosecución, *f.* **in p. of,** en cumplimiento de; en consecuencia de

pursuant /pər'suənt/ *a* and *adv* según; conforme (a), de acuerdo (con); en consecuencia (de)

pursue /pər'su/ *vt* perseguir; seguir; (search) buscar; (hunt) cazar; (a submarine, etc.) dar caza (a); (con- tinue) proseguir, continuar; (an occupation) dedicarse (a), ejercer

pursuer /pər'suər/ *n* perseguidor (-ra)

pursuit /pər'sut/ n perseguimiento, m; (search) busca, f; (hunt) caza, f; (performance) prosecución, f, desempeño, m; (employment) ocupación, f. **in p. of,** en busca de. **p. plane,** avión de caza, m

purulence /'pyʊrələns/ n purulencia, f

purulent /'pyʊrələnt/ a purulento

purvey /pər'vei/ vt proveer, surtir, suministrar; abastecer; procurar

purveyance /pər'veiəns/ n suministro, abastecimiento, m; provisión, f

purveyor /pər'veiər/ n suministrador (-ra), proveedor (-ra), bastecedor (-ra)

pus /pʌs/ n pus, m

push /pʊʃ/ n empujón, m; empellón, m; impulso, m; (of a person) empuje, m, energía, f; (attack) ataque, m; ofensiva, f; (effort) esfuerzo, m; crisis, f, momento crítico, m. **at a push,** Inf. en caso de necesidad; en un aprieto, si llegara al caso. **to give the p. to,** Inf. despedir (a). **p.-bicycle,** bicicleta, f. **p.-button,** botón, m; botón de llamada, m. **p.-cart,** carretilla de mano, f; (child's) cochecito de niño, m

push /pʊʃ/ vt empujar; (jostle) empellar, dar empellones (a); (a finger in one's eye, etc.) clavar; (a button) apretar; (Fig. a person) proteger, ayudar; dar publicidad (a); (a claim, etc.) insistir en; (compel) obligar. —vi empujar; dar empujones, empellar. **I am pushed for time,** Me falta tiempo. **He is pushed for money,** Está apurado por dinero. **I have pushed my finger in my eye,** Me he clavado el dedo en el ojo. **to p. against,** empujar contra; lanzarse contra; empellar, dar empellones (a). **to p. aside, away,** apartar con la mano; rechazar, alejar. **to p. back,** (hair, etc.) echar hacia atrás; (people) hacer retroceder; rechazar. **to p. by,** pasar. **to p. down,** hacer bajar; hacer caer; (demolish) derribar. **to p. forward,** vt empujar hacia delante, hacer avanzar; (a plan, etc.) llevar adelante. —vi adelantarse a empujones; avanzar; seguir el camino. **to p. oneself forward,** Fig. abrirse camino; entremeterse; darse importancia. **to p. in,** vt empujar; hacer entrar; clavar, hincar. —vi entrar a la fuerza; entremeterse. **to p. off,** vt apartar con la mano (a); Inf. quitar de encima (a). —vi Naut. desatracar; Inf. ponerse en camino. **to p. open,** empujar, abrir. **to p. out,** vt empujar hacia fuera; hacer salir; echar. —vi Naut. zarpar. **to p. through,** vt (business, etc.) despachar rápidamente; (a crowd) abrirse camino por. —vi aparecer, mostrarse. **to p. to,** cerrar. **to p. up,** empujar; hacer subir; (windows, etc.) levantar. **be pushing up the daises,** mirar los árboles de raíz

pushing /'pʊʃɪŋ/ a enérgico, emprendedor; ambicioso; agresivo. **by p. and shoving,** a empellones, a empujones

pusillanimity /ˌpyusələ'nɪmɪti/ n pusilanimidad, f

pusillanimous /ˌpyusə'lænəməs/ a pusilánime

puss /pʊs/ n micho (-cha). **P.! P.!** ¡Miz, Miz!

pustule /'pʌstʃul/ n pústula, f

put /pʊt/ vt poner; colocar; (pour out) echar; aplicar; emplear; (estimate) calcular; presentar; (ask) preguntar; (say) decir; (express) expresar; (a question) hacer; (a problem) plantear; (the weight) lanzar; (rank) estimar. **As the Spanish put it,** Como dicen los españoles. **If I may put it so,** Si puedo expresarlo así, Por así decirlo. **hard put to it,** en dificultades, apurado. **How will you put it to her?** ¿Cómo se lo vas a explicar a ella? **to put ashore,** echar en tierra (a). **to put a child to bed,** acostar a un niño. **to put in order,** arreglar; ordenar. **to put out of joint,** dislocar. **to put out of order,** estropear. **to put to death,** matar; (judicially) ajusticiar. **to put about,** vt (a rumor) diseminar, divulgar; (worry) preocupar. —vi Naut. virar, cambiar de rumbo. **to put aside,** poner a un lado; descartar; (omit) omitir, pasar por alto de; (fears, etc.) desechar. **to put away,** quitar; guardar; poner en salvo; arrinconar; (thoughts) desechar, ahuyentar; (save) ahorrar; (banish) despedir, alejar; (a wife) repudiar, divorciar; (food) tragar. **to put back,** vt echar hacia atrás; hacer retroceder; (replace) devolver, restituir; (the clock) retrasar; (retard) retardar, atrasar. —vi volver; Naut. volver a puerto. **to put down,** depositar; poner en el suelo; (the blinds) bajar; (an umbrella) cerrar; (a rebellion) sofocar; (gambling, etc.) suprimir; (humble) abatir,

humillar; degradar; (silence) hacer callar; (reduce) reducir, disminuir; (write) apuntar, anotar; (a name) inscribir; (to an account) poner a la cuenta de; (estimate) juzgar, creer; (impute) atribuir. **The book is so interesting that it's hard to put down,** El libro es tan interesante que es difícil dejarlo. **to put forth,** (leaves, flowers, sun's rays) echar; (a book) publicar, dar a luz; (a hand) alargar; (an arm) extender; (show) manifestar, mostrar; (strength, etc.) desplegar; (use) emplear. **to put forward,** avanzar; (a clock) adelantar; (a suggestion, etc.) hacer; (propose) proponer; (a case) presentar. **to put oneself forward,** ponerse en evidencia. **to put in,** poner dentro; (a hand, etc.) introducir; (liquids) echar en; (a government) poner en el poder; (an employment) nombrar, colocar; (insert) insertar; (a claim) presentar; (say) decir. **I shall put in two hours' work before bedtime,** Trabajaré por dos horas antes de acostarme. **He put in a good word for you,** Habló en tu favor. **to put in writing,** poner por escrito. **to put in for,** (an employment) solicitar (un empleo); (as a candidate) presentarse como candidato para. **to put into,** meter dentro (de); (words) expresar; (port) arribar, hacer escala en (un puerto). **to put off,** desechar; (garments) quitarse, despojarse (de); (postpone) diferir, aplazar; (evade) evadir, entretener; quitarse de encima (a), desembarazarse (de); (confuse) desconcertar; (discourage) desanimar; quitar el apetito (a). **to put on,** poner sobre; (clothes) ponerse; (pretend) fingir, afectar; poner; (a play) poner en escena; (the hands of a clock) adelantar; (weight) engordar, poner carnes; (add) añadir; (Sports. score) hacer; (bet) apostar; (the light) encender; (assume) tomar; (the brake) frenar; (abuse) abusar (de). engañar. **He put the kettle on the fire,** Puso la tetera en el fuego. **to put on airs and graces,** darse humos. **to put on probation,** dar el azul a, poner a prueba a. **to put on more trains,** poner más trenes. **put one's foot down,** ponerle a fulano el alto. **to put out,** vt (eject) echar, expulsar; hacer salir; poner en la calle; (a tenant) desahuciar; (one's hand) alargar; (one's arm) extender; (one's tongue) sacar; (eyes) saltar; (fire, light) apagar, extinguir; (leaves, etc.) echar; (horns) sacar; (head) asomar, sacar; (use) emplear; (give) entregar, dar; (at interest) dar a interés; (finish) terminar; (dislocate) dislocar; (worry) desconcertar; turbar; poner los nervios en punta (a); (anger) enojar; (inconvenience) incomodar; (a book) publicar; (a boat) echar al mar. —vi (of a ship) hacerse a la vela, zarpar. **to put out to grass,** mandar a pacer. **We put out to sea,** Nos hicimos a la mar. **to put the cart before the horse,** poner la carreta por delante de los bueyes. **to put through,** (perform) desempeñar; concluir, terminar; (thrust) meter; (subject to) someter a; (exercise) ejercitar; (on the telephone) poner en comunicación (con). **to put together,** juntar; (a machine, etc.) montar, armar. **to put two and two together,** atar cabos. **to put up,** vt (sails, a flag) izar; (raise a window) levantar, cerrar; (open a window, or an umbrella) abrir; (one's hands, etc.) poner en alto; (one's fists) alzar; (a prayer) ofrecer, hacer; (as a candidate) nombrar; (for sale) poner (a la venta); (the price) aumentar; (a prescription) preparar; (food) conservar; (pack) empaquetar; (a sword) envainar; (lodge) alojar; (a petition) presentar; (build) construir; Mech. montar; (Inf. plan) arreglar. —vi alojarse. **to put upon,** abusar (de); oprimir; (accuse) imputar, acusar (de). **to put up to,** incitar a, instigar (a); dar informaciones sobre; poner al corriente (de). **to put up with,** tolerar, soportar, aguantar; resignarse a; contentarse con, conformarse con

putative /'pyutətɪv/ a supuesto; (of relationship) putativo

putrefaction /ˌpyutrə'fækʃən/ n putrefacción, f

putrefy /'pyutrəˌfai/ vt pudrir. —vt pudrirse, descomponerse

putrid /'pyutrɪd/ a pútrido; Inf. apestoso

putt /pʌt/ n putt, m, y vi patear.

putting /'pʌtɪŋ/ n acción de poner, f; colocación, f. **p. forward of the clock,** adelanto de la hora, m. **p. off,** tardanza, dilación, f. **p. the weight,** lanzamiento del peso, m. **p. up,** (for office) candidatura, f. /'pʌtɪŋ/ **p. green,** pista de golf en miniatura, f

putty /'pʌti/ n masilla, f, vt enmasillar, rellenar con masilla
puzzle /'pʌzəl/ vt dejar perplejo; desconcertar; confundir; embrollar. —n problema, m; dificultad, f; enigma, m; (perplexity) perplejidad, f; (game) rompecabezas, m. **to p. out,** procurar resolver; encontrar la solución de. **to p. over,** pensar en, meditar sobre. **I am puzzled by...,** Me trae (or tiene) perplejo...
pygmy /'pɪgmi/ a and n pigmeo (-ea)
pyjamas /pə'dʒɑməz, -'dʒæməz/ n pijama, m
pylon /'pailɒn/ n pilón, m; poste, m; (at an airport) poste de señales, m
pylorus /pai'lɔrəs/ n píloro, m
pyorrhea /,paiə'riə/ n piorrea, f
pyramid /'pɪrəmɪd/ n pirámide, f

pyramidal /pɪ'ræmɪdl̩/ a piramidal
pyre /paiᵊr/ n pira, f
Pyrenean /,pɪərə'niən/ a pirineo, pirenaico
Pyrenees, the /'pɪərə,niz/ los Pirineos, m pl
pyrites /pai'raitiz/ n pirita, f
pyromancy /'pairə,mænsi/ n piromancia, f
pyrotechnic /,pairə'tɛknɪk/ a pirotécnico
pyrotechnics /,pairə'tɛknɪks/ n pirotecnia, f
pyrotechnist /,pairə'tɛknɪst/ n pirotécnico, m
Pyrrhic /'pɪrɪk/ a pírrico
Pythagorean /pɪ,θægə'riən/ a and n pitagórico (-ca)
Pythian /'pɪθiən/ a pitio
python /'paiθɒn/ n pitón, m
pythoness /'paiθənɪs/ n pitonisa, f

Q

q /kyu/ *n* (letter) cu, *f*
quack /kwæk/ *vi* (of a duck) graznar. —*n* (of a duck) graznido, *m;* (charlatan) charlatán, farsante, *m;* curandero, *m.* **q. doctor,** matasanos, medicastro, curandero, *m.* **q. medicine,** curanderismo, *m*
quackery /'kwækəri/ *n* charlatanería, *f,* charlatanismo, *m*
quadrangle /'kwɒd,ræŋgəl/ *n* cuadrángulo, *m;* (courtyard) patio, *m*
quadrangular /kwɒd'ræŋgyələr/ *a* cuadrangular
quadrant /'kwɒdrənt/ *n* (*Geom. Astron.* etc.) cuadrante, *m*
quadratic /kwɒ'drætɪk/ *a* cuadrático. **q. equation,** cuadrática, ecuación de segundo grado, *f*
quadrature /'kwɒdrətʃər/ *n* (*Math. Astron.*) cuadratura, *f*
quadrennial /kwɒ'drɛniəl/ *a* cuadrienal
quadrilateral /,kwɒdrə'lætərəl/ *a* and *n* cuadrilátero *m*
quadrille /kwɒ'drɪl/ *n* cuadrilla, *f;* (card game) cuatrillo, *m*
quadruped /'kwɒdru,pɛd/ *a* and *n* cuadrúpedo *m*
quadruple /kwɒ'drupəl/ *a* cuádruple. —*vt* cuadruplicar. —*n* cuádruplo, *m*
quadruplet /kwɒ'drʌplɪt/ *n* serie de cuatro cosas, *f;* bicicleta de cuatro asientos, *f;* uno (una) de cuatro niños (-as) gemelos (-as)
quadruplication /kwɒ,druplɪ'keɪʃən/ *n* cuadruplicación, *f*
quaff /kwɒf/ *vt* beber a grandes tragos, vaciar de un trago
quagmire /'kwæg,maiªr/ *n* tremedal, pantano, *m; Fig.* cenagal, *m*
quail /kweil/ *n* codorniz, *f;* (U.S.A.) parpayuela, *f.* —*vi* cejar, retroceder; temblar, acobardarse
quaint /kweint/ *a* pintoresco; curioso, raro; (eccentric) excéntrico, extravagante
quaintly /'kweintli/ *adv* de un modo pintoresco; curiosamente; con extravagancia
quaintness /'kweintnɪs/ *n* lo pintoresco; rareza, singularidad, *f;* (eccentricity) extravagancia, *f*
quake /kweik/ *vi* estremecerse, vibrar; temblar. —*n* estremecimiento, *m;* (of the earth) terremoto, *m.* **to q. with fear,** temblar de miedo
Quaker /'kweikər/ *n* cuáquero (-ra)
Quakerism /'kweikə,rɪzəm/ *n* cuaquerismo, *m*
quaking /'kweikɪŋ/ *a* temblón; tembloroso. —*n* temblor, *m;* estremecimiento, *m.* **q. ash,** álamo temblón, *m*
quakingly /'kweikɪŋli/ *adv* trémulamente
qualifiable /'kwɒlə,faiəbəl/ *a* calificable
qualification /,kwɒləfɪ'keɪʃən/ *n* calificación, *f;* requisito, *m;* capacidad, aptitud, *f;* (reservation) reservación, salvedad, *f*
qualified /'kwɒlə,faid/ *a* apto, competente; (of professions) con título universitario; habilitado; limitado
qualify /'kwɒlə,fai/ *vt* habilitar; calificar; modificar; suavizar; *vi* habilitarse; prepararse; llenar los requisitos
qualifying /'kwɒlə,faiɪŋ/ *a Gram.* calificativo
qualitative /'kwɒlɪ,teitɪv/ *a* cualitativo
quality /'kwɒlɪti/ *n* cualidad, *f;* calidad, *f;* propiedad, *f.* **This cloth is of good q.,** Esta tela es de buena calidad. **the q.,** la alta sociedad, la aristocracia
qualm /kwɑm/ *n* náusea, *f;* mareo, desmayo, *m;* (of conscience) escrúpulo, remordimiento, *m*
quandary /'kwɒndəri/ *n* incertidumbre, perplejidad, *f;* dilema, apuro, *m.* **to be in a q.,** estar perplejo
quantitative /'kwɒntɪ,teitɪv/ *a* cuantitativo
quantity /'kwɒntɪti/ *n* cantidad, *f;* gran cantidad, *f.* **unknown q.,** incógnita, *f*
quantum /'kwɒntəm/ *n* cantidad, *f;* tanto, *m.* **q. theory,** teoría de la quanta, *f*
quarantine /'kwɒrən,tin/ *n* cuarentena, *f, vt* someter a cuarentena
quarrel /'kwɒrəl/ *vi* pelear, disputar; (scold) reñir;

(find fault) criticar. —*n* pelea, disputa, *f;* (glazier's) diamante de vidriero, *m.* **to pick a q. with,** armar pleito con, reñir con. **to q. with,** reñir con, romper con; quejarse de
quarreller /'kwɒrələr/ *n* reñidor (-ra)
quarrelling /'kwɒrəlɪŋ/ *n* disputas, altercaciones, *f pl*
quarrelsome /'kwɒrəlsəm/ *a* pendenciero, peleador, belicoso
quarrelsomeness /'kwɒrəlsəmnɪs/ *n* belicosidad, pugnacidad, *f*
quarry /'kwɒri/ *n* cantera, *f; Fig.* mina, *f;* (prey) presa, *f;* víctima, *f.* —*vt* explotar una cantera; examinar
quarrying /'kwɒriɪŋ/ *n* explotación de canteras, *f;* cantería, *f*
quarryman /'kwɒrimən/ *n* cantero, *m*
quart /kwɔrt/ *n* cuarto de galón, *m*
quartan /'kwɔrtən/ *a* cuartanal. —*n* (fever) cuartana, *f*
quarter /'kwɔrtər/ *n* (fourth part) cuarta parte, *f,* cuarto, *m;* (of a year) trimestre, *m;* (of an hour, the moon, a ton, an animal, etc.) cuarto, *m;* (of the compass) cuarta, *f; Naut.* cuartelada, *f;* (of a town) barrio, *m;* (mercy) cuartel, *m; Herald.* cuartel, *m;* dirección, *f;* origen, *m,* fuente, *f; pl* **quarters,** vivienda, *f;* alojamiento, *m;* (barracks) cuartel, *m.* —*vt* cuartear; (a body) descuartizar, hacer cuartos (a); (troops) alojar; (in barracks) acuartelar; *Herald.* cuartelar. **a q. of an hour,** un cuarto de hora. **at close quarters,** de cerca. **hind quarters,** cuartos traseros, *m pl.* **It is a q. to four,** Son las cuatro menos cuarto. **It is a q. past four,** Son las cuatro y cuarto. **q.-day,** primer día de un trimestre, *m.* **q.-deck,** alcázar, *m;* cuerpo de oficiales de un buque, *m.* **q.-mile,** cuarto de milla, *m.* **q.-plate,** cuarto de placa, *m.* **q.-sessions,** sesión trimestral de los juzgados municipales, *f.* **q.-staff,** barra, *f.* **q.-tone,** cuarto de tono, *m*
quartering /'kwɔrtərɪŋ/ *n* (punishment) descuartizamiento, *m; Herald.* cantón, *m*
quarterly /'kwɔrtərli/ *a* trimestral, trimestre. —*n* publicación trimestral, *f, adv* trimestralmente
quartermaster /'kwɔrtər,mæstər/ *n Mil.* cabo furriel, *m; Nav.* maestre de víveres, cabo de mar, *m.* **q.-general,** intendente de ejército, *m*
quartet /kwɔr'tɛt/ *n* cuarteto, *m*
quarto /'kwɔrtou/ *n* papel en cuarto, *m;* libro en cuarto, *m.* **in q.,** en cuarto
quartz /kwɔrts/ *n* cuarzo, *m*
quash /kwɒʃ/ *vt Law.* anular, derogar; *Inf.* sofocar, reprimir
quasi /'kweizai, 'kwɑsi/ *a* and *adv* cuasi
quasimodo /,kwɑsə'moudou/ *n* cuasimodo, *m*
quatrain /'kwɒtrein/ *n* cuarteta, *f*
quaver /'kweivər/ *vi* vibrar; temblar; (trill) trinar, hacer quiebros. —*vt* decir con voz temblorosa. —*n* vibración, *f;* trémolo, *m;* (trill) trino, *m;* (musical note) corchea, *f*
quaveringly /'kweivərɪŋli/ *adv* con voz temblorosa
quavery /'kweivəri/ *a* trémulo, tembloroso
quay /ki, kei/ *n* muelle, *m*
queasiness /'kwizinɪs/ *n* náusea, *f;* escrupulosidad, *f*
queasy /'kwizi/ *a* propenso a la náusea; nauseabundo; delicado, escrupuloso
queen /kwin/ *n* reina, *f;* (in a Spanish pack of cards) caballo, *m;* (in a French or English pack and in chess) reina, *f.* **to q. it,** conducirse como una reina; mandar. **q. bee,** maestra, abeja reina, *f.* **q. cell,** maestril, *m.* **q. mother,** reina madre, *f.* **q. regent,** reina regente, *f*
queenliness /'kwinlɪnɪs/ *n* majestad de reina, *f*
queenly /'kwinli/ *a* de reina; regio
queer /kwiər/ *a* raro; extraño, singular; ridículo; (shady) sospechoso; (ill) malucho, algo enfermo; (mad) chiflado
queerly /'kwiªrli/ *adv* extrañamente; ridiculamente
queerness /'kwiªrnɪs/ *n* rareza, extrañeza, singularidad, *f;* ridiculez, *f*

quell /kwɛl/ vt subyugar; reprimir; apaciguar, calmar

quench /kwɛntʃ/ vt apagar; calmar; satisfacer. **to q. one's thirst,** apagar la sed

quenching /'kwɛntʃɪŋ/ n apagamiento, m; satisfacción, f

querulous /'kwɛrələs/ a quejumbroso

querulousness /'kwɛrələsnɪs/ n hábito de quejarse, m; quejumbre, f

query /'kwɪəri/ n pregunta, f; duda, f; punto de interrogación, m. —vt preguntar; dudar (de); poner en duda. —vi hacer una pregunta; expresar una duda

quest /kwɛst/ n busca, f; (adventure) demanda, f. **in q. of,** en busca de

question /'kwɛstʃən/ n pregunta, f; problema, m; asunto, m; cuestión, f; (discussion) debate, m, discusión, f. —vt and vi interrogar; examinar; poner en duda, dudar de; preguntarse; hacer preguntas. **beyond q.,** fuera de duda. **to ask a q.,** hacer una pregunta. **without q.,** sin duda. **It is out of the q.,** Es completamente imposible. **It is a q. of whether...,** Se trata de si... **q.-mark,** punto interrogante, m

questionable /'kwɛstʃənəbəl/ a cuestionable, discutible, dudoso; equívoco, sospechoso

questionableness /'kwɛstʃənəbəlnɪs/ n lo discutible; carácter dudoso, m; carácter sospechoso, m

questioner /'kwɛstʃənər/ n preguntador (-ra); interrogador (-ra)

questioning /'kwəstʃənɪŋ/ n preguntas, f pl; interrogatorio, m

questioningly /kwɛstʃənɪŋli/ adv interrogativamente

questionnaire /ˌkwɛstʃə'nɛər/ n cuestionario, m

quetzal /kɛt'sɑl/ n (money and Ornith.) quetzal, m

queue /kyu/ n coleta, f; cola, f, vi formar cola; hacer cola

quibble /'kwɪbəl/ n equívoco, subterfugio, m; sutileza, f; (pun) retruécano, m. —vi hacer uso de subterfugios; sutilizar

quibbler /'kwɪblər/ n sofista, mf

quibbling /'kwɪblɪŋ/ n sofistería, f, sofismas, m pl, sutilezas, f pl

quick /kwɪk/ a vivo; agudo; penetrante; sagaz; rápido, veloz; (ready) pronto; ágil, activo; (light) ligero. —adv rápidamente; (soon) pronto. —n carne viva, f; Fig. lo vivo. **Be q.!** ¡Date prisa! **He was very q.,** Lo hizo muy aprisa; Volvió (or Fue, according to sense) rápidamente. **the q. and the dead,** los vivos y los muertos. **to cut to the q.,** herir en lo más vivo. **q. march,** paso doble, m. **q.-sighted,** de vista aguda; perspicaz. **q. step,** paso rápido, m. **q.-tempered,** de genio vivo, colérico. **q. time,** compás rápido, m; Mil. paso doble, m. **q.-witted,** de ingenio agudo

quicken /'kwɪkən/ vt vivificar; animar; acelerar; excitar, avivar. —vi vivificarse; despertarse; renovarse; acelerarse; (stir) moverse. **to q. one's step,** acelerar el paso

quicklime /'kwɪk͵laim/ n cal viva, f

quickly /'kwɪkli/ adv rápidamente; (soon) pronto; (immediately) en seguida; (promptly) con presteza; vivamente

quickness /'kwɪknɪs/ n viveza, f; (of wit, etc.) agudeza, f; rapidez, velocidad, f; (promptness) prontitud, f; agilidad, f; (lightness) ligereza, f; (understanding) penetración, sagacidad, f

quicksand /'kwɪk͵sænd/ n arena movediza, f; Fig. cenagal, m

quicksilver /'kwɪk͵sɪlvər/ n azogue, mercurio, m, vt azogar

quiescence /kwi'esəns/ n reposo, m; quietud, tranquilidad, f; inactividad, f; pasividad, f

quiescent /kwi'esənt/ a quieto; inactivo; pasivo

quiet /'kwaiɪt/ a tranquilo; quieto; silencioso; quedo; monótono; inactivo; (informal) sin ceremonia; (simple) sencillo; (of the mind) sereno; (of colours, etc.) suave. —n tranquilidad, quietud, f; silencio, m; paz, f; (of mind) serenidad, f. —vt tranquilizar, sosegar; calmar. **to be q.,** callarse; no hacer ruido. **Be q.!** ¡Estate quieto! ¡A callar!

quietism /'kwaiɪ͵tɪzəm/ n quietismo, m

quietist /'kwaiɪtɪst/ n quietista, mf

quietistic /ˌkwaiɪ'tɪstɪk/ a quietista

quietly /'kwaiɪtli/ adv tranquilamente; en silencio; sin ruido; en calma; (simply) sencillamente; dulcemente

quietness /'kwaiɪtnɪs/ n tranquilidad, quietud, f; calma, f; paz, f; silencio, m

quietus /kwai'itəs/ n (quittance) quitanza, f, finiquito, m; golpe de gracia, m; muerte, f

quill /kwɪl/ n pluma de ave, f; (of a feather) cañón, m; (pen) pluma, f; (of a porcupine) púa, f. **q.-driver,** escribiente, mf

quilt /kwɪlt/ n colcha, f, edredón, m. —vt acolchar. **q. maker,** colchero, m

quilting /'kwɪltɪŋ/ n acolchamiento, m; colchadura, f

quince /kwɪns/ n (tree and fruit) membrillo, m. **q. cheese,** carne de membrillo, f. **q. jelly,** jalea de membrillo, f

quincentenary /ˌkwɪnsɛn'tɛnəri/ n quinto centenario, m

quinine /'kwainain/ n quinina, f

quinsy /'kwɪnzi/ n angina, f

quintessence /kwɪn'tesəns/ n quinta esencia, f

quintessential /ˌkwɪntə'sɛnʃəl/ a quintaesenciado

quintet /kwɪn'tet/ n quinteto, m

quintuple /'kwɪn'tupəl/ a quíntuplo

quintuplet /kwɪn'tʌplɪt/ n quintupleto, m; uno (una) de cinco niños (-as) gemelos (-as)

quip /kwɪp/ n agudeza, salida, f; (hint) indirecta, f; donaire, m, chanza, burla, f

quire /kwaiᵊr/ n (of paper) mano (de papel), f

quirk /kwɜrk/ n (quip) agudeza, salida, f; (quibble) sutileza, evasiva, f; (gesture) gesto, m

quit /kwɪt/ vt abandonar; dejar; renunciar (a). —vi marcharse, Inf. tomar las de Villadiego, poner pies en polvorosa; (slang) dejar de, cesar de. **notice to q.,** aviso de desahúcio, m

quite /kwait/ adv completamente, enteramente; totalmente; del todo; (very) muy; (fairly) bastante. **It is not q. the thing to do,** Esto es algo que no se hace. **Q. so!** ¡Claro!; ¡Eso es! Se comprende. **It is not q. as good as we hoped,** No es tan bueno como esperábamos. **Peter is q. grown-up,** Pedro está hecho un hombre (or es todo un hombre)

quits /kwɪts/ adv quito, descargado. **be q.,** estar en paz

quittance /'kwɪtns/ n quitanza, f; recibo, m; recompensa, f

quitter /'kwɪtər/ n desertor (-ra); cobarde, mf

quiver /'kwɪvər/ vi temblar; vibrar; estremecerse; palpitar; (of light) titilar. —n (for arrows) aljaba, f, carcaj, m. See also **quivering**

quivering /'kwɪvərɪŋ/ a tremulante; vibrante; palpitante. —n temblor, m; estremecimiento, m

quixotic /kwɪk'sɒtɪk/ a quijotesco

quixotism /'kwɪksə͵tɪzəm/ n quijotismo, m

quiz /kwɪz/ n examen parcial, m. —vt tomar el pelo (a); burlarse (de); (stare) mirar de hito en hito (a)

quizzical /'kwɪzɪkəl/ a burlón; cómico; estrafalario

quizzically /'kwɪzɪkli/ adv burlonamente; cómicamente

quoin /kɔin, kwɔin/ n piedra angular, f; ángulo, m; (wedge) cuña, f. —vt meter cuñas (a)

quoit /kwɔit/ n tejo, m; pl **quoits,** juego de tejos, m

quondam /'kwɒndəm/ a antiguo

quorum /'kwɔrəm/ n quórum, m. **to form a q.,** hacer un quórum

quota /'kwouta/ n cuota, f

quotable /'kwoutəbəl/ a citable; (Stock Exchange) cotizable

quota system n tablas diferenciales, f pl

quotation /kwou'teiʃən/ n citación, f; cita, f; Com. cotización, f. **q. mark,** comilla, f

quote /kwout/ vt citar; Com. cotizar. —n Inf. comilla, f

quoth /kwouθ/ vt **q. I,** dije yo. **q. he,** dijo él

quotient /'kwouʃənt/ n cociente, m. **intelligence q.,** cociente intelectual, m

R

r /ar/ *n* (letter) erre, *f*
rabbet /'ræbɪt/ *n* ranura, *f*, rebajo, *m.* —*vt* ensamblar a rebajo. **r.-joint,** junta a rebajo, *f*
rabbi /'ræbai/ *n* rabí, rabino, *m.* **grand r.,** gran rabino, *m*
rabbinical /rə'bɪnɪkəl/ *a* rabínico
rabbinism /'ræbə,nɪzəm/ *n* rabinismo, *m*
rabbit /'ræbɪt/ *n* conejo (-ja). —*a* conejuno, de conejo. —*vi* cazar conejos. **young r.,** gazapo, *m.* **r.-hutch,** jaula para conejos, *f.* **r.-warren,** conejera, *f*
rabble /'ræbəl/ *n* populacho, vulgo, *m,* plebe, *f*
Rabelaisian /,ræbə'leiziən/ *a* rabelasiano
rabid /'ræbɪd/ *a* rabioso; fanático; furioso, violento
rabies /'reibiz/ *n* rabia, hidrofobia, *f*
raccoon /ræ'kun/ *n* mapache, *m*
race /reis/ *n* carrera, *f;* (current) corriente, *f;* (prize) premio, *m;* (breed) raza, *f;* casta, estirpe, *f;* (family) linaje, *m,* familia, *f;* (scornful) ralea, *f;* (struggle) lucha, *f.* —*vi* tomar parte en una carrera; correr de prisa; asistir a concursos de carreras de caballos; (of a machine) dispararse. —*vt* (hacer) correr; competir en una carrera (con); desafiar a una carrera. **flat r.,** carrera llana, *f.* **mill-r.,** caz, *m.* **to run a r.,** tomar parte en una carrera; *Fig.* hacer una carrera. **r.-card,** programa de carreras de caballos, *m.* **r. hatred,** odio de razas, *m.* **r.-meeting,** concurso de carreras de caballos, *m.* **r. suicide,** suicidio de la raza, *m.* **r.-track,** pista, *f*
racecourse /'reis,kɔrs/ *n* hipódromo, *m;* estadio, *m*
racehorse /'reis,hɔrs/ *n* caballo de carrera, *m*
racer /'reisər/ *n* (horse) caballo de carreras, *m;* (person) carrerista, *mf;* (car) coche de carreras, *m;* (boat) yate de carreras, *m;* (bicycle) bicicleta de carreras, *f*
rachitic /rə'kɪtɪk/ *a* raquítico
racial /'reiʃəl/ *a* racial, de raza
racialism /'reiʃə,lɪzəm/ *n* rivalidad de razas, *f*
raciness /'reisinɪs/ *n* sabor, *m;* savia, *f,* pujanza, *f*
racing /'reisɪŋ/ *n* carreras, *f pl; Mech.* disparo, *m,* a de carreras; hípico. **r. calendar,** calendario de concursos de carreras de caballos, *m.* **r. car,** coche de carreras, *m.* **r. cycle,** bicicleta de carreras, *f*
rack /ræk/ *n* (for hay) percha (del pesebre), *f;* (in a railway compartment) rejilla, *f;* (for billiard cues) taquera, *f;* (for clothes) percha, *f;* (for torture) potro, *m; Mech.* cremallera, *f.* —*vt* poner en el potro, torturar; atormentar. **to be on the r.,** estar en el potro **to r. one's brains,** devanarse los sesos, quebrarse la cabeza. **r. and ruin,** ruina total, *f.* **r. railway,** ferrocarril de cremallera, *m,*
racket /'rækɪt/ *n Sports.* raqueta, *f;* (din) barahúnda, *f;* ruido, estrépito, *m;* confusión, *f;* (bustle) bullicio, *m,* agitación, *f;* (swindle) estafa, *f;* (binge) parranda, *f.* **to play rackets,** jugar a la raqueta
racking /'rækɪŋ/ *n* tortura, *f;* (of wine) trasiego, *m,* a torturante; (of a pain or cough) persistente
racoon /ræ'kun/ *n* mapache, *m*
racquet /'rækɪt/ *n* See **racket**
racy /'reisi/ *a* picante; sabroso
radar /'reidar/ *n* radar, *m*
raddled /'rædld/ *a* pintado de almagre; mal pintado
radial /'reidiəl/ *a* radial
radiance /'reidiəns/ *n* resplandor, brillo, *m,* luminosidad, *f*
radiant /'reidiənt/ *a* radiante; brillante, luminoso. —*n Geom.* línea radial, *f.* **r. heat,** calor radiante, *m*
radiantly /'reidiəntli/ *adv* con resplandor; brillantemente; con alegría
radiate /'reidi,eit/ *vi* radiar. —*vt* irradiar
radiation /,reidi'eiʃən/ *n* irradiación, *f; Geom.* radiación, *f*
radiator /'reidi,eitər/ *n* (for central heating and of a car) radiador, *m;* (stove) calorífero, *m*
radical /'rædɪkəl/ *a* radical. —*n* (*Math. Chem.*) radical, *m; Polit.* radical, *mf*
radicalism /'rædɪkə,lɪzəm/ *n* radicalismo, *m*
radio /'reidi,ou/ *n* radio, *f;* radiocomunicación, *f.* **r.**

amateur, r. enthusiast, radioaficionado (-da). **r. announcer,** locutor (-ra). **r. broadcast,** radioemisión, radiodifusión, *f.* **r. listener,** radiooyente, *mf* **r. receiver,** (technical) radiorreceptor, *m;* (usual word) aparato de radio, *m.* **r. transmitter,** radiotransmisor, *m*
radioactive /,reidiou'æktɪv/ *a* radiactivo
radioactive fallout *n* caída radiactiva, llovizna radiactiva, precipitación radiactiva, *f*
radioactivity /,reidiouæk'tɪvɪti/ *n* radiactividad, *f*
radiofrequency /,reidiou'frikwənsi/ *n* radiofrecuencia, *f*
radiolocation /,reidioulou'keiʃən/ radiolocación, *f*
radiologist /,reidi'ɒlɑgɪst/ *n* radiólogo, *m*
radiology /,reidi'ɒlədʒi/ *n* radiología, *f*
radiometer /,reidi'ɒmɪtər/ *n* radiómetro, *m*
radiometry /,reidi'ɒmɪtri/ *n* radiometría, *f*
radioscopy /,reidi'ɒskəpi/ *n* radioscopia, *f*
radiotherapeutics, radiotherapy /,reidiou,θerə'pyutɪks; ,reidiou'θerəpi/ *n* radioterapia, *f*
radish /'rædɪʃ/ *n* rábano, *m.* **horse-r.,** rábano picante, *m*
radium /'reidiəm/ *n* radio, *m*
radius /'reidiəs/ *n* (*Geom. Anat.*) radio, *m;* (of a wheel) rayo, *m;* (scope) alcance, *m*
raffia /'ræfiə/ *n* rafia, *f*
raffish /'ræfɪʃ/ *a* disoluto, libertino
raffle /'ræfəl/ *n* rifa, *f,* sorteo, *m;* lotería, *f.* —*vt* rifar, sortear
raffling /'ræflɪŋ/ *n* sorteo, *m,* rifa, *f*
raft /ræft/ *n* balsa, *f;* (timber) armadía, *f.* —*vt* transportar en balsa; cruzar en balsa
rafter /'ræftər/ *n* (of a roof) viga, traviesa, *f;* (raftsman) balsero, *m*
raftered /'ræftərd/ *a* con vigas
rag /ræg/ *n* jirón, guiñapo, *m;* (for cleaning) paño, trapo, *m;* (for papermaking) estraza, *f;* (of smoke, etc.) penacho, *m;* (newspaper) papelucho, *m;* **r. pl rags,** harapos, *m pl; Inf.* viejos hábitos, *m pl.* —*vt* (tease) tomar el pelo (a); burlarse de; hacer una broma pesada (a). **r.-and-bone-man, ragpicker,** andrajero, trapero (Mexico), pepinador, *m.* **r. doll,** muñeca de trapo, *f*
ragamuffin /'rægə,mʌfɪn/ *n* galopín, *m*
rage /reidʒ/ *n* (anger) cólera, rabia, ira, *f;* (of the elements) furia, violencia, *f;* (ardour) entusiasmo, ardor, *m;* (fashion) boga, moda, *f;* (craze) manía, *f;* (of the poet) furor, *m.* —*vi* (be angry) rabiar, estar furioso; (of the sea) encresparse, alborotarse, enfurecerse; (of wind, fire, animals) bramar, rugir; (of pain) rabiar; (be prevalent) prevalecer, desencadenarse. **to r. against,** protestar furiosamente contra; culpar amargamente (de). **to be all the r.,** *Inf.* ser la ultima moda. **to fly into a r.,** montar en cólera. **to put into a r.,** hacer rabiar
ragged /'rægɪd/ *a* harapiento, andrajoso; roto; (uneven) desigual; (rugged) peñascoso, áspero, escabroso; (serrated) serrado; dentellado; (of a coastline) accidentado; (unfinished) inacabado, sin terminar; (of style) descuidado, sin pulir
raggedness /'rægɪdnɪs/ *n* harapos, *m pl;* estado andrajoso, *m;* aspereza, escabrosidad, *f;* lo serrado; lo accidentado; (of style) falta de elegancia, tosquedad, *f*
raging /'reidʒɪŋ/ *a* furioso, rabioso; violento; (roaring) bramante; (of the sea) bravío; intenso. —*n* furia, *f;* violencia, *f;* intensidad, *f*
raglan /'ræglən/ *n* raglán, *m.* **r. sleeve,** manga raglán, *f*
ragout /ræ'gu/ *n* estofado, *m*
ragpicker /'ræg,pɪkər/ *n* trapero (-ra)
ragtime /'ræg,taim/ *n* música sincopada, *f*
raid /reid/ *n* incursión, correría, *f;* asalto, ataque, *m;* (by the police) razzia, *f;* (by aircraft) bombardeo, *m,* *vt* invadir; atacar, asaltar; apoderarse de; hacer una razzia en; (by aircraft) bombear, bombardear; (pil-

lage) pillar, saquear. **obliteration r.**, hombardeo de saturación, *m*

raider /'reidər/ *n* corsario, *m;* atacador, asaltador, *m;* (aircraft) avión enemigo, *m*

rail /reil/ *n* barra, *f;* antepecho, *m;* (of a staircase) barandilla, *f,* pasamano, *m;* (track) riel, *m;* (railway) ferrocarril, *m;* (of a ship) barandilla, *f;* (of a chair) travesaño, *m pl.* **rails,** (fence) cerca, barrera, palizada, *f.* —*vt* cercar con una palizada, poner cerca a; mandar por ferrocarril. **by r.**, por ferrocarril. **to run off the rails,** descarrilar. **to r. at,** protestar contra; prorrumpir en invectivas contra, injuriar de palabra (a)

railing /'reiliŋ/ *n* barandilla, *f;* antepecho, *m,* enrejado, *m;* (grille) reja, *f;* (jeers) burlas, *f pl;* insultos, *m pl,* injurias, *f pl;* quejas, *f pl*

raillery /'reiləri/ *n* jocosidad, tomadura de pelo, *f;* sátiras, *f pl*

railway /'reil,wei/ *n* ferrocarril, *m;* vía férrea, *f,* camino de hierro, *m, a* de ferrocarril, ferroviario. **elevated r.**, ferrocarril aéreo, *m.* **narrow gauge r.**, ferrocarril de vía estrecha, *m.* **r. buffet,** fonda, *f,* (or restaurante, *m*) de estación. **r. carriage,** departamento de tren, *m.* **r. company,** compañía de ferrocarriles, *f.* **r. crossing,** paso a nivel, *m.* **r. engine,** locomotora, *f.* **r. guard,** jefe del tren, *m.* **r. guide,** guía de ferrocarriles, *f.* **r. line,** vía férrea, *f.* **r. marshalling yard,** apartadero ferroviario, *m.* **r. passenger,** viajero (-ra) en un tren. **r. platform,** andén, *m.* **r. porter,** mozo de estación, *m.* **r. siding,** vía muerta, *f.* **r. signal,** disco de señales, *m.* **r. station,** estación (de ferrocarril), *f.* **r. system,** sistema ferroviario, *m.* **r. ticket,** billete de tren, *m*

railwayman /'reil,weimən/ *n* ferroviario, empleado de los ferrocarriles, *m*

raiment /'reimənt/ *n* ropa, *f; Poet.* hábitos, *m pl*

rain /rein/ *n* lluvia, *f.* —*vi* and *vt* llover. **a r. of arrows,** una lluvia de flechas. **fine r.,** llovizna, *f.* **to r. cats and dogs,** llover a cántaros. **to r. hard,** diluviar. **r. cloud,** nubarrón, *m.* **r.-gauge,** pluviómetro, *m*

rainbow /'rein,bou/ *n* arco iris, arco de San Martín, *m*

raincoat /'rein,kout/ *n* abrigo impermeable, *m*

raindrop /'rein,drɒp/ *n* gota de lluvia, *f*

rainfall /'rein,fɔl/ *n* cantidad llovida, *f;* (shower) aguacero, *m*

rainless /'reinlis/ *a* sin lluvia, seco

rainstorm /'rein,stɔrm/ *n* chaparrón, *m,* tempestad de lluvia, *f*

rainwater /'rein,wɔtər/ *n* lluvia, *f;* agua lluvia, *f*

rainy /'reini/ *a* lluvioso. **r. day,** día de lluvia, *m; Fig.* tiempo de escasez, *m*

raise /reiz/ *vt* levantar; alzar; (the hat) quitar; solevantar; (dough) fermentar; (erect) erigir, edificar; (dust) levantar; elevar; (promote) ascender; (increase) aumentar; hacer subir; (spirits, memories) evocar; (the dead) resucitar; (cause) causar; dar lugar (a); hacer concebir; (a question, a point) hacer; plantear; (breed or educate) criar; (a crop) cultivar; (an army) alistar; (gather together) juntar; (a subscription) hacer; (money, etc.) obtener, hallar; (a siege, etc.) levantar, alzar; (a laugh, a protest, etc.) suscitar, provocar; (utter) poner, dar; (a fund) abrir. **to r. oneself,** incorporarse. **He succeeded in raising himself,** Logró alzarse; Logró mejorar su posición. **He raised their hopes unduly,** Les hizo concebir esperanzas desmesuradas. **to r. an objection (to),** poner objeción (a). **to r. an outcry,** armar un alboroto. **to r. a point,** hacer una observación; plantear una cuestión. **to r. a siege,** levantar un sitio. **to r. Cain,** armar lo de Dios es Cristo. **to r. one's voice,** alzar la voz

raised /reizd/ *a* (in relief) en relieve; (embossed) de realce

raiser /'reizər/ *n* (breeder) criador (-ra); (cultivator) cultivador (-ra); (educator) educador (-ra); autor (-ra); fundador (-ra); (of objections, etc.) suscitador (-ra)

raisin /'reizin/ *n* pasa, *f*

raising /'reiziŋ/ *n* levantamiento, *m;* alzamiento, *m;* (of a building, monument) erección, *f;* elevación, *f;* (increase) aumento, *m;* provocación, *f;* fundación, *f;*

(breeding or education) crianza, *f;* (of spirits) evocación, *f;* (of the dead) resucitación, *f;* producción, *f;* (of crops) cultivo, *m*

rake /reik/ *n Agr.* rastrillo, *m,* rastra, *f;* (for the fire) hurgón, *m;* (croupier's) raqueta, *f;* (of a mast, funnel) inclinación, *f;* (person) tenorio, calavera, *m.* —*vt Agr.* rastrillar; (a fire, etc.) hurgar; (sweep) barrer; recoger; (ransack) buscar (en); (with fire) enfilar, tirar a lo largo de; (scan) escudriñar. —*vi* trabajar con el rastrillo; (slope) inclinarse. **r. off,** tajada, *f.* **to r. together,** juntar con el rastrillo; amontonar; ahorrar. **r. up,** (revive) resucitar, desenterrar

raking /'reikiŋ/ *n* rastrillaje, *m;* (the fire, etc.) hurgonada, *f*

rakish /'reikiʃ/ *a* (of a ship) de palos muy inclinados, (dissolute) disoluto, libertino; (dashing) elegante

rakishly /'reikiʃli/ *adv* disolutamente; elegantemente

rakishness /'reikiʃnis/ *n* (licentiousness) libertinaje, *m,* disipación, disolución, *f;* (elegance) elegancia, *f*

rally /'ræli/ *vt* reunir; *Mil.* rehacer; (faculties) concentrar; (tease) tomar el pelo (a). —*vi* reunirse; *Mil.* rehacerse; (revive) mejorar, recobrar las fuerzas; (of markets, etc.) mejorar *n* reunión, *f*

rallying /'ræliiŋ/ *n* reunión, *f;* (of faculties, etc.) concentración, *f;* (recovery) mejora, *f.* **r. point,** punto de reunión, *m*

ram /ræm/ *n Zool.* carnero, morueco, *m; Astron.* Aries, Carnero, *m;* (Mil. etc.) ariete, *m;* (tool) pisón, *m; Nav.* espolón, *m, vt* golpear con ariete o espolón; (of a gun) atacar; apisonar; meter a la fuerza; hacer tragar a la fuerza; (squeeze) apretar; (crowd) atestar

Ramadan /,ræmə'dɑn/ *n* ramadán, *m*

ramble /'ræmbəl/ *n* vagar, vagabundear; hacer una excursión. —*vt* errar por

rambler /'ræmblər/ *n* excursionista, *mf;* paseante, *mf; Bot.* rosa trepante, *f*

rambling /'ræmbliŋ/ *a* (of houses) encantado; laberíntico; (straggly) disperso; (of thought, etc.) incoherente, inconexo. —*n* vagabundeo, *m;* excursiones, *f pl;* paseo, *m;* (digression) digresiones, *f pl;* (delirium) desvaríos, *m pl*

ramification /,ræməfi'keiʃən/ *n* ramificación, *f*

ramify /'ræmə,fai/ *vi* ramificarse, tener ramificaciones. —*vt* ramificar; dividir en ramales

rammer /'ræmər/ *n* pisón de empedrador, *m;* baqueta (de fusil), *f;* (of a ship) espolón, *m*

ramp /ræmp/ *n* rampa, *f;* (swindle) estafa, *f;* (storm, commotion) tormenta, *f*

rampage /'ræmpeidʒ/ *vi* alborotarse; bramar

rampant /'ræmpənt/ *a* salvaje; *Herald.* rampante; (of persons) impaciente, furioso; (of plants, growth) lozano, exuberante; desenfrenado; (rife) prevaleciente, predominante

rampart /'ræmpart/ *n* muralla, *f;* terraplén, *m; Fig.* baluarte, *m.* —*vt* abaluartar, abastionar

ramrod /'ræm,rɒd/ *n* baqueta, *f*

ramshackle /'ræm,ʃækəl/ *a* destartalado, ruinoso; desvencijado; (badly made) mal hecho

ranch /ræntʃ/ *n* rancho, *m,* hacienda (de ganado), *f*

rancher /'ræntʃər/ *n* ranchero, *m*

rancid /'rænsid/ *a* rancio

rancidness /'rænsidnis/ *n* rancidez, *f*

rancor /'ræŋkər/ *n* rencor, encono, *m*

rancorous /'ræŋkərəs/ *a* rencoroso

random /'rændəm/ *n* azar, *m, a* fortuito, al azar; sin orden ni concierto. **at r.**, a la ventura, al azar; sin pensar; (of shooting) sin apuntar. **to talk at r.**, hablar a trochemoche

range /reindʒ/ *n* línea, hilera, *f;* (of mountains) cadena, *f;* serie, *f;* clase, *f;* variedad, *f;* (of goods) surtido, *m;* (of a gun, voice, vision, etc.) alcance, *m;* (area) extensión, área, *f;* esfera de actividad, *f;* (scope) alcance, *m;* (of voice, musical instrument) compás, *m;* (of colors) gama, *f;* (for shooting) campo de tiro, *m;* (for cooking) cocina económica, *f.* **at close r.**, de cerca. **out of r.**, fuera de alcance. **within r.**, al alcance. **r.-finder,** (of guns, cameras) telémetro, *m.* **r. of mountains,** cadena de montañas, *f;* sierra, *f*

range /reindʒ/ *vt Poet.* arreglar; alinear; ordenar; clasificar; (a gun, etc.) apuntar; (place oneself) ponerse; sumarse (a); (roam) recorrer; (scan) escudriñar. —*vi* extenderse; (roam) vagar; (of plants) crecer (en);

variar, fluctuar; oscilar, vacilar; (of guns, etc.) alcanzar; (of the mind) pasar (por); (include) incluir
ranger /'reɪndʒər/ n (wanderer) vagabundo, m; (keeper) guardabosque, m; *Mil.* batidor, m
ranging /'reɪndʒɪŋ/ n arreglo, m; alineación, f; ordenación, f; clasificación, f; (roving) vida errante, f
rank /ræŋk/ n línea, f; fila, f; grado, m; clase, f; rango, m; categoría, f; posición, f; calidad, f; distinción, f. —vt ordenar; clasificar; (estimate) estimar; poner (entre). —vi ocupar un puesto; tener un grado, rango, etc.; estar al nivel (de); ser igual (a); contarse (entre). —a (luxuriant) lozano, exuberante; fértil; (thick) espeso; (rancid) rancio; (complete) consumado; completo; (foul-smelling) fétido; *Fig.* repugnante, aborrecible; (very) muy. **of the first r.,** de primera calidad; de primera clase; de distinción. **the r. and file,** los soldados, la tropa; las masas, hombres de filas, m pl, mujeres de fila, f pl, la mayoría; los socios ordinarios (de un club, etc.). **to break ranks,** *Mil.* romper filas. **to rise from the ranks,** ascender de las filas. **to r. high,** ocupar alta posición; ser de los mejores (de). **to r. with,** estar al nivel de; (be numbered among) contarse entre, figurar entre
rankle /'ræŋkəl/ vi irritar, molestar; envenenarse la vida, hacerse odioso
rankly /'ræŋkli/ adv ranciamente; lozanamente; con exuberancia; abundantemente; groseramente
rankness /'ræŋknɪs/ n rancidez, f; olor rancio, m; fertilidad, lozanía, f; exuberancia, f, vigor, m; enormidad, f
ransack /'rænsæk/ vt (search) registrar; (pillage) saquear; *Fig.* buscar entre
ransacking /'rænsækɪŋ/ n (searching) registro, m; (sacking) saqueo, m
ransom /'rænsəm/ n rescate, m, redención, f; liberación, f. —vt rescatar, redimir
ransomer /'rænsəmər/ n rescatador (-ra)
ransoming /'rænsəmɪŋ/ n redención, f; liberación, f
rant /rænt/ vi declamar a gritos, vociferar; despotricar (contra); desvariar; hablar por hablar, hablar sin ton ni son. —n declamación, vociferación, f; desvarío, m
ranter /'ræntər/ n declamador (-ra); agitador populachero, m; predicador chillón, m
rap /ræp/ n golpecito, m; toque, m; (with the knocker) aldabada, f; (worthless trifle) ardite, maravedí, m. —vt and vi golpear; tocar. **He doesn't care a rap,** No le importa un ardite. **to rap at the door,** tocar a la puerta. **to rap with the knuckles,** golpear con los nudillos. **to rap out an oath,** proferir una blasfemia
rapacious /rə'peɪʃəs/ a rapaz
rapaciously /rə'peɪʃəsli/ adv con rapacidad
rapacity /rə'pæsɪti/ n rapacidad, f
rape /reɪp/ n (carrying off) rapto, m. **the Rape of the Sabine Women,** el Rapto de las Sabinas, m; *Law.* estupro, m; violación, f; *Bot.* nabo silvestre, m. —vt (carry off) raptar, robar; violar, forzar
rapid /'ræpɪd/ a rápido. —n rápido, m. **r. combustion,** combustión activa, f
rapidity /rə'pɪdɪti/ n rapidez, f
rapidly /'ræpɪdli/ adv rápidamente, con rapidez
rapier /'reɪpiər/ n estoque, m; espadín, m
rapine /'ræpɪn/ n rapiña, f
rapping /'ræpɪŋ/ n golpecitos, m pl; golpeo, m; toques, m pl; (of the knocker) aldabeo, m
rapscallion /ræp'skælyən/ n bribón, m
rapt /ræpt/ past part and a arrebatado; absorto; extático, extasiado
rapture /'ræptʃər/ n arrebato, m; éxtasis, m; transporte, m; embriaguez, f; entusiasmo, m
rapturous /'ræptʃərəs/ a embelesado; extático; entusiasta
rapturously /'ræptʃərəsli/ adv extáticamente; con entusiasmo
rare /rɛər/ a raro; extraordinario; exótico; infrecuente
raree show /'rɛəri/ n barracón de los fenómenos, barracón de las atracciones, m
rarefaction /,rɛərə'fækʃən/ n rarefacción, f
rarefy /'rɛərə,faɪ/ vt rarefacer. —vi rarefacerse
rareness /'rɛərnɪs/ n rareza, f; singularidad, f; infrecuencia, f

rarity /'rɛərɪti/ n raridad, f; (uncommonness and rare object) rareza, f
rascal /'ræskəl/ n sinvergüenza, m; truhán, bribón, pícaro, m; (affectionately) picaruelo, m
rascality /ræ'skælɪti/ n bellaquería, truhanería, f
rascally /'ræskəli/ a redomado; vil, ruin, canallesco
rash /ræʃ/ a temerario, precipitado; imprudente. —n erupción, f, salpullido, m
rasher /'ræʃər/ n magra, f; (of bacon) torrezno, m
rashly /'ræʃli/ adv temerariamente, precipitadamente; imprudentemente, con imprudencia
rashness /'ræʃnɪs/ n temeridad, precipitación, f; imprudencia, f
rasp /ræsp/ n escofina, f, rallo, m; sonido áspero, m. —vt raspar, escofinar; (get on one's nerves) poner los nervios en punta (a)
raspberry /'ræz,bɛri/ n frambuesa, f. **r.-cane,** frambueso, m. **r. jam,** mermelada de frambuesa, f
rasping /'ræspɪŋ/ a (of the voice) áspero, estridente
rat /ræt/ n rata, f; desertor, m; (black leg) esquirol, m. —vi cazar ratas; ser desertor; ser esquirol. **rat-catcher,** cazador de ratas, m. **rat poison,** matarratas, m, raticida, f. **rat-trap,** ratonera, f
ratable /'reɪtəbəl/ a sujeto a contribución; imponible; valuable
ratafia /,rætə'fiə/ n ratafía, f
rataplan /,rætə'plæn/ n rataplán, m
ratchet /'rætʃɪt/ n *Mech.* trinquete, m; (of a watch) disparador, m. **r.-drill,** carraca, f. **r.-wheel,** rueda dentada con trinquete, f
rate /reɪt/ n velocidad, f; razón, proporción, f; (of exchange) tipo, m; tanto, m; precio, m; clase, f; modo, m, manera, f; *Naut.* clasificación, f; (tax) contribución, f, impuesto, m; **rates,** (of a house) inquilinato, m. —vt tasar; estimar; fijar el precio (a); *Naut.* clasificar; imponer una contribución (de); (scold) reñir. **at a great r.,** rápidamente, velozmente. **at a r. of,** a razón de; a una velocidad de. **at any r.,** de todos modos; por lo menos; sea como fuere. **at this r.,** de este modo; a este paso; a esa cuenta; en esta proporción; (with seguir) así. **first-r.,** de primera clase. **rates and taxes,** contribuciones e impuestos, f pl. **r. of climb,** *Aer.* velocidad ascensional, f. **r. of exchange,** tipo de cambio, m. **r.-payer,** contribuyente, mf
rather /'ræðər/ adv más bien; antes; (more willingly) de mejor gana; (somewhat) algo, un poco; (perhaps) quizás; mejor dicho; (fairly) bastante; (very) muy; mucho; al contrario. **R.!** ¡Ya lo creo! **or r.,** o más bien. **anything r. than...,** todo menos... **He had r.,** Preferiría. **r. than,** antes que, en vez de
ratification /,rætɪfɪ'keɪʃən/ n ratificación, f; (of a bill) aprobación, f
ratifier /'rætə,faɪər/ n ratificador (-ra)
ratify /'rætə,faɪ/ vt ratificar
ratifying /'rætə,faɪɪŋ/ n ratificación, f, a ratificatorio
rating /'reɪtɪŋ/ n tasación, f; valuación, f; clasificación, f; impuesto, m, contribución, f; repartición de impuestos, f; (of a ship's company) graduación, f; (scolding) reprensión, f
ratio /'reɪʃou/ n razón, f; proporción, f. **in direct r.,** en razón directa
ratiocinate /,ræʃi'ɒsə,neɪt/ vi raciocinar
ratiocination /,ræʃi'ɒsə'neɪʃən/ n raciocinación, f
ration /'ræʃən, 'reɪʃən/ n ración, f. —vt racionar. **r.-book,** cartilla de racionamiento, f
rational /'ræʃənl/ a racional; razonable, juicioso. —n ser racional, m
rationalism /'ræʃənl,ɪzəm/ n racionalismo, m
rationalist /'ræʃənl,ɪst/ n racionalista, mf
rationalistic /,ræʃənl'ɪstɪk/ a racionalista
rationality /,ræʃə'nælɪti/ n racionalidad, f; justicia, f
rationalization /,ræʃənlə'zeɪʃən/ n racionalización, f; justificación, f
rationalize /'ræʃənl,aɪz/ vt hacer racional; concebir racionalmente; *Math.* quitar los radicales (a); justificar
rationing /'ræʃənɪŋ, 'reɪ-/ n racionamiento, m
rattan /ræ'tæn/ n rota, f, bejuco, m; junquillo, m
ratteen /ræ'tin/ n ratina, f
ratter /'rætər/ n perro ratonero, m; gato que caza ratas, m

ratting /ˈrætɪŋ/ *n* caza de ratas, *f;* deserción, *f*

rattle /ˈrætl/ *vi* hacer ruido; rechinar, crujir; (of loose windows, etc.) zangolotearse; (knock) golpear; tocar; (patter) bailar; sonar; (of the dying) dar un estertor. —*vt* (shake) sacudir; hacer vibrar; (jolt) traquetear; (do rapidly) acabar rápidamente; (confuse) aturdir, hacer perder la cabeza (a); desconcertar. **to r. along,** deslizarse (or correr) rápidamente. **to r. off,** (repeat) decir rápidamente; terminar apresuradamente. **to r. on about,** charlar mucho de, hablar sin cesar sobre

rattle /ˈrætl/ *n* rechinamiento, crujido, *m;* zangoloteo, *m;* ruido, *m;* son (de la lluvia, etc.), *m;* (in the throat) estertor, *m;* (of a rattlesnake) cascabel, *m;* (child's) sonajero, *m;* matraca, *f;* carraca, *f;* (chatter) charla, *f.* **r.-headed,** de cabeza de chorlito, casquivano

rattlesnake /ˈrætlˌsneɪk/ *n* serpiente de cascabel, *f,* crótalo, *m*

rattling /ˈrætlɪŋ/ *n* See **rattle**

raucous /ˈrɔkəs/ *a* ronco, estridente

raucousness /ˈrɔkəsnɪs/ *n* ronquedad, *f,* estridor, *m*

ravage /ˈrævɪdʒ/ *vt* devastar; (pillage) saquear; destruir; (spoil) estropear. —*n* devastación, *f;* destrucción, *f;* estrago, *m*

ravager /ˈrævɪdʒər/ *n* devastador (-ra); saqueador (-ra)

rave /reiv/ *vi* desvariar, delirar; (of the elements) bramar, rugir. **to r. about,** hablar con entusiasmo de; delirar por. **to r. against,** vociferar contra, despotricarse contra

ravel /ˈrævəl/ *vt* deshilar, destejer; *Fig.* enredar. **to r. out,** deshilarse; *Fig.* desenredarse, desenmarañarse

raven /ˈreivən/ *n* cuervo, *m, a* negro como el azabache

ravening /ˈrævənɪŋ/ *a* rapaz, salvaje

Ravenna /rəˈvɛnə/ Rávena, *f*

ravenous /ˈrævənəs/ *a* voraz

ravenously /ˈrævənəsli/ *adv* vorazmente

ravenousness /ˈrævənəsnɪs/ *n* voracidad, *f*

ravine /rəˈvin/ *n* cañada, *f,* barranco, cañón, *m*

raving /ˈreivɪŋ/ *n* delirio, *m,* desvaríos, *m pl.* —*a* delirante; violento; bravío

ravioli /ˌrævɪˈouli/ *n pl* ravioles, *m pl*

ravish /ˈrævɪʃ/ *vt* (carry off) arrebatar, raptar; extasiar, encantar; (rape) violar, forzar

ravisher /ˈrævɪʃər/ *n* raptador, *m;* violador, *m*

ravishing /ˈrævɪʃɪŋ/ *n* violación, *f, a* encantador

ravishment /ˈrævɪʃmənt/ *n* violación, *f;* arrobamiento, *m;* transporte, éxstasis, *m*

raw /rɔ/ *a* (of meat, etc., silk, leather, weather) crudo; bruto; (inexpert) bisoño; (of flesh) vivo; *Com.* en bruto. **raw-boned,** huesudo. **raw hand,** novato (-ta). **raw material,** primera materia, *f.* **raw materials,** materias primas, *f pl.* **raw score,** puntuación bruta, *f.* **raw silk,** seda cruda, seda en rama, *f.* **raw sugar,** azúcar bruto, *m*

rawhide /ˈrɔˌhaid/ *a* de cuero crudo

rawness /ˈrɔnɪs/ *n* crudeza, *f;* inexperiencia, *f;* (of weather) humedad, *f*

ray /rei/ *n* rayo, *m;* (line) raya, *f;* (radius) radio, *m;* (fish) raya, *f.* **cathode rays,** rayos católicos, *m pl*

rayon /ˈreiɒn/ *n* rayón, *m*

raze /reiz/ *vt* arrasar, asolar; demoler; (erase) borrar, tachar

razor /ˈreizər/ *n* navaja, *f.* **electric r.,** máquina de afeitar eléctrica, *f.* **safety r.,** máquina de afeitar, *f.* **slash with a r.,** navajada, *f.* **r. blade,** hoja de afeitar, *f.* **r. case,** navajero, *m.* **r. strop,** suavizador, *m*

re /ri, rei/ *n Mus.* re, *m; prep Law.* causa, *f; Com.* concerniente a

re /ri/ *prefix* (attached to verb) re-; (after the verb) de nuevo; (followed by infin.) volver a... **to re-count,** volver a contar, contar de nuevo, recontar

reabsorb /ˌriəbˈsɔrb, -ˈzɔrb/ *vt* resorber

reabsorption /ˌriəbˈsɔrpʃən, -ˈzɔrp-/ *n* reabsorción, resorción, *f*

reach /ritʃ/ *vt* (stretch out) alargar; extender; alcanzar; llegar hasta; (arrive at) llegar a; (achieve) lograr; obtener. —*vi* extenderse; alcanzar; penetrar. —*n* alcance, *m;* extensión, *f;* poder, *m;* capacidad, *f;* (of a river) tabla, *f.* **as far as the eye could r.,** hasta donde alcanzaba la vista. **He reached home very**

soon, Llegó muy pronto a casa. **out of r.,** fuera de alcance. **to r. a deadlock,** llegar a un punto muerto. **within r.,** al alcance. **within easy r.,** de fácil acceso; a corta distancia. **to r. after,** procurar alcanzar; hacer esfuerzos para obtener. **to r. back,** (of time) remontarse. **to r. down,** bajar. **r.-me-downs,** ropa hecha, *f*

react /riˈækt/ *vi* reaccionar. —*vt* hacer de nuevo; *Theat.* volver a representar

reaction /riˈækʃən/ *n* reacción, *f*

reactionary /riˈækʃəˌnɛri/ *a* and *n* reaccionario (-ia)

reactive /riˈæktɪv/ *a* reactivo

read /rid/ *vt* leer; (a riddle, etc.) adivinar; descifrar; interpretar; (study) estudiar; (the Burial Service, etc.) decir; (correct) corregir; (of thermometers, etc.) marcar. —*vi* leer; estudiar; (be written) estar escrito, decir. **The play acts better than it reads,** La comedia es mejor representada que leída. **to r. aloud,** leer en voz alta. **to r. between the lines,** leer entre líneas. **to r. proofs,** corregir pruebas. **to r. to oneself,** leer para sí. **to r. about,** leer; (learn) enterarse de. **to r. again,** volver a leer, leer otra vez. **to r. on,** continuar leyendo. **to r. out,** leer en alta voz. **to r. over,** leer; leerlo todo. **to r. over and over again,** leer muchas veces, leer y releer

read /red/ *past part* leído, etc. **well-r.,** releído; instruido, culto

readability /ˌridəˈbɪlɪti/ *n* legibilidad, *f;* interés, *m,* amenidad, *f*

readable /ˈridəbəl/ *a* legible; interesante

readdress /ˌriəˈdrɛs/ *vt* dirigir de nuevo (una carta, etc.); poner la nueva dirección en (una carta, etc.)

reader /ˈridər/ *n* lector (-ra); *Eccl.* lector, *m;* (proof) corrector de pruebas, *m;* (citation collector for a dictionary) cedulista, *mf;* (university) profesor (-ra) auxiliar a cátedra; (book) libro de lectura, *m.* **to be a great r.,** leer mucho. **the Spanish r.** (reader of Spanish books) el lector de español

readily /ˈrɛdli/ *adv* fácilmente; en seguida, inmediatamente; de buena gana, con placer

readiness /ˈrɛdinɪs/ *n* prontitud, expedición, *f;* buena voluntad, *f;* (of speech, etc.) facilidad, *f.* **in r.,** preparado. **r. of wit,** viveza de ingenio, *f*

reading /ˈridɪŋ/ *n* lectura, *f;* (erudition) conocimientos, *m pl;* (recital) declamación, *f;* (lecture) conferencia, *f;* (study) estudio, *m;* interpretación, *f;* (of a thermometer, etc.) registro, *m;* (of a will) apertura, *f.* **r.-book,** libro de lectura, *m.* **r.-desk,** atril, *m.* **r.-lamp,** lente para leer, *m,* carlita, *f.* **r.-lamp,** lámpara de sobremesa, *f.* **r.-matter,** material de lectura, *m.* **r.-room,** gabinete de lectura, *m,* sala de lectura, *f*

readjourn /ˌriəˈdʒɜrn/ *vt* (a meeting) suspender (la sesión) de nuevo

readjust /ˌriəˈdʒʌst/ *vt* reajustar, recomdar; *vi* reacomodarse

readjustment /ˌriəˈdʒʌstmənt/ *n* reajuste, *m,* reacomodación, *f*

readmission /ˌriədˈmɪʃən/ *n* readmisión, *f*

readmit /ˌriədˈmɪt/ *vt* readmitir

ready /ˈrɛdi/ *a* listo, preparado; dispuesto; pronto; (on the point of) a punto de; (easy) fácil; (near at hand) a la mano; (with money) contante; (with wit, etc.) vivo; (available) disponible; (nimble) ágil, ligero. **I am r. to do it,** Estoy dispuesto a hacerlo. **in r. cash,** en dinero contante. **to get r.,** prepararse; (dress) vestirse. **to make r.,** *vt* preparar; aprestar; *Print.* imponer. —*vi* prepararse, disponerse. **r.-made,** hecho; confeccionado. **r.-made clothing,** ropa hecha, *f.* **r. money,** dinero contante, *m.* **r.-witted,** de ingenio vivo

reaffirm /ˌriəˈfɜrm/ *vt* afirmar de nuevo; reiterar, volver a repetir

reaffirmation /ˌriæfərˈmeiʃən/ *n* reiteración, *f*

reagent /riˈeidʒənt/ *n* reactivo, *m*

real /ˈreiəl/ *a* real; verdadero; efectivo; (with silk, etc.) puro; sincero. **r. estate, r. property,** bienes raíces, *m pl*

realism /ˈriəˌlɪzəm/ *n* realismo, *m*

realist /ˈriəlɪst/ *n* realista, *mf*

realistic /ˌriəˈlɪstɪk/ *a* realista

reality /riˈælɪti/ *n* realidad, *f;* verdad, *f*

realizable /ˌriəˈlaizəbəl/ *a* realizable; factible

realization /ˌrɪələˈzeɪʃən/ n realización, f; comprensión, f

realize /ˈrɪəˌlaiz/ vt (understand) darse cuenta de, hacerse cargo de; realizar; (make real) dar vida a(); (accomplish) llevar a cabo; Com. realizar; (gain) adquirir

really /ˈrɪəli/ adv realmente; en verdad; en realidad; en efecto; (frankly) francamente. **R.?** ¿De veras?

realm /rɛlm/ n reino, m, dominios, m pl; Fig. esfera, f

realty /ˈrɪəlti/ n bienes raíces, m pl

ream /rim/ n resma, f

reanimate /ˌriˈænəˌmeit/ vt reanimar

reap /rip/ vt segar; Fig. cosechar, recoger

reaper /ˈripər/ n segador (-ra); (machine) segadora mecánica, f

reaping /ˈripɪŋ/ n siega, f; Fig. cosecha, f. **r.-machine,** segadora mecánica, f

reappear /ˌriəˈpɪər/ vi reaparecer

reappearance /ˌriəˈpɪərəns/ n reaparición, f

reapplication /ˌriæplɪˈkeiʃən/ n nueva aplicación, f; (of paint, etc.) otra capa, f; (for a post, etc.) neuva solicitud, f

reapply /ˌriəˈplai/ vt aplicar de nuevo; (paint, etc.) dar otra capa (de); (for a post, etc.) mandar una nueva solicitud

reappoint /ˌriəˈpɔint/ vt designar de nuevo

rear /rɪər/ vt (lift) alzar, levantar; (breed, educate) criar; (build) erigir, construir. —vi (of horses) encabritarse, corcovear

rear /rɪər/ n cola, f; parte de atrás, f; parte posterior, f; última fila, f; (background) fondo, m; Inf. trasera, f; Mil. retaguardia, f. —a de atrás; trasero; último; posterior; de última fila; Mil. de retaguardia. **in the r.,** por detrás; a la cola; a retaguardia. **to bring up the r.,** cerrar la marcha. **r.-admiral,** contra almirante, m. **r.-axle,** eje trasero, m. **r.-guard,** retaguardia, f. **r. lamp,** faro trasero, m. **r. rank,** última fila, f. **r. view,** vista por detrás, f; vista posterior, f

rearing /ˈrɪərɪŋ/ n (breeding) cría, f; (education) crianza, f

rearm /riˈɑrm/ vt rearmar. —vi rearmarse

rearmament /riˈɑrməmənt/ n rearmamento, m

rearrange /ˌriəˈreindʒ/ vt volver a arreglar; arreglar de otra manera; (a literary work) refundir, adaptar

rearrangement /ˌriəˈreindʒmənt/ n nuevo arroglo, m; (of a literary work) refundición, adaptación, f

reascend /ˌriəˈsɛnd/ vi and vt subir de nuevo, subir otra vez; montar de nuevo (sobre)

reason /ˈrizən/ n razón, f. **I have plenty of r. to...** No me faltarían motivos para... —vi and vt razonar. **to r. out of,** disuadir de. **by r. of,** a causa de, con motivo de; en virtud de. **for this r.,** por esto, por esta razón. **out of all r.,** fuera de razón. **to stand to r.,** ser lógico, estar puesto en razón. **with r.,** con razón. **r. of state,** razón de estado, f

reasonable /ˈrizənəbəl/ a razonable; racional

reasonableness /ˈrizənəbəlnɪs/ n lo razonable; moderación, f; justicia, f; racionalidad, f

reasonably /ˈrizənəbli/ adv razonablemente; con razón; bastante

reasoning /ˈrizənɪŋ/ n razonamiento, m

reassemble /ˌriəˈsɛmbəl/ vt reunir otra vez. —vi juntarse de nuevo

reassert /ˌriəˈsɜrt/ vt afirmar de nuevo, reiterar

reassertion /ˌriəˈsɜrʃən/ n reiteración, f

reassess /ˌriəˈsɛs/ vt tasar de nuevo; repartir de nuevo; (a work of art) hacer una nueva apreciación (de)

reassessment /ˌriəˈsɛsmənt/ n nueva tasación, f; nuevo repartimiento, m; (of a work of art) nueva estimación, f

reassume /ˌriəˈsum/ vt reasumir

reassumption /ˌriəˈsʌmpʃən/ n reasunción, f

reassurance /ˌriəˈsʊrəns/ n afirmación repetida, f; confianza restablecida, f

reassure /ˌriəˈʃʊr/ vt asegurar de nuevo; tranquilizar, confortar

reassuring /ˌriəˈʃʊrɪŋ/ a tranquilizador, consolador

rebate /ˈribeit/ n rebaja, f, descuento, m; reducción, f. —vt rebajar, descontar; reducir. **to r. pro rata,** ratear

rebec /ˈribɛk/ n Mus. rabel, m

rebel / n. ˈrɛbəl; v. rɪˈbɛl/ n rebelde, mf, insurrecto (-ta). —vi rebelarse, sublevarse. **r. leader,** cabecilla, m

rebellion /rɪˈbɛlyən/ n rebelión, f

rebellious /rɪˈbɛlyəs/ a rebelde; revoltoso; refractario

rebelliousness /rɪˈbɛlyəsnɪs/ n rebeldía, f

rebind /riˈbaind/ vt atar de nuevo; (a book) reencuadernar

rebirth /rɪˈbɜrθ/ n renacimiento, m

rebore /rɪˈbɔr/ vt (an engine) descarbonizar

reboring /rɪˈbɔrɪŋ/ n (of an engine) descarburación, f

reborn, to be /rɪˈbɔrn/ vi renacer; ser reincarnado

rebound /v. rɪˈbaund; n. ˈriˌbaund/ a (of books) reencuadernado. —vi rebotar; repercutir; (revive) reavivarse. —n rebote, resalto, m; reacción, f; rechazo, m

rebuff /rɪˈbʌf/ n repulsa, f, desaire, m; contrariedad, f. —vt rechazar; contrariar

rebuild /rɪˈbɪld/ vt reedificar

rebuilding /rɪˈbɪldɪŋ/ n reedificación, f

rebuke /rɪˈbyuk/ n reconvención, reprensión, censura, f, reproche, m, vt reprender, censurar, reprochar

rebukingly /rɪˈbyukɪŋli/ adv en tono de censura; con reprensión, con reprobación

rebut /rɪˈbʌt/ vt refutar

rebuttal /rɪˈbʌt/ n refutación, f

recalcitrance /rɪˈkælsɪtrəns/ n terquedad, obstinacia, f; rebeldía, f

recalcitrant /rɪˈkælsɪtrənt/ a reacio, recalcitrante

recall / v. rɪˈkɔl; n. also ˈrikɔl/ vt llamar; hacer volver; (dismiss) destituir; (ambassador, etc.) retirar; (remind or remember) recordar; (revoke) revocar. —n llamada, f; Mil. toque de llamada, m; (of ambassadors, etc.) retirada, f; (dismissal) destitución, f. **beyond r.,** irrevocable; (forgotten) olvidado

recant /rɪˈkænt/ vt retractar, retirar. —vi desdecirse (de), retractarse

recantation /ˌrikænˈteiʃən/ n recantación, f

recapitulate /ˌrikəˈpɪtʃəˌleit/ vt recapitular, resumir

recapitulation /ˌrikəˌpɪtʃəˈleiʃən/ n recapitulación, f

recapture /rɪˈkæptʃər/ vt volver a prender, hacer prisionero nuevamente; (a place) volver a tomar; (a ship) represar

recast /riˈkæst/ vt (metals, a literary work) refundir; (alter) cambiar; (reckon) volver a calcular

recasting /riˈkæstɪŋ/ n (metals, a literary work) refundición, f

recede /riˈsid/ vi retroceder; alejarse (de), separarse (de); desviarse (de); retirarse; desaparecer; (diminish) disminuir; (of prices) bajar

receding /riˈsidɪŋ/ a que retrocede, etc.

receipt /rɪˈsit/ n recibo, m; (for money) recibí, m; (recipe) receta, f; pl **receipts,** ingresos, m pl. —vt firmar (or extender) recibo. **on r. of,** al recibir. **to acknowledge the r. of,** acusar recibo de. **r. book,** libro talonario, m

receive /rɪˈsiv/ vt recibir, and vi recibir; admitir, aceptar; acoger; (money) percibir, cobrar; (lodge) hospedar, alojar; (contain) contener. **to be well received,** tener buena acogida

receiver /rɪˈsivər/ n recibidor (-ra); (of stolen goods) receptador (-ra); (in bankruptcies) síndico, m; (for other legal business) receptor, m; (of a telephone) auricular, m; Elec. receptor, m; Radio. radiorreceptor, m. **to hang up the r.,** colgar (el auricular)

receivership /rɪˈsivərˌʃɪp/ n sindicatura, f; receptoría, f

receiving /rɪˈsivɪŋ/ n recibimiento, m; (of money, etc.) cobranza, f, percibo, m; (of stolen goods) encubrimiento, m. —a que recibe; recipiente; de recepción. **r. set,** aparato de radio, m

recency /ˈrisənsi/ n lo reciente; novedad, f

recent /ˈrisənt/ a reciente; nuevo. **in r. years,** en estos últimos años

recently /ˈrisəntli/ adv recientemente; (before past participles) recién. **until r.,** hasta hace poco. **r. painted,** recién pintado

receptacle /rɪˈsɛptəkəl/ n receptáculo, recipiente, m; Bot. receptáculo, m

reception /rɪˈsɛpʃən/ n recepción, f; recibo, m; (welcome) acogida, f; (of evidence) recepción, f. **r. room,** pieza de recibo, f, gabinete, m

receptive /rɪˈsɛptɪv/ a receptivo; susceptible

receptiveness /rɪ'sɛptɪvnɛs/ n sensibilidad, susceptibilidad, f

recess /rɪ'sɛs, 'rises/ n (holiday) vacaciones, f pl; (during school hours) hora de recreo, f; (Fig. heart) seno, m, entrañas, f pl; (of the soul, heart) hondón, m; (in a coastline, etc.) depresión, f; (in a wall) nicho, m; (alcove) alcoba, f. **parliamentary r.,** interregno parlamentario, m

recessional /rɪ'sɛʃən/ n himno que se canta mientras se retiran los eclesiásticos y el coro, m

recharge /ri't∫ɑrdʒ/ vt (a gun, etc.) recargar; acusar de nuevo

recipe /'rɛsəpi/ n receta, f

recipient /rɪ'sɪpiənt/ n recibidor (-ra); el, m, (f, la) que recibe. —a recipiente; receptivo

reciprocal /rɪ'sɪprəkəl/ a recíproco

reciprocate /rɪ'sɪprə,keit/ vt reciprocar; Mech. producir movimiento de vaivén. —vi Mech. oscilar, tener movimiento alternativo; corresponder; ser recíproco

reciprocation /rɪ,sɪprə'keiʃən/ n reciprocación, f; reciprocidad, correspondencia, f

reciprocity /,rɛsə'prɒsɪti/ n reciprocidad, f

recital /rɪ'saitl/ n narración, relación, f; enumeración, f; recitación, f; Mus. recital, m

recitation /,rɛsɪ'teiʃən/ n recitación, f

recitative /,rɛsɪtə'tiv/ n recitado, m

recite /rɪ'sait/ vt recitar, repetir; narrar; declamar. —vi decir una recitación

reciter /rɪ,saitər/ n recitador (-ra); declamador (-ra)

reckless /'rɛklɪs/ a temerario, audaz; precipitado; descuidado (de); indiferente (a); excesivo; imprudente

recklessly /'rɛklɪsli/ adv temerariamente; descuidadamente; imprudentemente

recklessness /'rɛklɪsnɪs/ n temeridad, audacia, f; descuido, m; imprudencia, f; indiferencia, f

reckon /'rɛkən/ vt calcular, computar; contar; enumerar; (believe) considerar, juzgar; (attribute) atribuir; (think) creer (que). **to r. up,** echar cuentas, calcular. **to r. with,** contar con; tomar en serio

reckoner /'rɛkənər/ n calculador (-ra). **ready r.,** tablas matemáticas, f pl

reckoning /'rɛkənɪŋ/ n cálculo, m, calculación, f; cuenta, f; Fig. retribución, f, castigo, m; Naut. estima, f. **the day of r.,** el día de ajuste de cuentas; el día del juicio final. **to be out in one's r.,** equivocarse en el cálculo; engañarse en el juicio

reclaim /rɪ'kleim/ vt (land) entarquinar; (reform) reformar; (tame) domesticar; (claim) reclamar; (restore) restaurar

reclamation /,rɛklə'meiʃən/ n (of land) entarquinamiento, m; cultivo, m; (reform) reformación, f; (restoration) restauración, f; (claiming) reclamación, f

recline /rɪ'klain/ vt apoyar; recostar; reclinar; descansar, reposar. —vi recostarse, reclinarse; estar tumbado; apoyarse; descansar

reclining /rɪ'klainɪŋ/ n reclinación, f. —a inclinado; acostado; (of statues) yacente

recluse /'rɛklus, rɪ'klus/ a solitario, n recluso (-sa); solitario (-ia); ermitaño, m, anacoreta, mf

recognition /,rɛkəg'nɪʃən/ n reconocimiento, m

recognizable /,rɛkəg'naizəbəl/ a que puede reconocerse; identificable

recognizance /rɪ'kɒgnəzəns, -'kɒnə-/ n reconocimiento, m; Law. obligación, f

recognize /'rɛkəg,naiz/ vt reconocer; confesar

recoil /n. 'ri,kɔil; v. rɪ'kɔil/ n reculada, f; (of a gun) culatazo, m; (refusal) rechazo, m; (result) repercusión, f; (repugnance) aversión, repugnancia, f. —vi recular; retroceder; repercutir; sentir repugnancia

recoin /rɪ'kɔin/ vt acuñar de nuevo

recollect /,rɛkə'lɛkt/ vt acordarse de, recordar. **to r. oneself,** reponerse, recobrarse

recollection /,rɛkə'lɛkʃən/ n recuerdo, m, memoria, f

recommence /,rikə'mɛns/ vt and vi empezar de nuevo

recommend /,rɛkə'mɛnd/ vt recomendar; aconsejar; encargar

recommendable /,rɛkə'mɛndəbəl/ a recomendable

recommendation /,rɛkəmən'deiʃən/ n recomendación, f

recommendatory /,rɛkə'mɛndə,tɔri/ a recomendatario

recommender /,rɛkə'mɛndər/ n el, m, (f, la) que recomienda

recompense /'rɛkəm,pɛns/ n recompensa, f, vt recompensar

recomposition /,rikɒmpə'zɪʃən/ n recomposición, f

reconcilability /,rɛkən,sailə'bɪlɪti/ n posibilidad de reconciliación, f; compatibilidad, f

reconcilable /,rɛkən'sailəbəl/ a reconciliable; compatible; conciliable

reconcile /'rɛkən,sail/ vt reconciliar; (quarrels) componer, ajustar; (opposing theories, etc.) conciliar. **to r. oneself (to),** aceptar; acostumbrarse (a); resignarse (a)

reconciler /'rɛkən,sailər/ n reconciliador (-ra)

reconciliation /,rɛkən,sɪli'eiʃən/ n reconciliación, f; (of theories, etc.) conciliación, f

reconciliatory /,rɛkən'sɪliə,tɔri/ a reconciliador

recondite /'rɛkən,dait/ a recóndito

recondition /,rikən'dɪʃən/ vt reconditionar

reconnaissance /rɪ'kɒnəsəns, -zəns/ n reconocimiento, m; exploración, f. **r. flight,** vuelo de reconocimiento, m. **r. plane,** avión de reconocimiento, m

reconnoiter /,rikə'nɔitər/ vt Mil. reconocer; explorar. —vi Mil. practicar un reconocimiento; correr la campaña

reconnoitering /,rikə'nɔitərɪŋ/ n reconocimiento, m, a de reconocimiento

reconquer /ri'kɒŋkər/ vt reconquistar

reconquest /ri'kɒŋkwɛst/ n reconquista, f

reconsecrate /ri'kɒnsɪ,kreit/ vt consagrar de nuevo

reconsider /,rikən'sɪdər/ vt considerar de nuevo, volver a considerar; volver a discutir

reconsideration /,rikən,sɪdə'reiʃən/ n nueva consideración, f; nueva discusión, f

reconstitute /ri'kɒnstɪ,tut/ vt reconstituir

reconstitution /,rikɒnstɪ'tuʃən/ n reconstitución, f

reconstruct /,rikən'strʌkt/ vt reconstruir

reconstruction /,rikən'strʌkʃən/ n reconstrucción, f

reconversion /,rikən'vɜrʒən/ n reconversión, f

recopy /ri'kɒpi/ vt copiar de nuevo

record /v. rɪ'kɔrd; n. 'rɛkərd/ vt apuntar; inscribir; (recount) contar, escribir; recordar; registrar; (of thermometers, etc.) marcar, registrar; hacer un disco de gramófono de; (radio, cinema) impresionar. —n relación, f; crónica, f; historia, f; (soldier's) hoja de servicios, f; (past) antecedentes, m pl; documento, m; inscripción, f; (entry) partida, f; testimonio, m; (memory) recuerdo, m; registro, m; (gramophone) disco de gramófono, m; Sports. record, m, plusmarca, f; pl **records,** m pl; (notes) notas, f pl; (facts) datos, m pl; anales, m pl. **keeper of the records,** archivero, m. **off the r.,** confidencialmente. **on r.,** escrito; registrado; inscrito en los anales de la historia. **to break a r.,** supremar precedentes. **r.-holder,** plusmarquista, mf

recorder /rɪ'kɔrdər/ n registrador, m; archivero, m; Law. juez, m; (historian) historiador, m; Mus. caramillo, m; Mech. contador, indicador, m; (scientific) aparato registrador, m

recording /rɪ'kɔrdɪŋ/ a registrador. **r. apparatus,** (cinema, radio, gramophone) máquina de impresionar, f; (scientific) aparato registrador, m. **r. van,** carro de sonido, m

recount /rɪ'kaunt/ vt contar de nuevo; (tell) referir, narrar, contar

recoup /rɪ'kup/ vt compensar, indemnizar; recobrar, desquitarse de

recourse /'rikɔrs/ n recurso, m. **to have r. to,** recurrir, a

recover /rɪ'kʌvər/ vt (regain) recobrar; Fig. reconquistar; (retrieve) rescatar; Law. reivindicar. —vi reponerse; (in health) recobrar la salud, sanar, curarse; Law. ganar un pleito. **to r. consciousness,** volver en sí

recoverable /rɪ'kʌvərəbəl/ a recuperable

recovery /rɪ'kʌvəri/ n (regaining) recobro, m, recuperación, f; (of money) cobranza, f; (retrieval) rescate, m; Fig. reconquista, f; (from illness) mejoría, convalecencia, f; restablecimiento, m; Law. reivindicación, f

recreant /'rɛkriənt/ a traidor, falso, desleal. —n apóstata, mf traidor (-ra)

recreate /'rɛkri,eit/ vt recrear

recreation /ˌrɛkri'eiʃən/ n recreación, f; (break in schools) recreo, m. **r. hall,** sala de recreo, f

recreative /'rɛkri,eitɪv/ a recreativo

recriminate /rɪ'krɪmə,neit/ vi recriminar

recrimination /rɪˌkrɪmə'neiʃən/ n recriminación, reconvención, f

recriminator /rɪ'krɪmə,neitər/ n recriminador (-ra)

recriminatory /rɪ'krɪmənə,tɔri/ a recriminador

recross /ri'krɔs/ vt volver a cruzar, cruzar de nuevo

recrudesce /ˌrikru'dɛs/ vi recrudecer

recrudescence /ˌrikru'dɛsəns/ n recrudescencia, f

recrudescent /ˌrikru'dɛsənt/ a recrudescente

recruit /rɪ'krut/ n recluta, m. —vt reclutar; (restore) reponer

recruiting /rɪ'krutɪŋ/ n reclutamiento, m. **r. office,** caja de reclutamiento, f

recruiting flag n bandera de enganche, f

rectal /'rɛktl/ a rectal

rectangle /'rɛk,tæŋgəl/ n rectángulo, m

rectangular /rɛk'tæŋgyələr/ a rectangular

rectifiable /'rɛktə,faiəbəl/ a rectificable

rectification /ˌrɛktəfɪ'keiʃən/ n rectificación, f

rectifier /'rɛktə,faiər/ n rectificador, m

rectify /'rɛktə,fai/ vt rectificar

rectilinear /ˌrɛktl'ɪniər/ a rectilíneo

rectitude /'rɛktɪ,tud/ n rectitud, f

rector /'rɛktər/ n (of a university or school) rector, m; (priest) párroco, m

rectorship /'rɛktər,ʃip/ n rectorado, m

rectory /'rɛktəri/ n rectoral, rectoría, f

rectum /'rɛktəm/ n recto, m

recumbent /rɪ'kʌmbənt/ a recostado, reclinado; (of a statue) yacente

recuperable /rɪ'kupərəbəl/ a recuperable

recuperate /rɪ'kupə,reit/ vt recuperar, recobrar. —vi restablecerse, reponerse; recuperarse

recuperation /rɪkupə'reiʃən/ n recuperación, f

recuperative /rɪ'kupərətɪv/ a recuperativo

recur /rɪ'kɜr/ vi presentarse a la imaginación; volver (sobre); presentarse de nuevo, aparecer otra vez; repetirse; reproducirse

recurrence /rɪ'kɜrəns/ n reaparición, f; repetición, f

recurrent /rɪ'kɜrənt/ a periódico; Med. recurrente

red /rɛd/ a rojo; (of wine) tinto. —n color rojo, m; (in billiards) mingo, m, bola roja, f; Polit. rojo, m. **to catch red-handed,** coger con el hurto en las manos; coger con las manos en la masa, coger en el acto. **to grow red,** enrojecerse, ponerse rojo; volverse rojo. **red-berried,** con bayas rojas. **red cabbage,** lombarda, f. **red cedar,** cedro dulce, m. **red corpuscle,** glóbulo rojo, m. **Red Cross,** Cruz Roja, f. **red currant,** grosella, f. **red currant bush,** grosellero, m. **red-eyed,** con los ojos inyectados. **red fir,** pino silvestre, m. **red flush,** (in the sky) arrebol, m. **red-gold,** bermejo; (of hair, etc.) rojo. **red-haired,** pelirrojo, de pelo rojo. **red-handed,** con las manos ensangrentadas; Fig. en el acto. **red-head** (person) pelirrojo (-ja). **red-heat,** incandescencia, f. **red-hot,** candente, m. **red-lead,** minio, m. **red-letter,** de fiesta; extraordinario. **red-letter day,** día de fiesta, m; día extraordinario, m. **red mullet,** salmonete, m, trilla, f. **red ocher,** almagre, m. **red pepper,** pimiento, m; (cayenne) pimentón, m, **Red Sea,** mar Rojo, mar Bermejo, m. **red tape,** balduque, m; formulismo, m; burocracia, f. **red wine,** vino tinto, m

redbreast /'rɛd,brɛst/ n petirrojo, m

redden /'rɛdn/ vt rojear, enrojecer; pintar de rojo. —vi enrojecerse, ponerse rojo; volverse rojo

reddish /'rɛdɪʃ/ a rojizo

redeem /rɪ'dim/ vt (a mortgage, bonds, etc.) amortizar; (from pawn) desempeñar; (a promise, etc.) cumplir; libertar; redimir; compensar; (a fault) expiar; (reform) reformar; (rescue) rescatar

redeemable /rɪ'diməbəl/ a redimible; amortizable

redeemer /rɪ'dimər/ n rescatador (-ra); salvador (-ra); Theol. Redentor, m

redeeming /rɪ'dimɪŋ/ a redentor; compensatorio. **r. feature,** compensación, f; rasgo bueno, m. **There is no r. feature in his work,** No hay nada bueno en su obra

redemption /rɪ'dɛmpʃən/ n (of a mortgage, etc.)

amortización, f; (from pawn) desempeño, m; (of a promise, etc.) cumplimiento, m; (ransom, etc.) rescate, m; Theol. redención, f; compensación, f; (of a fault) expiación, f; reformación, f

redemptive /rɪ'dɛmptɪv/ a redentor

redescend /ˌridɪ'sɛnd/ vi bajar de nuevo

rediscovery /ˌridə'skʌvəri/ n nuevo descubrimiento, m

redistribute /ˌridɪ'stribyut/ vt distribuir de nuevo, volver a distribuir

redistribution /ˌridɪstrə'byuʃən/ n nueva distribución, f

redness /'rɛdnɪs/ n rojez, f, color rojo, m

redolent /'rɛdlənt/ a fragante, oloroso; Fig. evocador (de)

redouble /ri'dʌbəl/ vt redoblar. —vi redoblarse

redoubling /ri'dʌblɪŋ/ n redoblamiento, m

redoubt /rɪ'daut/ n reducto, m

redoubtable /rɪ'dautəbəl/ a formidable, terrible; valiente

redound /rɪ'daund/ vi redundar (en)

redress /rɪ'drɛs/ vt rectificar; reparar; remediar; hacer justicia (a); corregir

reduce /rɪ'dus/ vt reducir; disminuir; (in price) rebajar; abreviar; (exhaust, weaken) agotar; (impoverish) empobrecer; (degrade) degradar. **to r. to the ranks,** Mil. volver a las filas; degradar. **to be in reduced circumstances,** estar en la indigencia

reducible /rɪ'dusəbəl/ a reducible

reduction /rɪ'dʌkʃən/ n reducción, f; (in price) rebaja, f

redundance /rɪ'dʌndəns/ n redundancia, f

redundant /rɪ'dʌndənt/ a redundante; superfluo, excesivo

reduplicate /rɪ'dupli,keit/ vt reduplicar

reduplication /rɪ,dupli'keiʃən/ n reduplicación, f

reecho /ri'ɛkou/ vt repetir; devolver el son de, hacer reverberar. —vi repercutirse, reverberar

reed /rid/ n Bot. caña, f; (arrow) saeta, f; (pipe) caramillo, m; (in wind-instruments) lengüeta, f; Archit. junquillo, m; (in a loom) peine, m; (pastoral poetry) poesía bucólica, f. —vt (thatch) bardar con cañas

reedit /ri'ɛdit/ vt reeditar, volver a editar

reedy /'ridi/ a juncoso, lleno de cañas; (of the voice) silbante

reef /rif/ n arrecife, escollo, encalladero, m; Mineral. filón, m; Naut. rizo, m. —vt Naut. arrizar. **to take in reefs,** Naut. hacer el rizo. **r.-knot,** nudo de marino, m

reek /rik/ n humo, m; olor, m. —vi humear; oler (de); Fig. recordar, hacer pensar (en)

reeky /'riki/ a humoso

reel /ril/ n carrete, m; devanadera, f; (of a fishing rod) carrete, carretel, m; (cinema) cinta, f; (dance) baile escocés, m. —vt devanar. —vi tambalear, titubear; (of ships, etc.) cabecear; temblar; oscilar. **to r. about drunkenly,** (of persons) andar haciendo eses, arrimarse a las paredes. **to r. off,** recitar; enumerar; decir rápidamente

reelect /ˌrii'lɛkt/ vt reelegir

reelection /ˌrii'lɛkʃən/ n reelección, f

reeligible /ri'ɛlidʒəbəl/ a reelegible

reeling /'rilɪŋ/ n tambaleo, m; andar vacilante, m; (of a ship, etc.) cabeceo, m; oscilación, f

reembarcation /ˌriɛmbar'keiʃən/ n reembarque, m

reembark /ˌriɛm'bark/ vt reembarcar. —vi reembarcarse

reemerge /ˌrii'mɜrdʒ/ vi reaparecer

reemergence /ˌrii'mɜrdʒəns/ n reaparición, f

reenact /ˌrii'nækt/ vt revalidar (una ley); decretar de nuevo

reenactment /ˌrii'næktmənt/ n revalidación (de una ley), f; nuevo decreto, m

reengage /ˌriin'geidʒ/ vt contratar de nuevo

reengagement /ˌriin'geidʒmənt/ n nuevo contrato, m

reenlist /ˌriin'list/ vt and vi alistar(se) de nuevo

reenlistment /ˌriin'listmənt/ n reenganche, m

reenter /ri'ɛntər/ vt volver a entrar (en); reingresar (en)

reentry /ri'ɛntri/ n segunda entrada, f, reingreso, m

reequip /ˌriɪ'kwɪp/ vt equipar de nuevo
reestablish /ˌriɪ'stæblɪʃ/ vt restablecer; restaurar
reestablishment /ˌriɪ'stæblɪʃmənt/ n restablecimiento, m; restauración, f
reeve /riv/ vt Naut. laborear, guarnir
reexamination /ˌriɪgˌzæmɪ'neɪʃən/ n reexaminación, f; nuevo examen, m; Law. nuevo interrogatorio, m
reexamine /ˌriɪg'zæmɪn/ vt reexaminar; Law. interrogar de nuevo
reexport /ˌriɪk'spɔrt/ vt reexportar
reexportation /ˌriɪkspɔr'teɪʃən/ n reexportación, f
refashion /ri'fæʃən/ vt volver a hacer; formar de nuevo
refection /rɪ'fɛkʃən/ n refección, f
refectory /rɪ'fɛktəri/ n refectorio, m
refer /rɪ'fɜr/ vt atribuir (a); (send) enviar, remitir; (assign) referir (a), relacionar (con). —vi referirse (a); aludir (a); hablar (de)
referee /ˌrɛfə'ri/ n árbitro, m; Law. juez arbitrador, m; (reference) garante, mf fiador (-ra). —vi servir de árbitro
reference /'rɛfərəns/ n referencia, f; consulta, f; mención, f; alusión, f; (relation) relación, f; pl **references**, Com. referencias, f pl. **for r.,** para consulta. **in r. to,** con referencia a, respecto a, en cuanto a. **terms of r.,** puntos de consulta, m pl. **work of r.,** libro de consulta, m
reference book n libro de consulta, m
referendum /ˌrɛfə'rɛndəm/ n referéndum, m
refill /v. ri'fil; n. 'ri,fil/ vt rellenar; rehenchir; (pen) llenar de nuevo con tinta. —n (for a pencil) mina de recambio, f
refine /rɪ'faɪn/ vt refinar; (metals) acrisolar; (fats) clarificar; Fig. perfeccionar, pulir, refinar
refined /rɪ'faɪnd/ a refinado; fino; culto; cortés; elegante; delicado; (subtle) sutil; (affected) afectado
refinement /rɪ'faɪnmənt/ n refinamiento, m; finura, f; cultura, f; cortesía, f; elegancia, f; delicadeza, f; (subtlety) sutileza, f; (affectation) afectación, f
refiner /rɪ'faɪnər/ n refinador, m
refinery /rɪ'faɪnəri/ n refinería, f
refining /rɪ'faɪnɪŋ/ n refinación, f; Fig. refinamiento, m
refit /rɪ'fɪt/ vt reparar; Naut. embonar
refitting /rɪ'fɪtɪŋ/ n reparación, f; Naut. embonada, f
reflect /rɪ'flɛkt/ vt reflejar; reflexionar. —vi reflejar; reflexionar (sobre), pensar (en), meditar (sobre). **This offer reflects credit on him,** Esta oferta le hace honor. **to r. on, upon,** reflexionar sobre; (disparage) desacreditar; (affect unfavorably) perjudicar
reflecting /rɪ'flɛktɪŋ/ a reflector
reflection /rɪ'flɛkʃən/ n Phys. reflexión, f; reflejo, m; consideración, f, pensamiento, m; (aspersion) censura, f, reproche, m. **upon mature r.,** después de pensarlo bien
reflective /rɪ'flɛktɪv/ a Phys. reflector; reflexivo, pensativo, meditabundo
reflectively /rɪ'flɛktɪvli/ adv reflexivamente
reflector /rɪ'flɛktər/ n reflector, m; (shade) pantalla, f
reflex /'riflɛks/ a reflejo. —n reflejo, m; acción refleja, f. **r. action,** acción refleja, f
refloat /ri'floʊt/ vt (a ship) poner otra vex a flote, desvarar
reflux /'ri,flʌks/ n reflujo, m
reforestation n nuevas plantaciones, f pl
reform /rɪ'fɔrm/ n reforma, f. —a de reforma; reformista. —vt reformar; formar de nuevo. —vi reformarse
reformation /ˌrɛfər'meɪʃən/ n reformación, f; **Reformation,** Reforma, f
reformatory /rɪ'fɔrmə,tɔri/ a reformatorio, reformador. —n reformatorio, m, casa de corrección, f
reformer /rɪ'fɔrmər/ n reformador (-ra), reformista, mf
refract /rɪ'frækt/ vt refractar
refraction /rɪ'frækʃən/ n refracción, f
refractive /rɪ'fræktɪv/ a refringente
refractoriness /rɪ'fræktərɪnɪs/ n terquedad, obstinacia, f; rebeldía, indocilidad, f
refractory /rɪ'fræktəri/ a (of substances) refractario; recalcitrante, intratable, rebelde

refrain /rɪ'freɪn/ n estribillo, estrambote, m
refrain /rɪ'freɪn/ vi abstenerse (de), evitar
refresh /rɪ'frɛʃ/ vt refrescar
refreshing /rɪ'frɛʃɪŋ/ a refrescante; atractivo; estimulante; interesante
refreshment /rɪ'frɛʃmənt/ n (solace) solaz, reposo, m; recreación, f, deleite, m; (food and (or) drink) refresco, m. **r.-room,** (at a station) fonda, f
refrigerate /rɪ'frɪdʒə,reɪt/ vt refrigerar; enfriar; refrescar
refrigeration /rɪ,frɪdʒə'reɪʃən/ n refrigeración, f; enfriamiento, m. **r. chamber,** cámara frigorífica, f
refrigerative /rɪ'frɪdʒərətɪv/ a refrigerante, frigorífico
refrigerator /rɪ'frɪdʒə,reɪtər/ n refrigerador, m, nevera, f
refringent /rɪ'frɪndʒənt/ a refringente
refuel /ri'fyuəl/ vt (a furnace) cargar con carbón, etc.; (of a ship) tomar carbón; (of an airplane, motor vehicle) tomar bencina
refuge /'rɛfyudʒ/ n refugio, m; asilo, m; (resort) recurso, m; subterfugio, m; (traffic island) refugio para peatones, m. **to take r.,** refugiarse; resguardarse (de)
refugee /ˌrɛfyu'dʒi/ a refugiado. —n refugiado (-da)
refulgence /rɪ'fʌldʒəns/ n refulgencia, f
refulgent /rɪ'fʌldʒənt/ a refulgente
refund /rɪ'fʌnd/ vt reembolsar; devolver
refunding /ri'fʌndɪŋ/ n reembolso, m; devolución, f
refurbish /ri'fɜrbɪʃ/ vt restaurar; renovar; (a literary work) refundir
refurnish /ri'fɜrnɪʃ/ vt amueblar de nuevo
refusal /rɪ'fyuzəl/ n negativa, f; (rejection) rechazo, m; (option) opción, f; preferencia, f
refuse /rɪ'fyuz/ vt negar; (reject) rechazar. —vi negarse (a), rehusar; (of a horse) resistirse a saltar
refuse /'rɛfyus/ n desecho, m; desperdicios, m pl; residuo, m; basura, f. —a de desecho. **r. dump,** muladar, m
refutable /rɪ'fyutəbəl/ a refutable
refutation /ˌrɛfyʊ'teɪʃən/ n refutación, f
refute /rɪ'fyut/ vt refutar
regain /rɪ'geɪn/ vt recobrar, recuperar; cobrar; ganar de nuevo; Fig. reconquistar. **to r. one's breath,** cobrar aliento. **to r. consciousness,** volver en sí
regal /'rigəl/ a regio, real
regale /rɪ'geɪl/ vt regalar, agasajar; recrear, deleitar
regalia /rɪ'geɪliə/ n regalía, f; insignias reales, f pl; distintivos, m pl, insignias, f pl
regally /'rigəli/ adv regiamente
regard /rɪ'gard/ vt mirar; observar; considerar; (respect) respetar; (concern) importar, concernir; relacionarse con. —n mirada, f; atención, f; (esteem) aprecio, m, estimación, f; respeto, m; veneración, f; (relation) referencia, f; pl **regards,** recuerdos, saludos, m pl. **He has little r. for their feelings,** Le importan poco sus susceptibilidades. **With kindest regards,** Con mis saludos más afectuosos. **as regards, with r. to,** con referencia a, respecto a, en cuanto a
regardful /rɪ'gardfəl/ a atento (a), cuidadoso (de); que se preocupa (de)
regarding /rɪ'gardɪŋ/ prep tocante a, en cuanto a, respecto de
regardless /rɪ'gardlɪs/ a negligente (de); indiferente (a), insensible (a); que no se interesa (en); que no se inqueta (por); sin preocuparse (de)
regatta /rɪ'gætə, -'gatə/ n regata, f
regency /'ridʒənsi/ n regencia, f
regeneracy /rɪ'dʒɛnərəsi/ n regeneración, f
regenerate /rɪ'dʒɛnə,reɪt/ vt regenerar. —a regenerado
regeneration /rɪ,dʒɛnə'reɪʃən/ n regeneración, f
regenerative /rɪ'dʒɛnərətɪv/ a regenerador
regenerator /rɪ'dʒɛnə,reɪtər/ n regenerador (-ra)
regent /'ridʒənt/ n regente, mf
régime /rei'ʒim/ n régimen, m
regimen /'rɛdʒəmən/ n (Gram. Med.) régimen, m,
regiment /n. 'rɛdʒəmənt/ v. -,mɛnt/ n regimiento, m. —vt regimentar. **r. of the line,** tropa de línea, f
regimental /ˌrɛdʒə'mɛntḷ/ a de (un) regimiento, perteneciente a un regimiento
regimentation /ˌrɛdʒəmən'teɪʃən/ n regimentación, f

region /'riʤən/ n región, f
regional /'riʤən̩/ a regional
regionalism /'riʤən̩,ɪzəm/ n regionalismo, m
regionalist /'riʤən̩ɪst/ n regionalista, mf
regionalistic /'riʤən̩ɪstɪk/ a regionalista
register /'reʤəstər/ n (record and Mech. Mus. Print.) registro, m; (of ships, etc.) matrícula, f; lista, f. —vt registrar; matricular; (a ship) abanderar; inscribir; (one's child in a school) anotar (Argentina), inscribir; (of thermometers, etc.) marcar; (letters) certificar; (luggage) facturar; (in one's mind) grabar; (emotion) mostrar, manifestar. —vi (at a hotel, etc.) registrarse; Print. estar en registro. **cash r.**, caja registradora, f. **r. of births, marriages and deaths**, registro civil, m
registered letter /'reʤəstərd/ n carta certificada, f
registrar /'reʤə,strɑr/ n registrador, m; archivero, m; secretario, m; (of a school) jefe de inscripciones, secretario general (the latter has many more duties). **r. of births, marriages and deaths**, secretario del registro civil, m. **registrar's office**, oficina del registro civil, f
registration /,reʤə'streɪʃən/ n registro, m; inscripción, f; (of a vehicle, etc.) matrícula, f; Naut. abanderamiento, m; (of a letter, etc.) certificación, f. **r. number**, número de matrícula, m
registry /'reʤəstri/ n registro, m; inscripción, f; matrícula, f. **r. office**, oficina del registro civil, f; (for servants) agencia doméstica, f
regression /rɪ'greʃən/ n regresión, f, retroceso, m
regret /rɪ'gret/ vt sentir; lamentar, pesar; arrepentirse (de); (miss) echar de menos (a). —n sentimiento, pesar, m; (remorse) remordimiento, m. **I r. very much that...**, Me pesa mucho que..., Siento mucho que... **to send one's regrets**, mandar sus excusas
regretful /rɪ'gretfəl/ a lleno de pesar; arrepentido; lamentable, deplorable. **He was most r. that...**, Lamentaba mucho que...
regretfully /rɪ'gretfəli/ adv con pesar
regrettable /rɪ'gretəbəl/ a lamentable, deplorable; doloroso; (with loss, etc.) sensible
regrettably /rɪ'gretəbli/ adv lamentablemente; sensiblemente
regroup /ri'grup/ vt arreglar de nuevo; formar de nuevo; reorganizar
regular /'regyələr/ a regular; normal; (ordinary) corriente, común; (in order) en regla; (Gram. Bot. Eccl. Mil. Geom.) regular. —n Eccl. regular, m; (soldier) soldado de línea, m; (officer) militar de carrera, m; (client) parroquiano habitual, m
regularity /,regyə'lærɪti/ n regularidad,
regularization /,regyələrə'zeɪʃən/ n regularización, f
regularize /'regyələ,raɪz/ vt regularizar
regularly /'regyələrli/ adv regularmente
regulate /'regyə,leɪt/ vt regular; ajustar, arreglar; (direct) dirigir; reglamentar
regulation /,regyə'leɪʃən/ n regulación, f; arreglo, m; (rule) reglamento, m, a de reglamento; normal
regulative /'regyə,leɪtɪv/ a regulador
regulator /'regyə,leɪtər/ n Mech. regulador, m
regurgitate /rɪ'gɜrdʒɪ,teɪt/ vt and vi regurgitar
regurgitation /rɪ,gɜrdʒɪ'teɪʃən/ n regurgitación, f
rehabilitate /,rihə'bɪlɪ,teɪt/ vt rehabilitar
rehabilitation /,rihə,bɪlɪ'teɪʃən/ n rehabilitación, f
rehash /ri'hæʃ/ vt (a literary work, etc.) refundir
rehearing /ri'hɪrɪŋ/ n nueva audición, f, (of a case) revisión, f
rehearsal /rɪ'hɜrsəl/ n Theat. ensayo, m; recitación, f; relación, narración, f. **dress r.**, ensayo general, m
rehearse /rɪ'hɜrs/ vt Theat. ensayar; recitar; (narrate) narrar; enumerar
reheat /ri'hit/ vt recalentar
reign /rein/ n reinado, m. —vi reinar; predominar
reigning /'reinɪŋ/ a reinante; predominante
reimburse /,riɪm'bɜrs/ vt reembolsar
reimbursement /,riɪm'bɜrsmənt/ n reembolso, m
reimport /ri'ɪmpɔrt/ vt importar de nuevo, reimportar, n reimporte, m
reimportation /,riɪmpɔr'teɪʃən/ n reimportación, f
reimpose /,riɪm'pouz/ vt reimponer
reimposition /,riɪmpə'zɪʃən/ n reimposición, f

reimprison /,riɪm'prɪzən/ vt encarcelar de nuevo, reencarcelar
reimprisonment /,riɪm'prɪzənmənt/ n reencarcelamiento, m
rein /rein/ n rienda, f. —vt llevar las riendas (de); (hold back) refrenar. **to give r. to**, Fig. dar rienda suelta (a)
reincarnation /,riɪnkɑr'neɪʃən/ n reencarnación, f
reincorporate /,riɪn'kɔrpə,reɪt/ vt reincorporar
reincorporation /,riɪn,kɔrpə'reɪSən/ n reincorporación, f
reindeer /'rein,dɪər/ n reno, m
reinforce /,riɪn'fɔrs/ vt reforzar; (concrete) armar; fortalecer. **reinforced concrete**, n hormigón armado, m
reinforcement /,riɪn'fɔrsmənt/ n reforzamiento, m; (Mil. Nav. Fig.) refuerzo, m
reins. n See **rein**
reinsert /,riɪn'sɜrt/ vt volver a insertar
reinstall /,riɪn'stɔl/ vt reinstalar; rehabilitar
reinstallment /,riɪn'stɔlmənt/ n reinstalación, f; rehabilitación, f; restablecimiento, m
reinstate /,riɪn'steit/ vt reponer, restablecer; reinstalar; rehabilitar
reinstatement /,riɪn'steitmənt/ n restablecimiento, m; rehabilitación, f
reinsurance /,riɪn'ʃurəns/ n reaseguro, m
reinsure /,riɪn'ʃur, -'ʃɜr/ vt reasegurar
reintegrate /ri'ɪntə,greit/ vt reintegrar
reintegration /,riɪntə'greiʃən/ n reintegración, f
reinter /,riɪn'tɜr/ vt enterrar de nuevo
reinvest /,riɪn'vest/ vt reinvertir
reinvestment /,riɪn'vestmənt/ n reinversión, f
reinvigorate /,riɪn'vɪgə,reit/ vt reanimar, dar nuevo vigor (a)
reinvite /,riɪn'vait/ vt invitar de nuevo (a)
reissue /ri'ɪʃu/ n nueva emisión, f; (of a book, etc.) nueva edición, reimpresión, f. —vt hacer una nueva emisión (de); reeditar, publicar de nuevo
reiterate /ri'ɪtə,reit/ vt reiterar, repetir
reiteration /ri,ɪtə'reiʃən/ n reiteración, f
reiterative /ri'ɪtə,reitɪv/ a reiterativo
reject /v. rɪ'dʒɛkt/ vt rechazar, rehusar; repudiar; repulsar; desechar
rejection /rɪ'dʒɛkʃən/ n rechazamiento, m; repudiación, refutación, f; repulsa, f
rejoice /rɪ'dʒɔis/ vt alegrar, regocijar. —vi alegrarse (de), regocijarse (de), gloriarse (en)
rejoicing /rɪ'dʒɔisɪŋ/ n regocijo, júbilo, m, alegría, f; algazara, f, fiestas, f pl
rejoin /rɪ'dʒɔin/ vt and vi juntar de nuevo; volver a; reunirse con; (reply) contestar, replicar
rejoinder /rɪ'dʒɔindər/ n contestación, respuesta, f
rejuvenate /rɪ'dʒuvə,neit/ vt rejuvenecer
rejuvenation /rɪ,dʒuvə'neiʃən/ n rejuvenecimiento, m
rekindle /ri'kɪndl/ vt encender de nuevo; despertar, reavivar. —vi encenderse de nuevo; reavivarse
relapse /rɪ'læps; n. also 'rilæps/ n reincidencia, recaída, f; Med. recidiva, f. —vi reincidir (en); Med. recaer
relapsed /rɪ'læpst/ a relapso
relate /rɪ'leit/ vt (recount) relatar, narrar; relacionar; unir; (of kinship) emparentar. —vi ajustarse (a); referirse (a). **The first fact is not related to the second**, El primer hecho no tiene nada que ver con el segundo
related /rɪ'leitid/ a relacionado; (by kinship) emparentado. **John is well-r.**, Juan es de buena familia; Juan es de familia influyente; Juan tiene buenas relaciones
relater /rɪ,leitər/ n narrador (-ra)
relation /rɪ'leiʃən/ n (narrative) relación, narración, f; conexión, f; relación, f; (kinship) parentesco, m; (person) pariente (-ta). **in r. to**, con relación a, en cuanto a
relationship /rɪ'leiʃən,ʃɪp/ n parentesco, m; conexión, relación, f
relative /'relətɪv/ a relativo. —n pariente (-ta); pl **relatives**, parientes, m pl, parentela, f
relativism /'relətə,vɪzəm/ n relativismo, m
relativity /,relə'tɪvɪti/ n relatividad, f

relator /rɪ'leitər/ n Law. relator, m
relax /rɪ'læks/ vt relajar; aflojar; soltar; (make less severe) ablandar; (decrease) mitigar. —vi relajarse; aflojar; (rest) descansar
relaxation /ˌrilæk'seiʃən/ n relajación, f; aflojamiento, m; ablandamiento, m; mitigación, f; (rest) descanso, reposo, m; (pastime) pasatiempo, m; (amusement) diversión, f
relaxing /rɪ'læksɪŋ/ a relajante; (of climate) enervante
relay /'rilei; v. rɪ'lei/ n (of horses) parada, f; (shift) tanda, f; relevo, m; Elec. relais, m; Radio. redifusión, f. —vt enviar por posta; Elec. reemitir; Radio. retransmitir; (lay again) colocar de nuevo. **r. race,** carrera de equipo, carrera de relevos, f
release /rɪ'lis/ vt soltar; (hurl) lanzar; (set free) poner en libertad (a); librar (de); absolver; (surrender) renunciar (a); dar al público, poner en circulación; (lease again) realquilar. —n soltura, f; lanzamiento, m; liberación, f; (from pain) alivio, m; remisión, f; exoneración, f; publicación, f; (of films) representación, f; Law. soltura, f
relegate /'relɪˌgeit/ vt relegar
relegation /ˌrelɪ'geiʃən/ n relegación, f
relent /rɪ'lent/ vi ablandarse, enternecerse; ceder
relenting /rɪ'lentɪŋ/ n enternecimiento, desenojo, m
relentless /rɪ'lentlɪs/ a implacable, inexorable; despiadado
relentlessly /rɪ'lentlɪsli/ adv inexorablemente; sin piedad
relentlessness /rɪ'lentlɪsnɪs/ n inexorabilidad, f; falta de piedad, f
relet /ri'let/ vt realquilar
relevance /'relavəns/ n conexión, f; pertinencia, f; aplicabilidad, f
relevant /'relavənt/ a relativo; pertinente, a propósito, oportuno; aplicable
reliability /rɪˌlaiə'bɪlɪti/ n seguridad, f; formalidad, f; confianza, f; exactitud, f; veracidad, f
reliable /rɪ'laiəbəl/ a seguro; formal; digno de crédito, de confianza, solvente digno de confianza; exacto; veraz
reliably /rɪ'laiəbli/ adv seguramente; de una manera digna de confianza; exactamente
reliance /rɪ'laiəns/ n confianza, f. **to place r. on,** tener confianza en
reliant /rɪ'laiənt/ a confiado
relic /'relɪk/ n vestigio, rastro, m; Eccl. reliquia, f
relict /'relɪkt/ n viuda, f
relief /rɪ'lif/ n (alleviation) alivio, m; desahogo, m; (help) socorro, m, ayuda, f; beneficencia, f; Mil. relevo, m; (pleasure) placer, m, satisfacción, f; (consolation) consuelo, m; Law. remisión, f; Art. relieve, m. **high r.,** alto relieve, m. **low r.,** bajo relieve, m. **r. map,** mapa en relieve, m. **r. train,** tren de socorro, m
relieve /rɪ'liv/ vt aliviar; aligerar, suavizar; mitigar; (one's feelings, etc.) desahogar; (Mil. and to take the place of) relevar; (free) librar; (dismiss) destituir; (remove) quitar; (rob) robar; (help) socorrer, remediar; (redeem) redimir; (ornament) adornar; (from a wrong) hacer justicia (a)
relieving /rɪ'livɪŋ/ n alivio, m; aligeramiento, m; mitigación, f; (of the feelings) desahogo, m; Mil. relevo, m; (help) socorro, m. **r. arch,** sobrearco, m
relight /ri'lait/ vt volver a encender. —vi encenderse de nuevo
religion /rɪ'lidʒən/ n religión, f
religiosity /rɪˌlidʒi'ɒsɪti/ n religiosidad, f
religious /rɪ'lidʒəs/ a religioso; en religión; piadoso, crevente; devoto. —n religioso (-sa). **r. orders,** órdenes religiosas, f pl. **r. toleration,** libertad de cultos, f
religiousness /rɪ'lidʒəsnɪs/ n religiosidad, f
relinquish /rɪ'lɪŋkwɪʃ/ vt abandonar; (one's grip) soltar; renunciar; desistir (de), dejar (de); (a post) dimitir (de)
relinquishment /rɪ'lɪŋkwɪʃmənt/ n abandono, m; renuncia, f; dejamiento, m; (of a post) dimisión, f
reliquary /'relɪˌkweri/ n relicario, m
relish /'relɪʃ/ n gusto, m; sabor, m; (touch, smack) dejo, m; condimento, m; apetito, m, gana, f. —vt gustar de; comer con apetito; saborear, paladear; Fig.

seducir, atraer, gustar. —vi tener gusto (de). **I do not much r. the idea,** No me seduce la idea
relishing /'relɪʃɪŋ/ n saboreo, m; (enjoyment) goce, m, fruición, f; consideración, f
relive /ri'lɪv/ vt vivir de nuevo, volver a vivir
reload / ri'loud/ vt recargar
reluctance /rɪ'lʌktəns/ n repugnancia, desgana, f. **with r.,** a regañadientes, de mala gana
reluctant /rɪ'lʌktənt/ a poco dispuesto (a), que tiene repugnancia a (hacer algo), sin ganas; (forced) forzado; artificial; (hesitating) vacilante
reluctantly /rɪ'lʌktəntli/ adv de mala gana, con repugnancia, a disgusto
rely on /rɪ'lai/ vi contar con, confiar en, depender de
remain /rɪ'mein/ vi quedar; permanecer; (be left over) sobrar; continuar. **I r. yours faithfully...,** (in a letter) Queda de Vd. su att. s.s.... **It remains to be written,** Queda por escribir
remainder /rɪ'meindər/ n resto, m; restos, m pl, sobras, f pl; residuo, m. **The r. of the people went away,** Los demás se marcharon
remaining /rɪ'meinɪŋ/ pres part and a que queda; sobrante
remains /rɪ'meinz/ n pl restos, m pl; sobras, f pl, desperdicios, m pl; ruinas, f pl
remake /v. ri'meik/ vt rehacer; reformar
remand /rɪ'mænd/ vt Law. reencarcelar. —n Law. reencarcelamiento, m
remark /rɪ'mark/ n observación, f; nota, f; comentario, m. —vt and vi observar; notar. **to r. on,** comentar, hacer una observación sobre
remarkable /rɪ'markəbəl/ a notable, singular, extraordinario
remarkableness /rɪ'markəbəlnɪs/ n singularidad, f, lo extraordinario
remarkably /rɪ'markəbli/ adv singularmente
remarriage /'ri,mærɪdʒ/ n segundas nupcias, f pl, segundo casamiento, m
remarry /ri'mæri/ vt volver a casar (a). —vi casarse en segundas nupcias; volver a casarse
remediable /rɪ'midiəbəl/ a remediable
remedial /rɪ'midiəl/ a remediador; curativo, terapéutico
remedy /'remidi/ n remedio, m; recurso, m, vt remediar; curar
remember /rɪ'membər/ vt recordar; tener presente; acordarse de. —vi acordarse; no olvidarse. **R. me to your mother,** Dale recuerdos míos a tu madre. **If I r. rightly...,** Si bien me acuerdo... **And r. that I shall do no more!** ¡Y no olvides que no haré más!
remembrance /rɪ'membrəns/ n recuerdo, m; memoria, f; pl **remembrances,** recuerdos, m pl
remind /rɪ'maind/ vt recordar
reminder /rɪ'maindər/ n recuerdo, m; (warning) advertencia, f. **a gentle r.,** una indirecta, una insinuación
reminisce /ˌremə'nɪs/ vi Inf. recordar viejas historias
reminiscence /ˌremə'nɪsəns/ n reminiscencia, f, recuerdo, m
reminiscent /ˌremə'nɪsənt/ a evocador; que recuerda; de reminiscencia; que piensa en el pasado. **to be r. of,** recordar; Inf. oler a
reminiscently /ˌremə'nɪsəntli/ adv evocadoramente, como si recordara
remiss /rɪ'mɪs/ a negligente, descuidado
remission /rɪ'mɪʃən/ n remisión, f
remissly /rɪ'mɪsli/ adv negligentemente
remissness /rɪ'mɪsnɪs/ n negligencia, f, descuido, m
remit /rɪ'mɪt/ vt remitir; Com. remesar, enviar. —vi (pay) pagar
remittance /rɪ'mɪtns/ n remesa, f, envío, m
remitter /rɪ'mɪtər/ n remitente, mf
remnant /'remnənt/ n resto, m; (of fabric) retal, retazo, m; (relic) vestigio, m, reliquia, f. **r. sale,** saldo, m
remodel /ri'mɒdl/ vt rehacer; reformar; modelar de nuevo; (a play, etc.) refundir
remodeling /ri'mɒdlɪŋ/ n reformación, f; (of a play, etc.) refundición, f
remonstrance /rɪ'mɒnstrəns/ n protesta, f; reconvención, f

remonstrate /rɪ'mɒnstreit/ *vi* protestar, objetar. **to r. with,** reprochar, reconvenir

remorse /rɪ'mɔrs/ *n* remordimiento, *m*

remorseful /rɪ'mɔrsfəl/ *a* lleno de remordimientos; penitente, arrepentido

remorsefully /rɪ'mɔrsfəli/ *adv* con remordimiento

remorseless /rɪ'mɔrslɪs/ *a* sin conciencia, sin remordimientos; despiadado, inflexible

remorselessness /rɪ'mɔrslɪsnɪs/ *n* inexorabilidad, crueldad, dureza, *f*

remote /rɪ'mout/ *a* distante, lejano; remoto; aislado; ajeno; (slight) leve, vago. **r. control,** mando a distancia, *m*

remotely /rɪ'moutli/ *adv* remotamente

remoteness /rɪ'moutnɪs/ *n* distancia, *f*; aislamiento, *m*; alejamiento, *m*; (vagueness) vaguedad, *f*

remount /*v.* ri'maunt; *n.* 'ri,maunt/ *vt* subir de nuevo, montar de nuevo; *Mil.* remontar. —*vi* (go back to) remontar (a), derivarse (de). —*n Mil.* remonta, *f*

removable /rɪ'muvəbəl/ *a* que puede quitarse; (of collars, etc.) de quita y pon; transportable; (of officials, etc.) amovible

removal /rɪ'muvəl/ *n* acción de quitar o levantar, *f*; sacamiento, *m*; separación, *f*; eliminación, *f*; alejamiento, *m*; traslado, *m*; (from office, etc.) deposición, *f*; supresión, *f*; asesinato, *m*. **r. van,** carro de mudanzas, *m*

remove /rɪ'muv/ *vt* quitar; retirar; levantar; sacar; apartar; separar; eliminar; trasladar; (from office) destituir; suprimir; asesinar. —*vi* trasladarse. —*n* grado, *m*; distancia, *f*; (departure) partida, *f*. **to r. oneself,** quitarse de en medio. **to r. one's hat,** descubrirse. **first cousin once removed,** hijo de primo carnal, primo hermano del padre, primo hermano de la madre, *m*

remunerate /rɪ'myunə,reit/ *vt* remunerar

remuneration /rɪ,myunə'reiʃən/ *n* remuneración, *f*

remunerative /rɪ'myunərətɪv/ *a* remunerador

renaissance /'rɛnə,sans/ *n* renacimiento, *m*, *a* renacentista

Renaissance man /'rɛnə,sans/ *n* hombre del Renacimiento, *m*

Renaissance woman *n* mujer del Renacimiento, *f*

renal /'rinl/ *a* renal

rename /ri'neim/ *vt* poner otro nombre (a)

renascent /rɪ'næsənt, -'neisənt/ *a* renaciente, que renace

rend /rɛnd/ *vt* desgarrar, rasgar; *Fig.* lacerar; (split) hender; *Fig.* dividir. **to r. from,** arrancar (a). **to r. the air,** (with cries, etc.) llenar el aire

render /'rɛndər/ *vt* (return) devolver; dar; rendir; (make) hacer; (help, service) prestar; interpretar; (translate) traducir; (fat) derretir y clarificar

rendering /'rɛndərɪŋ/ *n* versión, *f*; interpretación, *f*

rendezvous /'rɑndə,vu, -dei-/ *n* cita, *f*; lugar de cita, *m*; reunión, *f*. —*vi* reunirse

rending /'rɛndɪŋ/ *n* desgarro, *m*; hendimiento, *m*

renegade /'rɛnɪ,geid/ *a* renegado. —*n* renegado (-da)

renew /rɪ'nu/ *vt* renovar; (resume) reanudar; (a lease, etc.) prorrogar

renewable /rɪ'nuəbəl/ *a* renovable

renewal /rɪ'nuəl/ *n* renovación, *f*; (resumption) reanudación, *f*; (of a lease, etc.) prorrogación, *f*

renewed /rɪ'nud/ *a* renovado; nuevo

rennet /'rɛnɪt/ *n* cuajo, *m*

renounce /rɪ'nauns/ *vt* renunciar; (a throne) abdicar; renegar (de), repudiar; abandonar. —*vi Law.* desistir; (cards) renunciar

renouncement /rɪ'naunsmənt/ *n* renuncia, *f*; (of a throne) abdicación, *f*; repudiación, *f*

renovate /'rɛnə,veit/ *vt* renovar; limpiar; restaurar

renovation /,rɛnə'veiʃən/ *n* renovación, *f*; limpiadura, *f*; restauración, *f*

renovator /'rɛnə,veitər/ *n* renovador (-ra)

renown /rɪ'naun/ *n* renombre, *m*, fama, *f*

renowned /rɪ'naund/ *a* renombrado, famoso

rent /rɛnt/ *n* (tear) rasgadura, *f*; desgarro, *m*; abertura, *f*; raja hendedura, *f*; (discord) división, *f*; (hire) alquiler, *m*; arrendamiento, *m*. —*vt* arrendar, alquilar. **r.-free,** sin pagar alquiler

rentable /'rɛntəbəl/ *a* alquilable, arrendable

rental /'rɛntl/ See **rent**

renter /'rɛntər/ *n* arrendador (-ra)

rentier *n* rentista, *mf*

renting /'rɛntɪŋ/ *n* alquiler, arrendamiento, *m*

renumber /ri'nʌmbər/ *vt* numerar de nuevo

renunciation /rɪ,nʌnsi'eiʃən/ *n* renunciación, renuncia, *f*

reoccupy /ri'ɒkyʊ,pai/ *vt* volver a ocupar, ocupar otra vez

reopen /ri'oupən/ *vt* abrir de nuevo, volver a abrir. —*vi* abrirse nuevamente, abrirse otra vez

reopening /ri'oupənɪŋ/ *n* reapertura, *f*

reorder /ri'ɔrdər/ *vt* ordenar de nuevo, *Com.* volver a pedir. —*n Com.* nuevo pedido, *m*

reorganization /,riɔrgənə'zeiʃən/ *n* reorganización, *f*

reorganize /ri'ɔrgə,naiz/ *vt* reorganizar

reorganizing /ri'ɔrgə,naizɪŋ/ *a* reorganizador

repack /ri'pæk/ *vt* reembalar; reenvasar; volver a hacer (una maleta)

repaint /ri'peint/ *vt* pintar de nuevo

repainting /ri'peintɪŋ/ *n* nueva pintura, *f*

repair /rɪ'pɛər/ *vt* arreglar (e.g. a machine) componer, remendar; reparar; restaurar; rehacer. —*vi* (with to) dirigirse a, ir a; acudir a. —*n* arreglo *m*, reparación, *f*; compostura, *f*; restauración, *f*. **to keep in r.,** conservar en buen estado

repairable /rɪ'pɛərəbəl/ *a* que se puede componer

repairer /rɪ'pɛərər/ *n* componedor (-ra); restaurador (-ra)

repairing /rɪ'pɛərɪŋ/ *a* reparador

reparable /'rɛpərəbəl/ *a* reparable; remediable

reparation /,rɛpə'reiʃən/ *n* reparación, *f*

repartee /,rɛpər'ti, -'tei, -ɑr-/ *n* respuestas, agudezas, *f pl; Inf.* dimes y diretes, *m pl*

repast /rɪ'pæst/ *n* comida, *f*; (light) colación, *f*

repatriate /*v.* ri'peitri,eit/ *vt* repatriar

repatriation /ri,peitri'eiʃən/ *n* repatriación, *f*

repay /rɪ'pei/ *vt* reembolsar; recompensar, pagar; pagar en la misma moneda. —*vi* pagar. **It well repays a visit,** Vale la pena de visitarse

repayable /rɪ'peiəbəl/ *a* reembolsable

repayment /rɪ'peimənt/ *n* reembolso, *m*; pago, retorno, *m*

repeal /rɪ'pil/ *n* abrogación, revocación, *f*, *vt* abrogar, rescindir, revocar

repeat /rɪ'pit/ *vt* repetir; reiterar; (renew) renovar; duplicar. —*n* repetición, *f*

repeated /rɪ'pitd/ *a* reiterado; redoblado

repeatedly /rɪ'pitdli/ *adv* reiteradamente, repetidamente

repeater /rɪ'pitər/ *n* repetidor (-ra); reloj de repetición, *m*; arma de repetición, *f*

repel /rɪ'pɛl/ *vt* repeler; ahuyentar; (spurn) rechazar; *Phys.* resistir; repugnar

repellent /rɪ'pɛlənt/ *a* repulsivo

repent /rɪ'pɛnt/ *vt* arrepentirse de. —*vi* arrepentirse

repentance /rɪ'pɛntns/ *n* arrepentimiento, *m*, penitencia, *f*

repentant /rɪ'pɛntnt/ *a* arrepentido, penitente, contrito

repentantly /rɪ'pɛntntli/ *adv* arrepentidamente, con contrición

repeople /ri'pipəl/ *vt* repoblar

repeopling /ri'pipəlɪŋ/ *n* repoblación, *f*

repercuss /,ripər'kʌs/ *vt* repercutir (en)

repercussion /,ripər'kʌʃən/ *n* repercusión, *f*

repercussive /,ripər'kʌsɪv/ *a* repercusivo

repertory /'rɛpər,tɔri/ *n* repertorio, *m*

repetition /,rɛpɪ'tɪʃən/ *n* repetición, *f*; recitación, *f*

repetitive /rɪ'pɛtɪtɪv/ *a* iterativo

repine /rɪ'pain/ *vi* afligirse (de); quejarse (de); padecer nostalgia

repining /rɪ'painɪŋ/ *n* pesares, *m pl*; quejas, *f pl*, descontento, *m*; nostalgia, *f*

replace /rɪ'pleis/ *vt* (put back) reponer, colocar de nuevo; restituir, devolver; (renew) renovar; (in a post, etc.) reemplazar, substituir

replaceable /rɪ'pleisəbəl/ *a* restituible; renovable; reemplazable

replacement /rɪ'pleismənt/ *n* reposición, *f*; restitución, devolución, *f*; renovación, *f*; reemplazo, *m*

replant /rɪ'plænt/ vt replantar
replanting /rɪ'plæntɪŋ/ n replantación, f
replenish /rɪ'plenɪʃ/ vt rellenar
replenishment /rɪ'plenɪʃmənt/ n relleno, m
replete /rɪ'plit/ a repleto
repletion /rɪ'pliʃən/ n repleción, f
replica /'replɪkə/ n réplica, f
reply /rɪ'plaɪ/ n respuesta, contestación, f, vi responder, contestar. **Awaiting your r.,** En espera de sus noticias. **in his r.,** en su respuesta
repolish /rɪ'pɒlɪʃ/ vt repulir
repopulate /rɪ'pɒpyəˌleɪt/ vt repoblar
repopulation /rɪˌpɒpyə'leɪʃən/ n repoblación, f
report /rɪ'pɔrt/ n (rumor) voz, f, rumor, m; (reputation) fama, f; (news) noticia, f; (journalistic) reportaje, m; (Mil. Nav. and from school) parte, f; (weather) boletín, m; (proceedings) actas, f pl; (statement) informe, m; relación, f; (of a gun, etc.) detonación, f; explosión, f. —vt dar cuenta de, relatar; informar; (measure) registrar; (Mil. Nav.) dar parte de; comunicar; (journalistic) hacer un reportaje de; (transcribe) transcribir; (accuse) denunciar; quejarse de. —vi presentar informe; ser reportero; (present oneself) presentarse, comparecer. **It is reported that...,** Se informa que...
report card n boletín de calificaciones, m
reporter /rɪ'pɔrtər/ n reportero (-ra); Law. relator, m
reporting /rɪ'pɔrtɪŋ/ n reporterismo, m
repose /rɪ'pouz/ n reposo, m; quietud, f; tranquilidad, serenidad, f. —vt reposar, descansar; reclinar; (place) poner. —vi reposar; tener confianza (en); basarse (en)
repository /rɪ'pɒzɪˌtɔri/ n repositorio, depósito, m; almacén, m; (furniture) guardamuebles, m; (person) depositario (-ia)
repoussé /ˌrəpu'seɪ/ n repujado, m. **to work in r.,** repujar
reprehend /ˌreprɪ'hend/ vt reprender, reprobar
reprehensible /ˌreprɪ'hensəbl/ a reprensible
reprehension /ˌreprɪ'henʃən/ n reprensión, f
represent /ˌreprɪ'zent/ vt representar; significar
representation /ˌreprɪzen'teɪʃən/ n representación, f
representational /ˌreprɪzen'teɪʃənl/ a Art. realista
representative /ˌreprɪ'zentətɪv/ a que representa; representativo. —n representante, mf
repress /rɪ'pres/ vt reprimir
repression /rɪ'preʃən/ n represión, f
repressive /rɪ'presɪv/ a represivo
reprieve /rɪ'priv/ vt Law. aplazar la ejecución (de); Fig. dar una tregua (a)
reprimand /'reprəˌmænd/ n reprimenda, f, vt reprender
reprint /n. 'riˌprɪnt; v. ri'prɪnt; / n reimpresión, tirada aparte, separata, f, vt reimprimir
reprinting /'riˌprɪntɪŋ/ n reimpresión, f
reprisal /rɪ'praɪzəl/ n represalia, f. **to take reprisals,** tomar represalias
reproach /rɪ'proutʃ/ n reproche, m; censura, f; (shame) vergüenza, f. —vt reprochar; censurar, echar en cara, afear
reproachful /rɪ'proutʃfəl/ a severo; lleno de reproches; de censura; (shameful) vergonzoso
reproachfully /rɪ'proutʃfəli/ adv con reprobación, con reprensión, severamente
reproachfulness /rɪ'proutʃfəlnɪs/ n severidad, f. **the r. of my gaze,** mi mirada llena de reproches
reprobate /'reprəˌbeɪt/ n réprobo (-ba)
reproduce /ˌriprə'dus/ vt reproducir. —vi reproducirse
reproducible /ˌriprə'dusəbəl/ a reproductible
reproduction /ˌriprə'dʌkʃən/ n reproducción, f
reproductive /ˌriprə'dʌktɪv/ a reproductor; de reproducción
reproof /rɪ'pruf/ n reconvención, f
reprove /rɪ'pruv/ vt censurar, culpar; reprender
reprovingly /rɪ'pruvɪŋli/. See **rebukingly**
reptile /'reptɪl, -taɪl/ a and n reptil, m
republic /rɪ'pʌblɪk/ n república, f. **the r. of letters,** la república de las letras
republican /rɪ'pʌblɪkən/ a and n republicano (-na)

republicanism /rɪ'pʌblɪkəˌnɪzəm/ n republicanismo, m
republish /rɪ'pʌblɪʃ/ vt publicar de nuevo; volver a editar
repudiate /rɪ'pyudiˌeɪt/ vt repudiar; negar, rechazar
repudiation /rɪˌpyudi'eɪʃən/ n repudiación, f
repugnance /rɪ'pʌgnəns/ n repugnacia, f
repugnant /rɪ'pʌgnənt/ a repugnante; contrario; opuesto. **to be r. to,** repugnar (a)
repulse /rɪ'pʌls/ vt repulsar, repeler; rebatir, refutar; (refuse) rechazar, n repulsa, f; refutación, f; rechazo, m
repulsion /rɪ'pʌlʃən/ n Phys. repulsión, f; repugnancia, aversión, f
repulsive /rɪ'pʌlsɪv/ a repulsivo, repugnante, repelente
repulsiveness /rɪ'pʌlsɪvnɪs/ n carácter repulsivo, m; aspecto repugnante, m
reputable /'repyətəbəl/ a honrado, respetable, formal
reputation /ˌrepyə'teɪʃən/ n reputación, f; fama, f, renombre, m. **to have the r. of,** ser reputado como, pasar por
reputed /rɪ'pyutɪd/ a supuesto; putativo
reputedly /rɪ'pyutɪdli/ adv según la opinión común, según dice la gente
request /rɪ'kwest/ n ruego, m, petición, f; instancia, f; solicitud, f; Com. demanda, f. —vt pedir, rogar; suplicar; solicitar. **in r.,** en boga; solicitado; en demanda, **on r.,** a solicitud. **r. stop,** (for buses) parada discrecional, f
requiem /'rekwiəm/ n réquiem, m. **r. mass,** misa de difuntos, f
require /rɪ'kwaɪər/ vt exigir, requerir; necesitar; (wish) desear; invitar. —vi ser necesario
required /rɪ'kwaɪərd/ a necesario; obligatorio
requirement /rɪ'kwaɪərmənt/ n deseo, m; requisito, m; formalidad, f; estipulación, f; necesidad, f
requisite /'rekwəzɪt/ n requisito, m. —a necesario, requisito, preciso. **to be r.,** ser necesario, ser menester hacer falta
requisition /ˌrekwə'zɪʃən/ vt Mil. requisar
requisitioning /ˌrekwə'zɪʃənɪŋ/ n requisa, f
requital /rɪ'kwaɪtl/ n recompensa, f; compensación, satisfacción, f
requite /rɪ'kwaɪt/ vt pagar, recompensar; (affection) corresponder a
reread /ri'rid/ vt releer
reredos /'rɪərdɒs/ n retablo, m
resale /'riˌseɪl/ n reventa, f
rescind /rɪ'sɪnd/ vt rescindir
rescission /rɪ'sɪʒən/ n rescisión, f
rescue /'reskyu/ vt salvar; librar; Mil. rescatar. —n socorro, m; salvamento, m; Mil. rescate, m. **to go to the r. of,** ir al socorro de. **r. party,** expedición de salvamento, f; Mil. expedición de rescate, f
rescuer /'reskyuər/ n salvador (-ra)
reseal /ri'sil/ vt resellar
research /rɪ'sɜrtʃ, 'risɜrtʃ/ n investigación, f, vt investigar
researcher /rɪsɜrtʃər, 'risɜrtʃər/ n investigador (-ra)
reseda /rɪ'sidə/ n Bot. reseda, f
resell /ri'sel/ vt revender
resemblance /rɪ'zembləns/ n parecido, m, semejanza, f. **The two sisters bear a strong r. to each other,** Las dos hermanas se parecen mucho
resemble /rɪ'zembəl/ vt parecerse (a). **Mary doesn't r. her mother,** María no se parece a su madre
resent /rɪ'zent/ vt resentirse de; ofenderse por, indignarse por; tomar a mal
resentful /rɪ'zentfəl/ a resentido; ofendido, indignado, agraviado; vengativo
resentfully /rɪ'zentfəli/ adv con resentimiento; con indignación
resentment /rɪ'zentmənt/ n resentimiento, m
reservation /ˌrezər'veɪʃən/ n reservación, f; reserva, f; territorio reservado, m; santuario, m. **mental r.,** reserva mental, f
reserve /rɪ'zɜrv/ n reserva, f. —vt reservar. —a de reserva. **without r.,** sin reserva
reserved /rɪ'zɜrvd/ a reservado; callado, taciturno. **r.**

compartment, reservado, *m.* **r. list,** (*Mil. Nav.*) sección de reserva, *f*

reservedly /rɪˈzɜrvɪdli/ *adv* con reserva

reservist /rɪˈzɜrvɪst/ *n* reservista, *mf*

reservoir /ˈrezər,vwɑr/ *n* depósito, *m;* cisterna, *f,* aljibe, tanque, *m*

reset /v. riˈset/ *vt* montar de nuevo

resettle /riˈsetl/ *vt* repoblar; rehabilitar; (a dispute) llegar a un nuevo acuerdo sobre

resettlement /riˈsetlmənt/ *n* repoblación, *f;* rehabilitación, *f;* (of a dispute) nuevo acuerdo, *m*

reshape /riˈʃeip/ *vt* reformar

reship /riˈʃɪp/ *vt* reembarcar

reshipment /riˈʃɪpmənt/ *n* reembarque, *m*

reshuffle /riˈʃʌfəl/ *vt* volver a barajar; *Fig.* cambiar

reside /rɪˈzaid/ *vi* residir, habitar; vivir

residence /ˈrezɪdəns/ *n* residencia, *f;* permanencia, estada, *f;* domicilio, *m*

resident /ˈrezɪdənt/ *a* residente; (of a servant) que duerme en casa; interno. —*n* residente, *mf;* (diplomacy) residente, *m*

residential /,rezɪˈdenʃəl/ *a* residencial

residue /ˈrezɪ,du/ *n* resto, *m;* (*Law., Chem.*) residuo, *m*

residuum /rɪˈzɪdʒuəm/ *n* residuo, *m*

resign /rɪˈzain/ *vt* renunciar (a); ceder; resignar. —*vi* dimitir. **to r. oneself,** resignarse

resignation /,rezɪgˈneiʃən/ *n* resignación, *f;* (from a post) dimisión, *f.* **to send in one's r.,** dimitir

resigned /rɪˈzaind/ *a* resignado

resignedly /rɪˈzainɪdli/ *adv* con resignación

resilience /rɪˈzɪlyəns/ *n* elasticidad, *f*

resilient /rɪˈzɪlyənt/ *a* elástico

resin /ˈrezɪn/ *n* resina, *f;* (solid, for violin bows, etc.) colofonia, *f*

resinous /ˈrezənəs/ *a* resinoso

resist /rɪˈzist/ *vt* and *vi* (bear) aguantar; (impede) impedir; (repel, ward off) resistir; rechazar; hacer frente (a); oponerse (a); negarse (a)

resistance /rɪˈzistəns/ *n* resistencia, *f;* aguante, *m,* tenacidad, *f;* oposición, *f;* repugnancia, *f.* **passive r.,** resistencia pasiva, *f.* **r. coil,** *Elec.* resistencia, *f.* **r. movement,** movimiento de resistencia, *m*

resistant /rɪˈzistənt/ *a* resistente

resister /rɪˈzistər/ *n* el, *m,* (f, la) que resiste

resole /riˈsoul/ *vt* remontar

resoling /riˈsoulɪŋ/ *n* remonta, *f*

resolute /ˈrezə,lut/ *a* resuelto, decidido

resolutely /,rezəˈlutli/ *adv* resueltamente

resolution /,rezəˈluʃən/ *n* resolución, *f;* (proposal placed before a legislative body, etc.) proposición, *f;* propósito, *m*

resolve /rɪˈzɒlv/ *vt* resolver; desarrollar, deshacer (an abbreviation, acronym, or initialism). —*vi* resolverse. —*n* propósito, *m;* (of character) resolución, firmeza, *f*

resonance /ˈrezənəns/ *n* resonancia, *f;* sonoridad, *f*

resonant /ˈrezənənt/ *a* resonante; reverberante, sonoro

resort /rɪˈzɔrt/ *n* recurso, *m;* punto de reunión. *m;* (frequentation) frecuentación, *f;* (gathering) concurrencia, *f;* reunión, *f.* —*vi* acudir (a), acogerse (a); hacer uso (de); pasar (a); (frequent) frecuentar, concurrir. **health r.,** balneario, *m.* **holiday r.,** playa de verano, *f;* pueblo de veraneo, *m.* **in the last r.,** en último recurso

resound /rɪˈzaund/ *vi* resonar, retumbar, retronar; *Fig.* tener fama, ser celebrado. —*vt* hacer reverberar; *Fig.* celebrar

resounding /rɪˈzaundɪŋ/ *a* retumbante, resonante

resource /ˈrisɔrs/ *n* recurso, *m;* (of character) inventiva, *f;* **pl resources;** recursos, fondos, *m pl*

resourceful /rɪˈsɔrsfəl/ *a* ingenioso

resourcefully /rɪˈsɔrsfəli/ *adv* ingeniosamente

resourcefulness /rɪˈsɔrsfəlnɪs/ *n* ingeniosidad, *f*

respect /rɪˈspekt/ *n* respeto, *m;* consideración, *f;* (reference, regard) respecto, *m;* *pl* **respects,** (greetings) saludos, *m pl;* homenaje, *m.* —*vt* respetar; honrar; (concern, regard) concernir, tocar (a). **in other respects,** por lo demás. **in r. of,** tocante a, respecto a. **in some respects,** desde algunos puntos de vista. **out of r. for,** por consideración a

respectability /rɪ,spektəˈbilɪti/ *n* respetabilidad, *f*

respectable /rɪˈspektəbəl/ *a* respetable; pasable; considerable

respectably /rɪˈspektəbli/ *adv* respetablemente

respected /rɪˈspektɪd/ *a* and *part* respetado; apreciado, estimado; digno de respeto, honrado

respectful /rɪˈspektfəl/ *a* respetuoso

respectfully /rɪˈspektfəli/ *adv* respetuosamente

respectfulness /rɪˈspektfəlnɪs/ *n* aire respetuoso, *m;* conducta respetuosa, *f*

respecting /rɪˈspektɪŋ/ *prep* con respecto a, en cuanto a, tocante a; a propósito de

respective /rɪˈspektɪv/ *a* respectivo; relativo

respectively /rɪˈspektɪvli/ *adv* respectivamente

respiration /,respəˈreiʃən/ *n* respiración, *f*

respirator /ˈrespə,reitər/ *n* respirador, *m*

respiratory /ˈrespərə,tɔri/ *a* respiratorio

respire /rɪˈspaiər/ *vt* and *vi* respirar; exhalar; descansar

respite /ˈrespɪt/ *n* tregua, pausa, *f;* respiro, *m;* *Law.* espera, *f.* —*vt* dar tregua (a); (postpone) aplazar; (relieve) aliviar

resplendence /rɪˈsplendəns/ *n* resplandor, *m,* refulgencia, *f,* esplendor, fulgor, *m*

resplendent /rɪˈsplendənt/ *a* resplandeciente, refulgente, relumbrante. **He was r. in a new uniform,** Lucía (or Ostentaba) un nuevo uniforme. **to be r.,** ser resplandeciente; relumbrar, refulgir

resplendently /rɪˈsplendəntli/ *adv* esplendorosamente

respond /rɪˈspɒnd/ *vi* responder; contestar; (obey) obedecer; reaccionar

respondent /rɪˈspɒndənt/ *n* (in a suit) demandado (-da)

response /rɪˈspɒns/ *n* respuesta, *f;* *Eccl.* responso, *m*

responsibility /rɪ,spɒnsəˈbilɪti/ *n* responsabilidad, *f*

responsible /rɪˈspɒnsəbəl/ *a* responsable

responsive /rɪˈspɒnsɪv/ *a* simpático, sensible, sensitivo

responsiveness /rɪˈspɒnsɪvnɪs/ *n* simpatía, *f;* sensibilidad, *f*

rest /rest/ *n* descanso, *m;* reposo, *m;* (the grave) última morada, *f;* tranquilidad, paz, *f;* inacción, *f;* (prop) soporte, apoyo, *m;* base, *f;* (for a lance) ristre, *m;* (for a rifle) apoyo, *m;* *Mus.* silencio, *m,* pausa, *f;* (in verse) cesura, *f.* **in r.,** en ristre. **the r.,** el resto; los demás, los otros. **to set at r.,** calmar, tranquilizar; (remove) quitar. **r.-cure,** cura de reposo, *f.* **r.-house,** hospedería, *f;* refugio, *m.* **r.-room, lounge,** sala de descanso, *f;* (toilet) excusado, retrete, *m;* (in theaters) saloncillo, *m*

rest /rest/ *vi* reposar, descansar; (lie down) acostarse, echarse; (stop) cesar, parar; estar en paz; apoyarse (en); descansar (sobre); posar; depender (de); (remain) quedar. —*vt* descansar; dar un descanso (a); (lean) apoyar; basar (en). **It rests with them,** Depende de ellos. **These valuable documents now rest in the Library of Congress,** Estos valiosos documentos han parado en la Biblioteca del Congresso. **May he r. in peace!** ¡Que en paz descanse! **to r. assured,** estar seguro. **to r. on one's oars,** cesar de remar; descansar

restate /riˈsteit/ *vt* repetir; afirmar de nuevo

restatement /riˈsteitmənt/ *n* repetición, *f*

restaurant /ˈrestərənt/ *n* restaurante, restorán, *m.* **r.-car,** coche-comedor, *m*

restful /ˈrestfəl/ *a* descansado; tranquilo, sosegado

resting /ˈrestɪŋ/ *n* reposo, *m.* **last r.-place,** última morada, *f.* **r.-place,** descansadero, *m;* refugio, *m*

restitution /,restɪˈtuʃən/ *n* restitución, *f*

restive /ˈrestɪv/ *a* (of a horse) repropio, ingobernable; inquieto, agitado; impaciente

restiveness /ˈrestɪvnɪs/ *n* inquietud, agitación, *f;* impaciencia, *f*

restless /ˈrestlɪs/ *a* agitado; inquieto, intranquilo; turbulento; sin reposo; (wakeful) desvelado; (ceaseless) incesante. **r. night,** noche desvelada, noche intranquila, *Inf.* noche toledana, *f*

restlessly /ˈrestlɪsli/ *adv* agitadamente; con inquietud; turbulentamente; incesantemente

restlessness /ˈrestlɪsnɪs/ *n* agitación, *f;* inquietud, intranquilidad, *f;* turbulencia, *f;* falta de reposo, *f;* (wakefulness) desvelo, *m;* movimiento incesante, *m*

restock /rɪ'stɒk/ vt (with goods) surtir de nuevo; proveer de nuevo; restablecer; repoblar

restoration /ˌrestə'reɪʃən/ n restauración, f; renovación, f; restablecimiento, m; (returning) restitución, f

restorative /rɪ'stɒrətɪv/ a and n restaurativo m

restore /rɪ'stɔr/ vt restaurar; restituir; devolver; restablecer; reponer; (repair) reformar, reparar; reconstruir; (to former rank, etc.) rehabilitar. **He restored the book to its place,** Devolvió el libro a su sitio

restorer /rɪ'stɔrər/ n restaurador (-ra)

restrain /rɪ'streɪn/ vt refrenar; reprimir; (restrict) limitar, restringir; (prevent) impedir; desviar; (detain) recluir. **to r. oneself,** contenerse

restrained /rɪ'streɪnd/ a moderado, mesurado; sobrio; (of emotion) contenido

restraining /rɪ'streɪnɪŋ/ a restrictivo; moderador, calmante

restraint /rɪ'streɪnt/ n freno, m; restricción, f; limitación, f; prohibición, f; compulsión, f; (reserve) reserva, f; moderación, f

restrict /rɪ'strɪkt/ vt restringir; limitar

restriction /rɪ'strɪkʃən/ n restricción, f; limitación, f

restrictive /rɪ'strɪktɪv/ a restrictivo

result /rɪ'zʌlt/ n resultado, m; consecuencia, resulta, f; solución, f. —vi resultar. **as the r. of,** de resultas de

resultant /rɪ'zʌltnt/ a resultante; consecuente. —n resultado, m; Mech. resultante, f

resume /rɪ'zum/ vt reasumir; (continue) reanudar, continuar; (summarize) resumir

résumé n resumen, m

resummon /rɪ'sʌmən/ vt convocar de nuevo (a); citar de nuevo (a)

resumption /rɪ'zʌmpʃən/ n (renewal) reanudación, f; reasunción, f

resurgence /rɪ'sɜrdʒəns/ n resurgimiento, m

resurrect /ˌrezə'rekt/ vt Inf. desenterrar; resucitar

resurrection /ˌrezə'rekʃən/ n resurrección, f

resuscitate /rɪ'sʌsɪˌteɪt/ vt and vi resucitar

resuscitation /rɪˌsʌsɪ'teɪʃən/ n resurrección, f; renovación, f; renacimiento, m

retail /'riteɪl/ n venta al por menor, reventa, f. —adv al por menor. —vt (goods) vender al por menor, revender; (tell) contar; repetir. **r. trade,** comercio al por menor, m

retailer /'riteɪlər/ n vendedor (-ra) al por menor; (of a story) narrador (-ra); el, m, (f, la) que cuenta algo

retain /rɪ'teɪn/ vt retener; guardar; conservar; (a barrister) ajustar; (hire) contratar

retainer /rɪ'teɪnər/ n (dependent) criado, dependiente, m; partidario, adherente, m; (fee) honorario, m; pl **retainers,** séquito, m, adherentes, m pl, gente, f

retaining wall /rɪ'teɪnɪŋ/ n muro de contención, m

retake /ˌri'teɪk/ vt volver a tomar; reconquistar

retaking /rɪ'teɪkɪŋ/ n reconquista, f

retaliate /rɪ'tæliˌeɪt/ vt vengarse de, desquitarse de. —vi vengarse, tomar represalias

retaliation /rɪˌtæli'eɪʃən/ n represalias, f pl; desquite, m, satisfacción, f. **law of r.,** talión, m,

retaliatory /rɪ'tæliə,tɔri/ a de represalias; de desquite

retard /rɪ'tɑrd/ vt retardar

retch /retʃ/ vi tener náuseas, procurar vomitar

retching n náusea, basca, f

retell /ˌri'tel/ vt repetir, volver a contar

retention /rɪ'tenʃən/ n retención, f; conservación, f

retentive /rɪ'tentɪv/ a retentivo

retentiveness /rɪ'tDntlvnIs/ n poder de retención, m; (memory) retentiva, f

reticence /'retəsəns/ n reticencia, reserva, f

reticent /'retəsənt/ a reservado, inexpresivo, taciturno

retina /'retnə, 'retnə/ n retina, f

retinue /'retn,u, -,yu/ n séquito, acompañamiento, m, comitiva, f

retire /rɪ'taɪ∂r/ vi retirarse; (to bed) recogerse, acostarse; (from a post) jubilarse. —vt retirar; jubilar. **to r. from a post,** Mil. rendir el puesto

retired /rɪ'taɪ∂rd/ a retirado; (remote) apartado, aislado; (hidden) escondido; (former) antiguo; (from employment, etc.) jubilado; (of an officer) retirado. **to place on the r. list,** jubilar; (Mil. Nav.) dar el retiro (a)

retirement /rɪ'taɪ∂rmənt/ n retirada, f; (solitude) apartamento, aislamiento, m; retiro, m; (superannuation) jubilación, f

retiring /rɪ'taɪ∂rɪŋ/ a que se retira; (from a post) dimitente; (with pension, etc.) de jubilación; (reserved) reservado; modesto

retort /rɪ'tɔrt/ vi replicar. —vt retorcer; devolver (una acusación, etc.). —n réplica, f; contestación, f; Chem. retorta, f

retouch /v. ri'tʌtʃ/ vt retocar

retrace /rɪ'treɪs/ vt volver a trazar; volver a andar (un camino); (one's steps) volver sobre sus pasos, volver atrás; (in memory) rememorar, recordar; buscar el origen (de); (recount) narrar, contar

retract /rɪ'trækt/ vt retractar, retirar; (draw back) retraer. —vi retractarse

retraction /rɪ'trækʃən/ n retracción, f

retranslate /rɪ'trænslet/ vt hacer una nueva traducción (de)

retransmission /ˌritrænsm'mɪʃən/ n retransmisión, f

retread /v. ri'tred/ vt pisar de nuevo; (tires) recauchetear

retreat /rɪ'trit/ n retirada, f; (Mil. signal) retreta, f; (refuge and Eccl.) retiro, m. —vi retirarse; retroceder; refugiarse

retreat house n casa de ejercicios, f

retreating /rɪ'tritɪŋ/ a que se retira; que retrocede; Mil. que se bate en retirada

retrench /rɪ'trentʃ/ vt reducir; disminuir; vi economizar, hacer economías

retrenchment /rɪ'trentʃmənt/ n disminución, reducción, f; economías, f pl

retrial /'rɪtraɪl/ n (of a person) nuevo proceso, m; (of a case) revisión, f

retribution /ˌretrə'byuʃən/ n retribución, f; justo castigo, m, pena merecida, f

retrievable /rɪ'trivəbəl/ a recuperable, que puede recobrarse; reparable

retrieval /rɪ'trivəl/ n recuperación, f; reparación, f; (of game) cobra, f; (of one's character) rehabilitación, f

retrieve /rɪ'triv/ vt (game, of dogs) cobrar; (regain) recobrar, recuperar; reparar; restaurar; reparar; restablecer; (one's character) rehabilitar. —vi cobrar la caza

retriever /rɪ'trivər/ n (dog) perdiguero (-ra)

retroactive /ˌretrou'æktɪv/ a retroactivo

retrocede /ˌretrə'sid/ vi retroceder

retrograde /'retrə,greɪd/ a retrógrado

retrogression /ˌretrə'greʃən/ n retrogradación, regresión, f; Med. retroceso, m

retrogressive /ˌretrə'gresɪv/ a retrógrado

retrospect /'retrə,spekt/ n mirada retrospectiva, f, examen del pasado, m. **in r.,** retrospectivamente

retrospection /ˌretrə'spekʃən/ n retrospección, f

retrospective /ˌretrə'spektɪv/ a retrospectivo

retrospectively /ˌretrə'spektɪvli/ adv retrospectivamente

retry /ˌri'traɪ/ vt (a case) rever; (a person) procesar de nuevo

return /rɪ'tɜrn/ vi regresar; volver; reaparecer; presentarse de nuevo; Law. revertir; (answer) contestar, responder. —vt (give back or put back) devolver; (a ball) restar; (a kindness, visit) pagar; restituir; (reciprocate) corresponder (a); recompensar; contestar (a); dar; rendir; (yield) producir; (a verdict) fallar, pronunciar; (report) dar parte de; anunciar; (exchange) cambiar; (elect) elegir. —n regreso, m; vuelta, f; (giving or putting back) devolución, f; pago, m; restitución, f; correspondencia, f; recompensa, f; (reply) respuesta, f; (reappearance) reaparición, f; reinstalación, f; repetición, f; (gain) ganancia, f; provecho, m; rendimiento, m; (exchange) cambio, m; (report) parte oficial, f; informe, m; lista, f; (election) elección, f; pl **returns,** tablas estadísticas, f pl; (of an election) resultados, m pl. **Many happy returns!** ¡Feliz cumpleaños! **by return mail,** a vuelta de correo. **on my (his, etc.) r.,** a la vuelta, cuando vuelva. **to r. like for like,** pagar en la misma moneda. **r. journey, r. trip,** viaje de vuelta, m. **r. match,** partido de vuelta, m. **r. ticket,** billete de ida y vuelta, m; billete de vuelta, m

returnable /rɪ'tɜrnəbəl/ a restituible; susceptible a

ser devuelto; (on approval) a prueba; *Law.* devolutivo

returning /rɪ'tɜrnɪŋ/ *a* que vuelve. —*n* See **return "Return to Sender"** «Al remitente»

reunion /ri'yunyən/ *n* reunión, *f*

reunite /ˌriyu'nait/ *vt* reunir. —*vi* reunirse

revaccinate /ri'væksə,neit/ *vt* revacunar

revaccination /ri,væksə'neiʃən/ *n* revacunación, *f*

reveal /rɪ'vil/ *vt* revelar; descubrir

revealer /rɪ'vilər/ *n* revelador (-ra)

revealing /rɪ'vilɪŋ/ *a* revelador. —*n* revelación, *f*; descubrimiento, *m*

reveille /'revəli; *Brit.* rɪ'væli/ *n Mil.* diana, *f*

revel /'revəl/ *vi* divertirse; regocijarse (en), gozarse (en); entregarse (a); (carouse) ir de parranda; emborracharse. —*n* algazara, jarana, *f*; *pl* **revels,** fiestas, festividades, *f pl*

revelation /ˌrevə'leiʃən/ *n* revelación, *f*; descubrimiento, *m*; (in the Bible) Apocalipsis, *m*

reveler /'revələr/ *n* convidado alegre, *m*; (at night) trasnochador (-ra); (drunk) borracho (-cha); (masked) máscara, *mf*

revelry /'revəlri/ *n* festividades, *f pl*, regocijo, *m*; orgías, *f pl*

revenge /rɪ'vɛndʒ/ *n* venganza, *f.* —*vt* vengarse de; desquitarse de

revengeful /rɪ'vɛndʒfəl/ *a* vengativo

revengefully /rɪ'vɛndʒfəli/ *adv* vengativamente

revengefulness /rɪ'vɛndʒfəlnɪs/ *n* deseo de venganza, *m*; carácter vengativo, *m*

revenger /rɪ'vɛndʒər/ *n* vengador (-ra)

revenue /'revən,yu, -ə,nu/ *n* rentas públicas, *f pl*; (treasury) fisco, *m*; *Com.* rédito, *m*, ingresos, *m pl*; beneficio, *m*. **Inland R.,** delegación de contribuciones, *f.* **r. officer,** agente fiscal, *m*

reverberate /rɪ'vɜrbə,reit/ *vt* and *vi* (of sound) retumbar, resonar; (of light, etc.) reverberar

reverberation /rɪ,vɜrbə'reiʃən/ *n* (reflection) reverberación, *f*; (of sound) retumbo, eco, *m*

revere /rɪ'viər/ *vt* reverenciar, venerar, honrar

reverence /'revərəns/ *n* reverencia, *f*, *vt* reverenciar

reverend /'revərənd/ *a* reverendo

reverent /'revərənt/ *a* reverente

reverently /'revərəntli/ *adv* reverentemente, con reverencia

reverie /'revəri/ *n* ensueño, *m*

reversal /rɪ'vɜrsəl/ *n* inversión, *f*; (of a verdict) revocación, *f*

reverse /rɪ'vɜrs/ *vt* invertir; (a steam engine) dar contra vapor (a); (a vehicle) poner en marcha atrás; (arms) llevar a la funerala; (a judgment, etc.) revocar, derogar. —*vi* (dancing) dar vueltas al revés. —*n* lo contrario, lo opuesto; (back) dorso, revés, *m*; (change) cambio, *m*; (check) revés, *m*, vicisitud, *f*; (loss) pérdida, *f*; (defeat) derrota, *f*; *Mech.* marcha atrás, *f*, *a* inverso; contrario, opuesto. **quite the r.,** todo lo contrario. **r. turn,** (of an engine) cambio de dirección, *m*; (in dancing) vuelta al revés, *f*

reversible /rɪ'vɜrsəbəl/ *a* reversible

reversion /rɪ'vɜrʒən, -ʃən/ *n* reversión, *f*; *Biol.* atavismo, *m*; (of offices) futura, *f*; (of property) reversión, *f*

revert /rɪ'vɜrt/ *vi Law.* revertir; volver (a)

review /rɪ'vyu/ *n* examen, análisis, *m*; juicio crítico, *m*; (journal and *Mil.*) revista, *f*; (criticism) revista, reseña, *f*; *Law.* revisión, *f.* —*vt* examinar, analizar; (*Mil.* etc.) pasar revista (a); revisar; repasar; (a book, etc.) reseñar; *Law.* revisar. —*vi* escribir revistas

review article *n* artículo de reseña, *m*

reviewer /rɪ'vyuər/ *n* revistero (-ra), crítico, *m*

revile /rɪ'vail/ *vt* injuriar, maldecir, difamar

reviler /rɪ'vailər/ *n* maldiciente, *m*, insultador (-ra)

reviling /rɪ'vailɪŋ/ *n* insultos, *m pl*, injurias, *f pl*

revisal /rɪ'vaizəl/ *n* revisión, *f*

revise /rɪ'vaiz/ *vt* revisar; repasar; corregir; (change) cambiar

reviser /rɪ'vaizər/ *n* revisor, *m*; corrector de pruebas, *m*

revision /rɪ'viʒən/ *n* revisión, *f*; repaso, *m*; corrección de pruebas, *f*

revisit /rɪ'vɪzɪt/ *vt* volver a visitar, visitar de nuevo

revival /rɪ'vaivəl/ *n* resurgimiento, *m*; renovación, *f*; (awakening) despertamiento, *m*; restablecimiento, *m*; resurrección, *f*; (of learning) renacimiento, *m*; *Theat.* reposición, *f*; (religious) despertar religioso, *m*

revive /rɪ'vaiv/ *vt* reponerse; restablecerse; resucitar; renovarse; renacer; cobrar fuerzas; (recover consciousness) volver en sí. —*vt* hacer revivir; resucitar; restablecer; renovar; restaurar; despertar; (fire, colors) avivar

reviver /rɪ'vaivər/ *n* resucitador (-ra)

revivification /rɪ,vɪvəfɪ'keiʃən/ *n* revivificación, *f*

revivify /rɪ'vɪvə,fai/ *vt* revivificar

revocable /'revəkəbəl, rɪ'vou-/ *a* revocable

revocation /ˌrevə'keiʃən/ *n* revocación, *f*

revoke /rɪ'vouk/ *vt* revocar, anular, derogar; (wills) quebrantar. —*vi* revocar, anular; (at cards) renunciar. —*n* (cards) renuncio, *m*

revolt /rɪ'voult/ *n* rebelión, *f*, *vi* rebelarse, sublevarse. —*vt* repugnar, indignar, dar asco (a)

revolting /rɪ'voultɪŋ/ *a* repugnante, asqueroso; (rebellious) rebelde

revolution /ˌrevə'luʃən/ *n* revolución, *f*; (turn) vuelta, *f*, giro, *m*

revolutionary /ˌrevə'luʃə,neri/ *a* and *n* revolucionario (-ia)

revolutionize /ˌrevə'luʃə,naiz/ *vt* revolucionar

revolve /rɪ'vɒlv/ *vi* dar vueltas, girar; suceder periódicamente. —*vt* hacer girar; (ponder) revolver, discurrir

revolver /rɪ'vɒlvər/ *n* revólver, *m*

revolving /rɪ'vɒlvɪŋ/ *a* giratorio; que vuelve; periódico. **r. chair,** silla giratoria, *f.* **r. door,** puerta giratoria, *f.* **r. stage,** escenario giratorio, *m*

revue /rɪ'vyu/ *n Theat.* revista, *f*

revulsion /rɪ'vʌlʃən/ *n* revulsión, *f*

revulsive /rɪ'vʌlsɪv/ *a Med.* revulsivo

rev up /rev/ *vt* (an engine) calentar

reward /rɪ'wɔrd/ *n* recompensa, *f*; retribución, *f.* —*vt* recompensar; satisfacer, premiar

rewarding /rɪ'wɔrdɪŋ/ *a* premiador; que recompensa. —*n* recompensación, *f.* **a rewarding experience,** una experiencia compensadora, *f*

rewrite /v. ri'rait/ *vt* escribir de nuevo; volver a escribir; redactar otra vez

rhapsody /'ræpsədi/ *n* rapsodia, *f*

rheostat /'riə,stæt/ *n* reóstato, *m*

rhetoric /'retərɪk/ *n* retórica, *f*

rhetorical /rɪ'tɔrɪkəl/ *a* retórico; declamatorio

rhetorician /ˌretə'rɪʃən/ *n* retórico (-ca)

rheumatic /ru'mætɪk/ *a* reumático. **r. fever,** reumatismo poliarticular agudo, *m*

rheumatism /'rumə,tɪzəm/ *n* reumatismo, reuma, *m*

rheumy /'rumi/ *a* catarroso; (of the eyes) legañoso

rhinestone /'rain,stoun/ *n* circón, *m*

Rhine, the /rain/ el Rin, *m*

rhinoceros /rai'nɒsərəs/ *n* rinoceronte, *m*

Rhodes /roudz/ Rodas, *f*

rhododendron /ˌroudə'dendrən/ *n* rododendro, *m*

rhubarb /'rubɑrb/ *n* ruibarbo, *m*

rhyme /raim/ *n* rima, *f*; verso, *m.* —*vi* and *vt* rimar. **without r. or reason,** sin ton ni son; a tontas y a locas

rhymer /'raimər/ *n* rimador (-ra)

rhyming /'raimɪŋ/ *a* rimador

rhythm /'rɪðəm/ *n* ritmo, *m*

rhythmic /'rɪðmɪk/ *a* rítmico

rib /rɪb/ *n* (*Anat. Bot. Aer. Naut. Archit.*) costilla, *f*; (of an umbrella or fan) varilla, *f*; (in cloth) cordoncillo, *m*, lista, *f*

ribald /'rɪbəld/ *a* escabroso, ribaldo, indecente

ribaldry /'rɪbəldri/ *n* ribaldería, escabrosidad, indecencia, *f*

ribbed /rɪbd/ *a* con costillas; (of cloth) listado, con listas

ribbon /'rɪbən/ *n* cinta, *f*; tira, *f*; (tatter) jirón, *m*. **to tear to ribbons,** hacer jirones

rice /rais/ *n* arroz, *m.* —*a* de arroz; con arroz. **r. field,** arrozal, *m.* **r.-paper,** papel de paja de arroz, *m.* **r.-pudding,** arroz con leche, *m*

rich /rɪtʃ/ *a* rico; opulento; (happy) dichoso; (of land, etc.) fértil; abundante; (of objects) magnífico, suntuoso, hermoso; precioso; (of food) exquisito;

suculento; (highly seasoned) muy sazonado; (creamy) con mucha nata; (of colours) brillante, vivo. **new r.**, ricacho (-cha). **newly-r.**, advenedizo. **to grow r.**, enriquecerse

riches /'rɪtʃɪz/ n riqueza, f

richly /'rɪtʃli/ adv ricamente; abundantemente; magníficamente; bien

richness /'rɪtʃnɪs/ n riqueza, f; opulencia, f; (of land, etc.) fertilidad, f; abundancia, f; (of objects) magnificencia, suntuosidad, hermosura, f; preciosidad, f; (of food) gusto exquisito, m; suculencia, f; (piquancy) gusto picante, m; (of colours) viveza, f

rickets /'rɪkɪts/ n raquitismo, m

rickety /'rɪkɪti/ a Med. raquítico; destartalado, desvencijado; (unsteady) tambaleante; cojo

rickshaw /'rɪkʃ ɔ/ n riksha, m

ricochet /ˌrɪkəˈʃei/ n rebote, m, vi rebotar

rid /rɪd/ vt librar (de). **to get rid of,** librarse de; quitarse de encima (a); perder, quitarse; (dismiss) despedir. **to rid oneself of,** librarse de, deshacerse de

riddance /'rɪdns/ n libramiento, m

riddle /'rɪdl/ n acertijo, m; enigma, problema, m; misterio, m; (sieve) tamiz de alambre, m; vt (guess) adivinar; (sift) cribar; (with holes) acribillar

ride /raid/ vi (a horse) montar a caballo, cabalgar; pasear a caballo; (a mule, a bicycle) montar en, pasear en; (a vehicle, train) ir en; (a carriage, car) andar en, pasear en; (float) flotar; (on the wind) dejarse llevar por el viento; ser llevado por el viento; (go) ir; (come) venir; (a distance) hacer... a caballo, en coche, etc.; Naut. estar al ancla; Mech. tener juego. —vt (a horse, mule, bicycle) montar; ir montado sobre; manejar; (a race) hacer; (float) flotar en; (cleave, the sea, etc.) surcar. —n paseo (a caballo, en bicicleta, en coche, etc.), m; viaje (en un autobús, de tren, etc.), f; (bridle path) camino de herradura, m; cabalgata, f; desfile a caballo, m. **a r. on horseback,** un paseo a caballo. **They gave me a r. in their car,** (e.g. to see the sights) Me llevaron a paseo en su auto, (a lift to a certain place) Me dieron un aventón. **ride at anchor,** estar fondeado. **to r. a bicycle,** montar en bicicleta. **to r. rough-shod over,** mandar a la baqueta (a), mandar a puntapiés (a). **to r. sidesaddle,** cabalgar a mujeriegas. **to r. at,** embestir con. **to r. away,** marcharse, alejarse; marcharse a caballo, etc. **to r. back,** volver; volver a caballo, en bicicleta, etc. **to r. behind,** seguir a caballo; ir inmediatamente detrás (de); (on the back seat) ocupar el asiento de atrás; (on the same animal) cabalgar en la grupa. **to r. down,** atropellar; (trample) pisotear, pasar por encima de. **to r. on,** seguir su camino. **to r. out,** salir a paseo en caballo, etc.; irse a paseo en coche, etc.; (a storm) hacer frente a, luchar con. **to r. over,** pasar por encima de. **to r. up,** vi llegar, acercarse; (of a tie, etc.) subir. —vt montar

rider /'raidər/ n cabalgador (-ra); jinete, m; persona que va en coche, etc., f; (on a bicycle) ciclista, mf; (on a motorcycle) motociclista, mf; (horsebreaker) domador de caballos, m; (clause) añadidura, f; corolario, m

ridge /rɪdʒ/ n cumbre, cima, f; (of mountains) cordillera, sierra, f; (of a roof, of a nose) caballete, m; Agr. lomo, caballón, m; (wrinkle) arruga, f; (on coins) cordoncillo, m. —vt surcar; formar lomos (en); (wrinkle) arrugar

ridicule /'rɪdɪˌkyul/ n ridículo, m, vt poner en ridículo, ridiculizar, burlarse (de), mofarse (de)

ridiculous /rɪˈdɪkyələs/ a ridículo, absurdo

ridiculously /rɪˈdɪkyələsli/ adv absurdamente

ridiculousness /rɪˈdɪkyələsnɪs/ n ridiculez, f

riding /'raidɪŋ/ a cabalgante; que va a caballo; montado (a, en, sobre); Naut. al ancla; (in compounds) de equitación; de montar. —n equitación, f; paseo a caballo; en bicicleta, etc., m; acción de ir a caballo, etc., f; (district) comarca, f. **r.-boots,** botas de montar, f pl. **r.-habit,** traje de montar, m; (woman's) amazona, f. **r.-master,** profesor de equitación, m. **r.-saddle,** silla de montar, f. **r.-school,** escuela de equitación, f

rife /raif/ a común; corriente; frecuente; prevalente; abundante; general. **r. with,** abundante en; lleno de

riffraff /'rɪf,ræf/ n desperdicios, m pl; (rabble) gentuza, canalla, f

rifle /'raifəl/ n rifle, fusil rayado, m. —vt robar; (a suitcase, etc.) desvalijar; (a gun) rayar. **r.-range,** campo de tiro, m. **r.-sling,** portafusil, m. **r.-shot,** fusilazo, m

rifleman /'raifəlmən/ n fusilero, m

rifler /'raiflər/ n saqueador (-ra)

rifling /'raiflɪŋ/ n (robbing) saqueo, robo, m; (of a suitcase, etc.) desvalijamiento, m

rift /rɪft/ n hendedura, abertura, f; grieta, f

rig /rɪg/ n Naut. aparejo, m; Inf. atavío, m. —vt (a ship) aparejar; equipar; (elections) falsificar. **to rig out,** proveer de; equipar con; ataviar. **to rig up,** arreglar; armar, construir

rigging /'rɪgɪŋ/ n (of a ship) aparejo, m

right /rait/ a recto; correcto; conveniente, debido; apropiado; exacto; (opposite of left hand) derecho; (straight) directo; en línea recta; razonable; (true) verdadero, genuino, legítimo; (just) justo; (prudent) prudente; (in health) sano. **All r.!** ¡Está bien! **I feel all r.,** Me siento perfectamente bien, Estoy bien. **He is the r. man for the job,** Él es el hombre que hace falta para el puesto. **It is the r. word,** Es la palabra apropiada. **on the r.,** a la derecha. **to be r.,** (of persons) tener razón. **to make r.,** poner en orden; arreglar. **r.-angle,** ángulo recto, m. **r.-angled,** rectangular. **r.-angled triangle,** triángulo rectángulo, m. **the R. Bank (of Paris),** la Orilla derecha, la Ribera derecha, f. **r. hand,** n (mano) derecha, diestra, f. —a de la mano derecha; (person) brazo derecho, m. —a de la mano derecha; de la derecha; a la derecha. **r.-handed,** derecho; diestro, hábil. **r. mind,** entero juicio, m. **r.-minded,** juicioso, prudente; honrado. **r.-of-way,** derecho a la vía, m

right /rait/ adv directamente; inmediatamente; derechamente; correctamente; debidamente; exactamente; bien; (quite, thoroughly) completamente; honradamente; (very) muy. **r. on,** adelante; en frente. **R. about face!** ¡Media vuelta a la derecha! **r. at the bottom,** al fondo; al final; el último (de la clase, etc.). **r. at the end of his speech,** al fin de su discurso. **r. away,** en seguida, inmediatamente

right /rait/ n razón, f; verdad, f; justicia, f; (good) bien, m; derecho, m; (not left side) derecha, f; (of political parties) derechas, f pl. **r. and wrong,** el bien y el mal. "**All rights reserved,**" «Derechos reservados.» **by rights,** por derecho. **It is on the r.,** Está a la derecha. **to exercise one's r.,** usar de su derecho. **r. of association,** derecho de asociación, m. **r. of way,** derecho de paso, m. **to be in the r.,** tener razón; estar en su derecho

right /rait/ vt enderezar; rectificar; corregir; poner en orden; Naut. enderezar; hacer justicia (a). **to r. wrongs,** deshacer agravios

righteous /'raitʃəs/ a recto, virtuoso, justo; justificado

righteously /'raitʃəsli/ adv virtuosamente; justamente

righteousness /'raitʃəsnɪs/ n rectitud, integridad, virtud, f; justicia, f

rightful /'raitfəl/ a justo; legítimo; verdadero

rightfully /'raitfəli/ adv justamente; legitimamente; verdaderamente

rightfulness /'raitfəlnɪs/ n justicia, f; legitimidad, f; verdad, f

rightly /'raitli/ adv justamente; debidamente; correctamente; bien. **r. or wrongly,** mal que bien

rightness /'raitnɪs/ n rectitud, f; derechura, f; justicia, f; exactitud, f

rigid /'rɪdʒɪd/ a rígido; inflexible; severo, riguroso

rigidity /rɪˈdʒɪdɪti/ n rigidez, f; inflexibilidad, f; severidad, f

rigmarole /'rɪgmə,roul/ n monserga, f, galimatías, m, jerigonza, f

rigor /'rɪgər/ n rigor, m

rigorous /'rɪgərəs/ a riguroso

rigorously /'rɪgərəsli/ adv rigurosamente

rile /rail/ vt Inf. irritar, sacar de tino (a)

rim /rɪm/ n borde, m; orilla, f; (of a wheel) llanta, f, aro, m

rime /raim/ n escarcha, f, vt cubrir con escarcha. See also **rhyme**

rind /raind/ *n* (of fruit) cáscara, corteza, *f*; (of cheese) costra, *f*; (of bacon) piel, *f*

ring /rɪŋ/ *n* círculo, *m*; (round the eyes) ojera, *f*; (for curtains, etc.) anilla, *f*; (for the finger) anillo, *m*, sortija, *f*; (for children's games, etc.) corro, *m*; (for the ears) arete, *m*; (of smoke and for the nose) anillo, *m*; (for hitching, etc.) argolla, *f*; (for boxing) cuadrilátero, *m*; (on a racecourse) picadero, *m*; (at a circus, bull-fight) ruedo, redondel, *m*; *Fig.* arena, *f*; (group) camarilla, *f*, grupo, *m*; (metallic sound) sonido metálico, *m*; resonancia, *f*; (tinkle) tintín, *m*; (of a bell) repique, tañido, son (de la campana), *m*; (of bells) juego de campanas, *m*; (of laughter, etc.) ruido, *m*; (of truth, etc.) apariencia, *f*. **r.-bolt,** *Naut.* cáncamo, *m*. **r. finger,** dedo anular, *m*. **r.-master,** director de circo, *m*

ring /rɪŋ/ *vt* (surround) cercar, rodear; (a bull, etc.) poner un anillo (a); (sound) hacer sonar; sonar; (a door bell, etc.) tocar, apretar; (bells) echar a vuelo; (announce by pealing the bells) anunciar, proclamar; sonar, tañer. —*vi* (of bells) sonar; (re-echo) resonar; (of the ears) zumbar; (tinkle) tintinar. **to r. the bell,** tocar la campana; tocar el timbre. **to r. off,** colgar el teléfono. **to r. up,** llamar por teléfono, telefonear

ringing /ˈrɪŋɪŋ/ *n* acción de tocar las campanas o el timbre, *f*; toque, *m*; repique, *m*; campanilleo, *m*; (in the ears) zumbido, *m*. —*a* resonante, sonoro. **r. signal,** señal de llamada, *f*. **the r. of the bells,** el son de las campanas

ringleader /ˈrɪŋˌlidər/ *n* cabecilla, *m*

ringlet /ˈrɪŋlɪt/ *n* rizo, bucle, *m*

ringworm /ˈrɪŋˌwɜrm/ *n* tiña, *f*

rink /rɪŋk/ *n* pista, *f*. **skating-r.,** sala de patinar, *f*; pista de patinar, *f*

rinse /rɪns/ *n* enjuague, *m*; enjuagadura, *f*; (of clothes) aclarado, *m*. —*vt* enjuagar; (clothes) aclarar; lavar

rinsing /ˈrɪnsɪŋ/ *n* See **rinse**; —*pl* **rinsings,** lavazas, *f pl, a* de aclarar

riot /ˈraɪət/ *n* motín, *m*; tumulto, *m*; desorden, *m*; exceso, *m*; orgía, *f*; disipación, *f*. —*vi* amotinarse; alborotarse; entregarse a la disipación (or al placer); (enjoy) gozar, disfrutar. **to run r.,** hacer excesos; perder el freno; desmandarse; *Fig.* extenderse por todas partes; crecer en abundancia, cubrir todo

rioter /ˈraɪətər/ *n* amotinador (-ra); alborotador (-ra)

riotous /ˈraɪətəs/ *a* sedicioso; bullicioso; disoluto; desordenado; desenfrenado

riotously /ˈraɪətəs/ *adv* sediciosamente; bulliciosamente; disolutamente; con exceso

riotousness /ˈraɪətəsnɪs/ *n* sedición, *f*; disolución, *f*; excesos, *m pl*, desenfreno, *m*; desorden, *m*

rip /rɪp/ *vt* rasgar; (unsew) descoser; (wood, etc.) partir; (make) hacer. —*vi* rasgarse. —*n* rasgón, *m*; rasgadura, *f*; desgarro, *m*; (libertine) calavera, *m*. **to rip off,** arrancar; quitar. **to rip open,** abrir; (an animal) abrir en canal

riparian /rɪˈpɛəriən/ *a* and *n* ribereño (-ña)

ripe /raɪp/ *a* maduro; preparado; perfecto; acabado

ripen /ˈraɪpən/ *vt* and *vi* madurar

ripeness /ˈraɪpənɪs/ *n* madurez, *f*

ripening /ˈraɪpənɪŋ/ *n* maduración, *f*

ripping /ˈrɪpɪŋ/ *n* rasgadura, *f*; (unstitching) deshiladura, *f*. —*a Inf.* estupendo

ripple /ˈrɪpəl/ *n* rizo, *m*; onda, *f*; (of sound) murmullo, *m*. —*vt* rizar. —*vi* rizarse; murmurar

rippling /ˈrɪplɪŋ/ *n* rizado, *m*; murmullo, *m*

rise /raɪz/ *vi* ascender; subir; levantarse; ponerse de pie; (of a meeting) suspenderse; (from the dead) resucitar; (grow) crecer; (swell) hincharse; (of sun, moon) salir; (of sound, gradient, price, stock exchange quotations) subir; (of river source) nacer; (in revolt) sublevarse, rebelarse; (to the mind) presentarse, surgir; (appear) aparecer; (of buildings, etc.) elevarse, alzarse; (in the world) mejorar de posición; (originate) originarse (en), proceder (de); (of mercury) alzarse; (of fish) picar. **He has risen in my estimation,** Ha ganado en mi estimación. **She rose early,** Se levantó temprano. **The color rose in her cheeks,** Se le subieron los colores a la cara. **to r. to the occasion,** estar al nivel de las circunstancias. **to r. to one's feet,** ponerse de pie. **to r. to the bait,**

morder el anzuelo. **to r. again,** levantarse de nuevo; resucitar; renovarse, suscitarse otra vez. **to r. above,** alzarse por encima de; mostrarse superior a

rise /raɪz/ *n* ascensión, *f*; subida, *f*; levantamiento, *m*; (in price, temperature) alza, *f*; (increase) aumento, *m*; (of the sun, moon) salida, *f*; (of a river) nacimiento, *m*; (origin) origen, *m*; (growth, development) desarrollo, crecimiento, *m*; (promotion) ascenso, *m*; (slope) cuesta, *f*; pendiente, *f*; (high ground) eminencia, altura, *f*. **to give r. to,** dar lugar a, causar. **r. and fall,** subida y baja, *f*; (of the voice) ritmo, *m*; (of music) cadencia, *f*; (of institutions) grandeza y decadencia, *f*. **r. to power,** subida al poder, *f*

riser /ˈraɪzər/ *n* el, *m*, (*f*, la) que se levanta; (of a step) contrahuella, *f*. **early r., early riser,** madrugador (-ra). **late r.,** el, *m*, (*f*, la) que se levanta tarde

risibility /ˌrɪzəˈbɪlɪti/ *n* risibilidad, *f*

risible /ˈrɪzəbəl/ *a* risible

rising /ˈraɪzɪŋ/ *n* subida, *f*; (of the source of rivers) nacimiento, *m*; (overflowing of rivers) crecimiento, *m*; (of sun, moon) salida, *f*; (from the dead) resurrección, *f*; (rebellion) sublevación, insurrección, *f*; (of the tide) crecida, *f*; (of bread) levadura, *f*; (of an assembly) suspensión, *f*; (of a theater curtain) subida, *f*; (literary) renacimiento, *m*, *a* creciente; naciente; saliente; (promising) de porvenir; (young) joven. **the r. generation,** los jóvenes, la generación joven. **He is r. forty,** Raya en los cuarenta. **He likes early r.,** Le gusta madrugar. **On the r. of the curtain...,** Al levantarse el telón... **the r. of the moon,** la salida de la luna, *f*. **the r. tide,** la marea creciente

risk /rɪsk/ *n* riesgo, *m*; peligro, *m*. —*vt* arriesgar; atreverse (a), osar. **at the r. of,** al riesgo de. **to take a r.,** tomar un riesgo; correr peligro. **to r. everything on the outcome,** jugar el todo por el todo

risk capital *n* capital-riesgo, *m*

riskiness /ˈrɪskɪnɪs/ *n* peligro, *m*

risky /ˈrɪski/ *a* arriesgado, peligroso

rissole /rɪˈsoʊl/ *n* risol, *m*, (*pl* risoles)

rite /raɪt/ *n* rito, *m*

rite of passage *n* rito de tránsito, *m*

ritual /ˈrɪtʃuəl/ *a* ritual. —*n* rito, *m*, ceremonia, *f*

ritualist /ˈrɪtʃuəlɪst/ *n* ritualista, *mf*

ritualistic /ˌrɪtʃuəˈlɪstɪk/ *a* ritualista

rival /ˈraɪvəl/ *n* rival, *mf a* competidor; rival. —*vt* rivalizar con, competir con

rivalry /ˈraɪvəlri/ *n* rivalidad, *f*

river /ˈrɪvər/ *n* río, *m*. —*a* del río; fluvial. **r.-basin,** cuenca de un río, *f*. **r.-bed,** lecho, cauce (de un río), *m*. **r. civilization,** civilización fluvial, *f*. **r.-god,** dios de los ríos, *m*. **r.-mouth,** ría, *f*. **r. port,** puerto fluvial, *m*

riverside /ˈrɪvərˌsaɪd/ *n* ribera, orilla de un río, *f*. —*a* de la(s) orilla(s) de un río; situado a la orilla de un río; ribereño

rivet /ˈrɪvɪt/ *n* remache, roblón, *m*. —*vt* remachar; clavar; *Fig.* fijar, concentrar; *Fig.* cautivar, absorber

riveter /ˈrɪvɪtər/ *n* remachador, *m*

riveting /ˈrɪvɪtɪŋ/ *n* remachado, remache, *m*; *Fig.* fijación, concentración, *f*; *Fig.* absorción, *f*. **r. machine,** remachadora, *f*

Riviera, the /ˌrɪviˈɛrə/ la Riviera, *f*

rivulet /ˈrɪvyəlɪt/ *n* riachuelo, arroyo, *m*

road /roʊd/ *n* camino, *m*; carretera, *f*; ruta, *f*; *pl* **roads,** *Naut.* rada, *f*. **high r.,** camino real, *m*. **main r.,** carretera, *f*. **secondary r.,** carretera de segunda clase, *f*. **on the r. to...,** en el camino de... **to get out of the r.,** *Inf.* quitarse de en medio. **to go by r.,** ir por carretera. **"R. up!"** «Carretera en reparaciones.» **r.-book,** guía de carreteras, *f*. **r. house,** albergue de carretera, *m*. **r. maker,** constructor de caminos, *m*; (navvy) peón caminero, *m*. **r. making,** construcción de caminos, *f*. **r. map,** mapa de carreteras, *m*. **r. sign,** señal de carretera, señal de tránsito, señal vial, *f*; poste indicador, *m*. **The r. to hell is paved with good intentions,** El camino del infierno está empedrado de buenas intenciones. **"R. Repairs,"** «Camino en Reparación»

roadmender /ˈroʊdˌmɛndər/ *n* peón caminero, *m*

roadside /ˈroʊdˌsaɪd/ *n* borde del camino, *m*, *a* al lado del camino

roadstead /ˈroʊdˌstɛd/ *n* rada, *f*

roadster /'roudstər/ n automóvil de turismo, m; bicicleta de carreras, f; caballo de aguante, m; buque fondeado en rada, m

roadway /'roud,wei/ n calzada, carretera, f

roam /roum/ vi vagar, vagabundear, andar errante. —vt errar por

roamer /'roumər/ n vagabundo (-da), hombre errante, m

roaming /'roumɪŋ/ n vagabundeo, m; excursiones, f pl, paseos, m pl; a errante, vagabundo; nómada

roan /roun/ a roano, sabino. —n caballo roano, m

roar /rɔr/ vi rugir; (of a bull, of the wind, of a person in anger) bramar; dar voces; (of the fire) crepitar; (of cannon) retumbar; (of thunder) estallar. —vt gritar. —n rugido, bramido, m; (shout) grito, m; (of the fire) crepitación, f; (of cannon, thunder) estallido, m; (noise) ruido, m. **to r. with laughter,** reírse a carcajadas

roaring /'rɔrɪŋ/ n (of horses) asma de los caballos, f, For other meanings, see under **roar.** a rugiente, bramante; Inf. magnífico. **to do a r. trade,** hacer un buen negocio

roast /roust/ n asado, m, carne asada, f. —a asado; tostado. —vt asar; (coffee and to warm one's feet, etc.) tostar; (metals) calcinar; (scold) desollar vivo (a). —vi asarse; tostarse. **r. beef,** rosbif, m

roaster /'roustər/ n asador, m; (for coffee or peanuts) tostador, m; (for chestnuts, etc.) tambor, m

roasting /'roustɪŋ/ n asación, f; (of coffee) tostado, m; (of metals) calcinación, f. **r. spit,** asador, m

rob /rɒb/ vt robar; quitar, privar (de). **They have robbed her of her pocketbook,** Le han robado la cartera

robber /'rɒbər/ n ladrón (-ona); (footpad) salteador de caminos, m; (brigand) bandido, m

robbery /'rɒbəri/ n robo, m. **It's daylight r.!** ¡Es un desuello! **to commit a r.,** cometer un robo. **r. with violence,** robo armado, m

robe /roub/ n traje talar, m, toga, f; (of a monk, nun) hábito, m; (of a priest, etc.) sotana, f; Poet. manto, m; (infant's) mantillas, f pl; pl robes, traje de ceremonia, m. —vt vestir; cubrir, revestir (de). —vi vestirse. **bath r.,** albornoz, m

robin /'rɒbɪn/ n petirrojo, m

robot /'roubat, -bɒt/ n hombre mecánico, m; Aer. piloto mecánico, m. **traffic r.,** torre del tráfico, f; aparato automático, m. **r. plane,** avión sin piloto, m

robust /rou'bʌst/ a robusto; fuerte, vigoroso. **to make r.,** robustecer

robustness /rou'bʌstnɪs/ n robustez, f; vigor, m, fuerza, f

rock /rɒk/ n roca, f; (in the sea) abrojo, escollo, m; peña, f, peñasco, m. **as firm as a r.,** como una roca. **to be on the rocks,** Inf. estar a la cuarta pregunta. **r. bottom,** n fondo, m. —a mínimo, más bajo. **r. crystal,** cuarzo, m. **r.-garden,** jardincito rocoso, jardín alpestre, m. **r.-plant,** planta alpestre, f. **r.-rose,** heliantemo, m. **r.-salt,** sal gema, f

rock /rɒk/ vt mecer; (shake) hacer temblar, sacudir; (to sleep) arrullar. —vi mecerse, balancearse; tambalearse; agitarse; temblar

rocker /'rɒkər/ n (of a chair, cradle) balancín, m; (chair) mecedora, f

rockery /'rɒkəri/ n jardincito rocoso, m

rocket /'rɒkɪt/ n cohete, volador, m. —vi lanzarse. **r.-launching aircraft,** avión lanzacohetes, f

rockiness /'rɒkɪnɪs/ n abundancia de rocas, f; fragosidad, escabrosidad, f

rocking /'rɒkɪŋ/ n balanceo, m; (staggering) tambaleo, m; oscilación, f; (of an infant) arrullo, m. **r.-chair,** mecedora, f. **r.-horse,** caballo balancín, caballo mecedor, m

rocky /'rɒki/ a rocoso; de roca; roqueño; (rough) fragoso, escabroso; (rugged) peñascoso, escarpado. **the R. Mountains,** las Montañas Rocosas, f pl

rococo /rə'koukou/ n rococó, m

rod /rɒd/ n vara, f; bastón de mando, m; (for fishing) caña, f; (measure) pértiga, f; (surveying) jalón, m; palo, m; (for punishment) vergajo, m; Mech. vástago, m. **connecting rod,** biela, f. **to fish with rod and line,** pescar con caña

rodent /'roudn̩t/ a and n roedor, m

roe /rou/ n (deer) corzo (-za); (of fish) hueva, f. **soft roes,** lechas, f pl

rogue /roug/ n bribón, pícaro, pillo, m; Law. vago, m; (affectionate) picaruelo (-la)

roguery /'rougəri/ n truhanería, picardía, f; (knaves) pícaros, m pl; (mischief) travesuras, f pl. **novel of r.,** novela picaresca, f

roguish /'rougɪʃ/ a picaresco, bellaco; (mischievous) travieso, juguetón; malicioso

roguishly /'rougɪʃli/ adv como un pícaro; con malicia

roguishness /'rougɪʃnɪs/ n picardía, bribonería, bellaquería, f; (mischievousness) travesuras, f pl; malicia, f

role /roul/ n papel, m

roll /roul/ n rollo, m; (list) rol, m, lista, f; (of bread) panecillo, m; (of a drum) redoble, m; (of thunder) tronido, m; (of cloth) pieza, f; (of tobacco) rollo, m; (of meat, etc.) pastel, m; (of a ship) balanceo, m; pl **rolls,** (records) archivos, m pl. **He has a nautical r.,** Tiene un andar de marinero. **to call the r.,** pasar lista. **r. film,** película fotográfica, f. **r. of honour,** lista de honor, f. **r.-on corset,** faja elástica, f, corsé de goma, m. **r.-top desk,** buró de cierre enrollable, m

roll /roul/ vi rodar; dar vueltas; (wallow) revolcarse; (of a ship) balancearse, bambolearse; (in money, etc.) nadar; (flow) correr, fluir; (Fig. of time) pasar tranquilamente; (of vehicle) rodar; pasar rodando; (of country) ondular; (of the sea) ondear; (of drums) redoblar; (of thunder) retumbar. —vt hacer rodar; arrollar; (a cigarette) liar; (metals) laminar; (move) mover; (the eyes) guiñar (los ojos); (the ground) apisonar; (pastry) aplanar; (of an organ) sonar; (a drum) redoblar. **Mary rolled her eyes heavenwards,** María puso los ojos en blanco. **to r. away,** alejarse; desaparecer; (of time) pasar. **to r. back,** volver, retirarse; desaparecer. **to r. by,** pasar rodando; desaparecer. **to r. down,** bajar rodando, rodar por. **to r. in,** llegar en gran cantidad (or en gran número). **to r. off,** caer de. **to r. on,** seguir su marcha; fluir sin cesar; seguir su curso; (of time) avanzar. **to r. out,** (metal) laminar; (pastry) aplanar; (bring out) sacar; desenrollar. **to r. over,** vt volcar; tumbar; dar la vuelta (a). —vi dar la vuelta; volverse al otro lado. **to r. up,** arrollar; envolver; (of hedgehogs, etc.) enroscarse, hacerse un ovillo

roll-call vote /'roul,kɔl/ n votación nominal, f

roller /'roulər/ n rodillo, m; cilindro, m; (wheel, castor) rueda, f; (for flattening the ground) apisonadora, f; Print. rodillo, m; (wave) ola grande, f. **r.-bandage,** venda, f. **r. canary,** canario de raza flauta, m. **r.-skate,** patín de ruedas, m. **r.-skating,** patinaje de ruedas, m. **r.-towel,** toalla continua, f

rollicking /'r`lɪkɪŋ/ a alegre, jovial; juguetón

rolling /'roulɪŋ/ a rodante; (of landscape) ondulante, quebrado. —n rodadura, f; (wallowing) revuelco, m; (of metals) laminación, f; (of a ship) balanceo, m; (rolling up) enrollamiento, m. **r.-pin,** rollo, rodillo de pastelero, m. **r.-stock,** material móvil ferroviario, m

Roman /'roumən/ a romano, de los romanos; (of noses and Print.) romano. —n romano (-na). **in R. fashion,** a la romana. **R. Catholic,** a católico; católico apostólico romano. —n el católico (-ca). **R. Catholicism,** catolicismo, m. **R. figures,** números romanos, m pl. **R. nose,** nariz romana, f. **R. road,** vía romana, f. **R. type,** Print. tipo romano, m

Romance /'roumæns/ a (of languages) romance. —n (language) romance, m

romance /rou'mæns/ n novela de caballería, f; romance, m; aventura, f; cuento, m, novela, f; romanticismo, m; Mus. romanza, f. —vi inventar ficciones; exagerar

romancer /rou'mænsər/ n romancerista, mf; mentiroso (-sa), embustero (-ra)

Romanesque /,roumə'nɛsk/ a románico; romanesco

Romanian /ru'meiniən, -'meinyən/ a rumano. —n rumano (-na); (language) rumano, m

romantic /rou'mæntɪk/ a and n romántico (-ca)

romantically /rou'mæntɪkli/ adv románticamente; de un modo romántico

romanticism /rou'mæntə,sɪzəm/ n romanticismo, m

romanticist /rou'mæntəsɪst/ n romántico (-ca)

Rome /roum/ n Roma, f

romp /rɒmp/ vi juguetear, brincar, retozar, loquear; correr rápidamente. —n locuelo (-la), saltaparedes, mf; (game) retozo, m. **The horse romped home easily,** El caballo ganó la carrera fácilmente
rompers /'rɒmpərz/ n mono, m
romping /'rɒmpɪŋ/ n juegos, m pl, travesuras, f pl
rondo /'rɒndou/ n rondó, m
rood /rud/ n cruz, f; crucifijo, m; cuarto de acre, m. **By the r.!** ¡Por mi santiguada!
roof /ruf/ n tejado, techado, m; (of a motor-car, bus) tejadillo, m; (of coaches, etc.) imperial, f; cubierta, f; (of the mouth) paladar, m; (bower) enramada, f; (of heaven) bóveda (del cielo), f. —vt techar, tejar; (shelter) abrigar. **r.-garden,** azotea, f. **r.-gutter,** canalera, f
roofer /'rufər/ n techador, m; constructor de tejados, m
rook /rʊk/ n chova, f, grajo, m; (chess) torre, f. —vt engañar, estafar; (overcharge) desollar vivo (a)
rookery /'rʊkəri/ n manada de grajos, f; colonia de grajos, aves marinas o focas, f
room /rum/ n (in a house) habitación, f, cuarto, m; sala, f, cámara, f; (behind a shop) trastienda, f; (space) sitio, espacio, m; lugar, m; (opportunity) oportunidad, f; (cause) motivo, m, causa, f. —vi alojarse. **bath-r.,** cuarto de baño, m. **dining-r.,** comedor, m. **drawing-r.,** salón, m. **There is no r. for us in this car,** No cabemos en este coche. **There is still r. for improvement,** Se puede mejorar todavía. **There isn't r. for anything else,** No cabe más. **to be r.,** caber, haber sitio. **to make r.,** hacer sitio
roomed /rumd/ a (in compounds) de... habitaciones; de... salas
roominess /'ruminɪs/ n espaciosidad, amplitud, amplitud de habitación, f; (of garments) holgura, f
rooming house /'rutɪd/ n casa de huéspedes, f
roommate /'rum,meit, 'rʊm-/ n compañero de cuarto, compañero de pieza, m
roomy /'rumi, 'rʊmi/ a espacioso, amplio; (of garments) holgado
roost /rust/ n percha de gallinero, f. —vi dormir en una percha; recogerse. **to rule the r.,** ser el amo del cotarro
rooster /'rustər/ n gallo, m,
root /rut or, sometimes, rʊt/ n raíz, f; Gram. radical, m; Mus. base, f; origen, m; explicación, f. —vt arraigar; Fig. fijar, clavar. —vi echar raíces; Fig. arraigarse; (of pigs, etc.) hozar, escarbar; revolver. **to r. out,** arrancar de raíz; Fig. desarraigar; (destroy) extirpar. **cubed r.,** raíz cúbica, f. **from the r.,** (entirely) de raíz. **square r.,** raíz cuadrada, f. **to cut close to the r.,** cortar a raíz
rooted a (in compounds) de raíces...; arraigado
rope /roup/ n soga, cuerda, f; (hawser) maroma, f; Naut. cabo, m; (tight-rope) cable, m, cuerda de volatinero, f; (string) ristra, sarta, f; hilo, m; pl **ropes,** (boxing) cuerdas del cuadrilátero, f pl. —vt encordelar, atar con cuerdas. **to r. in,** encerrar; (a person) enganchar, coger. **a r. of pearls,** una sarta de perlas. **to give a person plenty of r.,** dar mucha latitud (a). **to know the ropes,** conocer todos los trucos. **r.-ladder,** escala de cuerda, f. **r.-maker,** cordelero (-ra), soguero, m. **r.-making,** cordelería, soguería, f. **r.-trick,** truco de la cuerda, m. **r.-walk,** cordelería, f. **r.-yarn,** Naut. filástica, f
rosary /'rouzəri/ n rosario, m. **to say the r.,** rezar el rosario
rose /rouz/ n rosa, f; color de rosa, m; (rosette) roseta, f; Archit. rosetón, m; (of watering-can) pomo, m, roseta, f. —a de rosa, rosado. **to see the world through r.-colored spectacles,** ver las cosas en color de rosa. **to turn to r.,** volverse color de rosa, rosear. **r.-bay,** Bot. rododafne, adelfa, f. **r.-bush,** rosal, m. **r.-color,** color de rosa, rosa, m. **r.-colored,** de color de rosa, rosado. **r.-garden,** rosalera, rosaleda, f. **r. grower,** cultivador (-ra) de rosas. **r. hip,** escaramujo, m. **r. leaf,** hoja de rosa, f; pétalo de rosa, m. **r.-like,** como una rosa, de rosa. **r.-red,** de color de rosa; como una rosa. **climbing r.-tree,** rosal trepador, m. **dwarf r.-tree,** rosal bajo, m. **standard r.-tree,** rosal de tallo, m. **r.-water,** agua de rosas, f. **r.-window,** rosetón, m, rosa, f. **r.-wood,** palo de rosa, m

rosé a (of wines) rosado
rosebud /'rouz,bʌd/ n capullo de rosa, m
rosemary /'rouz,meəri/ n romero, m
rosin /'rɒzɪn/ n (solid, for violin-bows, etc.) colofonia, f; resina, f. —vt dar con colofonia; dar con resina
rosiness /'rouzɪnɪs/ n color de rosa, m
roster /'rɒstər/ n lista, f; registro, m, matrícula, f
rostrum /'rɒstrəm/ n tribuna, f; Zool. pico, m; (of a ship) espolón, m
rosy /'rouzi/ a róseo, rosado; sonrosado; Fig. de color de rosa, halagüeño; optimista. **r.-cheeked,** con (de) mejillas sonrosadas
rot /rɒt/ n putrefacción, podredumbre, f; (in trees) caries, f; (in sheep) comalía, f; (slang) patrañas, f pl, disparates, m pl, vi pudrirse; descomponerse; Fig. echarse a perder; (slang) decir disparates. —vt pudrir; Fig. corromper; (slang) tomar el pelo (a)
rota /'routə/ n lista, f; orden del día, m
rotary /'routəri/ a rotativo. **r. printing press,** rotativa, f
rotary telephone n teléfono de discado, m
rotate /'routeit/ vi girar, dar vueltas; alternarse. —vt hacer girar
rotating /'routeitɪŋ/ a rotativo; giratorio
rotation /rou'teiʃən/ n rotación, f; turno, m. **in r.,** por turnos. **r. of crops,** rotación de cultivos, f
rotatory /'routə,tɒri/ a rotatorio
rote /rout/ **to learn by r.** vt aprender de memoria, aprender por repetición; aprender de cotorra
rotogravure /,routəgrə'vyʊr/ n rotograbado, m
rotten /'rɒtn/ a putrefacto; podrido; (of bones, teeth) cariado; dañado; echado a perder; Fig. corrompido; (slang) pésimo. **to smell r.,** oler a podredumbre; apestar
rottenness /'rɒtn̩nɪs/ n putrefacción, podredumbre, f; Fig. corrupción, f
rotter /'rɒtər/ n (slang) perdido, m
rotting /'rɒtɪŋ/ n pudrición, f, a que se pudre
rotund /rou'tʌnd/ a rotundo
rotunda /rou'tʌndə/ n rotonda, f
rotundity /rou'tʌndɪti/ n redondez, f; rotundidad, f
roué /ru'ei, 'ruei/ n calavera, libertino, m
rouge /ruʒ/ n colorete, m, vt and vi pintar de rojo, poner(se) colorete
rough /rʌf/ a áspero; duro; (of country) fragoso, escabroso; (uneven) desigual; (stormy) borrascoso, tempestuoso; (of the sea) encrespado, bravo; (of movement) violento; (bristling) erizado; (of the hair) despeinado; (unpolished) tosco; basto; (unskilled) clumsy) torpe; (of sounds, tastes) áspero; (of persons) rudo, inculto; (severe) severo; (of behavior) brutal; (of manners) brusco; (rude) grosero; (approximate) aproximado. —adv duramente, mal. —n estado tosco, m; (person) matón, m. **in the r.,** en bruto; (roughed out) bosquejado. **to grow r.,** (of the sea) encresparse, embravecerse. **to take the r. with the smooth,** Fig. aceptar la realidad; tomar lo bueno con lo malo. **to r. it,** luchar contra las dificultades, pasar apuros; llevar una vida sencilla; vivir mal. **to r. out,** bosquejar. **r. and ready,** improvisado; provisional. **r. and tumble,** n camorra, pendencia, f. **r.-cast,** vt dar una primera capa de mezcla gruesa (a); bosquejar. **r. diamond,** diamante bruto (or en bruto), m. **r.-draft,** borrador, m; bosquejo, m. **r.-haired,** (of a dog) de pelo crespo. **r.-hewn,** modelado toscamente; desbastado; Fig. cerril, tosco. **r.-house,** jarana, f. **r.-rider,** domador (de caballos), m. **r. sketch,** bosquejo, esbozo, m. **r.-spoken,** malhablado
roughen /'rʌfən/ vt poner áspero. —vi ponerse áspero
roughly /'rʌfli/ adv rudamente, toscamente; (of tastes, sounds) brutalmente; bruscamente; (of tastes, sounds) ásperamente; (approximately) aproximadamente, más o menos
roughness /'rʌfnɪs/ n aspereza, f; dureza, f; tosquedad, f; rudeza, f; (of the sea, wind) braveza, f; violencia, f; (of manner) brusquedad, f; brutalidad, f; (vulgarity) grosería, f. **the r. of the way,** la aspereza del camino
roulette /ru'let/ n ruleta, f
round /raund/ a redondo; (plump) rollizo; rotundo, categórico; sonoro. **a r. sum,** una cantidad redonda;

un número redondo. **to walk at a r. pace,** andar a un buen paso. **r. dance,** baile en ruedo, *m.* **r.-faced,** carilleno, de cara redonda. **r.-house,** cuerpo de guardia, *m; Naut.* tumbadillo, *m.* **r.-shouldered,** cargado de espaldas. **r. table,** mesa redonda, *f;* (of King Arthur) Tabla Redonda, *f.* **r. trip,** viaje redondo, viaje de ida y vuelta, *m.* **r.-up,** rodeo de ganado, *m;* arresto, *m*

round /raund/ *n* círculo, *m;* esfera, *f;* redondez, *f;* (slice) rodaja, *f;* (of a ladder) peldaño, *m;* (patrol and *Mil.*) ronda, *f;* circuito, *m;* vuelta, *f,* giro, *m;* serie, *f;* rutina, *f;* (of ammunition) andanada, descarga, *f;* (of cartridge) cartucho con bala, *m;* (of applause, etc.) salva, *f;* (of golf) partido, *m;* (in a fight) asalto, *m; Sports.* vuelta, *f;* (of drinks) ronda, *f;* (doctor's) visitas, *f pl*

round /raund/ *vt* redondear; (*Fig.* complete) acabar, perfeccionar; (go round, e.g. a corner) dar vuelta (a), doblar, trasponer; rodear, cercar; (of a ship) doblar. —*vi* redondearse. **to r. off,** redondear; terminar; coronar. **to r. up,** (cattle) rodear. **to r. upon,** volverse contra

round /raund/ *adv* alrededor, en derredor; por todos lados; a la redonda, en torno; en circunferencia; en conjunto (**r. is not translated in Spanish, e.g.** *I shall come* **r.** *to your house,* Vendré a tu casa). —*prep* alrededor de. **all the year r.,** todo el año, el año entero. **r. about,** a la redonda de, al derredor de; (nearly) cerca de; (of time by the clock) a eso de. **The road is closed and we shall have to go r.,** El camino está cerrado y tendremos que dar una vuelta. **to come r.,** volver; dejarse persuadir; recobrar su buen humor. **to go r.,** (spin) dar vueltas; (of the wind) cambiar. **There is enough to go r.,** Hay bastante para todos

roundabout /a. ,raundə'baut, *n.* 'raundə,baut/ *a* indirecto; desviado; vago. —*n* tiovivo, *m;* (traffic) redondel, *m.* **He spoke in a r. way,** Hablaba con circunloquios. **We went there by a r. way,** Fuimos dando un rodeo

roundly /'raundli/ *adv* en redondo; rotundamente, claramente

roundness /'raundnıs/ *n* redondez, *f;* rotundidad, *f*

rouse /rauz/ *vt* despertar; animar; excitar; suscitar, provocar. **to r. oneself,** despertarse; animarse (a hacer algo)

rousing /'rauzıŋ/ *a* que despierta; (moving) emocionante; (enthusiastic) entusiasta; grande, bueno

rout /raut/ *n* (rabble) chusma, *f;* (party) sarao, *m;* (defeat) derrota, *f;* (meeting) reunión, *f.* —*vt* derrotar, poner en fuga; vencer

route /rut, raut/ *n* ruta, *f;* camino, *m;* itinerario, *m.* **r. march,** marcha de maniobras, *f*

routine /ru'tin/ *n* rutina, *f, a* rutinario, de rutina

rove /rouv/ *vi* vagar, errar

rover /'rouvər/ *n* vagabundo (-da), pirata, *m*

roving /'rouvıŋ/ *a* vagabundo; errante; ambulante

row /rou/ *n* (line) hilera, fila, hila, *f;* (in a theater, etc.) fila, *f;* (string) ristra, *f;* (in a boat) paseo en bote, *m;* (commotion) alboroto, *m;* (noise) ruido, *m;* (shindy) gresca, camorra, *f;* (scolding) regaño, *m, vi* (a boat) remar, bogar. —*vt* conducir remando; (scold) regañar. **to be a row,** (shindy) haber la de San Quintín. **to start a row,** (shindy) armar camorra.

rowboat /'rou,bout/ *n* bote de remos, *m*

rowdiness /'raudınıs/ *n* alboroto, *m*

rowdy /'raudi/ *a* alborotador. —*n* trafalmejas, *mf* rufián, *m*

rower /'rouər/ *n* remero (-ra), bogador (-ra)

rowing /'rouıŋ/ *n* que rema; de remos. —*n* deporte del remo, *m;* paseo en bote, *m.* **r.-boat,** bote de remos, *m.* **r.-club,** club náutico, *m.* **r.-seat,** bancada, *f.* **r.-stroke,** bogada, *f*

royal /'rɔiəl/ *a* real; regio. —*n Naut.* sobrejuanete, *m.* **r. academy,** real academia, *f.* **r. eagle,** águila real, *f.* **R. Highness,** Alteza Real, *f.* **r. letters patent,** cédula real, *f.* **R. Mail,** mala real, *f.* **R. Standard,** estandarte real, *m*

royalism /'rɔiə,lızəm/ *n* realismo, *m*

royalist /'rɔiəlıst/ *a* n realista, *mf*

royally /'rɔiəli/ *adv* realmente; regiamente

royalty /'rɔiəlti/ *n* realeza, *f;* miembro de la familia

real, *m;* tanto por ciento de los ingresos, *m;* derechos de autor, *m pl*

R.R. (abbrev. of *Railroad*) F.R. (abbrev. of *ferrocarril*)

rub /rʌb/ *vt* frotar, estregar; fregar; rozar; friccionar; (make sore) raspar. **to rub one's hands together,** frotarse las manos. **to rub the wrong way,** frotar a contrapelo. **to rub against,** rozar. **to rub along,** *Inf.* ir tirando. **to rub down,** (a horse) bruzar; limpiar; (dry) secar; (wear down) desgastar. **to rub in,** dar fricciones con; frotar con; (an idea, etc.) machacar. **to rub off,** *vt* quitar (frotando); borrar. —*vi* borrarse; separarse (de). **to rub out,** *vt* borrar. —*vi* borrarse. **to rub up,** (polish) limpiar; *Fig.* refrescar

rub /rʌb/ *n* frotación, *f;* roce, *m;* fricción, *f; Fig.* obstáculo, *m;* dificultad, *f.* **to give a rub,** frotar, etc.

rub-a-dub, rataplán, *m*

rubber /'rʌbər/ *a* de caucho, de goma. —*n* caucho, *m,* goma, *f;* (for erasing) goma de borrar, *f;* (masseur) masajista, *mf;* (at whist, etc.) partida, *f; pl* **rubbers,** zapatos de goma, chanclos, *m pl.* **synthetic r.,** caucho artificial, *m.* **r. band,** goma, banda de goma, *f.* **r. belt,** *Mech.* correa de transmisión de caucho, *f.* **r.-plant, tree,** cauchera, *f.* **r. plantation,** cauchal, *m.* **r. planter,** cauchero, *m.* **r. stamp,** estampilla, *f*

rubbing /'rʌbıŋ/ *n* frotación, *f;* fricción, *f;* roce, *m;* (of floors, dishes, etc.) fregado, *m*

rubbish /'rʌbıʃ/ *n* basura, *f;* desperdicios, *m pl,* desecho, *m;* (of goods) pacotilla, *f;* (nonsense) pamplinas, patrañas, *f pl,* disparates, *m pl.* **r. cart,** carro del basurero, *m*

rubbishy /'rʌbıʃi/ *a* sin valor, malo; (of goods) de pacotilla, de calidad inferior

rubble /'rʌbəl/ *n* escombros, *m pl;* cascote, *m;* piedra bruta, *f*

rubicund /'rubı,kʌnd/ *a* rubicundo

ruble /'rublei/ *n* rublo, *m*

rubric /'rubrık/ *n* rúbrica, *f*

ruby /'rubi/ *n* rubí, *m.* —*a* de rubíes; de rubí. **r. lips,** labios de rubí, *m pl*

rucksack /'rʌk,sæk, 'rʊk-/ *n* mochila, *f*

rudder /'rʌdər/ *n* timón, gobernalle, *m*

ruddiness /'rʌdinıs/ *n* rubicundez, *f;* rojez, *f;* frescura, *f*

ruddy /'rʌdi/ *a* rubicundo; rojo; frescote; (of animals) barcino

rude /rud/ *a* rudo; tosco; vigoroso; grosero, descortés

rudely /'rudli/ *adv* toscamente; groseramente

rudeness /'rudnıs/ *n* rudeza, *f;* tosquedad, *f;* grosería, incivilidad, descortesía, *f*

rudiment /'rudəmənt/ *n* rudimento, *m*

rudimentary /,rudə'mɛntəri/ *a* rudimentario

rue /ru/ *vt* lamentar, llorar. —*n Bot.* ruda, *f*

rueful /'rufəl/ *a* triste, melancólico; lamentable

ruefully /'rufəli/ *adv* tristemente

ruefulness /'rufəlnıs/ *n* tristeza, *f*

ruff /rʌf/ *n* golilla, lechuguilla, *f;* (of a bird) collarín de plumas, *m;* (of an animal) collarín de pelo, *m*

ruffian /'rʌfiən/ *n* rufián, *m*

ruffle /'rʌfəl/ *n Sew.* volante fruncido, *m;* (of a bird) collarín de plumas, *m;* (of an animal) collarín de pelo, *m;* (ripple) rizo, *m;* (annoyance) irritación, *f.* —*vt* (ripple) rizar; (pleat) fruncir; (feathers) erizar; (hair) despeinar; agitar; (annoy) irritar, incomodar

ruffling /'rʌflıŋ/ *n* (rippling) rizado, *m;* (pleating) fruncido, *m;* (of the temper) irritación, *f*

rug /rʌg/ *n* (floor) alfombra, *f;* manta de viaje, *f.* **rug strap,** portamantas, *m*

rugged /'rʌgıd/ *a* áspero, escabroso; escarpado, abrupto; (wrinkled) arrugado; tosco; (harsh) duro, severo; inculto; rudo; mal acabado; vigoroso

ruggedness /'rʌgıdnıs/ *n* aspereza, escabrosidad, *f;* lo escarpado; dureza, severidad, *f;* rudeza, *f;* vigor, *m*

ruin /'ruın/ *n* ruina, *f.* —*vt* arruinar; echar a perder, estropear por completo; (a woman) perder

ruination /,ruə'neiʃən/ *n* ruina, perdición, *f*

ruined /'ruınd/ *a* arruinado; en ruinas

ruinous /'ruənəs/ *a* ruinoso; en ruinas

ruinously /'ruənəsli/ *adv* ruinosamente

rule /rul/ *n* regla, *f;* gobierno, *m;* autoridad, *f;* mando, *m;* administración, *f;* (reign) reinado, *m;* (of a court, etc.) orden, *f;* (for measuring) regla, *f; Print.*

regleta, *f; pl* **rules,** reglas, *f pl;* reglamento, *m.* —*vt* gobernar; regentar, regir; (control) dominar; (of a chairman, etc.) disponer, decidir; (guide) guiar; (lines) reglar. —*vi* gobernar; (of a monarch) reinar; (of prices) mantenerse; estar en boga, prevalecer. **as a r.,** por regla general, en general. **slide-r.,** regla de cálculo, *f.* **to make it a r.,** tener por regla; tener por costumbre; tener por máxima. **to r. out,** excluir; *Law.* no admitir. **to r. over,** (of a king, etc.) reinar sobre. **r. of the road,** reglamento del tráfico, *m.* **r. of thumb,** regla empírica, *f;* rutina, *f*

ruler /'rʊlər/ *n* gobernador (-ra); soberano (-na); (master) amo (ama); (for ruling lines) regla, *f*

ruling /'rʊlɪŋ/ *a* regente; dominante; (current) vigente. —*n* gobierno, *m; Law.* decisión, *f,* fallo, *m;* (with lines) rayado, *m.* **r. pen,** tiralíneas, *m*

rum /rʌm/ *n* ron, *m*

rumble /'rʌmbəl/ *vi* retumbar, tronar; (of vehicles) rugir; crujir. —*n* retumbo, trueno, *m;* rugido, *m;* ruido sordo, *m;* rumor, *m;* crujido, *m*

rumbling /'rʌmblɪŋ/ *a* que retumba, etc. —*n* ruido sordo, *m;* retumbo, *m;* crujido, *m;* (in the bowels) rugido, *m*

ruminant /'rumənənt/ *a and n* rumiante, *mf*

ruminate /'rumə,neɪt/ *vi and vt* rumiar

rumination /,rumə'neɪʃən/ *n* rumia, *f;* meditación, reflexión, *f*

rummage /'rʌmɪdʒ/ *vt* revolver, desordenar, trastornar; explorar. **to r. out,** desenterrar

rumor /'rumər/ *n* rumor, *m,* fama, *f.* **It is rumored that...,** Hay rumores de que..., La voz corre que..., Se dice que...

rump /rʌmp/ *n* (of an animal) nalgas, ancas, *f pl;* cuarto trasero, *m;* (of a bird) rabadilla, *f;* (scornful) culo, *m,* posaderas, *f pl.* **r.-steak,** solomillo, *m*

rumple /'rʌmpəl/ *vt* arrugar; desordenar

run /rʌn/ *vi* correr; acudir; (flee) huir; (rush) precipitarse, lanzarse; (in a race) tomar parte en una carrera; competir; (pass over) deslizarse (por); (of machines) andar, marchar; (of traffic) circular; (leave, of trains, ships, lines) salir; (ply between) hacer el trayecto entre... y...; (flow) fluir, correr; (into the sea, of rivers) desembocar (en); (spurt) chorrear, manar; (drip) gotear; (leak) dejar fugar (el agua, etc.); (of colors) correrse; caer; (of tears) correr; derramarse; (of eyes) llorar; (melt) derretirse; (of a sore) supurar; (travel or go) ir; moverse; (work) trabajar; funcionar; (of editions of a book) agotarse; (of a play) representarse; (cross) cruzar; (elapse) correr; transcurrir, pasar; (become) hacerse; (of wording) decir; (be current) correr; (for parliament, etc.) hacerse candidato; (navigate) navegar; (spread) extenderse; (be) estar; ser; (of thoughts) pasar; (last) durar; (tend) tender (a). —*vt* (a race, a horse) correr; (drive) conducir; (a business, etc.) administrar; dirigir; (govern) gobernar, regir; (hunt) cazar; perseguir; (water, etc.) hacer correr; (pierce) clavar; introducir; (push) empujar; (one's hand, eye, etc.) pasar; (risks, etc.) correr; (possess) tener; establecer un servicio de (autobuses, etc.); (smuggle) hacer contrabando de. **The ship ran aground,** El barco encalló. **to run dry,** secarse; agotarse. **to run in the family,** estar en la familia. **to run into debt,** endeudarse, contraer deudas. **to run to seed,** granar; agotarse. **Steamers run daily between Barcelona and Mallorca,** Hay servicio diario de vapores entre Barcelona y Mallorca. **A stab of pain ran up his leg,** Sintió un dolor agudo en la pierna. **Feeling was running high,** Los ánimos estaban excitados. **My arrangements ran smoothly,** Mis planes marchaban bien. **Funds are running low,** El dinero escasea. **The tune runs in my head,** Tengo la canción metida en la cabeza. **The message runs like this,** El mensaje reza así, El mensaje dice así. **He ran his fingers through his hair,** Se mesaba los cabellos. **to run about,** andar de un lado a otro, correr por todas partes; (gad) corretear. **to run across,** cruzar corriendo; (meet) topar con, tropezar con. **to run after,** correr detrás (de); perseguir; buscar. **to run against,** (collide with) dar contra; (meet) tropezar con. **to run at,** abalanzarse hacia, precipitarse sobre; atacar. **to run away,** huir, escaparse; (slip away) escurrirse; (of a horse) dispararse, desbocarse. **to run away with,**

huir con, fugarse con; (carry off) arrebatar; (steal) llevarse; (imagine) imaginarse, figurarse, (of temper, etc.) dominar, poseer. **to run back,** volver corriendo; llegar corriendo; retroceder rápidamente, correr hacia atrás. **to run backwards,** correr hacia atrás; **to run backwards and forwards,** ir y venir. **to run behind,** correr detrás (de); quedarse atrás; (be late) estar atrasado. **to run down,** *vi* bajar corriendo; descender, bajar; (of a clock) parar; (of a battery) gastarse; (of liquids) correr; fluir; (drop by drop) destilar. —*vt* (capture) coger; alcanzar; (a person by a vehicle) atropellar; (a ship) echar a pique; (disparage) hablar mal de. **run-down,** (in health) agotado; (of a clock) parado. **to run for,** buscar corriendo; correr para coger (el autobús, etc.); (president, etc.) ser candidato para. **to run in,** *vi* entrar corriendo. —*vt* arrestar; hacer prisionero; *Print.* encerrar. **to run into,** tropezar con; chocar con; (plunge into) meterse de cabeza en; (of sums of money, etc.) ascender a; (of streets, rivers, etc.) desembocar en. **to run off,** *vi* escaparse corriendo; marcharse corriendo. —*vt* deslizarse por; (drain) vaciar; *Print.* imprimir; (compose) componer. **to run off with,** huir con. **to run on,** correr delante; continuar; (of the mind) pensar en, entregarse a; hablar sin cesar; *Print.* recorrer. **to run out,** *vi* salir corriendo; (of liquids) derramarse; salir; (end) acabarse; agotarse; (project) sobresalir. —*vt* (cricket) coger al lanzador fuera de la línea de saque. **to run out of,** no tener más de, haber terminado. **to run over,** *vi* rebosar; derramarse. —*vt* (of a vehicle) atropellar, pasar por encima de; (peruse) repasar; revisar. **run pell-mell,** salir pitando, salir volando, salvarse por pies. **to run through,** correr por; pasar por; recorrer; (go directly) ir directamente (a); (pierce) traspasar, pasar de parte a parte; (squander) derrochar, malbaratar; (read) hojear, leer por encima. **to run up,** *vt* (hoist) izar; hacer de prisa; construir rápidamente; (incur) incurrir. —*vi* subir corriendo; (of plants) trepar (por); (shrink) encogerse; (of expenses) aumentar. **to run up to time,** llegar a su hora. **to run up against,** tropezar con; (opposition, etc.) encontrar.

run /rʌn/ *n* carrera, corrida, *f;* (excursion) visita, excursión, *f;* (cricket) carrera, *f;* (walk) paseo, *m;* (by train or sea) viaje, *m;* (by bus, tram) trayecto, *m;* (sea crossing) travesía, *f;* (distance run) recorrido, *m;* (of events, etc.) curso, *m;* marcha, *f;* (of markets, etc.) tendencia, *f;* (rhythm) ritmo, *m;* dirección, *f;* distancia, *f; Mus.* serie de notas, *f;* serie, *f;* duración, *f; Theat.* serie de representaciones, *f;* (freedom to use) libre uso, *m;* (majority) mayoría, *f;* (on a bank) asedio, *m;* (on a book, etc.) d > f; (for sheep, etc.) terreno de pasto, *m;* (for fowls) gallinero, *m.* **a run of bad luck,** una temporada de mala suerte. **at a run,** corriendo. **in the long run,** a la larga, al fin y al cabo. **on the run,** en fuga; ocupado. **Prices came down with a run,** Los precios bajaron de golpe. **take-off run,** *Aer.* recorrido de despegue, *m*

runaway /'rʌnə,weɪ/ *a* fugitivo; (of a horse) desbocado

rune /run/ *n* runa, *f*

rung /rʌŋ/ *n* (of a ladder) peldaño, *f;* (of a chair) travesaño, *m;* (lath) listón, *m*

runic /'runɪk/ *a* rúnico

runner /'rʌnər/ *n* corredor (-ra); (carrier of sedan chair, etc.) silletero, *mf;* (smuggler) contrabandista, *m;* (courier) estafeta, *f;* (messenger) mensajero, *m;* (ring) anillo movible, pasador corredizo, *m;* rueda móvil, *f;* (of a sledge) patín, *m; Bot.* tallo rastrero, *m.* **r.-up,** el segundo

running /'rʌnɪŋ/ *a* corredor; (of water, bank accounts) corriente; (of a knot) corredizo; (of a sore) supurante; (continuous) continuo; (consecutive) consecutivo. —*n* carrera, *f;* marcha, *f;* funcionamiento, *m;* administración, *f;* gobierno, *m;* dirección, *f;* (flowing) derrame, *m;* (of trains, buses, etc.) servicio, *m;* (smuggling) contrabando, *m;* (of a sore) supuración, *f.* **six times r.,** seis veces consecutivas. **The car is in r. order,** El auto está en buen estado. **r. away,** fuga, *f.* **r.-board,** (of a car, etc.) estribo, *m;* (of a locomotive) plataforma, *f.* **r. costs,** gastos de mantenimiento, *m pl;* (railway) gastos de tracción, *m pl.* **r.**

fight, acción de retirada, *f.* **r.-knot,** lazo corredizo, *m.* **r. title,** *Print.* título de la columna, *m*

run-off match /'rʌnɔf/ *n* desempate, *m*

runway /'rʌn,weɪ/ *n* (for launching a ship) grada, *f;* (of an airfield) pista de aterrizaje, *f*

rupee /ru'pi, 'rupi/ *n* rupia, *f*

rupestrian /ru'pɛstriən/ *a* rupestre

rupture /'rʌptʃər/ *n* rompimiento, *m,* rotura, *f;* ruptura, *f; med* hernia, *f*

ruptured /'rʌptʃərd/ *a med* herniado, quebrado

rupturing /'rʌptʃərɪŋ/ *n* ruptura, *f*

rural /'rʊrəl/ *a* rural, campestre, del campo; agrario

ruse /ruz/ *n* artimaña, treta, ardid, *f*

rush /rʌʃ/ *n Bot.* junco, *m;* acometida, *f;* ataque, *m;* (of water) torrente, *m;* (bustle) bullicio, *m;* (speed) prisa, *f;* precipitación, *f;* acceso, *m;* (crowd) tropel, *m,* masa, *f;* (struggle) lucha, *f;* furia, *f.* —*vi* precipitarse, lanzarse; agolparse. —*vt* llevar rápidamente (a); despachar rápidamente; precipitar; (attack) asaltar, atacar; (capture) tomar, capturar; hacer de prisa; (a bill) hacer aprobar de prisa. **to r. upon,** abalanzarse hacia; embestir. **in a r.,** en tropel, en masa; de prisa. **to r. to a conclusion,** precipitarse a una conclusión. **r.-bottomed,** con asiento de enea. **r. hour,** hora de mayor circulación, *f,* hora de aglomeración, hora-pico (Argentina), hora brava (Argentina, informal). **r. order,** pedido urgente, *m*

rushy /'rʌʃi/ *a* juncoso

russet /'rʌsɪt/ *a* rojizo; rojo. **r. apple,** manzana asperiega, *f*

Russia /'rʌʃə/ Rusia, *f*

Russian /'rʌʃən/ *a* ruso. —*n* ruso (-sa); (language) ruso, *m.* **R. leather,** piel de Rusia, *f*

rust /rʌst/ *n* herrumbre, *f,* orín, *m;* moho, *m;* (disease) añublo, tizón, *m.* —*vt* aherrumbrar; enmohecer. —*vi* aherrumbrarse; enmohecerse

rustic /'rʌstɪk/ *a* rústico; campesino, aldeano; (scornful) palurdo, grosero. —*n* aldeano, *m;* (scornful) patán, *m*

rusticate /'rʌstɪ,keɪt/ *vi* rusticar, vivir en el campo. —*vt* enviar al campo

rustication /,rʌstɪ'keɪʃən/ *n* rusticación, *f*

rusticity /rʌ'stɪsɪti/ *n* rusticidad, *f*

rustiness /'rʌstɪnɪs/ *n* herrumbre, *f;* enmohecimiento, *m;* color rojizo, *m; Fig.* falta de práctica, *f*

rustle /'rʌsəl/ *n* susurro, *m;* murmurio, *m;* (of silk, a dress, etc.) frufrú, *m;* (of paper, etc.) crujido, *m.* —*vi* susurrar; murmurar; crujir. —*vt* (a paper) hacer crujir

rustless /'rʌstlɪs/ *a* inoxidable

rustling /'rʌslɪŋ/ *n* see **rustle**

rusty /'rʌsti/ *a* herrumbroso; enmohecido, mohoso; (red) rojizo, (worn out) usado, viejo; (out of practice) desacostumbrado; (forgotten) empolvorado, oxidado (e.g. *My Portuguese is rusty,* Mi portugués está empolvorado)

rut /rʌt/ *n* rodera, *f,* bache, surco, *m; fig* sendero trillado, *m; fig* rutina, *f;* (sexual appetite) celo, *m, vi* estar en celo

ruthless /'ruθlɪs/ *a* inhumano, insensible, despiadado; inexorable, inflexible

ruthlessly /'ruθlɪsnɪs/ *adv* inhumanamente; inflexiblemente, inexorablemente

ruthlessness *n* inhumanidad, *f;* inflexibilidad, inexorabilidad, *f*

Rwanda /ru'ɑndə/ Ruanda, *f*

rye /raɪ/ *n* centeno, *m.* **rye field,** centenar, *m*

S

s /ɛs/ n (letter) ese, f
sabbatarian /ˌsæbə'tɛəriən/ a sabatario
Sabbath /'sæbəθ/ n (Jewish) sábado, m; (Christian) domingo, m
sabbatical /sə'bætɪkəl/ a sabático
saber /'seibər/ n sable, m; (soldier) jinete, m. —vt dar sablazos (a), acuchillar. **s. cut, thrust,** sablazo, m
sable /'seibəl/ n (animal and fur) marta, f; herald sable, m. —a herald sable; poet negro
sabotage /'sæbəˌtɑʒ/ n sabotaje, m, vt cometer un acto de sabotaje en
saboteur /ˌsæbə'tɜr/ n saboteador, m
sac /sæk/ n biol saco, m
saccharin /'sækərɪn/ n sacarina, f
sachet /sæ'ʃei/ n sachet, m; bolsa, f. **handkerchief s.,** bolsa para pañuelos, f
sack /sæk/ n (bag) saco, m; mil saqueo, saqueamiento, saco, m. —vt meter en sacos; (dismiss) dar pasaporte (a), despedir; mil saquear. **to get the s.,** recibir el pasaporte. **to give the s.,** dar el pasaporte (a), poner de patitas en la calle (a). **s. coat,** saco, m
sackcloth /'sæk,klɔθ/ n harpillera, f. **to repent in s. and ashes,** ponerse cenizas en la cabeza
sacking /'sækɪŋ/ n harpillera, f; mil saqueo, m
sacrament /'sækrəmənt/ n sacramento, m; Eucaristía, f. **the Blessed S.,** el Santísimo Sacramento. **to receive the Holy S.,** comulgar. **to receive the last sacraments,** recibir los sacramentos, recibir la Extremaunción
sacramental /ˌsækrə'mɛntl/ a sacramental
sacramentalist /ˌsækrə'mɛntlɪst/ n sacramentario (-ia)
sacred /'seikrɪd/ a sagrado; sacro, santo; consagrado. **Nothing is s. to them,** No hay nada sagrado para ellos, No respetan nada. **the S. Heart of Jesus,** el Sagrado Corazón (de Jesús). **S. to the memory of...** Consagrado a la memoria de... **s. music,** música sagrada, f
sacredness /'seikrɪdnɪs/ n carácter sagrado, m; santidad, f; inviolabilidad, f
sacrifice /'sækrəˌfais/ n sacrificio, m. —vt and vi sacrificar. **s. of the mass,** sacrificio del altar, m
sacrificial /ˌsækrə'fɪʃəl/ a sacrificador; del sacrificio
sacrilege /'sækrəlɪdʒ/ n sacrilegio, m
sacrilegious /ˌsækrə'lɪdʒəs/ a sacrílego
sacristan /'sækrɪstən/ n sacristán, m
sacristy /'sækrɪsti/ n sacristía, f
sacrosanct /'sækrou,sæŋkt/ a sacrosanto
sacrum /'sækrəm, 'seikrəm/ n anat sacro, m
sad /sæd/ a triste; melancólico; (of a mistake) deplorable, funesto; Inf. redomado; (pensive) pensativo. **How s.!** ¡Qué lástima! ¡Qué triste! **It made me s.,** Me entristeció
sadden /'sædn/ vt entristecer, acongojar, afligir
saddle /'sædl/ n (riding) silla de montar, f; (of a bicycle, etc.) sillín, m; mech silla, f; Anat. espalda, f. —vt ensillar. **to s. with the responsibility of,** echar la responsabilidad de (a). **s. of mutton,** lomo de carnero, m. **s.-bag,** alforja, f. **s.-cloth,** mantilla de silla, f. **s.-tree,** arzón, m
saddler /'sædlər/ n sillero, guarnicionero, m
Sadducee /'sædʒə,si/ n saduceo (-ea)
sadism /'seidɪzəm/ n sadismo, m
sadist /'seidɪst/ n sadista, mf
sadistic /sə'dɪstɪk/ a sadístico
sadly /'sædli/ adv tristemente; (very) muy
sadness /'sædnɪs/ n tristeza, melancolía, f
safe /seif/ a al abrigo (de); seguro; salvo; (certain) cierto; prudente; digno de confianza. —n caja de caudales, f; (for food) alacena, f. **I stood beneath a tree s. from the rain,** Estaba de pie bajo un árbol, al abrigo de la lluvia. **to put something in a s. place,** poner algo en salvo; poner algo en un lugar seguro. **s. and sound,** sano y salvo. **s.-conduct,** salvoconducto, m. **s.-keeping,** lugar seguro, m; (of a person) buenas manos, f pl

safeguard /'seif,gɑrd/ n protección, garantía, f; precaución, f. —vt proteger, guardar; tomar precauciones (contra)
safely /'seifli/ adv seguramente; sin accidente, sin novedad, sano y salvo; sin peligro. **You may s. tell him,** Puedes decírselo con toda seguridad. **to put (something) away s.,** poner (algo) en un lugar seguro
safety /'seifti/ n seguridad, f. —a de seguridad; (of locks) de golpe. **a place of s.,** un lugar seguro. **in s.,** en salvo, en seguro; con seguridad. **to believe in s. first,** poner la seguridad en primer lugar. **to play for s.,** jugar seguro. **with complete s.,** con toda seguridad. **s.-belt,** (cinto) salvavidas, m. **s.-catch,** fiador, m. **s.-curtain,** telón de seguridad, telón contra incendios, m. **s.-fuse,** espoleta de seguridad, f. **s.-glass,** vidrio inastillable, m. **s.-island,** refugio para peatones, m. **s.-lamp,** lámpara de seguridad, f. **s.-latch,** pestillo de golpe, m. **s.-lock,** (of fire-arms) seguro, m; (of doors, etc.) cerradura de seguridad, f. **s.-pin,** imperdible, m. **s.-razor,** máquina de afeitar, f. **s.-valve,** válvula de seguridad, f
saffron /'sæfrən/ n azafrán, m, a azafranado, de color de azafrán
sag /sæg/ vi doblegarse, ceder; inclinarse; naut caer a sotavento; (of prices) bajar; (of spirits, etc.) flaquear
saga /'sɑgə/ n saga, f; epopeya, f
sagacious /sə'geiʃəs/ a sagaz, perspicaz; (of animals) sabio
sagacity /sə'gæsɪti/ n sagacidad, perspicacia, f; (of animals) sagacidad, f
sage /seidʒ/ n sabio, m; bot salvia, f. —a sabio; sagaz; cuerdo
Sagittarius /ˌsædʒɪ'tɛəriəs/ n Sagitario, m
Sahara, the /sə'hærə/ el Sáhara, m
said /sɛd/ a antedicho; tal dicho. **No sooner s. than done,** Dicho y hecho. **the s. Mr. Martínez,** el tal Sr. Martínez
sail /seil/ n (of a ship) vela, f; (sailing-ship) velero, m; (of a windmill) aspa, f; mech ala, f; (trip) paseo en barco, m. —vi navegar; ir en barco; dar un paseo en barco; (leave) salir en barco; zarpar; (of swans, etc.) deslizarse; (of clouds, etc.) flotar. —vt (a ship) gobernar; (the sea) navegar por. **She sailed into the room,** Entró majestuosamente en la sala. **The ship sailed at eight knots,** El buque navegaba a ocho nudos. **to go for a s.,** dar un paseo en barco. **to s. round the world,** dar la vuelta al mundo. **to s. the seas,** navegar por los mares. **to set s.,** darse a la vela, zarpar. **to take in the sails,** amainar. **s.-maker,** velero, m. **to s. into,** entrar en. **to s. round,** (the Cape, etc.) doblar. **to s. up,** subir en barco; (of a boat) ir río arriba
sailcloth /'seil,klɔθ/ n lona, f
sailing /'seilɪŋ/ n navegación, f; (departure) salida, f. **It's all plain s.,** Todo va viento en popa. **s.-boat,** bote de vela, m. **s.-ship,** buque de vela, velero, m
sailor /'seilər/ n marinero, m. **John is a bad s.,** Juan se marea fácilmente. **to be a good s.,** no marearse. **s.-blouse,** marinera, f. **s.-suit,** traje de marinero, m
saint /seint/ n santo (-ta); (before masculine names of Sts., excluding Sts. Dominic and Thomas) San; Inf. ángel, m. **All Saints' Day,** el día de Todos los Santos. **saint's day,** fiesta de un santo (or de una santa), f; (of a person) santo, m. **St. Bernard dog,** perro de San Bernardo, m. **St. John the Baptist,** San Juan Bautista. **St. Martin's summer,** el veranillo de San Martín. **St. Vitus's dance,** el baile de San Vito
sainthood /'seinthʊd/ n santidad, f
saintliness /'seintlɪnɪs/ n santidad, f
saintly /'seintli/ a de santo; de santa; santo; inf angelical
Saint Petersburg /seint 'pitərz,bɜrg/ San Petersburgo, m
sake /seik/ n amor, m; causa, f. **for God's s.,** por el amor de Dios. **for the s. of,** para; por amor de. **to talk for talking's s.,** hablar por hablar

salable /'seiləbəl/ a vendible
salaciousness /sə'leiʃəsnɪs/ n salacidad, f
salad /'sæləd/ n ensalada, f; (lettuce) lechuga, f. **fruit s.,** macedonia de frutas, f. **s.-bowl,** ensaladera, f. **s.-dressing,** aderezo, aliño, m, salsa para ensalada, f. **s.-oil,** aceite para ensaladas, m
salamander /'sælə,mændər/ n salamandra, f
salaried /'sælərid/ a a sueldo; (of posts) retribuido
salary /'sæləri/ n sueldo, salario, m
sale /seil/ n venta, f; (auction) almoneda, subasta pública, f. **clearance s.,** liquidación, f, saldo, m. **to be on s.,** estar de venta. **"Piano for s.,"** «Se vende un piano.» **s. price,** precio de venta, m; precio de saldo, m
sales contract n contrato de compraventa, m
salesman /'seilzmən/ n dependiente de tienda, m; (traveller) viajante, m
salesmanship /'seilzmən,ʃip/ n arte de vender, mf
salesroom /'seilz,rum/ n salón de ventas, m
saleswoman /'seilz,wumən/ n dependienta de tienda, vendedera, f
salient /'seiliənt/ a saliente; Fig. prominente, conspicuo, notable, n saliente, m. **s. angle,** ángulo saliente, m
saline /'seilin/ a salino. —n (marsh) saladar, m; med salino, m
saliva /sə'laivə/ n saliva, f
salivary /'sælə,veri/ a salival
salivate /'sælə,veit/ vi salivar
salivation /,sælə'veiʃən/ n salivación, f
sallow /'sælou/ a cetrino, oliváceo, lívido
sallowness /'sælounɪs/ n amarillez, lividez, f; palidez, f
sally /'sæli/ n (mil. etc) salida, f; (quip) ocurrencia, salida, f. —vi hacer una salida, salir. **to s. forth,** ponerse en camino
salmon /'sæmən/ n salmón, m; color de salmón, m. **s.-net,** salmonera, f. **s. trout,** trucha asalmonada, f
salon /sə'lɒn/ n salón, m
Salonika /sə'lɒnɪkə/ Salónica, f
saloon /sə'lun/ n sala, f; (of a steamer) cámara, f, salón, m; (on train, for sleeping) departamento de coche cama, m; (on train, for dining) coche comedor, m; auto coche cerrado, m. **billiard s.,** salón de billares, m. **dancing s.,** salón de baile, m. **hair-dresser's s.,** salón de peluquero, m. **s. bar,** bar, m
salsify /'sælsəfi/ n bot salsifí, m
salt /sɔlt/ n sal, f; (spice) sabor, m; (wit) sal, agudeza, f. —a salobre, salino; salado; (of land) salitroso. —vt (season) poner sal en; (cure) salar. **kitchen s.,** sal de cocina, f. **old s.,** inf lobo de mar, m. **rock s.,** sal gema, f. **sea s.,** sal marina, f. **to be not worth one's s.,** no merecer el pan que se come. **to take with a pinch of s.,** tomar con su grano de sal. **s.-cellar,** salero, m. **s. lagoon,** albufera, f. **s. lake,** lago salado, m. **s. marsh,** saladar, m. **s. meat,** carne salada, cecina, f. **s. merchant,** salinero, m. **s. mine,** mina de sal, f. **s.-spoon,** cucharita de sal, f. **s. water,** agua salada, f; agua de mar, f. **s.-water fish,** pez de mar, m. **s.-works,** salinas, f pl
saltiness /'sɔltinɪs/ n sabor de sal, m; salobridad, f
salting /'sɔltɪŋ/ n saladura, f; (salt marsh) saladar, m
saltless /'sɔltlɪs/ a sin sal, soso, insípido; Fig. soso
saltpeter /,sɔlt'pitər/ n salitre, m. **s. bed,** salitral, m. **s. works,** salitrería, f
salty /'sɔlti/ a salado; salobre
salubrious /sə'lubriəs/ a salubre, saludable, sano
salubriousness /sə'lubriəsnɪs/ n salubridad, f
salutary /'sælyə,teri/ a saludable, beneficioso
salutation /,sælyə'teiʃən/ n salutación, f, saludo, m
salute /sə'lut/ vt and vi saludar. —n saludo, m; (of guns) salva, f. **to fire a s.,** hacer salvas, saludar con... salvas. **The soldier saluted them,** El soldado les saludó. **to take the s.,** tomar el saludo. **saluting base,** puesto de mando, m
Salvadoran, Salvadorian /,sælvə'dɔrən; -'dɔriən/ a and n salvadoreño (-ña)
salvage /'sælvɪdʒ/ n salvamento, m, vt salvar
salvation /sæl'veiʃən/ n salvación, f. **to work out one's own s.,** salvar el alma. **the S. Army,** el Ejército de la Salvación, m
salve /sælv/ n pomada, f; fig bálsamo, m. —vt curar;

(overcome) vencer; (soothe) tranquilizar; naut salvar. **to s. one's conscience,** tranquilizar la conciencia
salver /'sælvər/ n salva, bandeja, f
salvo /'sælvou/ n (of guns or applause) salva, f; (reservation) salvedad, reservación, f. **s. of applause,** salva de aplausos, f
Samaritan /sə'mærɪtn/ a and n samaritano (-na)
same /seim/ a mismo; igual; parecido; idéntico. —adv lo mismo; del mismo modo. **all the s.,** sin embargo; con todo, a pesar de eso. **at the s. time,** al mismo tiempo; a la vez. **just the s.,** igual; (nevertheless) sin embargo. **He bowed deeply and I did the s.,** Él hizo una profunda reverencia y yo hice lo mismo. **They do not look at things the s. as we do,** No ven las cosas del mismo modo que nosotros. **If it is the s. to her,** Si le da igual. **It's all the s.,** Es igual, Lo mismo da, Es todo uno. **Ávila, capital of the province of the s. name,** Ávila, capital de la provincia de su nombre
"Same-Day Service" /'seimdei/ «En el día» (Argentina)
sameness /'seimnɪs/ n identidad, f; semejanza, f, parecido, m; monotonía, f
samovar /'sæmə,vɑr/ n samovar, m
sampan /'sæmpæn/ n (boat) champán, m
sample /'sæmpəl/ n muestra, f; prueba, f; ejemplo, m. —vt sacar una muestra de; (try) probar. **s. book,** muestrario, m
sampler /'sæmplər/ n probador, m; (of wines) catador, m; sew dechado, m
sanatorium /,sænə'tɔriəm/ n sanatorio, m
sanctification /,sæŋktəfɪ'keiʃən/ n santificación, f; consagración, f
sanctify /'sæŋktə,fai/ vt santificar; consagrar
sanctimonious /,sæŋktə'mouniəs/ a santurrón, mojigato, beato
sanctimoniousness /,sæŋktə'mouniəsnɪs/ n beatería, mojigatería, santurronería, f
sanction /'sæŋkʃən/ n sanción, f. —vt sancionar; autorizar. **to apply sanctions,** polit aplicar sanciones
sanctity /'sæŋktɪti/ n santidad, f; lo sagrado; inviolabilidad, f. **odor of s.,** olor de santidad, f
sanctuary /'sæŋktʃu,eri/ n santuario, m; (historical) sagrado, sagrado asilo, m; refugio, asilo, m. **to take s.,** acogerse a sagrado; refugiarse
sand /sænd/ n arena, f; (for drying writing) arenilla, f; granos de arena, m pl; pl **sands,** playa, f; (of life) horas de la vida, f pl. —vt arenar. **to plough the s.,** arar en el mar. **s.-bag,** n saco de arena, m. —vt (a building) proteger con sacos de arena; (a person) golpear con un saco de arena. **s.-bank,** banco de arena, m, barra, f. **to run on a s.-bank,** encallar. **s.-colored,** de color de arena. **s.-dune,** médano, m. **s.-paper,** n papel de lija, m. —vt pulir con papel de lija, lijar. **s.-pit,** arenal, m. **s. shoes,** alpargatas, f pl
sandal /'sændl/ n sandalia, f; (rope-soled) alpargata, f. **s.-wood,** sándalo, m
sandiness /'sændinɪs/ n naturaleza arenosa, f; (of hair) color bermejo, m
sandstone /'sænd,stoun/ n arenisca, f
sandstorm /'sænd,stɔrm/ n tempestad de arena, f; simún, m
sandwich /'sændwɪtʃ, 'sæn-/ n emparedado, bocadillo, m. —vt insertar. **I found myself sandwiched between two fat men,** Me encontré aplastado entre dos hombres gordos. **s.-man,** hombre sándwich, m
sandy /'sændi/ a arenoso; sabuloso; (of hair) rojo, rufo, bermejo. **a s. beach,** una playa arenosa
sane /sein/ a de juicio sano; razonable, prudente; sesudo. **He is a very s. person,** Es un hombre con mucho sentido común. **to be s.,** estar en su juicio; (of a policy, etc.) ser prudente, ser razonable
sangfroid /san'frwa/ n sangre fría, f; aplomo, m
sanguinary /'sæŋgwə,neri/ a sanguinario
sanguine /'sæŋgwɪn/ a (of complexion) rubicundo; sanguíneo; optimista, confiado. —n (drawing) sanguina, f. **to be s. about the future,** ser optimista acerca del porvenir, tener confianza en el porvenir
sanhedrin /sæn'hedrɪn/ n sanedrín, m
sanitary /'sænɪ,teri/ a sanitario; higiénico, **s. inspector,** inspector de sanidad, m. **s. napkin, s. towel,** ser-

villeta higiénica, toalla sanitaria, mf, paño higiénico, m

sanitation /ˌsænɪˈteɪʃən/ n higiene, f; sanidad pública, f; (apparatus) instalación sanitaria, f

sanity /ˈsænɪti/ n juicio sano, m; prudencia, f; (common sense) sentido común, m, sensatez, f

Sanskrit /ˈsænskrɪt/ a and n sánscrito, m

Santa Claus /ˈsæntə klɔz/ n (Spanish equivalent) los Reyes Magos, m pl

São Paulo /ˈsau ˈpaulou, -lʊ/ San Pablo, m

sap /sæp/ n (bot and fig) savia, f; mil zapa, f. —vt (undermine) debilitar, agotar; mil zapar

sapidity /sæˈpɪdɪti/ n sapidez, f

sapling /ˈsæplɪŋ/ n arbolillo, m

sapper /ˈsæpər/ n mil zapador, m

Sapphic /ˈsæfɪk/ a sáfico. **S. verse**, verso sáfico, m

sapphire /ˈsæfaɪ³r/ n zafiro, m. —a de zafiros; cerúleo, de zafiro

Saracen /ˈsærəsən/ a and n sarraceno (-na)

Saragossa /ˌsærəˈgɒsə/ Zaragoza, f

sarcasm /ˈsɑrkæzəm/ n sarcasmo, m

sarcastic /sɑrˈkæstɪk/ a sarcástico

sarcastically /sɑrˈkæstɪkli/ adv con sarcasmo, sarcásticamente

sarcophagus /sɑrˈkɒfəgəs/ n sarcófago, m

sardine /sɑrˈdin/ n sardina, f. **packed like sardines**, como sardinas en banasta. **s.-net**, sardinal, m

Sardinia /sɑrˈdɪniə/ Cerdeña, f

Sardinian /sɑrˈdɪniən/ a and n sardo (-da)

sardonic /sɑrˈdɒnɪk/ a sardónico

sarsaparilla /ˌsæspəˈrɪ, ˌsɑrspə-/ n zarzaparrilla, f

sash /sæʃ/ n (with uniform) faja, f; (belt) cinto, cinturón, m; (of a window) cerco, m. **s. window**, ventana de guillotina, f

Satan /ˈseɪtn/ n Satanás, m

satanic /səˈtænɪk, seɪ-/ a satánico

satchel /ˈsætʃəl/ n saquito de mano, m, bolsa, f; (school) vademécum, m; cartapacio, m, cartera, f

sate /seɪt/ vt saciar, hartar; satisfacer

sateen /sæˈtin/ n satén, m

satellite /ˈsætlˌaɪt/ n satélite, m

satiable /ˈseɪʃəbəl/ a saciable

satiate /v. ˈseɪʃiˌeɪt; -ɪt, -ˌeɪt/ vt saciar, hartar; satisfacer. —a harto; repleto

satiety /səˈtaɪɪti/ n saciedad, f

satin /ˈsætn/ n raso, m. —a de raso; (glossy) lustroso, terso. —vt (paper) satinar

satiny /ˈsætni/ a arrasado; lustroso, brillante

satire /ˈsætaɪ³r/ n sátira, f

satiric /səˈtɪərɪk/ a satírico

satirist /ˈsætərɪst/ n escritor (-ra) satírico (-ca)

satirize /ˈsætəˌraɪz/ vt satirizar

satisfaction /ˌsætɪsˈfækʃən/ n satisfacción, f; (contentment) contento, m, satisfacción, f; (for sin) expiación, f; (of a debt) pago, m; desquite, m; recompensa, f. **to demand s.**, pedir satisfacción. **to give** (someone) **s.**, dar contento (a), alegrar

satisfactorily /ˌsætɪsˈfæktərəli/ adv satisfactoriamente

satisfactoriness /ˌsætɪsˈfæktərɪnɪs/ n carácter satisfactorio, m, lo satisfactorio

satisfactory /ˌsætɪsˈfæktəri/ a satisfactorio; (for sin) expiatorio

satisfy /ˈsætɪsˌfaɪ/ vt satisfacer; (convince) convencer; (allay) tranquilizar, apaciguar. **I am satisfied with him**, Estoy satisfecho (Estoy contento) con él. **The explanation did not s. me**, La explicación no me convenció. **to s. oneself that...**, asegurarse de que... **to s. one's thirst**, apagar la sed

satisfying /ˈsætɪsˌfaɪŋ/ a que satisface; satisfactorio; (of food) nutritivo

satrap /ˈseɪtræp, ˈsæ-/ n sátrapa, m

saturate /ˈsætʃəˌreɪt/ vt saturar (de), empapar (de); chem saturar; fig imbuir; fig empapar. **to s. oneself in,** (a subject) empaparse en

saturation /ˌsætʃəˈreɪʃən/ n saturación, f. **s. point**, (chem etc.) punto de saturación, m

Saturday /ˈsætərˌdeɪ/ n sábado, m

Saturn /ˈsætərn/ n Saturno, m

saturnine /ˈsætərˌnaɪn/ a saturnino, taciturno

satyr /ˈseɪtər, ˈsætər/ n sátiro, m

sauce /sɔs/ n salsa, f; (thick fruit) compota, f; inf insolencia, f. **s.-boat**, salsera, f

saucepan /ˈsɔsˌpæn/ n cazuela, cacerola, f. **double s.**, baño de María, m

saucer /ˈsɔsər/ n platillo, m. **flying s.**, platillo volante, m. **s.-eyed**, con ojos redondos

sauciness /ˈsɔsɪnɪs/ n impertinencia, insolencia, f

saucy /ˈsɔsi/ a respondón, descarado; (cheerful) alegre; (of hats, etc.) coquetón, majo

sauerkraut /ˈsau³r,kraut/ n chucruta, f

saunter /ˈsɔntər/ vi pasearse, vagar, n paseo, m, vuelta, f

sausage /ˈsɔsɪdʒ/ n chorizo, m; salchicha, f. **s.-balloon**, globo cautivo, m. **s.-curl**, bucle, m. **s.-machine**, choricera, f. **s.-maker**, choricero (-ra)

savage /ˈsævɪdʒ/ a salvaje; feroz; (cruel) inhumano, cruel; (furious) furioso. —n salvaje, mf

savagely /ˈsævɪdʒli/ adv bárbaramente; ferozmente; furiosamente

savagery /ˈsævɪdʒri/ n salvajismo, m; ferocidad, f; brutalidad, crueldad, f

savannah /səˈvænə/ n sabana, f. **s. dweller**, sabanero (-ra)

save /seiv/ vt salvar; (keep) guardar; conservar; reservar; (money, one's clothes, etc.) ahorrar; (time) ganar; (avoid) evitar. —vi salvar; hacer economías; ahorrar. **He saved my life**, Me salvó la vida. **They have saved a room for me**, Me han reservado una habitación. **to s. appearances**, guardar las apariencias. **to s. oneself trouble**, ahorrarse molestias. **to s. the situation**, estar al nivel de las circunstancias

save /seiv/ prep salvo, excepto, menos. —conjunc sino, a menos que; con la excepción de. **all s. one**, todos menos uno. **all the conspirators s. he**, todos los conspiradores con la excepción de él

saving /ˈseivɪŋ/ a frugal, económico; (stingy) tacaño, avaricioso; (clause) condicional. —n salvación, f; (of money, time, etc.) ahorro, m, economía, f; pl **savings**, ahorros, m pl. —prep salvo, excepto, fuera de. —conjunc con excepción de que, fuera de que. **s. grace**, único mérito, m. **savings bank**, caja de ahorros, f. **savings fund**, montepío, m

savior /ˈseivyər/ n salvador (-ra). **the S.**, el Salvador, el Redentor

savor /ˈseivər/ n sabor, gusto, m; (aftertaste) dejo, m; (zest) salsa, f. —vi saber (a), tener sabor (de); fig oler (a). —vt saborear, paladear; (flavor) sazonar

savoriness /ˈseivərɪnɪs/ n buen sabor, m; (of a district) respetabilidad, f

savory /ˈseivari/ a sabroso, apetitoso; (not sweet) no dulce; (of places) respetable; (of reputation, etc.) bueno. —n entremés salado, m. **s. omelette**, tortilla, f

Savoy /səˈvɔi/ Saboya, f

saw /sɔ/ n (maxim) sentencia, f; (proverb) refrán, decir, m; (tool) sierra, f. —vt aserrar; (the air) cortar. —vi usar una sierra. **two-handled saw**, tronzador, m. **saw-fish**, pez sierra, m. **saw-mill**, molino de aserrar, m. **saw-pit**, aserradero, m

sawdust /ˈsɔˌdʌst/ n aserrín, m

sawhorse /ˈsɔˌhɔrs/ n caballete de aserrar, m

sawyer /ˈsɔyər/ n aserrador, m

Saxon /ˈsæksən/ a and n sajón (-ona)

Saxony /ˈsæksəni/ Sajonia, f

saxophone /ˈsæksəˌfoun/ n saxófono, saxofón m

say /sei/ vt decir; recitar. —vi decir. **Let us say that the house is worth $100,000**, Pongamos por ejemplo que la casa vale cien mil dólares. **He has no say in the matter**, No entra ni sale en el asunto. **I have said my say**, He dicho lo que quería. **They say**, Se dice, Dicen, La gente dice. **You don't say!** ¡Calle! ¿De veras? ¡Imposible! **that is to say...**, es decir...; esto es..., a saber... **to say one's prayers**, rezar, decir sus oraciones. **to say again**, volver a decir; decir otra vez, repetir. **to say over and over again**, repetir muchas veces, decir repetidamente. **What do you say to that?** ¿Qué dices a esto?

saying /ˈseiŋ/ n decir, m; (proverb) refrán, m; (maxim) sentencia, f. **As the s. is**, Como suele decirse; Según el refrán. **It goes without s.**, Huelga decir. **It's only a s.**, Es un decir, nada más

scab /skæb/ n (of a wound) costra, f; (disease) escabro, m; (blackleg) esquirol, m

scabbard /'skæbərd/ n vaina (de espada), f

scabby /'skæbi/ a costroso; (diseased) roñoso, sarnoso

scabies /'skeibiz/ n sarna, f. **s. mite,** arador de la sarna, m

scaffold /'skæfəld/ n (in building) andamio, m; (for execution) cadalso, patíbulo, m. **to go to the s.,** ir al patíbulo; acabar en el patíbulo

scaffolding /'skæfəldɪŋ/ n andamiada, f; (building, scaffold) andamio, m

scald /skɔld/ vt escaldar; quemar; (instruments) esterilizar. —n quemadura, escaldadura, f. **to s. oneself,** escaldarse. **scalding hot,** hirviendo

scale /skeil/ n (of a balance) platillo, m; zool escama, f; bot bráctea, f; bot hojuela, f; (flake) laminita, f; (mus, math) escala, f; (of charges, etc.) tarifa, f; (of salaries) escalafón, m; (of a thermometer) escala, f. —vt escalar; (fish) escamar. **major s.,** escala mayor, f. **minor s.,** escala menor, f. **on a grand s.,** en gran escala. **on a small s.,** en pequeña escala. **pair of scales,** balanza, f; (for heavy weights) báscula, f. **social s.,** escala social, f. **The Scales,** Astron. Libra, f. **to draw to s.,** dibujar a escala. **to turn the scales,** pesar; Fig. inclinar la balanza. **to s. down,** (Art. and of charges) reducir

scaling /'skeilɪŋ/ n (of fish) escamadura, f; (of buildings) desconchadura, f; (ascent) escalamiento, m

scallop /'skɒləp, 'skæl-/ n (ichth and badge) venera, f; concha, f; sew onda, f, festón, m. —vt Cul. guisar en conchas; sew ondear, festonear

scalp /skælp/ n anat pericráneo, m; (skin) cuero cabelludo, m; fig trofeo, m. —vt escalpar. **s.-hunter,** cazador de cabelleras, m

scalpel /'skælpəl/ n escalpelo, m

scaly /'skeili/ a escamoso, conchado; (of boilers) incrustado

scamp /skæmp/ n bribón, granuja, m, vt (work) frangollar

scamper /'skæmpər/ vi retozar, brincar; correr. —n carrerita, f. **to s. off,** salvarse por los pies, huir; marcharse corriendo

scan /skæn/ vt (verse) medir, escandir; (examine) escudriñar, examinar; (glance at) dar un vistazo (a)

scandal /'skændl/ n escándalo, m; maledicencia, f; (slander) calumnia, f. **to talk s.,** murmurar

scandalize /'skændl,aiz/ vt escandalizar

scandalous /'skændləs/ a escandaloso; infame; calumnioso

scandalously /'skændləsli/ adv escandalosamente

scandalousness /'skændləsnɪs/ n carácter escandaloso, m

Scandinavia /,skændə'neiviə/ Escandinavia, f

Scandinavian /,skændə'neiviən/ a escandinavo. —n escandinavo (-va);

scant /skænt/ a escaso; insuficiente

scantily /'skæntl̩i/ adv insuficientemente

scantiness /'skæntɪnɪs/ n escasez, f; insuficiencia, f

scanty /'skænti/ a insuficiente; escaso; (of hair) ralo; (of crops, etc.) pobre

scapegoat /'skeip,gout/ n víctima propiciatoria, f; cabeza de turco, f. **to be a s. for,** pagar el pato por

scapegrace /'skeip,greis/ n bribón, m

scapula /'skæpyələ/ n anat escápula, f

scapulary /'skæpyə,leri// n eccl escapulario, m

scar /skɑr/ n cicatriz, f; fig señal, f. —vt marcar con una cicatriz. **to s. over,** cicatrizarse

scarab /'skærəb/ n escarabajo, m; escarabajo sagrado, m

scarce /skeərs/ a escaso; insuficiente; raro. —adv poet apenas. **to make oneself s.,** largarse, pirarse, escabullirse; ausentarse, esconderse

scarcely /'skeərsli/ adv apenas; no bien; casi; (with difficulty) a duras penas, con dificultad. **It is s. likely he said that,** No es muy probable que lo hubiese dicho. **There were s. twenty people in the building,** Había apenas veinte personas en el edificio. **S. anyone likes his pictures,** Sus cuadros no le gustan a casi nadie

scarcity /'skeərsiti/ n escasez, insuficiencia, f; (famine) carestía, f; (rarity) rareza, f

scare /skeər/ vt asustar, espantar, llenar de miedo (a); intimidar. —n susto, pánico, m; alarma, f. **What a s. I got!** ¡Qué susto me he llevado! **to s. away,** ahuyentar

scarecrow /'skeər,krou/ n espantapájaros, m; Inf. estantigua, f, mamarracho, espantajo, m

scaremonger /'skeər,mʌŋgər/ n alarmista, mf

scarf /skɑrf/ n bufanda, f; (tie) corbata, f; mil faja, f

scarlatina /,skɑrlə'tinə/ n med escarlatina, f

scarlet /'skɑrlɪt/ n escarlata, f. —a de color escarlata. **to turn s.,** (of persons) enrojecerse. **s. fever,** escarlatina, f. **s. hat,** eccl capelo (cardenalicio), m. **s. runner,** bot judía verde, f

scatheless 'skeiðlɪs/ a ileso, sano y salvo

scathing /'skeiðɪŋ/ a mordaz, cáustico

scathingly /'skeiðɪŋli/ adv mordazmente, cáusticamente

scatter /'skætər/ vt esparcir, sembrar con; (benefits, etc.) derramar; (put to flight) derrotar; dispersar; disipar; fig frustrar; (squander) derrochar, desparramar. —vi dispersarse. **The crowd scattered,** La muchedumbre se dispersó. **s.-brained,** de cabeza de chorlito, atolondrado

scattered /'skætərd/ a disperso; esparcido

scattered showers n lluvias aisladas, f pl

scattering /'skætərɪŋ/ n dispersión, f; (defeat) derrota, f; esparcimiento, m; (small number) número pequeño, m

scavenge /'skævɪndʒ/ vt (streets) recoger la basura de, barrer

scavenger /'skævɪndʒər/ n (of the streets) barrendero, m; (dustman) basurero, m; zool animal que se alimenta de carne muerta, m; insecto que se alimenta de estiércol, m. —vt See **scavenge**

scenario /sɪ'neəri,ou, -'nɑr-/ n escenario, m

scene /sin/ n escena, f; teatro, lugar, m; espectáculo, m; (theat décor) decoración, f; (of a play) escena, f; (view) vista, perspectiva, f. **behind the scenes,** entre bastidores. **The s. is laid...,** La acción pasa... **to come on the s.,** entrar en escena. **to make a s.,** hacer una escena. **s.-painter,** n escenógrafo (-fa). **s.-shifter,** tramoyista, mf

scenery /'sinəri/ n theat decorado, m; (landscape) paisaje, m

scenic /'sinɪk/ a dramático; escénico; pintoresco. **s. railway,** montaña rusa, f

scenography /si'nɒgrəfi/ n escenografía, f

scent /sent/ vt perfumar; (smell) oler; (out) husmear, olfatear; (suspect) sospechar. —n perfume, m; fragancia, f; aroma, m; (smell) olor, m; (of hounds) viento, m; (of game, etc.) rastro, viento, m; (fig of person) nariz, f; (trail) pista, f. **to lose the s.,** perder la pista. **to s. danger,** oler el peligro. **to throw off the s.,** despistar. **s.-bottle,** frasco de perfume, m. **s.-spray,** pulverizador, m

scented /'sentɪd/ a perfumado; (of roses, etc.) de olor, oloroso; (in compounds) de... olfato. **s. sweet pea,** guisante de olor, m

scentless /'sentlɪs/ a sin olor; inodoro

scepter /'septər/ n cetro, m

sceptic /'skeptɪk/ n escéptico (-ca)

sceptical /'skeptɪkəl/ a escéptico

scepticism /'skeptə,sɪzm/ n escepticismo, m

schedule /'skedʒul/ n lista, m; programa, m; (of taxes) clase, f; (of trains, etc.) horario, m. —vt poner en una lista; inventariar

scheme /skim/ n plan, m; proyecto, m; diagrama, esquema, m; (summary) resumen, m; (of colors, etc.) combinación, f; (plot) intriga, maquinación, f. —vt proyectar. —vi planear, formar planes; (intrigue) intrigar, conspirar. **color s.,** combinación de colores, f

schemer /'skimər/ n (plotter) intrigante, mf

scheming /'skimɪŋ/ a intrigante; astuto. —n planes, proyectos, m pl; intrigas, maquinaciones, f pl

schism /'sɪzəm, 'skɪz-/ n cisma, mf

schismatic /sɪz'mætɪk, skɪz-/ a cismático. —n cismático (-ca)

scholar /'skɒlər/ n (at school) colegial (-la); (disciple) alumno (-na); (student) estudiante, mf; (learned person) erudito (-ta), hombre de letras, m; (scholarship holder) becario, m.

scholarly /'skɒlərli/ a de sabio, de hombre de letras; erudito

scholarship /'skɒlərˌʃip/ n erudición, f; saber, m; (exhibition) beca, f. **s. holder,** becario, m

scholastic /skə'læstik/ a escolar, escolástico; pedante; (medieval) escolástico. —n escolástico, m. **the s. profession,** el magisterio

school /skul/ n escuela, f; colegio, m; academia, f; educ departamento, m; (faculty) facultad, f; (of fish) banco, m. —vt enseñar, instruir; formar; disciplinar. **in s.,** en clase. **day s.,** escuela, f, colegio, m. **the Florentine s.,** (of painting) la escuela florentina. **the lower s.,** los alumnos del preparatorio. **private s.,** colegio particular, m. **s.-bag,** vademécum, f. **s.-book,** libro escolar, m. **s.-days,** los días de escuela; los años de colegio. **in his s.-days,** cuando él iba a la escuela. **s.-fees,** gastos de la enseñanza, m pl, cuota escolar, f.

schoolboy /'skul,bɔi/ n muchacho de escuela, colegial, m

school district n sector escolar, m

schoolfellow /'skul,felou/ n compañero de colegio, condiscípulo, m

schoolgirl /'skul,gɜrl/ n colegiala, f

schooling /'skuliŋ/ n educación, enseñanza, f

schoolmaster /'skul,mæstər/ n maestro de escuela, professor, m

schoolmistress /'skul,mistris/ n maestra de escuela, profesora, f

school of hard knocks n universidad sin tejados, f

schoolroom /'skul,rum/ n aula, sala de clase, salón de clase, m

schooner /'skunər/ n naut escuna, goleta, f

sciatic /sai'ætik/ a ciático

sciatica /sai'ætikə/ n ciática, f

science /'saiəns/ n ciencia, f

scientific /ˌsaiən'tifik/ a científico; exacto, sistemático

scientifically /ˌsaiən'tifikli/ adv científicamente

scientist /'saiəntist/ n hombre de ciencia, m, científico (-ca)

scimitar /'simitər, -ˌtɑr/ n cimitarra, f

scintilla /sin'tilə/ n fig átomo, vestigio, m

scintillate /'sintlˌeit/ vi centellear, lucir, chispear; (of persons) brillar

scion /'saiən/ n (sucker) acodo, m; (shoot) vástago, renuevo, m; (human) descendiente, mf. **s. of a noble race,** vástago de una raza noble, m

scissors /'sizərz/ n pl tijeras, f pl. **s.-sharpener,** amolador, m

sclerosis /sklɪ'rousis/ n med esclerosis, f

sclerotic /sklɪ'rɒtik/ a anat esclerótica, f

scoff /skɔf, skɒf/ n burla, mofa, f. —vi burlarse. **to s. at,** burlarse de, mofarse de

scoffer /'skɔfər, 'skɒf-/ n mofador (-ra); (at religion, etc.) incrédulo (-la)

scoffing /'skɔfiŋ, 'skɒf-/ a burlón. —n mofas, burlas, f pl

scold /skould/ n virago, f, vt reñir, reprender

scolding /'skouldiŋ/ n represión, increpación, f

sconce /skɒns/ n cubo de candelero, m; candelabro de pared, m; cornucopia, f

scone /skoun, skɒn/ n bollo, m

scoop /skup/ n pala de mano, f; cuchara de draga, f; (boat) achicador, m; (financial) golpe, m; (journalistic) éxito periodistico, m. —vt sacar con pala (de); sacar con cuchara (de); (shares, etc.) comprar, obtener. **to s. out,** vaciar; excavar; (bail) achicar

scooter /'skutər/ n (child's) patinete, patín del diablo, m; monopatín, m

scope /skoup/ n alcance, m; esfera de acción, f; lugar, m. **to give full s. to,** dar rienda suelta a. **to have full s.,** tener plena oportunidad; tener todas las facilidades. **within the s. of,** dentro del alcance de

scorbutic /skɔr'byutik/ a med escorbútico

scorch /skɔrtʃ/ vt chamuscar; (the skin) tostar; (of the sun) abrasar, quemar; (wither) agostar. **to s. along,** ir como un relámpago. **scorching,** a abrasador, ardiente; fig mordaz

score /skɔr/ n (scratch) rasguño, m; señal, f; (crossing out) raya, f; (reckoning) cuenta, f, escote, m; (notch) muesca, f; sports tanteo, m, puntuación, f; (point) punto, tanto, m; (twenty) veintena, f; (rea-

son) motivo, m, causa, f; respecto, m; mus partitura, f. —vt marcar; rayar; (erase) tachar, borrar; (cricket runs, etc.) hacer; (goals) marcar; (points) ganar; (reckon) apuntar. **s. a triumph,** apuntarse un triunfo; mus instrumentar; (for orchestra) orquestar. —vi (be fortunate) llevar la ventaja. **to pay off old scores,** ajustar cuentas viejas. **to s. off someone,** ganar un punto (a), triunfar de. **upon that s.,** a ese respecto; por esa causa. **Upon what s.?** ¿Con qué motivo? **s.-board,** marcador, m

scorer /'skɔrər/ n (of a goal, etc.) tanteador, m; (keeper of score) marcador, m

scoria /'skɔriə/ n escoria, f

scorn /skɔrn/ n desprecio, desdén, m. —vt despreciar, desdeñar; reírse de. **to s. to do,** no dignarse hacer

scornful /'skɔrnfəl/ a desdeñoso, despreciativo

scornfully /'skɔrnfəli/ adv desdeñosamente, con desprecio

Scorpion /'skɔrpiən/ n Escorpión, m

scorpion /'skɔrpiən/ n escorpión, alacrán, m; astron Escorpión, m

Scot /skɒt/ n escocés, m

scotch /skɒtʃ/ vt (kill) matar; (thwart) frustrar; (a wheel) calzar

Scotland /'skɒtlənd/ Escocia, f

Scotswoman /'skɒts,wumən/ n escocesa, f

Scottish /'skɒtiʃ/ a escocés

scoundrel /'skaundrəl/ n canalla, sinvergüenza, mf

scour /skauˀr/ vt (traverse) recorrer, batir; (pans, etc.) fregar, estregar; (free from) limpiar (de); (of water) arrastrar

scourge /skɜrdʒ/ vt azotar, flagelar; castigar, mortificar. —n disciplinas, f pl; fig verdugo, m, plaga, f

scout /skaut/ n mil batidor, explorador, m. —vi mil explorar, reconocer. —vt (flout) rechazar a mano airada, rechazar con desdén. **boy s.,** muchacho explorador, m

scowl /skaul/ vi fruncir el ceño. —n ceño, m. **to s. at,** mirar con ceño

scowling /'skauliŋ/ a amenazador

scragginess /'skræginis/ n magrez, flaqueza, f

scraggy /'skrægi/ a flaco, magro, descarnado

scramble /'skræmbəl/ vi trepar. —vt (throw) arrojar; (eggs) revolver. **scrambled eggs,** huevos revueltos, m pl. **to s. for,** andar a la rebatiña por; (for coins, etc.) luchar para. **to s. up,** escalar; subir a gatas

scrap /skræp/ n pedazo, m; fragmento, m; pizca, brizna, f; (shindy) suiza, camorra, f; (boxing) combate de boxeo, m; pl **scraps,** desperdicios, m pl; (food) restos de la comida, m pl. —vt desechar; (expunge) borrar; vi (fight) armar camorra. **a few scraps of news,** algunas noticias. **Do you mind not coming? Not a s.,** ¿Te importa no venir? Ni pizca. **s.-book,** álbum de recortes, m; **s.-heap,** depósito de basura, m; fig olvido, m. **s. iron,** chatarra, f, hierro viejo, m

scrape /skreip/ vt raspar, rascar, raer; (one's shoes) restregar; (a musical instrument) rascar. —n rasguño, m; ruido de raspar, m; (predicament) lío, apuro, m; dificultad, f. **to s. acquaintance with,** trabar amistad con. **to s. along,** inf ir tirando. **to s. away,** rascar; quitar. **to s. through,** (an examination) aprobar justo. **to s. together,** amontonar poco a poco

scrappy /'skræpi/ a escaso; fragmentario; (incoherent) descosido. **a s. meal,** una comida escasa

scratch /skrætʃ/ vt arañar; (the earth) escarbar; (rub) rascar; (a hole) hacer; (sketch) dibujar, trazar; (a horse) retirar de una carrera. —vi arañar; rascar; escarbar; (of a pen) rasguear; (back out) retirarse. —n arañazo, m; (of a pen) rasgueo, m; (in a race) línea de salida, f; (in games) cero, m; —a improvisado. **The dog scratched at the door,** El perro arañó la puerta. **to come up to s.,** estar al nivel de las circunstancias. **to s. one's head,** rascarse la cabeza. **to s. a person's eyes out,** sacar los ojos con las uñas (a). **to s. the surface of,** (a subject) tratar superficialmente. **to s. out,** tachar

scrawl /skrɔl/ vi hacer garabatos. —vt garabatear, garrapatear. —n garabato, m

scream /skrim/ vt and vi chillar. —n chillido, m. **It was a perfect s.** Era para morirse de risa. **to s. with laughter,** reírse a carcajadas, morirse de risa

screaming /'skrimɪŋ/ n chillidos, m pl. —a chillador; (piercing) penetrante, agudo; (funny) divertidísimo

screech /skritʃ/ vi chillar; (of owls, etc.) ulular; graznar. —n chillido, m, ululación, f; graznido, m. **s.-owl**, úlula, f

screed /skrid/ n arenga, f; cita larga, f

screen /skrin/ n biombo, m; (wire) tela metálica, f; (nonfolding) mampara, f; (ecol) cancel, m; (cinema, television) pantalla, f; (of trees, etc., and mil) cortina, f; (fig protection) abrigo, m. —vt proteger; (shelter) abrigar; (hide) esconder, ocultar; (a light) proteger con pantalla; (a film) proyectar; (sieve) cribar, cerner; (examine) investigar. **to s. from view**, ocultar la vista (de), esconder. **s. star**, estrella de la pantalla, f

screw /skru/ n tornillo, m; (propeller) hélice, f; vuelta de tornillo, f; presión, f; (miser) tacaño, m; (salary) salario, m. —vt atornillar; torcer; apretar, oprimir. **He has a s. loose,** Le falta un tornillo. **to s. down,** sujetar con tornillos. **to s. up,** cerrar con tornillos. **to s. up one's courage,** tomar coraje. **to s. up one's eyes,** desojarse, entornar los ojos. **s.-driver,** destornillador, m

scribble /'skrɪbəl/ vt escribir de prisa, vi garabatear, garrapatear; escribir, ser autor. —n garabato, garrapato, m; mala letra, letra ilegible, f; (note) billete, m

scribbler /'skrɪblər/ n el, m, (f, la) que tiene mala letra; (author) autor (-ra) malo (-la)

scribbling /'skrɪblɪŋ/ n garabateo, m. **s.-block,** bloque de papel, m

scribe /skraib/ n escribiente, copista, mf; (Jewish history) escriba, m

scrimmage /'skrɪmɪdʒ/ n reyerta, pelea, camorra, f; (Rugby) mêlée, f

script /skript/ n letra cursiva, f; print plumilla, f; manuscrito, m; law escritura, f; examen escrito, m; (film) escenario, m

scriptural /'skrɪptʃərəl/ a bíblico

Scripture /'skrɪptʃər/ n Sagrada Escritura, f. **Scriptures,** Escrituras, f pl; (of non-Christian religions) los libros sagrados

scrivener /'skrɪvnər/ n chupatintas, mf

scrofula /'skrɒfyələ/ n escrófula, f

scrofulous /'skrɒfyələs/ a escrofuloso

scroll /skroul/ n (of paper, etc.) rollo, m; pergamino, m; (flourish) rúbrica, f; (of an Ionic capital) voluta, f. **s. of fame,** lista de la fama, f

scrotum /'skroutəm/ n anat escroto, m

scrounge /skraundʒ/ vi sablear. —vt dar un sablazo (a); hurtar

scrounger /'skraundʒər/ n sablista, mf

scrub /skrʌb/ vt fregar; limpiar; restregar. —n fregado, m; limpieza, f; fricción, f; (brushwood) matorral, breñal, m, maleza, f

scrubbing /'skrʌbɪŋ/ n fregado, m. **s.-brush,** cepillo para el suelo, m

scrubby /'skrʌbi/ a (of plants) anémico; (of persons) insignificante, pobre; (of land) cubierto de maleza

scruff /skrʌf/ n nuca, f, pescuezo, m

scruple /'skrupəl/ n escrúpulo, m. —vi tener escrúpulos. **to have no scruples,** no tener escrúpulos

scrupulous /'skrupyələs/ a escrupuloso; exacto, meticuloso

scrupulously /'skrupyəlsli/ adv escrupulosamente; meticulosamente

scrupulousness /'skrupyələsnɪs/ n escrupulosidad, f; meticulosidad, f

scrutinize /'skrutn̩ˌaiz/ vt escudriñar, examinar; (votes) escrutar

scrutinizer /'skrutn̩ˌaizər/ n escudriñador (-ra); (of votes) escrutador (-ra)

scrutinizing /'skrutn̩ˌaizɪŋ/ escrutador

scrutiny /'skrutni/ n escrutinio, m

scud /skʌd/ vi correr; deslizarse; flotar. **to s. before the wind,** ir viento en popa

scuffle /'skʌfəl/ vi pelear, forcejear, andar a la rebatiña. —n refriega, pelea, sarracina, arrebatiña, f

scull /skʌl/ n remo, m, vi remar

scullery /'skʌləri/ n fregadero, m. **s. maid,** fregona, f

sculptor /'skʌlptər/ n escultor, m, escultora, f

sculptural /'skʌlptʃərəl/ a escultural, escultórico

sculpture /'skʌlptʃər/ n escultura, f, vt esculpir

scum /skʌm/ n espuma, f; (dregs) heces, f pl. —vt espumar. **s. of the earth,** las heces de la sociedad

scupper /'skʌpər/ n Naut. clava, f. —vt abrir las clavas (de); (frustrate) frustrar, destruir

scurrility /skə'rɪlɪti/ n grosería, indecencia, f

scurrilous /'skɜrələs/ a grosero, indecente

scurry /'skɜri/ vi echar a correr. —n fuga precipitada, f; (of rain) chaparrón, m; (of snow) remolino, m. **to s. off,** escabullirse. **to s. through,** hacer de prisa, terminar rápidamente

S-curve /'es.kɜrv/ n curva doble, f

scurvy /'skɜrvi/ a tiñoso, vil, ruin. —n escorbuto, m. **a s. trick,** una mala pasada

scuttle /'skʌtl̩/ n (trap-door) escotillón, m; naut escotilla, f; (for coal) carbonera, f; (flight) huida precipitada, f. —vt (a boat) echar a pique, vi (run away) escabullirse, apretar a correr

scythe /saið/ n dalle, m, guadaña, f, vt dallar, segar

sea /si/ n mar, m, or f; ola, f; multitud, f. **Black Sea,** Mar Negro. **Mediteranean Sea,** (Mar) Mediterráneo, m. **at sea,** en el mar; perplejo. **beyond the seas,** allende los mares. **by sea,** por mar. **by the sea,** a la orilla del mar. **high seas,** alta mar, f. **the seven seas,** todos los mares del mundo. **to go to sea,** hacerse marinero. **to put to sea,** hacerse a la mar, hacerse a la vela. **sea-anemone,** anémone de mar, f. **sea-bathing,** baños de mar, m pl. **sea-breeze,** brisa de mar, f. **sea captain,** capitán de mar, m. **sea chart,** carta de marear, f. **sea-coast,** litoral, m, costa marítima, f. **sea-cow,** manatí, m. **sea dog,** lobo de mar, m. **sea-fight,** combate naval, m. **sea-foam,** espuma de mar, f. **sea-girt,** rodeado por el mar. **sea-going,** de altura; navegante. **sea-going craft,** embarcación de alta mar, f. **sea-green,** verdemar, m. **sea-gull,** gaviota, f. **sea-horse,** caballo marino, m. **sea-legs,** piernas de marino, f pl. **sea-level,** nivel del mar, m. **sea-lion,** león marino, m. **sea-mist,** bruma, f. **sea-nymph,** nereida, f. **sea-power,** potencia naval, f. **sea-serpent,** serpiente de mar, f. **sea-sick,** mareado. **to be sea-sick,** marearse. **sea-sickness,** mal de mar, m. **sea-trip,** viaje por mar, m. **sea-urchin,** erizo de mar, m. **sea-wall,** dique de mar, m

seafarer /'si,fɛərər/ n (traveller) viajero (-ra) por mar; (sailor) marinero, m

seafaring /'si,fɛərɪŋ/ a marinero, marino. —n viajes por mar, m pl; vida del marinero, f

seal /sil/ n zool foca, f; lobo marino, m; piel de foca, f; sello, m; (stamp) estampillo, timbre, m; vt sellar; (stamp) estampar; (letters, etc.) cerrar; vi cazar focas. **His fate is sealed,** Su suerte está determinada. **His lips were sealed,** Sus labios estaban cerrados. **under my hand and s.,** firmado y sellado por mí. **s.-ring,** sortija de sello, f

sealing wax /'silɪŋ/ n lacre, m

sealskin /'sil,skɪn/ n piel de foca, f

seam /sim/ n sew costura, f; naut costura de los tablones, f; anat sutura, f; surg cicatriz, f; (wrinkle) arruga, f, surco, m; geol capa, f, yacimiento, m; mineral vena, f, filón, m. —vt coser; juntar; (a face) surcar, arrugar

seaman /'simən/ n marinero, m; hombre de mar, m; navegante, m. **able-bodied s.,** marinero práctico, m

seamanlike /'simən,laik/ a de marinero, marino; de buen marinero

seamanship /'simən,ʃɪp/ n marinería, f; náutica, f

seamstress /'simstrɪs/ n costurera, f

seamy /'simi/ a con costuras. **the s. side of life,** el lado peor de la vida

seance /'seians/ n sesión, junta, f; sesión de espiritistas, f

seaplane /'si,plein/ n hidroavión, hidroplano, m

seaport /'si,pɔrt/ n puerto de mar, m

sear /siər/ a marchito. —vt agostar, secar; (a wound) cauterizar; marchitar, ajar; (a conscience) endurecer

search /sɜrtʃ/ vt registrar; (a wound) explorar; examinar; escudriñar; investigar. —vi buscar. —n busca, f; (of luggage, etc.) reconocimiento, m. **in s. of,** en busca de. **to s. after, for,** buscar; ir al encuentro de. **to s. out,** ir en busca de; preguntar por. **right of s.,** (international law) derecho de visita, m. **s.-party,** pelotón de salvamento, m. **s.-warrant,** auto de reconocimiento, auto de registro domiciliario, orden de allanamiento, orden de cateo, *m*

searching /'sɜrtʃɪŋ/ *a* escrutador; penetrante; minucioso. **a s. look,** una mirada penetrante. **a s. wind,** un viento penetrante. **a s. question,** una pregunta perspicaz

searchlight /'sɜrtʃ‚lait/ *n* reflector, proyector, *m*

seashore /'si‚ʃɔr/ *n* playa, *f;* orilla del mar, *f*

seaside /'si‚said/ *n* orilla del mar, *f;* playa, *f.* **to go to the s.,** ir al mar, ir a la playa

season /'sizən/ *n* estación, *f;* sazón, *f;* temporada, *f;* tiempo, *m.* —*vt* (food) sazonar; (wood, wine) madurar; (accustom) acostumbrar, aclimatar; (with wit, etc.) salpimentar; (temper) templar, moderar. —*vi* madurarse. **at that s.,** a la sazón. **close s.,** veda, *f.* **in s.,** en sazón; a su tiempo. **out of s.,** fuera de sazón; fuera de tiempo, inoportuno. **the dead s.,** la estación muerta. **the autumn s.,** el otoño; (for social functions, etc.) la temporada de otoño. **s.-ticket,** billete de abono, *m*

seasonable /'sizənəbəl/ *a* de estación; tempestivo, oportuno

seasonably /'sizənəbli/ *adv* en sazón; oportunamente

seasonal /'sizənl/ *a* estacional; de temporada

seasonal worker *n* trabajador por temporada, *m*

seasoned /'sizənd/ *a* (of food) sazonado; (of wood, etc.) maduro. **highly-s.,** (of a dish) picante, con muchas especies

seasoning /'sizənɪŋ/ *n cul* condimento, *m;* madurez, *f;* aclimatación, *f; fig* salsa, sal, *f*

seat /sit/ *n* asiento, *m;* (bench) banco, *m;* (chair) silla, *f;* (in a cinema, etc.) localidad, *f;* (*theat* etc., ticket) entrada, *f;* (of a person) trasero, *m,* asentaderas, *f pl;* (of trousers) fondillos, *m pl;* (of government, etc.) sede, capital, *f;* (of war, etc.) teatro, *m;* (place) sitio, lugar, *m;* (house) casa solar, *f.* —*vt* sentar; poner en una silla (a); encontrar sitio; (of buildings) tener... asientos; (a chair) poner asiento (a). **The hall seats a thousand,** La sala tiene mil asientos, Hay mil asientos en la sala. **Please be seated!** ¡Haga el favor de sentarse! **to be seated,** estar sentado; sentarse. **to have a good s.,** (on a horse) caer bien a caballo. **to hold a s.,** in parliament, ser diputado a Cortes. **to keep one's s.,** permanecer sentado. **to take a s.,** tomar asiento, sentarse. **s.-back,** respaldo, *m.* **s. belt,** cinturón de seguridad, *m*

seater /'sitər/ *n* de... asientos. **four-s.,** automóvil de cuatro asientos, *m*

seaweed /'si‚wid/ *n* alga marina, *f*

seaworthy /'si‚wɜrði/ *a* (of a ship) en buen estado; marinero

sebaceous /sɪ'beiʃəs/ *a* sebáceo

secede /sɪ'sid/ *vi* retirarse (de); separarse (de)

secession /sɪ'sɛʃən/ *n* secesión, *f*

secessionist /sɪ'sɛnɪst/ *n* secesionista, *mf; polit* separatista, *mf.* —*a* secesionista; *polit* separatista

secluded /sɪ'kludɪd/ *a* apartado, retirado; solitario

seclusion /sɪ'kluʒən/ *n* reclusión, *f;* apartamiento, retiro, *m;* soledad, *f*

second /sɪ'kɒnd/ *a* segundo; otro; igual. —*adv* en segundo lugar; después. —*n* segundo, *m;* (in a duel) padrino, *m;* (helper) ayudante, *m;* (boxing) segundo, *m;* (railway compartment) departamento de segunda (clase), *m; mus* segunda, *f;* (of time) segundo, *m;* (moment) instante, momento, *m.* —*vt* secundar; (a motion) apoyar; *mil* ayudar. **the s. of May,** el dos de mayo. **James the S.,** Jaime el segundo. **on s. thoughts,** después de pensarlo bien. **every s. day,** cada dos días. **They live on the s. floor,** Viven en el primer piso (since the ground floor is not counted separately in Spanish speaking areas, the American second floor = the Spanish **primer piso**). **the s. largest,** el más grande menos uno. **to be s. to none,** no ser inferior a ninguno; (of persons) no ser inferior a nadie; no ceder a nadie. **to come off s.,** llegar el segundo; ser vencido. **seconds hand,** (of watch) segundero, *m.* **s.-in-command,** segundo, *m;* subjefe, *m.* **s.-best,** segundo. **My s.-best hat,** Mi sombrero número dos. **to come off s.-best,** salir mal parado, ser vencido. **s. class,** segunda clase, *f.* **s.-class,** de segunda clase; de calidad inferior; mediocre. **s.**

cousin, primo (-ma) segundo (-a). **s. gear,** segunda velocidad, *f.* **s.-hand,** *a* usado; de ocasión; no nuevo. —*adv* de segunda mano. **s.-hand car,** un coche de segunda mano. **s.-hand clothing,** ropa usada, *f.* **s.-hand clothing,** ropa usada, *f.* **s. lieutenant,** *mil* subteniente, segundo teniente, *m; nav* alférez de fragata, *m.* **s.-rate,** *a* inferior, mediocre. **s. sight,** doble vista, *f*

secondary /'sɛkən‚dɛri/ *a* secundario; subordinado; accesorio; poco importante. **s. education,** enseñanza secundaria, *f*

seconder /'sɛkəndər/ *n* ayudante, *m;* el, *m,* (f, la) que apoya una proposición

secondly /'sɛkəndli/ *adv* en segundo lugar

secrecy /'sikrəsi/ *n* secreto, *m;* reserva, *f,* silencio, *m.* **in the s. of one's own heart,** en lo más íntimo de su corazón

secret /'sikrɪt/ *a* secreto; clandestino; (of persons) reservado, taciturno; (secluded) remoto, apartado; oculto; misterioso. —*n* secreto, *m;* (key) clave, *f.* **a s. code,** un código secreto. **in s.,** en secreto, secretamente. **open s.,** secreto a voces. **to keep a s.,** guardar un secreto. **to keep s.,** tener secreto, ocultar. **s. drawer,** secreto, *m.*

secretaire /‚sɛkrɪ'tɛər/ *n* secréter, escritorio, *m*

secretarial /‚sɛkrɪ'tɛəriəl/ *a* de secretario. **s. college,** academia comercial, *f*

secretariat /‚sɛkrɪ'tɛəriət/ *n* secretaría, *f*

secretary /'sɛkrɪ‚tɛri/ *n* secretario (-ia). **private s.,** secretario (-ia) particular. **S. of State,** ministro, *m;* Ministro de Estado, *m*

secrete /sɪ'krit/ *vt* esconder, ocultar; *med* secretar

secretion /sɪ'kriʃən/ *n* escondimiento, *m; med* secreción, *f*

secretive /'sikrɪtɪv/ *a* reservado, callado

secretly /'sikrɪtli/ *adv* en secreto, secretamente; ocultamente, a escondidas

sect /sɛkt/ *n* secta, *f*

sectarian /sɛk'tɛəriən/ *a* and *n* sectario (-ia)

sectarianism /sɛk'tɛəriə‚nɪzəm/ *n* sectarismo, *m*

section /'sɛkʃən/ *n* sección, *f;* porción, *f;* subdivisión, *f;* (of a law) artículo, *m.* —*vt* seccionar. **conic s.,** sección cónica, *f*

sectional /'sɛkʃənl/ *a* en secciones. **s. bookcase,** biblioteca desmontable, *f*

sector /'sɛktər/ *n* sector, *m*

secular /'sɛkyələr/ *a* (very old) secular; (lay) seglar; laico; profano. **s. music,** música profana, *f.* **s. school,** escuela laica, *f*

secularization /‚sɛkyələrə'zeiʃən/ *n* secularización, *f*

secularize /'sɛkyələ‚raiz/ *vt* secularizar

secure /sɪ'kyʊr/ *a* seguro; (certain) asegurado; (safe) en seguridad; sano y salvo; (firm) firme; fijo; (confident (in)) confiado (en). —*vt* asegurar; (insure) garantizar; (lock) cerrar; (confine) prender; (acquire) adquirir, obtener; lograr, conseguir

securely /sɪ'kyʊrli/ *adv* seguramente; en seguridad, sin peligro; con confianza; (firmly) firmemente

security /sɪ'kyʊrɪti/ *n* seguridad, *f;* protección, defensa, *f;* garantía, *f;* (faith) confianza, *f; com* fianza, *f;* (person) fiador, *m; pl* **securities,** valores, títulos, *m pl.* **government securities,** papel del Estado, *m.* **to give s.,** *com* dar fianza. **to stand s. for,** *com* salir fiador de

sedan-chair /sɪ'dæn‚tʃɛər/ *n* silla de manos, *f*

sedate /sɪ'deit/ *a* tranquilo, sosegado; formal, serio, grave

sedately /sɪ'deitli/ *adv* sosegadamente; seriamente

sedateness /sɪ'deitnɪs/ *n* sosiego, *m,* tranquilidad, *f;* formalidad, compostura, *f*

sedative /'sɛdətɪv/ *a* and *n* sedativo, calmante *m*

sedentary /'sɛdn‚tɛri/ *a* sedentario

sediment /'sɛdəmənt/ *n* sedimento, *m*

sedimentation /‚sɛdəmən'teiʃən/ *n* sedimentación, *f*

sedition /sɪ'dɪʃən/ *n* sedición, *f*

seditious /sɪ'dɪʃəs/ *a* sedicioso

seduce /sɪ'dus/ *vt* seducir

seducer /sɪ'dusər/ *n* seductor, *m*

seduction /sɪ'dʌkʃən/ *n* seducción, *f*

seductive /sɪ'dʌktɪv/ *a* seductivo, atractivo; persuasivo

sedulous /'sɛdʒələs/ *a* asiduo, diligente

see /si/ *n* sede, *f.* **The Holy S.,** la Santa Sede, *f*

see /si/ *vt* and *vi* ver; mirar; (understand) comprender; (visit) visitar; (attend to) atender a; ocuparse de. **He sees the matter quite differently,** Él mira el asunto de un modo completamente distinto, Su punto de vista sobre el asunto es completamente distinto. **You are not fit to be seen,** No eres nada presentable. **See you next Tuesday!** ¡Hasta el miércoles que viene! **I see!** ¡Ya! ¡Ahora comprendo! **Let's see!** ¡Vamos a ver! **Shall I see you home?** ¿Quieres que te acompañe a casa? **to go and see,** ir a ver. **to see red,** echar chispas. **to see the sights,** visitar los monumentos. **to see life,** ver mundo. **to see service,** servir (en el ejército, etc.). **to see about,** atender a; pensar en; ocuparse de. **to see after,** cuidar de; atender (a); ocuparse de. **to see again,** volver a ver. **to see into,** investigar, examinar. **to see off,** (at the station, etc.) ir a despedir; acompañar. **to see out,** (a person) acompañar a la puerta; (a play, etc.) quedarse hasta el fin (de); no dejar el puesto. **to see over,** inspeccionar. **to see through,** (a house, etc.) inspeccionar; (a person) calarle las intenciones; (a mystery) penetrar; (a person through trouble) ayudar. **to see it through,** llevarlo al cabo; quedarse hasta el fin. **to see to,** atender a; ocuparse de; encargarse de. **to see to everything,** encargarse de todo

seed /sid/ *n* semilla, *f;* simiente, *f;* (of fruit) pepita, *f,* grano, *m; fig* germen, *m;* (offspring) prole, descendencia, *f* —*vi* granar. —*vt* sembrar. **s.-bed,** almáciga, *f,* semillero, *m.* **s.-pearl,** aljófar, *m.* **s.-plot,** sementera, *f; fig* semillero, *m.* **s.-time,** tiempo de sembrar, *m*

seedling /'sidlɪŋ/ *n* planta de semilla, *f*

seedsman /'sidzmən/ *n* tratante en semillas, *m*

seedy /'sidi/ *a* granado; (of clothes) raído, roto; (of persons) andrajoso, desharrapado; infeliz, desgraciado; (ill) indispuesto, malucho

seeing /'siɪŋ/ *n* vista, *f;* visión, *f.* **It is worth s.,** Vale la pena de verse. **s. that...,** visto que, dado que, como que. **S. is believing,** Ver es creer

seek /sik/ *vt* buscar; solicitar, pretender; (demand) pedir; (investigate) investigar; (to do something) procurar. tratar de. **They are much sought after,** Son muy populares, Están en demanda. **to s. after,** buscar; perseguir. **to s. for,** buscar

seeker /'siker/ *n* el, *m,* (*f,* la) que busca; investigador (-ra)

seem /sim/ *vi* parecer. **He seemed honest,** Parecía honrado. **It seemed to me,** Me pareció a mí. **It seems that they were both at home last night,** Parece ser que ambos estaban en casa anoche

seeming /'simɪŋ/ *a* aparente; supuesto

seemingly /'simɪŋli/ *adv* aparentemente; en apariencia

seemliness /'simlɪnɪs/ *n* decoro, *m*

seemly /'simli/ *a* decoroso, decente

seep /sip/ *vi* filtrar; rezumarse

seer /siər/ *n* profeta, *m*

seesaw /'si,sɔ/ *n* columpio, *m;* vaivén, *m.* —*vi* columpiarse; balancearse, oscilar. —*a* de vaivén, oscilante

seethe /sið/ *vi* hervir; *fig* bullir

segment /'sɛgmənt/ *n* segmento, *m*

segregate /*v.* 'sɛgrɪ,geit; *a.* -gɪt/ *vt* segregar. —*vi* segregarse. —*a* segregado

segregation /,sɛgrɪ'geiʃən/ *n* segregación, *f*

Seine, the /sen/ el Sena, *m*

seismic /'saizmɪk/ *a* sísmico

seismograph /'saizmə,græf/ *n* sismógrafo, *m*

seismological /,saizmə'lɒdʒɪkəl/ *a* sismológico

seismology /saiz'mɒlədʒi/ *n* sismología, *f*

seize /siz/ *vt law* embargar; apoderarse de; asir; (a person) prender; coger; (a meaning) comprender; (an occasion, etc.) aprovecharse de; (of emotions) dominar; (of illnesses) atacar. —*vi mech* atascarse. **He was seized by fear,** Le dominó el miedo. **to s. the opportunity,** aprovecharse de la oportunidad. **to s. upon a pretext,** valerse de un pretexto

seizure /'siʒər/ *n* asimiento, *m;* (of property) embargo, secuestro, *m;* (of a person) captura, *f;* arresto, *m; med* ataque, *m*

seldom /'sɛldəm/ *adv* rara vez, raramente; pocas veces

select /sɪ'lɛkt/ *a* escogido, selecto; exclusivista. —*vt* escoger

selection /sɪ'lɛkʃən/ *n* selección, *f.* **selections from Cervantes,** trozos escogidos de Cervantes, *m pl.* **to make a s. from,** escoger entre. **s. committee,** comité de selección, *m*

selective /sɪ'lɛktɪv/ *a* selectivo

self /sɛlf/ *n* mismo (-a), propio (-a); sí mismo (-a), se; personalidad, *f;* sí mismo (-a). **all by one's s.,** sin ayuda de nadie; solo; *inf* solito. **my other s.,** mi otro yo. **my better s.,** mi mejor parte. **the s.,** el yo. **s.-abasement,** humillación de sí mismo, *f.* **s.-acting,** automático. **s.-apparent,** evidente, patente. **s.-appointed,** nombrado por uno mismo. **s.-assertion,** presunción, *f.* **s.-assertive,** presumido. **s.-assurance,** confianza en sí mismo, *f;* aplomo, *m;* (impertinence) cara dura, frescura, *f.* **s.-centered,** egocéntrico. **s.-colored,** del mismo color; de su color natural. **s.-command,** dominio de sí mismo, *m;* sangre fría, ecuanimidad, *f.* **s.-complacent,** satisfecho de sí mismo, *f.* **s.-conceit,** vanidad, arrogancia, petulancia, *f.* **s.-confidence,** confianza en sí mismo, *f;* aplomo, *m.* **s.-confident,** seguro de sí mismo, lleno de confianza en sí mismo. **s.-conscious,** turbado, confuso, apocado. **s.-consciousness,** turbación, confusión, *f,* apocamiento, azoramiento, *m.* **s.-contained,** (of a person) reservado, poco comunicativo; dueño de sí mismo; (of things) completo; (of flats, etc.) independiente; con entrada independiente. **s.-contradictory,** contradictorio. **s.-control,** dominio de sí mismo, *m;* ecuanimidad, serenidad, sangre fría, *f.* **s.-controlled,** dueño de sí mismo; ecuánime, sereno. **s.-deception,** engaño de sí mismo, *m;* ilusiones, *f pl.* **s.-defense,** defensa propia, *f.* **s.-denial,** abnegación, *f;* renunciación, *f;* frugalidad, *f.* **s.-destruction,** suicidio, *m.* **s.-determination,** libre albedrío, *m;* (of peoples) autonomía, *f;* independencia, *f.* **s.-educating,** autodidacto. **s.-esteem,** respeto para uno mismo, *m;* amor propio, *m.* **s.-evident,** aparente, que salta a la vista. **s.-explanatory,** que se explica a sí mismo; evidente. **s.-generating,** autógeno. **s.-government,** (of a person) dominio de sí mismo, *m;* (of a state) autonomía, *f.* **s.-importance,** presunción, petulancia, *f.* **s.-important,** pagado de sí mismo. **to be s.-important,** darse importancia, darse tono. **s.-indulgence,** indulgencia con sí mismo, *f;* (of food, drink, etc.) excesos, *m pl,* falta de moderación, *f.* **s.-indulgent,** indulgente con sí mismo; dado a los placeres, sibarita. **s.-interest,** propio interés, *m.* **s.-knowledge,** conocimiento de sí mismo, *m.* **s.-love,** egolatría, *f.* **s.-made man,** hombre que ha llegado a su posición actual por sus propios esfuerzos, *m.* **self-medication,** automedicación, *f.* **s.-opinionated,** terco, obstinaz. **s.-portrait,** autorretrato, *m.* **s.-possessed,** dueño de sí mismo; reservado; de sangre fría. **s.-possession,** aplomo, *m,* sangre fría, serenidad, *f.* **s.-preservation,** protección de sí mismo, *f.* **s.-reliance,** independencia, *f;* confianza en sí mismo, *f.* **s.-reliant,** independiente; confiado en sí mismo. **s.-reproach,** remordimiento, *m.* **s.-respect,** respeto de sí mismo, *m;* amor propio, dignidad, *f.* **s.-respecting,** que se respeta; que tiene amor propio. **s.-restraint,** dominio de sí mismo, *m;* moderación, *f.* **s.-righteous,** farisaico. **s.-sacrifice,** abnegación, *f.* **s.-sacrificing,** abnegado. **s.-same,** mismo, idéntico. **s.-satisfaction,** satisfacción de sí mismo, *f;* vanidad, *f;* (of desires, etc.) satisfacción, indulgencia, *f.* **s.-satisfied,** satisfecho de sí mismo, pagado de sí mismo. **s.-seeking,** *a* egoísta, interesado. —*n* egoísmo, *m.* **s.-starter,** *Mech.* arranque automático, *m.* **s.-styled,** autodenominado, autotitulado, llamado por sí mismo. **s.-sufficiency,** suficiencia, *f;* presunción, *f.* **s.-sufficient,** que basta a sí mismo; contento de sí mismo. **s.-supporting,** que vive de su propio trabajo; (of an institution, business) independiente. **s.-taught,** autodidacto. **s.-willed,** voluntarioso

selfish /'sɛlfɪʃ/ *a* egoísta, interesado

selfishly /'sɛlfɪʃli/ *adv* interesadamente; por egoísmo

selfishness /'sɛlfɪʃnɪs/ *n* egoísmo, *m*

sell /sɛl/ *vt* vender. —*vi* vender; venderse. **They sold him to his enemies,** Le vendieron a sus enemigos. **House to s.,** «Se vende una casa.» **to s. at a loss,** malvender, vender con pérdida. **to s. for cash,** vender al contado. **to s. retail,** vender al por menor.

to s. **wholesale,** vender al por mayor. **to s. one's life
dearly,** vender cara la vida. **They sold the chair for
$10,** Vendieron la silla por diez dólares. **to s. off,**
(goods) liquidar, saldar. **to s. out,** vender; agotar.
The best edition is sold out, La mejor edición está
agotada. **All the nylons have been sold out,** Se han
vendido todas las medias de nilón (de cristal). **to s.
up,** vender
seller /'selər/ n vendedor (-ra), comerciante (en), m
selling /'selɪŋ/ n venta, f. **s. off,** liquidación, f. **s.
price,** precio de venta, m
selvage /'selvɪdʒ/ n (in cloth) orillo, m
semantics /sɪ'mæntɪks/ n semántica, f
semaphore /'semə,fɔr/ n semáforo, m, vt and vi
hacer señales semafóricas (a)
semaphoric /,semə'fɔrɪk/ a semafórico
semblance /'sembləns/ n apariencia, f. **to put on a
s. of woe,** aparentar ser triste
semen /'simən/ n semen, m, esperma, f
semester /sɪ'mestər/ n semestre, m
semi- prefix semi; medio. **s.-conscious,** medio consciente. **s.-detached house,** casa doble, f
semicircle /'semɪ,sɜrkəl/ n semicírculo, m
semicircular /,semɪ'sɜrkyələr/ a semicircular
semicolon /'semɪ,koulən/ n punto y coma, m
semidetached /,semɪdɪ'tætʃt, ,semaɪ-/ a (house)
apartado
semiformal /,semɪ'fɔrməl, ,semaɪ-/ a de media ceremonia
seminarist /'semɪnərɪst/ n seminarista, mf
seminary /'semə,neri/ n seminario, m; (for girls)
colegio interno, m
Semite /'semaɪt/ n semita, mf
Semitic /sə'mɪtɪk/ a semítico, semita
Semitism /'semɪ,tɪzəm/ n semitismo, m
semolina /,semə'linə/ n sémola, f
senate /'senɪt/ n senado, m
senator /'senətər/ n senador, m
senatorial /,senə'tɔriəl/ a senatorio
send /send/ vt enviar, mandar; com remitir; (a ball)
lanzar; (grant) conceder; permitir; (inflict) afligir
(con). **I sent Jane for it,** Envié a Juana a buscarlo.
He sent us word that he could not come, Nos
mandó un recado diciéndonos que no podía venir. **to
s. mad,** hacer enloquecer. **to s. packing,** mandar a
paseo. **to s. again,** volver a mandar. **to s. away,** vt
enviar; (dismiss) destituir; despedir; (scare off)
ahuyentar, vi enviar a otra parte. **to s. back,** (goods)
devolver; (persons) volver. **to s. down,** hacer bajar;
(rain, etc.) hacer, derramar; (a student) suspender,
expulsar. **to s. in,** mandar; (persons) hacer entrar, introducir; (food) servir; (a bill) presentar; (one's
name) dar. **Please s. him in!** ¡Sírvase de invitarle a
entrar! **to s. in one's resignation,** mandar su dimisión. **to s. off,** enviar, mandar; (goods) despachar;
(persons) destituir; (scare) ahuyentar. **s.-off,**
despedida, f. **a good s.-off,** una despedida afectuosa.
to s. on, (a letter) hacer seguir; (instructions) trasmitir. **to s. out,** hacer salir; mandar; (emit) despedir,
dar; (new shoots, etc.) echar. **to s. round,** (the hat,
etc.) hacer circular. **to s. up,** enviar arriba; mandar
subir, hacer subir; mandar, enviar; (a ball) lanzar
sender /'sendər/ n remitente, mf; elec transmisor, m
sending /'sendɪŋ/ n envío, m
Senegal /,senɪ'gɔl, -'gɑl/ Senegal, m
Senegalese /,senəgə'liz/ a and n senegalés (-esa)
senile /'sinaɪl/ a senil
senility /sɪ'nɪlɪti/ n senilidad, f
senior /'sinyər/ a mayor, de mayor edad; más antiguo. **Martinez s.,** Martínez padre. **Charles is Mary's
s. by five years,** Carlos es cinco años mayor que María. **s. member,** decano, m
seniority /sin'yɔrɪti/ n ancianidad, f; antigüedad, f
senna /'senə/ n bot sena, f
sensation /sen'seɪʃən/ n sensación, f; sentimiento, m;
impresión, f. **to create a s.,** causar una sensación
sensational /sen'seɪʃənl/ a sensacional
sensationalism /sen'seɪʃənl,ɪzəm/ n philos sensualismo, m; efectismo, m
sensationalist /sen'seɪʃənlɪst/ n philos sensualista,
mf; efectista, mf
sense /sens/ n sentido, m. —vt sentir. **in a s.,** hasta

cierto punto; desde un punto de vista. **in the full s.
of the word,** en toda la extensión de la palabra.
common s., sentido común, m. **He has no s. of
smell,** No tiene olfato. **the five senses,** los cinco sentidos. **to be out of one's senses,** estar fuera de sí,
estar trastornado. **You must be out of your senses!**
¡Debes de haber perdido el juicio! ¡Estás loco! **to
come to one's senses,** (after unconsciousness) volver
en sí; (after folly) recobrar el sentido común. **to talk
s.,** hablar con sentido común, hablar razonablemente.
s. organ, órgano de los sentidos, m. **have a good s.
of direction,** saber orientarse, tener buena orientación. **have no s. of smell,** ser incapaz de percibir
olores. **have no s. of taste,** ser incapaz de distinguir
gustos
senseless /'senslɪs/ a (unconscious) sin sentido, insensible; desmayado; (silly) necio, estúpido. **to
knock s.,** derribar, tumbar
senselessness /'senslɪsnɪs/ n falta de sentido común,
f; locura, absurdidad, f
sensibility /,sensə'bɪlɪti/ n sensibilidad, f
sensible /'sensəbəl/ a sensible; (conscious) consciente (de); sesudo. **to be s. of,** estar consciente de;
estar persuadido de
sensibly /'sensəbli/ adv sensiblemente; sesudamente,
cuerdamente
sensitive /'sensɪtɪv/ a sensitivo; susceptible (a); impresionable. **s. plant,** sensitiva, f
sensitivity /,sensɪ'tɪvɪti/ n sensibilidad, f; susceptibilidad, f; delicadeza, f
sensitize /'sensɪ,taɪz/ vt photo sensibilizar
sensory /'sensəri/ a sensorio
sensual /'senʃuəl/ a sensual; voluptuoso
sensualism /'senʃuə,lɪzəm/ n sensualismo, m
sensualist /'senʃuəlɪst/ n sensualista, mf
sensuality /,senʃu'ælɪti/ n sensualidad, f
sensually /'senʃuəli/ adv sensualmente
sensuous /'senʃuəs/ a sensorio
sensuousness /'senʃuəsnɪs/ n sensualidad, f
sentence /'sentns/ n law sentencia, f; (penalty) pena,
f; gram frase, f; (maxim) máxima, sentencia, f. —vt
sentenciar, condenar. **to pass s.,** pronunciar sentencia, fallar. **under s. of,** bajo pena de
sententious /sen'tenʃəs/ a sentencioso
sentient /'senʃənt/ a sensible
sentiment /'sentəmənt/ n sentimiento, m; (sentimentality) sentimentalismo, m; opinión, f
sentimental /,sentə'mentl/ a sentimental; (mawkish)
sensiblero
sentimentalist /,sentə'mentlɪst/ n romántico (-ca),
persona sentimental, f
sentimentality /,sentəmen'tælɪti/ n sentimentalismo,
m, sensiblería, f
sentimentalize /,sentə'mentl,aiz/ vt idealizar
sentimentally /,sentə'mentli/ adv sentimentalmente
sentinel /'sentnl/ n centinela, mf
sentry /'sentri/ n centinela, m. **to be on s. duty,** estar de guardia. **s.-box,** garita de centinela, f
separable /'sepərəbəl/ a separable
separate /a. 'separɪt; v. 'ʃreɪt/ a separado; distinto;
independiente. —vt separar; dividir. —vi separarse;
(of husband and wife) separarse de bienes y de cuerpos
separately /'sepərɪtli/ adv separadamente; aparte
separation /,sepə'reɪʃən/ n separación, f; law separación de bienes y de cuerpos, f
separatism /'sepərə,tɪzəm/ n separatismo, m
separatist /'sepərətɪst/ a and n separatista mf
Sephardic /sə'fardɪk/ a Sefaradí
sepia /'sipiə/ n (color and fish) sepia, f
September /sep'tembər/ n setiembre, septiembre, m
septic /'septɪk/ a séptico
septicemia /,septə'simiə/ n septicemia, f
septuagenarian /,septʃuədʒə'neəriən/ n setentón
(-ona); septuagenario (-ia)
septum /'septəm/ septo, tabique, m
sepulcher /'sepəlkər/ n sepulcro, m
sepulchral /sə'pʌlkrəl/ a sepulcral
sequel /'sikwəl/ n (of a story, etc.) continuación, f;
consecuencia, f; resultado, m
sequence /'sikwəns/ n sucesión, f; serie, f; orden,

mf; (at cards) serie, *f; gram* correspondencia, *f;* (*eccl* and cinema) secuencia, *f.* **s. of tenses,** correspondencia de los tiempos, *f*

sequestered /sɪˈkwestərd/ *a* aislado, remoto

sequestrate /sɪˈkwestreɪt/ *vt* secuestrar

sequestration /ˌsikwesˈtreɪʃən/ *n* secuestro, *m,*

sequin /ˈsikwɪn/ *n* lentejuela, *f*

seraglio /sɪˈrælyou/ *n* serrallo, *m*

seraph /ˈseraf/ *n* serafín, *m*

seraphic /sɪˈræfɪk/ *a* seráfico

seraphim /ˈserəfɪm/ *n* serafín, *m*

Serbia /ˈsɜrbiə/ Servia, *f*

Serbian /ˈsɜrbiən/ *a* servio. —*n* servio (-ia); (language) servio, *m*

serenade /ˌseraˈneɪd/ *n* serenata, *f, vt* dar una serenata (a)

serene /səˈrin/ *a* sereno. **His S. Highness,** Su Alteza Serenísima

serenity /səˈrenɪti/ *n* serenidad, *f;* tranquilidad, *f*

serf /sɜrf/ *n* siervo (-va)

serfdom /ˈsɜrfdəm/ *n* servidumbre, *f*

serge /sɜrdʒ/ *n* estameña, *f;* (silk) sarga, *f*

sergeant /ˈsɑrdʒənt/ *n mil* sargento, *m;* (police) sargento de policía, *m.* **s.-at-arms,** macero, *m.* **s.-major,** sargento instructor, *m*

serial /ˈsɪəriəl/ *a* en serie; (of a story) por entregas. —*n* novela por entregas, *f.* **s. number,** número de serie, *m*

sericulture /ˈsɜrɪˌkʌltʃər/ *n* sericultura, *f*

series /ˈsɪəriz/ *n* serie, *f;* cadena, *f; math* serie, progresión, *f.* **in s.,** en serie

serious /ˈsɪəriəs/ *a* serio; sincero; verdadero; (of illness, etc.) grave; importante. **He was s.** (not laughing) **when he said it,** Lo dijo en serio. **He is very s. about it,** Lo toma muy en serio. **to grow s.,** (of persons) ponerse serio; (of events) hacerse grave

seriously /ˈsɪəriəsli/ *adv* seriamente; en serio; gravemente. **to take** (something) **s.,** tomar (algo) en serio. **to take oneself s.,** tomarse muy en serio

seriousness /ˈsɪəriəsnɪs/ *n* seriedad, *f;* gravedad, *f.* **in all s.,** en serio, seriamente

sermon /ˈsɜrmən/ *n* sermón, *m*

sermonize /ˈsɜrməˌnaɪz/ *vt and vi* sermonear

serpent /ˈsɜrpənt/ *n* serpiente, *f; mus* serpentón, *m*

serpentine /ˈsɜrpənˌtin, -ˌtaɪn/ *a* serpentino; (of character) tortuoso. —*n mineral* serpentina, *f*

serrated /ˈsereɪtɪd/ *a* serrado; dentellado

serried /ˈserid/ *a* apretado, apiñado

serum /ˈsɪərəm/ *n* suero, *m*

servant /ˈsɜrvənt/ *n* servidor (-ra); (domestic) criado (-da); (employee) empleado (-da); (slave and *fig*) siervo (-va); *pl* **servants,** (domestic) servidumbre, *f,* servicio, *m.* **I remain your obedient s.,** Quedo de Vd. atento y seguro servidor (att. y s.s.). **civil s.,** empleado del estado, *m.* **general s.,** criada para todo, *f.* **man s.,** criado, *m.* **the s. problem,** el problema del servicio. **Your s., sir,** Servidor de Vd., señor. **s.-girl,** criada, *f*

serve /sɜrv/ *vt* servir (a); ser útil (a); satisfacer; (in a shop) despachar; (an apprenticeship, etc.) hacer; (a prison sentence) cumplir; (treat) tratar; (of stallion) cubrir; (a warrant, etc.) ejecutar; (a notice) entregar; (a ball) servir; (on a jury, etc.) formar parte de; *naut* aforrar. —*vi* servir; (*mil, nav*) hacer el servicio. —*n sports* saque, *m.* **It serves you right!** ¡Lo tienes merecido! **to s. at table,** servir a la mesa. **to s. as,** servir de. **to s. out,** distribuir; servir. **Serves 8,** (recipe) Da 8 porciones

server /ˈsɜrvər/ *n eccl* acólito, *m; sports* saque, *m;* (tray) bandeja, *f;* (for fish, etc.) pala, *f*

service /ˈsɜrvɪs/ *n* servicio, *m; eccl* oficio, *m;* servicio de mesa, *m;* (of a writ) entrega, *f; sports* saque, *m.* **coffee s.,** juego de café, *m.* **diplomatic s.,** cuerpo diplomático, *m.* **At your s.,** Para servir a Vd., A su disposición. **on active s.,** en acto de servicio; en el campo de batalla. **to go into s.,** (of servants) ir a servir. **to render s.,** prestar servicios. **s. tree,** serbal, *m*

serviceable /ˈsɜrvəsəbəl/ *a* (of persons) servicial; (of things) servible, utilizable; útil; práctico; (lasting) duradero

service road *n* vía de servicio, *f*

serviette /ˌsɜrviˈet/ *n* servilleta, *f.* **s. ring,** servilletero, *m*

servile /ˈsɜrvɪl/ *a* servil

servility /sərˈvɪlɪti/ *n* servilismo, *m*

serving /ˈsɜrvɪŋ/ *a* sirviente; al servicio (de). **s. maid,** criada, *f.* **s. table,** trinchero, *m*

servitude /ˈsɜrvɪˌtud/ *n* servidumbre, esclavitud, *f.* **penal s.,** cadena perpetua, *f*

session /ˈseʃən/ *n* sesión, *f;* junta, *f.* **petty sessions,** tribunal de primera instancia, *m*

set /set/ *vt* poner; colocar; fijar; (seeds, etc.) plantar; (bones) reducir, componer; (gems) engastar, montar; (a clock) regular; (sails) desplegar; (the teeth of a saw) trabar, triscar; (congeal) hacer coagular; (a trap) armar; (a snare) tender; (a razor) afilar; (make ready) preparar; (type) componer; (cause) hacer; *mus* poner en música; *mus* adaptar; (order) mandar; (prescribe) dar, asignar; (estimate) estimar, evaluar; (an example, etc.) dar; (establish) establecer, crear. —*vi* (of the sun, etc.) ponerse; (solidify) coagularse; solidificarse; (of tides) fluir; (of the wind) soplar; (of dogs) hacer punta. **The joke set him laughing,** El chiste le hizo reír. **to set an example,** dar ejemplo, dar el ejemplo. **set a precedent,** sentar precedente. **to set a person's mind at rest,** tranquilizar, sosegar. **to set a trap,** armar lazo. **to set at ease,** poner a sus anchas (a), hacer cómodo (a). **to set at naught,** despreciar. **to set eyes on,** poner los ojos en. **to set fire to,** pegar fuego a, incendiar. **to set free,** poner en libertad, librar (de). **to set in motion,** poner en marcha. **to set one's teeth,** apretar los dientes. **to set people talking,** dar que hablar a la gente. **to set the fashion,** fijar la moda; poner de moda. **to set the alarm at seven o'clock,** poner el despertador a las siete. **to set the table,** poner la mesa. **to set to work,** ponerse a trabajar. **to set about,** *vi* (begin) ponerse (a); empezar; (undertake) emprender. —*vt* (a rumor, etc.) divulgar. **They set about each other,** Empezaron a golpearse, Vinieron a las manos. **to set against,** indisponer (con), enemistar (con); hacer el enemigo (de), ser hostil (a); (balance) oponer, balancear. **to set oneself against,** oponerse a; atacar, luchar contra. **to set aside,** poner a un lado; apartar; (discard) desechar; (omit) omitir, pasar por alto de; dejar aparte, excluir; (keep) reservar; (money, etc.) ahorrar; (reject) rechazar; (quash) anular. **to set back,** retrasar; hacer retroceder. **set-back,** *n* revés, *m;* contrariedad, *f.* **to set before,** poner ante; (facts) exponer; (introduce) presentar. **to set down,** poner en tierra; depositar; (of a bus, etc.) dejar; (in writing) poner por escrito; anotar, apuntar; narrar, contar; (attribute) atribuir; (fix) fijar, formular; (believe to be) creer. **Passengers are set down at...,** Los viajeros pueden apearse en... **to set forth,** *vt* (one's opinions, etc.) exponer; publicar; (display) exhibir, mostrar; (make) hacer. —*vi* ponerse en camino. **to set going,** poner en marcha; echar a andar. **to set in,** empezar; (of the tide) fluir. **A reaction has set in,** Se ha hecho sentir una reacción. **to set off,** *vt* (explode) hacer estallar; (cause) hacer; (heighten) realzar; hacer resaltar; (counterbalance) contraponer. —*vi* partir; ponerse en camino. **set-off,** *n* contraste, *m,* contraposición, *f.* **to set off against,** contraponer. **to set on,** *vt* (a dog) azuzar; (incite) instigar, incitar. —*vi* atacar. **to set out,** *vt* (state) exponer, manifestar; (embellish) realzar; (display) arreglar, disponer. —*vi* ponerse en camino, partir. **to set over,** (rule) tener autoridad sobre, gobernar. **to set to,** (begin to) ponerse a, empezar a; (work) ponerse a trabajar. **set-to,** *n* lucha, *f;* (boxing) asalto, *m;* (quarrel) pelea, riña, *f.* **to set up,** *vt* (a monument, etc.) erigir, levantar; (fix) fijar; (apparatus, machinery) montar; (exalt) exaltar; (found) establecer; crear; (propound) exponer; (a howl, etc.) dar; (equip with) proveer de; instalar; (make strong) robustecer; fortificar; (type) componer; (raise) alzar. —*vi* establecerse; dárselas de. **He sets himself up as a painter,** Se las da de pintor. **to set** (a person) **up as a model,** poner como modelo (a). **to set up house,** poner casa. **to set up a business,** establecer un comercio. **set-up,** *n* establecimiento, *m;* arreglo, *m.* **to set upon,** atacar

set /set/ *n* (of sun, etc.) puesta, *f,* ocaso, *m;* (of the head, etc.) porte, *m;* (of a garment) corte, *m;* (of the tide, etc.) dirección, *f;* (slant) inclinación, *f;* (*fig* drift) tendencia, *f,* movimiento, *m;* (of the teeth of a saw) triscamiento, *m;* (of men, houses, etc.) grupo, *m;* (of tools, golf clubs, china, etc.) juego, *m;* (gang) pandilla, camarilla, *f;* clase, *f;* (*dance*) tanda, *f;* (tennis) partido, *f; theat* decoración, *f; radio* aparato de radio, *m,* radio, *f.* **coffee set,** juego de café, *m.* **all-mains set,** radio de corriente eléctrica, *f.* **battery set,** radio de batería, *f.* **portable set,** radio portátil, *f.* **the smart set,** el mundo elegante. **to have a shampoo and set,** hacerse lavar y marcar (el pelo). **to make a set,** hacer juego. **to make a dead set at,** hacer un ataque vigoroso (a), atacar resueltamente; procurar insinuarse en el favor de. **set of teeth,** dentadura, *f*

set /sɛt/ *a* fijo; inmóvil; (of a smile) forzado; (of a task) asignado; (of times) señalado, fijo; (prescribed) prescrito, establecido; (firm) firme; (resolved) resuelto; (well-known) consabido; (obstinate) terco, nada adaptable. **well set-up,** apuesto, bien plantado. **He is set on doing it,** Se empeña en **to be dead set against,** estar completamente opuesto a. **set phrase,** frase hecha, *f.* **set-square,** cartabón, *m*

settee /sɛ'ti/ *n* canapé, *m.* **s.-bed,** cama turca, *f*

setter /'sɛtər/ *n* (perro) séter, perdiguero, *m.* **s.-on,** instigador (-ra)

setting /'sɛtɪŋ/ *n* (of the sun, etc.) puesta, *f;* (of mortar, etc.) fraguado, *m;* (of a jelly) solidificación, *f;* (of jewels) engaste, *m,* montadura, *f;* (of bones) aliño, *m;* (of teeth of saw) traba, *f;* (of razor) afiladura, *f;* (of a trap) armadura, *f;* (of a machine, etc.) ajuste, *m;* (frame) marco, *m; mus* arreglo, *m; theat* decorado, *m;* (emplacement) lecho, *m.* **the s. sun,** el sol poniente. **s. free,** liberación, *f.* **s. off,** partida, salida, *f.* **s. out,** ida, marcha, *f;* principio, *m.* **s.-up,** creación, institución, *f,* establecimiento, *m;* (of a machine) montaje, *m; print* composición, *f*

settle /'sɛtl/ *vt* colocar; asegurar; afirmar; (a country) colonizar; (live in) establecer (en); (populate) poblar; (in a profession, etc.) dar; (install) instalar; (the imagination, etc.) sosegar, calmar; (resolve) resolver; (arrange) disponer, arreglar; (differences) componer, concertar; (an opponent, etc.) confundir; (a bill) saldar, pagar; (a claim) satisfacer; (liberty) depositar, clarificar; (end) poner fin (a). —*vi* establecerse; (of weather) serenarse; (to work, etc.) empezar a, ponerse a; aplicarse a; (decide) decidirse; (alight) posarse; (of foundations, etc.) asentarse; (of a ship) zozobrar; (of sediment) depositarse; (of liquid) clarificarse. **to s. accounts with,** *fig* ajustar cuentas con. **to s. down,** establecerse, arraigarse; adaptarse (a); (become calm) sosegarse, calmarse; sentar el juicio; (of foundations) asentarse; (of a ship) zozobrar; (of sediment) depositarse. **to s. in,** *vt* instalar. —*vi* instalarse. **to s. on,** (choose) escoger; (decide on) decidirse (a). **to s. a pension on,** señalar pensión (a). **to s. up,** *vt* (one's affairs) poner en orden; (bill) pagar, saldar. —*vi* llegar a un acuerdo; pagar cuentas

settled /'sɛtld/ *a* fijo; permanente; invariable; (of countries) colonizado; (of weather) sereno

settlement /'sɛtlmənt/ *n* (of a country) colonización, *f;* (of a dispute) arreglo, ajuste, *m;* (of a question) solución, *f;* decisión, *f;* (of a bill) saldo, pago, *m,* liquidación, *f;* (of an obligation) satisfacción, *f;* (colony) colonia, *f;* (creation) creación, institución, *f;* establecimiento, arraigo, *m.* **deed of s.,** escritura de donación, *f.* **marriage s.,** contrato matrimonial, *m;* **s. out of court,** arreglo pacífico, *m*

settler /'sɛtlər/ *n* colono, *m;* colonizador (-ra)

seven /'sɛvən/ *a* and *n* siete *m.* **It is s. o'clock,** Son las siete. **the s. deadly sins,** los siete pecados capitales

seventeen /'sɛvən'tin/ *a* diecisiete, diez y siete. —*n* diecisiete, *m.* **She is just s.,** Acaba de cumplir los diez y siete años

seventeenth /'sɛvən'tinθ/ *a* décimoséptimo; (of monarchs and of the month) diez y siete. —*n* décimoséptimo, *m.* **Louis the S.,** Luis diez y siete. **the s. of June,** el diez y siete de junio

seventh /'sɛvənθ/ *a* séptimo; (of the month) siete. —*n* séptimo, *m;* séptima parte, *f; mus* séptima, *f.* **Edward the S.,** Eduardo séptimo. **the s. of August,** el siete de agosto

seventieth /'sɛvəntiiθ/ *a* septuagésimo, setentavo. —*n* setentavo, *m*

seventy /'sɛvənti/ *a* and *n* setenta, *m*

sever /'sɛvər/ *vt* separar; romper; dividir

several /'sɛvərəl/ *a* distinto, diferente; respectivo; varios, *m pl,* (*f pl,* varias); algunos, *m pl,* (*f pl,* algunas)

severally /'sɛvərəli/ *adv* separadamente; individualmente; independientemente

severance /'sɛvərəns/ *n* separación, *f;* (of friendship, etc.) ruptura, *f*

severe /sə'vɪər/ *a* severo; riguroso; fuerte; duro; (of style) austero; (of pain) agudo; (of illness) grave

severely /sə'vɪərli/ *adv* severamente; intensamente; gravemente

severity /sə'vɛrɪti/ *n* severidad, *f;* intensidad, *f;* (of weather) inclemencia, *f;* (of illness) gravedad, *f*

sew /sou/ *vt* and *vi* coser. **to sew on,** coser, pegar

sewage /'suɪdʒ/ *n* aguas residuales, *f pl.* **s. system,** alcantarillado, *m*

sewer /'suər/ *n* alcantarilla, cloaca, *f,* albañal, *m*

sewing /'souɪŋ/ *n* costura, *f.* **s. bag,** costurero, *m.* **s. cotton,** hilo de coser, *m.* **s.-machine,** máquina de coser, *f.* **s. silk,** torzal, *m*

sex /sɛks/ *n* sexo, *m.* **the fair sex,** el bello sexo. **the weaker sex,** el sexo débil. **sex appeal,** atractivo, *m*

sexagenarian /ˌsɛksədʒə'nɛəriən/ *n* sexagenario (-ia)

sexless /'sɛkslɪs/ *a* neutro; frígido

sexologist /sɛk'sɒlədʒɪst/ *n* sexólogo (-ga)

sexology /sɛk'sɒlədʒi/ *n* sexología, *f*

sextant /'sɛkstənt/ *n* sextante, *m*

sexton /'sɛkstən/ *n* sacristán, *m;* sepulturero, *m;* (bell-ringer) campanero, *m*

sexual /'sɛkʃuəl/ *a* sexual

sexuality /ˌsɛkʃu'ælɪti/ *n* sexualidad, *f*

Sforza /'sfɔrtsə/ Esforcia, *f*

sh! /ʃ/ *interj* ¡Chitón! ¡Chis!

shabbily /'ʃæbəli/ *adv* (of dressing) pobremente; (of treatment) mezquinamente

shabbiness /'ʃæbɪnɪs/ *n* pobreza, *f;* estado andrajoso, *m;* (of behavior) mezquindad, ruindad, *f*

shabby /'ʃæbi/ *a* (of persons) desharrapado, andrajoso; (of garments) raído, roto; (of a neighborhood, etc.) pobre; (mean) ruin, mezquino

shack /ʃæk/ *n* choza, *f*

shackle /'ʃækəl/ *n* traba, *f; pl* **shackles,** grillos, *m pl,* esposas, *f pl; fig* cadenas, *f pl.* —*vt* poner esposas (a), encadenar; (a horse) apear; *fig* atar; (impede) estorbar

shad /ʃæd/ *n* sábalo, *m*

shade /ʃeid/ *n* sombra, *f;* (in a picture) toque de obscuro, *m;* (for the eyes) visera, *f;* (of a lamp) pantalla, *f;* (ghost) espectro, fantasma, *m;* (of color) matiz, *m;* (tinge) dejo, *m.* —*vt* sombrear, dar sombra (a); (the face, etc.) proteger, resguardar; (a drawing) esfumar. **in the s.,** a la sombra. **80° in the s.,** ochenta grados a la sombra. **to put** (a person) **in the s.,** eclipsar

shadiness /'ʃeidɪnɪs/ *n* sombra, *f*

shading /'ʃeidɪŋ/ *n* sombra, *f; art* degradación, *f*

shadow /'ʃædou/ *n* sombra, *f;* obscuridad, *f;* (in a picture) toque de obscuro, *m.* —*vt* sombrear; obscurecer; (a person) seguir la pista (a), proyectar una sombra. **to s. forth,** indicar; simbolizar. **s. show,** sombras chinescas, *f pl*

shadowy /'ʃædoui/ *a* umbroso; vago, indistinto, indefinido

shady /'ʃeidi/ *a* sombreado, umbrío; sombrío; (of persons, etc.) sospechoso. **It was s. in the wood,** Hacía sombra en el bosque

shaft /ʃæft/ *n* fuste, *m;* (arrow) flecha, saeta, *f,* dardo, *m;* (of a golf club, etc.) mango, *m;* (of a cart) vara, *f; mech* árbol, eje, *m;* (of a column and a feather) cañón, *m;* (of light) rayo, *m;* (of a mine) pozo, tiro, *m;* (air-shaft) conducto de aire, ventilador, *m.* **cam-s.,** árbol de levas, *m.* **driving s.,** árbol motor, *m*

shaggy /'ʃægi/ *a* peludo; lanudo

shagreen /ʃə'grin/ *n* chagrén, *m*

shah /ʃɑ, ʃɔ/ *n* cha, *m*

shake /ʃeik/ *vt* sacudir; agitar; hacer temblar; (weaken) debilitar, hacer flaquear. —*vi* estremecerse; temblar; (trill) trinar. **He managed to s. himself**

free, Consiguió librarse por una sacudida. **to s. hands,** darse la mano, estrecharse la mano. **to s. one's finger at,** señalar con el dedo (a). **to s. one's fist at,** amenazar con el puño (a). **to s. one's head,** mover la cabeza; negar con la cabeza. **to s. one's sides,** (with laughter) reírse a carcajadas. **to s. with fear,** temblar de miedo. **to s. down,** sacudir, hacer caer. **s.-down,** *n* cama improvisada, *f.* **to s. off,** sacudirse; librarse (de), perder; quitar de encima (a). **to s. out,** (unfurl) desplegar; sacudir. **to s. up,** agitar; sacudir, remover

shake /ʃeik/ *n* sacudida, *f;* (of the head) movimiento (de la cabeza), *m;* (of the hand) apretón (de manos), *m;* temblor, *m; mus* trino, gorjeo, *m.* **in two shakes,** *Inf.* en un periquete. **to give a person a good s.,** sacudir violentamente (a)

Shakespearean /ʃeik'spiəriən/ *a* shakespeariano

shakiness /'ʃeikinis/ *n* inestabilidad, *f;* poca firmeza, *f;* temblor, *m;* lo dudoso. **the s. of his voice,** su voz trémula

shaking /'ʃeikiŋ/ *n* sacudimiento, *m;* temblor, *m;* (of windows, etc.) zangoloteo, *m*

shaky /'ʃeiki/ *a* inestable; poco firme; (of hands, etc.) tembloroso; (of the voice) trémulo; (of gait) vacilante; dudoso

shale /ʃeil/ *n* esquisto, *m*

shall /ʃæl/ *unstressed* ʃəl/ *v aux* (expressing simple future) **I s. arrive tomorrow,** Llegaré mañana. **S. we go to the sea next week?** ¿Iremos al mar la semana próxima?; (expressing obligation, compulsion) **You s. not go out,** No has de salir, No quiero que salgas. **He s. see her immediately,** Tiene que verla en seguida; (as a polite formula) **S. I go?** ¿Quiere Vd. que vaya? **S. we buy the soap?** ¿Quiere Vd. que compremos el jabón? ¿Compraremos el jabón?

shallot /'ʃælət, ʃə'lɒt/ *n bot* chalote, *m,* ascalonia, *f*

shallow /'ʃælou/ *a* poco profundo; (of a receptacle) llano; (of persons) superficial, frívolo; (of knowledge, etc.) superficial, ligero, somero. *—n* bajío, *m*

shallowness /'ʃælounis/ *n* poca profundidad, *f;* superficialidad, *f*

sham /ʃæm/ *vt* fingir, simular. *—n* farsa, *f;* imitación, *f;* engaño, *m;* (person) farsante, *m.* *—a* fingido; falso; espurio. **to s. illness,** fingirse enfermo. **to s. dead,** hacer la mortecina. **You're just a s.,** Eres un farsante

sham battle *n mil* simulacro de combate, simulacro guerrero, *m*

shamble /'ʃæmbəl/ *vi* andar arrastrándose. *—n* andar pesado, *m; pl* **shambles,** matadero, *m; fig* carnicería, *f*

shambling /'ʃæmbliŋ/ *a* pesado, lento

shame /ʃeim/ *n* vergüenza, *f;* ignominia, *f;* deshonra, *f.* *—vt* avergonzar; deshonrar. **For s.!** ¡Qué vergüenza! **What a s.!** ¡Qué lástima! **to put to s.,** avergonzar

shamefaced /'ʃeim,feist/ *a* (bashful) vergonzoso, tímido; (ashamed) avergonzado

shamefacedly /,ʃeim'feisidli/ *adv* vergonzosamente, tímidamente; con vergüenza

shameful /'ʃeimfəl/ *a* vergonzoso, escandaloso; indecente

shamefully /'ʃeimfəli/ *adv* escandalosamente

shamefulness /'ʃeimfəlnis/ *n* vergüenza, infamia, *f;* indecencia, *f*

shameless /'ʃeimlis/ *a* desvergonzado; impúdico, indecente

shamelessly /'ʃeimlisli/ *adv* desvergonzadamente

shamelessness /'ʃeimlisnis/ *n* desvergüenza, poca vergüenza, *f;* impudicia, deshonestidad, *f*

shampoo /ʃæm'pu/ *n* champú, *m.* *—vt* dar un champú (a); dar un masaje (a). **dry s.,** champú seco, *m*

shamrock /'ʃæmrɒk/ *n* trébol blanco, *m*

shank /ʃæŋk/ *n* zanca, *f; mech* pierna, *f;* (handle) mango, *m;* (of a button) rabo, *m,* cola, *f.* **go on Shank's mare, ride on Shank's mare,** caminar en coche de San Francisco, ir en la boridad de Villadiego

shanty /'ʃænti/ *n* choza, *f*

shanty town *n* barriada (Peru), callampa, población, *f;* población callampa (Chile), *f.* Rancho (Venezuela), *m,* villa-miseria (Argentina), *f*

shape /ʃeip/ *n* forma, *f;* bulto, *m;* fantasma, *m;* (of a garment) corte, *m;* (of a person) talle, *m; cul* molde, *m;* (of a hat) forma, *f.* *—vt* formar; (a garment) cortar; (ideas) dar forma (a); adaptar; (stone, etc.) labrar; (one's life) dominar. *—vi* (of events) desarrollarse. **to go out of s.,** perder la forma. **to take s.,** tomar forma. **to s. one's course,** dirigirse (hacia, a); *naut* dar el rumbo. **to s. well,** prometer bien

shaped /ʃeipt/ *a* de forma de..., que tiene figura de... **pear-s.,** piriforme

shapeless /'ʃeiplis/ *a* informe; disforme

shapelessness /'ʃeiplisnis/ *n* informidad, *f;* deformidad, *f*

shapeliness /'ʃeiplinis/ *n* belleza de forma, *f;* simetría, *f*

shapely /'ʃeipli/ *a* bien formado; simétrico

share /ʃeər/ *n* porción, *f;* parte, *f;* cuota, *f;* contribución, *f;* (part ownership) interés, *m;* (in a company) acción, *f.* *—vt* distribuir; compartir; dividir; tomar parte en. *—vi* participar (de); tomar parte (en). **to fall to one's s.,** tocar, corresponder. **to go shares with,** dividir con, compartir con. **to take a s. in the conversation,** tomar parte en la conversación. **paid-up s.,** *com* acción liberada, *f.* **to s. out,** repartir, distribuir

shareholder /'ʃeər,houldər/ *n* accionista, *mf*

sharer /'ʃeərər/ *n* partícipe, *f*

shark /ʃɑrk/ *n ichth* tiburón, *m; inf* caimán, *m*

sharp /ʃɑrp/ *a* (of edges) afilado, cortante; (of points) punzante, puntiagudo; (of features, etc.) anguloso; (of bends, etc.) brusco; (of outlines, etc.) definido, distinto; (of pain, sound) agudo; (marked) marcado; (intense) intenso; (of winds, glance, etc.) penetrante; (of hearing) fino; (of appetite) bueno; (of showers) fuerte; (quick) rápido; (clever, etc.) vivo, listo; perspicaz; (of children) despierto, precoz; (unscrupulous) astuto, sin escrúpulos; (of criticism, remarks) mordaz; (of rebukes, sentences, etc.) severo; (of winters, etc.) riguroso; (of fighting) encarnizado; (of taste) picante; (sour) ácido; *mus* sostenido. *—adv* en punto; puntualmente. *—n mus* sostenido, *m.* **at five o'clock s.,** a las cinco en punto. **Look s.!** ¡Date prisa! **s.-edged,** afilado. **s.-eyed,** con ojos de lince; de mirada penetrante. **s.-featured,** de facciones angulosas. **s.-nosed,** de nariz puntiaguda. **s.-pointed,** puntiagudo. **s. practice,** procedimientos poco honrados, *m pl.* **s.-tongued,** de lengua áspera. **s. turn,** curva brusca, curva cerrada, *f.* **s.-witted,** de inteligencia viva, listo

sharpen /'ʃɑrpən/ *vt* (knives) afilar, amolar; (pencils, etc.) sacar punta (a); (wits, etc.) despabilar; (appetite) abrir. **This walk has sharpened my appetite,** Este paseo me ha abierto el apetito. **to s. one's claws,** afilarse las uñas

sharper /'ʃɑrpər/ *n inf* caballero de industria, timador, *m;* (at cards) fullero, *m*

sharply /'ʃɑrpli/ *adv* claramente; bruscamente; severamente; ásperamente

sharpness /'ʃɑrpnis/ *n* (of cold, etc.) intensidad, *f;* severidad, *f;* (cleverness) agudeza, perspicacia, *f;* (of a child) precocidad, *f;* (sarcasm, etc.) mordacidad, *f;* aspereza, *f;* brusquedad, *f*

sharpshooter /'ʃɑrpʃutər/ *n* franco tirador, *m*

sharpsighted /'ʃɑrp,saitid/ *a* de vista penetrante, listo, perspicaz

shatter /'ʃætər/ *vt* romper, quebrantar; hacer añicos; *fig* destrozar. **You have shattered my illusions,** Has destrozado todas mis ilusiones

shave /ʃeiv/ *vt* afeitar, rasurar; (wood, etc.) acepillar. *—vi* afeitarse; (of razors) afeitar. *—n* afeitada, *f.* **to have a s.,** hacerse afeitar. **to have a close s.,** *inf* escapar por un pelo

shaving /'ʃeiviŋ/ *n* afeitada, *f;* (of wood, etc.) viruta, acepilladura, *f.* **s.-bowl,** bacía, *f.* **s.-brush,** brocha de afeitar, *f.* **s.-glass,** espejo de afeitar, *m.* **s.-soap,** jabón de afeitar, *m.* **s.-stick,** barra de jabón de afeitar, *f*

shawl /ʃɔl/ *n* chal, mantón, rebozo, *m*

she /ʃi/ *pers pron* ella; la; (female) hembra, *f;* (translated by fem. ending in the case of animals, etc., e.g. *she bear,* osa, *she cat,* gata) **It is her,** Es ella. **she who is dancing,** la que baila

sheaf /ʃif/ *n* (of corn, etc.) gavilla, garba, *f;* (of arrows) haz, *m;* (of papers, etc.) paquete, atado, *m.* **to bind in sheaves,** agavillar

shear /ʃɪər/ *vt* (sheep) esquilar, trasquilar; tonsurar; cortar; (cloth) tundir

shearer /'ʃɪərər/ *n* (of sheep) esquilador, *m*

shearing /'ʃɪərɪŋ/ *n* (of sheep) esquileo, *m,* tonsura, *f;* (of cloth) tunda, *f.* **s. machine,** esquiladora, *f.* **s. season,** esquileo, *m*

shears /ʃɪərz/ *n pl* tijeras grandes, *f pl,* cizalla, *f*

sheath /ʃiθ/ *n* vaina, *f.* **s.-knife,** cuchillo de monte, *m*

sheathe /ʃið/ *vt* envainar; *naut* aforrar

shed /ʃed/ *vt* derramar; (skin, etc.) mudar; perder; (remove) quitarse, desprenderse de; (get rid of) deshacerse de. —*n* cobertizo, sotechado, *m;* cabaña, *f.* **to s. light on,** echar luz sobre, iluminar

sheen /ʃin/ *n* lustre, *m;* brillo, *m*

sheep /ʃip/ *n* oveja, *f;* carnero, *m;* ganado lanar, *m.* **He is the black s. of the family,** Es el garbanzo negro de la familia. **to cast sheep's eyes at,** lanzar miradas de carnero degollado. **s. breeder,** ganadero, *m.* **s.-dip,** desinfectante para ganado, *m.* **s.-dog,** perro de pastor, *m.* **s.-like,** ovejuno, de oveja. **s.-shearing,** esquileo, *m*

sheepfold /'ʃip,fould/ *n* aprisco, redil, *m*

sheepish /'ʃipiʃ/ *a* tímido, vergonzoso; estúpido

sheepishly /'ʃipiʃli/ *adv* tímidamente

sheepishness /'ʃipiʃnis/ *n* timidez, cortedad, *f;* estupidez, *f*

sheepskin /'ʃip,skin/ *n* piel de carnero, *f.* **s. jacket,** zamarra, *f*

sheer /ʃɪər/ *a* puro; completo, absoluto; (steep) escarpado, acantilado; a pico; (of fabrics) transparente; ligero, fino. —*adv* completamente; de un golpe; (perpendiculary) a pico. **to s. off,** desviarse; largarse, marcharse

sheet /ʃit/ *n* (bed) sábana, *f;* (shroud) mortaja, *f;* (of paper) hoja, *f;* cuartilla, *f;* (pamphlet) folleto, *m;* (news) periódico, *m,* hoja, *f;* (of metal, etc.) lámina, plancha, *f;* (of water, etc.) extensión, *f; naut* escota, *f.* —*vt* poner sábanas en; envolver en sábanas; (a corpse) amortajar. **to be as white as a s.,** estar pálido como un muerto. **s. bend,** (knot) nudo de tejedor, *m.* **s. glass,** vidrio en lámina, *m.* **s. iron,** hierro en planchas, *m*

sheik /ʃik/ *n* jeque, *m*

shekel /'ʃekəl/ *n* (coin) siclo, *m; pl* **shekels,** dinero, *m*

shelf /ʃelf/ *n* estante, anaquel, *m;* (reef) banco de arena, bajío, *m;* (of rock) escalón, *m.* **to be on the s.,** *inf* quedarse para tía, quedarse para vestir imágenes

shell /ʃel/ *n* (of small shellfish) concha, *f;* (of tortoise) coraza, *f;* (of insects, lobsters, etc.) caparazón, *m;* (of a nut) cáscara, *f;* (of an egg) cascarón, *m;* (of peas, beans) vaina, *f;* (*com* and *mus*) concha, *f;* (of a building) casco, *m;* (outside) exterior, *m;* (empty form) apariencia, *f; mil* granada, *f.* —*vt* pelar; (nuts) descascarar; (beans, etc.) desvainar; *mil* bombardear. **to be under s.-fire,** sufrir un bombardeo. **s. shock,** neurosis de guerra, *f*

shellfish /'ʃel,fiʃ/ *n* crustáceo, *m;* (as food) marisco, *m*

shelling /'ʃelɪŋ/ *n mil* bombardeo, *m*

shelter /'ʃeltər/ *n* abrigo, amparo, *m;* refugio, *m;* asilo, *m.* —*vt* dar asilo (a); abrigar; (defend) amparar, proteger; (hide) esconder. —*vi* refugiarse; resguardarse; esconderse

sheltered /'ʃeltərd/ *a* abrigado

sheltering /'ʃeltərɪŋ/ *a* protector

shelve /ʃelv/ *vt* (books) poner en un estante; (persons) destituir; (questions, etc.) aplazar, arrinconar; proveer de estantes, *vi* (slope) inclinarse, formar declive; (of sea bed) formar escalones

shelving /'ʃelvɪŋ/ *a* inclinado; (of ocean bed) acantilado

shepherd /'ʃepərd/ *n* pastor, *m.* —*vt* guardar; guiar, conducir. **s. boy,** zagal, *m.* **shepherd's pouch,** zurrón, *m*

shepherdess /'ʃepərdis/ *n* pastora, *f*

sherbet /'ʃɜrbit/ *n* sorbete, *m*

sheriff /'ʃerif/ *n* (in U.K.) sheriff, *m;* (U.S.A.) jefe de la policía, *m*

sherry /'ʃeri/ *n* (vino de) jerez, *m.* **dry s.,** jerez seco, *m*

Shetlands, the /'ʃetləndz/ las Islas de Shetland, *f pl*

shield /ʃild/ *n* escudo, *m;* (round) rodela, *f; herald* escudo de armas, *m; fig* defensa, *f,* amparo, *m.* —*vt* proteger, amparar. **to s. a person,** proteger a una persona. **to s. one's eyes from the sun,** proteger los ojos del sol. **s.-bearer,** escudero, *m*

shift /ʃift/ *vt* mover; trasladar; quitar, librarse de; cambiar. —*vi* moverse; (of the wind) girar; cambiar. —*n* cambio, *m;* (expedient) recurso, expediente, *m;* (dodge) artificio, *m,* trampa, *f;* (of workmen) tanda, *f,* turno, *m.* **to make s.,** arreglárselas (para hacer algo); procurar (hacer algo); (manage) ir tirando. **to s. for oneself,** componérselas, arreglárselas. **to s. the scenes,** *theat* cambiar de decoración. **to s. the helm,** *naut* cambiar el timón. **to work in shifts,** trabajar por turnos

shiftiness /'ʃiftinis/ *n* falta de honradez, informalidad, *f;* astucia, *f*

shifting /'ʃiftɪŋ/ *a* (of light, etc.) cambiante; (of sand, etc.) movedizo; (of wind) mudable; (of moods) voluble. **s. sand,** arena movediza, *f*

shiftless /'ʃiftlis/ *a* perezoso; sin energía, ineficaz

shiftlessness /'ʃiftlisnis/ *n* pereza, *f;* falta de energía, *f*

shifty /'ʃifti/ *a* (tricky) tramposo, astuto; (dishonest) informal, falso; (of gaze) furtivo. **s.-eyed,** *a* de mirada furtiva

Shiite /'ʃiait/ *a* and *n* chiita

shilling /'ʃilɪŋ/ *n* chelín, *m.* **nine shillings in the £,** nueve chelines por libra. **to cut off with a s.,** desheredar

shilly shally /'ʃili ʃæli/ *n* irresolución, vacilación, *f, vi* estar irresoluto, titubear, no saber qué hacer

shimmer /'ʃimər/ *vi* rielar; relucir. —*n* luz trémula, *f;* resplandor, *m;* viso, *m*

shin /ʃin/ *n* espinilla, *f;* (of beef) corvejón, *m.* **to s. up,** trepar

shindy /'ʃindi/ *n* suiza, reyerta, tasquera, *f.* **to kick up a s.,** armar camorra

shine /ʃain/ *vi* brillar; resplandecer, relucir, relumbrar. —*vt* (shoes) dar lustre (a). —*n* brillo, *m;* lustre, *m.* **in rain or s.,** en buen o mal tiempo. **to s. with happiness,** radiar felicidad. **to take the s. out of,** eclipsar

shingle /'ʃɪŋgəl/ *n* (pebbles) guijarros, *m pl;* cascajo, *m;* barda, *f;* (hair) pelo a la garçonne, *m; pl* **shingles,** *med* zona, *f,* herpe zóster, *m.* —*vt* (the hair) cortar a la garçonne

shining /'ʃainɪŋ/ *a* resplandeciente, brillante, reluciente; radiante. **s. with happiness,** radiante de felicidad. **s. example,** ejemplo notable, *m*

shintoism /'ʃintou,izəm/ *n* sintoísmo, *m*

shiny /'ʃaini/ *a* brillante; lustroso, terso; (of trousers, etc.) reluciente; (of paper) glaseado

ship /ʃip/ *n* buque, barco, *m;* (sailing) velero, *m.* —*vt* embarcar; (oars) armar. —*vi* embarcar; (as a member of crew) embarcarse. **on board s.,** a bordo. **to s. a sea,** embarcar agua. **to take s.,** embarcar. **to s. off,** mandar. **ship's boat,** lancha, *f.* **ship's boy,** grumete, *m.* **ship's carpenter,** carpintero de ribera, *m.* **ship's company,** tripulación, *f.* **s.-breaker,** desguazador, *m.* **s.-canal,** canal de navegación, *m.* **s.-load,** cargamento, *m*

shipbuilder /'ʃip,bildər/ *n* constructor de buques, arquitecto naval, *m*

shipbuilding /'ʃip,bildɪŋ/ *n* construcción naval, *f*

shipment /'ʃipmənt/ *n* embarque, *m;* despacho por mar, *m;* (consignment) remesa, *f*

shipowner /'ʃip,ounər/ *n* naviero, *m*

shipper /'ʃipər/ *n* naviero, *m;* importador, *m;* exportador, *m*

shipping /'ʃipɪŋ/ *n* embarque, *m;* buques, barcos, *m pl;* (of a country) marina, *f.* **s. agent,** consignatario de buques, *m.* **s. company,** compañía de navegación, *f.* **s. offices,** oficinas de una compañía de navegación, *f pl*

shipshape /'ʃip,ʃeip/ *a* en buen orden; bien arreglado

shipwreck /'ʃip,rek/ *n* naufragio, *m, vt* hacer naufragar, echar a pique

shipwrecked person /'ʃɪpˌrɛkt/ *n* náufrago (-ga). **to be shipwrecked**, naufragar
shipyard /'ʃɪpˌyɑrd/ *n* astillero, varadero, *m*
shire /ʃaɪər/ *n* condado, *m*
shirk /ʃɜrk/ *vt* eludir, esquivar; desentenderse de. —*vi* faltar al deber
shirker /'ʃɜrkər/ *n* gandul (-la); persona que no cumple con su deber, *f*
shirr /ʃɜr/ *vt* fruncir
shirt /ʃɜrt/ *n* camisa, *f.* **dress s.**, camisa de pechera dura, *f.* **hair-s.**, cilicio, *m.* **in one's s.-sleeves**, en mangas de camisa. **s.-blouse**, blusa sencilla, *f.* **s.-collar**, cuello de camisa, *m.* **s. factory** or **shop**, camisería, *f.* **shirt-front**, pechera, *f.* **s.-maker**, camisero (-ra)
shirting /'ʃɜrtɪŋ/ *n* tela para camisas, *f*
shiver /'ʃɪvər/ *vi* temblar, tiritar; dar diente con diente; (of a boat) zozobrar. —*vt* (break) hacer añicos, romper; (sails) sacudir. —*n* temblor, estremecimiento, *m;* escalofrío, *m;* (of glass, etc.) fragmento, *m,* astilla, *f.* **You give me the shivers**, Me das escalofríos
shivery /'ʃɪvəri/ *a* tembloroso; friolero. **I feel s.,** Tengo escalofríos
shoal /ʃoul/ *n* (of fish) banco, *m;* gran cantidad, *f;* (of people) multitud, muchedumbre, *f;* (water) bajo fondo, *m;* (sand-bank) banco, bajío, *m,* a poco profundo. **I know shoals of people in Valencia**, Conozco a muchísima gente de Valencia
shock /ʃɒk/ *n* choque, *m; elec* conmoción, *f; med* shock, *m;* (med stroke) conmoción cerebral, *f;* (fright) sobresalto, susto, *m.* —*vt* sacudir, dar una sacudida (a); chocar; escandalizar, horrorizar. —*vi* chocar. **electric s.**, conmoción eléctrica, *f.* **She is easily shocked**, Ella se escandaliza fácilmente. **s. of hair**, mata de pelo, *f.* **s. absorber**, *ech* amortiguador, *m; auto* amortiguador (de los muelles), *m.* **s. troops**, tropas de asalto, *f pl,* elementos de choque, *m pl*
shocking /'ʃɒkɪŋ/ *a* escandaloso; repugnante, horrible; espantoso. **How s.!** ¡Qué horror! **s. bad**, malísimo
shockingly /'ʃɒkɪŋli/ *adv* horriblemente
shod /ʃɒd/ *a* calzado; (of horses) herrado
shoddy /'ʃɒdi/ *n* pacotilla, *f.* —*a* de pacotilla; espurio, falso
shoe /ʃu/ *n* zapato, *m;* (horse) herradura, *f;* (*naut mech*) zapata, *f.* —*vt* (horses) herrar. **I should not like to be in his shoes**, No me gustaría estar en su pellejo. **That is quite another pair of shoes**, Eso es harina de otro costal. **to cast a s.**, (of horses) desherrarse, perder una herradura. **to put on one's shoes**, ponerse los zapatos, calzarse. **to remove one's shoes**, quitarse los zapatos, descalzarse. **wooden shoes**, zuecos, *m pl.* **s.-buckle**, hebilla de zapato, *f.* **s.-lace**, cordón de zapato, *m.* **s.-leather**, cuero para zapatos, *m;* calzado, *m.* **s.-scraper**, limpiabarros, *m,* estregadera, *f.* **s.-shop**, zapatería, *f*
shoeblack /'ʃuˌblæk/ *n* betún, *m;* (person) limpiabotas, *m*
shoehorn /'ʃuˌhɔrn/ *n* calzador, *m*
shoemaker /'ʃuˌmeɪkər/ *n* zapatero (-ra)
shoemaking /'ʃuˌmeɪkɪŋ/ *n* fabricación de calzado, zapatería, *f*
shoo /ʃu/ *interj* ¡fuera!; ¡zape! —*vt* ahuyentar
shoot /ʃut/ *vt* (throw) lanzar; precipitar; (empty) vaciar; (a rapid) salvar; (rays, etc.) echar; (an arrow, a gun, etc.) disparar; (a person, etc.) pegar un tiro (a); *sports* tirar; *mil* fusilar, pasar por las armas; (a film) hacer, impresionar. —*vi* lanzarse, precipitarse; (of pain) latir; (sprout) brotar; disparar; tirar; (at football) tirar a gol, chutar. **to s. a glance at**, lanzar una mirada (a). **I was shot in the foot**, Una bala me hirió en el pie. **to s. the sun**, *naut* tomar el sol. **to s. ahead**, tomar la delantera. **to s. at**, tirar a. **to s by**, pasar como una bala. **to s. down**, *aer* derribar; matar de un tiro. **to s. up**, (of children) espigarse; (of prices) subir mucho; (of cliffs, etc.) elevarse
shoot /ʃut/ *n* partida de caza, *f;* tiro, *m; bot* renuevo, retoño, *m*
shooting /'ʃutɪŋ/ *n* tiro, *m;* caza con escopeta, *f;* (of guns) tiroteo, *m;* (of an arrow) disparo, *m;* (of a film) rodaje, *m.* **to go s.**, ir a cazar con escopeta. **s.-box**,

pabellón de caza, *m.* **s. butts**, tiradero, *m.* **s. dog**, perro de caza, *m.* **s.-gallery**, tiro al blanco, *m.* **s. match**, concurso de tiro, *m.* **s. pain**, punzada de dolor, *f.* **s. party**, partida de caza, *f.* **s. practice**, ejercicios de tiro, *m pl.* **s.-range**, campo de tiro, *m.* **s. star**, estrella fugaz, *f*
shop /ʃɒp/ *n* tienda, *f;* (workshop) taller, *m.* —*vi* ir de compras, ir de tiendas; comprar. **to talk s.**, hablar de negocios. **s.-assistant**, dependiente (-ta). **s.-soiled**, deslucido. **s.-steward**, representante de los obreros de una fábrica o taller, *m.* **s. window**, escaparate, *m*
shopkeeper /'ʃɒpˌkipər/ *n* tendero (-ra)
shoplifter /'ʃɒpˌlɪftər/ *n* ladrón (-ona) de tiendas, ratero (-ra) de las tiendas
shoplifting /'ʃɒpˌlɪftɪŋ/ *n* ratería en las tiendas, *f*
shopper /'ʃɒpər/ *n* comprador (-ra)
shopping /'ʃɒpɪŋ/ *n* compra, *f;* compras, *f pl.* **to go s.**, ir de compras. **s. basket**, cesta para compras, *f.* **s. center**, centro comercial, *m*
shopwalker /'ʃɒpˌwɔkər/ *n* jefe de recepción, *m*
shore /ʃɔr/ *n* orilla, ribera, *f;* costa, *f;* (sands) playa, *f.* **off s.**, en alta mar. **on s.**, en tierra. **to come on s.**, desembarcar. **to s. up**, apuntalar, acodalar; *fig* apoyar
short /ʃɔrt/ *a* corto; (of persons) bajo; breve; (of temper) vivo; insuficiente; distante (de); (brusque) seco; (of money) alcanzado. —*adv* súbitamente; brevemente. —*n* (vowel) vocal breve, *m;* *pl* **shorts**, calzones cortos, *m pl.* **for s.**, para mayor brevedad. **for a s. time**, por poco tiempo. **in a s. time**, dentro de poco. **in s.**, en breve, en resumen, en pocas palabras. **on s. notice**, con poco tiempo de aviso. **s. of**, con la excepción de, menos. **to be s.**, faltar, ser escaso. **to be s. with someone**, tratar con sequedad (a). **to fall s. of expectations**, no cumplir las esperanzas. **to go s. of**, pasarse sin. **to grow s.**, escasear. **s.-circuit**, corto circuito, *m.* **s. cut**, atajo, *m.* **s.-haired**, pelicorto. **s.-handed**, falto de mano de obra. **s.-lived**, de vida corta; efímero, fugaz. **to be short-lived**, tener vida corta. **s.-sighted**, corto de vista. **s.-sightedness**, miopía, cortedad de vista, *f.* **s. story**, cuento, *m.* **s.-tempered**, irascible, irritable, de genio vivo. **s.-waisted**, corto de talle. **s.-winded**, corto de resuello; asmático
shortage /'ʃɔrtɪdʒ/ *n* falta, escasez, *f;* carestía, *f.* **water s.**, carestía de agua, *f*
shortcoming /'ʃɔrtˌkʌmɪŋ/ *n* defecto, *m;* imperfección, *f*
shorten /'ʃɔrtn/ *vt* acortar; reducir, disminuir; abreviar. —*vi* acortarse
shorthand /'ʃɔrtˌhænd/ *n* taquigrafía, estenografía, *f.* —*a* taquigráfico, estenográfico. **to take down in s.**, taquigrafiar. **s. writer**, estenógrafo (-fa); taquígrafo (-fa)
shortly /'ʃɔrtli/ *adv* dentro de poco, pronto; brevemente, en resumen, en pocas palabras; (curtly) bruscamente, secamente
shortness /'ʃɔrtnɪs/ *n* cortedad, *f;* brevedad, *f;* (of a person) pequeñez, *f;* (lack) falta, *f;* (of memory, sight) cortedad, *f;* brusqueness) sequedad, brusquedad, *f.* **s. of breath**, falta de aliento, respiración difícil, *f*
shot /ʃɒt/ *n* perdigón, *m; inf* perdigones, *m pl;* bala, *f;* (firing) tiro, *m;* (person) tirador (-ra); (stroke, etc.) golpe, *m,* tirada, *f;* (cinema) fotograma, *m.* —*a* (of silk) tornasolado. **at one s.**, de un tiro. **like a s.**, *fig* como una bala. **to exchange shots**, tirotearse. **to fire a s.**, disparar un tiro. **to have a s. at**, probar suerte. **s.-gun**, escopeta, *f.* **s. silk**, seda tornasolada, *f*
should /ʃʊd/ *v aux* (expressing future) **I s. like to go to the sea**, Me gustaría ir al mar; (expressing conditional) **I s. like to see them if I could**, Me gustaría verlos si pudiera; (expressing obligation) **You s. go at once**, Debes ir en seguida; (expressing probability) **They s. arrive tomorrow**, Seguramente llegarán mañana; (expressing doubt) **If the moment s. be opportune**, Si el momento fuera oportuno. **I s. just think so!** ¡Ya lo creo! ¡No lo dudo!
shoulder /'ʃoʊldər/ *n* hombro, *m;* (of mutton) espalda, *f;* (of a hill) falda, *f.* —*vt* echar al hombro, echar sobre sí; (a responsibility) cargar con, hacerse responsable para; (jostle) dar codazos (a). **s. to s.**, hombro a hombro. **S. arms!** ¡Armas al hombro! **s.-**

blade, omoplato, *m.* **s.-knot,** charretera, *f.* **s.-pad,** hombrera, *f.* **s.-strap,** *mil* dragona, *f;* (of a dress, etc.) tirante, *m;* (of a water carrier, etc.) correón, *m*

shouldered /'ʃouldərd/ *a* de hombros..., de espaldas... **round-s.,** cargado de espaldas

shout /ʃaut/ *vi* gritar, hablar a gritos. —*vt* gritar. —*n* grito, *m.* **shouts of applause,** aclamaciones, *f pl,* aplausos, *m pl.* **to s. from the housetops,** pregonar a los cuatro vientos. **to s. with laughter,** reírse a carcajadas. **to s. down,** silbar. **to s. out,** gritar

shouting /'ʃautɪŋ/ *n* gritos, *m pl,* vocerío, clamor, *m;* (applause) aclamaciones, *f pl*

shove /ʃʌv/ *vt* empujar; poner. —*n* empujón, *m.* **to s. along,** empujar. **to s. aside,** empujar a un lado; apartar a codazos. **to s. away,** rechazar. **to s. back,** hacer retroceder. **to s. forward,** hacer avanzar, empujar hacia adelante. **to s. off,** (a boat) echar afuera. **to s. out,** empujar hacia fuera

shovel /'ʃʌvəl/ *n* pala, *f.* —*vt* traspalar. **s. hat,** sombrero de teja, *m*

show /ʃou/ *vt* mostrar; hacer ver; (disclose) descubrir; revelar; (exhibit) exhibir; (indicate) indicar; (prove) demostrar, probar; (conduct) conducir, llevar, guiar; (explain) explicar; (oneself) presentarse. —*vi* mostrarse; verse; parecer. **to s. cause,** mostrar causa. **to s. fight,** ofrecer resistencia. **s. signs of,** dar señales de. **to s. itself,** declararse, asomarse, surgir. **to s. to the door,** acompañar a la puerta. **to s. in,** (a person) hacer entrar, introducir (en). **to s. off,** *vt* exhibir; realzar; (new clothes, etc.) lucir. —*vi* darse importancia; pavonearse. **to s. out,** (a person) acompañar a la puerta; (in anger) poner de patitas en la calle. **to s. through,** *vi* trasparentarse. —*vt* conducir por. **to s. up,** *vt* invitar a subir; (a fraud, etc.) descubrir; (a swindler) desenmascarar; (defects) revelar. —*vi* (stand out) destacarse; (be present) asomarse, asistir

show /ʃou/ *n* (exhibition) exposición, *f;* espectáculo, *m;* (sign) indicio, *m,* señal, *f;* (ostentation) pompa, *f,* aparato, *m,* ostentación, *f;* (appearance) apariencia, *f;* (affair) negocio, *m.* **to give the s. away,** echar los títeres a rodar. **to make a s. of,** hacer gala de. **s.-case,** escaparate, *m,* vitrina, *f.* **s. of hands,** votación por manos levantadas, *f.* **s.-room,** salón de muestras, *m*

showdown /'ʃou,daun/ *n* cartas boca arriba, *m*

shower /'ʃauər/ *n* chaparrón, chubasco, *m;* (of spray, etc.) chorro, *m;* (of stones, arrows, etc.) lluvia, *f;* (of honors) cosecha, *f,* (bridal) despedida de soltera, despedida de soltería, *f.* —*vt* derramar; rociar; mojar; llover. —*vi* chaparrear, llover. **s.-bath,** ducha, *f*

shower cap *n* gorro de ducha, *m*

showery /'ʃauəri/ *a* lluvioso

showily /'ʃouəli/ *adv* aparatosamente, con ostentación

showiness /'ʃouinɪs/ *n* ostentación, *f;* esplendor, *m,* magnificencia, *f*

showman /'ʃoumən/ *n* director de un espectáculo de feria, *m;* titiritero, *m;* pregonero, *m*

showy /'ʃoui/ *a* vistoso; ostentoso

shrapnel /'ʃræpnḷ/ *n* granada, *m,* granada de metralla, *f*

shred /ʃred/ *n* fragmento, *m;* (of cloth) jirón, *m;* brizna, *f; fig* pizca, *f.* —*vt* desmenuzar. **to tear in shreds,** hacer pedazos

shrew /ʃru/ *n zool* musaraña, *f;* (woman) fiera, *f*

shrewd /ʃrud/ *a* sagaz, perspicaz; prudente; (of the wind) penetrante; (pain) punzante. **to have a s. idea of,** tener una buena idea de. **a s. diplomat,** un fino diplomático

shrewdly /'ʃrudli/ *adv* sagazmente, con perspicacia; prudentemente

shrewdness /'ʃrudnɪs/ *n* sagacidad, perspicacia, *f;* prudencia, *f*

shrewish /'ʃruɪʃ/ *a* regañón

shrewishness /'ʃruɪʃnɪs/ *n* mal genio, *m*

shriek /ʃrik/ *vi* chillar, gritar. —*vt* decir a voces, gritar. —*n* chillido, *m;* grito agudo, *m.* **shrieks of laughter,** carcajadas, *f pl*

shrieking /'ʃrikɪŋ/ *n* gritos, chillidos, *m pl*

shrift /ʃrɪft/ **to give short,** enviar normala (a), enviar a paseo (a)

shrill /ʃrɪl/ *a* estridente, agudo

shrillness /'ʃrɪlnɪs/ *n* estridencia, *f*

shrimp /ʃrɪmp/ *n* camarón, *m,* gamba, *f, vi* pescar camarones

shrine /ʃrain/ *n* relicario, *m;* sepulcro de santo, *m;* templete, *m,* capilla, *f;* santuario, *m*

shrink /ʃrɪŋk/ *vi* encogerse; contraerse; disminuir, reducirse. —*vt* encoger; reducir, disminuir; desaparecer; disiparse. **I shrank from doing it,** Me repugnaba hacerlo. **to s. away from,** retroceder ante; recular ante; huir de. **to s. back,** recular (ante)

shrinkage /'ʃrɪŋkɪdʒ/ *n* encogimiento, *m;* contracción, *f;* reducción, disminución, *f*

shrinking /'ʃrɪŋkɪŋ/ *a* tímido

shrive /ʃraiv/ *vt* confesar

shrivel /'ʃrɪvəl/ *vi* avellanarse; (of persons, through old age) acartonarse, apergaminarse; (wither) marchitarse; arrugarse. —*vt* arrugar; secar, marchitar

shroud /ʃraud/ *n* sudario, *m,* mortaja, *f; Naut.* obenque, *m.* **to wrap in a s.,** amortajar

Shrove Tuesday /ʃrouv/ *n* martes de carnaval, *m*

shrub /ʃrʌb/ *n* arbusto, *m;* matajo, *m*

shrubbery /'ʃrʌbəri/ *n* arbustos, *m pl,* maleza, *f;* bosquecillo, *m*

shrug /ʃrʌg/ *vt* encogerse de hombros. —*n* encogimiento de hombros, *m*

shrunken /'ʃrʌŋkən/ *a* contraído; acartonado, apergaminado; seco, marchito. **shrunken head,** cabeza reducida, *f*

shudder /'ʃʌdər/ *vi* estremecerse; vibrar. —*n* estremecimiento, *m;* escalofrío, *m;* (of an engine, etc.) vibración, *f*

shuffle /'ʃʌfəl/ *vt* (the feet) arrastrar; (scrape) restregar; (cards) barajar; (papers) mezclar. —*vi* arrastrar los pies, arrastrarse; (cards) barajar; *fig* tergiversar. —*n* (of the cards) barajadura, *f; fig* evasiva, *f;* embuste, *m.* **to s. along,** andar arrastrando los pies

shuffling /'ʃʌflɪŋ/ *n* el arrastrar, *m,* (e.g. *the shuffling of chairs,* el arrastrar de sillas)

shun /ʃʌn/ *vt* evitar, rehuir, esquivar

shunt /ʃʌnt/ *vt rail* apartar; *elec* shuntar. —*vi rail* hacer maniobras

shunting /'ʃʌntɪŋ/ *n* (of trains) maniobras, *f pl*

shut /ʃʌt/ *vt* and *vi* cerrar. **to s. again,** volver a cerrar. **to s. down,** *vt* cerrar; (a machine) parar. —*vi* (of factories, etc.) cerrar. **to s. in,** encerrar; (surround) cercar, rodear. **to s. off,** (water, etc.) cortar; (isolate) aislar (de). **to s. out,** excluir; obstruir, impedir; negar la entrada (a). **to s. up,** *vt* cerrar; encerrar; *inf* hacer callar (a); *vi inf* callarse, cerrar la boca. **to s. oneself up,** encerrarse

shutter /'ʃʌtər/ *n* (window) contraventana, *f,* postigo, *m;* (of a camera) obturador, *m;* (of a fireplace) campana (de hogar), *f.* —*vt* poner contraventanas (a); cerrar los postigos de

shuttle /'ʃʌtḷ/ *n* (weaver's, and sewing-machine) lanzadera, *f,* (airplane service) puente aéreo, *m.* **s.-cock,** volante, gallito, *m*

shy /ʃai/ *a* (of animals) tímido, salvaje; (of persons) huraño, tímido; vergonzoso. —*vi* (of a horse) respingar; (of persons) asustarse (de). —*vt* (a ball, etc.) lanzar. —*n* (of a horse) respingo, *m;* (of a ball) lanzamiento, *m;* (try) prueba, tentativa, *f.* **to fight shy of,** procurar evitar. **to have a shy at,** probar

shyly /'ʃaili/ *adv* tímidamente; con vergüenza, vergonzosamente

shyness /'ʃainɪs/ *n* timidez, *f;* huraña, *f;* vergüenza, *f*

Siamese /,saiə'miz/ *a* siamés. —*n* siamés (-esa); (language) siamés, *m.* **S. cat,** gato siamés, *m*

Siberia /sai'bɪəriə/ Siberia, *f*

Siberian /sai'bɪəriən/ *a* and *n* siberiano (-na)

sic /sɪk/ *vt* atacar; abijar, azuzar (a dog); *adv* así (in academic prose)

Sicilian /sɪ'sɪlyən/ *a* and *n* siciliano (-na)

Sicily /'sɪsəli/ Sicilia, *f*

sick /sɪk/ *a* enfermo; mareado. **the s.,** los enfermos. **to be s.,** vomitar; estar enfermo. **to be s. of,** estar harto de. **to feel s.,** sentirse mareado. **to be on the s.-list,** estar enfermo. **s.-bed,** lecho de dolor, *m.* **s.-headache,** jaqueca, con náuseas, *f.* **s.-leave,** *mil* permiso por enfermedad, *m.* **s.-nurse,** enfermera, *f*

sicken /'sɪkən/ *vi* caer enfermo, enfermar; (feel sick) marearse; (recoil from) repugnar; (weary of) cansarse (de), aburrirse (de). —*vt* marear; dar asco (a), repugnar; cansar, aburrir. **It sickens me,** Me da asco. **He is sickening for measles,** Muestra síntomas de sarampión

sickening /'sıkənıŋ/ *a* nauseabundo; repugnante; (tedious) fastidioso

sickle /'sıkəl/ *n* hoz, segadera, *f*

sickliness /'sıklınıs/ *n* falta de salud, *f;* náusea, *f;* (paleness) palidez, *f*

sickly /'sıklı/ *a* enfermizo, achacoso, malucho; (of places, etc.) malsano; (pale) pálido; débil; (of a smell) nauseabundo; (mawkish) empalagoso

sickness /'sıknıs/ *n* enfermedad, *f;* mal, *m;* náusea, *f,* mareo, *m*

side /said/ *n* lado, *m;* (hand) mano, *f;* (of a river, etc.) orilla, *f,* margen, *m;* (of a person) costado, *m;* (of an animal) ijada, *f;* (of a hill) falda, pendiente, ladera, *f;* (of a ship) banda, *f,* costado, *m;* (aspect) aspecto, *m;* punto de vista, *m;* (party) partido, grupo, *m;* (team) equipo, *m;* (of descent) lado, *m.* —*a* lateral, de lado; oblicuo. **on all sides,** por todas partes. **on both sides,** por ambos lados. **s. by s.,** lado a lado. **the other s. of the picture,** el revés de la medalla. **to change sides,** cambiar de partido. **to pick sides,** escoger el equipo. **to put on s.,** darse tono, alzar el gallo. **to split one's sides,** desternillarse de risa, reírse a carcajadas. **to s. with,** declararse por, ponerse al lado de, tomar el partido de. **wrong s. out,** al revés. **s.-car,** sidecar, asiento lateral, *m.* **s.-chain,** *chem* cadena lateral, *f.* **s.-dish,** entremés, *m.* **s.-door,** puerta lateral, *f.* **s.-face,** *a* de perfil. —*n* perfil, *m.* **s.-glance,** mirada de soslayo, *f.* **s.-issue,** cuestión secundaria, *f.* **s.-line,** negocio accesorio, *m;* ocupación secundaria, *f; rail* vía secundaria, *f.* **s.-saddle,** silla de señora, silla de montar de lado, *f.* **s.-show,** (at a fair) barraca, *f,* puesto de feria, *m;* exhibición secundaria, *f;* función secundaria, *f.* **s.-table,** trinchero, *m.* **s.-track,** *n rail* apartadero, *m.* —*vt* desviar (de), apartar (de). **s.-view,** perfil, *m.* **s.-walk,** acera, *f.* **s.-whiskers,** patillas, *f pl*

sidelight /'said,lait/ *n* luz lateral, *f;* (on a ship) ojo de buey, *m; fig* información incidental, *f*

sidelong /'said,lɔŋ/ *adv* de lado, lateralmente; (of glances) de soslayo. —*a* oblicuo

side road *n* camino lateral, *m*

sideways /'said,weiz/ *adv* oblicuamente, de lado; (edgewise) de soslayo. —*a* de soslayo

siding /'saidıŋ/ *n rail* apartadero, *m*

sidle /'saidl/ *vi* andar (or ir) de lado. **to s. up to,** acercarse servilmente a; arrimarse (a)

siege /sidʒ/ *n* asedio, sitio, cerco, *m.* **to lay s. to,** poner cerco (a), sitiar, asediar cercar. **to raise a s.,** levantar un sitio

sienna /si'enə/ *n* tierra de siena natural, *f.* **burnt s.,** tierra de siena tostada, *f*

sieve /sıv/ *n* cedazo, tamiz, *m,* criba, *f, vt* tamizar, cerner, cribar

sift /sıft/ *vt* (sieve) cerner, cribar; (sugar, etc.) salpicar (con); (a question) escudriñar, examinar minuciosamente

sifting /'sıftıŋ/ *n* cribado, *m;* (of a question) investigación minuciosa, *f; pl* **siftings,** cerniduras, *f pl*

sigh /sai/ *vi* suspirar; (of the wind) susurrar. —*n* suspiro, *m;* (of the wind) susurro, *m.* **to s. for,** suspirar por; lamentar

sighing /'saiıŋ/ *n* suspiros, *m pl;* (of the wind) susurro, *m*

sight /sait/ *n* vista, *f;* visión, *f;* espectáculo, *m;* (fright) estantigua, *f.* —*vt* ver, divisar; (aim) apuntar. **front s.,** (of guns) alza, *f.* **short s.,** (of eyes) vista corta, *f.* **at first s.,** a primera vista. **in s.,** a la vista. **in s. of,** a vista de. **out of s.,** que no está a la vista; perdido de vista. **Out of s., out of mind,** Ojos que no ven, corazón que no siente. **to be lost to s.,** perderse de vista. **to lose s. of,** perder de vista (a). **to catch a s. of,** vislumbrar. **to come in s.,** aparecer, asomarse. **to know by s.,** conocer de vista (a). **s.-reading,** lectura a primera vista, *f*

sightly /'saitlı/ *a* hermoso; deleitable

sightseeing /'sait,siıŋ/ *n* turismo, *m.* **to go s.,** visitar los monumentos, ver los puntos de interés, *m*

sightseer /'sait,siər/ *n* curioso (-sa); turista, *mf*

sign /sain/ *n* señal, *f;* seña, *f;* indicio, *m;* (of the zo-diac and *mus*) signo, *m;* marca, *f; eccl* símbolo, *m;* (of a shop, etc.) muestra, *f,* rótulo, *m;* (symptom) síntoma, *m.* —*vt* firmar; indicar; *eccl* persignar. **as a s. of,** en señal de. **to converse by signs,** hablar por señas. **to make the s. of the cross over,** santiguar. **to show signs (of),** dar señas (de); indicar. **s.-painter,** pintor de muestras, *m*

signal /'sıgnl/ *n* señal, *f.* —*vt* señalar; hacer señas (a). —*vi* hacer señales. —*a* insigne, notable. **fog-s.,** señal de niebla, *f.* **landing s.,** *aer* señal de aterrizaje, *f.* **to give the s. for,** dar la señal para. **s.-box,** garita de señales, *f.* **s. code,** *naut* código de señales, *m*

signaler /'sıgnlər/ *n* señalador, *m*

signalize /'sıgnl,aiz/ *vt* señalar, distinguir

signalman /'sıgnlmən/ *n rail* guardavía, *m*

signatory /'sıgnə,tɔri/ *a* and *n* signatario (-ia)

signature /'sıgnətʃər/ *n* firma, *f;* (*mus* and *print*) signatura, *f*

signboard /'sain,bɔrd/ *n* letrero, *m,* muestra, *f*

signet /'sıgnıt/ *n* sello, *m.* **s.-ring,** anillo de sello, *m*

significance /sıg'nıfıkəns/ *n* significación, *f,* significado, *m;* importancia, *f*

significant /sıg'nıfıkənt/ *a* significativo, significante; expresivo; importante

significantly /sıg'nıfıkəntli/ *adv* significativamente; expresivamente

signify /'sıgnə,fai/ *vt* significar; querer decir; importar. —*vi* significar, tener importancia; importar

signpost /'sain,poust/ *n* indicador de dirección, *m*

Sikh /sik/ *n* sik, *mf* (*pl* siks)

silage /'sailıdʒ/ *n* forraje conservado en silo, *m*

silence /'sailəns/ *n* silencio, *m,* (*interj* ¡silencio! —*vt* hacer callar, imponer silencio (a); silenciar. **to keep s.,** guardar silencio, callarse. **to pass over in s.,** pasar en silencio (por), pasar por alto de. **S. gives consent,** Quien calla otorga

silencer /'sailənsər/ *n* (of fire-arms) silenciador, *m; auto* silenciador, silencioso, *m*

silent /'sailənt/ *a* silencioso. **to become s.,** enmudecer; callar. **to remain s.,** callarse, guardar silencio; permanecer silencioso. **s. partner,** *n* socio (-ia) comanditario (-ia)

silent film *n* película muda, *f*

silently /'sailəntli/ *adv* silenciosamente, en silencio

silhouette /,sılu'et/ *n* silueta, *f.* —*vt* representar en silueta; destacar. **in s.,** en silueta. **to be silhouetted against the sky,** destacarse contra el sielo

silica /'sılıkə/ *n* sílice, *f*

silk /sılk/ *n* seda, *f, a* de seda. **artificial s.,** seda artificial, *f.* **floss s.,** seda ocal, *f.* **sewing s.,** seda de coser, *f.* **twist s.,** seda cordelada, *f.* **as smooth as s.,** como una seda. **s. growing,** sericultura, *f.* **s. hat,** sombrero de copa, *m.* **s. merchandise,** sedería, *f.* **s. stocking,** media de seda, *f*

silken /'sılkən/ *a* de seda; sedoso

silkiness /'sılkınıs/ *n* carácter sedoso, *m;* suavidad, *f*

silk-screen process /'sılk,skrin/ *n* imprenta por tamiz, imprenta serigráfica, imprenta tamigráfica, impresión con estarcido de seda, *f,* proceso tamigráfico, *m,* serigrafía, tamigrafía, *f*

silkworm /'sılk,wɜrm/ *n* gusano de seda, *m*

silky /'sılki/ *a* sedoso; (of wine) suave

sill /sıl/ *n* (of a window) alféizar, antepecho, *m;* (of a door) umbral, *m*

silliness /'sılınıs/ *n* tontería, estupidez, *f*

silly /'sılı/ *a* tonto, estúpido; imbécil. —*n* tonto (-ta). **You are a s. ass,** Eres un imbécil

silo /'sailou/ *n* silo, *m*

silt /sılt/ *n* aluvión, *m,* sedimentación, *f.* **to s. up,** *vt* cegar (or obstruir) con aluvión. —*vi* cegarse con aluvión

silver /'sılvər/ *n* plata, *f.* —*a* de plata; argénteo; (of the voice, etc.) argentino. —*vt* platear; (mirrors) azogar; (hair) blanquear. **s. birch,** abedul, *m.* **s. fox,** zorro plateado, *m.* **s.-gry,** gris perla, *m.* **s.-haired,** de pelo entrecano. **s.-paper,** papel de estaño, *m.* **s.-plate,** *n* vajilla de plata, *f.* —*vt* platear. **s.-tongued,** de pico de oro; de voz argentina. **s. wedding,** bodas de plata, *f pl*

silversmith /'sılvər,smıθ/ *n* platero, *m.* **silversmith's shop,** platería, *f*

silvery /'sɪlvəri/ a plateado, argentado; (of sounds) argentino

simian /'sɪmiən/ a símico

similar /'sɪmələr/ a parecido (a), semejante (a); similar; geom semejante. **to be s. to,** asemejarse (a), parecerse (a)

similarity /ˌsɪmə'lærɪti/ n parecido, m, semejanza, similitud, f

similarly /'sɪmələrli/ adv de un modo parecido, asimismo

simile /'sɪməli/ n símil, m

simmer /'sɪmər/ vi hervir a fuego lento; fig estar a punto de estallar. **to s. down,** fig moderarse poco a poco. **to s. over,** fig estallar

simper /'sɪmpər/ vi sonreírse bobamente

simpering /'sɪmpərɪŋ/ n sonrisilla tonta, f

simperingly /'sɪmpərɪŋli/ adv con sonrisa necia

simple /'sɪmpəl/ a sencillo; simple; ingenuo, inocente; crédulo; (humble) humilde; (mere) mero. **s.-hearted,** inocente, cándido, sin malicia. **s.-minded,** ingenuo; crédulo. **s.-mindedness,** ingenuidad, f; credulidad, f

simpleton /'sɪmpəltən/ n primo (-ma); papanatas, m, tonto (-ta)

simplicity /sɪm'plɪsɪti/ n sencillez, f; simplicidad, candidez, f

simplifiable /ˌsɪmplə'faiəbəl/ a simplificable

simplification /ˌsɪmpləfɪ'keiʃən/ simplificación, f

simplify /'sɪmplə,fai/ vt simplificar

simply /'sɪmpli/ adv sencillamente; simplemente, meramente; absolutamente

simulacrum /ˌsɪmyə'leikrəm/ n simulacro, m

simulate /'sɪmyə,leit/ vt fingir, aparentar, simular

simulation /ˌsɪmyə'leiʃən/ n simulación, f, fingimiento, m

simultaneous /ˌsaiməl'teiniəs/ a simultáneo

simultaneously /ˌsaiməl'teiniəsli/ adv simultáneamente; al mismo tiempo (que)

simultaneousness /ˌsaiməl'teiniəsnɪs/ n simultaneidad, f

sin /sɪn/ n pecado, m, vi pecar; faltar (a)

since /sɪns/ adv desde entonces, desde (que). —prep desde. —conjunc desde que; ya que, puesto que. **a long time s.,** hace mucho. **not long s.,** hace poco. **How long is it s...?** ¿Cuánto tiempo hace que...? **s. then,** desde entonces

sincere /sɪn'sɪər/ a sincero

sincerely /sɪn'sɪərli/ adv sinceramente. **Yours s.,** Su afectísimo...

sincerity /sɪn'serɪti/ n sinceridad, f

sine /sain/ n math seno, m

sinecure /'saini,kyʊr/ n canonjía, sinecura, f, empleo de aviador (Mexican slang), m

sinew /'sɪnyu/ n tendón, m; pl **sinews,** nervio, m, fuerza, f

sinewy /'sɪnyui/ a (stringy) fibroso; musculoso, nervudo

sinful /'sɪnfəl/ a (of persons) pecador; (of thoughts, acts) pecaminoso

sinfulness /'sɪnfəlnɪs/ n pecado, m; culpabilidad, perversidad, maldad, f

sing /sɪŋ/ vi cantar; (of the ears) zumbar; (of wind, water) murmurar, susurrar; (of a cat) ronronear. —vt cantar. **to s. a child to sleep,** dormir a un niño cantando. **to s. another song,** inf bajar el tono. **to s. small,** hacerse el chiquito. **to s. the praises of,** hacer las alabanzas de. **to s. out,** vocear, gritar. **s.-song,** n canturía, f; concierto improvisado, m. —a monótono

Singapore /'sɪŋgə,pɔr/ Singapur, m

singe /sɪndʒ/ vt chamuscar; (a fowl) aperdigar; (hair) quemar las puntas de los cabellos

singer /'sɪŋər/ n cantor (-ra); (professional) cantante, mf; (bird) ave cantora, f

singing /'sɪŋɪŋ/ n canto, m; (of the ears) zumbido, m. —a cantante. **s.-bird,** ave cantora, f. **s.-master,** maestro de cantar, m

single /'sɪŋgəl/ a único; sencillo; solo; simple; (individual) particular; individual; (unmarried) soltero. —n (tennis) juego sencillo, individual, m. **in s. file,** de reata. **to s. out,** escoger; singularizar. **s. bed,** cama de monja, f. **s. bedroom,** habitación individual, habitación con una sola cama, f. **s.-breasted,** (of coats) recto. **s. combat,** combate singular, m. **s. entry,** Com. partida simple, f. **s.-handed,** de una mano; para una sola persona; sin ayuda, solo, en solitario. **s.-minded,** sin doblez, sincero de una sola idea. **s. ticket,** billete sencillo, m

singleness /'sɪŋgəlnɪs/ n celibato, m, soltería, f. **s. with s. of purpose,** con un solo objeto

singlet /'sɪŋglɪt/ n camiseta, f

singly /'sɪŋgli/ adv separadamente, uno a uno; a solas, solo; sin ayuda

singular /'sɪŋgyələr/ a and n singular, m

singularity /ˌsɪŋgyə'lærɪti/ n singularidad, f

singularly /'sɪŋgyələrli/ adv singularmente

sinister /'sɪnəstər/ a siniestro

sink /sɪŋk/ vi ir al fondo; bajar; hundirse; (of ships) irse a pique, naufragar; sumergirse; disminuir; caer (en); penetrar; (of persons, fires) morir; (of the sun, etc.) ponerse. —vt (a ship) echar a pique; sumergir; hundir; dejar caer; bajar; (wells) cavar; reducir, disminuir; (invest) invertir; (one's identity, etc.) tener secreto; (differences) olvidar; (engrave) grabar. **My heart sank,** Se me cayeron las alas del corazón. **He sank to his knees,** Cayó de rodillas. **He is sinking fast,** Está en las últimas. **Their words began to s. in,** Sus palabras empezaban a tener efecto (or hacer mella). **I found her sunk in thought,** La encontré ensimismada. **to s. one's voice,** bajar la voz. **to s. down on a chair,** dejarse caer en una silla. **to s. into misery,** caer en la miseria. **to s. under,** (a responsibility, etc.) estar agobiado bajo

sink /sɪŋk/ n (kitchen) fregadero, m; sumidero, m, sentina, f. **s. of iniquity,** sentina, f

sinker /'sɪŋkər/ n (engraver) grabador (-ra); (of a fishing line) plomada, f

sinking /'sɪŋkɪŋ/ n hundimiento, m; (of the sun) puesta, f; (of wells) cavadura, f; sumergimiento, m. **the s. of a boat,** el hundimiento de un buque. **with s. heart,** con la muerte en el alma. **s. fund,** fondo de amortización, m

sinless /'sɪnlɪs/ a sin pecado, inocente, puro

sinner /'sɪnər/ n pecador (-ra)

sinuosity /ˌsɪnyu'ɒsɪti/ n sinuosidad, f; flexibilidad, agilidad, f

sinuous /'sɪnyuəs/ a sinuoso, tortuoso; flexible, ágil

sinus /'sainəs/ n (anat etc.) seno, m

sip /sɪp/ vt sorber; (wine) saborear, paladear. —n sorbo, m

siphon /'saifən/ n sifón, m, vt sacar con sifón

sir /sɜr/ n señor, m; (British title) sir. **Dear s.,** Muy Señor mío

sire /saiər/ n (to a monarch) Señor, m; (father) padre, m; (stallion) semental, m. —vt procrear, engendrar

siren /'sairən/ n sirena, f. **s. suit,** mono, m

sirloin /'sɜrlɔin/ n solomillo, m

sirocco /sə'rɒkou/ n siroco, m

sister /'sɪstər/ n hermana, f; (before nun's christian name) Sor; (hospital) hermana del hospital, f; enfermera, f. **s. language,** lengua hermana, f. **s. ship,** buque gemelo, m. **s.-in-law,** cuñada, hermana política, f. **S. of Mercy,** Hermana de la Caridad, f

sisterhood /'sɪstər,hʊd/ n hermandad, f; comunidad de monjas, f

sisterly /'sɪstərli/ a de hermana

sit /sɪt/ vi sentarse; estar sentado; (of birds) posarse; (of hens) empollar; (in Parliament, etc.) ser diputado; (of a committee, etc.) celebrar sesión; (on a committee, etc.) formar parte de; (function) funcionar; (of garments, food, and fig) sentar. **to sit a horse,** mantenerse a caballo; montar a caballo. **to sit oneself,** sentarse, tomar asiento. **to sit by,** (a person) sentarse (or estar sentado) al lado de. **to sit for** (a portrait) servir de modelo para; hacerse retratar. **to sit tight,** no moverse. **to sit down,** sentarse; (besiege) sitiar. **to sit on,** sentarse (en or sobre); (eggs) empollar; (a committee, etc.) formar parte de; (investigate) investigar; (snub) dejar aplastado (a). **to sit out,** quedarse hasta el fin (de). **to sit out a dance,** conversar un baile. **to sit up,** incorporarse en la cama; tenerse derecho; (at night) velar; (of dogs, etc.) pedir. **to sit up and take notice,** abrir los ojos. **to sit up in bed,** incorporarse en la cama. **to sit up late,** estar de pie hasta muy tarde

sit-down strike /'sɪt,daun/ n huelga de brazos caídos, huelga de sentados, f
site /sait/ n sitio, local, m; (for building) solar, m
sitting /'sɪtɪŋ/ n asentada, f; (of Parliament, etc.) sesión, f; (for a portrait) estadia, f; (of eggs) nidada, f. **at a s.,** de una asentada. **s.-room,** sala de estar, f
situated /'sɪtʃu,eitɪd/ a situado. **How is he s.?** ¿Cómo está situado? ¿Cuál es su situación?
situation /,sɪtʃu'eiʃən/ n situación, f; (job) empleo, m
six /sɪks/ a and n seis, m. **It is six o'clock,** Son las seis. **Everything is at sixes and sevens,** Todo está en desorden. **six-foot,** de seis pies. **six hundred,** seiscientos (-as)
sixfold /'sɪks,fould/ a séxtuplo
sixteen /'sɪks'tin/ a and n diez y seis, dieciséis, m. **John is s.,** Juan tiene dieciséis años
sixteenth /'sɪks'tinθ/ a décimosexto; (of the month) (el) diez y seis; (of monarch) diez y seis. —n dieciseisavo, m
sixth /sɪksθ/ a sexto; (of the month) (el) seis; (of monarchs) sexto. —n seisavo, m; sexta parte, f; mus sexta, f. **Henry the S.,** Enrique sexto. **May the s.,** el seis de mayo
sixtieth /'sɪkstiɪθ/ a sexagésimo. —n sesentavo, m; sexagésima parte, f
sixty /'sɪksti/ a and n sesenta m. **John has turned s.,** Juan ha pasado los sesenta
sizable /'saizəbəl/ a bastante grande
size /saiz/ n tamaño, m; dimensión, f; (height) altura, f; (measurement) medida, f; talle, m; (in gloves, etc.) número, m; (glue) cola, f. —vt clasificar por tamaños; (glaze, etc.) encolar. **to s. up,** tomar las medidas (a).
sizzle /'sɪzəl/ vi chisporrotear, chirriar. —n chisporroteo, chirrido, m
skate /skeit/ n patín, m; ichth raya, f, vi patinar
skater /'skeitər/ n patinador (-ra)
skating /'skeitɪŋ/ n patinaje, m. **s. rink,** sala de patinar, f; pista de hielo, pista de patinar, f, patinadero, m
skein /skein/ n madeja, f
skeleton /'skelɪtn/ n esqueleto, m; (of a building) armadura, f; (of a literary work) esquema, m. **s. key,** ganzúa, f .
sketch /sketʃ/ n croquis, apunte, m; (for a literary work) esbozo, esquema, m; (article) cuadro, artículo, m; descripción, f; theat entremés, sainete, m. —vt dibujar; esbozar, bosquejar; trazar; describir. **s.-book,** álbum de croquis, m
sketchily /'sketʃəli/ adv incompletamente
sketching /'sketʃɪŋ/ n arte de dibujar, mf. **He likes s.,** Le gusta dibujar
sketchy /'sketʃi/ a bosquejado; incompleto; escaso
skewer /'skyuər/ n broqueta, f, vt espetar
ski /ski/ n esquí, m, vi esquiar
skid /skɪd/ n (of a vehicle) patinazo, m, vi patinar
skidding /'skɪdɪŋ/ n patinaje, m
skier /'skiər/ n esquiador, m
skiff /skɪf/ n esquife, m
skiing /'skiɪŋ/ n patinaje sobre la nieve, m, el esquiar. **to go s.,** ir a esquiar
skill /skɪl/ n habilidad, f
skilled /skɪld/ a hábil; experto
skilled worker n obrero calificado, m
skillful /'skɪlfəl/ a hábil
skim /skɪm/ vt espumar; (milk) desnatar; (touch lightly) deslizarse sobre, rozar; (a book) hojear
skimp /skɪmp/ vt escatimar; escasear; (work) frangollar. —vi ser parsimonioso
skimpy /'skɪmpi/ a escaso
skin /skɪn/ n tez, f, cutis, m; piel, f; (of fruit) pelleja, m, piel, f; (for wine) odre, pellejo, m; (on milk) espuma, f. —vt despellejar; pelar, mondar; (graze) hacerse daño (a); inf desollar. **next to one's s.,** sobre la piel. **to s. over,** cicatrizarse. **to have a thin s.,** fig ser muy susceptible. **to save one's s.,** salvar el pellejo. **s.-deep,** superficial. **s.-tight,** escurrido, muy ajustado
skinflint /'skɪn,flɪnt/ n avaro (-ra)
skinned /skɪnd/ a de... piel
skinny /'skɪni/ a flaco, descarnado, magro
skip /skɪp/ vi retozar, brincar, saltar; saltar a la comba; (bolt) largarse, escaparse. —vt saltar; (a book) hojear; (omit) omitir; pasar por alto de. —n brinco, pequeño salto, m
skipper /'skɪpər/ n naut patrón, m; (inf and sports) capitán, m
skirmish /'skɜrmɪʃ/ vi escaramuzar. —n escaramuza, f
skirt /skɜrt/ n falda, f; (edge) margen, borde, m, orilla, f; (of a jacket, etc.) faldón, m —vt ladear; (hug) rodear, ceñir
skit /skɪt/ n sátira, f; parodia, f
skittish /'skɪtɪʃ/ a (of a horse) retozón; (of persons) frívolo; caprichoso
skittle /'skɪtl/ n bolo, m; pl **skittles,** juego de bolos, m. **s. alley,** pista de bolos, bolera, f
skulk /skʌlk/ vi estar en acecho; esconderse; rondar
skull /skʌl/ n cráneo, m; calavera, f. **s.-cap,** gorro, casquete, m; (for ecclesiastics) solideo, m
skunk /skʌŋk/ n zool mofeta, f; chingue, mapurite, yaguré, zorrillo, zorrino, zorro hediondo, m
sky /skai/ n cielo, m. **to praise to the skies,** poner en los cuernos de la luna. **s.-blue,** n azul celeste, m. —a de color azul celeste, cerúleo. **s.-high,** hasta las nubes, hasta el cielo. **s.-line,** horizonte, m. **s.-scraper,** rascacielos, m. **s.-sign,** anuncio luminoso, m
skylight /'skai,lait/ n claraboya, f, tragaluz, m
slab /slæb/ n bloque, m; losa, f, plancha, f
slack /slæk/ a lento; flojo; (lazy) perezoso; negligente, descuidado; com encalmado; débil. —vi ser perezoso. **the s. season,** la estación muerta. **to be s. in one's work,** ser negligente en el trabajo. **to s. off,** disminuir sus esfuerzos; dejar de trabajar
slacken /'slækən/ vt and vi aflojar; disminuir, reducir. **The wind slackened,** El viento amainaba, El viento aflojaba. **to s. one's efforts,** disminuir sus esfuerzos. **to s. speed,** disminuir la velocidad
slackening /'slækənɪŋ/ n aflojamiento, m; disminución, f
slacker /'slækər/ n gandul (-la)
slackness /'slæknɪs/ n flojedad, f; pereza, falta de energía, f; negligencia, f; com desanimación, f
slacks /slæks/ n pl pantalones, m pl
slag /slæg/ n escoria, f. **s. heap,** escorial, m
slake /sleik/ vt (one's thirst and lime) apagar; satisfacer
slam /slæm/ vt cerrar de golpe; golpear. —n (of a door) portazo, m; golpe, m; (cards) capote, m. **He went out and slammed the door,** Salió dando un portazo
slander /'slændər/ n calumnia, f, vt calumniar
slanderer /'slændərər/ n calumniador (-ra)
slanderous /'slændərəs/ a calumnioso
slang /slæŋ/ n argot, m, jerga, f, vt poner como un trapo (a), llenar de insultos
slant /slænt/ vi estar al sesgo; inclinarse; ser oblicuo. —vt inclinar. —n inclinación, f; oblicuidad, f. **on the s.,** inclinado; oblicuo
slanting /'slæntɪŋ/ a al sesgo, inclinado; oblicuo
slap /slæp/ vt pegar con la mano. —n bofetada, f; palmada, f. **to s. on the back,** golpear en la espalda. **s.-dash,** (of persons) irresponsable, descuidado; (of work) chapucero, sin cuidado
slash /slæʃ/ vt (gash, also sleeves, etc.) acuchillar; cortar; (with a whip) dar latigazos (a). —n cuchillada, f; corte, m; latigazo, m
slashing /'slæʃɪŋ/ a mordaz, severo
slat /slæt/ n tablilla, f, vi (of sails) dar zapatazos, zapatear
slate /sleit/ n pizarra, f, esquisto, m; (for roofs and for writing) pizarra, f, vt (a roof) empizarrar; (censure) criticar severamente, censurar. **s.-colored,** apizarrado. **s. pencil,** pizarrín, m. **s. quarry,** pizarrería, f, pizarral, m
slater /'sleitər/ n pizarrero, m
slating /'sleitɪŋ/ n empizarrado, m; (criticism) crítica severa, censura, f; (scolding) peluca, f
slattern /'slætərn/ n pazpuerca, f
slatternly /'slætərnli/ a desgarbado, desaliñado
slaughter /'slɔtər/ n matanza, f; carnicería, f; —vt (animals) sacrificar, matar; matar, hacer una carnicería de. **s.-house,** matadero, m
slaughterer /'slɔtərər/ n jifero, carnicero, m
Slav /slɑv, slæv/ a and n eslavo (-va)

slave /sleiv/ *n* esclavo (-va). —*vi* trabajar mucho. **white s. traffic,** trata de blancas, *f.* **s.-bangle,** esclava, *f.* **s.-driver,** capataz de esclavos, negrero, *m; fig* negrero, sayón de esclavos, *m.* **s.-trade,** trata de esclavos, *f*

slaver /'sleivər/ *n* negrero, *m*

slaver /'slævər/ *vi* babear. —*n* baba, *f*

slavering /'slævərɪŋ/ *a* baboso

slavery /'sleivəri/ *n* esclavitud, *f;* trabajo muy arduo, *m*

slavish /'sleivɪʃ/ *a* de esclavo; servil

slavishly /'sleivɪʃli/ *adv* como esclava; servilmente

Slavonic /slə'vɒnɪk/ *a* eslavo. —*n* (language) eslavo, *m,* lengua eslava, *f*

slay /slei/ *vt* matar; asesinar

slayer /'sleiər/ *n* matador (-ra); asesino, *mf*

slaying /'sleiɪŋ/ *n* matanza, *f;* asesinato, *m*

sled /sled/ *n* trineo, *m,* rastra, *f*

sledge /sledʒ/ *n* trineo, *m.* —*vi* ir en trineo. —*vt* transportar por trineo. **s.-hammer,** acotillo, *m*

sleek /slik/ *a* liso, lustroso; (of general appearance) pulcro, bien aseado, elegante; (of manner) obsequioso

sleekness /'sliknɪs/ *n* lustre, *m,* lisura, *f;* (of an animal) gordura, *f;* elegancia, *f*

sleep /slip/ *n* sueño, *m.* —*vi* dormir; reposar, descansar. —*vt* dormir. **a deep s.,** un sueño pesado. **He walks in his s.,** Es un sonámbulo. **to court s.,** conciliar el sueño. **to go to s.,** dormirse; entumecerse. **My foot has gone to s.,** Se me ha dormido (*or* Se me ha entumecido) el pie. **to send a person to s.,** adormecer. **to s. like a top,** dormir como un lirón. **to s. oneself sober,** dormir la mona. **to s. in,** dormir tarde; dormir en casa. **to s. off,** (a cold, etc.) curarse... durmiendo; (drunkenness) dormirla. **to s. on,** *vt* (consider) dormir sobre, consultar con la almohada. —*vi* seguir durmiendo. **to s. out,** dormir fuera de casa; dormir al aire libre

sleeper /'slipər/ *n* durmiente, *mf; rail* traviesa, *f;* (on a train) coche cama, *m.* **to be a bad s.,** dormir mal. **to be a good s.,** dormir bien.

sleepily /'slipəli/ *adv* soñolientamente

sleepiness /'slipinɪs/ *n* somnolencia, *f;* letargo, *m*

sleeping /'slipɪŋ/ *a* durmiente. —*n* el dormir. **between s. and waking,** entre duerme y vela. **s.-bag,** saco-cama, *m.* **s.-car,** coche camas, *m.* **s.-draught,** narcótico, *m.* **s. partner,** *m* socio (-ia) comanditario (-ia). **s. sickness,** enfermedad del sueño, *f*

sleepless /'sliplɪs/ *a* (of persons) insomne, desvelado; (unremitting) incansable; (of the sea, etc.) en perpetuo movimiento. **to spend a s. night,** pasar una noche en vela, pasar una noche toledana, pasar una noche sin dormir

sleeplessness /'sliplɪsnɪs/ *n* insomnio, *m*

sleepwalker /'slip,wɔkər/ *n* sonámbulo (-la)

sleepwalking /'slip,wɔkɪŋ/ *n* sonambulismo, *m*

sleepy /'slipi/ *a* soñoliento; letárgico. **to be s.,** tener sueño. **s.-head,** lirón, *m,* marmota, *f*

sleet /slit/ *n* aguanieve, cellisca, nevisca, *f, vi* caer aguanieve, cellisquear, neviscar

sleeve /sliv/ *n* manga, *f;* (of a hose pipe, etc.) manguera, *f; mech* manguito, *m.* **to have something up one's s.,** traer algo en la manga

sleeved /slivd/ *a* con mangas...; de... manga(s)

sleeveless /'slivlɪs/ *a* sin manga

sleigh /slei/ *n* trineo, *m, vi* ir en trineo

sleight of hand /slait/ *n* prestidigitación, *f;* juego de manos, *m*

slender /'slɛndər/ *a* delgado; esbelto; tenue; escaso; pequeño; ligero. **Their means are very s.,** Sus recursos son muy escasos. **It is a very s. hope,** Es una esperanza muy remota

slenderness /'slɛndərnɪs/ *n* delgadez, *f;* esbeltez, *f;* tenuidad, *f;* escasez, *f*

sleuth /sluθ/ *n* (dog) sabueso, *m; inf* detective, *m*

slice /slais/ *n* lonja, tajada, *f;* (of fruit) raja, *f;* (of bread, etc.) rebanada, *f;* (share) parte, porción, *f;* (for fish, etc.) pala, *f.* —*vt* cortar en tajadas, etc.; rajar; cortar

slick /slɪk/ *a* hábil, diestro

slide /slaid/ *vi* deslizarse, resbalar; (over a question) pasar por alto de; (into a habit, etc.) caer (en). —*n*

resbalón, *m;* pista de hielo, *f;* (chute) tobogán, *m;* (of a microscope) portaobjetos, *m;* (lantern) diapositiva, *f;* (for the hair) pasador, *m;* (of rock, etc.) desprendimiento, *m; mech* guía, *f.* **to let things s.,** dejar rodar la bola. **s.-rule,** regla de cálculo, *f*

sliding /'slaidɪŋ/ *a* resbaladizo; corredizo; movible. **s. -door,** puerta corrediza, puerta de corradera, *f.* **s.-roof,** techo corredizo, *m.* **s.-scale,** escala graduada, *f;* **s.-seat,** asiento movible, *m;* (in a rowing-boat) bancada corrediza, *f*

slight /slait/ *a* delgado; débil, frágil; ligero; (small) pequeño; escaso; (trivial) insignificante, poco importante. —*vt* desairar, despreciar. —*n* desaire, desprecio, *m;* falta de respeto, *f*

slighting /'slaitɪŋ/ *a* despreciativo, de desprecio

slightingly /'slaitɪŋli/ *adv* con desprecio

slightly /'slaitli/ *adv* ligeramente; poco. **I only know her s.,** La conozco muy poco. **s. built,** de talle delgado

slightness /'slaitnɪs/ *n* (slimness) delgadez, *f;* ligereza, *f;* (triviality) poca importancia, insignificancia, *f*

slim /slɪm/ *a* delgado; escaso. —*vi* adelgazarse. **He has very s. chances of success,** Tiene muy pocas posibilidades de conseguir el éxito

slime /slaim/ *n* légamo, limo, lodo, cieno, *m;* (of a snail) limazo, *m; fig* cieno, *m*

sliminess /'slaiminɪs/ *n* limosidad, *f;* viscosidad, *f*

slimness /'slɪmnɪs/ *n* delgadez, *f;* escasez, *f*

slimy /'slaimi/ *a* limoso, legamoso; pecinoso, viscoso; (of persons) rastrero, servil

sling /slɪŋ/ *vt* arrojar, lanzar; tirar con honda; (a sword, etc.) suspender; (lift) embragar; (a limb) poner en cabestrillo. —*n* (for missiles) honda, *f; Naut* balso, *m;* (for a limb) cabestrillo, *m,* charpa, *f*

slink /slɪŋk/ *vi* (away, off) escurrirse, escabullirse

slip /slɪp/ *vi* resbalar, deslizar; (stumble) resbalar, tropezar; (fall) caer; (out of place) salirse; (become untied) desatarse; (steal away) escabullirse; (glide) deslizarse; (of years) correr, pasar; (skid) patinar. —*vt* deslizar; (garments, shoes) ponerse; (dogs, cables) soltar; (an arm round, etc.) pasar; *Rail* desacoplar; (escape) escaparse de; (free oneself of) librarse de. —*n* resbalón, *m;* (skid) patinazo, *m;* (stumble) tropezón, traspié, *m;* (oversight) inadvertencia, *f;* (mistake) falta, equivocación, *f;* (moral lapse) desliz, *m;* (petticoat) combinación, *f;* (cover) funda, *f; Bot* vástago, *m; Print* galerada, *f;* (of paper) papeleta, *f; pl* slips, *Naut* angullas, *f pl.* **It slipped my memory,** Se me fue de la memoria. **There's many a s. 'twixt the cup and the lip,** Del dicho al hecho hay muy gran trecho, De la mano a la boca desaparece la sopa. **to give** (someone) **the slip,** escaparse de. **You ought not to let the opportunity s.,** No debes perder la oportunidad. **to let s. a secret,** revelar un secreto. **to let s. an exclamation,** soltar (dar) una exclamación. **to s. into,** colarse en, deslizarse en. **to s. into,** colarse en, deslizarse en. **to s. into one's clothes,** vestirse rápidamente. **to s. on,** (a garment) ponerse. **to s. out,** salir a hurtadillas; escaparse; (of information) divulgarse. **s. of a boy,** mozalbete, joven imberbe, *m.* **s. of the tongue,** error de lengua, *m.* **s.-knot,** nudo corredizo, *m*

slipcover /'slɪp,kʌvər/ *n* cubierta, cubierta para muebles, funda, funda para muebles, *f*

slipper /'slɪpər/ *n* babucha, chinela, *f,* pantuflo, *m;* (heelless) chancleta, *f;* (dancing) zapatilla de baile, *f.* **s.-shaped,** achinelado

slippered /'slɪpərd/ *a* en zapatillas

slipperiness /'slɪpərinɪs/ *n* lo resbaladizo; (of persons) informalidad, *f*

slippery /'slɪpəri/ *a* resbaladizo; poco firme, inestable; (of persons) informal, sin escrúpulos

slipshod /'slɪpʃɒd/ *a* descuidado, negligente; poco correcto

slipway /'slɪpˌwei/ *n* surtida, *f,* angulias, *f pl*

slit /slɪt/ *vt* cortar; hender, rajar; (the throat) degollar. —*n* cortadura, *f;* resquicio, *m.* **to s. open,** abrir de un tajo

slither /'slɪðər/ *vi* resbalar; deslizarse

sliver /'slɪvər/ *n* raja, *f;* (of wood) astilla, *f;* (of cloth) tira, *f*

slobber /'slɒbər/ vi babear; (blubber) gimotear, n baba, f

sloe /slou/ n (fruit) endrina, f; (tree) endrino, m. **s.-colored**, endrino. **s.-eyed**, con ojos de mora

slog /slɒg/ vt golpear duramente. **to s. away**, batirse el cobre, trabajar como un negro

slogan /'slougən/ n grito de batalla, m; reclamo, m; frase hecha, f; mote, m

slop /slɒp/ n charco, m; pl **slops**, agua sucia, f; alimentos líquidos, m pl. —vi derramarse, verterse. —vt verter, derramar

slope /sloup/ n inclinación, f; pendiente, f; (of a mountain, etc.) falda, ladera, cuesta, f; vertiente, mf. —vi inclinarse; estar en declive; bajar (hacia). **to s. down**, declinar

sloping /'sloupɪŋ/ a inclinado; en declive; (of shoulders) caídos, m pl

sloppy /'slɒpi/ a casi líquido; (muddy) lodoso, lleno de barro; (of work) chapucero; (of persons) baboso, sobón. **s. sentiment**, sensiblería, f

slot /slɒt/ n ranura, muesca, f. **s.-machine**, máquina expendedora, f, expendedor, m; (in amusement arcades, etc.) tragaperras, m

sloth /slɒθ or, esp. for 2, slouθ/ n pereza, indolencia, f; zool perezoso, m

slothful /'slɒθfəl, 'slouθ-/ a perezoso, indolente

slouch /slautʃ/ n inclinación del cuerpo, f. —vi andar cabizbajo, andar arrastrando los pies. **to s. about**, vagar, golfear. **s.-hat**, sombrero gacho, m

slough /slʌf/ n (bog) cenagal, pantano, m, marisma, f; (of a snake) camisa, f. —vt (a skin) mudar; (prejudices, etc.) desechar

Slovak /'slouvɑk/ n eslovaco (-ca)

Slovakian /slou'vɑkiən/ a eslovaco

sloven /'slʌvən/ n puerco, m; (at work) chapucero, m

Slovene /slou'vin/ a and n esloveno (-na)

slovenliness /'slʌvənlɪnɪs/ n desaseo, desaliño, m; (carelessness) descuido, m, negligencia, f; (of work) chapucería, f

slovenly /'slʌvənli/ a desgarbado, desaseado; (careless) descuidado, negligente; (of work) chapucero

slow /slou/ a despacio; lento; (stupid) torpe; tardo; (of clocks) atrasado; (boring) aburrido; (inactive) flojo. —adv despacio, lentamente. **I was not s. to...**, No tardé en... **The clock is ten minutes s.**, El reloj lleva diez minutos de atraso. **to s. down**, aflojar el paso; ir más despacio. **s.-motion**, velocidad reducida, f. **s. train**, tren ómnibus, m. **s.-witted**, lerdo tardo

slowcoach /'slou,koutʃ/ n perezoso (-sa)

"Slow Down" «Moderar Su Velocidad»

slow learner n alumno de lento aprendizaje, m

slowly /'slouli/ adv despacio, lentamente; poco a poco

slowness /'slounɪs/ n lentitud, f; (delay) tardanza, f; (stupidity) torpeza, estupidez, f

slug /slʌg/ n babosa, f

sluggard /'slʌgərd/ n gandul (-la), perezoso (-a)

sluggish /'slʌgɪʃ/ a perezoso; (of the market) flojo; (of temperament, etc.) calmoso, flemático; (slow) lento

sluggishness /'slʌgɪʃnɪs/ n pereza, f; (of the market) flojedad, f; (slowness) lentitud, f

sluice /slus/ n esclusa, f; canal, m, acequia, f **to s. down**, lavar; echar agua sobre; (a person) dar una ducha (a), dar un baño (a). **s.-gate**, compuerta de esclusa, f; tajaderas, f pl, tablacho, m

slum /slʌm/ n barrio pobre, m, banda de miseria (Argentina), barriada (Peru), población (Chile), villamiseria (Argentina), f, tugurio (Colombia), m; pl **slums**, barrios bajos, m pl

slumber /'slʌmbər/ vi dormir; (go to sleep) dormirse, caer dormido; (be latent) estar latente. —n sueño, m

slump /slʌmp/ n com baja repentina, f; fig baja, racha mala, f. —vi com bajar repentinamente. **the s.**, la crisis económica. **to s. into an armchair**, dejarse caer en un sillón

slur /slɜr/ vt (words) comerse sílabas o letras (de); (in writing) unir (las palabras); (mus of notes) ligar. **to cast a s. on**, difamar, manchar. **to s. over**, pasar por alto de, omitir, suprimir

slush /slʌʃ/ n lodo, m; agua nieve, f; (sentimentality) ñoñería, f

slushy /'slʌʃi/ a lodoso, fangoso

slut /slʌt/ n pazpuerca, marrana, f

sly /slai/ a astuto, taimado, socarrón; disimulado; (arch) malicioso. **on the sly**, a hurtadillas

slyly /'slaili/ adv astutamente; disimuladamente; (archly) maliciosamente

slyness /'slainɪs/ n astucia, socarronería, f; disimulo, m; malicia, f

smack /smæk/ n (taste) sabor, gusto, m; (tinge) dejo, m; (blow) golpe, m; (with the hand) bofetada, palmada, f; (with a whip) latigazo, m; (crack of whip) restallido, chasquido, m; (kiss) beso sonado, m; (boat) lancha de pescar, f. —vi (taste of) tener gusto de, sabor a; (be tinged with) oler a. —vt (a whip) hacer restallar; (slap) pegar con la mano. **to s. one's lips over**, chuparse los dedos

small /smɔl/ a pequeño; menudo; menor; poco; (petty) mezquino, vulgar. —n parte estrecha, f. **a s. number**, un pequeño número. **to make a person look s.**, humillar. **to make oneself s.**, hacerse chiquito. **s.-arms**, armas portátiles, f pl. **s. change**, suelto, m. **s. craft**, embarcaciones menores, f pl. **s. fry**, pececillos, m pl; (children) gente menuda, f; gente sin importancia, f. **s. hours**, altas horas de la noche, f pl. **s.-minded**, adocenado, de cortos alcances. **s.-talk**, trivialidades, f pl, charla frívola, f

smallish /'smɔlɪʃ/ a bastante pequeño; más bien pequeño que grande

smallness /'smɔlnɪs/ n pequeñez, f; escasez, exigüidad, f

smallpox /'smɔl,pɒks/ n viruelas, f pl

smart /smɑrt/ vi picar; dolerse (de). —n escozor, m; dolor, m. —a severo; vivo; rápido; pronto; (competent) hábil; (clever) listo; (unscrupulous) cuco, astuto; (of personal appearance) majo; elegante, distinguido; (neat) aseado; (fashionable, etc.) de moda; de buen tono. **to s. for**, ser castigado por. **to s. under**, sufrir

smarten /'smɑrtn/ vt embellecer. —vi (up) ponerse elegante; mejorar. **I must go and s. myself up a little**, Tengo que arreglarme un poco

smartly /'smɑrtli/ adv severamente; vivamente; rápidamente; hábilmente; elegantemente

smartness /'smɑrtnɪs/ n viveza, f; prontitud, rapidez, f; (cleverness) despejo, m, habilidad, f; (wittiness) agudeza, f; (astuteness) cuquería, astucia, f; (of dress, etc.) elegancia, f; buen tono, m

smash /smæʃ/ vt romper, quebrar; (a ball, etc.) golpear; (annihilate) destruir; (an opponent) aplastar. —vi romperse, quebrarse; hacerse pedazos; (collide) chocar (con, contra); estallarse (contra); (financially) hacer bancarrota. —n rotura, f; quebrantamiento, m; estruendo, m; (financial) quiebra, ruina, f; (car, etc.) accidente, m; desastre, m, catástrofe, f. **to s. to atoms**, hacer trizas. **to s. up**, hacer pedazos. **s. and grab raid**, atraco a mano armada, m

smash hit n éxito arrollador, éxito rotundo, m

smattering /'smætərɪŋ/ n conocimiento superficial, m, tintura, f, barniz, m

smear /smɪər/ n mancha, f; biol frotis, m. —vt embadurnar (de); manchar (con), ensuciar (con); (oneself) untarse; (blur) borrar

smell /smɛl/ n (sense of) olfato, m; (odor) olor, m. —vt oler. —vi oler; tener olor; (disagreeably) oler mal, tener mal olor; (stink) apestar. **How good it smells!** ¡Qué bien huele! **to s. of**, oler a. **to s. out**, husmear

smelling /'smɛlɪŋ/ n olfateo, m. **s.-bottle**, frasco de sales, m. **s.-salts**, sales (inglesas), f pl

smelt /smɛlt/ vt fundir. —n ichth eperlano, m

smelter /'smɛltər/ n fundidor, m

smelting /'smɛltɪŋ/ n fundición, f. **s. furnace**, horno de fundición, m

smile /smail/ vi sonreír; reírse. —vt expresar con una sonrisa. —n sonrisa, f. **Mary smiled her thanks**, María dio las gracias con una sonrisa. **smile at adversity**, ponerse buena cara a mal tiempo. **to s. at threats**, reírse de las amenazas

smiling /'smailɪŋ/ a sonriente, risueño

smilingly /'smaɪlɪŋli/ adv sonriendo, con una sonrisa, con cara risueña

smirch /smɜrtʃ/ vt manchar. —n mancha, f

smirk /smɜrk/ vi sonreír con afectación; hacer visajes. —n sonrisa afectada, f

smirking /'smɜrkɪŋ/ a afectado; sonriente

smite /smaɪt/ vt golpear; (kill) matar; (punish) castigar; (pain) doler; (of bright light, sounds, etc.) herir; (cause remorse) remorder. **My conscience smites me,** Tengo remordimientos de conciencia. **to be smitten by,** inf estar prendado de. **I was smitten by a desire to smoke,** Me entraron deseos de fumar

smith /smɪθ/ n herrero, m. **smith's hammer,** destajador, m

smithereens /ˌsmɪðə'rinz/ n pl añicos, m pl

smithy /'smɪθi, 'smɪði/ n herrería, f

smock /smɒk/ n blusa, f; (child's) delantal, m

smoke /smouk/ n humo, m. —vi humear, echar humo; (tobacco) fumar. —vt ahumar; ennegrecer; (tobacco) fumar. **smoked glasses,** gafas ahumadas, f pl. **s. helmet,** casco respiratorio, m. **s.-screen,** cortina de humo, f. **s. signal,** ahumada, f. **s.-stack,** chimenea, f

smokeless /'smouklɪs/ a sin humo

smoker /'smoukər/ n fumador (-ra)

smoking /'smoukɪŋ/ a humeante. —n el fumar. **"S. Prohibited,"** «Se prohibe fumar.» **non-s. compartment,** rail departamento de no fumadores, m. **s.-carriage,** rail departamento para fumadores, m. **s.-room,** fumadero, m

smoky /'smouki/ a humeante; lleno de humo; (black) ahumado

smooth /smuð/ a liso; igual; (of the skin, etc.) suave; (of water) calmo, tranquilo; (flattering, etc.) lisonjero; obsequioso; afable. —vt allanar; (hair, etc.) alisar; (paths, etc.) igualar. **to s. down,** (a person) tranquilizar, calmar. **to s. over,** (faults) exculpar. **to s. the way for,** allanar el camino para. **s.-faced,** barbilampiño, lampiño, bien afeitado, todo afeitado; fig obsequioso, untuoso. **s.-haired,** de pelo liso. **s.-spoken,** de palabras lisonjeras; obsequioso

smoothly /'smuðli/ adv lisamente; (of speech) afablemente; con lisonjeras. **Everything was going s.,** Todo iba viento en popa

smoothness /'smuðnɪs/ n igualdad, f; lisura, f; (of skin, etc.) suavidad, f; (of water) calma, tranquilidad, f; (of manner, etc.) afabilidad, f

smother /'smʌðər/ vt ahogar, sofocar; (a fire) apagar; (cover) envolver, cubrir

smoulder /'smouldər/ vi arder sin llama, arder lentamente; (of passions, etc.) arder; estar latente

smouldering /'smouldərɪŋ/ a que arde lentamente; fig latente

smudge /smʌdʒ/ vt manchar, ensuciar; (blur) borrar. —n mancha, f

smug /smʌg/ a satisfecho de sí mismo, pagado de sí mismo; farisaico

smuggle /'smʌgəl/ vt pasar de contrabando. —vi hacer contrabando

smuggler /'smʌglər/ n contrabandista, mf

smuggling /'smʌglɪŋ/ n contrabando, m

smugly /'smʌgli/ adv con presunción, de un aire satisfecho

smugness /'smʌgnɪs/ n satisfacción de sí mismo, f; fariseísmo, m

smut /smʌt/ n copo de hollín, m; mancha, f; (disease) tizón, m

smutty /'smʌti/ a tiznado; ahumado; inf verde

snack /snæk/ n tentempié, piscolabis, bocado, m. **to take a s.,** tomar un piscolabis

snack bar n merendero, m

snaffle /'snæfəl/ n filete, m. —vt (a horse) refrenar. **s.-bridle,** bridón, m

snag /snæg/ n (of a tree) tocón, m; (of a tooth) raigón, m; (problem) busilis, m; obstáculo inesperado, m

snail /sneil/ n caracol, m. **at a snail's pace,** a paso de tortuga

snake /sneik/ n serpiente, f. **s.-charmer,** encantador de serpientes, m

snakelike /'sneik,laik/ a de serpiente; serpentino

snap /snæp/ vt morder; (break) romper; (one's fin-

gers) castañetear; (a whip) chasquear; (down a lid, etc.) cerrar de golpe; (beaks, etc.) cerrar ruidosamente; photo sacar una instantánea de. —vi partirse; quebrarse; hablar bruscamente. —n (bite) mordedura, f; golpe seco, m; chasquido, m; rotura, f; (clasp) cierre, m; (of weather) temporada, f; (spirit) vigor, brío, m; photo instantánea, f. **to s. at,** procurar morder; (an invitation, etc.) aceptar gustoso. **to s. one's fingers at,** fig burlarse de. **to s. up,** coger, agarrar; (a person) cortar la palabra (a), interrumpir. **s.-fastener,** botón de presión, m

snapdragon /'snæp,drægən/ n dragón, m, becerra, boca de dragón, f

snappily /'snæpəli/ adv irritablemente

snappishness /'snæpɪʃnɪs/ n irritabilidad, f

snappy /'snæpi/ a irritable; vigoroso

snapshot /'snæp,ʃɒt/ n instantánea, foto, f

snare /snɛr/ n cepo, lazo, m, trampa, f; fig red, f. —vt coger en el lazo; fig enredar

snarl /snɑrl/ vi (of dogs) regañar; (cats, etc.) gruñir. —n regañamiento, m; gruñido, m

snarling /'snɑrlɪŋ/ n regañamiento, m; gruñidos, m pl, a gruñidor

snatch /snætʃ/ vt asir; agarrar; (enjoy) disfrutar; (an opportunity) tomar, aprovecharse de. —n asimiento, agarro, m; (of time) rato, m; instante, m; (of song) fragmento, m. **to make a s. at,** procurar agarrar; alargar la mano hacia. **to s. a hurried meal,** comer aprisa. **to s. away,** arrebatar, quitar; (carry off) robar. **to s. up,** coger rápidamente; coger en brazos

sneak /snik/ vi deslizarse (en), colarse (en); (lurk) rondar; (inform) acusar. —n mandilón, m; (accuser) acusón (-ona). **to s. off,** escabullirse, irse a hurtadillas. **s.-thief,** n garduño (-ña)

sneaker /'snikər/ n (shoe) zapatilla de tenis, f

sneaking /'snikɪŋ/ a furtivo, ruin, mezquino; secreto

sneer /snɪər/ vi sonreír irónicamente; burlarse, mofarse. —n sonrisa sardónica, sonrisa de desprecio, f; burla, mofa, f. **to s. at,** mofarse de, burlarse de; hablar con desprecio de

sneering /'snɪərɪŋ/ a mofador, burlón

sneeringly /'snɪərɪŋli/ adv con una sonrisa sardónica, burlonamente

sneeze /sniz/ vi estornudar. —n estornudo, m. **It's not to be sneezed at,** No es moco de pavo

sniff /snɪf/ vi respirar fuertemente; resollar. —vt oler, olfatear; aspirar. **to s. at,** oler. **to s. out,** Inf. husmear

snigger /'snɪgər/ vi reírse por lo bajo, reírse disimuladamente. —n risa disimulada, f

snip /snɪp/ vt cortar con tijeras; cortar, quitar. —n tijeretada, f; (of cloth, etc.) recorte, pedacito, m

snipe /snaip/ n ornith agachadiza, f. **to s. at,** Mil. pacar

sniper /'snaipər/ n Mil. paco, m

snippet /'snɪpɪt/ n pedacito, fragmento, m; (of prose, etc.) trocito, m; (of news) noticia, f

snivel /'snɪvəl/ vi lloriquear, gimotear

sniveling /'snɪvəlɪŋ/ n lloriqueo, gimoteo, m. —a llorón; mocoso

snob /snɒb/ n esnob, mf

snobbery /'snɒbəri/ n snobismo, m

snobbish /'snɒbɪʃ/ a esnob

snood /snud/ n (for the hair) redecilla, f; (turkey's) moco (de pavo), m; (fishing) cendal, m

snoop /snup/ vi espiar; entremeterse

snooze /snuz/ vi dormitar, echar un sueño. —n sueñecito, m; (afternoon) siesta, f

snore /snɔr/ vi roncar. —n ronquido, m

snoring /'snɔrɪŋ/ n ronquidos, m pl

snort /snɔrt/ vi bufar; resoplar. —n bufido, m; resoplido, m

snout /snaut/ n hocico, m; (of a pig) jeta, f

snow /snou/ n nieve, f. —vi nevar. —vt nevar; fig inundar. **to s. under** (with), inundar con. **to be snowed up,** estar aprisionado por la nieve. **s.-blindness,** deslumbramiento causado por la nieve, m. **s.-boot,** bota para la nieve, f. **s.-bound,** aprisionado por la nieve; bloqueado por la nieve, f. **s.-capped,** coronado de nieve. **s.-clad,** cubierto de nieve, f. **s.-drift,** acumulación de nieve, f. **s.-field,** ventisquero, m. **s.-goggles,** gafas ahumadas, f pl. **s.-line,** límite de las nieves perpetuas, *m.* **s.-man,** figura de nieve, *f.* **s.-plough,** quitanieve, *m.* **s.-shoe,** raqueta de nieve, *f.* **s.-white,** blanco como la nieve

snowball /'snou,bɔl/ *n* bola de nieves, *f; bot* bola de nieve, *f*

snowdrop /'snou,drɒp/ *n* campanilla de invierno, violeta de febrero, *f*

snowfall /'snou,fɔl/ *n* nevada, *f*

snowflake /'snou,fleik/ *n* copo de nieve, *m*

snowstorm /'snou,stɔrm/ *n* ventisca, *f*

snowy /'snoui/ *a* nevoso; de nieve

snub /snʌb/ *vt* repulsar; desairar, tratar con desdén. —*n* repulsa, *f,* desaire, *m;* (nose) nariz respingona, *f.* **s.-nosed,** de nariz respingona

snuff /snʌf/ *vt* (breathe) oler, olfatear; inhalar; (a candle) atizar, despabilar. —*n* (of a candle) moco, *m,* despabiladura, *f;* (tobacco) rapé, *m.* **to take s.,** tomar rapé. **to s. out,** extinguir. **s.-box,** caja de rapé, tabaquera, *f*

snuffers /'snʌfərz/ *n pl* tenacillas, despabiladeras, *f pl*

snuffle /'snʌfəl/ *vi* hacer ruido con la nariz; respirar fuerte; (in speaking) ganguear

snuffling /'snʌflɪŋ/ *a* mocoso; (of the voice) gangoso

snug /snʌg/ *a* caliente; cómodo; (hidden) escondido, **to have a s. income,** tener el riñón bien cubierto, ser acomodado

snuggle /'snʌgəl/ *vi* hacerse un ovillo; acomodarse; ponerse cómodo. **to s. up to,** arrimarse a, apretarse contra

snugly /'snʌgli/ *adv* cómodamente

snugness /'snʌgnɪs/ *n* comodidad, *f*

so /sou/ *adv* así; de este modo, de esta manera; por lo tanto; tanto; (before adjs. and advs. but not before **más, mejor, menos, peor,** where **tanto** is used) tan; (in the same way) del mismo modo, de igual modo; (therefore) de modo que, de manera que; (also) también; (approximately) más o menos, aproximadamente. **Is that so?** ¿De veras? **if so...,** si así es... **He has not yet done so,** no lo ha hecho todavía. **I told you so!** ¡Ya te lo dije yo! **So be it!** ¡Así sea! **so far,** hasta aquí; hasta ahora. **So forth,** etcétera. **So long!** ¡Nos vemos! **so much,** tanto. **So much the worse for them,** Tanto peor para ellos. **to so speak,** por decirlo así. **so as to,** a fin de, para. **so long as,** con tal que, a condición de que. **so on,** etcétera. **so soon as,** tan pronto como. **so that,** de suerte que, de modo que, para que; con que. **so-and-so,** *n* fulano (-na); mengano (-na). **so-called,** así llamado, supuesto. **so-so,** así-así, regular

soak /souk/ *vt* remojar; empapar; (skins) abrevar. —*vi* estar en remojo. —*n* remojo, *m;* (rain) diluvio, *m;* (booze) borrachera, *f.* **to s. into,** filtrar en; penetrar. **to s. through,** penetrar; filtrar **so-called,** así llamado, supuesto. **so-so,** así, regular

soaked /soukt/ *a* remojado. **He is s. to the skin,** Está calado hasta los huesos

soaking /'soukɪŋ/ *n* remojo, *m;* empapamiento, *m,*

soap /soup/ *n* jabón, *m.* —*vt* jabonar; (flatter) enjabonar. **a tablet of s.,** una pastilla de jabón. **soft s.,** jabón blando, *m.* **toilet s.,** jabón de tocador, jaboncillo, *m.* **s.-bubble,** burbuja de jabón, *f.* **s. dish,** jabonera, *f.* **s. factory,** jabonería, *f.* **s.-flakes,** copos de jabón, *m pl*

soapbark tree /'soup,bark/ *n* quillay, palo de jabón, *m*

soap box *n lit* caja de jabón, *f; fig* tribuna callejera, *f*

soap opera /'ɒpərə/ *n* radionovela (on radio), telenovela (on television), *f,* serial lacrimógeno (derogatory), *m*

soapsuds /'soup,sʌdz/ *n pl* jabonaduras, *f pl*

soapy /'soupi/ *a* cubierto de jabón; jabonoso

soar /sɔr/ *vi* remontarse; *fig* elevarse; (of prices, etc.) subir de golpe

soaring /'sɔrɪŋ/ *n* remonte, vuelo, *m; fig* aspiración, *f;* (of prices, etc.) subida repentina, *f*

sob /sɒb/ *vi* sollozar. —*n* sollozo, *m.* **to sob one's heart out,** llorar a lágrima viva. **to sob out,** decir sollozando, decir entre sollozos

sobbing /'sɒbɪŋ/ *n* sollozos, *m pl, a* sollozante

sober /'soubər/ *a* sobrio; moderado; (of colors) obscuro. **s.-minded,** serio; reflexivo

sobriety /sə'braiɪti/ *n* sobriedad, *f;* moderación, *f;* seriedad, *f;* calma, tranquilidad, *f*

sobriquet /'soubrɪ,kei, -,kɛt/ *n* apodo, *m*

soccer /'sɒkər/ *n* fútbol (Asociación), *m*

sociability /,soʃə'bɪlɪti/ *n* sociabilidad, *f*

sociable /'souʃəbəl/ *a* sociable; amistoso

sociably /'souʃəbli/ *adv* sociablemente; amistosamente

social /'souʃəl/ *a* social; sociable. —*n* reunión, velada, *f.* **s.-democrat,** *a* and *n* socialdemócrata, *mf.* **s. event,** acontecimiento social, *m.* **s. insurance,** previsión social, *f.* **s. services,** servicios sociales, *m pl.* **s. work,** asistencia social, *f*

socialism /'souʃə,lɪzəm/ *n* socialismo, *m*

socialist /'souʃəlɪst/ *a* socialista, laborista. —*n* socialista, *mf*

socialization /,souʃələ'zeiʃən/ *n* socialización, *f*

socialize /'souʃə,laiz/ *vt* socializar

socially /'souʃəli/ *adv* socialmente

society /sə'saiɪti/ *n* sociedad, *f;* (fashionable) mundo elegante, *m,* alta sociedad, *f;* compañía, *f.* **to go into s.,** (of girls) ponerse de largo; entrar en el mundo elegante. **s. hostess,** dama de sociedad, *f.* **Society for the Prevention of Cruelty to Animals,** sociedad protectora de animales, *f.* **s. news,** noticias de sociedad, *f pl*

sociological /,sousiə'lɒdʒɪkəl/ *a* sociológico

sociologist /,sousi,plədʒɪst/ *n* sociólogo (-ga)

sociology /,sousi'plədʒi/ *n* sociología, *f*

sock /sɒk/ *n* calcetín, *m;* (for a shoe) plantilla, *f*

socket /'sɒkɪt/ *n mech* encaje, cubo, ojo, *m;* (of a lamp, and *elec*) enchufe, *m;* (of the eye) órbita, cuenca, *f;* (of a tooth) alvéolo, *m;* (of a joint) fosa, *f.* **His eyes started out of their sockets,** Sus ojos estaban fuera de su órbita

Socratic /sə'krætɪk/ *a* socrático

sod /sɒd/ *n* césped, *m;* (cut) tepe, *m*

soda /'soudə/ *n* sosa, *f.* **caustic s.,** sosa cáustica, *f.* **s.-ash,** carbonato sódico, *m.* **s.-fountain,** aparato de aguas gaseosas, *m.* **s.-water,** sifón, *f*

sodden /'sɒdn̩/ *a* saturado, empapado

sodium /'soudiəm/ *n* sodio, *m*

Sodomite /'soudə,mait/ *n* sodomita, *mf*

sodomy /'sɒdəmi/ *n* sodomía, *f*

sofa /'soufə/ *n* sofá, *m*

soft /sɔft/ *a* blando; suave; muelle; (flabby) flojo; (of disposition, etc.) dulce; (effeminate) muelle, afeminado; (lenient) indulgente; (easy) fácil; (silly) tonto. **to have a s. spot for,** (a person) tener una debilidad para. **s. coal,** carbón bituminoso, *m.* **s. drink,** bebida no alcohólica, *f.* **s. felt hat,** sombrero flexible, *m.* **s. fruit,** fruta blanda, *f.* **s.-boiled,** (of eggs) pasado por agua; (of persons) inocente, ingenuo. **s.-hearted,** de buen corazón; compasivo, bondadoso. **s.-heartedness,** buen corazón, *m,* bondad, *f.* **s.-spoken,** de voz suave; que habla con dulzura, meloso. **s. water,** agua blanda, *f*

soften /'sɔfən/ *vt* ablandar, reblandecer; (weaken) debilitar; (mitigate) mitigar, suavizar; (the heart, etc.) enternecer. —*vi* reblandecerse; enternecerse

softening /'sɔfənɪŋ/ *n* reblandecimiento, *m;* (relenting) enternecimiento, *m*

softly /'sɔftli/ *adv* suavemente; dulcemente, tiernamente; sin ruido, silenciosamente

softness /'sɔftnɪs/ *n* blandura, *f;* suavidad, *f;* (sweetness, etc.) dulzura, *f;* (of character) debilidad de carácter, *f;* (silliness) necedad, estupidez, *f*

soggy /'sɒgi/ *a* empapado de agua; saturado

soil /sɔil/ *n* tierra, *f;* (country) país, *m,* tierra, *f.* —*vt* ensuciar; *Fig.* manchar. **my native s.,** mi tierra, mi patria

soiled /sɔild/ *a* sucio. **s. linen,** ropa sucia, *f*

soirée /swɑ'rei/ *n* velada, *f*

sojourn /'soudʒɜrn/ *vi* morar, residir, permanecer. —*n* residencia, permanencia, *f*

sojourner /'soudʒɜrnər/ *n* morador (-ra), residente, *mf*

sol /sɒl/ *n mus* sol, *m.* **sol-fa,** *n* solfa, *f,* solfeo, *m.* —*vt* solfear

solace /'sɒlɪs/ *n* consuelo, solaz, *m.* —*vt* consolar; solazar

solar /'soulər/ *a* solar. **s. plexus,** *anat* plexo solar, *m*.
s. system, sistema solar, *m*

solder /'sɒdər/ *n* soldadura, *f, vt* soldar

soldering /'sɒdərɪŋ/ *n* soldadura, *f*

soldier /'souldʒər/ *n* soldado, *m; militar, m*. **He
wants to be a s.,** Quiere ser militar

soldierly /'souldʒərli/ *a* militar; marcial

soldiery /'souldʒəri/ *n* soldadesca, *f*

sole /soul/ *n* (of a foot) planta, *f;* (of a shoe) suela, *f;*
(of a plough) cepa, *f; ichth* lenguado, *m,* suela, *f.*
—*vt* (shoes) solar, poner suela (a). —*a* solo, único;
exclusivo. **s. right,** exclusiva, *f,* derecho exclusivo, *m*

solecism /'sɒlɪ,sɪzəm/ *n* solecismo, *m*

solely /'soulli/ *adv* sólo; únicamente, puramente;
meramente

solemn /'sɒləm/ *a* solemne; grave; serio; (sacred) sagrado. **Why do you look so s.?** ¿Por qué estás tan
serio?

solemnity /sə'lɛmnɪti/ *n* solemnidad, *f*

solemnization /,sɒləmnə'zeiʃən/ *n* solemnización,
celebración, *f*

solemnize /'sɒləm,naiz/ *vt* solemnizar

solemnly /'sɒləmli/ *adv* solemnemente; gravemente

solicit /sə'lɪsɪt/ *vt* solicitar; implorar, rogar encarecidamente

solicitation /sə,lɪsɪ'teiʃən/ *n* solicitación, *f*

solicitor /sə'lɪsɪtər/ *n* abogado (-da)

solicitous /sə'lɪsɪtəs/ *a* ansioso (de), deseoso (de);
solícito, atento; (worried) preocupado

solicitude /sə'lɪsɪ,tud/ *n* solicitud, *f,* cuidado, *m;*
(anxiety) preocupación, *f*

solid /'sɒlɪd/ *a* sólido; macizo; (of persons) serio, formal; (unanimous) unánime. —*n* sólido, *m*. **a s. meal,**
una comida fuerte. **He slept for ten s. hours,** Durmió
por diez horas seguidas. **solid-colored material,** tela
lisa, *f*. **s. food,** alimentos sólidos, *m pl*. **s. geometry,**
geometría del espacio, *f*. **solid gold,** oro de ley, *m*. **s.
tire,** llanta de goma maciza, *f*

solidarity /,sɒlɪ'dærɪti/ *n* solidaridad, *f*

solidification /sə,lɪdəfɪ'keiʃən/ *n* solidificación, *f*

solidify /sə'lɪdə,fai/ *vt* solidificar. —*vi* solidificarse;
congelarse

solidity /sə'lɪdɪti/ *n* solidez, *f;* unanimidad, *f*

solidly /'sɒlɪdli/ *adv* sólidamente

soliloquize /sə'lɪlə,kwaiz/ *vi* soliloquiar, hablar a solas

soliloquy /sə'lɪləkwi/ *n* soliloquio, *m*

solitaire /'sɒlɪ,tɛər/ *n* (diamond and game) solitario,
m

solitary /'sɒlɪ,tɛri/ *a* solitario; solo, aislado, único. **He
was in s. confinement for three months,** Estuvo incomunicado durante tres meses. **There is not a s.
one,** No hay ni uno

solitude /'sɒlɪ,tud/ *n* soledad, *f*

solo /'soulou/ *n* (performance and cards) solo, *m*. **to
sing a s.,** cantar un solo. **It was his first s. flight,**
Era su primer vuelo a solas

soloist /'soulouɪst/ *n* solista, *mf*

solstice /'sɒlstɪs, 'soul-/ *n* solsticio, *m*. **summer s.,**
solsticio vernal, *m*. **winter s.,** solsticio hiemal, *m*

solubility /,sɒlyə'bɪlɪti/ *n* solubilidad, *f*

soluble /'sɒlyəbəl/ *a* soluble

solution /sə'luʃən/ *n* solución, *f*

solvable /'sɒlvəbəl/ *a* que se puede resolver, soluble

solve /sɒlv/ *vt* resolver, hallar la solución de

solvency /'sɒlvənsi/ *n* solvencia, *f*

solvent /'sɒlvənt/ *a com* solvente; (chem and fig) disolvente. —*n* disolvente, *m*

somatic /sou'mætɪk/ *a* somático

somber /'sɒmbər/ *a* sombrío

somberly /'sɒmbərli/ *adv* sombríamente

somberness /'sɒmbərnɪs/ *n* lo sombrío; sobriedad, *f;*
melancolía, *f*

some /sʌm; *unstressed* səm/ *a* alguno (-a), algunos
(-as); (before a masculine sing. noun) algún; unos
(-as); un poco de, algo de; (as a partitive, often not
translated, e.g. *Give me s. wine,* Dame vino); (approximately) aproximadamente, unos (-as). —*pron*
algunos (-as), unos (-as); algo, un poco. **I should like
s. strawberries,** Me gustaría comer unas fresas. **s.
day,** algún día. **S. say yes, others no,** Algunos dicen

que sí, otros que no. **There are s. sixty people in the
garden,** Hay unas sesenta personas en el jardín

somebody, someone /'sʌmbɒdi; 'sʌm,wʌn/ *n* alguien, *mf*. **s. else,** otro (-a), otra persona, *f*. **S. or
other said that the book is worth reading,** No sé
quién dijo que el libro vale la pena de leerse. **to be
s.,** *inf* ser un personaje

somehow /'sʌm,hau/ *adv* de un modo u otro, de alguna manera. **S. I don't like them,** No sé por qué,
pero no me gustan

somersault /'sʌmər,sɔlt/ *n* salto mortal, *m, vi* dar un
salto mortal

something /'sʌm,θɪŋ/ *n* algo, *m,* alguna cosa, *f.*
—*adv* algún tanto. **Would you like s. else?** ¿Quiere
Vd. otra cosa? **He left s. like fifty thousand dollars,**
Dejó algo así como cincuenta mil dólares. **He has s.
to live for,** Tiene para que vivir

sometime /'sʌm,taim/ *adv* algún día, alguna vez; en
algún tiempo. —*a* ex-. **Come and see me s. soon,**
Ven a verme algún día de estos. **He will have to go
abroad s. or another,** Tarde o temprano, tiene que ir
al extranjero. **s. last month,** durante el mes pasado

sometimes /'sʌm,taimz/ *adv* algunas veces, a veces.
s. happy, s. sad, algunas veces feliz y otras triste, ora
feliz ora triste

somewhat /'sʌm,wʌt/ *adv* algo; algún tanto, un
tanto; un poco. **I am s. busy,** Estoy algo ocupado. **He
is s. of a lady-killer,** Tiene sus puntos de castigador,
Tiene algo de castigador

somewhere /'sʌm,wɛər/ *adv* en alguna parte. **s.
about,** por ahí. **s. else,** en otra parte

somnambulism /sɒm'næmbyə,lɪzəm/ *n* somnambulismo, *m*

somnambulist /sɒm'næmbyəlɪst/ *n* somnámbulo
(-la)

somnolence /'sɒmnələns/ *n* somnolencia, *f*

somnolent /'sɒmnələnt/ *a* soñoliento; soporífero

son /sʌn/ *n* hijo, *m*. **son-in-law,** yerno, hijo político,
m

sonata /sə'nɒtə/ *n* sonata, *f*

song /sɒŋ/ *n* canto, *m;* canción, *f;* (poem) poema,
verso, *m*. **It's nothing to make a s. about,** No es
para tanto. **to break into s.,** ponerse a cantar. **the S.
of Songs,** Cantar de los Cantares, *m*. **s.-bird,** ave ca-
nora, *f*. **s.-book,** libro de canciones, *m*. **s.-writer,**
compositor (-ra) de canciones

sonic /'sɒnɪk/ *a* sónico. **sonic boom,** estampido
sónico, *m*

sonnet /'sɒnɪt/ *n* soneto, *m*

sonorous /sə'nɔrəs/ *a* sonoro

sonorousness /sə'nɔrəsnɪs/ *n* sonoridad, *f*

soon /sun/ *adv* pronto; dentro de poco, luego. **as s.
as,** así que, en cuanto, luego que, no bien... **as s. as
possible,** lo antes posible, lo más pronto posible, con
la mayor antelación posible, cuanto antes. **s. after,**
poco después (de). **See you s.!** ¡Hasta pronto!
sooner or later, tarde o temprano. **the sooner the
better,** cuanto antes mejor. **No sooner had he left
the house, when...** Apenas hubo dejado la casa,
cuando... **Emily would sooner go to London,** Emilia
preferiría ir a Londres (A Emilia le gustaría más ir a
Londres)

soot /sʊt/ *n* hollín, *m, vt* cubrir de hollín

soothe /suð/ *vt* tranquilizar, calmar, (pain) aliviar,
mitigar

soothing /'suðɪŋ/ *a* calmante, tranquilizador, sosegador; (of powders, etc.) calmante

soothingly /'suðɪŋli/ *adv* con dulzura; suavemente;
como un consuelo

soothsayer /'suθ,seiər/ *n* adivino (-na), adivinador
(-ra)

soothsaying /'suθ,seiɪŋ/ *n* adivinanza, *f*

sooty /'sʊti/ *a* cubierto de hollín; negro como el hollín

sop /sɒp/ *n* sopa, *f;* (bribe) soborno, *m*

sophism /'sɒfɪzəm/ *n* sofisma, *m*

sophist /'sɒfɪst/ *n hist* sofista, *m;* (quibbler) sofista,
mf

sophistic /sə'fɪstɪk/ *a philos* sofista; (of persons, arguments) sofístico

sophisticated /sə'fɪstɪ,keitɪd/ *a* nada ingenuo; mundano; (cultured) culto

sophistication /sə͵fɪstɪ'keɪʃən/ n falta de simplicidad, f; mundanería, f; cultura, f
sophistry /'sɒfəstri/ n sofistería, f
Sophoclean /͵sɒfə'kliən/ a sofocleo
soporific /͵sɒpə'rɪfɪk/ a soporífico
sopping /'sɒpɪŋ/ a muy mojado. **s. wet,** hecho una sopa
soprano /sə'prænou/ n (voice and part) soprano, m; (singer) soprano, tiple, mf
sorcerer /'sɔrsərər/ n encantador, mago, brujo, m
sorceress /'sɔrsəris/ n hechicera, bruja, f
sorcery /'sɔrsəri/ n sortilegio, m, hechicería, brujería, f; encanto, m
sordid /'sɔrdɪd/ a sórdido; (of motives, etc.) ruin, vil
sordidness /'sɔrdɪdnɪs/ n sordidez, f; (of motives, etc.) vileza, bajeza, f
sordine /sɔrden/ n Mus. sordina, f
sore /sɔr/ a doloroso, malo; (sad) triste; (annoyed) enojado; (with need, etc.) extremo. —n llaga, f; (on horses, etc., caused by girths) matadura, f; Fig. herida, f; recuerdo doloroso, m. **to open an old s.,** Fig. renovar la herida. **running s.,** úlcera, f. **s. throat,** dolor de garganta, m
sorely /'sɔrli/ adv grandemente; muy; urgentemente. **He was s. tempted,** Tuvo grandes tentaciones
soreness /'sɔrnɪs/ n dolor, m; (resentment) amargura, f, resentimiento, m; (ill-feeling) rencor, m
sorrel /'sɔrəl, 'sɒr-/ n alazán. —n (horse) alazán, m; Bot. acedera, f
sorrow /'sɒrou/ n pesar, m, aflicción, pesadumbre, f; tristeza, f. —vi afligirse; entristecerse. **To my great s.,** Con gran pesar mío. **s.-stricken,** afligido, agobiado de pena
sorrowful /'sɒrəfəl/ a afligido, angustiado; triste
sorrowfully /'sɒrəfəli/ adv con pena, tristemente
sorrowing /'sɒrouɪŋ/ a afligido. —n aflicción, f, lamentación, f
sort /sɔrt/ n especie, f; clase, f; tipo, m. —vt separar (de); clasificar. **a s. of hat,** una especie de sombrero. **all sorts of,** toda clase de. **He is a good s.,** Es buen chico. **He is a queer s.,** Es un tipo raro. **in some s.,** hasta cierto punto. **I am out of sorts,** Estoy destemplado. **Nothing of the s.!** ¡Nada de eso!
sorter /'sɔrtər/ n oficial de correos, m; clasificador (-ra)
sorting /'sɔrtɪŋ/ n clasificación, f
sot /sɒt/ n zaque, pellejo, m
sotto voce /'sɒt'ou voutʃi/ adv a sovoz, en voz baja
soul /soul/ n alma, f; espíritu, m; (departed) ánima, f; (being) ser, m; (life) vida, f; (heart) corazón, m. **All Souls' Day,** Día de los Difuntos, m. **He is a good s.!** ¡Es un bendito! **She is a simple s.,** Ella es una alma de Dios. **without seeing a living s.,** sin ver un bicho viviente. **Upon my s.!** ¡Por mi vida! **s. in purgatory,** alma en pena, f. **s.-stirring,** emocionante
soulful /'soulfəl/ a sentimental, emocional; espiritual; romántico
soulless /'soullɪs/ a sin alma; mecánico
sound /saund/ n sonido, m; son, m; ruido, m; (strait) estrecho, m. —vi sonar; hacer ruido; resonar; (seem) parecer. —vt sonar; (the horn, the alarm, musical instrument) tocar; (express) expresar; proclamar; (praise) celebrar; Naut. hondear; Med. tentar; (the chest) auscultar; (try to discover) tentar, sondar; (experience) experimentar. **to the s. of,** al son de. **s.-box,** (of a gramophone) diafragma, m. **s.-detector,** fonolocalización de aviones, f. **s.-film,** película sonora, f. **s.-proof,** (of radio studios, etc.) aislado de todo sonido. **s.-track,** guía sonora, banda sonora, f. **s.-wave,** onda sonora, f
sound /saund/ a sano; (of a person) perspicaz; (reasonable) lógico, razonable; (of a policy, etc.) prudente; (of an argument, etc.) válido; (of an investment) seguro; (solvent) solvente; (good) bueno; (deep) profundo. —adv profundamente, bien
sounding /'saundɪŋ/ n Naut. sondeo, m; pl **soundings,** sondas, f pl. —a sonoro. **to take soundings,** sondar, echar la plomada. **s.-board,** tabla de armonía, f
soundless /'saundlɪs/ a sin ruido, silencioso
soundly /'saundli/ adv sanamente; juiciosamente; prudentemente; bien; (deeply) profundamente

soundness /'saundnɪs/ n (of a person) perspicacia, f; (of a policy, etc.) prudencia, f; (of an argument, etc.) validez, fuerza, f; (financial) solvencia, f
soup /sup/ n sopa, f. **clear s.,** consommé, m. **thick s.,** puré, m. **to be in the s.,** Inf. estar aviado. **s.-ladle,** cucharón, m. **s.-plate,** plato sopero, m. **s.-tureen,** sopera, f
sour /sauªr/ a ácido, agrio; (of milk) agrio; (of persons, etc.) agrio, desabrido. —vt agriar. **to go s.,** volverse agrio. **S. grapes!** ¡Están verdes!
source /sɔrs/ n (of a river, etc.) nacimiento, m; fuente, f; (of infection) foco, m. **to know from a good s.,** saber de buena tinta
sourly /'sauªrli/ adv agriamente
sourness /'sauªrnɪs/ n acidez, agrura, f; acrimonia, f
south /sauθ/ n sur, m; mediodía, m. —a del sur. —adv hacia el sur. **S. African,** a and n sudafricano (-na). **S. American,** a and n sudamericano (-na). **s.-east,** n sudeste, m. —a del sudeste. —adv hacia el sudeste. **s.-easter,** viento del sudeste, m. **s.-easterly,** a del sudeste; al sudeste. —adv hacia el sudeste. **s.-eastern,** del sudeste. **s.-s.-east,** n sudsudeste, m. **s.-s.-west,** sudsudoeste, m. **s.-west,** n sudoeste, m. —a del sudoeste. —adv hacia el sudoeste. **s.-west wind,** viento sudoeste, ábrego, m. **s.-westerly,** a del sudoeste. —adv hacia el sudoeste. **s.-western,** a del sudoeste
South Africa República Sudafricana, f
South America América del Sur, Sudamérica, f
southerly /'sʌðərli/ a del sur; hacia el sur. **The house has a s. aspect,** La casa está orientada al sur
southern /'sʌðərn/ a del sur; del mediodía; meridional. **S. Cross,** Cruz, f, Crucero, m. **s. express,** sudexpreso, m
southerner /'sʌðərnər/ n habitante del sur, m
South Sea Mar del Sur, Mar del Pacífico, m
southward /'sauθwərd/ Naut. 'sʌðərd/ a del sur; al sur. —adv hacia el sur
souvenir /͵suvə'nɪər/ n recuerdo, m
sovereign /'sɒvrɪn/ a soberano. —n soberano (-na); (coin) soberano, m
sovereignty /'sɒvrɪnti/ n soberanía, f
soviet /'souvi͵et/ n soviet, m, a soviético
Soviet Union, the la Unión Soviética, f
sow /sau/ n cerda, marrana, f; (of a wild boar) jabalina, f; (of iron) galápago, m
sow /sou/ vt sembrar; esparcir; diseminar
sower /'souər/ n sembrador (-ra)
sowing /'souɪŋ/ n sembradura, siembra, f. **s. machine,** sembradera, f
soya bean /'sɔiə/ n soja, f
spa /spɑ/ n balneario, m; (spring) manantial mineral, m, caldas, f pl
space /speis/ n espacio, m; (of time) temporada, f; intervalo, m; (Print., Mus.) espacio, m. —vt espaciar. **blank s.,** blanco, m. **s.-bar,** tecla de espacios, f, espaciador, m
spacious /'speiʃəs/ a espacioso; amplio
spaciousness /'speiʃəsnɪs/ n espaciosidad, f; amplitud, f
spade /speid/ n pala, azada, f; (cards) espada, f. **to call a s. a s.,** llamar al pan pan y al vino vino, llamar a las cosas por su nombre. **s.-work,** trabajo preparatorio, m, labor de pala, f
spaghetti /spə'geti/ n fideos, macarrones, m pl
Spain /spein/ España, f
span /spæn/ vt medir a palmos; rodear; medir; (cross) atravesar, cruzar. —n palmo, m; espacio, m, duración, f; (of a bridge) vano, m; (of wing, Aer., Zool.) envergadura, f; (distance) distancia, f. **single-s. bridge,** puente de vano único. **the brief s. of human life,** la corta duración de la vida humana
spangle /'spæŋgəl/ n lentejuela, f; (tinsel) oropel, m. —vt adornar con lentejuelas; sembrar (de), esparcir (de). **spangled with stars,** sembrado de estrellas
Spaniard /'spænyərd/ n español (-la). **a young S.,** un joven español
spaniel /'spænyəl/ n perro de aguas, perro sabueso español, m; (cocker) spaniel, m
Spanish /'spænɪʃ/ a español. —n (language) español, castellano, m. **a S. girl,** una muchacha española. **in S. fashion,** a la española. **S. American,** a and n his-

panoamericano (-na). **S. broom,** retama de olor, *f.* **S. fly,** cantárida, *f*

Spanish America Hispanoamérica, *f*

spank /spæŋk/ *vt* pegar con la mano, azotar. —*n* azotazo, *m.* **to s. along,** correr rápidamente; (of a horse) galopar

spanking /'spæŋkɪŋ/ *n* azotamiento, vapuleo, *m*

spanner /'spænər/ *n* llave inglesa, llave de tuercas, *f*

spar /spɑr/ *n Naut.* mastel, *m; Mineral.* espato, *m;* (boxing) boxeo, *m;* (quarrel) disputa, *f.* —*vi* boxear; (argue) disputar

spare /speər/ *a* (meager) frugal, escaso; (of persons) enjuto, flaco; (available) disponible; (extra) de repuesto. —*n* recambio, *m.* **s. part,** pieza de recambio, pieza de repuesto, *f.* **s. room,** cuarto de amigos, *m.* **s. time,** ratos de ocio, *m pl,* tiempo disponible, *m.* **s. wheel,** rueda de repuesto, *f*

spare /speər/ *vt* (expense, etc.) escatimar; ahorrar; (do without) pasarse sin; (give) dar; (a life, etc.) perdonar; (avoid) evitar; dispensar de; (grant) hacer gracia de; (time) dedicar. **I cannot s. her,** No puedo estar sin ella. **They have no money to s.,** No tienen dinero de sobra. **to be sparing of,** ser avaro de

sparingly /'speərɪŋli/ *adv* frugalmente; escasamente. **to eat s.,** comer con frugalidad

spark /spɑrk/ *n* chispa, *f;* (gallant) pisaverde, *m.* —*vi* chispear, echar chispas

sparking /'spɑrkɪŋ/ *a* chispeante. —*n* emisión de chispas, *f.* **s.-plug,** bujía de encendido, *f*

sparkle /'spɑrkəl/ *vi* centellear, rutilar, destellar; *Fig.* brillar; (of wines) ser espumoso. —*n* centelleo, destello, *m; Fig.* brillo, *m*

sparkling /'spɑrklɪŋ/ *a* rutilante, centelleante, reluciente; *Fig.* brillante, chispeante; (of wines) espumante

sparring match /'spɑrɪŋ/ *n* combate de boxeo amistoso, *m*

sparrow /'spærou/ *n* gorrión, *m.* **s.-hawk,** gavilán, esparaván, *m*

sparse /spɑrs/ *a* claro, ralo; esparcido

sparsely /'sparsli/ *adv* escasamente

Sparta /'spɑrtə/ Esparta, *f*

Spartan /'spɑrtn/ *a* and *n* espartano (-na)

spasm /'spæzəm/ *n* espasmo, *m;* ataque, *m;* acceso, *m*

spasmodic /spæz'mɒdɪk/ *a* espasmódico; intermitente

spasmodically /spæz'mɒdɪkli/ *adv* espasmódicamente

spat /spæt/ *n* (gaiter) polaina de tela, *f*

spate /speit/ *n* crecida, *f; Fig.* torrente, *m.* **in s.,** crecido

spatter /'spætər/ *vt* salpicar; (*Fig.* smirch) manchar. —*vi* rociar. —*n* salpicadura, *f;* rociada, *f*

spatula /'spætʃələ/ *n* espátula, *f*

spawn /spɒn/ *vt* and *vi* desovar; engendrar. —*n* huevas, *f pl,* freza, *f;* (offspring) producto, *m*

spawning /'spɒnɪŋ/ *n* desove, *m*

speak /spik/ *vi* hablar; pronunciar un discurso; (sound) sonar. —*vt* decir; (French, etc.) hablar. **She never spoke to him again,** Nunca volvió a dirigirle la palabra. **roughly speaking,** aproximadamente, más o menos. **Speaking for myself,** En cuanto a mí, Por mi parte. **without speaking,** sin decir nada, sin hablar. **to s. for,** (a person) hablar por. **to s. for itself,** hablar por sí mismo, ser evidente. **to s. one's mind,** decir lo que se piensa. **to s. of,** hablar de. **to s. out,** hablar claro; hablar alto. **to s. up for,** (a person) hablar en favor de (alguien)

speaker /'spikər/ *n* el, *m,* (*f,* la) que habla; (public) orador (-ra). **the S.,** el Presidente de la Cámara de los Comunes

speaking /'spikɪŋ/ *a* hablante; para hablar; elocuente, expresivo. —*n* habla, *f,* discurso, *m.* **They are not on s. terms,** No se hablan. **within s. distance,** al habla. **s.-trumpet,** portavoz, *m.* **s.-tube,** tubo acústico, *m*

spear /spɪər/ *n* lanza, *f;* (javelin) venablo, *m;* (harpoon) arpón, *m.* —*vt* herir con lanza, alancear; (fish) arponear. **s.-head,** punta de la lanza, *f.* **s.-thrust,** lanzada, *f*

special /'speʃəl/ *a* especial; particular; extraordinario. —*n* (train) tren extraordinario, *m.* **s. correspondent,**

corresponsal extraordinario, *m.* **s. friend,** amigo (-ga) del alma, amigo íntimo

specialist /'speʃəlɪst/ *n* especialista, *mf*

specialization /ˌspeʃələ'zeiʃən/ *n* especialización, *f*

specialize /'speʃə,laiz/ *vt* especializar. —*vi* especializarse

specially /'speʃəli/ *adv* especialmente; particularmente; sobre todo

specialty /ˌspeʃɪ'æliti/ *n* particularidad, *f;* especialidad, *f*

species /'spiʃiz, -siz/ *n* especie, *f;* raza, *f*

specific /spɪ'sɪfɪk/ *a* específico; explícito. —*n* específico, *m.* **s. gravity,** peso específico, *m,* densidad, *f*

specifically /spɪ'sɪfɪkli/ *adv* específicamente; explícitamente

specification /ˌspesəfɪ'keiʃən/ *n* especificación, *f*

specify /'spesə,fai/ *vt* especificar

specimen /'spesəmən/ *n* espécimen, *m;* ejemplo, *m; Inf.* tipo, *m*

specious /'spiʃəs/ *a* especioso

speciousness /'spiʃəsnɪs/ *n* plausibilidad, *f;* apariencia engañosa, *f*

speck /spek/ *n* pequeña mancha, *f;* punto, *m;* átomo, *m;* (on fruit) maca, *f*

speckle /'spekəl/ *vt* motear, manchar

speckled /'spekəld/ *a* abigarrado; con manchas

spectacle /'spektəkəl/ *n* espectáculo, *m;* escena, *f; pl* **spectacles,** gafas, *f pl,* anteojos, *m pl.* **s.-case,** cajita para las gafas, *f*

spectacled /'spektəkəld/ *a* con gafas, que lleva gafas

spectacular /spek'tækyələr/ *a* espectacular

spectator /'spekteitər/ *n* espectador (-ra)

specter /'spektər/ *n* espectro, fantasma, *m*

spectral /'spektrəl/ *a* espectral

spectroscope /'spektrə,skoup/ *n* espectroscopio, *m*

spectrum /'spektrəm/ *n Phys.* espectro, *m*

speculate /'spekyə,leit/ *vi* especular (sobre, acerca de); *Com.* especular (en)

speculation /ˌspekyə'leiʃən/ *n* especulación, *f*

speculative /'spekyə,lətɪv/ *a* especulativo

speculator /'spekyə,leitər/ *n* especulador (-ra)

speech /spitʃ/ *n* habla, *f;* palabra, *f;* (idiom) lenguaje, *m;* (language) idioma, *m; Gram.* oración, *f;* (address) discurso, *m;* disertación, *f.* **part of s.,** parte de la oración, *f.* **to make a s.,** pronunciar un discurso. **s. maker,** orador (-ra)

speechless /'spitʃlɪs/ *a* mudo; sin habla; descertado, turbado

speed /spid/ *n* prisa, rapidez, *f;* velocidad, *f.* —*vt* dar la bienvenida (a); conceder éxito (a); (accelerate) acelerar. —*vi* darse prisa; correr a toda prisa; (of arrows) volar. **at full s.,** a toda prisa; a toda velocidad; a todo correr. **maximum s.,** velocidad máxima, *f.* **with all s.,** a toda prisa. **s. of impact,** velocidad del choque, *f.* **s.-boat,** lancha de carrera, *f.* **s.-limit,** velocidad máxima, *f,* límite de velocidad, *m*

speedily /'spidli/ *adv* aprisa, rápidamente; prontamente

speediness /'spidɪnɪs/ *n* rapidez, prisa, celeridad, *f;* prontitud, *f*

speeding /'spidɪŋ/ *n* exceso de velocidad, *m.* **s. up,** aceleración, *f*

speedometer /spi'dɒmətər/ *n* cuentakilómetros, *m*

speedway /'spid,wei/ *n* autódromo, *m,* pista de ceniza, *f*

speedy /'spidi/ *a* rápido; pronto

spell /spel/ *n* ensalmo, hechizo, *m;* encanto, *m;* (bout) turno, *m;* (interval) rato, *m;* temporada, *f.* —*vt* (a word) deletrear; (a word in writing) escribir; (mean) significar; (be) ser. **a s. of good weather,** una temporada de buen tiempo. **by spells,** a ratos. **to learn to s.,** aprender la ortografía. **s.-bound,** encantado, fascinado; asombrado

spelling /'spelɪŋ/ *n* deletreo, *m;* ortografía, *f.* **s.-book,** silabario, *m;* **s. mistake,** falta de ortografía, *f*

spelling bee *n* certamen de deletreo, *m*

spend /spend/ *vt* gastar; (time, etc.) pasar; perder; consumir, agotar. —*vi* gastar, hacer gastos. **to s. oneself,** agotarse

spendthrift /'spɛnd‚θrɪft/ n derrochador (-ra), manirroto (-ta). —a despilfarrado, pródigo
spent /spɛnt/ a agotado, rendido. **The night is far s.,** La noche está avanzada. **s. bullet,** bala fría, f
sperm /spɜrm/ n Biol. esperma, f; (whale) cachalote, m
spermaceti /‚spɜrmə'sɛti/ n esperma de ballena, f
sphere /sfɪər/ n esfera, f. **s. of influence,** zona de influencia, f
spherical /'sfɛrɪkəl, 'sfɪər-/ a esférico
sphinx /sfɪŋks/ n esfinge, f. **s.-like,** de esfinge
spice /spais/ n especia, f; Fig. sabor, m; (trace) dejo, m. —vt especiar. **s. cupboard,** especiero, m
spick and span /'spɪk ən 'spæn/ a limpio como una patena; (brand-new) flamante; (of persons) muy compuesto
spicy /'spaisi/ a especiado; aromático; Fig. picante
spider /'spaidər/ n araña, f. **spider's web,** telaraña, f
spidery /'spaidəri/ a de araña; lleno de arañas. **s. writing,** letra de patas de araña, f
spigot /'spɪɡət/ n espiche, m
spike /spaik/ n punta (de hierro, etc.), f; escarpia, f; (for boots) clavo, m; Bot. espiga, f. —vt clavetear; (a cannon) clavar
spill /spɪl/ vt derramar. —n (fall) caída, f
spilling /'spɪlɪŋ/ n derramamiento, derrame, m
spin /spɪn/ vt hilar; (a cocoon) tejer; (a top) bailar; (a ball) tornear; (a coin) lanzar. —vi hilar; girar, bailar. —n vuelta, f; paseo, m. **to send spinning downstairs,** hacer rodar por la escalera (a). **to s. a yarn,** contar un cuento. **to s. out,** prolongar
spinach /'spɪnɪtʃ/ n espinaca, f
spinal /'spainl/ a espinal. **s. anaesthesia,** raquianestesia, f. **s. column,** columna vertebral, f
spindle /'spɪndl/ n huso, m; Mech. eje, m. **s.-shaped,** ahusado
spine /spain/ n Anat. espinazo, m, columna vertebral, f; Bot. espina, f; (of a porcupine, etc.) púa, f
spineless /'spainlɪs/ a Zool. invertebrado; Fig. débil
spinet /'spɪnɪt/ n espineta, f
spinner /'spɪnər/ n hilandero (-ra); máquina de hilar, f
spinney /'spɪni/ n arboleda, f; bosquecillo, m
spinning /'spɪnɪŋ/ n hilado, m; hilandería, f. **s.-machine,** máquina de hilar, f. **s.-top,** trompo, m, peonza, f. **s.-wheel,** rueca, f
spinster /'spɪnstər/ n soltera, f. **confirmed s.,** solterona, f
spiny /'spaini/ a con púas; espinoso
spiral /'spairəl/ a espiral; en espiral. —n espiral, f
spirally /'spairəli/ adv en espiral
spire /spaiər/ n (of a church) aguja, f; espira, f
spirit /'spɪrɪt/ n espíritu, m; alma, f; (ghost) aparecido, fantasma, m; (outstanding person) ingenio, m, inteligencia, f; (disposition) ánimo, m; (courage) valor, espíritu, m; (for a lamp, etc.) alcohol, m. **the Holy S.,** El Espíritu Santo. **to be in high spirits,** no caber de contento, saltar de alegría. **to be in low spirits,** estar desalentado, estar deprimido. **to be full of spirits,** ser bullicioso, tener mucha energía. **to keep up one's spirits,** sostener el valor. **to s. away,** quitar secretamente, hacer desaparecer; (kidnap) secuestrar. **s.-level,** nivel de burbuja, m. **s.-stove,** cocinilla, f
spirited /'spɪrɪtɪd/ a animado, vigoroso; fogoso, animoso, brioso
spiritless /'spɪrɪtlɪs/ a sin espíritu, apático; flojo, débil; (depressed) abatido, desalentado; (cowardly) sin valor, cobarde
spiritual /'spɪrɪtʃuəl/ a espiritual
spiritualism /'spɪrɪtʃuə‚lɪzəm/ n espiritismo, m; Philos. espiritualismo, m
spiritualist /'spɪrɪtʃuəlɪst/ n espiritista, mf; Philos. espiritualista, mf
spiritualistic /‚spɪrɪtʃuə'lɪstɪk/ a espiritista; Philos. espiritualista. **s. séance,** sesión espiritista, f
spirituality /‚spɪrɪtʃu'ælɪti/ ' n espiritualidad, f
spiritually /'spɪrɪtʃuəli/ adv espiritualmente
spirituous /'spɪrɪtʃuəs/ a espirituoso
spirt /spɜrt/ vi, vt, n. See **spurt**
spit /spɪt/ n (for roasting) espetón, asador, m; (sand-

bank) banco de arena, m; (of land) lengua de tierra, f; (spittle) saliva, f. **the spit of, the spit and image of, the spitting image of,** la imagen viva de, la segunda edición de, m. —vt (skewer) espetar; (saliva, etc.) escupir; (curses, etc.) vomitar. —vi escupir, expectorar; (of a cat) fufear, decir fu; (sputter) chisporrotear; (rain) lloviznar
spite /spait/ n malevolencia, mala voluntad, hostilidad, f; rencor, m, ojeriza, f. —vt contrariar, hacer daño (a). **He has a s. against them,** Les tiene rencor. **in s. of,** a pesar de; a despecho de
spiteful /'spaitfəl/ a rencoroso, malévolo
spitefully /'spaitfəli/ adv malévolo; con rencor; por maldad; por despecho
spitefulness /'spaitfəlnɪs/ n malevolencia, f; rencor, m
spitfire /'spɪt‚faiᵊr/ n cascarrabias, mf, furia, f
spittle /'spɪtl/ n saliva, f
splash /splæʃ/ vt salpicar (de); manchar (con). —vi derramarse, esparcirse; chapotear, chapalear. —n chapoteo, m; (of rain, etc.) chapaleteo, m; (stain or patch) mancha, f. **John was splashing about in the sea,** Juan chapoteaba en el mar. **to make a s.,** Fig. causar una sensación. **s.-board,** alero, m
spleen /splin/ n Anat. bazo, m; esplín, m
splendid /'splɛndɪd/ a espléndido; magnífico; glorioso; excelente
splendidly /'splɛndɪdli/ adv espléndidamente; magníficamente; excelentemente
splendor /'splɛndər/ n resplandor, m; magnificencia, f; (of exploits, etc.) esplendor, brillo, m
splice /splais/ vt (ropes, timbers) empalmar; (marry) unir, casar. —n empalme, m
splint /splɪnt/ n Surg. férula, f. **to put in a s.,** entablar
splinter /'splɪntər/ vt astillar, hacer astillas. —vi hacerse astillas
splintery /'splɪntəri/ a astilloso
split /splɪt/ vi henderse; resquebrajarse; (of seams) nacerse; abrirse; dividirse. —vt hender; partir; dividir; abrir; (the atom) escindir. —n hendedura, f; grieta, f; división, f; (in fabric) rasgón, m; (quarrel) ruptura, f. **to s. hairs,** andar en quisquillas, pararse en pelillos, utilizar. **I have a splitting headache,** Tengo un dolor de cabeza que me trae loco. **to s. one's sides,** reírse a carcajadas, desternillarse de risa. **to s. on a rock,** estrellarse contra una roca. **to s. the difference,** partir la diferencia. **The blow s. his head open,** El golpe le abrió la cabeza. **to s. on,** Inf. delatar, denunciar
splotch /splatʃ/ n mancha, f, borrón, m
splutter /'splʌtər/ vi chisporrotear; (of a person) balbucir. —n chisporroteo, m. **to s. out,** decir tartamudeando
spoil /spɔil/ n botín, despojo, m; (of war) trofeo, m. —vt estropear; echar a perder; (diminish) mitigar; (a child) mimar; (injure) dañar; (destroy) arruinar, destruir. —vi estropearse; echarse a perder. **to be spoiling for a fight,** tener ganas de pelearse. **You have spoilt my fun,** Me has aguado la fiesta. **s.-sport,** aguafiestas, mf
spoiled /spɔild/ a (of a child, etc.) mimado, consentido, malacostumbrado
spoke /spouk/ n (of a wheel) rayo, m; (of a ladder) travesaño, peldaño, m; Naut. cabilla (de la rueda del timón), f
spoken /'spoukən/ a hablado. **well-s.,** bien hablado; cortés
spokesman /'spouksmən/ n portavoz, m. **to be s.,** llevar la palabra
spoliation /‚spouli'eiʃən/ n expoliación, f; despojo, m
sponge /spʌndʒ/ n esponja, f; (cadger) gorrón (-ona); (cake) bizcocho, m. —vt limpiar con esponja. **to s.,** Inf. vivir de gorra. **s.-holder,** esponjera, f
sponger /'spʌndʒər/ n gorrón (-ona), vividor, m, sablista, mf
sponginess /'spʌndʒinɪs/ n esponjosidad, f
sponging n esponjadura, f; Inf. sablazo, m
spongy /'spʌndʒi/ a esponjoso
sponsor /'spɒnsər/ n garante, mf; valedor (-ra), patron (-na); (godfather) padrino, m; (godmother) madrina, f, (radio and TV) auspiciador, patrocinador, m

spontaneity /ˌspɒntə'niːɪti, -'neɪ-/ n espontaneidad, f

spontaneous /spɒn'teɪniəs/ a espontáneo. **s. combustion,** combustión espontánea, f

spontaneously /spɒn'teɪniəsli/ adv espontáneamente

spook /spuk/ n fantasma, espectro, m

spool /spul/ n (for thread) bobina, f, carrete, m; (in a sewing machine) canilla, f; (of a fishing rod) carrete, m

spoon /spun/ n cuchara, f. —vt sacar con cuchara. —vi (slang) besuquearse. **to s.-feed,** dar de comer con cuchara (a); tratar como un niño (a)

spoonful /'spunful/ n cucharada, f

spoor /spur, spɔr/ n pista, huella de animal, f; rastro, m

sporadic /spə'rædɪk/ a esporádico

spore /spɔr/ n Bot. espora, f; Zool. germen, m

sport /spɔrt/ n deporte, sport, m; deportismo, m; (jest) broma, f; (game) juego, m; (plaything) juguete, m; (pastime) pasatiempo, m. —vi jugar; recrearse, divertirse. —vt llevar; ostentar, lucir. **He is a s.,** Es un buen chico. **to make s. of,** burlarse de. **sports car,** coche de deporte, m. **sports ground,** campo de recreo, m. **sports jacket,** chaqueta de deporte, americana, f. **sports shirt,** camisa corta, f

sporting /'spɔrtɪv/ a deportista; caballeroso. **I think there is a s. chance,** Me parece que hay una posibilidad de éxito

sporting goods n artículos de deporte, efectos de deportes, m pl

sportive /'spɔrtɪv/ a juguetón; bromista

sportsman /'spɔrtsmən/ n deportista, m; aficionado al sport, m; Fig. caballero, señor, m; buen chico, m

sportsmanlike /'spɔrtsmən,laɪk/ a de deportista; caballeroso

sportsmanship /'spɔrtsmən,ʃɪp/ n deportividad, f

spot /spɒt/ n mancha, f; pinta, f; (on the face, etc.) peca, f; grano, m; (place) sitio, m; lugar, m; (of liquor) trago, m; (of food) bocado, m; (of rain) gota, f. —vt manchar; motear; (recognize) reconocer; (understand) darse cuenta de, comprender. **a tender s.,** Fig. debilidad, f. **on the s.,** en el acto. **s. ball,** (billiards) pinta, f. **s. cash,** dinero contante, m

spotless /'spɒtlɪs/ a saltando de limpio; sin mancha; inmaculado; puro; virgen

spotlight /'spɒt,laɪt/ n luz del proyector, f; proyector, m

spotted /'spɒtɪd/ a (stained) manchado; (of animals, etc.) con manchas; (of garments, etc.) con pintas

spotty /'spɒti/ a lleno de manchas; moteado; (pimply) con granos

spouse /spaus/ n esposo, m; esposa, f

spout /spaut/ vi chorrear; Inf. hablar incesantemente. —vt arrojar; vomitar; Inf. declamar, recitar. —n (of a jug, etc.) pico, m; (for water, etc.) tubo, m, cañería, f; canalón, m; (gust) ráfaga, nube, f. **down s.,** tubo de bajada, m

spouting /'spautɪŋ/ n chorreo, m; Inf. declamación, f

Sprachgefühl /'ʃpraxɡə,fil/ n sentido del idioma, m

sprain /spreɪn/ vt dislocar, torcer. —n dislocación, f, esguince, m. **Victoria has sprained her foot,** Victoria se ha torcido el pie

sprat /spræt/ n sardineta, f

sprawl /sprɔl/ vi recostarse (en); extenderse; (of plants) trepar. **He went sprawling,** Cayó cuan largo era

spray /spreɪ/ n (branch) ramo, m; (of water, etc.) rocío, m; (of the sea) espuma, f; (mechanical device) pulverizador, m. —vt pulverizar; rociar; regar; (the throat) jeringar

spread /spred/ vt tender; cubrir (de); poner; (stretch out) extender; (open out) desplegar; (of disease, etc.) propagar; diseminar; divulgar, difundir. —vi extenderse; propagarse; difundirse; divulgarse; (become general) generalizarse. —n extensión, f; expansión, f; propagación, f; divulgación, f; (Aer. and of birds) envergadura, f. **Carmen s. her hands to the fire,** Carmen extendió las manos al fuego. **The peacock s. its tail,** El pavo real hizo la rueda. **The dove s. its wings,** La paloma desplegó sus alas. **to s. out,** vt extender; desplegar; (scatter) esparcir, vi extenderse. **spread like wildfire,** correr como pólvora

en reguero, propagarse como un reguero de pólvora, ser un reguero de pólvora

spreading /'spredɪŋ/ n (of a disease) propagación, f; (of knowledge, etc.) divulgación, f; expansión, f; extensión, f

spreadsheet /'spred,ʃit/ n hoja de cálculo, f

spree /spri/ n juerga, parranda, f; excursión, f. **to go on the s.,** ir de juerga, ir de picos pardos

sprig /sprɪɡ/ n ramita, f; (of heather, etc.) espiga, f; (scion) vástago, m

sprightliness /'spraitlɪnɪs/ n vivacidad, f, despejo, m; energía, f

sprightly /'spraitli/ a vivaracho, despierto; enérgico

spring /sprɪŋ/ vi saltar, brincar; (become) hacerse; (seek) buscar; (of plants, water) brotar; (of tears) arrasar, llenar; (from) originarse (en), ser causado (por); inspirarse (en). —vt (a mine) volar; (a trap) soltar. **to s. a surprise,** dar una sorpresa. **to s. a surprise on a person,** coger a la imprevista (a). **to s. at a person,** precipitarse sobre. **to s. to one's feet,** ponerse de pie de un salto. **to s. back,** saltar hacia atrás; recular; volver a su sitio. **to s. open,** abrirse súbitamente. **to s. up,** (of plants) brotar, crecer; (of difficulties, etc.) surgir, asomarse

spring /sprɪŋ/ n (jump) salto, brinco, m; (of water) fuente, f; manantial, m; (season) primavera, f; (of a watch, etc.) resorte, m; (of a mattress, etc.) muelle, m. —a primaveral. —vt saltar, brincar. **at one s.,** en un salto. **to give a s.,** dar un salto. **s.-board,** trampolín, m. **s.-mattress,** colchón de muelles, m. **s.-tide,** marea viva, f

springiness /'sprɪŋɪnɪs/ n elasticidad, f

springlike /'sprɪŋ,laɪk/ a primaveral

springtime /'sprɪŋ,taɪm/ n primavera, f

sprinkle /'sprɪŋkəl/ vt esparcir; salpicar; rociar

sprinkling /'sprɪŋklɪŋ/ n salpicadura, f; rociadura, f; pequeño número, m. **a s. of snow,** una nevada ligera

sprint /sprɪnt/ vi sprintar. —n sprint, m

sprite /sprait/ n trasgo, m; hada, f

sprout /spraut/ vi brotar, despuntar, retoñar, tallecer; germinar. —vt salir. —n brote, retoño, pimpollo, m; germen, m. **Brussels sprouts,** coles de Bruselas, f pl

spruce /sprus/ a peripuesto, muy aseado, pulido; elegante, n Bot. pícea, f. **to s. oneself up,** arreglarse, ponerse elegante

spruceness /'sprusnɪs/ n aseo, buen parecer, m, elegancia, f

spry /sprai/ a activo, ágil

spur /spɜr/ n espuela, f; aguijada, f; (of a bird) espolón, m; Bot. espuela, f; (of a mountain range) espolón, estribo, m; Fig. estímulo, m. —vt espolear, picar con la espuela; calzarse las espuelas; Fig. estimular, incitar. **on the s. of the moment,** bajo el impulso del momento

spurious /'spyʊriəs/ a espurio; falso

spurn /spɜrn/ vt rechazar; tratar con desprecio; menospreciar

spurt /spɜrt/ vi (gush) chorrear, borbotar; brotar, surgir; (in racing, etc.) hacer un esfuerzo supremo. —vt hacer chorrear; lanzar. —n (jet) chorro, m; esfuerzo supremo, m

sputter /'spʌtər/ vi chisporrotear; crepitar; (of a pen) escupir; (of a person) balbucir

sputtering /'spʌtərɪŋ/ n chisporroteo, m; crepitación, f; (of a person) balbuceo, m

sputum /'spyutəm/ n esputo, m

spy /spai/ vt observar, discernir. —vi espiar, ser espía. —n espía, mf. **to spy out the land,** explorar el terreno. **to spy upon,** espiar; seguir los pasos (a). **spy-glass,** catalejo, m

spying /'spaiɪŋ/ n espionaje, m

squabble /'skwɒbəl/ n disputa, f; riña, f. —vi pelearse; disputar

squabbling /'skwɒblɪŋ/ n riñas, querellas, f pl; disputas, f pl

squad /skwɒd/ n escuadra, f; pelotón, m

squadron /'skwɒdrən/ n Mil. escuadrón, m; Nav. escuadra, f; Aer. escuadrilla, f; (of persons) pelotón, m. **s.-leader,** comandante, m

squalid /'skwɒlɪd/ a escuálido; (of quarrels, etc.) sórdido, mezquino

squall /skwɔl/ vi berrear; chillar. —n berrido, m;

chillido, *m;* (storm) chubasco, turbión, *m;* (storm) chubasco, turbión, *m; Fig.* tormenta, tempestad, *f*

squalor /'skwɒlər/ *n* escualidez, *f;* sordidez, mezquindad, *f*

squander /'skwɒndər/ *vt* derrochar, tirar, desperdiciar; (time, etc.) malgastar

squanderer /'skwɒndərər/ *n* derrochador (-ra)

squandering /'skwɒndərɪŋ/ *n* derroche, desperdicio, dispendio, *m;* (of time, etc.) pérdida, *f,* desperdicio, *m*

square /skwɛər/ *n Math.* cuadrado, *m;* rectángulo, *m;* (of a chessboard) escaque, *m;* (of a draughtboard and of graph paper) casilla, *f;* (in a town) plaza, *f;* (of troops) cuadro, *m, a* cuadrado; justo; igual; (honest) honrado, formal; (unambiguous) redondo, categórico; *Math.* cuadrado. **She wore a silk s. on her head,** Llevaba un pañuelo de seda en la cabeza. **five s. feet,** cinco pies cuadrados. **nine feet s.,** nueve pies en cuadro. **on the s.,** honradamente. **a s. dance,** contradanza, *f.* **a s. meal,** una buena comida. **s. dealing,** trato limpio, *m.* **The account is s.,** La cuenta está justa. **to get s. with,** desquitarse (de), vengarse de. **s. measure,** medida de superficie, *f.* **s. root,** raíz cuadrada, *f.* **s.-shouldered,** de hombros cuadrados

square /skwɛər/ *vt* cuadrar; escuadrar; (arrange) arreglar; (bribe) sobornar; (reconcile) acomodar; *Math.* cuadrar. —*vi* conformarse (con), cuadrar (con). **to s. the circle,** cuadrar el círculo. **to s. one's shoulders,** enderezarse. **to s. accounts with,** saldar cuentas con. **to s. up to,** (a person) avanzar belicosamente hacia

squarely /'skwɛərli/ *adv* en cuadro; directamente; sin ambigüedades, rotundamente; (honestly) de buena fe, honradamente

squareness /'skwɛərnɪs/ *n* cuadratura, *f;* (honesty) honradez, buena fe, *f*

squash /skwɒʃ/ *vt* aplastar. —*vi* aplastarse; apretarse. —*n* aplastamiento, *m;* (of fruit, etc.) pulpa, *f;* (of people) agolpamiento, *m;* muchedumbre, *f;* (drink) refresco (de limón, etc.), *m,* (sport) frontón con raqueta, *m*

squashy /'skwɒʃi/ *a* blando y húmedo

squat /skwɒt/ *vi* acuclillarse, agacharse, agazaparse ponerse en cuclillas; estar en cuclillas; (on land, etc.) apropiarse sin derecho. —*a* rechoncho

squatter /'skwɒtər/ *n* intruso (-sa); colono usurpador, *m*

squatter town *n.* See **shanty town**

squawk /skwɔk/ *vi* graznar; lanzar gritos agudos. —*n* graznido, *m;* grito agudo, *m*

squeak /skwik/ *vi* (of carts, etc.) chirriar, rechinar; (of shoes) crujir; (of persons, mice, etc.) chillar; (slang) cantar. —*n* chirrido, crujido, *m;* chillido, *m.* **to have a narrow s.,** escapar por un pelo

squeaking /'skwikɪŋ/ *n* chirrido, rechinamiento, *m;* crujido, *m;* (of humans, mice, etc.) chillidos, *m pl*

squeal /skwil/ *vi* lanzar gritos agudos, chillar; (complain) quejarse; (slang) cantar. —*n* grito agudo, chillido, *m*

squealing /'skwilɪŋ/ *n* gritos agudos, chillidos, *m pl*

squeamish /'skwimɪʃ/ *a* que se marea fácilmente; mareado; (nauseated) asqueado; delicado; remilgado

squeamishness /'skwimɪʃnɪs/ *n* tendencia a marearse, *f;* delicadeza, *f;* remilgos, *m pl*

squeeze /skwiz/ *vt* apretar; estrujar; (fruit) exprimir; (extort) arrancar; (money from) sangrar. —*n* (of the hand, etc.) apretón, *m;* estrujón, *m;* (of fruit juice) algunas gotas (de). **It was a tight s. in the car,** Íbamos muy apretados en el coche. **He was in a tight s.,** Se encontraba en un aprieto. **to s. one's way through the crowd,** abrirse camino a codazos por la muchedumbre. **to s. in,** *vt* hacer sitio para. —*vi* introducirse con dificultad (en)

squelch /skwɛltʃ/ *vi* gorgotear, chapotear. —*vt* aplastar

squib /skwɪb/ *n* (firework) rapapiés, buscapiés, *m;* (lampoon) pasquinada, *f*

squid /skwɪd/ *n* calamar, *m*

squint /skwɪnt/ *n* estrabismo, *m;* mirada furtiva, *f; Inf.* vistazo, *m,* mirada, *f.* —*vi* ser bizco; bizcar. **to s. at,** mirar de soslayo. **s.-eyed,** bizco. **to be s.-eyed,** mirar contra el gobierno

squire /skwaɪər/ *n* escudero, *m;* hacendado, *m.* —*vt* escoltar, acompañar

squirm /skwɜrm/ *vi* retorcerse; (with embarrassment) no saber dónde meterse. —*n* retorcimiento, *m.* **to s. along the ground,** arrastrarse por el suelo

squirrel /'skwɜrəl/ *n* ardilla, *f*

squirt /skwɜrt/ *vt* (liquids) lanzar. —*vi* chorrear, salir a chorros. —*n* chorro, *m;* (syringe) jeringa, *f*

stab /stæb/ *vt* apuñalar, dar de puñaladas (a); herir. —*n* puñalada, *f;* herida, *f;* (of pain, and *Fig.*) pinchzo, *m.* **a s. in the back,** una puñalada por la espalda

stability /stə'bɪlɪti/ *n* estabilidad, *f;* solidez, firmeza, *f*

stabilize /'steɪbə,laɪz/ *vt* estabilizar

stable /'steɪbəl/ *a* estable; fijo, firme. —*n* cuadra, caballeriza, *f;* (for cows, etc.) establo, *m.* —*vt* poner en la cuadra; alojar. **s.-boy,** mozo de cuadra, *m*

stack /stæk/ *n* (of hay) niara, *f,* almiar, *m;* (heap) montón, *m;* (of rifles) pabellón, *m;* (of a chimney) cañón, *m.* —*vt Agr.* hacinar; amontonar; *Mil.* poner (las armas) en pabellón

stacked /stækt/ *a* (woman) abultada de pechera

stadium /'steɪdiəm/ *n* estadio, *m*

staff /stæf/ *n* vara, *f;* (bishop's, and *Fig.*) báculo, *m;* (pilgrim's) bordón, *m;* (pole) palo, *m;* (flagstaff) asta, *f;* (of an office, etc.) personal, *m;* (editorial) redacción, *f;* (corps) cuerpo, *m; Mil.* plana mayor, *f,* estado mayor, *m; Mus.* pentagrama, *m.* —*vt* proveer de personal. **general s.,** estado mayor general, *m.* **s. officer,** *Mil.* oficial de estado mayor, *m*

stag /stæg/ *n* ciervo, *m.* **s.-beetle,** ciervo volante, *m.* **s.-hunting,** caza del ciervo, *f*

stage /steɪdʒ/ *n* (for workmen) andamio, *m;* (of a microscope) portaobjetos, *m; Theat.* escena, *f,* tablas, *f pl;* teatro, *m;* (of development, etc.) etapa, *f;* fase, *f.* —*vt Theat.* escenificar, poner en escena; *Theat.* representar; (a demonstration, etc.) arreglar. **by easy stages,** poco a poco; (of a journey) a pequeñas etapas. **to come on the s.,** salir a la escena. **to go on the s.,** hacerse actor (actriz), dedicarse al teatro. **s. carpenter,** tramoyista, *m.* **s.-coach,** diligencia, *f.* **s.-craft,** arte de escribir para el teatro, *f;* arte escénica, *f.* **s.-direction,** acotación, *f.* **s.-door,** entrada de los artistas, *f.* **s.-effect,** efecto escénico, *m.* **s.-fright,** miedo al público, *m.* **s.-hand,** tramoyista, sacasillas, metesillas y sacamuertos, *m.* **s. manager,** director de escena, *m.* **s.-whisper,** aparte, *m*

stagger /'stægər/ *vi* tambalear; andar haciendo eses; (hesitate) titubear, vacilar. —*vt* desconcertar. —*n* titubeo, tambaleo, *m; Aer.* decalaje, *m.* **staggered working hours,** horas de trabajo escalonadas, *f pl*

staggering /'stægərɪŋ/ *a* tambaleante; (surprising) asombroso, sorprendente; (dreadful) espantoso. **a s. blow,** un golpe que derriba

staging /'steɪdʒɪŋ/ *n* (scaffolding) andamio, *m; Theat.* producción, *f;* representación, *f;* decorado, *m*

stagnancy /'stægnənsi/ *n* (of water) estancación, *f;* (inactivity) estagnación, *f;* paralización, *f*

stagnant /'stægnənt/ *a* estancado; paralizado. **to be s.,** estar estancado. **s. water,** agua estancada, *f*

stagnate /'stægneɪt/ *vi* estancarse; estar estancado; (of persons) vegetar

stagnation /stæg'neɪʃən/ *n* (of water) estancación, *f;* estagnación, *f;* parálisis, *f*

staid /steɪd/ *a* serio, formal, juicioso

staidness /'steɪdnɪs/ *n* seriedad, formalidad, *f*

stain /steɪn/ *vt* manchar; (dye) teñir. —*n* mancha, *f;* colorante, *m.* **without a s.,** *Fig.* sin mancha. **stained glass,** vidrio de color, *m.* **s.-remover,** quitamanchas, *m*

stainless /'steɪnlɪs/ *a* sin mancha; inmaculado, puro

stair /stɛər/ *n* escalón, peldaño, *m;* escalera, *f; pl* **stairs,** escalera, *f.* **a flight of stairs,** una escalera, un tramo de escaleras. **below stairs,** escalera abajo. **s.-carpet,** alfombra de escalera, *f.* **s.-rod,** varilla para alfombra de escalera, *f*

staircase /'stɛər,keɪs/ *n* escalera, *f.* **spiral s.,** escalera de caracol, *f*

stake /steɪk/ *n* estaca, *f;* (for plants) rodrigón, *m;* (gaming) envite, *m,* apuesta, *f;* (in an undertaking) interés, *m; pl* **stakes,** (prize) premio, *m;* (race) carrera, *f.* —*vt* estacar; (plants) rodrigar; (bet) jugar. **at s.,**

en juego; en peligro. **to be burnt at the s.,** morir en la hoguera. **to s. one's all,** jugarse el todo por el todo. **to s. a claim,** hacer una reclamación. **to s. out,** jalonar

stalactite /stə'læktait/ n estalactita, f

stalagmite /stə'lægmait/ n estalagmita, f

stale /steil/ a no fresco; (of bread, etc.) duro, seco; (of air) viciado; viejo; pasado de moda; (tired) cansado

stalemate /'steil,meit/ n (chess, checkers) tablas, f pl; Fig. punto muerto, m. **to reach a s.,** llegar a un punto muerto

staleness /'steilnis/ n rancidez, f; (of bread, etc.) dureza, f; (of news, etc.) falta de novedad, f

stalk /stɔk/ n Bot. tallo, m; Bot. pedúnculo, m; (of a glass) pie, m. —vi andar majestuosamente; Fig. rondar. —vt (game) cazar al acecho; (a person) seguir los pasos (a)

stalking horse /'stɔkiŋ/ n boezuelo, m; Fig. pretexto, disfraz, m

stall /stɔl/ n (in a stable) puesto (individual), m; (stable) establo, m; (choir) silla de coro, f; (in a fair, etc.) barraca, f, puesto, m; Theat. butaca, f; (fingerstall) dedal, m. —vt (an engine) cortar accidentalmente. —vi Auto. pararse de pronto; Aer. perder velocidad; (of a cart, etc.) atascarse. **pit s.,** Theat. butaca de platea, f

stalling /'stɔliŋ/ n Auto. parada accidental, f; Aer. pérdida de velocidad, f. **Stop s.!** ¡Déje de rodeos!

stallion /'stælyən/ n semental, m

stalwart /'stɔlwərt/ a robusto, fornido; leal; valiente

stalwartness /'stɔlwərtnis/ n robustez, f; lealtad, f; valor, m

stamen /'steimən/ n Bot. estambre, m

stamina /'stæmənə/ n resistencia, f

stammer /'stæmər/ vi tartamudear; (hesitate in speaking) titubear, balbucir. —n tartamudez, f; titubeo, balbuceo, m

stammerer /'stæmərər/ n tartamudo (-da)

stammering /'stæməriŋ/ a tartamudo; balbuciente. —n tartamudeo, m; balbuceo, m

stamp /stæmp/ vt estampar; imprimir; (documents) timbrar; pegar el sello de correo (a); (characterize) sellar; (Fig. engrave) grabar; (coins) acuñar; (press) apisonar; (with the foot) golpear con los pies, patear; (in dancing) zapatear. —n (with the foot) patada, f, golpe con los pies, m; (mark, etc.) marca, f; (rubber, etc.) estampilla, f; matasellos, m; cuño, m; (for documents) póliza, f; timbre, m; (for letters) sello, m; (machine) punzón, m; mano de mortero, f; (Fig. sign) sello, m; (kind) temple, m, clase, f. **The events of that day are stamped on my memory,** Los acontecimientos de aquel día están grabados en mi memoria. **to s. out,** (a fire, etc.) extinguir, apagar; (resistance, etc.) vencer; destruir. **postage-s.,** sello de correos, m. **s.-album,** álbum de sellos, m. **s.-duty,** impuesto del timbre, m. **s.-machine,** expendedor automático de sellos de correo, m

stampede /stæm'pid/ n fuga precipitada, f; pánico, m. —vi huir precipitadamente; (of animals) salir de estampía; huir en desorden. —vt hacer perder la cabeza (a), sembrar el pánico entre

stamping /'stæmpiŋ/ n selladura, f; (of documents) timbrado, m; (of fabrics, etc.) estampado, m; (with the feet) pataleo, m; (in dancing) zapateo, m

stance /stæns/ n posición de los pies, f; postura, f

stanch /stɔntʃ/ vt restañar

stand /stænd/ vi estar de pie; ponerse de pie, incorporarse; estar; hallarse; sostenerse; ser; ponerse; (halt) parar; (remain) permanecer, quedar. —vt poner; (endure) resistir; tolerar; sufrir; (entertain) convidar. **S.!** ¡Alto! **as things s.,** tal como están las cosas. **I cannot s. any more,** No puedo más. **I cannot s. him,** No le puedo ver. **Nothing stands between them and ruin,** No hay nada entre ellos y la ruina. **I stand a drink,** Le convidé a un trago. **How do we s.?** ¿Cómo estamos? **It stands to reason that...,** Es lógico que... **Edward stands six feet,** Eduardo tiene seis pies de altura. **to s. accused of,** ser acusado de. **to s. godfather** (or **godmother**) **to,** sacar de pila (a). **to s. in need (of),** necesitar, tener necesidad (de). **to s. on end,** (of hair) ponerse de

punta, despeluzarse, **to s. one in good stead,** ser útil, ser ventajoso. **to s. one's ground,** no ceder, tenerse fuerte. **to s. to attention,** cuadrarse, permanecer en posición de firmes. **to s. well with,** tener buenas relaciones con, ser estimado de. **to s. aside,** tenerse a un lado; apartarse; (in favor of someone) retirarse. **to s. back,** quedarse atrás; recular, retroceder. **to s. by,** estar de pie cerca de; estar al lado de; estar presente (sin intervenir); ser espectador; estar preparado; (one's friends) ayudar, proteger; (a promise, etc.) atenerse (a); ser fiel (a); (of a ship) mantenerse listo. **s.-by,** n recurso, m. **to s. for,** representar; simbolizar; (mean) significar; (Parliament, etc.) presentarse como candidato; (put up with) tolerar, sufrir. **to s. in,** colaborar. **to s. in with,** estar de acuerdo con, ser partidario de; compartir. **to s. off,** mantenerse a distancia. **to s. out,** (in relief, and Fig. of persons) destacarse; (be firm) resistir, mantenerse firme; Naut. gobernar más afuera. **S. out of the way!** ¡Quítate del medio! **to s. over,** (be postponed) quedar aplazado. **to s. up,** estar de pie; ponerse de pie, incorporarse; tenerse derecho. **to s. up against,** resistir; oponerse a. **to s. up for,** defender; volverpor. **to s. up to,** hacer cara a

stand /stænd/ n puesto, m; posición, actitud, f; (for taxis, etc.) punto, m; (in a market, etc.) puesto, m; Sports. tribuna, f; (for a band) quiosco, m; (of a dish, etc.) pie, m; Mech. sostén, m; (opposition) resistencia, oposición, f. **to make a s. against,** oponerse resueltamente (a); ofrecer resistencia (a). **to take one's s.,** fundarse (en), apoyarse (en). **to take up one's s. by the fire,** ponerse cerca del fuego

standard /'stændərd/ n (flag) estandarte, m, bandera, f; (for gold, weights, etc.) marco, m; norma, f; convención, regla, f; (of a lamp) pie, m; (pole) poste, m; columna, f; (level) nivel, m. —a corriente; normal; típico; clásico. **It is a s. type,** Es un tipo corriente. **gold s.,** patrón de oro, m. **s. author,** autor clásico, m. **s. formula,** fórmula clásica, f. **s. of living,** nivel de vida, m. **s.-bearer,** abanderado, m. **s.-lamp,** lámpara vertical, f

standardization /,stændərdə'zeiʃən/ n (of armaments, etc.) unificación de tipos, f; (of dyestuffs, medicinals, etc.) control, m, estandardización, f

standardize /'stændər,daiz/ vt hacer uniforme; controlar

standing /'stændiŋ/ a de pie, derecho; permanente, fijo; constante. —n posición, f; reputación, f; importancia, f; antigüedad, f. **It is a quarrel of long s.,** Es una riña antigua. **s. committee,** comisión permanente, f. **s. room,** sitio para estar de pie, m. **s. water,** agua estancada, f. **standoffish,** frío, etiquetero; altanero. **stand-offishness,** frialdad, f; altanería, f.

standpoint, punto de vista, m

standstill /'stænd,stil/ n parada, f; pausa, f. **at a s.,** parado; (of industry) paralizado

stanza /'stænzə/ n estrofa, estancia, f

staple /'steipəl/ n (fastener) grapa, f; (of wool, etc.) hebra, fibra, f; producto principal (de un país), m; (raw material) materia prima, f; a principal; más importante; corriente

stapler /'steiplər/ (device) cosepapeles, engrapador, m, atrochadora (Argentina), f

star /stɑr/ n (all meanings) estrella, f; (asterisk) asterisco, m. —vt estrellar, sembrar de estrellas; marcar con asterisco. —vi (Theat. cinema) presentarse como estrella, ser estrella. **stars and stripes,** las barras y las estrellas. **to be born under a lucky s.,** tener estrella. **to see stars,** ver estrellas. **s.-gazing,** observación de las estrellas, f; ensimismamiento, m. **s.-spangled,** estrellado, tachonado de estrellas, sembrado de estrellas. **s.-turn,** gran atracción, f

starboard /'stɑrbərd/ n Naut. estribor, m

starch /stɑrtʃ/ n almidón, m, las harinas, f pl, vt almidonar

starchy /'stɑrtʃi/ a almidonado; (of food) feculento; Fig. tieso, entonado; etiquetero

stare /stɛər/ vi mirar fijamente; abrir mucho los ojos. —n mirada fija, f. **stony s.,** mirada dura, f. **to s. at,** (a person) clavar la mirada en; mirar de hito en hito (a). **The explanation stares one in the face,** La explicación salta a la vista (o está evidente). **to s. into**

space, mirar las telarañas. **to s. out of countenance,** avergonzar con la mirada

starfish /'stɑr,fɪʃ/ n estrella de mar, f

staring /'stɛərɪŋ/ a (of colors) chillón, llamativo, encendido. **s. eyes,** ojos saltones, m pl; ojos espantados, m pl

stark /stɑrk/ a rígido; Poet. poderoso; absoluto. **s. staring mad,** loco de atar. **s.-naked,** en cueros vivos, en pelota

starless /'stɑrlɪs/ a sin estrellas

starlight /'stɑr,laɪt/ n luz de las estrellas, f, a estrellado

starry /'stɑri/ a estrellado, sembrado de estrellas

start /stɑrt/ vi estremecerse, asustarse; saltar; (set out) salir; ponerse en camino; (of a train, a race) arrancar; ponerse en marcha; Aer. despegar; (begin) empezar; (of timbers) combarse. —vt empezar; (a car, etc.) poner en marcha; (a race) dar la señal de partida; (a hare, etc.) levantar; (cause) provocar, causar; (a discussion, etc.) abrir; iniciar. —n (fright) susto, m; (setting out) partida, salida, f; (beginning) principio, comienzo, m; (starting-point of a race) arrancadero, m; Aer. despegue, m; (advantage) ventaja, f. **at the s.,** al principio. **for a s.,** para empezar. **from s. to finish,** desde el principio hasta el fin. **She started to cry,** Se puso a llorar. **He has started his journey to Canada,** Ha empezado su viaje al Canadá. **I started up the engine,** Puse el motor en marcha. **to get a s.,** asustarse; tomar la delantera. **to give (a person) a s.,** asustar, dar un susto (a); dar la ventaja (a). **to give (a person) a s. in life,** ayudar a alguien a situarse en la vida. **to make a fresh s. (in life),** hacer vida nueva, empezar la vida de nuevo. **to s. after,** lanzarse en busca de; salir tras. **to s. back,** retroceder; emprender el viaje de regreso; marcharse. **to s. off,** salir, partir; ponerse en camino. **to s. up,** incorporarse bruscamente, ponerse de pie de un salto; (appear) surgir, aparecer. —vt (an engine) poner en marcha

starter /'stɑrtər/ n iniciador (-ra); (for a race) starter, juez de salida, m; (competitor in a race) corredor, m; (of a car, etc.) arranque, m

starting /'stɑrtɪŋ/ n (setting out) salida, partida, f; (beginning) principio, m; (fear) estremecimiento, m; susto, m. **s.-gear,** palanca de arranque, f. **s.-handle,** manivela de arranque, f. **s.-point,** punto de partida, m; Fig. arrancadero, punto de arranque, m. **s.-post,** puesto de salida, m

startle /'stɑrtl/ vt asustar, sobresaltar, alarmar. **The news startled him out of his indifference,** Las noticias le hicieron salir de su indiferencia

startling /'stɑrtlɪŋ/ a alarmante; (of dress, etc.) exagerado; (of colors) chillón

starvation /stɑr'veɪʃən/ n hambre, f; Med. inanición, f. **s. diet,** régimen de hambre, m. **s. wage,** ración de hambre, f

starve /stɑrv/ vi morir de hambre; pasar hambre, no tener bastante que comer; no comer. —vt matar de hambre; privar de alimentos (a). **I am simply starving,** Tengo una hambre canina, Me muero de hambre. **to s. with cold,** vi morir de frío. —vt matar de frío

starved /stɑrvd/ a muerto de hambre, hambriento. **s. of affection,** hambriento de cariño

starving /'stɑrvɪŋ/ a que muere de hambre, hambriento

state /steɪt/ n estado, m; condición, f; (anxiety) agitación, ansiedad, f; (social) rango, m; (pomp) magnificencia, pompa, f; (government, etc.) Estado, m; nación, f. —a de Estado; de gala, de ceremonia. **the married s.,** el estado matrimonial. **s. of war,** estado de guerra. **in s.,** con gran pompa. **to lie in s.,** (of a body) estar expuesto. **s. apartments,** habitaciones de gala, f pl. **s. banquet,** comida de gala, f. **s. coach,** coche de gala, m. **s. control,** control por el Estado, m. **S. Department,** Ministerio de Estado, m. **s. education,** instrucción pública, f. **State of the Union message,** Mensaje al Congreso, m. **s. papers,** documentos de Estado, m pl

state /steɪt/ vt decir (que), afirmar (que); (one's case, etc.) exponer; explicar; Math. proponer

statecraft /'steɪt,kræft/ n arte de gobernar, m

stated /'steɪtɪd/ a arreglado, indicado; fijo. **the s.**

date, la fecha indicada. **at s. intervals,** a intervalos fijos

statehood /'steɪthʊd/ n estadidad, f

stateliness /'steɪtlɪnɪs/ n dignidad, f; majestad, f

stately /'steɪtli/ a majestuoso; imponente; noble; digno

statement /'steɪtmənt/ n afirmación, declaración, f; resumen, m; exposición, f; Law. deposición, f; Com. estado de cuenta, m. **to make a s.,** hacer una declaración

stateroom /'steɪt,rum/ n sala de recepción, f; (on a ship) camarote, m

statesman /'steɪtsmən/ n hombre de estado, m

statesmanlike /'steɪtsmən,laɪk/ a de hombre de estado

statesmanship /'steɪtsmən,ʃɪp/ n arte de gobernar, m

static /'stætɪk/ a estático

statics /'stætɪks/ n estática, f

station /'steɪʃən/ n (place) puesto, sitio, m; (Rail. and Eccl.) estación, f; (social) posición social, f; Naut. apostadero, m; Surv. punto de marca, m. —vt estacionar, colocar, poner. **to s. oneself,** colocarse. **Stations of the Cross,** Estaciones, f pl. **s.-master,** jefe de la estación, m

stationary /'steɪʃə,nɛri/ a estacionario; inmóvil; Astron. estacional

stationer /'steɪʃənər/ n papelero (-ra). **stationer's shop,** papelería, f

stationery /'steɪʃə,nɛri/ n papelería, f, efectos de escritorio, m pl; papel de escribir, m

station wagon n psicorre, coche camioneta, coche rural, m

statistical /stə'tɪstɪkəl/ a estadístico

statistician /,stætɪ'stɪʃən/ n estadista, m

statistics /stə'tɪstɪks/ n estadística, f

statuary /'stætʃu,ɛri/ a estatuario. —n estatuaria, f; estatuas, f pl; (sculptor) estatuario, m

statue /'stætʃu/ n estatua, f; imagen, f

statuesque /,stætʃu'esk/ a escultural

statuette /,stætʃu'et/ n figurilla, f

stature /'stætʃər/ n estatura, f; (moral, etc.) valor, m

status /'steɪtəs, 'stætəs/ n (Law. etc.) estado, m; posición, f; rango, m. **What is his s. as a physicist?** ¿Cómo se le considera entre los físicos? **social s.,** posición social, f; rango social, m

statute /'stætʃut/ n ley, f; acto legislativo, m; estatuto, m; regla, f. **s. book,** código legal, m

statutory /'stætʃu,tɔri/ a establecido; reglamentario; estatutario

staunch /stɔntʃ/ a leal, fiel; firme, constante. —vt restañar

staunchness /'stɔntʃnɪs/ n lealtad, fidelidad, f; firmeza, f

stave /steɪv/ n (of a barrel, etc.) duela, f; (of a ladder) peldaño, m; (stanza) estrofa, f; Mus. pentagrama, m. **to s. in,** abrir boquete en; romper a golpes; quebrar. **to s. off,** apartar, alejar; (delay) aplazar, diferir; (avoid) evitar; (thirst, etc.) dominar

stay /steɪ/ vt detener; (a judgment, etc.) suspender. —vi permanecer; quedarse; detenerse; (of weather, etc.) durar; (lodge) hospedarse, vivir. **to come to s.,** venir a ser permanente. **to s. a person's hand,** detenerle el brazo. **to s. at home,** quedarse en casa. **s.-at-home,** a casero. —n persona casera, f. **to s. the course,** terminar la carrera. **S.! Say no more!** ¡Calle! ¡No diga más! **to s. away,** ausentarse. **to s. up,** no acostarse; velar. **to s. with,** quedarse con; alojarse con; quedarse en casa de, vivir con

stay /steɪ/ n estancia, permanencia, f; residencia, f; (restraint) freno, m; Law. suspensión, f; (endurance) aguante, m, resistencia, f; Naut. estay, m; (prop) puntal, m; Fig. apoyo, soporte, m; pl **stays,** corsé, m

stead /sted/ n lugar, m. **in the s. of,** en el lugar de, como substituto de. **It has stood me in good s.,** Me ha sido muy útil

steadfast /'sted,fæst/ a fijo; constante; firme; tenaz. **s. gaze,** mirada fija, f

steadfastly /'sted,fæstli/ adv fijamente; con constancia; firmemente; tenazmente

steadfastness /'sted,fæstnɪs/ n fijeza, f; constancia, f; firmeza, f; tenacidad, f

steadily /'stedli/ adv firmemente; (without stopping)

sin parar; continuamente; (assiduously) diligentemente; (uniformly) uniformemente. **Prices have gone up s.,** Los precios no han dejado de subir. **He looked at it s.,** Lo miraba sin pestañear (or fijamente)

steadiness /'stɛdɪnɪs/ n estabilidad, f; firmeza, f; constancia, f; (of persons) seriedad, formalidad, f; (of workers) diligencia, asiduidad, f

steady /'stɛdi/ a firme; seguro; fijo; constante; uniforme; continuo; estacionario; (of persons) serio, formal, juicioso; (of workers) diligente, asiduo. —vt afirmar; (persons) hacer más serio (a); (nerves, etc.) calmar, fortificar. **a s. job,** un empleo seguro. **S.! ¡Calma!** Naut. **¡Seguro! He steadied himself against the table,** Se apoyó en la mesa

steak /steik/ n tajada, f; biftec, m

steal /stil/ vt robar, hurtar; tomar. —vi robar, ser ladrón; (glide) deslizarse; (overwhelm) dominar, ganar insensiblemente (a). **to s. a kiss,** robar un beso. **to s. a look at,** mirar de soslayo (or de lado). **to s. away,** escurrirse, escabullirse; marcharse a hurtadillas. **to s. in,** deslizarse en, colarse en

stealthily /'stɛlθəli/ adv a hurtadillas; a escondidas, furtivamente

stealthiness /'stɛlθɪnɪs/ n carácter furtivo, m

stealthy /'stɛlθi/ a furtivo; cauteloso

steam /stim/ n vapor, m. —vi echar vapor. —vt Cul. cocer al vapor; (clothes) mojar; (windows, etc.) empañar. **to have the s. up,** estar bajo presión. **The windows are steamed,** Los cristales están empañados. **s.-boiler,** caldera de vapor, f. **s.-engine,** máquina de vapor, f. **s.-hammer,** maza de fragua, f. **s.-heat,** calefacción por vapor, f. **s.-roller,** Lit. apisonadora, Fig. fuerza arrolladora, f

steamboat /'stim,bout/ n vapor, m

steamer /'stimər/ n Cul. marmita al vacío, f; Naut. buque de vapor, m

steamship /'stim,ʃip/ n buque de vapor, piróscafo, m

steamy /'stimi/ a lleno de vapor

steed /stid/ n corcel, m

steel /stil/ n (metal, and Poet. sword) acero, m; (for sharpening) afilón, m. —a de acero; acerado. —vt acerar; Fig. endurecer. **to be made of s.,** Fig. ser de bronce. **He cannot s. himself to do it,** No puede persuadirse a hacerlo. **to s. one's heart,** hacerse duro de corazón. **cold s.,** arma blanca, f. **stainless s.,** acero inoxidable, m. **s.-engraving,** grabado en acero, m

steel mill n fábrica de acero, f

steep /stip/ a acantilado, escarpado; precipitoso; (of stairs, etc.) empinado; (of price) exorbitante. —vt (soak) remojar, empapar; Fig. absorber; (in a subject) empaparse (en). —n remojo, m. **It's a bit s.!** Inf. ¡Es un poco demasiado!

steeping /'stipɪŋ/ n remojo, m, maceración, f

steeple /'stipəl/ n campanario, m, torre, f; aguja, f

steeplechase /'stipəl,tʃeis/ n steeplechase, m, carrera de obstáculos, f

steepness /'stipnɪs/ n carácter escarpado, m, lo precipitoso

steer /stɪər/ vt Naut. gobernar; (a car, etc.) conducir; Fig. guiar, conducir. —vi Naut. timonear; Naut. navegar; Auto. conducir. —n Zool. novillo, m. **to s. clear of,** evitar. **to s. one's way through the crowd,** abrirse paso entre la muchedumbre

steerage /'stɪərɪdʒ/ n gobierno, m; (stern) popa, f; (quarters) entrepuente, m. **to go s.,** viajar en tercera clase

steering /'stɪərɪŋ/ n Naut. gobierno, m; (tiller, etc.) gobernalle, timón, m; (of a vehicle) conducción, f. **s.-column,** barra de dirección, f. **s.-wheel,** Auto. volante de dirección, m; Naut. rueda del timón, f

stellar /'stɛlər/ a estelar

stem /stem/ n (of a tree) tronco, m; (of a plant) tallo, m; (of a glass, etc.) pie, m; (Mus. of a note) rabo, m; (of a pipe) tubo, m; (of a word) radical, m. —vt (check) contener; (the tide) ir contra; (the current) vencer; (dam) estancar. **from s. to stern,** de proa a popa

stench /stentʃ/ n tufo, hedor, m, hediondez, f

stencil /'stɛnsəl/ n patrón para estarcir, m; estarcido, m. —vt estarcir

stenographer /stə'nɒɡrəfər/ n estenógrafo (-fa), taquígrafo (-fa)

stenography /stə'nɒɡrəfi/ n estenografía, taquigrafía, f

stentorian /stɛn'tɔriən/ a estentóreo

step /step/ n paso, m; (footprint) huella, f; (measure) medida, f; (of a stair, etc.) escalón, peldaño, m, grada, f; (of a ladder) peldaño, m; (of vehicles) estribo, m; (grade) escalón, m; Mus. intervalo, m. **at every s.,** a cada paso. **flight of steps,** escalera, f; (before a building, etc.) escalinata, f. **in steps,** en escalones. **to bend one's steps towards,** dirigirse hacia. **to keep in s.,** llevar el paso. **to take a s.,** dar un paso. **to take steps,** tomar medidas. **s. by s.,** paso a paso; poco a poco. **s.-dance,** baile típico, m. **s.-ladder,** escalera de tijera, f

step /step/ vi dar un paso; pisar; andar. **Please s. in!** Sírvase de entrar. **Will you s. this way, please?** ¡Haga el favor de venir por aquí! **to s. aside,** ponerse a un lado; desviarse; Fig. retirarse (en favor de). **to s. in,** entrar; intervenir (en); (meddle) entrometerse. **He stepped into the train,** Subió al tren. **to s. on,** pisar. **to s. on board,** Naut. ir a bordo. **to s. out,** salir; (from a vehicle) bajar; (a dance) bailar. **He stepped out a moment ago,** Salió hace un instante

stepbrother /'stɛp,brʌðər/ n hermanastro, medio hermano, m

stepchild /'stɛp,tʃaild/ n hijastro (-ra)

stepdaughter /'stɛp,dɔtər/ n hijastra, f

stepfather /'stɛp,faðər/ n padrastro, m

stepmother /'stɛp,mʌðər/ n madrastra, f

steppe /stɛp/ n estepa, f

steppingstone /'stɛpɪŋ,stoun/ n pasadera, f; Fig. escabel, escalón, m

stepsister /'stɛp,sɪstər/ n hermanastra, media hermana, f

stepson /'stɛp,sʌn/ n hijastro, m

stereotype /'stɛriə,taip/ n estereotipia, f, clisé, m, vt (Print. and Fig.) estereotipar

sterile /'stɛrɪl/ a estéril; árido

sterility /stə'rɪlɪti/ n esterilidad, f; aridez, f

sterilization /,stɛrələ'zeifən/ n esterilización, f

sterilize /'stɛrə,laiz/ vt esterilizar

sterilizer /'stɛrə,laizər/ n esterilizador, m

sterling /'stɜrlɪŋ/ a esterlina f; Fig. genuino. **pound s.,** libra esterlina, f

stern /stɜrn/ a severo, austero; duro. —n Naut. popa, f

sternly /'stɜrnli/ adv con severidad, severamente, duramente

sternness /'stɜrnnɪs/ n severidad, f; dureza, f

sternum /'stɜrnəm/ n Anat. esternón, m

stethoscope /'stɛθə,skoup/ n estetoscopio, m

stevedore /'stivɪ,dɔr/ n estibador, m

stew /stu/ vt guisar a la cazuela, estofar; (mutton, etc.) hervir; (fruit) cocer. —n estofado, m; Inf. agitación, f. **to be in a s.,** Inf. sudar la gota gorda. **stewed fruit,** compota de frutas, f. **s.-pot,** cazuela, olla, f, puchero, m

steward /'stuərd/ n administrador, m; mayordomo, m; (provision) despensero, m; Naut. camarero, m

stewardess /'stuərdɪs/ n Naut. camarera, f

stick /stɪk/ vt clavar (en), hundir (en); (put) poner; sacar; (stamps, etc.) pegar; fijar; (endure) resistir; tolerar. —vi clavarse, hundirse; estar clavado; pegarse; (remain) quedar; (in the mud, etc.) atascarse, embarrancarse, (on a reef) encallarse; (in the throat, etc.) atravesarse; (stop) detenerse. **It sticks in my throat,** Inf. No lo puedo tragar. **Friends always s. together,** Los amigos no se abandonan. **The nickname stuck to him,** El apodo se le quedó. **to s. at,** persistir en; desistir (ante); pararse (ante); tener escrúpulos sobre. **to s. at nothing,** no tener escrúpulos. **He stuck at his work,** Siguió trabajando. **to s. down,** pegar. **to s. out,** vi proyectar; sobresalir. —vt (one's chest) inflar; (one's tongue) sacar. **His ears s. out,** Tiene las orejas salientes. **to s. to,** (one's job) no dejar; (one's plans) adherirse (a); (one's principles) ser fiel (a); (one's friends) no abandonar; (one's word, etc.) cumplir; atenerse a. **to s. up,** vi (of hair) erizarse, ponerse de punta; salirse. —vt clavar; (a notice) fijar. **to s. up for,** (a person) defender

stick /stɪk/ n estaca, f; (for the fire) leña, f; (walking-s.) bastón, m; (of office) vara, f; (of sealing-wax, etc.) barra, *f;* palo, *m;* (baton) batuta, *f;* (of celery) tallo, *m.* **in a cleft s.,** entre la espada y la pared. **to give** (a person) **the s.,** dar palo (a)

stickiness /'stɪkɪnɪs/ *n* viscosidad, *f*

sticking plaster *n* esparadrapo, *m*

stick-in-the-mud /'stɪkɪnðə,mʌd/ *n* chapado a la antigua, *m*

stickler /'stɪklər/ *n* rigorista, *mf.* **to be a s. for etiquette,** ser etiquetero

sticky /'stɪki/ *a* pegajoso, viscoso; *Fig.* difícil

stiff /stɪf/ *a* rígido; inflexible; tieso; (of paste, etc.) espeso; (of manner) distante; (of a bow, etc.) frío; (of a person) almidonado, etiquetero; severo; (of examinations, etc.) difícil; (strong) fuerte; (of price, etc.) alto, exorbitante; (of a shirt front, etc.) duro. **s. with cold,** aterido de frío. **s. neck,** torticolis, *m.* **s.-necked,** terco, obstinaz

stiffen /'stɪfən/ *vt* reforzar; atiesar; (paste, etc.) hacer más espeso; (*Fig.* strengthen) robustecer; (make more obstinate) hacer más tenaz. —*vi* atiesarse; endurecerse; (straighten oneself) enderezarse; (of manner) volverse menos cordial; (become firmer) robustecerse; (become more obstinate) hacerse más tenaz. **The breeze stiffened,** Refrescó el viento

stiffly /'stɪfli/ *adv* tiesamente; rígidamente; obstinadamente

stiffness /'stɪfnɪs/ *n* rigidez, *f;* tiesura, *f;* dureza, *f;* (of manner) frialdad, *f;* (obstinacy) terquedad, obstinación, *f;* (of an examination, etc.) dificultad, *f*

stifle /'staɪfəl/ *vt* ahogar, sofocar; apagar; suprimir

stifling /'staɪflɪŋ/ *a* sofocante, bochornoso

stigma /'stɪgmə/ *n* estigma, *m*

stigmatize /'stɪgmə,taɪz/ *vt* estigmatizar

stile /staɪl/ *n* (nearest equivalent) portilla con escalones, *f*

stiletto /stɪ'lɛtou/ *n* estilete, *m*

still /stɪl/ *a* tranquilo; inmóvil; quedo; silencioso; (of wine) no espumoso. —*n* silencio, *m.* **in the s. of the night,** en el silencio de la noche. **Keep s.!** ¡Estate quieto! **to keep s.,** quedarse inmóvil, no moverse. **s.-birth,** nacimiento de un niño muerto, *m.* **s.-born,** nacido muerto. **s. life,** *Art.* bodegón, *m,* naturaleza muerta, *f*

still /stɪl/ *vt* hacer callar, acallar; calmar, tranquilizar; apaciguar; (pain) aliviar

still /stɪl/ *adv* todavía, aún; (nevertheless) sin embargo, no obstante; (always) siempre. **I think she s. visits them every week,** Me parece que sigue visitándoles cada semana. **s. and all,** con todo y eso. **s. more,** aún más

still /stɪl/ *n* alambique, *m.* **salt water s.,** adrazo, *m*

stillness /'stɪlnɪs/ *n* quietud, tranquilidad, *f;* silencio, *m.* **in the s. of the night,** en el silencio de la noche

stilt /stɪlt/ *n* zanco, *m*

stilted /'stɪltɪd/ *a* ampuloso, campanudo, hinchado

stimulant /'stɪmyələnt/ *a* and *n* estimulante, *m*

stimulate /'stɪmyə,leɪt/ *vt* estimular; incitar (a), excitar (a)

stimulating /'stɪmyə,leɪtɪŋ/ *a* estimulante; (encouraging) alentador; (inspiring) sugestivo, inspirador

stimulation /,stɪmyə'leɪʃən/ *n* excitación, *f;* (stimulus) estímulo, *m*

stimulus /'stɪmyələs/ *n* estímulo, *m;* *Med.* estimulante, *m;* (incentive) impulso, incentivo, *m;* acicate, aguijón, *m*

sting /stɪŋ/ *vt* picar, pinchar; (of snakes, etc.) morder; (of hot dishes) resquemar; (of hail, etc.) azotar; (pain) atormentar; (provoke) provocar (a), incitar (a). —*n* (*Zool.* organ) aguijón, *m;* *Bot.* púa, *f;* (of a scorpion) uña, *f;* (of a serpent) colmillo, *m;* (pain and wound) pinchazo, *m;* (serpent's) mordedura, *f;* (stimulus) acicate, estímulo, *m;* (torment) tormento, dolor, *m*

stingily /'stɪndʒəli/ *adv* avaramente, tacañamente

stinginess /'stɪndʒɪnɪs/ *n* tacañería, avaricia, *f*

stinging /'stɪŋɪŋ/ *a* picante; *Fig.* mordaz; (of blows) que duele

stingy /'stɪndʒi/ *a* tacaño, avaro, mezquino

stink /stɪŋk/ *vi* apestar, heder, oler mal. —*n* tufo, *m,* hediondez, *f*

stinking /'stɪŋkɪŋ/ *a* apestoso, hediondo, fétido, mal oliente

stint /stɪnt/ *vt* escatimar; limitar. —*n* límite, *m,* restricción, *f.* **without s.,** sin límite; sin restricción

stipend /'staɪpɛnd/ *n* estipendio, salario, *m*

stipple /'stɪpəl/ *vt Art.* puntear. —*n* punteado, *m*

stipulate /'stɪpyə,leɪt/ *vi* estipular, poner como condición. —*vt* estipular, especificar. **They stipulated for a five-day week,** Pusieron como condición (*or* Estipularon) que trabajasen cinco días por semana

stipulation /,stɪpyə'leɪʃən/ *n* estipulación, *f;* condición, *f*

stir /stɜr/ *vt* agitar; revolver; (the fire) atizar; (move) mover; (emotionally) conmover, impresionar; (the imagination) estimular. —*vi* moverse. —*n* movimiento, *m;* conmoción, *f;* (bustle) bullicio, *m;* sensación, *f.* **to make a s.,** causar una sensación. **to s. one's coffee,** revolver el café. **to s. up discontent,** fomentar el descontento

stirring /'stɜrɪŋ/ *a* conmovedor, emocionante, impresionante; (of times, etc.) turbulento, agitado

stirrup /'stɜrəp, 'stɪr-/ *n* estribo, *m.* **s.-cup,** última copa, *f.* **s.-pump,** bomba de mano (para líquidos), *f*

stitch /stɪtʃ/ *n* (action) puntada, *f;* (result) punto, *m;* *Surg.* punto de sutura, *m;* (pain) punzada, *f,* pinchazo, *m.* —*vt* coser; *Surg.* suturar

stoat /stout/ *n* armiño, *m;* (weasel) comadreja, *f*

stock /stɒk/ *n* (of a tree) tronco, *m;* (of a rifle) culata, *f;* (handle) mango, *m;* (of a horse's tail) nabo, *m;* (stem for grafting etc.) injerto, *m;* (race) raza, *f;* (lineage) linaje, *m,* estirpe, *f;* (supply) provisión, *f;* reserva, *f;* (of merchandise) surtido, *m;* *Cul.* caldo, *m;* (collar) alzacuello, *m;* *Bot.* alhelí, *m;* (government) papel del estado, *m,* valores públicos, *m pl;* (financial) valores, *m pl,* (of a company) capital, *m;* pl stocks, *Hist.* cepo, *m;* (of goods) existencias, *f pl,* stock, *m,* a corriente; (of the repertorio. **in s.** en existencia. **lives.,** ganado *m.* **rolling-s.,** *Rail.* materia móvil ferroviario, *m.* **s. phrase** frase hecha, *f.* **s. size,** talla corriente, *f.* **to lay in a s.,** hacer provisión de, almacenar. **to stand s.-still,** quedarse completamente inmóvil. **to take s.,** *Com.* hacer inventario. **to take s. of,** inventariar; examinar, considerar. **s.-breeder,** ganadero, *m.* **s.-broker,** corredor de bolsa, bolsista, *m.* **s. exchange,** bolsa, *f.* **s.-in-hand,** *Com.* existencias, *f pl.* **s.-in-trade** (*Com.* etc.) capital, *m.* **s.-raising,** cría de ganados, ganadería, *f.* **s.-taking,** *Com.* inventario, *m*

stock /stɒk/ *vt* proveer (de), abastecer (de); (of shops) tener existencia de

stockade /stɒ'keɪd/ *n* estacada, empalizada, *f,* *vt* empalizar

stocking /'stɒkɪŋ/ *n* media, *f.* **nylon stockings,** medias de cristal (or de nilón), *f pl*

stocky /'stɒki/ *a* rechoncho, doblado, achaparrado

stodgy /'stɒdʒi/ *a* (of food) indigesto; (of style, etc.) pesado, amazacotado

stoic /'stouɪk/ *a* and *n* estoico (-ca)

stoical /'stouɪkəl/ *a* estoico

stoicism /'stouə,sɪzəm/ *n* estoicismo, *m*

stoke /stouk/ *vt* (a furnace, etc.) cargar, alimentar; (a fire) echar carbón, etc., en. **s.-hole,** cuarto de fogoneros, *m;* *Naut.* cámara de calderas, *f*

stoker /'stoukər/ *n* fogonero, *m;* (mechanical) cargador, *m*

stole /stoul/ *n* (*Eccl.* and of fur, etc.) estola, *f*

stolid /'stɒlɪd/ *a* impasible, imperturbable

stolidity /stə'lɪdɪti/ *n* imperturbabilidad, impasibilidad, *f*

stolidly /'stɒlɪdli/ *adv* imperturbablemente

stomach /'stʌmək/ *n* estómago, vientre, *m;* apetito, *m;* (courage) corazón, valor, *m.* —*vt* digerir; (tolerate) tragar, sufrir. **s.ache,** dolor de estómago, *m*

stone /stoun/ *n* piedra, *f;* (gem) piedra preciosa, *f;* (of cherries, etc.) hueso, *m;* (of grapes, etc.) pepita, *f;* *Med.* cálculo, *m.* —*a* de piedra. —*vt* apedrear; (a wall, etc.) revestir de piedra; (fruit) deshuesar. **to pave with stones,** empedrar. **to leave no s. unturned,** no dejar piedra sin remover. **within a stone's throw,** a corta distancia, a un paso. **S. Age,** edad de piedra, *f.* **s.-breaker,** cantero, picapedrero, *m.* **s.-cold,** muy frío, completamente frío **s.-deaf,** *a* completamente sordo. **s.-fruit,** fruta de hueso, *f.* **s.-**

mason, mazonero, albañil, *m;* picapedrero, *m.* **s.-quarry,** pedrera, cantera, *f*

stonily /'stounḷi/ *adv* fríamente; fijamente, sin pestañear

stoniness /'stouninıs/ *n* lo pedregoso; (of hearts, etc.) dureza, *f;* (of stares, etc.) fijeza, inmovilidad, *f*

stoning /'stouniŋ/ *n* apedreamiento, *m,* lapidación, *f*

stony /'stouni/ *a* pedregoso; (of hearts, etc.) duro, insensible, empedernido; (of a stare, etc.) fijo, duro

stool /stul/ *n* banquillo, taburete, *m;* (feces) excremento, *m*

stoop /stup/ *vi* inclinarse, doblarse; encorvarse; ser cargado de espaldas; andar encorvado; (demean oneself) rebajarse (a). —*vt* inclinar, doblar. —*n* inclinación, *f;* cargazón de espaldas, *f*

stooping /'stupiŋ/ *a* inclinado, doblado; (of shoulders) cargado

stop /stɒp/ *vt* (a hole) obstruir, atascar; (a leak) cegar, tapar; (a tooth) empastar; (stanch) restañar; (the traffic, etc.) parar; detener; (prevent) evitar; (discontinue) cesar (de), dejarse de; (cut off) cortar; (end) poner fin (a), acabar con; (payment) suspender. —*vi* parar; detenerse; cesar; terminar; (stay) quedarse, permanecer. **I stopped myself from saying what I thought,** Me abstuve de decir lo que pensaba, Me mordí la lengua. **They stopped the food-supply,** Cortaron las provisiones. **to s. beating about the bush,** dejarse de historias. **to s. one's ears,** *Fig.* taparse los oídos. **to s. payments,** suspender pagos

stop /stɒp/ *n* parada, *f;* pausa, *f;* interrupción, *f;* cesación, *f;* (of an organ) registro, *m.* **"Stop,"** (road sign) «Alto.» **full s.,** *Gram.* punto, *m.* **tram s.,** parada de tranvía, *f.* **to come to a full s.,** pararse de golpe; cesar súbitamente. **to put a s. to,** poner fin a, poner coto a, acabar con. *f pl.* **s.-watch,** cronógrafo, *m*

stopgap /'stɒp,gæp/ *n* (person) tapaagujeros, *m;* substituto, *m*

stoppage /'stɒpıdʒ/ *n* parada, *f;* cesación, *f;* suspensión, *f;* interrupción, *f;* pausa, *f;* (obstruction) impedimento, *m;* obstrucción, *f.* **s. of work,** suspensión de trabajo, *f*

stopper /'stɒpər/ *n* tapón, *m;* obturador, *m, vt* cerrar con tapón, taponar

stopping /'stɒpiŋ/ *n* parada, *f;* cesación, *f;* suspensión, *f;* (of a tooth) empaste, *m.* **without s.,** sin parar. **without s. to draw breath,** de un aliento. **s.-place,** paradero, *m;* (of buses, etc.) parada, *f.* **s. train,** tren ómnibus, *m.* **s. up,** obturación, *f*

storage /'stɒrıdʒ/ *n* almacenamiento, *m;* (charge) almacenaje, *m;* (place) depósito, *m.* **cold s.,** cámara frigorífica, *f.* **s. battery,** acumulador, *m*

store /stɒr/ *n* provisión, *f;* abundancia, *f;* reserva, *f;* (of knowledge, etc.) tesoro, *m;* (for furniture, etc.) depósito, almacén, *m; pl* **stores,** (shop) almacenes, *m pl;* (food) provisiones, *f pl;* (*Mil.* etc.) pertrechos, *m pl.* —*vt* proveer; guardar, acumular; tener en reserva; (furniture, etc.) almacenar; (hold) caber en, tomar. **in s.,** en reserva; en depósito, en almacén. **to set s. by,** estimar en mucho; dar importancia a. **to set little s. by,** estimar en poco; conceder poca importancia a. **s.-room,** despensa, *f*

storehouse /'stɒr,haus/ *n* almacén, *m; Fig.* mina, *f,* tesoro, *m*

storied /'stɒrid/ *a* de...pisos. **two-s.,** de dos pisos

stork /stɒrk/ *n* cigüeña, *f*

storm /stɒrm/ *n* tempestad, tormenta, *f,* temporal, *m; Fig.* tempestad, *f; Mil.* asalto, *m.* —*vt Mil.* tomar por asalto, asaltar. —*vi* (of persons) bramar de cólera. **to take by s.,** tomar por asalto; *Fig.* cautivar, conquistar. **s. cloud,** nubarrón, *m.* **s.-signal,** señal de temporal, *f.* **s.-tossed,** *a* sacudido por la tempestad. **s. troops,** tropas de asalto, *f pl.* **s. window,** contravidriera, *f*

stormily /'stɒrməli/ *adv* tempestuosamente; con tormenta

storming /'stɒrmiŋ/ *n* (*Mil.* etc.) asalto, *m;* violencia, *f.* **s.-party,** pelotón de asalto, *m*

stormy /'stɒrmi/ *a* tempestuoso; de tormenta; (of life, etc.) borrascoso; (of meetings, etc.) tempestuoso

story /'stɒri/ *n* historia, *f;* cuento, *m;* anécdota, *f;* (funny) chiste, *m;* (plot) argumento, enredo, *m;* (fib) mentira, *f;* (floor) piso *m.* **It's always the same old s.,** Es siempre la misma canción (or historia). **That is**

quite another s., Eso es harina de otro costal. **short s.,** cuento, *m.* **s. book,** libro de cuentos, *m.* **s. teller,** cuentista, *mf;* (fibber) mentiroso (-sa)

stoup /stup/ *n* copa, *f;* pila de agua bendita, *f*

stout /staut/ *a* fuerte; (brave) intrépido, indómito; (fat) gordo, grueso; (firm) sólido, firme; (decided) resuelto; vigoroso. —*n* (drink) cerveza negra, *f.* **s.-hearted,** valiente, intrépido

stove /stouv/ *n* estufa, *f;* (open, for cooking) cocina económica, *f;* (gas, etc., for cooking) cocina, *f,* fogón, *m.* **s. pipe,** tubo de la chimenea, *m*

stow /stou/ *vt* meter, poner; colocar; (hide) esconder; (cargo) estibar, arrimar

stowaway /'stouə,wei/ *n* polizón, llovido, *m, vi* embarcarse secretamente

straddle /'strædḷ/ *vi* (*Nav.* etc.) graduar el tiro. —*vt* montar a horcajadas en. **s.-legged,** patiabierto

strafe /streif/ *vt* bombardear concentradamente; castigar; reñir

straggle /'strægəl/ *vi* rezagarse; vagar en desorden; dispersarse; estar esparcido; extenderse

straggler /'stræglər/ *n* rezagado (-da)

straggling /'strægliŋ/ *a* disperso; esparcido

straight /streit/ *a* derecho; recto; (of hair) lacio; directo; (tidy) en orden; (frank) franco; (honest) honrado. —*adv* derecho; en línea recta; directamente. **Keep s. on!** ¡Siga Vd. derecho! **to go s. to the point,** dejarse de rodeos, ir al grano. **To look s. in the eyes,** mirar derecho en los ojos. **s. away,** inmediatamente, en seguida. **s. out,** sin rodeos

straighten /'streitn/ *vt* enderezar; poner derecho; poner en orden; arreglar. —*vi* ponerse derecho; enderezarse. **to s. one's face,** componer el semblante. **to s. the line,** *Mil.* rectificar el frente. **to s. out,** poner en orden; *Fig.* desenredar. **to s. oneself up,** erguirse

straightforward /,streit'fɔrwərd/ *a* honrado, sincero; franco; (simple) sencillo. **s. answer,** respuesta directa, *f*

straightforwardly /,streit,fɔrwərdli/ *adv* honradamente; francamente

straightforwardness /,streit'fɔrwərdnıs/ *n* honradez, integridad, *f;* franqueza, *f;* (simplicity) sencillez, *f*

straightness /'streitnıs/ *n* derechura, rectitud, *f;* (of persons) honradez, probidad, *f*

straightway /'streit'wei, -,wei/ *adv* al instante, inmediatamente

strain /strein/ *vt* estirar; forzar; esforzar; (one's eyes) quebrarse; (one's ears) aguzar (el oído); (a muscle, etc.) torcer; (a friendship) pedir demasiado (a), exigir demasiado (de); (a person's patience, etc.) abusar (de); (words) tergiversar; (embrace) abrazar estrechamente (a); (filter) filtrar; *Cul.* colar. —*vi* hacer un gran esfuerzo, esforzarse (para). —*n* tirantez, *f;* tensión, *f;* (effort) esfuerzo, *m;* (sprain) torcedura, *f;* (nervous) tensión nerviosa, *f; Mech.* esfuerzo, *m;* (breed) raza, *f; Biol.* cepa, *f;* (tendency) tendencia, *f;* (heredity) herencia, *f;* rasgo, *m,* vena, *f;* (style) estilo, *m; Mus.* melodía, *f;* (of mirth, etc.) rasgo, *m;* (poetry) poesía, *f.* **to s. a point,** hacer una excepción. **to s. after effect,** buscar demasiado el efecto

strained /streind/ *a* tenso; (of muscles, etc.) torcido; (of smiles, etc.) forzado. **s. relations,** *Polit.* estado de tirantez, *m*

strainer /'streinər/ *n* filtro, *m;* coladero, *m*

strait /streit/ *n Geog.* estrecho, *m.* **to be in great straits,** estar en un apuro. **s. laced,** *Fig.* de manga estrecha, *f*

straiten /'streitn/ *vt* estrechar; limitar, **in straitened circumstances,** en la necesidad

Strait of Magellan /mə'dʒelən/ Estrecho de Magallanes, *m*

Straits Settlements Establecimientos del Estrecho, *m pl*

strand /strænd/ *n* (shore) playa, *f;* (of a river) ribera, orilla, *f;* (of rope) cabo, ramal, *m;* (of thread, etc.) hebra, *f;* (of hair) trenza, *f.* —*vt* and *vi* (a ship) encallar, varar. **to be stranded,** hallarse abandonado; (by missing a train, etc.) quedarse colgado. **to leave stranded,** abandonar, dejar plantado (a)

strange /streindʒ/ *a* (unknown) desconocido; nuevo; (exotic, etc.) extraño, singular; extraordinario; raro;

exótico. **I felt very s. in a s. country,** Me sentía muy solo en un país desconocido. **He is a very s. person,** Es una persona muy rara

strangely /'streindʒli/ adv extrañamente, singularmente; de un modo raro

strangeness /'streindʒnɪs/ n novedad, f; singularidad, f; rareza, f

stranger /'streindʒər/ n desconocido (-da); (from a foreign country) extranjero (-ra); (from another region, etc.) forastero (-ra).

strangle /'stræŋgəl/ vt estrangular; (a sob, etc.) ahogar

stranglehold /'stræŋgəl,hould/ n collar de fuerza, m. **to have a s. (on),** tener asido por la garganta; paralizar

strap /stræp/ n correa, f; tirante de botas, m, vt atar con correas

strapping /'stræpɪŋ/ a rozagante, robusto

stratagem /'strætədʒəm/ n estratagema, f, ardid, m

strategic /strə'tidʒɪk/ a estratégico

strategist /'strætɪdʒɪst/ n estratego, m

strategy /'strætɪdʒi/ n estrategia, f

stratification /,strætəfɪ'keiʃən/ n estratificación, f

stratosphere /'strætə,sfɪər/ n estratosfera, f

stratum /'streitəm, 'strætəm/ n Geol. estrato, m, capa, f; (social, etc.) estrato, m

straw /strɔ/ n paja, f. **I don't care a s.,** No se me da un bledo. **to be not worth a s.,** no valer un ardite. **to be the last s.,** ser el colmo. **to drink through a s.,** sorber con una paja. **s. hat,** sombrero de paja, m. **s.-colored,** pajizo

strawberry /'strɔ,beri/ n (plant and fruit, especially small or wild) fresa, f; (large cultivated) fresón, m. **s. bed,** fresal, m. **s. ice,** helado de fresa, m

stray /strei/ vi errar, vagar; perderse; (from a path, etc., also Fig.) descarriarse. —n animal perdido, m; niño (-ña) sin hogar. —a descarriado, perdido; errante; (sporadic) esporádico

stray bullet n bala perdida, f

streak /strik/ n raya, f; (in wood and stone) vena, f; (of light) rayo, m; (of humor, etc.) rasgo, m. —vt rayar. **like a s. of lightning,** como un relámpago

streaky /'striki/ a rayado; (of bacon) entreverado

stream /strim/ n arroyo, riachuelo, m; río, m; (current) corriente, f; (of words, etc.) torrente, m. —vi correr, fluir; manar, brotar; (float) flotar, ondear. —vt (blood, etc.) manar, echar. **The tears streamed down Jean's cheeks,** Las lágrimas corrían por las mejillas de Juana. **s.-lined,** fuselado

streamer /'strimər/ n gallardete, m, serpentina, f; (on a hat, etc.) cinta colgante, f, siguemepollo, m

stream-of-consciousness n escritura automática, f, fluir de la conciencia, m, flujo de la subconciencia, monólogo interior, m

street /strit/ n calle, f. **the man in the s.,** el hombre medio. **at s. level,** a ras de suelo. **s. arab,** golfo, m. **s. cries,** gritos de vendedores ambulantes, m pl. **s. entertainer,** saltabanco, m. **s. brawl, s. fight,** algarada callejera, f. **s. fighting,** luchas en las calles, f pl. **s. musician,** músico ambulante, m. **s.-sweeper,** barrendero, m. **s.-walker,** buscona, prostituta, f

strength /strɛŋkθ, strɛnθ/ n fuerza, f; (of colors, etc.) intensidad, f; (of character) firmeza (de carácter), f; (of will) resolución, decisión, f; Mil. complemento, m. **by sheer s.,** a viva fuerza. **on the s. of,** confiando en, en razón de

strengthen /'strɛŋkθən, 'strɛn-/ vt fortificar; consolidar; reforzar. —vi fortificarse; consolidarse; reforzarse

strengthening /'strɛŋkθənɪŋ, 'strɛn-/ a fortificante; tonificante. —n refuerzo, m; fortificación, f; consolidación, f

strenuous /'strɛnyuəs/ a activo, enérgico; vigoroso; (arduous) arduo

strenuously /'strɛnyuəsli/ adv enérgicamente, vigorosamente

strenuousness /'strɛnyuəsnɪs/ n energía, f; vigor, m; (arduousness) arduidad, f

streptococcus /,strɛptə'kɒkəs/ n Med. estreptococo, m

streptomycin /,strɛptə,maisɪn/ n Med. estreptomicina, f

stress /strɛs/ n tensión, f; impulso, m; importancia, f, énfasis, m; Gram. acento (tónico), m; acentuación, f; Mech. esfuerzo, m. —vt acentuar; poner énfasis en, insistir en. **under s. of circumstance,** impulsado por las circunstancias. **times of s.,** tiempos turbulentos, m pl. **to lay great s. on,** insistir mucho en; dar gran importancia a

stretch /strɛtʃ/ vt (make bigger) ensanchar; (pull) estirar; (one's hand, etc.) alargar, extender; (knock down) tumbar. —vi ensancharse; dar de sí; ceder; extenderse. **to s. oneself,** estirarse, desperezarse. **to s. as far as,** llegar hasta, extenderse hasta. **to s. a point,** hacer una concesión. **to s. one's legs,** estirar las piernas

stretch /strɛtʃ/ n estirón, m; tensión, f; (of country, etc.) extensión, f; (scope) alcance, m. **by a s. of the imagination,** con un esfuerzo de imaginación. **He can sleep for hours at a s.,** Puede dormir durante horas enteras

stretcher /'strɛtʃər/ n (for gloves) ensanchador, m; dilatador, m; (for canvas) bastidor, m; (for wounded, etc.) camilla, f. **s.-bearer,** camillero, m

strew /stru/ vt esparcir; derramar

stricken /'strɪkən/ a (wounded) herido; (ill) enfermo; (with grief) afligido, agobiado de dolor. **s. in years,** entrado en años

strict /strɪkt/ a exacto; estricto; escrupuloso; severo

strictly /'strɪktli/ adv exactamente; estrictamente; severamente, con severidad. **s. speaking,** en rigor, en realidad

strictness /'strɪktnɪs/ n exactitud, f; escrupulosidad, f; rigor, m; severidad, f

stricture /'strɪktʃər/ n Fig. crítica severa, censura, f. **to pass strictures on,** criticar severamente

stride /straid/ vi andar a pasos largos, dar zancadas; cruzar a grandes trancos. —vt cruzar de un tranco; poner una pierna en cada lado de. —n zancada, f; paso largo, tranco, m. **to s. up and down,** dar zancadas

strident /'straidnt/ a estridente; (of colors) chillón

strife /straif/ n lucha, f, conflicto, m

strike /straik/ vt golpear; pegar, dar una bofetada (a); (wound) herir; (a coin) acuñar; (a light) encender; (of a snake) morder; (a blow) asestar, dar; (of ships, a rock, etc.) chocar contra; estrellarse contra; (flags) bajar, arriar; (a tent) desmontar; (camp) levantar; (come upon) llegar a; (discover) encontrar por casualidad, tropezar con; hallar, descubrir; (seem) parecer; (impress) impresionar; (of ideas) ocurrirse; (an attitude) tomar, adoptar; (of a clock) dar; (a balance) hacer; (a bargain) cerrar, llegar a; (level) nivelar; (cuttings) enraizar. —vi golpear; (of a clock) dar la hora; (of a ship) encallar; (go) ir; (penetrate) penetrar; (of a cutting) arraigar; (sound) sonar. **He struck the table with his fist,** Golpeó la mesa con el puño. **I was very much struck by the city's beauty,** La belleza de la ciudad me impresionó mucho. **The news struck fear into their hearts,** La noticia les llenó el corazón de miedo. **The clock struck three,** El reloj dio las tres. **The hour has struck,** Fig. Ha llegado la hora. **How did the house s. you?** ¿Qué te pareció la casa? **to s. a bargain,** cerrar un trato. **to s. a blow,** asestar un golpe. **to s. across country,** ir a campo traviesa. **to s. an attitude,** tomar una actitud. **to s. home,** dar en el blanco; herir; herir en lo más vivo; hacerse sentir. **to s. at,** asestar un golpe (a); acometer, embestir; atacar. **to s. down,** derribar; (of illness) acometer. **to s. off,** (a head, etc.) cortar; (a name) borrar, tachar; (print) imprimir. **to s. out,** vi asestar un golpe (a); (of a swimmer) nadar; echarse, lanzarse. —vt (a word, etc.) borrar, rayar; (begin) iniciar. **to s. through,** (cross out) rayar, tachar; (of the sun's rays, etc.) penetrar. **to s. up,** vt tocar; empezar a cantar; (a friendship) trabar. —vi empezar a tocar. **to s. up a march,** Mil. batir la marcha

strike /straik/ n huelga, f. —vi declararse en huelga. **go-slow s.,** tortuguismo, m. **lock-out s.,** huelga patronal, f. **sit-down s.,** huelga de brazos caídos, f. **to go on s.,** declararse en huelga. **s.-breaker,** esquirol, m. **s.-pay,** subsidio de huelga, m

striker /'straikər/ n huelguista, mf

striking /'straikiŋ/ a notable, sorprendente; (impressive) impresionante; que llama la atención; llamativo

string /striŋ/ n bramante, m; cuerda, f; (ribbon) cinta, f; (of beads, etc.) sarta, f; (of onions) ristra, f; (of horses, etc.) reata, f; hilera, f; (of a bridge) cable, m; (of oaths, lies) sarta, serie, f; (of beans) fibra, f. —vt encordar; (beads, etc.) ensartar; (beans) quitar las fibras (de). **He is all strung up,** Se le crispan los nervios. **the strings,** los instrumentos de cuerda. **a s. of pearls,** un collar de perlas. **for strings,** *Mus.* para arco. **to pull strings,** *Fig.* manejar los hilos. **to s. up,** (an instrument) templar; (a person) pender, ahorcar. **s. bean,** judía verde, f

stringed /striŋd/ a (of musical instruments) de cuerda. **s. instrument,** instrumento de cuerda, m

stringency /'strindʒənsi/ n severidad, f; estrechez, f

stringent /'strindʒənt/ a estricto, severo

stringy /'striŋi/ a fibroso; filamentoso; correoso; arrugado

strip /strip/ vt desnudar; despojar (de), quitar; robar; (a cow) ordeñar hasta agotar la leche. —vi desnudarse. —n (tatter) jirón, m; tira, lista, f; (of wood) listón, m; (of earth) pedazo, m; (Geog. of land) zona, f. **to s. off,** vt quitar; (bark from a tree) descortezar; (one's clothes) despojarse de. —vi desprenderse, separarse

stripe /straip/ n raya, lista, f; (Mil. etc.) galón, m; (lash) azote, m. —vt rayar. **the stripes of the tiger,** las rayas del tigre

striped /straipt, 'straipid/ a listado, a rayas; con rayas. **s. trousers,** pantalón de corte, m

stripling /'stripliŋ/ n joven imberbe, pollo, mancebo, m

strive /straiv/ vi esforzarse (a); pugnar (por, para); trabajar (por); (fight against) luchar contra; pelear con. **He was striving to understand,** Pugnaba por (or Se esforzaba a) comprender

stroke /strouk/ n (blow) golpe, m; (of the oars) golpe del remo, m, remada, f; (at billards) tacada, f; (in golf) tirada, f; (in swimming) braza, f; (of a clock) campanada, f; (of a pen) rasgo de la pluma, m; (of a brush) pincelada, f; *Mech.* golpe de émbolo, m; (caress) caricia con la mano, f. —vt acariciar con la mano. **on the s. of six,** al acabar de dar las seis. **to have a s.,** tener un ataque de apoplejía. **s. of genius,** rasgo de ingenio, m. **s. of good luck,** racha de buena suerte, f

stroll /stroul/ vi pasearse, vagar. —n vuelta, f, paseo, m. **to go for a s.,** dar una vuelta

stroller /'stroulər/ n paseante, mf

strolling /'strouliŋ/ a errante; ambulante. **s. player,** n cómico (-ca) ambulante

strong /strɔŋ/ a fuerte; vigoroso; robusto; enérgico; firme; poderoso; (of colours) intenso, vivo; (of tea, coffee) cargado; *Gram.* fuerte. **The government took s. measures,** El gobierno tomó medidas enérgicas. **They gave very s. reasons,** Alegaron unas razones muy poderosas. **Grammar is not his s. point,** La gramática no es su punto fuerte. **The enemy is s. in numbers,** El enemigo es numéricamente fuerte. **The society is four thousand s.,** La sociedad tiene cuatro mil miembros. **s. box,** caja de caudales, f. **s. man,** hombre fuerte, m; (in a circus) hércules, m. **s.-minded,** de espíritu fuerte; independiente. **s. room,** cámara acorazada, f

stronghold /'strɔŋ,hould/ n fortaleza, f; refugio, m

strongly /'strɔŋli/ adv vigorosamente; fuertemente; firmemente

strop /strɔp/ n (razor) suavizador, m, vt suavizar

strophe /'stroufi/ n estrofa, f

structural /'strʌktʃərəl/ a estructural

structurally /'strʌktʃərəli/ adv estructuralmente, desde el punto de vista de la estructura

structure /'strʌktʃər/ n estructura, f; edificio, m; construcción, f

struggle /'strʌgəl/ vi luchar; pelear; disputarse. —n lucha, f; combate, m; conflicto, m. **to s. to one's feet,** luchar por levantarse. **without a s.,** sin luchar

struggling /'strʌgliŋ/ a pobre, indigente, que lucha para vivir

strum /strʌm/ vt (a stringed instrument) rascar; tocar mal

strumpet /'strʌmpit/ n ramera, f

strut /strʌt/ vi pavonearse. —vt (prop) apuntalar. —n pavonada, f; (prop) puntal, m. **to s. out,** salir de un paso majestuoso

strychnine /'striknin/ n estricnina, f

stub /stʌb/ n (of a tree) tocón, m; (of a pencil, candle, etc.) cabo, m; pedazo, fragmento, m; (of a cigarette or cigar) colilla, f. **s.-book,** talonario, m

stubble /'stʌbəl/ n rastrojo, m; (beard) barba de tres días, f

stubborn /'stʌbərn/ a inquebrantable, tenaz; persistente; (pig-headed) terco, testarudo

stubbornness /'stʌbərnis/ n tenacidad, f; terquedad, testarudez, f

stucco /'stʌkou/ n estuco, m, vt estucar

stud /stʌd/ n (of horses) caballeriza, f; (nail) tachón, m; (for collars) pasador para camisas, m. —vt tachonar; sembrar. **dress s.,** botón de la pechera, m. **s.-farm,** potrero, m

student /'studnt/ n estudiante, mf. —a estudiantil

studied /'stʌdid/ a estudiado; calculado; (of style) cerebral, reflexivo; (intentional) deliberado

studio /'studi,ou/ n estudio, m. **broadcasting s.,** estudio de emisión, m

studious /'studiəs/ a estudioso, aplicado; (deliberate) intencional, deliberate; (eager) solícito, ansioso

studiously /'studiəsli/ adv estudiosamente; con intención, deliberadamente; solícitamente

study /'stʌdi/ n estudio, m; solicitud, f, cuidado, m; investigación, f; (room) gabinete, cuarto de trabajo, m. —vt ocuparse de, cuidar de, atender a; considerar; estudiar; examinar; (the stars) observar; (try) procurar. —vi estudiar. **in a brown s.,** en Babia. **to make a s. of,** hacer un estudio de, estudiar. **to s. for an examination,** prepararse para un examen

stuff /stʌf/ n substancia, materia, f; (fabric) tela, f, paño, m; (rubbish) cachivaches, m pl, cosas, f pl. —a de estofa. —vt henchir; llenar; *Cul.* rellenar; (with food) ahitar (de); (cram) atestar, apretar; (furniture) rehenchir; (an animal, bird) disecar; (put) meter, poner. **S. and nonsense!** ¡Patrañas! **to be poor s.,** ser de pacotilla; no valer para nada

stuffed animal /stʌft/ n animal disecado, m

stuffiness /'stʌfinis/ n mala ventilación, f; falta de aire, f; calor, m

stuffing /'stʌfiŋ/ n (of furniture) rehenchimiento, m; *Cul.* relleno, m

stuffy /'stʌfi/ a mal ventilado, poco aireado, ahogado

stultify /'stʌltə,fai/ vt hacer inútil; invalidar; hacer ridículo

stumble /'stʌmbəl/ vi tropezar; dar un traspié; (in speaking) tartamudear. —n tropezón, m; traspié, m. **to s. through a speech,** pronunciar un discurso a tropezones. **to s. against,** tropezar contra. **to s. upon, across,** tropezar con; encontrar por casualidad

stumbling block n tropiezo, impedimento, m

stump /stʌmp/ n (of a tree) tocón, m; (of an arm, leg) muñón, m; (of a pencil, candle) cabo, m; (of a tooth) raigón, m; (of a cigar) colilla, f; (cricket) poste, montante, m; *Art.* esfumino, m; (leg) pata, f. —vt (disconcert) desconcertar, m; *Art.* esfumar; recorrer. **to s. up,** *Inf.* pagar

stun /stʌn/ vt dejar sin sentido (a); aturdir de un golpe (a); (astound) pasmar

stunning /'stʌniŋ/ a aturdidor; que pasma; *Inf.* estupendo

stunt /stʌnt/ vt impedir el crecimiento de; encanijar. —n (advertising) anuncio de reclamo, m; recurso (para conseguir algo), m; proeza, f

stunted /'stʌntid/ a (of trees, etc.) enano; (of children) encanijado; (of intelligence) inmaduro

stupefaction /,stupə'fækʃən/ n estupefacción, f; estupor, m

stupefy /'stupə,fai/ vt atontar, embrutecer; causar estupor (a), asombrar

stupendous /stu'pendəs/ a asombroso; enorme

stupid /'stupid/ a (with sleep, etc.) atontado; (silly) estúpido, tonto. —n tonto (-ta)

stupidity /stu'piditi/ n estupidez, f; tontería, f

stupor /'stupər/ n estupor, m

sturdiness /'stərdinis/ n robustez, f, vigor, m; firmeza, tenacidad, f

sturdy /'stɜrdi/ a robusto, vigoroso, fuerte; firme, tenaz

sturgeon /'stɜrdʒən/ n Ichth. esturión, m

stutter /'stʌtər/ vi tartamudear. —vt balbucir. —n tartamudeo, m

stutterer /'stʌtərər/ n tartamudo (-da)

stuttering /'stʌtərɪŋ/ a tartamudo; balbuciente. —n tartamudeo, m

sty /stai/ n (pig) pocilga, f; Med. orzuelo, m

Stygian /'stɪdʒiən/ a estigio

style /stail/ n (for etching) buril, m; (Lit., Art., Archit., etc.) estilo, m; (fashion) moda, f; (model) modelo, m; (behavior, etc.) tono, m; elegancia, f; (kind) especie, clase, f; (designation) tratamiento, m; vt llamar, nombrar. **the latest styles from Madrid,** los últimos modelos de Madrid. **He has a very individual s.,** Su estilo es muy personal. **They live in great s.,** Viven en gran lujo

stylet /'stailɪt/ n estilete, m

stylish /'stailɪʃ/ a elegante

stylishness /'stailɪʃnɪs/ n elegancia, f

stylist /'stailɪst/ n estilista, mf

stylize /'stailaiz/ vt estilizar

suasion /'sweiʒən/ n persuasión, f

suasive /'sweisɪv/ a suasorio, persuasivo

suave /swɑv/ a afable, cortés, urbano; (of wine) suave

suavity /'swɒvɪti/ n afabilidad, urbanidad, f

subaltern /sʌb'ɔltərn/ n Mil. subalterno, m, a subalterno, subordinado

subcommittee /'sʌbkə,mɪti/ n subcomisión, f

subconscious /sʌb'kɒnʃəs/ a subconsciente. **the s.,** la subconsciencia

subconsciously /sʌb'kɒnʃəsli/ adv subconscientemente

subcutaneous /,sʌbkyu'teiniəs/ a subcutáneo

subdivide /,sʌbdɪ'vaid/ vt subdividir. —vi subdividirse

subdivision /'sʌbdɪ,vɪʒən/ n subdivisión, f

subdominant /sʌb'dɒmənənt/ n Mus. subdominante, f

subdue /səb'du/ vt subyugar, sojuzgar, vencer; (one's passions) dominar; (colors, voices) suavizar; (lessen) mitigar; apagar

subdued /səb'dud/ a (of colors) apagado; (of persons) sumiso; (depressed) deprimido, melancólico. **in a s. voice,** en voz baja

subheading /'sʌb,hedɪŋ/ n subtítulo, m

subhuman /sʌb'hyumən/ a subhumano

subject /n. 'sʌbdʒɪkt; v. səb'dʒekt/ a sujeto; sometido (a); expuesto (a). —n (of a country) súbdito (-ta); sujeto, m; (of study) asignatura, materia, f; (theme) tema, m; (Gram., Philos.) sujeto, m. —vt subyugar; someter. **It can only be done s. to his consent,** Podrá hacerse únicamente si él lo consiente. **to change the s.,** cambiar de conversación. **to s. to criticism,** criticar (a). **s.-matter,** materia, m; (of a letter) contenido, m

subjection /səb'dʒekʃən/ n sujeción, f; sometimiento, m. **He was in a state of complete s.,** Estaba completamente sumiso. **to bring into s.,** subyugar

subjective /səb'dʒektɪv/ a subjetivo

subjectiveness /səb'dʒektɪvnɪs/ n subjetividad, f

subjectivism /səb'dʒektə,vɪzəm/ n subjetivismo, m

subjoin /səb'dʒɔin/ vt añadir, adjuntar

subjugate /'sʌbdʒə,geit/ vt subyugar, someter

subjugation /,sʌbdʒə'geiʃən/ n subyugación, f

subjunctive /səb'dʒʌŋktɪv/ a and n subjuntivo m

sublet /v. sʌb'let; n. 'sʌb,let/ vt subarrendar. —n subarriendo, m

sublimate /v. 'sʌblə,meit/ n. -mɪt/ vt sublimar. —n sublimado, m

sublimation /,sʌblɪ'meiʃən/ n sublimación, f

sublime /sə'blaim/ a sublime; absoluto, completo; extremo. **the s.,** lo sublime

sublimely /sə'blaimli/ adv sublimemente; completamente

submachine gun /,sʌbmə'ʃin/ n pistola ametralladora, metralleta, f, subfusil ametrallador, m

submarine /,sʌbmə'rin/ a submarino. —n

submarino, m. **midget s.,** submarino enano, submarino de bolsillo, m. **s. chaser,** cazasubmarino, m

submerge /səb'mɜrdʒ/ vt sumergir; inundar. —vi sumergirse. **The submarine submerged,** El submarino se sumergió

submergence /səb'mɜrdʒəns/ n sumergimiento, m, sumersión, f; hundimiento, m

submersible /səb'mɜrsəbəl/ a sumergible

submersion /səb'mɜrʒən/ n sumersión, f; hundimiento, m

submission /səb'mɪʃən/ n sometimiento, m; sumisión, resignación, f; docilidad, f

submissive /səb'mɪsɪv/ a sumiso, dócil, manso

submissively /səb'mɪsɪvli/ adv sumisamente, con docilidad

submissiveness /səb'mɪsɪvnɪs/ n sumisión, docilidad, f

submit /səb'mɪt/ vt someterse (a); doblarse ante; (a scheme, etc.) someter; presentar; (urge) proponer. —vi someterse; resignarse; (surrender) rendirse, entregarse. **to s. to arbitration,** someter a arbitraje

subnormal /sʌb'nɔrməl/ a anormal

subordinate /adj., n. sə'bɔrdṇɪt; v. -dṇ,eit/ a subordinado; subalterno, inferior; secundario. —n subordinado (-da). —vt subordinar

subordination /sə,bɔrdṇ'eiʃən/ n subordinación, f

suborn /sə'bɔrn/ vt sobornar, cohechar

subplot /'sʌb,plɒt/ n intriga secundaria, trama secundaria, f

subpoena /sə'pinə/ n citación, f, vt citar

subscribe /səb'skraib/ vt and vi subscribir; (to a periodical, etc.) abonarse (a)

subscriber /səb'skraibər/ n subscriptor (-ra); abonado (-da)

subscription /səb'skrɪpʃən/ n subscripción, f; (to a periodical, series of concerts, etc.) abono, m; (to a club) cuota, f

subsection /'sʌb,sekʃən/ n subsección, f

subsequent /'sʌbsɪkwənt/ a consiguiente, subsecuente; posterior. **s. to,** después de, posterior a. **s. upon,** de resultas de

subsequently /'sʌbsɪkwəntli/ adv más tarde; subsiguientemente; posteriormente

subservience /səb'sɜrviens/ n servilidad, f; utilidad, f

subservient /səb'sɜrviənt/ a servil; subordinado; útil

subside /səb'said/ vi (of water) bajar; (of ground) hundirse; (of foundations) asentarse; disminuir; calmarse; (be quiet) callarse. **to s. into a chair,** dejarse caer en un sillón

subsidence /səb'saidṇs/ n hundimiento, m; desplome, derrumbamiento, m; (of floods) bajada, f; (of anger, etc.) apaciguamiento, m

subsidiary /səb'sɪdi,ɛri/ a subsidiario

subsidize /'sʌbsɪ,daiz/ vt subvencionar

subsidy /'sʌbsɪdi/ n subvención, f, subsidio, m; prima, f

subsist /səb'sɪst/ vi subsistir

subsistence /səb'sɪstəns/ n subsistencia, f

subsoil /'sʌb,sɔil/ n subsuelo, m

substance /'sʌbstəns/ n substancia, f

substantial /səb'stænʃəl/ a substancial; sólido; importante

substantially /səb'stænʃəli/ adv substancialmente; sólidamente

substantiate /səb'stænʃi,eit/ vt establecer, verificar; justificar

substantiation /səb,stænʃi'eiʃən/ n comprobación, verificación, f; justificación, f

substantive /'sʌbstəntɪv/ a real, independiente; Gram. substantivo. —n Gram. substantivo, m

substitute /'sʌbstɪ,tut/ n substituto (-ta); (material) substituto, m. —vt substituir, reemplazar. **to be a s. for,** hacer las veces de

substitution /,sʌbstɪ'tuʃən/ n substitución, f, reemplazo, m

substratum /'sʌb,streitəm, -,strætəm/ n substrato, m

subterfuge /'sʌbtər,fyudʒ/ n subterfugio, m; evasiva, f

subterranean /,sʌbtə'reiniən/ a subterráneo

subtitle /'sʌb,taitḷ/ n subtítulo, m; (on films) guión, m

subtle /'sʌtḷ/ *a* sutil; delicado; penetrante; (crafty) astuto

subtlety /'sʌtḷti/ *n* sutileza, *f;* delicadeza, *f;* (craftiness) astucia, *f*

subtly /'sʌtli/ *adv* sutilmente; con delicadeza

subtract /səb'trækt/ *vt* restar, substraer

subtraction /səb'trækʃən/ *n* resta, substracción, *f*

suburb /'sʌbərb/ *n* suburbio, *m;* *pl* **suburbs,** las afueras, *f pl* los arrabales, *m pl*

suburban /sə'bərbən/ *a* suburbano

subvention /səb'vɛnʃən/ *n* subvención, *f*

subversion /səb'vɜrʒən/ *n* subversión, *f*

subversive /səb'vɜrsɪv/ *a* subversivo

subvert /səb'vɜrt/ *vt* subvertir

subway /'sʌb,wei/ *n* (passageway) pasaje subterráneo, *m;* (underground railway) metro (Spain, Puerto Rico), subte (Argentina), *m*

succeed /sək'sid/ *vt* seguir (a); suceder (a); heredar. —*vi* seguir (a); suceder (a); (be successful) tener éxito. **I did not s. in doing it,** No logré hacerlo. **to s. to the throne,** subir al trono

succeeding /sək'sidɪŋ/ *a* subsiguiente; futuro; consecutivo; sucesivo

success /sək'sɛs/ *n* éxito, *m;* triunfo, *m.* **to be a s.,** tener éxito. **The film was a great s.,** La película tuvo mucho éxito

successful /sək'sɛsfəl/ *a* que tiene éxito; afortunado, venturoso; próspero.

successfully /sək'sɛsfəli/ *adv* con éxito; prósperamente

succession /sək'sɛʃən/ *n* sucesión, *f;* (series) serie, *f;* (inheritance) herencia, *f;* (descendants) descendencia, *f.* **in s.,** sucesivamente

successive /sək'sɛsɪv/ *a* sucesivo

successor /sək'sɛsər/ *n* sucesor (-ra)

succinct /sək'sɪŋkt/ *a* sucinto, conciso

succinctly /sək'sɪŋktli/ *adv* sucintamente, brevemente, en pocas palabras

succor /'sʌkər/ *vt* socorrer, auxiliar. —*n* socorro, *m,* ayuda, *f*

succulence /'sʌkyələns/ *n* suculencia, *f*

succulent /'sʌkyələnt/ *a* suculento

succumb /sə'kʌm/ *vi* sucumbir; someterse, ceder

such /sʌtʃ/ *a* tal; parecido, semejante; así; tanto; (before an adjective, adverb) tan. —*n* el, *m,* (*f,* la) que, los, *m pl,* (*f pl,* las) que; tal. **s. men,** tales hombres. **I have never seen s. magnificence,** Nunca no he visto tanta magnificencia. **s. an important man,** un hombre tan importante. **s. pictures as these,** cuadros como estos. **S. is life!** ¡Así es la vida! **science as s.,** la ciencia como tal. **s.-and-s.,** tal y tal

suchlike /'sʌtʃ,laik/ *a* parecido, semejante; de esta clase

suck /sʌk/ *vt* chupar; (the breast) mamar; sorber; (of a vacuum cleaner, etc.) aspirar. —*n* chupada, *f;* succión, *f.* **to s. down,** tragar. **to s. up,** aspirar; absorber

sucker /'sʌkər/ *n* *Zool.* ventosa, *f;* *Bot.* acodo, mugrón, *m;* (greenhorn) primo, *m;* (pig) lechón, *m*

suckle /'sʌkəl/ *vt* amamantar, dar el pecho (a)

suckling pig /'sʌklɪŋ/ *n* lechón, cochinillo, *m*

suction /'sʌkʃən/ *n* succión, *f;* aspiración, *f.* **s.-pump,** bomba aspirante, *f*

Sudanese /,sudn'iz/ *a* and *n* sudanés (-esa)

Sudan, the /su'dæn/ el Sudán, *m*

sudden /'sʌdn/ *a* súbito; (unexpected) inesperado, impensado; (of bends) brusco. **all of a s.,** de repente; súbitamente

suddenly /'sʌdn̩li/ *adv* súbitamente; de pronto, de repente

suddenness /'sʌdn̩nɪs/ *n* carácter repentino, *m;* (of a bend, etc.) brusquedad, *f*

suds /sʌdz/ *n pl* jabonaduras, *f pl;* espuma, *f*

sue /su/ *vt* *Law.* proceder contra, pedir en juicio; *Law.* demandar; (beg) suplicar. **to sue for peace,** pedir la paz

suede /sweid/ *n* ante, *m.* **s. glove,** guante de ante, *m*

suet /'suɪt/ *n* sebo, *m*

Suez Canal, the /'su'ɛz/ el Istmo de Suez, *m*

suffer /'sʌfər/ *vt* sufrir, padecer; pasar, experimentar; (tolerate) tolerar, sufrir; (allow) permitir. —*vi* sufrir.

She suffers from her environment, es la víctima de su medio ambiente

sufferance /'sʌfərəns/ *n* tolerancia, *f.* **on s.,** por tolerancia

sufferer /'sʌfərər/ *n* enfermo (-ma); víctima, *f*

suffering /'sʌfərɪŋ/ *n* sufrimiento, padecimiento, *m;* dolor, *m.* —*a* sufriente

suffice /sə'fais/ *vi* ser suficiente, bastar. —*vt* satisfacer

sufficiency /sə'fɪʃənsi/ *n* suficiencia, *f;* (of money) subsistencia, *f*

sufficient /sə'fɪʃənt/ *a* suficiente, bastante. **to be s.,** bastar, ser suficiente

sufficiently /sə'fɪʃəntli/ *adv* suficientemente, bastante

suffix /'sʌfɪks/ *n* *Gram.* sufijo, *m*

suffocate /'sʌfə,keit/ *vt* ahogar, sofocar, asfixiar. —*vi* sofocarse, asfixiarse

suffocating /'sʌfə,keitɪŋ/ *a* sofocante, asfixiante

suffocation /,sʌfə'keiʃən/ *n* sofocación, asfixia, *f;* ahogo, *m*

suffrage /'sʌfrɪdʒ/ *n* sufragio, *m;* voto, *m.* **universal s.,** sufragio universal, *m*

suffragette /,sʌfrə'dʒɛt/ *n* sufragista, *f*

suffuse /sə'fyuz/ *vt* bañar, inundar, cubrir

sugar /'ʃʊgər/ *n* azúcar, *m.* —*vt* azucarar. **brown s.,** azúcar moreno, *m.* **loaf s.,** azúcar de pilón, *m.* **white s.,** azúcar blanco, *m.* **to s. the pill,** dorar la píldora. **s.-almond,** peladilla, *f.* **s.-basin,** azucarera, *f.* **s.-beet,** remolacha, *f.* **s.-candy,** azúcar candi, *m.* **s.-cane,** caña de azúcar, *f.* **s.-cane syrup,** miel de caña, *f.* **s.-paste,** alfeñique, *m,* alcorza, *f.* **s.-refinery,** fábrica de azúcar, *f.* **s.-tongs,** tenacillas para azúcar, *f pl*

sugary /'ʃʊgəri/ *a* azucarado; *Fig.* meloso, almibarado

suggest /səg'dʒɛst/ *vt* implicar; indicar, dar a entender; sugerir; (advise) aconsejar; (hint) insinuar; (evoke) evocar. **I suggested they should go to London,** Les aconsejé que fueran a Londres. **An idea suggested itself to him,** Se le ocurrió una idea

suggestion /səg'dʒɛstʃən/ *n* sugestión, *f;* insinuación, *f*

suggestive /səg'dʒɛstɪv/ *a* sugestivo; estimulante

suicidal /,suə'saidḷ/ *a* suicida. **s. tendency,** tendencia suicida, tendencia al suicidio, *f*

suicide /'suə,said/ *n* (act) suicidio, *m;* (person) suicida, *mf.* **to commit s.,** darse la muerte, quitarse la vida suicidarse

suit /sut/ *n* (request) petición, súplica, *f;* oferta de matrimonio, *f; Law.* pleito, *m;* (of clothes) traje, *m;* (cards) palo, *m;* (of cards held) serie, *f, vt* convenir; sentar; ir bien (a); venir bien (a); (adapt) adaptar. **S. yourself!** ¡Haz lo que quieras! **The arrangement suits me very well,** El arreglo me viene muy bien. **The climate doesn't s. me,** El clima no me sienta bien. **The color does not s. you,** El color no te va bien. **to follow s.,** seguir el ejemplo (de); (cards) jugar el mismo palo. **s.-case,** maleta, *f*

suitability /,sutə'bɪlɪti/ *n* conveniencia, *f;* aptitud, *f*

suitable /'sutəbəl/ *a* conveniente; apropiado; apto; a propósito. **Not s. for children,** No apto para menores. **to make s. for,** adaptar a las necesidades de

suitably /'sutəbli/ *adv* convenientemente; apropiadamente

suite /swit/ *n* (of retainers, etc.) séquito, acompañamiento, *m;* (of furniture, etc.) juego, *m; Mus.* suite, *f.* **private s.,** habitaciones particulares, *f pl.* **s. of rooms,** apartamiento, *m*

suitor /'sutər/ *n* *Law.* demandante, *m;* pretendiente, *m*

sulk /sʌlk/ *vi* ponerse malhumorado, ser mohíno

sulkiness /'sʌlkɪnɪs/ *n* mohína, *f,* mal humor, *m*

sulky /'sʌlki/ *a* mohíno, malhumorado

sullen /'sʌlən/ *a* taciturno, hosco; malhumorado, sombrío; (of a landscape, etc.) triste, sombrío

sullenly /'sʌlənli/ *adv* taciturnamente, hoscamente

sullenness /'sʌlənnɪs/ *n* taciturnidad, hosquedad, *f,* mal humor, *m*

sully /'sʌli/ *vt* desdorar, empañar; manchar

sulphur /'sʌlfər/ *n* azufre, *m*

sulphuric /sʌl'fyurɪk/ *a* sulfúrico

sulphurous /'sʌlfərəs/ *a* sulfuroso

sultan /'sʌltn/ *n* sultán, *m*

sultriness /'sʌltrɪnɪs/ *n* bochorno, calor sofocante, *m*

sultry /'sʌltri/ a bochornoso, sofocante

sum /sʌm/ n suma, f; total, m; cantidad, f; (in arithmetic) problema (de aritmética), m. —vt sumar, calcular. **in sum,** en suma; en resumen. **to sum up,** recapitular; resumir; (a person) tomar las medidas (a)

summarily /sə'meərəli/ adv someramente; Law. sumariamente

summarize /'sʌmə,raiz/ vt resumir brevemente; compendiar

summary /'sʌməri/ a somero; Law. sumario. —n resumen, sumario, compendio, m. **summary records,** actas resumidas, f pl

summer /'sʌmər/ n verano, estío, m. **to spend the s.,** veranear. **s.-house,** cenador, m. **s.-time,** verano, m; hora de verano, f. **s. wheat,** trigo tremesino, m

summing-up /'sʌmɪŋ,ʌp/ n recapitulación, f

summit /'sʌmɪt/ n cima, cumbre, f; Fig. apogeo, m

summitry /'sʌmɪtri/ n diplomacia en la cumbre, f

summon /'sʌmən/ vt llamar, hacer venir; mandar, requerir; Law. citar. **to s. up one's courage,** cobrar ánimos

summons /'sʌmənz/ n llamamiento, m; Mil. intimación, f; Law. citación, f. —vt Law. citar

sump /sʌmp/ n (of a motor-car) pozo colector, m; Mineral. sumidero, m

sumptuous /'sʌmptʃuəs/ a suntuoso, lujoso, magnífico

sumptuousness /'sʌmptʃuəsnɪs/ n suntuosidad, magnificencia, f

sun /sʌn/ n sol, m. **The sun was shining,** Hacía sol, El sol brillaba. **to bask in the sun,** tomar el sol. **sunbathing,** baños de sol, m pl. **sun-blind,** toldo para el sol, m. **sun-bonnet,** capelina, f. **sun-glasses,** gafas ahumadas, f pl. **sun-helmet,** casco colonial, m. **sunspot,** Astron. mancha del sol, f; (freckle) peca, f. **sun-worship,** adoración del sol, f

sunbeam /'sʌn,bim/ n rayo de sol, m

sunburn /'sʌn,bɜrn/ n quemadura del sol, f; bronceado, m

sunburnt /'sʌn,bɜrnt/ a quemado por el sol; bronceado, tostado por el sol

sundae /'sʌndei/ n helado de frutas, m

Sunday /'sʌndei/ n domingo, m. **in his S. best,** en su traje dominguero, endomingado. **S. school,** escuela dominical, f

Sunday's child n niño nacido de pies, niño nacido un domingo, niño mimado de la fortuna

sunder /'sʌndər/ vt dividir en dos, hender; separar

sundial /'sʌn,daiəl/ n reloj de sol, reloj solar, m

sundown /'sʌn,daun/ n puesta del sol, f

sundry /'sʌndri/ a varios (-as). —n pl **sundries,** artículos diversos, m pl; Com. varios, m pl. **all and s.,** todo el mundo, todos y cada uno

sunflower /'sʌn,flauər/ n girasol, tornasol, m, trompeta de amor, f

sunken /'sʌŋkən/ a (of eyes, etc.) hundido

sunless /'sʌnlɪs/ a sin sol

sun letter n letra solar, f

sunlight /'sʌn,lait/ n luz del sol, f, rayos del sol, m pl. **artificial s.,** sol artificial, m. **in the s.,** al sol

sunny /'sʌni/ a de sol; bañado de sol; asoleado; expuesto al sol; (face) risueño; (of disposition, etc.) alegre. **to be s.,** hacer sol

sunrise /'sʌn,raiz/ n salida del sol, f. **from s. to sunset,** de sol a sol

sunset /'sʌn,set/ n puesta del sol, f. **at s.,** a la caída (or puesta) del sol

sunshade /'sʌn,ʃeid/ n parasol, quitasol, m, sombrilla, f

sunshine /'sʌn,ʃain/ n luz del sol, f. **in the s.,** al sol

sunstroke /'sʌn,strouk/ n insolación, f

sup /sʌp/ vt sorber. —vi cenar. —n sorbo, m

super /'supər/ n (actor) comparsa, mf; (film) superproducción, f; (of a beehive) alza, f

superabundance /,supərə'bʌndəns/ n superabundancia, sobreabundancia, f

superabundant /,supərə'bʌndənt/ a superabundante, sobreabundante. **to be s.,** sobreabundar

superannuate /,supər'ænyu,eit/ vt (retire) jubilar

superannuated /,supər'ænyu,eitid/ a (retired) jubilado; (out-of-date) anticuado

superannuation /,supər,ænyu'eiʃən/ n (retirement and pension) jubilación, f

superb /su'pərb/ a magnífico, espléndido

superbly /su'pərbli/ adv magníficamente

supercargo /'supər'kargou/ n Naut. sobrecargo, m

supercharger /'supər,tʃardʒər/ n (Auto., Aer.) compresor, m

supercilious /,supər'siliəs/ a altanero, altivo, orgulloso; desdeñoso

superciliousness /,supər'siliəsnɪs/ n altanería, altivez, f, orgullo, m; desdén, m

superficial /,supər'fiʃəl/ a superficial

superficiality /,supər,fiʃi'ælɪti/ n superficialidad, f

superficially /,supər'fiʃəli/ adv superficialmente

superfine /,supər'fain/ a superfino

superfluity /,supər'fluɪti/ n superfluidad, f

superfluous /su'pərfluəs/ a superfluo. **to be s.,** sobrar

superfortress /'supər,fɔrtrɪs/ n Aer. superfortaleza volante, f

superhuman /,supər'hyumən/ a sobrehumano

superimpose /,supərɪm'pouz/ vt sobreponer

superintend /,supərɪn'tend/ vt superentender, dirigir

superintendent /,supərɪn'tendənt/ n superintendente, mf; director (-ra); (school) inspector; (police) subjefe de la policía, m

superior /sə'pɪəriər/ a superior; (in number) mayor; (smug) desdeñoso. —n superior (-ra). **Mother S.,** (madre) superiora, f. **s. to,** superior a; encima de

superiority /sə,pɪəri'ɔrɪti/ n superioridad, f

superlative /sə'pɜrlətɪv/ a extremo, supremo; Gram. superlativo. —n Gram. superlativo, m

superlatively /sə'pɜrlətɪvli/ adv en sumo grado, superlativamente

superman /'supər,mæn/ n superhombre, m

supermarket /'supər,markɪt/ n supermercado, m

supernatural /,supər'nætʃərəl/ a sobrenatural

supernumerary /,supər'numə,reri/ a and n supernumerario (-ia)

superposition /,supərpə'zɪʃən/ n superposición, f

superscribe /'supər,skraib/ vt sobrescribir; poner el sobrescrito (a)

superscription /,supər'skrɪpʃən/ n (on letters, documents) sobrescrito, m; leyenda, f

supersede /,supər'sid/ vt reemplazar; suplantar

supersensible /,supər'sensəbəl/ a suprasensible

superstition /,supər'stɪʃən/ n superstición, f

superstitious /,supər'stɪʃəs/ a supersticioso

supertax /'supər,tæks/ n impuesto suplementario, m

supervene /,supər'vin/ vi sobrevenir

supervise /,supər,vaiz/ vt superentender, vigilar; dirigir

supervision /,supər'vɪʒən/ n superintendencia, f; dirección, f

supervisor /'supər,vaizər/ n superintendente, mf; inspector (-ra); director (-ra)

supine /a. su'pain; n. 'supain/ a supino; indolente, negligente. —n Gram. supino, m

supper /'sʌpər/ n cena, f. **the Last S.,** la Última Cena. **to have s.,** cenar. **s.-time,** hora de cenar, f

supplant /sə'plænt/ vt suplantar; usurpar; reemplazar

supplanter /sə'plæntər/ n suplantador (-ra)

supple /'sʌpəl/ a flexible; dócil, manso; (fawning) adulador, servil, lisonjero

supplement /'sʌpləmənt/ n suplemento, m; (of a book) apéndice, m

supplementary /,sʌplə'mentəri/ a suplementario; adicional

suppleness /'sʌpəlnɪs/ n flexibilidad, f; docilidad, f; servilidad, f

suppliant /'sʌpliənt/ a and n suplicante, mf

supplicate /'sʌpli,keit/ vt and vi suplicar

supplication /, s½pli'keiʃən/ n suplicación, f; súplica, f

supply /sə'plai/ vt proveer (de); suministrar; proporcionar, dar; (a deficiency) suplir; (a post) llenar; (a post temporarily) reemplazar. —n suministro, surtimiento, m; provisión, f; (of electricity, etc.) suministro, m; Com. oferta, f; (person) substituto (-ta); pl **supplies,** Com. existencias, f pl; Mil. pertrechos, m pl;

víveres, *m pl*, provisiones, *f pl*. **s. and demand,** oferta y demanda, *f*

support /sə'pɔrt/ *vt* apoyar, sostener; mantener; (endure) durar; (a cause) apoyar, defender; (corroborate) confirmar, vindicar. —*n* apoyo, *m;* sostén, *m;* soporte, *m*. **to speak in s. of,** defender, abogar por. **to s. oneself,** ganarse la vida, mantenerse

supporter /sə'pɔrtər/ *n* apoyo, *m;* defensor (-ra); partidario (-ia)

suppose /sə'pouz/ *vt* suponer; imaginar(se); creer. **always supposing,** dado que, en el caso de que. **Supposing he had gone out?** ¿Y si hubiera salido? **I don't s. they will go to Spain,** No creo que vayan a España. **He is supposed to be clever,** Tiene fama de listo

supposed /sə'pouzd, -'pouzɪd/ *a* supuesto; que se llama a sí mismo

supposition /ˌsʌpə'zɪʃən/ *n* suposición, hipótesis, *f*

suppress /sə'prɛs/ *vt* reprimir; (yawns, etc.) ahogar; contener; (heresies, rebellions, books, etc.) suprimir; (dissemble) disimular, esconder; (a heckler, etc.) hacer callar

suppressed /sə'prɛst/ *a* reprimido; contenido; disimulado

suppression /sə'prɛʃən/ *n* represión, *f;* supresión, *f;* disimulación, *f*

suppurate /'sʌpyəˌreit/ *vi* supurar

suppuration /ˌsʌpyə'reiʃən/ *n* supuración, *f*

supremacy /sə'prɛməsi/ *n* supremacía, *f*

supreme /sə'prim/ *a* supremo; sumo. **with s. indifference,** con suma indiferencia. **s. court,** tribunal supremo, *m*

surcharge /sɜr'tʃɑrdʒ/ *n* sobrecarga, *f*

sure /ʃʊr/ *a* seguro; cierto. —*adv* seguramente. **Be s. to...!** ¡Ten cuidado de...! ¡No dejes de...! **to be s.,** seguramente, sin duda; ¡claro!; (fancy!) ¡no me digas!; ¡qué sorpresa! **I am not so s. of that,** No diría yo tanto. **Come on Thursday for s.,** Venga el jueves sin falta. **It is s. to rain tomorrow,** Seguramente va a llover mañana. **to make s. of,** asegurarse de. **to be (or feel) s.,** estar seguro. **s.-footed,** de pie firme, seguro

surely /'ʃʊrli/ *adv* seguramente; sin duda, ciertamente; por supuesto

sureness /'ʃʊrnɛs/ *n* seguridad, *f;* certeza, *f*

surety /'ʃʊrti/ *n* garantía, fianza, *f;* (person) garante, *mf*. **to go s. for,** ser fiador (de), salir garante (por)

surf /sɜrf/ *n* resaca, *f;* rompiente, *m;* oleaje, *m*. **s.-board,** aquaplano, *m*. **s.-riding,** patinaje sobre las olas, *m*

surface /'sɜrfɪs/ *n* superficie, *f;* exterior, *m*. —*a* superficial. —*vi* (of a submarine) salir a la superficie. **on the s.,** en apariencia

surface mail *n* correo por vía ordinaria, servicio ordinario, servicio per vía de superficie, *m*

surfeit /'sɜrfɪt/ *n* exceso, *m*, superabundancia, *f;* saciedad, *f*. —*vt* hartar; saciar

surge /sɜrdʒ/ *vi* (of waves) embravecerse, hincharse; (of crowds) agitarse, bullir; (of emotions) despertarse. —*n* (of sea, crowd, blood) oleada, *f;* (of anger) ola, *f*. **The blood surged into his face,** La sangre se le subió a las mejillas

surgeon /'sɜrdʒən/ *n* cirujano, *m;* (*Nav., Mil.*) médico, *m*

surgery /'sɜrdʒəri/ *n* cirugía, *f;* (doctor's) consultorio, *m;* (dispensary) dispensario, *m*

surgical /'sɜrdʒɪkəl/ *a* quirúrgico

surliness /'sɜrlinɪs/ *n* mal genio, *m*, taciturnidad, *f;* brusquedad, *f*

surly /'sɜrli/ *a* taciturno, huraño, malhumorado; brusco

surmise /sər'maiz/ *n* conjetura, suposición, *f*. —*vt* conjeturar, adivinar; imaginar, suponer. —*vi* hacer conjeturas

surmount /sər'maunt/ *vt* superar, vencer; coronar

surname /'sɜrˌneim/ *n* apellido, *m*, *vt* denominar, nombrar

surpass /sər'pæs/ *vt* superar, exceder; aventajarse (a); eclipsar

surpassing /sər'pæsɪŋ/ *a* sin par, incomparable

surplus /'sɜrplʌs/ *n* exceso, sobrante, *m;* (*Com.* of ac-

counts) superávit, *m*. **sale of s. stock,** liquidación de saldos, *f*

surprise /sər'praiz, sə-/ *n* sorpresa, *f;* asombro, *m*. —*vt* sorprender; asombrar. **to s.** (someone) **in the act,** coger en el acto. **to take** (a person) **by s.,** sorprender (a). **He was surprised into admitting it,** Cogido a la imprevista, lo confesó

surprising /sər'praizɪŋ, sə-/ *a* sorprendente

surrealism /sə'riəˌlɪzəm/ *n* surrealismo, *m*

surrealist /sə'riəlɪst/ *a* and *n* surrealista, *mf*

surrender /sə'rɛndər/ *vt* rendir, entregar; (goods) ceder, renunciar (a). —*vi* rendirse, entregarse; abandonarse. —*n* rendición, capitulación, *f;* entrega, *f;* (of goods) cesión, *f;* (of an insurance policy) rescate, *m*. **to s. oneself to remorse,** abandonarse (or entregarse) al remordimiento. **to s. unconditionally,** entregarse a discreción

surreptitious /ˌsɜrəp'tɪʃəs/ *a* subrepticio

surreptitiously /ˌsɜrəp'tɪʃəsli/ *adv* subrepticiamente, a hurtadillas

surround /sə'raund/ *vt* rodear; cercar; *Mil.* asediar, sitiar. —*n* borde, *m*. **Peter was surrounded by his friends,** Pedro estaba rodeado por sus amigos

surrounding /sə'raundɪŋ/ *a* (que está) alrededor de; vecino. **the s. country,** los alrededores

surroundings /sə'raundɪŋz/ *n pl* cercanías, *f pl*, alrededores, *m pl;* (environment) medio, *m;* (medio) ambiente, *m*

surtax /'sɜrˌtæks/ *n* impuesto suplementario, *m*

surveillance /sər'veiləns/ *n* vigilancia, *f*

survey /*v.* sə'vei; *n.* 'sɜrvei/ *vt* contemplar, mirar; (events, etc.) pasar en revista; estudiar; (land, etc.) apear; (a house, etc.) inspeccionar. —*n* vista general, *f;* inspección, *f;* (of facts, etc.) examen, *m;* estudio, *m;* (of land, etc.) apeo, *m;* (of literature, etc.) bosquejo, breve panorama, *m*

surveying /sər'veiɪŋ/ *n* agrimensura, *f*

surveyor /sər'veiər/ *n* agrimensor, *m;* (superintendent) inspector, *m;* superintendente, *m*

survival /sər'vaivəl/ *n* supervivencia, *f*. **s. of the fittest,** supervivencia de los más aptos, *f*

survive /sər'vaiv/ *vt* sobrevivir a. —*vi* sobrevivir; (of customs) subsistir, durar

survivor /sər'vaivər/ *n* sobreviviente, *mf*

susceptibility /səˌsɛptə'bɪlɪti/ *n* susceptibilidad, *f;* tendencia, *f;* *pl* **susceptibilities,** sensibilidad, *f*

susceptible /sə'sɛptəbəl/ *a* susceptible; impresionable; sensible; (to love) enamoradizo. **He is s. to bronchitis,** Es susceptible a la bronquitis

suspect /*a., n.* 'sʌspɛkt; *v.* sə'spɛkt/ *a* and *n* sospechoso (-sa). —*vt* sospechar; dudar; imaginar, suponer. —*vi* tener sospechas

suspend /sə'spɛnd/ *vt* suspender. **suspended animation,** muerte aparente, *f*

suspender /sə'spɛndər/ *n* liga, *f;* *pl* **suspenders,** (braces) tirantes del pantalón, *m pl*. **s.-belt,** faja, *f*

suspense /sə'spɛns/ *n* incertidumbre, *f*. **to keep** (a person) **in s.,** dejar en la incertidumbre (a)

suspension /sə'spɛnʃən/ *n* suspensión, *f*. **s.-bridge,** puente colgante, *m*. **s. of payments,** suspensión de pagos, *f*,

suspicion /sə'spɪʃən/ *n* sospecha, *f;* (touch) dejo, *m;* cantidad muy pequeña, *f*. **to be above s.,** estar por encima de toda sospecha. **to be under s.,** estar bajo sospecha. **I had no suspicions...,** No sospechaba...

suspicious /sə'spɪʃəs/ *a* (by nature) suspicaz; sospechoso. **to make s.,** hacer sospechar

suspiciously /sə'spɪʃəsli/ *adv* suspicazmente, desconfiadamente; de un modo sospechoso. **It seems s. like...,** Tiene toda la apariencia de...

suspiciousness /sə'spɪʃəsnɪs/ *n* carácter sospechoso, *m*, lo sospechoso; suspicacia, *f*

sustain /sə'stein/ *vt* sostener; mantener; sustentar; apoyar; corroborar, confirmar; (a note) prolongar. **to s. injuries,** recibir heridas

sustenance /'sʌstənəns/ *n* mantenimiento, *m;* sustento, *m*, alimentos, *m pl*

suture /'sutʃər/ *n* sutura, *f*

svarabhakti /ˌsfarə'bakti/ *a* esvarabático

svelte /svɛlt/ *a* esbelto, gentil

swab /swɒb/ *vt* *Naut.* lampacear; limpiar con lampazo; *Surg.* tamponar. —*n* lampazo, *m; Surg.* torunda, *f*, tampón, *m*

swaddle /'swɒdl/ *vt* envolver; (infants) fajar

swaddling clothes /'swɒdlɪŋ/ *n pl* pañales, *m pl.* **to be still in s. clothes,** *Fig.* estar en mantillas, estar en pañales

swag /swæg/ *n* botín, *m*

swagger /'swægər/ *vi* fanfarronear, pavonearse; darse importancia. —*n* pavoneo, *m;* aire importante, *m;* (coat) tonto, *m.* —*a* majo; de última moda

swaggering /'swægərɪŋ/ *a* fanfarrón, jactancioso; importante

Swahili /swɑ'hili/ suaili; *n* suaili, *m*

swain /swein/ *n* zagal, *m;* enamorado, *m;* pretendiente, amante, *m*

swallow /'swɒlou/ *vt* tragar, engullir. —*n* trago, *m;* sorbo, *m; Ornith.* golondrina, *f.* **to s. an insult (a story),** tragar un insulto (una historia). **to s. one's words,** retractarse. **to s. one's pride,** bajar la cerviz, humillarse. **to s. up,** tragar; absorber.

swamp /swɒmp/ *n* pantano, *m,* marisma, *f.* —*vt* sumergir; (a boat) echar a pique, hundir; (inundate) inundar

swampy /'swɒmpi/ *a* pantanoso

swan /swɒn/ *n* cisne, *m.* **swan's down,** plumón de cisne, *m.* **s.-song,** canto del cisne, *m*

swank /swæŋk/ *n* pretensiones, *f pl,* *vi* darse humos

sward /swɔrd/ *n* césped, *m,* hierba, *f*

swarm /swɔrm/ *n* enjambre, *m;* (of people) muchedumbre, multitud, *f;* tropel, *m.* —*vi* (of bees) enjambrar; (of other insects) pulular; (of people) hormiguear, bullir, pulular. —*vt* (climb) trepar. **to s. with,** estar infestado de

swarthiness /'swɔrðinɪs/ *n* tez morena, *f;* color moreno, *m*

swarthy /'swɔrði/ *a* moreno

swashbuckler /'swɒʃˌbʌklər, 'swɔʃ-/ *n* perdonavidas, matasiete, *m*

swashbuckling /'swɒʃˌbʌklɪŋ/ *a* matamoros, valentón, fanfarrón

swastika /'swɒstɪkə/ *n* esvástica, cruz gamada, *f*

swathe /swɒð/ *vt* envolver; fajar; (with bandages) vendar

swathing /'swɒðɪŋ/ *n* envoltura, *f;* (bandages) vendas, *f pl*

sway /swei/ *vi* balancearse; oscilar; (stagger, of persons) bambolearse; (totter, of things) tambalearse; (of carriages) cabecear; (gracefully, in walking) cimbrarse. —*vt* balancear, mecer; oscilar; hacer tambalear; (influence) influir, inclinar; (govern) regir, gobernar. —*n* balanceo, *m;* oscilación, *f;* vaivén, *m;* tambaleo, *m;* (influence) ascendiente, dominio, *m,* influencia, *f;* (rule) imperio, poder, *m.* **to hold s. over,** gobernar, regir

swear /swɛər/ *vt* jurar; (*Law.* etc.) declarar bajo juramento. —*vi* jurar; (curse) echar pestes, blasfemar. **to s. at,** maldecir. **to s. by,** jurar por; poner fe implícita en. **to be sworn in,** prestar juramento. **to s. in,** tomar juramento (a). **to s. to,** atestiguar

sweat /swɛt/ *n* sudor, *m; Inf.* trabajo arduo, *m.* —*vi* sudar. —*vt* sudar; hacer sudar; (workers) explotar. **by the s. of one's brow,** con el sudor de la frente, con el sudor del rostro. **s.-gland,** glándula sudorípara, *f*

sweated /'swɛtɪd/ *a* (of persons) explotado; (of labor) mal retribuido

sweater /'swɛtər/ *n* suéter, jersey, *m*

sweating /'swɛtɪŋ/ *n* transpiración, *f;* (of workers) explotación, *f*

sweaty /'swɛti/ *a* sudoroso

Swede /swid/ *n* sueco (-ca); (vegetable) naba, *f*

Sweden /'swidn/ Suecia, *f*

Swedish /'swidɪʃ/ *a* sueco. —*n* (language) sueco, *m*

sweep /swip/ *vi* extenderse (por); (cleave) surcar; pasar rápidamente (por); invadir; dominar; andar majestuosamente; (with a brush) barrer. —*vt* barrer; pasar (por); (the strings of a musical instrument) rasguear; (the sea) navegar por; (mines) barrer; (the horizon, etc.) examinar; (a chimney) deshollinar; (with a brush) barrer; (remove) arrebatar; quitar; llevarse; (abolish) suprimir. **to s. along,** *vt* (of the current, crowds, etc.) arrastrar. —*vi* pasar majestuosamente;

correr rápidamente (por). **to s. aside,** apartar con la mano; abandonar; (a protest) desoír, no hacer caso de. **to s. away,** barrer; (remove) llevarse; destruir; suprimir. **to s. down,** *vt* barrer; (carry) arrastrar. —*vi* (of cliffs, etc.) bajar; (of an enemy) abalanzarse (sobre); lanzarse (por). **to s. off,** barrer; (a person) llevarse sin perder tiempo; arrebatar con violencia (a). **to be swept off one's feet,** ser arrastrado (por); perder el balance; (of emotion) ser dominado por. **to s. up,** recoger, barrer

sweep /swip/ *n* barredura, *f;* (of a chimney) deshollinador, *m;* (of the tide) curso, *m;* (of a scythe, etc.) golpe, *m;* (range) alcance, *m;* (fold) pliegue, *m;* (curve) curva, *f;* (of water, etc.) extensión, *f;* (of wings) envergadura, *f.* **with a s. of the arm,** con un gesto del brazo. **to make a clean s. of,** hacer tabla rasa de

sweeping /'swipɪŋ/ *a* completo; comprensivo; demasiado general; radical. **a s. judgment,** un juicio demasiado general. **s. change,** cambio radicale, *m pl.* **s. brush,** escoba, *f*

sweepings /'swipɪŋz/ *n pl* barreduras, *f pl;* residuos, *m pl;* (of society) heces, *f pl*

sweepstake /'swip,steik/ *n* lotería, *f*

sweet /swit/ *a* dulce; (of scents) oloroso, fragante; (of sounds) melodioso, dulce; (charming) encantador; amable; (pretty) bonito. —*n* bombón, *m;* golosina, *f;* (at a meal) (plato) dulce, *m;* dulzura, *f;* (beloved) amor, *m,* querido (-da). **How s. it smells!** ¡Qué buen olor tiene! **the sweets of life,** las dulzuras de la vida. **s.-pea,** guisante de olor, *m,* haba de las Indias, *f.* **s.-potato,** batata, *f.* **s.-scented,** perfumado, fragante. **s.-tempered,** amable, de carácter dulce. **s.-toothed,** goloso. **s.-william,** *Bot.* clavel de la China, clavel de ramillete, clavel de San Isidro, ramillete de Constantinopla, *m,* minutisa, *f*

sweetbread /'swit,brɛd/ *n* lechecillas, *f pl*

sweeten /'switn/ *vt* azucarar; endulzar. **Cervantes sweetens one's bitter moments,** Cervantes endulza los momentos ásperos

sweetheart /'swit,hɑrt/ *n* amante, *mf,* amado (-da); (as address) querido (-da)

sweetish /'switɪʃ/ *a* algo dulce

sweetly /'switli/ *adv* dulcemente; (of scents) olorosamente; (of sounds) melodiosamente; (of behavior, etc.) amablemente

sweetmeat /'swit,mit/ *n* bombón, dulce, *m*

sweetness /'switnɪs/ *n* dulzura, *f;* (of scents) buen olor, *m,* fragancia, *f;* (of sounds) melodía, dulzura, *f;* (of character) bondad, amabilidad, *f*

sweet potato *n* batata, *f,* boniato, buniato, camote, *m*

sweet sixteen *n* (age) los dieciséis abriles, *m pl;* (party) quinceañera (at age fifteen) *f*

swell /swɛl/ *vi* hincharse; (of the sea) entumecerse; crecer; aumentarse. —*vt* hinchar; aumentar. —*n* (of the sea) oleada, *f,* oleaje, *m;* (of the ground) ondulación, *f;* (of sound) crescendo, *m;* (increase) aumento, *m;* (dandy) pisaverde, elegante, *m;* (important person) pájaro gordo, *m;* (at games, etc.) espada, *m.* —*a* estupendo; elegantísimo; de primera, excelente. **to suffer from swelled head,** tener humos, darse importancia. **This foot is swollen,** Este pie está hinchado (or tumefacto). **The refugees have swelled the population,** Los refugiados han aumentado la población. **eyes swollen with tears,** ojos arrasados de lágrimas. **to s. with pride,** hincharse de orgullo

swelling /'swɛlɪŋ/ *n* hinchazón, *f; Med.* tumefacción, *f;* (bruise, etc.) chichón, *m*

swelter /'swɛltər/ *vi* abrasarse; arder. —*n* bochorno, calor sofocante, *m*

swerve /swɜrv/ *vi* desviarse; apartarse (de); torcerse. —*n* desvío, *m*

swift /swɪft/ *a* rápido, veloz; pronto. —*adv* velozmente, rápidamente. —*n Ornith.* vencejo, *m.* **s.-flowing,** (of rivers, etc.) de corriente rápida. **s.-footed,** de pies ligeros

swiftly /'swɪftli/ *adv* rápidamente, velozmente

swiftness /'swɪftnɪs/ *n* rapidez, velocidad, *f;* prontitud, *f*

swim /swɪm/ *vi* nadar; flotar; (glide) deslizarse; (fill) inundarse. —*vt* (a horse) hacer nadar; pasar a nado; nadar. —*n* natación, *f.* **eyes swimming with tears,**

ojos inundados de lágrimas. **He enjoys a s.,** Le gusta nadar. **My head swims,** Se me va la cabeza. **Everything swam before my eyes,** Todo parecía bailar ante mis ojos. **to be in the s.,** formar parte (de), ser (de); (be up to date) estar al corriente. **to s. with the tide,** ir con la corriente

swimmer /'swɪmər/ n nadador (-ra). **He is a bad s.,** Él nada mal

swimming /'swɪmɪŋ/ n natación, f; (of the head) vértigo, m. **s.-bath,** piscina, f. **s.-costume,** traje de baño, m. **s.-pool,** piscina al aire libre, f

swindle /'swɪndl/ vt engañar, estafar; defraudar (de). —n estafa, f, timo, m; engaño, m; impostura, f

swindler /'swɪndlər/ n estafador (-ra), trampeador (-ra); engañador (-ra)

swine /swaɪn/ n cerdo, puerco, m; (person) cochino (-na). **a herd of s.,** una manada de cerdos

swineherd /'swaɪn,hɜrd/ n porquero, m

swing /swɪŋ/ vi balancearse; oscilar; (hang) colgar, pender; columpiarse; girar; dar la vuelta; (of a boat) bornear. —vt balancear; (hang) colgar; (rock) mecer; (in a swing, etc.) columpiar; hacer oscilar; (raise) subir. —n oscilación, f; vaivén, m; balanceo, m; (rhythm) ritmo, m; (seat, etc.) columpio, m; (reach) alcance, m. **The door swung open,** La puerta se abrió silenciosamente. **He swung the car round,** Dio la vuelta al auto. **He swung himself into the saddle,** Montó de un salto. **to be in full s.,** estar a toda marcha. **to go with a s.,** tener mucho éxito. **s.-bridge,** puente giratorio, m. **s.-door,** puerta giratoria, f

swinging /'swɪŋɪŋ/ a oscilante; pendiente; rítmico. —n balanceo, m; oscilación, f; vaivén, m; ritmo, m. **s. stride,** andar rítmico, m

swinish /'swaɪnɪʃ/ a porcuno, de cerdo; cochino, sucio

swipe /swaɪp/ vt golpear duro; aplastar. —n golpe fuerte, m

swirl /swɜrl/ vi arremolinarse. —n remolino, m

swish /swɪʃ/ vt (of an animal's tail) agitar, mover, menear; (of a cane) blandir; (thrash) azotar. —vi silbar; (of water) susurrar; (of a dress, etc.) crujir. —n silbo, m; (of water) susurro, murmullo, m; (of a dress, etc.) crujido, m

Swiss /swɪs/ a and n suizo (-za)

switch /swɪtʃ/ n vara, f; (riding) látigo, m; (of hair) trenza, f; Elec. interruptor, m; Rail. aguja, f; (Rail. siding) desviadero, m. —vt azotar; (a train) desviar; Elec. interrumpir; (transfer) trasladar; (of an animal, its tail) remover, mover rápidamente. **to s. off,** (Elec. and telephone) cortar; (Radio. and Auto.) desconectar. **to s. on,** conectar; (a light) poner (la luz); (a radio) encender

switchback /'swɪtʃ,bæk/ n subida en zigzag, f; (amusement) montañas rusas, f pl

switchboard /'swɪtʃ,bɔrd/ n cuadro de distribución, m

Switzerland /'swɪtsərlənd/ Suiza, f

swivel /'swɪvəl/ n torniquete, m; anillo móvil, m; pivote, m. —vi girar sobre un eje; dar una vuelta. **s.-chair,** silla giratoria, f. **s.-door,** puerta giratoria, f

swoon /swun/ vi desvanecerse, desmayarse. —n desmayo, desvanecimiento, m

swoop /swup/ vi calarse, abatirse; (of robbers, etc.) abalanzarse (sobre). —n calada, f. **at one fell s.,** de un solo golpe

sword /sɔrd/ n espada, f; sable, m. **to measure swords with,** cruzar espadas con. **to put to the s.,** pasar a cuchillo (a). **s.-arm,** brazo derecho, m. **s.-cut,** sablazo, m. **s.-dance,** danza de espadas, f. **s.-fish,** pez espada, pez sierra, espadarte, m, jifia, f. **s.-play,** esgrima, f; manejo de la espada, m. **s.-thrust,** golpe de espada, m; estocada, f

swordsman /'sɔrdzmən/ n espadachín, m; esgrimidor, m

swordsmanship /'sɔrdzmən,ʃɪp/ n manejo de la espada, m; esgrima, f

sybarite /'sɪbə,raɪt/ a and n sibarita, mf

sybaritic /,sɪbə'rɪtɪk/ a sibarítico, sibarita

sycamore /'sɪkə,mɔr/ n sicomoro, m; falso plátano, m

sycophancy /'sɪkəfənsi/ n servilismo, m

sycophant /'sɪkəfənt/ n sicofanta, m

syllabic /sɪ'læbɪk/ a silábico

syllable /'sɪləbəl/ n sílaba, f

syllabus /'sɪləbəs/ n programa, m; compendio, m

syllogism /'sɪlə,dʒɪzəm/ n silogismo, m

sylph /sɪlf/ n sílfide, f, silfo, m; (woman) sílfide, f; (hummingbird) colibrí, m. **s.-like,** de sílfide; como una sílfide

sylvan /'sɪlvən/ a selvático, silvestre; rústico

symbiosis /,sɪmbi'oʊsɪs/ n simbiosis, f

symbol /'sɪmbəl/ n símbolo, emblema, m; Math. símbolo, m; (of rank, etc.) insignia, f

symbolical /sɪm'bɒlɪkəl/ a simbólico

symbolism /'sɪmbə,lɪzəm/ n simbolismo, m

symbolist /'sɪmbəlɪst/ n simbolista, mf

symbolize /'sɪmbə,laɪz/ vt simbolizar

symmetrical /sɪ'mɛtrɪkəl/ a simétrico

symmetry /'sɪmɪtri/ n simetría, f

sympathetic /,sɪmpə'θɛtɪk/ a simpático; compasivo; (of the public, etc.) bien dispuesto. —n Anat. gran simpático, m. **s. words,** palabras de simpatía, f pl. **s. ink,** tinta simpática, f

sympathetically /,sɪmpə'θɛtɪkli/ adv simpáticamente; con compasión

sympathize /'sɪmpə,θaɪz/ vi simpatizar (con); (understand) comprender; (condole) compadecerse (de), condolerse (de); dar el pésame

sympathizer /'sɪmpə,θaɪzər/ n partidario (-ia)

sympathy /'sɪmpəθi/ n simpatía, f; compasión, f. **Paul is in s. with their aims,** Pablo está de acuerdo con sus objetos. **Please accept my s.,** (on a bereavement) Le acompaño a Vd. en su sentimiento

symphonic /sɪm'fɒnɪk/ a sinfónico

symphony /'sɪmfəni/ n sinfonía, f

symposium /sɪm'poʊziəm/ n colección de artículos, f

symptom /'sɪmptəm/ n síntoma, m; señal, f, indicio, m. **to show symptoms of,** dar indicios de

symptomatic /,sɪmptə'mætɪk/ a sintomático

synagogue /'sɪnə,gɒg/ n sinagoga, f

synchronization /,sɪŋkrənə'zeɪʃən/ n sincronización, f

synchronize /'sɪŋkrə,naɪz/ vi coincidir, tener lugar simultáneamente; sincronizarse. —vt sincronizar

synchronous /'sɪŋkrənəs/ a sincrónico

syncopate /'sɪŋkə,peɪt/ vt (Gram. Mus.) sincopar

syncopation /,sɪŋkə'peɪʃən/ n Mus. síncopa, f

syndical /'sɪndɪkəl/ a sindical

syndicalism /'sɪndɪkə,lɪzəm/ n sindicalismo, m

syndicalist /'sɪndɪkəlɪst/ n sindicalista, mf

syndicate /n. 'sɪndɪkɪt; v. -,keɪt/ n sindicato, m, vt sindicar

syndication /,sɪndɪ'keɪʃən/ n sindicación, f

synod /'sɪnəd/ n Eccl. sínodo, m

synonym /'sɪnənɪm/ n sinónimo, m

synonymous /sɪ'nɒnəməs/ a sinónimo

synopsis /sɪ'nɒpsɪs/ n sinopsis, f

synoptic /sɪ'nɒptɪk/ a sinóptico

syntax /'sɪntæks/ n sintaxis, f

synthesis /'sɪnθəsɪs/ n síntesis, f

synthetic /sɪn'θɛtɪk/ a sintético

synthetize /'sɪnθə,taɪz/ vt sintetizar

syphilis /'sɪfəlɪs/ n sífilis, f

syphilitic /,sɪfə'lɪtɪk/ a and n sifilítico (-ca)

Syracuse /'sɪrə,kyus, -,kyuz/ Siracusa, f

syren /'saɪrən/ n. See **siren**

Syria /'sɪəriə/ Siria, f

Syrian /'sɪəriə/ a and n siríaco (-ca), sirio (-ia)

syringe /sə'rɪndʒ/ n jeringa, f, vt jeringar

syrup /'sɪrəp, 'sɜr-/ n jarabe, m; (for bottling fruit, etc.) almíbar, m

syrupy /'sɪrəpi, 'sɜr-/ a siroposo

system /'sɪstəm/ n sistema, m; régimen, m; método, m; (body) organismo, m. **He has no s. in his work,** No tiene método en su trabajo. **the nervous s.,** el sistema nervioso. **the feudal s.,** el feudalismo, el sistema feudal

systematic /,sɪstə'mætɪk/ a sistemático, metódico

systematically /,sɪstə'mætɪkli/ adv sistemáticamente, metódicamente

systematization /,sɪstəmətə'zeɪʃən/ n sistematización, f

systematize /'sɪstəmə,taɪz/ vt sistematizar

systole /'sɪstə,li/ n Med. sístole, f

T

t /ti/ n (letter) te, f. —*a* en T, en forma de T. **T bandage,** vendaje en T, m. **T square,** regla T, f

tab /tæb/ n oreja, f

tabby /'tæbi/ n gato romano, m; (female) gata, f; Inf. vieja chismosa, f

tabernacle /'tæbər,nækəl/ n tabernáculo, m; templo, m; Archit. templete, m; Eccl. custodia, f

tabes /'teibiz/ n Med. tabes, f

table /'teibəl/ n mesa, f; (food) comida, mesa, f; (of the law, weights, measures, contents, etc.) tabla, f; (of land) meseta, f; (of prices) lista, tarifa, f. —vt (parliament) poner sobre la mesa; enumerar, apuntar, hacer una lista de. **to clear the t.,** alzar (or levantar) la mesa. **to lay the t.,** cubrir (or poner) la mesa. **to have a table d'hôte meal,** tomar el menú. **to rise from the t.,** levantarse de la mesa. **to sit down at the t.,** ponerse a la mesa. **The tables are turned,** Se volvió la tortilla. **side t.,** aparador, trinchero, m. **small t.,** mesilla, f. **t. of contents,** tabla de materias, f, índice, índice de materias, índice general, m. **t.-centrepiece,** centro de mesa, m. **t.-cloth,** mantel, m. **t.-companion,** comensal, mf. **t.-knife,** cuchillo de mesa, m. **t.-lamp,** quinqué, m; lampara de mesa, f. **t.-land,** meseta, f. **t.-leg,** pata de una mesa, f. **t.-linen,** mantelería, f. **t.-napkin,** servilleta, f. **t.-runner,** camino de mesa, m. **t.-spoon,** cuchara para los legumbres, f. **t.-talk,** conversación de sobremesa, f. **t.-turning,** mesas que dan vueltas, f pl. **t.-ware,** artículos para la mesa, m pl

tableau /tæ'blou/ n cuadro, m. **tableaux vivants,** cuadros vivos, m pl

tablespoonful /'teibəlspun,fʊl/ n cucharada, f

tablet /'tæblɪt/ n tabla, f; (with inscription) tarjeta, losa, lápida, f; Med. comprimido, m, tableta, f; (of soap, chocolate) pastilla, f. **writing t.,** taco de papel, m

tabloid /'tæblɔid/ n comprimido, m, pastilla, f

taboo /tə'bu, tæ-/ n tabú, m. —a prohibido, tabú. —vt declarar tabú, prohibir

tabor /'teibər/ n Mus. tamboril, tamborín, m. **t. player,** tamborilero, m

tabouret /,tæbə'ret/ n (stool) taburete, m; (for embroidery) tambor de bordar, m; Mus. tamborilete, m

tabulate /'tæbyə,leit/ vt resumir en tablas; hacer una lista de, catalogar

tabulation /,tæbyə'leiʃən/ n distribución en tablas, f

tacit /'tæsɪt/ a tácito

taciturn /'tæsɪ,tɜrn/ a taciturno, sombrío, reservado, de pocas palabras

taciturnity /,tæsɪ'tɜrnɪti/ n taciturnidad, f; reserva, f

tack /tæk/ n (nail) tachuela, puntilla, f; Sew. hilván, embaste, m; Naut. amura, f; Naut. puño de amura, m; Naut. bordada, f; Fig. cambio de política, m. —vt clavar con tachuelas; Sew. hilvanar, embastar; Fig. añadir. —vi Naut. virar; Fig. cambiar de política, adoptar un nuevo plan de acción. **t. puller,** sacabrocas, m

tackle /'tækəl/ n aparejo, m; maniobra, f; Naut. cuadernal, m, jarcia, f; (gear) aparejos, avíos, m pl; (football) carga, f. —vt agarrar, asir; Fig. atacar, abordar; (football) cargar; (undertake) emprender; (a problem) luchar con. **t.-block,** polea, f

tackling /'tæklɪŋ/ n aparejo, m, maniobra, f; Naut. cordaje, m

tacky /'tæki/ a pegajoso, viscoso

tact /tækt/ n tacto, m, discreción, diplomacia, delicadeza, f

tactful /'tæktfəl/ a lleno de tacto, diplomático, discreto

tactfully /'tæktfəli/ adv discretamente, diplomáticamente

tactical /'tæktɪkəl/ a táctico

tactically /'tæktɪkli/ adv según la táctica; del punto de vista táctico

tactician /tæk'tɪʃən/ n táctico, m

tactics /'tæktɪks/ n pl táctica, f

tactile /'tæktɪl/ a táctil; tangible

tactless /'tæktlɪs/ a que no tiene tacto, sin tacto alguno, indiscreto

tactlessly /'tæktlɪsli/ adv impolíticamente, indiscretamente

tactlessness n falta de tacto, f

tadpole /'tædpoul/ n renacuajo, m

taffeta /'tæfɪtə/ n tafetán, m

tag /tæg/ n herrete, m; (label) marbete, m, etiqueta, f; (of tail) punta del rabo, f; (of boot) tirador de bota, m; (game) marro, m; (rag) arrapiezo, m; (quotation) cita bien conocida, f; (of song, poem) refrán, m. **to play t.,** jugar al marro

Tagus /'teigəs/ el Tajo, m

Tahiti /tə'hiti/ Taití, Tahití, m

tail /teil/ n cola, f, rabo, m; (plait) trenza, f; (wisp of hair) mechón, m; (of a comet) cola, cabellera, f; (of a note in music) rabito, m; (of a coat) faldón, m; (of a kite) cola, f; (of the eye), rabo, m; (retinue) séquito, m, banda, f; (of an aeroplane) cola, f; (end) fin, m; (of coin) cruz, f; (line) fila, cola, f. —vt seguir de cerca, pisarle (a uno) los talones. **to t. after,** seguir de cerca. **to t. away,** disminuir; desaparecer, perderse de vista. **to t. on,** juntar. **to turn t.,** volver la espalda, poner los pies en polvorosa. **with the t. between the legs,** con el rabo entre piernas. **t.-board,** (of a cart) escalera, f. **t.-coat,** frac, m. **t.-end,** extremo, m; fin, m; lo último. **t.-feather,** pena, f. **t.-fin,** aleta caudal, f; Aer. timón de dirección, m. **t.-light,** farol trasero, m. **t.-piece,** (of a violin, etc.) cola, f; Print. marmosete, culo de lámpara, m. **t. spin** Aer. barrena de cola, f. **t. wind,** viento de cola, m

tailed /teild/ a de rabo. **big-t.,** rabudo, de cola grande. **long-t.,** rabilargo. **short-t.,** rabicorto

tailless /'teillɪs/ a rabón, sin rabo

tailor /'teilər/ n sastre (-ra). **t.-made,** m traje sastre, m, a de hechura de sastre. **tailor's shop,** sastrería, f

tailoring /'teilərɪŋ/ n sastrería, f; (work) corte, m

taint /teint/ n corrupción, f; infección, f; (blemish) mancha, f; (tinge) dejo, m. —vt corromper, pervertir; inficionar; (meat) corromper. —vi corromperse, inficionarse; (meat) corromperse

take /teik/ vt tomar; (receive) aceptar; (remove) quitar; (pick up) coger; (grab) asir, agarrar; Math. restar; (carry) llevar; (a person) traer, llevar; (guide) conducir, guiar; (win) ganar; (earn) cobrar, percibir; obtener; (make prisoner) hacer prisionero, prender; (a town, etc.) tomar, rendir, conquistar; (appropriate) apoderarse de, apropiarse; (steal) robar, hurtar; (ensnare) coger, cazar con trampas; (fish) pescar, coger; (a trick, in cards) hacer (una baza); (an illness) contraer, coger; (by surprise) sorprender, coger desprevenido (a); (attract) atraer; (drink) beber; (a meal) tomar; (select) escoger; (hire) alquilar; (suppose) suponer; (use) emplear, usar; (impers., require) necesitarse, hacer falta; (purchase) comprar; (assume) adoptar, asumir; (a leap) dar (un salto); (a walk) dar (un paseo); (a look) echar (un vistazo); (measures) tomar (medidas); (the chair) presidir; (understand) comprender; (a photograph) sacar (una fotografía); (believe) creer; (consider) considerar; (a note) apuntar; (jump over) saltar; (time) tomar, emplear. **I t. size three in shoes,** Calzo el número tres. **to t. to be,** (believe) suponer; (mistake) creer equivocadamente. **to t. (a thing) badly,** tomarlo (or llevarlo) a mal. **The book took me two hours to read,** Necesité dos horas para leer el libro, Leí el libro en dos horas. **And this, I t. it, is Mary?** ¿Y supongo que ésta será María? **to be taken with,** ser entusiasta de; (of persons) estar prendado de. **to t. aback,** desconcertar, coger desprevenido (a). **to t. again,** volver a tomar; llevar otra vez; (a photograph) retratar otra vez. **to t. along,** llevar; traer. **to t. away,** quitar; llevarse. **to t. back,** devolver; (retract) retractar; (receive) recibir (algo) devuelto. **to t. down,** bajar; (a building) derribar; (machinery) desmontar; (hair) deshacerse (el cabello); (swallow) tragar; (in writing) apuntar;

(humble) quitar los humos (a), humillar. **to t. for,** creer, imaginar; (a walk, etc.) llevar a; (mistake) creer erróneamente; tomar por. **Whom do you t. me for?** ¿Por quién me tomas? **to. t. for granted (assume),** dar por descontado, dar por lecho, dar por sentado, dar por supuesto; (underestimate) no hacer caso de, tratar con indiferencia. **t. the lion's share (of),** llevarse la parte del león (de), llevarse la tajada del león (de). **t. shape,** cobrar perfiles más nítidos, estructurarse con más nitidez, ir adquiriendo consistencia, tomar forma. **t. the law into one's own hands,** tomar la justicia por la mano. **to t. from,** privar, quitar de; (subtract) restar; substraer de. **to t. in,** (believe) tragar, creer; (sail) acortar las velas; (deceive) engañar; (lead in) hacer entrar; (accept) recibir, aceptar. **to t. off,** quitar; (surgically) amputar; (one's hat, etc.) quitarse (el sombrero); (eyes) sacar; (take away) llevarse; (mimic) imitar; (ridicule) ridiculizar; (unstick) despegar; (discount) descontar. **to t. on,** emprender; aceptar; (at sports) jugar. **to t. on oneself,** encargarse de, tomar por su cuenta, asumir. **to t. out,** sacar; extraer; (remove) quitar; (outside) llevar fuera; (for a walk) llevar a paseo; (obtain) obtener, sacar; (tire) agotar, rendir. **to t. over,** tomar posesión de; asumir; (show) mostrar, conducir por. **t. the bull by the horns,** ir al toro por los cuernos. **take seriously,** tomar en serio. **to t. up,** subir; (pick up) recoger; tomar; (a challenge, etc.) aceptar; (a dress, etc.) acortar; (absorb) absorber; (of space) ocupar; (of time) ocupar, hacer perder; (buy) comprar; (adopt) dedicarse a; (arrest) arrestar, prender; (criticize) censurar, criticar; (begin) empezar; (resume) continuar

take /teik/ *vt* tomar; (be successful) tener éxito; (of vaccination, etc.) prender; (a good (bad) photograph) salir bien (mal). **to t. after,** salir a, parecerse a; (of conduct) seguir el ejemplo de; **to t. off,** salir; *Aer.* despegar. **to t. on,** *Inf.* lamentarse. **to t. to,** dedicarse a; darse a; (of persons) tomar cariño a; (grow accustomed) acostumbrarse a. **to t. up with,** hacerse amigo de

take /teik/ *n* toma, *f;* cogida, *f; Print.* tomada, *f; Theat.* taquilla, *f.* **t.-in,** engaño, *m.* **t.-off,** *Aer.* (recorrido de) despegue, *m;* caricatura, *f;* sátira, *f*

taker /'teikər/ *n* tomador (-ra)

taking /'teikiŋ/ *n* toma, *f;* secuestro, *m, n pl* **takings,** ingresos, *m pl; Theat.* taquilla, entrada, *f.* —*a* atractivo, encantador; simpático; (of disease) contagioso

talc /tælk/ *n Mineral.* talco, *m*

talcum powder /'tælkəm/ *n* talco, polvo de talco, *m*

tale /teil/ *n* (recital) narración, historia, *f;* relato, *m;* cuento, *m;* leyenda, historia, fábula, *f;* (number) cuenta, *f,* número, *m;* (gossip) chisme, *m.* **old wives' t.,** cuento de viejas, *m.* **to tell a t.,** contar una historia. **to tell tales,** contar cuentos; revelar secretos, chismear

talebearer /'teil,bɛərər/ *n* correveidile, *mf;* chismoso (-sa), soplón (-ona)

talebearing /'teil,bɛəriŋ/ *n* el chismear, *m*

talent /'tælənt/ *n* (coin) talento, *m;* (ability) ingenio, *m;* habilidad, *f.* **the best t. in Spain,** la flor de la cultura española

talented /'tæləntid/ *a* talentoso, ingenioso

talisman /'tælismən/ *n* talismán, *m*

talit /'talis, talit/ *taled, m*

talk /tɔk/ *vi* and *vt* hablar, decir. **to t. business,** hablar de negocios. **to t. for talking's sake,** hablar por hablar. **to t. French,** hablar francés. **to t. nonsense,** decir disparates. **to t. too much,** hablar demasiado; *Inf.* hablar por los codos, irse (a uno) la lengua. **to t. about,** hablar de; conversar sobre. **to t. at,** decir algo a alguien para que lo entienda otro. **Are you talking at me?** ¿Lo dices por mí? **to t. away,** seguir hablando; disipar. **to t. into,** persuadir, inducir (a). **to t. of,** hablar de; charlar sobre. **to t. on,** hablar acerca de (or sobre); (continue) seguir hablando. **to t. out of,** disuadir de. **to t. out of turn,** meterse donde no le llaman, meter la pata. **to t. over,** hablar de; discutir, considerar. **to t. round,** persuadir. **to t. to,** (address) hablar a; (consult) hablar con; (scold) reprender. **to t. to each other,** hablarse. **to t. up,** hablar claro

talk /tɔk/ *n* conversación, *f;* (informal lecture) charla, *f;* (empty words) palabras, *f pl;* (notoriety) escándalo, *m;* rumor, *m.* **There is t. of...,** Se dice que...; Se habla de que. **to give a t.,** dar una charla. **to indulge in small t.,** hablar de cosas sin importancia, hablar de naderías

talkative /'tɔkətɪv/ *a* locuaz, gárrulo, hablador, decidor. **to be very t.,** ser muy locuaz; *Inf.* tener mucha lengua

talkativeness /'tɔkətɪvnɪs/ *n* locuacidad, garrulidad, *f*

talker /'tɔkər/ *n* hablador (-ra), conversador (-ra); (lecturer) orador (-ra); (in a derogatory sense) fanfarrón (-ona), charlatán (-ana). **to be a good t.,** hablar bien, ser buen conversacionista

talking /'tɔkiŋ/ *a* que habla, hablante; (of birds, dolls, etc.) parlero. **to give a good t. to,** dar una peluca (a). **t.-film,** película sonora, *f.* **t.-machine,** fonógrafo, *m*

tall /tɔl/ *a* alto; (of stories) exagerado. **five feet tall,** de cinco pies de altura

tallboy /'tɔl,bɔi/ *n* cómoda alta, *f*

tallness /'tɔlnɪs/ *n* altura, *f;* estatura, talla, *f;* (of stories) lo exagerado

tallow /'tælou/ *n* sebo, *m.* **t. candle,** vela de sebo, *f.* **t. chandler,** velero (-ra). **t.-faced,** con cara de color de cera

tallowy /'tæloui/ *a* seboso

tally /'tæli/ *n* tarja, tara, *f;* cuenta, *f.* —*vt* llevar la cuenta (de). —*vi* estar conforme, cuadrar

Talmud /'talmud/ *n* Talmud, *m*

Talmudic /tal'mudɪk/ *a* talmúdico

tamable /'teiməbəl/ *a* domable, domesticable

tambour /'tæmbʊr, tæm'bʊr/ *n Mus.* tambor, *m;* (for embroidery) tambor (or bastidor) para bordar, *m*

tambourine /,tæmbə'rin/ *n* pandereta, *f*

tame /teim/ *a* domesticado, manso; (spiritless) sumiso; (dull) aburrido, soso. —*vt* domar, domesticar; (curb) reprimir, gobernar, domar, suavizar. **to grow t.,** domesticarse

tameness /'teimnɪs/ *n* mansedumbre, *f;* sumisión, timidez, *f*

tamer /'teimər/ *n* domador (-ra)

taming /'teimiŋ/ *n* domadura, *f.* **The T. of the Shrew,** La Fierecilla Domada

tamp /tæmp/ *vt* apisonar; (in blasting) atacar (un barreno)

tamper /'tæmpər/ *vi* (with) descomponer, estropear; (meddle with) meterse con; (witnesses) sobornar; (documents) falsificar

tampon /'tæmpɒn/ *n Surg.* tampón, tapón, *m, vt* taponar

tan /tæn/ *vt* curtir, adobar; (of sun) tostar, quemar; (slang) zurrar. —*vi* tostarse por el sol. —*n* color café claro, *m;* bronceado, cutis tostado, *m.* —*a* de color café claro

tandem /'tændəm/ *n* tándem, *m*

tang /tæŋ/ *n* (of sword, etc.) espiga, *f;* (flavor) fuerte sabor, *m;* (sound) retintín, *m*

tangent /'tændʒənt/ *a* and *n* tangente *f.* **to go off on a t.,** *Fig.* salir por la tangente

tangerine /,tændʒə'rin/ *a* and *n* tangerino (-na). **t. orange,** naranja mandarina, *f*

tangible /'tændʒəbəl/ *a* tangible; *Fig.* real

Tangier /tæn'dʒiər/ *n* Tánger, *m*

tangle /'tæŋgəl/ *n* embrollo, enredo, nudo, *m;* (of streets) laberinto, *m; Fig.* confusión, *f.* —*vt* embrollar, enmarañar; (entangle) enredar; *Fig.* poner en confusión, complicar. —*vi* enmarañarse

tank /tæŋk/ *n* tanque, depósito (de agua, etc.), *m;* cisterna, *f;* (as a reservoir) aljibe, estanque, *m; Mil.* tanque, carro de asalto, *m*

tankard /'tæŋkərd/ *n* pichel, bock, *m*

tanker /'tæŋkər/ *n* petrolero, *m*

tanned /tænd/ *a* bronceado, quemado por el sol, dorado por el sol

tanner /'tænər/ *n* curtidor, *m;* (slang) medio chelín, *m.* **tanner's scraper,** descarnador, *m.* **tanner's vat,** noque, *m*

tannery /'tænəri/ *n* curtiduría, *f*

tannic /'tænɪk/ a Chem. tánico. **t. acid,** ácido tánico, m

tannin /'tænɪn/ n Chem. tanino, m

tanning /'tænɪŋ/ n curtido, adobamiento, m

tantalize /'tæntḷ,aiz/ vt tentar, atormentar, provocar

tantalizing /'tæntḷ,aizɪŋ/ a tentador, atormentador; provocativo

tantamount /'tæntə,maunt/ a equivalente, igual. **to be t. to,** ser equivalente a

tantrum /'tæntrəm/ n pataleta, rabieta, f, berrinche, m

taoism /'dauɪzəm/ n taoísmo, m

taoist /'daust/ n taoísta, mf

tap /tæp/ n (blow) pequeño golpe, toque ligero, m; palmadita, f; (for drawing water, etc.) grifo, m, llave, f; (of a barrel) canilla, f; (brew of liquor) clase de vino, f; (tap-room) bar con mostrador, m; (tool) macho de terraja, m; (piece of leather on shoe) tapa, f; pl **taps,** Mil. toque de apagar las luces, m. —vt (strike) golpear ligeramente, dar una palmadita a; (pierce) horadar; (a barrel) decentar; Surg. hacer una puntura en; (trees) sangrar; Elec. derivar (una corriente); (of water, current) tomar; (information) descubrir; (telephone) escuchar las conversaciones telefónicas. —vi golpear ligeramente. **to tap at the door,** llamar suavemente a la puerta. **on tap,** en tonel. **screw-tap,** terraja, f. **tap-dance,** claqué, m. **tap-root,** raíz pivotante, f

tape /teip/ n (linen) cinta de hilo, f; (cotton) cinta de algodón, f; (telegraph machine) cinta de papel, f; (surveying) cinta para medir, f. **adhesive t.,** cinta adhesiva, f. **red t.,** balduque, m; Fig. burocracia, f; formulismo, m. **t.-machine,** telégrafo de cotizaciones, bancarias, m. **t.-measure,** cinta métrica, f

taper /'teipər/ n bujía, cerilla, f; Eccl. cirio, m. —vi ahusarse, rematar en punta. —vt afilar

tapering /'teipərɪŋ/ a cónico, piramidal; (of fingers) afilado

tapestried /'tæpəstrid/ a cubierto de tapices, tapizado

tapestry /'tæpəstri/ n tapiz, m. **t. weaver,** tapicero, m

tapeworm /'teip,wɜrm/ n tenia, lombriz solitaria, f

tapioca /,tæpi'oukə/ n tapioca, f

tapir /'teipər/ n Zool. danta, f

tar /tɑr/ n alquitrán, m, brea, f. —vt embrear, alquitranar. **to tar and feather,** emplumar. **coal t.,** alquitrán mineral, m

tarantella /,tærən'telə/ n tarantela, f

tarantula /tə'ræntʃələ/ n tarántula, f

tardily /'tardḷi/ adv tardíamente; lentamente

tardiness /'tardɪnɪs/ n tardanza, lentitud, f

tardy /'tardi/ a (late) tardío; (slow) lento; (reluctant) desinclinado

tare /teər/ n Bot. yero, m; (in the Bible) cizaña, f; Com. tara, f; (of a vehicle) peso en vacío, m

target /'targɪt/ n blanco (de tiro), m; (shield) rodela, tarja, f. **t. practice,** tiro al blanco, m

tariff /'tærɪf/ n tarifa, f. **to put a t. on,** tarifar

tarlatan /'tarlətn/ n tarlatana, f

tarmac /'tarmæk/ n alquitranado, m

tarn /tarn/ n lago de montaña, m

tarnish /'tarnɪʃ/ n deslustre, m. —vt deslustrar, empañar; Fig. obscurecer, manchar. —vi deslustrarse

tarpaulin /tar'pɔlɪn, 'tarpəlɪn/ n alquitranado, encerado, m

tarred /tard/ a alquitranado, embreado

tarring /'tarɪŋ/ n embreadura, f

tarry /'tari/ vi tardar, detenerse

tart /tart/ a ácido, acerbo, agridulce; Fig. áspero. —n tarta, f; pastelillo de fruta, m

tartan /'tartn/ n Naut. tartana, f; (plaid) tartán, m

tartar /'tartər/ n Chem. tártaro, m; (in teeth) sarro, tártaro, m; **cream of t.,** (cremor) tártaro, m. **t. emetic,** tártaro emético, m. **Tartar,** a and n tártaro (-ra)

Tartary /'tartəri/ Tartaria, f

tartly /'tartli/ adv ásperamente, agriamente

tartness /'tartnɪs/ n acidez, f; Fig. aspereza, f

task /tæsk/ n tarea, labor, f; empresa, f; misión, f. **to take to t.,** regañar, censurar. **t.-force,** (naval or military) contingente, m

taskmaster /'tæsk,mæstər/ n el que señala una tarea; amo, m

tassel /'tæsəl/ n borla, f; (of corn) panoja, espiga, f

taste /teist/ n gusto, m; (flavor) sabor, m; (specimen) ejemplo, m, idea, f; (small quantity) un poco, muy poco; (liking) afición, inclinación, f; (of drink) sorbo, trago, m; (tinge) dejo, m. —vt (appraise) probar; gustar, percibir el gusto de; (experience) experimentar, conocer. —vi tener gusto, tener sabor. **a matter of t.,** cuestión de gusto. **Each to his own t.,** Entre gustos no hay disputa. **He had not tasted a bite,** No había probado bocado. **in bad (good) t.,** de mal (buen) gusto; de mal (buen) tono. **to have a t. for,** ser aficionado a, gustar de. **to t.,** Cul. a gusto, a sabor. **to t. of,** tener gusto de, saber a

tasted /'teistid/ a (in compounds) de sabor...

tasteful /'teistfəl/ a de buen gusto

tastefully /'teistfəli/ adv con buen gusto

tastefulness /'teistfəlnɪs/ n buen gusto, m

tasteless /'teistlɪs/ a insípido, soso, insulso; de mal gusto

tastelessness /'teistlɪsnɪs/ n insipidez, insulsez, f; mal gusto, m

taster /'teistər/ n catador, m; (vessel) catavino, m

tasting /'teistɪŋ/ n saboreo, m, gustación, f, a (in compounds) de sabor...

tasty /'teisti/ a apetitoso, sabroso

tatter /'tætər/ n andrajo, harapo, m; jirón, m. **to tear in tatters,** hacer jirones

tattered /'tætərd/ a andrajoso, haraposo

tatting /'tætɪŋ/ n frivolité, m

tattoo /tæ'tu/ n tatuaje, m; Mil. retreta, f; (display) parada militar, f. —vt tatuar

tattooing /tæ'tuɪŋ/ n tatuaje, m; tamboreo, m

taunt /tɔnt/ n mofa, f, insulto, escarnio, m. —vt insultar, atormentar. **to t. with,** echar en cara

taunting /'tɔntɪŋ/ a insultante, burlón, insolente

tauntingly /'tɔntɪnli/ adv burlonamente, insolentemente

Taurus /'tɔrəs/ n tauro, toro, m

taut /tɔt/ a tieso, tirante, tenso; en regla; Naut. **to make t.,** tesar

tauten /'tɔtn/ vt tesar; poner tieso

tautness /'tɔtnɪs/ n tensión, f

tautological /,tɔtḷ'pdʒɪkəl/ a tautológico

tautology /tɔ'tɒlədʒi/ n tautología, f

tavern /'tævərn/ n taberna, f; (inn) mesón, m, posada, f. **t.-keeper,** tabernero, m

tawdrily /'tɔdrɪli/ adv llamativamente, de un modo cursi

tawdriness /'tɔdrɪnɪs/ n charrería, f

tawdry /'tɔdri/ a chillón, charro, cursi

tawny /'tɔni/ a leonado

tax /tæks/ n contribución, gabela, imposición, f; Fig. carga, f; vt imponer contribuciones (a); Law. tasar; Fig. cargar, abrumar. **to tax with,** tachar (de), acusar (de). **direct (indirect) tax,** contribución directa (indirecta), f. **tax-collector,** recaudador de contribuciones, m. **tax-free,** libre de impuestos. **tax-rate,** tarifa de impuestos, f, cupo, m. **tax-register,** lista de contribuyentes, f

taxable /'tæksəbəl/ a imponible, sujeto a impuestos

taxation /tæk'seiʃən/ n imposición de contribuciones (or impuestos), f

tax evasion n evasión tributaria, f

taxi /'tæksi/ n taxi, m. —vi ir en un taxi; Aer. correr por tierra. **t. driver,** chófer o un taxi, taxista, m. **t. rank, taxi stand,** parada de taxis, f

taxidermist /'tæksɪ,dɜrmɪst/ n taxidermista, mf

taxidermy /'tæksɪ,dɜrmi/ n taxidermia, f

taximeter /'tæksi,mitər/ n taxímetro, m

taxpayer /'tæks,peiər/ n contribuyente, mf

taxpaying /'tæks,peiɪŋ/ a tributario, que paga contribuciones

tax reform n reforma impositiva, reforma tributaria, f

tea /ti/ n (liquid) té, m; (meal) merienda, f. **to have tea,** tomar el té, merendar. **tea-caddy,** bote para té, m. **tea-chest,** caja para té, f. **tea-cosy,** cubretetera, m. **tea-cup,** taza para té, f. **tea-dance,** té baile, m. **tea-kettle** or **tea-pot,** tetera, f. **tea-leaf,** hoja de té, f. **tea-party,** reunión para tomar el té, f. **tea-room,** salón de té, *m.* **tea-rose,** rosa de té, *f.* **tea-set,** juego de té, *m.* **tea-strainer,** colador de té, *m.* **tea-time,** hora de té, *f.* **tea-urn,** samovar, *m,* tetera para hacer té, *f.* **tea-waggon,** carrito para el té, *m*

teach /titʃ/ *vt* (a person) enseñar, instruir; (a subject) enseñar; (to lecture on) ser profesor de; (a lesson) dar una lección (de). —*vi* (be a teacher) dedicarse a la enseñanza. **to teach at...,** desempeñor una cátedra en... **to t. a person Spanish,** enseñar el castellano a alguien. **to t. how to,** enseñar a (followed by infin.)

teachability /ˌtitʃə'bɪlɪti/ *n* docilidad, *f*
teachable /'titʃəbəl/ *a* educable; dócil
teacher /'titʃər/ *n* preceptor, *m;* profesor, maestro, *m.* **woman t.,** profesora, maestra, *f*
teaching /'titʃɪŋ/ *n* enseñanza, *f;* (belief) doctrina, *f,* a docente. **t. profession,** magisterio, *m*
teaching method *n* método didáctico, *f*
teak /tik/ *n Bot.* teca, *f;* (wood) madera de teca, *f*
team /tim/ *n* (of horses) tiro, *m;* (of oxen, mules) par, *m,* pareja, yunta, *f; Sports.* partido, equipo, *m;* compañía, *f,* grupo, *m.* —*vt* enganchar, uncir. **t.-work,** cooperación, *f*
teamster /'timstər/ *n* gañán, *m*
tear /tɪər/ *vt* rasgar; romper; lacerar; (in pieces) hacer pedazos, despedazar; (scratch) arañar; *Fig.* atormentar. **to t. asunder,** romper; desmembrar. **to t. away,** arrancar, quitar violentamente. **to t. down,** derribar, echar abajo. **to t. off,** arrancar; desgajar. **to t. oneself away,** arrancarse, desgarrarse. **to t. one's hair,** arrancarse los pelos, mesarse. **to t. open,** abrir apresuradamente. **to t. up,** hacer pedazos; (uproot) arrancar, desarraigar.
tear /tɛər/ *vi* rasgarse; romper; correr precipitadamente. **to t. along,** correr rápidamente (por). **to t. away,** marcharse corriendo. **to t. down,** bajar corriendo. **to t. into,** entrar corriendo en. **to t. off,** irse precipitadamente, marcharse corriendo. **to t. up,** subir corriendo; llegar corriendo; atravesar rápidamente
tear /tɛər/ *n* lágrima, *f;* (drop) gota, *f.* **with tears in one's eyes,** con lágrimas en los ojos. **to shed tears,** llorar, lagrimear. **to wipe away one's tears,** secarse las lágrimas. **t.-drop,** lágrima, *f.* **t.-duct,** conductor lacrimal, *m.* **t.-gas,** gas lacrimante, *m.* **t.-stained,** mojado de lágrimas
tear /tɛər/ *n* (rent) rasgón, *m*
tearful /'tɪərfəl/ *a* lloroso, lacrimoso
tearfully /'tɪərfəli/ *adv* con lágrimas en los ojos
tearing *n* rasgadura, *f,* desgarro, *m*
tearjerker /'tɪərˌdʒɜrkər/ *n* drama lacrimón, *m*
tease /tiz/ *vt* (card) cardar; (annoy) fastidiar, irritar, molestar; (chaff) tomar el pelo (a), embromar; (pester) importunar. —*n* bromista, *mf*
teasel /'tizəl/ *n Bot.* cardencha, *f,* *vt* cardar
teaser /'tizər/ *n* (problem) rompecabezas, *m;* (person) bromista, *mf*
teaspoon /'tiˌspun/ *n* cucharita, *f*
teaspoonful /'tispun,fʊl/ *n* cucharadita, *f*
teat /tit, tɪt/ *n* pezón, *m;* (of animals) teta, *f*
technical /'tɛknɪkəl/ *a* técnico. **t. offence,** *Law.* cuasidelito, *m.* **t. school,** escuela industrial, *m*
technicality /ˌtɛknɪ'kælɪti/ *n* carácter técnico, *m;* tecnicismo, *m;* detalle técnico, *m*
technician /tɛk'nɪʃən/ *n* técnico, *m*
technicolor /'tɛknɪˌkʌlər/ *n* tecnicolor, *m*
technique /tɛk'nik/ *n* técnica, *f;* ejecución, *f;* mecanismo, *m*
technological /ˌtɛknə'lɒdʒɪkəl/ *a* tecnológico
technologist /tɛk'nɒlədʒɪst/ *n* tecnólogo, *m*
technology /tɛk'nɒlədʒi/ *n* tecnología, *f*
teddy bear /'tɛdi/ *n* osito de trapo, *m*
tedious /'tidiəs/ *a* aburrido, tedioso, pesado
tediously /'tidiəsli/ *adv* aburridamente
tediousness /'tidiəsnɪs/ *n* aburrimiento, *m,* pesadez, *f*
tedium /'tidiəm/ *n* tedio, *m,* monotonía, *f*
tee /ti/ *n Sports.* meta, *f;* (golf) tee, *m;* (letter) te, *f;* cosa en forma de te, *f.* —*vt* (golf) colocar la pelota en el tee
teem /tim/ *vi* rebosar (de), abundar (en); pulular, hormiguear, estar lleno (de); (with rain) diluviar
teeming /'timɪŋ/ *a* prolífico, fecundo. **t. with,** abundante en, lleno de

teens /tinz/ *n pl* números y años desde trece hasta diez y nueve; edad de trece a diez y nueve años de edad. **to be still in one's t.,** no haber cumplido aún los veinte
teeter /'titər/ *vi* balancearse, columpiarse
teethe /tið/ *vi* endentecer, echar los dientes
teething /'tiðɪŋ/ *n* dentición, *f.* **t.-ring,** chupador, *m*
teetotal /ti'toutl/ *a* abstemio
teetotalism /ti'toutl,ɪzəm/ *n* abstinencia completa de bebidas alcohólicas, *f*
teetotaller /'ti,toutlər/ *n* abstemio (-ia)
teetotum /ti'toutəm/ *n* perinola, *f*
telecast /'tɛlɪ,kæst/ *vt* teledifundir
telecommunication /ˌtɛlɪkə,myunɪ'keɪʃən/ *n* telecomunicación, *f*
telegram /'tɛlɪ,græm/ *n* telegrama, *f*
telegraph /'tɛlɪ,græf/ *n* telégrafo, *m.* —*vi* telegrafiar; *Fig.* hacer señas. —*vt* telegrafiar, enviar por telégrafo. **t. line,** línea telegráfica, *f.* **t. office,** central de telégrafos, *f.* **t. pole,** poste telegráfico, *m.* **t. wire,** hilo telegráfico, *m*
telegraphic /ˌtɛlɪ'græfɪk/ *a* telegráfico
telegraphist /tə'lɛgrəfɪst/ *n* telegrafista, *mf*
telegraphy /tə'lɛgrəfi/ *n* telegrafía, *f.* **wireless t.,** telegrafía sin hilos, *f*
telemetry /tə'lɛmɪtri/ *n* telemetría, *f*
teleology /ˌtɛli'ɒlədʒi/ *n* teleología, *f*
telepathic /ˌtɛlə'pæθɪk/ *a* telepático
telepathy /tə'lɛpəθi/ *n* telepatía, *f*
telephone /'tɛləˌfoun/ *n* teléfono, *m.* —*vi* telefonear. —*vt* telefonear, llamar por teléfono. **to be on the t.,** (speaking) estar communicando; (of subscribers) tener teléfono. **dial t.,** teléfono automático, *m.* **t. call,** comunicación telefónica, *f;* conversación telefónica, *f.* **t. call box,** teléfono público, *m.* **t. directory,** guía de teléfonos, *f.* **t. exchange,** central telefónica, *f.* **t. number,** número de teléfono, *m.* **t. operator,** telefonista, *mf.* **t. receiver,** receptor telefónico, *m.* **t. wire,** hilo telefónico, *m*
telephonic /ˌtɛlə'fɒnɪk/ *a* telefónico
telephonist /tə'lɛfənɪst/ *n* telefonista, *mf*
telephony /tə'lɛfəni/ *n* telefonía, *f.* **wireless t.,** telefonía sin hilos, *f*
teleprinter /'tɛlə,prɪntər/ *n* teletipo, *m*
telescope /'tɛlə,skoup/ *n* telescopio, catalejo, *m.* —*vt* enchufar. —*vi* enchufarse, meterse una cosa dentro de otra
telescopic /ˌtɛlə'skɒpɪk/ *a* telescópico; de enchufe
televise /'tɛlə,vaiz/ *vt* trasmitir por televisión
television /'tɛlə,vɪʒən/ *n* televisión, *f.* **on television,** por televisión. **I saw her on television,** La vi por televisión
television series *n* serie televisiva, *f*
tell /tɛl/ *vt* contar, narrar; decir; revelar; expresar; (the time, of clocks) marcar; (inform) comunicar, informar; (show) indicar, manifestar; (explain) explicar; distinguir; (order) mandar; (compute) contar. —*vi* decir; (have effect) producir efecto. **We cannot t.,** No sabemos. **Who can t.?** ¿Quién sabe? **T. that to the marines!,** ¡Cuéntaselo a tu tía! **to t. its own tale,** hacer ver por sí mismo lo que hay. **to t. again,** volver a decir; contar otra vez. **to t. off,** regañar, reñir; (on a mission) despachar, mandar. **to t. on,** delatar. **to t. upon,** afectar
teller /'tɛlər/ *n* narrador (-ra); (of votes) escrutador (-ra) de votos; (payer) pagador; (bank) cajero (-ra), *m*
telling /'tɛlɪŋ/ *a* notable, significante. —*n* narración, *f*
telltale /'tɛl,teil/ *n* chismoso (-sa), soplón (-ona); (informer) acusón (-ona); *Fig.* indicio, *m,* señal, *f,* a revelador
temerity /tə'mɛrɪti/ *n* temeridad, *f*
temper /'tɛmpər/ *n* (of metals) temple, *m;* (nature) naturaleza, *f,* carácter, *m;* espíritu, *m;* (mood) humor, *m;* (anger) mal genio, *m.* —*vt* (of metals) templar; moderar, mitigar; mezclar. —*vi* templarse. **bad (good) t.,** mal (buen) humor. **to keep one's t.,** no enojarse, no impacientarse. **to lose one's t.,** enojarse, perder la paciencia
tempera /'tɛmpərə/ *n Art.* templa, *f.* **in t.,** al temple, *m*
temperament /'tɛmpərəmənt, -prəmənt/ *n* tempera-·

mento, *m;* modo de ser, natural, *m,* naturaleza, índole, *f; Mus.* temple, *m*

temperamental /ˌtempərə'mentḷ, -prə'men-/ *a* natural, innato; caprichoso

temperamentally /ˌtempərə'mentḷi, -prə'men- *adv* por naturaleza

temperance /'tempərəns/ *n* moderación, templanza, *f;* sobriedad, abstinencia, *f*

temperate /'tempərit/ *a* moderado; sobrio; (of regions) templado. **t. zone,** zona templada, *f*

temperately /'tempəritli/ *adv* sobriamente

temperateness /'tempəritnis/ *n* moderación, sobriedad, mesura, *f;* (of regions) templanza, *f*

temperature /'tempərətʃər/ *n* temperatura, *f.* **to have a t.,** tener fiebre

tempered /'tempərd/ *a* de humor..., de genio... **to be good (bad) t.,** ser de buen (mal) humor

tempering /'tempəriŋ/ *n* temperación, *f*

tempest /'tempist/ *n* tempestad, borrasca, *f,* temporal, *m; Fig.* tormenta, *f*

tempest in a teapot borrasca en un vaso de agua, *m*

tempestuous /tem'pestʃuəs/ *a* tempestuoso, borrascoso; *Fig.* impetuoso, violento

tempestuousness /tem'pestʃuəsnis/ *n* lo tempestuoso; *Fig.* impetuosidad, violencia, *f*

temple /'tempəl/ *n* templo, *m; Anat.* sien, *f*

tempo /'tempou/ *n Mus.* tiempo, *m*

temporal /'tempərəl/ *a* temporal; (transient) transitorio, fugaz; *Anat.* temporal. —*n Anat.* hueso temporal, *m*

temporality /ˌtempə'ræliti/ *n* temporalidad, *f*

temporarily /ˌtempə'reərəli/ *adv* provisionalmente

temporariness /'tempə,rerinis/ *n* interinidad, *f*

temporary /'tempə,reri/ *a* provisional, interino

temporize /'tempə,raiz/ *vi* ganar tiempo; contemporizar

temporizing /'tempə,raiziŋ/ *n* contemporización, *f, a* contemporizador

tempt /tempt/ *vt* tentar; atraer, seducir

temptation /temp'teiʃən/ *n* tentación, *f;* aliciente, atractivo, *m*

tempter /'temptər/ *n* tentador (-ra)

tempting /'temptiŋ/ *a* tentador, atrayente; seductor

ten /ten/ *a* diez; (of the clock) las diez, *f pl;* (of age) diez años, *m pl,* n diez, *m;* (a round number) decena, *f;* **ten-millionth,** *a* and *n* diezmillonésimo *m.* **ten months old,** diezmesino. **ten syllable,** decasílabo. **ten thousand,** *a* and *n* diez mil *m.* **There are ten thousand soldiers,** Hay diez mil soldados. **ten-thousandth,** *a* and *n* diezmilésimo *m*

tenable /'tenəbəl/ *a* sostenible, defendible

tenacious /tə'neiʃəs/ *a* tenaz; (stubborn) porfiado, obstinaz, terco; (sticky) adhesivo. **to be t. of life,** estar muy apegado a la vida

tenaciously /tə'neiʃəsli/ *adv* tenazmente; porfiadamente

tenacity /tə'næsiti/ *n* tenacidad, *f;* porfía, *f;* tesón, *m*

tenancy /'tenənsi/ *n* inquilinato, *m;* tenencia, *f*

tenant /'tenənt/ *n* arrendatario (-ia), inquilino (-na); habitante, *m;* morador (-ra)

tench /tentʃ/ *n Ichth.* tenca, *f*

tend /tend/ *vt* cuidar, atender; guardar; vigilar. —*vi* tender; inclinarse (a), propender (a)

tendency /'tendənsi/ *n* tendencia, inclinación, propensión, *f;* proclividad, *f*

tendentious /ten'denʃəs/ *a* tendencioso

tender /'tendər/ *n* guardián, *m; Com.* oferta, propuesta, *f; Naut.* falúa, *f;* (of a railway engine) ténder, *m.* **legal t.,** moneda corriente, *f*

tender /'tendər/ *a* tierno; delicado; (of conscience) escrupuloso; (of a subject) espinoso; compasivo, afectuoso, sensible; muelle, blando. **t.-hearted,** compasivo, tierno de corazón

tender /'tendər/ *vt* ofrecer; dar; presentar. —*vi* hacer una oferta. **to t. condolences,** dar el pésame. **to t. one's resignation,** presentar la dimisión. **to t. thanks,** dar las gracias

tenderly /'tendərli/ *adv* tiernamente

tenderness /'tendərnis/ *n* ternura, *f;* sensibilidad, *f;* delicadeza, *f;* dulzura, *f;* indulgencia, *f;* compasivi-

dad, benevolencia, *f;* escrupulosidad, *f;* mimo, cariño, *m*

tendon /'tendən/ *n Anat.* tendón, *m.* **t. of Achilles,** tendón de Aquiles, *m*

tenement /'tenəmənt/ *n* casa de vecindad, *f;* vivienda, *f; Poet.* morada, *f*

Teneriffe /ˌtenə'rif/ Tenerife, *f*

tenet /'tenit/ *n* principio, dogma, *m,* doctrina, *f*

tenfold /a.'ten,fould/ *adv.* -'fould/ *a* décuplo. —*adv* diez veces

tennis /'tenis/ *n* tenis, *m.* **to play t.,** jugar al tenis. **t. ball,** pelota de tenis, *f.* **t. court,** campo de tenis, *m,* cancha de tenis, pista de tenis, *f.* **tennis club,** club de tenis, *m.* **t. racket,** raqueta de tenis, *f;* **tennis shoe,** zapatilla de tenis, *f*

tenon /'tenən/ *n* espiga, *f, vt* espigar

tenor /'tenər/ *n* curso, *m;* tenor, contenido, *m; Mus.* tenor, *m; Mus.* alto, *m;* (mus. instrument) viola, *f.* —*a Mus.* de tenor

tense /tens/ *n Gram.* tiempo, *m.* —*a* tirante, estirado, tieso; tenso

tenseness /'tensnis/ *n* tirantez, *f;* tensión, *f*

tensile /'tensəl/ *a* tensor; extensible

tension /'tenʃən/ *n* tensión, *f; Elec.* voltaje, *m,* tensión, *f;* (of sewing-machine) tensahílo, *m.* **state of t.,** (diplomatic) estado de tirantez, *m*

tent /tent/ *n* tienda (de campaña), *f;* (bell) pabellón, *m; Surg.* tienda, *f.* **oxygen t.,** tienda oxígena, *f.* **to pitch tents,** armar las tiendas de campaña; acamparse. **to strike tents,** plegar tiendas. **t. fly,** toldo de tienda, *m.* **t. maker,** tendero, *m.* **t. peg,** clave que sujeta las cuerdas de una tienda, *f.* **t. pole,** mástil (or montante) de tienda, *m*

tentacle /'tentəkəl/ *n* tentáculo, *m*

tentative /'tentətiv/ *a* tentativo, interino, provisional, de prueba, *n* tentativa, *f,* ensayo, *m*

tentatively /'tentətivli/ *adv* por vía de ensayo, experimentalmente

tenth /tenθ/ *a* décimo; (of monarchs) diez; (of the month) (el) diez. —*n* décimo, *m;* (part) décima parte, *f; Mus.* decena, *f*

tenthly /'tenθli/ *adv* en décimo lugar

tenuity /tə'nuiti/ *n* tenuidad, *f;* sutilidad, *f;* delgadez, *f*

tenuous /'tenyuəs/ *a* tenue; sutil; delgado; fino

tenure /'tenyər/ *n* tenencia, posesión, *f;* (duration) duración, *f;* (of office) administración, *f*

tepid /'tepid/ *a* tibio

tepidity /tə'piditi/ *n* tibieza, *f*

tercentenary /ˌtɜrsen'tenəri/ *n* tercer centenario, *m*

tercet /'tɜrsit/ *n* terceto, *m*

term /tɜrm/ *n* (limit) límite, fin, *m;* (period) plazo, tiempo, período, *m;* (schools, universities) trimestre, *m;* (Math. Law. Logic.) término, *m;* (word) expresión, palabra, *f* pl. **terms,** (conditions) condiciones, *f pl;* (charges) precios, *m, pl,* tarifa, *f;* (words) términos, *m pl,* palabras, *f pl.* —*vt* llamar, calificar. **for a t. of years,** por un plazo de años. **in plain terms,** en palabras claras. **on equal terms,** en condiciones iguales. **to be on bad (good) terms with,** estar en (or tener) malas (buenas) relaciones con. **to come to terms,** llegar a un acuerdo; hacer las paces. **What are your terms?** ¿Cuáles son sus condiciones? (price) ¿Cuáles son sus precios? **terms of sale,** condiciones de venta, *f pl*

termagant /'tɜrməgənt/ *n* arpía, fiera, *f*

terminable /'tɜrmənəbəl/ *a* terminable

terminal /'tɜrmənl/ *a* terminal, final; (of schools, universities) trimestre. —*n* término, *m; Elec.* borne, *m;* (schools, universities) examen de fin de trimestre, *m;* (railway) estación terminal, *f;* (Archit. and figure) término, *m; Archit.* remate, *m*

terminate /'tɜrmə,neit/ *vt* limitar; terminar, concluir, poner fin (a). —*vi* terminarse, concluirse (por); cesar

termination /ˌtɜrmə'neiʃən/ *n* terminación, conclusión, *f;* fin, *m; Gram.* terminación, *f;* cabo, remate, *m*

terminology /ˌtɜrmə'nɒlədʒi/ *n* nomenclatura, terminología, *f*

terminus /'tɜrmənəs/ *n* (railway) estación terminal, *f;* (Archit. and figure) término, *m; Archit.* remate, *m; Myth.* Término

termite /'tɜrmait/ *n Ent.* termita, *m*

term paper *n* trabajo de examen, *m*
terms of trade *n* relación de los precios de intercambio, *f*
terrace /'terəs/ *n* terraza, *f*, *vt* terraplenar
terraced /'terəst/ *a* en terrazas; con terrazas
terracotta /ˌterə'kɒtə/ *n* terracota, *f*
terrain /tə'rein/ *n* terreno, campo, *m*, región, *f*
terrapin /'terəpin/ *n* tortuga de agua dulce, *f*
terrestrial /tə'restriəl/ *a* terrestre, terrenal
terrible /'terəbəl/ *a* terrible, pavoroso, espantoso; *Inf.* tremendo
terribleness /'terəbəlnɪs/ *n* terribilidad, *f*, lo horrible
terrier /'teriər/ *n* terrier, *m; Inf.* soldado del ejército territorial, *m*
terrific /tə'rɪfɪk/ *a* espantoso, terrible; *Inf.* atroz, tremendo
terrify /'terəˌfai/ *vt* aterrorizar, espantar, horrorizar
terrifying /'terəˌfaiɪŋ/ *a* aterrador, espantoso
territorial /ˌterɪ'tɔriəl/ *a* territorial. —*n* soldado del ejército territorial, *m*
territoriality /ˌterɪˌtɔri'ælɪti/ *n* territorialidad, *f*
territory /'terɪˌtɔri/ *n* región, comarca, *f*; (state) territorio, *m;* jurisdicción, *f.* **mandated territory,** territorio bajo mandato, *m pl*
terror /'terər/ *n* terror, pavor, espanto, *m.* **the Reign of T.,** el Reinado del Terror, *m.* **t.-stricken,** espantado, muerto de miedo
terrorism /'terəˌrɪzəm/ *n* terrorismo, *m*
terrorist /'terərɪst/ *n* terrorista, *m*
terrorization /ˌterərə'zeiʃən/ *n* aterramiento, *m*
terrorize /'terəˌraiz/ *vt* aterrorizar
terse /tɜrs/ *a* conciso, sucinto; seco, brusco
tersely /'tɜrsli/ *adv* concisamente; secamente
terseness /'tɜrsnɪs/ *n* concisión, *f;* brusquedad, *f*
tertiary /'tɜrʃiˌeri, -ʃəri/ *a* tercero; *Geol.* terciario. —*n Eccl.* terciario, *m*
tessera /'tesərə/ *n* tesela, *f*
test /test/ *n* (proof) prueba, *f;* examen, *m;* investigación, *f;* (standard) criterio, *m*, piedra de toque, *f; Chem.* análisis, *m;* (trial) ensayo, *m; Zool.* concha, *f.* —*vt Chem.* ensayar; probar, poner a prueba; examinar; (eyes) graduar (la vista). **to put to the t.,** poner a prueba. **to stand the t.,** soportar la prueba. **t. match,** partido internacional de cricket, *m.* **t. meal,** *Med.* comida de prueba, *f.* **t. pilot,** *Aer.* piloto de pruebas, *m.* **t. tube,** tubo de ensayo, *m*
testament /'testəmənt/ *n* testamento, *m.* **the New T.,** el Nuevo Testamento, *m.* **the Old T.,** el Antiguo Testamento, *m*
testamentary /ˌtestə'mentəri/ *a* testamentario
testate /'testeit/ *a* testado
testator /'testeitər/ *n* testador, *m*, **(testatrix,** testadora, *f)*
testicle /'testɪkəl/ *n* testículo, *m*
testification /ˌtestəfɪ'keiʃən/ *n* testificación, *f*
testify /'testəˌfai/ *vt* and *vi* declarar, atestar; *Law.* atestiguar, testificar, dar fe
testily /'testɪli/ *adv* malhumoradamente
testimonial /ˌtestə'mouniəl/ *n* recomendación, *f;* certificado, *m;* (tribute) homenaje, *m*
testimony /'testəˌmouni/ *n* testimonio, *m*, declaración, *f;* (proof) prueba, *f.* **in t. whereof,** en fe de lo cual. **to bear t.,** atestar
testiness /'testinɪs/ *n* mal humor, *m*, irritación, *f*
testing grounds /'testɪŋ/ *n* campo de experimentación, campo de pruebas, *m*
testy /'testi/ *a* enojadizo, irritable, irascible, quisquilloso
tetanus /'tetənəs/ *n* tétano, *m*
tether /'teðər/ *n* traba, atadura, maniota, *f.* —*vt* atar con una correa. **to be at the end of one's t.,** acabarse la resistencia; acabarse la paciencia
Teuton /'tutn/ *n* teutón (-ona)
Teutonic /tu'tɒnɪk/ *a* teutónico
text /tekst/ *n* texto, *m;* (subject) tema, *m;* (motto) lema, *m;* (of a musical composition) letra, *f.* **t.-book,** libro de texto, *m*
textile /'tekstail/ *a* textil, de tejer. —*n* textil, *m*, materia textil, *f;* tejido, *m*
textual /'tekstʃuəl/ *a* textual

texture /'tekstʃər/ *n* (material and *Biol.*) tejido, *m;* textura, *f*
Thailand /'tai,lænd/ Tailandia, *f*
thalamus /'θæləməs/ *n* (*Anat., Bot.*) tálamo, *m*
Thames, the /temz/ *n* el Támesis, *m.* **to set the T. on fire,** descubrir la pólvora
than /ðæn, ðen; *unstressed* ðən, ən/ *conjunc* que; (between **more, less,** or **fewer** and a number) de; (in comparisons of inequality) que, but que becomes(*a*) del (de la, de los, de las) que if the point of comparison is a noun in the principal clause, which has to be supplied mentally to fill up the ellipsis; (*b*) de lo que if there is no noun to act as a point of comparison, e.g. **He was older than I thought,** Era más viejo de lo que yo pensaba. **They have less than they deserve,** Tienen menos de lo que merecen. **They lose more money than (the money) they earn,** Pierden más dinero del que ganan. **He will meet with more opposition than he thought,** Va a encontrar más oposición de la que pensaba. **I have more books than you,** Tengo más libros que tú. **She has fewer than nine and more than five,** Ella tiene menos de nueve y más de cinco
thank /θæŋk/ *vt* agradecer, dar las gracias (a). **to t. for,** agradecer. **I will t. you to be more polite,** Le agradecería que fuese más cortés. **He has himself to t. for it,** Él mismo tiene la culpa de ello. **No, t. you,** No, muchas gracias. **T. goodness!** ¡Gracias a Dios!
thank /θæŋks/ *n* (now in pl. only, **thanks)** gracias, *f pl.* **a vote of thanks,** un voto de gracias. **Many thanks!** ¡Muchas gracias! **to return thanks,** dar las gracias. **thanks to,** merced a, debido a. **thanks to you,** gracias a tí. **t.-offering,** ofrecimiento en acción de gracias, *m*
thankful /'θæŋkfəl/ *a* agradecido. **I am t. to see,** Me alegro de ver, Me es grato ver
thankfully /'θæŋkfəli/ *adv* con gratitud, agradecido
thankfulness /'θæŋkfəlnɪs/ *n* agradecimiento, *m;* gratitud, *f*
thankless /'θæŋklɪs/ *a* ingrato; desagradecido; desagradable
thanksgiving /ˌθæŋks'gɪvɪŋ/ *n* acción de gracias, *f.* **t. service,** servicio de acción de gracias, *m.* **Thanksgiving (Day),** *n* día de acción de dar gracias, día de gracias, *m*
that /ðæt; *unstressed* ðət/ *dem a* ese, *m;* esa, *f;* aquel, *m;* aquella, *f, dem. pron* ése, *m;* ésa, *f;* eso, *neut;* aquél, *m;* aquélla, *f;* aquello, *neut;* (standing for a noun) el, *m;* la, *f;* lo, *neut* **All t. there is,** Todo lo que hay. **His temperament is t. of his mother,** Su temperamento es el de su madre. **We have not come to t. yet,** Todavía no hemos llegado a ese punto. **T. is what I want to know,** Eso es lo que quiero saber. **with t.,** con eso; (thereupon) en eso. **Go t. way,** Vaya Vd. por allí; Tome Vd. aquel camino. **T. is to say...,** Es decir.... **What do you mean by t.?** ¿Qué quieres decir con eso? **The novel is not as bad as all t.,** La novela no es tan mala como tú piensas (*or* como dicen, etc.)
that /ðæt; *unstressed* ðət/ *pron rel* que; el cual, *m;* la cual, *f;* lo cual, *neut;* (of persons) a quien, *mf;* a quienes, *mf pl;* (with from) de quien, *mf;* de quienes, *mf pl;* (of place) donde. **The letter t. I sent you,** la carta que te mandé. **The box t. John put them in,** la caja en la cual les puso Juan. **The last time t. I saw her,** La última vez que la vi
that /ðæt; *unstressed* ðət/ *conjunc* que; (of purpose) para que; afin de que; (before infin.) para; (because) porque. **O t. he would come!** ¡Ojalá que viniese! **so t.,** para que; (before infin.) para; (as a result) de manera que; de modo que. **It is better t. he should not come,** Es mejor que no venga. **now t.,** ahora que
thatch /θætʃ/ *n* barda, *f, vt* bardar
thaw /θɔ/ *n* deshielo, *m.* —*vt* deshelar; derretir. —*vi* deshelarse; derretirse
the /*stressed* ði; *unstressed before a consonant* ðə, *unstressed before a vowel* ði/ *def art* el, *m;* la, *f;* lo, *neut;* los, *m pl;* las, *f pl;* (before feminine sing. noun beginning with stressed a or ha) el; (untranslated between the name and number of a monarch, pope, ruler, e.g. *Charles the Tenth,* Carlos diez). —*adv* (before a comparative) cuanto, tanto más. **at the** or

to the, al, *m,* (also before feminine sing. noun beginning with a or ha); a la, *f;* a lo, *neut;* a los, *m pl;* a las, *f pl.* **from the** or **of the,** del, *m,* (also before feminine sing. noun beginning with stressed a or ha); de la, *f;* de lo, *neut;* de los, *m pl;* de las, *f pl.* **the one,** see one. **The sooner the better,** Cuanto antes mejor. **The room will be all the warmer,** El cuarto estará tanto más caliente

theater /'θiətər/ *n* teatro, *m;* (lecture) anfiteatro, *m;* (drama) teatro, *m,* obra dramática, *f;* (scene) teatro, *m,* escena, *f.* **t. attendant,** acomodador (-ra)

theater-in-the-round /'θiətərɪnðə'raund/ *n* teatro circular, teatro en círculo, *m*

Theatine /θi'ətin, ,tɪn/ *a* and *n* Eccl. teatino *m*

theatrical /θi'ætrɪkəl/ *a* teatral. —*n pl* **theatricals,** funciones teatrales, *f pl.* **amateur theatricals,** función de aficionados, *f.* **t. company,** compañía de teatro, *f.* **t. costumier,** mascarero (-ra), alquilador (-ra) de disfraces. **t. manager,** empresario de teatro, *m*

theatricality /θi,ætrɪ'kælɪti/ *n* teatralidad, *f*

Theban *a* and *n* tebeo (-ea), tebano (-na)

Thebes /θibz/ Tebas, *f*

thee /ði/ *pers pron* te; (after prep.) tí. **with t.,** contigo

theft /θɛft/ *n* robo, hurto, *m*

their /ðɛr; *unstressed* ðər/ *poss a* su, *mf sing;* sus, *pl;* de ellos, *m pl;* de ellas, *f pl.* **They have t. books,** Tienen sus libros. **I have t. books,** Tengo los libros de ellos

theirs /ðɛrz/ *poss pron* (el) suyo, *m;* (la) suya, *f;* (los) suyos, *m pl;* (las) suyas, *f pl;* de ellos, *m pl;* de ellas, *f pl.* **These hats are t.,** Estos sombreros son los suyos

them /ðɛm; *unstressed* ðəm, əm/ *pers pron* ellos, *m pl;* ellas, *f pl;* (as object of a verb) los, *m pl;* las, *f pl;* (to them) les

thematic /θi'mætɪk/ *a* temático

theme /θim/ *n* tema, asunto, *m;* tesis, *f; Mus.* tema, motivo, *m*

themselves /ðəm'sɛlvz, ,ðɛm-/ *pers pron pl* ellos mismos, *m pl;* ellas mismas, *f pl, reflexive pron* sí; sí mismos; (with a reflexive verb) se. **They t. told me about it,** Ellos mismos me lo dijeron. **They left it for t.,** Lo dejaron para sí (mismos)

then /ðɛn/ *adv* (of future time) entonces; (of past time) a la sazón, en aquella época, entonces; (next, afterwards) luego, después, en seguida; (in that case) en este caso, entonces; (therefore) por consiguiente. —*a* de entonces. —*n* entonces, *m.* —*conjunc* (moreover) además; pues. **And what t.?** ¿Y qué pasó después?; ¿Y qué pasará ahora?; ¿Y qué más? **by t.,** por entonces. **now and t.,** de vez en cuando. **now... t.,** ya... ya, ora... ora. **since t.,** desde aquel tiempo; desde entonces; desde aquella ocasión. **until t.,** hasta entonces; hasta aquella época. **well t.,** bien, pues. **t. and there,** en el acto, en seguida; allí mismo

thence /ðɛns/ *adv* desde allí, de allí; (therefore) por eso, por esa razón, por consiguiente

thenceforth /,ðɛns'fɔrθ/ *adv* de allí en adelante, desde entonces

theocracy /θi'ɒkrəsi/ *n* teocracia, *f*

theocratic /,θiə'krætɪk/ *a* teocrático

theologian /,θiə'loudʒən/ *n* teólogo, *m*

theological /,θiə'lɒdʒɪkəl/ *a* teológico, teologal

theologize /θi'ɒlə,dʒaiz/ *vi* teologizar

theology /θi'ɒlədʒi/ *n* teología, *f*

theorem /'θiərəm/ *n* teorema, *m*

theoretical /,θiə'rɛtɪkəl/ *a* teórico

theoretically /,θiə'rɛtɪkli/ *adv* teóricamente, en teoría

theorist /'θiərɪst/ *n* teórico, *m*

theorize /'θiə,raiz/ *vi* teorizar

theory /'θiəri/ *n* teoría, *f*

theosophical /,θiə'sɒfɪkəl/ *a* teosófico

theosophist /θi'ɒsəfɪst/ *n* teósofo, *m*

theosophy /θi'ɒsəfi/ *n* teosofía, *f*

therapeutic /,θɛrə'pyutɪk/ *a* terapéutico. —*n* **therapeutics,** terapéutica, *f*

therapeutist /,θɛrə'pyutɪst/ *n* terapeuta, *mf*

therapy /'θɛrəpi/ *suffix* terapia, *f*

there /ðɛr; *unstressed* ðər/ *adv* allí; ahí, allá; (at that point) en eso; (used pronominally as subject of verb) haber, e.g. T. *was once a king,* Hubo una vez un rey;

What is t. to do here? ¿Qué hay que hacer aquí? —*interj* ¡vaya!; (I told you so!) ¡ya ves! ¡ya te lo dije yo!; (in surprise) ¡toma! **about t.,** cerca de allí. **down t.,** allí abajo. **in t.,** allí dentro. **out t.,** allí fuera. **over t.,** ahí; allá a lo lejos. **up t.,** allí arriba. **T. came a time when...,** Llegó la hora cuando... **T. it is!** ¡Allí está! **t. is** or **t. are,** hay. **t. was** or **t. were,** había, hubo. **t. may be,** puede haber, quizás habrá. **t. must be,** tiene que haber. **t. will be,** habrá. **T., t.!** (to a child, etc.) ¡Vamos!

thereabouts /'ðɛərə,bauts/ *adv* (near to a place) cerca de allí, por ahí, allí cerca; (approximately) aproximadamente, cerca de

thereafter /,ðɛər'æftər/ *adv* después, después de eso

thereby /,ðɛər'bai/ *adv* (near to that place) por allí cerca; (by that means) con lo cual, de este modo

therefore /'ðɛər,fɔr/ *adv* por lo tanto, por eso, así, por consiguiente; por esta razón

therein /,ðɛər'ɪn/ *adv* (inside) allí dentro; (in this, that particular) en estre, en eso, en ese particular

thereinafter /,ðɛərɪn'æftər/ *adv* posteriormente, más adelante

thereupon /'ðɛərə,pɒn/ *adv* (in consequence) por consiguiente, por lo tanto; (at that point) luego, en eso; (immediately afterwards) inmediatamente después, en seguida

thermal /'θɜrməl/ *a* termal. **t. springs,** aguas termales, termas, *f pl*

thermodynamics /,θɜrmoudai'næmɪks/ *n* termodinámica, *f*

thermoelectric /,θɜrmouɪ'lɛktrɪk/ *a* termoeléctrico

thermometer /θər'mɒmitər/ *n* termómetro, *m*

Thermopylae /θər'mɒpə,li/ Termópilas, *f*

thermos flask /'θɜrməs/ *n* termos, *m*

thermostat /'θɜrmə,stæt/ *n* termostato, *m*

thermostatic /,θɜrmə'stætɪk/ *a* termostático

thesaurus /θɪ'sɔrəs/ *n* tesoro, tesauro, *m*

these /ðiz/ *dem pron pl* of **this,** éstos, *m pl;* éstas, *f pl, dem a* estos, *m pl;* estas, *f pl.* **Aren't t. your flowers?** ¿No son éstas tus flores? **T. pictures have been sold,** Estos cuadros han se han vendito

thesis /'θisɪs/ *n* tesis, *f*

Thespian /'θɛspiən/ *a* dramático

Thessaly /'θɛsəli/ Tesalia, *f*

they /ðei/ *pers pron* ellos, *m pl;* ellas, *f pl;* (people) se (followed by sing. verb). **T. say,** Dicen, Se dice

thick /θɪk/ *a* espeso; (big) grueso, (wall) grueso, (string, cord) gordo; (vapors) denso; (muddy) turbio; (dense, close) tupido apretado; (numerous) numeroso, repetido, continuo; (full of) lleno (de); (of voice) velado, indistinto; (obtuse) estúpido, lerdo; (friendly) íntimo. —*adv* densamente; continuamente, sin cesar. **three feet t.,** de tres pies de espesor. **That's a bit t.!** ¡Eso es un poco demasiado! **to be as t. as thieves,** estar unidos como los dedos de la mano. **t.-lipped,** con labios gruesos, bezudo. **t.-headed,** estúpido, lerdo. **t.-skinned,** de piel gruesa; *Zool.* paquidermo; *Fig.* sin vergüenza, insensible. **t. stroke,** (of letters) grueso, *m*

thick /θɪk/ *n* espesor, *m;* parte gruesa, *f;* lo más denso; (of a fight) lo más reñido; centro, *m.* **in the t. of,** en el centro (de), en medio de

thicken /'θɪkən/ *vt* espesar; (increase) aumentar, multiplicar; *Cul.* espesar. —*vi* espesarse; condensar; aumentar, multiplicarse; (of a mystery, etc.) complicarse; hacerse más denso; *Cul.* espesarse

thickening /'θɪkənɪŋ/ *n* hinchamiento, *m;* gordura, *f;* (Cul. and of paints) espesante, *m*

thicket /'θɪkɪt/ *n* matorral, soto, *m;* maleza, *f;* (grove) boscaje, *m*

thickly /'θɪkli/ *adv* densamente; espesamente; continuamente, sin cesar; (of speech) indistintamente

thickness /'θɪknɪs/ *n* espesor, *m;* grueso, *m;* densidad, *f;* (of liquids) consistencia, *f;* (layer) capa, *f;* (of speech) dificultad (en el hablar), *f*

thickset /'θɪk'sɛt/ *a* doblado

thief /θif/ *n* ladrón (-ona); (in a candle) moco de vela, *m.* **Stop t.!** ¡Ladrones! **thieves' den,** *Fig.* cueva de ladrones, *f*

thieve /θiv/ *vi* hurtar, robar. —*vt* robar

thievish /'θivɪʃ/ *a* ladrón

thigh /θai/ n muslo, m. **t.-bone,** fémur, m

thimble /'θimbəl/ n dedal, m

thimbleful /'θimbəl‚ful/ n lo que cabe en un dedal; Fig. dedada, f

thin /θin/ a delgado; (lean) flaco; (small) pequeño; delicado; fino; (of air, light) tenue, sutil; (clothes) ligero; (sparse) escaso; transparente; (watery) aguado; (of wine) bautizado; (not close) claro; (of arguments) flojo. —vt adelgazar; aclarar; Agr. limpiar; reducir. —vi adelgazarse; afilarse; reducirse. **somewhat t.,** (of persons) delgaducho, algo flaco. **to grow t.,** enflaquecer; afilarse. **to make t.,** hacer adelgazar volver flaco. **t.-clad,** ligero de ropa; mal vestido. **t.-faced,** de cara delgada. **t.-lipped,** de labios apretados. **t.-skinned,** de piel fina; Fig. sensitivo, sensible

thine /ðain/ See **theirs.** poss pron (el) tuyo, m; (la) tuya, f; (los) tuyos, m pl; (las) tuyas, f pl; tu, mf; tus, mf pl; de tí. **The fault is t.,** La culpa es tuya, La culpa es de tí

thing /θiŋ/ n cosa, f; objeto, artículo, m; (affair) asunto, m; (contemptuous) sujeto, tipo, m; (creature) ser, m, criatura, f; pl **things,** (belongings) efectos, trastos, m pl; (luggage) equipaje, m; (clothes) trapitos, m pl; (circumstances) circunstancias, condiciones, f pl. **above all things,** ante todo, sobre todo. **a very pretty little t.,** (child) una pequeña muy mona. **as things are,** tal como están las cosas. **for one t.,** en primer lugar. **Her behavior is not quite the t.,** La conducta de ella no está bien vista. **The bad t. is that...,** Lo malo es que... **The good t. is that...,** Menos mal que...; Lo bueno es que... **No such t.!** ¡No hay tal!; ¡Nada de eso! **Poor t.!** ¡Pobrecito!; (woman) ¡Pobre mujer!; (man) ¡Pobre hombre! **to be just the t.,** venir al pelo. **with one t. and another,** entre unas cosas y otras. **I like things Spanish,** Me gusta lo español

think /θiŋk/ vt and vi pensar; (believe) creer; (deem) considerar, juzgar; imaginar; (suspect) sospechar; (opine) ser de opinión (que). **And to t. that...!** ¡Y pensar que...! **As you t. fit,** Como usted quiera, Como a usted le parezca bien. **He thought as much,** Se lo figuraba. **He little thought that...!** ¡Cuán lejos estaba de pensar que...! **He thinks nothing of...,** No le importa...; Desprecia..., Tiene una opinión bastante mala de.... **I don't t. so,** No lo creo. **I should t. not!** ¡Claro que no! **¡Eso sí que no! I should t. so!** ¡Claro! ¡Ya lo creo! **It makes me t. of...,** Me hace pensar en... **One might t.,** Podría creerse... **to t. better of something,** cambiar de opinión, considerar mejor. **to t. highly (badly) of,** tener buen (mal) concepto sobre. **to t. over carefully,** pensarlo bien, considerar detenidamente; Inf. consultar con la almohada. **to t. proper,** creer conveniente. **to t. to oneself,** pensar para sí (or entre sí). **to t. too much of oneself,** pensar demasiado en sí; tener demasiada buena opinión de sí mismo; tener humos. **What do you t. about it?** ¿Qué te parece? **to t. about,** (of persons) pensar en; (of things) pensar de (or sobre); meditar, considerar, reflexionar sobre. **to t. for,** pensar por. **to t. of,** pensar en; pensar de (or sobre). **What do you t. of this?** ¿Qué te parece esto? **to t. out,** idear, proyectar, hacer planes para; (a problem) resolver. **to t. over,** pensar; reflexionar sobre, meditar sobre. **I shall t. it over,** Lo pensaré.

thinker /'θiŋkər/ n pensador, m

thinking /'θiŋkiŋ/ n pensamiento, m, reflexión, f; meditación, f; juicio, m; opinión, f; parecer, m. —a pensador; inteligente; racional; serio. **To my way of t.,** Según pienso yo, A mi parecer. **way of t.,** modo de pensar, m

thinly /'θinli/ adv delgadamente; esparcidamente; (lightly) ligeramente; poco numeroso

thinness /'θinnis/ n delgadez, f; (leanness) flaqueza, f; sutileza, tenuidad, f; (lack) escasez, f; pequeño número, m; poca consistencia, f

third /θɜrd/ a tercero (tercer before m, sing noun); (of monarchs) tercero; (of the month) (el) tres. —n tercio, m, tercera parte, f; Mus. tercera, f. **T. time lucky!** ¡A la tercera va la vencida! **t. class,** n tercera clase, f. —a de tercera clase. **t. party,** tercera persona, f. **t.-party insurance,** seguro contra tercera persona, m. **t. person,** tercero (-ra); Gram. tercera persona, f. **t.-rate,** de tercera clase

thirdly /'θɜrdli/ adv en tercer lugar

thirst /θɜrst/ n sed, f; Fig. deseo, m, ansia, f; entusiasmo, m. **to satisfy one's t.,** apagar (or matar) la sed

thirsty /'θɜrsti/ a sediento. **to be t.,** tener sed. **to make t.,** dar sed.

thirteen /'θɜr'tin/ a and n trece m. **t. hundred,** a and n mil trescientos m

thirteenth /'θɜr'tinθ/ a décimotercio; (of monarchs) trece; (of month) (el) trece, m, n décimotercio, trezavo, m

thirtieth /'θɜrtiəθ/ a trigésimo; (of month) (el) treinta. m. —n treintavo, m

thirty /'θɜrti/ a and n treinta, m. **t.-first,** treinta y uno

this /ðis/ dem a este, m; esta, f, dem pron éste, m; ésta, f; esto, neut. by **t. time,** a esta hora, ya. **like t.,** de este modo, así. **T. is Wednesday,** Hoy es miércoles. **What is all t.?** ¿Qué es todo esto?

thistle /'θisəl/ n cardo, m. **t.-down,** papo de cardo, vilano de cardo, m

thither /'θiðər, 'ðiδ-/ adv allá, hacia allá; a ese fin. —a más remoto

thong /θɔŋ/ n correa, tira, f

thoracic /θɔ'ræsik/ a torácico

thorax /'θɔræks/ n tórax, m

thorn /θɔrn/ n espina, f; (tree) espino, m; Fig. abrojo, m, espina, f. **to be a t. in the flesh of,** ser una espina en el costado de. **t. brake,** espinar, m

thornless /'θɔrnlis/ a sin espinas

thorny /'θɔrni/ a espinoso; Fig. difícil, arduo

thorough /'θɜrou/ a completo; perfecto; (conscientious) concienzudo; (careful) cuidadoso. **t.-bred,** (of animals) de pura raza, de casta; (of persons) bien nacido. **t.-paced,** cabal, consumado

thoroughfare /'θɜrə‚feər/ n vía pública, f. **"No t.,"** «Prohibido el paso», «Calle cerrada»

thoroughly /'θɜrəli/ adv completamente; (of knowing a subject) a fondo; concienzudamente

thoroughness /'θɜrənis/ n perfección, f; minuciosidad, f

those /ðouz/ dem a pl of **that,** esos, m pl; esas, f pl; aquellos, m pl; aquellas, f pl, dem pron ésos, m pl; ésas, f pl; aquéllos, m pl; aquéllas, f pl; (standing for a noun) los, m pl; las, f pl. **t. who,** quienes, mf pl; los que, m pl; las que, f pl. **t. that** or **which,** los que, m pl; las que, f pl. **Your eyes are t. of your mother,** Tus ojos son los de tu madre

thou /θau/ pers pron tú

though /ðou/ conjunc (followed by subjunc. when doubt is implied or uncertain future time) aunque, bien que; (nevertheless) sin embargo, no obstante; (in spite of) a pesar de que; (but) pero. **as t.,** como si (followed by subjunc.). **even t.,** aunque (followed by subjunc.)

thought /θɔt/ n pensamiento, m; meditación, reflexión, f; some **thoughts on...** algunas reflexiones sobre...; opinión, f; consideración, f; idea, f, propósito, m; (care) cuidado, m, solicitud, f; Inf. pizca, f. **on second thought,** después de pensarlo bien. **The t. struck him,** Se le ocurrió la idea. **to collect one's thoughts,** orientarse; informarse (de). **t.-reading,** adivinación del pensamiento, f. **t.-transference,** telepatía, transmisión del pensamiento, f

thoughtful /'θɔtfəl/ a pensativo, meditabundo; serio; especulativo; (provident) previsor; (kind) atento, solícito; cuidadoso; (anxious) inquieto, intranquilo

thoughtfully /'θɔtfəli/ adv pensativamente; seriamente; (providently) con previsión; (kindly) atentamente, solícitamente

thoughtfulness /'θɔtfəlnis/ n natural reflexivo, m, seriedad, f; (kindness) solicitud, atención, f; (forethought) previsión, f

thoughtless /'θɔtlis/ a irreflexivo; (careless) descuidado, negligente; (unkind) inconsiderado; (silly) necio, estúpido

thoughtlessly /'θɔtlisli/ adv sin pensar, irreflexivamente; negligentemente

thoughtlessness /'θɔtlisnis/ n irreflexión, f; descuido, *m*, negligencia, *f*; (unkindness) inconsideración, *f*; (silliness) neciedad, *f*

thousand /'θauzənd/ *a* mil. —*n* mil, *m*; millar, *m*. **one t.,** mil, *m*. **one t. three hundred,** *a* mil trescientos, *m pl*; mil trescientas, *f pl*. —*n* mil trescientos, *m pl*. **two (three) t.,** dos (tres) mil. **by thousands,** por millares; por miles. **t.-fold,** mil veces más

thousandth /'θauzəndθ/ *a* and *n* milésimo *m*

Thrace /θreis/ Tracia, *f*

thrall /θrɔl/ *n* esclavo (-va); esclavitud, *f*

thrash /θræʃ/ *vt* azotar, apalear; *Agr.* trillar, desgranar; *Inf.* triunfar sobre, derrotar. —*vi Agr.* trillar el grano; arrojarse, agitarse. *Fig.* **to t. out,** ventilar

thrashing /'θræʃɪŋ/ *n* apaleamiento, *m*, paliza, *f*; *Agr.* See **threshing**

thread /θred/ *n* hilo, *m*; (fibre) hebra, fibra, *f*, filamento, *m*; (of a screw) filete, *m*; *Fig.* hilo, *m*, *a* de hilo. —*vt* (a needle) enhebrar; (beads) ensartar; (make one's way) colarse a través de, atravesar; pasar por. **to hang by a t.,** pender de un hilo. **to lose the t. of,** *Fig.* perder el hilo de

threadbare /'θred,beər/ *a* raído; muy usado; *Fig.* trivial, viejo

threadlike /'θred,laik/ *a* como un hilo, filiforme

threadworm /'θred,wɜrm/ *n m*, lombriz intestinal, *f*

threat /θret/ *n* amenaza, *f*

threaten /'θretṇ/ *vt* and *vi* amenazar. **to t. with,** amenazar con

threatening /'θretṇɪŋ/ *a* amenazador. —*n* amenazas, *f pl*

threateningly /'θretṇɪŋli/ *adv* con amenazas

three /θri/ *a* and *n* tres *m*; (of the clock) las tres, *f pl*; (of one's age) tres años, *m pl*. **t.-color process,** tricromía, *f*. **t.-colored,** tricolor. **t.-cornered,** triangular; (of hats) de tres picos, tricornio. **t.-cornered hat,** sombrero de tres picos, tricornio, *m*. **t. decker,** *Naut.* navío de tres puentes, *m*; novela larga, *f*. **t. deep,** en tres hileras. **t. hundred,** *a* and *n* trescientos *m*. **t.-hundredth,** *a* and *n* tricentésimo *m*. **t.-legged,** de tres patas. **t.-legged stool,** banqueta, *f*. **t.-per-cents,** accion al tres por ciento (3%), *f*. **t.-phase,** *Elec.* trifásico. **t.-ply,** (of yarn) triple; (of wood) de tres capas. **t.-quarter,** de tres cuartos. **t. quarters of an hour,** tres cuartos de hora, *m pl*. **t.-sided,** trilátero. **t. speed gear box,** cambio de marcha de tres velocidades, *m*. **t.-stringed,** *Mus.* de tres cuerdos. **t. thousand,** *a* tres mil, *mf pl*; *n* tres mil, *m*

threefold /'θri,fould/ *a* triple

Three Musketeers, the los Tres Mosqueteros

threescore /'θri'skɔr/ *a* and *n* sesenta, *m pl*

threesome /'θrisəm/ *n* partido de tres, *m*

threnody /'θrenədi/ *n* treno, *m*

thresh /θreʃ/ *vt* trillar, desgranar. —*vi* trillar el grano. **to t. out,** ventilar

threshing /'θreʃɪŋ/ *n* trilla, *f*. **t. floor,** era, *f*. **t. machine,** trilladora, *f*

threshold /'θreʃould/ *n* umbral, *m*; *Psychol.* limen, *m*; *Fig.* comienzo, principio, *m*; (entrance) entrada, *f*. **to cross the t.,** atravesar (or pisar) los umbrales

thrice /θrais/ *adv* tres veces

thrift /θrift/ *n* frugalidad, parsimonia, *f*

thriftless /'θriftlis/ *a* malgastador, manirroto

thrifty /'θrifti/ *a* frugal, económico

thrill /θril/ *n* estremecimiento, *m*; emoción, *f*. —*vt* conmover, emocionar; penetrar. —*vi* estremecerse, emocionarse

thriller /'θrilər/ *n* libro, *m*, (or comedia, *f*) sensacional; (detective novel) novela policíaca, *f*

thrilling /'θrilɪŋ/ *a* sensacional, espeluznante; (moving) emocionante, conmovedor

thrive /θraiv/ *vi* prosperar, medrar; enriquecerse, tener éxito; (grow) desarrollarse, robustecerse; florecer; (of plants) acertar

thriving /'θraivɪŋ/ *a* próspero; floreciente; robusto, vigoroso

throat /θrout/ *n* garganta, *f*; orificio, *m*; (narrow entry) paso, *m*. **sore t.,** dolor de garganta, *m*. **to cut one's t.,** cortarse la garganta. **to take by the t.,** asir (or agarrar) por la garganta

throat cancer *n* cáncer de la garganta, *m*

throaty /'θrouti/ *a* indistinto, ronco

throb /θrɒb/ *n* latido, *m*; pulsación, *f*; vibración, *f*; *Fig.* estremecimiento, *m*. —*vi* palpitar, latir; vibrar

throbbing /'θrɒbɪŋ/ *n* pulsación, *f*; vibración, *f*. —*a* palpitante; vibrante. **t. pain,** dolor pungente, *m*

throe /θrou/ *n* dolor, *m*, agonía, angustia, *f*. **in the throes of,** en medio de; luchando con; en las garras de. **throes of childbirth,** dolores de parto, *m pl*. **throes of death,** agonía de la muerte, *f*

thrombosis /θrɒm'bousɪs/ *n Med.* trombosis, *f*

throne /θroun/ *n* trono, *m*; (royal power) corona, *f*, poder real, *m*. —*vt* elevar al trono. **speech from the t.,** el discurso de la corona, *m*

throng /θrɔŋ/ *n* muchedumbre, multitud, *f*. —*vi* apiñarse remolinarse, acudir. —*vt* atestar, llenar de bote en bote

throstle /'θrɒsəl/ *n Ornith.* tordo, malvís, *m*

throttle /'θrɒtl/ *n Mech.* regulador, *m*; *Auto.* estrangulador, *m*; *Inf.* garganta, *f*. —*vt* estrangular; *Fig.* ahogar, suprimir. **to open (close) the t.,** abrir (cerrar) el estrangulador

throttling /'θrɒtlɪŋ/ *n* estrangulación, *f*

through /θru/ *prep* por; al través de; de un lado a otro de; por medio de; (between) entre; por causa de; gracias a. —*adv* al través; de un lado a otro; (whole) entero, todo; (from beginning to end) desde el principio hasta el fin; (to the end) hasta el fin. —*a* (of passages, etc.) que va desde... hasta...; (of trains) directo. **to look t. the window,** mirar por la ventana, asomarse a la ventana. **to be wet t.,** estar calado hasta los huesos; estar muy mojado. **to carry t.,** llevar a cabo. **to fall t.,** caer por; (fail) fracasar. **to sleep the whole night t.,** dormir durante toda la noche, dormir la noche entera. **t. and t.,** completamente. **through the length and breadth of,** a lo largo y a lo ancho de, hasta los últimos rincones de. **t. traffic,** tráfico directo, *m*. **t. train,** tren directo, *m*

throughout /θru'aut/ *prep* por todo; durante todo. —*adv* completamente; (from beginning to end) desde el principio hasta el fin; (everywhere) en todas partes

throw /θrou/ *vt* arrojar, lanzar, echar; (fire) disparar; (pottery) plasmar; (knock down) derribar; (slough) mudar (la piel); (cast off) despojarse de; (a rider) desmontar; (a glance) echar, dirigir (una mirada, etc.); (silk) torcer; (dice) echar; (light) dirigir, enfocar. **to t. oneself at the head of,** echarse a la cabeza de. **to t. open,** abrir de par en par; abrir. **to t. overboard,** *Naut.* echar al mar; desechar; (desert) abandonar. **to t. about,** esparcir, desparramar; derrochar. **to t. aside,** echar a un lado, desechar; abandonar, dejar. **to t. away,** tirar; desechar; (spend) malgastar, derrochar; (waste) sacrificar; (of opportunities) malograr, perder. **to t. back,** devolver; echar hacia atrás. **to t. down,** derribar, dar en el suelo con; echar abajo; (arms) rendir. **to t. down the glove,** arrojar el guante. **to t. oneself down,** tumbarse, echarse; (descend) echarse abajo. **to t. oneself down from,** arrojarse de. **to t. in,** echar dentro; (give extra) añadir; (the clutch) embragar; insertar; (a remark) hacer (una observación). **to t. off,** despojarse de; quitarse; (refuse) rechazar; sacudirse; (get rid of) despedir; (renounce) renunciar; (exhale) emitir, despedir; (verses) improvisar. **to t. on,** echar sobre; (garments) ponerse. **to t. oneself upon,** lanzarse sobre. **to t. out,** expeler; hacer salir; plantar en la calle; (utter) proferir, soltar; (one's chest) inflar. **to t. over,** (desert) abandonar, dejar. **to t. up,** (build) levantar; lanzar en el aire; (a post, etc.) renunciar a; abandonar; vomitar

throw /θrou/ *n* echada, *f*; tiro, *m*; (at dice) lance, *m*; jugada, *f*; (wrestling) derribo, *m*. **within a stone's t.,** a tiro de piedra. **t.-back,** retroceso, *m*; *Biol.* atavismo, *m*

thrower /'θrouər/ *n* tirador (-ra), lanzador (-ra)

throwing /'θrouɪŋ/ *n* lanzamiento, *m*, lanzada, *f*. **t. the hammer,** lanzamiento del martillo, *m*

thrum /θrʌm/ *vt* and *vi* tocar mal; (of keyed instruments) teclear; (of stringed instruments) rascar las cuerdas (de)

thrush /θrʌʃ/ *n Ornith.* tordo, *m*

thrust /θrʌst/ *n* empujón, *m*; (with a sword) estocada, *f*; (fencing) golpe, *m*; (with a lance) bote, *m*; ataque, *m*; asalto, *m*. —*vt* empujar; (put) meter; (insert) introducir; (pierce) atravesar; (out, through, of the head, etc.) asomar. —*vi* acometer, atacar, embestir; meterse, introducirse; (intrude) entrometerse; (fencing) dar un golpe. **to t. aside**, empujar a un lado; (proposals) rechazar. **to t. back**, hacer retroceder, empujar hacia atrás; (words) tragarse; (thoughts) apartar, rechazar. **to t. down**, empujar hacia abajo; hacer bajar; *Fig.* reprimir. **to t. forward**, empujar hacia delante; hacer seguir. **to t. oneself forward**, adelantarse; *Fig.* ponerse delante de los otros, darse importancia. **to t. in**, introducir; (stick) hincar; (insert) intercalar. **to t. on**, hacer seguir; empujar sobre; (garments) ponerse rápidamente. **to t. oneself in**, introducirse; entrometerse. **to t. out**, echar fuera; hacer salir; echar; expulsar; (the tongue) sacar (la lengua); (the head, etc.) asomar. **to t. through**, atravesar; (pierce) traspasar. **to t. one's way through**, abrirse paso por. **to t. upon**, imponer, hacer aceptar

thud /θʌd/ *n* sonido sordo, *m;* golpe sordo, *m*

thug /θʌg/ *n* asesino, criminal, *m*

thumb /θʌm/ *n* pulgar, *m.* —*vt* hojear; ensuciar con los dedos. **under the t. of,** *Fig.* en el poder de. **t. index,** índice pulgar, *m.* **t.-mark,** huella del dedo, *f.* **t.-screw,** tornillo de orejas, *m,* **t.-stall,** dedil, *m.* **t.-tack,** chinche, *m*

thump /θʌmp/ *n* golpe, porrazo, *m.* —*vt* and *vi* golpear, aporrear; (the ground, of rabbits) zapatear

thunder /ˈθʌndər/ *n* trueno, *m;* (of hooves, etc.) estampido, *m;* estruendo, *m.* —*vi* tronar; retumbar; *Fig.* fulminar. —*vt* gritar en una voz de trueno, rugir. **to t. along,** avanzar como el trueno; galopar ruidosamente. **t.-clap,** trueno, *m.* **t.-cloud,** nube de tormenta, *f,* nubarrón, *m.* **t.-storm,** tronada, *f.* **t. struck,** muerto, estupefacto. **to be thunderstruck,** quedarse frío

thunderbolt /ˈθʌndərˌboult/ *n* rayo, *m*

thunderer /ˈθʌndərər/ *n* fulminador, *m.* **the Thunderer,** Júpiter tonante, Júpiter tronante, *m;* el «Times» londinense, *m*

Thuringia /θʊˈrɪndʒiə/ Turingia, *f*

Thursday /ˈθɜrzdei/ *n* jueves, *m.* **Holy T.,** Jueves Santo, *m*

thus /ðʌs/ *adv* así; de este modo; en estos términos; hasta este punto. **t. far,** hasta ahora; hasta este punto; hasta aquí. **Thus it is that...,** Así es que...

thwack /θwæk/ *n* golpe, *m; vt* golpear

thwart /θwɔrt/ *vt* frustrar, impedir

thy /ðai/ *poss a* tu, *mf;* tus, *m pl,* and *f pl*

thyme /taim/ *n Bot.* tomillo, *m*

thymus /ˈθaiməs/ *n Anat.* timo, *m*

thyroid /ˈθairɔid/ *a* tiroideo. **t. gland,** tiroides, *f*

thyself /ðaiˈself/ *poss pron* tu mismo, *m;* tu misma, *f;* (with prep.) tí mismo, *m;* tí misma, *f;* (in a reflexive verb) te

tiara /tiˈærə, -ˈɑrə/ *n* tiara, *f*

Tiberias /taiˈbɪəriəs/ Tiberíades, *f*

Tibetan /tɪˈbɛtn/ *a* and *n* tibetano (-na); (language) tibetano, *m*

tibia /ˈtɪbiə/ *n Anat.* tibia, *f*

tic /tɪk/ *n* (twitch) tic nervioso, *m*

tick /tɪk/ *n Ent.* ácaro, *m;* (sound) tictac, *m;* (cover) funda de colchón, *f; Inf.* fiado, crédito, *m;* (mark) marca, *f vi* hacer tictac. —*vt* poner una marca contra. **on t.,** *Inf.* al fiado. **to t. off,** poner una marca contra; *Inf.* reñir. **to t. over,** *Auto.* andar, marchar

ticket /ˈtɪkɪt/ *n* billete, *m;* (for an entertainment) entrada, localidad, *f;* (label) etiqueta, *f;* (pawn) papeleta de empeño, *f;* (for luggage) talón, *m; (Polit. U.S.A.)* candidatura, *f, vt* marcar. **to take one's t.,** sacar el billete (or for entertainment) la entrada, *f).* **excursion t.,** billete de excursión, *m.* **return t.,** billete de ida y vuelta, *m.* **season t.,** billete de abono, *m.* **single t.,** billete sencillo, *m.* **t. agency,** (for travel) agencia de viajes, *f;* (for entertainments) agencia de teatros, *f.* **t. collector or inspector,** revisor, *m.* **t. holder,** tenedor de billete, *m;* abonado (-da). **t. office,** (railway) despacho de billetes, *m;* taquilla, *f.* **t.-of-leave,** libertad condicional, *f.* **t. punch,** sacabocados, *m;* (on tramcars) clasificador de billetes, *m*

ticking /ˈtɪkɪŋ/ *n* (sound) tictac, *m;* (cloth) cotí, *m*

tickle /ˈtɪkəl/ *vt* hacer cosquillas (a), cosquillear; irri-

tar; (gratify) halagar; (amuse) divertir. —*vi* tener cosquillas; hacer cosquillas; ser irritante

ticklish /ˈtɪklɪʃ/ *a* cosquilloso; (of persons) difícil, vidrioso; (of affairs) espinoso, delicado

tidal /ˈtaidl/ *a* de marea. **t. wave,** marejada, *f; Fig.* ola popular, *f*

tidbit /ˈtɪd,bɪt/ *n* See **titbit**

tiddlywinks /ˈtɪdli,wɪŋks/ *n* juego de la pulga, *m*

tide /taid/ *n* marea, *f;* (season) tiempo, *m,* estación, *f;* (trend) corriente, *f;* (progress) curso, *m;* marcha, *f.* —*vi* (with over) vencer, superar; aguardar la ocasión. **to go against the t.,** ir contra la corriente. **to go with the t.,** seguir la corriente. **high t.,** marea alta, *f.* **low t.,** marea baja, *f,* bajamar, *m.* **neap t.,** marea muerta, *f.* **t. mark,** lengua del agua, *f*

tideless /ˈtaidlɪs/ *a* sin mareas

tidily /ˈtaidli/ *adv* aseadamente; en orden, metódicamente

tidiness /ˈtaidnɪs/ *n* aseo, *m;* buen orden, *m*

tidings /ˈtaidɪŋz/ *n pl* noticias, nuevas, *f pl*

tidy /ˈtaidi/ *a* aseado; metódico, en orden; pulcro; *Inf.* considerable. —*vt* poner en orden, asear; limpiar; (oneself) arreglarse

tie /tai/ *n* lazo, *m,* atadura, *f;* (knot) nudo, *m;* (for the neck) corbata, *f; Sports.* empate, *m; Mus.* ligado, *m; Archit.* tirante, *m;* (spiritual bond) lazo, *m;* (burden) carga, responsabilidad, *f,* **tie clasp,** pisa corbata, *mf.* **tie-pin,** alfiler de corbata, *m.* **tie seller,** corbatero (-ra)

tie /tai/ *vt* atar; (bind) ligar; (lace) lacear; (a knot) hacer; (with a knot) anudar; (unite) unir; *(Fig.* bind) constreñir, obligar; (limit) limitar, restringir; (occupy) ocupar, entretener; (hamper) estorbar, impedir. —*vi* atarse; *Sports.* empatar. **to tie one's tie,** hacer la corbata. **to tie down,** atar; limitar; obligar. **They tied him down to a chair,** Le ataron a una silla. **to tie together,** enlazar, ligar; unir. **to tie up,** liar, atar; (wrap) envolver; recoger; *Naut.* amarrar, atracar; (restrict) limitar, restringir; (invest) invertir

tie-breaker /ˈtai,breikər/ *n* desempate, *m*

tier /tɪər/ *n* fila, hilera, *f.* **in tiers,** en gradas, (of a dress) en volantes

tiff /tɪf/ *n* disgusto, *m*

tiger /ˈtaigər/ *n* tigre, *m.* **t.-cat,** gato (-ta) atigrado (-da). **t.-lily,** tigridia, *f*

tigerish /ˈtaigərɪʃ/ *a* atigrado, de tigre; salvaje, feroz

tight /tait/ *a* apretado; (not leaky) hermético, impermeable; (taut) tieso, tirante; (narrow) estrecho; (trim) compacto; (of clothes) muy ajustado; (shut) bien cerrado; *Naut.* estanco; (risky) peligroso, difícil; (miserly) tacaño; (of money, goods) escaso; **to be t.-fisted,** ser como un puño. **to hold t.,** agarrar fuerte. **t. corner,** *Fig.* aprieto, lance apretado, *m.* **t.-rope,** cuerda de volatinero, *f.* **t.-rope walker,** alambrista, equilibrista, *mf;* volatinero (-ra), bailarín de la cuerda floja, *m.* **t.-rope walker's pole,** balancín, *m*

tighten /ˈtaitn/ *vt* estrechar, apretar; (stretch) estirar; (of saddle girths) cinchar. —*vi* estrecharse; estirarse

tightly /ˈtaitli/ *adv* estrechamente

tightness /ˈtaitnɪs/ *n* estrechez, *f;* tirantez, tensión, *f;* (feeling of constriction) opresión, *f;*

tights /taits/ *n pl* mallas, *f pl*

tigress /ˈtaigrɪs/ *n* tigresa, *f*

tile /tail/ *n* teja, *f;* (for flooring) baldosa, losa, *f;* (ornamental) azulejo, *m;* (hat) chistera, *f.* —*vt* tejar; embaldosar. **t. floor,** enlosado, embaldosado, *m.* **t. manufacturer,** tejero, *m.* **t. works** or **yard,** tejar, *m,* (Colombia) galpón *m*

tiler /ˈtailər/ *n* solador, *m;* tejero, *m*

till /tɪl/ *n* (for money) cajón, *m.* —*vt Agr.* cultivar, labrar. —*prep* hasta. —*conjunc* hasta que

tillable /ˈtɪləbəl/ *a* laborable

tillage /ˈtɪlɪdʒ/ *n* labranza, *f,* cultivo, *m;* tierra de labrantío, *f*

tiller /ˈtɪlər/ *n Agr.* labrador, *m; Bot.* mugrón, renuevo, vástago, *m; Naut.* caña del timón, *f*

tilling /ˈtɪlɪŋ/ *n Agr.* cultivo, laboreo, *m*

tilt /tɪlt/ *n* inclinación, *f;* ladeo, *m;* (fight) torneo, *m,* justa, *f.* —*vt* inclinar; ladear; (a drinking vessel) empinar. —*vi* inclinarse; ladearse; (fight) justar. **to t. against,** *Fig.* arremeter contra, atacar. **at full t.,** a

todo correr. **t. hammer,** martinete de báscula, *m.* **t.-
yard,** palestra, *f*

tilting /'tɪltɪŋ/ *n* incinación, *f;* (fighting) justas, *f pl.*
—*a* inclinado

timber /'tɪmbər/ *n* madera de construcción, *f;* (trees)
árboles de monte, *m pl;* bosque, *m;* (beam) viga, *f;
Naut.* cuaderna, *f.* —*vt* enmaderar. **t. line,** límite del
bosque maderable, *m.* **t. merchant,** maderero, *m.* **t.
wolf,** lobo gris, *m.* **t. work,** maderaje, *m.* **t. yard,**
maderería, *f,* corral de madera, *m*

timbered /'tɪmbərd/ *a* enmaderado; (with trees) arbolado

timbre /'tæmbər, 'tɪm-/ *n Mus.* timbre, *m*

timbrel /'tɪmbrəl/ *n Mus.* tamborete, tamboril, *m*

time /taim/ *n* (in general) tiempo, *m;* (epoch) época,
edad, *f;* tiempos, *m pl;* (of the year) estación, *f;* (by
the clock) hora, *f;* (lifetime) vida, *f;* (particular moment of time) momento, *m;* (occasion) sazón, ocasión, *f;* (day) día, *m;* (time allowed) plazo, *m;* (in
repetition) vez, *f; Mus.* compás, *m; Mil.* paso, *m.*
—*vt* ajustar al tiempo; hacer con oportunidad; (regulate) regular; calcular el tiempo que se emplea en
hacer una cosa; (a blow) calcular. **all the t.,** todo el
tiempo; continuamente, sin cesar. **a long t.,** mucho
tiempo. **a long t. ago,** mucho tiempo ha, hace
mucho tiempo. **at a t.,** a la vez, al mismo tiempo; (of
period) en una época. **at any t.,** a cualquier hora; en
cualquier momento; (when you like) cuando gustes.
at no t., jamás, nunca. **at some t.,** alguna vez; en alguna época. **at some t. or another,** un día u otro; en
una u otra ocasión; en alguna época. **at that t.,** en
aquella época; en la sazón; en aquel instante. **at the
one t.,** de una vez. **at the present t.,** en la actualidad, al presente. **at the proper t.,** a su debido
tiempo; a la hora señalada; a la hora conveniente. **at
the same t.,** al mismo tiempo. **at the same t. as,**
mientras, a medida que; al mismo instante que, **at
times,** a veces, en ocasiones. **behind the times,** *Fig.*
atrasado de noticias; pasado de moda. **behind t.,**
atrasado. **by that t.,** para entonces. **every t.,** cada
vez; siempre. **for some t.,** durante algún tiempo. **for
some t. past,** de algún tiempo a esta parte. **for the t.
being,** de momento, por ahora, por lo pronto. **from
this t.,** desde hoy; desde esta fecha. **from this t. forward,** de hoy en adelante. **from t. to t.,** de vez en
cuando, de cuando en cuando, de tarde en tarde. **in a
month's t.,** en un mes. **in a short t.,** en breve, dentro de poco. **in good t.,** puntualmente; temprano. **in
my t.,** en mis días, en mis tiempos. **in olden times,**
antiguamente, en otros tiempos. **in the course of t.,**
andando el tiempo, en el transcurso de los años. **in
the t. of,** en la época de. **in t.,** (promptly) a tiempo;
con el tiempo. **in t. to come,** en el porvenir. **It is t.
to...,** Es hora de.... **many times,** frecuentemente,
muchas veces. **Once upon a t.,** Érase una vez, Una
vez había, Érase que érase, Érase que se era. **Since t.
out of mind,** Desde tiempo inmemorial. **the last
(next) t.,** la última (próxima) vez. **this t. of year,**
esta estación del año. **T. hangs heavy on his hands,**
El tiempo se le hace interminable. **T. flies,** El tiempo
vuela. **T. will tell!** ¡El tiempo lo dirá! ¡Veremos lo
que veremos! **What t. is it?** ¿Qué hora es? **The t. is...,**
La hora es... **within a given t.,** dentro de un plazo
dado. **to be out of t.,** estar fuera de compás. **to gain
t.,** ganar tiempo. **to have a good t.,** pasarlo bien,
divertirse. **to have a bad t.,** pasarlo mal; *Inf.* tener
un mal cuarto de hora. **to have no t. to,** no tener
tiempo para + noun or pronoun, no tener tiempo de
+ infinitive. **to keep t.,** guardar el compás. **to kill t.,**
engañar (or entretener) el tiempo. **to mark t.,** marcar
el paso; *Fig.* hacer tiempo. **to pass the t.,** pasar el
rato; pasar el tiempo. **to pass the t. of day,** saludar.
to serve one's t., (to a trade) servir el aprendizaje;
(in prison) cumplir su condena; *Mil.* hacer el servicio
militar. **to take t.,** tomar tiempo para. **to take t.
by the forelock,** asir la ocasión por la melena. **to
waste t.,** perder el tiempo. **t. exposure,** pose, *f.* **t.-
fuse,** espoleta de tiempo, espoleta graduada, *f.* **t.-
honored,** tradicional, consagrado por el tiempo. **t.-
keeper,** capataz, *m;* reloj, *m.* **t.-saving,** que ahorra el
tiempo. **t.-server,** lameculos, *mf.* **t.-signal,** señales
horarias, *f pl.* **t.-table,** horario, *m;* itinerario, pro-

grama, *m* (railway) guía de ferrocarriles, *f.* **t. to
come,** porvenir, *m,* lo venidero

timed /taimd/ *a* calculado; **(ill-)** intempestivo;
(well-) oportuno

timeless /'taimlɪs/ *a* eterno

timeliness /'taimlinɪs/ *n* tempestividad, oportunidad,
f

timely /'taimli/ *a* oportuno

timepiece /'taim,pis/ *n* reloj, *m*

time zone *n* huso esférico, huso horario, *m*

timid /'tɪmɪd/ *a* tímido, asustadizo, medroso; (shy)
vergonzoso

timidity /tɪ'mɪdɪti/ *n* timidez, *f;* vergüenza, *f*

timing /'taimɪŋ/ *n* medida del tiempo, *f; Mech.* regulación, *f;* (timetable) horario, *f*

timorous /'tɪmərəs/ *a* timorato, apocado, asustadizo

timorousness /'tɪmərəsnɪs/ *n* encogimiento, *m,* timidez, *f*

tin /tɪn/ *n* (metal) estaño, *m;* (container) lata, *f;*
(sheet) hojalata, *f;* (money) plata, *f.* —*vt* estañar;
(place in tins) envasar en lata; cubrir con hojalata,
hoja de aluminio, *f.* **tin-foil,** papel de estaño, *m.* **tin
hat,** casco de acero, *m.* **tin opener,** abrelatas, abridor
de latas, *m.* **tin-plate,** hojalata, *f.* **tin soldier,** soldado
de plomo, *m.* **tin ware,** hojalatería, *f*

tincture /'tɪŋktʃər/ *n* tintura, *f,* tinte, *m; Med.* tintura,
f; (trace) dejo, *m;* (veneer) capa, *f.* —*vt* teñir, tinturar

tinder /'tɪndər/ *n* yesca, *f.* **t. box,** yescas, lumbres, *f
pl*

tinge /tɪndʒ/ *n* tinte, matiz, *m; Fig.* dejo, toque, *m.*
—*vt* matizar, tinturar; *Fig.* tocar

tingle /'tɪŋgəl/ *n* picazón, comezón, *f;* (thrill) estremecimiento, *m.* —*vi* picar; (of ears) zumbar;
(thrill) estremecerse (de); vibrar

tingling /'tɪŋglɪŋ/ *n* picazón, *f;* (of the ears) zumbido, *m;* (thrill) estremecimiento, *m*

tinker /'tɪŋkər/ *n* calderero remendón, *m.* —*vt*
remendar. —*vi* chafallar. **to t. with,** jugar con

tinkle /'tɪŋkəl/ *n* tilín, retintín, *m;* campanilleo, *m;*
cencerreo, *m.* —*vi* tintinar. —*vt* hacer tintinar

tinkling /'tɪŋklɪŋ/ *n* retintín, tintineo, *m;* campanilleo, *m*

tinned /tɪnd/ *a* (of food) en lata, en conserva

tinsel /'tɪnsəl/ *n* oropel, *m;* (cloth) lama de oro o
plata, *f,* brocadillo, *m; Fig.* oropel, *m.* —*a* de oropel;
de brocadillo; *Fig.* charro. —*vt* adornar con oropel

tinsmith /'tɪn,smɪθ/ *n* hojalatero, estañador, *m*

tint /tɪnt/ *n* tinta, *f,* color, *m;* matiz, *m;* tinte, *m.*
—*vt* colorar, teñir; matizar

tinting /'tɪntɪŋ/ *n* tintura, *f,* teñido, *m*

tiny /'taini/ *a* diminuto, minúsculo, menudo, chiquito

tip /tɪp/ *n* punta, *f;* cabo, *m,* extremidad, *f;* (of an
umbrella, etc.) regatón, *m;* (of a lance) borne, *m;* (of
a cigarette) boquilla, *f;* (of a shoe) puntera, *f;* (of a
finger) yema, *f;* (for rubbish) depósito de basura, *m;*
(gratuity) propina, *f;* (information) informe oportuno,
m; (tap) golpecito, *m.* **to have on the tip of one's
tongue,** tener en la punta de la lengua. **tip-cart,** volquete, *m.* **tip-up seat,** asiento plegable, *m*

tip /tɪp/ *vt* inclinar; volcar, voltear; (drinking vessel)
empinar; poner regatón, etc. (a); *Poet.* tocar, golpear
ligeramente; (reward) dar propina (a). —*vi* inclinarse;
(topple) tambalearse; (reward) dar propina. **to tip
the wink,** guiñar el ojo a (a). **to tip off,** (liquids)
echar; hacer caer; (inform) decir en secreto; informar
oportunamente. **to tip over,** volcar; hacer caer.
—*vi* volcarse, caer; (of a boat) zozobrar. **to tip up,** *vt*
(a seat) levantar; (money) proporcionar (el dinero);
(upset) volcar; hacer perder el equilibrio. —*vi*
volcarse; (of a seat) levantarse; (lose the balance)
perder el equilibrio

tipple /'tɪpəl/ *n* bebida, *f.* —*vt* beber, sorber. —*vi*
empinar el codo

tippler /'tɪplər/ *n* borracho (-cha)

tipsily /'tɪpsəli/ *adv* como borracho

tipsiness /'tɪpsinɪs/ *n* borrachera, *f*

tipsy /'tɪpsi/ *a* achispado, algo borracho. **to be t.,** estar entre dos luces, estar entre dos velas

tiptoe /'tɪp,tou/ **(on)** *adv* de puntillas; *Fig.* excitado,
ansioso. **to stand on t.,** ponerse de puntillas, empinarse

tirade /'taireid/ *n* diatriba, *f*

tire /taiᵊr/ n (of a cart, etc.) llanta, f; Auto. neumático, m; (of a perambulator, etc.) rueda de goma, f. **balloon t.,** neumático balón, m. **pneumatic t.,** neumático, m. **slack t.,** neumático desinflado, m. **solid t.,** neumático macizo, m. **spare t.,** neumático de recambio (or de repuesto), m. **t. burst,** estallido de un neumático, m. **t. valve,** válvula de cámara (del neumático), f

tire /taiᵊr/ vt cansar, fatigar; (bore) aburrir. —vi cansarse, fatigarse; aburrirse. **to be tired of,** estar cansado de. **to grow tired,** empezar a cansarse. **to t. out,** rendir de cansancio

tired /taiᵊrd/ a cansado, fatigado. **to be sick and t. of,** estar hasta la coronilla (de), (of persons) con. **t. of,** cansado de; disgustado de

tiredness /'taiᵊrdnɪs/ n cansancio, m, fatiga, f; aburrimiento, m

tireless /'taiᵊrlɪs/ a infatigable, incansable

tirelessly /'taiᵊrlɪsli/ adv sin tregua, sin cesar

tiresome /'taiᵊrsəm/ a fastidioso, molesto, pesado; (dull) aburrido

tiresomeness /'taiᵊrsəmnɪs/ n pesadez, f, fastidio, m; tedio, aburrimiento, m

tiring /'taiᵊrɪŋ/ a fatigoso

tissue /'tɪʃu/ n (cloth) tisú, m, lama, f; (paper) pañuelito m; Biol. tejido, m; (series) serie, sarta, f. **t. paper,** papel de seda, m

tit /tɪt/ n Ornith. paro, m. **tit for tat,** tal para cual

Titan /'taitn/ n titán, m

titanic /tai'tænɪk/ a titánico

titbit /'tɪt,bɪt/ n golosina, f

tithe /taið/ n décima, f; fracción, pequeña parte, f, vt diezmar. **t. gatherer,** diezmero (-ra)

titillate /'tɪtl,eit/ vt titilar, estimular

titivate /'tɪtə,veit/ vi arreglarse

title /'taitl/ n título, m; (right) derecho, m; documento, m. **to give a t. to,** intitular; ennoblecer. **t. deed,** títulos de propiedad, m. **t. page,** portada, f. **t. role,** papel principal, m

titter /'tɪtər/ vi reírse disimuladamente. —n risa disimulada, f

tittle /'tɪtl/ n adarme, tilde, ápice, m

titular /'tɪtʃələr/ a titular; nominal

to /tu/ unstressed tʊ, tə/ prep a; (as far as) hasta; (in the direction of) en dirección a, hacia; (with indirect object) a; (until) hasta; (compared with) en comparación con, comparado con; (against) contra; (according to) según; (as) como; (in) en; (so that, in order to, for the purpose of) para; (indicating possession) a, de; (of time by the clock) menos; (by) por; (before verbs of motion or which imply motion) a (sometimes para); (before some other verbs) de; en; (before verbs of beginning, inviting, exhorting, obliging) a; (indicating indirect object) a; (before a subjunctive or infinitive indicating future action or obligation) que. **To** is often not translated. With most Spanish infinitives no separate translation is necessary, e.g. leer, decir, to read, to speak. Some verbs are always followed by a preposition (e.g. to begin to speak, empezar a hablar, etc.). **to come to,** volver en sí. **to lie to,** Naut. ponerse a la capa. **to and from,** de un lado a otro. **face to face,** cara a cara. **He has been a good friend to them,** Ha sido un buen amigo para ellos. **That is new to me,** Eso es nuevo para mí. **He went to London,** Se fue a Londres. **to go to France (Canada),** ir a Francia (al Canadá). **the road to Madrid,** la carretera de Madrid. **She kept the secret to herself,** Guardó el secreto para sí. **to go to the dentist,** ir al dentista. **We give it to them,** Se lo damos a ellos. **It belongs to me,** Pertenece a mí. **What does it matter to you?** ¿Qué te importa a tí? **I wish to see him,** Quiero verle. **They did it to help us,** Lo hicieron para ayudarnos. **I have to go to see her,** Tengo que ir a verla. **to this day,** hasta hoy, hasta el presente. **It is a quarter to six,** Son las seis menos cuarto. **to the last shilling,** hasta el último chelín. **the next to me,** el que me sigue. **closed to the public,** cerrado para el público

toad /toud/ n sapo, m

toadstool /'toud,stul/ n hongo, m. **poisonous t.,** seta venenosa, f

toady /'toudi/ n lameculos, mf adulador (-ra). —vt lamer el culo (a), adular

toast /toust/ n Cul. tostada, f; (drink) brindis, m. —vt tostar; brindar, beber a la salud de. —vi brindar. **buttered t.,** mantecada, f. **t.-rack,** portatostadas, m

toaster /'toustər/ n (device) tostador, m; (person) brindador, m

toasting /'toustɪŋ/ n tostadura, f, tueste, m, a de tostar. **t.-fork,** tostadera, f

tobacco /tə'bækou/ n tabaco, m. —a tabacalero. **black** or **cut t.,** picadura, f. **leaf t.,** tabaco de hoja, m. **mild t.,** tobaco flojo, m. **pipe t.,** tabaco de pipa, m. **plug t.,** tabaco para mascar, m. **strong t.,** tabaco fuerte, m. **Turkish t.,** tabaco turco, m. **Virginian t.,** tabaco rubio, m. **t.-pipe,** pipa (de tabaco), f. **t.-pipe cleaner,** escobillón para limpiar pipas, m. **t. plantation,** tabacal, m. **t. planter,** tabacalero (-ra). **t. poisoning,** tabaquismo, m. **t.-pouch** or **jar,** tabaquera, f

tobacconist /tə'bækənɪst/ n tabaquero (-ra). **tobacconist's shop,** tabaquería, f

toboggan /tə'bɒgən/ n tobogán, m. —vi ir en tobogán. **t. run,** pista de tobogán, f

tocsin /'tɒksɪn/ n rebato, m

today /tə'dei/ adv hoy; ahora, actualmente, al presente, hoy día. —n el día de hoy. **from t.,** desde hoy. **from t. forward,** de hoy en adelante

toddle /'tɒdl/ vi hacer pinos, empezar a andar; (stroll) dar una vuelta; (leave) marcharse

toddy /'tɒdi/ n ponche, m

toe /tou/ n dedo del pie, m; (cloven) pezuña, f; uña, f; (of furniture) base, f, pie, m; (of stockings, shoes) punta, f. **He stepped on my toe,** Me pisó el dedo del pie. **big toe,** dedo pulgar del pie, dedo gordo del pie, m. **little toe,** dedo pequeño del pie, m. **to toe the line,** ponerse en la raya; Fig. cumplir con su deber. **toe-cap,** puntera, f. **toe-dancing,** baile de puntillas, m. **toe-nail,** uña del dedo del pie, f

toffee /'tɒfi/ n caramelo, m

toga /'tougə/ n toga, f

together /tə'gɛðər/ adv junto; (uninterruptedly) sin interrupción; (in concert) simultáneamente, a la vez, al mismo tiempo; (consecutively) seguido. **t. with,** con; junto con; en compañía de; (simultaneously) a la vez que

toil /tɔil/ n labor, f, trabajo, m —pl. **toils,** lazos, m pl; Fig. redes, f pl. —vi trabajar, afanarse. **to t. along,** caminar penosamente (por); adelantar con dificultad. **to t. up,** subir penosamente

toiler /'tɔilər/ n trabajador (-ra)

toilet /'tɔilɪt/ n tocado, m; atavío, m; vestido, m; (w.c.) retrete, excusado, m; (for ladies) tocador, m. **to make one's t.,** arreglarse. **t. case,** neceser, m. **t.-paper,** papel higiénico, m. **t.-powder,** polvos de arroz, m pl. **t. roll,** rollo de papel higiénico, m. **t.-set,** juego de tocador, m. **t. soap,** jabón de olor, jabón de tocador, m

toiling /'tɔilɪŋ/ n trabajo duro, m, a laborioso, trabajador

token /'toukən/ n señal, muestra, f; prueba, f; (presage) síntoma, indicio, m; (remembrance) recuerdo, m. **as a t. of,** en señal de; como recuerdo de

Tokyo /'touki,ou/ Tokio, m

tolerable /'tɒlərəbəl/ a tolerable, soportable, llevadero; (fairly good) mediano, mediocre, regular

tolerably /'tɒlərəbli/ adv bastante

tolerance /'tɒlərəns/ n tolerancia, f; paciencia, indulgencia, f

tolerant /'tɒlərənt/ a tolerante; indulgente

tolerate /'tɒlə,reit/ vt tolerar, sufrir, soportar; permitir

toleration /,tɒlə'reiʃən/ n tolerancia, f; indulgencia, paciencia, f. **religious t.,** libertad de cultos, f

toll /toul/ n (of a bell) tañido, doble, m; (for passage) peaje, portazgo, m; (for grinding) derecho de molienda, m. —vt and vi doblar, tañer. **to t. the hour,** dar la hora. **t. call,** conferencia telefónica interurbana, llamada a larga distancia, f. **t. gate,** barrera de peaje, f. **t. house,** oficina de portazgos, f

toll booth n caseta de pago, f

tolling /'toulɪŋ/ n tañido, clamor (de las campanas), m

Tom /tɒm/ n Tomás, m; (cat) gato, m. **Tom, Dick and Harry,** Fulano, Zutano y Mengano

tomahawk /'tɒmə,hɔk/ n hacha de guerra de los indios, f

tomato /tə'meitou/ n tomate, jitomate, (Mexico) m. **t. plant,** tomatera, f. **t. sauce,** salsa de tomate, f

tomb /tum/ n tumba, f, sepulcro, m

tombac /'tɒmbæk/ n tombac, m, tumbaga, f

tomboy /'tɒm,bɔi/ n muchachote, torbellino, m

tombstone /'tum,stoun/ n piedra mortuoria, f, monumento funerario, m

tome /toum/ n tomo, volumen, m

tomfoolery /,tɒm'fuləri/ n necedad, tontería, f; payasada, f

tommy gun /'tɒmi/ n pistola automática

tomorrow /tə'mɔrou/ adv and n mañana, f. **a fortnight t.,** mañana en quince. **the day after t.,** pasado mañana. **t. afternoon (morning),** mañana por la tarde (mañana). **T. is Friday,** Mañana es viernes

ton /tʌn/ n tonelada, f

tonality /tou'næliti/ n tonalidad, f

tone /toun/ n tono, m; (Mus. Med. Art.) tono, m; (of the voice) acento, m, entonación, f; (of musical instruments) sonido, m; (shade) matiz, m. —vt entonar; Photo. virar. **to t. down,** vt (Art. Mus.) amortiguar; Fig. suavizar, modificar. —vi (Art. Mus.) amortiguarse; Fig. suavizarse, modificarse. **to t. in with,** (of colors) vt armonizar con. —vi armonizarse, corresponder en tono o matiz. **to t. up,** vt subir de color, intensificar el color de; Med. entonar, robustecer. **t. poem,** poema sinfónico, m

tonelessly /'tounlisli/ adv sin tono; apáticamente

tongs /tɒŋz/ n pl tenazas, f pl; tenacillas, f pl. **curling t.,** tenacillas para el pelo, f pl. **sugar t.,** tenacillas para azúcar, f pl

tongue /tʌŋ/ n Anat. lengua, f; (language) idioma, m, lengua, f; (speech) modo de hablar, m, habla, f; Mus. lengüeta, f; (of buckle) diente, m; (of shoe) oreja, f; (of land) lengua, f; (of a bell) badajo, m; (flame) lengua, f. **My t. ran away with me,** Inf. Se me fue la mula. **to give t.,** ladrar. **to hold one's t.,** cerrar el pico, tener la boca. **t. of fire,** lengua de fuego, f. **t. tied,** con impedimento en el habla; turbado, confuso; mudo. **t.-twister,** trabalenguas, m

-tongued a de voz...

tonic /'tɒnik/ a tónico. —n Med. tónico, reconstituyente, m; Mus. tónica, f

tonight /tə'nait/ adv and n esta noche

tonnage /'tʌnidʒ/ n tonelaje, porte, m; (duty) derecho de tonelaje, m

tonner /'tʌnər/ n Naut. de... toneladas

tonsil /'tɒnsəl/ n amígdala, f

tonsillitis /,tɒnsə'laitis/ n amigdalitis, f

tonsure /'tɒnʃər/ n Eccl. tonsura, f, vt tonsurar

tonsured /'tɒnʃərd/ a tonsurado

too /tu/ adv demasiado; (very) muy; también; además. **too hard,** demasiado difícil, demasiado rígido; (of persons) demasiado duro. **too much,** demasiado. **too often,** con demasiada frecuencia

tool /tul/ n herramienta, f; utensilio, m; instrumento, m; (person) criatura, f. —vt labrar con herramienta; (a book) estampar en seco. **t.-bag,** capacho, m. **t. box,** caja de herramientas, f

tooling /'tulɪŋ/ n (of books) estampación en seco, f

toot /tut/ n sonido de bocina, m, vi sonar una bocina

tooth /tuθ/ n diente, m; muela, f; (of comb) púa, f; (taste) gusto, paladar, m; (cog) diente de rueda, m; (of saw) diente, m. —vt dentar; mellar. —vi Mech. engranar. **armed to the teeth,** armado hasta los dientes. **double t.,** muela, f. **false teeth,** dentadura postiza, f. **set of teeth,** dentadura, f. **to cut one's teeth,** echar los dientes. **to have a sweet t.,** ser muy goloso. **to show one's teeth,** enseñar los dientes. **t.-brush,** cepillo para los dientes, m. **t. drawing,** extracción de un diente, f. **t.-paste,** pasta dentífrica, f

toothache /'tuθ,eik/ n dolor de muelas, m

toothed /tuθt/ a con dientes; dentado

toothless /'tuθlis/ a desdentado, sin dientes; (of combs) sin púas

toothpick /'tuθ,pik/ n mondadientes, m

top /tɒp/ n (summit) cima, cumbre, f; (of a tree) copa, f; (of the head) coronilla, f; (of a page) cabeza,

f; (crest) copete, m, cresta, f; (surface) superficie, f; (of a wall) coronamiento, m; (tip) punta, f; (point) ápice, m; (of a tram, bus) imperial, baca, f; (of a wave) cresta, f; (acme) auge, m; (of a class) primero (de la clase), m; (highest rank) último grado, m; (of a plant) hojas, f pl; (of a piano) cima, f; Naut. cofa, f; (head of a bed, etc.) cabeza, f; (lid) tapadera, f; (toy) trompo, peón, m; (humming) trompa, f, a más alto; máximo; (chief) principal, primero. —vt (cover) cubrir de; (cut off) desmochar; (come level with) llegar a la cima de; (rise above) elevarse por encima de (de), coronar, dominar; (be superior to) exceder, aventajar; (golf) topear. **at the top,** a la cabeza; a la cumbre. **from top to bottom,** de arriba abajo. **on top of,** encima de; (besides) en adición a, además de. **to be top-dog,** ser un gallito. **to sleep like a top,** dormir como un lirón. **top boots,** botas de campaña, f pl. **top-dog,** vencedor, m; poderoso, m. **top-hat,** sombrero de copa, m. **top-heavy,** más pesado por arriba que por abajo

topaz /'toupæz/ n topacio, jacinto occidental, m

topcoat /'tɒp,kout/ n sobretodo, gabán, m

top floor n piso alto, m

topic /'tɒpik/ n asunto, tema, m

topical /'tɒpikəl/ a tópico; actual

topknot /'tɒp,nɒt/ n cresta, f, penacho, m; (of birds) moño, m; copete, m

topmast /'tɒp,mæst, Naut. -məst/ n mastelero, m

topmost /'tɒp,moust/ a más alto; más importante

topographer /tə'pɒgrəfər/ n topógrafo, m

topographical /,tɒpə'græfikəl/ a topográfico

topography /tə'pɒgrəfi/ n topografía, f

topple /'tɒpəl/ vi tambalearse, estar al punto de caer. **to t. down,** volcarse; derribarse; caer. **to t. over,** vi venirse abajo; perder el equilibrio. —vt derribar, hacer caer

topsail /'tɒp,seil; Naut. -səl/ n gavia, f

topsy-turvy /'tɒpsi'tɜrvi/ a desordenado. —adv en desorden, patas arriba, de arriba abajo

toque /touk/ n toca, f

torch /tɔrtʃ/ n antorcha, hacha, tea, f. **electric t.,** lamparilla eléctrica, f. **t.-bearer,** hachero, m

torchlight /'tɔrtʃ,lait/ n luz de antorcha, f. **by t.,** a la luz de las antorchas

torment /v. tɔr'mɛnt, n. 'tɔrmɛnt/ n tormento, m, angustia, f; (torture) tortura, f; suplicio, m; mortificación, f; disgusto, m. —vt atormentar, martirizar; (torture) torturar; molestar

tormentor /tɔr'mɛntər/ n atormentador (-ra)

tornado /tɔr'neidou/ n tornado, m

torpedo /tɔr'pidou/ n torpedo, m; Ichth. pez torpedo, m. —vt torpedear. **self-propelling t.,** torpedo automóvil, m. **t.-boat,** torpedero, m. **t.-boat destroyer,** cazatorpedero, contratorpedero, m. **t. netting,** red contra torpedos, f. **t. station,** base de torpederos, f. **t. tube,** tubo lanzatorpedos, m

torpedoing /tɔr'pidouɪŋ/ n torpedeamiento, torpedeo, m

torpid /'tɔrpid/ a aletargado, entorpecido; (of the mind) torpe, tardo, apático

torpidity, torpor /tɔr'piditi, 'tɔrpər/ n letargo, m; apatía, f

torrent /'tɔrənt/ n torrente, m

torrential /tə'rɛnʃəl/ a torrencial

torrid /'tɔrid/ a tórrido. **t. zone,** zona tórrida, f

torsion /'tɔrʃən/ n torsión, f

torso /'tɔrsou/ n torso, m

tort /tɔrt/ n Law. tuerto, m

tortoise /'tɔrtəs/ n tortuga, f. **t.-shell,** carey, m. —a de carey

tortuous /'tɔrtʃuəs/ a tortuoso

tortuousness /'tɔrtʃuəsnis/ n tortuosidad, f

torture /'tɔrtʃər/ n tortura, f, tormento, m; angustia, f. —vt torturar, dar tormento (a); martirizar

torturer /'tɔrtʃərər/ n atormentador (-ra)

torturing /'tɔrtʃərɪŋ/ a torturador, atormentador; angustioso

toss /tɒs/ n sacudimiento, m, sacudida, f; (of the head) movimiento (de cabeza), m; (bull fighting) cogida, f; (from a horse) caída de caballo, f. —vt echar, lanzar; agitar, sacudir; (of bulls) acornear. —vi agitarse; (of plumes, etc.) ondear; (in a boat) balancearse a la merced de las olas; jugar a cara o cruz. **to t. in a blanket**, mantear, dar una manta (a). **to t. aside**, echar a un lado; abandonar. **to t. off**, beber de un trago. **to t. up**, jugar a cara o cruz

tot /tɒt/ n (child) nene (-na), crío (-ía); (of drink) vaso pequeño, m. **to tot up**, sumar

total /'toutl/ a total; absoluto, completo, entero. —n total, m, suma, f. —vt sumar. —vi ascender (a). **t. employment**, ocupación total, f. **t. war**, guerra total, f

totalitarian /tou,tælɪ'teəriən/ a totalitario

totality /tou'tælɪti/ n totalidad, f

totally /'toutli/ adv totalmente, completamente

totem /'toutəm/ n tótem, m

totemism /'toutə,mɪzəm/ n totemismo, m

totter /'totər/ vi (of persons) bambolearse; tambalear, estar al punto de caer; Fig. aproximarse a su fin

tottering /'totərɪŋ/ a vacilante; tambaleante. —n bamboleo, m; tambaleo, m

toucan /'tukæn/ n Ornith. tucán, m

touch /tʌtʃ/ vt tocar; (brush against) rozar; (reach) alcanzar; (musical instruments) tocar; (move) emocionar, enternecer; (spur on) aguijar; (food) tomar; (affect) influir, afectar; (arouse) despertar, estimular; (equal) compararse con, igualar; (consider) tratar ligeramente (de); (money) dar un sablazo (a). —vi tocarse; imponer las manos para curar. **I have not touched a bite**, No he probado un bocado. **This touches me dearly**, Esto me toca de cerca. **to t. at**, hacer escala en, tocar en (un puerto). **to t. off**, descargar. **to t. up**, retocar; corregir. **to t. upon**, (a subject) tratar superficialmente de, tratar ligeramente de; hablar de; considerar

touch /tʌtʃ/ n (sense of) tacto, m; (contact) toque, contacto, m; (brushing) roce, m; (tap) golpe ligero, m; palmadita, f; (of an illness) ataque ligero, m; Mus. dedeo, m; (little) dejo, m; (test) prueba, f, toque, m; Art. toque, m, pincelada, f. **by the t.**, a tiento. **in t. with**, en relaciones con; en comunicación con; al corriente de. **to give the finishing t.**, dar la última pincelada; dar el último toque. **t.-line**, (football) línea de toque, línea lateral, f. **t.-me-not**, Inf. erizo, m. **t.-stone**, piedra de toque, f

touched /tʌtʃt/ a emocionado, conmovido

touchiness /'tʌtʃɪnɪs/ n susceptibilidad, f

touching /'tʌtʃɪŋ/ a patético, conmovedor. —prep tocante a, acerca de. —n tocamiento, m

touchy /'tʌtʃi/ a susceptible, quisquilloso, vidrioso

tough /tʌf/ a (hard) duro; vigoroso, fuerte, robusto; resistente; (of character) tenaz, firme; (of a job) difícil; espinoso. —n chulo, m

toughen /'tʌfən/ vt endurecer. —vi endurecerse

toughness /'tʌfnɪs/ n dureza, f; vigor, m, fuerza, f; resistencia, f; tenacidad, firmeza, f; dificultad, f

Toulouse /tu'luz/ Tolosa, f

toupee /tu'pei/ n tupé, m

tour /tʊr/ n viaje, m, excursión, f. —vi viajar. —vt viajar por. **circular t.**, viaje redondo, m. **on t.**, Theat. en tour, de gira

touring /'tʊrɪŋ/ a de turismo. —n turismo, m; viaje, m. **t. car**, coche de turismo, m

tourist /'tʊrɪst/ n turista, mf; viajero (-ra). **t. agency**, agencia de turismo, f, patronato de turismo, m. **t. ticket**, billete kilométrico, m

tournament /'tʊrnəmənt/ n torneo, m, justa, f; (of games) concurso, m

tourniquet /'tɜrnɪkɪt, 'tʊr-/ n torniquete, m

tousle /'tauzəl, -səl/ vt despeinar; desordenar el pelo

tout /taut/ n buhonero, m. **to t. for**, pescar, solicitar

tow /tou/ n remolque, m; (rope) estopa, f. —vt (Naut. Auto.) remolcar. **on tow**, a remolque. **tow-path**, camino de sirga, m. **tow rope**, cable de remolque, m

towage /'touɪdʒ/ n remolque, m; (fee) derechos de remolque, m pl

towards /tɔrdz/ prep hacia, en dirección a; (of time) sobre, cerca de; (concerning) tocante a; (with persons) para, con

towel /'tauəl/ n toalla, f. **roller t.**, toalla continua, f. **t. rail**, toallero, m

toweling /'tauəlɪŋ/ n tela para toallas, f

tower /'tauər/ n torre, f; (fortress) fortaleza, f; (bel-fry) campanario, m; (large) torreón, m. —vi elevarse. **to t. above**, destacarse sobre, sobresalir; Fig. sobrepujar, superar

towered /'tauərd/ a torreado; de las... torres. **high t.**, de las altas torres

towering /'tauərɪŋ/ a elevado; dominante; orgulloso; Fig. violento, terrible

town /taun/ n población, f, pueblo, m; ciudad, f. **t. clerk**, secretario de ayuntamiento, m. **t. council**, concejo municipal, m. **t. councilor**, concejero municipal, m. **t. crier**, pregonero, m. **t. hall**, (casa de) ayuntamiento, casa consistorial, f. **t. house**, casa de ciudad, f **t. planning**, urbanismo, m; reforma urbana, f. **t. wall**, muralla, f

"Town Ahead" «Poblado Próximo»

townsman /'taunzmən/ n ciudadano, m

town worthy n persona principal de la ciudad, f

toxic /'tɒksɪk/ a tóxico

toxicological /,tɒksɪkə'lɒdʒɪkəl/ a toxicológico

toxicologist /,tɒksɪ'kɒlədʒɪst/ n toxicólogo, m

toxicology /,tɒksɪ'kɒlədʒi/ n toxicología, f

toxin /'tɒksɪn/ n toxina, f

toy /tɔi/ n juguete, m. —vi (with) jugar con; acariciar. **toy maker**, fabricante de juguetes, m

toyshop /'tɔiˌʃɒp/ n juguetería, tienda de juguetes, f

trace /treis/ n huella, pista, f, rastro, m; vestigio, m; indicio, m, evidencia, f; (of a harness) tirante, m; (touch) dejo, m; (of fear, etc.) sombra, f. —vt trazar; (through transparent paper) calcar; seguir la pista (de); (write) escribir; (discern) distinguir; investigar; descubrir; determinar; (walk) atravesar, recorrer. **to t. back**, (of ancestry, etc.) hacer remontar (a)

traceable /'treisəbəl/ a que se puede trazar; atribuible

tracer /'treisər/ n trazador (-ra). **t. bullet**, bala luminosa, f

tracery /'treisəri/ n tracería, f

trachea /'treikiə/ n Anat. tráquea, f

trachoma /trə'koumə/ n Med. tracoma, f

tracing /'treisɪŋ/ n calco, m; trazo, m; seguimiento, m. **t.-paper**, papel de calcar, m

track /træk/ n huella, f, rastro, m; (for racing, etc.) pista, f; (of wheels) rodada, f; (railway) vía, f; (of a boat) estela, f; (path) senda, vereda, f; (sign) señal, evidencia, f; (course) ruta, f. —vt rastrear, seguir la pista (de); Naut. sirgar. **to t. down**, seguir y capturar. **double t.**, vía doble, f. **off the t.**, extraviado; (of a train) descarrilado; Fig. por los cerros de Úbeda. **side t.**, desviadero, m. **to keep t. of**, Inf. no perder de vista (a); seguir las fortunas de

trackless /'træklɪs/ a sin camino; sin huella; (of trams, etc.) sin rieles; (untrodden) no pisado

tract /trækt/ n tracto, m; región, f; Anat. vía, f; (written) tratado, m

tractability /,træktə'bɪlɪti/ n docilidad, f

tractable /'træktəbəl/ a dócil

traction /'trækʃən/ n tracción, f. **t.-engine**, máquina de arrastre (or de tracción), f

tractor /'træktər/ n máquina de arrastre, f; tractor, m

trade /treid/ n comercio, m; tráfico, m; negocio, m; industria, f; (calling) oficio, m, profesión, f; (dealers) comerciantes, mf pl. —vi comerciar, traficar. —vt cambiar. **to t. on**, explotar, aprovecharse de. **by t.**, de oficio, por profesión. **t.-mark**, marca de fábrica, f. **t.-name**, razón social, f. **t. price**, precio para el comerciante, m. **t. union**, sindicato, m. **T. Union Congress**, Congreso de Sindicatos, m. **t. unionism**, sistema de sindicatos obreros, m. **t.-winds**, vientos alisios, m pl

trader /'treidər/ n comerciante, traficante, mf; mercader, m; (boat) buque mercante, m

tradesman /'treidzmən/ n tendero, m. **tradesmen's entrance**, puerta de servicio, f

trading /'treidɪŋ/ n comercio, tráfico, m. —a mercantil, comercial, mercante. **t. ship**, buque mercante, m. **t. station**, factoría, f

tradition /trə'dɪʃən/ n tradición, f

traditional /trə'dɪʃənl/ a tradicional; del lugar

traditionalism /trə'dɪʃənlˌɪzəm/ n tradicionalismo, m

traditionalist /trə'dɪʃənlɪst/ n tradicionalista, mf

traditionally /trə'dɪʃənli/ adv según la tradición, tradicionalmente

traduce /trə'dus/ *vt* calumniar, denigrar, vituperar

traducer /trə'dusər/ *n* calumniador (-ra)

traffic /'træfɪk/ *n* comercio, negocio, tráfico, *m;* (in transit) transporte, *m;* (in movement) circulación, *f.* —*vi* comerciar, traficar, negociar. **to cause a block in the t.,** interrumpir la circulación. **t. block,** obstrución del tráfico, *f,* atasco en la circulación, *m.* **t. indicator,** (on a car) indicador de dirección, *m.* **t. island,** refugio para peatones, salvavidas, *m.* **t. light,** disco, *m,* luz (de tráfico), *f,* semáforo, *m.* **t. roundabout,** redondel, *m*

trafficker /'træfɪkər/ *n* traficante, *mf*

tragedian /trə'dʒidiən/ *n* trágico, *m*

tragedy /'trædʒɪdi/ *n* tragedia, *f*

tragic /'trædʒɪk/ *a* trágico

tragicomedy /,trædʒɪ'kɒmɪdi/ *n* tragicomedia, *f*

tragicomic /,trædʒɪ'kɒmɪk/ *a* tragicómico

trail /treɪl/ *n* rastro, *m,* pista, huella, *f;* (path) sendero, *m;* (of a comet) cola, cabellera, *f.* —*vt* rastrear, seguir el rastro de; (drag) arrastrar; (the anchor) garrar. —*vi* arrastrar; (of plants) trepar. **on the t. of,** en busca de; siguiendo el rastro de; **put somebody on the t. of...** darle a fulano la pista de...

trailer /'treɪlər/ *n* cazador (-ra); perseguidor (-ra); *Auto.* remolque, *m;* (cinema) anuncio de próximas atracciones, *m; Bot.* talle rastrero, *m*

train /treɪn/ *n* (railway) tren, *m;* (of a dress) cola, *f;* (retinue) séquito, *m;* (procession) desfile, *m,* comitiva, *f;* (series) serie, sucesión, *f;* (of gunpowder) reguero de pólvora, *m.* **down t.,** tren descendente, *m.* **excursion t.,** tren de excursionistas, *m.* **express t.,** exprés, tren expreso, *m.* **fast t.,** rápido, *m.* **goods t.,** tren de mercancías, *m.* **mail t.,** tren correo, *m.* **next t.,** próximo tren, *m.* **passenger t.,** tren de pasajeros, *m.* **stopping t.,** tren ómnibus, *m.* **through t.,** tren directo, *m.* **up t.,** tren ascendente, *m.* **t.-bearer,** paje que lleva la cola, *m;* dama de honor, *f;* (of a cardinal, etc.) caudatario, *m.* **t.-ferry,** buque transbordador, *m.* **t.-oil,** aceite de ballena, *m.* **t. service,** servicio de trenes, *m*

train /treɪn/ *vt* educar; adiestrar; enseñar; *Sports.* entrenar; (firearms) apuntar; (plants) guiar; (accustom) habituar, acostumbrar; (a horse for racing) entrenar; (circus) amaestrar. —*vi* educarse; adiestrarse; *Sports.* entrenarse

trainer /'treɪnər/ *n* (of men and racehorses) entrenador, *m;* (of performing animals) domador, *m*

training /'treɪnɪŋ/ *n* educación, *f;* enseñanza, instrucción, *f; Sports.* entrenamiento, *m.* **t.-college,** escuela normal, *f.* **t.-ship,** buque escuela, *m*

trait /treɪt/ *n* rasgo, *m,* característica, *f*

traitor /'treɪtər/ *n* traidor, *m*

traitress /'treɪtrɪs/ *n* traidora, *f*

trajectory /trə'dʒɛktəri/ *n* trayectoria, *f*

tram /træm/ *n* tranvía, *m.* —*a* tranviario. **t. conductor,** cobrador de tranvía, *m.* **t. depot,** cochera de tranvías, *f.* **t. stop,** parada de tranvía, *f.*

trammel /'træməl/ *n* (of a horse) traba, *f; Fig.* obstáculo, estorbo, *m.* —*vt* travar; *Fig.* estorbar, impedir

tramp /træmp/ *n* (person) vagabundo (-da); vago (-ga); (walk) caminata, *f,* paseo largo, *m;* ruido de pasos, *m; Naut.* vapor volandero, *m.* —*vi* ir a pie; patear; vagabundear. —*vt* vagar por

trample /'træmpəl/ *n* pisoteo, *m;* (of feet) ruido de pasos, *m.* —*vt* pisotear, pisar, hollar. —*vi* pisar fuerte. **to t. on,** *Fig.* atropellar humillar

trance /træns/ *n* rapto, arrobamiento, *m; Med.* catalepsia, *f*

tranquil /'træŋkwɪl/ *a* tranquilo, apacible; sereno, sosegado

tranquility /træŋ'kwɪlɪti/ *n* tranquilidad, paz, quietud, *f;* serenidad, *f,* sosiego, *m;* calma, *f*

tranquilize /'træŋkwə,laɪz/ *vt* tranquilizar, sosegar, calmar

tranquilizer /'træŋkwə,laɪzər/ *n* calmante, *m*

tranquilizing /'træŋkwə,laɪzɪŋ/ *a* sosegador, tranquilizador

trans- *prefix* trans-. **t.-Pyrenean,** *a* traspirenaico. **to t. -ship,** trasbordar. **t.-shipment,** trasbordo, *m.* **t.- Siberian,** trasiberiano

trans- *prefix* trans-. **t.-Pyrenean,** *a* traspirenaico. **to t. -ship,** trasbordar. **t.-shipment,** trasbordo, *m.* **t.- Siberian,** trasiberiano

transact /træn'sækt/ *vt* despachar, hacer. —*vi* despachar un negocio

transaction /træn'sækʃən/ *n* desempeño, *m;* negocio, *m;* transacción, operación, *f; pl* **transactions** (of a society) actas, *f pl*

transatlantic /,trænsət'læntɪk/ *a* transatlántico. **t. liner,** transatlántico, *m*

transcend /træn'sɛnd/ *vt* exceder, superar, rebasar. —*vi* trascender

transcendence /træn'sɛndəns/ *n* superioridad, *f;* trascendencia, *f*

transcendental /,trænsɛn'dɛntl̩/ *a* trascendental

transcontinental /,trænskɒntn̩'ɛntl̩/ *a* transcontinental

transcribe /træn'skraib/ *vt* trascribir, copiar; *Mus.* trascribir, adaptar

transcriber /træn'skraibər/ *n* copiador (-ra); *Mus.* adaptador (-ra)

transcript /'trænskrɪpt/ *n* traslado, trasunto, *m;* (student's) certificado de estudios, certificado de materias aprobadas, *m,* constancia de estudios, copia del expediente académico, hoja de estudios, *f*

transcription /træn'skrɪpʃən/ *n* trascripción, copia, *f,* trasunto, *m; Mus.* trascripción, adaptación, *f,* arreglo, *m*

transept /'trænsɛpt/ *n Archit.* transepto, crucero, *m*

transfer /*v.* træns'fɜr, *n.* 'trænsfər/ *n* traslado, *m;* trasferencia, *f,* traspaso, *m; Law.* cesión, enajenación, *f;* (picture) calcomanía, *f.* —*vt* trasladar; trasferir; pasar; *Law.* enajenar, ceder; estampar; calcografiar. —*vi* trasbordarse. **deed of t.,** escritura de cesión, *f.* **t. -paper,** papel de calcar, *m*

transferable /træns'fɜrəbəl/ *a* trasferible

transferee /,trænsfə'ri/ *n* cesionario (-ia)

transference /træns'fɜrəns/ *n* traslado, *m;* transferencia, *f; Law.* cesión, enajenación, *f*

transferor /træns'fɜrər/ *n* cesionista, *mf*

transfiguration /,trænsfɪgyə'reɪʃən/ *n* trasfiguración, *f*

transfigure /træns'fɪgyər/ *vt* trasfigurar, trasformar

transfix /træns'fɪks/ *vt* traspasar; *Fig.* paralizar

transfixion /træns'fɪkʃən/ *n* trasfixión, *f*

transform /træns'fɔrm/ *vt* trasformar; convertir, cambiar. **It is completely transformed,** Está completamente trasformado

transformation /,trænsfər'meɪʃən/ *n* trasformación, *f;* conversión, *f,* cambio, *m*

transformative /træns'fɔrmətɪv/ *a* trasformador

transformer /træns'fɔrmər/ *n Elec.* trasformador, *m*

transfuse /træns'fyuz/ *vt* trasfundir

transfusion /træns'fyuʒən/ *n* trasfusión, *f.* **blood t.,** trasfusión de sangre, *f*

transgress /træns'grɛs/ *vt* exceder, sobrepasar; (violate) contravenir, violar, pecar contra. —*vi* pecar

transgression /træns'grɛʃən/ *n* contravención, trasgresión, *f;* pecado, *m*

transgressor /træns'grɛsər/ *n* trasgresor (-ra), pecador (-ra)

transient /'trænʃənt, -ʒənt/ *a* transitorio, fugaz, pasajero; perecedero

transiently /'trænʃəntli, -ʒənt-/ *adv* pasajeramente

transit /'trænsɪt/ *n* tránsito, paso, *m;* trasporte, *m; Astron.* tránsito, *m.* **in t.,** de tránsito

transition /træn'zɪʃən/ *n* transición, *f;* cambio, *m;* tránsito, paso, *m*

transitional /træn'zɪʃənl̩/ *a* de transición, transitorio

transitive /'trænsɪtɪv/ *a Gram.* transitivo, activo. **t. verb,** verbo transitivo, verbo activo, *m*

transitively /'trænsɪtɪvli/ *adv* transitivamente

transitorily /,trænsɪ'tɔrəli/ *adv* transitoriamente; provisionalmente

transitoriness /'trænsɪ,tɔrɪnɪs/ *n* brevedad, *f,* lo fugaz

transitory /'trænsɪ,tɔri/ *a* transitorio, fugaz, pasajero, breve

translatable /træns'leɪtəbəl/ *a* traducible

translate /træns'leɪt/ *vt* traducir; interpretar; (transfer) trasladar

translation /træns'leɪʃən/ *n* traducción, *f;* versión, *f;* traslado, *m*

translator /trænsˈleɪtər/ n traductor (-ra)
translucence /trænsˈlusəns/ n traslucidez, f
translucent /trænsˈlusənt/ a traslúcido, trasparente
transmigrate /trænsˈmaɪgreɪt/ vi trasmigrar
transmigration /ˌtrænsmaɪˈgreɪʃən/ n trasmigración, f
transmissibility /ˌtrænsˌmɪsəˈbɪlɪti/ n trasmisibilidad, f
transmissible /trænsˈmɪsəbəl/ a trasmisible
transmission /trænsˈmɪʃən/ n trasmisión, f
transmit /trænsˈmɪt/ vt trasmitir; remitir, dar
transmitter /trænsˈmɪtər/ n trasmisor (-ra); *Radio.* radiotrasmisor, m; *Elec.* trasmisor, m
transmutable /trænsˈmyutəbəl/ a trasmutable
transmutation /ˌtrænsmyuˈteɪʃən/ n trasmutación, f
transmute /trænsˈmyut/ vt trasmutar
transoceanic /ˌtrænsouʃiˈænɪk/ a transoceánico
transom /ˈtrænsəm/ n travesaño, m; *Naut.* yugo de popa, m
transpacific /ˌtrænspəˈsɪfɪk/ a traspacífico
transparency /trænsˈpɛərənsi/ n trasparencia; diafanidad, f; (picture) trasparente, m
transparent /trænsˈpɛərənt/ a trasparente; diáfano; (of style) claro, limpio
transpiration /ˌtrænspəˈreɪʃən/ n traspiración, f
transpire /trænˈspaɪər/ vi traspirar; rezumarse; hacerse público; *Inf.* acontecer. —vt exhalar
transplant /trænsˈplænt/ vt trasplantar
transplantation /ˌtrænsplænˈteɪʃən/ n trasplante, m, trasplantación, f,
transport /v. trænsˈpɔrt, n. ˈtrænspɔrt/ n trasporte, m; *Naut.* navío de trasporte, m; *Aer.* avión de trasporte, m; (fit) acceso, paroxismo, m. —vt trasportar; (convicts) deportar; *Fig.* (joy) colmar; (rage) llenar
transportable /trænsˈpɔrtəbəl/ a trasportable
transportation /ˌtrænspərˈteɪʃən/ n trasporte, m; (convicts) deportación, f
transporter /træns,pɔrtər/ n trasportador (-ra)
transpose /trænsˈpouz/ vt trasponer; *Mus.* trasportar
transposition /ˌtrænspəˈzɪʃən/ n trasposición, f
transversal /trænsˈvɜrsəl/ a n trasversal, m
transverse /trænsˈvɜrs/ a trasverso, trasversal
transversely /trænsˈvɜrsli/ adv trasversalmente
trap /træp/ n trampa, f; cepo, m; (net) lazo, m, red, f; (for mice, rats) ratonera, f; *Mech.* sifón de depósito, m; pequeño carruaje de dos ruedas, m; (door) puerta caediza, f; *Theat.* escotillón, m; pl **traps**, trastos, m pl; equipaje, m. —vt coger con trampa; hacer caer en el lazo; *Fig.* tender el lazo. —vi armar una trampa; armar lazo. **to fall into a t.,** *Fig.* caer en la trampa. **to pack one's traps,** liar el hato
trapeze /træˈpiz/ n trapecio (de gimnasia), m
trapper /ˈtræpər/ n cazador de animales de piel, m
trappings /ˈtræpɪŋz/ n pl arneses, jaeces, m pl; arreos, aderezos, m pl, galas, f pl
trash /træʃ/ n paja, hojarasca, f; (of sugar, etc.) bagazo, m; trastos viejos, m pl; cachivaches, m pl; (literary) paja, f
trashy /ˈtræʃi/ a de ningún valor, inútil, despreciable
traumatic /trɑˈmætɪk/ a *Med.* traumático
traumatism /ˈtraumə,tɪzəm/ n *Med.* traumatismo, m
travail /trəˈveɪl/ n dolores de parto, m pl. —vi estar de parto; trabajar
travel /ˈtrævəl/ n el viajar, viajes, m pl. —vi viajar; ver mundo; (of traffic) circular, pasar, ir. —vt viajar por; recorrer; (with number of miles) hacer. **to t. over,** viajar por; recorrer. **t. worn,** fatigado por el viaje
travel agent n agente de viajes, mf
traveled /ˈtrævəld/ a que ha viajado, que ha visto muchas partes
traveler /ˈtrævələr/ n viajero (-ra); pasajero (-ra). **commercial t.,** viajante, mf **traveler's check,** cheque de viajeros, m. **traveler's joy,** *Bot.* clemátide, f
traveling /ˈtrævəlɪŋ/ n viajes, m pl. —a viajar; para (or de) viajar; (itinerant) ambulante. **t. crane,** grúa móvil, f. **t. expenses,** gastos de viaje, m pl. **t. requisites,** objetos de viaje, m pl. **t. rug,** manta, f. **t. show,** circo ambulante, m
traversable /trəˈvɜrsəbəl/ a atravesable, transitable, practicable
traverse /n., a. ˈtrævɜrs; v. trəˈvɜrs/ n travesaño, m; *Law.* negación, f; (*Mil. Archit.*) través, m; (crossing)

travesía, f, a transversal. —vt atravesar, cruzar; *Law.* negar
travesty /ˈtrævəsti/ n parodia, f, vt parodiar
trawl /trɔl/ vt rastrear. —vi pescar a la rastra. **t.-net,** red de arrastre, f
trawler /ˈtrɔlər/ n barco barredero, m; pescador a la rastra, m
trawling /ˈtrɔlɪŋ/ n pesca a la rastra, f
tray /treɪ/ n bandeja, f; (of a balance) platillo, m; (in a wardrobe, etc.) cajón, m; (trough) artesa, f
treacherous /ˈtretʃərəs/ a traidor, falso, pérfido, fementido; (of memory) infiel; engañoso; (of ice, etc.) peligroso
treacherously /ˈtretʃərəsli/ adv traidoramente, a traición
treachery /ˈtretʃəri/ n perfidia, traición, falsedad, f
treacle /ˈtrikəl/ n melado, m
tread /tred/ n pisada, f; paso, m; (of a stair) peldaño, m; (of tire) pastilla, f; (walk) andar, porte, m, vi pisar; (trample) pisotear; hollar; (oppress) oprimir. —vt hollar; (a path) abrir; recorrer; caminar por; bailar. **to t. the grapes,** pisar las uvas. **to t. the stage,** pisar las tablas. **to t. under foot,** hollar; pisotear. **to t. on,** pisar. **to t. on one's heels,** pisarle los talones a uno; seguir de cerca. **to t. out,** (a measure) bailar
treading /ˈtredɪŋ/ n pisoteo, m
treadle /ˈtredl/ n pedal, m; (of a loom) cárcola, f
treadmill /ˈtred,mɪl/ n molino de rueda de escalones, m; *Fig.* rueda, f
treason /ˈtrizən/ n traición, f. **high t.,** alta traición, lesa majestad, f
treasonable /ˈtrizənəbəl/ a desleal, traidor
treasonably /ˈtrizənəbli/ adv traidoramente
treasure /ˈtrɛʒər/ n tesoro, m; riqueza, f, caudal, m; *Fig.* perla, f. —vt atesorar; acumular (or guardar) riquezas; (a memory) guardar. **t. trove,** tesoro hallado, m
treasurer /ˈtrɛʒərər/ n tesorero (-ra)
treasury /ˈtrɛʒəri/ n tesorería, f; (government department) Ministerio de Hacienda, m; (anthology) tesoro, m. **t. bench,** banco del Gobierno, m
treat /trit/ n (pleasure) gusto, placer, m; (present) obsequio, m; (entertainment) fiesta, f. —vt tratar; *Med.* tratar, curar; (regale) obsequiar. —vi (stand host) convidar; (of) tratar de, versar sobre; (with) negociar con
treatise /ˈtritɪs/ n tesis, monografía, disertación, f, tratado, m
treatment /ˈtritmənt/ n tratamiento, m; (of persons) conducta hacia, f, modo de obrar con, m; *Med.* tratamiento, m; (*Lit., Art.*) procedimiento, m, técnica, f
treaty /ˈtriti/ n tratado, pacto, m; (bargain) contrato, m
treble /ˈtrebəl/ n *Mus.* tiple, m; voz de tiple, f. —a triple; *Mus.* sobreagudo. —vt triplicar; vi triplicarse. **t. clef,** clave de sol, f
trebling /ˈtreblɪŋ/ n triplicación, f
tree /tri/ n árbol, m; (for shoes) horma, f; (of a saddle) arzón, m. **breadfruit t.,** árbol del pan, m. **Judas t.,** árbol de amor, m. **t. of knowledge,** árbol de la ciencia, m. **t.-covered,** arbolado. **t.-frog,** rana de San Antonio, f
treeless /ˈtrilɪs/ a sin árboles
trefoil /ˈtrifɔɪl/ n trébol, trifolio, m
trek /trek/ vi caminar, andar
trellis /ˈtrelɪs/ n enrejado, m; (for plants) espaldera, f. —vt cercar con un enrejado; construir espalderas
tremble /ˈtrembəl/ vi temblar; estremecerse; trepidar; vibrar; (sway) oscilar; (of flags) ondear; agitarse; ser tembloroso. **His fate trembled in the balance,** Su suerte estaba en la balanza. **to t. all over,** temblar de pies a cabeza
trembling /ˈtremblɪŋ/ n temblor, m; estremecimiento, m; trepidación, f; vibración, f; (fear) agitación, ansiedad, f; temor, m. —a tembloroso; trémulo
tremendous /trɪˈmɛndəs/ a terrible, espantoso; formidable; grande; importante; *Inf.* tremendo; enorme
tremendously /trɪˈmɛndəsli/ adv terriblemente; *Inf.* enormemente
tremor /ˈtrɛmər/ n temblor, movimiento sísmico, m; (thrill) estremecimiento, m; vibración, f

tremulous /'trɛmyələs/ a trémulo, tembloroso; vacilante; tímido

tremulously /'trɛmyələsli/ adv trémulamente; tímidamente

tremulousness /'trɛmyələsnɪs/ n lo tembloroso; vacilación, f; timidez, f

trench /trɛntʃ/ n zanja, f, foso, m; (for irrigation) acequia, f; Mil. trinchera, f. —vt hacer zanjas (en); acequiar; Mil. atrincherar. **t.-fever,** tifus exantemático, m. **t.-foot,** pie de trinchera, m. **t.-mortar,** mortero de trinchera, m

trenchant /'trɛntʃənt/ a mordaz

trencher /'trɛntʃər/ n trinchero, m

trend /trɛnd/ n curso, rumbo, m; Fig. tendencia, f; dirección, f. —vi Fig. tender

trepan /trɪ'pæn/ vt Surg. trepanar

trepanning /trɪ'pænɪŋ/ n Surg. trepanación, f

trepidation /ˌtrɛpɪ'deɪʃən/ n trepidación, f

trespass /'trɛspəs, -pæs/ n violación de propiedad, f; ofensa, f; pecado, m; (in the Lord's Prayer) deuda, f. —vi (on land) entrar sin derecho, violar la propiedad; (upon) entrar sin permiso en; (with patience, etc.) abusar de; (against) pecar contra, infringir

trespasser /'trɛspəsər, -pæs-/ n violador (-ra) de la ley de propiedad. **"Trespassers will be prosecuted,"** «Entrada prohibida,» «Prohibido el paso»

tress /trɛs/ n (plait) trenza, f; rizo, bucle, m; pl **tresses,** cabellera, f

trestle /'trɛsəl/ n caballete, m; armazón, m. **trestle-table,** mesa de caballete, f

triad /'traɪæd/ n terna, f; Mus. acorde, m

trial /'traɪəl/ n prueba, f, ensayo, m; examen, m; (experiment) tentativa, f, experimento, m; (misfortune) desgracia, pena, f; (nuisance) molestia, f; Law. vista de una causa, f. **on t.,** a prueba; Law. en proceso. **to bring to t.,** procesar. **to stand one's t.,** ser procesado. **t. run,** marcha de ensayo, f. **t. trip,** Naut. viaje de ensayo, m

trial and error n tanteos, m. **by trial and error,** por tanteos.

triangle /'traɪˌæŋɡəl/ n triángulo, m. **acute-angled t.,** triángulo acutángulo, m. **obtuse-angled t.,** triángulo obtusángulo, m. **right-angled t.,** triángulo rectángulo, m. **the eternal t.,** el eterno triángulo

triangular /traɪ'æŋɡyələr/ a triangular, triángulo

triangulation /traɪˌæŋɡyə'leɪʃən/ n (in surveying) triangulación, f

tribal /'traɪbəl/ a tribal

tribe /traɪb/ n tribu, f

tribesman /'traɪbzmən/ n miembro de una tribu, m

tribulation /ˌtrɪbyə'leɪʃən/ n tribulación, f; pena, aflicción, desgracia, f

tribunal /traɪ'byunl/ n (seat) tribunal, m; (court) juzgado, m; (confessional) confesionario, m

tribunate /'trɪbyənɪt/ n tribunado, m

tribune /'trɪbyun/ n (person) tribuno, m; tribuna, f

tribunicial a tribúnico

tributary /'trɪbyəˌtɛri/ a and n tributario m

tribute /'trɪbyut/ n tributo, m; contribución, imposición, f

trice /traɪs/ n tris, soplo, m. **in a t.,** en un periquete, en un avemaría, en dos trancos

tricentennial /ˌtraɪsɛn'tɛniəl/ a de trescientos años; n tercer centenario, tricentenario, m

trick /trɪk/ n (swindle) estafa, f, engaño, m; (ruse) truco, m, estratagema, ardid, f; (mischief) travesura, f; burla, f; (illusion) ilusión, f; (habit) costumbre, f; (affectation) afectación, f; (jugglery) juego de manos, m; (knack) talento, m; (at cards) baza, f. —vt engañar, estafar; (with out) adornar, ataviar; (with into) inducir fraudulentamente. —vi trampear. **dirty t.,** Inf. mala pasada, perrada, f. **His memory plays him tricks,** La memoria le engaña. **to play a t. on,** gastar una broma (a). **to play tricks,** hacer travesuras. **t. riding,** acrobacia ecuestre, f

trickery /'trɪkəri/ n maullería, superchería, f; fraude, engaño, m

trickle /'trɪkəl/ n chorrito, hilo (de agua, etc.) m. —vi gotear. **to t. down,** deslizar por, correr por, escurrir por

trickling /'trɪklɪŋ/ n goteo, m; (sound) murmullo, m

trickster /'trɪkstər/ n embustero (-ra), trampeador (-ra). **to be a t.,** ser buena maula

tricky /'trɪki/ a informal, maullero; (of things) difícil, complicado; (clever) ingenioso

tricolor /'traɪˌkʌlər/ a tricolor

tricycle /'traɪsɪkəl/ n triciclo, m

tried /traɪd/ a probado

triennial /traɪ'ɛniəl/ a trienal

trifle /'traɪfəl/ n (object) baratija, fruslería, f; pequeñez, tontería, bagatela, f; Culin, f; (small amount) pequeña cantidad, f, muy poco (de); (adverbially) algo. —vi entretenerse, jugar. —vt (away) malgastar. **to t. with,** jugar con

trifler /'traɪflər/ n persona frívola, f; (with affections) seductor (-ra)

trifling /'traɪflɪŋ/ a insignificante, sin importancia, trivial

trigger /'trɪɡər/ n (of a fire-arm) gatillo, m; Mech. tirador, m

trigonometric /ˌtrɪɡənə'mɛtrɪk/ a trigonométrico

trigonometry /ˌtrɪɡə'nɒmɪtri/ n trigonometría, f

trilingual /traɪ'lɪŋɡwəl/ a trilingüe

trill /trɪl/ n trino, m, vi trinar

trillion /'trɪlyən/ n trillón, m

trilogy /'trɪlədʒi/ n trilogía, f

trim /trɪm/ a aseado; bien arreglado; bien ajustado; elegante; bonito; (of sail) orientado. **She has a t. waist,** Inf. Tiene un talle juncal. —n orden, m; buen estado, m; buena condición, f; (toilet) atavío, m. —vt arreglar; (tidy) asear; pulir; (ornament) ornar, adornar; (adapt) ajustar, adaptar; Sew. aguarnecer; (lamps) despabilar; (a fire) atizar; (hair, moustache) atusar, recortar; (trees) mondar, atusar; alisar; (sails) templar, orientar; (distribute weight in a boat) equilibrar; (of quill pens) tajar. —vi (waver) nadar entre dos aguas. **to t. oneself up,** arreglarse

trimly /'trɪmli/ adv aseadamente; lindamente

trimmer /'trɪmər/ n guarnecedor (-ra); contemporizador (-ra)

trimming /'trɪmɪŋ/ n arreglo, m; guarnición, f; (on a dress) pasamanería, f; adorno, m; Agr. poda, f; adaptación, f, ajuste, m; pl **trimmings,** accesorios, m pl

trimness /'trɪmnɪs/ n aseo, buen orden, m; buen estado, m; elegancia, lindeza, f; (slimness) esbeltez, f

Trinidad and Tobago /'trɪnɪdæd; tə'beɪɡou/ Trinidad, f, y Tobago, m

Trinidadian /ˌtrɪni'deɪdiən/ n and a trinitario

Trinity /'trɪnɪti/ n Trinidad, f

trinket /'trɪŋkɪt/ n joya, alhaja, f; dije, m, chuchería, baratija, f

trinomial /traɪ'noumiəl/ a Math. de tres términos. —n Math. trinomio, m

trio /'triou/ n trío, m

trip /trɪp/ n excursión, f; viaje, m; (slip) traspié, tropiezo, m; (in wrestling) zancadilla, f; (mistake) desliz, m. —vi (stumble) tropezar, caer; (move nimbly) andar airosamente, ir (or correr) ligeramente; (frolic) bailar, saltar; (wrestling, games) echar la zancadilla; (err) equivocarse; cometer un desliz. —vt (up) hacer caer; echar la zancadilla (a); coger en una falta; hacer desdecirse; coger en un desliz; Naut. levantar (el ancla)

tripartite /traɪ'pɑrtaɪt/ a tripartito

tripartition /ˌtraɪpɑr'tɪʃən/ n tripartición, f

tripe /traɪp/ n callos, m pl

triple /'trɪpəl/ a triple. —vt triplicar. —vi triplicarse

triplet /'trɪplɪt/ n Poet. terceto, m; Mus. tresillo, m; cada uno (una) de tres hermanos (hermanas) gemelos (-as)

triplicate /a. 'trɪplɪkɪt, v. -ˌkeɪt/ a triplicado. —vt triplicar

triplication /ˌtrɪplɪ'keɪʃən/ n triplicación, f

tripod /'traɪpɒd/ n trípode, m

Tripoli /'trɪpəli/ Trípoli, m

tripper /'trɪpər/ n turista, excursionista, mf

tripping /'trɪpɪŋ/ a ligero, ágil

trippingly /'trɪpɪŋli/ adv ligeramente

triptych /'trɪptɪk/ n tríptico, m

trite /traɪt/ a vulgar, trivial

triteness /'traɪtnɪs/ n trivialidad, vulgaridad, f

triumph /'traiəmf/ n triunfo, m. —vi triunfar; (over) triunfar de, vencer

triumphal /trai'ʌmfəl/ a triunfal. **t. arch,** arco de triunfo, m

triumphant /trai'ʌmfənt/ a triunfante, victorioso

triumvirate /trai'ʌmvərit/ n triunvirato, m

trivet /'trivit/ n trébedes, f pl, trípode, m

trivial /'triviəl/ a trivial, frívolo; insignificante, sin importancia

triviality /,trivi'æliti/ n trivialidad, frivolidad, f; insignificancia, f

trochlea /'troklia/ n Anat. tróclea, f

trodden /'trodṇ/ a trillado, batido

troglodyte /'troglə,dait/ a and n troglodita, mf

Trojan /'troudʒən/ a and n troyano (-na). **the T. War,** la guerra de Troya, f

trolley /'troli/ n Elec. trole, m; (for children) carretón, m. **t.-bus,** trolebús, m. —n **trolley car** tranvía, m. **t.-pole,** trole, f

trollop /'troləp/ n tarasca, ramera, f

trombone /trom'boun/ n trombón, m. **t. player,** trombón, m

troop /trup/ n banda, muchedumbre, f; Theat. compañía, f; (of cavalry) escuadrón, m; pl **troops,** Mil. tropas, f pl; ejército, m. —vi ir en tropel, congregarse; (with away) marcharse en tropel, retirarse; (with out) salir en masa. **fresh troops,** tropas frescas, f pl. **storm troops,** tropas de asalto, f pl. **t.-ship,** transporte de guerra, m

trooper /'trupər/ n soldado de caballería, m

trope /troup/ n tropo, m.

trophy /'troufi/ n trofeo, m

tropic /'tropik/ a and n trópico, m.

tropical /'tropikəl/ a tropical

tropism /'troupizəm/ n tropismo, m

trot /trot/ n trote, m. —vi trotar. **to t. out,** Inf. sacar a relucir

troth /troθ/ n fe, f; palabra, f. **to plight one's t.,** dar palabra de matrimonio, desposarse

trotting /'trotiŋ/ a trotón. —n trote, m

troubadour /'trubə,dɔr/ n trovador, m, a trovadoresco

trouble /'trʌbəl/ n (grief) aflicción, angustia, f; (difficulty) dificultad, f; (effort) esfuerzo, f; pena, desgracia, f; (annoyance) disgusto, sinsabor, m; (unrest) confusión, f, disturbio, m; (illness) enfermedad, f; mal, m; (disagreement) desavenencia, f. **The t. is....,** Lo malo es; La dificultad está en que... **to be in t.,** estar afligido; estar en un apuro, estar entre la espada y la pared. **to be not worth the t.,** no valer la pena. **to stir up t.,** revolver el río; armar un lío. **to take the t. to,** tomarse la molestia de

trouble /'trʌbəl/ vt turbar; agitar; afligir, inquietar; (badger) importunar; (annoy) molestar; (cost an effort) costar trabajo (e.g., Learning Spanish did not t. him much, No le costó mucho trabajo aprender el castellano). —vi preocuparse; darse la molestia; inquietarse

troubled /'trʌbəld/ a agitado; inquieto; preocupado; (of life) accidentado, borrascoso. **to fish in t. waters,** pescar en agua turbia, pescar en río revuelto

troublesome /'trʌbəlsəm/ a difficultoso; molesto; inconveniente; importuno; fastidioso

trough /trof/ n gamella, f; (for kneading bread) artesa, f; (of the waves) seno, m; (meteorological) mínimo, m. **drinking t.,** abrevadero, m. **stone t.,** pila, f

trounce /trauns/ vt zurrar, apalear; Fig. fustigar

troupe /trup/ n compañía, f

trousers /'trauzərz/ n pl pantalones, m pl. **plus four t.,** pantalones de golf, m pl. **striped t.,** pantalón de corte, m. **t. pocket,** bolsillo del pantalón, m. **t. press,** prensa para pantalones, f

trousseau /'trusou/ n ajuar de novia, m

trout /traut/ n trucha, f

trowel /'trauəl/ n Agr. almocafre, m; (mason's) paleta, f, palustre, m

Troy /trɔi/ Troya, f

troy weight /trɔi/ n peso de joyería, m

troy weight n peso de joyería, m

truant /'truənt/ n novillero, m; haragán (-ana). —a

haragán, perezoso. **to play t.,** (from school) hacer novillos; ausentarse

truce /trus/ n tregua, f; suspensión, cesación, f

truck /trʌk/ n (lorry) camión, m; carretilla de mano, f; (railway) vagón de carga, m; (intercourse) relaciones, f pl; (trash) cachivaches, m pl, cosas sin valor, f pl

truckage /'trʌkidʒ/ n camionaje, m; acarreo, m

truckle /'trʌkəl/ vi humillarse, no levantar los ojos. **t. bed,** carriola, f

truculence /'trʌkyələns/ n truculencia, agresividad, f

truculent /'trʌkyələnt/ a truculento, agresivo

trudge /trʌdʒ/ vi caminar a pie; andar con dificultad, caminar lentamente, andar trabajosamente, n caminata, f

true /tru/ a verdadero; real; leal, sincero; fiel; exacto; honesto; genuino; auténtico; alineado, a plomo. **That is t. of....** —adv es propio de.... **t.-bred,** de casta legítima. **t.-hearted,** leal, fiel, sincero

truffle /'trʌfəl/ n trufa, f. **to stuff with truffles,** trufar

truism /'truizəm/ n perogrullada, f

truly /'truli/ adv lealmente; realmente, verdaderamente; en efecto, por cierto; sinceramente, de buena fe. **Yours t.,** su seguro servidor (su s.s.)

trump /trʌmp/ n (cards) triunfo, m; son de la trompeta, m; Inf. gran persona, joya, f. —vt ganar con el triunfo. **to t. up,** inventar. **t.-card,** naipe de triunfo, m

trumpery /'trʌmpəri/ a de pacotilla; ineficaz. —n oropel, m

trumpet /'trʌmpit/ n trompeta, f. —vt trompetear; Fig. pregonar. —vi (of elephant) barritar. **ear-t.,** trompetilla (acústica), f. **speaking t.,** portavoz, m. **t. blast,** trompetazo, m. **t. shaped,** en trompeta

trumpeter /'trʌmpitər/ n trompetero, trompeta, m

trumpeting /'trʌmpitiŋ/ n trompeteo, m; (of elephant) barrito, m

truncate /'trʌŋkeit/ a truncado. —vt truncar

truncheon /'trʌntʃən/ n porra (de goma), f; bastón de mando, m. **blow with a t.,** porrazo, m

trundle /'trʌndl/ vt and vi rodar

trunk /trʌŋk/ n (Anat. Bot.) tronco, m; (elephant's) trompa, f; (railway) línea principal, f; baúl, m; cofre, m; pl **trunks,** (Elizabethan, etc.) trusas, f pl; calzoncillos cortos, m pl. **wardrobe t.,** baúl mundo, m. **t.-call,** conferencia telefónica, f. **t.-line,** tronco, m. **t.-road,** carretera de primera clase, carretera mayor, f

truss /trʌs/ n Med. braguero, m; (of straw, etc.) haz, m; (of blossom) racimo, m; (framework) armazón, f. —vt atar; Cul. espetar; (a building) apuntalar

trust /trʌst/ n fe, confianza, f; deber, m; Law. fideicomiso, m; (credit) crédito, m; esperanza, expectación, f; Com. trust, m. —vt tener confianza en; confiar en; esperar; creer; Com. dar crédito (a). —vi confiar; Com. dar crédito. **in t.,** en confianza, fideicomiso; en administración, en depósito. **on t.,** al fiado

trustee /trʌ'sti/ n guardián, m; Law. fideicomisario, depositario, consignatario, m

trustful /'trʌstfəl/ a confiado

trustingly /'trʌstiŋli/ adv confiadamente

trust release n extinción de fideicomiso, f

trustworthiness /'trʌst,wɜrðinis/ n honradez, probidad, integridad, f; (of statements) exactitud, f

trustworthy /'trʌst,wɜrði/ a digno de confianza, honrado; fidedigno, seguro; exacto

trusty /'trʌsti/ a leal, fiel; firme, seguro

truth /truθ/ n verdad, f; realidad, f; exactitud, f. **the plain t.,** la pura verdad. **to tell the t.,** decir la verdad

truthful /'truθfəl/ a veraz; exacto, verdadero

truthfulness /'truθfəlnis/ n veracidad, f; exactitud, f

try /trai/ vt and vi procurar, tratar de; (test) probar, ensayar; (a case, Law.) ver (el pleito); (strain) poner a prueba; (tire) cansar, fatigar; (annoy) molestar, exasperar; (afflict) hacer sufrir, afligir; (attempt) intentar; (judge) juzgar; (the weight of) tomar a pulso; (assay) refinar. —n tentativa, f; (football) tiro, m. **Try as he would....,** Por más que hizo... **to try hard to,** hacer un gran esfuerzo para. **to try one's luck,** probar fortuna. **to try on clothes,** probarse (un vestido, etc.). **to try out,** poner a prueba, probar. **to try to,** tratar de, procurar

trying /'traɪɪŋ/ *a* molesto; fatigoso; irritante; (painful) angustioso, penoso

tryst /trɪst/ *n* cita, *f;* lugar de cita, *m.* —*vt* citar. —*vi* citarse

tsar /zɑr, tsɑr/ *n* zar, *m*

tsarina /zɑ'rinə, tsɑ-/ *n* zarina, *f*

tsetse fly /tset'se, 'tsitsi/ *n* mosca tsetsé, *f*

tub /tʌb/ *n* cuba, *f,* artesón, *m;* cubeta, *f.* —*vi* bañarse. **tub thumper,** Inf. gerundio, *m*

tuba /'tubə/ *n* Mus. tuba, *f*

tube /tub/ *n* tubo, *m;* (railway) metro, ferrocarril subterráneo, *m;* tubo, *m;* Anat. trompa, *f.* **Eustachian t.,** Anat. trompa de Eustaquio, *f.* **Fallopian t.,** trompa de Falopio, *f.* **inner t.,** Auto. cámara de aire, *f.* **speaking t.,** tubo acústico, *m.* **test t.,** tubo de ensayo, *m*

tuber /'tubər/ *n* tubérculo, *m*

tubercular /tu'bɜrkyələr/ *a* tuberculoso

tuberculosis /tu,bɜrkyə'lousɪs/ *n* tuberculosis, *f*

tuberose /'tub,rouz/ *n* nardo, *m,* tuberosa, *f*

tubing /'tubɪŋ/ *n* tubería, *f*

tubular /'tubyələr/ *a* tubular

tuck /tʌk/ *n* Sew. alforza, *f;* pliegue, *m.* —*vt* recoger; Sew. alforzar. —*vi* hacer alforzas. **to t. in,** (in bed) arropar; Inf. tragar. **to t. under,** poner debajo; doblar. **to t. up,** (in bed) arropar; (skirt) sofaldar; (sleeves) arremangar

tucker /'tʌkər/ *n* camisolín, *m*

Tuesday /'tuzdei/ *n* martes, *m.* **Shrove T.,** martes de carnaval, *m*

tuft /tʌft/ *n* (bunch) manojo, *m;* (on the head) copete, moño, *m,* cresta, *f;* (tassel) borla, *f;* mechón, *m*

tug /tʌg/ *n* tirón, *m;* sacudida, *f;* (boat) remolcador, *m.* —*vt* tirar de; halar; sacudir. —*vi* tirar con fuerza. **to give a tug,** dar una sacudida. **tug of war,** Lit. lucha de la cuerda, *f;* Fig. estira y afloja, *m sing*

tuition /tu'ɪʃən/ *n* (teaching) instrucción, enseñanza, *f;* lecciones, *f pl;* (fee) cuota, *f*

tulip /'tulɪp/ *n* tulipán, *m.* **t. wood,** palo de rosa, *m*

tulle /tul/ *n* tul, *m*

tumble /'tʌmbəl/ *n* caída, *f;* (somersault) tumbo, *m;* voltereta, *f.* —*vi* caer; (acrobats) voltear, dar saltos. —*vt* hacer caer; desarreglar. **to t. down,** venirse abajo; caer por. **to t. down,** ruinoso, destartalado. **to t. off,** caer de. **to t. out,** *vt* hacer salir; arrojar. —*vi* salir apresuradamente. **to t. over,** *vt* tropezar con. —*vi* volcarse. **to t. to,** Inf. caer en la cuenta

tumbler /'tʌmblər/ *n* (acrobat) volteador (-ra); vaso para beber, *m*

tumbrel /'tʌmbrəl/ *n* carreta, *f*

tumefaction /,tumə'fækʃən/ *n* tumefacción, *f*

tumid /'tumɪd/ *a* túmido, hinchado

tumor /'tumər/ *n* tumor, *m*

tumult /'tumʌlt/ *n* alboroto, tumulto, *m;* conmoción, agitación, *f;* confusión, *f*

tumultuous /tu'mʌltʃuəs/ *a* tumultuoso, alborotado; ruidoso; confuso; turbulento, violento

tumulus /'tumyələs/ *n* túmulo, *m*

tun /tʌn/ *n* tonel, *m,* cuba, *f, vt* entonelar, embarrilar

tuna /'tʌni/ *n* atún, *m*

tune /tun/ *n* melodía, *f;* son, *m;* armonía, *f;* Fig. tono, *m;* Inf. suma, *f.* —*vt* Mus. afinar, templar; Radio. sintonizar; (up, an engine) ajustar (un motor). —*vi* (in) sintonizar el receptor; (up, Mus.) templar (afinar) los instrumentos. **in t.,** Mus. afinado, templado; Fig. armonioso; (agreement) de acuerdo, conforme. **out of t.,** Mus. desafinado, destemplado. **to be out of t.,** desentonar, discordar; Fig. no armonizar, no estar en armonía. **to go out of t.,** desafinar. **to put out of t.,** destemplar. **to change one's t.,** Inf. bajar el tono

tuneful /'tunfəl/ *a* melodioso

tunefully /'tunfəli/ *adv* melodiosamente, armoniosamente

tunefulness /'tunfəlnɪs/ *n* melodía, *f*

tuneless /'tunlɪs/ *a* disonante, discordante

tuner /'tunər/ *n* afinador, templador, *m;* Radio. sintonizador, *m*

tungsten /'tʌŋstən/ *n* tungsteno, *m*

tunic /'tunɪk/ *n* túnica, *f*

tuning /'tunɪŋ/ *n* afinación, *f;* Radio. sintonización, *f.* **t. fork,** diapasón normal, *m.* **t. key,** templador, *m*

Tunis /'tunɪs/ Túnez, *m*

Tunisian /tu'niʒən/ *a and n* tunecino (-na)

tunnel /'tʌnl/ *n* túnel, *m.* —*vt* hacer (or construir) un túnel por. —*vi* hacer un túnel

tunneling /'tʌnlɪŋ/ *n* construcción de túneles, *f;* horadación, *f*

turban /'tɜrbən/ *n* turbante, *m*

turbid /'tɜrbɪd/ *a* turbio; Fig. confuso, **to make t.,** enturbiar

turbine /'tɜrbɪn, -bain/ *n* turbina, *f*

turbulence /'tɜrbyələns/ *n* turbulencia, *f;* desorden, *m;* agitación, *f*

turbulent /'tɜrbyələnt/ *a* turbulento; alborotado; (stormy) borrascoso; agitado

tureen /tu'rin/ *n* sopera, *f*

turf /tɜrf/ *n* césped, *m;* (fuel) turba, *f;* (racing) carreras de caballos, *f pl*

turgid /'tɜrdʒɪd/ *a* turgente, hinchado; (of style) pomposo

turgidity /tər'dʒɪdɪti/ *n* turgencia, *f;* pomposidad, *f*

Turk /tɜrk/ *n* turco (-ca). **Turk's head,** (duster) deshollinador, *m;* Naut. cabeza de turco, *f*

Turkey /'tɜrki/ Turquía, *f*

turkey /'tɜrki/ *n* (cock) pavo, *m;* (hen) pava, *f;* **t. red,** rojo turco, *m*

Turkish /'tɜrkɪʃ/ *a* turco. —*n* (language) turco, idioma turco, *m.* **T. bath,** baño turco, *m.* **T. slipper,** babucha, *f.* **T. towel,** toalla rusa, *f*

turmeric /'tɜrmərɪk/ *n* cúrcuma, *f.* **t. paper,** papel de cúrcuma, *m*

turmoil /'tɜrmɔil/ *n* alboroto, tumulto, desorden, *m*

turn /tɜrn/ *n* turno, *m;* (twist) torcimiento, *m;* (bend) recodo, *m,* vuelta, *f;* (in a river) meandro, *m;* (in a road) viraje, *m;* (revolution) vuelta, revolución, *f;* (direction) dirección, *f;* (in spiral stair) espira, *f;* Theat. número, *m;* (change) cambio, *m;* vicisitud, *f;* (appearance) aspecto, *m;* (service) servicio, *m;* (nature) índole, naturaleza, *f;* (of phrase) giro, *m,* expresión, *f;* (walk) vuelta, *f,* paseo, *m;* (talent) talento, *m.* **a sharp t.,** (in a road) un viraje rápido. **at every t.,** a cada instante; en todas partes. **bad t.,** flaco servicio, *m.* **by turns,** por turnos. **good t.,** servicio, favor, *m.* **in its turn,** a su vez. **in t.,** sucesivamente. **Now it's my t.,** Ahora me toca a mí. **The affair has taken a new t.,** El asunto ha cambiado de aspecto. **turn of the century,** vuelta del siglo, *f.* **to a t.,** Cul. a la perfección. **to have a t. for,** tener talento para. **to take turns at,** alternar en. **t.-table,** (railway) plataforma, *f;* (of a gramophone) disco giratorio, *m.* **t. up,** barahúnda, conmoción, *f;* (of trousers) dobladillo (del pantalón), *m*

turn /tɜrn/ *vt* (on a lathe) tornear; (revolve) dar vueltas a, girar; (a key, door handle, etc.) torcer; (the leaves of a book) hojear; (the brain) trastornar; (a screw) enroscar; (the stomach) revolver (el estómago), marear; (go round) doblar, dar la vuelta a; (change) cambiar, mudar; (translate) traducir, verter; (dissuade) disuadir; (deflect) desviar; (apply) adaptar; (direct, move) volver; (concentrate) dirigir; concentrar; (turn over) volver del revés al derecho; (upside-down) volver lo de arriba abajo; (make) hacer, volver; (make sour) volver agrio; (transform) transformar convertir; Mil. envolver. **He has turned thirty,** Ha cumplido los treinta. **He said it without turning a hair,** Lo dijo sin pestañear. **He turned his head,** Volvió la cabeza. **They have turned the corner,** Han doblado la esquina; Fig. Han pasado la crisis. **"Please t. over,"** «A la vuelta (de la página).» **to t. a deaf ear to,** no dar oídos a, no hacer caso de. **to t. one's hand to,** aplicarse a. **to t. to account,** sacar ventaja (de). **to t. adrift,** dejar a la merced de las olas; echar de casa, poner en la calle; abandonar. **to t. against,** causar aversión, hacer hostil. **to t. aside,** desviar. **to t. away,** despedir; rechazar; (the head, etc.) volver; desviar. **to t. back,** hacer volver; enviar de nuevo; (raise) alzar; (fold) doblar; (the clock) retrasar. **to t. down,** (lower) bajar; (gas) bajar; (a glass, etc.) poner boca abajo; (reject) rechazar; (a suitor) dar calabazas (a). **to t. from,** alejar de, desviar de. **to t. in,**

doblar hacia dentro; entregar. **to t. in one's toes,** ser patizambo. **to t. inside out,** volver al revés. **to t. into,** (enter) entrar en; (change) cambiar en, transformar en; convertir en; (translate) traducir a. **to t. off,** (dismiss) despedir; (from) desviarse de, dejar; (light) apagar; (water) cortar; *Mech.* cerrar; (disconnect) desconectar; (avoid) evitar; (refuse) rechazar. **to t. off the tap,** (water, gas) cerrar la llave (del agua, del gas). **to t. on,** (light) encender; (water, gas, etc.) abrir la llave (del agua, del gas); (steam) dar (vapor); (electric current) establecer (la corriente eléctrica); (eyes) fijar. **to t. out,** (expel) expeler, echar; (dismiss) despedir; (animals) echar al campo; (produce) producir; (dress) vestir; (equip) equipar, guarnecer; (a light) apagar. **to t. over,** (the page) volver (la hoja); (transfer) ceder, traspasar; revolver; (upset) volcar; considerar, pensar. **to t. round,** dar vuelta (a); girar; (empty) descargar. **to t. up,** levantar; apuntar; hacia arriba; (the earth) labrar, cavar; (a glass) poner boca arriba; (one's sleeves, skirt) arremangar; (fold) doblar. **to t. up one's nose at,** mirar con desprecio. **to t. upon,** atacar, volverse contra, acometer; depender de, estribar en. **to t. upside down,** volver lo de arriba abajo; revolver; revolcar

turn /tɜrn/ *vi* (in a lathe) tornear; (revolve) girar, dar vueltas; (depend) depender (de); torcer; volverse; dar la vuelta; girar sobre los talones; dirigirse (a, hacia); (move) mudar de posición; (deviate) desviarse (de); (be changed) convertirse (en); (become) hacerse, venir a ser; (begin) meterse a; (take to) dedicarse a; (seek help) acudir; (change behavior) enmendarse, corregirse; (the stomach) revolver (el estómago); (go sour) agriarse, avinagrarse; (rebel) sublevarse. **He turned to the left,** Dio la vuelta a la izquierda; Torció hacia la izquierda. **My head turns,** (with giddiness) Se me va la cabeza. **to t. about,** voltearse, dar la vuelta. **to t. against,** coger aversión (a), disgustarse con; volverse hostil (a). **to t. aside,** desviarse; dejar el camino. **to t. away,** volver la cabeza; apartarse; alejarse. **to t. back,** volver atrás; volver de nuevo; retroceder; volver sobre sus pasos. **to t. down,** doblarse; reducirse. **to t. from,** alejarse de; apartarse de, huir de. **to t. in,** doblarse hacia dentro; (retire) acostarse. **to t. into,** transformarse en; convertirse en. **to t. off,** (depart from) desviarse (de); (fork) torcer, bifurcarse. **to t. out,** estar vuelto hacia fuera; (leave one) salir de casa; (rise) levantarse (de la cama); (arrive) llegar, presentarse; (attend) asistir, acudir; (result) resultar. **to t. over,** mudar (or cambiar) de posición, revolverse; (upset) voltearse, volcarse. **to t. round,** girar; volverse; cambiar de frente; cambiar de dirección, dar la vuelta; (*Auto., Aer.*) virar; (change views) cambiar de opinión; (change sides) cambiar de partido. **to t. round and round,** dar vueltas, girar. **to t. to,** (apply to) acudir a; (begin) ponerse a; (become) convertirse en; (face) dirigirse hacia; (address) dirigirse a. **to t. up,** (crop up), surgir, aparecer; (arrive) llegar; (happen) acontecer; (be found again) volver a hallarse, reaparecer; (cards) venir; (of hats) levantar el ala; (of hair, etc.) doblarse. **His nose turns up,** Tiene la nariz respingona

turncoat /'tɜrn‚kout/ *n* desertor (-ra), renegado (-da). **to become a t.,** volver la casaca

turned-up /'tɜrnd'ʌp/ *a* (of hats) con el ala levantada; (of noses) respingona

turner /'tɜrnər/ *n* (craftsman) tornero, torneador, *m*

turnery /'tɜrnəri/ *n* tornería, *f*

turning /'tɜrnɪŋ/ *n* (bend) vuelta, *f;* (turnery) tornería, *f;* (of milk, etc.) agrura, *f; pl* **turnings,** *Sew.* ensanche, *m.* **t.-point,** punto decisivo, *m,* crisis, *f*

turnip /'tɜrnɪp/ *n* nabo, *m.* **t. field,** nabar, *m*

turnover /'tɜrn‚ouvər/ *n Com.* ventas, *f pl; Cul.* pastelillo, *m*

turnpike /'tɜrn‚paik/ *n* barrera de portazgo, *f*

turnstile /'tɜrn‚stail/ *n* torniquete, *m*

turpentine /'tɜrpən‚tain/ *n* aguarrás, *m,* trementina, *f*

turpitude /'tɜrpɪ‚tud/ *n* infamia, maldad, *f*

turquoise /'tɜrkɔiz, -‚kwɔiz/ *n* turquesa, *f*

turret /'tɜrɪt/ *n* torrecilla, almenilla, *f; Naut.* torre blindada, *f*

turreted /'tɜrɪtɪd/ *a* con torres, guarnecido de torres; en forma de torre

turtle /'tɜrtl/ *n* tortuga (dove) tórtolo (-la); (sea) tortuga de mar, *f.* **to turn t.,** voltearse patas arriba; *Naut.* zozobrar. **t. soup,** sopa de tortuga, *f*

Tuscan /'tʌskən/ *a* and *n* toscano (-na)

Tuscany /'tʌskəni/ Toscana, *f*

tusk /tʌsk/ *n* colmillo, *m*

tussle /'tʌsəl/ *n* lucha, *f;* agarrada, *f.* —*vi* luchar, pelear; tener una agarrada

tutelage /'tutlɪdʒ/ *n* tutela, *f*

tutelar /'tutlər/ *a* tutelar

tutor /'tutər/ *n* (private) ayo, *m;* profesor (-ra); (Roman law) tutor, *m;* (supervisor of studies) preceptor. —*vt* enseñar, instruir. —*vi* ser profesor, dar clases

tutorial /tu'tɔriəl/ *n* (university) seminario, *m;* (private) clase particular, *f*

tutoring /'tutərɪŋ/ *n* enseñanza, instrucción, *f*

twaddle /'twɒdl/ *n* disparates, *m pl,* tonterías, patrañas, *f pl*

twain /twein/ *a* and *n* dos, *m*

twang /twæŋ/ *n* punteado de una cuerda, *m;* (of a guitar) zumbido, *m;* (in speech) gangueo, *m.* —*vt* puntear; (las cuerdas de un instrumento) rasguear. —*vi* zumbar. **to speak with a t.,** hablar con una voz gangosa

tweak /twik/ *n* pellizco, *m;* sacudida, *f,* tirón, *m.* —*vt* pellizcar; sacudir, tirar

tweed /twid/ *n* mezcla, *f,* cheviot, *m*

tweezers /'twizərz/ *n pl* pinzas, tenacillas, *f pl*

twelfth /twelfθ/ *a* duodécimo; (of the month) (el) doce; (of monarchs) doce. —*n* duodécimo, *m;* (part) dozavo, *m,* duodécima parte, *f.* **T.-night,** Día de Reyes, *m,* Epifanía, *f*

twelve /twelv/ *a* and *n* doce *m;* (of age) doce años, *m pl.* **t. o'clock,** las doce; (mid-day) mediodía, *m;* (midnight) media noche, *f,* las doce de la noche. **t.-syllabled,** dodecasílabo

twentieth /'twentiɪθ/ *a* vigésimo; (of the month) (el) veinte; (of monarchs) veinte, *n* vigésimo, *m;* (part) vientavo, *m,* vigésima parte, *f*

twenty /'twenti/ *a* veinte; (of age) veinte años, *m pl, n* veinte, *m;* (score) veintena, *f.* **t.-first,** vigésimo primero; (of date) (el) veintiuno, *m,* (In modern Spanish the ordinals above *décimo* "tenth" are generally replaced by the cardinals, e.g. *the twenty-ninth chapter,* el capítulo veintinueve.)

twice /twais/ *adv* dos veces. **t. as many** or **as much,** el doble

twiddle /'twɪdl/ *vt* jugar con; hacer girar. —*vi* girar; vibrar. —*n* vuelta, *f.* **to t. one's thumbs,** dar vuelta a los pulgares, estar mano sobre mano

twig /twɪg/ *n* ramita, pequeña rama, *f*

twilight /'twai‚lait/ *n* crepúsculo, *m;* media luz, *f.* —*a* crepuscular. **in the t.,** en el crepúsculo; en la media luz. **t. sleep,** parto sin dolor, *m*

twin /twɪn/ *a* gemelo, mellizo; doble. —*n* gemelo (-la), mellizo (-za); (of objects) pareja, *f,* par, *m.* **t.-engined,** bimotor. **t. screw,** (*Naut. Aer.*) de dos hélices

twine /twain/ *n* bramante, cordel, *m;* guita, *f.* —*vt* enroscar; (weave) tejer; (encircle) ceñir; (round, about) abrazar. —*vi* (of plants) trepar; entrelazarse; (wind) serpentear

twinge /twɪndʒ/ *n* punzada, *f,* dolor agudo, *m; Fig.* remordimiento, tormento, *m.* —*vi* causar un dolor agudo

twining /'twainɪŋ/ *a Bot.* trepante, voluble. **t. plant,** planta enredadera (or trepante), *f*

twinkle /'twɪŋkəl/ *vi* centellear, chispear, titilar; (of eyes) brillar; (of feet) moverse rápidamente, bailar. —*n* (in the eye) chispa, *f*

twinkling /'twɪŋklɪŋ/ *n* centelleo, *m;* titilación, *f;* (of the eye) brillo, *m;* (glimpse) vislumbre, *m; Fig.* instante, momento, *m.* —*a* titilante, centelleador. **in a t.,** en un dos por tres. **in the t. of an eye,** en un abrir y cerrar de ojos

twin-tailed comet /'twɪn‚teild/ *n* ceratias, *m*

twirl /twɜrl/ *n* rotación, vuelta, *f;* pirueta, *f.* —*vi* hacer girar; voltear; torcer; (a stick, etc.) dar vueltas (a). —*vi* girar, dar vueltas; dar piruetas

twirp /twɜrp/ *n Inf.* renacuajo, *m*

twist /twɪst/ n (skein) mecha, f; trenza, f; (yarn) torzal, m; (of tobacco) rollo, m; (of bread) rosca de pan, f; (act of twisting) torcimiento, m, torsión, f; (in a road, etc.) recodo, m, curva, vuelta, f; (pull) sacudida, f; (contortion) regate, esguince, m; (in a winding stair) espira, f; (in ball games) efecto, m; (in a person's nature) peculiaridad, f; falta de franqueza, f; (to words) interpretación, f. —vt torcer; enroscar; (plait) trenzar; (wring) estrujar; (weave) tejer; (encircle) ceñir; (a stick, etc.) dar vueltas a; (of hands) crispar; (distort) interpretar mal, torcer. —vi torcerse; enroscarse; (wind) serpentear; dar vueltas; (coil) ensortijarse; (writhe) undular, retorcerse; (of a stair) dar vueltas

twisted /'twɪstɪd/ a torcido; (of persons) contrahecho

twisting /'twɪstɪŋ/ n torcimiento, m; torcedura, f; serpenteo, m; (interlacing) entrelazamiento, m. —a sinuoso, serpenteado

twit /twɪt/ (**with**) vt echar en cara

twitch /twɪtʃ/ n sacudida, f, tirón, m; (nervous) contracción nerviosa, f. —vt tirar bruscamente, quitar rápidamente; agarrar; (ears, etc.) mover; (hands) &crispar, retorcer. —vi crisparse; (of ears, nose) moverse

twitching /'twɪtʃɪŋ/ n sacudida, f; (contraction) crispamiento, m, contracción nerviosa, f; (pain) punzada, f; (of conscience) remordimiento, m

twitter /'twɪtər/ n piada, f, gorjeo, m. —vi piar, gorjear

two /tu/ a and n dos, m; (of the clock) (las) dos, f pl; (of age) dos años, m pl. —a de dos. **in two,** en dos partes. **in two's,** de dos en dos. **one or two,** uno o dos; algunos, m pl; algunas, f pl. **two against two,** dos a dos. **two by two,** de dos en dos, a pares. **Two can live as cheaply as one,** Donde come uno comen dos. **to put two and two together,** atar cabos. **two-edged,** de dos filos. **two-faced,** de dos caras; Fig. de ·dos haces. **to be two-faced,** hacer a dos caras. **two-headed,** de dos cabezas; bicéfalo. **two hundred,** a and n doscientos, m. **two hundredth,** a ducentésimo. —n ducentésima parte, f; doscientos, m. **two-legged,** bípedo. **two-ply,** de dos hilos. **two-seater,** a de dos asientos. **two-speed gear box,** cambio de marcha de

dos velocidades, m. **two-step,** paso doble, m. **two of a kind,** (well-matched) tal para cual. **two-way switch,** Elec. interruptor de dos direcciones, m

twofold /a. 'tu,fould; adv. -'fould/ a doble. —adv doblemente, dos veces

twosome /'tusəm/ n partido de dos, m

two's words theory n teoría de los dos gladios, f

tying /'taiŋ/ n ligadura, f; atadura, f

tympanum /'tɪmpənəm/ n (Anat., Archit.) tímpano, m

type /taip/ n tipo, m; Print. carácter, m, letra de imprenta, f, tipo, m. —vt and vi escribir a máquina. **t. case,** caja de imprenta, f. **t. founder,** fundidor de letras de imprenta, m. **t. foundry,** fundición de tipos, f. **t.-setter,** cajista, mf **t.-setting,** composición tipográfica, f

typewrite /'taip,rait/ vt and vi escribir a máquina

typewriter /'taip,raitər/ n máquina de escribir, f

typewriting /'taip,raitɪŋ/ n mecanografía, f, a mecanográfico

typewritten /'taip,rɪtn/ a escrito a máquina

typhoid /'taifɔid/ n tifoidea, fiebre tifoidea, f

typhoon /tai'fun/ n tifón, m

typhus /'taifəs/ n tifus, m

typical /'tɪpɪkəl/ a típico, característico; simbólico

typify /'tɪpə,fai/ vt simbolizar, representar; ser ejemplo de

typist /'taipɪst/ n mecanografista, mf; mecanógrafo (-fa)

typographer /tai'pɒgrəfər/ n tipógrafo, m

typographic /,taipə'græfɪk/ a tipográfico

typography /tai'pɒgrəfi/ n tipografía, f

tyrannical /tɪ'rænɪkəl/ a tiránico, despótico

tyrannization /,tɪrənə'zeifən/ n tiranización, f

tyrannize /'tɪrə,naiz/ vi tiranizar

tyranny /'tɪrəni/ n tiranía, f, despotismo, m

tyrant /'tairənt/ n déspota, m, tirano (-na)

Tyre /taiər/ Tiro, m

Tyrolese /,tairə'liz/ a and n tirolés (-esa)

Tyrol, the /tɪ'roul/ el Tirol

Tyrrhenian /tɪ'riniən/ a tirreno

Tyrrhenian Sea, the el Mar Tirreno, m

u /yu/ n (letter) u, f. **U-boat,** submarino, m. **u-shaped,** en forma de U
ubiquitous /yu'bɪkwɪtəs/ a ubicuo, omnipresente
ubiquity /yu'bɪkwɪti/ n ubicuidad, omnipresencia, f
udder /'ʌdər/ n ubre, teta, mama, f
ugh /ux, ʌg/ interj ¡uf!
ugliness /'ʌglinɪs/ n fealdad, f; (moral) perversidad, f; (of a situation) peligro, m, lo difícil
ugly /'ʌgli/ a (morally) repugnante, asqueroso, perverso; (of a situation) peligroso, difícil; (of a wound) grave, profundo; (of a look) amenazador; Inf. desagradable; (of weather) borrascoso. **to make u.,** afear, hacer feo
Ukraine /yu'krein/ Ucrania, f
Ukrainian /yu'kreiniən/ a and n ucranio (-ia)
ukulele /ˌyukə'leili/ n Mus. ucelele, m
ulcer /'ʌlsər/ n úlcera, f
ulcerate /'ʌlsəˌreit/ vt ulcerar. —vi ulcerarse
ulceration /ˌʌlsə'reiʃən/ n ulceración, f
ulcerous /'ʌlsərəs/ a ulceroso
ulterior /ʌl'tɪəriər/ a (of place) ulterior; (of time) posterior, ulterior; (of motives) interesado, oculto; **ulterior motive,** segunda intención, f
ultimate /'ʌltəmɪt/ a último; fundamental, esencial
ultimately /'ʌltəmɪtli/ adv por fin, al final; esencialmente
ultimatum /ˌʌltə'meitəm/ n ultimátum, m
ultimo /'ʌltəˌmou/ adv del mes anterior
ultra /'ʌltrə/ a exagerado, extremo. —prefix ultra-. **u-red,** ultrarrojo. **u.-violet,** ultravioleta
ultramarine /ˌʌltrəmə'rin/ a ultramarino. —n azul de ultramar, m
ultramontane /ˌʌltrəmɒn'tein/ a ultramontano
ululation /ˌʌlyə'leiʃən/ n ululación, f, ululato, m
umbilical /ʌm'bɪlɪkəl/ a umbilical
umbilicus /ʌm'bɪlɪkəs/ n ombligo, m
umbra /'ʌmbrə/ n Astron. cono de sombra, m
umbrage /'ʌmbrɪdʒ/ n Poet. sombra, f; resentimiento, enfado, m. **to take u.,** ofenderse, resentirse
umbrella /ʌm'brelə/ n paraguas, m. **u. maker,** paragüero (-ra). **u. shop,** paragüería, f. **u. stand,** paragüero, m
umpire /'ʌmpaiᵊr/ n Sports. árbitro, m; Law. juez arbitrador, tercero en discordia, m. —vt arbitrar
un- prefix Used before adjectives, adverbs, abstract nouns, verbs and translated in Spanish by **in-, des-, nada, no, poco, sin,** as well as in other ways
unabashed /ˌʌnə'bæʃt/ a desvergonzado, descarado, insolente; (calm) sereno, sosegado
unabashedly /ˌʌnə'bæʃɪdli/ adv sin rubor
unabated /ˌʌnə'beitɪd/ a no disminuido; cabal, entero
unabbreviated /ˌʌnə'brivi,eitɪd/ a íntegro, sin abreviar
unable /ʌn'eibəl/ a incapaz, impotente; (physical defect) imposibilitado. **to be u. to,** no poder, serle a uno imposible. **to be u. to control,** no poder controlar
unabridged /ˌʌnə'brɪdʒd/ a. See **unabbreviated**
unaccented /ʌn'æksentɪd/ a sin acento
unacceptability /ˌʌnæk,septə'bɪlɪti/ n lo inaceptable
unacceptable /ˌʌnæk,septəbəl/ a inaceptable
unaccepted /ˌʌnæk,septɪd/ a rechazado, no aceptado
unaccommodating a poco complaciente, nada servicial
unaccompanied /ˌʌnə'kʌmpənid/ a solo, sin compañía; Mus. sin acompañamiento
unaccomplished /ˌʌnə'kɒmplɪʃt/ a incompleto, sin terminar, inacabado; (not clever) sin talento
unaccountability /ˌʌnə,kauntə'bɪlɪti/ n lo inexplicable; falta de responsabilidad, irresponsabilidad, f
unaccountable /ˌʌnə'kauntəbəl/ a inexplicable; irresponsable
unaccountably /ˌʌnə'kauntəbli/ adv inexplicablemente, extrañamente

unaccredited /ˌʌnæ'kredɪtɪd/ a no acreditado, extraoficial
unaccustomed /ˌʌnə'kʌstəmd/ a no habituado; (unusual)ʸ desacostumbrado, insólito, inusitado
unacknowledged /ˌʌnæk'nɒlɪdʒd/ a no reconocido; (of letter) sin contestación, por contestar; no correspondido, sin devolver; (of crimes, etc.) inconfeso, no declarado
unacquainted /ˌʌnə'kweintɪd/ a que no conoce; que desconoce, que ignora; no habituado. **to be u. with,** no conocer; ignorar; no estar acostumbrado a
unadaptable /ˌʌnə'dæptəbəl/ a inadaptable (also of persons)
unadorned /ˌʌnə'dɔrnd/ a sin adorno sencillo, que no tiene adornos
unadulterated /ˌʌnə'dʌltə,reitɪd/ a sin mezcla, no adulterado, natural; genuino, verdadero; puro
unadventurous /ˌʌnæd'ventʃərəs/ a nada aventurero, que no busca aventuras, tímido; tranquilo, sin incidente
unadvisability /ˌʌnæd,vaizə'bɪlɪti/ n imprudencia, f; inoportunidad, f
unadvisable /ˌʌnæd,vaizə'bəl/ a imprudente; inoportuno, no conveniente
unadvisedly /ˌʌnæd,vaizɪdli/ adv imprudentemente
unaffected /ˌʌnə'fektɪd/ a natural, llano, sin melindres; impasible; genuino, sincero. **u. by,** no afectado por
unaffectedly /ˌʌnə'fektɪdli/ adv sin afectación
unaffectedness /ˌʌnə'fektɪdnɪs/ n naturalidad, sencillez, f; sinceridad, franqueza, f
unaffiliated /ˌʌnə'fɪli,eitɪd/ a no afiliado
unafraid /ˌʌnə'freid/ a sin temor
unaided a sin ayuda, solo a solas
unaired /ʌn'eərd/ a sin ventilar, no ventilado; húmedo, sin airear
unalloyed /ˌʌnə'lɔid/ a sin mezcla, puro
unalterability /ʌn,ɔltərə'bɪlɪti/ n lo inalterable; constancia, f
unalterable /ʌn'ɔltərəbəl/ a inalterable; invariable, constante
unambiguous /ˌʌnæm'bɪgyuəs/ a no ambiguo, nada dudoso, claro
unambitious /ˌʌnæm'bɪʃəs/ a sin ambición; modesto
unamusing /ˌʌnə'myuzɪŋ/ a nada divertido
unanimity /ˌyunə'nɪmɪti/ n unanimidad, f
unanimous /yu'nænəməs/ a unánime
unanimously /yu'nænəməsli/ adv unánimemente, por unanimidad. **carried u.,** adoptado por unanimidad
unanswerability /ʌn,ænsərə'bɪlɪti/ n imposibilidad de negar, f; lo irrefutable
unanswerable /ʌn'ænsərəbəl/ a incontestable, incontrovertible, incontrastable, irrefutable
unanswered /ʌn'ænsərd/ a no contestado, sin contestar; (unrequited) no correspondido
unapparent /ˌʌnə'pærənt/ a no aparente
unappealable /ˌʌnə'piləbəl/ a inapelable
unappeasable /ˌʌnə'pizəbəl/ a implacable
unappeased /ˌʌnə'pizd/ a no satisfecho; implacable
unappetizing /ʌn'æpɪ,taizɪŋ/ a no apetitoso; (unattractive) repugnante, feo
unappreciated /ˌʌnə'priʃi,eitɪd/ a desestimado, no apreciado, tenido en poco; (misunderstood) mal comprendido
unapproachable /ˌʌnə'proutʃəbəl/ a inaccesible
unapproachableness /ˌʌnə'proutʃəbəlnɪs/ n inaccesibilidad, f
unappropriated /ˌʌnə'proupri,eitɪd/ a no concedido; libre
unapproved /ˌʌnə'pruvd/ a sin aprobar, no aprobado
unarm /ʌn'ɑrm/ vt desarmar. —vi desarmarse, quitarse las armas
unarmed /ʌn'ɑrmd/ a desarmado; indefenso; (Zool., Bot.) inerme

unarranged /ˌʌnə'reindʒd/ a no arreglado, sin clasificar; (accidental) fortuito, casual

unartistic /ˌʌnar'tıstık/ a no artístico

unascertainable /ˌʌnæsər'teinəbəl/ a no verificable

unashamed /ˌʌnə'ʃeimd/ a sin vergüenza; tranquilo, sereno; insolente, descarado

unasked /ʌn'æskt/ a sin pedir; no solicitado; espontáneo; (uninvited) no convidado

unassailable /ˌʌnə'seiləbəl/ a inexpugnable; irrefutable; incontestable

unassisted /ˌʌnə'sıstıd/ a. See **unaided**

unassuming /ˌʌnə'sumıŋ/ a modesto, sin pretensiones

unattached /ˌʌnə'tætʃt/ a suelto; *Law.* no embargado; *Mil.* de reemplazo; independiente

unattainable /ˌʌnə'teinəbəl/ a inasequible, irrealizable

unattainableness /ˌʌnə'teinəbəlnıs/ n imposibilidad de alcanzar (or realizar), f; inaccesibilidad

unattended /ˌʌnə'tendıd/ a solo, sin acompañamiento; (of ill person) sin tratamiento; (of entertainment, etc.) no concurrido

unattested /ˌʌnə'testıd/ a sin atestación

unattractive /ˌʌnə'træktıv/ a poco atrayente, desagradable, antipático, feo

unattractiveness /ˌʌnə'træktıvnıs/ n fealdad, falta de hermosura, f; lo desagradable

unauthentic /ˌʌnɔ'θentık/ a no auténtico, sin autenticidad; apócrifo

unauthorized /ʌn'ɔθə,raizd/ a no autorizado

unavailable ˌ½nə'veiləbəl/ a inaprovechable

unavailing /ˌʌnə'veilıŋ/ a inútil, vano

unavenged /ˌʌnə'vendʒd/ a no vengado, sin castigo

unavoidable /ˌʌnə'vɔidəbəl/ a inevitable, preciso, necesario. **to be u.,** no poder evitarse, no tener remedio

unavoidableness /ˌʌnə'vɔidəbəlnıs/ n inevitabilidad, necesidad, f

unavoidably /ˌʌnə'vɔidəbli/ adv irremediablemente

unaware /ˌʌnə'weər/ a ignorante; inconsciente. **to be u. of,** ignorar, desconocer; no darse cuenta de

unawareness /ˌʌnə'weərnıs/ n ignorancia, f, desconocimiento, m; inconsciencia, f

unawares /ˌʌnə'weərz/ adv (by mistake) sin querer, inadvertidamente; (unprepared) de sorpresa, de improviso, inopinadamente. **He caught me u.,** Me cogió desprevenido

unbalance /ʌn'bæləns/ vt desequilibrar, hacer perder el equilibrio; *Fig.* trastornar

unbalanced /ʌn'bælanst/ a desequilibrado; *Fig.* trastornado; *Com.* no balanceado

unbaptized /ʌn'bæptaizd/ a no bautizado, sin bautizar

unbar /ʌn'bɑr/ vt desatrancar; *Fig.* abrir

unbearable /ʌn'beərəbəl/ a intolerable, insufrible, inaguantable, inllevable, insoportable

unbearably /ʌn'beərəbli/ adv insoportablemente

unbeatable /ʌn'bitəbəl/ a inmejorable

unbeaten /ʌn'bitn/ a (of paths) no frecuentado, no pisado; (of armies) no derrotado, no batido; invicto

unbecoming /ˌʌnbı'kʌmıŋ/ a impropio, inapropiado, inconveniente; indecoroso, indigno; indecente; (of clothes) que no va bien, que sienta mal

unbelief /ˌʌnbı'lif/ n incredulidad, f

unbelievable /ˌʌnbı'livəbəl/ a increíble

unbelievably /ˌʌnbı'livəbli/ adv increíblemente

unbeliever /ˌʌnbı'livər/ n incrédulo (-la), descreído (-da)

unbeloved /ˌʌnbı'lʌvd/ a no amado

unbend /ʌn'bend/ vt desencorvar, enderezar; entretenerse, descansar; (*Naut.* of sails) desenvergar; (*Naut.* of cables) desamarrar. —vi enderezarse; mostrarse afable

unbending /ʌn'bendıŋ/ a inflexible, rígido, tieso; *Fig.* inexorable, inflexible, duro, terco; (amiable) afable, jovial

unbiased /ʌn'baiəst/ a imparcial, ecuánime

unbidden /ʌn'bıdn/ a espontáneo; (uninvited) no convidado, no invitado

unbind /ʌn'baind/ vt desligar, desatar; (bandages) desvendar; (books) desencuadernar

unbleached /ʌn'blitʃt/ a crudo, sin blanquear

unblemished /ʌn'blemıʃt/ a no manchado; (pure) sin mancha, inmaculado, puro

unblessed /ʌn'blest/ a no bendecido, no consagrado; (accursed) maldito; (unhappy) desdichado

unblushing /ʌn'blʌʃıŋ/ a desvergonzado, insolente

unbolt /ʌn'boult/ vt descerrojar, desempernar

unborn /ʌn'bɔrn/ a sin nacer, no nacido todavía; venidero

unbosom /ʌn'buzəm/ vt confesar, declarar. **to u. oneself,** abrir su pecho (a) or (con)

unbought /ʌn'bɔt/ a no comprado; gratuito, libre; (not bribed) no sobornado

unbound /ʌn'baund/ a suelto, libre; (of books) en rama, no encuadernado

unbounded /ʌn'baundıd/ a ilimitado, infinito; inmenso

unbowed /ʌn'baud/ a erguido; no encorvar; (undefeated) invicto

unbreakable /ʌn'breikəbəl/ a irrompible, inquebrantable

unbridled /ʌn'braidld/ a desenfrenado, violento; licencioso

unbroken /ʌn'broukən/ a no quebrantado, intacto, entero; continuo, incesante; no interrumpido; (of soil) virgen; (of a horse) indomado, inviolado; (of the spirit) indómito; (of a record) no batido

unbrotherly /ʌn'brʌðərli/ a poco fraternal, indigno de hermanos

unbuckle /ʌn'bʌkəl/ vt deshebillar

unburden /ʌn'bərdn/ vt descargar; aliviar. **to u. one-self,** (express one's feelings) desahogarse

unburied /ʌn'berid/ a insepulto

unburnt /ʌn'bərnt/ a no quemado; incombusto

unbusinesslike /ʌn'bıznıs,laik/ a informal; poco comercial, descuidado

unbutton /ʌn'bʌtn/ vt desabrochar, desabotonar

uncalled /ʌn'kɔld/ a no llamado, no invitado. **u.-for,** impertinente; innecesario

uncannily /ʌn'kænļi/ adv misteriosamente

uncanniness /ʌn'kænınıs/ n lo misterioso

uncanny /ʌn'kæni/ a misterioso, horroroso, pavoroso

uncared-for /ʌn'keərd,fɔr/ a abandonado, desatendido, desamparado

uncarpeted /ʌn'karpıtıd/ a sin alfombra

uncaught /ʌn'kɔt/ a no prendido, libre

unceasing /ʌn'sisıŋ/ a continuo, incesante, sin cesar, constante

unceasingly /ʌn'sisıŋli/ adv incesantemente, sin cesar

uncensored /ʌn'sensərd/ a no censurado

unceremonious /ˌʌnserə'mouniəs/ a sin ceremonia, familiar; descortés, brusco

unceremoniousness /ˌʌnserə'mouniəsnıs/ n falta de ceremonia, familiaridad, f; incivilidad, descortesía, f

uncertain /ʌn'sərtn/ a incierto, dudoso, inseguro; precario; (hesitant) indeciso, vacilante, irresoluto

uncertainly /ʌn'sərtņli/ adv inciertamente

uncertainty /ʌn'sərtņti/ n incertidumbre, duda, f; inseguridad, f; irresolución, f

uncertificated /ˌʌnsər'tıfı,keitıd/ a sin certificado (of teachers, etc.) sin título

uncertified /ʌn'sərtə,faid/ a sin garantía; no garantizado; (of lunatics) sin certificar

unchain /ʌn'tʃein/ vt desencadenar

unchallenged /ʌn'tʃæləndʒd/ a incontestable

unchangeable /ʌn'tʃeindʒəbəl/ a invariable, inalterable, inmutable

unchangeableness /ʌn'tʃeindʒəbəlnıs/ n invariabilidad, inalterabilidad, f

unchanging /ʌn'tʃeindʒıŋ/ a inmutable, invariable

uncharitable /ʌn'tʃærıtəbəl/ a nada caritativo, duro; intolerante, intransigente

uncharitableness /ʌn'tʃærıtəbəlnıs/ n falta de caridad, f; intolerancia, intransigencia

uncharitably /ʌn'tʃærıtəbli/ adv sin caridad; con intolerancia

unchaste /ʌn'tʃeist/ a incasto, incontinente; deshonesto, impuro, lascivo

unchecked /ʌn'tʃekt/ a desenfrenado; (unproved) no comprobado; *Com.* no confrontado

unchivalrous /ʌnʃ'ʃɪvəlrəs/ a nada galante, nada caballeroso

unchristened /ʌn'krɪsənd/ a no bautizado, sin bautizar

unchristian /ʌn'krɪstʃən/ a (heathen) pagano; poco cristiano, indigno de un cristiano, nada caritativo

uncircumcised /ʌn'sɜrkəm,saizd/ a incircunciso

uncircumscribed /ʌn'sɜrkəm,skraibd/ a incircunscripto

uncivil /ʌn'sɪvəl/ a descortés, incivil

uncivilizable /ʌn'sɪvə,laizəbəl/ a reacio a la civilización

uncivilized /ʌn'sɪvə,laizd/ a no civilizado, bárbaro, salvaje, inculto

uncivilly /ʌn'sɪvəli/ adv descortésmente

unclad /ʌn'klæd/ a sin vestir; desnudo

unclasp /ʌn'klæsp/ vt (jewelery) desengarzar; desabrochar; (of hands) soltar, separar

unclassifiable /ʌn'klæsə,faiəbəl/ a inclasificable

unclassified /ʌn'klæsə,faid/ a sin clasificar

uncle /'ʌŋkəl/ n tío, m; (pawnbroker) prestamista, m

unclean /ʌn'klin/ a sucio, puerco, inmundo; desaseado; impuro, obsceno; (ritually) poluto

uncleanliness /ʌn'klɛnlinɪs/ n suciedad, porquería, f; desaseo, m; falta de limpieza, f

uncleanly /ʌn'klɛnli/ a sucio, puerco; desaseado

uncleanness /ʌn'klinnɪs/ n suciedad, f; impureza, obscenidad, inmoralidad, f

unclench /ʌn'klɛntʃ/ vt (of hands) abrir

Uncle Tom's Cabin La Cabaña del Tío Tom

unclouded /ʌn'klaudɪd/ a sin nubes, despejado, claro

uncoil /ʌn'kɔil/ vt desarrollar. —vi desovillarse; (of snakes) desanillarse

uncollected /ˌʌnkə'lɛktɪd/ a disperso; no cobrado; (in confusion) confuso, desordenado

uncolored /ʌn'kʌlərd/ a incoloro; Fig. imparcial, objetivo, sencillo

uncombed /ʌn'koumd/ a despeinado, sin peinar

uncomfortable /ʌn'kʌmftəbəl/ a incómodo; (anxious) intranquilo, inquieto, desasosegado, preocupado; (awkward) molesto, difícil, desagradable. **to be u.**, (people) estar incómodo; (anxious) estar preocupado; (of things) ser incómodo

uncomfortableness /ʌn'kʌmfərtəbəlnɪs/ n incomodidad, f; malestar, m; intranquilidad, preocupación, f; dificultad, f; lo desagradable

uncomfortably /ʌn'kʌmfərtəbli/ adv incómodamente; intranquilamente; desagradablemente

uncomforted /ʌn'kʌmfərtɪd/ a desconsolado, sin consuelo

uncommercial /ˌʌnkə'mɜrʃəl/ a no comercial

uncommon /ʌn'kɒmən/ a poco común, extraordinario, singular, raro, extraño; infrecuente; insólito

uncommonly /ʌn'kɒmənli/ adv extraordinariamente, muy; infrecuentemente, raramente

uncommonness /ʌn'kɒmənnɪs/ n infrecuencia, rareza, f; singularidad, f

uncommunicative /ˌʌnkə'myunɪkətɪv/ a reservado, poco expresivo

uncommunicativeness /ˌʌnkə'myunɪkətɪvnɪs/ n reserva, f

uncomplaining /ˌʌnkəm'pleinɪŋ/ a resignado, que no se queja

uncomplainingly /ˌʌnkəm'pleinɪŋli/ adv con resignación

uncompliant /ˌʌnkəm'plaiant/ a sordo, inflexible

uncomplicated /ʌn'kɒmplɪ,keitɪd/ a sencillo, sin complicaciones

uncomplimentary /ˌʌnkɒmplə'mɛntəri/ a descortés, poco halagüeño, ofensivo

uncompromising /ʌn'kɒmprə,maizɪŋ/ a inflexible, estricto, intolerante; irreconciliable

unconcealed /ˌʌnkən'sild/ a no oculto; abierto

unconcern /ˌʌnkən'sɜrn/ n indiferencia, frialdad, f, desapego, m; (lack of interest) apatía, despreocupación, f; (nonchalance) desenfado, m, frescura, f

unconcerned /ˌʌnkən'sɜrnd/ a indiferente, frío, despegado; apático, despreocupado; desenfadado, fresco

unconcernedly / ˌʌnkən'sɜrnɪdli/ adv con indiferencia; sin preocuparse; con desenfado

unconditional /ˌʌnkən'dɪʃənl/ a incondicional, absoluto. **u. surrender**, rendición incondicional, f

unconditionally /ˌʌnkən'dɪʃənli/ adv incondicionalmente; Mil. a discreción

unconfessed /ˌʌnkən'fɛst/ a inconfeso

unconfined /ˌʌnkən'faind/ a suelto, libre; ilimitado; sin estorbo

unconfirmed /ˌʌnkən'fɜrmd/ a no confirmado; (report) sin confirmar

uncongenial /ˌʌnkən'dʒinyəl/ a incompatible, antipático; desagradable, repugnante

uncongeniality /ˌʌnkən,dʒini'ælɪti/ n incompatibilidad, antipatía, f; repugnancia, f; lo desagradable

unconnected /ˌʌnkə'nɛktɪd/ a inconexo; Mech. desconectado; (relationship) sin parentesco; (confused) incoherente

unconquerable /ʌn'kɒŋkərəbəl/ a invencible, indomable, inconquistable

unconquered /ʌn'kɒŋkərd/ a no vencido

unconscientious /ˌʌnkɒnʃɪ'ɛnʃəs/ a poco concienzudo

unconscionable /ʌn'kɒnʃənəbəl/ a excesivo, desmedido; sin conciencia

unconscious /ʌn'kɒnʃəs/ a inconsciente; (senseless) insensible, sin sentido; espontáneo; (unaware) ignorante. **to be u. of,** ignorar; perder la consciencia de. **to become u.,** perder el sentido

unconsciously /ʌn'kɒnʃəsli/ adv inconscientemente, involuntariamente

unconsciousness /ʌn'kɒnʃəsnɪs/ n inconsciencia, f; (hypnosis, swoon) insensibilidad, f; (unawareness) ignorancia, falta de conocimiento, f

unconsecrated /ʌn'kɒnsɪ,kreitɪd/ a no consagrado

unconsidered /ˌʌnkən'sɪdərd/ a indeliberado; sin importancia, trivial

unconstitutional /ˌʌnkɒnstɪ'tuʃənl/ a anticonstitucional, inconstitucional

unconstitutionally /ˌʌnkɒnstɪ'tuʃənli/ adv inconstitucionalmente

unconstrained /ˌʌnkən'streind/ a libre; voluntario; sin freno

uncontaminated /ˌʌnkən'tæmɪ'neitɪd/ a incontaminado; puro, sin mancha, impoluto

uncontested /ˌʌnkən'tɛstɪd/ a sin oposición

uncontradicted /ˌʌnkɒntrə'dɪktɪd/ a sin contradicción; incontestable

uncontrollable /ˌʌnkən'trouləbəl/ a irrefrenable, incontrolable, inmanejable; (temper) ingobernable; indomable

uncontrolled /ˌʌnkən'trould/ a libre, no controlado; desenfrenado, desgobernado

unconventional /ˌʌnkən'vɛnʃənl/ n poco convencional; bohemio, excéntrico, extravagante; original

unconventionality /ˌʌnkən,vɛnʃə'nælɪti/ n excentricidad, extravagancia, independencia de ideas, f; (of a design) originalidad, f

unconversant /ˌʌnkən'vɜrsənt/ a poco familiar, poco versado (en)

unconverted /ˌʌnkən'vɜrtɪd/ a no convertido; sin transformar

unconvinced /ˌʌnkən'vɪnst/ a no convencido

unconvincing /ˌʌnkən'vɪnsɪŋ/ a no convincente, poco convincente, que no me (nos, etc.) convence; frívolo

uncooked /ʌn'kʊkt/ a crudo, no cocido, sin cocer

uncork /ʌn'kɔrk/ vt destapar, descorchar, quitar el corcho

uncorrected /ˌʌnkə'rɛktɪd/ a sin corregir, no corregido

uncorroborated /ˌʌnkə'rɒbə,reitɪd/ a no confirmado, sin confirmar

uncorrupted /ˌʌnkə'rʌptɪd/ a incorrupto; puro, no pervertido; (unbribed) no sobornado, honrado

uncorruptible /ˌʌnkə'rʌptəbəl/ a incorruptible

uncountable /ʌn'kauntəbəl/ a innumerable

uncounted /ʌn'kauntɪd/ a no contado, sin cuenta

uncouple /ʌn'kʌpəl/ vt soltar; desenganchar, desconectar

uncouth /ʌn'kuθ/ a grosero, chabacano, tosco, patán

uncouthness /ʌn'kuθnɪs/ n grosería, tosquedad, patanería, f

uncover /ʌn'kʌvər/ *vt* descubrir; (remove lid of) destapar; (remove coverings of) desabrigar, desarropar; (leave unprotected) desamparar; (disclose) revelar, dejar al descubierto. —*vi* descubrirse, quitar el sombrero

uncovered /ʌn'kʌvərd/ *a* descubierto; desnudo; sin cubierta

uncreated /ʌnkri'eitid/ *a* increado

uncritical /ʌn'krɪtɪkəl/ *a* sin sentido crítico, poco juicioso

uncross /ʌn'krɔs/ *vt* (of legs) descruzar

uncrossed /ʌn'krɔst/ *a* (of check) sin cruzar

uncrowned /ʌn'kraund/ *a* antes de ser coronado; sin corona

unction /'ʌŋkʃən/ *n* unción, *f;* untadura, *f,* untamiento, *m;* (unguent) ungüento, *m;* (zeal) fervor, *m;* (flattery) insinceridad, hipocresía, *f;* (relish) gusto, entusiasmo, *m.* **extreme u.,** extremaunción, *f*

unctuous /'ʌŋktʃuəs/ *a* untuoso, craso; insincero, zalamero

uncultivable /ʌn'kʌltəvəbəl/ *a* incultivable

uncultivated /ʌn'kʌltə,veitid/ *a* inculto, yermo; (barbarous) salvaje, bárbaro; (uncultured) inculto, tosco; no cultivado

uncultured /ʌn'kʌltʃərd/ *a* inculto, iletrado

uncurbed /ʌn'kɜrbd/ *a* sin freno; *Fig.* desenfrenado

uncurl /ʌn'kɜrl/ *vt* desrizar *vi* desrizarse; desovillarse

uncurtained /ʌn'kɜrtṇd/ *a* sin cortinas; con las cortinas recogidas

uncut /ʌn'kʌt/ *a* sin cortar, no cortado; (of gems) sin labrar

undamaged /ʌn'dæmɪdʒd/ *a* indemne, sin daño

undated /ʌn'deitid/ *a* sin fecha

undaunted /ʌn'dɔntid/ *a* intrépido, atrevido

undeceive /ʌndɪ'siv/ *vt* desengañar, desilusionar

undecided /ʌndɪ'saidid/ *a* (of question) pendiente, indeciso; dudoso; vacilante, irresoluto

undecipherable /ʌndɪ'saifərəbəl/ *a* indescifrable; ilegible

undeclared /ʌndɪ'kleərd/ *a* no declarado

undefended /ʌndɪ'fendɪd/ *a* indefenso

undeferable /ʌndɪ'fɜrəbəl/ *a* inaplazable

undefiled /ʌndɪ'faild/ *a* impoluto, incontaminado; puro

undefinable /ʌndɪ'fainəbəl/ *a* indefinible; inefable, vago

undefined /ʌndɪ'faind/ *a* indefinido; indeterminado

undelivered /ʌndɪ'lɪvərd/ *a* no recibido; (speech) no pronunciado; (not sent) no enviado

undemonstrative /ʌndə'mɒnstrətɪv/ *a* poco expresivo, reservado

undeniable /ʌndɪ'naiəbəl/ *a* incontestable, innegable, indudable; excelente; inequívoco, evidente

undeniably /ʌndɪ'naiəbli/ *adv* indudablemente

undenominational /ʌndɪ,nɒmə'neiʃənḷ/ *a* sin denominación

undependable /ʌndɪ'pendəbəl/ *a* indigno de confianza

under /'ʌndər/ *prep* debajo de; bajo; (in) en; (less than) menos de, menos que; (at the orders of) a las órdenes de, al mando de; (in less time than) en menos de; (under the weight of) bajo el peso de; (at the foot of) al abrigo de; (for less than) por menos de; (at the time of) en la época de, en tiempos de; (according to) según, conforme a, en virtud de (e.g. *under the law,* en virtud de la ley); (of monarchs) bajo (or durante) el reinado de; (of rank) inferior a; (in virtue of) en virtud de; (of age) menor de; (with penalty, pretext, etc.) so; en; a (see below for examples); (*Agr.* of fields) plantado de, sembrado de. **u. arms,** bajo las armas. **u. contract,** bajo contrato. **u. cover,** al abrigo, bajo cubierto. **u. cover of,** bajo pretexto de, so color de. **u. fire,** bajo fuego. **u. oath,** bajo juramento. **u. pain of,** so pena de. **u. sail,** a la vela. **u. separate cover,** bajo cubierta separada, en sobre apartado, por separado. **u. steam,** al vapor. **u. way,** en camino; en marcha; en preparación. **to be u. an obligation,** deber favores; (to) tener obligacion de; estar obligado a

under /'ʌndər/ *a* inferior; (of rank) subalterno, subordinado; bajo, bajero. —*adv* debajo; abajo; más abajo; menos; (for less) para menos; (ill) mal; (insufficient)

insuficiente. **to bring u.,** someter. **to keep u.,** dominar, subyugar

underact /ʌndər'ækt/ *vt* hacer un papel sin fogosidad

underarm /'ʌndər,ɑrm/ *n* sobaco, *m.* —*a* sobacal; (of bowling) de debajo del brazo. **to serve u.,** sacar por debajo

underbid /ʌndər'bɪd/ *vt* ofrecer menos que

underbred /ʌndər'bred/ *a* mal criado, mal educado

undercharge /ʌndər'tʃɑrdʒ/ *vt* cobrar menos de lo debido

underclothes /'ʌndər,klouz, -,klouðz/ *n* ropa interior, *f,* paños menores, *m pl*

undercurrent /'ʌndər,kɜrənt/ *n* corriente submarina, *f; Fig.* tendencia oculta, *f*

undercut /'ʌndər,kʌt/ *n* (of meat) filete, *m*

underdeveloped /,ʌndərdɪ'veləpt/ *a* de desarrollo atrasado; *Photo.* no revelado lo suficiente

underdog /'ʌndər,dɔg/ *n* víctima, *f;* débil, paciente, *m.* **underdogs,** los de abajo, *m pl*

underdone /'ʌndər'dʌn/ *a* (of meat) crudo, medio asado

underdress /,ʌndər'dres/ *vt* and *vi* vestir(se) sin bastante elegancia

underestimate /,ʌndər'estə,meit/ *vt* tasar en menos; desestimar, menospreciar

underfeed /,ʌndər'fid/ *vt* alimentar insuficientemente

underfoot /,ʌndər'fut/ *adv* debajo de los pies, en el suelo

undergo /,ʌndər'gou/ *vt* sufrir, padecer, pasar por. **undergo surgery,** someterse a la cirugía

undergraduate /,ʌndər'grædʒuit/ *n* estudiante no graduado, *m*

underground /*a., n.* 'ʌndər,graund; *adv.* -'graund/ *a* subterráneo; *Fig.* oculto, secreto. —*adv* bajo tierra, debajo de la tierra; *Fig.* en secreto, ocultamente. —*n* sótano, *m;* metro, ferrocarril subterráneo, *m*

undergrown /'ʌndər,groun/ *a* enclenque

undergrowth /'ʌndər,grouθ/ *n* maleza, *f*

underhand /'ʌndər,hænd/ *adv Fig.* bajo mano, ocultamente, a escondidas. —*a Fig.* secreto, oculto

underlie /,ʌndər'lai/ *vt* estar debajo de; servir de base a, caracterizar

underline /'ʌndər,lain/ *vt* subrayar

underling /'ʌndərlɪŋ/ *n* subordinado (-da)

underlying /,ʌndər'laiŋ/ *a* fundamental, básico, esencial

undermentioned /,ʌndər'menʃən/d *a* abajo citado

undermine /,ʌndər'main/ *vt* socavar, excavar; minar, destruir poco a poco

undermining /'ʌndər,mainɪŋ/ *n* socava, excavación, *f;* destrucción, *f, a* minador

underneath /,ʌndər'niθ/ *adv* debajo. —*prep* bajo, debajo de

undernourished /,ʌndər'nɜrɪʃt/ *a* mal alimentado

undernourishment /,ʌndər'nɜrɪʃmənt/ *n* desnutrición, *f*

underpaid /,ʌndər'peid/ *a* insuficientemente retribuido, mal pagado

underpass /'ʌndər,pæs, -,pɑs/ *n* pasaje por debajo, *m*

underpay /,ʌndər'pei/ *vt* pagar mal, remunerar (or retribuir) deficientemente

underpayment /'ʌndər,peimənt/ *n* retribución mezquina, *f,* pago insuficiente, *m*

underpin /,ʌndər'pɪn/ *vt* apuntalar, socalzar

underpopulated /,ʌndər'pɒpyə,leitid/ *a* con baja densidad de población

underprivileged /'ʌndər'prɪvəlɪdʒd/ *a* menesteroso, pobre, necesitado

underrate /,ʌndər'reit/ *vt* tasar en menos; tener en poco, desestimar, menospreciar

underripe /'ʌndər,raip/ *a* verde

undersecretary /'ʌndər,sekrə,teri/ *n* subsecretario (-ia)

undersell /,ʌndər'sel/ *vt* vender a un precio más bajo que

underside /'ʌndər,said/ *n* revés, envés, *m*

undersigned /'ʌndər,saind/ *a* infrascrito, suscrito. **the u.,** el abajo firmado, el infrascrito

undersized /,ʌndər'saizd/ *a* muy pequeño, enclenque, enano

underskirt /'ʌndər,skɜrt/ *n* enagua, *f;* refajo, *m*

underslung /'ʌndər'slʌŋ/ *a* Auto. con bajo centro de gravedad

understand /ˌʌndər'stænd/ *vt* comprender, entender; (know) saber; (be acquainted with) conocer; (hear) oír, tener entendido; (mean) sobrentender. —*vi* comprender, entender; oír, tener entendido. **to u. each other,** comprenderse. **It being understood that...,** Bien entendido que...

understandable /ˌʌndər'stændəbəl/ *a* comprensible; inteligible. **It is very u. why he does not wish to come,** Se comprende muy bien por qué no quiere venir

understanding /ˌʌndər'stændɪŋ/ *n* (intelligence) entendimiento, *m,* inteligencia, *f;* (agreement) acuerdo, *m;* (knowledge) conocimiento, *m;* (wisdom) comprensión, sabiduría, *f.* —*a* inteligente; sabio; (sympathetic) comprensivo, simpático. **to come to an u.,** ponerse de acuerdo

understandingly /ˌʌndərstændɪŋ/ *adv* con inteligencia; con conocimiento (de); con simpatía

understate /ˌʌndər'steit/ *vt* decir menos que, rebajar, describir sin énfasis

understatement /'ʌndərsteitmənt/ *n* moderación, *f*

understudy /'ʌndər,stʌdi/ *n* sobresaliente, *mf.* —*vt* sustituir

undertake /ˌʌndər'teik/ *vt* comprometerse a, encargarse de; emprender, abarcar, acometer

undertaker /'ʌndər,teikər/ *n* empresario, director de pompas fúnebres, *m*

undertaking /ˌʌndər'teikɪŋ/ *n* empresa, tarea, *f;* garantía, promesa, *f;* (funerals) funeraria, *f*

undertone /'ʌndər,toun/ *n* voz baja, *f; Art.* color tenue (or apagado), *m.* **in an u.,** en voz baja

undervalue /ˌʌndər'vælyu/ *vt* tasar en menos; tener en poco, despreciar

underwater /'ʌndər'wɔtər/ *a* subacuático, submarino. **underwater flipper,** aleta de bucear

underweight /'ʌndər'weit/ *a* de bajo peso, que pesa menos de lo debido, flaco

underworld /'ʌndər,wɜrld/ *n* (hell) infierno, averno, *m;* (slums) hampa, *f,* fondos bajos de la sociedad, *m pl;* heces de la sociedad, *f pl*

underwrite /ˌʌndər'rait/ *vt Com.* asegurar contra riesgos; reasegurar; obligarse a comprar todas las acciones de una compañía no subscritas por el público, mediante un pago convenido

underwriter /'ʌndər,raitər/ *n* asegurador, *m;* reasegurador, *m*

underwriting /'ʌndər,raitɪŋ/ *n* aseguro, *m;* reaseguro, *m*

undeserved /ˌʌndɪ'zɜrvd/ *a* inmerecido, no merecido

undeserving /ˌʌndɪ'zɜrvɪŋ/ *a* indigno, desmerecedor; que no merece

undesirable /ˌʌndɪ'zaiᵊrəbəl/ *a* no deseable; nocivo, pernicioso; (unsuitable) inconveniente

undesired /ˌʌndɪ'zaiᵊrd/ *a* no deseado; no solicitado, no buscado

undesirous /ˌʌndɪ'zaiᵊrəs/ *a* no deseoso

undestroyed /ˌʌndɪ'strɔid/ *a* sin destruir, no destruido, intacto

undetected /ˌʌndɪ'tɛktɪd/ *a* no descubierto

undeveloped /ˌʌndɪ'vɛləpt/ *a* no desarrollado; rudimentario; inmaturo; (of a country) no explotado, virgen; *Photo.* no revelado; (of land) sin cultivar

undeviating /ʌn'divi,eitɪŋ/ *a* directo; constante, persistente

undigested /ˌʌndɪ'dʒɛstɪd/ *a* no digerido, indigesto

undignified /ʌn'dɪgnə,faid/ *a* sin dignidad; poco serio; indecoroso

undiluted /ˌʌndɪ'lutɪd/ *a* sin diluir, puro

undiminished /ˌʌndɪ'mɪnɪʃt/ *a* no disminuido, sin disminuir, cabal, íntegro

undimmed /ʌn'dɪmd/ *a* no obscurecido, brillante

undiplomatic /ˌʌndɪplə'mætɪk/ *a* impolítico, indiscreto

undirected /ˌʌndɪ'rɛktɪd/ *a* sin dirección; (of letters) sin señas

undiscernible /ˌʌndɪ'sɜrnəbəl/ *a* imperceptible, invisible

undiscerning /ˌʌndɪ'sɜrnɪŋ/ *a* sin percepción, obtuso, sin discernimiento

undisciplined /ʌn'dɪsəplɪnd/ *a* indisciplinado

undisclosed /ˌʌndɪ'sklouzd/ *a* no revelado, secreto

undiscouraged /ˌʌndɪ'skʌrɪdʒd/ *a* animoso, sin flaquear, sin desaliento

undiscovered /ˌʌndɪ'skʌvərd/ *a* no descubierto, ignoto

undiscriminating /ˌʌndɪ'skrɪmə,neitɪŋ/ *a* sin distinción; sin sentido crítico

undisguised /ˌʌndɪ'skaizd/ *a* sin disfraz; abierto, claro

undismayed /ˌʌndɪs'meid/ *a* intrépido, impávido; sin desaliento

undisposed /ˌʌndɪ'spouzd/ *a* desinclinado; (of property) no enajenado, no invertido

undisputed /ˌʌndɪ'spyutɪd/ *a* incontestable, indisputable

undistinguishable /ˌʌndɪ'stɪŋgwɪʃəbəl/ *a* indistinguible

undistinguished /ˌʌndɪ'stɪŋgwɪʃt/ *a* (of writers) poco conocido; indistinto; sin distinción

undisturbed /ˌʌndɪ'stɜrbd/ *a* sin tocar; tranquilo, sereno, impasible

undivided /ˌʌndɪ'vaidɪd/ *a* indiviso, íntegro; junto; completo, entero

undo /ʌn'du/ *vt* anular; reparar; desatar, deshacer; desasir; abrir

undoing /ʌn'duɪŋ/ *n* anulación, *f;* (reparation) reparación, *f;* (opening) abrir, *m;* ruina, *f*

undomesticated /ˌʌndə'mɛstɪ,keitɪd/ *a* salvaje, no domesticado; poco casero

undone /ʌn'dʌn/ *a* and *part* sin hacer; deshecho; arruinado, perdido. **I am undone!** ¡Estoy perdido! **to come u.,** desatarse. **to leave u.,** dejar sin hacer

undoubted /ʌn'dautɪd/ *a* indudable, evidente, incontestable

undoubtedly /ʌn'dautɪdli/ *adv* sin duda

undrained /ʌn'dreind/ *a* sin drenaje

undramatic /ˌʌndrə'mætɪk/ *a* no dramático

undreamed /ʌn'drimd/ *a* no soñado. **u. of,** inopinado, no imaginado

undress /ʌn'drɛs/ *vt* desnudar, desvestir. —*vi* desnudarse. —*n* traje de casa, *m;* paños menores, *m pl; Mil.* traje de cuartel, *m*

undressed /ʌn'drɛst/ *a* desnudo; en paños menores; (of wounds) sin curar; *Com.* en rama, en bruto

undrinkable /ʌn'drɪŋkəbəl/ *a* impotable

undue /ʌn'du/ *a* excesivo, indebido; injusto; impropio; (of a bill of exchange) por vencer

undulant /'ʌndʒələnt/ *a* ondulante. **u. fever,** fiebre mediterránea, fiebre de Malta, *f*

undulate /'ʌndʒə,leit/ *vi* ondular, ondear

undulating /'ʌndʒə,leitɪŋ/ *a* ondulante

undulation /ˌʌndʒə'leiʃən/ *n* ondulación, undulación, *f,* ondeo, *m;* fluctuación, *f*

undulatory /'ʌndʒələ,tɔri/ *a* ondulatorio, undoso

unduly /ʌn'duli/ *adv* excesivamente, demasiado, indebidamente; injustamente

undutiful /ʌn'dutəfəl/ *a* desobediente, irrespetuoso

undutifulness /ʌn'dutəfəlnɪs/ *n* desobediencia, falta de respeto, *f*

undying /ʌn'daiɪŋ/ *a* inmortal, imperecedero; eterno

unearned /ʌn'ɜrnd/ *a* no ganado; inmerecido

unearth /ʌn'ɜrθ/ *vt* desenterrar; *Fig.* descubrir, sacar a luz

unearthing /ʌn'ɜrθɪŋ/ *n* desenterramiento, *m; Fig.* descubrimiento, *m,* revelación, *f*

unearthly /ʌn'ɜrθli/ *a* sobrenatural; misterioso, aterrador, espantoso

uneasily /ʌn'daiɪŋ/ *adv* con dificultad; incómodamente; inquietamente

uneasiness /ʌn'izɪnɪs/ *n* malestar, *m;* (discomfort) incomodidad, *f;* (anxiety) inquietud, intranquilidad, *f,* desasosiego, *m*

uneasy /ʌn'izi/ *a* incómodo; inseguro; inquieto, intranquilo, desasosegado; aturdido, turbado. **to become u.,** inquietarse

uneatable /ʌn'itəbəl/ *a* incomible

uneaten /ʌn'itn/ *a* no comido

uneconomical /ˌʌnɛkə'nɒmɪkəl/ *a* poco económico, costoso, caro

unedifying /ʌn'ɛdə,faiɪŋ/ *a* poco edificante

unedited /ʌn'ɛdɪtɪd/ *a* inédito

uneducated /ʌnˈɛdʒəˌkeitɪd/ *a* ignorante; ineducado, inculto, indocto

unembarrassed /ˌʌnɛmˈbærəst/ *a* sereno, tranquilo, imperturbable; (financially) sin deudas, acomodado

unemotional /ˌʌnɪˈmouʃənl/ *a* frío, impasible

unemployable /ˌʌnɛmˈplɔiəbəl/ *a* sin uso, inservible; (of persons) inútil para el trabajo

unemployed /ˌʌnɛmˈplɔid/ *a* sin empleo; (out of work) sin trabajo, parado; desocupado, ocioso; inactivo. —*n* paro obrero, *m.* **the u.,** los sin trabajo, los cesantes, los desocupados

unemployment /ˌʌnɛmˈplɔimənt/ *n* paro forzoso, *m.* **u. benefit,** subvención contra el paro obrero, *f.* **u. insurance,** seguro contra el paro obrero, *m,*

unencumbered /ˌʌnɛnˈkʌmbərd/ *a* libre, independiente; (of estates) libre de gravamen; (untaxable) saneado

unending /ʌnˈɛndɪŋ/ *a* perpetuo, eterno, sin fin; inacabable, constante, continuo, incesante

unendurable /ˌʌnɛnˈdurəbəl/ *a* insoportable, insufrible, intolerable

unenlightened /ˌʌnɛnˈlaitn̩d/ *a* ignorante

unenterprising /ʌnˈɛntərˌpraizɪŋ/ *a* poco emprendedor, tímido

unenthusiastic /ˌʌnɛnˌθuziˈæstɪk/ *a* sin entusiasmo, tibio

unenviable /ʌnˈɛnviəbəl/ *a* no envidiable

unequal /ʌnˈikwəl/ *a* desigual; inferior; (out of proportion) desproporcionado; injusto; insuficiente; incapaz; (of ground) escabroso. **to be u. to the task,** ser incapaz de la tarea; no tener fuerzas para la tarea

unequalled /ʌnˈikwəld/ *a* sin igual, incomparable, sin par, único

unequally /ʌnˈikwəli/ *adv* desigualmente

unequivocal /ˌʌnɪˈkwɪvəkəl/ *a* inequívoco; redondo, claro, franco

unerring /ʌnˈɜrɪŋ, -ˈɛr-/ *a* infalible; seguro

unerringly /ʌnˈɜrɪŋli, -ˈɛr-* *adv* infaliblemente; sin equivocarse

unessential /ˌʌnəˈsɛnʃəl/ *a* no esencial

unesthetic /ˌʌnɛsˈθɛtɪk/ *a* antiestético

uneven /ʌnˈivən/ *a* desigual; (of roads) escabroso, quebrado; (of numbers) impar, irregular

unevenly /ʌnˈivənli/ *adv* desigualmente

unevenness /ʌnˈivənnɪs/ *n* desigualdad, *f*; desnivel, *m,* irregularidad, *f.* **the unevenness of the terrain,** lo desigual del terreno, lo accidentado del terreno, *m*

uneventful /ˌʌnɪˈvɛntfəl/ *a* sin incidentes, sin acontecimientos notables; tranquilo

unexaggerated /ˌʌnɪgˈzædʒəˌreitɪd/ *a* nada exagerado

unexamined /ˌʌnɪgˈzæmɪnd// *a* no examinado, sin examinar

unexampled /ˌʌnɪgˈzæmpəld/ *a* sin igual, sin par

unexceptionable /ˌʌnɪkˈsɛpʃənəbəl/ *a* intachable, irreprensible; correcto; impecable, perfecto

unexhausted /ˌʌnɪgˈzɔstɪd/ *a* no agotado; inexhausto

unexpected /ˌʌnɪkˈspɛktɪd/ *a* inesperado, imprevisto, inopinado, impensado; repentino, súbito

unexpectedly /ˌʌnɪkˈspɛktɪdli/ *adv* inesperadamente; de repente

unexpectedness /ˌʌnɪkˈspɛktɪdnɪs/ *n* lo inesperado

unexpired /ˌʌnɪkˈspaiᵊrd/ *a* (of bill of exchange) no vencido; (of lease) no caducado

unexplored /ˌʌnɪkˈsplɔrd/ *a* inexplorado

unexpressed /ˌʌnɪkˈsprɛst/ *a* no expresado; tácito, sobrentendido

unexpurgated /ʌnˈɛkspərˌgeitɪd/ *a* sin expurgar, completo

unfading /ʌnˈfeidɪŋ/ *a* inmarcesible, inmarchitable; eterno, inmortal

unfailing /ʌnˈfeilɪŋ/ *a* inagotable; inexhausto; seguro; indefectible

unfailingly /ʌnˈfeilɪŋli/ *adv* siempre, constantemente; sin faltar

unfair /ʌnˈfɛər/ *a* injusto; vil, bajo, soez; de mala fe, engañoso; (of play) sucio

unfairly /ʌnˈfɛərli/ *adv* injustamente; de mala fe

unfairness /ʌnˈfɛərnɪs/ *n* injusticia, *f*; mala fe, *f*

unfaithful /ʌnˈfeiθfəl/ *a* infiel; desleal; inexacto, incorrecto. **to be u. to,** ser infiel a; faltar a

unfaithfulness /ʌnˈfeiθfəlnɪs/ *n* infidelidad, *f*; deslealtad, *f*; inexactitud, *f*

unfaltering /ʌnˈfɔltərɪŋ/ *a* sin vacilar; resuelto, firme

unfamiliar /ˌʌnfəˈmɪlyər/ *a* poco familiar; desconocido. **to be u. with,** ser ignorante de

unfashionable /ʌnˈfæʃənəbəl/ *a* pasado de moda, fuera de moda; poco elegante

unfashionableness /ʌnˈfæʃənəbəlnɪs/ *n* falta de elegancia, *f*

unfashionably /ʌnˈfæʃənəbli/ *adv* contra la tendencia de la moda; sin elegancia

unfasten /ʌnˈfæsən/ *vt* desatar; desabrochar, desenganchar; abrir; aflojar; soltar

unfathomable /ʌnˈfæðəməbəl/ *a* insondable; impenetrable, inescrutable

unfavorable /ʌnˈfeivərəbəl/ *a* desfavorable, adverso, contrario

unfavorably /ʌnˈfeivərəbli/ *adv* desfavorablemente

unfeathered /ʌnˈfɛðərd/ *a* implume, sin plumas

unfeeling /ʌnˈfilɪŋ/ *a* insensible, impasible, frío; duro, cruel

unfeigned /ʌnˈfeind/ *a* sincero, natural, verdadero

unfenced /ʌnˈfɛnst/ *a* descercado, sin tapia; abierto

unfermented /ˌʌnfərˈmɛntɪd/ *a* no fermentado;

unfetter /ʌnˈfɛtər/ *vt* desencadenar, destrabar; poner en libertad, librar

unfilial /ʌnˈfɪliəl/ *a* poco filial, desobediente

unfinished /ʌnˈfɪnɪʃt/ *a* incompleto, inacabado; sin acabar; imperfecto

unfit /ʌnˈfɪt/ *a* incapaz; incompetente, inepto; (unsuitable) impropio; (useless) inservible, inadecuado; (unworthy) indigno; (ill) enfermo, malo. —*vt* inhabilitar, incapacitar. **u. for human consumption,** impropio para el consumo humano

unfitness /ʌnˈfɪtnɪs/ *n* incapacidad, *f*; incompetencia, ineptitud, *f*; impropiedad, *f*; falta de mérito, *f*; falta de salud, *f*

unfix /ʌnˈfɪks/ *vt* desprender, despegar, descomponer; soltar. **to come unfixed,** desprenderse

unflagging /ʌnˈflægɪŋ/ *a* incansable, infatigable; persistente, constante

unflattering /ʌnˈflætərɪŋ/ *a* poco halagüeño

unflinching /ʌnˈflɪntʃɪŋ/ *a* inconmovible, resuelto, firme

unfold /ʌnˈfould/ *vt* desplegar, desdoblar; tender; abrir; (plans) revelar, descubrir; contar, manifestar. —*vi* abrirse

unfolding /ʌnˈfouldɪŋ/ *a* que se abre. —*n* despliegue, *m*; revelación, *f*; narración, *f*

unforced /ʌnˈfɔrst/ *a* libre; espontáneo; fácil; natural

unforeseen /ˌʌnfɔrˈsin/ *a* imprevisto, inesperado

unforgettable /ˌʌnfərˈgɛtəbəl/ *a* involvidable

unforgivable /ˌʌnfərˈgɪvəbəl/ *a* inexcusable, imperdonable

unforgiving /ˌʌnfərˈgɪvɪŋ/ *a* implacable, que no perdona, inexorable

unforgotten /ˌʌnfərˈgɒtn̩/ *a* no olvidado

unformed /ʌnˈfɔrmd/ *a* informe; rudimentario; inmaturo; (inexperienced) inexperto, sin experiencia

unfortunate /ʌnˈfɔrtʃənɪt/ *a* desdichado, infortunado, desgraciado, desventurado. —*n* desdichado (-da); pobre, *mf*; (prostitute) perdida, *f*

unfortunately /ʌnˈfɔrtʃənɪtli/ *adv* por desdicha, desgraciadamente

unfounded /ʌnˈfaundɪd/ *a* infundado, inmotivado, sin fundamento, injustificado

unframed /ʌnˈfreimd/ *a* sin marco

unfrequented /ʌnˈfrikwəntɪd/ *a* poco frecuentado, solitario, retirado, aislado

unfriendliness /ʌnˈfrɛndlinɪs/ *n* hostilidad, falta de amistad, frialdad, *f*; huraña, insociabilidad, *f*

unfriendly /ʌnˈfrɛndli/ *a* hostil, enemigo; (of things, events) perjudicial; huraño, insociable

unfrock /ʌnˈfrɒk/ *vt* degradar, exclaustrar

unfruitful /ʌnˈfrutfəl/ *a* estéril, infecundo; infructuoso, improductivo, vano

unfulfilled /ˌʌnfəlˈfild/ *a* incumplido, sin cumplir; malogrado

unfurl /ʌnˈfɜrl/ *vt* desplegar; *Naut.* izar (las velas)

unfurnished /ʌnˈfɜrnɪʃt/ *a* desamueblado, sin muebles; desprovisto (de), sin

ungainliness /ʌn'geinlinɪs/ n falta de gracia, torpeza, f, desgarbo, m

ungainly /ʌn'geinli/ a desgarbado

ungallant /ʌn'gælənt/ a poco caballeroso, nada galante

ungenerous /ʌn'dʒɛnərəs/ a poco generoso; avaro, tacaño, mezquino; injusto

ungentlemanly /ʌn'dʒɛntḷmənli/ a poco caballeroso, indigno de un caballero

unglazed /ʌn'gleizd/ a sin vidriar; (paper) sin satinar; deslustrado

ungloved /ʌn'glʌvd/ a sin guante(s)

unglue /ʌn'glu/ vt desencolar, despegar

ungodliness /ʌn'gɒdlinɪs/ n impiedad, f

ungodly /ʌn'gɒdli/ a impío, irreligioso

ungovernable /ʌn'gʌvərnəbəl/ a ingobernable, indomable; irrefrenable

ungraceful /ʌn'greisfəl/ a desagraciado, desgarbado, sin gracia

ungracious /ʌn'greiʃəs/ a desagradable, poco cortés, desdeñoso

ungraciousness /ʌn'greiʃəsnɪs/ n descortesía, aspereza, inurbanidad, f

ungrammatical /ˌʌngrə'mætɪkəl/ a antigramatical, incorrecto

ungrateful /ʌn'greitfəl/ a ingrato, desagradecido; desagradable, odioso

ungratefulness /ʌn'greitfəlnɪs/ n ingratitud, f; lo desagradable

ungrounded /ʌn'graundɪd/ a infundado; sin motivo

ungrudging /ʌn'grʌdʒɪŋ/ a no avaro, liberal; generoso, magnánimo

ungrudgingly /ʌn'grʌdʒɪŋli/ adv de buena gana

unguarded /ʌn'gardɪd/ a indefenso, sin protección; descuidado; indiscreto, imprudente; sin reflexión

unguided /ʌn'gaidɪd/ a sin guía

unhallowed /ʌn'hæloud/ a impío, profano

unhampered /ʌn'hæmpərd/ a desembarazado, libre

unhappily /ʌn'hæpəli/ adv desafortunadamente, por desgracia

unhappiness /ʌn'hæpinɪs/ n infelicidad, desgracia, desdicha, tristeza, f

unhappy /ʌn'hæpi/ a infeliz, desgraciado, desdichado, triste; (ill-fated) aciago, funesto, malhadado; (remark) inoportuno, inapropiado

unharmed /ʌn'harmd/ a ileso, sano y salvo; (of things) indemne, sin daño

unharness /ʌn'harnɪs/ vt desaparejar; desenganchar; desarmar

unhealthiness /ʌn'hɛlθinɪs/ n falta de salud, f; (of place) insalubridad, f

unhealthy /ʌn'hɛlθi/ a enfermizo; malsano, insalubre

unheard /ʌn'hɜrd/ a no oído; sin ser escuchado; desconocido. **u.-of**, inaudito, no imaginado

unheeding /ʌn'hidiŋ/ a distraído; desatento, sin prestar atención (a); descuidado

unhelpful /ʌn'hɛlpfəl/ a poco servicial; inútil

unhesitating /ʌn'hɛzɪˌteitiŋ/ a resuelto, decidido; pronto, inmediato

unhesitatingly /ʌn'hɛzɪˌteitiŋli/ adv sin vacilar

unhinge /ʌn'hindʒ/ vt desgoznar, desquiciar; (of the mind) trastornar

unhitch /ʌn'hitʃ/ vt desenganchar; descolgar

unholy /ʌn'houli/ a impío, sacrílego

unhonored /ʌn'ɒnərd/ a sin que se reconociese sus méritos; despreciado; (check) protestado

unhook /ʌn'hʊk/ vt desenganchar; desabrochar; descolgar

unhoped-for /ʌn'houptfɔr/ a inesperado

unhurt /ʌn'hɜrt/ a ileso, incólume, sano y salvo; (of things) sin daño

unicellular /ˌyunə'sɛlyələr/ a unicelular

unicolored /'yunɪˌkʌlərd/ a unicolor

unicorn /'yunɪˌkɔrn/ n unicornio, m

unidentified /ˌʌnai'dɛntəˌfaid/ a no reconocido, no identificado

unification /ˌyunəfɪ'keiʃən/ n unificación, f

uniform /'yunəˌfɔrm/ a uniforme; igual, constante, invariable; homogéneo. —n uniforme, m. **in full u.**, de gran uniforme. **to make u.**, uniformar, igualar, hacer uniforme

uniformity /ˌyunə'fɔrmɪti/ n uniformidad, igualdad, f

uniformly /'yunəˌfɔrmli/ adv uniformemente

unify /'yunəˌfai/ vt unificar; unir

unilateral /ˌyunə'lætərəl/ a unilateral

unimaginable /ˌʌnɪ'mædʒənəbəl/ a inimaginable, no imaginable

unimaginative /ˌʌnɪ'mædʒənətɪv/ a sin imaginación

unimpaired /ˌʌnɪm'pɛərd/ a no disminuido; sin alteración; intacto, entero; sin menoscabo

unimpeachable /ˌʌnɪm'pitʃəbəl/ a irreprochable, intachable

unimportance /ˌʌnɪm'pɔrtṇs/ n no importancia, insignificancia, trivialidad, f

unimportant /ˌʌnɪm'pɔrtṇt/ a sin importancia, nada importante, insignificante, trivial

unimpressive /ˌʌnɪm'prɛsɪv/ a poco impresionante; nada conmovedor; (of persons) insignificante

uninflammable /ˌʌnɪn'flæməbəl/ a no inflamable, incombustible

uninfluenced /ˌʌnɪn'fluənsd/ a no afectado (por), libre (de)

uninformed /ˌʌnɪn'fɔrmd/ a ignorante

uninhabitable /ˌʌnɪn'hæbɪtəbəl/ a inhabitable

uninhabited /ˌʌnɪn'hæbɪtɪd/ a deshabitado, inhabitado, vacío, desierto

uninjured /ʌn'ɪndʒərd/ a ileso; sin daño

uninspired /ˌʌnɪn'spaiᵊrd/ a sin inspiración; pedestre, mediocre

uninstructive /ˌʌnɪn'strʌktɪv/ a nada instructivo

uninsured /ˌʌnɪn'ʃʊrd/ a no asegurado

unintelligent /ˌʌnɪn'tɛlɪdʒənt/ a nada inteligente, corto de alcances, tonto

unintelligibility /ˌʌnɪnˌtɛlɪdʒə'bɪlɪti/ n incomprensibilidad, f, lo ininteligible

unintelligible /ˌʌnɪn'tɛlɪdʒəbəl/ a ininteligible, incomprensible

unintentional /ˌʌnɪn'tɛnʃənḷ/ a involuntario, inadvertido

unintentionally /ˌʌnɪn'tɛnʃənḷi/ adv sin querer, involuntariamente

uninterested /ʌn'ɪntərəstɪd/ a no interesado, despreocupado

uninteresting /ʌn'ɪntərəstɪŋ/ a sin interés, poco interesante, soso

uninterrupted /ˌʌnɪntə'rʌptɪd/ a ininterrum pido, sin interrupción; continuo, incesante

uninvited /ˌʌnɪn'vaitɪd/ a no invitado, no convidado, sin invitación; (unlooked-for) no buscado

uninviting /ˌʌnɪn'vaitɪŋ/ a poco atrayente; inhospitalario

union /'yunyən/ n unión, f; Mech. manguito de unión, m; conexión, f; (poverty) asociación, f; (of trade) gremio de oficios, m; sindicato (obrero), m; (workhouse) asilo, m; (U.S.A.) Estados Unidos de América, m pl

unionism /'yunyəˌnɪzəm/ n unionismo, m

unionist /'yunyənɪst/ n Polit. unionista, mf

unique /yu'nik/ a único, sin igual, sin par

uniqueness /yu'niknɪs/ n unicidad, f; lo singular

unisexual /ˌyunə'sɛkʃuəl/ a unisexual

unison /'yunəsən/ n unisonancia, f. **in u.**, al unísono

unit /'yunɪt/ n unidad, f. **u. bookcase**, librería en secciones, f

Unitarian /ˌyunɪ'tɛəriən/ a and n unitario (-ia)

Unitarianism /ˌyunɪ'tɛəriəˌnɪzəm/ n unitarismo, m

unite /yu'nait/ vt unir, juntar; combinar, incorporar; (of countries) unificar; (of energies, etc.) reunir. —vi unirse, juntarse; reunirse, concertarse; convenirse

united /yu'naitɪd/ a unido; junto. **the U. Nations**, las Naciones Unidas, f pl

unitedly /yu'naitɪdli/ adv unidamente; armoniosamente, de acuerdo

United States of America los Estados Unidos, m pl

unity /'yunɪti/ n unidad, f; Math. la unidad; unión, f; conformidad, armonía, f. **the three unities**, las tres unidades

universal /ˌyunə'vɜrsəl/ a universal; general; común. **to make u.**, universalizar, generalizar. **u. joint**, junta universal, f; Auto. cardán, m

universality /ˌyunəvər'sælɪti/ n universalidad, f

universalize /ˌyunə'vɜrsəˌlaiz/ vt universalizar

universe /'yunə,vɜrs/ n universo, m; creación, f, mundo, m

university /,yunə'vɜrsɪti/ n universidad, f. —a universitario. **u. degree,** grado universitario, m

unjust /ʌn'dʒʌst/ a injusto

unjustifiable /ʌn,dʒʌstə'faiəbəl/ a injustificable, indisculpable, inexcusable

unjustifiably /ʌn,dʒʌstə'faiəbli/ adv injustificadamente, inexcusablemente

unjustly /ʌn'dʒʌstli/ adv injustamente, sin razón

unkempt /ʌn'kɛmpt/ a despeinado; desaseado, sucio

unkind /ʌn'kaind/ a nada bondadoso, nada amable; poco complaciente; duro, cruel; desfavorable, nada propicio

unkindly /ʌn'kaindli/ adv sin bondad; con dureza, cruelmente

unkindness /ʌn'kaindnɪs/ n falta de bondad, f; severidad, crueldad, dureza, f, rigor, m; acto de crueldad, m

unknowable /ʌn'nouəbəl/ a impenetrable, incomprehensible, insondable

unknowingly /ʌn'nouɪŋli/ adv sin querer, involuntariamente; sin saberlo; insensiblemente

unknown /ʌn'noun/ a ignoto, desconocido; Math. incógnito. —n lo desconocido, misterio, m; Math. incógnita, f; (person) desconocido (-da), forastero (-ra). Math. **u. quantity,** incógnita, f

unlabeled /ʌn'leibəld/ a sin etiqueta

unlace /ʌn'leis/ vt desenlazar; desatar

unladylike /ʌn'leidi,laik/ a indigno (or impropio) de una dama; vulgar, ordinario, cursi

unlamented /,ʌnlə'mɛntɪd/ a no llorado, no lamentado

unlatch /ʌn'lætʃ/ vt alzar el pestillo de, abrir

unlawful /ʌn'lɔfəl/ a ilegal, ilícito

unlawfulness /ʌn'lɔfəlnɪs/ n ilegalidad, f

unlearn /ʌn'lɜrn/ vt olvidar, desaprender

unleash /ʌn'liʃ/ vt soltar

unleavened /ʌn'lɛvənd/ a ázimo, sin levadura

unless /ʌn'lɛs/ conjunc a no ser que, a menos que, como no, si no (all followed by subjunc.); salvo, excepto, con excepción de

unlicensed /ʌn'laisənst/ a no autorizado, sin licencia

unlike /ʌn'laik/ a disímil, desemejante; distinto, diferente. —prep a distinción de, a diferencia de, al contrario de. **They are quite u.,** No se parecen nada

unlikeliness /ʌn'laiklinɪs/ n improbabilidad, f

unlikely /ʌn'laikli/ a improbable, inverosímil; arriesgado

unlikeness /ʌn'laiknɪs/ n desemejanza, diferencia, f

unlimited /ʌn'lɪmɪtɪd/ a ilimitado, infinito, inmenso; sin restricción; excesivo, exagerado. **unlimited telephone,** teléfono no medido (Argentina)

unlined /ʌn'laind/ a no forrado, sin forro; sin rayas; (of face) sin arrugas

unlit /ʌn'lɪt/ a no iluminado, oscuro, sin luz

unload /ʌn'loud/ vt descargar; aligerar; Naut. hondear; (of shares) deshacerse de. —vi descargar

unloading /ʌn'loudɪŋ/ n descarga, f, descargue, m

unlock /ʌn'lɒk/ vt desencerrar, abrir; Fig. revelar, descubrir

unlooked-for /ʌn'luktfɔr/ a inopinado, inesperado

unloose /ʌn'lus/ vt desatar; soltar; poner en libertad

unlovable /ʌn'lʌvəbəl/ a indigno del querer; antipático, poco amable; repugnante

unloveliness /ʌn'lʌvlinɪs/ n falta de hermosura, fealdad, f

unlovely /ʌn'lʌvli/ a nada hermoso, feo; desagradable

unluckily /ʌn'lʌkəli/ adv desafortunadamente, por desgracia

unluckiness /ʌn'lʌkinɪs/ n mala suerte, f; (unsuitability) inoportunidad, f; lo nefasto, lo malo

unlucky /ʌn'lʌki/ a de mala suerte; desdichado, desgraciado, infeliz; (ill-omened) funesto, nefasto, fatal; inoportuno, inconveniente

unmanageable /ʌn'mænɪdʒəbəl/ a indomable, indócil; ingobernable, inmanejable; (unwieldy) difícil de manejar, pesado

unmannerliness /ʌn'mænərlinɪs/ n mala crianza, descortesía, f

unmannerly /ʌn'mænərli/ a mal educado, descortés

unmarketable /ʌn'markɪtəbəl/ a invendible

unmarriageable /ʌn'mærɪdʒəbəl/ a incasable

unmarried /ʌn'mærid/ a soltero, célibe

unmask /ʌn'mæsk/ vt desenmascarar; Fig. quitar la careta (a). —vi quitarse la máscara; Fig. quitarse la careta, descubrirse

unmeaning /ʌn'minɪŋ/ a sin sentido, vacío, sin significación

unmelodious /,ʌnmə'loudiəs/ a sin melodía, discorde

unmendable /ʌn'mɛndəbəl/ a incomponible

unmentionable /ʌn'mɛnʃənəbəl/ a que no se puede mencionar; indigno de mencionarse

unmerciful /ʌn'mɜrsɪfəl/ a sin piedad, sin compasión; cruel, despiadado, duro

unmerited /ʌn'mɛrɪtɪd/ a inmerecido, desmerecido

unmethodical /,ʌnmə'θɒdɪkəl/ a poco metódico

unmindful /ʌn'maindfəl/ a olvidadizo; desatento; negligente. **u. of,** sin pensar en, olvidando

unmistakable /,ʌnmɪ'steikəbəl/ a inequívoco; manifiesto, evidente, indudable

unmistakably /,ʌnmɪ'steikəbli/ adv indudablemente

unmitigated /ʌn'mɪtɪ,geitɪd/ a no mitigado; completo, absoluto; (of rogue) redomado

unmixed /ʌn'mɪkst/ a sin mezcla; puro, sencillo; (free) limpio

unmoor /ʌn'mʊr/ vt desamarrar

unmoral /ʌn'mɔrəl, -'mɒr-/ a amoral, no moral; sin fin didáctico

unmounted /ʌn'mauntɪd/ a desmontado

unmoved /ʌn'muvd/ a fijo; (unemotional) impasible, frío; (determined) firme, inflexible, inexorable

unmuffle /ʌn'mʌfəl/ vt desembozar, descubrir

unmusical /ʌn'myuzikəl/ a sin afición a la música; sin oído (para la música); inarmónico

unnamable /ʌn'neiməbəl/ a que no se puede nombrar, innominable

unnatural /ʌn'nætʃərəl/ a desnaturalizado; (of vices, etc.) contra natural; innatural; (of style) rebuscado; artificial; inhumano, cruel

unnaturalness /ʌn'nætʃərəlnɪs/ n lo monstruoso; lo innatural; artificialidad, f; inhumanidad, f

unnavigable /ʌn'nævɪgəbəl/ a innavegable, no navegable

unnecessarily /,ʌnnɛsə'sɛrəli/ adv inútilmente, innecesariamente, sin necesidad

unnecessariness /ʌn'nɛsə,sɛrinɪs/ n inutilidad, f; superfluidad, f; lo innecesario

unnecessary /ʌn'nɛsə,sɛri/ a innecesario, superfluo, inútil

unneighborly /ʌn'neibərli/ a de mala vecindad, impropio de vecinos, poco servicial

unnerve /ʌn'nɜrv/ vt acobardar quitar el valor, desanimar

unnoticed /ʌn'noutɪst/ a inadvertido, no observado

unobliging /ʌnə'blaidʒɪŋ/ a nada servicial

unobservable /,ʌnbə'zɜrvəbəl/ a inobservable

unobservant /,ʌnəb'zɜrvənt/ a desobservante

unobserved /,ʌnəb'zɜrvd/ a sin ser notado, desapercibido

unobstructed /,ʌnəb'strʌktɪd/ a no obstruido; sin obstáculos; libre

unobtainable /,ʌnəb'teinəbəl/ a inalcanzable, inasequible

unobtrusive /,ʌnəb'trusɪv/ a discreto, modesto

unobtrusiveness /,ʌnəb'trusɪvnɪs/ n discreción, modestia, f

unoccupied /ʌn'ɒkyə,paid/ a (at leisure) desocupado, ocioso, sin ocupación; vacío, vacante, libre; (untenanted) deshabitado

unofficial /,ʌnə'fɪʃəl/ a no oficial

unopened /ʌn'oupənd/ a sin abrir, cerrado; (of exhibitions, etc.) no inaugurado

unopposed /,ʌnə'pouzd/ a sin oposición

unorganized /ʌn'ɔrgə,naizd/ a inorganizado; Biol. inorgánico

unoriginal /,ʌnə'rɪdʒənl/ a poco original

unorthodox /ʌn'ɔrθə,dɒks/ a heterodoxo

unostentatious /,ʌnɒstən'teiʃəs/ a sencillo, modesto, sin ostentación

unostentatiousness /ˌʌnɒstən'teiʃəsnis/ n sencillez, modestia, falta de ostentación, f

unpack /ʌn'pæk/ vt desempaquetar; (trunks) vaciar; (bales) desembalar. —vi desempaquetar; deshacer las maletas

unpacking /ʌn'pækiŋ/ n desembalaje, m

unpaid /ʌn'peid/ a sin pagar, no pagado

unpalatable /ʌn'pælətəbəl/ a de mal sabor; desagradable

unparalleled /ʌn'pærə,lɛld/ a sin paralelo, sin par, sin igual

unpardonable /ʌn'pardṇəbəl/ a imperdonable, inexcusable, irremisible

unparliamentary /ˌʌnparlə'mɛntəri/ a poco parliamentario

unpatriotic /ˌʌnpeitri'ɒtik/ a antipatriótico

unpaved /ʌn'peivd/ a sin empedrar

unperceived /ˌʌnpər'sivd/ a inadvertido, sin ser notado

unperturbed /ˌʌnpər'tɜrbd/ a impasible, sin alterarse, sereno

unpleasant /ʌn'plɛzənt/ a desagradable, desapacible; ofensivo; (troublesome) enfadoso, molesto

unpleasantly /ʌn'plɛzəntli/ adv desagradablemente

unpleasantness /ʌn'plɛzəntnis/ n lo desagradable; disgusto, sinsabor, m; (disagreement) disputa, riña, f

unpleasing /ʌn'pliziŋ/ a nada placentero; desagradable, sin atractivos

unplug /ʌn'plʌg/ vt desenchufar

unpoetic, unpoetical, /ˌʌnpou'ɛtik; ˌʌnpou'ɛtikəl/ a poco poético

unpolished /ʌn'pɒliʃt/ a sin pulir, tosco, mate; Fig. inculto, cerril. **u. diamond,** diamante en bruto, m

unpolluted /ˌʌnpə'lutid/ a impoluto, incontaminado; puro, sin pervertir

unpopular /ʌn'pɒpyələr/ a impopular

unpopularity /ˌʌnpɒpyə'lærɪti/ n impopularidad, f

unpractical /ʌn'præktɪkəl/ a impracticable, imposible; (of persons) sin sentido práctico

unpracticed /ʌn'præktɪst/ a no practicado; inexperto, inhábil

unpraiseworthy /ʌn'preiz,wɜrði/ a inmeritorio

unprecedented /ʌn'prɛsɪ,dɛntɪd/ a sin precedente, inaudito

unprejudiced /ʌn'prɛdʒədɪst/ a sin prejuicios, imparcial

unpremeditated /ˌʌnpri'mɛdɪ,teitɪd/ a sin premeditación, indeliberado, impremeditado

unprepared /ˌʌnprɪ'pɛərd/ a sin preparación, no preparado; desprevenido; desapercibido (unready)

unpreparedness /ˌʌnprɪ'pɛərɪdnɪs/ n falta de preparación, imprevisión, f, desapercibimiento, m

unprepossessing /ˌʌnpripə'zɛsiŋ/ a poco atrayente, antipático

unpresentable /ˌʌnprɪ'zɛntəbəl/ a impresentable

unpretentious /ˌʌnprɪ'tɛnʃəs/ a sin pretensiones, modesto

unpriced /ʌn'praist/ a sin precio

unprincipled /ʌn'prɪnsəpəld/ a sin consciencia, sin escrúpulos

unprinted /ʌn'prɪntɪd/ a sin imprimir, no impreso

unprocurable /ˌʌnprou'kyurəbəl/ a inalcanzable, inasequible

unproductive /ˌʌnprə'dʌktɪv/ a improductivo; infructuoso, estéril

unproductiveness /ˌʌnprə'dʌktɪvnɪs/ n infructuosidad, f; esterilidad, f

unprofessional /ˌʌnprə'fɛʃənḷ/ a sin profesión; contrario a la ética profesional

unprofitable /ʌn'prɒfɪtəbəl/ a improductivo, infructuoso; sin provecho; inútil; nada lucrativo

unprogressive /ˌʌnprə'grɛsɪv/ a reaccionario

unpromising /ʌn'prɒməsiŋ/ a poco halagüeño

unpronounceable /ˌʌnprə'naunsəbəl/ a impronunciable

unpropitious /ˌʌnprə'pɪʃəs/ a desfavorable, nada propicio, nada halagüeño

unprosperous /ʌn'prɒspərəs/ a impróspero

unprotected /ˌʌnprə'tɛktɪd/ a sin protección; (of persons) indefenso, desválido

unproved /ʌn'pruvd/ a no probado, sin demostrar

unprovided /ˌʌnprə'vaidɪd/ a desapercibido, desprovisto. **u. for,** sin provisión (para); sin medios de vida, desamparado

unprovoked /ˌʌnprə'voukt/ a no provocado, sin provocación; sin motivo

unpublished /ʌn'pʌblɪʃt/ a inédito, no publicado, sin publicar

unpunctual /ʌn'pʌŋktʃuəl/ a no puntual, retrasado

unpunctuality /ʌnˌpʌŋktʃu'ælɪti/ n falta de puntualidad, f, retraso, m

unpunctually /ʌn'pʌŋktʃuəli/ adv sin puntualidad, tarde, con retraso

unpunishable /ʌn'pʌnɪʃə bəl/ a no punible

unpunished /ʌn'pʌnɪʃt/ a impune, sin castigo

unpurchasable /ʌn'pɜrtʃɪsəbəl/ a que no puede comprarse

unqualified /ʌn'kwɒlɪˌfaid/ a incapaz, incompetente; (with professions) sin título; (downright) incondicional, absoluto

unquenchable /ʌn'kwɛntʃəbəl/ a inextinguible, inapagable; insaciable

unquestionable /ʌn'kwɛstʃənəbəl/ a indiscutible, indudable, indubitable

unquestionably /ʌn'kwɛstʃənəbli/ adv indudablemente

unquiet /ʌn'kwaiɪt/ a inquieto, intranquilo; agitado

unravel /ʌn'rævəl/ vt deshilar; destejer; (a mystery, etc.) desentrañar, desembrollar, descifrar

unraveling /ʌn'rævəliŋ/ n deshiladura, f; aclaración, f

unreadable /ʌn'ridəbəl/ a ilegible

unreadiness /ʌn'rɛdɪnɪs/ n falta de preparación, f, desapercibimiento, m; lentitud, f

unready /ʌn'rɛdi/ a desapercibido, desprevenido; lento

unreal /ʌn'riəl/ a irreal; falso, imaginario, ilusorio; ficticio; artificial; insincero, hipócrita; ideal; incorpóreo

unreality /ˌʌnri'ælɪti/ n irrealidad, f; falsedad, f; artificialidad, f; lo quimérico

unreasonable /ʌn'rizənəbəl/ a irrazonable, irracional; disparatado, extravagante; (with price, etc.) exorbitante, excesivo

unreasonableness /ʌn'rizənəbəlnɪs/ n irracionalidad, f; exorbitancia, f

unreasonably /ʌn'rizənəbli/ adv irracionalmente

unreasoning /ʌn'rizəniŋ/ a irracional; sin motivo, sin causa

unreceipted /ˌʌnrɪ'sitɪd/ a sin recibo

unrecognizable /ʌn'rɛkəgˌnaizəbəl/ a que no puede reconocerse; imposible de reconocer

unrecognized /ʌn'rɛkəgˌnaizd/ a no reconocido

unreconciled /ʌn'rɛkənˌsaild/ a no resignado, no reconciliado

unrectified /ʌn'rɛktəˌfaid/ a no corregido, sin rectificar

unredeemed /ˌʌnrɪ'dimd/ a no redimido; no mitigado; (of pledges) sin desempeñar

unrefined /ˌʌnrɪ'faind/ a no refinado, impuro; inculto, grosero

unreformed /ˌʌnrɪ'fɔrmd/ a no reformado

unrefuted /ˌʌnrɪ'fyutɪd/ a no refutado

unregenerate /ˌʌnrɪ'dʒɛnərɪt/ a no regenerado

unregretted /ˌʌnrɪ'grɛtɪd/ a no llorado, sin lamentar

unrehearsed /ˌʌnrɪ'hɜrst/ a sin preparación; Theat. sin ensayar; (extempore) improvisado

unrelated /ˌʌnrɪleitɪd/ a inconexo; (of persons) sin parentesco

unrelenting /ˌʌnrɪ'lɛntiŋ/ a implacable, inflexible, inexorable

unreliability /ˌʌnrɪˌlaiə'bɪlɪti/ n incertidumbre, f; el no poder confiar en, informalidad, inestabilidad, f

unreliable /ˌʌnrɪˌlaiəbəl/ a incierto, dudoso, indigno de confianza; (of persons) informal

unrelieved /ˌʌnrɪ'livd/ a no aliviado; absoluto, completo, total

unremitting /ˌʌnrɪ'mɪtiŋ/ a incansable

unremunerative /ˌʌnrɪ'myunərətɪv/ a sin remuneración, no remunerado

unrepealed /ˌʌnrɪ'pild/ a vigente

unrepentant /ˌʌnrɪ'pɛntṇt/ a impenitente

unrepresentative /ˌʌnrɛprɪ'zɛntətɪv/ a poco representativo

unrepresented /ˌʌnrɛprɪ'zɛntɪd/ a sin representación

unrequited /ˌʌnrɪ'kwaitɪd/ a no correspondido

unreserved /ˌʌnrɪ'zɜrvd/ a no reservado; expresivo, comunicativo, expansivo, franco

unreservedly /ˌʌnrɪ'zɜrvɪdli/ adv sin reserva; con toda franqueza

unresisting /ˌʌnrɪ'zɪstɪŋ/ a sin oponer resistencia

unresolved /ˌʌnrɪ'zɒlvd/ a sin resolverse, vacilante; incierto, dudoso, inseguro; sin solución

unresponsive /ˌʌnrɪ'spɒnsɪv/ a flemático; insensible, sordo

unresponsiveness /ˌʌnrɪ'spɒnsɪvnɪs/ n flema, f; insensibilidad, f

unrest /ʌn'rɛst/ n desasosiego, m, agitación, inquietud, f

unrestful /ʌn'rɛstfəl/ a agitado, inquieto, intranquilo

unrestrained /ˌʌnrɪ'streind/ a desenfrenado; ilimitado, sin límites; sin reserva

unrestricted /ˌʌnrɪ'strɪktɪd/ a sin restricción; ilimitado

unrevealed /ˌʌnrɪ'vild/ a no revelado, por descubrir, no descubierto

unrewarded /ˌʌnrɪ'wɔrdɪd/ a sin premio, no recompensado

unrighteous /ʌn'raitʃəs/ a injusto, malo, perverso

unrighteousness /ʌn'raitʃəsnɪs/ n injusticia, f; maldad, perversidad, f

unripe /ʌn'raip/ a verde, inmaturo

unripeness /ʌn'raipnɪs/ n falta de madurez, f

unrivaled /ʌn'raivəld/ a sin igual, sin par

unroll /ʌn'roul/ vt desarrollar. —vi desarrollarse; (unfold) desplegarse (a la vista)

unromantic /ˌʌnrou'mæntɪk/ a poco (or nada) romántico

unruffled /ʌn'rʌfəld/ a sereno, plácido, ecuánime; no arrugado; (of hair) liso

unruliness /ʌn'rulinɪs/ n turbulencia, indisciplina, f; insubordinación, rebeldía, f

unruly /ʌn'ruli/ a ingobernable, revoltoso; refractario, rebelde; (of hair) indomable

unsaddle /ʌn'sædl/ vt desensillar; derribar (del caballo, etc.)

unsafe /ʌn'seif/ a inseguro; peligroso; arriesgado; (to eat) nocivo

unsafeness /ʌn'seifnɪs/ n inseguridad, f; peligro, riesgo, m

unsaid /ʌn'sɛd/ a sin decir, no dicho

unsalable /½n'seiləbəl/ a invendible

unsalaried /ʌn'sælərid/ a no asalariado

unsalted /ʌn'sɔltɪd/ a no salado, sin sal

unsanctioned /ʌn'sæŋkʃənd/ a no permitido, sin sancionar

unsanitary /ʌn'sænɪteri/ a antihigiénico

unsatisfactoriness /ˌʌnsætɪs'fæktərinɪs/ n lo insatisfactorio

unsatisfactory /ˌʌnsætɪs'fæktəri/ a poco (or nada) satisfactorio; no aceptable

unsatisfied /ʌn'sætɪs,faid/ a no satisfecho; descontento; no convencido; (hungry) no harto; Com. no saldado

unsatisfying /ʌn'sætɪs,faiɪŋ/ a que no satisface

unsavoriness /ʌn'seivərinɪs/ n insipidez, f, mal sabor, m; lo desagradable; sordidez, suciedad, f

unsavory /ʌn'seivəri/ a insípido, de mal sabor; desagradable; sórdido, sucio

unscalable /ʌn'skeiləbəl/ a inascendible, virgen

unscathed /ʌn'skeiðd/ a sin daño, ileso

unscented /ʌn'sɛntɪd/ a sin perfume, sin olor, no fragante

unscholarly /ʌn'skɒlərli/ a nada erudito; indigno de un erudito

unscientific /ˌʌnsaiən'tɪfɪk/ a no científico

unscrew /ʌn'skru/ vt destornillar. —vi destornillarse

unscrewing /ʌn'skruɪŋ/ n destornillamiento, m

unscrupulous /ʌn'skrupyələs/ a sin escrúpulos, poco escrupuloso, desaprensivo

unscrupulousness /ʌn'skrupyələsnɪs/ n falta de escrúpulos, desaprensión, f

unseal /ʌn'sil/ vt desellar, romper (or quitar) el sello (de)

unseasonable /ʌn'sizənəbəl/ a intempestivo, fuera de sazón; inoportuno, inconveniente. **at an u. hour,** a una hora inconveniente, a deshora

unseasonableness /ʌn'sizənəbəlnɪs/ n lo intempestivo, inoportunidad, f

unseasonably /ʌn'sizənəbli/ /adv intempestivamente; a deshora; inoportunamente

unseasoned /ʌn'sizənd/ a Cul. sin sazonar, soso; (wood) verde; no maduro, sin madurar

unseat /ʌn'sit/ vt (from horse) tirar, echar al suelo; Polit. desituir

unseaworthy /'ʌn'si,wɜrði/ a innavegable

unseemliness /ʌn'simlinɪs/ n falta de decoro, f; indecencia, f

unseemly /ʌn'simli/ a indecoroso, indigno; indecente; impropio

unseen /ʌn'sin/ a no visto, invisible; inadvertido; secreto, oculto. —n versión al libro abierto, f. **the u.,** lo invisible

unselfish /ʌn'sɛlfɪʃ/ a desinteresado, abnegado, nada egoísta; generoso

unselfishness /ʌn'sɛlfɪʃnɪs/ n abnegación, f; desinterés, m; generosidad, f

unsentimental /ˌʌnsɛntə'mɛntl̩/ a no sentimental

unserviceable /ʌn'sɜrvɪsəbəl/ a inservible, inútil, que no sirve para nada, sin utilidad

unsettle /ʌn'sɛtl/ vt desarreglar; desorganizar; hacer inseguro; agitar, perturbar

unsettled /ʌn'sɛtld/ a inconstante, variable; Com. pendiente, sin pagar; incierto; sin resolver; (of estates) sin solucionar

unshackle /ʌn'ʃækəl/ vt desencadenar

unshakable /ʌn'ʃeikəbəl/ a inconmovible, firme

unshapely /ʌn'ʃeipli/ a desproporcionado

unshaven /ʌn'ʃeivən/ a sin afeitar

unsheathe /ʌn'ʃið/ vt desenvainar, sacar

unsheltered /ʌn'ʃɛltərd/ a desabrigado, desamparado; no protegido, sin protección; (of places) sin abrigo, expuesto; (from) sin defensa contra

unship /ʌn'ʃɪp/ vt desembarcar; (the oars) desarmar

unshod /ʌn'ʃɒd/ a descalzo; (of a horse) sin herraduras

unshorn /ʌn'ʃɔrn/ a sin esquilar; intonso

unshrinkable /ʌn'ʃrɪŋkəbəl/ a que no se encoge

unshrinking /ʌn'ʃrɪŋkɪŋ/ a intrépido; resoluto, sin vacilar

unsightly /ʌn'saitli/ a feo, horrible, repugnante, antiestético

unsinkable /ʌn'sɪŋkəbəl/ a insumergible

unskilled /ʌn'skɪld/ a inexperto, inhábil, imperito, torpe

unsmokable /ʌn'smoukəbəl/ a (of tobacco) infumable

unsociability /ˌʌnsouʃə'bɪliti/ n insociabilidad, huraña, esquivez, f

unsociable /ʌn'souʃəbəl/ a insociable, huraño, esquivo, arisco

unsocial /ʌn'souʃəl/ a insocial, antisocial

unsold /ʌn'sould/ a no vendido, sin vender

unsolder /ʌn'sɒdər/ vt desoldar, desestañar

unsoldierly /ʌn'souldʒərli/ a indigno de un soldado; poco marcial

unsophisticated /ˌʌnsə'fɪstɪ,keitɪd/ a ingenuo, inocente, cándido

unsought /ʌn'sɔt/ a no solicitado; no buscado

unsound /ʌn'saund/ a enfermo; defectuoso; (rotten) podrido; (fallacious) erróneo, poco convincente; (of persons) informal, indigno de confianza; (of religious views) heterodoxo. **of u. mind,** insano

unsoundness /ʌn'saundnɪs/ n lo defectuoso; mal estado, m; falsedad, f; informalidad, f; heterodoxia, f

unsparing /ʌn'spɛərɪŋ/ a severo, implacable; generoso, pródigo

unspeakable /ʌn'spikəbəl/ a indecible, inefable; que no puede mencionarse, horrible

unspecified /ʌn'spɛsə,faid/ a no especificado

unspoiled /ʌn'spɔilt/ a intacto; ileso, indemne; no corrompido, no estropeado; (of children) no mimado

unspoken /ʌn'spoukən/ a no pronunciado

unsportsmanlike /ʌnˈspɔrtsmən,laik/ *a* indigno de un cazador; indigno de un deportista; nada caballeroso. **to play in an u. way,** jugar sucio

unstable /ʌnˈsteibəl/ *a* inestable; variable; inconstante; vacilante, irresoluto

unstained /ʌnˈsteind /*a* no manchado; no teñido; inmaculado, sin mancha

unstamped /ʌnˈstæmpt/ *a* sin sello; no sellado

unstatesmanlike /ʌnˈsteitsmən,laik/ *a* impropio (*or* indigno) de un hombre de estado

unsteadiness /ʌnˈstedinis/ *n* inestabilidad, falta de firmeza, *f;* inconstancia, *f*

unsteady /ʌnˈstedi/ *a* inestable, inseguro; inconstante

unstick /ʌnˈstik/ *vt* despegar

unstitch /ʌnˈstitʃ/ *vt* desapuntar

unstressed /ʌnˈstrest/ *a* sin énfasis; (of syllables) sin acento

unstudied /ʌnˈstʌdid/ *a* no estudiado; natural, espontáneo

unsubstantial /ˌʌnsəbˈstænʃəl/ *a* insubstancial; ligero; irreal, imaginario; incorpóreo; aparente

unsuccessful /ˌʌnsəkˈsesfəl/ *a* sin éxito; infructuoso. **to be u.,** no tener éxito

unsuccessfully /ˌʌnsəkˈsesfəli/ *adv* en vano, sin éxito

unsuitability /ˌʌnsutəˈbiliti/ *n* impropiedad, *f;* inconveniencia, incongruencia, *f;* incapacidad, *f;* inoportunidad, *f*

unsuitable /ʌnˈsutəbəl/ *a* inapropiado; inconveniente; impropio; inservible; incapaz; inoportuno

unsung /ʌnˈsʌŋ/ *a* no cantado; no celebrado en verso

unsupported /ˌʌnsəˈpɔrtid/ *a* sin apoyo; sin defensa; no favorecido

unsurmountable /ˌʌnsərˈmauntəbəl/ *a* insuperable, infranqueable

unsurpassable /ˌʌnsərˈpæsəbəl/ *a* inmejorable, insuperable

unsurpassed /ˌʌnsərˈpæst/ *a* sin par

unsuspecting /ˌʌnsəˈspektiŋ/ *a* no suspicaz, confiado, no receloso

unswerving /ʌnˈswɜrviŋ/ *a* directo; sin vacilar, constante

unsymmetrical /ˌʌnsiˈmetrikəl/ *a* asimétrico

unsympathetic /ˌʌnsimpəˈθetik/ *a* indiferente, incompasivo; antipático

unsystematic /ˌʌnsistəˈmætik/ *a* sin sistema, asistemático, no metódico

untalented /ʌnˈtæləntid/ *a* sin talento

untamed /ʌnˈteimd/ *a* indomado, cerril, bravío, no domesticado; desenfrenado, violento

unteach /ʌnˈtitʃ/ *vt* desenseñar

untenable /ʌnˈtenəbəl/ *a* insostenible

untenanted /ʌnˈtenəntid/ *a* desalquilado, deshabitado; vacío, desierto

unthankful /ʌnˈθæŋkfəl/ *a* ingrato, desagradecido

unthinkable /ʌnˈθiŋkəbəl/ *a* inconcebible; imposible

unthinking /ʌnˈθiŋkiŋ/ *a* sin reflexión; desatento; indiscreto

unthinkingly /ʌnˈθiŋkiŋli/ *adv* sin pensar

unthread /ʌnˈθred/ *vt* deshebrar

untidily /ʌnˈtaidli/ *adv* en desorden, sin aseo

untidiness /ʌnˈtaidinis/ *n* desorden, *m;* desaseo, desaliño, *m;* falta de pulcritud, *f*

untidy /ʌnˈtaidi/ *a* desarreglado; desaseado; abandonado; en desorden, sin concierto

untie /ʌnˈtai/ *vt* desatar, desanudar; (knots) deshacer

until /ʌnˈtil/ *prep* hasta. —*conjunc* hasta que. (The subjunc. is required in clauses referring to future time, e.g. *No venga usted hasta que le avise yo,* Don't come until I tell you. In clauses referring to past or present time the indicative is generally used, e.g. *No la reconocí hasta que se volvió,* I didn't recognize her until she turned round)

untilled /ʌnˈtild/ *a* sin cultivar

untimeliness /ʌnˈtaimlinis/ *n* inoportunidad, *f;* lo prematuro

untimely /ʌnˈtaimli/ *a* inoportuno, intempestivo; prematuro

untiring /ʌnˈtaiˀriŋ/ *a* incansable, infatigable

unto /ˈʌntu; *unstressed* -tə/ *prep* hacia

untold /ʌnˈtould/ *a* no revelado; no narrado; sin decir, no dicho; incalculable

untouchable /ʌnˈtʌtʃəbəl/ *a* que no puede tocarse, intangible; (of castes) intocable

untouched /ʌnˈtʌtʃt/ *a* sin tocar; intacto, incólume

untrained /ʌnˈtreind/ *a* indisciplinado; inexperto; no adiestrado

untranslatable /ˌʌntrænsˈleitəbəl/ *a* intraducible

untraveled /ʌnˈtrævəld/ *a* no frecuentado; (of persons) provinciano

untried /ʌnˈtraid/ *a* no experimentado. **u. knight,** caballero novel, *m*

untrodden /ʌnˈtrɒdn̩/ *a* no hollado, no frecuentado; inexplorado, virgen

untroubled /ʌnˈtrʌbəld/ *a* tranquilo, sosegado

untrue /ʌnˈtru/ *a* mentiroso, falso, engañoso; ficticio, imaginario; traidor, desleal; infiel

untrustworthiness /ʌnˈtrʌst,wɜrðinis/ *n* incertidumbre, inseguridad, *f;* (of persons) informalidad, *f*

untrustworthy /ʌnˈtrʌst,wɜrði/ *a* indigno de confianza; incierto, dudoso; desleal

untruth /ʌnˈtruθ/ *n* mentira, falsedad, *f;* ficción, *f*

untruthful /ʌnˈtruθfəl/ *a* mentiroso; falso

untruthfulness /ʌnˈtruθfəlnis/ *n* falsedad, *f*

untwist /ʌnˈtwist/ *vt* destorcer

unused /ʌnˈyuzd/ *a* no empleado; /ʌnˈyust/ desacostumbrado; inusitado; (postage stamp) sin sellar

unusual /ʌnˈyuʒuəl/ *a* fuera de lo común, desacostumbrado; extraño, raro, peregrino, extraordinario

unusually /ʌnˈyuʒuəli/ *adv* excepcionalmente; infrecuentemente

unusualness /ʌnˈyuʒuəlnis/ *n* lo insólito; rareza, *f*

unutterable /ʌnˈʌtərəbəl/ *a* indecible, inexpresable

unvarnished /ʌnˈvɑrniʃt/ *a* sin barnizar; *Fig.* sencillo

unvarying /ʌnˈvɛəriŋ/ *a* invariable, constante, uniforme

unveil /ʌnˈveil/ *vt* quitar el velo; (memorial) descubrir; *Fig.* revelar. —*vi* quitarse el velo; revelarse, quitarse la careta

unventilated /ʌnˈventɪˌleitɪd/ *a* sin ventilación; sin aire, ahogado; (of topics) no discutido

unverifiable /ʌn,vɛrəˈfaiəbəl/ *a* que no puede verificarse

unverified /ʌn,vɛrəˈfaid/ *a* sin verificar

unvisited /ʌn ˈvɪsɪtɪd/ *a* no visitado; no frecuentado

unvoiced /ʌnˈvɔist/ *a* no expresado

unwanted /ʌnˈwɒntid/ *a* no deseado; superfluo, de más

unwarlike /ʌnˈwɔr,laik/ *a* nada marcial, pacífico

unwarranted /ʌnˈwɔrəntid/ *a* sin garantía; inexcusable, injustificable

unwary /ʌnˈwɛəri/ *a* incauto, imprudente

unwashed /ʌnˈwɒʃt/ *a* sin lavar; sucio

unwatched /ʌnˈwɒtʃt/ *a* no vigilado

unwavering /ʌnˈweivəriŋ/ *a* resuelto, firme; inexorable; (gaze) fijo

unwaveringly /ʌnˈweivəriŋli/ *adv* sin vacilar; inexorablemente

unwearied /ʌnˈwiərid/ *a* incansable; infatigable

unwelcome /ʌnˈwelkəm/ *a* mal acogido; inoportuno; desagradable

unwell /ʌnˈwel/ *a* indispuesto

unwholesome /ʌnˈhoulsəm/ *a* malsano, nocivo, insalubre

unwholesomeness /ʌnˈhoulsəmnis/ *n* insalubridad, *f*

unwieldiness /ʌnˈwildinis/ *n* pesadez, dificultad de manejarse, *f*

unwieldy /ʌnˈwildi/ *a* pesado, abultado, difícil de manejar

unwilling /ʌnˈwiliŋ/ *a* desinclinado, reluctante

unwillingly /ʌnˈwiliŋli/ *adv* de mala gana

unwillingness /ʌnˈwiliŋnis/ *n* falta de inclinación, repugnancia, *f*

unwind /ʌnˈwaind/ *vt* desenvolver; (thread) desdevanar, desovillar. —*vi* desarrollarse; desdevanarse

unwise /ʌnˈwaiz/ *a* imprudente, indiscreto, incauto; (lacking wisdom) tonto

unwisely /ʌnˈwaizli/ *adv* imprudentemente, indiscretamente

unwitting /ʌnˈwitiŋ/ *a* inconsciente

unwittingly /ʌnˈwitiŋli/ *adv* sin darse cuenta

unwomanly /ʌnˈwumənli/ *a* poco femenino

unwonted /ʌnˈwɒntid/ *a* insólito, inusitado

unworkable /ʌnˈwɜrkəbəl/ a impráctico
unworkmanlike /ʌnˈwɜrkmənˌlaik/ a chapucero, charanguero
unworldly /ʌnˈwɜrldli/ a poco, mundano, espiritual
unworn /ʌnˈwɔrn/ a sin llevar, nuevo
unworthiness /ʌnˈwɜrðinis/ n indignidad, f
unworthy /ʌnˈwɜrði/ a indigno
unwounded /ʌnˈwundid/ a no herido, sin herida, ileso
unwrap /ʌnˈræp/ vt desenvolver, desempapelar
unwritten /ʌnˈritn/ a no escrito. **u. law,** ley consuetudinaria, f
unyielding /ʌnˈyildɪŋ/ a duro, firme; (of persons) inflexible, terco, resuelto, obstinado
unyoke /ʌnˈyouk/ vt desuncir, quitar el yugo
up /ʌp/ adv (high) arriba, en alto; (higher) hacia arriba; (out of bed) levantado; (standing) de pie; (finished) concluido, terminado; (of time) llegado; (excited) agitado; (rebellious) sublevado; (of sun, etc.) salido; (come or gone up) subido; (of universities) en residencia; (for discussion) bajo consideración; (abreast of) al lado, al nivel; (incapable) incapaz, incompetente; (ill) enfermo, indispuesto. **"Up,"** (on elevators) «Para subir.» (For various idiomatic uses of **up** after verbs, see verbs themselves.) a (in a few expressions only) ascendente. —prep en lo alto de; hacia arriba de; a lo largo de; (with country) en el interior de; (with current) contra. **to be up in arms,** sublevarse, rebelarse. **to be very hard up,** ser muy pobre, estar a la cuarta pregunta. **to drink up,** beberlo todo. **to go or come up,** subir. **to lay up,** acumular. **to speak up,** hablar en voz alta. **He has something up his sleeve,** Tiene algo en la manga. **It is all up,** Todo se acabó, Mi gozo en el pozo. **It is not up to much,** Vale muy poco; No es muy fuerte. **It is up to you,** Tú dirás, Tú harás lo que te parezca. **What is he up to?** ¿Qué está tramando? **What's up?** ¿Qué pasa? ¿Qué hay? **up and down,** adv bajando y subiendo, de arriba abajo; de un lado a otro; por todas partes. **up-and-down,** a fluctuante; (of roads) undulante; (of life) accidentado, borrascoso. **ups and downs,** vicisitudes, f pl, altibajos, m pl. **up-grade,** subida, f. **up in,** versado en, perito en. **well up in,** fuerte en. **up North,** al norte; en el norte; hacia el norte. **up there,** allí arriba, allí en lo alto. **up to,** hasta; (aware) al corriente de, informado de. **up to date,** adv hasta la fecha. **up-to-date,** a de última moda; al día. **up to now,** hasta ahora. **up train,** tren ascendente. **Up with...!** ¡Arriba! **Up you go!** (to children) ¡Upa!
upbraid /ʌpˈbreid/ vt reprender, echar en cara
upbringing /ˈʌpˌbrɪŋɪŋ/ n crianza, educación, f
upcountry /n., a ˈʌpˌkʌntri; adv. ʌpˈkʌntri/ n tierra adentro, f; lo interior (de un país). —a de tierra adentro, del interior. —adv tierra adentro, hacia el interior
update /ʌpˈdeit/ vt actualizar, poner al día
upheaval /ʌpˈhivəl/ n solevantamiento, m; trastorno, m
uphill /a, adv. ˈʌpˈhil; n. ˈʌpˌhil/ a ascendente; (penoso, fatigoso, difícil. —adv cuesta arriba, pecho arriba
uphold /ʌpˈhould/ vt sostener, apoyar; (help) ayudar, consolar; (protect) defender; (countenance) aprobar; Law. confirmar
upholder /ʌpˈhouldər/ n sostenedor (-ra), defensor (-ra)
upholster /ʌpˈhoulstər, əˈpoul-/ vt entapizar, tapizar
upholsterer /ʌpˈhoulstərər; əˈpoulʎ/ n tapicero, m
upholstery /ʌpˈhoulstəri, əˈpoulʎ/ n tapicería, f; (of car) almohadillado, m
upkeep /ˈʌpˌkip/ n mantenimiento, m, conservación, f
upland /ˈʌplənd/ n tierra alta, f, a alto, elevado
uplift /v. ʌpˈlift; n. ˈʌpˌlift/ vt elevar. —n elevación, f; Inf. fervor, m
upon /əˈpɒn/ prep. See **on**
upper /ˈʌpər/ a compar superior; alto; de arriba. —n (of shoe) pala, f, Sports. **u.-cut,** golpe de abajo arriba, upper-cut, m. **U. Egypt,** Alto Egipto, m. **u. hand,** dominio, m; superioridad, ventaja, f. **u. house,** cámara alta, f; senado, m. **u. ten,** los diez primeros

upper classes a clases altas, capas altas, f·pl
uppermost /ˈʌpərˌmoust/ a más alto, más elevado; predominante, principal; más fuerte. —adv en primer lugar; en lo más alto. **to be u.,** predominar
upright /ˈʌpˌrait/ a recto, derecho; vertical; (honorable) honrado, digno, recto. —n (stanchion) mástil, soporte, palo derecho, montante, m. —adv en pie; derecho
uprightly /ˈʌpˌraitli/ adv rectamente, honradamente
uprightness /ˈʌpˌraitnis/ n rectitud, honradez, probidad, f
uprising /ˈʌpˌraizɪŋ/ n insurrección, sublevación, f
uproar /ˈʌpˌrɔr/ n alboroto, tumulto, estrépito, m, conmoción, f
uproarious /ʌpˈrɔriəs/ a tumultuoso, estrepitoso
uproot /ʌpˈrut/ vt desarraigar; Fig. arrancar; (destroy) extirpar
uprooting /ʌpˈrutɪŋ/ n desarraigo, m; arranque, m; extirpación, f
upset /v. ʌpˈset; n. ˈʌpˌset/ vt volcar; (overthrow) derribar, echar abajo; (frustrate) contrariar; desarreglar; (distress) trastornar, turbar; (of food) hacer mal. —vi volcarse. —n vuelco, m; trastorno, m. **u. price,** tipo de subasta, m
upsetting /ʌpˈsetɪŋ/ a turbante, inquietante
upshot /ˈʌpˌʃɒt/ n resultado, m; consecuencia, f
upside /ˈʌpˌsaid/ n lado superior, m; parte superior, f; (of trains) andén ascendente, m. **u. down,** al revés, de arriba abajo; en desorden
upstairs /ˈʌpˈstɛərz/ adv arriba, en el piso de arriba; (with go or come) al piso de arriba
upstanding /ʌpˈstændɪŋ/ a gallardo, guapo. **an u. young man (woman),** un buen mozo (una buena moza)
upstart /ˈʌpˌstart/ n arribista, mf; advenedizo (-za), insolente, mf; presuntuoso (-sa)
upstream /ˈʌpˈstrim/ a and adv contra la corriente, agua arriba, río arriba
upturned /ˈʌpˌtɜrnd/ a (of noses) respingada
upward /ˈʌpwərd/ a ascendente, hacia arriba
upwards /ˈʌpwərdz/ adv hacia arriba, en adelante. **u. of,** más de
Urals, the /ˈyʊrəlz/ los Urales, m pl
uranium /yʊˈreiniəm/ n Mineral. uranio, m
Uranus /ˈyʊrənəs, yʊˈrei-/ n Astron. Urano, m
urban /ˈɜrbən/ a urbano, ciudadano
urbane /ɜrˈbein/ a cortés, urbano, fino
urbanity /ɜrˈbæniti/ n urbanidad, cortesía, finura, f
urbanization /ˌɜrbənəˈzeiʃən/ n urbanización, f
urbanize /ˈɜrbəˌnaiz/ vt urbanizar
urban renewal n renovación urbana, renovación urbanística, f
urchin /ˈɜrtʃin/ n galopín, granuja, pilluelo, m
ureter /yuˈritər/ n Anat. uréter, m
urethra /yuˈriθrə/ n Anat. uretra, f
urge /ɜrdʒ/ vt empujar, impeler; incitar, estimular, azuzar, animar; pedir con urgencia, recomendar con ahínco, instar, insistir (en). —n instinto, impulso, m; deseo, m; ambición, f
urgency /ˈɜrdʒənsi/ n urgencia, f; importancia, perentoriedad, f
urgent /ˈɜrdʒənt/ a urgente; importante, apremiante, perentorio. **to be u.,** urgir
urgently /ˈɜrdʒəntli/ adv urgentemente
uric /ˈyʊrik/ a úrico
urinal /ˈyʊrənl/ n orinal, urinario, m
urinalysis /ˌyʊrəˈnæləsis/ n análisis de orina, urinálisis, m
urinary /ˈyʊrəˌnɛri/ a urinario
urinary tract n conducto urinario, m, vías urinarias, f pl
urinate /ˈyʊrəˌneit/ vi orinar
urine /ˈyʊrin/ n orín, m
urn /ɜrn/ n urna, f; (for coffee) cafetera, f; (for tea) tetera, f
Ursa /ˈɜrsə/ n Astron. osa, f. **U. Major,** osa mayor, f. **U. Minor,** osa menor, f
urticaria /ˌɜrtiˈkɛəriə/ n Med. urticaria, f
Uruguayan /ˌyʊrəˈgweiən/ a and n uruguayo (-ya)
us /ʌs/ pron nos; (with prep.) nosotros. **He came toward us,** Vino hacia nosotros

usable /'yuzəbəl/ *a* aprovechable, servible

usage /'yusɪdʒ/ *n* (handling) tratamiento, *m*; uso, *m*, costumbre, *f*

use /yus/ *n* uso, *m*; manejo, empleo, *m*; (custom) costumbre práctica, *f*; (need) necesidad, *f*; (usefulness) aprovechamiento, *m*; *Law.* usufructo, *m*. **directions for use,** direcciones para el uso, *f pl,* **for the use of...,** para uso de... **in use,** en uso. **out of use,** anticuado; fuera de moda. **to be of no use,** no servir; ser inútil. **to have no use for,** no tener necesidad de; *Inf.* tener en poco. **to make use of,** servirse de, aprovechar. **to put to use,** poner en uso, poner en servicio

use /yuz/ *vt* usar; (employ) emplear; (utilize) servirse de, utilizar; (handle) manejar; hacer uso de; (consume) gastar, consumir; (treat) tratar; practicar. **to use up,** agotar, acabar con; consumir. —*vi impers* acostumbrar, soler (e.g. *It used to happen that...,* Solía ocurrir que...). **(Used to** and the verb which follows are often translated simply by the imperfect tense of the following verb, e.g. *I used to see her every day,* La veía todos los días. Use of the verbs *acostumbrar* or *soler* to translate used to adds emphasis to the statement)

used /yuzd/ *a* and *past part* /yust/ acostumbrado, habituado, empleado; (clothes) usado; (postage stamp) sellado, de. **to become u. to,** acostumbrarse a

useful /'yusfəl/ *a* útil; provechoso; servicial

usefully /'yusfəli/ *adv* útilmente; con provecho

usefulness /'yusfəlnɪs/ *n* utilidad, *f*; valor, *m*

useless /'yuslɪs/ *a* inútil; vano, infructuoso. **to render u.,** inutilizar

uselessness /'yuslɪsnɪs/ *n* inutilidad, *f*

user /'yuzər/ *n* el, *m*, (*f,* la) que usa, comprador (-ra)

usher /'ʌʃər/ *n* ujier, *m*; (in a theater) acomodador (-ra). —*vt* introducir, anunciar; acomodar

usual /'yuʒuəl/ *a* usual, acostumbrado, habitual; normal, común. **as u.,** como siempre. **in the u. form,** *Com.* al usado; como de costumbre. **with their usual courtesy,** con la cortesía que les es característica

usually /'yuʒuəli/ *adv* por lo general, ordinariamente.

We u. go out on Sundays, Acostumbramos salir los domingos

usurer /'yuʒərər/ *n* usurero (-ra)

usurious /yu'ʒʊriəs/ *a* usurario

usurp /yu'sɜrp/ *vt* usurpar; asumir, arrogarse

usurpation /,yusər'peiʃən/ *n* usurpación, *f*; arrogación, *f*

usurper /yu'sɜrpər/ *n* usurpador (-ra)

usurping /yu'sɜrpɪŋ/ *a* usurpador

usury /'yuʒəri/ *n* usura, *f*. **to practice u.,** usurear, dar (or tomar) a usura

utensil /yu'tɛnsəl/ *n* utensilio, instrumento, *m*; herramienta, *f*. **kitchen utensils,** batería de cocina, *f*

uterine /'yutərɪn/ *a* *Med.* uterino

uterus /'yutərəs/ *n* útero, *m*

utilitarian /yu,tɪlɪ'tɛəriən/ *a* utilitario

utilitarianism /yu,tɪlɪ'tɛəriə,nɪzəm/ *n* utilitarismo, *m*

utility /yu'tɪlɪti/ *n* utilidad, *f*; ventaja, *f*, beneficio, provecho, *m*. **u. goods,** artículos fabricados bajo la autorizacion del gobierno, *m pl*

utilizable /,yutɪl'aizəbəl/ *a* utilizable, aprovechable

utilization ,yutWə'zeiSən/ *n* empleo, aprovechamiento, *m*

utilize /'yutɪ,aiz/ *vt* utilizar, servirse de; aprovechar

utmost /'ʌt,moust/ *a* (outermost) (farthest) más remoto, más distante; (greatest) mayor, más grande. —*n* lo más; todo lo posible. **to do one's u.,** hacer todo lo posible, hacer todo lo que uno pueda

utopian /yu'toupiən/ *a* utópico

utter /'ʌtər/ *a* completo, total; terminate, absoluto; sumo, extremo. **He is an u. fool,** Es un tonto de capirote

utter /'ʌtər/ *vt* pronunciar, proferir, decir, hablar; (a sigh, cry, etc.) dar; (express) manifestar, expresar, explicar; (coin) poner en circulación; (a libel) publicar; (disclose) revelar, descubrir

utterance /'ʌtərəns/ *n* expresión, manifestación, *f*; pronunciación, *f*; (style) lenguaje, *m*

utterly /'ʌtərli/ *adv* enteramente, completamente

uttermost /'ʌtər,moust/ *a.* See **utmost**

uvula /'yuvyələ/ *n* *Anat.* úvula, *f*

uxorious /ʌk'sɔriəs/ *a* uxorio

V

v /vi/ n (letter) ve, f; pieza en forma de V, f
vacancy /'veikənsi/ n vacío, m; vacancia, f; (mental) vacuidad, f; (of offices, posts) vacante, f; (leisure) desocupación, ociosidad, f; (gap, blank) vacío, m, laguna, f
vacant /'veikənt/ a vacío; despoblado, deshabitado; (free) libre; (of offices, etc.) vacante; (leisured) ocioso; (absent-minded) distraído; (vague) vago; (foolish) estúpido, estólido
vacantly /'veikəntli/ adv distraídamente; estúpidamente
vacate /'veikeit/ vt dejar vacío; (a post) dejar; (a throne) renunciar a; dejar vacante; Mil. evacuar; Law. anular, rescindir
vacation /vei'keiʃən/ n (of offices) vacante, f; (holiday) vacaciones, f pl, f. **the long v.**, las vacaciones de verano. **to be on a v.**, estar de vacaciones
vaccinate /'væksə,neit/ vt vacunar
vaccination /,væksə'neiʃən/ n vacunación, f
vaccine /væk'sin/ n vacuna, f
vacillate /'væsə,leit/ vi (sway) oscilar; (hesitate) vacilar, titubear, dudar
vacillating /'væsə,leitɪŋ/ a vacilante
vacillation n vacilación, f
vacuity /væ'kyuti/ n vacuidad, f
vacuous /'vækyuəs/ a desocupado, ocioso; estúpido, vacío
vacuum /'vækyum/ n vacío, m. **v. brake**, freno al vacío, m. **v. cleaner**, aspirador de polvo, m. **v. flask**, termos, m. **v. pump**, bomba neumática, f. **vacuum-shelf dryer**, secador al vacío, m
vade mecum /'vei'di mikəm, 'va-/ n vademécum, m
vagabond /'vægə,bɒnd/ n vagabundo (-da); vago, m; (beggar) mendigo (-ga). —a vagabundo, errante
vagabondage /'vægə,bɒndidʒ/ n vagabundeo, m, vagancia, f
vagary /və'gɛəri, 'veigəri/ n (whim) capricho, antojo, m, extravagancia, f; (of the mind) divagación, f
vagina /və'dʒainə/ n vagina, f
vaginal /'vædʒənl/ a vaginal
vagrancy /'veigrənsi/ n vagancia, f
vagrant /'veigrənt/ n vago, m, a vagabundo, errante
vague /veig/ a vago; indistinto; equívoco, ambiguo; (uncertain) incierto
vaguely /'veigli/ adv vagamente
vagueness /'veignis/ n vaguedad, f
vain /vein/ a vano; (fruitless) infructuoso; (useless) inútil; (unsubstantial) fútil, insubstancial; fantástico; (empty) vacío; (worthless) despreciable; (conceited) vanidoso, presumido. **in v.**, en vano, en balde, inútilmente. **v. about**, orgulloso de
vainglorious /vein'glɔriəs, -'glour-/ a vanaglorioso
vaingloriousness /vein'glɔriəsnis/ n vanagloria, f
vainly /'veinli/ adv vanamente; inútilmente; (conceitedly) vanidosamente, con vanidad
valance /'væləns/ n cenefa, f
vale /veil/ n (valley) valle, m. —interj ¡adiós! —n (good-bye) vale, m
valediction /,vælɪ'dikʃən/ n despedida, f; vale, m
valedictory /,vælɪ'diktəri/ a de despedida
Valencian /və'lɛnʃən/ a and n valenciano (-na)
valency /'veilənsi/ n Chem. valencia, f
valet /væ'lei, 'vælɪt/ n criado, m. **v. de chambre**, ayuda de cámara, m
valetudinarian /,vælɪ,tudn'ɛəriən/ a valetudinario
Valhalla /væl'hælə, val'halə/ n el Valhala, m
valiant /'vælyənt/ a valiente, esforzado, animoso, bravo
valiantly /'vælyəntli/ adv valientemente
valid /'vælɪd/ a válido, valedero; (of laws in force) vigente
validate /'vælɪ,deit/ vt validar
validation /,vælɪ'deiʃən/ n validación, f
validity /və'lɪdɪti/ n validez, f
validly /'vælɪdli/ adv válidamente
valise /və'lis/ n valija, f, saco de viaje, m

Valkyrie /væl'kɪəri/ n Valquiria, f
valley /'væli/ n valle, m
valor /'vælər/ n valor, m, valentía, f
valorous /'vælərəs/ a valoroso, esforzado, intrépido
valuable /'vælyuəbəl/ a valioso; costoso; precioso; estimable; excelente. —n pl **valuables**, objetos de valor, m pl
valuableness /'vælyuəbəlnis/ n valor, m
valuation /,vælyu'eiʃən/ n valuación, tasación, f; estimación, f
valuator /'vælyu,eitər/ n tasador, m
value /'vælyu/ n valor, m; precio, m; estimación, f; importancia, f; (Gram. Mus.) valor, m; pl **values**, valores morales, principios, m pl. —vt tasar, valorar; estimar; apreciar; tener en mucho; hacer caso de; considerar. **to be of v.**, ser de valor
valued /'vælyud/ a apreciado, estimado; precioso
valueless /'vælyulɪs/ a sin valor; insignificante
valuer /'vælyuər/ n tasador, m
valve /vælv/ n (Elec., Mech., Anat.) válvula, f; (Bot., Zool.) valva, f
valved /vælvd/ a con válvulas; (in compounds) de... válvulas
valvular /'vælvyələr/ a valvular
vamp /væmp/ n (of a shoe) pala (de zapato), f; (patch) remiendo, m; Mus. acompañamiento improvisado, m; Inf. aventurera, f. —vt (of shoes) poner palas (a); (patch) remendar; Mus. improvisar un acompañamiento; (of a woman) fascinar, engatusar
vampire /'væmpaiᵊr/ n vampiro, m
van /væn/ n (Mil., Nav., Fig.) vanguardia, f; camión, m; (for delivery) camión de reparto, m; (for furniture) conductora de muebles, f; (removal) carro de mudanzas, m; (mail) camión postal, m; (for bathing) caseta de baño, f; (for guard on trains) furgón de equipajes, m; (railroad car) vagón, m
vandal /'vændl/ a and n vándalo (-la); bárbaro (-ra)
vandalism /'vændl,izəm/ n vandalismo, m
Vandyke /væn'daik/ n cuadro de Vandyke, m. **V. beard**, perilla, f. **V. collar**, cuello de encaje, m
vane /vein/ n (weathercock) veleta, f; (of a windmill) aspa, f; (of a propeller) paleta, f; (of a feather) barba, f; (of a surveying instrument) pínula, f
vanguard /'væn,gard/ n vanguardia, f. **in the v.**, a vanguardia; Fig. en la vanguardia
vanilla /və'nɪlə/ n vainilla, f
vanish /'vænɪʃ/ vi desaparecer; desvanecerse; disiparse
vanishing /'vænɪʃɪŋ/ n desaparición, f; disipación, f. **v. cream**, crema desvanecedora, f. **v. point**, punto de la vista, m
vanity /'vænɪti/ n vanidad, f. **v. case**, polvera de bolsillo, f
vanquish /'væŋkwɪʃ/ vt vencer, derrotar
vanquisher /'væŋkwɪʃər/ n vencedor (-ra)
vantage /'væntɪdʒ, 'van-/ n ventaja (also in tennis), f. **v.-ground**, posición ventajosa, f, sitial de privilegio, m
vapid /'væpɪd/ a insípido, insulso; (of speeches, etc.) soso, aburrido, insípido
vapidity /væ'pɪdɪti/ n insipidez, sosería, f
vapor /'veipər/ n vapor, m; pl **vapors**, (hysteria) vapores, m pl. —vi (boast) jactarse, baladronear; decir disparates. **v. bath**, baño de vapor, m
vaporizable /,veipə'raizəbəl/ a vaporizable
vaporization /,veipərə'zeiʃən/ n vaporización, f
vaporize /'veipə,raiz/ vt vaporizar. —vi vaporizarse
vaporizer /'veipə,raizər/ n vaporizador, m
vaporous /'veipərəs/ a vaporoso
variability /,veəriə'bɪlɪti/ n variabilidad, f
variable /'veəriəbəl/ a variable. —n Math. variable, f
variably /'veəriəbli/ adv variablemente
variance /'veəriəns/ n variación, f, cambio, m; desacuerdo, m, disensión, f; diferencia, contradicción, f. **at v.**, en desacuerdo, reñidos; hostil (a), opuesto (a); (of things) distinto (de), en contradicción (con)

variant /'vɛəriənt/ n variante, f
variation /,vɛəri'eiʃən/ n variación, f; cambio, m; variedad, f; diferencia, f; (Mus. magnetism) variación, f
varicose /'væri,kous/ a varicoso
varied success /'vɛərid/ éxito vario, m
variegate /'vɛərii,geit/ vt abigarrar, matizar, salpicar
variegated /'vɛərii,geitid/ a abigarrado; variado; mezclado
variegation /,vɛərii'geiʃən/ n abigarramiento, m; diversidad de colores, f
variety /və'raiiti/ n variedad, f; diversidad, f; (choice) surtido, m. **v. show,** función de variedades, f
various /'vɛəriəs/ a vario, diverso; diferente
variously /'vɛəriəsli/ adv diversamente
varix /'vɛəriks/ n várice, f
varnish /'vɑrniʃ/ n barniz, m. —vt barnizar; (pottery) vidriar; (conceal) disimular. **copal v.,** barniz copal, m. **japan v.,** charol japonés, m. **lacquer v.,** laca, f. **v. remover,** (for nails) quitaesmalte, m
varnishing /'vɑrniʃiŋ/ n barnizado, m; (of pottery) vidriado, m
vary /'vɛəri/ vt variar; cambiar; diversificar; modificar. —vi variar; (be different) ser distinto (de); (deviate) desviarse (de); (disagree) estar en desacuerdo, distar, estar en contradicción. **to v. directly (indirectly),** Math. variar en razón directa (inversa)
varying /'vɛəriiŋ/ a variante, cambiante, diverso
vascular /'væskyələr/ a vascular
vase /veis, veiz, vɑz/ n vaso, jarrón, m; urna, f
vaseline /'væsə,lin/ n vaselina, f
vassal /'væsəl/ n vasallo (-lla); esclavo (-va), siervo (-va). —a tributario
vast /væst/ a vasto, extenso; enorme; grande. —n vastedad, inmensidad, f
vastly /'væstli/ adv enormemente; muy; con mucho
vastness /'væstnis/ n vastedad, extensión, f; inmensidad, f; enormidad, f, gran tamaño, m; grandeza, f
vat /væt/ n cuba, tina, f; alberca, f, estanque, m. **dyeing vat,** cuba de tintorero, f. **tanning vat,** noque, m. **wine vat,** lagar, m
Vatican /'vætikən/ a and n Vaticano, m
vaticinate /və'tisə,neit/ vt and vi vaticinar, profetizar
vaticination /və,tisə'neiʃən/ n vaticinio, m, predicción, f
vaudeville /'vɔdvil/ n vodevil, m, zarzuela cómica, f
vault /vɔlt/ n Archit. bóveda, f; caverna, f; (for wine) bodega, cueva, f; (in a bank) cámara acorazada, f; (in a church) cripta, f; sepultura, f; (of the sky) bóveda celeste, f; (leap) salto, m; voltereta, f. —vi (jump) saltar; (with a pole) saltar con pértiga; saltar por encima de; voltear. —vt Archit. abovedar; saltar
vaulted /'vɔltid/ a abovedado
vaulter /'vɔltər/ n saltador (-ra)
vaulting /'vɔltiŋ/ n construcción de bóvedas, f; bóvedas, f pl; edificio abovedado, m; (jumping) salto, m. **v.-horse,** potro de madera, m
vaunt /vɔnt/ vi jactarse (de), hacer gala (de); triunfar (sobre). —vt ostentar, sacar a relucir; (praise) alabar. —n jactancia, f
veal /vil/ n ternera, f. **v.-cutlet,** chuleta de ternera, f
vector /'vɛktər/ n vector, m
Veda /'veidə/ n Veda, m
veer /viər/ vi (of the wind) girar; (of a ship) virar; Fig. cambiar (de opinión, etc.). —vt virar
vegetable /'vɛdʒtəbəl/ n vegetal, m; legumbre, f; pl **vegetables,** (green and generally cooked) verduras, f pl; (raw green) hortalizas, f pl. **v. dish,** fuente de legumbres, f. **v. garden,** huerto de legumbres, m; **v. ivory,** marfil vegetal, m. **v. kingdom,** reino vegetal, m. **v. soup,** sopa de hortelano, f
vegetal /'vɛdʒitl/ a vegetal
vegetarian /,vɛdʒi'tɛəriən/ a and n vegetariano (-na)
vegetarianism /,vɛdʒi'tɛəriə,nizəm/ n vegetarianismo, m
vegetate /'vɛdʒi,teit/ vi vegetar
vegetation /,vɛdʒi'teiʃən/ n vegetación, f
vehemence /'viəməns/ n vehemencia, f; violencia, f; impetuosidad, f; pasión, f, ardor, m
vehement /'viəmənt/ a vehemente; violento; impetuoso; apasionado

vehemently /'viəməntli/ adv con vehemencia; violentamente; con impetuosidad; apasionadamente
vehicle /'viikəl/ n vehículo, m; (means) medio, m; instrumento, m
vehicular /vi'hikyələr/ a vehicular, de los vehículos; de los coches. **v. traffic,** circulación de los coches, f; los vehículos
veil /veil/ n velo, m; (curtain) cortina, f; (disguise) disfraz, m; (excuse) pretexto, m; (appearance) apariencia, f. —vt velar; cubrir con un velo; (hide) tapar, encubrir; (dissemble) disimular; (disguise) disfrazar. **to take the v.,** tomar el velo, profesar
vein /vein/ n (Anat., Bot.) vena, f; (Geol., Mineral.) veta, f, filón, m; (in wood) fibra, hebra, f; (Fig. streak) rasgo, m; (inspiration) vena, f; (mood) humor, m
veined, veiny /veind/ 'veini/ a venoso; de venas; veteado
velar /'vilər/ a velar
vellum /'vɛləm/ n vitela, f
velocity /və'lɒsiti/ n velocidad, f; rapidez, f
velodrome /'vilə,droum/ n velódromo, m
velours /və'lur/ n terciopelo, m
velvet /'vɛlvit/ n terciopelo, m, a hecho de terciopelo; aterciopelado
velveteen /,vɛlvi'tin/ n pana, f, velludillo, m
velvety /'vɛlviti/ a aterciopelado
venal /'vinl/ a venal
venality /vi'næliti/ n venalidad, f
vend /vɛnd/ vt vender
vendor /'vɛndər/ n vendedor (-ra)
veneer /və'niər/ vt chapear, taracear; (conceal) disimular, disfrazar. —n taraceado, chapeado, m; (plate) chapa, hoja para chapear, f; (Fig. gloss) barniz, m, apariencia, f
venerability /,vɛnərə'biliti/ n venerabilidad, respetabilidad, f
venerable /'vɛnərəbəl/ a venerable
venerate /'vɛnə,reit/ vt venerar, reverenciar
veneration /,vɛnə'reiʃən/ n veneración, f
venerator /'vɛnə,reitər/ n venerador (-ra)
venereal /və'niəriəl/ a venéreo. **v. disease,** enfermedad venérea, f
Venetian /və'niʃən/ a and n veneciano (-na). **v. blinds,** persianas, celosías, f pl
Venezuelan /,vɛnə'zweilən/ a and n venezolano (-na)
vengeance /'vɛndʒəns/ n venganza, f
vengeful /'vɛndʒfəl/ a vengativo
venial /'viniəl/ a venial
veniality /,vini'æliti/ n venialidad, f
Venice /'vɛnis/ Venecia, f
venison /'vɛnəsən/ n venado, m
venom /'vɛnəm/ n veneno, m
venomous /'vɛnəməs/ a venenoso; maligno, malicioso
venomously /'vɛnəməsli/ adv con malignidad, maliciosamente
venomousness /'vɛnəməsnis/ n venenosidad, f; malignidad, f
venous /'vinəs/ a venoso
vent /vɛnt/ n abertura, f; salida, f; (air-hole) respiradero, m; (in pipes) ventosa, f; (in fire-arms) oído, m; Anat. ano, m; (Fig. outlet) desahogo, m; expresión, f. —vt dejar escapar; (pierce) agujerear; (discharge) emitir, vomitar; (relieve) desahogar; expresar, dar expresión (a), dar rienda suelta (a)
venter /'vɛntər/ n Law. vientre, m
ventilate /'vɛntl,eit/ vt ventilar; discutir
ventilation /,vɛntl'eiʃən/ n ventilación, f
ventilator /'vɛntl,eitər/ n ventilador, m
ventricle /'vɛntrikəl/ n ventrículo, m
ventriloquism /vɛn'trilə,kwizəm/ n ventriloquia, f
ventriloquist /vɛn'triləkwist/ n ventrílocuo (-ua)
venture /'vɛntʃər/ n ventura, f; riesgo, m; aventura, f; especulación, f. —vt arriesgar, aventurar; (stake) jugar; (state) expresar. —vi aventurarse; (dare) atreverse, osar; permitirse. **at a v.,** a la ventura. **to v. on,** arriesgarse a; probar ventura con; lanzarse a; (a remark) permitirse. **to v. out,** atreverse a salir

venturesome /'vɛntʃərsəm/ *a* atrevido, audaz; (dangerous) arriesgado, peligroso

venturesomeness /'vɛntʃərsəmnɪs/ *n* atrevimiento, *m*, temeridad, *f*; (risk) riesgo, peligro, *m*

Venus /'vinəs/ *n* (planet) Venus, *m*; (woman) venus, *f*

veracious /və'reɪʃəs/ *a* veraz, verídico; verdadero

veracity /və'ræsɪti/ *n* veracidad, *f*; verdad, *f*

veranda /və'rændə/ *n* veranda, *f*

verb /vɜrb/ *n* verbo, *m*. **auxiliary v.**, verbo auxiliar, *m*. **intransitive v.**, verbo intransitivo (neutro), *m*. **reflexive v.**, verbo reflexivo, *m*. **transitive v.**, verbo transitivo, *m*

verbal /'vɜrbəl/ *a* verbal

verbally /'vɜrbəli/ *adv* de palabra, verbalmente

verbatim /vər'beitɪm/ *a* textual. —*adv* textualmente, palabra por palabra

verbiage /'vɜrbiɪdʒ/ *n* verbosidad, palabrería, *f*

verbose /vər'bous/ *a* verboso, prolijo

verbosity /vər'bɒsɪti/ *n* verbosidad, *f*

verdancy /'vɜrdnsi/ *n* verdura, *f*; verdor, *m*

verdant /'vɜrdnt/ *a* verde

verdict /'vɜrdɪkt/ *n* Law. veredicto, fallo, *m*, sentencia, *f*; opinión, *f*, juicio, *m*. **to bring in a v.**, fallar sentencia

verdigris /'vɜrdɪ,gris/ *n* cardenillo, verdín, *m*

verdure /'vɜrdʒər/ *n* verdura, *f*, verdor, *m*; Fig. lozanía, *f*

verge /vɜrdʒ/ *n* (wand) vara, *f*; (edge) margen, borde, *m*; (of a lake, etc.) orilla, *f*; (horizon) horizonte, *m*; Fig. víspera, *f*, punto, *m*. **on the v. of**, al margen de, a la orilla de. **to be on the v. of**, Fig. estar a punto de; estar en vísperas de

verger /'vɜrdʒər/ *n* macero, *m*; (in a church) pertiguero, *m*

verifiable /,vɛrə'faiəbəl/ *a* verificable

verification /,vɛrəfɪ'keiʃən/ *n* verificación, *f*

verifier /'vɛrə,faiər/ *n* verificador (-ra)

verify /'vɛrə,fai/ *vt* verificar, confirmar; probar

verily /'vɛrəli/ *adv* de veras, en verdad

verisimilitude /,vɛrəsɪ'mɪlɪ,tud/ *n* verosimilitud, *f*

veritable /'vɛrɪtəbəl/ *a* verdadero

veritably /'vɛrɪtəbli/ *adv* verdaderamente

verity /'vɛrɪti/ *n* verdad, *f*

vermicelli /,vɜrmɪ'tʃɛli/ *n* fideos, *m pl*

vermilion /vər'mɪlyən/ *n* bermellón, *m*

vermin /'vɜrmɪn/ *n* bichos dañinos, *m pl*; (insects) parásitos, *m pl*

vermouth /vər'muθ/ *n* vermut, *m*

vernacular /vər'nækyələr/ *a* vernáculo; nativo; vulgar. —*n* lengua popular, *f*; lenguaje vulgar, *m*

versatile /'vɜrsətl/ *a* Zool. versátil; inconstante, voluble; (clever) de muchos talentos; de muchos intereses; adaptable; completo, cabal

versatility /,vɜrsə'tɪlɪti/ *n* (cleverness) muchos talentos, *m pl*; adaptabilidad, *f*

verse /vɜrs/ *n* verso, *m*; (stanza) estrofa, *f*; (in the Bible) versículo, *m*; (poetry) poesía, *f*, versos, *m pl*. **to make verses**, escribir versos

versed /vɜrst/ *a* versado, experimentado

versicle /'vɜrsɪkəl/ *n* versículo, *m*

versification /,vɜrsəfɪ'keiʃən/ *n* versificación, *f*

versifier /'vɜrsə,faiər/ *n* versificador (-ra)

versify /'vɜrsə,fai/ *vt and vi* versificar

version /'vɜrʒən/ *n* versión, *f*; traducción, *f*; interpretación, *f*

versus /'vɜrsəs/ *prep* contra

vertebra /'vɜrtəbrə/ *n* vértebra, *f*

vertebral /'vɜrtəbrəl/ *a* vertebral

vertebrate /'vɜrtəbrɪt/ *n* vertebrado, *m*

vertex /'vɜrtɛks/ *n* (Geom., Anat.) vértice, *m*; Astron. cenit, *m*; cumbre, *f*

vertical /'vɜrtɪkəl/ *a* vertical

verticality /,vɜrtɪ'kælɪti/ *n* verticalidad, *f*

vertiginous /vər'tɪdʒənəs/ *a* vertiginoso

vertigo /'vɜrtɪ,gou/ *n* vértigo, *m*

verve /vɜrv/ *n* brío, *m*, fogosidad, *f*

very /'vɛri/ *a* mismo; (mere) mero; (true) verdadero; (with adjective and comparative) más grande; Inf. mismísimo; (complete) perfecto, completo. **The v. thought of it made him laugh,** Sólo con pensarlo se

rió (*or* La mera idea le hizo reír). **this v. minute,** este mismísimo instante. **the v. day,** el mismo día

very /'vɛri/ *adv* muy; mucho; demasiado; (exactly) exactamente; completamente; absolutamente. **He is v. worried,** Está muy preocupado. **He is not v. well,** (i.e. rather ill) Está bastante bien. **This cloth is the v. best,** Esta tela es la mejor que hay. **I like it v. much,** Me gusta muchísimo. **He is v. much pleased,** Está muy contento. **so v. little,** tan poco; tan pequeño. **v. well,** muy bien

vesicle /'vɛsɪkəl/ *n* vesícula, *f*

vesper /'vɛspər/ *n* estrella vespertina, *f*, héspero, *m*; *pl* **vespers,** Eccl. vísperas, *f pl*

vessel /'vɛsəl/ *n* vasija, *f*, recipiente, *m*; (boat) barco, buque, *m*; (Anat., Bot.) vaso, *m*

vest /vɛst/ *n* camiseta, *f*; (waistcoat) chaleco, *m*. —*vt* vestir; (with authority, etc.) revestir de; (property, etc.) hacer entrega de, ceder. —*vi* tener validez; (dress) vestirse. **vested interests,** intereses creados, *m pl*. **v.-pocket,** bolsillo del chaleco, *m*. **v.-pocket camera,** cámara de bolsillo, *f*

vestal /'vɛstl/ *a* vestal; virgen, casto. —*n* vestal, *f*; virgen, *f*

vestibule /'vɛstə,byul/ *n* vestíbulo, *m*; (anteroom) antecámara, *f*; (of a theatre box) antepalco, *m*; Anat. vestíbulo, *m*

vestige /'vɛstɪdʒ/ *n* vestigio, rastro, *m*; sombra, *f*; Biol. rudimento, *m*

vestment /'vɛstmənt/ *n* hábito, *m*; Eccl. vestidura, *f*

vestry /'vɛstri/ *n* vestuario, *m*, sacristía, *f*

vesture /'vɛstʃər/ *n* traje, hábito, *m*, vestidura, *f*

Vesuvius /və'suviəs/ Vesubio, *m*

veteran /'vɛtərən/ *a* veterano; de los veteranos; aguerrido; anciano; experimentado. —*n* veterano (-na)

veterinary /'vɛtərə,nɛri/ *a* veterinario. **v. science,** veterinaria, *f*. **v. surgeon,** veterinario, *m*

veto /'vitou/ *n* veto, *m*; prohibición, *f*. —*vt* poner el veto; prohibir

vex /vɛks/ *vt* contrariar, irritar; enojar; (make impatient) impacientar; fastidiar; (afflict) afligir, acongojar; (worry) inquietar

vexation /vɛk'seiʃən/ *n* contrariedad, irritación, *f*; enojo, enfado, *m*; (impatience) impaciencia, *f*; fastidio, *m*; aflicción, *f*; inquietud, *f*; disgusto, *m*

vexatious /vɛk'seiʃəs/ *a* irritante; enojoso, enfadoso; fastidioso, molesto

vexatiousness /vɛk'seiʃəsnɪs/ *n* fastidio, *m*, molestia, *f*; incomodidad, *f*; contrariedad, *f*

vexed /vɛkst/ *a* discutido; contencioso; (thorny) espinoso, difícil

vexing /'vɛksɪŋ/ *a* irritante; molesto; enfadoso

via /'vaiə, 'viə/ *n* vía, *f*, prep por, por la vía de

viability /,vaiə'bɪlɪti/ *n* viabilidad, *f*

viable /'vaiəbəl/ *a* viable

viaduct /'vaiə,dʌkt/ *n* viaducto, *m*

vial /'vaiəl/ *n* frasco, *m*, ampolleta, *f*

vibrant /'vaibrənt/ *a* vibrante

vibrate /'vaibreit/ *vi* vibrar; (of machines) trepidar; oscilar. —*vt* hacer vibrar, vibrar

vibration /vai'breiʃən/ *n* vibración, *f*; trepidación, *f*; oscilación, *f*

vibrator /'vaibreitər/ *n* Elec. vibrador, *m*; Radio. oscilador, *m*

vicar /'vɪkər/ *n* vicario, *m*; (of a parish) cura, *m*. **v.-general,** vicario general, *m*

vicarious /vai'kɛəriəs/ *a* vicario; sufrido por otro; experimentado por otro

vicariously /vai'kɛəriəsli/ *adv* por delegación; por substitución. **I know it only vicariously,** Lo conozco sólo por referencia

vice /vais/ *n* vicio, *m*; defecto, *m*; (in a horse) vicio, resabio, *m*; (tool) tornillo de banco, *m*, prefix **vice. v.-admiral,** vicealmirante, *m*. **v.-chairman,** vicepresidente (-ta). **v.-chancellor,** vicecanciller, *m*. **v.-consul,** vicecónsul, *m*. **v.-consulate,** vice-consulado, *m*. **v.-president,** vicepresidente (-ta)

viceroy /'vaisrɔi/ *n* virrey, *m*

vice versa /'vaisə,vɜrsə, 'vais-/ *adv* viceversa

vicinity /vɪ'sɪnɪti/ *n* vecindad, *f*; (nearness) cercanía, proximidad, *f*. **to be in the v. of,** estar en la vecindad de

vicious /'vɪʃəs/ a vicioso. **v. circle,** círculo vicioso, m
viciousness /'vɪʃəsnɪs/ n viciosidad, f; (in a horse) resabios, m pl
vicissitude /vɪ'sɪsɪ,tud/ n vicisitud, f
vicissitudinous /vɪ,sɪsɪ'tudnəs/ a accidentado, vicisitudinario
victim /'vɪktəm/ n víctima, f
victimization /,vɪktəmə'zeɪʃən/ n sacrificio, m; tormento, m
victimize /'vɪktə,maɪz/ vt hacer víctima (de); sacrificar; ser víctima (de), sufrir; (cheat) estafar, engañar
victor /'vɪktər/ n víctor, vencedor, m
victoria /vɪk'tɔriə/ n victoria, f
Victorian /vɪk'tɔriən/ a victoriano
victorious /vɪk'tɔriəs/ a victorioso, triunfante. **to be v.,** triunfar, salir victorioso
victoriously /vɪk'tɔriəsli/ adv victoriosamente, triunfalmente
victory /'vɪktəri/ n victoria, f
victual /'vɪtl/ n vitualla, vianda, f; pl **victuals,** víveres, m pl, provisiones, f pl. —vt avituallar; abastecer. —vi tomar provisiones
victualler /'vɪtlər/ n abastecedor (-ra), proveedor (-ra)
victualling /'vɪtlɪŋ/ n abastecimiento, m
vide /wɪde, 'vaɪdi, 'videi/ Latin imperative véase, véanse
videlicet /wɪ'deɪlɪ,ket, vi'deləsɪt/ adv a saber
video /'vɪdi,ou/, n vídeo, m
videotape /'vɪdiou,teip/ n videograbación, videocinta, f
vie /vai/ vi (with) competir con; rivalizar con; (with a person for) disputar; luchar con
Vienna /vi'ɛnə/ Viena, f
Viennese /,viə'niz/ a and n vienés (-esa)
view /vyu/ n vista, f; perspectiva, f, panorama, m; (landscape) paisaje, m; escena, f; inspección, f; (judgment) opinión, f, parecer, m; consideración, f; (appearance) apariencia, f; aspecto, m; (purpose) propósito, m, intención, f; (sight) alcance de la vista, m; (show) exposición, f. —vt examinar; inspeccionar; (look at) mirar; (see) ver, contemplar; considerar. **in v. of,** en vista de. **in my v.,** en mi opinión, según creo yo. **on v.,** a la vista. **to keep in v.,** no perder de vista; Fig. no olvidar, tener presente. **to take a different v.,** pensar de un modo distinto. **to v. a house,** inspeccionar una casa. **with a v. to,** con el propósito de. **v.-finder,** enfocador, m. **v.-point,** punto de vista, m
viewer /'vyuər/ n espectador (-ra); examinador (-ra)
viewing /'vyuɪŋ/ n inspección, f, examen, m
vigil /'vɪdʒəl/ n vela, vigilia, f; Eccl. vigilia, f
vigilance /'vɪdʒələns/ n vigilancia, f, desvelo, m
vigilant /'vɪdʒələnt/ a vigilante, desvelado
vigilantly /'vɪdʒələntli/ adv vigilantemente
vignette /vɪn'yet/ n viñeta, f
vigor /'vɪgər/ n vigor, m, fuerza, f
vigorous /'vɪgərəs/ a vigoroso, enérgico, fuerte
vigorously /'vɪgərəsli/ adv con vigor
Viking /'vaikɪŋ/ n vikingo, m
vile /vail/ a vil; bajo; despreciable; infame; Inf. horrible
vilely /'vailli/ adv vilmente; Inf. mal, horriblemente
vileness /'vailnɪs/ n vileza, f; bajeza, f; infamia, f
vilification /,vɪləfɪ'keiʃən/ n vilipendio, m, difamación, f
vilifier /'vɪlə,faiər/ n difamador (-ra)
vilify /'vɪlə,fai/ vt vilipendiar, difamar
villa /'vɪlə/ n villa, torre, casa de campo, f; hotel, m
village /'vɪlɪdʒ/ n aldea, f, pueblo, m
villager /'vɪlɪdʒər/ n aldeano (-na)
villain /'vɪlən/ n Hist. villano, m; malvado, m
villainous /'vɪlənəs/ a malvado; infame; vil
villainously /'vɪlənəsli/ adv vilmente
villainy /'vɪləni/ n vileza, infamia, maldad, f
vindicate /'vɪndɪ,keit/ vt vindicar, justificar; defender
vindication /,vɪndɪ'keiʃən/ n vindicación, justificación, f; defensa, f
vindicative /vɪn'dɪkətɪv/ a vindicativo, vindicador, justificativo
vindicator /'vɪndɪ,keitər/ n vindicador (-ra)
vindictive /vɪn'dɪktɪv/ a vengativo; rencoroso

vindictively /vɪn'dɪktɪvli/ adv vengativamente; rencorosamente
vindictiveness /vɪn'dɪktɪvnɪs/ n deseo de venganza, m; rencor, m
vine /vain/ n vid, parra, f; (twining plant) enredadera, f. **v.-arbor,** emparrado, m. **v.-branch,** sarmiento, m. **v.-clad,** cubierto de parras. **v.-grower,** vinicultor, m. **v.-growing,** vinicultura, f. **v.-leaf,** hoja de parra, f. **v.-pest,** filoxera, f. **v.-stock,** cepa, f
vinegar /'vɪnɪgər/ n vinagre, m. **v.-cruet,** vinagrera, f. **v.-sauce,** vinagreta, f
vinegary /'vɪnɪgəri/ a vinagroso
vineyard /'vɪnyərd/ n viña, f, viñedo, m. **v.-keeper,** viñador, m
vinification /,vɪnəfɪ'keiʃən/ n vinificación, f
vinosity /vai'nɒsɪti/ n vinosidad, f
vinous /'vainəs/ a vinoso
vintage /'vɪntɪdʒ/ n vendimia, f; (of wine) cosecha (de vino), f
vintner /'vɪntnər/ n vinatero, m
viola /vi'oulə/ n (Mus., Bot.) viola, f. **v. player,** viola, mf
violate /'vaiə,leit/ vt (desecrate) profanar; (infringe) contravenir, infringir; (break) romper; (ravish) violar
violation /,vaiə'leiʃən/ n profanación, f; (infringement) contravención, f; (rape) violación, f
violator /'vaiə,leitər/ n violador (-ra); (ravisher) violador, m
violence /'vaiələns/ n violencia, f
violent /'vaiələnt/ a violento
violently /'vaiələntli/ adv con violencia
violet /'vaiəlɪt/ n violeta, f. —a violado, **v. color,** violeta, color violado, m
violin /,vaiə'lɪn/ n violín, m
violinist /,vaiə'lɪnɪst/ n violinista, mf
violoncellist /,vaiələn'tʃɛlɪst/ n violoncelista, mf
violoncello /,vaiələn'tʃɛlou/ n violoncelo, m
viper /'vaipər/ n víbora, f
viperish /'vaipərɪʃ/ a viperino
virago /vɪ'rɑgou/ n virago, f,
Virgilian /vər'dʒɪliən/ a virgiliano
virgin /'vɜrdʒɪn/ n virgen, f; (sign of the zodiac) Virgo, m. —a virginal; (untouched) virgen. **the V.,** la Virgen. **v. soil,** tierra virgen, f
virginal /'vɜrdʒənl/ a virginal
virginity /vər'dʒɪnɪti/ n virginidad, f
Virgo /'vɜrgou/ n Virgo, m
virile /'vɪrəl/ a viril
virility /və'rɪlɪti/ n virilidad, f
virtual /'vɜrtʃuəl/ a virtual
virtue /'vɜrtʃu/ n virtud, f
virtuosity /,vɜrtʃu'ɒsɪti/ n virtuosidad, f
virtuoso /,vɜrtʃu'ousou/ n virtuoso (-sa)
virtuous /'vɜrtʃuəs/ a virtuoso
virulence /'vɪryələns/ n virulencia, f
virulent /'vɪryələnt/ a virulento
virulently /'vɪryələntli/ adv con virulencia
virus /'vairəs/ n virus, m
visa /'vizə/ n visado, m
visage /'vɪzɪdʒ/ n cara, f, rostro, m; semblante, aspecto, m
viscera /'vɪsərə/ n víscera, f
visceral /'vɪsərəl/ a visceral
viscid /'vɪsɪd/ a viscoso
viscosity /vɪ'skɒsɪti/ n viscosidad, f
viscount /'vai,kaunt/ n vizconde, m
viscountess /'vai,kauntɪs/ n vizcondesa, f
viscous /'vɪskəs/ a viscoso
visé /'vizei/ n visado, m, vt visar
visibility /,vɪzə'bɪlɪti/ n visibilidad, f. **poor v.,** mala visibilidad, f
visible /'vɪzəbəl/ a visible; aparente, evidente
visibly /'vɪzəbli/ adv visiblemente; a ojos vistas
Visigoth /'vɪzɪ,gɒθ/ n visigodo (-da)
Visigothic /,vɪzɪ'gɒθɪk/ a visigodo, visigótico
vision /'vɪʒən/ n visión, f; (eyesight) vista, f. **field of v.,** campo visual, m
visionary /'vɪʒə,neri/ a and n visionario (-ia)
visit /'vɪzɪt/ n visita, f; (inspection) inspección, f; (doctor's) visita de médico, f. —vt visitar; hacer una visita (a); ir a ver; inspeccionar; (frequent) frecuen-

tar; (Biblical) visitar. **to be visited by an epidemic,** sufrir una epidemia. **to go visiting,** ir de visita. **to pay a v.,** hacer una visita

visitation /ˌvɪzɪ'teɪʃən/ n visita, f; Eccl. visitación, f; (inspection) inspección, f; (punishment) castigo, m

visiting /'vɪzɪtɪŋ/ a de visita. **v. card,** tarjeta de visita, f. **v. card case,** tarjetero, m. **visiting hours,** horas de visita, f pl

visitor /'vɪzɪtər/ n visita, f; (official) visitador, m

visor /'vaɪzər/ n visera, f

vista /'vɪstə/ n vista, perspectiva, f

visual /'vɪʒuəl/ a visual. **the v. arts,** las artes visuales

visualize /'vɪʒuə,laɪz/ vt and vi imaginarse, ver mentalmente

vital /'vaɪtl/ a vital; esencial; trascendental

vitalism /'vaɪtl,ɪzəm/ n vitalismo, m

vitality /vaɪ'tælɪti/ n vitalidad, f

vitalize /'vaɪtl,aɪz/ vt vitalizar, vivificar; reanimar

vitals /'vaɪtlz/ n pl partes vitales, f pl; Fig. entrañas, f pl

vitamin /'vaɪtəmɪn/ n vitámina, f

vitiate /'vɪʃi,eɪt/ vt viciar; corromper, contaminar

viticultural /ˌvɪtɪ'kʌltʃərl/ a vitícola

viticulture /'vɪtɪ,kʌltʃər/ n viticultura, f

vitreous /'vɪtriəs/ a vítreo, vidrioso

vitrification /ˌvɪtrəfɪ'keɪʃən/ n vitrificación, f

vitrify /'vɪtrə,faɪ/ vt vitrificar. —vi vitrificarse

vitriol /'vɪtriəl/ n vitriolo, ácido sulfúrico, m

vitriolic /ˌvɪtri'blɪk/ a vitriólico

Vitruvius /vɪ'truviəs/ Vitrubio, m

vituperable /vaɪ'tupərəbəl/ a vituperable

vituperate /vaɪ'tupə,reɪt/ vt vituperar

vituperation /vaɪ,tupə'reɪʃən/ n vituperio, m

vituperative /vaɪ'tupərətɪv/ a vituperador

vivacious /vɪ'veɪʃəs, vaɪ-/ a animado, vivaracho

vivaciously /vɪ'veɪʃəsli, vaɪ-/ adv animadamente

vivacity /vɪ'væsɪti, vaɪ-/ n vivacidad, animación, f

viva voce /'vaɪ'və vousi, 'vɪvə/ a oral. —n examen oral, m

vivid /'vɪvɪd/ a vivo; brillante; intenso; (of descriptions, etc.) gráfico

vividly /'vɪvɪdli/ adv vivamente; brillantemente

vividness /'vɪvɪdnɪs/ n vivacidad, f; intensidad, f; (strength) fuerza, f

vivification /ˌvɪvəfɪ'keɪʃən/ n vivificación, f

vivify /'vɪvə,faɪ/ vt vivificar, avivar

vivifying /'vɪvə,faɪɪŋ/ a vivificante

vivisection /ˌvɪvə'sekʃən/ n vivisección, f

vixen /'vɪksən/ n raposa, zorra, f; (woman) arpía, f

viz. a saber

vizier /vɪ'zɪər, 'vɪzyər/ n visir, m. **grand v.,** gran visir, m

vocabulary /vou'kæbyə,leri/ n vocabulario, m

vocal /'voukəl/ a vocal. **v. cords,** cuerdas vocales, f pl

vocalist /'voukəlɪst/ n cantante, mf. voz, f

vocalization /ˌvoukələ'zeɪʃən/ n vocalización, f

vocalize /'voukə,laɪz/ vt vocalizar

vocation /vou'keɪʃən/ n vocación, f; oficio, m; empleo, m; profesión, f

vocational /vou'keɪʃənl/ a profesional; práctico. **vocational guidance,** guía vocacional, orientación profesional, f. **v. training,** instrucción práctica, f; enseñanza de oficio, m

vociferate /vou'sɪfə,reɪt/ vt gritar. —vi vociferar, vocear

vociferation /vou,sɪfə'reɪʃən/ n vociferación, f

vociferous /vou'sɪfərəs/ a (noisy) ruidoso; vocinglero, clamoroso

vociferously /vou'sɪfərəsli/ adv ruidosamente; a gritos

vodka /'vɒdkə/ n vodca, f

vogue /voug/ n moda, f. **in v.,** en boga, de moda

voice /vɔɪs/ n voz, f. —vt expresar, interpretar; hacerse eco de; hablar. **in a loud v.,** en voz alta. **in a low v.,** en voz baja

voiced /vɔɪst/ a (in compounds) de voz...; hablado

void /vɔɪd/ a (empty) vacío; (vacant) vacante; deshabitado; (lacking in) privado (de), desprovisto (de); (without) sin; Law. inválido, nulo; sin valor. —n vacío, m. —vt evacuar; Law. anular; invalidar

voile /vɔɪl/ n espumilla, f

volatile /'vɒlətl/ a volátil; (light) ligero; (changeable) voluble, inconstante

volatility /ˌvɒlə'tɪlɪti/ n volatilidad, f; ligereza, f; volubilidad, f

volatilization /ˌvɒlətlə'zeɪʃən/ n volatilización, f

volatilize /'vɒlətl,aɪz/ vt volatilizar. —vi volatilizarse

volcanic /vɒl'kænɪk/ a volcánico

volcano /vɒl'keinou/ n volcán, m. **extinct v.,** volcán extinto, m

volition /vou'lɪʃən/ n volición, f; voluntad, f

volley /'vɒli/ n (of stones, etc.) lluvia, f; (of firearms) descarga, f; (of cannon, naval guns) andanada, f; Sports. voleo, m; (of words, etc.) torrente, m; (of applause and as a salute) salva, f. —vt Sports. volear; (abuse, etc.) dirigir. —vi lanzar una descarga, hacer una descarga

volt /voult/ n Elec. voltío, m; (of a horse and in fencing) vuelta, f. **v.-ampere,** voltamperio, m

voltage /'voultɪdʒ/ n voltaje, m. **v. control,** mando del voltaje, m

voltaic /vɒl'teiik/ a voltaico

Voltairian /voul'teəriən/ a volteriano

voltmeter /'voult,mitər/ n voltímetro, m

volubility /ˌvɒlyə'bɪlɪti/ n garrulidad, locuacidad, f

voluble /'vɒlyəbəl/ a gárrulo, locuaz

volume /'vɒlyum/ n (book) tomo, m; (amount, size, space) volumen, m; (of water) caudal (de río), m; (mass) masa, f; (of smoke) humareda, f, nubes de humo, f pl

volumed /'vɒlyumd/ a (in compounds) en... volúmenes, de... tomos

volumetric /ˌvɒlyə'metrɪk/ a volumétrico

voluminous /və'lumənəs/ a voluminoso

voluminousness /və'lumənəsnɪs/ n lo voluminoso

voluntarily /ˌvɒlən'terəli/ adv voluntariamente

voluntariness /ˌvɒlən'terinɪs/ n carácter voluntario, m

voluntary /'vɒlən,teri/ a voluntario; espontáneo; libre; (charitable) benéfico; (intentional) intencional, deliberado. —n solo de órgano, m

volunteer /ˌvɒlən'tɪər/ n Mil. voluntario (-ia). —a de voluntarios. —vt ofrecer; contribuir; expresar. —vi ofrecerse para hacer algo; Mil. alistarse, ofrecerse a servir como voluntario

volunteering /ˌvɒlən'tɪərɪŋ/ n voluntariado, m

voluptuary /və'lʌptʃu,eri/ n voluptuoso (-sa); sibarita, mf

voluptuous /və'lʌptʃuəs/ a voluptuoso

voluptuously /və'lʌptʃuəsli/ adv voluptuosamente

voluptuousness /və'lʌptʃuəsnɪs/ n voluptuosidad, f; sensualidad, f

volute /və'lut/ n Archit. voluta, f

vomit /'vɒmɪt/ vt and vi vomitar; arrojar, devolver. —n vómito, m

vomiting /'vɒmɪtɪŋ/ n vómito, m

voodoo /'vudu/ n vudú, m

voracious /vɔ'reɪʃəs/ a voraz

voracity /vɔ'ræsɪti/ n voracidad, f

vortex /'vɔrteks/ n torbellino, m, vorágine, f; Fig. vórtice, m

vortical /'vɔrtɪkəl/ a vortiginoso

votary /'voutəri/ n devoto (-ta), adorante, mf; partidario (-ia)

vote /vout/ n voto, m; (voting) votación, f; (suffrage) sufragio, m; (election) elección, f. —vt votar; asignar; nombrar; elegir; (consider) tener por. —vi votar, dar el voto. **casting v.,** voto de calidad, m. **to put to the v.,** poner a votación. **to v. down,** desechar, rechazar. **v. of confidence,** voto de confianza, m. **v. of thanks,** voto de gracias, m

voter /'voutər/ n votante, mf, votador (-ra); elector (-ra)

voting /'voutɪŋ/ n votación, f; elección, f. —a de votar; electoral. **v. paper,** papeleta de votación, f

votive /'voutɪv/ a votivo. **v. offering,** exvoto, m

vouch /vautʃ/ vi atestiguar; afirmar; garantizar; responder (de)

voucher /'vautʃər/ n (guarantor) fiador (-ra); (guarantee) garantía, f; (receipt) recibo, m; (proof) prueba, f; documento justificativo, m; vale, bono, m

vouchsafe /vautʃˈseif/ vt conceder, otorgar
vouchsafement /vautʃˈseifmənt/ n concesión, f, otorgamiento, m
vow /vau/ n voto, m; promesa solemne, f. —vt hacer voto (de), hacer promesa solemne (de); jurar. **to take a vow,** hacer un voto
vowel /ˈvauəl/ n vocal, f
voyage /ˈvɔiidʒ/ n viaje (por mar), m; travesía, f. —vi viajar por mar. **Good v.!** ¡Buen viaje!, Feliz viaje!
voyager /ˈvɔiidʒər/ n viajero (-ra)
vulcanite /ˈvʌlkə,nait/ n ebonita, f
vulcanization /,vʌlkənəˈzeifən/ n vulcanización, f
vulcanize /ˈvʌlkə,naiz/ vt vulcanizar
vulgar /ˈvʌlgər/ a vulgar; (ill-bred) ordinario, cursi; (in bad taste) de mal gusto; trivial; adocenado;

(coarse) grosero. —n vulgo, populacho, m. **v. fraction,** fracción común, f
vulgarism /ˈvʌlgə,rizəm/ n vulgarismo, m; vulgaridad, f
vulgarity /vʌlˈgærɪti/ n vulgaridad, f; grosería, f; mal tono, m, cursilería, f
vulgarize /ˈvʌlgə,raiz/ vt vulgarizar; popularizar
vulgarly /ˈvʌlgərli/ adv vulgarmente; comúnmente; groseramente
Vulgate /ˈvʌlgeit/ n Vulgata, f
vulnerability /,vʌlnərəˈbɪti/ n vulnerabilidad, f
vulnerable /ˈvʌlnərəbəl/ a vulnerable
vulpine /ˈvʌlpain/ a vulpino; astuto
vulture /ˈvʌltʃər/ n buitre, m
vulva /ˈvʌlvə/ n vulva, f

W

w /'dʌbəl,yu/ n ve doble, f
wabble /'wɒbəl/ vi. See **wobble**
wad /wɒd/ n (of straw, etc.) atado, m; (of notes, etc.) rollo, m; (in a gun) taco, m. —vt Sew. acolchar; (furniture) emborrar; (guns) atacar; (stuff) rellenar
wadding /'wɒdɪŋ/ n borra, f; (lining) entretela, f; (for guns) taco, m; (stuffing) relleno, m
waddle /'wɒdl/ n anadeo, m, vi anadear
waddling /'wɒdlɪŋ/ a patojo, que anadea
wade /weid/ vi and vt andar (en el agua, etc.); vadear; (paddle) chapotear. **to w. in,** entrar en (el agua, etc.); Fig. meterse en. **to w. through,** (a book) leer con dificultad; estudiar detenidamente; ir por
wader /'weidər/ n el, m, (f, la) que vadea; (bird) ave zancuda, f; pl **waders,** botas de vadear, f pl
wafer /'weifər/ n (host) hostia, f; (for sealing) oblea, f; (for ices) barquillo, m
waffle /'wɒfəl/ n Cul. fruta de sartén, f
waft /wɑft/ vt llevar por el aire o encima del agua; hacer flotar; (stir) mecer; (of the wind) traer. —n (fragrance) ráfaga de olor, f
wag /wæg/ n (of the tail) coleada, f; movimiento, m; meneo, m; (jester) bromista, mf. —vt mover ligeramente; agitar; (of the tail) menear (la cola), colear. —vi menearse; moverse; oscilar; (of the world) ir. **And thus the world wags,** Y así va el mundo
wage /weidʒ/ vt emprender; sostener; hacer. **to w. war,** hacer guerra. —n pl. **wages,** salario, m
wager /'weidʒər/ n (bet) apuesta, f; (test) prueba, f, vt (bet) apostar; (pledge) empeñar. **to lay a w.,** hacer una apuesta
waggish /'wægɪʃ/ a zumbón, jocoso; cómico
waggishness /'wægɪʃnɪs/ n jocosidad, f
waggle /'wægəl/ vt menear; mover; agitar; oscilar. —vi menearse; moverse; agitarse; oscilar. —n meneo, movimiento, m; oscilación, f
Wagnerian /vɑg'nɪəriən/ a wagneriano
wagon /'wægən/ n carro, m; carreta, f; (railway) vagón, m. **w.-lit,** coche cama, m. **w.-load,** carretada, f; vagón, m
wagoner /'wægənər/ n carretero, m
waif /weif/ n niño (-ña) sin hogar; animal perdido o abandonado, m; objeto extraviado, m; objeto sin dueño, m. **waifs and strays,** niños abandonados, m pl
wail /weil/ n lamento, gemido, m; (complaint) queja, f. —vi lamentarse, gemir; quejarse (de). —vt lamentar, deplorar
wailer /'weilər/ n lamentador (-ra)
wailing /'weilɪŋ/ n lamentaciones, f pl, gemidos, m pl, a lamentador, plañidero
wainscot /'weinskət, -skɒt/ n entablado de madera, m. —vt enmaderar; poner friso de madera (a)
waist /weist/ n cintura, f; (blouse) blusa, f; (belt) cinturón, m; (bodice) corpiño, m; (narrowest portion) cuello, m, garganta, f; Naut. combés, m. **w.-band,** pretina, f. **w.-deep,** hasta la cintura. **w.-line,** cintura, f. **w. measurement,** medida de la cintura, f. **w.-coat,** chaleco, m. **w. strap,** trincha, f
wait /weit/ vi and vt esperar, aguardar; (serve) servir. **to keep waiting,** hacer esperar. **to w. at table,** servir a la mesa. **to w. on oneself,** servirse a sí mismo; cuidarse a sí mismo; hacer las cosas por sí solo. **to w. one's time,** aguardar la ocasión. **to w. for,** (until) esperar hasta que; (of persons) esperar (a), aguardar (a); (in ambush) acechar. **to w. upon,** (serve) servir (a); (visit) visitar; presentar sus respetos (a); (Fig. accompany) acompañar; (follow) seguir a
waiter /'weitər/ n camarero, mozo, m; (tray) bandeja, f
waiting /'weitɪŋ/ n espera, f. —a que espera; de espera; de servicio. **lady-in-w.,** dama de servicio, f. **w.-**maid, camarera, doncella, f. **w.-room,** (of a bus station, etc.) sala de espera, f; (of an office) antesala, f
waitress /'weitrɪs/ n camarera, f
waive /weiv/ vt renunciar (a); desistir (de)
wake /weik/ vi estar despierto; despertarse; (watch) velar. —vt despertar; (a corpse) velar (a). —n vela, f; vigilia, f; (of a corpse) velatorio, m; (holiday) fiesta, f; (of a ship) estela, f. **in the w. of,** Naut. en la estela de; después de; seguido por
wakeful /'weikfəl/ a vigilante; (awake) despierto. **to be w.,** pasar la noche en vela
wakefulness /'weikfəlnɪs/ n vigilancia, f; (sleeplessness) insomnia, f
waken /'weikən/ vi despertarse. —vt despertar; (call) llamar
waking /'weikɪŋ/ a despierto; de vela. —n despertar, m; (watching) vela, f
wale /weil/ n (weal) verdugo, m, huella de azote, f, vt azotar
Wales /weilz/ (País de) Gales, m
walk /wɔk/ n (pace) paso, m; (modo de) andar, m; (journey on foot) paseo, m, vuelta, f; (long) caminata, f; (promenade) paseo, m, avenida, f; (path) senda, f; (rank) clase social, f; esfera, f; profesión, f; ocupación, f. **quick w.,** paseo rápido, m; (pace) andar rápido, m. **to go for a w.,** ir de paseo. **to take a w.,** dar un paseo (or una vuelta), pasear. **to take for a w.,** llevar a paseo, sacar a paseo. **w.-out,** (strike) huelga, f. **w.-over,** triunfo, m, (or victoria, f) fácil. **w. past,** desfile, m
walk /wɔk/ vi andar; caminar; ir a pie; (take a walk) pasear, dar un paseo; (of ghosts) aparecer; (behave) conducirse. —vt hacer andar; (take for a walk) sacar a paseo; andar de una parte a otra (de), recorrer; (a specified distance) hacer a pie, andar; (a horse) llevar al paso. **to w. abroad,** dar un paseo; salir. **to w. arm in arm,** ir de bracero. **to w. past,** pasar; (in procession) desfilar. **to w. quickly,** andar de prisa. **to w. slowly,** andar despacio, andar lentamente. **to w. the hospitals,** estudiar en los hospitales. **to w. the streets,** recorrer las calles; vagar por las calles. **to w. about,** pasearse; ir y venir. **to w. after,** seguir (a), ir detrás de. **to w. along,** andar por; recorrer. **to w. away,** marcharse, irse. **to w. away with,** (win) ganar, llevarse; (steal) quitar, tomar, alzarse con. **to w. back,** volver; volver a pie, regresar a pie. **to w. down,** bajar; bajar a pie; andar por. **to w. in,** entrar en; entrar a pie en; (walk about) pasearse en. **to w. on,** seguir andando; (step on) pisar. **to w. out,** salir. **to w. over,** andar por; llevar la victoria (a); triunfar fácilmente sobre. **to w. round,** dar la vuelta a. **to w. round and round,** dar vueltas. **to w. up,** subir andando; subir. **to w. up and down,** dar vueltas, ir y venir
walker /'wɔkər/ n (pedestrian) peatón, m; andador (-ra); (promenader) paseante, mf
walking /'wɔkɪŋ/ n el andar; (excursion on foot) paseo, m. —a andante; de andar; a pie; ambulante. **at a w. pace,** a un paso de andadura. **w. encyclopedia,** enciclopedia ambulante, f. **w. match,** marcha atlética, f. **w.-stick,** bastón, m. **w. tour,** excursión a pie, f
Walkyrie /wal'kiəri/ n valquiria, f
wall /wɔl/ n muro, m; (rampart) muralla, f; (Fig. and of an organ, cavity, etc.) pared, f. **partition w.,** tabique, m. **Walls have ears,** Las paredes oyen. **w. lizard,** lagartija, f. **w. map,** mapa mural, m. **w.-painting,** pintura mural, f. **w.-paper,** papel pintado, m. **w. socket,** Elec. enchufe, m.
wall /wɔl/ vt cercar con un muro; amurallar. **to w. in,** murar. **to w. up,** tapiar, tabicar
wallet /'wɒlɪt/ n cartera, f; bolsa de cuero, f
wallflower /'wɒl,flauər/ n alhelí, m
Walloon /wɒ'lun/ a and n valón (-ona)
wallop /'wɒləp/ n golpe, m, vt tundir, zurrar
wallow /'wɒlou/ vi revolcarse; encenagarse; (in riches, etc.) nadar (en). —n revuelco, m

walnut /'wɔl,nʌt/ n (tree and wood) nogal, m; (nut) nuez de nogal, f

walrus /'wɔlrəs/ n morsa, f

waltz /wɔlts/ n vals, m, vi valsar

wan /wɑn/ a ojeroso, descolorido; (of the sky, etc.) pálido, sin color

wand /wɒnd/ n vara, f; (conductor's) batuta, f. **magic w.,** varita mágica, f

wander /'wɒndər/ vi errar, vagar; (deviate) extraviarse; (from the subject) desviarse del asunto; divagar; (be delirious) delirar. —vt vagar por, errar por, recorrer

wanderer /'wɒndərər/ n vagabundo (-da); hombre, m, (f, mujer) errante; (traveler) viajero (-ra)

wandering /'wɒndərɪŋ/ a errante; vagabundo; nómada; (traveling) viajero; (delirious) delirante; (of thoughts, the mind) distraído; (of cells, kidneys, etc.) flotante. —n vagancia, f; viaje, m; (delirium) delirio, m; (digression) divagación, f; (of a river, etc.) meandro, m. **the w. Jew,** el judío errante

wane /wein/ vi (of the moon, etc.) menguar; (decrease) disminuir; (Fig. decay) decaer. —n (of the moon) menguante de la luna, f; mengua, f; disminución, f; decadencia, f

waning /'weinɪŋ/ a menguante

wanly /'wɑnli/ adv pálidamente; Fig. tristemente

wanness /'wɑnnɪs/ n palidez, f; Fig. tristeza, f

want /wɒnt/ vt (lack) carecer de, faltar; (need) necesitar, haber menester de; (require or wish) querer, desear; (demand) exigir; (ought) deber; (do without) pasarse sin. —vi hacer falta; carecer (de); (be poor) estar necesitado. **I don't w.,** No quiero, No me da la gana. **to be wanted,** hacer falta; (called) ser llamado. **You are wanted on the telephone,** Te llaman por teléfono

want /wɒnt/ n (lack) falta, f; escasez, carestía, f; (need) necesidad, f; (poverty) pobreza, indigencia, f; (absence) ausencia, f; (wish) deseo, m; exigencia, f. **in w. of,** por falta de; en la ausencia de. **to be in w.,** estar en la necesidad, ser indigente

wanted /'wɒntɪd/ se necesita; (advertisement) demanda, f. **Estelle wants me to write a letter,** Estrella quiere que escriba una carta. **What do you w. me to do?** ¿Qué quiere Vd. que haga?; ¿En qué puedo servirle? **What does Paul w.?** ¿Qué quiere Pablo?; (require) ¿Qué necesita Pablo? **He wants (needs) a holiday,** Le hacen falta unas vacaciones, Necesita unas vacaciones

wanting /'wɒntɪŋ/ a deficiente (en); falto (de); (scarce) escaso; ausente; (in intelligence) menguado. —prep (less) menos; (without) sin. **to be w.,** faltar. **to be w. in,** carecer de

wanton /'wɒntən/ a (playful) juguetón; (wilful) travieso; (loose) suelto, libre; (unrestrained) desenfrenado; extravagante; excesivo; caprichoso; (dishevelled) en desorden; (reckless) indiscreto; (of vegetation) lozano; (purposeless) inútil; imperdonable; frívolo; (unchaste) disoluto; lascivo. —n mujer disoluta, f; ramera, f; (child) niño (-ña) juguetón (-ona)

wantonly /'wɒntnli/ adv innecesariamente; sin motivo; excesivamente; lascivamente

war /wɑr/ n guerra, f. —a de guerra; guerrero. —vi guerrear. **at war with,** en guerra con. **cold war,** guerra tonta, f. **on a war footing,** en pie de guerra. **We are at war,** Estamos en guerra. **to be on the war-path,** Fig. Inf. buscar pendencia, tratar de armarla. **to declare war on,** declarar la guerra (a). **to make war on,** hacer la guerra (a). **war to the death,** guerra a muerte, f. **war correspondent,** corresponsal en el teatro de guerra, m. **war-cry,** alarido de guerra, grito de combate, grito de guerra m. **war-dance,** danza guerrera, f. **war horse,** caballo de batalla, m. **war loan,** empréstito de guerra, m. **war-lord,** adalid, caudillo, jefe militar, m. **war material,** pertrechos de guerra, m pl; municiones, f pl. **war memorial,** monumento a los caídos, m. **war minister,** Ministro de la Guerra, m. **war neurosis,** neurosis de guerra, f. **War Office,** Ministerio de la Guerra, m. **war plane,** avión de guerra, m. **war-ship,** barco (or buque) de guerra, m. **war-wearied,** agotado por la guerra

warble /'wɔrbəl/ vt and vi trinar; gorjear; murmurar. —n trino, m; gorjeo, m; murmurio, m

ward /wɔrd/ n protección, f; (of a minor) pupilo (-la); (of locks, keys) guarda, f; (of a city) barrio, distrito, m; (of a hospital, etc.) sala, f; (of a prison) celda, f; (fencing) guardia, f. **w.-room,** cuarto de los oficiales, m. **w. sister,** hermana de una sala de hospital, f

ward /wɔrd/ vt proteger, defender. **to w. off,** desviar; evitar

warden /'wɔrdn/ n guardián, m; director (-ra); (of a prison) alcaide, m; (of a church) mayordomo de la iglesia, m; (of a port) capitán, m

warder /'wɔrdər/ n (jailer) guardián, m; alabardero, guardia, m

wardress /'wɔrdrɪs/ n guardiana, f

wardrobe /'wɔrdroub/ n guardarropa, ropero, m; (clothes) ropa, f; Theat. vestuario, m. **w. trunk,** baúl mundo, m

ware /wɛər/ n mercadería, f; (pottery) loza, f; pl **wares,** mercancías, f pl

war effort n esfuerzo bélico, esfuerzo de guerra, esfuerzo guerrero, m

warehouse /n. 'wɛər,haus; v. -,hauz/ n almacén, m, vt almacenar

warehouseman /'wɛər,hausmən/ n almacenero, m

warfare /'wɔr,fɛər/ n guerra, f; lucha, f; arte militar, m, or f. **chemical w.,** guerra química, f

war head n (of torpedo) cabeza de combate, punto de combate, f; (of missile) detonante, m

war hero n héroe de guerra, m

war heroine n heroína de guerra, f

warily /'wɛərəli/ adv con cautela, cautelosamente; prudentemente

wariness /'wɛərɪnɪs/ n cautela f; prudencia, f

warlike /'wɔr,laik/ a belicoso, guerrero; militar, de guerra; marcial. **war-spirit,** espíritu belicoso, m, marcialidad, f

warm /wɔrm/ a caliente; (lukewarm) tibio; (hot) caluroso; (affectionate) cordial, cariñoso, afectuoso; (angry) acalorado; (enthusiastic) entusiasta, ardiente; (art) cálido; (of coats, etc.) de abrigo; (fresh) fresco, reciente, Inf. adinerado. —vt calentar; Fig. encender; entusiasmar. —vi calentarse; Fig. entusiasmarse (con). **to have a w. at the fire,** calentarse al lado del fuego. **to be w.,** (of things) estar caliente; (of coats, etc.) ser de abrigo; (of the weather) hacer calor; (of people) tener calor. **to grow w.,** calentarse; (grow angry) excitarse, agitarse; (of a discussion) hacerse acalorado. **to keep w.,** conservar caliente; calentar. **to keep oneself w.,** estar caliente, no enfriarse. **to w. up,** calentar. **w.-blooded,** de sangre caliente; ardiente. **w.-hearted,** de buen corazón; generoso; afectuoso, cordial. **w.-heartedness,** buen corazón, m; generosidad, f; cordialidad, f

warming /'wɔrmɪŋ/ n calentamiento, m; calefacción, f. —a calentador; para calentar. **w.-pan,** calentador, m

warmly /'wɔrmli/ adv (affectionately) cordialmente, afectuosamente; con entusiasmo; (angrily) acaloradamente. **to be w. wrapped up,** estar bien abrigado

warmonger /'wɔr,mʌŋgər/ n atizador de guerra, belicista, fautor de guerra, fomentador de guerra, propagador (-ra) de guerra

warmth /wɔrmθ/ n calor, m

warn /wɔrn/ vt advertir; prevenir; amonestar; (inform) avisar

warning /'wɔrnɪŋ/ n advertencia, f; aviso, m; amonestación, f; (lesson) lección, f; escarmiento, m; alarma, f. —a amonestador; de alarma. **to give w.,** prevenir, advertir; (dismiss) despedir. **to take w.,** escarmentar

warningly /'wɔrnɪŋli/ adv indicando el peligro; con alarma; con amenaza

warp /wɔrp/ vt torcer; combar; Naut. espiar; (the mind) pervertir. —vi torcerse; combarse, bornearse; Naut. espiarse. —n (in a fabric) urdimbre, f; (in wood) comba, f, torcimiento, m; Naut. espía, f. **w. and woof,** trama y urdimbre, f

warping /'wɔrpɪŋ/ n (of wood) combadura, f; (weaving) urdidura, f; Naut. espía, f; (of the mind) perversión, f. **w. frame,** urdidera, f

warrant /'wɔrənt, 'wɒr-/ n autoridad, f; justificación, f; autorización, f; garantía, f; decreto de prisión, m; orden, f; Com. orden de pago, f; Mil. nombramiento, m; motivo, m, razón, f. —vt justificar; autorizar; garantizar, responder por; asegurar. **pay w.**, boletín de pago, m

warrantable /'wɔrəntəbəl/ a justificable

warrantor /'wɔrən,tɔr/ n garante, mf

warranty /'wɔrənti/ n autorización, f; justificación, f; Law. garantía, f

warren /'wɔrən/ n (for hunting) vedado, m; (rabbit) conejera, f; vivar, m, madriguera, f

warrior /'wɔriər/ n guerrero, m; soldado, m

Warsaw /'wɔrsɔ/ Varsovia, f

wart /wɔrt/ n verruga, f

wary /'wɛəri/ a cauto, cauteloso; prudente

wash /wɒʃ/ vt lavar; (dishes) fregar; (lave) bañar; (clean) limpiar; (furrow) surcar; (wet) regar, humedecer; (with paint) dar una capa de color o de metal. —vi lavarse; lavar ropa. **Two of the crew were washed overboard**, El mar arrastró a dos de los tripulantes. **Will this material w.?** ¿Se puede lavar esta tela? ¿Es lavable esta tela? **to w. ashore**, echar a la playa. **w. away**, (remove by washing) quitar lavando; derrubiar; (water or waves) arrastrar, llevarse. **to w. one's hands**, lavarse las manos. **to look washed out**, estar ojeroso. **to w. down**, lavar; limpiar; (remove) llevarse; (accompany with drink) regar. **to w. off**, vt quitar lavando; hacer desaparecer; borrar; (of waves, etc.) llevarse; (of color) desteñir. —vi borrarse; desteñirse. **to w. up**, lavar los platos, fregar la vajilla; (cast up) desechar. **w. one's dirty laundry in public**, sacar los más sucios trapillos a la colada

wash /wɒʃ/ n lavadura, f, lavado, m; baño, m; (clothes) ropa para lavar, ropa sucia, f; colada, f; (of the waves) chapoteo, m; (lotion) loción, f; (coating) capa, f; (silt) aluvión, m. **w.-basin**, palangana, f; lavabo, m. **w.-board**, tabla de lavar, f. **w.-house**, lavadero, m. **w.-leather**, gamuza, badana, f. **w.-out**, fracaso, m. **w.-stand**, aguamanil, lavabo, m. **w.-tub**, cuba de lavar, f

washable /'wɒʃəbəl/ a lavable

washer /'wɒʃər/ n lavador (-ra); (washerwoman) lavandera, f; (machine) lavadora, f; Mech. arandela, f

washerwoman /'wɒʃər,wumən/ n lavandera, f

washing /'wɒʃɪŋ/ n lavamiento, m; ropa sucia, ropa para lavar, f; ropa limpia, f; ropa, f; (bleaching) blanqueadura, f; (toilet) abluciones, f pl; Eccl. lavatorio, m; pl **washings**, lavazas, f pl. **There is a lot of w. to be done**, Hay mucha ropa que lavar. **w.-board**, tabla de lavar, f. **w.-day**, día de colada, m. **w.-machine**, lavadora, máquina de lavar, f. **w.-soda**, carbonato sódico, m. **w.-up**, lavado de los platos, m. **w.-up machine**, fregador mecánico de platos, m

wasp /wɒsp/ n avispa, f. **wasp's nest**, avispero, m. **w.-waisted**, (of clothes) ceñido, muy ajustado

waspish /'wɒspɪʃ/ a enojadizo, irascible; malicioso; mordaz

wastage /'weistɪdʒ/ n desgaste, desperdicio, m

waste /weist/ vt desperdiciar, derrochar, malgastar; (time) perder; consumir; corroer; (devastate) asolar, devastar; echar a perder; malograr; disipar; agotar. —vi gastarse; consumirse; perderse. **to w. time**, perder el tiempo. **to w. away**, (of persons) demacrarse, consumirse

waste /weist/ n (wilderness) yermo, desierto, m; (vastness) inmensidad, vastedad, f; (loss) pérdida, f; (squandering) despilfarro, derroche, m; disminución, f; (refuse) desechos, m pl; (of cotton, etc.) borra, f; disipación, f. —a (of land) sin cultivar; yermo, inútil; desechado, de desecho; superfluo. **to lay w.**, devastar. **w. land**, yermo, m; tierras sin cultivar, f pl. **w. paper**, papel usado, papel de desecho, m. **w.-paper basket**, cesto para papeles, m. **w.-pipe**, desaguadero, tubo de desagüe, m

wasteful /'weistfəl/ a pródigo, derrochador, manirroto; antieconómico; ruinoso; inútil

wastefully /'weistfəli/ adv pródigamente; antieconómicamente; inútilmente

wastefulness /'weistfəlnɪs/ n prodigalidad, f, despil-

farro, m; pérdida, f; gasto inútil, m; falta de economía, f

waster /'weistər/ n gastador (-ra); disipador (-ra); (loafer) golfo, m

watch /wɒtʃ/ vi velar; mirar. —vt mirar; observar; guardar; (await) esperar; (spy upon) espiar, acechar. **to w. for**, buscar aguardar. **to w. over**, vigilar, guardar; (care for) cuidar; proteger

watch /wɒtʃ/ n (at night) vela, f; (wakefulness) desvelo, m; observación, vigilancia, f; (Mil. Naut.) guardia, f; (sentinel) centinela, m; (watchman) sereno, vigilante, m; (guard) ronda, f; (timepiece) reloj de bolsillo, m. **to be on the w.**, estar al acecho, estar al alerta, estar a la mira. **to keep w.**, vigilar. **dog w.**, media guardia, f. **pocket w.**, reloj de bolsillo, m. **wrist w.**, reloj de pulsera, m. **w.-case**, caja de reloj, relojera, f. **w.-chain**, cadena de reloj, leontina, f. **w.-dog**, perro guardián, m. **w.-glass**, cristal de reloj, m. **w.-making**, relojería, f. **w.-night**, noche vieja, f. **w.-spring**, muelle de reloj, m, espiral, f. **w.-tower**, vigía, atalaya, f

watcher /'wɒtʃər/ n observador (-ra); espectador (-ra); (at a sick bed) el, m, (f, la) que vela a un enfermo

watchful /'wɒtʃfəl/ a vigilante, alerto; observador; atento, cuidadoso

watchfully /'wɒtʃfəli/ adv vigilantemente; atentamente

watchfulness /'wɒtʃfəlnɪs/ n vigilancia, f; cuidado, m; desvelo, m

watching /'wɒtʃɪŋ/ n observación, f; (vigil) vela, f

watchmaker /'wɒtʃ,meikər/ n relojero (-ra). **watchmaker's shop**, relojería, f

watchman /'wɒtʃmən/ n vigilante, sereno, m; guardián, m

watchword /'wɒtʃ,wɜrd/ n (password) consigna, contraseña, f; (motto) lema, m

water /'wɔtər/ n agua, f; (tide) marea, f; (of precious stones) aguas, f pl; (urine) orina, f; (quality) calidad, clase, f. —a de agua; por agua; acuático; hidráulico. **fresh w.**, (not salt) agua dulce, f; agua fresca, f. **hard w.**, agua cruda, f. **high w.**, marea alta, f. **low w.**, marea baja, f. **of the first w.**, de primera clase. **running w.**, agua corriente, f. **soft w.**, agua blanda, f. **to make w.**, Naut. hacer agua; orinar. **to take the waters**, tomar las aguas. **under w.**, adv debajo del agua. —a acuático. **w.-bird**, ave acuática, f. **w. blister**, ampolla, f. **w.-boatman**, chinche de agua, f. **w.-borne**, flotante. **w.-bottle**, cantimplora, f. **w.-brash**, acedia, f. **w.-butt**, barril, m, pipa, f. **w.-carrier**, aguador (-ra). **w.-cart**, carro de regar, m. **w.-closet**, retrete, excusado, m. **w.-color**, acuarela, f. **w.-color painting**, pintura a la acuarela, f. **w.-colorist**, acuarelista, mf **w.-cooled**, enfriado por agua. **w.-cooler**, cantimplora, f. **w.-finder**, zahorí, m. **w. front**, (wharf) muelle, m; puerto, m; litoral, m. **w.-gauge**, indicador de nivel de agua, m, vara de aforar, f. **w.-glass**, vidrio soluble, silicato de sosa, m. **w. heater**, calentador de agua, m. **w.-ice**, helado, m. **w.-level**, nivel de las aguas, m. **w.-lily**, nenúfar, m, azucena de agua, f. **w.-line**, lengua de agua, f; (of a ship) línea de flotación, f. **w.-logged**, anegado en agua. **w.-main**, cañería maestra de agua, f. **w. man**, barquero, m. **w.-melon**, sandía, f. **w. mill**, aceña, f. **w.-nymph**, náyade, f. **w.-pipe**, cañería del agua, f. **w. pitcher**, jarro, m. **w. plant**, planta acuática, f. **w.-polo**, polo acuático, m. **w.-power**, fuerza hidráulica, f. **w.-rate**, cupo del consumo de agua, m. **w. snake**, culebra de agua, f. **w. softener**, generador de agua dulce, m; purificador de agua, m. **w. spaniel**, perro (-rra) de aguas. **w. sprite**, ondina, f. **w.-supply**, abastecimiento de agua, m; traída de aguas, f. **w. tank**, depósito para agua, m. **w. tower**, arca de agua, f. **w. wave**, ondulado al agua, m. **w.-way**, canal, río m, o vía f, navegable. **w.-wheel**, rueda hidráulica, f, azud, m; (for irrigation) aceña, f. **w. wings**, nadaderas, f pl

water /'wɔtər/ vt (irrigate, sprinkle) regar; (moisten) mojar; (cattle, etc.) abrevar; (wine, etc.) aguar; diluir con agua; (bathe) bañar. —vi (of animals) beber agua; (of engines, etc.) tomar agua; (of the eyes, mouth) hacerse agua. **My mouth waters**, Se me hace agua la boca

watercourse /'wɔtər,kɔrs/ n corriente de agua, f; cauce, m; lecho de un río, m
watercress /'wɔtər,krɛs/ n berro, mastuerzo, m
watered /'wɔtərd/ a regado, abundante en agua; (of silk) tornasolado
watered-down /'wɔtərd'daun/ Fig. pasado por agua
waterfall /'wɔtər,fɔl/ n salto de agua, m, cascada, catarata, f
wateriness /'wɔtərinıs/ n humedad, f; acuosidad, f
watering /'wɔtərıŋ/ n riego, m; irrigación, f; (of eyes) lagrimeo, m; (of cattle, etc.) el abrevar (a); Naut. aguada, f. **w.-can**, regadera, f. **w.-cart**, carro de regar, m. **w.-place**, (for animals) aguadero, m; (for cattle) abrevadero, m; (spa) balneario, m; (by the sea) playa de veraneo, f
watermark /'wɔtər,mɑrk/ n (in paper) filigrana, f; nivel del agua, m. —vt filigranar
waterproof /'wɔtər,pruf/ a impermeable; a prueba de agua. —n impermeable, m. —vt hacer impermeable, impermeabilizar
water-repellent /'wɔtərrı,pɛlənt/ a repelente al agua
watershed /'wɔtər,ʃɛd/ n vertiente, f; línea divisoria de las aguas, f; (river-basin) cuenca, f
waterspout /'wɔtər,spaut/ n bomba marina, manga, trompa, f
watertight /'wɔtər,tait/ a impermeable, estanco; a prueba de agua; (of arguments, etc.) irrefutable
watertightness /'wɔtər,taitnıs/ n impermeabilidad, f
waterworks /'wɔtər,wɜrks/ n establecimiento para la distribución de las aguas, m; obras hidráulicas, f pl
watery /'wɔtəri/ a (wet) húmedo; acuoso; (of the sky) de lluvia; (of eyes) lagrimoso, lloroso; (sodden) mojado; (of soup, etc.) claro; insípido
watt /wɒt/ n vatio, m. **w. hour**, vatio hora, m. **w.-meter**, vatímetro, m
wattage /'wɒtıdʒ/ n vatiaje, m
wattle /'wɒtl/ n zarzo, m; (of turkey) barba, f; (of fish) barbilla, f
wave /weiv/ vi ondear; ondular; flotar; hacer señales. —vt (brandish) blandir; agitar; (the hair) ondular; ondear; hacer señales (de). **They waved goodby to him,** Le hicieron adiós con la mano; Le hicieron señas de despedida; Se despidieron de él agitando el pañuelo
wave /weiv/ n (of the sea) ola, f; Phys. onda, f; (in hair or a surface) ondulación, f; (movement) movimiento, m; (of anger, etc.) ráfaga, f. **long w.**, onda larga, f. **medium w.**, onda media, f. **short w.**, onda corta, f. **sound w.**, onda sonora, f. **to have one's hair waved,** hacerse ondular el pelo. **w. band**, franja undosa, escala de longitudes de onda, f. **w. crest**, cresta de la ola, cabrilla, f. **w.-length**, longitud de onda, f
wavelet /'weivlıt/ n pequeña ola, olita, f; (ripple) rizo (del agua), m
wave of immigration una imigración, f
waver /'weivər/ vi ondear; oscilar; (hesitate) vacilar, titubear; (totter) tambalearse; (weaken) flaquear
waverer /'weivərər/ n irresoluto (-ta), vacilante, m
wavering /'weivərıŋ/ n vacilación, irresolución, f. —a oscilante; vacilante; irresoluto; flotante
waving /'weivıŋ/ n ondulación, f; oscilación, f; agitación, f; movimiento, m. —a ondulante; oscilante; que se balancea
wavy /'weivi/ a ondulado; flotante
wax /wæks/ n cera, f; (cobblers') cerote, m; (in the ear) cerilla, f. —a de cera. —vt encerar. —vi crecer; hacerse; ponerse. **to wax enthusiastic,** entusiasmarse. **waxed paper,** papel encerado, m. **wax chandler,** cerero, m. **wax doll,** muñeca de cera, f. **wax modeling,** modelado en cera, m, ceroplástica, f. **wax taper,** blandón, m
waxen /'wæksən/ a de cera; como la cera; de color de cera
waxing /'wæksıŋ/ n enceramiento, m; (of the moon) crecimiento, m; aumento, m
wax museum n museo de cera, m
waxwork /'wæks,wɜrk/ n figura de cera, f
waxy /'wæksi/ a. See **waxen**
way /wei/ n camino, m; senda, f; paso, m; ruta, f; (railway, etc.) vía, f; dirección, f; rumbo, m; distancia, f; (journey) viaje, m; (sea crossing) travesía, f;

avance, progreso, m; (Naut. etc.) marcha, f; método, m; modo, m; (means) medio, m; manera, f; (habit) costumbre, f; (behavior) conducta, f, modo de obrar, m; (line of business, etc.) ramo, m; (state) estado, m, condición, f; (course) curso, m; (respect) punto de vista, m; (particular kind) género, m; (scale) escala, f. **a long way off,** a gran distancia, a lo lejos. **a short way off,** a poca distancia, no muy lejos. **by way of,** pasando por; por vía de; como; por medio de; a modo de. **by the way,** de paso; durante el viaje; durante la travesía; a propósito, entre paréntesis. **in a small way,** en pequeña escala. **in a way,** hasta cierto punto; desde cierto punto de vista. **in many ways,** de muchos modos; por muchas cosas. **in no way,** de ningún modo; nada. **in the way,** en el medio. **in the way of,** en cuanto a, tocante a; en materia de. **I went out of my way to,** Dejé el camino para; Me di la molestia de. **Is this the way to...?** ¿Es este el camino a...? **Make way!** ¡Calle! **Milky Way,** vía láctea, f. **on the way,** en camino; al paso; durante el viaje. **out of the way,** puesto a un lado; arrinconado; apartado, alejado; (imprisoned) en prisión; fuera del camino; remoto; (unusual) original. **over the way,** en frente; al otro lado (de la calle, etc.). **right of w.,** derecho de paso, m. **The ship left on its way to...,** El barco zarpó con rumbo a... the **Way of the Cross,** vía crucis, f. **This way!** ¡Por aquí!; De este modo, Así. **this way and that,** en todas direcciones, por todos lados. **"This way to...,"** «Dirección a...» A... **under way,** en camino; en marcha; en preparación. **to bar the way,** cerrar el paso. **to be in the way,** estorbar. **to be out of the way of doing,** haber perdido la costumbre de hacer (algo). **to clear the way,** abrir paso, abrir calle; Fig. preparar el terreno. **to force one's way through,** abrirse paso por. **to find a way,** encontrar un camino; Fig. encontrar medios. **to find one's way,** hallar el camino; orientarse. **to get into the way of,** contraer la costumbre de. **to get under way,** Naut. zarpar, hacerse a la vela; ponerse en marcha. **to give way,** ceder; (break) romper. **to go a long way,** ir lejos; contribuir mucho (a). **to have one's own way,** salir con la suya. **to keep out of the way,** vt and vi esconder(se); mantener(se) alejado; mantener(se) apartado. **to lose one's way,** perder el camino; desorientarse; Fig. extraviarse. **to make one's way,** abrirse paso. **to make one's way down,** bajar. **to make one's way round,** dar la vuelta a. **to make one's way up,** subir. **to make way,** hacer lugar; hacer sitio; dar paso (a). **to pay one's way,** ganarse la vida; pagar lo que se debe. **to prepare the way for,** preparar el terreno para. **to put out of the way,** poner a un lado; apartar; (kill) matar; (imprison) poner en la cárcel; hacer cautivo (a). **to see one's way,** poder ver el camino; poder orientarse; ver el modo de hacer algo; ver cómo se puede hacer algo. **ways and means,** medios y arbitrios, m pl. **way back,** camino de regreso, m; vuelta, f. **way down,** bajada, f. **way in,** entrada, f. **way out,** salida, f. **way round,** camino alrededor, m; solución, f; modo de evitar..., m. **way through,** paso, m. **way up,** subida, f
wayfarer /'wei,fɛərər/ n transeúnte, mf; viajero (-ra)
wayfaring /'wei,fɛərıŋ/ a que va de viaje; errante, ambulante
waylay /'wei,lei/ vt asechar, salir al paso (de)
wayside /'wei,said/ n borde del camino, m. —a (of flowers) silvestre; (by the side of the road) en la carretera
wayward /'weiwərd/ a caprichoso; desobediente; voluntarioso; travieso; rebelde
waywardness /'weiwərdnıs/ n desobediencia, indocilidad, f; voluntariedad, f; travesura, f; rebeldía, f
we /wi/ pron nosotros, m pl; nosotras, f pl, (Usually omitted except for emphasis or for clarity.) **We are in the garden,** Estamos en el jardín. **We have come, but they are not here,** Nosotros hemos venido pero ellos no están aquí
weak /wik/ a débil; flojo; frágil; delicado; (insecure) inseguro; (of arguments) poco convincente; (of prices, markets, etc.) flojo, en baja. **w.-eyed,** de vista floja. **w.-kneed,** débil de rodillas; Fig. sin voluntad.

w.-minded, sin carácter; pusilánime; **w. spot**, debilidad, *f;* flaco, *m;* lado débil, *m;* desventaja, *f*

weaken /'wikən/ *vt* debilitar; (diminish) disminuir. —*vi* debilitarse; flaquear, desfallecer; (give way) ceder

weakening /'wikənɪŋ/ *n* debilitación, *f.* —*a* debilitante; enervante

weaker /'wikər/ *a compar* más débil. **the w. sex**, el sexo débil

weakling /'wiklɪŋ/ *n* ser delicado, *m,* persona débil, *f;* cobarde, *m; Inf.* alfeñique, *m*

weakly /'wikli/ *a* enfermizo, delicado, enclenque. —*adv* débilmente

weakness /'wiknɪs/ *n* debilidad, *f;* imperfección, *f*

weal /wil/ *n* bienestar, *m;* prosperidad, *f;* (blow) verdugo, *m*

wealth /wɛlθ/ *n* riqueza, *f;* abundancia, *f;* bienes, *m pl*

wealthy /'wɛlθi/ *a* rico, adinerado, acaudalado; abundante (en)

wean /win/ *vt* destetar, ablactar; separar (de); privar (de); enajenar el afecto de; (of ideas) desaferrar (de)

weaning /'winɪŋ/ *n* ablactación, *f,* destete, *m*

weapon /'wepən/ *n* arma, *f;* pl **weapons**, (*Zool., Bot.*) medios de defensa, *m* pl. **steel w.**, arma blanca, *f*

wear /wɛər/ *n* uso, *m;* gasto, *m;* deterioro, *m;* (fashion) moda, boga, *f.* **for hard w.**, para todo uso. **for one's own w.**, para su propio uso. **for evening w.**, para llevar de noche. **for summer w.**, para llevar en verano. **w. and tear**, uso y desgaste, *m;* deterioro natural, *m*

wear /wɛər/ *vt* llevar; llevar puesto; traer; usar; (have) tener; (exhibit) mostrar; (be clad in) vestir; (waste) gastar; deteriorar; (make) hacer; (exhaust) agotar, cansar, consumir. —*vi* (last) durar; (of persons) conservar(se); (of time) correr; avanzar. **She wears well**, Está bien conservada. **to w. one's heart on one's sleeve**, tener el corazón en la mano. **to w. the trousers**, *Fig. Inf.* llevar los pantalones. **to w. well**, durar mucho. **to w. away**, *vt* gastar, roer; (rub out) borrar; consumir. —*vi* (of time) pasar lentamente, transcurrir despacio. **to w. down**, gastar; consumir; reducir; agotar las fuerzas de; destruir; (tire) fatigar. **to w. off**, *vt* destruir; borrar. —*vi* quitarse; borrarse; *Fig.* desaparecer, pasar. **to w. on**, (of time) transcurrir, correr, pasar. **to w. out**, *vt* usar; romper con el uso; consumir, acabar con; (exhaust) agotar; (tire) rendir. —*vi* usarse; romperse con el uso; consumirse

wearable /'wɛərəbəl/ *a* que se puede llevar

wearer /'wɛərər/ *n* el, *m,* (f. la) que lleva alguna cosa

weariness /'wɪərɪnɪs/ *n* cansancio, *m,* fatiga, lasitud, *f;* aburrimiento, *m;* aversión, repugnancia, *f*

wearing /'wɛərɪŋ/ *n* uso, *m;* desgaste, *m.* —*a* (tiring) agotador; cansado. **w. apparel**, ropa, *f*

wearisome /'wɪərɪsəm/ *a* cansado; laborioso; aburrido, tedioso, pesado

wearisomely /'wɪərɪsəmli/ *adv* tediosamente

wearisomeness /'wɪərɪsəmnɪs/ *n* cansancio, *m;* aburrimiento, tedio, hastío, *m*

weary /'wɪəri/ *a* cansado, fatigado; aburrido; hastiado; impaciente; tedioso, enfadoso. —*vt* cansar, fatigar; aburrir; hastiar; molestar. —*vi* cansarse, fatigarse; aburrirse. **to w. for**, anhelar, suspirar por; (miss) echar de menos (a). **to w. of**, aburrirse de; (things) impacientarse de; (people) impacientarse con

weasel /'wizəl/ *n* comadreja, *f*

weather /'wɛðər/ *n* tiempo, *m;* intemperie, *f;* (storm) tempestad, *f.* —*a Naut.* del lado del viento; de barlovento. —*vt* (of rain, etc.) desgastar; curtir; secar al aire; *Naut.* pasar a barlovento; (bear) aguantar, capear; (survive) sobrevivir a; luchar con. —*vi* curtirse a la intemperie. **Andrew is a little under the w.**, Andrés está algo destemplado; (with drink) Andrés tiene una mona; (depressed) Andrés está melancólico. **to be bad (good) w.**, hacer mal (buen) tiempo. **What is the w. like?** ¿Qué tiempo hace? ¿Cómo está el tiempo? **w.-beaten**, curtido por la intemperie. **w. chart**, carta meteorológica, *f.* **w. conditions**, condiciones meteorológicas, *f* pl. **w. forecast**, pronóstico del tiempo, *m.* **w.-hardened**, endurecido a la intemperie.

w. prophet, meteorologista, *mf* **w. report**, boletín meteorológico, *m.* **w.-worn**, gastado por la intemperie; curtido por la intemperie

weathercock /'wɛðərkɒk/ *n* veleta, *f*

weathering /'wɛðərɪŋ/ *n* desintegración por la acción atmosférica, *f*

weather-resistant /'wɛðərɪˌzɪstənt/ *a* resistente a la intemperie

weave /wiv/ *vt* tejer; trenzar; entrelazar; *Fig.* tejer. —*vi* tejer. —*n* tejido, *m;* textura, *f*

weaver /'wivər/ *n* tejedor (-ra)

weaving /'wivɪŋ/ *n* tejido, *m;* tejeduría, *f.* **w. machine**, telar, *m*

web /wɛb/ *n* tejido, *m;* tela, *f;* (network) red, *f;* (spider's) telaraña, *f;* (of a feather) barba, *f;* (of birds, etc.) membrana interdigital, *f;* (of intrigue) red, *f;* (snarl) lazo, *m,* trampa, *f.* **web-foot**, pie palmado, *m.* **web-footed**, palmípedo.

webbed /wɛbd/ *a* (of feet) unido por una membrana

wed /wɛd/ *vt* casarse con; (join in marriage, cause to marry) casar; *Fig.* unir. —*vi* estar casado; casarse

wedded /'wɛdɪd/ *a* casado; matrimonial, conyugal; *Fig.* unido (a); aficionado (a), entusiasta (de), devoto (de); aferrado (a). **to be w. to one's own opinion**, estar aferrado a su propia opinión

wedding /'wɛdɪŋ/ *n* boda, *f,* casamiento, *m;* (with golden, etc.) bodas, *f* pl; (union) enlace, *m, a* de boda, nupcial, matrimonial, conyugal; de novios, de la novia. **golden w.**, bodas de oro, *f* pl. **silver w.**, bodas de plata, *f* pl. **w. bouquet**, ramo de la novia, *m.* **w.-breakfast**, banquete de bodas, *m.* **w.-cake**, torta de la boda, *f,* pan de la boda, *m.* **w.-day**, día de la boda, *m.* **w.-march**, marcha nupcial, *f.* **w.-present**, regalo de boda, regalo de la boda, *m.* **w.-ring**, anillo de la boda, *m.* **w. trip**, viaje de novios, *m*

wedge /wɛdʒ/ *n* cuña, *f;* (under a wheel) calza, alzaprima, *f; Mil.* cuña, mella, *f;* (of cheese) pedazo, *m.* —*vt* acuñar, meter cuñas; (a wheel) calzar; (fix) sujetar. **to be the thin end of the w.**, ser el principio, ser el primer paso. **to drive a w.**, *Mil.* hacer mella, practicar una cuña. **to w. oneself in**, introducirse con dificultad (en). **w.-shaped**, cuneiforme

wedlock /'wɛdˌlɒk/ *n* matrimonio, *m*

Wednesday /'wɛnzdeɪ/ *n* miércoles, *m*

wee /wi/ *a* pequeñito, chiquito. **a wee bit**, un poquito

weed /wid/ *n* mala hierba, *f;* tabaco, *m;* (cigar) cigarro, *m;* (person) madeja, *f;* (*Fig.* evil) cizaña, *f.* —*vt* carpir, desherbar, sachar, sallar, escardar; *Fig.* extirpar, arrancar. **w.-grown**, cubierto de malas hierbas. **to w. out**, extirpar; quitar

weeder /'widər/ *n* (person) escardador (-ra); (implement) sacho, *m*

weeding /'widɪŋ/ *n* (also *Fig.*) escarda, *f*

weedy /'widi/ *a* lleno de malas hierbas; *Fig.* raquítico

week /wik/ *n* semana, *f.* **in a w.**, de hoy en ocho (días); en una semana; después de una semana. **once a w.**, una vez por semana. **a w. ago**, hace una semana. **Michael will come a w. from today**, Miguel llegará hoy en ocho. **w. in, w. out**, semana tras semana. **w.-day**, día de trabajo, día laborable, día de la semana que no sea el domingo. **on weekdays**, entre semana, *m.* **w.-end**, fin de semana, *m.* **w.-end case**, saco de noche, *m*

weekly /'wikli/ *a* semanal, semanario; de cada semana. —*adv* semanalmente, cada semana. —*n* semanario, *m,* revista semanal, *f*

weep /wip/ *vt* and *vi* llorar. **to w. for**, (a person) llorar (a); (on account of) llorar por; (with happiness, etc.) llorar de. **They wept for joy**, Lloraron de alegría

weeping /'wipɪŋ/ *n* lloro, llanto, *m,* lágrimas, *f* pl. —*a* lloroso, que llora; (of trees) llorón. **w.-willow**, sauce llorón, *m*

weevil /'wivəl/ *n* gorgojo, *m*

weigh /wei/ *vt* pesar; (consider) considerar, ponderar, tomar en cuenta; comparar; (the anchor) levar. —*vi* pesar; ser de importancia. **to w. anchor**, zarpar, levar el ancla, hacerse a la vela. **to w. down**, pesar sobre; sobrecargar; hacer inclinarse bajo; *Fig.* agobiar. **to be weighed down**, hundirse por su propio peso; *Fig.* estar agobiado. **to w. out**, pesar. **to w. with**, influir (en). **w.-bridge**, báscula, *f*

weighing /'weɪɪŋ/ n pesada, f; (weight) peso, m; (of the anchor) leva, f; (consideration) ponderación, consideración, f. **w.-machine,** báscula, f

weight /weɪt/ n peso, m; (heaviness) pesantez, f; cargo, m; (of a clock and as part of a system) pesa, f; Fig. peso, m, importancia, f. —vt cargar; (a stick) emplomar; aumentar el peso (de); poner un peso (a). **gross w.,** peso bruto, m. **heavy w.,** peso pesado, m. **light w.,** peso ligero, m. **middle w.,** peso medio, m. **net w.,** peso neto, m. **to lose w.,** adelgazar. **loss of w.,** (of a person) adelgazamiento, m. **to put on w.,** cobrar carnes, hacerse más gordo. **to put the w.,** Sports. lanzar el peso. **to throw one's w. about,** Inf. darse importancia. **to try the w. of,** sopesar. **weights and measures,** pesas y medidas, f pl. **weightlifting,** halterofilia, f

weighty /'weɪti/ a pesado; (influential) influyente; importante, de peso; grave

weir /wɪər/ n presa, esclusa, f; (for fish) cañal, m

weird /wɪərd/ a misterioso, sobrenatural; fantástico; mágico; (queer) raro, extraño. **the W. Sisters,** las Parcas

weirdly /'wɪərdli/ adv misteriosamente; fantásticamente; (queerly) de un modo raro, extrañamente

weirdness /'wɪərdnɪs/ n misterio, m; cualidad fantástica, f; lo sobrenatural; (queerness) rareza, f

welcome /'wɛlkəm/ a bienvenido; (pleasant) grato, agradable. —n bienvenida, f; buena acogida, f; (reception) acogida, f. —vt dar la bienvenida (a); acoger con alegría, acoger con entusiasmo; agasajar, festejar; (receive) acoger, recibir; recibir con gusto. **W.!** ¡Bienvenido! **to bid w.,** dar la bienvenida (a). **You are w.,** Estás bienvenido. **You are w. to it,** Está a su disposición

welcoming /'wɛlkəmɪŋ/ a acogedor, cordial, amistoso

weld /wɛld/ vt soldar; combinar; unificar

welder /'wɛldər/ n soldador, m

welding /'wɛldɪŋ/ n soldadura, f; unión, fusión, f

welfare /'wɛl,fɛər/ n bienestar, bien, m; (health) salud, f; prosperidad, f; intereses, m pl. **w. state,** estado benefactor, estado de beneficencia, estado socializante, m. **w. work,** trabajo social, m

well /wɛl/ a bien; bien de salud; bueno; conveniente; (advantageous) provechoso; favorable; (happy) feliz; (healed) curado; (recovered) repuesto. **I am very w.,** Estoy muy bien. **to get w.,** ponerse bien. **to make w.,** curar. **w. enough,** bastante bien

well /wɛl/ adv bien; (very) muy; favorablemente; convenientemente; (easily) sin dificultad. **as w.,** también. **as w. as,** tan bien como; además de. **That is all very w. but...,** Todo eso está muy bien pero... **to be w. up in,** estar versado en. **to get on w. with,** llevarse bien con. **Very w.!** ¡Está bien!; Muy bien. **w. and good,** bien está. **w. now,** ahora bien. **w. then,** conque; pues bien. **w.-advised,** bien aconsejado; prudente. **w.-aimed,** certero. **w.-appointed,** bien provisto; (furnished) bien amueblado. **w.-attended,** concurrido. **w.-balanced,** bien equilibrado. **w.-behaved,** bien educado; (of animals) manso. **w.-being,** bienestar, m; felicidad, f. **w.-born,** bien nacido, de buena familia. **w.-bred,** bien criado, bien educado; (of animals) de pura raza. **w.-chosen,** bien escogido. **w.-defined,** bien definido. **w.-deserved,** bien merecido. **w.-disposed,** bien dispuesto; favorable; bien intencionado. **w.-doing,** n el obrar bien; obras de caridad, f pl, a bondadoso, caritativo. **w.-done,** a bien hecho. —interj ¡bravo! **w.-educated,** instruido, culto. **w.-favored,** guapo, de buen parecer. **w.-founded,** bien fundado. **w.-groomed,** elegante. **w.-grounded,** bien fundado; bien instruido. **w.-informed,** instruido; culto; ilustrado. **w.-intentioned,** bien intencionado. **w.-known,** bien conocido, notorio. **w.-meaning,** bien intencionado. **w.-modulated,** armonioso. **w.-off,** acomodado, adinerado; feliz. **w.-read,** culto, instruido. **w.-shaped,** bien hecho; bien formado. **w.-shaped nose,** nariz perfilada, f. **w.-spent,** bien empleado. **w.-spoken,** bien hablado; bien dicho. **w.-stocked,** bien provisto. **w.-suited,** apropiado. **w.-timed,** oportuno. **w.-to-do,** acomodado, rico. **w.-wisher,** amigo (-ga). **w.-worn,** raído; (of paths) trillado

well /wɛl/ n pozo, m; (of a stair) caja, f; cañón de es-

calera, m; (fountain) fuente, f, manantial, m; (of a fishing boat) vivar, m; (of a ship) sentina, f. **w.-sinker,** pocero, m

well /wɛl/ vi chorrear, manar, brotar, fluir

Welsh /wɛlʃ/ a galés, de Gales. —n (language) galés, m. **the W.,** los galeses

Welshman /'wɛlʃmən/ n galés, m

Welshwoman /'wɛlʃ,wʊmən/ n galesa, f

welt /wɛlt/ n (of shoe) vira, f, cerquillo, m; (in knitting) ribete, m; (weal) verdugo, m

Weltanschauung /'vɛltənʃaʊəŋ/ n cosmovisión, postura de vida, f

welter /'wɛltər/ vi revolcarse; bañarse (en), nadar (en). —n confusión, f, tumulto, m; mezcla, f. **w.-weight,** peso welter, m

wench /wɛntʃ/ n mozuela, muchacha, f

wend /wɛnd/ vt dirigir, encaminar. —vi ir. **to w. one's way,** dirigir sus pasos, seguir su camino

Wesleyan /'wɛsliən/ a wesleyano, metodista. —n metodista, mf

west /wɛst/ n oeste, m; poniente, m; occidente, m. —a del oeste; occidental. —adv hacia el oeste, a poniente; al occidente. **W. Indian,** de las Antillas, de las Indias Occidentales. **w.-north-w.,** oesnorueste, m. **w.-south-w.,** oessudueste, m. **w. wind,** viento del oeste, poniente, m

westerly /'wɛstərli/ a del oeste; hacia el oeste; occidental

western /'wɛstərn/ a occidental; del oeste. —n (novel) novela caballista, f; (film) película del oeste, f

westernized /'wɛstər,naɪzd/ a influido por el occidente

westernmost /'wɛstərn,moʊst/ a más al oeste

West Indies Indias Occidentales, f pl

westward /'wɛstwərd/ a que está al oeste. —adv hacia el oeste; hacia el occidente

wet /wɛt/ a mojado; húmedo; (rainy) lluvioso. —vt mojar; humedecer. —n (rain) lluvia, f. **"Mind the wet paint!"** «¡Cuidado, recién pintado!» **to be wet,** estar mojado; (of the weather) llover. **to get wet,** mojarse. **wet blanket,** Fig. aguafiestas, mf **wet through,** (of persons) calado, hecho una sopa. **wet-nurse,** nodriza, f

wetness /'wɛtnɪs/ n humedad, f; (rain) lluvia, f

wetting /'wɛtɪŋ/ n mojada, f; humectación, f; (soaking) remojo, m

whack /wæk/ n golpe, m; (try) tentativa, f; (portion) porción, parte, f. —vt golpear, aporrear, pegar

whale /weɪl/ n ballena, f. **sperm w.,** cachalote, m. **w.-oil,** aceite de ballena, m

whalebone /'weɪl,boʊn/ n barbas de ballena, f pl, ballena, f

whaler /'weɪlər/ n (man) ballenero, pescador de ballenas, m; (boat) buque ballenero, m

whaling /'weɪlɪŋ/ a ballenero. —n pesca de ballenas, f. **w.-gun,** cañón arponero, m

wharf /wɔrf/ n muelle, embarcadero, descargadero, m, vt amarrar al muelle

what /wʌt; unstressed wət/ a pron (interrogative and exclamatory) qué; cómo; (relative) que; el que, m; la que, f; lo que, neut; los que, m pl; las que, f pl; (which, interrogative) cuál, mf; cuáles, mf pl; (how many) cuantos, m pl; cuantas, f pl; (interrogative and exclamatory) cuántos, m pl; cuántas, f pl; (how much, interrogative and exclamatory) cuánto, m; cuánta, f. **And w. not,** Y qué sé yo qué más. **Make w. changes you will,** Haz los cambios que quieras. **W. confidence he had...,** La confianza que tenía... **W. is this called?** ¿Cómo se llama esto? **W. did they go there for?** ¿Por qué fueron? **W. do you take me for?** ¿Por quién me tomas? **That was not w. he said,** No fue eso lo que dijo. **to know what's w.,** saber cuántas son cinco. **You have heard the latest news, w.?** Has oído las últimas noticias, ¿verdad? **W. a pity!** ¡Qué lástima! **W., do you really believe it?** ¿Lo crees de veras? **W. else?** ¿Qué más? **W. for?** ¿Para qué? **what's-his-name,** fulano (-na) de tal, m. **W. ho!** ¡Hola! **W. if...?** ¿Qué será si...? **W. is the matter?** ¿Qué pasa? ¿Qué hay? **w. though...,** aun cuando...; ¿Qué importa qué? **w. with one thing, w. with another,** entre una cosa y otra. **What's more;...** Es más,...

whatever /wʌt'evər/ *a pron* cuanto; todo lo que; cualquier cosa que; cualquier. **W. sacrifice is necessary,** Cualquier sacrificio que sea necesario. **W. I have is yours,** Todo lo que tenga es vuestro. **W. happens,** Venga lo que venga. **It is of no use w.,** No sirve absolutamente para nada

wheal /wil/ *n.* See **weal**

wheat /wit/ *n* trigo, *m.* —*a* de trigo. **summer w.,** trigo tremesino, *m.* **whole w.,** *a* de trigo entero. **w.-ear,** espiga de trigo, *f.* **w.-field,** trigal, *m.* **w.-sheaf,** gavilla de trigo, *f*

wheaten /'witn/ *a* de trigo; del color del trigo

wheedle /'widl/ *vt* lagotear, engatusar; (flatter) halagar; (with out) sacar con mimos

wheedling /'widlɪŋ/ *a* zalamero, mimoso; marrullero. —*n* lagotería, *f*, mimos, *m pl;* (flattery) halagos, *m pl;* marrullería, *f*

wheel /wil/ *n* rueda, *f;* (bicycle) bicicleta, *f;* (for steering a ship) timón, *m;* rueda del timón, *f;* (for steering a car) volante, *m;* (for spinning) rueca, *f;* (potter's) rueda de alfarero, *f;* (of birds) vuelo, *m;* (turn) vuelta, *f; Mil.* conversión, *f.* **Catherine w.,** (firework) rueda de Santa Catalina, *f.* **back w.,** rueda trasera, *f.* **front w.,** rueda delantera, *f.* **to break on the w.,** enrodar. **to go on wheels,** ir en ruedas; *Fig.* ir viento en popa. **to take the w.,** (in a ship) tomar el timón; tomar el volante. **w. of fortune,** rueda de la fortuna, *f.* **w.-chair,** silla de ruedas, *f.* **w.-house,** timonera, *f.* **w.-mark,** rodada, *f*

wheel /wil/ *vt* hacer rodar; (push) empujar; (drive) conducir; transportar; llevar; pasear; (turn) hacer girar. —*vi* girar; dar vueltas; ir en bicicleta. **to w. about,** cambiar de frente; volverse; cambiar de rumbo

wheelbarrow /'wil,bærou/ *n* carretilla, *f*

wheeled /wild/ *a* de... ruedas; con ruedas. **w. chair,** silla de ruedas, *f*

wheeling /'wilɪŋ/ *n* rodaje, *m; Mil.* conversión, *f;* (of birds) vuelos, *m pl,* vueltas, *f pl.* **free-w.,** rueda libre, *f*

wheelwright /'wil,rait/ *n* carpintero de carretas, ruedero, *m*

wheeze /wiz/ *vi* ser asmático, jadear, respirar fatigosamente, resollar

wheezing /'wizɪŋ/ *n* resuello, jadeo, *m;* respiración fatigada, *f*

whelp /welp/ *n* cachorro (-rra). —*vi and vt* parir

when /wen; *unstressed* wən/ *adv* cuando (interrogative, cuándo); (as soon as) tan pronto como, en cuanto; (meaning "and then") y luego, y entonces; (although) aunque. **I will see you w.** I return, Te veré cuando vuelva. **W. he came to see me he was already ill,** Cuando vino a verme estaba enfermo ya. **We returned a week ago, since w. I have not been out,** Volvimos hace ocho días y desde entonces no he salido. **Since w.?** ¿Desde cuándo?

whence /wens/ *adv* de donde (interrogative, de dónde); a donde (interrogative a dónde); por donde, de que; por lo que. **W. does he come?** ¿De dónde viene? **W. comes it that?** ¿Cómo es que...?

whenever /wen'evər/ *adv* cuando quiera que, siempre que; cada vez que, todas las veces que; cuando

where /wɛər/ *adv pron* donde (interrogative, dónde); en donde; en que (interrogative, en qué); (to where with verbs of motion) a donde (interrogative, a dónde); (from where with verbs of motion) de donde (interrogative, de dónde). **W. are you going to?** ¿A dónde va Vd.? **This is w. we get out,** (of a bus, etc.) Nos apeamos aquí

whereabouts /'wɛərə,bauts/ *adv* (interrogative) dónde; (relative) donde. —*n* paradero, *m*

whereas /wɛər'æz/ *conjunc* (inasmuch as) visto que, ya que; (although) mientras (que)

whereat /wɛər'æt/ *adv* por lo cual; a lo cual

whereby /wɛər'bai/ *adv* cómo; por qué; por el cual, con el cual

wherefore /'wɛər,fɔr/ *adv* (why) por qué; por lo cual. —*n* porqué, *m*

wherein /wɛər'ɪn/ *adv* en donde (interrogative, en dónde); en que (interrogative, en qué)

whereinto /wɛər'ɪntu/ *adv* en donde; dentro del cual; en lo cual

whereof /wɛər'ʌv/ *adv* de que; (whose) cuyo

whereon /wɛər'ɒn/ *adv* sobre que; en qué

whereto /wɛər'tu/ *adv* adonde; a lo que

whereupon /,wɛərə'pɒn/ *adv* dónde; sobre lo cual, con lo cual; en consecuencia de lo cual

wherever /wɛər'evər/ *adv* dondequiera (que), en cualquier sitio; adondequiera (que). **Sit w. you like,** Siéntate donde te parezca bien

wherewith /wɛər'wɪθ, -'wɪð/ *adv* con que (interrogative, con qué)

wherewithal /'wɛərwɪð,ɔl, -wɪθ-/ *n* lo necesario; dinero necesario, *m*

whet /wet/ *vt* (knives, etc.) afilar, amolar, aguzar; (curiosity, etc.) excitar, estimular

whether /'weðər/ *conjunc* si; que; sea que, ya que. **W. he will or no,** Que quiera, que no quiera. **w. or not,** si o no

whetstone /'wet,stoun/ *n* afiladera, amoladera, piedra de amolar, *f*

whetting /'wetɪŋ/ *n* aguzadura, amoladura, *f;* (of curiosity, etc.) estimulación, excitación, *f*

whey /wei/ *n* suero (de la leche), *m*

which /wɪtʃ/ *a and pron* cuál; cuáles, *mf pl;* que (interrogative, qué); el cual, *m;* la cual, *f;* lo cual, *neut;* los cuales, *m pl;* las cuales, *f pl;* el que, *m;* la que, *f;* lo que, *neut;* los que, *m pl;* las que, *f pl;* (who) quien. **all of w.,** todo lo cual, etc. **in w.,** en donde, en el que; donde. **the w.,** el cual, la cual, etc. **W. would you like?** ¿Cuál quieres? **The documents w. I have seen,** Los documentos que he visto. **W. way have we to go?** ¿Por dónde hemos de ir?

whichever /wɪtʃ'evər/ *a and pron* cualquiera (que), *mf;* cualesquiera, *mf pl;* el que, *m;* la que, *f;* (of persons only) quienquiera (que), *mf;* quienesquiera (que), *mf pl* **Give me w. you like,** Dame el que quieras. **I shall take w. of you would like to come,** Me llevaré a cualquiera de Vds. que guste de venir

whiff /wɪf/ *n* (of air) soplo, *m;* vaho, *m;* fragancia, *f*

while /wail/ *n* rato, *m;* momento, *m;* tiempo, *m.* **after a w.,** al cabo de algún tiempo, después de algún tiempo. **a little w. ago,** hace poco. **all this w.,** en todo este tiempo. **at whiles,** a ratos, de vez en cuando. **between whiles,** de cuando en cuando; entre tanto. **It is worth your w. to do it,** Vale la pena de hacerse. **Mary smiled the w.,** María mientras tanto se sonreía. **once in a w.,** de vez en cuando; en ocasiones

while /wail/ *conjunc* mientras (que); al (followed by an infinitive); al mismo tiempo que; a medida que; (although) aunque; si bien. **w. I was walking down the street,** mientras andaba por la calle, al andar yo por la calle. —*vt* **to w.** (away), pasar, entretener. **to w. away the time,** pasar el rato

whim /wɪm/ *n* capricho, antojo, *m;* manía, *f;* extravagancia, *f;* fantasía, *f*

whimper /'wɪmpər/ *n* quejido, sollozo, gemido, *m, vi* lloriquear, quejarse, sollozar, gemir

whimpering /'wɪmpərɪŋ/ *n* lloriqueo, llanto, *m, a* que lloriquea

whimsical /'wɪmzɪkəl/ *a* antojadizo, caprichoso; fantástico

whimsicality /,wɪmzɪ'kælɪti/ *n* capricho, *m,* extravagancia, *f;* fantasía, *f*

whimsically /'wɪmzɪkli/ *adv* caprichosamente; fantásticamente

whine /wain/ *vi* gimotear, lloriquear; quejarse

whining /'wainɪŋ/ *n* gimoteo, lloriqueo, *m;* quejumbres, *f pl.* —*a* que lloriquea; quejumbroso

whinny /'wɪni/ *n* relincho, hin, *m, vi* relinchar

whip /wɪp/ *n* azotar; pegar; *Cul.* batir; *Sew.* sobrecoser; (ropes, etc.) ligar; (defeat) vencer. —*vi* moverse rápidamente. **to w. down,** *vi* bajar volando, bajar corriendo. —*vt* arrebatar (de). **to w. in,** entrar precipitadamente (en), penetrar apresuradamente (en). **to w. off,** cazar a latigazos, despachar a golpes; (remove) quitar rápidamente; (persons) llevar corriendo, llevar aprisa. **to w. open,** abrir rápidamente. **to w. out,** *vt* (draw) sacar rápidamente; (utter) saltar diciendo (que); proferir. —*vi* escabullirse, escaparse, salir apresuradamente. **to w. round,** volverse de repente. **to w. up,** *vt* (horses, etc.) avivar con el látigo;

(snatch) coger de repente agarrar; (gather) reunir. —*vi* (mount) subir corriendo

whip /wɪp/ *n* azote, zurriago, *m;* (riding) látigo, *m.* **blow with a w.,** latigazo, *m.* **to have the w.-hand,** mandar, tener la sartén por el mango; tener la ventaja. **w.-cord,** tralla del látigo, *f*

whippet /'wɪpɪt/ *n* especie de perro (-rra) lebrero (-ra)

whipping /'wɪpɪŋ/ *n* paliza, *f,* vapuleo, azotamiento, *m.* **w. post,** picota, *f.* **w. top,** trompo, *m,* peonza, *f*

whirl /wɜrl/ *n* vuelta, *f,* giro, *m;* rotación, *f; Fig.* torbellino, *m.* —*vi* girar; dar vueltas; (dance) bailar, danzar. —*vt* hacer girar; dar vueltas (a); (carry) llevar rápidamente. **to w. along,** volar (por), pasar aprisa (por); dejar atrás los vientos, correr velozmente. **to w. past,** pasar volando (por); pasar como una exhalación. **to w. through,** atravesar rápidamente, cruzar volando

whirligig /'wɜrlɪˌgɪg/ *n* perinola, *f;* (merry-go-round) tiovivo, *m*

whirlpool /'wɜrlˌpul/ *n* vórtice, remolino, *m; Fig.* vorágine, *f*

whirlwind /'wɜrlˌwɪnd/ *n* torbellino, *m,* manga de viento, *f*

whirr /wɜr/ *n* zumbido, *m;* (of wings) ruido (de las alas), *m.* —*vi* girar; zumbar

whirring /'wɜrɪŋ/ *n* zumbido, *m;* ruido, *m.* —*a* que gira; que zumba

whisk /wɪsk/ *n* cepillo, *m; Cul.* batidor, *m;* (movement) movimiento rápido, *m.* —*vt Cul.* batir; (wag) menear, mover rápidamente; (with off, away) quitar rápidamente; sacudirse; arrebatar; (take away a person) llevarse (a). —*vi* moverse rápidamente; andar rápidamente

whiskered /'wɪskərd/ *a* bigotudo

whiskers /'wɪskɑrz/ *n pl* mostacho, *m,* patillas, barbas, *f pl;* (of a feline) bigotes, *m pl*

whisky /'wɪs-/ *n* güisqui, *m*

whisper /'wɪspər/ *n* cuchicheo, *m;* (rumour) voz, *f;* (of leaves, etc.) susurro, murmullo, *m.* —*vi* and *vt* cuchichear, hablar al oído; (of leaves, etc.) susurrar; (of rumors) murmurar. **in a w.,** al oído, en un susurro

whisperer /'wɪspərərsol/ *n* cuchicheador (-ra); (gossip) murmurador (-ra)

whispering /'wɪspərɪŋ/ *n* cuchicheo, *m;* susurro, *m;* (gossip) murmurio, *m.* **w. gallery,** galería de los murmullos, *f. Inf.* sala de los secretos, *f*

whistle /'wɪsəl/ *n* (sound) silbido, silbo, *m;* (instrument) pito, silbato, *m; Inf.* gaznate, *m.* —*vi* and *vt* silbar. **blast on the w.,** pitido, *m.* **to w. for,** llamar silbando; *Inf.* esperar sentado, buscar en vano

whistler /'wɪslər/ *n* silbador (-ra)

whistling /'wɪslɪŋ/ *n* silbido, *m, a* silbador

whit /wɪt/ *n* pizca, *f,* bledo, *m.* **not a w.,** ni pizca

white /waɪt/ *a* blanco; pálido; puro. —*n* color blanco, blanco, *m;* (pigment) pintura blanca, *f;* (whiteness) blancura, *f;* (of egg) clara (del huevo), *f;* (person) blanco, *m.* **Elizabeth went w.,** Isabel se puso pálida. **the w.,** (billiards) la blanca. **the w. of the eye,** lo blanco del ojo. **w. ant,** hormiga blanca, termita, *f.* **w. cabbage,** repollo, *m.* **w. caps,** (of waves) cabrillas, *f pl;* (of mountains) picos blancos, *m pl.* **w. clover,** trébol blanco, *m.* **w. corpuscle,** glóbulo blanco, *m.* **w. currant,** grosella blanca, *f.* **w. elephant,** elefante (-ta) blanco (-ca). **w. ensign,** pabellón blanco, *m.* **w.-faced,** de cara pálida. **w. fish,** pescado blanco, *m.* **w. flag,** bandera blanca, *f.* **w.-haired,** de pelo blanco. **w. heat,** calor blanco, *m,* candencia, *f;* ardor, *m.* **w. horses,** cabrillas, palomas, *f pl.* **w.-hot,** incandescente. **W. House, the,** la Casa Blanca, *f.* **w. lead,** albayalde, *m.* **w. lie,** mentira inocente, mentira oficiosa, mentira piadosa, la mentirilla, *f.* **w. man,** blanco, hombre de raza blanca, *m.* **the white man's burden,** la misión sagrada de la civilización blanca, *f.* **w. meat,** carne blanca, pechuga, *f.* **w. paper,** libro blanco, *m.* **w. sauce,** salsa blanca, *f.* **w. slave,** víctima de la trata de blancas, *f.* **w. slavery,** trata de blancas, *f.* **w. sugar,** azúcar blanco, azúcar de flor, *m.* **w. woman,** mujer de raza blanca, *f*

whiten /'waɪtn/ *vt* blanquear. —*vi* blanquearse

whiteness /'waɪtnɪs/ *n* blancura, *f;* palidez, *f;* pureza, *f;* Poet. nieve, *f*

whitening /'waɪtn̩ɪŋ/ *n* blanqueo, *m;* blanco de España, *m;* blanco para los zapatos, *m*

whitewash /'waɪt,wɒʃ/ *vt* blanquear, jalbegar, encalar; (Fig. of faults) disculpar, justificar

whitewashing /'waɪt,wɒʃɪŋ/ *n* blanqueo, *m,* encaladura, *f*

whither /'wɪðər/ *adv* (interrogative) adónde; (with a clause) adonde

whithersoever /ˌwɪðərsou'ɛvər/ *adv* adondequiera

whiting /'waɪtɪŋ/ *n* blanco de España, *m;* blanco para los zapatos, *m;* (fish) pescadilla, *f,* merlango, *m*

whitish /'waɪtɪʃ/ *a* blanquecino

whitlow /'wɪtlou/ *n* panadizo, *m*

Whitsun /'wɪtsən/ *a* de Pentecostés.

Whitsunday /'wɪt'sʌndeɪ/ *n* domingo de Pentecostés, *m*

Whitsuntide /'wɪtsən,taɪd/ *n* pascua de Pentecostés, *f*

whittle /'wɪtl/ *n* navaja, *f.* —*vt* cercenar, cortar; (sharpen) afilar, sacar punta (a); tallar; Fig. reducir. **to w. away, down,** Fig. reducir a nada

whizz /wɪz/ *n* silbido, zumbido, *m, vi* silbar, zumbar

whizzing /'wɪzɪŋ/ *n* silbido, *m, a* que zumba

who /hu/ *pron* (interrogative) quién, *mf;* quiénes, *mf pl;* (relative) quien, *mf;* quienes, *mf pl;* que; (in elliptical constructions the person that, etc.) el que, *m;* la que, *f;* los que, *m pl;* las que, *f pl*

whoa /wou/ *interj* ¡so!

whoever /hu'ɛvər/ *pron* quienquiera (que); cualquiera (que); quien.

whole /houl/ *a* (healthy) sano; (uninjured) ileso, entero; todo. —*n* todo, *m;* total, *m;* totalidad, *f;* conjunto, *m.* **on the w.,** por regla general, en general; en conjunto. **the w. week,** la semana entera, toda la semana. **w.-hearted,** sincero, genuino; entusiasta. **w.-heartedly,** de todo corazón. **w.-heartedness,** sinceridad, *f;* entusiasmo, *m.* **w. length,** a de cuerpo entero. **w. number,** número entero, *m*

wholemeal /'houl'mil/ *n* harina de trigo entero, *f, a* de trigo entero

wholeness /'houlnɪs/ *n* totalidad, *f;* integridad, *f;* todo, *m*

wholesale /'houl,seɪl/ *a Com.* al por mayor; en grueso; Fig. general; en masa. —*n* venta al por mayor, *f.* **w. price,** precio al por mayor, *m.* **w. trade,** comercio al por mayor, *m*

wholesaler /'houl,seɪlər/ *n* comerciante al por mayor, *mf* mercader de grueso, *m*

wholesome /'houlsəm/ *a* sano; saludable; (edifying) edificante

wholesomeness /'houlsəmnɪs/ *n* sanidad, *f;* lo sano; lo saludable

wholly /'houli/ *adv* completamente, enteramente, totalmente; integralmente; del todo

whom /hum/ *pron* quien, *mf;* a quienes, *mf pl;* (interrogative) a quién, *mf;* a quiénes, *mf pl;* al que, *m;* a la que, *f;* a los que, *m pl;* a las que, *f pl.* **from w.,** de quien; (interrogative) de quién. **the man w. you saw,** el hombre a quien viste

whoop /wup, wʊp/ *n* alarido, grito, *m;* estertor de la tos ferina, *m.* —*vi* dar gritos, chillar; /hup/ (whooping-cough) toser

whooping cough /'hupɪŋ/ *n* tos ferina, coqueluche, *f*

whore /hɔr/ *n* puta, ramera, *f*

whorl /wɜrl, wɔrl/ *n* (of a shell) espira, *f; Bot.* verticilo, *m;* (of a spindle) tortera, *f*

whorled /wɜrld, wɔrld/ *a Bot.* verticilado; (of shells) en espira

whose /huz/ *pron* cuyo, *m;* cuya, *f;* cuyos, *m pl;* cuyas, *f pl;* de quien, *mf;* de quienes, *mf pl;* (interrogative) de quién, de quiénes; **W. daughter is she?** ¿De quién es ella la hija? **This is the writer w. name I always forget,** Este es el autor cuyo nombre siempre olvido

whosoever /ˌhusou'ɛvər/ *pron.* See **whoever**

why /waɪ/ *adv* (interrogative) por qué; (on account of which) por el cual, *m;* por la cual, *f;* por lo cual, *neut;* por los cuales, *m pl;* por las cuales, *f pl;* (how) cómo. —*n* ni porqué, *m.;* ¡cómo!; ¡cómo!; ¡vaya! si. **not to know the why or wherefore,** no saber ni el porqué ni el cómo, no saber ni el qué ni el por qué. **Why! I have just come,** ¡Si no hago más de llegar! **Why not?** ¿Por qué no? ¡Cómo no!

wick /wɪk/ n mecha, torcida, f

wicked /'wɪkɪd/ a malo; malvado, perverso; pecaminoso; malicioso; (mischievous) travieso

wickedly /'wɪkɪdli/ adv mal; perversamente; maliciosamente

wickedness /'wɪkɪdnɪs/ n maldad, f; perversidad, f; pecado, m; (mischievousness) travesura, f

wicker /'wɪkər/ n mimbre, m, a de mimbre

wicket /'wɪkɪt/ n postigo, portillo, m; (half-door) media puerta, f; (at cricket) meta, f. **w.-keeper,** guardameta, m

wide /waid/ a ancho; (in measurements) de ancho; vasto; extenso; grande; amplio; (loose) holgado; (distant) lejos; liberal; general, comprensivo. —adv lejos; completamente. **far and w.,** por todas partes. **to be too w.,** ser muy ancho; estar muy ancho; (of garments) venir muy ancho. **two feet w.,** dos pies de ancho. **w.-awake,** muy despierto; despabilado; vigilante. **w.-eyed,** con los ojos muy abiertos; asombrado. **w.-open,** abierto de par en par

widely /'waidli/ adv extensamente; generalmente; (very) muy

widen /'waidn̩/ vt ensanchar; extender. —vi ensancharse; extenderse

widening /'waidnɪŋ/ n ensanche, m; extensión, f

widespread /'waid'spred/ a universal, generalizado; extenso; esparcido. **to become w.,** generalizarse

widow /'wɪdou/ n viuda, f. —vt dejar viuda; dejar viudo; Fig. privar. **to be a grass w.,** estar viuda. **to become a w.,** enviudar, perder al esposo. **widow's pension,** viudedad, f. **widow's weeds,** luto de viuda, m

widowed /'wɪdoud/ a viudo

widower /'wɪdouər/ n viudo, m. **to become a w.,** perder a la esposa, enviudar

widowhood /'wɪdou‚hud/ n viudez, f

width /wɪdθ/ n anchura, f; (of cloth) ancho, m; (of mind) liberalismo, m. **double w.,** (cloth) doble ancho, m

wield /wild/ vt (a scepter) empuñar; (power, etc.) ejercer; (a pen, sword) manejar

wife /waif/ n esposa, mujer, f; mujer, f; comadre, f. **husband and w.,** los cónyuges, los esposos. **old wives' tale,** cuento de viejas, m. **The Merry Wives of Windsor,** Las alegres comadres de Windsor. **to take to w.,** contraer matrimonio con, tomar como esposa (a)

wifely /'waifli/ a de esposa, de mujer casada; de mujer de su casa; conyugal

wig /wɪg/ n peluca, f; (hair) cabellera, f. **top wig,** peluquín, m. **wigmaker,** peluquero, m

wigged /wɪgd/ a con peluca, de peluca

wigging /'wɪgɪŋ/ n (scolding) peluca, f

wigwam /'wɪgwɒm/ n tienda de indios, f

wild /waild/ a (of animals, men, land) salvaje; (barren) desierto, yermo; (mountainous) riscoso, montañoso; (of plants, birds) silvestre; montés; (disarranged) en desorden, desarreglado; (complete) absoluto, completo; (dissipated) disipado; vicioso; (foolish) alocado; (of the sea) bravío; (of weather, etc.) borrascoso; (mad with delight, etc.) loco; (frantic, mad) frenético, loco; (with "talk," etc.) extravagante; insensato, desatinado; (shy) arisco; (incoherent) inconexo, incoherente; (frightened) alarmado, espantado; (wilful) travieso, indomable. —n tierra virgen, f; desierto, m; soledad, f. **It made me w.,** (angry) Me hizo rabiar. **to run w.,** volver al estado silvestre; (of persons) llevar una vida de salvajes; volverse loco. **to shoot w.,** errar el tiro. **to spread like w. fire,** propagarse como el fuego. **w. beast,** fiera, f. **w. boar,** jabalí, m. **w. cat,** gato montés, m. **w. duck,** pato silvestre, m. **w. goat,** cabra montesa, f. **w.-goose chase,** caza infructuosa, f; empresa quimérica, f. **w. oats,** avenas locas, f pl; Fig. indiscreciones de la juventud, f pl. **to sow one's w. oats,** andarse a la flor del berro

wilderness /'wɪldərnɪs/ n desierto, m; yermo, páramo, despoblado, m; soledad, f; (jungle) selva, f; (maze) laberinto, m; infinidad, f

wildly /'waildli/ adv en un estado salvaje; sin cultivo;

(rashly) desatinadamente; sin reflexión, sin pensar; (incoherently) incoherentemente; (stupidly, of looking, etc.) tontamente; (in panic) con ojos espantados, con terror en los ojos, alarmado

wildness /'waildnɪs/ n salvajez, f; estado silvestre, m; naturaleza silvestre, f; (ferocity) ferocidad, f; (of the wind, sea) braveza, f; (of the wind) violencia, f; (impetuosity) impetuosidad, f; (of statements, etc.) extravagancia, f; (incoherence) incoherencia, f; (disorder) desorden, m; (wilfulness, of children) travesuras, f pl; (of the expression) gesto espantado, m

wile /wail/ n estratagema, f, engaño, m, ardid, f

wilily /'wailɪli/ adv astutamente

wiliness /'wailɪnɪs/ n astucia, f

will /wɪl/ n voluntad, f; albedrío, m; (wish) deseo, m; (pleasure) discreción, f, placer, m; (legal document) testamento, m. **against my w.,** contra mi voluntad. **at w.,** a voluntad; a gusto; a discreción. **free w.,** libre albedrío, m. **of one's own free w.,** por su propia voluntad. **iron w.,** voluntad de hierro, f. **last w. and testament,** última disposición, última voluntad, f. **to do with a w.,** hacer con toda el alma, hacer con entusiasmo. **to make one's w.,** otorgar (hacer) su testamento. **w.-power,** fuerza de voluntad, f

will /wɪl/ vt querer; disponer, ordenar; (bequeath) legar, dejar en testamento, mandar; (oblige) sugestionar (a una persona) para que haga algo; hipnotizar. —vi aux querer; (As a sign of the future it is not translated separately in Spanish) **I w. come tomorrow,** Vendré mañana. **John does not approve, but I w. go,** Juan no lo aprueba pero yo quiero ir. **Do what you w.,** Haga lo que a Vd. le parezca bien, Haga lo que Vd. quiera; Haga lo que haga. **Boys w. be boys,** Los niños son siempre niños. **He w. not (won't) do it,** No lo hará; No quiere hacerlo

willful /'wɪlfəl/ a rebelde, voluntarioso; (of children) travieso; (of crimes, etc.) premeditado

willfully /'wɪlfəli/ adv voluntariosamente; intencionadamente; (of committing crimes) con premeditación

willfulness /'wɪlfəlnɪs/ n rebeldía, f; (obstinacy) terquedad, obstinación, f

William the Silent /'wɪlyəm/ Guillermo el Taciturno

willing /'wɪlɪŋ/ a dispuesto, inclinado; (serviceable) servicial; deseoso; espontáneo; complaciente; gustoso; (willingly) de buena gana. **to be w.,** estar dispuesto (a), querer; consentir (en)

willingly /'wɪlɪŋli/ adv de buena gana, con gusto

willingness /'wɪlɪŋnɪs/ n buena voluntad, f; deseo de servir, m; complacencia, f; (consent) consentimiento, m

will-o'-the-wisp /'wɪləðə'wɪsp/ n fuego fatuo, m

willow /'wɪlou/ n sauce, m. **weeping w.,** sauce llorón, m. **w.-pattern china,** porcelana de estilo chino, f. **w. tree,** sauce, m

willowy /'wɪloui/ a lleno de sauces; (slim) cimbreño, esbelto, alto y delgado

willy nilly /'wɪli 'nɪli/ adv de buen o mal grado, mal que bien

wilt /wɪlt/ vi (of plants) marchitarse, secarse; Fig. languidecer; ajarse. —vt marchitar; Fig. ajar; hacer languidecer

wily /'waili/ a astuto, chuzón

wimple /'wɪmpəl/ n toca, f

win /wɪn/ vt ganar; (reach) alcanzar, lograr; (a victory, etc.) llevarse; conquistar. —vi ganar; triunfar. —n triunfo, m. **to win back,** volver a ganar; recobrar

wince /wɪns/ vi retroceder, recular; (flinch) quejarse; (of a horse) respingar. —n respingo, m. **without wincing,** sin quejarse; estoicamente

winch /wɪntʃ/ n cabria, f; (handle) manubrio, f

wind /wɪnd/ n viento, m; aire, m; (flatulence) flatulencia, f; (breath) respiración, f, aliento, m; (idle talk) paja, f. **breath of w.,** soplo de viento, m. **following w.,** viento en popa, m. **high w.,** viento alto, viento fuerte, m. **land w.,** viento terrenal, m. **It's an ill w. that blows nobody good,** No hay mal que por bien no venga. **There is something in the w.,** Hay algo en el aire, Se trama algo. **to get w. of,** husmear. **to sail before the w.,** navegar de viento en popa. **The w. stiffened,** Refrescó el viento. **You took the w. out of his sails,** Le deshinchaste las velas. **w.-instrument,** instrumento de viento, m. **w.-proof,** a prueba del viento. **w.-swept,** expuesto a todos los vientos. **w. storm,** ventarrón, *m*

wind /waind/ *vi* serpentear; desfilar lentamente; torcerse. —*vt* (turn) dar vueltas (a); (a handle) manejar, mover; (a watch) dar cuerda (a); (wool, etc.) devanar, ovillar; (wrap) envolver; (of arms, embrace) rodear (con); (a horn) tocar. **to w. off,** devanar; desenrollar. **to w. round,** (wrap) envolver; (skirt) rodear; (embrace) ceñir con (los brazos); (pass by) pasar por; deslizarse por; (of snakes) enroscarse. **to w. up,** (a watch) dar cuerda (a); (thread) devanar; (conclude) concluir; *Com.* liquidar; (excite) agitar, emocionar

windbag /'wɪnd,bæg/ *n* pandero, *m*, sacamuelas, *mf*
winder /'waindər/ *n* (person) devanador (-ra); (machine) devanadera, *f*; (of a clock) llave, *f*
windfall /'wɪnd,fɔl/ *n* fruta caída del árbol, *f*; (good luck) breva, *f*; ganancia inesperada, lotería, *f*
windiness /'wɪndɪnɪs/ *n* tiempo ventoso, *m*; situación expuesta a todos los vientos, *f*; (of speech) pomposidad, verbosidad, *f*
winding /'waindɪŋ/ *a* tortuoso; (e.g., road) sinuoso; serpentino; en espiral. —*n* tortuosidad, *f*; meandro, recoveco, *m*, vuelta, curva, *f*. **w. sheet,** mortaja, *f*, sudario, *m*. **w. stair,** escalera de caracol, *f*. **w.-up,** conclusión, *f*; *Com.* liquidación, *f*
windlass /'wɪndləs/ *n* torno, *m*
windless /'wɪndlɪs/ *a* sin viento
windmill /'wɪnd,mɪl/ *n* molino de viento, *m*
window /'wɪndou/ *n* ventana, *f*; (of a shop) escaparate, *m*; (in a train, car, bank, etc.) ventanilla, *f*; (booking office) taquilla, *f*; (of a church) vidriera, *f*. **casement w.,** ventana, *f*. **sash w.,** ventana de guillotina, *f*. **small w.,** ventanilla, *f*. **stained glass w.,** vidriera, *f*. **to lean out of the w.,** asomarse a la ventana. **to look out of the w.,** mirar por la ventana. **w. blind,** (Venetian) persiana, *f*; transparente, *m*; (against the sun) toldo, *m*. **w.-dresser,** decorador (-ra) de escaparates. **w. frame,** marco de ventana, *m*. **w.-pane,** cristal (de ventana), *m*. **w.-shutter,** contraventana, *f*. **w.-sill,** repisa de la ventana, *f*, alféizar, *m*
windpipe /'wɪnd,paip/ *n* tráquea, *f*
windscreen /'wɪnd,skrin/ *n* parabrisas, guardabrisa, *m*. **w.-wiper,** limpiaparabrisas, limpiavidrios, *m*
windward /'wɪndwərd/ *n* barlovento, *m*. —*a* de barlovento. —*adv* a barlovento
windy /'wɪndi/ *a* ventoso; expuesto al viento; (of style) hinchado, pomposo. **it is w.,** Hace viento
wine /wain/ *n* vino, *m*; zumo fermentado (de algunas frutas), *m*. —*a* de vino; de vinos; para vino. **in w.,** *Cul.* en vino; (drunk) ebrio, borracho. **heavy w.,** vino fuerte, *m*. **light w.,** vino ligero, *m*. **local w.,** vino del país, *m*, **matured w.,** vino generoso, *m*. **red w.,** vino tinto, *m*. **thin w.,** vinillo, *m*. **white w.,** vino blanco, *m*. **w.-cellar,** bodega, cueva, *f*. **w.-colored,** de color de vino. **w.-cooler,** cubo para enfriar vinos, *m*. **w. country,** tierra de vino, *f*. **w. decanter,** garrafa para vino, *f*. **w.-grower,** vinicultor (-ra). **w.-growing,** *n* vinicultura, *f*. —*a* vinícola. **w. lees,** zupia, *f*. **w. merchant,** comerciante en vinos, *mf*. vinatero, *m*. **w.-press,** lagar, *m*. **w.-taster,** catavinos, *m*. **w. waiter,** bodeguero, *m*
wineskin /'wain,skɪn/ *n* bota, *f*, odre, pellejo, *m*
wing /wɪŋ/ *n* (of a bird and *Zool. Archit. Aer. Mil. Bot.*) ala, *f*; (flight) vuelo, *m*; *Theat.* bastidor, *m*; *Fig.* protección, *f*. —*vt* dar alas (a); llevar sobre las alas; (wound) herir en el ala; herir en el brazo; volar por. —*vi* volar. **beating of wings,** batir de alas, aleteo, *m*. **in the wings,** *Theat.* entre bastidores. **on the w.,** al vuelo. **to clip a (person's) wings,** cortar (or quebrar) las alas (a). **under his w.,** bajo su protección. **w.-case,** élitro (de un insecto), *m*. **w. chair,** sillón con orejas, *m*. **w.-commander,** teniente coronel de aviación, *m*. **w.-span,** (*Zool.* and *Aer.*) envergadura, *f*. **w.-spread,** extensión del ala, *f*. **w.-tip,** punta del ala, *f*
winged /wɪŋd/ *esp. Literary* 'wɪŋɪd/ *a* alado, con alas; (in compounds) de alas...; (swift) alado; (of style) elevado, alado
wink /wɪŋk/ *vi* (blink) pestañear; (as a signal, etc.) guiñar; (of stars, etc.) titilar, parpadear, centellear. —*vt* guiñar (el ojo). —*n* pestañeo, *m*; guiño, *m*. **not**

to sleep a w., no pegar los ojos. **to take forty winks,** echar una siesta. **to w. at,** guiñar el ojo (a); (ignore) hacer la vista gorda
winking /'wɪŋkɪŋ/ *n* (blinking) parpadeo, *m;* (as a signal) guiños, *m pl;* (of stars, etc.) titilación, *f*, pestañeo, *m.* —*a* (of stars, etc.) titilante. **like w.,** en un abrir y cerrar de ojos.
winner /'wɪnər/ *n* ganador (-ra); vencedor (-ra)
winning /'wɪnɪŋ/ *a* ganador; vencedor; (attractive) encantador. —*n* ganancia, *f*. **w. number,** número galardonado, número premiado, número vencedor, *m*. **w.-post,** meta, *f*. **w. side,** *Sports.* equipo vencedor, *m;* (politics, etc.) partido vencedor, *m*
winnings /'wɪnɪŋz/ *n* ganancias, *f pl*
winnow /'wɪnou/ *vt* aventar, abalear; *Fig.* separar
winnower /'wɪnouər/ *n* aventador (-ra)
winnowing /'wɪnouɪŋ/ *n* abaleo, aventamiento, *m;* *Fig.* separación, *f*. **w. fork,** bieldo, *m*. **w. machine,** aventador mecánico, *m*
winsome /'wɪnsəm/ *a* sanduguero; dulce, encantador
winsomeness /'wɪnsəmnɪs/ *n* sandunga, *f*; encanto, *m*, dulzura, *f*
winter /'wɪntər/ *n* invierno, *m*. —*a* de invierno; hiemal. —*vi* pasar el invierno, invernar. —*vt* (of cattle, etc.) guardar en invierno. **in w.,** en invierno, durante el invierno. **w. clothes,** ropa de invierno, *f*. **w. palace,** palacio de invierno, *m*. **w. quarters,** invernadero, *m*. **w. season,** invierno, *m;* temporada de invierno, *f*. **w. sleep,** invernada, *f*. **w. solstice,** solsticio hiemal, *m*. **w. sports,** deportes de nieve, *m pl*. **w. wheat,** trigo de invierno, *m*
wintry /'wɪntri/ *a* de invierno; invernal; (of a smile, etc.) glacial
wipe /waip/ *vt* limpiar; (rub) frotar; (dry) secar; (remove) quitar. —*n* limpión, *m*; (blow) golpe de lado, *m*. **to w. one's eyes,** enjugarse las lagrimas. **to w. off, out,** limpiar; (remove) quitar; (erase) borrar; (kill) destruir completamente, exterminar; (a military force) destrozar; (a debt) cancelar
wire /waiⁿr/ *n* alambre, *m*; hilo metálico, *m*; telégrafo (eléctrico), *m*; *Inf.* telegrama, *m*. —*vt* atar con alambre; (fence) alambrar; (snare) coger con lazo de alambre; (of electrical equipment, etc.) instalar; (telegraph) telegrafiar. —*vi* (telegraph) telegrafiar. **barbed w.,** alambre espinoso, *m*. **live w.,** alambre cargado (de electricidad), *m;* (person) fuerza viva, *f*. **w.-cutters,** cortaalambres, *m pl*. **w.-entanglement,** *Mil.* alambrada, *f*. **w. fence,** alambrera, *f*, cercado de alambre, *m*. **w. gauze,** tela metálica, *f*. **w. nail,** punta de París, *f*. **w.-netting,** malla de alambre, *f*; alambrado, *m*. **w.-pulling,** influencias secretas, *f pl;* intrigas políticas, *f pl*
wiredraw /'waiⁿr,drɔ/ *vt* estirar (alambre), tirar (el hilo de hierro, plata, etc.); (arguments, etc.) sutilizar
wiredrawer /'waiⁿr,drɔər/ *n* estirador, *m*
wiredrawing /'waiⁿr,drɔɪŋ/ *n* tirado, *m;* *Fig.* sutileza, *f*
wireless /'waiⁿrlɪs/ *a* sin hilos; (of a message) radiotelegráfico; por radio. —*n* telegrafía sin hilos, *f*; radiotelefonía, *f;* (telegram) radiocomunicación, *f;* (broadcasting) radio, *f*. —*vt* radiotelegrafiar. **Let's listen to the w.,** Vamos a escuchar la radio. **portable w.,** radio portátil, *f*. **w. engineer,** ingeniero radiotelegrafista, *m*. **w. enthusiast,** radioaficionado (-da). **w. licence,** permiso de radiorreceptor, *m*. **w. operator,** radiotelegrafista, *mf*. **w. room,** cuarto de telegrafía sin hilos, *m*. **w. set,** aparato de radio, *m*. **w. station,** estación de radiotelegrafía, *f;* (broadcasting) radioemisora, *f*. **w. telegraph,** telégrafo sin hilos, *m*. **w. telegraphy,** telegrafía sin hilos, radiotelegrafía, *f*. **w. telephony,** telefonía sin hilos, *f*. **w. transmission,** radioemisión, *f*
wiretap /'waiⁿr,tæp/ *vi* poner escucha. —*vt* poner escucha a
wiring /'waiⁿrɪŋ/ *n* instalación de alambres eléctricos, *f*
wiry /'waiⁿri/ *a* semejante a un alambre; (of persons) nervudo
wisdom /'wɪzdəm/ *n* sabiduría, *f*; (learning) saber, *m;* (judgment) juicio, *m*. **Book of W.,** Libro de la Sabiduría, *m*. **w.-tooth,** muela del juicio, *f*

wise /waiz/ *a* sabio; juicioso, prudente; (informed) enterado, informado. **a w. man,** un sabio. **in no w.,** de ningún modo. **the W. Men of the East,** los magos. **w. guy,** *Inf.* toro corrido, *m*

wisely /'waizli/ *adv* sabiamente; prudentemente, con prudencia

wish /wɪʃ/ *n* deseo, *m.* **Best wishes for the New Year,** Los mejores deseos para el Año Nuevo. **w.-bone,** espoleta, *f*

wish /wɪʃ/ *vt* querer; desear; ansiar; (with "good morning', etc.) dar. **I w. he were here!** ¡Ojalá que estuviera aquí! **Theresa wishes us to go,** Teresa quiere que vayamos. **I w. it had happened otherwise,** Quisiera que las cosas hubiesen pasado de otra manera. **I w. you would make less noise,** Me gustaría que hicieses menos ruido. **I only w. one thing,** Solamente deseo una cosa. **I w. you good luck,** Te deseo mucha suerte. **I wished him a merry Christmas,** Le deseé unas Pascuas muy felices, Le felicité las Pascuas. **to w. a prosperous New Year,** desear un próspero Año Nuevo. **to w. good-by,** despedirse (de). **to w. good day,** dar los buenos días. **to w. for,** desear

wisher /'wɪʃər/ *n* el que, *m,* (*f,* la que) desea, deseador (-ra)

wishful /'wɪʃfəl/ *a* deseoso; ansioso; ávido. **w. thinking,** ilusiones, *f pl;* optimismo injustificado, optimismo exagerado, *m*

wisp /wɪsp/ *n* mechón, *m;* jirón, *m;* trozo, pedazo, *m*

wistaria /wɪ'stɪəriə, -'stɛər-/ *n* vistaria, *f*

wistful /'wɪstfəl/ *a* ansioso; triste; patético; (envious) envidioso; (regretful) de pesar; (remorseful) de remordimiento; (thoughtful) pensativo

wistfully /'wɪstfəli/ *adv* con ansia; tristemente; patéticamente; con envidia; con pesar; con remordimiento; pensativo

wistfulness /'wɪstfəlnɪs/ *n* ansia, *f;* tristeza, *f;* (envy) envidia, *f;* (regret) pesar, *m;* (remorse) remordimiento, *m;* (thoughtfulness) lo pensativo, lo distraído

wit /wɪt/ *n* (reason) juicio, *m;* agudeza, gracia, *f,* rasgo de ingenio, *m;* ingenio, *m;* inteligencia, *f,* talento, *m;* (person) hombre de ingenio, *m;* mujer de ingenio, *f.* **my five wits,** mis cinco sentidos. **to be at one's wits' end,** no saber qué hacer. **to live by one's wits,** ser caballero de industria. **to lose one's wits,** perder el juicio

witch /wɪtʃ/ *n* bruja, *f.* **witches' sabbath,** aquelarre, *m.* **w.-doctor,** hechizador, mago, *m.* **witch-hazel,** carpe, *m;* loción de carpe, *f*

witchcraft /'wɪtʃˌkræft/ *n* brujería, *f;* sortilegio, encantamiento, *m*

witchery /'wɪtʃəri/ *n* brujería, *f; Fig.* encanto, *m,* magia, *f*

with /wɪθ, wɪð/ *prep* con; en compañía de; en casa de; (against) contra; (among) entre; en; (by) por; (towards) hacia; para con; (according to) según; (notwithstanding) a pesar de; a; (concerning) con respecto a; en el caso de. **Rose is w. Antony,** Rosa está con Antony. **He was w. his dog,** Estaba acompañado por su perro. **He pulled at it w. both hands,** Lo tiró con las dos manos. **filled w. fear,** lleno de miedo. **to shiver w. cold,** temblarse de frío. **the girl w. golden hair,** la muchacha del pelo dorado. **They killed it w. one blow,** Lo mataron de un solo golpe. **It rests w. you to decide,** Tú tienes que decidirlo; Te toca a tí decidirlo. **to begin w.,** *adv* para empezar; *v* empezar por. **w. all speed,** a toda prisa. **to part w.,** desprenderse de; (of people) despedirse de; separarse de. **w. that...,** (at once) en esto... (disease and poverty, etc.) **are still with us,** están todavía en el mundo

withal /wɪð'ɔl, wɪθ-/ *adv* además; al mismo tiempo. —*prep* con

withdraw /wɪð'drɔ, wɪθ-/ *vt* retirar; (words) retractar; (remove) quitar, privar (de); (a legal action) apartar. —*vi* retirarse; retroceder; apartarse; irse

withdrawal /wɪð'drɔəl, wɪθ-/ *n* retirada, *f;* (retirement) retiro, *m;* apartamiento, *m*

withdrawn /wɪð'drɔn, wɪθ-/ *a* (abstracted) ensimismado, meditabundo

wither /'wɪðər/ *vi* marchitarse, secarse, ajarse. —*vt* marchitar, secar, ajar; *Fig.* hacer languidecer, matar; (snub) avergonzar

withered /'wɪðərd/ *a* marchito, mustio; muerto; (of persons) acartonado, seco

witheredness /'wɪðərdnɪs/ *n* marchitez, *f;* sequedad, *f*

withering /'wɪðərɪŋ/ *a* que marchita; (scorching) abrasador, ardiente; (scornful) despreciativo, desdeñoso; (biting) mordaz, cáustico

withers /'wɪðərz/ *n* cruz, *f*

withhold /wɪθ'hould, wɪð-/ *vt* retener; detener; (restrain) refrenar; apartar; (refuse) negar; abstenerse de; (refuse to reveal) ocultar

withholding /wɪθ'houldɪŋ, wɪð-/ *n* detención, *f;* (refusal) negación, *f*

within /wɪð'ɪn, wɪθ-/ *adv* dentro, adentro; en el interior; en casa; *Fig.* en su interior. **He stayed w.,** Se quedó dentro. **Is Mrs. González w.?** ¿Está en casa la Sra. González?

within /wɪð'ɪn, wɪθ-/ *prep* dentro de; el interior de; en; entre; (within range of) al alcance de; a la distancia de; (near) cerca de; a poco de; (of time) en el espacio de, en; dentro de; (almost) por poco, casi. **He was w. an inch of being killed,** Por poco le matan. **to be w. hearing,** estar al alcance de la voz. **seen from w.,** visto desde dentro. **twice w. a fortnight,** dos veces en quince días. **w. himself,** por sus adentros, entre sí. **w. an inch of,** *Fig.* a dos dedos de. **w. a few miles of Edinburgh,** a unas millas de Edimburgo. **w. a short distance,** en una corta distancia; a poca distancia

without /wɪð'aut, wɪθ-/ *prep* sin; falto de; (outside) fuera de; (beyond) más allá de. —*adv* exteriormente; por fuera; hacia afuera; fuera. **It goes w. saying,** No hay que decir. **w. more ado,** sin más ni más. **w. my knowledge,** sin que yo lo supiese. **w. regard for,** sin miramientos por. **w. saying more,** sin decir más. **without batting an eyelash,** sin sobresaltos

withstand /wɪθ'stænd, wɪð-/ *vt* resistir, oponerse (a); soportar

withstanding /wɪθ'stændɪŋ, wɪð-/ *n* resistencia, oposición (a), *f*

witless /'wɪtlɪs/ *a* sin seso, tonto, necio

witness /'wɪtnɪs/ *n* (evidence) testimonio, *m;* (person) testigo, *mf;* espectador (-ra). **in w. whereof,** en fe de lo cual. **to bear w.,** atestiguar, dar testimonio. **to bring forward witnesses,** hacer testigos. **w. my hand,** en fe de lo cual, firmo. **w.-box,** puesto de los testigos, *m.* **w. for the defence,** testigo de descargo, *mf.* **w. for the prosecution,** testigo de cargo, *mf*

witness /'wɪtnɪs/ *vt* (show) mostrar, señalar; (see) ser testigo de, ver, presenciar; *Law.* atestiguar. —*vi* dar testimonio; servir de testigo

witticism /'wɪtəˌsɪzəm/ *n* rasgo de ingenio, donaire, *m,* agudeza, *f*

wittily /'wɪtli/ *adv* ingeniosamente, donairosamente, agudamente

wittiness /'wɪtnɪs/ *n* viveza de ingenio, donosura, *f*

witty /'wɪti/ *a* salado, gracioso. **w. sally,** agudeza, *f*

wizard /'wɪzərd/ *n* mago, hechicero, *m*

wizardry /'wɪzərdri/ *n* magia, *f*

wizened /'wɪzənd/ *a* seco, arrugado; (of persons) acartonado

wobble /'wɒbəl/ *vi* tambalearse, balancearse; (quiver) temblar; oscilar; *Mech.* galopar; (stagger) titubear; *Fig.* vacilar

wobbly /'wɒbli/ *a* que se bambolea; inestable; *Fig.* vacilante

woe /wou/ *n* dolor, *m;* congoja, aflicción, *f;* mal, desastre, infortunio, *m.* **Woe is me!** ¡Ay de mí! ¡Desdichado de mí!

woebegone /'woubɪˌgɔn/ *a* angustiado

woeful /'woufəl/ *a* triste; doloroso; funesto

woefully /'woufəli/ *adv* tristemente; dolorosamente

wolf /wulf/ *n* lobo (-ba). **a w. in sheep's clothing,** un lobo en piel de cordero. **to cry w.,** gritar «el lobo!» **to keep the w. from the door,** ponerse a cubierto del hambre. **w.-cub,** lobezno, *m.* **w.-hound,** perro lobo, *m.* **w. pack,** manada de lobos, *f*

wolfish /'wulfɪʃ/ *a* lobuno, de lobo

wolfram /'wulfrəm, 'vɒl-/ *n* volframio, *m*

woman /'wumən/ *n* mujer, *f;* hembra, *f;* (lady-in-waiting) dama de servicio, *f.* **a fine figure of a w.,** una real hembra. **w. doctor,** médica, *f.* **w.-hater,** misógino, *m.* **w. of the town,** mujer de la vida airada, *f.* **w. of the world,** mujer de mundo, *f*

womanhood /'wʊmənˌhʊd/ *n* feminidad, *f;* sexo feminino, *m*

womanish /'wʊmənɪʃ/ *a* afeminado

womankind /'wʊmənˌkaind/ *n* el sexo femenino, las mujeres

womanliness /'wʊmənlɪnɪs/ *n* feminidad, *f;* carácter femenino, *m*

womanly /'wʊmənli/ *a* femenino, de mujer

womb /wum/ *n* útero, *m*, matriz, *f; Fig.* seno, *m*

women's dormitory /'wɪmɪnz/ *n* residencia para señoritas, *f*

wonder /'wʌndər/ *n* maravilla, *f;* prodigio, *m;* portento, milagro, *m;* (surprise) sorpresa, *f;* admiración, *f;* asombro, *m;* (problem) enigma, *m;* misterio, *m.* —*vi* admirarse, asombrarse, maravillarse; sorprenderse. —*vt* (ask oneself) preguntarse; desear saber. **I wondered what the answer would be,** Me preguntaba qué sería la respuesta. **It is no w. that...,** No es mucho que..., No es sorprendente que... **It is one of the wonders of the world,** Es una de las maravillas del mundo. **to work wonders,** hacer milagros. **to w. at,** asombrarse de, maravillarse de; sorprenderse de. **w.-working,** milagroso

wonderful /'wʌndərfəl/ *a* maravilloso; magnífico; asombroso; *Inf.* estupendo

wonderfully /'wʌndərfli/ *adv* maravillosamente; admirablemente

wondering /'wʌndərɪŋ/ *a* de asombro, sorprendido; perplejo

wonderingly /'wʌndərɪŋli/ *adv* con asombro

wonderland /'wʌndərˌlænd/ *n* mundo fantástico, *m;* reino de las hadas, *m;* país de las maravillas, *m.* **"Alice in W.,"** Alicia en el país de las maravillas

wonderment /'wʌndərmənt/ *n.* See **wonder**

wondrous /'wʌndrəs/ *a* maravilloso. —*adv* extraordinariamente

wont /wɔnt, wount/ *n* costumbre, *f.* —*vi* soler. **as he was w.,** Como solía

won't /wount/. See **will not**

wonted /'wɔntɪd, 'woun-/ *a* sólito, acostumbrado

woo /wu/ *vt* galantear; hacer la corte (a), solicitar amores a; cortejar; *Fig.* solicitar; perseguir

wood /wʊd/ *n* bosque, *m;* madera, *f;* (for the fire, etc.) leña, *f;* (cask) barril, *m.* —*a* de madera; (of the woods) selvático. **dead w.,** ramas muertas, *f pl; Fig.* paja, *f.* **w. alcohol,** alcohol metílico, *m.* **w.-anemone,** anémona de los bosques, *f.* **w.-block floor,** entarimado, *m.* **w.-borer,** xiló-fago, *m.* **w.-carver,** tallista, *mf* **w.-carving,** talla en madera, *f.* **w.-craft,** conocimiento del campo, *m.* **w.-cut,** grabado en madera, *m.* **w.-cutter,** leñador, *m.* **w.-engraver,** grabador (-ra) en madera. **w.-engraving,** grabado al boj, *m.* **w.-fibre,** fibra de madera, *f.* **w.-louse,** cochinilla, *f.* **w.-nymph,** ninfa de los bosques, *f.* **w.-pigeon,** paloma torcaz, *f.* **w.-pile,** pila de leña, leñera, *f.* **w.-pulp,** pulpa de madera, *f.* **w.-shaving,** acepilladura, *f.* **w.-splinter,** tasquil, *m,* astilla, *f.* **w.-wind,** *Mus.* madera, *f.* **w.-worm,** carcoma, *f*

wooded /'wʊdɪd/ *a* provisto de árboles, plantado de árboles, arbolado

wooden /'wʊdn/ *a* de madera; de palo; (of smiles) mecánico; (stiff) indiferente, sin emoción; (clumsy) torpe; (of character) inflexible. **He has a w. leg,** Tiene una pata de palo. **w. beam,** madero, *m;* viga de madera, *f.* **w. bridge,** pontón, *m.* **w. galley,** *Print.* galerín, *m*

woodland /*n.* 'wʊdˌlænd; *a* -lənd/ *n* bosques, *m pl.* —*a* de bosque; silvestre

woodpecker /'wʊdˌpɛkər/ *n* pájaro carpintero, picamaderos, *m*

woodshed /'wʊdˌʃɛd/ *n* leñera, *f*

woodwork /'wʊdˌwɜrk/ *n* maderaje, *m;* molduras, *f pl;* carpintería, *f*

woody /'wʊdi/ *a* leñoso; arbolado, con árboles. **w. tissue,** tejido leñoso, *m*

wooer /'wuər/ *n* pretendiente, galanteador, *m*

woof /wuf/ *n* trama, *f*

wooing /'wuɪŋ/ *n* galanteo, *m*

wool /wʊl/ *n* lana, *f.* —*a* de lana; lanar. **to go w.-gathering,** estar distraído. **to pull the w. over a person's eyes,** engañar como a un chino. **w.-bearing,** lanar. **w.-carding,** cardadura de lana, *f.* **w.-growing,** cría de ganado lanar, *f.* **w. merchant,** comerciante en lanas, *mf,* lanero, *m.* **w.-pack,** fardo de lana, *m.* **w. trade,** comercio de lana, *m*

woollen /'wʊlən/ *a* de lana; lanar. —*n* paño de lana, *m;* género de punta de lana, *m*

woolliness /'wʊlɪnɪs/ *n* lanosidad, *f*

woolly /'wʊli/ *a* lanudo, lanoso; de lana; *Bot.* velloso; (of hair) lanoso, crespo. —*n* género de punta de lana, *m;* (sweater) jersey, *m*

word /wɜrd/ *n* palabra, *f; Gram.* vocablo, *m; Theol.* verbo, *m;* (maxim) sentencia, *f,* dicho, *m;* (message) recado, *m;* (news) aviso, *m,* noticias, *f pl;* (Mil. command) voz de mando, *f;* (order) orden, *f;* (password) contraseña, *f;* (term) término, *m.* —*vt* expresar; formular; (draw up) redactar; escribir. **He was as good as his w.,** Fue hombre de palabra. **I do not know how to w. this letter,** No sé cómo redactar esta carta. **in a w.,** en una palabra; en resumidas cuentas. **by w. of mouth,** de palabra. **I give you my w. for it,** Le doy mi palabra de honor. **in other words,** en otros términos; en efecto. **the W. (of God),** el Verbo (de Dios). **to have a w. with,** hablar con; conversar con; entablar conversación con. **to leave w.,** dejar recado. **to have words with,** tener palabras con. **to keep one's w.,** cumplir su palabra

word index *n* índice de vocablos, *m*

wordiness /'wɜrdɪnɪs/ *n* palabrería, verbosidad, *f*

wording /'wɜrdɪŋ/ *n* fraseología, *f;* expresión, *f;* estilo, *m;* (terms) términos, *m pl;* (drawing up) redacción, *f*

word processing /'wɜrd ˌprɒsɛsɪŋ/ *n* tratamiento de textos, procesamiento de textos, *m*

wordy /'wɜrdi/ *a* verboso, prolijo

work /wɜrk/ *n* trabajo, *m;* (sewing) labor, *f;* (literary, artistic production and theological) obra, *f;* (behavior) acción, *f,* acto, *m;* (employment) empleo, *m;* (business affairs) negocios, *m pl; pl* **works,** obras, fortificaciones, *f, pl;* obras públicas, *f pl;* construcciones, *f pl;* (of a machine) mecanismo, *m;* motor, *m;* (factory) fábrica, *f,* taller, *m.* **w. of art,** obra de arte. **w. accident,** accidente del trabajo, *m.* **w.-bag,** bolsa de costura, *f,* saco de labor, *m.* **w.-box,** (on legs) costurero, *m;* (small) neceser de costura, *m.* **w.-people,** obreros (-as). **w.-room,** taller, *m;* (study) estudio, *m;* (for sewing) cuarto de costura, *m.* **w.-table,** banco de taller, *m;* (for writing) mesa de escribir, *f*

work /wɜrk/ *vi* trabajar; *Sew.* hacer labor de aguja, coser; (embroider) bordar; *Mech.* funcionar, marchar; (succeed) tener éxito; ser eficaz; (be busy) estar ocupado; (be employed) tener empleo; (of the face) demudarse, torcerse; (ferment) fermentar; (operate) obrar *vt* trabajar; operar, hacer funcionar; mover; (control) manejar; (a mine) explotar; (embroider) bordar; (wood) tallar; (a problem) resolver; calcular; (iron, etc.) labrar; (the soil) cultivar; (a ship) maniobrar; (do) hacer; (bring about) efectuar; traer consigo; producir; (agitate oneself) agitarse, emocionarse, excitarse. **to w. in repoussé,** repujar. **to w. loose,** desprenderse. **to w. one's passage,** trabajar por el pasaje. **to w. overtime,** trabajar horas extraordinarias. **to w. two ways,** ser espada de dos filos. **to w. at,** trabajar en; ocuparse en; dedicarse a; elaborar. **to w. in,** *vt* introducir; insinuar. —*vi* combinarse. **to w. into,** penetrar en. **to w. off,** usar, emplear; (get rid of) deshacerse de, librarse de. **to w. on, upon,** influir en; obrar sobre; estar ocupado en. **to w. out,** *vt* calcular; resolver; (a mine, topic, etc.) agotar; (develop) elaborar, desarrollar; trazar, planear; (find) encontrar. —*vi* llegar (a); resultar; venir a ser. **to w. up,** crear; (promote) fomentar; producir; (excite) agitar, excitar; (fashion) dar forma (a), labrar; (finish) terminar

workable /'wɜrkəbəl/ *a* laborable; factible, practicable; (of a mine) explotable

workableness /'wɜrkəbəlnɪs/ *n* practicabilidad, *f*

workaday /'wɜrkəˌdei/ *a* de todos los días; prosaico

workbench /'wɜrkˌbɛntʃ/ banco de mecánico, *f,*

banco de taller, banco de trabajo, *m,* mesa de trabajo, *f*

workday /'wɜrk,dei/ *n* día de trabajo, día laborable, *m*

worker /'wɜrkər/ *n* trabajador (-ra); (manual) obrero (-ra); (of a machine) operario (-ia). **w.-ant,** hormiga obrera, *f.* **w.-bee,** abeja obrera, *f*

workhouse /'wɜrk,haus/ *n* asilo, *m*

working /'wɜrkɪŋ/ *a* de trabajo; (of capital) de explotación; trabajador, que trabaja; obrero. —*n* trabajo, *m;* (of a machine, organism, institution) funcionamiento, *m;* explotación, *f;* (of a mine) laboreo, *m;* (of a ship) maniobra, *f;* (of metal, stone, wood) labra, *f;* operación, *f;* (result) efecto, resultado, *m;* (calculation) cálculo, *m.* **"Not w.,"** «No funciona.» **to be in w. order,** funcionar bien. **w.-class,** clase obrera, *f;* pueblo, *m.* **w.-clothes,** ropa de trabajo, *f.* **w.-day,** día de trabajo, *m.* **w.-hours,** horas de trabajo, horas hábiles, *f pl.* **w. hypothesis,** postulado, *m.* **w.-man,** obrero, *m;* trabajador, *m.* **w.-out,** elaboración, *f;* ensayo, *m.* **w.-plan,** plan de trabajo, *m.* **w.-woman,** obrera, *f;* trabajadora, *f*

workless /'wɜrklɪs/ *a* sin trabajo

workman /'wɜrkmən/ *n* obrero, *m;* (agricultural) labrador, *m*

workmanlike /'wɜrkmən,laik/ *a* bien hecho, bien acabado; (clever) hábil

workmanship /'wɜrkmən,ʃɪp/ *n* trabajo, *m;* manufactura, *f;* hechura, *f;* (cleverness) habilidad, *f*

works /wɜrks/ *n* fábrica, *f*

workshop /'wɜrk,ʃɒp/ *n* taller, *m*

world /wɜrld/ *n* mundo, *m.* **For all the w. as if...,** Exactamente como si... **to see the w.,** ver mundo. **to treat the w. as one's oyster,** ponerse el mundo por montera. **w. without end,** por los siglos de los siglos. **w.-power,** potencia mundial, gran potencia, *f.* **w.-wide,** mundial, universal

world almanac *n* compendio mundial, *m*

worldliness /'wɜrldlɪnɪs/ *n* mundanería, *f,* conocimiento del mundo, *m;* frivolidad, vanidad mundana, *f;* egoísmo, *m;* prudencia, *f*

worldly /'wɜrldli/ *a* de este mundo; mundano; humano; profano; frívolo. **to be w.-wise,** tener mucho mundo

worm /wɜrm/ *n* gusano, *m;* lombriz, *f; Chem.* serpentín, *m;* (of a screw) tornillo sinfín, *m;* (person) gusano, *m; Fig.* gusano roedor, remordimiento, *m.* **intestinal w.,** lombriz intestinal, *f,* gusano de la conciencia. **w.-eaten,** carcomido. **w.-hole,** picadura de gusano, lombriguera, *f.* **w.-powder,** polvos antihelmínticos, *m pl.* **w.-shaped,** vermiforme

worm /wɜrm/ *vt* (a dog) dar un vermífugo (a). —*vi* arrastrarse como un gusano. **to w. one's way into,** deslizarse en; *Fig.* insinuarse en, introducirse en. **to w. out,** (secrets, information) sonsacar

wormwood /'wɜrm,wʊd/ *n* ajenjo, *m*

wormy /'wɜrmi/ *a* gusanoso, lleno de gusanos

worn /wɔrn/ *a* (of garments) raído; estropeado; gastado; (of paths) trillado; (of the face) arrugado, cansado. **w. out,** acabado; muy usado; (tired) rendido; (exhausted) agotado

worrier /'wɜriər/ *n* inquietador (-ra); receloso (-sa); aprensivo (-va)

worry /'wɜri/ *n* preocupación, inquietud, ansiedad, *f;* problema, cuidado, *m.* —*vt* (prey) zamarrear; preocupar, inquietar; molestar; importunar. —*vi* estar preocupado, estar intranquilo, inquietarse. **Don't worry,** Pierda cuidado, No pase cuidado

worrying /'wɜriɪŋ/ *a* inquietante, perturbador; molesto

worse /wɜrs/ *a compar* peor; inferior. —*adv* peor; menos. —*n* lo peor. **so much the w.,** tanto peor. **to be w. off,** estar peor; estar en peores circunstancias; ser menos feliz. **to be the w. for wear,** ser muy usado; estar ajado; ser ya viejo. **to grow w.,** empeorarse; (of an ill person) ponerse peor. **w. and w.,** de mal en peor, peor que peor. **w. than ever,** peor que nunca

worsen /'wɜrsən/ *vt* agravar, hacer peor; exasperar. —*vi* agravarse, empeorarse; exasperarse

worsening /'wɜrsənɪŋ/ *n* agravación, *f,* empeoramiento, *m;* exasperación, *f*

worship /'wɜrʃɪp/ *n* culto, *m;* adoración, *f;* veneración, *f.* —*vt* adorar; reverenciar. —*vi* adorar; rezar; dar culto (a). **place of w.,** edificio de culto, *m.* **Your W.,** vuestra merced

worshipful /'wɜrʃɪpfəl/ *a* venerable, respetable

worshipper /'wɜrʃɪpər/ *n* adorador (-ra); *pl* **worshippers,** (in a church, etc.) fieles, *m pl,* congregación, *f*

worshipping /'wɜrʃɪpɪŋ/ *n* adoración, *f,* culto, *m*

worst /wɜrst/ *a* el (la, etc.) peor; más malo. —*adv* el (la, etc.) peor. —*n* el (la, etc.) peor; lo peor. —*vt* vencer, derrotar; triunfar sobre **If the w. comes to the w.,** En el peor de los casos. **The w. of it is that...,** Lo peor es que... **to have the w. of it,** salir perdiendo, llevar la peor parte

worsted /'wʊstɪd, 'wɜrstɪd/ *n* estambre, *m, a* de estambre

worth /wɜrθ/ *n* valor, *m;* precio, *m;* mérito, *m, a* (que) vale; de precio de; cuyo valor es de; equivalente a; (que) merece; digno de. **He bought six hundred pesetas w. of sweets,** Compró seiscientas pesetas de dulces. **He sang for all he was w.,** Cantó con toda su alma. **It is w. seeing,** Es digno de verse, Vale la pena de verse. **to be w.,** valer. **to be w. while,** valer la pena, merecer la pena

worthily /'wɜrðili/ *adv* dignamente

worthiness /'wɜrðinɪs/ *n* mérito, valor, *m*

worthless /'wɜrθlɪs/ *a* sin valor; sin mérito; inútil; malo; (of persons) vil, despreciable, indigno

worthlessness /'wɜrθlɪsnɪs/ *n* falta de valor, *f,* falta de mérito, *f;* inutilidad, *f;* (of persons) bajeza, vileza, *f*

worthy /'wɜrði/ *a* digno de respeto, benemérito, respetable; digno, merecedor; meritorio. —*n* varón ilustre, hombre célebre, *m;* héroe, *m;* (*Inf. Ironic.*) tío, *m.* **to be w. of,** ser digno de, merecer

would /wʊd/ *unstressed* wəd/ *preterite* and *subjunctive* of **will.** (indicating a conditional tense) **They w. come if...,** Vendrían si...; (indicating an imperfect tense) **Often he w. sing,** Muchas veces cantaba, **Now and then a blackbird w. whistle,** De vez en cuando silbó un mirlo; (expressing wish, desire) **What w. they?** ¿Qué quieren? **The place where I w. be,** El lugar donde quisiera estar. **W. I were at home!** ¡Ojalá que estuviese en casa! **I thought that I w. tell you,** Se me ocurrió la idea de decírselo. **It w. seem that...,** Parece ser que..., Según parece...; Se diría que... **He said that he w. never have done it,** Dijo que no lo hubiera hecho nunca. **They w. have been killed if he had not rescued them,** Habrían sido matados si él no los hubiese salvado. **He w. go,** Se empeñó en ir. **He w. not do it,** Rehusó hacerlo, Se resistió a hacerlo; No quiso hacerlo. **This w. probably be the house,** Sin duda esta sería la casa. **W. you be good enough to...,** Tenga Vd. la bondad de..., Haga el favor de...

would-be /'wʊdbi/ *a* supuesto; llamado; aspirante (a); en esperanza de (followed by infin.); (frustrated) frustrado, malogrado

wound /wund/ *n* herida, *f.* —*vt* herir; (the feelings) lastimar, lacerar. **deep w.,** herida penetrante, *f.* **the wounded,** los heridos

wounding /'wundɪŋ/ *n* herida, *f, a Fig.* lastimador

wraith /reiθ/ *n* fantasma, espectro, *m,* sombra, *f*

wrangle /'ræŋgəl/ *vi* discutir; altercar, disputar acaloradamente; reñir; (bargain) regatear. —*n* argumento, *m;* disputa, *f,* altercado, *m;* riña, *f*

wrangler /'ræŋglər/ *n* disputador (-ra); (Cambridge University) laureado en matemáticas, *m*

wrangling /'ræŋglɪŋ/ *n* disputas, *f pl,* altercación, *f;* (bargaining) regateo, *m*

wrap /ræp/ *vt* envolver; arrollar; cubrir; abrigar; (conceal) ocultar. —*n* envoltorio, *m;* abrigo, *m;* (for a person) estar embelesado con

wrapper /'ræpər/ *n* envoltura, *f;* embalaje, *m;* (of a newspaper) faja, *f;* (of a book) sobrecubierta, *f;* (dressing-gown) bata, *f,* salto de cama, *m*

wrapping /'ræpɪŋ/ *n* envoltura, cubierta, *f.* **w.-paper,** papel de envolver, *m*

wrath /ræθ/ *n* ira, *f*

wrathful /'ræθfəl/ *a* airado
wreak /rik/ *vt* ejecutar; (anger, etc.) descargar. **to w. one's vengeance,** vengarse
wreath /riθ/ *n* guirnalda, *f;* corona, *f;* trenza, *f.* **funeral w.,** corona funeraria, *f*
wreathe /rið/ *vt* trenzar; (entwine) entrelazar (de); (garland) coronar (de), enguirnaldar (con); (encircle) ceñir, rodear; (a face in smiles) iluminar
wreck /rɛk/ *n* naufragio, *m;* buque naufragado, *m;* destrucción, *f; Fig.* ruina, *f;* (remains) restos, *m pl;* (person) sombra, *f.* —*vt* hacer naufragar; destruir; *Fig.* arruinar; hacer fracasar. **I am a complete w.,** *Inf.* Estoy hecho una ruina. **to be wrecked,** irse a pique, naufragar; *Fig.* arruinarse; frustrarse
wreckage /'rɛkɪdʒ/ *n* naufragio, *m;* restos de naufragio, *m pl;* ruinas, *f pl;* (of a car, plane, etc.) restos, *m pl;* accidente, *m*
wrecked /rɛkt/ *a* naufragado
wrecker /'rɛkər/ *n* destructor (-ra); (of ships) raquero, *m*
wren /rɛn/ *n* reyezuelo, *m*
wrench /rɛntʃ/ *n* (jerk) arranque, *m;* (pull) tirón, *m;* (sprain) torcedura, *f;* (tool) llave, *f;* (pain) dolor, *m.* —*vt* arrancar; forzar; torcer; dislocar. **He has wrenched his arm,** Se ha torcido el brazo
wrest /rɛst/ *vt* arrebatar, arrancar
wrestle /'rɛsəl/ *vi* luchar. —*n* lucha grecorromana, *f; Fig.* lucha, *f.* **to w. with,** *Fig.* luchar con; luchar contra
wrestler /'rɛslər/ *n* luchador, *m*
wrestling /'rɛslɪŋ/ *n* lucha grecorromana, *f.* **all-in-w.,** lucha libre, *f.* **w.-match,** lucha, *f*
wretch /rɛtʃ/ *n* infeliz, *mf;* (ruffian) infame, *m;* (playful) picaruelo (-la). **a poor w.,** un pobre diablo
wretched /'rɛtʃɪd/ *a* (unhappy) infeliz, desdichado; miserable; pobre; (ill) enfermo; horrible; malo; mezquino; despreciable; lamentable
wretchedly /'rɛtʃɪdli/ *adv* tristemente; pobremente; muy mal; ruinmente
wretchedness /'rɛtʃɪdnɪs/ *n* infelicidad, desdicha, *f;* miseria, pobreza, *f;* escualidez, *f;* ruindad, *f*
wriggle /'rɪgəl/ *vi* agitarse, moverse; menearse; serpear, culebrear; retorcerse. —*n* See under **wriggling. to w. into,** insinuarse en, deslizarse dentro (de). **to w. out,** escaparse. **to w. out of a difficulty,** extricarse de una dificultad
wriggling /'rɪglɪŋ/ *n* meneo, *m;* retorcimiento, *m;* serpenteo, culebreo, *m*
wring /rɪŋ/ *vt* torcer; estrujar; exprimir; arrancar; (force) forzar. **to w. one's hands,** restregarse las manos. **to w. the neck of,** torcer el pescuezo (a). **to w. out,** exprimir; estrujar
wringer /'rɪŋər/ *n* torcedor (-ra); (for clothes) exprimidor de ropa, *m*
wringing /'rɪŋɪŋ/ *n* torsión, *f.* **w.-machine,** exprimidor de ropa, *m*
wrinkle /'rɪŋkəl/ *n* arruga, *f;* pliegue, *m; Inf.* noción, *f.* —*vt* arrugar. —*vi* arrugarse. **to w. one's brow,** (frown) fruncir el ceño; (in perplexity) arrugar la frente
wrinkling /'rɪŋklɪŋ/ *n* arrugamiento, *m*
wrinkly /'rɪŋkli/ *a* arrugado
wrist /rɪst/ *n* muñeca, *f.* **w.-band,** tira del puño de la camisa, *f.* **w. bandage,** pulsera, *f*
wristlet /'rɪstlɪt/ *n* pulsera, *f;* manguito elástico, *m.* **w. watch,** reloj de pulsera, *m*
writ /rɪt/ *n;* escritura, *f; Law.* decreto judicial, mandamiento, *m;* orden, *f;* título ejecutorio, *m;* hábeas corpus, *m.* **Holy W.,** la Sagrada Escritura. **to issue a w.,** dar orden. **to serve a w.,** notificar una orden. **w. of privilege,** auto de excarcelación, *m*
write /rait/ *vt and vi* escribir; *Fig.* mostrar. **He writes a good hand,** Tiene buena letra. **I shall w. to them**

for a list, Les escribiré pidiendo una lista. **to w. back,** contestar por escrito; contestar a una carta. **to w. down,** poner por escrito; anotar, apuntar; describir. **to w. for,** escribir para; escribir para pedir algo; escribir algo en vez de otra persona. **to w. off,** escribir; escribir rápidamente; cancelar. **to w. on,** seguir escribiendo; escribir sobre. **to w. out,** copiar; redactar. **to w. over again,** escribir de nuevo, escribir otra vez, volver a escribir. **to w. up,** redactar; *Com.* poner al día; (praise) escribir alabando
writer /'raitər/ *n* escritor (-ra); autor (-ra). **the present w.,** el que, *m,* (*f,* la que) esto escribe. **writer's cramp,** calambre del escribiente, *m*
writhe /raið/ *vi* retorcerse
writhing /'raiðɪŋ/ *n* retorsión, *f*
writing /'raitɪŋ/ *n* escritura, *f;* (work) escrito, *m;* inscripción, *f;* documento, *m;* (style) estilo, *m;* (hand) letra, *f;* el arte de escribir; trabajo literario, *m.* **in one's own w.,** de su propia letra. **in w.,** por escrito. **w.-case,** escribanía, *f.* **w.-desk,** escritorio, *m.* **w.-pad,** taco de papel, *m.* **w.-paper,** papel de escribir, *m.* **w.-table,** mesa de escribir, *f*
written /'rɪtn/ *a* escrito
wrong /rɔŋ/ *a* injusto; mal; equivocado, erróneo; inexacto; falso; incorrecto; desacertado; inoportuno. **It is the w. one,** No es el que hacía falta; No es el que quería. **to be in the w. place,** estar mal situado; estar mal colocado. **to be w.,** estar mal; no tener razón; (mistaken) estar equivocado; (of deeds or things) estar mal hecho; (be unjust) ser injusto; (of clocks) andar mal. **to do w.,** hacer mal; obrar mal. **to get out of bed on the w. side,** levantarse del izquierdo. **to go w.,** (of persons) descarriarse; (of affairs) ir mal; salir mal; frustrarse; (of apparatus) estropearse, no funcionar. **We have taken the w. road,** Nos hemos equivocado de camino. **You were very w. to...,** Has hecho muy mal en... **w.-headed,** terco, obstinado; disparatado. **w.-headedness,** terquedad, obstinación, *f.* **w. number,** (telephone) número errado, *m.* **w. side,** revés, *m;* lado malo, *m.* **w. side out,** al envés; al revés
wrong /rɔŋ/ *adv* mal; injustamente; sin razón; incorrectamente; equivocadamente; (inside out) al revés. **to get it w.,** (a sum) calcular mal; (misunderstand) comprender mal
wrong /rɔŋ/ *n* mal, *m;* injusticia, *f;* perjuicio, *m;* ofensa, *f,* agravio, *m;* culpa, *f;* error, *m.* **to be in the w.,** no tener razon; haber hecho mal. **to put one in the w.,** echar la culpa (a), hacer responsable (de)
wrong /rɔŋ/ *vt* hacer mal (a); perjudicar; ser injusto con; ofender
wrongdoer /'rɔŋ,duər/ *n* malhechor (-ra); pecador (-ra); perverso (-sa)
wrongdoing /'rɔŋ,duɪŋ/ *n* maldad, maleficencia, *f;* pecado, *m;* injusticia, *f*
wrongful /'rɔŋfəl/ *a* injusto; perjudicial; falso
wrongfully /'rɔŋfəli/ *adv* injustamente; falsamente
wrongly /'rɔŋli/ *adv* injustamente; erróneamente, equivocadamente; perversamente; mal
wrongness /'rɔŋnɪs/ *n* mal, *m;* injusticia, *f;* falsedad, *f;* inexactitud, *f,* error, *m*
wrought /rɔt/ *a* forjado; labrado; (hammered) batido; trabajado. **w. iron,** hierro dulce, hierro forjado, *m.* **w. up,** muy excitado, muy agitado, muy nervioso
wry /rai/ *a* torcido; tuerto; triste; pesimista; desilusionado; irónico. **wry face,** mueca *f,* de desengaño, de ironía, de disgusto, etc. **make a wry face,** torcer el gesto. **wry neck,** *Ornith.* torcecuello, *m*
wryly /'raili/ *adv* tristemente; irónicamente
Wuthering Heights /'wʌðərɪŋ/ Cumbres borrascosas
wye /wai/ *n* (letter) ye, i griega, *f;* horquilla, cosa en forma de Y, *f*

XYZ

x /ɛks/ n equis, f

x-ray /'ɛks,reɪ/ vt tomar una radiografía (de). **x-ray,** rayo x, m pl. **x-ray examination,** examen con rayos x, m. **x-ray photograph,** radiografía, f

xylophone /'zaɪlə,foʊn/ n xilófono, m

y /waɪ/ n (letter) i griega, ye, f

yacht /yɒt/ n yate, m. **y. club,** club marítimo, m. **y. race,** regata de yates, f

yachting /'yɒtɪŋ/ n navegación en yate, f, paseo en yate, m

yachtsman /'yɒtsmən/ n deportista náutico, balandrista, balandrismo, m

yank /yæŋk/ n tirón, m, sacudida, f. —vt dar un tirón (a); sacar de un tirón

Yankee /'yæŋki/ a and n yanqui, mf

yap /yæp/ vi ladrar. —n ladrido, m

yapper /'yæpər/ n (yapping dog) gozque, gozquejo, m

yapping /'yæpɪŋ/ n ladridos, m pl, a que ladra

yard /yɑrd/ n (measure) yarda, f; Naut. verga, f; corral, m; (courtyard) patio, m. —vt acorralar. **goods y.,** estación de mercancías, f. **y.-arm,** penol (de la verga), m. **y.-stick,** vara de medir de una yarda, f

yarn /yɑrn/ n hilaza, f; hilo, m; (story) historia, f, cuento, m. **to spin a y.,** contar una historia

yaw /yɔ/ vi Naut. guiñar; Aer. serpentear. —n Naut. guiñada, f; Aer. serpenteo, m

yawl /yɔl/ n yola, f; bote, m

yawn /yɔn/ vi bostezar; quedarse con la boca abierta; (of chasms, etc.) abrirse. —n bostezo, m. **to stifle a y.,** ahogar un bostezo

yawning /'yɔnɪŋ/ a abierto. —n bostezos, m pl

ye /ði/ spelling pron. yi/ pers pron vos, vosotros

yea /yeɪ/ adv en verdad, ciertamente; y aun... no sólo... sino. —n sí, m

year /yɪər/ n año, m; pl **years,** años, m pl, edad, f. **We are getting on in years,** Nos vamos haciendo viejos. **He is five years old,** Tiene cinco años. **all the y. round,** todo el año, el año entero. **by the y.,** al año. **every other y.,** cada dos años, un año sí y otro no. **in after years,** en años posteriores. **last y.,** el año pasado. **next y.,** el año próximo. el año que viene. **y. after y.,** año tras año. **New Y.,** Año Nuevo, m. **to see the New Y. in,** ver empezar el Año Nuevo. **New Year's Day,** día de Año Nuevo, m. **(A) Happy New Y.!** ¡Feliz Año Nuevo! **y.-book,** anuario, m

yearling calf /'yɪərlɪŋ/ n becerra f

yearly /'yɪərli/ a anual. —adv anualmente, cada año; una vez al año

yearn /yɜrn/ vi anhelar, suspirar (por); desear vivamente

yearning /'yɜrnɪŋ/ n sed, ansia, f; anhelo, deseo vehemente, m. —a ansioso; anhelante; (tender) tierno

yeast /yist/ n levadura, f

yell /yɛl/ vi and vt chillar; gritar. —n chillido, m; grito, m

yelling /'yɛlɪŋ/ n chillidos, m pl; gritos, m pl, gritería, f

yellow /'yɛloʊ/ a amarillo; (of hair) rubio; (cowardly) cobarde; (newspaper) amarillista, sensacionalista. **to turn y.,** vt ponerse amarillo; amarillear. —vt volver amarillo. **y. fever,** fiebre amarilla, f. **y.-hammer,** Ornith. emberizo, m

yellowing /'yɛloʊɪŋ/ n amarilleo, m

yellowish /'yɛloʊɪʃ/ a amarillento

yellowness /'yɛloʊnɪs/ n amarillez, f

yellow pages n páginas amarillas, páginas doradas, f pl

yelp /yɛlp/ vi gañir. —n gañido, m

yelping /'yɛlpɪŋ/ n gañidos, m pl

yen /yɛn/ n (currency) yen, m; (desire) deseovivo, m

yeoman /'yoʊmən/ n pequeño propietario rural, m; soldado de caballería, m. **Y. of the Guard,** alabardero de la Casa Real, m

yes /yɛs/ adv sí. **Yes?** ¿De verdad? ¿Y qué pasó después? ¿Y entonces? **to say yes,** decir que sí; dar el sí. **yes-man,** amenista, sacristán de amén, m

yesterday /'yɛstər,deɪ/ adv ayer. —n ayer, m. **the day before y.,** anteayer

yet /yɛt/ adv aún, todavía. **as yet,** hasta ahora; todavía. **He has not come yet,** No ha venido todavía. **yet again,** otra vez

yet /yɛt/ conjunc sin embargo, no obstante, con todo; pero. **The book is well written and yet I do not like it,** El libro está bien escrito, y sin embargo no me gusta

yew /yu/ n tejo, m; madera de tejo, f

Yiddish /'yɪdɪʃ/ n yídis, yídish, yídico, m; a yídico

yield /yild/ vt producir; dar; (grant) otorgar; (afford) ofrecer; (surrender) ceder. —vi producir; (submit) rendirse, someterse; (of disease) responder; (give way) flaquear, doblegarse; dar de sí; (consent) consentir (en); (to circumstances, etc.) ceder (a), sucumbir (a). —n producción, f, producto, m; Com. rédito, m; (crop) cosecha, f. **to y. to temptation,** ceder a la tentación. **to y. up,** entregar; devolver

yielding /'yildɪŋ/ a flexible; (soft) blando; dócil, sumiso; fácil; condescendiente

yogurt /'yoʊgərt/ n yogur, m

yoke /yoʊk/ n yugo, m; (of oxen) yunta, f; (for pails) balancín, m; (of a garment) canesú, m; Fig. férula, f, yugo, m. —vt uncir, acoplar. **to throw off the y.,** sacudir el yugo

yokel /'yoʊkəl/ n patán, rústico, m

yolk /yoʊk/ n (of an egg) yema, f

yonder /'yɒndər/ a aquel, m; aquella, f; aquellos, m pl; aquellas, f pl. —adv allí; allí a lo lejos

yore /yɔr/ n in days of y., antaño; en otro tiempo

you /yu/ unstressed yʊ, yə/ pers pron nominative (polite form) usted (Vd.), mf; ustedes (Vds.), mf pl; (familiar form) sing tu, mf; (pl) vosotros, m pl; vosotras, f pl; (one) uno, m; una, f; se (followed by 3rd pers. sing. of verb). —pers pron acc (polite form) le, m; la, f; les, m pl; las, f pl; a usted, a ustedes; (informal form) te, mf, os, mf pl; (after most prepositions) si, mf; vosotros, m pl; vosotras, f pl. **Are you there?** (telephone) ¡Oiga! **I gave the parcel to you,** Te (os) di el paquete; Di el paquete a usted (a ustedes). **I shall wait for you in the garden,** Te (os) esperaré en el jardín; Esperaré a Vds. (a Vd.) en el jardín. **This present is for you,** Este regalo es para ti (para vosotros, para Vd. (Vds.)). **Away with you!** ¡Vete! ¡Marchaos! **Between you and me,** Entre tú y yo. **you can't eat your cake and have it too,** no hay rosa sin espinas. **You never can tell,** No se sabe nunca, Uno no sabe nunca

young /yʌŋ/ a joven; nuevo, reciente; inexperto; poco avanzado. —n cría, f, hijuelos, m pl. **y. blood,** Inf. pollo pera, m. **y. girl,** jovencita, f. **y. man** joven, m. **y. people,** jóvenes, m pl. **in his y. days,** en su juventud. **The night is y.,** La noche está poca avanzada. **to grow y. again,** rejuvenecer. **with y.,** (of animals) preñada f

younger /'yʌŋgər/ a más joven; menor. **Peter is his y. brother,** Pedro es su hermano menor. **to look y.,** parecer más joven

youngish /'yʌŋgɪʃ/ a bastante joven

youngster /'yʌŋstər/ n jovencito, chico, muchacho, m; niño, m

your /yʊr, yɔr/ unstressed yər/ a poss (polite form) su (pl sus), de usted (Vd.), (pl de ustedes (Vds.)); (familiar form) tu (pl vuestro). **I have y. papers,** Tengo tus (vuestros) papeles; Tengo los papeles de Vd. (or de Vds.). **Is y. mother?** ¿Cómo está su (tu) madre? **It is y. turn,** Te toca a ti, Le toca a Vd.

yours /yʊrz, yɔrz/ pron poss (polite form) (el) suyo, m; (la) suya, f; (los) suyos, m pl; (las) suyas, f pl; el, m; la, f; lo, neut; los, m pl; las, f pl; de usted (Vd.), mf sing or de ustedes (Vds.), mf pl; (familiar form) (el) tuyo, m; (la) tuya, f; (los) tuyos, m pl; (las) tuyas, f pl; (el) vuestro, m; (la) vuestra, f; (los) vuestros, m pl; (las) vuestras, f pl. **This is a picture of y.,**

(addressing one person), Este es uno de los cuadros de usted (Vd.), Este es uno de tus cuadros. **This hat is mine, it is not y.,** Este sombrero es el mío, no es el tuyo. **The horse is y.,** El caballo es tuyo (de Vd.). **Y. affectionately,** Un abrazo de tu amigo... **Y. faithfully,** Queda de Vd. su att. (atentísimo) s.s. (seguro servidor). **Y. sincerely,** Queda de Vd. su aff. (afectuoso)

yourself /yʊr'self, yɔr- yər-/ pers pron (familiar form sing) tú mismo, m; tú misma, f; (after a preposition) tí, mf; (polite form) usted (Vd.) mismo, m; usetd misma, f; pl **yourselves,** (familiar form) vosotros mismos, m pl; vosotras mismas, f pl; (polite form) ustedes (Vds.) mismos, m pl; ustedes mismas, f pl. **This is for y.,** Esto es para ti; Esto es para Vd.

youth /yuθ/ n juventud, f; (man) joven, chico, mozalbete, m; (collectively) jóvenes, m pl, juventud, f

youthful /'yuθfəl/ a joven, juvenil; de la juventud

yowl /yaul/ n gañido, aullido, m. —vi gañir, aullar

Yucatan /,yukə'tæn/ a yucateco

yucca /'yʌkə/ n Bot. yuca, f

Yugoslav /'yugou,slɑv/ n yugoeslavo (-va). —a yugoeslavo

Yugoslavia /,yugou'slaviə/ Yugoeslavia, f

Yukon, the /'yukɒn/ el Yukón, m

Yule /yul/ n Navidad, f. **y.-log,** leño de Navidad, m. **y-tide,** Navidades, f pl

z /zi/ n (letter) zeda, zeta, f

zeal /zil/ n celo, entusiasmo, m; ardor, fervor, m

zealot /'zɛlət/ n fanático (-ca)

zealous /'zɛləs/ a celoso, entusiasta

zealously /'zɛləsli/ adv con entusiasmo

zebra /'zibrə/ n cebra, f

zenith /'zinıθ/ n cenit, m; Fig. apogeo, punto culminante, m

zephyr /'zɛfər/ n céfiro, m, brisa, f

zero /'zɪərou/ n cero, m. **below z.,** bajo cero. **z. hour,** hora cero, f

zest /zɛst/ n sabor, gusto, m; entusiasmo, m. **to eat with z.,** comer con buen apetito. **to enter on with z.,** emprender con entusiasmo

zigzag /'zɪg,zæg/ n zigzag, m. —a and adv en zigzag. —vi zigzaguear, hacer zigzags, serpentear; (of persons) andar haciendo eses

Zimbabwe /zɪm'bɑbweɪ/ Zimbabue

zinc /zɪŋk/ n cinc, m. **z. oxide,** óxido de cinc, m

Zion /'zaiən/ n Sión, m

Zionism /'zaiə,nızəm/ n sionismo, m

Zionist /'zaiənıst/ n and a sionista

zip /zɪp/ n (of a bullet) silbido, m; Inf. energía, f. **zip fastener,** cierre de cremallera, m

zip code n código postal, m

zipper /'zɪpər/ n cremallera, f, cierre relámpago, cierre, cerrador, m

zircon /'zɜrkɒn/ n circón, m

zither /'zıθər/ n cítara, f

zodiac /'zoudi,æk/ n zodiaco, m

zone /zoun/ n zona, f; faja, f

zoo /zu/ n jardín zoológico, m

zoological /,zouə'lɒdʒɪkəl/ a zoológico. **Z. garden,** jardín zoológico, m

zoologist /zou'ɒlədʒɪst/ n zoólogo, m

zoology /zou'ɒlədʒi/ n zoología, f

zoom /zum/ n zumbido, m. —vi zumbar; Aer. empinarse

Zulu /'zulu/ a and n zulú mf

Zuyder Zee, the /'zaidər 'zei, 'zi/ el Zuyderzée, m

Spanish Irregular Verbs

Infinitive	Present	Future	Preterit	Past Part.
andar	ando	andaré	anduve	andado
caber	quepo	cabré	cupe	cabido
caer	caigo	caeré	caí	caído
conducir	conduzco	conduciré	conduje	conducido
dar	doy	daré	di	dado
decir	digo	diré	dije	dicho
estar	estoy	estaré	estuve	estado
haber	he	habré	hube	habido
hacer	hago	haré	hice	hecho
ir	voy	iré	fui	ido
jugar	juego	jugaré	jugué	jugado
morir	muero	moriré	morí	muerto
oir	oigo	oiré	oí	oído
poder	puedo	podré	pude	podido
poner	pongo	pondré	puse	puesto
querer	quiero	querré	quise	querido
saber	sé	sabré	supe	sabido
salir	salgo	saldré	salí	salido
ser	soy	seré	fui	sido
tener	tengo	tendré	tuve	tenido
traer	traigo	traeré	traje	traído
valer	valgo	valdré	valí	valido
venir	vengo	vendré	vine	venido
ver	veo	veré	vi	visto

Las formas del verbo inglés

1. Se forma la 3ª persona singular del tiempo presente exactamente al igual que el plural de los sustantivos, añadiendo **-es** o **-s** a la forma sencilla según las mismas reglas, así:

(1)	teach	pass	wish	fix	buzz		
	teaches	passes	wishes	fixes	buzzes		

(2)	place	change	judge	please	freeze		
	places	changes	judges	pleases	freezes		

(3a)	find	sell	clean	hear	love	buy	know
	finds	sells	cleans	hears	loves	buys	knows

(3b)	think	like	laugh	stop	hope	meet	want
	thinks	likes	laughs	stops	hopes	meets	wants

(4)	cry	try	dry	carry	deny		
	cries	tries	dries	carries	denies		

Cinco verbos muy comunes tienen 3ª persona singular irregular:

(5)	go	do	say	have	be
	goes	does	says	has	is

2. Se forman el tiempo pasado y el participio de modo igual, añadiendo a la forma sencilla la terminación **-ed** o **-d** según las reglas que siguen:

(1) Si la forma sencilla termina en **-d** o **-t,** se le pone **-ed** como sílaba aparte:

end	fold	need	load	want	feast	wait	light
ended	folded	needed	loaded	wanted	feasted	waited	lighted

(2) Si la forma sencilla termina en cualquier otra consonante, se añade también **-ed** pero sin hacer sílaba aparte:

(2a)
bang	sail	seem	harm	earn	weigh
banged	sailed	seemed	harmed	earned	weighed

(2b)
lunch	work	look	laugh	help	pass
lunched	worked	looked	laughed	helped	passed

(3) Si la forma sencilla termina en **-e,** se le pone sólo **-d:**

(3a)
hate	taste	waste	guide	fade	trade
hated	tasted	wasted	guided	faded	traded

(3b)
free	judge	rule	name	dine	scare
freed	judged	ruled	named	dined	scared

(3c)
place	force	knife	like	hope	base
placed	forced	knifed	liked	hoped	based

(4) Una **-y** final que sigue a cualquier consonante se cambia en **-ie** al añadir la **-d** del pasado/participio:

cry	try	dry	carry	deny
cried	tried	dried	carried	denied

3. Varios verbos muy comunes forman el tiempo pasado y el participio de manera irregular. Pertenecen a tres grupos.

(1) Los que tienen una sola forma irregular para tiempo pasado y participio, como los siguientes:

bend	bleed	bring	build	buy	catch	creep	deal
bent	bled	brought	built	bought	caught	crept	dealt

dig	feed	feel	fight	find	flee	get	hang
dug	fed	felt	fought	found	fled	got	hung

have	hear	hold	keep	lead	leave	lend	lose
had	heard	held	kept	led	left	lent	lost

make	mean	meet	say	seek	sell	send	shine
made	meant	met	said	sought	sold	sent	shone

shoot	sit	sleep	spend	stand	strike	sweep	teach
shot	sat	slept	spent	stood	struck	swept	taught

(2) Los que tienen una forma irregular para el tiempo pasado y otra forma irregular para el participio, como los siguientes:

be	beat	become	begin	bite
was	beat	became	began	bit
been	beaten	become	begun	bitten
blow	break	choose	come	do
blew	broke	chose	came	did
blown	broken	chosen	come	done
draw	drink	drive	eat	fall
drew	drank	drove	ate	fell
drawn	drunk	driven	eaten	fallen
fly	forget	freeze	give	go
flew	forgot	froze	gave	went
flown	forgotten	frozen	given	gone
grow	hide	know	ride	ring
grew	hid	knew	rode	rang
grown	hidden	known	ridden	rung
rise	run	see	shake	shrink
rose	ran	saw	shook	shrank
risen	run	seen	shaken	shrunk
sing	sink	speak	steal	swear
sang	sank	spoke	stole	swore
sung	sunk	spoken	stolen	sworn
swim	tear	throw	wear	write
swam	tore	threw	wore	wrote
swum	torn	thrown	worn	written

(3) Los que no varían del todo, la forma sencilla funcionando también como pasado/participio; entre éstos son de mayor frecuencia:

bet	burst	cast	cost	cut
hit	hurt	let	put	quit
read	set	shed	shut	slit
spit	split	spread	thrust	wet

Numbers/Números

Cardinal/Cardinales

one	1	uno, una
two	2	dos
three	3	tres
four	4	cuatro
five	5	cinco
six	6	seis
seven	7	siete
eight	8	ocho
nine	9	nueve
ten	10	diez
eleven	11	once
twelve	12	doce
thirteen	13	trece
fourteen	14	catorce
fifteen	15	quince
sixteen	16	dieciséis
seventeen	17	diecisiete
eighteen	18	dieciocho
nineteen	19	diecinueve
twenty	20	veinte
twenty-one	21	veinte y uno (or veintiuno)
twenty-two	22	veinte y dos (or veintidós)
thirty	30	treinta
thirty-one	31	treinta y uno
thirty-two	32	treinta y dos
forty	40	cuarenta
fifty	50	cincuenta
sixty	60	sesenta
seventy	70	setenta
eighty	80	ochenta
ninety	90	noventa

one hundred	100	cien
one hundred one	101	ciento uno
one hundred two	102	ciento dos
two hundred	200	doscientos, -as
three hundred	300	trescientos, -as
four hundred	400	cuatrocientos, -as
five hundred	500	quinientos, -as
six hundred	600	seiscientos, -as
seven hundred	700	setecientos, -as
eight hundred	800	ochocientos, -as
nine hundred	900	novecientos, -as
one thousand	1,000	mil
two thousand	2,000	dos mil
one hundred thousand	100,000	cien mil
one million	1,000,000	un millón
two million	2,000,000	dos millones

Ordinal/Ordinales

first	1st / 1°	primero
second	2nd / 2°	segundo
third	3rd / 3°	tercero
fourth	4th / 4°	cuarto
fifth	5th / 5°	quinto
sixth	6th / 6°	sexto
seventh	7th / 7°	séptimo
eighth	8th / 8°	octavo
ninth	9th / 9°	noveno
tenth	10th / 10°	décimo

Days of the Week/Días de la Semana

Sunday	domingo	Thursday	jueves
Monday	lunes	Friday	viernes
Tuesday	martes	Saturday	sábado
Wednesday	miércoles		

Months/Meses

January	enero	July	julio
February	febrero	August	agosto
March	marzo	September	septiembre
April	abril	October	octubre
May	mayo	November	noviembre
June	junio	December	diciembre

Weights and Measures/Pesos y Medidas

1 centímetro	=	.3937 inches	1 kilolitro	=	264.18 gallons
1 metro	=	39.37 inches	1 inch	=	2.54 centímetros
1 kilómetro	=	.621 mile	1 foot	=	.305 metros
1 centigramo	=	.1543 grain	1 mile	=	1.61 kilómetros
1 gramo	=	15.432 grains	1 grain	=	.065 gramos
1 kilogramo	=	2.2046 pounds	1 pound	=	.455 kilogramos
1 tonelada	=	2.204 pounds	1 ton	=	.907 toneladas
1 centilitro	=	.338 ounces	1 ounce	=	2.96 centilitros
1 litro	=	1.0567 quart (liquid);	1 quart	=	1.13 litros
		.908 quart (dry)	1 gallon	=	4.52 litros

Signs/Señales

Caution	Precaución	**No smoking**	Prohibido fumar
Danger	Peligro	**No admittance**	Entrada prohibida
Exit	Salida	**One way**	Dirección única
Entrance	Entrada	**No entry**	Dirección prohibida
Stop	Alto	**Women**	Señoras, Mujeres, Damas
Closed	Cerrado	**Men**	Señores, Hombres, Caballeros
Open	Abierto	**Ladies' Room**	El cuarto de damas
Slow	Despacio	**Men's Room**	El servicio

Useful Phrases/Locuciones Útiles

Good day, Good morning. Buenos días.
Good afternoon. Buenas tardes.
Good night, Good evening. Buenas noches.
Hello. ¡Hola!
Welcome! ¡Bienvenido!
See you later. Hasta luego.
Goodbye. ¡Adiós!
How are you? ¿Cómo está usted?
I'm fine, thank you. Estoy bien, gracias.
I'm pleased to meet you. Mucho gusto en conocerle.
May I introduce . . . Quisiera presentar . . .
Thank you very much. Muchas gracias.
You're welcome. De nada *or* No hay de qué.
Please. Por favor.
Excuse me. Con permiso.
Good luck. ¡Buena suerte!
To your health. ¡Salud!

Please help me. Ayúdeme, por favor.
I don't know. No sé.

I don't understand. No entiendo.
Do you understand? ¿Entiende usted?
I don't speak Spanish. No hablo español.
Do you speak English? ¿Habla usted inglés?
How do you say . . . in Spanish? ¿Cómo se dice . . . en español?
What do you call this? ¿Cómo se llama esto?
Speak slowly, please. Hable despacio, por favor.
Please repeat. Repita, por favor.
I don't like it. No me gusta.
I am lost. Ando perdido; Me he extraviado.

What is your name? ¿Cómo se llama usted?
My name is . . . Me llamo . . .
I am an American. Soy norteamericano.
Where are you from? ¿De dónde es usted?
I'm from . . . Soy de . . .

How is the weather? ¿Qué tiempo hace?

It's cold (hot) today. Hace frío (calor) hoy.

What time is it? ¿Qué hora es?

How much is it? ¿Cuánto es?

It is too much. Es demasiado.

What do you wish? ¿Qué desea usted?

I want to buy . . . Quiero comprar . . .

May I see something better? ¿Podría ver algo mejor?

May I see something cheaper? ¿Podría ver algo menos caro?

It is not exactly what I want. No es exactamente lo que quiero.

I'm hungry. Tengo hambre.

I'm thirsty. Tengo sed.

Where is there a restaurant? ¿Dónde hay un restaurante?

I have a reservation. Tengo una reservación.

I would like . . . Quisiera . . .; Me gustaría . . .

Please give me . . . Por favor, déme usted . . .

Please bring me . . . Por favor, tráigame usted . . .

May I see the menu? ¿Podría ver el menú?

The bill, please. La cuenta, por favor.

Is service included in the bill? ¿El servicio está incluido en la cuenta?

Where is there a hotel? ¿Dónde hay un hotel?

Where is the post office? ¿Dónde está el correo?

Is there any mail for me? ¿Hay correo para mí?

Where can I mail this letter? ¿Dónde puedo echar esta carta al correo?

Take me to . . . Lléveme a . . .

I believe I am ill. Creo que estoy enfermo.

Please call a doctor. Por favor, llame al médico.

Please call the police. Por favor, llame a la policía.

I want to send a telegram. Quiero poner un telegrama.

As soon as possible. Cuanto antes.

Round trip. Ida y vuelta.

Please help me with my luggage. Por favor, ayúdeme con mi equipaje.

Where can I get a taxi? ¿Dónde se puede encontrar un taxi?

What is the fare to . . . ¿Cuánto es el pasaje hasta . . . ?

Please take me to this address. Por favor, lléveme a esta dirección.

Where can I change my money? ¿Dónde puedo cambiar mi dinero?

Where is the nearest bank? ¿Dónde está el banco más cercano?

Can you accept my check? ¿Puede aceptar usted mi cheque?

Do you accept traveler's checks? ¿Aceptan cheques de viaje?

What is the postage? ¿Cuánto es el franqueo?

Where is the nearest drugstore? ¿Dónde está la farmacia más cercana?

Where is the men's (women's) room? ¿Dónde está el servicio de caballeros (de señoras)?

Please let me off at. . . Por favor, déjeme bajar en . . .

Right away. ¡Pronto!

Help. ¡Socorro!

Who is it? ¿Quién es?

Just a minute! ¡Un momento no más!

Come in. ¡Pase usted!

Pardon me. Dispense usted.

Stop. ¡Pare!

Look out. ¡Cuidado!

Hurry. ¡De prisa! *or* ¡Dése prisa!

Go on. ¡Siga!

To (on, at) the right. A la derecha.

To (on, at) the left. A la izquierda.

Straight ahead. Adelante.